The COMPLETE ETHIOPIAN BIBLE

In ENGLISH

ALL APOCRYPHAL TEXTS INCLUDING BOOKS OF ENOCH WISDOM JUBILEES & OTHERS

By Dr Lewis Spencer

This edition of The Complete Ethiopian Bible was meticulously edited to the highest precision, drawing upon historical texts and extensive scholarly research. Special acknowledgment is due to the Oxford Theology Society for their invaluable support and contributions, ensuring the utmost accuracy and integrity of this work.

Dear Reader,

This book is a labour of love and dedication by many devoted individuals. If this work has enriched your understanding and faith, your thoughts would mean the world to me. Please consider leaving a review via the QR code to support this publication and future endeavours.

Thank you!

Dr Lewis Spencer

CONTENTS

OLD TESTAMENT

GENESIS

CHAPTER 1

1 In [the] beginning God created the heavens and the earth, **2** and the earth was formless and void, and darkness [was] on the face of the deep, and the Spirit of God [was] fluttering on the face of the waters, **3** and God says, "Let light be"; and light is. **4** And God sees that the light [is] good, and God separates between the light and the darkness, **5** and God calls the light "Day," and the darkness He has called "Night"; and there is an evening, and there is a morning—day one. **6** And God says, "Let an expanse be in the midst of the waters, and let it be separating between waters and waters." **7** And God makes the expanse, and it separates between the waters which [are] under the expanse, and the waters which [are] above the expanse: and it is so. **8** And God calls the expanse "Heavens"; and there is an evening, and there is a morning—[the] second day. **9** And God says, "Let the waters under the heavens be collected to one place, and let the dry land be seen": and it is so. **10** And God calls the dry land "Earth," and the collection of the waters He has called "Seas"; and God sees that [it is] good. **11** And God says, "Let the earth yield tender grass, herb sowing seed, fruit-tree (whose seed [is] in itself) making fruit after its kind, on the earth": and it is so. **12** And the earth brings forth tender grass, herb sowing seed after its kind, and tree making fruit (whose seed [is] in itself) after its kind; and God sees that [it is] good; **13** and there is an evening, and there is a morning—[the] third day. **14** And God says, "Let luminaries be in the expanse of the heavens, to make a separation between the day and the night, then they have been for signs, and for appointed times, and for days and years, **15** and they have been for luminaries in the expanse of the heavens to give light on the earth": and it is so. **16** And God makes the two great luminaries, the great luminary for the rule of the day, and the small luminary—and the stars—for the rule of the night; **17** and God gives them in the expanse of the heavens to give light on the earth, **18** and to rule over day and over night, and to make a separation between the light and the darkness; and God sees that [it is] good; **19** and there is an evening, and there is a morning—[the] fourth day. **20** And God says, "Let the waters teem with the teeming living creature, and let [the] bird fly above the earth on the face of the expanse of the heavens." **21** And God creates the great dragons, and every living creature that is creeping, which the waters have teemed with, after their kind, and every bird with wing, after its kind, and God sees that [it is] good. **22** And God blesses them, saying, "Be fruitful, and multiply, and fill the waters in the seas, and let the bird multiply in the earth": **23** and there is an evening, and there is a morning—[the] fifth day. **24** And God says, "Let the earth bring forth the living creature after its kind, livestock and creeping thing, and beast of the earth after its kind": and it is so. **25** And God makes the beast of the earth after its kind, and the livestock after their kind, and every creeping thing of the ground after its kind, and God sees that [it is] good. **26** And God says, "Let Us make man in Our image, according to Our likeness, and let them rule over [the] fish of the sea, and over [the] bird of the heavens, and over livestock, and over all the earth, and over every creeping thing that is creeping on the earth." **27** And God creates the man in His image; in the image of God He created him, a male and a female He created them. **28** And God blesses them, and God says to them, "Be fruitful, and multiply, and fill the earth, and subdue it, and rule over [the] fish of the sea, and over [the] bird of the heavens, and over every living thing that is creeping on the earth." **29** And God says, "Behold, I have given to you every herb sowing seed, which [is] on the face of all the earth, and every tree in which [is] the fruit of a tree sowing seed, to you it is for food; **30** and to every beast of the earth, and to every bird of the heavens, and to every creeping thing on the earth, in which [is] breath of life, every green herb [is] for food": and it is so. **31** And God sees all that He has done, and behold, [it is] very good; and there is an evening, and there is a morning—the sixth day.

CHAPTER 2

1 And the heavens and the earth are completed, and all their host; **2** and God completes by the seventh day His work which He has made, and ceases by the seventh day from all His work which He has made. **3** And God blesses the seventh day, and sanctifies it, for in it He has ceased from all His work which God had created for making. **4** These [are] the generations of the heavens and of the earth in their being created, in the day of Yhwh God's making the earth and the heavens; **5** and no shrub of the field is yet in the earth, and no herb of the field yet sprouts, for Yhwh God has not rained on the earth, and there is not a man to serve the ground, **6** and a mist goes up from the earth, and has watered the whole face of the ground. **7** And Yhwh God forms the man—dust from the ground, and breathes into his nostrils breath of life, and the man becomes a living creature. **8** And Yhwh God plants a garden in Eden, at the east, and He sets there the man whom He has formed; **9** and Yhwh God causes to sprout from the ground every tree desirable for appearance, and good for food, and the Tree of Life in the midst of the garden, and the Tree of the Knowledge of Good and Evil. **10** And a river is going out from Eden to water the garden, and from there it is parted, and has become four chief [rivers]; **11** the name of the first [is] Pison, it [is] that which is surrounding the whole land of Havilah where the gold [is], **12** and the gold of that land [is] good; the bdellium and the shoham stone [are] there; **13** and the name of the second river [is] Gihon, it [is] that which is surrounding the whole land of Cush; **14** and the name of the third river [is] Hiddekel, it [is] that which is going east of Asshur; and the fourth river is the Euphrates. **15** And Yhwh God takes the man, and causes him to rest in the Garden of Eden, to serve it and to keep it. **16** And Yhwh God lays a charge on the man, saying, "From every tree of the garden eating you eat; **17** but from the Tree of the Knowledge of Good and Evil, you do not eat from it, for in the day of your eating from it—dying you die." **18** And Yhwh God says, "[It is] not good for the man to be alone; I make him a helper as his counterpart." **19** And Yhwh God forms from the ground every beast of the field, and every bird of the heavens, and brings [them] to the man, to see what he calls it; and whatever the man calls a living creature, that [is] its name. **20** And the man calls names to all the livestock, and to bird of the heavens, and to every beast of the field; but for man a helper has not been found as his counterpart. **21** And Yhwh God causes a deep sleep to fall on the man, and he sleeps, and He takes one of his ribs, and closes up flesh in its stead. **22** And Yhwh God builds up the rib which He has taken out of the man into a woman, and brings her to the man; **23** and the man says, "This at last! Bone of my bone, and flesh of my flesh!" For this is called Woman, for this has been taken from Man; **24** therefore a man leaves his father and his mother, and has cleaved to his wife, and they have become one flesh. **25** And both of them are naked, the man and his wife, and they are not ashamed of themselves.

CHAPTER 3

1 And the serpent has been cunning above every beast of the field which Yhwh God has made, and he says to the woman, "Is it true that God has said, You do not eat from every tree of the garden?" **2** And the woman says to the serpent, "From the fruit of the trees of the garden we eat, **3** but from the fruit of the tree which [is] in the midst of the garden, God has said, You do not eat of it, nor touch it, lest you die." **4** And the serpent says to the woman, "Dying, you do not die, **5** for God knows that in the day of your eating of it—your eyes have been opened, and you have been as God, knowing good and evil." **6** And the woman sees that the tree [is] good for food, and that it [is] pleasant to the eyes, and the tree is desirable to make [one] wise, and she takes from its fruit and eats, and also gives [some] to her husband with her, and he eats; **7** and the eyes of them both are opened, and they know that they [are] naked, and they sew fig-leaves, and make girdles for themselves. **8** And they hear the sound of Yhwh God walking up and down in the garden at the breeze of the day, and the man and his wife hide themselves from the face of Yhwh God in the midst of the trees of the garden. **9** And Yhwh God calls to the man and says to him, "Where [are] you?" **10** and he says, "I have heard Your sound in the garden, and I am afraid, for I am naked, and I hide myself." **11** And He says, "Who has declared to you that you [are] naked? Have you eaten from the tree of which I have commanded you not to eat?" **12** and the man says, "The woman whom You placed with me—she has given to me from the tree, and I eat." **13** And Yhwh God says to the woman, "What [is] this you have done?" And the woman says, "The serpent has caused me to forget, and I eat." **14** And Yhwh God says to the serpent, "Because you have done this, cursed [are] you above all the livestock, and above every beast of the field: on your belly you go, and dust you eat, [for] all days of your life; **15** and I put enmity between you and the woman, and between your seed and her Seed; He bruises your head, and you bruise His heel." **16** To the woman He said, "Multiplying I multiply your sorrow and your conception; you will bear children in sorrow, and your desire [is] toward your Man [[*or* husband]], and He [[*or* he]] will rule over you." **17** And to the man He said, "Because you have listened to the voice of your wife, and eat from the tree concerning which I have charged you, saying, You do not eat of it, cursed [is] the ground on your account; in sorrow you eat of it [for] all days of your life, **18** and it brings forth thorn and bramble for you, and you have eaten the herb of the field; **19** by the sweat of your face you eat bread until your return to the ground, for you have been taken out of it, for dust you [are], and to dust you return." **20** And the man calls his wife's name Eve, for she has been mother of all living. **21** And Yhwh God makes coats of skin [for] the man and his wife, and clothes them. **22** And Yhwh God says, "Behold, the man was as one of Us, as to the knowledge of good and evil; and now, lest he send forth his hand, and has also taken from the Tree of Life, and eaten, and lived for all time." **23** Yhwh God sends him forth from the Garden of Eden to serve the ground from which he has been taken; **24** indeed, He casts out the man, and causes the cherubim to dwell at the east of the Garden of Eden with the sword of flame whirling around to guard the way of the Tree of Life.

CHAPTER 4

1 And the man knew his wife Eve, and she conceives and bears Cain, and says, "I have acquired a man by Yhwh"; **2** and she adds to bear his brother, even Abel. And Abel is feeding a flock, and Cain has been servant of the ground. **3** And it comes to pass at the end of days that Cain brings from the fruit of the ground a present to Yhwh; **4** and Abel, he has brought, he also, from the female firstlings of his flock, and from their fat ones; and Yhwh looks to Abel and to his present, **5** and to Cain and to his present He has not looked; and it is very displeasing to Cain, and his countenance is fallen. **6** And Yhwh says to Cain, "Why do you have displeasure? and why has your countenance fallen? **7** Is there not, if you do well, acceptance? and if you do not do well, sin [[*or* a sin-offering]] is lying at the opening, and its [[*or* His]] desire [is] for you, and you rule over it [[*or* by Him]]." **8** And Cain says to his brother Abel, [["Let us go into the field";]] and it comes to pass in their being in the field, that Cain rises up against his brother Abel, and slays him. **9** And Yhwh says to Cain, "Where [is] your brother Abel?" And he says, "I have not known; am I my brother's keeper?" **10** And He says, "What have you done? the voice of your brother's blood is crying to Me from the ground; **11** and now, cursed [are] you from the ground, which has opened her mouth to receive the blood of your brother from your hand; **12** when you till the ground, it will not add to give its strength to you—a wanderer, even a trembling one, you are in the earth." **13** And Cain says to Yhwh, "My punishment is too great than to bear; **14** behold, You have driven me today from off the face of the ground, and from Your face I am hid; and I have been a wanderer, even a trembling one, in the earth, and it has been—everyone finding me will slay me." **15** And Yhwh says to him, "Therefore, of any slayer of Cain it is required sevenfold"; and Yhwh sets to Cain a token that none finding him will slay him. **16** And Cain goes out from before Yhwh, and dwells in the land, moving about east of Eden; **17** and Cain knows his wife, and she conceives, and bears Enoch; and he is building a city, and he calls the name of the city, according to the name of his son—Enoch. **18** And born to Enoch is Irad; and Irad has begotten Mehujael; and Mehujael has begotten Methusael; and Methusael has begotten Lamech. **19** And Lamech takes to himself two wives, the name of the first Adah, and the name of the second Zillah. **20** And Adah bears Jabal, he has been father of those inhabiting tents and [having] purchased livestock; **21** and the name of his brother [is] Jubal, he has been father of everyone handling harp and pipe. **22** And Zillah, she also bears Tubal-Cain, an instructor of every craftsman in bronze and iron; and a sister of Tubal-Cain [is] Naamah. **23** And Lamech says to his wives: "Adah and Zillah, hear my voice; Wives of Lamech, give ear

[to] my saying: For I have slain a man for my wound, || Even a young man for my hurt; **24** For sevenfold is required for Cain, || And for Lamech seventy-sevenfold." **25** And Adam again knows his wife, and she bears a son, and calls his name Seth, "for God has appointed for me another seed instead of Abel": for Cain had slain him. **26** And to Seth, to him also a son has been born, and he calls his name Enos; then a beginning was made of preaching in the Name of Yhwh.

CHAPTER 5

1 This [is] an account of the generations of Adam. In the day of God's creating man, in the likeness of God He has made him; **2** a male and a female He has created them, and He blesses them, and calls their name Man, in the day of their being created. **3** And Adam lives one hundred and thirty years [[*or* two hundred and thirty years]], and begets [a son] in his likeness, according to his image, and calls his name Seth. **4** And the days of Adam after his begetting Seth are eight hundred years [[*or* seven hundred years]], and he begets sons and daughters. **5** And all the days of Adam which he lived are nine hundred and thirty years, and he dies. **6** And Seth lives one hundred and five years [[*or* two hundred and five years]], and begets Enos. **7** And Seth lives after his begetting Enos eight hundred and seven years [[*or* seven hundred and seven years]], and begets sons and daughters. **8** And all the days of Seth are nine hundred and twelve years, and he dies. **9** And Enos lives ninety years [[*or* one hundred and ninety years]], and begets Cainan. **10** And Enos lives after his begetting Cainan eight hundred and fifteen years [[*or* seven hundred and fifteen years]], and begets sons and daughters. **11** And all the days of Enos are nine hundred and five years, and he dies. **12** And Cainan lives seventy years [[*or* one hundred and seventy years]], and begets Mahalaleel. **13** And Cainan lives after his begetting Mahalaleel eight hundred and forty years [[*or* seven hundred and forty years]], and begets sons and daughters. **14** And all the days of Cainan are nine hundred and ten years, and he dies. **15** And Mahalaleel lives sixty-five years [[*or* one hundred and sixty-five years]], and begets Jared. **16** And Mahalaleel lives after his begetting Jared eight hundred and thirty years [[*or* seven hundred and thirty years]], and begets sons and daughters. **17** And all the days of Mahalaleel are eight hundred and ninety-five years, and he dies. **18** And Jared lives one hundred and sixty-two years, and begets Enoch. **19** And Jared lives after his begetting Enoch eight hundred years, and begets sons and daughters. **20** And all the days of Jared are nine hundred and sixty-two years, and he dies. **21** And Enoch lives sixty-five years [[*or* one hundred and sixty-five years]], and begets Methuselah. **22** And Enoch habitually walks with God after his begetting Methuselah three hundred years [[*or* two hundred years]], and begets sons and daughters. **23** And all the days of Enoch are three hundred and sixty-five years. **24** And Enoch habitually walks with God, and he is not, for God has taken him. **25** And Methuselah lives one hundred and eighty-seven years, and begets Lamech. **26** And Methuselah lives after his begetting Lamech seven hundred and eighty-two years, and begets sons and daughters. **27** And all the days of Methuselah are nine hundred and sixty-nine years, and he dies. **28** And Lamech lives one hundred and eighty-two years [[*or* one hundred and eighty-eight years]], and begets a son, **29** and calls his name Noah, saying, "This [one] comforts us concerning our work, and concerning the labor of our hands, because of the ground which Yhwh has cursed." **30** And Lamech lives after his begetting Noah five hundred and ninety-five years [[*or* five hundred and sixty-five years]], and begets sons and daughters. **31** And all the days of Lamech are seven hundred and seventy-seven years [[*or* seven hundred and fifty-three years]], and he dies. **32** And Noah is a son of five hundred years, and Noah begets Shem, Ham, and Japheth.

CHAPTER 6

1 And it comes to pass that mankind has begun to multiply on the face of the ground, and daughters have been born to them, **2** and the sons of God see that they, the daughters of men, [are] beautiful, and they take women for themselves of all whom they have chosen. **3** And Yhwh says, "My Spirit does not strive in man for all time, for indeed, he [is] flesh, but his days have been one hundred and twenty years." **4** The giants were in the earth in those days, and even afterward, when sons of God come in to the daughters of men, and they have borne to them those who [were] the mighty from of old, the men of renown. **5** And Yhwh sees that the wickedness of man [is] abundant in the earth, and every imagination of the thoughts of his heart [is] only evil every day; **6** and Yhwh regrets that He has made man in the earth, and He grieves Himself—to His heart. **7** And Yhwh says, "I wipe away man whom I have created from off the face of the ground, from man to beast, to creeping thing, and to bird of the heavens, for I have regretted that I have made them." **8** And Noah found grace in the eyes of Yhwh. **9** These [are] the generations of Noah: Noah [is] a righteous man; he has been perfect among his generations; Noah has habitually walked with God. **10** And Noah begets three sons: Shem, Ham, and Japheth. **11** And the earth is corrupt before God, and the earth is filled [with] violence. **12** And God sees the earth, and behold, it has been corrupted, for all flesh has corrupted its way on the earth. **13** And God said to Noah, "An end of all flesh has come before Me, for the earth has been full of violence from their presence; and behold, I am destroying them with the earth. **14** Make an ark of gopher-wood for yourself; you make rooms within the Ark, and you have covered it from inside and from outside with pitch; **15** and this [is] how you do it: three hundred cubits [is] the length of the Ark, fifty cubits its breadth, and thirty cubits its height; **16** you make a window for the Ark, and you finish it to a cubit from above; and you put the opening of the Ark in its side; you make it [with] lower, second, and third [stories]. **17** And I, behold, I am bringing in the flood of waters on the earth, to destroy from under the heavens all flesh in which [is] a living spirit; all that [is] in the earth expires. **18** And I have established My covenant with you, and you have come into the Ark—you, and your sons, and your wife, and your son's wives with you; **19** and of all that lives, of all flesh, you bring two from every [kind] into the Ark, to keep alive with you; they are male and female. **20** From the bird after its kind, and from the livestock after its kind, [and] from every creeping thing of the ground after its kind, two of every [kind] they come to you, to keep alive. **21** And you, take for yourself from all food that is eaten; and you have gathered [it] to yourself, and it has been for you and for them for food." **22** And Noah does according to all that God has commanded him; so he has done.

CHAPTER 7

1 And Yhwh says to Noah, "Come, you and all your house, into the Ark, for I have seen you [are] righteous before Me in this generation; **2** you take seven pairs from all the clean beasts to yourself, a male and its female; and of the beasts which are not clean—two, a male and its female; **3** also, seven pairs from [each] bird of the heavens, a male and a female, to keep alive seed on the face of all the earth; **4** for after seven more days I am sending rain on the earth [for] forty days and forty nights, and have wiped away all the substance that I have made from off the face of the ground." **5** And Noah does according to all that Yhwh has commanded him. **6** And Noah [is] a son of six hundred years, and the flood of waters has been on the earth. **7** And Noah goes—and his sons, and his wife, and his sons' wives with him—into the Ark, out of the presence of the waters of the flood; **8** from the clean beast, and from the beast that [is] not clean, and from the bird, and of everything that is creeping on the ground, **9** they have come to Noah two by two into the Ark, a male and a female, as God has commanded Noah. **10** And it comes to pass, after seven days, that waters of the flood have been on the earth. **11** In the six hundredth year of the life of Noah, in the second month, on the seventeenth day of the month, on this day all [the] fountains of the great deep have been broken up, and the network of the heavens has been opened, **12** and the shower is on the earth [for] forty days and forty nights. **13** On this very same day Noah, and Shem, and Ham, and Japheth, sons of Noah, and Noah's wife, and the three wives of his sons with them, went into the Ark— **14** they, and every living creature after its kind, and every beast after its kind, and every creeping thing that is creeping on the earth after its kind, and every bird after its kind (every bird, every wing). **15** And they come to Noah, into the Ark, two by two of all the flesh in which [is] a living spirit; **16** and they that are coming in, male and female of all flesh, have come in as God has commanded him, and Yhwh closes [it] for him. **17** And the flood is on the earth [for] forty days, and the waters multiply and lift up the Ark, and it is raised up from off the

earth; **18** and the waters are mighty and multiply exceedingly on the earth; and the Ark goes on the face of the waters. **19** And the waters have been very, very mighty on the earth, and all the high mountains are covered which [are] under the whole heavens; **20** the waters prevailed from above the mountains, and cover [them] fifteen cubits; **21** and all flesh expires that is moving on the earth, among bird, and among livestock, and among beast, and among every teeming thing which is teeming on the earth, and all mankind; **22** all in whose nostrils [is] breath of a living spirit—of all that [is] in the dry land—have died. **23** And all the substance that is on the face of the ground is wiped away—from man to beast, to creeping thing, and to bird of the heavens; indeed, they are wiped away from the earth, and only Noah is left, and those who [are] with him in the Ark; **24** and the waters are mighty on the earth [for] one hundred and fifty days.

CHAPTER 8

1 And God remembers Noah, and every living thing, and all the livestock which [are] with him in the Ark, and God causes a wind to pass over the earth, and the waters subside, **2** and the fountains of the deep and the network of the heavens are closed, and the shower is restrained from the heavens. **3** And the waters return from off the earth, going on and returning; and the waters are lacking at the end of one hundred and fifty days. **4** And the Ark rests, in the seventh month, on the seventeenth day of the month, on mountains of Ararat; **5** and the waters have been going and decreasing until the tenth month; in the tenth [month], on the first of the month, the heads of the mountains appeared. **6** And it comes to pass, at the end of forty days, that Noah opens the window of the Ark which he made, **7** and he sends forth the raven, and it goes out, going out and turning back until the drying of the waters from off the earth. **8** And he sends forth the dove from him to see whether the waters have been lightened from off the face of the ground, **9** and the dove has not found rest for the sole of her foot, and she turns back to him, to the Ark, for waters [are] on the face of all the earth, and he puts out his hand, and takes her, and brings her in to him, into the Ark. **10** And he stays yet seven more days, and adds to send forth the dove from the Ark; **11** and the dove comes to him at evening, and behold, an olive leaf [is] torn off in her mouth; and Noah knows that the waters have been lightened from off the earth. **12** And he stays yet seven more days, and sends forth the dove, and it did not add to return to him anymore. **13** And it comes to pass in the six hundredth and first year, in the first [month], on the first of the month, the waters have been dried from off the earth; and Noah turns aside the covering of the Ark, and looks, and behold, the face of the ground has been dried. **14** And in the second month, on the twenty-seventh day of the month, the earth has become dry. **15** And God speaks to Noah, saying, "Go out from the Ark, you, and your wife, and your sons, and your sons' wives with you; **16** every living thing that [is] with you, of all flesh, among bird, and among livestock, and among every creeping thing which is creeping on the earth, bring out with you; **17** and they have teemed in the earth, and been fruitful, and have multiplied on the earth." **18** And Noah goes out, and his sons, and his wife, and his sons' wives with him; **19** every beast, every creeping thing, and every bird; every creeping thing on the earth, after their families, have gone out from the Ark. **20** And Noah builds an altar to Yhwh, and takes from every clean beast and from every clean bird, and causes burnt-offerings to ascend on the altar; **21** and Yhwh smells the refreshing fragrance, and Yhwh says to His heart, "I do not continue to disfavor the ground because of man anymore, though the imagination of the heart of man [is] evil from his youth; and I do not continue to strike all living anymore, as I have done; **22** during all [the] days of the earth, seed-time and harvest, and cold and heat, and summer and winter, and day and night never cease."

CHAPTER 9

1 And God blesses Noah and his sons, and says to them, "Be fruitful, and multiply, and fill the earth; **2** and your fear and your dread is on every beast of the earth, and on every bird of the heavens, on all that creeps on the ground, and on all fishes of the sea—into your hand they have been given. **3** Every creeping thing that is alive, to you it is for food; as the green herb I have given to you the whole; **4** only flesh in its life—its blood—you do not eat. **5** And only your blood for your lives do I require; from the hand of every living thing I require it, and from the hand of man, from the hand of every man's brother I require the life of man; **6** whoever sheds man's blood, by man is his blood shed: for in the image of God has He made man. **7** And you, be fruitful and multiply, teem in the earth, and multiply in it." **8** And God speaks to Noah, and to his sons with him, saying, **9** "And I, behold, I am establishing My covenant with you, and with your seed after you, **10** and with every living creature which [is] with you, among bird, among livestock, and among every beast of the earth with you, from all who are going out of the Ark—to every beast of the earth. **11** And I have established My covenant with you, and all flesh is not cut off anymore by waters of a flood, and there is not a flood to destroy the earth anymore." **12** And God says, "This is a token of the covenant which I am giving between Me and you, and every living creature that [is] with you, to continuous generations; **13** My bow I have given in the cloud, and it has been for a token of a covenant between Me and the earth; **14** and it has come to pass (in My sending a cloud over the earth) that the bow has been seen in the cloud, **15** and I have remembered My covenant which is between Me and you, and every living creature among all flesh, and the waters no longer become a flood to destroy all flesh; **16** and the bow has been in the cloud, and I have seen it—to remember the perpetual covenant between God and every living creature among all flesh which [is] on the earth." **17** And God says to Noah, "This [is] a token of the covenant which I have established between Me and all flesh that [is] on the earth." **18** And the sons of Noah who are going out of the Ark are Shem, and Ham, and Japheth; and Ham is father of Canaan. **19** These three [are] sons of Noah, and from these has all the earth been overspread. **20** And Noah remains a man of the ground, and plants a vineyard, **21** and drinks of the wine, and is drunken, and uncovers himself in the midst of the tent. **22** And Ham, father of Canaan, sees the nakedness of his father, and declares to his two brothers outside. **23** And Shem takes—Japheth also—the garment, and they place on the shoulder of them both, and go backward, and cover the nakedness of their father; and their faces [are] backward, and their father's nakedness they have not seen. **24** And Noah awakens from his wine, and knows that which his young son has done to him, **25** and says: "Cursed [is] Canaan, || Servant of servants he is to his brothers." **26** And he says: "Blessed of my God Yhwh [is] Shem, || And Canaan is servant to him. **27** God gives beauty to Japheth, || And he dwells in tents of Shem, || And Canaan is servant to him." **28** And Noah lives after the flood three hundred and fifty years; **29** and all the days of Noah are nine hundred and fifty years, and he dies.

CHAPTER 10

1 And these [are] the generations of the sons of Noah, Shem, Ham, and Japheth: and sons are born to them after the flood. **2** Sons of Japheth [are] Gomer, and Magog, and Madai, and Javan, and Tubal, and Meshech, and Tiras. **3** And sons of Gomer [are] Ashkenaz, and Riphath, and Togarmah. **4** And sons of Javan [are] Elishah, and Tarshish, Kittim, and Dodanim. **5** By these the islands of the nations have been parted in their lands, each by his tongue, by their families, in their nations. **6** And sons of Ham [are] Cush, and Mitzraim, and Phut, and Canaan. **7** And sons of Cush [are] Seba, and Havilah, and Sabtah, and Raamah, and Sabtechah; and sons of Raamah [are] Sheba and Dedan. **8** And Cush has begotten Nimrod; **9** he has begun to be a hero in the land; he has been a hero in hunting before Yhwh; therefore it is said, "As Nimrod the hero [in] hunting before Yhwh." **10** And the first part of his kingdom is Babel, and Erech, and Accad, and Calneh, in the land of Shinar; **11** from that land he has gone out to Asshur, and builds Nineveh, even the broad places of the city, and Calah, **12** and Resen, between Nineveh and Calah; it [is] the great city. **13** And Mitzraim has begotten the Ludim, and the Anamim, and the Lehabim, and the Naphtuhim, **14** and the Pathrusim, and the Casluhim (from where have come out Philistim), and the Caphtorim. **15** And Canaan has begotten Sidon his firstborn, and Heth, **16** and the Jebusite, and the Amorite, and the Girgashite, **17** and the Hivite, and the Arkite, and the Sinite, **18** and the Arvadite, and the Zemarite, and the Hamathite; and afterward the families of the Canaanite have been scattered. **19** And the border of the Canaanite is from Sidon, [in] your coming toward Gerar, to

Gaza; [in] your coming toward Sodom, and Gomorrah, and Admah, and Zeboim, to Lasha. **20** These [are] sons of Ham, by their families, by their tongues, in their lands, in their nations. **21** As for Shem, father of all sons of Eber, the older brother of Japheth, he has also begotten. **22** Sons of Shem [are] Elam, and Asshur, and Arphaxad, and Lud, and Aram. **23** And sons of Aram [are] Uz, and Hul, and Gether, and Mash. **24** And Arphaxad has begotten Salah, and Salah has begotten Eber. **25** And two sons have been born to Eber; the name of the first [is] Peleg (for in his days the earth has been divided), and his brother's name [is] Joktan. **26** And Joktan has begotten Almodad, and Sheleph, and Hazarmaveth, and Jerah, **27** and Hadoram, and Uzal, and Diklah, **28** and Obal, and Abimael, and Sheba, **29** and Ophir, and Havilah, and Jobab; all these [are] sons of Joktan; **30** and their dwelling is from Mesha, [in] your coming toward Sephar, a mountain of the east. **31** These [are] sons of Shem, by their families, by their tongues, in their lands, by their nations. **32** These [are] families of the sons of Noah, by their generations, in their nations, and by these the nations have been parted in the earth after the flood.

CHAPTER 11

1 And the whole earth is of one language, and of the same words, **2** and it comes to pass, in their journeying from the east, that they find a valley in the land of Shinar and dwell there; **3** and they each say to his neighbor, "Give help, let us make bricks, and burn [them] thoroughly": and the brick is to them for stone, and the bitumen has been to them for mortar. **4** And they say, "Give help, let us build for ourselves a city and tower with its head in the heavens, and make for ourselves a name, lest we be scattered over the face of all the earth." **5** And Yhwh comes down to see the city and the tower which the sons of men have built; **6** and Yhwh says, "Behold, the people [is] one, and one language [is] to them all, and this it has dreamed of doing; and now, nothing is restrained from them of that which they have purposed to do. **7** Give help, let us go down there and confuse their language, so that a man will not understand the language of his companion." **8** And Yhwh scatters them from there over the face of all the earth, and they cease to build the city; **9** therefore [one] has called its name Babel, for there Yhwh has confused the language of all the earth, and from there Yhwh has scattered them over the face of all the earth. **10** These [are] the generations of Shem: Shem [is] a son of one hundred years, and begets Arphaxad two years after the flood. **11** And Shem lives after his begetting Arphaxad five hundred years, and begets sons and daughters. **12** And Arphaxad has lived thirty-five years [[or one hundred and thirty-five years]], and begets Salah. **13** And Arphaxad lives after his begetting Salah four hundred and three years [[or four hundred and thirty years]], and begets sons and daughters. **14** And Salah has lived thirty years [[or one hundred and thirty years]], and begets Eber. **15** And Salah lives after his begetting Eber four hundred and three years [[or three hundred and thirty years]], and begets sons and daughters. **16** And Eber lives thirty-four years [[or one hundred and thirty-four years]], and begets Peleg. **17** And Eber lives after his begetting Peleg four hundred and thirty years [[or three hundred and seventy years]], and begets sons and daughters. **18** And Peleg lives thirty years [[or one hundred and thirty years]], and begets Reu. **19** And Peleg lives after his begetting Reu two hundred and nine years, and begets sons and daughters. **20** And Reu lives thirty-two years [[or one hundred and thirty-two years]], and begets Serug. **21** And Reu lives after his begetting Serug two hundred and seven years, and begets sons and daughters. **22** And Serug lives thirty years [[or one hundred and thirty years]], and begets Nahor. **23** And Serug lives after his begetting Nahor two hundred years, and begets sons and daughters. **24** And Nahor lives twenty-nine years [[or seventy-nine years]], and begets Terah. **25** And Nahor lives after his begetting Terah one hundred and nineteen years [[or one hundred and twenty-nine years]], and begets sons and daughters. **26** And Terah lives seventy years, and begets Abram, Nahor, and Haran. **27** And these [are] the generations of Terah: Terah has begotten Abram, Nahor, and Haran; and Haran has begotten Lot; **28** and Haran dies in the presence of Terah his father, in the land of his birth, in Ur of the Chaldees. **29** And Abram and Nahor take to themselves wives; the name of Abram's wife [is] Sarai, and the name of Nahor's wife [is] Milcah, daughter of Haran, father of Milcah, and father of Iscah. **30** And Sarai is barren—she has no child.

31 And Terah takes his son Abram, and Lot, son of Haran, his son's son, and his daughter-in-law Sarai, wife of his son Abram, and they go out with them from Ur of the Chaldees, to go toward the land of Canaan; and they come to Haran, and dwell there. **32** And the days of Terah are two hundred and five years, and Terah dies in Haran.

CHAPTER 12

1 And Yhwh says to Abram, "Go for yourself, from your land, and from your family, and from the house of your father, to the land which I show you. **2** And I make you become a great nation, and bless you, and make your name great; and be a blessing. **3** And I bless those blessing you, and I curse him who is cursing you, and all families of the ground have been blessed in you." **4** And Abram goes on, as Yhwh has spoken to him, and Lot goes with him, and Abram [is] a son of seventy-five years in his going out from Haran. **5** And Abram takes his wife Sarai, and his brother's son Lot, and all their substance that they have gained, and the persons that they have obtained in Haran; and they go out to go toward the land of Canaan; and they come to the land of Canaan. **6** And Abram passes over into the land, to the place of Shechem, to the oak of Moreh; and the Canaanite [is] then in the land. **7** And Yhwh appears to Abram and says, "To your seed I give this land"; and there he builds an altar to Yhwh, who has appeared to him. **8** And he removes from there toward a mountain at the east of Beth-El, and stretches out the tent (Beth-El at the west, and Hai at the east), and he builds an altar to Yhwh there, and preaches in the Name of Yhwh. **9** And Abram journeys, going on and journeying toward the south. **10** And there is a famine in the land, and Abram goes down toward Egypt to sojourn there, for the famine [is] grievous in the land; **11** and it comes to pass as he has drawn near to enter Egypt, that he says to his wife Sarai, "Now behold, I have known that you [are] a woman of beautiful appearance; **12** and it has come to pass that the Egyptians see you, and they have said, This [is] his wife; and they have slain me, and you they keep alive. **13** please say you [are] my sister, so that it is well with me because of you, and my soul has lived for your sake." **14** And it comes to pass, at the entering of Abram into Egypt, that the Egyptians see the woman that she [is] exceedingly beautiful; **15** and princes of Pharaoh see her, and praise her to Pharaoh, and the woman is taken [to] Pharaoh's house; **16** and to Abram he has done good because of her, and he has sheep and oxen, and male donkeys, and menservants, and handmaids, and female donkeys, and camels. **17** And Yhwh plagues Pharaoh and his house—great plagues—for the matter of Sarai, Abram's wife. **18** And Pharaoh calls for Abram and says, "What [is] this you have done to me? why have you not declared to me that she [is] your wife? **19** Why have you said, she [is] my sister, and I take her to myself for a wife? and now, behold, your wife, take and go." **20** And Pharaoh charges men concerning him, and they send him away, and his wife, and all that he has.

CHAPTER 13

1 And Abram goes up from Egypt (he and his wife, and all that he has, and Lot with him) toward the south; **2** and Abram [is] exceedingly wealthy in livestock, in silver, and in gold. **3** And he goes on his journeys from the south, even to Bethel, to the place where his tent had been at the commencement, between Bethel and Hai— **4** to the place of the altar which he made there at the first, and there Abram preaches in the Name of Yhwh. **5** And also to Lot, who is going with Abram, there has been sheep and oxen and tents; **6** and the land has not permitted them to dwell together, for their substance has been much, and they have not been able to dwell together; **7** and there is a strife between those feeding Abram's livestock and those feeding Lot's livestock; and the Canaanite and the Perizzite [are] then dwelling in the land. **8** And Abram says to Lot, "Please let there not be strife between me and you, and between my shepherds and your shepherds, for we [are] men—brothers. **9** Is not all the land before you? Please be parted from me; if to the left, then I to the right; and if to the right, then I to the left." **10** And Lot lifts up his eyes, and sees the whole circuit of the Jordan that it [is] all a watered country (before Yhwh's destroying Sodom and Gomorrah, as Yhwh's garden, as the land of Egypt), in your coming toward Zoar, **11** and Lot chooses for himself the whole circuit of the Jordan; and Lot journeys from the east, and they are parted—a man from his companion; **12** Abram has dwelt in the land of Canaan, and Lot has dwelt in the cities of the circuit, and moves [his] tent to Sodom; **13** and the men of Sodom [are] evil, and sinners before Yhwh exceedingly. **14** And Yhwh said to Abram, after Lot's being parted from him, "Now lift up your eyes and look from the place where you [are], northward, and southward, and eastward, and westward; **15** for the whole of the land which you are seeing, I give it to you and to your Seed for all time. **16** And I have set your seed as dust of the earth, so that, if one is able to number the dust of the earth, even your seed is numbered; **17** rise, go up and down through the land, to its length, and to its breadth, for to you I give it." **18** And Abram moves [his] tent, and comes, and dwells among the oaks of Mamre, which [are] in Hebron, and builds there an altar to Yhwh.

CHAPTER 14

1 And it comes to pass in the days of Amraphel king of Shinar, Arioch king of Ellasar, Chedorlaomer king of Elam, and Tidal king of nations, **2** they have made war with Bera king of Sodom, and with Birsha king of Gomorrah, Shinab king of Admah, and Shemeber king of Zeboim, and the king of Bela, which [is] Zoar. **3** All these have been joined together to the Valley of Siddim, which [is] the Salt Sea; **4** [for] twelve years they served Chedorlaomer, and the thirteenth year they rebelled. **5** And in the fourteenth year came Chedorlaomer, and the kings who [are] with him, and they strike the Rephaim in Ashteroth Karnaim, and the Zuzim in Ham, and the Emim in Shaveh Kiriathaim, **6** and the Horites in their Mount Seir, to El-Paran, which [is] by the wilderness; **7** and they turn back and come to En-Mishpat, which [is] Kadesh, and strike the whole field of the Amalekite, and also the Amorite who is dwelling in Hazezon-Tamar. **8** And the king of Sodom goes out, and the king of Gomorrah, and the king of Admah, and the king of Zeboim, and the king of Bela, which [is] Zoar; and they set in array [for] battle with them in the Valley of Siddim, **9** with Chedorlaomer king of Elam, and Tidal king of nations, and Amraphel king of Shinar, and Arioch king of Ellasar; four kings with the five. **10** And the Valley of Siddim [is] full of bitumen-pits; and the kings of Sodom and Gomorrah flee, and fall there, and those left have fled to the mountain. **11** And they take the whole substance of Sodom and Gomorrah, and the whole of their food, and go away; **12** and they take Lot, Abram's brother's son (seeing he is dwelling in Sodom), and his substance, and go away. **13** And one who is escaping comes and declares to Abram the Hebrew, and he is dwelling among the oaks of Mamre the Amorite, brother of Eshcol, and brother of Aner, and they [are] Abram's allies. **14** And Abram hears that his brother has been taken captive, and he draws out his trained servants, three hundred and eighteen, and pursues to Dan. **15** And he divides himself against them by night, he and his servants, and strikes them, and pursues them to Hobah, which [is] at the left of Damascus; **16** and he brings back the whole of the substance, and he has also brought back his brother Lot and his substance, and also the women and the people. **17** And the king of Sodom goes out to meet him (after his turning back from the striking of Chedorlaomer, and of the kings who [are] with him), to the Valley of Shaveh, which [is] the king's valley. **18** And Melchizedek king of Salem has brought out bread and wine, and he [is] priest of God Most High; **19** and he blesses him and says, "Blessed [is] Abram to God Most High, possessing the heavens and earth; **20** and blessed [is] God Most High, who has delivered your adversaries into your hand"; and he gives to him a tenth of all. **21** And the king of Sodom says to Abram, "Give to me the persons, and take the substance to yourself," **22** and Abram says to the king of Sodom, "I have lifted up my hand to Yhwh, God Most High, possessing the heavens and earth— **23** from a thread even to a shoe-strap I do not take of anything which you have, that you do not say, I have made Abram rich; **24** save only that which the young men have eaten, and the portion of the men who have gone with me—Aner, Eshcol, and Mamre—they take their portion."

CHAPTER 15

1 After these things the word of Yhwh has been to Abram

in a vision, saying, "Do not fear, Abram, I [am] a shield to you, your reward [is] exceedingly great." **2** And Abram says, "Lord Yhwh, what do You give to me, and I am going childless? and an acquired son in my house is Demmesek Eliezer." **3** And Abram says, "Behold, to me You have not given seed, and behold, a servant will be my heir." **4** And behold, the word of Yhwh [is] to him, saying, "This [one] will not be your heir; but he who comes out from your bowels, he will be your heir"; **5** and He brings him out outside and says, "Now look attentively toward the heavens and count the stars, if you are able to count them"; and He says to him, "Thus is your seed." **6** And he has believed in Yhwh, and He reckons it to him—righteousness. **7** And He says to him, "I [am] Yhwh who brought you out from Ur of the Chaldees, to give to you this land to possess it"; **8** and he says, "Lord Yhwh, whereby do I know that I possess it?" **9** And He says to him, "Take for Me a heifer of three years, and a female goat of three years, and a ram of three years, and a turtle-dove, and a young bird"; **10** and he takes all these to Him, and separates them in the midst, and puts each piece opposite its fellow, but the bird he has not divided; **11** and the ravenous birds come down on the carcasses, and Abram causes them to turn back. **12** And the sun is about to go in, and deep sleep has fallen on Abram, and behold, a terror of great darkness is falling on him; **13** and He says to Abram, "knowing—know that your seed is a sojourner in a land not theirs, and they have served them, and they have afflicted them four hundred years, **14** and the nation also whom they serve I judge, and after this they go out with great substance; **15** and you come to your fathers in peace; you are buried in a good old age; **16** and the fourth generation turns back here, for the iniquity of the Amorite is not yet complete." **17** And it comes to pass—the sun has gone in, and thick darkness has been and behold, a furnace of smoke, and a lamp of fire, which has passed over between those pieces. **18** In that day has Yhwh made with Abram a covenant, saying, "To your seed I have given this land, from the River of Egypt to the great river, the Euphrates River, **19** with the Kenite, and the Kenizzite, and the Kadmonite, **20** and the Hittite, and the Perizzite, and the Rephaim, **21** and the Amorite, and the Canaanite, and the Girgashite, and the Jebusite."

CHAPTER 16

1 And Sarai, Abram's wife, has not borne to him, and she has a handmaid, an Egyptian, and her name [is] Hagar; **2** and Sarai says to Abram, "Now behold, Yhwh has restrained me from bearing, please go in to my handmaid; perhaps I am built up from her"; and Abram listens to the voice of Sarai. **3** And Sarai, Abram's wife, takes Hagar the Egyptian, her handmaid, at the end of the tenth year of Abram's dwelling in the land of Canaan, and gives her to her husband Abram—to him for a wife, **4** and he goes in to Hagar, and she conceives, and she sees that she has conceived, and her mistress is lightly esteemed in her eyes. **5** And Sarai says to Abram, "My violence [is] for you; I have given my handmaid into your bosom, and she sees that she has conceived, and I am lightly esteemed in her eyes; Yhwh judges between me and you." **6** And Abram says to Sarai, "Behold, your handmaid [is] in your hand, do to her that which is good in your eyes"; and Sarai afflicted her, and she flees from her presence. **7** And the Messenger of Yhwh finds her by the fountain of water in the wilderness, by the fountain in the way [to] Shur, **8** and He says, "Hagar, Sarai's handmaid, from where have you come, and to where do you go?" And she says, "From the presence of Sarai, my mistress, I am fleeing." **9** And the Messenger of Yhwh says to her, "Return to your mistress, and humble yourself under her hands"; **10** and the Messenger of Yhwh says to her, "Multiplying I multiply your seed, and it is not numbered from multitude"; **11** and the Messenger of Yhwh says to her, "Behold you [are] conceiving, and bearing a son, and have called his name Ishmael, for Yhwh has listened to your affliction; **12** and he is a wild-donkey man, his hand against everyone, and everyone's hand against him—and before the face of all his brothers he dwells." **13** And she calls the Name of Yhwh who is speaking to her, "You [are], O God, my beholder"; for she said, "Even here have I looked behind my beholder?" **14** therefore has one called the well, "The well of the Living One, my beholder"; behold, between Kadesh and Bered. **15** And Hagar bears a son to Abram; and Abram calls the name of his son, whom Hagar has borne, Ishmael; **16** and Abram [is] a son of eighty-six years in Hagar's bearing Ishmael to Abram.

CHAPTER 17

1 And Abram is a son of ninety-nine years, and Yhwh appears to Abram, and says to him, "I [am] God Almighty, habitually walk before Me, and be perfect; **2** and I give My covenant between Me and you, and multiply you very exceedingly." **3** And Abram falls on his face, and God speaks with him, saying, **4** "I—behold, My covenant [is] with you, and you have become father of a multitude of nations; **5** and your name is no longer called Abram, but your name has been Abraham, for father of a multitude of nations have I made you; **6** and I have made you exceedingly fruitful, and made you become nations, and kings go out from you. **7** And I have established My covenant between Me and you, and your seed after you, throughout their generations, for a perpetual covenant, to become God to you, and to your seed after you; **8** and I have given to you, and to your seed after you, the land of your sojournings, the whole land of Canaan, for a continuous possession, and I have become their God." **9** And God says to Abraham, "And you keep My covenant, you and your seed after you, throughout their generations; **10** this [is] My covenant which you keep between Me and you, and your seed after you: every male of you [is] to be circumcised; **11** and you have circumcised the flesh of your foreskin, and it has become a token of a covenant between Me and you. **12** And a son of eight days is circumcised by you; every male throughout your generations, born in the house, or bought with money from any son of a stranger, who is not of your seed; **13** he is certainly circumcised who [is] born in your house, or bought with your money; and My covenant has become in your flesh a perpetual covenant; **14** and an uncircumcised one, a male, the flesh of whose foreskin is not circumcised, indeed, that person has been cut off from his people; My covenant he has broken." **15** And God says to Abraham, "Sarai your wife—you do not call her name Sarai, for Sarah [is] her name; **16** and I have blessed her, and have also given to you a son from her; and I have blessed her, and she has become nations—kings of peoples are from her." **17** And Abraham falls on his face, and laughs, and says in his heart, "Is one born to the son of one hundred years? or does Sarah—daughter of ninety years—bear?" **18** And Abraham says to God, "O that Ishmael may live before You"; **19** and God says, "Your wife Sarah is certainly bearing a son to you, and you have called his name Isaac, and I have established My covenant with him, for a perpetual covenant, to his seed after him. **20** As for Ishmael, I have heard you; behold, I have blessed him, and made him fruitful, and multiplied him, very exceedingly; twelve princes does he beget, and I have made him become a great nation; **21** and My covenant I establish with Isaac, whom Sarah does bear to you at this appointed time in the next year"; **22** and He finishes speaking with him, and God goes up from Abraham. **23** And Abraham takes his son Ishmael, and all those born in his house, and all those bought with his money—every male among the men of Abraham's house and circumcises the flesh of their foreskin, in this very same day, as God has spoken with him. **24** And Abraham [is] a son of ninety-nine years in the flesh of his foreskin being circumcised; **25** and his son Ishmael [is] a son of thirteen years in the flesh of his foreskin being circumcised; **26** in this very same day Abraham has been circumcised, and his son Ishmael; **27** and all the men of his house—born in the house, and bought with money from the son of a stranger—have been circumcised with him.

CHAPTER 18

1 And Yhwh appears to him among the oaks of Mamre, and he is sitting at the opening of the tent, about the heat of the day; **2** and he lifts up his eyes and looks, and behold, three men standing by him, and he sees, and runs to meet them from the opening of the tent, and bows himself toward the earth, **3** and he says, "My Lord, if now I have found grace in Your eyes, please do not pass on from Your servant; **4** please let a little water be accepted, and wash Your feet, and recline under the tree; **5** and I bring a piece of bread, and support Your heart; afterward pass on, for therefore You have passed over to Your servant"; and they say, "So may you do as you have spoken." **6** And Abraham hurries toward the tent, to Sarah, and says, "Hurry three measures of flour-meal, knead, and make cakes"; **7** and Abraham ran to the herd, and takes a son of the herd, tender and good, and gives to the young man, and he hurries to prepare it; **8** and he takes butter and milk, and the son of the herd which he has prepared, and sets before them; and he is standing by them under the tree, and they eat. **9** And they say to him, "Where [is] Sarah your wife?" And he says, "Behold—in the tent"; **10** and He says, "Returning I return to you, about the time of life, and behold, to Sarah your wife a son." And Sarah is listening at the opening of the tent, which is behind him; **11** and Abraham and Sarah [are] aged, entering into days—the way of women has ceased to be to Sarah; **12** and Sarah laughs in her heart, saying, "After I have waxed old have I had pleasure? My lord [is] also old!" **13** And Yhwh says to Abraham, "Why [is] this? Sarah has laughed, saying, Is it really true—I bear—and I am aged? **14** Is anything too wonderful for Yhwh? at the appointed time I return to you, about the time of life, and Sarah has a son." **15** And Sarah denies, saying, "I did not laugh"; for she has been afraid; and He says, "No, but you did laugh." **16** And the men rise from there, and look on the face of Sodom, and Abraham is going with them to send them away; **17** and Yhwh said, "Am I concealing from Abraham that which I am doing, **18** and Abraham certainly becomes a great and mighty nation, and blessed in him have been all nations of the earth? **19** for I have known him, that he commands his children, and his house after him (and they have kept the way of Yhwh), to do righteousness and judgment, that Yhwh may bring on Abraham that which He has spoken concerning him." **20** And Yhwh says, "The cry of Sodom and Gomorrah—because great; and their sin—because exceedingly grievous: **21** I go down now, and see whether according to its cry which is coming to Me they have done completely—and if not—I know"; **22** and the men turn from there, and go toward Sodom; and Abraham is yet standing before Yhwh. **23** And Abraham draws near and says, "Do You also consume righteous with wicked? **24** perhaps there are fifty righteous in the midst of the city; do You also consume, and not bear with the place for the sake of the fifty righteous who [are] in its midst? **25** Far be it from You to do according to this thing, to put to death the righteous with the wicked; that it has been—as the righteous so the wicked—far be it from You; does the Judge of all the earth not do justice?" **26** And Yhwh says, "If I find in Sodom fifty righteous in the midst of the city, then have I borne with all the place for their sake." **27** And Abraham answers and says, "Now behold, I have willed to speak to the Lord, and I [am] dust and ashes; **28** perhaps there are lacking five of the fifty righteous—do You destroy for five the whole of the city?" And He says, "I do not destroy [it], if I find there forty-five." **29** And he adds again to speak to Him and says, "Perhaps there are found there forty?" And He says, "I do not do [it], because of the forty." **30** And he says, "Please let it not be displeasing to the Lord, and I speak: perhaps there are found there thirty?" And He says, "I do not do [it], if I find there thirty." **31** And he says, "Now behold, I have willed to speak to the Lord: perhaps there are found there twenty?" And He says, "I do not destroy [it], because of the twenty." **32** And he says, "Please let it not be displeasing to the Lord, and I speak only this time: perhaps there are found there ten?" And He says, "I do not destroy [it], because of the ten." **33** And Yhwh goes on, when He has finished speaking to Abraham, and Abraham has turned back to his place.

CHAPTER 19

1 And two of the messengers come toward Sodom at evening, and Lot is sitting at the gate of Sodom, and Lot sees, and rises to meet them, and bows himself—face to the earth, **2** and he says, "Now behold, my lords, please turn aside to the house of your servant, and lodge, and wash your feet—then you have risen early and gone on your way"; and they say, "No, but we lodge in the broad place." **3** And he presses on them greatly, and they turn aside to him, and come into his house; and he makes a banquet for them, and has baked unleavened things; and they eat. **4** Before they lie down, the men of the city—men of Sodom—have surrounded the house, from young even to aged, all the people from the extremity; **5** and they call to Lot and say to him, "Where [are] the men who have come to you tonight? bring them out to us, and we know them." **6** And Lot goes out to them, to the opening, and the door has shut behind him, **7** and says, "Please, my brothers, do not do evil; **8** now behold, I have two daughters who have not known anyone; please let me bring them out to you, and do to them as [is] good in your eyes; only do nothing to these men,

for therefore they have come in within the shadow of my roof." **9** And they say, "Come near here"; they also say, "This one has come to sojourn, and he certainly judges! Now, we do evil to you more than [to] them"; and they press against the man, against Lot greatly, and come near to break the door. **10** And the men put forth their hand, and bring in Lot to them, into the house, and have shut the door; **11** and the men who [are] at the opening of the house they have struck with blindness, from small even to great, and they weary themselves to find the opening. **12** And the men say to Lot, "Whom have you here still? son-in-law, your sons also, and your daughters, and all whom you have in the city, bring out from this place; **13** for we are destroying this place, for their cry has been great [before] the face of Yhwh, and Yhwh does send us to destroy it." **14** And Lot goes out and speaks to his sons-in-law, those taking his daughters, and says, "Rise, go out from this place, for Yhwh is destroying the city"; and he is as [one] mocking in the eyes of his sons-in-law. **15** And when the dawn has ascended, then the messengers press on Lot, saying, "Rise, take your wife, and your two daughters who are found present, lest you are consumed in the iniquity of the city." **16** And he lingers, and the men lay hold on his hand, and on the hand of his wife, and on the hand of his two daughters, through the mercy of Yhwh to him, and they bring him out, and cause him to rest outside the city. **17** And it comes to pass, when he has brought them outside, that he says, "Escape for your life; do not look behind you, nor stand in all the circuit; escape to the mountain, lest you are consumed." **18** And Lot says to them, "Oh not [so], my lord; **19** now behold, your servant has found grace in your eyes, and you make great your kindness which you have done with me by saving my life, and I am unable to escape to the mountain, lest the evil cleave [to] me and I have died; **20** now behold, this city [is] near to flee there, and it [is] little; please let me escape there (is it not little?) that my soul may live." **21** And he says to him, "Behold, I have also accepted your face for this thing, without overthrowing the city [for] which you have spoken; **22** hurry, escape there, for I am not able to do anything until your entering there"; therefore he calls the name of the city Zoar. **23** The sun has gone out on the earth, and Lot has entered into Zoar, **24** and Yhwh has rained on Sodom and on Gomorrah brimstone and fire from Yhwh, from the heavens; **25** and He overthrows these cities, and all the circuit, and all the inhabitants of the cities, and that which is shooting up from the ground. **26** And his wife looks from behind him, and she becomes a pillar of salt! **27** And Abraham rises early in the morning to the place where he has stood [before] the face of Yhwh; **28** and he looks on the face of Sodom and Gomorrah, and on all the face of the land of the circuit, and sees, and behold, the smoke of the land went up as smoke of the furnace. **29** And it comes to pass, in God's destroying the cities of the circuit, that God remembers Abraham, and sends Lot out of the midst of the overthrow in the overthrowing of the cities in which Lot dwelt. **30** And Lot goes up out of Zoar, and dwells in the mountain, and his two daughters with him, for he has been afraid of dwelling in Zoar, and he dwells in a cave, he and his two daughters. **31** And the firstborn says to the younger, "Our father [is] old, and there is not a man in the earth to come in to us, as [is] the way of all the earth; **32** come, we cause our father to drink wine, and lie with him, and preserve a seed from our father." **33** And they cause their father to drink wine on that night; and the firstborn goes in and lies with her father, and he has not known in her lying down or in her rising up. **34** And it comes to pass, on the next day, that the firstborn says to the younger, "Behold, I have lain with my father last night: we also cause him to drink wine tonight, then go in, lie with him, and we preserve a seed from our father." **35** And they cause their father to drink wine on that night also, and the younger rises and lies with him, and he has not known in her lying down or in her rising up. **36** And the two daughters of Lot conceive from their father, **37** and the firstborn bears a son and calls his name Moab: he [is] father of Moab to this day. **38** As for the younger, she has also born a son and calls his name Ben-Ammi: he [is] father of the sons of Ammon to this day.

CHAPTER 20

1 And Abraham journeys from there toward the land of the south, and dwells between Kadesh and Shur, and sojourns in Gerar; **2** and Abraham says concerning his wife Sarah, "She is my sister"; and Abimelech king of Gerar sends and takes Sarah. **3** And God comes to Abimelech in a dream of the night and says to him, "Behold, you [are] a dead man, because of the woman whom you have taken—and she married to a husband." **4** And Abimelech has not drawn near to her, and he says, "Lord, do you also slay a righteous nation? **5** Has he not himself said to me, She [is] my sister! And she, even she herself, said, He [is] my brother; in the integrity of my heart, and in the innocence of my hands, I have done this." **6** And God says to him in the dream, "Indeed, I have known that in the integrity of your heart you have done this, and I withhold you, even I, from sinning against Me, therefore I have not permitted you to come against her; **7** and now send back the man's wife, for he [is] inspired, and he prays for you, and you live; and if you do not send back, know that dying you die, you and all that you have." **8** And Abimelech rises early in the morning, and calls for all his servants, and speaks all these words in their ears; and the men fear exceedingly; **9** and Abimelech calls for Abraham and says to him, "What have you done to us? and what have I sinned against you, that you have brought on me, and on my kingdom, a great sin? works which are not done you have done with me." **10** Abimelech also says to Abraham, "What have you seen that you have done this thing?" **11** And Abraham says, "Because I said, Surely the fear of God is not in this place, and they have slain me for the sake of my wife; **12** and also, she is truly my sister, daughter of my father, only not daughter of my mother, and she becomes my wife; **13** and it comes to pass, when God has caused me to wander from my father's house, that I say to her, This [is] your kindness which you do with me: at every place to where we come, say of me, He [is] my brother." **14** And Abimelech takes sheep and oxen, and servants and handmaids, and gives to Abraham, and sends back his wife Sarah to him; **15** and Abimelech says, "Behold, my land [is] before you, where it is good in your eyes, dwell"; **16** and to Sarah he has said, "Behold, I have given one thousand pieces of silver to your brother; behold, it is to you a covering of eyes, to all who are with you"; and by all this she is reasoned with. **17** And Abraham prays to God, and God heals Abimelech and his wife, and his handmaids, and they bear: **18** for Yhwh restraining had restrained every womb of the house of Abimelech, because of Sarah, Abraham's wife.

CHAPTER 21

1 And Yhwh has looked after Sarah as He has said, and Yhwh does to Sarah as He has spoken; **2** and Sarah conceives, and bears a son to Abraham, to his old age, at the appointed time that God has spoken of with him; **3** and Abraham calls the name of his son who is born to him, whom Sarah has borne to him—Isaac; **4** and Abraham circumcises his son Isaac, [being] a son of eight days, as God has commanded him. **5** And Abraham [is] a son of one hundred years in his son Isaac being born to him, **6** and Sarah says, "God has made laughter for me; everyone who is hearing laughs for me." **7** She also says, "Who has said to Abraham, Sarah has suckled sons, that I have born a son for his old age?" **8** And the boy grows, and is weaned, and Abraham makes a great banquet in the day of Isaac's being weaned; **9** and Sarah sees the son of Hagar the Egyptian, whom she has borne to Abraham, mocking, **10** and she says to Abraham, "Cast out this handmaid and her son; for the son of this handmaid has no possession with my son—with Isaac." **11** And the thing is very wrong in the eyes of Abraham, for his son's sake; **12** and God says to Abraham, "Let it not be wrong in your eyes because of the youth, and because of your handmaid: all that Sarah says to you—listen to her voice, for in Isaac is a seed called to you. **13** As for the son of the handmaid also, for a nation I set him, because he [is] your seed." **14** And Abraham rises early in the morning, and takes bread, and a bottle of water, and gives to Hagar (placing [it] on her shoulder), also the boy, and sends her out; and she goes on, and goes astray in the wilderness of Beer-Sheba; **15** and the water is consumed from the bottle, and she places the boy under one of the shrubs. **16** And she goes and sits by herself opposite [him], far off, about a bow-shot, for she said, "Do not let me look on the death of the boy"; and she sits opposite [him], and lifts up her voice, and weeps. **17** And God hears the voice of the youth; and the messenger of God calls to Hagar from the heavens and says to her, "What to you, Hagar? Do not fear; for God has listened to the voice of the youth where he [is]; **18** rise, lift up the youth, and lay hold on him with your hand, for I set him for a great nation." **19** And God opens her eyes, and she sees a well of water, and she goes and fills the bottle [with] water, and causes the youth to drink; **20** and God

is with the youth, and he grows, and dwells in the wilderness, and is an archer; **21** and he dwells in the wilderness of Paran, and his mother takes for him a wife from the land of Egypt. **22** And it comes to pass at that time that Abimelech speaks—Phichol also, head of his host—to Abraham, saying, "God [is] with you in all that you are doing; **23** and now, swear to me by God here: you do not lie to me, or to my continuator, or to my successor; according to the kindness which I have done with you—do with me, and with the land in which you have sojourned." **24** And Abraham says, "I swear." **25** And Abraham reasoned with Abimelech concerning the matter of a well of water which Abimelech's servants have violently taken away, **26** and Abimelech says, "I have not known who has done this thing, and even you did not declare to me, and I also, I have not heard except today." **27** And Abraham takes sheep and oxen, and gives to Abimelech, and they make, both of them, a covenant; **28** and Abraham sets seven lambs of the flock by themselves. **29** And Abimelech says to Abraham, "What [are] they—these seven lambs which you have set by themselves?" **30** And he says, "For—the seven lambs you accept from my hand, so that it becomes a witness for me that I have dug this well"; **31** therefore he has called that place "Beer-Sheba," for both of them have sworn there. **32** And they make a covenant in Beer-Sheba, and Abimelech rises—Phichol also, head of his host—and they return to the land of the Philistines; **33** and [Abraham] plants a tamarisk in Beer-Sheba, and preaches there in the Name of Yhwh, the perpetual God; **34** and Abraham sojourns in the land of the Philistines many days.

CHAPTER 22

1 And it comes to pass after these things that God has tried Abraham and says to him, "Abraham"; and he says, "Here I [am]." **2** And He says, "Now take your son, your only one, whom you have loved, even Isaac, and go for yourself to the land of Moriah, and cause him to ascend there for a burnt-offering on one of the mountains of which I speak to you." **3** And Abraham rises early in the morning, and saddles his donkey, and takes two of his young men with him, and his son Isaac, and he cleaves the wood of the burnt-offering, and rises and goes to the place of which God has spoken to him. **4** On the third day—Abraham lifts up his eyes, and sees the place from afar; **5** and Abraham says to his young men, "Remain by yourselves here with the donkey, and I and the youth go over there and worship, and return to you." **6** And Abraham takes the wood of the burnt-offering, and places on his son Isaac, and he takes in his hand the fire, and the knife; and they go on both of them together. **7** And Isaac speaks to his father Abraham and says, "My father," and he says, "Here I [am], my son." And he says, "Behold, the fire and the wood, and where the lamb for a burnt-offering?" **8** and Abraham says, "God provides for Himself the lamb for a burnt-offering, my son"; and they go on both of them together. **9** And they come to the place of which God has spoken to him, and there Abraham builds the altar, and arranges the wood, and binds his son Isaac, and places him on the altar above the wood; **10** and Abraham puts forth his hand, and takes the knife—to slaughter his son. **11** And the Messenger of Yhwh calls to him from the heavens and says, "Abraham, Abraham"; and he says, "Here I [am]"; **12** and He says, "Do not put forth your hand to the youth, nor do anything to him, for now I have known that you are fearing God, and have not withheld your son, your only one, from Me." **13** And Abraham lifts up his eyes, and looks, and behold, a ram behind, seized in a thicket by its horns; and Abraham goes, and takes the ram, and causes it to ascend for a burnt-offering instead of his son; **14** and Abraham calls the name of that place "Yhwh-Jireh," because it is said this day in the mountain, "Yhwh provides." **15** And the Messenger of Yhwh calls to Abraham a second time from the heavens, **16** and says, "I have sworn by Myself—a declaration of Yhwh—that because you have done this thing, and have not withheld your son, your only one, **17** that blessing I bless you, and multiplying I multiply your seed as stars of the heavens, and as sand which [is] on the seashore; and your Seed possesses the gate of His enemies; **18** and all nations of the earth have blessed themselves in your Seed, because you have listened to My voice." **19** And Abraham turns back to his young men, and they rise and go together to Beer-Sheba; and Abraham dwells in Beer-Sheba. **20** And it comes to pass after these things that it is declared to Abraham, saying, "Behold, Milcah has borne, even she, sons to your brother Nahor: 21 his firstborn Huz, and his brother Buz; and Kemuel father of Aram, 22 and Chesed, and Hazo, and Pildash, and Jidlaph, and Bethuel; 23 and Bethuel has begotten Rebekah"; Milcah has borne these eight to Nahor, Abraham's brother; 24 and his concubine, whose name [is] Reumah, she also has borne Tebah, and Gaham, and Tahash, and Maachah.

CHAPTER 23

1 And the life of Sarah is one hundred and twenty-seven years—years of the life of Sarah; 2 and Sarah dies in Kirjath-Arba, which [is] Hebron, in the land of Canaan, and Abraham goes to mourn for Sarah, and to lament her. 3 And Abraham rises up from the presence of his dead, and speaks to the sons of Heth, saying, 4 "A sojourner and a settler I [am] with you; give to me a possession of a burying-place with you, and I bury my dead from before me." 5 And the sons of Heth answer Abraham, saying to him, 6 "Hear us, my lord; a prince of God [are] you in our midst; in the choice of our burying-places bury your dead: none of our burying-places do we withhold from you, from burying your dead." 7 And Abraham rises and bows himself to the people of the land, to the sons of Heth, 8 and he speaks with them, saying, "If it is your desire to bury my dead from before me, hear me, and meet for me with Ephron, son of Zoar; 9 and he gives to me the cave of Machpelah, which he has, which [is] in the extremity of his field; for full money does he give it to me, in your midst, for a possession of a burying-place." 10 And Ephron is sitting in the midst of the sons of Heth, and Ephron the Hittite answers Abraham in the ears of the sons of Heth, of all those entering the gate of his city, saying, 11 "No, my lord, hear me: the field I have given to you, and the cave that [is] in it, to you I have given it; before the eyes of the sons of my people I have given it to you—bury your dead." 12 And Abraham bows himself before the people of the land, 13 and speaks to Ephron in the ears of the people of the land, saying, "Only—if you would hear me—I have given the money of the field—accept from me, and I bury my dead there." 14 And Ephron answers Abraham, saying to him, 15 "My lord, hear me: the land—four hundred shekels of silver; between me and you, what [is] it? Bury your dead." 16 And Abraham listens to Ephron, and Abraham weighs to Ephron the silver which he has spoken of in the ears of the sons of Heth, four hundred silver shekels, passing with the merchant. 17 And established are the field of Ephron, which [is] in Machpelah, which [is] before Mamre, the field and the cave which [is] in it, and all the trees which [are] in the field, which [are] around all its border, 18 to Abraham by purchase, before the eyes of the sons of Heth, among all entering the gate of his city. 19 And after this Abraham has buried his wife Sarah at the cave of the field of Machpelah before Mamre (which [is] Hebron), in the land of Canaan; 20 and established are the field, and the cave which [is] in it, to Abraham for a possession of a burying-place, from the sons of Heth.

CHAPTER 24

1 And Abraham [is] old, he has entered into days, and Yhwh has blessed Abraham in all [things]; 2 and Abraham says to his servant, the eldest of his house, who is ruling over all that he has, "Please put your hand under my thigh, 3 and I cause you to swear by Yhwh, God of the heavens and God of the earth, that you do not take a wife for my son from the daughters of the Canaanite, in the midst of whom I am dwelling; 4 but to my land and to my family you go, and have taken a wife for my son, for Isaac." 5 And the servant says to him, "It may be the woman is not willing to come after me to this land; do I at all cause your son to return to the land from where you came out?" 6 And Abraham says to him, "Take heed to yourself lest you cause my son to return there; 7 Yhwh, God of the heavens, who has taken me from the house of my father, and from the land of my birth, and who has spoken to me, and who has sworn to me, saying, To your seed I give this land, He sends His messenger before you, and you have taken a wife for my son from there; 8 and if the woman is not willing to come after you, then you have been acquitted from this my oath: only you do not cause my son to return there." 9 And the servant puts his hand under the thigh of Abraham his lord, and swears to him concerning this matter. 10 And the servant takes ten camels of the camels of his lord and goes, also of all the goods

of his lord in his hand, and he rises, and goes to Aram-Naharaim, to the city of Nahor; 11 and he causes the camels to kneel at the outside of the city, at the well of water, at evening, at the time of the coming out of the women who draw water. 12 And he says, "Yhwh, God of my lord Abraham, please cause to meet before me this day—(and do kindness with my lord Abraham; 13 behold, I am standing by the fountain of water, and daughters of the men of the city are coming out to draw water; 14 and it has been, the young person to whom I say, Please incline your pitcher and I drink, and she has said, Drink, and I also water your camels)—her [whom] You have decided for Your servant, for Isaac; and by it I know that You have done kindness with my lord." 15 And it comes to pass, before he has finished speaking, that behold, Rebekah (who was born to Bethuel, son of Milcah, wife of Nahor, brother of Abraham) is coming out, and her pitcher on her shoulder, 16 and the young person [is] of very good appearance, a virgin, and a man has not known her; and she goes down to the fountain, and fills her pitcher, and comes up. 17 And the servant runs to meet her and says, "Please let me swallow a little water from your pitcher"; 18 and she says, "Drink, my lord"; and she hurries, and lets down her pitcher on her hand, and gives him drink. 19 And she finishes giving him drink and says, "Also for your camels I draw until they have finished drinking"; 20 and she hurries, and empties her pitcher into the drinking-trough, and runs again to the well to draw, and draws for all his camels. 21 And the man, wondering at her, remains silent, to know whether Yhwh has made his way prosperous or not. 22 And it comes to pass, when the camels have finished drinking, that the man takes a golden ring (whose weight [is] a bekah), and two bracelets for her hands (whose weight [is] ten [bekahs] of gold), 23 and says, "Whose daughter [are] you? Please declare to me, is the house of your father a place for us to lodge in?" 24 And she says to him, "I [am] daughter of Bethuel, son of Milcah, whom she has borne to Nahor." 25 She also says to him, "Both straw and provender [are] abundant with us, also a place to lodge in." 26 And the man bows, and pays respect to Yhwh, 27 and says, "Blessed [is] Yhwh, God of my lord Abraham, who has not left off His kindness and His truth with my lord—I [being] in the way, Yhwh has led me to the house of my lord's brothers." 28 And the young person runs, and declares to the house of her mother according to these words. 29 And Rebekah has a brother, and his name [is] Laban, and Laban runs to the man who [is] outside, to the fountain; 30 indeed, it comes to pass, when he sees the ring, and the bracelets on the hands of his sister, and when he hears the words of his sister Rebekah, saying, "Thus has the man spoken to me," that he comes to the man, and behold, he is standing by the camels by the fountain. 31 And he says, "Come in, O blessed one of Yhwh! Why do you stand outside—and I have prepared the house and place for the camels?" 32 And he brings in the man into the house, and looses the camels, and gives straw and provender for the camels, and water to wash his feet, and the feet of the men who [are] with him: 33 and sets before him to eat; but he says, "I do not eat until I have spoken my word"; and he says, "Speak." 34 And he says, "I [am] Abraham's servant; 35 and Yhwh has blessed my lord exceedingly, and he is great; and He gives to him flock, and herd, and silver, and gold, and menservants, and maidservants, and camels, and donkeys; 36 and Sarah, my lord's wife, bears a son to my lord, after she has been aged, and he gives to him all that he has. 37 And my lord causes me to swear, saying, You do not take a wife to my son from the daughters of the Canaanite, in whose land I am dwelling; 38 If not—to the house of my father you go, and to my family, and you have taken a wife for my son. 39 And I say to my lord, It may be the woman does not come after me; 40 and he says to me, Yhwh, before whom I have habitually walked, sends His messenger with you, and has prospered your way, and you have taken a wife for my son from my family, and from the house of my father; 41 then you are acquitted from my oath, when you come to my family; and if they do not give [one] to you, then you have been acquitted from my oath. 42 And I come to the fountain today, and I say, Yhwh, God of my lord Abraham, now if You are making prosperous my way in which I am going— 43 (behold, I am standing by the fountain of water), then the virgin is coming out to draw, and I have said to her, Please let me drink a little water from your pitcher, 44 and she has said to me, Both drink, and I also draw for your camels—she is the woman whom Yhwh has decided for my lord's son. 45 Before I finish speaking to my heart, then behold, Rebekah is coming out, and her pitcher [is] on her shoulder, and she goes down to the fountain and draws; and I say to her,

15

please let me drink, **46** and she hurries and lets down her pitcher from off her and says, Drink, and I also water your camels; and I drink, and she has also watered the camels. **47** And I ask her, and say, whose daughter [are] you? and she says, Daughter of Bethuel, son of Nahor, whom Milcah has borne to him, and I put the ring on her nose, and the bracelets on her hands, **48** and I bow, and pay respect before Yhwh, and I bless Yhwh, God of my lord Abraham, who has led me in the true way to receive the daughter of my lord's brother for his son. **49** And now, if you are dealing kindly and truly with my lord, declare to me; and if not, declare to me; and I turn to the right or to the left." **50** And Laban answers—Bethuel also—and they say, "The thing has gone out from Yhwh; we are not able to speak to you bad or good; **51** behold, Rebekah [is] before you, take and go, and she is a wife to your lord's son, as Yhwh has spoken." **52** And it comes to pass, when the servant of Abraham has heard their words, that he bows himself toward the earth before Yhwh; **53** and the servant takes out vessels of silver, and vessels of gold, and garments, and gives to Rebekah; precious things also he has given to her brother and to her mother. **54** And they eat and drink, he and the men who [are] with him, and lodge all night; and they rise in the morning, and he says, "Send me to my lord"; **55** and her brother says—her mother also—"Let the young person abide with us a week or ten days, afterward she goes." **56** And he says to them, "Do not delay me, seeing Yhwh has prospered my way; send me away, and I go to my lord"; **57** and they say, "Let us call for the young person, and inquire of her mouth"; **58** and they call for Rebekah, and say to her, "Do you go with this man?" And she says, "I go." **59** And they send away their sister Rebekah, and her nurse, and Abraham's servant, and his men; **60** and they bless Rebekah, and say to her, "You [are] our sister; become thousands of myriads, and your seed possesses the gate of those hating it." **61** And Rebekah and her young women arise, and ride on the camels, and go after the man; and the servant takes Rebekah and goes. **62** And Isaac has come in from the entrance of the Well of the Living One, my Beholder; and he is dwelling in the land of the south, **63** and Isaac goes out to meditate in the field, at the turning of the evening, and he lifts up his eyes, and looks, and behold, camels are coming. **64** And Rebekah lifts up her eyes, and sees Isaac, and comes down off the camel; **65** and she says to the servant, "Who [is] this man who is walking in the field to meet us?" And the servant says, "It [is] my lord"; and she takes the veil, and covers herself. **66** And the servant recounts to Isaac all the things that he has done, **67** and Isaac brings her into the tent of his mother Sarah, and he takes Rebekah, and she becomes his wife, and he loves her, and Isaac is comforted after [the death of] his mother.

CHAPTER 25

1 And Abraham adds and takes a wife, and her name [is] Keturah; **2** and she bears to him Zimran, and Jokshan, and Medan, and Midian, and Ishbak, and Shuah. **3** And Jokshan has begotten Sheba and Dedan; and the sons of Dedan were Asshurim, and Letushim, and Leummim; **4** and the sons of Midian [are] Ephah, and Epher, and Enoch, and Abidah, and Eldaah: all these [are] sons of Keturah. **5** And Abraham gives all that he has to Isaac; **6** and to the sons of the concubines whom Abraham has, Abraham has given gifts, and sends them away from his son Isaac (in his being yet alive) eastward, to the east country. **7** And these [are] the days of the years of the life of Abraham, which he lived, one hundred and seventy-five years; **8** and Abraham expires, and dies in a good old age, aged and satisfied, and is gathered to his people. **9** And his sons Isaac and Ishmael bury him at the cave of Machpelah, at the field of Ephron, son of Zoar the Hittite, which [is] before Mamre— **10** the field which Abraham bought from the sons of Heth—there Abraham has been buried, and his wife Sarah. **11** And it comes to pass after the death of Abraham, that God blesses his son Isaac; and Isaac dwells by the Well of the Living One, my Beholder. **12** And these [are] the generations of Ishmael, Abraham's son, whom Hagar the Egyptian, Sarah's handmaid, has borne to Abraham; **13** and these [are] the names of the sons of Ishmael, by their names, according to their births: firstborn of Ishmael, Nebajoth; and Kedar, and Adbeel, and Mibsam, **14** and Mishma, and Dumah, and Massa, **15** Hadar, and Tema, Jetur, Naphish, and Kedemah: **16** these are sons of Ishmael, and these [are] their names, by their villages, and by their towers; twelve princes according to their peoples. **17** And these [are] the years of the life of Ishmael, one

hundred and thirty-seven years; and he expires, and dies, and is gathered to his people; **18** and they dwell from Havilah to Shur, which [is] before Egypt, in [your] going toward Asshur; in the presence of all his brothers has he fallen. **19** And these [are] the generations of Isaac, Abraham's son: Abraham has begotten Isaac; **20** and Isaac is a son of forty years in his taking Rebekah, daughter of Bethuel the Aramean, from Padan-Aram, sister of Laban the Aramean, to him for a wife. **21** And Isaac makes plea to Yhwh before his wife, for she [is] barren: and Yhwh accepts his plea, and his wife Rebekah conceives, **22** and the children struggle together within her, and she says, "If [it is] right—why [am] I thus?" And she goes to seek Yhwh. **23** And Yhwh says to her, "Two nations [are] in your womb, and two peoples from your bowels are parted; and the [one] people is stronger than the [other] people; and the older serves the younger." **24** And her days to bear are fulfilled, and behold, twins [are] in her womb; **25** and the first comes out all red as a hairy robe, and they call his name Esau; **26** and afterward his brother has come out, and his hand is taking hold on Esau's heel, and one calls his name Jacob; and Isaac [is] a son of sixty years in her bearing them. **27** And the youths grew, and Esau is a man acquainted [with] hunting, a man of the field; and Jacob [is] a plain man, inhabiting tents; **28** and Isaac loves Esau, for [his] game [is] in his mouth; and Rebekah is loving Jacob. **29** And Jacob boils stew, and Esau comes in from the field, and he [is] weary; **30** and Esau says to Jacob, "Please let me eat some of this red-red thing, for I [am] weary"; therefore [one] has called his name Edom; **31** and Jacob says, "Sell your birthright to me today." **32** And Esau says, "Behold, I am going to die, and what is this to me—a birthright?" **33** and Jacob says, "Swear to me today": and he swears to him, and sells his birthright to Jacob; **34** and Jacob has given bread and stew of lentils to Esau, and he eats, and drinks, and rises, and goes; and Esau despises the birthright.

CHAPTER 26

1 And there is a famine in the land, besides the first famine which was in the days of Abraham, and Isaac goes to Abimelech king of the Philistines, to Gerar. **2** And Yhwh appears to him and says, "Do not go down toward Egypt, dwell in the land concerning which I speak to you, **3** sojourn in this land, and I am with you, and bless you, for to you and to your seed I give all these lands, and I have established the oath which I have sworn to your father Abraham; **4** and I have multiplied your seed as stars of the heavens, and I have given to your seed all these lands; and all nations of the earth have blessed themselves in your Seed; **5** because that Abraham has listened to My voice, and keeps My charge, My commands, My statutes, and My laws." **6** And Isaac dwells in Gerar; **7** and men of the place ask him of his wife, and he says, "She [is] my sister": for he has been afraid to say, "My wife—lest the men of the place kill me for Rebekah, for she [is] of good appearance." **8** And it comes to pass, when the days have been prolonged to him there, that Abimelech king of the Philistines looks through the window, and sees, and behold, Isaac is playing with his wife Rebekah. **9** And Abimelech calls for Isaac and says, "Behold, she [is] surely your wife; and how could you have said, She [is] my sister?" And Isaac says to him, "Because I said, Lest I die for her." **10** And Abimelech says, "What [is] this you have done to us? as a little thing one of the people had lain with your wife, and you had brought on us guilt"; **11** and Abimelech commands all the people, saying, "He who comes against this man or against his wife, dying does die." **12** And Isaac sows in that land, and finds in that year a hundredfold, and Yhwh blesses him; **13** and the man is great, and goes on, going on and becoming great, until he has been very great, **14** and he has possession of a flock, and possession of a herd, and an abundant service; and the Philistines envy him, **15** and all the wells which his father's servants dug in the days of his father Abraham, the Philistines have stopped them, and fill them with dust. **16** And Abimelech says to Isaac, "Go from us; for you have become much mightier than we"; **17** and Isaac goes from there, and encamps in the Valley of Gerar, and dwells there; **18** and Isaac turns back, and digs the wells of water which they dug in the days of his father Abraham, which the Philistines have stopped after the death of Abraham, and he calls to them names according to the names which his father called them. **19** And Isaac's servants dig in the valley, and find there a well of living water, **20** and shepherds of Gerar strive with shepherds of Isaac, saying, "The water [is] ours"; and he calls the name of the well "Strife," because they have striven habitually with him; 21 and they dig another well, and they strive also for it, and he calls its name "Hatred." 22 And he removes from there, and digs another well, and they have not striven for it, and he calls its name "Enlargements," and says, "For—now has Yhwh given enlargement to us, and we have been fruitful in the land." 23 And he goes up from there [to] Beer-Sheba, 24 and Yhwh appears to him during that night and says, "I [am] the God of your father Abraham, do not fear, for I [am] with you, and have blessed you, and have multiplied your seed, because of My servant Abraham"; 25 and he builds there an altar, and preaches in the Name of Yhwh, and stretches out there his tent, and there Isaac's servants dig a well. 26 And Abimelech has gone to him from Gerar, and Ahuzzath his friend, and Phichol head of his host; 27 and Isaac says to them, "Why have you come to me, and you have hated me, and you send me away from you?" 28 And they say, "We have certainly seen that Yhwh has been with you, and we say, Now let there be an oath between us, between us and you, and let us make a covenant with you; 29 do no evil with us, as we have not touched you, and as we have only done good with you, and send you away in peace; you [are] now blessed of Yhwh." 30 And he makes a banquet for them, and they eat and drink, 31 and rise early in the morning, and swear to one another, and Isaac sends them away, and they go from him in peace. 32 And it comes to pass during that day that Isaac's servants come and declare to him concerning the circumstances of the well which they have dug, and say to him, "We have found water"; 33 and he calls it Shebah, [oath,] therefore the name of the city [is] Beer-Sheba, [Well of the Oath,] to this day. 34 And Esau is a son of forty years, and he takes a wife, Judith, daughter of Beeri the Hittite, and Bashemath, daughter of Elon the Hittite, 35 and they are a bitterness of spirit to Isaac and to Rebekah

CHAPTER 27

1 And it comes to pass that Isaac [is] aged, and his eyes are too dim for seeing, and he calls [for] his older son Esau and says to him, "My son"; and he says to him, "Here I [am]." 2 And he says, "Now behold, I have become aged, I have not known the day of my death; 3 and now, please take up your instruments, your quiver, and your bow, and go out to the field, and hunt provision for me, 4 and make tasteful things for me, [such] as I have loved, and bring [them] to me, and I eat, so that my soul blesses you before I die." 5 And Rebekah is listening while Isaac is speaking to his son Esau; and Esau goes to the field to hunt game—to bring in; 6 and Rebekah has spoken to her son Jacob, saying, "Behold, I have heard your father speaking to your brother Esau, saying, 7 Bring game for me, and make tasteful things for me, and I eat, and bless you before Yhwh before my death. 8 And now, my son, listen to my voice, to that which I am commanding you: 9 Now go to the flock, and take for me two good kids of the goats from there, and I make them tasteful things for your father, [such] as he has loved; 10 and you have taken [them] to your father, and he has eaten, so that his soul blesses you before his death." 11 And Jacob says to his mother Rebekah, "Behold, my brother Esau [is] a hairy man, and I [am] a smooth man, 12 it may be my father feels me, and I have been in his eyes as a deceiver, and have brought on me disapproval, and not a blessing"; 13 and his mother says to him, "On me your disapproval, my son; only listen to my voice, and go, take for me." 14 And he goes, and takes, and brings to his mother, and his mother makes tasteful things, [such] as his father has loved; 15 and Rebekah takes the desirable garments of Esau her older son, which [are] with her in the house, and puts them on Jacob her younger son; 16 and she has put the skins of the kids of the goats on his hands, and on the smooth of his neck, 17 and she gives the tasteful things, and the bread which she has made, into the hand of her son Jacob. 18 And he comes to his father and says, "My father"; and he says, "Here I [am]; who [are] you, my son?" 19 And Jacob says to his father, "I [am] Esau your firstborn; I have done as you have spoken to me; please rise, sit and eat of my game, so that your soul blesses me." 20 And Isaac says to his son, "What [is] this you have hurried to find, my son?" And he says, "That which your God Yhwh has caused to come before me." 21 And Isaac says to Jacob, "Please come near, and I feel you, my son, whether you [are] he, my son Esau, or not." 22 And Jacob comes near to his father Isaac, and

he feels him, and says, "The voice [is] the voice of Jacob, and the hands hands of Esau." 23 And he has not discerned him, for his hands have been hairy, as the hands of his brother Esau, and he blesses him, 24 and says, "You are he—my son Esau?" And he says, "I [am]." 25 And he says, "Bring [it] near to me, and I eat of my son's game, so that my soul blesses you"; and he brings [it] near to him, and he eats; and he brings wine to him, and he drinks. 26 And his father Isaac says to him, "Please come near and kiss me, my son"; 27 and he comes near, and kisses him, and he smells the fragrance of his garments, and blesses him, and says, "See, the fragrance of my son [is] as the fragrance of a field which Yhwh has blessed; 28 and God gives to you of the dew of the heavens, and of the fatness of the earth, and abundance of grain and wine; 29 peoples serve you, and nations bow themselves to you, be mighty over your brothers, and the sons of your mother bow themselves to you; those who curse you [are] cursed, and those who bless you [are] blessed." 30 And it comes to pass, as Isaac has finished blessing Jacob, and Jacob is only just going out from the presence of his father Isaac, that his brother Esau has come in from his hunting; 31 and he also makes tasteful things, and brings to his father, and says to his father, "Let my father arise, and eat of his son's game, so that your soul blesses me." 32 And his father Isaac says to him, "Who [are] you?" And he says, "I [am] your son, your firstborn, Esau"; 33 and Isaac trembles a very great trembling and says, "Who, now, [is] he who has provided game, and brings to me, and I eat of all before you come in, and I bless him? Indeed, he is blessed." 34 When Esau hears the words of his father, then he cries a very great and bitter cry, and says to his father, "Bless me, me also, O my father"; 35 and he says, "Your brother has come with subtlety, and takes your blessing." 36 And he says, "Is it because he whose name is called Jacob takes me by the heel these two times? He has taken my birthright; and behold, now he has taken my blessing"; he also says, "Have you not kept back a blessing for me?" 37 And Isaac answers and says to Esau, "Behold, a mighty one have I set him over you, and all his brothers have I given to him for servants, and [with] grain and wine have I sustained him; and for you now, what will I do, my son?" 38 And Esau says to his father, "One blessing have you my father? bless me, me also, O my father"; and Esau lifts up his voice, and weeps. 39 And his father Isaac answers and says to him, "Behold, of the fatness of the earth is your dwelling, and of the dew of the heavens from above; 40 and by your sword you live, and your brother serves you; and it has come to pass, when you rule, that you have broken his yoke from off your neck." 41 And Esau hates Jacob, because of the blessing with which his father blessed him, and Esau says in his heart, "The days of mourning [for] my father draw near, and I slay my brother Jacob." 42 And the words of Esau her older son are declared to Rebekah, and she sends and calls for Jacob her younger son, and says to him, "Behold, your brother Esau is comforting himself in regard to you—to slay you; 43 and now, my son, listen to my voice, and rise, flee for yourself to my brother Laban, to Haran, 44 and you have dwelt with him some days, until your brother's fury turns back, 45 until your brother's anger turns back from you, and he has forgotten that which you have done to him, and I have sent and taken you from there; why am I bereaved even of you both the same day?" 46 And Rebekah says to Isaac, "I have been disgusted with my life because of the presence of the daughters of Heth; if Jacob takes a wife of the daughters of Heth, like these—from the daughters of the land—why do I live?"

CHAPTER 28

1 And Isaac calls to Jacob, and blesses him, and commands him, and says to him, "You must not take a wife of the daughters of Canaan; 2 rise, go to Padan-Aram, to the house of your mother's father Bethuel, and take for yourself a wife from there, from the daughters of your mother's brother Laban; 3 and God Almighty bless you, and make you fruitful, and multiply you, and you have become an assembly of peoples; 4 and He gives to you the blessing of Abraham, to you and to your seed with you, to cause you to possess the land of your sojournings, which God gave to Abraham." 5 And Isaac sends Jacob away, and he goes to Padan-Aram, to Laban, son of Bethuel the Aramean, brother of Rebekah, mother of Jacob and Esau. 6 And Esau sees that Isaac has blessed Jacob, and has sent him to Padan-Aram to take to himself from there a wife—in his blessing him that he lays a charge on him, saying,

You must not take a wife from the daughters of Canaan— **7** that Jacob listens to his father and to his mother, and goes to Padan-Aram— **8** and Esau sees that the daughters of Canaan are evil in the eyes of his father Isaac, **9** and Esau goes to Ishmael, and takes Mahalath, daughter of Ishmael, Abraham's son, sister of Nebajoth, to his wives, to himself, for a wife. **10** And Jacob goes out from Beer-Sheba, and goes toward Haran, **11** and he touches at a [certain] place, and lodges there, for the sun has gone in, and he takes of the stones of the place, and makes [them] his pillows, and lies down in that place. **12** And he dreams, and behold, a ladder set up on the earth, and its head is touching the heavens; and behold, messengers of God are going up and coming down by it; **13** and behold, Yhwh is standing on it, and He says, "I [am] Yhwh, God of your father Abraham, and God of Isaac; the land on which you are lying, to you I give it, and to your seed; **14** and your seed has been as the dust of the land, and you have broken forth westward, and eastward, and northward, and southward, and all families of the ground have been blessed in you and in your seed. **15** And behold, I [am] with you, and have kept you wherever you go, and have caused you to return to this ground; for I do not leave you until I have surely done that which I have spoken to you." **16** And Jacob awakens out of his sleep and says, "Surely Yhwh is in this place, and I did not know"; **17** and he fears and says, "How fearful [is] this place; this is nothing but a house of God, and this a gate of the heavens." **18** And Jacob rises early in the morning, and takes the stone which he has made his pillows, and makes it a standing pillar, and pours oil on its top, **19** and he calls the name of that place Bethel, [house of God,] and yet, Luz [is] the name of the city at the first. **20** And Jacob vows a vow, saying, "Seeing God is with me, and has kept me in this way which I am going, and has given to me bread to eat, and a garment to put on— **21** when I have turned back in peace to the house of my father, and Yhwh has become my God, **22** then this stone which I have made a standing pillar is a house of God, and all that You give to me—tithing I tithe to You."

better for me to give her to you than to give her to another man; dwell with me"; **20** and Jacob serves for Rachel seven years; and they are in his eyes as some days, because of his loving her. **21** And Jacob says to Laban, "Give up my wife, for my days have been fulfilled, and I go in to her"; **22** and Laban gathers all the men of the place, and makes a banquet. **23** And it comes to pass in the evening, that he takes his daughter Leah, and brings her to him, and he goes in to her; **24** and Laban gives his maidservant Zilpah to her, to his daughter Leah, [for] a maidservant. **25** And it comes to pass in the morning, that behold, it [is] Leah; and he says to Laban, "What [is] this you have done to me? Have I not served with you for Rachel? and why have you deceived me?" **26** And Laban says, "It is not done so in our place, to give the younger before the firstborn; **27** fulfill the period of seven [for] this one, and we also give to you this one, for the service which you serve with me yet seven other years." **28** And Jacob does so, and fulfills the period of seven [for] this one, and he gives his daughter Rachel to him for a wife for him; **29** and Laban gives his maidservant Bilhah to his daughter Rachel for a maidservant for her. **30** And he also goes in to Rachel, and he also loves Rachel more than Leah; and he serves with him yet seven other years. **31** And Yhwh sees that Leah [is] the hated one, and He opens her womb, and Rachel [is] barren; **32** and Leah conceives, and bears a son, and calls his name Reuben, for she said, "Because Yhwh has looked on my affliction; because now does my husband love me." **33** And she conceives again, and bears a son, and says, "Because Yhwh has heard that I [am] the hated one, He also gives to me even this [one]"; and she calls his name Simeon. **34** And she conceives again and bears a son, and says, "Now [is] the time, my husband is joined to me, because I have born to him three sons," therefore has [one] called his name Levi. **35** And she conceives again and bears a son, and this time says, "I praise Yhwh"; therefore, has she called his name Judah; and she ceases from bearing.

CHAPTER 29

1 And Jacob lifts up his feet, and goes toward the land of the sons of the east; **2** and he looks, and behold, a well in the field, and behold, there [are] three droves of a flock crouching by it, for they water the droves from that well, and the great stone [is] on the mouth of the well. **3** (When all the droves have been gathered there, and they have rolled the stone from off the mouth of the well, and have watered the flock, then they have turned back the stone on the mouth of the well to its place.) **4** And Jacob says to them, "My brothers, where [are] you from?" And they say, "We [are] from Haran." **5** And he says to them, "Have you known Laban, son of Nahor?" And they say, "We have known." **6** And he says to them, "Does he have peace?" And they say, "Peace; and behold, his daughter Rachel is coming with the flock." **7** And he says, "Behold, the day [is] still great, [it is] not time for the livestock to be gathered; water the flock, and go, delight yourselves." **8** And they say, "We are not able, until all the droves be gathered together, and they have rolled away the stone from the mouth of the well, and we have watered the flock." **9** He is yet speaking with them, and Rachel has come with the flock which her father has, for she [is] shepherdess; **10** and it comes to pass, when Jacob has seen Rachel, daughter of his mother's brother Laban, and the flock of his mother's brother Laban, that Jacob comes near and rolls the stone from off the mouth of the well, and waters the flock of his mother's brother Laban. **11** And Jacob kisses Rachel, and lifts up his voice, and weeps, **12** and Jacob declares to Rachel that he [is] her father's brother, and that he [is] Rebekah's son, and she runs and declares [it] to her father. **13** And it comes to pass, when Laban hears the report of his sister's son Jacob, that he runs to meet him, and embraces him, and kisses him, and brings him into his house; and he recounts to Laban all these things, **14** and Laban says to him, "You [are] surely my bone and my flesh"; and he dwells with him a month of days. **15** And Laban says to Jacob, "Is it because you [are] my brother that you have served me for nothing? declare to me what your hire [is]." **16** And Laban has two daughters, the name of the older [is] Leah, and the name of the younger Rachel, **17** and the eyes of Leah [are] tender, and Rachel has been beautiful of form and beautiful of appearance. **18** And Jacob loves Rachel and says, "I serve you seven years for Rachel your younger daughter": **19** and Laban says, "It is

CHAPTER 30

1 And Rachel sees that she has not borne to Jacob, and Rachel is envious of her sister, and says to Jacob, "Give me sons, and if there is none—I die." **2** And Jacob's anger burns against Rachel, and he says, "Am I instead of God who has withheld from you the fruit of the womb?" **3** And she says, "Behold, my handmaid Bilhah, go in to her, and she bears on my knees, and I am built up, even I, from her"; **4** and she gives Bilhah her maidservant to him for a wife, and Jacob goes in to her; **5** and Bilhah conceives, and bears a son to Jacob, **6** and Rachel says, "God has decided for me, and has also listened to my voice, and gives a son to me"; therefore she has called his name Dan. **7** And Bilhah, Rachel's maidservant, conceives again, and bears a second son to Jacob, **8** and Rachel says, "With wrestlings of God I have wrestled with my sister, indeed, I have prevailed"; and she calls his name Napthali. **9** And Leah sees that she has ceased from bearing, and she takes Zilpah her maidservant, and gives her to Jacob for a wife; **10** and Zilpah, Leah's maidservant, bears a son to Jacob, **11** and Leah says, "A troop is coming"; and she calls his name Gad. **12** And Zilpah, Leah's maidservant, bears a second son to Jacob, **13** and Leah says, "Because of my happiness, for daughters have pronounced me blessed"; and she calls his name Asher. **14** And Reuben goes in the days of wheat-harvest, and finds love-apples in the field, and brings them to his mother Leah, and Rachel says to Leah, "Please give to me of the love-apples of your son." **15** And she says to her, "Is your taking my husband a little thing, that you have also taken the love-apples of my son?" And Rachel says, "He therefore lies with you tonight, for your son's love-apples." **16** And Jacob comes in from the field at evening; and Leah goes to meet him and says, "You come in to me, for [in] hiring I have hired you with my son's love-apples"; and he lies with her during that night. **17** And God listens to Leah, and she conceives, and bears a son to Jacob, a fifth, **18** and Leah says, "God has given my hire, because I have given my maidservant to my husband"; and she calls his name Issachar. **19** And Leah conceives again, and she bears a sixth son to Jacob, **20** and Leah says, "God has endowed me—a good dowry; this time my husband dwells with me, for I have borne six sons to him"; and she calls his name Zebulun; **21** and afterward she has borne a daughter, and calls her name Dinah. **22** And God remembers Rachel, and God listens to her, and opens her womb, **23** and she conceives and bears a son, and says, "God has gathered up my reproach"; **24** and she calls his name Joseph, saying, "Yhwh is adding to me another son." **25** And it comes to pass, when Rachel has borne Joseph, that Jacob says to Laban, "Send me away, and I go to my place, and to my land; **26** give up my wives and my children, for whom I have served you, and I go; for you have known my service which I have served you." **27** And Laban says to him, "Now if I have found grace in your eyes—I have observed diligently that Yhwh blesses me for your sake." **28** He also says, "Define your hire to me, and I give." **29** And he says to him, "You have known that which I have served you [in], and that which your substance was with me; **30** for [it is] little which you have had at my appearance, and it breaks forth into a multitude, and Yhwh blesses you at my coming; and now, when do I make, I also, for my own house?" **31** And he says, "What do I give to you?" And Jacob says, "You do not give me anything; if you do this thing for me, I turn back; I have delight; I watch your flock; **32** I pass through all your flock today to turn aside every speckled and spotted sheep from there, and every brown sheep among the lambs, and speckled and spotted among the goats—and it has been my hire; **33** and my righteousness has answered for me in the day to come, when it comes in for my hire before your face—everyone which is not speckled and spotted among [my] goats, and brown among [my] lambs—it is stolen with me." **34** And Laban says, "Behold, O that it were according to your word"; **35** and he turns aside during that day the striped and the spotted male goats, and all the speckled and the spotted female goats, everyone that [has] white in it, and every brown one among the lambs, and he gives into the hand of his sons, **36** and sets a journey of three days between himself and Jacob; and Jacob is feeding the rest of the flock of Laban. **37** And Jacob takes to himself a rod of fresh poplar and almond and plane-tree, and peels in them white peelings, making bare the white that [is] on the rods, **38** and sets up the rods which he has peeled in the gutters in the watering troughs (where the flock comes to drink), in front of the flock, that they may conceive in their coming to drink; **39** and the flocks conceive at the rods, and the flock bears striped, speckled, and spotted ones. **40** And Jacob has parted the lambs, and he puts the face of the flock toward the striped, also all the brown in the flock of Laban, and he sets his own droves by themselves, and has not set them near Laban's flock. **41** And it has come to pass, whenever the strong ones of the flock conceive, that Jacob sets the rods before the eyes of the flock in the gutters, to cause them to conceive by the rods, **42** and when the flock is feeble, he does not set [them]; and the feeble ones have been Laban's, and the strong ones Jacob's. **43** And the man increases very exceedingly, and has many flocks, and maidservants, and menservants, and camels, and donkeys.

CHAPTER 31

1 And he hears the words of Laban's sons, saying, "Jacob has taken all that our father has; indeed, from that which our father has, he has made all this glory"; **2** and Jacob sees the face of Laban, and behold, it is not with him as before. **3** And Yhwh says to Jacob, "Return to the land of your fathers, and to your family, and I am with you." **4** And Jacob sends and calls for Rachel and for Leah to the field to his flock; **5** and says to them, "I am beholding your father's face—that it is not toward me as before, and the God of my father has been with me, **6** and you have known that with all my power I have served your father, **7** and your father has played on me, and has changed my hire ten times; and God has not permitted him to do evil with me. **8** If he says thus: The speckled are your hire, then all the flock bore speckled ones; and if he says thus: The striped are your hire, then all the flock bore striped; **9** and God takes away the substance of your father, and gives to me. **10** And it comes to pass at the time of the flock conceiving, that I lift up my eyes and see in a dream, and behold, the male goats, which are going up on the flock, [are] striped, speckled, and spotted; **11** and the Messenger of God says to me in the dream, Jacob, and I say, Here I [am]. **12** And He says, Now lift up your eyes and see [that] all the male goats which are going up on the flock [are] striped, speckled, and spotted, for I have seen all that Laban is doing to you; **13** I [am] the God of Bethel where you have anointed a standing pillar, where you have vowed a vow to me; now, arise, go out from this land, and return to the land of your birth." **14** And Rachel answers—Leah also—and says to him, "Have we yet a portion and inheritance in the house of our father? **15** have we not been reckoned strangers to him? for he has sold us, and he also utterly consumes our money; **16** for all the wealth which God has taken away from our father, it [is] ours, and our children's; and now, all that God has said to you—do." **17** And Jacob rises, and lifts up his sons and his wives on the camels, **18** and leads all his livestock, and all his substance which he has acquired, the livestock of his getting, which he has acquired in Padan-Aram, to go to his father Isaac, to the land of Canaan. **19** And Laban has gone to shear his flock, and Rachel steals the teraphim which her father has; **20** and Jacob deceives the heart of Laban the Aramean, because he has not declared to him that he is fleeing; **21** and he flees, he and all that he has, and rises, and passes over the River, and sets his face [toward] the Mount of Gilead. **22** And it is told to Laban on the third day that Jacob has fled, **23** and he takes his brothers with him, and pursues after him a journey of seven days, and overtakes him in the Mount of Gilead. **24** And God comes to Laban the Aramean in a dream of the night and says to him, "Take heed to yourself lest you speak with Jacob from good to evil." **25** And Laban overtakes Jacob; and Jacob has fixed his tent in the mountain; and Laban with his brothers have fixed [theirs] in the Mount of Gilead. **26** And Laban says to Jacob, "What have you done that you deceive my heart, and lead away my daughters as captives of the sword? **27** Why have you hidden yourself to flee, and deceive me, and have not declared to me, and I send you away with joy and with songs, with tambourine and with harp, **28** and have not permitted me to kiss my sons and my daughters? Now you have acted foolishly in doing [so]; **29** my hand is to God to do evil with you, but the God of your father last night has spoken to me, saying, Take heed to yourself from speaking with Jacob from good to evil. **30** And now, you have certainly gone, because you have been very desirous for the house of your father; why have you stolen my gods?" **31** And Jacob answers and says to Laban, "Because I was afraid, for I said, Lest you violently take away your daughters from me; **32** with whomsoever you find your gods—he must not live; before our brothers discern for yourself what [is] with me, and take to yourself": and Jacob has not known that Rachel has stolen them. **33** And Laban goes into the tent of Jacob, and into the tent of Leah, and into the tent of the two handmaidens, and has not found; and he goes out from the tent of Leah, and goes into the tent of Rachel. **34** And Rachel has taken the teraphim, and puts them in the furniture of the camel, and sits on them; and Laban feels all the tent, and has not found; **35** and she says to her father, "Let it not be displeasing in the eyes of my lord that I am not able to rise at your presence, for the way of women [is] on me"; and he searches, and has not found the teraphim. **36** And it is displeasing to Jacob, and he strives with Laban; and Jacob answers and says to Laban, "What [is] my transgression? what my sin, that you have burned after me? **37** for you have felt all my vessels: what have you found of all the vessels of your house? set here before my brothers, and your brothers, and they decide between us both. **38** These twenty years I [am] with you: your ewes and your female goats have not miscarried, and the rams of your flock I have not eaten; **39** the torn I have not brought to you—I repay it—from my hand you seek it; I have been deceived by day, and I have been deceived by night; **40** I have been [thus]: drought has consumed me in the day, and frost by night, and my sleep wanders from my eyes. **41** This [is] to me twenty years in your house: I have served you fourteen years for your two daughters, and six years for your flock; and you change my hire ten times; **42** unless the God of my father, the God of Abraham, and the Fear of Isaac, had been for me, surely now you had sent me away empty; God has seen my affliction and the labor of my hands, and reproves last night." **43** And Laban answers and says to Jacob, "The daughters [are] my daughters, and the sons my sons, and the flock my flock, and all that you are seeing [is] mine; and to my daughters—what do I to these today, or to their sons whom they have born? **44** and now, come, let us make a covenant, I and you, and it has been for a witness between me and you." **45** And Jacob takes a stone, and lifts it up [for] a standing pillar; **46** and Jacob says to his brothers, "Gather stones," and they take stones, and make a heap; and they eat there on the heap; **47** and Laban calls it Jegar-Sahadutha; and Jacob has called it Galeed. **48** And Laban says, "This heap [is] witness between me and you today"; therefore has he called its name Galeed; **49** Mizpah also, for he said, "Yhwh watches between me and you, for we are hidden from one another; **50** if you afflict my daughters, or take wives beside my daughters—there is no man with us—

see, God [is] witness between me and you." ⁵¹ And Laban says to Jacob, "Behold, this heap, and behold, the standing pillar which I have cast between me and you; ⁵² this heap [is] witness, and the standing pillar [is] witness, that I do not pass over this heap to you, and that you do not pass over this heap and this standing pillar to me—for evil; ⁵³ the God of Abraham and the God of Nahor, judges between us—the God of their father," and Jacob swears by the Fear of his father Isaac. ⁵⁴ And Jacob sacrifices a sacrifice on the mountain, and calls to his brothers to eat bread, and they eat bread, and lodge on the mountain; ⁵⁵ and Laban rises early in the morning, and kisses his sons and his daughters, and blesses them; and Laban goes on, and turns back to his place.

CHAPTER 32

¹ And Jacob has gone on his way, and messengers of God come on him; ² and Jacob says, when he has seen them, "This [is] the camp of God"; and he calls the name of that place "Two Camps." ³ And Jacob sends messengers before him to his brother Esau, toward the land of Seir, the field of Edom, ⁴ and commands them, saying, "Thus you say to my lord, to Esau, Thus said your servant Jacob: I have sojourned with Laban, and I linger until now; ⁵ and I have ox, and donkey, flock, and manservant, and maidservant, and I send to declare to my lord, to find grace in his eyes." ⁶ And the messengers return to Jacob, saying, "We came to your brother, to Esau, and he is also coming to meet you, and four hundred men with him"; ⁷ and Jacob fears exceedingly, and is distressed, and he divides the people who [are] with him, and the flock, and the herd, and the camels, into two camps, ⁸ and says, "If Esau comes to one camp, and has struck it—then the camp which is left has been for an escape." ⁹ And Jacob says, "God of my father Abraham and God of my father Isaac, Yhwh who says to me, Return to your land and to your family, and I do good with you: ¹⁰ I have been unworthy of all the kind acts and of all the truth which You have done with your servant—for with my staff I passed over this Jordan, and now I have become two camps. ¹¹ Please deliver me from the hand of my brother, from the hand of Esau: for I am fearing him, lest he come and has struck me—mother beside sons; ¹² and You have said, I certainly do good with you, and have set your seed as the sand of the sea, which is not numbered because of the multitude." ¹³ And he lodges there during that night, and takes from that which is coming into his hand, a present for his brother Esau: ¹⁴ female goats two hundred, and male goats twenty, ewes two hundred, and rams twenty, ¹⁵ suckling camels and their young ones thirty, cows forty, and bullocks ten, female donkeys twenty, and foals ten; ¹⁶ and he gives into the hand of his servants every drove by itself, and says to his servants, "Pass over before me, and a space you put between drove and drove." ¹⁷ And he commands the first, saying, "When my brother Esau meets you, and has asked you, saying, Whose [are] you? and to where do you go? and whose [are] these before you? ¹⁸ then you have said, Your servant Jacob's: it [is] a present sent to my lord, to Esau; and behold, he also [is] behind us." ¹⁹ And he commands also the second, also the third, also all who are going after the droves, saying, "According to this manner do you speak to Esau in your finding him, ²⁰ and you have also said, Behold, your servant Jacob [is] behind us"; for he said, "I pacify his face with the present which is going before me, and afterward I see his face; it may be he lifts up my face"; ²¹ and the present passes over before his face, and he has lodged during that night in the camp. ²² And he rises in that night, and takes his two wives, and his two maidservants, and his eleven children, and passes over the passage of Jabbok; ²³ and he takes them, and causes them to pass over the brook, and he causes that which he has to pass over. ²⁴ And Jacob is left alone, and One wrestles with him until the ascending of the dawn; ²⁵ and He sees that He is not able for him, and He comes against the hollow of his thigh, and the hollow of Jacob's thigh is disjointed in his wrestling with Him; ²⁶ and He says, "Send Me away, for the dawn has ascended": and he says, "I do not send You away, except You have blessed me." ²⁷ And He says to him, "What [is] your name?" And he says, "Jacob." ²⁸ And He says, "Your name is no longer called Jacob, but Israel; for you have reigned with God and with men, and prevail." ²⁹ And Jacob asks and says, "Please declare Your Name"; and He says, "Why [is] this, you ask for My Name?" And He blesses him there. ³⁰ And Jacob calls the name of the place Peniel: "For I have seen God face to face, and my life is delivered"; ³¹ and

the sun rises on him when he has passed over Penuel, and he is halting on his thigh; ³² therefore the sons of Israel do not eat the sinew which shrank, which [is] on the hollow of the thigh, to this day, because He came against the hollow of Jacob's thigh, against the sinew which shrank.

CHAPTER 33

¹ And Jacob lifts up his eyes, and looks, and behold, Esau is coming, and with him four hundred men; and he divides the children to Leah, and to Rachel, and to the two maidservants; ² and he sets the maidservants and their children first, and Leah and her children behind, and Rachel and Joseph last. ³ And he himself passed over before them, and bows himself to the earth seven times, until his drawing near to his brother, ⁴ and Esau runs to meet him, and embraces him, and falls on his neck, and kisses him, and they weep; ⁵ and he lifts up his eyes, and sees the women and the children, and says, "What [are] these to you?" And he says, "The children with whom God has favored your servant." ⁶ And the maidservants draw near, they and their children, and bow themselves; ⁷ and Leah also draws near, and her children, and they bow themselves; and afterward Joseph has drawn near with Rachel, and they bow themselves. ⁸ And he says, "What to you [is] all this camp which I have met?" And he says, "To find grace in the eyes of my lord." ⁹ And Esau says, "I have abundance, my brother, that which you have, let it be for yourself." ¹⁰ And Jacob says, "No, please, now if I have found grace in your eyes, then you have received my present from my hand, because that I have seen your face, as the seeing of the face of God, and you are pleased with me; ¹¹ please receive my blessing which is brought to you, because God has favored me, and because I have all [things]"; and he presses on him, and he receives [it], ¹² and says, "Let us journey and go on, and I go on before you." ¹³ And he says to him, "My lord knows that the children [are] tender, and the suckling flock and the herd [are] with me; when they have beaten them one day, then all the flock has died. ¹⁴ Please let my lord pass over before his servant, and I lead on gently, according to the foot of the work which [is] before me, and to the foot of the children, until I come to my lord, to Seir." ¹⁵ And Esau says, "Please let me place with you some of the people who [are] with me"; and he said, "Why [is] this? I find grace in the eyes of my lord." ¹⁶ And Esau turns back on that day on his way to Seir; ¹⁷ and Jacob has journeyed to Succoth, and builds a house for himself, and has made shelters for his livestock, therefore he has called the name of the place Succoth. ¹⁸ And Jacob comes safe [to the] city of Shechem, which [is] in the land of Canaan, in his coming from Padan-Aram, and encamps before the city, ¹⁹ and he buys the portion of the field where he has stretched out his tent, from the hand of the sons of Hamor, father of Shechem, for one hundred kesitah; ²⁰ and he sets up there an altar, and proclaims at it God—the God of Israel.

CHAPTER 34

¹ And Dinah, daughter of Leah, whom she has borne to Jacob, goes out to look on the daughters of the land, ² and Shechem, son of Hamor the Hivite, a prince of the land, sees her, and takes her, and lies with her, and humbles her; ³ and his soul cleaves to Dinah, daughter of Jacob, and he loves the young person, and speaks to the heart of the young person. ⁴ And Shechem speaks to his father Hamor, saying, "Take for me this girl for a wife." ⁵ And Jacob has heard that he has defiled his daughter Dinah, and his sons were with his livestock in the field, and Jacob kept silent until their coming. ⁶ And Hamor, father of Shechem, goes out to Jacob to speak with him; ⁷ and the sons of Jacob came in from the field when they heard, and the men grieve themselves, and it [is] very displeasing to them, for folly he has done against Israel, to lie with the daughter of Jacob—and so it is not done. ⁸ And Hamor speaks with them, saying, "Shechem, my son, his soul has cleaved to your daughter; please give her to him for a wife, ⁹ and join in marriage with us; you give your daughters to us, and you take our daughters for yourselves, ¹⁰ and you dwell with us, and the land is before you; dwell and trade [in] it, and have possessions in it." ¹¹ And Shechem says to her father and to her brothers, "Let me find grace in your eyes, and that which you say to me, I give; ¹² multiply on me dowry and gift

exceedingly, and I give as you say to me, and give to me the young person for a wife." ¹³ And the sons of Jacob answer Shechem and his father Hamor deceitfully, and they speak (because he defiled their sister Dinah), ¹⁴ and say to them, "We are not able to do this thing, to give our sister to one who has a foreskin, for it [is] a reproach to us. ¹⁵ Only for this we consent to you: if you are as we, to have every male of you circumcised, ¹⁶ then we have given our daughters to you, and we take your daughters for ourselves, and we have dwelt with you, and have become one people; ¹⁷ and if you do not listen to us to be circumcised, then we have taken our daughter, and have gone." ¹⁸ And their words are good in the eyes of Hamor, and in the eyes of Shechem, Hamor's son; ¹⁹ and the young man did not delay to do the thing, for he had delight in Jacob's daughter, and he is honorable above all the house of his father. ²⁰ And Hamor comes—his son Shechem also—to the gate of their city, and they speak to the men of their city, saying, ²¹ "These men are peaceable with us; then let them dwell in the land, and trade [in] it; and the land, behold, [is] wide before them; their daughters let us take to ourselves for wives, and our daughters give to them. ²² Only for this do the men consent to us, to dwell with us, to become one people, in every male of us being circumcised, as they are circumcised; ²³ their livestock, and their substance, and all their beasts—are they not ours? only let us consent to them, and they dwell with us." ²⁴ And to Hamor, and to his son Shechem, do all those going out of the gate of his city listen, and every male is circumcised, all those going out of the gate of his city. ²⁵ And it comes to pass, on the third day, in their being pained, that two of the sons of Jacob, Simeon and Levi, Dinah's brothers, take each his sword, and come in against the city confidently, and slay every male; ²⁶ and Hamor, and his son Shechem, they have slain by the mouth of the sword, and they take Dinah out of Shechem's house, and go out. ²⁷ Jacob's sons have come in on the wounded, and they spoil the city, because they had defiled their sister; ²⁸ their flock and their herd, and their donkeys, and that which [is] in the city, and that which [is] in the field, have they taken; ²⁹ and all their wealth, and all their infants, and their wives they have taken captive, and they spoil also all that [is] in the house. ³⁰ And Jacob says to Simeon and to Levi, "You have troubled me, by causing me to stink among the inhabitants of the land, among the Canaanite, and among the Perizzite: and I [am] few in number, and they have been gathered against me, and have struck me, and I have been destroyed, I and my house." ³¹ And they say, "Does he make our sister as a harlot?"

CHAPTER 35

¹ And God says to Jacob, "Rise, go up to Bethel, and dwell there, and make there an altar to God, who appeared to you in your fleeing from the face of your brother Esau." ² And Jacob says to his household, and to all who [are] with him, "Turn aside the gods of the stranger which [are] in your midst, and cleanse yourselves, and change your garments; ³ and we rise, and go up to Bethel, and I make there an altar to God, who is answering me in the day of my tribulation, and is with me in the way that I have gone." ⁴ And they give to Jacob all the gods of the stranger that [are] in their hand, and the rings that [are] in their ears, and Jacob hides them under the oak which [is] by Shechem; ⁵ and they journey, and the terror of God is on the cities which [are] around them, and they have not pursued after the sons of Jacob. ⁶ And Jacob comes to Luz which [is] in the land of Canaan (it [is] Bethel), he and all the people who [are] with him, ⁷ and he builds there an altar, and proclaims at the place the God of Bethel: for there had God been revealed to him, in his fleeing from the face of his brother. ⁸ And Deborah, Rebekah's nurse, dies, and she is buried at the lower part of Bethel, under the oak, and he calls its name "Oak of Weeping." ⁹ And God appears to Jacob again, in his coming from Padan-Aram, and blesses him; ¹⁰ and God says to him, "Your name [is] Jacob: your name is no longer called Jacob, but Israel is your name"; and He calls his name Israel. ¹¹ And God says to him, "I [am] God Almighty; be fruitful and multiply, a nation and an assembly of nations is from you, and kings from your loins go out; ¹² and the land which I have given to Abraham and to Isaac—to you I give it, indeed to your seed after you I give the land." ¹³ And God goes up from him, in the place where He has spoken with him. ¹⁴ And Jacob sets up a standing pillar in the place where He has spoken with him, a standing pillar of stone, and he pours on it an oblation, and he

pours on it oil; ¹⁵ and Jacob calls the name of the place where God spoke with him Bethel. ¹⁶ And they journey from Bethel, and there is yet a distance of land before entering Ephratha, and Rachel bears, and is sharply pained in her bearing; ¹⁷ and it comes to pass, in her being sharply pained in her bearing, that the midwife says to her, "Do not fear, for this also [is] a son for you." ¹⁸ And it comes to pass in the going out of her soul (for she died), that she calls his name Ben-Oni; and his father called him Benjamin. ¹⁹ And Rachel dies, and is buried in the way to Ephratha, which [is] Beth-Lehem, ²⁰ and Jacob sets up a standing pillar over her grave; which [is] the standing pillar of Rachel's grave to this day. ²¹ And Israel journeys, and stretches out his tent beyond the Tower of Edar; ²² and it comes to pass in Israel's dwelling in that land, that Reuben goes, and lies with his father's concubine Bilhah; and Israel hears. ²³ And the sons of Jacob are twelve. Sons of Leah: Jacob's firstborn Reuben, and Simeon, and Levi, and Judah, and Issachar, and Zebulun. ²⁴ Sons of Rachel: Joseph and Benjamin. ²⁵ And sons of Bilhah, Rachel's maidservant: Dan and Naphtali. ²⁶ And sons of Zilpah, Leah's maidservant: Gad and Asher. These [are] sons of Jacob, who have been born to him in Padan-Aram. ²⁷ And Jacob comes to his father Isaac, at Mamre, the city of Arba (which [is] Hebron), where Abraham and Isaac have sojourned. ²⁸ And the days of Isaac are one hundred and eighty years, ²⁹ and Isaac expires, and dies, and is gathered to his people, aged and satisfied with days; and his sons Esau and Jacob bury him.

CHAPTER 36

¹ And these [are] the generations of Esau, who [is] Edom. ² Esau has taken his wives from the daughters of Canaan: Adah daughter of Elon the Hittite, and Aholibamah daughter of Anah, daughter of Zibeon the Hivite, ³ and Bashemath daughter of Ishmael, sister of Nebajoth. ⁴ And Adah bears to Esau, Eliphaz; and Bashemath has borne Reuel; ⁵ and Aholibamah has borne Jeush, and Jaalam, and Korah. These [are] sons of Esau, who were born to him in the land of Canaan. ⁶ And Esau takes his wives, and his sons, and his daughters, and all the persons of his house, and his livestock, and all his beasts, and all his substance which he has acquired in the land of Canaan, and goes into the country from the face of his brother Jacob; ⁷ for their substance was more abundant than to dwell together, and the land of their sojournings was not able to bear them because of their livestock; ⁸ and Esau dwells in Mount Seir: Esau is Edom. ⁹ And these [are] the generations of Esau, father of Edom, in Mount Seir. ¹⁰ These [are] the names of the sons of Esau: Eliphaz son of Adah, wife of Esau; Reuel son of Bashemath, wife of Esau. ¹¹ And the sons of Eliphaz are Teman, Omar, Zepho, and Gatam, and Kenaz; ¹² and Timnath was concubine to Eliphaz son of Esau, and she bears to Eliphaz, Amalek; these [are] sons of Adah wife of Esau. ¹³ And these [are] sons of Reuel: Nahath and Zerah, Shammah and Mizzah; these were sons of Bashemath wife of Esau. ¹⁴ And these have been the sons of Aholibamah daughter of Anah, daughter of Zibeon, wife of Esau; and she bears to Esau, Jeush and Jaalam and Korah. ¹⁵ These [are] chiefs of the sons of Esau: sons of Eliphaz, firstborn of Esau: Chief Teman, Chief Omar, Chief Zepho, Chief Kenaz, ¹⁶ Chief Korah, Chief Gatam, Chief Amalek; these [are] chiefs of Eliphaz, in the land of Edom; these [are] sons of Adah. ¹⁷ And these [are] sons of Reuel son of Esau: Chief Nahath, Chief Zerah, Chief Shammah, Chief Mizzah; these [are] chiefs of Reuel, in the land of Edom; these [are] sons of Bashemath wife of Esau. ¹⁸ And these [are] sons of Aholibamah wife of Esau: Chief Jeush, Chief Jaalam, Chief Korah; these [are] chiefs of Aholibamah daughter of Anah, wife of Esau. ¹⁹ These [are] sons of Esau (who [is] Edom), and these their chiefs. ²⁰ These [are] sons of Seir the Horite, the inhabitants of the land: Lotan, and Shobal, and Zibeon, and Anah, ²¹ and Dishon, and Ezer, and Dishan; these [are] chiefs of the Horites, sons of Seir, in the land of Edom. ²² And the sons of Lotan are Hori and Heman; and a sister of Lotan [is] Timna. ²³ And these [are] sons of Shobal: Alvan and Manahath, and Ebal, Shepho and Onam. ²⁴ And these [are] sons of Zibeon, both Ajah and Anah: it [is] Anah that has found the Imim in the wilderness, in his feeding the donkeys of his father Zibeon. ²⁵ And these [are] sons of Anah: Dishon, and Aholibamah daughter of Anah. ²⁶ And these [are] sons of Dishon: Hemdan, and Eshban, and Ithran, and Cheran. ²⁷ These [are] sons of Ezer: Bilhan, and Zaavan, and Akan. ²⁸ These [are] sons of Dishan: Uz and Aran. ²⁹ These [are] chiefs of the Horite: Chief

Lotan, Chief Shobal, Chief Zibeon, Chief Anah, **30** Chief Dishon, Chief Ezer, Chief Dishan: these [are] chiefs of the Horite in reference to their chiefs in the land of Seir. **31** And these [are] the kings who have reigned in the land of Edom before the reigning of a king over the sons of Israel. **32** And Bela son of Beor reigns in Edom, and the name of his city [is] Dinhabah; **33** and Bela dies, and Jobab son of Zerah from Bozrah reigns in his stead; **34** and Jobab dies, and Husham from the land of the Temanite reigns in his stead. **35** And Husham dies, and Hadad son of Bedad reigns in his stead (who strikes Midian in the field of Moab), and the name of his city [is] Avith; **36** and Hadad dies, and Samlah of Masrekah reigns in his stead; **37** and Samlah dies, and Saul from Rehoboth of the River reigns in his stead; **38** and Saul dies, and Ba'al-hanan son of Achbor reigns in his stead; **39** and Ba'al-hanan son of Achbor dies, and Hadar reigns in his stead, and the name of his city [is] Pau; and his wife's name [is] Mehetabel daughter of Matred, daughter of Me-zahab. **40** And these [are] the names of the chiefs of Esau, according to their families, according to their places, by their names: Chief Timnah, Chief Alvah, Chief Jetheth, **41** Chief Aholibamah, Chief Elah, Chief Pinon, **42** Chief Kenaz, Chief Teman, Chief Mibzar, **43** Chief Magdiel, Chief Iram: these [are] chiefs of Edom, in reference to their dwellings, in the land of their possession; he [is] Esau father of Edom.

CHAPTER 37

1 And Jacob dwells in the land of his father's sojourning—in the land of Canaan. **2** These [are] the generations of Jacob: Joseph, a son of seventeen years, has been enjoying himself with his brothers among the flock (and he [is] a youth), with the sons of Bilhah, and with the sons of Zilpah, his father's wives, and Joseph brings in an account of their evil to their father. **3** And Israel has loved Joseph more than any of his sons, for he [is] a son of his old age, and has made for him a long coat; **4** and his brothers see that their father has loved him more than any of his brothers, and they hate him, and have not been able to speak [to] him peaceably. **5** And Joseph dreams a dream, and declares to his brothers, and they add still more to hate him. **6** And he says to them, "Please hear this dream which I have dreamed: **7** that, behold, we are binding bundles in the midst of the field, and behold, my bundle has arisen, and has also stood up, and behold, your bundles are all around, and they bow themselves to my bundle." **8** And his brothers say to him, "Do you certainly reign over us? do you certainly rule over us?" And they add still more to hate him, for his dreams, and for his words. **9** And he dreams yet another dream, and recounts it to his brothers, and says, "Behold, I have dreamed a dream again, and behold, the sun and the moon, and eleven stars, are bowing themselves to me." **10** And he recounts to his father, and to his brothers; and his father pushes against him, and says to him, "What [is] this dream which you have dreamed? do we certainly come, I, and your mother, and your brothers—to bow ourselves to you, to the earth?" **11** and his brothers are zealous against him, and his father has watched the matter. **12** And his brothers go to feed the flock of their father in Shechem, **13** and Israel says to Joseph, "Are your brothers not feeding in Shechem? come, and I send you to them"; and he says to him, "Here I [am]"; **14** and he says to him, "Now go see the peace of your brothers, and the peace of the flock, and bring me back word"; and he sends him from the Valley of Hebron, and he comes to Shechem. **15** And a man finds him, and behold, he is wandering in the field, and the man asks him, saying, "What do you seek?" **16** and he says, "I am seeking my brothers, please declare to me where they are feeding." **17** And the man says, "They have journeyed from this, for I have heard some saying, Let us go to Dothan," and Joseph goes after his brothers, and finds them in Dothan. **18** And they see him from afar, even before he draws near to them, and they conspire against him to put him to death. **19** And they say to one another, "Behold, this man of the dreams comes; **20** and now, come, and we slay him, and cast him into one of the pits, and have said, An evil beast has devoured him; and we see what his dreams are." **21** And Reuben hears, and delivers him out of their hand, and says, "Let us not strike the life"; **22** and Reuben says to them, "Shed no blood; cast him into this pit which [is] in the wilderness, and do not put forth a hand on him," in order to deliver him out of their hand, to bring him back to his father. **23** And it comes to pass, when Joseph has come to his brothers, that they strip Joseph of his coat, the long coat which [is] on him, **24** and take him and cast him into the pit, and the pit [is] empty, there is no water in it. **25** And they sit down to eat bread, and they lift up their eyes, and look, and behold, a caravan of Ishmaelites coming from Gilead, and their camels carrying spices, and balm, and myrrh, going to take [them] down to Egypt. **26** And Judah says to his brothers, "What gain when we slay our brother, and have concealed his blood? **27** Come, and we sell him to the Ishmaelites, and our hands are not on him, for he [is] our brother—our flesh"; and his brothers listen. **28** And Midianite merchantmen pass by and they draw out and bring up Joseph out of the pit, and sell Joseph to the Ishmaelites for twenty pieces of silver, and they bring Joseph into Egypt. **29** And Reuben returns to the pit, and behold, Joseph is not in the pit, and he tears his garments, **30** and he returns to his brothers and says, "The boy is not, and I—to where am I going?" **31** And they take the coat of Joseph, and slaughter a kid of the goats, and dip the coat in the blood, **32** and send the long coat, and they bring [it] to their father, and say, "We have found this; please discern whether it [is] your son's coat or not." **33** And he discerns it and says, "My son's coat! An evil beast has devoured him; torn—Joseph is torn!" **34** And Jacob tears his raiment, and puts sackcloth on his loins, and becomes a mourner for his son many days, **35** and all his sons and all his daughters rise to comfort him, and he refuses to comfort himself, and says, "For I go down to my son mourning, to Sheol," and his father weeps for him. **36** And the Midianites have sold him to Egypt, to Potiphar, a eunuch of Pharaoh, head of the executioners.

CHAPTER 38

1 And it comes to pass, at that time, that Judah goes down from his brothers, and turns aside to a man, an Adullamite, whose name [is] Hirah; **2** and Judah sees there the daughter of a man, a Canaanite, whose name [is] Shuah, and takes her, and goes in to her. **3** And she conceives, and bears a son, and he calls his name Er; **4** and she conceives again, and bears a son, and calls his name Onan; **5** and she adds again, and bears a son, and calls his name Shelah; and he was in Chezib in her bearing him. **6** And Judah takes a wife for Er, his firstborn, and her name [is] Tamar; **7** and Er, Judah's firstborn, is evil in the eyes of Yhwh, and Yhwh puts him to death. **8** And Judah says to Onan, "Go in to the wife of your brother, and marry her, and raise up seed to your brother"; **9** and Onan knows that the seed is not [reckoned] his; and it has come to pass, if he has gone in to his brother's wife, that he has destroyed [it] to the earth, so as not to give seed to his brother; **10** and that which he has done is evil in the eyes of Yhwh, and He puts him also to death. **11** And Judah says to his daughter-in-law Tamar, "Abide [as] a widow at your father's house, until my son Shelah grows up"; for he said, "Lest he die—even he—like his brothers"; and Tamar goes and dwells at her father's house. **12** And the days are multiplied, and the daughter of Shuah, Judah's wife, dies; and Judah is comforted, and goes up to his sheep-shearers, he and Hirah his friend the Adullamite, to Timnath. **13** And it is declared to Tamar, saying, "Behold, your husband's father is going up to Timnath to shear his flock"; **14** and she turns aside the garments of her widowhood from off her, and covers herself with a veil, and wraps herself up, and sits in the opening of Enayim, which [is] by the way to Timnath, for she has seen that Shelah has grown up, and she has not been given to him for a wife. **15** And Judah sees her, and reckons her for a harlot, for she has covered her face, **16** and he turns aside to her by the way and says, "Please come, let me come in to you," for he has not known that she [is] his daughter-in-law; and she says, "What do you give to me, that you may come in to me?" **17** and he says, "I send a kid of the goats from the flock." And she says, "Do you give a pledge until you send [it]?" **18** and he says, "What [is] the pledge that I give to you?" And she says, "Your seal, and your ribbon, and your staff which [is] in your hand"; and he gives to her, and goes in to her, and she conceives to him; **19** and she rises, and goes, and turns aside her veil from off her, and puts on the garments of her widowhood. **20** And Judah sends the kid of the goats by the hand of his friend the Adullamite, to receive the pledge from the hand of the woman, and he has not found her; **21** And he asks the men of her place, saying, "Where [is] the separated one—she in Enayim, by the way?" And they say, "There has not been in this [place] a separated one." **22** And he turns back to Judah and says, "I have not found her; and the men of the place also have said, There has not been in this [place] a separated one," **23** and Judah says, "Let her take to herself, lest we become despised; behold, I sent this kid, and you have not found her." **24** And it comes to pass about three months [after], that it is declared to Judah, saying, "Your daughter-in-law Tamar has committed fornication; and also, behold, she has conceived by fornication": and Judah says, "Bring her out—and she is burned." **25** She is brought out, and she has sent to her husband's father, saying, "To a man whose these [are], I [am] pregnant"; and she says, "Please discern whose these [are]— the seal, and the ribbons, and the staff." **26** And Judah discerns and says, "She has been more righteous than I, because that I did not give her to my son Shelah"; and he has not added to know her again. **27** And it comes to pass in the time of her bearing, that behold, twins [are] in her womb; **28** and it comes to pass in her bearing, that [one] gives out a hand, and the midwife takes and binds on his hand a scarlet thread, saying, "This has come out first." **29** And it comes to pass as he draws back his hand, that behold, his brother has come out, and she says, "What! You have broken forth—the breach [is] on you"; and he calls his name Perez; **30** and afterward his brother has come out, on whose hand [is] the scarlet thread, and he calls his name Zerah.

CHAPTER 39

1 And Joseph has been brought down to Egypt, and Potiphar, a eunuch of Pharaoh, head of the executioners, an Egyptian man, buys him out of the hands of the Ishmaelites who have brought him there. **2** And Yhwh is with Joseph, and he is a prosperous man, and he is in the house of his lord the Egyptian, **3** and his lord sees that Yhwh is with him, and all that he is doing Yhwh is causing to prosper in his hand, **4** and Joseph finds grace in his eyes and serves him, and he appoints him over his house, and all that he has he has given into his hand. **5** And it comes to pass from the time that he has appointed him over his house, and over all that he has, that Yhwh blesses the house of the Egyptian for Joseph's sake, and the blessing of Yhwh is on all that he has, in the house, and in the field; **6** and he leaves all that he has in the hand of Joseph, and he has not known anything that he has, except the bread which he is eating. And Joseph is of a handsome form, and of a handsome appearance. **7** And it comes to pass after these things, that his lord's wife lifts up her eyes to Joseph and says, "Lie with me"; **8** and he refuses and says to his lord's wife, "Behold, my lord has not known what [is] with me in the house, and all that he has he has given into my hand; **9** none is greater in this house than I, and he has not withheld from me anything, except you, because you [are] his wife; and how will I do this great evil? Then I have sinned against God." **10** And it comes to pass at her speaking to Joseph day [by] day, that he has not listened to her, to lie near her, to be with her; **11** and it comes to pass about this day, that he goes into the house to do his work, and there is none of the men of the house there in the house, **12** and she catches him by his garment, saying, "Lie with me"; and he leaves his garment in her hand, and flees, and goes outside. **13** And it comes to pass, when she sees that he has left his garment in her hand, and flees outside, **14** that she calls for the men of her house, and speaks to them, saying, "See, he has brought a man to us, a Hebrew, to play with us; he has come in to me, to lie with me, and I call with a loud voice, **15** and it comes to pass, when he hears that I have lifted up my voice and call, that he leaves his garment near me, and flees, and goes outside." **16** And she places his garment near her, until the coming in of his lord to his house. **17** And she speaks to him according to these words, saying, "The Hebrew servant whom you have brought to us, has come in to me to play with me; **18** and it comes to pass, when I lift my voice and call, that he leaves his garment near me, and flees outside." **19** And it comes to pass, when his lord hears the words of his wife, which she has spoken to him, saying, "According to these things has your servant done to me," that his anger burns; **20** and Joseph's lord takes him, and puts him to the round-house, a place where the king's prisoners [are] bound; and he is there in the round-house. **21** And Yhwh is with Joseph, and stretches out kindness to him, and puts his grace in the eyes of the chief of the round-house; **22** and the chief of the round-house gives into the hand of Joseph all the prisoners who [are] in the round-house, and of all that they are doing there, he has been doer; **23** the chief of the round-house does not see anything under his hand, because Yhwh [is] with him, and that which he is doing Yhwh is causing to prosper.

CHAPTER 40

1 And it comes to pass, after these things—the butler of the king of Egypt and the baker have sinned against their lord, against the king of Egypt; **2** and Pharaoh is angry against his two eunuchs, against the chief of the butlers, and against the chief of the bakers, **3** and puts them in confinement in the house of the chief of the executioners, into the round-house, the place where Joseph [is] a prisoner, **4** and the chief of the executioners charges Joseph with them, and he serves them; and they are in confinement [for some] days. **5** And they dream a dream both of them, each his dream in one night, each according to the interpretation of his dream, the butler and the baker whom the king of Egypt has, who [are] prisoners in the round-house. **6** And Joseph comes to them in the morning, and sees them, and behold, they [are] morose; **7** and he asks Pharaoh's eunuchs who [are] with him in confinement in the house of his lord, saying, "Why [are] your faces sad today?" **8** And they say to him, "We have dreamed a dream, and there is no interpreter of it"; and Joseph says to them, "Are interpretations not with God? Please recount to me." **9** And the chief of the butlers recounts his dream to Joseph and says to him, "In my dream, then behold, a vine [is] before me! **10** and in the vine [are] three branches, and it [is] as it were flourishing; gone up has its blossom, its clusters have ripened grapes; **11** and Pharaoh's cup [is] in my hand, and I take the grapes and press them into the cup of Pharaoh, and I give the cup into the hand of Pharaoh." **12** And Joseph says to him, "This [is] its interpretation: the three branches are three days; **13** yet, within three days Pharaoh lifts up your head, and has put you back on your station, and you have given the cup of Pharaoh into his hand, according to the former custom when you were his butler. **14** Surely if you have remembered me with you, when it is well with you, and have please done kindness with me, and have made mention of me to Pharaoh, then you have brought me out from this house, **15** for I was really stolen from the land of the Hebrews; and here also I have done nothing that they have put me in the pit [for]." **16** And the chief of the bakers sees that he has interpreted good, and he says to Joseph, "I also [am] in a dream, and behold, three baskets of white bread [are] on my head, **17** and in the highest basket [are] of all [kinds] of Pharaoh's food, work of a baker; and the birds are eating them out of the basket, from off my head." **18** And Joseph answers and says, "This [is] its interpretation: the three baskets are three days; **19** yet, within three days Pharaoh lifts up your head from off you, and has hanged you on a tree, and the birds have eaten your flesh from off you." **20** And it comes to pass, on the third day, Pharaoh's birthday, that he makes a banquet to all his servants, and lifts up the head of the chief of the butlers, and the head of the chief of the bakers among his servants, **21** and he puts back the chief of the butlers to his butlership, and he gives the cup into the hand of Pharaoh; **22** and the chief of the bakers he has hanged, as Joseph has interpreted to them; **23** and the chief of the butlers has not remembered Joseph, but forgets him.

CHAPTER 41

1 And it comes to pass, at the end of two years of days that Pharaoh is dreaming, and behold, he is standing by the River, **2** and behold, from the River coming up are seven cows, of beautiful appearance, and fat [in] flesh, and they feed among the reeds; **3** and behold, seven other cows are coming up after them out of the River, of bad appearance, and lean [in] flesh, and they stand near the cows on the edge of the River, **4** and the cows of bad appearance and lean [in] flesh eat up the seven cows of beautiful appearance, and fat—and Pharaoh awakens. **5** And he sleeps, and dreams a second time, and behold, seven ears are coming up on one stalk, fat and good, **6** and behold, seven ears, thin, and blasted with an east wind, are springing up after them; **7** and the thin ears swallow the seven fat and full ears—and Pharaoh awakens, and behold, a dream. **8** And it comes to pass in the morning, that his spirit is moved, and he sends and calls all the enchanters of Egypt, and all its wise men, and Pharaoh recounts to them his dream, and there is no interpreter of them to Pharaoh. **9** And the chief of the butlers speaks with Pharaoh, saying, "I mention my sin this day: **10** Pharaoh has been angry against his servants, and puts me in confinement in the house of the chief of the executioners, me and the chief of the bakers; **11** and we dream a dream in one night, I and he, each according to the interpretation of his dream we have dreamed. **12** And there [is] with us a youth, a Hebrew, servant to the chief of the executioners, and we recount to him, and he interprets to us our dreams, [to] each according to his dream has he interpreted, **13** and it comes to pass, as he has interpreted to us so it has been, me he put back on my station, and him he hanged." **14** And Pharaoh sends and calls Joseph, and they cause him to run out of the pit, and he shaves, and changes his garments, and comes to Pharaoh. **15** And Pharaoh says to Joseph, "I have dreamed a dream, and there is no interpreter of it, and I have heard concerning you, saying, You understand a dream to interpret it," **16** and Joseph answers Pharaoh, saying, "Without me—God answers Pharaoh with peace." **17** And Pharaoh speaks to Joseph: "In my dream, behold, I am standing by the edge of the River, **18** and behold, out of the River coming up are seven cows, fat [in] flesh, and of beautiful form, and they feed among the reeds; **19** and behold, seven other cows are coming up after them, thin, and of very bad form, and lean [in] flesh; I have not seen like these in all the land of Egypt for badness. **20** And the lean and the bad cows eat up the first seven fat cows, **21** and they come in to their midst, and it has not been known that they have come in to their midst, and their appearance [is] bad as at the commencement; and I awake. **22** And I see in my dream, and behold, seven ears are coming up on one stalk, full and good; **23** and behold, seven ears, withered, thin, blasted with an east wind, are springing up after them; **24** and the thin ears swallow the seven good ears; and I tell [it] to the enchanters, and there is none declaring [it] to me." **25** And Joseph says to Pharaoh, "The dream of Pharaoh is one: that which God is doing he has declared to Pharaoh; **26** the seven good cows are seven years, and the seven good ears are seven years, the dream is one; **27** and the seven thin and bad cows which are coming up after them are seven years, and the seven empty ears, blasted with an east wind, are seven years of famine; **28** this [is] the thing which I have spoken to Pharaoh: God has shown Pharaoh what He is doing. **29** Behold, seven years are coming of great abundance in all the land of Egypt, **30** and seven years of famine have arisen after them, and all the plenty is forgotten in the land of Egypt, and the famine has finished the land, **31** and the plenty is not known in the land because of that famine afterward, for it [is] very grievous. **32** And because of the repeating of the dream to Pharaoh twice, surely the thing is established by God, and God is hurrying to do it. **33** And now, let Pharaoh provide a man, intelligent and wise, and set him over the land of Egypt; **34** let Pharaoh make and appoint overseers over the land, and receive a fifth of the land of Egypt in the seven years of plenty, **35** and they gather all the food of these good years that are coming, and heap up grain under the hand of Pharaoh—food in the cities; and they have kept [it], **36** and the food has been for a store for the land, for the seven years of famine which are in the land of Egypt; and the land is cut off by the famine." **37** And the thing is good in the eyes of Pharaoh, and in the eyes of all his servants, **38** and Pharaoh says to his servants, "Do we find like this, a man in whom the Spirit of God [is]?" **39** and Pharaoh says to Joseph, "After God's causing you to know all this, there is none intelligent and wise as you; **40** you are over my house, and at your mouth do all my people kiss; only in the throne I am greater than you." **41** And Pharaoh says to Joseph, "See, I have put you over all the land of Egypt." **42** And Pharaoh turns aside his seal-ring from off his hand, and puts it on the hand of Joseph, and clothes him [with] garments of fine linen, and places a chain of gold on his neck, **43** and causes him to ride in the second chariot which he has, and they proclaim before him, "Bow the knee!" And [he] set him over all the land of Egypt. **44** And Pharaoh says to Joseph, "I [am] Pharaoh, and without you a man does not lift up his hand and his foot in all the land of Egypt"; **45** and Pharaoh calls Joseph's name Zaphnath-Paaneah, and he gives to him Asenath daughter of Poti-Pherah, priest of On, for a wife, and Joseph goes out over the land of Egypt. **46** And Joseph [is] a son of thirty years in his standing before Pharaoh king of Egypt, and Joseph goes out from the presence of Pharaoh, and passes over through all the land of Egypt; **47** and the land makes in the seven years of plenty by handfuls. **48** And he gathers all the food of the seven years which have been in the land of Egypt, and puts food in the cities; the food of the field which [is] around [each] city has he put in its midst; **49** and Joseph gathers grain as sand of the sea, multiplying exceedingly, until he has ceased to number, for there is no number. **50** And to Joseph were born two sons before the year of famine comes,

whom Asenath daughter of Poti-Pherah, priest of On, has borne to him, **51** and Joseph calls the name of the firstborn Manasseh: "For God has made me to forget all my labor, and all the house of my father"; **52** and the name of the second he has called Ephraim: "For God has caused me to be fruitful in the land of my affliction." **53** And the seven years of plenty are completed which have been in the land of Egypt, **54** and the seven years of famine begin to come, as Joseph said, and famine is in all the lands, but in all the land of Egypt has been bread; **55** and all the land of Egypt is famished, and the people cry to Pharaoh for bread, and Pharaoh says to all the Egyptians, "Go to Joseph; that which he says to you—do." **56** And the famine has been over all the face of the land, and Joseph opens all [places] which have [grain] in them, and sells to the Egyptians; and the famine is severe in the land of Egypt, **57** and all the earth has come to Egypt, to buy, to Joseph, for the famine was severe in all the earth.

CHAPTER 42

1 And Jacob sees that there is grain in Egypt, and Jacob says to his sons, "Why do you look at each other?" **2** he also says, "Behold, I have heard that there is grain in Egypt, go down there, and buy for us from there, and we live and do not die"; **3** and the ten brothers of Joseph go down to buy grain in Egypt, **4** and Benjamin, Joseph's brother, Jacob has not sent with his brothers, for he said, "Lest harm meet him." **5** And the sons of Israel come to buy in the midst of those coming, for the famine has been in the land of Canaan, **6** and Joseph is the ruler over the land, he who is selling to all the people of the land, and Joseph's brothers come and bow themselves to him—face to the earth. **7** And Joseph sees his brothers, and discerns them, and makes himself strange to them, and speaks sharp things with them, and says to them, "From where have you come?" And they say, "From the land of Canaan—to buy food." **8** And Joseph discerns his brothers, but they have not discerned him, **9** and Joseph remembers the dreams which he dreamed of them and says to them, "You [are] spies; you have come to see the nakedness of the land." **10** And they say to him, "No, my lord, but your servants have come to buy food; **11** we [are] all of us sons of one man, we [are] right men; your servants have not been spies"; **12** and he says to them, "No, but you have come to see the nakedness of the land"; **13** and they say, "Your servants [are] twelve brothers; we [are] sons of one man in the land of Canaan, and behold, the young one [is] with our father today, and one is not." **14** And Joseph says to them, "This [is] that which I have spoken to you, saying, You [are] spies, **15** by this you are proved: [as] Pharaoh lives, if you go out from this—except by your young brother coming here; **16** send one of you, and let him bring your brother, and you, remain bound, and let your words be proved, whether truth be with you: and if not, [as] Pharaoh lives, surely you [are] spies"; **17** and he gathers them into confinement [for] three days. **18** And Joseph says to them on the third day, "Do this and live; I fear God! **19** if you [are] right men, let one of your brothers be bound in the house of your confinement, and you, go, carry in grain [for] the famine of your houses, **20** and you bring your young brother to me, and your words are established, and you do not die"; and they do so. **21** And they say to one another, "Truly we [are] guilty concerning our brother, because we saw the distress of his soul, in his making supplication to us, and we did not listen: therefore this distress has come on us." **22** And Reuben answers them, saying, "Did I not speak to you, saying, Do not sin against the boy? and you did not listen; and his blood also, behold, it is required." **23** And they have not known that Joseph understands, for the interpreter [is] between them; **24** and he turns around from them, and weeps, and turns back to them, and speaks to them, and takes Simeon from them, and binds him before their eyes. **25** And Joseph commands, and they fill their vessels [with] grain, also to put back the money of each of them into his sack, and to give to them provision for the way; and one does to them so. **26** And they lift up their grain on their donkeys, and go from there, **27** and the one opens his sack to give provender to his donkey at a lodging-place, and he sees his money, and behold, it [is] in the mouth of his bag, **28** and he says to his brothers, "My money has been put back, and also, behold, in my bag": and their heart goes out, and they tremble, to one another saying, "What [is] this God has done to us!" **29** And they come to their father Jacob, to the land of Canaan, and they declare to him all the things meeting them, saying, **30** "The man, the lord of the land, has spoken with us sharp things, and makes us as spies of the land; ³¹ and we say to him, We [are] right men, we have not been spies, ³² we [are] twelve brothers, sons of our father, one is not, and the young one [is] today with our father in the land of Canaan. ³³ And the man, the lord of the land, says to us, By this I know that you [are] right men—leave one of your brothers with me, and take [for] the famine of your houses and go, ³⁴ and bring your young brother to me, and I know that you [are] not spies, but you [are] right men; I give your brother to you, and you trade with the land." ³⁵ And it comes to pass, they are emptying their sacks, and behold, the bundle of each man's silver [is] in his sack, and they see their bundles of silver, they and their father, and are afraid; ³⁶ and their father Jacob says to them, "You have bereaved me; Joseph is not, and Simeon is not, and Benjamin you take—all these [things] have been against me." ³⁷ And Reuben speaks to his father, saying, "You put to death my two sons, if I do not bring him to you; give him into my hand, and I bring him back to you"; ³⁸ and he says, "My son does not go down with you, for his brother [is] dead, and he by himself is left; when harm has met him in the way in which you go, then you have brought down my grey hairs in sorrow to Sheol."

CHAPTER 43

¹ And the famine [is] severe in the land; ² and it comes to pass, when they have finished eating the grain which they brought from Egypt, that their father says to them, "Return, buy for us a little food." ³ And Judah speaks to him, saying, "The man protesting protested to us, saying, You do not see my face without your brother [being] with you; ⁴ if you are sending our brother with us, we go down, and buy for you food, ⁵ and if you are not sending—we do not go down, for the man said to us, You do not see my face without your brother [being] with you." ⁶ And Israel says, "Why did you do evil to me, by declaring to the man that you had yet a brother?" ⁷ and they say, "The man asked diligently concerning us, and concerning our family, saying, Is your father yet alive? have you a brother? and we declare to him according to the tenor of these things; do we certainly know that he will say, Bring down your brother?" ⁸ And Judah says to his father Israel, "Send the youth with me, and we arise, and go, and live, and do not die, both we, and you, and our infants. ⁹ I am guarantor [for] him, from my hand you require him; if I have not brought him to you, and set him before you—then I have sinned against you all the days; ¹⁰ for if we had not lingered, surely now we had returned these two times." ¹¹ And their father Israel says to them, "If so, now, do this: take of the praised thing of the land in your vessels, and take down to the man a present, a little balm, and a little honey, spices and myrrh, nuts and almonds; ¹² and double money take in your hand, even the money which is brought back in the mouth of your bags, you take back in your hand, it may be it [is] an oversight. ¹³ And take your brother, and rise, return to the man; ¹⁴ and God Almighty give to you mercies before the man, so that he has sent to you your other brother and Benjamin; and I, when I am bereaved—I am bereaved." ¹⁵ And the men take this present, double money also they have taken in their hand, and Benjamin; and they rise, and go down to Egypt, and stand before Joseph; ¹⁶ and Joseph sees Benjamin with them and says to him who [is] over his house, "Bring the men into the house, and slaughter an animal, and make ready, for the men eat with me at noon." ¹⁷ And the man does as Joseph has said, and the man brings in the men into the house of Joseph, ¹⁸ and the men are afraid because they have been brought into the house of Joseph, and they say, "For the matter of the money which was put back in our bags at the commencement are we brought in—to roll himself on us, and to throw himself on us, and to take us for servants—our donkeys also." ¹⁹ And they come near to the man who [is] over the house of Joseph, and speak to him at the opening of the house, ²⁰ and say, "O my lord, we really come down at the commencement to buy food; ²¹ and it comes to pass, when we have come to the lodging-place, and open our bags, that behold, each one's money [is] in the mouth of his bag, our money in its weight, and we bring it back in our hand; ²² and other money have we brought down in our hand to buy food; we have not known who put our money in our bags." ²³ And he says, "Peace to you, do not fear: your God and the God of your father has given to you hidden treasure in your bags, your money came to me"; and he brings out Simeon to them. ²⁴ And the man brings in the men into Joseph's house, and

gives water, and they wash their feet; and he gives provender for their donkeys, ²⁵ and they prepare the present until the coming of Joseph at noon, for they have heard that there they eat bread. ²⁶ And Joseph comes into the house, and they bring to him the present which [is] in their hand, into the house, and bow themselves to him, to the earth; ²⁷ and he asks of them of peace and says, "Is your father well? the aged man of whom you have spoken, is he yet alive?" ²⁸ and they say, "Your servant our father [is] well, he is yet alive"; and they bow, and pay respect. ²⁹ And he lifts up his eyes and sees his brother Benjamin, his mother's son, and says, "Is this your young brother, of whom you have spoken to me?" And he says, "God favor you, my son." ³⁰ And Joseph hurries, for his bowels have been moved for his brother, and he seeks to weep, and enters the inner chamber, and weeps there; ³¹ and he washes his face, and goes out, and refrains himself, and says, "Place bread." ³² And they place for him by himself, and for them by themselves, and for the Egyptians who are eating with him by themselves: for the Egyptians are unable to eat bread with the Hebrews, for it [is] an abomination to the Egyptians. ³³ And they sit before him, the firstborn according to his birthright, and the young one according to his youth, and the men wonder one at another; ³⁴ and he lifts up gifts from before him to them, and the gift of Benjamin is five hands more than the gifts of all of them; and they drink, indeed, they drink abundantly with him.

CHAPTER 44

¹ And he commands him who [is] over his house, saying, "Fill the bags of the men [with] food, as they are able to carry, and put the money of each in the mouth of his bag; ² and my cup, the silver cup, you put in the mouth of the bag of the young one, and his grain-money"; and he does according to the word of Joseph which he has spoken. ³ The morning is bright, and the men have been sent away, they and their donkeys— ⁴ they have gone out of the city—they have not gone far off—and Joseph has said to him who [is] over his house, "Rise, pursue after the men; and you have overtaken them, and you have said to them: Why have you repaid evil for good? ⁵ Is this not that with which my lord drinks? and he observes diligently with it; you have done evil [in] that which you have done." ⁶ And he overtakes them, and speaks to them these words, ⁷ and they say to him, "Why does my lord speak according to these words? far be it from your servants to do according to this word; ⁸ behold, the money which we found in the mouth of our bags we brought back to you from the land of Canaan, and how do we steal from the house of your lord silver or gold? ⁹ with whomsoever of your servants it is found, he has died, and we also are to my lord for servants." ¹⁰ And he says, "Now also, according to your words, so it [is]; he with whom it is found becomes my servant, and you are acquitted"; ¹¹ and they hurry and take down each his bag to the earth, and each opens his bag; ¹² and he searches—at the eldest he has begun, and at the youngest he has completed—and the cup is found in the bag of Benjamin; ¹³ and they tear their garments, and each loads his donkey, and they return to the city. ¹⁴ And Judah and his brothers come to the house of Joseph, and he is yet there, and they fall to the earth before him; ¹⁵ and Joseph says to them, "What [is] this deed that you have done? have you not known that a man like me diligently observes?" ¹⁶ And Judah says, "What do we say to my lord? what do we speak? and how do we justify ourselves? God has found out the iniquity of your servants; behold, we [are] servants to my lord, both we, and he in whose hand the cup has been found"; ¹⁷ and he says, "Far be it from me to do this; the man in whose hand the cup has been found, he becomes my servant; and you, go up in peace to your father." ¹⁸ And Judah comes near to him and says, "O my lord, please let your servant speak a word in the ears of my lord, and do not let your anger burn against your servant—for you are as Pharaoh. ¹⁹ My lord has asked his servants, saying, Do you have a father or brother? ²⁰ and we say to my lord, We have a father, an aged one, and a child of old age, a little one; and his brother died, and he is left alone of his mother, and his father has loved him. ²¹ And you say to your servants, Bring him down to me, and I set my eye on him; ²² and we say to my lord, The youth is not able to leave his father, when he has left his father, then he has died; ²³ and you say to your servants, If your young brother does not come down with you, you do not add to see my face. ²⁴ And it comes to pass, that we have come up to your servant my father, that we declare to him the words of my lord; ²⁵ and our father says,

Return, buy for us a little food, **26** and we say, We are not able to go down; if our young brother is with us, then we have gone down; for we are not able to see the man's face, and our young brother not with us. **27** And your servant my father says to us, You have known that my wife bore two to me, **28** and one goes out from me, and I say, Surely he is torn—torn! And I have not seen him since; **29** when you have taken also this from my presence, and harm has met him, then you have brought down my grey hairs with evil to Sheol. **30** And now, at my coming to your servant my father, and the youth not with us (and his soul is bound up in his soul), **31** then it has come to pass, when he sees that the youth is not, that he has died, and your servants have brought down the grey hairs of your servant our father with sorrow to Sheol; **32** for your servant obtained the youth by guarantee from my father, saying, If I do not bring him to you— then I have sinned against my father all the days. **33** And now, please let your servant abide instead of the youth [as] a servant to my lord, and the youth goes up with his brothers, **34** for how do I go up to my father, and the youth not with me? lest I look on the evil which finds my father."

CHAPTER 45

1 And Joseph has not been able to refrain himself before all those standing by him, and he calls, "Put out every man from me"; and no man has stood with him when Joseph makes himself known to his brothers, **2** and he gives forth his voice in weeping, and the Egyptians hear, and the house of Pharaoh hears. **3** And Joseph says to his brothers, "I [am] Joseph, is my father yet alive?" And his brothers have not been able to answer him, for they have been troubled at his presence. **4** And Joseph says to his brothers, "Please come near to me," and they come near; and he says, "I [am] your brother Joseph, whom you sold into Egypt; **5** and now, do not be grieved, nor let it be displeasing in your eyes that you sold me here, for God has sent me before you to preserve life. **6** Because these two years the famine [is] in the heart of the land, and yet five years [remain in] which there is neither plowing nor harvest; **7** and God sends me before you, to place a remnant of you in the land, and to give life to you by a great escape; **8** and now, you have not sent me here, but God, and He sets me for a father to Pharaoh, and for lord to all his house, and ruler over all the land of Egypt. **9** Hurry, and go up to my father, then you have said to him, Thus said your son Joseph: God has set me for lord to all Egypt; come down to me, do not stay, **10** and you have dwelt in the land of Goshen, and been near to me, you and your sons, and your son's sons, and your flock, and your herd, and all that you have, **11** and I have nourished you there— for yet [are] five years of famine—lest you become poor, you and your household, and all that you have. **12** And behold, your eyes are seeing, and the eyes of my brother Benjamin, that [it is] my mouth which is speaking to you; **13** and you have declared to my father all my glory in Egypt, and all that you have seen, and you have hurried, and have brought down my father here." **14** And he falls on the neck of his brother Benjamin, and weeps, and Benjamin has wept on his neck; **15** and he kisses all his brothers, and weeps over them; and afterward his brothers have spoken with him. **16** And the sound has been heard in the house of Pharaoh, saying, "The brothers of Joseph have come"; and it is good in the eyes of Pharaoh, and in the eyes of his servants, **17** and Pharaoh says to Joseph, "Say to your brothers, This you do: load your beasts, and go, enter the land of Canaan, **18** and take your father, and your households, and come to me, and I give to you the good of the land of Egypt, and you eat the fat of the land. **19** Indeed, you have been commanded: this you do, take for yourselves out of the land of Egypt, wagons for your infants, and for your wives, and you have brought your father, and come; **20** and your eye has no pity on your vessels, for the good of all the land of Egypt [is] yours." **21** And the sons of Israel do so, and Joseph gives wagons to them by the command of Pharaoh, and he gives to them provision for the way; **22** to all of them has he given—to each changes of garments, and to Benjamin he has given three hundred pieces of silver, and five changes of garments; **23** and to his father he has sent thus: ten donkeys carrying of the good things of Egypt, and ten female donkeys carrying grain and bread, even food for his father for the way. **24** And he sends his brothers away, and they go; and he says to them, "Do not be angry in the way." **25** And they go up out of Egypt, and come to the land of Canaan, to their father Jacob, **26** and they declare to him, saying, "Joseph [is] yet alive," and that he [is] ruler over all the land of Egypt; and his heart ceases, for he has not given credence to them. **27** And they speak to him all the words of Joseph, which he has spoken to them, and he sees the wagons which Joseph has sent to carry him away, and the spirit of their father Jacob lives; **28** and Israel says, "Enough! My son Joseph [is] yet alive; I go and see him before I die."

CHAPTER 46

1 And Israel journeys, and all that he has, and comes to Beer-Sheba, and sacrifices sacrifices to the God of his father Isaac; **2** and God speaks to Israel in visions of the night and says, "Jacob, Jacob"; and he says, "Here I [am]." **3** And He says, "I [am] God, God of your father, do not be afraid of going down to Egypt, for I set you there for a great nation; **4** I go down with you to Egypt, and I also certainly bring you up, and Joseph puts his hand on your eyes." **5** And Jacob rises from Beer-Sheba, and the sons of Israel carry away their father Jacob, and their infants, and their wives, in the wagons which Pharaoh has sent to carry him, **6** and they take their livestock, and their goods which they have acquired in the land of Canaan, and come into Egypt—Jacob, and all his seed with him, **7** his sons, and his sons' sons with him, his daughters, and his sons' daughters, indeed, all his seed he brought with him into Egypt. **8** And these [are] the names of the sons of Israel who are coming into Egypt: Jacob and his sons, Jacob's firstborn, Reuben. **9** And sons of Reuben: Enoch, and Phallu, and Hezron, and Carmi. **10** And sons of Simeon: Jemuel, and Jamin, and Ohad, and Jachin, and Zohar, and Shaul son of the Canaanite. **11** And sons of Levi: Gershon, Kohath, and Merari. **12** And sons of Judah: Er, and Onan, and Shelah, and Perez, and Zerah (and Er and Onan die in the land of Canaan). And sons of Perez are Hezron and Hamul. **13** And sons of Issachar: Tola, and Phuvah, and Job, and Shimron. **14** And sons of Zebulun: Sered, and Elon, and Jahleel. **15** These [are] sons of Leah whom she bore to Jacob in Padan-Aram, and his daughter Dinah; all the persons of his sons and his daughters [are] thirty-three. **16** And sons of Gad: Ziphion, and Haggi, Shuni, and Ezbon, Eri, and Arodi, and Areli. **17** And sons of Asher: Jimnah, and Ishuah, and Isui, and Beriah, and their sister Serah. And sons of Beriah: Heber and Malchiel. **18** These [are] sons of Zilpah, whom Laban gave to his daughter Leah, and she bears these to Jacob— sixteen persons. **19** Sons of Rachel, Jacob's wife: Joseph and Benjamin. **20** And born to Joseph in the land of Egypt (whom Asenath daughter of Poti-Pherah, priest of On, has borne to him) [are] Manasseh and Ephraim. **21** And sons of Benjamin: Belah, and Becher, and Ashbel, Gera, and Naaman, Ehi, and Rosh, Muppim, and Huppim, and Ard. **22** These [are] sons of Rachel, who were born to Jacob; all the persons [are] fourteen. **23** And sons of Dan: Hushim. **24** And sons of Naphtali: Jahzeel, and Guni, and Jezer, and Shillem. **25** These [are] sons of Bilhah, whom Laban gave to his daughter Rachel; and she bears these to Jacob—all the persons [are] seven. **26** All the persons who are coming to Jacob to Egypt, coming out of his thigh, apart from the wives of Jacob's sons, all the persons [are] sixty-six. **27** And the sons of Joseph who have been born to him in Egypt [are] two persons. All the persons of the house of Jacob who are coming into Egypt [are] seventy. **28** And Judah he has sent before him to Joseph, to direct before him to Goshen, and they come into the land of Goshen; **29** and Joseph harnesses his chariot, and goes up to meet his father Israel, to Goshen, and appears to him, and falls on his neck, and weeps on his neck again; **30** and Israel says to Joseph, "Let me die this time, after my seeing your face, for you [are] yet alive." **31** And Joseph says to his brothers, and to the house of his father, "I go up, and declare to Pharaoh, and say to him, My brothers, and the house of my father who [are] in the land of Canaan have come to me; **32** and the men [are] feeders of a flock, for they have been men of livestock; and their flock, and their herd, and all that they have, they have brought. **33** And it has come to pass, when Pharaoh calls for you and has said, What [are] your works? **34** that you have said, Your servants have been men of livestock from our youth, even until now, both we and our fathers, in order that you may dwell in the land of Goshen, for the abomination of the Egyptians is everyone feeding a flock."

CHAPTER 47

[1] And Joseph comes and declares [it] to Pharaoh, and says, "My father, and my brothers, and their flock, and their herd, and all they have, have come from the land of Canaan, and behold, they [are] in the land of Goshen." [2] And out of his brothers he has taken five men, and sets them before Pharaoh; [3] and Pharaoh says to his brothers, "What [are] your works?" And they say to Pharaoh, "Your servants [are] feeders of a flock, both we and our fathers"; [4] and they say to Pharaoh, "We have come to sojourn in the land, for there is no pasture for the flock which your servants have, for the famine in the land of Canaan [is] grievous; and now, please let your servants dwell in the land of Goshen." [5] And Pharaoh speaks to Joseph, saying, "Your father and your brothers have come to you: [6] the land of Egypt is before you; cause your father and your brothers to dwell in the best of the land—they dwell in the land of Goshen, and if you have known, and there are among them men of ability, then you have set them [as] heads over the livestock I have." [7] And Joseph brings in his father Jacob, and causes him to stand before Pharaoh; and Jacob blesses Pharaoh. [8] And Pharaoh says to Jacob, "How many [are] the days of the years of your life?" [9] And Jacob says to Pharaoh, "The days of the years of my sojournings [are] one hundred and thirty years; few and evil have been the days of the years of my life, and they have not reached the days of the years of the life of my fathers, in the days of their sojournings." [10] And Jacob blesses Pharaoh, and goes out from before Pharaoh. [11] And Joseph settles his father and his brothers, and gives a possession to them in the land of Egypt, in the best of the land, in the land of Rameses, as Pharaoh commanded; [12] and Joseph nourishes his father, and his brothers, and all the house of his father [with] bread, according to the mouth of the infants. [13] And there is no bread in all the land, for the famine [is] very grievous, and the land of Egypt and the land of Canaan are feeble because of the famine; [14] and Joseph gathers all the silver that is found in the land of Egypt and in the land of Canaan, for the grain that they are buying, and Joseph brings the silver into the house of Pharaoh. [15] And the silver is consumed out of the land of Egypt and out of the land of Canaan, and all the Egyptians come to Joseph, saying, "Give bread to us—why do we die before you, though the money has ceased?" [16] and Joseph says, "Give your livestock; and I give to you for your livestock, if the money has ceased." [17] And they bring in their livestock to Joseph, and Joseph gives to them bread, for the horses, and for the livestock of the flock, and for the livestock of the herd, and for the donkeys; and he tends them with bread, for all their livestock, during that year. [18] And that year is finished, and they come to him on the second year, and say to him, "We do not hide from my lord, that since the money has been finished, and possession of the livestock [is] to my lord, there has not been left before my lord except our bodies, and our ground; [19] why do we die before your eyes, both we and our ground? buy us and our ground for bread, and we and our ground are servants to Pharaoh; and give seed, and we live, and do not die, and the ground is not desolate." [20] And Joseph buys all the ground of Egypt for Pharaoh, for the Egyptians have each sold his field, for the famine has been severe on them, and the land becomes Pharaoh's; [21] as for the people, he has removed them to cities from the [one] end of the border of Egypt even to its [other] end. [22] Only the ground of the priests he has not bought, for the priests have a portion from Pharaoh, and they have eaten their portion which Pharaoh has given to them, therefore they have not sold their ground. [23] And Joseph says to the people, "Behold, I have bought you today and your ground for Pharaoh; behold, seed for you, and you have sown the ground, [24] and it has come to pass in the increases, that you have given a fifth to Pharaoh, and four of the parts are for yourselves, for seed of the field, and for your food, and for those who [are] in your houses, and for food for your infants." [25] And they say, "You have revived us; we find grace in the eyes of my lord, and have been servants to Pharaoh"; [26] and Joseph sets it for a statute to this day, concerning the ground of Egypt, [that] Pharaoh has a fifth; only the ground of the priests alone has not become Pharaoh's. [27] And Israel dwells in the land of Egypt, in the land of Goshen, and they have possession in it, and are fruitful, and multiply exceedingly; [28] and Jacob lives in the land of Egypt seventeen years, and the days of Jacob, the years of his life, are one hundred and forty-seven years. [29] And the days of Israel are near to die, and he calls for his son, for Joseph, and says to him, "Now if I have found grace in your eyes, please put your hand under my thigh, and you have done kindness and truth with me; please do not bury me in Egypt, [30] and I have lain

with my fathers, and you have carried me out of Egypt, and buried me in their burying-place." And he says, "I do according to your word"; [31] and he says, "Swear to me"; and he swears to him, and Israel bows himself on the head of the bed.

CHAPTER 48

[1] And it comes to pass, after these things, that [one] says to Joseph, "Behold, your father is sick"; and he takes his two sons with him, Manasseh and Ephraim. [2] And [one] declares [it] to Jacob and says, "Behold, your son Joseph is coming to you"; and Israel strengthens himself, and sits on the bed. [3] And Jacob says to Joseph, "God Almighty has appeared to me, in Luz, in the land of Canaan, and blesses me, [4] and says to me, Behold, I am making you fruitful, and have multiplied you, and given you for an assembly of peoples, and given this land to your seed after you, a continuous possession. [5] And now, your two sons, who are born to you in the land of Egypt, before my coming to you to Egypt, they [are] mine; Ephraim and Manasseh, as Reuben and Simeon, they are mine; [6] and your family which you have begotten after them are yours; by the name of their brothers they are called in their inheritance. [7] And I—in my coming in from Padan-[Aram] Rachel has died by me in the land of Canaan, in the way, while yet a distance of land to enter Ephrata, and I bury her there in the way of Ephrata, which [is] Beth-Lehem." [8] And Israel sees the sons of Joseph and says, "Who [are] these?" [9] and Joseph says to his father, "They [are] my sons, whom God has given to me in this [place]"; and he says, "Please bring them to me, and I bless them." [10] And the eyes of Israel have been heavy from age—he is unable to see; and he brings them near to him, and he kisses them and cleaves to them; [11] and Israel says to Joseph, "I had not thought [possible] to see your face, and behold, God has also showed me your seed." [12] And Joseph brings them out from between his knees, and bows himself on his face to the earth; [13] and Joseph takes them both, Ephraim in his right hand toward Israel's left, and Manasseh in his left toward Israel's right, and brings [them] near to him. [14] And Israel puts out his right hand and places [it] on the head of Ephraim, who [is] the younger, and his left hand on the head of Manasseh; he has guided his hands wisely, for Manasseh [is] the firstborn. [15] And he blesses Joseph and says, "God, before whom my fathers Abraham and Isaac habitually walked: God who is feeding me from my being to this day: [16] the Messenger who is redeeming me from all evil blesses the youths, and my name is called on them, and the name of my fathers Abraham and Isaac; and they increase into a multitude in the midst of the land." [17] And Joseph sees that his father sets his right hand on the head of Ephraim, and it is wrong in his eyes, and he supports the hand of his father to turn it aside from off the head of Ephraim to the head of Manasseh; [18] and Joseph says to his father, "Not so, my father, for this [is] the firstborn; set your right hand on his head." [19] And his father refuses and says, "I have known, my son, I have known; he also becomes a people, and he also is great, and yet, his young brother is greater than he, and his seed is the fullness of the nations"; [20] and he blesses them in that day, saying, "By you does Israel bless, saying, God set you as Ephraim and as Manasseh"; and he sets Ephraim before Manasseh. [21] And Israel says to Joseph, "Behold, I am dying, and God has been with you, and has brought you back to the land of your fathers; [22] and I have given to you one portion above your brothers, which I have taken out of the hand of the Amorite by my sword and by my bow."

CHAPTER 49

[1] And Jacob calls to his sons and says, "Be gathered together, and I declare to you that which happens with you in the latter end of the days. [2] Be assembled, and hear, sons of Jacob, || And listen to your father Israel. [3] Reuben! You [are] my firstborn, || My power, and beginning of my strength, || The abundance of exaltation, || And the abundance of strength; [4] Unstable as water, you are not abundant; For you have gone up your father's bed; Then you have defiled [it]: He went up my couch! [5] Simeon and Levi [are] brothers! Instruments of violence—their espousals! [6] Into their secret, do not come, O my soul! Do not be united to their assembly, O my glory; For in their anger they slew a man, || And in their self-will eradicated a prince. [7] Cursed [is] their anger, for [it is]

fierce, || And their wrath, for [it is] sharp; I divide them in Jacob, || And I scatter them in Israel. **8** Judah! Your brothers praise you! Your hand [is] on the neck of your enemies, || Sons of your father bow themselves to you. **9** A lion's whelp [is] Judah, || For prey, my son, you have gone up; He has bent, he has crouched as a lion, || And as a lioness; who causes him to arise? **10** The scepter does not turn aside from Judah, || And a lawgiver from between his feet, || Until his Seed comes; And His [is] the obedience of peoples. **11** Binding to the vine his donkey, || And to the choice vine the colt of his donkey, || He has washed in wine his clothing, || And in the blood of grapes his covering; **12** Red [are] eyes with wine, || And white [are] teeth with milk! **13** Zebulun dwells at a haven of the seas, || And he [is] for a haven of ships; And his side [is] to Sidon. **14** Issachar [is] a strong donkey, || Crouching between the two folds; **15** And he sees rest, that [it is] good, || And the land, that [it is] pleasant, || And he inclines his shoulder to bear, || And is a servant for tribute. **16** Dan judges his people, || As one of the tribes of Israel; **17** Dan is a serpent by the way, a viper by the path, || Which is biting the horse's heels, || And its rider falls backward. **18** For Your salvation I have waited, Yhwh! **19** Gad! A troop assaults him, || But he assaults last. **20** Out of Asher his bread [is] fat; And he gives delicacies of a king. **21** Naphtali [is] a doe sent away, || Who is giving beautiful young ones. **22** Joseph [is] a fruitful son; A fruitful son by a fountain, || Daughters step over the wall; **23** And embitter him indeed, they have striven, || Indeed, archers hate him; **24** And his bow abides in strength, || And strengthened are the arms of his hands || By the hands of the Mighty One of Jacob, || From where is a shepherd, a son of Israel. **25** By the God of your father who helps you, || And the Mighty One who blesses you, || Blessings of the heavens from above, || Blessings of the deep lying under, || Blessings of breasts and womb— **26** Your father's blessings have been mighty || Above the blessings of my progenitors, || To the limit of the perpetual heights || They are for the head of Joseph, || And for the crown of the one || Separate [from] his brothers. **27** Benjamin! A wolf tears; In the morning he eats prey, || And at evening he apportions spoil." **28** All these [are] the twelve tribes of Israel, and this [is] that which their father has spoken to them, and he blesses them; each according to his blessing he has blessed them. **29** And he commands them and says to them, "I am being gathered to my people; bury me by my fathers, at the cave which [is] in the field of Ephron the Hittite; **30** in the cave which [is] in the field of Machpelah, which [is] on the front of Mamre, in the land of Canaan, which Abraham bought with the field from Ephron the Hittite for a possession of a burying-place; **31** (there they buried Abraham and his wife Sarah; there they buried Isaac and his wife Rebekah; and there I buried Leah); **32** the purchase of the field and of the cave which [is] in it, [is] from sons of Heth." **33** And Jacob finishes commanding his sons, and gathers up his feet to the bed, and expires, and is gathered to his people.

CHAPTER 50

1 And Joseph falls on his father's face, and weeps over him, and kisses him; 2 and Joseph commands his servants, the physicians, to embalm his father, and the physicians embalm Israel; 3 and they fulfill for him forty days, for so they fulfill the days of the embalmed, and the Egyptians weep for him seventy days. 4 And the days of his weeping pass away, and Joseph speaks to the house of Pharaoh, saying, "Now if I have found grace in your eyes, please speak in the ears of Pharaoh, saying, 5 My father caused me to swear, saying, Behold, I am dying; in my burying-place which I have prepared for myself in the land of Canaan, there you bury me; and now, please let me go up and bury my father, then I return"; 6 and Pharaoh says, "Go up and bury your father, as he caused you to swear." 7 And Joseph goes up to bury his father, and all [the] servants of Pharaoh go up with him, [the] elderly of his house, and all [the] elderly of the land of Egypt, 8 and all the house of Joseph, and his brothers, and the house of his father; only their infants, and their flock, and their herd, have they left in the land of Goshen; 9 and there go up with him both chariot and horsemen, and the camp is very great. 10 And they come to the threshing-floor of Atad, which [is] beyond the Jordan, and they lament there, a lamentation great and very grievous; and he makes for his father a mourning seven days, 11 and the inhabitant of the land, the Canaanite, sees the mourning in the threshing-floor of Atad and says, "A grievous mourning [is] this

to the Egyptians"; therefore [one] has called its name "The mourning of the Egyptians," which [is] beyond the Jordan. 12 And his sons do to him so as he commanded them, 13 and his sons carry him away to the land of Canaan, and bury him in the cave of the field of Machpelah, which Abraham bought with the field for a possession of a burying-place, from Ephron the Hittite, on the front of Mamre. 14 And Joseph turns back to Egypt, he and his brothers, and all who are going up with him to bury his father, after his burying his father. 15 And the brothers of Joseph see that their father is dead, and say, "Perhaps Joseph hates us, and certainly returns to us all the evil which we did with him." 16 And they give a charge for Joseph, saying, "Your father commanded before his death, saying, 17 Thus you say to Joseph: Ah, now, please bear with the transgression of your brothers and their sin, for they have done you evil; and now, please bear with the transgression of the servants of the God of your father"; and Joseph weeps in their speaking to him. 18 And his brothers also go and fall before him, and say, "Behold, we [are] to you for servants." 19 And Joseph says to them, "Do not fear, for [am] I in the place of God? 20 As for you, you devised evil against me, [but] God devised it for good, in order to do as [at] this day, to keep alive a numerous people; 21 and now, do not fear: I nourish you and your infants"; and he comforts them, and speaks to their heart. 22 And Joseph dwells in Egypt, he and the house of his father, and Joseph lives one hundred and ten years, 23 and Joseph looks on Ephraim's sons of a third [generation]; sons also of Machir, son of Manasseh, have been born on the knees of Joseph. 24 And Joseph says to his brothers, "I am dying, and God certainly inspects you, and has caused you to go up from this land, to the land which He has sworn to Abraham, to Isaac, and to Jacob." 25 And Joseph causes the sons of Israel to swear, saying, "God certainly inspects you, and you have brought up my bones from this [place]." 26 And Joseph dies, a son of one hundred and ten years, and they embalm him, and he is put into a coffin in Egypt.

EXODUS

CHAPTER 1

1 And these [are] the names of the sons of Israel who are coming into Egypt; each man and his household have come with Jacob: **2** Reuben, Simeon, Levi, and Judah, **3** Issachar, Zebulun, and Benjamin, **4** Dan, and Naphtali, Gad, and Asher. **5** And all the persons coming out of the thigh of Jacob are seventy persons; as for Joseph, he was in Egypt. **6** And Joseph dies, and all his brothers, and all that generation; **7** and the sons of Israel have been fruitful, and they teem, and multiply, and are very, very mighty, and the land is filled with them. **8** And there rises a new king over Egypt, who has not known Joseph, **9** and he says to his people, "Behold, the people of the sons of Israel [are] more numerous and mightier than we. **10** Give help! Let us act wisely concerning it, lest it multiply, and it has come to pass, when war happens, that it has been joined, even it, to those hating us, and has fought against us, and has gone up out of the land." **11** And they set princes of tribute over it, so as to afflict it with their burdens, and it builds the store-cities of Pithom and Rameses for Pharaoh; **12** and as they afflict it, so it multiplies, and so it breaks forth, and they are distressed because of the sons of Israel; **13** and the Egyptians cause the sons of Israel to serve with rigor, **14** and make their lives bitter in hard service, in clay, and in brick, and in every [kind] of service in the field; all their service in which they have served [is] with rigor. **15** And the king of Egypt speaks to the midwives, the Hebrewesses (of whom the name of the first [is] Shiphrah, and the name of the second Puah), **16** and says, "When you cause the Hebrew women to bear, and have looked on the children, if it [is] a son, then you have put him to death; and if it [is] a daughter, then she has lived." **17** And the midwives fear God, and have not done as the king of Egypt has spoken to them, and they keep the boys alive; **18** and the king of Egypt calls for the midwives and says to them, "Why have you done this thing, and keep the boys alive?" **19** And the midwives say to Pharaoh, "Because the Hebrew women [are] not as the Egyptian women, for they [are] lively; before the midwife comes to them—they have borne!" **20** And God does good to the midwives, and the people multiply, and are very mighty; **21** and it comes to pass, because the midwives have feared God, that He makes households for them; **22** and Pharaoh lays a charge on all his people, saying, "Every son who is born—you cast him into the River, and every daughter you keep alive."

CHAPTER 2

1 And there goes a man of the house of Levi, and he takes the daughter of Levi, **2** and the woman conceives, and bears a son, and she sees him, that he [is] beautiful, and she hides him [for] three months, **3** and she has not been able to hide him anymore, and she takes an ark of rushes for him, and covers it with bitumen and with pitch, and puts the boy in it, and puts [it] in the weeds by the edge of the River; **4** and his sister stations herself far off, to know what is done to him. **5** And a daughter of Pharaoh comes down to bathe at the River, and her girls are walking by the side of the River, and she sees the ark in the midst of the weeds, and sends her handmaid, and she takes it, **6** and opens, and sees him—the boy, and behold, a child weeping! And she has pity on him and says, "This is [one] of the Hebrews' children." **7** And his sister says to the daughter of Pharaoh, "Do I go? when I have called a suckling woman of the Hebrews for you, then she suckles the boy for you"; **8** and the daughter of Pharaoh says to her, "Go"; and the virgin goes, and calls the mother of the boy, **9** and the daughter of Pharaoh says to her, "Take this boy away, and suckle him for me, and I give your hire"; and the woman takes the boy, and suckles him. **10** And the boy grows, and she brings him to the daughter of Pharaoh, and he is to her for a son, and she calls his name Moses, and says, "Because I have drawn him from the water." **11** And it comes to pass, in those days, that Moses is grown, and he goes out to his brothers, and looks on their burdens, and sees a man, an Egyptian, striking a man, a Hebrew, [one] of his brothers, **12** and he turns here and there, and sees that there is no man, and strikes the Egyptian, and hides him in the sand. **13** And he goes out on the second day, and behold, two men, Hebrews, are striving, and he says to the wrongdoer, "Why do you strike your neighbor?" **14** and he says, "Who set you for a head and judge over us? Are you saying [it] to slay me as you have slain the Egyptian?" And Moses fears and says, "Surely the thing has been known." **15** And Pharaoh hears of this thing, and seeks to slay Moses, and Moses flees from the face of Pharaoh, and dwells in the land of Midian, and dwells by the well. **16** And to a priest of Midian [are] seven daughters, and they come and draw, and fill the troughs to water the flock of their father, **17** and the shepherds come and drive them away, and Moses arises, and saves them, and waters their flock. **18** And they come to their father Reuel, and he says, "Why have you hurried to come in today?" **19** and they say, "A man, an Egyptian, has delivered us out of the hand of the shepherds, and has also diligently drawn for us, and waters the flock"; **20** and he says to his daughters, "And where [is] he? why [is] this [that] you left the man? call for him, and he eats bread." **21** And Moses is willing to dwell with the man, and he gives his daughter Zipporah to Moses, **22** and she bears a son, and he calls his name Gershom, for he said, "I have been a sojourner in a strange land." **23** And it comes to pass during these many days, that the king of Egypt dies, and the sons of Israel sigh because of the service, and cry, and their cry goes up to God, because of the service; **24** and God hears their groaning, and God remembers His covenant with Abraham, with Isaac, and with Jacob; **25** and God sees the sons of Israel, and God knows.

CHAPTER 3

1 And Moses has been feeding the flock of his father-in-law Jethro, priest of Midian, and he leads the flock behind the wilderness, and comes to the mountain of God, to Horeb; **2** and the Messenger of Yhwh appears to him in a flame of fire, out of the midst of the bush, and he sees, and behold, the bush is burning with fire, and the bush is not consumed. **3** And Moses says, "Now I turn aside and see this great appearance. Why is the bush not burned?" **4** and Yhwh sees that he has turned aside to see, and God calls to him out of the midst of the bush and says, "Moses! Moses!" And he says, "Here I [am]." **5** And He says, "Do not come near here. Cast your shoes from off your feet, for the place on which you are standing is holy

ground." **6** He also says, "I [am] the God of your father, God of Abraham, God of Isaac, and God of Jacob"; and Moses hides his face, for he is afraid to look toward God. **7** And Yhwh says, "I have certainly seen the affliction of My people who [are] in Egypt, and I have heard their cry because of its exactors, for I have known its pains; **8** and I go down to deliver it out of the hand of the Egyptians, and to cause it to go up out of the land to a land good and broad, to a land flowing with milk and honey—to the place of the Canaanite, and the Hittite, and the Amorite, and the Perizzite, and the Hivite, and the Jebusite. **9** And now, behold, the cry of the sons of Israel has come to Me, and I have also seen the oppression with which the Egyptians are oppressing them, **10** and now, come, and I send you to Pharaoh; and bring out My people, the sons of Israel, from Egypt." **11** And Moses says to God, "Who [am] I, that I go to Pharaoh, and that I bring out the sons of Israel from Egypt?" **12** and He says, "Because I am with you, and this [is] the sign to you that I have sent you: in your bringing out the people from Egypt—you serve God on this mountain." **13** And Moses says to God, "Behold, I am coming to the sons of Israel, and have said to them, The God of your fathers has sent me to you, and they have said to me, What [is] His Name? what do I say to them?" **14** And God says to Moses, "I am that which I am." He also says, "Thus you say to the sons of Israel: I am has sent me to you." **15** And God says again to Moses, "Thus you say to the sons of Israel: Yhwh, God of your fathers, God of Abraham, God of Isaac, and God of Jacob, has sent me to you; this [is] My Name for all time, and this [is] My memorial, to generation [and] generation. **16** Go, and you have gathered the elderly of Israel, and have said to them: Yhwh, God of your fathers, has appeared to me, God of Abraham, Isaac, and Jacob, saying, I have certainly inspected you, and that which is done to you in Egypt; **17** and I say [that] I bring you up out of the affliction of Egypt to the land of the Canaanite, and the Hittite, and the Amorite, and the Perizzite, and the Hivite, and the Jebusite, to a land flowing [with] milk and honey. **18** And they have listened to your voice, and you have entered, you and [the] elderly of Israel, to the king of Egypt, and you have said to him: Yhwh, God of the Hebrews, has met with us; and now, please let us go a journey of three days into the wilderness, and we sacrifice to our God Yhwh. **19** And I have known that the king of Egypt does not permit you to go, unless by a strong hand, **20** and I have put forth My hand, and have struck Egypt with all My wonders, which I do in its midst—and afterward he sends you away. **21** And I have given the grace of this people in the eyes of the Egyptians, and it has come to pass, when you go, you do not go empty; **22** and [every] woman has asked from her neighbor, and from her who is sojourning in her house, [for] vessels of silver, and vessels of gold, and garments, and you have put [them] on your sons and on your daughters, and have spoiled the Egyptians."

CHAPTER 4

1 And Moses answers and says, "And if they do not give credence to me, nor listen to my voice, and say, Yhwh has not appeared to you?" **2** And Yhwh says to him, "What [is] this in your hand?" And he says, "A rod"; **3** and He says, "Cast it to the earth"; and he casts it to the earth, and it becomes a serpent—and Moses flees from its presence. **4** And Yhwh says to Moses, "Put forth your hand, and lay hold on the tail of it"; and he puts forth his hand, and lays hold on it, and it becomes a rod in his hand— **5** "so that they believe that Yhwh, God of their fathers, has appeared to you, God of Abraham, God of Isaac, and God of Jacob." **6** And Yhwh says to him again, "Now put your hand into your bosom"; and he puts his hand into his bosom, and he brings it out, and behold, his hand [is] leprous as snow; **7** and He says, "Put your hand back into your bosom"; and he puts his hand back into his bosom, and he brings it out from his bosom, and behold, it has turned back as his flesh— **8** "and it has come to pass, if they do not give credence to you, and do not listen to the voice of the first sign, that they have given credence to the voice of the latter sign. **9** And it has come to pass, if they do not give credence even to these two signs, nor listen to your voice, that you have taken of the waters of the River, and have poured [it] on the dry land, and the waters which you take from the River have been, indeed, they have become blood on the dry land." **10** And Moses says to Yhwh, "O my Lord, I [am] not a man of words, either yesterday, or before, or since Your speaking to Your servant, for I [am] slow of mouth, and slow of tongue." **11** And Yhwh says to him, "Who appointed a mouth for man? or who appoints the mute, or deaf, or open, or blind? is it not I, Yhwh? **12** and now, go, and I am with your mouth, and have directed you that which you speak"; **13** and he says, "O my Lord, please send by the hand [of another that] You send." **14** And the anger of Yhwh burns against Moses, and He says, "Is Aaron the Levite not your brother? I have known that he speaks well, and also, behold, he is coming out to meet you; when he has seen you, then he has rejoiced in his heart, **15** and you have spoken to him, and have set the words in his mouth, and I am with your mouth, and with his mouth, and have directed you that which you do; **16** and he, he has spoken to the people for you, and it has come to pass, he is to you for a mouth, and you are to him for God; **17** and you take this rod in your hand, with which you do the signs." **18** And Moses goes and turns back to his father-in-law Jethro, and says to him, "Please let me go, and I return to my brothers who [are] in Egypt, and I see whether they are yet alive." And Jethro says to Moses, "Go in peace." **19** And Yhwh says to Moses in Midian, "Go, return to Egypt, for all the men who seek your life have died"; **20** and Moses takes his wife, and his sons, and causes them to ride on the donkey, and turns back to the land of Egypt, and Moses takes the rod of God in his hand. **21** And Yhwh says to Moses, "In your going to return to Egypt, see—all the wonders which I have put in your hand—that you have done them before Pharaoh, and I strengthen his heart, and he does not send the people away; **22** and you have said to Pharaoh, Thus said Yhwh: My son, My firstborn [is] Israel, **23** and I say to you, send My son away, and he serves Me; and [if] you refuse to send him away, behold, I am slaying your son, your firstborn." **24** And it comes to pass in the way, in a lodging place, that Yhwh meets him, and seeks to put him to death; **25** and Zipporah takes a flint, and cuts off the foreskin of her son, and causes [it] to touch his feet, and says, "You [are] surely a bridegroom of blood to me"; **26** and He desists from him. Then she said, "A bridegroom of blood," in reference to the circumcision. **27** And Yhwh says to Aaron, "Go into the wilderness to meet Moses"; and he goes, and meets him on the mountain of God, and kisses him, **28** and Moses declares to Aaron all the words of Yhwh with which He has sent him, and all the signs with which He has charged him. **29** And Moses goes—Aaron also—and they gather all the elderly of the sons of Israel, **30** and Aaron speaks all the words which Yhwh has spoken to Moses, and does the signs before the eyes of the people; **31** and the people believe when they hear that Yhwh has looked after the sons of Israel, and that He has seen their affliction; and they bow and pay respect.

CHAPTER 5

1 And afterward Moses and Aaron have entered, and they say to Pharaoh, "Thus said Yhwh, God of Israel: Send My people away, and they keep a celebration for Me in the wilderness"; **2** and Pharaoh says, "Who [is] Yhwh, that I listen to His voice to send Israel away? I have not known Yhwh, and I also do not send Israel away." **3** And they say, "The God of the Hebrews has met with us; please let us go a journey of three days into the wilderness, and we sacrifice to our God Yhwh, lest He meet us with pestilence or with sword." **4** And the king of Egypt says to them, "Why, Moses and Aaron, do you free the people from its works? go to your burdens." **5** Pharaoh also says, "Behold, the people of the land [are] numerous now, and you have caused them to cease from their burdens!" **6** And on that day Pharaoh commands the exactors among the people and its authorities, saying, **7** "You do not add to give straw to the people for the making of the bricks as before—they go and have gathered straw for themselves; **8** and you put on them the proper quantity of the bricks which they are making before, you do not diminish from it, for they are remiss, therefore they are crying, saying, Let us go, let us sacrifice to our God; **9** let the service be heavy on the men, and let them work at it, and not be dazzled by lying words." **10** And the exactors of the people, and its authorities, go out, and speak to the people, saying, "Thus said Pharaoh: I do not give you straw, **11** you—go, take straw for yourselves where you can find [it], for there is nothing diminished of your service." **12** And the people are scattered over all the land of Egypt, to gather stubble for straw, **13** and the exactors are making haste, saying, "Complete your works, the matter of a day in its day, as when there is straw." **14** And the authorities of the sons of Israel, whom the exactors of Pharaoh have placed over them, are beaten, saying, "Why have you not completed your portion in making brick as before,

both yesterday and today?" **15** And the authorities of the sons of Israel come in and cry to Pharaoh, saying, "Why do you do thus to your servants? **16** Straw is not given to your servants, and they are saying to us, Make bricks, and behold, your servants are struck—and your people have sinned." **17** And he says, "Remiss—you are remiss, therefore you are saying, Let us go, let us sacrifice to Yhwh; **18** and now, go, serve; and straw is not given to you, and you give the [required] measure of bricks." **19** And the authorities of the sons of Israel see them in affliction, saying, "You do not diminish from your bricks; the matter of a day in its day." **20** And they meet Moses and Aaron standing to meet them in their coming out from Pharaoh, **21** and say to them, "Yhwh look on you, and judge, because you have caused our fragrance to stink in the eyes of Pharaoh, and in the eyes of his servants—to give a sword into their hand to slay us." **22** And Moses turns back to Yhwh and says, "Lord, why have You done evil to this people? why [is] this [that] You have sent me? **23** and since I have come to Pharaoh to speak in Your Name, he has done evil to this people, and You have not delivered Your people at all."

CHAPTER 6

1 And Yhwh says to Moses, "Now you see that which I do to Pharaoh, for with a strong hand he sends them away, indeed, with a strong hand he casts them out of his land." **2** And God speaks to Moses and says to him, "I [am] Yhwh, **3** and I appear to Abraham, to Isaac, and to Jacob, as God Almighty; as for My Name Yhwh, I have not been known to them; **4** and I have also established My covenant with them, to give the land of Canaan to them, the land of their sojournings, wherein they have sojourned; **5** and I have also heard the groaning of the sons of Israel, whom the Egyptians are causing to serve, and I remember My covenant. **6** Therefore say to the sons of Israel: I [am] Yhwh, and I have brought you out from under the burdens of the Egyptians, and have delivered you from their service, and have redeemed you by an outstretched arm, and by great judgments, **7** and have taken you to Myself for a people, and I have been to you for God, and you have known that I [am] your God Yhwh, who is bringing you out from under the burdens of the Egyptians; **8** and I have brought you to the land which I have lifted up My hand to give it to Abraham, to Isaac, and to Jacob, and have given it to you—a possession; I [am] Yhwh." **9** And Moses speaks so to the sons of Israel, and they did not listen to Moses, for anguish of spirit, and for harsh service. **10** And Yhwh speaks to Moses, saying, **11** "Go in, speak to Pharaoh king of Egypt, and he sends the sons of Israel out of his land"; **12** and Moses speaks before Yhwh, saying, "Behold, the sons of Israel have not listened to me, and how does Pharaoh hear me, and I of uncircumcised lips?" **13** And Yhwh speaks to Moses and to Aaron, and charges them for the sons of Israel, and for Pharaoh king of Egypt, to bring out the sons of Israel from the land of Egypt. **14** These [are] heads of the house of their fathers. Sons of Reuben firstborn of Israel: Enoch, and Phallu, Hezron, and Carmi; these [are] families of Reuben. **15** And sons of Simeon: Jemuel, and Jamin, and Ohad, and Jachin, and Zohar, and Shaul, son of the Canaanite; these [are] families of Simeon. **16** And these [are] the names of the sons of Levi, as to their births: Gershon, and Kohath, and Merari; and the years of the life of Levi [are] one hundred and thirty-seven years. **17** The sons of Gershon: Libni and Shimi, as to their families. **18** And the sons of Kohath: Amram, and Izhar, and Hebron, and Uzziel; and the years of the life of Kohath [are] one hundred and thirty-three years. **19** And the sons of Merari: Mahli and Mushi; these [are] families of Levi, as to their births. **20** And Amram takes his aunt Jochebed to himself for a wife, and she bears Aaron and Moses to him; and the years of the life of Amram [are] one hundred and thirty-seven years. **21** And sons of Izhar: Korah, and Nepheg, and Zichri. **22** And sons of Uzziel: Mishael, and Elzaphan, and Sithri. **23** And Aaron takes Elisheba daughter of Amminadab, sister of Naashon, to himself for a wife, and she bears to him Nadab, and Abihu, Eleazar, and Ithamar. **24** And sons of Korah: Assir, and Elkanah, and Abiasaph; these [are] families of the Korahite. **25** And Eleazar, Aaron's son, has taken to himself [one] of the daughters of Putiel for a wife for himself, and she bears Phinehas to him; these [are] heads of the fathers of the Levites, as to their families. **26** This [is] Aaron—and Moses—to whom Yhwh said, "Bring out the sons of Israel from the land of Egypt, by their hosts"; **27** these are they who are speaking to Pharaoh king of Egypt, to bring out the sons of Israel from Egypt, this [is]

Moses—and Aaron. **28** And it comes to pass in the day of Yhwh's speaking to Moses in the land of Egypt, **29** that Yhwh speaks to Moses, saying, "I [am] Yhwh, speak to Pharaoh king of Egypt all that I am speaking to you." **30** And Moses says before Yhwh, "Behold, I [am] of uncircumcised lips, and how does Pharaoh listen to me?"

CHAPTER 7

1 And Yhwh says to Moses, "See, I have given you [as] a god to Pharaoh, and your brother Aaron is your prophet; **2** you speak all that I command you, and your brother Aaron speaks to Pharaoh, and he has sent the sons of Israel out of his land. **3** And I harden the heart of Pharaoh, and have multiplied My signs and My wonders in the land of Egypt, **4** and Pharaoh does not listen, and I have put My hand on Egypt, and have brought out My hosts, My people, the sons of Israel, from the land of Egypt by great judgments; **5** and the Egyptians have known that I [am] Yhwh, in My stretching out My hand against Egypt; and I have brought out the sons of Israel from their midst." **6** And Moses does—Aaron also—as Yhwh commanded them; so have they done; **7** and Moses [is] a son of eighty years, and Aaron [is] a son of eighty-three years, in their speaking to Pharaoh. **8** And Yhwh speaks to Moses and to Aaron, saying, **9** "When Pharaoh speaks to you, saying, Give a wonder for yourselves; then you have said to Aaron, Take your rod and cast [it] before Pharaoh—it becomes a dragon." **10** And Moses goes in—Aaron also—to Pharaoh, and they do so as Yhwh has commanded; and Aaron casts his rod before Pharaoh and before his servants, and it becomes a dragon. **11** And Pharaoh also calls for wise men and for sorcerers; and the enchanters of Egypt, they also, with their [enchanting] flames, do so, **12** and they each cast down his rod, and they become dragons, and the rod of Aaron swallows their rods; **13** and the heart of Pharaoh is strong, and he has not listened to them, as Yhwh has spoken. **14** And Yhwh says to Moses, "The heart of Pharaoh has been hard, he has refused to send the people away; **15** go to Pharaoh in the morning, behold, he is going out to the water, and you have stood to meet him by the edge of the River, and the rod which was turned to a serpent you take in your hand, **16** and you have said to him: Yhwh, God of the Hebrews, has sent me to you, saying, Send My people away, and they serve Me in the wilderness; and behold, you have not listened until now. **17** Thus said Yhwh: By this you know that I [am] Yhwh; behold, I am striking with the rod which [is] in my hand, on the waters which [are] in the River, and they have been turned to blood, **18** and the fish that [are] in the River die, and the River has stunk, and the Egyptians have been wearied of drinking waters from the River." **19** And Yhwh says to Moses, "Say to Aaron, Take your rod, and stretch out your hand against the waters of Egypt, against their streams, against their rivers, and against their ponds, and against all their collections of waters; and they are blood—and there has been blood in all the land of Egypt, both in [vessels of] wood, and in [those of] stone." **20** And Moses and Aaron do so, as Yhwh has commanded, and he lifts up [his hand] with the rod, and strikes the waters which [are] in the River, before the eyes of Pharaoh and before the eyes of his servants, and all the waters which [are] in the River are turned to blood, **21** and the fish which [is] in the River has died, and the River stinks, and the Egyptians have not been able to drink water from the River; and the blood is in all the land of Egypt. **22** And the enchanters of Egypt do so with their secrets, and the heart of Pharaoh is strong, and he has not listened to them, as Yhwh has spoken, **23** and Pharaoh turns and goes into his house, and has not set his heart even to this; **24** and all the Egyptians seek water all around the River to drink, for they have not been able to drink of the waters of the River. **25** And seven days are completed after Yhwh's striking the River.

CHAPTER 8

1 And Yhwh says to Moses, "Go to Pharaoh, and you have said to him, Thus said Yhwh: Send My people away, and they serve Me; **2** and if you are refusing to send [them] away, behold, I am striking all your border with frogs; **3** and the River has teemed [with] frogs, and they have gone up and gone into your house, and into the inner chamber of your bed, and on your couch, and into the house of your servants, and among your people, and into your ovens, and into your kneading-troughs; **4** indeed, on you, and on your people, and on all your servants the frogs go up." **5** And Yhwh says to Moses, "Say to Aaron, Stretch out your hand, with your rod, against the streams, against the rivers, and against the ponds, and cause the frogs to come up against the land of Egypt." **6** And Aaron stretches out his hand against the waters of Egypt, and the frog comes up, and covers the land of Egypt; **7** and the enchanters do so with their secrets, and cause the frogs to come up against the land of Egypt. **8** And Pharaoh calls for Moses and for Aaron and says, "Make supplication to Yhwh, that he may turn aside the frogs from me, and from my people, and I send the people away, and they sacrifice to Yhwh." **9** And Moses says to Pharaoh, "Beautify yourself over me; when do I make supplication for you, and for your servants, and for your people, to cut off the frogs from you and from your houses—only in the River they remain?" **10** and he says, "Tomorrow." And he says, "According to your word [it is], so that you know that there is none like our God Yhwh, **11** and the frogs have turned aside from you, and from your houses, and from your servants, and from your people; only in the River they remain." **12** And Moses—Aaron also—goes out from Pharaoh, and Moses cries to Yhwh concerning the matter of the frogs which He has set on Pharaoh; **13** and Yhwh does according to the word of Moses, and the frogs die out of the houses, out of the courts, and out of the fields, **14** and they heap them up together, and the land stinks. **15** And Pharaoh sees that there has been a respite, and he has hardened his heart, and has not listened to them, as Yhwh has spoken. **16** And Yhwh says to Moses, "Say to Aaron, Stretch out your rod, and strike the dust of the land, and it has become gnats in all the land of Egypt." **17** And they do so, and Aaron stretches out his hand with his rod, and strikes the dust of the land, and the gnats are on man and on beast; all the dust of the land has been gnats in all the land of Egypt. **18** And the enchanters do so with their secrets, to bring out the gnats, and they have not been able, and the gnats are on man and on beast; **19** and the enchanters say to Pharaoh, "It [is] the finger of God"; and the heart of Pharaoh is strong, and he has not listened to them, as Yhwh has spoken. **20** And Yhwh says to Moses, "Rise early in the morning, and station yourself before Pharaoh, behold, he is going out to the waters, and you have said to him, Thus said Yhwh: Send My people away, and they serve Me; **21** for if you are not sending My people away, behold, I am sending against you, and against your servants, and against your people, and against your houses, the beetle, and the houses of the Egyptians have been full of the beetle, and also the ground on which they are. **22** And I have separated in that day the land of Goshen, in which My people are staying, that the beetle is not there, so that you know that I [am] Yhwh in the midst of the land, **23** and I have put a division between My people and your people; this sign is tomorrow." **24** And Yhwh does so, and the grievous beetle enters the house of Pharaoh, and the house of his servants, and in all the land of Egypt the land is corrupted from the presence of the beetle. **25** And Pharaoh calls to Moses and to Aaron and says, "Go, sacrifice to your God in the land"; **26** and Moses says, "[It is] not right to do so—for us to sacrifice the abomination of the Egyptians to our God Yhwh; behold, we sacrifice the abomination of the Egyptians before their eyes—and they do not stone us! **27** We go a journey of three days into the wilderness and have sacrificed to our God Yhwh as He says to us." **28** And Pharaoh says, "I send you away, and you have sacrificed to your God Yhwh in the wilderness, only do not go very far off; make supplication for me"; **29** and Moses says, "Behold, I am going out from you, and have made supplication to Yhwh, and tomorrow the beetle has turned aside from Pharaoh, from his servants, and from his people; only, do not let Pharaoh add to deceive in not sending the people away to sacrifice to Yhwh." **30** And Moses goes out from Pharaoh, and makes supplication to Yhwh, **31** and Yhwh does according to the word of Moses, and turns aside the beetle from Pharaoh, from his servants, and from his people—there has not been one left; **32** and Pharaoh also hardens his heart at this time, and has not sent the people away.

CHAPTER 9

1 And Yhwh says to Moses, "Go to Pharaoh, and you have spoken to him, Thus said Yhwh, God of the Hebrews: Send My people away, and they serve Me, **2** for if you are refusing to send [them] away, and are still keeping hold on them, **3** behold, the hand of Yhwh is on your livestock which [are] in the field, on horses, on donkeys, on camels, on herd, and on flock—a very grievous pestilence. **4** And Yhwh has separated between the livestock of Israel and the livestock of Egypt, and there does not die a thing of all the sons of Israel; **5** and Yhwh sets an appointed time, saying, Tomorrow Yhwh does this thing in the land." **6** And Yhwh does this thing on the next day, and all the livestock of Egypt die, and of the livestock of the sons of Israel not one has died; **7** and Pharaoh sends, and behold, not even one of the livestock of Israel has died, and the heart of Pharaoh is hard, and he has not sent the people away. **8** And Yhwh says to Moses and to Aaron, "Take for yourselves the fullness of your handfuls—soot of a furnace, and Moses has sprinkled it toward the heavens, before the eyes of Pharaoh, **9** and it has become small dust over all the land of Egypt, and it has become on man and on livestock a boil breaking forth [with] blisters in all the land of Egypt." **10** And they take the soot of the furnace, and stand before Pharaoh, and Moses sprinkles it toward the heavens, and it is a boil [with] blisters breaking forth on man and on beast; **11** and the enchanters have not been able to stand before Moses because of the boil, for the boil has been on the enchanters, and on all the Egyptians. **12** And Yhwh strengthens the heart of Pharaoh, and he has not listened to them, as Yhwh has spoken to Moses. **13** And Yhwh says to Moses, "Rise early in the morning, and station yourself before Pharaoh, and you have said to him, Thus said Yhwh, God of the Hebrews: Send My people away, and they serve Me, **14** for at this time I am sending all My plagues to your heart, and on your servants, and on your people, so that you know that there is none like Me in all the earth, **15** for now I have put forth My hand, and I strike you, and your people, with pestilence, and you are hidden from the earth. **16** And yet for this I have caused you to stand, so as to show you My power, and for the sake of declaring My Name in all the earth; **17** still you are exalting yourself against My people—so as not to send them away; **18** behold, I am raining very grievous hail about [this] time tomorrow, such as has not been in Egypt from the day of its founding and until now. **19** And now, send, strengthen your livestock and all that you have in the field; every man and beast which is found in the field, and is not gathered into the house—the hail has come down on them, and they have died." **20** He who is fearing the word of Yhwh among the servants of Pharaoh has caused his servants and his livestock to flee to the houses; **21** and he who has not set his heart to the word of Yhwh leaves his servants and his livestock in the field. **22** And Yhwh says to Moses, "Stretch forth your hand toward the heavens, and there is hail in all the land of Egypt, on man, and on beast, and on every herb of the field in the land of Egypt." **23** And Moses stretches out his rod toward the heavens, and Yhwh has given voices and hail, and fire goes toward the earth, and Yhwh rains hail on the land of Egypt, **24** and there is hail, and fire catching itself in the midst of the hail, very grievous, such as has not been in all the land of Egypt since it has become a nation. **25** And the hail strikes all that [is] in the field in all the land of Egypt, from man even to beast, and the hail has struck every herb of the field, and it has broken every tree of the field; **26** only in the land of Goshen, where the sons of Israel [are], there has been no hail. **27** And Pharaoh sends, and calls for Moses and for Aaron, and says to them, "I have sinned this time—Yhwh [is] the righteous, and I and my people [are] the wicked, **28** make supplication to Yhwh, and plead that there be no voices of God and hail, and I send you away, and you do not add to remain." **29** And Moses says to him, "At my going out of the city, I spread my palms to Yhwh—the voices cease, and there is no more hail, so that you know that the earth [is] Yhwh's; **30** but you and your servants—I have known that you are not yet afraid of the face of Yhwh God." **31** And the flax and the barley have been struck, for the barley [is] budding, and the flax forming flowers, **32** and the wheat and the rye have not been struck, for they are late. **33** And Moses goes out from Pharaoh, [from] the city, and spreads his hands to Yhwh, and the voices and the hail cease, and rain has not been poured out to the earth; **34** and Pharaoh sees that the rain has ceased, and the hail and the voices, and he continues to sin, and hardens his heart, he and his servants; **35** and the heart of Pharaoh is strong, and he has not sent the sons of Israel away, as Yhwh has spoken by the hand of Moses.

CHAPTER 10

1 And Yhwh says to Moses, "Go to Pharaoh, for I have declared his heart hard, and the heart of his servants, so that I set these signs of Mine in their midst, **2** and so that you recount in the ears of your son, and of your son's son, that which I have done in Egypt, and My signs which I have set among them, and you have known that I [am] Yhwh." **3** And Moses comes in—Aaron also—to Pharaoh, and they say to him, "Thus said Yhwh, God of the Hebrews: Until when have you refused to be humbled at My presence? send My people away, and they serve Me, **4** for if you are refusing to send My people away, behold, tomorrow I am bringing in the locust into your border, **5** and it has covered the eye of the land, and none is able to see the land, and it has eaten the remnant of that which is escaped, which is left to you from the hail, and it has eaten every tree which is springing out of the field for you; **6** and they have filled your houses, and the houses of all your servants, and the houses of all the Egyptians, which neither your fathers nor your father's fathers have seen, since the day of their being on the ground to this day." And he turns and goes out from Pharaoh. **7** And the servants of Pharaoh say to him, "Until when does this [one] become a snare to us? send the men away, and they serve their God Yhwh; do you not yet know that Egypt has perished?" **8** And Moses is brought back—Aaron also—to Pharaoh, and he says to them, "Go, serve your God Yhwh, but who—who [are] those going?" **9** And Moses says, "With our young ones, and with our aged ones, we go, with our sons, and with our daughters, with our flock, and our herd, we go, for we have a festival to Yhwh." **10** And he says to them, "Be it so, Yhwh [is] with you when I send you and your infants away; see—for evil [is] before your faces. **11** Not so! Go now, you who [are] men, and serve Yhwh, for that you are seeking"; and [one] casts them out from the presence of Pharaoh. **12** And Yhwh says to Moses, "Stretch out your hand against the land of Egypt for the locust, and it goes up against the land of Egypt, and eats every herb of the land—all that the hail has left." **13** And Moses stretches out his rod against the land of Egypt, and Yhwh has led an east wind over the land all that day, and all the night; the morning has been, and the east wind has lifted up the locust. **14** And the locust goes up against all the land of Egypt, and rests in all the border of Egypt—very grievous: before it there has not been such a locust as it, and after it there is none such; **15** and it covers the eye of all the land, and the land is darkened; and it eats every herb of the land, and all the fruit of the trees which the hail has left, and there has not been left any green thing in the trees, or in the herb of the field, in all the land of Egypt. **16** And Pharaoh hurries to call for Moses and for Aaron and says, "I have sinned against your God Yhwh, and against you, **17** and now, please bear with my sin, only this time, and make supplication to your God Yhwh, that He may turn aside from off me only this death." **18** And he goes out from Pharaoh, and makes supplication to Yhwh, **19** and Yhwh turns a very strong sea wind, and it lifts up the locust, and blows it into the Red Sea—there has not been left one locust in all the border of Egypt; **20** and Yhwh strengthens the heart of Pharaoh, and he has not sent the sons of Israel away. **21** And Yhwh says to Moses, "Stretch out your hand toward the heavens, and there is darkness over the land of Egypt, and the darkness is felt." **22** And Moses stretches out his hand toward the heavens, and there is darkness—thick darkness in all the land of Egypt [for] three days; **23** they have not seen one another, and none has risen from his place [for] three days; but there has been light for all the sons of Israel in their dwellings. **24** And Pharaoh calls to Moses and says, "Go, serve Yhwh, only your flock and your herd are stayed, your infants also go with you"; **25** and Moses says, "You also give sacrifices and burnt-offerings in our hand, and we have prepared for our God Yhwh; **26** and also our livestock go with us—there is not left a hoof, for we take from it to serve our God Yhwh; and we do not know how we serve Yhwh until our going there." **27** And Yhwh strengthens the heart of Pharaoh, and he has not been willing to send them away; **28** and Pharaoh says to him, "Go from me, take heed to yourself, do not add to see my face, for in the day you see my face you die"; **29** and Moses says, "You have spoken correctly, I do not add to see your face anymore."

CHAPTER 11

1 And Yhwh says to Moses, "One more plague I bring in on Pharaoh and on Egypt, afterward he sends you away from this; when he is sending you away, he surely casts you out from this [place] altogether; **2** now speak in the ears of the people, and they ask—each man from his neighbor, and each woman from her neighbor—[for] vessels of silver and vessels of gold." ³ And Yhwh gives the grace of the people in the eyes of the Egyptians; also the man Moses [is] very great in the land of Egypt, in the eyes of the servants of Pharaoh, and in the eyes of the people. ⁴ And Moses says, "Thus said Yhwh: About midnight I am going out into the midst of Egypt, ⁵ and every firstborn in the land of Egypt has died, from the firstborn of Pharaoh who is sitting on his throne, to the firstborn of the maidservant who [is] behind the millstones, and all the firstborn of beasts; ⁶ and there has been a great cry in all the land of Egypt, such as there has not been, and such as there is not again; ⁷ and against all the sons of Israel a dog does not sharpen its tongue, from man even to beast, so that you know that Yhwh makes a separation between the Egyptians and Israel. ⁸ And all these servants of yours have come down to me, and bowed themselves to me, saying, Go out, you and all the people who [are] at your feet; and afterward I go out"; and he goes out from Pharaoh in the heat of anger. ⁹ And Yhwh says to Moses, "Pharaoh does not listen to you, so as to multiply My wonders in the land of Egypt"; ¹⁰ and Moses and Aaron have done all these wonders before Pharaoh, and Yhwh strengthens Pharaoh's heart, and he has not sent the sons of Israel out of his land.

CHAPTER 12

¹ And Yhwh speaks to Moses and to Aaron in the land of Egypt, saying, ² "This month [is] the chief of months to you—it [is] the first of the months of the year to you; ³ speak to all the congregation of Israel, saying, In the tenth of this month they take to themselves, each man, a lamb for the house of the fathers, a lamb for a house. ⁴ And if the household is too few for a lamb, then he has taken, he and his neighbor who is near to his house, for the number of persons, each according to his eating you count for the lamb. ⁵ A lamb, a perfect one, a male, a son of a year, let [it] be to you; you take [it] from the sheep or from the goats. ⁶ And it has become a charge to you, until the fourteenth day of this month, and the whole assembly of the congregation of Israel has slaughtered it between the evenings; ⁷ and they have taken of the blood, and have put [it] on the two doorposts, and on the lintel over the houses in which they eat it. ⁸ And they have eaten the flesh in this night, a roast with fire; they eat it with unleavened things and bitters; ⁹ you do not eat of it raw, or boiled in water at all, but a roast with fire, its head with its legs, and with its innards; ¹⁰ and you do not leave of it until morning, and that which is remaining of it until morning you burn with fire. ¹¹ And thus you eat it: your loins girded, your sandals on your feet, and your staff in your hand, and you have eaten it in haste; it is Yhwh's Passover, ¹² and I have passed over through the land of Egypt during this night, and have struck every firstborn in the land of Egypt, from man even to beast, and I do judgments on all the gods of Egypt; I [am] Yhwh. ¹³ And the blood has become a sign for you on the houses where you [are], and I have seen the blood, and have passed over you, and a plague is not on you for destruction in My striking in the land of Egypt. ¹⁴ And this day has become a memorial to you, and you have kept it [for] a celebration to Yhwh throughout your generations—a continuous statute; you keep it [for] a celebration. ¹⁵ Seven days you eat unleavened things; only—in the first day you cause leaven to cease out of your houses; for anyone eating anything fermented from the first day until the seventh day, indeed, that person has been cut off from Israel. ¹⁶ And in the first day [is] a holy convocation, and in the seventh day you have a holy convocation; any work is not done in them, only that which is eaten by any person—it alone is done by you, ¹⁷ and you have observed the Unleavened Things, for in this very day I have brought out your hosts from the land of Egypt, and you have observed this day throughout your generations—a continuous statute. ¹⁸ In the first [month], on the fourteenth day of the month, in the evening, you eat unleavened things until the twenty-first day of the month, at evening; ¹⁹ seven days leaven is not found in your houses, for anyone eating anything fermented—that person has been cut off from the congregation of Israel, among the sojourners or among the natives of the land; ²⁰ you do not eat anything fermented—in all your dwellings you eat [only] unleavened things." ²¹ And Moses calls for all [the] elderly of Israel and says to them, "Draw out and take for yourselves [from] the flock, for your families, and slaughter the Passover-sacrifice; ²² and you have taken a bunch of hyssop, and have dipped [it] in the blood

which [is] in the basin, and have struck [it] on the lintel, and on the two doorposts, from the blood which [is] in the basin, and you, you do not go out—each from the opening of his house—until morning. ²³ And Yhwh has passed on to strike the Egyptians, and has seen the blood on the lintel, and on the two doorposts, and Yhwh has passed over the opening, and does not permit the destruction to come into your houses to strike. ²⁴ And you have observed this thing for a statute to you and to your sons for all time; ²⁵ and it has been, when you come to the land which Yhwh gives to you as He has spoken, that you have kept this service; ²⁶ and it has come to pass, when your sons say to you, What [is] this service you have? ²⁷ that you have said, It [is] a sacrifice of Passover to Yhwh, who passed over the houses of the sons of Israel in Egypt, in His striking the Egyptians, and our houses He delivered." ²⁸ And the people bow and pay respect, and the sons of Israel go and do as Yhwh commanded Moses and Aaron; so they have done. ²⁹ And it comes to pass, at midnight, that Yhwh has struck every firstborn in the land of Egypt, from the firstborn of Pharaoh who is sitting on his throne, to the firstborn of the captive who [is] in the prison-house, and every firstborn of beasts. ³⁰ And Pharaoh rises by night, he and all his servants, and all the Egyptians, and there is a great cry in Egypt, for there is not a house where there is not [one] dead, ³¹ and he calls for Moses and for Aaron by night and says, "Rise, go out from the midst of my people, both you and the sons of Israel, and go, serve Yhwh according to your word; ³² take both your flock and your herd as you have spoken, and go; then you have also blessed me." ³³ And the Egyptians are urgent on the people, hastening to send them away out of the land, for they said, "We are all dead"; ³⁴ and the people take up their dough before it is fermented, their kneading-troughs [are] bound up in their garments on their shoulder. ³⁵ And the sons of Israel have done according to the word of Moses, and they ask for vessels of silver and vessels of gold, and garments, from the Egyptians; ³⁶ and Yhwh has given the grace of the people in the eyes of the Egyptians, and they cause them to ask, and they spoil the Egyptians. ³⁷ And the sons of Israel journey from Rameses to Succoth, about six hundred thousand men on foot, apart from infants; ³⁸ and a great rabble has also gone up with them, and flock and herd—very much livestock. ³⁹ And they bake unleavened cakes with the dough which they have brought out from Egypt, for it has not fermented; for they have been cast out of Egypt, and have not been able to delay, and also they have not made provision for themselves. ⁴⁰ And the dwelling of the sons of Israel [in] which they have dwelt in Egypt [is] four hundred and thirty years; ⁴¹ and it comes to pass, at the end of four hundred and thirty years—indeed, it comes to pass on this very same day—all the hosts of Yhwh have gone out from the land of Egypt. ⁴² It [is] a night of watchings to Yhwh, to bring them out from the land of Egypt; it [is] this night of watchings to Yhwh to all the sons of Israel throughout their generations. ⁴³ And Yhwh says to Moses and Aaron, "This [is] a statute of the Passover; any son of a stranger does not eat of it; ⁴⁴ and any man's servant, the purchase of money, when you have circumcised him—then he eats of it; ⁴⁵ a settler or hired servant does not eat of it; ⁴⁶ it is eaten in one house, you do not carry out of the house [any] of the flesh outside, and you do not break a bone of it; ⁴⁷ all the congregation of Israel keeps it. ⁴⁸ And when a sojourner sojourns with you, and has made a Passover to Yhwh, every male of his [is] to be circumcised, and then he comes near to keep it, and he has been as a native of the land, but any uncircumcised one does not eat of it; ⁴⁹ one law is to a native, and to a sojourner who is sojourning in your midst." ⁵⁰ And all the sons of Israel do as Yhwh commanded Moses and Aaron; so they have done. ⁵¹ And it comes to pass on this very same day, Yhwh has brought out the sons of Israel from the land of Egypt by their hosts.

CHAPTER 13

¹ And Yhwh speaks to Moses, saying, ² "Sanctify to Me every firstborn, opening any womb among the sons of Israel, among man and among beast; it [is] Mine." ³ And Moses says to the people, "Remember this day [in] which you have gone out from Egypt, from the house of servants, for by strength of hand Yhwh has brought you out from this, and anything fermented is not eaten; ⁴ you are going out today, in the month of Abib. ⁵ And it has been, when Yhwh brings you to the land of the Canaanite, and of the Hittite, and of the Amorite, and of the Hivite, and of the Jebusite, which He has sworn to your

fathers to give to you, a land flowing with milk and honey, that you have done this service in this month. **6** Seven days you eat unleavened things, and in the seventh day [is] a celebration to Yhwh; **7** unleavened things are eaten the seven days, and anything fermented is not seen with you; indeed, leaven is not seen with you in all your border. **8** And you have declared to your son in that day, saying, [It is] because of what Yhwh did to me, in my going out from Egypt, **9** and it has been to you for a sign on your hand, and for a memorial between your eyes, so that the Law of Yhwh is in your mouth, for by a strong hand Yhwh has brought you out from Egypt; **10** and you have kept this statute at its appointed time from days to days. **11** And it has been, when Yhwh brings you to the land of the Canaanite as He has sworn to you and to your fathers, and has given it to you, **12** that you have caused everyone opening a womb to pass over to Yhwh, and every firstling—the increase of beasts which you have: the males [are] Yhwh's. **13** And every firstling of a donkey you ransom with a lamb, and if you do not ransom [it], then you have beheaded it; and you ransom every firstborn of man among your sons. **14** And it has been, when your son asks you hereafter, saying, What [is] this? that you have said to him, By strength of hand Yhwh has brought us out from Egypt, from a house of servants; **15** indeed, it comes to pass, when Pharaoh has been pained to send us away, that Yhwh slays every firstborn in the land of Egypt, from the firstborn of man even to the firstborn of beast; therefore I am sacrificing to Yhwh all opening a womb who [are] males, and I ransom every firstborn of my sons; **16** and it has been for a token on your hand, and for frontlets between your eyes, for by strength of hand Yhwh has brought us out of Egypt." **17** And it comes to pass in Pharaoh's sending the people away, that God has not led them the way of the land of the Philistines, for it [is] near; for God said, "Lest the people sigh in their seeing war, and have turned back toward Egypt"; **18** and God turns around the people the way of the wilderness of the Red Sea, and the sons of Israel have gone up by fifties from the land of Egypt. **19** And Moses takes the bones of Joseph with him, for he certainly caused the sons of Israel to swear, saying, "God certainly inspects you, and you have brought up my bones from this [place] with you." **20** And they journey from Succoth, and encamp in Etham at the extremity of the wilderness, **21** and Yhwh is going before them by day in a pillar of a cloud, to lead them in the way, and by night in a pillar of fire, to give light to them, to go by day and by night; **22** He does not remove the pillar of the cloud by day, and the pillar of the fire by night, [from] before the people.

have seen the Egyptians today, you add no more to see them for all time; **14** Yhwh fights for you, and you keep silent." **15** And Yhwh says to Moses, "Why do you cry to Me? Speak to the sons of Israel, and they journey; **16** and you, lift up your rod, and stretch out your hand toward the sea, and cleave it, and the sons of Israel go into the midst of the sea on dry land. **17** And I—behold, I am strengthening the heart of the Egyptians, and they go in after them, and I am honored by Pharaoh, and by all his force, by his chariots, and by his horsemen; **18** and the Egyptians have known that I [am] Yhwh, in My being honored by Pharaoh, by his chariots, and by his horsemen." **19** And the Messenger of God, who is going before the camp of Israel, journeys and goes at their rear; and the pillar of the cloud journeys from their front, and stands at their rear, **20** and comes in between the camp of the Egyptians and the camp of Israel, and the cloud and the darkness are, and he enlightens the night, and the one has not drawn near to the other all the night. **21** And Moses stretches out his hand toward the sea, and Yhwh causes the sea to go on by a strong east wind all the night, and makes the sea become dry ground, and the waters are cleaved, **22** and the sons of Israel go into the midst of the sea on dry land, and the waters [are] a wall to them, on their right and on their left. **23** And the Egyptians pursue, and go in after them (all the horses of Pharaoh, his chariots, and his horsemen) into the midst of the sea, **24** and it comes to pass, in the morning watch, that Yhwh looks to the camp of the Egyptians through the pillar of fire and of the cloud, and troubles the camp of the Egyptians, **25** and turns aside the wheels of their chariots, and they lead them with difficulty, and the Egyptians say, "Let us flee from the face of Israel, for Yhwh is fighting for them against the Egyptians." **26** And Yhwh says to Moses, "Stretch out your hand toward the sea, and the waters turn back on the Egyptians, on their chariots, and on their horsemen." **27** And Moses stretches out his hand toward the sea, and the sea turns back, at the turning of the morning, to its perennial flow, and the Egyptians are fleeing at its coming, and Yhwh shakes off the Egyptians in the midst of the sea, **28** and the waters turn back, and cover the chariots and the horsemen, even all the force of Pharaoh, who are coming in after them into the sea—there has not been left even one of them. **29** And the sons of Israel have gone on dry land in the midst of the sea, and the waters [are] a wall to them, on their right and on their left; **30** and Yhwh saves Israel out of the hand of the Egyptians in that day, and Israel sees the Egyptians dead on the seashore, **31** and Israel sees the great hand with which Yhwh has worked against the Egyptians, and the people fear Yhwh, and remain steadfast in Yhwh, and in His servant Moses.

CHAPTER 14

1 And Yhwh speaks to Moses, saying, **2** "Speak to the sons of Israel, and they turn back and encamp before Pi-Hahiroth, between Migdol and the sea, before Ba'al-Zephon; you encamp in front of it by the sea, **3** and Pharaoh has said of the sons of Israel, They are entangled in the land, the wilderness has shut on them; **4** and I have strengthened the heart of Pharaoh, and he has pursued after them, and I am honored by Pharaoh, and by all his force, and the Egyptians have known that I [am] Yhwh"; and they do so. **5** And it is declared to the king of Egypt that the people have fled, and the heart of Pharaoh and of his servants is turned against the people, and they say, "What [is] this we have done, that we have sent Israel away from our service?" **6** And he harnesses his chariot, and he has taken his people with him, **7** and he takes six hundred chosen chariots, even all the chariots of Egypt, and captains over them all; **8** and Yhwh strengthens the heart of Pharaoh king of Egypt, and he pursues after the sons of Israel, and the sons of Israel are going out with a high hand, **9** and the Egyptians pursue after them, and all the chariot horses of Pharaoh, and his horsemen, and his force, overtake them, encamping by the sea, by Pi-Hahiroth, before Ba'al-Zephon. **10** And Pharaoh has drawn near, and the sons of Israel lift up their eyes, and behold, the Egyptians are journeying after them, and they fear exceedingly, and the sons of Israel cry to Yhwh. **11** And they say to Moses, "Because there are no graves in Egypt, have you taken us away to die in a wilderness? what is this you have done to us—to bring us out from Egypt? **12** Is this not the word which we spoke to you in Egypt, saying, Cease from us, and we serve the Egyptians; for [it is] better for us to serve the Egyptians than to die in a wilderness?" **13** And Moses says to the people, "Do not fear, station yourselves, and see the salvation of Yhwh, which He does for you today; for as you

CHAPTER 15

1 Then Moses sings—and the sons of Israel—this song to Yhwh, and they speak, saying, "I sing to Yhwh, || For triumphing He has triumphed; The horse and its rider He has thrown into the sea. **2** My strength and song is Yah, || And He is become my salvation: This [is] my God, and I glorify Him; God of my father, and I exalt Him. **3** Yhwh [is] a man of battle; Yhwh [is] His Name. **4** Chariots of Pharaoh and his force || He has cast into the sea; And the choice of his captains || Have sunk in the Red Sea! **5** The depths cover them; They went down into the depths as a stone. **6** Your right hand, O Yhwh, || Has become honorable in power; Your right hand, O Yhwh, || Crushes an enemy. **7** And in the abundance of Your excellence || You throw down Your withstanders, || You send forth Your wrath—It consumes them as stubble. **8** And by the wind of Your anger || Waters have been heaped together; Flowings have stood as a heap; Depths have been congealed || In the heart of a sea. **9** The enemy said, I pursue, I overtake; I apportion spoil; My soul is filled with them; I draw out my sword; My hand destroys them— **10** You have blown with Your wind || The sea has covered them; They sank as lead in mighty waters. **11** Who [is] like You among the gods, O Yhwh? Who [is] like You— honorable in holiness—Fearful in praises—doing wonders? **12** You have stretched out Your right hand—Earth swallows them! **13** You have led forth in Your kindness || The people whom You have redeemed. You have led on in Your strength || To Your holy habitation. **14** Peoples have heard, they are troubled; Pain has seized inhabitants of Philistia. **15** Then chiefs of Edom have been troubled; Mighty ones of Moab—Trembling seizes them! All inhabitants of Canaan have melted! **16** Terror and dread fall on them; By the greatness of Your arm || They are still as a stone, || Until Your people pass over, O Yhwh; Until the people pass over || Whom You have purchased. **17** You bring them in, and plant them || In a mountain of Your inheritance, || A fixed place for Your dwelling You have made, O Yhwh; A sanctuary, O Lord, Your hands have established; **18** Yhwh reigns—[for] all time and forever!" **19** For the horse of Pharaoh has gone in with his chariots and with his horsemen into the sea, and Yhwh turns back the waters of the sea on them, and the sons of Israel have gone on dry land in the midst of the sea. **20** And Miriam the inspired one, sister of Aaron, takes the timbrel in her hand, and all the women go out after her, with timbrels and with choruses; **21** and Miriam answers to them: "Sing to Yhwh, || For triumphing He has triumphed; The horse and its rider He has thrown into the sea!" **22** And Moses causes Israel to journey from the Red Sea, and they go out to the wilderness of Shur, and they go three days in the wilderness, and have not found water, **23** and they come to Marah, and have not been able to drink the waters of Marah, for they [are] bitter; therefore [one] has called its name Marah. **24** And the people murmur against Moses, saying, "What do we drink?" **25** and he cries to Yhwh, and Yhwh shows him a tree, and he casts [it] into the waters, and the waters become sweet. He has made a statute for them there, and an ordinance, and He has tried them there, **26** and He says, "If you really listen to the voice of your God Yhwh, and do that which is right in His eyes, and have listened to His commands, and kept all His statutes, none of the sickness which I laid on the Egyptians do I lay on you, for I, Yhwh, am healing you." **27** And they come to Elim, and there [are] twelve fountains of water, and seventy palm trees; and they encamp there by the waters.

CHAPTER 16

1 And they journey from Elim, and all the congregation of the sons of Israel come to the wilderness of Sin, which [is] between Elim and Sinai, on the fifteenth day of the second month of their going out from the land of Egypt. **2** And all the congregation of the sons of Israel murmur against Moses and against Aaron in the wilderness; **3** and the sons of Israel say to them, "Oh that we had died by the hand of Yhwh in the land of Egypt, in our sitting by the flesh-pot, in our eating bread to satiety—for you have brought us out to this wilderness to put all this assembly to death with hunger." **4** And Yhwh says to Moses, "Behold, I am raining bread from the heavens for you— and the people have gone out and gathered the matter of a day in its day—so that I try them whether they walk in My law or not; **5** and it has been on the sixth day, that they have prepared that which they bring in, and it has been double above that which they gather day [by] day." **6** And Moses says—Aaron also—to all the sons of Israel, "Evening—and you have known that Yhwh has brought you out from the land of Egypt; **7** and morning—and you have seen the glory of Yhwh, in His hearing your murmurings against Yhwh, and what [are] we, that you murmur against us?" **8** And Moses says, "In Yhwh's giving to you flesh to eat in the evening, and bread in the morning to satiety—in Yhwh's hearing your murmurings, which you are murmuring against Him, and what [are] we? your murmurings [are] not against us, but against Yhwh." **9** And Moses says to Aaron, "Say to all the congregation of the sons of Israel, Come near before Yhwh, for He has heard your murmurings"; **10** and it comes to pass, when Aaron is speaking to all the congregation of the sons of Israel, that they turn toward the wilderness, and behold, the glory of Yhwh is seen in the cloud. **11** And Yhwh speaks to Moses, saying, **12** "I have heard the murmurings of the sons of Israel; speak to them, saying, Between the evenings you eat flesh, and in the morning you are satisfied [with] bread, and you have known that I [am] your God Yhwh." **13** And it comes to pass in the evening, that the quail comes up, and covers the camp, and in the morning there has been the lying of dew around the camp, **14** and the lying of the dew goes up, and behold, on the face of the wilderness [is] a thin, bare thing, thin as hoarfrost on the earth. **15** And the sons of Israel see, and say to one another, "What [is] it?" For they have not known what it [is]; and Moses says to them, "It [is] the bread which Yhwh has given to you for food. **16** This [is] the thing which Yhwh has commanded: Gather of it, each according to his eating, an omer for the counted head; and the number of your persons, take, each, for those in his tent." **17** And the sons of Israel do so, and they gather, he who is [gathering] much, and he who is [gathering] little; **18** and they measure with an omer, and he who is [gathering] much has nothing over, and he who is [gathering] little has no

lack, each according to his eating they have gathered. **19** And Moses says to them, "Let no man leave of it until morning"; **20** and they have not listened to Moses, and some of them leave of it until morning, and it brings up worms and stinks; and Moses is angry with them. **21** And they gather it morning by morning, each according to his eating; when the sun has been warm, then it has melted. **22** And it comes to pass on the sixth day, they have gathered a second bread, two omers for one, and all the princes of the congregation come in, and declare [it] to Moses. **23** And he says to them, "It [is] that which Yhwh has spoken: A rest—a holy Sabbath to Yhwh—[is] tomorrow; that which you bake, bake; and that which you boil, boil; and all that is remaining, let [it] rest for yourselves for preservation until the morning." **24** And they let it rest until the morning, as Moses has commanded, and it has not stunk, and a worm has not been in it. **25** And Moses says, "Eat it today, for today [is] a Sabbath to Yhwh; today you do not find it in the field: **26** six days you gather it, and in the seventh day—the Sabbath—there is none in it." **27** And it comes to pass on the seventh day, some of the people have gone out to gather, and have not found. **28** And Yhwh says to Moses, "How long have you refused to keep My commands and My laws? **29** see, because Yhwh has given the Sabbath to you, therefore He is giving to you on the sixth day bread of two days; each abide [in] his place, no one goes out from his place on the seventh day." **30** And the people rest on the seventh day, **31** and the house of Israel calls its name Manna, and it [is] as white coriander seed; and its taste [is] as a cake with honey. **32** And Moses says, "This [is] the thing which Yhwh has commanded: Fill the omer with it, for a charge for your generations, so that they see the bread which I have caused you to eat in the wilderness, in My bringing you out from the land of Egypt." **33** And Moses says to Aaron, "Take one pot, and put the fullness of the omer of manna [in] there, and let it rest before Yhwh, for a charge for your generations"; **34** as Yhwh has given command to Moses, so Aaron lets it rest before the Testimony, for a charge. **35** And the sons of Israel have eaten the manna [for] forty years, until their coming to the land to be inhabited; they have eaten the manna until their coming to the extremity of the land of Canaan. **36** and the omer is a tenth of the ephah.

CHAPTER 17

1 And all the congregation of the sons of Israel journey from the wilderness of Sin, on their journeys, by the command of Yhwh, and encamp in Rephidim, and there is no water for the people to drink; **2** and the people strive with Moses, and say, "Give us water, and we drink." And Moses says to them, "Why do you strive with me? Why do you try Yhwh?" **3** and the people thirst for water there, and the people murmur against Moses, and say, "Why [is] this [that] you have brought us up out of Egypt to put us to death, also our sons and our livestock, with thirst?" **4** And Moses cries to Yhwh, saying, "What do I do to this people? yet a little, and they have stoned me." **5** And Yhwh says to Moses, "Pass over before the people, and take with you from [the] elderly of Israel, and take your rod in your hand, with which you have struck the River, and you have gone. **6** Behold, I am standing before you there on the rock in Horeb, and you have struck on the rock, and waters have come out from it, and the people have drunk." And Moses does so before the eyes of [the] elderly of Israel, **7** and he calls the name of the place Massah, and Meribah, because of the strife of the sons of Israel, and because of their trying Yhwh, saying, "Is Yhwh in our midst or not?" **8** And Amalek comes, and fights with Israel in Rephidim, **9** and Moses says to Joshua, "Choose men for us, and go out, fight with Amalek: tomorrow I am standing on the top of the hill, and the rod of God in my hand." **10** And Joshua does as Moses has said to him, to fight with Amalek, and Moses, Aaron, and Hur have gone up [to] the top of the height; **11** and it has come to pass, when Moses lifts up his hand, that Israel has been mighty, and when he lets his hands rest, that Amalek has been mighty. **12** And the hands of Moses [are] heavy, and they take a stone and set [it] under him, and he sits on it, and Aaron and Hur have taken hold on his hands, one on this [side] and one on that [side]; and his hands are steadfast until the going in of the sun; **13** and Joshua weakens Amalek and his people by the mouth of the sword. **14** And Yhwh says to Moses, "Write this, a memorial in a Scroll, and set [it] in the ears of Joshua, that I utterly wipe away the remembrance of Amalek from under the heavens"; **15** and Moses builds an altar, and calls its name Yhwh-Nissi, **16** and says, "Because a hand [is] on the throne of Yah, war [is] to Yhwh with Amalek from generation [to] generation."

CHAPTER 18

¹ And Jethro priest of Midian, father-in-law of Moses, hears all that God has done for Moses and for His people Israel, that Yhwh has brought out Israel from Egypt, ² and Jethro, father-in-law of Moses, takes Zipporah, wife of Moses, after her parting, ³ and her two sons, of whom the name of one [is] Gershom, for he said, "I have been a sojourner in a strange land"; ⁴ and the name of the other [is] Eliezer, for, "The God of my father [is] for my help, and He delivers me from the sword of Pharaoh." ⁵ And Jethro, father-in-law of Moses, comes, and his sons, and his wife, to Moses, to the wilderness where he is encamping—the mountain of God; ⁶ and he says to Moses, "I, your father-in-law Jethro, am coming to you, and your wife, and her two sons with her." ⁷ And Moses goes out to meet his father-in-law, and bows himself, and kisses him, and they ask of one another of welfare, and come into the tent; ⁸ and Moses recounts to his father-in-law all that Yhwh has done to Pharaoh, and to the Egyptians, on account of Israel, all the travail which has found them in the way, and [how] Yhwh delivers them. ⁹ And Jethro rejoices for all the good which Yhwh has done to Israel, whom He has delivered from the hand of the Egyptians; ¹⁰ and Jethro says, "Blessed [is] Yhwh, who has delivered you from the hand of the Egyptians, and from the hand of Pharaoh—who has delivered this people from under the hand of the Egyptians; ¹¹ now I have known that Yhwh [is] greater than all the gods, for in the thing they have acted proudly—[He is] above them!" ¹² And Jethro, father-in-law of Moses, takes a burnt-offering and sacrifices [it] for God; and Aaron comes in, and all [the] elderly of Israel, to eat bread with the father-in-law of Moses, before God. ¹³ And it comes to pass on the next day, that Moses sits to judge the people, and the people stand before Moses from the morning to the evening; ¹⁴ and the father-in-law of Moses sees all that he is doing for the people and says, "What [is] this thing which you are doing for the people? Why are you sitting by yourself, and all the people standing by you from morning until evening?" ¹⁵ And Moses says to his father-in-law, "Because the people come to me to seek God; ¹⁶ when they have a matter, it has come to me, and I have judged between a man and his neighbor, and made known the statutes of God, and His laws." ¹⁷ And the father-in-law of Moses says to him, "The thing which you are doing [is] not good; ¹⁸ you surely wear away, both you, and this people which [is] with you, for the thing is too heavy for you, you are not able to do it by yourself. ¹⁹ Now listen to my voice, I counsel you, and God is with you: be for the people before God, and you have brought in the things to God; ²⁰ and you have warned them [concerning] the statutes and the laws, and have made known to them the way in which they go, and the work which they do. ²¹ And you provide out of all the people men of ability, fearing God, men of truth, hating dishonest gain, and have placed [these] over them [for] heads of thousands, heads of hundreds, heads of fifties, and heads of tens, ²² and they have judged the people at all times; and it has come to pass, they bring every great matter to you, and they judge every small matter themselves; and lighten it from off yourself, and they have borne with you. ²³ If you do this thing, and God has commanded you, then you have been able to stand, and all this people also goes to its place in peace." ²⁴ And Moses listens to the voice of his father-in-law, and does all that he said, ²⁵ and Moses chooses men of ability out of all Israel, and makes them chiefs over the people [for] heads of thousands, heads of hundreds, heads of fifties, and heads of tens, ²⁶ and they have judged the people at all times; they bring the hard matter to Moses, and they judge every small matter themselves. ²⁷ And Moses sends his father-in-law away, and he goes away to his own land.

CHAPTER 19

¹ In the third month of the going out of the sons of Israel from the land of Egypt, in this day they have come into the wilderness of Sinai, ² and they journey from Rephidim, and enter the wilderness of Sinai, and encamp in the wilderness; and Israel encamps there before the mountain. ³ And Moses has gone up to God, and Yhwh calls to him out of the mountain,

saying, "Thus you say to the house of Jacob, and declare to the sons of Israel: ⁴ You have seen that which I have done to the Egyptians, and [how] I carry you on eagles' wings and bring you to Myself. ⁵ And now, if you really listen to My voice, then you have kept My covenant, and have been a special treasure to Me more than all the peoples, for all the earth [is] Mine; ⁶ and you are to Me a kingdom of priests and a holy nation: these [are] the words which you speak to the sons of Israel." ⁷ And Moses comes, and calls for [the] elderly of the people, and sets before them all these words which Yhwh has commanded him; ⁸ and all the people answer together and say, "All that Yhwh has spoken we do"; and Moses returns the words of the people to Yhwh. ⁹ And Yhwh says to Moses, "Behold, I am coming to you in the thickness of the cloud, so that the people hear in My speaking with you, and also believe in you for all time"; and Moses declares the words of the people to Yhwh. ¹⁰ And Yhwh says to Moses, "Go to the people and you have sanctified them today and tomorrow, and they have washed their garments, ¹¹ and have been prepared for the third day; for on the third day Yhwh comes down on Mount Sinai before the eyes of all the people. ¹² And you have made a border [for] the people all around, saying, Take heed to yourselves, going up into the mountain or coming against its extremity; whoever is coming against the mountain is certainly put to death; ¹³ a hand does not come against him, for he is certainly stoned or shot through, whether beast or man—it does not live; in the prolonging of the ram's horn they go up into the mountain." ¹⁴ And Moses comes down from the mountain to the people, and sanctifies the people, and they wash their garments; ¹⁵ and he says to the people, "Be prepared for the third day, do not come near to a woman." ¹⁶ And it comes to pass, on the third day, while it is morning, that there are voices, and lightnings, and a heavy cloud on the mountain, and the sound of a very strong horn; and all the people who [are] in the camp tremble. ¹⁷ And Moses brings out the people from the camp to meet God, and they station themselves at the lower part of the mountain, ¹⁸ and Mount Sinai [is] wholly [in] smoke from the presence of Yhwh, who has come down on it in fire, and its smoke goes up as smoke of the furnace, and the whole mountain trembles exceedingly; ¹⁹ and the sound of the horn is going on, and [is] very strong; Moses speaks, and God answers him with a voice. ²⁰ And Yhwh comes down on Mount Sinai, to the top of the mountain, and Yhwh calls for Moses to the top of the mountain, and Moses goes up. ²¹ And Yhwh says to Moses, "Go down, protest to the people, lest they break through to Yhwh to see, and many of them have fallen; ²² and also the priests who are coming near to Yhwh sanctify themselves, lest Yhwh break forth on them." ²³ And Moses says to Yhwh, "The people [are] unable to come up to Mount Sinai, for You have protested to us, saying, Make a border [for] the mountain, then you have sanctified it." ²⁴ And Yhwh says to him, "Go, descend, then you have come up, you and Aaron with you; and the priests and the people do not break through to come up to Yhwh, lest He break forth on them." ²⁵ And Moses goes down to the people and speaks to them.

CHAPTER 20

¹ And God speaks all these words, saying, ² "I [am] your God Yhwh, who has brought you out of the land of Egypt, out of a house of servants. ³ You have no other Gods before Me. ⁴ You do not make a carved image for yourself, or any likeness which [is] in the heavens above, or which [is] in the earth beneath, or which [is] in the waters under the earth. ⁵ You do not bow yourself to them, nor serve them: for I, your God Yhwh, [am] a zealous God, charging iniquity of fathers on sons, on a third and on a fourth [generation] of those hating Me, ⁶ and doing kindness to thousands, of those loving Me and keeping My commands. ⁷ You do not take up the Name of your God Yhwh for a vain thing, for Yhwh does not acquit him who takes up His Name for a vain thing. ⁸ Remember the Sabbath day to sanctify it; ⁹ six days you labor and have done all your work, ¹⁰ and the seventh day [is] a Sabbath to your God Yhwh; you do not do any work, you, and your son, and your daughter, your manservant, and your handmaid, and your livestock, and your sojourner who is within your gates— ¹¹ for [in] six days Yhwh has made the heavens and the earth, the sea, and all that [is] in them, and rests in the seventh day; therefore Yhwh has blessed the Sabbath day and sanctifies it. ¹² Honor your father and your mother, so that your days are prolonged on the ground which your God Yhwh is giving to you. ¹³ You do not

murder. **14** You do not commit adultery. **15** You do not steal. **16** You do not answer [with] a false testimony against your neighbor. **17** You do not desire the house of your neighbor, you do not desire the wife of your neighbor, or his manservant, or his handmaid, or his ox, or his donkey, or anything which [is] your neighbor's." **18** And all the people are seeing the voices, and the flames, and the sound of the horn, and the mountain smoking; and the people see, and move, and stand far off, **19** and say to Moses, "Speak with us, and we hear, and do not let God speak with us, lest we die." **20** And Moses says to the people, "Do not fear, for God has come to try you, and in order that His fear may be before your faces—that you do not sin." **21** And the people stand far off, and Moses has drawn near to the thick darkness where God [is]. **22** And Yhwh says to Moses, "Thus you say to the sons of Israel: You have seen that I have spoken with you from the heavens; **23** you do not make gods of silver and gods of gold [to be] with Me—you do not make [any idol] for yourselves. **24** You make an altar of earth for Me, and you have sacrificed on it your burnt-offerings and your peace-offerings, your flock and your herd; in every place where I cause My Name to be remembered I come to you, and have blessed you. **25** And if you make an altar of stones for Me, you do not build them of hewn work; when you have waved your tool over it, then you defile it; **26** neither do you go up by steps on My altar, that your nakedness is not revealed on it.

CHAPTER 21

1 And these [are] the judgments which you set before them: **2** When you buy a Hebrew servant, he serves [for] six years, and in the seventh he goes out as a freeman for nothing; **3** if he comes in by himself, he goes out by himself; if he [is] owner of a wife, then his wife has gone out with him; **4** if his lord gives a wife to him, and she has borne sons or daughters to him—the wife and her children are her lord's, and he goes out by himself. **5** And if the servant really says: I have loved my lord, my wife, and my sons—I do not go out free, **6** then his lord has brought him near to God, and has brought him near to the door, or to the doorpost, and his lord has bored his ear with an awl, and he has served him for all time. **7** And when a man sells his daughter for a handmaid, she does not go out according to the going out of the menservants; **8** if [it is] evil in the eyes of her lord, so that he has not betrothed her, then he has let her be ransomed; he has no power to sell her to a strange people, in his dealing treacherously with her. **9** And if he betroths her to his son, he does to her according to the right of daughters. **10** If he takes another [woman] for him, he does not withdraw her food, her covering, and her habitation; **11** and if he does not do these three for her, then she has gone out for nothing, without money. **12** He who strikes a man so that he has died is certainly put to death; **13** as for him who has not laid wait, but God has brought [him] to his hand, I have even set a place for you to where he flees. **14** And when a man presumes against his neighbor to slay him with subtlety, you take him from My altar to die. **15** And he who strikes his father or his mother is certainly put to death. **16** And he who steals a man, and has sold him, and he has been found in his hand, is certainly put to death. **17** And he who is reviling his father or his mother is certainly put to death. **18** And when men contend, and a man has struck his neighbor with a stone, or with the fist, and he does not die, but has fallen on the bed; **19** if he rises, and has gone up and down outside on his staff, then the striker has been acquitted; he only gives [for] his cessation, and he is thoroughly healed. **20** And when a man strikes his manservant or his handmaid with a rod, and he has died under his hand—he is certainly avenged; **21** only if he remains a day, or two days, he is not avenged, for he [is] his money. **22** And when men strive, and have struck a pregnant woman, and her children have come out, and there is no harm [to them], he is certainly fined as the husband of the woman lays on him, and he has given through the judges; **23** and if there is harm [to them], then you have given life for life, **24** eye for eye, tooth for tooth, hand for hand, foot for foot, **25** burning for burning, wound for wound, stripe for stripe. **26** And when a man strikes the eye of his manservant, or the eye of his handmaid, and has destroyed it, he sends him away as a freeman for his eye; **27** and if he knocks out a tooth of his manservant or a tooth of his handmaid, he sends him away as a freeman for his tooth. **28** And when an ox gores man or woman, and they have died, the ox is certainly stoned, and his flesh is not eaten, and the owner of the ox [is] acquitted; **29** and if the ox is [one] accustomed to

gore before, and it has been testified to its owner, and he does not watch it, and it has put to death a man or woman, the ox is stoned, and its owner is also put to death. **30** If atonement is laid on him, then he has given the ransom of his life, according to all that is laid on him; **31** whether it gores a son or gores a daughter, according to this judgment it is done to him. **32** If the ox gores a manservant or a handmaid, he gives thirty silver shekels to their lord, and the ox is stoned. **33** And when a man opens a pit, or when a man digs a pit, and does not cover it, and an ox or donkey has fallen [in] there— **34** the owner of the pit repays, he gives back money to its owner, and the dead is his. **35** And when a man's ox strikes the ox of his neighbor and it has died, then they have sold the living ox, and halved its money, and they also halve the dead one; **36** or, [if] it has been known that the ox is [one] accustomed to gore before, and its owner does not watch it, he certainly repays ox for ox, and the dead is his.

CHAPTER 22

1 When a man steals an ox or sheep, and has slaughtered it or sold it, he repays [with] five of the herd for the ox, and four of the flock for the sheep. **2** If in the breaking through, the thief is found, and he has been struck and has died, there is no blood for him; **3** if the sun has risen on him, blood [is] for him, he certainly repays; if he has nothing, then he has been sold for his theft; **4** if the theft is certainly found alive in his hand, whether ox, or donkey, or sheep—he repays double. **5** When a man depastures a field or vineyard, and has sent out his beast, and it has pastured in the field of another, he repays [with] the best of his field, and the best of his vineyard. **6** When fire goes forth and has found thorns, and a stack, or the standing grain, or the field has been consumed, he who causes the burning certainly repays. **7** When a man gives silver or vessels to his neighbor to keep, and it has been stolen out of the man's house; if the thief is found, he repays double. **8** If the thief is not found, then the master of the house has been brought near to God [to see] whether he has not put forth his hand against the work of his neighbor. **9** For every matter of transgression, for ox, for donkey, for sheep, for raiment, for any lost thing of which it is said that it is his, the matter of them both comes to God; he whom God condemns repays double to his neighbor. **10** When a man gives to his neighbor a donkey, or ox, or sheep, or any beast to keep, and it has died, or has been hurt, or taken captive, [with] none seeing— **11** an oath of Yhwh is between them both, that he has not put forth his hand against the work of his neighbor, and its owner has accepted, and he does not repay; **12** but if it is certainly stolen from him, he repays to its owner; **13** if it is certainly torn, he brings it in [as] a witness; he does not repay the torn thing. **14** And when a man asks for [anything] from his neighbor, and it has been hurt or has died—its owner not being with it—he certainly repays; **15** if its owner [is] with it, he does not repay—if it [is] a hired thing, it has come for its hire. **16** And when a man entices a virgin who [is] not betrothed, and has lain with her, he certainly endows her to himself for a wife; **17** if her father utterly refuses to give her to him, he weighs out money according to the dowry of virgins. **18** You do not keep a witch alive. **19** Whoever lies with a beast is certainly put to death. **20** He who is sacrificing to a god, except to Yhwh alone, is devoted. **21** And you do not oppress a sojourner, nor crush him, for you have been sojourners in the land of Egypt. **22** You do not afflict any widow or orphan; **23** if you really afflict him, surely if he cries to Me at all, I certainly hear his cry; **24** and My anger has burned, and I have slain you by the sword, and your wives have been widows, and your sons orphans. **25** If you lend money [to] My poor people [who are] with you, you are not as a usurer to him; you do not lay usury on him; **26** if you take the garment of your neighbor in pledge at all, you return it to him during the going in of the sun: **27** for it is his only covering, it [is] his garment for his skin; wherein does he lie down? and it has come to pass, when he cries to Me, that I have heard, for I [am] gracious. **28** You do not revile God, and you do not curse a prince among your people. **29** You do not delay your fullness and your liquids; you give the firstborn of your sons to Me; **30** so you do to your ox [and] to your sheep; it is with its mother [for] seven days, on the eighth day you give it to Me. **31** And you are holy men to Me, and you do not eat flesh torn in the field, you cast it to a dog.

CHAPTER 23

¹ You do not lift up a vain report; you do not put your hand with a wicked man to be a violent witness. ² You are not after many to [do] evil, nor do you testify concerning a strife, to turn aside after many to cause [others] to turn aside; ³ and you do not honor a poor man in his strife. ⁴ When you meet your enemy's ox or his donkey going astray, you certainly turn it back to him; ⁵ when you see the donkey of him who is hating you crouching under its burden, then you have ceased from leaving [it] to it—you certainly leave [it] with him. ⁶ You do not turn aside the judgment of your poor in his strife; ⁷ you keep far off from a false matter, and you do not slay an innocent and righteous man; for I do not justify a wicked man. ⁸ And you do not take a bribe, for the bribe binds the open-[eyed] and perverts the words of the righteous. ⁹ And you do not oppress a sojourner, since you have known the soul of the sojourner, for you have been sojourners in the land of Egypt. ¹⁰ And [for] six years you sow your land and have gathered its increase; ¹¹ and [in] the seventh you release it, and have left it, and the needy of your people have eaten, and the beast of the field eats their remainder; so you do to your vineyard [and] to your olive-yard. ¹² Six days you do your work, and on the seventh day you rest, so that your ox and your donkey rest, and the son of your handmaid and the sojourner is refreshed; ¹³ and in all that which I have said to you—take heed; and you do not mention the name of other gods; it is not heard on your mouth. ¹⁴ You keep a celebration to Me three times in a year: ¹⁵ you keep the Celebration of Unleavened Things (you eat unleavened things [for] seven days as I have commanded you, at the time appointed [in] the month of Abib; for in it you have come forth out of Egypt, and you do not appear [in] My presence empty); ¹⁶ and the Celebration of Harvest, the first-fruits of your works which you sow in the field; and the Celebration of the Ingathering in the outgoing of the year, in your gathering your works out of the field. ¹⁷ Three times in a year all your males appear before [the] face of the Lord Yhwh. ¹⁸ You do not sacrifice the blood of My sacrifice on a fermented thing, and the fat of My festival does not remain until morning; ¹⁹ the beginning of the first-fruits of your ground you bring into the house of your God Yhwh; you do not boil a kid in its mother's milk. ²⁰ Behold, I am sending a Messenger before you to keep you in the way, and to bring you to the place which I have prepared; ²¹ be watchful because of His presence, and listen to His voice, do not rebel against Him, for He does not bear with your transgression, for My Name [is] in His heart; ²² for if you listen diligently to His voice, and have done all that which I speak, then I have been at enmity with your enemies, and have distressed those distressing you. ²³ For My Messenger goes before you, and has brought you to the Amorite, and the Hittite, and the Perizzite, and the Canaanite, the Hivite, and the Jebusite, and I have cut them off. ²⁴ You do not bow yourself to their gods, nor serve them, nor do according to their doings, but utterly devote them, and thoroughly break their standing pillars. ²⁵ And you have served your God Yhwh, and He has blessed your bread and your water, and I have turned aside sickness from your heart; ²⁶ there is not a miscarrying and barren one in your land; I fulfill the number of your days. ²⁷ I send My terror before you, and I have put to death all the people among whom you come, and I have given the neck of all your enemies to you. ²⁸ And I have sent the hornet before you, and it has cast out the Hivite, the Canaanite, and the Hittite from before you; ²⁹ I do not cast them out from before you in one year, lest the land be a desolation, and the beast of the field has multiplied against you; ³⁰ I cast them out little [by] little from before you, until you are fruitful, and have inherited the land. ³¹ And I have set your border from the Red Sea, even to the sea of the Philistines, and from the wilderness to the River; for I give the inhabitants of the land into your hand, and you have cast them out from before you. ³² You do not make a covenant with them and with their gods; ³³ they do not dwell in your land, lest they cause you to sin against Me when you serve their gods, when it becomes a snare to you."

CHAPTER 24

¹ And He said to Moses, "Come up to Yhwh, you, and Aaron, Nadab, and Abihu, and seventy from [the] elderly of Israel, and you have bowed yourselves far off"; ² and Moses has drawn near to Yhwh by himself; and they do not draw near, and the people do not go up with him. ³ And Moses comes in, and recounts to the people all the words of Yhwh, and all the judgments, and all the people answer [with] one voice, and say, "All the words which Yhwh has spoken we do." ⁴ And Moses writes all the words of Yhwh, and rises early in the morning, and builds an altar under the hill, and twelve standing pillars for the twelve tribes of Israel; ⁵ and he sends the youths of the sons of Israel, and they cause burnt-offerings to ascend, and sacrifice sacrifices of peace-offerings to Yhwh—calves. ⁶ And Moses takes half of the blood and puts [it] in basins, and he has sprinkled half of the blood on the altar; ⁷ and he takes the Scroll of the Covenant, and proclaims [it] in the ears of the people, and they say, "All that which Yhwh has spoken we do, and we obey." ⁸ And Moses takes the blood and sprinkles [it] on the people, and says, "Behold, the blood of the covenant which Yhwh has made with you, concerning all these things." ⁹ And Moses goes up, Aaron also, Nadab and Abihu, and seventy from [the] elderly of Israel, ¹⁰ and they see the God of Israel, and under His feet [is] as the work of a pavement of sapphire, and as the substance of the heavens for purity; ¹¹ and He has not put forth His hand to those of the sons of Israel who are near, and they see God, and eat and drink. ¹² And Yhwh says to Moses, "Come up to Me [on] the mountain and be there, and I give to you the tablets of stone, and the Law, and the command, which I have written to direct them." ¹³ And Moses rises—his minister Joshua also—and Moses goes up to the mountain of God; ¹⁴ and he has said to the elderly, "Abide for us in this [place] until we return to you, and behold, Aaron and Hur [are] with you—he who has matters comes near to them." ¹⁵ And Moses goes up to the mountain, and the cloud covers the mountain; ¹⁶ and the glory of Yhwh dwells on Mount Sinai, and the cloud covers it [for] six days, and He calls to Moses on the seventh day from the midst of the cloud. ¹⁷ And the appearance of the glory of Yhwh [is] as a consuming fire on the top of the mountain, before the eyes of the sons of Israel; ¹⁸ and Moses goes into the midst of the cloud, and goes up to the mountain, and Moses is on the mountain forty days and forty nights.

CHAPTER 25

¹ And Yhwh speaks to Moses, saying, ² "Speak to the sons of Israel, and they take a raised-offering for Me; you take My raised-offering from every man whose heart impels him. ³ And this [is] the raised-offering which you take from them: gold, and silver, and bronze, ⁴ and blue, and purple, and scarlet, and linen, and goats' [hair], ⁵ and rams' skins made red, and tachashim skins, and shittim wood, ⁶ oil for the light, spices for the anointing oil, and for the incense of the spices, ⁷ shoham stones, and stones for setting for an ephod, and for a breastplate. ⁸ And they have made a sanctuary for Me, and I have dwelt in their midst; ⁹ according to all that which I am showing you, the pattern of the Dwelling Place, and the pattern of all its vessels, even so you make [it]. ¹⁰ And they have made an ark of shittim wood; two cubits and a half its length, and a cubit and a half its breadth, and a cubit and a half its height; ¹¹ and you have overlaid it [with] pure gold, you overlay it inside and outside, and you have made a ring of gold on it all around. ¹² And you have cast four rings of gold for it, and have put [them] on its four feet, even two rings on its one side, and two rings on its second side; ¹³ and you have made poles of shittim wood, and have overlaid them [with] gold, ¹⁴ and have brought the poles into the rings on the sides of the Ark, to carry the Ark by them; ¹⁵ the poles are in the rings of the Ark, they are not turned aside from it; ¹⁶ and you have put the Testimony which I give to you into the Ark. ¹⁷ And you have made a propitiatory covering of pure gold, two cubits and a half its length, and a cubit and a half its breadth; ¹⁸ and you have made two cherubim of gold; you make them beaten work at the two ends of the propitiatory covering; ¹⁹ and make one cherub at the end on this [side] and one cherub at the end on that [side]; at the propitiatory covering you make the cherubim on its two ends. ²⁰ And the cherubim have been spreading out wings on high, covering over the propitiatory covering with their wings, and their faces [are] toward one another—the faces of the cherubim are toward the propitiatory covering. ²¹ And you have put the propitiatory covering on the Ark above, and you put the Testimony which I give to you into the Ark; ²² and I have met with you there, and have spoken with you from off the propitiatory covering (from between the two cherubim, which [are] on the Ark of the Testimony) all that which I

command you concerning the sons of Israel. ²³ And you have made a table of shittim wood, two cubits its length, and a cubit its breadth, and a cubit and a half its height, ²⁴ and have overlaid it [with] pure gold, and have made a crown of gold for it all around, ²⁵ and have made a border of a handbreadth for it all around, and have made a crown of gold for its border all around. ²⁶ And you have made four rings of gold for it, and have put the rings on the four corners, which [are] at its four feet; ²⁷ close by the border are the rings for places for poles to carry the table; ²⁸ and you have made the poles of shittim wood, and have overlaid them with gold, and the table has been carried with them; ²⁹ and you have made its dishes, and its bowls, and its covers, and its cups, with which they pour out; you make them of pure gold; ³⁰ and you have put Bread of the Presentation on the table before Me continually. ³¹ And you have made a lampstand of pure gold; the lampstand is made of beaten work; its base, and its branch, its calyxes, its knobs, and its flowers are of the same; ³² and six branches are coming out of its sides, three branches of the lampstand out of the first side, and three branches of the lampstand out of the second side; ³³ three calyxes made like almonds in one branch, a knob and a flower, and three calyxes made like almonds in one branch, a knob and a flower—so for the six branches which are coming out from the lampstand. ³⁴ And in the lampstand [are] four calyxes made like almonds, its knobs and its flowers; ³⁵ and a knob under two branches of the same, and a knob under two branches of the same, and a knob under two branches of the same, for the six branches which are coming out of the lampstand; ³⁶ their knobs and their branches are of the same, all of it one beaten work of pure gold; ³⁷ and you have made its seven lamps, and [one] has caused its lamps to go up, and it has given light over [and] beyond its front. ³⁸ And its snuffers and its snuff dishes [are] of pure gold; ³⁹ he makes it of a talent of pure gold, with all these vessels. ⁴⁰ Now see and make [them] by their pattern which you are shown on the mountain."

CHAPTER 26

¹ "And you make the Dwelling Place [with] ten curtains of twined linen, and blue, and purple, and scarlet; [with] cherubim, the work of a designer, you make them; ² the length of the one curtain [is] twenty-eight by the cubit, and the breadth of the one curtain [is] four by the cubit, one measure [is] for all the curtains; ³ five of the curtains are joining to one another, and five curtains are joining to one another. ⁴ And you have made loops of blue on the edge of the first curtain, at the end in the joining; and so you make in the edge of the outermost curtain, in the joining of the second. ⁵ You make fifty loops in the first curtain, and you make fifty loops in the edge of the curtain which [is] in the joining of the second, causing the loops to take hold to one another; ⁶ and you have made fifty hooks of gold, and have joined the curtains to one another by the hooks, and the Dwelling Place has been one. ⁷ And you have made curtains of goats' [hair] for a tent over the Dwelling Place; you make eleven curtains: ⁸ the length of one curtain [is] thirty by the cubit, and the breadth of one curtain [is] four by the cubit; one measure [is] for the eleven curtains; ⁹ and you have joined the five curtains apart, and the six curtains apart, and have doubled the six curtains at the front of the tent. ¹⁰ And you have made fifty loops on the edge of the first curtain, the outermost in the joining, and fifty loops on the edge of the curtain which is joining the second; ¹¹ and you have made fifty hooks of bronze, and have brought in the hooks into the loops, and have joined the tent, and it has been one. ¹² And the excess remaining in the curtains of the tent—the half of the curtain which is remaining—has spread over the back part of the Dwelling Place; ¹³ and the cubit on this [side], and the cubit on that [side], in the remaining [part] of the length of the curtains of the tent, is spread out over the sides of the Dwelling Place, on this [side] and on that [side], to cover it; ¹⁴ and you have made a covering for the tent of rams' skins made red, and a covering of tachashim skins above. ¹⁵ And you have made the boards for the Dwelling Place of shittim wood, standing up; ¹⁶ ten cubits [is] the length of the board, and a cubit and a half the breadth of one board; ¹⁷ two handles [are] to one board, joined to one another; so you make for all the boards of the Dwelling Place; ¹⁸ and you have made the boards of the Dwelling Place—twenty boards for the south side southward; ¹⁹ and you make forty sockets of silver under the twenty boards, two sockets under one board for its two

handles, and two sockets under the other board for its two handles. ²⁰ And for the second side of the Dwelling Place, for the north side, [are] twenty boards, ²¹ and their forty sockets of silver, two sockets under one board, and two sockets under another board. ²² And for the sides of the Dwelling Place westward, you make six boards. ²³ And you make two boards for the corners of the Dwelling Place in the two sides. ²⁴ And they are pairs beneath, and together they are pairs above its head to one ring; so is it for them both, they are for the two corners. ²⁵ And they have been eight boards, and their sockets of silver [are] sixteen sockets, two sockets under one board, and two sockets under another board. ²⁶ And you have made bars of shittim wood: five for the boards of the first side of the Dwelling Place, ²⁷ and five bars for the boards of the second side of the Dwelling Place, and five bars for the boards of the side of the Dwelling Place at the two sides, westward; ²⁸ and one has caused the middle bar in the midst of the boards to reach from end to end; ²⁹ and you overlay the boards [with] gold, and you make their rings of gold [for] places for bars, and have overlaid their bars with gold; ³⁰ and you have raised up the Dwelling Place according to its fashion which you have been shown on the mountain. ³¹ And you have made a veil of blue, and purple, and scarlet, and twined linen, the work of a designer; he makes it [with] cherubim; ³² and you have put it on four pillars of shittim wood, overlaid [with] gold, their pegs [are] of gold, on four sockets of silver. ³³ And you have put the veil under the hooks, and have brought in the Ark of the Testimony there within the veil; and the veil has made a separation for you between the holy and the Holy of Holies. ³⁴ And you have put the propitiatory covering on the Ark of the Testimony in the Holy of Holies. ³⁵ And you have set the table at the outside of the veil, and the lampstand opposite the table on the side of the Dwelling Place southward, and you put the table on the north side. ³⁶ And you have made a covering for the opening of the tent of blue, and purple, and scarlet, and twined linen, the work of an embroiderer; ³⁷ and you have made five pillars of shittim [wood] for the covering, and have overlaid them [with] gold, their pegs [are] of gold, and you have cast five sockets of bronze for them."

CHAPTER 27

¹ "And you have made the altar of shittim wood, five cubits the length, and five cubits the breadth—the altar is square—and three cubits [is] its height. ² And you have made its horns on its four corners, its horns are of the same, and you have overlaid it [with] bronze. ³ And you have made its pots to remove its ashes, and its shovels, and its bowls, and its forks, and its fire-pans, even all its vessels you make of bronze. ⁴ And you have made a grate of network of bronze for it, and have made four rings of bronze on the net on its four extremities, ⁵ and have put it under the rim of the altar beneath, and the net has been up to the middle of the altar. ⁶ And you have made poles for the altar, poles of shittim wood, and have overlaid them [with] bronze. ⁷ And the poles have been brought into the rings, and the poles have been on the two sides of the altar in carrying it. ⁸ You make it hollow [with] boards; as it has been showed [to] you on the mountain, so do they make [it]. ⁹ And you have made the court of the Dwelling Place: for the south side southward, hangings for the court of twined linen, the length of the first side [is] one hundred by the cubit, ¹⁰ and its twenty pillars and their twenty sockets [are] of bronze, the pegs of the pillars and their fillets [are] of silver; ¹¹ and so for the north side in length, hangings of one hundred [cubits] in length, and its twenty pillars and their twenty sockets [are] of bronze, the pegs of the pillars and their fillets [are] of silver. ¹² And [for] the breadth of the court at the west side [are] hangings of fifty cubits, their pillars ten, and their sockets ten. ¹³ And the breadth of the court at the east side, eastward, [is] fifty cubits. ¹⁴ And the hangings at the side [are] fifteen cubits, their pillars three, and their sockets three. ¹⁵ And at the second side [are] hangings of fifteen [cubits], their pillars three, and their sockets three. ¹⁶ And for the gate of the court [is] a covering of twenty cubits of blue, and purple, and scarlet, and twined linen, the work of an embroiderer; their pillars four, their sockets four. ¹⁷ All the pillars of the court all around [are] filleted [with] silver, their pegs [are] silver, and their sockets bronze. ¹⁸ The length of the court [is] one hundred by the cubit, and the breadth fifty by fifty, and the height five cubits, of twined linen, and their sockets [are] bronze; ¹⁹ for all the vessels of the Dwelling Place, in all its service, and all its pins,

and all the pins of the court, [are] bronze. ²⁰ And you command the sons of Israel, and they bring pure oil of beaten olive to you for the light, to cause the lamp to go up continually. ²¹ In the Tent of Meeting, at the outside of the veil, which [is] over the Testimony, Aaron—his sons also—arrange it from evening until morning before Yhwh. [It is] a continuous statute for their generations, from the sons of Israel."

CHAPTER 28

¹ "And you, bring your brother Aaron near to you, and his sons with him, from the midst of the sons of Israel, for his being priest to Me, [even] Aaron, Nadab, and Abihu, Eleazar, and Ithamar, sons of Aaron; ² and you have made holy garments for your brother Aaron, for glory and for beauty; ³ and you speak to all the wise of heart, whom I have filled [with] a spirit of wisdom, and they have made the garments of Aaron to sanctify him for his being priest to Me. ⁴ And these [are] the garments which they make: a breastplate, and an ephod, and an upper robe, and an embroidered coat, a turban, and a girdle; indeed, they have made holy garments for your brother Aaron, and for his sons, for his being priest to Me. ⁵ And they take the gold, and the blue, and the purple, and the scarlet, and the linen, ⁶ and have made the ephod of gold, blue, and purple, and scarlet, and twined linen, the work of a designer; ⁷ it has two shoulders joining at its two ends, and it is joined. ⁸ And the girdle of his ephod which [is] on him, according to its work, is of the same, of gold, blue, and purple, and scarlet, and twined linen. ⁹ And you have taken the two shoham stones, and have engraved the names of the sons of Israel on them; ¹⁰ six of their names on the first stone, and the names of the remaining six on the second stone, according to their births; ¹¹ the work of an engraver of stone, [as] engravings of a signet—you engrave the names of the sons of Israel on the two stones; encompassing, you make them [with] filigrees of gold. ¹² And you have set the two stones on the shoulders of the ephod—stones of memorial to the sons of Israel—and Aaron has borne their names before Yhwh, on his two shoulders, for a memorial. ¹³ And you have made filigrees of gold, ¹⁴ and you make them [with] two chains of pure gold [as] wreathed work, work of thick bands, and you have put the thick chains on the filigrees. ¹⁵ And you have made a breastplate of judgment, the work of a designer; you make it according to the work of the ephod; you make it of gold, blue, and purple, and scarlet, and twined linen; ¹⁶ it is square, doubled, a span its length, and a span its breadth. ¹⁷ And you have set settings of stone in it, four rows of stone: a row of sardius, topaz, and carbuncle [is] the first row; ¹⁸ and the second row [is] emerald, sapphire, and diamond; ¹⁹ and the third row [is] opal, agate, and amethyst; ²⁰ and the fourth row [is] beryl, and onyx, and jasper; they are embroidered with gold in their settings, ²¹ and the stones are according to the names of the sons of Israel, twelve according to their names, [as] engravings of a signet, each with his name; they are for the twelve tribes. ²² And you have made wreathed chains on the breastplate, [the] work of thick bands of pure gold; ²³ and you have made two rings of gold on the breastplate, and have put the two rings on the two ends of the breastplate; ²⁴ and you have put the two thick bands of gold on the two rings at the ends of the breastplate; ²⁵ and you put the two ends of the two thick bands on the two filigrees, and you have put [them] on the shoulders of the ephod toward the front of its face. ²⁶ And you have made two rings of gold, and have set them on the two ends of the breastplate, on its border, which [is] toward the side of the ephod within it; ²⁷ and you have made two rings of gold, and have put them on the two shoulders of the ephod, from beneath, in front of its face, close by its joining, above the girdle of the ephod, ²⁸ and they bind the breastplate by its rings to the rings of the ephod with a ribbon of blue, to be above the girdle of the ephod, and the breastplate is not loosed from the ephod. ²⁹ And Aaron has borne the names of the sons of Israel in the breastplate of judgment, on his heart, in his going into the holy place, for a memorial before Yhwh continually. ³⁰ And you have put the Lights and the Perfections into the breastplate of judgment, and they have been on the heart of Aaron, in his going in before Yhwh, and Aaron has borne the judgment of the sons of Israel on his heart before Yhwh continually. ³¹ And you have made the upper robe of the ephod completely of blue, ³² and the opening for his head has been in its midst; there is a border for its opening all around—the work of a weaver—[and] there is as the opening of a [linen] habergeon for it; it is not torn. ³³

And you have made on its hem pomegranates of blue, and purple, and scarlet, on its hem all around, and bells of gold in their midst all around; ³⁴ a bell of gold and a pomegranate [and] a bell of gold and a pomegranate [are] on the hems of the upper robe all around. ³⁵ And it has been on Aaron to minister in, and its sound has been heard in his coming into the holy place before Yhwh, and in his going out, and he does not die. ³⁶ And you have made a flower of pure gold, and have engraved the engravings of a signet on it: Holy to Yhwh; ³⁷ and you have put it on a blue ribbon, and it has been on the turban—it is toward the front of the face of the turban; ³⁸ and it has been on the forehead of Aaron, and Aaron has borne the iniquity of the holy things which the sons of Israel hallow, even all their holy gifts; and it has been on his forehead continually for a pleasing thing for them before Yhwh. ³⁹ And you have embroidered the coat of linen, and have made a turban of linen, and you make a girdle—the work of an embroiderer. ⁴⁰ And you make coats for the sons of Aaron, and you have made girdles for them, and you make caps for them, for glory and for beauty; ⁴¹ and you have clothed your brother Aaron with them, and his sons with him, and have anointed them, and have consecrated their hand, and have sanctified them, and they have been priests to Me. ⁴² And make linen trousers for them to cover the naked flesh; they are from the loins even to the thighs; ⁴³ and they have been on Aaron and on his sons in their going into the Tent of Meeting, or in their drawing near to the altar to minister in the holy place, and they do not bear iniquity nor have they died; [it is] a continuous statute to him and to his seed after him."

CHAPTER 29

¹ "And this [is] the thing which you do to them, to hallow them, for being priests to Me: take one bullock, a son of the herd, and two rams, perfect ones, ² and unleavened bread, and unleavened cakes anointed with oil; you make them of fine wheat flour, ³ and you have put them on one basket, and have brought them near in the basket, also the bullock and the two rams. ⁴ And you bring Aaron and his sons near to the opening of the Tent of Meeting, and have bathed them with water; ⁵ and you have taken the garments, and have clothed Aaron with the coat, and the upper robe of the ephod, and the ephod, and the breastplate, and have girded him with the girdle of the ephod, ⁶ and have set the turban on his head, and have put the holy crown on the turban, ⁷ and have taken the anointing oil, and have poured [it] on his head, and have anointed him. ⁸ And you bring his sons near, and have clothed them [with] coats, ⁹ and have girded them [with] a girdle (Aaron and his sons), and have bound caps on them; and the priesthood has been theirs by a continuous statute, and you have consecrated the hand of Aaron, and the hand of his sons, ¹⁰ and have brought the bullock near before the Tent of Meeting, and Aaron has laid—his sons also—their hands on the head of the bullock. ¹¹ And you have slaughtered the bullock before Yhwh, at the opening of the Tent of Meeting, ¹² and have taken of the blood of the bullock, and have put [it] on the horns of the altar with your finger, and you pour out all the blood at the foundation of the altar; ¹³ and you have taken all the fat which is covering the innards, and the redundance on the liver, and the two kidneys, and the fat which [is] on them, and have made incense on the altar; ¹⁴ and the flesh of the bullock, and his skin, and his dung, you burn with fire at the outside of the camp; it [is] a sin-offering. ¹⁵ And you take the first ram, and Aaron and his sons have laid their hands on the head of the ram, ¹⁶ and you have slaughtered the ram, and have taken its blood, and have sprinkled [it] around the altar, ¹⁷ and you cut the ram into its pieces, and have washed its innards, and its legs, and have put [them] on its pieces, and on its head; ¹⁸ and you have made incense with the whole ram on the altar. It [is] a burnt-offering to Yhwh, a refreshing fragrance; it [is] a fire-offering to Yhwh. ¹⁹ And you have taken the second ram, and Aaron has laid—his sons also—their hands on the head of the ram, ²⁰ and you have slaughtered the ram, and have taken of its blood, and have put [it] on the tip of the right ear of Aaron, and on the tip of the right ear of his sons, and on the thumb of their right hand, and on the great toe of their right foot, and have sprinkled the blood around the altar; ²¹ and you have taken of the blood which [is] on the altar, and of the anointing oil, and have sprinkled [it] on Aaron, and on his garments, and on his sons, and on the garments of his sons with him, and he has been hallowed, he and his garments, and his sons, and the

garments of his sons with him. **22** And you have taken from the ram the fat, and the fat tail, and the fat which is covering the innards, and the redundance on the liver, and the two kidneys, and the fat which [is] on them, and the right leg, for it [is] a ram of consecration, **23** and one round cake of bread, and one cake of oiled bread, and one thin cake out of the basket of the unleavened things which [is] before Yhwh; **24** and you have set the whole on the hands of Aaron, and on the hands of his sons, and have waved them [for] a wave-offering before Yhwh; **25** and you have taken them out of their hand, and have made incense on the altar beside the burnt-offering, for refreshing fragrance before Yhwh; it [is] a fire-offering to Yhwh. **26** And you have taken the breast from the ram of the consecration which [is] for Aaron, and have waved it [for] a wave-offering before Yhwh, and it has become your portion; **27** and you have sanctified the breast of the wave-offering, and the leg of the raised-offering, which has been waved, and which has been lifted up from the ram of the consecration, of that which [is] for Aaron, and of that which [is] for his sons; **28** and it has been for Aaron and for his sons, by a continuous statute from the sons of Israel, for it [is] a raised-offering; and it is a raised-offering from the sons of Israel, from the sacrifices of their peace-offerings—their raised-offering to Yhwh. **29** And the holy garments which are Aaron's are for his sons after him, to be anointed in them and to consecrate their hand in them; **30** [for] seven days the priest in his stead (of his sons) puts them on when he goes into the Tent of Meeting to minister in the holy place. **31** And you take the ram of the consecration and have boiled its flesh in the holy place; **32** and Aaron has eaten—his sons also—the flesh of the ram, and the bread which [is] in the basket, at the opening of the Tent of Meeting; **33** and they have eaten those things by which there is atonement to consecrate their hand, to sanctify them; and a stranger does not eat [them], for they [are] holy; **34** and if there is left of the flesh of the consecration or of the bread until the morning, then you have burned that which is left with fire; it is not eaten, for it [is] holy. **35** And you have done thus to Aaron and to his sons, according to all that I have commanded you, [for] seven days you consecrate their hand; **36** and a bullock, a sin-offering, you prepare daily for the atonements, and you have atoned for the altar in your making atonement on it, and have anointed it to sanctify it; **37** [for] seven days you make atonement for the altar, and have sanctified it, and the altar has been most holy; all that is coming against the altar is holy. **38** And this [is] that which you prepare on the altar: two lambs, sons of a year, daily continually; **39** you prepare the first lamb in the morning, and you prepare the second lamb between the evenings; **40** and a tenth part of fine flour mixed with a fourth part of a hin of beaten oil, and a fourth part of a hin of wine [for] a drink-offering, [is] for the first lamb. **41** And you prepare the second lamb between the evenings; according to the present of the morning, and according to its drink-offering, you prepare for it, for refreshing fragrance, a fire-offering to Yhwh— **42** a continual burnt-offering for your generations [at] the opening of the Tent of Meeting before Yhwh, to where I meet with you to speak to you there, **43** and I have met with the sons of Israel there, and it has been sanctified by My glory. **44** And I have sanctified the Tent of Meeting and the altar, and I sanctify Aaron and his sons for being priests to Me, **45** and I have dwelt in the midst of the sons of Israel, and have become their God, **46** and they have known that I [am] their God Yhwh, who has brought them out of the land of Egypt, that I may dwell in their midst; I [am] their God Yhwh."

up between the evenings, he makes incense [on] it; [it is] a continual incense before Yhwh throughout your generations. **9** You do not cause strange incense to go up on it—and burnt-offering and present; and you do not pour out a drink-offering on it; **10** and Aaron has made atonement on its horns once in a year, by the blood of the sin-offering of atonements; once in a year he makes atonement for it, throughout your generations; it [is] most holy to Yhwh." **11** And Yhwh speaks to Moses, saying, **12** "When you take up the census of the sons of Israel for their numbers, then they have each given an atonement [for] his soul to Yhwh in their being numbered, and there is no plague among them in their being numbered. **13** This they give, everyone passing over to those numbered, half a shekel, by the shekel of the holy place (the shekel [is] twenty gerahs); half a shekel [is] the raised-offering to Yhwh; **14** everyone passing over to those numbered, from a son of twenty years and upwards, gives the raised-offering of Yhwh; **15** the rich do not multiply, and the poor do not diminish from the half-shekel, to give the raised-offering of Yhwh, to make atonement for your souls. **16** And you have taken the atonement-money from the sons of Israel, and have given it for the service of the Tent of Meeting; and it has been to the sons of Israel for a memorial before Yhwh, to make atonement for your souls." **17** And Yhwh speaks to Moses, saying, **18** "And you have made a laver of bronze (and its base of bronze), for washing; and you have put it between the Tent of Meeting and the altar, and have put water [in] there, **19** and Aaron and his sons have washed their hands and their feet from it; **20** they wash [with] water in their going into the Tent of Meeting, and do not die; or in their drawing near to the altar to minister, to make incense [as] a fire-offering to Yhwh, **21** then they have washed their hands and their feet, and they do not die, and it has been a continuous statute to them, to him and to his seed, throughout their generations." **22** And Yhwh speaks to Moses, saying, **23** "And you, take [these] principal spices for yourself: five hundred [shekels] of liquid myrrh, and the half of that—two hundred and fifty [shekels]—of spice cinnamon, and two hundred and fifty [shekels] of spice-cane, **24** and five hundred [shekels] of cassia, by the shekel of the holy place, and a hin of olive oil; **25** and you have made it a holy anointing oil, a compound mixture, work of a compounder; it is a holy anointing oil. **26** And with it you have anointed the Tent of Meeting, and the Ark of the Testimony, **27** and the table and all its vessels, and the lampstand and its vessels, and the altar of incense, **28** and the altar of burnt-offering and all its vessels, and the laver and its base; **29** and you have sanctified them, and they have been most holy; all that is coming against them is holy; **30** and you anoint Aaron and his sons, and have sanctified them for being priests to Me. **31** And you speak to the sons of Israel, saying, This is a holy anointing oil to Me, throughout your generations; **32** it is not poured on [the] flesh of man, and you make nothing [else] like it in its proportion; it [is] holy—it is holy to you; **33** a man who compounds [any] like it, or who puts of it on a stranger, has even been cut off from his people." **34** And Yhwh says to Moses, "Take to yourself spices—stacte, and onycha, and galbanum—spices and pure frankincense; they are part for part; **35** and you have made it an incense, a compound, work of a compounder, salted, pure, holy; **36** and you have beaten [some] of it small, and have put of it before the Testimony in the Tent of Meeting, to where I meet with you; it is most holy to you. **37** As for the incense which you make, you do not make [any] for yourselves in its proportion; it is holy to you for Yhwh; **38** a man who makes [any] like it—to be refreshed by it—has even been cut off from his people."

CHAPTER 30

1 "And you have made an altar [for] making incense; you make it of shittim wood; **2** a cubit its length and a cubit its breadth (it is square), and two cubits its height; its horns [are] of the same. **3** And you have overlaid it with pure gold—its top, and around its sides, and its horns; and you have made a crown of gold for it all around; **4** and you make two rings of gold for it, under its crown on its two ribs; you make [them] on its two sides, and they have become places for poles to carry it with them. **5** And you have made the poles of shittim wood, and have overlaid them with gold; **6** and you have put it before the veil, which [is] by the Ark of the Testimony, before the propitiatory covering which [is] over the Testimony, where I meet with you. **7** And Aaron has made incense on it, incense of spices, morning by morning; in his making the lamps right, he makes incense [on] it, **8** and in Aaron's causing the lamps to go

CHAPTER 31

1 And Yhwh speaks to Moses, saying, **2** "See, I have called by name Bezaleel, son of Uri, son of Hur, of the tribe of Judah, **3** and I fill him [with] the Spirit of God, in wisdom, and in understanding, and in knowledge, and in all work, **4** to devise inventions to work in gold, and in silver, and in bronze, **5** and in a carving of stone for settings, and in a carving of wood to work in all work. **6** And I, behold, have given with him Aholiab, son of Ahisamach, of the tribe of Dan, and I have given wisdom in the heart of every wise-hearted one, and they have made all that which I have commanded you. **7** The Tent of Meeting, and the Ark of Testimony, and the propitiatory covering which [is] on it, and all the vessels of the tent, **8** and the table and its vessels, and the pure lampstand and all its vessels, and the altar of the incense, **9** and the altar of the burnt-offering and all its vessels, and the laver and its base, **10** and the colored garments, and the holy garments for Aaron the priest, and the garments of his sons, for acting as priests in; **11** and the anointing oil, and the incense of the spices for the holy place; according to all that I have commanded you—they do." **12** And Yhwh speaks to Moses, saying, **13** "And you, speak to the sons of Israel, saying, Surely you keep My Sabbaths, for it [is] a sign between Me and you throughout your generations, to know that I, Yhwh, am sanctifying you; **14** and you have kept the Sabbath, for it [is] holy to you, he who is defiling it is certainly put to death—for any who does work in it—that person has even been cut off from the midst of his people. **15** [For] six days work is done, and in the seventh day [is] a Sabbath of holy rest to Yhwh; any who does work in the Sabbath day is certainly put to death, **16** and the sons of Israel have observed the Sabbath; to keep the Sabbath throughout their generations [is] a perpetual covenant— **17** it [is] a sign between Me and the sons of Israel for all time; for [in] six days Yhwh made the heavens and the earth, and in the seventh day He has ceased and is refreshed." **18** And He gives to Moses, when He finishes speaking with him in Mount Sinai, two tablets of the Testimony, tablets of stone, written by the finger of God.

CHAPTER 32

1 And the people see that Moses is delaying to come down from the mountain, and the people assemble against Aaron, and say to him, "Rise, make gods for us, who go before us, for this Moses—the man who brought us up out of the land of Egypt—we have not known what has happened to him." **2** And Aaron says to them, "Break off the rings of gold which [are] in the ears of your wives, your sons, and your daughters, and bring [them] to me"; **3** and all the people break off the rings of gold which [are] in their ears, and bring [them] to Aaron, **4** and he receives [it] from their hand, and fashions it with an engraving tool, and makes it [into] a molten calf, and they say, "These [are] your gods, O Israel, who brought you up out of the land of Egypt!" **5** And Aaron sees, and builds an altar before it, and Aaron calls, and says, "A festival to Yhwh—tomorrow"; **6** and they rise early on the next day, and cause burnt-offerings to ascend, and bring peace-offerings near; and the people sit down to eat and to drink, and rise up to play. **7** And Yhwh says to Moses, "Go, descend, for your people whom you have brought up out of the land of Egypt have done corruptly, **8** they have quickly turned aside from the way that I have commanded them; they have made a molten calf for themselves, and bow themselves to it, and sacrifice to it, and say, These [are] your gods, O Israel, who brought you up out of the land of Egypt!" **9** And Yhwh says to Moses, "I have seen this people, and behold, it [is] a stiff-necked people; **10** and now, leave Me alone, and My anger burns against them, and I consume them, and I make you become a great nation." **11** And Moses appeases the face of his God Yhwh and says, "Why, O Yhwh, does Your anger burn against Your people, whom You have brought forth out of the land of Egypt with great power and with a strong hand? **12** why do the Egyptians speak, saying, He brought them out in calamity to slay them among mountains, and to consume them from off the face of the ground? turn back from the heat of Your anger, and relent from this calamity against Your people. **13** Be mindful of Abraham, of Isaac, and of Israel, Your servants, to whom You have sworn by Yourself, and to whom You speak: I multiply your seed as stars of the heavens, and all this land, as I have said, I give to your seed, and they have inherited [it] for all time"; **14** and Yhwh relents from the evil which He has spoken of doing to His people. **15** And Moses turns, and goes down from the mountain, and the two tablets of the Testimony [are] in his hand, tablets written on both their sides; they [are] written on this [side] and on that [side]; **16** and the tablets are the work of God, and the writing is the writing of God, engraved on the tablets. **17** And Joshua hears the voice of the people in their shouting and says to Moses, "A noise of battle in the camp!" **18** and he says, "It is not the voice of the crying of might, nor is it the voice of the crying of weakness—I am hearing a voice of singing." **19** And it comes to pass, when he has drawn near to the camp, that he sees the calf, and the dancing, and the anger of Moses burns, and he casts the tablets out of his hands, and breaks them below the mountain; **20** and he takes the calf which they have made, and burns [it] with fire, and grinds [it] until [it is] small, and scatters [it] on the face of the waters, and causes the sons of Israel to drink. **21** And Moses says to Aaron, "What

has this people done to you, that you have brought in a great sin on it?" **22** and Aaron says, "Do not let the anger of my lord burn; you have known the people, that it [is beset] with evil; **23** and they say to me, Make gods for us, who go before us, for this Moses—the man who brought us up out of the land of Egypt—we have not known what has happened to him; **24** and I say to them, Whoever has gold, let them break [it] off, and they give [it] to me, and I cast it into the fire, and this calf comes out." **25** And Moses sees the people, that it [is] unbridled, for Aaron has made it unbridled for contempt among its withstanders, **26** and Moses stands in the gate of the camp and says, "Who [is] for Yhwh? [Come] to me!" And all the sons of Levi are gathered to him; **27** and he says to them, "Thus said Yhwh, God of Israel: Each put his sword by his thigh, pass over and turn back from gate to gate through the camp, and each slay his brother, and each his friend, and each his relation." **28** And the sons of Levi do according to the word of Moses, and there falls of the people on that day about three thousand men, **29** and Moses says, "Consecrate your hand to Yhwh today, for a man [is] against his son, and against his brother, so as to bring a blessing on you today." **30** And it comes to pass, on the next day, that Moses says to the people, "You have sinned a great sin, and now I go up to Yhwh, perhaps I can atone for your sin." **31** And Moses turns back to Yhwh and says, "Ah, now this people has sinned a great sin, that they make a god of gold for themselves; **32** and now, if You take away their sin—and if not—please blot me out of Your scroll which You have written." **33** And Yhwh says to Moses, "Whoever has sinned against Me—I blot him out of My scroll; **34** and now, go, lead the people wherever I have spoken to you of; behold, My Messenger goes before you, and in the day of my charging—then I have charged their sin on them." **35** And Yhwh plagues the people because they made the calf which Aaron made.

CHAPTER 33

1 And Yhwh speaks to Moses, "Go, ascend from this [place], you and the people, whom you have brought up out of the land of Egypt, to the land which I have sworn to Abraham, to Isaac, and to Jacob, saying, I give it to your seed. **2** And I have sent a Messenger before you, and have cast out the Canaanite, the Amorite, and the Hittite, and the Perizzite, the Hivite, and the Jebusite. **3** [Go up] to a land flowing with milk and honey, for I do not go up in your midst, for you [are] a stiff-necked people—lest I consume you in the way." **4** And the people hear this sad thing, and mourn; and none puts his ornaments on him. **5** And Yhwh says to Moses, "Say to the sons of Israel: You [are] a stiff-necked people; [in] one moment I could come up into your midst and could have consumed you; and now, put down your ornaments from off you, and I know what I do to you"; **6** and the sons of Israel take off their ornaments at Mount Horeb. **7** And Moses takes the tent, and has stretched it out at the outside of the camp, far off from the camp, and has called it, "Tent of Meeting"; and it has come to pass, everyone seeking Yhwh goes out to the Tent of Meeting, which [is] at the outside of the camp. **8** And it has come to pass, at the going out of Moses to the tent, all the people rise, and have stood, each at the opening of his tent, and have looked expectingly after Moses, until his going into the tent. **9** And it has come to pass, at the going in of Moses to the tent, the pillar of the cloud comes down, and has stood at the opening of the tent, and He has spoken with Moses; **10** and all the people have seen the pillar of the cloud standing at the opening of the tent, and all the people have risen and bowed themselves, each at the opening of his tent. **11** And Yhwh has spoken to Moses face to face, as a man speaks to his friend; and he has turned back to the camp, and his minister Joshua, son of Nun, a youth, does not depart out of the tent. **12** And Moses says to Yhwh, "See, You are saying to me, Bring up this people, and You have not caused me to know whom You send with me; and You have said, I have known you by name, and you have also found grace in My eyes. **13** And now, if, please, I have found grace in Your eyes, please cause me to know Your way, and I know You, so that I find grace in Your eyes, and consider that this nation [is] Your people"; **14** and He says, "My presence goes, and I have given rest to you." **15** And he says to Him, "If Your presence is not going—do not take us up from this [place]; **16** and in what is it known now, that I have found grace in Your eyes—I and Your people—is it not in Your going with us? and we have been distinguished—I and Your people—from all the people who [are] on the face of the ground." **17** And Yhwh says to Moses, "Even this thing which you have spoken I do; for you have found grace in My eyes, and I know you by name." 18 And he says, "Please show me Your glory"; 19 and He says, "I cause all My goodness to pass before your face, and have called concerning the Name of Yhwh before you, and favored him whom I favor, and loved him whom I love." 20 He also says, "You are unable to see My face, for man does not see Me and live"; 21 Yhwh also says, "Behold, a place [is] by Me, and you have stood on the rock, 22 and it has come to pass, in the passing by of My glory, that I have set you in a cleft of the rock, and spread out My hands over you until My passing by, 23 and I have turned aside My hands, and you have seen My back parts, and My face is not seen."

CHAPTER 34

1 And Yhwh says to Moses, "Hew for yourself two tablets of stone like the first, and I have written on the tablets the words which were on the first tablets which you have broken; 2 and be prepared at morning, and you have come up in the morning to Mount Sinai, and have stood before Me there, on the top of the mountain, 3 and no man comes up with you, and also no man is seen in all the mountain, also the flock and the herd do not feed toward the front of that mountain." 4 And he hews two tablets of stone like the first, and Moses rises early in the morning, and goes up to Mount Sinai as Yhwh commanded him, and takes [the] two tablets of stone in his hand. 5 And Yhwh comes down in a cloud, and stations Himself with him there, and calls in the Name of Yhwh, 6 and Yhwh passes over before his face, and calls: "Yhwh, Yhwh God, merciful and gracious, slow to anger, and abundant in kindness and truth, 7 keeping kindness for thousands, taking away iniquity, and transgression, and sin, and not entirely acquitting, charging iniquity of fathers on sons and on sons' sons, on a third and on a fourth [generation]." 8 And Moses hurries, and bows to the earth, and pays respect, 9 and says, "Now if I have found grace in Your eyes, O my Lord, please let my Lord go in our midst (for it [is] a stiff-necked people), and you have forgiven our iniquity and our sin, and have inherited us." 10 And He says, "Behold, I am making a covenant. I do wonders before all your people, which have not been done in all the earth, or in any nation, and all the people in whose midst you [are in] have seen the work of Yhwh, for it [is] fearful—that which I am doing with you. 11 Observe for yourself that which I am commanding you today. Behold, I am casting out from before you the Amorite, and the Canaanite, and the Hittite, and the Perizzite, and the Hivite, and the Jebusite; 12 take heed to yourself lest you make a covenant with the inhabitant of the land into which you are going, lest it become a snare in your midst; 13 for you break down their altars, and you shatter their standing pillars, and you cut down its Asherim; 14 for you do not bow yourselves to another god—for Yhwh, whose Name [is] Zealous, is a zealous God. 15 Lest you make a covenant with the inhabitant of the land, and they have gone whoring after their gods, and have sacrificed to their gods, and [one] has called to you, and you have eaten of his sacrifice, 16 and you have taken of their daughters for your sons, and their daughters have gone whoring after their gods, and have caused your sons to go whoring after their gods; 17 you do not make a molten god for yourself. 18 You keep the Celebration of Unleavened Things; [for] seven days you eat unleavened things, as I have commanded you, at an appointed time, [in] the month of Abib: for in the month of Abib you came out from Egypt. 19 All opening a womb [are] Mine, and every firstling of your livestock born a male, [whether] ox or sheep; 20 and you ransom the firstling of a donkey with a lamb; and if you do not ransom, then you have beheaded it; you ransom every firstborn of your sons, and they do not appear before Me empty. 21 [For] six days you work, and on the seventh day you rest; in plowing-time and in harvest you rest. 22 And you observe [the] Celebration of Weeks for yourself, of [the] first-fruits of wheat-harvest; and the Celebration of Ingathering at the revolution of the year. 23 Three times in a year all your males appear before the Lord Yhwh, God of Israel; 24 for I dispossess nations from before you, and have enlarged your border, and no man desires your land in your going up to appear before your God Yhwh three times in a year. 25 You do not slaughter the blood of My sacrifice with a fermented thing; and the sacrifice of the Celebration of the Passover does not remain until morning. 26 You bring the first of the first-fruits of the land into the house of your God Yhwh. You do not boil a kid in its mother's milk." 27 And Yhwh says to Moses, "Write these words for yourself, for I have made a covenant with you and with Israel according to the tenor of these words." 28 And he is there with Yhwh forty days and forty nights; he has not eaten bread, and he has not drunk water; and he writes on the tablets the matters of the covenant—the Ten Commandments. 29 And it comes to pass, when Moses is coming down from Mount Sinai (and the two tablets of the Testimony [are] in the hand of Moses in his coming down from the mountain), that Moses has not known that the skin of his face has shone in His speaking with him, 30 and Aaron sees—all the sons of Israel also—Moses, and behold, the skin of his face has shone, and they are afraid of coming near to him. 31 And Moses calls to them, and Aaron and all the princes in the congregation return to him, and Moses speaks to them; 32 and afterward all the sons of Israel have come near, and he charges them with all that Yhwh has spoken with him in Mount Sinai. 33 And Moses finishes speaking with them, and puts a veil on his face; 34 and in the going in of Moses before Yhwh to speak with Him, he turns aside the veil until his coming out; and he has come out and has spoken to the sons of Israel that which he is commanded; 35 and the sons of Israel have seen the face of Moses, that the skin of the face of Moses has shone, and Moses has put back the veil on his face until his going in to speak with Him.

CHAPTER 35

1 And Moses assembles all the congregation of the sons of Israel and says to them, "These [are] the things which Yhwh has commanded—to do them: 2 [For] six days work is done, and on the seventh day there is a holy [day] for you, a Sabbath of rest to Yhwh; any who does work in it is put to death; 3 you do not burn a fire in any of your dwellings on the Sabbath day." 4 And Moses speaks to all the congregation of the sons of Israel, saying, "This [is] the thing which Yhwh has commanded, saying, 5 Take a raised-offering for Yhwh from among you; everyone whose heart [is] willing brings it [as] the raised-offering of Yhwh: gold, and silver, and bronze, 6 and blue, and purple, and scarlet, and linen, and goats' [hair], 7 and rams' skins made red, and tachashim skins, and shittim wood, 8 and oil for the light, and spices for the anointing oil, and for the spice-incense, 9 and shoham stones, and stones for settings, for an ephod, and for a breastplate. 10 And all the wise-hearted among you come in, and make all that Yhwh has commanded: 11 the Dwelling Place, its tent, and its covering, its hooks, and its boards, its bars, its pillars, and its sockets, 12 the Ark and its poles, the propitiatory covering, and the veil of the covering, 13 the table and its poles, and all its vessels, and the Bread of the Presentation, 14 and the lampstand for the light, and its vessels, and its lamps, and the oil for the light, 15 and the altar of incense, and its poles, and the anointing oil, and the spice-incense, and the covering of the opening at the opening of the Dwelling Place, 16 the altar of burnt-offering and the bronze grate which it has, its poles, and all its vessels, the laver and its base, 17 the hangings of the court, its pillars, and their sockets, and the covering of the gate of the court, 18 the pins of the Dwelling Place, and the pins of the court, and their cords, 19 the colored garments, to do service in the holy place, the holy garments for Aaron the priest, and the garments of his sons to act as priest in." 20 And all the congregation of the sons of Israel go out from the presence of Moses, 21 and they come in—every man whom his heart has lifted up, and everyone whom his spirit has made willing—they have brought in the raised-offering of Yhwh for the work of the Tent of Meeting, and for all its service, and for the holy garments. 22 And they come in—the men with the women—every willing-hearted one—they have brought in nose-ring, and earring, and seal-ring, and necklace, all golden goods, even everyone who has waved a wave-offering of gold to Yhwh. 23 And every man with whom has been found blue, and purple, and scarlet, and linen, and goats' [hair], and rams' skins made red, and tachashim skins, have brought [them] in; 24 everyone lifting up a raised-offering of silver and bronze has brought in the raised-offering of Yhwh; and everyone with whom has been found shittim wood for any work of the service brought [it] in. 25 And every wise-hearted woman has spun with her hands, and they bring in yarn—of the blue, and the purple, [and] the scarlet—and the linen; 26 and all the women whose heart has lifted them up in wisdom, have spun the goats' [hair]. 27 And the princes have brought in the shoham stones, and the stones for settings, for the ephod, and for the breastplate, 28 and the spices, and the

oil for the light, and for the anointing oil, and for the spice-incense; **29** every man and woman of the sons of Israel (whom their heart has made willing to bring in for all the work which Yhwh commanded to be done by the hand of Moses) brought in a willing-offering to Yhwh. **30** And Moses says to the sons of Israel, "See, Yhwh has called Bezaleel, son of Uri, son of Hur, of the tribe of Judah, by name, **31** and He fills him [with] the Spirit of God, in wisdom, in understanding, and in knowledge, and in all work, **32** even to devise inventions to work in gold, and in silver, and in bronze, **33** and in a carving of stones for settings, and in a carving of wood to work in any work of design. **34** And He has put [it] in his heart to direct, he and Aholiab, son of Ahisamach, of the tribe of Dan; **35** He has filled them with wisdom of heart to do every work, of engraver, and designer, and embroiderer (in blue, and in purple, in scarlet, and in linen), and weaver, who does any work, and of designers of designs."

CHAPTER 36

1 And Bezaleel, and Aholiab, and every wise-hearted man, in whom Yhwh has given wisdom and understanding to know to do every work of the service of the holy place, have done according to all that Yhwh commanded. **2** And Moses calls to Bezaleel, and to Aholiab, and to every wise-hearted man in whose heart Yhwh has given wisdom, everyone whom his heart lifted up, to come near to the work to do it. **3** And they take from before Moses all the raised-offering which the sons of Israel have brought in for the work of the service of the holy place to do it; and still they have brought to him a willing-offering morning by morning. **4** And all the wise men, who are doing all the work of the holy place, each come from his work which they are doing, **5** and speak to Moses, saying, "The people are multiplying to bring in more than sufficient for the service of the work which Yhwh commanded [us] to do." **6** And Moses commands, and they cause a voice to pass over through the camp, saying, "Do not let man or woman make anymore work for the raised-offering of the holy place"; and the people are restrained from bringing, **7** and the work has been sufficient for them, for all the work, to do it, and to leave. **8** And all the wise-hearted ones among the doers of the work make the Dwelling Place; he has made them [with] ten curtains of twined linen, and blue, and purple, and scarlet, [with] cherubim, the work of a designer. **9** The length of one curtain [is] twenty-eight by the cubit, and the breadth of one curtain [is] four by the cubit; one measure [is] for all the curtains. **10** And he joins the five curtains to one another, and the [other] five curtains he has joined to one another; **11** and he makes loops of blue on the edge of one curtain, at the end, in the joining; so he has made in the edge of the outmost curtain, in the joining of the second; **12** he has made fifty loops in the first curtain, and he has made fifty loops in the end of the curtain which [is] in the joining of the second; the loops are taking hold on one another. **13** And he makes fifty hooks of gold, and joins the curtains to one another by the hooks, and the Dwelling Place is one. **14** And he makes curtains of goats' [hair] for a tent over the Dwelling Place; eleven curtains he has made them; **15** the length of one curtain [is] thirty by the cubit, and the breadth of one curtain [is] four cubits; one measure [is] for the eleven curtains; **16** and he joins the five curtains apart, and the six curtains apart. **17** And he makes fifty loops on the outer edge of the curtain, in the joining; and he has made fifty loops on the edge of the curtain which is joining the second; **18** and he makes fifty hooks of bronze to join the tent—to be one; **19** and he makes a covering for the tent of rams' skins made red, and a covering of tachashim skins above. **20** And he makes the boards for the Dwelling Place of shittim wood, standing up; **21** ten cubits [is] the length of the [one] board, and a cubit and a half the breadth of the [one] board; **22** two handles [are] to one board, joined to one another; so he has made for all the boards of the Dwelling Place. **23** And he makes the boards for the Dwelling Place; twenty boards for the south side southward; **24** and he has made forty sockets of silver under the twenty boards: two sockets under one board for its two handles, and two sockets under the other board for its two handles. **25** And for the second side of the Dwelling Place, for the north side, he has made twenty boards, **26** and their forty sockets of silver: two sockets under one board, and two sockets under the other board; **27** and for the sides of the Dwelling Place westward, he has made six boards; **28** and he has made two boards for the corners of the Dwelling Place, in the two sides; **29** and they have been

twins below, and together they are twins at its head, at one ring; so he has done to both of them at the two corners; **30** and there have been eight boards; and their sockets of silver [are] sixteen sockets, two sockets under one board. **31** And he makes bars of shittim wood: five for the boards of the first side of the Dwelling Place, **32** and five bars for the boards of the second side of the Dwelling Place, and five bars for the boards of the Dwelling Place, for the sides westward; **33** and he makes the middle bar to enter into the midst of the boards from end to end; **34** and he has overlaid the boards with gold, and he has made their rings of gold, places for bars, and he overlays the bars with gold. **35** And he makes the veil of blue, and purple, and scarlet, and twined linen; he has made it [with] cherubim—the work of a designer; **36** and he makes four pillars of shittim [wood] for it, and overlays them with gold; their pegs [are] of gold; and he casts four sockets of silver for them. **37** And he makes a covering for the opening of the tent, of blue, and purple, and scarlet, and twined linen, the work of an embroiderer, **38** also its five pillars, and their pegs; and he overlaid their tops and their fillets [with] gold, and their five sockets [are] bronze.

CHAPTER 37

1 And Bezaleel makes the Ark of shittim wood; two cubits and a half its length, and a cubit and a half its breadth, and a cubit and a half its height; **2** and he overlays it with pure gold inside and outside, and makes a wreath of gold for it all around; **3** and he casts four rings of gold for it on its four feet, even two rings on its one side, and two rings on its second side; **4** and he makes poles of shittim wood, and overlays them with gold, **5** and he brings in the poles into the rings, by the sides of the Ark, to carry the Ark. **6** And he makes a propitiatory covering of pure gold, two cubits and a half its length, and a cubit and a half its breadth; **7** and he makes two cherubim of gold; he has made them of beaten work at the two ends of the propitiatory covering— **8** one cherub at the end on this [side] and one cherub at the end on that [side]; he has made the cherubim from [above] the propitiatory covering, at its two ends; **9** and the cherubim are spreading out wings on high, covering over the propitiatory covering with their wings, and their faces [are] toward one another; the faces of the cherubim have been toward the propitiatory covering. **10** And he makes the table of shittim wood; two cubits its length, and a cubit its breadth, and a cubit and a half its height, **11** and overlays it with pure gold, and makes a wreath of gold for it all around. **12** And he makes a border for it of a handbreadth around, and makes a wreath of gold around for its border; **13** and he casts four rings of gold for it, and puts the rings on the four corners which [are] at its four feet; **14** the rings have been close by the border, places for poles to carry the table. **15** And he makes the poles of shittim wood, and overlays them with gold, to carry the table; **16** and he makes the vessels which [are] on the table, its dishes, and its bowls, and its cups, and the cups by which they pour out, of pure gold. **17** And he makes the lampstand of pure gold; he has made the lampstand of beaten work, its base, and its branch, its calyxes, its knobs, and its flowers, have been of the same; **18** and six branches are coming out of its sides, three branches of the lampstand out of its one side, and three branches of the lampstand out of its second side; **19** three calyxes, made like almonds, in one branch, a knob and a flower; and three calyxes, made like almonds, in another branch, a knob and a flower; so for the six branches which are coming out of the lampstand. **20** And in the lampstand [are] four calyxes, made like almonds, its knobs, and its flowers, **21** and a knob under the two branches of the same, and a knob under the two branches of the same, and a knob under the two branches of the same, [are] for the six branches which are coming out of it; **22** their knobs and their branches have been of the same; all of it one beaten work of pure gold. **23** And he makes its seven lamps, and its snuffers, and its snuff-dishes, of pure gold; **24** he has made it of a talent of pure gold, and with all its vessels. **25** And he makes the incense-altar of shittim wood, a cubit its length, and a cubit its breadth (square), and two cubits its height; its horns have been of the same; **26** and he overlays it with pure gold, around its top and its sides, and its horns; and he makes a wreath of gold for it all around; **27** and he has made two rings of gold for it under its wreath, at its two corners, at its two sides, for places for poles to carry it with them. **28** And he makes the poles of shittim wood, and overlays them with gold; **29** and he makes the holy anointing oll, and the pure spice-incense—work of a compounder.

CHAPTER 38

1 And he makes the altar of burnt-offering of shittim wood; five cubits its length, and five cubits its breadth (square), and three cubits its height; **2** and he makes its horns on its four corners; its horns have been of the same; and he overlays it with bronze; **3** and he makes all the vessels of the altar, the pots, and the shovels, and the sprinkling-pans, the forks, and the fire-pans; he has made all its vessels of bronze. **4** And he makes a bronze grate of network for the altar, under its rim beneath, to its midst; **5** and he casts four rings for the four ends of the bronze grate—places for bars; **6** and he makes the poles of shittim wood, and overlays them with bronze; **7** and he brings in the poles into the rings on the sides of the altar, to carry it with them; he made it hollow [with] boards. **8** And he makes the laver of bronze, and its base of bronze, with the mirrors of the women assembling, who have assembled at the opening of the Tent of Meeting. **9** And he makes the court: at the south side southward, the hangings of the court of twined linen, one hundred by the cubit, **10** their pillars [are] twenty, and their bronze sockets twenty, the pegs of the pillars and their fillets [are] silver; **11** and at the north side, one hundred by the cubit, their pillars [are] twenty, and their sockets of bronze twenty; the pegs of the pillars and their fillets [are] silver; **12** and at the west side [are] hangings, fifty by the cubit; their pillars [are] ten, and their sockets ten; the pegs of the pillars and their fillets [are] silver; **13** and at the east side eastward, fifty cubits. **14** The hangings on the side [are] fifteen cubits, their pillars three, and their sockets three, **15** and at the second side at the gate of the court, on this [side] and on that [side]—hangings of fifteen cubits, their pillars three, and their sockets three; **16** all the hangings of the court around [are] of twined linen, **17** and the sockets for the pillars of bronze, the pegs of the pillars and their fillets of silver, and the overlaying of their tops of silver, and all the pillars of the court are filleted with silver. **18** And the covering of the gate of the court [is] the work of an embroiderer, of blue, and purple, and scarlet, and twined linen; and twenty cubits [is] the length, and the height with the breadth [is] five cubits, corresponding to the hangings of the court; **19** and their pillars [are] four, and their sockets of bronze four, their pegs [are] of silver, and the overlaying of their tops and their fillets [are] of silver; **20** and all the pins for the Dwelling Place, and for the court all around, [are] of bronze. **21** These are the numberings of the Dwelling Place (the Dwelling Place of Testimony), which has been numbered by the command of Moses, the service of the Levites, by the hand of Ithamar son of Aaron the priest. **22** And Bezaleel son of Uri, son of Hur, of the tribe of Judah, has made all that Yhwh commanded Moses; **23** and with him [is] Aholiab son of Ahisamach, of the tribe of Dan, an engraver, and designer and embroiderer in blue, and in purple, and in scarlet, and in linen. **24** All the gold which is prepared for the work in all the work of the holy place (and it is the gold of the wave-offering) [is] twenty-nine talents, and seven hundred and thirty shekels, by the shekel of the holy place. **25** And the silver of those numbered of the congregation [is] one hundred talents, and one thousand and seven hundred and seventy-five shekels, by the shekel of the holy place; **26** a bekah for the counted head (half a shekel, by the shekel of the holy place), for everyone who is passing over to those numbered, from a son of twenty years and upwards, for six hundred thousand and three thousand and five hundred and fifty. **27** And one hundred talents of silver are for casting the sockets of the holy place, and the sockets of the veil; one hundred sockets for the hundred talents, a talent for a socket; **28** and [from] the one thousand and seven hundred and seventy-five [shekels] he has made pegs for the pillars, and overlaid their tops, and filleted them. **29** And the bronze of the wave-offering [is] seventy talents, and two thousand and four hundred shekels; **30** and he makes with it the sockets of the opening of the Tent of Meeting, and the bronze altar, and the bronze grate which it has, and all the vessels of the altar, **31** and the sockets of the court all around, and the sockets of the gate of the court, and all the pins of the Dwelling Place, and all the pins of the court all around.

CHAPTER 39

1 And of the blue, and the purple, and the scarlet, they made colored garments, to minister in the holy place; and they make the holy garments which [are] for Aaron, as Yhwh has commanded Moses. **2** And he makes the ephod, of gold, blue, and purple, and scarlet, and twined linen, **3** and they expand the plates of gold, and have cut off wires to work in the midst of the blue, and in the midst of the purple, and in the midst of the scarlet, and in the midst of the linen—the work of a designer; **4** they have made shoulder-pieces for it, joining; it is joined at its two ends. **5** And the girdle of his ephod which [is] on it is of the same, according to its work, of gold, blue, and purple, and scarlet, and twined linen, as Yhwh has commanded Moses. **6** And they prepare the shoham stones, set [with] filigrees of gold, engraved with engravings of a signet—the names of the sons of Israel on [them]; **7** and he sets them on the shoulders of the ephod—stones of memorial for the sons of Israel, as Yhwh has commanded Moses. **8** And he makes the breastplate, the work of a designer, like the work of the ephod, of gold, blue, and purple, and scarlet, and twined linen; **9** it has been square; they have made the breastplate double, a span its length, and a span its breadth, doubled. **10** And they fill four rows of stones in it: a row of a sardius, a topaz, and a carbuncle [is] the first row; **11** and the second row an emerald, a sapphire, and a diamond; **12** and the third row an opal, an agate, and an amethyst; **13** and the fourth row a beryl, an onyx, and a jasper—set [with] filigrees of gold in their settings. **14** And the stones, according to the names of the sons of Israel, are twelve, according to their names, engravings of a signet, each according to his name, for the twelve tribes. **15** And they make wreathed chains on the breastplate, [the] work of thick bands of pure gold; **16** and they make two filigrees of gold, and two rings of gold, and put the two rings on the two ends of the breastplate, **17** and they put the two thick bands of gold on the two rings on the ends of the breastplate; **18** and they have put the two ends of the two thick bands on the two filigrees, and they put them on the shoulders of the ephod, toward the front of its face. **19** And they make two rings of gold, and set [them] on the two ends of the breastplate, on its border, which [is] on the side of the ephod within; **20** and they make two rings of gold, and put them on the two shoulders of the ephod below, in front of its front, close by its joining, above the girdle of the ephod; **21** and they bind the breastplate by its rings to the rings of the ephod, with a ribbon of blue, to be above the girdle of the ephod, and the breastplate is not loosed from off the ephod, as Yhwh has commanded Moses. **22** And he makes the upper robe of the ephod, the work of a weaver, completely of blue; **23** and the opening of the upper robe [is] in its midst, as the opening of a [linen] habergeon, [with] a border for its opening all around; it is not torn; **24** and they make on the hems of the upper robe pomegranates of blue, and purple, and scarlet, twined. **25** And they make bells of pure gold, and put the bells in the midst of the pomegranates, on the hems of the upper robe, all around, in the midst of the pomegranates; **26** a bell and a pomegranate [and] a bell and a pomegranate [are] on the hems of the upper robe all around, to minister in, as Yhwh has commanded Moses. **27** And they make the coats of linen, the work of a weaver, for Aaron and for his sons, **28** and the turban of linen, and the beautiful caps of linen, and the linen trousers, of twined linen, **29** and the girdle of twined linen, and blue, and purple, and scarlet, the work of an embroiderer, as Yhwh has commanded Moses. **30** And they make the flower of the holy crown of pure gold, and write a writing on it, engravings of a signet: "Holy to Yhwh"; **31** and they put a ribbon of blue on it, to put [it] on the turban above, as Yhwh has commanded Moses. **32** And all the service of the Dwelling Place of the Tent of Meeting is completed; and the sons of Israel do according to all that Yhwh has commanded Moses; so they have done. **33** And they bring in the Dwelling Place to Moses, the tent, and all its vessels, its hooks, its boards, its bars, and its pillars, and its sockets; **34** and the covering of rams' skins, which are made red, and the covering of tachashim skins, and the veil of the covering; **35** the Ark of the Testimony and its poles, and the propitiatory covering; **36** the table, all its vessels, and the Bread of the Presentation; **37** the pure lampstand, its lamps, the lamps of arrangement, and all its vessels, and the oil for the light; **38** And the golden altar, and the anointing oil, and the spice-incense, and the covering of the opening of the tent; **39** the bronze altar and the bronze grate which it has, its poles, and all its vessels, the laver and its base; **40** the hangings of the court, its pillars, and its sockets; and the covering for the gate of the court, its cords, and its pins; and all the vessels of the service of the Dwelling Place, for the Tent of Meeting; **41** the colored clothes to minister in the holy place, the holy garments for Aaron the priest, and the garments of his sons, to act as priest in. **42** According to all that Yhwh has commanded Moses, so the sons of Israel have done all the service; **43** and Moses sees all the work, and behold, they have done it as Yhwh has commanded; so they have done. And Moses blesses them.

CHAPTER 40

1 And Yhwh speaks to Moses, saying, **2** "On the first day of the month, in the first month, you raise up the Dwelling Place of the Tent of Meeting, **3** and have set the Ark of the Testimony [in] there, and have covered over the Ark with the veil, **4** and have brought in the table, and set its arrangement in order, and have brought in the lampstand, and caused its lamps to go up. **5** And you have put the golden altar for incense before the Ark of the Testimony, and have put the covering of the opening to the Dwelling Place, **6** and have put the altar of the burnt-offering before the opening of the Dwelling Place of the Tent of Meeting, **7** and have put the laver between the Tent of Meeting and the altar, and have put water [in] there. **8** And you have set the court all around, and have placed the covering of the gate of the court, **9** and have taken the anointing oil, and anointed the Dwelling Place, and all that [is] in it, and hallowed it, and all its vessels, and it has been holy; **10** and you have anointed the altar of the burnt-offering, and all its vessels, and sanctified the altar, and the altar has been most holy; **11** and you have anointed the laver and its base, and sanctified it. **12** And you have brought Aaron and his sons near to the opening of the Tent of Meeting, and have bathed them with water; **13** and you have clothed Aaron with the holy garments, and anointed him, and sanctified him, and he has acted as priest to Me. **14** And you bring his sons near, and have clothed them with coats, **15** and anointed them as you have anointed their father, and they have acted as priests to Me, and their anointing has been to them for a continuous priesthood throughout their generations." **16** And Moses does according to all that Yhwh has commanded him; so he has done. **17** And it comes to pass, in the first month, in the second year, on the first of the month, the Dwelling Place has been raised up; **18** and Moses raises up the Dwelling Place, and sets its sockets, and places its boards, and places its bars, and raises its pillars, **19** and spreads the tent over the Dwelling Place, and puts the covering of the tent on it above, as Yhwh has commanded Moses. **20** And he takes and puts the Testimony into the Ark, and sets the poles on the Ark, and puts the propitiatory covering on the Ark above; **21** and brings the Ark into the Dwelling Place, and places the veil of the covering, and covers over the Ark of the Testimony, as Yhwh has commanded Moses. **22** And he puts the table in the Tent of Meeting, on the side of the Dwelling Place northward, at the outside of the veil, **23** and sets in order the arrangement of bread on it, before Yhwh, as Yhwh has commanded Moses. **24** And he puts the lampstand in the Tent of Meeting, opposite the table, on the side of the Dwelling Place southward, **25** and causes the lamps to go up before Yhwh, as Yhwh has commanded Moses. **26** And he sets the golden altar in the Tent of Meeting, before the veil, **27** and makes incense on it—spice-incense—as Yhwh has commanded Moses. **28** And he sets the covering [at] the opening of the Dwelling Place, **29** and he has set the altar of the burnt-offering [at] the opening of the Dwelling Place of the Tent of Meeting, and causes the burnt-offering to go up on it, and the present, as Yhwh has commanded Moses. **30** And he puts the laver between the Tent of Meeting and the altar, and puts water [in] there for washing, **31** and Moses and Aaron and his sons have washed their hands and their feet at the same; **32** in their going into the Tent of Meeting, and in their drawing near to the altar, they wash, as Yhwh has commanded Moses. **33** And he raises up the court all around the Dwelling Place, and around the altar, and places the covering of the gate of the court; and Moses completes the work. **34** And the cloud covers the Tent of Meeting, and the glory of Yhwh has filled the Dwelling Place; **35** and Moses has not been able to go into the Tent of Meeting, for the cloud has dwelt on it, and the glory of Yhwh has filled the Dwelling Place. **36** And in the going up of the cloud from off the Dwelling Place the sons of Israel journey in all their journeys; **37** and if the cloud does not go up then they do not journey, until the day of its going up. **38** For the cloud of Yhwh [is] on the Dwelling Place by day, and fire is in it by night, before the eyes of all the house of Israel in all their journeys.

LEVITICUS

CHAPTER 1

1 And Yhwh calls to Moses, and speaks to him out of the Tent of Meeting, saying, **2** "Speak to the sons of Israel, and you have said to them: Any man of you, when he brings an offering near to Yhwh out of the livestock—out of the herd or out of the flock—you bring your offering near. **3** If his offering [is] a burnt-offering out of the herd, he brings a male near, a perfect one, to the opening of the Tent of Meeting; he brings it near at his pleasure before Yhwh; **4** and he has laid his hand on the head of the burnt-offering, and it has been accepted for him to make atonement for him; **5** and he has slaughtered the son of the herd before Yhwh; and sons of Aaron, the priests, have brought the blood near, and sprinkled the blood around the altar, which [is] at the opening of the Tent of Meeting. **6** And he has stripped the burnt-offering, and has cut it into its pieces; **7** and the sons of Aaron the priest have put fire on the altar, and arranged wood on the fire; **8** and sons of Aaron, the priests, have arranged the pieces, with the head and the fat, on the wood, which [is] on the fire, which [is] on the altar; **9** and he washes its innards and its legs with water; and the priest has made incense with the whole on the altar, a burnt-offering, a fire-offering of refreshing fragrance to Yhwh. **10** And if his offering [is] out of the flock—out of the sheep or out of the goats—he brings a male near, a perfect one, for a burnt-offering, **11** and he has slaughtered it by the side of the altar northward, before Yhwh; and sons of Aaron, the priests, have sprinkled its blood around the altar; **12** and he has cut it into its pieces, and its head and its fat, and the priest has arranged them on the wood, which [is] on the fire, which [is] on the altar; **13** and he washes the innards and the legs with water, and the priest has brought the whole near, and has made incense on the altar; it [is] a burnt-offering, a fire-offering of refreshing fragrance to Yhwh. **14** And if his offering [is] a burnt-offering out of the bird to Yhwh, then he has brought his offering near out of the turtle-doves or out of the young pigeons, **15** and the priest has brought it near to the altar, and has wrung off its head, and has made incense on the altar, and its blood has been wrung out by the side of the altar; **16** and he has turned aside its crop with its feathers, and has cast it near the altar, eastward, to the place of ashes; **17** and he has cleaved it with its wings (he does not separate [it]), and the priest has made it an incense on the altar, on the wood, which [is] on the fire; it [is] a burnt-offering, a fire-offering of refreshing fragrance to Yhwh."

CHAPTER 2

1 "And when a person brings an offering near, a present to Yhwh, [and] his offering is of flour, then he has poured oil on it, and has put frankincense on it; **2** and he has brought it to the sons of Aaron, the priests, and one [of the priests] has taken from there the fullness of his hand of its flour and of its oil, besides all its frankincense, and the priest has made incense with its memorial on the altar, a fire-offering of refreshing fragrance to Yhwh; **3** and the remnant of the present [is] for Aaron and for his sons, most holy, of the fire-offerings of Yhwh. **4** And when you bring an offering near, a present baked in an oven, [it is of] unleavened cakes of flour mixed with oil, or thin unleavened cakes anointed with oil. **5** And if your offering [is] a present [made] on the griddle, it is of flour, mixed with oil, unleavened; **6** divide it into parts, and you have poured oil on it; it [is] a present. **7** And if your offering [is] a present [made] on the frying-pan, it is made of flour with oil, **8** and you have brought in the present which is made of these to Yhwh, and [one] has brought it near to the priest, and has brought it near to the altar, **9** and the priest has lifted up from the present its memorial, and has made incense on the altar, a fire-offering of refreshing fragrance to Yhwh; **10** and the remnant of the present [is] for Aaron and for his sons, most holy, of the fire-offerings of Yhwh. **11** No present which you bring near to Yhwh is made fermented, for you do not make incense [as] a fire-offering to Yhwh with any leaven or any honey. **12** An offering of first-[fruits]—you bring them near to Yhwh, but they do not go up on the altar for refreshing fragrance. **13** And every offering—your present—you season with salt, and you do not let the salt of the covenant of your God cease from your present; you bring salt near with all your offerings. **14** And if you bring a present of first-fruits near to Yhwh, you bring the present of your first-fruits near of green ears, roasted with fire, beaten out [grain] of a fruitful field, **15** and you have put oil on it, and laid frankincense on it, [for] it [is] a present; **16** and the priest has made incense with its memorial from its beaten out [grain], and from its oil, besides all its frankincense, [as] a fire-offering to Yhwh."

CHAPTER 3

1 "And if his offering [is] a sacrifice of peace-offerings, if he is bringing near out of the herd, whether male or female, he brings a perfect one near before Yhwh, **2** and he has laid his hand on the head of his offering, and has slaughtered it at the opening of the Tent of Meeting, and sons of Aaron, the priests, have sprinkled the blood around the altar. **3** And he has brought near from the sacrifice of the peace-offerings a fire-offering to Yhwh, the fat which is covering the innards, and all the fat which [is] on the innards, **4** and the two kidneys, and the fat which [is] on them, which [is] on the flanks, and the redundance on the liver above the kidneys—he turns it aside, **5** and sons of Aaron have made it an incense on the altar, on the burnt-offering which [is] on the wood, which [is] on the fire, [as] a fire-offering of refreshing fragrance to Yhwh. **6** And if his offering [is] out of the flock for a sacrifice of peace-offerings to Yhwh, male or female, he brings a perfect one near; **7** if he is bringing a sheep near [for] his offering, then he has brought it near before Yhwh, **8** and has laid his hand on the head of his offering, and has slaughtered it before the Tent of Meeting, and sons of Aaron have sprinkled its blood around the altar. **9** And he has brought near from the sacrifice of the peace-offerings a fire-offering to Yhwh, its fat, the whole fat tail close by the bone—he turns it aside, and the fat which is covering the innards, and all the fat which [is] on the innards, **10** and the two kidneys, and the fat which [is] on them, which [is] on the flanks, and the redundance on the liver above the kidneys—he turns it aside, **11** and the priest has made it an incense on the altar [as] bread of a fire-offering to Yhwh. **12** And if his offering [is] a goat, then he has brought it near before Yhwh, **13** and has laid his hand on its head, and has slaughtered it before the Tent of Meeting, and sons of Aaron have sprinkled its blood around the altar; **14** and he has brought his offering near from it, a fire-offering to Yhwh, the fat which is covering the innards, and all the fat which [is] on the innards, **15** and the two kidneys, and the fat which [is] on them, which [is] on the flanks, and the redundance on the liver above the kidneys—he turns it aside, **16** and the priest has made them an incense on the altar [as] bread of a fire-offering, for refreshing fragrance; all the fat [is] Yhwh's. **17** [This is] a continuous statute throughout your generations in all your dwellings: you do not eat any fat or any blood."

CHAPTER 4

1 And Yhwh speaks to Moses, saying, **2** "Speak to the sons of Israel, saying, When a person sins through ignorance against any of the commands of Yhwh [regarding things] which are not to be done, and has done [something] against one of these— **3** if the priest who is anointed sins according to the guilt of the people, then he has brought near for his sin which he has sinned a bullock, a son of the herd, a perfect one, to Yhwh, for a sin-offering, **4** and he has brought in the bullock to the opening of the Tent of Meeting before Yhwh, and has laid his hand on the head of the bullock, and has slaughtered the bullock before Yhwh. **5** And the priest who is anointed has taken of the blood of the bullock, and has brought it into the Tent of Meeting, **6** and the priest has dipped his finger in the blood, and sprinkled of the blood seven times before Yhwh, at the front of the veil of the holy place; **7** and the priest has put of the blood on the horns of the altar of spice-incense before Yhwh, which [is] in the Tent of Meeting, and he pours out all the blood of the bullock at the foundation of the altar of the burnt-offering, which [is] at the opening of the Tent of Meeting. **8** And he lifts up from it all the fat of the bullock of the sin-offering, the fat which is covering over the innards, and all the fat which [is] on the innards, **9** and the two kidneys, and the fat which [is] on

them, which [is] on the flanks, and the redundance on the liver above the kidneys—he turns it aside, **10** as it is lifted up from the ox of the sacrifice of the peace-offerings; and the priest has made them an incense on the altar of the burnt-offering. **11** And the skin of the bullock, and all its flesh, with its head, and with its legs, and its innards, and its dung— **12** he has even brought out the whole bullock to the outside of the camp, to a clean place, to the place of the pouring out of the ashes, and he has burned it on the wood with fire; it is burned beside the place of the pouring out of the ashes. **13** And if all the congregation of Israel errs ignorantly, and the thing has been hidden from the eyes of the assembly, and they have done [something against] one of all the commands of Yhwh [regarding things] which are not to be done, and have been guilty; **14** when the sin which they have sinned concerning it has been known, then the assembly has brought a bullock near, a son of the herd, for a sin-offering, and they have brought it in before the Tent of Meeting; **15** and the elderly of the congregation have laid their hands on the head of the bullock, before Yhwh, and [one] has slaughtered the bullock before Yhwh. **16** And the priest who is anointed has brought in of the blood of the bullock to the Tent of Meeting, **17** and the priest has dipped his finger in the blood, and has sprinkled seven times before Yhwh at the front of the veil, **18** and he puts [some] of the blood on the horns of the altar which [is] before Yhwh, which [is] in the Tent of Meeting; and he pours out all the blood at the foundation of the altar of the burnt-offering, which [is] at the opening of the Tent of Meeting; **19** and he lifts up all its fat from it, and has made incense on the altar. **20** And he has done to the bullock as he has done to the bullock of the sin-offering, so he does to it; and the priest has made atonement for them, and it has been forgiven them; **21** and he has brought out the bullock to the outside of the camp, and has burned it as he has burned the first bullock; it [is] a sin-offering of the assembly. **22** When a prince sins, and has done [something against] one of all the commands of his God Yhwh [regarding things] which are not to be done, through ignorance, and has been guilty, **23** or his sin wherein he has sinned has been made known to him, then he has brought in his offering, a kid of the goats, a male, a perfect one, **24** and he has laid his hand on the head of the goat, and has slaughtered it in the place where he slaughters the burnt-offering before Yhwh; it [is] a sin-offering. **25** And the priest has taken of the blood of the sin-offering with his finger, and has put [it] on the horns of the altar of the burnt-offering, and he pours out its blood at the foundation of the altar of the burnt-offering, **26** and he makes incense on the altar with all its fat, as the fat of the sacrifice of the peace-offerings; and the priest has made atonement for him because of his sin, and it has been forgiven him. **27** And if any person of the people of the land sins through ignorance, by his doing [something against] one of the commands of Yhwh [regarding things] which are not to be done, and has been guilty, **28** or his sin which he has sinned has been made known to him, then he has brought in his offering, a kid of the goats, a perfect one, a female, for his sin which he has sinned, **29** and he has laid his hand on the head of the sin-offering, and has slaughtered the sin-offering in the place of the burnt-offering. **30** And the priest has taken of its blood with his finger, and has put [it] on the horns of the altar of the burnt-offering, and he pours out all its blood at the foundation of the altar, **31** and he turns aside all its fat, as the fat has been turned aside from off the sacrifice of the peace-offerings, and the priest has made incense on the altar for refreshing fragrance to Yhwh; and the priest has made atonement for him, and it has been forgiven him. **32** And if he brings in a sheep [for] his offering, a female for a sin-offering, he brings in a perfect one, **33** and he has laid his hand on the head of the sin-offering, and has slaughtered it for a sin-offering in the place where he slaughters the burnt-offering. **34** And the priest has taken of the blood of the sin-offering with his finger, and has put [it] on the horns of the altar of the burnt-offering, and he pours out all its blood at the foundation of the altar, **35** and he turns aside all its fat, as the fat of the sheep is turned aside from the sacrifice of the peace-offerings, and the priest has made them an incense on the altar, according to the fire-offerings of Yhwh, and the priest has made atonement for him, for his sin which he has sinned, and it has been forgiven him."

CHAPTER 5

1 "And when a person sins, and has heard the voice of an oath, and he [is] witness, or has seen, or has known—if he does not declare [it], then he has borne his iniquity. **2** Or when a person comes against anything unclean, or against a carcass of an unclean beast, or against a carcass of unclean livestock, or against a carcass of an unclean teeming creature, and it has been hidden from him, then he [is] unclean and guilty; **3** or when he comes against [the] uncleanness of man, even any of his uncleanness whereby he is unclean, and it has been hidden from him, and he has known, then he has been guilty. **4** Or when a person swears, speaking wrongfully with the lips to do evil, or to do good, even anything which man speaks wrongfully with an oath, and it has been hid from him—when he has known then he has been guilty of one of these; **5** and it has been when he is guilty of one of these, that he has confessed concerning that which he has sinned, **6** and has brought in his guilt-offering to Yhwh for his sin which he has sinned, a female out of the flock, a lamb, or a kid of the goats, for a sin-offering, and the priest has made atonement for him because of his sin. **7** And if his hand does not reach to the sufficiency of a lamb, then he has brought in his guilt-offering—he who has sinned—two turtle-doves or two young pigeons to Yhwh, one for a sin-offering and one for a burnt-offering; **8** and he has brought them to the priest, and has brought near that which [is] for a sin-offering first, and has wrung off its head from its neck, and does not separate [it], **9** and he has sprinkled of the blood of the sin-offering on the side of the altar, and that which is left of the blood is wrung out at the foundation of the altar; it [is] a sin-offering. **10** And he makes the second a burnt-offering, according to the ordinance, and the priest has made atonement for him because of his sin which he has sinned, and it has been forgiven him. **11** And if his hand does not reach to two turtle-doves, or to two young pigeons, then he has brought in his offering—he who has sinned—a tenth of an ephah of flour for a sin-offering; he puts no oil on it, nor does he put frankincense on it, for it [is] a sin-offering, **12** and he has brought it to the priest, and the priest has taken a handful from it of the fullness of his hand—its memorial—and has made incense on the altar, according to the fire-offerings of Yhwh; it [is] a sin-offering. **13** And the priest has made atonement for him, for his sin which he has sinned against one of these, and it has been forgiven him, and [the remnant] has been for the priest, like the present." **14** And Yhwh speaks to Moses, saying, **15** "When a person commits a trespass, and has sinned through ignorance against the holy things of Yhwh, then he has brought in his guilt-offering to Yhwh, a ram, a perfect one, out of the flock, at your valuation [in] silver—shekels by the shekel of the holy place—for a guilt-offering. **16** And that which he has sinned against the holy thing he repays, and is adding to it its fifth, and has given it to the priest, and the priest makes atonement for him with the ram of the guilt-offering, and it has been forgiven him. **17** And when any person sins, and has done [something against] one of all the commands of Yhwh [regarding things] which are not to be done, and has not known, then he has been guilty, and has borne his iniquity. **18** Then he has brought in a ram, a perfect one, out of the flock, at your valuation, for a guilt-offering, to the priest; and the priest has made atonement for him, for his ignorance in which he has erred and he has not known, and it has been forgiven him; **19** it [is] a guilt-offering; he has certainly been guilty before Yhwh."

CHAPTER 6

1 And Yhwh speaks to Moses, saying, **2** "When any person sins, and has committed a trespass against Yhwh, and has lied to his fellow concerning a deposit, or concerning fellowship, or concerning violent robbery, or has oppressed his fellow; **3** or has found a lost thing, and has lied concerning it, and has sworn to a falsehood, concerning one of all [these] which man does, sinning in them: **4** then it has been, when he sins and has been guilty, that he has returned the plunder which he has violently taken away, or the thing which he has gotten by oppression, or the deposit which has been deposited with him, or the lost thing which he has found; **5** or all that concerning which he swears falsely, he has even repaid it in its principal, and he is adding to it its fifth; he gives it to him whose it [is] in the day of his guilt-offering. **6** And he brings his guilt-offering to Yhwh, a ram, a perfect one, out of the flock, at your valuation, for a guilt-offering, to the priest, **7** and the priest has made atonement for him before Yhwh, and it has been forgiven him, concerning one thing of all that he does, by being guilty therein." **8** And Yhwh speaks to Moses, saying, **9** "Command Aaron and his sons, saying, This [is] a law of the burnt-offering: the burnt-offering on [the] burning pile [remains] on the altar all the night until the morning, and the fire of the altar is burning on it. **10** And the priest has put on his long robe of fine linen, and he puts his fine linen trousers on his flesh, and has lifted up the ashes which the fire consumes with the burnt-offering on the altar, and has put them near the altar; **11** and he has stripped off his garments, and has put on other garments, and has brought out the ashes to the outside of the camp, to a clean place. **12** And the fire on the altar is burning on it, it is not quenched, and the priest has burned wood on it morning by morning, and has arranged the burnt-offering on it, and has made incense on it [with] the fat of the peace-offerings; **13** fire is continually burning on the altar, it is not quenched. **14** And this [is] a law of the present: sons of Aaron have brought it near before Yhwh to the front of the altar, **15** and [one] has lifted up of it with his hand from the flour of the present, and from its oil, and all the frankincense which [is] on the present, and has made incense on the altar of refreshing fragrance—its memorial to Yhwh. **16** And Aaron and his sons eat the remnant of it; it is eaten [with] unleavened things in a holy place—they eat it in the court of the Tent of Meeting. **17** It is not baked [with] anything fermented; I have given it [for] their portion out of My fire-offerings; it [is] most holy, like the sin-offering, and like the guilt-offering. **18** Every male among the sons of Aaron eats it—a continuous statute throughout your generations, out of the fire-offerings of Yhwh. All that comes against them is holy." **19** And Yhwh speaks to Moses, saying, **20** "This [is] an offering of Aaron and of his sons, which they bring near to Yhwh in the day of his being anointed: a tenth of the ephah of flour [for] a continual present, half of it in the morning, and half of it in the evening; **21** it is made on a griddle with oil—you bring it in stirred; you bring baked pieces of the present near [for] a refreshing fragrance to Yhwh. **22** And the priest who is anointed in his stead, from among his sons, makes it; [it is] a continuous statute of Yhwh; it is completely burned as incense; **23** and every present of a priest is a whole burnt-offering; it is not eaten." **24** And Yhwh speaks to Moses, saying, **25** "Speak to Aaron and to his sons, saying, This [is] a law of the sin-offering: in the place where the burnt-offering is slaughtered, the sin-offering is slaughtered before Yhwh; it [is] most holy. **26** The priest who is making atonement with it eats it; it is eaten in a holy place, in the court of the Tent of Meeting; **27** all that comes against its flesh is holy, and when [any] of its blood is sprinkled on the garment, that on which it is sprinkled you wash in the holy place; **28** and an earthen vessel in which it is boiled is broken, and if it is boiled in a bronze vessel, then it is scoured and rinsed with water. **29** Every male among the priests eats it—it [is] most holy; **30** and no sin-offering, [any] of whose blood is brought into the Tent of Meeting to make atonement in the holy place, is eaten; it is burned with fire."

CHAPTER 7

1 "And this [is] a law of the guilt-offering: it [is] most holy; **2** in the place where they slaughter the burnt-offering they slaughter the guilt-offering, and he sprinkles its blood on the altar all around, **3** and he brings near all its fat from it, the fat tail, and the fat which is covering the innards, **4** and the two kidneys, and the fat which [is] on them, which [is] on the flanks, and the redundance on the liver above the kidneys—he turns it aside; **5** and the priest has made them an incense on the altar, a fire-offering to Yhwh; it [is] a guilt-offering. **6** Every male among the priests eats it; it is eaten in a holy place—it [is] most holy; **7** as [is] a sin-offering, so [is] a guilt-offering; one law [is] for them; the priest who makes atonement by it—it is his. **8** And the priest who is bringing any man's burnt-offering near, the skin of the burnt-offering which he has brought near, it is the priest's, his own; **9** and every present which is baked in an oven, and all done in a frying-pan, and on a griddle, [is] the priest's who is bringing it near; it is his; **10** and every present, mixed with oil or dry, is for all the sons of Aaron—one as another. **11** And this [is] a law of the sacrifice of the peace-offerings which [one] brings near to Yhwh: **12** if he brings it near for a thank-offering, then he has brought near with the sacrifice of thank-offering unleavened cakes mixed with oil, and thin unleavened cakes anointed with oil, and of stirred flour cakes mixed with oil; **13** besides the cakes, he brings fermented bread near [with] his offering, besides the sacrifice of thank-offering of his peace-offerings; **14** and he has brought near from it one [cake] from every offering [as] a raised-offering to Yhwh for the priest who is sprinkling the blood of the peace-offerings; it is for him; **15** as for the flesh of the sacrifice of the thank-offering of his peace-offerings, it is eaten in the day of his offering; he does not leave of it until morning. **16** And if the sacrifice of his offering [is] a vow or free-will offering, it is eaten in the day of his bringing his sacrifice near; and on the next day the remnant of it is also eaten; **17** and the remnant of the flesh of the sacrifice is burned with fire on the third day; **18** and if any of the flesh of the sacrifice of his peace-offerings is eaten at all on the third day, it is not pleasing; it is not reckoned for him who is bringing it near; it is an abomination, and the person who is eating of it bears his iniquity. **19** And the flesh which comes against any unclean thing is not eaten; it is burned with fire; as for the flesh, every clean one eats of the flesh; **20** and the person who eats of the flesh of the sacrifice of the peace-offerings which [are] Yhwh's, and his uncleanness [is] on him, indeed, that person has been cut off from his people. **21** And when a person comes against anything unclean, of the uncleanness of man, or of the uncleanness of beasts, or of any unclean teeming creature, and has eaten of the flesh of the sacrifice of the peace-offerings which [are] Yhwh's, indeed, that person has been cut off from his people." **22** And Yhwh speaks to Moses, saying, **23** "Speak to the sons of Israel, saying, You do not eat any fat of ox, and sheep, and goat; **24** and the fat of a carcass, and the fat of a torn thing, is prepared for any work, but you certainly do not eat it; **25** for whoever eats the fat of the beast, of which [one] brings near [as] a fire-offering to Yhwh, indeed, the person who eats [it] has been cut off from his people. **26** And you do not eat any blood in all your dwellings, of bird, or of beast; **27** any person who eats any blood, indeed, that person has been cut off from his people." **28** And Yhwh speaks to Moses, saying, **29** "Speak to the sons of Israel, saying, He who is bringing the sacrifice of his peace-offerings near to Yhwh brings in his offering to Yhwh from the sacrifice of his peace-offerings; **30** his own hands bring in the fire-offerings of Yhwh, the fat beside the breast—he brings it in with the breast to wave it [as] a wave-offering before Yhwh. **31** And the priest has made incense with the fat on the altar, and the breast has been Aaron's and his sons; **32** and you give the right leg to the priest [as] a raised-offering of the sacrifices of your peace-offerings; **33** he from the sons of Aaron who is bringing the blood of the peace-offerings and the fat near—the right leg is for a portion for him. **34** For I have taken the breast of the wave-offering and the leg of the raised-offering from the sons of Israel, from the sacrifices of their peace-offerings, and I give them to Aaron the priest, and to his sons, by a continuous statute, from the sons of Israel." **35** This [is] an anointed portion [for] Aaron, and an anointed portion [for] his sons out of the fire-offerings of Yhwh, in the day he has brought them near to act as priest of Yhwh, **36** which Yhwh has commanded to give to them from the sons of Israel, in the day of His anointing them—a continuous statute throughout their generations. **37** This [is] the law for burnt-offering, for present, and for sin-offering, and for guilt-offering, and for consecrations, and for a sacrifice of the peace-offerings, **38** which Yhwh has commanded Moses in Mount Sinai, in the day of His commanding the sons of Israel to bring their offerings near to Yhwh, in the wilderness of Sinai.

CHAPTER 8

1 And Yhwh speaks to Moses, saying, **2** "Take Aaron and his sons with him, and the garments, and the anointing oil, and the bullock of the sin-offering, and the two rams, and the basket of unleavened things, **3** and assemble all the congregation to the opening of the Tent of Meeting." **4** And Moses does as Yhwh has commanded him, and the congregation is assembled to the opening of the Tent of Meeting, **5** and Moses says to the congregation, "This [is] the thing which Yhwh has commanded to do." **6** And Moses brings Aaron and his sons near, and bathes them with water, **7** and puts the coat on him, and girds him with the girdle, and clothes him with the upper robe, and puts the ephod on him, and girds him with the girdle of the ephod, and binds [it] to him with it, **8** and puts the breastplate on him, and puts the Lights and the Perfections into the breastplate, **9** and puts the turban on his head, and puts the golden flower of the holy crown on the turban, toward the front of its face, as Yhwh has commanded Moses. **10** And Moses takes the anointing oil, and anoints the

Dwelling Place, and all that [is] in it, and sanctifies them; **11** and he sprinkles of it on the altar seven times, and anoints the altar, and all its vessels, and the laver, and its base, to sanctify them; **12** and he pours of the anointing oil on the head of Aaron, and anoints him to sanctify him. **13** And Moses brings the sons of Aaron near, and clothes them [with] coats, and girds them [with] girdles, and binds caps to them, as Yhwh has commanded Moses. **14** And he brings the bullock of the sin-offering near, and Aaron lays—his sons also—their hands on the head of the bullock of the sin-offering, **15** and [one] slaughters, and Moses takes the blood, and puts [it] around the horns of the altar with his finger, and cleanses the altar, and he has poured out the blood at the foundation of the altar, and sanctifies it, to make atonement on it. **16** And he takes all the fat that [is] on the innards, and the redundance on the liver, and the two kidneys, and their fat, and Moses makes incense on the altar, **17** and the bullock, and its skin, and its flesh, and its dung, he has burned with fire, at the outside of the camp, as Yhwh has commanded Moses. **18** And he brings the ram of the burnt-offering near, and Aaron and his sons lay their hands on the head of the ram, **19** and [one] slaughters, and Moses sprinkles the blood around the altar; **20** and he has cut the ram into its pieces, and Moses makes incense with the head, and the pieces, and the fat, **21** and he has washed the innards and the legs with water, and Moses makes incense with the whole ram on the altar; it [is] a burnt-offering for refreshing fragrance; it [is] a fire-offering to Yhwh, as Yhwh has commanded Moses. **22** And he brings the second ram near, a ram of the consecrations, and Aaron and his sons lay their hands on the head of the ram, **23** and [one] slaughters, and Moses takes of its blood, and puts [it] on the tip of the right ear of Aaron, and on the thumb of his right hand, and on the great toe of his right foot; **24** and he brings the sons of Aaron near, and Moses puts of the blood on the tip of their right ear, and on the thumb of their right hand, and on the great toe of their right foot. And Moses sprinkles the blood around the altar, **25** and takes the fat, and the fat tail, and all the fat that [is] on the innards, and the redundance on the liver, and the two kidneys, and their fat, and the right leg; **26** and out of the basket of unleavened things, which [is] before Yhwh, he has taken one unleavened cake, and one cake of oiled bread, and one thin cake, and puts [them] on the fat, and on the right leg; **27** and he puts the whole on the hands of Aaron, and on the hands of his sons, and waves them [as] a wave-offering before Yhwh. **28** And Moses takes them from off their hands, and makes incense on the altar, on the burnt-offering—they [are] consecrations for refreshing fragrance; it [is] a fire-offering to Yhwh; **29** and Moses takes the breast, and waves it [as] a wave-offering before Yhwh; it has been for Moses for a portion of the ram of the consecrations, as Yhwh has commanded Moses. **30** And Moses takes of the anointing oil, and of the blood which [is] on the altar, and sprinkles [them] on Aaron, on his garments, and on his sons, and on the garments of his sons with him, and he sanctifies Aaron, his garments, and his sons, and the garments of his sons with him. **31** And Moses says to Aaron and to his sons, "Boil the flesh at the opening of the Tent of Meeting, and there you eat it and the bread which [is] in the basket of the consecrations, as I have commanded, saying, Aaron and his sons eat it. **32** And the remnant of the flesh and of the bread you burn with fire; **33** and you do not go out from the opening of the Tent of Meeting [for] seven days, until the day of the fullness, the days of your consecration—for seven days he consecrates your hand; **34** as he has done on this day, Yhwh has commanded to do, to make atonement for you; **35** and you abide at the opening of the Tent of Meeting by day and by night [for] seven days, and you have kept the charge of Yhwh, and do not die, for so I have been commanded." **36** And Aaron does—his sons also—all the things which Yhwh has commanded by the hand of Moses.

CHAPTER 9

1 And it comes to pass on the eighth day, Moses has called for Aaron and for his sons, and for [the] elderly of Israel, **2** and he says to Aaron, "Take a calf for yourself, a son of the herd, for a sin-offering, and a ram for a burnt-offering, perfect ones, and bring [them] near before Yhwh. **3** And you speak to the sons of Israel, saying, Take a kid of the goats for a sin-offering, and a calf, and a lamb, sons of a year, perfect ones, for a burnt-offering, **4** and a bullock and a ram for peace-offerings, to sacrifice before Yhwh, and a present mixed with oil; for today

Yhwh has appeared to you." **5** And they take that which Moses has commanded to the front of the Tent of Meeting, and all the congregation draws near and stands before Yhwh; **6** and Moses says, "This [is] the thing which Yhwh has commanded; do [it], and the glory of Yhwh appears to you." **7** And Moses says to Aaron, "Draw near to the altar, and make your sin-offering, and your burnt-offering, and make atonement for yourself, and for the people, and make the offering of the people, and make atonement for them, as Yhwh has commanded." **8** And Aaron draws near to the altar, and slaughters the calf of the sin-offering, which [is] for himself; **9** and the sons of Aaron bring the blood near to him, and he dips his finger in the blood, and puts [it] on the horns of the altar, and he has poured out the blood at the foundation of the altar; **10** and the fat, and the kidneys, and the redundance of the liver, of the sin-offering, he has made incense on the altar, as Yhwh has commanded Moses; **11** and he has burned the flesh and the skin with fire, at the outside of the camp. **12** And he slaughters the burnt-offering, and the sons of Aaron have presented the blood to him, and he sprinkles it around the altar; **13** and they have presented the burnt-offering to him, by its pieces, and the head, and he makes incense on the altar; **14** and he washes the innards and the legs, and makes incense for the burnt-offering on the altar. **15** And he brings the offering of the people near, and takes the goat of the sin-offering which [is] for the people, and slaughters it, and makes it a sin-offering, like the first; **16** and he brings the burnt-offering near, and makes it, according to the ordinance; **17** and he brings the present near, and fills his palm with it, and makes incense on the altar, apart from the burnt-offering of the morning. **18** And he slaughters the bullock and the ram, a sacrifice of the peace-offerings, which [are] for the people, and sons of Aaron present the blood to him (and he sprinkles it around the altar), **19** and the fat of the bullock, and of the ram, the fat tail, and the covering [of the innards], and the kidneys, and the redundance on the liver, **20** and they set the fat on the breasts, and he makes incense with the fat on the altar; **21** and Aaron has waved the breasts and the right leg [as] a wave-offering before Yhwh, as He has commanded Moses. **22** And Aaron lifts up his hand toward the people, and blesses them, and comes down from making the sin-offering, and the burnt-offering, and the peace-offerings. **23** And Moses goes in—Aaron also—to the Tent of Meeting, and they come out, and bless the people, and the glory of Yhwh appears to all the people; **24** and fire comes out from before Yhwh, and consumes the burnt-offering and the fat on the altar; and all the people see, and cry aloud, and fall on their faces.

CHAPTER 10

1 And the sons of Aaron, Nadab and Abihu, each take his censer, and put fire in them, and put incense on it, and bring strange fire near before Yhwh, which He has not commanded them; **2** and fire goes out from before Yhwh and consumes them, and they die before Yhwh. **3** And Moses says to Aaron, "It [is] that which Yhwh has spoken, saying, By those drawing near to Me I am sanctified, and in the face of all the people I am honored"; and Aaron is silent. **4** And Moses calls to Mishael and to Elzaphan, sons of Uzziel, uncle of Aaron, and says to them, "Come near, carry your brothers from the front of the holy place to the outside of the camp"; **5** and they come near, and carry them in their coats to the outside of the camp, as Moses has spoken. **6** And Moses says to Aaron and his sons, to Eleazar and to Ithamar, "You do not uncover your heads, and you do not tear your garments, that you do not die, and He is angry on all the congregation; as for your brothers, the whole house of Israel, they lament the burning which Yhwh has kindled; **7** and you do not go out from the opening of the Tent of Meeting, lest you die, for the anointing oil of Yhwh [is] on you"; and they do according to the word of Moses. **8** And Yhwh speaks to Aaron, saying, **9** "You do not drink wine and strong drink, you and your sons with you, in your going into the Tent of Meeting, and you do not die—a continuous statute throughout your generations, **10** so as to make a separation between the holy and the common, and between the unclean and the pure; **11** and to teach the sons of Israel all the statutes which Yhwh has spoken to them by the hand of Moses." **12** And Moses speaks to Aaron and his sons, to Eleazar and to Ithamar, who are left, "Take the present that is left from the fire-offerings of Yhwh, and eat it unleavened near the altar, for it [is] most holy, **13** and you have eaten it in the holy place, for it

[is] your portion, and the portion of your sons, from the fire-offerings of Yhwh; for so I have been commanded. **14** And you eat the breast of the wave-offering and the leg of the raised-offering in a clean place, you, and your sons, and your daughters with you; they have been given for your portion and the portion of your sons, out of the sacrifices of peace-offerings of the sons of Israel; **15** the leg of the raised-offering, and breast of the wave-offering, besides fire-offerings of the fat, they bring in to wave [as] a wave-offering before Yhwh, and it has been to you, and to your sons with you, by a continuous statute, as Yhwh has commanded." **16** And Moses has diligently sought the goat of the sin-offering, and behold, it is burned, and he is angry against Eleazar and against Ithamar, sons of Aaron, who are left, saying, **17** "Why have you not eaten the sin-offering in the holy place, for it [is] most holy—and He has given it to you to take away the iniquity of the congregation, to make atonement for them before Yhwh? **18** behold, its blood has not been brought into the holy place within; eating you eat it in the holy place, as I have commanded." **19** And Aaron speaks to Moses, "Behold, today they have brought their sin-offering and their burnt-offering near before Yhwh; and [things] like these meet me, yet I have eaten a sin-offering today; is it good in the eyes of Yhwh?" **20** And Moses listens, and it is good in his eyes.

CHAPTER 11

1 And Yhwh speaks to Moses and to Aaron, saying to them, **2** "Speak to the sons of Israel, saying, This [is] the beast which you eat out of all the beasts which [are] on the earth: **3** any dividing a hoof, and cleaving the cleft of the hooves, bringing up the cud, among the beasts—you eat it. **4** Only, this you do not eat, of those bringing up the cud, and of those dividing the hoof: the camel, though it is bringing up the cud, yet the hoof is not dividing—it [is] unclean to you; **5** and the hyrax, though it is bringing up the cud, yet the hoof is not divided—it [is] unclean to you; **6** and the hare, though it is bringing up the cud, yet the hoof has not divided—it [is] unclean to you; **7** and the sow, though it is dividing the hoof, and cleaving the cleft of the hoof, yet it does not bring up the cud—it [is] unclean to you. **8** You do not eat of their flesh, and you do not come against their carcass—they [are] unclean to you. **9** This you eat of all which [are] in the waters: anything that has fins and scales in the waters, in the seas, and in the brooks, them you eat; **10** and anything that does not have fins and scales in the seas, and in the brooks, of any teeming creature of the waters, and of any creature which lives, which [is] in the waters—they [are] an abomination to you; **11** indeed, they are an abomination to you; you do not eat of their flesh, and you detest their carcass. **12** Anything that does not have fins and scales in the waters—it [is] an abomination to you. **13** And these you detest of the bird—they are not eaten, they [are] an abomination: the eagle, and the bearded vulture, and the osprey, **14** and the kite, and the falcon after its kind, **15** every raven after its kind, **16** and the ostrich, and the nightjar [[*or* male ostrich]], and the seagull, and the hawk after its kind, **17** and the little owl, and the cormorant, and the great owl, **18** and the waterhen, and the pelican, and the Egyptian vulture, **19** and the stork, the heron after its kind, and the hoopoe, and the bat. **20** Every teeming creature which is flying, which is going on four [legs]—it [is] an abomination to you. **21** Only, this you eat of any teeming thing which is flying, which is going on four, which has legs above its feet, to move with them on the earth; **22** these of them you eat: the locust after its kind, and the bald locust after its kind, and the cricket after its kind, and the grasshopper after its kind; **23** and every teeming thing which is flying, which has four feet—it [is] an abomination to you. **24** And you are made unclean by these; anyone who is coming against their carcass is unclean until the evening; **25** and anyone who is lifting up of their carcass washes his garments, and has been unclean until the evening— **26** even every beast which is dividing the hoof, and is not cloven-footed, and is not bringing up the cud—they [are] unclean to you; anyone who is coming against them is unclean. **27** And anything going on its paws, among all the beasts which are going on four—they [are] unclean to you; anyone who is coming against their carcass is unclean until the evening; **28** and he who is lifting up their carcass washes his garments, and has been unclean until the evening—they [are] unclean to you. **29** And this [is] the unclean to you among the teeming things which are teeming on the earth: the weasel, and the muroid, and the tortoise [[*or* large lizard]] after its kind, **30** and the gecko [[or ferret]], and the chameleon, and the lizard, and the snail, and the mole; **31** these [are] the unclean to you among all which are teeming; anyone who is coming against them in their death is unclean until the evening. **32** And anything on which anyone of them falls, in their death, is unclean, of any vessel of wood or garment or skin or sack, any vessel in which work is done is brought into water, and has been unclean until the evening, then it has been clean; **33** and any earthen vessel, into the midst of which [any] one of them falls, all that [is] in its midst is unclean, and you break it. **34** Of all the food which is eaten, that on which comes [such] water, is unclean, and all drink which is drunk in any [such] vessel is unclean; **35** and anything on which [any] of their carcass falls is unclean; oven or double pots, it is broken down, they [are] unclean, indeed, they are unclean to you. **36** Only, a fountain or pit, a collection of water, is clean, but that which is coming against their carcass is unclean; **37** and when [any] of their carcass falls on any sown seed which is sown—it [is] clean; **38** and when water is put on the seed, and [any] of its carcass has fallen on it—it [is] unclean to you. **39** And when any of the beasts which are for food for you dies, he who is coming against its carcass is unclean until the evening; **40** and he who is eating of its carcass washes his garments, and has been unclean until the evening; and he who is lifting up its carcass washes his garments, and has been unclean until the evening. **41** And every teeming thing which is teeming on the earth is an abomination, it is not eaten; **42** anything going on the belly, and any going on four, to every multiplier of feet, to every teeming thing which is teeming on the earth—you do not eat them, for they [are] an abomination; **43** you do not make yourselves abominable with any teeming thing which is teeming, nor do you make yourselves unclean with them, so that you have been unclean with them. **44** For I [am] your God Yhwh, and you have sanctified yourselves, and you have been holy, for I [am] holy; and you do not defile your persons with any teeming thing which is creeping on the earth; **45** for I [am] Yhwh who am bringing you up out of the land of Egypt to become your God; and you have been holy, for I [am] holy. **46** This [is] a law of the beasts, and of the bird, and of every living creature which is moving in the waters, and of every creature which is teeming on the earth, **47** to make separation between the unclean and the pure, and between the beast that is eaten, and the beast that is not eaten."

CHAPTER 12

1 And Yhwh speaks to Moses, saying, **2** "Speak to the sons of Israel, saying, A woman when she gives seed, and has borne a male, then she has been unclean [for] seven days; she is unclean according to the days of separation for her sickness; **3** and in the eighth day the flesh of his foreskin is circumcised; **4** and she abides in the blood of her cleansing [for] thirty-three days; she does not come against any holy thing, and she does not go into the sanctuary, until the fullness of the days of her cleansing. **5** And if she bears a female, then she has been unclean [for] two weeks, as in her separation; and she abides by the blood of her cleansing [for] sixty-six days. **6** And in the fullness of the days of her cleansing for son or for daughter she brings in a lamb, a son of a year, for a burnt-offering, and a young pigeon or a turtle-dove for a sin-offering, to the opening of the Tent of Meeting, to the priest; **7** and he has brought it near before Yhwh, and has made atonement for her, and she has been cleansed from the fountain of her blood; this [is] the law of her who is bearing, in regard to a male or to a female. **8** And if her hand does not find the sufficiency of a sheep, then she has taken two turtle-doves or two young pigeons, one for a burnt-offering and one for a sin-offering, and the priest has made atonement for her, and she has been cleansed."

CHAPTER 13

1 And Yhwh speaks to Moses and to Aaron, saying, **2** "When a man has a rising, or scab, or bright spot in the skin of his flesh, and it has become a leprous plague in the skin of his flesh, then he has been brought to Aaron the priest, or to one of his sons the priests; **3** and the priest has seen the plague in the skin of the flesh, and the hair in the plague has turned white, and the appearance of the plague [is] deeper than the skin of his flesh—it [is] a plague of leprosy, and the priest has

seen him, and has pronounced him unclean. **4** And if the bright spot is white in the skin of his flesh, and its appearance is not deeper than the skin, and its hair has not turned white, then the priest has shut up [him who has] the plague [for] seven days. **5** And the priest has seen him on the seventh day, and behold, the plague has stood in his eyes, the plague has not spread in the skin, and the priest has shut him up [for] a second seven days. **6** And the priest has seen him on the second seventh day, and behold, the plague has faded, and the plague has not spread in the skin, and the priest has pronounced him clean; it [is] a scab, and he has washed his garments, and has been clean. **7** And if the scab spreads greatly in the skin, after his being seen by the priest for his cleansing, then he has been seen a second time by the priest; **8** and the priest has seen, and behold, the scab has spread in the skin, and the priest has pronounced him unclean; it [is] leprosy. **9** When a plague of leprosy is in a man, then he has been brought to the priest, **10** and the priest has seen, and behold, a white rising in the skin, and it has turned the hair white, and a quickening of raw flesh [is] in the rising— **11** it [is] an old leprosy in the skin of his flesh, and the priest has pronounced him unclean; he does not shut him up, for he [is] unclean. **12** And if the leprosy breaks out greatly in the skin, and the leprosy has covered all the skin of [him who has] the plague, from his head even to his feet, to all that appears to the eyes of the priest, **13** then the priest has seen, and behold, the leprosy has covered all his flesh, and he has pronounced [him who has] the plague clean; it has all turned white; he [is] clean. **14** And in the day of raw flesh being seen in him, he is unclean; **15** and the priest has seen the raw flesh, and has pronounced him unclean; the raw flesh is unclean—it [is] leprosy. **16** Or when the raw flesh turns back, and has been turned to white, then he has come to the priest, **17** and the priest has seen him, and behold, the plague has been turned to white, and the priest has pronounced clean [him who has] the plague; he [is] clean. **18** And when flesh has in it, in its skin, an ulcer, and it has been healed, **19** and there has been in the place of the ulcer a white rising, or a bright white spot, reddish, then it has been seen by the priest; **20** and the priest has seen, and behold, its appearance [is] lower than the skin, and its hair has turned white, and the priest has pronounced him unclean; it [is] a plague of leprosy—it has broken out in an ulcer. **21** And if the priest sees it, and behold, there is no white hair in it, and it is not lower than the skin, and has faded, then the priest has shut him up [for] seven days; **22** and if it spreads greatly in the skin, then the priest has pronounced him unclean—it [is] a plague; **23** and if the bright spot stays in its place—it has not spread—it [is] an inflammation of the ulcer; and the priest has pronounced him clean. **24** Or when flesh has a fiery burning in its skin, and the quickening of the burning, the bright white spot, has been reddish or white, **25** and the priest has seen it, and behold, the hair has turned white in the bright spot, and its appearance [is] deeper than the skin, it [is] leprosy; it has broken out in the burning, and the priest has pronounced him unclean; it [is] a plague of leprosy. **26** And if the priest sees it, and behold, there is no white hair on the bright spot, and it is not lower than the skin, and it has faded, then the priest has shut him up [for] seven days; **27** and the priest has seen him on the seventh day, [and] if it spreads greatly in the skin, then the priest has pronounced him unclean; it [is] a plague of leprosy. **28** And if the bright spot stays in its place, it has not spread in the skin, and has faded; it [is] a rising of the burning, and the priest has pronounced him clean; for it [is] inflammation of the burning. **29** And when a man (or a woman) has a plague in him, in the head or in the beard, **30** then the priest has seen the plague, and behold, its appearance is deeper than the skin, and a thin, shining hair [is] in it, and the priest has pronounced him unclean; it [is] a scale—it [is] a leprosy of the head or of the beard. **31** And when the priest sees the scaly plague, and behold, its appearance is not deeper than the skin, and there is no black hair in it, then the priest has shut up [him who has] the scaly plague [for] seven days. **32** And the priest has seen the plague on the seventh day, and behold, the scale has not spread, and a shining hair has not been in it, and the appearance of the scale is not deeper than the skin, **33** then he has shaved himself, but he does not shave the scale; and the priest has shut up [him who has] the scale [for] a second seven days. **34** And the priest has seen the scale on the seventh day, and behold, the scale has not spread in the skin, and its appearance is not deeper than the skin, and the priest has pronounced him clean, and he has washed his garments, and has been clean. **35** And if the scale spreads greatly in the skin after his cleansing, **36** and the priest has seen him, and behold, the scale has spread in the skin, the priest does not seek for the shining hair—he is unclean; **37** and if in his eyes the scale has stayed, and black hair has sprung up in it, the scale has been healed—he [is] clean—and the priest has pronounced him clean. **38** And when a man or woman has bright spots in the skin of their flesh, white bright spots, **39** and the priest has seen, and behold, white [and] faded bright spots [are] in the skin of their flesh—it [is] a freckled spot broken out in the skin; he [is] clean. **40** And when a man's head [is] polished, he [is] bald; he [is] clean; **41** and if his head is polished from the corner of his face, he [is] bald of the forehead; he [is] clean. **42** And when there is in the bald back of the head, or in the bald forehead, a reddish-white plague, it [is] a leprosy breaking out in the bald back of the head, or in the bald forehead; **43** and the priest has seen him, and behold, the rising of the reddish-white plague in the bald back of the head, or in the bald forehead, [is] as the appearance of leprosy, in the skin of the flesh, **44** he [is] a leprous man—he [is] unclean; the priest pronounces him utterly unclean; his plague [is] in his head. **45** As for the leper in whom [is] the plague, his garments are torn, and his head is uncovered, and he covers over the upper lip, and he calls, Unclean! Unclean! **46** He is unclean all the days that the plague [is] in him; he [is] unclean. He dwells alone; his dwelling [is] at the outside of the camp. **47** And when there is a plague of leprosy in any garment—in a garment of wool, or in a garment of linen, **48** or in the warp, or in the woof, of linen or of wool, or in a skin, or in any work of skin— **49** and the plague has been greenish or reddish in the garment, or in the skin, or in the warp, or in the woof, or in any vessel of skin, it [is] a plague of leprosy, and it has been shown [to] the priest. **50** And the priest has seen the plague, and has shut up [that which has] the plague [for] seven days; **51** and he has seen the plague on the seventh day, and the plague has spread in the garment, or in the warp, or in the woof, or in the skin, of all that is made of skin for work, the plague [is] a fretting leprosy; it [is] unclean. **52** And he has burned the garment, or the warp, or the woof, in wool or in linen, or any vessel of skin in which the plague is; for it [is] a fretting leprosy; it is burned with fire. **53** And if the priest sees, and behold, the plague has not spread in the garment, or in the warp, or in the woof, or in any vessel of skin, **54** then the priest has commanded, and they have washed that in which the plague [is], and he has shut it up [for] a second seven days. **55** And the priest has seen [that which has] the plague after it has been washed, and behold, the plague has not changed its aspect, and the plague has not spread—it [is] unclean; you burn it with fire; it [is] a fretting in its back-part or in its front-part. **56** And if the priest has seen, and behold, the plague has faded after it has been washed, then he has torn it out of the garment, or out of the skin, or out of the warp, or out of the woof; **57** and if it is still seen in the garment, or in the warp, or in the woof, or in any vessel of skin, it [is] a fretting; you burn it with fire—that in which the plague [is]. **58** And the garment, or the warp, or the woof, or any vessel of skin which you wash when the plague has turned aside from them, then it has been washed a second time, and has been clean. **59** This [is] the law of a plague of leprosy [in] a garment of wool or of linen, or of the warp or of the woof, or of any vessel of skin, to pronounce it clean or to pronounce it unclean."

CHAPTER 14

1 And Yhwh speaks to Moses, saying, **2** "This is a law of the leper, in the day of his cleansing, that he has been brought to the priest, **3** and the priest has gone out to the outside of the camp, and the priest has seen, and behold, the plague of leprosy has ceased from the leper, **4** and the priest has commanded, and he has taken for him who is to be cleansed, two clean living birds, and cedar wood, and scarlet, and hyssop. **5** And the priest has commanded, and he has slaughtered one bird on an earthen vessel, over running water; **6** [as for] the living bird, he takes it, and the cedar wood, and the scarlet, and the hyssop, and has dipped them and the living bird in the blood of the slaughtered bird, over the running water, **7** and he has sprinkled on him who is to be cleansed from the leprosy seven times, and has pronounced him clean, and has sent out the living bird over the face of the field. **8** And he who is to be cleansed has washed his garments, and has shaved all his hair, and has bathed with water, and has been clean, and afterward he comes into the camp, and has dwelt at the outside of his tent [for] seven days. **9** And it has been, on the seventh day—he shaves all his hair, his head, and his beard, and his eyebrows, even all his hair he shaves, and he has washed his garments, and has bathed his flesh with water, and has been clean. **10** And on the eighth day he takes two lambs, perfect ones, and one ewe-lamb, daughter of a year, a perfect one, and three-tenth parts of flour [for] a present, mixed with oil, and one log of oil. **11** And the priest who is cleansing has caused the man who is to be cleansed to stand with them before Yhwh, at the opening of the Tent of Meeting, **12** and the priest has taken one male lamb, and has brought it near for a guilt-offering, also the log of oil, and has waved them [as] a wave-offering before Yhwh. **13** And he has slaughtered the lamb in the place where he slaughters the sin-offering and the burnt-offering, in the holy place; for like the sin-offering, the guilt-offering is for the priest; it [is] most holy. **14** And the priest has taken of the blood of the guilt-offering, and the priest has put [it] on the tip of the right ear of him who is to be cleansed, and on the thumb of his right hand, and on the great toe of his right foot; **15** and the priest has taken of the log of oil, and has poured [it] on the left palm of the priest, **16** and the priest has dipped his right finger in the oil which [is] on his left palm, and has sprinkled of the oil with his finger seven times before Yhwh. **17** And of the remainder of the oil which [is] on his palm, the priest puts [it] on the tip of the right ear of him who is to be cleansed, and on the thumb of his right hand, and on the great toe of his right foot, on the blood of the guilt-offering; **18** and the remnant of the oil which [is] on the palm of the priest, he puts [it] on the head of him who is to be cleansed, and the priest has made atonement for him before Yhwh. **19** And the priest has made the sin-offering, and has made atonement for him who is to be cleansed from his uncleanness, and afterward he slaughters the burnt-offering; **20** and the priest has caused the burnt-offering to ascend, also the present, on the altar, and the priest has made atonement for him, and he has been clean. **21** And if he [is] poor, and his hand is not reaching [these things], then he has taken one lamb [for] a guilt-offering, for a wave-offering, to make atonement for him, and one-tenth part of flour mixed with oil for a present, and a log of oil, **22** and two turtle-doves, or two young pigeons, which his hand reaches to, and one has been a sin-offering and one a burnt-offering; **23** and he has brought them in on the eighth day for his cleansing to the priest, to the opening of the Tent of Meeting, before Yhwh. **24** And the priest has taken the lamb of the guilt-offering, and the log of oil, and the priest has waved them [as] a wave-offering before Yhwh; **25** and he has slaughtered the lamb of the guilt-offering, and the priest has taken of the blood of the guilt-offering, and has put [it] on the tip of the right ear of him who is to be cleansed, and on the thumb of his right hand, and on the great toe of his right foot; **26** and the priest pours of the oil on the left palm of the priest; **27** and the priest has sprinkled with his right finger of the oil which [is] on his left palm, seven times before Yhwh. **28** And the priest has put of the oil which [is] on his palm, on the tip of the right ear of him who is to be cleansed, and on the thumb of his right hand, and on the great toe of his right foot, on the place of the blood of the guilt-offering; **29** and he puts the remnant of the oil which [is] on the palm of the priest on the head of him who is to be cleansed, to make atonement for him, before Yhwh. **30** And he has made one of the turtle-doves or of the young pigeons (from that which his hand reaches to, **31** [even] that which his hand reaches to), one a sin-offering and one a burnt-offering, besides the present, and the priest has made atonement for him who is to be cleansed before Yhwh. **32** This [is] a law of him in whom [is] a plague of leprosy, whose hand does not reach to his cleansing." **33** And Yhwh speaks to Moses and to Aaron, saying, **34** "When you come into the land of Canaan, which I am giving to you for a possession, and I have put a plague of leprosy in a house [in] the land of your possession, **35** then he whose the house [is] has come in and declared [it] to the priest, saying, Some plague has appeared to me in the house; **36** and the priest has commanded, and they have prepared the house before the priest comes in to see the plague (that all which [is] in the house is not unclean), and afterward the priest comes in to see the house; **37** and he has seen the plague, and behold, the plague [is] in the walls of the house, hollow streaks, greenish or reddish, and their appearance [is] lower than the wall, **38** and the priest has gone out of the house to the opening of the house, and has shut up the house [for] seven days. **39** And the priest has turned back on the seventh day, and has seen, and behold, the plague has spread in the walls of the house, **40** and the priest has commanded, and they have drawn out the stones in which the plague [is], and have cast them to the outside of the city, to an unclean place; **⁴¹** and he causes the house to be scraped all around inside, and they have poured out the clay which they have scraped off, at the outside of the city, at an unclean place; **⁴²** and they have taken other stones, and brought [them] to the place of the stones, and he takes other clay and has coated the house. **⁴³** And if the plague returns, and has broken out in the house, after he has drawn out the stones, and after the scraping of the house, and after the coating, **⁴⁴** then the priest has come in and seen, and behold, the plague has spread in the house; it [is] a fretting leprosy in the house; it [is] unclean. **⁴⁵** And he has broken down the house, its stones, and its wood, and all the clay of the house, and he has brought [them] forth to the outside of the city, to an unclean place. **⁴⁶** And he who is going into the house all the days he has shut it up, is unclean until the evening; **⁴⁷** and he who is lying in the house washes his garments; and he who is eating in the house washes his garments. **⁴⁸** And if the priest certainly comes in, and has seen, and behold, the plague has not spread in the house after the coating of the house, then the priest has pronounced the house clean, for the plague has been healed. **⁴⁹** And he has taken two birds, and cedar wood, and scarlet, and hyssop for the cleansing of the house; **⁵⁰** and he has slaughtered one bird on an earthen vessel, over running water; **⁵¹** and he has taken the cedar wood, and the hyssop, and the scarlet, and the living bird, and has dipped them in the blood of the slaughtered bird, and in the running water, and has sprinkled against the house seven times. **⁵²** And he has cleansed the house with the blood of the bird, and with the running water, and with the living bird, and with the cedar wood, and with the hyssop, and with the scarlet; **⁵³** and he has sent the living bird away to the outside of the city to the face of the field, and has made atonement for the house, and it has been clean. **⁵⁴** This [is] the law for every plague of the leprosy and for scale, **⁵⁵** and for leprosy of a garment, and of a house, **⁵⁶** and for a rising, and for a scab, and for a bright spot— **⁵⁷** to direct in the day of being unclean, and in the day of being clean; this [is] the law of the leprosy."

CHAPTER 15

¹ And Yhwh speaks to Moses and to Aaron, saying, **²** "Speak to the sons of Israel, and you have said to them: When there is discharging out of the flesh of any man, he [is] unclean [from] his discharge; **³** and this is his uncleanness in his discharge—his flesh has run with his discharge, or his flesh has stopped from his discharge; it [is] his uncleanness. **⁴** Every bed on which he who has the discharging lies is unclean, and every vessel on which he sits is unclean; **⁵** and anyone who comes against his bed washes his garments, and has bathed with water, and been unclean until the evening. **⁶** And he who is sitting on the vessel on which he sits who has the discharging, washes his garments, and has bathed with water, and been unclean until the evening. **⁷** And he who is coming against the flesh of him who has the discharging, washes his garments, and has bathed with water, and been unclean until the evening. **⁸** And when he who has the discharging spits on him who is clean, then he has washed his garments, and has bathed with water, and been unclean until the evening. **⁹** And all the saddle on which he who has the discharging rides is unclean; **¹⁰** and anyone who is coming against anything which is under him is unclean until the evening, and he who is carrying them washes his garments, and has bathed with water, and been unclean until the evening. **¹¹** And anyone against whom he who has the discharging comes (and has not rinsed his hands with water) has even washed his garments, and bathed with water, and been unclean until the evening. **¹²** And the earthen vessel which he who has the discharging comes against is broken; and every wooden vessel is rinsed with water. **¹³** And when he who has the discharging is clean from his discharge, then he has numbered seven days for himself for his cleansing, and has washed his garments, and has bathed his flesh with running water, and been clean. **¹⁴** And on the eighth day he takes two turtle-doves or two young pigeons for himself, and has come in before Yhwh to the opening of the Tent of Meeting, and has given them to the priest; **¹⁵** and the priest has made them, one a sin-offering and one a burnt-offering; and the priest has made atonement for him before Yhwh, because of his discharge. **¹⁶** And when a man's seed [from] intercourse goes out from him, then he has bathed all his flesh with water, and

been unclean until the evening. **¹⁷** And any garment, or any skin on which there is seed [from] intercourse, has also been washed with water, and been unclean until the evening. **¹⁸** And a woman with whom a man lies with seed [from] intercourse, they also have bathed with water, and been unclean until the evening. **¹⁹** And when a woman has discharging—blood is her discharge in her flesh—she is in her separation [for] seven days, and anyone who is coming against her is unclean until the evening. **²⁰** And anything on which she lies in her separation is unclean, and anything on which she sits is unclean; **²¹** and anyone who is coming against her bed washes his garments, and has bathed with water, and been unclean until the evening. **²²** And anyone who is coming against any vessel on which she sits washes his garments, and has washed with water, and been unclean until the evening. **²³** And if it [is] on the bed, or on the vessel on which she is sitting, in his coming against it, he is unclean until the evening. **²⁴** And if a man really lies with her, and her separation is on him, then he has been unclean [for] seven days, and all the bed on which he lies is unclean. **²⁵** And when a woman's discharge of blood flows many days within the time of her separation, or when it flows over her separation—all the days of the discharge of her uncleanness are as the days of her separation; she [is] unclean. **²⁶** Every bed on which she lies all the days of her discharge is as the bed of her separation to her, and every vessel on which she sits is unclean as the uncleanness of her separation; **²⁷** and anyone who is coming against them is unclean, and has washed his garments, and has bathed with water, and been unclean until the evening. **²⁸** And if she has been clean from her discharge, then she has numbered seven days for herself, and afterward she is clean; **²⁹** and on the eighth day she takes two turtle-doves or two young pigeons for herself, and has brought them to the priest, to the opening of the Tent of Meeting; **³⁰** and the priest has made one a sin-offering and one a burnt-offering, and the priest has made atonement for her before Yhwh, because of the discharge of her uncleanness. **³¹** And you have separated the sons of Israel from their uncleanness, and they do not die in their uncleanness, in their defiling My Dwelling Place which [is] in their midst. **³²** This [is] the law for him who has the discharging, and of him whose seed [from] intercourse goes out from him, to become unclean with it, **³³** and of her who is sick in her separation, and of him who has the discharging (his discharge, of the male or of the female), and of a man who lies with an unclean woman."

CHAPTER 16

¹ And Yhwh speaks to Moses after the death of the two sons of Aaron, in their drawing near before Yhwh, and they die; **²** indeed, Yhwh says to Moses, "Speak to your brother Aaron, and he does not come in at all times to the holy place within the veil, to the front of the propitiatory covering, which [is] on the Ark, and he does not die, for I am seen in a cloud on the propitiatory covering. **³** With this Aaron comes into the holy place: with a bullock, a son of the herd, for a sin-offering, and a ram for a burnt-offering; **⁴** he puts on a holy linen coat, and linen trousers are on his flesh, and he girds himself with a linen girdle, and he wraps himself up with a linen turban; they [are] holy garments; and he has bathed his flesh with water and put them on. **⁵** And from the congregation of the sons of Israel he takes two kids of the goats for a sin-offering and one ram for a burnt-offering; **⁶** and Aaron has brought the bullock of the sin-offering near, which is his own, and has made atonement for himself and for his house; **⁷** and he has taken the two goats, and has caused them to stand before Yhwh, at the opening of the Tent of Meeting. **⁸** And Aaron has given lots over the two goats, one lot for Yhwh and one lot for a goat of departure; **⁹** and Aaron has brought the goat near, on which the lot for Yhwh has gone up, and has made it a sin-offering. **¹⁰** And the goat on which the lot for a goat of departure has gone up is caused to stand living before Yhwh to make atonement by it, to send it away for a goat of departure into the wilderness. **¹¹** And Aaron has brought the bullock of the sin-offering near, which is his own, and has made atonement for himself and for his house, and has slaughtered the bullock of the sin-offering which [is] his own, **¹²** and has taken the fullness of the censer of burning coals of fire from off the altar, from before Yhwh, and the fullness of his hands of thin spice-incense, and has brought [it] within the veil; **¹³** and he has put the incense on the fire before Yhwh, and the cloud of the incense has covered the propitiatory covering which [is] on the Testimony, and he does not die. **¹⁴**

And he has taken of the blood of the bullock, and has sprinkled with his finger on the front of the propitiatory covering eastward; even at the front of the propitiatory covering he sprinkles seven times of the blood with his finger. **15** And he has slaughtered the goat of the sin-offering which [is] the people's, and has brought in its blood to the inside of the veil, and has done with its blood as he has done with the blood of the bullock, and has sprinkled it on the propitiatory covering, and at the front of the propitiatory covering, **16** and he has made atonement for the holy place because of the uncleanness of the sons of Israel, and because of their transgressions in all their sins; and so he does for the Tent of Meeting which is dwelling with them in the midst of their uncleannesses. **17** And no man is in the Tent of Meeting in his going in to make atonement in the holy place, until his coming out; and he has made atonement for himself, and for his house, and for all the assembly of Israel. **18** And he has gone out to the altar which [is] before Yhwh, and has made atonement for it; and he has taken of the blood of the bullock and of the blood of the goat, and has put [it] around the horns of the altar; **19** and he has sprinkled on it of the blood with his finger seven times, and has cleansed it, and has hallowed it from the uncleannesses of the sons of Israel. **20** And he has ceased from making atonement [for] the holy place, and the Tent of Meeting, and the altar, and has brought the living goat near; **21** and Aaron has laid his two hands on the head of the living goat, and has confessed over it all the iniquities of the sons of Israel, and all their transgressions in all their sins, and has put them on the head of the goat, and has sent [it] away by the hand of a ready man into the wilderness; **22** and the goat has borne on himself all their iniquities to a land of separation. And he has sent the goat away into the wilderness, **23** and Aaron has come into the Tent of Meeting, and has stripped off the linen garments which he had put on in his going into the holy place, and has placed them there; **24** and he has bathed his flesh with water in the holy place, and has put on his garments, and has come out, and has made his burnt-offering, and the burnt-offering of the people, and has made atonement for himself and for the people; **25** and with the fat of the sin-offering he makes incense on the altar. **26** And he who is sending the goat away for a goat of departure washes his garments, and has bathed his flesh with water, and afterward he comes into the camp. **27** And the bullock of the sin-offering and the goat of the sin-offering, whose blood has been brought in to make atonement in the holy place, [one] brings out to the outside of the camp, and they have burned their skins, and their flesh, and their dung with fire; **28** and he who is burning them washes his garments, and has bathed his flesh with water, and afterward he comes into the camp. **29** And it has been for a continuous statute to you, in the seventh month, on the tenth of the month, you humble yourselves, and do no work—the native and the sojourner who is sojourning in your midst; **30** for on this day he makes atonement for you, to cleanse you; you are clean from all your sins before Yhwh; **31** it [is] a Sabbath of rest for you, and you have humbled yourselves—a continuous statute. **32** And the priest whom he anoints, and whose hand he consecrates to act as priest instead of his father, has made atonement, and has put on the linen garments, the holy garments; **33** and he has made atonement [for] the holy sanctuary; and [for] the Tent of Meeting, even [for] the altar he makes atonement; indeed, he makes atonement for the priests and for all the people of the assembly. **34** And this has been for a continuous statute to you, to make atonement for the sons of Israel, because of all their sins, once in a year"; and he does as Yhwh has commanded Moses.

CHAPTER 17

1 And Yhwh speaks to Moses, saying, **2** "Speak to Aaron and to his sons, and to all the sons of Israel; and you have said to them: This [is] the thing which Yhwh has commanded, saying, **3** Any man of the house of Israel who slaughters ox, or lamb, or goat in the camp, or who slaughters [it] at the outside of the camp, **4** and has not brought it in to the opening of the Tent of Meeting to bring an offering near to Yhwh before the Dwelling Place of Yhwh, blood is reckoned to that man—he has shed blood—and that man has been cut off from the midst of his people; **5** so that the sons of Israel bring in their sacrifices which they are sacrificing on the face of the field, indeed, they have brought them to Yhwh, to the opening of the Tent of Meeting, to the priest, and they have sacrificed sacrifices of

peace-offerings to Yhwh with them. **6** And the priest has sprinkled the blood on the altar of Yhwh, at the opening of the Tent of Meeting, and has made incense with the fat for refreshing fragrance to Yhwh; **7** and they do not sacrifice their sacrifices anymore to the goat [idols] after which they are going whoring; this is a continuous statute to them, throughout their generations. **8** And you say to them: Any man of the house of Israel, or of the sojourners who sojourns in your midst, who causes burnt-offering or sacrifice to ascend, **9** and does not bring it in to the opening of the Tent of Meeting to make it to Yhwh—that man has been cut off from his people. **10** And any man of the house of Israel, or of the sojourners who is sojourning in your midst, who eats any blood, I have even set My face against the person who is eating the blood, and have cut him off from the midst of his people; **11** for the life of the flesh is in the blood, and I have given it to you on the altar, to make atonement for your souls; for it [is] the blood which makes atonement for the soul. **12** Therefore I have said to the sons of Israel: No person among you eats blood, and the sojourner who is sojourning in your midst does not eat blood; **13** and any man of the sons of Israel, or of the sojourners who is sojourning in your midst, who hunts game, beast or bird, which is eaten—has even poured out its blood and covered it with dust; **14** for [it is] the life of all flesh, its blood is for its life; and I say to the sons of Israel: You do not eat [the] blood of any flesh, for the life of all flesh is its blood; anyone eating it is cut off. **15** And any person who eats a carcass or torn thing, among natives or among sojourners, has washed his garments and bathed with water, and been unclean until the evening— then he has been clean; **16** and if he does not wash, and does not bathe his flesh—then he has borne his iniquity."

CHAPTER 18

1 And Yhwh speaks to Moses, saying, **2** "Speak to the sons of Israel, and you have said to them: I [am] your God Yhwh; **3** you do not do according to the work of the land of Egypt in which you have dwelt, and you do not do according to the work of the land of Canaan to where I am bringing you in, and you do not walk in their statutes. **4** You do My judgments and you keep My statutes, to walk in them; I [am] your God Yhwh. **5** And you have kept My statutes and My judgments which man does and lives in them; I [am] Yhwh. **6** None of you draws near to any relation of his flesh to uncover nakedness; I [am] Yhwh. **7** You do not uncover the nakedness of your father and the nakedness of your mother, she [is] your mother; you do not uncover her nakedness. **8** You do not uncover the nakedness of the wife of your father; it [is] the nakedness of your father. **9** The nakedness of your sister, daughter of your father, or daughter of your mother, born at home or born outside—you do not uncover their nakedness. **10** The nakedness of your son's daughter, or of your daughter's daughter—you do not uncover their nakedness; for theirs [is] your nakedness. **11** The nakedness of a daughter of your father's wife, begotten of your father, she [is] your sister—you do not uncover her nakedness. **12** You do not uncover the nakedness of a sister of your father; she [is] a relation of your father. **13** You do not uncover the nakedness of your mother's sister, for she [is] your mother's relation. **14** You do not uncover the nakedness of your father's brother; you do not draw near to his wife; she [is] your aunt. **15** You do not uncover the nakedness of your daughter-in-law; she [is] your son's wife; you do not uncover her nakedness. **16** You do not uncover the nakedness of your brother's wife; it [is] your brother's nakedness. **17** You do not uncover the nakedness of a woman and her daughter, nor do you take her son's daughter and her daughter's daughter, to uncover her nakedness; they [are] her relations; it [is] wickedness. **18** And you do not take a woman [in addition] to her sister, to be an adversary, to uncover her nakedness beside her, in her life. **19** And you do not draw near to a woman in the separation of her uncleanness to uncover her nakedness. **20** And you do not give your seed [from] intercourse to the wife of your fellow, to become unclean with her. **21** And you do not give from your seed to pass over to the Molech, nor do you defile the Name of your God; I [am] Yhwh. **22** And you do not lie with a male as one lies with a woman; it [is] an abomination. **23** And you do not commit your intercourse with any beast, to become unclean with it; and a woman does not stand before a beast to mate with it; it [is] perversion. **24** Do not defile yourselves with all these, for with all these the nations have been defiled which I am sending away from before you; ²⁵ and the land is defiled, and I charge its iniquity on it, and the land vomits out its inhabitants. ²⁶ And you have kept My statutes and My judgments, and do not do [any] of all these abominations, the native and the sojourner who is sojourning in your midst, ²⁷ for the men of the land who [are] before you have done all these abominations and the land is defiled, ²⁸ and the land does not vomit you out in your defiling it, as it has vomited out the nation which [is] before you; ²⁹ for anyone who does [any] of all these abominations—even the persons who are doing [so]—have been cut off from the midst of their people; ³⁰ and you have kept My charge, so as not to do [any] of the abominable statutes which have been done before you, and you do not defile yourselves with them; I [am] your God Yhwh."

CHAPTER 19

¹ And Yhwh speaks to Moses, saying, ² "Speak to all the congregation of the sons of Israel, and you have said to them: You are holy, because I, your God Yhwh, [am] holy. ³ You each fear his mother and his father, and you keep My Sabbaths; I [am] your God Yhwh. ⁴ You do not turn to the idols, and you do not make a molten god for yourselves; I [am] your God Yhwh. ⁵ And when you sacrifice a sacrifice of peace-offerings to Yhwh, you sacrifice it at your pleasure; ⁶ it is eaten in the day of your sacrificing [it], and on the next day, and that which is left to the third day is burned with fire, ⁷ and if it is really eaten on the third day, it [is] an abomination, it is not pleasing, ⁸ and he who is eating it bears his iniquity, for he has defiled the holy thing of Yhwh, and that person has been cut off from his people. ⁹ And in your reaping the harvest of your land you do not completely reap the corner of your field, and you do not gather the gleaning of your harvest, ¹⁰ and you do not glean your vineyard, even the omitted part of your vineyard you do not gather, you leave them for the poor and for the sojourner; I [am] your God Yhwh. ¹¹ You do not steal, nor feign, nor lie—each against his fellow. ¹² And you do not swear by My Name for falsehood, or you have defiled the Name of your God; I [am] Yhwh. ¹³ You do not oppress your neighbor, nor take plunder; the wages of the hired worker do not remain with you until morning. ¹⁴ You do not revile the deaf; and you do not put a stumbling block before the blind; and you have been afraid of your God; I [am] Yhwh. ¹⁵ You do not do perversity in judgment; you do not lift up the face of the poor, nor honor the face of the great; you judge your fellow in righteousness. ¹⁶ You do not go slandering among your people; you do not stand against the blood of your neighbor; I [am] Yhwh. ¹⁷ You do not hate your brother in your heart; you certainly reprove your fellow, and do not permit sin on him. ¹⁸ You do not take vengeance, nor watch the sons of your people; and you have had love for your neighbor as yourself; I [am] Yhwh. ¹⁹ You keep My statutes. You do not cause your livestock to mate [with] two kinds; you do not sow your field with two kinds; and a garment of two kinds, mixed material, does not go up on you. ²⁰ And when a man lies with a woman with seed [from] intercourse, and she [is] a maidservant, betrothed to a man, and not really ransomed, or freedom has not been given to her, there is an investigation; they are not put to death, for she [is] not free. ²¹ And he has brought in his guilt-offering to Yhwh, to the opening of the Tent of Meeting, a ram [for] a guilt-offering, ²² and the priest has made atonement for him with the ram of the guilt-offering before Yhwh, for his sin which he has sinned, and it has been forgiven him because of his sin which he has sinned. ²³ And when you come into the land and have planted all [kinds] of trees [for] food, then you have reckoned its fruit as uncircumcised, it is uncircumcised to you [for] three years, it is not eaten, ²⁴ and in the fourth year all its fruit is holy—praises for Yhwh. ²⁵ And in the fifth year you eat its fruit—to add to you its increase; I [am] your God Yhwh. ²⁶ You do not eat with the blood. You do not enchant, nor observe clouds. ²⁷ You do not round the corner of your head, nor destroy the corner of your beard. ²⁸ And you do not put a cutting for the soul in your flesh; and a writing, a cross-mark, you do not put on yourself; I [am] Yhwh. ²⁹ You do not defile your daughter to cause her to go whoring, that the land does not go whoring, and the land has been full of wickedness. ³⁰ You keep My Sabbaths and you revere My sanctuary; I [am] Yhwh. ³¹ You do not turn to those having familiar spirits, and you do not seek for wizards, to become unclean by them; I [am] your God Yhwh. ³² You rise up at the presence of grey hairs, and you

have honored the presence of an old man, and have been afraid of your God; I [am] Yhwh. ³³ And when a sojourner sojourns with you in your land, you do not oppress him; ³⁴ the sojourner who is sojourning with you is to you as a native among you, and you have had love for him as for yourself, for you have been sojourners in the land of Egypt; I [am] your God Yhwh. ³⁵ You do not do perversity in the judgment, in the measure, in the weight, and in the liquid measure; ³⁶ you have righteous balances, righteous weights, a righteous ephah, and a righteous hin; I [am] your God Yhwh, who has brought you out from the land of Egypt; ³⁷ and you have observed all my statutes, and all my judgments, and have done them; I [am] Yhwh."

CHAPTER 20

¹ And Yhwh speaks to Moses, saying, ² "And you say to the sons of Israel: Any man of the sons of Israel, and of the sojourners who is sojourning in Israel, who gives to the Molech from his seed, is certainly put to death; the people of the land stone him with stone; ³ and I set My face against that man, and have cut him off from the midst of his people, for he has given to the Molech from his seed, so as to defile My sanctuary, and to defile My holy Name. ⁴ And if the people of the land really hide their eyes from that man, in his giving to the Molech from his seed, so as not to put him to death, ⁵ then I have set My face against that man and against his family, and have cut him off, and all who are going whoring after him, even going whoring after the Molech, from the midst of their people. ⁶ And the person who turns to those having familiar spirits, and to the wizards, to go whoring after them, I have even set My face against that person, and cut him off from the midst of his people. ⁷ And you have sanctified yourselves, and you have been holy, for I [am] your God Yhwh; ⁸ and you have kept My statutes, and have done them; I [am] Yhwh, sanctifying you. ⁹ For any man who reviles his father and his mother is certainly put to death; he has reviled his father and his mother: his blood [is] on him. ¹⁰ And a man who commits adultery with a man's wife—who commits adultery with the wife of his neighbor—the adulterer and the adulteress are surely put to death. ¹¹ And a man who lies with his father's wife—he has uncovered the nakedness of his father—both of them are certainly put to death; their blood [is] on them. ¹² And a man who lies with his daughter-in-law—both of them are certainly put to death; they have done perversion; their blood [is] on them. ¹³ And a man who lies with a male as one lies with a woman—both of them have done an abomination; they are certainly put to death; their blood [is] on them. ¹⁴ And a man who takes the woman and her mother—it [is] wickedness; they burn him and them with fire, and there is no wickedness in your midst. ¹⁵ And a man who commits his intercourse with a beast is certainly put to death, and you slay the beast. ¹⁶ And a woman who draws near to any beast to mate with it—you have even slain the woman and the beast; they are certainly put to death; their blood [is] on them. ¹⁷ And a man who takes his sister, a daughter of his father or daughter of his mother, and he has seen her nakedness, and she sees his nakedness—it is a shame; and they have been cut off before the eyes of the sons of their people; he has uncovered the nakedness of his sister; he bears his iniquity. ¹⁸ And a man who lies with a sick woman and has uncovered her nakedness, her fountain he has made bare, and she has uncovered the fountain of her blood—even both of them have been cut off from the midst of their people. ¹⁹ And you do not uncover the nakedness of your mother's sister and your father's sister, because his relation he has made bare; they bear their iniquity. ²⁰ And a man who lies with his aunt, he has uncovered the nakedness of his uncle; they bear their sin; they die childless. ²¹ And a man who takes his brother's wife—it [is] impurity; he has uncovered the nakedness of his brother; they are childless. ²² And you have kept all My statutes and all My judgments, and have done them, and the land does not vomit you out to where I am bringing you in to dwell in it; ²³ and you do not walk in the statutes of the nation which I am sending away from before you, for they have done all these, and I am wearied with them. ²⁴ And I say to you, You possess their ground, and I give it to you to possess it—a land flowing with milk and honey. I [am] your God Yhwh, who has separated you from the peoples. ²⁵ And you have made separation between the pure beasts and the unclean, and between the unclean bird and the pure, and you do not make yourselves abominable by beast or by bird,

or by anything which creeps [on] the ground which I have separated to you for unclean. **26** And you have been holy to Me, for I, Yhwh, [am] holy; and I separate you from the peoples to become Mine. **27** And a man or woman, when there is a familiar spirit in them, or who [are] wizards, are certainly put to death; they stone them with stone; their blood [is] on them."

CHAPTER 21

1 And Yhwh says to Moses, "Speak to the priests, sons of Aaron, and you have said to them: No one defiles himself for a [dead] person among his people, **2** except for his relation who [is] near to him: for his mother, and for his father, and for his son, and for his daughter, and for his brother, **3** and for his sister, the virgin, who is near to him, who has not been to a man; he is defiled for her. **4** A master [priest] does not defile himself among his people—to defile himself; **5** they do not make baldness on their head, and they do not shave the corner of their beard, and they do not make a cutting in their flesh; **6** they are holy to their God, and they do not defile the Name of their God, for the fire-offerings of Yhwh, bread of their God, they are bringing near, and have been holy. **7** They do not take a woman of harlotry, or defiled, and they do not take a woman cast out from her husband, for he [is] holy to his God; **8** and you have sanctified him, for he is bringing the bread of your God near. He is holy to you, for I, Yhwh, sanctifying you, [am] holy. **9** And when a daughter of any priest defiles herself by going whoring—she is defiling her father; she is burned with fire. **10** And the high priest of his brothers, on whose head the anointing oil is poured, and who has consecrated his hand to put on the garments, does not uncover his head, nor tear his garments, **11** nor does he come beside any dead person; he does not defile himself for his father and for his mother; **12** nor does he go out from the sanctuary, nor does he defile the sanctuary of his God, for the separation of the anointing oil of his God [is] on him; I [am] Yhwh. **13** And he takes a wife in her virginity; **14** a widow, or cast out, or defiled, [or] a harlot—these he does not take, but he takes a virgin of his own people [for] a wife, **15** and he does not defile his seed among his people; for I [am] Yhwh, sanctifying him." **16** And Yhwh speaks to Moses, saying, **17** "Speak to Aaron, saying, No man of your seed throughout their generations in whom there is blemish draws near to bring the bread of his God near, **18** for no man in whom [is] a blemish draws near: a man blind, or lame, or disfigured, or deformed, **19** or a man in whom there is a breach in the foot, or a breach in the hand, **20** or hunchbacked, or a dwarf, or [with] a defect in his eye, or [with] an itch, or [with] a scab, or [with] a broken testicle. **21** No man in whom is blemish (of the seed of Aaron the priest) comes near to bring the fire-offerings of Yhwh near; blemish [is] in him; he does not come near to bring the bread of his God near. **22** Bread of his God—from the most holy things and from the holy things—he eats; **23** only, he does not come toward the veil, and he does not draw near to the altar; for blemish [is] in him; and he does not defile My sanctuaries; for I [am] Yhwh, sanctifying them." **24** And Moses speaks to Aaron, and to his sons, and to all the sons of Israel.

CHAPTER 22

1 And Yhwh speaks to Moses, saying, **2** "Speak to Aaron and to his sons, and they are separated from the holy things of the sons of Israel, and they do not defile My holy Name in what they are hallowing to Me; I [am] Yhwh. **3** Say to them: Throughout your generations, any man who draws near, out of all your seed, to the holy things which the sons of Israel sanctify to Yhwh, and his uncleanness [is] on him—indeed, that person has been cut off from before My face; I [am] Yhwh. **4** Any man of the seed of Aaron, and he is leprous or has discharging—he does not eat of the holy things until he is clean; and he who is coming against any uncleanness of a person, or a man whose seed [from] intercourse goes out from him, **5** or a man who comes against any teeming thing which is unclean to him, or against a man who is unclean to him, even any of his uncleanness— **6** the person who comes against it has even been unclean until the evening, and does not eat of the holy things, but has bathed his flesh with water, **7** and the sun has gone in, and he has been clean, and afterward he eats of the holy things, for it [is] his food; **8** he does not eat a carcass or torn thing, to become unclean with it; I [am] Yhwh. **9** And

they have kept My charge, and bear no sin for it, that they have died for it when they defile it; I [am] Yhwh sanctifying them. **10** And no stranger eats of the holy thing; a settler [with] a priest and a hired worker does not eat of the holy thing; **11** but when a priest buys a person, the purchase of his money, he eats of it, also one born in his house; they eat of his bread. **12** And a priest's daughter, when she is a strange man's, she does not eat of the raised-offering of the holy things; **13** but a priest's daughter, when she is a widow, or cast out, and has no seed, and has turned back to the house of her father, as [in] her youth, she eats of her father's bread; but no stranger eats of it. **14** And when a man eats of a holy thing through ignorance, then he has added its fifth part to it, and has given [it] to the priest, with the holy thing; **15** and they do not defile the holy things of the sons of Israel—that which they lift up to Yhwh, **16** or have caused them to bear the iniquity of the guilt-offering in their eating their holy things; for I [am] Yhwh, sanctifying them." **17** And Yhwh speaks to Moses, saying, **18** "Speak to Aaron, and to his sons, and to all the sons of Israel, and you have said to them: Any man of the house of Israel, or of the sojourners in Israel, who brings his offering near, of all his vows, or of all his willing offerings which they bring near to Yhwh for a burnt-offering— **19** [you bring near] at your pleasure a perfect one, a male of the herd, of the sheep or of the goats; **20** nothing in which [is] blemish do you bring near, for it is not for a pleasing thing for you. **21** And when a man brings a sacrifice of peace-offerings near to Yhwh, to complete a special vow, or for a willing-offering, of the herd or of the flock, it is perfect for a pleasing thing: no blemish is in it. **22** Blind, or broken, or maimed, or [having] an oozing sore [[or a defect of the eye]], or itch, or scab—you do not bring these near to Yhwh, and you do not make a fire-offering from them on the altar to Yhwh. **23** As for an ox or sheep [that] is deformed or stunted—you make it a willing-offering, but it is not pleasing for a vow. **24** As for bruised, or beaten, or torn, or cut—you do not bring [it] near to Yhwh; and in your land you do not do it. **25** And you do not bring the bread of your God near from the hand of a son of a stranger, from any of these, for their corruption [is] in them; blemish [is] in them; they are not pleasing for you." **26** And Yhwh speaks to Moses, saying, **27** "When ox, or lamb, or goat is born, and it has been under its mother [for] seven days, then from the eighth day and from now on, it is pleasing for an offering, a fire-offering to Yhwh; **28** but an ox or sheep—you do not slaughter it and its young one in one day. **29** And when you sacrifice a sacrifice of thanksgiving to Yhwh, you sacrifice at your pleasure; **30** it is eaten on that day—you do not leave of it until morning; I [am] Yhwh. **31** And you have kept my commands and have done them; I [am] Yhwh; **32** and you do not defile My holy Name, and I have been hallowed in the midst of the sons of Israel; I [am] Yhwh, sanctifying you, **33** who am bringing you up out of the land of Egypt, to become your God; I [am] Yhwh."

CHAPTER 23

1 And Yhwh speaks to Moses, saying, **2** "Speak to the sons of Israel, and you have said to them: Appointed times of Yhwh, which you proclaim [as] holy convocations, these [are] My appointed times. **3** [For] six days work is done, and in the seventh day [is] a Sabbath of rest, a holy convocation; you do no work; it [is] a Sabbath to Yhwh in all your dwellings. **4** These [are] appointed times of Yhwh, holy convocations, which you proclaim in their appointed times: **5** in the first month, on the fourteenth of the month, between the evenings, [is] the Passover to Yhwh; **6** and on the fifteenth day of this month [is] the Celebration of Unleavened Things to Yhwh; [for] seven days you eat unleavened things; **7** on the first day you have a holy convocation, you do no servile work; **8** and you have brought a fire-offering near to Yhwh [for] seven days; in the seventh day [is] a holy convocation; you do no servile work." **9** And Yhwh speaks to Moses, saying, **10** "Speak to the sons of Israel, and you have said to them: When you come into the land which I am giving to you, and have reaped its harvest, and have brought in the sheaf, the beginning of your harvest to the priest, **11** then he has waved the sheaf before Yhwh for your acceptance; on the next day of the Sabbath the priest waves it. **12** And you have prepared a lamb, a perfect one, a son of a year, in the day of your waving the sheaf for a burnt-offering to Yhwh, **13** and its present [is] two-tenth parts of flour mixed with oil, a fire-offering to Yhwh, a refreshing fragrance, and its drink-offering [is] a fourth of the hin of wine. **14** And you do not eat bread and roasted grain and full ears until this very day, until your bringing in the offering of your God—a continuous statute throughout your generations, in all your dwellings. **15** And you have numbered for yourselves from the day after the Sabbath, from the day of your bringing in the sheaf of the wave-offering: they are seven perfect Sabbaths; **16** you number fifty days to the day after the seventh Sabbath, and you have brought a new present near to Yhwh; you bring in two [loaves] of bread out of your dwellings [for] a wave-offering; they are of two-tenth parts of flour; they are baked [with] yeast—first-[fruits] to Yhwh. **18** And you have brought near, besides the bread, seven lambs, perfect ones, sons of a year, and one bullock, a son of the herd, and two rams; they are a burnt-offering to Yhwh, with their present and their drink-offerings, a fire-offering of refreshing fragrance to Yhwh. **19** And you have prepared one kid of the goats for a sin-offering, and two lambs, sons of a year, for a sacrifice of peace-offerings, **20** and the priest has waved them, besides the bread of the first-[fruits], [as] a wave-offering before Yhwh, besides the two lambs; they are holy to Yhwh for the priest; **21** and you have proclaimed in this very day [that] it is a holy convocation for yourselves, you do no servile work—a continuous statute in all your dwellings, throughout your generations. **22** And in your reaping the harvest of your land you do not complete the corner of your field in your reaping, and you do not gather the gleaning of your harvest, you leave them for the poor and for the sojourner; I [am] your God Yhwh." **23** And Yhwh speaks to Moses, saying, **24** "Speak to the sons of Israel, saying, In the seventh month, on the first of the month, you have a Sabbath, a memorial of shouting, a holy convocation; **25** you do no servile work, and you have brought a fire-offering near to Yhwh." **26** And Yhwh speaks to Moses, saying, **27** "Only—on the tenth of this seventh month is the Day of Atonements; you have a holy convocation, and you have humbled yourselves, and have brought a fire-offering near to Yhwh; **28** and you do no work in this very day, for it is a day of atonements, to make atonement for you, before your God Yhwh. **29** For any person who is not humbled in this very day has even been cut off from his people; **30** and any person who does any work in this very day, I have even destroyed that person from the midst of his people; **31** you do no work—a continuous statute throughout your generations in all your dwellings. **32** It [is] a Sabbath of rest for yourselves, and you have humbled yourselves in the ninth of the month at evening; you keep your Sabbath from evening until evening." **33** And Yhwh speaks to Moses, saying, **34** "Speak to the sons of Israel, saying, In the fifteenth day of this seventh month [is the] Celebration of Shelters [for] seven days to Yhwh; **35** the first day [is] a holy convocation, you do no servile work; **36** [for] seven days you bring a fire-offering near to Yhwh, on the eighth day you have a holy convocation, and you have brought a fire-offering near to Yhwh; it [is] a restraint, you do no servile work. **37** These [are] appointed times of Yhwh, which you proclaim [as] holy convocations, to bring a fire-offering near to Yhwh, a burnt-offering, a present, a sacrifice, and drink-offerings, a thing of a day in its day, **38** apart from the Sabbaths of Yhwh, and apart from your gifts, and apart from all your vows, and apart from all your willing-offerings, which you give to Yhwh. **39** Only—on the fifteenth day of the seventh month, in your gathering the increase of the land, you keep the celebration of Yhwh [for] seven days; on the first day [is] a Sabbath, and on the eighth day a Sabbath; **40** and you have taken for yourselves on the first day the fruit of beautiful trees, branches of palms, and boughs of thick trees, and willows of a brook, and have rejoiced before your God Yhwh [for] seven days. **41** And you have kept it [as] a celebration to Yhwh, seven days in a year—a continuous statute throughout your generations; in the seventh month you keep it [as] a celebration. **42** You dwell in shelters [for] seven days; all who are natives in Israel dwell in shelters, **43** so that your generations know that I caused the sons of Israel to dwell in shelters in My bringing them out of the land of Egypt; I [am] your God Yhwh." **44** And Moses speaks to the sons of Israel [concerning] the appointed times of Yhwh.

CHAPTER 24

1 And Yhwh speaks to Moses, saying, **2** "Command the sons of Israel, and they bring pure oil of beaten olive to you for the lamp, to cause a light to go up continually; **3** Aaron arranges it at the outside of the veil of the Testimony, in the Tent of Meeting, from evening until morning before Yhwh continually—

a continuous statute throughout your generations; **4** he arranges the lights on the pure lampstand before Yhwh continually. **5** And you have taken flour, and have baked twelve cakes with it, two-tenth parts are in one cake, **6** and you have set them [in] two rows (six in the row) on the pure table before Yhwh, **7** and you have put pure frankincense on the row, and it has been with the bread for a memorial, a fire-offering to Yhwh. **8** On each Sabbath day he arranges it before Yhwh continually, from the sons of Israel—a perpetual covenant; **9** and it has been for Aaron and for his sons, and they have eaten it in the holy place, for it [is] most holy to him, from the fire-offerings of Yhwh—a continuous statute." **10** And a son of an Israeli woman goes out (and he [is] son of an Egyptian man) in the midst of the sons of Israel, and the son of the Israeli woman and a man of Israel strive in the camp, **11** and the son of the Israeli woman execrates the Name and reviles; and they bring him to Moses; and his mother's name [is] Shelomith daughter of Dibri, of the tribe of Dan; **12** and he causes him to rest in confinement —to explain to them by the mouth of Yhwh. **13** And Yhwh speaks to Moses, saying, **14** "Bring out the reviler to the outside of the camp; and all those hearing have laid their hands on his head, and all the congregation has stoned him. **15** And you speak to the sons of Israel, saying, When any man reviles his God—then he has borne his sin; **16** and he who is execrating the Name of Yhwh is certainly put to death; all the congregation certainly casts stones at him; as a sojourner so a native, in his execrating the Name, he is put to death. **17** And when a man strikes any soul of man, he is certainly put to death. **18** And he who strikes a beast repays it, body for body. **19** And when a man puts a blemish in his fellow, as he has done so it is done to him; **20** breach for breach, eye for eye, tooth for tooth; as he puts a blemish in a man so it is done in him. **21** And he who strikes a beast repays it, and he who strikes [the life of] man is put to death. **22** One judgment is for you; as a sojourner so is a native; for I [am] your God Yhwh." **23** And Moses speaks to the sons of Israel, and they bring out the reviler to the outside of the camp, and stone him [with] stone; and the sons of Israel have done as Yhwh has commanded Moses.

CHAPTER 25

1 And Yhwh speaks to Moses, in Mount Sinai, saying, **2** "Speak to the sons of Israel, and you have said to them: When you come into the land which I am giving to you, then the land has kept a Sabbath to Yhwh. **3** [For] six years you sow your field, and [for] six years you prune your vineyard, and have gathered its increase, **4** and in the seventh year is a Sabbath of rest for the land, a Sabbath to Yhwh; you do not sow your field, and you do not prune your vineyard; **5** you do not reap the spontaneous growth of your harvest, and you do not gather the grapes of your separated thing; it is a year of rest for the land. **6** And the Sabbath [increase] of the land has been for you for food, to you, and to your manservant, and to your handmaid, and to your hired worker, and to your settler, who are sojourning with you; **7** and for your livestock, and for the beast which [is] in your land, is all its increase for [them] to eat. **8** And you have numbered seven Sabbaths of years for yourself, seven times seven years, and the days of the seven Sabbaths of years have been forty-nine years for you, **9** and you have caused a horn of shouting to pass over in the seventh month, on the tenth of the month; in the Day of Atonements you cause a horn to pass over through all your land; **10** and you have hallowed the year, the fiftieth year; and you have proclaimed liberty in the land to all its inhabitants; it is a Jubilee for you; and you have turned back each to his possession; indeed, you return each to his family. **11** It [is] a Jubilee, the fiftieth year, it is a year for you; you do not sow, nor reap its spontaneous growth, nor gather its separated things; **12** for it [is] a Jubilee—it is holy to you; you eat its increase from the field; **13** you return each to his possession in this Year of the Jubilee. **14** And when you sell anything to your fellow, or buy from the hand of your fellow, you do not oppress one another; **15** you buy from your fellow by the number of years after the Jubilee; he sells to you by the number of the years of increase; **16** you multiply its price according to the multitude of the years, and you diminish its price according to the fewness of the years; for [it is] a number of increases [that] he is selling to you; **17** and you do not oppress one another, and you have been afraid of your God; for I [am] your God Yhwh. **18** And you have done My statutes, and you keep My judgments, and have done them, and you have dwelt on the land confidently, ¹⁹ and the land has given its fruit, and you have eaten to satiety, and have dwelt confidently on it. ²⁰ And when you say, What do we eat in the seventh year, behold, do we not sow, nor gather our increase? ²¹ then I have commanded My blessing on you in the sixth year, and it has made the increase for three years; ²² and you have sown [in] the eighth year, and have eaten of the old increase; you eat the old until the ninth year, until the coming in of its increase. ²³ And the land is not sold—to extinction, for the land [is] Mine, for you [are] sojourners and settlers with Me; ²⁴ and in all the land of your possession you give a redemption for the land. ²⁵ When your brother becomes poor, and has sold his possession, then his redeemer who is near to him has come, and he has redeemed the sold thing of his brother; ²⁶ and when a man has no redeemer, and his own hand has attained [means], and he has found [it] as sufficient [for] its redemption, ²⁷ then he has reckoned the years of its sale, and has given back that which is over to the man to whom he sold [it], and he has returned to his possession. ²⁸ And if his hand has not found sufficiency to give back to him, then his sold thing has been in the hand of him who buys it until the Year of Jubilee; and it has gone out in the Jubilee, and he has returned to his possession. ²⁹ And when a man sells a dwelling-house [in] a walled city, then his right of redemption has been until the completion of a year from its selling; his right of redemption is [during these] days; ³⁰ and if it is not redeemed to him until the fullness of a perfect year, then the house which [is] in a walled city has been established to extinction to him buying it, throughout his generations; it does not go out in the Jubilee. ³¹ And a house of the villages which have no surrounding wall is reckoned on the field of the country; there is redemption for it, and it goes out in the Jubilee. ³² As for cities of the Levites—houses of the cities of their possession—continuous redemption is for the Levites; ³³ as for him who redeems from the Levites, then the sale of a house (and [in] the city of his possession) has gone out in the Jubilee, for the houses of the cities of the Levites are their possession in the midst of the sons of Israel. ³⁴ And a field, a outskirt of their cities, is not sold; for it [is] a continuous possession for them. ³⁵ And when your brother has become poor, and his hand has failed with you, then you have kept hold on him, sojourner and settler, and he has lived with you; ³⁶ you take no usury or increase from him; and you have been afraid of your God; and your brother has lived with you; ³⁷ you do not give your money to him in usury, and you do not give your food for increase. ³⁸ I [am] your God Yhwh, who has brought you out of the land of Egypt to give the land of Canaan to you, to become your God. ³⁹ And when your brother becomes poor with you, and he has been sold to you, you do not lay servile service on him; ⁴⁰ he is as a hired worker [and] as a settler with you; he serves with you until the Year of the Jubilee— ⁴¹ then he has gone out from you, he and his sons with him, and has turned back to his family; and he turns back to the possession of his fathers. ⁴² For they [are] My servants, whom I have brought out from the land of Egypt: they are not sold [with] the sale of a servant; ⁴³ you do not rule over him with rigor, and you have been afraid of your God. ⁴⁴ And your manservant and your handmaid whom you have [are] from the nations who [are] around you; you buy manservant and handmaid from them, ⁴⁵ and also from the sons of the settlers who are sojourning with you, you buy from them, and from their families who [are] with you, which they have begotten in your land, and they have been to you for a possession; ⁴⁶ and you have taken them for an inheritance for your sons after you, to inherit [for] a possession; you lay service on them for all time, but on your brothers, the sons of Israel, each with his brother—you do not rule over him with rigor. ⁴⁷ And when the hand of a sojourner or settler with you attains [riches], and your brother with him has become poor, and he has been sold to a sojourner, a settler with you, or to the root of the family of a sojourner, ⁴⁸ after he has been sold, there is a right of redemption for him; one of his brothers redeems him, ⁴⁹ or his uncle or a son of his uncle redeems him, or any of the relations of his flesh, of his family, redeems him, or [if] his own hand has attained [means] then he has been redeemed. ⁵⁰ And he has reckoned with his buyer from the year of his being sold to him until the Year of Jubilee, and the money of his sale has been by the number of years; it is with him as the days of a hired worker. ⁵¹ If many years still [remain], he gives back his redemption [money] according to them, from the money of his purchase. ⁵² And if few are left of the years until the Year of Jubilee, then he has reckoned with him [and] he gives back his redemption [money] according to his years;

⁵³ as a hired worker, year by year, he is with him, and he does not rule him with rigor before your eyes. ⁵⁴ And if he is not redeemed in these [years], then he has gone out in the Year of Jubilee, he and his sons with him. ⁵⁵ For the sons of Israel [are] servants to Me; they [are] My servants whom I have brought out of the land of Egypt; I [am] your God Yhwh."

CHAPTER 26

¹ "You do not make idols for yourselves; and you do not set up carved image or standing image for yourselves; and you do not put a stone of imagery in your land, to bow yourselves to it; for I [am] your God Yhwh. ² You keep My Sabbaths and you revere My sanctuary; I [am] Yhwh. ³ If you walk in My statutes, and you keep My commands, and have done them, ⁴ then I have given your rains in their season, and the land has given her produce, and the tree of the field gives its fruit; ⁵ and the threshing has reached to you, [and] the gathering, and the gathering reaches the sowing-[time]; and you have eaten your bread to satiety, and have dwelt confidently in your land. ⁶ And I have given peace in the land, and you have lain down, and there is none causing trembling; and I have caused evil beasts to cease out of the land, and the sword does not pass over into your land. ⁷ And you have pursued your enemies, and they have fallen before you by the sword; ⁸ and five of you have pursued one hundred, and one hundred of you pursue a myriad; and your enemies have fallen before you by the sword. ⁹ And I have turned to you, and have made you fruitful, and have multiplied you, and have established My covenant with you; ¹⁰ and you have eaten old [store], and you bring out the old because of the new. ¹¹ And I have given My Dwelling Place in your midst, and My soul does not loathe you; ¹² and I have habitually walked in your midst, and have become your God, and you become My people; ¹³ I [am] your God Yhwh, who has brought you out of the land of the Egyptians, from being their servants; and I break the bars of your yoke and cause you to go erect. ¹⁴ And if you do not listen to Me and do not do all these commands, ¹⁵ and if you kick at My statutes, and if your soul loathes My judgments, so as not to do all My commands—to your breaking My covenant— ¹⁶ I also do this to you: I have even appointed trouble over you, the consumption, and the burning fever, consuming eyes, and causing pain of soul; and you have sowed your seed in vain, and your enemies have eaten it; ¹⁷ and I have set My face against you, and you have been struck before your enemies; and those hating you have ruled over you, and you have fled when there is none pursuing you. ¹⁸ And if up to these you [still] do not listen to Me—then I have added to discipline you sevenfold for your sins; ¹⁹ and I have broken the pride of your strength, and have made your heavens as iron, and your earth as bronze; ²⁰ and your strength has been consumed in vain, and your land does not give her produce, and the tree of the land does not give its fruit. ²¹ And if you walk with Me [in] opposition, and are not willing to listen to Me, then I have added to you a plague sevenfold, according to your sins, ²² and sent the beast of the field against you, and it has bereaved you; and I have cut off your livestock, and have made you few, and your ways have been desolate. ²³ And if by these you are not instructed by Me, and have walked with Me [in] opposition, ²⁴ then I have walked—I also—with you in opposition, and have struck you, even I, sevenfold for your sins; ²⁵ and I have brought in a sword on you, executing the vengeance of a covenant; and you have been gathered to your cities, and I have sent pestilence into your midst, and you have been given into the hand of an enemy. ²⁶ In My breaking your staff of bread, then ten women have baked your bread in one oven, and have given back your bread by weight; and you have eaten and are not satisfied. ²⁷ And if for this you do not listen to Me, and have walked with Me in opposition, ²⁸ then I have walked with you in the fury of opposition, and have disciplined you, even I, sevenfold for your sins. ²⁹ And you have eaten [the] flesh of your sons; and you eat [the] flesh of your daughters. ³⁰ And I have destroyed your high places, and cut down your images, and have put your carcasses on the carcasses of your idols, and My soul has loathed you; ³¹ and I have made your cities a ruin, and have made your sanctuaries desolate, and I do not smell your refreshing fragrance; ³² and I have made the land desolate, and your enemies who are dwelling in it have been astonished at it. ³³ And I scatter you among nations, and have drawn out a sword after you, and your land has been a desolation, and your cities are a ruin. ³⁴ Then the land enjoys its Sabbaths all the days of the

desolation—and you [are] in the land of your enemies; then the land rests, and has enjoyed its Sabbaths; ³⁵ it rests all the days of the desolation [for] that which it has not rested in your Sabbaths, in your dwelling on it. ³⁶ And those who are left of you—I have also brought a faintness into their heart in the lands of their enemies, and the sound of a leaf driven away has pursued them, and they have fled [as in] flight from a sword—and they have fallen, and there is none pursuing. ³⁷ And they have stumbled on one another, as from the face of a sword, and there is none pursuing, and you have no standing before your enemies, ³⁸ and you have perished among the nations, and the land of your enemies has consumed you. ³⁹ And those who are left of you—they consume away in their iniquity, in the lands of your enemies; and also in the iniquities of their fathers, they consume away with them. ⁴⁰ And [if] they have confessed their iniquity and the iniquity of their fathers, in their trespass which they have trespassed against Me, and also that they have walked with Me in opposition, ⁴¹ when I also walk in opposition to them, and have brought them into the land of their enemies—if then their uncircumcised heart is humbled, and then they accept the punishment of their iniquity— ⁴² then I have remembered My covenant [with] Jacob, and also My covenant [with] Isaac, and also My covenant [with] Abraham I remember, and I remember the land. ⁴³ And the land is left by them, and enjoys its Sabbaths, in the desolation without them, and they accept the punishment of their iniquity, because, even because, they have kicked against My judgments, and their soul has loathed My statutes, ⁴⁴ and also even this, in their being in the land of their enemies, I have not rejected them, nor have I loathed them, to consume them, to break My covenant with them; for I [am] their God Yhwh— ⁴⁵ then I have remembered for them the covenant of the ancestors, whom I brought forth out of the land of Egypt before the eyes of the nations to become their God; I [am] Yhwh." ⁴⁶ These [are] the statutes, and the judgments, and the laws, which Yhwh has given between Him and the sons of Israel in Mount Sinai, by the hand of Moses.

is sanctifying it—then he has added a fifth of the money of your valuation to it, and it has been established to him; 20 and if he does not redeem the field, or if he has sold the field to another man, it is not redeemed anymore; 21 and the field has been, in its going out in the Jubilee, holy to Yhwh as a field which is devoted; his possession is for the priest. 22 And if he sanctifies a field of his purchase to Yhwh, which [is] not of the fields of his possession, 23 then the priest has reckoned to him the amount of your valuation up to the Year of Jubilee, and he has given your valuation in that day [as] a holy thing to Yhwh; 24 in the Year of the Jubilee the field returns to him from whom he bought it, to him who [has] the possession of the land. 25 And all your valuation is by the shekel of the holy place: the shekel is twenty gerahs. 26 Only, a firstling which is Yhwh's firstling among beasts—no man sanctifies it, whether ox or sheep; it [is] Yhwh's. 27 And if [from] among the unclean beast, then he has ransomed [it] at your valuation, and he has added its fifth to it; and if it is not redeemed, then it has been sold at your valuation. 28 Only, no devoted thing which a man devotes to Yhwh of all that he has, of man, and beast, and of the field of his possession, is sold or redeemed; every devoted thing is most holy to Yhwh. 29 No devoted thing, which is devoted of man, is ransomed, it is surely put to death. 30 And all the tithe of the land, of the seed of the land, of the fruit of the tree, is Yhwh's; [it is] holy to Yhwh. 31 And if a man really redeems [any] of his tithe, he adds its fifth to it. 32 And all the tithe of the herd and of the flock—all that passes by under the rod—the tenth is holy to Yhwh; 33 he does not inquire between good and bad, nor does he exchange it; and if he really exchanges it, then it has been [holy] and its exchange is holy; it is not redeemed." 34 These [are] the commands which Yhwh has commanded Moses for the sons of Israel in Mount Sinai.

NUMBERS

CHAPTER 27

1 And Yhwh speaks to Moses, saying, **2** "Speak to the sons of Israel, and you have said to them: When a man makes a special vow in your valuation of persons to Yhwh, **3** then your valuation has been of the male from a son of twenty years even to a son of sixty years, and your valuation has been fifty shekels of silver by the shekel of the holy place. **4** And if it [is] a female, then your valuation has been thirty shekels; **5** and if from a son of five years even to a son of twenty years, then your valuation of the male has been twenty shekels, and for the female, ten shekels; **6** and if from a son of a month even to a son of five years, then your valuation of the male has been five shekels of silver, and for the female your valuation [is] three shekels of silver; **7** and if from a son of sixty years and above, if a male, then your valuation has been fifteen shekels, and for a female, ten shekels. **8** And if he is poorer than your valuation, then he has presented himself before the priest, and the priest has valued him; according to that which the hand of him who is vowing reaches, the priest values him. **9** And if [it is] a beast of which they bring near [as] an offering to Yhwh, all that [one] gives of it to Yhwh is holy; **10** he does not change it nor exchange it, a good for a bad, or a bad for a good; and if he really exchanges beast for beast, then it has been [holy] and its exchange is holy. **11** And if [it is] any unclean beast of which they do not bring near [as] an offering to Yhwh, then he has presented the beast before the priest, **12** and the priest has valued it, whether good or bad; according to your valuation, O priest, so it is; **13** and if he really redeems it, then he has added its fifth to your valuation. **14** And when a man sanctifies his house [as] a holy thing to Yhwh, then the priest has valued it, whether good or bad; as the priest values it so it stands; **15** and if he who is sanctifying redeems his house, then he has added a fifth of the money of your valuation to it, and it has become his. **16** And if a man sanctifies to Yhwh from a field of his possession, then your valuation has been according to its seed—a homer of barley-seed at fifty shekels of silver; **17** if he sanctifies his field from the Year of the Jubilee, according to your valuation it stands; **18** and if he sanctifies his field after the Jubilee, then the priest has reckoned the money to him according to the years which are left, to the Year of the Jubilee, and it has been diminished from your valuation. **19** And if he really redeems the field—he who

CHAPTER 1

1 And Yhwh speaks to Moses in the wilderness of Sinai, in the Tent of Meeting, on the first of the second month, in the second year of their going out of the land of Egypt, saying, **2** "Take a census of all the congregation of the sons of Israel by their families, by the house of their fathers, in the number of names—every male by their counted heads; **3** from a son of twenty years and upward, everyone going out to the host in Israel, you number them by their hosts, you and Aaron; **4** and with you there is a man for a tribe, each is a head of the house of his fathers. **5** And these [are] the names of the men who stand with you: for Reuben, Elizur son of Shedeur; **6** for Simeon, Shelumiel son of Zurishaddai; **7** for Judah, Nahshon son of Amminadab; **8** for Issachar, Nathaneel son of Zuar; **9** for Zebulun, Eliab son of Helon; **10** for the sons of Joseph: for Ephraim, Elishama son of Ammihud; for Manasseh, Gamaliel son of Pedahzur; **11** for Benjamin, Abidan son of Gideoni; **12** for Dan, Ahiezer son of Ammishaddai; **13** for Asher, Pagiel son of Ocran; **14** for Gad, Eliasaph son of Deuel; **15** for Naphtali, Ahira son of Enan." **16** These [are] those called of the congregation, princes of the tribes of their fathers; they [are] heads of the thousands of Israel. **17** And Moses takes—Aaron also—these men, who were defined by name, **18** and they assembled all the congregation on the first of the second month, and they declare their births, by their families, by the house of their fathers, in the number of names from a son of twenty years and upward, by their counted heads, **19** as Yhwh has commanded Moses; and he numbers them in the wilderness of Sinai. **20** And the sons of Reuben, Israel's firstborn—their births, by their families, by the house of their fathers, in the number of names, by their counted heads, every male from a son of twenty years and upward, everyone going out to the host— **21** their numbered ones, for the tribe of Reuben, are forty-six thousand and five hundred. **22** Of the sons of Simeon—their births, by their families, by the house of their fathers, its numbered ones in the number of names, by their counted heads, every male from a son of twenty years and upward, everyone going out to the host— **23** their numbered ones, for the tribe of Simeon, [are] fifty-nine thousand and three hundred. **24** Of the sons of Gad—their births, by their families, by the house of their fathers, in the number of names, from a son of twenty years and upward, everyone going out to the host— **25** their numbered ones, for the tribe of Gad, [are] forty-five thousand and six hundred and fifty. **26** Of the sons of Judah—their births, by their families, by the house of their fathers, in the number of names, from a son of twenty years and upward, everyone going out to the host— **27** their numbered ones, for the tribe of Judah, [are] seventy-four thousand and six hundred. **28** Of the sons of Issachar—their births, by their families, by the house of their fathers, in the number of names, from a son of twenty years and upward, everyone going out to the host— **29** their numbered ones, for the tribe of Issachar, [are] fifty-four thousand and four hundred. **30** Of the sons of Zebulun—their births, by their families, by the house of their fathers, in the number of names, from a son of twenty years and upward, everyone going out to the host— **31** their numbered ones, for the tribe of Zebulun, [are] fifty-seven thousand and four hundred. **32** Of the sons of Joseph: of the sons of Ephraim— their births, by their families, by the house of their fathers, in the number of names, from a son of twenty years and upward, everyone going out to the host— **33** their numbered ones, for the tribe of Ephraim, [are] forty thousand and five hundred. **34** Of the sons of Manasseh—their births, by their families, by the house of their fathers, in the number of names, from a son of twenty years and upward, everyone going out to the host— **35** their numbered ones, for the tribe of Manasseh, [are] thirty-two thousand and two hundred. **36** Of the sons of Benjamin— their births, by their families, by the house of their fathers, in the number of names, from a son of twenty years and upward, everyone going out to the host— **37** their numbered ones, for the tribe of Benjamin, [are] thirty-five thousand and four hundred. **38** Of the sons of Dan—their births, by their families, by the house of their fathers, in the number of names, from a son of twenty years and upward, everyone going out to the host— **39** their numbered ones, for the tribe of Dan, [are] sixty-two thousand and seven hundred. **40** Of the sons of Asher— their births, by their families, by the house of their fathers, in the number of names, from a son of twenty years and upward, everyone going out to the host— **41** their numbered ones, for the tribe of Asher, [are] forty-one thousand and five hundred. **42** Of the sons of Naphtali—their births, by their families, by the house of their fathers, in the number of names, from a son of twenty years and upward, everyone going out to the host— **43** their numbered ones, for the tribe of Naphtali, [are] fifty-three thousand and four hundred. **44** These [are] those numbered, whom Moses numbered—Aaron also—and the princes of Israel, twelve men, each one has been [the representative] for the house of his fathers. **45** And they are, all those numbered of the sons of Israel, by the house of their fathers, from a son of twenty years and upward, everyone going out to the host in Israel, **46** indeed, all those numbered are six hundred thousand and three thousand and five hundred and fifty. **47** And the Levites, for the tribe of their fathers, have not numbered themselves in their midst, **48** seeing Yhwh speaks to Moses, saying, **49** "Only the tribe of Levi you do not number, and you do not take up their census in the midst of the sons of Israel; **50** and you, appoint the Levites over the Dwelling Place of the Testimony, and over all its vessels, and over all that it has; they carry the Dwelling Place, and all its vessels, and they serve it; and they encamp around the Dwelling Place. **51** And in the journeying of the Dwelling Place, the Levites take it down, and in the encamping of the Dwelling Place, the Levites raise it up; and the stranger who is coming near is put to death." **52** And the sons of Israel have encamped, each by his camp, and each by his standard, by their hosts; **53** and the Levites encamp around the Dwelling Place of the Testimony; and there is no wrath on the congregation of the sons of Israel, and the Levites have kept the charge of the Dwelling Place of the Testimony. **54** And the sons of Israel do according to all that Yhwh has commanded Moses; so they have done.

CHAPTER 2

1 And Yhwh speaks to Moses and to Aaron, saying, **2** "The sons of Israel encamp, each by his standard, with ensigns of the house of their fathers; they encamp around, from in sight of the Tent of Meeting." **3** And those encamping eastward toward the sun-rising [are] of the standard of the camp of Judah, by their hosts; and the prince of the sons of Judah [is] Nahshon, son of Amminadab; **4** and his host, and their numbered ones, [are] seventy-four thousand and six hundred. **5** And those encamping by him [are] of the tribe of Issachar; and the prince of the sons of Issachar [is] Nethaneel son of

Zuar; **6** and his host, and its numbered ones, [are] fifty-four thousand and four hundred. **7** The tribe of Zebulun [is with them]; and the prince of the sons of Zebulun [is] Eliab son of Helon; **8** and his host, and its numbered ones, [are] fifty-seven thousand and four hundred. **9** All those numbered of the camp of Judah [are] one hundred thousand and eighty thousand and six thousand and four hundred, by their hosts; they journey first. **10** The standard of the camp of Reuben [is] southward, by their hosts; and the prince of the sons of Reuben [is] Elizur son of Shedeur; **11** and his host, and its numbered ones, [are] forty-six thousand and five hundred. **12** And those encamping by him [are of] the tribe of Simeon; and the prince of the sons of Simeon [is] Shelumiel son of Zurishaddai; **13** and his host, and their numbered ones, [are] fifty-nine thousand and three hundred. **14** And the tribe of Gad [is with him]; and the prince of the sons of Gad [is] Eliasaph son of Reuel; **15** and his host, and their numbered ones, [are] forty-five thousand and six hundred and fifty. **16** All those numbered of the camp of Reuben [are] one hundred thousand and fifty-one thousand and four hundred and fifty, by their hosts; and they journey second. **17** And the Tent of Meeting has journeyed [with] the camp of the Levites in the middle of the camps; as they encamp so they journey, each at his station by their standards. **18** The standard of the camp of Ephraim, by their hosts, [is] westward; and the prince of the sons of Ephraim [is] Elishama son of Ammihud; **19** and his host, and their numbered ones, [are] forty thousand and five hundred. **20** And by him [is] the tribe of Manasseh; and the prince of the sons of Manasseh [is] Gamaliel son of Pedahzur; **21** and his host, and their numbered ones, [are] thirty-two thousand and two hundred. **22** And the tribe of Benjamin [is with them]; and the prince of the sons of Benjamin [is] Abidan son of Gideoni; **23** and his host, and their numbered ones, [are] thirty-five thousand and four hundred. **24** All those numbered of the camp of Ephraim [are] one hundred thousand and eight thousand and one hundred, by their hosts; and they journey third. **25** The standard of the camp of Dan [is] northward, by their hosts; and the prince of the sons of Dan [is] Ahiezer son of Ammishaddai; **26** and his host, and their numbered ones, [are] sixty-two thousand and seven hundred. **27** And those encamping by him [are of] the tribe of Asher; and the prince of the sons of Asher [is] Pagiel son of Ocran; **28** and his host, and their numbered ones, [are] forty-one thousand and five hundred. **29** And the tribe of Naphtali [is with them]; and the prince of the sons of Naphtali [is] Ahira son of Enan; **30** and his host, and their numbered ones, [are] fifty-three thousand and four hundred. **31** All those numbered of the camp of Dan [are] one hundred thousand and fifty-seven thousand and six hundred; they journey at the rear by their standards. **32** These [are] those numbered of the sons of Israel by the house of their fathers; all those numbered of the camps by their hosts [are] six hundred thousand and three thousand and five hundred and fifty. **33** And the Levites have not numbered themselves in the midst of the sons of Israel, as Yhwh has commanded Moses. **34** And the sons of Israel do according to all that Yhwh has commanded Moses; so they have encamped by their standards, and so they have journeyed, each by his families, by the house of his fathers.

CHAPTER 3

1 And these [are] the generations of Aaron and Moses, in the day of Yhwh's speaking with Moses in Mount Sinai. **2** And these [are] the names of the sons of Aaron: the firstborn Nadab, and Abihu, Eleazar, and Ithamar; **3** these [are] the names of the sons of Aaron, the anointed priests, whose hand he has consecrated for acting as priest. **4** And Nadab dies— Abihu also—before Yhwh, in their bringing strange fire near before Yhwh, in the wilderness of Sinai, and they did not have sons; and Eleazar—Ithamar also—acts as priest in the presence of their father Aaron. **5** And Yhwh speaks to Moses, saying, **6** "Bring the tribe of Levi near, and you have caused it to stand before Aaron the priest, and they have served him, **7** and kept his charge, and the charge of all the congregation before the Tent of Meeting, to do the service of the Dwelling Place; **8** and they have kept all the vessels of the Tent of Meeting, and the charge of the sons of Israel, to do the service of the Dwelling Place; **9** and you have given the Levites to Aaron and to his sons; they are surely given to him out of the sons of Israel. **10** And you appoint Aaron and his sons, and they have kept their priesthood, and the stranger who comes near is put to death." **11** And Yhwh speaks to Moses, saying, **12** "And I, behold, have taken the Levites from the midst of the sons of Israel instead of every firstborn opening a womb among the sons of Israel, and the Levites have been Mine; **13** for every firstborn [is] Mine, in the day of My striking every firstborn in the land of Egypt I have sanctified to Myself every firstborn in Israel, from man to beast; they are Mine; I [am] Yhwh." **14** And Yhwh speaks to Moses in the wilderness of Sinai, saying, **15** "Number the sons of Levi by the house of their fathers, by their families; every male from a son of a month and upward—you number them." **16** And Moses numbers them according to the command of Yhwh, as he has been commanded. **17** And these are the sons of Levi by their names: Gershon, and Kohath, and Merari. **18** And these [are] the names of the sons of Gershon by their families: Libni and Shimei. **19** And the sons of Kohath by their families: Amram, and Izhar, Hebron, and Uzziel. **20** And the sons of Merari by their families: Mahli and Mushi; these are the families of the Levites, by the house of their fathers. **21** Of Gershon—the family of the Libnite and the family of the Shimite; these are the families of the Gershonite. **22** Their numbered ones, in number, every male from a son of a month and upward, their numbered ones [are] seven thousand and five hundred. **23** The families of the Gershonite encamp westward behind the Dwelling Place. **24** And the prince of a father's house for the Gershonite [is] Eliasaph son of Lael. **25** And the charge of the sons of Gershon in the Tent of Meeting [is] the Dwelling Place, and the tent, its covering, and the veil at the opening of the Tent of Meeting, **26** and the hangings of the court, and the veil at the opening of the court, which [is] by the Dwelling Place and by the altar all around, and its cords, to all its service. **27** And of Kohath—the family of the Amramite, and the family of the Izharite, and the family of the Hebronite, and the family of the Uzzielite; these are families of the Kohathite. **28** In number, all the males, from a son of a month and upward, [are] eight thousand and six hundred, keeping the charge of the holy place. **29** The families of the sons of Kohath encamp southward by the side of the Dwelling Place. **30** And the prince of a father's house for the families of the Kohathite [is] Elizaphan son of Uzziel. **31** And their charge [is] the Ark, and the table, and the lampstand, and the altars, and the vessels of the holy place with which they serve, and the veil, and all its service. **32** And Eleazar son of Aaron the priest [is] the prince of the princes of the Levites, [with] the oversight of the keepers of the charge of the holy place. **33** Of Merari—the family of the Mahlite and the family of the Mushite; these [are] the families of Merari. **34** And their numbered ones, in number, all the males from a son of a month and upward, [are] six thousand and two hundred. **35** And the prince of a father's house for the families of Merari [is] Zuriel son of Abihail; they encamp northward by the side of the Dwelling Place. **36** And the oversight [and] charge of the sons of Merari [are] the boards of the Dwelling Place, and its bars, and its pillars, and its sockets, and all its vessels, and all its service, **37** and the pillars of the court all around, and their sockets, and their pins, and their cords. **38** And those encamping before the Dwelling Place eastward, before the Tent of Meeting, at the east, [are] Moses and Aaron, and his sons, keeping the charge of the sanctuary for the charge of the sons of Israel, and the stranger who comes near is put to death. **39** All those numbered of the Levites whom Moses numbered—Aaron also—by the command of Yhwh, by their families, every male from a son of a month and upward, [are] twenty-two thousand. **40** And Yhwh says to Moses, "Number every firstborn male of the sons of Israel from a son of a month and upward, and take up the number of their names; **41** and you have taken the Levites for Me (I [am] Yhwh), instead of every firstborn among the sons of Israel, and the livestock of the Levites instead of every firstling among the livestock of the sons of Israel." **42** And Moses numbers, as Yhwh has commanded him, all the firstborn among the sons of Israel. **43** And every firstborn male, by the number of names, from a son of a month and upward, of their numbered ones, are twenty-two thousand two hundred and seventy-three. **44** And Yhwh speaks to Moses, saying, **45** "Take the Levites instead of every firstborn among the sons of Israel, and the livestock of the Levites instead of their livestock; and the Levites have been Mine; I [am] Yhwh. **46** And [from] those ransomed of the two hundred and seventy-three of the firstborn of the sons of Israel, who are more than the Levites, **47** you have even taken five shekels apiece by the counted head—you take by the shekel of the holy place; the shekel [is] twenty gerahs; **48** and you have given the money to Aaron and to his sons, whereby those over and above are ransomed." **49** And Moses takes the ransom money from those over and above those ransomed by the Levites; **50** he has taken the money from the firstborn of the sons of Israel—one thousand and three hundred and sixty-five, by the shekel of the holy place; **51** and Moses gives the money of those ransomed to Aaron and to his sons, according to the command of Yhwh, as Yhwh has commanded Moses.

CHAPTER 4

1 And Yhwh speaks to Moses and to Aaron, saying, **2** "Take a census of the sons of Kohath from the midst of the sons of Levi, by their families, by the house of their fathers; **3** from a son of thirty years and upward, even until a son of fifty years, everyone going in to the host, to do work in the Tent of Meeting. **4** This [is] the service of the sons of Kohath in the Tent of Meeting [for] the most holy things: **5** when Aaron and his sons have come in, in the journeying of the camp, and have taken down the veil of the hanging, and have covered the Ark of the Testimony with it, **6** then they have put a covering of tachash skin on it, and have spread a garment completely of blue above, and have placed its poles. **7** And they spread a garment of blue over the table of the presence, and have put the dishes, and the spoons, and the bowls, and the cups of the drink-offering on it, and the bread of continuity is on it, **8** and they have spread a garment of scarlet over them, and have covered it with a covering of tachash skin, and have placed its poles, **9** and have taken a garment of blue, and have covered the lampstand of the lamp, and its lights, and its snuffers, and its snuff-dishes, and all its oil vessels with which they minister to it; **10** and they have put it and all its vessels into a covering of tachash skin, and have put [it] on the bar. **11** And they spread a garment of blue over the golden altar, and have covered it with a covering of tachash skin, and have placed its poles, **12** and have taken all the vessels of ministry with which they minister in the holy place, and have put [them] into a garment of blue, and have covered them with a covering of tachash skin, and have put [them] on the bar, **13** and have removed the ashes of the altar, and have spread a garment of purple over it, **14** and have put on it all its vessels with which they minister on it—the censers, the hooks, and the shovels, and the bowls, all the vessels of the altar—and have spread a covering of tachash skin on it, and have placed its poles. **15** And Aaron has finished—his sons also—covering the holy place, and all the vessels of the holy place, in the journeying of the camp, and afterward the sons of Kohath come in to carry [it], and they do not come to the holy thing, lest they have died; these [things are] the burden of the sons of Kohath in the Tent of Meeting. **16** And the oversight of Eleazar, son of Aaron the priest, [is] the oil of the lamp, and the spice-incense, and the present of continuity, and the anointing oil, the oversight of all the Dwelling Place and of all [that is] in it, in the sanctuary and in its vessels." **17** And Yhwh speaks to Moses and to Aaron, saying, **18** "You do not cut off the tribe of the families of the Kohathite from the midst of the Levites; **19** but do this for them, and they have lived and do not die in their drawing near [to] the Holy of Holies: Aaron and his sons go in, and have set them, each man to his service, and to his burden, **20** and they do not go in to see when the holy thing is swallowed, lest they have died." **21** And Yhwh speaks to Moses, saying, **22** "Also take a census of the sons of Gershon by the house of their fathers, by their families; **23** from a son of thirty years and upward, until a son of fifty years, you number them—everyone who is going in to serve the host, to do the service in the Tent of Meeting. **24** This [is] the service of the families of the Gershonite, to serve and for burden: **25** and they have carried the curtains of the Dwelling Place, and the Tent of Meeting, its covering, and the covering of the tachash [skin] which [is] on it above, and the veil at the opening of the Tent of Meeting, **26** and the hangings of the court, and the veil at the opening of the gate of the court which [is] by the Dwelling Place, and by the altar all around, and their cords, and all the vessels of their service, and all that is made for them—and they have served. **27** By the command of Aaron and his sons is all the service of the sons of the Gershonite, in all their burden and in all their service; and you have laid a charge on them concerning the charge of all their burden. **28** This [is] the service of the families of the sons of the Gershonite in the Tent of Meeting; and their charge [is] under the hand of Ithamar son of Aaron the priest. **29** The sons of Merari, by their families, by the house of their fathers—you number them; **30** from a son of thirty years and upward even to a son of fifty years, you number them—everyone who is going in to the host, to do the service of the Tent of Meeting.

31 And this [is] the charge of their burden, of all their service in the Tent of Meeting: the boards of the Dwelling Place, and its bars, and its pillars, and its sockets, **32** and the pillars of the court all around, and their sockets, and their pins, and their cords, of all their vessels, and of all their service; and you number the vessels of the charge of their burden by name. **33** This [is] the service of the families of the sons of Merari, for all their service, in the Tent of Meeting, by the hand of Ithamar son of Aaron the priest." **34** And Moses numbers—Aaron also, and the princes of the congregation—the sons of the Kohathite, by their families, and by the house of their fathers, **35** from a son of thirty years and upward even to a son of fifty years, everyone who is going in to the host, for service in the Tent of Meeting, **36** and their numbered ones, by their families, are two thousand seven hundred and fifty. **37** These [are] those numbered of the families of the Kohathite, everyone who is serving in the Tent of Meeting, whom Moses and Aaron numbered by the command of Yhwh, by the hand of Moses. **38** And those numbered of the sons of Gershon, by their families, and by the house of their fathers, **39** from a son of thirty years and upward even to a son of fifty years, everyone who is going in to the host, for service in the Tent of Meeting, **40** even their numbered ones, by their families, by the house of their fathers, are two thousand and six hundred and thirty. **41** These [are] those numbered of the families of the sons of Gershon, everyone who is serving in the Tent of Meeting, whom Moses and Aaron numbered by the command of Yhwh. **42** And those numbered of the families of the sons of Merari, by their families, by the house of their fathers, **43** from a son of thirty years and upward even to a son of fifty years, everyone who is going in to the host, for service in the Tent of Meeting, **44** even their numbered ones, by their families, are three thousand and two hundred. **45** These [are] those numbered of the families of the sons of Merari, whom Moses and Aaron numbered by the command of Yhwh, by the hand of Moses. **46** All those numbered, whom Moses numbered—Aaron also, and the princes of Israel—of the Levites, by their families, and by the house of their fathers, **47** from a son of thirty years and upward even to a son of fifty years, everyone who is going in to do the work of the service, even the service of burden in the Tent of Meeting, **48** even their numbered ones are eight thousand and five hundred and eighty; **49** he has numbered them by the command of Yhwh, by the hand of Moses, each man by his service, and by his burden, with his numbered ones, as Yhwh has commanded Moses.

CHAPTER 5

1 And Yhwh speaks to Moses, saying, **2** "Command the sons of Israel, and they send out of the camp every leper, and everyone with discharging, and everyone defiled by a body; **3** you send out from male even to female; you send them to the outside of the camp and they do not defile their camps in the midst of which I dwell." **4** And the sons of Israel do so, and they send them out to the outside of the camp; as Yhwh has spoken to Moses so the sons of Israel have done. **5** And Yhwh speaks to Moses, saying, **6** "Speak to the sons of Israel: Man or woman, when they do any of the sins of man, by committing a trespass against Yhwh, and that person [is] guilty, **7** and they have confessed their sin which they have done, then he has restored his guilt in its principal, and is adding its fifth to it, and has given [it] to him in reference to whom he has been guilty. **8** And if the man has no redeemer to restore the guilt to, the guilt which is restored [is] to Yhwh for the priest, apart from the ram of the atonements, whereby he makes atonement for him. **9** And every raised-offering of all the holy things of the sons of Israel, which they bring near to the priest, becomes his; **10** and any man's hallowed things become his; that which any man gives to the priest becomes his." **11** And Yhwh speaks to Moses, saying, **12** "Speak to the sons of Israel, and you have said to them: When any man's wife turns aside, and has committed a trespass against him, **13** and a man has lain with her [with] the seed [from] intercourse, and it has been hid from the eyes of her husband, and concealed, and she has been defiled, and there is no witness against her, and she has not been caught, **14** and a spirit of jealousy has passed over him, and he has been jealous [for] his wife, and she has been defiled—or a spirit of jealousy has passed over him, and he has been jealous [for] his wife, and she has not been defiled— **15** then the man has brought in his wife to the priest, and he has brought in her offering for her—a tenth of the ephah of barley

meal; he does not pour oil on it, nor does he put frankincense on it, for it [is] a present of jealousy, a present of memorial, causing remembrance of iniquity. **16** And the priest has brought her near, and has caused her to stand before Yhwh, **17** and the priest has taken holy water in an earthen vessel, and the priest takes of the dust which is on the floor of the Dwelling Place, and has put [it] into the water, **18** and the priest has caused the woman to stand before Yhwh, and has uncovered the woman's head, and has given the present of the memorial into her hands (it [is] a present of jealousy), and the bitter waters which cause the curse are in the hand of the priest. **19** And the priest has caused her to swear, and has said to the woman, If no man has lain with you, and if you have not turned aside [to] uncleanness under your husband, be free from these bitter waters which cause the curse; **20** and you, if you have turned aside under your husband, and if you have been defiled, and a man commits his intercourse with you besides your husband— **21** then the priest has caused the woman to swear with an oath of execration, and the priest has said to the woman—Yhwh gives you for an execration and for a curse in the midst of your people, in Yhwh's giving your thigh to fall and your belly to swell, **22** and these waters which cause the curse have gone into your bowels to cause the belly to swell and the thigh to fall; and the woman has said, Amen, Amen. **23** And the priest has written these execrations in a scroll, and has blotted [them] out with the bitter waters, **24** and has caused the woman to drink the bitter waters which cause the curse, and the waters which cause the curse have entered into her for bitter things. **25** And the priest has taken the present of jealousy out of the hand of the woman, and has waved the present before Yhwh, and has brought it near to the altar; **26** and the priest has taken a handful of the present, its memorial, and has made incense on the altar, and afterward causes the woman to drink the water; **27** indeed, he has caused her to drink the water, and it has come to pass, if she has been defiled and commits a trespass against her husband, that the waters which cause the curse have gone into her for bitter things, and her belly has swelled, and her thigh has fallen, and the woman has become an execration in the midst of her people. **28** And if the woman has not been defiled, and is clean, then she has been acquitted, and has been sown [with] seed. **29** This [is] the law of jealousies when a wife turns aside under her husband and has been defiled, **30** or when a spirit of jealousy passes over a man and he has been jealous of his wife, then he has caused the woman to stand before Yhwh, and the priest has done to her all this law, **31** and the man has been acquitted from iniquity, and that woman bears her iniquity."

CHAPTER 6

1 And Yhwh speaks to Moses, saying, **2** "Speak to the sons of Israel, and you have said to them: When a man or woman does extraordinarily by vowing a vow of a Nazarite, to be separate to Yhwh, **3** he keeps separate from wine and strong drink; he does not drink vinegar of wine and vinegar of strong drink, and he does not drink any juice of grapes, and he does not eat moist or dry grapes; **4** all [the] days of his separation he does not eat of anything which is made of the wine-vine, from kernels even to husk. **5** All [the] days of the vow of his separation a razor does not pass over his head; he is holy until the fullness of the days [in] which he separates himself to Yhwh; the upper part of the hair of his head has grown up. **6** All [the] days of his keeping separate to Yhwh, he does not go near a dead person; **7** for his father, or for his mother, for his brother, or for his sister—he does not become unclean for them at their death, for the separation of his God [is] on his head; **8** all [the] days of his separation he [is] holy to Yhwh. **9** And when the dead dies beside him in an instant, suddenly, and he has defiled the head of his separation, then he has shaved his head in the day of his cleansing; on the seventh day he shaves it, **10** and on the eighth day he brings in two turtle-doves or two young pigeons to the priest, to the opening of the Tent of Meeting, **11** and the priest has prepared one for a sin-offering and one for a burnt-offering, and has made atonement for him because of that which he has sinned by the body, and he has hallowed his head on that day; **12** and he has separated to Yhwh the days of his separation, and he has brought in a lamb, a son of a year, for a guilt-offering, and the former days are fallen, for his separation has been defiled. **13** And this [is] the law of the Nazarite: in the day of the fullness of the days of his separation, he is brought to the opening of the Tent of Meeting,

14 and he has brought his offering near to Yhwh—one male lamb, a son of a year, a perfect one, for a burnt-offering, and one female lamb, a daughter of a year, a perfect one, for a sin-offering, and one ram, a perfect one, for peace-offerings, 15 and a basket of unleavened things of flour, cakes mixed with oil, and thin cakes of unleavened things anointed with oil, and their present, and their drink-offerings. 16 And the priest has brought [them] near before Yhwh, and has made his sin-offering and his burnt-offering; 17 and he makes the ram [as] a sacrifice of peace-offerings to Yhwh, besides the basket of unleavened things; and the priest has made its present and its drink-offering. 18 And the Nazarite has shaved (at the opening of the Tent of Meeting) the head of his separation, and has taken the hair of the head of his separation, and has put [it] on the fire which [is] under the sacrifice of the peace-offerings. 19 And the priest has taken the boiled shoulder from the ram, and one unleavened cake out of the basket, and one thin unleavened cake, and has put [them] on the palms of the Nazarite after his shaving [the hair of] his separation; 20 and the priest has waved them [as] a wave-offering before Yhwh; it [is] holy to the priest, besides the breast of the wave-offering, and besides the leg of the raised-offering; and afterward the Nazarite drinks wine. 21 This [is] the law of the Nazarite who vows his offering to Yhwh for his separation, apart from that which his hand attains; according to his vow which he vows so he does by the law of his separation." 22 And Yhwh speaks to Moses, saying, 23 "Speak to Aaron and to his sons, saying, Thus you bless the sons of Israel, saying to them: 24 Yhwh bless you and keep you; 25 Yhwh cause His face to shine on you, || And favor you; 26 Yhwh lift up His countenance on you, || And appoint for you—peace. 27 And they have put My Name on the sons of Israel, and I bless them."

CHAPTER 7

1 And it comes to pass on the day [when] Moses [was] finishing to set up the Dwelling Place, that he anoints it, and sanctifies it, and all its vessels, and the altar, and all its vessels, and he anoints them, and sanctifies them, 2 and the princes of Israel (heads of the house of their fathers, they [are] princes of the tribes, they who are standing over those numbered) bring near, 3 indeed, they bring their offering before Yhwh of six covered wagons and twelve oxen—a wagon for two of the princes, and an ox for one—and they bring them near before the Dwelling Place. 4 And Yhwh speaks to Moses, saying, 5 "Receive [these] from them, and they have been [used] for doing the service of the Tent of Meeting, and you have given them to the Levites, each according to his service." 6 And Moses takes the wagons and the oxen, and gives them to the Levites. 7 He has given the two wagons and the four oxen to the sons of Gershon, according to their service, 8 and he has given the four wagons and the eight oxen to the sons of Merari, according to their service, by the hand of Ithamar son of Aaron the priest, 9 but he has not given [any] to the sons of Kohath, for the service of the holy place [is] on them, [which] they carry on the shoulder. 10 And the princes bring the dedication of the altar near in the day of its being anointed, indeed, the princes bring their offering near before the altar. 11 And Yhwh says to Moses, "One prince a day, one prince a day—they bring their offering near for the dedication of the altar." 12 And he who is bringing his offering near on the first day is Nahshon son of Amminadab, of the tribe of Judah. 13 And his offering [is] one silver dish, its weight one hundred and thirty [shekels], [and] one silver bowl of seventy shekels, by the shekel of the holy place, both of them full of flour mixed with oil for a present; 14 one golden spoon of ten [shekels], full of incense; 15 one bullock, a son of the herd, one ram, one lamb, a son of a year, for a burnt-offering; 16 one kid of the goats for a sin-offering; 17 and for a sacrifice of the peace-offerings: two oxen, five rams, five male goats, five lambs, sons of a year; this [is] the offering of Nahshon son of Amminadab. 18 On the second day Nethaneel son of Zuar, prince of Issachar, has brought [an offering] near. 19 He has brought his offering near: one silver dish, its weight one hundred and thirty [shekels], [and] one silver bowl of seventy shekels, by the shekel of the holy place, both of them full of flour mixed with oil for a present; 20 one golden spoon of ten [shekels], full of incense; 21 one bullock, a son of the herd, one ram, one lamb, a son of a year, for a burnt-offering; 22 one kid of the goats for a sin-offering; 23 and for a sacrifice of the peace-offerings: two oxen, five rams, five male goats, five lambs, sons of a year; this [is] the offering of Nethaneel son of Zuar. 24 On the third day, Eliab son of Helon, prince of the sons of Zebulun— 25 his offering [is] one silver dish, its weight one hundred and thirty [shekels], [and] one silver bowl of seventy shekels, by the shekel of the holy place, both of them full of flour mixed with oil for a present; 26 one golden spoon of ten [shekels], full of incense; 27 one bullock, a son of the herd, one ram, one lamb, a son of a year, for a burnt-offering; 28 one kid of the goats for a sin-offering; 29 and for a sacrifice of the peace-offerings: two oxen, five rams, five male goats, five lambs, sons of a year; this [is] the offering of Eliab son of Helon. 30 On the fourth day, Elizur son of Shedeur, prince of the sons of Reuben— 31 his offering [is] one silver dish, its weight one hundred and thirty [shekels], [and] one silver bowl of seventy shekels, by the shekel of the holy place, both of them full of flour mixed with oil for a present; 32 one golden spoon of ten [shekels], full of incense; 33 one bullock, a son of the herd, one ram, one lamb, a son of a year, for a burnt-offering; 34 one kid of the goats for a sin-offering; 35 and for a sacrifice of the peace-offerings: two oxen, five rams, five male goats, five lambs, sons of a year; this [is] the offering of Elizur son of Shedeur. 36 On the fifth day, Shelumiel son of Zurishaddai, prince of the sons of Simeon— 37 his offering [is] one silver dish, its weight one hundred and thirty [shekels], [and] one silver bowl of seventy shekels, by the shekel of the holy place, both of them full of flour mixed with oil for a present; 38 one golden spoon of ten [shekels], full of incense; 39 one bullock, a son of the herd, one ram, one lamb, a son of a year, for a burnt-offering; 40 one kid of the goats for a sin-offering; 41 and for a sacrifice of the peace-offerings: two oxen, five rams, five male goats, five lambs, sons of a year; this [is] the offering of Shelumiel son of Zurishaddai. 42 On the sixth day, Eliasaph son of Deuel, prince of the sons of Gad— 43 his offering [is] one silver dish, its weight one hundred and thirty [shekels], [and] one silver bowl of seventy shekels, by the shekel of the holy place, both of them full of flour mixed with oil for a present; 44 one golden spoon of ten [shekels], full of incense; 45 one bullock, a son of the herd, one ram, one lamb, a son of a year, for a burnt-offering; 46 one kid of the goats for a sin-offering; 47 and for a sacrifice of the peace-offerings: two oxen, five rams, five male goats, five lambs, sons of a year; this [is] the offering of Eliasaph son of Deuel. 48 On the seventh day, Elishama son of Ammihud, prince of the sons of Ephraim— 49 his offering [is] one silver dish, its weight one hundred and thirty [shekels], [and] one silver bowl of seventy shekels, by the shekel of the holy place, both of them full of flour mixed with oil for a present; 50 one golden spoon of ten [shekels], full of incense; 51 one bullock, a son of the herd, one ram, one lamb, a son of a year, for a burnt-offering; 52 one kid of the goats for a sin-offering; 53 and for a sacrifice of the peace-offerings: two oxen, five rams, five male goats, five lambs, sons of a year; this [is] the offering of Elishama son of Ammihud. 54 On the eighth day, Gamaliel son of Pedahzur, prince of the sons of Manasseh— 55 his offering [is] one silver dish, its weight one hundred and thirty [shekels], [and] one silver bowl of seventy shekels, by the shekel of the holy place, both of them full of flour mixed with oil for a present; 56 one golden spoon of ten [shekels], full of incense; 57 one bullock, a son of the herd, one ram, one lamb, a son of a year, for a burnt-offering; 58 one kid of the goats for a sin-offering; 59 and for a sacrifice of the peace-offerings: two oxen, five rams, five male goats, five lambs, sons of a year; this [is] the offering of Gamaliel son of Pedahzur. 60 On the ninth day, Abidan son of Gideoni, prince of the sons of Benjamin— 61 his offering [is] one silver dish, its weight one hundred and thirty [shekels], [and] one silver bowl of seventy shekels, by the shekel of the holy place, both of them full of flour mixed with oil for a present; 62 one golden spoon of ten [shekels], full of incense; 63 one bullock, a son of the herd, one ram, one lamb, a son of a year, for a burnt-offering; 64 one kid of the goats for a sin-offering; 65 and for a sacrifice of the peace-offerings: two oxen, five rams, five male goats, five lambs, sons of a year; this [is] the offering of Abidan son of Gideoni. 66 On the tenth day, Ahiezer son of Ammishaddai, prince of the sons of Dan— 67 his offering [is] one silver dish, its weight one hundred and thirty [shekels], [and] one silver bowl of seventy shekels, by the shekel of the holy place, both of them full of flour mixed with oil for a present; 68 one golden spoon of ten [shekels], full of incense; 69 one bullock, a son of the herd, one ram, one lamb, a son of a year, for a burnt-offering; 70 one kid of the goats for a sin-offering; 71 and for a sacrifice of the peace-offerings: two oxen, five rams, five male goats, five lambs, sons of a year; this [is] the offering of Ahiezer son of Ammishaddai. 72 On the

eleventh day, Pagiel son of Ocran, prince of the sons of Asher— **73** his offering [is] one silver dish, its weight one hundred and thirty [shekels], [and] one silver bowl of seventy shekels, by the shekel of the holy place, both of them full of flour mixed with oil for a present; **74** one golden spoon of ten [shekels], full of incense; **75** one bullock, a son of the herd, one ram, one lamb, a son of a year, for a burnt-offering; **76** one kid of the goats for a sin-offering; **77** and for a sacrifice of the peace-offerings: two oxen, five rams, five male goats, five lambs, sons of a year; this [is] the offering of Pagiel son of Ocran. **78** On the twelfth day, Ahira son of Enan, prince of the sons of Naphtali— **79** his offering [is] one silver dish, its weight one hundred and thirty [shekels], [and] one silver bowl of seventy shekels, by the shekel of the holy place, both of them full of flour mixed with oil for a present; **80** one golden spoon of ten [shekels], full of incense; **81** one bullock, a son of the herd, one ram, one lamb, a son of a year, for a burnt-offering; **82** one kid of the goats for a sin-offering; **83** and for a sacrifice of the peace-offerings: two oxen, five rams, five male goats, five lambs, sons of a year; this [is] the offering of Ahira son of Enan. **84** This [is] the dedication of the altar, in the day of its being anointed by the princes of Israel: twelve silver dishes, twelve silver bowls, twelve golden spoons; **85** each silver dish [is] one hundred and thirty [shekels], and each bowl seventy; all the silver of the vessels [is] two thousand and four hundred [shekels], by the shekel of the holy place; **86** twelve golden spoons full of incense, ten [shekels] each spoon, by the shekel of the holy place; all the gold of the spoons [is] one hundred and twenty [shekels]; **87** all the oxen for burnt-offering [are] twelve bullocks; twelve rams, twelve lambs, sons of a year, and their present, and twelve kids of the goats for sin-offering; **88** and all the oxen for the sacrifice of the peace-offerings [are] twenty-four bullocks; sixty rams, sixty male goats, sixty lambs, sons of a year; this is the dedication of the altar in the day of its being anointed. **89** And in the entering of Moses into the Tent of Meeting to speak with Him, indeed, he hears the voice speaking to him from off the propitiatory covering which [is] on the Ark of the Testimony, from between the two cherubim; and He speaks to him.

CHAPTER 8

1 And Yhwh speaks to Moses, saying, **2** "Speak to Aaron, and you have said to him: In your causing the lights to go up, the seven lights give light toward the front of the face of the lampstand." **3** And Aaron does so; he has caused its lights to go up toward the front of the face of the lampstand, as Yhwh has commanded Moses. **4** And this [is] the work of the lampstand: beaten work of gold; from its thigh to its flower it [is] beaten work; as the appearance which Yhwh showed Moses, so he has made the lampstand. **5** And Yhwh speaks to Moses, saying, **6** "Take the Levites from the midst of the sons of Israel, and you have cleansed them. **7** And thus you do to them to cleanse them: sprinkle waters of atonement on them, and they have caused a razor to pass over all their flesh, and have washed their garments, and cleansed themselves, **8** have taken a bullock, a son of the herd, and its present, flour mixed with oil, and you take a second bullock, a son of the herd, for a sin-offering; **9** and you have brought the Levites near before the Tent of Meeting, and you have assembled all the congregation of the sons of Israel, **10** and you have brought the Levites near before Yhwh, and the sons of Israel have laid their hands on the Levites, **11** and Aaron has waved the Levites [as] a wave-offering before Yhwh, from the sons of Israel, and they have been [consecrated] for doing the service of Yhwh. **12** And the Levites lay their hands on the head of the bullocks, and make one a sin-offering and one a burnt-offering to Yhwh, to atone for the Levites. **13** And you have caused the Levites to stand before Aaron, and before his sons, and have waved them [as] a wave-offering to Yhwh; **14** and you have separated the Levites from the midst of the sons of Israel, and the Levites have become Mine; **15** and afterward the Levites come in to serve the Tent of Meeting, and you have cleansed them, and have waved them [as] a wave-offering. **16** For they are certainly given to Me out of the midst of the sons of Israel, instead of him who opens any womb—the firstborn of all; I have taken them for Myself from the sons of Israel; **17** for every firstborn among the sons of Israel [is] Mine, among man and among beast; in the day of My striking every firstborn in the land of Egypt I sanctified them for Myself; **18** and I take the Levites instead of every firstborn among the sons of Israel. **19** And I give the Levites [as] gifts to Aaron and to his sons, from the midst of the sons of Israel, to do the service of the sons of Israel in the Tent of Meeting, and to make atonement for the sons of Israel, and there is no plague among the sons of Israel in the sons of Israel drawing near to the holy place." **20** And Moses does—Aaron also, and all the congregation of the sons of Israel—to the Levites according to all that Yhwh has commanded Moses concerning the Levites; so the sons of Israel have done to them. **21** And the Levites cleanse themselves, and wash their garments, and Aaron waves them [as] a wave-offering before Yhwh, and Aaron makes atonement for them to cleanse them, **22** and afterward the Levites have gone in to do their service in the Tent of Meeting, before Aaron and before his sons; as Yhwh has commanded Moses concerning the Levites, so they have done to them. **23** And Yhwh speaks to Moses, saying, **24** "This [is] who [is] for the Levites: from a son of twenty-five years and upward he goes in to serve the host in the service of the Tent of Meeting, **25** and from a son of fifty years he returns from the host of the service, and does not serve anymore, **26** and he has ministered with his brothers in the Tent of Meeting, to keep the charge, and does not do service; thus you do to the Levites concerning their charge."

CHAPTER 9

1 And Yhwh speaks to Moses, in the wilderness of Sinai, in the second year of their going out of the land of Egypt, in the first month, saying, **2** "Also, the sons of Israel prepare the Passover in its appointed time; **3** in the fourteenth day of this month between the evenings you prepare it in its appointed time; you prepare it according to all its statutes and according to all its ordinances." **4** And Moses speaks to the sons of Israel to prepare the Passover, **5** and they prepare the Passover in the first [month], on the fourteenth day of the month, between the evenings, in the wilderness of Sinai; according to all that Yhwh has commanded Moses, so the sons of Israel have done. **6** And there are men who have been defiled by the body of a man, and they have not been able to prepare the Passover on that day, and they come near before Moses and before Aaron on that day, **7** and those men say to him, "We are defiled by the body of a man; why are we withheld so as not to bring the offering of Yhwh near in its appointed time, in the midst of the sons of Israel?" **8** And Moses says to them, "Stand, and I hear what Yhwh has commanded concerning you." **9** And Yhwh speaks to Moses, saying, **10** "Speak to the sons of Israel, saying, Though any man is unclean by a body or in a distant journey (of you or of your generations), he has still prepared a Passover to Yhwh; **11** they prepare it in the second month, on the fourteenth day, between the evenings; they eat it with unleavened and bitter things; **12** they do not leave of [it] until morning; and they do not break a bone in it; they prepare it according to all the statute of the Passover. **13** And the man who is clean, and has not been on a journey, and has ceased to prepare the Passover, indeed, that person has been cut off from his people; because he has not brought the offering of Yhwh near in its appointed time, that man bears his sin. **14** And when a sojourner sojourns with you, then he has prepared a Passover to Yhwh—according to the statute of the Passover and according to its ordinance, so he does; one statute is for you, indeed, for a sojourner and for a native of the land." **15** And in the day of the raising up of the Dwelling Place, the cloud has covered the Dwelling Place, even the Tent of the Testimony; and in the evening there is as an appearance of fire on the Dwelling Place until morning; **16** so it is continually; the cloud covers it, also the appearance of fire by night. **17** And according to the going up of the cloud from off the tent, then afterward the sons of Israel journey; and in the place where the cloud dwells, there the sons of Israel encamp; **18** by the command of Yhwh the sons of Israel journey, and by the command of Yhwh they encamp; all the days that the cloud dwells over the Dwelling Place they encamp. **19** And in the cloud prolonging itself over the Dwelling Place many days, then the sons of Israel have kept the charge of Yhwh, and do not journey. **20** And so when the cloud is over the Dwelling Place [for] a number of days: by the command of Yhwh they encamp, and by the command of Yhwh they journey. **21** And so when the cloud is from evening until morning, when the cloud has gone up in the morning, then they have journeyed; whether by day or by night, when the cloud has gone up, then they have journeyed. **22** Whether two days, or a month, or days, in the cloud prolonging itself over the Dwelling Place, to dwell over it, the sons of Israel encamp and do not journey; and in its being lifted up they journey. **23** By the command of Yhwh they encamp, and by the command of Yhwh they journey; they have kept the charge of Yhwh, by the command of Yhwh in the hand of Moses.

CHAPTER 10

1 And Yhwh speaks to Moses, saying, **2** "Make two trumpets of silver for yourself; you make them of beaten work, and they have been for you for the convocation of the congregation, and for the journeying of the camps; **3** and they have blown with them, and all the congregation has assembled to you at the opening of the Tent of Meeting. **4** And if they blow with one, then the princes, heads of the thousands of Israel, have assembled to you; **5** and you have blown—a shout, and the camps which are encamping eastward have journeyed. **6** And you have blown—a second shout, and the camps which are encamping southward have journeyed; they blow a shout for their journeys. **7** And in the assembling of the assembly you blow, and do not shout; **8** and sons of Aaron, the priests, blow with the trumpets; and they have been for a continuous statute to you throughout your generations. **9** And when you go into battle in your land against the adversary who is distressing you, then you have shouted with the trumpets, and you have been remembered before your God Yhwh, and you have been saved from your enemies. **10** And in the day of your gladness, and in your appointed times, and in the beginnings of your months, you have also blown with the trumpets over your burnt-offerings, and over the sacrifices of your peace-offerings, and they have been for a memorial to you before your God; I [am] your God Yhwh." **11** And it comes to pass, in the second year, in the second month, on the twentieth of the month, the cloud has gone up from off the Dwelling Place of the Testimony, **12** and the sons of Israel journey in their journeys from the wilderness of Sinai, and the cloud dwells in the wilderness of Paran; **13** and they journey at first by the command of Yhwh in the hand of Moses. **14** And the standard of the camp of the sons of Judah journeys in the first [place], by their hosts, and over its host [is] Nahshon son of Amminadab. **15** And over the host of the tribe of the sons of Issachar [is] Nathaneel son of Zuar. **16** And over the host of the tribe of the sons of Zebulun [is] Eliab son of Helon. **17** And the Dwelling Place has been taken down, and the sons of Gershon and the sons of Merari have journeyed, carrying the Dwelling Place. **18** And the standard of the camp of Reuben has journeyed, by their hosts, and over its host [is] Elizur son of Shedeur. **19** And over the host of the tribe of the sons of Simeon [is] Shelumiel son of Zurishaddai. **20** And over the host of the tribe of the sons of Gad [is] Eliasaph son of Deuel. **21** And the Kohathites have journeyed, carrying the Dwelling Place, and the [others] have raised up the Dwelling Place until their coming in. **22** And the standard of the camp of the sons of Ephraim has journeyed, by their hosts, and over its host [is] Elishama son of Ammihud. **23** And over the host of the tribe of the sons of Manasseh [is] Gamalial son of Pedahzur. **24** And over the host of the tribe of the sons of Benjamin [is] Abidan son of Gideoni. **25** And the standard of the camp of the sons of Dan has journeyed (rearward to all the camps), by their hosts, and over its host [is] Ahiezer son of Ammishaddai. **26** And over the host of the tribe of the sons of Asher [is] Pagiel son of Ocran. **27** And over the host of the tribe of the sons of Naphtali [is] Ahira son of Enan. **28** These [are] the journeys of the sons of Israel by their hosts when they journey. **29** And Moses says to Hobab son of Raguel the Midianite, father-in-law of Moses, "We are journeying to the place of which Yhwh has said, I give it to you; go with us, and we have done good to you, for Yhwh has spoken good concerning Israel." **30** And he says to him, "I do not go; but I go to my land and to my family." **31** And he says, "Please do not forsake us, because you have known our encamping in the wilderness, and you have been to us for eyes; **32** and it has come to pass, when you go with us—indeed, it has come to pass—that good which Yhwh does kindly with us, we have done it kindly to you." **33** And they journey from the mountain of Yhwh a journey of three days; and the Ark of the Covenant of Yhwh is journeying before them [for] the journey of three days, to spy out a resting place for them; **34** and the cloud of Yhwh [is] on them by day, in their journeying from the camp. **35** And it comes to pass in the journeying of the Ark, that Moses says, "Rise, O Yhwh, and Your enemies are scattered, and those hating You flee from

Your presence." **36** And in its resting he says, "Return, O Yhwh, [to] the myriads, the thousands of Israel."

CHAPTER 11

1 And the people are evil, as those sighing habitually in the ears of Yhwh, and Yhwh hears, and His anger burns, and the fire of Yhwh burns among them, and consumes in the extremity of the camp. **2** And the people cry to Moses, and Moses prays to Yhwh, and the fire is quenched; **3** and he calls the name of that place Taberah, for the fire of Yhwh has "burned" among them. **4** And the rabble who [are] in its midst have lusted greatly, and the sons of Israel also turn back and weep, and say, "Who gives us flesh? **5** We have remembered the fish which we eat in Egypt for nothing, the cucumbers, and the melons, and the leeks, and the onions, and the garlic; **6** and now our soul [is] dry, there is not anything, except the manna, before our eyes." **7** And the manna is as coriander seed, and its aspect as the aspect of bdellium; **8** the people have turned aside and gathered [it], and ground [it] with millstones, or beat [it] in a mortar, and boiled [it] in a pan, and made it cakes, and its taste has been as the taste of the moisture of oil. **9** And in the descending of the dew on the camp by night, the manna descends on it. **10** And Moses hears the people weeping by its families, each at the opening of his tent, and the anger of Yhwh burns exceedingly, and in the eyes of Moses [it is] evil. **11** And Moses says to Yhwh, "Why have You done evil to Your servant? and why have I not found grace in Your eyes—to put the burden of all this people on me? **12** I—have I conceived all this people? I—have I begotten it, that You say to me, Carry it in your bosom, as the one supporting carries the nursing suckling, to the ground which You have sworn to its fathers? **13** From where do I have flesh to give to all this people? for they weep to me, saying, Give flesh to us, and we eat. **14** I am not able—I alone—to bear all this people, for [it is] too heavy for me; **15** and if thus You are doing to me—please slay me; slay, if I have found grace in your eyes, and do not let me look on my affliction." **16** And Yhwh says to Moses, "Gather to Me seventy men from [the] elderly of Israel, whom you have known that they are [the] elderly of the people, and its authorities; and you have taken them to the Tent of Meeting, and they have stationed themselves there with you, **17** and I have come down and spoken with you there, and have kept back of the Spirit which [is] on you, and have put [that One] on them, and they have borne some of the burden of the people with you, and you do not bear [it] alone. **18** And you say to the people: Sanctify yourselves for tomorrow, and you have eaten flesh, for you have wept in the ears of Yhwh, saying, Who gives us flesh? for we [had] good in Egypt; and Yhwh has given flesh to you, and you have eaten. **19** You do not eat one day, nor two days, nor five days, nor ten days, nor twenty days, **20** [but] even to a month of days, until it comes out from your nostrils, and it has become an abomination to you, because that you have loathed Yhwh, who [is] in your midst, and weep before Him, saying, Why is this [that] we have come out of Egypt!" **21** And Moses says, "Six hundred thousand footmen [are] the people in whose midst I [dwell]; and You, You have said, I give flesh to them, and they have eaten [for] a month of days! **22** Is flock and herd slaughtered for them, that one has found [enough] for them? Are all the fishes of the sea gathered for them, that one has found [enough] for them?" **23** And Yhwh says to Moses, "Has the hand of Yhwh become short? now you see whether My word meets you or not." **24** And Moses goes out, and speaks the words of Yhwh to the people, and gathers seventy men from [the] elderly of the people, and causes them to stand around the tent, **25** and Yhwh comes down in the cloud, and speaks to him, and keeps back of the Spirit which [is] on him, and puts [that One] on the seventy elderly men; and it comes to pass at the resting of the Spirit on them, that they prophesy, and they have never done [so] again. **26** And two of the men are left in the camp, the name of the first [is] Eldad and the name of the second Medad, and the spirit rests on them (and they are among those written, but they have not gone out to the tent), and they prophesy in the camp; **27** and the young man runs, and declares [it] to Moses, and says, "Eldad and Medad are prophesying in the camp." **28** And Joshua son of Nun, minister of Moses, [one] of his young men, answers and says, "My lord Moses, restrain them." **29** And Moses says to him, "Are you zealous for me? O that all Yhwh's people were prophets! That Yhwh would put His Spirit on them!" **30** And Moses is gathered to the camp, he and [the] elderly of Israel. **31** And a spirit has journeyed from Yhwh, and cuts off quails from the sea, and leaves [them] by the camp, as a day's journey here and as a day's journey there, around the camp, and about two cubits above the face of the land. **32** And the people rise all that day, and all the night, and all the day after, and gather the quails—he who has least has gathered ten homers—and they spread them out for themselves around the camp. **33** The flesh is yet between their teeth—it is not yet cut off—and the anger of Yhwh has burned among the people, and Yhwh strikes [with] a very great striking among the people; **34** and [one] calls the name of that place Kibroth-Hattaavah, for there they have buried the people who lust. **35** From Kibroth-Hattaavah the people have journeyed to Hazeroth, and they are in Hazeroth.

CHAPTER 12

1 And Miriam speaks—Aaron also—against Moses concerning the circumstance of the Cushite woman whom he had taken, for he had taken a Cushite woman; **2** and they say, "Has Yhwh only spoken by Moses? Has he not also spoken by us?" And Yhwh hears. **3** And the man Moses [is] very humble, more than any of the men who [are] on the face of the ground. **4** And Yhwh suddenly says to Moses, and to Aaron, and to Miriam, "Come out, you three, to the Tent of Meeting"; and those three come out. **5** And Yhwh comes down in the pillar of the cloud, and stands at the opening of the tent, and calls Aaron and Miriam, and both of them come out. **6** And He says, "Now hear My words: If your prophet is of Yhwh, || I make Myself known to him in a vision; I speak with him in a dream. **7** Not so My servant Moses; He [is] steadfast in all My house. **8** I speak with him mouth to mouth, || Even [by] an appearance, and not in riddles; And he beholds the form of Yhwh attentively. Now why have you not been afraid || To speak against My servant—against Moses?" **9** And the anger of Yhwh burns against them, and He goes on, **10** and the cloud has turned aside from off the tent, and behold, Miriam [is] leprous as snow; and Aaron turns to Miriam, and behold, leprous! **11** And Aaron says to Moses, "O my lord, please do not lay [this] sin on us [in] which we have been foolish, and [in] which we have sinned; **12** please do not let her be as [one] dead, when in his coming out from the womb of his mother—the half of his flesh is consumed." **13** And Moses cries to Yhwh, saying, "O God, please give healing to her! Please!" **14** And Yhwh says to Moses, "But [if] her father had but spat in her face—is she not ashamed [for] seven days? she is shut out [for] seven days at the outside of the camp, and afterward she is gathered." **15** And Miriam is shut out at the outside of the camp [for] seven days, and the people have not journeyed until Miriam is gathered; **16** and afterward the people have journeyed from Hazeroth, and they encamp in the wilderness of Paran.

CHAPTER 13

1 And Yhwh speaks to Moses, saying, **2** "Send men for yourself, and they spy out the land of Canaan, which I am giving to the sons of Israel; one man—you send one man for the tribe of his fathers, everyone a prince among them." **3** And Moses sends them from the wilderness of Paran by the command of Yhwh; all of them [are] men, [and] they are heads of the sons of Israel, **4** and these [are] their names: for the tribe of Reuben, Shammua son of Zaccur; **5** for the tribe of Simeon, Shaphat son of Hori; **6** for the tribe of Judah, Caleb son of Jephunneh; **7** for the tribe of Issachar, Igal son of Joseph; **8** for the tribe of Ephraim, Oshea son of Nun; **9** for the tribe of Benjamin, Palti son of Raphu; **10** for the tribe of Zebulun, Gaddiel son of Sodi; **11** for the tribe of Joseph (for the tribe of Manasseh), Gaddi son of Susi; **12** for the tribe of Dan, Ammiel son of Gemalli; **13** for the tribe of Asher, Sethur son of Michael; **14** for the tribe of Naphtali, Nahbi son of Vopshi; **15** for the tribe of Gad, Geuel son of Machi. **16** These [are] the names of the men whom Moses has sent to spy out the land; and Moses calls Hoshea son of Nun, Joshua. **17** And Moses sends them to spy out the land of Canaan and says to them, "Go up this [way] into the south, and you have gone up the mountain, **18** and have seen the land, what it [is], and the people which is dwelling on it, whether it [is] strong or feeble, [and] whether it [is] few or many; **19** and what the land [is] in which it is dwelling, whether it [is] good or bad; and what [are] the cities in which it is dwelling, whether in camps or in fortresses. **20**

And what the land [is], whether it [is] fat or lean; whether there is wood in it or not; and you have strengthened yourselves, and have taken of the fruit of the land"; now the days [are] days of the first-fruits of grapes. **21** And they go up and spy out the land, from the wilderness of Zin to Rehob at the going in to Hamath; **22** and they go up by the south, and come to Hebron, and there [are] Ahiman, Sheshai, and Talmai, children of Anak (and Hebron was built seven years before Zoan in Egypt), **23** and they come to the Brook of Eshcol, and cut down a branch and one cluster of grapes there, and they carry it on a staff by two, also [some] of the pomegranates, and of the figs. **24** That place has been called the Brook of Eshcol, because of the cluster which the sons of Israel cut from there. **25** And they return from spying out the land at the end of forty days. **26** And they go and come to Moses, and to Aaron, and to all the congregation of the sons of Israel, to the wilderness of Paran, to Kadesh; and they bring them and all the congregation back word, and show them the fruit of the land. **27** And they recount to him, and say, "We came to the land to where you have sent us, and it is indeed flowing with milk and honey—and this [is] its fruit; **28** only, surely the people which is dwelling in the land [is] strong; and the cities are fortified [and] very great; and we have also seen children of Anak there. **29** Amalek is dwelling in the land of the south, and the Hittite, and the Jebusite, and the Amorite are dwelling in the hill country, and the Canaanite is dwelling by the sea, and by the side of the Jordan." **30** And Caleb stills the people concerning Moses and says, "Let us certainly go up—and we have possessed it; for we are thoroughly able to [do] it." **31** And the men who have gone up with him said, "We are not able to go up against the people, for it [is] stronger than we"; **32** and they bring out an evil account of the land which they have spied out to the sons of Israel, saying, "The land into which we passed over to spy it out is a land eating up its inhabitants; and all the people whom we saw in its midst [are] men of stature; **33** and there we saw the giants, sons of Anak, of the giants; and we are as grasshoppers in our own eyes—and so we were in their eyes."

CHAPTER 14

1 And all the congregation lifts up, and they give forth their voice, and the people weep during that night; **2** and all the sons of Israel murmur against Moses and against Aaron, and all the congregation says to them, "O that we had died in the land of Egypt, or in this wilderness, O that we had died! **3** and why is Yhwh bringing us to this land to fall by the sword, [that] our wives and our infants become a prey? Is it not good for us to return to Egypt?" **4** And they say to one another, "Let us appoint a head and return to Egypt." **5** And Moses falls—Aaron also—on their faces, before all the assembly of the congregation of the sons of Israel. **6** And Joshua son of Nun and Caleb son of Jephunneh, of those spying out the land, have torn their garments, **7** and they speak to all the congregation of the sons of Israel, saying, "The land into which we have passed over to spy it out [is] a very, very good land; **8** if Yhwh has delighted in us, then He has brought us into this land, and has given it to us, a land which is flowing with milk and honey; **9** only, do not rebel against Yhwh: and you, do not fear the people of the land, for they [are] our bread; their defense has turned aside from off them, and Yhwh [is] with us; do not fear them." **10** And all the congregation says to stone them with stones, and the glory of Yhwh has appeared in the Tent of Meeting to all the sons of Israel. **11** And Yhwh says to Moses, "Until when does this people despise Me? and until when do they not believe in Me, for all the signs which I have done in its midst? **12** I strike it with pestilence, and dispossess it, and make you become a nation greater and mightier than it." **13** And Moses says to Yhwh, "Then the Egyptians have heard! For with Your power You have brought up this people out of their midst, **14** and they have said [it] to the inhabitant of this land, they have heard that You, Yhwh, [are] in the midst of this people, that You are seen eye to eye—O Yhwh, and Your cloud is standing over them—and in a pillar of cloud You are going before them by day, and in a pillar of fire by night. **15** And You have put to death this people as one man, and the nations who have heard Your fame have spoken, saying, **16** From Yhwh's want of ability to bring in this people to the land which He has sworn to them, He slaughters them in the wilderness. **17** And now, please let the power of my Lord be great, as You have spoken, saying, **18** Yhwh [is] slow to anger and of great kindness, bearing away iniquity and transgression, and not entirely acquitting, charging iniquity of fathers on sons, on a third and on a fourth [generation]— **19** please forgive the iniquity of this people, according to the greatness of Your kindness, and as You have borne with this people from Egypt, even until now." **20** And Yhwh says, "I have forgiven according to your word, **21** but nevertheless, as I live, indeed, the whole earth is filled [with] the glory of Yhwh, **22** for all the men who are seeing My glory and My signs which I have done in Egypt and in the wilderness, and try Me these ten times, and have not listened to My voice— **23** they do not see the land which I have sworn to their fathers, indeed, none of those despising Me see it; **24** but My servant Caleb, because there has been another spirit with him, and he is fully after Me—I have brought him into the land to where he has entered, and his seed possesses it. **25** And the Amalekite and the Canaanite are dwelling in the valley; tomorrow turn and journey for yourselves into the wilderness—the way of the Red Sea." **26** And Yhwh speaks to Moses and to Aaron, saying, **27** "Until when [do I bear] with this evil congregation—they who are murmuring against Me? the murmurings of the sons of Israel, which they are murmuring against Me, I have heard; **28** say to them: As I live—a declaration of Yhwh—if, as you have spoken in My ears, do I not do so to you? **29** Your carcasses fall in this wilderness, even all your numbered ones, to all your number, from a son of twenty years and upward, who have murmured against Me; **30** you do not come into the land [for] which I have lifted up My hand to cause you to dwell in it, except Caleb son of Jephunneh and Joshua son of Nun. **31** As for your infants—of whom you have said, They become a spoil—I have even brought them in, and they have known the land which you have kicked against; **32** as for you—your carcasses fall in this wilderness, **33** and your sons are shepherding in the wilderness [for] forty years, and have borne your whoredoms until your carcasses are consumed in the wilderness; **34** by the number of the days [in] which you spied out the land, forty days—a day for a year, a day for a year— you bear your iniquities [for] forty years, and you have known My opposition; **35** I, Yhwh, have spoken; if, nonetheless, I do not do this to all this evil congregation who are meeting against Me— they are consumed in this wilderness, and there they die." **36** Then the men whom Moses has sent to spy out the land, [who] then return and cause all the congregation to murmur against him by bringing out an evil account concerning the land, **37** even the men bringing out an evil account of the land, they die by the plague before Yhwh; **38** and Joshua son of Nun and Caleb son of Jephunneh have lived, of those men who go to spy out the land. **39** And Moses speaks these words to all the sons of Israel, and the people mourn exceedingly, **40** and they rise early in the morning, and go up to the top of the mountain, saying, "Here we [are], and we have come up to the place which Yhwh has spoken of, for we have sinned." **41** And Moses says, "Why [is] this [that] you are transgressing the command of Yhwh? For it does not prosper; **42** do not go up, for Yhwh is not in your midst, and you are not struck before your enemies; **43** for the Amalekite and the Canaanite [are] there before you, and you have fallen by the sword, because that you have turned back from after Yhwh, and Yhwh is not with you." **44** And they presume to go up to the top of the mountain, but the Ark of the Covenant of Yhwh, and Moses, have not departed out of the midst of the camp. **45** And the Amalekite and the Canaanite who are dwelling in that mountain come down and strike them, and beat them down to Hormah.

CHAPTER 15

1 And Yhwh speaks to Moses, saying, **2** "Speak to the sons of Israel, and you have said to them: When you come into the land of your dwellings, which I am giving to you, **3** then you have prepared a fire-offering to Yhwh, a burnt-offering or a sacrifice, for separating a vow or free-will offering, or in your appointed things, to make a refreshing fragrance to Yhwh, out of the herd or out of the flock. **4** And he who is bringing his offering near to Yhwh has brought a present of a tenth part of flour mixed with a fourth of the hin of oil; **5** and you prepare a fourth of the hin of wine for a drink-offering, with the burnt-offering or for the sacrifice, for one lamb; **6** or for a ram you prepare a present of two-tenth parts of flour mixed with a third of the hin of oil; **7** and you bring a third part of the hin of wine near for a drink-offering—a refreshing fragrance to Yhwh. **8** And when you make a son of the herd a burnt-offering, or a sacrifice for separating a vow, or peace-offerings to Yhwh, **9**

then he has brought near for the son of the herd a present of three-tenth parts of flour mixed with a half of the hin of oil; **10** and you bring a half of the hin of wine near for a drink-offering, [for] a fire-offering of refreshing fragrance to Yhwh; **11** thus it is done for one ox, or for one ram, or for a lamb of the sheep or of the goats. **12** According to the number that you prepare, so you do to each, according to their number; **13** every native does thus with these, for bringing a fire-offering near of refreshing fragrance to Yhwh; **14** and when a sojourner sojourns with you, or whoever [is] in your midst throughout your generations, and he has made a fire-offering of refreshing fragrance to Yhwh, as you do so he does. **15** One statute is for you of the congregation and for the sojourner who is sojourning, a continuous statute throughout your generations: as you [are] so is the sojourner before Yhwh; **16** one law and one ordinance is for you and for the sojourner who is sojourning with you." **17** And Yhwh speaks to Moses, saying, **18** "Speak to the sons of Israel, and you have said to them: In your coming into the land to where I am bringing you in, **19** then it has been, in your eating of the bread of the land, you raise up a raised-offering to Yhwh; **20** you raise up a cake of the first of your dough [as] a raised-offering; as the raised-offering of a threshing-floor, so you raise it up. **21** You give to Yhwh from the first of your dough [as] a raised-offering throughout your generations. **22** And when you err, and do not do all these commands which Yhwh has spoken to Moses— **23** the whole that Yhwh has charged on you by the hand of Moses, from the day that Yhwh has commanded and from now on, throughout your generations— **24** then it has been, if from the eyes of the congregation it has been done through ignorance, that all the congregation has prepared one bullock, a son of the herd, for a burnt-offering, for refreshing fragrance to Yhwh, and its present, and its drink-offering, according to the ordinance, and one kid of the goats for a sin-offering. **25** And the priest has made atonement for all the congregation of the sons of Israel, and it has been forgiven them, for it [is] ignorance, and they have brought in their offering, a fire-offering to Yhwh, and their sin offering before Yhwh for their ignorance; **26** and it has been forgiven to all the congregation of the sons of Israel and to the sojourner who is sojourning in their midst, for that all the people [did it] through ignorance. **27** And if one person sins through ignorance, then he has brought a female goat near, daughter of a year, for a sin-offering; **28** and the priest has made atonement for the person who is erring, in his sinning through ignorance before Yhwh, by making atonement for him, and it has been forgiven him; **29** one law is for yourselves—for the native among the sons of Israel and for the sojourner who is sojourning in their midst— for him who is doing [anything] through ignorance. **30** And the person who does [evil] with a high hand—of the native or of the sojourner—he is reviling Yhwh, and that person has been cut off from the midst of his people; **31** because he despised the word of Yhwh and has broken His command, that person is certainly cut off; his iniquity [is] on him." **32** And the sons of Israel are in the wilderness, and they find a man gathering wood on the Sabbath day, **33** and those finding him gathering wood bring him near to Moses, and to Aaron, and to all the congregation, **34** and they place him in confinement, for it [is] not explained what is [to be] done to him. **35** And Yhwh says to Moses, "The man is certainly put to death [by] all the congregation stoning him with stones at the outside of the camp." **36** And all the congregation brings him out to the outside of the camp and stone him with stones, and he dies, as Yhwh has commanded Moses. **37** And Yhwh speaks to Moses, saying, **38** "Speak to the sons of Israel, and you have commanded to them, and they have made fringes on the skirts of their garments for themselves, throughout their generations, and they have put a ribbon of blue on the fringe of the skirt, **39** and it has been to you for a fringe, and you have seen it, and have remembered all the commands of Yhwh, and have done them, and you do not search after your heart and after your eyes, after which you are going whoring, **40** so that you remember and have done all My commands, and you have been holy to your God. **41** I [am] your God Yhwh, who has brought you out from the land of Egypt to become your God; I [am] your God Yhwh."

CHAPTER 16

1 And Korah, son of Izhar, son of Kohath, son of Levi, takes both Dathan and Abiram sons of Eliab, and On son of Peleth, sons of Reuben, **2** and they rise up before Moses with men of the sons of Israel, two hundred and fifty princes of the congregation, called of the convention, men of renown, **3** and they are assembled against Moses and against Aaron, and say to them, "Enough of you! For all the congregation—all of them [are] holy, and Yhwh [is] in their midst; and why do you lift yourselves up above the assembly of Yhwh?" **4** And Moses hears, and falls on his face, **5** and he speaks to Korah and to all his congregation, saying, "Indeed, [in the] morning Yhwh may cause [you] to know those who are His and him who is holy, and has brought [him] near to Him; even him whom He fixes on He brings near to Him. **6** Do this: take censers for yourselves—Korah and all his company— **7** and put fire in them and put incense on them before Yhwh tomorrow, and it has been, the man whom Yhwh chooses, he [is] the holy one—enough of you, sons of Levi!" **8** And Moses says to Korah, "Now hear, sons of Levi; **9** is it little to you that the God of Israel has separated you from the congregation of Israel to bring you near to Himself, to do the service of the Dwelling Place of Yhwh, and to stand before the congregation to serve them? **10** Indeed, He brings you near, and all your brothers, the sons of Levi, with you—and you have also sought the priesthood! **11** Therefore, you and all your congregation are meeting against Yhwh; and Aaron, what [is] he, that you murmur against him?" **12** And Moses sends to call for Dathan and for Abiram, sons of Eliab, and they say, "We do not come up! **13** Is it little that you have brought us up out of a land flowing with milk and honey, to put us to death in a wilderness, that you also certainly make yourself prince over us? **14** Indeed, you have not brought us into a land flowing with milk and honey, nor do you give an inheritance of field and vineyard to us; do you pick out the eyes of these men? we do not come up!" **15** And it is very displeasing to Moses, and he says to Yhwh, "Do not turn to their present; I have not taken one donkey from them, nor have I afflicted one of them." **16** And Moses says to Korah, "You and all your congregation, be [present] before Yhwh—you, and they, and Aaron—tomorrow; **17** and let each take his censer and you have put incense on them, and each has brought his censer near before Yhwh—two hundred and fifty censers; indeed, you and Aaron, each [with] his censer." **18** And they each take his censer, and put fire on them, and lay incense on them, and they stand at the opening of the Tent of Meeting with Moses and Aaron. **19** And Korah assembles all the congregation against them at the opening of the Tent of Meeting, and the glory of Yhwh is seen by all the congregation. **20** And Yhwh speaks to Moses and to Aaron, saying, **21** "Be separated from the midst of this congregation, and I consume them in a moment"; **22** and they fall on their faces, and say, "God, God of the spirits of all flesh—one man sins, and are You angry against all the congregation?" **23** And Yhwh speaks to Moses, saying, **24** "Speak to the congregation, saying, Go up from around the dwelling place of Korah, Dathan, and Abiram." **25** And Moses rises, and goes to Dathan and Abiram, and [the] elderly of Israel go after him, **26** and he speaks to the congregation, saying, "Now turn aside from the tents of these wicked men, and do not come against anything that they have, lest you are consumed in all their sins." **27** And they go up from the dwelling place of Korah, Dathan, and Abiram, from all around, and Dathan and Abiram have come out, standing at the opening of their tents, with their wives, and their sons, and their infants. **28** And Moses says, "By this you know that Yhwh has sent me to do all these works, that [they are] not from my own heart; **29** if these die according to the death of all men, or the charge of all men is charged on them, Yhwh has not sent me; **30** but if Yhwh does a strange thing, and the ground has opened her mouth and swallowed them and all that they have, and they have gone down alive to Sheol, then you have known that these men have despised Yhwh." **31** And it comes to pass at his finishing speaking all these words, that the ground which [is] under them cleaves, **32** and the earth opens her mouth and swallows them, and their houses, and all the men who [are] for Korah, and all the goods, **33** and they go down—they and all that they have—alive to Sheol, and the earth closes over them, and they perish from the midst of the assembly; **34** and all Israel who [are] around them have fled at their voice, for they said, "Lest the earth swallow us"; **35** and fire has come out from Yhwh and consumes the two hundred and fifty men bringing the incense near. **36** And Yhwh speaks to Moses, saying, **37** "Say to Eleazar son of Aaron the priest to lift up the censers from the midst of the burning and scatter the fire away, for they have been hallowed. **38** [As for] the censers of these sinners against their own souls, indeed, they have made them [into]

spread-out plates [for] a covering for the altar, for they have brought them near before Yhwh, and they are hallowed; and they become a sign to the sons of Israel." **39** And Eleazar the priest takes the bronze censers which they who are burned had brought near, and they spread them out [for] a covering for the altar— **40** a memorial to the sons of Israel, so that a stranger who is not of the seed of Aaron does not draw near to make incense before Yhwh, and is not as Korah and as his congregation, as Yhwh has spoken by the hand of Moses to him. **41** And on the next day all the congregation of the sons of Israel murmurs against Moses and against Aaron, saying, "You have put the people of Yhwh to death." **42** And it comes to pass, in the congregation being assembled against Moses and against Aaron, that they turn toward the Tent of Meeting, and behold, the cloud has covered it and the glory of Yhwh is seen; **43** and Moses comes—Aaron also—to the front of the Tent of Meeting. **44** And Yhwh speaks to Moses, saying, **45** "Get up from the midst of this congregation, and I consume them in a moment"; and they fall on their faces, **46** and Moses says to Aaron, "Take the censer and put fire on it from off the altar, and place incense, and go quickly to the congregation and make atonement for them, for the wrath has gone out from the presence of Yhwh—the plague has begun." **47** And Aaron takes [it] as Moses has spoken, and runs to the midst of the assembly, and behold, the plague has begun among the people; and he gives the incense, and makes atonement for the people, **48** and stands between the dead and the living, and the plague is restrained; **49** and those who die by the plague are fourteen thousand and seven hundred, apart from those who die for the matter of Korah; **50** and Aaron turns back to Moses, to the opening of the Tent of Meeting, and the plague has been restrained.

CHAPTER 17

1 And Yhwh speaks to Moses, saying, **2** "Speak to the sons of Israel, and take a rod from each of them, for a father's house, from all their princes, for the house of their fathers—twelve rods; you write the name of each on his rod, **3** and you write Aaron's name on the tribe of Levi; for one rod [is] for the head of their fathers' house. **4** And you have placed them in the Tent of Meeting before the Testimony, where I meet with you. **5** And it has come to pass, the man's rod on whom I fix flourishes, and I have caused the murmurings of the sons of Israel, which they are murmuring against you, to cease from off Me." **6** And Moses speaks to the sons of Israel, and all their princes give to him one rod for a prince, one rod for a prince, for their fathers' house—twelve rods; and the rod of Aaron [is] in the midst of their rods; **7** and Moses places the rods before Yhwh in the Tent of the Testimony. **8** And it comes to pass, on the next day, that Moses goes into the Tent of the Testimony, and behold, the rod of Aaron has flourished for the house of Levi, and brings out a bud, and blossoms [with] a blossom, and produces almonds; **9** and Moses brings out all the rods from before Yhwh to all the sons of Israel, and they look, and each takes his rod. **10** And Yhwh says to Moses, "Put back the rod of Aaron before the Testimony, for a charge, for a sign to the sons of rebellion, and you remove their murmurings from off Me, and they do not die"; **11** and Moses does as Yhwh has commanded him; so he has done. **12** And the sons of Israel speak to Moses, saying, "Behold, we have expired, we have perished, all of us have perished! **13** Any who is at all drawing near to the Dwelling Place of Yhwh dies; have we not been consumed—to expire?"

CHAPTER 18

1 And Yhwh says to Aaron, "You, and your sons, and the house of your father with you, bear the iniquity of the sanctuary; and you and your sons with you bear the iniquity of your priesthood; **2** and also your brothers, the tribe of Levi, the tribe of your father, bring near with you, and they are joined to you, and serve you, even you and your sons with you, before the Tent of the Testimony. **3** And they have kept your charge, and the charge of all the tent; only, they do not come near to the vessels of the holy place and to the altar, and they do not die, either they or you; **4** and they have been joined to you and have kept the charge of the Tent of Meeting for all the service of the tent; and a stranger does not come near to you; **5** and you have kept the charge of the holy place and the charge of the altar, and there is no more wrath against the sons of Israel. **6** And I, behold, have taken your brothers the Levites from the midst of the sons of Israel; they are a gift given to you by Yhwh to do the service of the Tent of Meeting; **7** and you and your sons with you keep your priesthood for everything of the altar and within the veil, and you have served; I make your priesthood a gift [for] service; and the stranger who is coming near is put to death." **8** And Yhwh speaks to Aaron: "And I, behold, have given to you the charge of My raised-offerings, of all the hallowed things of the sons of Israel—I have given them to you and to your sons for the anointing, by a continuous statute. **9** This is yours from the most holy things, from the fire: all their offering, of all their present, and of all their sin-offering, and of all their guilt-offering, which they give back to Me, is most holy to you and to your sons; **10** you eat it among the most holy things; every male eats it; it is holy to you. **11** And this [is] yours: the raised-offering of their gift, with all the wave-offerings of the sons of Israel; I have given them to you, and to your sons, and to your daughters with you, by a continuous statute; every clean one in your house eats it; **12** all the best of the oil, and all the best of the new wine, and wheat—their first-[fruits] which they give to Yhwh—I have given them to you. **13** The first-fruits of all that [is] in their land, which they bring to Yhwh, are yours; every clean one in your house eats it; **14** every devoted thing in Israel is yours; **15** everyone opening a womb of all flesh which they bring near to Yhwh, among man and among beast, is yours; only, you certainly ransom the firstborn of man, and you ransom the firstling of the unclean beast. **16** And their ransomed ones from a son of a month, you ransom with your valuation [for] five shekels of silver, by the shekel of the holy place; it [is] twenty gerahs. **17** Only, the firstling of a cow, or the firstling of a sheep, or the firstling of a goat, you do not ransom, they [are] holy: you sprinkle their blood on the altar, and you make incense of their fat [as] a fire-offering of refreshing fragrance to Yhwh; **18** and their flesh is yours, as the breast of the wave-offering and as the right leg are yours. **19** All the raised-offerings of the holy things, which the sons of Israel lift up to Yhwh, I have given to you, and to your sons, and to your daughters with you, by a continuous statute—a covenant of salt; it [is] continuous before Yhwh to you and to your seed with you." **20** And Yhwh says to Aaron, "You do not inherit in their land, and you do not have a portion in their midst: I [am] your portion and your inheritance in the midst of the sons of Israel; **21** and to the sons of Levi, behold, have given all the tenth in Israel for inheritance in exchange for their service which they are serving—the service of the Tent of Meeting. **22** And the sons of Israel no longer come near to the Tent of Meeting, to bear sin, to die, **23** and the Levites have done the service of the Tent of Meeting, and they bear their iniquity; [it is] a continuous statute throughout your generations that they have no inheritance in the midst of the sons of Israel; **24** but the tithe of the sons of Israel which they lift up to Yhwh, a raised-offering, I have given to the Levites for inheritance; therefore I have said of them, They have no inheritance in the midst of the sons of Israel." **25** And Yhwh speaks to Moses, saying, **26** "And you speak to the Levites, and you have said to them: When you take the tithe from the sons of Israel which I have given to you from them for your inheritance, then you have lifted up the raised-offering of Yhwh from it, a tithe of the tithe; **27** and your raised-offering has been reckoned to you as grain from the threshing-floor and as the fullness from the wine-vat; **28** so you lift up—you also—the raised-offering of Yhwh from all your tithes which you receive from the sons of Israel; and you have given the raised-offering of Yhwh from it to Aaron the priest; **29** out of all your gifts you lift up every raised-offering of Yhwh, out of all its fat—its hallowed part—out of it. **30** And you have said to them: In your lifting up its fat out of it, then it has been reckoned to the Levites as increase of a threshing-floor and as increase of a wine-vat; **31** and you have eaten it in every place, you and your households, for it [is] your hire in exchange for your service in the Tent of Meeting; **32** and you bear no sin for it in your lifting up its fat out of it, but you do not defile the holy things of the sons of Israel, and you do not die."

CHAPTER 19

1 And Yhwh speaks to Moses and to Aaron, saying, **2** "This [is] a statute of the law which Yhwh has commanded, saying, Speak to the sons of Israel, and they bring a red cow to you, a perfect one, in which there is no blemish, on which no yoke has gone up; **3** and you have given it to Eleazar the priest, and he has brought it out to the outside of the camp, and has slaughtered it before him. **4** And Eleazar the priest has taken of its blood with his finger, and has sprinkled [it] toward the front of the face of the Tent of Meeting from its blood seven times; **5** and [one] has burned the cow before his eyes; her skin, and her flesh, and her blood, besides her dung, he burns; **6** and the priest has taken cedar wood, and hyssop, and scarlet, and has cast [them] into the midst of the burning of the cow; **7** and the priest has washed his garments, and has bathed his flesh with water, and afterward comes into the camp, and the priest is unclean until the evening; **8** and he who is burning it washes his garments with water, and has bathed his flesh with water, and is unclean until the evening. **9** And a clean man has gathered the ashes of the cow, and has placed [them] at the outside of the camp in a clean place, and it has become a charge for the congregation of the sons of Israel for waters of separation—it [is for] sin; **10** and he who is gathering the ashes of the heifer has washed his garments and is unclean until the evening; and it has been to the sons of Israel and to the sojourner who is sojourning in their midst for a continuous statute. **11** He who is coming against the dead body of any man is unclean [for] seven days; **12** he cleanses himself for it on the third day and on the seventh day, [and] he is clean; and if he does not cleanse himself on the third day and on the seventh day, he is not clean. **13** Anyone who is coming against the dead, against the body of man who dies, and does not cleanse himself, he has defiled the Dwelling Place of Yhwh, and that person has been cut off from Israel, for water of separation is not sprinkled on him; he is unclean; his uncleanness [is] still on him. **14** This [is] the law when a man dies in a tent: everyone who is coming into the tent and all that [is] in the tent are unclean [for] seven days; **15** and every open vessel which has no covering of thread on it is unclean. **16** And everyone on the face of the field who comes against the pierced of a sword, or against the dead, or against a bone of man, or against a grave, is unclean [for] seven days, **17** and for the unclean person they have taken from the ashes of the burning of the [cow], and he has put running water over it into a vessel; **18** and a clean person has taken hyssop, and has dipped [it] in water, and has sprinkled [it] on the tent, and on all the vessels, and on the persons who have been there, and on him who is coming against a bone, or against one pierced, or against the dead, or against a grave. **19** And the clean has sprinkled [it] on the unclean on the third day and on the seventh day, and has cleansed him on the seventh day, and he has washed his garments, and has bathed with water, and has been clean in the evening. **20** And the man who is unclean and does not cleanse himself, indeed, that person has been cut off from the midst of the assembly; for he has defiled the sanctuary of Yhwh; water of separation is not sprinkled on him; he [is] unclean. **21** And it has been for a continuous statute to them, that he who is sprinkling the water of separation washes his garments, and he who is coming against the water of separation is unclean until the evening, **22** and all against which the unclean person comes is unclean, and the person who is coming against [it] is unclean until the evening."

CHAPTER 20

1 And the sons of Israel, all the congregation, come [into] the wilderness of Zin in the first month, and the people abide in Kadesh; and Miriam dies there and is buried there. **2** And there has been no water for the congregation, and they are assembled against Moses and against Aaron, **3** and the people strive with Moses and speak, saying, "And oh that we had expired when our brothers expired before Yhwh! **4** and why have you brought in the assembly of Yhwh to this wilderness to die there, we and our beasts? **5** and why have you brought us up out of Egypt to bring us to this evil place? [It is] not a place of seed, and fig, and vine, and pomegranate; and there is no water to drink." **6** And Moses and Aaron go in from the presence of the assembly to the opening of the Tent of Meeting and fall on their faces, and the glory of Yhwh is seen by them. **7** And Yhwh speaks to Moses, saying, **8** "Take the rod and assemble the congregation—you and your brother Aaron—and you have spoken to the rock before their eyes, and it has given its water, and you have brought out water to them from the rock, and have watered the congregation and their beasts." **9** And Moses takes the rod from before Yhwh as He has commanded him, **10** and Moses and Aaron assemble the assembly to the front of the rock, and he says to them, "Now hear, O rebels, do we bring out water to you from this rock?" **11** and Moses lifts up his hand and strikes the rock with his rod twice; and much water comes out, and the congregation drinks, and their beasts [drink]. **12** And Yhwh says to Moses and to Aaron, "Because you have not believed in Me to sanctify Me before the eyes of the sons of Israel, therefore you do not bring in this assembly to the land which I have given to them." **13** These [are] the waters of Meribah, because the sons of Israel have "striven" with Yhwh, and He is sanctified among them. **14** And Moses sends messengers from Kadesh to the king of Edom, "Thus said your brother Israel: You have known all the travail which has found us, **15** that our fathers go down to Egypt, and we dwell in Egypt [for] many days, and the Egyptians do evil to us and to our fathers; **16** then we cry to Yhwh, and He hears our voice, and sends a Messenger, and is bringing us out of Egypt; and behold, we [are] in Kadesh, a city [in] the extremity of your border. **17** Please let us pass over through your land; we do not pass over through a field or through a vineyard, nor do we drink waters of a well; we go the way of the king, we do not turn aside [to] the right or left until we pass over your border." **18** And Edom says to him, "You do not pass over through me, lest I come out to meet you with the sword." **19** And the sons of Israel say to him, "We go in the highway, and if we drink of your waters—I and my livestock—then I have given their price; only, let me pass over on my feet, nothing [more]." **20** And he says, "You do not pass over"; and Edom comes out to meet him with many people and with a strong hand; **21** and Edom refuses to permit Israel to pass over through his border, and Israel turns aside from off him. **22** And the sons of Israel, all the congregation, journey from Kadesh and come to Mount Hor, **23** and Yhwh speaks to Moses and to Aaron in Mount Hor, on the border of the land of Edom, saying, **24** "Aaron is gathered to his people, for he does not go into the land which I have given to the sons of Israel, because that you provoked My mouth at the waters of Meribah. **25** Take Aaron and his son Eleazar, and cause them to go up Mount Hor, **26** and strip Aaron of his garments, and you have clothed his son Eleazar [with] them, and Aaron is gathered, and dies there." **27** And Moses does as Yhwh has commanded, and they go up to Mount Hor before the eyes of all the congregation, **28** and Moses strips Aaron of his garments, and clothes his son Eleazar with them, and Aaron dies there on the top of the mountain; and Moses comes down—Eleazar also—from the mountain, **29** and all the congregation sees that Aaron has expired, and all the house of Israel laments Aaron [for] thirty days.

coming out of the border of the Amorite, for Arnon [is] the border of Moab, between Moab and the Amorite; **14** therefore it is said in [the] scroll of the Wars of Yhwh: "Waheb in Suphah, || And the brooks of Arnon; **15** And the spring of the brooks, || Which turned aside to the dwelling of Ar, || And has leaned to the border of Moab." **16** And from there [they journeyed] to Beer; it [is] the well [concerning] which Yhwh said to Moses, "Gather the people, and I give water to them." **17** Then Israel sings this song: "Spring up, O well, || Let all answer to it! **18** A well—princes have dug it, || Nobles of the people have prepared it, || With the lawgiver, with their staffs." And from the wilderness [they journeyed] to Mattanah, **19** and from Mattanah to Nahaliel, and from Nahaliel to Bamoth, **20** and from Bamoth, in the valley which [is] in the field of Moab, [to] the top of Pisgah, which has looked on the front of the wilderness. **21** And Israel sends messengers to Sihon king of the Amorite, saying, **22** "Let me pass through your land, we do not turn aside into a field or into a vineyard; we do not drink waters of a well; we go in the king's way until we pass over your border." **23** And Sihon has not permitted Israel to pass through his border, and Sihon gathers all his people, and comes out to meet Israel in the wilderness, and comes to Jahaz, and fights against Israel. **24** And Israel strikes him by the mouth of the sword, and possesses his land from Arnon to Jabbok—to the sons of Ammon; for the border of the sons of Ammon [is] strong. **25** And Israel takes all these cities, and Israel dwells in all the cities of the Amorite, in Heshbon and in all its villages; **26** for Heshbon is a city of Sihon king of the Amorite, and he has fought against the former king of Moab, and takes all his land out of his hand as far as Arnon; **27** therefore those using allegories say: "Enter Heshbon, || Let the city of Sihon be built and ready, **28** For fire has gone out from Heshbon, || A flame from the city of Sihon, || It has consumed Ar of Moab, || Owners of the high places of Arnon. **29** Woe to you, O Moab, || You have perished, O people of Chemosh! He has given his sons [as] fugitives, || And his daughters into captivity, || To Sihon king of the Amorite! **30** And we shoot them; Heshbon has perished as far as Dibon, || And we make desolate as far as Nophah, || Which [is] as far as Medeba." **31** And Israel dwells in the land of the Amorite, **32** and Moses sends to spy out Jaazer, and they capture its villages, and dispossess the Amorite who [is] there, **33** and turn and go up the way of Bashan, and Og king of Bashan comes out to meet them, he and all his people, to battle [at] Edrei. **34** And Yhwh says to Moses, "Do not fear him, for into your hand I have given him, and all his people, and his land, and you have done to him as you have done to Sihon king of the Amorite, who is dwelling in Heshbon." **35** And they strike him, and his sons, and all his people, until he has no remnant left to him, and they possess his land.

CHAPTER 21

1 And the Canaanite, king of Arad, dwelling in the south, hears that Israel has come the way of the Atharim, and he fights against Israel, and takes [some] of them captive. **2** And Israel vows a vow to Yhwh and says, "If You certainly give this people into my hand, then I have devoted their cities"; **3** and Yhwh listens to the voice of Israel and gives up the Canaanite, and he devotes them and their cities, and calls the name of the place Hormah. **4** And they journey from Mount Hor, the way of the Red Sea, to go around the land of Edom, and the soul of the people is short in the way, **5** and the people speak against God and against Moses, "Why have you brought us up out of Egypt to die in a wilderness? for there is no bread, and there is no water, and our soul has been weary of this light bread." **6** And Yhwh sends the burning serpents among the people, and they bite the people, and many people of Israel die; **7** and the people come to Moses and say, "We have sinned, for we have spoken against Yhwh and against you; pray to Yhwh that He turns the serpent aside from us"; and Moses prays in behalf of the people. **8** And Yhwh says to Moses, "Make a burning [serpent] for yourself, and set it on an ensign; and it has been, everyone who is bitten and has seen it—he has lived." **9** And Moses makes a serpent of bronze, and sets it on the ensign, and it has been, if the serpent has bitten any man, and he has looked expectingly to the serpent of bronze—he has lived. **10** And the sons of Israel journey and encamp in Oboth. **11** And they journey from Oboth and encamp in Ije-Abarim, in the wilderness that [is] on the front of Moab, at the rising of the sun. **12** From there they have journeyed and encamp in the Valley of Zared. **13** From there they have journeyed and encamp beyond Arnon, which [is] in the wilderness which is

CHAPTER 22

1 And the sons of Israel journey and encamp in the plains of Moab beyond the Jordan, [by] Jericho. **2** And Balak son of Zippor sees all that Israel has done to the Amorite, **3** and Moab is exceedingly afraid of the presence of the people, for it [is] numerous; and Moab is distressed by the presence of the sons of Israel, **4** and Moab says to [the] elderly of Midian, "Now the assembly licks up all that is around us, as the ox licks up the green thing of the field." And Balak son of Zippor [is] king of Moab at that time, **5** and he sends messengers to Balaam son of Beor, to Pethor, which [is] by the River of the land of the sons of his people, to call for him, saying, "Behold, a people has come out of Egypt; behold, it has covered the eye of the land, and it is abiding in front of me; **6** and now, come, please curse this people for me, for it [is] mightier than I. It may be I prevail, [and] we strike it, and I cast it out from the land; for I have known that which you bless is blessed, and that which you curse is cursed." **7** And [the] elderly of Moab and [the] elderly of Midian go with divinations in their hand, and they come to Balaam and speak the words of Balak to him, **8** and he says to them, "Lodge here tonight, and I have brought you back word, as Yhwh speaks to me"; and the princes of Moab abide with Balaam. **9** And God comes to Balaam and says, "Who [are] these men with you?" **10** And Balaam says to God, "Balak, son of Zippor, king of Moab, has sent to me: **11** Behold, the people that is coming out from Egypt and covers the eye of the land—now come, pierce it for me; it may be I am able to fight against it and have cast it out"; **12** and God says to Balaam, "You do not go with them; you do not curse the people, for it

[is] blessed." **13** And Balaam rises in the morning and says to the princes of Balak, "Go to your land, for Yhwh is refusing to permit me to go with you"; **14** and the princes of Moab rise, and come to Balak, and say, "Balaam is refusing to come with us." **15** And Balak adds yet to send princes, more numerous and honored than these, **16** and they come to Balaam and say to him, "Thus said Balak son of Zippor: Please do not be withheld from coming to me, **17** for I honor you very greatly, and all that you say to me I do; and come, please pierce this people for me." **18** And Balaam answers and says to the servants of Balak, "If Balak gives to me the fullness of his house of silver and gold, I am not able to pass over the command of my God Yhwh, to do a little or a great thing; **19** and now, please abide in this [place], you also, tonight, then I know what Yhwh is adding to speak with me." **20** And God comes to Balaam by night and says to him, "If the men have come to call for you, rise, go with them, and only the thing which I speak to you—do it." **21** And Balaam rises in the morning, and saddles his donkey, and goes with the princes of Moab, **22** and the anger of God burns because he is going, and the Messenger of Yhwh stations Himself in the way for an adversary to him, and he is riding on his donkey, and two of his servants [are] with him, **23** and the donkey sees the Messenger of Yhwh standing in the way with His drawn sword in His hand, and the donkey turns aside out of the way and goes into a field, and Balaam strikes the donkey to turn it aside into the way. **24** And the Messenger of Yhwh stands in a narrow path of the vineyards, [with] a wall on this [side] and a wall on that [side], **25** and the donkey sees the Messenger of Yhwh, and is pressed to the wall, and presses Balaam's foot to the wall, and he adds to strike her; **26** and the Messenger of Yhwh adds to pass over, and stands in a narrow place where there is no way to turn aside [to] the right or left, **27** and the donkey sees the Messenger of Yhwh, and crouches under Balaam, and the anger of Balaam burns, and he strikes the donkey with a staff. **28** And Yhwh opens the mouth of the donkey, and she says to Balaam, "What have I done to you that you have struck me these three times?" **29** and Balaam says to the donkey, "Because you have rolled yourself against me; oh that there were a sword in my hand, for now I had slain you"; **30** and the donkey says to Balaam, "Am I not your donkey on which you have ridden since [I became] yours, even to this day? have I at all been accustomed to do thus to you?" And he says, "No." **31** And Yhwh uncovers the eyes of Balaam, and he sees the Messenger of Yhwh standing in the way with His drawn sword in His hand, and he bows and pays respect, to his face; **32** and the Messenger of Yhwh says to him, "Why have you struck your donkey these three times? behold, I have come out for an adversary, for [your] way has been perverse before Me, **33** and the donkey sees Me and turns aside at My presence these three times; unless she had turned aside from My presence, surely I had also slain you now, and kept her alive." **34** And Balaam says to the Messenger of Yhwh, "I have sinned, for I did not know that You [are] standing to meet me in the way; and now, if [it is] evil in Your eyes, I turn back by myself." **35** And the Messenger of Yhwh says to Balaam, "Go with the men; and only the word which I speak to you—it you speak"; and Balaam goes with the princes of Balak. **36** And Balak hears that Balaam has come, and goes out to meet him, to a city of Moab, which [is] on the border of Arnon, which [is] in the extremity of the border; **37** and Balak says to Balaam, "Did I not diligently send to you to call for you? why did you not come to me? am I not truly able to honor you?" **38** And Balaam says to Balak, "Behold, I have come to you; now, am I able to speak anything at all? the word which God sets in my mouth—it I speak." **39** And Balaam goes with Balak, and they come to Kirjath-Huzoth, **40** and Balak sacrifices oxen and sheep, and sends [some] to Balaam and to the princes who [are] with him; **41** and it comes to pass in the morning, that Balak takes Balaam and causes him to go up [to] the high places of Ba'al, and he sees the extremity of the people from there.

CHAPTER 23

1 And Balaam says to Balak, "Build seven altars for me in this [place], and prepare seven bullocks and seven rams for me in this [place]." **2** And Balak does as Balaam has spoken, and Balak—Balaam also—offers a bullock and a ram on the altar, **3** and Balaam says to Balak, "Station yourself by your burnt-offering and I go on, it may be Yhwh comes to meet me, and the thing which He shows me I have declared to you", and he goes [to] a high place. **4** And God comes to Balaam, and he says to Him, "I have arranged the seven altars, and I offer a bullock and a ram on the altar"; **5** and Yhwh puts a word in the mouth of Balaam and says, "Return to Balak, and thus you speak." **6** And he returns to him, and behold, he is standing by his burnt-offering, he and all the princes of Moab. **7** And he takes up his allegory and says: "Balak king of Moab leads me from Aram; From mountains of the east. Come—curse Jacob for me, || And come—be indignant [with] Israel. **8** How do I pierce [when] God has not pierced? And how am I indignant [when] Yhwh has not been indignant? **9** For from the top of rocks I see him, || And from heights I behold him; Behold a people! He dwells alone, || And does not reckon himself among nations. **10** Who has counted the dust of Jacob, || And the number of the fourth of Israel? Let me die the death of upright ones, || And let my last end be like his!" **11** And Balak says to Balaam, "What have you done to me? I have taken you to pierce my enemies, and behold, you have certainly blessed"; **12** and he answers and says, "That which Yhwh puts in my mouth—do I not take heed to speak it?" **13** And Balak says to him, "Come! Come to another place with me, from where you see it—you see only its extremity, and you do not see all of it, and pierce it for me there"; **14** and he takes him [to] the field of Zophim, to the top of Pisgah, and builds seven altars, and offers a bullock and a ram on the altar. **15** And he says to Balak, "Station yourself here by your burnt-offering, and I meet [Him] there"; **16** and Yhwh comes to Balaam, and sets a word in his mouth, and says, "Return to Balak, and thus you speak." **17** And he comes to him, and behold, he is standing by his burnt-offering, and the princes of Moab [are] with him, and Balak says to him: "What has Yhwh spoken?" **18** And he takes up his allegory and says: "Rise, Balak, and hear; Give ear to me, son of Zippor! **19** God [is] not a man—and lies, || And a son of man—and relents! Has He said—and He does not do [it]? And spoken—and He does not confirm it? **20** Behold, I have received [only] to bless; Indeed, He blesses, and I cannot reverse it. **21** He has not beheld iniquity in Jacob, || Nor has He seen perverseness in Israel; His God Yhwh [is] with him, || And a shout of a king [is] in him. **22** God is bringing them out from Egypt, || As the swiftness of a wild ox for him; **23** For no enchantment [is] against Jacob, || Nor divination against Israel; At the time it is said of Jacob and Israel, || O what God has worked! **24** Behold, the people rises as a lioness, || And he lifts himself up as a lion; He does not lie down until he eats prey, || And drinks blood of pierced ones." **25** And Balak says to Balaam, "Neither pierce it at all, nor bless it at all"; **26** and Balaam answers and says to Balak, "Have I not spoken to you, saying, All that Yhwh speaks—I do it?" **27** And Balak says to Balaam, "Please come, I take you to another place; it may be it is right in the eyes of God to pierce it for me from there." **28** And Balak takes Balaam to the top of Peor, which is looking on the front of the wilderness, **29** and Balaam says to Balak, "Build seven altars for me in this [place], and prepare seven bullocks and seven rams for me in this [place]"; **30** and Balak does as Balaam said, and he offers a bullock and a ram on an altar.

CHAPTER 24

1 And Balaam sees that [it is] good in the eyes of Yhwh to bless Israel, and he has not gone as time by time to seek enchantments, and he sets his face toward the wilderness; **2** and Balaam lifts up his eyes, and sees Israel dwelling by its tribes, and the Spirit of God is on him, **3** and he takes up his allegory and says: "An affirmation of Balaam son of Beor, || And an affirmation of the man whose eyes are shut, **4** An affirmation of him who is hearing sayings of God, || Who sees a vision of the Almighty, || Falling—and eyes uncovered: **5** How good have been your tents, O Jacob, || Your dwelling places, O Israel; **6** They have been stretched out as valleys, || As gardens by a river; As aloes Yhwh has planted, || As cedars by waters; **7** He makes water flow from his buckets, || And his seed [is] in many waters; And his King [is] higher than Gog [[or Agag]], || And his kingdom is exalted. **8** God is bringing him out of Egypt, || As the swiftness of a wild ox for him, || He eats up nations—his adversaries, || And he breaks their bones, || And he strikes [with] his arrows. **9** He has bent, he has lain down as a lion, || And as a lioness, who raises him up? He who is blessing you [is] blessed, || And he who is cursing you [is] cursed." **10** And the anger of Balak burns against Balaam, and he strikes his hands; and Balak says to Balaam, "I called you to pierce my enemies, and behold, you have certainly blessed these three times; **11** and now, flee for yourself to your place;

I have said, I greatly honor you, and behold, Yhwh has kept you back from honor." **12** And Balaam says to Balak, "Did I not also speak to your messengers whom you have sent to me, saying, **13** If Balak gives to me the fullness of his house of silver and gold, I am not able to pass over the command of Yhwh, to do good or evil of my own heart; that which Yhwh speaks—it I speak? **14** and now, behold, I am going to my people; come, I counsel you [concerning] that which this people does to your people in the latter end of the days." **15** And he takes up his allegory and says: "An affirmation of Balaam son of Beor, || And an affirmation of the man whose eyes [are] shut; **16** An affirmation of him who is hearing sayings of God, || And knowing knowledge of the Most High; He sees a vision of the Almighty, || Falling—and eyes uncovered: **17** I see Him, but not now; I behold Him, but not near; A star has proceeded from Jacob, || And a scepter has risen from Israel, || And has struck corners of Moab, || And has destroyed all sons of Seth. **18** And Edom has been a possession, || And Seir has been a possession [for] his enemies, || And Israel is doing valiantly; **19** And [One] rules out of Jacob, || And has destroyed a remnant from the city." **20** And he sees Amalek, and takes up his allegory, and says: "Amalek [is] first [among] nations, || But his latter end—destruction forever." **21** And he sees the Kenite, and takes up his allegory, and says: "Your dwelling [is] enduring, || And your nest is being set in a rock, **22** But the Kenite is for a burning; Until when does Asshur keep you captive?" **23** And he takes up his allegory and says: "Woe! Who lives when God does this? **24** But ships [come] from the side of Chittim, || And they have humbled Asshur, || And they have humbled Eber, || But it is also perishing forever." **25** And Balaam rises, and goes, and turns back to his place, and Balak has also gone on his way.

CHAPTER 25

1 And Israel dwells in Shittim, and the people begin to go whoring to daughters of Moab, **2** and they call for the people to the sacrifices of their gods, and the people eat and bow themselves to their gods, **3** and Israel is joined to Ba'al-Peor, and the anger of Yhwh burns against Israel. **4** And Yhwh says to Moses, "Take all the chiefs of the people and hang them before Yhwh in sight of the sun; and the fierceness of the anger of Yhwh turns back from Israel." **5** And Moses says to [the] judges of Israel, "Each slays his men who are joined to Ba'al-Peor." **6** And behold, a man of the sons of Israel has come, and brings a Midianitess to his brothers before the eyes of Moses and before the eyes of all the congregation of the sons of Israel, who are weeping at the opening of the Tent of Meeting; **7** and Phinehas, son of Eleazar, son of Aaron the priest, sees, and rises from the midst of the congregation, and takes a javelin in his hand, **8** and goes in after the man of Israel to the hollow place, and pierces them both, the man of Israel and the woman—to her belly, and the plague is restrained from the sons of Israel; **9** and the dead by the plague are twenty-four thousand. **10** And Yhwh speaks to Moses, saying, **11** "Phinehas, son of Eleazar, son of Aaron the priest, has turned back My fury from the sons of Israel by his being zealous with My zeal in their midst, and I have not consumed the sons of Israel in My zeal. **12** Therefore say, Behold, I am giving My covenant of peace to him, **13** and it has been to him and to his seed after him [for] a covenant of a continuous priesthood, because that he has been zealous for his God, and makes atonement for the sons of Israel." **14** And the name of the man of Israel who is struck, who has been struck with the Midianitess, [is] Zimri son of Salu, prince of the house of a father of the Simeonite; **15** and the name of the woman who is struck, the Midianitess, [is] Cozbi daughter of Zur; he [is] head of peoples of a father's house in Midian. **16** And Yhwh speaks to Moses, saying, **17** "Distress the Midianites, and you have struck them, **18** for they are adversaries to you with their frauds, [with] which they have acted fraudulently to you, concerning the matter of Peor and concerning the matter of Cozbi, daughter of a prince of Midian, their sister, who is struck in the day of the plague for the matter of Peor."

CHAPTER 26

1 And it comes to pass, after the plague, that Yhwh speaks to Moses and to Eleazar son of Aaron the priest, saying, **2** "Take a census of all the congregation of the sons of Israel, from a son of twenty years and upward, by the house of their fathers, everyone going out to the host in Israel." **3** And Moses speaks—Eleazar the priest also—with them in the plains of Moab by the Jordan, [near] Jericho, saying, **4** "From a son of twenty years and upward," as Yhwh has commanded Moses and the sons of Israel who are coming out from the land of Egypt. **5** Reuben, firstborn of Israel—sons of Reuben: of Enoch [is] the family of the Enochite; of Pallu the family of the Palluite; **6** of Hezron the family of the Hezronite; of Carmi the family of the Carmite. **7** These [are] families of the Reubenite, and their numbered ones are forty-three thousand and seven hundred and thirty. **8** And the son of Pallu [is] Eliab; **9** and the sons of Eliab [are] Nemuel, and Dathan, and Abiram; this [is that] Dathan and Abiram, called ones of the congregation, who have striven against Moses and against Aaron in the congregation of Korah, in their striving against Yhwh, **10** and the earth opens her mouth, and swallows them and Korah, in the death of the congregation, in the fire consuming the two hundred and fifty men, and they become a sign; **11** but the sons of Korah did not die. **12** Sons of Simeon by their families: of Nemuel [is] the family of the Nemuelite; of Jamin the family of the Jaminite; of Jachin the family of the Jachinite; **13** of Zerah the family of the Zerahite; of Shaul the family of the Shaulite. **14** These [are] families of the Simeonite—twenty-two thousand and two hundred. **15** Sons of Gad by their families: of Zephon [is] the family of the Zephonite; of Haggi the family of the Haggite; of Shuni the family of the Shunite; **16** of Ozni the family of the Oznite; of Eri the family of the Erite: **17** of Arod the family of the Arodite; of Areli the family of the Arelite. **18** These [are] families of the sons of Gad by their numbered ones—forty thousand and five hundred. **19** Sons of Judah [are] Er and Onan; and Er dies—Onan also—in the land of Canaan. **20** And sons of Judah by their families are: of Shelah the family of the Shelanite; of Perez the family of the Perezite; of Zerah the family of the Zerahite; **21** and sons of Perez are: of Hezron the family of the Hezronite; of Hamul the family of the Hamulite. **22** These [are] families of Judah by their numbered ones—seventy-six thousand and five hundred. **23** Sons of Issachar by their families: of Tola [is] the family of the Tolaite; of Pua the family of the Punite; **24** of Jashub the family of the Jashubite; of Shimron the family of the Shimronite. **25** These [are] families of Issachar by their numbered ones—sixty-four thousand and three hundred. **26** Sons of Zebulun by their families: of Sered [is] the family of the Sardite; of Elon the family of the Elonite; of Jahleel the family of the Jahleelite. **27** These [are] families of the Zebulunite by their numbered ones—sixty thousand and five hundred. **28** Sons of Joseph by their families [are] Manasseh and Ephraim. **29** Sons of Manasseh: of Machir [is] the family of the Machirite; and Machir has begotten Gilead; of Gilead [is] the family of the Gileadite. **30** These [are] sons of Gilead: of Jeezer [is] the family of the Jeezerite; of Helek the family of the Helekite; **31** and of Asriel the family of the Asrielite; and of Shechem the family of the Shechemite; **32** and of Shemida the family of the Shemidaite; and of Hepher the family of the Hepherite. **33** And Zelophehad son of Hepher had no sons, but [only] daughters, and the names of the daughters of Zelophehad [are] Mahlah, and Noah, Hoglah, Milcah, and Tirzah. **34** These [are] families of Manasseh, and their numbered ones [are] fifty-two thousand and seven hundred. **35** These [are] sons of Ephraim by their families: of Shuthelah [is] the family of the Shuthelhite; of Becher the family of the Bachrite; of Tahan the family of the Tahanite. **36** And these [are] sons of Shuthelah: of Eran the family of the Eranite. **37** These [are] families of the sons of Ephraim by their numbered ones—thirty-two thousand and five hundred. These [are] sons of Joseph by their families. **38** Sons of Benjamin by their families: of Bela [is] the family of the Belaite; of Ashbel the family of the Ashbelite; of Ahiram the family of the Ahiramite; **39** of Shupham the family of the Shuphamite; of Hupham family of the Huphamite. **40** And sons of Bela are Ard and Naaman: [of Ard is] the family of the Ardite; of Naaman the family of the Naamite. **41** These [are] sons of Benjamin by their families, and their numbered ones [are] forty-five thousand and six hundred. **42** These [are] sons of Dan by their families: of Shuham [is] the family of the Shuhamite; these [are] families of Dan by their families; **43** all the families of the Shuhamite by their numbered ones—sixty-four thousand and four hundred. **44** Sons of Asher by their families: of Jimna [is] the family of the Jimnite; of Jesui the family of the Jesuite; of Beriah the family of the Beriite. **45** Of sons of Beriah: of Heber [is] the family of the Heberite; of Malchiel the family of the Malchielite. **46** And the name of the daughter of Asher [is]

Sarah. **47** These [are] families of the sons of Asher by their numbered ones—fifty-three thousand and four hundred. **48** Sons of Naphtali by their families: of Jahzeel [is] the family of the Jahzeelite; of Guni the family of the Gunite; **49** of Jezer the family of the Jezerite; of Shillem the family of the Shillemite. **50** These [are] families of Naphtali by their families, and their numbered ones [are] forty-five thousand and four hundred. **51** These [are] numbered ones of the sons of Israel—six hundred thousand and one thousand seven hundred and thirty. **52** And Yhwh speaks to Moses, saying, **53** "The land is apportioned to these by inheritance, by the number of names; **54** to the many you increase their inheritance, and to the few you diminish their inheritance; each is given his inheritance according to his numbered ones. **55** Surely the land is apportioned by lot; they inherit by the names of the tribes of their fathers; **56** their inheritance is apportioned according to the lot between many and few." **57** And these [are] numbered ones of the Levite by their families: of Gershon [is] the family of the Gershonite; of Kohath the family of the Kohathite; of Merari the family of the Merarite. **58** These [are] families of the Levite: the family of the Libnite, the family of the Hebronite, the family of the Mahlite, the family of the Mushite, the family of the Korathite. And Kohath has begotten Amram, **59** and the name of Amram's wife is Jochebed, daughter of Levi, whom has been born to Levi in Egypt; and she bears to Amram Aaron, and Moses, and their sister Miriam. **60** And born to Aaron [are] Nadab, and Abihu, Eleazar, and Ithamar; **61** and Nadab dies—Abihu also—in their bringing strange fire near before Yhwh. **62** And their numbered ones are twenty-three thousand, every male from a son of a month and upwards, for they have not numbered themselves in the midst of the sons of Israel, because an inheritance has not been given to them in the midst of the sons of Israel. **63** These [are] those numbered by Moses and Eleazar the priest, who have numbered the sons of Israel in the plains of Moab by the Jordan, [near] Jericho; **64** and among these there has not been a man of those numbered by Moses and Aaron the priest, who numbered the sons of Israel in the wilderness of Sinai, **65** for Yhwh said of them, "They certainly die in the wilderness"; and there has not been left a man of them, except Caleb son of Jephunneh and Joshua son of Nun.

CHAPTER 27

1 And daughters of Zelophehad son of Hepher, son of Gilead, son of Machir, son of Manasseh, of the families of Manasseh son of Joseph, draw near—and these [are] the names of his daughters: Mahlah, Noah, and Hoglah, and Milcah, and Tirzah— **2** and stand before Moses, and before Eleazar the priest, and before the princes, and all the congregation, at the opening of the Tent of Meeting, saying, **3** "Our father died in the wilderness, and he was not in the midst of the congregation who were gathered together against Yhwh in the congregation of Korah, but he died for his own sin, and had no sons; **4** why is the name of our father withdrawn from the midst of his family because he has no son? give a possession to us in the midst of the brothers of our father"; **5** and Moses brings their cause near before Yhwh. **6** And Yhwh speaks to Moses, saying, **7** "The daughters of Zelophehad are speaking correctly; you certainly give to them a possession of an inheritance in the midst of their father's brothers, and have caused the inheritance of their father to pass over to them. **8** And you speak to the sons of Israel, saying, When a man dies and has no son, then you have caused his inheritance to pass over to his daughter; **9** and if he has no daughter, then you have given his inheritance to his brothers; **10** and if he has no brothers, then you have given his inheritance to his father's brothers; **11** and if his father has no brothers, then you have given his inheritance to his relation who is near to him of his family, and he has possessed it"; and it has been to the sons of Israel for a statute of judgment, as Yhwh has commanded Moses. **12** And Yhwh says to Moses, "Go up to this Mount Abarim, and see the land which I have given to the sons of Israel; **13** and you have seen it, and you have been gathered to your people, also you, as your brother Aaron has been gathered, **14** because you provoked My mouth in the wilderness of Zin, in the strife of the congregation—to sanctify Me at the waters before their eyes"; they [are] the waters of Meribah, in Kadesh, in the wilderness of Zin. **15** And Moses speaks to Yhwh, saying, **16** "Yhwh, God of the spirits of all flesh, appoint a man over the congregation, **17** who goes out before them, and who comes in before them, and who takes them out, and who brings

them in, and the congregation of Yhwh is not as sheep which have no shepherd." **18** And Yhwh says to Moses, "Take Joshua son of Nun to yourself, a man in whom [is] the Spirit, and you have laid your hand on him, **19** and have caused him to stand before Eleazar the priest and before all the congregation, and have charged him before their eyes, **20** and have put of your splendor on him, so that all the congregation of the sons of Israel listens. **21** And he stands before Eleazar the priest, and he has inquired before Yhwh for him by the judgment of the Lights; at his word they go out, and at his word they come in, he and all the sons of Israel with him—even all the congregation." **22** And Moses does as Yhwh has commanded him, and takes Joshua and causes him to stand before Eleazar the priest and before all the congregation, **23** and lays his hands on him and charges him, as Yhwh has spoken by the hand of Moses.

CHAPTER 28

1 And Yhwh speaks to Moses, saying, **2** "Command the sons of Israel, and you have said to them: My offering, My bread for My fire-offerings, My refreshing fragrance, you take heed to bring near to Me in its appointed time. **3** And you have said to them: This [is] the fire-offering which you bring near to Yhwh: two lambs, sons of a year, perfect ones, daily, [for] a continual burnt-offering; **4** you prepare the first lamb in the morning, and you prepare the second lamb between the evenings; **5** and a tenth of the ephah of flour for a present mixed with a fourth of the hin of beaten oil; **6** [it is] a continual burnt-offering, which was made in Mount Sinai for refreshing fragrance, [for] a fire-offering to Yhwh. **7** And its drink-offering [is] a fourth of the hin for one lamb; pour out a drink-offering of strong drink to Yhwh in the holy place. **8** And you prepare the second lamb between the evenings; as the present of the morning and as its drink-offering, you prepare [it as] a fire-offering of refreshing fragrance to Yhwh. **9** And on the Sabbath day, two lambs, sons of a year, perfect ones, and two-tenth parts of flour, a present mixed with oil, and its drink-offering— **10** the burnt-offering of the Sabbath in its Sabbath, besides the continual burnt-offering and its drink-offering. **11** And in the beginnings of your months you bring a burnt-offering near to Yhwh: two bullocks, sons of the herd, and one ram, seven lambs, sons of a year, perfect ones; **12** and three-tenth parts of flour, a present mixed with oil, for one bullock, and two-tenth parts of flour, a present mixed with oil, for one ram; **13** and a tenth—a tenth part of flour, a present mixed with oil, for one lamb, [for] a burnt-offering, a refreshing fragrance, a fire-offering to Yhwh; **14** and their drink-offerings are a half of the hin for a bullock, and a third of the hin for a ram, and a fourth of the hin for a lamb, of wine; this [is] the burnt-offering of every month for the months of the year. **15** And one kid of the goats is prepared for a sin-offering to Yhwh, besides the continual burnt-offering and its drink-offering. **16** And in the first month, on the fourteenth day of the month, [is] the Passover to Yhwh; **17** and in the fifteenth day of this month [is] a festival; [for] seven days unleavened bread is eaten. **18** In the first day [is] a holy convocation; you do no servile work; **19** and you have brought a fire-offering near, a burnt-offering to Yhwh: two bullocks, sons of the herd, and one ram, and seven lambs, sons of a year, they are perfect ones for you; **20** and their present of flour mixed with oil—you prepare three-tenth parts for a bullock and two-tenth parts for a ram; **21** you prepare a tenth—a tenth part for one lamb, for the seven lambs, **22** and one goat [for] a sin-offering, to make atonement for you. **23** Apart from the burnt-offering of the morning, which [is] for the continual burnt-offering, you prepare these; **24** like these you prepare bread of a fire-offering daily [for] seven days, a refreshing fragrance to Yhwh; it is prepared besides the continual burnt-offering and its drink-offering. **25** And on the seventh day you have a holy convocation; you do no servile work. **26** And on the day of the first-fruits, in your bringing a new present near to Yhwh, in your weeks, you have a holy convocation; you do no servile work. **27** And you have brought a burnt-offering near for refreshing fragrance to Yhwh: two bullocks, sons of the herd, one ram, seven lambs, sons of a year, **28** and their present, flour mixed with oil, three-tenth parts for one bullock, two-tenth parts for one ram, **29** a tenth—a tenth part for one lamb, for the seven lambs; **30** one kid of the goats to make atonement for you; **31** apart from the continual burnt-offering and its present, you prepare [them] and their drink-offerings; they are perfect ones for you."

CHAPTER 29

[1] "And in the seventh month, on the first of the month, you have a holy convocation; you do no servile work; it is a day of shouting to you; [2] and you have prepared a burnt-offering for refreshing fragrance to Yhwh: one bullock, a son of the herd, one ram, seven lambs, sons of a year, perfect ones; [3] and their present of flour mixed with oil: three-tenth parts for the bullock, two-tenth parts for the ram, [4] and one-tenth part for one lamb, for the seven lambs; [5] and one kid of the goats [for] a sin-offering, to make atonement for you; [6] apart from the burnt-offering of the month and its present, and the continual burnt-offering and its present, and their drink-offerings, according to their ordinance, for refreshing fragrance, a fire-offering to Yhwh. [7] And on the tenth of this seventh month you have a holy convocation, and you have humbled your souls; you do no work; [8] and you have brought a burnt-offering near to Yhwh, a refreshing fragrance: one bullock, a son of the herd, one ram, seven lambs, sons of a year; they are perfect ones for you; [9] and their present of flour mixed with oil: three-tenth parts for the bullock, two-tenth parts for one ram, [10] a tenth—a tenth part for one lamb, for the seven lambs, [11] one kid of the goats [for] a sin-offering, apart from the sin-offering of the atonements, and the continual burnt-offering and its present, and their drink-offerings. [12] And on the fifteenth day of the seventh month you have a holy convocation; you do no servile work; and you have celebrated a festival to Yhwh [for] seven days, [13] and have brought a burnt-offering near, a fire-offering of refreshing fragrance, to Yhwh: thirteen bullocks, sons of the herd, two rams, fourteen lambs, sons of a year; they are perfect ones; [14] and their present of flour mixed with oil: three-tenth parts for one bullock, for the thirteen bullocks, two-tenth parts for one ram, for the two rams, [15] and a tenth—a tenth part for one lamb, for the fourteen lambs; [16] and one kid of the goats [for] a sin-offering, apart from the continual burnt-offering, its present, and its drink-offering. [17] And on the second day: twelve bullocks, sons of the herd, two rams, fourteen lambs, sons of a year, perfect ones; [18] and their present and their drink-offerings for the bullocks, for the rams, and for the sheep, in their number, according to the ordinance; [19] and one kid of the goats [for] a sin-offering, apart from the continual burnt-offering, and its present, and their drink-offerings. [20] And on the third day: eleven bullocks, two rams, fourteen lambs, sons of a year, perfect ones; [21] and their present and their drink-offerings for the bullocks, for the rams, and for the lambs, in their number, according to the ordinance; [22] and one goat [for] a sin-offering, apart from the continual burnt-offering, and its present, and its drink-offering. [23] And on the fourth day: ten bullocks, two rams, fourteen lambs, sons of a year, perfect ones; [24] their present and their drink-offerings for the bullocks, for the rams, and for the lambs, in their number, according to the ordinance; [25] and one kid of the goats [for] a sin-offering, apart from the continual burnt-offering, its present, and its drink-offering. [26] And on the fifth day: nine bullocks, two rams, fourteen lambs, sons of a year, perfect ones; [27] and their present and their drink-offerings for the bullocks, for the rams, and for the lambs, in their number, according to the ordinance; [28] and one goat [for] a sin-offering, apart from the continual burnt-offering, and its present, and its drink-offering. [29] And on the sixth day: eight bullocks, two rams, fourteen lambs, sons of a year, perfect ones; [30] and their present and their drink-offerings for the bullocks, for the rams, and for the lambs, in their number, according to the ordinance; [31] and one goat [for] a sin-offering, apart from the continual burnt-offering, its present, and its drink-offering. [32] And on the seventh day: seven bullocks, two rams, fourteen lambs, sons of a year, perfect ones; [33] and their present and their drink-offerings for the bullocks, for the rams, and for the lambs, in their number, according to the ordinance; [34] and one goat [for] a sin-offering, apart from the continual burnt-offering, its present, and its drink-offering. [35] On the eighth day you have a restraint; you do no servile work; [36] and you have brought a burnt-offering near, a fire-offering of refreshing fragrance, to Yhwh: one bullock, one ram, seven lambs, sons of a year, perfect ones; [37] their present and their drink-offerings for the bullock, for the ram, and for the lambs, in their number, according to the ordinance; [38] and one goat [for] a sin-offering, apart from the continual burnt-offering, and its present, and its drink-offering. [39] You prepare these to Yhwh in your appointed times—apart from your vows and your free-will offerings—for your burnt-offerings, and for your presents, and for your drink-offerings, and for your peace-offerings." [40] And Moses speaks to the sons of Israel according to all that Yhwh has commanded Moses.

CHAPTER 30

[1] And Moses speaks to the heads of the tribes of the sons of Israel, saying, "This [is] the thing which Yhwh has commanded: [2] When a man vows a vow to Yhwh, or has sworn an oath to bind a bond on his soul, he does not defile his word; he does according to all that is going out from his mouth. [3] And when a woman vows a vow to Yhwh, and has bound a bond in the house of her father in her youth, [4] and her father has heard her vow and her bond which she has bound on her soul, and her father has kept silent to her, then all her vows have been established, and every bond which she has bound on her soul is established. [5] And if her father has disallowed her in the day of his hearing, none of her vows and her bonds which she has bound on her soul are established, and Yhwh is propitious to her, for her father has disallowed her. [6] And if she is having a husband, and her vows [are] on her, or a wrongful utterance [on] her lips which she has bound on her soul, [7] and her husband has heard, and in the day of his hearing he has kept silent to her, then her vows have been established, and her bonds which she has bound on her soul are established. [8] And if in the day of her husband's hearing he disallows her, then he has broken her vow which [is] on her, and the wrongful utterance of her lips which she has bound on her soul, and Yhwh is propitious to her. [9] As for the vow of a widow or cast-out woman, all that she has bound on her soul is established on her. [10] And if she has vowed [in] the house of her husband, or has bound a bond on her soul with an oath, [11] and her husband has heard, and has kept silent to her—he has not disallowed her—then all her vows have been established, and every bond which she has bound on her soul is established. [12] And if her husband certainly breaks them in the day of his hearing, none of the outgoing of her lips concerning her vows, or concerning the bond of her soul, is established—her husband has broken them—and Yhwh is propitious to her. [13] Every vow and every oath—a bond to humble a soul—her husband establishes it, or her husband breaks it; [14] and if her husband certainly keeps silent to her from day to day, then he has established all her vows or all her bonds which [are] on her; he has established them, for he has kept silent to her in the day of his hearing; [15] and if he indeed breaks them after his hearing, then he has borne her iniquity." [16] These [are] the statutes which Yhwh has commanded Moses between a man and his wife, between a father and his daughter, in her youth, [in] the house of her father.

CHAPTER 31

[1] And Yhwh speaks to Moses, saying, [2] "Execute the vengeance of the sons of Israel against the Midianites—afterward you are gathered to your people." [3] And Moses speaks to the people, saying, "Arm men from [among] you for the war, and they are against Midian, to put the vengeance of Yhwh on Midian; [4] one thousand for a tribe—you send one thousand for a tribe, of all the tribes of Israel, to the war." [5] And there are given out of the thousands of Israel one thousand for a tribe—twelve thousand armed ones [for] war; [6] and Moses sends them, one thousand for a tribe, to the war; [he sent] them and Phinehas son of Eleazar the priest to the war, with the holy vessels and the trumpets of shouting in his hand. [7] And they war against Midian, as Yhwh has commanded Moses, and slay every male; [8] and they have slain the kings of Midian besides their pierced ones: Evi, and Rekem, and Zur, and Hur, and Reba—five kings of Midian; and they have slain Balaam son of Beor with the sword. [9] And the sons of Israel take the women of Midian and their infants captive; and they have plundered all their livestock, and all their substance, and all their wealth; [10] and they have burned all their cities, with their habitations, and all their towers, with fire. [11] And they take all the spoil and all the prey, among man and among beast; [12] and they bring in the captives, and the prey, and the spoil to Moses, and to Eleazar the priest, and to the congregation of the sons of Israel, to the camp, to the plains of Moab, which [are] by the Jordan, [near] Jericho. [13] And

Moses, and Eleazar the priest, and all the princes of the congregation, go out to meet them, to the outside of the camp, ¹⁴ and Moses is angry against the inspectors of the force, chiefs of the thousands, and chiefs of the hundreds, who are coming in from the warfare of battle. ¹⁵ And Moses says to them, "Have you kept every female alive? ¹⁶ behold, they have been to the sons of Israel, through the word of Balaam, to cause a trespass against Yhwh in the matter of Peor, and the plague is in the congregation of Yhwh. ¹⁷ And now, slay every male among the infants, indeed, slay every woman knowing a man by the lying of a male; ¹⁸ and all the infants among the women who have not known the lying of a male you have kept alive for yourselves. ¹⁹ And you, encamp at the outside of the camp [for] seven days; any who has slain a person, and any who has come against a pierced one, cleanse yourselves on the third day and on the seventh day—you and your captives; ²⁰ and every garment, and every skin vessel, and every work of goats' [hair], and every wooden vessel, you yourselves cleanse." ²¹ And Eleazar the priest says to the men of war who go to battle, "This [is] the statute of the law which Yhwh has commanded Moses: ²² only the gold, and the silver, the bronze, the iron, the tin, and the lead, ²³ everything which may go into fire, you cause to pass over through fire, and it has been clean; it is surely cleansed with the water of separation; and all that may not go into fire, you cause to pass over through water; ²⁴ and you have washed your garments on the seventh day and have been clean, and afterward you come into the camp." ²⁵ And Yhwh speaks to Moses, saying, ²⁶ "Take up the sum of the prey of the captives, among man and among beast, you, and Eleazar the priest, and the heads of the fathers of the congregation; ²⁷ and you have halved the prey between those handling the battle, who go out to the war, and all the congregation; ²⁸ and you have raised a tribute to Yhwh from the men of battle, who go out to the war, one body out of five hundred, of man, and of the herd, and of the donkeys, and of the flock; ²⁹ you take from their half and have given [it] to Eleazar the priest [as] a raised-offering of Yhwh. ³⁰ And from the sons of Israel's half you take one possession out of fifty, of man, of the herd, of the donkeys, and of the flock, of all the livestock, and you have given them to the Levites keeping the charge of the Dwelling Place of Yhwh." ³¹ And Moses does—Eleazar the priest also—as Yhwh has commanded Moses. ³² And the prey, the remainder of the spoil which the people of the host have spoiled, is six hundred thousand and seventy thousand and five thousand of the flock; ³³ and seventy-two thousand of the herd; ³⁴ and sixty-one thousand donkeys; ³⁵ and of mankind—of the women who have not known the lying of a male—all the persons [are] thirty-two thousand. ³⁶ And the half, the portion of those who go out into the war, is [in] number three hundred thousand and thirty thousand and seven thousand and five hundred of the flock. ³⁷ And the tribute to Yhwh of the sheep is six hundred seventy-five; ³⁸ and the herd [is] thirty-six thousand, and their tribute to Yhwh [is] seventy-two; ³⁹ and the donkeys [are] thirty thousand and five hundred, and their tribute to Yhwh [is] sixty-one; ⁴⁰ and of mankind [are] sixteen thousand, and their tribute to Yhwh [is] thirty-two persons. ⁴¹ And Moses gives the tribute—Yhwh's raised-offering—to Eleazar the priest, as Yhwh has commanded Moses. ⁴² And of the sons of Israel's half, which Moses halved from the men who war— ⁴³ and the congregation's half is three hundred thousand and thirty thousand [and] seven thousand and five hundred of the flock; ⁴⁴ and thirty-six thousand of the herd; ⁴⁵ and thirty thousand and five hundred donkeys; ⁴⁶ and sixteen thousand of mankind— ⁴⁷ Moses takes from the sons of Israel's half one possession from the fifty, of man and of beast, and gives them to the Levites keeping the charge of the Dwelling Place of Yhwh, as Yhwh has commanded Moses. ⁴⁸ And the inspectors whom the thousands of the host have (heads of the thousands and heads of the hundreds), draw near to Moses, ⁴⁹ and they say to Moses, "Your servants have taken up the sum of the men of war who [are] with us, and not a man of us has been missed; ⁵⁰ and we bring Yhwh's offering near, each of that which he has found of vessels of gold—chain, and bracelet, seal-ring, [ear]-ring, and bead—to make atonement for ourselves before Yhwh." ⁵¹ And Moses receives—Eleazar the priest also—the gold from them, every vessel of workmanship; ⁵² and all the gold of the raised-offering which they have lifted up to Yhwh is sixteen thousand seven hundred and fifty shekels, from heads of the thousands and from heads of the hundreds; ⁵³ (the men of the host have each taken spoil for himself); ⁵⁴ and Moses takes—Eleazar the priest also—the gold from the heads of the thousands and of the hundreds, and they

bring it into the Tent of Meeting [as] a memorial for the sons of Israel before Yhwh.

CHAPTER 32

¹ And much livestock has [belonged] to the sons of Reuben and to the sons of Gad—very many; and they see the land of Jazer and the land of Gilead, and behold, the place [is] a place [for] livestock; ² and the sons of Gad and the sons of Reuben come in and speak to Moses, and to Eleazar the priest, and to the princes of the congregation, saying, ³ "Ataroth, and Dibon, and Jazer, and Nimrah, and Heshbon, and Elealeh, and Shebam, and Nebo, and Beon, ⁴ the land which Yhwh has struck before the congregation of Israel, is a land for livestock, and your servants have livestock." ⁵ And they say, "If we have found grace in your eyes, let this land be given to your servants for a possession; cause us not to pass over the Jordan." ⁶ And Moses says to the sons of Gad and to the sons of Reuben, "Do your brothers go to the battle, and you—do you sit here? ⁷ and why discourage the heart of the sons of Israel from passing over to the land which Yhwh has given to them? ⁸ Thus your fathers did in my sending them from Kadesh-Barnea to see the land; ⁹ and they go up to the Valley of Eshcol, and see the land, and discourage the heart of the sons of Israel so as not to go into the land which Yhwh has given to them; ¹⁰ and the anger of Yhwh burns in that day, and He swears, saying, ¹¹ They do not see—the men who are coming up out of Egypt from a son of twenty years and upward—the ground which I have sworn to Abraham, to Isaac, and to Jacob, for they have not been fully after Me, ¹² except Caleb son of Jephunneh the Kenezite and Joshua son of Nun, for they have been fully after Yhwh; ¹³ and the anger of Yhwh burns against Israel, and He causes them to wander in the wilderness [for] forty years, until the consumption of all the generation which is doing evil in the eyes of Yhwh. ¹⁴ And behold, you have risen in the stead of your fathers, an increase of sinful men, to add yet to the fury of the anger of Yhwh toward Israel; ¹⁵ when you turn back from after Him, then He has added yet to leave him in the wilderness, and you have done corruptly to all this people." ¹⁶ And they come near to him and say, "We build folds for the flock here for our livestock, and cities for our infants; ¹⁷ but we are armed, hastening before the sons of Israel until we have brought them to their place; and our infants have dwelt in the cities of defense because of the inhabitants of the land; ¹⁸ we do not return to our houses until the sons of Israel have each inherited his inheritance, ¹⁹ for we do not inherit with them across the Jordan and beyond, for our inheritance has come to us beyond the Jordan at the [sun]-rising." ²⁰ And Moses says to them, "If you do this thing, if you are armed before Yhwh for battle, ²¹ and every armed one of you has passed over the Jordan before Yhwh, until His dispossessing His enemies from before Him, ²² and the land has been subdued before Yhwh, then afterward you return, and have been acquitted by Yhwh and by Israel, and this land has been to you for a possession before Yhwh. ²³ And if you do not do so, behold, you have sinned against Yhwh, and know that your sin finds you; ²⁴ build for yourselves cities for your infants and folds for your flock, and that which is going out from your mouth you do." ²⁵ And the sons of Gad and the sons of Reuben speak to Moses, saying, "Your servants do as my lord is commanding; ²⁶ our infants, our wives, our livestock, and all our beasts, are there in cities of Gilead, ²⁷ and your servants pass over, every armed one of the host, before Yhwh, to battle, as my lord is saying." ²⁸ And Moses commands Eleazar the priest, and Joshua son of Nun, and the heads of the fathers of the tribes of the sons of Israel concerning them; ²⁹ and Moses says to them, "If the sons of Gad and the sons of Reuben pass over the Jordan with you, everyone armed for battle, before Yhwh, and the land has been subdued before you, then you have given the land of Gilead to them for a possession; ³⁰ and if they do not pass over armed with you, then they have possessions in your midst in the land of Canaan." ³¹ And the sons of Gad and the sons of Reuben answer, saying, "That which Yhwh has spoken to your servants, so we do; ³² we pass over armed before Yhwh [to] the land of Canaan, and with us [is] the possession of our inheritance beyond the Jordan." ³³ And Moses gives to them—to the sons of Gad, and to the sons of Reuben, and to the half of the tribe of Manasseh son of Joseph—the kingdom of Sihon king of the Amorite and the kingdom of Og king of Bashan, the land by its cities, in the borders, the cities of the surrounding land. ³⁴ And the sons of Gad build Dibon, and Ataroth, and Aroer, ³⁵ and

Atroth, Shophan, and Jaazer, and Jogbehah, **36** and Beth-Nimrah, and Beth-Haran, cities of defense, and sheepfolds. **37** And the sons of Reuben have built Heshbon, and Elealeh, and Kirjathaim, **38** and Nebo, and Ba'al-Meon (changed in name), and Shibmah, and they call the names of the cities which they have built by [these] names. **39** And sons of Machir son of Manasseh go to Gilead, and capture it, and dispossess the Amorite who [is] in it; **40** and Moses gives Gilead to Machir son of Manasseh, and he dwells in it. **41** And Jair son of Manasseh has gone and captures their towns, and calls them "Towns of Jair"; **42** and Nobah has gone and captures Kenath and its villages, and calls it Nobah, by his own name.

CHAPTER 33

1 These [are] the journeys of the sons of Israel who have come out of the land of Egypt, by their hosts, by the hand of Moses and Aaron; **2** and Moses writes their outgoings, by their journeys, by the command of Yhwh; and these [are] their journeys, by their outgoings: **3** And they journey from Rameses in the first month, on the fifteenth day of the first month; from the day after the Passover the sons of Israel have gone out with a high hand before the eyes of all the Egyptians— **4** and the Egyptians are burying those whom Yhwh has struck among them, every firstborn, and Yhwh has done judgments on their gods. **5** And the sons of Israel journey from Rameses and encamp in Succoth. **6** And they journey from Succoth and encamp in Etham, which [is] in the extremity of the wilderness. **7** And they journey from Etham and turn back over Pi-Hahiroth, which [is] on the front of Ba'al-Zephon, and they encamp before Migdol. **8** And they journey from Pi-Hahiroth, and pass over through the midst of the sea into the wilderness, and go a journey of three days in the wilderness of Etham, and encamp in Marah. **9** And they journey from Marah and come to Elim, and twelve fountains of waters and seventy palm trees [are] in Elim, and they encamp there. **10** And they journey from Elim and encamp by the Red Sea. **11** And they journey from the Red Sea and encamp in the wilderness of Sin. **12** And they journey from the wilderness of Sin and encamp in Dophkah. **13** And they journey from Dophkah and encamp in Alush. **14** And they journey from Alush and encamp in Rephidim; and there was no water there for the people to drink. **15** And they journey from Rephidim and encamp in the wilderness of Sinai. **16** And they journey from the wilderness of Sinai and encamp in Kibroth-Hattaavah. **17** And they journey from Kibroth-Hattaavah and encamp in Hazeroth. **18** And they journey from Hazeroth and encamp in Rithmah. **19** And they journey from Rithmah and encamp in Rimmon-Parez. **20** And they journey from Rimmon-Parez and encamp in Libnah. **21** And they journey from Libnah and encamp in Rissah. **22** And they journey from Rissah and encamp in Kehelathah. **23** And they journey from Kehelathah and encamp in Mount Shapher. **24** And they journey from Mount Shapher and encamp in Haradah. **25** And they journey from Haradah and encamp in Makheloth. **26** And they journey from Makheloth and encamp in Tahath. **27** And they journey from Tahath and encamp in Tarah. **28** And they journey from Tarah and encamp in Mithcah. **29** And they journey from Mithcah and encamp in Hashmonah. **30** And they journey from Hashmonah and encamp in Moseroth. **31** And they journey from Moseroth and encamp in Bene-Jaakan. **32** And they journey from Bene-Jaakan and encamp at Hor-Hagidgad. **33** And they journey from Hor-Hagidgad and encamp in Jotbathah. **34** And they journey from Jotbathah and encamp in Ebronah. **35** And they journey from Ebronah and encamp in Ezion-Gaber. **36** And they journey from Ezion-Gaber and encamp in the wilderness of Zin, which [is] Kadesh. **37** And they journey from Kadesh and encamp in Mount Hor, in the extremity of the land of Edom. **38** And Aaron the priest goes up to Mount Hor by the command of Yhwh, and dies there in the fortieth year of the going out of the sons of Israel from the land of Egypt, in the fifth month, on the first of the month; **39** and Aaron [is] a son of one hundred and twenty-three years in his dying on Mount Hor. **40** And the Canaanite, king of Arad, who is dwelling in the south in the land of Canaan, hears of the coming of the sons of Israel. **41** And they journey from Mount Hor and encamp in Zalmonah. **42** And they journey from Zalmonah and encamp in Punon. **43** And they journey from Punon and encamp in Oboth. **44** And they journey from Oboth and encamp in Ije-Abarim, in the border of Moab. **45** And they journey from Iim and encamp in Dibon-Gad. **46** And they journey from Dibon-Gad and encamp in Almon-Diblathaim. **47** And they journey from Almon-Diblathaim and encamp in the mountains of Abarim, before Nebo. **48** And they journey from the mountains of Abarim and encamp in the plains of Moab by the Jordan, [near] Jericho. **49** And they encamp by the Jordan, from Beth-Jeshimoth as far as Abel-Shittim in the plains of Moab. **50** And Yhwh speaks to Moses in the plains of Moab by the Jordan, [near] Jericho, saying, **51** "Speak to the sons of Israel, and you have said to them: When you are passing over the Jordan to the land of Canaan, **52** then you have dispossessed all the inhabitants of the land from before you, and have destroyed all their imagery, indeed, you destroy all their molten images, and you lay waste [to] all their high places, **53** and you have possessed the land and dwelt in it, for I have given the land to you to possess it. **54** And you have inherited the land by lot, by your families; to the many you increase their inheritance, and to the few you diminish their inheritance; to where the lot goes out to him, it is his; you inherit by the tribes of your fathers. **55** And if you do not dispossess the inhabitants of the land from before you, then it has been [that] those whom you let remain of them [are] for pricks in your eyes and for thorns in your sides, and they have distressed you on the land in which you are dwelling, **56** and it has come to pass, as I thought to do to them, I do to you."

CHAPTER 34

1 And Yhwh speaks to Moses, saying, **2** "Command the sons of Israel, and you have said to them: When you are coming into the land of Canaan—this [is] the land which falls to you by inheritance, the land of Canaan, by its borders— **3** then the south quarter has been to you from the wilderness of Zin, by the sides of Edom, indeed, the south border has been to you from the extremity of the Salt Sea eastward; **4** and the border has turned around to you from the south to the ascent of Akrabbim, and has passed on to Zin, and its outgoings have been from the south to Kadesh-Barnea, and it has gone out at Hazar-Addar, and has passed on to Azmon; **5** and the border has turned around from Azmon to the Brook of Egypt, and its outgoings have been at the sea. **6** As for the west border, even the Great Sea has been a border to you; this is the west border to you. **7** And this is the north border to you: from the Great Sea you mark out for yourselves Mount Hor; **8** from Mount Hor you mark out to go to Hamath, and the outgoings of the border have been to Zedad; **9** and the border has gone out to Ziphron, and its outgoings have been at Hazar-Enan; this is the north border to you. **10** And you have marked out for yourselves for the border eastward, from Hazar-Enan to Shepham; **11** and the border has gone down from Shepham to Riblah, on the east of Ain, and the border has gone down, and has struck against the shoulder of the Sea of Chinnereth eastward; **12** and the border has gone down to the Jordan, and its outgoings have been at the Salt Sea; this is the land for you by its borders all around." **13** And Moses commands the sons of Israel, saying, "This [is] the land which you inherit by lot, which Yhwh has commanded to give to the nine tribes and the half of the tribe; **14** for the tribe of the sons of Reuben, by the house of their fathers, and the tribe of the children of Gad, by the house of their fathers, have received [their inheritance]; and [those of] the half of the tribe of Manasseh have received their inheritance; **15** the two tribes and the half of the tribe have received their inheritance beyond the Jordan, [near] Jericho, eastward, at the [sun]-rising." **16** And Yhwh speaks to Moses, saying, **17** "These [are] the names of the men who give the inheritance of the land to you: Eleazar the priest and Joshua son of Nun. **18** And one prince—you take one prince from a tribe to give the land by inheritance. **19** And these [are] the names of the men: of the tribe of Judah, Caleb son of Jephunneh; **20** and of the tribe of the sons of Simeon, Shemuel son of Aminihud; **21** of the tribe of Benjamin, Elidad son of Chislon; **22** and a prince of the tribe of the sons of Dan, Bukki son of Jogli; **23** of the sons of Joseph, a prince of the tribe of the sons of Manasseh, Hanniel son of Ephod; **24** and a prince of the tribe of the sons of Ephraim, Kemuel son of Shiphtan; **25** and a prince of the tribe of the sons of Zebulun, Elizaphan son of Parnach; **26** and a prince of the tribe of the sons of Issachar, Paltiel son of Azzan; **27** and a prince of the tribe of the sons of Asher, Ahihud son of Shelomi; **28** and a prince of the tribe of the sons of Naphtali, Pedahel son of Ammihud." **29** These [are] those whom Yhwh has commanded to give the sons of Israel inheritance in the land of Canaan.

CHAPTER 35

1 And Yhwh speaks to Moses in the plains of Moab by the Jordan, [near] Jericho, saying, **2** "Command the sons of Israel, and they have given to the Levites cities to inhabit from the inheritance of their possession; you also give [the] outskirt around them, of the cities, to the Levites. **3** And the cities have been for them to inhabit, and their outskirts are for their livestock, and for their goods, and for all their beasts. **4** And the outskirts of the cities which you give to the Levites [are], from the wall of the city and outside, one thousand cubits around. **5** And you have measured from the outside of the city: the east quarter—two thousand by the cubit, and the south quarter—two thousand by the cubit, and the west quarter—two thousand by the cubit, and the north quarter—two thousand by the cubit; and the city [is] in the midst; this is the outskirts of the cities to them. **6** And the cities which you give to the Levites [are] the six cities of refuge, which you give for the fleeing there of the manslayer, and besides them you give forty-two cities; **7** all the cities which you give to the Levites [are] forty-eight cities, them and their outskirts. **8** And the cities which you give [are] from the possession of the sons of Israel; from the many you multiply, and from the few you diminish; each, according to his inheritance which they inherit, gives to the Levites from his cities." **9** And Yhwh speaks to Moses, saying, **10** "Speak to the sons of Israel, and you have said to them: When you are passing over the Jordan to the land of Canaan, **11** and have prepared cities for yourselves—they are cities of refuge to you—then a manslayer, striking a person through ignorance, has fled there, **12** and the cities have been for a refuge to you from the redeemer, and the manslayer does not die until his standing before the congregation for judgment. **13** As for the cities which you give, six [are] cities of refuge to you; **14** three of the cities you give from beyond the Jordan, and three of the cities you give in the land of Canaan; they are cities of refuge. **15** For sons of Israel, and for a sojourner, and for a settler in their midst, are these six cities for a refuge, for the fleeing there of anyone striking a person through ignorance. **16** And if he has struck him with an instrument of iron, and he dies, he [is] a murderer: the murderer is certainly put to death. **17** And if he has struck him with a stone [in] the hand, with which he could die, and he dies, he [is] a murderer: the murderer is certainly put to death. **18** Or [if] he has struck him with a wooden instrument [in] the hand, with which he could die, and he dies, he [is] a murderer: the murderer is certainly put to death. **19** The redeemer of blood puts the murderer to death himself; in his coming against him he puts him to death. **20** And if he pushes him in hatred, or has cast [anything] at him by lying in wait, and he dies, **21** or he has struck him with his hand in enmity, and he dies, the striker is certainly put to death; he [is] a murderer; the redeemer of blood puts the murderer to death in his coming against him. **22** And if, in an instant, without enmity, he has pushed him, or has cast any instrument at him without lying in wait, **23** or with any stone with which he could die, without seeing, indeed, causes [it] to fall on him, and he dies, and he [is] not his enemy, nor seeking his evil, **24** then the congregation has judged between the striker and the redeemer of blood by these judgments. **25** And the congregation has delivered the manslayer out of the hand of the redeemer of blood, and the congregation has caused him to return to the city of his refuge, to where he has fled, and he has dwelt in it until the death of the chief priest who has been anointed with the holy oil. **26** And if the manslayer indeed goes out [from] the border of the city of his refuge to where he flees, **27** and the redeemer of blood has found him at the outside of the border of the city of his refuge, and the redeemer of blood has slain the manslayer, blood [is] not [reckoned] to him; **28** for he dwells in the city of his refuge until the death of the chief priest; and after the death of the chief priest the manslayer turns back to the city of his possession. **29** And these things have been for a statute of judgment to you throughout your generations, in all your dwellings. **30** Whoever strikes a person, by the mouth of witnesses [one] slays the murderer; and one witness does not testify against a person to cause [him] to die. **31** And you take no atonement for the life of a murderer who [is] condemned to die, for he is certainly put to death; **32** and you take no atonement for him [who had] to flee to the city of his refuge, to return to dwell in the land, until the death of the priest. **33** And you do not profane the land which you [are] in, for blood profanes the land; as for the land, it is not pardoned for blood which is shed in it except by the blood of him who sheds it; **34** and you do not defile the land in which you are dwelling, in the midst of which I dwell, for I, Yhwh, dwell in the midst of the sons of Israel."

CHAPTER 36

1 And the heads of the fathers of the families of the sons of Gilead, son of Machir, son of Manasseh, of the families of the sons of Joseph, come near and speak before Moses and before the princes, heads of the fathers of the sons of Israel, 2 and say, "Yhwh commanded my lord to give the land for inheritance by lot to the sons of Israel, and my lord has been commanded by Yhwh to give the inheritance of our brother Zelophehad to his daughters. 3 Now [if] they have been [given] to one from the sons of the [other] tribes of the sons of Israel for wives, and their inheritance has been withdrawn from the inheritance of our fathers, and has been added to the inheritance of the tribe which is theirs, and it is withdrawn from the lot of our inheritance, 4 and if it is the Jubilee of the sons of Israel, then their inheritance has been added to the inheritance of the tribe which is theirs, and their inheritance is withdrawn from the inheritance of the tribe of our fathers." 5 And Moses commands the sons of Israel by the command of Yhwh, saying, "The tribe of the sons of Joseph is speaking correctly; 6 this [is] the thing which Yhwh has commanded concerning the daughters of Zelophehad, saying, To those good in their eyes let them be for wives; only, let them be for wives to a family of the tribe of their fathers; 7 and the inheritance of the sons of Israel does not turn around from tribe to tribe; for each of the sons of Israel cleaves to the inheritance of the tribe of his fathers. 8 And every daughter possessing an inheritance from the tribes of the sons of Israel is for a wife to one from the family of the tribe of her father, so that the sons of Israel each possess the inheritance of his fathers, 9 and the inheritance does not turn around from [one] tribe to another tribe; for each of the tribes of the sons of Israel cleaves to his inheritance." 10 As Yhwh has commanded Moses, so the daughters of Zelophehad have done, 11 and Mahlah, Tirzah, and Hoglah, and Milcah, and Noah, daughters of Zelophehad, are for wives to the sons of their fathers' brothers; 12 they have been for wives [to men] from the families of the sons of Manasseh, son of Joseph, and their inheritance is with the tribe of the family of their father. 13 These [are] the commands and the judgments which Yhwh has commanded by the hand of Moses concerning the sons of Israel, in the plains of Moab by the Jordan, [near] Jericho.

DEUTERONOMY

CHAPTER 1

1 These [are] the words which Moses has spoken to all Israel beyond the Jordan in the wilderness, in the plain opposite Suph, between Paran, and Tophel, and Laban, and Hazeroth, and Di-Zahab. **2** [It takes] eleven days [to go] from Horeb, the way of Mount Seir, to Kadesh-Barnea. **3** And it comes to pass in the fortieth year, in the eleventh month, on the first of the month, Moses has spoken to the sons of Israel according to all that Yhwh has commanded him concerning them, **4** after his striking Sihon king of the Amorite who is dwelling in Heshbon, and Og king of Bashan who is dwelling in Ashtaroth in Edrei. **5** Beyond the Jordan, in the land of Moab, Moses has begun to explain this law, saying, **6** "Our God Yhwh has spoken to us in Horeb, saying, For you dwell at this mountain long enough; **7** turn and journey for yourselves, and go to the mountain of the Amorite, and to all its neighboring places in the plain, in the hill-country, and in the low country, and in the south, and in the haven of the sea, the land of the Canaanite, and of Lebanon, as far as the great river, the Euphrates River; **8** see, I have set the land before you; go in and possess the land which Yhwh has sworn to your fathers, to Abraham, to Isaac, and to Jacob, to give to them and to their seed after them. **9** And I speak to you at that time, saying, I am not able to bear you by myself; **10** your God Yhwh has multiplied you, and behold, today you [are] as the stars of the heavens for multitude; **11** Yhwh, God of your fathers, is adding to you, as you [are], one thousand times, and blesses you as He has spoken to you. **12** How do I bear your pressure, and your burden, and your strife by myself? **13** Provide wise and understanding men for yourselves that are known to your tribes, and I set them for your heads; **14** and you answer me and say, The thing which you have spoken [is] good to do. **15** And I take the heads of your tribes, wise men that are known, and I appoint them [as] heads over you, princes of thousands, and princes of hundreds, and princes of fifties, and princes of tens, and authorities for your tribes. **16** And I command your judges at that time, saying, Listen between your brothers—then you have judged [in] righteousness between a man, and his brother, and his sojourner; **17** you do not discern faces in judgment; you hear the little as well as the great; you arc not afraid of the face of any, for the judgment is God's, and the thing which is too hard for you, you bring near to me, and I have heard it. **18** And I command you at that time all the things which you do. **19** And we journey from Horeb, and go [through] all that great and fearful wilderness which you have seen, the way of the hill-country of the Amorite, as our God Yhwh has commanded us, and we come to Kadesh-Barnea. **20** And I say to you, You have come to the hill-country of the Amorite, which our God Yhwh is giving to us; **21** see, your God Yhwh has set the land before you; go up, possess, as Yhwh, God of your fathers, has spoken to you; do not fear, nor be frightened. **22** And you come near to me, all of you, and say, Let us send men before us, and they search the land for us, and they bring us back word [concerning] the way in which we go up into it, and the cities to which we come in; **23** and the thing is good in my eyes, and I take twelve men from you, one man for the tribe. **24** And they turn and go up to the hill-country, and come to the Valley of Eshcol, and spy it out, **25** and they take in their hand from the fruit of the land, and bring [it] down to us, and bring us back word, and say, The land is good which our God Yhwh is giving to us. **26** And you have not been willing to go up, and you provoke the mouth of your God Yhwh, **27** and murmur in your tents, and say, In Yhwh's hating us He has brought us out of the land of Egypt, to give us into the hand of the Amorite—to destroy us; **28** to where are we going up? our brothers have melted our heart, saying, [The] people [are] greater and taller than we; [the] cities [are] great and fortified up to the heavens, and we have also seen sons of Anakim there. **29** And I say to you, Do not be terrified, nor be afraid of them; **30** your God Yhwh, who is going before you—He fights for you, according to all that He has done with you in Egypt before your eyes, **31** and in the wilderness where you have seen that your God Yhwh has carried you, as a man carries his son, in all the way which you have gone until your coming to this place. **32** And in this thing you are not steadfast in your God Yhwh, **33** who is going before you in the way to search out for you a place for your encamping, in fire by night, to show you in the way in which you go, and in a cloud by day. **34** And Yhwh hears the voice of your words, and is angry, and swears, saying, **35** Not one of these men of this evil generation sees the good land which I have sworn to give to your fathers, **36** except Caleb son of Jephunneh—he sees it, and to him I give the land on which he has trodden, and to his sons, because that he has been fully after Yhwh. **37** Moreover, Yhwh has been angry with me for your sake, saying, Indeed, you do not go in there; **38** Joshua son of Nun, who is standing before you, he goes in there; strengthen him, for he causes Israel to inherit [it]. **39** And your infants, of whom you have said, They are for a prey, and your sons who today have not known good and evil, they go in there, and I give it to them, and they possess it; **40** but you, turn and journey for yourselves toward the wilderness, the way of the Red Sea. **41** And you answer and say to me, We have sinned against Yhwh; we go up and we have fought, according to all that which our God Yhwh has commanded us; and you each gird on his weapons of war, and you are ready to go up into the hill-country; **42** and Yhwh says to me, Say to them, You do not go up, nor fight, for I am not in your midst, and you are not struck before your enemies. **43** And I speak to you, and you have not listened, and provoke the mouth of Yhwh, and act proudly, and go up into the hill-country; **44** and the Amorite who is dwelling in that hill-country comes out to meet you, and they pursue you as the bees do, and strike you in Seir, even to Hormah. **45** And you return and weep before Yhwh, and Yhwh has not listened to your voice, nor has He given ear to you; **46**

and you dwell in Kadesh [for] many days, according to the days which you had dwelt."

CHAPTER 2

1 "And we turn and journey into the wilderness, the way of the Red Sea, as Yhwh has spoken to me, and we go around Mount Seir [for] many days. **2** And Yhwh speaks to me, saying, **3** For you go around this mountain long enough; turn for yourselves northward. **4** And the people command you, saying, You are passing over into the border of your brothers, sons of Esau, who are dwelling in Seir, and they are afraid of you; and you have been very watchful; **5** you do not strive with them, for I do not give [any] of their land to you—even the treading of the sole of a foot; I have given Mount Seir to Esau for a possession. **6** You buy food from them with money, and have eaten; and you also buy water from them with money, and have drunk. **7** For your God Yhwh has blessed you in all the work of your hands; He has known your walking in this great wilderness these forty years; your God Yhwh [is] with you; you have not lacked anything. **8** And we pass by from our brothers, sons of Esau, who are dwelling in Seir, by the way of the plain, by Elath and by Ezion-Gaber, and we turn and pass over the way of the wilderness of Moab; **9** and Yhwh says to me, Do not distress Moab, nor stir yourself up against them [in] battle, for I do not give [any] of their land to you [for] a possession; for I have given Ar to the sons of Lot [for] a possession. **10** The Emim have formerly dwelt in it, a people great, and numerous, and tall as the Anakim; **11** they are reckoned [as] Rephaim, they also, as the Anakim; and the Moabites call them Emim. **12** And the Horim have formerly dwelt in Seir, but the sons of Esau dispossess them, and destroy them from before them, and dwell in their stead, as Israel has done to the land of his possession which Yhwh has given to them. **13** Now rise and pass over the Brook of Zered for yourselves; and we pass over the Brook of Zered. **14** And the days which we have walked from Kadesh-Barnea until we have passed over the Brook of Zered [are] thirty-eight years, until the consumption of all the generation of the men of battle from the midst of the camp, as Yhwh has sworn to them; **15** and indeed the hand of Yhwh has been against them, to destroy them from the midst of the camp until they are consumed. **16** And it comes to pass, when all the men of battle have finished dying from the midst of the people, **17** that Yhwh speaks to me, saying, **18** Today you are passing over the border of Moab, even Ar, **19** and [when] you have come near the sons of Ammon, you do not distress them, nor stir yourself up against them, for I do not give [any] of the land of the sons of Ammon to you [for] a possession; for I have given it to the sons of Lot [for] a possession. **20** It is reckoned [as] a land of Rephaim, even it; Rephaim formerly dwelt in it, and the Ammonites call them Zamzummim, **21** a people great, and numerous, and tall as the Anakim, and Yhwh destroys them before them, and they dispossess them, and dwell in their stead, **22** as He has done for the sons of Esau who are dwelling in Seir, when He destroyed the Horim from before them, and they dispossess them, and dwell in their stead to this day. **23** As for the Avim who are dwelling in villages as far as Gaza, the Caphtorim—who are coming out from Caphtor—have destroyed them, and dwell in their stead. **24** Rise, journey, and pass over the Brook of Arnon; see, I have given into your hand Sihon king of Heshbon, the Amorite, and his land; begin to possess [it], and stir yourself up against him [in] battle. **25** This [is] the day I begin to put your dread and your fear on the face of the peoples under the whole heavens, who hear your fame, and have trembled and been pained because of you. **26** And I send messengers from the wilderness of Kedemoth to Sihon king of Heshbon, [with] words of peace, saying, **27** Let me pass over through your land; in the way—in the way I go, I do not turn aside [to the] right or left. **28** You sell me food for money, and I have eaten; and you give to me water for money, and I have drunk; only, let me pass over on my feet, **29** as the sons of Esau who are dwelling in Seir and the Moabites who are dwelling in Ar have done for me, until I pass over the Jordan to the land which our God Yhwh is giving to us. **30** And Sihon king of Heshbon has not been willing to let us pass over by him, for your God Yhwh has hardened his spirit and strengthened his heart, so as to give him into your hand as at this day. **31** And Yhwh says to me, See, I have begun to give Sihon and his land before your faces; begin to possess—to possess his land. **32** And Sihon comes out to meet us, he and all his people, to the battle at Jahaz; **33** and our God Yhwh gives him before our faces, and we strike him, and his sons, and all his people; **34** and we capture all his cities at that time, and devote the whole city—men, and the women, and the infants; we have not left a remnant; **35** only, we have spoiled the livestock for ourselves, and the spoil of the cities which we have captured. **36** From Aroer, which [is] by the edge of the Brook of Arnon, and the city which [is] by the brook, even to Gilead, there has not been a city which [is] too high for us; our God Yhwh has given the whole before our faces. **37** Only, you have not drawn near to the land of the sons of Ammon—any part of the Brook of Jabbok, and cities of the hill-country, and anything which our God Yhwh has [not] commanded."

CHAPTER 3

1 "And we turn and go up the way to Bashan, and Og king of Bashan comes out to meet us, he and all his people, to the battle [at] Edrei. **2** And Yhwh says to me, Do not fear him, for I have given him, and all his people, and his land into your hand, and you have done to him as you have done to Sihon king of the Amorite who is dwelling in Heshbon. **3** And our God Yhwh indeed gives Og king of Bashan and all his people into our hands, and we strike him until there has been no remnant left to him; **4** and we capture all his cities at that time; there has not been a city which we have not taken from them—sixty cities, all the region of Argob, the kingdom of Og in Bashan. **5** All these [are] cities fortified with high walls, double gates, and bar, apart from very many cities of the open place; **6** and we devote them, as we have done to Sihon king of Heshbon, devoting [the] men, the women, and the infants of every city; **7** and all the livestock, and the spoil of the cities, we have spoiled for ourselves. **8** And at that time we take the land out of the hand of the two kings of the Amorite, which is beyond the Jordan, from the Brook of Arnon to Mount Hermon **9** (Sidonians call Hermon Sirion, and the Amorites call it Senir), **10** all the cities of the plain, and all Gilead, and all Bashan, as far as Salchah and Edrei, cities of the kingdom of Og in Bashan. **11** For only Og king of Bashan had been left of the remnant of the Rephaim; behold, his bedstead [is] a bedstead of iron. Is it not in Rabbath of the sons of Ammon? Its length [is] nine cubits and its breadth [is] four cubits, by the cubit of a man. **12** And this land, [which] we had possessed at that time, from Aroer, which [is] by the Brook of Arnon, and the half of Mount Gilead and its cities, I have given to the Reubenite and to the Gadite; **13** and the rest of Gilead and all Bashan, the kingdom of Og, I have given to the half tribe of Manasseh; all the region of Argob, with all Bashan—it is called the land of [the] Rephaim. **14** Jair son of Manasseh has taken all the region of Argob, as far as the border of Geshuri and Maachathi ([namely] Bashan), and calls them by his own name, Havoth-Jair, to this day. **15** And I have given Gilead to Machir. **16** And to the Reubenite and to the Gadite I have given from Gilead even to the Brook of Arnon, the middle of the valley and the border, even to the Brook of Jabbok, the border of the sons of Ammon, **17** and the plain, and the Jordan, and the border, from Chinnereth even to the Sea of the Plain (the Salt Sea), under the Springs of Pisgah, at the [sun]-rising. **18** And at that time I command you, saying, Your God Yhwh has given this land to you to possess it; you pass over armed before your brothers the sons of Israel, all the sons of might. **19** Only your wives, and your infants, and your livestock—I have known that you have much livestock—dwell in your cities which I have given to you, **20** until Yhwh gives rest to your brothers like yourselves, and they also have possessed the land which your God Yhwh is giving to them beyond the Jordan; then you have each turned back to his possession which I have given to you. **21** And I have commanded Joshua at that time, saying, Your eyes are seeing all that which your God Yhwh has done to these two kings—so Yhwh does to all the kingdoms to where you are passing over; **22** do not fear them, for your God Yhwh—He is fighting for you. **23** And to Yhwh I beg for grace at that time, saying, **24** Lord Yhwh, You have begun to show Your servant Your greatness and Your strong hand; for who [is] a god in the heavens or in earth who does according to Your works and according to Your might? **25** Please let me pass over and see the good land which [is] beyond the Jordan, this good hill-country, and Lebanon. **26** And Yhwh shows Himself angry with me for your sake, and has not listened to me, and Yhwh says to me, Enough of you; do not add to speak to Me about this thing anymore; **27** go up [to] the top of Pisgah, and lift up your eyes westward, and northward, and southward, and eastward, and see with your eyes, for you do not pass over this Jordan; **28** and charge Joshua, and strengthen him, and harden him, for he passes over before this people, and he causes them to inherit the land which you see. **29** And we dwell in a valley opposite Beth-Peor."

CHAPTER 4

1 "And now, O Israel, listen to the statutes and to the judgments which I am teaching you to do, so that you live, and have gone in, and possessed the land which Yhwh God of your fathers is giving to you. **2** You do not add to the word which I am commanding you, nor diminish from it, to keep the commands of your God Yhwh which I am commanding you. **3** Your eyes are seeing that which Yhwh has done in Ba'al-Peor, for every man who has gone after Ba'al-Peor, your God Yhwh has destroyed him from your midst; **4** and you who are cleaving to your God Yhwh [are] alive today—all of you. **5** See, I have taught you statutes and judgments, as my God Yhwh has commanded me, to do so in the midst of the land to where you are going in to possess it; **6** and you have kept and done [them] (for it [is] your wisdom and your understanding) before the eyes of the peoples who hear all these statutes, and they have said, Surely a people wise and understanding [is] this great nation. **7** For which [is] the great nation that has God [so] near to it, as our God Yhwh, in all we have called to Him? **8** and which [is] the great nation which has righteous statutes and judgments according to all this law which I am setting before you today? **9** Only, take heed to yourself, and watch your soul exceedingly, lest you forget the things which your eyes have seen, and lest they turn aside from your heart all [the] days of your life; and you have made them known to your sons and to your sons' sons. **10** [Never forget] the day when you have stood before your God Yhwh in Horeb, in Yhwh's saying to me, Assemble the people to Me, and I cause them to hear My words, so that they learn to fear Me all the days that they are alive on the ground, and they teach their sons; **11** and you draw near and stand under the mountain, and the mountain is burning with fire to the heart of the heavens, [with] darkness, cloud, and thick darkness, **12** and Yhwh speaks to you out of the midst of the fire; you are hearing a voice of words, but you are seeing no likeness, only a voice; **13** and He declares His covenant to you, which He has commanded you to do, the Ten Commandments, and He writes them on two tablets of stone. **14** And Yhwh has commanded me at that time to teach you statutes and judgments, for your doing them in the land to where you are passing over to possess it. **15** And you have been very watchful of your souls, for you have not seen any likeness in the day of Yhwh's speaking to you in Horeb out of the midst of the fire, **16** lest you do corruptly, and have made for yourselves a carved image, a likeness of any figure: a form of male or female, **17** a form of any beast which [is] in the earth, a form of any winged bird which flies in the heavens, **18** a form of any creeping thing on the ground, a form of any fish which [is] in the waters below the earth. **19** And lest you lift up your eyes to the heavens, and have seen the sun, and the moon, and the stars, all the host of the heavens, and have been drawn away, and have bowed yourself to them and served them, which your God Yhwh has apportioned to all the peoples under all the heavens. **20** And Yhwh has taken you, and He is bringing you out from the iron furnace, from Egypt, to be to Him for a people, an inheritance, as [at] this day. **21** And Yhwh has showed Himself angry with me because of your words, and swears to my not passing over the Jordan, and to my not going into the good land which your God Yhwh is giving to you [for] an inheritance; **22** for I am dying in this land; I am not passing over the Jordan, but you are passing over and have possessed this good land. **23** Take heed to yourselves lest you forget the covenant of your God Yhwh which He has made with you, and have made a carved image for yourselves, a likeness of anything [concerning] which your God Yhwh has charged you; **24** for your God Yhwh is a consuming fire—a zealous God. **25** When you beget sons and sons' sons, and you have become old in the land, and have done corruptly, and have made a carved image, a likeness of anything, and have done evil in the eyes of Yhwh to provoke Him to anger, **26** I have caused the heavens and the earth to testify against you this day, that you perish utterly quickly from off the land to where you are passing over the Jordan to possess it; you do not prolong days on it, but are utterly destroyed; **27** and Yhwh has scattered you among the peoples, and you have been left few in number among the nations to where Yhwh leads you, **28** and you have served gods there, work of man's hands, wood and stone, which do not see, nor hear, nor eat, nor smell. 29 And you have sought your God Yhwh from there, and have found [Him] when you seek Him with all your heart and with all your soul. 30 In the distress of yours, when all these things have found you in the latter end of the days, and you have turned back to your God Yhwh and have listened to His voice— 31 for your God Yhwh [is] a merciful God—He does not fail you, nor destroy you, nor forget the covenant of your fathers which He has sworn to them. 32 For ask now of the former days which have been before you, from the day that God created man on the earth, and from the [one] end of the heavens even to the [other] end of the heavens, whether there has been as this great thing, or [if anything] has been heard like it. 33 Has a people heard the voice of God speaking out of the midst of the fire, as you have heard, you—and live? 34 Or has God tried to go in to take a nation for Himself from the midst of a nation, by trials, by signs, and by wonders, and by war, and by a strong hand, and by an outstretched arm, and by great terrors, according to all that your God Yhwh has done to you in Egypt before your eyes? 35 You—you have been shown [it], to know that He, Yhwh, [is] God; there is none else besides Him. 36 He has caused you to hear His voice from the heavens, to instruct you; and on earth He has showed you His great fire, and you have heard His words out of the midst of the fire. 37 And because that He has loved your fathers, He also fixes on their seed after them, and brings you out in His presence, by His great power, from Egypt, 38 to dispossess nations greater and stronger than you from your presence, to bring you in to give their land to you [for] an inheritance, as [at] this day. 39 And you have known today, and have turned [it] back to your heart, that He, Yhwh, [is] God in the heavens above and on the earth below—there is none else; 40 and you have kept His statutes and His commands which I am commanding you today, so that it is well for you, and for your sons after you, and so that you prolong days on the ground which your God Yhwh is giving to you—all the days." 41 Then Moses separates three cities beyond the Jordan, toward the sun-rising, 42 for the fleeing there of the manslayer who slays his neighbor unknowingly, and he is not hating him before, and he has fled to one of these cities and he has lived: 43 Bezer in the wilderness, in the land of the plain, for the Reubenite; and Ramoth in Gilead for the Gadite; and Golan in Bashan for the Manassite. 44 And this [is] the law which Moses has set before the sons of Israel; 45 these [are] the testimonies, and the statutes, and the judgments, which Moses has spoken to the sons of Israel in their coming out of Egypt, 46 beyond the Jordan, in the valley opposite Beth-Peor, in the land of Sihon, king of the Amorite, who is dwelling in Heshbon, whom Moses and the sons of Israel have struck in their coming out of Egypt; 47 and they possess his land and the land of Og king of Bashan, two kings of the Amorite who [are] beyond the Jordan, [toward] the sun-rising, 48 from Aroer, which [is] by the edge of the Brook of Arnon, even to Mount Zion, which [is] Hermon— 49 and all the plain beyond the Jordan eastward, even to the Sea of the Plain, below the Springs of Pisgah.

CHAPTER 5

1 And Moses calls to all Israel and says to them, "Hear, O Israel, the statutes and the judgments which I am speaking in your ears today, and you have learned them and have observed to do them. 2 Our God Yhwh made a covenant with us in Horeb; 3 Yhwh has not made this covenant with our fathers, but with us, we—these here—all of us living today. 4 Yhwh has spoken with you face to face on the mountain, out of the midst of the fire; 5 I am standing between Yhwh and you, at that time, to declare the word of Yhwh to you, for you have been afraid from the presence of the fire, and you have not gone up into the mountain; for [He] says: 6 I, Yhwh, [am] your God who has brought you out from the land of Egypt, from a house of servants. 7 You have no other gods in My presence. 8 You do not make a carved image for yourself, any likeness which [is] in the heavens above, or which [is] in the earth beneath, or which [is] in the waters under the earth. 9 You do not bow yourself to them, nor serve them: for I, your God Yhwh, [am] a zealous God, charging iniquity of fathers on sons, and on a third and on a fourth [generation] of those hating Me, 10 and doing kindness to thousands, of those loving Me and of those keeping My commands. 11 You do not take up the Name of your God Yhwh for a vain thing, for Yhwh does not acquit him who takes up His Name for a vain thing. 12 Observe the

Sabbath day to sanctify it, as your God Yhwh has commanded you; 13 six days you labor and have done all your work, 14 and the seventh day [is] a Sabbath to your God Yhwh; you do not do any work, you, and your son, and your daughter, and your manservant, and your handmaid, and your ox, and your donkey, and all your livestock, and your sojourner who [is] within your gates, so that your manservant and your handmaid rest like yourself. 15 And you have remembered that you have been a servant in the land of Egypt, and your God Yhwh brings you out from there by a strong hand and by an outstretched arm; therefore your God Yhwh has commanded you to keep the Sabbath day. 16 Honor your father and your mother, as your God Yhwh has commanded you, so that your days are prolonged, and so that it is well with you on the ground which your God Yhwh is giving to you. 17 You do not murder. 18 You do not commit adultery. 19 You do not steal. 20 You do not answer [with] a false testimony against your neighbor. 21 You do not desire your neighbor's wife, nor do you covet your neighbor's house, his field, and his manservant, and his handmaid, his ox, and his donkey, and anything which [is] your neighbor's. 22 Yhwh has spoken these words to all your assembly in the mountain, out of the midst of the fire, [and] of the cloud, and of the thick darkness, [with] a great voice; and He has not added; and He writes them on two tablets of stone and gives them to me. 23 And it comes to pass, as you hear the voice out of the midst of the darkness and of the mountain burning with fire, that you come near to me, all [the] heads of your tribes and your elderly, 24 and say, Behold, our God Yhwh has showed us His glory and His greatness; and we have heard His voice out of the midst of the fire; this day we have seen that God speaks with man—and he has lived. 25 And now, why do we die? for this great fire consumes us if we add to hear the voice of our God Yhwh anymore—then we have died. 26 For who of all flesh [is] he who has heard the voice of the living God speaking out of the midst of the fire like us, and lives? 27 Draw near and hear all that which our God Yhwh says, and you, you speak to us all that which our God Yhwh speaks to you, and we have listened and done it. 28 And Yhwh hears the voice of your words in your speaking to me, and Yhwh says to me, I have heard the voice of the words of this people which they have spoken to you; they have done well [in] all that they have spoken. 29 O that their heart had been thus to them, to fear Me and to keep My commands [for] all the days, that it may be well with them and with their sons for all time! 30 Go, say to them, Return for yourselves, to your tents; 31 and you, stand here with Me, and let Me speak to you all the command, and the statutes, and the judgments which you teach them, and they have done [them] in the land which I am giving to them to possess it. 32 And you have observed to do as your God Yhwh has commanded you, you do not turn aside [to] the right or left; 33 in all the way which your God Yhwh has commanded you—walk, so that you live, and [it is] well with you, and you have prolonged days in the land which you possess."

CHAPTER 6

1 "And this [is] the command, the statutes and the judgments which your God Yhwh has commanded to teach you to do in the land which you are passing over there to possess it, 2 so that you fear your God Yhwh, to keep all His statutes and His commands which I am commanding you, you, and your son, and your son's son, all [the] days of your life, and so that your days are prolonged. 3 And you have heard, O Israel, and observed to do [them], that it may be well with you, and that you may multiply exceedingly, as Yhwh, God of your fathers, has spoken to you, [in] the land flowing with milk and honey. 4 Hear, O Israel: Our God Yhwh—Yhwh [is] one! 5 And you have loved your God Yhwh with all your heart, and with all your soul, and with all your might. 6 And these words which I am commanding you today have been on your heart, 7 and you have repeated them to your sons, and spoken of them in your sitting in your house, and in your walking in the way, and in your lying down, and in your rising up, 8 and have bound them for a sign on your hand, and they have been for frontlets between your eyes, 9 and you have written them on doorposts of your house and on your gates. 10 And it has been, when your God Yhwh brings you into the land which He has sworn to your fathers, to Abraham, to Isaac, and to Jacob, to give to you great and good cities which you have not built, 11 and houses full of all good things which you have not filled, and wells dug which you have not dug, vineyards and olive-yards which you

have not planted, that you have eaten and been satisfied. **12** Take heed to yourself lest you forget Yhwh who has brought you out of the land of Egypt, out of a house of servants. **13** You fear your God Yhwh, and you serve Him, and you swear by His Name. **14** You do not go after other gods, of the gods of the peoples who [are] around you, **15** for your God Yhwh [is] a zealous God in your midst—lest the anger of your God Yhwh burns against you, and He has destroyed you from off the face of the ground. **16** You do not try your God Yhwh as you tried [Him] in Massah. **17** You diligently keep the commands of your God Yhwh, and His testimonies and His statutes which He has commanded you, **18** and you have done that which is right and good in the eyes of Yhwh, so that it is well with you, and you have gone in and possessed the good land which Yhwh has sworn to your fathers, **19** to drive away all your enemies from your presence, as Yhwh has spoken. **20** When your son asks you hereafter, saying, What [are] the testimonies, and the statutes, and the judgments which our God Yhwh has commanded you? **21** then you have said to your son, We have been servants of Pharaoh in Egypt, and Yhwh brings us out of Egypt by a high hand; **22** and Yhwh gives signs and wonders, great and severe, on Egypt, on Pharaoh, and on all his house, before our eyes; **23** and He has brought us out from there, in order to bring us in, to give to us the land which He had sworn to our fathers. **24** And Yhwh commands us to do all these statutes, to fear our God Yhwh, for good to ourselves [for] all the days, to keep us alive, as [at] this day; **25** and it is righteousness for us when we observe to do all this command before our God Yhwh, as He has commanded us."

CHAPTER 7

1 "When your God Yhwh brings you into the land to where you are going in to possess it, and He has cast out many nations from your presence, the Hittite, and the Girgashite, and the Amorite, and the Canaanite, and the Perizzite, and the Hivite, and the Jebusite, seven nations more numerous and mighty than you, **2** and your God Yhwh has given them before you, then you have struck them—you utterly devote them— you do not make a covenant with them, nor do you favor them. **3** And you do not join in marriage with them; you do not give your daughter to his son, and you do not take his daughter to your son, **4** for he turns aside your son from after Me, and they have served other gods; and the anger of Yhwh has burned against you and has destroyed you quickly. **5** But thus you do to them: you break down their altars, and you shatter their standing pillars, and you cut down their Asherim, and you burn their carved images with fire. **6** For you [are] a holy people to your God Yhwh; your God Yhwh has fixed on you, to be to Him for a peculiar people, out of all the peoples who [are] on the face of the ground. **7** Yhwh has delighted in you and fixes on you, not because of your being more numerous than any of the peoples, for you [are] the least of all the peoples, **8** but because of Yhwh's loving you, and because of His keeping the oath which He has sworn to your fathers; Yhwh has brought you out by a strong hand, and ransoms you from a house of servants, from the hand of Pharaoh king of Egypt. **9** And you have known that He, your God Yhwh, [is] God, the faithful God keeping the covenant and the kindness with those loving Him and with those keeping His commands, for one thousand generations, **10** and repaying to those hating Him to their face, to destroy them; He does not delay to him who is hating Him, He repays [it] to him to his face. **11** And you have kept the command, and the statutes, and the judgments, which I am commanding you today to do them. **12** And it has been, because you hear these judgments, and have kept and done them, that your God Yhwh has kept the covenant and the kindness with you which He has sworn to your fathers, **13** and has loved you, and blessed you, and multiplied you, and has blessed the fruit of your womb, and the fruit of your ground, your grain, and your new wine, and your oil, the increase of your oxen, and the wealth of your flock, on the ground which He has sworn to your fathers to give to you. **14** Blessed are you above all the peoples; there is not a barren man or a barren woman in you—nor among your livestock; **15** and Yhwh has turned aside every sickness from you, and none of the evil diseases of Egypt (which you have known) does He put on you, and He has put them on all hating you. **16** And you have consumed all the peoples whom your God Yhwh is giving to you; your eye has no pity on them, and you do not serve their gods, for it [is] a snare to you. **17** When you say in your heart, These nations [are] more numerous than I,

how am I able to dispossess them? **18** You are not afraid of them; you surely remember that which your God Yhwh has done to Pharaoh and to all of Egypt, **19** the great trials which your eyes have seen, and the signs, and the wonders, and the strong hand, and the outstretched arm, with which your God Yhwh has brought you out; so does your God Yhwh do to all the peoples of whose presence you are afraid. **20** And your God Yhwh also sends the locust among them, until the destruction of those who are left, even those who are hidden from your presence; **21** you are not terrified by their presence, for your God Yhwh [is] in your midst, a God great and fearful. **22** And your God Yhwh has cast out these nations from your presence little [by] little (you are not able to consume them quickly, lest the beast of the field multiplies against you), **23** and your God Yhwh has given them before you, and confused them [with] a great destruction until their being destroyed; **24** and He has given their kings into your hand, and you have destroyed their name from under the heavens; no man stations himself in your presence until you have destroyed them. **25** You burn the carved images of their gods with fire; you do not desire the silver and gold on them, nor have you taken [it] for yourself, lest you are snared by it, for it [is] an abomination [to] your God Yhwh; **26** and you do not bring in an abomination to your house, or you have been devoted like it—you utterly detest it and you utterly abhor it; for it [is] devoted."

CHAPTER 8

1 "All the command which I am commanding you today you observe to do, so that you live, and have multiplied, and gone in, and possessed the land which Yhwh has sworn to your fathers; **2** and you have remembered all the way which your God Yhwh has caused you to go these forty years in the wilderness, in order to humble you to try you, to know that which [is] in your heart, whether you keep His commands or not. **3** And He humbles you, and causes you to hunger, and causes you to eat the manna (which you have not known, even your fathers have not known), in order to cause you to know that man does not live by bread alone, but man lives by everything proceeding [from] the mouth of Yhwh. **4** Your raiment has not worn out from off you, and your foot has not swelled these forty years, **5** and you have known with your heart that as a man disciplines his son, your God Yhwh is disciplining you, **6** and you have kept the commands of your God Yhwh, to walk in His ways and to fear Him. **7** For your God Yhwh is bringing you into a good land, a land of brooks of waters, of fountains, and of depths coming out in valley and in mountain; **8** a land of wheat, and barley, and vine, and fig, and pomegranate; a land of oil olive and honey; **9** a land in which you eat bread without scarcity—you do not lack anything in it; a land whose stones [are] iron, and you dig bronze out of its mountains. **10** And you have eaten and been satisfied, and have blessed your God Yhwh on the good land which he has given to you. **11** Take heed to yourself lest you forget your God Yhwh so as not to keep His commands, and His judgments, and His statutes which I am commanding you today; **12** lest you eat and have been satisfied, and build good houses and have inhabited [them], **13** and your herd and your flock are multiplied, and silver and gold are multiplied to you, and all that is yours is multiplied, **14** and your heart has been high, and you have forgotten your God Yhwh who is bringing you out of the land of Egypt, out of a house of servants; **15** who is causing you to go in the great and the terrible wilderness [with] burning serpent, and scorpion, and thirst—where there is no water; who is bringing out waters to you from the flinty rock; **16** who is causing you to eat manna in the wilderness, which your fathers have not known, in order to humble you, and in order to try you, to do you good in your latter end; **17** and you have said in your heart, My power and the might of my hand have made this wealth for me. **18** And you have remembered your God Yhwh, for it [is] He who is giving power to you to make wealth, in order to establish His covenant which He has sworn to your fathers, as [at] this day. **19** And it has been, if you really forget your God Yhwh, and have gone after other gods, and served them, and bowed yourself to them, I have testified against you today that you utterly perish. **20** As the nations whom Yhwh is destroying from your presence, so you perish, because you do not listen to the voice of your God Yhwh."

CHAPTER 9

1 "Hear, O Israel: You are passing over the Jordan today to go in to possess nations greater and mightier than yourself, cities great and fortified up to the heavens, **2** a people great and tall, sons of Anakim, whom you have known, and [of whom] you have heard: Who stations himself before sons of Anak? **3** And you have known today that your God Yhwh [is] He who is passing over before you [as] a consuming fire; He destroys them, and He humbles them before you, and you have dispossessed them, and destroyed them quickly, as Yhwh has spoken to you. **4** You do not speak in your heart (in your God Yhwh's driving them away from before you), saying, In my righteousness Yhwh has brought me in to possess this land; but in Yhwh dispossessing these nations from your presence, [it is because of] their being wicked. **5** [It is] not in your righteousness and in the uprightness of your heart [that] you are going in to possess their land, but in Yhwh dispossessing these nations from your presence, [it is because of] their being wicked, and in order to establish the word which Yhwh has sworn to your fathers, to Abraham, to Isaac, and to Jacob; **6** and you have known that [it is] not in your righteousness [that] your God Yhwh is giving this good land to you to possess it, for you [are] a people stiff of neck. **7** Remember [and] do not forget that [with] which you have made your God Yhwh angry in the wilderness; from the day that you have come out of the land of Egypt until your coming to this place, you have been rebellious against Yhwh; **8** even in Horeb you have made Yhwh angry, and Yhwh shows Himself angry against you—to destroy you. **9** In my going up into the mountain to receive the tablets of stone (tablets of the covenant which Yhwh has made with you), then I abide on the mountain forty days and forty nights; I have not eaten bread and I have not drunk water; **10** and Yhwh gives to me the two tablets of stone written with the finger of God, and on them [is] according to all the words which Yhwh has spoken with you on the mountain, out of the midst of the fire, in the day of the assembly. **11** And it comes to pass, at the end of forty days and forty nights, Yhwh has given the two tablets of stone to me—tablets of the covenant. **12** Then Yhwh says to me, Rise, go down, hurry from here, for your people whom you have brought out of Egypt have done corruptly; they have quickly turned aside from the way which I have commanded them—they have made a molten thing for themselves! **13** And Yhwh speaks to me, saying, I have seen this people, and behold, it [is] a people stiff of neck. **14** Desist from Me, and I destroy them, and blot out their name from under the heavens, and I make you become a nation mightier and more numerous than it. **15** And I turn and come down from the mountain, and the mountain is burning with fire, and the two tablets of the covenant [are] on my two hands, **16** and I see, and behold, you have sinned against your God Yhwh; you have made a molten calf for yourselves; you have quickly turned aside from the way which Yhwh has commanded you. **17** And I lay hold on the two tablets, and cast them out of my two hands, and break them before your eyes, **18** and I throw myself before Yhwh, as at first, [for] forty days and forty nights; I have not eaten bread and I have not drunk water, because of all your sins which you have sinned by doing evil in the eyes of Yhwh, to make Him angry. **19** For I have been afraid because of the anger and the fury with which Yhwh has been angry against you, to destroy you; and Yhwh also listens to me at this time. **20** And Yhwh has showed Himself very angry with Aaron, to destroy him, and I also pray for Aaron at that time. **21** And I have taken your sin, the calf which you have made, and I burn it with fire, and beat it, grinding well until it [is] small as dust, and I cast its dust into the brook which is going down out of the mountain. **22** And in Taberah, and in Massah, and in Kibroth-Hattaavah, you have been making Yhwh angry; **23** also in Yhwh's sending you from Kadesh-Barnea, saying, Go up and possess the land which I have given to you; then you provoke the mouth of your God Yhwh, and have not given credence to Him, nor listened to His voice. **24** You have been rebellious against Yhwh from the day of my knowing you. **25** And I throw myself before Yhwh—the forty days and the forty nights when I had thrown myself—because Yhwh has commanded to destroy you; **26** and I pray to Yhwh, and say, Lord Yhwh, do not destroy Your people and Your inheritance whom You have ransomed in Your greatness, whom You have brought out of Egypt with a strong hand; **27** be mindful of Your servants, of Abraham, of Isaac, and of Jacob; do not turn to the stiffness of this people, and to its wickedness, and to its sin, **28** lest the land from which You have brought us out says,

Because of Yhwh's want of ability to bring them into the land of which He has spoken to them, and because of His hating them, He brought them out to put them to death in the wilderness. **29** And they [are] Your people and Your inheritance, whom You have brought out by Your great power and by Your outstretched arm!"

CHAPTER 10

1 "At that time Yhwh has said to me, Hew two tablets of stone for yourself like the first, and come up to Me into the mountain, and you have made an ark of wood for yourself, **2** and I write on the tablets the words which were on the first tablets, which you have broken, and you have placed them in the Ark. **3** And I make an ark of shittim wood, and hew two tablets of stone like the first, and go up to the mountain with the two tablets in my hand. **4** And He writes on the tablets according to the first writing, the Ten Commandments, which Yhwh has spoken to you in the mountain, out of the midst of the fire, in the day of the assembly, and Yhwh gives them to me, **5** and I turn and come down from the mountain, and put the tablets in the Ark which I had made, and they are there, as Yhwh commanded me. **6** And the sons of Israel have journeyed from Beeroth of the sons of Jaakan to Mosera; Aaron died there, and he is buried there, and his son Eleazar acts as priest in his stead. **7** From there they journeyed to Gudgodah, and from Gudgodah to Jotbathah, a land of brooks of water. **8** At that time Yhwh has separated the tribe of Levi to carry the Ark of the Covenant of Yhwh, to stand before Yhwh, to serve Him, and to bless in His Name to this day; **9** therefore there has not been a portion and inheritance for Levi with his brothers; Yhwh Himself [is] his inheritance, as your God Yhwh has spoken to him. **10** And I have stood in the mountain, as the former days, [for] forty days and forty nights, and Yhwh also listens to me at that time; Yhwh has not willed to destroy you. **11** And Yhwh says to me, Rise, go to journey before the people, and they go in and possess the land which I have sworn to their fathers to give to them. **12** And now, O Israel, what is your God Yhwh asking from you, except to fear your God Yhwh, to walk in all His ways, and to love Him, and to serve your God Yhwh with all your heart and with all your soul, **13** to keep the commands of Yhwh, and His statutes which I am commanding you today, for good for you? **14** Behold, the heavens, even the heavens of the heavens, [belong] to your God Yhwh, [as does] the earth and all that [is] in it. **15** Only, Yhwh has delighted in your fathers, to love them, and He fixes on their seed after them—on you, out of all the peoples, as [at] this day. **16** And you have circumcised the foreskin of your heart, and you do not harden your neck anymore. **17** For He, your God Yhwh, [is] God of the gods and Lord of the lords—the great, the mighty, and the fearful God, who does not accept by appearances, nor takes a bribe; **18** He is doing the judgment of fatherless and widow, and loving the sojourner, to give bread and raiment to him. **19** And you have loved the sojourner, for you were sojourners in the land of Egypt. **20** You fear your God Yhwh, you serve Him, and you cleave to Him, and you swear by His Name. **21** He [is] your praise, and He [is] your God, who has done these great and fearful [things] with you which your eyes have seen. **22** Your fathers went down to Egypt with seventy persons, and now your God Yhwh has made you as [the] stars of the heavens for multitude."

CHAPTER 11

1 "And you have loved your God Yhwh, and kept His charge, and His statutes, and His judgments, and His commands, [for] all the days; **2** and you have known today—for it is not your sons who have not known and who have not seen the discipline of your God Yhwh, His greatness, His strong hand, and His outstretched arm; **3** and His signs and His doings which He has done in the midst of Egypt, to Pharaoh king of Egypt and to all his land; **4** and that which He has done to the force of Egypt, to its horses, and to its chariot, when He has caused the waters of the Red Sea to flow against their faces in their pursuing after them, and Yhwh destroys them, to this day; **5** and that which He has done to you in the wilderness until your coming to this place; **6** and that which He has done to Dathan and to Abiram, sons of Eliab, sons of Reuben, when the earth has opened her mouth and swallows them, and their houses, and their tents, and all that lives which is at their feet, in the midst of all Israel— **7** but [it is] your eyes which are seeing all the great work of Yhwh which He has done. **8** And you have kept all the command which I am commanding you today, so that you are strong, and have gone in, and possessed the land to where you are passing over to possess it, **9** and so that you prolong days on the ground which Yhwh has sworn to your fathers to give to them and to their seed—a land flowing with milk and honey. **10** For the land to where you are going in to possess it is not as the land of Egypt from where you have come out, where you sow your seed and have watered with your foot, as a garden of the green herb; **11** but the land to where you are passing over to possess it [is] a land of hills and valleys—it drinks water of the rain of the heavens— **12** a land which your God Yhwh is searching; the eyes of your God Yhwh [are] continually on it, from the beginning of the year even to the latter end of the year. **13** And it has been, if you listen diligently to My commands which I am commanding you today, to love your God Yhwh, and to serve Him with all your heart and with all your soul, **14** then I have given the rain of your land in its season—autumn rain and spring rain—and you have gathered your grain, and your new wine, and your oil, **15** and I have given herbs in your field for your livestock, and you have eaten and been satisfied. **16** Take heed to yourselves lest your heart be enticed, and you have turned aside, and served other gods, and bowed yourselves to them, **17** and the anger of Yhwh has burned against you, and He has restrained the heavens and there is no rain, and the ground does not give her increase, and you have perished quickly from off the good land which Yhwh is giving to you. **18** And you have placed these words of mine on your heart and on your soul, and have bound them for a sign on your hand, and they have been for frontlets between your eyes; **19** and you have taught them to your sons by speaking of them in your sitting in your house, and in your going in the way, and in your lying down, and in your rising up, **20** and have written them on the doorposts of your house and on your gates, **21** so that your days are multiplied, and the days of your sons, on the ground which Yhwh has sworn to your fathers to give to them, as the days of the heavens above the earth. **22** For if you diligently keep all this command which I am commanding you to do—to love your God Yhwh, to walk in all His ways, and to cleave to Him— **23** then Yhwh has dispossessed all these nations from before you, and you have possessed nations greater and mightier than you. **24** Every place on which the sole of your foot treads is yours: from the wilderness and Lebanon, from the river, the Euphrates River, even to the Western Sea, is your border. **25** No man stations himself in your presence; your God Yhwh puts your dread and your fear on the face of all the land on which you tread, as He has spoken to you. **26** See, today I am setting before you a blessing and a reviling: **27** the blessing when you listen to the commands of your God Yhwh which I am commanding you today; **28** and the reviling if you do not listen to the commands of your God Yhwh, and have turned aside from the way which I am commanding you today, to go after other gods which you have not known. **29** And it has been, when your God Yhwh brings you into the land to where you are going in to possess it, that you have given the blessing on Mount Gerizim and the reviling on Mount Ebal; **30** are they not beyond the Jordan, behind the way of the going in of the sun, in the land of the Canaanite who is dwelling in the plain opposite Gilgal, near the oaks of Moreh? **31** for you are passing over the Jordan to go in to possess the land which your God Yhwh is giving to you; and you have possessed it, and dwelt in it, **32** and observed to do all the statutes and the judgments which I am setting before you today."

CHAPTER 12

1 "These [are] the statutes and the judgments which you observe to do in the land which Yhwh, God of your fathers, has given to you to possess it, all the days that you are living on the ground. **2** You utterly destroy all the places where the nations which you are dispossessing served their gods, on the high mountains, and on the heights, and under every green tree; **3** and you have broken down their altars, and shattered their standing pillars, and you burn their Asherim with fire, and you cut down carved images of their gods, and have destroyed their name out of that place. **4** You do not do so to your God Yhwh; **5** rather—that you seek after the place which your God Yhwh chooses out of all your tribes to put His Name there, for

His Dwelling Place, and you have entered there, **6** and have brought in there your burnt-offerings, and your sacrifices, and your tithes, and the raised-offering of your hand, and your vows, and your free-will offerings, and the firstlings of your herd and of your flock; **7** and you have eaten there before your God Yhwh, and have rejoiced in every putting forth of your hand, you and your households, with which your God Yhwh has blessed you. **8** You do not do according to all that we are doing here today—each [doing] anything that is right in his own eyes— **9** for until now you have not come to the rest and to the inheritance which your God Yhwh is giving to you. **10** When you have passed over the Jordan, and have dwelt in the land which your God Yhwh is causing you to inherit, and He has given rest to you from all your surrounding enemies, and you have dwelt confidently, **11** then it has been, the place on which your God Yhwh fixes to cause His Name to dwell there, there you bring in all that which I am commanding you: your burnt-offerings, and your sacrifices, your tithes, and the raised-offering of your hand, and all the choice of your vows which you vow to Yhwh. **12** And you have rejoiced before your God Yhwh, you, and your sons, and your daughters, and your menservants, and your handmaids, and the Levite who [is] within your gates, for he has no part and inheritance with you. **13** Take heed to yourself lest you cause your burnt-offerings to ascend in any place which you see; **14** rather—that in the place which Yhwh chooses in one of your tribes, there you cause your burnt-offerings to ascend, and there you do all that which I am commanding you. **15** Nevertheless, you slaughter anything of the desire of your soul, and have eaten [its] flesh according to the blessing of your God Yhwh which He has given to you in all your gates; the unclean and the clean eat it, as [if] the roe and as [if] the deer. **16** Only, you do not eat the blood—you pour it on the earth as water; **17** you are not able to eat within your gates the tithe of your grain, and of your new wine, and your oil, and the firstlings of your herd and of your flock, and any of your vows which you vow, and your free will offerings, and a raised-offering of your hand; **18** but you eat it before your God Yhwh in the place which your God Yhwh fixes on, you, and your son, and your daughter, and your manservant, and your handmaid, and the Levite who [is] within your gates, and you have rejoiced before your God Yhwh in every putting forth of your hand; **19** take heed to yourself lest you forsake the Levite [for] all your days on your ground. **20** When your God Yhwh enlarges your border, as He has spoken to you, and you have said, Let me eat flesh—for your soul desires to eat flesh—you eat flesh of all the desire of your soul. **21** When the place is far from you [in] which your God Yhwh chooses to put His Name there, then you have sacrificed from your herd and from your flock which Yhwh has given to you, as I have commanded you, and have eaten within your gates, of all the desire of your soul; **22** only, as the roe and the deer is eaten, so do you eat it; the unclean and the clean alike eat it. **23** Only, be sure not to eat the blood, for the blood [is] the life, and you do not eat the life with the flesh; **24** you do not eat it—you pour it on the earth as water; **25** you do not eat it, in order that it may be well with you and with your sons after you when you do that which [is] right in the eyes of Yhwh. **26** Only, your holy things which you have, and your vows, you take up, and have gone to the place which Yhwh chooses, **27** and you have made your burnt-offerings— the flesh and the blood—on the altar of your God Yhwh; and the blood of your sacrifices is poured out by the altar of your God Yhwh, and you eat the flesh. **28** Observe, and you have obeyed all these words which I am commanding you, in order that it may be well with you and with your sons after you for all time, when you do that which [is] good and right in the eyes of your God Yhwh. **29** When your God Yhwh cuts off the nations—to where you are going in to possess them—from your presence, and you have possessed them, and have dwelt in their land— **30** take heed to yourself lest you are ensnared after them, after their being destroyed out of your presence, and lest you inquire about their gods, saying, How do these nations serve their gods, that I also do so? **31** You do not do so to your God Yhwh; for every abomination that Yhwh has hated they have done for their gods, for they even burn their sons and their daughters with fire for their gods. **32** The whole thing which I am commanding you, you observe to do it; you do not add to it, nor diminish from it."

CHAPTER 13

¹ "When a prophet or a dreamer of a dream arises in your midst, and he has given a sign or wonder to you, ² and the sign and the wonder has come to pass, which he has spoken of to you, saying, Let us go after other gods (which you have not known) and serve them, ³ you do not listen to the words of that prophet or to that dreamer of the dream, for your God Yhwh is trying you to know whether you are loving your God Yhwh with all your heart and with all your soul; ⁴ you walk after your God Yhwh, and you fear Him, and you keep His commands, and you listen to His voice, and you serve Him, and you cleave to Him. ⁵ And that prophet or that dreamer of the dream is put to death, for he has spoken apostasy against your God Yhwh (who is bringing you out of the land of Egypt, and has ransomed you out of a house of servants), to drive you out of the way in which your God Yhwh has commanded you to walk, and you have put away evil from your midst. ⁶ When your brother, son of your mother, or your son, or your daughter, or the wife of your bosom, or your friend who [is] as your own soul, moves you in secret, saying, Let us go and serve other gods (which you have not known, you and your fathers, ⁷ of the gods of the peoples who [are] around you, who are near to you, or who are far off from you, from the end of the earth even to the [other] end of the earth), ⁸ you do not consent to him, nor listen to him, nor does your eye have pity on him, nor do you spare, nor do you cover him over. ⁹ But you surely kill him; your hand is on him in the first place to put him to death, and the hand of all the people last; ¹⁰ and you have stoned him with stones and he has died, for he has sought to drive you away from your God Yhwh, who is bringing you out of the land of Egypt, out of a house of servants; ¹¹ and all Israel hears and fears, and does not add to do like this evil thing in your midst. ¹² When you hear [someone] in one of your cities, which your God Yhwh is giving to you to dwell there, saying, ¹³ Men, sons of worthlessness, have gone out of your midst, and they force away the inhabitants of their city, saying, Let us go and serve other gods (which you have not known), ¹⁴ then you have inquired, and searched, and asked diligently, and behold, [if] truth, the thing is established; this abomination has been done in your midst— ¹⁵ you surely strike the inhabitants of that city by the mouth of the sword, devoting it and all that [is] in it, even its livestock, by the mouth of the sword. ¹⁶ And you gather all its spoil into the midst of its broad place, and have completely burned the city and all its spoil with fire for your God Yhwh, and it has been a continuous heap, it is not built anymore; ¹⁷ and nothing from any of that [which is] devoted stays in your hand, so that Yhwh turns back from the fierceness of His anger, and has given mercies to you, and loved you, and multiplied you, as He has sworn to your fathers, ¹⁸ because you listen to the voice of your God Yhwh, to keep all his commands which I am commanding you today, to do that which [is] right in the eyes of your God Yhwh."

CHAPTER 14

¹ "You [are] sons of your God Yhwh; you do not cut yourselves, nor make baldness between your eyes for the dead; ² for you [are] a holy people to your God Yhwh, and Yhwh has fixed on you to be to Him for a people, a peculiar treasure, out of all the peoples who [are] on the face of the ground. ³ You do not eat any abomination; ⁴ this [is] the beast which you eat: ox, lamb of the sheep, or kid of the goats, ⁵ deer, and roe, and fallow deer, and wild goat, and ibex, and antelope, and zemer; ⁶ and every beast dividing the hoof, and cleaving the cleft into two hooves, bringing up the cud, among the beasts— you eat it. ⁷ Only, this you do not eat, of those dividing up the cud, and of those dividing the cloven hoof: the camel, and the hare, and the hyrax, for they are bringing up the cud, but the hoof has not divided—they [are] unclean to you; ⁸ and the sow, for it is dividing the hoof, and not [bringing] up the cud—it [is] unclean to you; you do not eat of their flesh, and you do not come against their carcass. ⁹ This you eat of all which [are] in the waters: anything which has fins and scales you eat; ¹⁰ and anything which does not have fins and scales you do not eat— it [is] unclean to you. ¹¹ Any clean bird you eat; ¹² and these [are] they of which you do not eat: the eagle, and the bearded vulture, and the osprey, ¹³ and the kite, and the falcon, and the vulture after its kind, ¹⁴ and every raven after its kind; ¹⁵ and the ostrich, and the nightjar [[or male ostrich]], and the seagull, and the hawk after its kind; ¹⁶ the little owl, and the great owl, and the waterhen, ¹⁷ and the pelican, and the Egyptian vulture, and the cormorant, ¹⁸ and the stork, and the heron after its kind, and the hoopoe, and the bat. ¹⁹ And every teeming thing which is flying—it [is] unclean to you; they are not eaten; ²⁰ any clean bird you eat. ²¹ You do not eat of any carcass; you give it to the sojourner who [is] within your gates, and he has eaten it; or sell [it] to a stranger; for you [are] a holy people to your God Yhwh. You do not boil a kid in its mother's milk. ²² You certainly tithe all the increase of your seed which the field is bringing forth year by year; ²³ and you have eaten before your God Yhwh, in the place where He chooses to cause His Name to dwell, the tithe of your grain, of your new wine, and of your oil, and the firstlings of your herd, and of your flock, so that you learn to fear your God Yhwh [for] all the days. ²⁴ And when the way is too much for you, that you are not able to carry it—when the place is too far off from you which your God Yhwh chooses to put His Name there, when your God Yhwh blesses you— ²⁵ then you have given [it] in money, and have bound up the money in your hand, and gone to the place on which your God Yhwh fixes; ²⁶ and you have given the money for anything which your soul desires, for oxen, and for sheep, and for wine, and for strong drink, and for anything which your soul asks for, and you have eaten before your God Yhwh there, and you have rejoiced, you and your house. ²⁷ As for the Levite who [is] within your gates, you do not forsake him, for he has no portion and inheritance with you. ²⁸ At the end of three years you bring out all the tithe of your increase in that year, and have placed [it] within your gates; ²⁹ and the Levite has come in—for he has no part and inheritance with you—and the sojourner, and the fatherless, and the widow, who [are] within your gates, and they have eaten, and been satisfied, so that your God Yhwh blesses you in all the work of your hand which you do."

CHAPTER 15

¹ "At the end of seven years you make a release, ² and this [is] the matter of the release: every owner of a loan [is] to release his hand which he lifts up against his neighbor, he does not exact of his neighbor and of his brother, but has proclaimed a release to Yhwh; ³ of the stranger you may exact, but that which is yours with your brother your hand releases, ⁴ except there is an end [when] no poor [are] with you; for Yhwh greatly blesses you in the land which your God Yhwh is giving to you [for] an inheritance to possess it, ⁵ only if you listen diligently to the voice of your God Yhwh, to observe to do all this command which I am commanding you today. ⁶ For your God Yhwh has blessed you as He has spoken to you; and you have lent [to] many nations, but you have not borrowed; and you have ruled over many nations, but they do not rule over you. ⁷ When there is with you any poor of one of your brothers, in one of your cities, in your land which your God Yhwh is giving to you, you do not harden your heart, nor shut your hand from your needy brother; ⁸ for you certainly open your hand to him, and certainly lend him sufficiency for his lack which he lacks. ⁹ Take heed to yourself lest there be a worthless word in your heart, saying, The seventh year [is] near, the year of release; and your eye is evil against your needy brother, and you do not give to him, and he has called to Yhwh concerning you, and it has been sin in you; ¹⁰ you certainly give to him, and your heart is not sad in your giving to him, for because of this thing your God Yhwh blesses you in all your works and in every putting forth of your hand; ¹¹ because the poor does not cease out of the land, therefore I am commanding you, saying, You certainly open your hand to your brother, to your poor and to your needy one in your land. ¹² When your brother is sold to you, a Hebrew or a Hebrewess, and he has served you [for] six years, then in the seventh year you send him away free from you. ¹³ And when you send him away free from you, you do not send him away empty; ¹⁴ you certainly adorn him from your flock, and from your threshing-floor, and from your wine-vat; you give to him [from] that which your God Yhwh has blessed you [with], ¹⁵ and you have remembered that you have been a servant in the land of Egypt, and your God Yhwh ransoms you; therefore I am commanding you this thing today. ¹⁶ And it has been, when he says to you, I do not go out from you, because he has loved you and your house, because [it is] good for him with you, ¹⁷ then you have taken the awl, and have put [it] through his ear, and through the door, and he has been a perpetual servant to you; and you also do so to your handmaid. ¹⁸ It is not hard in your eyes in your sending him away free from you; for [his worth has been] double the hire of a hired worker [when] he has served you six years; and your God

Yhwh has blessed you in all that you do. ¹⁹ Every firstling that is born in your herd and in your flock—you sanctify the male to your God Yhwh; you do not work with the firstling of your ox, nor shear the firstling of your flock; ²⁰ you eat it before your God Yhwh year by year, in the place which Yhwh chooses, you and your house. ²¹ And when there is a blemish in it, [or it is] lame or blind, [or has] any evil blemish, you do not sacrifice it to your God Yhwh; ²² you eat it within your gates, the unclean and the clean alike, as the roe and as the deer. ²³ Only, you do not eat its blood—you pour it on the earth as water."

CHAPTER 16

¹ "Observe the month of Abib, and you have made a Passover to your God Yhwh, for in the month of Abib your God Yhwh has brought you out of Egypt by night; ² and you have sacrificed a Passover to your God Yhwh, of the flock and of the herd, in the place which Yhwh chooses to cause His Name to dwell there. ³ You do not eat any fermented thing with it; [for] seven days you eat unleavened things with it, bread of affliction (for you have come out of the land of Egypt in haste), so that you remember the day of your coming out of the land of Egypt all [the] days of your life; ⁴ and leaven is not seen with you in all your border [for] seven days, and there does not remain [any] of the flesh which you sacrifice at evening on the first day until morning. ⁵ You are not able to sacrifice the Passover within any of your gates which your God Yhwh is giving to you, ⁶ except at the place which your God Yhwh chooses to cause His Name to dwell—there you sacrifice the Passover in the evening, at the going in of the sun, the season of your coming out of Egypt; ⁷ and you have cooked and eaten in the place on which your God Yhwh fixes, and have turned in the morning and gone to your tents; ⁸ [for] six days you eat unleavened things, and on the seventh day [is] a restraint to your God Yhwh, you do no work. ⁹ You number seven weeks for yourself; you begin to number seven weeks from the beginning of the sickle among the standing grain, ¹⁰ and you have observed the Celebration of Weeks to your God Yhwh, a tribute of a free-will offering of your hand, which you give as your God Yhwh blesses you. ¹¹ And you have rejoiced before your God Yhwh, you, and your son, and your daughter, and your manservant, and your handmaid, and the Levite who [is] within your gates, and the sojourner, and the fatherless, and the widow, who [are] in your midst, in the place which your God Yhwh chooses to cause His Name to dwell there, ¹² and you have remembered that you have been a servant in Egypt, and have observed and done these statutes. ¹³ You observe the Celebration of Shelters for yourself [for] seven days, in your ingathering of your threshing-floor and of your wine-vat; ¹⁴ and you have rejoiced in your celebration, you, and your son, and your daughter, and your manservant, and your handmaid, and the Levite, and the sojourner, and the fatherless, and the widow, who [are] within your gates. ¹⁵ [For] seven days you celebrate before your God Yhwh in the place which Yhwh chooses, for your God Yhwh blesses you in all your increase and in every work of your hands, and you have been only rejoicing. ¹⁶ Three times in a year all of your males appear before your God Yhwh in the place which He chooses: in the Celebration of Unleavened Things, and in the Celebration of Weeks, and in the Celebration of Shelters; and they do not appear before Yhwh empty; ¹⁷ each [gives] according to the gift of his hand, according to the blessing of your God Yhwh, which He has given to you. ¹⁸ You set for yourself judges and authorities within all your gates which your God Yhwh is giving to you, for your tribes; and they have judged the people [with] a righteous judgment. ¹⁹ You do not turn aside judgment; you do not discern faces, nor take a bribe, for the bribe blinds the eyes of the wise and perverts the words of the righteous. ²⁰ Righteousness—you pursue righteousness, so that you live and have possessed the land which your God Yhwh is giving to you. ²¹ You do not plant an Asherah of any trees for yourself near the altar of your God Yhwh, which you make for yourself, ²² and you do not raise up any standing image for yourself which your God Yhwh is hating."

CHAPTER 17

¹ "You do not sacrifice to your God Yhwh ox or sheep in which there is a blemish—any bad thing; for it [is] an abomination [to] your God Yhwh. ² When there is found in your midst, in one of your cities which your God Yhwh is giving to you, a man or a woman who does evil in the eyes of your God Yhwh by transgressing His covenant, ³ and he goes and serves other gods, and bows himself to them, and to the sun, or to the moon, or to any of the host of the heavens, which I have not commanded, ⁴ and it has been declared to you, and you have heard, and have searched diligently, and behold, [if] truth, the thing is established; this abomination has been done in Israel— ⁵ then you have brought out that man or that woman who has done this evil thing, to your gates—the man or the woman—and you have stoned them with stones, and they have died. ⁶ By the mouth of two witnesses or three witnesses is he who is being put to death put to death; he is not put to death by the mouth of one witness; ⁷ the hand of the witnesses is on him in the first place to put him to death, and the hand of all the people last; and you have put away evil out of your midst. ⁸ When anything is too hard for you for judgment, between blood and blood, between plea and plea, and between stroke and stroke—matters of strife within your gates—then you have risen and gone up to the place on which your God Yhwh fixes, ⁹ and have come to the priests, the Levites, and to the judge who is in those days, and have inquired, and they have declared the word of judgment to you, ¹⁰ and you have done according to the tenor of the word which they declare to you ([they] of that place which Yhwh chooses); and you have observed to do according to all that they direct you. ¹¹ According to the tenor of the law which they direct you, and according to the judgment which they say to you, you do; you do not turn aside from the word which they declare to you [to] the right or left. ¹² And the man who acts with presumption, so as not to listen to the priest (who is standing to serve your God Yhwh there), or to the judge, even that man has died, and you have put away evil from Israel, ¹³ and all the people hear and fear, and do not presume anymore. ¹⁴ When you come into the land which your God Yhwh is giving to you, and have possessed it, and dwelt in it, and you have said, Let me set a king over me like all the nations which [are] around me ¹⁵ you certainly set a king over you on whom Yhwh fixes; you set a king over you from the midst of your brothers; you are not able to set a stranger over you, who is not your brother. ¹⁶ Only, he does not multiply horses for himself, nor cause the people to return to Egypt, so as to multiply horses, seeing Yhwh has said to you, You do not add to return in this way anymore. ¹⁷ And he does not multiply wives for himself, and his heart does not turn aside, and he does not exceedingly multiply silver and gold for himself. ¹⁸ And it has been, when he sits on the throne of his kingdom, that he has written a copy of this law for himself, on a scroll, from [that] before the priests, the Levites, ¹⁹ and it has been with him, and he has read in it all [the] days of his life, so that he learns to fear his God Yhwh, to keep all the words of this law and these statutes—to do them, ²⁰ so that his heart is not high above his brothers, and so as not to turn aside from the command [to] the right or left, so that he prolongs days over his kingdom, he and his sons in the midst of Israel."

CHAPTER 18

¹ "There is not for the priests, the Levites—all the tribe of Levi—a portion and inheritance with Israel; they eat fire-offerings of Yhwh, even His inheritance, ² and he has no inheritance in the midst of his brothers; Yhwh Himself [is] his inheritance, as He has spoken to him. ³ And this is the priest's right from the people, from those sacrificing a sacrifice, whether ox or sheep, he has even given to the priest the leg, and the two cheeks, and the stomach; ⁴ you give to him the first of your grain, of your new wine, and of your oil, and the first of the fleece of your flock; ⁵ for your God Yhwh has fixed on him, out of all your tribes, to stand to serve in the Name of Yhwh—him and his sons continually. ⁶ And when the Levite comes from one of your cities, out of all Israel where he has sojourned, and has come with all the desire of his soul to the place which Yhwh chooses, ⁷ then he has ministered in the Name of his God Yhwh like all his brothers, the Levites, who are standing there before Yhwh. ⁸ They eat portion like portion, apart from his sold things from the fathers. ⁹ When you are coming into the land which your God Yhwh is giving to you, you do not learn to do according to the abominations of those nations. ¹⁰ There is not found in you one causing his son and his daughter to pass over into fire, a user of divinations, an observer of clouds, and an enchanter, and a sorcerer, ¹¹ and a

charmer, and one inquiring from a familiar spirit, and a wizard, and one seeking to the dead. **12** For everyone doing these [is] an abomination [to] Yhwh, and because of these abominations your God Yhwh is dispossessing them from your presence. **13** You must be perfect with your God Yhwh, **14** for these nations whom you are possessing listen to observers of clouds and to diviners; but you—your God Yhwh has not permitted you so. **15** Your God Yhwh raises up for you a Prophet like me out of your midst, out of your brothers—you must listen to Him, **16** according to all that you asked from your God Yhwh in Horeb, in the day of the assembly, saying, Do not let me add to hear the voice of my God Yhwh, and do not let me see this great fire anymore, and I do not die; **17** and Yhwh says to me, They have done well [in] what they have spoken; **18** I raise up for them a Prophet like you out of the midst of their brothers, and I have given My words in His mouth, and He has spoken to them all that which I command Him; **19** and it has been [that] the man who does not listen to My words which He speaks in My Name, I require [it] of him. **20** Only, the prophet who presumes to speak a word in My Name, which I have not commanded him to speak, and who speaks in the name of other gods, indeed, that prophet has died. **21** And when you say in your heart, How do we know the word which Yhwh has not spoken? **22** That which the prophet speaks in the Name of Yhwh, and the thing is not, and does not come—it [is] the word which Yhwh has not spoken; the prophet has spoken it in presumption; you are not afraid of him."

CHAPTER 19

1 "When your God Yhwh cuts off the nations whose land your God Yhwh is giving to you, and you have dispossessed them, and dwelt in their cities and in their houses, **2** you separate three cities for yourself in the midst of your land which your God Yhwh is giving to you to possess it. **3** You prepare the way for yourself, and have divided into three parts the border of your land which your God Yhwh causes you to inherit, and it has been for the fleeing there of every manslayer. **4** And this [is] the matter of the manslayer who flees there, and has lived: he who strikes his neighbor unknowingly, and is not hating him before— **5** even he who comes into a forest with his neighbor to hew wood, and his hand has driven with an axe to cut the tree, and the iron has slipped from the wood, and has met his neighbor, and he has died—he flees to one of these cities, and has lived, **6** lest the redeemer of blood pursue after the manslayer when his heart is hot and has overtaken him, because the way is great, and has struck his life, and he has no sentence of death, for he is not hating him before; **7** therefore I am commanding you, saying, You separate three cities for yourself. **8** And if your God Yhwh enlarges your border, as He has sworn to your fathers, and has given to you all the land which He has spoken to give to your fathers— **9** when you keep all this command to do it, which I am commanding you today, to love your God Yhwh and to walk in His ways [for] all the days—then you have added three more cities for yourself to these three; **10** and [do this] lest innocent blood is shed in the midst of your land which your God Yhwh is giving to you [for] an inheritance, and there has been blood on you. **11** And when a man is hating his neighbor, and has lain in wait for him, and risen against him, and struck his life, and he has died, then he has fled to one of these cities, **12** and [the] elderly of his city have sent and taken him from there, and given him into the hand of the redeemer of blood, and he has died; **13** your eye has no pity on him, and you have put away the innocent blood from Israel, and it is well with you. **14** You do not remove a border of your neighbor, which they of former times have made, in your inheritance, which you inherit in the land which your God Yhwh is giving to you to possess it. **15** One witness does not rise against a man for any iniquity and for any sin, in any sin which he sins; by the mouth of two witnesses or by the mouth of three witnesses is a thing established. **16** When a violent witness rises against a man to testify against him apostasy, **17** then both of the men who have the strife have stood before Yhwh, before the priests and the judges who are in those days, **18** and the judges have searched diligently, and behold, the witness [is] a false witness who has testified a falsehood against his brother, **19** then you have done to him as he devised to do to his brother, and you have put away evil out of your midst, **20** and those who are left hear and fear, and do not add to do according to this evil thing in your midst anymore. **21** And your eye does not pity—life for life, eye for

eye, tooth for tooth, hand for hand, foot for foot."

CHAPTER 20

1 "When you go out to battle against your enemy, and have seen horse and chariot—a people more numerous than you— you are not afraid of them, for your God Yhwh [is] with you, who is bringing you up out of the land of Egypt; **2** and it has been, in your drawing near to the battle, that the priest has come near, and spoken to the people, **3** and said to them, Hear, O Israel: You are drawing near today to battle against your enemies, do not let your hearts be tender, do not fear, nor make haste, nor be terrified at their presence, **4** for your God Yhwh [is] He who is going with you, to fight for you with your enemies—to save you. **5** And the authorities have spoken to the people, saying, Who [is] the man that has built a new house and has not dedicated it? Let him go and return to his house, lest he die in battle and another man dedicate it. **6** And who [is] the man that has planted a vineyard and has not made it common? Let him go and return to his house, lest he die in battle, and another man make it common. **7** And who [is] the man that has betrothed a woman and has not taken her? Let him go and return to his house, lest he die in battle, and another man take her. **8** And the authorities have added to speak to the people and said, Who [is] the man that is afraid and tender of heart? Let him go and return to his house, and the heart of his brothers does not melt like his heart. **9** And it has come to pass, as the authorities finish to speak to the people, that they have appointed princes of the hosts at the head of the people. **10** When you draw near to a city to fight against it, then you have called to it for peace, **11** and it has been, if it answers you [with] peace, and has opened to you, then it has come to pass, all the people who are found in it are for tributaries to you, and have served you. **12** And if it does not make peace with you, and has made war with you, then you have laid siege against it, **13** and your God Yhwh has given it into your hand, and you have struck every male of it by the mouth of the sword. **14** Only, the women, and the infants, and the livestock, and all that is in the city, all its spoil, you seize for yourself, and you have eaten the spoil of your enemies which your God Yhwh has given to you. **15** So you do to all the cities which are very far off from you, which are not of the cities of these nations. **16** Only, of the cities of these peoples which your God Yhwh is giving to you [for] an inheritance, you do not keep alive any [that are] breathing; **17** for you certainly devote the Hittite, and the Amorite, the Canaanite, and the Perizzite, the Hivite, and the Jebusite, as your God Yhwh has commanded you, **18** so that they do not teach you to do according to all their abominations which they have done for their gods, and you have sinned against your God Yhwh. **19** When you lay siege to a city [for] many days to fight against it, to capture it, you do not destroy its trees to force an axe against them, for you eat of them, and you do not cut them down—for the tree of the field [is] man's—to go in at your presence in the siege. **20** Only, the tree of which you know that it [is] not a fruit-tree, you destroy it, and have cut [it] down, and have built a bulwark against the city which is making war with you until you have subdued it."

CHAPTER 21

1 "When one is found slain, fallen in a field on the ground which your God Yhwh is giving to you to possess it, [and] it is not known who has struck him, **2** then your elderly and yours [of those] judging have gone out and measured to the cities which [are] around the slain one, **3** and it has been, the city which [is] near to the slain one, even [the] elderly of that city have taken a heifer of the herd, which has not been worked with, which has not drawn in a yoke, **4** and [the] elderly of that city have brought down the heifer to a hard valley, which is not tilled nor sown, and have beheaded the heifer there in the valley. **5** And the priests, sons of Levi, have come near—for your God Yhwh has fixed on them to serve Him and to bless in the Name of Yhwh, and by their mouth is every strife and every stroke— **6** and all [the] elderly of that city, who are near to the slain one, wash their hands over the heifer which is beheaded in the valley, **7** and they have answered and said, Our hands have not shed this blood, and our eyes have not seen— **8** receive atonement for Your people Israel, whom You have ransomed, O Yhwh, and do not permit innocent blood in the midst of Your people Israel; and the blood has been pardoned to them, **9** and you put away the innocent blood out of your midst, for you do that which [is] right in the eyes of Yhwh. **10** When you go out to battle against your enemies, and your God Yhwh has given them into your hand, and you have taken captive its captivity, **11** and have seen a woman of beautiful form in the captivity, and have delighted in her, and have taken [her] to yourself for a wife, **12** then you have brought her into the midst of your household, and she has shaved her head, and prepared her nails, **13** and turned aside the raiment of her captivity from off her, and has dwelt in your house, and lamented her father and her mother [for] a month of days, and afterward you go in to her and have married her, and she has been to you for a wife. **14** And it has been, if you have not delighted in her, that you have sent her away at her desire, and surely you do not sell her for money; you do not tyrannize over her, because that you have humbled her. **15** When a man has two wives, one loved and the other hated, and they have borne sons to him (the loved one and the hated one), and the firstborn son has been to the hated one, **16** then it has been, in the day of his causing his sons to inherit that which he has, he is not able to declare firstborn the son of the loved one, in the face of the son of the hated one—the firstborn. **17** But the firstborn, son of the hated one, he acknowledges, to give to him a double portion of all that is found with him, for he [is] the beginning of his strength; to him [is] the right of the firstborn. **18** When a man has a son apostatizing and being rebellious—he is not listening to the voice of his father and to the voice of his mother, and they have disciplined him, and he does not listen to them— **19** then his father and his mother have laid hold on him, and they have brought him out to [the] elderly of his city, and to the gate of his place, **20** and have said to [the] elderly of his city, Our son—this one—is apostatizing and being rebellious; he is not listening to our voice—a glutton and drunkard. **21** Then all the men of his city have stoned him with stones and he has died, and you have put away the evil out of your midst, and all Israel hears and fears. **22** And when there is a sin in a man [with] a judgment of death, and he has been put to death, and you have hanged him on a tree, **23** his corpse does not remain on the tree, for you certainly bury him in the day—for he who is hanged [becomes] a curse of God—and you do not defile your ground which your God Yhwh is giving to you [for] an inheritance."

CHAPTER 22

1 "You do not see the ox of your brother or his sheep driven away, and have hidden yourself from them, you certainly turn them back to your brother; **2** and if your brother [is] not near to you, and you have not known him, then you have removed it to the midst of your house, and it has been with you until your brother seeks it, and you have given it back to him; **3** and so you do to his donkey, and so you do to his garment, and so you do to any lost thing of your brother's, which is lost by him, and you have found it; you are not able to hide yourself. **4** You do not see the donkey of your brother, or his ox, falling in the way, and have hid yourself from them; you certainly raise [them] up for him. **5** Anything of a man is not on a woman, nor does a man put on the garment of a woman, for anyone doing these [is] an abomination [to] your God Yhwh. **6** When a bird's nest comes before you in the way, in any tree, or on the earth, [with] brood or eggs, and the mother is sitting on the brood or on the eggs, you do not take the mother with the young ones; **7** you certainly send the mother away, and take the young ones for yourself, so that it is well with you and you have prolonged days. **8** When you build a new house, then you have made a parapet for your roof, and you do not put blood on your house when one falls from it. **9** You do not sow your vineyard [with] two kinds [of seed], lest the fullness of the seed which you sow and the increase of the vineyard be separated. **10** You do not plow with an ox and with a donkey together. **11** You do not put on mixed material, wool and linens together. **12** You make fringes for yourself on the four skirts of your covering with which you cover [yourself]. **13** When a man takes a wife, and has gone in to her, and hated her, **14** and laid evil deeds of words against her, and brought out an evil name against her, and said, I have taken this woman, and I draw near to her, and I have not found proofs of virginity in her; **15** then the father of

the girl, and her mother, have taken and brought out the girl's proofs of virginity to [the] elderly of the city in the gate, **16** and the father of the girl has said to the elderly, I have given my daughter to this man for a wife, and he hates her; **17** and behold, he has laid evil deeds of words, saying, I have not found proofs of virginity for your daughter—and these [are] the proofs of virginity of my daughter! And they have spread out the garment before [the] elderly of the city. **18** And [the] elderly of that city have taken the man, and discipline him, **19** and fined him one hundred pieces of silver, and given [them] to the father of the girl, because he has brought out an evil name on a virgin of Israel; and she is to him for a wife—he is not able to send her away [for] all his days. **20** And if this thing has been truth—proofs of virginity have not been found for the girl— **21** then they have brought out the girl to the opening of her father's house, and the men of her city have stoned her with stones and she has died, for she has done folly in Israel, to go whoring [in] her father's house; and you have put away evil out of your midst. **22** When a man is found lying with a woman married to a husband, then both of them have died—the man who is lying with the woman, and the woman; and you have put away evil out of Israel. **23** When there is a girl, a virgin, betrothed to a man, and a man has found her in a city and lain with her, **24** then you have brought them both out to the gate of that city, and stoned them with stones, and they have died: the girl, because that she has not cried in a city; and the man, because that he has humbled his neighbor's wife; and you have put away evil out of your midst. **25** And if the man finds the girl who is betrothed in a field, and the man has laid hold on her, and lain with her, then the man who has lain with her has died alone; **26** and you do not do anything to the girl—the girl has no deadly sin; for as a man rises against his neighbor and has murdered him, [taking] a life, so [is] this thing; **27** for he found her in a field, [and when] she has cried—the girl who is betrothed—then she has no savior. **28** When a man finds a girl, a virgin who is not betrothed, and has caught her, and lain with her, and they have been found, **29** then the man who is lying with her has given fifty pieces of silver to the father of the girl, and she is to him for a wife; because that he has humbled her, he is not able to send her away [for] all his days. **30** A man does not take his father's wife, nor uncover his father's skirt."

CHAPTER 23

1 "No one wounded, bruised, or cut in the genitals enters into the assembly of Yhwh; **2** a bastard does not enter into the assembly of Yhwh; even a tenth generation of him does not enter into the assembly of Yhwh. **3** An Ammonite and a Moabite do not enter into the assembly of Yhwh; even a tenth generation of them do not enter into the assembly of Yhwh—for all time, **4** because that they have not come before you with bread and with water in the way, in your coming out from Egypt, and because he has hired against you Balaam son of Beor, of Pethor of Aram-Naharaim, to revile you; **5** and your God Yhwh has not been willing to listen to Balaam, and your God Yhwh turns the reviling to a blessing for you, because your God Yhwh has loved you; **6** you do not seek their peace and their good all your days—for all time. **7** You do not detest an Edomite, for he [is] your brother; you do not detest an Egyptian, for you have been a sojourner in his land; **8** sons who are begotten of them, a third generation of them, enter into the assembly of Yhwh. **9** When a camp goes out against your enemies, then you have kept from every evil thing. **10** When there is a man who is not clean in you, from an accident at night, then he has gone out to the outside of the camp; he does not come into the midst of the camp; **11** and it has been, at the turning of the evening, he bathes with water, and at the going in of the sun he comes into the midst of the camp. **12** And you have a station at the outside of the camp, and you have gone out there outside; **13** and you have a peg on your staff, and it has been, in your sitting outside, that you have dug with it, and turned back, and covered your filth. **14** For your God Yhwh is walking up and down in the midst of your camp, to deliver you and to give your enemies before you, and your camp has been holy, and He does not see the nakedness of anything in you, and has turned back from after you. **15** You do not shut up a servant to his lord, who escapes to you from his lord; **16** he dwells with you in your midst, in the place which he chooses within one of your gates, where it is pleasing to him; you do not oppress him. **17** There is not a whore among the daughters of Israel, nor is there a whoremonger among the sons of Israel; **18** you do not bring the wage of a whore or the price of a dog into the house of your God Yhwh for any vow; for even both of them [are] an abomination [to] your God Yhwh. **19** You do not lend in usury to your brother—usury of money, usury of food, usury of anything which is lent on usury. **20** You may lend in usury to a stranger, but you do not lend in usury to your brother, so that your God Yhwh blesses you in every putting forth of your hand on the land to where you go in to possess it. **21** When you vow a vow to your God Yhwh, you do not delay to complete it; for your God Yhwh certainly requires it from you, lest it has been sin in you. **22** And when you refrain to vow, it is not sin in you. **23** You keep and have done the utterance of your lips, as you have vowed to your God Yhwh, a free-will offering which you have spoken with your mouth. **24** When you come into the vineyard of your neighbor, then you have eaten grapes according to your desire, your sufficiency, but you do not put [any] into your vessel. **25** When you come in among the standing grain of your neighbor, then you have plucked the ears with your hand, but you do not wave a sickle over the standing grain of your neighbor."

CHAPTER 24

1 "When a man takes a wife and has married her, and it has been, if she does not find grace in his eyes (for he has found nakedness in her of anything), then he has written a writing of divorce for her, and given [it] into her hand, and sent her out of his house; **2** when she has gone out of his house, and has gone and been another man's, **3** and the latter man has hated her, and written a writing of divorce for her, and given [it] into her hand, and sent her out of his house, or when the latter man dies, who has taken her to himself for a wife, **4** her former husband who sent her away is not able to return to take her to be to him for a wife, after that she has become defiled; for it [is] an abomination before Yhwh, and you do not cause the land to sin which your God Yhwh is giving to you [for] an inheritance. **5** When a man takes a new wife, he does not go out into the host, and [one] does not pass over to him for anything; he is free at his own house [for] one year, and his wife, whom he has taken, he has made glad. **6** No one takes millstones and rider in pledge, for it [is one's] life he is taking in pledge. **7** When a man is found stealing a person from his brothers, from the sons of Israel, and has tyrannized over him and sold him, then that thief has died, and you have put away evil out of your midst. **8** Take heed in the plague of leprosy, to watch greatly, and to do according to all that the priests, the Levites, teach you; you observe to do as I have commanded them; **9** remember that which your God Yhwh has done to Miriam in the way, in your coming out of Egypt. **10** When you lift up a debt of anything on your brother, you do not go into his house to obtain his pledge; **11** you stand at the outside, and the man on whom you are lifting [it] up is bringing out the pledge to you at the outside. **12** And if he is a poor man, you do not lie down with his pledge; **13** you certainly give back the pledge to him at the going in of the sun, and he has lain down in his own raiment and has blessed you; and it is righteousness to you before your God Yhwh. **14** You do not oppress a hired worker, poor and needy, of your brothers or of your sojourner who is in your land within your gates; **15** you give his hire in his day, and the sun does not go in on it, for he [is] poor, and he is supporting his life on it, lest he cries against you to Yhwh, and it has been sin in you. **16** Fathers are not put to death for sons, and sons are not put to death for fathers—they are each put to death for his own sin. **17** You do not turn aside the judgment of a fatherless sojourner, nor take the garment of a widow in pledge; **18** and you have remembered that you have been a servant in Egypt, and your God Yhwh ransoms you from there; therefore, I am commanding you to do this thing. **19** When you reap your harvest in your field, and have forgotten a sheaf in a field, you do not return to take it; it is for the sojourner, for the fatherless, and for the widow, so that your God Yhwh blesses you in all the work of your hands. **20** When you beat your olive, you do not examine the branch behind you; it is for the sojourner, for the fatherless, and for the widow. **21** When you cut your vineyard, you do not glean behind you; it is for the sojourner, for the fatherless, and for the widow; **22** and you have remembered that you have been a servant in the land of Egypt; therefore, I am commanding you to do this thing."

CHAPTER 25

1 "When there is a strife between men, and they have come near to the judgment, and they have judged, and declared righteous the righteous, and declared wrong the wrongdoer, **2** then it has come to pass, if the wrongdoer is to be struck, that the judge has caused him to fall down, and [one] has struck him in his presence, according to the sufficiency of his wrongdoing, by number; **3** he strikes him forty [times]; he is not adding, lest he is adding to strike him above these many stripes, and your brother be lightly esteemed in your eyes. **4** You do not muzzle an ox in its threshing. **5** When brothers dwell together, and one of them has died and has no son, the wife of the dead is not given to a strange man; her husband's brother goes in to her, and has taken her to him for a wife, and performs the duty of her husband's brother; **6** and it has been, the firstborn which she bears rises for the name of his dead brother, and his name is not wiped away out of Israel. **7** And if the man does not delight to take his brother's wife, then his brother's wife has gone up to the gate, to the elderly, and said, My husband's brother is refusing to raise up a name for his brother in Israel; he has not been willing to perform the duty of my husband's brother; **8** and [the] elderly of his city have called for him, and spoken to him, and he has stood and said, I have no desire to take her. **9** Then his brother's wife has drawn near to him before the eyes of the elderly, and drawn his shoe from off his foot, and spat in his face, and answered and said, Thus it is done to the man who does not build up the house of his brother; **10** and his name has been called in Israel, The house of him whose shoe is drawn off. **11** When men strive together with one another, and the wife of one has drawn near to deliver her husband out of the hand of his striker, and has put forth her hand, and laid hold on his private parts, **12** then you have cut off her hand; your eye does not spare. **13** You do not have [both] a great stone and a small stone in your bag. **14** You do not have a great ephah and a small ephah in your house. **15** You have a complete and just stone, [and] you have a complete and just ephah, so that they prolong your days on the ground which your God Yhwh is giving to you; **16** for anyone doing these things, anyone doing iniquity, [is] an abomination [to] your God Yhwh. **17** Remember that which Amalek has done to you in the way in your going out from Egypt, **18** that he has met you in the way, and strikes among you all those feeble behind you (when you [were] weary and fatigued), and is not fearing God. **19** And it has been, in your God Yhwh giving rest to you from all your surrounding enemies, in the land which your God Yhwh is giving to you [for] an inheritance to possess it, you blot out the remembrance of Amalek from under the heavens—you do not forget."

CHAPTER 26

1 "And it has been, when you come into the land which your God Yhwh is giving to you [for] an inheritance, and you have possessed it and dwelt in it, **2** that you have taken from the first of all the fruits of the ground, which you bring in out of your land which your God Yhwh is giving to you, and have put [it] in a basket, and gone to the place which your God Yhwh chooses to cause His Name to dwell there. **3** And you have come to the priest who is in those days, and have said to him, I have declared to your God Yhwh today that I have come into the land which Yhwh has sworn to our fathers to give to us; **4** and the priest has taken the basket out of your hand and placed it before the altar of your God Yhwh. **5** And you have answered and said before your God Yhwh, My father [is] a perishing Aramean! And he goes down to Egypt, and sojourns there with few men, and becomes a great, mighty, and populous nation there; **6** and the Egyptians do us evil, and afflict us, and put hard service on us; **7** and we cry to Yhwh, God of our fathers, and Yhwh hears our voice, and sees our affliction, and our labor, and our oppression; **8** and Yhwh brings us out from Egypt by a strong hand, and by an outstretched arm, and by great fear, and by signs, and by wonders, **9** and He brings us to this place, and gives this land to us—a land flowing with milk and honey. **10** And now, behold, I have brought in the first of the fruits of the ground which you have given to me, O Yhwh. (And you have placed it before your God Yhwh, and bowed yourself before your God Yhwh, **11** and rejoiced in all the good which your God Yhwh has given to you and to your house—you, and the Levite, and the sojourner who [is] in your midst.) **12** When you complete to tithe all the tithe of your increase in the third year, the year of the tithe, then you have given to the Levite, to the sojourner, to the fatherless, and to the widow, and they have eaten within your gates and been satisfied, [13] and you have said before your God Yhwh, I have put away the separated thing out of the house, and have also given it to the Levite, and to the sojourner, and to the orphan, and to the widow, according to all Your command which You have commanded me; I have not passed over from Your commands, nor have I forgotten. [14] I have not eaten of it in my affliction, nor have I put away of it for uncleanness, nor have I given of it for the dead; I have listened to the voice of my God Yhwh; I have done according to all that You have commanded me; [15] look from Your holy habitation, from the heavens, and bless Your people Israel and the ground which You have given to us, as You have sworn to our fathers—a land flowing [with] milk and honey. [16] This day your God Yhwh is commanding you to do these statutes and judgments; and you have listened and done them with all your heart and with all your soul. [17] Today you have proclaimed Yhwh to be to you for God, that [you are] to walk in His ways, and to keep His statutes, and His commands, and His judgments, and to listen to His voice. [18] And today Yhwh has proclaimed you to be to Him for a people, a peculiar treasure, as He has spoken to you, that [you are] to keep all His commands, [19] so as to make you highest above all the nations whom He has made for a praise, and for a name, and for beauty, and for your being a holy people to your God Yhwh, as He has spoken."

CHAPTER 27

[1] And Moses and [the] elderly of Israel command the people, saying, "Keep all the command which I am commanding you today; [2] and it has been, in the day that you pass over the Jordan to the land which your God Yhwh is giving to you, that you have raised up great stones for yourself, and plastered them with plaster, [3] and written on them all the words of this law in your passing over, so that you go into the land which your God Yhwh is giving to you—a land flowing with milk and honey, as Yhwh, God of your fathers, has spoken to you. [4] And it has been, in your passing over the Jordan, you raise up these stones which I am commanding you today, in Mount Ebal, and you have plastered them with plaster, [5] and built an altar there to your God Yhwh, an altar of stones; you do not wave iron over them. [6] You build the altar of your God Yhwh [with] complete stones, and have caused burnt-offerings to ascend on it to your God Yhwh, [7] and sacrificed peace-offerings, and eaten there, and rejoiced before your God Yhwh, [8] and written on the stones all the words of this law, well engraved." [9] And Moses speaks—the priests, the Levites, also—to all Israel, saying, "Keep silent and hear, O Israel: This day you have become a people for your God Yhwh; [10] and you have listened to the voice of your God Yhwh, and done His commands and His statutes which I am commanding you today." [11] And Moses commands the people on that day, saying, [12] "These stand on Mount Gerizzim to bless the people, in your passing over the Jordan: Simeon, and Levi, and Judah, and Issachar, and Joseph, and Benjamin. [13] And these stand, for the reviling, on Mount Ebal: Reuben, Gad, and Asher, and Zebulun, Dan, and Naphtali." [14] And the Levites have answered and said to every man of Israel [with] a loud voice: [15] "Cursed [is] the man who makes a carved and molten image, an abomination [to] Yhwh, work of the hands of a craftsman, and has put [it] in a secret place." And all the people have answered and said, "Amen." [16] "Cursed [is] he who is making light of his father and his mother." And all the people have said, "Amen." [17] "Cursed [is] he who is removing his neighbor's border." And all the people have said, "Amen." [18] "Cursed [is] he who is causing the blind to err in the way." And all the people have said, "Amen." [19] "Cursed [is] he who is turning aside the judgment of fatherless, sojourner, and widow." And all the people have said, "Amen." [20] "Cursed [is] he who is lying with his father's wife, for he has uncovered his father's skirt." And all the people have said, "Amen." [21] "Cursed [is] he who is lying with any beast." And all the people have said, "Amen." [22] "Cursed [is] he who is lying with his sister, daughter of his father or daughter of his mother." And all the people have said, "Amen." [23] "Cursed [is] he who is lying with his mother-in-law." And all the people have said, "Amen." [24] "Cursed [is] he who is striking his neighbor in secret." And all the people have said, "Amen." [25] "Cursed [is] he who is taking a bribe to strike a person, innocent blood."

And all the people have said, "Amen." [26] "Cursed [is] he who does not establish the words of this law, to do them." And all the people have said, "Amen."

CHAPTER 28

[1] "And it has been, if you listen diligently to the voice of your God Yhwh, to observe to do all His commands which I am commanding you today, that your God Yhwh has made you highest above all the nations of the earth, [2] and all these blessings have come on you and overtaken you, because you listen to the voice of your God Yhwh: [3] Blessed [are] you in the city, and blessed [are] you in the field. [4] Blessed [is] the fruit of your womb, and the fruit of your ground, and the fruit of your livestock, the increase of your oxen, and the wealth of your flock. [5] Blessed [is] your basket and your kneading-trough. [6] Blessed [are] you in your coming in, and blessed [are] you in your going out. [7] Yhwh makes your enemies, who are rising up against you, to be struck before your face; in one way they come out to you, and in seven ways they flee before you. [8] Yhwh commands the blessing with you in your storehouses, and in every putting forth of your hand, and has blessed you in the land which your God Yhwh is giving to you. [9] Yhwh establishes you to Himself for a holy people, as He has sworn to you, when you keep the commands of your God Yhwh and have walked in His ways; [10] and all the peoples of the land have seen that the Name of Yhwh is called by you, and they have been afraid of you. [11] And Yhwh has made you abundant in good, in the fruit of the womb, and in the fruit of your livestock, and in the fruit of your ground, on the ground which Yhwh has sworn to your fathers to give to you. [12] Yhwh opens his good treasure to you—the heavens—to give the rain of your land in its season, and to bless all the work of your hand, and you have lent to many nations, and you do not borrow. [13] And Yhwh has set you for head and not for tail; and you have been only above, and are not beneath, for you listen to the commands of your God Yhwh, which I am commanding you today, to keep and to do, [14] and you do not turn aside from all the words which I am commanding you today [to] the right or left, to go after other gods, to serve them. [15] And it has been, if you do not listen to the voice of your God Yhwh, to observe to do all His commands and His statutes which I am commanding you today, that all these revilings have come on you and overtaken you: [16] Cursed [are] you in the city, and cursed [are] you in the field. [17] Cursed [is] your basket and your kneading-trough. [18] Cursed [is] the fruit of your body, and the fruit of your land, the increase of your oxen, and the wealth of your flock. [19] Cursed [are] you in your coming in, and cursed [are] you in your going out. [20] Yhwh sends the curse, the trouble, and the rebuke on you, in every putting forth of your hand which you do, until you are destroyed, and until you perish quickly, because of the evil of your doings [by] which you have forsaken Me. [21] Yhwh causes the pestilence to cleave to you until He consumes you from off the ground to where you are going in to possess it. [22] Yhwh strikes you with consumption, and with fever, and with inflammation, and with extreme burning, and with sword, and with blasting, and with mildew, and they have pursued you until you perish [23] And your heavens which [are] over your head have been bronze, and the earth which [is] under you iron; [24] Yhwh gives dust and ashes [for] the rain of your land; it comes down on you from the heavens until you are destroyed. [25] Yhwh makes you struck before your enemies; in one way you go out to them, and in seven ways you flee before them, and you have been for a trembling to all kingdoms of the earth; [26] and your carcass has been for food for every bird of the heavens and for the beast of the earth, and there is none causing [them] to tremble. [27] Yhwh strikes you with the ulcer of Egypt, and with lumps, and with scurvy, and with itch, of which you are not able to be healed. [28] Yhwh strikes you with madness, and with blindness, and with astonishment of heart; [29] and you have been groping at noon, as the blind gropes in darkness; and you do not cause your ways to prosper; and you have been only oppressed and plundered [for] all the days, and there is no savior. [30] You betroth a woman, and another man lies with her; you build a house, and do not dwell in it; you plant a vineyard, and do not make it common; [31] your ox [is] slaughtered before your eyes, and you do not eat of it; your donkey [is] violently taken away from before you, and it is not given back to you; your sheep [are] given to your enemies, and there is no savior for you. [32] Your sons and your daughters [are] given to another people, and your eyes are looking and

consumed for them all the day, but your hand is not to God! **33** A people whom you have not known eat the fruit of your ground and all your labor; and you have been only oppressed and bruised [for] all the days; **34** and you have been mad because of the sight of your eyes which you see. **35** Yhwh strikes you with a severe ulcer on the knees and on the legs (of which you are not able to be healed), from the sole of your foot even to your crown. **36** Yhwh causes you and your king whom you raise up over you to go to a nation which you have not known, you and your fathers, and you have served other gods there—wood and stone; **37** and you have been for an astonishment, for an allegory, and for a byword among all the peoples to where Yhwh leads you. **38** You take much seed out into the field, and you gather little in, for the locust consumes it; **39** you plant vineyards and have labored, but you do not drink wine, nor gather [grapes], for the worm consumes it; **40** olives are yours in all your border, but you do not pour out oil, for your olive falls off. **41** You beget sons and daughters, but they are not with you, for they go into captivity; **42** the locust possesses all your trees and the fruit of your ground; **43** the sojourner who [is] in your midst goes up very high above you, and you go down very low; **44** he lends [to] you, and you do not lend [to] him; he is for head and you are for tail. **45** And all these curses have come on you, and pursued you, and overtaken you, until you are destroyed, because you have not listened to the voice of your God Yhwh, to keep His commands and His statutes which he has commanded you; **46** and they have been on you for a sign and for a wonder, also on your seed—for all time. **47** Because that you have not served your God Yhwh with joy and with gladness of heart, because of the abundance of all things— **48** you have served your enemies, whom Yhwh sends against you, in hunger, and in thirst, and in nakedness, and in lack of all things; and He has put a yoke of iron on your neck until He has destroyed you. **49** Yhwh lifts up a nation against you from afar, from the end of the earth—it flies as the eagle—a nation whose tongue you have not heard, **50** a nation of fierce countenance, which does not accept the face of the aged and does not favor the young; **51** and it has eaten the fruit of your livestock and the fruit of your ground, until you are destroyed; which does not leave to you grain, new wine, and oil, the increase of your oxen, and the wealth of your flock, until it has destroyed you. **52** And it has laid siege to you in all your gates until your walls come down—the high and the fortified ones in which you are trusting, in all your land; indeed, it has laid siege to you in all your gates, in all your land which your God Yhwh has given to you. **53** And you have eaten the fruit of your body, [the] flesh of your sons and your daughters (whom your God Yhwh has given to you), in the siege and in the constriction with which your enemies constrict you. **54** The man who is tender in you, and who [is] very delicate—his eye is evil against his brother, and against the wife of his bosom, and against the remnant of his sons whom he leaves, **55** against giving to one of them of the flesh of his sons whom he eats, because he has nothing left for himself in the siege and in the constriction with which your enemy constricts you in all your gates. **56** The tender woman in you, and the delicate, who has not tried the sole of her foot to place on the ground because of delicateness and because of tenderness—her eye is evil against the husband of her bosom, and against her son, and against her daughter, **57** and against her seed which comes out from between her feet, even against her sons whom she bears, for she eats them in secret, in the lacking of everything, in the siege and in the constriction with which your enemy constricts you within your gates. **58** If you do not observe to do all the words of this law which are written in this scroll, to fear this honored and fearful Name—your God Yhwh— **59** then Yhwh has made your strokes extraordinary, and the strokes [against] your seed [are] great strokes that are persisting and severe sicknesses that are persisting. **60** And He has brought back all the diseases of Egypt on you, from the presence of which you have been afraid, and they have cleaved to you. **61** Also every sickness and every stroke which is not written in the scroll of this law—Yhwh causes them to go up on you until you are destroyed, **62** and you have been left with few men, whereas that you would have been as stars of the heavens for multitude, for you have not listened to the voice of your God Yhwh. **63** And it has been, as Yhwh has rejoiced over you to do you good and to multiply you, so Yhwh rejoices over you to destroy you and to lay you waste; and you have been pulled away from off the ground to where you are going in to possess it; **64** and Yhwh has scattered you among all the peoples, from the end of the earth even to the [other] end of the earth; and you have served other gods there which you

have not known, you and your fathers—wood and stone. **65** And you do not rest among those nations, indeed, there is no resting place for the sole of your foot, and Yhwh has given to you a trembling heart, and failing of eyes, and grief of soul there; **66** and your life has been hanging in suspense before you, and you have been afraid by night and by day, and you do not have assurance in your life; **67** in the morning you say, O that it were evening! And in the evening you say, O that it were morning! (from the fear of your heart, with which you are afraid, and from the sight of your eyes which you see.) **68** And Yhwh has brought you back to Egypt in ships, by the way of which I said to you, You do not add to see it anymore; and you have sold yourselves to your enemies there, for menservants and for maidservants, and there is no buyer."

CHAPTER 29

1 These [are] the words of the covenant which Yhwh has commanded Moses to make with the sons of Israel in the land of Moab, apart from the covenant which He made with them in Horeb. **2** And Moses calls to all Israel and says to them, "You have seen all that which Yhwh has done before your eyes in the land of Egypt, to Pharaoh, and to all his servants, and to all his land— **3** the great trials which your eyes have seen, the signs, and those great wonders. **4** And Yhwh has not given to you a heart to know, and eyes to see, and ears to hear, until this day. **5** And I cause you to go in a wilderness [for] forty years; your garments have not been consumed from off you, and your shoe has not worn away from off your foot; **6** you have not eaten bread, and you have not drunk wine and strong drink, so that you know that I [am] your God Yhwh. **7** And you come to this place, and Sihon king of Heshbon—also Og king of Bashan—comes out to meet us to battle, and we strike them, **8** and take their land, and give it for an inheritance to the Reubenite, and to the Gadite, and to the half of the tribe of the Manassite; **9** and you have kept the words of this covenant and done them, so that you cause all that you do to prosper. **10** You are standing today, all of you, before your God Yhwh: your heads, your tribes, your elderly, and your authorities, every man of Israel, **11** your infants, your wives, and your sojourner who [is] in the midst of your camps, from the hewer of your wood to the drawer of your water, **12** for your passing over into the covenant of your God Yhwh, and into His oath which your God Yhwh is making with you today, **13** in order to establish you to Himself for a people today, and He Himself is your God, as He has spoken to you, and as He has sworn to your fathers, to Abraham, to Isaac, and to Jacob. **14** And I am not making this covenant and this oath with you alone, **15** but with him who is here with us, standing before our God Yhwh today, and with him who is not here with us today, **16** for you have known how you dwelt in the land of Egypt, and how we passed by through the midst of the nations which you have passed by; **17** and you see their abominations, and their idols of wood and stone, silver and gold, which [are] with them, **18** lest there be among you a man or woman, or family or tribe, whose heart is turning from our God Yhwh today, to go to serve the gods of those nations, lest there be in you a root bearing the fruit of gall and wormwood; **19** and it has been, in his hearing the words of this oath, that he has blessed himself in his heart, saying, I have peace, though I go on in the stubbornness of my heart—in order to sweep away the watered with the thirsty. **20** Yhwh is not willing to be propitious to him, for then the anger of Yhwh smokes, also His zeal, against that man, and all the oath which is written in this scroll has lain down on him, and Yhwh has blotted out his name from under the heavens, **21** and Yhwh has separated him for calamity out of all the tribes of Israel, according to all the oaths of the covenant which is written in this Scroll of the Law. **22** And the latter generation of your sons who rise after you, and the stranger who comes in from a far-off land, have said, when they have seen the strokes of that land and its sicknesses which Yhwh has sent into it: **23** The whole land is burned [with] brimstone and salt, it is not sown, nor does it shoot up, nor does any herb go up on it there, like the overthrow of Sodom and Gomorrah, Admah and Zeboim, which Yhwh overturned in His anger and in His fury. **24** Indeed, all the nations have said, Why has Yhwh done thus to this land? why the heat of this great anger? **25** And they have said, Because that they have forsaken the covenant of Yhwh, God of their fathers, which He made with them in His bringing them out of the land of Egypt, **26** and they go and serve other gods, and bow themselves to them—gods which they have not known, and which He has not apportioned to them; **27** and the anger of Yhwh burns against that land, to bring in on it all the reviling that is written in this scroll, **28** and Yhwh plucks them from off their ground in anger, and in fury, and in great wrath, and casts them into another land, as [at] this day. **29** The things hidden [belong] to our God Yhwh, and the things revealed [belong] to us and to our sons for all time, to do all the words of this law."

CHAPTER 30

1 "And it has been, when all these things come on you, the blessing and the reviling, which I have set before you, and you have brought [them] back to your heart among all the nations to where your God Yhwh has driven you away, **2** and have turned back to your God Yhwh and listened to His voice, according to all that I am commanding you today, you and your sons, with all your heart and with all your soul— **3** then your God Yhwh has turned back [to] your captivity and pitied you, indeed, He has turned back and gathered you out of all the peoples to where your God Yhwh has scattered you. **4** If your outcast is in the extremity of the heavens, your God Yhwh gathers you from there and He takes you from there; **5** and your God Yhwh has brought you into the land which your fathers have possessed, and you have inherited it, and He has done you good, and multiplied you above your fathers. **6** And your God Yhwh has circumcised your heart and the heart of your seed, to love your God Yhwh with all your heart and with all your soul, for the sake of your life; **7** and your God Yhwh has put all this oath on your enemies and on those hating you, who have pursued you. **8** And you turn back, and have listened to the voice of Yhwh, and have done all His commands which I am commanding you today; **9** and your God Yhwh has made you abundant in every work of your hand, in the fruit of your body, and in the fruit of your livestock, and in the fruit of your ground, for good; for Yhwh turns back to rejoice over you for good, as He rejoiced over your fathers, **10** for you listen to the voice of your God Yhwh, to keep His commands and His statutes which are written in the scroll of this law, for you turn back to your God Yhwh with all your heart and with all your soul. **11** For this command which I am commanding you today, it is not too wonderful for you, nor [is] it far off. **12** It is not in the heavens, saying, Who goes up into the heavens for us, and takes it for us, and causes us to hear it, that we may do it? **13** And it [is] not beyond the sea, saying, Who passes over beyond the sea for us, and takes it for us, and causes us to hear it, that we may do it? **14** For the word is very near to you, in your mouth, and in your heart—to do it. **15** See, today I have set before you life and good, and death and evil, **16** in that today I am commanding you to love your God Yhwh, to walk in His ways, and to keep His commands, and His statutes, and His judgments; and you have lived and multiplied, and your God Yhwh has blessed you in the land to where you are going in to possess it. **17** And if your heart turns, and you do not listen, and have been drawn away, and have bowed yourself to other gods and served them, **18** I have declared to you this day that you certainly perish, you do not prolong days on the ground which you are passing over the Jordan to go in there to possess it. **19** I have caused the heavens and the earth to testify against you today—I have set before you life and death, the blessing and the reviling, and you have fixed on life, so that you live, you and your seed, **20** to love your God Yhwh, to listen to His voice, and to cleave to Him (for He [is] your life and the length of your days), to dwell on the ground which Yhwh has sworn to your fathers, to Abraham, to Isaac, and to Jacob, to give to them."

CHAPTER 31

1 And Moses goes and speaks these words to all Israel, **2** and he says to them, "I [am] a son of one hundred and twenty years today; I am not able to go out and to come in anymore, and Yhwh has said to me, You do not pass over this Jordan. **3** Your God Yhwh—He is passing over before you; He destroys these nations from before you, and you have possessed them; Joshua—he is passing over before you, as Yhwh has spoken. **4** And Yhwh has done to them as he has done to Sihon and to Og, kings of the Amorite, and to their land, whom He destroyed. **5** And Yhwh has given them before your face, and

you have done to them according to all the command which I have commanded you, **6** be strong and courageous, do not fear, nor be terrified because of them, for your God Yhwh [is] He who is going with you; He does not fail you nor forsake you." **7** And Moses calls for Joshua and says to him before the eyes of all Israel, "Be strong and courageous, for you go in with this people to the land which Yhwh has sworn to their fathers to give to them, and you cause them to inherit it; **8** and Yhwh [is] He who is going before you, He Himself is with you; He does not fail you nor forsake you; do not fear, nor be frightened." **9** And Moses writes this law and gives it to the priests (sons of Levi, those carrying the Ark of the Covenant of Yhwh), and to all [the] elderly of Israel, **10** and Moses commands them, saying, "At the end of seven years, in the appointed time, the year of release, in the Celebration of Shelters, **11** in the coming in of all Israel to see the face of Yhwh in the place which He chooses, you proclaim this law before all Israel in their ears. **12** Assemble the people, the men, and the women, and the infants, and your sojourner who [is] within your gates, so that they hear, and so that they learn, and have feared your God Yhwh, and observed to do all the words of this law; **13** and their sons, who have not known, hear and have learned to fear your God Yhwh [for] all the days which you are living on the ground to where you are passing over the Jordan to possess it." **14** And Yhwh says to Moses, "Behold, your days have drawn near to die; call Joshua, and station yourselves in the Tent of Meeting, and I charge him"; and Moses goes— Joshua also—and they station themselves in the Tent of Meeting, **15** and Yhwh is seen in the tent in a pillar of a cloud; and the pillar of the cloud stands at the opening of the tent. **16** And Yhwh says to Moses, "Behold, you are lying down with your fathers, and this people has risen and gone whoring after the gods of the stranger of the land, into the midst of which it has entered, and it has forsaken Me and broken My covenant which I made with it; **17** and My anger has burned against it in that day, and I have forsaken them, and hidden My face from them, and it has been for consumption, and many evils and distresses have found it, and it has said in that day, [Is] it not because my God is not in my midst that these evils have found me? **18** and I certainly hide My face in that day for all the evil which it has done, for it has turned to other gods. **19** And now, write this song for yourselves, and teach it [to] the sons of Israel; put it in their mouths, so that this song is to Me for a witness against the sons of Israel. **20** When I bring them to the ground flowing with milk and honey, which I have sworn to their fathers, and they have eaten, and been satisfied, and been fat, and have turned to other gods, and they have served them, and despised Me, and broken My covenant, **21** then it has been, when many evils and distresses meet it, that this song has testified to its face for a witness; for it is not forgotten out of the mouth of its seed, for I have known its imagining which it is doing today, before I bring them into the land of which I have sworn." **22** And Moses writes this song on that day, and teaches it [to] the sons of Israel. **23** Then He commands Joshua son of Nun, and says, "Be strong and courageous, for you bring in the sons of Israel to the land which I have sworn to them, and I am with you." **24** And it comes to pass, when Moses finishes to write the words of this law on a scroll, until their completion, **25** that Moses commands the Levites carrying the Ark of the Covenant of Yhwh, saying, **26** "Take this Scroll of the Law, and you have set it on the side of the Ark of the Covenant of your God Yhwh, and it has been against you for a witness there; **27** for I have known your rebellion and your stiff neck; behold, in my being yet alive with you today, you have been rebelling against Yhwh, and surely also after my death. **28** Assemble to me all the elderly of your tribes, and your authorities, and I speak these words in their ears, and cause the heavens and the earth to testify against them, **29** for I have known that you act very corruptly after my death, and have turned aside from the way which I commanded you, and evil has met you in the latter end of the days, because you do evil in the eyes of Yhwh, to make Him angry with the work of your hands." **30** And Moses speaks the words of this song in the ears of all the assembly of Israel, until their completion:

CHAPTER 32

1 "Give ear, O heavens, and I speak; And you hear, O earth, sayings of my mouth! **2** My doctrine drops as rain; My sayings flow as dew; As storms on the tender grass, || And as showers on the herb, **3** For I proclaim the Name of Yhwh; Ascribe greatness to our God! **4** The Rock—His work [is] perfect, || For all His ways [are] just; God of steadfastness, and without iniquity; Righteous and upright [is] He. **5** It has done corruptly to Him; Their blemish is not of His sons, || A generation perverse and crooked! **6** Do you act thus to Yhwh, || O people foolish and not wise? Is He not your Father—He who bought you? He made you, and establishes you. **7** Remember days of old—Understand the years of many generations—Ask your father, and he tells you; Your elderly, and they say to you: **8** In the Most High causing nations to inherit, || In His separating sons of Adam—He sets up the borders of the peoples || By the number of the sons of God [[or sons of Israel]]. **9** For Yhwh's portion [is] His people, || Jacob [is] the line of His inheritance. **10** He finds him in a land—a desert, || And in a void—a howling wilderness, || He turns him around—He causes him to understand—He keeps him as the apple of His eye. **11** As an eagle wakes up its nest, || Flutters over its young ones, || Spreads its wings [and] takes them, || Carries them on its pinions— **12** Yhwh alone leads him, || And there is no strange god with him. **13** He makes him ride on high places of earth, || And he eats increase of the fields, || And He makes him suck honey from a rock, || And oil out of the flint of a rock; **14** Butter of the herd, and milk of the flock, || With fat of lambs, and rams of sons of Bashan, || And male goats, with fat of kidneys of wheat; And of the blood of the grape you drink wine! **15** And Yeshurun waxes fat, and kicks: You have been fat, you have been thick, || You have been covered. And he leaves God who made him, || And dishonors the Rock of his salvation. **16** They make Him zealous with strangers, || They make Him angry with abominations. **17** They sacrifice to the demons, not God, || To gods they have not known, || New ones—they came from the vicinity; Your fathers have not feared them! **18** You forget the Rock that begot you, || And neglect God who forms you. **19** And Yhwh sees and despises—For the provocation of His sons and His daughters. **20** And He says: I hide My face from them, || I see what their latter end [is]; For they [are] a contrary generation, || Sons in whom is no steadfastness. **21** They have made Me jealous by [what is] not God, || They made Me angry by their vanities; And I make them jealous by [what is] not a people, || I make them angry by a foolish nation. **22** For a fire has been kindled in My anger, || And it burns to the lowest [part] of Sheol, || And consumes earth and its increase, || And sets on fire [the] foundations of mountains. **23** I heap calamities on them, || I consume My arrows on them. **24** Exhausted by famine, || And consumed by heat and bitter destruction—I also send the teeth of beasts on them, || With poison of fearful things of the dust. **25** The sword destroys from outside, || And out of the inner-chambers—terror, || Both youth and virgin, || Suckling with man of grey hair. **26** I have said: I blow them away, || I cause their remembrance to cease from man; **27** If I do not fear the anger of an enemy, || Lest their adversaries know—Lest they say, Our hand is high, || And Yhwh has not worked all this. **28** For they [are] a nation lost to counsels, || And there is no understanding in them. **29** If only they were wise, || They would deal wisely [with] this, || They would attend to their latter end! **30** How does one pursue a thousand, || And two cause a myriad to flee, || If not that their Rock has sold them, || And Yhwh has shut them up? **31** For their rock [is] not as our Rock || (And our enemies [are] judges!) **32** For their vine [is] of the vine of Sodom, || And of the fields of Gomorrah; Their grapes [are] grapes of gall—They have bitter clusters; **33** The poison of dragons [is] their wine || And the fierce venom of cobras. **34** Is it not laid up with Me? Sealed among My treasures? **35** Vengeance and retribution [are] Mine, || At the due time—their foot slides; For near is a day of their calamity, || And things prepared for them have hastened. **36** For Yhwh judges His people, || And gives comfort over His servants. For He sees the going away of power, || And none is restrained and left. **37** And He has said, Where [are] their gods—The rock in which they trusted? **38** Who eat the fat of their sacrifices, || [And] drink the wine of their drink-offering? Let them arise and help you, || Let it be a hiding place for you! **39** See, now, that I [am] He, || And there is no god besides Me; I put to death and I keep alive; I have struck and I heal; And there is not a deliverer from My hand, **40** For I lift up My hand to the heavens, || And have said, I live for all time! **41** If I have sharpened the brightness of My sword, || And My hand lays hold on judgment, || I return vengeance to My adversaries, || And to those hating Me—I repay! **42** I make My arrows drunk with blood, || And My sword devours flesh, || From the blood of the pierced and captive, || From the head of the leaders of the enemy. **43** Sing, O nations, [with] His people, || For He avenges the blood of His servants, || And He turns back vengeance on His adversaries, || And has pardoned His land [and] His people."

44 And Moses comes and speaks all the words of this song in the ears of the people, he and Hoshea son of Nun; **45** and Moses finishes to speak all these words to all Israel, **46** and says to them, "Set your heart to all the words which I am testifying against you today, that you command your sons to observe to do all the words of this law, **47** for it [is] not a vain thing for you, for it [is] your life, and by this thing you prolong days on the ground to where you are passing over the Jordan to possess it." **48** And Yhwh speaks to Moses on this very same day, saying, **49** "Go up to this Mount Abarim, Mount Nebo, which [is] in the land of Moab, which [is] on the front of Jericho, and see the land of Canaan which I am giving to the sons of Israel for a possession; **50** and die on the mountain to where you are going up, and be gathered to your people, as your brother Aaron has died on Mount Hor and is gathered to his people; **51** because you trespassed against Me in the midst of the sons of Israel at the waters of Meribath-Kadesh, the wilderness of Zin, because you did not sanctify Me in the midst of the sons of Israel. **52** Indeed, you see the land before [you], but you do not go in there to the land which I am giving to the sons of Israel."

CHAPTER 33

1 And this [is] the blessing [with] which Moses the man of God blessed the sons of Israel before his death, **2** and he says: "Yhwh has come from Sinai, || And has risen from Seir for them; He has shone from Mount Paran, || And has come [with] myriads of holy ones; At His right hand [came] a fiery law [[or a flaming fire]] for them. **3** Indeed, He [is] loving the peoples; All His holy ones [are] in Your hand, || And they sat down at Your foot, || [Each] lifts up Your words. **4** Moses has commanded a law for us, || A possession of the assembly of Jacob. **5** And He is King in Yeshurun, || In the heads of the people gathering together, || The tribes of Israel! **6** Let Reuben live, and not die, || And let his men be an [incalculable] number. **7** And this [is] for Judah, and he says: Hear, O Yhwh, the voice of Judah, || And You bring him in to his people; His hand has striven for him, || And You are a help from his adversaries. **8** And of Levi he said: Your Perfections and your Lights [are] for your pious one, || Whom You have tried in Massah, || You strive with him at the waters of Meribah; **9** Who is saying of his father and his mother, || I have not seen him; And he has not discerned his brothers, || And he has not known his sons; For they have observed Your saying, || And they keep Your covenant. **10** They teach Your judgments to Jacob, || And Your law to Israel; They put incense in Your nose, || And whole burnt-offering on Your altar. **11** Bless, O Yhwh, his strength, || And accept the work of his hands, || Strike the loins of his withstanders, || And of those hating him—that they do not rise! **12** Of Benjamin he said: The beloved of Yhwh dwells confidently by Him, || Covering him over every day; Indeed, he dwells between His shoulders. **13** And of Joseph he said: His land [is] blessed [by] Yhwh, || By a precious thing of the heavens, || By dew, and by the deep crouching beneath, **14** And by a precious thing—fruits of the sun, || And by a precious thing—cast forth by the months, **15** And by a chief thing—of the ancient mountains, || And by a precious thing—of the continuous heights, **16** And by a precious thing—of earth and its fullness, || And the good pleasure of Him who is dwelling in the bush; Let it come for the head of Joseph, || And for the crown of him [who is] separate from his brothers. **17** His splendor [is] a firstling of his ox, || And his horns [are] horns of a wild ox; With them he pushes the peoples || Altogether to the ends of the earth; And they [are] the myriads of Ephraim, || And they [are] the thousands of Manasseh. **18** And of Zebulun he said: Rejoice, O Zebulun, in your going out, || And, O Issachar, in your tents; **19** They call peoples [to] the mountain, || There they sacrifice righteous sacrifices; For they suck up the abundance of the seas, || And hidden things hidden in the sand. **20** And of Gad he said: Blessed is he who is enlarging Gad, || He dwells as a lioness, || And has torn the arm—also the crown! **21** And he provides the first part for himself, || For there the portion of the lawgiver is covered, || And he comes [with] the heads of the people; He has done the righteousness of Yhwh, || And His judgments with Israel. **22** And of Dan he said: Dan [is] a lion's whelp; He leaps from Bashan. **23** And of Naphtali he said: O Naphtali, satisfied with pleasure, || And full of the blessing of Yhwh, || Possess [the] west and [the] south. **24** And of Asher he said: Asher [is] blessed with sons, || Let him be accepted by his brothers, || And dipping his foot in oil. **25** Iron and bronze [are] your shoes, || And as your days—your strength. **26** [There is] none like the God of Yeshurun, || Riding the heavens to your help, || And in His excellence the skies. **27** The eternal God [is] a habitation, || And beneath [are] continuous arms. And He casts out the enemy from your presence and says, Destroy! **28** And Israel dwells [in] confidence alone; The eye of Jacob [is] to a land of grain and wine; Also His heavens drop down dew. **29** O your blessedness, O Israel! Who is like you? A people saved by Yhwh, || The shield of your help, || And He who [is] the sword of your excellence! And your enemies are subdued for you, || And you tread on their high places."

CHAPTER 34

1 And Moses goes up from the plains of Moab to Mount Nebo, the top of Pisgah, which [is] on the front of Jericho, and Yhwh shows him all the land—Gilead to Dan, **2** and all Naphtali, and the land of Ephraim, and Manasseh, and all the land of Judah to the Western Sea, **3** and the south, and the circuit of the Valley of Jericho, the city of palms, to Zoar. **4** And Yhwh says to him, "This [is] the land which I have sworn to Abraham, to Isaac, and to Jacob, saying, I give it to your seed; I have caused you to see with your eyes, but you do not pass over there." **5** And Moses, servant of the Lord, dies there in the land of Moab, according to the command of Yhwh; **6** and He buries him in a valley in the land of Moab, opposite Beth-Peor, and no man has known his burying place to this day. **7** And Moses [is] a son of one hundred and twenty years when he dies; his eye has not become dim, nor has his moisture fled. **8** And the sons of Israel lament Moses in the plains of Moab [for] thirty days; and the days of weeping [and] mourning for Moses are completed. **9** And Joshua son of Nun is full of the spirit of wisdom, for Moses had laid his hands on him, and the sons of Israel listen to him, and do as Yhwh commanded Moses. **10** And there has not arisen a prophet in Israel like Moses anymore, whom Yhwh has known face to face, **11** in reference to all the signs and the wonders which Yhwh sent him to do in the land of Egypt, to Pharaoh, and to all his servants, and to all his land, **12** and in reference to all the strong hand and to all the great fear which Moses did before the eyes of all Israel.

JOSHUA

CHAPTER 1

1 And it comes to pass after the death of Moses, servant of Yhwh, that Yhwh speaks to Joshua son of Nun, minister of Moses, saying, **2** "My servant Moses is dead, and now, rise, pass over this Jordan, you and all this people, to the land which I am giving to them, to the sons of Israel. **3** Every place on which the sole of your foot treads, I have given it to you, as I have spoken to Moses. **4** From this wilderness and Lebanon, and to the great river, the Euphrates River, all the land of the Hittites, and to the Great Sea—the going in of the sun—is your border. **5** No man stations himself before you all [the] days of your life; as I have been with Moses, I am with you, I do not fail you, nor forsake you; **6** be strong and courageous, for you cause this people to inherit the land which I have sworn to their fathers to give to them. **7** Only, be strong and very courageous, to observe to do according to all the Law which Moses My servant commanded you; you do not turn aside from it right or left, so that you act wisely in every [place] to where you go; **8** the scroll of this Law does not depart out of your mouth, and you have meditated in it by day and by night, so that you observe to do according to all that is written in it, for then you cause your way to prosper, and then you act wisely. **9** Have I not commanded you? be strong and courageous; do not be terrified nor frightened, for your God Yhwh [is] with you in every [place] to where you go." **10** And Joshua commands the authorities of the people, saying, **11** "Pass over into the midst of the camp, and command the people, saying, Prepare provision for yourselves, for within three days you are passing over this Jordan, to go in to possess the land which your God Yhwh is giving to you to possess it." **12** And to the Reubenite, and to the Gadite, and to the half of the tribe of Manasseh, Joshua has spoken, saying, **13** "Remember the word which Moses, servant of Yhwh, commanded you, saying, Your God Yhwh is giving rest to you, and He has given this land to you; **14** your wives, your infants, and your substance, abide in the land which Moses has given to you beyond the Jordan, and you pass over by fifties, before your brothers, all the mighty men of valor, and have helped them, **15** until Yhwh gives rest to your brothers as to yourselves, and they have possessed, even they, the land which your God Yhwh is giving to them; then you have turned back to the land of your possession, and have possessed it, which Moses, servant of Yhwh, has given to you beyond the Jordan, [at] the sun-rising." **16** And they answer Joshua, saying, "All that you have commanded us we do; and to every [place] to where you send us, we go; **17** according to all that we listened to [from] Moses, so we listen to you; surely your God Yhwh is with you as He has been with Moses. **18** Any man who provokes your mouth, and does not hear your words, in all that you command him, is put to death; only, be strong and courageous."

CHAPTER 2

1 And Joshua son of Nun silently sends two men, spies, from Shittim, saying, "Go, see the land—and Jericho"; and they go and come into the house of a woman, a harlot, and her name [is] Rahab, and they lie down there. **2** And it is told to the king of Jericho, saying, "Behold, men have come in here tonight, from the sons of Israel, to search the land." **3** And the king of Jericho sends to Rahab, saying, "Bring out the men who are coming to you, who have come into your house, for they have come to search the entirety of the land." **4** And the woman takes the two men, and hides them, and says thus: "The men came to me, and I have not known where they [are] from; **5** and it comes to pass—the gate is to [be] shut—in the dark, and the men have gone out; I have not known to where the men have gone; pursue, hurry after them, for you overtake them"; **6** and she has caused them to go up on the roof, and hides them with the flax wood, which is arranged for her on the roof. **7** And the men have pursued after them the way of the Jordan, by the fords, and they have shut the gate afterward when the pursuers have gone out after them. **8** And before they lie down, she has gone up to them on the roof, **9** and she says to the men, "I have known that Yhwh has given the land to you, and that your terror has fallen on us, and that all the inhabitants of the land have melted at your presence. **10** For we have heard how Yhwh dried up the waters of the Red Sea at your presence, in your going out of Egypt, and that which you have done to the two kings of the Amorite who [are] beyond the Jordan; to Sihon and to Og whom you devoted. **11** And we hear, and our heart melts, and there has not stood anymore spirit in [any] man from your presence, for He, your God Yhwh, [is] God in the heavens above and on the earth below. **12** And now, please swear to me by Yhwh—because I have done kindness with you—that you have done, even you, kindness with the house of my father, and have given a true token to me, **13** and have kept alive my father, and my mother, and my brothers, and my sisters, and all that they have, and have delivered our souls from death." **14** And the men say to her, "Our soul to die for yours; if you do not declare this—our matter, then it has been, in Yhwh's giving this land to us, that we have done kindness and truth with you." **15** And she causes them to go down by a rope through the window, for her house [is] in the side of the wall, and she [is] dwelling in the wall; **16** and she says to them, "Go to the mountain, lest the pursuers come on you; and you have been hidden there three days until the turning back of the pursuers, and afterward you go on your way." **17** And the men say to her, "We are acquitted of this, your oath, which you have caused us to swear: **18** behold, we are coming into the land, bind this line of scarlet thread to the window by which you have caused us to go down, and gather your father, and your mother, and your brothers, and all the house of your father to you, to the house; **19** and it has been, anyone who goes out from the doors of your house outside, his blood [is] on his head, and we are innocent; and anyone who is with you in the house, his blood [is] on our head, if a hand is on him; **20** and if you declare this—our matter, then we have been acquitted from your oath which you have caused us to swear." **21** And she says, "According to your words, so it [is]"; and she sends them away, and they go; and she binds the scarlet line to the window. **22** And they go, and come to the mountain, and abide there three days until the pursuers have turned back; and the pursuers seek in all the way, and have not found. **23** And the two men turn back, and come down from the hill, and pass over, and come to Joshua son of Nun, and recount to him all that has come on them; **24** and they say to Joshua, "Surely Yhwh has given all the land into our hand; and also, all the inhabitants of the land have melted at our presence."

CHAPTER 3

1 And Joshua rises early in the morning, and they journey from Shittim, and come to the Jordan, he and all the sons of Israel, and they lodge there before they pass over. **2** And it comes to pass, at the end of three days, that the authorities pass over into the midst of the camp, **3** and command the people, saying, "When you see the Ark of the Covenant of your God Yhwh, and the priests, the Levites, carrying it, then you journey from your place, and have gone after it; **4** only, a distance is between you and it, about two thousand cubits by measure; you do not come near to it, so that you know the way in which you go, for you have not passed over in the way before." **5** And Joshua says to the people, "Sanctify yourselves, for tomorrow Yhwh does wonders in your midst." **6** And Joshua speaks to the priests, saying, "Take up the Ark of the Covenant, and pass over before the people"; and they take up the Ark of the Covenant, and go before the people. **7** And Yhwh says to Joshua, "This day I begin to make you great in the eyes of all Israel, so that they know that as I was with Moses I am with you; **8** and you, command the priests carrying the Ark of the Covenant, saying, When you come to the extremity of the waters of the Jordan, stand in the Jordan." **9** And Joshua says to the sons of Israel, "Come near here, and hear the words of your God Yhwh"; **10** and Joshua says, "By this you know that the living God [is] in your midst, and He certainly dispossesses from before you the Canaanite, and the Hittite, and the Hivite, and the Perizzite, and the Girgashite, and the Amorite, and the Jebusite: **11** behold, the Ark of the Covenant of the Lord of all the earth is passing over before you into the Jordan; **12** and now, take for yourselves twelve men out of the tribes of Israel, one man—one man for a tribe; **13** and it has been, at the resting of the soles of the feet of the priests carrying the Ark of Yhwh, Lord of all the earth, in the waters of the Jordan, the waters of the Jordan are cut off—the waters which are coming down from above—and they stand—one heap." **14** And it comes to pass, in the journeying of the people from their tents to pass over the Jordan, and of the priests carrying the Ark of the Covenant before the people, **15** and at those carrying the Ark coming to the Jordan, and the feet of the priests carrying the Ark have been dipped in the extremity of the waters (and the Jordan is full over all its banks all the days of harvest)— **16** that the waters stand; those coming down from above have risen—one heap, very far above Adam, the city which [is] at the side of Zaretan; and those going down by the Sea of the Plain (the Salt Sea), have been completely cut off; and the people have passed through opposite Jericho; **17** and the priests carrying the Ark of the Covenant of Yhwh stand on dry ground in the midst of the Jordan—established, and all Israel are passing over on dry ground until all the nation has completed to pass over the Jordan.

CHAPTER 4

1 And it comes to pass, when all the nation has completed to pass over the Jordan, that Yhwh speaks to Joshua, saying, **2** "Take for yourselves twelve men out of the people, one man— one man out of a tribe; **3** and command them, saying, Take up for yourselves from this [place], from the midst of the Jordan, from the established standing-place of the feet of the priests, twelve stones, and you have removed them over with you, and placed them in the lodging-place in which you lodge tonight." **4** And Joshua calls to the twelve men whom he prepared out of the sons of Israel, one man—one man out of a tribe; **5** and Joshua says to them, "Pass over before the Ark of your God Yhwh into the midst of the Jordan, and each of you lift up one stone on his shoulder, according to the number of the tribes of the sons of Israel, **6** so that this is a sign in your midst when your children ask hereafter, saying, What [are] these stones to you? **7** that you have said to them, Because the waters of the Jordan were cut off, at the presence of the Ark of the Covenant

of Yhwh; in its passing over into the Jordan the waters of the Jordan were cut off; and these stones have been for a memorial to the sons of Israel for all time." **8** And the sons of Israel do so as Joshua commanded, and take up twelve stones out of the midst of the Jordan, as Yhwh has spoken to Joshua, according to the number of the tribes of the sons of Israel, and remove them over with them to the lodging-place, and place them there, **9** even the twelve stones Joshua has raised up out of the midst of the Jordan, the place of the standing of the feet of the priests carrying the Ark of the Covenant, and they are there to this day. **10** And the priests carrying the Ark are standing in the midst of the Jordan until the completion of the whole thing which Yhwh commanded Joshua to speak to the people, according to all that Moses commanded Joshua, and the people hurry and pass over. **11** And it comes to pass, when all the people have completed to pass over, that the Ark of Yhwh passes over, and the priests, in the presence of the people; **12** and the sons of Reuben, and the sons of Gad, and the half of the tribe of Manasseh, pass over, by fifties, before the sons of Israel, as Moses had spoken to them; **13** about forty thousand, armed ones of the host, passed over before Yhwh for battle, to the plains of Jericho. **14** On that day Yhwh has made Joshua great in the eyes of all Israel, and they fear him, as they feared Moses, all [the] days of his life. **15** And Yhwh speaks to Joshua, saying, **16** "Command the priests carrying the Ark of the Testimony, and they come up out of the Jordan." **17** And Joshua commands the priests, saying, "Come up out of the Jordan." **18** And it comes to pass, in the coming up of the priests carrying the Ark of the Covenant of Yhwh out of the midst of the Jordan—the soles of the feet of the priests have been drawn up into the dry ground—and the waters of the Jordan return to their place, and go over all its banks as before. **19** And the people have come up out of the Jordan on the tenth of the first month, and encamp in Gilgal, in the extremity east of Jericho; **20** and these twelve stones, which they have taken out of the Jordan, Joshua has raised up in Gilgal. **21** And he speaks to the sons of Israel, saying, "When your sons ask their fathers hereafter, saying, What [are] these stones? **22** then you have caused your sons to know, saying, Israel passed over this Jordan on dry land; **23** because your God Yhwh dried up the waters of the Jordan at your presence, until your passing over, as your God Yhwh did to the Red Sea which He dried up at our presence until our passing over; **24** so that all the people of the land know the hand of Yhwh—that it [is] strong, so that you have feared your God Yhwh [for] all the days."

CHAPTER 5

1 And it comes to pass, when all the kings of the Amorite which [are] beyond the Jordan, toward the sea, and all the kings of the Canaanite which [are] by the sea, hear how that Yhwh has dried up the waters of the Jordan at the presence of the sons of Israel until their passing over, that their heart is melted, and there has not been anymore spirit in them because of the presence of the sons of Israel. **2** At that time Yhwh said to Joshua, "Make knives of flint for yourself, and return, circumcise the sons of Israel a second time"; **3** and Joshua makes knives of flint for himself, and circumcises the sons of Israel at the height of the foreskins. **4** And this [is] the thing [for] which Joshua circumcises [them]: all the people who are coming out of Egypt, who are males, all the men of war have died in the wilderness, in the way, in their coming out of Egypt, **5** for all the people who are coming out were circumcised, and all the people who [are] born in the wilderness, in the way, in their coming out from Egypt, they have not circumcised; **6** for forty years the sons of Israel have gone in the wilderness, until all the nation of the men of war who are coming out of Egypt, who did not listen to the voice of Yhwh, to whom Yhwh has sworn not to show them the land which Yhwh swore to their fathers to give to us, a land flowing with milk and honey, are consumed; **7** and He raised up their sons in their stead, Joshua has circumcised them, for they have been uncircumcised, for they have not circumcised them in the way. **8** And it comes to pass, when all the nation has completed to be circumcised, that they abide in their places in the camp until their recovering; **9** and Yhwh says to Joshua, "Today I have rolled the reproach of Egypt from off you"; and [one] calls the name of that place Gilgal to this day. **10** And the sons of Israel encamp in Gilgal, and make the Passover on the fourteenth day of the month, at evening, in the plains of Jericho; **11** and they eat of the old grain of the land on the next day of the Passover, unleavened things and roasted [grain], on this very same day; **12** and the manna ceases on the next day in their eating of the old grain of the land, and there has been no more manna for [the] sons of Israel, and they eat of the increase of the land of Canaan in that year. **13** And it comes to pass in Joshua's being by Jericho, that he lifts up his eyes, and looks, and behold, [there is] one standing in front of him, and his drawn sword [is] in his hand, and Joshua goes to him, and says to him, "Are you for us or for our adversaries?" **14** And He says, "No, for I [am] Prince of Yhwh's host; now I have come"; and Joshua falls on his face to the earth, and pays respect, and says to Him, "What is my Lord speaking to His servant?" **15** And the Prince of Yhwh's host says to Joshua, "Cast off your shoe from off your foot, for the place on which you are standing is holy"; and Joshua does so.

CHAPTER 6

1 And Jericho shuts itself up, and is shut up, because of the presence of the sons of Israel—none going out, and none coming in. **2** And Yhwh says to Joshua, "See, I have given Jericho and its king into your hand—mighty men of valor, **3** and you have surrounded the city—all the men of battle—going around the city once; thus you do [for] six days; **4** and seven priests carry seven horns of the rams before the Ark, and on the seventh day you go around the city seven times, and the priests blow with the horns, **5** and it has been, in the prolonging of the horn of the ram, in your hearing the voice of the horn, all the people shout [with] a great shout, and the wall of the city has fallen under it, and the people have gone up, each straight before him." **6** And Joshua son of Nun calls to the priests and says to them, "Carry the Ark of the Covenant, and seven priests carry seven horns of the rams before the Ark of Yhwh"; **7** and He said to the people, "Pass over, and go around the city, and he who is armed passes over before the Ark of Yhwh." **8** And it comes to pass, when Joshua speaks to the people, that the seven priests carrying seven horns of the rams before Yhwh have passed over and blown with the horns, and the Ark of the Covenant of Yhwh is going after them; **9** and he who is armed is going before the priests blowing the horns, and he who is gathering up is going after the Ark, going on and blowing with the horns; **10** and Joshua has commanded the people, saying, "Do not shout, nor cause your voice to be heard, nor does a word go out from your mouth, until the day of my saying to you, Shout! Then you have shouted." **11** And the Ark of Yhwh goes around the city, going around once, and they come into the camp, and lodge in the camp. **12** And Joshua rises early in the morning, and the priests carry the Ark of Yhwh, **13** and seven priests carrying seven horns of the rams before the Ark of Yhwh are walking, going on, and they have blown with the horns—and he who is armed is going before them, and he who is gathering up is going behind the Ark of Yhwh—going on and blowing with the horns. **14** And they go around the city once on the second day, and return to the camp; thus they have done [for] six days. **15** And it comes to pass, on the seventh day, that they rise early, at the ascending of the dawn, and go around the city, according to this manner, seven times; (only on that day have they gone around the city seven times); **16** and it comes to pass, at the seventh time, the priests have blown with the horns, and Joshua says to the people, "Shout! For Yhwh has given the city to you; **17** and the city has been devoted, it and all that [is] in it, to Yhwh; only Rahab the harlot lives, she and all who [are] with her in the house, for she hid the messengers whom we sent; **18** and surely you have kept from the devoted thing, lest you devote [yourselves], and have taken from the devoted thing, and have made the camp of Israel become a devoted thing, and have troubled it; **19** and all the silver and gold, and vessels of bronze and iron—it [is] holy to Yhwh; it comes into the treasury of Yhwh." **20** And the people shout, and blow with the horns, and it comes to pass, when the people hear the voice of the horn, that the people shout [with] a great shout, and the wall falls under it, and the people goes up into the city, each straight before him, and they capture the city; **21** and they devote all that [is] in the city, from man even to woman, from young even to aged, even to ox, and sheep, and donkey, by the mouth of the sword. **22** And Joshua said to the two men who are spying out the land, "Go into the house of the woman, the harlot, and bring out the woman from there, and all whom she has, as you have sworn to her." **23** And the young men, those spying, go in and bring out Rahab, and her father, and her mother, and her brothers, and all whom she has; indeed, they

have brought out all her relatives, and place them at the outside of the camp of Israel. **24** And they have burned the city with fire, and all that [is] in it; only, the silver and the gold, and the vessels of bronze, and of iron, they have given [to] the treasury of the house of Yhwh; **25** and Rahab the harlot, and the house of her father, and all whom she has, Joshua has kept alive; and she dwells in the midst of Israel to this day, for she hid the messengers whom Joshua sent to spy out Jericho. **26** And Joshua adjures [them] at that time, saying, "Cursed [is] the man before Yhwh who raises up and has built this city, [even] Jericho; he lays its foundation in his firstborn, and he sets up its doors in his youngest." **27** And Yhwh is with Joshua, and his fame is in all the land.

CHAPTER 7

1 And the sons of Israel commit a trespass in the devoted thing, and Achan, son of Carmi, son of Zabdi, son of Zerah, of the tribe of Judah, takes from the devoted thing, and the anger of Yhwh burns against the sons of Israel. **2** And Joshua sends men from Jericho to Ai, which [is] near Beth-Aven, on the east of Bethel, and speaks to them, saying, "Go up and spy out the land"; and the men go up and spy Ai, **3** and they return to Joshua, and say to him, "Do not let all the people go up; let about two thousand men, or about three thousand men, go up, and they strike Ai; do not cause all the people to labor there; for they [are] few." **4** So about three thousand men of the people go up from there, and they flee before the men of Ai, **5** and the men of Ai strike about thirty-six men from them, and pursue them before the gate to Shebarim, and they strike them in Morad; and the heart of the people is melted, and becomes water. **6** And Joshua tears his garments, and falls on his face to the earth before the Ark of Yhwh until the evening, he and [the] elderly of Israel, and they cause dust to go up on their head. **7** And Joshua says, "Aah! Lord Yhwh, why have You caused this people to pass over the Jordan at all, to give us into the hand of the Amorite to destroy us? And oh that we had been willing—and we dwell beyond the Jordan! **8** Oh, Lord, what do I say, after that Israel has turned the neck before its enemies? **9** and the Canaanite and all the inhabitants of the land hear, and have come around against us, and cut off our name from the earth; and what do You do for Your great Name?" **10** And Yhwh says to Joshua, "Rise, for you—why this—[that] you [are] falling on your face? **11** Israel has sinned, and they have also transgressed My covenant which I commanded them, and also taken of the devoted thing, and also stolen, and also deceived, and also put [it] among their vessels, **12** and the sons of Israel have not been able to stand before their enemies; they turn the neck before their enemies, for they have become a devoted thing; I do not add to be with you—if you do not destroy the devoted thing from your midst. **13** Rise, sanctify the people, and you have said, Sanctify yourselves for tomorrow; for thus said Yhwh, God of Israel: A devoted thing [is] in your midst, O Israel, you are not able to stand before your enemies until your turning aside the devoted thing from your midst; **14** and you have been brought near in the morning by your tribes, and it has been [that] the tribe which Yhwh captures draws near by families, and the family which Yhwh captures draws near by households, and the household which Yhwh captures draws near by men; **15** and it has been, he who is captured with the devoted thing is burned with fire, he and all that he has, because he has transgressed the covenant of Yhwh, and because he has done folly in Israel." **16** And Joshua rises early in the morning, and brings Israel near by its tribes, and the tribe of Judah is captured; **17** and he brings the family of Judah near, and he captures the family of the Zerahite; and he brings the family of the Zerahite near by men, and Zabdi is captured; **18** and he brings his household near by men, and Achan—son of Carmi, son of Zabdi, son of Zerah, of the tribe of Judah—is captured. **19** And Joshua says to Achan, "My son, please give glory to Yhwh, God of Israel, and give thanks to Him, and now declare to me what you have done—do not hide [it] from me." **20** And Achan answers Joshua and says, "Truly I have sinned against Yhwh, God of Israel, and I have done thus and thus; **21** and I see among the spoil a good robe of Shinar, and two hundred shekels of silver, and one wedge of gold, whose weight [is] fifty shekels, and I desire them, and take them; and behold, they [are] hid in the earth, in the midst of my tent, and the silver [is] under it." **22** And Joshua sends messengers, and they run to the tent, and behold, it is hidden in his tent, and the silver [is] under it; **23** and they take them out of the midst of the tent, and bring them to Joshua, and to all the sons of Israel, and pour them out before Yhwh. **24** And Joshua takes Achan son of Zerah, and the silver, and the robe, and the wedge of gold, and his sons, and his daughters, and his ox, and his donkey, and his flock, and his tent, and all that he has, and all Israel with him, and they brought them up [to] the Valley of Achor. **25** And Joshua says, "Why have you troubled us? Yhwh troubles you this day!" And all Israel cast stone at him, and they burn them with fire, and they stone them with stones, **26** and they raise up a great heap of stones over him to this day, and Yhwh turns back from the heat of His anger, therefore [one] has called the name of that place "Valley of Achor" until this day.

CHAPTER 8

1 And Yhwh says to Joshua, "Do not fear, nor be frightened, take with you all the people of war, and rise, go up to Ai; see, I have given into your hand the king of Ai, and his people, and his city, and his land, **2** and you have done to Ai and to her king as you have done to Jericho and to her king; only spoil its spoil and its livestock for yourselves; for you set an ambush for the city at its rear." **3** And Joshua rises, and all the people of war, to go up to Ai, and Joshua chooses thirty thousand men, mighty men of valor, and sends them away by night, **4** and commands them, saying, "See, you are ones lying in wait against the city, at the rear of the city, you do not go very far off from the city, and all of you have been prepared, **5** and I and all the people who [are] with me draw near to the city, and it has come to pass, when they come out to meet us as at the first, and we have fled before them, **6** and they have come out after us until we have drawn them out of the city, for they say, They are fleeing before us as at the first, and we have fled before them, **7** and you rise from the ambush, and have occupied the city, and your God Yhwh has given it into your hand; **8** and it has been, when you capture the city, you burn the city with fire, you do according to the word of Yhwh, see, I have commanded you." **9** And Joshua sends them away, and they go to the ambush, and abide between Bethel and Ai, on the west of Ai; and Joshua lodges on that night in the midst of the people. **10** And Joshua rises early in the morning, and inspects the people, and goes up, he and [the] elderly of Israel, before the people to Ai; **11** and all the people of war who [are] with him have gone up, and draw near and come in before the city, and encamp on the north of Ai; and the valley [is] between him and Ai. **12** And he takes about five thousand men, and sets them [for] an ambush between Bethel and Ai, on the west of the city; **13** and they set the people, all the camp which [is] on the north of the city, and its rear on the west of the city, and that night Joshua goes on into the midst of the valley. **14** And it comes to pass, when the king of Ai sees [it], that he hurries, and rises early, and the men of the city go out to meet Israel for battle, he and all his people, at the appointed time, at the front of the plain, and he has not known that an ambush [is] against him, on the rear of the city. **15** And Joshua and all Israel [seem] struck before them, and flee the way of the wilderness, **16** and all the people who [are] in the city are called to pursue after them, and they pursue after Joshua, and are drawn away out of the city, **17** and there has not been a man left in Ai and Bethel who has not gone out after Israel, and they leave the city open, and pursue after Israel. **18** And Yhwh says to Joshua, "Stretch out with the javelin which [is] in your hand toward Ai, for I give it into your hand"; and Joshua stretches out with the javelin which [is] in his hand toward the city, **19** and the ambush has risen [with] haste, out of its place, and they run at the stretching out of his hand, and go into the city, and capture it, and hurry, and burn the city with fire. **20** And the men of Ai look behind them, and see, and behold, the smoke of the city has gone up to the heavens, and there has not been power in them to flee here and there—and the people who are fleeing to the wilderness have turned against the pursuer— **21** and Joshua and all Israel have seen that the ambush has captured the city, and that the smoke of the city has gone up, and they turn back and strike the men of Ai; **22** and these have come out from the city to meet them, and they are in the midst of Israel, some on this [side], and some on that [side], and they strike them until he has not left a remnant and escaped one to them; **23** and they have caught the king of Ai alive, and bring him near to Joshua. **24** And it comes to pass, at Israel's finishing to slay all the inhabitants of Ai in the field, in the wilderness in which they pursued them (and all of them fall by the mouth of the sword

until their consumption), that all of Israel turns back to Ai, and strikes it by the mouth of the sword; **25** and all who fall during the day, of men and of women, are twelve thousand—all men of Ai. **26** And Joshua has not brought back his hand which he stretched out with the javelin until he has devoted all the inhabitants of Ai; **27** only the livestock and the spoil of that city has Israel spoiled for themselves, according to the word of Yhwh which He commanded Joshua. **28** And Joshua burns Ai, and makes it a continuous heap—a desolation to this day; **29** and he has hanged the king of Ai on the tree until evening, and at the going in of the sun Joshua has commanded, and they take down his carcass from the tree, and cast it to the opening of the gate of the city, and raise a great heap of stones over it until this day. **30** Then Joshua builds an altar to Yhwh, God of Israel, in Mount Ebal, **31** as Moses, servant of Yhwh, commanded the sons of Israel, as it is written in the Scroll of the Law of Moses—an altar of whole stones, over which he has not waved iron—and they cause burnt-offerings to go up on it to Yhwh, and sacrifice peace-offerings; **32** and he writes there on the stones a copy of the Law of Moses, which he has written in the presence of the sons of Israel. **33** And all Israel, and its elderly, and authorities, and his judges, are standing on this [side] and on that [side] of the Ark, before the priests, the Levites, carrying the Ark of the Covenant of Yhwh, the sojourner as well as the native, half of them in front of Mount Gerizim, and the half of them in front of Mount Ebal, as Moses servant of Yhwh had commanded to bless the people of Israel at the first. **34** And afterward he has proclaimed all the words of the Law, the blessing and the reviling, according to all that is written in the Scroll of the Law; **35** there has not been a thing of all that Moses commanded which Joshua has not proclaimed before all the assembly of Israel, and the women, and the infants, and the sojourner who is going in their midst.

CHAPTER 9

1 And it comes to pass, when all the kings who [are] beyond the Jordan, in the hill-country, and in the low-country, and in every haven of the Great Sea, toward Lebanon, the Hittite, and the Amorite, the Canaanite, the Perizzite, the Hivite, and the Jebusite, hear— **2** that they gather themselves together to fight with Joshua, and with Israel—[with] one mouth. **3** And the inhabitants of Gibeon have heard that which Joshua has done to Jericho and to Ai, **4** and they work, even they, with subtlety, and go, and feign to be ambassadors, and take old sacks for their donkeys, and wine-bottles, old, and split, and bound up, **5** and sandals, old and patched, on their feet, and old garments on them, and all the bread of their provision is dry—it was crumbs. **6** And they go to Joshua, to the camp at Gilgal, and say to him, and to the men of Israel, "We have come from a far-off land, and now, make a covenant with us"; **7** and the men of Israel say to the Hivite, "It may be [that] you are dwelling in our midst, so how do we make a covenant with you?" **8** and they say to Joshua, "We [are] your servants." And Joshua says to them, "Who [are] you? and where do you come from?" **9** And they say to him, "Your servants have come from a very far-off land, for the Name of your God Yhwh, for we have heard His fame, and all that He has done in Egypt, **10** and all that He has done to the two kings of the Amorite who [are] beyond the Jordan, to Sihon king of Heshbon, and to Og king of Bashan, who [is] in Ashtaroth. **11** And our elderly, and all the inhabitants of our land speak to us, saying, Take provision in your hand for the way, and go to meet them, and you have said to them: We [are] your servants, and now, make a covenant with us; **12** this bread of ours—we provided ourselves with it hot out of our houses, on the day of our coming out to go to you, and now, behold, it is dry, and has been crumbs; **13** and these [are] the wine-bottles which we filled, new, and behold, they have split; and these, our garments and our sandals, have become old, from the exceeding greatness of the way." **14** And the men take of their provision, and have not asked the mouth of Yhwh; **15** and Joshua makes peace with them, and makes a covenant with them, to keep them alive; and the princes of the congregation swear to them. **16** And it comes to pass, that at the end of three days after they have made a covenant with them, that they hear that they [are] their neighbors—that they are dwelling in their midst. **17** And the sons of Israel journey and come to their cities on the third day—and their cities [are] Gibeon, and Chephirah, and Beeroth, and Kirjath-Jearim— **18** and the sons of Israel have not struck them, for the princes of the congregation have sworn to them by Yhwh, God of Israel, and all the congregation murmur against the princes. **19** And all the princes say to all the congregation, "We have sworn to them by Yhwh, God of Israel; and now, we are not able to come against them; **20** we do this to them, and have kept them alive, and wrath is not on us, because of the oath which we have sworn to them." **21** And the princes say to them, "They live, and are hewers of wood and drawers of water for all the congregation, as the princes spoke to them." **22** And Joshua calls for them, and speaks to them, saying, "Why have you deceived us, saying, We are very far from you, yet you [are] dwelling in our midst? **23** and now you are cursed, and none of you is cut off [from being] a servant, even hewers of wood and drawers of water, for the house of my God." **24** And they answer Joshua and say, "Because it was certainly declared to your servants that your God Yhwh commanded His servant Moses to give all the land to you, and to destroy all the inhabitants of the land from before you; and we fear greatly for ourselves because of you, and we do this thing; **25** and now, behold, we [are] in your hand, as [it is] good, and as [it is] right in your eyes to do to us—do." **26** And he does to them so, and delivers them from the hand of the sons of Israel, and they have not slain them; **27** and on that day Joshua makes them hewers of wood and drawers of water for the congregation, and for the altar of Yhwh, to this day, at the place which He chooses.

CHAPTER 10

1 And it comes to pass, when Adoni-Zedek king of Jerusalem hears that Joshua has captured Ai, and devotes it (as he had done to Jericho and to her king so he has done to Ai and to her king), and that the inhabitants of Gibeon have made peace with Israel, and are in their midst— **2** that they are greatly afraid, because Gibeon [is] a great city, as one of the royal cities, and because it [is] greater than Ai, and all its men [are] heroes **3** And Adoni-Zedek king of Jerusalem sends to Hoham king of Hebron, and to Piram king of Jarmuth, and to Japhia king of Lachish, and to Debir king of Eglon, saying, **4** "Come up to me, and help me, and we strike Gibeon, for it has made peace with Joshua, and with the sons of Israel." **5** And five kings of the Amorite (the king of Jerusalem, the king of Hebron, the king of Jarmuth, the king of Lachish, the king of Eglon) are gathered together, and go up, they and all their camps, and encamp against Gibeon, and fight against it. **6** And the men of Gibeon send to Joshua, to the camp at Gilgal, saying, "Do not let your hand cease from your servants; come up to us [with] haste, and give safety to us, and help us; for all the kings of the Amorite, dwelling in the hill-country, have been assembled against us." **7** And Joshua goes up from Gilgal, he, and all the people of war with him, even all the mighty men of valor. **8** And Yhwh says to Joshua, "Do not be afraid of them, for I have given them into your hand, there does not stand a man of them in your presence." **9** And Joshua comes to them suddenly (all the night he has gone up from Gilgal), **10** and Yhwh crushes them before Israel, and strikes them [with] a great striking at Gibeon, and pursues them the way of the ascent of Beth-Horon, and strikes them to Azekah, and to Makkedah. **11** And it comes to pass, in their fleeing from the face of Israel—they [are] in the descent of Beth-Horon—and Yhwh has cast great stones on them out of the heavens, to Azekah, and they die; more are they who have died by the hailstones than they whom the sons of Israel have slain by the sword. **12** Then Joshua speaks to Yhwh in the day of Yhwh's giving up the Amorites before the sons of Israel, and he says before the eyes of Israel, "Sun—stand still in Gibeon; and moon—in the Valley of Ajalon"; **13** and the sun stands still, and the moon has stood—until the nation takes vengeance [on] its enemies; is it not written on the Scroll of the Upright, "and the sun stands in the midst of the heavens, and has not hurried to go in—as a perfect day?" **14** And there has not been like that day before it or after it, for Yhwh's listening to the voice of a man; for Yhwh is fighting for Israel. **15** And Joshua turns back, and all Israel with him, to the camp at Gilgal. **16** And these five kings flee, and are hidden in a cave at Makkedah, **17** and it is declared to Joshua, saying, "The five kings have been found hidden in a cave at Makkedah." **18** And Joshua says, "Roll great stones to the mouth of the cave, and appoint men over it to watch them; **19** and you, do not stand, pursue after your enemies, and you have struck them from the rear; do not permit them to go into their cities, for your God Yhwh has given them into your hand." **20** And it comes to pass, when Joshua and the sons of Israel finish to strike them [with] a very great

striking until they are consumed, and the remnant who have remained of them go into the fortified cities, **21** that all the people return to the camp, to Joshua, [at] Makkedah, in peace; none moved his tongue sharply against the sons of Israel. **22** And Joshua says, "Open the mouth of the cave, and bring out to me these five kings from the cave"; **23** and they do so, and bring out to him these five kings from the cave: the king of Jerusalem, the king of Hebron, the king of Jarmuth, the king of Lachish, the king of Eglon. **24** And it comes to pass, when they bring out these kings to Joshua, that Joshua calls to every man of Israel, and says to the captains of the men of war, who have gone with him, "Draw near, set your feet on the necks of these kings"; and they draw near, and set their feet on their necks. **25** And Joshua says to them, "Do not fear, nor be frightened; be strong and courageous; for thus does Yhwh do to all your enemies with whom you are fighting"; **26** and Joshua strikes them afterward, and puts them to death, and hangs them on five trees; and they are hanging on the trees until the evening. **27** And it comes to pass, at the time of the going in of the sun, Joshua has commanded, and they take them down from off the trees, and cast them into the cave where they had been hid, and put great stones on the mouth of the cave until this very day. **28** And Joshua has captured Makkedah on that day, and he strikes it by the mouth of the sword, and he has devoted its king, them and every person who [is] in it—he has not left a remnant; and he does to the king of Makkedah as he did to the king of Jericho. **29** And Joshua passes over, and all Israel with him, from Makkedah [to] Libnah, and fights with Libnah; **30** and Yhwh also gives it into the hand of Israel, and its king, and [Joshua] strikes it by the mouth of the sword, and every person who [is] in it—he does not leave a remnant in it; and he does to its king as he did to the king of Jericho. **31** And Joshua passes over, and all Israel with him, from Libnah to Lachish, and encamps against it, and fights against it. **32** And Yhwh gives Lachish into the hand of Israel, and [Joshua] captures it on the second day, and strikes it by the mouth of the sword, and every person who [is] in it, according to all that he did to Libnah. **33** Then Horam king of Gezer has come up to help Lachish, and Joshua strikes him and his people, until he has not left a remnant to him. **34** And Joshua passes over, and all Israel with him, from Lachish to Eglon, and they encamp against it, and fight against it, **35** and capture it on that day, and strike it by the mouth of the sword, and every person who [is] in it he has devoted on that day, according to all that he did to Lachish. **36** And Joshua goes up, and all Israel with him, from Eglon to Hebron, and they fight against it, **37** and capture it, and strike it by the mouth of the sword, and its king, and all its cities, and every person who [is] in it—he has not left a remnant— according to all that he did to Eglon—and devotes it, and every person who [is] in it. **38** And Joshua turns back, and all Israel with him, to Debir, and fights against it, **39** and captures it, and its king, and all its cities, and they strike them by the mouth of the sword, and devote every person who [is] in it—he has not left a remnant; as he did to Hebron so he did to Debir, and to its king, and as he did to Libnah, and to its king. **40** And Joshua strikes all the land of the hill-country, and of the south, and of the low-country, and of the springs, and all their kings—he has not left a remnant, and he has devoted all that breathe, as Yhwh, God of Israel, commanded. **41** And Joshua strikes them from Kadesh-Barnea, even to Gaza, and all the land of Goshen, even to Gibeon; **42** and Joshua has captured all these kings and their land [at] one time, for Yhwh, God of Israel, is fighting for Israel. **43** and Joshua turns back, and all Israel with him, to the camp at Gilgal.

CHAPTER 11

1 And it comes to pass, when Jabin king of Hazor hears, that he sends to Jobab king of Madon, and to the king of Shimron, and to the king of Achshaph, **2** and to the kings who [are] on the north in the hill-country, and in the plain south of Chinneroth, and in the low country, and in the elevations of Dor, on the west, **3** [to] the Canaanite on the east, and on the west, and the Amorite, and the Hittite, and the Perizzite, and the Jebusite in the hill-country, and the Hivite under Hermon, in the land of Mizpeh— **4** and they go out, they and all their camps with them, a people numerous, as the sand which [is] on the seashore for multitude, and [with] very many horse and charioteer; **5** and all these kings are met together, and they come and encamp together at the waters of Merom, to fight with Israel. **6** And Yhwh says to Joshua, "Do not be afraid of their presence, for about this time tomorrow I am giving all of them slain before Israel; hamstring their horses, and burn their chariots with fire." **7** And Joshua comes, and all the people of war with him, against them by the waters of Merom, and they suddenly fall on them; **8** and Yhwh gives them into the hand of Israel, and they strike them and pursue them to the great Sidon, and to Misrephoth-Maim, and to the Valley of Mizpeh eastward, and they strike them, until he has not left a remnant to them; **9** and Joshua does to them as Yhwh commanded to him; he has hamstrung their horses, and burned their chariots with fire. **10** And Joshua turns back at that time, and captures Hazor, and he has struck its king by the sword; for Hazor [was] formerly head of all these kingdoms; **11** and they strike every person who [is] in it by the mouth of the sword; he has devoted—he has not left anyone breathing, and he has burned Hazor with fire; **12** and all the cities of these kings, and all their kings, Joshua has captured, and he strikes them by the mouth of the sword; he devoted them, as Moses, servant of Yhwh, commanded. **13** Only, all the cities which are standing by their hill, Israel has not burned them—except Joshua has burned Hazor, only; **14** and all the spoil of these cities, and the livestock, the sons of Israel have spoiled for themselves; only, they have struck every man by the mouth of the sword, until their destroying them; they have not left anyone breathing. **15** As Yhwh commanded His servant Moses, so Moses commanded Joshua, and so Joshua has done; he has not turned aside a thing of all that Yhwh commanded Moses. **16** And Joshua takes all this land: the hill-country, and all the south, and all the land of Goshen, and the low country, and the plain, even the hill-country of Israel and its low lands, **17** from the Mount of Halak, which is going up [to] Seir, and to Ba'al-Gad, in the Valley of Lebanon, under Mount Hermon; and he has captured all their kings, and he strikes them, and puts them to death. **18** Joshua has made war with all these kings [for] many days; **19** there has not been a city which made peace with the sons of Israel except the Hivite, inhabitants of Gibeon; they have taken the whole in battle; **20** for it has been from Yhwh to strengthen their heart, to meet in battle with Israel, in order to devote them, so that they have no grace, but in order to destroy them, as Yhwh commanded Moses. **21** And Joshua comes at that time, and cuts off the Anakim from the hill-country, from Hebron, from Debir, from Anab, and from all the hill-country of Judah, and from all the hill-country of Israel; Joshua has devoted them with their cities. **22** There has not been Anakim left in the land of the sons of Israel; only in Gaza, in Gath, and in Ashdod, were they left. **23** And Joshua takes the whole of the land, according to all that Yhwh has spoken to Moses, and Joshua gives it for an inheritance to Israel according to their divisions, by their tribes; and the land has rest from war.

CHAPTER 12

1 And these [are] kings of the land whom the sons of Israel have struck, and possess their land beyond the Jordan, at the sun-rising, from the Brook of Arnon to Mount Hermon, and all the plain eastward: **2** Sihon, king of the Amorite, who is dwelling in Heshbon, ruling from Aroer which [is] on the border of the Brook of Arnon, and the middle of the brook, and half of Gilead, and to the Brook of Jabok, the border of the sons of Ammon; **3** and the plain to the Sea of Chinneroth eastward, and to the Sea of the Plain (the Salt Sea) eastward, the way to Beth-Jeshimoth, and from the south under the Springs of Pisgah. **4** And the border of Og king of Bashan (of the remnant of the Rephaim), who is dwelling in Ashtaroth and in Edrei, **5** and ruling in Mount Hermon, and in Salcah, and in all Bashan, to the border of the Geshurite, and the Maachathite, and the half of Gilead, the border of Sihon king of Heshbon. **6** Moses, servant of Yhwh, and the sons of Israel have struck them, and Moses, servant of Yhwh, gives it—a possession to the Reubenite, and to the Gadite, and to the half of the tribe of Manasseh. **7** And these [are] kings of the land whom Joshua and the sons of Israel have struck beyond the Jordan westward, from Ba'al-Gad, in the Valley of Lebanon, and to the Mount of Halak, which is going up to Seir; and Joshua gives it to the tribes of Israel—a possession according to their divisions; **8** in the hill-country, and in the low country, and in the plain, and in the springs, and in the wilderness, and in the south; the Hittite, the Amorite, and the Canaanite, the Perizzite, the Hivite, and the Jebusite: **9** the king of Jericho, one; the king of Ai, which [is] beside Bethel, one; **10** the king of Jerusalem, one; the king of Hebron, one; **11** the king of

Jarmuth, one; the king of Lachish, one; **12** the king of Eglon, one; the king of Gezer, one; **13** the king of Debir, one; the king of Geder, one; **14** the king of Hormah, one; the king of Arad, one; **15** the king of Libnah, one; the king of Adullam, one; **16** the king of Mekkedah, one; the king of Beth-El, one; **17** the king of Tappuah, one; the king of Hepher, one; **18** the king of Aphek, one; the king of Lasharon, one; **19** the king of Madon, one; the king of Hazor, one; **20** the king of Shimron-Meron, one; the king of Achshaph, one; **21** the king of Taanach, one; the king of Megiddo, one; **22** the king of Kedesh, one; the king of Jokneam of Carmel, one; **23** the king of Dor, at the elevation of Dor, one; the king of the nations of Gilgal, one; **24** the king of Tirzah, one; all the kings [are] thirty-one.

CHAPTER 13

1 And Joshua is old, entering into days, and Yhwh says to him, "You have become aged, you have entered into days; as for the land, very much has been left to possess. **2** This [is] the land that is left: all the circuits of the Philistines, and all Geshuri, **3** from Sihor which [is] on the front of Egypt, and to the border of Ekron northward (it is reckoned to the Canaanite), five princes of the Philistines, the Gazathite, and the Ashdothite, the Eshkalonite, the Gittite, and the Ekronite, also the Avim; **4** from the south, all the land of the Canaanite, and Mearah, which [is] to the Sidonians, to Aphek, to the border of the Amorite; **5** and the land of the Giblite, and all Lebanon, at the sun-rising, from Ba'al-Gad under Mount Hermon, to the going in to Hamath: **6** all the inhabitants of the hill-country, from Lebanon to Misrephoth-Maim, all the Sidonians: I dispossess them before the sons of Israel; only, cause it to fall to Israel for an inheritance, as I have commanded you. **7** And now, apportion this land for an inheritance to the nine tribes, and half of the tribe of Manasseh." **8** With [the other half], the Reubenite and the Gadite have received their inheritance, which Moses has given to them beyond the Jordan eastward, as Moses servant of Yhwh has given to them; **9** from Aroer, which [is] on the edge of the Brook of Arnon, and the city which [is] in the midst of the brook, and all the plain of Medeba to Dihon, **10** and all the cities of Sihon king of the Amorite, who reigned in Heshbon, to the border of the sons of Ammon, **11** and Gilead, and the border of the Geshurite, and of the Maachathite, and all Mount Hermon, and all Bashan to Salcah; **12** all the kingdom of Og in Bashan, who reigned in Ashtaroth and in Edrei; he was left of the remnant of the Rephaim, and Moses strikes them, and dispossesses them; **13** and the sons of Israel did not dispossess the Geshurite, and the Maachathite; and Geshur and Maachath dwell in the midst of Israel to this day. **14** Only, he has not given an inheritance to the tribe of Levi; fire-offerings of Yhwh, God of Israel, [are] its inheritance, as He has spoken to it. **15** And Moses gives to the tribe of the sons of Reuben, for their families; **16** and the border is to them from Aroer, which [is] on the edge of the Brook of Arnon, and the city which [is] in the midst of the brook, and all the plain by Medeba, **17** Heshbon, and all its cities which [are] in the plain, Dibon, and Bamoth-Ba'al, and Beth-Ba'al-Meon, **18** and Jahazah, and Kedemoth, and Mephaath, **19** and Kirjathaim, and Sibmah, and Zareth-Shahar, on the mountain of the valley, **20** and Beth-Peor, and the Springs of Pisgah, and Beth-Jeshimoth, **21** and all the cities of the plain, and all the kingdom of Sihon king of the Amorite, who reigned in Heshbon, whom Moses struck, with the princes of Midian, Evi, and Rekem, and Zur, and Hur, and Reba, princes of Sihon, inhabitants of the land. **22** And the sons of Israel have slain Balaam, son of Beor, the diviner, with the sword, among their wounded ones. **23** And the border of the sons of Reuben is the Jordan, and [its] border; this [is] the inheritance of the sons of Reuben, for their families, the cities and their villages. **24** And Moses gives to the tribe of Gad, to the sons of Gad, for their families; **25** and the border to them is Jazer, and all the cities of Gilead, and half of the land of the sons of Ammon, to Aroer which [is] on the front of Rabbah, **26** and from Heshbon to Ramath-Mispeh, and Betonim, and from Mahanaim to the border of Debir, **27** and in the valley, Beth-Aram, and Beth-Nimrah, and Succoth, and Zaphon, the rest of the kingdom of Sihon king of Heshbon, the Jordan and [its] border, to the extremity of the Sea of Chinnereth, beyond the Jordan eastward. **28** This [is] the inheritance of the sons of Gad, for their families, the cities and their villages. **29** And Moses gives to the half-tribe of Manasseh; and it is to the half-tribe of the sons of Manasseh, for their families. **30** And their border is from

Mahanaim, all Bashan, all the kingdom of Og king of Bashan, and all the small towns of Jair, which [are] in Bashan—sixty cities; ³¹ and half of Gilead, and Ashteroth, and Edrei, cities of the kingdom of Og in Bashan, [are] to the sons of Machir, son of Manasseh, to the half of the sons of Machir, for their families. ³² These [are] they whom Moses caused to inherit in the plains of Moab beyond the Jordan, [by] Jericho, eastward; ³³ and Moses did not give an inheritance to the tribe of Levi; Yhwh, God of Israel, Himself, [is] their inheritance, as He has spoken to them.

CHAPTER 14

¹ And these [are] they of the sons of Israel who inherited in the land of Canaan, whom Eleazar the priest, and Joshua son of Nun, and the heads of the fathers of the tribes of the sons of Israel, caused to inherit; ² their inheritance [is] by lot, as Yhwh commanded by the hand of Moses, for the nine tribes and the half-tribe; ³ for Moses has given the inheritance of two of the tribes, and of half of the tribe, beyond the Jordan, and he has not given an inheritance to the Levites in their midst; ⁴ for the sons of Joseph have been two tribes, Manasseh and Ephraim, and they have not given a portion to the Levites in the land, except cities to dwell in, and their outskirts for their livestock, and for their possessions; ⁵ as Yhwh commanded Moses, so the sons of Israel have done, and they apportion the land. ⁶ And the sons of Judah come near to Joshua in Gilgal, and Caleb son of Jephunneh the Kenezzite says to him, "You have known the word that Yhwh has spoken to Moses, the man of God, concerning me and concerning you in Kadesh-Barnea: ⁷ I [was] a son of forty years in Moses, servant of Yhwh, sending me from Kadesh-Barnea, to spy out the land, and I bring him back word as with my heart; ⁸ and my brothers who have gone up with me have caused the heart of the people to melt, and I have been fully after my God Yhwh; ⁹ and Moses swears in that day, saying, Nevertheless—the land on which your foot has trodden, it is to you for an inheritance, and to your sons—for all time, for you have been fully after my God Yhwh. ¹⁰ And now, behold, Yhwh has kept me alive, as He has spoken, these forty-five years, since Yhwh spoke this word to Moses when Israel went in the wilderness; and now, behold, I [am] a son of eighty-five years today; ¹¹ yet today I [am] strong as in the day of Moses' sending me; as my power [was] then, so [is] my power now, for battle, and to go out, and to come in. ¹² And now, give this hill-country to me, of which Yhwh spoke in that day, for you heard in that day, for Anakim [are] there, and great, fortified cities; if [it] so be [that] Yhwh [is] with me, then I have dispossessed them, as Yhwh has spoken." ¹³ And Joshua blesses him, and gives Hebron to Caleb son of Jephunneh for an inheritance, ¹⁴ therefore Hebron has been to Caleb son of Jephunneh the Kenezzite for an inheritance to this day, because that he was fully after Yhwh, God of Israel; ¹⁵ and the name of Hebron [was] formerly Kirjath-Arba (the man [was] the greatest among the Anakim); and the land has rest from war.

CHAPTER 15

¹ And the lot for the tribe of the sons of Judah, for their families, is to the border of Edom; the wilderness of Zin southward, at the extremity of the south; ² and to them the south border is at the extremity of the Salt Sea, from the bay which is looking southward; ³ and it has gone out to the south to Maaleh-Akrabbim, and passed over to Zin, and gone up on the south to Kadesh-Barnea, and passed over [to] Hezron, and gone up to Adar, and turned around to Karkaa, ⁴ and passed over [to] Azmon, and gone out [at] the Brook of Egypt, and the outgoings of the border have been at the sea; this is the south border to you. ⁵ And the east border [is] the Salt Sea, to the extremity of the Jordan, and the border at the north quarter [is] from the bay of the sea, at the extremity of the Jordan; ⁶ and the border has gone up [to] Beth-Hoglah, and passed over on the north of Beth-Arabah, and the border has gone up [to] the stone of Bohan son of Reuben: ⁷ and the border has gone up toward Debir from the Valley of Achor, and northward looking to Gilgal, which [is] opposite the ascent of Adummim, which [is] on the south of the brook, and the border has passed over to the waters of En-Shemesh, and its outgoings have been to En-Rogel; ⁸ and the border has gone up the Valley of the

Son of Hinnom, to the side of the Jebusite on the south (it [is] Jerusalem), and the border has gone up to the top of the hill-country which [is] on the front of the Valley of Hinnom westward, which [is] in the extremity of the Valley of the Rephaim northward; ⁹ and the border has been marked out, from the top of the hill-country to the fountain of the waters of Nephtoah, and has gone out to the cities of Mount Ephron, and the border has been marked out [to] Ba'alah (it [is] Kirjath-Jearim); ¹⁰ and the border has gone around from Ba'alah westward, to Mount Seir, and passed over to the side of Mount Jearim (it [is] Chesalon), on the north, and gone down [to] Beth-Shemesh, and passed over to Timnah; ¹¹ and the border has gone out to the side of Ekron northward, and the border has been marked out [to] Shicron, and has passed over to Mount Ba'alah, and gone out [to] Jabneel; and the outgoings of the border have been at the sea. ¹² And the west border [is] to the Great Sea, and [its] border; this [is] the border of the sons of Judah all around for their families. ¹³ And to Caleb son of Jephunneh he has given a portion in the midst of the sons of Judah, according to the command of Yhwh to Joshua, [even] the city of Arba, father of Anak—it [is] Hebron. ¹⁴ And Caleb is dispossessing there the three sons of Anak: Sheshai, and Ahiman, and Talmai, children of Anak, ¹⁵ and he goes up there to the inhabitants of Debir; and the name of Debir [was] formerly Kirjath-Sepher. ¹⁶ And Caleb says, "He who strikes Kirjath-Sephar, and has captured it—I have given my daughter Achsah to him for a wife." ¹⁷ And Othniel son of Kenaz, brother of Caleb, captures it, and he gives his daughter Achsah to him for a wife. ¹⁸ And it comes to pass, in her coming in, that she persuades him to ask [for] a field from her father, and she comes down off the donkey, and Caleb says to her, "What do you [want]?" ¹⁹ And she says, "Give a blessing to me; when you have given me the land of the south, then you have given springs of waters to me"; and he gives the upper springs and the lower springs to her. ²⁰ This [is] the inheritance of the tribe of the sons of Judah, for their families. ²¹ And the cities at the extremity of the tribe of the sons of Judah are to the border of Edom in the south, Kabzeel, and Eder, and Jagur, ²² and Kinah, and Dimonah, and Adadah, ²³ and Kedesh, and Hazor, and Ithnan, ²⁴ Ziph, and Telem, and Bealoth, ²⁵ and Hazor, Hadattah, and Kerioth, Hezron (it [is] Hazor), ²⁶ Amam, and Shema, and Moladah, ²⁷ and Hazar-Gaddah, and Heshmon, and Beth-Palet, ²⁸ and Hazar-Shual, and Beer-Sheba, and Bizjothjah, ²⁹ Ba'alah, and Iim, and Azem, ³⁰ and Eltolad, and Chesil, and Hormah, ³¹ and Ziklag, and Madmannah, and Sansannah, ³² and Lebaoth, and Shilhim, and Ain, and Rimmon; all the cities [are] twenty-nine, and their villages. ³³ In the low country: Eshtaol, and Zoreah, and Ashnah, ³⁴ and Zanoah, and En-Gannim, Tappuah, and Enam, ³⁵ Jarmuth, and Adullam, Socoh, and Azekah, ³⁶ and Sharaim, and Adithaim, and Gederah, and Gederothaim; fourteen cities and their villages. ³⁷ Zenan, and Hadashah, and Migdal-Gad, ³⁸ and Dilean, and Mizpeh, and Joktheel, ³⁹ Lachish, and Bozkath, and Eglon, ⁴⁰ and Cabbon, and Lahmam, and Kithlish, ⁴¹ and Gederoth, Beth-Dagon, and Naamah, and Makkedah; sixteen cities and their villages. ⁴² Libnah, and Ether, and Ashan, ⁴³ and Jiphtah, and Ashnah, and Nezib, ⁴⁴ and Keilah, and Achzib, and Mareshah; nine cities and their villages. ⁴⁵ Ekron and its towns and its villages, ⁴⁶ from Ekron and westward, all that [are] by the side of Ashdod, and their villages. ⁴⁷ Ashdod, its towns and its villages, Gaza, its towns and its villages, to the Brook of Egypt, and the Great Sea, and [its] border. ⁴⁸ And in the hill-country: Shamir, and Jattir, and Socoh, ⁴⁹ and Dannah, and Kirjath-Sannah (it [is] Debir), ⁵⁰ and Anab, and Eshtemoh, and Anim, ⁵¹ and Goshen, and Holon, and Giloh; eleven cities and their villages. ⁵² Arab, and Dumah, and Eshean, ⁵³ and Janum, and Beth-Tappuah, and Aphekah, ⁵⁴ and Humtah, and Kirjath-Arba (it [is] Hebron), and Zior; nine cities and their villages. ⁵⁵ Maon, Carmel, and Ziph, and Juttah, ⁵⁶ and Jezreel, and Jokdeam, and Zanoah, ⁵⁷ Cain, Gibeah, and Timnah; ten cities and their villages. ⁵⁸ Halhul, Beth-Zur, and Gedor, ⁵⁹ and Maarath, and Beth-Anoth, and Eltekon; six cities and their villages. ⁶⁰ Kirjath-Ba'al (it [is] Kirjath-Jearim), and Rabbah; two cities and their villages. ⁶¹ In the wilderness: Beth-Arabah, Middin, and Secacah, ⁶² and Nibshan, and the City of Salt, and En-Gedi; six cities and their villages. ⁶³ As for the Jebusites, inhabitants of Jerusalem, the sons of Judah have not been able to dispossess them, and the Jebusite dwells with the sons of Judah in Jerusalem to this day.

CHAPTER 16

¹ And the lot for the sons of Joseph goes out from Jordan [by] Jericho, to the waters of Jericho on the east, to the wilderness going up from Jericho in the hill-country of Beth-El, ² and has gone out from Beth-El to Luz, and passed over to the border of Archi [to] Ataroth, ³ and gone down westward to the border of Japhleti, to the border of the lower Beth-Horon, and to Gezer, and its outgoings have been at the sea. ⁴ And the sons of Joseph—Manasseh and Ephraim—inherit. ⁵ And the border of the sons of Ephraim is by their families; and the border of their inheritance is on the east, Atroth-Addar to the upper Beth-Horon; ⁶ and the border has gone out at the sea, to Michmethah on the north, and the border has gone around eastward [to] Taanath-Shiloh, and passed over it eastward to Janohah, ⁷ and gone down from Janohah [to] Ataroth, and to Naarath, and touched against Jericho, and gone out at the Jordan. ⁸ From Tappuah the border goes westward to the Brook of Kanah, and its outgoings have been at the sea: this [is] the inheritance of the tribe of the sons of Ephraim, for their families. ⁹ And the separate cities of the sons of Ephraim [are] in the midst of the inheritance of the sons of Manasseh, all the cities and their villages; ¹⁰ and they have not dispossessed the Canaanite who is dwelling in Gezer, and the Canaanite dwells in the midst of Ephraim to this day, and is for forced labor—serving.

CHAPTER 17

¹ And the lot is for the tribe of Manasseh (for he [is] firstborn of Joseph), for Machir firstborn of Manasseh, father of Gilead, for he has been a man of war, and his are Gilead and Bashan. ² And there is [a lot] for the sons of Manasseh who are left, for their families; for the sons of Abiezer, and for the sons of Helek, and for the sons of Asriel, and for the sons of Shechem, and for the sons of Hepher, and for the sons of Shemida; these [are] the children of Manasseh son of Joseph—the males—by their families. ³ As for Zelophehad, son of Hepher, son of Gilead, son of Machir, son of Manasseh, he has no children except daughters, and these [are] the names of his daughters: Mahlah, and Noah, Hoglah, Milcah, and Tirzah, ⁴ and they draw near before Eleazar the priest, and before Joshua son of Nun, and before the princes, saying, "Yhwh commanded Moses to give an inheritance to us in the midst of our brothers"; and he gives to them, at the command of Yhwh, an inheritance in the midst of the brothers of their father. ⁵ And ten portions fall [to] Manasseh, apart from the land of Gilead and Bashan, which [are] beyond the Jordan; ⁶ for the daughters of Manasseh have inherited an inheritance in the midst of his sons, and the land of Gilead has been for the sons of Manasseh who are left. ⁷ And the border of Manasseh is from Asher to Michmethah, which [is] on the front of Shechem, and the border has gone on to the right, to the inhabitants of En-Tappuah. ⁸ The land of Tappuah has been for Manasseh, and Tappuah to the border of Manasseh for the sons of Ephraim. ⁹ And the border has come down [to] the Brook of Kanah, southward of the brook; these cities of Ephraim [are] in the midst of the cities of Manasseh, and the border of Manasseh [is] on the north of the brook, and its outgoings are at the sea. ¹⁰ Southward [is] for Ephraim and northward for Manasseh, and the sea is his border, and in Asher they meet on the north, and in Issachar on the east. ¹¹ And in Issachar and in Asher, Manasseh has Beth-Shean and its towns, and Ibleam and its towns, and the inhabitants of Dor and its towns, and the inhabitants of En-Dor and its towns, and the inhabitants of Taanach and its towns, and the inhabitants of Megiddo and its towns—three counties. ¹² And the sons of Manasseh have not been able to occupy these cities, and the Canaanite is desirous to dwell in this land, ¹³ and it comes to pass, when the sons of Israel have been strong, that they put the Canaanite to forced labor, and have not utterly dispossessed him. ¹⁴ And the sons of Joseph speak with Joshua, saying, "Why have you given an inheritance to me—one lot and one portion, and I [am] a numerous people? Yhwh has blessed me until now." ¹⁵ And Joshua says to them, "If you [are] a numerous people, go up to the forest for yourself, then you have created [a place] for yourself there in the land of the Perizzite and of the Rephaim, when Mount Ephraim has been narrow for you." ¹⁶ And the sons of Joseph say, "The mountain is not enough for us, and a chariot of iron [is] with every Canaanite who is dwelling in the land of the valley—to him who [is] in Beth-Shean and its towns, and to him who [is] in the Valley of Jezreel." ¹⁷ And Joshua speaks to the house of Joseph, to Ephraim and to Manasseh, saying, "You [are] a numerous people, and have great power; you do not have [only] one lot, ¹⁸ because the mountain is yours; because it [is] a forest—you have created it, and its outgoings have been yours; because you dispossess the Canaanite, though it has chariots of iron—though it [is] strong."

CHAPTER 18

¹ And all the congregation of the sons of Israel is assembled [at] Shiloh, and they cause the Tent of Meeting to dwell there, and the land has been subdued before them. ² And there are seven tribes left among the sons of Israel who have not shared their inheritance, ³ and Joshua says to the sons of Israel, "Until when are you remiss to go in to possess the land which He, Yhwh, God of your fathers, has given to you? ⁴ Give three men from you for [each] tribe, and I send them, and they rise and go up and down through the land, and describe it according to their inheritance, and come to me, ⁵ and they have divided it into seven portions—Judah stays by its border on the south, and the house of Joseph stays by their border on the north— ⁶ and you describe the land [in] seven portions, and have brought [it] to me here, and I have cast a lot for you here before our God Yhwh; ⁷ for there is no portion for the Levites in your midst, for the priesthood of Yhwh [is] their inheritance, and Gad, and Reuben, and half of the tribe of Manasseh received their inheritance beyond the Jordan eastward, which Moses, servant of Yhwh, gave to them." ⁸ And the men rise and go; and Joshua commands those who are going to describe the land, saying, "Go, and walk up and down through the land, and describe it, and return to me, and here I cast a lot for you before Yhwh in Shiloh." ⁹ And the men go, and pass over through the land, and describe it by cities, in seven portions, on a scroll, and they come to Joshua, to the camp [at] Shiloh. ¹⁰ And Joshua casts a lot for them in Shiloh before Yhwh, and there Joshua apportions the land to the sons of Israel, according to their divisions. ¹¹ And a lot goes up [for] the tribe of the sons of Benjamin, for their families; and the border of their lot goes out between the sons of Judah and the sons of Joseph. ¹² And the border is for them at the north side from the Jordan, and the border has gone up to the side of Jericho on the north, and gone up through the hill-country westward, and its outgoings have been at the wilderness of Beth-Aven; ¹³ and the border has gone over there to Luz, to the side of Luz (it [is] Beth-El) southward, and the border has gone down [to] Atroth-Addar, by the hill that [is] on the south of the lower Beth-Horon; ¹⁴ and the border has been marked out, and has gone around to the corner of the sea southward, from the hill which [is] at the front of Beth-Horon southward, and its outgoings have been to Kirjath-Ba`al (it [is] Kirjath-Jearim), a city of the sons of Judah: this [is] the west quarter. ¹⁵ And the south quarter [is] from the end of Kirjath-Jearim, and the border has gone out westward, and has gone out to the fountain of the waters of Nephtoah; ¹⁶ and the border has come down to the extremity of the hill which [is] on the front of the Valley of the Son of Hinnom, which [is] in the Valley of the Rephaim northward, and has gone down the Valley of Hinnom to the side of Jebusi southward, and gone down [to] En-Rogel, ¹⁷ and has been marked out on the north, and gone out to En-Shemesh, and gone out to Geliloth, which [is] opposite the ascent of Adummim, and gone down [to] the stone of Bohan son of Reuben, ¹⁸ and passed over to the side in front of the Arabah northward, and gone down to Arabah; ¹⁹ and the border has passed over to the side of Beth-Hoglah northward, and the outgoings of the border have been to the north bay of the Salt Sea, to the south extremity of the Jordan; this [is] the south border; ²⁰ and the Jordan borders it at the east quarter; this [is] the inheritance of the sons of Benjamin, by its borders all around, for their families. ²¹ And the cities for the tribe of the sons of Benjamin, for their families, have been Jericho, and Beth-Hoglah, and the Valley of Keziz, ²² and Beth-Arabah, Zemaraim, and Beth-El, ²³ and Avim, and Parah, and Ophrah, ²⁴ and Chephar-Haammonai, and Ophni, and Gaba; twelve cities and their villages. ²⁵ Gibeon, and Ramah, and Beeroth, ²⁶ and Mizpeh, and Chephirah, and Mozah, ²⁷ and Rekem, and Irpeel, and Taralah, ²⁸ and Zelah, Eleph, and Jebusi (it [is] Jerusalem), Gibeath, Kirjath; fourteen cities and their villages. This [is] the inheritance of the sons of Benjamin, for their

families.

CHAPTER 19

¹ And the second lot goes out for Simeon, for the tribe of the sons of Simeon, for their families; and their inheritance is in the midst of the inheritance of the sons of Judah, ² and they have in their inheritance Beer-Sheba, and Sheba, and Moladah, ³ and Hazar-Shual, and Balah, and Azem, ⁴ and Eltolad, and Bethul, and Hormah, ⁵ and Ziklag, and Beth-Marcaboth, and Hazar-Susah, ⁶ and Beth-Lebaoth, and Sharuhen; thirteen cities and their villages. ⁷ Ain, Remmon, and Ether, and Ashan; four cities and their villages; ⁸ also all the villages which [are] around these cities, to Ba'alath-Beer, Ramoth of the south. This [is] the inheritance of the tribe of the sons of Simeon, for their families; ⁹ out of the portion of the sons of Judah [is] the inheritance of the sons of Simeon, for the portion of the sons of Judah has been too much for them, and the sons of Simeon inherit in the midst of their inheritance. ¹⁰ And the third lot goes up for the sons of Zebulun, for their families; and the border of their inheritance is to Sarid, ¹¹ and their border has gone up toward the sea, and Maralah, and come against Dabbasheth, and come to the brook which [is] on the front of Jokneam, ¹² and turned back from Sarid eastward, at the sun-rising, by the border of Chisloth-Tabor, and gone out to Daberath, and gone up to Japhia, ¹³ and there it has passed over eastward, to the east, to Gittah-Hepher, [to] Ittah-Kazin, and gone out [to] Rimmon-Methoar to Neah; ¹⁴ and the border has gone around it, from the north to Hannathon; and its outgoings have been [in] the Valley of Jiphthah-El, ¹⁵ and Kattath, and Nahallal, and Shimron, and Idalah, and Beth-Lehem; twelve cities and their villages. ¹⁶ This [is] the inheritance of the sons of Zebulun, for their families, these cities and their villages. ¹⁷ The fourth lot has gone out for Issachar, for the sons of Issachar, for their families; ¹⁸ and their border is [at] Jezreel, and Chesulloth, and Shunem, ¹⁹ and Haphraim, and Shihon, and Anaharath, ²⁰ and Rabbith, and Kishion, and Abez, ²¹ and Remeth, and En-Gannim, and En-Haddah, and Beth-Pazzez; ²² and the border has touched against Tabor, and Shahazimah, and Beth-Shemesh, and the outgoings of their border have been [at] the Jordan; sixteen cities and their villages. ²³ This [is] the inheritance of the tribe of the sons of Issachar, for their families, the cities and their villages. ²⁴ And the fifth lot goes out for the tribe of the sons of Asher, for their families; ²⁵ and their border is Helkath, and Hali, and Beten, and Achshaph, ²⁶ and Alammelech, and Amad, and Misheal; and it touches against Carmel westward, and against Shihor-Libnath; ²⁷ and has turned back, at the sun-rising, [to] Beth-Dagon, and come against Zebulun, and against the Valley of Jiphthah-El toward the north of Beth-Emek, and Neiel, and has gone out to Cabul on the left, ²⁸ and Hebron, and Rehob, and Hammon, and Kanah, to great Sidon; ²⁹ and the border has turned back to Ramah, and to the fortified city Tyre; and the border has turned back to Hosah, and its outgoings are at the sea, from the coast to Achzib, ³⁰ and Ummah, and Aphek, and Rehob; twenty-two cities and their villages. ³¹ This [is] the inheritance of the tribe of the sons of Asher, for their families, these cities and their villages. ³² The sixth lot has gone out for the sons of Naphtali—for the sons of Naphtali, for their families; ³³ and their border is from Heleph, from Allon in Zaanannim, and Adami, Nekeb, and Jabneel, to Lakkum, and its outgoings are [at] the Jordan; ³⁴ and the border has turned back westward [to] Aznoth-Tabor, and gone out there to Hukkok, and touched against Zebulun on the south, and it has touched against Asher on the west, and against Judah [at] the Jordan, at the sun-rising; ³⁵ and the cities of defense [are] Ziddim, Zer, and Hammath, Rakkath, and Chinnereth, ³⁶ and Adamah, and Ramah, and Hazor, ³⁷ and Kedesh, and Edrei, and En-Hazor, ³⁸ and Iron, and Migdal-El, Horem, and Beth-Anath, and Beth-Shemesh; nineteen cities and their villages. ³⁹ This [is] the inheritance of the tribe of the sons of Naphtali, for their families, the cities and their villages. ⁴⁰ The seventh lot has gone out for the tribe of the sons of Dan, for their families; ⁴¹ and the border of their inheritance is Zorah, and Eshtaol, and Ir-Shemesh, ⁴² and Shalabbin, and Aijalon, and Jethlah, ⁴³ and Elon, and Thimnathah, and Ekron, ⁴⁴ and Eltekeh, and Gibbethon, and Ba'alath, ⁴⁵ and Jehud, and Bene-Barak, and Gath-Rimmon, ⁴⁶ and Me-Jarkon, and Rakkon, with the border in front of Joppa. ⁴⁷ And the border of the sons of Dan goes out from them, and the sons of Dan go up and fight with Leshem, and capture it, and strike it by the mouth of the sword, and possess it, and dwell in it, and call

Leshem, Dan, according to the name of their father Dan. ⁴⁸ This [is] the inheritance of the tribe of the sons of Dan, for their families, these cities and their villages. ⁴⁹ And they finish to give the land in inheritance, by its borders, and the sons of Israel give an inheritance to Joshua son of Nun in their midst; ⁵⁰ by the command of Yhwh they have given to him the city which he asked for, Timnath-Serah, in the hill-country of Ephraim, and he builds the city and dwells in it. ⁵¹ These [are] the inheritances which Eleazar the priest, and Joshua son of Nun, and the heads of the fathers of the tribes of the sons of Israel, have caused to inherit by lot, in Shiloh, before Yhwh, at the opening of the Tent of Meeting; and they finish to apportion the land.

CHAPTER 20

¹ And Yhwh speaks to Joshua, saying, ² "Speak to the sons of Israel, saying, Give cities of refuge for yourselves, as I have spoken to you by the hand of Moses, ³ for the fleeing there of a manslayer striking life through ignorance, without knowledge; and they have been for a refuge to you from the redeemer of blood. ⁴ When [one] has fled to one of these cities, and has stood [at] the opening of the gate of the city, and has spoken his matter in the ears of [the] elderly of that city, then they have gathered him into the city to them, and have given a place to him, and he has dwelt with them. ⁵ And when the redeemer of blood pursues after him, then they do not shut up the manslayer into his hand, for he has struck his neighbor without knowledge, and is not hating him until now; ⁶ and he has dwelt in that city until his standing before the congregation for judgment, until the death of the chief priest who is in those days—then the manslayer turns back and has come to his city, and to his house, to the city from where he fled." ⁷ And they sanctify Kedesh in Galilee, in the hill-country of Naphtali, and Shechem in the hill-country of Ephraim, and Kirjath-Arba (it [is] Hebron), in the hill-country of Judah; ⁸ and beyond the Jordan, [at] Jericho eastward, they have given Bezer in the wilderness, in the plain, out of the tribe of Reuben, and Ramoth in Gilead out of the tribe of Gad, and Golan in Bashan out of the tribe of Manasseh. ⁹ These have been cities of meeting for all the sons of Israel, and for a sojourner who is sojourning in their midst, for the fleeing there of anyone striking life through ignorance, and he does not die by the hand of the redeemer of blood until his standing before the congregation.

CHAPTER 21

¹ And the heads of the fathers of the Levites draw near to Eleazar the priest, and to Joshua son of Nun, and to the heads of the fathers of the tribes of the sons of Israel, ² and they speak to them in Shiloh, in the land of Canaan, saying, "Yhwh commanded by the hand of Moses to give to us cities to dwell in, and their outskirts for our livestock." ³ And the sons of Israel give to the Levites, out of their inheritance, at the command of Yhwh, these cities and their outskirts: ⁴ and the lot goes out for the families of the Kohathite, and there are for the sons of Aaron the priest (of the Levites), out of the tribe of Judah, and out of the tribe of Simeon, and out of the tribe of Benjamin, thirteen cities by lot, ⁵ and for the sons of Kohath who are left, out of the families of the tribe of Ephraim, and out of the tribe of Dan, and out of the half-tribe of Manasseh, ten cities by lot. ⁶ And for the sons of Gershon, out of the families of the tribe of Issachar, and out of the tribe of Asher, and out of the tribe of Naphtali, and out of the half-tribe of Manasseh in Bashan, [are] thirteen cities by lot. ⁷ For the sons of Merari, for their families, out of the tribe of Reuben, and out of the tribe of Gad, and out of the tribe of Zebulun, [are] twelve cities. ⁸ And the sons of Israel give these cities and their outskirts to the Levites, as Yhwh commanded by the hand of Moses, by lot. ⁹ And they give out of the tribe of the sons of Judah, and out of the tribe of the sons of Simeon, these cities which are called by name; ¹⁰ and they are for the sons of Aaron, of the families of the Kohathite, of the sons of Levi, for the first lot has been theirs; ¹¹ and they give to them the city of Arba father of Anak (it [is] Hebron), in the hill-country of Judah, and its outskirts around it; ¹² and they have given the field of the city and its villages to Caleb son of Jephunneh for his possession. ¹³ And to the sons of Aaron the priest they have given the city of refuge [for] the manslayer, Hebron and its outskirts, and Libnah and its

outskirts, **14** and Jattir and its outskirts, and Eshtemoa and its outskirts, **15** and Holon and its outskirts, and Debir and its outskirts, **16** and Ain and its outskirts, and Juttah and its outskirts, Beth-Shemesh and its outskirts; nine cities out of these two tribes. **17** And out of the tribe of Benjamin, Gibeon and its outskirts, Geba and its outskirts, **18** Anathoth and its outskirts, and Almon and its outskirts—four cities; **19** all the cities of the sons of Aaron the priests, [are] thirteen cities and their outskirts. **20** And for the families of the sons of Kohath, the Levites, who are left of the sons of Kohath, even the cities of their lot are of the tribe of Ephraim; **21** and they give to them the city of refuge [for] the manslayer, Shechem and its outskirts, in the hill-country of Ephraim, and Gezer and its outskirts, **22** and Kibzaim and its outskirts, and Beth-Horon and its outskirts—four cities. **23** And out of the tribe of Dan, Eltekeh and its outskirts, Gibbethon and its outskirts, **24** Aijalon and its outskirts, Gath-Rimmon and its outskirts—four cities. **25** And out of the half-tribe of Manasseh, Taanach and its outskirts, and Gath-Rimmon and its outskirts—two cities; **26** all the cities [are] ten and their outskirts, for the families of the sons of Kohath who are left. **27** And for the sons of Gershon, of the families of the Levites, out of the half-tribe of Manasseh, the city of refuge [for] the manslayer, Golan in Bashan and its outskirts, and Beeshterah and its outskirts—two cities. **28** And out of the tribe of Issachar, Kishon and its outskirts, Dabarath and its outskirts, **29** Jarmuth and its outskirts, En-Gannim and its outskirts—four cities. **30** And out of the tribe of Asher, Mishal and its outskirts, Abdon and its outskirts, **31** Helkath and its outskirts, and Rehob and its outskirts—four cities. **32** And out of the tribe of Naphtali, the city of refuge [for] the manslayer, Kedesh in Galilee and its outskirts, and Hammoth-Dor and its outskirts, and Kartan and its outskirts—three cities; **33** all the cities of the Gershonite, for their families, [are] thirteen cities and their outskirts. **34** And for the families of the sons of Merari, the Levites, who are left, [are,] out of the tribe of Zebulun, Jokneam and its outskirts, Kartah and its outskirts, **35** Dimnah and its outskirts, Nahalal and its outskirts—four cities. **36** And out of the tribe of Reuben, Bezer and its outskirts, and Jahazah and its outskirts, **37** Kedemoth and its outskirts, and Mephaath and its outskirts—four cities. **38** And out of the tribe of Gad, the city of refuge [for] the manslayer, Ramoth in Gilead and its outskirts, and Mahanaim and its outskirts, **39** Heshbon and its outskirts, Jazer and its outskirts—four cities [in] all. **40** All the cities for the sons of Merari, for their families, who are left of the families of the Levites—their lot is twelve cities. **41** All the cities of the Levites in the midst of the possession of the sons of Israel [are] forty-eight cities, and their outskirts. **42** These cities are each city and its outskirts around it; so to all these cities. **43** And Yhwh gives to Israel the whole of the land which He has sworn to give to their fathers, and they possess it, and dwell in it; **44** and Yhwh gives rest to them all around, according to all that which He has sworn to their fathers, and there has not stood a man in their presence of all their enemies, Yhwh has given the whole of their enemies into their hand; **45** there has not fallen a thing of all the good thing which Yhwh spoke to the house of Israel—the whole has come.

CHAPTER 22

1 Then Joshua calls for the Reubenite, and for the Gadite, and for the half-tribe of Manasseh, **2** and says to them, "You have kept the whole of that which Moses, servant of Yhwh, commanded you, and you listen to my voice, to all that I have commanded you; **3** you have not left your brothers these many days to this day, and have kept the charge—the command of your God Yhwh. **4** And now, your God Yhwh has given rest to your brothers, as He spoke to them; and now, turn, and go for yourselves to your tents, to the land of your possession, which Moses, servant of Yhwh, has given to you beyond the Jordan. **5** Only, be very watchful to do the command and the Law which Moses, servant of Yhwh, commanded you, to love your God Yhwh, and to walk in all His ways, and to keep His commands, and to cleave to Him, and to serve Him, with all your heart, and with all your soul." **6** And Joshua blesses them, and sends them away, and they go to their tents. **7** And to the half-tribe of Manasseh Moses has given, in Bashan, and to its [other] half Joshua has given with their brothers beyond the Jordan westward; and also when Joshua has sent them away to their tents, then he blesses them, **8** and speaks to them, saying, "Turn back to your tents with great riches, and with very much livestock, with silver, and with gold, and with bronze, and with iron, and with very much raiment; divide the spoil of your enemies with your brothers." **9** And the sons of Reuben, and the sons of Gad, and the half-tribe of Manasseh, turn back and go from the sons of Israel out of Shiloh, which [is] in the land of Canaan, to go to the land of Gilead, to the land of their possession, in which they have possession, according to the command of Yhwh, by the hand of Moses; **10** and they come to the districts of the Jordan, which [are] in the land of Canaan, and the sons of Reuben, and the sons of Gad, and the half-tribe of Manasseh, build an altar there by the Jordan—a great altar in appearance. **11** And the sons of Israel hear, saying, "Behold, the sons of Reuben, and the sons of Gad, and the half-tribe of Manasseh, have built the altar at the frontier of the land of Canaan, in the districts of the Jordan, at the passage of the sons of Israel." **12** And the sons of Israel hear, and all the congregation of the sons of Israel is assembled at Shiloh, to go up against them to war; **13** and the sons of Israel send to the sons of Reuben, and to the sons of Gad, and to the half-tribe of Manasseh—to the land of Gilead—Phinehas son of Eleazar the priest, **14** and ten princes with him, one prince—one prince for a house of a father, for all the tribes of Israel, and each of them a head of a house of their fathers, for the thousands of Israel. **15** And they come to the sons of Reuben, and to the sons of Gad, and to the half-tribe of Manasseh, to the land of Gilead, and speak with them, saying, **16** "Thus said all the congregation of Yhwh: What [is] this trespass which you have trespassed against the God of Israel, to turn back today from after Yhwh, by your building an altar for yourselves, for your rebelling today against Yhwh? **17** Is the iniquity of Peor little to us, from which we have not been cleansed until this day—and the plague is in the congregation of Yhwh, **18** that you turn back today from after Yhwh? and it has been [that] you rebel against Yhwh today, and tomorrow He is angry against all the congregation of Israel. **19** And surely, if the land of your possession is unclean, pass over for yourselves to the land of the possession of Yhwh, where the Dwelling Place of Yhwh has dwelt, and have possession in our midst; and do not rebel against Yhwh, and do not rebel against us, by your building an altar for yourselves, besides the altar of our God Yhwh. **20** Did Achan son of Zerah not commit a trespass in the devoted thing, and there was wrath on all the congregation of Israel? and he alone did not expire in his iniquity." **21** And the sons of Reuben, and the sons of Gad, and the half-tribe of Manasseh, answer and speak with the heads of the thousands of Israel: **22** "The God of gods—Yhwh, the God of gods—Yhwh, He is knowing, and Israel—he knows, if [we are] in rebellion, and if in trespass against Yhwh, do not save us this day! **23** [If we] are building an altar for ourselves to turn back from after Yhwh, and if to cause burnt-offering and present to go up on it, and if to make peace-offerings on it—Yhwh Himself requires [it]. **24** And nevertheless, we have done it from fear of [this] thing, saying, Hereafter your sons speak to our sons, saying, And what have you to [do with] Yhwh God of Israel? **25** for Yhwh has put a border between us and you, O sons of Reuben, and sons of Gad—Jordan; you have no portion in Yhwh—and your sons have caused our sons to cease, not to fear Yhwh. **26** And we say, Now let us prepare to build the altar for ourselves—not for burnt-offering, nor for sacrifice— **27** but it [is] a witness between us and you, and between our generations after us, to do the service of Yhwh before Him with our burnt-offerings, and with our sacrifices, and with our peace-offerings, and your sons do not say hereafter to our sons, You have no portion in Yhwh. **28** And we say, And it has been, when they say [so] to us, and to our generations hereafter, that we have said, See the pattern of the altar of Yhwh, which our fathers made—not for burnt-offering nor for sacrifice—but it [is] a witness between us and you. **29** Far be it from us to rebel against Yhwh, and to turn back from after Yhwh today, to build an altar for burnt-offering, for present, and for sacrifice, apart from the altar of our God Yhwh, which [is] before His Dwelling Place." **30** And Phinehas the priest, and the princes of the congregation, and the heads of the thousands of Israel, who [are] with him, hear the words which the sons of Reuben, and the sons of Gad, and the sons of Manasseh have spoken, and it is good in their eyes. **31** And Phinehas son of Eleazar the priest says to the sons of Reuben, and to the sons of Gad, and to the sons of Manasseh, "Today we have known that Yhwh [is] in our midst, because you have not committed this trespass against Yhwh—then you have delivered the sons of Israel out of the hand of Yhwh." **32** And Phinehas son of Eleazar the priest, and the princes, turn back from the sons of Reuben, and from the sons of Gad, out of the land of Gilead, to the land of Canaan, to the sons of Israel, and bring them back word; **33** and the thing is good in the eyes of the sons of Israel, and the sons of Israel bless God, and have not spoken to go up against them to war, to destroy the land which the sons of Reuben, and the sons of Gad, are dwelling in. **34** And the sons of Reuben and the sons of Gad proclaim concerning the altar, that, "[It is] a witness between us that Yhwh [is] God."

CHAPTER 23

1 And it comes to pass, many days after that Yhwh has given rest to Israel from all their surrounding enemies, that Joshua is old, entering into days, **2** and Joshua calls for all Israel, for his elderly, and for his heads, and for his judges, and for his authorities, and says to them, "I have become old; I have entered into days; **3** and you have seen all that your God Yhwh has done to all these nations because of you, for your God Yhwh [is] He who is fighting for you; **4** see, I have caused these nations who are left to fall to you for an inheritance to your tribes, from the Jordan (and all the nations which I cut off), and the Great Sea [at] the [setting] sun. **5** As for your God Yhwh, He thrusts them from your presence, and has dispossessed them from before you, and you have possessed their land, as your God Yhwh has spoken to you, **6** and you have been very strong to keep and to do the whole that is written in the Scroll of the Law of Moses, so as not to turn aside from it right or left, **7** so as not to go in among these nations, these who are left with you; and you do not make mention of the name of their gods, nor do you swear, nor do you serve them, nor do you bow yourselves to them; **8** but you cleave to your God Yhwh, as you have done until this day. **9** And Yhwh is dispossessing great and mighty nations from before you; as for you, none has stood in your presence until this day; **10** one man of you pursues a thousand, for your God Yhwh [is] He who is fighting for you, as He has spoken to you; **11** and you have been very watchful for yourselves to love your God Yhwh. **12** But—if you turn back at all and have cleaved to the remnant of these nations, these who are left with you, and intermarried with them, and gone in to them, and they to you, **13** certainly know that your God Yhwh is not continuing to dispossess these nations from before you, and they have been to you for a trap, and for a snare, and for a scourge, in your sides, and for thorns in your eyes, until you perish from off this good ground which your God Yhwh has given to you. **14** And behold, I am going, today, in the way of all the earth, and you have known—with all your heart, and with all your soul—that there has not fallen one thing of all the good things which your God Yhwh has spoken concerning you; the whole have come to you; there has not failed of it one thing. **15** And it has been, as there has come on you all the good thing which your God Yhwh has spoken to you, so Yhwh brings on you the whole of the evil thing, until His destroying you from off this good ground which your God Yhwh has given to you; **16** in your transgressing the covenant of your God Yhwh which He commanded you, and you have gone and served other gods, and bowed yourselves to them, then the anger of Yhwh has burned against you, and you have perished quickly from off the good land which He has given to you."

CHAPTER 24

1 And Joshua gathers all the tribes of Israel to Shechem, and calls for [the] elderly of Israel, and for his heads, and for his judges, and for his authorities, and they station themselves before God. **2** And Joshua says to all the people, "Thus said Yhwh, God of Israel: Beyond the River your fathers have dwelt of old—Terah father of Abraham and father of Nachor—and they serve other gods; **3** and I take your father Abraham from beyond the River, and cause him to go through all the land of Canaan, and multiply his seed, and give Isaac to him. **4** And I give Jacob and Esau to Isaac; and I give Mount Seir to Esau, to possess it; and Jacob and his sons have gone down to Egypt. **5** And I send Moses and Aaron, and plague Egypt, as I have done in its midst, and afterward I have brought you out. **6** And I bring out your fathers from Egypt, and you go to the sea, and the Egyptians pursue after your fathers, with chariot and with horsemen, to the Red Sea; **7** and they cry to Yhwh, and He sets thick darkness between you and the Egyptians, and brings the sea over him, and covers them, and your eyes see that

which I have done in Egypt; and you dwell in a wilderness [for] many days. **8** And I bring you into the land of the Amorite who is dwelling beyond the Jordan, and they fight with you, and I give them into your hand, and you possess their land, and I destroy them out of your presence. **9** And Balak son of Zippor, king of Moab, rises and fights against Israel, and sends and calls for Balaam son of Beor, to revile you, **10** and I have not been willing to listen to Balaam, and he greatly blesses you, and I deliver you out of his hand. **11** And you pass over the Jordan, and come to Jericho, and the possessors of Jericho fight against you—the Amorite, and the Perizzite, and the Canaanite, and the Hittite, and the Girgashite, the Hivite, and the Jebusite—and I give them into your hand. **12** And I send the hornet before you, and it casts them out from your presence—two kings of the Amorite—not by your sword, nor by your bow. **13** And I give a land to you for which you have not labored, and cities which you have not built, and you dwell in them; you are eating of vineyards and olive-yards which you have not planted. **14** And now, fear Yhwh, and serve Him, in perfection and in truth, and turn aside the gods which your fathers served beyond the River, and in Egypt, and serve Yhwh; **15** and if [it is] wrong in your eyes to serve Yhwh—choose for yourselves today whom you serve—whether the gods whom your fathers served, which [are] beyond the River, or the gods of the Amorite in whose land you are dwelling; but me and my house—we serve Yhwh." **16** And the people answer and say, "Far be it from us to forsake Yhwh, to serve other gods; **17** for our God Yhwh [is] He who is bringing us and our fathers up out of the land of Egypt, out of a house of servants, and who has done these great signs before our eyes, and keeps us in all the way in which we have gone, and among all the peoples through whose midst we passed; **18** and Yhwh casts out the whole of the peoples, even the Amorite inhabiting the land, from our presence; we also serve Yhwh, for He [is] our God." **19** And Joshua says to the people, "You are not able to serve Yhwh, for He [is] a most holy God; He [is] a zealous God; He does not bear with your transgression and with your sins. **20** When you forsake Yhwh, and have served gods of a stranger, then He has turned back and done harm to you, and consumed you, after that He has done good to you." **21** And the people say to Joshua, "No, but we serve Yhwh!" **22** And Joshua says to the people, "You are witnesses against yourselves, that you have chosen Yhwh for yourselves, to serve Him," and they say, "Witnesses!" **23** "And now, turn aside the gods of the stranger which [are] in your midst, and incline your heart to Yhwh, God of Israel." **24** And the people say to Joshua, "We serve our God Yhwh, and we listen to His voice." **25** And Joshua makes a covenant with the people on that day, and lays a statute and an ordinance on it, in Shechem. **26** And Joshua writes these words in the Scroll of the Law of God, and takes a great stone, and raises it up there under the oak which [is] in the sanctuary of Yhwh. **27** And Joshua says to all the people, "Behold, this stone is for a witness against us, for it has heard all the sayings of Yhwh which He has spoken with us, and it has been for a witness against you, lest you lie against your God." **28** And Joshua sends the people away, each to his inheritance. **29** And it comes to pass, after these things, that Joshua son of Nun, servant of Yhwh, dies, a son of one hundred and ten years, **30** and they bury him in the border of his inheritance, in Timnath-Serah, which [is] in the hill-country of Ephraim, on the north of the hill of Gaash. **31** And Israel serves Yhwh all [the] days of Joshua, and all [the] days of the elderly who prolonged days after Joshua, and who knew all the work of Yhwh which He did to Israel. **32** And the bones of Joseph, which the sons of Israel brought up out of Egypt, they buried in Shechem, in the portion of the field which Jacob bought from the sons of Hamor father of Shechem, with one hundred kesitah; and they are for an inheritance to the sons of Joseph. **33** And Eleazar son of Aaron died, and they bury him in a hill of his son Phinehas, which was given to him in the hill-country of Ephraim.

JUDGES

CHAPTER 1

1 And it comes to pass after the death of Joshua, that the sons of Israel ask of Yhwh, saying, "Who goes up for us to the Canaanite, at the commencement, to fight against it?" **2** And Yhwh says, "Judah goes up; behold, I have given the land into his hand." **3** And Judah says to his brother Simeon, "Go up with me into my lot, and we fight against the Canaanite—and I have gone, even I, with you into your lot"; and Simeon goes with him. **4** And Judah goes up, and Yhwh gives the Canaanite and the Perizzite into their hand, and they strike them in Bezek—ten thousand men; **5** and they find Adoni-Bezek in Bezek, and fight against him, and strike the Canaanite and the Perizzite. **6** And Adoni-Bezek flees, and they pursue after him, and seize him, and cut off his thumbs and his great toes, **7** and Adoni-Bezek says, "Seventy kings—their thumbs and their great toes cut off—have been gathering under my table; as I have done so God has repaid to me"; and they bring him to Jerusalem, and he dies there. **8** And the sons of Judah fight against Jerusalem, and capture it, and strike it by the mouth of the sword, and they have sent the city into fire; **9** and afterward the sons of Judah have gone down to fight against the Canaanite inhabiting the hill-country, and the south, and the low country; **10** and Judah goes to the Canaanite who is dwelling in Hebron (and the name of Hebron [was] formerly Kirjath-Arba), and they strike Sheshai, and Ahiman, and Talmai. **11** And he goes there to the inhabitants of Debir (and the name of Debir [was] formerly Kirjath-Sepher), **12** and Caleb says, "He who strikes Kirjath-Sepher and has captured it—then I have given my daughter Achsah to him for a wife." **13** And Othniel son of Kenaz, younger brother of Caleb, captures it, and he gives his daughter Achsah to him for a wife. **14** And it comes to pass in her coming in, that she persuades him to ask from her father the field, and she comes down off the donkey, and Caleb says to her, "What do you [want]?" **15** And she says to him, "Give a blessing to me; when you have given me the south land—then you have given springs of water to me"; and Caleb gives the upper springs and the lower springs to her. **16** And the sons of the Kenite, father-in-law of Moses, have gone up out of the city of palms with the sons of Judah [to] the wilderness of Judah, which [is] in the south of Arad, and they go and dwell with the people. **17** And Judah goes with his brother Simeon, and they strike the Canaanite inhabiting Zephath, and devote it; and [one] calls the name of the city Hormah. **18** And Judah captures Gaza and its border, and Askelon and its border, and Ekron and its border; **19** and Yhwh is with Judah, and he occupies the hill-country, but not to dispossess the inhabitants of the valley, for they have chariots of iron. **20** And they give Hebron to Caleb, as Moses has spoken, and he dispossesses the three sons of Anak there. **21** And the sons of Benjamin have not dispossessed the Jebusite inhabiting Jerusalem; and the Jebusite dwells with the sons of Benjamin, in Jerusalem, until this day. **22** And the house of Joseph goes up—even they—to Beth-El, and Yhwh [is] with them; **23** and the house of Joseph causes [men] to spy out Beth-El (and the name of the city [was] formerly Luz), **24** and the watchers see a man coming out from the city, and say to him, "Please show us the entrance of the city, and we have done kindness with you." **25** And he shows them the entrance of the city, and they strike the city by the mouth of the sword, and they have sent the man and all his family away; **26** and the man goes to the land of the Hittites, and builds a city, and calls its name Luz—it [is] its name to this day. **27** And Manasseh has not occupied Beth-Shean and its towns, and Taanach and its towns, and the inhabitants of Dor and its towns, and the inhabitants of Iblaim and its towns, and the inhabitants of Megiddo and its towns, and the Canaanite is desirous to dwell in that land; **28** and it comes to pass, when Israel has been strong, that he sets the Canaanite to forced labor, and has not utterly dispossessed it. **29** And Ephraim has not dispossessed the Canaanite who is dwelling in Gezer, and the Canaanite dwells in its midst, in Gezer. **30** Zebulun has not dispossessed the inhabitants of Kitron, and the inhabitants of Nahalol, and the Canaanite dwells in its midst, and they become forced labor. **31** Asher has not dispossessed the inhabitants of Accho, and the inhabitants of Sidon, and Ahlab, and Achzib, and Helbah, and Aphik, and Rehob; **32** and the Asherite dwells in the midst of the Canaanite, the inhabitants of the land, for it has not dispossessed them. **33** Naphtali has not dispossessed the inhabitants of Beth-Shemesh, and the inhabitants of Beth-Anath, and he dwells in the midst of the Canaanite, the inhabitants of the land; and the inhabitants of Beth-Shemesh and of Beth-Anath were for forced labor for them. **34** And the Amorites press the sons of Dan to the mountain, for they have not permitted them to go down to the valley; **35** and the Amorite is desirous to dwell in Mount Heres, in Aijalon, and in Shaalbim, and the hand of the house of Joseph is heavy, and they are for forced labor; **36** and the border of the Amorite [is] from the ascent of Akrabbim, from the rock and upward.

CHAPTER 2

1 And the Messenger of Yhwh goes up from Gilgal to Bochim, **2** and says, "I cause you to come up out of Egypt, and bring you into the land which I have sworn to your fathers, and say, I do not break My covenant with you for all time; and you make no covenant with the inhabitants of this land—you break down their altars; and you have not listened to My voice—what [is] this you have done? **3** And I have also said, I do not cast them out from your presence, and they have been for adversaries to you, and their gods are for a snare to you." **4** And it comes to pass, when the Messenger of Yhwh speaks these words to all the sons of Israel, that the people lift up their voice and weep, **5** and they call the name of that place Bochim, and sacrifice to Yhwh there. **6** And Joshua sends the people away, and the sons of Israel go, each to his inheritance, to possess the land; **7** and the people serve Yhwh all [the] days of Joshua, and all [the] days of [the] elderly who prolonged days after Joshua, who saw all the great work of Yhwh which He did to Israel. **8** And Joshua son of Nun, servant of Yhwh, dies, a son of one hundred and ten years, **9** and they bury him in the border of his inheritance, in Timnath-Heres, in the hill-country of Ephraim, on the north of Mount Gaash; **10** and all that generation have also been gathered to their fathers, and another generation rises after them who have not known Yhwh, and even the work which He has done to Israel. **11** And the sons of Israel do evil in the eyes of Yhwh, and serve the Ba'alim, **12** and forsake Yhwh, God of their fathers, who brings them out from the land of Egypt, and go after other gods (of the gods of the peoples who [are] around them), and bow themselves to them, and provoke Yhwh, **13** indeed, they forsake Yhwh, and do service to Ba'al and to Ashtaroth. **14** And the anger of Yhwh burns against Israel, and He gives them into the hand of spoilers, and they spoil them, and He sells them into the hand of their surrounding enemies, and they have not been able to stand before their enemies anymore; **15** in every [place] where they have gone out, the hand of Yhwh has been against them for calamity, as Yhwh has spoken, and as Yhwh has sworn to them, and they are greatly distressed. **16** And Yhwh raises up judges, and they save them from the hand of their spoilers; **17** and they have also not listened to their judges, but have gone whoring after other gods, and bow themselves to them; they have turned aside [with] haste out of the way [in] which their fathers walked to obey the commands of Yhwh—they have not done so. **18** And when Yhwh raised up judges for them—then Yhwh was with the judge, and saved them out of the hand of their enemies all [the] days of the judge; for Yhwh sighs, because of their groaning from the presence of their oppressors, and of those thrusting them away. **19** And it has come to pass, when the judge dies—they turn back and have done corruptly above their fathers, to go after other gods, to serve them, and to bow themselves to them; they have not fallen from their doings, and from their stiff way. **20** And the anger of Yhwh burns against Israel, and He says, "Because that this nation has transgressed My covenant which I commanded their fathers, and have not listened to My voice— **21** I also do not continue to dispossess any from before them of the nations which Joshua has left when he dies, **22** in order to try Israel by them, whether they are keeping the way of Yhwh, to go in it, as their fathers kept [it], or not." **23** And Yhwh leaves these nations, so as not to dispossess them quickly, and did not give them into the hand of Joshua.

CHAPTER 3

1 And these [are] the nations which Yhwh left, to try Israel by them, all who have not known all the wars of Canaan; **2** (only for the sake of the generations of the sons of Israel knowing, to teach them war, only those who formerly have not known them)— **3** five princes of the Philistines, and all the Canaanite, and the Zidonian, and the Hivite inhabiting Mount Lebanon, from Mount Ba'al-Hermon to the entering in of Hamath; **4** and they are to prove Israel by them, to know whether they obey the commands of Yhwh that He commanded their fathers by the hand of Moses. **5** And the sons of Israel have dwelt in the midst of the Canaanite, the Hittite, and the Amorite, and the Perizzite, and the Hivite, and the Jebusite, **6** and take their daughters to them for wives, and have given their daughters to their sons, and they serve their gods; **7** and the sons of Israel do evil in the eyes of Yhwh, and forget their God Yhwh, and serve the Ba'alim and the Asheroth. **8** And the anger of Yhwh burns against Israel, and He sells them into the hand of Chushan-Rishathaim king of Aram-Naharaim, and the sons of Israel serve Chushan-Rishathaim eight years; **9** and the sons of Israel cry to Yhwh, and Yhwh raises a savior to the sons of Israel, and he saves them—Othniel son of Kenaz, Caleb's younger brother; **10** and the Spirit of Yhwh is on him, and he judges Israel, and goes out to battle, and Yhwh gives Chushan-Rishathaim king of Aram into his hand, and his hand is strong against Chushan-Rishathaim; **11** and the land rests forty years. And Othniel son of Kenaz dies, **12** and the sons of Israel add to do evil in the eyes of Yhwh; and Yhwh strengthens Eglon king of Moab against Israel, because that they have done evil in the eyes of Yhwh; **13** and he gathers the sons of Ammon and Amalek to himself, and goes and strikes Israel, and they possess the city of palms; **14** and the sons of Israel serve Eglon king of Moab eighteen years. **15** And the sons of Israel cry to Yhwh, and Yhwh raises a savior to them, Ehud son of Gera, a Benjamite (a man [with] his right hand bound), and the sons of Israel send a present by his hand to Eglon king of Moab; **16** and Ehud makes a sword for himself, and it has two mouths (its length [is] a cubit), and he girds it under his long robe on his right thigh; **17** and he brings the present near to Eglon king of Moab, and Eglon [is] a very fat man. **18** And it comes to pass, when he has finished to bring the present near, that he sends the people carrying the present away, **19** and he himself has turned back from the carved images which [are] at Gilgal and says, "I have a secret word for you, O king"; and he says, "Hush!" And all those standing by him go out from him. **20** And Ehud has come to him, and he is sitting in the cool upper chamber which he has for himself, and Ehud says, "I have a word of God for you"; and he rises from off the throne; **21** and Ehud puts forth his left hand, and takes the sword from off his right thigh, and thrusts it into his belly; **22** and the hilt also goes in after the blade, and the fat shuts on the blade, that he has not drawn the sword out of his belly, and he goes out [through] the antechamber **[[**or and the dung came out**]]**. **23** And Ehud goes out at the porch, and shuts the doors of the upper chamber on him, and has bolted [it]; **24** and he has gone out, and his servants have come in, and look, and behold, the doors of the upper chamber are bolted, and they say, "He is surely covering his feet, [relieving himself,] in the cool inner chamber." **25** And they stay until confounded, and behold, he is not opening the doors of the upper chamber, and they take the key, and open, and behold, their lord is fallen to the earth—dead. **26** And Ehud escaped during their lingering, and has passed by the images, and escapes to Seirath. **27** And it comes to pass, in his coming in, that he blows with a horn in the hill-country of Ephraim, and the sons of Israel go down with him from the hill-country, and he before them; **28** and he says to them, "Pursue after me, for Yhwh has given your enemies, the Moabites, into your hand"; and they go down after him, and capture the passages of the Jordan toward Moab, and have not permitted a man to pass over. **29** And they strike Moab at that time, about ten thousand men, all robust, and everyone a man of valor, and no man has escaped; **30** and Moab is humbled in that day under the hand of Israel; and the land rests [for] eighty years. **31** And after him has been Shamgar son of Anath, and he strikes the Philistines—six hundred men—with an ox-goad, and he also saves Israel.

CHAPTER 4

1 And the sons of Israel add to do evil in the eyes of Yhwh when Ehud is dead, **2** and Yhwh sells them into the hand of Jabin king of Canaan, who has reigned in Hazor, and Sisera [is] the head of his host, and he is dwelling in Harosheth of the nations; **3** and the sons of Israel cry to Yhwh, for he has nine hundred chariots of iron, and he has oppressed the sons of Israel mightily [for] twenty years. **4** And Deborah, a woman, a prophetess, wife of Lapidoth, she is judging Israel at that time, **5** and she is dwelling under the palm-tree of Deborah, between Ramah and Beth-El, in the hill-country of Ephraim, and the sons of Israel go up to her for judgment. **6** And she sends and calls for Barak son of Abinoam, out of Kedesh-Naphtali, and

says to him, "Has Yhwh, God of Israel, not commanded? go, and you have drawn toward Mount Tabor, and have taken with you ten thousand men, out of the sons of Naphtali, and out of the sons of Zebulun, **7** and I have drawn to you, to the Brook of Kishon, Sisera, head of the host of Jabin, and his chariot, and his multitude, and have given him into your hand." **8** And Barak says to her, "If you go with me, then I have gone; and if you do not go with me, I do not go"; **9** and she says, "I certainly go with you; only, surely your glory is not on the way which you are going, for Yhwh sells Sisera into the hand of a woman"; and Deborah rises and goes with Barak to Kedesh. **10** And Barak calls Zebulun and Naphtali to Kedesh, and he goes up—ten thousand men [are] at his feet—and Deborah goes up with him. **11** And Heber the Kenite has been separated from the Kenite, from the sons of Hobab father-in-law of Moses, and he stretches out his tent to the oak in Zaanaim, which [is] by Kedesh. **12** And they declare to Sisera that Barak son of Abinoam has gone up to Mount Tabor, **13** and Sisera calls all his chariots, nine hundred chariots of iron, and all the people who [are] with him, from Harosheth of the nations, to the Brook of Kishon. **14** And Deborah says to Barak, "Rise, for this [is] the day in which Yhwh has given Sisera into your hand; has Yhwh not gone out before you?" And Barak goes down from Mount Tabor, and ten thousand men after him. **15** And Yhwh destroys Sisera, and all the chariots, and all the camp, by the mouth of the sword, before Barak, and Sisera comes down from off the chariot, and flees on his feet. **16** And Barak has pursued after the chariots and after the camp, to Harosheth of the nations, and all the camp of Sisera falls by the mouth of the sword—there has not been left even one. **17** And Sisera has fled on his feet to the tent of Jael wife of Heber the Kenite, for [there is] peace between Jabin king of Hazor and the house of Heber the Kenite; **18** and Jael goes out to meet Sisera and says to him, "Turn aside, my lord, turn aside to me, do not fear"; and he turns aside to her, into the tent, and she covers him with a mantle. **19** And he says to her, "Please give me a little water to drink, for I am thirsty"; and she opens the bottle of milk, and gives him to drink, and covers him. **20** And he says to her, "Stand at the opening of the tent, and it has been, if any comes in, and has asked you and said, Is there a man here? that you have said, There is not." **21** And Jael wife of Heber takes the pin of the tent, and takes the hammer in her hand, and goes to him gently, and strikes the pin into his temples, and it fastens in the earth—and he has been fast asleep, and is weary—and he dies. **22** And behold, Barak is pursuing Sisera, and Jael comes out to meet him, and says to him, "Come, and I show you the man whom you are seeking"; and he comes to her, and behold, Sisera is fallen—dead, and the pin [is] in his temples. **23** And God humbles Jabin king of Canaan before the sons of Israel on that day, **24** and the hand of the sons of Israel goes, going on and becoming hard on Jabin king of Canaan, until they have cut off Jabin king of Canaan.

CHAPTER 5

1 And Deborah sings—also Barak son of Abinoam—on that day, saying, **2** "For freeing leaders in Israel, || For a people willingly offering themselves, || Bless Yhwh. **3** Hear, you kings; give ear, you princes, || I sing to Yhwh, || I sing praise to Yhwh, God of Israel. **4** Yhwh, in Your going forth out of Seir, || In Your stepping out of the field of Edom, || The earth trembled and the heavens dropped, || And thick clouds dropped water. **5** Hills flowed from the face of Yhwh, || This one—Sinai—From the face of Yhwh, God of Israel. **6** In the days of Shamgar son of Anath—In the days of Jael—The ways have ceased, || And those going in the paths go [in] crooked ways. **7** Villages ceased in Israel—they ceased, || Until I arose—Deborah, || That I arose, a mother in Israel. **8** He chooses new gods, || Then war [is] at the gates! A shield is not seen—and a spear || Among forty thousand in Israel. **9** My heart [is] to the lawgivers of Israel, || Who are offering themselves willingly among the people, || Bless Yhwh! **10** Riders on white donkeys—Sitters on a long robe—And walkers by the way—meditate! **11** By the voice of shouters || Between the places of drawing water, || There they give out righteous acts of Yhwh, || Righteous acts of His villages in Israel, || Then the people of Yhwh have gone down to the gates. **12** Awake, awake, Deborah; Awake, awake, utter a song; Rise, Barak, and take your captivity captive, || Son of Abinoam. **13** Then him who is left of the majestic ones He caused to rule the people of Yhwh, || He caused me to rule among the mighty. **14** From Ephraim [are] those whose root [is] in Amalek, || After you, Benjamin, among your peoples, || From Machir lawgivers came down, || And from Zebulun those drawing with the reed of a writer. ¹⁵ And princes in Issachar [are] with Deborah, || Indeed, Issachar [is] right with Barak, || Into the valley he was sent on his feet. In the divisions of Reuben, || The decrees of heart [are] great! ¹⁶ Why have you abided between the boundaries, || To hear lowings of herds? For the divisions of Reuben, || The searchings of heart [are] great! ¹⁷ Gilead dwelt beyond the Jordan, || And why does Dan sojourn [in] ships? Asher has abided at the haven of the seas, || And dwells by his creeks. ¹⁸ Zebulun [is] a people who exposed its soul to death, || Naphtali also—on high places of the field. ¹⁹ Kings came—they fought; Then kings of Canaan fought, || In Taanach, by the waters of Megiddo; They did not take gain of money! ²⁰ They fought from the heavens: The stars fought with Sisera from their highways. ²¹ The Brook of Kishon swept them away, || The most ancient brook—the Brook of Kishon. You tread down strength, O my soul! ²² Then the horse-heels were broken, || By gallopings—gallopings of its mighty ones. ²³ Curse Meroz, said a messenger of Yhwh, || Cursing, curse its inhabitants! For they did not come to the help of Yhwh, || To the help of Yhwh among the mighty! ²⁴ Above women is Jael, || The wife of Heber the Kenite, || She is blessed above women in the tent. ²⁵ He asked for water—she gave milk; She brought butter near in a lordly dish. ²⁶ She sends forth her hand to the pin, || And her right hand to the laborers' hammer, || And she hammered Sisera—she struck his head, || Indeed, she struck, and it passed through his temple. ²⁷ He bowed between her feet—He fell, he lay down; He bowed between her feet, he fell; Where he bowed, there he fell—destroyed. ²⁸ She has looked out through the window—Indeed, she cries out—the mother of Sisera, || Through the lattice: Why is his chariot delaying to come? Why have the steps of his chariot tarried? ²⁹ The wise ones, her princesses, answer her, || Indeed, she returns her sayings to herself: ³⁰ Do they not find? They apportion spoil, || A female—two females—for every head, || Spoil of finger-work for Sisera, || Spoil of embroidered finger-work, || Finger-work—a pair of embroidered things, || For the necks of the spoil! ³¹ So do all Your enemies perish, O Yhwh, || And those loving Him [are] || As the going out of the sun in its might!" And the land rests [for] forty years.

CHAPTER 6

¹ And the sons of Israel do evil in the eyes of Yhwh, and Yhwh gives them into the hand of Midian [for] seven years, ² and the hand of Midian is strong against Israel, [so] the sons of Israel have made for themselves the nooks which [are] in the mountains, and the caves, and the strongholds [to hide] from the presence of Midian. ³ And it has been, if Israel has sowed, that Midian has come up, and Amalek, and the sons of the east, indeed, they have come up against him, ⁴ and encamp against them, and destroy the increase of the land until your entering Gaza; and they leave no sustenance in Israel, either sheep, or ox, or donkey; ⁵ for they and their livestock come up, with their tents; they come in as the fullness of the locust for multitude, and of them and of their livestock there is no number, and they come into the land to destroy it. ⁶ And Israel is very weak from the presence of Midian, and the sons of Israel cry to Yhwh. ⁷ And it comes to pass, when the sons of Israel have cried to Yhwh concerning Midian, ⁸ that Yhwh sends a man, a prophet, to the sons of Israel, and he says to them, "Thus said Yhwh, God of Israel: I have brought you up out of Egypt, and I bring you out from a house of servants, ⁹ and I deliver you out of the hand of the Egyptians, and out of the hand of all your oppressors, and I cast them out from your presence, and I give their land to you, ¹⁰ and I say to you, I [am] your God Yhwh, you do not fear the gods of the Amorite in whose land you are dwelling—and you have not listened to My voice." ¹¹ And the Messenger of Yhwh comes and sits under the oak which [is] in Ophrah, which [is] to Joash the Abi-Ezrite, and his son Gideon is beating out wheat in the winepress, to remove [it] from the presence of the Midianites; ¹² and the Messenger of Yhwh appears to him and says to him, "Yhwh [is] with you, O mighty man of valor." ¹³ And Gideon says to Him, "O my Lord, [if] Yhwh is indeed with us, then why has all this found us? and where [are] all His wonders which our fathers recounted to us, saying, Has Yhwh not brought us up out of Egypt? and now Yhwh has left us, and gives us into the hand of Midian." ¹⁴ And Yhwh turns to him and says, "Go in this—your power; and you have saved Israel out of the hand of Midian—have I not sent you?" ¹⁵ And he says to Him, "O my Lord, with what do I save Israel? behold, my chief [is] weak in Manasseh, and I [am] the least in the house of my father." ¹⁶ And Yhwh says to him, "Because I am with you—you have struck the Midianites as one man." ¹⁷ And he says to Him, "Now if I have found grace in Your eyes, then You have done a sign for me that You are speaking with me. ¹⁸ Please do not move from here until my coming to You, and I have brought out my present, and put it before You"; and He says, "I abide until your return." ¹⁹ And Gideon has gone in, and prepares a kid of the goats, and an ephah of flour [worth] of unleavened things; he has put the flesh in a basket, and he has put the broth in a pot, and he brings [them] out to Him, to the place of the oak, and brings [them] near. ²⁰ And the Messenger of God says to him, "Take the flesh and the unleavened things, and place [them] on this rock—and pour out the broth"; and he does so. ²¹ And the Messenger of Yhwh puts forth the end of the staff which [is] in His hand, and comes against the flesh, and against the unleavened things, and the fire goes up out of the rock and consumes the flesh and the unleavened things—and the Messenger of Yhwh has gone from his eyes. ²² And Gideon sees that He [is] the Messenger of Yhwh, and Gideon says, "Aah, Lord Yhwh! For so I have looked on the Messenger of Yhwh face to face!" ²³ And Yhwh says to him, "Peace to you; do not fear; you do not die." ²⁴ And Gideon builds an altar to Yhwh there, and calls it Yhwh-Shalom, it [is] yet in Ophrah of the Abi-Ezrites to this day. ²⁵ And it comes to pass, on that night, that Yhwh says to him, "Take the young ox which your father has, and the second bullock of seven years, and you have thrown down the altar of Ba'al which your father has, and cut down the Asherah which [is] by it, ²⁶ and you have built an altar to your God Yhwh on the top of this stronghold, by the arrangement, and have taken the second bullock, and caused a burnt-offering to ascend with the wood of the Asherah which you cut down." ²⁷ And Gideon takes ten men of his servants, and does as Yhwh has spoken to him, and it comes to pass, because he has been afraid of the house of his father, and the men of the city, to do [it] by day, that he does [it] by night. ²⁸ And the men of the city rise early in the morning, and behold, the altar of Ba'al has been broken down, and the Asherah which is by it has been cut down, and the second bullock has been offered on the altar which is built. ²⁹ And they say to one another, "Who has done this thing?" And they inquire and seek, and they say, "Gideon son of Joash has done this thing." ³⁰ And the men of the city say to Joash, "Bring out your son, and he dies, because he has broken down the altar of Ba'al, and because he has cut down the Asherah which [is] by it." ³¹ And Joash says to all who have stood against him, "You, do you plead for Ba'al? you—do you save him? he who pleads for him is put to death during the morning; if he [is] a god he pleads against him himself, because he has broken down his altar." ³² And he calls him, on that day, Jerubba'al, saying, "The Ba'al pleads against him, because he has broken down his altar." ³³ And all Midian and Amalek and the sons of the east have gathered together, and pass over, and encamp in the Valley of Jezreel, ³⁴ and the Spirit of Yhwh has clothed Gideon, and he blows with a horn, and Abi-Ezer is called after him; ³⁵ and he has sent messengers into all Manasseh, and it is also called after him; and he has sent messengers into Asher, and into Zebulun, and into Naphtali, and they come up to meet them. ³⁶ And Gideon says to God, "If You are Savior of Israel by my hand, as You have spoken, ³⁷ behold, I am placing the fleece of wool in the threshing-floor: if dew is only on the fleece, and dryness on all the earth—then I have known that You save Israel by my hand, as You have spoken"; ³⁸ and it is so, and he rises early on the next day, and presses the fleece, and wrings dew out of the fleece—the fullness of the bowl of waters. ³⁹ And Gideon says to God, "Do not let Your anger burn against me, and I only speak this time; please let me try only this time with the fleece—please let there be only dryness on the fleece, and let there be dew on all the earth." ⁴⁰ And God does so on that night, and there is only dryness on the fleece, and there has been dew on all the earth.

CHAPTER 7

¹ And Jerubba'al (he [is] Gideon) rises early, and all the people who [are] with him, and they encamp by the well of Harod, and the camp of Midian has been on the south of him, on the height of Moreh, in the valley. ² And Yhwh says to Gideon, "The people who [are] with you [are] too many for My

giving Midian into their hand, lest Israel beautify itself against Me, saying, My hand has given salvation to me, [3] and now, please call in the ears of the people, saying, Whoever [is] afraid and trembling, let him turn back and go early from Mount Gilead"; and there return twenty-two thousand of the people, and ten thousand have been left. [4] And Yhwh says to Gideon, "The people [are] yet too many; bring them down to the water, and I refine him for you there; and it has been, he of whom I say to you, This goes with you—he goes with you; and any of whom I say to you, This does not go with you—he does not go." [5] And he brings the people down to the water, and Yhwh says to Gideon, "Everyone who laps of the water with his tongue as the dog laps—you set him apart; also everyone who bows on his knees to drink." [6] And the number of those lapping with their hand to their mouth is three hundred men, and all the rest of the people have bowed down on their knees to drink water. [7] And Yhwh says to Gideon, "I save you by the three hundred men who are lapping, and have given Midian into your hand, and all the people go, each to his place." [8] And the people take the provision in their hand, and their horns, and he has sent every man of Israel away, each to his tents; and he has kept hold on the three hundred men, and the camp of Midian has been by him in the lower part of the valley. [9] And it comes to pass, on that night, that Yhwh says to him, "Rise, go down into the camp, for I have given it into your hand; [10] and if you are afraid to go down—go down, you and your young man Phurah, to the camp, [11] and you have heard what they speak, and afterward your hands are strengthened, and you have gone down against the camp." And he goes down, he and his young man Phurah, to the extremity of the fifties who [are] in the camp, [12] and Midian, and Amalek, and all the sons of the east are lying in the valley, as the locust for multitude, and of their camels there is no number, as sand which [is] on the seashore for multitude. [13] And Gideon comes in, and behold, a man is recounting a dream to his companion, and says, "Behold, I have dreamed a dream, and behold, a cake of barley-bread is turning itself over into the camp of Midian, and it comes to the tent, and strikes it, and it falls, and turns it upwards, and the tent has fallen." [14] And his companion answers and says, "This is nothing except the sword of Gideon son of Joash, a man of Israel; God has given Midian and all the camp into his hand." [15] And it comes to pass, when Gideon hears the narration of the dream and its interpretation, that he bows himself, and turns back to the camp of Israel, and says, "Rise, for Yhwh has given the camp of Midian into your hand." [16] And he divides the three hundred men [into] three detachments, and puts horns into the hand of all of them, and empty pitchers, and lamps within the pitchers. [17] And he says to them, "Look at me, and thus do; and behold, I am coming into the extremity of the camp—and it has been—as I do so you do; [18] and I have blown with a horn—I and all who [are] with me, and you have blown with horns, even you, around all the camp, and have said, For Yhwh and for Gideon!" [19] And Gideon comes—and the hundred men who [are] with him—into the extremity of the camp, [at] the beginning of the middle watch (they had just posted watchmen), and they blow with horns—also dashing in pieces the pitchers which [are] in their hand; [20] and the three detachments blow with horns, and break the pitchers, and keep hold with their left hand on the lamps, and with their right hand on the horns to blow, and they cry, "The sword of Yhwh and of Gideon!" [21] And they each stand in his place, around the camp, and all the camp runs, and they shout, and flee; [22] and the three hundred blow the horns, and Yhwh sets the sword of each against his companion, even through all the camp; and the camp flees to Beth-Shittah, at Zererath, to the border of Abel-Meholah, by Tabbath. [23] And the men of Israel are called from Naphtali, and from Asher, and from all Manasseh, and pursue after Midian. [24] And Gideon has sent messengers into all the hill-country of Ephraim, saying, "Come down to meet Midian, and capture the waters from them as far as Beth-Barah, and the Jordan"; and every man of Ephraim is called, and they capture the waters as far as Beth-Barah, and the Jordan, [25] and they capture two of the heads of Midian, Oreb and Zeeb, and slay Oreb at the rock of Oreb, and they have slain Zeeb at the wine-vat of Zeeb, and they pursue into Midian; and they have brought the heads of Oreb and Zeeb to Gideon beyond the Jordan.

CHAPTER 8

[1] And the men of Ephraim say to him, "What [is] this thing you have done to us—not to call for us when you went to fight with Midian?" And they strive with him severely; [2] and he says to them, "What have I now done like you? Are the gleanings of Ephraim not better than the harvest of Abi-Ezer? [3] God has given the heads of Midian, Oreb and Zeeb, into your hand; and what have I been able to do like you?" Then their temper desisted from off him in his speaking this thing. [4] And Gideon comes to the Jordan, passing over, he and the three hundred men who [are] with him—wearied, yet pursuing— [5] and he says to the men of Succoth, "Please give cakes of bread to the people who [are] at my feet, for they [are] wearied, and I am pursuing after Zebah and Zalmunna, kings of Midian." [6] And the heads of Succoth say, "Is the hand of Zebah and Zalmunna now in your hand, that we give bread to your host?" [7] And Gideon says, "Therefore—in Yhwh's giving Zebah and Zalmunna into my hand—I have threshed your flesh with the thorns of the wilderness, and with the threshing instruments." [8] And he goes up there [to] Penuel, and speaks to them thus; and the men of Penuel answer him as the men of Succoth answered. [9] And he also speaks to the men of Penuel, saying, "In my turning back in peace, I break down this tower." [10] And Zebah and Zalmunna [are] in Karkor, and their camps with them, about fifteen thousand, all who are left of all the camp of the sons of the east; and those falling [are] one hundred and twenty thousand men, drawing sword. [11] And Gideon goes up the way of those who dwell in tents, on the east of Nobah and Jogbehah, and strikes the camp, and the camp was confident; [12] and Zebah and Zalmunna flee, and he pursues after them, and captures the two kings of Midian, Zebah and Zalmunna, and he has caused all the camp to tremble. [13] And Gideon son of Joash turns back from the battle, at the going up of the sun, [14] and captures a young man of the men of Succoth, and asks him, and he describes to him the heads of Succoth, and its elderly—seventy-seven men. [15] And he comes to the men of Succoth and says, "Behold Zebah and Zalmunna, with whom you reproached me, saying, Is the hand of Zebah and Zalmunna now in your hand that we give bread to your men who [are] wearied?" [16] And he takes the elderly of the city, and [the] thorns of the wilderness, and the threshing instruments, and teaches the men of Succoth by them, [17] and he has broken down the Tower of Penuel, and slays the men of the city. [18] And he says to Zebah and to Zalmunna, "What manner of men [were they] whom you slew in Tabor?" And they say, "As you—so they, [each] one as the form of the king's sons." [19] And he says, "They [were] my brothers—sons of my mother; Yhwh lives, if you had kept them alive—I would not kill you." [20] And he says to his firstborn Jether, "Rise, slay them"; and the young man has not drawn his sword, for he has been afraid, for he [is] yet a youth. [21] And Zebah and Zalmunna say, "Rise and fall on us; for as the man—his might"; and Gideon rises, and slays Zebah and Zalmunna, and takes the crescents which [are] on the necks of their camels. [22] And the men of Israel say to Gideon, "Rule over us, both you, and your son, and your son's son, for you have saved us from the hand of Midian." [23] And Gideon says to them, "I do not rule over you, nor does my son rule over you; Yhwh rules over you." [24] And Gideon says to them, "Let me ask a petition of you, and each give to me the ring of his prey, for they have rings of gold, for they [are] Ishmaelites." [25] And they say, "We certainly give"; and they spread out the garment, and each casts the ring of his prey there; [26] and the weight of the rings of gold which he asked for is one thousand and seven hundred [shekels] of gold, apart from the crescents, and the pendants, and the purple garments, which [are] on the kings of Midian, and apart from the chains which [are] on the necks of their camels, [27] and Gideon makes it into an ephod, and sets it up in his city, in Ophrah, and all Israel go whoring after it there, and it is for a snare to Gideon and to his house. [28] And Midian is humbled before the sons of Israel, and have not added to lift up their head; and the land rests [for] forty years in the days of Gideon. [29] And Jerubba'al son of Joash goes and dwells in his own house, [30] and there have been seventy sons of Gideon, coming out of his loin, for he had many wives; [31] and his concubine, who [is] in Shechem, has borne to him—even she—a son, and he appoints his name Abimelech. [32] And Gideon son of Joash dies, in a good old age, and is buried in the burying-place of his father Joash, in Ophrah of the Abi-Ezrite. [33] And it comes to pass, when Gideon [is] dead, that the sons of Israel turn back and go whoring after the Ba'alim, and set Ba'al-Berith over them for a god; [34] and the sons of Israel have not remembered their God Yhwh, who is delivering them out of the hand of all their surrounding enemies, [35] neither have they done kindness

with the house of Jerubba'al—Gideon—according to all the good which he did with Israel.

CHAPTER 9

¹ And Abimelech son of Jerubba'al goes to Shechem, to his mother's brothers, and speaks to them, and to all the family of the house of his mother's father, saying, ² "Now speak in the ears of all the masters of Shechem, Which [is] good for you—seventy men ruling over you (all the sons of Jerubba'al), or one man ruling over you? And you have remembered that I [am] your bone and your flesh." ³ And his mother's brothers speak concerning him, in the ears of all the masters of Shechem, all these words, and their heart inclines after Abimelech, for they said, "He [is] our brother"; ⁴ and they give seventy [pieces] of silver out of the house of Ba'al-Berith to him, and Abimelech hires vain and unstable men with them, and they go after him; ⁵ and he goes into the house of his father at Ophrah, and slays his brothers, sons of Jerubba'al, seventy men, on one stone; and Jotham, youngest son of Jerubba'al, is left, for he was hidden. ⁶ And all the masters of Shechem are gathered together, and all the house of Millo, and come and cause Abimelech to reign for king at the oak of the camp which [is] in Shechem; ⁷ and they declare [it] to Jotham, and he goes and stands on the top of Mount Gerizim, and lifts up his voice, and calls, and says to them, "Listen to me, O masters of Shechem, and God listens to you: ⁸ The trees have diligently gone to anoint a king over them, and they say to the olive, Reign over us. ⁹ And the olive says to them, Have I ceased from my fatness, by which they honor gods and men, that I have gone to stagger over the trees? ¹⁰ And the trees say to the fig, Come, reign over us. ¹¹ And the fig says to them, Have I ceased from my sweetness, and my good increase, that I have gone to stagger over the trees? ¹² And the trees say to the vine, Come, reign over us. ¹³ And the vine says to them, Have I ceased from my new wine, which is making gods and men glad, that I have gone to stagger over the trees? ¹⁴ And all the trees say to the bramble, Come, reign over us. ¹⁵ And the bramble says to the trees, If in truth you are anointing me for king over you, come, take refuge in my shadow; and if not—fire comes out from the bramble, and devours the cedars of Lebanon. ¹⁶ And now, if you have acted in truth and in sincerity when you make Abimelech king; and if you have done good with Jerubba'al, and with his house; and if you have done to him according to the deed of his hands— ¹⁷ because my father has fought for you, and casts his life away from [him], and delivers you from the hand of Midian; ¹⁸ and you have risen against the house of my father today, and slay his sons, seventy men, on one stone, and cause Abimelech son of his handmaid to reign over the masters of Shechem, because he [is] your brother— ¹⁹ indeed, if in truth and in sincerity you have acted with Jerubba'al and with his house this day, rejoice in Abimelech, and he rejoices—even he—in you; ²⁰ and if not—fire comes out from Abimelech and devours the masters of Shechem and the house of Millo, and fire comes out from the masters of Shechem and from the house of Millo, and devours Abimelech." ²¹ And Jotham hurries, and flees, and goes to Beer, and dwells there, from the face of his brother Abimelech. ²² And Abimelech is prince over Israel [for] three years, ²³ and God sends an evil spirit between Abimelech and the masters of Shechem, and the masters of Shechem deal treacherously with Abimelech, ²⁴ for [the] coming in of [the] violence [against] seventy sons of Jerubba'al, and to place their blood on their brother Abimelech, who slew them, and on the masters of Shechem, who strengthened his hands to slay his brothers. ²⁵ And the masters of Shechem set ambushes for him on the top of the hills, and rob everyone who passes over by them in the way, and it is declared to Abimelech. ²⁶ And Gaal son of Ebed comes—also his brothers—and they pass over into Shechem, and the masters of Shechem trust in him, ²⁷ and go out into the field, and gather their vineyards, and tread, and make praises, and go into the house of their god, and eat and drink, and revile Abimelech. ²⁸ And Gaal son of Ebed says, "Who [is] Abimelech, and who [is] Shechem, that we serve him? is [he] not son of Jerubba'al? and his commander Zebul? The men of Hamor father of Shechem serve you, and why do we serve him—we? ²⁹ and oh that this people were in my hand—then I turn Abimelech aside"; and he says to Abimelech, "Increase your host, and come out." ³⁰ And Zebul, prince of the city, hears the words of Gaal son of Ebed, and his anger burns, ³¹ and he sends messengers to Abimelech deceitfully, saying, "Behold, Gaal son of Ebed and his brothers are coming into Shechem, and behold, they are fortifying the city against you; ³² and now, rise by night, you and the people who [are] with you, and lay wait in the field, ³³ and it has been, in the morning, about the rising of the sun, you rise early, and have pushed against the city; and behold, he and the people who [are] with him are going out to you—and you have done to him as your hand finds." ³⁴ And Abimelech rises, and all the people who [are] with him, by night, and they lay wait against Shechem—four detachments; ³⁵ and Gaal son of Ebed goes out, and stands at the opening of the gate of the city, and Abimelech rises—also the people who [are] with him—from the ambush, ³⁶ and Gaal sees the people and says to Zebul, "Behold, people are coming down from the top of the hills"; and Zebul says to him, "You are seeing the shadow of the hills like men." ³⁷ And Gaal adds yet to speak and says, "Behold, people are coming down from the high part of the land, and another detachment is coming by the way of the oak of Meonenim." ³⁸ And Zebul says to him, "Where [is] your mouth now, in that you say, Who [is] Abimelech that we serve him? is this not the people against which you have kicked? Please go out now and fight against it." ³⁹ And Gaal goes out before the masters of Shechem, and fights against Abimelech, ⁴⁰ and Abimelech pursues him, and he flees from his presence, and many fall wounded—to the opening of the gate. ⁴¹ And Abimelech abides in Arumah, and Zebul casts out Gaal and his brothers from dwelling in Shechem. ⁴² And it comes to pass, on the next day, that the people go out to the field, and they declare [it] to Abimelech, ⁴³ and he takes the people, and divides them into three detachments, and lays wait in a field, and looks, and behold, the people are coming out from the city, and he rises against them, and strikes them. ⁴⁴ And Abimelech and the detachments who [are] with him pushed on, and stand at the opening of the gate of the city, and the two detachments have pushed against all who are in the field, and strike them, ⁴⁵ and Abimelech has fought against the city all that day, and captures the city, and has slain the people who [are] in it, and he breaks down the city, and sows it [with] salt. ⁴⁶ And all the masters of the Tower of Shechem hear, and go into the high place of the house of the god Berith, ⁴⁷ and it is declared to Abimelech that all the masters of the Tower of Shechem have gathered themselves together, ⁴⁸ and Abimelech goes up to Mount Zalmon, he and all the people who [are] with him, and Abimelech takes the great axe in his hand, and cuts off a bough of the trees, and lifts it up, and sets [it] on his shoulder, and says to the people who [are] with him, "What you have seen me do—hurry, do as I [have done]." ⁴⁹ And every one of the people cuts down his bough and goes after Abimelech, and sets [them] at the high place, and burns the high place with fire by these, and also all the men of the Tower of Shechem die—about one thousand men and women. ⁵⁰ And Abimelech goes to Thebez, and encamps against Thebez, and captures it, ⁵¹ and a strong tower has been in the midst of the city, and all the men and the women flee there, and all the masters of the city, and they shut [it] behind them, and go up on the roof of the tower. ⁵² And Abimelech comes to the tower, and fights against it, and draws near to the opening of the tower to burn it with fire, ⁵³ and a certain woman casts a piece of a millstone on the head of Abimelech, and breaks his skull, ⁵⁴ and he calls quickly to the young man carrying his weapons and says to him, "Draw your sword, and you have put me to death, lest they say of me—A woman slew him"; and his young man pierced him through, and he dies. ⁵⁵ And the men of Israel see that Abimelech [is] dead, and each one goes to his place; ⁵⁶ and God turns back the evil of Abimelech which he did to his father to slay his seventy brothers; ⁵⁷ and God has returned all the evil of the men of Shechem on their [own] head, and the cursing of Jotham son of Jerubba'al comes to them.

CHAPTER 10

¹ And there rises after Abimelech, to save Israel, Tola son of Puah, son of Dodo, a man of Issachar, and he is dwelling in Shamir, in the hill-country of Ephraim, ² and he judges Israel [for] twenty-three years, and he dies, and is buried in Shamir. ³ And there rises Jair the Gileadite after him, and he judges Israel [for] twenty-two years, ⁴ and he has thirty sons riding on thirty donkey-colts, and they have thirty cities (they call them Havoth-Jair to this day), which [are] in the land of Gilead; ⁵ and Jair dies, and is buried in Kamon. ⁶ And the sons of Israel add to do evil in the eyes of Yhwh, and serve the Ba'alim, and

Ashtaroth, and the gods of Aram, and the gods of Sidon, and the gods of Moab, and the gods of the sons of Ammon, and the gods of the Philistines, and forsake Yhwh, and have not served Him; **7** and the anger of Yhwh burns against Israel, and He sells them into the hand of the Philistines, and into the hand of the sons of Ammon, **8** and they crush and oppress the sons of Israel in that year; [and for] eighteen years—all the sons of Israel [who] are beyond the Jordan, in the land of the Amorite, which [is] in Gilead. **9** And the sons of Ammon pass over the Jordan to also fight against Judah, and against Benjamin, and against the house of Ephraim, and Israel has great distress. **10** And the sons of Israel cry to Yhwh, saying, "We have sinned against You, because we have even forsaken our God, and serve the Ba'alim." **11** And Yhwh says to the sons of Israel, "[Have I] not [saved you] from the Egyptians, and from the Amorite, from the sons of Ammon, and from the Philistines? **12** And the Zidonians, and Amalek, and Maon have oppressed you, and you cry to Me, and I save you out of their hand; **13** and you have forsaken Me, and serve other gods, therefore I do not add to save you. **14** Go and cry to the gods on which you have fixed; they save you in the time of your tribulation." **15** And the sons of Israel say to Yhwh, "We have sinned, do to us according to all that is good in Your eyes; only please deliver us this day." **16** And they turn aside the gods of the stranger out of their midst, and serve Yhwh, and His soul is grieved with the misery of Israel. **17** And the sons of Ammon are called together, and encamp in Gilead, and the sons of Israel are gathered together, and encamp in Mizpah. **18** And the people—heads of Gilead— say to one another, "Who [is] the man that begins to fight against the sons of Ammon? he is for head to all inhabitants of Gilead."

CHAPTER 11

1 And Jephthah the Gileadite has been a mighty man of valor, and he [is the] son of a harlot woman; and Gilead begets Jephthah, **2** and the wife of Gilead bears sons to him, and the wife's sons grow up and cast Jephthah out, and say to him, "You do not inherit in the house of our father; for you [are the] son of another woman." **3** And Jephthah flees from the face of his brothers, and dwells in the land of Tob; and vain men gather themselves together to Jephthah, and they go out with him. **4** And it comes to pass, after a time, that the sons of Ammon fight with Israel, **5** and it comes to pass, when the sons of Ammon have fought with Israel, that [the] elderly of Gilead go to take Jephthah from the land of Tob; **6** and they say to Jephthah, "Come, and you have been for a captain to us, and we fight against the sons of Ammon." **7** And Jephthah says to [the] elderly of Gilead, "Have you not hated me? and you cast me out from the house of my father, and why have you come to me now when you are in distress?" **8** and [the] elderly of Gilead say to Jephthah, "Therefore, now, we have turned back to you; and you have gone with us, and have fought against the sons of Ammon, and you have been for head to us—to all the inhabitants of Gilead." **9** And Jephthah says to [the] elderly of Gilead, "If you are taking me back to fight against the sons of Ammon, and Yhwh has given them before me—am I for a head to you?" **10** And [the] elderly of Gilead say to Jephthah, "Yhwh is listening between us—if we do not do so according to your word." **11** And Jephthah goes with [the] elderly of Gilead, and the people set him over them for head and for captain, and Jephthah speaks all his words before Yhwh in Mizpeh. **12** And Jephthah sends messengers to the king of the sons of Ammon, saying, "What [is this] to me and to you, that you have come to me, to fight in my land?" **13** And the king of the sons of Ammon says to the messengers of Jephthah, "Because Israel took my land in his coming up out of Egypt, from Arnon, and to the Jabbok, and to the Jordan; and now, restore them in peace." **14** And Jephthah adds yet and sends messengers to the king of the sons of Ammon, **15** and says to him, "Thus said Jephthah: Israel did not take the land of Moab, and the land of the sons of Ammon, **16** for in their coming up out of Egypt, Israel goes in the wilderness to the Red Sea, and comes to Kadesh, **17** and Israel sends messengers to the king of Edom, saying, Please let me pass over through your land, and the king of Edom did not listen; and [Israel] has also sent to the king of Moab, and he has not been willing; and Israel abides in Kadesh, **18** and he goes through the wilderness, and goes around the land of Edom and the land of Moab, and comes in at the rising of the sun of the land of Moab, and they encamp beyond Arnon, and have not come into the border of Moab, for Arnon [is] the

border of Moab. **19** And Israel sends messengers to Sihon, king of the Amorite, king of Heshbon, and Israel says to him, Please let us pass over through your land, to my place, **20** and Sihon has not trusted Israel to pass over through his border, and Sihon gathers all his people, and they encamp in Jahaz, and fight with Israel; **21** and Yhwh, God of Israel, gives Sihon and all his people into the hand of Israel, and they strike them, and Israel possesses all the land of the Amorite, the inhabitant of that land, **22** and they possess all the border of the Amorite from Arnon, and to the Jabbok, and from the wilderness, and to the Jordan. **23** And now, Yhwh, God of Israel, has dispossessed the Amorite from the presence of His people Israel, and you would possess it! **24** That which your god Chemosh causes you to possess—do you not possess it? and all that which our God Yhwh has dispossessed from our presence—we possess it. **25** And now, [are] you at all better than Balak son of Zippor, king of Moab? did he strive with Israel at all? did he fight against them at all? **26** In Israel's dwelling in Heshbon and in its towns, and in Aroer and in its towns, and in all the cities which [are] by the sides of Arnon [for] three hundred years—and why have you not delivered them in that time? **27** And I have not sinned against you, and you are doing evil with me—to fight against me. Yhwh, the Judge, judges between the sons of Israel and the sons of Ammon today." **28** And the king of the sons of Ammon has not listened to the words of Jephthah which he sent to him, **29** and the Spirit of Yhwh is on Jephthah, and he passes over Gilead and Manasseh, and passes over Mizpeh of Gilead, and he has passed over from Mizpeh of Gilead to the sons of Ammon. **30** And Jephthah vows a vow to Yhwh and says, "If You give the sons of Ammon into my hand at all— **31** then it has been, that which comes out from the doors of my house at all to meet me in my turning back in peace from the sons of Ammon—it has been for Yhwh, or I have offered up a burnt-offering for it." **32** And Jephthah passes over to the sons of Ammon to fight against them, and Yhwh gives them into his hand, **33** and he strikes them from Aroer, and to [where] you are going in to Minnith—twenty cities—and to the meadow of the vineyards, [with] a very great striking; and the sons of Ammon are humbled at the presence of the sons of Israel. **34** And Jephthah comes into Mizpeh, to his house, and behold, his daughter is coming out to meet him with timbrels, and with choruses, and except her alone, he has no son or daughter. **35** And it comes to pass, when he sees her, that he tears his garments and says, "Aah! My daughter, you have caused me to bend greatly, and you have been among those troubling me; and I have opened my mouth to Yhwh, and I am not able to turn back." **36** And she says to him, "My father, you have opened your mouth to Yhwh, do to me as it has gone out from your mouth, after that Yhwh has done vengeance for you on your enemies, on the sons of Ammon." **37** And she says to her father, "Let this thing be done to me; desist from me [for] two months, and I go on, and have gone down on the hills, and I weep for my virginity—I and my friends." **38** And he says, "Go"; and he sends her away [for] two months, and she goes, she and her friends, and she weeps for her virginity on the hills; **39** and it comes to pass at the end of two months that she turns back to her father, and he does to her his vow which he has vowed, and she did not know a man; and it is a statute in Israel: **40** from time to time the daughters of Israel go to talk to the daughter of Jephthah the Gileadite, four days in a year.

CHAPTER 12

1 And the men of Ephraim are called together, and pass over northward, and say to Jephthah, "Why have you passed over to fight against the sons of Ammon, and have not called on us to go with you? We burn your house with fire over you." **2** And Jephthah says to them, "I have been a man of great strife (I and my people) with the sons of Ammon, and I call you, and you have not saved me out of their hand, **3** and I see that you are not a savior, and I put my life in my hand, and pass over to the sons of Ammon, and Yhwh gives them into my hand— and why have you come up to me this day to fight against me?" **4** And Jephthah gathered all the men of Gilead, and fights with Ephraim, and the men of Gilead strike Ephraim, because they said, "You Gileadites [are] fugitives of Ephraim, in the midst of Ephraim—in the midst of Manasseh." **5** And Gilead captures the passages of the Jordan to Ephraim, and it has been, when [any of] the fugitives of Ephraim say, "Let me pass over," and the men of Gilead say to him, "[Are] you an Ephraimite?" And he says, "No"; **6** that they say to him, "Now say, Shibboleth"; and he says, "Sibboleth," and is not prepared to speak right—and they seize him, and slaughter him at the passages of the Jordan, and there fall at that time, of Ephraim, forty-two chiefs. **7** And Jephthah judged Israel [for] six years, and Jephthah the Gileadite dies, and is buried in [one of] the cities of Gilead. **8** And after him Ibzan of Beth-Lehem judges Israel, **9** and he has thirty sons, and thirty daughters he gave away [in marriage], and thirty daughters he brought in from outside for his sons; and he judges Israel [for] seven years. **10** And Ibzan dies, and is buried in Beth-Lehem. **11** And after him Elon the Zebulunite judges Israel, and he judges Israel [for] ten years, **12** and Elon the Zebulunite dies, and is buried in Aijalon, in the land of Zebulun. **13** And after him, Abdon son of Hillel, the Pirathonite, judges Israel, **14** and he has forty sons, and thirty grandsons, riding on seventy donkey-colts, and he judges Israel [for] eight years. **15** And Abdon son of Hillel, the Pirathonite, dies, and is buried in Pirathon, in the land of Ephraim, in the hill-country of the Amalekite.

CHAPTER 13

1 And the sons of Israel add to do evil in the eyes of Yhwh, and Yhwh gives them into the hand of the Philistines [for] forty years. **2** And there is a certain man of Zorah, of the family of the Danite, and his name [is] Manoah, his wife [is] barren, and has not borne; **3** and the Messenger of Yhwh appears to the woman and says to her, "Now behold, you [are] barren and have not borne; when you have conceived, then you have borne a son. **4** And now, please take heed and do not drink wine and strong drink, and do not eat any unclean thing, **5** for behold, you are conceiving and bearing a son, and a razor does not go up on his head, for the youth is a Nazarite to God from the womb, and he begins to save Israel out of the hand of the Philistines." **6** And the woman comes and speaks to her husband, saying, "A Man of God has come to me, and His appearance [is] as the appearance of the Messenger of God, very fearful, and I have not asked Him where He [is] from, and he has not declared His Name to me; **7** and He says to me, Behold, you are pregnant, and bearing a son, and now do not drink wine and strong drink, and do not eat any unclean thing, for the youth is a Nazarite to God from the womb until the day of his death." **8** And Manoah makes plea to Yhwh and says, "O my Lord, the Man of God whom You sent, please let Him come in again to us, and direct us what we do to the youth who is born." **9** And God listens to the voice of Manoah, and the Messenger of God comes again to the woman, and she [is] sitting in a field, and her husband Manoah is not with her, **10** and the woman hurries, and runs, and declares [it] to her husband, and says to him, "Behold, He has appeared to me—the Man who came on [that] day to me." **11** And Manoah rises, and goes after his wife, and comes to the Man, and says to Him, "Are you the Man who spoke to the woman?" And He says, "I [am]." **12** And Manoah says, "Now let Your words come to pass; what is the custom of the youth—and his work?" **13** And the Messenger of Yhwh says to Manoah, "Of all that I said to the woman let her take heed; **14** she does not eat of anything which comes out from the wine-vine, and she does not drink wine and strong drink, and she does not eat any unclean thing; she observes all that I have commanded her." **15** And Manoah says to the Messenger of Yhwh, "Please let us detain You, and we prepare a kid of the goats before You." **16** And the Messenger of Yhwh says to Manoah, "If you detain Me—I do not eat of your bread; and if you prepare a burnt-offering—offer it to Yhwh"; for Manoah has not known that He [is] the Messenger of Yhwh. **17** And Manoah says to the Messenger of Yhwh, "What [is] Your Name? when Your words come to pass, then we have honored You." **18** And the Messenger of Yhwh says to him, "Why do you ask this, My Name, since it [is] incomprehensible?" **19** And Manoah takes the kid of the goats, and the present, and offers on the rock to Yhwh, and He is doing wonderfully, and Manoah and his wife are looking on, **20** and it comes to pass, in the going up of the flame from off the altar toward the heavens, that the Messenger of Yhwh goes up in the flame of the altar, and Manoah and his wife are looking on, and they fall on their faces to the earth, **21** and the Messenger of Yhwh has not added again to appear to Manoah, and to his wife, then Manoah has known that He [is] the Messenger of Yhwh. **22** And Manoah says to his wife, "We certainly die, for we have seen God." **23** And his wife says to him, "If Yhwh were desirous to put us to death, He had not received burnt-offering and present from our hands, nor

showed us all these things, nor caused us to hear [anything] like this as [at this] time." **24** And the woman bears a son, and calls his name Samson, and the youth grows, and Yhwh blesses him, **25** and the Spirit of Yhwh begins to move him in the camp of Dan, between Zorah and Eshtaol.

CHAPTER 14

1 And Samson goes down to Timnath, and sees a woman in Timnath of the daughters of the Philistines, **2** and comes up and declares [it] to his father and to his mother, and says, "I have seen a woman in Timnath, of the daughters of the Philistines; and now, take her for me for a wife." **3** And his father says to him—also his mother, "Is there no woman among the daughters of your brothers, and among all my people, that you are going to take a woman from the uncircumcised Philistines?" And Samson says to his father, "Take her for me, for she is right in my eyes." **4** And his father and his mother have not known that it [is] from Yhwh, that He is seeking a meeting of the Philistines; and the Philistines are ruling over Israel at that time. **5** And Samson goes down—also his father and his mother, to Timnath, and they come to the vineyards of Timnath, and behold, a lion's whelp roars at meeting him, **6** and the Spirit of Yhwh prospers over him, and he tears it as the tearing of a kid, and there is nothing in his hand, and he has not declared to his father and to his mother that which he has done. **7** And he goes down and speaks to the woman, and she is right in the eyes of Samson; **8** and he turns back after [some] days to take her, and turns aside to see the carcass of the lion, and behold, a swarm of bees [are] in the body of the lion—and honey. **9** And he takes it down on to his hands, and goes on, going and eating; and he goes to his father, and to his mother, and gives to them, and they eat, and he has not declared to them that he took down the honey from the body of the lion. **10** And his father goes down to the woman, and Samson makes a banquet there, for so the young men does; **11** and it comes to pass, when they see him, that they take thirty companions, and they are with him. **12** And Samson says to them, "Now let me put forth a riddle to you; if you certainly declare it to me [in] the seven days of the banquet, and have found [it] out, then I have given thirty linen shirts and thirty changes of garments to you; **13** and if you are not able to declare [it] to me, then you have given thirty linen shirts and thirty changes of garments to me." And they say to him, "Put forth your riddle, and we hear it!" **14** And he says to them: "Out of the eater came forth something to eat, || And out of the strong came forth [something] sweet"; and they were not able to declare the riddle [in] three days. **15** And it comes to pass, on the seventh day, that they say to Samson's wife, "Entice your husband, that he declare the riddle to us, lest we burn you and the house of your father with fire; have you not called for us [here] to rob us?" **16** And Samson's wife weeps for it and says, "You have only hated me, and have not loved me; you have put forth the riddle to the sons of my people, but have not declared it to me"; and he says to her, "Behold, I have not declared [it] to my father and to my mother—and I declare [it] to you?" **17** And she weeps for it the seven days [in] which their banquet has been, and it comes to pass on the seventh day that he declares [it] to her, for she has distressed him; and she declares the riddle to the sons of her people. **18** And the men of the city say to him on the seventh day, before the sun goes in: "What [is] sweeter than honey? And what [is] stronger than a lion?" And he says to them: "Unless you had plowed with my heifer, || You had not found out my riddle." **19** And the Spirit of Yhwh prospers over him, and he goes down to Ashkelon, and strikes down thirty of their men, and takes their armor, and gives the changes to those declaring the riddle; and his anger burns, and he goes up to the house of his father; **20** and Samson's wife becomes his companion's, who had attended to him.

CHAPTER 15

1 And it comes to pass after [some] days, in the days of wheat-harvest, that Samson looks after his wife, with a kid of the goats, and says, "I go in to my wife, to the inner chamber"; and her father has not permitted him to go in, **2** and her father says, "I certainly said that you surely hated her, and I give her to your companion; is her younger sister not better than she? Please let her be to you instead of her." **3** And Samson says of them, "I am more innocent this time than the Philistines, though I am doing evil with them." **4** And Samson goes and catches three hundred foxes, and takes torches, and turns tail to tail, and puts a torch between the two tails, in the midst, **5** and kindles fire in the torches, and sends [them] out into the standing grain of the Philistines, and burns [it] from heap even to standing grain, even to vineyard [and] olive-yard. **6** And the Philistines say, "Who has done this?" And they say, "Samson, son-in-law of the Timnite, because he has taken away his wife, and gives her to his companion"; and the Philistines go up, and burn her and her father with fire. **7** And Samson says to them, "Though you do thus, nevertheless I am avenged on you, and afterward I cease!" **8** And he strikes them hip and thigh [with] a great striking, and goes down and dwells in the cleft of the rock of Etam. **9** And the Philistines go up, and encamp in Judah, and are spread out in Lehi, **10** and the men of Judah say, "Why have you come up against us?" And they say, "We have come up to bind Samson, to do to him as he has done to us." **11** And three thousand men of Judah go down to the cleft of the rock of Etam, and say to Samson, "Have you now known that the Philistines are rulers over us? and what [is] this you have done to us?" And he says to them, "As they did to me, so I did to them." **12** And they say to him, "We have come down to bind you—to give you into the hand of the Philistines." And Samson says to them, "Swear to me, lest you fall on me yourselves." **13** And they speak to him, saying, "No, but we certainly bind you, and have given you into their hand, and we certainly do not put you to death"; and they bind him with two thick bands, new ones, and bring him up from the rock. **14** He has come to Lehi—and the Philistines have shouted at meeting him—and the Spirit of Yhwh prospers over him, and the thick bands which [are] on his arms are as flax which they burn with fire, and his bands are melted from off his hands, **15** and he finds a fresh jawbone of a donkey, and puts forth his hand and takes it, and strikes down one thousand men with it. **16** And Samson says, "With the jawbone of a donkey, heap on heaps—I have struck down one thousand men with the jawbone of a donkey!" **17** And it comes to pass, when he finishes speaking, that he casts away the jawbone out of his hand, and calls that place Ramath-Lehi; **18** and he thirsts exceedingly, and calls to Yhwh, and says, "You have given this great salvation by the hand of Your servant; and now, I die with thirst, and have fallen into the hand of the uncircumcised." **19** And God cleaves the hollow place which [is] in Lehi, and waters come out of it, and he drinks, and his spirit comes back, and he revives; therefore [one] has called its name "The fountain of him who is calling," which [is] in Lehi to this day. **20** And he judges Israel in the days of the Philistines [for] twenty years.

CHAPTER 16

1 And Samson goes to Gaza, and sees a woman there, a harlot, and goes in to her; **2** [it is told] to the Gazathites, saying, "Samson has come in here"; and they go around and lay wait for him all the night at the gate of the city, and keep themselves silent all the night, saying, "Until the morning light—then we have slain him." **3** And Samson lies down until the middle of the night, and rises in the middle of the night, and lays hold on the doors of the gate of the city, and on the two side-posts, and removes them with the bar, and puts [them] on his shoulders, and takes them up to the top of the hill, which [is] on the front of Hebron. **4** And it comes to pass afterward that he loves a woman in the Valley of Sorek, and her name [is] Delilah, **5** and the princes of the Philistines come up to her, and say to her, "Entice him, and see wherein his great power [is], and wherein we are able for him—and we have bound him to afflict him, and each one of us gives eleven hundred pieces of silver to you." **6** And Delilah says to Samson, "Please declare to me wherein your great power [is], and with what you are bound, to afflict you." **7** And Samson says to her, "If they bind me with seven green cords which have not been dried, then I have been weak, and have been as one of mankind." **8** And the princes of the Philistines bring up to her seven green cords which have not been dried, and she binds him with them. **9** And the ambush is abiding with her in an inner chamber, and she says to him, "Philistines [are] on you, Samson!" And he breaks the cords as a thread of tow is broken in its touching fire, and his power has not been known. **10** And Delilah says to Samson, "Behold, you have played on me, and speak lies to me; now, please declare to me with what you are bound." **11** And he says to her, "If they certainly bind me with

thick bands, new ones, by which work has not been done, then I have been weak, and have been as one of mankind." **12** And Delilah takes thick bands, new ones, and binds him with them, and says to him, "Philistines [are] on you, Samson!" And the ambush is abiding in an inner chamber, and he breaks them from off his arms as a thread. **13** And Delilah says to Samson, "Until now you have played on me, and speak lies to me; declare to me with what you are bound." And he says to her, "If you weave the seven locks of my head with the web." **14** And she fixes [it] with the pin and says to him, "Philistines [are] on you, Samson!" And he awakens out of his sleep, and pulls out the pin of the loom, and with the web. **15** And she says to him, "How do you say, I have loved you, and your heart is not with me? these three times you have played on me, and have not declared to me wherein your great power [is]." **16** And it comes to pass, because she distressed him with her words all the days, and urges him, and his soul is grieved to death, **17** that he declares all his heart to her, and says to her, "A razor has not gone up on my head, for I [am] a Nazarite to God from the womb of my mother; if I have been shaven, then my power has turned aside from me, and I have been weak, and have been as all of mankind." **18** And Delilah sees that he has declared all his heart to her, and she sends and calls for the princes of the Philistines, saying, "Come up this time, for he has declared all his heart to me"; and the princes of the Philistines have come up to her, and bring up the money in their hand. **19** and she makes him sleep on her knees, and calls for a man, and shaves the seven locks of his head, and begins to afflict him, and his power turns aside from off him; **20** and she says, "Philistines [are] on you, Samson!" And he awakens out of his sleep and says, "I go out as time by time, and shake free"; but he has not known that Yhwh has turned aside from off him. **21** And the Philistines seize him, and pick out his eyes, and bring him down to Gaza, and bind him with two bronze chains; and he is grinding in the prison-house. **22** And the hair of his head begins to shoot up when he has been shaven, **23** and the princes of the Philistines have been gathered together to sacrifice a great sacrifice to their god Dagon, and to rejoice; and they say, "Our god has given our enemy Samson into our hand." **24** And the people see him, and praise their god, for they said, "Our god has given into our hand our enemy, and he who is laying waste to our land, and who multiplied our wounded." **25** And it comes to pass, when their heart [is] glad, that they say, "Call for Samson, and he entertains for us"; and they call for Samson out of the prison-house, and he entertains before their faces, and they cause him to stand between the pillars. **26** And Samson says to the young man who is keeping hold on his hand, "Let me also feel the pillars on which the house is established, and I lean on them." **27** And the house has been full of the men and the women, and all the princes of the Philistines [are] there, and about three thousand men and women [are] on the roof, who are watching Samson entertain. **28** And Samson calls to Yhwh and says, "Lord Yhwh, please remember me and please strengthen me only this time, O God; and I am avenged—vengeance at once—because of my two eyes, on the Philistines." **29** And Samson turns aside [to] the two middle pillars, on which the house is established, and on which it is supported, [to] one with his right hand and one with his left; **30** and Samson says, "Let me die with the Philistines," and he inclines himself powerfully, and the house falls on the princes, and on all the people who [are] in it, and the dead whom he has put to death in his death are more than those whom he put to death in his life. **31** And his brothers come down, and all the house of his father, and lift him up, and bring him up, and bury him between Zorah and Eshtaol, in the burying-place of his father Manoah; and he has judged Israel [for] twenty years.

CHAPTER 17

1 And there is a man of the hill-country of Ephraim, and his name [is] Micah, **2** and he says to his mother, "The eleven hundred pieces of silver which have been taken of yours, and [of which] you have sworn, and also spoken in my ears; behold, the silver [is] with me, I have taken it"; and his mother says, "Blessed [is] my son of Yhwh." **3** And he gives back the eleven hundred pieces of silver to his mother, and his mother says, "I had certainly sanctified the silver to Yhwh, from my hand, for my son, to make a carved image, and a molten image; and now, I give it back to you." **4** And he gives back the money to his mother, and his mother takes two hundred pieces of silver, and gives them to a refiner, and he makes them a carved image, and a molten image, and it is in the house of Micah. **5** As for the man Micah, he has a house of gods, and he makes an ephod, and teraphim, and consecrates the hand of one of his sons, and he is for a priest to him; **6** in those days there is no king in Israel, each does that which is right in his own eyes. **7** And there is a young man of Beth-Lehem-Judah, of the family of Judah, and he [is] a Levite, and he [is] a sojourner there. **8** And the man goes out of the city, out of Beth-Lehem-Judah, to sojourn where he finds, and comes to the hill-country of Ephraim, to the house of Micah, to work his way. **9** And Micah says to him, "Where do you come from?" And he says to him, "I [am] a Levite of Beth-Lehem-Judah, and I am going to sojourn where I find." **10** And Micah says to him, "Dwell with me, and be for a father and for a priest to me, and I give ten pieces of silver to you for the days, and a suit of garments, and your sustenance"; and the Levite goes [in]. **11** And the Levite is willing to dwell with the man, and the young man is to him as one of his sons. **12** And Micah consecrates the hand of the Levite, and the young man is for a priest to him, and he is in the house of Micah, **13** and Micah says, "Now I have known that Yhwh does good to me, for the Levite has been for a priest to me."

CHAPTER 18

1 In those days there is no king in Israel, and in those days the tribe of the Danite is seeking an inheritance to inhabit for itself, for [that] has not fallen to it to that day in the midst of the tribes of Israel by inheritance. **2** And the sons of Dan send, out of their family, five of their men—men, sons of valor—from Zorah, and from Eshtaol, to traverse the land, and to search it, and they say to them, "Go, search the land"; and they come into the hill-country of Ephraim, to the house of Micah, and lodge there. **3** They [are] with the household of Micah, and they have discerned the voice of the young man, the Levite, and turn aside there, and say to him, "Who has brought you here? and what are you doing in this [place]? And why are you here?" **4** And he says to them, "Thus and thus has Micah done to me; and he hires me, and I am for a priest to him." **5** And they say to him, "Please ask of God, and we know whether our way on which we are going is prosperous." **6** And the priest says to them, "Go in peace; before Yhwh [is] your way in which you go." **7** And the five men go, and come to Laish, and see the people which [is] in its midst, dwelling confidently, according to the custom of Zidonians, quiet and confident; and there is none putting to shame in the land in [any] thing, possessing restraint, and they [are] far off from the Zidonians, and have no word with [any] man. **8** And they come to their brothers at Zorah and Eshtaol, and their brothers say to them, "What [did] you [find]?" **9** And they say, "Rise, and we go up against them, for we have seen the land, and behold—very good; and you are keeping silent! Do not be slothful to go—to enter to possess the land. **10** When you go, you come to a confident people, and the land [is] large on both hands, for God has given it into your hand, a place where there is no lack of anything which [is] in the land." **11** And there journey there, of the family of the Danite, from Zorah, and from Eshtaol, six hundred men girded with weapons of war. **12** And they go up and encamp in Kirjath-Jearim, in Judah, therefore they have called that place, "Camp of Dan," until this day; behold, behind Kirjath-Jearim. **13** And they pass over there [to] the hill-country of Ephraim, and come to the house of Micah. **14** And the five men, those going to traverse the land of Laish, answer and say to their brothers, "Have you known that in these houses there is an ephod, and teraphim, and carved image, and molten image? and now, know what you do." **15** And they turn aside there, and come to the house of the young man, the Levite, the house of Micah, and ask of him of welfare— **16** (and the six hundred men girded with their weapons of war, who [are] of the sons of Dan, are standing at the opening of the gate)— **17** indeed, the five men, those going to traverse the land, go up—they have come in there—they have taken the carved image, and the ephod, and the teraphim, and the molten image—and the priest is standing at the opening of the gate, and the six hundred men who are girded with weapons of war— **18** indeed, these have entered the house of Micah, and take the carved image, the ephod, and the teraphim, and the molten image; and the priest says to them, "What are you doing?" **19** and they say to him, "Keep silent, lay your hand on your mouth, and go with us, and be for a father and for a priest to us: is it better your being a priest

for the house of one man, or your being priest for a tribe and for a family in Israel?" **20** And the heart of the priest is glad, and he takes the ephod, and the teraphim, and the carved image, and goes into the midst of the people, **21** and they turn and go, and put the infants, and the livestock, and the baggage, before them. **22** They have been far off from the house of Micah—and the men who [are] in the houses which [are] near the house of Micah have been called together, and overtake the sons of Dan, **23** and call to the sons of Dan, and they turn their faces around, and say to Micah, "What [is this] to you that you have been called together?" **24** And he says, "You have taken my gods which I made, and the priest, and you go; and what more do I [have]? and what [is] this you say to me, What [is this] to you?" **25** And the sons of Dan say to him, "Do not let your voice be heard with us, lest men bitter in soul fall on you, and you have gathered your life, and the life of your household"; **26** and the sons of Dan go on their way, and Micah sees that they are stronger than he, and turns, and goes back to his house. **27** And they have taken that which Micah had made, and the priest whom he had, and come in against Laish, against a people quiet and confident, and strike them by the mouth of the sword, and have burned the city with fire, **28** and there is no deliverer, for it [is] far off from Sidon, and they have no word with [any] man, and it [is] in the valley which [is] by Beth-Rehob; and they build the city, and dwell in it, **29** and call the name of the city Dan, by the name of their father Dan, who was born to Israel; and yet Laish [is] the name of the city at the first. **30** And the sons of Dan raise up the carved image for themselves, and Jonathan son of Gershom, son of Manasseh, he and his sons have been priests for the tribe of the Danite, until the day of the expulsion of [the people] of the land. **31** And they appoint for themselves the carved image of Micah, which he had made, all the days of the house of God being in Shiloh.

CHAPTER 19

1 And it comes to pass in those days, when there is no king in Israel, that there is a man, a Levite, a sojourner in the sides of the hill-country of Ephraim, and he takes a wife for himself, a concubine, out of Beth-Lehem-Judah; **2** and his concubine commits whoredom against him, and she goes from him to the house of her father, to Beth-Lehem-Judah, and is there four months of days. **3** And her husband rises and goes after her, to speak to her heart, to bring her back, and his young man [is] with him, and a couple of donkeys; and she brings him into the house of her father, and the father of the young woman sees him, and rejoices to meet him. **4** And his father-in-law keeps hold on him, father of the young woman, and he abides with him three days, and they eat and drink, and lodge there. **5** And it comes to pass, on the fourth day, that they rise early in the morning, and he rises to go, and the father of the young woman says to his son-in-law, "Support your heart with a morsel of bread, and afterward you go on." **6** And both of them sit, and eat and drink together, and the father of the young woman says to the man, "Please be willing and lodge all night, and let your heart be glad." **7** And the man rises to go, and his father-in-law presses on him, and he turns back and lodges there. **8** And he rises early in the morning, on the fifth day, to go, and the father of the young woman says, "Please support your heart"; and they have tarried until the turning of the day, and both of them eat. **9** And the man rises to go, he, and his concubine, and his young man, but his father-in-law, father of the young woman, says to him, "Now behold, the day has fallen toward evening, please lodge all night; behold, the declining of the day! Lodge here and let your heart be glad—and you have risen early tomorrow for your journey, and you have gone to your tent." **10** And the man has not been willing to lodge all night, and he rises, and goes, and comes in until [he is] opposite Jebus (it [is] Jerusalem), and a couple of saddled donkeys [are] with him; and his concubine [is] with him. **11** They [are] near Jebus, and the day has greatly gone down, and the young man says to his lord, "Please come, and we turn aside to this city of the Jebusite and lodge in it." **12** And his lord says to him, "Let us not turn aside to the city of a stranger, that is not of the sons of Israel there, but we have passed over to Gibeah." **13** And he says to his young man, "Come, and we draw near to one of the places, and have lodged in Gibeah, or in Ramah." **14** And they pass over, and go on, and the sun goes in on them near Gibeah, which is of Benjamin; **15** and they turn aside there to go in to lodge in Gibeah, and he goes in and sits in a broad place of the city, and there is no man gathering them into the house to lodge. **16** And behold, an old man has come from his work in the field in the evening, and the man [is] of the hill-country of Ephraim, and he [is] a sojourner in Gibeah, and the men of the place [are] Benjamites. **17** And he lifts up his eyes, and sees the man, the traveler, in a broad place of the city, and the old man says, "To where do you go? and where do you come from?" **18** And he says to him, "We are passing over from Beth-Lehem-Judah to the sides of the hill-country of Ephraim—I [am] from there, and I go to Beth-Lehem-Judah, and I am going to the house of Yhwh, and there is no man gathering me into the house, **19** and there is both straw and provender for our donkeys, and there is also bread and wine for me, and for your handmaid, and for the young man with your servants; there is no lack of anything." **20** And the old man says, "Peace to you; only, all your lack [is] on me, but do not lodge in the broad place." **21** And he brings him into his house, and mixes [food] for the donkeys, and they wash their feet, and eat and drink. **22** They are making their heart glad, and behold, men of the city, men—sons of worthlessness—have gone around the house, beating on the door, and they speak to the old man, the master of the house, saying, "Bring out the man who has come into your house, and we know him." **23** And the man, the master of the house, goes out to them and says to them, "No, my brothers, please do not do evil after that this man has come into my house; do not do this folly; **24** behold, my daughter, the virgin, and his concubine, please let me bring them out and you humble them, and do that which is good in your eyes to them, and do not do this foolish thing to this man." **25** And the men have not been willing to listen to him, and the man takes hold on his concubine and brings [her] out to them outside, and they know her and roll themselves on her all the night until the morning, and they send her away in the ascending of the dawn; **26** and the woman comes in at the turning of the morning, and falls at the opening of the man's house where her lord [is], until the light. **27** And her lord rises in the morning, and opens the doors of the house, and goes out to go on his way, and behold, the woman, his concubine, is fallen at the opening of the house, and her hands [are] on the threshold, **28** and he says to her, "Rise, and we go"; but there is no answering, and he takes her on the donkey, and the man rises and goes to his place, **29** and comes into his house, and takes the knife, and lays hold on his concubine, and cuts her in pieces to her bones—into twelve pieces, and sends her into all the border of Israel. **30** And it has come to pass, everyone who sees has said, "There has not been—indeed, there has not been seen [anything] like this, from the day of the coming up of the sons of Israel out of the land of Egypt until this day; set your [heart] on it, take counsel, and speak."

CHAPTER 20

1 And all the sons of Israel go out, and the congregation is assembled as one man, from Dan even to Beer-Sheba, and the land of Gilead, to Yhwh, at Mizpeh. **2** And the chiefs of all the people, of all the tribes of Israel, station themselves in the assembly of the people of God, four hundred thousand footmen drawing sword. **3** And the sons of Benjamin hear that the sons of Israel have gone up to Mizpeh. And the sons of Israel say, "Speak! How has this evil been?" **4** And the man, the Levite, husband of the woman who has been murdered, answers and says, "My concubine and I went into Gibeah, which [is] of Benjamin, to lodge; **5** and the masters of Gibeah rise against me—and they go around the house against me by night—they thought to slay me, and they have humbled my concubine, and she dies; **6** and I lay hold on my concubine, and cut her in pieces, and send her into all the country of the inheritance of Israel; for they have done wickedness and folly in Israel; **7** behold, you [are] all sons of Israel; give for yourselves a word and counsel here." **8** And all the people rise as one man, saying, "None of us goes to his tent, and none of us turns aside to his house; **9** and now, this [is] the thing which we do to Gibeah: [we go up] against it by lot! **10** and we have taken ten men of one hundred, of all the tribes of Israel, and one hundred of a thousand, and a thousand of a myriad, to receive provision for the people, to do, at their coming to Gibeah of Benjamin, according to all the folly which it has done in Israel." **11** And every man of Israel is gathered to the city, as one man—companions. **12** And the tribes of Israel send men among all the tribes of Benjamin, saying, "What [is] this evil which has been

among you? **13** And now, give up the men—sons of worthlessness—which [are] in Gibeah, and we put them to death, and we put away evil from Israel." And [the sons of] Benjamin have not been willing to listen to the voice of their brothers, the sons of Israel; **14** and the sons of Benjamin are gathered out of the cities to Gibeah, to go out to battle with the sons of Israel. **15** And the sons of Benjamin number themselves on that day; out of the cities [are] twenty-six thousand men drawing sword, apart from the inhabitants of Gibeah, [who] numbered themselves, seven hundred chosen men; **16** among all this people [are] seven hundred chosen men, their right hand bound, each of these slinging with a stone at the hair, and he does not err. **17** And the men of Israel numbered themselves, apart from Benjamin, four hundred thousand men, drawing sword, each of these a man of war. **18** And they rise and go up to Beth-El, and ask of God, and the sons of Israel say, "Who goes up for us at the commencement to battle with the sons of Benjamin?" And Yhwh says, "Judah—at the commencement." **19** And the sons of Israel rise in the morning, and encamp against Gibeah, **20** and the men of Israel go out to battle with Benjamin, and the men of Israel set themselves in array [for] battle with them, against Gibeah, **21** and the sons of Benjamin come out from Gibeah, and destroy twenty-two thousand men in Israel on that day—to the earth. **22** And the people, the men of Israel, strengthen themselves, and add to set in array [for] battle in the place where they arranged themselves on the first day. **23** And the sons of Israel go up and weep before Yhwh until the evening, and ask of Yhwh, saying, "Do I add to draw near to battle with the sons of my brother Benjamin?" And Yhwh says, "Go up against him." **24** And the sons of Israel draw near to the sons of Benjamin on the second day, **25** and Benjamin comes out to meet them from Gibeah on the second day, and destroy eighteen thousand men among the sons of Israel again—to the earth; all these are drawing sword. **26** And all the sons of Israel go up, even all the people, and come to Beth-El, and weep, and sit there before Yhwh, and fast on that day until the evening, and cause burnt-offerings and peace-offerings to ascend before Yhwh. **27** And the sons of Israel ask of Yhwh—and the Ark of the Covenant of God [is] there in those days, **28** and Phinehas son of Eleazar, son of Aaron, is standing before it in those days, saying, "Do I add to go out to battle again with the sons of my brother Benjamin, or do I cease?" And Yhwh says, "Go up, for tomorrow I give him into your hand." **29** And Israel sets ones lying in wait against Gibeah, all around, **30** and the sons of Israel go up against the sons of Benjamin on the third day, and arrange themselves against Gibeah, as time by time. **31** And the sons of Benjamin come out to meet the people; they have been drawn away out of the city, and begin to strike [some] of the people—wounded as time by time—in the highways (of which one is going up to Beth-El, and the other to Gibeah in the field), [are] about thirty men of Israel. **32** And the sons of Benjamin say, "They are struck before us as at the beginning"; but the sons of Israel said, "Let us flee, and draw them away out of the city, to the highways." **33** And all the men of Israel have risen from their place, and arrange themselves at Ba'al-Tamar, and the ambush of Israel is coming forth out of its place, out of the meadow of Gibeah. **34** And they come in from the front against Gibeah—ten thousand chosen men out of all Israel—and the battle [is] grievous, and they have not known that the calamity is reaching toward them. **35** And Yhwh strikes Benjamin before Israel, and the sons of Israel destroy in Benjamin, on that day, twenty-five thousand and one hundred men; all these [are] drawing sword. **36** And the sons of Benjamin see that they have been struck—and the men of Israel give place to Benjamin, for they have trusted in the ambush which they had set against Gibeah, **37** and the ambush has hurried, and pushes against Gibeah, and the ambush draws itself out, and strikes the whole of the city by the mouth of the sword. **38** And the appointed sign of the men of Israel with the ambush was their causing a great volume of smoke to go up from the city. **39** And the men of Israel turn in battle, and Benjamin has begun to strike the wounded among the men of Israel, about thirty men, for they said, "Surely they are utterly struck before us, as [at] the first battle"; **40** but the volume has begun to go up from the city—a pillar of smoke—and Benjamin turns behind, and behold, the perfection of the city has gone up toward the heavens. **41** And the men of Israel have turned, and the men of Benjamin are troubled, for they have seen that the calamity has struck against them— **42** and they turn before the men of Israel to the way of the wilderness, and the battle has followed them; and those who [are] from the cities are destroying them in their midst; **43** they have surrounded the Benjamites—they have pursued them—they have trodden them down with ease as far as the front of Gibeah, at the sunrising. **44** And eighteen thousand men of Benjamin fall—all these [were] men of valor; **45** and they turn and flee toward the wilderness, to the rock of Rimmon; and they glean five thousand of their men in the highways, and follow after them to Gidom, and strike two thousand [more] of their men. **46** And all those falling of Benjamin are twenty-five thousand men drawing sword, on that day—all these [were] men of valor; **47** but six hundred men turn and flee into the wilderness, to the rock of Rimmon, and they dwell in the rock of Rimmon four months. **48** And the men of Israel have turned back to the sons of Benjamin, and strike them by the mouth of the sword out of the city—men even to livestock, even to all that is found; they have also sent all the cities which are found into the fire.

CHAPTER 21

1 And the men of Israel have sworn in Mizpeh, saying, "None of us gives his daughter to Benjamin for a wife." **2** And the people come to Beth-El, and sit there until the evening before God, and lift up their voice, and weep [with] a great weeping, **3** and say, "Why, O Yhwh, God of Israel, has this been in Israel—to be lacking one tribe from Israel today?" **4** And it comes to pass on the next day, that the people rise early, and build an altar there, and cause burnt-offerings and peace-offerings to ascend. **5** And the sons of Israel say, "Who [is] he that has not come up in the assembly to Yhwh out of all the tribes of Israel?" For the great oath has been concerning him who has not come up to Yhwh to Mizpeh, saying, "He is surely put to death." **6** And the sons of Israel sigh concerning their brother Benjamin, and say, "Today there has been one tribe cut off from Israel, **7** what do we do for them—for those who are left—for wives, since we have sworn by Yhwh not to give to them from our daughters for wives?" **8** And they say, "Who is [that] one out of the tribes of Israel who has not come up to Yhwh to Mizpeh?" And behold, none has come to the camp from Jabesh-Gilead—to the assembly. **9** And the people numbered themselves, and behold, there is no man from the inhabitants of Jabesh-Gilead. **10** And the congregation sends twelve thousand men of the sons of valor there, and commands them, saying, "Go—and you have struck the inhabitants of Jabesh-Gilead by the mouth of the sword, even the women and the infants. **11** And this [is] the thing which you do; every male, and every woman knowing the lying of a male, you devote." **12** And they find four hundred young women, virgins, out of the inhabitants of Jabesh-Gilead, who have not known man by the lying of a male, and they bring them to the camp at Shiloh, which [is] in the land of Canaan. **13** And all the congregation sends [word] and speaks to the sons of Benjamin who [are] in the rock of Rimmon, and proclaims peace to them; **14** and Benjamin turns back at that time, and they give to them the women whom they have kept alive of the women of Jabesh-Gilead, and they have not found for [all of] them so. **15** And the people sighed concerning Benjamin, for Yhwh had made a breach among the tribes of Israel. **16** And [the] elderly of the congregation say, "What do we do to the remnant for wives—for the women have been destroyed out of Benjamin?" **17** And they say, "A possession of an escaped party [is] to Benjamin, and a tribe is not blotted out from Israel; **18** and we are not able to give wives to them out of our daughters, for the sons of Israel have sworn, saying, Cursed [is] he who is giving a wife to Benjamin." **19** And they say, "Behold, a festival of Yhwh [is] in Shiloh, from time to time, which [is] on the north of Beth-El, at the rising of the sun, by the highway which is going up from Beth-El to Shechem, and on the south of Lebonah." **20** And they command the sons of Benjamin, saying, "Go—and you have laid wait in the vineyards, **21** and have seen, and behold, if the daughters of Shiloh come out to dance in dances—then you have gone out from the vineyards, and each caught his wife out of the daughters of Shiloh for yourselves, and have gone to the land of Benjamin; **22** and it has been, when their fathers or their brothers come in to plead to us, that we have said to them, Favor us [by] them, for we have not each taken his wife in battle, for you have not given [wives] to them at this time, [so] you are [not] guilty." **23** And the sons of Benjamin do so, and take women according to their number, out of the dancers whom they have seized; and they go, and return to their inheritance, and build the cities, and dwell in them. **24** And the sons of Israel go up and down there at that time, each to his tribe, and to his family; and they each go out there to his inheritance. **25** In those days there is no king in Israel; each does that which is right in his own eyes.

RUTH

CHAPTER 1

1 And it comes to pass, in [the] days [when] the ones judging judge, that there is a famine in the land, and there goes a man from Beth-Lehem-Judah to sojourn in the fields of Moab, he, and his wife, and his two sons. **2** And the name of the man [is] Elimelech, and the name of his wife Naomi, and the name of his two sons Mahlon and Chilion, Ephraimites from Beth-Lehem-Judah; and they come into the fields of Moab, and are there. **3** And Elimelech husband of Naomi dies, and she is left, she and her two sons; **4** and they take to them wives, Moabitesses: the name of the first [is] Orpah, and the name of the second Ruth; and they dwell there about ten years. **5** And they die also, both of them—Mahlon and Chilion—and the woman is left of her two children and of her husband. **6** And she rises, she and her daughters-in-law, and turns back from the fields of Moab, for she has heard in the fields of Moab that God has looked after His people—to give to them bread. **7** And she goes out from the place where she has been, and her two daughters-in-law with her, and they go in the way to return to the land of Judah. **8** And Naomi says to her two daughters-in-law, "Go, return, each to the house of her mother; Yhwh does with you kindness as you have done with the dead, and with me; **9** Yhwh grants to you, and you find rest each in the house of her husband"; and she kisses them, and they lift up their voice and weep. **10** And they say to her, "Surely with you we go back to your people." **11** And Naomi says, "Turn back, my daughters; why do you go with me? are there yet to me sons in my bowels that they have been to you for husbands? **12** Turn back, my daughters, go, for I am too aged to be to a husband; though I had said, There is for me hope, also, I have been tonight to a husband, and also I have borne sons: **13** do you wait for them until they grow up? Do you shut yourselves up for them, not to be to a husband? no, my daughters, for more bitter to me than to you, for the hand of Yhwh has gone out against me." **14** And they lift up their voice, and weep again, and Orpah kisses her mother-in-law, and Ruth has cleaved to her. **15** And she says, "Behold, your sister-in-law has turned back to her people, and to her god, turn back after your sister-in-law." **16** And Ruth says, "Do not urge me to leave you—to turn back from after you; for to where you go I go, and where you lodge I lodge; your people [is] my people, and your God my God. **17** Where you die I die, and there I am buried; thus does Yhwh to me, and thus He adds—for death itself parts between me and you." **18** And she sees that she is strengthening herself to go with her, and she ceases to speak to her; **19** and the two of them go until their coming to Beth-Lehem; and it comes to pass at their coming to Beth-Lehem, that all the city is moved at them, and they say, "Is this Naomi?" **20** And she says to them, "Do not call me Naomi; call me Mara, for the Almighty has dealt very bitterly to me, **21** I went out full, and Yhwh has brought me back empty, why do you call me Naomi, and Yhwh has testified against me, and the Almighty has done evil to me?" **22** And Naomi turns back, and Ruth the Moabitess, her daughter-in-law, with her, who has turned back from the fields of Moab, and they have come to Beth-Lehem at the commencement of barley-harvest.

CHAPTER 2

1 And Naomi has an acquaintance of her husband's, a man mighty in wealth, of the family of Elimelech, and his name [is] Boaz. **2** And Ruth the Moabitess says to Naomi, "Please let me go into the field, and I gather among the ears of grain after him in whose eyes I find grace"; and she says to her, "Go, my daughter." **3** And she goes and comes and gathers in a field after the reapers, and her chance happens—the portion of the field is Boaz's who [is] of the family of Elimelech. **4** And behold, Boaz has come from Beth-Lehem, and says to the reapers,

"Yhwh [is] with you"; and they say to him, "Yhwh blesses you." **5** And Boaz says to his young man who is set over the reapers, "Whose [is] this young person?" **6** And the young man who is set over the reapers answers and says, "A young woman—Moabitess—she [is], who came back with Naomi from the fields of Moab, **7** and she says, Please let me glean and I have gathered among the sheaves after the reapers; and she comes and remains since the morning and until now; she sat in the house a little [while]." **8** And Boaz says to Ruth, "Have you not heard, my daughter? Do not go to glean in another field, and also, do not pass over from here, and thus you cleave to my young women: **9** your eyes [are] on the field which they reap, and you have gone after them; have I not charged the young men not to touch you? when you are thirsty then you have gone to the vessels, and have drunk from that which the young men draw." **10** And she falls on her face, and bows herself to the earth, and says to him, "Why have I found grace in your eyes, to discern me, and I a stranger?" **11** And Boaz answers and says to her, "It has been thoroughly declared to me all that you have done with your mother-in-law, after the death of your husband, and you leave your father, and your mother, and the land of your birth, and come to a people which you have not known before. **12** Yhwh repays your work, and your reward is complete from Yhwh, God of Israel, under whose wings you have come to take refuge." **13** And she says, "Let me find grace in your eyes, my lord, because you have comforted me, and because you have spoken to the heart of your maidservant, and I am not as one of your maidservants." **14** And Boaz says to her, "At meal-time come near here, and you have eaten of the bread, and dipped your morsel in the vinegar." And she sits at the side of the reapers, and he reaches to her roasted grain, and she eats, and is satisfied, and leaves. **15** And she rises to glean, and Boaz charges his young men, saying, "Even between the sheaves she gleans, and you do not cause her to blush; **16** and also you surely cast to her of the handfuls—and have left, and she has gleaned, and you do not push against her." **17** And she gleans in the field until the evening, and beats out that which she has gleaned, and it is about an ephah of barley; **18** and she takes [it] up, and goes into the city, and her mother-in-law sees that which she has gleaned, and she brings out and gives to her that which she left from her satiety. **19** And her mother-in-law says to her, "Where have you gleaned today? and where have you worked? may he who is discerning you be blessed." And she declares to her mother-in-law with whom she has worked, and says, "The name of the man with whom I have worked today [is] Boaz." **20** And Naomi says to her daughter-in-law, "Blessed [is] he of Yhwh who has not forsaken His kindness with the living and with the dead"; and Naomi says to her, "The man is a relation of ours; he [is] of our redeemers." **21** And Ruth the Moabitess says, "Also he surely said to me, Near the young people whom I have you cleave until they have completed the whole of the harvest which I have." **22** And Naomi says to her daughter-in-law Ruth, "Good, my daughter, that you go out with his young women, and they do not come against you in another field." **23** And she cleaves to the young women of Boaz to glean, until the completion of the barley-harvest, and of the wheat-harvest, and she dwells with her mother-in-law.

CHAPTER 3

1 And her mother-in-law Naomi says to her, "My daughter, do I not seek rest for you, that it may be well with you? **2** and now, is not Boaz of our acquaintance, with whose young women you have been? behold, he is winnowing the threshing-floor of barley tonight, **3** and you have bathed, and anointed yourself, and put your garments on you, and gone down to the threshing-floor; do not let yourself be known to the man until he completes to eat and to drink; **4** and it comes to pass, when he lies down, that you have known the place where he lies down, and have gone in, and uncovered his feet, and lain down—and he declares to you that which you do." **5** And she says to her, "All that you say—I do." **6** And she goes down [to] the threshing-floor, and does according to all that her mother-in-law commanded her **7** And Boaz eats and drinks, and his heart is glad; and he goes in to lie down at the end of the heap; and she comes in gently, and uncovers his feet, and lies down. **8** And it comes to pass, at the middle of the night, that the man trembles, and turns himself, and behold, a woman is lying at his feet. **9** And he says, "Who [are] you?" And she says, "I [am] Ruth your handmaid, and you have spread your skirt over your

handmaid, for you [are] a redeemer." **10** And he says, "Blessed [are] you of Yhwh, my daughter, you have dealt more kindly at the latter end than at the beginning—not to go after the young men, either poor or rich. **11** And now, my daughter, do not fear, all that you say I do to you, for all the gate of my people knows that you [are] a virtuous woman. **12** And now, surely, true, that I [am] a redeemer, but also there is a redeemer nearer than I. **13** Lodge tonight, and it has been in the morning, if he redeems you, well: he redeems; and if he does not delight to redeem you, then I have redeemed you—I; Yhwh lives! Lie down until the morning." **14** And she lies down at his feet until the morning, and rises before one discerns another; and he says, "Let it not be known that the woman has come into the floor." **15** And he says, "Give the covering which [is] on you, and keep hold on it"; and she keeps hold on it, and he measures six [measures] of barley, and lays [it] on her; and he goes into the city. **16** And she comes to her mother-in-law, and she says, "Who [are] you, my daughter?" And she declares to her all that the man has done to her. **17** And she says, "These six [measures] of barley he has given to me, for he said, You do not go in empty to your mother-in-law." **18** And she says, "Sit still, my daughter, until you know how the matter falls, for the man does not rest except he has completed the matter today."

CHAPTER 4

1 And Boaz has gone up to the gate, and sits there, and behold, the redeemer is passing by of whom Boaz had spoken, and he says, "Turn aside, sit down here, such a one, such a one"; and he turns aside and sits down. **2** And he takes ten men from [the] elderly of the city, and says, "Sit down here"; and they sit down. **3** And he says to the redeemer, "A portion of the field which [is] to our brother, to Elimelech, has Naomi sold, who has come back from the fields of Moab; **4** and I said, I uncover your ear, saying, Buy before the inhabitants and before [the] elderly of my people; if you redeem—redeem, and if none redeems—declare [it] to me and I know, for there is none except you to redeem, and I after you." And he says, "I redeem [it]." **5** And Boaz says, "In the day of your buying the field from the hand of Naomi, then from Ruth the Moabitess, wife of the dead, you have bought [it], to raise up the name of the dead over his inheritance." **6** And the redeemer says, "I am not able to redeem [it] for myself, lest I destroy my inheritance; redeem for yourself—you—my right of redemption, for I am not able to redeem." **7** And this [is] formerly in Israel for redemption and for exchanging, to establish anything: a man has drawn off his sandal, and given [it] to his neighbor, and this [is] the Testimony in Israel. **8** And the redeemer says to Boaz, "Buy [it] for yourself," and draws off his sandal. **9** And Boaz says to the elderly, and [to] all the people, "You [are] witnesses today that I have bought all that [belonged] to Elimelech, and all that [belonged] to Chilion and Mahlon, from the hand of Naomi; **10** and also Ruth the Moabitess, wife of Mahlon, I have bought to myself for a wife, to raise up the name of the dead over his inheritance; and the name of the dead is not cut off from among his brothers, and from the gate of his place; witnesses you [are] today." **11** And all the people who [are] in the gate say—also the elderly, "Witnesses! Yhwh makes the woman who is coming to your house as Rachel and as Leah, both of whom built the house of Israel; and you do virtuously in Ephrathah, and proclaim the name in Beth-Lehem; **12** and let your house be as the house of Perez (whom Tamar bore to Judah), of the seed which Yhwh gives to you of this young woman." **13** And Boaz takes Ruth, and she becomes his wife, and he goes in to her, and Yhwh gives conception to her, and she bears a son. **14** And the women say to Naomi, "Blessed [is] Yhwh who has not let a redeemer cease to you today, and his name is proclaimed in Israel, **15** and he has been to you for a restorer of life, and for a nourisher of your old age, for your daughter-in-law who has loved you—who is better to you than seven sons—has borne him." **16** And Naomi takes the boy, and lays him in her bosom, and is to him for a nurse; **17** and the neighboring women give a name to him, saying, "There has been a son born to Naomi," and they call his name Obed; he [is] father of Jesse, father of David. **18** And these are generations of Perez: Perez begot Hezron, **19** and Hezron begot Ram, and Ram begot Amminidab, **20** and Amminidab begot Nahshon, and Nahshon begot Salmon, **21** and Salmon begot Boaz, and Boaz begot Obed, **22** and Obed begot Jesse, and Jesse begot David.

1 SAMUEL

CHAPTER 1

¹ And there is a certain man of Ramathaim-Zophim, of the hill-country of Ephraim, and his name [is] Elkanah, son of Jeroham, son of Elihu, son of Tohu, son of Zuph, an Ephraimite, ² and he has two wives, the name of the first [is] Hannah, and the name of the second Peninnah, and Peninnah has children, and Hannah has no children. ³ And that man has gone up out of his city from time to time, to bow himself, and to sacrifice, before Yhwh of Hosts, in Shiloh, and there [are] two sons of Eli, Hophni and Phinehas, priests of Yhwh. ⁴ And the day comes, and Elkanah sacrifices, and he has given portions to his wife Peninnah, and to all her sons and her daughters, ⁵ and he gives a certain portion to Hannah—double, for he has loved Hannah, and Yhwh has shut her womb; ⁶ and her rival has also provoked her greatly, so as to make her tremble, for Yhwh has shut up her womb. ⁷ And so is done year by year, from the time of her going up into the house of Yhwh, so she provokes her, and she weeps, and does not eat. ⁸ And her husband Elkanah says to her, "Hannah, why do you weep? and why do you not eat? and why is your heart afflicted? am I not better to you than ten sons?" ⁹ And Hannah rises after eating in Shiloh, and after drinking, and Eli the priest is sitting on the throne by the doorpost of the temple of Yhwh. ¹⁰ And she is bitter in soul, and prays to Yhwh, and weeps greatly, ¹¹ and vows a vow, and says, "Yhwh of Hosts, if You certainly look on the affliction of Your handmaid, and have remembered me, and do not forget Your handmaid, and have given to Your handmaid seed of men—then I have given him to Yhwh all [the] days of his life, and a razor does not go up on his head." ¹² And it has been, when she multiplied praying before Yhwh, that Eli is watching her mouth, ¹³ and Hannah, she is speaking over her heart—only her lips are moving, and her voice is not heard, and Eli reckons her to be drunken. ¹⁴ And Eli says to her, "Until when are you drunken? turn aside your wine from you." ¹⁵ And Hannah answers and says, "No, my lord, I [am] a woman sharply pained in spirit, and I have not drunk wine and strong drink, and I pour out my soul before Yhwh; ¹⁶ do not put your handmaid before a daughter of worthlessness, for from the abundance of my meditation, and of my provocation, I have spoken until now." ¹⁷ And Eli answers and says, "Go in peace, and the God of Israel gives your petition which you have asked of Him." ¹⁸ And she says, "Let your handmaid find grace in your eyes"; and the woman goes on her way, and eats, and her face has not been [downcast] for herself anymore. ¹⁹ And they rise early in the morning, and bow themselves before Yhwh, and turn back, and come to their house in Ramah, and Elkanah knows his wife Hannah, and Yhwh remembers her; ²⁰ and it comes to pass, at the revolution of the days, that Hannah conceives, and bears a son, and calls his name Samuel, for, "I have asked for him from Yhwh." ²¹ And the man Elkanah goes up, and all his house, to sacrifice to Yhwh the sacrifice of the days, and his vow. ²² And Hannah has not gone up, for she said to her husband, "Until the youth is weaned—then I have brought him in, and he has appeared before the face of Yhwh, and dwelt there for all time." ²³ And her husband Elkanah says to her, "Do that which is good in your eyes; abide until your weaning him; only, let Yhwh establish His word"; and the woman abides and suckles her son until she has weaned him, ²⁴ and she causes him to go up with her when she has weaned him, with three bullocks, and one ephah of flour, and a bottle of wine, and she brings him into the house of Yhwh at Shiloh, and the youth [is but] a youth. ²⁵ And they slaughter the bullock, and bring in the youth to Eli, ²⁶ and she says, "O my lord, your soul lives! My lord, I [am] the woman who stood with you in this [place], to pray to Yhwh; ²⁷ I prayed for this youth, and Yhwh gives to me my petition which I asked of Him; ²⁸ and I also have called him to Yhwh, all the days that he has lived—he is called to Yhwh"; and he bows himself there before Yhwh.

CHAPTER 2

¹ And Hannah prays and says: "My heart has exulted in Yhwh, || My horn has been high in Yhwh, || My mouth has been large over my enemies, || For I have rejoiced in Your salvation. ² There is none holy like Yhwh, || For there is none except You, || And there is no rock like our God. ³ You do not multiply—you speak haughtily—The old saying goes out from your mouth, || For Yhwh [is] a God of knowledge, || And actions are weighed by Him. ⁴ Bows of the mighty are broken, || And the stumbling have girded on strength. ⁵ The satiated hired themselves for bread, || And the hungry have ceased. While the barren has borne seven, || And she abounding with sons has languished. ⁶ Yhwh puts to death, and keeps alive, || He brings down to Sheol, and brings up. ⁷ Yhwh dispossesses, and He makes rich, || He makes low, indeed, He makes high. ⁸ He raises the poor from the dust, || He lifts up the needy from a dunghill, || To cause [them] to sit with nobles, || Indeed, He causes them to inherit a throne of glory, || For the fixtures of earth [are] of Yhwh, || And He sets the habitable world on them. ⁹ He keeps the feet of His saints, || And the wicked are silent in darkness, || For man does not become mighty by power. ¹⁰ Yhwh—His adversaries are broken down, || He thunders against them in the heavens: Yhwh judges the ends of the earth, || And gives strength to His king, || And exalts the horn of His anointed." ¹¹ And Elkanah goes to Ramath, to his house, and the youth has been serving Yhwh [in] the presence of Eli the priest; ¹² and the sons of Eli [are] sons of worthlessness, they have not known Yhwh. ¹³ And the custom of the priests with the people [is that when] any man is sacrificing a sacrifice, then the servant of the priest has come in when the flesh is boiling, and [with] the hook of three teeth in his hand, ¹⁴ and has struck [it] into the pan, or kettle, or cauldron, or pot; all that the hook brings up the priest takes for himself; thus they do to all Israel who are coming in there in Shiloh. ¹⁵ Also, before they make incense with the fat, then the priest's servant has come in and said to the man who is sacrificing, "Give flesh to roast for the priest, and he does not take boiled flesh from you, but raw"; ¹⁶ and the man says to him, "Let them surely make incense with the fat according to the [custom] today, then take to yourself as your soul desires"; and he has said to him, "Surely you give now; and if not—I have taken by strength." ¹⁷ And the sin of the young men is very great [in] the presence of Yhwh, for the men have despised the offering of Yhwh. ¹⁸ And Samuel is ministering [in] the presence of Yhwh, a youth girt [with] an ephod of linen; ¹⁹ and his mother makes a small upper coat for him, and she has brought it up to him from time to time, in her coming up with her husband to sacrifice the sacrifice of the time. ²⁰ And Eli blessed Elkanah and his wife, and said, "Yhwh appoints seed of this woman for you, for the petition which she asked for Yhwh"; and they have gone to their place. ²¹ When Yhwh has looked after Hannah, then she conceives and bears three sons and two daughters; and the youth Samuel grows up with Yhwh. ²² And Eli [is] very old, and has heard all that his sons do to all Israel, and how that they lie with the women who are assembling [at] the opening of the Tent of Meeting, ²³ and he says to them, "Why do you do things like these? for I am hearing of your evil words from all the people—these! ²⁴ No, my sons; for the report which I am hearing is not good, causing the people of Yhwh to transgress. ²⁵ If a man sins against a man, then God has judged him; but if a man sins against Yhwh, who prays for him?" And they do not listen to the voice of their father, though Yhwh has delighted to put them to death. ²⁶ And the youth Samuel is going on and growing up, and [is] good with both Yhwh, and also with men. ²⁷ And a man of God comes to Eli and says to him, "Thus said Yhwh: Was I really revealed to the house of your father in their being in Egypt, before Pharaoh's house, ²⁸ even to choose him out of all the tribes of Israel for a priest for Myself, to go up on My altar, to make incense, to bear an ephod before Me, and I give to the house of your father all the fire-offerings of the sons of Israel? ²⁹ Why do you kick at My sacrifice and at My offering, which I commanded [in] My habitation, and honor your sons above Me, to make yourselves fat from the first part of every offering of Israel, of My people? ³⁰ Therefore—a declaration of Yhwh, God of Israel—I certainly said, Your house and the house of your father walk up and down before Me for all time; and now—a declaration of Yhwh—Far be it from Me! For he who is honoring Me, I honor, and those despising Me, are lightly esteemed. ³¹ Behold, days [are] coming, and I have cut off your arm, and the arm of the house of your father, that an old man is not in your house; ³² and you have beheld an adversary [in My] habitation, in all that He does good with Israel, and there is not an old man in your house all the days. ³³ And the man of yours

I do not cut off from My altar—[My purpose is] to consume your eyes, and to grieve your soul; and all the increase of men [in] your house die; **34** and this [is] the sign to you that comes to your two sons, to Hophni and Phinehas—in one day both of them die; **35** and I have raised up a steadfast priest for Myself; he does as in My heart and in My soul; and I have built a steadfast house for him, and he has walked up and down before My anointed all the days; **36** and it has been, everyone who is left in your house comes to bow himself to him for a wage of silver and a cake of bread, and has said, Please admit me to one of the priest's offices, to eat a morsel of bread."

CHAPTER 3

1 And the youth Samuel is serving Yhwh before Eli, and the word of Yhwh has been precious in those days—there is no vision breaking forth. **2** And it comes to pass, at that time, that Eli is lying down in his place, and his eyes have begun [to be] faded—he is not able to see. **3** And the lamp of God is not yet extinguished, and Samuel is lying down in the temple of Yhwh, where the Ark of God [is], **4** and Yhwh calls to Samuel, and he says, "Here I [am]." **5** And he runs to Eli and says, "Here I [am], for you have called for me"; and he says, "I did not call; turn back, lie down"; and he goes and lies down. **6** And Yhwh adds to call Samuel again, and Samuel rises and goes to Eli, and says, "Here I [am], for you have called for me"; and he says, "I have not called, my son, turn back, lie down." **7** And Samuel has not yet known Yhwh, and the word of Yhwh is not yet revealed to him. **8** And Yhwh adds to call Samuel the third time, and he rises and goes to Eli, and says, "Here I [am], for you have called for me"; and Eli understands that Yhwh is calling to the youth. **9** And Eli says to Samuel, "Go, lie down, and it has been, if He calls to you, that you have said, Speak, Yhwh, for Your servant is hearing"; and Samuel goes and lies down in his place. **10** And Yhwh comes, and stations Himself, and calls as time by time, "Samuel, Samuel"; and Samuel says, "Speak, for Your servant is hearing." **11** And Yhwh says to Samuel, "Behold, I am doing a thing in Israel, at which the two ears of everyone hearing it tingle. **12** In that day I establish to Eli all that I have spoken to his house, beginning and completing; **13** and I have declared to him that I am judging his house for all time, for the iniquity which he has known, for his sons are making themselves vile, and he has not restrained them, **14** and therefore I have sworn to the house of Eli: the iniquity of the house of Eli is not atoned for, by sacrifice, and by offering— for all time." **15** And Samuel lies until the morning, and opens the doors of the house of Yhwh, and Samuel is afraid of declaring the vision to Eli. **16** And Eli calls Samuel and says, "Samuel, my son"; and he says, "Here I [am]." **17** And he says, "What [is] the word which He has spoken to you? Please do not hide it from me; so God does to you, and so does He add, if you hide from me a word of all the words that He has spoken to you." **18** And Samuel declares to him the whole of the words, and has not hid from him; and he says, "It [is] Yhwh; that which is good in His eyes He does." **19** And Samuel grows up, and Yhwh has been with him, and has not let any of his words fall to the earth; **20** and all Israel knows, from Dan even to Beer-Sheba, that Samuel is established for a prophet to Yhwh. **21** And Yhwh adds to appear in Shiloh, for Yhwh has been revealed to Samuel, in Shiloh, by the word of Yhwh.

CHAPTER 4

1 And the word of Samuel is to all Israel, and Israel goes out to meet the Philistines for battle, and they encamp by Eben-Ezer, and the Philistines have encamped in Aphek, **2** and the Philistines set themselves in array to meet Israel, and the battle spreads itself, and Israel is struck before the Philistines, and they strike among the ranks in the field about four thousand men. **3** And the people come into the camp, and [the] elderly of Israel say, "Why has Yhwh struck us today before the Philistines? we take the Ark of the Covenant of Yhwh from Shiloh to ourselves, and it comes into our midst, and He saves us out of the hand of our enemies." **4** And the people send to Shiloh, and they take from there the Ark of the Covenant of Yhwh of Hosts, inhabiting the cherubim, and there [are] two sons of Eli with the Ark of the Covenant of God, Hophni and Phinehas. **5** And it comes to pass, at the coming in of the Ark of the Covenant of Yhwh to the camp, that all Israel shouts

[with] a great shout, and the earth is moved. **6** And the Philistines hear the noise of the shouting, and say, "What [is] the noise of this great shout in the camp of the Hebrews?" And they perceive that the Ark of Yhwh has come into the camp. **7** And the Philistines are afraid, for they said, "God has come into the camp"; and they say, "Woe to us, for there has been nothing like this before. **8** Woe to us, who delivers us out of the hand of these majestic gods? these [are] the gods who are striking the Egyptians with every plague in the wilderness. **9** Strengthen yourselves, and become men, O Philistines, lest you do service to Hebrews, as they have done to you—then you have become men, and have fought." **10** And the Philistines fight, and Israel is struck, and they each flee to his tents, and the slaughter is very great, and thirty thousand footmen of Israel fall; **11** and the Ark of God has been taken, and the two sons of Eli, Hophni and Phinehas, have died. **12** And a man of Benjamin runs out of the ranks, and comes into Shiloh, on that day, and his long robes [are] torn, and earth [is] on his head; **13** and he comes in, and behold, Eli is sitting on the throne by the side of the way, watching, for his heart has been trembling for the Ark of God, and the man has come into the city and declares [it], and all the city cries out. **14** And Eli hears the noise of the cry and says, "What [is] the noise of this tumult?" And the man hurried, and comes in, and tells Eli. **15** And Eli is a son of ninety-eight years, and his eyes have stood, and he has not been able to see. **16** And the man says to Eli, "I [am] he who has come out of the ranks, and I have fled out of the ranks today"; and he says, "What has been the matter, my son?" **17** And he who is bearing tidings answers and says, "Israel has fled before the Philistines, and also a great slaughter has been among the people, and also your two sons have died—Hophni and Phinehas—and the Ark of God has been captured." **18** And it comes to pass, at his mentioning the Ark of God, that he falls backward from off the throne, by the side of the gate, and his neck is broken, and he dies, for the man [is] old and heavy, and he has judged Israel [for] forty years. **19** And his daughter-in-law, wife of Phinehas, [is] pregnant, about to bear, and she hears the report of the taking of the Ark of God, that her father-in-law and her husband have died, and she bows, and bears, for her pains have turned on her. **20** And at the time of her death, the women who are standing by her say, "Do not fear, for you have borne a son," she has not answered, nor set her heart [to it]; **21** and she calls the youth Ichabod, saying, "Glory has removed from Israel," because of the taking of the Ark of God, and because of her father-in-law and her husband. **22** And she says, "Glory has removed from Israel, for the Ark of God has been taken."

CHAPTER 5

1 And the Philistines have taken the Ark of God, and bring it in from Eben-Ezer to Ashdod, **2** and the Philistines take the Ark of God and bring it into the house of Dagon, and set it near Dagon. **3** And the Ashdodites rise early on the next day, and behold, Dagon is fallen on its face to the earth, before the Ark of Yhwh; and they take Dagon, and put it back in its place. **4** And they rise early in the morning on the next day, and behold, Dagon is fallen on its face to the earth, before the Ark of Yhwh, and the head of Dagon, and the two palms of its hands are cut off at the threshold, only Dagon's [body] has been left of him; **5** therefore the priests of Dagon, and all those coming into the house of Dagon, do not tread on the threshold of Dagon, in Ashdod, until this day. **6** And the hand of Yhwh is heavy on the Ashdodites, and He makes them desolate, and strikes them with lumps, Ashdod and its borders. **7** And the men of Ashdod see that [it is] so, and have said, "The Ark of the God of Israel does not abide with us, for His hand has been hard on us, and on our god Dagon." **8** And they send and gather all the princes of the Philistines to them, and say, "What do we do to the Ark of the God of Israel?" And they say, "Let the Ark of the God of Israel be brought around to Gath"; and they bring around the Ark of the God of Israel; **9** and it comes to pass after they have brought it around, that the hand of Yhwh is against the city—a very great destruction; and He strikes the men of the city, from small and to great; and lumps break forth on them. **10** And they send the Ark of God to Ekron, and it comes to pass, at the coming in of the Ark of God to Ekron, that the Ekronites cry out, saying, "They have brought around the Ark of the God of Israel to us, to put us and our people to death." **11** And they send and gather all the princes of the Philistines, and say, "Send the Ark of the God of Israel away, and it turns back to its place, and it does not put us and our people to death"; for there has been a deadly destruction throughout all the city, the hand of God has been very heavy there, **12** and the men who have not died have been struck with lumps, and the cry of the city goes up into the heavens.

CHAPTER 6

1 And the Ark of Yhwh is in the field of the Philistines [for] seven months, **2** and the Philistines call for priests and for diviners, saying, "What do we do to the Ark of Yhwh? let us know with what we send it to its place." **3** And they say, "If you are sending the Ark of the God of Israel away, you do not send it away empty; for you certainly send back a guilt-offering to Him; then you are healed, and it has been known to you why His hand does not turn aside from you." **4** And they say, "What [is] the guilt-offering which we send back to Him?" And they say, "The number of the princes of the Philistines—five golden lumps, and five golden muroids—for one plague [is] to you all, and to your princes, **5** and you have made images of your lumps, and images of your muroids that are corrupting the land, and have given glory to the God of Israel; it may be [that] He lightens His hand from off you, and from off your gods, and from off your land; **6** and why do you harden your heart as the Egyptians and Pharaoh hardened their heart? do they not—when He has rolled Himself on them—send them away, and they go? **7** And now, take and make one new cart, and two suckling cows, on which a yoke has not gone up, and you have bound the cows in the cart, and caused their young ones to turn back from after them to the house, **8** and you have taken the Ark of Yhwh, and put it on the cart, and the vessels of gold which you have returned to Him—a guilt-offering—you put in a coffer on its side, and have sent it away, and it has gone; **9** and you have seen if it goes up the way of its own border, to Beth-Shemesh—He has done this great evil to us; and if not, then we have known that His hand has not come against us; it has been an accident to us." **10** And the men do so, and take two suckling cows, and bind them in the cart, and they shut up their young ones in the house; **11** and they place the Ark of Yhwh on the cart, and the coffer, and the golden muroids, and the images of their lumps. **12** And the cows go straight in the way, on the way to Beth-Shemesh, they have gone in one highway, going and lowing, and have not turned aside right or left; and the princes of the Philistines are going after them to the border of Beth-Shemesh. **13** And the Beth-Shemeshites are reaping their wheat-harvest in the valley, and they lift up their eyes, and see the Ark, and rejoice to see [it]. **14** And the cart has come into the field of Joshua the Beth-Shemeshite, and stands there, and there [is] a great stone, and they cleave the wood of the cart, and they have caused the cows to ascend [as] a burnt-offering to Yhwh. **15** And the Levites have taken down the Ark of Yhwh, and the coffer which [is] with it, in which [are] the vessels of gold, and place [them] on the great stone; and the men of Beth-Shemesh have caused burnt-offerings to ascend and sacrifice sacrifices in that day to Yhwh; **16** and the five princes of the Philistines have seen [it], and return [to] Ekron, on that day. **17** And these [are] the golden lumps which the Philistines have sent back—a guilt-offering to Yhwh: one for Ashdod, one for Gaza, one for Ashkelon, one for Gath, one for Ekron; **18** and the golden muroids—the number of all the cities of the Philistines, for the five princes, from the fortified city even to a village of the open place, and to the great stone [[or great meadow]] on which they placed the Ark of Yhwh—[are] in the field of Joshua the Beth-Shemeshite to this day. **19** And He strikes among the men of Beth-Shemesh, for they looked into the Ark of Yhwh, indeed, He strikes seventy men [out] of fifty thousand men [[or fifty thousand and seventy men]] among the people; and the people mourn, because Yhwh struck among the people [with] a great striking. **20** And the men of Beth-Shemesh say, "Who is able to stand before Yhwh, this holy God? and to whom does He go up from us?" **21** And they send messengers to the inhabitants of Kirjath-Jearim, saying, "The Philistines have sent back the Ark of Yhwh; come down, take it up with you."

CHAPTER 7

1 And the men of Kirjath-Jearim come and bring up the Ark of Yhwh, and bring it into the house of Abinadab, in the height,

and they have sanctified his son Eleazar to keep the Ark of Yhwh. **2** And it comes to pass, from the day of the dwelling of the Ark in Kirjath-Jearim, that the days are multiplied—indeed, they are twenty years—and all the house of Israel wails after Yhwh. **3** And Samuel speaks to all the house of Israel, saying, "If you are turning back to Yhwh with all your heart—turn aside the gods of the stranger from your midst, and Ashtaroth; and prepare your heart for Yhwh, and serve Him only, and He delivers you out of the hand of the Philistines." **4** And the sons of Israel turn aside the Ba'alim and Ashtaroth, and serve Yhwh alone; **5** and Samuel says, "Gather all Israel to Mizpeh, and I pray to Yhwh for you." **6** And they are gathered to Mizpeh, and draw water, and pour out before Yhwh, and fast on that day, and say there, "We have sinned against Yhwh"; and Samuel judges the sons of Israel in Mizpeh. **7** And the Philistines hear that the sons of Israel have gathered themselves to Mizpeh; and the princes of the Philistines go up against Israel, and the sons of Israel hear, and are afraid of the presence of the Philistines. **8** And the sons of Israel say to Samuel, "Do not keep silent for us from crying to our God Yhwh, and He saves us out of the hand of the Philistines." **9** And Samuel takes a fat lamb, and causes it to go up—a whole burnt-offering to Yhwh; and Samuel cries to Yhwh for Israel, and Yhwh answers him; **10** and Samuel is causing the burnt-offering to go up—and the Philistines have drawn near to battle against Israel—and Yhwh thunders with a great noise, on that day, on the Philistines, and troubles them, and they are struck before Israel. **11** And the men of Israel go out from Mizpeh, and pursue the Philistines, and strike them to the place of Beth-Car. **12** And Samuel takes a stone, and sets [it] between Mizpeh and Shen, and calls its name Eben-Ezer, saying, "Until now Yhwh has helped us." **13** And the Philistines are humbled, and have not added anymore to come into the border of Israel, and the hand of Yhwh is on the Philistines all the days of Samuel. **14** And the cities which the Philistines have taken from Israel are restored to Israel—from Ekron even to Gath—and Israel has delivered their border out of the hand of the Philistines; and there is peace between Israel and the Amorite. **15** And Samuel judges Israel all the days of his life, **16** and he has gone from year to year, and gone around Beth-El, and Gilgal, and Mizpeh, and judged Israel [in] all these places; **17** and his returning [is] to Ramath, for his house [is] there, and he has judged Israel there, and he builds an altar to Yhwh there.

CHAPTER 8

1 And it comes to pass, when Samuel [is] aged, that he makes his sons judges over Israel. **2** And the name of his firstborn son is Joel, and the name of his second Abiah, judges in Beer-Sheba: **3** and his sons have not walked in his ways, and turn aside after the dishonest gain, and take a bribe, and turn aside judgment. **4** And all [the] elderly of Israel gather themselves together, and come to Samuel at Ramath, **5** and say to him, "Behold, you have become aged, and your sons have not walked in your ways; now, appoint a king to us, to judge us, like all the nations." **6** And the thing is evil in the eyes of Samuel when they have said, "Give a king to us, to judge us"; and Samuel prays to Yhwh. **7** And Yhwh says to Samuel, "Listen to the voice of the people, to all that they say to you, for they have not rejected you, but they have rejected Me from reigning over them. **8** According to all the works that they have done from the day of My bringing them up out of Egypt, even to this day, when they forsake Me, and serve other gods—so they are also doing to you. **9** And now, listen to their voice; only, surely you certainly protest to them, and have declared to them the custom of the king who reigns over them." **10** And Samuel speaks all the words of Yhwh to the people who are asking [for] a king from him, **11** and says, "This is the custom of the king who reigns over you: he takes your sons, and has appointed for himself among his chariots, and among his horsemen, and they have run before his chariots; **12** also to appoint for himself heads of thousands, and heads of fifties; also to plow his plowing, and to reap his reaping; and to make instruments of his war, and instruments of his charioteer. **13** And he takes your daughters for perfumers, and for cooks, and for bakers; **14** and your fields, and your vineyards, and your olive-yards—he takes the best, and has given to his servants. **15** And he tithes your seed and your vineyards, and has given to his eunuchs, and to his servants. **16** And your menservants and your maidservants, and the best of your young men and your donkeys, he takes, and has prepared for his own work; **17**

he tithes your flock, and you are for servants to him. **18** And you have cried out in that day because of the king whom you have chosen for yourselves, and Yhwh does not answer you in that day." **19** And the people refuse to listen to the voice of Samuel, and say, "No, but a king is over us, **20** and we have been, even we, like all the nations; and our king has judged us, and gone out before us, and fought our battles." **21** And Samuel hears all the words of the people, and speaks them in the ears of Yhwh; **22** and Yhwh says to Samuel, "Listen to their voice, and you have caused a king to reign over them." And Samuel says to the men of Israel, "Go, each man, to his city."

CHAPTER 9

1 And there is a man of Benjamin, and his name [is] Kish, son of Abiel, son of Zeror, son of Bechorath, son of Aphiah, a Benjamite, a mighty man of valor, **2** and he has a son, and his name [is] Saul, a choice youth and handsome, and there is not a man among the sons of Israel more handsome than he—from his shoulder and upward, higher than any of the people. **3** And the donkeys of Kish, father of Saul, are lost, and Kish says to his son Saul, "Now take one of the young men with you, and rise, go, seek the donkeys." **4** And he passes over through the hill-country of Ephraim, and passes over through the land of Shalisha, and they have not found [them]; and they pass over through the land of Shaalim, and they are not; and he passes over through the land of Benjamin, and they have not found [them]. **5** They have come to the land of Zuph, and Saul has said to his young man who [is] with him, "Come, and we return, lest my father leave off from the donkeys, and has been sorrowful for us." **6** And he says to him, "Now behold, a man of God [is] in this city, and the man is honored; all that he speaks certainly comes; now, we go there, it may be he declares to us our way on which we have gone." **7** And Saul says to his young man, "And behold, we go, and what do we bring to the man? for the bread has gone from our vessels, and there is no present to bring to the man of God—what [is] with us?" **8** And the young man adds to answer Saul and says, "Behold, there is found a fourth of a shekel of silver with me: and I have given to the man of God, and he has declared our way to us." **9** Formerly in Israel, thus said the man in his going to seek God: "Come and we go to the seer." For the "prophet" of today is formerly called "the seer." **10** And Saul says to his young man, "Your word [is] good; come, we go"; and they go to the city where the man of God [is]. **11** They are going up in the ascent of the city, and have found young women going out to draw water, and say to them, "Is the seer in this [place]?" **12** And they answer them and say, "He is; behold, before you! Hurry, now, for he has come to the city today, for the people [have] a sacrifice today in a high place. **13** At your going into the city so you find him, before he goes up to the high place to eat; for the people do not eat until his coming, for he blesses the sacrifice; afterward, they who are called eat, and now, go up, for you should find him at this time." **14** And they go up to the city; they are coming into the midst of the city, and behold, Samuel is coming out to meet them, to go up to the high place; **15** and Yhwh had uncovered the ear of Samuel one day before the coming of Saul, saying, **16** "At this time tomorrow, I send to you a man out of the land of Benjamin—and you have anointed him for leader over My people Israel, and he has saved My people out of the hand of the Philistines; for I have seen My people, for its cry has come to Me." **17** When Samuel has seen Saul, then Yhwh has answered him, "Behold, the man of whom I have spoken to you; this [one] restrains My people." **18** And Saul draws near to Samuel in the midst of the gate and says, "Please declare to me where this seer's house [is]." **19** And Samuel answers Saul and says, "I [am] the seer; go up before me into the high place, and you have eaten with me today, and I have sent you away in the morning, and all that [is] in your heart I declare to you. **20** And as for the donkeys which are lost from you [for] three days as of today, do not set your heart to them, for they have been found; and to whom [is] all the desire of Israel? is it not to you and to all your father's house?" **21** And Saul answers and says, "Am I not a Benjamite—of the smallest of the tribes of Israel? and my family the least of all the families of the tribe of Benjamin? and why have you spoken to me according to this word?" **22** And Samuel takes Saul, and his young man, and brings them into the chamber, and gives a place to them at the head of those called; and they [are] about thirty men. **23** And Samuel says to the cook, "Give the portion which I gave to you, of which I said

to you, Set it by you." **24** (And the cook lifts up the leg, and that which [is] on it, and sets [it] before Saul), and he says, "Behold, that which is left; [it] is set before your face—eat, for it is kept for you for this appointed time, [at my] saying, I have called the people"; and Saul eats with Samuel on that day. **25** And they come down from the high place to the city, and he speaks with Saul on the roof. **26** And they rise early, and it comes to pass, at the ascending of the dawn, that Samuel calls to Saul, on the roof, saying, "Rise, and I send you away"; and Saul rises, and they go out, both of them—he and Samuel, outside. **27** They are going down in the extremity of the city, and Samuel has said to Saul, "Say to the young man that he should pass on before us (and he passes on), and you, stand at this time, and I cause you to hear the word of God."

CHAPTER 10

1 And Samuel takes the vial of the oil, and pours [it] on his head, and kisses him, and says, "Is it not because Yhwh has appointed you over His inheritance for leader? **2** In your going from me today—then you have found two men by the grave of Rachel, in the border of Benjamin, at Zelzah, and they have said to you, The donkeys have been found which you have gone to seek; and behold, your father has left the matter of the donkeys, and has sorrowed for you, saying, What do I do for my son? **3** And you have passed on there, and beyond, and have come to the oak of Tabor, and three men going up to God to Beth-El have found you there, one carrying three kids, and one carrying three cakes of bread, and one carrying a bottle of wine, **4** and they have asked of your welfare, and given two loaves to you, and you have received from their hand. **5** Afterward you come to the hill of God, where the garrison of the Philistines [is], and it comes to pass, at your coming in there to the city, that you have met a band of prophets coming down from the high place, and before them stringed instrument, and tambourine, and pipe, and harp, and they are prophesying; **6** and the Spirit of Yhwh has prospered over you, and you have prophesied with them, and have turned into a [new] man; **7** and it has been, when these signs come to you— do for yourself as your hand finds, for God [is] with you. **8** And you have gone down before me to Gilgal, and behold, I am going down to you, to cause burnt-offerings to ascend, to sacrifice sacrifices of peace-offerings; you wait [for] seven days until my coming to you, and I have made known to you that which you do." **9** And it has been, at his turning his shoulder to go from Samuel, that God turns to him another heart, and all these signs come on that day, **10** and they come in there to the height, and behold, a band of prophets [is there] to meet him, and the Spirit of God prospers over him, and he prophesies in their midst. **11** And it comes to pass, all knowing him before, see, and behold, he has prophesied with prophets, and the people say to one another, "What [is] this [that] has happened to the son of Kish? is Saul also among the prophets?" **12** And a man there answers and says, "And who [is] their father?" Therefore it has been for an allegory, "Is Saul also among the prophets?" **13** And he ceases from prophesying, and comes to the high place, **14** and the uncle of Saul says to him, and to his young man, "To where did you go?" And he says, "To seek the donkeys; and we see that they are not, and we come to Samuel." **15** And the uncle of Saul says, "Please declare to me what Samuel said to you." **16** And Saul says to his uncle, "He certainly declared to us that the donkeys were found"; and of the matter of the kingdom he has not declared to him that which Samuel said. **17** And Samuel calls the people to Yhwh to Mizpeh, **18** and says to the sons of Israel, "Thus said Yhwh, God of Israel: I have brought up Israel out of Egypt, and I deliver you out of the hand of the Egyptians, and out of the hand of all the kingdoms who are oppressing you; **19** and you have rejected your God today, who [is] Himself your Savior out of all your evils and your distresses, and you say, No, but you set a king over us; and now, station yourselves before Yhwh, by your tribes, and by your thousands." **20** And Samuel brings all the tribes of Israel near, and the tribe of Benjamin is captured, **21** and he brings the tribe of Benjamin near by its families, and the family of Matri is captured, and Saul son of Kish is captured, and they seek him, and he has not been found. **22** And they ask again of Yhwh, "Has the man come here yet?" And Yhwh says, "Behold, he has been hidden near the vessels." **23** And they run and bring him there, and he stationed himself in the midst of the people, and he is higher than any of the people from his shoulder and upward. **24** And Samuel says to all the people,

"Have you seen him on whom Yhwh has fixed, for there is none like him among all the people?" And all the people shout, and say, "Let the king live!" ²⁵ And Samuel speaks to the people the right of the kingdom, and writes in a scroll, and places [it] before Yhwh; and Samuel sends all the people away, each to his house. ²⁶ And Saul has also gone to his house, to Gibeah, and the force goes with him whose heart God has touched; ²⁷ and the sons of worthlessness have said, "How can this one save us?" And they despise him, and have not brought a present to him; and he is as one being deaf.

CHAPTER 11

¹ And Nahash the Ammonite comes up, and encamps against Jabesh-Gilead, and all the men of Jabesh say to Nahash, "Make a covenant with us, and we serve you." ² And Nahash the Ammonite says to them, "For this I cut [a covenant] with you, in picking out every right eye of yours—and I have set it [for] a reproach on all Israel." ³ And [the] elderly of Jabesh say to him, "Leave us alone [for] seven days, and we send messengers into all the border of Israel: and if there is none saving us—then we have come out to you." ⁴ And the messengers come to Gibeah of Saul, and speak the words in the ears of the people, and all the people lift up their voice and weep; ⁵ and behold, Saul has come out of the field after the herd, and Saul says, "What [is that] to the people, that they weep?" And they recount the words of the men of Jabesh to him. ⁶ And the Spirit of God prospers over Saul, in his hearing these words, and his anger burns greatly, ⁷ and he takes a couple of oxen, and cuts them in pieces, and sends [them] through all the border of Israel, by the hand of the messengers, saying, "He who is not coming out after Saul and after Samuel—thus it is done to his oxen"; and the fear of Yhwh falls on the people, and they come out as one man. ⁸ And he inspects them in Bezek, and the sons of Israel are three hundred thousand, and the men of Judah thirty thousand. ⁹ And they say to the messengers who are coming, "Thus you say to the men of Jabesh-Gilead: Tomorrow you have safety—by the heat of the sun"; and the messengers come and declare [it] to the men of Jabesh, and they rejoice; ¹⁰ and the men of Jabesh say [to the Ammonites], "Tomorrow we come out to you, and you have done to us according to all that [is] good in your eyes." ¹¹ And it comes to pass, on the next day, that Saul puts the people in three detachments, and they come into the midst of the camp in the morning-watch, and strike Ammon until the heat of the day; and it comes to pass that those left are scattered, and there have not been left two of them together. ¹² And the people say to Samuel, "Who is he that says, Saul reigns over us? give up the men, and we put them to death." ¹³ And Saul says, "There is no man put to death on this day, for today Yhwh has worked salvation in Israel." ¹⁴ And Samuel says to the people, "Come and we go to Gilgal, and renew the kingdom there"; ¹⁵ and all the people go to Gilgal, and cause Saul to reign there before Yhwh in Gilgal, and sacrifice sacrifices of peace-offerings there before Yhwh, and Saul rejoices there—and all the men of Israel—very greatly.

CHAPTER 12

¹ And Samuel says to all Israel, "Behold, I have listened to your voice, to all that you said to me, and I cause a king to reign over you, ² and now, behold, the king is habitually walking before you, and I have become aged and gray-headed, and my sons, behold, they [are] with you, and I have habitually walked before you from my youth until this day. ³ Behold, here I [am]; testify against me before Yhwh, and before His anointed; whose ox have I taken, and whose donkey have I taken, and whom have I oppressed; whom have I bruised, and of whose hand have I taken a ransom, and hide my eyes with it? And I restore [it] to you." ⁴ And they say, "You have not oppressed us, nor have you crushed us, nor have you taken anything from the hand of anyone." ⁵ And he says to them, "Yhwh [is] a witness against you, and His anointed [is] a witness this day, that you have not found anything in my hand"; and they say, "A witness." ⁶ And Samuel says to the people, "Yhwh [is] He who made Moses and Aaron, and who brought up your fathers out of the land of Egypt! ⁷ and now, station yourselves, and I judge you before Yhwh, with all the righteous acts of Yhwh, which He did with you, and with your

fathers. ⁸ When Jacob has come to Egypt, and your fathers cry to Yhwh, then Yhwh sends Moses and Aaron, and they bring out your fathers from Egypt, and cause them to dwell in this place, ⁹ and they forget their God Yhwh, and He sells them into the hand of Sisera, head of the host of Hazor, and into the hand of the Philistines, and into the hand of the king of Moab, and they fight against them, ¹⁰ and they cry to Yhwh, and say, We have sinned, because we have forsaken Yhwh, and serve the Ba'alim, and Ashtaroth, and now, deliver us out of the hand of our enemies, and we serve You. ¹¹ And Yhwh sends Jerubba'al, and Bedan, and Jephthah, and Samuel, and delivers you out of the hand of your surrounding enemies, and you dwell confidently. ¹² And you see that Nahash king of the sons of Ammon has come against you, and you say to me, No, but a king reigns over us; and your God Yhwh [is] your king! ¹³ And now, behold the king whom you have chosen—whom you have asked for! And behold, Yhwh has placed a king over you. ¹⁴ If you fear Yhwh, and have served Him, and listened to His voice, then you do not provoke the mouth of Yhwh, and you have been—both you and the king who has reigned over you—after your God Yhwh. ¹⁵ And if you do not listen to the voice of Yhwh—then you have provoked the mouth of Yhwh, and the hand of Yhwh has been against you, and against your fathers. ¹⁶ Also now, station yourselves and see this great thing which Yhwh is doing before your eyes; ¹⁷ is it not wheat-harvest today? I call to Yhwh, and He gives voices and rain; and know and see that your evil is great which you have done in the eyes of Yhwh, to ask [for] a king for yourselves." ¹⁸ And Samuel calls to Yhwh, and Yhwh gives voices and rain on that day, and all the people greatly fear Yhwh and Samuel; ¹⁹ and all the people say to Samuel, "Pray for your servants to your God Yhwh, and we do not die, for we have added evil to all our sins to ask [for] a king for ourselves." ²⁰ And Samuel says to the people, "Do not fear; you have done all this evil; only, do not turn aside from after Yhwh—and you have served Yhwh with all your heart, ²¹ and you do not turn aside after the vain things which do not profit nor deliver, for they [are] vain, ²² for Yhwh does not leave His people, on account of His great Name; for Yhwh has been pleased to make you for a people to Him. ²³ I, also, far be it from me to sin against Yhwh, by ceasing to pray for you, and I have directed you in the good and upright way; ²⁴ only, fear Yhwh, and you have served Him in truth with all your heart, for see that which He has made great with you; ²⁵ and if you really do evil, both you and your king are consumed."

CHAPTER 13

¹ Saul [is] a son of [[thirty]] years in his reigning, and he has reigned over Israel [forty]-two years, ² then Saul chooses for himself three thousand [men] out of Israel; and two thousand are with Saul in Michmash, and in the hill-country of Beth-El; and one thousand have been with Jonathan in Gibeah of Benjamin; and he has sent each one of the remnant of the people to his tents. ³ And Jonathan strikes the garrison of the Philistines which [is] in Geba, and the Philistines hear, and Saul has blown with a horn through all the land, saying, "Let the Hebrews hear." ⁴ And all Israel have heard, saying, "Saul has struck the garrison of the Philistines," and also, "Israel has been abhorred by the Philistines"; and the people are called after Saul to Gilgal. ⁵ And the Philistines have been gathered to fight with Israel; thirty thousand chariots, and six thousand horsemen, and a people as the sand which [is] on the seashore for multitude; and they come up and encamp in Michmash, east of Beth-Aven. ⁶ And the men of Israel have seen that they are distressed, that the people have been oppressed, and the people hide themselves in caves, and in thickets, and in rocks, and in high places, and in pits. ⁷ And Hebrews have passed over the Jordan to the land of Gad and Gilead; and Saul [is] yet in Gilgal, and all the people have trembled after him. ⁸ And he waits seven days, according to the appointment with Samuel, and Samuel has not come to Gilgal, and the people are scattered from off him. ⁹ And Saul says, "Bring the burnt-offering and the peace-offerings near to me"; and he causes the burnt-offering to ascend. ¹⁰ And it comes to pass at his completing to cause the burnt-offering to ascend, that behold, Samuel has come, and Saul goes out to meet him, to bless him; ¹¹ and Samuel says, "What have you done?" And Saul says, "Because I saw that the people were scattered from off me, and you had not come at the appointment of the days, and the Philistines are gathered to Michmash, ¹² and I say, Now the Philistines come down to me to Gilgal, and I have not appeased

the face of Yhwh; and I force myself, and cause the burnt-offering to ascend." **13** And Samuel says to Saul, "You have been foolish; you have not kept the command of your God Yhwh, which He commanded you, for now Yhwh had established your kingdom over Israel for all time; **14** and now, your kingdom does not stand, Yhwh has sought [for] a man for Himself according to His own heart, and Yhwh charges him for leader over His people, for you have not kept that which Yhwh commanded you." **15** And Samuel rises, and goes up from Gilgal to Gibeah of Benjamin; and Saul inspects the people who are found with him, about six hundred men, **16** and Saul, and his son Jonathan, and the people who are found with them, are abiding in Gibeah of Benjamin, and the Philistines have encamped in Michmash. **17** And the destroyer goes out from the camp of the Philistines—three detachments: one detachment turns to the way of Ophrah, to the land of Shual, **18** and one detachment turns the way of Beth-Horon, and one detachment turns the way of the border which is looking on the Valley of the Zeboim, toward the wilderness. **19** And a craftsman is not found in all the land of Israel, for the Philistines said, "Lest the Hebrews make sword or spear"; **20** and all Israel goes down to the Philistines, to each sharpen his plowshare, and his coulter, and his axe, and his mattock; **21** and there has been the file for mattocks, and for coulters, and for three-pronged rakes, and for the axes, and to set up the goads. **22** And it has been, in the day of battle, that there has not been found a sword and spear in the hand of any of the people who [are] with Saul and with Jonathan—but it is found with Saul and with his son Jonathan. **23** And the station of the Philistines goes out to the passage of Michmash.

CHAPTER 14

1 And the day comes that Jonathan son of Saul says to the young man carrying his weapons, "Come, and we pass over to the station of the Philistines, which [is] on the other side of this"; and he has not declared [it] to his father. **2** And Saul is abiding at the extremity of Gibeah, under the pomegranate which [is] in Migron, and the people who [are] with him [are] about six hundred men, **3** and Ahiah, son of Ahitub, brother of Ichabod, son of Phinehas son of Eli priest of Yhwh in Shiloh, [was] bearing an ephod; and the people did not know that Jonathan has gone. **4** And between the passages where Jonathan sought to pass over to the station of the Philistines [is] the edge of a rock on one side, and the edge of a rock on the other side, and the name of one is Bozez, and the name of the other Seneh. **5** One edge [is] fixed on the north in front of Michmash, and the one on the south in front of Gibeah. **6** And Jonathan says to the young man carrying his weapons, "Come, and we pass over to the station of these uncircumcised; it may be Yhwh works for us, for there is no restraint to Yhwh to save by many or by few." **7** And the bearer of his weapons says to him, "Do all that [is] in your heart; turn for yourself; behold, I [am] with you, as your own heart." **8** And Jonathan says, "Behold, we are passing over to the men, and are revealed to them; **9** if they thus say to us, Stand still until we have come to you, then we have stood in our place, and do not go up to them; **10** and if they thus say, Come up against us, then we have gone up, for Yhwh has given them into our hand, and this [is] the sign to us." **11** And both of them are revealed to the station of the Philistines, and the Philistines say, "Behold, Hebrews are coming out of the holes where they have hid themselves." **12** And the men of the station answer Jonathan, and the bearer of his weapons, and say, "Come up to us, and we cause you to know something." And Jonathan says to the bearer of his weapons, "Come up after me, for Yhwh has given them into the hand of Israel." **13** And Jonathan goes up on his hands, and on his feet, and the bearer of his weapons after him; and they fall before Jonathan, and the bearer of his weapons is putting [them] to death after him. **14** And the first striking which Jonathan and the bearer of his weapons have struck is of about twenty men, in about half a furrow of a yoke of a field, **15** and there is a trembling in the camp, in the field, and among all the people, the station and the destroyers have trembled—even they, and the earth shakes, and it becomes a trembling of God. **16** And the watchmen of Saul in Gibeah of Benjamin see, and behold, the multitude has melted away, and it goes on, and is beaten down. **17** And Saul says to the people who [are] with him, "Now inspect and see; who has gone from us?" And they inspect, and behold, Jonathan and the bearer of his weapons are not. **18** And Saul says to Ahiah, "Bring the Ark

of God near"; for the Ark of God has been with the sons of Israel on that day. **19** And it comes to pass, while Saul spoke to the priest, that the noise which [is] in the camp of the Philistines goes on, going on and becoming great, and Saul says to the priest, "Remove your hand." **20** And Saul is called, and all the people who [are] with him, and they come to the battle, and behold, the sword of each has been against his neighbor—a very great destruction. **21** And the Hebrews [who] have been with the Philistines before the day prior, who had gone up with them into the camp, have turned around, even they, to be with Israel who [are] with Saul and Jonathan, **22** and all the men of Israel, who are hiding themselves in the hill-country of Ephraim, have heard that the Philistines have fled, and they pursue—even they—after them in battle. **23** And Yhwh saves Israel on that day, and the battle has passed over to Beth-Aven. **24** And the men of Israel have been distressed on that day, and Saul adjures the people, saying, "Cursed [is] the man who eats food until the evening, and I have been avenged of my enemies"; and none of the people have tasted food. **25** And all [those of] the land have come into a forest, and there is honey on the face of the field; **26** and the people come into the forest, and behold, the honey dropped, and none is moving his hand to his mouth, for the people feared the oath. **27** And Jonathan has not heard of his father's adjuring the people, and puts forth the end of the rod, which [is] in his hand, and dips it in the honeycomb, and brings back his hand to his mouth—and his eyes see! **28** And a man of the people answers and says, "Your father certainly adjured the people, saying, Cursed [is] the man who eats food today; and the people are weary." **29** And Jonathan says, "My father has troubled the land; now see that my eyes have become bright because I tasted a little of this honey. **30** How much more if the people had well eaten today of the spoil of its enemies which it has found, for now the striking has not been great among the Philistines." **31** And they strike on that day among the Philistines from Michmash to Aijalon, and the people are very weary, **32** and the people make toward the spoil, and take sheep, and oxen, and sons of the herd, and slaughter on the earth, and the people eat with the blood. **33** And they declare to Saul, saying, "Behold, the people are sinning against Yhwh, to eat with the blood." And he says, "You have dealt treacherously, roll a great stone to me today." **34** And Saul says, "Be scattered among the people, and you have said to them: Each bring his ox to me, and each his sheep; and you have slain [them] in this place, and eaten, and you do not sin against Yhwh to eat with the blood." And all the people bring [them]—each one [with] his ox in his hand, that night—and slaughter [them] there. **35** And Saul builds an altar to Yhwh; with it he has begun to build altars to Yhwh. **36** And Saul says, "Let us go down after the Philistines by night, and we prey on them until the morning light, and do not leave a man of them." And they say, "Do all that is good in your eyes." And the priest says, "Let us draw near to God here." **37** And Saul asks of God, "Do I go down after the Philistines? do You give them into the hand of Israel?" And He has not answered him on that day. **38** And Saul says, "Everyone draw near here, the chiefs of the people, and know and see in what this sin has been today; **39** for Yhwh lives, who is saving Israel: surely if it is in my son Jonathan, surely he certainly dies"; and none is answering him out of all the people. **40** And he says to all Israel, "You are on one side, and I and my son Jonathan are on another side"; and the people say to Saul, "Do that which is good in your eyes." **41** And Saul says to Yhwh, God of Israel, "Give perfection"; and Jonathan and Saul are captured, and the people went out. **42** And Saul says, "Cast between me and my son Jonathan"; and Jonathan is captured. **43** And Saul says to Jonathan, "Declare to me, what have you done?" And Jonathan declares to him and says, "I certainly tasted a little honey with the end of the rod that [is] in my hand; behold, I die!" **44** And Saul says, "Thus God does, and thus does He add, for you certainly die, Jonathan." **45** And the people say to Saul, "Does Jonathan die who worked this great salvation in Israel? Certainly not! Yhwh lives, if there falls to the earth [even one] hair from his head, for with God he has worked this day"; and the people rescue Jonathan, and he has not died. **46** And Saul goes up from after the Philistines, and the Philistines have gone to their place; **47** and Saul captured the kingdom over Israel, and he fights all around against all his enemies, against Moab, and against the sons of Ammon, and against Edom, and against the kings of Zobah, and against the Philistines, and wherever he turns he distresses [them]. **48** And he makes a force, and strikes Amalek, and delivers Israel out of the hand of its spoiler. **49** And the sons of Saul are Jonathan, and Ishui, and Melchi-

Shua; as for the name of his two daughters, the name of the firstborn [is] Merab, and the name of the younger Michal; **50** and the name of the wife of Saul [is] Ahinoam, daughter of Ahimaaz; and the name of the head of his host [is] Abner son of Ner, uncle of Saul; **51** and Kish [is] the father of Saul, and Ner, the father of Abner, [is] the son of Ahiel. **52** And the war is severe against the Philistines all the days of Saul; when Saul has seen any mighty man, and any son of valor, then he gathers him to himself.

CHAPTER 15

1 And Samuel says to Saul, "Yhwh sent me to anoint you for king over His people, over Israel; and now, listen to the voice of the words of Yhwh. **2** Thus said Yhwh of Hosts: I have looked after that which Amalek did to Israel, that which he laid for him in the way in his going up out of Egypt. **3** Now go, and you have struck Amalek, and devoted all that he has, and you have no pity on him, and have put to death from man to woman, from infant to suckling, from ox to sheep, from camel to donkey." **4** And Saul summons the people, and inspects them in Telaim, two hundred thousand footmen, and ten thousand [are] men of Judah. **5** And Saul comes to a city of Amalek, and lays wait in a valley; **6** and Saul says to the Kenite, "Go, turn aside, go down from the midst of Amalek, lest I consume you with it, and you did kindness with all the sons of Israel, in their going up out of Egypt"; and the Kenite turns aside from the midst of Amalek. **7** And Saul strikes Amalek from Havilah [to] your going to Shur, which [is] on the front of Egypt, **8** and he catches Agag king of Amalek alive, and he has devoted all the people by the mouth of the sword; **9** and Saul has pity—also the people—on Agag, and on the best of the flock, and of the herd, and of the seconds, and on the lambs, and on all that [is] good, and have not been willing to devote them; and all the work, despised and wasted—it they devoted. **10** And the word of Yhwh is to Samuel, saying—**11** "I have regretted that I caused Saul to reign for king, for he has turned back from after Me, and he has not performed My words"; and it is displeasing to Samuel, and he cries to Yhwh all the night. **12** And Samuel rises early to meet Saul in the morning, and it is declared to Samuel, saying, "Saul has come to Carmel, and behold, he is setting up a monument to himself, and goes around, and passes over, and goes down to Gilgal." **13** And Samuel comes to Saul, and Saul says to him, "Blessed [are] you of Yhwh; I have performed the word of Yhwh." **14** And Samuel says, "And what [is] the noise of this flock in my ears—and the noise of the herd which I am hearing?" **15** And Saul says, "They have brought them from Amalek, because the people had pity on the best of the flock, and of the herd, in order to sacrifice to your God Yhwh, and we have devoted the remnant." **16** And Samuel says to Saul, "Desist, and I declare to you that which Yhwh has spoken to me tonight"; and he says to him, "Speak." **17** And Samuel says, "Are you not, if you [are] little in your own eyes, head of the tribes of Israel? and Yhwh anoints you for king over Israel, **18** and Yhwh sends you in the way, and says, Go, and you have devoted the sinners, the Amalekite, and fought against them until they are consumed; **19** and why have you not listened to the voice of Yhwh—and fly to the spoil, and do evil in the eyes of Yhwh?" **20** And Saul says to Samuel, "Because—I have listened to the voice of Yhwh, and I go in the way which Yhwh has sent me, and bring in Agag king of Amalek, and I have devoted Amalek; **21** and the people take of the spoil of the flock and herd, the first part of the devoted thing, for sacrifice to your God Yhwh in Gilgal." **22** And Samuel says, "Has Yhwh had delight in burnt-offerings and sacrifices as [in] listening to the voice of Yhwh? behold, listening is better than sacrifice; to give attention than fat of rams; **23** for rebellion [is as] a sin of divination, and stubbornness [is as] iniquity and teraphim; because you have rejected the word of Yhwh, He also rejects you from [being] king." **24** And Saul says to Samuel, "I have sinned, for I passed over the command of Yhwh, and your words; because I have feared the people, I also listen to their voice; **25** and now, please bear with my sin, and return with me, and I bow myself to Yhwh." **26** And Samuel says to Saul, "I do not return with you; for you have rejected the word of Yhwh, and Yhwh rejects you from being king over Israel." **27** And Samuel turns around to go, and he lays hold on the skirt of his upper robe—and it is torn! **28** And Samuel says to him, "Yhwh has torn the kingdom of Israel from you today, and given it to your neighbor who is better than you; **29** and also, the Preeminence of Israel does not lie nor relent, for He [is] not a man that He should relent." **30** And he says, "I have sinned; now please honor me before [the] elderly of my people and before Israel, and return with me; and I have bowed myself to your God Yhwh." **31** And Samuel turns back after Saul, and Saul bows himself to Yhwh; **32** and Samuel says, "Bring Agag king of Amalek to me," and Agag comes to him daintily, and Agag says, "Surely the bitterness of death has turned aside." **33** And Samuel says, "As your sword bereaved women—so is your mother bereaved above women"; and Samuel hews Agag in pieces before Yhwh in Gilgal. **34** And Samuel goes to Ramath, and Saul has gone to his house—to Gibeah of Saul. **35** And Samuel has not added to see Saul until the day of his death, for Samuel mourned for Saul, and Yhwh regretted that He had caused Saul to reign over Israel.

CHAPTER 16

1 And Yhwh says to Samuel, "Until when are you mourning for Saul, and I have rejected him from reigning over Israel? fill your horn with oil and go, I send you to Jesse the Beth-Lehemite, for I have seen among his sons a king for Myself." **2** And Samuel says, "How do I go? when Saul has heard, then he has slain me." And Yhwh says, "You take a heifer of the herd in your hand, and have said, I have come to sacrifice to Yhwh; **3** and you have called for Jesse in the sacrifice, and I cause you to know that which you do, and you have anointed for Me him of whom I speak to you." **4** And Samuel does that which Yhwh has spoken, and comes to Beth-Lehem, and [the] elderly of the city tremble to meet him, and [one] says, "Is your coming peace?" **5** and he says, "Peace; I have come to sacrifice to Yhwh, sanctify yourselves, and you have come in with me to the sacrifice"; and he sanctifies Jesse and his sons, and calls them to the sacrifice. **6** And it comes to pass, in their coming in, that he sees Eliab and says, "Surely His anointed [is] here before Yhwh." **7** And Yhwh says to Samuel, "Do not look at his appearance, and at the height of his stature, for I have rejected him; for [it is] not as man sees—for man looks at the eyes, and Yhwh looks at the heart." **8** And Jesse calls to Abinadab, and causes him to pass by before Samuel; and he says, "Indeed, Yhwh has not fixed on this [one]." **9** And Jesse causes Shammah to pass by, and he says, "Indeed, Yhwh has not fixed on this [one]." **10** And Jesse causes seven of his sons to pass by before Samuel, and Samuel says to Jesse, "Yhwh has not fixed on these." **11** And Samuel says to Jesse, "Are the young men finished?" And he says, "Yet the youngest has been left; and behold, he delights himself among the flock"; and Samuel says to Jesse, "Send and take him, for we do not turn around until his coming in here." **12** And he sends, and brings him in, and he [is] ruddy, with beautiful eyes, and of good appearance; and Yhwh says, "Rise, anoint him, for this [is] he." **13** And Samuel takes the horn of oil, and anoints him in the midst of his brothers, and the Spirit of Yhwh prospers over David from that day and onward; and Samuel rises and goes to Ramath. **14** And the Spirit of Yhwh turned aside from Saul, and a spirit of sadness from Yhwh terrified him; **15** and the servants of Saul say to him, "Now behold, a spirit of sadness [from] God is terrifying you; **16** now let our lord command your servants before you [that] they seek a skillful man playing on a harp, and it has come to pass, in the spirit of sadness [from] God being on you, that he has played with his hand and [it is] well with you." **17** And Saul says to his servants, "Now provide for me a man playing well—then you have brought [him] to me." **18** And one of the servants answers and says, "Behold, I have seen a son of Jesse the Beth-Lehemite, skillful in playing, and a mighty, virtuous man, and a man of battle, and intelligent in word, and a man of form, and Yhwh [is] with him." **19** And Saul sends messengers to Jesse and says, "Send to me your son David, who [is] with the flock." **20** And Jesse takes a donkey, bread, and a bottle of wine, and one kid of the goats, and sends [them] by the hand of his son David to Saul. **21** And David comes to Saul, and stands before him, and he loves him greatly; and he is a bearer of his weapons. **22** And Saul sends to Jesse, saying, "Please let David stand before me, for he has found grace in my eyes." **23** And it has come to pass, in the spirit of [sadness from] God being on Saul, that David has taken the harp, and played with his hand, and Saul has refreshment and gladness, and the spirit of sadness has turned aside from off him.

CHAPTER 17

¹ And the Philistines gather their camps to battle, and are gathered to Shochoh, which [is] to Judah, and encamp between Shochoh and Azekah, in Ephes-Dammim; ² and Saul and the men of Israel have been gathered, and encamp by the Valley of Elah, and set in array [for] battle to meet the Philistines. ³ And the Philistines are standing on the mountain on this [side], and Israel is standing on the mountain on that [side], and the valley [is] between them. ⁴ And a man goes out, the champion from the camps of the Philistines, his name [is] Goliath, from Gath; his height [is] six cubits and a span [[or four cubits and a span]], ⁵ and a helmet of bronze [is] on his head, and he is clothed [with] a scaled coat of mail, and the weight of the coat of mail [is] five thousand shekels of bronze, ⁶ and a frontlet of bronze [is] on his feet, and a javelin of bronze between his shoulders, ⁷ and the wood of his spear [is] like a weavers' beam, and the flame of his spear [is] six hundred shekels of iron, and the bearer of the buckler is going before him. ⁸ And he stands and calls to the ranks of Israel, and says to them, "Why do you come out to set in array for battle? [Am] I not the Philistine, and you the servants of Saul? choose a man for yourselves, and let him come down to me; ⁹ if he is able to fight with me, and has struck me, then we have been for servants to you; and if I prevail against him, and have struck him, then you have been for servants to us, and have served us." ¹⁰ And the Philistine says, "I have reproached the ranks of Israel this day; give a man to me and we fight together!" ¹¹ And Saul hears—and all Israel—these words of the Philistine, and they are broken down and greatly afraid. ¹² And David [is] son of this Ephraimite of Beth-Lehem-Judah, whose name [is] Jesse, and he has eight sons, and the man has become aged among men in the days of Saul; ¹³ and the three eldest sons of Jesse go, they have gone after Saul to battle; and the name of his three sons who have gone into battle [are] Eliab the firstborn, and his second Abinadab, and the third Shammah. ¹⁴ And David is the youngest, and the three eldest have gone after Saul, ¹⁵ and David is going and returning from Saul, to feed the flock of his father at Beth-Lehem. ¹⁶ And the Philistine draws near, morning and evening, and stations himself [for] forty days. ¹⁷ And Jesse says to his son David, "Now take an ephah of this roasted [grain] and these ten loaves for your brothers, and run to the camp to your brothers; ¹⁸ and take these ten cuttings of the cheese to the head of the one thousand, and inspect your brothers for welfare, and receive their pledge." ¹⁹ And Saul, and they, and all the men of Israel, [are] in the Valley of Elah, fighting with the Philistines. ²⁰ And David rises early in the morning, and leaves the flock to a keeper, and lifts up, and goes, as Jesse commanded him, and he comes to the path, and to the force which is going out to the rank, and they have shouted for battle; ²¹ and Israel and the Philistines set in array rank to meet rank. ²² And David lets down the goods from off him on the hand of a keeper of the goods, and runs into the rank, and comes and asks of his brothers of [their] welfare. ²³ And he is speaking with them, and behold, a man, the champion, is coming up, his name [is] Goliath the Philistine, from Gath, out of the ranks of the Philistines, and he speaks according to those words, and David hears; ²⁴ and all the men of Israel, when they see the man, flee from his presence, and are greatly afraid. ²⁵ And the men of Israel say, "Have you seen this man who is coming up? For he is coming up to reproach Israel, and it has been—the man who strikes him, the king enriches him with great riches, and he gives his daughter to him, and makes his father's house free in Israel." ²⁶ And David speaks to the men who are standing by him, saying, "What is done to the man who strikes this Philistine, and has turned aside reproach from Israel? for who [is] this uncircumcised Philistine that he has reproached the ranks of the living God?" ²⁷ And the people speak to him according to this word, saying, "Thus it is done to the man who strikes him." ²⁸ And Eliab, his eldest brother, hears when he speaks to the men, and the anger of Eliab burns against David, and he says, "Why [is] this—[that] you have come down? and to whom have you left those few sheep in the wilderness? I have known your pride, and the evil of your heart—for you have come down to see the battle." ²⁹ And David says, "What have I done now? is it not a word?" ³⁰ And he turns around from him to another, and says according to this word, and the people return him word as the first word. ³¹ And the words which David has spoken are heard, and they declare [them] before Saul, and he receives him; ³² and David says to Saul, "Let no man's heart fall because of him, your servant goes, and has fought with this Philistine." ³³

And Saul says to David, "You are not able to go to this Philistine, to fight with him, for you [are] a youth, and he [has been] a man of war from his youth." ³⁴ And David says to Saul, "Your servant has been a shepherd among the sheep for his father, and the lion has come—and the bear—and has taken away a sheep out of the drove, ³⁵ and I have gone out after him, and struck him, and delivered [it] out of his mouth, and he rises against me, and I have taken hold on his beard, and struck him, and put him to death. ³⁶ Your servant has struck both the lion and the bear, and this uncircumcised Philistine has been as one of them, for he has reproached the ranks of the living God." ³⁷ And David says, "Yhwh, who delivered me out of the paw of the lion, and out of the paw of the bear, He delivers me from the hand of this Philistine." And Saul says to David, "Go, and Yhwh is with you." ³⁸ And Saul clothes David with his long robe, and has put a helmet of bronze on his head, and clothes him with a coat of mail. ³⁹ And David girded his sword above his long robe, and begins to go, for he has not tried [it]; and David says to Saul, "I am not able to go with these, for I had not tried"; and David turns them aside from off him. ⁴⁰ And he takes his staff in his hand, and chooses five smooth stones for himself from the brook, and puts them in the shepherds' vessel that he has, even in the leather pouch, and his sling [is] in his hand, and he draws near to the Philistine. ⁴¹ And the Philistine goes on, going and drawing near to David, and the man carrying the buckler [is] before him, ⁴² and the Philistine looks attentively, and sees David, and despises him, for he was a youth, and ruddy, with a handsome appearance. ⁴³ And the Philistine says to David, "Am I a dog that you are coming to me with sticks?" And the Philistine reviles David by his gods, ⁴⁴ and the Philistine says to David, "Come to me, and I give your flesh to the bird of the heavens, and to the beast of the field." ⁴⁵ And David says to the Philistine, "You are coming to me with sword, and with spear, and with buckler, and I am coming to you in the Name of Yhwh of Hosts, God of the ranks of Israel, which you have reproached! ⁴⁶ This day Yhwh shuts you up into my hand—and I have struck you, and turned aside your head from off you, and given the carcass of the camp of the Philistines this day to the bird of the heavens, and to the beast of the earth, and all the earth knows that God is for Israel! ⁴⁷ and all this assembly knows that Yhwh does not save by sword and by spear, for the battle [is] Yhwh's, and He has given you into our hand." ⁴⁸ And it has come to pass, that the Philistine has risen, and goes, and draws near to meet David, and David hurries and runs to the rank to meet the Philistine, ⁴⁹ and David puts forth his hand into the vessel, and takes a stone from there, and slings, and strikes the Philistine on his forehead, and the stone sinks into his forehead, and he falls on his face to the earth. ⁵⁰ And David is stronger than the Philistine with a sling and with a stone, and strikes the Philistine, and puts him to death, and there is no sword in the hand of David, ⁵¹ and David runs and stands over the Philistine, and takes his sword, and draws it out of its sheath, and puts him to death, and cuts off his head with it; and the Philistines see that their hero [is] dead, and flee. ⁵² And the men of Israel rise—also Judah—and shout, and pursue the Philistines until you enter the valley, and to the gates of Ekron, and the wounded of the Philistines fall in the way of Shaaraim, even to Gath, and to Ekron, ⁵³ and the sons of Israel return from burning after the Philistines, and spoil their camps. ⁵⁴ And David takes the head of the Philistine, and brings it to Jerusalem, and he has put his weapons in his own tent. ⁵⁵ And when Saul sees David going out to meet the Philistine, he has said to Abner, head of the host, "Whose son [is] this—the youth, Abner?" And Abner says, "Your soul lives, O king, I have not known." ⁵⁶ And the king says, "Ask whose son this [is]—the young man." ⁵⁷ And when David turns back from striking the Philistine, then Abner takes him and brings him in before Saul, and the head of the Philistine [is] in his hand; ⁵⁸ and Saul says to him, "Whose son [are] you, O youth?" And David says, "Son of your servant Jesse, the Beth-Lehemite."

CHAPTER 18

¹ And it comes to pass, when he finishes to speak to Saul, that the soul of Jonathan has been bound to the soul of David, and Jonathan loves him as his own soul. ² And Saul takes him on that day, and has not permitted him to return to the house of his father. ³ And Jonathan makes—David also—a covenant, because he loves him as his own soul, ⁴ and Jonathan strips himself of the upper robe which [is] on him, and gives it to

David, and his long robe, even to his sword, and to his bow, and to his girdle. **5** And David goes out wherever Saul sends him; he acted wisely, and Saul sets him over the men of war, and it is good in the eyes of all the people, and also in the eyes of the servants of Saul. **6** And it comes to pass, in their coming in, in David's returning from striking the Philistine, that the women come out from all the cities of Israel to sing—also the dancers—to meet Saul the king, with tambourines, with joy, and with three-stringed instruments; **7** and the women answer—those playing, and say, "Saul has struck among his thousands, || And David among his myriads." **8** And it is exceedingly displeasing to Saul, and this thing is evil in his eyes, and he says, "They have given myriads to David, and they have given the thousands to me, and what more [is there] for him but the kingdom?" **9** And Saul is eyeing David from that day and from then on. **10** And it comes to pass, on the next day, that the spirit of sadness [from] God prospers over Saul, and he prophesies in the midst of the house, and David is playing with his hand, as [he did] day by day, and the javelin [is] in the hand of Saul, **11** and Saul casts the javelin and says, "I strike through David, even through the wall"; and David turns around out of his presence twice. **12** And Saul is afraid of the presence of David, for Yhwh has been with him, and He has turned aside from Saul; **13** and Saul turns him aside from him, and appoints him to himself [for] head of one thousand, and he goes out and comes in, before the people. **14** And David is acting wisely in all his ways, and Yhwh [is] with him, **15** and Saul sees that he is acting very wisely, and is afraid of him, **16** and all Israel and Judah love David when he is going out and coming in before them. **17** And Saul says to David, "Behold, my elder daughter Merab—I give her to you for a wife; only, be for a son of valor to me, and fight the battles of Yhwh"; and Saul said, "Do not let my hand be on him, but let the hand of the Philistines be on him." **18** And David says to Saul, "Who [am] I? and what [is] my life—the family of my father in Israel—that I am son-in-law of the king?" **19** And it comes to pass, at the time of the giving of Merab daughter of Saul to David, that she has been given to Adriel the Meholathite for a wife. **20** And Michal daughter of Saul loves David, and they declare [it] to Saul, and the thing is right in his eyes, **21** and Saul says, "I give her to him, and she is for a snare to him, and the hand of the Philistines is on him"; and Saul says to David, "By the second—you become my son-in-law today." **22** And Saul commands his servants, "Speak to David gently, saying, Behold, the king has delighted in you, and all his servants have loved you, and now, be son-in-law of the king." **23** And the servants of Saul speak these words in the ears of David, and David says, "Is it a light thing in your eyes to be son-in-law of the king—and I a poor man, and lightly esteemed?" **24** And the servants of Saul declare [it] to him, saying, "David has spoken according to these words." **25** And Saul says, "Thus you say to David, There is no delight for the king in dowry, but in one hundred foreskins of the Philistines—to be avenged on the enemies of the king"; and Saul thought to cause David to fall by the hand of the Philistines. **26** And his servants declare these words to David, and the thing is right in the eyes of David, to be son-in-law of the king; and the days have not been full, **27** and David rises and goes, he and his men, and strikes two hundred men among the Philistines, and David brings in their foreskins, and they set them before the king, to be son-in-law of the king; and Saul gives his daughter Michal to him for a wife. **28** And Saul sees and knows that Yhwh [is] with David, and Michal daughter of Saul has loved him, **29** and Saul adds to be afraid of the presence of David still; and Saul is an enemy of David [for] all the days. **30** And the princes of the Philistines come out, and it comes to pass from the time of their coming out, David has acted more wisely than any of the servants of Saul, and his name is very precious.

CHAPTER 19

1 And Saul speaks to his son Jonathan, and to all his servants, to put David to death, **2** and Jonathan son of Saul delighted in David exceedingly, and Jonathan declares [it] to David, saying, "My father Saul is seeking to put you to death, and now, please take heed in the morning, and you have abided in a secret place and been hidden, **3** and I go out, and have stood by the side of my father in the field where you [are], and I speak of you to my father, and have seen what [is coming], and have declared [it] to you." **4** And Jonathan speaks good of David to his father Saul and says to him, "Do not let

the king sin against his servant, against David, because he has not sinned against you, and because his works [are] very good for you; **5** indeed, he puts his life in his hand, and strikes the Philistine, and Yhwh works a great salvation for all Israel; you have seen, and rejoice, and why do you sin against innocent blood, to put David to death for nothing?" **6** And Saul listens to the voice of Jonathan, and Saul swears, "Yhwh lives—he does not die." **7** And Jonathan calls for David, and Jonathan declares all these words to him, and Jonathan brings in David to Saul, and he is before him as before. **8** And there adds to be war, and David goes out and fights against the Philistines, and strikes among them [with] a great striking, and they flee from his face. **9** And a spirit of sadness [from] Yhwh is to Saul, and he is sitting in his house, and his javelin [is] in his hand, and David is playing with the hand, **10** and Saul seeks to strike with the javelin through David, and through the wall, and he frees himself from the presence of Saul, and he strikes the javelin through the wall; and David has fled and escapes during that night. **11** And Saul sends messengers to the house of David to watch him, and to put him to death in the morning; and his wife Michal declares [it] to David, saying, "If you are not delivering your life tonight—tomorrow you are put to death." **12** And Michal causes David to go down through the window, and he goes on, and flees, and escapes; **13** and Michal takes the teraphim, and lays [it] on the bed, and she has put the mattress of goats' [hair for] his pillows, and covers [it] with a garment. **14** And Saul sends messengers to take David, and she says, "He [is] sick." **15** And Saul sends the messengers to see David, saying, "Bring him up in the bed to me in order to put him to death." **16** And the messengers come in, and behold, the teraphim [are] on the bed, and the mattress of goats' [hair for] his pillows. **17** And Saul says to Michal, "Why have you thus deceived me—that you send my enemy away, and he escapes?" And Michal says to Saul, "He said to me, Send me away. Why do I put you to death?" **18** And David has fled, and escapes, and comes to Samuel at Ramath, and declares to him all that Saul has done to him, and he goes, he and Samuel, and they dwell in Naioth. **19** And it is declared to Saul, saying, "Behold, David [is] in Naioth in Ramah." **20** And Saul sends messengers to take David, and they see the assembly of the prophets prophesying, and Samuel standing, set over them, and the Spirit of God is on Saul's messengers, and they prophesy—they also. **21** And they declare [it] to Saul, and he sends other messengers, and they prophesy—they also; and Saul adds and sends messengers a third time, and they prophesy—they also. **22** And he goes—he also—to Ramath, and comes to the great well which [is] in Sechu, and asks and says, "Where [are] Samuel and David?" And [one] says, "Behold, in Naioth in Ramah." **23** And he goes there—to Naioth in Ramah, and the Spirit of God is on him also; and he goes, going on, and he prophesies until his coming to Naioth in Ramah, **24** and he strips off—he also—his garments, and prophesies—he also—before Samuel, and falls down naked all that day and all the night; therefore they say, "Is Saul also among the prophets?"

CHAPTER 20

1 And David flees from Naioth in Ramah, and comes, and says before Jonathan, "What have I done? what [is] my iniquity? and what [is] my sin before your father, that he is seeking my life?" **2** And he says to him, "Far be it! You do not die; behold, my father does not do anything great or small and does not uncover my ear; and why does my father hide this thing from me? this [thing] is not." **3** And David swears again and says, "Your father has certainly known that I have found grace in your eyes, and he says, Do not let Jonathan know this, lest he is grieved; and yet, Yhwh lives, and your soul lives, but—as a step between me and death." **4** And Jonathan says to David, "What does your soul [desire]? Command and I do it for you." **5** And David says to Jonathan, "Behold, the new moon [is] tomorrow; and I certainly sit with the king to eat; and you have sent me away, and I have been hidden in a field until the third evening; **6** if your father looks after me at all, then you have said, David earnestly asked of me to run to his city of Beth-Lehem, for there [is] a sacrifice of the days for all the family. **7** If thus he says: Good; [there is] peace for your servant; and if it is very displeasing to him—know that the evil has been determined by him; **8** and you have done kindness to your servant, for you have brought your servant into a covenant of Yhwh with you—and if there is iniquity in me, put me to death yourself; for why [is] this [that] you bring me to your father?" **9** And Jonathan says, "Far be it from you! For I certainly do not know that the evil has been determined by my father to come on you, and I do not declare it to you." **10** And David says to Jonathan, "Who declares [it] to me? or what [if] your father answers you sharply?" **11** And Jonathan says to David, "Come, and we go out into the field"; and both of them go out into the field. **12** And Jonathan says to David, "Yhwh, God of Israel, [is my witness]—when I search out my father about [this] time tomorrow [or] the third [day], and behold, [there is] good toward David, and I do not then send to you, and have uncovered your ear— **13** thus Yhwh does to Jonathan, and thus He adds; when the evil concerning you is good to my father, then I have uncovered your ear, and sent you away, and you have gone in peace, and Yhwh is with you, as he was with my father; **14** and not only while I am alive do you do the kindness of Yhwh with me, and I do not die, **15** but you do not cut off your kindness from my house for all time, nor in Yhwh's cutting off the enemies of David, each one from off the face of the ground." **16** So Jonathan cuts [a covenant] with the house of David, and Yhwh has sought [it] from the hand of the enemies of David; **17** and Jonathan adds to cause David to swear, because he loves him, for he has loved him [as] the love [for] his own soul. **18** And Jonathan says to him, "Tomorrow [is] the new moon, and you have been looked after, for your seat is looked after; **19** and on the third day you certainly come down, and have come to the place where you were hidden in the day of the work, and have remained near the stone of Ezel. **20** And I shoot three of the arrows at the side, sending out at a mark for myself; **21** and behold, I send the youth, [saying], Go, find the arrows. If I say to the youth at all, Behold, the arrows [are] on this side of you—take them and come, for [there is] peace for you, and there is no [adverse] word—[as] Yhwh lives. **22** And if thus I say to the young man, Behold, the arrows [are] beyond you—go, for Yhwh has sent you away; **23** as for the thing which you and I have spoken, behold, Yhwh [is] between me and you for all time." **24** And David is hidden in the field, and it is the new moon, and the king sits down by the food to eat, **25** and the king sits on his seat, as time by time, on a seat by the wall, and Jonathan rises, and Abner sits at the side of Saul, and David's place is looked after. **26** And Saul has not spoken anything on that day, for he said, "It [is] an accident; he is not clean—surely not clean." **27** And it comes to pass on the second day of the new moon, that David's place is looked after, and Saul says to his son Jonathan, "Why has the son of Jesse not come in, either yesterday or today, to the food?" **28** And Jonathan answers Saul, "David has earnestly asked [permission] from me [to go] to Beth-Lehem, **29** and he says, Please send me away, for we have a family sacrifice in the city, and my brother has given command to me himself, and now, if I have found grace in your eyes, please let me go away and see my brothers; therefore he has not come to the table of the king." **30** And the anger of Saul burns against Jonathan, and he says to him, "Son of a perverse [woman] of rebellion! Have I not known that you are fixing on the son of Jesse to your own shame, and to the shame of the nakedness of your mother? **31** for all the days that the son of Jesse lives on the ground you are not established, you and your kingdom; and now, send and bring him to me, for he [is] a son of death." **32** And Jonathan answers his father Saul and says to him, "Why is he put to death? what has he done?" **33** And Saul casts the javelin at him to strike him, and Jonathan knows that it has been determined by his father to put David to death. **34** And Jonathan rises from the table in the heat of anger, and has not eaten food on the second day of the new moon, for he has been grieved for David, for his father put him to shame. **35** And it comes to pass in the morning, that Jonathan goes out into the field for the appointment with David, and a little youth [is] with him. **36** And he says to his youth, "Now run, find the arrows which I am shooting"; the youth is running, and he has shot the arrow, causing [it] to pass over him. **37** And the youth comes to the place of the arrow which Jonathan has shot, and Jonathan calls after the youth, and says, "Is the arrow not beyond you?" **38** and Jonathan calls after the youth, "Speed, hurry, do not stand"; and Jonathan's youth gathers the arrows, and comes to his lord. **39** And the youth has not known anything, only Jonathan and David knew the word. **40** And Jonathan gives his weapons to the youth whom he has and says to him, "Go, carry into the city." **41** The youth has gone, and David has risen from Ezel, at the south, and falls on his face to the earth, and bows himself three times, and they kiss one another, and they weep with one another, until David exerted himself; **42** and Jonathan says to David, "Go in peace,

in that we have sworn—the two of us—in the Name of Yhwh, saying, Yhwh is between me and you, and between my seed and your seed—for all time"; and he rises and goes; and Jonathan has gone into the city.

CHAPTER 21

1 And David comes to Nob, to Ahimelech the priest, and Ahimelech trembles at meeting David and says to him, "Why [are] you alone, and no man [is] with you?" **2** And David says to Ahimelech the priest, "The king has commanded me [on] a matter, and he says to me, Let no man know anything of the matter about which I send you, and which I have commanded you; and [my] young men know [to go] to such and such a place. **3** And now, what is there under your hand? Give five loaves into my hand, or that which is found." **4** And the priest answers David and says, "There is no common bread under my hand, but there is holy bread; if only the youths have been kept from women." **5** And David answers the priest and says to him, "Surely, if women have been restrained from us as before in my going out, then the vessels of the young men are holy, and it [is] a common way; and also, surely it is sanctified today in the vessel." **6** And the priest gives the holy thing to him, for there was no bread there except the Bread of the Presentation, which is turned aside from the presence of Yhwh to put hot bread [there] in the day of its being taken away. **7** And there [is] a man of the servants of Saul detained before Yhwh on that day, and his name [is] Doeg the Edomite, chief of the shepherds whom Saul has. **8** And David says to Ahimelech, "And is there not spear or sword here under your hand? for I have taken neither my sword nor my vessels in my hand, for the matter of the king was urgent." **9** And the priest says, "The sword of Goliath the Philistine, whom you struck in the Valley of Elah, behold, it is wrapped in a garment behind the ephod, if you take it to yourself, take; for there is none other except it in this [place]." And David says, "There is none like it—give it to me." **10** And David rises and flees on that day from the face of Saul, and comes to Achish king of Gath; **11** and the servants of Achish say to him, "Is this not David, the king of the land? is it not of this one [that] they sing in dances, saying, Saul struck among his thousands, and David among his myriads?" **12** And David lays these words in his heart, and is exceedingly afraid of the face of Achish king of Gath, **13** and changes his behavior before their eyes, and feigns himself mad in their hand, and scribbles on the doors of the gate, and lets down his spittle to his beard. **14** And Achish says to his servants, "Behold, you see a man acting as a madman; why do you bring him to me? **15** Am I lacking madmen, that you have brought in this one to act as a madman before me? does this one come into my house?"

CHAPTER 22

1 And David goes from there, and escapes to the cave of Adullam, and his brothers hear, and all the house of his father, and they go down to him there; **2** and every man in distress gathers themselves to him, and every man who has an exactor, and every man bitter in soul, and he is for head over them, and there are about four hundred men with him. **3** And David goes from there to Mizpeh of Moab and says to the king of Moab, "Please let my father and my mother come out with you, until I know what God does for me"; **4** and he leads them before the king of Moab, and they dwell with him all the days of David's being in the fortress. **5** And the prophet Gad says to David, "You do not abide in a fortress, go, and you have entered the land of Judah for yourself"; and David goes and enters the forest of Hareth. **6** And Saul hears that David has become known, and the men who [are] with him, and Saul is abiding in Gibeah, under the grove in Ramah, and his spear [is] in his hand, and all his servants [are] standing by him. **7** And Saul says to his servants who are standing by him, "Now hear, sons of Benjamin; does the son of Jesse also give fields and vineyards to all of you? Does he appoint all of you [to be] heads of thousands and heads of hundreds? **8** for all of you have conspired against me, and there is none uncovering my ear about my son's cutting [a covenant] with the son of Jesse, and there is none of you grieving for me, and uncovering my ear, that my son has raised up my servant against me, to lie in wait as [at] this day." **9** And Doeg the Edomite answers, who is set over the servants of Saul, and says, "I have seen the son of Jesse coming to Nob, to Ahimelech son of Ahitub, **10** and he inquires of Yhwh for him, and has given provision to him, and has given the sword of Goliath the Philistine to him." **11** And the king sends to call Ahimelech son of Ahitub, the priest, and all the house of his father, the priests, who [are] in Nob, and all of them come to the king; **12** and Saul says, "Now hear, son of Ahitub"; and he says, "Here I [am], my lord." **13** And Saul says to him, "Why have you conspired against me, you and the son of Jesse, by your giving bread and a sword to him, and to inquire of God for him, to rise against me, to lie in wait, as [at] this day?" **14** And Ahimelech answers the king and says, "And who among all your servants [is] as David—faithful, and son-in-law of the king, and has turned aside to your council, and is honored in your house? **15** Today have I begun to inquire of God for him? far be it from me! Do not let the king lay anything against his servant, against any of the house of my father, for your servant has known nothing of all this, little or much." **16** And the king says, "You surely die, Ahimelech, you and all the house of your father." **17** And the king says to the runners, those standing by him, "Turn around, and put the priests of Yhwh to death, because their hand [is] also with David, and because they have known that he is fleeing, and have not uncovered my ear"; and the servants of the king have not been willing to put forth their hand to come against the priests of Yhwh. **18** And the king says to Doeg, "Turn around, and come against the priests"; and Doeg the Edomite turns around, and comes against the priests himself, and in that day puts to death eighty-five men bearing a linen ephod, **19** and Nob, the city of the priests, he has struck by the mouth of the sword, from man and to woman, from infant and to suckling, and ox, and donkey, and sheep, by the mouth of the sword. **20** And one son of Ahimelech, son of Ahitub, escapes, and his name [is] Abiathar, and he flees after David, **21** and Abiathar declares to David that Saul has slain the priests of Yhwh. **22** And David says to Abiathar, "I have known on that day when Doeg the Edomite [is] there, that he certainly declares [it] to Saul; I have brought [it] around to every person of the house of your father; **23** dwell with me; do not fear; for he who seeks my life seeks your life; for you [are my] charge with me."

CHAPTER 23

1 And they declare to David, saying, "Behold, the Philistines are fighting against Keilah, and they are spoiling the threshing-floors." **2** And David inquires of Yhwh, saying, "Do I go? And have I struck among these Philistines?" And Yhwh says to David, "Go, and you have struck among the Philistines, and saved Keilah." **3** And David's men say to him, "Behold, we here in Judah are afraid; and how much more when we go to Keilah, to the ranks of the Philistines?" **4** And David adds again to inquire of Yhwh, and Yhwh answers him and says, "Rise, go down to Keilah, for I am giving the Philistines into your hand." **5** And David goes, and his men, to Keilah, and fights with the Philistines, and leads away their livestock, and strikes among them [with] a great striking, and David saves the inhabitants of Keilah. **6** And it comes to pass, in the fleeing of Abiathar son of Ahimelech to David, to Keilah, an ephod came down in his hand. **7** And it is declared to Saul that David has come to Keilah, and Saul says, "God has made him known for my hand, for he has been shut in, to enter into a city of doors and bar." **8** And Saul summons all the people to the battle, to go down to Keilah, to lay siege to David and to his men. **9** And David knows that Saul is devising the evil against him and says to Abiathar the priest, "Bring the ephod near." **10** And David says, "Yhwh, God of Israel, Your servant has certainly heard that Saul is seeking to come to Keilah, to destroy the city on my account. **11** Do the possessors of Keilah shut me up into his hand? does Saul come down as Your servant has heard? Yhwh, God of Israel, please declare [it] to Your servant." And Yhwh says, "He comes down." **12** And David says, "Do the possessors of Keilah shut me up and my men into the hand of Saul?" And Yhwh says, "They shut [you] up." **13** And David rises—and his men—about six hundred men, and they go out from Keilah, and go up and down where they go up and down; and it has been declared to Saul that David has escaped from Keilah, and he ceases to go out. **14** And David abides in the wilderness, in fortresses, and abides in the hill-country, in the wilderness of Ziph; and Saul seeks him [for] all the days, and God has not given him into his hand. **15** And David sees that Saul has come out to seek his life, and David [is] in the wilderness of Ziph, in

a forest. **16** And Jonathan son of Saul rises, and goes to David [in the] forest, and strengthens his hand in God, **17** and says to him, "Do not fear, for the hand of my father Saul does not find you, and you reign over Israel, and I am to you for second, and also so knows my father Saul." **18** And both of them make a covenant before Yhwh; and David abides in the forest, and Jonathan has gone to his house. **19** And the Ziphites go up to Saul at Gibeah, saying, "Is David not hiding himself with us in fortresses, in the forest, in the height of Hachilah, which [is] on the south of the desolate place? **20** And now, by all the desire of your soul, O king, to come down, come down, and ours [is] to shut him up into the hand of the king." **21** And Saul says, "Blessed [are] you of Yhwh, for you have pity on me; **22** now go prepare yet, and know and see his place where his foot is; who has seen him there? for [one] has said to me, He is very cunning. **23** And see and know of all the hiding places where he hides himself, and you have turned back prepared to me, and I have gone with you, and it has been, if he is in the land, that I have searched him out through all the thousands of Judah." **24** And they rise and go to Ziph before Saul, and David and his men [are] in the wilderness of Maon, in the plain, at the south of the desolate place. **25** And Saul and his men go to seek, and they declare [it] to David, and he goes down the rock, and abides in the wilderness of Maon; and Saul hears, and pursues after David [to] the wilderness of Maon. **26** And Saul goes on this side of the mountain, and David and his men on that side of the mountain, and David is hurried to go from the face of Saul, and Saul and his men are surrounding David and his men, to catch them. **27** And a messenger has come to Saul, saying, "Hurry, and come, for the Philistines have pushed against the land." **28** And Saul turns back from pursuing after David, and goes to meet the Philistines, therefore they have called that place "The Rock of Divisions." **29** And David goes up there, and abides in fortresses [at] En-gedi.

CHAPTER 24

1 And it comes to pass, when Saul has turned back from after the Philistines, that they declare to him, saying, "Behold, David [is] in the wilderness of En-gedi." **2** And Saul takes three thousand chosen men out of all Israel, and goes to seek David and his men, on the front of the rocks of the wild goats, **3** and he comes to folds of the flock, on the way, and there [is] a cave, and Saul goes in to cover his feet; and David and his men are abiding in the sides of the cave. **4** And the men of David say to him, "Behold, the day of which Yhwh said to you, Behold, I am giving your enemy into your hand, and you have done to him as it is good in your eyes"; and David rises and cuts off the skirt of the upper robe which [is] on Saul with stealth. **5** And it comes to pass afterward that the heart of David strikes him, because that he has cut off the skirt which [is] on Saul, **6** and he says to his men, "Far be it from me, by Yhwh; I do not do this thing to my lord—to the anointed of Yhwh—to put forth my hand against him, for he [is] the anointed of Yhwh." **7** And David subdues his men by words, and has not permitted them to rise against Saul; and Saul has risen from the cave, and goes on the way; **8** and David rises afterward, and goes out from the cave, and calls after Saul, saying, "My lord, O king!" And Saul looks attentively behind him, and David bows—face to the earth—and pays respect. **9** And David says to Saul, "Why do you hear the words of man, saying, Behold, David is seeking your calamity? **10** Behold, this day your eyes have seen how that Yhwh has given you into my hand today in the cave; and [one] said to slay you, and [my eye] has pity on you, and I say, I do not put forth my hand against my lord, for he [is] the anointed of Yhwh. **11** And my father, see, indeed see the skirt of your upper robe in my hand; for by cutting off the skirt of your upper robe, and I have not slain you, know and see that there is not evil and transgression in my hand, and I have not sinned against you, and you are hunting my soul to take it! **12** Yhwh judges between me and you, and Yhwh has avenged me of you, and my hand is not on you; **13** as the allegory of the ancients says, Wickedness goes out from the wicked, and my hand is not on you. **14** After whom has the king of Israel come out? after whom are you pursuing? After a dead dog! After one flea! **15** And Yhwh has been for judge, and has judged between me and you, indeed, He sees and pleads my cause, and delivers me out of your hand." **16** And it comes to pass, when David completes to speak these words to Saul, that Saul says, "Is this your voice, my son David?" And Saul lifts up his voice, and weeps. **17** And he says to David, "You [are] more righteous than I; for you have done me good, and I have done you evil; [18] and you have declared today how that you have done good with me, how that Yhwh shut me up into your hand, and you did not slay me, [19] and that a man finds his enemy, and has sent him away in a good manner; and Yhwh repays you good for that which you did to me this day. [20] And now, behold, I have known that you certainly reign, and the kingdom of Israel has stood in your hand; [21] and now, swear to me by Yhwh [that] you do not cut off my seed after me, nor do you destroy my name from the house of my father." [22] And David swears to Saul, and Saul goes to his house, and David and his men have gone up to the fortress.

CHAPTER 25

[1] And Samuel dies, and all Israel is gathered, and mourns for him, and buries him in his house, in Ramah; and David rises and goes down to the wilderness of Paran. [2] And [there is] a man in Maon, and his work [is] in Carmel; and the man [is] very great, and he has three thousand sheep and one thousand goats; and he is shearing his flock in Carmel. [3] And the name of the man [is] Nabal, and the name of his wife [is] Abigail, and the woman [is] of good understanding, and of beautiful form, and the man [is] hard and evil [in his] doings; and he [is] a Calebite. [4] And David hears in the wilderness that Nabal is shearing his flock, [5] and David sends ten young men, and David says to the young men, "Go up to Carmel, and you have come to Nabal, and asked of him in my name of welfare, [6] and said thus to the living: and peace to you, and peace to your house, and peace to all that you have! [7] and now, I have heard that you have shearers; now, the shepherds whom you have have been with us, we have not put them to shame, nor has anything been looked after by them, all the days of their being in Carmel. [8] Ask your young men, and they declare [it] to you, and the young men find grace in your eyes, for we have come on a good day; please give that which your hand finds to your servants and to your son, to David." [9] And the young men of David come in, and speak to Nabal according to all these words, in the name of David—and rest. [10] And Nabal answers the servants of David and says, "Who [is] David, and who [is] the son of Jesse? Have servants been multiplied today who are each breaking away from his master? [11] And have I taken my bread, and my water, and my flesh, which I slaughtered for my shearers, and have given [it] to men whom I have not known where they [are] from?" [12] And the young men of David turn on their way, and turn back, and come in, and declare to him according to all these words. [13] And David says to his men, "Each gird on his sword"; and they each gird on his sword, and David also girds on his sword, and about four hundred men go up after David, and two hundred have remained by the vessels. [14] And one young man of the youths has declared [it] to Abigail wife of Nabal, saying, "Behold, David has sent messengers out of the wilderness to bless our lord, and he flies on them; [15] and the men [are] very good to us, and have not put us to shame, and we have not looked after anything all the days we have gone up and down with them, in our being in the field; [16] they have been a wall to us both by night and by day, all the days of our being with them, feeding the flock. [17] And now, know and consider what you do; for evil has been determined against our lord, and against all his house, and he [is] too much a son of worthlessness to be spoken to." [18] And Abigail hurries, and takes two hundred loaves, and two bottles of wine, and five sheep, prepared, and five measures of roasted grain, and one hundred bunches of raisins, and two hundred bunches of figs, and sets [them] on the donkeys. [19] And she says to her young men, "Pass over before me; behold, I am coming after you"; and she has not declared [it] to her husband Nabal; [20] and it has come to pass, she is riding on the donkey and is coming down in the secret part of the hill-country, and behold, David and his men are coming down to meet her, and she meets them. [21] And David said, "Surely in vain I have kept all that this [one] has in the wilderness, and nothing has been looked after of all that he has, and he turns back to me evil for good; [22] thus God does to the enemies of David, and thus He adds, if I leave of all that he has until the morning light—of those sitting on the wall." [23] And Abigail sees David, and hurries and comes down from off the donkey, and falls on her face before David, and bows herself to the earth, [24] and falls at his feet and says, "On me, my lord, the iniquity; and please let your handmaid speak in your ear, and hear the words of your handmaid. [25] Please do not let my lord set his heart to this man of worthlessness, on Nabal, for as his name [is] so [is] he; Nabal [is] his name, and folly [is] with him; and I, your handmaid, did not see the young men of my lord whom you sent; [26] and now, my lord, Yhwh lives, and your soul lives, in that Yhwh has withheld you from coming in with blood, and to save your hand from yourself—now let your enemies be as Nabal, even those seeking evil toward my lord. [27] And now, this blessing which your maidservant has brought to my lord—it has been given to the young men who are going up and down at the feet of my lord. [28] Please bear with the transgression of your handmaid, for Yhwh certainly makes a steadfast house for my lord; for my lord has fought the battles of Yhwh, and evil is not found in you [all] your days. [29] And man rises to pursue you and to seek your soul, and the soul of my lord has been bound in the bundle of life with your God Yhwh; as for the soul of your enemies, He slings them out in the midst of the hollow of the sling. [30] And it has been, when Yhwh does to my lord according to all the good which He has spoken concerning you, and appointed you for leader over Israel, [31] that this is not to you for a stumbling-block, and for an offense of heart to my lord—either to shed blood for nothing, or my lord's restraining himself; and Yhwh has done good to my lord, and you have remembered your handmaid." [32] And David says to Abigail, "Blessed [is] Yhwh, God of Israel, who has sent you to meet me this day, [33] and blessed [is] your discretion, and blessed [are] you in that you have restrained me this day from coming in with blood, and to restrain my hand to myself. [34] And yet, Yhwh lives, God of Israel, who has kept me back from doing evil with you, for unless you had hurried, and come to meet me, surely there had not been left to Nabal until the morning light, of those sitting on the wall." [35] And David receives from her hand that which she has brought to him, and he has said to her, "Go up in peace to your house; see, I have listened to your voice, and accept your face." [36] And Abigail comes to Nabal, and behold, he has a banquet in his house, like a banquet of the king, and the heart of Nabal [is] glad within him, and he [is] drunk to excess, and she has not declared anything to him, little or much, until the morning light. [37] And it comes to pass in the morning, when the wine is gone out from Nabal, that his wife declares these things to him, and his heart dies within him, and he has been as a stone. [38] And it comes to pass [in] about ten days, that Yhwh strikes Nabal and he dies, [39] and David hears that Nabal [is] dead and says, "Blessed [is] Yhwh who has pleaded the cause of my reproach from the hand of Nabal, and His servant has kept back from evil, and Yhwh has turned back the wickedness of Nabal on his own head"; and David sends and speaks with Abigail, to take her to himself for a wife. [40] And the servants of David come to Abigail at Carmel, and speak to her, saying, "David has sent us to you to take you to himself for a wife." [41] And she rises and bows herself—face to the earth—and says, "Behold, your handmaid [is] for a maidservant to wash the feet of the servants of my lord." [42] And Abigail hurries and rises, and rides on the donkey; and [there are] five of her young women who are going at her feet; and she goes after the messengers of David, and is to him for a wife. [43] And David has taken Ahinoam from Jezreel, and they are—even both of them—for wives to him; [44] and Saul gave his daughter Michal, David's wife, to Phalti son of Laish, who [is] of Gallim.

CHAPTER 26

[1] And the Ziphites come to Saul at Gibeah, saying, "Is David not hiding himself in the height of Hachilah, on the front of the desert?" [2] And Saul rises, and goes down to the wilderness of Ziph, and with him [are] three thousand men, chosen ones of Israel, to seek David in the wilderness of Ziph. [3] And Saul encamps in the height of Hachilah, which [is] on the front of the desert, by the way, and David is abiding in the wilderness, and he sees that Saul has come into the wilderness after him; [4] and David sends spies, and knows that Saul has come to Nachon, [5] and David rises, and comes to the place where Saul has encamped, and David sees the place where Saul has lain, and Abner son of Ner, head of his host, and Saul is lying in the path, and the people are encamping around him. [6] And David answers and says to Ahimelech the Hittite, and to Abishai son of Zeruiah, brother of Joab, saying, "Who goes down with me to Saul, to the camp?" And Abishai says, "I go down with you." [7] And David comes—and Abishai—by night to the people, and behold, Saul is lying sleeping in the path, and his spear is pressed into the earth by his pillow, and Abner and the people

are lying around him. **8** And Abishai says to David, "God has shut up your enemy into your hand today; and now, please let me strike him with [the] spear, even into the earth, at once— and not repeat [it] to him." **9** And David says to Abishai, "Do not destroy him; for who has put forth his hand against the anointed of Yhwh and been acquitted?" **10** And David says, "Yhwh lives; except Yhwh strikes him, or his day comes that he has died, or he goes down into battle and has been consumed— **11** far be it from me, by Yhwh, from putting forth my hand against the anointed of Yhwh; and now, please take the spear which [is] by his pillow, and the jug of water, and we go away." **12** And David takes the spear, and the jug of water by the pillow of Saul, and they go away, and there is none seeing, and there is none knowing, and there is none awaking, for all of them are sleeping, for a deep sleep [from] Yhwh has fallen on them. **13** And David passes over to the other side, and stands on the top of the hill far off—great [is] the place between them; **14** and David calls to the people, and to Abner son of Ner, saying, "Do you not answer, Abner?" And Abner answers and says, "Who [are] you [who] have called to the king?" **15** And David says to Abner, "Are you not a man? and who [is] like you in Israel? but why have you not watched over your lord the king? for one of the people had come in to destroy the king, your lord. **16** This thing which you have done is not good; Yhwh lives, but you [are] sons of death, in that you have not watched over your lord, over the anointed of Yhwh; and now, see where the king's spear [is], and the jug of water which [is] by his pillow." **17** And Saul discerns the voice of David and says, "Is this your voice, my son David?" And David says, "My voice, my lord, O king!" **18** and he says, "Why [is] this—my lord is pursuing after his servant? for what have I done, and what evil [is] in my hand? **19** And now, please let my lord the king hear the words of his servant: if Yhwh has moved you against me, let Him accept a present; but if [merely] the sons of men, they [are] cursed before Yhwh, for today they have cast me out from being admitted into the inheritance of Yhwh, saying, Go, serve other gods. **20** And now, do not let my blood fall to the earth before the face of Yhwh, for the king of Israel has come out to seek one flea, as [one] pursues the partridge in mountains." **21** And Saul says, "I have sinned; return, my son David, for I do evil to you no more, because that my soul has been precious in your eyes this day; behold, I have acted foolishly, and err very greatly." **22** And David answers and says, "Behold, the king's spear; and let one of the young men pass over, and receive it; **23** and Yhwh turns each back to his righteousness and his faithfulness, in that Yhwh has given you into [my] hand today, and I have not been willing to put forth my hand against the anointed of Yhwh, **24** and behold, as your soul has been great in my eyes this day, so is my soul great in the eyes of Yhwh, and He delivers me out of all distress." **25** And Saul says to David, "Blessed [are] you, my son David, also working you work, and also prevailing you prevail." And David goes on his way, and Saul has turned back to his place.

CHAPTER 27

1 And David says to his heart, "Now I am consumed by the hand of Saul one day; there is nothing better for me than that I diligently escape to the land of the Philistines, and Saul has been despairing of me—of seeking me anymore in all the border of Israel, and I have escaped out of his hand." **2** And David rises, and passes over, he and six hundred men who [are] with him, to Achish son of Maoch king of Gath; **3** and David dwells with Achish in Gath, he and his men, each one with his household, [even] David and his two wives, Ahinoam the Jezreelitess, and Abigail wife of Nabal the Carmelitess. **4** And it is declared to Saul that David has fled to Gath, and he has not added to seek him anymore. **5** And David says to Achish, "Now if I have found grace in your eyes, they give a place to me in one of the cities of the field, and I dwell there, indeed, why does your servant dwell in the royal city with you?" **6** And Achish gives Ziklag to him in that day, therefore Ziklag has been for the kings of Judah until this day. **7** And the number of the days which David has dwelt in the field of the Philistines [is one year] of days and four months; **8** and David and his men go up, and they push toward the Geshurite, and the Gerizite, and the Amalekite (for they are inhabitants of the land from of old), as you come to Shur and to the land of Egypt, **9** and David has struck the land, and does not keep alive man and woman, and has taken sheep, and oxen, and donkeys, and camels, and garments, and turns back, and comes to Achish. **10** And Achish

says, "To where have you pushed today?" And David says, "Against the south of Judah, and against the south of the Jerahmeelite, and to the south of the Kenite." **11** David keeps alive neither man nor woman, to bring in [word] to Gath, saying, "Lest they declare [it] against us, saying, Thus David has done, and thus [is] his custom all the days that he has dwelt in the fields of the Philistines." **12** And Achish believes in David, saying, "He has made himself utterly abhorred among his people in Israel, and has been for a perpetual servant to me."

CHAPTER 28

1 And it comes to pass in those days, that the Philistines gather their camps for the war, to fight against Israel, and Achish says to David, "You certainly know that you go out with me into the camp, you and your men." **2** And David says to Achish, "Therefore you know that which your servant does." And Achish says to David, "Therefore I appoint you keeper of my head [for] all the days." **3** And Samuel has died, and all Israel mourns for him, and buries him in Ramah, even in his city, and Saul has turned aside those having familiar spirits, and the wizards, out of the land. **4** And the Philistines are gathered, and come in, and encamp in Shunem, and Saul gathers all Israel, and they encamp in Gilboa, **5** and Saul sees the camp of the Philistines, and fears, and his heart trembles greatly, **6** and Saul inquires of Yhwh, and Yhwh has not answered him, either by the dreams, or by the Lights, or by the prophets. **7** And Saul says to his servants, "Seek a woman for me possessing a familiar spirit, and I go to her, and inquire of her"; and his servants say to him, "Behold, a woman possessing a familiar spirit [is] in En-dor." **8** And Saul disguises himself and puts on other garments, and goes, he and two of the men with him, and they come to the woman by night, and he says, "Please divine to me by the familiar spirit, and cause him whom I say to you to come up to me." **9** And the woman says to him, "Behold, you have known that which Saul has done, that he has cut off those having familiar spirits, and the wizards, out of the land; and why are you laying a snare for my soul—to put me to death?" **10** And Saul swears to her by Yhwh, saying, "Yhwh lives, punishment does not meet you for this thing." **11** And the woman says, "Whom do I bring up to you?" And he says, "Bring up Samuel to me." **12** And the woman sees Samuel, and cries with a loud voice, and the woman speaks to Saul, saying, "Why have you deceived me? For you [are] Saul!" **13** And the king says to her, "Do not fear; for what have you seen?" And the woman says to Saul, "I have seen gods coming up out of the earth." **14** And he says to her, "What [is] his form?" And she says, "An aged man is coming up, and he [is] covered with an upper robe"; and Saul knows that he [is] Samuel, and bows—face to her earth—and pays respect. **15** And Samuel says to Saul, "Why have you troubled me, to bring me up?" And Saul says, "I have great distress, and the Philistines are fighting against me, God has turned aside from me, and has not answered me anymore, either by the hand of the prophets, or by dreams; and I call for you to let me know what I [should] do." **16** And Samuel says, "And why do you ask me, and Yhwh has turned aside from you, and is your enemy? **17** And Yhwh does for Himself as He has spoken by my hand, and Yhwh tears the kingdom out of your hand, and gives it to your neighbor—to David. **18** Because you have not listened to the voice of Yhwh, nor did the fierceness of His anger on Amalek—therefore Yhwh has done this thing to you this day; **19** indeed, Yhwh also gives Israel into the hand of the Philistines with you, and tomorrow you and your sons [are] with me; Yhwh also gives the camp of Israel into the hand of the Philistines." **20** And Saul hurries and falls—the fullness of his stature—to the earth, and fears greatly because of the words of Samuel; also power was not in him, for he had not eaten bread all the day, and all the night. **21** And the woman comes to Saul, and sees that he has been greatly troubled, and says to him, "Behold, your maidservant has listened to your voice, and I put my soul in my hand, and I obey your words which you have spoken to me; **22** and now, please listen, you also, to the voice of your maidservant, and I set a morsel of bread before you; and eat, and there is power in you when you go in the way." **23** And he refuses and says, "I do not eat"; and his servants urge him on, and also the woman, and he listens to their voice, and rises from the earth, and sits on the bed. **24** And the woman has a calf of the stall in the house, and she hurries and slaughters it, and takes flour, and kneads, and bakes it [into] unleavened things, **25** and brings [them] near before Saul, and before his servants, and they eat, and rise, and go on during that night.

CHAPTER 29

1 And the Philistines gather all their camps to Aphek, and Israel is encamping at a fountain which [is] in Jezreel, **2** and the princes of the Philistines are passing on by hundreds, and by thousands, and David and his men are passing on in the rear with Achish. **3** And the heads of the Philistines say, "What [are] these Hebrews?" And Achish says to the heads of the Philistines, "Is this not David, servant of Saul king of Israel, who has been with me these days or these years, and I have not found anything in him [wrong] from the day of his falling away until this day?" **4** And the heads of the Philistines are angry against him, and the heads of the Philistines say to him, "Send back the man, and he turns back to his place to where you have appointed him, and does not go down with us into battle, and is not for an adversary to us in battle; and with what does this one reconcile himself to his lord—is it not with the heads of those men? **5** Is this not David, of whom they answer in choruses, saying, Saul has struck among his thousands, and David among his myriads?" **6** And Achish calls to David and says to him, "Yhwh lives, surely you [are] upright, and good in my eyes is your going out, and your coming in with me in the camp, for I have not found evil in you from the day of your coming to me until this day; but you are not good in the eyes of the princes; **7** and now, return, and go in peace, and you do no evil in the eyes of the princes of the Philistines." **8** And David says to Achish, "But what have I done? and what have you found in your servant from the day that I have been before you until this day—that I do not go in and have fought against the enemies of my lord the king?" **9** And Achish answers and says to David, "I have known that you [are] good in my eyes as a messenger of God; only, the princes of the Philistines have said, He does not go up with us into battle; **10** and now, rise early in the morning—and the servants of your lord who have come with you. When you have risen early in the morning, and have light, then go." **11** And David rises early, he and his men, to go in the morning, to return to the land of the Philistines, and the Philistines have gone up to Jezreel.

CHAPTER 30

1 And it comes to pass, in the coming in of David and his men to Ziklag on the third day, that the Amalekites have pushed toward the south, and to Ziklag, and strike Ziklag, and burn it with fire, **2** and they take the women who [are] in it captive; they have not put anyone to death from small to great, and they lead [them] away, and go on their way. **3** And David comes in—and his men—to the city, and behold, [it is] burned with fire, and their wives, and their sons, and their daughters have been taken captive. **4** And David lifts up—and the people who [are] with him—their voice and weep, until they have no power to weep. **5** And the two wives of David have been taken captive, Ahinoam the Jezreelitess, and Abigail wife of Nabal the Carmelite; **6** and David has great distress, for the people have said to stone him, for the soul of all the people has been bitter, each for his sons and for his daughters; and David strengthens himself in his God Yhwh. **7** And David says to Abiathar the priest, son of Ahimelech, "Please bring the ephod near to me"; and Abiathar brings the ephod near to David, **8** and David inquires of Yhwh, saying, "I pursue after this troop—do I overtake it?" And He says to him, "Pursue, for you certainly overtake, and certainly deliver." **9** And David goes on, he and six hundred men who [are] with him, and they come to the Brook of Besor, and those left have stood still, **10** and David pursues, he and four hundred men (and two hundred men stand still who have been too faint to pass over the Brook of Besor), **11** and they find a man, an Egyptian, in the field, and take him to David, and give bread to him, and he eats, and they cause him to drink water, **12** and give to him a piece of a bunch of dried figs, and two bunches of raisins, and he eats, and his spirit returns to him, for he has not eaten bread nor drunk water [for] three days and three nights. **13** And David says to him, "Whose [are] you? and where [are] you from?" And he says, "I [am] an Egyptian youth, servant to a man, an Amalekite, and my lord forsakes me, for I have been sick [for]

three days, **14** we pushed [to] the south of the Cherethite, and against that which [is] to Judah, and against the south of Caleb, and we burned Ziklag with fire." **15** And David says to him, "Do you bring me down to this troop?" And he says, "Swear to me by God [that] you do not put me to death, nor do you shut me up into the hand of my lord, and I bring you down to this troop." **16** And he brings him down, and behold, they are spread out over the face of all the earth, eating, and drinking, and celebrating, with all the great spoil which they have taken out of the land of the Philistines, and out of the land of Judah. **17** And David strikes them from the twilight even to the evening of the next day, and there has not escaped of them a man, except four hundred young men who have ridden on the camels and flee. **18** And David delivers all that the Amalekites have taken; David has also delivered his two wives. **19** And nothing of theirs has lacked, from small to great, and to sons and daughters, and from the spoil, even to all that they had taken to themselves, David has brought back the whole, **20** and David takes the whole of the flock and of the herd [that] they have led on before these livestock, and they say, "This [is] David's spoil." **21** And David comes to the two hundred men who were too faint to go after David, and whom they cause to abide at the Brook of Besor, and they go out to meet David, and to meet the people who [are] with him, and David approaches the people, and asks of them of welfare. **22** And every bad and worthless man, of the men who have gone with David, answers, indeed, they say, "Because that they have not gone with us we do not give to them of the spoil which we have delivered, except each his wife and his children, and they lead away and go." **23** And David says, "You do not do so, my brothers, with that which Yhwh has given to us, and He preserves us, and gives the troop which comes against us into our hand; **24** and who listens to you in this thing? for as the portion of him who was brought down into battle, so also [is] the portion of him who is abiding by the vessels—they share alike." **25** And it comes to pass from that day and forward, that he appoints for a statute and for an ordinance for Israel to this day. **26** And David comes to Ziklag, and sends of the spoil to [the] elderly of Judah, to his friends, saying, "Behold, a blessing for you of the spoil of the enemies of Yhwh," **27** to those in Beth-El, and to those in South Ramoth, and to those in Jattir, **28** and to those in Aroer, and to those in Siphmoth, and to those in Eshtemoa, **29** and to those in Rachal, and to those in the cities of the Jerahmeelites, and to those in the cities of the Kenites, **30** and to those in Hormah, and to those in Chor-Ashan, and to those in Athach, **31** and to those in Hebron, and to all the places where David—he and his men—had gone up and down.

CHAPTER 31

1 And the Philistines are fighting against Israel, and the men of Israel flee from the face of the Philistines, and fall wounded in Mount Gilboa, **2** and the Philistines follow Saul and his sons, and the Philistines strike Jonathan, and Abinadab, and Malchishua, the sons of Saul. **3** And the battle is hard against Saul, and the archers find him—men with bow—and he is greatly pained by the archers; **4** and Saul says to the bearer of his weapons, "Draw your sword, and pierce me with it, lest they come—these uncircumcised—and have pierced me, and rolled themselves on me"; and the bearer of his weapons has not been willing, for he is greatly afraid, and Saul takes the sword, and falls on it. **5** And the bearer of his weapons sees that Saul [is] dead, and he falls—he also—on his sword, and dies with him; **6** and Saul dies, and three of his sons, and the bearer of his weapons, also all his men, together on that day. **7** And they see—the men of Israel, who [are] beyond the valley, and who [are] beyond the Jordan—that the men of Israel have fled, and that Saul and his sons have died, and they forsake the cities and flee, and Philistines come in, and dwell in them. **8** And it comes to pass on the next day, that the Philistines come to strip the wounded, and they find Saul and his three sons fallen on Mount Gilboa, **9** and they cut off his head, and strip off his weapons, and send [them] into the land of the surrounding Philistines, to proclaim tidings [in] the house of their idols, and [among] the people; **10** and they place his weapons [in] the house of Ashtaroth, and they have fixed his body on the wall of Beth-Shan. **11** And they hear regarding it—the inhabitants of Jabesh-Gilead—that which the Philistines have done to Saul, **12** and all the men of valor arise, and go all the night, and take the body of Saul, and the bodies of his sons, from the wall of Beth-Shan, and come to Jabesh, and burn them there, **13** and they take their bones, and bury [them] under the tamarisk in Jabesh, and fast seven days.

2 SAMUEL

CHAPTER 1

1 And it comes to pass after the death of Saul, that David has returned from striking the Amalekite, and David dwells in Ziklag [for] two days, **2** and it comes to pass, on the third day, that behold, a man has come in out of the camp from Saul, and his garments [are] torn, and earth [is] on his head; and it comes to pass in his coming to David, that he falls to the earth and pays respect. **3** And David says to him, "Where do you come from?" And he says to him, "I have escaped out of the camp of Israel." **4** And David says to him, "What has been the matter? Please declare [it] to me." And he says, "That the people have fled from the battle, and also a multitude of the people have fallen, and they die; and also Saul and his son Jonathan have died." **5** And David says to the youth who is declaring [it] to him, "How have you known that Saul and his son Jonathan [are] dead?" **6** And the youth who is declaring [it] to him says, "I happened to meet in Mount Gilboa, and behold, Saul is leaning on his spear; and behold, the chariots and those possessing horses have followed him; **7** and he turns behind him, and sees me, and calls to me, and I say, Here I [am]. **8** And he says to me, Who [are] you? and I say to him, I [am] an Amalekite. **9** And he says to me, Please stand over me and put me to death, for the arrow has seized me, for all my soul [is] still in me. **10** And I stand over him, and put him to death, for I knew that he does not live after his falling, and I take the crown which [is] on his head, and the bracelet which [is] on his arm, and bring them to my lord here." **11** And David takes hold on his garments, and tears them, and also all the men who [are] with him, **12** and they mourn, and weep, and fast until the evening, for Saul, and for his son Jonathan, and for the people of Yhwh, and for the house of Israel, because they have fallen by the sword. **13** And David says to the youth who is declaring [it] to him, "Where [are] you from?" And he says, "I [am] the son of a sojourner, an Amalekite." **14** And David says to him, "How were you not afraid to put forth your hand to destroy the anointed of Yhwh?" **15** And David calls to one of the youths and says, "Draw near—fall on him"; and he strikes him, and he dies; **16** and David says to him, "Your blood [is] on your own head, for your mouth has testified against you, saying, I put to death the anointed of Yhwh." **17** And David laments with this lamentation over Saul, and over his son Jonathan; **18** and he says to teach the sons of Judah "The Bow"; behold, it is written on the Scroll of the Upright: **19** "The beauty of Israel || [Is] wounded on your high places; How the mighty have fallen! **20** Do not declare [it] in Gath, || Do not proclaim the tidings in the streets of Ashkelon, || Lest they rejoice—The daughters of the Philistines, || Lest they exult—The daughters of the uncircumcised! **21** Mountains of Gilboa! No dew nor rain be on you, || And fields of raised-offerings! For there has become loathsome || The shield of the mighty, || The shield of Saul— without the anointed with oil. **22** From the blood of the wounded, || From the fat of the mighty, || The bow of Jonathan || Has not turned backward; And the sword of Saul does not return empty. **23** Saul and Jonathan! They are loved and pleasant in their lives, || And in their death they have not been parted. They have been lighter than eagles, || They have been mightier than lions! **24** Daughters of Israel! Weep for Saul, || Who is clothing you [in] scarlet with delights. Who is lifting up ornaments of gold on your clothing. **25** How the mighty have fallen || In the midst of the battle! Jonathan [was] wounded on your high places! **26** I am in distress for you, my brother Jonathan, || You were very pleasant to me; Your love was wonderful to me, || Above the love of women! **27** How the mighty have fallen, || Indeed, the weapons of war perish!"

CHAPTER 2

1 And it comes to pass afterward, that David inquires of Yhwh, saying, "Do I go up into one of the cities of Judah?" And

Yhwh says to him, "Go up." And David says, "To where do I go up?" And He says, "To Hebron." **2** And David goes up there, and also his two wives, Ahinoam the Jezreelitess, and Abigail wife of Nabal the Carmelite; **3** and David has brought up his men who [are] with him—a man and his household—and they dwell in the cities of Hebron. **4** And the men of Judah come, and anoint David there for king over the house of Judah; and they declare to David, saying, "The men of Jabesh-Gilead [are] they who buried Saul." **5** And David sends messengers to the men of Jabesh-Gilead and says to them, "Blessed [are] you of Yhwh, in that you have done this kindness with your lord, with Saul, that you bury him. **6** And now Yhwh does kindness and truth with you, and I also do this good with you because you have done this thing; **7** and now your hands are strong, and be for sons of valor, for your lord Saul [is] dead, and the house of Judah has also anointed me for king over them." **8** And Abner, son of Ner, head of the host which Saul has, has taken Ish-Bosheth, son of Saul, and causes him to pass over to Mahanaim, **9** and causes him to reign over Gilead, and over the Ashurite, and over Jezreel, and over Ephraim, and over Benjamin, and over Israel—all of it. **10** Ish-Bosheth son of Saul [is] a son of forty years in his reigning over Israel, and he has reigned [for] two years; only the house of Judah has been after David. **11** And the number of the days that David has been king in Hebron, over the house of Judah, is seven years and six months. **12** And Abner son of Ner goes out, and servants of Ish-Bosheth son of Saul, from Mahanaim to Gibeon. **13** And Joab son of Zeruiah, and servants of David, have gone out, and they meet by the pool of Gibeon together, and sit down, these by the pool on this [side], and these by the pool on that [side]. **14** And Abner says to Joab, "Now let the youths rise and play before us"; and Joab says, "Let them rise." **15** And they rise and pass over, in number twelve of Benjamin, even of Ish-Bosheth son of Saul, and twelve of the servants of David. **16** And they each lay hold on the head of his companion, and his sword [is] in the side of his companion, and they fall together, and [one] calls that place Helkath-Hazzurim, which [is] in Gibeon, **17** and the battle is very hard on that day, and Abner is struck, and the men of Israel, before the servants of David. **18** And there are three sons of Zeruiah there: Joab, and Abishai, and Asahel; and Asahel [is] light on his feet, as one of the roes which [are] in the field, **19** and Asahel pursues after Abner, and has not turned aside to go to the right or to the left, from after Abner. **20** And Abner looks behind him and says, "Are you he—Asahel?" And he says, "I [am]." **21** And Abner says to him, "Turn aside to your right hand or to your left, and seize one of the youths for yourself, and take his armor for yourself"; and Asahel has not been willing to turn aside from after him. **22** And Abner adds again, saying to Asahel, "Turn aside from after me, why do I strike you to the earth? and how do I lift up my face to your brother Joab?" **23** And he refuses to turn aside, and Abner strikes him with the back part of the spear to the fifth [rib], and the spear comes out from behind him, and he falls there, and dies under it; and it comes to pass, everyone who has come to the place where Asahel has fallen and dies—they stand still. **24** And Joab and Abishai pursue after Abner, and the sun has gone in, and they have come to the height of Ammah, which [is] on the front of Giah, the way of the wilderness of Gibeon. **25** And the sons of Benjamin gather themselves together after Abner, and become one troop, and stand on the top of a certain height, **26** and Abner calls to Joab and says, "Does the sword consume forever? have you not known that it is bitterness in the latter end? and until when do you not say to the people to turn back from after their brothers?" **27** And Joab says, "God lives! For unless you had spoken, surely then from the morning each of the people had gone up from after his brother." **28** And Joab blows with a horn, and all the people stand still, and no longer pursue after Israel, nor have they added to fight anymore. **29** And Abner and his men have gone through the plain all that night, and pass over the Jordan, and go on [through] all Bithron, and come to Mahanaim. **30** And Joab has turned back from after Abner, and gathers all the people, and there are lacking of the servants of David nineteen men, and Asahel; **31** and the servants of David have struck of Benjamin, even among the men of Abner, three hundred and sixty men—they died. **32** And they lift up Asahel, and bury him in the burying-place of his father, which [is] in Beth-Lehem, and they go all the night—Joab and his men—and [dawn's light] shines on them in Hebron.

CHAPTER 3

1 And the war is long between the house of Saul and the house of David, and David is going on and [is] strong, and the house of Saul is going on and [is] weak. **2** And there are sons born to David in Hebron, and his firstborn is Amnon, of Ahinoam the Jezreelitess, **3** and his second [is] Chileab, of Abigail wife of Nabal the Carmelite, and the third [is] Absalom son of Maacah daughter of Talmai king of Geshur, **4** and the fourth [is] Adonijah son of Haggith, and the fifth [is] Shephatiah son of Abital, **5** and the sixth [is] Ithream, of Eglah wife of David; these have been born to David in Hebron. **6** And it comes to pass, in the war being between the house of Saul and the house of David, that Abner has been strengthening himself in the house of Saul, **7** and Saul has a concubine, and her name [is] Rizpah daughter of Aiah, and [Ish-Bosheth] says to Abner, "Why have you gone in to the concubine of my father?" **8** And it is exceedingly displeasing to Abner, because of the words of Ish-Bosheth, and he says, "[Am] I the head of a dog—that in reference to Judah, today I do kindness with the house of your father Saul, to his brothers, and to his friends, and have not delivered you into the hand of David—that you charge against me iniquity concerning the woman today? **9** thus God does to Abner, and thus He adds to him, surely as Yhwh has sworn to David—surely so I do to him: **10** to cause the kingdom to pass over from the house of Saul, and to raise up the throne of David over Israel, and over Judah, from Dan even to Beer-Sheba." **11** And he is not able to return a word [to] Abner anymore, because of his fearing him. **12** And Abner sends messengers to David for himself, saying, "Whose [is] the land?" [And] saying, "Make your covenant with me, and behold, my hand [is] with you, to bring around all Israel to you." **13** And [David] says, "Good I make a covenant with you; only, one thing I am asking of you, that is, you do not see my face, except [that] you first bring in Michal daughter of Saul in your coming in to see my face." **14** And David sends messengers to Ish-Bosheth son of Saul, saying, "Give up my wife Michal, whom I betrothed to myself with one hundred foreskins of the Philistines." **15** And Ish-Bosheth sends, and takes her from a man, from Phaltiel son of Laish, **16** and her husband goes with her, going on and weeping behind her, to Bahurim, and Abner says to him, "Go, return"; and he turns back. **17** And the word of Abner was with [the] elderly of Israel, saying, "Thus far you have been seeking David for king over you, **18** and now, do [it], for Yhwh has spoken of David saying, [It is] by the hand of my servant David to save My people Israel out of the hand of the Philistines, and out of the hand of all their enemies." **19** And Abner also speaks in the ears of Benjamin, and Abner also goes to speak in the ears of David in Hebron all that [is] good in the eyes of Israel, and in the eyes of all the house of Benjamin, **20** and Abner comes to David, to Hebron, and twenty men [are] with him, and David makes a banquet for Abner and for the men who [are] with him. **21** And Abner says to David, "I arise, and go, and gather the whole of Israel to my lord the king, and they make a covenant with you, and you have reigned over all that your soul desires"; and David sends Abner away, and he goes in peace. **22** And behold, the servants of David, and Joab, have come from the troop, and they have brought much spoil with them, and Abner is not with David in Hebron, for he has sent him away, and he goes in peace; **23** and Joab and all the host that [were] with him have come, and they declare to Joab, saying, "Abner son of Ner has come to the king, and he sends him away, and he goes in peace." **24** And Joab comes to the king and says, "What have you done? behold, Abner has come to you! Why [is] this—you have sent him away, and he is really gone? **25** You have known Abner son of Ner, that he came to deceive you, and to know your going out and your coming in, and to know all that you are doing." **26** And Joab goes out from David, and sends messengers after Abner, and they bring him back from the well of Sirah, and David did not know. **27** And Abner turns back to Hebron, and Joab turns him aside to the midst of the gate to speak with him quietly, and strikes him there in the fifth [rib]—and he dies—for the blood of his brother Asahel. **28** And David hears afterward and says, "My kingdom and I [are] acquitted by Yhwh for all time, from the blood of Abner son of Ner; **29** it stays on the head of Joab, and on all the house of his father, and there is not cut off from the house of Joab one who has discharging, and leprous, and laying hold on a staff, and falling by a sword, and lacking bread." **30** And Joab and his brother Abishai slew Abner because that he put their brother Asahel to death in Gibeon, in battle. **31** And David says to Joab, and to all the people who [are] with him, "Tear your garments, and gird on sackcloth, and mourn before Abner"; and King David is going after the bier. **32** And they bury Abner in Hebron, and the king lifts up his voice, and weeps at the grave of Abner, and all the people weep; **33** and the king laments for Abner and says, "Does Abner die as the death of a fool? **34** Your hands not bound, || And your feet not brought near to chains! You have fallen as one falling before sons of evil!" And all the people add to weep over him. **35** And all the people come to cause David to eat bread while yet day, and David swears, saying, "Thus God does to me, and thus He adds, for—before the going in of the sun, I taste no bread or any other thing." **36** And all the people have discerned [it], and it is good in their eyes, as all that the king has done is good in the eyes of all the people; **37** and all the people know, even all Israel, in that day, that it has not been from the king—to put Abner son of Ner to death. **38** And the king says to his servants, "Do you not know that a prince and a great one has fallen this day in Israel? **39** and today I [am] tender, and an anointed king: and these men, sons of Zeruiah, [are] too hard for me; Yhwh repays to the doer of the evil according to his evil."

CHAPTER 4

1 And the son of Saul hears that Abner [is] dead in Hebron, and his hands are feeble, and all of Israel has been troubled. **2** And two men, heads of troops, have been [to] the son of Saul, the name of the first [is] Baanah, and the name of the second Rechab, sons of Rimmon the Beerothite, of the sons of Benjamin, for Beeroth is also reckoned to Benjamin, **3** and the Beerothites flee to Gittaim, and are sojourners there to this day. **4** And to Jonathan son of Saul [is] a son—lame; he was a son of five years at the coming in of the rumor of [the death of] Saul and Jonathan, out of Jezreel, and his nurse lifts him up, and flees, and it comes to pass in her hastening to flee, that he falls, and becomes lame, and his name [is] Mephibosheth. **5** And the sons of Rimmon the Beerothite, Rechab and Baanah, go, and come in at the heat of the day to the house of Ish-Bosheth, and he is lying down—the lying down of noon; **6** and they have come there, to the midst of the house, taking wheat, and they strike him to the fifth [rib], and Rechab and his brother Baanah have escaped; **7** indeed, they come into the house, and he is lying on his bed, in the inner part of his bed-chamber, and they strike him, and put him to death, and turn his head aside, and they take his head, and go the way of the plain all the night, **8** and bring in the head of Ish-Bosheth to David in Hebron, and say to the king, "Behold, the head of Ish-Bosheth, son of Saul, your enemy, who sought your life; and Yhwh gives vengeance to my lord the king this day, of Saul and of his seed." **9** And David answers Rechab and his brother Baanah, sons of Rimmon the Beerothite, and says to them, "Yhwh lives, who has redeemed my soul out of all adversity, **10** when one is declaring to me, saying, Behold, Saul is dead, and he was as a bearer of tidings in his own eyes, then I take hold on him, and slay him in Ziklag, instead of my giving to him [for] the tidings. **11** Also—when wicked men have slain the righteous man in his own house, on his bed; and now, do I not require his blood from your hand, and have taken you away from the earth?" **12** And David commands the young men, and they slay them, and cut off their hands and their feet, and hang [them] over the pool in Hebron, and they have taken the head of Ish-Bosheth, and bury [it] in the burying-place of Abner in Hebron.

CHAPTER 5

1 And all the tribes of Israel come to David, to Hebron, and speak, saying, "Behold, we [are] your bone and your flesh; **2** also thus far, in Saul's being king over us, you have been he who is bringing out and bringing in Israel, and Yhwh says to you, You feed My people Israel, and you are for leader over Israel." **3** And all [the] elderly of Israel come to the king, to Hebron, and King David makes a covenant with them in Hebron before Yhwh, and they anoint David for king over Israel. **4** A son of thirty years [is] David in his being king; he has reigned [for] forty years; **5** he reigned over Judah in Hebron [for] seven years and six months, and in Jerusalem he reigned [for] thirty-three years, over all Israel and Judah. **6** And the king goes, and his men, to Jerusalem, to the Jebusite, the inhabitant of the land, and they speak to David, saying, "You do not come in here, except [that] you turn aside the blind and the lame," saying, "David does not come in here." **7** And David captures the fortress of Zion, it [is] the City of David. **8** And on that day David says, "Anyone striking the Jebusite, let him go up by the watercourse (and the lame and the blind—the hated of David's soul)." Therefore they say, "The blind and lame—he does not come into the house." **9** And David dwells in the fortress, and calls it the City of David, and David builds all around, from Millo and inward, **10** and David goes, going on and becoming great, and Yhwh, God of Hosts, [is] with him. **11** And Hiram king of Tyre sends messengers to David, and cedar-trees, and craftsmen of wood, and craftsmen of stone, for walls, and they build a house for David, **12** and David knows that Yhwh has established him for king over Israel, and that He has lifted up his kingdom, because of His people Israel. **13** And again David takes concubines and wives out of Jerusalem, after his coming from Hebron, and again there are born to David sons and daughters. **14** And these [are] the names of those born to him in Jerusalem: Shammuah, and Shobab, and Nathan, and Solomon, **15** and Ibhar, and Elishua, and Nepheg, and Japhia, **16** and Elishama, and Eliada, and Eliphalet. **17** And the Philistines hear that they have anointed David for king over Israel, and all the Philistines come up to seek David, and David hears, and goes down to the fortress, **18** and the Philistines have come, and are spread out in the Valley of Rephaim. **19** And David asks of Yhwh, saying, "Do I go up to the Philistines? do You give them into my hand?" And Yhwh says to David, "Go up, for I certainly give the Philistines into your hand." **20** And David comes to Ba'al-Perazim, and David strikes them there, and says, "Yhwh has broken forth [on] my enemies before me, as the breaking forth of waters"; therefore he has called the name of that place Ba'al-Perazim. **21** And they forsake their idols there, and David and his men lift them up. **22** And the Philistines add again to come up, and are spread out in the Valley of Rephaim, **23** and David asks of Yhwh, and He says, "You do not go up, turn around to their rear, and you have come to them from the front [[or in front]] of the mulberries, **24** and it comes to pass, in your hearing the sound of a stepping in the tops of the mulberries, then you move sharply, for then Yhwh has gone out before you to strike in the camp of the Philistines." **25** And David does so, as Yhwh commanded him, and strikes the Philistines from Geba to your coming to Gazer.

CHAPTER 6

1 And again David gathered every chosen one in Israel—thirty thousand, **2** and David rises and goes, and all the people who [are] with him, from Ba'ale-Judah, to bring up the Ark of God from there, whose name has been called—the Name of Yhwh of Hosts, inhabiting the cherubim—on it. **3** And they cause the Ark of God to ride on a new cart, and lift it up from the house of Abinadab, which [is] in the height, and Uzzah and Ahio sons of Abinadab are leading the new cart; **4** and they lift it up from the house of Abinadab, which [is] in the height, with the Ark of God, and Ahio is going before the Ark, **5** and David and all the house of Israel are playing before Yhwh, with all kinds of [instruments] of fir-wood, even with harps, and with psalteries, and with timbrels, and with horns, and with cymbals. **6** And they come to the threshing-floor of Nachon, and Uzzah puts forth [his hand] to the Ark of God, and lays hold on it, for they released the oxen; **7** and the anger of Yhwh burns against Uzzah, and God strikes him there for the error, and he dies there by the Ark of God. **8** And it is displeasing to David, because that Yhwh has broken forth a breach on Uzzah, and [one] calls that place Perez-Uzzah to this day; **9** and David fears Yhwh on that day and says, "How does the Ark of Yhwh come to me?" **10** And David has not been willing to turn aside the Ark of Yhwh to himself, to the City of David, and David turns it aside to the house of Obed-Edom the Gittite, **11** and the Ark of Yhwh inhabits the house of Obed-Edom the Gittite [for] three months, and Yhwh blesses Obed-Edom and all his house. **12** And it is declared to King David, saying, "Yhwh has blessed the house of Obed-Edom, and all that he has, because of the Ark of God"; and David goes and brings up the Ark of God from the house of Obed-Edom to the City of David with joy. **13** And it comes to pass, when those carrying the Ark of Yhwh have stepped six steps, that he sacrifices an ox and a fatling. **14** And David is dancing with all [his] strength before Yhwh, and David is girded with a linen ephod, **15** and David and all the house of Israel are bringing up the Ark of Yhwh with shouting, and with the voice of a horn, **16** and it has come to pass, the Ark of Yhwh

has come into the City of David, and Michal daughter of Saul has looked through the window and sees King David moving and dancing before Yhwh, and she despises him in her heart. **17** And they bring in the Ark of Yhwh, and set it up in its place, in the midst of the tent which David has spread out for it, and David causes burnt-offerings and peace-offerings to ascend before Yhwh. **18** And David finishes from causing the burnt-offering and the peace-offerings to ascend, and blesses the people in the Name of Yhwh of Hosts, **19** and he apportions to all the people, to all the multitude of Israel, from man and to woman, to each, one cake of bread, and one eshpar, and one ashisha, and all the people go, each to his house. **20** And David turns back to bless his house, and Michal daughter of Saul goes out to meet David and says, "How honorable was the king of Israel today, who was uncovered today before the eyes of the handmaids of his servants, as one of the vain ones is openly uncovered!" **21** And David says to Michal, "Before Yhwh, who fixed on me above your father, and above all his house, to appoint me leader over the people of Yhwh, and over Israel—indeed, I played before Yhwh; **22** and I have been more vile than this, and have been low in my eyes, and with the handmaids whom you have spoken of, I am honored with them." **23** As for Michal daughter of Saul, she had no child until the day of her death.

CHAPTER 7

1 And it comes to pass, when the king sat in his house, and Yhwh has given rest to him all around, from all his enemies, **2** that the king says to Nathan the prophet, "Now see, I am dwelling in a house of cedars, but the Ark of God is dwelling in the midst of the curtain." **3** And Nathan says to the king, "All that [is] in your heart—go, do, for Yhwh [is] with you." **4** And it comes to pass in that night, that the word of Yhwh is to Nathan, saying, **5** "Go, and you have said to My servant, to David, Thus said Yhwh: Do you build for Me a house for My dwelling in? **6** for I have not dwelt in a house even from the day of My bringing up the sons of Israel out of Egypt, even to this day, and am walking up and down in a tent and in a dwelling place. **7** During all [the time] that I have walked up and down among all the sons of Israel, have I spoken a word with one of the tribes of Israel, which I commanded to feed my people Israel, saying, Why have you not built a house of cedars for Me? **8** and now, thus you say to My servant, to David, Thus said Yhwh of Hosts: I have taken you from the pasture, from after the flock, to be leader over My people, over Israel; **9** and I am with you wherever you have gone, and I cut off all your enemies from your presence, and have made a great name for you, as the name of the great ones who [are] in the earth, **10** and I have appointed a place for My people, for Israel, and have planted it, and it has dwelt in its place, and it is not troubled anymore, and the sons of perverseness do not add to afflict it anymore, as in the beginning, **11** even from the day that I appointed judges over My people Israel; and I have given rest to you from all your enemies, and Yhwh has declared to you that Yhwh makes a house for you. **12** When your days are full, and you have lain with your fathers, then I have raised up your seed after you which goes out from your bowels, and have established his kingdom; **13** he builds a house for My Name, and I have established the throne of his kingdom for all time. **14** I am to him for a father, and he is to Me for a son; whom in his dealing perversely I have even reproved with a rod of men, and with strokes of the sons of Adam, **15** and My kindness does not turn aside from him, as I turned it aside from Saul, whom I turned aside from before you, **16** and your house and your kingdom [are] steadfast before you for all time, your throne is established for all time." **17** According to all these words, and according to all this vision, so spoke Nathan to David. **18** And King David comes in and sits before Yhwh, and says, "Who [am] I, Lord Yhwh? and what [is] my house, that You have brought me here? **19** And yet this [is] little in Your eyes, Lord Yhwh, and You also speak concerning the house of Your servant far off; and this [is] the law of the man, Lord Yhwh. **20** And what does David add more to speak to You? and You, You have known Your servant, Lord Yhwh. **21** Because of Your word, and according to Your heart, You have done all this greatness, to cause Your servant to know [it]. **22** Therefore You have been great, Yhwh God, for there is none like You, and there is no God except You, according to all that we have heard with our ears. **23** And who [is] as Your people, as Israel—one nation in the earth, whom God has gone to redeem for a people for

Himself, and to make for Himself a name—and to do for Yourself the greatness—even fearful things for Your land, at the presence of Your people, whom You have redeemed for Yourself out of Egypt—[among the] nations and their gods? **24** Indeed, You establish Your people Israel for Yourself, for a people for Yourself for all time, and You, Yhwh, have been to them for God. **25** And now, Yhwh God, the word which You have spoken concerning Your servant, and concerning his house, establish for all time, and do as You have spoken. **26** And Your Name is great for all time, saying, Yhwh of Hosts [is] God over Israel, and the house of Your servant David is established before You, **27** for You, Yhwh of Hosts, God of Israel, have uncovered the ear of Your servant, saying, I build a house for you, therefore Your servant has found his heart to pray this prayer to You. **28** And now, Lord Yhwh, You [are] God Himself, and Your words are truth, and You speak this goodness to Your servant, **29** and now, begin and bless the house of Your servant, to be before You for all time, for You, Lord Yhwh, have spoken, and by Your blessing the house of Your servant is blessed for all time."

CHAPTER 8

1 And it comes to pass afterward that David strikes the Philistines, and humbles them, and David takes the bridle of the metropolis out of the hand of the Philistines. **2** And he strikes Moab, and measures them with a line, causing them to lie down on the earth, and he measures two lines to put to death, and the fullness of the line to keep alive, and the Moabites are for servants to David, bearers of a present. **3** And David strikes Hadadezer son of Rehob, king of Zobah, in his going to bring back his power by the River [Euphrates]; **4** and David captures from him one thousand and seven hundred horsemen, and twenty thousand footmen, and David utterly destroys the whole of the charioteers; he leaves only one hundred of their charioteers. **5** And Aram of Damascus comes to give help to Hadadezer king of Zobah, and David strikes twenty-two thousand men of Aram; **6** and David puts garrisons in Aram of Damascus, and Aram is for a servant to David, carrying a present; and Yhwh saves David wherever he has gone; **7** and David takes the shields of gold which were on the servants of Hadadezer, and brings them to Jerusalem; **8** and from Betah, and from Berothai, cities of Hadadezer, King David has taken very much bronze. **9** And Toi king of Hamath hears that David has struck all the force of Hadadezer, **10** and Toi sends his son Joram to King David to ask of him of welfare, and to bless him (because that he has fought against Hadadezer, and strikes him, for Hadadezer had been a man of wars [with] Toi), and in his hand have been vessels of silver, and vessels of gold, and vessels of bronze, **11** also King David sanctified them to Yhwh, with the silver and the gold which he sanctified of all the nations which he subdued: **12** of Aram, and of Moab, and of the sons of Ammon, and of the Philistines, and of Amalek, and of the spoil of Hadadezer son of Rehob king of Zobah. **13** And David makes a name in his turning back from his striking Aram in the Valley of Salt—eighteen thousand; **14** and he puts garrisons in Edom—he has put garrisons in all of Edom, and all Edom are servants to David; and Yhwh saves David wherever he has gone. **15** And David reigns over all Israel, and David is doing judgment and righteousness to all his people, **16** and Joab son of Zeruiah [is] over the host, and Jehoshaphat son of Ahilud [is] remembrancer, **17** and Zadok son of Ahitub, and Ahimelech son of Abiathar, [are] priests, and Seraiah [is] scribe, **18** and Benaiah son of Jehoiada [is over] both the Cherethite and the Pelethite, and the sons of David have been ministers.

CHAPTER 9

1 And David says, "Is there yet any left of the house of Saul, and I do with him kindness because of Jonathan?" **2** And the house of Saul has a servant, and his name [is] Ziba, and they call for him to David; and the king says to him, "Are you Ziba?" And he says, "Your servant." **3** And the king says, "Is there not yet a man of the house of Saul, and I do with him the kindness of God?" And Ziba says to the king, "Jonathan has yet a son—lame." **4** And the king says to him, "Where [is] he?" And Ziba says to the king, "Behold, he [is] in the house of Machir, son of Ammiel, in Behold Debar." **5** And King David sends, and

takes him out of the house of Machir son of Ammiel, of Behold-Debar, **6** and Mephibosheth son of Jonathan, son of Saul, comes to David, and falls on his face, and pays respect, and David says, "Mephibosheth"; and he says, "Behold, your servant." **7** And David says to him, "Do not be afraid; for I certainly do with you kindness because of your father Jonathan, and have given back to you all the field of your father Saul, and you continually eat bread at my table." **8** And he bows himself and says, "What [is] your servant, that you have turned to the dead dog—such as I?" **9** And the king calls to Ziba servant of Saul and says to him, "All that was of Saul and of all his house, I have given to the son of your lord, **10** and you have served the land for him, you and your sons, and your servants, and have brought in, and there has been bread for the son of your lord, and he has eaten it; and Mephibosheth, son of your lord, continually eats bread at my table"; and Ziba has fifteen sons and twenty servants. **11** And Ziba says to the king, "According to all that my lord the king commands his servant, so your servant does." "As for Mephibosheth," [says the king,] "he is eating at my table as one of the sons of the king." **12** And Mephibosheth has a young son, and his name [is] Micha, and everyone dwelling in the house of Ziba [are] servants to Mephibosheth. **13** And Mephibosheth is dwelling in Jerusalem, for he is continually eating at the table of the king, and he [is] lame [in] his two feet.

CHAPTER 10

1 And it comes to pass afterward, that the king of the sons of Ammon dies, and his son Hanun reigns in his stead, **2** and David says, "I do kindness with Hanun son of Nahash, as his father did kindness with me"; and David sends to comfort him by the hand of his servants concerning his father, and the servants of David come into the land of the sons of Ammon. **3** And the heads of the sons of Ammon say to their lord Hanun, "Is David honoring your father in your eyes because he has sent comforters to you? for has David not sent his servants to you to search the city, and to spy it, and to overthrow it?" **4** And Hanun takes the servants of David, and shaves off the half of their beard, and cuts off their long robes in the midst—to their buttocks, and sends them away; **5** and they declare [it] to David, and he sends to meet them, for the men have been greatly ashamed, and the king says, "Abide in Jericho until your beard springs up—then you have returned." **6** And the sons of Ammon see that they have been abhorred by David, and the sons of Ammon send and hire Aram of Beth-Rehob, and Aram of Zoba, twenty thousand footmen, and the king of Maacah [with] one thousand men, and Ish-Tob [with] twelve thousand men; **7** and David hears, and sends Joab, and all the host—the mighty men. **8** And the sons of Ammon come out, and set in array [for] battle, at the opening of the gate, and Aram of Zoba, and Rehob, and Ish-Tob, and Maacah, [are] by themselves in the field; **9** and Joab sees that the front of the battle has been to him before and behind, and he chooses [out] of all the chosen in Israel, and sets in array to meet Aram, **10** and he has given the rest of the people into the hand of his brother Abishai, and sets in array to meet the sons of Ammon. **11** And he says, "If Aram is stronger than I, then you have been for salvation to me, and if the sons of Ammon are stronger than you, then I have come to give salvation to you; **12** be strong and strengthen yourself for our people, and for the cities of our God, and Yhwh does that which is good in His eyes." **13** And Joab draws near, and the people who [are] with him, to battle against Aram, and they flee from his presence; **14** and the sons of Ammon have seen that Aram has fled, and they flee from the presence of Abishai, and go into the city; and Joab turns back from the sons of Ammon, and comes to Jerusalem. **15** And Aram sees that it is struck before Israel, and they are gathered together; **16** and Hadadezer sends, and brings out Aram which [is] beyond the River, and they come to Helam, and Shobach, head of the host of Hadadezer, [is] before them. **17** And it is declared to David, and he gathers all Israel, and passes over the Jordan, and comes to Helam, and Aram sets itself in array to meet David, and they fight with him; **18** and Aram flees from the presence of Israel, and David slays seven hundred charioteers and forty thousand horsemen of Aram, and he has struck Shobach, [the] head of its host, and he dies there. **19** And all the kings—servants of Hadadezer—see that they have been struck before Israel, and make peace with Israel, and serve them; and Aram is afraid to help the sons of Ammon anymore.

CHAPTER 11

1 And it comes to pass, at the revolution of the year—at the time of the going out of the messengers—that David sends Joab, and his servants with him, and all Israel, and they destroy the sons of Ammon, and lay siege against Rabbah, but David is dwelling in Jerusalem. **2** And it comes to pass, at evening-time, that David rises from off his bed, and walks up and down on the roof of the king's house, and sees a woman bathing from the roof, and the woman [is] of very good appearance, **3** and David sends and inquires about the woman, and [someone] says, "Is this not Bathsheba, daughter of Eliam, wife of Uriah the Hittite?" **4** And David sends messengers, and takes her, and she comes to him, and he lies with her—and she is purifying herself from her uncleanness—and she turns back to her house; **5** and the woman conceives, and sends, and declares [it] to David, and says, "I [am] conceiving." **6** And David sends to Joab, [saying], "Send Uriah the Hittite to me," and Joab sends Uriah to David; **7** and Uriah comes to him, and David asks of the prosperity of Joab, and of the prosperity of the people, and of the prosperity of the war. **8** And David says to Uriah, "Go down to your house, and wash your feet"; and Uriah goes out of the king's house, and there goes out a gift from the king after him, **9** and Uriah lies down at the opening of the king's house, with all the servants of his lord, and has not gone down to his house. **10** And they declare [it] to David, saying, "Uriah has not gone down to his house"; and David says to Uriah, "Have you not come from a journey? why have you not gone down to your house?" **11** And Uriah says to David, "The ark, and Israel, and Judah, are abiding in shelters, and my lord Joab, and the servants of my lord, are encamping on the face of the field; and should I go to my house to eat and to drink, and to lie with my wife? [By] your life and the life of your soul—if I do this thing." **12** And David says to Uriah, "Also abide in this [place] today, and tomorrow I send you away"; and Uriah abides in Jerusalem on that day and on the next day, **13** and David calls for him, and he eats before him, and drinks, and he causes him to drink, and he goes out in the evening to lie on his bed with the servants of his lord, and he has not gone down to his house. **14** And it comes to pass in the morning that David writes a letter to Joab and sends [it] by the hand of Uriah; **15** and he writes in the letter, saying, "Place Uriah in front of the face of the most severe battle, and you have turned back from after him, and he has been struck, and has died." **16** And it comes to pass in Joab's watching of the city, that he appoints Uriah to the place where he knew that valiant men [were]; **17** and the men of the city go out and fight with Joab, and [some] of the people, from the servants of David, fall; and Uriah the Hittite also dies. **18** And Joab sends and declares to David all the matters of the war, **19** and commands the messenger, saying, "At your finishing all the matters of the war to speak to the king, **20** then, it has been, if the king's fury ascends, and he has said to you, Why did you draw near to the city to fight? did you not know that they shoot from off the wall? **21** Who struck Abimelech son of Jerubbesheth? did a woman not cast a piece of a rider from the wall on him, and he dies in Thebez? why did you draw near to the wall? that you have said, Also—your servant Uriah the Hittite is dead." **22** And the messenger goes, and comes in, and declares to David all that with which Joab sent him, **23** and the messenger says to David, "Surely the men have been mighty against us, and come out to us into the field, and we are on them to the opening of the gate, **24** and those shooting shoot at your servants from off the wall, and [some] of the servants of the king are dead, and also, your servant Uriah the Hittite is dead." **25** And David says to the messenger, "Thus you say to Joab, Do not let this thing be evil in your eyes; for thus and thus the sword devours; strengthen your warfare against the city, and throw it down; so you strengthen him." **26** And the wife of Uriah hears that her husband Uriah [is] dead, and laments for her lord; **27** and the mourning passes by, and David sends and gathers her to his house, and she is to him for a wife, and bears a son to him; and the thing which David has done is evil in the eyes of Yhwh.

CHAPTER 12

1 And Yhwh sends Nathan to David, and he comes to him, and says to him: "Two men have been in one city, one rich and one poor. **2** The rich has very many flocks and herds, **3** but the poor one has nothing, except one little ewe-lamb which he has bought and keeps alive. And it grows up together with him and with his sons. It eats of his morsel, and it drinks from his cup, and it lies in his bosom, and it is as a daughter to him. **4** And a traveler comes to the rich man, and he spares to take from his own flock, and from his own herd, to prepare for the traveling [man] who has come to him; and he takes the ewe-lamb of the poor man and prepares it for the man who has come to him." **5** And the anger of David burns against the man exceedingly, and he says to Nathan, "Yhwh lives, surely the man who is doing this [is] a son of death, **6** and [for] the ewe-lamb he repays fourfold, because that he has done this thing, and because that he had no pity." **7** And Nathan says to David, "You [are] the man! Thus said Yhwh, God of Israel: I anointed you for king over Israel, and I delivered you out of the hand of Saul; **8** and I give to you the house of your lord, and the wives of your lord, into your bosom, and I give the house of Israel and Judah to you; and if [that is] too little, then I add such and such [things] to you. **9** Why have you despised the word of Yhwh, to do evil in His eyes? You have struck Uriah the Hittite by the sword, and you have taken his wife for a wife for yourself, and you have slain him by the sword of the sons of Ammon. **10** And now, the sword does not turn aside from your house for all time, because you have despised Me, and take the wife of Uriah the Hittite to be for a wife for yourself; **11** thus said Yhwh: Behold, I am raising up calamity against you, out of your [own] house, and have taken your wives before your eyes, and given [them] to your neighbor, and he has lain with your wives before the eyes of this sun; **12** for you have done [it] in secret, and I do this thing before all Israel, and before the sun." **13** And David says to Nathan, "I have sinned against Yhwh." And Nathan says to David, "Also—Yhwh has caused your sin to pass away; you do not die; **14** only, because you have caused the enemies of Yhwh to greatly despise by this thing, also—the son who is born to you surely dies." **15** And Nathan goes to his house, and Yhwh strikes the boy, whom the wife of Uriah has borne to David, and it is incurable; **16** and David seeks God for the youth, and David keeps a fast, and has gone in and lodged, and lain on the earth. **17** And [the] elderly of his house rise against him, to raise him up from the earth, and he has not been willing, nor has he eaten bread with them; **18** and it comes to pass on the seventh day, that the boy dies, and the servants of David fear to declare to him that the boy is dead, for they said, "Behold, in the boy being alive we spoke to him, and he did not listen to our voice; and how do we say to him, The boy is dead? Then he has done evil." **19** And David sees that his servants are whispering, and David understands that the boy is dead, and David says to his servants, "Is the boy dead?" And they say, "Dead." **20** And David rises from the earth, and bathes and anoints [himself], and changes his raiment, and comes into the house of Yhwh, and bows himself, and comes to his house, and asks and they place bread for him, and he eats. **21** And his servants say to him, "What [is] this thing you have done? because of the living boy you have fasted and you weep, and when the boy is dead you have risen and eat bread." **22** And he says, "While the boy is alive I have fasted and I weep, for I said, Who knows [if] Yhwh pities me and the boy has lived? **23** And now, he has died, why [is] this—I fast? am I able to bring him back again? I am going to him, and he does not return to me." **24** And David comforts his wife Bathsheba, and goes in to her, and lies with her, and she bears a son, and he calls his name Solomon; and Yhwh has loved him, **25** and sends by the hand of Nathan the prophet, and calls his name Jedidiah, because of Yhwh. **26** And Joab fights against Rabbah of the sons of Ammon, and captures the royal city, **27** and Joab sends messengers to David and says, "I have fought against Rabbah—I have also captured the city of waters; **28** and now, gather the rest of the people, and encamp against the city, and capture it, lest I capture the city, and my name has been called on it." **29** And David gathers all the people, and goes to Rabbah, and fights against it, and captures it; **30** and he takes the crown of their king from off his head, and its weight [is] a talent of gold, and precious stones, and it is on the head of David; and he has brought out the spoil of the city—very much; **31** and he has brought out the people who [are] in it, and sets [them] to the saw, and to cutting instruments of iron, and to axes of iron, and has caused them to pass over into the brick-kiln; and so he does to all the cities of the sons of Ammon; and David turns back, and all the people, to Jerusalem.

CHAPTER 13

[1] And it comes to pass afterward that Absalom son of David has a beautiful sister, and her name [is] Tamar, and Amnon son of David loves her. [2] And Amnon has distress—even to become sick, because of his sister Tamar, for she [is] a virgin, and it is hard in the eyes of Amnon to do anything to her. [3] And Amnon has a friend, and his name [is] Jonadab, son of Shimeah, David's brother, and Jonadab [is] a very wise man, [4] and says to him, "Why [are] you thus lean, O king's son, morning by morning? do you not declare [it] to me?" And Amnon says to him, "Tamar—sister of my brother Absalom—I am loving." [5] And Jonadab says to him, "Lie down on your bed, and feign yourself sick, and your father has come in to see you, and you have said to him: Please let my sister Tamar come in and give me bread to eat; and she has made the food before my eyes so that I see [it], and have eaten from her hand." [6] And Amnon lies down, and feigns himself sick, and the king comes in to see him, and Amnon says to the king, "Please let my sister Tamar come, and she makes two cakes before my eyes, and I eat from her hand." [7] And David sends to Tamar, to the house, saying, "Now go to the house of your brother Amnon and make food for him." [8] And Tamar goes to the house of her brother Amnon, and he is lying down, and she takes the dough, and kneads, and makes cakes before his eyes, and cooks the cakes, [9] and takes the frying-pan, and pours out before him, and he refuses to eat, and Amnon says, "Have everyone go out from me"; and everyone goes out from him. [10] And Amnon says to Tamar, "Bring the food into the inner chamber, and I eat from your hand"; and Tamar takes the cakes that she has made and brings [them] to her brother Amnon [in] the inner chamber, [11] and she brings [them] near to him to eat, and he lays hold on her, and says to her, "Come, lie with me, my sister." [12] And she says to him, "No, my brother, do not humble me, for it is not done so in Israel; do not do this folly. [13] And I—to where do I cause my reproach to go? and you are as one of the fools in Israel; and now, please speak to the king; for he does not withhold me from you." [14] And he has not been willing to listen to her voice, and is stronger than she, and humbles her, and lies with her. [15] And Amnon hates her—a very great hatred—that greater [is] the hatred with which he has hated her than the love with which he loved her, and Amnon says to her, "Rise, go." [16] And she says to him, "Because of the circumstances this evil is greater than the other that you have done with me—to send me away"; and he has not been willing to listen to her, [17] and calls his young man, his servant, and says, "Now send this one away from me outside, and bolt the door after her." [18] And a long coat [is] on her, for such upper robes daughters of the king who [are] virgins put on—and his servant takes her outside, and has bolted the door after her. [19] And Tamar takes ashes for her head, and has torn the long coat that [is] on her, and puts her hand on her head, and goes, going on and crying; [20] and her brother Absalom says to her, "Has your brother Amnon been with you? and now, my sister, keep silent, he [is] your brother; do not set your heart to this thing"; and Tamar dwells—but desolate—in the house of her brother Absalom. [21] And King David has heard all these things, and it is very displeasing to him; [22] and Absalom has not spoken with Amnon either evil or good, for Absalom is hating Amnon, because that he humbled his sister Tamar. [23] And it comes to pass, after two years of days, that Absalom has shearers in Ba'al-Hazor, which [is] near Ephraim, and Absalom calls for all the sons of the king. [24] And Absalom comes to the king and says, "Now behold, your servant has shearers, please let the king go—and his servants—with your servant." [25] And the king says to Absalom, "No, my son, please let us not all go, and we are not too heavy on you"; and he presses on him, and he has not been willing to go, and he blesses him. [26] And Absalom says, "If not, please let my brother Amnon go with us"; and the king says to him, "Why does he go with you?" [27] and Absalom urges for him, and he sends Amnon and all the sons of the king with him. [28] And Absalom commands his young men, saying, "Now see, when the heart of Amnon [is] glad with wine, and I have said to you, Strike Amnon, that you have put him to death; do not fear; is it not because I have commanded you? be strong, indeed, become sons of valor." [29] And the young men of Absalom do to Amnon as Absalom commanded, and all the sons of the king rise, and they ride, each on his mule, and flee. [30] And it comes to pass—they [are] in the way—and the report has come to David, saying, "Absalom has struck all the sons of the king, and there is not left [even] one of them"; [31] and the king rises, and tears his garments, and lies on the earth, and all his servants are standing by [with] torn garments. [32] And Jonadab son of Shimeah, David's brother, answers and says, "Do not let my lord say, The whole of the young men, the sons of the king, they have put to death; for Amnon alone [is] dead, for it has been appointed by the command of Absalom from the day of his humbling his sister Tamar; [33] and now, do not let my lord the king lay the word to his heart, saying, All the sons of the king have died, for Amnon alone [is] dead." [34] And Absalom flees, and the young man who is watching lifts up his eyes and looks, and behold, many people are coming by the way behind him, on the side of the hill. [35] And Jonadab says to the king, "Behold, the sons of the king have come; as the word of your servant, so it has been." [36] And it comes to pass at his finishing to speak, that behold, the sons of the king have come, and they lift up their voice, and weep, and also the king and all his servants have wept—a very great weeping. [37] And Absalom has fled, and goes to Talmai, son of Ammihud, king of Geshur, and [David] mourns for his son all the days. [38] And Absalom has fled, and goes to Geshur, and is there [for] three years; [39] and King David determines to go out to Absalom, for he has been comforted for Amnon, for [he is] dead.

CHAPTER 14

[1] And Joab son of Zeruial knows that the heart of the king [is] on Absalom, [2] and Joab sends to Tekoah, and takes a wise woman from there, and says to her, "Please feign yourself a mourner, and now put on garments of mourning, and do not anoint yourself with oil, and you have been as a woman mourning for the dead [for] these many days, [3] and you have gone to the king, and spoken to him, according to this word", and Joab puts the words into her mouth. [4] And the woman of Tekoah speaks to the king, and falls on her face to the earth, and pays respect, and says, "Save, O king." [5] And the king says to her, "What do you [want]?" And she says, "I [am] truly a widow woman, and my husband dies, [6] and your maidservant has two sons; and both of them strive in a field, and there is no deliverer between them, and one strikes the other, and puts him to death; [7] and behold, the whole family has risen against your maidservant, and say, Give up him who strikes his brother, and we put him to death for the life of his brother whom he has slain, and we also destroy the heir; and they have quenched my coal which is left—so as not to set a name and remnant on the face of the ground for my husband." [8] And the king says to the woman, "Go to your house, and I give charge concerning you." [9] And the woman of Tekoah says to the king, "On me, my lord, O king, [is] the iniquity, and on the house of my father; and the king and his throne [are] innocent." [10] And the king says, "He who speaks to you, and you have brought him to me, then he does not add to come against you anymore." [11] And she says, "Please let the king remember by your God Yhwh, that the redeemer of blood does not add to destroy, and they do not destroy my son"; and he says, "Yhwh lives; if there falls [even one] hair of your son to the earth." [12] And the woman says, "Please let your maidservant speak a word to my lord the king"; and he says, "Speak." [13] And the woman says, "And why have you thought thus concerning the people of God? indeed, the king is speaking this thing as a guilty one, in that the king has not brought back his outcast; [14] for we surely die, and [are] as water which is running down to the earth, which is not gathered, and God does not accept a person, and has devised plans in that the outcast is not outcast by Him. [15] And now that I have come to speak this word to my lord the king, [it is] because the people made me afraid, and your maidservant says, Please let me speak to the king; it may be the king does the word of his handmaid, [16] for the king listens to deliver his handmaid out of the paw of the man [seeking] to destroy me and my son together out of the inheritance of God, [17] and your maidservant says, Please let the word of my lord the king be for ease; for as a messenger of God so [is] my lord the king, to understand the good and the evil; and your God Yhwh is with you." [18] And the king answers and says to the woman, "Please do not hide from me the thing that I am asking you"; and the woman says, "Please let my lord the king speak." [19] And the king says, "Is the hand of Joab with you in all this?" And the woman answers and says, "Your soul lives, my lord, O king, none [turn] to the right or to the left from all that my lord the king has spoken; for your servant Joab commanded me, and he put all these words in the mouth of your maidservant. [20] Your servant Joab has done this

thing in order to bring around the appearance of the thing, and my lord [is] wise, according to the wisdom of a messenger of God, to know all that [is] in the land." **21** And the king says to Joab, "Now behold, you have done this thing; and go, bring back the young man Absalom." **22** And Joab falls on his face to the earth, and pays respect, and blesses the king, and Joab says, "Today your servant has known that I have found grace in your eyes, my lord, O king, in that the king has done the word of his servant." **23** And Joab rises and goes to Geshur, and brings in Absalom to Jerusalem, **24** and the king says, "Let him turn around to his house, and he does not see my face." And Absalom turns around to his house, and he has not seen the face of the king. **25** And there was no man [so] beautiful in all Israel like Absalom, to praise greatly; from the sole of his foot even to his crown there was no blemish in him; **26** and in his shaving his head—and it has been at the end of year by year that he shaves [it], for it [is] heavy on him, and he has shaved it—he has even weighed out the hair of his head—two hundred shekels by the king's weight. **27** And there are born to Absalom three sons and one daughter, and her name [is] Tamar; she was a woman of beautiful appearance. **28** And Absalom dwells in Jerusalem [for] two years of days, and he has not seen the face of the king; **29** and Absalom sends to Joab, to send him to the king, and he has not been willing to come to him; and he sends again a second time, and he has not been willing to come. **30** And he says to his servants, "See, the portion of Joab [is] by the side of mine, and he has barley there; go and burn it with fire"; and the servants of Absalom burn the portion with fire. **31** And Joab rises and comes to Absalom in the house, and says to him, "Why have your servants burned the portion that I have with fire?" **32** And Absalom says to Joab, "Behold, I sent to you, saying, Come here, and I send you to the king to say, Why have I come in from Geshur? [It was] good for me while I [was] there—and now, let me see the king's face, and if there is iniquity in me then you have put me to death." **33** And Joab comes to the king, and declares [it] to him, and he calls to Absalom, and he comes to the king, and bows himself to him, on his face, to the earth, before the king, and the king gives a kiss to Absalom.

CHAPTER 15

1 And it comes to pass afterward that Absalom prepares a chariot and horses for himself, and fifty men are running before him; **2** and Absalom has risen early, and stood by the side of the way of the gate, and it comes to pass, every man who has a pleading to come to the king for judgment, that Absalom calls to him and says, "Of what city [are] you?" And he says, "Your servant [is] of one of the tribes of Israel." **3** And Absalom says to him, "See, your matters [are] good and straightforward—and there is none listening to you from the king." **4** And Absalom says, "Who makes me judge in the land, that every man who has a plea and judgment comes to me? Then I have declared him righteous." **5** And it has come to pass, in the drawing near of anyone to bow himself to him, that he has put forth his hand, and laid hold on him, and given a kiss to him; **6** and Absalom does according to this thing to all Israel who come in for judgment to the king, and Absalom steals the heart of the men of Israel. **7** And it comes to pass, at the end of forty years, that Absalom says to the king, "Please let me go, and I complete my vow that I vowed to Yhwh in Hebron, **8** for your servant has vowed a vow in my dwelling in Geshur, in Aram, saying, If Yhwh certainly brings me back to Jerusalem, then I have served Yhwh." **9** And the king says to him, "Go in peace"; and he rises and goes to Hebron, **10** and Absalom sends spies through all the tribes of Israel, saying, "At your hearing the voice of the horn, then you have said, Absalom has reigned in Hebron." **11** And two hundred men have gone with Absalom out of Jerusalem, invited ones, and they are going in their simplicity, and have not known anything; **12** and Absalom sends Ahithophel the Gilonite, a counselor of David, out of his city, out of Gilo, in his sacrificing sacrifices; and the conspiracy is strong, and the people are going and increasing with Absalom. **13** And he who is declaring tidings comes to David, saying, "The heart of the men of Israel has been after Absalom." **14** And David says to all his servants who [are] with him in Jerusalem, "Rise, and we flee, for we have no escape from the face of Absalom; hurry to go, lest he hurries, and has overtaken us, and forced evil on us, and struck the city by the mouth of the sword." **15** And the servants of the king say to the king, "According to all that my lord the king chooses—behold, your

servants do." **16** And the king goes out, and all his household at his feet, and the king leaves ten women—concubines—to keep the house. **17** And the king goes out, and all the people at his feet, and they stand still at the farthest off house. **18** And all his servants are passing on at his side, and all the Cherethite, and all the Pelethite, and all the Gittites, six hundred men who came at his feet from Gath, are passing on at the front of the king. **19** And the king says to Ittai the Gittite, "Why do you go—you also—with us? Return and abide with the king, for you [are] a stranger, and also an exile, you—to your place. **20** Your coming in [was only] yesterday, and should I move you to go with us today, since I am going over [to] where [I do not know where] I am going? Return, and take your brothers back. Kindness and truth [be] with you." **21** And Ittai answers the king and says, "Yhwh lives, and my lord the king lives, surely in the place where my lord the king is—if for death, if for life, surely your servant [is] there." **22** And David says to Ittai, "Go and pass over"; and Ittai the Gittite passes over, and all his men, and all the infants who [are] with him. **23** And all the land is weeping [with] a great voice, and all the people are passing over; and the king is passing over through the Brook of Kidron, and all the people are passing over on the front of the way of the wilderness; **24** and behold, also Zadok, and all the Levites with him, are carrying the Ark of the Covenant of God, and they make the Ark of God firm, and Abiathar goes up, until the completion of all the people to pass over out of the city. **25** And the king says to Zadok, "Take back the Ark of God to the city; if I find grace in the eyes of Yhwh, then He has brought me back, and shown me it and His habitation; **26** and if thus He says, I have not delighted in you; here I [am], He does to me as [is] good in His eyes." **27** And the king says to Zadok the priest, "Are you a seer? Return to the city in peace, and your son Ahimaaz, and Jonathan son of Abiathar, your two sons with you; **28** see, I am lingering in the plains of the wilderness until the coming in of a word from you to declare to me." **29** And Zadok takes back—and Abiathar—the Ark of God to Jerusalem, and they abide there. **30** And David is going up in the ascent of the [Mount of] Olives, going up and weeping, and he has the head covered, and he is going barefooted, and all the people who [are] with him have each covered his head, and have gone up, going up and weeping; **31** and David declared, saying, "Ahithophel [is] among the conspirators with Absalom"; and David says, "Please make the counsel of Ahithophel foolish, O Yhwh." **32** And it comes to pass, David has come to the top, where he bows himself to God, and behold, Hushai the Archite [is there] to meet him, with [with] his coat torn, and earth on his head; **33** and David says to him, "If you have passed on with me then you have been for a burden on me, **34** and if you return to the city and have said to Absalom, I am your servant, O king; I [am] also servant of your father until now, and presently, I [am] also your servant; then you have made void the counsel of Ahithophel for me; **35** and are Zadok and Abiathar the priests not with you there? and it has been, the whole of the matter that you hear from the house of the king you declare to Zadok and to Abiathar the priests. **36** Behold, their two sons [are] there with them: Ahimaaz to Zadok, and Jonathan to Abiathar, and you have sent to me by their hand anything that you hear." **37** And Hushai, David's friend, comes to the city, and Absalom comes to Jerusalem.

CHAPTER 16

1 And David has passed on a little from the top, and behold, Ziba, servant of Mephibosheth, [is there] to meet him, and a couple of donkeys [are] saddled, and on them [are] two hundred loaves, and one hundred bunches of raisins, and one hundred of summer-fruit, and a bottle of wine. **2** And the king says to Ziba, "What [are] these to you?" And Ziba says, "The donkeys for the household of the king to ride on, and the bread and the summer-fruit for the young men to eat, and the wine for the wearied to drink in the wilderness." **3** And the king says, "And where [is] the son of your lord?" And Ziba says to the king, "Behold, he is abiding in Jerusalem, for he said, Today the house of Israel gives back the kingdom of my father to me." **4** And the king says to Ziba, "Behold, all that Mephibosheth has [is] for you"; and Ziba says, "I have bowed myself—I find grace in your eyes, my lord, O king." **5** And King David has come to Bahurim, and behold, a man there is coming out, of the family of the house of Saul, and his name [is] Shimei, son of Gera, he comes out, coming out and reviling; **6** and he stones David with stones, and all the servants of King

David, and all the people, and all the mighty men on his right and on his left. **7** And thus said Shimei in his reviling: "Go out, go out, O man of blood, and man of worthlessness! **8** Yhwh has turned back on you all the blood of the house of Saul, in whose stead you have reigned, and Yhwh gives the kingdom into the hand of your son Absalom; and behold, you [are] in your evil, for you [are] a man of blood." **9** And Abishai son of Zeruiah says to the king, "Why does this dead dog revile my lord the king? Please let me pass over and I turn aside his head." **10** And the king says, "And what do I [have to do] with you, O sons of Zeruiah? for let him revile; even because Yhwh has said to him, Revile David; and who says, Why have You done so?" **11** And David says to Abishai, and to all his servants, "Behold, my son who came out of my bowels is seeking my life, and also surely now the Benjamite; leave him alone, and let him revile, for Yhwh has commanded [so] to him; **12** it may be Yhwh looks on my affliction, and Yhwh has turned back good to me for his reviling this day." **13** And David goes with his men in the way, and Shimei is going at the side of the hill opposite him, going on, and he reviles, and stones with stones close by him, and has dusted with dust. **14** And the king comes in, and all the people who [are] with him, wearied, and they are refreshed there. **15** And Absalom and all the people, the men of Israel, have come to Jerusalem, and Ahithophel with him, **16** and it comes to pass, when Hushai the Archite, David's friend, has come to Absalom, that Hushai says to Absalom, "Let the king live! Let the king live!" **17** And Absalom says to Hushai, "[Is] this your kindness with your friend? why have you not gone with your friend?" **18** And Hushai says to Absalom, "No, for he whom Yhwh has chosen, and this people, even all the men of Israel, I am his, and I abide with him; **19** and secondly, for whom do I labor? is it not before his son? as I served before your father, so I am before you." **20** And Absalom says to Ahithophel, "Give counsel for yourself [for] what we do." **21** And Ahithophel says to Absalom, "Go in to the concubines of your father, whom he left to keep the house, and all Israel has heard that you have been abhorred by your father, and the hands of all who [are] with you have been strong." **22** And they spread out the tent for Absalom on the roof, and Absalom goes in to the concubines of his father before the eyes of all Israel. **23** And the counsel of Ahithophel which he counseled in those days [is] as [when] one inquires at the word of God; so [is] all the counsel of Ahithophel both to David and to Absalom.

CHAPTER 17

1 And Ahithophel said to Absalom, "Please let me choose twelve thousand men, and I arise and pursue after David tonight, **2** and come on him, and he [will be] weary and feeble-handed, and I have caused him to tremble, and all the people who [are] with him have fled, and I have struck the king by himself, **3** and I bring back all the people to you—as the turning back of the whole [except] the man whom you are seeking—[then] all the people are [at] peace." **4** And the word is right in the eyes of Absalom, and in the eyes of all [the] elderly of Israel. **5** And Absalom says, "Now call for Hushai the Archite also, and we hear what [is] in his mouth—even he." **6** And Hushai comes to Absalom, and Absalom speaks to him, saying, "According to this word Ahithophel has spoken; do we do his word? if not, you—speak." **7** And Hushai says to Absalom, "The counsel that Ahithophel has counseled [is] not good at this time." **8** And Hushai says, "You have known your father and his men, that they [are] heroes, and they are bitter in soul as a bereaved bear in a field, and your father [is] a man of war, and does not lodge with the people; **9** behold, now, he is hidden in one of the pits, or in one of the places, and it has been at the falling among them at the commencement, that the hearer has heard and said, There has been a slaughter among the people who [are] after Absalom; **10** and he also, the son of valor, whose heart [is] as the heart of the lion, utterly melts, for all Israel knows that your father is a hero, and those with him [are] sons of valor. **11** So that I have counseled: let all Israel be diligently gathered to you, from Dan even to Beer-Sheba, as the sand that [is] by the sea for multitude, and you yourself are going in the midst; **12** and we have come to him in one of the places where he is found, and we [are] on him as the dew falls on the ground, and there has not been left of him and of all the men who [are] with him even one. **13** And if he is gathered to a city, then they have caused all Israel to carry ropes to that city, and we have drawn it to the brook until there has not even been found a stone there." **14** And Absalom says—

and all the men of Israel, "The counsel of Hushai the Archite [is] better than the counsel of Ahithophel"; and Yhwh willed to make void the good counsel of Ahithophel for the sake of Yhwh's bringing the calamity to Absalom. **15** And Hushai says to Zadok and to Abiathar the priests, "Thus and thus Ahithophel has counseled Absalom and the elderly of Israel, and thus and thus I have counseled; **16** and now, send quickly, and declare [it] to David, saying, Do not lodge in the plains of the wilderness tonight, and also, certainly pass over, lest there is a swallowing up of the king and of all the people who are with him." **17** And Jonathan and Ahimaaz are standing at En-Rogel, and the maidservant has gone and declared [it] to them—and they go and have declared [it] to King David—for they are not able to be seen to go into the city. **18** And a youth sees them, and declares [it] to Absalom; and both of them go on quickly, and come to the house of a man in Bahurim, and he has a well in his court, and they go down there, **19** and the woman takes and spreads the covering over the face of the well, and spreads the ground grain on it, and the thing has not been known. **20** And the servants of Absalom come to the woman at the house, and say, "Where [are] Ahimaaz and Jonathan?" And the woman says to them, "They passed over the brook of water"; and they seek, and have not found, and return to Jerusalem. **21** And it comes to pass, after their going on, that they come up out of the well, and go and declare [it] to King David, and say to David, "Rise, and pass over the waters quickly, for thus has Ahithophel counseled against you." **22** And David rises, and all the people who [are] with him, and they pass over the Jordan, until the morning light, until not one has been lacking who has not passed over the Jordan. **23** And Ahithophel has seen that his counsel was not done, and he saddles the donkey, and rises and goes to his house, to his city, and gives charge to his household, and strangles himself, and dies, and he is buried in the burying-place of his father. **24** And David came to Mahanaim, and Absalom passed over the Jordan, he and all the men of Israel with him; **25** and Absalom has set Amasa over the host instead of Joab, and Amasa [is] a man's son whose name is Ithra the Israeli who has gone in to Abigail, daughter of Nahash, sister of Zeruiah, mother of Joab; **26** and Israel encamps with Absalom [in] the land of Gilead. **27** And it comes to pass at the coming in of David to Mahanaim, that Shobi son of Nahash, from Rabbah of the sons of Ammon, and Machir son of Ammiel, from Behold-Debar, and Barzillai the Gileadite, from Rogelim, **28** [have brought] bed, and basin, and earthen vessel, and wheat, and barley, and flour, and roasted [grain], and beans, and lentiles, and roasted [pulse], **29** and honey, and butter, and sheep, and cheese of cows; they have brought [these] near for David, and for the people who [are] with him to eat, for they said, "Your people [are] hungry, and weary, and thirsty, in the wilderness."

CHAPTER 18

1 And David inspects the people who [are] with him, and sets over them heads of thousands and heads of hundreds, **2** and David sends the third of the people by the hand of Joab, and the third by the hand of Abishai, son of Zeruiah, brother of Joab, and the third by the hand of Ittai the Gittite, and the king says to the people, "I certainly go out—I also—with you." **3** And the people say, "You do not go out, for if we utterly flee, they do not set [their] heart on us; and if half of us die, they do not set [their] heart to us—for [you are] now like ten thousand of us; and now, [it is] better that you are for a helper to us from the city." **4** And the king says to them, "That which is good in your eyes I do"; and the king stands at the side of the gate, and all the people have gone out by hundreds and by thousands, **5** and the king charges Joab, and Abishai, and Ittai, saying, "[Deal] gently—for me, for the youth, for Absalom"; and all the people heard in the king's charging all the heads concerning Absalom. **6** And the people go out into the field to meet Israel, and the battle is in a forest of Ephraim; **7** and the people of Israel are struck there before the servants of David, and the striking there is great on that day—twenty thousand; **8** and the battle there is scattered over the face of all the land, and the forest multiplies to devour among the people more than those whom the sword has devoured in that day. **9** And Absalom meets before the servants of David, and Absalom is riding on the mule, and the mule comes in under an entangled bough of the great oak, and his head takes hold on the oak, and he is placed between the heavens and the earth, and the mule that [is] under him has passed on. **10** And one man sees, and declares [it] to Joab, and says, "Behold, I saw Absalom hanging in an oak." **11** And Joab says to the man who is declaring [it] to him, "And behold, you have seen—and why did you not strike him there to the earth—and [it would be] on me to give to you ten pieces of silver and one girdle?" **12** And the man says to Joab, "Indeed, though I am weighing on my hand one thousand pieces of silver, I do not put forth my hand to the son of the king; for in our ears the king has charged you, and Abishai, and Ittai, saying, Observe who [is] against the youth—against Absalom; **13** or I had done a vain thing against my soul, and no matter is hid from the king, and you would station yourself opposite from [me]." **14** And Joab says, "[It is] not right [that] I linger before you"; and he takes three darts in his hand, and strikes them into the heart of Absalom, while he [is] alive, in the midst of the oak. **15** And they go around—ten youths carrying weapons of Joab—and strike Absalom, and put him to death. **16** And Joab blows with a horn, and the people turn back from pursuing after Israel, for Joab has kept back the people; **17** and they take Absalom and cast him into the great pit in the forest, and set up a very great heap of stones over him, and all Israel has fled—each to his tent. **18** And Absalom has taken, and sets up for himself in his life, the standing-pillar that [is] in the king's valley, for he said, "I have no son to cause my name to be remembered"; and he calls the standing-pillar by his own name, and it is called "The Monument of Absalom" to this day. **19** And Ahimaaz son of Zadok said, "Please let me run, and I bear the king tidings, for Yhwh has delivered him out of the hand of his enemies"; **20** and Joab says to him, "You are not a man of tidings this day, but you have borne tidings on another day, and this day you do not bear tidings, because the king's son [is] dead." **21** And Joab says to Cushi, "Go, declare to the king that which you have seen"; and Cushi bows himself to Joab, and runs. **22** And Ahimaaz son of Zadok adds again and says to Joab, "And whatever it is, please let me run, I also, after the Cushite." And Joab says, "Why [is] this—you are running, my son, and [there are] no tidings found from you?" **23** "And whatever happens," he said, "let me run." And he says to him, "Run"; and Ahimaaz runs the way of the circuit, and passes by the Cushite. **24** And David is sitting between the two gates, and the watchman goes to the roof of the gate, to the wall, and lifts up his eyes, and looks, and behold, a man running by himself. **25** And the watchman calls, and declares [it] to the king, and the king says, "If [he is] by himself, tidings [are] in his mouth"; and he comes, coming on and drawing near. **26** And the watchman sees another man running, and the watchman calls to the gatekeeper, and says, "Behold, a man running by himself"; and the king says, "This one is also bearing tidings." **27** And the watchman says, "I see the running of the first as the running of Ahimaaz son of Zadok." And the king says, "This [is] a good man, and he comes with good tidings." **28** And Ahimaaz calls and says to the king, "Peace"; and he bows himself to the king, on his face, to the earth, and says, "Blessed [is] your God Yhwh who has shut up the men who lifted up their hand against my lord the king." **29** And the king says, "Peace to the youth—for Absalom?" And Ahimaaz says, "I saw the great multitude, at the sending away of the servant of the king, even your servant [by] Joab, and I have not known what [it is]." **30** And the king says, "Turn around, station yourself here"; and he turns around and stands still. **31** And behold, the Cushite has come, and the Cushite says, "Let tidings be proclaimed, my lord, O king; for today Yhwh has delivered you out of the hand of all those rising up against you." **32** And the king says to the Cushite, "Peace to the youth—for Absalom?" And the Cushite says, "Let them be—as the youth—the enemies of my lord the king, and all who have risen up against you for evil." **33** And the king trembles, and goes up on the upper chamber of the gate, and weeps, and thus he has said in his going, "My son Absalom! My son! My son Absalom! Oh that I had died for you, Absalom, my son, my son!"

CHAPTER 19

1 And it is declared to Joab, "Behold, the king is weeping and mourning for Absalom"; **2** and the salvation on that day becomes mourning to all the people, for the people have heard on that day, saying, "The king has been grieved for his son." **3** And the people steals away, on that day, to go into the city, as the people steal away, who are ashamed, in their fleeing in battle; **4** and the king has covered his face, indeed, the king cries [with] a loud voice, "My son Absalom! Absalom, my son,

my son!" **5** And Joab comes into the house to the king and says, "Today you have put to shame the faces of all your servants, those delivering your life today, and the life of your sons, and of your daughters, and the life of your wives, and the life of your concubines, **6** to love your enemies, and to hate those loving you, for today you have declared that you have no princes and servants, for today I have known that if Absalom [were] alive, and all of us dead today, that then it were right in your eyes. **7** And now, rise, go out and speak to the heart of your servants, for I have sworn by Yhwh, that [if] you are not going out—there does not lodge a man with you tonight; and this [is] worse for you than all the evil that has come on you from your youth until now." **8** And the king rises, and sits in the gate, and they have declared to all the people, saying, "Behold, the king is sitting in the gate"; and all the people come in before the king, and Israel has fled, each to his tents. **9** And it comes to pass, all the people are contending through all the tribes of Israel, saying, "The king delivered us out of the hand of our enemies, indeed, he himself delivered us out of the hand of the Philistines, and now he has fled out of the land because of Absalom, **10** and Absalom whom we anointed over us [is] dead in battle, and now, why are you silent—to bring back the king?" **11** And King David sent to Zadok and to Abiathar the priests, saying, "Speak to [the] elderly of Judah, saying, Why are you last to bring back the king to his house, since the word of all Israel has come to the king, to his house; **12** you [are] my brothers, you [are] my bone and my flesh, and why are you last to bring back the king? **13** And say to Amasa, Are you not my bone and my flesh? Thus God does to me, and thus He adds, if you are not head of the host before me instead of Joab [for] all the days." **14** And he inclines the heart of all the men of Judah as one man, and they send to the king, "Return, you and all your servants." **15** And the king turns back, and comes to the Jordan, and Judah has come to Gilgal, to go to meet the king, to bring the king over the Jordan, **16** and Shimei son of Gera, the Benjamite, who [is] from Bahurim, hurries, and comes down with the men of Judah, to meet King David, **17** and one thousand men [are] with him from Benjamin, and Ziba servant of the house of Saul, and his fifteen sons and his twenty servants with him, and they have gone prosperously over the Jordan before the king. **18** And the ferry-boat has passed over to carry over the household of the king, and to do that which [is] good in his eyes, and Shimei son of Gera has fallen before the king in his passing over into the Jordan, **19** and he says to the king, "Do not let my lord impute iniquity to me; neither remember that which your servant did perversely in the day that my lord the king went out from Jerusalem—for the king to set [it] to his heart; **20** for your servant has known that I have sinned; and behold, I have come today, first of all the house of Joseph, to go down to meet my lord the king." **21** And Abishai son of Zeruiah answers and says, "Is Shimei not put to death for this—because he reviled the anointed of Yhwh?" **22** And David says, "And what do I [have to do] with you, O sons of Zeruiah, that today you are for an adversary to me? Is any man put to death in Israel today? for have I not known that today I [am] king over Israel?" **23** And the king says to Shimei, "You do not die"; and the king swears to him. **24** And Mephibosheth son of Saul has come down to meet the king—and he did not prepare his feet, nor did he prepare his upper lip, indeed, he did not wash his garments, even from the day of the going away of the king, until the day that he came in peace— **25** and it comes to pass, when he has come to Jerusalem to meet the king, that the king says to him, "Why did you not go with me, Mephibosheth?" **26** And he says, "My lord, O king, my servant deceived me, for your servant said, I saddle the donkey for myself, and ride on it, and go with the king, for your servant [is] lame; **27** and he utters slander against your servant to my lord the king, and my lord the king [is] as a messenger of God; and do that which is good in your eyes, **28** for all the house of my father have been nothing except men of death before my lord the king, and you set your servant among those eating at your table, and what right do I have anymore—even to cry anymore to the king?" **29** And the king says to him, "Why do you speak anymore of your matters? I have said, You and Ziba—share the field." **30** And Mephibosheth says to the king, "Indeed, let him take the whole, after that my lord the king has come in peace to his house." **31** And Barzillai the Gileadite has gone down from Rogelim, and passes over the Jordan with the king, to send him away over the Jordan; **32** and Barzillai [is] very aged, a son of eighty years, and he has sustained the king in his abiding in Mahanaim, for he [is] a very great man; **33** and the king says to Barzillai, "Pass over with me, and I have sustained you in Jerusalem with me." **34** And Barzillai says to the king, "How many [are] the days of the years of my life, that I go up with the king to Jerusalem? **35** I [am] a son of eighty years today; do I know between good and evil? does your servant taste that which I am eating, and that which I drink? do I listen anymore to the voice of male and female singers? and why is your servant for a burden to my lord the king anymore? **36** As a little thing, your servant passes over the Jordan with the king, and why does the king repay me this repayment? **37** Please let your servant turn back again, and I die in my own city, near the burying-place of my father and of my mother—and behold, your servant Chimham, let him pass over with my lord the king, and do to him that which [is] good in your eyes." **38** And the king says, "Chimham goes over with me, and I do to him that which [is] good in your eyes, indeed, all that you fix on me I do to you." **39** And all the people pass over the Jordan, and the king has passed over, and the king gives a kiss to Barzillai, and blesses him, and he turns back to his place. **40** And the king passes over to Gilgal, and Chimham has passed over with him, and all the people of Judah, and they bring over the king, and also the half of the people of Israel. **41** And behold, all the men of Israel are coming to the king, and they say to the king, "Why have our brothers, the men of Judah, stolen you—and they bring the king and his household over the Jordan, and all the men of David with him?" **42** And all the men of Judah answer against the men of Israel, "Because the king [is] near to us, and why [is] this [that] you are displeased about this matter? have we eaten of the king's [substance] at all? Has he lifted up a gift to us?" **43** And the men of Israel answer the men of Judah, and say, "We have ten parts in the king, and also more than you in David; and why have you lightly esteemed us, that our word has not been first to bring back our king?" And the word of the men of Judah is sharper than the word of the men of Israel.

CHAPTER 20

1 And there happened to be a man of worthlessness there, and his name [is] Sheba, son of Bichri, a Benjamite, and he blows with a horn and says, "We have no portion in David, and we have no inheritance in the son of Jesse; each [goes] to his tents, O Israel." **2** And every man of Israel goes up from after David, after Sheba son of Bichri, and the men of Judah have cleaved to their king, from the Jordan even to Jerusalem. **3** And David comes to his house at Jerusalem. And the king takes the ten women-concubines whom he had left to keep the house, and puts them in a house of ward and sustains them, and he has not gone in to them, and they are shut up to the day of their death, living in widowhood. **4** And the king says to Amasa, "Call the men of Judah for me [within] three days, and you, stand here," **5** and Amasa goes to call Judah, and tarries beyond the appointed time that he had appointed him; **6** and David says to Abishai, "Now Sheba son of Bichri does evil to us more than Absalom; you, take the servants of your lord, and pursue after him, lest he has found fortified cities for himself, and delivered himself [from] our eye." **7** And the men of Joab go out after him, and the Cherethite, and the Pelethite, and all the mighty men, and they go out from Jerusalem to pursue after Sheba son of Bichri; **8** they [are] near the great stone that [is] in Gibeon, and Amasa has gone before them, and Joab [is] girded; he has put his long robe on him, and on it a girdle—a sword [is] fastened on his loins in its sheath; and he has gone out, and it falls. **9** And Joab says to Amasa, "Are you [in] peace, my brother?" And the right hand of Joab lays hold on the beard of Amasa to give a kiss to him; **10** and Amasa has not been watchful of the sword that [is] in the hand of Joab, and he strikes him with it to the fifth [rib], and sheds out his bowels to the earth, and he has not repeated [it] to him, and he dies; and Joab and his brother Abishai have pursued after Sheba son of Bichri. **11** And a man has stood by him, of the young men of Joab, and says, "He who has delight in Joab, and he who [is] for David—after Joab!" **12** And Amasa is rolling himself in blood, in the midst of the highway, and the man sees that all the people have stood still, and he brings around Amasa out of the highway to the field, and casts a garment over him when he has seen that everyone who has come by him has stood still. **13** When he has been removed out of the highway, every man has passed on after Joab, to pursue after Sheba son of Bichri. **14** And he passes over through all the tribes of Israel to Abel, and to Beth-Maachah, and to all the Berites, and they are assembled, and also go in after him, **15** and they go in and lay

siege against him, in Abel of Beth-Maachah, and cast up a mound against the city, and it stands in a trench, and all the people who are [are] with Joab are destroying, to cause the wall to fall. **16** And a wise woman calls out of the city, "Hear! Hear! Please say to Joab, Come near here, and I speak to you." **17** And he comes near to her, and the woman says, "Are you Joab?" And he says, "I [am]." And she says to him, "Hear the words of your handmaid"; and he says, "I am hearing." **18** and she speaks, saying, "They spoke often in former times, saying, Let them diligently inquire at Abel, and so they finished. **19** I [am] of the peaceable, faithful ones of Israel; you are seeking to destroy a city and mother in Israel; why do you swallow up the inheritance of Yhwh?" **20** And Joab answers and says, "Far be it—far be it from me; I do not swallow up nor destroy. **21** The matter [is] not so; for a man of the hill-country of Ephraim—Sheba son of Bichri [is] his name—has lifted up his hand against the king, against David; give him up by himself, and I go away from the city." And the woman says to Joab, "Behold, his head is cast to you over the wall." **22** And the woman comes to all the people in her wisdom, and they cut off the head of Sheba son of Bichri, and cast [it] to Joab, and he blows with a horn, and they are scattered from the city, each [goes] to his tents, and Joab has turned back to Jerusalem to the king. **23** And Joab [is] over all the host of Israel, and Benaiah son of Jehoiada [is] over the Cherethite, and over the Pelethite, **24** and Adoram [is] over the tribute, and Jehoshaphat son of Ahilud [is] the remembrancer, **25** and Sheva [is] scribe, and Zadok and Abiathar [are] priests, **26** and also, Ira the Jairite has been minister to David.

CHAPTER 21

1 And there is a famine in the days of David [for] three years, year after year, and David seeks the face of Yhwh, and Yhwh says, "[This is] for Saul and for the bloody house, because that he put the Gibeonites to death." **2** And the king calls for the Gibeonites and says to them—as for the Gibeonites, they [are] not of the sons of Israel, but of the remnant of the Amorite, and the sons of Israel had sworn to them, and Saul seeks to strike them in his zeal for the sons of Israel and Judah— **3** indeed, David says to the Gibeonites, "What do I do for you? and with what do I make atonement? and bless the inheritance of Yhwh." **4** And the Gibeonites say to him, "We have no silver and gold by Saul and by his house, and we have no man to put to death in Israel"; and he says, "What you are saying I do to you." **5** And they say to the king, "The man who consumed us, and who devised against us—we have been destroyed from stationing ourselves in all the border of Israel— **6** let there be given to us seven men of his sons, and we have hanged them before Yhwh, in the height of Saul, the chosen of Yhwh." And the king says, "I give"; **7** and the king has pity on Mephibosheth son of Jonathan, son of Saul, because of the oath of Yhwh that [is] between them, between David and Jonathan son of Saul; **8** and the king takes the two sons of Rizpah daughter of Aiah, whom she bore to Saul, Armoni and Mephibosheth, and the five sons of Michal daughter of Saul whom she bore to Adriel son of Barzillai the Meholathite, **9** and gives them into the hand of the Gibeonites, and they hang them in the hill before Yhwh; and the seven fall together, and they have been put to death in the days of harvest, in the first [days], the commencement of barley-harvest. **10** And Rizpah daughter of Aiah takes the sackcloth, and stretches it out for herself on the rock, from the commencement of harvest until water has been poured out on them from the heavens, and has not permitted a bird of the heavens to rest on them by day, or the beast of the field by night. **11** And it is declared to David that which Rizpah daughter of Aiah, concubine of Saul, has done, **12** and David goes and takes the bones of Saul, and the bones of his son Jonathan, from the possessors of Jabesh-Gilead, who had stolen them from the broad place of Beth-Shan, where the Philistines hanged them, in the day of the Philistines striking Saul in Gilboa; **13** and he brings up there the bones of Saul, and the bones of his son Jonathan, and they gather the bones of those hanged, **14** and bury the bones of Saul and of his son Jonathan in the land of Benjamin, in Zelah, in the burying-place of his father Kish, and do all that the king commanded, and God accepts the plea for the land afterward. **15** And again the Philistines have war with Israel, and David goes down, and his servants with him, and they fight with the Philistines; and David is weary, **16** and Ishbi-Benob, who [is] among the children of the giant—the weight of his spear [is] three hundred [shekels in] weight of bronze, and he is girded with a new one—speaks of striking David, **17** and Abishai son of Zeruiah gives help to him, and strikes the Philistine, and puts him to death; then the men of David swear to him, saying, "You do not go out with us to battle again, nor quench the lamp of Israel." **18** And it comes to pass afterward that the battle is again in Gob with the Philistines. Then Sibbechai the Hushathite has struck Saph, who [is] among the children of the giant. **19** And the battle is again in Gob with the Philistines, and Elhanan son of Jaare-Oregim, the Beth-Lehemite, strikes [a brother of] Goliath the Gittite, and the wood of his spear [is] like a weavers' beam. **20** And the battle is again in Gath, and there is a man of [great] stature, and the fingers of his hands [are] six, and the toes of his feet [are] six—twenty-four in number, and he has also been born to the giant, **21** and he reproaches Israel, and Jonathan son of Shimeah, David's brother, strikes him; **22** these four have been born to the giant in Gath, and they fall by the hand of David, and by the hand of his servants.

CHAPTER 22

1 And David speaks the words of this song to Yhwh in the day Yhwh has delivered him out of the hand of all his enemies, and out of the hand of Saul, **2** and he says: "Yhwh [is] my rock, || And my bulwark, and a deliverer to me, **3** My God [is] my rock—I take refuge in Him; My shield, and the horn of my salvation, || My high tower, and my refuge! My Savior, You save me from violence! **4** I call on Yhwh, [who is worthy] to be praised: And I am saved from my enemies. **5** When the breakers of death surrounded me, || The streams of the worthless terrify me, **6** The cords of Sheol have surrounded me, || The snares of death have been before me. **7** In my adversity I call on Yhwh, || And I call to my God, || And He hears my voice from His temple, || And my cry [is] in His ears, **8** And the earth shakes and trembles, || Foundations of the heavens are troubled, || And are shaken, for He has wrath! **9** Smoke has gone up by His nostrils, || And fire devours from His mouth; Brands have been kindled by it. **10** And He inclines the heavens and comes down, || And thick darkness [is] under His feet. **11** And He rides on a cherub and flies, || And is seen on the wings of the wind. **12** And He sets darkness around Him [for His] dwelling places, || Darkness of waters [and] thick clouds of the skies. **13** From the brightness before Him || Brands of fire were kindled! **14** Yhwh thunders from the heavens, || And the Most High gives forth His voice. **15** And He sends forth arrows, and scatters them; Lightning, and troubles them; **16** And the streams of the sea are seen, || [The] foundations of the world are revealed, || By the rebuke of Yhwh, || From the breath of the spirit of His anger. **17** He sends from above—He takes me, || He draws me out of many waters. **18** He delivers me from my strong enemy, || From those hating me, || For they were stronger than me. **19** They are before me in a day of my calamity, || And Yhwh is my support, **20** And He brings me out to a large place, || He draws me out for He delighted in me. **21** Yhwh repays me, || According to my righteousness, || According to the cleanness of my hands, He returns to me. **22** For I have kept the ways of Yhwh, || And have not done wickedly against my God. **23** For all His judgments [are] before me, || As for His statutes, I do not turn from them. **24** And I am perfect before Him, || And I keep myself from my iniquity. **25** And Yhwh returns to me, || According to my righteousness, || According to my cleanness before His eyes. **26** With the kind You show Yourself kind, || With the perfect man You show Yourself perfect, **27** With the pure You show Yourself pure, || And with the perverse You show Yourself a wrestler. **28** And You save the poor people, || But Your eyes on the high cause [them] to fall. **29** For You [are] my lamp, O Yhwh, || And Yhwh lightens my darkness. **30** For by You I run [against] a troop, || By my God I leap a wall. **31** God—His way [is] perfect, || The saying of Yhwh is tried, || He [is] a shield to all those trusting in Him. **32** For who is God except Yhwh? And who [is the] Rock except our God? **33** God—my bulwark, [my] strength, || And He makes my way perfect; **34** Making my feet like does, || And causes me to stand on my high places, **35** Teaching my hands for battle, || And a bow of bronze was brought down by my arms, **36** And You give the shield of Your salvation to me, || And Your lowliness makes me great. **37** You enlarge my step under me, || And my ankles have not slipped. **38** I pursue my enemies and destroy them, || And I do not turn until they are consumed. **39** And I consume them, and strike them, || And

they do not rise, and fall under my feet. **40** And You gird me [with] strength for battle, || You cause my withstanders to bow under me. **41** And my enemies—You give to me the neck, || Those hating me—and I cut them off. **42** They look, and there is no savior; To Yhwh, and He has not answered them. **43** And I beat them as dust of the earth, || As mire of the streets I beat them small—I spread them out! **44** And You deliver me || From the strivings of my people, || You place me for a head of nations; A people I have not known serve me. **45** Sons of a stranger feign obedience to me, || At the hearing of the ear they listen to me. **46** Sons of a stranger fade away, || And gird themselves by their close places. **47** Yhwh lives, and blessed [is] my Rock, || And exalted is my God—The Rock of my salvation. **48** God—who is giving vengeance to me, || And bringing down peoples under me, **49** And bringing me forth from my enemies, || Indeed, You raise me up above my withstanders. You deliver me from a man of violence. **50** Therefore I confess You, O Yhwh, among nations, || And I sing praise to Your Name. **51** Magnifying the salvations of His king, || And doing loving-kindness to His anointed, || To David, and to his seed—for all time!"

CHAPTER 23

1 And these [are] the last words of David: "A declaration of David son of Jesse, || And a declaration of the man raised up— Concerning the anointed of the God of Jacob, || And the sweetness of the songs of Israel: **2** The Spirit of Yhwh has spoken by me, || And His word [is] on my tongue. **3** He said— the God of Israel—to me, || He spoke—the Rock of Israel: He who is ruling over man [is] righteous, || He is ruling in the fear of God. **4** And he rises as the light of morning, || A morning sun [with] no clouds! By the shining, by the rain, || Tender grass of the earth! **5** For though my house [is] not so with God; So He made a perpetual covenant with me, || Arranged in all things, and kept; For all my salvation, and all desire, || For He has not caused [it] to spring up. **6** As for the worthless—All of them [are] driven away as a thorn, || For they are not taken away by hand; **7** And the man who comes against them || Is filled with iron and the staff of a spear, || And they are utterly burned with fire || In the cessation." **8** These [are] the names of the mighty ones whom David has: sitting in the seat [is] the Tachmonite, head of the captains—he [is] Adino, who hardened himself against eight hundred—wounded at one time. **9** And after him [is] Eleazar son of Dodo, son of Ahohi, of the three mighty men with David; in their exposing themselves among the Philistines—they have been gathered there to battle, and the men of Israel go up— **10** he has arisen, and strikes among the Philistines until his hand has been weary, and his hand cleaves to the sword, and Yhwh works a great salvation on that day, and the people turn back after him only to strip off. **11** And after him [is] Shammah son of Agee the Hararite, and the Philistines are gathered into a company, and there is a portion of the field full of lentils there, and the people have fled from the presence of the Philistines, **12** and he stations himself in the midst of the portion, and delivers it, and strikes the Philistines, and Yhwh works a great salvation. **13** And three of the thirty heads go down and come to the harvest, to David, to the cave of Adullam, and the company of the Philistines are encamping in the Valley of Rephaim, **14** and David [is] then in a fortress, and the station of the Philistines [is] then in Beth-Lehem, **15** and David longs and says, "Who gives me a drink of the water of the well of Beth-Lehem, which [is] by the gate?" **16** And the three mighty ones cleave through the camp of the Philistines, and draw water out of the well of Beth-Lehem, which [is] by the gate, and take [it] up, and bring [it] to David; and he was not willing to drink it, and pours it out to Yhwh, **17** and says, "Far be it from me, O Yhwh, to do this; is it the blood of the men who are going with their lives?" And he was not willing to drink it; the three mighty ones did these [things]. **18** And Abishai brother of Joab, son of Zeruiah, he [is] head of three, and he is lifting up his spear against three hundred—wounded, and he has a name among three. **19** Is he not the honored of the three? and he becomes their head; and he has not come to the [first] three. **20** And Benaiah son of Jehoiada (son of a man of valor, great in deeds from Kabzeel), has struck two lion-like men of Moab, and he has gone down and struck the lion in the midst of the pit in a day of snow. **21** And he has struck the Egyptian man, a man of appearance, and a spear [is] in the hand of the Egyptian, and he goes down to him with a rod, and takes the spear violently away out of the hand of the Egyptian, and slays him with his own spear. ²² Benaiah son of Jehoiada has done these [things], and has a name among the three mighty ones. ²³ He is honored more than the thirty, but he did not come to the three; and David sets him over his guard. ²⁴ Asahel brother of Joab [is] of the thirty; Elhanan son of Dodo of Beth-Lehem, ²⁵ Shammah the Harodite, Elika the Harodite, ²⁶ Helez the Paltite, Ira son of Ikkesh the Tekoite, ²⁷ Abiezer the Annethothite, Mebunnai the Hushathite, ²⁸ Zalmon the Ahohite, Maharai the Netophathite, ²⁹ Heleb son of Baanah the Netophathite, Ittai son of Ribai from Gibeah of the sons of Benjamin, ³⁰ Benaiah the Pirathonite, Hiddai of the brooks of Gaash, ³¹ Abi-Albon the Arbathite, Azmaveth the Barhumite, ³² Eliahba the Shaalbonite, of the sons of Jashen, Jonathan, ³³ Shammah the Hararite, Ahiam son of Sharar the Hararite, ³⁴ Eliphelet son of Ahasbai, son of the Maachathite, Eliam son of Ahithophel the Gilonite, ³⁵ Hezrai the Carmelite, Paarai the Arbite, ³⁶ Igal son of Nathan from Zobah, Bani the Gadite, ³⁷ Zelek the Ammonite, Naharai the Beerothite, bearer of the weapons of Joab son of Zeruiah, ³⁸ Ira the Ithrite, Gareb the Ithrite, ³⁹ Uriah the Hittite: thirty-seven in all.

CHAPTER 24

¹ And the anger of Yhwh adds to burn against Israel, and [an adversary] moves David about them, saying, "Go, number Israel and Judah." ² And the king says to Joab, head of the host that [is] with him, "Now go to and fro through all the tribes of Israel, from Dan even to Beer-Sheba, and inspect the people; then I have known the number of the people." ³ And Joab says to the king, "Indeed, your God Yhwh adds to the people, as they are, one hundred times, and the eyes of my lord the king are seeing; and my lord the king, why is he desirous of this thing?" ⁴ And the word of the king is severe toward Joab, and against the heads of the force, and Joab goes out, and the heads of the force, [from] before the king to inspect the people, even Israel; ⁵ and they pass over the Jordan, and encamp in Aroer, on the right of the city that [is] in the midst of the Brook of Gad, and to Jazer, ⁶ and they come to Gilead, and to the land of Tahtim-Hodshi, and they come to Dan-Jaan, and around to Sidon, ⁷ and they come to the fortress of Tyre, and all the cities of the Hivite, and of the Canaanite, and go out to the south of Judah, to Beer-Sheba. ⁸ And they go to and fro through all the land, and come in to Jerusalem at the end of nine months and twenty days, ⁹ and Joab gives the account of the inspection of the people to the king, and Israel is eight hundred thousand men of valor, drawing sword, and the men of Judah five hundred thousand men. ¹⁰ And the heart of David strikes him, after that he has numbered the people, and David says to Yhwh, "I have greatly sinned in that which I have done, and now, O Yhwh, please cause the iniquity of Your servant to pass away, for I have acted very foolishly." ¹¹ And David rises in the morning, and the word of Yhwh has been to Gad the prophet, seer of David, saying, ¹² "Go, and you have spoken to David, Thus said Yhwh: I am lifting up three [choices] for you, choose one of them, and I do [it] to you." ¹³ And Gad comes to David, and declares [it] to him, and says to him, "Does seven years of famine come to you in your land? or are you fleeing before your adversary [for] three months—and he is pursuing you? or is there pestilence [for] three days in your land? now, know and see what word I take back to Him sending me." ¹⁴ And David says to Gad, "I have great distress; please let us fall into the hand of Yhwh, for His mercies [are] many, but do not let me fall into the hand of man." ¹⁵ And Yhwh gives a pestilence on Israel from the morning even to the time appointed, and there dies of the people, from Dan even to Beer-Sheba, seventy thousand men, ¹⁶ and the messenger puts forth his hand to Jerusalem to destroy it, and Yhwh sighs concerning the calamity, and says to the messenger who is destroying among the people, "Enough, now, cease your hand"; and the messenger of Yhwh was near the threshing-floor of Araunah the Jebusite. ¹⁷ And David speaks to Yhwh when he sees the messenger who is striking among the people, and says, "Behold, I have sinned, indeed, I have done perversely; and these—the flock—what have they done? Please let Your hand be on me and on the house of my father." ¹⁸ And Gad comes to David on that day and says to him, "Go up, raise an altar to Yhwh in the threshing-floor of Araunah the Jebusite"; ¹⁹ and David goes up, according to the word of Gad, as Yhwh commanded. ²⁰ And Araunah looks, and sees the king and his servants passing over to him, and Araunah goes out and bows himself to the king [with] his face to the earth. ²¹ And Araunah

says, "Why has my lord the king come to his servant?" And David says, "To buy the threshing-floor from you, to build an altar to Yhwh, and the plague is restrained from the people." ²² And Araunah says to David, "Let my lord the king take [it] and cause that which is good in his eyes to ascend; see, [here are] the oxen for a burnt-offering, and the threshing instruments, and the instruments of the oxen, for wood"; ²³ Araunah has given the whole [as] a king to a king; and Araunah says to the king, "Your God Yhwh accepts you." ²⁴ And the king says to Araunah, "No, for I surely buy from you for a price, and I do not cause burnt-offerings to ascend to my God Yhwh for nothing"; and David buys the threshing-floor and the oxen for fifty shekels of silver, ²⁵ and David builds an altar to Yhwh there, and causes burnt-offerings and peace-offerings to ascend, and Yhwh accepts the plea for the land, and the plague is restrained from Israel.

1 KINGS

CHAPTER 1

¹ And King David [is] old, entering into days, and they cover him with garments, and he has no heat, ² and his servants say to him, "Let them seek [for] a young woman, a virgin, for my lord the king, and she has stood before the king, and is a companion to him, and has lain in your bosom, and my lord the king has heat." ³ And they seek [for] a beautiful young woman in all the border of Israel, and find Abishag the Shunammite, and bring her to the king, ⁴ and the young woman [is] very, very beautiful, and she is a companion to the king, and serves him, and the king has not known her. ⁵ And Adonijah son of Haggith is lifting himself up, saying, "I reign"; and he prepares for himself a chariot and horsemen, and fifty men running before him, ⁶ and his father has not grieved him [all] his days, saying, "Why have you done this?" And he also [is] of a very good form, and [his mother] bore him after Absalom. ⁷ And his words are with Joab son of Zeruiah, and with Abiathar the priest, and they help after Adonijah; ⁸ and Zadok the priest, and Benaiah son of Jehoiada, and Nathan the prophet, and Shimei, and Rei, and the mighty ones whom David has, have not been with Adonijah. ⁹ And Adonijah sacrifices sheep and oxen and fatlings near the stone of Zoheleth that [is] by En-Rogel, and calls all his brothers, sons of the king, and for all the men of Judah, servants of the king; ¹⁰ and he has not called Nathan the prophet, and Benaiah, and the mighty ones, and his brother Solomon. ¹¹ And Nathan speaks to Bathsheba, mother of Solomon, saying, "Have you not heard that Adonijah son of Haggith has reigned, and our lord David has not known? ¹² and now, come, please let me counsel you, and deliver your life and the life of your son Solomon; ¹³ go and enter in to King David, and you have said to him: Have you not, my lord, O king, sworn to your handmaid, saying, Surely your son Solomon reigns after me, and he sits on my throne? and why has Adonijah reigned? ¹⁴ Behold, you are yet speaking there with the king, and I come in after you, and have completed your words." ¹⁵ And Bathsheba comes in to the king, [into] the inner chamber, and the king [is] very aged, and Abishag the Shunammite is serving the king; ¹⁶ and Bathsheba bows and pays respect to the king, and the king says, "What do you [want]?" ¹⁷ And she says to him, "My lord, you have sworn by your God Yhwh to your handmaid, [saying], Surely your son Solomon reigns after me, and he sits on my throne; ¹⁸ and now, behold, Adonijah has reigned, and now, my lord, O king, you have not known; ¹⁹ and he sacrifices ox, and fatling, and sheep in abundance, and calls for all the sons of the king, and for Abiathar the priest, and for Joab head of the host—and he has not called for your servant Solomon. ²⁰ And you, my lord, O king, the eyes of all Israel [are] on you, to declare to them who sit on the throne of my lord the king after him; ²¹ and it has been, when my lord the king lies with his fathers, that I have been, I and my son Solomon—[reckoned] sinners." ²² And behold, she is yet speaking with the king, and Nathan the prophet has come in; ²³ and they declare to the king, saying, "Behold, Nathan the prophet"; and he comes in before the king, and bows himself to the king, on his face to the earth. ²⁴ And Nathan says, "My lord, O king, you have said, Adonijah reigns after me, and he sits on my throne; ²⁵ for he has gone down today, and sacrifices ox, and fatling, and sheep, in abundance, and calls for all the sons of the king, and for the heads of the host, and for Abiathar

the priest, and behold, they are eating and drinking before him, and they say, Let King Adonijah live! **26** But he has not called for me, your servant, and for Zadok the priest, and for Benaiah, son of Jehoiada, and for your servant Solomon; **27** if this thing has been from my lord the king, then you have not caused your servant to know who sits on the throne of my lord the king after him." **28** And King David answers and says, "Call for Bathsheba for me"; and she comes in before the king, and stands before the king. **29** And the king swears and says, "Yhwh lives, who has redeemed my soul out of all adversity; **30** surely as I swore to you by Yhwh, God of Israel, saying, Surely your son Solomon reigns after me, and he sits on my throne in my stead; surely so I do this day." **31** And Bathsheba bows—face to the earth—and pays respect to the king, and says, "Let my lord, King David, live for all time." **32** And King David says, "Call for Zadok the priest, and for Nathan the prophet, and for Benaiah son of Jehoiada for me"; and they come in before the king. **33** And the king says to them, "Take the servants of your lord with you, and you have caused my son Solomon to ride on my own mule, and caused him to go down to Gihon, **34** and Zadok the priest has anointed him there—and Nathan the prophet—for king over Israel, and you have blown with a horn and said, Let King Solomon live; **35** and you have come up after him, and he has come in and has sat on my throne, and he reigns in my stead, and I have appointed him to be leader over Israel, and over Judah." **36** And Benaiah son of Jehoiada answers the king and says, "Amen! So does Yhwh, God of my lord the king, say; **37** as Yhwh has been with my lord the king, so is He with Solomon, and makes his throne greater than the throne of my lord King David." **38** And Zadok the priest goes down, and Nathan the prophet, and Benaiah son of Jehoiada, and the Cherethite, and the Pelethite, and they cause Solomon to ride on the mule of King David, and cause him to go to Gihon, **39** and Zadok the priest takes the horn of oil out of the tent, and anoints Solomon, and they blow with a horn, and all the people say, "Let King Solomon live." **40** And all the people come up after him, and the people are piping with pipes, and rejoicing [with] great joy, and the earth splits with their voice. **41** And Adonijah hears, and all those called who [are] with him, and they have finished to eat, and Joab hears the noise of the horn and says, "Why [is] the noise of the city roaring?" **42** He is yet speaking, and behold, Jonathan son of Abiathar the priest has come in, and Adonijah says, "Come in, for you [are] a man of valor, and you bear good tidings." **43** And Jonathan answers and says to Adonijah, "Truly our lord King David has caused Solomon to reign, **44** and the king sends with him Zadok the priest, and Nathan the prophet, and Benaiah son of Jehoiada, and the Cherethite, and the Pelethite, and they cause him to ride on the king's mule, **45** and they anoint him—Zadok the priest and Nathan the prophet—for king in Gihon, and have come up there rejoicing, and the city is moved; it [is] the noise that you have heard. **46** And also Solomon has sat on the throne of the kingdom, **47** and also the servants of the king have come into bless our lord King David, saying, Your God makes the name of Solomon better than your name, and his throne greater than your throne; and the king bows himself on the bed, **48** and also thus the king has said, Blessed [is] Yhwh, God of Israel, who has given [one] sitting on my throne today, and my eyes are seeing." **49** And they tremble, and rise—all those called who [are] for Adonijah—and go, each on his way; **50** and Adonijah fears because of Solomon, and rises, and goes, and lays hold on the horns of the altar. **51** And it is declared to Solomon, saying, "Behold, Adonijah fears King Solomon, and behold, he has laid hold on the horns of the altar, saying, Let King Solomon swear to me as today—he does not put his servant to death by the sword." **52** And Solomon says, "If he becomes a virtuous man—there does not fall [even one] hair of his to the earth, and if evil is found in him—then he has died." **53** And King Solomon sends, and they bring him down from off the altar, and he comes in and bows himself to King Solomon, and Solomon says to him, "Go to your house."

CHAPTER 2

1 And the days of David to die draw near, and he charges his son Solomon, saying, **2** "I am going in the way of all the earth, and you have been strong, and become a man, **3** and you have kept the charge of your God Yhwh, to walk in His ways, to keep His statutes, His commands, and His judgments, and His testimonies, as it is written in the Law of Moses, so that you do wisely [in] all that you do, and wherever you turn,

4 so that Yhwh establishes His word which He spoke to me, saying, If your sons observe their way to walk before Me in truth, with all their heart, and with all their soul; saying, A man of yours is never cut off from the throne of Israel. **5** And also, you have known that which he did to me—Joab son of Zeruiah—that which he did to two heads of the hosts of Israel, to Abner son of Ner, and to Amasa son of Jether—that he slays them, and makes the blood of war in peace, and puts the blood of war in his girdle, that [is] on his loins, and in his sandals that [are] on his feet; **6** and you have done according to your wisdom, and do not let his old age go down in peace to Sheol. **7** And you do kindness to the sons of Barzillai the Gileadite, and they have been among those eating at your table, for so they drew near to me in my fleeing from the face of your brother Absalom. **8** And behold, Shimei son of Gera, the Benjamite of Bahurim, [is] with you, and he reviled me—a grievous reviling—in the day of my going to Mahanaim; and he has come down to meet me at the Jordan, and I swear to him by Yhwh, saying, I do not put you to death by the sword; **9** and now, do not acquit him, for you [are] a wise man, and you have known that which you do to him, and have brought down his old age with blood to Sheol." **10** And David lies down with his fathers, and is buried in the City of David, **11** and the days that David has reigned over Israel [are] forty years; he has reigned seven years in Hebron, and he has reigned thirty-three years in Jerusalem. **12** And Solomon has sat on the throne of his father David, and his kingdom is established greatly, **13** and Adonijah son of Haggith comes to Bathsheba, mother of Solomon, and she says, "Is your coming peace?" And he says, "Peace." **14** And he says, "I have a word for you," and she says, "Speak." **15** And he says, "You have known that the kingdom was mine, and all Israel had set their faces toward me for reigning, and the kingdom is turned around, and is my brother's, for it was his from Yhwh; **16** and now, I am asking one petition of you—do not turn back my face"; and she says to him, "Speak." **17** And he says, "Please speak to Solomon the king, for he does not turn back your face, and he gives Abishag the Shunammite to me for a wife." **18** And Bathsheba says, "Good; I speak to the king for you." **19** And Bathsheba comes to King Solomon to speak to him for Adonijah, and the king rises to meet her, and bows himself to her, and sits on his throne, and places a throne for the mother of the king, and she sits at his right hand. **20** And she says, "I ask one small petition of you, do not turn back my face"; and the king says to her, "Ask, my mother, for I do not turn back your face." **21** And she says, "Let Abishag the Shunammite be given to your brother Adonijah for a wife." **22** And King Solomon answers and says to his mother, "And why are you asking [for] Abishag the Shunammite for Adonijah? also ask [for] the kingdom for him—for he [is] my elder brother—even for him, and for Abiathar the priest, and for Joab son of Zeruiah." **23** And King Solomon swears by Yhwh, saying, "Thus God does to me, and thus He adds—surely Adonijah has spoken this word against his [own] soul; **24** and now, Yhwh lives, who has established me, and causes me to sit on the throne of my father David, and who has made a house for me as He spoke—surely Adonijah is put to death today." **25** And King Solomon sends by the hand of Benaiah son of Jehoiada, and he falls on him, and he dies. **26** And the king said to Abiathar the priest, "Go to Anathoth, to your fields; for you [are] a man of death, but I do not put you to death in this day, because you have carried the Ark of Lord Yhwh before my father David, and because you were afflicted in all that my father was afflicted in." **27** And Solomon casts out Abiathar from being priest of Yhwh, to fulfill the word of Yhwh which He spoke concerning the house of Eli in Shiloh. **28** And the report has come to Joab—for Joab has turned aside after Adonijah, though he did not turn aside after Absalom—and Joab flees to the tent of Yhwh, and lays hold on the horns of the altar. **29** And it is declared to King Solomon that Joab has fled to the tent of Yhwh, and behold, [is] near the altar; and Solomon sends Benaiah son of Jehoiada, saying, "Go, fall on him." **30** And Benaiah comes into the tent of Yhwh and says to him, "Thus said the king: Come out"; and he says, "No, but I die here." And Benaiah brings back word [to] the king, saying, "Thus spoke Joab, indeed, thus he answered me." **31** And the king says to him, "Do as he has spoken, and fall on him, and you have buried him, and turned aside the causeless blood which Joab shed from off me, and from off the house of my father; **32** and Yhwh has turned back his blood on his own head, [on him] who has fallen on two men more righteous and better than he, and slays them with the sword—and my father David did not know—Abner son of Ner, head of the host of Israel, and Amasa son of Jether, head of the host of Judah; **33** indeed, their blood has turned back on the head of Joab, and on the head of his seed for all time; and for David, and for his seed, and for his house, and for his throne, there is peace for all time, from Yhwh." **34** And Benaiah son of Jehoiada goes up and falls on him, and puts him to death, and he is buried in his own house in the wilderness, **35** and the king puts Benaiah son of Jehoiada over the host in his stead, and the king has put Zadok the priest in the stead of Abiathar. **36** And the king sends and calls for Shimei, and says to him, "Build a house for yourself in Jerusalem, and you have dwelt there, and do not go out [from] there anywhere; **37** and it has been, in the day of your going out, and you have passed over the Brook of Kidron, you certainly know that you surely die—your blood is on your head." **38** And Shimei says to the king, "The word [is] good; as my lord the king has spoken so your servant does"; and Shimei dwells in Jerusalem many days. **39** And it comes to pass, at the end of three years, that two of the servants of Shimei flee to Achish son of Maachah, king of Gath, and they declare to Shimei, saying, "Behold, your servants [are] in Gath"; **40** and Shimei rises, and saddles his donkey, and goes to Gath, to Achish, to seek his servants, and Shimei goes and brings his servants from Gath. **41** And it is declared to Solomon that Shimei has gone from Jerusalem to Gath, and returns, **42** and the king sends and calls for Shimei, and says to him, "Have I not caused you to swear by Yhwh—and I testify against you, saying, In the day of your going out, and you have gone anywhere, you certainly know that you surely die; and you say to me, The word I have heard [is] good? **43** and why have you not kept the oath of Yhwh, and the charge that I charged on you?" **44** And the king says to Shimei, "You have known all the evil that your heart has known, which you did to my father David, and Yhwh has turned back your evil on your head, **45** and King Solomon [is] blessed, and the throne of David is established before Yhwh for all time." **46** And the king charges Benaiah son of Jehoiada, and he goes out and falls on him, and he dies, and the kingdom is established in the hand of Solomon.

CHAPTER 3

1 And Solomon joins in marriage with Pharaoh king of Egypt, and takes the daughter of Pharaoh, and brings her to the City of David, until he completes to build his own house, and the house of Yhwh, and the wall of Jerusalem all around. **2** Only, the people are sacrificing in high places, for there has not been built a house for the Name of Yhwh until those days. **3** And Solomon loves Yhwh, to walk in the statutes of his father David—only, he is sacrificing and making incense in high places— **4** and the king goes to Gibeon, to sacrifice there, for it [is] the great high place; Solomon causes one thousand burnt-offerings to ascend on that altar. **5** Yhwh has appeared to Solomon in Gibeon, in a dream of the night, and God says, "Ask—what do I give to you?" **6** And Solomon says, "You have done with Your servant, my father David, great kindness, as he walked before You in truth and in righteousness, and in uprightness of heart with You, and You keep this great kindness for him, and give to him a son sitting on his throne, as [at] this day. **7** And now, O Yhwh my God, You have caused Your servant to reign instead of my father David; and I [am] a little child, I do not know [how] to go out and to come in; **8** and Your servant [is] in the midst of your people, whom You have chosen, a people numerous, that is not numbered nor counted for multitude, **9** and You have given an understanding heart to Your servant, to judge Your people, to discern between good and evil; for who is able to judge this great people of Yours?" **10** And the thing is good in the eyes of the Lord, that Solomon has asked this thing, **11** and God says to him, "Because that you have asked for this thing, and have not asked for many days for yourself, nor asked for riches for yourself, nor asked for the life of your enemies, and have asked for discernment for yourself to understand judgment, **12** behold, I have done according to your words; behold, I have given a wise and understanding heart to you, that there has not been [one] like you before you, and after you there does not arise [one] like you; **13** and also, that which you have not asked for I have given to you, both riches and honor, that there has not been a man like you among the kings [for] all your days; **14** and if you walk in My ways to keep My statutes, and My commands, as your father David walked, then I have prolonged your days." **15** And Solomon awakens, and behold, [it was] a dream; and

he comes to Jerusalem, and stands before the Ark of the Covenant of Yhwh, and causes burnt-offerings to ascend, and makes peace-offerings, and he makes a banquet for all his servants. **16** Then two women, harlots, come to the king, and they stand before him, **17** and the first woman says, "O my lord, this woman and I are dwelling in one house, and I bring forth with her, in the house; **18** and it comes to pass on the third day of my bringing forth, that this woman also brings forth, and we [are] together, there is no stranger with us in the house, except the two of us, in the house. **19** And the son of this woman dies at night, because she has lain on him, **20** and she rises in the middle of the night, and takes my son from beside me—and your handmaid is asleep—and lays him in her bosom, and she has laid her dead son in my bosom; **21** and I rise in the morning to suckle my son, and behold, [he is] dead; and I consider in the morning concerning it, and behold, it was not my son whom I bore." **22** And the other woman says, "No, but my son [is] the living, and your son the dead"; and this [one] says, "No, but your son [is] the dead, and my son the living." And they speak before the king. **23** And the king says, "This [one] says, This [is] my son, the living, and your son [is] the dead; and that [one] says, No, but your son [is] the dead, and my son the living." **24** And the king says, "Take a sword for me"; and they bring the sword before the king, **25** and the king says, "Cut the living child into two, and give half to one, and half to the other." **26** And the woman whose son [is] the living one says to the king (for her bowels yearned over her son), indeed, she says, "O my lord, give the living child to her, and do not put him to death at all"; and this [one] says, "Let him be neither mine or yours—cut [him]." **27** And the king answers and says, "Give the living child to her [who wants him], and do not put him to death at all; she [is] his mother." **28** And all [in] Israel hear of the judgment that the king has judged, and fear because of the king, for they have seen that the wisdom of God [is] in his heart to do judgment.

CHAPTER 4

1 And King Solomon is king over all Israel, **2** and these [are] the heads whom he has: Azariah son of Zadok [is] the priest; **3** Elihoreph and Ahiah sons of Shisha [are] scribes; Jehoshaphat son of Ahilud [is] remembrancer; **4** and Benaiah son of Jehoiada [is] over the host; and Zadok and Abiathar [are] priests; **5** and Azariah son of Nathan [is] over the officers; and Zabud son of Nathan [is] minister, friend of the king; **6** and Ahishar [is] over the household, and Adoniram son of Abda [is] over the tribute. **7** And Solomon has twelve officers over all Israel, and they have sustained the king and his household—a month in the year is on each one for sustenance; **8** and these [are] their names: Ben-Hur in the hill-country of Ephraim; **9** Ben-Dekar in Makaz, and Shaalbim, and Beth-Shemesh, and Elon-Beth-Hanan; **10** Ben-Hesed, in Aruboth, has Sochoh and all the land of Hepher; **11** Ben-Abinadab [has] all the elevation of Dor; Taphath daughter of Solomon became his wife; **12** Baana Ben-Ahilud [has] Taanach and Megiddo, and all Beth-Shean, which [is] by Zartanah beneath Jezreel, from Beth-Shean to Abel-Meholah, to beyond Jokneam; **13** Ben-Geber, in Ramoth-Gilead, has the small towns of Jair son of Manasseh, which [are] in Gilead; he has a portion of Argob that [is] in Bashan—sixty great cities [with] wall and bronze bar; **14** Ahinadab son of Iddo [has] Mahanaim; **15** Ahimaaz [is] in Naphtali; he also has taken Basemath daughter of Solomon for a wife; **16** Baanah Ben-Hushai [is] in Asher, and in Aloth; **17** Jehoshaphat Ben-Paruah [is] in Issachar; **18** Shimei Ben-Elah [is] in Benjamin; **19** Geber Ben-Uri [is] in the land of Gilead, the land of Sihon king of the Amorite, and of Og king of Bashan: and [he is] the one officer who [is] in the land. **20** Judah and Israel [are] many, as the sand that [is] by the sea for multitude, eating and drinking and rejoicing. **21** And Solomon has been ruling over all the kingdoms, from the River [to] the land of the Philistines and to the border of Egypt: they are bringing a present near, and serving Solomon, all [the] days of his life. **22** And the provision of Solomon for one day is thirty cors of flour, and sixty cors of meal, **23** ten fat oxen, and twenty feeding oxen, and one hundred sheep, apart from deer, and roe, and fallow-deer, and fatted beasts of the stalls, **24** for he is ruling over all beyond the river, from Tiphsah and to Gaza, over all the kings beyond the River, and he has peace from all his surrounding servants. **25** And Judah dwells—and Israel—in confidence, each under his vine, and under his fig tree, from Dan even to Beer-Sheba, all the days of Solomon. **26** And

Solomon has forty thousand stalls of horses for his chariots, and twelve thousand horsemen. **27** And these officers have sustained King Solomon and everyone drawing near to the table of King Solomon, each [in] his month; they let nothing be lacking. **28** And the barley and the straw, for horses and for dromedaries, they bring to the place where they are, each according to his ordinance. **29** And God gives very much wisdom and understanding to Solomon, and breadth of heart, as the sand that [is] on the edge of the sea; **30** and the wisdom of Solomon is greater than the wisdom of any of the sons of the east, and [greater] than all the wisdom of Egypt; **31** and he is wiser than all men, [wiser] than Ethan the Ezrahite, and Heman, and Chalcol, and Darda, sons of Mahol, and his name is in all the surrounding nations. **32** And he speaks three thousand allegories, and his songs [are] one thousand and five; **33** and he speaks concerning the trees, from the cedar that [is] in Lebanon, even to the hyssop that is coming out in the wall, and he speaks concerning the livestock, and concerning the bird, and concerning the creeping things, and concerning the fishes, **34** and there come out [those] of all the peoples to hear the wisdom of Solomon, from all kings of the earth who have heard of his wisdom.

CHAPTER 5

1 And Hiram king of Tyre sends his servants to Solomon, for he heard that they had anointed him for king instead of his father, for Hiram was loving toward David all the days; **2** and Solomon sends to Hiram, saying, **3** "You have known my father David, that he has not been able to build a house for the Name of his God Yhwh, because of the wars that have been all around him, until Yhwh's putting them under the soles of his feet. **4** And now, my God Yhwh has given rest to me all around, there is no adversary nor evil occurrence, **5** and behold, I am saying to build a house for the Name of my God Yhwh, as Yhwh spoke to my father David, saying, Your son whom I appoint in your stead on your throne, he builds the house for My Name. **6** And now, command, and they cut down cedars for me out of Lebanon, and my servants are with your servants, and I give the hire of your servants to you according to all that you say, for you have known that there is not a man among us acquainted with cutting wood, like the Sidonians." **7** And it comes to pass at Hiram's hearing the words of Solomon, that he rejoices exceedingly and says, "Blessed [is] Yhwh today, who has given to David a wise son over this numerous people." **8** And Hiram sends to Solomon, saying, "I have heard that which you have sent to me, I do all your desire concerning cedar-wood and fir-wood; **9** my servants bring [them] down from Lebanon to the sea, and I make them floats in the sea to the place that you send to me, and I have spread them out there; and you take [them] up, and you execute my desire, to give the food [for] my house." **10** And Hiram is giving cedar-trees and fir-trees to Solomon—all his desire, **11** and Solomon has given twenty thousand cors of wheat to Hiram, [the] food for his house, and twenty cors of beaten oil; thus Solomon gives to Hiram year by year. **12** And Yhwh has given wisdom to Solomon as He spoke to him, and there is peace between Hiram and Solomon, and both of them make a covenant. **13** And King Solomon lifts up a tribute out of all Israel, and the tribute is thirty thousand men, **14** and he sends them to Lebanon, ten thousand a month, by changes; they are in Lebanon [for] a month [and] two months in their own house; and Adoniram [is] over the tribute. **15** And King Solomon has seventy thousand bearing burdens, and eighty thousand hewing in the mountain, **16** apart from the three thousand and three hundred heads of the officers of Solomon who [are] over the work—those ruling over the people who are working in the business. **17** And the king commands, and they bring great stones, precious stones, [and] hewn stones, to lay the foundation of the house; **18** and the builders of Solomon, and the builders of Hiram, and the Giblites hew [them], and prepare the wood and the stones to build the house.

CHAPTER 6

1 And it comes to pass, in the four hundred and eightieth year of the going out of the sons of Israel from the land of Egypt, in the fourth year—in the month of Ziv, it [is] the second month—of the reigning of Solomon over Israel, that he builds the house for Yhwh. **2** As for the house that King Solomon has built for Yhwh, its length [is] sixty cubits, and its breadth twenty, and its height thirty cubits. **3** As for the porch on the front of the temple of the house, its length [is] twenty cubits on the front of the breadth of the house; its breadth [is] ten by the cubit on the front of the house; **4** and he makes frames of narrowing windows for the house. **5** And he builds a couch against the wall of the house all around, [even] the walls of the house all around, of the temple and of the oracle, and makes sides all around. **6** The lowest couch, its breadth [is] five by the cubit; and the middle, its breadth [is] six by the cubit; and the third, its breadth [is] seven by the cubit, for he has put withdrawings of the house all around outside—not to lay hold on the walls of the house. **7** And the house, in its being built, has been built of perfect stone [that was] brought; and hammer and the axe—any instrument of iron—was not heard in the house in its being built. **8** The opening of the middle side [is] at the right shoulder of the house, and with windings they go up on the middle one, and from the middle one to the third. **9** And he builds the house, and completes it, and covers the house [with] beams and rows of cedars. **10** And he builds the couch against all the house, its breadth [is] five cubits, and it takes hold of the house by cedar-wood. **11** And the word of Yhwh is to Solomon, saying, **12** "This house that you are building—if you walk in My statutes, and do My judgments, indeed, have done all My commands, to walk in them, then I have established My word with you, which I spoke to your father David, **13** and have dwelt in the midst of the sons of Israel, and do not forsake My people Israel." **14** And Solomon builds the house and completes it; **15** and he builds the walls of the house within with beams of cedar, from the floor of the house to the walls of the ceiling; he has overlaid the inside with wood, and covers the floor of the house with ribs of fir. **16** And he builds the twenty cubits on the sides of the house with ribs of cedar, from the floor to the walls; and he builds for it within, for the oracle, for the Holy of Holies. **17** And [this area of] the house was forty by the cubit; it [is the area of] the temple before My face. **18** And the cedar for the house within [is] carvings of knobs and openings of flowers; the whole [is] cedar, there is not a stone seen. **19** And he has prepared the oracle in the midst of the house within, to put the Ark of the Covenant of Yhwh there. **20** And before the oracle [is] twenty cubits in length, and twenty cubits in breadth, and its height [is] twenty cubits; and he overlays it with gold refined, and overlays the altar with cedar. **21** And Solomon overlays the house within with gold refined, and causes [it] to pass over in chains of gold before the oracle, and overlays it with gold. **22** And he has overlaid the whole of the house with gold, until the completion of all the house; and the whole of the altar that the oracle has, he has overlaid with gold. **23** And he makes two cherubim of the oil-tree within the oracle; their height [is] ten cubits; **24** and the first wing of the cherub [is] five cubits, and the second wing of the cherub five cubits—ten cubits from the ends of his wings even to the ends of his wings; **25** and the second cherub [is] ten by the cubit; one measure and one form [are] of the two cherubim, **26** the height of the first cherub [is] ten by the cubit, and so [is] the second cherub; **27** and he sets the cherubim in the midst of the inner house, and they spread out the wings of the cherubim, and a wing of the first comes against the wall, and a wing of the second cherub is coming against the second wall, and their wings [stretched] into the midst of the house, coming wing against wing; **28** and he overlays the cherubim with gold, **29** and he has carved all around the walls of the house with engravings of carvings, cherubim, and palm trees, and openings of flowers, inside and outside. **30** And he has overlaid the floor of the house with gold, inside and outside; **31** as for the opening of the oracle, he made doors of the oil-tree; the lintel [and] doorposts [are] a fifth [of the wall]. **32** And the two doors [are] of the oil-tree, and he has carved on them carvings of cherubim, and palm-trees, and openings of flowers, and overlaid with gold, and he causes the gold to go down on the cherubim and on the palm-trees. **33** And so he has made for the opening of the temple, doorposts of the oil-tree, from the fourth [of the wall]. **34** And the two doors [are] of fir-tree, the two sides of the first door are revolving, and the two hangings of the second door are revolving. **35** And he has carved cherubim, and palms, and openings of flowers, and overlaid the carved work with straightened gold. **36** And he builds the inner court, three rows of hewn work, and a row of beams of cedar. **37** In the fourth year the house of Yhwh has been founded, in the month of Ziv, **38** and in the eleventh year, in the month of Bul (the eighth month), the house has been finished in all its matters, and in all its ordinances, and he builds it [in] seven years.

CHAPTER 7

¹ And Solomon has built his own house [in] thirteen years, and he finishes all his house. ² And he builds the House of the Forest of Lebanon; its length [is] one hundred cubits, and its breadth fifty cubits, and its height thirty cubits, on four rows of cedar pillars, and cedar-beams on the pillars; ³ and [it is] covered with cedar above, on the sides that [are] on the forty-five pillars, fifteen in the row. ⁴ And frames [are] in three rows, and window [is] toward window three times. ⁵ And all the openings and the doorposts [are of] square frame; and window [is] toward window three times. ⁶ And he has made the porch of the pillars; its length fifty cubits, and its breadth thirty cubits, and the porch [is] before them, and pillars and a thick place [are] before them. ⁷ And the porch of the throne where he judges—the porch of judgment—he has made, and [it is] covered with cedar from the floor to the floor. ⁸ As for his house where he dwells, the other court [is] within the porch—it has been as this work; and he makes a house for the daughter of Pharaoh—whom Solomon has taken—like this porch. ⁹ All these [are] of precious stones, according to the measures of hewn work, sawn with a saw, inside and outside, even from the foundation to the coping, and at the outside, to the great court. ¹⁰ And the foundation [is] of precious stones, great stones, stones of ten cubits, and stones of eight cubits; ¹¹ and precious stones [are] above, according to the measures of hewn work, and cedar; ¹² and the great court around [is] three rows of hewn work, and a row of cedar-beams, even for the inner court of the house of Yhwh, and for the porch of the house. ¹³ And King Solomon sends and takes Hiram out of Tyre— ¹⁴ he [is the] son of a woman, a widow, of the tribe of Naphtali, and his father [is] a man of Tyre, a worker in bronze, and he is filled with the wisdom and the understanding, and the knowledge to do all work in bronze—and he comes to King Solomon, and does all his work. ¹⁵ And he forms the two pillars of bronze; eighteen cubits [is] the height of the first pillar, and a cord of twelve cubits goes around the second pillar. ¹⁶ And he has made two chapters to put on the tops of the pillars, cast in bronze; five cubits the height of the first capital, and five cubits the height of the second capital. ¹⁷ Nets of network, wreaths of chain-work [are] for the chapters that [are] on the top of the pillars, seven for the first capital, and seven for the second capital. ¹⁸ And he makes the pillars, and two rows around on the one network, to cover the chapters that [are] on the top, with the pomegranates, and so he has made for the second capital. ¹⁹ And the chapters that [are] on the top of the pillars [are] of lily-work in the porch, four cubits; ²⁰ and the chapters on the two pillars also [have pomegranates] above, close by the protuberance that [is] beside the net; and the pomegranates [are] two hundred, in rows around on the second capital. ²¹ And he raises up the pillars for the porch of the temple, and he raises up the right pillar, and calls its name Jachin, and he raises up the left pillar, and calls its name Boaz; ²² and on the top of the pillars [is] lily-work; and the work of the pillars [is] completed. ²³ And he makes the molten sea, ten by the cubit from its edge to its edge; [it is] round all about, and its height [is] five by the cubit, and a line of thirty by the cubit surrounds it around; ²⁴ and knobs beneath its brim around are going around it, ten by the cubit, going around the sea; the knobs [are] in two rows, cast in its being cast. ²⁵ It is standing on twelve oxen, three facing the north, and three facing the west, and three facing the south, and three facing the east, and the sea [is] on them above, and all their back parts [are] inward. ²⁶ And its thickness [is] a handbreadth, and its edge [is] as the work of the edge of a cup, [as] flowers of lilies; it contains two thousand baths. ²⁷ And he makes the ten bases of bronze; the length of the one base [is] four by the cubit, and its breadth [is] four by the cubit, and its height [is] three by the cubit. ²⁸ And this [is] the work of the base: they have borders, and the borders [are] between the joinings; ²⁹ and on the borders that [are] between the joinings [are] lions, oxen, and cherubim, and on the joinings a base above, and beneath the lions and the oxen [are] additions—sloping work. ³⁰ And four wheels of bronze [are] for the one base, and axles of bronze; and its four corners have shoulders—the molten shoulders [are] under the laver, beside each addition. ³¹ And its mouth within the capital and above [is] by the cubit, and its mouth [is] round, the work of the base, a cubit and half a cubit;

and also on its mouth [are] carvings and their borders, square, not round. ³² And the four wheels [are] under the borders, and the spokes of the wheels [are] in the base, and the height of the one wheel [is] a cubit and half a cubit. ³³ And the work of the wheels [is] as the work of the wheel of a chariot, their spokes, and their axles, and their felloes, and their naves; the whole [is] molten. ³⁴ And four shoulders [are] for the four corners of the one base; its shoulders [are] out of the base. ³⁵ And in the top of the base [is] the half of a cubit in the height all around; and on the top of the base its spokes and its borders [are] of the same. ³⁶ And he engraves on the tablets of its spokes, and on its borders, cherubim, lions, and palm-trees, according to the void space of each, and additions all around. ³⁷ Thus he has made the ten bases; they all have one casting, one measure, one form. ³⁸ And he makes ten lavers of bronze; the one laver contains forty baths [and] the one laver [is] four by the cubit; one laver on the one base [is] for [each of] the ten bases; ³⁹ and he puts the five bases on the right side of the house, and five on the left side of the house, and he has put the sea on the right side of the house eastward—from toward the south. ⁴⁰ And Hiram makes the lavers, and the shovels, and the bowls; and Hiram completes to do all the work that he made for King Solomon, [for] the house of Yhwh: ⁴¹ two pillars, and bowls of the chapters that [are] on the top of the two pillars, and the two nets to cover the two bowls of the chapters that [are] on the top of the pillars; ⁴² and the four hundred pomegranates for the two nets (two rows of pomegranates for the one net to cover the two bowls of the chapters that [are] on the front of the pillars); ⁴³ and the ten bases, and the ten lavers on the bases; ⁴⁴ and the one sea, the twelve oxen under the sea, ⁴⁵ and the pots, and the shovels, and the bowls; and all these vessels, that Hiram has made for King Solomon [for] the house of Yhwh, [are] of polished bronze. ⁴⁶ The king has cast them in the circuit of the Jordan, in the thick soil of the ground, between Succoth and Zarthan. ⁴⁷ And Solomon places the whole of the vessels; because of the very great abundance, the weight of the bronze has not been searched out. ⁴⁸ And Solomon makes all the vessels that [are] in the house of Yhwh: the altar of gold, and the table of gold (on which [is] the Bread of the Presentation), ⁴⁹ and the lampstands, five on the right, and five on the left, before the oracle, of refined gold, and the flowers, and the lamps, and the tongs, of gold, ⁵⁰ and the basins, and the snuffers, and the bowls, and the spoons, and the censers, of refined gold, and the hinges for the doors of the inner-house, for the Holy of Holies, for the doors of the house of the temple, of gold. ⁵¹ And it is complete—all the work that King Solomon has made [for] the house of Yhwh, and Solomon brings in the sanctified things of his father David; he has put the silver, and the gold, and the vessels in the treasuries of the house of Yhwh.

CHAPTER 8

¹ Then Solomon assembles the elderly of Israel, and all the heads of the tribes, princes of the fathers of the sons of Israel, to King Solomon, to Jerusalem, to bring up the Ark of the Covenant of Yhwh from the City of David—it [is] Zion; ² and all the men of Israel are assembled to King Solomon, in the month of Ethanim, in the festival (the seventh month). ³ And all [the] elderly of Israel come in, and the priests lift up the Ark, ⁴ and bring up the Ark of Yhwh, and the Tent of Meeting, and all the holy vessels that [are] in the tent, indeed, the priests and the Levites bring them up. ⁵ And King Solomon and all the congregation of Israel who are assembled to him [are] with him before the Ark, sacrificing sheep and oxen, that are not counted nor numbered for multitude. ⁶ And the priests bring in the Ark of the Covenant of Yhwh to its place, to the oracle of the house, to the Holy of Holies, to the place of the wings of the cherubim; ⁷ for the cherubim are spreading forth two wings to the place of the Ark, and the cherubim cover over the Ark, and over its poles from above; ⁸ and they lengthen the poles, and the heads of the poles are seen from the holy [place] on the front of the oracle, and are not seen outside, and they are there to this day. ⁹ There is nothing in the Ark, only the two tablets of stone which Moses put there in Horeb when Yhwh covenanted with the sons of Israel in their going out of the land of Egypt. ¹⁰ And it comes to pass, in the going out of the priests from the holy [place], that the cloud has filled the house of Yhwh, ¹¹ and the priests have not been able to stand to minister because of the cloud, for the glory of Yhwh has filled the house of Yhwh. ¹² Then Solomon said, "Yhwh has said [He is] to dwell

in thick darkness; **13** I have surely built a house of habitation for You; a fixed place for Your abiding for all ages." **14** And the king turns his face around, and blesses the whole assembly of Israel; and all the assembly of Israel is standing. **15** And he says, "Blessed [is] Yhwh, God of Israel, who spoke by His mouth with my father David, and by His hand has fulfilled [it], saying, **16** From the day that I brought out My people, even Israel, from Egypt, I have not fixed on a city out of all the tribes of Israel, to build a house for My Name being there; and I fix on David to be over My people Israel. **17** And it is with the heart of my father David to build a house for the Name of Yhwh, God of Israel, **18** and Yhwh says to my father David, Because that it has been with your heart to build a house for My Name, you have done well that it has been with your heart; **19** only, you do not build the house, but your son who is coming out from your loins, he builds the house for My Name. **20** And Yhwh establishes His word which He spoke, and I am risen up instead of my father David, and I sit on the throne of Israel, as Yhwh spoke, and build the house for the Name of Yhwh, God of Israel, **21** and I set a place for the Ark there, where the covenant of Yhwh [is], which He made with our fathers in His bringing them out from the land of Egypt." **22** And Solomon stands before the altar of Yhwh, in front of all the assembly of Israel, and spreads his hands toward the heavens, **23** and says, "Yhwh, God of Israel, there is not a God like You, in the heavens above and on the earth below, keeping the covenant and the kindness for Your servants, those walking before You with all their heart, **24** which You have kept for Your servant, my father David, that which You spoke to him; indeed, You speak with Your mouth, and with Your hand have fulfilled [it], as [at] this day. **25** And now, Yhwh, God of Israel, keep for Your servant, my father David, that which You spoke to him, saying, A man of yours is never cut off from before My face, sitting on the throne of Israel—only, if your sons watch their way, to walk before Me as you have walked before Me. **26** And now, O God of Israel, please let Your word be established which You have spoken to Your servant, my father David. **27** But is it true [that] God dwells on the earth? behold, the heavens and the heavens of the heavens cannot contain You, how much less this house which I have built! **28** Then You have turned to the prayer of Your servant, and to his supplication, O Yhwh my God, to listen to the cry and to the prayer which Your servant is praying before You today, **29** for Your eyes being open toward this house night and day, toward the place of which You have said, My Name is there; to listen to the prayer which Your servant prays toward this place. **30** Then You have listened to the supplication of Your servant, and of Your people Israel, which they pray toward this place; indeed, You listen in the place of Your dwelling, in the heavens—and You have listened, and have forgiven, **31** that which a man sins against his neighbor, and he has lifted up an oath on him to cause him to swear, and the oath has come in before Your altar in this house, **32** then You hear in the heavens, and have done, and have judged Your servants, to declare wicked the wicked, to put his way on his [own] head, and to declare righteous the righteous, to give him according to his righteousness. **33** In Your people Israel being struck before an enemy, because they sin against You, and they have turned back to You, and have confessed Your Name, and prayed, and made supplication to You in this house, **34** then you hear in the heavens, and have forgiven the sin of Your people Israel, and brought them back to the ground that You gave to their fathers. **35** In the heavens being restrained, and there is no rain, because they sin against You, and they have prayed toward this place, and confessed Your Name, and turn back from their sin, for You afflict them, **36** then You hear in the heavens, and have forgiven the sin of Your servants, and of Your people Israel, for You direct them [to] the good way in which they go, and have given rain on Your land which You have given to Your people for inheritance. **37** Famine—when it is in the land; pestilence—when it is [in the land]; blasting, mildew, locust; caterpillar—when it is [in the land]; when its enemy has distressed it in the land [in] its gates, any plague, any sickness— **38** any prayer, any supplication that [is] of any man of all Your people Israel, each who knows the plague of his own heart, and has spread his hands toward this house, **39** then You hear in the heavens, the settled place of Your dwelling, and have forgiven, and have done, and have given to each according to all his ways, whose heart You know (for You have known—You alone—the heart of all the sons of man), **40** so that they fear You all the days that they are living on the face of the ground that You have given to our fathers. **41** And also, to the stranger who is not of Your people Israel, and has come from a far-off land for Your Name's sake— **42** for they hear of Your great Name, and of Your strong hand, and of Your outstretched arm—and he has come in and prayed toward this house, **43** You hear in the heavens, the settled place of Your dwelling, and have done according to all that the stranger calls to You for, in order that all the peoples of the earth may know Your Name, to fear You like Your people Israel, and to know that Your Name has been called on this house which I have built. **44** When Your people go out to battle against its enemy, in the way that You send them, and they have prayed to Yhwh [in] the way of the city which you have fixed on, and of the house which I have built for Your Name, **45** then You have heard their prayer and their supplication in the heavens, and have maintained their cause. **46** When they sin against You (for there is not a man who does not sin), and You have been angry with them, and have given them up before an enemy, and they have taken captive their captivity to the land of the enemy far off or near; **47** and they have turned [it] back to their heart in the land to where they have been taken captive, and have turned back, and made supplication to You in the land of their captors, saying, We have sinned and done perversely—we have done wickedly; **48** indeed, they have turned back to You with all their heart and with all their soul, in the land of their enemies who have taken them captive, and have prayed to You [in] the way of their land, which You gave to their fathers, the city which You have chosen, and the house which I have built for Your Name: **49** then You have heard in the heavens, the settled place of Your dwelling, their prayer and their supplication, and have maintained their cause, **50** and have forgiven Your people who have sinned against You, even all their transgressions which they have transgressed against You, and have given them mercies before their captors, and they have had mercy [on] them— **51** for they [are] Your people and Your inheritance, whom You brought out of Egypt, out of the midst of the furnace of iron— **52** for Your eyes being open to the supplication of Your servant, and to the supplication of Your people Israel, to listen to them in all they call to You for; **53** for You have separated them to Yourself for an inheritance, out of all the peoples of the earth, as You spoke by the hand of Your servant Moses, in Your bringing out our fathers from Egypt, O Lord Yhwh." **54** And it comes to pass, at Solomon's finishing to pray to Yhwh all this prayer and supplication, he has risen from before the altar of Yhwh, from bending on his knees and [having] his hands spread out to the heavens, **55** and he stands and blesses all the assembly of Israel [with] a loud voice, saying, **56** "Blessed [is] Yhwh who has given rest to His people Israel, according to all that He has spoken; not [even] one word has fallen of all His good word, which He spoke by the hand of His servant Moses. **57** Our God Yhwh is with us as He has been with our fathers; He does not forsake us nor leave us; **58** to incline our heart to Himself, to walk in all His ways, and to keep His commands, and His statutes, and His judgments, which He commanded our fathers; **59** and these, my words, with which I have made supplication before Yhwh, are near to our God Yhwh by day and by night, to maintain the cause of His servant, and the cause of His people Israel, the matter of a day in its day, **60** that all the peoples of the earth may know that He, Yhwh, [is] God; there is none else; **61** and your heart has been perfect with our God Yhwh, to walk in His statutes, and to keep His commands, as [at] this day." **62** And the king and all Israel with him are sacrificing a sacrifice before Yhwh; **63** and Solomon sacrifices the sacrifice of peace-offerings, which he has sacrificed to Yhwh: twenty-two thousand oxen and one hundred and twenty thousand sheep; and the king and all the sons of Israel dedicate the house of Yhwh. **64** On that day the king has sanctified the middle of the court that [is] before the house of Yhwh, for he has made the burnt-offering, and the present, and the fat of the peace-offerings there; for the altar of bronze that [is] before Yhwh [is] too small to contain the burnt-offering, and the present, and the fat of the peace-offerings. **65** And Solomon makes, at that time, the festival— and all Israel with him, a great assembly from the entering in of Hamath to the Brook of Egypt—before our God Yhwh, [for] seven days and seven [more] days—fourteen days. **66** On the eighth day he has sent the people away, and they bless the king, and go to their tents, rejoicing and glad of heart for all the good that Yhwh has done to His servant David, and to His people Israel.

CHAPTER 9

¹ And it comes to pass, at Solomon's finishing to build the house of Yhwh, and the house of the king, and all the desire of Solomon that he delighted to do, ² that Yhwh appears to Solomon a second time, as He appeared to him in Gibeon, ³ and Yhwh says to him, "I have heard your prayer and your supplication with which you have made supplication before Me; I have hallowed this house that you have built to put My Name there for all time, and My eyes and My heart have been there [for] all the days. ⁴ And you—if you walk before Me as your father David walked, in simplicity of heart, and in uprightness, to do according to all that I have commanded you, [and] you keep My statutes and My judgments, ⁵ then I have established the throne of your kingdom over Israel for all time, as I spoke to your father David, saying, A man of yours is never cut off from [being] on the throne of Israel. ⁶ If you at all turn back— you and your sons—from after Me, and do not keep My commands [and] My statutes that I have set before you, and have gone and served other gods, and bowed yourselves to them, ⁷ then I have cut off Israel from the face of the ground that I have given to them, and the house that I have hallowed for My Name I send away from My presence, and Israel has been for an allegory and for a byword among all the peoples; ⁸ as for this house [that] is high, everyone passing by it is astonished, and has hissed, and they have said, Why has Yhwh done this to this land and to this house? ⁹ and they have said, Because that they have forsaken their God Yhwh, who brought out their fathers from the land of Egypt, and they lay hold on other gods, and bow themselves to them and serve them; therefore Yhwh has brought all this calamity on them." ¹⁰ And it comes to pass, at the end of twenty years, that Solomon has built the two houses, the house of Yhwh, and the house of the king. ¹¹ Hiram king of Tyre has assisted Solomon with cedar-trees, and with fir-trees, and with gold, according to all his desire; then King Solomon gives to Hiram twenty cities in the land of Galilee. ¹² And Hiram comes out from Tyre to see the cities that Solomon has given to him, and they have not been right in his eyes, ¹³ and he says, "What [are] these cities that you have given to me, my brother?" And one calls them the land of Cabul to this day. ¹⁴ And Hiram sends one hundred and twenty talents of gold to the king. ¹⁵ And this [is] the matter of the tribute that King Solomon has lifted up, to build the house of Yhwh, and his own house, and Millo, and the wall of Jerusalem, and Hazor, and Megiddo, and Gezer ¹⁶ (Pharaoh king of Egypt has gone up and captures Gezer, and burns it with fire, and he has slain the Canaanite who is dwelling in the city, and gives it [as] presents to his daughter, wife of Solomon). ¹⁷ And Solomon builds Gezer, and the lower Beth-Horon, ¹⁸ and Ba'alath, and Tadmor in the wilderness, in the land, ¹⁹ and all the cities of stores that King Solomon has, and the cities of the chariots, and the cities of the horsemen, and the desire of Solomon that he desired to build in Jerusalem, and in Lebanon, and in all the land of his dominion. ²⁰ The whole of the people that is left of the Amorite, the Hittite, the Perizzite, the Hivite, and the Jebusite, who [are] not of the sons of Israel— ²¹ their sons who are left behind them in the land, whom the sons of Israel have not been able to devote—he has even lifted up a tribute of service [on] them to this day. ²² And Solomon has not appointed a servant out of the sons of Israel, for they [are] the men of war, and his servants, and his heads, and his captains, and the heads of his chariots, and his horsemen. ²³ These [are] the five hundred and fifty heads of the officers who [are] over the work of Solomon, those ruling among the people who are laboring in the work. ²⁴ Only, the daughter of Pharaoh went up out of the City of David to her house that [Solomon] built for her; then he built Millo. ²⁵ And Solomon caused burnt-offerings and peace-offerings to ascend three times in a year on the altar that he built for Yhwh, and he burned it as incense with that which [is] before Yhwh, and finished the house. ²⁶ And King Solomon has made a navy in Ezion-Geber, that is beside Eloth, on the edge of the Sea of Suph, in the land of Edom. ²⁷ And Hiram sends his servants in the navy, shipmen knowing the sea, with servants of Solomon, ²⁸ and they come to Ophir, and take four hundred and twenty talents of gold from there, and bring [it] to King Solomon.

CHAPTER 10

¹ And the queen of Sheba is hearing of the fame of Solomon concerning the Name of Yhwh, and comes to try him with enigmas, ² and she comes to Jerusalem, with a very great company, camels carrying spices, and very much gold, and precious stone, and she comes to Solomon, and speaks to him all that has been with her heart, ³ And Solomon declares to her all her matters—there has not been a thing hid from the king that he has not declared to her. ⁴ And the queen of Sheba sees all the wisdom of Solomon, and the house that he built, ⁵ and the food of his table, and the sitting of his servants, and the standing of his ministers, and their clothing, and his butlers, and his burnt-offering that he causes to ascend in the house of Yhwh, and there has not been anymore spirit in her. ⁶ And she says to the king, "The word that I heard in my land has been true concerning your matters and your wisdom; ⁷ and I gave no credence to the words until I have come, and my eyes see, and behold, not [even] half was declared to me; you have added wisdom and goodness to the report that I heard. ⁸ O the blessedness of your men, O the blessedness of your servants— these—who are standing before you continually, who are hearing your wisdom! ⁹ Your God Yhwh is blessed, who delighted in you, to put you on the throne of Israel; in Yhwh's loving Israel for all time He sets you for king, to do judgment and righteousness." ¹⁰ And she gives to the king one hundred and twenty talents of gold, and very many spices, and precious stone; there never again came in abundance like that spice that the queen of Sheba gave to King Solomon. ¹¹ And also, the navy of Hiram that bore gold from Ophir, brought in very much almug-trees and precious stone from Ophir; ¹² and the king makes the almug-trees a support for the house of Yhwh, and for the house of the king, and harps and psalteries for singers; there have not come such almug-trees, nor have there been seen [such] to this day. ¹³ And King Solomon gave to the queen of Sheba all her desire that she asked, apart from that which he gave to her as a memorial of King Solomon, and she turns and goes to her land, she and her servants. ¹⁴ And the weight of the gold that has come to Solomon in one year is six hundred sixty six talents of gold, ¹⁵ apart from [that of] the tourists, and of the traffic of the merchants, and of all the kings of Arabia, and of the governors of the land. ¹⁶ And King Solomon makes two hundred bucklers of alloyed gold—six hundred [shekels] of gold go up on the one buckler; ¹⁷ and three hundred shields of alloyed gold—three pounds of gold go up on the one shield; and the king puts them [in] the House of the Forest of Lebanon. ¹⁸ And the king makes a great throne of ivory, and overlays it with refined gold; ¹⁹ the throne has six steps, and a round top [is] to the throne behind it, and hands [are] on this [side] and on that, to the place of the sitting, and two lions are standing near the hands, ²⁰ and twelve lions are standing there on the six steps, on this [side] and on that; it has not been made so for any kingdom. ²¹ And all the drinking vessels of King Solomon [are] of gold, and all the vessels of the House of the Forest of Lebanon [are] of refined gold—there are none of silver; it was not reckoned in the days of Solomon for anything, ²² for the king has a navy of Tarshish at sea with a navy of Hiram; once in three years the navy of Tarshish comes, carrying gold, and silver, ivory, and apes, and peacocks [[or monkeys]]. ²³ And King Solomon is greater than any of the kings of the earth for riches and for wisdom, ²⁴ and all the earth is seeking the presence of Solomon, to hear his wisdom that God has put into his heart, ²⁵ and they are each bringing his present, vessels of silver, and vessels of gold, and garments, and armor, and spices, horses, and mules, the matter of a year in a year. ²⁶ And Solomon gathers chariots, and horsemen, and he has one thousand and four hundred chariots, and twelve thousand horsemen, and he places them in the cities of the chariot, and with the king in Jerusalem. ²⁷ And the king makes the silver in Jerusalem as stones, and he has made the cedars as the sycamores that [are] in the low country, for abundance. ²⁸ And the outgoing of the horses that King Solomon has [is] from Egypt, and from Keveh; merchants of the king take from Keveh at a price; ²⁹ and a chariot comes up and comes out of Egypt for six hundred pieces of silver, and a horse for one hundred and fifty, and so for all the kings of the Hittites, and for the kings of Aram; they bring out by their hand.

CHAPTER 11

¹ And King Solomon has loved many strange women, and the daughter of Pharaoh, females of Moab, Ammon, Edom, Sidon, [and] of the Hittites, ² of the nations of which Yhwh said to the sons of Israel, "You do not go in to them, and they do not go in to you; surely they turn aside your heart after their gods"; Solomon has cleaved to them for love. ³ And he has

seven hundred wives, princesses, and three hundred concubines; and his wives turn aside his heart. **4** And it comes to pass, at the time of Solomon's old age, his wives have turned aside his heart after other gods, and his heart has not been perfect with his God Yhwh, like the heart of his father David. **5** And Solomon goes after Ashtoreth goddess of the Zidonians, and after Milcom the abomination of the Ammonites; **6** and Solomon does evil in the eyes of Yhwh, and has not been fully after Yhwh, like his father David. **7** Then Solomon builds a high place for Chemosh the abomination of Moab, in the hill that [is] on the front of Jerusalem, and for Molech the abomination of the sons of Ammon; **8** and so he has done for all his strange women, who are perfuming and sacrificing to their gods. **9** And Yhwh shows Himself angry with Solomon, for his heart has turned aside from Yhwh, God of Israel, who had appeared to him twice, **10** and given a charge to him concerning this thing, not to go after other gods; and he has not kept that which Yhwh commanded, **11** and Yhwh says to Solomon, "Because that this has been with you, and you have not kept My covenant and My statutes that I charged on you, I surely tear the kingdom from you, and have given it to your servant. **12** Only, I do not do it in your days, for the sake of your father David; I tear it out of the hand of your son; **13** only, I do not tear away all of the kingdom; I give one tribe to your son, for the sake of My servant David, and for the sake of Jerusalem that I have chosen." **14** And Yhwh raises up an adversary against Solomon, Hadad the Edomite; he [is] of the seed of the king in Edom; **15** and it comes to pass, in David's being with Edom, in the going up of Joab head of the host to bury the slain, that he strikes every male in Edom— **16** for six months Joab abided there, and all Israel, until the cutting off of every male in Edom— **17** and Hadad flees, he and certain Edomites, of the servants of his father, with him, to go to Egypt, and Hadad [is] a little youth, **18** and they rise out of Midian, and come into Paran, and take men with them out of Paran, and come into Egypt, to Pharaoh king of Egypt, and he gives a house to him, and has commanded bread for him, and has given land to him. **19** And Hadad finds grace in the eyes of Pharaoh exceedingly, and he gives to him a wife, the sister of his own wife, sister of Tahpenes the mistress; **20** and the sister of Tahpenes bears to him his son Genubath, and Tahpenes weans him within the house of Pharaoh, and Genubath is in the house of Pharaoh in the midst of the sons of Pharaoh. **21** And Hadad has heard in Egypt that David has lain with his fathers, and that Joab head of the host is dead, and Hadad says to Pharaoh, "Send me away, and I go to my land." **22** And Pharaoh says to him, "But what are you lacking with me, that behold, you are seeking to go to your own land?" And he says, "Nothing, but you certainly send me away." **23** And God raises an adversary against him, Rezon son of Eliadah, who has fled from Hadadezer king of Zobah, his lord, **24** and gathers men to himself, and is head of a troop in David's slaying them, and they go to Damascus, and dwell in it, and reign in Damascus; **25** and he is an adversary against Israel all the days of Solomon (besides the evil that Hadad [did]), and he cuts off in Israel, and reigns over Aram. **26** And Jeroboam son of Nebat, an Ephraimite of Zereda—the name of whose mother [is] Zeruah, a widow woman—servant to Solomon, he also lifts up a hand against the king; **27** and this [is] the thing [for] which he lifted up a hand against the king: Solomon built Millo—he shut up the breach of the city of his father David, **28** and the man Jeroboam [is] mighty in valor, and Solomon sees that the young man is doing business, and appoints him over all the burden of the house of Joseph. **29** And it comes to pass, at that time, that Jeroboam has gone out from Jerusalem, and Ahijah the Shilonite, the prophet, finds him in the way, and he is covering himself with a new garment; and both of them [are] by themselves in a field, **30** and Ahijah lays hold on the new garment that [is] on him, and tears it [into] twelve pieces, **31** and says to Jeroboam, "Take ten pieces for yourself, for thus said Yhwh, God of Israel: Behold, I am tearing the kingdom out of the hand of Solomon, and have given the ten tribes to you, **32** but he has the one tribe for My servant David's sake, and for Jerusalem's sake, the city which I have fixed on, out of all the tribes of Israel, **33** because they have forsaken Me, and bow themselves to Ashtoreth, goddess of the Zidonians, to Chemosh god of Moab, and to Milcom god of the sons of Ammon, and have not walked in My ways, to do that which [is] right in My eyes, and My statutes and My judgments, like his father David. **34** And I do not take the whole of the kingdom out of his hand, for I make him prince all [the] days of his life, for the sake of My servant David whom I chose, who kept My commands and My statutes; **35** and I have taken the kingdom out of the hand of his son, and given it to you—the ten tribes; **36** and to his son I give one tribe, for there being a lamp before Me for My servant David in Jerusalem [for] all the days, the city that I have chosen for Myself to put My Name there. **37** And I take you, and you have reigned over all that your soul desires, and you have been king over Israel; **38** and it has been, if you hear all that I command you, and have walked in My ways, and done that which is right in My eyes, to keep My statutes and My commands, as My servant David did, that I have been with you, and have built a steadfast house for you, as I built for David, and have given Israel to you, **39** and I humble the seed of David for this; only, not [for] all the days." **40** And Solomon seeks to put Jeroboam to death, and Jeroboam rises and flees to Egypt, to Shishak king of Egypt, and he is in Egypt until the death of Solomon. **41** And the rest of the matters of Solomon, and all that he did, and his wisdom, are they not written on the scroll of the matters of Solomon? **42** And the days that Solomon has reigned in Jerusalem over all Israel [are] forty years, **43** and Solomon lies with his fathers, and is buried in the city of his father David, and his son Rehoboam reigns in his stead.

CHAPTER 12

1 And Rehoboam goes to Shechem, for all Israel has come to Shechem to make him king. **2** And it comes to pass, at Jeroboam son of Nebat's hearing (and he [is] yet in Egypt where he has fled from the presence of Solomon the king, and Jeroboam dwells in Egypt), **3** that they send and call for him; and they come—Jeroboam and all the assembly of Israel—and speak to Rehoboam, saying, **4** "Your father hardened our yoke, and you, now, lighten [some] of the hard service of your father, and his heavy yoke that he put on us, and we serve you." **5** And he says to them, "Yet go [for] three days, and come back to me"; and the people go. **6** And King Rehoboam consults with the elderly who have been standing in the presence of his father Solomon, in his being alive, saying, "How are you counseling to answer this people?" **7** And they speak to him, saying, "If, today, you are a servant of this people, and have served them, and answered them, and spoken good words to them, then they have been servants to you [for] all the days." **8** And he forsakes the counsel of the elderly which they counseled him, and consults with the boys who have grown up with him, who are standing before him; **9** and he says to them, "What are you counseling, and we answer this people, who have spoken to me, saying, Lighten [some] of the yoke that your father put on us?" **10** And they speak to him—the boys who had grown up with him—saying, "Thus you say to this people who have spoken to you, saying, Your father made our yoke heavy, and you, make [it] light on us; thus you speak to them, My little [finger] is thicker than the loins of my father; **11** and now, my father laid a heavy yoke on you, and I add to your yoke; my father disciplined you with whips, and I discipline you with scorpions." **12** And they come—Jeroboam and all the people—to Rehoboam, on the third day, as the king had spoken, saying, "Come back to me on the third day." **13** And the king answers the people sharply, and forsakes the counsel of the elderly which they counseled him, **14** and speaks to them, according to the counsel of the boys, saying, "My father made your yoke heavy, and I add to your yoke; my father disciplined you with whips, and I discipline you with scorpions"; **15** and the king did not listen to the people, for the revolution was from Yhwh, in order to establish His word that Yhwh spoke by the hand of Ahijah the Shilonite to Jeroboam son of Nebat. **16** And all Israel sees that the king has not listened to them, and the people send the king back word, saying, "What portion do we have in David? indeed, there is no inheritance in the son of Jesse; [return] to your tents, O Israel; now see your house, O David!" And Israel goes to its tents. **17** As for the sons of Israel, those dwelling in the cities of Judah—Rehoboam reigns over them. **18** And King Rehoboam sends Adoram who [is] over the tribute, and all Israel casts stones at him, and he dies; and King Rehoboam has strengthened himself to go up into a chariot to flee to Jerusalem; **19** and Israel transgresses against the house of David to this day. **20** And it comes to pass, at all Israel hearing that Jeroboam has returned, that they send and call him to the congregation, and cause him to reign over all Israel; none has been after the house of David except the tribe of Judah alone. **21** And Rehoboam comes to Jerusalem, and assembles all the house of Judah and the tribe of Benjamin, one hundred and eighty thousand chosen warriors, to fight with the house of Israel, to bring back the kingdom to Rehoboam son of Solomon, 22 And the word of God is to Shemaiah a man of God, saying, 23 "Speak to Rehoboam son of Solomon, king of Judah, and to all the house of Judah and Benjamin, and the rest of the people, saying, 24 Thus said Yhwh: You do not go up nor fight with your brothers the sons of Israel; let each return to his house, for this thing has been from Me"; and they hear the word of Yhwh, and turn back to go according to the word of Yhwh. 25 And Jeroboam builds Shechem in the hill-country of Ephraim, and dwells in it, and goes out there, and builds Penuel; 26 and Jeroboam says in his heart, "Now the kingdom turns back to the house of David— 27 if this people goes up to make sacrifices in the house of Yhwh in Jerusalem, then the heart of this people has turned back to their lord, to Rehoboam king of Judah, and they have slain me, and turned back to Rehoboam king of Judah." 28 And the king takes counsel, and makes two calves of gold, and says to them, "Enough of you from going up to Jerusalem; behold, your gods, O Israel, which brought you up out of the land of Egypt." 29 And he sets the one in Beth-El, and the other he has put in Dan, 30 and this thing becomes a sin, and the people go before the one—to Dan. 31 And he makes the house of high places, and makes priests from the extremities of the people, who were not of the sons of Levi; 32 and Jeroboam makes a festival in the eighth month, on the fifteenth day of the month, like the festival that [is] in Judah, and he offers on the altar—so he did in Beth-El—to sacrifice to the calves which he made, and he has appointed in Beth-El the priests of the high places that he made. 33 And he offers up on the altar that he made in Beth-El, on the fifteenth day of the eighth month, in the month that he devised from his own heart, and he makes a festival for the sons of Israel, and offers on the altar—to make incense.

CHAPTER 13

1 And behold, a man of God has come from Judah, by the word of Yhwh, to Beth-El, and Jeroboam is standing by the altar—to make incense; 2 and he calls against the altar, by the word of Yhwh, and says, "Altar! Altar! Thus said Yhwh: Behold, a son is born to the house of David—Josiah [is] his name—and he has sacrificed on you the priests of the high places who are making incense on you, and bones of man are burned on you." 3 And he has given a sign on that day, saying, "This [is] the sign that Yhwh has spoken, Behold, the altar is torn, and the ashes that [are] on it [are] poured forth." 4 And it comes to pass, at the king's hearing the word of the man of God that he calls against the altar in Beth-El, that Jeroboam puts forth his hand from off the altar, saying, "Catch him"; and his hand that he has put forth against him is dried up, and he is not able to bring it back to himself, 5 and the altar is torn, and the ashes [are] poured forth from the altar, according to the sign that the man of God had given by the word of Yhwh. 6 And the king answers and says to the man of God, "Please appease the face of your God Yhwh, and pray for me, and my hand comes back to me"; and the man of God appeases the face of Yhwh, and the hand of the king comes back to him, and it is as at the beginning. 7 And the king speaks to the man of God, "Come in with me to the house, and refresh yourself, and I give a gift to you." 8 And the man of God says to the king, "If you give to me the half of your house, I do not go in with you, nor do I eat bread, nor do I drink water, in this place; 9 for so He commanded me by the word of Yhwh, saying, You do not eat bread nor drink water, nor return in the way that you have come." 10 And he goes on in another way, and has not turned back in the way in which he came in to Beth-El. 11 And a certain aged prophet is dwelling in Beth-El, and his son comes and recounts to him every deed that the man of God has done today in Beth-El, the words that he has spoken to the king—indeed, they recount them to their father. 12 And their father says to them, "Where [is] this—the way he has gone?" And his sons see the way that the man of God who came from Judah has gone. 13 And he says to his sons, "Saddle the donkey for me," and they saddle the donkey for him, and he rides on it, 14 and goes after the man of God, and finds him sitting under the oak, and says to him, "Are you the man of God who has come from Judah?" And he says, "I [am]." 15 And he says to him, "Come with me to the house and eat bread." 16 And he says, "I am not able to return with you, and to go in with you, nor do I eat bread or drink water with you in this place, 17 for [there is] a word to me by the word of Yhwh, You do not eat bread nor

drink water there [and] you do not return to go in the way in which you came " 18 And he says to him, "I [am] also a prophet like you, and a messenger spoke to me by the word of Yhwh, saying, Bring him back with you to your house, and he eats bread and drinks water." He has lied to him. 19 And he turns back with him, and eats bread in his house, and drinks water. 20 And it comes to pass—they are sitting at the table—and [there] is a word of Yhwh to the prophet who brought him back, 21 and he calls to the man of God who came from Judah, saying, "Thus said Yhwh: Because that you have provoked the mouth of Yhwh, and have not kept the command that your God Yhwh charged you, 22 and turn back and eat bread and drink water in the place of which He said to you, You do not eat bread nor drink water—your carcass does not come into the burying-place of your fathers." 23 And it comes to pass, after his eating bread, and after his drinking, that he saddles the donkey for him, for the prophet whom he had brought back, 24 and he goes, and a lion finds him in the way, and puts him to death, and his carcass is cast in the way, and the donkey is standing near it, and the lion is standing near the carcass. 25 And behold, men are passing by, and see the carcass cast in the way, and the lion standing near the carcass, and they come and speak [of it] in the city in which the old prophet is dwelling. 26 And the prophet who brought him back out of the way hears and says, "It [is] the man of God who provoked the mouth of Yhwh, and Yhwh gives him to the lion, and it destroys him, and puts him to death, according to the word of Yhwh that he spoke to him." 27 And he speaks to his sons saying, "Saddle the donkey for me," and they saddle [it]. 28 And he goes and finds his carcass cast in the way, and the donkey and the lion are standing near the carcass—the lion has not eaten the carcass nor destroyed the donkey. 29 And the prophet takes up the carcass of the man of God, and places it on the donkey, and brings it back, and the old prophet comes to the city to mourn and to bury him, 30 and he places his carcass in his own grave, and they mourn for him, "Oh, my brother!" 31 And it comes to pass, after his burying him, that he speaks to his sons, saying, "At my death—you have buried me In the burying place in which the man of God is buried; place my bones near his bones; 32 for the word certainly comes to pass that he called by the word of Yhwh concerning the altar which [is in] Beth-El, and concerning all the houses of the high places that [are] in cities of Samaria." 33 After this thing Jeroboam has not turned from his evil way, and turns back, and makes priests of high places from the extremities of the people; he who is desirous—he consecrates his hand, and he is of the priests of the high places. 34 And in this thing is the sin of the house of Jeroboam, even to cut [it] off, and to destroy [it] from off the face of the ground.

CHAPTER 14

1 At that time Abijah son of Jeroboam was sick, 2 and Jeroboam says to his wife, "Now rise and change yourself, and they do not know that you [are the] wife of Jeroboam, and you have gone to Shiloh; behold, Ahijah the prophet [is] there; he spoke to me of [being] king over this people; 3 and you have taken in your hand ten loaves, and crumbs, and a bottle of honey, and have gone to him; he declares to you what becomes of the youth." 4 And the wife of Jeroboam does so, and rises, and goes to Shiloh, and enters the house of Ahijah, and Ahijah is not able to see, for his eyes have stood because of his age. 5 And Yhwh said to Ahijah, "Behold, the wife of Jeroboam is coming to seek a word from you concerning her son, for he is sick; thus and thus you speak to her, and it comes to pass at her coming in, that she is making herself strange." 6 And it comes to pass, at Ahijah's hearing the sound of her feet [as] she came to the opening, that he says, "Come in, wife of Jeroboam, why is this [that] you are making yourself strange? and I am sent to you [with] a sharp thing. 7 Go, say to Jeroboam, Thus said Yhwh, God of Israel: Because that I have made you high out of the midst of the people, and appoint you leader over my people Israel, 8 and tear the kingdom from the house of David, and give it to you—and you have not been as My servant David who kept My commands, and who walked after Me with all his heart, to only do that which [is] right in My eyes, 9 and you do evil above all who have been before you, and go, and make other gods and molten images for yourself to provoke Me to anger, and you have cast Me behind your back— 10 therefore, behold, I am bringing calamity to the house of Jeroboam, and have cut off to Jeroboam those sitting

on the wall—shut up and left—in Israel, and have put away the posterity of the house of Jeroboam, as one puts away the dung until its consumption; ¹¹ the dogs eat him who dies of Jeroboam in a city, and birds of the heavens eat him who dies in a field, for Yhwh has spoken. ¹² And you, rise, go to your house; in the going in of your feet to the city, the boy has died; ¹³ and all Israel has mourned for him, and buried him, for this one—by himself—of Jeroboam comes to a grave, because there has been found in him a good thing toward Yhwh, God of Israel, in the house of Jeroboam. ¹⁴ And Yhwh has raised up for Himself a king over Israel who cuts off the house of Jeroboam this day—and what? Even now! ¹⁵ And Yhwh has struck Israel as the reed is moved by the waters, and has plucked Israel from off this good ground that He gave to their fathers, and scattered them beyond the River, because that they made their Asherim, provoking Yhwh to anger; ¹⁶ and He gives up Israel because of the sins of Jeroboam that he sinned, and that he caused Israel to sin." ¹⁷ And the wife of Jeroboam rises, and goes, and comes to Tirzah; she has come to the threshold of the house, and the youth dies; ¹⁸ and they bury him, and all Israel mourns for him, according to the word of Yhwh that he spoke by the hand of His servant Ahijah the prophet. ¹⁹ And the rest of the matters of Jeroboam, how he fought, and how he reigned, behold, they are written on the scroll of the Chronicles of the Kings of Israel. ²⁰ And the days that Jeroboam reigned [are] twenty-two years, and he lies with his fathers, and his son Nadab reigns in his stead. ²¹ And Rehoboam son of Solomon has reigned in Judah; Rehoboam [is] a son of forty-one years in his reigning, and he has reigned seventeen years in Jerusalem, the city that Yhwh chose to set His Name there, out of all the tribes of Israel, and the name of his mother [is] Naamah the Ammonitess. ²² And Judah does evil in the eyes of Yhwh, and they make Him zealous above all that their fathers did by their sins that they have sinned. ²³ And they build—they also—for themselves high places, and standing-pillars, and Asherim, on every high height, and under every green tree; ²⁴ and a whoremonger has also been in the land; they have done according to all the abominations of the nations that Yhwh dispossessed from the presence of the sons of Israel. ²⁵ And it comes to pass, in the fifth year of King Rehoboam, Shishak king of Egypt has gone up against Jerusalem, ²⁶ and he takes the treasures of the house of Yhwh, and the treasures of the house of the king, indeed, he has taken the whole; and he takes all the shields of gold that Solomon made. ²⁷ And King Rehoboam makes shields of bronze in their stead, and has made [them] a charge on the hand of the heads of the runners, those keeping the opening of the house of the king, ²⁸ and it comes to pass, from the going in of the king to the house of Yhwh, the runners carry them, and have brought them back to the chamber of the runners. ²⁹ And the rest of the matters of Rehoboam and all that he did, are they not written on the scroll of the Chronicles of the Kings of Judah? ³⁰ And there has been war between Rehoboam and Jeroboam [for] all the days; ³¹ and Rehoboam lies with his fathers, and is buried with his fathers in the City of David, and the name of his mother [is] Naamah the Ammonitess, and his son Abijam reigns in his stead.

CHAPTER 15

¹ And in the eighteenth year of King Jeroboam son of Nebat, Abijam has reigned over Judah; ² he has reigned three years in Jerusalem, and the name of his mother [is] Maachah daughter of Abishalom; ³ and he walks in all the sins of his father that he did before him, and his heart has not been perfect with his God Yhwh, as the heart of his father David; ⁴ but for David's sake his God Yhwh has given to him a lamp in Jerusalem, to raise up his son after him, and to establish Jerusalem, ⁵ in that David did that which [is] right in the eyes of Yhwh, and did not turn aside from all that He commanded him all [the] days of his life—except in the matter of Uriah the Hittite; ⁶ and there has been war between Rehoboam and Jeroboam all the days of his life. ⁷ And the rest of the matters of Abijam and all that he did, are they not written on the scroll of the Chronicles of the Kings of Judah? And there has been war between Abijam and Jeroboam; ⁸ and Abijam lies with his fathers, and they bury him in the City of David, and his son Asa reigns in his stead. ⁹ And in the twentieth year of Jeroboam king of Israel, Asa has reigned over Judah, ¹⁰ and he has reigned forty-one years in Jerusalem, and the name of his mother [is] Maachah daughter of Abishalom. ¹¹ And Asa does that which [is] right in the eyes

of Yhwh, like his father David, ¹² and removes the whoremongers out of the land, and turns aside all the idols that his fathers made; ¹³ and also his mother Maachah—he turns her aside from being mistress, in that she made a horrible thing for an Asherah, and Asa cuts down her horrible thing, and burns [it] by the Brook of Kidron; ¹⁴ but the high places have not been removed; only, the heart of Asa has been perfect with Yhwh [for] all his days, ¹⁵ and he brings in the sanctified things of his father, and his own sanctified things, to the house of Yhwh: silver, and gold, and vessels. ¹⁶ And there has been war between Asa and Baasha king of Israel [for] all their days, ¹⁷ and Baasha king of Israel goes up against Judah, and builds Ramah, not to permit anyone going out and coming in to Asa king of Judah. ¹⁸ And Asa takes all the silver and the gold that are left in the treasures of the house of Yhwh, and the treasures of the house of the king, and gives them into the hand of his servants, and King Asa sends them to Ben-Hadad, son of Tabrimmon, son of Hezion king of Aram, who is dwelling in Damascus, saying, ¹⁹ "A covenant [is] between me and you, between my father and your father; behold, I have sent a reward of silver and gold to you; go, break your covenant with Baasha king of Israel, and he goes up from off me." ²⁰ And Ben-Hadad listens to King Asa, and sends the heads of the forces that he has against cities of Israel, and strikes Ijon, and Dan, and Abel-Beth-Maachah, and all Chinneroth, besides all the land of Naphtali; ²¹ and it comes to pass at Baasha's hearing, that he ceases from building Ramah, and dwells in Tirzah. ²² And King Asa has summoned all Judah—there is none exempt—and they lift up the stones of Ramah, and its wood, that Baasha has built, and King Asa builds with them Geba of Benjamin, and Mizpah. ²³ And the rest of all the matters of Asa, and all his might, and all that he did, and the cities that he built, are they not written on the scroll of the Chronicles of the Kings of Judah? Only, at the time of his old age he was diseased in his feet; ²⁴ and Asa lies with his fathers, and is buried with his fathers in the city of his father David, and his son Jehoshaphat reigns in his stead. ²⁵ And Nadab son of Jeroboam has reigned over Israel, in the second year of Asa king of Judah, and he reigns over Israel two years, ²⁶ and does evil in the eyes of Yhwh, and goes in the way of his father, and in his sin that he made Israel to sin. ²⁷ And Baasha son of Ahijah, of the house of Issachar, conspires against him, and Baasha strikes him in Gibbethon, which [belonged] to the Philistines—and Nadab and all Israel are laying siege against Gibbethon— ²⁸ indeed, Baasha puts him to death in the third year of Asa king of Judah, and reigns in his stead. ²⁹ And it comes to pass, at his reigning, he has struck the whole house of Jeroboam, he has not left any breathing to Jeroboam until his destroying him, according to the word of Yhwh, that He spoke by the hand of His servant Ahijah the Shilonite, ³⁰ because of the sins of Jeroboam that he sinned, and that he caused Israel to sin, by his provocation with which he provoked Yhwh, God of Israel, to anger. ³¹ And the rest of the matters of Nadab and all that he did, are they not written on the scroll of the Chronicles of the Kings of Israel? ³² And there has been war between Asa and Baasha king of Israel [for] all their days. ³³ In the third year of Asa king of Judah, Baasha son of Ahijah has reigned over all Israel in Tirzah, twenty-four years, ³⁴ and he does evil in the eyes of Yhwh, and walks in the way of Jeroboam, and in his sin that he caused Israel to sin.

CHAPTER 16

¹ And a word of Yhwh is to Jehu son of Hanani, against Baasha, saying, ² "Because that I have raised you up out of the dust, and appoint you leader over My people Israel, and you walk in the way of Jeroboam, and cause My people Israel to sin—to provoke Me to anger with their sins; ³ behold, I am putting away the posterity of Baasha, even the posterity of his house, and have given up your house as the house of Jeroboam son of Nebat; ⁴ the dogs eat him who dies of Baasha in a city, and [the] bird of the heavens eats him who dies of his in a field." ⁵ And the rest of the matters of Baasha, and that which he did, and his might, are they not written on the scroll of the Chronicles of the Kings of Israel? ⁶ And Baasha lies with his fathers, and is buried in Tirzah, and his son Elah reigns in his stead. ⁷ And also by the hand of Jehu son of Hanani the prophet a word of Yhwh has been concerning Baasha, and concerning his house, and concerning all the evil that he did in the eyes of Yhwh to provoke Him to anger with the work of his hands, to be like the house of Jeroboam, and concerning that for which

he struck him. **8** In the twenty-sixth year of Asa king of Judah, Elah son of Baasha has reigned over Israel in Tirzah, two years; **9** and his servant Zimri conspires against him (head of the half of the chariots) and he [is] in Tirzah drinking—a drunkard in the house of Arza, who [is] over the house in Tirzah. **10** And Zimri comes in and strikes him, and puts him to death, in the twenty-seventh year of Asa king of Judah, and reigns in his stead; **11** and it comes to pass in his reigning, at his sitting on his throne, he has struck the whole house of Baasha; he has not left to him any sitting on the wall, and of his redeemers, and of his friends. **12** And Zimri destroys the whole house of Baasha, according to the word of Yhwh that He spoke concerning Baasha, by the hand of Jehu the prophet, **13** concerning all the sins of Baasha, and the sins of his son Elah, that they sinned, and that they caused Israel to sin to provoke Yhwh, God of Israel, with their vanities. **14** And the rest of the matters of Elah and all that he did, are they not written on the scroll of the Chronicles of the Kings of Israel? **15** In the twenty-seventh year of Asa king of Judah, Zimri has reigned seven days in Tirzah; and the people are encamping against Gibbethon, which [belonged] to the Philistines; **16** and the people who are encamping hear, saying, "Zimri has conspired, and also has struck the king"; and all Israel causes Omri head of the host to reign over Israel on that day in the camp. **17** And Omri goes up, and all Israel with him, from Gibbethon, and they lay siege to Tirzah. **18** And it comes to pass, at Zimri's seeing that the city has been captured, that he comes into a high place of the house of the king, and burns the house of the king over himself with fire, and he dies, **19** for his sins that he sinned, to do evil in the eyes of Yhwh, to walk in the way of Jeroboam, and in his sin that he did, to cause Israel to sin; **20** and the rest of the matters of Zimri and his conspiracy that he made, are they not written on the scroll of the Chronicles of the Kings of Israel? **21** Then the sons of Israel are parted into halves; half of the people have been after Tibni son of Ginath to cause him to reign, and the [other] half after Omri; **22** and the people that are after Omri are stronger than the people that are after Tibni son of Ginath, and Tibni dies, and Omri reigns. **23** In the thirty-first year of Asa king of Judah, Omri has reigned over Israel twelve years; he has reigned in Tirzah six years, **24** and he buys the Mount of Samaria from Shemer with two talents of silver, and builds [on] the mountain, and calls the name of the city that he has built by the name of Shemer, lord of the hill—Samaria. **25** And Omri does evil in the eyes of Yhwh, and does evil above all who [are] before him, **26** and walks in all the way of Jeroboam son of Nebat, and in his sin that he caused Israel to sin, to provoke Yhwh, God of Israel, with their vanities. **27** And the rest of the matters of Omri that he did and his might that he exercised, are they not written on the scroll of the Chronicles of the Kings of Israel? **28** And Omri lies with his fathers, and is buried in Samaria, and his son Ahab reigns in his stead. **29** And Ahab son of Omri has reigned over Israel in the thirty-eighth year of Asa king of Judah, and Ahab son of Omri reigns over Israel in Samaria twenty-two years, **30** and Ahab son of Omri does evil in the eyes of Yhwh above all who [are] before him. **31** And it comes to pass, as if it had been trivial—his walking in the sins of Jeroboam son of Nebat—that he takes a wife, Jezebel daughter of Ethba'al, king of the Zidonians, and goes and serves Ba'al, and bows himself to it, **32** and raises up an altar for Ba'al in the house of the Ba'al, which he built in Samaria; **33** and Ahab makes the Asherah, and Ahab adds to do so as to provoke Yhwh, God of Israel, above all the kings of Israel who have been before him. **34** In his days Hiel the Beth-Elite has built Jericho; he laid its foundation with Abiram his firstborn, and he set up its doors with Segub his youngest, according to the word of Yhwh that He spoke by the hand of Joshua son of Nun.

CHAPTER 17

1 And Elijah the Tishbite, of the inhabitants of Gilead, says to Ahab, "Yhwh, God of Israel, lives, before whom I have stood, there is not dew and rain these years, except according to my word." **2** And the word of Yhwh is to him, saying, **3** "Go from this [place]; and you have turned for yourself eastward, and been hidden by the Brook of Cherith that [is] on the front of the Jordan, **4** and it has been [that] you drink from the brook, and I have commanded the ravens to sustain you there." **5** And he goes and does according to the word of Yhwh, indeed, he goes and dwells by the Brook of Cherith, that [is] on the front of the Jordan, **6** and the ravens are bringing bread and flesh to

him in the morning, and bread and flesh in the evening, and he drinks from the brook. **7** And it comes to pass, at the end of [the] days, that the brook dries up, for there has been no rain in the land, **8** and the word of Yhwh is to him, saying, **9** "Rise, go to Zarephath, that [belongs] to Sidon, and you have dwelt there; behold, I have commanded a widow woman to sustain you there." **10** And he rises, and goes to Zarephath, and comes to the opening of the city, and behold, there [is] a widow woman gathering sticks, and he calls to her and says, "Please bring a little water to me in a vessel, and I drink." **11** And she goes to bring [it], and he calls to her and says, "Please bring a morsel of bread to me in your hand." **12** And she says, "Your God Yhwh lives, I do not have a cake, but the fullness of the hand of meal in a pitcher, and a little oil in a dish; and behold, I am gathering two sticks, and have gone in and prepared it for myself, and for my son, and we have eaten it—and died." **13** And Elijah says to her, "Do not fear, go, do according to your word, only make a little cake for me there, in the first place, and you have brought [it] out to me; and for you and for your son make [it] last; **14** for thus said Yhwh, God of Israel: The pitcher of meal is not consumed, and the dish of oil is not lacking, until the day of Yhwh's giving a shower on the face of the ground." **15** And she goes, and does according to the word of Elijah, and she eats, she and he and her household [for many] days; **16** the pitcher of meal was not consumed, and the dish of oil did not lack, according to the word of Yhwh that He spoke by the hand of Elijah. **17** And it comes to pass, after these things, the son of the woman, mistress of the house, has been sick, and his sickness is very severe until no breath has been left in him. **18** And she says to Elijah, "What [is this] to me and to you, O man of God? you have come to me to cause my iniquity to be remembered, and to put my son to death!" **19** And he says to her, "Give your son to me"; and he takes him out of her bosom, and takes him up to the upper chamber where he is abiding, and lays him on his own bed, **20** and cries to Yhwh and says, "My God Yhwh, have You also brought calamity on the widow with whom I am sojourning, to put her son to death?" **21** And he stretches himself out on the boy three times, and calls to Yhwh and says, "O Yhwh my God, please let the soul of this boy return into his midst"; **22** and Yhwh listens to the voice of Elijah, and the soul of the boy turns back into his midst, and he lives. **23** And Elijah takes the boy, and brings him down from the upper chamber of the house, and gives him to his mother, and Elijah says, "See, your son lives!" **24** And the woman says to Elijah, "Now [by] this I have known that you [are] a man of God, and the word of Yhwh in your mouth [is] truth."

CHAPTER 18

1 And the days are many, and the word of Yhwh has been to Elijah in the third year, saying, "Go, appear to Ahab, and I give rain on the face of the ground"; **2** and Elijah goes to appear to Ahab. And the famine is severe in Samaria, **3** and Ahab calls to Obadiah, who [is] over the house—and Obadiah has been fearing Yhwh greatly, **4** and it comes to pass, in Jezebel's cutting off the prophets of Yhwh, that Obadiah takes one hundred prophets, and hides them, fifty men in a cave, and has sustained them with bread and water— **5** and Ahab says to Obadiah, "Go through the land, to all fountains of waters, and to all the brooks, perhaps we find hay, and keep alive horse and mule, and do not cut off any of the livestock." **6** And they apportion the land to themselves, to pass over into it; Ahab has gone in one way by himself, and Obadiah has gone in another way by himself; **7** and Obadiah [is] in the way, and behold, Elijah [is there] to meet him; and he discerns him, and falls on his face and says, "Are you he—my lord Elijah?" **8** And he says to him, "I [am]; go, say to your lord, Behold, Elijah." **9** And he says, "What have I sinned, that you are giving your servant into the hand of Ahab—to put me to death? **10** Your God Yhwh lives, if there is a nation and kingdom to where my lord has not sent to seek [for] you; and they said, He is not, then he caused the kingdom and the nation to swear, that it does not find you; **11** and now, you are saying, Go, say to your lord, Behold, Elijah; **12** and it has been, I go from you, and the Spirit of Yhwh lifts you up to where I do not know, and I have come to declare to Ahab, and he does not find you, and he has slain me; and your servant is fearing Yhwh from my youth. **13** Has it not been declared to my lord that which I have done in Jezebel's slaying the prophets of Yhwh, that I hide one hundred men of the prophets of Yhwh, fifty by fifty in a cave, and sustained them with bread and water? **14** and now you are saying, Go, say to my lord, Behold, Elijah—and he has slain me!" **15** And Elijah says, "Yhwh of Hosts lives, before whom I have stood, surely I appear to him today." **16** Obadiah goes to meet Ahab, and declares [it] to him, and Ahab goes to meet Elijah. **17** [And it] comes to pass, at Ahab's seeing Elijah that Ahab says to him, "Are you he—the troubler of Israel?" **18** And he says, "I have not troubled Israel, but you and the house of your father, in your forsaking the commands of Yhwh, and you go after the Ba'alim; **19** and now, send, gather all Israel to me, to the Mount of Carmel, and the four hundred and fifty prophets of Ba'al, and the four hundred prophets of Asherah who are eating at the table of Jezebel." **20** And Ahab sends among all the sons of Israel, and gathers the prophets to the Mount of Carmel; **21** and Elijah comes near to all the people and says, "Until when are you leaping on the two branches? If Yhwh [is] God, go after Him; and if Ba'al, go after him"; and the people have not answered him a word. **22** And Elijah says to the people, "I have been left, by myself, a prophet of Yhwh; and the prophets of Ba'al [are] four hundred and fifty men; **23** and let them give two bullocks to us, and they choose one bullock for themselves, and cut it in pieces, and place [it] on the wood, and place no fire; and I prepare the other bullock, and have put [it] on the wood, and I do not place fire— **24** and you have called in the name of your god, and I call in the Name of Yhwh, and it has been, the god who answers by fire—He [is] the God." And all the people answer and say, "The word [is] good." **25** And Elijah says to the prophets of Ba'al, "Choose one bullock for yourselves, and prepare [it] first, for you [are] the multitude, and call in the name of your god, and place no fire." **26** And they take the bullock that [one] gave to them, and prepare [it], and call in the name of Ba'al from the morning even until the noon, saying, "O Ba'al, answer us!" And there is no voice, and there is none answering; and they leap on the altar that one had made. **27** And it comes to pass, at noon, that Elijah mocks at them and says, "Call with a loud voice, for he [is] a god, for he is meditating, or pursuing, or on a journey; it may be he is asleep, and awakes." **28** And they call with a loud voice, and cut themselves, according to their ordinance, with swords and with spears, until a flowing of blood [is] on them; **29** and it comes to pass, at the passing by of the noon, that they feign themselves prophets until the going up of the present, and there is no voice, and there is none answering, and there is none attending. **30** And Elijah says to all the people, "Come near to me"; and all the people come near to him, and he repairs the altar of Yhwh that is broken down; **31** and Elijah takes twelve stones, according to the number of the tribes of the sons of Jacob, to whom the word of Yhwh was, saying, "Israel is your name"; **32** and he builds an altar with the stones, in the Name of Yhwh, and makes a trench, as about the space of two measures of seed, around the altar. **33** And he arranges the wood, and cuts the bullock in pieces, and places [it] on the wood, and says, "Fill four pitchers of water, and pour [them] on the burnt-offering, and on the wood"; **34** and he says, "Do [it] a second time"; and they do [it] a second time; and he says, "Do [it] a third time"; and they do [it] a third time; **35** and the water goes around the altar, and he has also filled the trench with water. **36** And it comes to pass, at the going up of the [evening] present, that Elijah the prophet comes near and says, "Yhwh, God of Abraham, Isaac, and Israel, let it be known today that You [are] God in Israel, and that I, Your servant, have done the whole of these things by Your word; **37** answer me, O Yhwh, answer me, and this people [then] knows that You [are] Yhwh God; and You have turned their heart backward." **38** And a fire falls [from] Yhwh, and consumes the burnt-offering, and the wood, and the stones, and the dust, and it has licked up the water that [is] in the trench. **39** And all the people see, and fall on their faces, and say, "Yhwh, He [is] the God! Yhwh, He [is] the God!" **40** And Elijah says to them, "Catch the prophets of Ba'al; do not let a man escape from them"; and they catch them, and Elijah brings them down to the Brook of Kishon, and slaughters them there. **41** And Elijah says to Ahab, "Go up, eat and drink, because of the sound of the noise of the shower." **42** And Ahab goes up to eat, and to drink, and Elijah has gone up to the top of Carmel, and he stretches himself out on the earth, and he places his face between his knees, **43** and says to his young man, "Now go up, look attentively [toward] the way of the sea"; and he goes up and looks attentively, and says, "There is nothing"; and he says, "Turn back," seven times. **44** And it comes to pass, at the seventh, that he says, "Behold, a little thickness as the palm of a man is coming up out of the sea." And he says, "Go up,

say to Ahab, Bind and go down, and the shower does not restrain you." **45** And it comes to pass, in the meantime, that the heavens have become black—thick clouds and wind—and the shower is great; and Ahab rides, and goes to Jezreel, **46** and the hand of Yhwh has been on Elijah, and he girds up his loins, and runs before Ahab, until your entering Jezreel.

CHAPTER 19

1 And Ahab declares to Jezebel all that Elijah did, and all of how he slew all the prophets by the sword, **2** and Jezebel sends a messenger to Elijah, saying, "Thus do the gods do, and thus do they add—surely about this time tomorrow, I make your life as the life of one of them." **3** And he fears, and rises, and goes for his life, and comes to Beer-Sheba, that [is] Judah's, and leaves his young man there, **4** and he himself has gone a day's journey into the wilderness, and comes and sits under a certain broom tree, and desires his soul to die, and says, "Enough, now, O Yhwh, take my soul, for I [am] not better than my fathers." **5** And he lies down and sleeps under a certain broom tree, and behold, a messenger is reaching toward him and says to him, "Rise, eat"; **6** and he looks attentively, and behold, at his bolster [is] a cake [on] burning stones, and a dish of water, and he eats, and drinks, and turns, and lies down. **7** And the messenger of Yhwh turns back a second time, and is reaching toward him, and says, "Rise, eat, for the way is too great for you"; **8** and he rises, and eats, and drinks, and goes in the power of that food [for] forty days and forty nights, to the mountain of God—Horeb. **9** And he comes in there, to the cave, and lodges there, and behold, the word of Yhwh [is] to him, and says to him, "What are you [doing] here, Elijah?" **10** And he says, "I have been very zealous for Yhwh, God of Hosts, for the sons of Israel have forsaken Your covenant—they have thrown down Your altars, and they have slain Your prophets by the sword, and I am left, I, by myself, and they seek my life—to take it." **11** And He says, "Go out, and you have stood on the mountain before Yhwh." And behold, Yhwh is passing by, and a wind—great and strong—is tearing mountains, and shattering rocks before Yhwh, [but] Yhwh [is] not in the wind; and after the wind [is] a shaking, [but] Yhwh [is] not in the shaking; **12** and after the shaking [is] a fire, [but] Yhwh [is] not in the fire; and after the fire [is] a voice [like] a small whisper; **13** and it comes to pass, at Elijah's hearing [it], that he wraps his face in his robe, and goes out, and stands at the opening of the cave, and behold, a voice [speaks] to him, and it says, "What are you [doing] here, Elijah?" **14** And he says, "I have been very zealous for Yhwh, God of Hosts; for the sons of Israel have forsaken Your covenant, they have thrown down Your altars, and they have slain Your prophets by the sword, and I am left, I, by myself, and they seek my life—to take it." **15** And Yhwh says to him, "Go, return on your way to the wilderness of Damascus, and you have gone in, and anointed Hazael for king over Aram, **16** and you anoint Jehu son of Nimshi for king over Israel, and you anoint Elisha son of Shaphat, of Abel-Meholah, for prophet in your stead. **17** And it has been, he who has escaped from the sword of Hazael, Jehu puts to death, and he who has escaped from the sword of Jehu, Elisha puts to death; **18** and I have left in Israel seven thousand—all the knees that have not bowed to Ba'al, and every mouth that has not kissed him." **19** And he goes there, and finds Elisha son of Shaphat, and he is plowing; twelve yoke [are] before him, and he [is] with the twelfth; and Elijah passes over to him, and casts his robe at him, **20** and he forsakes the ox, and runs after Elijah, and says, "Please let me give a kiss to my father and to my mother, and I go after you." And he says to him, "Go, turn back, for what have I done to you?" **21** And he turns back from after him, and takes the yoke of the ox, and sacrifices it, and with [the] instruments of the ox he has boiled its flesh, and gives to the people, and they eat, and he rises, and goes after Elijah, and serves him.

CHAPTER 20

1 And Ben-Hadad king of Aram has gathered all his force, and thirty-two kings [are] with him, and horse and chariot, and he goes up and lays siege against Samaria, and fights with it, **2** and sends messengers to Ahab king of Israel, to the city, **3** and says to him, "Thus said Ben-Hadad: Your silver and your gold are mine, and your wives and your sons—the best—are mine." **4** And the king of Israel answers and says, "According to your word, my lord, O king; I [am] yours, and all that I have." **5** And the messengers turn back and say, "Thus spoke Ben-Hadad, saying, Surely I sent to you, saying, Your silver, and your gold, and your wives, and your sons, you give to me; **6** for if, at this time tomorrow, I send my servants to you, then they have searched your house, and the houses of your servants, and it has been [that] every desirable thing of your eyes they place in their hand, and have taken [them] away." **7** And the king of Israel calls to all [the] elderly of the land and says, "Please know and see that this [one] is seeking evil, for he sent to me for my wives, and for my sons, and for my silver, and for my gold, and I did not withhold from him." **8** And all the elderly and all the people say to him, "Do not listen, nor consent." **9** And he says to the messengers of Ben-Hadad, "Say to my lord the king, All that you sent to your servant for at the first I do, and this thing I am not able to do"; and the messengers go and take him back word. **10** And Ben-Hadad sends to him and says, "Thus the gods do to me, and thus do they add, if the dust of Samaria suffice for handfuls for all the people who [are] at my feet." **11** And the king of Israel answers and says, "Speak: Do not let him who is girding on boast himself as him who is loosing [his armor]." **12** And it comes to pass at the hearing of this word—and he is drinking, he and the kings, in the shelters—that he says to his servants, "Set yourselves"; and they set themselves against the city. **13** And behold, a certain prophet has come near to Ahab king of Israel and says, "Thus said Yhwh: Have you seen all this great multitude? behold, I am giving it into your hand today, and you have known that I [am] Yhwh." **14** And Ahab says, "By whom?" And he says, "Thus said Yhwh: By the young men of the heads of the provinces"; and he says, "Who directs the battle?" And he says, "You." **15** And he inspects the young men of the heads of the provinces, and they are two hundred and thirty-two, and after them he has mustered all the people, all the sons of Israel—seven thousand, **16** and they go out at noon, and Ben-Hadad is drinking—drunk in the shelters, he and the kings, the thirty-two kings helping him. **17** And the young men of the heads of the provinces go out at the first, and Ben-Hadad sends, and they declare to him, saying, "Men have come out of Samaria." **18** And he says, "If they have come out for peace, catch them alive; and if they have come out for battle, catch them alive." **19** And these have gone out of the city—the young men of the heads of the provinces—and the force that [is] after them, **20** and each strikes his man, and Aram flees, and Israel pursues them, and Ben-Hadad king of Aram escapes on a horse—and the horsemen; **21** and the king of Israel goes out, and strikes the horses, and the charioteers, and has struck among the Arameans a great striking. **22** And the prophet comes near to the king of Israel and says to him, "Go, strengthen yourself, and know and see that which you do, for at the turn of the year the king of Aram is coming up against you." **23** And the servants of the king of Aram said to him, "Their gods [are] gods of hills, therefore they were stronger than us; and yet, we fight with them in the plain—are we not stronger than they? **24** And this thing you do: turn aside each of the kings out of his place, and set captains in their stead; **25** and you, number for yourself a force as the force that is fallen from you, and horse for horse, and chariot for chariot, and we fight with them in the plain; are we not stronger than they?" And he listens to their voice, and does so. **26** And it comes to pass at the turn of the year, that Ben-Hadad inspects the Arameans, and goes up to Aphek, to battle with Israel, **27** and the sons of Israel have been inspected, and supported, and go to meet them, and the sons of Israel encamp before them, like two flocks of goats, and the Arameans have filled the land. **28** And a man of God comes near, and speaks to the king of Israel and says, "Thus said Yhwh: Because that the Arameans have said, Yhwh [is] God of [the] hills, but He [is] not God of [the] valleys—I have given the whole of this great multitude into your hand, and you have known that I [am] Yhwh." **29** And they encamp opposite one another [for] seven days, and it comes to pass on the seventh day, that the battle draws near, and the sons of Israel strike one hundred thousand footmen of Aram in one day. **30** And those left flee to Aphek, into the city, and the wall falls on twenty-seven chief men who are left, and Ben-Hadad has fled, and comes into the city, into the innermost part. **31** And his servants say to him, "Now behold, we have heard that the kings of the house of Israel—that they are kind kings; please let us put sackcloth on our loins and ropes on our heads, and we go out to the king of Israel; it may be he keeps you alive." **32** And they gird sackcloth on their loins, and ropes

[are] on their heads, and they come to the king of Israel, and say, "Your servant Ben-Hadad has said, Please let me live"; and he says, "Is he still alive? he [is] my brother." **33** And the men observe diligently, and hurry, and catch [the word] from him, and say, "Your brother Ben-Hadad"; and he says, "Go in, bring him"; and Ben-Hadad comes out to him, and he causes him to come up on the chariot. **34** And he says to him, "The cities that my father took from your father, I give back, and you make streets for yourself in Damascus, as my father did in Samaria; and I, with a covenant, send you away"; and he makes a covenant with him, and sends him away. **35** And a certain man of the sons of the prophets said to his neighbor by the word of Yhwh, "Please strike me"; and the man refuses to strike him, **36** and he says to him, "Because that you have not listened to the voice of Yhwh, behold, you are going from me, and the lion has struck you"; and he goes from him, and the lion finds him, and strikes him. **37** And he finds another man and says, "Please strike me"; and the man strikes him, striking and wounding, **38** and the prophet goes and stands for the king on the way, and disguises himself with ashes on his eyes. **39** And it comes to pass—the king is passing by—that he has cried to the king and says, "Your servant went out into the midst of the battle, and behold, a man has turned aside and brings a man to me, and says, Keep this man; if he is at all missing, then your life has been for his life, or you weigh out a talent of silver; **40** and it comes to pass, your servant is working here and there, and he is not!" And the king of Israel says to him, "Your judgment [is] right; you have determined [it]." **41** And he hurries and turns aside the ashes from off his eyes, and the king of Israel discerns him, that he [is] of the prophets, **42** and he says to him, "Thus said Yhwh: Because you have sent away the man I devoted, out of [your] hand, even your life has been for his life, and your people for his people"; **43** and the king of Israel goes to his house, sulky and angry, and comes to Samaria.

CHAPTER 21

1 And it comes to pass after these things, a vineyard has been to Naboth the Jezreelite, that [is] in Jezreel, near the palace of Ahab king of Samaria, **2** and Ahab speaks to Naboth, saying, "Give your vineyard to me, and it is for a garden of green herbs for me, for it [is] near by my house, and I give to you a better vineyard than it in its stead; if [this is] good in your eyes, I give to you its price [in] silver." **3** And Naboth says to Ahab, "Far be it from me, by Yhwh, my giving the inheritance of my fathers to you"; **4** and Ahab comes to his house, sulky and angry, because of the word that Naboth the Jezreelite has spoken to him when he says, "I do not give the inheritance of my fathers to you," and he lies down on his bed, and turns around his face, and has not eaten bread. **5** And his wife Jezebel comes to him, and speaks to him, "Why [is] this [that] your spirit [is] sulky, and you are not eating bread?" **6** And he says to her, "Because I speak to Naboth the Jezreelite, and say to him, Give your vineyard to me for money, or if you desire, I give a vineyard to you in its stead; and he says, I do not give my vineyard to you." **7** And his wife Jezebel says to him, "You now execute rule over Israel! Rise, eat bread, and let your heart be glad—I give the vineyard of Naboth the Jezreelite to you." **8** And she writes letters in the name of Ahab, and seals with his seal, and sends the letters to the elderly and to the nobles who are in his city, those dwelling with Naboth, **9** and she writes in the letters, saying, "Proclaim a fast, and cause Naboth to sit at the head of the people, **10** and cause two men—sons of worthlessness—to sit opposite him, and they testify of him, saying, You have blessed [[*or* cursed]] God and [the] king; and they have brought him out, and stoned him, and he dies." **11** And the men of his city, the elderly and the nobles who are dwelling in his city, do as Jezebel has sent to them, as written in the letters that she sent to them, **12** they have proclaimed a fast, and caused Naboth to sit at the head of the people, **13** and two men—sons of worthlessness—come in, and sit opposite him, and the men of worthlessness testify of him, even Naboth, before the people, saying, "Naboth blessed [[*or* cursed]] God and [the] king"; and they take him out to the outside of the city, and stone him with stones, and he dies; **14** and they send to Jezebel, saying, "Naboth was stoned, and is dead." **15** And it comes to pass, at Jezebel's hearing that Naboth has been stoned, and is dead, that Jezebel says to Ahab, "Rise, possess the vineyard of Naboth the Jezreelite, that he refused to give to you for money, for Naboth is not alive but dead." **16**

And it comes to pass, at Ahab's hearing that Naboth is dead, that Ahab rises to go down to the vineyard of Naboth the Jezreelite, to possess it. **17** And the word of Yhwh is to Elijah the Tishbite, saying, **18** "Rise, go down to meet Ahab king of Israel, who [is] in Samaria—behold, in the vineyard of Naboth, to where he has gone down to possess it, **19** and you have spoken to him, saying, Thus said Yhwh: Have you murdered, and also possessed? and you have spoken to him, saying, Thus said Yhwh: In the place where the dogs licked the blood of Naboth, the dogs lick your blood, even yours." **20** And Ahab says to Elijah, "Have you found me, O my enemy?" And he says, "I have found—because of your selling yourself to do evil in the eyes of Yhwh; **21** behold, I am bringing calamity on you, and have taken away your posterity, and cut off from Ahab those sitting on the wall, and restrained, and left, in Israel, **22** and given up your house like the house of Jeroboam son of Nebat, and like the house of Baasha son of Ahijah, for the provocation with which you have provoked [Me], and cause Israel to sin. **23** And Yhwh has also spoken of Jezebel, saying, The dogs eat Jezebel in the bulwark of Jezreel; **24** the dogs eat him who dies of Ahab in a city, and [the] bird of the heavens eats him who dies in a field; **25** surely there has been none like Ahab, who sold himself to do evil in the eyes of Yhwh, whom his wife Jezebel has moved, **26** and he does very abominably to go after the idols, according to all that the Amorite did whom Yhwh dispossessed from the presence of the sons of Israel." **27** And it comes to pass, at Ahab's hearing these words, that he tears his garments, and puts sackcloth on his flesh, and fasts, and lies in sackcloth, and goes gently. **28** And the word of Yhwh is to Elijah the Tishbite, saying, **29** "Have you seen that Ahab has been humbled before Me? because that he has been humbled before Me, I do not bring in the calamity in his days; I bring in the calamity on his house in the days of his son."

CHAPTER 22

1 And they sit still three years; there is no war between Aram and Israel. **2** And it comes to pass in the third year, that Jehoshaphat king of Judah comes down to the king of Israel, **3** and the king of Israel says to his servants, "Have you not known that Ramoth-Gilead [is] ours? and we are keeping silent from taking it out of the hand of the king of Aram!" **4** And he says to Jehoshaphat, "Do you go with me to battle [against] Ramoth-Gilead?" And Jehoshaphat says to the king of Israel, "As I am, so [are] you; as my people, so your people; as my horses, so your horses." **5** And Jehoshaphat says to the king of Israel, "Please seek the word of Yhwh today"; **6** and the king of Israel gathers the prophets, about four hundred men, and says to them, "Do I go to battle against Ramoth-Gilead, or do I refrain?" And they say, "Go up, and the Lord gives [it] into the hand of the king." **7** And Jehoshaphat says, "[Is there] not a prophet of Yhwh still here that we may seek from him?" **8** And the king of Israel says to Jehoshaphat, "Yet one man [remains] to seek Yhwh from him, and I have hated him, for he does not prophesy good concerning me, but evil—Micaiah son of Imlah"; and Jehoshaphat says, "Do not let the king say so." **9** And the king of Israel calls to a certain eunuch and says, "Hurry along Micaiah son of Imlah." **10** And the king of Israel and Jehoshaphat king of Judah are sitting, each on his throne, clothed with garments, in a threshing-floor, at the opening of the Gate of Samaria, and all the prophets are prophesying before them. **11** And Zedekiah son of Chenaanah makes horns of iron for himself and says, "Thus said Yhwh: By these you push the Arameans until they are consumed"; **12** and all the prophets are prophesying so, saying, "Go up to Ramoth-Gilead, and prosper, and Yhwh has given [it] into the hand of the king." **13** And the messenger who has gone to call Micaiah has spoken to him, saying, "Now behold, the words of the prophets, with one mouth, [are] good toward the king; please let your word be as the word of one of them—and you have spoken good." **14** And Micaiah says, "Yhwh lives; surely that which Yhwh says to me—it I speak." **15** And he comes to the king, and the king says to him, "Micaiah, do we go to Ramoth-Gilead, to battle, or do we refrain?" And he says to him, "Go up, and prosper, and Yhwh has given [it] into the hand of the king." **16** And the king says to him, "How many times am I adjuring you that you speak nothing to me but truth in the Name of Yhwh?" **17** And he says, "I have seen all Israel scattered on the hills as sheep that have no shepherd, and Yhwh says, These have no master; let them return—each to his house in peace." **18** And the king of Israel says to Jehoshaphat, "Have I not said to you, He does

not prophesy of me good, but evil?" **19** And he says, "Therefore, hear a word of Yhwh! I have seen Yhwh sitting on His throne, and all the host of the heavens standing by Him, on His right and on His left; **20** and Yhwh says, Who entices Ahab, and he goes up and falls in Ramoth-Gilead? and this one says thus, and that one is saying thus. **21** And the spirit goes out and stands before Yhwh, and says, I entice him; and Yhwh says to him, By what? **22** and he says, I go out, and have been a spirit of falsehood in the mouth of all his prophets; and He says, You entice, and also you are able; go out and do so. **23** And now, behold, Yhwh has put a spirit of falsehood in the mouth of all these prophets of yours, and Yhwh has spoken calamity concerning you." **24** And Zedekiah son of Chenaanah draws near and strikes Micaiah on the cheek, and says, "Where [is] this [that] the spirit [from] Yhwh has passed over from me to speak with you?" **25** And Micaiah says, "Behold, you are seeing on that day when you go into the innermost chamber to be hidden." **26** And the king of Israel says, "Take Micaiah, and turn him back to Amon head of the city, and to Joash son of the king, **27** and you have said, Thus said the king: Place this one in the house of restraint, and cause him to eat bread of oppression, and water of oppression, until my coming in peace." **28** And Micaiah says, "If you return in peace at all, Yhwh has not spoken by me"; and he says, "Hear, O peoples, all of them." **29** And the king of Israel goes up—and Jehoshaphat king of Judah—to Ramoth-Gilead. **30** And the king of Israel says to Jehoshaphat to disguise himself, and to go into battle, "And you, put on your garments." And the king of Israel disguises himself, and goes into battle. **31** And the king of Aram commanded the thirty-two heads of the charioteers whom he has, saying, "You do not fight with small or with great, but with the king of Israel by himself." **32** And it comes to pass, at the heads of the charioteers seeing Jehoshaphat, that they said, "He [is] surely the king of Israel!" And they turn aside to him to fight, and Jehoshaphat cries out, **33** and it comes to pass, at the heads of the charioteers seeing that he [is] not the king of Israel, that they turn back from after him. **34** And a man has drawn with a bow in his simplicity, and strikes the king of Israel between the joinings and the coat of mail, and he says to his charioteer, "Turn your hand, and take me out from the camp, for I have become sick." **35** And the battle increases on that day, and the king has been caused to stand in the chariot, in front of Aram, and he dies in the evening, and the blood of the wound runs out to the midst of the chariot, **36** and he causes the cry to pass over through the camp, at the going in of the sun, saying, "Each to his city, and each to his land!" **37** And the king dies, and comes into Samaria, and they bury the king in Samaria; **38** and [one] rinses the chariot by the pool of Samaria, and the dogs lick his blood when they had washed the armor, according to the word of Yhwh that He spoke. **39** And the rest of the matters of Ahab, and all that he did, and the house of ivory that he built, and all the cities that he built, are they not written on the scroll of the Chronicles of the Kings of Israel? **40** And–Ahab lies with his fathers, and his son Ahaziah reigns in his stead. **41** And Jehoshaphat son of Asa has reigned over Judah in the fourth year of Ahab king of Israel, **42** Jehoshaphat [is] a son of thirty-five years in his reigning, and he has reigned twenty-five years in Jerusalem, and the name of his mother [is] Azubah daughter of Shilhi. **43** And he walks in all the way of his father Asa, he has not turned aside from it, to do that which [is] right in the eyes of Yhwh; only, the high places have not been removed—the people are still sacrificing and making incense in high places. **44** And Jehoshaphat makes peace with the king of Israel; **45** and the rest of the matters of Jehoshaphat, and his might that he exercised, and with which he fought, are they not written on the scroll of the Chronicles of the Kings of Judah? **46** And the remnant of the whoremongers who were left in the days of his father Asa he took away out of the land; **47** and there is no king in Edom; he set up a king. **48** Jehoshaphat made ships of Tarshish to go to Ophir for gold, and they did not go, for the ships were broken in Ezion-Geber. **49** Then Ahaziah son of Ahab said to Jehoshaphat, "Let my servants go with your servants in the ships"; and Jehoshaphat was not willing. **50** And Jehoshaphat lies with his fathers, and is buried with his fathers in the city of his father David, and his son Jehoram reigns in his stead. **51** Ahaziah son of Ahab has reigned over Israel in Samaria in the seventeenth year of Jehoshaphat king of Judah, and reigns over Israel two years, **52** and does evil in the eyes of Yhwh, and walks in the way of his father, and in the way of his mother, and in the way of Jeroboam son of Nebat who caused Israel to sin, **53** and serves the Ba'al, and bows himself to it, and provokes Yhwh, God of Israel, according to all that his father had done.

2 KINGS

CHAPTER 1

¹ And Moab transgresses against Israel after the death of Ahab, ² and Ahaziah falls through the lattice in his upper chamber that [is] in Samaria, and is sick, and sends messengers, and says to them, "Go, inquire of Ba'al-Zebub god of Ekron if I recover from this sickness." ³ And a messenger of Yhwh has spoken to Elijah the Tishbite, "Rise, go up to meet the messengers of the king of Samaria, and speak to them, Is it because that there is not a God in Israel—you are going to inquire of Ba'al-Zebub god of Ekron? ⁴ and therefore, thus said Yhwh: The bed to where you have gone up, you do not come down from it, for you certainly die"; and Elijah goes on. ⁵ And the messengers return to him, and he says to them, "What [is] this—you have turned back!" ⁶ And they say to him, "A man has come up to meet us and says to us, Go, return to the king who sent you, and you have said to him, Thus said Yhwh: Is it because there is not a God in Israel—you are sending to inquire of Ba'al-Zebub god of Ekron? therefore, the bed to where you have gone up, you do not come down from it, for you certainly die." ⁷ And he says to them, "What [is] the fashion of the man who has come up to meet you, and speaks these words to you?" ⁸ And they say to him, "A hairy man, and a girdle of skin girt around his loins"; and he says, "He [is] Elijah the Tishbite." ⁹ And he sends to him a head of fifty and his fifty, and he goes up to him (and behold, he is sitting on the top of the hill), and he speaks to him, "O man of God, the king has spoken, Come down." ¹⁰ And Elijah answers and speaks to the head of the fifty, "And if I [am] a man of God, fire comes down from the heavens and consumes you and your fifty"; and fire comes down from the heavens and consumes him and his fifty. ¹¹ And he turns and sends to him another head of fifty and his fifty, and he answers and speaks to him, "O man of God, thus said the king: Hurry, come down." ¹² And Elijah answers and speaks to them, "If I [am] a man of God, fire comes down from the heavens and consumes you and your fifty"; and fire of God comes down from the heavens and consumes him and his fifty. ¹³ And he turns and sends a third head of fifty and his fifty, and the third head of fifty goes up, and comes in, and bows on his knees before Elijah, and makes supplication to him, and speaks to him, "O man of God, please let my soul and the soul of your servants—these fifty—be precious in your eyes. ¹⁴ Behold, fire has come down from the heavens and consumes the two heads of the former fifties and their fifties; and now, let my soul be precious in your eyes." ¹⁵ And a messenger of Yhwh speaks to Elijah, "Go down with him, do not be afraid of him"; and he rises and goes down with him to the king, ¹⁶ and speaks to him, "Thus said Yhwh: Because that you have sent messengers to inquire of Ba'al-Zebub god of Ekron—is it because there is not a God in Israel to inquire of His word? therefore, the bed to where you have gone up—you do not come down from it, for you certainly die." ¹⁷ And he dies, according to the word of Yhwh that Elijah spoke, and Jehoram reigns in his stead, in the second year of Jehoram son of Jehoshaphat king of Judah, for he had no son. ¹⁸ And the rest of the matters of Ahaziah that he did, are they not written on the scroll of the Chronicles of the Kings of Israel?

CHAPTER 2

¹ And it comes to pass, at Yhwh's taking up Elijah to the heavens in a whirlwind, that Elijah goes, and Elisha, from Gilgal, ² and Elijah says to Elisha, "Please abide here, for Yhwh has sent me to Beth-El"; and Elisha says, "Yhwh lives, and your soul lives, if I leave you"; and they go down to Beth-El. ³ And sons of the prophets who [are] in Beth-El come out to Elisha, and say to him, "Have you known that today Yhwh is taking your lord from your head?" And he says, "I also have known—keep silent." ⁴ And Elijah says to him, "Elisha, please abide here, for Yhwh has sent me to Jericho"; and he says, "Yhwh lives, and your soul lives, if I leave you"; and they come to

Jericho. ⁵ And sons of the prophets who [are] in Jericho come near to Elisha, and say to him, "Have you known that today Yhwh is taking your lord from your head?" And he says, "I also have known—keep silent." ⁶ And Elijah says to him, "Please abide here, for Yhwh has sent me to the Jordan"; and he says, "Yhwh lives, and your soul lives, if I leave you"; and both of them go on— ⁷ and fifty men of the sons of the prophets have gone on, and stand opposite [them] far off—and both of them have stood by the Jordan. ⁸ And Elijah takes his robe, and wraps [it] together, and strikes the waters, and they are halved, here and there, and both of them pass over on dry land. ⁹ And it comes to pass, at their passing over, that Elijah has said to Elisha, "Ask what I do for you before I am taken from you." And Elisha says, "Indeed, please let there be a double portion of your spirit to me"; ¹⁰ and he says, "You have asked a hard thing; if you see me taken from you, it is to you so; and if not, it is not." ¹¹ And it comes to pass, they are going, going on and speaking, and behold, a chariot of fire and horses of fire [appear], and they separate between them both, and Elijah goes up to the heavens in a whirlwind. ¹² And Elisha is seeing, and he is crying, "My father! My father! The chariot of Israel and its horsemen!" And he has not seen him again; and he takes hold on his garments and tears them into two pieces. ¹³ And he takes up the robe of Elijah that fell from off him, and turns back and stands on the edge of the Jordan, ¹⁴ and he takes the robe of Elijah that fell from off him, and strikes the waters, and says, "Where [is] Yhwh, God of Elijah—even He?" And he strikes the waters, and they are halved, here and there, and Elisha passes over. ¹⁵ And they see him—the sons of the prophets who [are] in Jericho—from opposite [them], and they say, "The spirit of Elijah has rested on Elisha"; and they come to meet him, and bow themselves to him to the earth, ¹⁶ and say to him, "Now behold, there are fifty men with your servants, sons of valor: please let them go, and they seek your lord, lest the Spirit of Yhwh has taken him up, and casts him on one of the hills or into one of the valleys"; and he says, "You do not send." ¹⁷ And they press on him, until he is ashamed, and he says, "Send"; and they send fifty men, and they seek three days, and have not found him; ¹⁸ and they return to him—and he is abiding in Jericho—and he says to them, "Did I not say to you, Do not go?" ¹⁹ And the men of the city say to Elisha, "Now behold, the site of the city [is] good, as my lord sees, and the waters [are] bad, and the earth sterile." ²⁰ And he says, "Bring a new dish to me, and place salt there"; and they bring [it] to him, ²¹ and he goes out to the source of the waters, and casts salt there, and says, "Thus said Yhwh: I have given healing to these waters; there is not anymore death and sterility there." ²² And the waters are healed to this day, according to the word of Elisha that he spoke. ²³ And he goes up from there to Beth-El, and he is going up in the way, and little youths have come out from the city, and scoff at him, and say to him, "Go up, bald-head! Go up, bald-head!" ²⁴ And he looks behind him, and sees them, and declares them vile in the Name of Yhwh, and two bears come out of the forest and ripped apart forty-two of the boys. ²⁵ And he goes from there to the hill of Carmel, and from there he has turned back to Samaria.

CHAPTER 3

¹ And Jehoram son of Ahab has reigned over Israel, in Samaria, in the eighteenth year of Jehoshaphat king of Judah, and he reigns twelve years, ² and does evil in the eyes of Yhwh, only not like his father, and like his mother, and he turns aside the standing-pillar of Ba'al that his father made; ³ surely he has cleaved to the sins of Jeroboam son of Nebat that he caused Israel to sin; he has not turned aside from it. ⁴ And Mesha king of Moab was a sheep-master, and he rendered to the king of Israel one hundred thousand lambs and one hundred thousand rams, [with] wool, ⁵ and it comes to pass at the death of Ahab, that the king of Moab transgresses against the king of Israel. ⁶ And King Jehoram goes out from Samaria in that day, and inspects all Israel, ⁷ and goes and sends to Jehoshaphat king of Judah, saying, "The king of Moab has transgressed against me; do you go with me to Moab for battle?" And he says, "I go up, as I, so you; as my people, so your people; as my horses, so your horses." ⁸ And he says, "Where [is] this—the way we go up?" And he says, "The way of the wilderness of Edom." ⁹ And the king of Israel goes, and the king of Judah, and the king of Edom, and they turn around the way seven days, and there has been no water for the camp, and for the livestock that [are] at their feet, ¹⁰ and the king of Israel says, "Aah! For Yhwh has

called for these three kings to give them into the hand of Moab." ¹¹ And Jehoshaphat says, "Is there not a prophet of Yhwh here, and we seek Yhwh by him?" And one of the servants of the king of Israel answers and says, "Here [is] Elisha son of Shaphat, who poured water on the hands of Elijah." ¹² And Jehoshaphat says, "The word of Yhwh is with him"; and the king of Israel goes down to him, and Jehoshaphat, and the king of Edom. ¹³ And Elisha says to the king of Israel, "And what do I [have to do] with you? go to the prophets of your father, and to the prophets of your mother"; and the king of Israel says to him, "No, for Yhwh has called for these three kings to give them into the hand of Moab." ¹⁴ And Elisha says, "Yhwh of Hosts lives, before whom I have stood; for unless I am lifting up the face of Jehoshaphat king of Judah, I do not look to you, nor see you; ¹⁵ and now, bring a musician to me"; and it has been, at the playing of the musician, that the hand of Yhwh is on him, ¹⁶ and he says, "Thus said Yhwh: Make this valley ditches—ditches; ¹⁷ for thus said Yhwh: You do not see wind, nor do you see rain, and that valley is full of water, and you have drunk—you, and your livestock, and your beasts. ¹⁸ And this has been light in the eyes of Yhwh, and he has given Moab into your hand, ¹⁹ and you have struck every fortified city, and every choice city, and you cause every good tree to fall, and you stop all fountains of waters, and you mar every good portion with stones." ²⁰ And it comes to pass in the morning, at the ascending of the [morning] present, that behold, waters are coming in from the way of Edom, and the land is filled with the waters, ²¹ and all of Moab has heard that the kings have come up to fight against them, and they are called together, from everyone girding on a girdle and upward, and they stand by the border. ²² And they rise early in the morning, and the sun has shone on the waters, and the Moabites see, from opposite [them], [that] the waters [are] red as blood, ²³ and say, "This [is] blood; the kings have been surely destroyed, and they each strike his neighbor; and now for spoil, Moab!" ²⁴ And they come to the camp of Israel, and Israel rises, and strikes the Moabites, and they flee from their face; and they enter into Moab, so as to strike Moab, ²⁵ and they break down the cities, and they each cast his stone [on] every good portion, and have filled it, and they stop every fountain of water, and they cause every good tree to fall—until one had left its stones in Kir-Haraseth, and the slingers go around and strike it. ²⁶ And the king of Moab sees that the battle has been too strong for him, and he takes with him seven hundred men drawing sword, to cleave through to the king of Edom, and they have not been able, ²⁷ and he takes his son, the firstborn who reigns in his stead, and causes him to ascend [as] a burnt-offering on the wall, and there is great wrath against Israel, and they journey from off him, and return to the land.

CHAPTER 4

¹ And a certain woman of the wives of the sons of the prophets has cried to Elisha, saying, "Your servant, my husband, is dead, and you have known that your servant was fearing Yhwh, and the lender has come to take my two children to himself for servants." ² And Elisha says to her, "What do I do for you? declare to me, what do you have in the house?" And she says, "Your maidservant has nothing in the house except a pot of oil." ³ And he says, "Go, ask [for] vessels for yourself from outside, from all your neighbors—empty vessels—let [them] not be few; ⁴ and you have entered, and have shut the door on you, and on your sons, and have poured it into all these vessels, and the full ones you remove." ⁵ And she goes from him, and shuts the door on her, and on her sons; they are bringing [them] near to her, and she is pouring [it] out, ⁶ and it comes to pass, at the filling of the vessels, that she says to her son, "Bring another vessel near to me," and he says to her, "There is not another vessel"; and the oil stays. ⁷ And she comes and declares [it] to the man of God, and he says, "Go, sell the oil, and repay your loan; and you [and] your sons live off the rest." ⁸ And the day comes that Elisha passes over to Shunem, and there [is] a great woman, and she lays hold on him to eat bread, and it comes to pass, at the time of his passing over, he turns aside there to eat bread, ⁹ and she says to her husband, "Now behold, I have known that he is a holy man of God, passing over by us continually; ¹⁰ please let us make a little upper chamber of the wall, and we set for him there a bed, and a table, and a high seat, and a lampstand; and it has been, in his coming to us, he turns aside there." ¹¹

And the day comes that he comes in there, and turns aside to the upper chamber, and lies there, ¹² and he says to his young man Gehazi, "Call for this Shunammite"; and he calls for her, and she stands before him. ¹³ And he says to him, "Now say to her, Behold, you have troubled yourself concerning us with all this trouble; what can [I] do for you? is it to speak for you to the king, or to the head of the host?" And she says, "I am dwelling in the midst of my people." ¹⁴ And he says, "And what can [I] do for her?" And Gehazi says, "Truly she has no son, and her husband [is] aged." ¹⁵ And he says, "Call for her"; and he calls for her, and she stands at the opening, ¹⁶ and he says, "At this season, according to the time of life, you are embracing a son"; and she says, "No, my lord, O man of God, do not lie to your maidservant." ¹⁷ And the woman conceives and bears a son, at this season, according to the time of life that Elisha spoke of to her. ¹⁸ And the boy grows, and the day comes that he goes out to his father, to the reapers, ¹⁹ and he says to his father, "My head, my head"; and he says to the young man, "Carry him to his mother"; ²⁰ and he carries him, and brings him to his mother, and he sits on her knees until the noon, and dies. ²¹ And she goes up, and lays him on the bed of the man of God, and shuts [the door] on him, and goes out, ²² and calls to her husband and says, "Please send one of the young men and one of the donkeys to me, and I run to the man of God, and return." ²³ And he says, "Why are you going to him today? [It is] neither new moon nor Sabbath!" And she says, "Peace [to you]!" ²⁴ And she saddles the donkey and says to her young man, "Lead, and go, do not restrain riding for me, except I have commanded [so] to you." ²⁵ And she goes, and comes to the man of God, to the hill of Carmel, and it comes to pass, at the man of God's seeing her from within view, that he says to his young man Gehazi, "Behold, this Shunammite; ²⁶ now please run to meet her, and say to her, Is there peace to you? is there peace to your husband? is there peace to the boy?" And she says, "Peace." ²⁷ And she comes to the man of God, to the hill, and lays hold on his feet, and Gehazi comes near to thrust her away, and the man of God says, "Leave her alone, for her soul [is] bitter to her, and Yhwh has hidden [it] from me, and has not declared [it] to me." ²⁸ And she says, "Did I ask for a son from my lord? did I not say, Do not deceive me?" ²⁹ And he says to Gehazi, "Gird up your loins, and take my staff in your hand, and go; when you meet a man, you do not greet him; and when a man greets you, you do not answer him; and you have laid my staff on the face of the youth." ³⁰ And the mother of the youth says, "Yhwh lives, and your soul lives—if I leave you"; and he rises and goes after her. ³¹ And Gehazi has passed on before them, and lays the staff on the face of the youth, and there is no voice, and there is no attention, and he turns back to meet him, and declares to him, saying, "The youth has not awoken." ³² And Elisha comes into the house, and behold, the youth is dead, laid on his bed, ³³ and he goes in and shuts the door on them both, and prays to Yhwh. ³⁴ And he goes up, and lies down on the boy, and puts his mouth on his mouth, and his eyes on his eyes, and his hands on his hands, and stretches himself on him, and the flesh of the boy becomes warm; ³⁵ and he turns back and walks in the house, once here and once there, and goes up and stretches himself on him, and the youth sneezes until seven times, and the youth opens his eyes. ³⁶ And he calls to Gehazi and says, "Call to this Shunammite"; and he calls her, and she comes to him, and he says, "Lift up your son." ³⁷ And she goes in, and falls at his feet, and bows herself to the earth, and lifts up her son, and goes out. ³⁸ And Elisha has turned back to Gilgal, and the famine [is] in the land, and the sons of the prophets are sitting before him, and he says to his young man, "Set on the great pot, and boil stew for the sons of the prophets." ³⁹ And one goes out to the field to gather herbs, and finds a vine of the field, and gathers gourds of the field from it—the fullness of his garment—and comes in and splits [them] into the pot of stew, for they did not know [them]; ⁴⁰ and they pour out for the men to eat, and it comes to pass at their eating of the stew, that they have cried out, and say, "Death [is] in the pot, O man of God!" And they have not been able to eat. ⁴¹ And he says, "Then bring a meal"; and he casts into the pot and says, "Pour out for the people, and they eat"; and there was no bad thing in the pot. ⁴² And a man has come from Ba'al-Shalishah, and brings to the man of God bread of first-fruits, twenty loaves of barley, and full ears of grain in its husk, and he says, "Give to the people, and they eat." ⁴³ And his minister says, "How do I give this before one hundred men?" And he says, "Give to the people, and they eat, for thus said Yhwh: Eat and leave"; ⁴⁴ and he gives before them, and they eat and leave, according to the word of Yhwh.

CHAPTER 5

1 And Naaman, head of the host of the king of Aram, was a great man before his lord, and accepted of face, for Yhwh had given salvation to Aram by him, and the man was mighty in valor, [but] leprous. **2** And the Arameans have gone out [by] troops, and they take a little girl captive out of the land of Israel, and she is before the wife of Naaman, **3** and she says to her mistress, "O that my lord [were] before the prophet who [is] in Samaria; then he recovers him from his leprosy." **4** And [one] goes in and declares [it] to his lord, saying, "Thus and thus the girl who [is] from the land of Israel has spoken." **5** And the king of Aram says, "Go, enter, and I send a letter to the king of Israel"; and he goes and takes in his hand ten talents of silver, and six thousand [pieces] of gold, and ten changes of garments. **6** And he brings in the letter to the king of Israel, saying, "And now, at the coming in of this letter to you, behold, I have sent my servant Naaman to you, and you have recovered him from his leprosy." **7** And it comes to pass, at the king of Israel's reading the letter, that he tears his garments and says, "Am I God, to put to death and to keep alive, that this [one] is sending to me to recover a man from his leprosy? for surely know now, and see, for he is presenting himself to me." **8** And it comes to pass, at Elisha the man of God's hearing that the king of Israel has torn his garments, that he sends to the king, saying, "Why have you torn your garments? Please let him come to me, and he knows that there is a prophet in Israel." **9** And Naaman comes, with his horses and with his chariot, and stands at the opening of the house for Elisha; **10** and Elisha sends a messenger to him, saying, "Go, and you have washed seven times in the Jordan, and your flesh turns back to you—and be clean." **11** And Naaman is angry, and goes on and says, "Behold, I said, He certainly comes out to me, and has stood and called in the Name of his God Yhwh, and waved his hand over the place, and recovered the leper. **12** Are not Abana and Pharpar, rivers of Damascus, better than all the waters of Israel? do I not wash in them and I have been clean?" And he turns and goes on in fury. **13** And his servants come near, and speak to him, and say, "My father, the prophet had spoken a great thing to you—do you not do [it]? and surely, when he has said to you, Wash, and be clean." **14** And he goes down and dips in the Jordan seven times, according to the word of the man of God, and his flesh turns back as the flesh of a little youth, and is clean. **15** And he turns back to the man of God, he and all his camp, and comes in, and stands before him, and says, "Now behold, I have known that there is not a God in all the earth except in Israel; and now, please take a blessing from your servant." **16** And he says, "Yhwh lives, before whom I have stood—if I take [it]"; and he presses on him to take, and he refuses. **17** And Naaman says, "If not, please let a couple of mules' burden of earth be given to your servant, for your servant makes no more burnt-offering and sacrifice to other gods, but [only sacrifices] to Yhwh. **18** For in this thing may Yhwh be propitious to your servant, in the coming in of my lord into the house of Rimmon to bow himself there, and he was supported by my hand, and I bowed myself [in] the house of Rimmon; for my bowing myself in the house of Rimmon, may Yhwh now be propitious to your servant in this thing." **19** And he says to him, "Go in peace." And he goes from him a distance of land, **20** and Gehazi, servant of Elisha the man of God, says, "Behold, my lord has spared this Aramean Naaman, not to receive from his hand that which he brought; for Yhwh lives; if I have run after him, then I have taken something from him." **21** And Gehazi pursues after Naaman, and Naaman sees one running after him, and comes down off the chariot to meet him, and says, "Is there peace?" **22** And he says, "Peace; my lord has sent me, saying, Behold, now, this, two young men of the sons of the prophets have come to me from the hill-country of Ephraim; please give a talent of silver and two changes of garments to them." **23** And Naaman says, "Be pleased, take two talents"; and he urges him, and binds two talents of silver in two purses, and two changes of garments, and gives [them] to two of his young men, and they carry [them] before him; **24** and he comes to the high place, and takes [them] out of their hand, and lays [them] up in the house, and sends the men away, and they go. **25** And he has come in, and stands by his lord, and Elisha says to him, "From where—Gehazi?" And he says, "Your servant did not go here or there." **26** And he says to him, "My heart did not go when the man turned from off his chariot to meet you; is it a time to take silver, and to take garments, and olives, and vines, and flock, and herd, and menservants, and maidservants? **27** indeed, the leprosy of Naaman cleaves to you and to your seed for all time"; and he goes out from before him—leprous as snow.

CHAPTER 6

1 And sons of the prophet say to Elisha, "Now behold, the place where we are dwelling before you is too narrow for us; **2** please let us go to the Jordan, and we each take one beam from there, and we make a place there for ourselves to dwell there"; and he says, "Go." **3** And the one says, "Please be willing, and go with your servants"; and he says, "I go." **4** And he goes with them, and they come to the Jordan, and cut down the trees, **5** and it comes to pass, the one is felling the beam, and the iron [ax head] has fallen into the water, and he cries and says, "Aah! My lord, for it was borrowed!" **6** And the man of God says, "To where has it fallen?" And he shows him the place, and he cuts a stick, and casts [it] there, and causes the iron to swim, **7** and says, "Raise [it] up for yourself"; and he puts forth his hand and takes it. **8** And the king of Aram has been fighting against Israel, and takes counsel with his servants, saying, "At such and such a place [is] my encamping." **9** And the man of God sends to the king of Israel, saying, "Take heed of passing by this place, for the Arameans are coming down there"; **10** and the king of Israel sends to the place of which the man of God spoke to him, and warned him, and he is preserved there not [just] once and not [just] twice. **11** And the heart of the king of Aram is tossed about concerning this thing, and he calls to his servants and says to them, "Do you not declare to me who of us [is] for the king of Israel?" **12** And one of his servants says, "No, my lord, O king, for Elisha the prophet, who [is] in Israel, declares to the king of Israel the words that you speak in the inner part of your bed-chamber." **13** And he says, "Go and see where he [is], and I send and take him"; and it is declared to him, saying, "Behold—in Dothan." **14** And he sends horses and chariot, and a heavy force there, and they come in by night, and go around against the city. **15** And the servant of the man of God rises early, and goes out, and behold, a force is surrounding the city, and horse and chariot, and his young man says to him, "Aah! My lord, how do we do?" **16** And he says, "Do not fear, for more [are] they who [are] with us than they who [are] with them." **17** And Elisha prays and says, "Yhwh, please open his eyes, and he sees"; and Yhwh opens the eyes of the young man, and he sees, and behold, the hill is full of horses and chariots of fire around Elisha. **18** And they come down to it, and Elisha prays to Yhwh and says, "Please strike this nation with blindness"; and He strikes them with blindness, according to the word of Elisha. **19** And Elisha says to them, "This [is] not the way, nor [is] this the city; come after me, and I lead you to the man whom you seek"; and he leads them to Samaria. **20** And it comes to pass, at their coming to Samaria, that Elisha says, "Yhwh, open the eyes of these, and they see"; and Yhwh opens their eyes, and they see, and behold, [they are] in the midst of Samaria! **21** And the king of Israel says to Elisha at his seeing them, "My father, do I strike, do I strike?" **22** And he says, "You do not strike; are you striking those whom you have taken captive with your sword and with your bow? set bread and water before them, and they eat, and drink, and go to their lord." **23** And he prepares great provision for them, and they eat and drink, and he sends them away, and they go to their lord: and troops of Aram have not added to come into the land of Israel anymore. **24** And it comes to pass afterward, that Ben-Hadad king of Aram gathers all his camp, and goes up, and lays siege to Samaria, **25** and there is a great famine in Samaria, and behold, they are laying siege to it, until the head of a donkey is at eighty pieces of silver, and a forth of the cab of dove's dung at five pieces of silver. **26** And it comes to pass, the king of Israel is passing by on the wall, and a woman has cried to him, saying, "Save, my lord, O king." **27** And he says, "Yhwh does not save you—from where do I save you? out of the threshing-floor or out of the wine-vat?" **28** And the king says to her, "What is [troubling] you?" And she says, "This woman said to me, Give your son, and we eat him today, and we eat my son tomorrow; **29** and we boil my son and eat him, and I say to her on the next day, Give your son, and we eat him; and she hides her son." **30** And it comes to pass, at the king's hearing the words of the woman, that he tears his garments, and he is passing by on the wall, and the people see, and behold, the sackcloth [is] within on his flesh. **31** And he says, "Thus God does to me and thus He adds, if the head of Elisha son of Shaphat remains on him this day." **32** And Elisha is sitting in his house, and the elderly are sitting with him, and [the king] sends a man from before him; before the messenger comes to him, even he himself said to the elderly, "Have you seen that this son of the murderer has sent [him] to turn aside my head? see, at the coming in of the messenger, shut the door, and you have held him fast at the door, is not the sound of the feet of his lord behind him?" **33** He is yet speaking with them, and behold, the messenger is coming down to him, and he says, "Behold, this [is] the calamity from Yhwh; why do I wait for Yhwh anymore?"

CHAPTER 7

1 And Elisha says, "Hear a word of Yhwh! Thus said Yhwh: About this time tomorrow, a measure of fine flour [is] at a shekel, and two measures of barley at a shekel, in the Gate of Samaria." **2** And the captain whom the king has, by whose hand he has been supported, answers the man of God and says, "Behold, Yhwh is making windows in the heavens—will this thing be?" And he says, "Behold, you are seeing it with your eyes, and you do not eat thereof." **3** And four men have been leprous at the opening of the gate, and they say to one another, "Why are we sitting here until we have died? **4** If we have said, We go into the city, then the famine [is] in the city and we have died there; and if we have sat here, then we have died; and now, come and we go down to the camp of Aram; if they keep us alive, we live, and if they put us to death—we have died." **5** And they rise in the twilight, to go to the camp of Aram, and they come to the extremity of the camp of Aram, and behold, there is not a man there, **6** seeing Yhwh has caused the camp of Aram to hear a noise of chariot and a noise of horse—a noise of great force, and they say to one another, "Behold, the king of Israel has hired against us the kings of the Hittites, and the kings of Egypt, to come against us." **7** And they rise and flee in the twilight, and forsake their tents, and their horses, and their donkeys—the camp as it [is]—and flee for their life. **8** And these lepers come to the extremity of the camp, and come into one tent, and eat, and drink, and lift up silver, and gold, and garments, and garments from there, and go and hide; and they turn back and go into another tent, and lift up from there, and go and hide. **9** And they say to one another, "We are not doing right this day; it [is] a day of tidings, and we are keeping silent; and we have waited until the morning light, then punishment has found us; and now, come and we go in and declare [it] to the house of the king." **10** And they come in, and call to the gatekeeper of the city, and declare for themselves, saying, "We have come to the camp of Aram, and behold, there is no man or sound of man there, but the bound horse, and the bound donkey, and tents as they [are]." **11** and he calls the gatekeepers, and they declare [it] to the house of the king within. **12** And the king rises by night and says to his servants, "Now let me declare to you that which the Arameans have done to us; they have known that we are famished, and they go out from the camp to be hidden in the field, saying, When they come out from the city, then we catch them alive, and we enter into the city." **13** And one of his servants answers and says, "Then please let them take five of the horses that are left, that have been left in it—behold, they [are] as all the multitude of Israel who have been left in it; behold, they are as all the multitude of Israel who have been consumed—and we send and see." **14** And they take two chariot-horses, and the king sends [them] after the camp of Aram, saying, "Go, and see." **15** And they go after them to the Jordan, and behold, all the way is full of garments and vessels that the Arameans have cast away in their haste, and the messengers return and declare [it] to the king. **16** And the people go out and spoil the camp of Aram, and there is a measure of fine flour at a shekel, and two measures of barley at a shekel, according to the word of Yhwh. **17** And the king has appointed the captain, by whose hand he is supported, over the gate, and the people tread him down in the gate, and he dies, as the man of God spoke, which he spoke in the coming down of the king to him, **18** indeed, it comes to pass, according to the speaking of the man of God to the king, saying, "Two measures of barley at a shekel, and a measure of fine flour at a shekel are, at this time tomorrow, in the Gate of Samaria"; **19** and the captain answers the man of God and says, "And behold, Yhwh is making windows in the heavens—will this thing be?" And he says, "Behold, you are

seeing it with your eyes, and you do not eat thereof"; **20** and it comes to him so, and the people tread him down in the gate, and he dies.

CHAPTER 8

1 And Elisha spoke to the woman whose son he had revived, saying, "Rise and go, you and your household, and sojourn where you sojourn, for Yhwh has called for a famine, and also, it is coming to the land [for] seven years." **2** And the woman rises, and does according to the word of the man of God, and goes, she and her household, and sojourns in the land of the Philistines [for] seven years. **3** And it comes to pass, at the end of seven years, that the woman turns back from the land of the Philistines, and goes out to cry to the king for her house and for her field. **4** And the king is speaking to Gehazi, servant of the man of God, saying, "Please recount to me the whole of the great things that Elisha has done." **5** And it comes to pass, he is recounting to the king how he had revived the dead, and behold, the woman whose son he had revived is crying to the king for her house and for her field, and Gehazi says, "My lord, O king, this [is] the woman, and this [is] her son, whom Elisha revived." **6** And the king inquires of the woman, and she recounts to him, and the king appoints a certain eunuch to her, saying, "Give back all that she has, and all the increase of the field from the day of her leaving the land even until now." **7** And Elisha comes to Damascus, and Ben-Hadad king of Aram is sick, and it is declared to him, saying, "The man of God has come here." **8** And the king says to Hazael, "Take a present in your hand, and go to meet the man of God, and you have sought Yhwh by him, saying, Do I revive from this sickness?" **9** And Hazael goes to meet him, and takes a present in his hand, even of every good thing of Damascus, a burden of forty camels, and he comes in and stands before him, and says, "Your son Ben-Hadad, king of Aram, has sent me to you, saying, Do I revive from this sickness?" **10** And Elisha says to him, "Go, say, You certainly do not revive, seeing [that] Yhwh has showed me that he surely dies." **11** And he sets his face, indeed, he sets [it] until he is ashamed, and the man of God weeps. **12** And Hazael says, "Why is my lord weeping?" And he says, "Because I have known the evil that you do to the sons of Israel—you send their fortifications into fire, and you slay their young men with sword, and you dash their sucklings to pieces, and you rip up their pregnant women." **13** And Hazael says, "But what [is] your servant—the dog, that he does this great thing?" And Elisha says, "Yhwh has showed me you—king of Aram." **14** And he goes from Elisha, and comes to his lord, and he says to him, "What did Elisha say to you?" And he says, "He said to me, You certainly recover." **15** And it comes to pass on the next day, that he takes the coarse cloth, and dips [it] in water, and spreads [it] on his face, and he dies, and Hazael reigns in his stead. **16** And in the fifth year of Joram son of Ahab, king of Israel—and Jehoshaphat [is] king of Judah—Jehoram son of Jehoshaphat, king of Judah, has reigned; **17** he was a son of thirty-two years in his reigning, and he has reigned eight years in Jerusalem. **18** And he walks in the way of the kings of Israel, as the house of Ahab did, for a daughter of Ahab was to him for a wife, and he does evil in the eyes of Yhwh, **19** and Yhwh was not willing to destroy Judah, for the sake of His servant David, as He said to him, to give a lamp to him—to his sons [for] all the days. **20** In his days Edom has revolted from under the hand of Judah, and they cause a king to reign over them, **21** and Joram passes over to Zair, and all the chariots with him, and he himself has risen by night, and strikes Edom that is coming around to him, and the heads of the chariots, and the people flee to their tents; **22** and Edom revolts from under the hand of Judah until this day; then Libnah revolts at that time. **23** And the rest of the matters of Joram and all that he did, are they not written on the scroll of the Chronicles of the Kings of Judah? **24** And Joram lies with his fathers, and is buried with his fathers in the City of David, and his son Ahaziah reigns in his stead. **25** In the twelfth year of Joram son of Ahab, king of Israel, Ahaziah son of Jehoram, king of Judah, has reigned; **26** Ahaziah [is] a son of twenty-two years in his reigning, and he has reigned one year in Jerusalem, and the name of his mother [is] Athaliah daughter of Omri, king of Israel, **27** and he walks in the way of the house of Ahab, and does evil in the eyes of Yhwh, like the house of Ahab, for he [is] son-in-law of the house of Ahab. **28** And he goes with Joram son of Ahab to battle with Hazael king of Aram in Ramoth-Gilead, and the Arameans strike Joram, **29** and Joram the king turns back to be healed in Jezreel of the wounds with which the Arameans strike him in Ramah, in his fighting with Hazael king of Aram, and Ahaziah son of Jehoram, king of Judah, has gone down to see Joram son of Ahab in Jezreel, for he is sick.

CHAPTER 9

¹ And Elisha the prophet has called to one of the sons of the prophets and says to him, "Gird up your loins, and take this vial of oil in your hand, and go to Ramoth-Gilead, ² and you have gone in there, and see Jehu son of Jehoshaphat, son of Nimshi, there, and you have gone in, and caused him to rise out of the midst of his brothers, and brought him into the inner part of an inner-chamber, ³ and taken the vial of oil, and poured [it] on his head, and said, Thus said Yhwh: I have anointed you for king to Israel; and you have opened the door, and fled, and do not wait." ⁴ And the young man goes—the young man the prophet—to Ramoth-Gilead, ⁵ and comes in, and behold, chiefs of the force are sitting, and he says, "I have a word for you, O chief!" And Jehu says, "To which of all of us?" And he says, "To you, O chief." ⁶ And he rises and comes into the house, and he pours the oil on his head, and says to him, "Thus said Yhwh, God of Israel: I have anointed you for king to the people of Yhwh, to Israel, ⁷ and you have struck the house of your lord Ahab, and I have required the blood of My servants the prophets, and the blood of all the servants of Yhwh, from the hand of Jezebel; ⁸ and all the house of Ahab has perished, and I have cut off from Ahab those sitting on the wall, and restrained, and left, in Israel, ⁹ and I have given up the house of Ahab like the house of Jeroboam son of Nebat, and as the house of Baasha son of Ahijah, ¹⁰ and dogs eat Jezebel in the portion of Jezreel, and there is none burying"; and he opens the door and flees. ¹¹ And Jehu has gone out to the servants of his lord, and [one] says to him, "Is there peace? why did this madman come to you?" And he says to them, "You have known the man and his talk." ¹² And they say, "False! Declare to us now"; and he says, "He spoke thus and thus to me, saying, Thus said Yhwh: I have anointed you for king to Israel." ¹³ And they hurry—each [one]—and take his garment, and put [it] under him at the top of the stairs, and blow with a horn, and say, "Jehu has reigned!" ¹⁴ And Jehu son of Jehoshaphat, son of Nimshi, conspires against Joram. And Joram was keeping in Ramoth-Gilead, he and all Israel, from the presence of Hazael king of Aram, ¹⁵ and King Joram turns back to be healed in Jezreel, of the wounds with which the Arameans strike him in his fighting with Hazael king of Aram. And Jehu says, "If it is your mind, do not let an escaped one go out from the city, to go to declare [it] in Jezreel." ¹⁶ And Jehu rides, and goes to Jezreel, for Joram is lying there, and Ahaziah king of Judah has gone down to see Joram. ¹⁷ And the watchman is standing on the tower in Jezreel, and sees the company of Jehu in his coming, and says, "I see a company"; and Joram says, "Take a rider and send [him] to meet them, and let him say, Is there peace?" ¹⁸ and the rider on the horse goes to meet him and says, "Thus said the king: Is there peace?" And Jehu says, "And what is peace to you? turn around behind me." And the watchman declares, saying, "The messenger came to them, and he has not returned." ¹⁹ And he sends a second rider on a horse, and he comes to them and says, "Thus said the king: Is there peace?" And Jehu says, "And what is peace to you? turn around behind me." ²⁰ And the watchman declares, saying, "He came to them, and he has not returned, and the driving [is] like the driving of Jehu son of Nimshi, for he drives with madness." ²¹ And Jehoram says, "Harness"; and his chariot is harnessed, and Jehoram king of Israel goes out, and Ahaziah king of Judah, each in his chariot, and they go out to meet Jehu, and find him in the portion of Naboth the Jezreelite. ²² And it comes to pass, at Jehoram's seeing Jehu, that he says, "Is there peace, Jehu?" And he says, "What [is] the peace, while the whoredoms of your mother Jezebel, and her witchcrafts, are many?" ²³ And Jehoram turns his hands and flees, and says to Ahaziah, "Deceit, O Ahaziah!" ²⁴ And Jehu has filled his hand with a bow, and strikes Jehoram between his arms, and the arrow goes out from his heart, and he bows down in his chariot. ²⁵ And [Jehu] says to his captain Bidkar, "Lift up, cast him into the portion of the field of Naboth the Jezreelite—for remember, you and I were riding together after his father Ahab, and Yhwh lifted this burden on him: ²⁶ Have I not seen the blood of Naboth and the blood of his sons last night—a declaration of Yhwh—indeed, I have repaid to you in this portion—a declaration of Yhwh—and now, lift up, cast him

into the portion, according to the word of Yhwh." ²⁷ And Ahaziah king of Judah has seen, and flees the way of the garden-house, and Jehu pursues after him, and says, "Strike him—also him—in the chariot," in the going up to Gur, that [is] Ibleam, and he flees to Megiddo, and dies there, ²⁸ and his servants carry him to Jerusalem in a chariot, and bury him in his burying-place with his fathers in the City of David. ²⁹ And in the eleventh year of Joram son of Ahab, Ahaziah reigned over Judah. ³⁰ And Jehu comes to Jezreel, and Jezebel has heard, and puts her eyes in paint and beautifies her head, and looks out through the window. ³¹ And Jehu has come into the gate, and she says, "Was there peace [for] Zimri—slayer of his lord?" ³² And he lifts up his face to the window and says, "Who [is] with me? Who?" And two [or] three eunuchs look out to him; ³³ and he says, "Let her go"; and they let her go, and [some] of her blood is sprinkled on the wall, and on the horses, and he treads her down. ³⁴ And he comes in, and eats, and drinks, and says, "Now look after this cursed one and bury her, for she [is] a king's daughter." ³⁵ And they go to bury her, and have not found [anything] of her except the skull, and the feet, and the palms of the hands. ³⁶ And they turn back, and declare [it] to him, and he says, "It [is] the word of Yhwh that He spoke by the hand of this servant, Elijah the Tishbite, saying, In the portion of Jezreel the dogs eat the flesh of Jezebel, ³⁷ and the carcass of Jezebel has been as dung on the face of the field in the portion of Jezreel, that they do not say, This [is] Jezebel."

CHAPTER 10

¹ And Ahab has seventy sons in Samaria, and Jehu writes letters, and sends [them] to Samaria, to the heads of Jezreel, the elderly, and to those supporting Ahab, saying, ² "And now, at the coming in of this letter to you, and sons of your lord [are] with you, and the chariots and the horses, and a fortified city, and the armor, [are] with you, ³ that you have seen the best and the most upright of the sons of your lord, and have set [him] on the throne of his father, and fight for the house of your lord." ⁴ And they fear very greatly, and say, "Behold, the two kings have not stood before him, and how do we stand—we?" ⁵ And he who [is] over the house, and he who [is] over the city, and the elderly, and those supporting, send to Jehu, saying, "We [are] your servants, and all that you say to us we do; we do not make anyone king—do that which [is] good in your eyes." ⁶ And he writes a letter to them a second time, saying, "If you [are] for me, and are listening to my voice, take the heads of the men—the sons of your lord; and come to me about this time tomorrow, to Jezreel"; and the sons of the king [are] seventy men, with the great ones of the city—those bringing them up. ⁷ And it comes to pass, at the coming in of the letter to them, that they take the sons of the king, and slaughter seventy men, and put their heads in baskets, and send [them] to him at Jezreel, ⁸ and the messenger comes in, and declares [it] to him, saying, "They have brought in the heads of the sons of the king," and he says, "Make them two heaps at the opening of the gate until the morning." ⁹ And it comes to pass in the morning, that he goes out, and stands, and says to all the people, "You are righteous; behold, I have conspired against my lord, and slay him—and who struck all these? ¹⁰ Now you know that nothing falls of the word of Yhwh to the earth that Yhwh spoke against the house of Ahab, and Yhwh has done that which He spoke by the hand of His servant Elijah." ¹¹ And Jehu strikes all those left to the house of Ahab in Jezreel, and all his great men, and his acquaintances, and his priests, until he has not left a remnant to him. ¹² And he rises, and comes in and goes to Samaria; he [is] at the shepherds' shearing-house in the way, ¹³ and Jehu has found the brothers of Ahaziah king of Judah and says, "Who [are] you?" And they say, "We [are] brothers of Ahaziah, and we go down to greet the sons of the king and the sons of the mistress." ¹⁴ And he says, "Catch them alive"; and they catch them alive, and slaughter them at the pit of the shearing-house, forty-two men, and he has not left [even one] man of them. ¹⁵ And he goes there, and finds Jehonadab son of Rechab to meet him, and blesses him, and says to him, "Is your heart right, as my heart [is] with your heart?" And Jehonadab says, "It is." "Then it is; give your hand"; and he gives his hand, and he causes him to come up into the chariot to him, ¹⁶ and says, "Come with me, and look on my zeal for Yhwh"; and they cause him to ride in his chariot. ¹⁷ And he comes to Samaria, and strikes all those left to Ahab in Samaria, until his destroying him, according to the word of Yhwh that He spoke to Elisha. ¹⁸

And Jehu gathers the whole of the people and says to them, "Ahab served Ba'al a little—Jehu serves him much: ¹⁹ and now, all the prophets of Ba'al, all his servants, and all his priests, call to me; do not let a man be lacking, for I have a great sacrifice for Ba'al; everyone who is lacking—he does not live"; and Jehu has done [it] in subtlety, in order to destroy the servants of Ba'al. ²⁰ And Jehu says, "Sanctify a restraint for Ba'al"; and they proclaim [it]. ²¹ And Jehu sends into all Israel, and all the servants of Ba'al come in, and there has not been left a man who has not come in; and they come into the house of Ba'al, and the house of Ba'al is full—mouth to mouth. ²² And he says to him who [is] over the wardrobe, "Bring out clothing for all those serving Ba'al"; and he brings out the clothing to them. ²³ And Jehu goes in—and Jehonadab son of Rechab—to the house of Ba'al, and says to the servants of Ba'al, "Search and see, lest there be [any] from the servants of Yhwh here with you—but [only] the servants of Ba'al by themselves." ²⁴ And they come in to make sacrifices and burnt-offerings, and Jehu has set eighty men for himself in an out-place, and says, "The man who lets [any] of the men whom I am bringing into your hand escape—his soul for his soul." ²⁵ And it comes to pass, at his finishing to make the burnt-offering, that Jehu says to the runners and to the captains, "Go in, strike them, let none come out"; and they strike them by the mouth of the sword, and the runners and the captains cast [them] out; and they go to the city, to the house of Ba'al, ²⁶ and bring out the standing-pillars of the house of Ba'al, and burn them, ²⁷ and break down the standing-pillar of Ba'al, and break down the house of Ba'al, and appoint it for a latrine to this day. ²⁸ And Jehu destroys Ba'al out of Israel, ²⁹ only [not]—the sins of Jeroboam son of Nebat, that he caused Israel to sin, Jehu has not turned aside from after them—the calves of gold that [are] at Beth-El and in Dan. ³⁰ And Yhwh says to Jehu, "Because that you have done well, to do that which [is] right in My eyes—according to all that [is] in My heart you have done to the house of Ahab—the sons of the fourth [generation] sit on the throne of Israel for you." ³¹ And Jehu has not taken heed to walk in the Law of Yhwh, God of Israel, with all his heart; he has not turned aside from the sins of Jeroboam that he caused Israel to sin. ³² In those days Yhwh has begun to cut off [some] in Israel, and Hazael strikes them in all the border of Israel, ³³ from the Jordan, at the sun-rising: the whole land of Gilead, of the Gadite, and the Reubenite, and the Manassite (from Aroer, that [is] by the Brook of Arnon), even Gilead and Bashan. ³⁴ And the rest of the matters of Jehu, and all that he did, and all his might, are they not written on the scroll of the Chronicles of the Kings of Israel? ³⁵ And Jehu lies with his fathers, and they bury him in Samaria, and his son Jehoahaz reigns in his stead. ³⁶ And the days that Jehu has reigned over Israel in Samaria [are] twenty-eight years.

CHAPTER 11

¹ And Athaliah [is] mother of Ahaziah, and she has seen that her son [is] dead, and she rises, and destroys all the seed of the kingdom; ² and Jehosheba daughter of king Joram, sister of Ahaziah, takes Joash son of Ahaziah, and steals him out of the midst of the sons of the king who are put to death, him and his nurse, in the inner part of the bed-chambers, and they hide him from the presence of Athaliah, and he has not been put to death, ³ and he is with her, in the house of Yhwh, hiding himself, six years, and Athaliah is reigning over the land. ⁴ And in the seventh year Jehoiada has sent and takes the heads of the hundreds, of the executioners and of the runners, and brings them to him, into the house of Yhwh, and makes a covenant with them, and causes them to swear in the house of Yhwh, and shows them the son of the king, ⁵ and commands them, saying, "This [is] the thing that you do; the third of you [are] going in on the Sabbath, and keepers of the charge of the house of the king, ⁶ and the third [is] at the Gate of Sur, and the third at the gate behind the runners, and you have kept the charge of the house pulled down; ⁷ and two parts of you, all going out on the Sabbath—they have kept the charge of the house of Yhwh about the king, ⁸ and you have surrounded the king all around, each with his weapons in his hand, and he who is coming to the ranges is put to death; and be with the king in his going out and in his coming in." ⁹ And the heads of the hundreds do according to all that Jehoiada the priest commanded, and take—each [one]—his men going in on the Sabbath, with those going out on the Sabbath, and come to Jehoiada the priest, ¹⁰ and the priest gives to the heads of

the hundreds the spears and the shields that King David had, that [are] in the house of Yhwh. ¹¹ And the runners stand, each with his weapons in his hand, from the right shoulder of the house to the left shoulder of the house, by the altar and by the house, by the king all around; ¹² and he brings out the son of the king, and puts the crown on him, and the Testimony, and they make him king, and anoint him, and strike the hand, and say, "Let the king live." ¹³ And Athaliah hears the voice of the runners [and] of the people, and she comes to the people [in] the house of Yhwh, ¹⁴ and looks, and behold, the king is standing by the pillar, according to the ordinance, and the heads and the trumpets [are] by the king, and all the people of the land are rejoicing and blowing with trumpets, and Athaliah tears her garments, and calls, "Conspiracy! Conspiracy!" ¹⁵ And Jehoiada the priest commands the heads of the hundreds, inspectors of the force, and says to them, "Bring her out to the outside of the ranges, and him who is going after her, put to death by the sword": for the priest had said, "Do not let her be put to death in the house of Yhwh." ¹⁶ And they make sides for her, and she enters the way of the entering in of the horses to the house of the king, and is put to death there. ¹⁷ And Jehoiada makes the covenant between Yhwh and the king and the people, to be for a people to Yhwh, and between the king and the people. ¹⁸ And all the people of the land go to the house of Ba'al, and break it down; they have thoroughly broken its altars and its images, and they have slain Mattan priest of Ba'al before the altars; and the priest sets inspectors over the house of Yhwh, ¹⁹ and takes the heads of the hundreds, and the executioners, and the runners, and all the people of the land, and they bring down the king from the house of Yhwh, and come by the way of the gate of the runners, to the house of the king, and he sits on the throne of the kings. ²⁰ And all the people of the land rejoice, and the city [is] quiet, and they have put Athaliah to death by the sword in the house of the king; ²¹ Jehoash is a son of seven years in his reigning.

CHAPTER 12

¹ In the seventh year of Jehu, Jehoash has reigned, and he has reigned forty years in Jerusalem, and the name of his mother [is] Zibiah of Beer-Sheba, ² and Jehoash does that which is right in the eyes of Yhwh all his days in which Jehoiada the priest directed him, ³ only, the high places have not been removed—the people are still sacrificing and making incense in high places. ⁴ And Jehoash says to the priests, "All the money of the sanctified things that is brought into the house of Yhwh, the money of him who is passing over, the money of each of the souls—his valuation, all the money that goes up on the heart of a man to bring into the house of Yhwh, ⁵ the priests take to themselves, each from his acquaintance, and they strengthen the breach of the house in all [places] there where a breach is found." ⁶ And it comes to pass, in the twenty-third year of King Jehoash, the priests have not strengthened the breach of the house, ⁷ and King Jehoash calls to Jehoiada the priest, and to the priests, and says to them, "Why are you not strengthening the breach of the house? and now, receive no money from your acquaintances, but give it for the breach of the house." ⁸ And the priests do not consent to receive money from the people, nor to strengthen the breach of the house, ⁹ and Jehoiada the priest takes a chest, and pierces a hole in its lid, and puts it near the altar, on the right side, as one comes into the house of Yhwh, and the priests keeping the threshold have put all the money there that is brought into the house of Yhwh. ¹⁰ And it comes to pass, at their seeing that the money [is] abundant in the chest, that there goes up a scribe of the king, and of the high priest, and they bind [it] up, and count the money that is found [in] the house of Yhwh, ¹¹ and have given the weighed money into the hands of those doing the work, those inspecting the house of Yhwh, and they bring it out to those working in the wood, and to builders who are working in the house of Yhwh, ¹² and to those [repairing] the wall, and to hewers of stone, and to buy wood and hewn stones to strengthen the breach of the house of Yhwh, and for all that goes out on the house, to strengthen it. ¹³ Only, there is not made for the house of Yhwh basins of silver, snuffers, bowls, trumpets, any vessel of gold, and vessel of silver, out of the money that is brought into the house of Yhwh; ¹⁴ for they give it to those doing the work, and they have strengthened the house of Yhwh with it, ¹⁵ and they do not reckon with the men into whose hand they give the money to give to those doing the work, for they are dealing in faithfulness. ¹⁶ The money of

a trespass-offering and the money of sin-offerings is not brought into the house of Yhwh—it is for the priests. **17** Then Hazael king of Aram goes up and fights against Gath, and captures it, and Hazael sets his face to go up against Jerusalem; **18** and Jehoash king of Judah takes all the sanctified things that Jehoshaphat, and Jehoram, and Ahaziah, his fathers, kings of Judah, had sanctified, and his own sanctified things, and all the gold that is found in the treasures of the house of Yhwh and of the house of the king, and sends [them] to Hazael king of Aram, and he goes up from off Jerusalem. **19** And the rest of the matters of Joash and all that he did, are they not written on the scroll of the Chronicles of the Kings of Judah? **20** And his servants rise, and make a conspiracy, and strike Joash in the house of Millo, that is going down to Silla. **21** Indeed, Jozachar son of Shimeath, and Jehozabad son of Shemer, his servants, have struck him, and he dies, and they bury him with his fathers in the City of David, and his son Amaziah reigns in his stead.

CHAPTER 13

1 In the twenty-third year of Joash son of Ahaziah, king of Judah, Jehoahaz son of Jehu has reigned over Israel in Samaria, seventeen years, **2** and he does evil in the eyes of Yhwh, and goes after the sins of Jeroboam son of Nebat, that he caused Israel to sin—he did not turn aside from it, **3** and the anger of Yhwh burns against Israel, and He gives them into the hand of Hazael king of Aram, and into the hand of Ben-Hadad son of Hazael, all the days. **4** And Jehoahaz appeases the face of Yhwh, and Yhwh listens to him, for He has seen the oppression of Israel, for the king of Aram has oppressed them— **5** and Yhwh gives a savior to Israel, and they go out from under the hand of Aram, and the sons of Israel dwell in their tents as before; **6** only, they have not turned aside from the sins of the house of Jeroboam that he caused Israel to sin, therein they walked, and also, the Asherah has remained in Samaria— **7** for he did not leave to Jehoahaz of the people except fifty horsemen, and ten chariots, and ten thousand footmen, for the king of Aram has destroyed them, and makes them as dust for threshing. **8** And the rest of the matters of Jehoahaz, and all that he did, and his might, are they not written on the scroll of the Chronicles of the Kings of Israel? **9** And Jehoahaz lies with his fathers, and they bury him in Samaria, and his son Joash reigns in his stead. **10** In the thirty-seventh year of Joash king of Judah, Jehoash son of Jehoahaz has reigned over Israel in Samaria, sixteen years, **11** and he does evil in the eyes of Yhwh, he has not turned aside from all the sins of Jeroboam son of Nebat that he caused Israel to sin, therein he walked. **12** And the rest of the matters of Joash, and all that he did, and his might with which he fought with Amaziah king of Judah, are they not written on the scroll of the Chronicles of the Kings of Israel? **13** And Joash lies with his fathers, and Jeroboam has sat on his throne, and Joash is buried in Samaria with the kings of Israel. **14** And Elisha has been sick with his sickness in which he dies, and Joash king of Israel comes down to him and weeps on his face, and says, "My father, my father, the chariot of Israel, and its horsemen." **15** And Elisha says to him, "Take bow and arrows": and he takes bow and arrows for himself. **16** And he says to the king of Israel, "Place your hand on the bow"; and he places his hand, and Elisha puts his hands on the hands of the king, **17** and says, "Open the window eastward"; and he opens, and Elisha says, "Shoot," and he shoots; and he says, "An arrow of salvation from Yhwh, and an arrow of salvation against Aram, and you have struck Aram, in Aphek, until consuming." **18** And he says, "Take the arrows," and he takes; and he says to the king of Israel, "Strike to the earth"; and he strikes three times, and stays. **19** And the man of God is angry against him and says, "By striking five or six times then you had struck Aram until consuming; but now you [only] strike Aram three times." **20** And Elisha dies, and they bury him, and troops of Moab come into the land at the coming in of the year, **21** and it comes to pass, they are burying a man, and behold, they have seen the troop, and cast the man into the grave of Elisha, and the man goes and comes against the bones of Elisha, and lives, and rises on his feet. **22** And Hazael king of Aram has oppressed Israel all the days of Jehoahaz, **23** and Yhwh favors them, and pities them, and turns to them for the sake of His covenant with Abraham, Isaac, and Jacob, and has not been willing to destroy them, nor to cast them from His presence as yet. **24** And Hazael king of Aram dies, and his son Ben-Hadad reigns in

his stead, **25** and Jehoash son of Jehoahaz turns and takes the cities out of the hand of Ben-Hadad son of Hazael that he had taken out of the hand of his father Jehoahaz in war; Joash has struck him three times, and he brings back the cities of Israel.

CHAPTER 14

1 In the second year of Joash son of Jehoahaz, king of Israel, Amaziah son of Joash, king of Judah, has reigned; **2** he was a son of twenty-five years in his reigning, and he has reigned twenty-nine years in Jerusalem, and the name of his mother [is] Jehoaddan of Jerusalem, **3** and he does that which [is] right in the eyes of Yhwh, only not like his father David; he has done according to all that his father Joash did, **4** only, the high places have not been removed—the people are still sacrificing and making incense in high places. **5** And it comes to pass, when the kingdom has been strong in his hand, that he strikes his servants, those striking his father the king, **6** and the sons of those striking [him] he has not put to death, as it is written in the Scroll of the Law of Moses that Yhwh commanded, saying, "Fathers are not put to death for sons, and sons are not put to death for fathers, but each is put to death for his own sin." **7** He has struck ten thousand of Edom in the Valley of Salt, and seized Selah in war, and [one] calls its name Joktheel to this day, **8** then Amaziah has sent messengers to Jehoash son of Jehoahaz, son of Jehu, king of Israel, saying, "Come, we look one another in the face." **9** And Jehoash king of Israel sends to Amaziah king of Judah, saying, "The thorn that [is] in Lebanon has sent to the cedar that [is] in Lebanon, saying, Give your daughter to my son for a wife; and a beast of the field that [is] in Lebanon passes by, and treads down the thorn. **10** You have certainly struck Edom, and your heart has lifted you up; be honored, and abide in your house; and why do you stir yourself up in evil, that you have fallen, you and Judah with you?" **11** And Amaziah has not listened, and Jehoash king of Israel goes up, and they look one another in the face, he and Amaziah king of Judah, in Beth-Shemesh, that [is] Judah's, **12** and Judah is struck before Israel, and they each flee to his tent. **13** And Jehoash king of Israel caught Amaziah king of Judah, son of Jehoash, son of Ahaziah, in Beth-Shemesh, and they come to Jerusalem, and he bursts through the wall of Jerusalem, at the Gate of Ephraim to the Corner Gate, four hundred cubits, **14** and has taken all the gold and the silver, and all the vessels that are found in the house of Yhwh, and in the treasures of the house of the king, and the sons of the pledges, and turns back to Samaria. **15** And the rest of the matters of Jehoash that he did, and his might, and how he fought with Amaziah king of Judah, are they not written on the scroll of the Chronicles of the Kings of Israel? **16** And Jehoash lies with his fathers, and is buried in Samaria with the kings of Israel, and his son Jeroboam reigns in his stead. **17** And Amaziah son of Joash, king of Judah, lives after the death of Jehoash son of Jehoahaz, king of Israel, fifteen years, **18** and the rest of the matters of Amaziah, are they not written on the scroll of the Chronicles of the Kings of Judah? **19** And they make a conspiracy against him in Jerusalem, and he flees to Lachish, and they send after him to Lachish, and put him to death there, **20** and lift him up on the horses, and he is buried in Jerusalem with his fathers in the City of David. **21** And all the people of Judah take Azariah, and he [is] a son of sixteen years, and cause him to reign instead of his father Amaziah; **22** he has built Elath, and brings it back to Judah, after the lying of the king with his fathers. **23** In the fifteenth year of Amaziah son of Joash, king of Judah, Jeroboam son of Joash, king of Israel, has reigned in Samaria, forty-one years, **24** and he does evil in the eyes of Yhwh; he has not turned aside from all the sins of Jeroboam son of Nebat that he caused Israel to sin. **25** He has brought back the border of Israel, from the entering in of Hamath to the sea of the desert, according to the word of Yhwh, God of Israel, that He spoke by the hand of His servant Jonah son of Amittai the prophet, who [is] of Gath-Hepher, **26** for Yhwh has seen the very bitter affliction of Israel, and there is none restrained, and there is none left, and there is no helper for Israel; **27** and Yhwh has not spoken to blot out the name of Israel from under the heavens, and saves them by the hand of Jeroboam son of Joash. **28** And the rest of the matters of Jeroboam, and all that he did, and his might with which he fought, and with which he brought back Damascus, and Hamath of Judah, into Israel, are they not written on the scroll of the Chronicles of the Kings of Israel? **29** And Jeroboam lies with his fathers, with the kings of Israel, and his son Zechariah reigns in his stead.

CHAPTER 15

¹ In the twenty-seventh year of Jeroboam king of Israel, Azariah son of Amaziah, king of Judah, has reigned; ² he was a son of sixteen years in his reigning, and he has reigned fifty-two years in Jerusalem, and the name of his mother [is] Jecholiah of Jerusalem, ³ and he does that which [is] right in the eyes of Yhwh, according to all that his father Amaziah did, ⁴ only, the high places have not been removed—the people are still sacrificing and making incense in high places. ⁵ And Yhwh strikes the king, and he is a leper to the day of his death, and he dwells in a separate house, and Jotham son of the king [is] over the house, judging the people of the land. ⁶ And the rest of the matters of Azariah and all that he did, are they not written on the scroll of the Chronicles of the Kings of Judah? ⁷ And Azariah lies with his fathers, and they bury him with his fathers in the city of David, and his son Jotham reigns in his stead. ⁸ In the thirty-eighth year of Azariah king of Judah, Zechariah son of Jeroboam has reigned over Israel in Samaria, six months, ⁹ and he does evil in the eyes of Yhwh as his fathers did; he has not turned aside from the sins of Jeroboam son of Nebat that he caused Israel to sin. ¹⁰ And Shallum son of Jabesh conspires against him, and strikes him before the people, and puts him to death, and reigns in his stead. ¹¹ And the rest of the matters of Zechariah, behold, they are written on the scroll of the Chronicles of the Kings of Israel. ¹² It [is] the word of Yhwh that He spoke to Jehu, saying, "Sons of the fourth [generation] sit on the throne of Israel for you"; and it is so. ¹³ Shallum son of Jabesh has reigned in the thirty-ninth year of Uzziah king of Judah, and he reigns a month of days in Samaria; ¹⁴ and Menahem son of Gadi goes up from Tirzah and comes to Samaria, and strikes Shallum son of Jabesh in Samaria, and puts him to death, and reigns in his stead. ¹⁵ And the rest of the matters of Shallum and his conspiracy that he made, behold, they are written on the scroll of the Chronicles of the Kings of Israel. ¹⁶ Then Menahem strikes Tiphsah, and all who [are] in it, and its borders from Tirzah, for it did not open [to him], and he strikes [it], [and] he has ripped up all its pregnant women. ¹⁷ In the thirty-ninth year of Azariah king of Judah, Menahem son of Gadi has reigned over Israel in Samaria, ten years. ¹⁸ And he does evil in the eyes of Yhwh; he has not turned aside from the sins of Jeroboam son of Nebat that he caused Israel to sin, all his days. ¹⁹ Pul king of Asshur has come against the land, and Menahem gives one thousand talents of silver to Pul, for his hand being with him to strengthen the kingdom in his hand. ²⁰ And Menahem brings out the silver [from] Israel, [from] all the mighty men of wealth, to give to the king of Asshur, fifty shekels of silver for each one, and the king of Asshur turns back and has not stayed there in the land. ²¹ And the rest of the matters of Menahem and all that he did, are they not written on the scroll of the Chronicles of the Kings of Israel? ²² And Menahem lies with his fathers, and his son Pekahiah reigns in his stead. ²³ In the fiftieth year of Azariah king of Judah, Pekahiah son of Menahem has reigned over Israel in Samaria, two years, ²⁴ and he does evil in the eyes of Yhwh; he has not turned aside from the sins of Jeroboam son of Nebat that he caused Israel to sin. ²⁵ And Pekah son of Remaliah, his captain, conspires against him, and strikes him in Samaria, in the high place of the house of the king with Argob and Arieh; and fifty men of the sons of the Gileadites [were] with him, and he puts him to death, and reigns in his stead. ²⁶ And the rest of the matters of Pekahiah and all that he did, behold, they are written on the scroll of the Chronicles of the Kings of Israel. ²⁷ In the fifty-second year of Azariah king of Judah, Pekah son of Remaliah has reigned over Israel in Samaria, twenty years, ²⁸ and he does evil in the eyes of Yhwh, he has not turned aside from the sins of Jeroboam son of Nebat that he caused Israel to sin. ²⁹ In the days of Pekah king of Israel, Tiglath-Pileser king of Asshur has come, and takes Ijon, and Abel-Beth-Maachah, and Janoah, and Kedesh, and Hazor, and Gilead, and Galilee, all the land of Naphtali, and removes them to Asshur. ³⁰ And Hoshea son of Elah makes a conspiracy against Pekah son of Remaliah, and strikes him, and puts him to death, and reigns in his stead, in the twentieth year of Jotham son of Uzziah. ³¹ And the rest of the matters of Pekah and all that he did, behold, they are written on the scroll of the Chronicles of the Kings of Israel. ³² In the second year of Pekah son of Remaliah, king of Israel, Jotham son of Uzziah, king of Judah, has reigned. ³³ He was a son of twenty-five years in his reigning, and he has reigned sixteen years in Jerusalem, and the name of his mother [is] Jerusha daughter of Zadok, ³⁴ and he does that which [is] right in the eyes of Yhwh; he has done according to all that his father Uzziah did. ³⁵ Only, the high places have not been removed—the people are still sacrificing and making incense in high places; he has built the high gate of the house of Yhwh. ³⁶ And the rest of the matters of Jotham and all that he did, are they not written on the scroll of the Chronicles of the Kings of Judah? ³⁷ In those days Yhwh has begun to send Rezin king of Amram and Pekah son of Remaliah against Judah. ³⁸ And Jotham lies with his fathers, and is buried with his fathers in the city of his father David, and his son Ahaz reigns in his stead.

CHAPTER 16

¹ In the seventeenth year of Pekah son of Remaliah, Ahaz son of Jotham, king of Judah, has reigned. ² Ahaz [is] a son of twenty years in his reigning, and he has reigned sixteen years in Jerusalem, and he has not done that which [is] right in the eyes of his God Yhwh, like his father David, ³ and he walks in the way of the kings of Israel, and he has also caused his son to pass over into fire, according to the abominations of the nations that Yhwh dispossessed from the presence of the sons of Israel, ⁴ and he sacrifices and makes incense in high places, and on the heights, and under every green tree. ⁵ Then Rezin king of Aram, and Pekah son of Remaliah, king of Israel, go up to Jerusalem, to battle, and they lay siege to Ahaz, and they have not been able to fight. ⁶ At that time Rezin king of Aram has brought back Elath to Aram, and casts out the Jews from Elath, and the Arameans have come to Elath, and dwell there to this day. ⁷ And Ahaz sends messengers to Tiglath-Pileser king of Asshur, saying, "I [am] your servant and your son; come up and save me out of the hand of the king of Aram, and out of the hand of the king of Israel, who are rising up against me." ⁸ And Ahaz takes the silver and the gold that is found in the house of Yhwh, and in the treasures of the house of the king, and sends to the king of Asshur [as] a bribe. ⁹ And the king of Asshur listens to him, and the king of Asshur goes up to Damascus, and seizes it, and removes [the people of] it to Kir, and he has put Rezin to death. ¹⁰ And King Ahaz goes to meet Tiglath-Pileser king of Asshur [at] Damascus, and sees the altar that [is] in Damascus, and King Ahaz sends to Urijah the priest the likeness of the altar, and its pattern, according to all its work, ¹¹ and Urijah the priest builds the altar according to all that King Ahaz has sent from Damascus; so Urijah the priest did until the coming in of King Ahaz from Damascus. ¹² And the king comes in from Damascus, and the king sees the altar, and the king draws near on the altar, and offers on it, ¹³ and burns his burnt-offering and his present as incense, and pours out his drink-offering, and sprinkles the blood of the peace-offerings that he has, on the altar. ¹⁴ As for the altar of bronze that [is] before Yhwh—he brings [it] near from the front of the house, from between the altar and the house of Yhwh, and puts it on the side of the altar, northward. ¹⁵ And King Ahaz commands him—Urijah the priest—saying, "On the great altar burn as incense the burnt-offering of the morning, and the present of the evening, and the burnt-offering of the king, and his present, and the burnt-offering of all the people of the land, and their present, and their drink-offerings; and all the blood of the burnt-offering, and all the blood of the sacrifice, you sprinkle on it, and the altar of bronze is for me to inquire [by]." ¹⁶ And Urijah the priest does according to all that King Ahaz commanded. ¹⁷ And King Ahaz cuts off the borders of the bases, and turns aside the laver from off them, and he has taken down the sea from off the bronze oxen that [are] under it, and puts it on a pavement of stones. ¹⁸ And the covered place for the Sabbath that they built in the house, and the entrance of the king outside, he turned [from] the house of Yhwh, because of the king of Asshur. ¹⁹ And the rest of the matters of Ahaz that he did, are they not written on the scroll of the Chronicles of the Kings of Judah? ²⁰ And Ahaz lies with his fathers, and is buried with his fathers in the City of David, and his son Hezekiah reigns in his stead.

CHAPTER 17

¹ In the twelfth year of Ahaz king of Judah, Hoshea son of Elah has reigned over Israel in Samaria, nine years, ² and he

does evil in the eyes of Yhwh, only, not as the kings of Israel who were before him; **³** Shalmaneser king of Asshur came up against him, and Hoshea is a servant to him, and renders a present to him. **⁴** And the king of Asshur finds in Hoshea a conspiracy, in that he has sent messengers to So king of Egypt, and has not caused a present to go up to the king of Asshur, as year by year, and the king of Asshur restrains him, and binds him in a house of restraint. **⁵** And the king of Asshur goes up into all the land, and he goes up to Samaria, and lays siege against it [for] three years; **⁶** in the ninth year of Hoshea, the king of Asshur has captured Samaria, and removes Israel to Asshur, and causes them to dwell in Halah, and in Habor, [by] the river Gozan, and [in] the cities of the Medes. **⁷** And it comes to pass, because the sons of Israel have sinned against their God Yhwh—who brings them up out of the land of Egypt, from under the hand of Pharaoh king of Egypt—and fear other gods, **⁸** and walk in the statutes of the nations that Yhwh dispossessed from the presence of the sons of Israel, and of the kings of Israel that they made; **⁹** and the sons of Israel covertly do things that [are] not right against their God Yhwh, and build high places for themselves in all their cities, from a tower of the watchers to the fortified city, **¹⁰** and set up standing-pillars and Asherim for themselves on every high height, and under every green tree, **¹¹** and make incense there in all high places, like the nations that Yhwh removed from their presence, and do evil things to provoke Yhwh, **¹²** and serve the idols, of which Yhwh said to them, "You do not do this thing." **¹³** And Yhwh testifies against Israel, and against Judah, by the hand of every prophet, and every seer, saying, "Turn back from your evil ways, and keep My commands, My statutes, according to all the Law that I commanded your fathers, and that I sent to you by the hand of My servants the prophets"; **¹⁴** and they have not listened, and harden their neck, like the neck of their fathers, who did not remain steadfast in their God Yhwh, **¹⁵** and reject His statutes and His covenant that He made with their fathers, and His testimonies that He testified against them, and go after the vain thing, and become vain, and after the nations that are around them, of whom Yhwh commanded them not to do like them. **¹⁶** And they forsake all the commands of their God Yhwh, and make a molten image for themselves—two calves, and make an Asherah, and bow themselves to all the host of the heavens, and serve Ba`al, **¹⁷** and cause their sons and their daughters to pass over through fire, and divine divinations, and use enchantments, and sell themselves to do evil in the eyes of Yhwh, to provoke Him. **¹⁸** And Yhwh shows Himself very angry against Israel, and turns them aside from His presence; none has been left, only the tribe of Judah by itself. **¹⁹** Also Judah has not kept the commands of their God Yhwh, and they walk in the statutes of Israel that they had made. **²⁰** And Yhwh kicks against all the seed of Israel, and afflicts them, and gives them into the hand of spoilers, until He has cast them out of His presence, **²¹** for He has torn Israel from the house of David, and they make Jeroboam son of Nebat king, and Jeroboam drives Israel from after Yhwh, and has caused them to sin a great sin, **²²** and the sons of Israel walk in all the sins of Jeroboam that he did, they have not turned aside from them, **²³** until Yhwh has turned Israel aside from His presence, as He spoke by the hand of all His servants the prophets, and Israel is removed from off its land to Asshur, to this day. **²⁴** And the king of Asshur brings in [people] from Babylon and from Cutha, and from Ava, and from Hamath, and Sepharvaim, and causes [them] to dwell in the cities of Samaria instead of the sons of Israel, and they possess Samaria, and dwell in its cities; **²⁵** and it comes to pass, at the commencement of their dwelling there, they have not feared Yhwh, and Yhwh sends the lions among them, and they are destroying among them. **²⁶** And they speak to the king of Asshur, saying, "The nations that you have removed and place in the cities of Samaria have not known the custom of the God of the land, and He sends the lions among them, and behold, they are destroying them, as they do not know the custom of the God of the land." **²⁷** And the king of Asshur commands, saying, "Cause one of the priests to go there whom you removed from there, and they go and dwell there, and he teaches them the custom of the God of the land." **²⁸** And one of the priests whom they removed from Samaria comes in, and dwells in Beth-El, and he is teaching them how they fear Yhwh, **²⁹** and each nation is making its gods, and they place [them] in the houses of the high places that the Samaritans have made—each nation in their cities where they are dwelling. **³⁰** And the men of Babylon have made Succoth-Benoth, and the men of Cuth have made Nergal, and the men of Hamath have made Ashima, **³¹** and the Avites have made Nibhaz and Tartak, and the Sepharvites are burning their sons with fire to Adrammelech and Anammelech, gods of Sepharvim. **³²** And they are fearing Yhwh, and make for themselves from their extremities priests of high places, and they are working for them in the house of the high places. **³³** They are fearing Yhwh, and they are serving their gods, according to the custom of the nations from where they removed them. **³⁴** To this day they are doing according to the former customs—they are not fearing Yhwh, and are not doing according to their statutes, and according to their ordinances, and according to the Law, and according to the command, that Yhwh commanded the sons of Jacob whose name He made Israel, **³⁵** and Yhwh makes a covenant with them and charges them, saying, "You do not fear other gods, nor bow yourselves to them, nor serve them, nor sacrifice to them, **³⁶** but Yhwh who brought you up out of the land of Egypt with great power, and with an outstretched arm, Him you fear, and to Him you bow yourselves, and to Him you sacrifice; **³⁷** and the statutes, and the judgments, and the Law, and the command, that He wrote for you, you observe to do all the days, and you do not fear other gods; **³⁸** and you do not forget the covenant that I have made with you, and you do not fear other gods; **³⁹** but you fear your God Yhwh, and He delivers you out of the hand of all your enemies"; **⁴⁰** and they have not listened, but they are doing according to their former custom, **⁴¹** and these nations are fearing Yhwh, and they have served their carved images, both their sons and their sons' sons; as their fathers did, they are doing to this day.

CHAPTER 18

¹ And it comes to pass, in the third year of Hoshea son of Elah, king of Israel, Hezekiah son of Ahaz, king of Judah, has reigned; **²** he was a son of twenty-five years in his reigning, and he has reigned twenty-nine years in Jerusalem, and the name of his mother [is] Abi daughter of Zechariah. **³** And he does that which [is] right in the eyes of Yhwh, according to all that his father David did, **⁴** he has turned aside the high places, and broken in pieces the standing-pillars, and cut down the Asherah, and beaten down the bronze serpent that Moses made, for up to these days the sons of Israel were making incense to it, and he calls it "a piece of bronze." **⁵** In Yhwh, God of Israel, he has trusted, and after him there has not been like him among all the kings of Judah, nor [among any] who were before him; **⁶** and he cleaves to Yhwh, he has not turned aside from after Him, and keeps His commands that Yhwh commanded Moses. **⁷** And Yhwh has been with him; in every place where he goes out he acts wisely, and he rebels against the king of Asshur, and has not served him; **⁸** he has struck the Philistines, even to Gaza and its borders, from a tower of watchers to the fortified city. **⁹** And it comes to pass, in the fourth year of King Hezekiah—it [is] the seventh year of Hoshea son of Elah, king of Israel—Shalmaneser king of Asshur has come up against Samaria and lays siege to it, **¹⁰** and they capture it at the end of three years; in the sixth year of Hezekiah—it [is] the ninth year of Hoshea king of Israel—Samaria has been captured, **¹¹** and the king of Asshur removes Israel to Asshur, and placed them in Halah, and in Habor [by] the river Gozan, and [in] cities of the Medes, **¹²** because that they have not listened to the voice of their God Yhwh, and transgress His covenant—all that He commanded Moses, servant of Yhwh—indeed, they have not listened nor done [it]. **¹³** And in the fourteenth year of King Hezekiah, Sennacherib king of Asshur has come up against all the fortified cities of Judah, and seizes them, **¹⁴** and Hezekiah king of Judah sends to the king of Asshur at Lachish, saying, "I have sinned, turn back from off me; that which you put on me I bear"; and the king of Asshur lays on Hezekiah king of Judah three hundred talents of silver and thirty talents of gold, **¹⁵** and Hezekiah gives all the silver that is found in the house of Yhwh and in the treasures of the house of the king; **¹⁶** at that time Hezekiah has cut off the doors of the temple of Yhwh, and the pillars that Hezekiah king of Judah had overlaid, and gives them to the king of Asshur. **¹⁷** And the king of Asshur sends Tartan, and the chief of the eunuchs, and the chief of the butlers, from Lachish, to King Hezekiah, with a heavy force, to Jerusalem, and they go up and come to Jerusalem, and they go up, and come in and stand by the conduit of the upper pool that [is] in the highway of the fuller's field. **¹⁸** And they call to the king, and Eliakim son of Hilkiah, who [is] over the house, and Shebna the scribe, and Joah son of Asaph, the remembrancer, go out to them. **19** And the chief of the butlers says to them, "Now say to Hezekiah, Thus said the great king, the king of Asshur: What [is] this confidence in which you have confided? **20** You have said: Only a word of the lips! Counsel and might [are] for battle; now, on whom have you trusted that you have rebelled against me? **21** Now behold, you have trusted for yourself on the staff of this broken reed, on Egypt; which a man leans on, and it has gone into his hand and pierced it! So [is] Pharaoh king of Egypt to all those trusting on him. **22** And when you say to me, We have trusted in our God Yhwh, is it not He whose high places and whose altars Hezekiah has turned aside, and says to Judah and to Jerusalem, You bow yourselves before this altar in Jerusalem? **23** And now, please give a pledge for yourself to my lord the king of Asshur, and I give two thousand horses to you, if you are able to give riders for yourself on them. **24** And how do you turn back the face of one captain of the least of the servants of my lord, that you trust for yourself on Egypt for chariot and for horsemen? **25** Have I now come up without Yhwh against this place to destroy it? Yhwh said to me, Go up against this land, and you have destroyed it." **26** And Eliakim son of Hilkiah says—and Shebna and Joah—to the chief of the butlers, "Please speak to your servants [in] Aramaic, for we are understanding, but do not speak with us [in] Jewish, in the ears of the people who [are] on the wall." **27** And the chief of the butlers says to them, "For your lord, and to you, has my lord sent me to speak these words? is it not for the men—those sitting on the wall—to eat their own dung and to drink their own water, with you?" **28** And the chief of the butlers stands and calls with a great voice [in] Jewish, and speaks and says, "Hear a word of the great king, the king of Asshur— **29** thus said the king: Do not let Hezekiah lift you up, for he is not able to deliver you out of his hand; **30** and do not let Hezekiah make you trust in Yhwh, saying, Yhwh certainly delivers us, and this city is not given into the hand of the king of Asshur. **31** Do not listen to Hezekiah, for thus said the king of Asshur: Make a blessing with me, and come out to me, and each eat of his vine, and each [eat] of his fig tree, and each drink the waters of his own well, **32** until my coming in, and I have taken you to a land like your own land, a land of grain and new wine, a land of bread and vineyards, a land of olive oil, and honey; and live, and do not die; and do not listen to Hezekiah when he persuades you, saying, Yhwh delivers us. **33** Have each of the gods of the nations ever delivered his land out of the hand of the king of Asshur? **34** Where [are] the gods of Hamath and Arpad? where [are] the gods of Sepharvaim, Hena, and Ivvah, that they have delivered Samaria out of my hand? **35** Who [are] they] among all the gods of the lands that have delivered their land out of my hand, that Yhwh delivers Jerusalem out of my hand?" **36** And the people have kept silent, and have not answered him a word, for the command of the king is, saying, "Do not answer him." **37** And Eliakim son of Hilkiah, who [is] over the house, comes in, and Shebna the scribe, and Joah son of Asaph, the remembrancer, to Hezekiah, with torn garments, and they declare to him the words of the chief of the butlers.

CHAPTER 19

1 And it comes to pass, at King Hezekiah's hearing, that he tears his garments, and covers himself with sackcloth, and enters the house of Yhwh, **2** and sends Eliakim, who [is] over the house, and Shebna the scribe, and the elderly of the priests, covering themselves with sackcloth, to Isaiah the prophet, son of Amoz, **3** and they say to him, "Thus said Hezekiah: This day [is] a day of distress, and rebuke, and despising; for sons have come to the birth, and there is not power to bring forth. **4** It may be your God Yhwh hears all the words of the chief of the butlers with which the king of Asshur his lord has sent him to reproach the living God, and has decided concerning the words that your God Yhwh has heard, and you have lifted up prayer for the remnant that is found." **5** And the servants of King Hezekiah come to Isaiah, **6** and Isaiah says to them, "Thus you say to your lord, Thus said Yhwh: Do not be afraid because of the words that you have heard, with which the servants of the king of Asshur have reviled Me. **7** Behold, I am giving a spirit in him, and he has heard a report, and has turned back to his land, and I have caused him to fall by the sword in his land." **8** And the chief of the butlers turns back and finds the king of Asshur fighting against Libnah, for he has heard that he has journeyed from Lachish. **9** And he hears concerning Tirhakah king of Cush, saying, "Behold, he

has come out to fight with you"; and he turns and sends messengers to Hezekiah, saying, **10** "Thus you speak to Hezekiah king of Judah, saying, Do not let your God in whom you are trusting lift you up, saying, Jerusalem is not given into the hand of the king of Asshur. **11** Behold, you have heard that which the kings of Asshur have done to all the lands—to devote them; and are you delivered? **12** did the gods of the nations deliver them whom my fathers destroyed—Gozan, and Haran, and Rezeph, and the sons of Eden, who [are] in Thelassar? **13** Where [is] the king of Hamath, and the king of Arpad, and the king of the city of Sepharvaim, Hena, and Ivvah?" **14** And Hezekiah takes the letters out of the hand of the messengers and reads them, and goes up to the house of Yhwh, and Hezekiah spreads it before Yhwh. **15** And Hezekiah prays before Yhwh and says, "O Yhwh, God of Israel, inhabiting the cherubim, You [are] God Himself—You alone—to all the kingdoms of the earth: You have made the heavens and the earth. **16** Incline, O Yhwh, Your ear, and hear; open, O Yhwh, Your eyes, and see; and hear the words of Sennacherib with which he has sent him to reproach the living God. **17** Truly, O Yhwh, kings of Asshur have laid waste the nations and their land, **18** and have put their gods into fire, for they [are] no gods, but work of the hands of man, wood and stone, and destroy them. **19** And now, O our God Yhwh, please save us out of his hand, and all kingdoms of the earth know that You [are] Yhwh God—You alone." **20** And Isaiah son of Amoz sends to Hezekiah, saying, "Thus said Yhwh, God of Israel: That which you have prayed to Me concerning Sennacherib king of Asshur I have heard; **21** this [is] the word that Yhwh spoke concerning him: Trampled on you—laughed at you || Has the virgin daughter of Zion; Shaken the head behind you || Has the daughter of Jerusalem! **22** Whom have you reproached and reviled? And against whom lifted up a voice? Indeed, you lift up your eyes on high—Against the Holy One of Israel! **23** By the hand of your messengers || You have reproached the Lord, and say, || In the multitude of my chariots I have come up to a high place of mountains—The sides of Lebanon, || And I cut down the height of its cedars, || The choice of its firs, || And I enter the lodging of its extremity, || The forest of its Carmel. **24** I have dug, and drunk strange waters, || And I dry up with the sole of my steps || All floods of a bulwark. **25** Have you not heard from afar [that] I made it, || From days of old that I formed it? Now I have brought it in, || And it becomes a desolation, || Ruinous heaps [are] fortified cities, **26** And their inhabitants [are] feeble-handed, || They were broken down, and are dried up, || They have been the herb of the field, || And the greenness of the tender grass, || Grass of the roofs, || And blasted grain—before it has risen up! **27** And your sitting down, and your going out, || And your coming in, I have known, || And your anger toward Me; **28** Because of your anger toward Me, || And your noise—it came up into My ears, || I have put My hook in your nose, || And My bridle in your lips, || And have caused you to turn back || In the way in which you came. **29** And this [is] the sign to you, || Food of the year [is] the spontaneous growth, || And in the second year the self-produced, || And in the third year you sow, and reap, || And plant vineyards, and eat their fruits. **30** And it has continued—The escaped of the house of Judah || That has been left—to take root beneath, || And has made fruit upward. **31** For a remnant goes out from Jerusalem, || And an escape from Mount Zion; The zeal of Yhwh [of Hosts] does this. **32** Therefore, thus said Yhwh, || Concerning the king of Asshur: He does not come into this city, || Nor does he shoot an arrow there, || Nor does he come before it with shield, || Nor does he pour out a mound against it. **33** In the way that he comes in—In it he turns back, || And to this city he does not come in, || A declaration of Yhwh— **34** And I have covered over this city, || To save it for My own sake, || And for the sake of My servant David." **35** And it comes to pass, in that night, that a messenger of Yhwh goes out, and strikes one hundred eighty-five thousand in the camp of Asshur, and they rise early in the morning, and behold, all of them [are] dead corpses. **36** And Sennacherib king of Asshur journeys, and goes, and turns back, and dwells in Nineveh; **37** and it comes to pass, he is bowing himself in the house of his god Nisroch, and [his sons] Adramelech and Sharezar have struck him with the sword, and they have escaped to the land of Ararat, and his son Esar-Haddon reigns in his stead.

CHAPTER 20

1 In those days Hezekiah has been sick to death, and Isaiah son of Amoz the prophet comes to him and says to him, "Thus said Yhwh: Give a charge to your house, for you are dying, and do not live." **2** And he turns around his face to the wall, and prays to Yhwh, saying, **3** "Ah, now, O Yhwh, please remember how I have habitually walked before You in truth and with a perfect heart, and I have done that which [is] good in Your eyes"; and Hezekiah weeps [with] a great weeping. **4** And it comes to pass, [when] Isaiah has not [yet] gone out to the middle court, that the word of Yhwh has been to him, saying, **5** "Return, and you have said to Hezekiah, leader of My people, Thus said Yhwh, God of your father David: I have heard your prayer, I have seen your tear, behold, I give healing to you. On the third day you go up to the house of Yhwh; **6** and I have added fifteen years to your days, and I deliver you and this city out of the hand of the king of Asshur, and have covered over this city for My own sake, and for the sake of My servant David." **7** And Isaiah says, "Take a cake of figs"; and they take and lay [it] on the boil, and he revives. **8** And Hezekiah says to Isaiah, "What [is] the sign that Yhwh gives healing to me, that I have gone up to the house of Yhwh on the third day?" **9** And Isaiah says, "This [is] the sign to you from Yhwh, that Yhwh does the thing that He has spoken—[will] the shadow have gone on ten degrees, or does it turn back ten degrees?" **10** And Hezekiah says, "It has been light for the shadow to incline ten degrees; no, but let the shadow turn backward ten degrees." **11** And Isaiah the prophet calls to Yhwh, and He brings back the shadow by the degrees that it had gone down in the degrees of Ahaz—backward ten degrees. **12** At that time Berodach-Baladan son of Baladan, king of Babylon, has sent letters and a present to Hezekiah, for he heard that Hezekiah had been sick; **13** and Hezekiah listens to them, and shows them all the house of his treasury, the silver, and the gold, and the spices, and the good ointment, and all the house of his vessels, and all that has been found in his treasuries; there has not been a thing that Hezekiah has not showed them in his house and in all his dominion. **14** And Isaiah the prophet comes to King Hezekiah and says to him, "What did these men say? and from where do they come to you?" And Hezekiah says, "They have come from a far-off land—from Babylon." **15** And he says, "What did they see in your house?" And Hezekiah says, "They saw all that [is] in my house; there has not been a thing that I have not showed them among my treasures." **16** And Isaiah says to Hezekiah, "Hear a word of Yhwh: **17** Behold, days are coming, and all that [is] in your house, and [all] that your father has treasured up until this day, has been carried to Babylon; there is not a thing left, said Yhwh; **18** and of your sons who go out from you, whom you beget, they take away, and they have been eunuchs in the palace of the king of Babylon." **19** And Hezekiah says to Isaiah, "The word of Yhwh that you have spoken [is] good"; and he says, "Why not, if there is peace and truth in my days?" **20** And the rest of the matters of Hezekiah, and all his might, and how he made the pool, and the conduit, and brings in the waters to the city, are they not written on the scroll of the Chronicles of the Kings of Judah? **21** And Hezekiah lies with his fathers, and his son Manasseh reigns in his stead.

CHAPTER 21

1 Manasseh [is] a son of twelve years in his reigning, and he has reigned fifty-five years in Jerusalem, and the name of his mother [is] Hephzi-Bah; **2** and he does evil in the eyes of Yhwh, according to the abominations of the nations that Yhwh dispossessed from the presence of the sons of Israel, **3** and he turns and builds the high places that his father Hezekiah destroyed, and raises altars for Ba'al, and makes an Asherah, as Ahab king of Israel did, and bows himself to all the host of the heavens, and serves them. **4** And he has built altars in the house of Yhwh, of which Yhwh said, "In Jerusalem I put My Name." **5** And he builds altars to all the host of the heavens in the two courts of the house of Yhwh; **6** and he has caused his son to pass through fire, and observed clouds, and used enchantment, and dealt with a familiar spirit and wizards; he has multiplied to do evil in the eyes of Yhwh—to provoke to anger. **7** And he sets the carved image of the Asherah that he made in the house of which Yhwh said to David and to his son Solomon, "In this house, and in Jerusalem, that I have chosen out of all the tribes of Israel, I put My Name for all time; **8** and I do not add to cause the foot of Israel to move from the ground that I gave to their fathers, only, if they observe to do according to all that I commanded them, and to all the Law that My servant Moses commanded them." **9** And they have not

listened, and Manasseh causes them to err, to do evil above the nations that Yhwh destroyed from the presence of the sons of Israel. **10** And Yhwh speaks by the hand of his servants the prophets, saying, **11** "Because that Manasseh king of Judah has done these abominations—he has done evil above all that the Amorites have done who [are] before him, and also causes Judah to sin by his idols— **12** therefore, thus said Yhwh, God of Israel: Behold, I am bringing in calamity on Jerusalem and Judah, that whoever hears of it, his two ears tingle. **13** And I have stretched out the line of Samaria over Jerusalem, and the plummet of the house of Ahab, and wiped Jerusalem as one wipes the dish—he has wiped, and has turned [it] on its face. **14** And I have left the remnant of My inheritance, and given them into the hand of their enemies, and they have been for a prey and for a spoil to all their enemies, **15** because that they have done evil in My eyes, and are provoking Me to anger from the day that their fathers came out of Egypt, even to this day." **16** And also, Manasseh has shed very much innocent blood, until he has filled Jerusalem mouth to mouth, apart from his sin that he has caused Judah to sin, to do evil in the eyes of Yhwh. **17** And the rest of the matters of Manasseh, and all that he did, and his sin that he sinned, are they not written on the scroll of the Chronicles of the Kings of Judah? **18** And Manasseh lies with his fathers, and is buried in the garden of his house, in the garden of Uzza, and his son Amon reigns in his stead. **19** Amon [is] a son of twenty-two years in his reigning, and he has reigned two years in Jerusalem, and the name of his mother [is] Meshullemeth daughter of Haruz of Jotbah, **20** and he does evil in the eyes of Yhwh, as his father Manasseh did, **21** and walks in all the way that his father walked in, and serves the idols that his father served, and bows himself to them, **22** and forsakes Yhwh, God of his fathers, and has not walked in the way of Yhwh. **23** And the servants of Amon conspire against him, and put the king to death in his own house, **24** and the people of the land strike all those conspiring against King Amon, and the people of the land cause his son Josiah to reign in his stead. **25** And the rest of the matters of Amon that he did, are they not written on the scroll of the Chronicles of the Kings of Judah? **26** and [one] buries him in his burying-place in the garden of Uzza, and his son Josiah reigns in his stead.

CHAPTER 22

1 Josiah [is] a son of eight years in his reigning, and he has reigned thirty-one years in Jerusalem, and the name of his mother [is] Jedidah daughter of Adaiah of Boskath, **2** and he does that which is right in the eyes of Yhwh, and walks in all the way of his father David, and has not turned aside [to] the right or left. **3** And it comes to pass, in the eighteenth year of King Josiah, the king has sent Shaphan son of Azaliah, son of Meshullam, the scribe, to the house of Yhwh, saying, **4** "Go up to Hilkiah the high priest, and he completes the silver that is brought into the house of Yhwh, that the keepers of the threshold have gathered from the people, **5** and they give it into the hand of those doing the work, the overseers, in the house of Yhwh, and they give it to those doing the work, that [are] in the house of Yhwh, to strengthen the breach of the house, **6** to craftsmen, and to builders, and [to repairers of] the wall, and to buy wood and hewn stones to strengthen the house; **7** only, the silver that is given into their hand is not reckoned with them, for they are dealing in faithfulness." **8** And Hilkiah the high priest says to Shaphan the scribe, "I have found [the] Scroll of the Law in the house of Yhwh"; and Hilkiah gives the scroll to Shaphan, and he reads it. **9** And Shaphan the scribe comes to the king, and brings the king back word, and says, "Your servants have poured out the silver that has been found in the house, and give it into the hand of those doing the work, the inspectors, in the house of Yhwh." **10** And Shaphan the scribe declares to the king, saying, "Hilkiah the priest has given a scroll to me"; and Shaphan reads it before the king. **11** And it comes to pass, at the king's hearing the words of the Scroll of the Law, that he tears his garments, **12** and the king commands Hilkiah the priest, and Ahikam son of Shaphan, and Achbor son of Michaiah, and Shaphan the scribe, and Asahiah servant of the king, saying, **13** "Go, seek Yhwh for me, and for the people, and for all Judah, concerning the words of this scroll that is found, for great [is] the fury of Yhwh that is kindled against us, because that our fathers have not listened to the words of this scroll, to do according to all that is written for us." **14** And Hilkiah the priest goes, and Ahikam, and Achbor, and Shaphan, and Asahiah, to Huldah the prophetess, wife of Shallum, son of

Tikvah, son of Harhas, keeper of the garments, and she is dwelling in Jerusalem in the second [quarter], and they speak to her. **15** And she says to them, "Thus said Yhwh, God of Israel: Say to the man who has sent you to me, **16** Thus said Yhwh: Behold, I am bringing in calamity to this place and on its inhabitants, all the words of the scroll that the king of Judah has read, **17** because that they have forsaken Me, and make incense to other gods, so as to provoke Me to anger with every work of their hands, and My wrath has been kindled against this place, and it is not quenched. **18** And to the king of Judah, who is sending you to seek Yhwh, thus you say to him, Thus said Yhwh, God of Israel: The words that you have heard— **19** because your heart [is] tender, and you are humbled because of Yhwh, in your hearing that which I have spoken against this place, and against its inhabitants, to be for a desolation, and for a reviling, and you tear your garments and weep before Me—I also have heard—a declaration of Yhwh— **20** therefore, behold, I am gathering you to your fathers, and you have been gathered to your grave in peace, and your eyes do not look on any of the calamity that I am bringing in on this place"; and they bring the king back word.

CHAPTER 23

1 And the king sends, and they gather all [the] elderly of Judah and Jerusalem to him, **2** and the king goes up to the house of Yhwh, and every man of Judah, and all the inhabitants of Jerusalem, with him, and the priests, and the prophets, and all the people, from small to great, and he reads in their ears all the words of the Scroll of the Covenant that is found in the house of Yhwh. **3** And the king stands by the pillar, and makes the covenant before Yhwh, to walk after Yhwh, and to keep His commands, and His testimonies, and His statutes, with all the heart, and with all the soul, to establish the words of this covenant that are written on this scroll, and all the people stand in the covenant. **4** And the king commands Hilkiah the high priest, and the priests of the second order, and the keepers of the threshold, to bring out from the temple of Yhwh all the vessels that are made for Ba'al, and for the Asherah, and for all the host of the heavens, and he burns them at the outside of Jerusalem, in the fields of Kidron, and has carried their ashes to Beth-El. **5** And he has caused to cease the idolatrous priests whom the kings of Judah have appointed (and they make incense in high places, in cities of Judah and outskirts of Jerusalem), and those making incense to Ba'al, to the sun, and to the moon, and to the twelve signs, and to all the host of the heavens. **6** And he brings out the Asherah from the house of Yhwh to the outside of Jerusalem, to the Brook of Kidron, and burns it at the Brook of Kidron, and beats it small to dust, and casts its dust on the grave of the sons of the people. **7** And he breaks down the houses of the whoremongers that [are] in the house of Yhwh, where the women are weaving houses for the Asherah. **8** And he brings in all the priests out of the cities of Judah, and defiles the high places where the priests have made incense, from Geba to Beer-Sheba, and has broken down the high places of the gates that [are] at the opening of the Gate of Joshua, head of the city, that [is] on a man's left hand at the gate of the city; **9** only, the priests of the high places do not come up to the altar of Yhwh in Jerusalem, but they have eaten unleavened things in the midst of their brothers. **10** And he has defiled Topheth that [is] in the Valley of the Son of Hinnom, so that no man causes his son and his daughter to pass over through fire to Molech. **11** And he causes to cease the horses that the kings of Judah have given to the sun from the entering in of the house of Yhwh, by the chamber of Nathan-Melech the eunuch, that [is] in the outskirts; and he has burned the chariots of the sun with fire. **12** And the altars that [are] on the top of the upper chamber of Ahaz, that the kings of Judah made, and the altars that Manasseh made in the two courts of the house of Yhwh, the king has broken down, and removes from there, and has cast their dust into the Brook of Kidron. **13** And the high places that [are] on the front of Jerusalem, that [are] on the right of the Mount of Corruption, that Solomon king of Israel had built to Ashtoreth, abomination of the Zidonians, and Chemosh, abomination of Moab, and to Milcom, abomination of the sons of Ammon, the king has defiled. **14** And he has broken the standing-pillars in pieces, and cuts down the Asherim, and fills their place with bones of men; **15** and also the altar that [is] in Beth-El, the high place that Jeroboam son of Nebat made, by which he made Israel sin, both that altar and the high place he has broken down, and burns the high

place—he has beat it small to dust, and has burned the Asherah. **16** And Josiah turns, and sees the graves that [are] there on the mountain, and sends and takes the bones out of the graves, and burns [them] on the altar, and defiles it, according to the word of Yhwh that the man of God proclaimed, who proclaimed these things. **17** And he says, "What [is] this sign that I see?" And the men of the city say to him, "The grave of the man of God who has come from Judah, and proclaims these things that you have done concerning the altar of Beth-El." **18** And he says, "Leave him alone, let no man touch his bones"; and they let his bones escape with the bones of the prophet who came out of Samaria. **19** And also all the houses of the high places that [are] in the cities of Samaria, that the kings of Israel made to provoke to anger, Josiah has turned aside, and does to them according to all the deeds that he did in Beth-El. **20** And he slays all the priests of the high places who [are] there by the altars, and burns the bones of man on them, and turns back to Jerusalem. **21** And the king commands the whole of the people, saying, "Make a Passover to your God Yhwh, as it is written on this scroll of the covenant." **22** Surely there has not been made like this Passover from the days of the ones judging who judged Israel, even all the days of the kings of Israel, and of the kings of Judah; **23** but in the eighteenth year of King Josiah, this Passover has been made to Yhwh in Jerusalem. **24** And also, those having familiar spirits, and the wizards, and the teraphim, and the idols, and all the abominations that were seen in the land of Judah, and in Jerusalem, Josiah has put away, in order to establish the words of the Law that are written on the scroll that Hilkiah the priest has found in the house of Yhwh. **25** And like him there has not been before him a king who turned back to Yhwh with all his heart, and with all his soul, and with all his might, according to all the Law of Moses, and after him there has none risen like him. **26** Only, Yhwh has not turned back from the fierceness of His great anger with which His anger burned against Judah, because of all the provocations with which Manasseh provoked him, **27** and Yhwh says, "I also turn Judah aside from my presence, as I turned Israel aside, and I have rejected this city that I have chosen—Jerusalem, and the house of which I said, My Name is there." **28** And the rest of the matters of Josiah and all that he did, are they not written on the scroll of the Chronicles of the Kings of Judah? **29** In his days Pharaoh Necho king of Egypt has come up against the king of Asshur, by the Euphrates River, and King Josiah goes out to meet him, and [Pharaoh Necho] puts him to death in Megiddo when he sees him. **30** And his servants cause him to ride dying from Megiddo, and bring him to Jerusalem, and bury him in his own grave, and the people of the land take Jehoahaz son of Josiah, and anoint him, and cause him to reign instead of his father. **31** Jehoahaz [is] a son of twenty-three years in his reigning, and he has reigned three months in Jerusalem, and the name of his mother [is] Hamutal daughter of Jeremiah of Libnah, **32** and he does evil in the eyes of Yhwh, according to all that his fathers did, **33** and Pharaoh Necho binds him in Riblah, in the land of Hamath, from reigning in Jerusalem, and he puts a fine on the land—one hundred talents of silver, and a talent of gold. **34** And Pharaoh Necho causes Eliakim son of Josiah to reign instead of his father Josiah, and turns his name to Jehoiakim, and he has taken Jehoahaz away, and he comes to Egypt, and dies there. **35** And Jehoiakim has given the silver and the gold to Pharaoh; only he valued the land to give the silver by the command of Pharaoh; from each, according to his valuation, he exacted the silver and the gold, from the people of the land, to give to Pharaoh Necho. **36** Jehoiakim [is] a son of twenty-five years in his reigning, and he has reigned eleven years in Jerusalem, and the name of his mother [is] Zebudah daughter of Pedaiah of Rumah, **37** and he does evil in the eyes of Yhwh, according to all that his fathers did.

CHAPTER 24

1 In his days Nebuchadnezzar king of Babylon has come up, and Jehoiakim is a servant to him [for] three years; and he turns and rebels against him, **2** and Yhwh sends against him the troops of the Chaldeans, and the troops of Aram, and the troops of Moab, and the troops of the sons of Ammon, and He sends them against Judah to destroy it, according to the word of Yhwh that He spoke by the hand of His servants the prophets; **3** only, by the command of Yhwh it has been against Judah to turn [them] aside from His presence, for the sins of Manasseh, according to all that he did, **4** and also the innocent blood that he has shed, and he fills Jerusalem with innocent blood, and Yhwh was not willing to forgive. **5** And the rest of the matters of Jehoiakim and all that he did, are they not written on the scroll of the Chronicles of the Kings of Judah? **6** And Jehoiakim lies with his fathers, and his son Jehoiachin reigns in his stead. **7** And the king of Egypt has not added anymore to go out from his own land, for the king of Babylon has taken, from the Brook of Egypt to the Euphrates River, all that had been to the king of Egypt. **8** Jehoiachin [is] a son of eighteen years in his reigning, and he has reigned three months in Jerusalem, and the name of his mother [is] Nehushta daughter of Elnathan of Jerusalem, **9** and he does evil in the eyes of Yhwh, according to all that his fathers did. **10** At that time servants of Nebuchadnezzar king of Babylon have come up to Jerusalem, and the city goes into siege, **11** and Nebuchadnezzar king of Babylon comes against the city, and his servants are laying siege to it, **12** and Jehoiachin king of Judah goes out to the king of Babylon, he, and his mother, and his servants, and his chiefs, and his eunuchs, and the king of Babylon takes him in the eighth year of his reign, **13** and brings out from there all the treasures of the house of Yhwh, and the treasures of the house of the king, and cuts in pieces all the vessels of gold that Solomon king of Israel made in the temple of Yhwh, as Yhwh had spoken. **14** And he has removed all Jerusalem, and all the chiefs, and all the mighty men of valor—ten thousand [is] the expulsion—and every craftsman and smith; none has been left except the poor of the people of the land. **15** And he removes Jehoiachin to Babylon, and the mother of the king, and the wives of the king, and his eunuchs, and the mighty ones of the land—he has caused a removal to go from Jerusalem to Babylon, **16** and all the men of valor, seven thousand, and the craftsmen and the smiths, one thousand, the whole [are] mighty men, warriors; and the king of Babylon brings them in a captivity to Babylon. **17** And the king of Babylon causes his father's brother Mattaniah to reign in his stead, and turns his name to Zedekiah. **18** Zedekiah [is] a son of twenty-one years in his reigning, and he has reigned eleven years in Jerusalem, and the name of his mother [is] Hamutal daughter of Jeremiah of Libnah, **19** and he does evil in the eyes of Yhwh according to all that Jehoiakim did, **20** for by the anger of Yhwh it has been against Jerusalem and against Judah, until He [finally] cast them out from His presence. And Zedekiah rebels against the king of Babylon.

CHAPTER 25

1 And it comes to pass, in the ninth year of his reign, in the tenth month, on the tenth of the month, Nebuchadnezzar king of Babylon has come, he and all his force, against Jerusalem, and encamps against it, and builds a surrounding fortification against it. **2** And the city enters into siege until the eleventh year of King Zedekiah. **3** On the ninth of the month, when the famine is severe in the city, then there has not been bread for the people of the land. **4** And the city is broken up, and all the men of war [go] by night the way of the gate, between the two walls that [are] by the garden of the king, and the Chaldeans [are] against the city all around, and [the king] goes the way of the plain. **5** And the force of the Chaldeans pursue after the king, and overtake him in the plains of Jericho, and all his force have been scattered from him; **6** and they seize the king, and bring him up to the king of Babylon, to Riblah, and they speak judgment with him. **7** And they have slaughtered the sons of Zedekiah before his eyes, and he has blinded the eyes of Zedekiah, and binds him with bronze chains, and they bring him to Babylon. **8** And in the fifth month, on the seventh of the month (it [is] the nineteenth year of King Nebuchadnezzar king of Babylon), Nebuzaradan chief of the executioners, servant of the king of Babylon, has come to Jerusalem, **9** and he burns the house of Yhwh, and the house of the king, and all the houses of Jerusalem, indeed, he has burned every great house with fire; **10** and all the forces of the Chaldeans, who [are] with the chief of the executioners, have broken down the walls of Jerusalem all around. **11** And the rest of the people, those left in the city, and those falling who have fallen to the king of Babylon, and the rest of the multitude, Nebuzaradan chief of the executioners has removed; **12** and of the poor of the land the chief of the executioners has left for vinedressers and for farmers. **13** And the pillars of bronze that [are] in the house of Yhwh, and the bases, and the sea of bronze, that [is] in the house of Yhwh, the Chaldeans have broken in pieces, and carry away their bronze to Babylon. **14** And the pots, and the shovels,

and the snuffers, and the spoons, and all the vessels of bronze with which they minister, they have taken; **15** and the fire-pans, and the bowls that [are] wholly of silver, the chief of the executioners has taken. **16** The two pillars, the one sea, and the bases that Solomon made for the house of Yhwh, there was no weighing of the bronze of all these vessels; **17** eighteen cubits [is] the height of the one pillar, and the capital on it [is] of bronze, and the height of the capital [is] three cubits, and the net and the pomegranates [are] on the capital all around—the whole [is] of bronze; and the second pillar has like these, with the net. **18** And the chief of the executioners takes Seraiah the head priest, and Zephaniah the second priest, and the three keepers of the threshold; **19** and he has taken out of the city a certain eunuch who is appointed over the men of war, and five men of those seeing the king's face who have been found in the city, and the head scribe of the host who musters the people of the land, and sixty men of the people of the land who are found in the city; **20** and Nebuzaradan chief of the executioners takes them, and causes them to go to the king of Babylon, to Libnah, **21** and the king of Babylon strikes them, and puts them to death in Riblah, in the land of Hamath, and he removes Judah from off its land. **22** And the people that are left in the land of Judah whom Nebuchadnezzar king of Babylon has left—he appoints Gedaliah son of Ahikam, son of Shaphan, over them. **23** And all the heads of the forces hear—they and the men—that the king of Babylon has appointed Gedaliah, and they come to Gedaliah, to Mizpah, even Ishmael son of Nethaniah, and Johanan son of Kareah, and Seraiah son of Tanhumeth the Netophathite, and Jaazaniah son of the Maachathite—they and their men; **24** and Gedaliah swears to them and to their men, and says to them, "Do not be afraid of the servants of the Chaldeans, dwell in the land and serve the king of Babylon, and it is good for you." **25** And it comes to pass, in the seventh month, Ishmael son of Nathaniah has come, son of Elishama of the seed of the kingdom, and ten men with him, and they strike Gedaliah, and he dies, and the Jews and the Chaldeans who have been with him in Mizpah. **26** And all the people rise, from small even to great, and the heads of the forces, and come to Egypt, for they have been afraid of the presence of the Chaldeans. **27** And it comes to pass, in the thirty-seventh year of the expulsion of Jehoiachin king of Judah, in the twelfth month, on the twenty-seventh of the month, Evil-Merodach king of Babylon has lifted up, in the year of his reigning, the head of Jehoiachin king of Judah, out of the house of restraint, **28** and speaks good things with him and puts his throne above the throne of the kings who [are] with him in Babylon, **29** and has changed the garments of his restraint, and he has eaten bread continually before him all [the] days of his life, **30** and his allowance—a continual allowance—has been given to him from the king, the matter of a day in its day, all [the] days of his life.

1 CHRONICLES

CHAPTER 1

1 Adam, Seth, Enosh, **2** Kenan, Mahalaleel, Jered, **3** Enoch, Methuselah, Lamech, **4** Noah, Shem, Ham, and Japheth. **5** Sons of Japheth: Gomer and Magog, and Madai, and Javan, and Tubal, and Meshech, and Tiras. **6** And sons of Gomer: Ashchenaz, and Riphath, and Togarmah. **7** And sons of Javan: Elisha, and Tarshishah, Kittim, and Dodanim. **8** Sons of Ham: Cush, and Mizraim, Put, and Canaan. **9** And sons of Cush: Seba and Havilah, and Sabta, and Raamah, and Sabtecka. And sons of Raamah: Sheba and Dedan. **10** And Cush begot Nimrod: he began to be a mighty one in the land. **11** And Mizraim begot the Ludim, and the Anamim, and the Lehabim, and the Naphtuhim, **12** and the Pathrusim, and the Casluhim (from whom the Philistim came out), and the Caphtorim. **13** And Canaan begot Sidon his firstborn, and Heth, **14** and the Jebusite, and the Amorite, and the Girgashite, **15** and the Hivite, and the Arkite, and the Sinite, **16** and the Arvadite, and the Zemarite, and the Hamathite. **17** Sons of Shem: Elam and Asshur, and Arphaxad, and Lud, and Aram, and Uz, and Hul, and Gether, and Meshech. **18** And Arphaxad begot Shelah, and Shelah begot Eber. **19** And two sons have been born to Eber, the name of the first [is]

Peleg, for in his days the earth has been divided, and the name of his brother is Joktan. 20 And Joktan begot Almodad, and Sheleph, and Hazarmaveth, and Jerah, 21 and Hadoram, and Uzal, and Diklah, 22 and Ebal, and Abimael, and Sheba, 23 and Ophir, and Havilah, and Jobab; all these [are] sons of Joktan. 24 Shem, Arphaxad, Shelah, 25 Eber, Peleg, Reu, 26 Serug, Nahor, Terah, 27 Abram—he [is] Abraham. 28 Sons of Abraham: Isaac and Ishmael. 29 These [are] their generations: [the] firstborn of Ishmael [was] Nebaioth, then Kedar, and Adheel, and Mibsam, 30 Mishma, and Dumah, Massa, Hadad, and Tema, 31 Jetur, Naphish, and Kedema. These are sons of Ishmael. 32 And sons of Keturah, Abraham's concubine: she bore Zimran, and Jokshan, and Medan, and Midian, and Ishbak, and Shuah. And sons of Jokshan: Sheba and Dedan. 33 And sons of Midian: Ephah and Epher, and Enoch, and Abida, and Eldaah; all these [are] sons of Keturah. 34 And Abraham begets Isaac. Sons of Isaac: Esau and Israel. 35 Sons of Esau: Eliphaz, Reuel, and Jeush, and Jaalam, and Korah. 36 Sons of Eliphaz: Teman, and Omar, Zephi, and Gatam, Kenaz, and Timna, and Amalek. 37 Sons of Reuel: Nahath, Zerah, Shammah, and Mizzah. 38 And sons of Seir: Lotan, and Shobal, and Zibeon, and Anah, and Dishon, and Ezar, and Dishan. 39 And sons of Lotan: Hori and Homam, and sister of Lotan [is] Timna. 40 Sons of Shobal: Alian, and Manahath, and Ebal, Shephi, and Onam. And sons of Zideon: Aiah and Anah. 41 The sons of Anah: Dishon. And sons of Dishon: Amram, and Eshban, and Ithran, and Cheran. 42 Sons of Ezer: Bilhan, and Zavan, Jakan. Sons of Dishan: Uz and Aran. 43 And these [are] the kings who reigned in the land of Edom before the reigning of a king of the sons of Israel: Bela son of Beor, and the name of his city [is] Dinhabah. 44 And Bela dies, and Jobab son of Zerah from Bozrah reigns in his stead; 45 and Jobab dies, and Husham from the land of the Temanite reigns in his stead; 46 and Husham dies, and Hadad son of Bedad reigns in his stead (who strikes Midian in the field of Moab) and the name of his city [is] Avith; 47 and Hadad dies, and Samlah from Masrekah reigns in his stead; 48 and Samlah dies, and Shaul from Rehoboth of the River reigns in his stead; 49 and Shaul dies, and Ba'al-Hanan son of Achbor reigns in his stead; 50 and Ba'al-Hanan dies, and Hadad reigns in his stead, and the name of his city [is] Pai, and the name of his wife [is] Mehetabel daughter of Matred, daughter of Me-Zahab; Hadad also dies. 51 And chiefs of Edom are: Chief Timnah, Chief Aliah, Chief Jetheth, 52 Chief Aholibamah, Chief Elah, Chief Pinon, 53 Chief Kenaz, Chief Teman, Chief Mibzar, 54 Chief Magdiel, Chief Iram. These [are] chiefs of Edom.

in Caleb-Ephratah, then the wife of Hezron, Abijah, even bears to him Asshur, father of Tekoa. 25 And sons of Jerahmeel, firstborn of Hezron, are: the firstborn Ram, and Bunah, and Oren, and Ozem, Ahijah. 26 And Jerahmeel has another wife, and her name [is] Atarah, she [is] mother of Onam. 27 And sons of Ram, firstborn of Jerahmeel, are Maaz, and Jamin, and Eker. 28 And sons of Onam are Shammai and Jada. And sons of Shammai: Nadab and Abishur. 29 And the name of the wife of Abishur [is] Abihail, and she bears Ahban and Molid to him. 30 And sons of Nadab: Seled and Appaim; and Seled dies without sons. 31 And sons of Appaim: Ishi. And sons of Ishi: Sheshan. And sons of Sheshan: Ahlai. 32 And sons of Jada, brother of Shammai: Jether and Jonathan; and Jether dies without sons. 33 And sons of Jonathan: Peleth and Zaza. These were sons of Jerahmeel. 34 And Sheshan had no sons, but daughters, and Sheshan has a servant, an Egyptian, and his name [is] Jarha, 35 and Sheshan gives his daughter to his servant Jarha for a wife, and she bears Attai to him; 36 and Attai begot Nathan, and Nathan begot Zabad, 37 and Zabad begot Ephlal, and Ephlal begot Obed, 38 and Obed begot Jehu, 39 and Jehu begot Azariah, and Azariah begot Helez, and Helez begot Eleasah, 40 and Eleasah begot Sismai, and Sismai begot Shallum, 41 and Shallum begot Jekamiah, and Jekamiah begot Elishama. 42 And sons of Caleb brother of Jerahmeel: Mesha his firstborn, he [is] father of Ziph; and sons of Mareshah: Abi-Hebron. 43 And sons of Hebron: Korah, and Tappuah, and Rekem, and Shema. 44 And Shema begot Raham father of Jorkoam, and Rekem begot Shammai. 45 And a son of Shammai [is] Maon, and Maon [is] father of Beth-Zur. 46 And Ephah concubine of Caleb bore Haran, and Moza, and Gazez; and Haran begot Gazez. 47 And sons of Jahdai: Regem, and Jotham, and Geshem, and Pelet, and Ephah, and Shaaph. 48 The concubine of Caleb, Maachah, bore Sheber and Tirhanah; 49 and she bears Shaaph father of Madmannah, Sheva father of Machbenah, and father of Gibea; and a daughter of Caleb [is] Achsa. 50 These were sons of Caleb son of Hur, firstborn of Ephrathah: Shobal father of Kirjath-Jearim, 51 Salma father of Beth-Lehem, Hareph father of Beth-Gader. 52 And there are sons to Shobal father of Kirjath-Jearim: Haroeh, half of the Menuhothite; 53 and the families of Kirjath-Jearim: the Ithrite, and the Puhite, and the Shumathite, and the Mishraite. The Zorathite and the Eshtaolite went out from these. 54 Sons of Salma: Beth-Lehem, and the Netophathite, Atroth, Beth-Joab, and half of the Menuhothite, the Zorite; 55 and the families of the scribes, the inhabitants of Jabez: Tirathites, Shimeathites, Suchathites. They [are] the Kenites, those coming of Hammath father of the house of Rechab.

CHAPTER 2

1 These [are] sons of Israel: Reuben, Simeon, Levi, and Judah, Issachar, and Zebulun, 2 Dan, Joseph, and Benjamin, Naphtali, Gad, and Asher. 3 Sons of Judah: Er, and Onan, and Shelah, three have been born to him of a daughter of Shua the Canaanitess. And Er, firstborn of Judah, is evil in the eyes of Yhwh, and He puts him to death. 4 And his daughter-in-law Tamar has borne Perez and Zerah to him. All the sons of Judah [are] five. 5 Sons of Perez: Hezron, and Hamul. 6 And sons of Zerah: Zimri, and Ethan, and Heman, and Calcol, and Dara; all of them five. 7 And sons of Carmi: Achar, troubler of Israel, who trespassed in the devoted thing. 8 And sons of Ethan: Azariah. 9 And sons of Hezron who were born to him: Jerahmeel, and Ram, and Chelubai. 10 And Ram begot Amminadab, and Amminadab begot Nahshon, prince of the sons of Judah; 11 and Nahshon begot Salma, and Salma begot Boaz, 12 and Boaz begot Obed, and Obed begot Jesse; 13 and Jesse begot his firstborn Eliab, and Abinadab the second, and Shimea the third, 14 Nethaneel the fourth, Raddai the fifth, 15 Ozem the sixth, David the seventh, 16 and their sisters Zeruiah and Abigail. And sons of Zeruiah: Abishai, and Joab, and Asah-El—three. 17 And Abigail has borne Amasa, and the father of Amasa [is] Jether the Ishmaelite. 18 And Caleb son of Hezron has begotten Azubah, Isshah, and Jerioth; and these [are] her sons: Jesher, and Shobab, and Ardon. 19 And Azubah dies, and Caleb takes Ephrath to himself, and she bears Hur to him. 20 And Hur begot Uri, and Uri begot Bezaleel. 21 And afterward Hezron has gone in to a daughter of Machir father of Gilead, and he has taken her, and he [is] a son of sixty years, and she bears Segub to him. 22 And Segub begot Jair, and he has twenty-three cities in the land of Gilead, 23 and he takes Geshur and Aram, the small villages of Jair, from them, with Kenath and its small towns, sixty cities—all these [belonged to] the sons of Machir father of Gilead. 24 And after the death of Hezron

CHAPTER 3

1 And these were sons of David, who were born to him in Hebron: the firstborn Amnon, of Ahinoam the Jezreelitess; second Daniel, of Abigail the Carmelitess; 2 the third Absalom, son of Maachah daughter of Talmai king of Geshur; the fourth Adonijah, son of Haggith; 3 the fifth Shephatiah, of Abital; the sixth Ithream, of his wife Eglah. 4 Six have been borne to him in Hebron, and he reigns seven years and six months there, and he has reigned thirty-three years in Jerusalem. 5 And these were born to him in Jerusalem: Shimea, and Shobab, and Nathan, and Solomon—four, of Bathsheba daughter of Ammiel. 6 Also Ibhar, and Elishama, and Eliphelet, 7 and Nogah, and Nepheg, and Japhia, 8 and Elishama, and Eliada, and Eliphelet—nine. 9 All [are] sons of David, apart from sons of the concubines, and their sister Tamar. 10 And the son of Solomon [is] Rehoboam, Abijah his son, Asa his son, Jehoshaphat his son, 11 Joram his son, Ahaziah his son, Joash his son, 12 Amaziah his son, Azariah his son, Jotham his son, 13 Ahaz his son, Hezekiah his son, Manasseh his son, 14 Amon his son, Josiah his son. 15 And sons of Josiah: the firstborn Johanan, the second Jehoiakim, the third Zedekiah, the fourth Shallum. 16 And sons of Jehoiakim: Jeconiah his son, Zedekiah his son. 17 And sons of Jeconiah: Assir; Salathiel his son; 18 also Malchiram and Pedaiah, and Shenazzar, Jecamiah, Hoshama, and Nedabiah. 19 And sons of Pedaiah: Zerubbabel and Shimei. And sons of Zerubbabel: Meshullam, and Hananiah, and their sister Shelomith, 20 and Hashubah, and Ohel, and Berechiah, and Hasadiah, Jushab-Hesed—five. 21 And sons of Hananiah: Pelatiah, and Jesaiah, sons of Rephaiah, sons of Arnan, sons of Obadiah, sons of Shechaniah. 22 And sons of Shechaniah: Shemaiah; and sons of Shemaiah: Hattush, and Igeal, and Bariah, and Neariah, and Shaphat—six. 23 And sons of Neariah: Elioenai, and Hezekiah, and Azrikam—three. 24 And sons of

Elioenai: Hodaiah, and Eliashib, and Pelaiah, and Akkub, and Johanan, and Delaiah, and Anani—seven.

CHAPTER 4

1 Sons of Judah: Perez, Hezron, and Carmi, and Hur, and Shobal. **2** And Reaiah son of Shobal begot Jahath, and Jahath begot Ahumai and Lahad; these [are] families of the Zorathite. **3** And these [are] of the father of Etam: Jezreel, and Ishma, and Idbash; and the name of their sister [is] Hazzelelponi; **4** and Penuel [is] father of Gedor, and Ezer father of Hushah. These [are] sons of Hur, firstborn of Ephratah, father of Beth-Lehem. **5** And to Ashhur father of Tekoa were two wives, Helah and Naarah; **6** and Naarah bears to him Ahuzzam, and Hepher, and Temeni, and Haahashtari: these [are] sons of Naarah. **7** And sons of Helah: Zereth, and Zohar, and Ethnan. **8** And Coz begot Anub, and Zobebah, and the families of Aharhel son of Harum. **9** And Jabez is honored above his brothers, and his mother called his name Jabez, saying, "Because I have brought forth with grief." **10** And Jabez calls to the God of Israel, saying, "If blessing You bless me, then You have made my border great, and Your hand has been with me, and You have kept [me] from evil—not to grieve me"; and God brings in that which he asked. **11** And Chelub brother of Shuah begot Mehir; he [is] father of Eshton. **12** And Eshton begot Beth-Rapha, and Paseah, and Tehinnah father of Ir-Nahash; these [are] men of Rechah. **13** And sons of Kenaz: Othniel and Seraiah; and sons of Othniel: Hathath. **14** And Meonothai begot Ophrah, and Seraiah begot Joab father of the Valley of the Craftsmen, for they were craftsmen. **15** And sons of Caleb son of Jephunneh: Iru, Elah, and Naam; and sons of Elah: even Kenaz. **16** And sons of Jehaleleel: Ziph and Ziphah, Tiria, and Asareel. **17** And sons of Ezra: Jether, and Mered, and Epher, and Jalon. And she bears Miriam, and Shammai, and Ishbah father of Eshtemoa. **18** And his wife Jehudijah bore Jered father of Gedor, and Heber father of Socho, and Jekuthiel father of Zanoah. And these [are] sons of Bithiah daughter of Pharaoh, whom Mered took, **19** and sons of the wife of Hodiah sister of Naham: Abi-Keilah the Garmite, and Eshtemoa the Maachathite. **20** And sons of Shimon: Amnon, and Rinnah, Ben-Hanon, and Tilon; and sons of Ishi: Zoheth, and Ben-Zoheth. **21** Sons of Shelah son of Judah: Er father of Lecah, and Laadah father of Mareshah, and the families of the house of the service of fine linen, of the house of Ashbea; **22** and Jokim, and the men of Chozeba, and Joash, and Saraph, who ruled over Moab and Jashubi-Lehem; and these things [are] ancient. **23** They [are] the potters and inhabitants of Netaim and Gedera; they dwelt there with the king in his work. **24** Sons of Simeon: Nemuel, and Jamin, Jarib, Zerah, Shaul; **25** Shallum his son, Mibsam his son, Mishma his son. **26** And sons of Mishma: Hammuel his son, Zacchur his son, Shimei his son. **27** And to Shimei [are] sixteen sons and six daughters, and to his brothers there are not many sons, and none of their families have multiplied as much as the sons of Judah. **28** And they dwell in Beer-Sheba, and Moladah, and Hazar-Shaul, **29** and in Bilhah, and in Ezem, and in Tolad, **30** and in Bethuel, and in Hormah, and in Ziklag, **31** and in Beth-Marcaboth, and in Hazar-Susim, and in Beth-Birei, and in Shaarim; these [are] their cities until the reigning of David. **32** And their villages [are] Etam, and Ain, Rimmon, and Tochen, and Ashan—five cities, **33** and all their villages that [are] around these cities to Ba`al; these [are] their dwellings, and they have their genealogy: **34** even Meshobab, and Jamlech, and Joshah son of Amaziah, **35** and Joel, and Jehu son of Josibiah, son of Seraiah, son of Asiel, **36** and Elioenai, and Jaakobah, and Jeshohaiah, and Asaiah, and Adiel, and Jesimiel, and Benaiah, **37** and Ziza son of Shiphi, son of Allon, son of Jedaiah, son of Shimri, son of Shemaiah. **38** These who are coming in by name [are] princes in their families, and the house of their fathers has broken forth into a multitude; **39** and they go to the entrance of Gedor, to the east of the valley, to seek pasture for their flock, **40** and they find pasture, fat and good, and the land broad of sides, and quiet, and safe, for those dwelling there before are of Ham. **41** And these who are written by name come in the days of Hezekiah king of Judah, and strike their tents, and the habitations that have been found there, and devote them to destruction to this day, and dwell in their stead, because pasture for their flock [is] there. **42** And of them, of the sons of Simeon, five hundred men have gone to Mount Seir, and Pelatiah, and Neariah, and Rephaiah, and Uzziel, sons of Ishi, at their head, **43** and they strike the remnant of those escaped of Amalek, and dwell there to this day.

CHAPTER 5

1 As for sons of Reuben, firstborn of Israel—for he [is] the firstborn, and on account of his profaning the bed of his father his birthright has been given to the sons of Joseph son of Israel, and [he is] not to be reckoned by genealogy for the birthright, **2** for Judah has been mighty over his brother, and for leader above him, and the birthright [is] to Joseph— **3** sons of Reuben, firstborn of Israel: Enoch, and Pallu, Hezron, and Carmi. **4** Sons of Joel: Shemaiah his son, Gog his son, Shimei his son, **5** Micah his son, Reaiah his son, Ba`al his son, **6** Beerah his son, whom Tilgath-Pilneser king of Asshur removed; he [is] prince of the Reubenite. **7** And his brothers, by their families, in the genealogy of their generations, [are] heads: Jeiel, and Zechariah, **8** and Bela son of Azaz, son of Shema, son of Joel— he is dwelling in Aroer, even to Nebo and Ba`al-Meon; **9** and he dwelt at the east even to the entering in of the wilderness, even from the Euphrates River, for their livestock were multiplied in the land of Gilead. **10** And they have made war with the Hagarites in the days of Saul, who fall by their hand, and they dwell in their tents over all the face of the east of Gilead. **11** And the sons of Gad have dwelt opposite them in the land of Bashan to Salcah: **12** Joel the head, and Shapham the second, and Jaanai and Shaphat in Bashan; **13** and their brothers of the house of their fathers [are] Michael, and Meshullam, and Sheba, and Jorai, and Jachan, and Zia, and Heber—seven. **14** These [are] sons of Abihail son of Huri, son of Jaroah, son of Gilead, son of Michael, son of Jeshishai, son of Jahdo, son of Buz; **15** Ahi son of Abdiel, son of Guni, [is] head of the house of their fathers; **16** and they dwell in Gilead in Bashan, and in her small towns, and in all outskirts of Sharon, on their outskirts; **17** all of them reckoned themselves by genealogy in the days of Jotham king of Judah, and in the days of Jeroboam king of Israel. **18** Sons of Reuben, and the Gadite, and the half of the tribe of Manasseh, of sons of valor, men carrying shield and sword, and treading bow, and taught in battle, [are] forty-four thousand and seven hundred and sixty, going out to the host. **19** And they make war with the Hagarites, and Jetur, and Naphish, and Nodab, **20** and they are helped against them, and the Hagarites are given into their hand, and all who [are] with them, for they cried to God in battle, and He received their plea, because they trusted in Him. **21** And they take their livestock captive—fifty thousand of their camels, and two hundred and fifty thousand sheep, and two thousand donkeys, and one hundred thousand of mankind; **22** for many have fallen pierced, for the battle [is] of God; and they dwell in their stead until the expulsion. **23** And the sons of the half of the tribe of Manasseh dwelt in the land, from Bashan to Ba`al-Hermon, and Senir, and Mount Hermon; they have multiplied. **24** And these [are] heads of the house of their fathers: even Epher, and Ishi, and Eliel, and Azriel, and Jeremiah, and Hodaviah, and Jahdiel, men mighty in valor, men of renown, heads of the house of their fathers. **25** And they trespass against the God of their fathers, and go whoring after the gods of the peoples of the land whom God destroyed from their presence; **26** and the God of Israel stirs up the spirit of Pul king of Asshur, and the spirit of Tilgath-Pilneser king of Asshur, and he removes them—even the Reubenite, and the Gadite, and the half of the tribe of Manasseh—and brings them to Halah, and Habor, and Hara, and the River of Gozan to this day.

CHAPTER 6

1 Sons of Levi: Gershon, Kohath, and Merari. **2** And the sons of Kohath: Amram, Izhar, and Hebron, and Uzziel. **3** And sons of Amram: Aaron, and Moses, and [his daughter] Miriam. And sons of Aaron: Nadab, and Abihu, Eleazar, and Ithamar. **4** Eleazar begot Phinehas, Phinehas begot Abishua, **5** and Abishua begot Bukki, and Bukki begot Uzzi, **6** and Uzzi begot Zerahiah, and Zerahiah begot Meraioth, **7** Meraioth begot Amariah, and Amariah begot Ahitub, **8** and Ahitub begot Zadok, and Zadok begot Ahimaaz, **9** and Ahimaaz begot Azariah, and Azariah begot Johanan, **10** and Johanan begot Azariah—him who acted as priest in the house that Solomon built in Jerusalem. **11** And Azariah begets Amariah, and Amariah begot Ahitub, **12** and Ahitub begot Zadok, and Zadok begot Shallum, **13** and Shallum begot Hilkiah, and Hilkiah begot Azariah, **14** and Azariah begot Seraiah, and Seraiah begot Jehozadak; **15** and Jehozadak has gone in Yhwh's removing Judah and Jerusalem by the hand of

Nebuchadnezzar. **16** Sons of Levi: Gershom, Kohath, and Merari. **17** And these [are] names of sons of Gershom: Libni and Shimei. **18** And sons of Kohath: Amram, and Izhar, and Hebron, and Uzziel. **19** Sons of Merari; Mahli and Mushi. And these [are] families of the Levite according to their fathers; **20** of Gershom: Libni his son, Jahath his son, Zimmah his son, **21** Joah his son, Iddo his son, Zerah his son, Jeaterai his son. **22** Sons of Kohath: Amminadab his son, Korah his son, Assir his son, **23** Elkanah his son, and Ebiasaph his son, and Assir his son, **24** Tahath his son, Uriel his son, Uzziah his son, and Shaul his son. **25** And sons of Elkanah: Amasai and Ahimoth. **26** Elkanah—sons of Elkanah: Zophai his son, and Nahath his son, **27** Eliab his son, Jeroham his son, Elkanah his son. **28** And sons of Samuel: the firstborn Vashni, and the second Abijah. **29** Sons of Merari: Mahli, Libni his son, Shimei his son, Uzzah his son, **30** Shimea his son, Haggiah his son, Asaiah his son. **31** And these [are] they whom David stationed over the parts of the song of the house of Yhwh, from the resting of the Ark, **32** and they are ministering before the Dwelling Place of the Tent of Meeting, in song, until the building by Solomon of the house of Yhwh in Jerusalem; and they stand according to their ordinance over their service. **33** And these [are] those standing, and their sons, of the sons of the Kohathite: Heman the singer, son of Joel, son of Shemuel, **34** son of Elkanah, son of Jeroham, son of Eliel, son of Toah, **35** son of Zuph, son of Elkanah, son of Mahath, son of Amasai, **36** son of Elkanah, son of Joel, son of Azariah, son of Zephaniah, **37** son of Tahath, son of Assir, son of Ebiasaph, son of Korah, **38** son of Izhar, son of Kohath, son of Levi, son of Israel. **39** And his brother Asaph, who is standing on his right—Asaph, son of Berachiah, son of Shimea, **40** son of Michael, son of Baaseiah, son of Malchiah, **41** son of Ethni, son of Zerah, son of Adaiah, **42** son of Ethan, son of Zimmah, son of Shimei, **43** son of Jahath, son of Gershom, son of Levi. **44** And sons of Merari, their brothers, on the left: Ethan son of Kishi, son of Abdi, son of Malluch, **45** son of Hashabiah, son of Amaziah, son of Hilkiah, **46** son of Amzi, son of Bani, son of Shamer, **47** son of Mahli, son of Mushi, son of Merari, son of Levi. **48** And their brothers the Levites are put to all the service of the Dwelling Place of the house of God. **49** And Aaron and his sons are making incense on the altar of the burnt-offering, and on the altar of the incense, for all the work of the Holy of Holies, and to make atonement for Israel, according to all that Moses servant of God commanded. **50** And these [are] sons of Aaron: Eleazar his son, Phinehas his son, Abishua his son, **51** Bukki his son, Uzzi his son, Zerahiah his son, **52** Meraioth his son, Amariah his son, Ahitub his son, **53** Zadok his son, Ahimaaz his son. **54** And these [are] their dwellings, throughout their towers, in their borders, of the sons of Aaron, of the family of the Kohathite, for the lot was theirs; **55** and they give to them Hebron in the land of Judah and its outskirts around it; **56** and they gave the field of the city and its villages to Caleb son of Jephunneh. **57** And they gave the cities of refuge to the sons of Aaron: Hebron, and Libnah and its outskirts, and Jattir, and Eshtemoa and its outskirts, **58** and Hilen and its outskirts, Debir and its outskirts, **59** and Ashan and its outskirts, and Beth-Shemesh and its outskirts. **60** And from the tribe of Benjamin: Geba and its outskirts, and Allemeth and its outskirts, and Anathoth and its outskirts. All their cities [are] thirteen cities among their families. **61** And to the sons of Kohath, those left of the family of the tribe, from the half of the tribe, the half of Manasseh, by lot, [are] ten cities. **62** And to the sons of Gershom, for their families, from the tribe of Issachar, and from the tribe of Asher, and from the tribe of Naphtali, and from the tribe of Manasseh in Bashan, [are] thirteen cities. **63** To the sons of Merari, for their families, from the tribe of Reuben, and from the tribe of Gad, and from the tribe of Zebulun, by lot, [are] twelve cities. **64** And the sons of Israel give the cities and their outskirts to the Levites. **65** And they give by lot from the tribe of the sons of Judah, and from the tribe of the sons of Simeon, and from the tribe of the sons of Benjamin, these cities which they call by name; **66** and some of the families of the sons of Kohath have cities of their border from the tribe of Ephraim; **67** and they give the cities of refuge to them: Shechem and its outskirts in the hill-country of Ephraim, and Gezer and its outskirts, **68** and Jokmeam and its outskirts, and Beth-Horan and its outskirts, **69** and Aijalon and its outskirts, and Gath-Rimmon and its outskirts; **70** and from the half tribe of Manasseh: Aner and its outskirts, and Bileam and its outskirts, for the family of the sons of Kohath who are left. **71** To the sons of Gershom from the family of the half of the tribe of Manasseh: Golan in Bashan and its outskirts, and Ashtaroth and its outskirts; **72** and from the tribe of Issachar:

Kedesh and its outskirts, Daberath and its outskirts, **73** and Ramoth and its outskirts, and Anem and its outskirts; **74** and from the tribe of Asher: Mashal and its outskirts, and Abdon and its outskirts, **75** and Hukok and its outskirts, and Rehob and its outskirts; **76** and from the tribe of Naphtali: Kedesh in Galilee and its outskirts, and Hammon and its outskirts, and Kirjathaim and its outskirts. **77** To the sons of Merari who are left, from the tribe of Zebulun: Rimmon and its outskirts, Tabor and its outskirts; **78** and from beyond the Jordan by Jericho, at the east of the Jordan, from the tribe of Reuben: Bezer in the wilderness and its outskirts, and Jahzah and its outskirts, **79** and Kedemoth and its outskirts, and Mephaath and its outskirts; **80** and from the tribe of Gad: Ramoth in Gilead and its outskirts, and Mahanaim and its outskirts, **81** and Heshbon and its outskirts, and Jazer and its outskirts.

CHAPTER 7

1 And sons of Issachar: Tola, and Puah, Jashub, and Shimron—four. **2** And sons of Tola: Uzzi, and Rephaiah, and Jeriel, and Jahmai, and Jibsam, and Shemuel, heads of the house of their fathers, [even] of Tola, mighty men of valor in their generations; their number in the days of David [is] twenty-two thousand and six hundred. **3** And sons of Uzzi: Izrahiah; and sons of Izrahiah: Michael, and Obadiah, and Joel, Ishiah, Hamishah—all of them heads. **4** And beside them, by their generations, of the house of their fathers, [are] thirty-six thousand troops of the host of battle, for they multiplied wives and sons; **5** and their brothers of all the families of Issachar, mighty men of valor, listed by their genealogy, [are] eighty-seven thousand for the whole. **6** Of Benjamin: Bela, and Becher, and Jediael—three. **7** And sons of Bela: Ezbon, and Uzzi, and Uzziel, and Jerimoth, and Iri—five; heads of a house of fathers, mighty men of valor, with their genealogy, twenty-two thousand and thirty-four. **8** And sons of Becher: Zemirah, and Joash, and Eliezar, and Elioenai, and Omri, and Jerimoth, and Abijah, and Anathoth, and Alameth. All these [are] sons of Becher, **9** with their genealogy, after their generations, heads of a house of their fathers, mighty men of valor, twenty thousand and two hundred. **10** And sons of Jediael: Bilhan; and sons of Bilhan: Jeush, and Benjamin, and Ehud, and Chenaanah, and Zethan, and Tarshish, and Ahishahar. **11** All these [are] sons of Jediael, even heads of the fathers, mighty in valor, seventeen thousand and two hundred going out to the host for battle. **12** And Shuppim and Huppim [are] sons of Ir, [and] Hushim [is] the son of Aher. **13** Sons of Naphtali: Jahziel, and Guni, and Jezer, and Shallum, sons of Bilhah. **14** Sons of Manasseh: Ashriel, whom Jaladah his Aramean concubine bore, with Machir father of Gilead. **15** And Machir took wives for Huppim and for Shuppim, and the name of the first [is] Maachah, and the name of the second Zelophehad, and Zelophehad has daughters. **16** And Maachah wife of Machir bears a son and calls his name Peresh, and the name of his brother [is] Sheresh, and his sons [are] Ulam and Rakem. **17** And son of Ulam: Bedan. These [are] sons of Gilead son of Machir, son of Manasseh. **18** And his sister Hammolecheth bore Ishhod, and Abiezer, and Mahalah. **19** And the sons of Shemida are Ahian, and Shechem, and Likhi, and Aniam. **20** And sons of Ephraim: Shuthelah, and Bered his son, and Tahath his son, and Eladah his son, and Tahath his son, **21** and Zabad his son, and Shuthelah his son, and Ezer, and Elead; and men of Gath who are born in the land have slain them because they came down to take their livestock. **22** And their father Ephraim mourns many days, and his brothers come to comfort him, **23** and he goes in to his wife, and she conceives and bears a son, and he calls his name Beriah, because his house had been in calamity— **24** and his daughter [is] Sherah, and she builds Beth-Horon, the lower and the upper, and Uzzen-Sherah— **25** Rephah [is] his son, and Resheph, and Telah his son, and Tahan his son, **26** Laadan his son, Ammihud his son, Elishama his son, **27** Nun his son, Joshua his son. **28** And their possession and their dwellings [are] Beth-El and its small towns, and Naaran to the east, and Gezer and its small towns to the west, and Shechem and its small towns, as far as Gaza and its small towns; **29** and by the parts of the sons of Manasseh [are] Beth-Shean and its small towns, Taanach and its small towns, Megiddo and its small towns, Dor and its small towns; the sons of Joseph, son of Israel, dwelt in these. **30** Son of Asher: Imnah, and Ishve, and Ishvi, and Beriah, and their sister Serah. **31** And sons of Beriah: Heber and Malchiel—he [is] father of Birzavith. **32** And Heber begot Japhlet, and Shomer, and Hotham, and their sister Shua. 33 And sons of Japhlet: Pasach, and Bimhal, and Ashvath; these [are] sons of Japhlet. 34 and sons of Shamer: Ahi, and Rohgah, Jehubbah, and Aram. 35 And [each] son of his brother Helem: Zophah, and Imna, and Shelesh, and Amal. 36 Sons of Zophah: Suah, and Harnepher, and Shual, and Beri, and Imrah, 37 Bezer, and Hod, and Shamma, and Shilshah, and Ithran, and Beera. 38 And sons of Jether: Jephunneh, and Pispah, and Ara. 39 And sons of Ulla: Arah, and Hanniel, and Rezia. 40 All these [are] sons of Asher, heads of the house of the fathers, chosen ones, mighty in valor, heads of the princes, with their genealogy, for the host, for battle, their number [is] twenty-six thousand men.

CHAPTER 8

1 And Benjamin begot Bela his firstborn, Ashbel the second, and Aharah the third, 2 Nohah the fourth, and Rapha the fifth. 3 And there are sons to Bela: Addar, and Gera, 4 and Abihud, and Abishua, and Naaman, and Ahoah, 5 and Gera, and Shephuphan, and Huram. 6 And these [are] sons of Ehud—they are heads of fathers to the inhabitants of Geba, and they remove them to Manahath: 7 even Naaman, and Ahiah, and Gera, who removed them and begot Uzza and Ahihud. 8 And Shaharaim begot in the field of Moab after his sending them away; Hushim and Baara [are] his wives. 9 And he begets of his wife Hodesh: Jobab, and Zibia, and Mesha, and Malcham, 10 and Jeuz, and Shachiah, and Mirmah. These [are] his sons, heads of fathers. 11 And of Hushim he begot Ahitub and Elpaal. 12 And sons of Elpaal: Eber, and Misheam, and Shamer (he built Ono and Lod and its small towns), 13 and Beriah and Shema (they [are] the heads of fathers to the inhabitants of Aijalon— they caused the inhabitants of Gath to flee), 14 and Ahio, Shashak, and Jeremoth, 15 and Zebadiah, and Arad, and Ader, 16 and Michael, and Ispah, and Joha, sons of Beriah, 17 and Zebadiah, and Meshullam, and Hezeki, and Heber, 18 and Ishmerai, and Jezliah, and Jobab, sons of Elpaal; 19 and Jakim, and Zichri, and Zabdi, 20 and Elienai, and Zillethai, and Eliel, 21 and Adaiah, and Beraiah, and Shimrath, sons of Shimei; 22 and Ishpan, and Heber, and Eliel, 23 and Abdon, and Zichri, and Hanan, 24 and Hananiah, and Elam, and Antothijah, 25 and Iphedeiah, and Penuel, sons of Shashak; 26 and Shamsherai, and Shehariah, and Athaliah, 27 and Jaareshiah, and Eliah, and Zichri, sons of Jeroham. 28 These [are] heads of fathers, by their generations, [the] heads. These dwelt in Jerusalem. 29 And the father of Gibeon has dwelt in Gibeon, and the name of his wife [is] Maachah; 30 and his son, the firstborn, [is] Abdon, and Zur, and Kish, and Ba'al, and Nadab, 31 and Gedor, and Ahio, and Zacher; 32 and Mikloth begot Shimeah. And they also dwelt opposite their brothers—with their brothers in Jerusalem. 33 And Ner begot Kish, and Kish begot Saul, and Saul begot Jonathan, and Malchi-Shua, and Abinadab, and Esh-Ba'al. 34 And a son of Jonathan [is] Merib-Ba'al, and Merib-Ba'al begot Micah; 35 and sons of Micah: Pithon, and Melech, and Tarea, and Ahaz: 36 and Ahaz begot Jehoadah, and Jehoadah begot Alemeth, and Azmaveth, and Zimri; and Zimri begot Moza, 37 and Moza begot Binea, Raphah his son, Eleasah his son, Azel his son. 38 And to Azel [are] six sons, and these [are] their names: Azrikam, Bocheru, and Ishmael, and Sheariah, and Obadiah, and Hanan. All these [are] sons of Azel. 39 And sons of his brother Eshek: Ulam his firstborn, Jehush the second, and Eliphelet the third. 40 And the sons of Ulam are men mighty in valor, treading bow, and multiplying sons and son's sons— one hundred and fifty. All these [are] of the sons of Benjamin.

CHAPTER 9

1 And all [those of] Israel have reckoned themselves by genealogy, and behold, they are written on the scroll of the kings of Israel and Judah—they were removed to Babylon for their trespass. 2 And the first inhabitants, who [are] in their possession, in their cities, of Israel, [are] the priests, the Levites, and the Nethinim. 3 And those who dwelt in Jerusalem of the sons of Judah, and of the sons of Benjamin, and of the sons of Ephraim and Manasseh: 4 Uthai son of Ammihud, son of Omri, son of Imri, son of Bani, of the sons of Perez, son of Judah. 5 And of the Shilonite: Asaiah the firstborn, and his sons. 6 And of the sons of Zerah: Jeuel, and their brothers—six hundred and ninety. 7 And of the sons of Benjamin: Sallu son of Meshullam, son of Hodaviah, son of Hassenuah, 8 and

Ibneiah son of Jeroham, and Elah son of Uzzi, son of Michri, and Meshullam son of Shephatiah, son of Reuel, son of Ibnijah. 9 And their brothers, according to their generations, [are] nine hundred and fifty-six. All these [are] men, heads of fathers, according to the house of their fathers. 10 And of the priests: Jedaiah, and Jehoiarib, and Jachin, 11 and Azariah son of Hilkiah, son of Meshullam, son of Zadok, son of Meraioth, son of Ahitub, leader in the house of God; 12 and Adaiah son of Jeroham, son of Pashhur, son of Malchijah, and Maasai son of Adiel, son of Jahzerah, son of Meshullam, son of Meshillemith, son of Immer. 13 And their brothers, heads of the house of their fathers, [are] one thousand and seven hundred and sixty, mighty in valor, for the work of the service of the house of God. 14 And of the Levites: Shemaiah son of Hashshub, son of Azrikam, son of Hashabiah, of the sons of Merari; 15 and Bakbakkar, Heresh, and Galal, and Mattaniah son of Micah, son of Zichri, son of Asaph; 16 and Obadiah son of Shemariah, son of Galal, son of Jeduthun, and Berechiah son of Asa, son of Elkanah, who is dwelling in the villages of the Netophathite. 17 And the gatekeepers [are] Shallum, and Akkub, and Talmon, and Ahiman, and their brothers—Shallum [is] the head; 18 and until now they [are] at the gate of the king eastward; they [are] the gatekeepers for the companies of the sons of Levi. 19 And Shallum son of Kore, son of Ebiasaph, son of Korah, and his brothers, of the house of his father, the Korahites, [are] over the work of the service, keepers of the thresholds of the tent, and their fathers [are] over the camp of Yhwh, keepers of the entrance; 20 and Phinehas son of Eleazar has been leader over them formerly; Yhwh [is] with him. 21 Zechariah son of Meshelemiah [is] gatekeeper at the opening of the Tent of Meeting. 22 All of those who are chosen for gatekeepers at the thresholds [are] two hundred and twelve; they [are] in their villages, by their genealogy; they whom David and Samuel the seer appointed in their office. 23 And they and their sons [are] over the gates of the house of Yhwh, even of the house of the tent, by watches. 24 The gatekeepers are at [the] four sides: east, west, north, and south. 25 And their brothers in their villages [are] to come in with these for seven days from time to time. 26 For the four chiefs of the gatekeepers in office, they are Levites, and they have been over the chambers, and over the treasuries of the house of God, 27 and they lodge around the house of God, for the watch [is] on them, and they [are] over the opening, even morning by morning. 28 And [some] of them [are] over the vessels of service, for they bring them in by number, and by number they take them out. 29 And [some] of them are appointed over the vessels, even over all the vessels of the holy place, and over the fine flour, and the wine, and the oil, and the frankincense, and the spices. 30 And [some] of the sons of the priests are mixing the mixture for spices. 31 And Mattithiah of the Levites (he [is] the firstborn to Shallum the Korahite), [is] in office over the work of the pans. 32 And of the sons of the Kohathite, [some] of their brothers [are] over the bread of the arrangement, to prepare [it] Sabbath by Sabbath. 33 And these who sing, heads of fathers of the Levites, in the chambers, [are] free, for [they are] over them in the work by day and by night. 34 These heads of the fathers of the Levites [are] heads throughout their generations. These have dwelt in Jerusalem. 35 And the father of Gibeon, Jehiel, has dwelt in Gibeon, and the name of his wife [is] Maachah; 36 and his son, the firstborn, [is] Abdon and Zur, and Kish, and Ba'al, and Ner, and Nadab, 37 and Gedor, and Ahio, and Zechariah, and Mikloth. 38 And Mikloth begot Shimeam, and they have also dwelt opposite their brothers—with their brothers in Jerusalem. 39 And Ner begot Kish, and Kish begot Saul, and Saul begot Jonathan, and Malchi-Shua, and Abinadab, and Esh-Ba'al. 40 And a son of Jonathan [is] Merib-Ba'al, and Merib-Ba'al begot Micah. 41 And sons of Micah: Pithon, and Melech, and Tahrea, 42 and Ahaz—he begot Jaarah, and Jaarah begot Alemeth, and Azmaveth, and Zimri, and Zimri begot Moza, 43 and Moza begot Binea, and Rephaiah his son, Eleasah his son, Azel his son. 44 And to Azel [are] six sons, and these [are] their names: Azrikam, Bocheru, and Ishmael, and Sheariah, and Obadiah, and Hanan; these [are] sons of Azel.

CHAPTER 10

1 And the Philistines have fought with Israel, and the men of Israel flee from the face of the Philistines, and fall wounded in Mount Gilboa, 2 and the Philistines pursue after Saul, and after his sons, and the Philistines strike Jonathan, and Abinadab, and Malchi-Shua, sons of Saul. 3 And the battle [is]

heavy on Saul, and those shooting with the bow find him, and he is wounded by those shooting, **4** and Saul says to the bearer of his weapons, "Draw your sword and pierce me with it, lest these uncircumcised come and have abused me." And the bearer of his weapons has not been willing, for he fears exceedingly, and Saul takes the sword, and falls on it; **5** and the bearer of his weapons sees that Saul [is] dead, and falls, he also, on the sword, and dies; **6** and Saul dies, and his three sons, and all his house—they died together. **7** And all the men of Israel who [are] in the valley see that they have fled and that Saul and his sons have died, and they forsake their cities and flee, and the Philistines come and dwell in them. **8** And it comes to pass, on the next day, that the Philistines come to strip the wounded, and find Saul and his sons fallen in Mount Gilboa, **9** and strip him, and carry away his head and his weapons, and send [them] into the land of the surrounding Philistines to proclaim tidings [to] their idols and the people; **10** and they put his weapons in the house of their gods, and have fixed his skull in the house of Dagon. **11** And all Jabesh-Gilead hears of all that the Philistines have done to Saul, **12** and all the men of valor rise and carry away the body of Saul, and the bodies of his sons, and bring them to Jabesh, and bury their bones under the oak in Jabesh, and fast seven days. **13** And Saul dies because of his trespass that he trespassed against Yhwh, against the word of Yhwh that he did not keep, and also for asking to inquire of a familiar spirit; **14** and he did not inquire of Yhwh, and He puts him to death, and turns around the kingdom to David son of Jesse.

CHAPTER 11

1 And all Israel is gathered to David at Hebron, saying, "Behold, we [are] your bone and your flesh; **2** even in time past, even in Saul's being king, it is you who are taking out and bringing in Israel, and your God Yhwh says to you: You feed My people Israel, and you are leader over My people Israel." **3** And all [the] elderly of Israel come to the king at Hebron, and David makes a covenant with them in Hebron before Yhwh, and they anoint David for king over Israel, according to the word of Yhwh by the hand of Samuel. **4** And David goes, and all Israel, to Jerusalem—it [is] Jebus—and the Jebusite [is] there, the inhabitants of the land. **5** And the inhabitants of Jebus say to David, "You do not come in here"; and David captures the fortress of Zion—it [is] the City of David. **6** And David says, "Whoever strikes the Jebusite first becomes head and prince"; and Joab son of Zeruiah goes up first and becomes head. **7** And David dwells in the fortress, therefore they have called it the City of David; **8** and he builds the city all around, from Millo, and to the circumference, and Joab restores the rest of the city. **9** And David goes, going on and becoming great, and Yhwh of Hosts [is] with him. **10** And these [are] heads of the mighty ones whom David has, who are strengthening themselves with him in his kingdom, with all Israel, to cause him to reign, according to the word of Yhwh, over Israel. **11** And this [is] an account of the mighty ones whom David has: Jashobeam son of a Hachmonite [is] head of the thirty, he is lifting up his spear against three hundred—wounded, at one time. **12** And after him [is] Eleazar son of Dodo the Ahohite, he [is] among the three mighty; **13** he has been with David in Pas-Dammim, and the Philistines have been gathered there to battle, and a portion of the field is full of barley, and the people have fled from the face of the Philistines, **14** and they station themselves in the midst of the portion, and deliver it, and strike the Philistines, and Yhwh saves [with] a great salvation. **15** And three of the thirty heads go down on the rock to David, to the cave of Adullam, and the host of the Philistines is encamping in the Valley of Rephaim, **16** and David [is] then in the fortress, and the station of the Philistines [is] then in Beth-Lehem, **17** and David longs and says, "Who gives me water to drink from the well of Beth-Lehem that [is] at the gate!" **18** And the three break through the camp of the Philistines, and draw water from the well of Beth-Lehem that [is] at the gate, and carry and bring [it] to David, and David has not been willing to drink it, and pours it out to Yhwh, **19** and says, "Far be it from me, by my God, to do this; do I drink the blood of these men with their lives? for with their lives they have brought it"; and he was not willing to drink it; these [things] the three mighty ones did. **20** And Abishai brother of Joab, he has been head of the three: and he is lifting up his spear against three hundred—wounded, and has a name among three. **21** Of the three he is more honored than the [other] two, and becomes their head; but he has not come to

the [first] three. **22** Benaiah son of Jehoiada, son of a man of valor, of great deeds, from Kabzeel: he has struck the two lion-like Moabites, and he has gone down and struck the lion in the midst of the pit, in the day of snow. **23** And he has struck the man, the Egyptian, a man of [great] measure—five by the cubit—and in the hand of the Egyptian [is] a spear like a weavers' beam, and he goes down to him with a rod, and violently takes away the spear out of the hand of the Egyptian, and slays him with his own spear. **24** These [things] Benaiah son of Jehoiada has done, and has a name among the three mighty ones. **25** Of the thirty, behold, he [is] honored, but he has not come to the [first] three, and David sets him over his guard. **26** And the mighty ones of the forces [are] Asahel brother of Joab, Elhanan son of Dodo of Beth-Lehem, **27** Shammoth the Harorite, Helez the Pelonite, **28** Ira son of Ikkesh the Tekoite, Abi-Ezer the Annethothite, **29** Sibbecai the Hushathite, Ilai the Ahohite, **30** Maharai the Netophathite, Heled son of Baanah the Netophathite, **31** Ithai son of Ribai of Gibeah, of the sons of Benjamin, Benaiah the Pirathonite, **32** Hurai of the brooks of Gaash, Abiel the Arbathite, **33** Azmaveth the Baharumite, Eliahba the Shaalbonite, **34** the sons of Hashem the Gizonite, Jonathan son of Shage the Hararite, **35** Ahiam son of Sacar the Hararite, Eliphal son of Ur, **36** Hepher the Mecherathite, Ahijah the Pelonite, **37** Hezor the Carmelite, Naarai son of Ezbai, **38** Joel brother of Nathan, Mibhar son of Haggeri, **39** Zelek the Ammonite, Naharai the Berothite, bearer of the weapons of Joab son of Zeruiah, **40** Ira the Ithrite, Gareb the Ithrite, **41** Uriah the Hittite, Zabad son of Ahlai, **42** Adina son of Shiza the Reubenite, head of the Reubenites, and thirty by him, **43** Hanan son of Maachah, and Joshaphat the Mithnite, **44** Uzzia the Ashterathite, Shama and Jehiel sons of Hothan the Aroerite, **45** Jediael son of Shimri, and his brother Joha the Tizite, **46** Eliel the Mahavite, and Jeribai, and Joshaviah, sons of Elnaam, and Ithmah the Moabite, **47** Eliel, and Obed, and Jaasiel the Mesobaite.

CHAPTER 12

1 And these [are] those coming to David at Ziklag, while shut up because of Saul son of Kish, and they [are] among the mighty ones, helping the battle, **2** armed with bow, right and left handed, with stones, and with arrows, with bows, of the brothers of Saul, of Benjamin. **3** The head [is] Ahiezer, and Joash, sons of Shemaab the Gibeathite, and Jeziel, and Pelet, sons of Azmaveth, and Berachah, and Jehu the Antothite, **4** and Ishmaiah the Gibeonite, a mighty one among the thirty, and over the thirty, and Jeremiah, and Jahaziel, and Johanan, and Josabad the Gederathite. **5** Eluzai, and Jerimoth, and Bealiah, and Shemariah, and Shephatiah the Haruphite; **6** Elkanah, and Jesiah, and Azareel, and Joezer, and Jashobeam the Korahites, **7** and Joelah, and Zebadiah, sons of Jeroham of Gedor. **8** And of the Gadite there have been separated to David, to the fortress, to the wilderness, mighty men of valor, men of the host for battle, setting in array buckler and spear, and their faces [are as] the face of the lion, and as roes on the mountains for speed: **9** Ezer the head, Obadiah the second, Eliab the third, **10** Mishmannah the fourth, Jeremiah the fifth, **11** Attai the sixth, Eliel the seventh, **12** Johanan the eighth, Elzabad the ninth, **13** Jeremiah the tenth, Machbannai the eleventh. **14** These [are] of the sons of Gad, heads of the host; the least [is] one of one hundred, and the greatest, of one thousand; **15** these [are] they who have passed over the Jordan in the first month—and it is full over all its banks—and cause all [those in] the valley to flee to the east and to the west. **16** And [some] from the sons of Benjamin and Judah came to David at the stronghold, **17** and David goes out before them, and answers and says to them, "If you have come to me for peace, to help me, I have a heart to unite with you; and if to betray me to my adversaries—without violence in my hands—the God of our fathers sees and reproves." **18** And the Spirit has clothed Amasai, head of the captains: "To you, O David, and with you, O son of Jesse—peace! Peace to you, and peace to your helper, for your God has helped you"; and David receives them, and puts them among the heads of the troop. **19** And [some] from Manasseh have defected to David in his coming with the Philistines against Israel to battle—and they did not help them, for by counsel the princes of the Philistines sent him away, saying, "He defects with our heads to his master Saul." **20** In his going to Ziglag there have fallen to him from Manasseh: Adnah, and Jozabad, and Jediael, and Michael, and Jozabad, and Elihu, and Zillthai, heads of the thousands who [are] of Manasseh; **21** and they have helped with David over the troop, for all of them [are] mighty men of valor, and they are captains in the host, **22** for at that time, day by day, they come to David to help him, until it is a great camp, like a camp of God. **23** And these [are] the numbers of the head, of the armed men of the host; they have come to David at Hebron to turn around the kingdom of Saul to him, according to the mouth of Yhwh. **24** The sons of Judah, carrying buckler and spear, [are] six thousand and eight hundred, armed ones of the host. **25** Of the sons of Simeon, mighty men of valor for the host, [are] seven thousand and one hundred. **26** Of the sons of Levi [are] four thousand and six hundred; **27** and Jehoiada [is] the leader of the Aaronite, and with him [are] three thousand and seven hundred, **28** and Zadok, a young man, a mighty man of valor, and of the house of his father [are] twenty-two heads. **29** And of the sons of Benjamin, brothers of Saul, [are] three thousand, and until now their greater part are keeping the charge of the house of Saul. **30** And of the sons of Ephraim [are] twenty thousand and eight hundred, mighty men of valor, men of renown, according to the house of their fathers. **31** And of the half of the tribe of Manasseh [are] eighteen thousand, who have been defined by name, to come to cause David to reign. **32** And of the sons of Issachar, having understanding for the times, to know what Israel should do; their heads [are] two hundred, and all their brothers [are] at their command. **33** Of Zebulun, going forth to the host, arranging battle with all instruments of battle, [are] fifty thousand, and keeping rank without a double heart. **34** And of Naphtali, one thousand heads, and with them, with buckler and spear, [are] thirty-seven thousand. **35** And of the Danite, arranging battle, [are] twenty-eight thousand and six hundred. **36** And of Asher, going forth to the host, to arrange battle, [are] forty thousand. **37** And from beyond the Jordan, of the Reubenite, and of the Gadite, and of the half of the tribe of Manasseh, with all instruments of the host for battle, [are] one hundred and twenty thousand. **38** All these [are] men of war, keeping rank—they have come to Hebron with a perfect heart, to cause David to reign over all Israel, and also all the rest of Israel [are] of one heart, to cause David to reign, **39** and they are there, with David, three days, eating and drinking, for their brothers have prepared for them. **40** And also those near to them—to Issachar, and Zebulun, and Naphtali—are bringing in bread on donkeys, and on camels, and on mules, and on oxen—food of fine flour, fig-cakes and grape-cakes, and wine, and oil, and oxen, and sheep, in abundance, for joy [is] in Israel.

CHAPTER 13

1 And David consults with the heads of the thousands and of the hundreds, [and] with every leader, **2** and David says to all the assembly of Israel, "If it is good to you, and it has broken forth from our God Yhwh—we send to our brothers, those left in all the lands of Israel, and the priests and the Levites with them in the cities of their outskirts, and they are gathered to us, **3** and we bring around the Ark of our God to us, for we did not seek Him in the days of Saul." **4** And all the assembly says to do so, for the thing is right in the eyes of all the people. **5** And David assembles all Israel from Shihor of Egypt even to the entering in of Hamath, to bring in the Ark of God from Kirjath-Jearim, **6** and David goes up, and all Israel, to Ba'alah, to Kirjath-Jearim that [belongs] to Judah, to bring up from there the Ark of God, Yhwh, inhabiting the cherubim, where the Name is called on. **7** And they place the Ark of God on a new cart from the house of Abinadab, and Uzza and Ahio are leading the cart, **8** and David and all Israel are playing before God, with all strength, and with songs, and with harps, and with psalteries, and with timbrels, and with cymbals, and with trumpets. **9** And they come to the threshing-floor of Chidon, and Uzza puts forth his hand to seize the Ark, for the oxen were released, **10** and the anger of Yhwh is kindled against Uzza, and He strikes him, because that he has put forth his hand on the Ark, and he dies there before God. **11** And it is displeasing to David, because Yhwh has made a breach on Uzza, and one calls that place "Breach of Uzza" to this day. **12** And David fears God on that day, saying, "How do I bring the Ark of God to me?" **13** And David has not turned aside the Ark to himself, to the City of David, and turns it aside to the house of Obed-Edom the Gittite. **14** And the Ark of God dwells with the household of Obed-Edom, in his house, three months, and Yhwh blesses the house of Obed-Edom, and all that he has.

CHAPTER 14

1 And Huram king of Tyre sends messengers to David, and cedar-wood, and craftsmen of walls, and craftsmen of wood, to build a house for him. **2** And David knows that Yhwh has established him for king over Israel, because of the lifting up on high of his kingdom, for the sake of His people Israel. **3** And David takes wives again in Jerusalem, and David begets sons and daughters again; **4** and these [are] the names of the children whom he has in Jerusalem: Shammua, and Shobab, Nathan, and Solomon, **5** and Ibhar, and Elishua, and Elpalet, **6** and Nogah, and Nepheg, and Japhia, **7** and Elishama, and Beeliada, and Eliphalet. **8** And the Philistines hear that David has been anointed for king over all Israel, and all the Philistines go up to seek David, and David hears, and goes out before them. **9** And the Philistines have come, and rush into the Valley of Rephaim, **10** and David asks of God, saying, "Do I go up against the Philistines—and have You given them into my hand?" And Yhwh says to him, "Go up, and I have given them into your hand." **11** And they go up into Ba'al-Perazim, and David strikes them there, and David says, "God has broken up my enemies by my hand, like the breaking up of waters"; therefore they have called the name of that place Ba'al-Perazim. **12** And they leave their gods there, and David commands, and they are burned with fire. **13** And the Philistines add again, and rush into the valley, **14** and David asks again of God, and God says to him, "Do not go up after them, turn around from them, and you have come to them from the front [[*or* in front]] of the mulberries; **15** and it comes to pass, when you hear the sound of the stepping at the heads of the mulberries, then you go out into battle, for God has gone out before you to strike the camp of the Philistines." **16** And David does as God commanded him, and they strike the camp of the Philistines from Gibeon even to Gazer; **17** and the name of David goes out into all the lands, and Yhwh has put his fear on all the nations.

CHAPTER 15

1 And he makes houses for himself in the City of David, and prepares a place for the Ark of God, and stretches out a tent for it. **2** Then David said, "None [are] to carry the Ark of God, except the Levites, for Yhwh has fixed on them to carry the Ark of God and to serve Him for all time." **3** And David assembles all Israel to Jerusalem, to bring up the Ark of Yhwh to its place that he had prepared for it. **4** And David gathers the sons of Aaron and the Levites— **5** of sons of Kohath: Uriel the chief and one hundred and twenty of his brothers; **6** of sons of Merari: Asaiah the chief and two hundred and twenty of his brothers; **7** of sons of Gershom: Joel the chief and one hundred and thirty of his brothers; **8** of sons of Elizaphan: Shemaiah the chief and two hundred of his brothers; **9** of sons of Hebron: Eliel the chief and eighty of his brothers; **10** of sons of Uzziel: Amminadab the chief and one hundred and twelve of his brothers. **11** And David calls to Zadok and to Abiathar the priests, and to the Levites, to Uriel, Asaiah, and Joel, Shemaiah, and Eliel, and Amminadab, **12** and says to them, "You [are] heads of the fathers of the Levites; sanctify yourselves, you and your brothers, and you have brought up the Ark of Yhwh, God of Israel, to [the place] I have prepared for it; **13** because you [did] not [do it] at the first, our God Yhwh made a breach on us, because we did not seek Him according to the ordinance." **14** And the priests and the Levites sanctify themselves to bring up the Ark of Yhwh, God of Israel; **15** and sons of the Levites carry the Ark of God, as Moses commanded, according to the word of Yhwh, above them with poles on their shoulder. **16** And David says to the heads of the Levites to appoint their brothers the singers, with instruments of song, psalteries, and harps, and cymbals, sounding, to lift up with the voice for joy. **17** And the Levites appoint Heman son of Joel, and of his brothers, Asaph son of Berechiah, and of the sons of Merari their brothers, Ethan son of Kushaiah; **18** and with them their brothers, the seconds [in rank]: Zechariah, Ben, and Jaaziel, and Shemiramoth, and Jehiel, and Unni, Eliab, and Benaiah, and Maaseiah, and Mattithiah, and Elipheleh, and Mikneiah; and Obed-Edom and Jeiel the gatekeepers; **19** and the singers, Heman, Asaph, and Ethan, [are] to sound with cymbals of bronze; **20** and Zechariah, and Aziel, and Shemiramoth, and Jeheil, and Unni, and Eliab, and Maaseiah, and Benaiah, with psalteries over the girls' [voices], **21** and Mattithiah, and Elipheleh, and Mikneiah, and Obed-Edom, and Jeiel, and Azaziah, to oversee with harps on the eighth. **22** And Chenaniah, head of the Levites, [is] over the burden; he instructs about the burden, for he [is] intelligent. **23** And Berechiah and Elkanah [are] gatekeepers for the Ark. **24** And Shebaniah, and Joshaphat, and Nethaneel, and Amasai, and Zechariah, and Benaiah, and Eliezer the priests, are blowing with trumpets before the Ark of God; and Obed-Edom and Jehiah [are] gatekeepers for the Ark. **25** And it is David, and [the] elderly of Israel, and the heads of the thousands, who are going to bring up the Ark of the Covenant of Yhwh from the house of Obed-Edom with joy; **26** and it comes to pass, in God's helping the Levites carrying the Ark of the Covenant of Yhwh, that they sacrifice seven bullocks and seven rams. **27** And David is wrapped in an upper robe of fine linen, and all the Levites who are carrying the Ark, and the singers, and Chenaniah head of the burden of the singers; and an Ephod of linen [is] on David. **28** And all of Israel is bringing up the Ark of the Covenant of Yhwh with shouting, and with the sound of a horn, and with trumpets, and with cymbals, sounding with psalteries and harps, **29** and it comes to pass, the Ark of the Covenant of Yhwh is entering into the City of David, and Michal daughter of Saul is looking through the window, and sees King David dancing and playing, and despises him in her heart.

CHAPTER 16

1 And they bring in the Ark of God, and set it up in the midst of the tent that David has stretched out for it, and they bring burnt-offerings and peace-offerings near before God; **2** and David ceases from offering the burnt-offering and the peace-offerings, and blesses the people in the Name of Yhwh, **3** and gives a portion to every man of Israel, both man and woman: to each a cake of bread, and a measure of wine, and a grape-cake. **4** And he puts before the Ark of Yhwh, those ministering from the Levites, even to make mention of, and to thank, and to give praise to Yhwh, God of Israel: **5** Asaph the head, and his second Zechariah; Jeiel, and Shemiramoth, and Jehiel, and Mattithiah, and Eliab, and Benaiah, and Obed-Edom, and Jeiel, with instruments of psalteries, and with harps; and Asaph is sounding with cymbals; **6** and Benaiah and Jahaziel the priests [are] continually [sounding] with trumpets before the Ark of the Covenant of God. **7** On that day, at that time, David has given at the beginning to give thanks to Yhwh by the hand of Asaph and his brothers: **8** "Give thanks to Yhwh, call on His Name, || Make His doings known among the peoples. **9** Sing to Him, sing psalms to Him, || Meditate on all His wonders. **10** Boast yourselves in His Holy Name, || The heart of those seeking Yhwh rejoices. **11** Seek Yhwh and His strength, || Seek His face continually. **12** Remember His wonders that He did, || His signs, and the judgments of His mouth, **13** O seed of Israel, His servant, || O sons of Jacob, His chosen ones! **14** He [is] our God Yhwh, || His judgments [are] in all the earth. **15** Remember His covenant for all time, || The word He commanded—To one thousand generations, **16** Which He has made with Abraham, || And His oath—to Isaac, **17** And He establishes it to Jacob for a statute, || To Israel [for] a perpetual covenant, **18** Saying, To you I give the land of Canaan, || The portion of your inheritance, **19** When you were few in number, || As a little thing, and sojourners in it. **20** And they go up and down, || From nation to nation, || And from a kingdom to another people. **21** He has not permitted any to oppress them, || And reproves kings on their account: **22** Do not come against My anointed ones, || And do no evil against My prophets. **23** Sing to Yhwh, all the earth, || Proclaim His salvation from day to day. **24** Recount His glory among nations, || His wonders among all the peoples. **25** For great [is] Yhwh, and greatly praised, || And He [is] fearful above all gods. **26** For all gods of the peoples [are] nothing, || And Yhwh has made the heavens. **27** Splendor and majesty [are] before Him, || Strength and joy [are] in His place. **28** Ascribe to Yhwh, you families of peoples, || Ascribe to Yhwh glory and strength. **29** Ascribe to Yhwh the glory of His Name, || Lift up a present, and come before Him. Bow yourselves to Yhwh, || In the beauty of holiness. **30** Be pained before Him, all the earth; Also, the world is established, || It is not moved! **31** The heavens rejoice, and the earth is glad, || And they say among nations, Yhwh has reigned! **32** The sea roars, and its fullness, || The field exults, and all that [is] in it, **33** Then trees of the forest sing, || From the presence of Yhwh, || For He has come to judge the earth! **34** Give thanks to Yhwh, for [He is] good, || For His kindness [is] for all time, **35** And say, Save us, O God of our salvation, || And gather us, and deliver us from the nations, || To give thanks to Your Holy Name, || To triumph in Your praise. **36** Blessed [is] Yhwh, God of Israel, || From age to age"; And all the people say, "Amen," and have given praise to Yhwh. **37** And he leaves there [those] of Asaph and of his brothers, before the Ark of the Covenant of Yhwh, to minister before the Ark continually, according to the matter of a day in its day; **38** both Obed-Edom and their sixty-eight brothers, and Obed-Edom son of Jeduthun, and Hosah, for gatekeepers; **39** and Zadok the priest, and his brothers the priests, before the Dwelling Place of Yhwh, in a high place that [is] in Gibeon, **40** to cause burnt-offerings to ascend continually to Yhwh on the altar of burnt-offering, morning and evening, and for all that is written in the Law of Yhwh that He charged on Israel. **41** And with them [are] Heman and Jeduthun, and the rest of those chosen, who were defined by name, to give thanks to Yhwh, for His kindness [is] for all time; **42** and with them—Heman and Jeduthun—[are] trumpets and cymbals for those sounding, and instruments of the song of God, and the sons of Jeduthun [are] at the gate. **43** And all the people go, each to his house, and David turns around to bless his house.

CHAPTER 17

1 And it comes to pass as David sat in his house, that David says to Nathan the prophet, "Behold, I am dwelling in a house of cedars, and the Ark of the Covenant of Yhwh [is] under curtains"; **2** and Nathan says to David, "All that [is] in your heart do, for God [is] with you." **3** And it comes to pass on that night that a word of God is to Nathan, saying, **4** "Go, and you have said to My servant David, Thus said Yhwh: You do not build for Me the house to dwell in. **5** For I have not dwelt in a house from the day that I brought up Israel until this day, and I am [going] from tent to tent, and from the Dwelling Place. **6** Wherever I have walked up and down among all Israel, have I spoken a word with one of [the] judges of Israel, whom I commanded to feed My people, saying, Why have you not built a house of cedars for Me? **7** And now, thus you say to My servant, to David, Thus said Yhwh of Hosts: I have taken you from the habitation, from after the sheep, to be leader over My people Israel, **8** and I am with you wherever you have walked, and I cut off all your enemies from your presence, and have made a name for you like the name of the great ones who [are] in the earth. **9** And I have prepared a place for My people Israel, and planted it, and it has dwelt in its place, and is not troubled anymore, and the sons of perverseness do not add to wear it out as at first, **10** indeed, even from the days that I appointed judges over My people Israel. And I have humbled all your enemies, and I declare to you that Yhwh builds a house for you. **11** And it has come to pass, when your days have been fulfilled to go with your fathers, that I have raised up your seed after you, who is of your sons, and I have established his kingdom; **12** he builds a house for Me, and I have established his throne for all time; **13** I am to him for a father, and he is to Me for a son, and I do not turn aside My kindness from him as I turned it aside from him who was before you, **14** and I have established him in My house, and in My kingdom for all time, and his throne is established for all time." **15** According to all these words, and according to all this vision, so spoke Nathan to David. **16** And David the king comes in and sits before Yhwh, and says, "Who [am] I, O Yhwh God, and what [is] my house, that You have brought me here? **17** And this is small in Your eyes, O God, and You speak concerning the house of Your servant far off, and have seen me as a type of the man who is on high, O Yhwh God! **18** What more does David add to You for the honor of Your servant; and You have known Your servant. **19** O Yhwh, for Your servant's sake, and according to Your own heart You have done all this greatness, to make known all these great things. **20** O Yhwh, there is none like You, and there is no god except You, according to all that we have heard with our ears. **21** And who [is] as Your people Israel, one nation in the earth whom God has gone to ransom to Himself for a people, to make a great and fearful name for Yourself, to cast out nations from the presence of Your people whom You have ransomed out of Egypt? **22** Indeed, You appoint Your people Israel to Yourself for a people for all time, and You, O Yhwh, have been to them for God. **23** And now, O Yhwh, let the word that You have spoken concerning Your servant, and concerning his house, be steadfast for all time, and do as You have spoken; **24** and let it be steadfast, and Your Name is great for all time, saying, Yhwh of Hosts, God of Israel, [is] God to Israel, and the house of Your servant David is established before You; 25 for You, O my God, have uncovered the ear of Your servant—to build a house for him, therefore Your servant has found [desire] to pray before You. 26 And now, Yhwh, You [are] God Himself, and You speak this goodness concerning Your servant; 27 and now, You have been pleased to bless the house of Your servant, to be before You for all time; for You, O Yhwh, have blessed, and it is blessed for all time."

CHAPTER 18

1 And it comes to pass after this, that David strikes the Philistines, and humbles them, and takes Gath and its small towns out of the hand of the Philistines; 2 and he strikes Moab, and the Moabites are servants to David, bringing a present. 3 And David strikes Hadarezer king of Zobah, at Hamath, in his going to establish his power by the Euphrates River, 4 and David captures from him one thousand chariots, and seven thousand horsemen, and twenty thousand footmen, and David utterly destroys all the chariots, and leaves of them [only] one hundred chariots. 5 And Aram of Damascus comes to give help to Hadarezer king of Zobah, and David strikes twenty-two thousand men in Aram, 6 and David puts [garrisons] in Aram of Damascus, and the Arameans are for servants to David, carrying a present, and Yhwh gives salvation to David wherever he has gone. 7 And David takes the shields of gold that have been on the servants of Hadarezer, and brings them to Jerusalem; 8 and from Tibhath, and from Chun, cities of Hadarezer, David has taken very much bronze; with it Solomon has made the bronze sea, and the pillars, and the vessels of bronze. 9 And Tou king of Hamath hears that David has struck the whole force of Hadarezer king of Zobah, 10 and he sends his son Hadoram to King David, to ask of him of peace, and to bless him, because that he has fought against Hadarezer and strikes him (for Hadarezer had been a man of wars with Tou); and [with him were] all kinds of vessels, of gold, and silver, and bronze; 11 King David has also sanctified them to Yhwh with the silver and the gold that he has taken from all the nations, from Edom, and from Moab, and from the sons of Ammon, and from the Philistines, and from Amalek. 12 And Abishai son of Zeruiah has struck Edom in the Valley of Salt—eighteen thousand, 13 and he puts garrisons in Edom, and all the Edomites are servants to David; and Yhwh saves David wherever he has gone. 14 And David reigns over all Israel, and he is doing judgment and righteousness to all his people, 15 and Joab son of Zeruiah [is] over the host, and Jehoshaphat son of Ahilud [is] remembrancer, 16 and Zadok son of Ahitub and Abimelech son of Abiathar [are] priests, and Shavsha [is] scribe, 17 and Benaiah son of Jehoiada [is] over the Cherethite and the Pelethite, and the chief sons of David [are] at the hand of the king.

CHAPTER 19

1 And it comes to pass after this, that Nahash king of the sons of Ammon dies, and his son reigns in his stead, 2 and David says, "I do kindness with Hanun son of Nahash, for his father did kindness with me"; and David sends messengers to comfort him concerning his father. And the servants of David come to the land of the sons of Ammon, to Hanun, to comfort him, 3 and the heads of the sons of Ammon say to Hanun, "Is David honoring your father in your eyes because he has sent comforters to you? Have his servants not come to you in order to search, and to overthrow, and to spy out the land?" 4 And Hanun takes the servants of David and shaves them, and cuts their long robes in the midst, to the buttocks, and sends them away. 5 And [some] go and declare to David concerning the men, and he sends to meet them—for the men have been greatly ashamed—and the king says, "Dwell in Jericho until your beard is grown, then you have returned." 6 And the sons of Ammon see that they have made themselves abhorred by David, and Hanun and the sons of Ammon send one thousand talents of silver, to hire for themselves, from Aram-Naharaim, and from Aram-Maachah, and from Zobah, chariots and horsemen; 7 and they hire for themselves thirty-two thousand chariots, and the king of Maachah and his people, and they come in and encamp before Medeba, and the sons of Ammon have been gathered out of their cities, and come to the battle.

8 And David hears, and sends Joab, and all the host of the mighty men, 9 and the sons of Ammon come out and set in array [for] battle at the opening of the city, and the kings who have come [are] by themselves in the field. 10 And Joab sees that the front of the battle has been to him, before and behind, and he chooses out of all the choice in Israel, and sets in array to meet Aram, 11 and he has given the remnant of the people into the hand of his brother Abishai, and they set in array to meet the sons of Ammon. 12 And he says, "If Aram is stronger than me, then you have been for salvation to me; and if the sons of Ammon are stronger than you, then I have saved you; 13 be strong, and we strengthen ourselves, for our people, and for the cities of our God, and Yhwh does that which is good in His eyes." 14 And Joab draws near, and the people who [are] with him, before Aram to battle, and they flee from his face; 15 and the sons of Ammon have seen that Aram has fled, and they flee—they also—from the face of his brother Abishai, and go into the city. And Joab comes to Jerusalem. 16 And Aram sees that they have been struck before Israel, and send messengers, and bring out Aram that [is] beyond the River, and Shophach head of the host of Hadarezer [is] before them. 17 And it is declared to David, and he gathers all Israel, and passes over the Jordan, and comes to them, and sets in array against them; indeed, David sets in array [for] battle to meet Aram, and they fight with him; 18 and Aram flees from the face of Israel, and David slays seven thousand charioteers and forty thousand footmen of Aram, and he has put Shophach head of the host to death. 19 And the servants of Hadarezer see that they have been struck before Israel, and they make peace with David and serve him, and Aram has not been willing to help the sons of Ammon anymore.

CHAPTER 20

1 And it comes to pass, at the time of the turn of the year—at the time of the going out of the messengers—that Joab leads out the force of the host, and destroys the land of the sons of Ammon, and comes in and besieges Rabbah—David is abiding in Jerusalem—and Joab strikes Rabbah, and breaks it down. 2 And David takes the crown of their king from off his head, and finds it [to be] a talent of gold [in] weight, and [with] precious stone in it, and it is on the head of David; and he has brought out very much spoil of the city, 3 and he has brought out the people who [are] in it, and sets [them] to the saw, and to cutting instruments of iron, and to axes; and thus David does to all cities of the sons of Ammon, and David turns back—and all the people—to Jerusalem. 4 And it comes to pass after this, that war remains in Gezer with the Philistines; then Sibbechai the Hushathite has struck Sippai, of the children of the giant, and they are humbled. 5 And there is war with the Philistines again, and Elhanan son of Jair strikes Lahmi, brother of Goliath the Gittite, the wood of whose spear [is] like a weavers' beam. 6 And there is war in Gath again, and there is a man of [great] measure, and his fingers and his toes [are] six and six—twenty-four [total], and he has also been born to the giant. 7 And he reproaches Israel, and Jonathan son of Shimea, brother of David, strikes him. 8 These were born to the giant in Gath, and they fall by the hand of David, and by the hand of his servants.

CHAPTER 21

1 Then Satan stands up against Israel, and persuades David to number Israel, 2 and David says to Joab and to the heads of the people, "Go, number Israel from Beer-Sheba even to Dan, and bring [the account] to me, and I know their number." 3 And Joab says, "Yhwh adds to His people as they are one hundred times; are they not, my lord, O king, all of them for servants to my lord? why does my lord seek this? why is he for a cause of guilt to Israel?" 4 And the word of the king [is] severe against Joab, and Joab goes out, and goes up and down in all Israel, and comes to Jerusalem. 5 And Joab gives the account of the numbering of the people to David, and all Israel is one million and one hundred thousand, each drawing sword, and Judah [is] four hundred and seventy thousand, each drawing sword. 6 And he has not numbered Levi and Benjamin in their midst, for the word of the king was abominable with Joab. 7 And it is evil in the eyes of God concerning this thing, and He strikes Israel, 8 and David says to God, "I have sinned

exceedingly in that I have done this thing; and now, please cause the iniquity of Your servant to pass away, for I have acted very foolishly." **9** And Yhwh speaks to Gad, seer of David, saying, **10** "Go, and you have spoken to David, saying, Thus said Yhwh: I am extending three [choices] to you; choose one of these for yourself, and I do [it] to you." **11** And Gad comes to David and says to him, "Thus said Yhwh: Take for yourself— **12** either famine for three years, or three months to be consumed from the face of your adversaries (even [for] the sword of your enemies to overtake), or three days of the sword of Yhwh (even pestilence in the land, and a messenger of Yhwh destroying in all the border of Israel); and now, see; what word do I return to Him who is sending me?" **13** And David says to Gad, "I am greatly distressed, please let me fall into the hand of Yhwh, for His mercies [are] very many, and do not let me fall into the hand of man." **14** And Yhwh gives a pestilence in Israel, and there falls from Israel seventy thousand men, **15** and God sends a messenger to Jerusalem to destroy it, and as he is destroying, Yhwh has seen, and is comforted concerning the calamity, and says to the messenger who [is] destroying, "Enough now, cease your hand." And the messenger of Yhwh is standing by the threshing-floor of Ornan the Jebusite, **16** and David lifts up his eyes, and sees the messenger of Yhwh standing between the earth and the heavens, and his sword [is] drawn in his hand, stretched out over Jerusalem, and David falls, and the elderly, covered with sackcloth, on their faces. **17** And David says to God, "Did I not command to number the people? Indeed, it [is] I who have sinned, and done great evil: and these, the flock, what did they do? O Yhwh, my God, please let Your hand be on me, and on the house of my father, and not on Your people—to be plagued." **18** And the messenger of Yhwh commanded to Gad to say to David, "Surely David goes up to raise an altar to Yhwh in the threshing-floor of Ornan the Jebusite." **19** And David goes up by the word of Gad, that he spoke in the Name of Yhwh. **20** And Ornan turns back and sees the messenger, and his four sons [are] with him hiding themselves, and Ornan is threshing wheat. **21** And David comes to Ornan, and Ornan looks attentively and sees David, and goes out from the threshing-floor, and bows himself to David— face to the earth. **22** And David says to Ornan, "Give the place of the threshing-floor to me, and I build an altar to Yhwh in it; give it to me for full price, and the plague is restrained from the people." **23** And Ornan says to David, "Take [it] to yourself, and my lord the king does that which is good in his eyes; see, I have given the oxen for burnt-offerings, and the threshing instruments for wood, and the wheat for a present; I have given the whole." **24** And King David says to Ornan, "No, for I surely buy [it] for full price; for I do not lift up that which is yours to Yhwh, so as to offer a burnt-offering without cost." **25** And David gives to Ornan six hundred shekels of gold [in] weight for the place; **26** and David builds an altar to Yhwh there, and offers burnt-offerings and peace-offerings, and calls to Yhwh, and He answers him from the heavens with fire on the altar of the burnt-offering. **27** And Yhwh speaks to the messenger, and he turns back his sword to its sheath. **28** At that time, when David sees that Yhwh has answered him in the threshing-floor of Ornan the Jebusite, then he sacrifices there; **29** and the Dwelling Place of Yhwh that Moses made in the wilderness, and the altar of the burnt-offering, [are] at that time at a high place in Gibeon; **30** and David is not able to go before it to seek God, for he has been afraid because of the sword of the messenger of Yhwh.

CHAPTER 22

1 And David says, "This is the house of Yhwh God, and this [is] the altar for burnt-offering for Israel." **2** And David says to gather the sojourners who [are] in the land of Israel, and appoints hewers to hew hewn-stones to build a house of God. **3** And David has prepared iron in abundance for nails for leaves of the gates and for couplings, and bronze in abundance—there is no weighing, **4** and cedar-trees without number, for the Zidonians and the Tyrians brought in cedar-trees in abundance to David. **5** And David says, "My son Solomon [is] a youth and tender, and the house to be built for Yhwh [is] to be made exceedingly great, for renown and for beauty to all the lands; now let me prepare for it"; and David prepares in abundance before his death. **6** And he calls for his son Solomon, and charges him to build a house for Yhwh, God of Israel, **7** and David says to his son Solomon, "As for me, it has been with my heart to build a house for the Name of my God Yhwh, **8** and

the word of Yhwh [is] against me, saying, You have shed blood in abundance, and you have made great wars; you do not build a house for My Name, for you have shed much blood to the earth before Me. **9** Behold, a son is born to you; he is a man of rest, and I have given rest to him from all his surrounding enemies, for Solomon is his name, and I give peace and quietness to Israel in his days; **10** he builds a house for My Name, and he is to Me for a son, and I [am] to him for a father, and I have established the throne of his kingdom over Israel for all time. **11** Now my son, Yhwh is with you, and you have prospered, and have built the house of your God Yhwh, as He spoke concerning you. **12** Only, may Yhwh give wisdom and understanding to you, and charge you concerning Israel, even to keep the Law of your God Yhwh; **13** then you prosper, if you observe to do the statutes and the judgments that Yhwh charged Moses with concerning Israel; be strong and courageous; do not fear, nor be cast down. **14** And behold, in my affliction I have prepared for the house of Yhwh one hundred thousand talents of gold, and one million talents of silver; and of bronze and of iron there is no weighing, for it has been in abundance; and I have prepared wood and stones, and you add to them. **15** And with you in abundance [are] workmen, hewers and craftsmen of stone and of wood, and every skillful man for every work. **16** Of the gold, of the silver, and of the bronze, and of the iron, there is no number; arise and do, and Yhwh is with you." **17** And David gives charge to all heads of Israel to give help to his son Solomon, [saying], **18** "Is your God Yhwh not with you? indeed, He has given rest to you all around, for He has given the inhabitants of the land into my hand, and the land has been subdued before His people. **19** Now give your heart and your soul to seek for your God Yhwh, and rise and build the sanctuary of Yhwh God, to bring in the Ark of the Covenant of Yhwh, and the holy vessels of God, to the house that is built for the Name of Yhwh."

CHAPTER 23

1 And David was old and satisfied with days, and he causes his son Solomon to reign over Israel, **2** and gathers all the heads of Israel, and the priests, and the Levites; **3** and the Levites are numbered from a son of thirty years and upward, and their number, for their counted heads, is of thirty-eight thousand mighty men. **4** Of these, twenty-four thousand [are] to preside over the work of the house of Yhwh, and six thousand officers and judges, **5** and four thousand gatekeepers, and four thousand giving praise to Yhwh, "with instruments that I made for praising," [says David.] **6** And David distributes them into divisions of the sons of Levi—of Gershon, Kohath, and Merari. **7** Of the Gershonite: Laadan and Shimei. **8** Sons of Laadan: the head [is] Jehiel, and Zetham, and Joel—three. **9** Sons of Shimei: Shelomith, and Haziel, and Haran—three; these [are] heads of the fathers of Laadan. **10** And sons of Shimei: Jahath, Zina, and Jeush, and Beriah; these [are] the four sons of Shimei. **11** And Jahath is the head, and Zizah the second, and Jeush and Beriah have not multiplied sons, and they become the house of a father by one numbering. **12** Sons of Kohath: Amram, Izhar, Hebron, and Uzziel—four. **13** Sons of Amram: Aaron and Moses; and Aaron is separated for his sanctifying the Holy of Holies, he and his sons, for all time, to make incense before Yhwh, to serve Him, and to bless in His Name for all time. **14** As for Moses, the man of God, his sons are called after the tribe of Levi. **15** Sons of Moses: Gershom and Eliezer. **16** Sons of Gershom: Shebuel the head. **17** And sons of Eliezer are Rehabiah the head, and Eliezer had no other sons, and the sons of Rehabiah have multiplied exceedingly. **18** Sons of Izhar: Shelomith the head. **19** Sons of Hebron: Jeriah the head, Amariah the second, Jahaziel the third, and Jekameam the fourth. **20** Sons of Uzziel: Micah the head, and Ishshiah the second. **21** Sons of Merari: Mahli and Mushi; sons of Mahli: Eleazar and Kish. **22** And Eleazar dies, and he had no sons, but daughters, and their brothers, sons of Kish, take them. **23** Sons of Mushi: Mahli, and Eder, and Jerimoth—three. **24** These [are] sons of Levi, by the house of their fathers, heads of the fathers, by their appointments, in the number of names, by their counted heads, doing the work for the service of the house of Yhwh, from a son of twenty years and upward, **25** for David said, "Yhwh, God of Israel, has given rest to His people, and He dwells in Jerusalem for all time"; **26** and also of the Levites, "None [are] to carry the Dwelling Place and all its vessels for its service"; **27** for by the last words of David they [took] the number of the sons of Levi from a son of twenty years and upward, **28** for their station [is] at the side of the sons of Aaron, for the service of the house of Yhwh, over the courts, and over the chambers, and over the cleansing of every holy thing, and the work of the service of the house of God, **29** and for the bread of the arrangement, and for fine flour for present, and for the thin unleavened cakes, and for [the work of] the pan, and for that which is stirred, and for all [liquid] measure and [solid] measure; **30** and to stand, morning by morning, to give thanks, and to give praise to Yhwh, and so at evening; **31** and for all the burnt-offerings—burnt-offerings to Yhwh for Sabbaths, for new moons, and for appointed times, by number, according to the ordinance on them continually, before Yhwh. **32** And they have kept the charge of the Tent of Meeting, and the charge of the holy place, and the charge of their brothers, the sons of Aaron, for the service of the house of Yhwh.

CHAPTER 24

1 And [these are] their divisions, of the sons of Aaron. [The] sons of Aaron [are] Nadab, and Abihu, Eleazar, and Ithamar. **2** And Nadab dies—and Abihu—in the presence of their father, and they had no sons, and Eleazar and Ithamar act as priests. **3** And David distributes them—and Zadok of the sons of Eleazar, and Ahimelech of the sons of Ithamar—according to their office in their service; **4** and there are found of the sons of Eleazar more for heads of the mighty men than of the sons of Ithamar; and they distribute them. Of the sons of Eleazar, heads for [each] house of [their] fathers—sixteen; and of the sons of Ithamar, for [each] house of their fathers—eight. **5** And they distribute them by lots, with one another, for they have been princes of the holy place and princes of God, from the sons of Eleazar and from the sons of Ithamar. **6** And Shemaiah son of Nethaneel the scribe, of the Levites, writes them before the king, and the princes, and Zadok the priest, and Ahimelech son of Abiathar, and heads of the fathers for priests and for Levites, one house of a father being taken possession of for Eleazar and one being taken possession of for Ithamar. **7** And the first lot goes out for Jehoiarib, for Jedaiah the second, **8** for Harim the third, for Seorim the fourth, **9** for Malchijah the fifth, for Mijamin the sixth, **10** for Hakkoz the seventh, for Abijah the eighth, **11** for Jeshuah the ninth, for Shecaniah the tenth, **12** for Eliashib the eleventh, for Jakim the twelfth, **13** for Huppah the thirteenth, for Jeshebeab the fourteenth, **14** for Bilgah the fifteenth, for Immer the sixteenth, **15** for Hezir the seventeenth, for Aphses the eighteenth, **16** for Pethahiah the nineteenth, for Jehezekel the twentieth, **17** for Jachin the twenty-first, for Gamul the twenty-second, **18** for Delaiah the twenty-third, for Maaziah the twenty-fourth. **19** These [are] their appointments for their service, to come into the house of Yhwh, according to their ordinance by the hand of their father Aaron, as Yhwh God of Israel commanded them. **20** And of the sons of Levi who are left—of sons of Amram: Shubael; of sons of Shubael: Jehdeiah. **21** Of Rehabiah, of sons of Rehabiah: the head Ishshiah. **22** Of the Izharite: Shelomoth; of sons of Shelomoth: Jahath. **23** And sons of Jeriah: Amariah the second, Jahaziel the third, Jekameam the fourth. **24** Sons of Uzziel: Michah; of sons of Michah: Shamir. **25** Ishshiah [is] a brother of Michah; of sons of Ishshiah: Zechariah; **26** sons of Merari: Mahli and Mushi; sons of Jaaziah: Beno; **27** sons of Merari, of Jaaziah: Beno, and Shoham, and Zaccur, and Ibri. **28** Of Mahli: Eleazar, who had no sons; **29** of Kish, sons of Kish: Jerahmeel. **30** And sons of Mushi [are] Mahli, and Eder, and Jerimoth; these [are] sons of the Levites, for the house of their fathers, **31** and they also cast lots just as their brothers, the sons of Aaron, before David the king, and Zadok, and Ahimelech, and heads of the fathers for priests and for Levites; the chief father just as his younger brother.

CHAPTER 25

1 And David and the heads of the host separate for service, of the sons of Asaph, and Heman, and Jeduthun, who are prophesying with harps, with psalteries, and with cymbals; and the number of the workmen is according to their service. **2** Of sons of Asaph: Zaccur, and Joseph, and Nethaniah, and Asharelah; sons of Asaph [are] by the side of Asaph, who is prophesying by the side of the king. **3** Of Jeduthun, sons of Jeduthun: Gedaliah, and Zeri, and Jeshaiah, [and Shimei, and]

Hashabiah, and Mattithiah, six, by the side of their father Jeduthun; he is prophesying with a harp, for giving of thanks and of praise for Yhwh. **4** Of Heman, sons of Heman: Bukkiah, Mattaniah, Uzziel, Shebuel, and Jerimoth, Hananiah, Hanani, Eliathah, Giddalti, and Romamti-Ezer, Joshbekashah, Mallothi, Hothir, Mahazioth; **5** all these [are] sons of Heman, seer of the king in the things of God, to lift up a horn; and God gives fourteen sons and three daughters to Heman. **6** All these [are] by the side of their father in the song of the house of Yhwh, with cymbals, psalteries, and harps, for the service of the house of God; by the side of the king [are] Asaph, and Jeduthun, and Heman. **7** And their number, with their brothers taught in the song of Yhwh—all who are intelligent—[is] two hundred and eighty-eight. **8** And they cause lots to fall, charge next to [charge], the small as well as the great, the intelligent with the learner. **9** And the first lot goes out for Asaph to Joseph; the second, Gedaliah—him, and his brothers and his sons—twelve; **10** the third, Zaccur, his sons and his brothers—twelve; **11** the fourth to Izri, his sons and his brothers—twelve; **12** the fifth, Nethaniah, his sons and his brothers—twelve; **13** the sixth, Bukkiah, his sons and his brothers—twelve; **14** the seventh, Jesharelah, his sons and his brothers—twelve; **15** the eighth, Jeshaiah, his sons and his brothers—twelve; **16** the ninth, Mattaniah, his sons and his brothers—twelve; **17** the tenth, Shimei, his sons and his brothers—twelve; **18** eleventh, Azareel, his sons and his brothers—twelve; **19** the twelfth to Hashabiah, his sons and his brothers—twelve; **20** for the thirteenth, Shubael, his sons and his brothers—twelve; **21** for the fourteenth, Mattithiah, his sons and his brothers—twelve; **22** for the fifteenth to Jeremoth, his sons and his brothers—twelve; **23** the sixteenth to Hananiah, his sons and his brothers—twelve; **24** the seventeenth to Joshbekashah, his sons and his brothers—twelve; **25** the eighteenth to Hanani, his sons and his brothers—twelve; **26** the nineteenth to Mallothi, his sons and his brothers—twelve; **27** the twentieth to Eliathah, his sons and his brothers—twelve; **28** the twenty-first to Hothir, his sons and his brothers—twelve; **29** the twenty-second to Giddalti, his sons and his brothers—twelve; **30** the twenty-third to Mahazioth, his sons and his brothers—twelve; **31** the twenty-fourth to Romamti-Ezer, his sons and his brothers—twelve.

CHAPTER 26

1 For the divisions of the gatekeepers, of the Korahites: Meshelemiah son of Kore, of the sons of Asaph; **2** and sons of Meshelemiah: Zechariah the firstborn, Jediael the second, Zebadiah the third, Jathniel the fourth, **3** Elam the fifth, Jehohanan the sixth, Elioenai the seventh. **4** And moreover, sons of Obed-Edom: Shemaiah the firstborn, Jehozabad the second, Joah the third, and Sacar the fourth, and Nethaneel the fifth, **5** Ammiel the sixth, Issachar the seventh, Peullethai the eighth, for God has blessed him. **6** And sons have been born to his son Shemaiah, who are ruling throughout the house of their father, for they [are] mighty men of valor. **7** Sons of Shemaiah: Othni, and Rephael, and Obed, [and] Elzabad; his brothers Elihu and Semachiah [are] sons of valor. **8** All these [are] of the sons of Obed-Edom; they, and their sons, and their brothers, men of valor with might for service—sixty-two of Obed-Edom. **9** And sons and brothers of Meshelemiah, sons of valor—eighteen; **10** and of Hosah, of the sons of Merari, [are these] sons: Shimri the head (though he was not firstborn, yet his father sets him for head), **11** Hilkiah the second, Tebaliah the third, Zechariah the fourth; all the sons and brothers of Hosah—thirteen. **12** For these [are] the divisions of the gatekeepers, of the heads of the mighty ones, [with] charges just as their brothers, to minister in the house of Yhwh, **13** and they cause lots to fall, the small as well as the great, according to the house of their fathers, for every gate. **14** And the lot falls eastward to Shelemiah; and [for] his son Zechariah, a counselor with understanding, they cause lots to fall, and his lot goes out northward; **15** to Obed-Edom southward, and to his sons, the house of the gatherings; **16** to Shuppim and to Hosah to the west, with Shallecheth Gate, in the highway, the ascent, watch next to watch; **17** to the east [are] six Levites, to the north [are] four each day, to the south [are] four each day, and for the gatherings, two by two; **18** at Parbar, to the west, [are] four at the highway, two at Parbar. **19** These are the divisions of the gatekeepers, of the sons of the Korahite, and of the sons of Merari. **20** And of the Levites, Ahijah [is] over the treasures of the house of God, even for the treasures of the holy things. **21** Sons of Laadan, sons of the Gershonite, of

Laadan, heads of the fathers of Laadan the Gershonite: Jehieli. **22** Sons of Jehieli: Zetham and his brother Joel, over the treasures of the house of Yhwh. **23** Of the Amramite, of the Izharite, of the Hebronite, of [the] Uzzielite— **24** and Shebuel son of Gershom, son of Moses, [is] president over the treasures. **25** And his brothers, of Eliezer: Rehabiah his son, and Jeshaiah his son, and Joram his son, and Zichri his son, and Shelomith his son. **26** This Shelomith and his brothers [are] over all the treasures of the holy things that David the king, and heads of the fathers, even heads of thousands, and of hundreds, and heads of the host, sanctified; **27** from the battles and from the spoil, they sanctified to strengthen the house of Yhwh; **28** and all that Samuel the seer, and Saul son of Kish, and Abner son of Ner, and Joab son of Zeruiah sanctified, everyone sanctifying [anything—it is] by the side of Shelomith and his brothers. **29** Of the Izharite, Chenaniah and his sons [are] for the outward work over Israel, for officers and for judges. **30** Of the Hebronite, Hashabiah and his brothers, one thousand and seven hundred sons of valor, [are] over the inspection of Israel, beyond the Jordan westward, for all the work of Yhwh, and for the service of the king. **31** Of the Hebronite, Jerijah [is] the head of the Hebronite, according to the generations of his fathers. In the fortieth year of the reign of David they have been sought out, and there are found among them mighty men of valor, in Jazer of Gilead— **32** and his brothers, two thousand and seven hundred sons of valor, [are] heads of the fathers, and King David appoints them over the Reubenite, and the Gadite, and the half of the tribe of the Manassite, for every matter of God and matter of the king.

CHAPTER 27

1 And the sons of Israel, after their number, heads of the fathers, and princes of the thousands and of the hundreds, and their officers, those serving the king in any matter of the divisions, that are coming in and going out month by month throughout all months of the year, [are] twenty-four thousand in each division. **2** Over the first division for the first month [is] Jashobeam son of Zabdiel, and twenty-four thousand [are] on his division; **3** [he was] of the sons of Perez, [and] the head of all princes of the hosts for the first month. **4** And over the division of the second month [is] Dodai the Ahohite, and Mikloth [is] also president of his division, and twenty-four thousand [are] on his division. **5** Head of the third host, for the third month, [is] Benaiah son of Jehoiada, the head priest, and twenty-four thousand [are] on his division. **6** This Benaiah [is] a mighty one of the thirty, and over the thirty, and his son Ammizabad [is in] his division. **7** The fourth, for the fourth month, [is] Asahel brother of Joab, and his son Zebadiah after him, and twenty-four thousand [are] on his division. **8** The fifth, for the fifth month, [is] the prince Shamhuth the Izrahite, and twenty-four thousand [are] on his division. **9** The sixth, for the sixth month, [is] Ira son of Ikkesh the Tekoite, and twenty-four thousand [are] on his division. **10** The seventh, for the seventh month, [is] Helez the Pelonite, of the sons of Ephraim, and twenty-four thousand [are] on his division. **11** The eighth, for the eighth month, [is] Sibbecai the Hushathite, of the Zerahite, and twenty-four thousand [are] on his division. **12** The ninth, for the ninth month, [is] Abiezer the Antothite, of the Benjamite, and twenty-four thousand [are] on his division. **13** The tenth, for the tenth month, [is] Maharai the Netophathite, of the Zerahite, and twenty-four thousand [are] on his division. **14** Eleventh, for the eleventh month, [is] Benaiah the Pirathonite, of the sons of Ephraim, and twenty-four thousand [are] on his division. **15** The twelfth, for the twelfth month, [is] Heldai the Netophathite, of Othniel, and twenty-four thousand [are] on his division. **16** And over the tribes of Israel: the leader of the Reubenite [is] Eliezer son of Zichri; of the Simeonite, Shephatiah son of Maachah; **17** of the Levite, Hashabiah son of Kemuel; of the Aaronite, Zadok; **18** of Judah, Elihu, of the brothers of David; of Issachar, Omri son of Michael; **19** of Zebulun, Ishmaiah son of Obadiah; of Naphtali, Jerimoth son of Azriel; **20** of the sons of Ephraim, Hoshea son of Azaziah; of the half of the tribe of Manasseh, Joel son of Pedaiah; **21** of the half of Manasseh in Gilead, Iddo son of Zechariah; of Benjamin, Jaasiel son of Abner; of Dan, Azareel son of Jeroham. **22** These [are the] heads of the tribes of Israel. **23** But David has not taken up their number from a son of twenty years and under, for Yhwh had said [He would] multiply Israel as the stars of the heavens. **24** Joab son of Zeruiah has begun to number, but has not finished; and there is wrath against Israel for this, and the

number has not gone up in the account of the Chronicles of King David. **25** And Azmaveth son of Adiel [is] over the treasures of the king; and Jonathan son of Uzziah [is] over the treasures in the field, in the cities, and in the villages, and in the towers; **26** and Ezri son of Chelub [is] over workmen of the field for the service of the ground; **27** and Shimei the Ramathite [is] over the vineyards; and Zabdi the Shiphmite [is] over what [is] in the vineyards for the treasures of wine; **28** and Ba'al-Hanan the Gederite [is] over the olives and the sycamores that [are] in the low country; and Joash [is] over the treasures of oil; **29** and Shitrai the Sharonite [is] over the herds that are feeding in Sharon; and Shaphat son of Adlai [is] over the herds in the valleys; **30** and Obil the Ishmaelite [is] over the camels; and Jehdeiah the Meronothite [is] over the donkeys; **31** and Jaziz the Hagerite [is] over the flock; all these [are] heads of the substance that King David has. **32** And Jonathan, David's uncle, [is] counselor, a man of understanding, [and] he is also a scribe; and Jehiel son of Hachmoni [is] with the sons of the king; **33** and Ahithophel [is] counselor to the king; and Hushai the Archite [is] the friend of the king; **34** and after Ahithophel [is] Jehoiada son of Benaiah, and Abiathar; and the head of the host of the king [is] Joab.

CHAPTER 28

1 And David assembles all the heads of Israel, heads of the tribes, and heads of the divisions who are serving the king, and heads of the thousands, and heads of the hundreds, and heads of all the substance and possessions of the king, and of his sons, with the officers and the mighty ones, and of every mighty man of valor—to Jerusalem. **2** And David the king rises on his feet and says, "Hear me, my brothers and my people, I [had it] with my heart to build a house of rest for the Ark of the Covenant of Yhwh, and for the footstool of our God, and I prepared to build, **3** and God has said to me, You do not build a house for My Name, for you [are] a man of wars, and you have shed blood. **4** And Yhwh, God of Israel, fixes on me out of all the house of my father to be for king over Israel for all time, for He has fixed on Judah for a leader, and in the house of Judah, the house of my father, and among the sons of my father, He has been pleased with me to make [me] king over all Israel; **5** and out of all my sons—for Yhwh has given many sons to me—He also fixes on my son Solomon, to sit on the throne of the kingdom of Yhwh over Israel, **6** and says to me, Your son Solomon builds My house and My courts, for I have fixed on him [to be] to Me for a son, and I am to him for a father. **7** And I have established his kingdom for all time, if he is strong to do My commands and My judgments, as at this day. **8** And now, before the eyes of all Israel, the assembly of Yhwh, and in the ears of our God, keep and seek all the commands of your God Yhwh, so that you possess this good land, and have caused your sons to inherit after you for all time. **9** And you, my son Solomon, know the God of your father, and serve Him with a perfect heart and with a willing mind, for Yhwh is seeking all hearts, and He is understanding every imagination of the thoughts; if you seek Him, He is found by you, and if you forsake Him, He casts you off forever. **10** See, now, for Yhwh has fixed on you to build a house for a sanctuary; be strong, and do." **11** And David gives to his son Solomon the pattern of the porch, and of its houses, and of its treasures, and of its upper chambers, and of its innermost chambers, and of the house of the atonement; **12** and the pattern of all that has been with him by the Spirit, for the courts of the house of Yhwh, and for all the surrounding chambers, for the treasures of the house of God, and for the treasures of the things sacrificed; **13** and for the divisions of the priests and of the Levites, and for all the work of the service of the house of Yhwh, and for all vessels of service of the house of Yhwh, **14** even gold by weight, for [things of] gold, for all instruments of every service; for all instruments of silver by weight, for all instruments of every service; **15** and [by] weight for the lampstands of gold, and their lamps of gold, by weight [for] lampstand and lampstand, and its lamps; and for the lampstands of silver, by weight for a lampstand and its lamps, according to the service of lampstand and lampstand; **16** and the gold [by] weight for tables of the arrangement, for table and table, and silver for the tables of silver; **17** and the forks, and the bowls, and the cups of pure gold, and for the basins of gold, by weight for basin and basin, and for the basins of silver, by weight for basin and basin, **18** and for the altar of incense, refined gold by weight, and for the pattern of the chariot of the cherubim of gold, spreading and covering over the Ark of the Covenant of Yhwh. **19** The whole [is] in writing from the hand of Yhwh, "He caused me to understand all the work of the pattern," [said David.] **20** And David says to his son Solomon, "Be strong and courageous, and do; do not fear nor be frightened, for Yhwh God, my God, [is] with you; He does not fail you, nor forsake you, to the completion of all the work of the service of the house of Yhwh. **21** And behold, divisions of the priests and of the Levites [are] for all the service of the house of God; and with you in all work [is] every willing one with wisdom, for every service; and the heads and all the people [are] according to all your words."

CHAPTER 29

1 And David the king says to all the assembly, "My son Solomon—the one on whom God has fixed—[is] young and tender, and the work [is] great, for the palace is not for man, but for Yhwh God; **2** and with all my power I have prepared for the house of my God, the gold for [things of] gold, and the silver for [things of] silver, and the bronze for [things of] bronze, the iron for [things of] iron, and the wood for [things of] wood, shoham stones, and settings, and stones of painting and of diverse colors, and all [kinds of] precious stone, and stones of white marble, in abundance. **3** And again, because of my delighting in the house of my God, the substance I have— a peculiar treasure of gold and silver—I have given for the house of my God, even over and above all I have prepared for the holy house: **4** three thousand talents of gold, of the gold of Ophir, and seven thousand talents of refined silver, to overlay the walls of the houses, **5** even gold for [things of] gold, and silver for [things of] silver, and for all the work by the hand of craftsmen; and who [is] he that is offering to willingly consecrate his hand to Yhwh today?" **6** And the heads of the fathers, and the heads of the tribes of Israel, and the heads of the thousands, and of the hundreds, and of the heads of the work of the king, offer willingly. **7** And they give for the service of the house of God five thousand talents and ten thousand drams of gold, and ten thousand talents of silver, and eighteen thousand talents of bronze, and one hundred thousand talents of iron; **8** and he with whom stones are found has given [them] to the treasury of the house of Yhwh, by the hand of Jehiel the Gershonite. **9** And the people rejoice because of their offering willingly, for with a perfect heart they have offered willingly to Yhwh; and David the king has also rejoiced [with] great joy. **10** And David blesses Yhwh before the eyes of all the assembly, and David says, "Blessed [are] You, Yhwh, God of Israel, our Father, from age even to age. **11** To You, O Yhwh, [is] the greatness, and the might, and the beauty, and the victory, and the splendor, because of all in the heavens and in the earth; to You, O Yhwh, [is] the kingdom, and He who is lifting up Himself over all for head; **12** and the riches, and the honor [are] from before You, and You are ruling over all, and in Your hand [is] power and might, and [it is] in Your hand to make great and to give strength to all. **13** And now, our God, we are giving thanks to You, and giving praise to Your beautiful Name; **14** indeed, because who [am] I, and who [are] my people, that we retain power to offer thus willingly? but the whole [is] from You, and we have given to You out of Your [own] hand. **15** for we [are] sojourners and settlers before You, like all our fathers; our days on the land [are] as a shadow, and there is none abiding. **16** O our God Yhwh, all this store [with] which we have prepared to build a house for You, for Your Holy Name, [is] out of Your [own] hand, and the whole [is] of You. **17** And I have known, my God, that You are trying the heart, and desire uprightness; I, in the uprightness of my heart, have willingly offered all these; and now, I have seen Your people who are found here with joy to offer willingly to You. **18** O Yhwh, God of Abraham, Isaac, and Israel, our fathers, keep this for all time for the imagination of the thoughts of the heart of Your people, and prepare their heart for You; **19** and give a perfect heart to my son Solomon, to keep Your commands, Your testimonies, and Your statutes, and to do the whole, even to build the palace [for] which I have prepared." **20** And David says to all the assembly, "Now bless your God Yhwh"; and all the assembly blesses Yhwh, God of their fathers, and bows and pays respect to Yhwh and to the king. **21** And they sacrifice sacrifices to Yhwh, and cause burnt-offerings to ascend to Yhwh on that next day: one thousand bullocks, one thousand rams, one thousand lambs, and their oblations, and sacrifices in abundance for all Israel. **22** And they eat and drink before Yhwh on that day with great joy, and cause Solomon son of David to reign a second time, and anoint [him] before Yhwh for leader, and Zadok for priest. **23** And Solomon sits on the throne of Yhwh for king instead of his father David, and prospers, and all of Israel listens to him, **24** and all the heads, and the mighty men, and also all the sons of King David have given a hand under Solomon the king; **25** and Yhwh makes Solomon exceedingly great before the eyes of all Israel, and puts on him the splendor of the kingdom that has not been on any king over Israel before him. **26** And David son of Jesse has reigned over all Israel, **27** and the days that he has reigned over Israel [are] forty years; he reigned in Hebron seven years, and he reigned in Jerusalem thirty-three; **28** and he dies in a good old age, satisfied with days, riches, and honor, and his son Solomon reigns in his stead. **29** And the matters of David the king, the first and the last, behold, they are written beside the matters of Samuel the seer, and beside the matters of Nathan the prophet, and beside the matters of Gad the seer, **30** with all his reign, and his might, and the times that went over him, and over Israel, and over all kingdoms of the lands.

2 CHRONICLES

CHAPTER 1

1 And Solomon son of David strengthens himself over his kingdom, and his God Yhwh [is] with him, and makes him exceedingly great. **2** And Solomon says to all Israel, to heads of the thousands, and of the hundreds, and to the ones judging, and to every honorable one of all Israel, heads of the fathers, **3** and they go—Solomon, and all the assembly with him—to the high place that [is] in Gibeon, for God's Tent of Meeting has been there, that Moses, servant of Yhwh, made in the wilderness, **4** but David had the Ark of God brought up from Kirjath-Jearim to the [place] David had prepared for it, for he stretched out a tent for it in Jerusalem; **5** and the altar of bronze that Bezaleel son of Uri, son of Hur made, he put before the Dwelling Place of Yhwh; and Solomon and the assembly seek Him [there]. **6** And Solomon goes up there, on the altar of bronze, before Yhwh, that [is] at the Tent of Meeting, and causes one thousand burnt-offerings to ascend on it. **7** In that night God has appeared to Solomon and says to him, "Ask— what do I give to you?" **8** And Solomon says to God, "You have done great kindness with my father David, and have caused me to reign in his stead. **9** Now, O Yhwh God, Your word with my father David is steadfast, for You have caused me to reign over a people [as] numerous as the dust of the earth; **10** now, give wisdom and knowledge to me, and I go out before this people, and I come in, for who judges this—Your great people?" **11** And God says to Solomon, "Because that this has been with your heart, and you have not asked for riches, wealth, and honor, and the life of those hating you, and also have not asked for many days, and ask for wisdom and knowledge for yourself, so that you judge My people over which I have caused you to reign— **12** the wisdom and the knowledge is given to you, and riches and wealth and honor I [also] give to you, that there has not been so to the kings who [are] before you, and after you it is not so." **13** And Solomon comes in to Jerusalem [from] the high place that [is] in Gibeon, from before the Tent of Meeting, and reigns over Israel, **14** and Solomon gathers chariots and horsemen, and he has one thousand and four hundred chariots, and twelve thousand horsemen, and he places them in the cities of the chariots, and with the king in Jerusalem. **15** And the king makes the silver and the gold in Jerusalem as stones, and the cedars he made as sycamores that [are] in the low country, for abundance. **16** And the source of the horses that [are] for Solomon [is] from Egypt and from Keva; merchants of the king take [them] from Keva at a price, **17** and they come up, and bring out a chariot from Egypt for six hundred pieces of silver, and a horse for one hundred and fifty, and so for all the kings of the Hittites and the kings of Aram—they bring [them] out by their hand.

CHAPTER 2

1 And Solomon says to build a house for the Name of Yhwh, and a house for his kingdom, **2** and Solomon numbers seventy thousand men bearing burden, and eighty thousand men hewing in the mountain, and three thousand and six hundred overseers over them. **3** And Solomon sends to Huram king of Tyre, saying, "When you have dealt with my father David, then you send cedars to him to build a house for him to dwell in; **4** behold, I am building a house for the Name of my God Yhwh, to sanctify [it] to Him, to make incense before Him, incense of spices, and a continual arrangement, and burnt-offerings at morning and at evening, at Sabbaths, and at new moons, and at appointed times of our God Yhwh; this [is] on Israel for all time. **5** And the house that I am building [is] great, for our God [is] greater than all gods; **6** and who retains strength to build a house for Him, since the heavens, even the heavens of the heavens, do not contain Him? and who [am] I that I build a house for Him, except to make incense before Him? **7** And now, send a wise man to me to work in gold, and in silver, and in bronze, and in iron, and in purple, and crimson, and blue, and knowing to engrave engravings with the wise men who [are] with me in Judah and in Jerusalem, whom my father David prepared; **8** and send to me cedar-trees, firs, and algums from Lebanon, for I have known that your servants know to cut down trees of Lebanon, and behold, my servants [are] with your servants, **9** even to prepare trees in abundance for me, for the house that I am building [is] great and wonderful. **10** And behold, I have given to your servants, to hewers, to those cutting the trees, twenty thousand cors of beaten wheat, and twenty thousand cors of barley, and twenty thousand baths of wine, and twenty thousand baths of oil." **11** And Huram king of Tyre answers in writing, and sends [it] to Solomon: "In the love of Yhwh for His people, He has set you [as] king over them." **12** And Huram says, "Blessed [is] Yhwh, God of Israel, who made the heavens and the earth, who has given a wise son to David the king, knowing wisdom and understanding, who builds a house for Yhwh, and a house for his kingdom. **13** And now, I have sent a wise man having understanding, of [my] father Huram **14** (son of a woman of the daughters of Dan, and his father a man of Tyre), knowing to work in gold, and in silver, in bronze, in iron, in stones, and in wood, in purple, in blue, and in fine linen, and in crimson, and to engrave any engraving, and to devise any invention that is given to him, with your wise men, and the wise men of my lord, your father David. **15** And now, the wheat, and the barley, the oil, and the wine, as my lord said, let him send to his servants, **16** and we cut trees out of Lebanon, according to all your need, and bring them to you—floats by sea, to Joppa, and you take them up to Jerusalem." **17** And Solomon numbers all the men, the sojourners who [are] in the land of Israel, after the numbering with which his father David numbered them, and they are found [to be] one hundred and fifty thousand and three thousand and six hundred; **18** and he makes from them seventy thousand burden-bearers, and eighty thousand hewers in the mountain, and three thousand and six hundred overseers, to cause the people to work.

CHAPTER 3

1 And Solomon begins to build the house of Yhwh in Jerusalem, on the mount of Moriah where He appeared to his father David, in the place that David had prepared, in the threshing-floor of Ornan the Jebusite, **2** and he begins to build in the second [day], in the second month, in the fourth year of his reign. **3** And [in] these Solomon has been instructed to build the house of God: the length [in] cubits by the former measure [is] sixty cubits, and the breadth twenty cubits. **4** As for the porch that [is] on the front, the length [is] by the front of the breadth of the house—twenty cubits, and the height one hundred and twenty [[*or* twenty]], and he overlays it within with pure gold. **5** And he has covered the large house with fir-trees, and he covers it with fine gold, and causes palms and chains to ascend on it, **6** and he overlays the house with precious stone for beauty, and the gold [is] gold of Parvaim, **7** and he covers the house, the beams, the thresholds, and its walls, and its doors, with gold, and has engraved cherubim on the walls. **8** And he makes the most holy house: its length by the front of the breadth of the house—twenty cubits, and its breadth twenty cubits, and he covers it with six hundred talents of fine gold; **9** and the weight of the nails [is] fifty shekels of gold, and he has covered the upper chambers with gold. **10** And he makes two cherubim in the most holy house, image work, and he overlays them with gold; **11** as for the wings of the

cherubim, their length [is] twenty cubits, the wing of the one [is] five cubits, touching the wall of the house, and the other wing [is] five cubits, touching the wing of the other cherub. **12** And the wing of the other cherub [is] five cubits touching the wall of the house, and the other wing [is] five cubits, adhering to the wing of the other cherub. **13** The wings of these cherubim are spreading forth twenty cubits, and they are standing on their feet and their faces [are] inward. **14** And he makes the veil of blue, and purple, and crimson, and fine linen, and causes cherubim to go up on it. **15** And he makes two pillars at the front of the house, thirty-five cubits in length, and the ornament that [is] on their heads [is] five cubits. **16** And he makes chains in the oracle, and puts [them] on the heads of the pillars, and makes one hundred pomegranates, and puts [them] on the chains. **17** And he raises up the pillars on the front of the temple, one on the right and one on the left, and calls the name of that on the right Jachin, and the name of that on the left Boaz.

CHAPTER 4

1 And he makes an altar of bronze: twenty cubits its length, and twenty cubits its breadth, and ten cubits its height. **2** And he makes the molten sea; ten by the cubit, from its edge to its edge, round in encompassment, and its height [is] five by the cubit, and a line of thirty by the cubit surrounds it around. **3** And the likeness of oxen [is] under it, encompassing it all around, ten to the cubit, surrounding the sea around; two rows of oxen are cast in its being cast. **4** It is standing on twelve oxen, three facing the north, and three facing the west, and three facing the south, and three facing the east, and the sea [is] on them above, and all their back parts [are] within. **5** And its thickness [is] a handbreadth, and its lip as the work of the lip of a cup flowered with lilies; holding [within]—it contains three thousand baths. **6** And he makes ten lavers, and puts five on the right, and five on the left, to wash with them; they purge the work of the burnt-offering with them; and the sea [is] for priests to wash with. **7** And he makes the ten lampstands of gold, according to their ordinance, and places [them] in the temple, five on the right, and five on the left. **8** And he makes ten tables, and places [them] in the temple, five on the right, and five on the left; and he makes one hundred bowls of gold. **9** And he makes the court of the priests, and the great court, and doors for the court, and he has overlaid their doors with bronze. **10** And he has placed the sea on the right shoulder eastward, from toward the south. **11** And Huram makes the pots, and the shovels, and the bowls, and Huram finishes to make the work that he made for King Solomon in the house of God; **12** two pillars, and the bowls, and the crowns on the heads of the two pillars, and the two networks to cover the two bowls of the crowns that [are] on the heads of the pillars; **13** and the four hundred pomegranates for the two networks, two rows of pomegranates for the one network, to cover the two bowls of the crowns that [are] on the front of the pillars. **14** And he has made the bases; and he has made the lavers on the bases; **15** the one sea, and the twelve oxen under it, **16** and the pots, and the shovels, and the forks, and all their vessels, his father Huram has made for King Solomon, for the house of Yhwh, of bronze purified. **17** The king has cast them in the circuit of the Jordan, in the thick soil of the ground, between Succoth and Zeredathah. **18** And Solomon makes all these vessels in great abundance, that the weight of the bronze has not been searched out. **19** And Solomon makes all the vessels that [are for] the house of God, and the altar of gold, and the tables, and on them [is] Bread of the Presentation; **20** and the lampstands, and their lamps, for their burning according to the ordinance, before the oracle, of gold refined; **21** and the flowers, and the lamps, and the tongs of gold—it [is] the perfection of gold; **22** and the snuffers, and the bowls, and the spoons, and the censers, of gold refined, and the opening of the house, its innermost doors to the Holy of Holies, and the doors of the house to the temple, of gold.

CHAPTER 5

1 And all the work that Solomon made for the house of Yhwh is finished, and Solomon brings in the sanctified things of his father David, and the silver, and the gold, and all the vessels he has put among the treasures of the house of God. **2**

Then Solomon assembles the elderly of Israel, and all the heads of the tribes, princes of the fathers of the sons of Israel, to Jerusalem, to bring up the Ark of the Covenant of Yhwh from the City of David—it [is] Zion. ³ And all the men of Israel are assembled to the king in the celebration—it [is] the seventh month; ⁴ and all [the] elderly of Israel come in, and the Levites lift up the Ark, ⁵ and they bring up the Ark, and the Tent of Meeting, and all the holy vessels that [are] in the tent; the priests, the Levites, have brought them up; ⁶ and King Solomon and all the congregation of Israel who are convened to him before the Ark are sacrificing sheep and oxen that are not counted nor numbered from multitude. ⁷ And the priests bring in the Ark of the Covenant of Yhwh to its place, to the oracle of the house, to the Holy of Holies, to the place of the wings of the cherubim; ⁸ and the cherubim are spreading out wings over the place of the Ark, and the cherubim cover over the Ark, and over its poles, from above; ⁹ and they lengthen the poles, and the heads of the poles are seen out of the Ark on the front of the oracle, and they are not seen outside; and it is there to this day. ¹⁰ There is nothing in the Ark but the two tablets that Moses gave in Horeb, where Yhwh covenanted with the sons of Israel, in their going out from Egypt. ¹¹ And it comes to pass, in the going out of the priests from the holy place—for all the priests who are present have sanctified themselves, there is none to watch by divisions, ¹² and the Levites, the singers, to all of them, to Asaph, to Heman, to Jeduthun, and to their sons, and to their brothers, clothed in white linen, with cymbals, and with psalteries, and harps, are standing on the east of the altar, and with them one hundred and twenty priests blowing with trumpets— ¹³ indeed, it comes to pass, trumpeters and singers [are] as one, to sound [with] one voice—to praise and to give thanks to Yhwh, and at the lifting up of the sound with trumpets, and with cymbals, and with instruments of song, and at giving praise to Yhwh, [saying], "For [He is] good, for His kindness [is] for all time," that the house is filled with a cloud—the house of Yhwh, ¹⁴ and the priests have not been able to stand to minister from the presence of the cloud, for the glory of Yhwh has filled the house of God.

CHAPTER 6

¹ Then Solomon said, "Yhwh said [He would] dwell in thick darkness, ² and I have built a house of habitation for You, and a fixed place for Your dwelling for all ages." ³ And the king turns around his face, and blesses the whole assembly of Israel, and the whole assembly of Israel is standing, ⁴ and he says, "Blessed [is] Yhwh, God of Israel, who has spoken with His mouth with my father David, and with His hands has fulfilled [it], saying, ⁵ From the day that I brought out My people from the land of Egypt, I have not fixed on a city out of any of the tribes of Israel to build a house for my name being there, and I have not fixed on a man to be leader over My people Israel; ⁶ and I fix on Jerusalem for My Name being there, and I fix on David to be over My people Israel. ⁷ And it is with the heart of my father David to build a house for the Name of Yhwh God of Israel, ⁸ and Yhwh says to my father David, Because that it has been with your heart to build a house for My Name, you have done well that it has been with your heart, ⁹ but you do not build the house, for your son who comes forth out from your loins, he builds the house for My Name. ¹⁰ And Yhwh establishes His word that He spoke, and I rise up in the stead of my father David, and sit on the throne of Israel, as Yhwh spoke, and I build the house for the Name of Yhwh, God of Israel, ¹¹ and I place the Ark there, where the covenant of Yhwh [is] that He made with the sons of Israel." ¹² And he stands before the altar of Yhwh, in front of all the assembly of Israel, and spreads out his hand— ¹³ for Solomon has made a scaffold of bronze, and puts it in the midst of the court, five cubits its length, and five cubits its breadth, and three cubits its height, and he stands on it, and kneels on his knees in front of all the assembly of Israel, and spreads forth his hands toward the heavens— ¹⁴ and says, "O Yhwh God of Israel, there is not like You a god in the heavens and in the earth, keeping the covenant and the kindness for Your servants who are walking before You with all their heart; ¹⁵ who has kept for Your servant, my father David, that which You spoke to him; indeed, You speak with Your mouth, and with Your hand have fulfilled [it], as at this day. ¹⁶ And now, O Yhwh, God of Israel, keep for Your servant, my father David, that which You spoke to him, saying, A man of yours is never cut off from before My face, sitting on the throne of Israel—only, if your sons watch their

way to walk in My law, as you have walked before Me. ¹⁷ And now, O Yhwh, God of Israel, let Your word be steadfast that You have spoken to Your servant, to David. ¹⁸ For is it true [that] God dwells with man on the earth? Behold, the heavens, and the heavens of the heavens, do not contain You, how much less this house that I have built? ¹⁹ And You have turned to the prayer of Your servant, and to his supplication, O Yhwh my God, to listen to the cry and to the prayer that Your servant is praying before You, ²⁰ for Your eyes being open toward this house by day and by night, toward the place that You have said to put Your Name there, to listen to the prayer that Your servant prays toward this place. ²¹ And You have listened to the supplications of Your servant, and of Your people Israel, that they pray toward this place, and You hear from the place of Your dwelling, from the heavens, and have listened, and forgiven. ²² If a man sins against his neighbor, and he has lifted up an oath on him to cause him to swear, and the oath has come in before Your altar in this house— ²³ then You hear from the heavens, and have done, and have judged Your servants, to give back to the wicked, to put his way on his head, and to declare righteous the righteous, to give to him according to his righteousness. ²⁴ And if Your people Israel is struck before an enemy because they sin against You, and they have turned back and confessed Your Name, and prayed and made supplication before You in this house— ²⁵ then You hear from the heavens and have forgiven the sin of Your people Israel, and caused them to return to the ground that You have given to them, and to their fathers. ²⁶ In the heavens being restrained and there is no rain because they sin against You, and they have prayed toward this place and confessed Your Name, [and] they turn back from their sin because You afflict them— ²⁷ then You hear in the heavens, and have forgiven the sin of Your servants, and of Your people Israel, because You direct them to the good way in which they walk, and have given rain on Your land that You have given to Your people for an inheritance. ²⁸ Famine, when it is in the land, [and] pestilence, when it is [in the land], blasting and mildew, locust and caterpillar, when they are [in the land], when its enemies have distressed it in the land—its gates, any plague and any sickness; ²⁹ any prayer, any supplication that is for any man, and for all Your people Israel, when they each know his own plague, and his own pain, and he has spread out his hands toward this house— ³⁰ then You hear from the heavens, the settled place of Your dwelling, and have forgiven, and have given to each according to all his ways (because You know his heart, for You alone have known the heart of the sons of men), ³¹ so that they fear You, to walk in Your ways, all the days that they are living on the face of the ground that You have given to our fathers. ³² And also, to the stranger who is not of Your people Israel, and he has come from a far-off land for the sake of Your great Name, and Your strong hand, and Your outstretched arm, and they have come in and prayed toward this house— ³³ then You hear from the heavens, from the settled place of Your dwelling, and have done according to all that the stranger calls to You for, so that all the peoples of the earth know Your Name, so as to fear You, as Your people Israel, and to know that Your Name is called on this house that I have built. ³⁴ When Your people go out to battle against its enemies in the way that You send them, and they have prayed to You [in] the way of this city that You have fixed on, and the house that I have built for Your Name— ³⁵ then You have heard their prayer and their supplication from the heavens, and have maintained their cause. ³⁶ When they sin against You—for there is not a man who does not sin—and You have been angry with them, and have given them before an enemy, and their captors have taken them captive to a land far off or near; ³⁷ and they have turned [it] back to their heart in the land to where they have been taken captive, and have turned back and made supplication to You in the land of their captivity, saying, We have sinned, we have done perversely, and have done wickedly; ³⁸ indeed, they have turned back to You with all their heart, and with all their soul, in the land of their captivity, to where they have taken them captive, and they have prayed [in] the way of their land that You have given to their fathers, and of the city that You have chosen, and of the house that I have built for Your Name— ³⁹ then You have heard from the heavens, from the settled place of Your dwelling, their prayer and their supplications, and have maintained their cause, and forgiven Your people who have sinned against You. ⁴⁰ Now my God, I implore You, let Your eyes be open and Your ears attentive to the prayer of this place. ⁴¹ And now, rise, O Yhwh God, to Your rest, You and the Ark of Your strength; Your priests, O Yhwh God, are clothed with salvation, and Your saints rejoice in the goodness. **42** O Yhwh God, do not turn back the face of Your anointed, be mindful of the kind acts of Your servant David."

CHAPTER 7

1 And at Solomon's finishing to pray, then the fire has come down from the heavens and consumes the burnt-offering and the sacrifices, and the glory of Yhwh has filled the house, **2** and the priests have not been able to go into the house of Yhwh, because the glory of Yhwh has filled the house of Yhwh. **3** And all the sons of Israel are looking on the descending of the fire, and the glory of Yhwh on the house, and they bow—faces to the earth—on the pavement, and pay respect, and give thanks to Yhwh, [saying], "For [He is] good, for His kindness [is] for all time!" **4** And the king and all the people are sacrificing a sacrifice before Yhwh, **5** and King Solomon sacrifices the sacrifice: twenty-two thousand of the herd and one hundred and twenty thousand of the flock; and the king and all the people dedicate the house of God. **6** And the priests are standing over their charges, and the Levites with instruments of the song of Yhwh that David the king made, to give thanks to Yhwh, for His kindness [is] for all time, in David's praising by their hand—and the priests are blowing trumpets opposite them, and all of Israel is standing. **7** And Solomon sanctifies the middle of the court that [is] before the house of Yhwh, for he has made the burnt-offerings and the fat of the peace-offerings there, for the altar of bronze that Solomon made has not been able to contain the burnt-offering, and the present, and the fat. **8** And Solomon makes the celebration at that time [for] seven days, and all Israel with him—a very great assembly—from the entering in of Hamath to the Brook of Egypt. **9** And they make a restraint on the eighth day, because they have made the dedication of the altar [for] seven days, and the celebration [for] seven days. **10** And on the twenty-third day of the seventh month he has sent the people to their tents, rejoicing, and glad in heart, for the goodness that Yhwh has done to David, and to Solomon, and to His people Israel. **11** And Solomon finishes the house of Yhwh, and the house of the king; and all that has come on the heart of Solomon to do in the house of Yhwh, and in his own house, he has caused to prosper. **12** And Yhwh appears to Solomon by night and says to him, "I have heard your prayer, and have fixed on this place for Myself for a house of sacrifice. **13** If I restrain the heavens and there is no rain, and if I lay charge on the locust to consume the land, and if I send pestilence among My people— **14** and My people on whom My Name is called are humbled, and pray, and seek My face, and turn back from their evil ways, then I hear from the heavens, and forgive their sin, and heal their land. **15** Now My eyes are open and My ears attentive to the prayer of this place; **16** and now, I have chosen and sanctified this house for My Name being there for all time; indeed, My eyes and My heart have been there [for] all the days. **17** And you, if you walk before Me as your father David walked, even to do according to all that I have commanded you, and keep My statutes and My judgments— **18** then I have established the throne of your kingdom, as I covenanted with your father David, saying, A man of yours is never cut off [from] ruling in Israel; **19** and if you turn back—you—and have forsaken My statutes and My commands that I have placed before you, and have gone and served other gods, and bowed yourselves to them—then I have plucked them from off My ground that I have given to them, **20** and this house that I have sanctified for My Name, I cast from before My face, and make it for a proverb and for a byword among all the peoples. **21** And this house that has been high is an astonishment to everyone passing by it, and he has said, Why has Yhwh done thus to this land and to this house? **22** and they have said, Because that they have forsaken Yhwh, God of their fathers, who brought them out from the land of Egypt, and lay hold on other gods, and bow themselves to them, and serve them, therefore He has brought all this calamity on them."

CHAPTER 8

1 And it comes to pass at the end of twenty years that Solomon has built the house of Yhwh and his own house. **2** As for the cities that Huram has given to Solomon, Solomon has built them, and he causes the sons of Israel to dwell there. **3** And Solomon goes to Hamath-Zobah, and lays hold on it; **4** and he builds Tadmor in the wilderness, and all the cities of store that he has built in Hamath. **5** And he builds Beth-Horon the upper, and Beth-Horon the lower—cities of defense, with walls, double gates, and bar— **6** and Ba'alath, and all the cities of store that Solomon had, and all the cities of the chariot, and the cities of the horsemen, and all the desire of Solomon that he desired to build in Jerusalem, and in Lebanon, and in all the land of his dominion. **7** All the people who are left of the Hittite, and the Amorite, and the Perizzite, and the Hivite, and the Jebusite, who are not of Israel— **8** of their sons who have been left after them in the land, whom the sons of Israel did not consume—Solomon lifts up a tribute to this day. **9** And Solomon has made none of the sons of Israel servants for his work, but they [are] men of war, and heads of his captains, and heads of his charioteers, and of his horsemen; **10** and these [are] heads of the officers whom King Solomon has, two hundred and fifty who are rulers among the people. **11** And Solomon has brought up the daughter of Pharaoh from the City of David to the house that he built for her, for he said, "My wife does not dwell in the house of David king of Israel, for they are holy to whom the Ark of Yhwh has come." **12** Then Solomon has caused burnt-offerings to ascend to Yhwh on the altar of Yhwh that he built before the porch, **13** even by the matter of a day in its day, to cause to ascend according to the command of Moses, on Sabbaths, and on new moons, and on appointed times, three times in a year—in the Celebration of Unleavened Things, and in the Celebration of Weeks, and in the Celebration of Shelters. **14** And he establishes, according to the ordinance of his father David, the divisions of the priests over their service, and of the Levites over their charges, to praise and to minister before the priests, according to the matter of a day in its day, and the gatekeepers in their divisions at every gate, for so [is] the command of David the man of God. **15** And they have not turned aside [from] the command of the king concerning the priests and the Levites, in reference to any matter, and to the treasures. **16** And all the work of Solomon is prepared until the day of the foundation of the house of Yhwh, and until its completion; the house of Yhwh is perfect. **17** Then Solomon has gone to Ezion-Geber, and to Elath, on the border of the sea, in the land of Edom; **18** and Huram sends to him, by the hand of his servants, ships and servants knowing the sea, and they go with servants of Solomon to Ophir, and take four hundred and fifty talents of gold from there, and bring it to King Solomon.

CHAPTER 9

1 And the queen of Sheba has heard of the fame of Solomon, and comes to Jerusalem to try Solomon with acute sayings, with a very great company, and camels carrying spices and gold in abundance, and precious stone; and she comes to Solomon, and speaks with him all that has been with her heart, **2** and Solomon declares all her matters to her, and there has not been hid a thing from Solomon that he has not declared to her. **3** And the queen of Sheba sees the wisdom of Solomon, and the house that he has built, **4** and the food of his table, and the sitting of his servants, and the standing of his ministers, and their clothing, and his stewards, and their clothing, and his burnt-offering that he offered up in the house of Yhwh, and there has not been anymore spirit in her. **5** And she says to the king, "The word [is] true that I heard in my land concerning your matters and concerning your wisdom, **6** and I have given no credence to their words until I have come and my eyes see, and behold, there has not been declared to me the half of the abundance of your wisdom—you have added to the report that I heard. **7** O the blessedness of your men, and the blessedness of your servants these who are standing before you continually, and hearing your wisdom. **8** Let your God Yhwh be blessed who has delighted in you to put you on His throne for king for your God Yhwh; in the love of your God to Israel, to establish it for all time, He has put you over them for king, to do judgment and righteousness." **9** And she gives to the king one hundred and twenty talents of gold, and spices in great abundance, and precious stone; and there has not been any such spice as the queen of Sheba has given to King Solomon. **10** And also, servants of Huram, and servants of Solomon, who brought in gold from Ophir, have brought in algum-trees and precious stone. **11** And the king makes the algum-trees [into] staircases for the house of Yhwh, and for the house of the king, and harps and psalteries for singers; and there have been none seen like these before in the land of Judah. **12** And King Solomon has given to the queen of Sheba all her desire that she asked, apart from that which she had brought to the king, and she turns and goes to her land, she and her servants. **13** And the weight of the gold that is coming to Solomon in one year is six hundred and sixty-six talents of gold, **14** apart from [what] the tourists and the merchants are bringing in; and all the kings of Arabia, and the governors of the land, are bringing in gold and silver to Solomon. **15** And King Solomon makes two hundred bucklers of alloyed gold—he causes six hundred [shekels] of alloyed gold to go up on the one buckler; **16** and three hundred shields of alloyed gold—he causes three hundred [shekels] of gold to go up on the one shield, and the king puts them in the House of the Forest of Lebanon. **17** And the king makes a great throne of ivory, and overlays it with pure gold; **18** and six steps [are] to the throne, and a footstool of gold, [and] they are fastened to the throne; and [places for] hands [are] on this [side] and on that [side] on the place of the sitting, and two lions are standing near the hands, **19** and twelve lions are standing there on the six steps on this [side] and on that [side]: it has not been made so for any kingdom. **20** And all the drinking vessels of King Solomon [are] of gold, and all the vessels of the House of the Forest of Lebanon [are] of refined gold—silver is not reckoned in the days of Solomon for anything; **21** for ships of the king are going to Tarshish with servants of Huram: once in three years the ships of Tarshish come carrying gold, and silver, ivory, apes, and peacocks [[or monkeys]]. **22** And King Solomon becomes greater than any of the kings of the earth for riches and wisdom; **23** and all the kings of the earth are seeking the presence of Solomon to hear his wisdom that God has put in his heart, **24** and they are each bringing in his present, vessels of silver, and vessels of gold, and garments, harness, and spices, horses, and mules, a rate year by year. **25** And there are four thousand stalls for horses and chariots, and twelve thousand horsemen for Solomon, and he placed them in cities of the chariot, and with the king in Jerusalem. **26** And he is ruling over all the kings from the River even to the land of the Philistines, and to the border of Egypt. **27** And the king makes the silver in Jerusalem as stones, and he has made the cedars as sycamores that [are] in the low country, for abundance, **28** and they are bringing out horses from Egypt to Solomon, and from all the lands. **29** And the rest of the matters of Solomon, the first and the last, are they not written beside the matters of Nathan the prophet, and beside the prophecy of Ahijah the Shilonite, and with the visions of Iddo the seer concerning Jeroboam son of Nebat? **30** And Solomon reigns in Jerusalem over all Israel [for] forty years, **31** and Solomon lies with his fathers, and they bury him in the city of his father David, and his son Rehoboam reigns in his stead.

CHAPTER 10

1 And Rehoboam goes to Shechem, for all of Israel has come [to] Shechem to cause him to reign. **2** And it comes to pass, at Jeroboam son of Nebat—who [is] in Egypt because he has fled from the face of Solomon the king—hearing, that Jeroboam turns back out of Egypt; **3** and they send and call for him, and Jeroboam comes in, and all of Israel, and they speak to Rehoboam, saying, **4** "Your father made our yoke sharp, and now, make light [some] of the sharp service of your father, and [some] of his heavy yoke that he put on us, and we serve you." **5** And he says to them, "Yet three days—then return to me"; and the people go. **6** And King Rehoboam consults with the aged men who have been standing before his father Solomon in his being alive, saying, "How are you counseling to answer this people?" **7** And they speak to him, saying, "If you become good to this people, and have been pleased with them, and spoken to them good words, then they have been servants to you [for] all the days." **8** And he forsakes the counsel of the aged men that they counseled him, and consults with the boys who have grown up with him, those standing before him, **9** and he says to them, "What are you counseling, and we answer this people that have spoken to me, saying, Make light [some] of the yoke that your father put on us?" **10** And the boys who have grown up with him speak with him, saying, "Thus you say to the people who have spoken to you, saying, Your father made our yoke heavy, and you, make light [some] of our yoke; thus you say to them, My little finger is thicker than the loins of my father; **11** and now, my father laid a heavy yoke on you, and I add to your yoke; my father disciplined you with whips, and I—

with scorpions." **12** And Jeroboam comes in, and all the people, to Rehoboam on the third day, as the king spoke, saying, "Return to me on the third day." **13** And the king answers them sharply, and King Rehoboam forsakes the counsel of the aged men, **14** and speaks to them according to the counsel of the boys, saying, "My father made your yoke heavy, and I add to it; my father disciplined you with whips, and I—with scorpions." **15** And the king has not listened to the people, for the revolution has been from God, for the sake of Yhwh's establishing His word that He spoke by the hand of Abijah the Shilonite to Jeroboam son of Nebat. **16** And all Israel have seen that the king has not listened to them, and the people send back [word to] the king, saying, "What portion do we have in David? indeed, there is no inheritance in a son of Jesse; [go], each to your tents, O Israel! Now see your house, O David!" And all [in] Israel go to their tents. **17** As for the sons of Israel who are dwelling in the cities of Judah—Rehoboam reigns over them. **18** And King Rehoboam sends Hadoram, who [is] over the tribute, and the sons of Israel cast stones at him, and he dies; and King Rehoboam has strengthened himself to go up into a chariot to flee to Jerusalem; **19** and Israel transgresses against the house of David to this day.

CHAPTER 11

1 And Rehoboam comes to Jerusalem, and assembles the house of Judah and Benjamin—one hundred and eighty thousand chosen warriors—to fight with Israel, to bring back the kingdom to Rehoboam. **2** And a word of Yhwh is to Shemaiah, a man of God, saying, **3** "Speak to Rehoboam son of Solomon king of Judah, and to all Israel in Judah and Benjamin, saying, **4** Thus said Yhwh: You do not go up nor fight with your brothers! Let each return to his house, for this thing has been from Me"; and they hear the words of Yhwh, and turn back from going against Jeroboam. **5** And Rehoboam dwells in Jerusalem, and builds cities for a bulwark in Judah, **6** indeed, he builds Beth-Lehem, and Etam, and Tekoa, **7** and Beth-Zur, and Shocho, and Adullam, **8** and Gath, and Mareshah, and Ziph, **9** and Adoraim, and Lachish, and Azekah, **10** and Zorah, and Aijalon, and Hebron, that [are] in Judah and in Benjamin, cities of bulwarks. **11** And he strengthens the bulwarks, and puts leaders in them, and treasures of food, and oil, and wine, **12** and in each and every city [he puts] bucklers and spears, and strengthens them very greatly; and he has Judah and Benjamin. **13** And the priests and the Levites that [are] in all Israel have stationed themselves by him, out of all their border, **14** for the Levites have left their outskirts and their possession, and they come to Judah and to Jerusalem, for Jeroboam and his sons have cast them off from acting as priests for Yhwh, **15** and he establishes for himself priests for high places, and for goat [idols] and for calf [idols] that he made. **16** And after them, out of all the tribes of Israel, those giving their heart to seek Yhwh, God of Israel, have come to Jerusalem to sacrifice to Yhwh, God of their father. **17** And they strengthen the kingdom of Judah, and strengthen Rehoboam son of Solomon, for three years, because they walked in the way of David and Solomon for three years. **18** And Rehoboam takes a wife for himself, Mahalath, child of Jerimoth son of David, [and of] Abigail daughter of Eliab son of Jesse. **19** And she bears sons to him: Jeush, and Shamaria, and Zaham. **20** And after her he has taken Maachah daughter of Absalom, and she bears to him Abijah, and Attai, and Ziza, and Shelomith. **21** And Rehoboam loves Maachah daughter of Absalom above all his wives and his concubines—for he has taken eighteen wives and sixty concubines—and he begets twenty-eight sons and sixty daughters. **22** And Rehoboam appoints Abijah son of Maachah for head, for leader among his brothers, for to cause him to reign. **23** And he has understanding, and disperses from all his sons to all lands of Judah and Benjamin, to all cities of the bulwarks, and gives provision in abundance to them; and he asks for a multitude of wives [for them].

CHAPTER 12

1 And it comes to pass, at the establishing of the kingdom of Rehoboam, and at his strengthening himself, he has forsaken the Law of Yhwh, and all Israel with him. **2** And it comes to pass, in the fifth year of King Rehoboam, Shishak king of Egypt has come up against Jerusalem—because they trespassed against Yhwh— **3** with one thousand and two hundred chariots, and with sixty thousand horsemen, and there is no number to the people who have come with him out of Egypt—Lubim, Sukkiim, and Cushim— **4** and he captures the cities of the bulwarks that [are] of Judah, and comes to Jerusalem. **5** And Shemaiah the prophet has come to Rehoboam and the heads of Judah who have been gathered to Jerusalem [to escape] from the presence of Shishak, and says to them, "Thus said Yhwh: You have forsaken Me, and also, I have left you in the hand of Shishak"; **6** and the heads of Israel are humbled—and the king—and they say, "Yhwh [is] righteous." **7** And when Yhwh sees that they have been humbled, a word of Yhwh has been [sent] to Shemaiah, saying, "They have been humbled; I do not destroy them, and I have given to them as a little thing for an escape, and I do not pour out My fury in Jerusalem by the hand of Shishak; **8** but they become servants to him, and they know My service, and the service of the kingdoms of the lands." **9** And Shishak king of Egypt comes up against Jerusalem, and takes the treasures of the house of Yhwh and the treasures of the house of the king—he has taken the whole—and he takes the shields of gold that Solomon had made; **10** and King Rehoboam makes shields of bronze in their stead, and has given [them] a charge on the hand of the heads of the runners who are keeping the opening of the house of the king; **11** and it comes to pass, from the time of the going in of the king to the house of Yhwh, the runners have come in and lifted them up, and brought them back to the chamber of the runners. **12** And in his being humbled, the wrath of Yhwh has turned back from him, so as not to destroy to completion; and also, there have been good things in Judah. **13** And King Rehoboam strengthens himself in Jerusalem and reigns; for Rehoboam [is] a son of forty-two years in his reigning, and he has reigned seventeen years in Jerusalem, the city that Yhwh has chosen to put His Name there, out of all the tribes of Israel, and the name of his mother [is] Naamah the Ammonitess, **14** and he does evil, for he has not prepared his heart to seek Yhwh. **15** And the matters of Rehoboam, the first and the last, are they not written among the matters of Shemaiah the prophet, and of Iddo the seer, concerning genealogy? And the wars of Rehoboam and Jeroboam [are for] all the days; **16** and Rehoboam lies with his fathers, and is buried in the City of David, and his son Abijah reigns in his stead.

CHAPTER 13

1 In the eighteenth year of King Jeroboam, Abijah reigns over Judah; **2** he has reigned three years in Jerusalem (and the name of his mother [is] Michaiah daughter of Uriel, from Gibeah), and there has been war between Abijah and Jeroboam. **3** And Abijah directs the war with a force of mighty men of war, four hundred thousand chosen men, and Jeroboam has set in array [for] battle with him, with eight hundred thousand chosen men, mighty men of valor. **4** And Abijah rises up on the hill of Zemaraim that [is] in the hill-country of Ephraim, and says, "Hear me, Jeroboam and all Israel! **5** Is it not for you to know that Yhwh, God of Israel, has given the kingdom over Israel to David for all time, to him and to his sons—a covenant of salt? **6** and Jeroboam, son of Nebat, servant of Solomon son of David, rises up and rebels against his lord! **7** And vain men are gathered to him, sons of worthlessness, and they strengthen themselves against Rehoboam son of Solomon, and Rehoboam was a youth, and tender of heart, and has not strengthened himself against them. **8** And now you are saying to strengthen yourselves before the kingdom of Yhwh in the hand of the sons of David, and you [are] a numerous multitude, and calves of gold [are] with you that Jeroboam has made for you for gods. **9** Have you not cast out the priests of Yhwh, the sons of Aaron, and the Levites, and make priests for yourselves like the peoples of the lands? everyone who has come to fill his hand with a bullock, a son of the herd, and seven rams, even he has been a priest for [those which are] not gods! **10** As for us, Yhwh [is] our God, and we have not forsaken Him, and priests are ministering to Yhwh, sons of Aaron and the Levites, in the work, **11** and are making incense to Yhwh, burnt-offerings morning by morning, and evening by evening, and incense of spices, and the arrangement of bread [is] on the pure table, and the lampstand of gold, and its lamps, to burn evening by evening, for we are keeping the charge of our God Yhwh, and you have forsaken Him. **12** And behold, with us—at [our] head—[is] God, and His priests and trumpets of shouting to shout against you; O sons

of Israel, do not fight with Yhwh, God of your fathers, for you do not prosper." **13** And Jeroboam has brought around the ambush to come in from behind them, and they are before Judah, and the ambush [is] behind them. **14** And Judah turns, and behold, the battle [is] against them, before and behind, and they cry to Yhwh, and the priests are blowing with trumpets, **15** and the men of Judah shout; and it comes to pass, at the shouting of the men of Judah, that God has struck Jeroboam and all Israel before Abijah and Judah. **16** And the sons of Israel flee from the face of Judah, and God gives them into their hand, **17** and Abijah and his people strike among them a great striking, and five hundred thousand chosen men of Israel fall wounded. **18** And the sons of Israel are humbled at that time, and the sons of Judah are strong, for they have leaned on Yhwh, God of their fathers. **19** And Abijah pursues after Jeroboam and captures cities from him: Beth-El and its small towns, and Jeshanah and its small towns, and Ephraim and its small towns. **20** And Jeroboam has not retained power anymore in the days of Abijah, and Yhwh strikes him, and he dies. **21** And Abijah strengthens himself, and takes fourteen wives for himself, and begets twenty-two sons and sixteen daughters; **22** and the rest of the matters of Abijah, and his ways, and his words, are written in the commentary of the prophet Iddo.

CHAPTER 14

1 And Abijah lies with his fathers, and they bury him in the City of David, and his son Asa reigns in his stead. In his days the land was quiet [for] ten years. **2** And Asa does that which is good and that which is right in the eyes of his God Yhwh, **3** and turns aside the altars of the stranger, and the high places, and breaks the standing-pillars, and cuts down the Asherim, **4** and commands to Judah to seek Yhwh, God of their fathers, and to do the Law and the command; **5** and he turns aside the high places and the images out of all cities of Judah, and the kingdom is quiet before him. **6** And he builds cities of bulwarks in Judah, for the land has quiet; and there is no war with him in these years, because Yhwh has given rest to him. **7** And he says to Judah, "Let us build these cities, and surround [them] with wall, and towers, double gates, and bars, while the land [is] before us, because we have sought our God Yhwh, we have sought, and He gives rest to us all around"; and they build and prosper. **8** And Asa has a force of three hundred thousand from Judah carrying buckler and spear, and two hundred and eighty thousand from Benjamin carrying shield and treading bow; all these [are] mighty men of valor. **9** And Zerah the Cushite comes out to them with a force of one million [men] and three hundred chariots, and he comes to Mareshah, **10** and Asa goes out before him, and they set in array [for] battle in the Valley of Zephathah at Mareshah. **11** And Asa calls to his God Yhwh and says, "Yhwh, it is nothing for You to help, between the mighty and those who have no power; help us, O Yhwh, our God, for we have leaned on You, and in Your Name we have come against this multitude; O Yhwh, You [are] our God; do not let mortal man prevail against You!" **12** And Yhwh strikes the Cushim before Asa and before Judah, and the Cushim flee, **13** and Asa and the people who [are] with him pursue them even to Gerar, and there falls [many] from the Cushim, for they have no preserving, because they have been broken before Yhwh and before His camp; and [those of Judah] carry away very much spoil, **14** and strike all the cities around Gerar, for a fear of Yhwh has been on them, and they spoil all the cities, for abundant spoil has been in them; **15** and they have also struck tents of livestock, and they capture sheep in abundance, and camels, and return to Jerusalem.

CHAPTER 15

1 And the Spirit of God has been on Azariah son of Oded, **2** and he goes out before Asa and says to him, "Hear me, Asa, and all Judah and Benjamin; Yhwh [is] with you—in your being with Him, and if you seek Him, He is found by you, and if you forsake Him, He forsakes you; **3** and many days [are] to Israel without [the] true God, and without a teaching priest, and without law, **4** and it turns back in its distress to Yhwh, God of Israel, and they seek Him, and He is found by them, **5** and in those times there is no peace for him who is going out, and for him who is coming in, for many troubles [are] on all the inhabitants of the lands, **6** and they have been beaten down, nation by nation, and city by city, for God has troubled them with every adversity, **7** and you, be strong, and do not let your hands be feeble, for there is a reward for your work." **8** And at Asa's hearing these words, and the prophecy of Oded the prophet, he has strengthened himself, and causes the abominations to pass away out of all the land of Judah and Benjamin, and out of the cities that he has captured from the hill-country of Ephraim, and renews the altar of Yhwh that [is] before the porch of Yhwh, **9** and gathers all Judah and Benjamin, and the sojourners with them out of Ephraim, and Manasseh, and out of Simeon—for they have defected to him from Israel in abundance, in their seeing that his God Yhwh [is] with him. **10** And they are gathered to Jerusalem in the third month of the fifteenth year of the reign of Asa, **11** and sacrifice to Yhwh on that day from the spoil they have brought in—seven hundred oxen and seven thousand sheep, **12** and they enter into a covenant to seek Yhwh, God of their fathers, with all their heart and with all their soul, **13** and everyone who does not seek for Yhwh, God of Israel, is put to death, from small to great, from man to woman. **14** And they swear to Yhwh with a loud voice, and with shouting, and with trumpets, and with horns, **15** and all Judah rejoices concerning the oath, for they have sworn with all their heart, and they have sought Him with all their goodwill, and He is found by them, and Yhwh gives rest to them all around. **16** And also Maachah, mother of Asa the king—he has removed her from [being] mistress, in that she has made for an Asherah a horrible thing, and Asa cuts down her horrible thing, and beats [it] small, and burns [it] by the Brook of Kidron: **17** yet the high places have not been removed from Israel; only, the heart of Asa has been perfect all his days. **18** And he brings in the sanctified things of his father, and his own sanctified things, to the house of God: silver, and gold, and vessels. **19** And war has not been until the thirty-fifth year of the reign of Asa.

CHAPTER 16

1 In the thirty-sixth year of the reign of Asa, Baasha king of Israel has come up against Judah, and builds Ramah, so as not to permit any going out and coming in to Asa king of Judah. **2** And Asa brings out silver and gold from the treasures of the house of Yhwh and of the house of the king, and sends [them] to Ben-Hadad king of Aram, who is dwelling in Damascus, saying, **3** "A covenant [is] between me and you, and between my father and your father, behold, I have sent silver and gold to you; go, break your covenant with Baasha king of Israel, and he goes up from off me." **4** And Ben-Hadad listens to King Asa, and sends the heads of the forces that he has to cities of Israel, and they strike Ijon, and Dan, and Abel-Maim, and all the stores, cities of Naphtali. **5** And it comes to pass, at Baasha's hearing, that he ceases from building Ramah, and lets his work rest; **6** and Asa the king has taken all Judah, and they carry away the stones of Ramah and its wood that Baasha has built [with], and he builds Geba and Mizpah with them. **7** And at that time Hanani the seer has come to Asa king of Judah and says to him, "Because of your leaning on the king of Aram, and you have not leaned on your God Yhwh, therefore the force of the king of Aram has escaped from your hand. **8** Did the Cushim and the Lubim not become a very great force for multitude, for chariot, and for horsemen? and in your leaning on Yhwh He gave them into your hand, **9** for Yhwh—His eyes go to and fro in all the earth, to show Himself strong [for] a people whose heart [is] perfect toward Him; you have been foolish concerning this, because from now on there are wars with you." **10** And Asa is angry at the seer, and puts him [in] the house of stocks, for [he is] in a rage with him for this; and Asa oppresses [some] of the people at that time. **11** And behold, the matters of Asa, the first and the last, behold, they are written on the scroll of the kings of Judah and Israel. **12** And Asa is diseased— in the thirty-ninth year of his reign—in his feet, until his disease is excessive; and also in his disease he has not sought Yhwh, but among physicians. **13** And Asa lies with his fathers, and dies in the forty-first year of his reign, **14** and they bury him in [one of] his graves that he had prepared for himself in the City of David, and they cause him to lie on a bed that [one] has filled [with] spices, and various kinds of mixtures, with perfumed work; and they burn a very great burning for him.

CHAPTER 17

1 And his son Jehoshaphat reigns in his stead, and he strengthens himself against Israel, **2** and puts a force in all the fortified cities of Judah, and puts garrisons in the land of Judah, and in the cities of Ephraim that his father Asa had captured. **3** And Yhwh is with Jehoshaphat, for he has walked in the first ways of his father David, and has not sought for the Ba'alim, **4** for he has sought for the God of his father, and he has walked in His commands, and not according to the work of Israel. **5** And Yhwh establishes the kingdom in his hand, and all Judah gives a present to Jehoshaphat, and he has riches and honor in abundance, **6** and his heart is high in the ways of Yhwh, and again he has turned aside the high places and the Asherim out of Judah. **7** And in the third year of his reign he has sent for his heads, for Ben-Hail, and for Obadiah, and for Zechariah, and for Nethaneel, and for Michaiah, to teach in cities of Judah; **8** and with them the Levites: Shemaiah, and Nethaniah, and Zebadiah, and Asahel, and Shemiramoth, and Jonathan, and Adonijah, and Tobijath, and Tob-Adonijah—the Levites; and with them Elishama and Jehoram, the priests. **9** And they teach in Judah, and the Scroll of the Law of Yhwh [is] with them, and they go around into all cities of Judah, and teach among the people. **10** And there is a fear of Yhwh on all kingdoms of the lands that [are] around Judah, and they have not fought with Jehoshaphat; **11** and [some] from the Philistines are bringing a present to Jehoshaphat, and silver [as] tribute; also, the Arabians are bringing to him a flock of seven thousand and seven hundred rams, and seven thousand and seven hundred male goats. **12** And Jehoshaphat is going on and becoming very great, and he builds palaces and cities of store in Judah, **13** and he has much work in cities of Judah; and men of war, mighty men of valor, [are] in Jerusalem. **14** And these [are] their numbers, for the house of their fathers—of Judah, heads of thousands: Adnah the head, and with him three hundred thousand mighty men of valor; **15** and at his hand [is] Jehohanan the head, and with him two hundred and eighty thousand; **16** and at his hand [is] Amasiah son of Zichri, who is willingly offering himself to Yhwh, and with him two hundred thousand mighty men of valor. **17** And of Benjamin, mighty men of valor: Eliada, and with him two hundred thousand armed with bow and shield; **18** and at his hand [is] Jehozabad, and with him one hundred and eighty thousand armed ones of the host. **19** These [are] those serving the king, apart from those whom the king put in the fortress cities in all of Judah.

CHAPTER 18

1 And Jehoshaphat has riches and honor in abundance, and joins affinity to Ahab, **2** and goes down at the end of [certain] years to Samaria to [visit] Ahab, and Ahab sacrifices sheep and oxen in abundance for him and for the people who [are] with him, and persuades him to go up to Ramoth-Gilead. **3** And Ahab king of Israel says to Jehoshaphat king of Judah, "Do you go with me [to] Ramoth-Gilead?" And he says to him, "As I—so you, and as your people—my people, and [we go] with you into the battle." **4** And Jehoshaphat says to the king of Israel, "Please seek the word of Yhwh this day." **5** And the king of Israel gathers the prophets, four hundred men, and says to them, "Do we go to Ramoth-Gilead to battle, or do I refrain?" And they say, "Go up, and God gives [it] into the hand of the king." **6** And Jehoshaphat says, "[Is there] not still a prophet of Yhwh here, and we seek from him?" **7** And the king of Israel says to Jehoshaphat, "[There is] still one man to seek Yhwh from him, and I have hated him, for he is not prophesying of good concerning me, but of evil [for] all his days, he [is] Micaiah son of Imlah"; and Jehoshaphat says, "Do not let the king say so." **8** And the king of Israel calls to a certain officer and says, "Hurry Micaiah son of Imlah." **9** And the king of Israel and Jehoshaphat king of Judah are sitting, each on his throne, clothed with garments, and they are sitting in a threshing-floor at the opening of the Gate of Samaria, and all the prophets are prophesying before them. **10** And Zedekiah son of Chenaanah makes horns of iron for himself and says, "Thus said Yhwh: **11** With these you push Aram until you have consumed them." And all the prophets are prophesying so, saying, "Go up [to] Ramath-Gilead and prosper, and Yhwh has given [it] into the hand of the king." **12** And the messenger who has gone to call for Micaiah has spoken to him, saying, "Behold, the words of the prophets [as] one mouth [are] good toward the king, and please let your word be like one of theirs: and you have spoken good." **13** And Micaiah says "Yhwh lives, surely that which my God says, I speak it." **14** And he comes to the king, and the king says to him, "Micaiah, do we go to Ramoth-Gilead to battle, or do I refrain?" And he says, "Go up, and prosper, and they are given into your hand." **15** And the king says to him, "How many times am I adjuring you that you speak to me only truth in the Name of Yhwh?" **16** And he says, "I have seen all Israel scattered on the mountains, as sheep that have no shepherd, and Yhwh says, There are no masters for these, they each return to his house in peace." **17** And the king of Israel says to Jehoshaphat, "Did I not say to you [that] he does not prophesy good concerning me, but rather of evil?" **18** And [Micaiah] says, "Therefore, hear a word of Yhwh: I have seen Yhwh sitting on His throne, and all the host of the heavens standing on His right and His left; **19** and Yhwh says, Who entices Ahab king of Israel, and he goes up and falls in Ramoth-Gilead? And this speaker says thus, and that speaker thus. **20** And the spirit goes out, and stands before Yhwh, and says, I entice him; and Yhwh says to him, With what? **21** and he says, I go out, and have become a spirit of falsehood in the mouth of all his prophets. And He says, You entice, and also, you are able; go out and do so. **22** And now, behold, Yhwh has put a spirit of falsehood in the mouth of these prophets of yours, and Yhwh has spoken calamity concerning you." **23** And Zedekiah son of Chenaanah comes near and strikes Micaiah on the cheek, and says, "Where [is] this—the way the spirit [from] Yhwh passed over from me to speak with you?" **24** And Micaiah says, "Behold, you see in that day that you enter into the innermost chamber to be hidden." **25** And the king of Israel says, "Take Micaiah, and turn him back to Amon head of the city, and to Joash son of the king, **26** and you have said, Thus said the king: Put this [one] in the house of restraint, and cause him to eat bread of oppression, and water of oppression, until my return in peace." **27** And Micaiah says, "If you certainly return in peace, Yhwh has not spoken by me"; and he says, "Hear, O peoples, all of them!" **28** And the king of Israel goes up—and Jehoshaphat king of Judah—to Ramoth-Gilead; **29** and the king of Israel says to Jehoshaphat to disguise himself, and to go into battle, "And you, put on your garments." And the king of Israel disguises himself, and they go into battle. **30** And the king of Aram has commanded the heads of the charioteers whom he has, saying, "You do not fight with small or with great, except with the king of Israel by himself." **31** And it comes to pass at the heads of the charioteers seeing Jehoshaphat, that they have said, "He is the king of Israel," and they turn around against him to fight, and Jehoshaphat cries out, and Yhwh has helped him, and God entices them from him; **32** indeed, it comes to pass, at the heads of the charioteers seeing that it has not been the king of Israel—they turn back from after him. **33** And a man has drawn with a bow in his simplicity, and strikes the king of Israel between the joinings and the coat of mail, and he says to the charioteer, "Turn your hand, and you have brought me out of the camp, for I have become [gravely] sick." **34** And the battle increases on that day, and the king of Israel has been propped up in the chariot in front of Aram until the evening, and he dies at the time of the going in of the sun.

CHAPTER 19

1 And Jehoshaphat king of Judah turns back to his house in peace, to Jerusalem, **2** and Jehu son of Hanani the seer goes out to his presence and says to King Jehoshaphat, "Do you love to give help to the wicked and to those hating Yhwh? and for this, wrath [is] against you from before Yhwh, **3** but good things have been found with you, for you have put away the Asheroth out of the land, and have prepared your heart to seek God." **4** And Jehoshaphat dwells in Jerusalem, and he turns back and goes out among the people from Beer-Sheba to the hill-country of Ephraim, and brings them back to Yhwh, God of their fathers. **5** And he establishes judges in the land, in all the fortified cities of Judah, for every city, **6** and says to the ones judging, "See what you are doing—for you do not judge for man, but for Yhwh, who [is] with you in the matter of judgment; **7** and now, let fear of Yhwh be on you, observe and do, for there is not perverseness with our God Yhwh, and favoring by appearance, and taking of a bribe." **8** And also in Jerusalem, Jehoshaphat has appointed of the Levites, and of the priests, and of the heads of the fathers of Israel, for the judgment of Yhwh, and for strife; and they return to Jerusalem, **9** and he lays a charge on them, saying, "Thus do you do in the fear of Yhwh, in faithfulness, and with a perfect heart, **10** and any strife that comes to you of your brothers who are dwelling in their cities, between blood and blood, between law and command, statutes, and judgments, then you have warned them and they do not become guilty before Yhwh, and wrath has not been on you and on your brothers; thus do you do, and you are not guilty. **11** And behold, Amariah the head priest [is] over you for every matter of Yhwh, and Zebadiah son of Ishmael, the leader of the house of Judah, [is] for every matter of the king, and the Levites [are] officers before you; be strong and do, and Yhwh is with the good."

CHAPTER 20

1 And it comes to pass after this, the sons of Moab have come in, and the sons of Ammon, and with them of the peoples, to battle against Jehoshaphat. **2** And [some] come in and declare [it] to Jehoshaphat, saying, "A great multitude has come against you from beyond the sea, from Aram, and behold, they [are] in Hazezon-Tamar—it [is] En-Gedi." **3** And Jehoshaphat fears, and sets his face to seek for Yhwh, and proclaims a fast over all Judah; **4** and Judah is gathered to inquire of Yhwh; also, from all the cities of Judah they have come to seek Yhwh. **5** And Jehoshaphat stands in the assembly of Judah and Jerusalem, in the house of Yhwh, at the front of the new court, **6** and says, "O Yhwh, God of our fathers, are You not God in the heavens? indeed, You are ruling over all kingdoms of the nations, and power and might [are] in Your hand, and there is none with You to station himself. **7** Are You not our God? You have dispossessed the inhabitants of this land from before Your people Israel, and give it to the seed of Your friend Abraham for all time, **8** and they dwell in it, and build a sanctuary in it for You, for Your Name, saying, **9** If evil comes on us—sword, judgment, and pestilence, and famine—we stand before this house, and before You, for Your Name [is] in this house, and cry to You out of our distress, and You hear and save. **10** And now, behold, sons of Ammon, and Moab, and Mount Seir, whom You did not grant to Israel to go in against in their coming out of the land of Egypt, for they turned aside from off them and did not destroy them, **11** and behold, they are repaying to us—to come to drive us out of Your possession that You have caused us to possess. **12** O our God, do You not execute judgment on them? for there is no power in us before this great multitude that has come against us, and we do not know what we do, but our eyes [are] on You." **13** And all Judah is standing before Yhwh, also their infants, their wives, and their sons. **14** And the Spirit of Yhwh has been on Jahaziel, son of Zechariah, son of Benaiah, son of Jeiel, son of Mattaniah, the Levite, of the sons of Asaph, in the midst of the assembly, **15** and he says, "Attend, all Judah, and you inhabitants of Jerusalem, and O King Jehoshaphat, Thus said Yhwh to you: You do not fear, nor be afraid of the face of this great multitude, for the battle [is] not for you, but for God. **16** Tomorrow, go down against them, behold, they are coming up by the ascent of Ziz, and you have found them in the end of the valley, the front of the wilderness of Jeruel. **17** [It is] not for you to fight in this; station yourselves, stand, and see the salvation of Yhwh with you, O Judah and Jerusalem—do not be afraid nor fear—tomorrow go out before them, and Yhwh [is] with you." **18** And Jehoshaphat bows—face to the earth—and all Judah and the inhabitants of Jerusalem have fallen before Yhwh, to bow themselves to Yhwh. **19** And the Levites, of the sons of the Kohathites, and of the sons of the Korahites, rise to give praise to Yhwh, God of Israel, with a loud voice on high. **20** And they rise early in the morning, and go out to the wilderness of Tekoa, and in their going out Jehoshaphat has stood and says, "Hear me, O Judah and inhabitants of Jerusalem, remain steadfast in your God Yhwh, and be steadfast; remain steadfast in His prophets and prosper." **21** And he takes counsel with the people, and appoints singers for Yhwh, and those giving praise for the honor of holiness, in the going out before the armed [men], and saying, "Give thanks to Yhwh, for His kindness [is] for all time." **22** And at the time they have begun with singing and praise, Yhwh has put ambushes against the sons of Ammon, Moab, and Mount Seir, who are coming in to Judah, and they are struck, **23** and the sons of Ammon stand up, and Moab, against the inhabitants of Mount Seir, to devote and to destroy, and at their finishing with the inhabitants of Seir, they helped, a man against his neighbor, to destroy. **24** And Judah has come to the watchtower in the wilderness, and they look toward the multitude, and behold, they [are] carcasses fallen to the earth, and none [had] an escape, **25** and Jehoshaphat comes in, and his people, to seize their spoil, and they find among them, in abundance, both goods and carcasses, and desirable vessels, and they take spoil for themselves without prohibition, and they are seizing the spoil [for] three days, for it [is] abundant. **26** And on the fourth day they have been assembled at the Valley of Blessing, for there they blessed Yhwh: therefore they have called the name of that place, "Valley of Blessing," to this day. **27** And they return, every man of Judah and Jerusalem, and Jehoshaphat at their head, to go back to Jerusalem with joy, for Yhwh has made them rejoice over their enemies. **28** And they come to Jerusalem with psalteries, and with harps, and with trumpets, to the house of Yhwh. **29** And there is a fear of God on all kingdoms of the lands in their hearing that Yhwh has fought with the enemies of Israel, **30** and the kingdom of Jehoshaphat is quiet, and his God gives rest to him all around. **31** And Jehoshaphat reigns over Judah, a son of thirty-five years in his reigning, and he has reigned twenty-five years in Jerusalem, and the name of his mother [is] Azubah daughter of Shilhi. **32** And he walks in the way of his father Asa, and has not turned aside from it, to do that which is right in the eyes of Yhwh. **33** Only, the high places have not been removed, and still the people have not prepared their heart for the God of their fathers. **34** And the rest of the matters of Jehoshaphat, the first and the last, behold, they are written among the matters of Jehu son of Hanani, who has been mentioned on the scroll of the kings of Israel. **35** And after this Jehoshaphat king of Judah has joined himself with Ahaziah king of Israel (he did wickedly in doing [this]), **36** and he joins him with himself to make ships to go to Tarshish, and they make ships in Ezion-Geber, **37** and Eliezer son of Dodavah, of Mareshah, prophesies against Jehoshaphat, saying, "For your joining yourself with Ahaziah, Yhwh has broken up your works"; and the ships are broken, and have not retained [power] to go to Tarshish.

CHAPTER 21

1 And Jehoshaphat lies with his fathers, and is buried with his fathers in the City of David, and his son Jehoram reigns in his stead. **2** And he has brothers, sons of Jehoshaphat: Azariah, and Jehiel, and Zechariah, and Azariah, and Michael, and Shephatiah; all these [are] sons of Jehoshaphat king of Israel, **3** and their father gives to them many gifts of silver and of gold, and of precious things, with fortified cities in Judah, and he has given the kingdom to Jehoram, for he [is] the firstborn. **4** And Jehoram rises up over the kingdom of his father, and strengthens himself, and slays all his brothers with the sword, and also of the heads of Israel. **5** Jehoram [is] a son of thirty-two years in his reigning, and he has reigned eight years in Jerusalem, **6** and he walks in the way of the kings of Israel, as the house of Ahab did, for a daughter of Ahab has been to him for a wife, and he does evil in the eyes of Yhwh, **7** and Yhwh has not been willing to destroy the house of David, for the sake of the covenant that He made with David, and as He had said to give a lamp to him and to his sons [for] all the days. **8** In his days Edom has revolted from under the hand of Judah, and they cause a king to reign over them; **9** and Jehoram passes over with his heads, and all the chariots with him, and it comes to pass, he has risen by night and strikes the Edomites who are coming around against him, and the princes of the chariots, **10** and Edom revolts from under the hand of Judah to this day; then Libnah revolts at that time from under his hand, because he has forsaken Yhwh, God of his fathers; **11** also, he has made high places on the mountains of Judah, and causes the inhabitants of Jerusalem to commit whoredom, and compels Judah. **12** And a writing from Elijah the prophet comes to him, saying, "Thus said Yhwh, God of your father David: Because that you have not walked in the ways of your father Jehoshaphat, and in the ways of Asa king of Judah, **13** and you walk in the way of the kings of Israel, and cause Judah and the inhabitants of Jerusalem to commit whoredom like the whoredoms of the house of Ahab, and also your brothers, the house of your father, who are better than yourself, you have slain; **14** behold, Yhwh is striking [with] a great striking among your people, and among your sons, and among your wives, and among all your goods— **15** and you, with many sicknesses, with disease of your bowels, until your bowels come out by the sickness, day by day." **16** And Yhwh wakes up against Jehoram the spirit of the Philistines and of the Arabians, who [are] beside the Cushim, **17** and they come up into Judah, and break

into it, and take captive all the substance that is found at the house of the king, and also his sons, and his wives, and there has not been left to him a son except Jehoahaz the youngest of his sons. **18** And after all this Yhwh has plagued him in his bowels by a disease for which there is no healing, **19** and it comes to pass, from days to days, and at the time of the going out of the end of two years, his bowels have gone out with his sickness, and he dies of severe diseases, and his people have not made for him a burning like the burning of his fathers. **20** He was a son of thirty-two [years] in his reigning, and he has reigned eight years in Jerusalem, and he goes without desire, and they bury him in the City of David, and not in the graves of the kings.

CHAPTER 22

1 And the inhabitants of Jerusalem cause his youngest son Ahaziah to reign in his stead (for the troop had slain all the chiefly that came in with the Arabians to the camp), and Ahaziah son of Jehoram, king of Judah, reigns. **2** Ahaziah [is] a son of twenty-two years in his reigning, and he has reigned one year in Jerusalem, and the name of his mother [is] Athaliah daughter of Omri; **3** he has also walked in the ways of the house of Ahab, for his mother has been his counselor to do wickedly. **4** And he does evil in the eyes of Yhwh, like the house of Ahab, for they have been his counselors, after the death of his father, for destruction to him. **5** Also, he has walked in their counsel, and goes with Jehoram son of Ahab, king of Israel, to battle against Hazael king of Aram in Ramoth-Gilead, and they of Ramah strike Joram; **6** and he turns back to be healed in Jezreel because of the wounds with which they had struck him in Ramah, in his fighting with Hazael king of Aram. And Azariah son of Jehoram, king of Judah, has gone down to see Jehoram son of Ahab in Jezreel, for he [is] sick; **7** and to come to Joram has been from God [for] the destruction of Ahaziah; and in his coming he has gone out with Jehoram to Jehu son of Nimshi, whom Yhwh anointed to cut off the house of Ahab. **8** And it comes to pass, in Jehu's executing judgment with the house of Ahab, that he finds the heads of Judah and sons of the brothers of Ahaziah, ministers of Ahaziah, and slays them. **9** And he seeks Ahaziah, and they capture him (and he is hiding himself in Samaria), and bring him to Jehu, and put him to death, and bury him, for they said, "He [is] son of Jehoshaphat, who sought Yhwh with all his heart"; and there is none of the house of Ahaziah to retain power for the kingdom. **10** And Athaliah mother of Ahaziah has seen that her son is dead, and she rises and destroys the whole seed of the kingdom of the house of Judah. **11** And Jehoshabeath daughter of the king takes Joash son of Ahaziah, and steals him from the midst of the sons of the king who are put to death, and puts him and his nurse into the inner part of the bed-chambers, and Jehoshabeath daughter of King Jehoram, wife of Jehoiada the priest, because she has been sister of Ahaziah, hides him from the face of Athaliah, and she has not put him to death. **12** And he is with them in the house of God hiding himself [for] six years, and Athaliah is reigning over the land.

CHAPTER 23

1 And in the seventh year Jehoiada has strengthened himself, and takes the heads of the hundreds, even Azariah son of Jeroham, and Ishmael son of Jehohanan, and Azariah son of Obed, and Maaseiah son of Adaiah, and Elishaphat son of Zichri, into the covenant with him. **2** And they go around in Judah, and gather the Levites out of all the cities of Judah, and heads of the fathers of Israel, and come to Jerusalem, **3** and all the assembly make a covenant in the house of God with the king, and he says to them, "Behold, the son of the king reigns, as Yhwh spoke concerning the sons of David. **4** This [is] the thing that you do: the third of you, going in on the Sabbath, of the priests, and of the Levites, [are] for gatekeepers of the thresholds, **5** and the third [are] at the house of the king, and the third at the Foundation Gate, and all the people [are] in the courts of the house of Yhwh. **6** And none enter the house of Yhwh except the priests, and those ministering of the Levites (they go in for they [are] holy), and all the people keep the watch of Yhwh; **7** and the Levites have surrounded the king all around, each with his weapon in his hand, and he who has gone into the house is put to death; and be with the king in his coming in and in his going out." **8** And the Levites and all Judah do according to all that Jehoiada the priest has commanded, and each takes his men going in on the Sabbath, with those going out on the Sabbath, for Jehoiada the priest has not let away the divisions. **9** And Jehoiada the priest gives to the heads of the hundreds the spears, and the shields, and the bucklers that [are] King David's, that [are] in the house of God; **10** and he stations the whole of the people, and each [with] his dart in his hand, from the right shoulder of the house to the left shoulder of the house, at the altar, and at the house, by the king, all around. **11** And they bring out the son of the king, and put the crown on him, and [give him] the Testimony, and cause him to reign; and Jehoiada and his sons anoint him, and say, "Let the king live!" **12** And Athaliah hears the voice of the people who are running, and who are praising the king, and she comes to the people [in] the house of Yhwh, **13** and sees, and behold, the king is standing by his pillar in the entrance, and the heads, and the trumpets [are] by the king, and all the people of the land rejoicing and shouting with trumpets, and the singers with instruments of song, and the teachers, to praise, and Athaliah tears her garments and says, "Conspiracy! Conspiracy!" **14** And Jehoiada the priest brings out the heads of the hundreds, inspectors of the force, and says to them, "Take her out from within the rows, and he who has gone after her is put to death by the sword"; for the priest said, "Do not put her to death [in] the house of Yhwh." **15** And they make sides for her, and she comes to the entrance of the Horse Gate at the house of the king, and they put her to death there. **16** And Jehoiada makes a covenant between him, and between all the people, and between the king, to be for a people to Yhwh; **17** and all the people enter the house of Ba'al, and break it down, indeed, they have broken his altars and his images, and they have slain Mattan priest of Ba'al before the altars. **18** And Jehoiada puts the offices of the house of Yhwh into the hand of the priests, the Levites, whom David had apportioned over the house of Yhwh, to cause the burnt-offerings of Yhwh to ascend, as written in the Law of Moses, with joy, and with singing, by the hands of David; **19** and he stations the gatekeepers over the gates of the house of Yhwh, and the unclean in anything do not go in. **20** And he takes the heads of the hundreds, and the majestic ones, and the rulers among the people, and all the people of the land, and brings down the king from the house of Yhwh, and they come in through the high gate to the house of the king, and cause the king to sit on the throne of the kingdom. **21** And all the people of the land rejoice, and the city has been quiet, and they have put Athaliah to death by the sword.

CHAPTER 24

1 Joash [is] a son of seven years in his reigning, and he has reigned forty years in Jerusalem, and the name of his mother [is] Zibiah of Beer-Sheba. **2** And Joash does that which is right in the eyes of Yhwh all the days of Jehoiada the priest. **3** And Jehoiada takes two wives for him, and he begets sons and daughters. **4** And it comes to pass after this, it has been with the heart of Joash to renew the house of Yhwh, **5** and he gathers the priests and the Levites, and says to them, "Go out to the cities of Judah, and gather money from all Israel to strengthen the house of your God sufficiently year by year, and you, hurry to the matter"; and the Levites have not hurried. **6** And the king calls for Jehoiada the head and says to him, "Why have you not required of the Levites to bring in out of Judah and out of Jerusalem the tribute of Moses, servant of Yhwh, and of the assembly of Israel, for the Tent of the Testimony? **7** for sons of Athaliah, the wicked one, have broken up the house of God, and also, they have prepared all the holy things of the house of Yhwh for Ba'alim." **8** And the king commands, and they make one chest, and put it at the gate of the house of Yhwh outside, **9** and give an intimation in Judah and in Jerusalem to bring to Yhwh the tribute of Moses, servant of God, [laid] on Israel in the wilderness. **10** And all the heads, and all the people rejoice, and they bring in, and cast into the chest, to completion. **11** And it comes to pass, at the time one brings in the chest for the inspection of the king by the hand of the Levites, and at their seeing that the money [is] abundant, that a scribe of the king has come in, and an officer of the head-priest, and they empty the chest, and take it up and turn it back to its place; thus they have done day by day, and gather money in abundance. **12** And the king and Jehoiada give it to the doers of the work of the service of the house of Yhwh, and they are

hiring hewers and craftsmen to renew the house of Yhwh, and also—to craftsmen in iron and bronze to strengthen the house of Yhwh. **13** And those doing the business work, and there goes up lengthening to the work by their hand, and they establish the house of God by its proper measure, and strengthen it. **14** And at their completing [it], they have brought in the rest of the money before the king and Jehoiada, and they make [with] it vessels for the house of Yhwh, vessels of serving, and of offering up, and spoons, even vessels of gold and silver; and they are causing burnt-offerings to ascend in the house of Yhwh continually, all the days of Jehoiada. **15** And Jehoiada is aged and satisfied with days, and dies—a son of one hundred and thirty years in his death, **16** and they bury him in the City of David with the kings, for he has done good in Israel, and with God and his house. **17** And after the death of Jehoiada, heads of Judah have come in, and bow themselves to the king; then the king has listened to them, **18** and they forsake the house of Yhwh, God of their fathers, and serve the Asherim and the idols, and there is wrath on Judah and Jerusalem for this guilt of theirs. **19** And He sends among them prophets, to bring them back to Yhwh, and they testify against them, and they have not given ear; **20** and the Spirit of God has clothed Zechariah son of Jehoiada the priest, and he stands above the people, and says to them, "Thus said God: Why are you transgressing the commands of Yhwh, and do not prosper? because you have forsaken Yhwh, He forsakes you." **21** And they conspire against him, and stone him [with] stone by the command of the king, in the court of the house of Yhwh, **22** and Joash the king has not remembered the kindness that his father Jehoiada did with him, and slays his son, and in his death he said, "Yhwh sees and requires." **23** And it comes to pass, at the turn of the year, the force of Aram has come up against him, and they come to Judah and Jerusalem, and destroy all the heads of the people from the people, and they have sent all their spoil to the king of Damascus, **24** for with few men the force of Aram has come in, and Yhwh has given into their hand a mighty force for multitude, because they have forsaken Yhwh, God of their fathers; and they have executed judgments with Joash. **25** And in their going from him—for they left him with many diseases—his servants themselves have conspired against him for the blood of the sons of Jehoiada the priest, and slay him on his bed, and he dies; and they bury him in the City of David, and have not buried him in the graves of the kings. **26** And these [are] those conspiring against him: Zabad son of Shimeath the Ammonitess, and Jehozabad son of Shimrith the Moabitess. **27** As for his sons, and the greatness of the burden on him, and the foundation of the house of God, behold, they are written on the commentary of the scroll of the Kings; and his son Amaziah reigns in his stead.

CHAPTER 25

1 Amaziah [was] a son of twenty-five years [when] he has reigned, and he has reigned twenty-nine years in Jerusalem, and the name of his mother [is] Jehoaddan of Jerusalem, **2** and he does that which is right in the eyes of Yhwh—only, not with a perfect heart. **3** And it comes to pass, when the kingdom has been strong on him, that he slays his servants, those striking his father the king, **4** and he has not put their sons to death, but [did] as is written in the Law, in the Scroll of Moses, whom Yhwh commanded, saying, "Fathers do not die for sons, and sons do not die for fathers, but they each die for his own sin." **5** And Amaziah gathers Judah and appoints them according to the house of the fathers, for heads of the thousands and for heads of the hundreds, for all Judah and Benjamin; and he inspects them from a son of twenty years and upward, and finds them [to be] three hundred thousand chosen ones, going forth to the host, holding spear and buckler. **6** And he hires out of Israel one hundred thousand mighty men of valor, with one hundred talents of silver; **7** and a man of God has come to him, saying, "O king, the host of Israel does not go with you; for Yhwh is not with Israel—all the sons of Ephraim; **8** but if you are going, do [it], be strong for battle, God causes you to stumble before an enemy, for there is power in God to help, and to cause to stumble." **9** And Amaziah says to the man of God, "But what to do about the hundred talents that I have given to the troop of Israel?" And the man of God says, "Yhwh has more to give to you than this." **10** And Amaziah separates them, of the troop that has come to him from Ephraim, to go to their own place; and their anger burns mightily against Judah, and they return to their place in the heat of anger. **11**

And Amaziah has strengthened himself, and leads his people, and goes to the Valley of Salt, and strikes ten thousand of the sons of Seir. [1][2] And the sons of Judah have taken captive ten thousand alive, and they bring them to the top of the rock, and cast them from the top of the rock, and all of them have been broken. [13] And the sons of the troop that Amaziah has sent back from going with him to battle—they rush against cities of Judah, from Samaria even to Beth-Horon, and strike three thousand of them, and seize much prey. [14] And it comes to pass after the coming in of Amaziah from striking the Edomites, that he brings in the gods of the sons of Seir, and establishes them for gods for himself, and bows himself before them, and he makes incense to them. [15] And the anger of Yhwh burns against Amaziah, and He sends a prophet to him, and he says to him, "Why have you sought the gods of the people that have not delivered their people out of your hand?" [16] And it comes to pass, in his speaking to him, that he says to him, "Have we appointed you for a counselor to the king? For you [must] cease; why do they strike you?" And the prophet ceases and says, "I have known that God has counseled to destroy you, because you have done this and have not listened to my counsel." [17] And Amaziah king of Judah takes counsel, and sends to Joash son of Jehoahaz, son of Jehu, king of Israel, saying, [18] "Come, we look one another in the face." And Joash king of Israel sends to Amaziah king of Judah, saying, "The thorn that [is] in Lebanon has sent to the cedar that [is] in Lebanon, saying, Give your daughter to my son for a wife; and a beast of the field that [is] in Lebanon passes by and treads down the thorn. [19] You have said, Behold, I have struck Edom; and your heart has lifted you up to boast; now, abide in your house, do you stir yourself up in evil, that you have fallen, you and Judah with you?" [20] And Amaziah has not listened, for it [is] from God in order to give them into [their] hand, because they have sought the gods of Edom; [21] and Joash king of Israel goes up, and they look one another in the face, he and Amaziah king of Judah, in Beth-Shemesh, that [is] Judah's, [22] and Judah is struck before Israel, and they flee—each to his tents. [23] And Joash king of Israel has caught Amaziah king of Judah, son of Joash, son of Jehoahaz, in Beth-Shemesh, and brings him to Jerusalem, and breaks down in the wall of Jerusalem from the Gate of Ephraim to the Corner Gate—four hundred cubits, [24] and [takes] all the gold, and the silver, and all the vessels that are found in the house of God with Obed-Edom, and the treasures of the house of the king, and the sons of the pledges, and turns back to Samaria. [25] And Amaziah son of Joash, king of Judah, lives after the death of Joash son of Jehoahaz, king of Israel, fifteen years; [26] and the rest of the matters of Amaziah, the first and the last, behold, are they not written on the scrolls of the kings of Judah and Israel? [27] And from the time that Amaziah has turned aside from after Yhwh—they make a conspiracy against him in Jerusalem, and he flees to Lachish, and they send after him to Lachish, and put him to death there, [28] and lift him up on the horses, and bury him with his fathers in the city of Judah.

CHAPTER 26

[1] And all the people of Judah take Uzziah (and he [is] a son of sixteen years), and cause him to reign instead of his father Amaziah. [2] He has built Eloth, and restores it to Judah after the king's lying with his fathers. [3] Uzziah [is] a son of sixteen years in his reigning, and he has reigned fifty-two years in Jerusalem, and the name of his mother [is] Jecholiah of Jerusalem. [4] And he does that which is right in the eyes of Yhwh, according to all that his father Amaziah did, [5] and he is as one seeking God in the days of Zechariah who has understanding in visions of God: and in the days of his seeking Yhwh, God has caused him to prosper. [6] And he goes forth and fights with the Philistines, and breaks down the wall of Gath, and the wall of Jabneh, and the wall of Ashdod, and builds cities [around] Ashdod, and among the Philistines. [7] And God helps him against the Philistines, and against the Arabians who are dwelling in Gur-Ba`al and the Mehunim. [8] And the Ammonites give a present to Uzziah, and his name goes to the entering in of Egypt, for he strengthened himself greatly. [9] And Uzziah builds towers in Jerusalem, by the Corner Gate, and by the Valley Gate, and by the angle, and strengthens them; [10] and he builds towers in the wilderness, and digs many wells, for he had much livestock, both in the low country and in the plain, farmers and vinedressers in the mountains, and in Carmel; for he was a lover of the ground. [11] And Uzziah has a force making war,

going forth to the host, by troops, in the number of their reckoning by the hand of Jeiel the scribe and Maaseiah the officer, by the hand of Hananiah [one] of the heads of the king. [12] The whole number of heads of the fathers of the mighty men of valor [is] two thousand and six hundred; [13] and by their hand [is] the force of the host—three hundred thousand and seven thousand and five hundred warriors, with mighty power to give help to the king against the enemy. [14] And Uzziah prepares for them, for all the host, shields, and spears, and helmets, and coats of mail, and bows, even to stones of the slings. [15] And he makes inventions in Jerusalem—a device of an inventor—to be on the towers, and on the corners, to shoot with arrows and with great stones, and his name goes out to a distance, for he has been wonderfully helped until he has been strong. [16] And at his being strong his heart has been high to destruction, and he trespasses against his God Yhwh, and goes into the temple of Yhwh to make incense on the altar of incense. [17] And Azariah the priest goes in after him, and with him eighty priests of Yhwh, sons of valor, [18] and they stand up against Uzziah the king, and say to him, "[It is] not for you, O Uzziah, to make incense to Yhwh, but for priests, sons of Aaron, who are sanctified to make incense; go forth from the sanctuary, for you have trespassed, indeed, for you [will] not [have] honor from Yhwh God." [19] And Uzziah is angry, and in his hand [is] a censer to make incense, and in his being angry with the priests—the leprosy has risen in his forehead, before the priests, in the house of Yhwh, from beside the altar of incense. [20] And Azariah the head priest looks toward him, and all the priests, and behold, he [is] leprous in his forehead, and they hurry him there, and also he himself has hurried to go out, for Yhwh has plagued him. [21] And Uzziah the king is a leper to the day of his death, and inhabits a separate house—a leper, for he has been cut off from the house of Yhwh, and his son Jotham [is] over the house of the king, judging the people of the land. [22] And the rest of the matters of Uzziah, the first and the last, Isaiah son of Amoz the prophet has written; [23] and Uzziah lies with his fathers, and they bury him with his fathers in the field of the burying place that the kings have, for they said, "He [is] a leper"; and his son Jotham reigns in his stead.

CHAPTER 27

[1] Jotham [is] a son of twenty-five years in his reigning, and he has reigned sixteen years in Jerusalem, and the name of his mother [is] Jerushah daughter of Zadok. [2] And he does that which is right in the eyes of Yhwh, according to all that his father Uzziah did; only, he has not come into the temple of Yhwh; and again the people are doing corruptly. [3] He has built the Upper Gate of the house of Yhwh, and in the wall of Ophel he has built abundantly; [4] and he has built cities in the hill-country of Judah, and he has built palaces and towers in the forests. [5] And he has fought with the king of the sons of Ammon, and prevails over them, and the sons of Ammon give to him in that year one hundred talents of silver, and ten thousand cors of wheat, and ten thousand of barley; the sons of Ammon have returned this to him both in the second year and in the third. [6] And Jotham strengthens himself, for he has prepared his ways before his God Yhwh. [7] And the rest of the matters of Jotham, and all his battles, and his ways, behold, they are written on the scroll of the kings of Israel and Judah. [8] He was a son of twenty-five years in his reigning, and he has reigned sixteen years in Jerusalem; [9] and Jotham lies with his fathers, and they bury him in the City of David, and his son Ahaz reigns in his stead.

CHAPTER 28

[1] Ahaz [is] a son of twenty years in his reigning, and he has reigned sixteen years in Jerusalem, and he has not done that which is right in the eyes of Yhwh, as his father David, [2] and walks in the ways of the kings of Israel, and has also made molten images for Ba`alim, [3] and has made incense himself in the Valley of the Son of Hinnom, and burns his sons with fire according to the abominations of the nations that Yhwh dispossessed from the presence of the sons of Israel, [4] and sacrifices and makes incense in high places, and on the heights, and under every green tree. [5] And his God Yhwh gives him into the hand of the king of Aram, and they strike him, and take captive a great captivity from him, and bring [them] to

Damascus, and he has also been given into the hand of the king of Israel, and he strikes him [with] a great striking. **6** And Pekah son of Remaliah slays one hundred and twenty thousand in Judah in one day (the whole [are] sons of valor), because of their forsaking Yhwh, God of their fathers. **7** And Zichri, a mighty one of Ephraim, slays Maaseiah son of the king, and Azrikam leader of the house, and Elkanah second to the king. **8** And the sons of Israel take captive of their brothers: two hundred thousand wives, sons, and daughters; and they have also seized much spoil from them, and they bring in the spoil to Samaria. **9** And there has been a prophet of Yhwh there (Oded [is] his name), and he goes out before the host that has come to Samaria, and says to them, "Behold, in the fury of Yhwh, God of your fathers, against Judah, He has given them into your hand, and you slay among them in rage—it has come to the heavens; **10** and now you are saying to subdue sons of Judah and Jerusalem for menservants and for maidservants for yourselves; but are there not causes of guilt with you before your God Yhwh? **11** and now, hear me, and send back the captives whom you have taken captive of your brothers, for the heat of the anger of Yhwh [is] on you." **12** And certain of the heads of the sons of Ephraim (Azariah son of Johanan, Berechiah son of Meshillemoth, and Jehizkiah son of Shallum, and Amasa son of Hadlai), rise up against those coming in from the host, **13** and say to them, "You do not bring in the captives here, for guilt against Yhwh [is already] on us, you are saying to add to our sin and to our guilt. For abundant [is] the guilt we have, and the fierceness of anger on Israel." **14** And the armed men leave the captives and the prey before the heads and all the assembly; **15** and the men who have been expressed by name rise and take hold on the captives, and they have clothed all their naked ones from the spoil, indeed, they clothe them, and shoe them, and cause them to eat and drink, and anoint them, and lead them on donkeys, even every feeble one, and bring them to Jericho, the city of palms, near their brothers, and return to Samaria. **16** At that time King Ahaz has sent to the king of Asshur to give help to him; **17** and again the Edomites have come, and strike in Judah, and take captive a captivity. **18** And the Philistines have rushed against the cities of the low country, and of the south of Judah, and capture Beth-Shemesh, and Aijalon, and Gederoth, and Shocho and its villages, and Timnah and its villages, and Gimzo and its villages, and dwell there, **19** for Yhwh has humbled Judah because of Ahaz king of Israel, for he made free with Judah, even to commit a trespass against Yhwh. **20** And Tilgath-Pilneser king of Asshur comes to him, and does distress him, and has not strengthened him, **21** though Ahaz has taken a portion [out] of the house of Yhwh, and [out] of the house of the king, and of the princes, and gives to the king of Asshur, yet it is no help to him. **22** And in the time of his distress—he adds to trespass against Yhwh (this King Ahaz), **23** and he sacrifices to the gods of Damascus [which were] those striking him, and says, "Because the gods of the kings of Aram are helping them, I sacrifice to them, and they help me," and they have been to him to cause him to stumble, and to all Israel. **24** And Ahaz gathers the vessels of the house of God, and cuts in pieces the vessels of the house of God, and shuts the doors of the house of Yhwh, and makes altars for himself in every corner in Jerusalem. **25** And in each and every city of Judah he has made high places to make incense to other gods, and provokes Yhwh, God of his fathers. **26** And the rest of his matters, and all his ways, the first and the last, behold, they are written on the scroll of the kings of Judah and Israel. **27** And Ahaz lies with his fathers, and they bury him in the city, in Jerusalem, but have not brought him to the graves of the kings of Israel, and his son Hezekiah reigns in his stead.

CHAPTER 29

1 Hezekiah [was] a son of twenty-five years [when] he has reigned, and he has reigned twenty-nine years in Jerusalem, and the name of his mother [is] Abijah daughter of Zechariah; **2** and he does that which is right in the eyes of Yhwh, according to all that his father David did. **3** He, in the first year of his reign, in the first month, has opened the doors of the house of Yhwh, and strengthens them, **4** and brings in the priests and the Levites, and gathers them to the broad place to the east. **5** And he says to them, "Hear me, O Levites, now sanctify yourselves, and sanctify the house of Yhwh, God of your fathers, and bring out the impurity from the holy place, **6** for our fathers have trespassed, and done that which is evil in the

eyes of our God Yhwh, and forsake him, and turn around their faces from the Dwelling Place of Yhwh, and give the neck. **7** They have also shut the doors of the porch, and quench the lamps, and they have not made incense, and have not caused burnt-offering to ascend in the holy place to the God of Israel, **8** and the wrath of Yhwh is on Judah and Jerusalem, and He gives them for a trembling, for an astonishment, and for a hissing, as you are seeing with your eyes. **9** And behold, our fathers have fallen by the sword, and our sons, and our daughters, and our wives [are] in captivity for this. **10** Now [it is] with my heart to make a covenant before Yhwh, God of Israel, and the fierceness of His anger turns back from us. **11** My sons, do not be at rest now, for Yhwh has fixed on you to stand before Him, to serve Him, and to be ministering and making incense to Him." **12** And the Levites rise—Mahath son of Amasai, and Joel son of Azariah, of the sons of the Kohathite; and of the sons of Merari: Kish son of Abdi, and Azariah son of Jehalelel; and of the Gershonite: Joah son of Zimmah, and Eden son of Joah; **13** and of the sons of Elizaphan: Shimri and Jeiel; and of the sons of Asaph: Zechariah and Mattaniah; **14** and of the sons of Heman: Jehiel and Shimei; and of the sons of Jeduthun: Shemaiah and Uzziel— **15** and they gather their brothers, and sanctify themselves, and come in, according to the command of the king in the matters of Yhwh, to cleanse the house of Yhwh, **16** and the priests come into the inner part of the house of Yhwh to cleanse [it], and bring out all the uncleanness that they have found in the temple of Yhwh to the court of the house of Yhwh, and the Levites receive [it], to take [it] out to the Brook of Kidron outside. **17** And they begin to sanctify on the first of the first month, and on the eighth day of the month they have come to the porch of Yhwh, and they sanctify the house of Yhwh in eight days, and on the sixteenth day of the first month they have finished. **18** And they come in to Hezekiah the king within, and say, "We have cleansed all the house of Yhwh, and the altar of the burnt-offering, and all its vessels, and the table of the arrangement, and all its vessels, **19** and all the vessels that King Ahaz cast away in his reign—in his trespass—we have prepared and sanctified, and behold, they [are] before the altar of Yhwh." **20** And Hezekiah the king rises early, and gathers the heads of the city, and goes up to the house of Yhwh; **21** and they bring in seven bullocks, and seven rams, and seven lambs, and seven young male goats, for a sin-offering for the kingdom, and for the sanctuary, and for Judah; and he commands to sons of Aaron, the priests, to cause [them] to ascend on the altar of Yhwh. **22** And they slaughter the oxen, and the priests receive the blood, and sprinkle on the altar; and they slaughter the rams, and sprinkle the blood on the altar; and they slaughter the lambs, and sprinkle the blood on the altar; **23** and they bring the male goats of the sin-offering near before the king and the assembly, and they lay their hands on them; **24** and the priests slaughter them, and make a sin-offering with their blood on the altar, to make atonement for all Israel, that "For all Israel," said the king, "[is] the burnt-offering and the sin-offering." **25** And he appoints the Levites in the house of Yhwh with cymbals, with psalteries, and with harps, by the command of David, and of Gad, seer of the king, and of Nathan the prophet, for the command [is] by the hand of Yhwh, by the hand of His prophets; **26** and the Levites stand with the instruments of David, and the priests with the trumpets. **27** And Hezekiah commands to cause the burnt-offering to ascend on the altar; and at the time the burnt-offering began, the song of Yhwh began, and the trumpets, and with [the] hands of [the] instruments of David king of Israel. **28** And all the assembly are worshiping, and the singers singing, and the trumpeters blowing; the whole [is] until the completion of the burnt-offering. **29** And at the completion of the offering up, the king and all those found with him have bowed, and pay respect. **30** And Hezekiah the king commands—and the princes—to the Levites [to cause them] to give praise to Yhwh in the words of David, and of Asaph the seer, and they praise—to joy, and they bow, and pay respect. **31** And Hezekiah answers and says, "Now you have filled your hand for Yhwh, come near, and bring in sacrifices and thank-offerings to the house of Yhwh"; and the assembly brings in sacrifices and thank-offerings, and every willing-hearted one—burnt-offerings. **32** And the number of the burnt-offerings that the assembly has brought in is seventy oxen, one hundred rams, [and] two hundred lambs; for all these [are] a burnt-offering to Yhwh. **33** And the sanctified things [are] six hundred oxen and three thousand sheep. **34** Only, the priests have become few, and have not been able to strip the whole of the burnt-offerings, and their brothers the

Levites strengthen them until the completion of the work, and until the priests sanctify themselves, for the Levites [are] more upright of heart to sanctify themselves than the priests. **35** And also, burnt-offerings [are] in abundance, with fat of the peace-offerings, and with oblations for the burnt-offering; and the service of the house of Yhwh is established, **36** and Hezekiah and all the people rejoice because of God's giving preparation to the people, for the thing has been suddenly.

CHAPTER 30

1 And Hezekiah sends to all Israel and Judah, and he has also written letters to Ephraim and Manasseh, [to cause them] to come to the house of Yhwh in Jerusalem, to make a Passover to Yhwh, God of Israel. **2** And the king takes counsel, and his heads, and all the assembly in Jerusalem, to make the Passover in the second month, **3** for they have not been able to make it at that time, for the priests have not sanctified themselves sufficiently, and the people have not been gathered to Jerusalem. **4** And the thing is right in the eyes of the king, and in the eyes of all the assembly, **5** and they establish the thing, to cause an intimation to pass over into all Israel, from Beer-Sheba even to Dan, to come to make a Passover to Yhwh, God of Israel, in Jerusalem; for they had not done as it is written for a long time. **6** And the runners go with letters from the hand of the king and his heads into all Israel and Judah, even according to the command of the king, saying, "O sons of Israel, turn back to Yhwh, God of Abraham, Isaac, and Israel, and He turns back to the escaped part that is left of you from the hand of the kings of Asshur; **7** and do not be like your fathers and like your brothers, who trespassed against Yhwh, God of their fathers, and He gives them to desolation, as you see. **8** Now do not harden your neck like your fathers, give a hand to Yhwh, and come into His sanctuary that He has sanctified for all time, and serve your God Yhwh, and the fierceness of His anger turns back from you; **9** for in your turning back to Yhwh, your brothers and your sons have mercies before their captors, even to return to this land, for your God Yhwh [is] gracious and merciful, and He does not turn aside the face from you if you turn back to Him." **10** And the runners are passing over from city to city in the land of Ephraim and Manasseh, even to Zebulun, but they are laughing at them and mocking at them, **11** only, certain from Asher, and Manasseh, and from Zebulun, have been humbled, and come to Jerusalem. **12** Also, in Judah the hand of God has been to give one heart to them to do the command of the king and of the heads in the matter of Yhwh; **13** and many people are gathered to Jerusalem to make the Celebration of Unleavened Things in the second month—a mighty assembly for multitude. **14** And they arise and turn aside the altars that [are] in Jerusalem, and they have turned aside all the incense altars, and cast [them] into the Brook of Kidron; **15** and they slaughter the Passover-offering on the fourteenth of the second month, and the priests and the Levites have been ashamed, and sanctify themselves, and bring in burnt-offerings to the house of Yhwh. **16** And they stand on their station according to their ordinance, according to the Law of Moses the man of God; the priests are sprinkling the blood out of the hand of the Levites, **17** for many [are] in the assembly who have not sanctified themselves, and the Levites [are] over the slaughtering of the Passover-offerings for everyone not clean, to sanctify [him] to Yhwh: **18** for a multitude of the people, many from Ephraim, and Manasseh, Issachar, and Zebulun, have not been cleansed, but have eaten the Passover otherwise than it is written; but Hezekiah prayed for them, saying, "Yhwh, who [is] good, receives atonement for everyone **19** who has prepared his heart to seek God—Yhwh, God of his fathers—yet not according to the cleansing of the holy place"; **20** and Yhwh listens to Hezekiah and heals the people. **21** And the sons of Israel, those found in Jerusalem, make the Celebration of Unleavened Things [for] seven days with great joy; and the Levites and the priests are giving praise to Yhwh day by day with instruments of praise before Yhwh. **22** And Hezekiah speaks to the heart of all the Levites, those giving good understanding concerning Yhwh, and they eat the appointed thing [for] seven days; sacrificing sacrifices of peace-offerings, and making confession to Yhwh, God of their fathers. **23** And all the assembly take counsel to keep [it] another seven days, and they keep [it for] seven days [with] joy; **24** for Hezekiah king of Judah has presented one thousand bullocks and seven thousand sheep to the assembly; and the heads have presented one thousand

bullocks and ten thousand sheep to the assembly; and priests sanctify themselves in abundance. **25** And all the assembly of Judah rejoices, and the priests, and the Levites, and all the assembly, those coming in from Israel, and the sojourners—those coming in from the land of Israel and those dwelling in Judah, **26** and there is great joy in Jerusalem; for from the days of Solomon son of David, king of Israel, there is not like this in Jerusalem, **27** and the priests, the Levites, rise and bless the people, and their voice is heard, and their prayer comes into His holy habitation in the heavens.

CHAPTER 31

1 And at the completion of all this, all [those of] Israel who are found present have gone out to the cities of Judah, and break the standing-pillars, and cut down the Asherim, and break down the high places and the altars, out of all Judah and Benjamin, and in Ephraim and Manasseh, even to completion, and all the sons of Israel return, each to his possession, to their cities. **2** And Hezekiah appoints the divisions of the priests and of the Levites, by their divisions, each according to his service, of the priests and of the Levites, for burnt-offering and for peace-offerings, to minister and to give thanks, and to give praise in the gates of the camps of Yhwh. **3** And a portion of the king, from his substance, [is] for burnt-offerings, for burnt-offerings of the morning and of the evening, and the burnt-offerings of Sabbaths, and of new moons, and of appointed times, as it is written in the Law of Yhwh. **4** And he commands to the people, to the inhabitants of Jerusalem, to give the portion of the priests and of the Levites, so that they are strengthened in the Law of Yhwh; **5** and at the spreading forth of the thing, the sons of Israel have multiplied the first-fruit of grain, new wine, and oil, and honey, and of all the increase of the field, and they have brought in the tithe of the whole in abundance. **6** And the sons of Israel and Judah, those dwelling in cities of Judah, have also brought in a tithe of herd and flock, and a tithe of the holy things that are sanctified to their God Yhwh, and they set [them in] heaps of heaps. **7** In the third month they have begun to lay the foundation of the heaps, and in the seventh month they have finished. **8** And Hezekiah and the heads come in and see the heaps, and bless Yhwh and His people Israel, **9** and Hezekiah inquires at the priests and the Levites concerning the heaps, **10** and Azariah the head priest, of the house of Zadok, speaks to him and says, "From the beginning of the bringing of the raised-offering to the house of Yhwh, [there is enough] to eat, and to be satisfied, and to leave abundantly, for Yhwh has blessed His people, and that left [is] this store." **11** And Hezekiah commands to prepare chambers in the house of Yhwh, and they prepare, **12** and they bring in the raised-offering, and the tithe, and the holy things faithfully; and over them is a leader, Conaniah the Levite, and his brother Shimei [is] second; **13** and Jehiel, and Azaziah, and Nahath, and Asahel, and Jerimoth, and Jozabad, and Eliel, and Ismachiah, and Mahath, and Benaiah, [are] inspectors under the hand of Conaniah and his brother Shimei, by the appointment of Hezekiah the king, and Azariah leader of the house of God. **14** And Kore son of Imnah the Levite, the gatekeeper at the east, [is] over the willing-offerings of God, to give the raised-offering of Yhwh, and the most holy things. **15** And by his hand [are] Eden, and Miniamin, and Jeshua, and Shemaiah, Amariah, and Shechaniah, in cities of the priests, faithfully to give to their brothers in divisions, as the great so the small, **16** apart from their genealogy, to males from a son of three years and upward, to everyone who has gone into the house of Yhwh, by the matter of a day in its day, for their service in their charges, according to their divisions; **17** and the genealogy of the priests by the house of their fathers, and of the Levites, from a son of twenty years and upward, in their charges, in their divisions; **18** and to the genealogy among all their infants, their wives, and their sons, and their daughters to all the congregation, for in their faithfulness they sanctify themselves in holiness. **19** And for sons of Aaron, the priests, in the fields of the outskirt of their cities, in each and every city, [are] men who have been defined by name, to give portions to every male among the priests, and to everyone who reckoned himself by genealogy among the Levites. **20** And Hezekiah does thus in all Judah, and does that which is good, and that which is right, and that which is true, before his God Yhwh; **21** and in every work that he has begun for the service of the house of God, and for the Law, and for the command, to seek for his God with all his heart, he has worked and prospered.

CHAPTER 32

¹ After these things and this truth, Sennacherib king of Asshur has come, indeed, he comes to Judah, and encamps against the cities of the bulwarks, and says to break into them himself. ² And Hezekiah sees that Sennacherib has come, and his face [is] to the battle against Jerusalem, ³ and he takes counsel with his heads and his mighty ones, to stop the waters of the fountains that [are] at the outside of the city—and they help him, ⁴ and many people are gathered, and they stop all the fountains and the brook that is rushing into the midst of the land, saying, "Why do the kings of Asshur come, and have found much water?" ⁵ And he strengthens himself, and builds the whole of the wall that is broken, and causes [it] to ascend to the towers, and at the outside of the wall [builds] another, and strengthens Millo [in] the City of David, and makes darts in abundance, and shields. ⁶ And he puts heads of war over the people, and gathers them to him, to the broad place of a gate of the city, and speaks to their heart, saying, ⁷ "Be strong and courageous, do not be afraid, nor be cast down from the face of the king of Asshur, and from the face of all the multitude that [is] with him, for with us [are] more than with him. ⁸ With him [is] an arm of flesh, but with us [is] our God Yhwh to help us and to fight our battles"; and the people are supported by the words of Hezekiah king of Judah. ⁹ After this Sennacherib king of Asshur has sent his servants to Jerusalem—and he [is] by Lachish, and all his power with him—against Hezekiah king of Judah and against all Judah who [are] in Jerusalem, saying, ¹⁰ "Thus said Sennacherib king of Asshur: On what are you trusting and abiding in the bulwark in Jerusalem? ¹¹ Is Hezekiah not persuading you to give you up to die by famine and by thirst, saying, Our God Yhwh delivers us from the hand of the king of Asshur? ¹² Has Hezekiah himself not turned aside His high places and His altars, and speaks to Judah and to Jerusalem, saying, You bow yourselves before one altar and you make incense on it? ¹³ Do you not know what I have done—I and my fathers—to all peoples of the lands? Were the gods of the nations of the lands at all able to deliver their land out of my hand? ¹⁴ Who among all the gods of these nations whom my fathers have devoted to destruction [is] he who has been able to deliver his people out of my hand, that your God is able to deliver you out of my hand? ¹⁵ And now, do not let Hezekiah lift you up, nor persuade you thus, nor give credence to him, for no god of any nation and kingdom is able to deliver his people from my hand and from the hand of my fathers: also, surely your God does not deliver you from my hand!" ¹⁶ And again his servants have spoken against Yhwh God and against His servant Hezekiah, ¹⁷ and he has written letters to give reproach to Yhwh, God of Israel, and to speak against Him, saying, "As the gods of the nations of the lands that have not delivered their people from my hand, so the God of Hezekiah does not deliver His people from my hand." ¹⁸ And they call with a great voice [in] Jewish against the people of Jerusalem who [are] on the wall, to frighten them and to trouble them, that they may capture the city, ¹⁹ and they speak against the God of Jerusalem as against the gods of the peoples of the land—work of the hands of man. ²⁰ And Hezekiah the king prays, and Isaiah son of Amoz the prophet, concerning this, and they cry to the heavens, ²¹ and Yhwh sends a messenger and cuts off every mighty man of valor—both leader and head—in the camp of the king of Asshur, and he turns back with shame of face to his land and enters the house of his god, and those coming out of his bowels have caused him to fall there by the sword. ²² And Yhwh saves Hezekiah and the inhabitants of Jerusalem from the hand of Sennacherib king of Asshur and from the hand of all, and He leads them around; ²³ and many are bringing in an offering to Yhwh, to Jerusalem, and precious things to Hezekiah king of Judah, and he is lifted up before the eyes of all the nations after this. ²⁴ In those days Hezekiah has been sick even to death, and he prays to Yhwh, and He speaks to him and has appointed a wonder for him; ²⁵ and Hezekiah has not returned according to the deed [done] to him, for his heart has been lofty, and there is wrath on him and on Judah and Jerusalem; ²⁶ and Hezekiah is humbled for the loftiness of his heart, he and the inhabitants of Jerusalem, and the wrath of Yhwh has not come on them in the days of Hezekiah. ²⁷ And Hezekiah has very much riches and honor, and he has made treasures for himself of silver, and of gold, and of precious stone, and of spices, and of shields, and of all [kinds] of desirable vessels, ²⁸ and storehouses for the increase of grain, and new wine, and oil, and stalls for all kinds of livestock, and herds for stalls; ²⁹ and he has made cities for himself, and possessions of flocks and herds in abundance, for God has given very much substance to him. ³⁰ And Hezekiah himself has stopped the upper source of the waters of Gihon, and directs them beneath to the west of the City of David, and Hezekiah prospers in all his work; ³¹ and so with the ambassadors of the heads of Babylon, those sending to him to inquire of the wonder that has been in the land, God has left him to try him, to know all in his heart. ³² And the rest of the matters of Hezekiah and his kind acts, behold, they are written in the vision of Isaiah son of Amoz the prophet, on the scroll of the kings of Judah and Israel. ³³ And Hezekiah lies with his fathers, and they bury him in the highest of the graves of the sons of David, and all Judah and the inhabitants of Jerusalem have done honor to him at his death, and his son Manasseh reigns in his stead.

CHAPTER 33

¹ Manasseh is a son of twelve years in his reigning, and he has reigned fifty-five years in Jerusalem; ² and he does evil in the eyes of Yhwh, like the abominations of the nations that Yhwh dispossessed from the presence of the sons of Israel, ³ and he turns and builds the high places that his father Hezekiah has broken down, and raises altars for Ba'alim, and makes Asherim, and bows himself to all the host of the heavens, and serves them. ⁴ And he has built altars in the house of Yhwh of which Yhwh had said, "My Name is in Jerusalem for all time." ⁵ And he builds altars for all the host of the heavens in the two courts of the house of Yhwh. ⁶ And he has caused his sons to pass over through fire in the Valley of the Son of Hinnom, and observed clouds and used enchantments and witchcraft, and dealt with a familiar spirit, and a wizard; he has multiplied to do evil in the eyes of Yhwh, to provoke him to anger. ⁷ And he places the carved image of the idol that he made in the house of God, of which God said to David, and to his son Solomon, "In this house, and in Jerusalem that I have chosen out of all the tribes of Israel, I put My Name for all time, ⁸ and I do not add to turn aside the foot of Israel from off the ground that I appointed to your fathers, only, if they watch to do all that I have commanded them—to all the Law, and the statutes, and the ordinances by the hand of Moses." ⁹ And Manasseh causes Judah and the inhabitants of Jerusalem to err, to do evil above the nations that Yhwh destroyed from the presence of the sons of Israel. ¹⁰ And Yhwh speaks to Manasseh and to his people, and they have not attended, ¹¹ and Yhwh brings in against them the heads of the host that the king of Asshur has, and they capture Manasseh among the thickets, and bind him with bronze chains, and cause him to go to Babylon. ¹² And when he is in distress he has appeased the face of his God Yhwh, and is exceedingly humbled before the God of his fathers, ¹³ and prays to Him, and He accepts his plea, and hears his supplication, and brings him back to Jerusalem, to his kingdom, and Manasseh knows that He, Yhwh, [is] God. ¹⁴ And after this he has built an outer wall for the City of David, on the west of Gihon, in the valley, and at the entering in at the Fish Gate, and it has gone around to the tower, and he makes it exceedingly high, and he puts heads of the force in all the cities of the bulwarks in Judah. ¹⁵ And he turns aside the gods of the stranger, and the idol, out of the house of Yhwh, and all the altars that he had built on the mountain of the house of Yhwh and in Jerusalem, and casts [them] to the outside of the city. ¹⁶ And he builds the altar of Yhwh, and sacrifices on it sacrifices of peace-offerings and thank-offering, and commands to Judah to serve Yhwh, God of Israel; ¹⁷ but still the people are sacrificing in high places, only—to their God Yhwh. ¹⁸ And the rest of the matters of Manasseh, and his prayer to his God, and the matters of the seers, those speaking to him in the Name of Yhwh, God of Israel, behold, they are [on the scroll of] the matters of the kings of Israel; ¹⁹ and his prayer, and his plea, and all his sin, and his trespass, and the places in which he had built high places, and established the Asherim and the carved images before his being humbled, behold, they are written beside the matters of Hozai. ²⁰ And Manasseh lies with his fathers, and they bury him in his own house, and his son Amon reigns in his stead. ²¹ Amon [is] a son of twenty-two years in his reigning, and he has reigned two years in Jerusalem, ²² and he does evil in the eyes of Yhwh, as his father Manasseh did, and Amon has sacrificed to all the carved images that his father Manasseh had made, and serves them, ²³ and has not been

humbled before Yhwh, like the humbling of his father Manasseh, for Amon himself has multiplied guilt. **24** And his servants conspire against him and put him to death in his own house, **25** and the people of the land strike all those conspiring against King Amon, and the people of the land cause his son Josiah to reign in his stead.

CHAPTER 34

1 Josiah [is] a son of eight years in his reigning, and he has reigned thirty-one years in Jerusalem, **2** and he does that which is right in the eyes of Yhwh, and walks in the ways of his father David, and has not turned aside [to] the right or left. **3** And in the eighth year of his reign (and he [is] yet a youth), he has begun to seek for the God of his father David, and in the twelfth year he has begun to cleanse Judah and Jerusalem from the high places, and the Asherim, and the carved images, and the molten images. **4** And they break down the altars of the Ba'alim before him, and he has cut down the images that [are] on high above them, and the Asherim, and the carved images, and the molten images, he has broken and beaten small, and strews [them] on the surface of the graves of those sacrificing to them, **5** and he has burned the bones of the priests on their altars, and cleanses Judah and Jerusalem, **6** and in the cities of Manasseh, and Ephraim, and Simeon, even to Naphtali, with their tools, all around. **7** And he breaks down the altars and the Asherim, and he has beaten down the carved images very small, and he has cut down all the images in all the land of Israel, and turns back to Jerusalem. **8** And in the eighteenth year of his reign, to purify the land and the house, he has sent Shaphan son of Azaliah, and Maaseiah head of the city, and Joah son of Johaz the remembrancer, to strengthen the house of his God Yhwh. **9** And they come to Hilkiah the high priest, and they give the money that is brought into the house of God, that the Levites, keeping the threshold, have gathered from the hand of Manasseh, and Ephraim, and from all the remnant of Israel, and from all Judah, and Benjamin, and the inhabitants of Jerusalem, **10** and they give [it] into the hand of the workmen, those appointed over the house of Yhwh, and they give it [to] the workmen who are working in the house of Yhwh, to repair and to strengthen the house; **11** and they give [it] to craftsmen and to builders to buy hewn stones, and wood for couplings and for beams [for] the houses that the kings of Judah had destroyed. **12** And the men are working faithfully in the business, and over them are appointed Jahath and Obadiah, the Levites, of the sons of Merari, and Zechariah and Meshullam, of the sons of the Kohathite, to overlook; and of the Levites, everyone understanding about instruments of song, **13** and over the burden-bearers, and overseers of everyone doing work for every service; and of the Levites [are] scribes, and officers, and gatekeepers. **14** And in their bringing out the money that is brought into the house of Yhwh, Hilkiah the priest has found the Scroll of the Law of Yhwh by the hand of Moses, **15** and Hilkiah answers and says to Shaphan the scribe, "I have found [the] Scroll of the Law in the house of Yhwh"; and Hilkiah gives the scroll to Shaphan, **16** and Shaphan brings in the scroll to the king, and brings the king back word again, saying, "All that has been given into the hand of your servants they are doing, **17** and they pour out the money that is found in the house of Yhwh, and give it into the hand of those appointed and into the hands of those doing the work." **18** And Shaphan the scribe declares [it] to the king, saying, "Hilkiah the priest has given a scroll to me"; and Shaphan reads in it before the king. **19** And it comes to pass, at the king's hearing the words of the Law, that he tears his garments, **20** and the king commands Hilkiah, and Ahikam son of Shaphan, and Abdon son of Micah, and Shaphan the scribe, and Asaiah, servant of the king, saying, **21** "Go, seek Yhwh for me, and for him who is left in Israel and in Judah, concerning the words of the scroll that is found, for great [is] the fury of Yhwh that is poured on us, because that our fathers did not keep the word of Yhwh to do according to all that is written on this scroll." **22** And Hilkiah goes, and they of the king, to Huldah the prophetess, wife of Shallum son of Tikvath, son of Hasrah, keeper of the garments, and she is dwelling in Jerusalem in the Second [Quarter], and they speak to her thus. **23** And she says to them, "Thus said Yhwh, God of Israel: Say to the man who has sent you to me, **24** Thus said Yhwh: Behold, I am bringing in calamity on this place and on its inhabitants, all the execrations that are written on the scroll that they read before the king of Judah, **25** because that they have forsaken Me, and

make incense to other gods, so as to provoke Me with all the works of their hands, and My fury is poured out on this place, and it is not quenched. **26** And to the king of Judah who is sending you to inquire of Yhwh, thus you say to him, Thus said Yhwh God of Israel, whose words you have heard: **27** Because your heart [is] tender, and you are humbled before God in your hearing His words concerning this place and concerning its inhabitants, and are humbled before Me, and tear your garments, and weep before Me, indeed, I have also heard [you]—a declaration of Yhwh. **28** Behold, I am gathering you to your fathers, and you have been gathered to your graves in peace, and your eyes do not look on all the calamity that I am bringing on this place and, on its inhabitants,"; and they bring the king back word. **29** And the king sends and gathers all the elderly of Judah and Jerusalem, **30** and the king goes up to the house of Yhwh, and [to] every man of Judah, and the inhabitants of Jerusalem, and the priests, and the Levites, even all the people, from great even to small, and he reads in their ears all the words of the scroll of the covenant that is found in the house of Yhwh. **31** And the king stands on his station, and makes the covenant before Yhwh to walk after Yhwh, and to keep His commands, and His testimonies, and His statutes, with all his heart and with all his soul, to do the words of the covenant that are written on this scroll. **32** And he presents everyone who is found in Jerusalem and Benjamin, and the inhabitants of Jerusalem do according to the covenant of God, the God of their fathers. **33** And Josiah turns aside all the abominations out of all the lands that the sons of Israel have, and causes everyone who is found in Israel to serve, to serve their God Yhwh; all his days they did not turn aside from after Yhwh, God of their fathers.

CHAPTER 35

1 And Josiah makes a Passover to Yhwh in Jerusalem, and they slaughter the Passover-offering on the fourteenth of the first month, **2** and he stations the priests over their charges, and strengthens them for the service of the house of Yhwh, **3** and says to the Levites who are teaching all Israel, who are sanctified to Yhwh, "Put the holy Ark in the house that Solomon son of David, king of Israel, built; it is not a burden on the shoulder to you. Now serve your God Yhwh and His people Israel, **4** and prepare, by the house of your fathers, according to your divisions, by the writing of David king of Israel, and by the writing of his son Solomon, **5** and stand in the holy place, by the divisions of the house of the fathers of your brothers, sons of the people, and the portion of the house of a father of the Levites, **6** and slaughter the Passover-offering and sanctify yourselves, and prepare for your brothers, to do according to the word of Yhwh by the hand of Moses." **7** And Josiah lifts up to the sons of the people a flock of lambs and young goats, the whole for Passover-offerings, for everyone who is found, to the number of thirty thousand, and three thousand oxen: these [are] from the substance of the king. **8** And his heads, for a willing-offering to the people, to the priests and to the Levites, have lifted up; Hilkiah, and Zechariah, and Jehiel, leaders in the house of God, have given two thousand and six hundred to the priests for Passover-offerings, and three hundred oxen; **9** and Conaniah, and Shemaiah, and Nethaneel, his brothers, and Hashabiah, and Jeiel, and Jozabad, heads of the Levites, have lifted up five thousand to the Levites for Passover-offerings, and five hundred oxen. **10** And the service is prepared, and the priests stand on their station, and the Levites on their divisions, according to the command of the king, **11** and they slaughter the Passover-offering, and the priests sprinkle out of their hand, and the Levites are stripping [them]; **12** and they turn aside the burnt-offering to put them by the divisions of the house of the fathers of the sons of the people, to bring near to Yhwh, as it is written in the scroll of Moses—and so for the oxen. **13** And they cook the Passover with fire according to the ordinance, and they have cooked the sanctified things in pots, and in kettles, and in pans—for all the sons of the people. **14** And afterward they have prepared for themselves and for the priests; for the priests, sons of Aaron, [are occupied] in the offering up of the burnt-offering and of the fat until night; and the Levites have prepared for themselves and for the priests, sons of Aaron. **15** And the singers, sons of Asaph, [are] on their station according to the command of David, and Asaph, and Heman, and Jeduthun seer of the king, and the gatekeepers [are] at every gate; it is not for them to turn aside from off their service, for their brothers the Levites have prepared for them. **16** And all the service of Yhwh is prepared on that day to keep the Passover and to cause burnt-offering to ascend on the altar of Yhwh, according to the command of King Josiah. **17** And the sons of Israel who are found make the Passover at that time, and the Celebration of Unleavened Things, [for] seven days. **18** And there has not been made a Passover like it in Israel from the days of Samuel the prophet, and none of the kings of Israel made such a Passover as Josiah has made, and the priests, and the Levites, and all Judah and Israel who are found, and the inhabitants of Jerusalem. **19** In the eighteenth year of the reign of Josiah this Passover has been made. **20** After all this, when Josiah has prepared the house, Necho king of Egypt has come up to fight against Carchemish by the Euphrates, and Josiah goes forth to meet him; **21** and he sends messengers to him, saying, "And what do I [have to do] with you, O king of Judah? I do not come against you today, but to the house with which I have war, and God commanded to hurry me; cease for yourself from God who [is] with me, and He does not destroy you." **22** And Josiah has not turned around his face from him, but has disguised himself to fight against him, and has not listened to the words of Necho, from the mouth of God, and comes to fight in the Valley of Megiddo; **23** and the archers shoot at King Josiah, and the king says to his servants, "Remove me, for I have become very sick." **24** And his servants remove him from the chariot, and cause him to ride on the second chariot that he has, and cause him to go to Jerusalem, and he dies, and is buried in the graves of his fathers, and all Judah and Jerusalem are mourning for Josiah, **25** and Jeremiah laments for Josiah, and all the male and female singers speak in their lamentations of Josiah to this day, and set them for a statute on Israel, and behold, they are written beside the Lamentations. **26** And the rest of the matters of Josiah and his kind acts, according as it is written in the Law of Yhwh, **27** even his matters, the first and the last, behold, they are written on the scroll of the kings of Israel and Judah.

CHAPTER 36

1 And the people of the land take Jehoahaz son of Josiah and cause him to reign instead of his father in Jerusalem. 2 Jehoahaz [is] a son of twenty-three years in his reigning, and he has reigned three months in Jerusalem, 3 and the king of Egypt turns him aside in Jerusalem, and fines the land one hundred talents of silver, and a talent of gold; 4 and the king of Egypt causes his brother Eliakim to reign over Judah and Jerusalem, and turns his name to Jehoiakim; and Necho has taken his brother Jehoahaz and brings him to Egypt. 5 Jehoiakim [is] a son of twenty-five years in his reigning, and he has reigned eleven years in Jerusalem, and he does evil in the eyes of his God Yhwh; 6 Nebuchadnezzar king of Babylon has come up against him, and binds him in bronze chains to take him away to Babylon. 7 And Nebuchadnezzar has brought from the vessels of the house of Yhwh to Babylon, and puts them in his temple in Babylon. 8 And the rest of the matters of Jehoiakim, and his abominations that he has done, and that which is found against him, behold, they are written on the scroll of the kings of Israel and Judah, and his son Jehoiachin reigns in his stead. 9 Jehoiachin [is] a son of eight years in his reigning, and he has reigned three months and ten days in Jerusalem, and he does evil in the eyes of Yhwh; 10 and at the turn of the year King Nebuchadnezzar has sent and brings him to Babylon with the desirable vessels of the house of Yhwh, and causes his brother Zedekiah to reign over Judah and Jerusalem. 11 Zedekiah [is] a son of twenty-one years in his reigning, and he has reigned eleven years in Jerusalem; 12 and he does evil in the eyes of his God Yhwh, he has not been humbled before Jeremiah the prophet [speaking] from the mouth of Yhwh; 13 and he has also rebelled against King Nebuchadnezzar who had caused him to swear by God, and he hardens his neck and strengthens his heart against turning back to Yhwh, God of Israel. 14 Also, all the heads of the priests and the people have multiplied to commit a trespass according to all the abominations of the nations, and they defile the house of Yhwh that He has sanctified in Jerusalem. 15 And Yhwh, God of their fathers, sends to them by the hand of His messengers—rising early and sending—for He has had pity on His people and on His habitation, 16 but they are mocking at the messengers of God, and despising His words, and acting deceitfully with His prophets, until the going up of the fury of Yhwh against His people—until there is no healing. 17 And He causes the king of the Chaldeans to go up against them, and he slays their chosen

ones by the sword in the house of their sanctuary, and has had no pity on young man and virgin, old man and very aged—He has given the whole into his hand. 18 And all the vessels of the house of God, the great and the small, and the treasures of the house of Yhwh, and the treasures of the king and of his princes—he has brought the whole to Babylon. 19 And they burn the house of God, and break down the wall of Jerusalem, and they have burned all its palaces with fire, and all its desirable vessels—to destruction. 20 And he removes those left of the sword to Babylon, and they are to him and to his sons for servants, until the reigning of the kingdom of Persia, 21 to fulfill the word of Yhwh in the mouth of Jeremiah, until the land has enjoyed its Sabbaths; all the days of the desolation it kept Sabbath—to the fullness of seventy years. 22 And in the first year of Cyrus king of Persia, at the completion of the word of Yhwh in the mouth of Jeremiah, Yhwh has awoken the spirit of Cyrus king of Persia, and he causes an intimation to pass over into all his kingdom, and also in writing, saying, 23 "Thus said Cyrus king of Persia: Yhwh, God of the heavens, has given all kingdoms of the earth to me, and He has laid a charge on me to build a house for Him in Jerusalem which [is] in Judah; who is among you of all His people? His God Yhwh [is] with him, and he goes up!

EZRA

CHAPTER 1

1 And in the first year of Cyrus king of Persia, at the completion of the word of Yhwh from the mouth of Jeremiah, has Yhwh awoken the spirit of Cyrus king of Persia, and he causes an intimation to pass over into all his kingdom, and also in writing, saying, **2** "Thus said Cyrus king of Persia: Yhwh, God of the heavens, has given all kingdoms of the earth to me, and He has laid a charge on me to build a house for Him in Jerusalem, that [is] in Judah; **3** who [is] among you of all His people? His God is with him, and he goes up to Jerusalem, that [is] in Judah, and builds the house of Yhwh, God of Israel (He [alone is] God), that [is] in Jerusalem. **4** And everyone who is left, of any of the places where he [is] a sojourner, the men of his place assist him with silver, and with gold, and with goods, and with beasts, along with a free-will offering for the house of God, that [is] in Jerusalem." **5** And heads of the fathers of Judah and Benjamin rise, and the priests and the Levites, even everyone whose spirit God has awoken, to go up to build the house of Yhwh, that [is] in Jerusalem; **6** and all those around them have strengthened [them] with their hands, with vessels of silver, with gold, with goods, and with beasts, and with precious things, apart from all that has been offered willingly. **7** And King Cyrus has brought out the vessels of the house of Yhwh that Nebuchadnezzar has brought out of Jerusalem, and puts them in the house of his gods; **8** indeed, Cyrus king of Persia brings them out by the hand of Mithredath the treasurer, and numbers them to Sheshbazzar the prince of Judah. **9** And this [is] their number: dishes of gold thirty, dishes of silver one thousand, knives twenty-nine, **10** basins of gold thirty, basins of silver (seconds) four hundred and ten, other vessels one thousand. **11** All the vessels of gold and of silver [are] five thousand and four hundred; the whole has Sheshbazzar brought up with the going up of the expulsion from Babylon to Jerusalem.

CHAPTER 2

1 And these [are] sons of the province who are going up—of the captives of the expulsion that Nebuchadnezzar king of Babylon removed to Babylon, and they return to Jerusalem and Judah, each to his city— **2** who have come in with Zerubbabel, Jeshua, Nehemiah, Seraiah, Reelaiah, Mordecai, Bilshan, Mispar, Bigvai, Rehum, Baanah. The number of the men of the people of Israel: **3** sons of Parosh, two thousand one hundred seventy-two; **4** sons of Shephatiah, three hundred seventy-two; **5** sons of Arah, seven hundred seventy-five; **6** sons of Pahath-Moab, of the sons of Jeshua [and] Joab, two thousand eight hundred and twelve; **7** sons of Elam, one thousand two hundred fifty-four; **8** sons of Zattu, nine hundred and forty-five;

⁹ sons of Zaccai, seven hundred and sixty; ¹⁰ sons of Bani, six hundred forty-two; ¹¹ sons of Bebai, six hundred twenty-three; ¹² sons of Azgad, one thousand two hundred twenty-two; ¹³ sons of Adonikam, six hundred sixty-six; ¹⁴ sons of Bigvai, two thousand fifty-six; ¹⁵ sons of Adin, four hundred fifty-four; ¹⁶ sons of Ater of Hezekiah, ninety-eight; ¹⁷ sons of Bezai, three hundred twenty-three; ¹⁸ sons of Jorah, one hundred and twelve; ¹⁹ sons of Hashum, two hundred twenty-three; ²⁰ sons of Gibbar, ninety-five; ²¹ sons of Beth-Lehem, one hundred twenty-three; ²² sons of Netophah, fifty-six; ²³ men of Anathoth, one hundred twenty-eight; ²⁴ sons of Azmaveth, forty-two; ²⁵ sons of Kirjath-Arim, Chephirah, and Beeroth, seven hundred and forty-three; ²⁶ sons of Ramah and Gaba, six hundred twenty-one; ²⁷ men of Michmas, one hundred twenty-two; ²⁸ men of Beth-El and Ai, two hundred twenty-three; ²⁹ sons of Nebo, fifty-two; ³⁰ sons of Magbish, one hundred fifty-six; ³¹ sons of another Elam, one thousand two hundred fifty-four; ³² sons of Harim, three hundred and twenty; ³³ sons of Lod, Hadid, and Ono, seven hundred twenty-five; ³⁴ sons of Jericho, three hundred forty-five; ³⁵ sons of Senaah, three thousand and six hundred and thirty. ³⁶ The priests: sons of Jedaiah, of the house of Jeshua, nine hundred seventy-three; ³⁷ sons of Immer, one thousand fifty-two; ³⁸ sons of Pashhur, one thousand two hundred forty-seven; ³⁹ sons of Harim, one thousand and seventeen. ⁴⁰ The Levites: sons of Jeshua and Kadmiel, of the sons of Hodaviah, seventy-four. ⁴¹ The singers: sons of Asaph, one hundred twenty-eight. ⁴² Sons of the gatekeepers: sons of Shallum, sons of Ater, sons of Talmon, sons of Akkub, sons of Hatita, sons of Shobai, the whole [are] one hundred thirty-nine. ⁴³ The Nethinim: sons of Ziha, sons of Hasupha, sons of Tabbaoth, ⁴⁴ sons of Keros, sons of Siaha, sons of Padon, ⁴⁵ sons of Lebanah, sons of Hagabah, sons of Akkub, ⁴⁶ sons of Hagab, sons of Shalmai, sons of Hanan, ⁴⁷ sons of Giddel, sons of Gahar, sons of Reaiah, ⁴⁸ sons of Rezin, sons of Nekoda, sons of Gazzam, ⁴⁹ sons of Uzza, sons of Paseah, sons of Besai, ⁵⁰ sons of Asnah, sons of Mehunim, sons of Nephusim, ⁵¹ sons of Bakbuk, sons of Hakupha, sons of Harhur, ⁵² sons of Bazluth, sons of Mehida, sons of Harsha, ⁵³ sons of Barkos, sons of Sisera, sons of Thamah, ⁵⁴ sons of Neziah, sons of Hatipha. ⁵⁵ Sons of the servants of Solomon: sons of Sotai, sons of Sophereth, sons of Peruda, ⁵⁶ sons of Jaalah, sons of Darkon, sons of Giddel, ⁵⁷ sons of Shephatiah, sons of Hattil, sons of Pochereth of Zebaim, sons of Ami. ⁵⁸ All the Nethinim, and the sons of the servants of Solomon [are] three hundred ninety-two. ⁵⁹ And these [are] those going up from Tel-Melah, Tel-Harsa, Cherub, Addan, Immer, and they have not been able to declare the house of their fathers, and their seed, whether they [are] of Israel: ⁶⁰ sons of Delaiah, sons of Tobiah, sons of Nekoda, six hundred fifty-two. ⁶¹ And of the sons of the priests: sons of Habaiah, sons of Koz, sons of Barzillai (who took a wife from the daughters of Barzillai the Gileadite, and is called by their name); ⁶² these have sought their register among those reckoning themselves by genealogy, and they have not been found, and they are redeemed from the priesthood, ⁶³ and the Tirshatha says to them that they do not eat of the most holy things until the standing up of a priest with [the] Lights and with [the] Perfections. ⁶⁴ All the assembly together [is] forty-two thousand three hundred sixty, ⁶⁵ apart from their servants and their handmaids; these [are] seven thousand three hundred thirty-seven: and of them [are] two hundred male and female singers. ⁶⁶ Their horses [are] seven hundred thirty-six, their mules, two hundred forty-five, ⁶⁷ their camels, four hundred thirty-five, donkeys, six thousand seven hundred and twenty. ⁶⁸ And some of the heads of the fathers in their coming to the house of Yhwh that [is] in Jerusalem, have offered willingly for the house of God, to establish it on its base; ⁶⁹ according to their power they have given to the treasure of the work; of gold, sixty-one thousand drams, and of silver, five thousand pounds, and of priests' coats, one hundred. ⁷⁰ And the priests dwell, and the Levites, and of the people, and the singers, and the gatekeepers, and the Nethinim, in their cities; even all Israel in their cities.

CHAPTER 3

¹ And the seventh month comes, and the sons of Israel [are] in the cities, and the people are gathered, as one man, to Jerusalem. ² And Jeshua son of Jozadak rises, and his brothers the priests, and Zerubbabel son of Shealtiel, and his brothers, and they build the altar of the God of Israel, to cause to ascend on it burnt-offerings, as it is written in the Law of Moses, the man of God. ³ And they establish the altar on its bases, because of the fear on them of the peoples of the lands, and he causes burnt-offerings to ascend on it to Yhwh, burnt-offerings for the morning and for the evening. ⁴ And they make the Celebration of the Shelters as it is written, and the burnt-offering of the day daily in number according to the ordinance, the matter of a day in its day; ⁵ and after this a continual burnt-offering, and for new moons, and for all appointed times of Yhwh that are sanctified; and for everyone who is willingly offering a willing-offering to Yhwh. ⁶ From the first day of the seventh month they have begun to cause burnt-offerings to ascend to Yhwh, and the temple of Yhwh has not been founded, ⁷ and they give money to hewers and to craftsmen, and food, and drink, and oil to Zidonians and to Tyrians, to bring in cedar-trees from Lebanon to the Sea of Joppa, according to the permission of Cyrus king of Persia concerning them. ⁸ And in the second year of their coming to the house of God, to Jerusalem, in the second month, began Zerubbabel son of Shealtiel, and Jeshua son of Jozadak, and the remnant of their brothers the priests and the Levites, and all those coming from the captivity to Jerusalem, and they appoint the Levites from a son of twenty years and upward, to overlook the work of the house of Yhwh. ⁹ And Jeshua stands, [and] his sons, and his brothers, Kadmiel and his sons, sons of Judah together, to overlook those doing the work in the house of God; the sons of Henadad, [and] their sons and their brothers the Levites. ¹⁰ And those building have founded the temple of Yhwh, and they appoint the priests, clothed, with trumpets, and the Levites, sons of Asaph, with cymbals, to praise Yhwh, by means of [the instruments of] David king of Israel. ¹¹ And they respond in praising and in giving thanks to Yhwh, "For [He is] good, for His kindness [is] for all time over Israel!" And all the people have shouted [with] a great shout in giving praise to Yhwh, because the house of Yhwh has been founded. ¹² And many of the priests, and the Levites, and the heads of the fathers, the aged men who had seen the first house—in this house being founded before their eyes—are weeping with a loud voice, and many with a shout, in joy, lifting up the voice; ¹³ and the people are not discerning the noise of the shout of joy from the noise of the weeping of the people, for the people are shouting [with] a great shout, and the noise has been heard to a distance.

CHAPTER 4

¹ And adversaries of Judah and Benjamin hear that the sons of the captivity are building a temple to Yhwh, God of Israel, ² and they draw near to Zerubbabel, and to heads of the fathers, and say to them, "Let us build with you; for, like you, we seek to your God, and we are not sacrificing since the days of Esar-Haddon king of Asshur, who brought us up here." ³ And Zerubbabel says to them, also Jeshua, and the rest of the heads of the fathers of Israel, "Not for you, and for us, to build a house to our God; but we ourselves together build to Yhwh God of Israel, as King Cyrus, king of Persia, commanded us." ⁴ And it comes to pass, the people of the land are making the hands of the people of Judah feeble, and troubling them in building, ⁵ and are hiring against them counselors to make void their counsel all the days of Cyrus king of Persia, even until the reign of Darius king of Persia. ⁶ And in the reign of Ahasuerus, in the commencement of his reign, they have written an accusation against the inhabitants of Judah and Jerusalem; ⁷ and in the days of Artaxerxes have Bishlam, Mithredath, Tabeel, and the rest of his companions written to Artaxerxes king of Persia, and the writing of the letter is written in Aramaic, and interpreted in Aramaic. ⁸ Rehum counselor, and Shimshai scribe have written a letter concerning Jerusalem to Artaxerxes the king, thus: ⁹ Then Rehum counselor, and Shimshai scribe, and the rest of their companions, Dinaites, and Apharsathchites, Tarpelites, Apharsites, Archevites, Babylonians, Susanchites (who are Elamites), ¹⁰ and the rest of the nations that the great and honorable Asnapper removed and set in the city of Samaria, and the rest beyond the river, and at such a time: ¹¹ This [is] a copy of a letter that they have sent to him, to Artaxerxes the king: "Your servants, men beyond the river, and at such a time; ¹² be it known to the king, that the Jews who have come up from you to us, have come to Jerusalem, the rebellious and base city they are building, and the walls they have finished, and the foundations they join. ¹³ Now let it be known to the king, that if this city is built and the walls finished, that they do not give toll, tribute, and custom;

and at length it causes loss [to] the kings. **14** Now because that the salt of the palace [is] our salt, and we have no patience to see the nakedness of the king, therefore we have sent and made known to the king; **15** so that he seeks in the scroll of the records of your fathers, and you find in the scroll of the records, and know, that this city [is] a rebellious city, and causing loss [to] kings and provinces, and makers of sedition [are] in its midst from the days of old, therefore this city has been ruined. **16** We are making known to the king that, if this city be built and the walls finished, by this means you have no portion beyond the river." **17** The king has sent an answer to Rehum counselor, and Shimshai scribe, and the rest of their companions who are dwelling in Samaria, and the rest beyond the river, "Peace, and at such a time: **18** The letter that you sent to us, explained, has been read before me, **19** and by me a decree has been made, and they sought, and have found that this city is lifting up itself against kings from the days of old, and rebellion and sedition is made in it, **20** and mighty kings have been over Jerusalem, even rulers over all beyond the river, and toll, tribute, and custom is given to them. **21** Now make a decree to cause these men to cease, and this city is not built, until a decree is made by me. **22** And beware of negligence in doing this; why does the hurt become great to the loss of the kings?" **23** Then from the time that a copy of the letter of King Artaxerxes is read before Rehum, and Shimshai the scribe, and their companions, they have gone in haste to Jerusalem, to the Jews, and caused them to cease by force and strength; **24** then ceased the service of the house of God that [is] in Jerusalem, and it ceased until the second year of the reign of Darius king of Persia.

CHAPTER 5

1 And the prophets have prophesied (Haggai the prophet, and Zechariah son of Iddo) to the Jews who [are] in Judah and in Jerusalem, in the Name of the God of Israel—to them. **2** Then Zerubbabel son of Shealtiel, and Jeshua son of Jozadak, have risen, and begun to build the house of God, that [is] in Jerusalem, and with them are the prophets of God supporting them. **3** At that time have come to them Tatnai, governor beyond the river, and Shethar-Boznai, and their companions, and thus they are saying to them, "Who has made for you a decree to build this house, and to finish this wall?" **4** Then we have said thus to them, "What [are] the names of the men who are building this building?" **5** And the eye of their God has been on [the] elders of [the] Jews, and they have not caused them to cease until [the] matter goes to Darius, and then they send back a letter concerning this thing. **6** The copy of a letter that Tatnai, governor beyond the river, has sent, and Shethar-Boznai and his companions, the Apharsachites who [are] beyond the river, to Darius the king. **7** A letter they have sent to him, and thus is it written in it: **8** "To Darius the king, all peace! Be it known to the king that we have gone to the province of Judah, to the great house of God, and it is built [with] rolled stones, and wood is placed in the walls, and this work is done speedily, and prospering in their hand. **9** Then we have asked of these elders, thus we have said to them, Who has made for you a decree to build this house, and to finish this wall? **10** And also their names we have asked of them, to let you know, that we might write the names of the men who [are] at their head. **11** And thus they have returned us word, saying, We [are] servants of the God of the heavens and earth, and are building the house that was built many years before this, that a great king of Israel built and finished: **12** but after that our fathers made the God of the heavens angry, he gave them into the hand of Nebuchadnezzar king of Babylon the Chaldean, and this house he destroyed, and the people he removed to Babylon; **13** but in the first year of Cyrus king of Babylon, Cyrus the king made a decree to build this house of God, **14** and also, the vessels of the house of God, of gold and silver, that Nebuchadnezzar had taken forth out of the temple that [is] in Jerusalem, and brought them to the temple of Babylon, them has Cyrus the king brought forth out of the temple of Babylon, and they have been given to [one], Sheshbazzar [is] his name, whom he made governor, **15** and said to him, Lift up these vessels, go, put them down in the temple that [is] in Jerusalem, and the house of God is built on its place. **16** Then this Sheshbazzar has come—he has laid the foundations of the house of God that [is] in Jerusalem, and from there even until now it has been building, and is not finished. **17** And now, if it is good to the king, let a search be made in the treasure-house of the king, that [is] there in Babylon, whether it be that there was a decree made by Cyrus the king to build this house of God in Jerusalem, and the will of the king concerning this thing he sends to us."

CHAPTER 6

1 Then Darius the king made a decree, and they sought in the house of the scrolls of the treasuries placed there in Babylon, **2** and there has been found at Achmetha, in a palace that [is] in the province of Media, a scroll, and a record thus written within it [is]: **3** "In the first year of Cyrus the king, Cyrus the king has made a decree concerning the house of God in Jerusalem: let the house be built in the place where they are sacrificing sacrifices, and its foundations strongly laid; its height sixty cubits, its breadth sixty cubits; **4** three rows of rolled stones, and a row of new wood, and let the outlay be given out of the king's house. **5** And also, the vessels of the house of God, of gold and silver, that Nebuchadnezzar took forth out of the temple that [is] in Jerusalem, and brought to Babylon, let be given back, and go to the temple that [is] in Jerusalem, [each] to its place, and put [them] down in the house of God. **6** Now Tatnai, governor beyond the river, Shethar-Boznai, and their companions, the Apharsachites, who [are] beyond the river, be far from here; **7** let alone the work of this house of God, let the governor of the Jews, and [the] elders of the Jews, build this house of God on its place. **8** And a decree is made by me concerning that which you do with [the] elders of these Jews to build this house of God, that of [the] riches of [the] king, that [are] of [the] tribute beyond [the] river, let the outlay be given speedily to these men, that they do not cease; **9** and what they are needing—both young bullocks, and rams, and lambs for burnt-offerings to the God of the heavens, wheat, salt, wine, and oil according to the saying of the priests who [are] in Jerusalem—let be given to them day by day without fail, **10** that they are bringing sweet savors near to the God of the heavens, and praying for the life of the king, and of his sons. **11** And a decree is made by me, that anyone who changes this thing, let wood be pulled down from his house, and being raised up, let him be struck on it, and let his house be made a dunghill for this. **12** And God, who caused His Name to dwell there, casts down any king and people that puts forth his hand to change, to destroy this house of God that [is] in Jerusalem; I Darius have made a decree; let it be done speedily." **13** Then Tatnai, governor beyond the river, Shethar-Boznai, and their companions, according to that which Darius the king has sent, so they have done speedily; **14** and [the] elders of [the] Jews are building and prospering through [the] prophecy of Haggai [the] prophet, and Zechariah son of Iddo, and they have built and finished by [the] decree of [the] God of Israel, and by [the] decree of Cyrus, and Darius, and Artaxerxes king of Persia. **15** And this house has gone out until the third day of the month Adar, that is [in] the sixth year of the reign of Darius the king. **16** And the sons of Israel have made, [and] the priests, and the Levites, and the rest of the sons of the captivity, a dedication of this house of God with joy, **17** and have brought near for the dedication of this house of God: one hundred bullocks, two hundred rams, four hundred lambs; and twelve young male goats for a sin-offering for all Israel according to the number of the tribes of Israel; **18** and they have established the priests in their divisions, and the Levites in their courses, over the service of God that [is] in Jerusalem, as it is written in the scroll of Moses. **19** And the sons of the captivity make the Passover on the fourteenth of the first month, **20** for the priests and the Levites have been purified together—all of them [are] pure—and they slaughter the Passover for all the sons of the captivity, and for their brothers the priests, and for themselves. **21** And the sons of Israel, those returning from the captivity, and everyone who is separated from the uncleanness of the nations of the land to them, to seek to Yhwh, God of Israel, eat, **22** and they make the Celebration of Unleavened Things seven days with joy, for Yhwh made them to rejoice, and turned around the heart of the king of Asshur to them, to strengthen their hands in the work of the house of God, the God of Israel.

CHAPTER 7

1 And after these things, in the reign of Artaxerxes king of

Persia, Ezra son of Seraiah, son of Azariah, son of Hilkiah, **2** son of Shallum, son of Zadok, son of Ahitub, **3** son of Amariah, son of Azariah, son of Meraioth, **4** son of Zerahiah, son of Uzzi, son of Bukki, **5** son of Abishua, son of Phinehas, son of Eleazar, son of Aaron the head priest; **6** Ezra himself has come up from Babylon, and he [is] a scribe ready in the Law of Moses, that Yhwh God of Israel gave, and the king gives to him—according to the hand of his God Yhwh on him—all his request. **7** And there go up of the sons of Israel, and of the priests, and the Levites, and the singers, and the gatekeepers, and the Nethinim, to Jerusalem, in the seventh year of Artaxerxes the king. **8** And he comes to Jerusalem in the fifth month, that [is in] the seventh year of the king, **9** for on the first of the month he has founded the ascent from Babylon, and on the first of the fifth month he has come to Jerusalem, according to the good hand of his God on him, **10** for Ezra has prepared his heart to seek the Law of Yhwh, and to do, and to teach in Israel statute and judgment. **11** And this [is] a copy of the letter that King Artaxerxes gave to Ezra the priest, the scribe, a scribe of the words of the commands of Yhwh, and of His statutes on Israel: **12** "Artaxerxes, king of kings, to Ezra the priest, a perfect scribe of the Law of the God of the heavens, and at such a time: **13** By me has been made a decree that everyone who is willing, in my kingdom, of the people of Israel and of its priests and Levites, to go to Jerusalem with you, go; **14** because that from the king and his seven counselors you are sent, to inquire concerning Judah and concerning Jerusalem, with the Law of God that [is] in your hand, **15** and to carry silver and gold that the king and his counselors willingly offered to the God of Israel, whose dwelling place [is] in Jerusalem, **16** and all the silver and gold that you find in all the province of Babylon, with the free-will offerings of the people, and of the priests, offering willingly, for the house of their God that [is] in Jerusalem, **17** therefore you speedily buy with this money, bullocks, rams, lambs, and their presents, and their drink-offerings, and bring them near to the altar of the house of your God that [is] in Jerusalem, **18** and that which to you and to your brothers is good to do with the rest of the silver and gold, according to the will of your God you do. **19** And the vessels that are given to you, for the service of the house of your God, make perfect before the God of Jerusalem; **20** and the rest of the necessary things of the house of your God, that it falls to you to give, you give from the treasure-house of the king. **21** And by me—I Artaxerxes the king—is made a decree to all treasurers who [are] beyond the river, that all that Ezra the priest, scribe of the Law of the God of the heavens, asks of you, be done speedily: **22** To silver one hundred talents, and to wheat one hundred cors, and to wine one hundred baths, and to oil one hundred baths, and salt without reckoning; **23** all that [is] by the decree of the God of the heavens, let be done diligently for the house of the God of the heavens; for why is there wrath against the kingdom of the king and his sons? **24** And to you we are making known, that on any of the priests and Levites, singers, gatekeepers, Nethinim, and servants of the house of God, tribute and custom is no authority to lift up. **25** And you, Ezra, according to the wisdom of your God, that [is] in your hand, appoint magistrates—even judges who may be judging—judging all the people who are beyond the river, to all knowing the Law of your God, and he who has not known, you cause to know; **26** and any who does not do the Law of your God, and the law of the king, judgment is done speedily on him, whether to death, or to banishment, or to confiscation of riches, and to bonds." **27** Blessed [is] Yhwh, God of our fathers, who has given such a thing as this in the heart of the king, to beautify the house of Yhwh that [is] in Jerusalem, **28** and to me has stretched out kindness before the king and his counselors, and before all the mighty heads of the king: and I have strengthened myself as the hand of my God Yhwh [is] on me, and I gather out of Israel heads to go up with me.

CHAPTER 8

1 And these [are] heads of their fathers, and the genealogy of those going up with me, in the reign of Artaxerxes the king, from Babylon. **2** From the sons of Phinehas: Gershom; from the sons of Ithamar: Daniel; from the sons of David: Hattush; **3** from the sons of Shechaniah, from the sons of Pharosh: Zechariah, and with him, reckoning themselves by genealogy, of males one hundred and fifty. **4** From the sons of Pahath-Moab: Elihoenai son of Zerahiah, and with him two hundred

who are males. **5** From the sons of Shechaniah: the son of Jahaziel, and with him three hundred who are males. **6** And from the sons of Adin: Ebed son of Jonathan, and with him fifty who are males. **7** And from the sons of Elam: Jeshaiah son of Athaliah, and with him seventy who are males. **8** And from the sons of Shephatiah: Zebadiah son of Michael, and with him eighty who are males. **9** From the sons of Joab: Obadiah son of Jehiel, and with him two hundred and eighteen who are males. **10** And from the sons of Shelomith, the son of Josiphiah, and with him one hundred and sixty who are males. **11** And from the sons of Bebai: Zechariah son of Bebai, and with him twenty-eight who are males. **12** And from the sons of Azgad: Johanan son of Hakkatan, and with him one hundred and ten who are males. **13** And from the younger sons of Adonikam—and these [are] their names—Eliphelet, Jeiel, and Shemaiah, and with them sixty who are males. **14** And from the sons of Bigvai, Uthai and Zabbud, and with them seventy who are males. **15** And I gather them to the river that is going to Ahava, and we encamp there three days; and I consider about the people, and about the priests, and of the sons of Levi I have found none there; **16** and I send for Eliezer, for Ariel, for Shemaiah, and for Elnathan, and for Jarib, and for Elnathan, and for Nathan, and for Zechariah, and for Meshullam, heads, and for Joiarib, and for Elnathan, men of understanding; **17** and I charge them for Iddo the head, in the place Casiphia, and put in their mouth words to speak to Iddo, [and] his brothers the Nethinim, in the place Casiphia, to bring to us servants for the house of our God. **18** And they bring to us, according to the good hand of our God on us, a man of understanding, of the sons of Mahli, son of Levi, son of Israel, and Sherebiah, and his sons, and his brothers, eighteen; **19** and Hashabiah, and with him Jeshaiah, of the sons of Merari, his brothers, and their sons, twenty; **20** and from the Nethinim, whom David and the heads gave for the service of the Levites, two hundred and twenty Nethinim, all of them defined by name. **21** And I proclaim there a fast, by the river Ahava, to afflict ourselves before our God, to seek from Him a right way for us, and for our infants, and for all our substance, **22** for I was ashamed to ask from the king a force and horsemen to help us because of the enemy in the way, for we spoke to the king, saying, "The hand of our God [is] on all seeking Him for good, and His strength and His wrath [is] on all forsaking Him." **23** And we fast, and seek from our God for this, and He accepts our plea. **24** And I separate from the heads of the priests, twelve, even Sherebiah, Hashabiah, and with them of their brothers ten, **25** and I weigh to them the silver, and the gold, and the vessels, a raised-offering of the house of our God, that the king, and his counselors, and his heads, and all Israel—those present—lifted up; **26** and I weigh to their hand six hundred and fifty talents of silver, and one hundred talents of vessels of silver, one hundred talents of gold, **27** and twenty basins of gold, of one thousand drams, and two vessels of good shining bronze, desirable as gold. **28** And I say to them, "You [are] holy to Yhwh, and the vessels [are] holy, and the silver and the gold [are] a willing-offering to Yhwh, God of your fathers; **29** watch, and keep, until you weigh before the heads of the priests, and of the Levites, and the heads of the fathers of Israel, in Jerusalem, in the chambers of the house of Yhwh." **30** And the priests and the Levites took the weight of the silver, and of the gold, and of the vessels, to bring to Jerusalem to the house of our God. **31** And we journey from the river Ahava, on the twelfth of the first month, to go to Jerusalem, and the hand of our God has been on us, and He delivers us from the hand of the enemy and the one lying in wait by the way; **32** and we come to Jerusalem, and dwell there three days. **33** And on the fourth day has been weighed the silver, and the gold, and the vessels, in the house of our God, to the hand of Meremoth son of Uriah the priest, and with him Eleazar son of Phinehas, and with them Jozabad son of Jeshua, and Noadiah son of Binnui, the Levites: **34** by number, by weight of everyone, and all the weight is written at that time. **35** Those coming in of the captives—sons of the expulsion—have brought burnt-offerings near to the God of Israel: twelve bullocks for all Israel, ninety-six rams, seventy-seven lambs, twelve young male goats for a sin-offering—the whole a burnt-offering to Yhwh; **36** and they give the laws of the king to the lieutenants of the king and the governors beyond the river, and they have lifted up the people and the house of God.

CHAPTER 9

¹ And at the completion of these things, the heads have drawn near to me, saying, "The people of Israel, and the priests, and the Levites, have not been separated from the peoples of the lands, as to their abominations, even the Canaanite, the Hittite, the Perizzite, the Jebusite, the Ammonite, the Moabite, the Egyptian, and the Amorite, ² for they have taken of their daughters to them, and to their sons, and the holy seed have mingled themselves among the peoples of the lands, and the hand of the heads and of the seconds have been first in this trespass." ³ And at my hearing this word, I have torn my garment and my upper robe, and pluck out of the hair of my head, and of my beard, and sit astonished, ⁴ and to me are gathered everyone trembling at the words of the God of Israel, because of the trespass of the expulsion, and I am sitting astonished until the present of the evening. ⁵ And at the present of the evening I have risen from my affliction, and at my tearing my garment and my upper robe, then I bow down on my knees, and spread out my hands to my God Yhwh, ⁶ and say, "O my God, I have been ashamed, and have blushed to lift up, O my God, my face to You, for our iniquities have increased over the head, and our guilt has become great to the heavens. ⁷ From the days of our fathers we [are] in great guilt to this day, and in our iniquities we have been given—we, our kings, our priests—into the hand of the kings of the lands, with sword, with captivity, and with spoiling, and with shame of face, as [at] this day. ⁸ And now, as a small moment grace has been from our God Yhwh, to leave an escape for us, and to give to us a nail in His holy place, by our God's enlightening our eyes, and by giving us a little quickening in our servitude; ⁹ for we [are] servants, and in our servitude our God has not forsaken us, and stretches out to us kindness before the kings of Persia, to give to us a quickening to lift up the house of our God, and to cause its ruins to cease, and to give to us a wall in Judah and in Jerusalem. ¹⁰ And now, what do we say, O our God, after this? for we have forsaken Your commands, ¹¹ that You have commanded by the hands of Your servants the prophets, saying, The land into which you are going to possess it, [is] a land of impurity, by the impurity of the people of the lands, by their abominations with which they have filled it—from mouth to mouth—by their uncleanness; ¹² and now, your daughters you do not give to their sons, and their daughters you do not take to your sons, and you do not seek their peace, and their good—for all time, so that you are strong, and have eaten the good of the land, and given possession to your sons for all time. ¹³ And after all that has come on us for our evil works, and for our great guilt (for You, O our God, have kept back of the rod from our iniquities, and have given to us an escape like this), ¹⁴ do we turn back to break Your commands, and to join ourselves in marriage with the people of these abominations? Are You not angry against us—even to consumption—until there is no remnant and escaped part? ¹⁵ O Yhwh, God of Israel, You [are] righteous, for we have been left an escape, as [it is] this day; behold, we [are] before You in our guilt, for there is none to stand before You concerning this."

CHAPTER 10

¹ And at Ezra's praying, and at his making confession, weeping and casting himself down before the house of God, there have been gathered to him out of Israel a very great assembly—men and women and children—for the people have wept, multiplying weeping. ² And Shechaniah son of Jehiel, of the sons of Elam, answers and says to Ezra, "We have trespassed against our God, and we settle strange women of the peoples of the land; and now there is hope for Israel concerning this, ³ and now, let us make a covenant with our God, to cause all the women to go out, and that which is born of them, by the counsel of the Lord, and of those trembling at the command of our God, and according to law it is done; ⁴ rise, for on you [is] the matter, and we [are] with you; be strong, and do." ⁵ And Ezra rises, and causes the heads of the priests, the Levites, and all Israel, to swear to do according to this word—and they swear. ⁶ And Ezra rises from before the house of God, and goes to the chamber of Jehohanan son of Eliashib; indeed, he goes there, bread he has not eaten, and water he has not drunk, for he is mourning because of the trespass of the expulsion. ⁷ And they cause a voice to pass over into Judah and Jerusalem, to all sons of the expulsion, to be gathered to Jerusalem, ⁸ and everyone who does not come in by the third day, according to the counsel of the heads and the

elderly, all his substance is devoted, and himself separated from the assembly of the expulsion. ⁹ And all the men of Judah and Benjamin are gathered to Jerusalem by the third day, it [is] the ninth month, on the twentieth of the month, and all the people sit in the broad place of the house of God, trembling on account of the matter and of the showers. ¹⁰ And Ezra the priest rises and says to them, "You have trespassed, and you settle strange women, to add to the guilt of Israel; ¹¹ and now, make confession to Yhwh, God of your fathers, and do His good pleasure, and be separated from the peoples of the land, and from the strange women." ¹² And all the assembly answers and says [with] a great voice, "Right; according to your word—on us to do; ¹³ but the people [are] many, and [it is] the time of showers, and there is no power to stand outside, and the work [is] not for one day, nor for two, for we have multiplied to transgress in this thing. ¹⁴ Please let our heads of all the assembly stand; and all who [are] in our cities, who have settled strange wives, come in at [the] appointed times, and with them [the] elderly of city and city, and judges in it, until the turning back of the fury of the wrath of our God from us, for this thing." ¹⁵ Only Jonathan son of Asahel, and Jahaziah son of Tikvah, stood against this, and Meshullam, and Shabbethai the Levite, helped them. ¹⁶ And the sons of the expulsion do so, and Ezra the priest, [and] men, heads of the fathers, for the house of their fathers, are separated, even all of them by name, and they sit on the first day of the tenth month, to examine the matter; ¹⁷ and they finish with all the men who have settled strange women to the first day of the first month. ¹⁸ And there are found of the sons of the priests that have settled strange women: of the sons of Jeshua son of Jozadak, and his brothers, Maaseiah, and Eliezer, and Jarib, and Gedaliah; ¹⁹ and they give their hand to send out their wives, and being guilty, a ram of the flock for their guilt. ²⁰ And of the sons of Immer: Hanani and Zebadiah; ²¹ and of the sons of Harim: Maaseiah, and Elijah, and Shemaiah, and Jehiel, and Uzziah; ²² and of the sons of Pashhur: Elioenai, Maaseiah, Ishmael, Nethaneel, Jozabad, and Elasah. ²³ And of the Levites: Jozabad, and Shimei, and Kelaiah (he [is] Kelita), Pethahiah, Judah, and Eliezer. ²⁴ And of the singers: Eliashib. And of the gatekeepers: Shallum, and Telem, and Uri. ²⁵ And of Israel: of the sons of Parosh: Ramiah, and Jeziah, and Malchijah, and Miamin, and Eleazar, and Malchijah, and Benaiah. ²⁶ And of the sons of Elam: Mattaniah, Zechariah, and Jehiel, and Abdi, and Jeremoth, and Elijah. ²⁷ And of the sons of Zattu: Elioenai, Eliashib, Mattaniah, and Jeremoth, and Zabad, and Aziza. ²⁸ And of the sons of Bebai: Jehohanan, Hananiah, Zabbai, Athlai. ²⁹ And of the sons of Bani: Meshullam, Malluch, and Adaiah, Jashub, and Sheal, and Ramoth. ³⁰ And of the sons of Pahath-Moab: Adna, and Chelal, Benaiah, Maaseiah, Mattaniah, Bezaleel, and Binnui, and Manasseh. ³¹ And of the sons of Harim: Eliezer, Ishijah, Malchiah, Shemaiah, Shimeon, ³² Benjamin, Malluch, Shemariah. ³³ Of the sons of Hashum: Mattenai, Mattathah, Zabad, Eliphelet, Jeremai, Manasseh, Shimei. ³⁴ Of the sons of Bani: Maadai, Amram, and Uel, ³⁵ Benaiah, Bedeiah, Cheluhu, ³⁶ Vaniah, Meremoth, Eliashib, ³⁷ Mattaniah, Mattenai, and Jaasau, ³⁸ and Bani, and Binnui, Shimei, ³⁹ and Shelemiah, and Nathan, and Adaiah, ⁴⁰ Machnadbai, Shashai, Sharai, ⁴¹ Azareel, and Shelemiah, Shemariah, ⁴² Shallum, Amariah, Joseph. ⁴³ Of the sons of Nebo: Jeiel, Mattithiah, Zabad, Zebina, Jadau, and Joel, Benaiah; ⁴⁴ all these have taken strange women, and there are of them women who adopt sons.

NEHEMIAH

CHAPTER 1

¹ Words of Nehemiah son of Hachaliah. And it comes to pass, in the month of Chisleu, the twentieth year, and I have been in Shushan the palace, ² and Hanani, one of my brothers, he and men of Judah come in, and I ask them concerning the Jews, the escaped part that have been left of the captivity, and concerning Jerusalem; ³ and they say to me, "Those left, who have been left of the captivity there in the province, [are] in great evil, and in reproach, and the wall of Jerusalem is broken down, and its gates have been burned with fire." ⁴ And it comes to pass, at my hearing these words, I have sat down, and I weep and mourn [for] days, and I am fasting and praying

before the God of the heavens. **5** And I say, "Ah, now, O Yhwh, God of the heavens, God, the great and the fearful, keeping the covenant and kindness for those loving Him, and for those keeping His commands, **6** please let Your ear be attentive and Your eyes open, to listen to the prayer of Your servant, that I am praying before You today, by day and by night, concerning the sons of Israel, Your servants, and confessing concerning the sins of the sons of Israel, that we have sinned against You; indeed, I and the house of my father have sinned; **7** we have acted very corruptly against You, and have not kept the commands, and the statutes, and the judgments, that You commanded Your servant Moses. **8** Please remember the word that You commanded Your servant Moses, saying, You trespass—I scatter you among peoples; **9** and you have turned back to Me, and kept My commands, and done them—if your outcast is in the end of the heavens, there I gather them, and have brought them to the place that I have chosen to cause My Name to dwell there. **10** And they [are] Your servants, and Your people, whom You have ransomed by Your great power, and by Your strong hand. **11** Ah, now, O Lord, please let Your ear be attentive to the prayer of Your servant, and to the prayer of Your servants, those delighting to fear Your Name; and please give prosperity to Your servant today, and give him for mercies before this man"; and I have been butler to the king.

CHAPTER 2

1 And it comes to pass, in the month of Nisan, the twentieth year of Artaxerxes the king, wine [is] before him, and I lift up the wine, and give to the king, and I had not been sad before him; **2** and the king says to me, "Why [is] your face sad, and you not sick? this is nothing except sadness of heart"; and I fear very much, **3** and say to the king, "Let the king live for all time! Why should my face not be sad, when the city, the place of the graves of my fathers, [is] a desolation, and its gates have been consumed with fire?" **4** And the king says to me, "For what are you seeking?" And I pray to the God of the heavens, **5** and say to the king, "If [it is] good to the king, and if your servant is pleasing before you, that you send me to Judah, to the city of the graves of my fathers, and I have built it." **6** And the king says to me (and the queen is sitting near him), "How long is your journey? and when do you return?" And it is good before the king, and he sends me away, and I set to him a time. **7** And I say to the king, "If [it is] good to the king, let letters be given to me for the governors beyond the River, that they let me pass over until I come to Judah: **8** and a letter to Asaph, keeper of the paradise that the king has, that he give to me trees for beams [for] the gates of the palace that the house has, and for the wall of the city, and for the house into which I enter"; and the king gives to me, according to the good hand of my God on me. **9** And I come to the governors beyond the River, and give to them the letters of the king; and the king sends with me heads of a force, and horsemen; **10** and Sanballat the Horonite hears, and Tobiah the servant, the Ammonite, and it is evil to them—a great evil—that a man has come to seek good for the sons of Israel. **11** And I come to Jerusalem, and I am there three days, **12** and I rise by night, I and a few men with me, and have not declared to a man what my God is giving to my heart to do for Jerusalem, and there is no beast with me except the beast on which I am riding. **13** And I go out through the Valley Gate by night, and to the front of the Dragon Fountain, and to the Refuse Gate, and I am inspecting the walls of Jerusalem, that are broken down, and its gates consumed with fire. **14** And I pass over to the Fountain Gate, and to the King's Pool, and there is no place for the beast under me to pass over, **15** and I am going up through the brook by night, and am inspecting the wall, and turn back, and come in through the Valley Gate, and turn back. **16** And the prefects have not known to where I have gone, and what I am doing; and to the Jews, and to the priests, and to the nobles, and to the prefects, and to the rest of those doing the work, until now I have not declared [it]; **17** and I say to them, "You are seeing the evil that we are in, in that Jerusalem [is] desolate, and its gates have been burned with fire; come and we build the wall of Jerusalem, and we are not a reproach anymore." **18** And I declare to them the hand of my God that is good on me, and also the words of the king that he said to me, and they say, "Let us rise, and we have built"; and they strengthen their hands for good. **19** And Sanballat the Horonite hears, and Tobiah the servant, the Ammonite, and Geshem the Arabian,

and they mock at us, and despise us, and say, "What [is] this thing that you are doing? Are you rebelling against the king?" **20** And I return them word, and say to them, "The God of the heavens—He gives prosperity to us, and we His servants rise and have built; and to you there is no portion, and right, and memorial in Jerusalem."

CHAPTER 3

1 And Eliashib the high priest rises, and his brothers the priests, and they build the Sheep Gate; they have sanctified it, and set up its doors, even to the Tower of Meah they have sanctified it, to the Tower of Hananeel; **2** and by his hand men of Jericho have built; and by their hand Zaccur son of Imri has built; **3** and sons of Hassenaah have built the Fish Gate; they have walled it, and set up its doors, its locks, and its bars. **4** And by their hand Merimoth son of Urijah, son of Koz, has strengthened; and by his hand Meshullam son of Berechiah, son of Meshezabeel, has strengthened; and by his hand Zadok son of Baana has strengthened; **5** and by his hand the Tekoites have strengthened, and their majestic ones have not brought in their neck to the service of their Lord. **6** And Jehoiada son of Paseah and Meshullam son of Besodeiah have strengthened the Old Gate; they have walled it, and set up its doors, and its locks, and its bars. **7** And by their hand Melatiah the Gibeonite has strengthened, and Jadon the Meronothite, men of Gibeon and of Mizpah, [belonging] to the throne of the governor beyond the River. **8** By his hand Uzziel son of Harhaiah of the refiners has strengthened; and by his hand Hananiah son of [one of] the compounders has strengthened; and they leave Jerusalem to the broad wall. **9** And by their hand Rephaiah son of Hur, head of the half of the district of Jerusalem, has strengthened. **10** And by their hand Jedaiah son of Harumaph has strengthened, and opposite his own house; and by his hand Hattush son of Hashabniah has strengthened. **11** A second measure Malchijah son of Harim has strengthened, and Hashub son of Pahath-Moab, even the Tower of the Furnaces. **12** And by his hand Shallum son of Halohesh, head of the half of the district of Jerusalem, has strengthened, he and his daughters. **13** Hanun has strengthened the Valley Gate, and the inhabitants of Zanoah; they have built it, and set up its doors, its locks, and its bars, and one thousand cubits in the wall to the Refuse Gate. **14** And Malchijah son of Rechab, head of the district of Beth-Haccerem, has strengthened the Refuse Gate; he builds it, and sets up its doors, its locks, and its bars. **15** And Shallum son of Col-Hozeh, head of the district of Mizpah, has strengthened the Fountain Gate: he builds it, and covers it, and sets up its doors, its locks, and its bars, and the wall of the pool of Siloah, to the garden of the king, and to the steps that are going down from the City of David. **16** After him Nehemiah son of Azbuk, head of the half of the district of Beth-Zur, has strengthened to opposite the graves of David, and to the pool that is made, and to the house of the mighty ones. **17** After him the Levites have strengthened, [and] Rehum son of Bani; by his hand Hashabiah, head of the half of the district of Keilah, has strengthened for his district. **18** After him their brothers have strengthened, [and] Bavvai son of Henadad, head of the half of the district of Keilah. **19** And Ezer son of Jeshua, head of Mizpah, strengthens, by his hand, a second measure, from in front of the ascent of the armory at the angle. **20** After him Baruch son of Zabbai has hurried to strengthen a second measure from the angle to the opening of the house of Eliashib the high priest. **21** After him Meremoth son of Urijah, son of Koz, has strengthened a second measure, from the opening of the house of Eliashib even to the completion of the house of Eliashib. **22** And after him the priests, men of the circuit, have strengthened. **23** After them Benjamin has strengthened, and Hashub, opposite their house; after him Azariah son of Maaseiah, son of Ananiah, has strengthened near his house. **24** After him Binnui son of Henadad has strengthened a second measure, from the house of Azariah to the angle, and to the corner. **25** Palal son of Uzai [strengthened] from opposite the angle, and the tower that is going out from the upper house of the king that [is] at the court of the prison; after him Pedaiah son of Parosh [strengthened]. **26** And the Nethinim have been dwelling in Ophel, to opposite the Water Gate at the east, and the tower that goes out. **27** After him the Tekoites have strengthened a second measure, from opposite the great tower that goes out, and to the wall of Ophel. **28** From above the Horse Gate the priests have strengthened, each opposite his house. **29** After them Zadok son of Immer has strengthened opposite his house; and after him Shemaiah son of Shechaniah, keeper of the East Gate, has strengthened. ³⁰ After him Hananiah son of Shelemiah has strengthened, and Hanun the sixth son of Zalaph, a second measure; after him Meshullam son of Berechiah has strengthened opposite his chamber. ³¹ After him Malchijah son of the refiner has strengthened, to the house of the Nethinim, and of the merchants, opposite the Miphkad Gate, and to the ascent of the corner. ³² And between the ascent of the corner and the Sheep Gate, the refiners and the merchants have strengthened.

CHAPTER 4

¹ And it comes to pass, when Sanballat has heard that we are building the wall, that it is displeasing to him, and he is very angry and mocks at the Jews, ² and says before his brothers and the force of Samaria, indeed, he says, "What [are] the weak Jews doing? are they left to themselves? do they sacrifice? do they complete in a day? do they revive the stones out of the heaps of the rubbish—and they are burned?" ³ And Tobiah the Ammonite [is] by him and says, "Also, that which they are building—if a fox goes up, then it has broken down their stone wall." ⁴ Hear, O our God, for we have been despised; and return their reproach on their own head, and give them for a spoil in a land of captivity; ⁵ and do not cover over their iniquity, and do not let their sin be blotted out from before You, for they have provoked [You] to anger in front of those building. ⁶ And we build the wall, and all the wall is joined—to its half, and the people have a heart to work. ⁷ And it comes to pass, when Sanballat has heard, and Tobiah, and the Arabians, and the Ammonites, and the Ashdodites, that lengthening has gone up to the walls of Jerusalem, that the breeches have begun to be stopped, then it is very displeasing to them, ⁸ and they conspire, all of them together, to come to fight against Jerusalem, and to do to it injury. ⁹ And we pray to our God, and appoint a watch against them, by day and by night, because of them. ¹⁰ And Judah says, "The power of the burden-bearers has become feeble, and the rubbish [is] abundant, and we are not able to build on the wall." ¹¹ And our adversaries say, "They do not know, nor see, until we come into their midst, and have slain them, and caused the work to cease." ¹² And it comes to pass, when the Jews have come who are dwelling near them, that they say to us ten times from all the places to where you return—[they are] against us. ¹³ And I appoint at the lowest of the places, at the back of the wall, in the clear places, indeed, I appoint the people, by their families, with their swords, their spears, and their bows. ¹⁴ And I see, and rise up, and say to the nobles, and to the prefects, and to the rest of the people, "Do not be afraid of them; remember the Lord, the great and the fearful, and fight for your brothers, your sons, and your daughters, your wives, and your houses." ¹⁵ And it comes to pass, when our enemies have heard that it has been known to us, and God frustrates their counsel, and we return, all of us, to the wall, each to his work; ¹⁶ indeed, it comes to pass, from that day, half of my servants are working in the business, and half of them are keeping hold of both the spears, the shields, and the bows, and the coats of mail; and the heads [are] behind all the house of Judah. ¹⁷ The builders on the wall, and the bearers of the burden, those loading, [each] with one of his hands is working in the business, and one is laying hold of the missile. ¹⁸ And the builders [are] each with his sword, girded on his loins, and building, and he who is blowing with a horn [is] beside me. ¹⁹ And I say to the nobles, and to the prefects, and to the rest of the people, "The work is abundant, and large, and we are separated on the wall, far off from one another; ²⁰ in the place that you hear the voice of the horn there you are gathered to us; our God fights for us." ²¹ And we are working in the business, and half of them are keeping hold of the spears, from the going up of the dawn until the coming forth of the stars. ²² Also, at that time I said to the people, "Let each lodge with his servant in the midst of Jerusalem, and they have been a watch for us by night, and [for] the work by day": ²³ and there are none—I, and my brothers, and my servants, the men of the watch who [are] after me—there are none of us putting off our garments, each [has] his vessel of water.

CHAPTER 5

¹ And there is a great cry of the people and their wives, concerning their brothers the Jews, ² indeed, there are [those] who are saying, "Our sons, and our daughters, we—are many, and we receive grain, and eat, and live." ³ And there are [those] who are saying, "Our fields, and our vineyards, and our houses, we are pledging, and we receive grain for the famine." ⁴ And there are [those] who are saying, "We have borrowed money for the tribute of the king, [on] our fields, and our vineyards; ⁵ and now, as the flesh of our brothers [is] our flesh, as their sons [are] our sons, and behold, we are subduing our sons and our daughters for servants, and there are [those] of our daughters subdued, and our hand has no might, and our fields and our vineyards [are] to others." ⁶ And it is very displeasing to me when I have heard their cry and these words, ⁷ and my heart reigns over me, and I strive with the nobles, and with the prefects, and say to them, "You are exacting usury on one another"; and I set against them a great assembly, ⁸ and say to them, "We have acquired our brothers the Jews, those sold to the nations, according to the ability that [is] in us, and you also sell your brothers, and they have been sold to us!" And they are silent, and have not found a word. ⁹ And I say, "The thing that you are doing [is] not good; do you not walk in the fear of our God, because of the reproach of the nations our enemies? ¹⁰ And also, I, my brothers, and my servants, are exacting silver and grain on them; please let us leave off this usury. ¹¹ Please give back to them, as today, their fields, their vineyards, their olive-yards, and their houses, and the hundredth [part] of the money, and of the grain, of the new wine, and of the oil, that you are exacting of them." ¹² And they say, "We give back, and we seek nothing from them; so we do as you are saying." And I call the priests, and cause them to swear to do according to this thing; ¹³ also, I have shaken my lap, and I say, "Thus God shakes out every man from his house and from his labor who does not perform this thing; indeed, thus is he shaken out and empty"; and all the assembly says, "Amen," and praises Yhwh; and the people do according to this thing. ¹⁴ Also, from the day that he appointed me to be their governor in the land of Judah, from the twentieth year even to the thirty-second year of Artaxerxes the king—twelve years—I, and my brothers, have not eaten the bread of the governor: ¹⁵ the former governors who [are] before me have made themselves heavy on the people, and take of them in bread and wine, besides forty shekels in silver; also, their servants have ruled over the people—and I have not done so, because of the fear of God. ¹⁶ And also, in the work of this wall I have done mightily, even a field we have not bought, and all my servants are gathered there for the work; ¹⁷ and of the Jews, and of the prefects, one hundred and fifty men, and those coming to us of the nations that [are] around us, [are] at my table; ¹⁸ and that which has been prepared for one day [is] one ox, six fat sheep, also birds have been prepared for me, and once in ten days of all wines abundantly, and with this, the bread of the governor I have not sought, for heavy is the service on this people. ¹⁹ Remember for me, O my God, for good, all that I have done for this people.

CHAPTER 6

¹ And it comes to pass, when it has been heard by Sanballat, and Tobiah, and by Geshem the Arabian, and by the rest of our enemies, that I have built the wall, and there has not been left in it a breach (also, until that time I had not set up the doors in the gates), ² that Sanballat sends, also Geshem, to me, saying, "Come and we meet together in the villages, in the Valley of Ono"; and they are thinking to do to me evil. ³ And I send to them messengers, saying, "A great work I am doing, and I am not able to come down; why does the work cease when I let it alone, and have come down to you?" ⁴ and they send to me, according to this word, four times, and I return them [word] according to this word. ⁵ And Sanballat sends to me, according to this word, a fifth time, his servant, and an open letter in his hand; ⁶ it is written in it, "Among the nations it has been heard, and Gashmu is saying: You and the Jews are thinking to rebel, therefore you are building the wall, and you have been to them for a king—according to these words! ⁷ And also, you have appointed prophets to call for you in Jerusalem, saying, A king [is] in Judah, and now it is heard by the king according to these words; and now come, and we take counsel together." ⁸ And I send to him, saying, "It has not been according to these words that you are saying, for from your own heart you are devising them"; ⁹ for all of them are

making us afraid, saying, "Their hands are too feeble for the work, and it is not done"; and now, strengthen my hands. [10] And I have entered the house of Shemaiah son of Delaiah, son of Mehetabeel—and he is restrained—and he says, "Let us meet at the house of God, at the inside of the temple, and we shut the doors of the temple, for they are coming to slay you—indeed, by night they are coming to slay you." [11] And I say, "A man such as I—does he flee? and who as I, that goes into the temple, and lives? I do not go in." [12] And I discern, and behold, God has not sent him, for in the prophecy he has spoken to me both Tobiah and Sanballat hired him, [13] so that he [is] a hired worker, that I may fear and do so, and I had sinned, and it had been to them for an evil name that they may reproach me. [14] Be mindful, O my God, of Tobiah, and of Sanballat, according to these his works, and also, of Noadiah the prophetess, and of the rest of the prophets who have been making me afraid. [15] And the wall is completed in the twenty-fifth of Elul, on the fifty-second day; [16] and it comes to pass, when all our enemies have heard, and all the nations who are all around us see, that they fall greatly in their own eyes, and know that by our God has this work been done. [17] Also, in those days the nobles of Judah are multiplying their letters going to Tobiah, and those of Tobiah are coming to them; [18] for many in Judah are sworn to him, for he [is] son-in-law to Shechaniah son of Arah, and his son Jehohanan has taken the daughter of Meshullam son of Berechiah; [19] also, they have been speaking of his good deeds before me, and they have been taking my words out to him; Tobiah has sent letters to make me afraid.

CHAPTER 7

[1] And it comes to pass, when the wall has been built, that I set up the doors, and the gatekeepers are appointed, and the singers, and the Levites, [2] and I charge my brother Hanani, and Hananiah head of the palace, concerning Jerusalem, for he [is] as a man of truth, and fearing God above many— [3] and I say to them, "Do not let the gates of Jerusalem be opened until the heat of the sun, and while they are standing by let them shut the doors, and fasten, and appoint guards of the inhabitants of Jerusalem, each at his watch, and each in front of his house." [4] And the city [is] broad on both sides, and great, and the people [are] few in its midst, and there are no houses built; [5] and my God puts it to my heart, and I gather the nobles, and the prefects, and the people, for the genealogy, and I find a scroll of the genealogy of those coming up at the beginning, and I find written in it: [6] These [are] sons of the province, those coming up of the captives of the expulsion that Nebuchadnezzar king of Babylon removed—and they return to Jerusalem and to Judah, each to his city— [7] who are coming in with Zerubbabel, Jeshua, Nehemiah, Azariah, Raamiah, Nahamani, Mordecai, Bilshan, Mispereth, Bigvai, Nehum, Baanah. The number of the men of the people of Israel: [8] sons of Parosh, two thousand one hundred and seventy-two; [9] sons of Shephatiah, three hundred seventy-two; [10] sons of Arah, six hundred fifty-two; [11] sons of Pahath-Moab, of the sons of Jeshua and Joab, two thousand and eight hundred [and] eighteen; [12] sons of Elam, one thousand two hundred fifty-four; [13] sons of Zattu, eight hundred forty-five; [14] sons of Zaccai, seven hundred and sixty; [15] sons of Binnui, six hundred forty-eight; [16] sons of Bebai, six hundred twenty-eight; [17] sons of Azgad, two thousand three hundred twenty-two; [18] sons of Adonikam, six hundred sixty-seven; [19] sons of Bigvai, two thousand sixty-seven; [20] sons of Adin, six hundred fifty-five; [21] sons of Ater of Hezekiah, ninety-eight; [22] sons of Hashum, three hundred twenty-eight; [23] sons of Bezai, three hundred twenty-four; [24] sons of Hariph, one hundred [and] twelve; [25] sons of Gibeon, ninety-five; [26] men of Beth-Lehem and Netophah, one hundred eighty-eight; [27] men of Anathoth, one hundred twenty-eight; [28] men of Beth-Azmaveth, forty-two; [29] men of Kirjath-Jearim, Chephirah, and Beeroth, seven hundred forty-three; [30] men of Ramah and Gaba, six hundred twenty-one; [31] men of Michmas, one hundred and twenty-two; [32] men of Bethel and Ai, one hundred twenty-three; [33] men of the other Nebo, fifty-two; [34] sons of the other Elam, one thousand two hundred fifty-four; [35] sons of Harim, three hundred and twenty; [36] sons of Jericho, three hundred forty-five; [37] sons of Lod, Hadid, and Ono, seven hundred and twenty-one; [38] sons of Senaah, three thousand nine hundred and thirty. [39] The priests: sons of Jedaiah, of the house of Jeshua, nine hundred seventy-three; [40] sons of Immer, one thousand fifty-two; [41] sons of Pashur, one thousand two hundred forty-seven; [42] sons of Harim, one thousand and seventeen. [43] The Levites: sons of Jeshua, of Kadmiel, of sons of Hodevah, seventy-four. [44] The singers: sons of Asaph, one hundred forty-eight. [45] The gatekeepers: sons of Shallum, sons of Ater, sons of Talmon, sons of Akkub, sons of Hatita, sons of Shobai: one hundred thirty-eight. [46] The Nethinim: sons of Ziha, sons of Hasupha, sons of Tabbaoth, [47] sons of Keros, sons of Sia, sons of Padon, [48] sons of Lebanah, sons of Hagaba, sons of Shalmai, [49] sons of Hanan, sons of Giddel, sons of Gahar, [50] sons of Reaiah, sons of Rezin, sons of Nekoda, [51] sons of Gazzam, sons of Uzza, sons of Phaseah, [52] sons of Bezai, sons of Meunim, sons of Nephishesim, [53] sons of Bakbuk, sons of Hakupha, sons of Harhur, [54] sons of Bazlith, sons of Mehida, sons of Harsha, [55] sons of Barkos, sons of Sisera, sons of Tamah, [56] sons of Neziah, sons of Hatipha. [57] Sons of the servants of Solomon: sons of Sotai, sons of Sophereth, sons of Perida, [58] sons of Jaala, sons of Darkon, sons of Giddel, [59] sons of Shephatiah, sons of Hattil, sons of Pochereth of Zebaim, sons of Amon. [60] All the Nethinim and the sons of the servants of Solomon [are] three hundred ninety-two. [61] And these [are] those coming up from Tel-Melah, Tel-Harsha, Cherub, Addon, and Immer—and they have not been able to declare the house of their fathers, and their seed, whether they [are] of Israel— [62] sons of Delaiah, sons of Tobiah, sons of Nekoda, six hundred forty-two. [63] And of the priests: sons of Habaiah, sons of Koz, sons of Barzillai (who has taken a wife from the daughters of Barzillai the Gileadite, and is called by their name). [64] These have sought their register among those reckoning themselves by genealogy, and it has not been found, and they are redeemed from the priesthood, [65] and the Tirshatha says to them that they do not eat of the most holy things until the standing up of the priest with [the] Lights and Perfections. [66] All the assembly together [is] forty-two thousand three hundred and sixty, [67] apart from their servants and their handmaids—these [are] seven thousand three hundred thirty-seven; and of them [are] male and female singers, two hundred forty-five. [68] Their horses [are] seven hundred thirty-six; their mules, two hundred [and] forty-five; [69] camels, four hundred thirty-five; donkeys, six thousand seven hundred and twenty. [70] And from the extremity of the heads of the fathers they have given to the work; the Tirshatha has given to the treasure, one thousand drams of gold, fifty bowls, five hundred and thirty priests' coats. [71] And of the heads of the fathers they have given to the treasure of the work, twenty thousand drams of gold, and two thousand and two hundred pounds of silver. [72] And that which the rest of the people have given [is] twenty thousand drams of gold, and two thousand pounds of silver, and sixty-seven priests' coats. [73] And they dwell—the priests, and the Levites, and the gatekeepers, and the singers, and [some] of the people, and the Nethinim, and all Israel—in their cities, and the seventh month comes, and the sons of Israel [are] in their cities.

CHAPTER 8

[1] And all the people are gathered as one man to the broad place that [is] before the Water Gate, and they say to Ezra the scribe to bring the Scroll of the Law of Moses, that Yhwh commanded Israel. [2] And Ezra the priest brings the Law before the assembly, both of men and women, and everyone intelligent to hear, on the first day of the seventh month, [3] and he reads in it before the broad place that [is] before the Water Gate, from the light until the middle of the day, in front of the men, and the women, and those intelligent, and the ears of all the people [are] toward the Scroll of the Law. [4] And Ezra the scribe stands on a tower of wood that they made for the purpose, and Mattithiah stands near him, and Shema, and Anaiah, and Urijah, and Hilkiah, and Maaseiah, on his right; and on his left Pedaiah, and Mishael, and Malchijah, and Hashum, and Hashbaddana, Zechariah, Meshullam. [5] And Ezra opens the scroll before the eyes of all the people—for he has been above all the people—and at his opening [it] all the people have stood up, [6] and Ezra blesses Yhwh, the great God, and all the people answer, "Amen, Amen," with lifting up of their hands, and they bow and pay respect to Yhwh—faces to the earth. [7] And Jeshua, and Bani, and Sherebiah, Jamin, Akkub, Shabbethai, Hodijah, Maaseiah, Kelita, Azariah, Jozabad, Hanan, Pelaiah, and the Levites, giving the people understanding in the Law, and the people, [are] on their station, [8] and they read in the Scroll, in the Law of God, explaining—so as to give the meaning, and they give

understanding to the convocation. ⁹ And Nehemiah—he [is] the Tirshatha—says (and Ezra the priest, the scribe, and the Levites who are instructing the people) to all the people, "Today is holy to your God Yhwh, do not mourn, nor weep": for all the people are weeping at their hearing the words of the Law. ¹⁰ And he says to them, "Go, eat fat things, and drink sweet things, and send portions to him for whom nothing is prepared, for today [is] holy to our Lord, and do not be grieved, for the joy of Yhwh is your strength." ¹¹ And the Levites are keeping all the people silent, saying, "Be silent, for today [is] holy, and do not be grieved." ¹² And all the people go to eat, and to drink, and to send portions, and to make great joy, because they have understood concerning the words that they made known to them. ¹³ And on the second day have been gathered heads of the fathers of all the people, the priests, and the Levites, to Ezra the scribe, even to act wisely concerning the words of the Law. ¹⁴ And they find written in the Law that Yhwh commanded by the hand of Moses, that the sons of Israel dwell in shelters in the celebration, in the seventh month, ¹⁵ and that they proclaim and cause to pass over all their cities (and in Jerusalem), saying, "Go out to the mountain, and bring leaves of the olive, and leaves of the oil tree, and leaves of the myrtle, and leaves of the palms, and leaves of thick trees, to make shelters as it is written." ¹⁶ And the people go out, and bring in, and make for themselves shelters, each on his roof, and in their courts, and in the courts of the house of God, and in the broad place of the Water Gate, and in the broad place of the Gate of Ephraim. ¹⁷ And they make—all the assembly of the captives of the captivity—shelters, and they sit in shelters; for the sons of Israel had not done, from the days of Jeshua son of Nun, so to that day, and there is very great joy. ¹⁸ And he reads in the Scroll of the Law of God day by day, from the first day until the last day, and they make a celebration seven days, and on the eighth day a restraint, according to the ordinance.

CHAPTER 9

¹ And in the twenty-fourth day of this month the sons of Israel have been gathered with fasting, and with sackcloth, and earth on them; ² and the seed of Israel are separated from all sons of a stranger, and stand and confess concerning their sins, and the iniquities of their fathers, ³ and rise up on their station, and read in the Scroll of the Law of their God Yhwh a fourth of the day, and a fourth they are confessing and bowing themselves to their God Yhwh. ⁴ And there stand up on the ascent, of the Levites, Jeshua, and Bani, Kadmiel, Shebaniah, Bunni, Sherebiah, Bani, Chenani, and they cry with a loud voice to their God Yhwh. ⁵ And the Levites say, [even] Jeshua, and Kadmiel, Bani, Hashabniah, Sherebiah, Hodijah, Shebaniah, Pethahiah, "Rise, bless your God Yhwh, from age to age, || And they bless the Name of Your glory || That [is] exalted above all blessing and praise. ⁶ You [are] He, O Yhwh, Yourself—You have made the heavens, || The heavens of the heavens, and all their host, || The earth and all that [are] on it, || The seas and all that [are] in them, || And You are keeping all of them alive, || And the host of the heavens are bowing themselves to You. ⁷ You [are] He, O Yhwh God, || Who fixed on Abraham, || And brought him out from Ur of the Chaldeans, || And made his name Abraham, ⁸ And found his heart steadfast before You, || So as to make with him the covenant, || To give the land of the Canaanite, || The Hittite, the Amorite, and the Perizzite, and the Jebusite, and the Girgashite, || To give [it] to his seed. And You establish Your words, || For You [are] righteous, ⁹ And see the affliction of our fathers in Egypt, || And their cry have heard by the Sea of Suph, ¹⁰ And give signs and wonders on Pharaoh, || And on all his servants, || And on all the people of his land, || For You have known that they have acted proudly against them, || And You make to Yourself a name as [at] this day. ¹¹ And You have cleaved the sea before them, || And they pass over into the midst of the sea on the dry land, || And their pursuers You have cast into the depths, || As a stone, into the strong waters. ¹² And by a pillar of cloud You have led them by day, || And by a pillar of fire by night, || To lighten to them the way in which they go. ¹³ And on Mount Sinai You have come down, || Even to speak with them from the heavens, || And You give to them right judgments, || And true laws, good statutes and commands. ¹⁴ And Your holy Sabbath You have made known to them, || And commands, and statutes, and law, || You have commanded for them, || By the hand of Your servant Moses; ¹⁵ And bread from the heavens You have given to them for their hunger, || And

water from a rock have brought out to them for their thirst, || And say to them to go in to possess the land || That You have lifted up Your hand to give to them. ¹⁶ And they and our fathers have acted proudly, || And harden their neck, || And have not listened to Your commands, ¹⁷ Indeed, they refuse to listen, || And have not remembered Your wonders that You have done with them, || And harden their neck and appoint a head, || To turn back to their service, in their rebellion; And You [are] a God of pardons, || Gracious, and merciful, long-suffering, and abundant in kindness, || And have not forsaken them. ¹⁸ Also, when they have made to themselves a molten calf, || And say, This [is] your god || That brought you up out of Egypt, || And do great despisings, ¹⁹ and You, in Your abundant mercies, || Have not forsaken them in the wilderness—The pillar of the cloud has not turned aside from off them by day, || To lead them in the way, || And the pillar of the fire by night, || To give light to them and the way in which they go. ²⁰ And Your good Spirit You have given, || To cause them to act wisely; And Your manna You have not withheld from their mouth, || And water You have given to them for their thirst, ²¹ And forty years You have nourished them in a wilderness; They have not lacked; Their garments have not worn out, || And their feet have not swelled. ²² And You give to them kingdoms, and peoples, || And apportion them to the corner, || And they possess the land of Sihon, || And the land of the king of Heshbon, || And the land of Og king of Bashan. ²³ And You have multiplied their sons as the stars of the heavens, || And bring them into the land || That You have said to their fathers to go in to possess. ²⁴ And the sons come in, and possess the land, || And You humble the inhabitants of the land—the Canaanites—before them, || And give them into their hand, and their kings, || And the peoples of the land, || To do with them according to their pleasure. ²⁵ And they capture fortified cities, and fat ground, || And possess houses full of all good, || Dug-wells, vineyards, and olive-yards, || And fruit-trees in abundance, || And they eat, and are satisfied, || And become fat, || And delight themselves in Your great goodness. ²⁶ And they are disobedient, || And rebel against You, || And cast Your law behind their back, || And Your prophets they have slain, || Who testified against them, || To bring them back to You, || And they do great despisings, ²⁷ And You give them into the hand of their adversaries, || And they distress them, || And in the time of their distress they cry to You, || And You, from the heavens, hear, || And according to Your abundant mercies, || Give saviors to them, || And they save them out of the hand of their adversaries. ²⁸ And when they have rest, || They turn back to do evil before You, || And You leave them in the hand of their enemies, || And they rule over them; And they return, and call You, || And You hear from the heavens, || And deliver them many times, || According to Your mercies, ²⁹ And testify against them, || To bring them back to Your law; And they have acted proudly, || And have not listened to Your commands, || And against Your judgments have sinned—Which man does and has lived in them—And they give a stubborn shoulder, || And have hardened their neck, || And have not listened. ³⁰ And You draw over them many years, || And testify against them by Your Spirit, || By the hand of Your prophets, || And they have not given ear, || And You give them into the hand of peoples of the lands, ³¹ and in Your abundant mercies || You have not made them a consumption, || Nor have forsaken them; For a God, gracious and merciful, [are] You. ³² And now, O our God—God, the great, the mighty, || And the fearful, || Keeping the covenant and the kindness—Do not let all the travail that has found us be little before You, || For our kings, for our heads, and for our priests, || And for our prophets, and for our fathers, || And for all Your people, || From the days of the kings of Asshur to this day; ³³ And You [are] righteous concerning all that has come on us, || For You have done truth, || And we have done wickedly; ³⁴ And our kings, our heads, || Our priests, and our fathers, || Have not done Your law, || Nor attended to Your commands, || And to Your testimonies, || That You have testified against them; ³⁵ And they, in their kingdom, || And in Your abundant goodness, || That You have given to them, || And in the land, the large and the fat, || That You have set before them, || Have not served You, || Nor turned back from their evil doings. ³⁶ Behold, we—today—[are] servants, || And the land that You have given to our fathers, || To eat its fruit and its good, || Behold, we [are] servants on it, ³⁷ And its increase it is multiplying to the kings || Whom You have set over us || In our sins; And over our bodies they are ruling, || And over our livestock, || According to their pleasure, || And we [are] in great distress. **38** And for all this we are making a steadfast covenant, || And are writing, || And over him who is sealed || [Are] our heads, our Levites, [and] our priests."

CHAPTER 10

1 And over those sealed [are] Nehemiah the Tirshatha, son of Hachaliah, and Zidkijah, **2** Seraiah, Azariah, Jeremiah, **3** Pashhur, Amariah, Malchijah, **4** Huttush, Shebaniah, Malluch, **5** Harim, Meremoth, Obadiah, **6** Daniel, Ginnethon, Baruch, **7** Meshullam, Abijah, Mijamin, **8** Maaziah, Bilgai, Shemaiah; these [are] the priests. **9** And the Levites: both Jeshua son of Azaniah, Binnui of the sons of Henadad, Kadmiel, **10** and their brothers: Shebaniah, Hodijah, Kelita, Pelaiah, Hanan, **11** Micha, Rehob, Hashabiah, **12** Zaccur, Sherebiah, Shebaniah, **13** Hodijah, Bani, Beninu. **14** Heads of the people: Parosh, Pahath-Moab, Elam, Zatthu, Bani, **15** Bunni, Azgad, Bebai, **16** Adonijah, Bigvai, Adin, **17** Ater, Hizkijah, Azzur, **18** Hodijah, Hashum, Bezai, **19** Hariph, Anathoth, Nebai, **20** Magpiash, Meshullam, Hezir, **21** Meshezabeel, Zadok, Jaddua, **22** Pelatiah, Hanan, Anaiah, **23** Hoshea, Hananiah, Hashub, **24** Hallohesh, Pilha, Shobek, **25** Rehum, Hashabnah, Maaseiah, **26** and Ahijah, Hanan, Anan, **27** Malluch, Harim, Baanah. **28** And the rest of the people, the priests, the Levites, the gatekeepers, the singers, the Nethinim, and everyone who has been separated from the peoples of the lands to the Law of God, their wives, their sons, and their daughters, every knowing intelligent one, **29** are laying hold on their brothers, their majestic ones, and coming into an execration and an oath, to walk in the Law of God, that was given by the hand of Moses, servant of God, and to observe and to do all the commands of Yhwh our Lord, and His judgments, and His statutes; **30** and that we do not give our daughters to the peoples of the land, and we do not take their daughters to our sons; **31** and the peoples of the land who are bringing in the wares and any grain on the Sabbath day to sell, we do not receive of them on the Sabbath, and on a holy day, and we leave the seventh year, and usury on every hand. **32** And we have appointed for ourselves commands, to put on ourselves the third of a shekel in a year, for the service of the house of our God, **33** for bread of the arrangement, and the continual present, and the continual burnt-offering of the Sabbaths, of the new moons, for appointed times, and for holy things, and for sin-offerings, to make atonement for Israel, even all the work of the house of our God. **34** And we have caused the lots to fall for the offering of wood, [among] the priests, the Levites, and the people, to bring into the house of our God, by the house of our fathers, at times appointed, year by year, to burn on the altar of our God Yhwh, as it is written in the Law, **35** and to bring in the first-fruits of our ground, and the first-fruits of all fruit of every tree, year by year, to the house of Yhwh, **36** and the firstlings of our sons, and of our livestock, as it is written in the Law, and the firstlings of our herds and our flocks, to bring into the house of our God, to the priests who are ministering in the house of our God. **37** And the beginning of our dough, and our raised-offerings, and the fruit of every tree, of new wine, and of oil, we bring to the priests, into the chambers of the house of our God, and the tithe of our ground to the Levites; and they—the Levites—have the tithes in all the cities of our tillage; **38** and the priest, son of Aaron, has been with the Levites in the tithing of the Levites, and the Levites bring up the tithe of the tithe to the house of our God to the chambers, to the treasure-house; **39** for they bring to the chambers—the sons of Israel and the sons of Levi—the raised-offering of the grain, the new wine, and the oil, and there [are] vessels of the sanctuary, and the priests, those ministering, and the gatekeepers, and the singers, and we do not forsake the house of our God.

CHAPTER 11

1 And the heads of the people dwell in Jerusalem, and the rest of the people have caused lots to fall to bring in one out of ten to dwell in Jerusalem the holy city, and nine parts in the cities, **2** and the people give a blessing to all the men who are offering themselves willingly to dwell in Jerusalem. **3** And these [are] heads of the province who have dwelt in Jerusalem, and in cities of Judah, they have dwelt each in his possession in their cities; Israel, the priests, and the Levites, and the Nethinim, and the sons of the servants of Solomon. **4** And in Jerusalem have dwelt of the sons of Judah, and of the sons of Benjamin. Of the sons of Judah: Athaiah son of Uzziah, son of Zechariah, son of Amariah, son of Shephatiah, son of Mahalaleel, of the sons of Perez; **5** and Masseiah son of Baruch, son of Col-Hozeh, son of Hazaiah, son of Adaiah, son of Joiarib, son of Zechariah, son of Shiloni; **6** all the sons of Perez who are dwelling in Jerusalem [are] four hundred sixty-eight, men of valor. **7** And these [are] sons of Benjamin: Sallu son of Meshullam, son of Joed, son of Pedaiah, son of Kolaiah, son of Maaseiah, son of Ithiel, son of Jesaiah; **8** and after him Gabbai, Sallai, nine hundred twenty-eight. **9** And Joel son of Zichri [is] inspector over them, and Judah son of Senuah [is] over the city—second. **10** Of the priests: Jedaiah son of Joiarib, Jachin, **11** Seraiah son of Hilkiah, son of Meshullam, son of Zadok, son of Meraioth, son of Ahitub, leader of the house of God, **12** and their brothers doing the work of the house [are] eight hundred twenty-two; and Adaiah son of Jeroham, son of Pelaliah, son of Amzi, son of Zechariah, son of Pashhur, son of Malchiah, **13** and his brothers, heads of fathers, two hundred forty-two; and Amashsai son of Azareel, son of Ahazai, son of Meshillemoth, son of Immer, **14** and their brothers, one hundred twenty-eight mighty men of valor; and an inspector over them [is] Zabdiel, son of [one of] the great men. **15** And of the Levites: Shemaiah son of Hashub, son of Azrikam, son of Hashabiah, son of Bunni, **16** and Shabbethai, and Jozabad, [are] over the outward work of the house of God, of the heads of the Levites, **17** and Mattaniah son of Micha, son of Zabdi, son of Asaph, [is] head—at the commencement he gives thanks in prayer; and Bakbukiah [is] second among his brothers, and Abda son of Shammua, son of Galal, son of Jeduthun. **18** All the Levites, in the holy city, [are] two hundred eighty-four. **19** And the gatekeepers, Akkub, Talmon, and their brothers, those watching at the gates, [are] one hundred seventy-two. **20** And the rest of Israel, of the priests, of the Levites, [are] in all cities of Judah, each in his inheritance; **21** and the Nethinim are dwelling in Ophel, and Ziha and Gishpa [are] over the Nethinim. **22** And the overseer of the Levites in Jerusalem [is] Uzzi son of Bani, son of Hashabiah, son of Mattaniah, son of Micha—of the sons of Asaph, the singers [who are] for the front of the work of the house of God, **23** for the command of the king [is] on them, and support [is] for the singers, a matter of a day in its day. **24** And Pethahiah son of Meshezabeel, of the sons of Zerah, son of Judah, [is] by the hand of the king, for every matter of the people. **25** And at the villages with their fields, of the sons of Judah there have dwelt, in Kirjath-Arba and its small towns, and in Dibon and its small towns, and in Jekabzeel and its villages, **26** and in Jeshua, and in Moladah, and in Beth-Phelet, **27** and in Hazar-Shaul, and in Beer-Sheba and its small towns, **28** and in Ziklag, and in Mekonah and in its small towns, **29** and En-Rimmon, and in Zareah, and in Jarmuth, **30** Zanoah, Adullam, and their villages, Lachish and its fields, Azekah and its small towns; and they encamp from Beer-Sheba to the Valley of the Hinnom. **31** And of Benjamin [are] at Geba, Michmash, and Aija, and Beth-El, and its small towns, **32** Anathoth, Nob, Ananiah, **33** Hazor, Ramah, Gittaim, **34** Hadid, Zeboim, Neballat, **35** Lod, and Ono, the Valley of the Craftsmen. **36** And of the Levites, the divisions of Judah [are] for Benjamin.

CHAPTER 12

1 And these [are] the priests and the Levites who came up with Zerubbabel son of Shealtiel, and Jeshua: Seraiah, Jeremiah, Ezra, **2** Amariah, Malluch, Hattush, **3** Shechaniah, Rehum, Meremoth, **4** Iddo, Ginnethoi, Abijah, **5** Miamin, Maadiah, Bilgah, **6** Shemaiah, and Joiarib, Jedaiah, **7** Sallu, Amok, Hilkiah, Jedaiah; these [are] heads of the priests and of their brothers in the days of Jeshua. **8** And the Levites: Jeshua, Binnui, Kadmiel, Sherebiah, Judah, Mattaniah, he [is] over the thanksgiving, and his brothers, **9** and Bakbukiah and Unni, their brothers, [are] opposite them in charges. **10** And Jeshua has begotten Joiakim, and Joiakim has begotten Eliashib, and Eliashib has begotten Joiada, **11** and Joiada has begotten Jonathan, and Jonathan has begotten Jaddua. **12** And in the days of Joiakim have been priests, heads of the fathers: of Seraiah, Meraiah; of Jeremiah, Hananiah; **13** of Ezra, Meshullam; of Amariah, Jehohanan; **14** of Melicu, Jonathan; of Shebaniah, Joseph; **15** of Harim, Adna; of Meraioth, Helkai; **16** of Iddo, Zechariah; of Ginnethon, Meshullam; **17** of Abijah, Zichri; of Miniamin; of Moadiah, Piltai; **18** of Bilgah, Shammua; of Shemaiah, Jonathan; **19** and of Joiarib, Mattenai; of Jedaiah, Uzzi; **20** of Sallai, Kallai; of Amok, Eber; **21** of Hilkiah,

Hashabiah; of Jedaiah, Nethaneel. **22** The Levites, in the days of Eliashib, Joiada, and Johanan, and Jaddua, are written, heads of fathers, and of the priests, in the kingdom of Darius the Persian. **23** Sons of Levi, heads of the fathers, are written on the scroll of the Chronicles even until the days of Johanan son of Eliashib; **24** and heads of the Levites: Hashabiah, Sherebiah, and Jeshua son of Kadmiel, and their brothers, [are] opposite them, to give praise, to give thanks, by command of David the man of God, charge close by charge. **25** Mattaniah, and Bakbukiah, Obadiah, Meshullam, Talmon, Akkub, [are] gatekeepers, keeping watch in the gatherings of the gates. **26** These [are] in the days of Joiakim son of Jeshua, son of Jozadak, and in the days of Nehemiah the governor, and of Ezra the priest, the scribe. **27** And at the dedication of the wall of Jerusalem they sought the Levites out of all their places, to bring them to Jerusalem, to make the dedication even with gladness, and with thanksgivings, and with singing, [with] cymbals, psalteries, and with harps; **28** and sons of the singers are gathered together even from the circuit around Jerusalem, and from the villages of Netophathi, **29** and from the house of Gilgal, and from fields of Geba and Azmaveth, the singers have built for villages for themselves around Jerusalem; **30** and the priests and the Levites are cleansed, and they cleanse the people, and the gates, and the wall. **31** And I bring up the heads of Judah on the wall, and appoint two great thanksgiving companies and processions. At the right, on the wall, to the Refuse Gate; **32** and after them goes Hoshaiah, and half of the heads of Judah, **33** and Azariah, Ezra, and Meshullam, **34** Judah, and Benjamin, and Shemaiah, and Jeremiah; **35** and of the sons of the priests with trumpets, Zechariah son of Jonathan, son of Shemaiah, son of Mattaniah, son of Michaiah, son of Zaccur, son of Asaph, **36** and his brothers Shemaiah, and Azarael, Milalai, Gilalai, Maai, Nethaneel, and Judah, Hanani, with instruments of song of David the man of God, and Ezra the scribe [is] before them; **37** and by the Fountain Gate and in front of them, they have gone up by the steps of the City of David, at the going up of the wall beyond the house of David, and to the Water Gate eastward. **38** And the second thanksgiving company that is going opposite, and I after it, and half of the people on the wall from beyond the Tower of the Furnaces and to the broad wall, **39** and from beyond the Gate of Ephraim, and by the Old Gate, and by the Fish Gate, and the Tower of Hananeel, and the Tower of Meah, and to the Sheep Gate—and they have stood at the Prison Gate. **40** And the two thanksgiving companies stand in the house of God, and I and half of the prefects with me, **41** and the priests, Eliakim, Maaseiah, Miniamin, Michaiah, Elioenai, Zechariah, Hananiah, with trumpets, **42** and Masseiah, and Shemaiah, and Eleazar, and Uzzi, and Jehohanan, and Malchijah, and Elam, and Ezer, and the singers sound, and Jezrahiah the inspector; **43** and they sacrifice on that day great sacrifices and rejoice, for God has made them rejoice [with] great joy, and also, the women and the children have rejoiced, and the joy of Jerusalem is heard—to a distance. **44** And certain are appointed on that day over the chambers for treasures, for raised-offerings, for first-fruits, and for tithes, to gather into them out of the fields of the cities the portions of the law for priests, and for Levites, for the joy of Judah [is] over the priests, and over the Levites, who are standing up. **45** And the singers and the gatekeepers keep the charge of their God, even the charge of the cleansing—according to the command of David [and] his son Solomon, **46** for in the days of David and Asaph of old [were] heads of the singers, and a song of praise and thanksgiving to God. **47** And all Israel in the days of Zerubbabel, and in the days of Nehemiah, are giving the portions of the singers, and of the gatekeepers, the matter of a day in its day, and are sanctifying to the Levites, and the Levites are sanctifying to the sons of Aaron.

CHAPTER 13

1 On that day there was read in the scroll of Moses, in the ears of the people, and it has been found written in it that an Ammonite and Moabite does not come into the assembly of God for all time, **2** because they have not come before the sons of Israel with bread and with water, and hire against them Balaam to revile them, and our God turns the reviling into a blessing. **3** And it comes to pass, at their hearing the Law, that they separate all the mixed people from Israel. **4** And before this Eliashib the priest, appointed over chambers of the house of our God, [is] a relation of Tobiah, **5** and he makes for him a

great chamber, and there they were formerly putting the present, the frankincense, and the vessels, and the tithe of the grain, the new wine, and the oil—the commanded thing of the Levites, and the singers, and the gatekeepers—and the raised-offering of the priests. **6** And during all this I was not in Jerusalem, for in the thirty-second year of Artaxerxes king of Babylon I came to the king, and at the end of days I have asked of the king, **7** and I come to Jerusalem, and understand concerning the evil that Eliashib has done for Tobiah, to make to him a chamber in the courts of the house of God, **8** and it is very displeasing to me, and I cast all the vessels of the house of Tobiah outside, out of the chamber, **9** and I command, and they cleanse the chambers, and I bring back there the vessels of the house of God with the present and the frankincense. **10** And I know that the portions of the Levites have not been given, and they flee each to his field—the Levites and the singers, doing the work. **11** And I strive with the prefects, and say, "Why has the house of God been forsaken?" And I gather them, and set them on their station; **12** and all Judah has brought in the tithe of the grain, and of the new wine, and of the oil, to the treasuries. **13** And I appoint treasurers over the treasuries, Shelemiah the priest, and Zadok the scribe, and Pedaiah of the Levites; and by their hand [is] Hanan son of Zaccur, son of Mattaniah, for they have been reckoned steadfast, and on them [it is] to give a portion to their brothers. **14** Be mindful of me, O my God, for this, and do not blot out my kind acts that I have done, for the house of my God, and for its charges. **15** In those days I have seen in Judah those treading wine-vats on Sabbath, and bringing in the sheaves, and loading on the donkeys, and also, wine, grapes, and figs, and every burden, indeed, they are bringing into Jerusalem on the Sabbath day, and I testify in the day of their selling provision. **16** And the Tyrians have dwelt in it, bringing in fish, and every ware, and selling on Sabbath to the sons of Judah and in Jerusalem. **17** And I strive with the nobles of Judah, and say to them, "What [is] this evil thing that you are doing, and defiling the Sabbath day? **18** Thus did not your fathers do? and our God brings in on us all this evil, and on this city, and you are adding fierceness on Israel, to defile the Sabbath." **19** And it comes to pass, when the gates of Jerusalem have been dark before the Sabbath, that I command, and the doors are shut, and I command that they do not open them until after the Sabbath; and of my servants I have stationed at the gates; there does not come in a burden on the Sabbath day. **20** And they lodge—the merchants and sellers of all ware—at the outside of Jerusalem, once or twice, **21** and I testify against them, and say to them, "Why are you lodging in front of the wall? if you repeat [it], I put forth a hand on you"; from that time they have not come in on the Sabbath. **22** And I command to the Levites that they be cleansed, and coming in, keeping the gates, to sanctify the Sabbath day. Also, this, remember for me, O my God, and have pity on me, according to the abundance of Your kindness. **23** Also, in those days, I have seen the Jews [who] have settled women of Ashdod, of Ammon, of Moab. **24** And of their sons, half are speaking Ashdoditish—and are not knowing to speak Jewish—and according to the language of people and people. **25** And I strive with them, and declare them vile, and strike certain of them, and pluck off their hair, and cause them to swear by God, "You do not give your daughters to their sons, nor do you take of their daughters to your sons, and to yourselves. **26** By these did not Solomon king of Israel sin? and among the many nations there was no king like him, and he was beloved by his God, and God makes him king over all Israel—even him [whom] the strange women caused to sin. **27** And do we listen to you to do all this great evil, to trespass against our God, to settle strange women?" **28** And [one] of the sons of Joiada son of Eliashib the high priest, [is] son-in-law to Sanballat the Horonite, and I cause him to flee from off me. **29** Be mindful of them, O my God, for the redeemed of the priesthood, and the covenant of the priesthood, and of the Levites. **30** And I have cleansed them from every stranger, and appoint charges to priests and to Levites, each in his work, **31** and for the wood-offering at appointed times, and for first-fruits. Be mindful of me, O my God, for good.

ESTHER

CHAPTER 1

¹ And it comes to pass, in the days of Ahasuerus—he [is] Ahasuerus who is reigning from Hodu even to Cush, one hundred twenty-seven provinces— ² in those days, at the sitting of King Ahasuerus on the throne of his kingdom, that [is] in Shushan the palace, ³ in the third year of his reign, he has made a banquet to all his heads and his servants; of the force of Persia and Media, the chiefs and heads of the provinces [are] before him, ⁴ in his showing the wealth of the glory of his kingdom, and the glory of the beauty of his greatness, many days—one hundred eighty days. ⁵ And at the fullness of these days the king has made a banquet to all the people who are found in Shushan the palace, from great even to small, [for] seven days, in the court of the garden of the house of the king— ⁶ white linen, white cotton, and blue, fastened with cords of fine linen and purple on rings of silver, and pillars of marble, couches of gold, and of silver, on a pavement of smaragdus, and white marble, and mother-of-pearl, and black marble— ⁷ and the giving of drink in vessels of gold, and the vessels [are] various vessels, and the royal wine [is] abundant, as a memorial of the king. ⁸ And the drinking [is] according to law, none is pressing, for so the king has appointed for every chief one of his house, to do according to the pleasure of man and man. ⁹ Also Vashti the queen has made a banquet for women, in the royal house that King Ahasuerus has. ¹⁰ On the seventh day, as the heart of the king is glad with wine, he has commanded to Mehuman, Biztha, Harbona, Bigtha, and Abagtha, Zethar, and Carcas, the seven eunuchs who are ministering in the presence of King Ahasuerus, ¹¹ to bring in Vashti the queen before the king, with a royal crown, to show the peoples and the heads her beauty, for she [is] of good appearance, ¹² and the queen Vashti refuses to come in at the word of the king that [is] by the hand of the eunuchs, and the king is very angry, and his fury has burned in him. ¹³ And the king says to wise men, knowing the times—for so [is] the word of the king before all knowing law and judgment, ¹⁴ and he who is near to him [is] Carshena, Shethar, Admatha, Tarshish, Meres, Marsena, Memucan, seven heads of Persia and Media seeing the face of the king, who are sitting first in the kingdom— ¹⁵ "According to law, what should [I] do with Queen Vashti, because that she has not done the saying of King Ahasuerus by the hand of the eunuchs?" ¹⁶ And Memucan says before the king and the heads, "Queen Vashti has not done perversely against the king by himself, but against all the heads, and against all the peoples that [are] in all provinces of King Ahasuerus; ¹⁷ for the word of the queen goes forth to all the women, to render their husbands contemptible in their eyes, in their saying, King Ahasuerus commanded to bring in Vashti the queen before him, and she did not come; ¹⁸ indeed, this day princesses of Persia and Media, who have heard the word of the queen, say [so] to all heads of the king, even according to the sufficiency of contempt and wrath. ¹⁹ If to the king [it be] good, there goes forth a royal word from before him, and it is written with the laws of Persia and Media, and does not pass away, that Vashti does not come in before King Ahasuerus, and the king gives her royalty to her companion who [is] better than she; ²⁰ and the sentence of the king that he makes has been heard in all his kingdom—for it [is] great—and all the wives give honor to their husbands, from great even to small." ²¹ And the thing is good in the eyes of the king, and of the princes, and the king does according to the word of Memucan, ²² and sends letters to all provinces of the king, to province and province according to its writing, and to people and people according to its tongue, for every man being head in his own house—and speaking according to the language of his people.

CHAPTER 2

¹ After these things, at the ceasing of the fury of King Ahasuerus, he has remembered Vashti, and that which she did, and that which has been decreed concerning her; ² and servants of the king, his ministers, say, "Let them seek for the king young women, virgins, of good appearance, ³ and the king appoints inspectors in all provinces of his kingdom, and they gather every young woman—virgin, of good appearance—to Shushan the palace, to the house of the women, to the hand of Hegai eunuch of the king, keeper of the women, and to give their purifications, ⁴ and the young woman who is good in the

eyes of the king reigns instead of Vashti"; and the thing is good in the eyes of the king, and he does so. ⁵ A man, a Jew, there has been in Shushan the palace, and his name [is] Mordecai son of Jair, son of Shimei, son of Kish, a Benjamite— ⁶ who had been removed from Jerusalem with the expulsion that was removed with Jeconiah king of Judah, whom Nebuchadnezzar king of Babylon removed— ⁷ and he is supporting Hadassah—she [is] Esther—daughter of his uncle, for she has neither father nor mother, and the young woman [is] of beautiful form, and of good appearance, and at the death of her father and her mother Mordecai has taken her to himself for a daughter. ⁸ And it comes to pass, in the word of the king, even his law, being heard, and in many young women being gathered to Shushan the palace, to the hand of Hegai, that Esther is taken to the house of the king, to the hand of Hegai, keeper of the women, ⁹ and the young woman is good in his eyes, and she receives kindness before him, and he hurries her purifications and her portions—to give to her, and the seven young women who are provided—to give to her, from the house of the king, and he changes her and her young women to a good [place in] the house of the women. ¹⁰ Esther has not declared her people, and her family, for Mordecai has laid a charge on her that she does not declare [it]; ¹¹ and during every day Mordecai is walking up and down before the court of the house of the women to know the welfare of Esther, and what is done with her. ¹² And in the drawing near of the turn of each young woman to come in to King Ahasuerus, at the end of there being to her—according to the law of the women—twelve months, for so they fulfill the days of their purifications; six months with oil of myrrh, and six months with perfumes, and with the purifications of women, ¹³ and with this the young woman has come in to the king, all that she says is given to her to go in with her out of the house of the women to the house of the king; ¹⁴ in the evening she has gone in, and in the morning she has turned back to the second house of the women, to the hand of Shaashgaz eunuch of the king, keeper of the concubines; she does not come in anymore to the king except the king has delighted in her, and she has been called by name. ¹⁵ And in the drawing near of the turn of Esther—daughter of Abihail, uncle of Mordecai, whom he had taken to himself for a daughter—to come in to the king, she has not sought a thing except that which Hegai eunuch of the king, keeper of the women, says, and Esther is receiving grace in the eyes of all seeing her. ¹⁶ And Esther is taken to King Ahasuerus, to his royal house, in the tenth month—it [is] the month of Tebeth—in the seventh year of his reign, ¹⁷ and the king loves Esther above all the women, and she receives grace and kindness before him above all the virgins, and he sets a royal crown on her head, and causes her to reign instead of Vashti, ¹⁸ and the king makes a great banquet to all his heads and his servants—the banquet of Esther—and has made a release to the provinces, and gives gifts as a memorial of the king. ¹⁹ And in the virgins being gathered a second time, then Mordecai is sitting in the gate of the king; ²⁰ Esther is not declaring her family and her people, as Mordecai has laid a charge on her, and the saying of Mordecai Esther is doing as when she was truly with him. ²¹ In those days, when Mordecai is sitting in the gate of the king, has Bigthan been angry, and Teresh (two of the eunuchs of the king, the keepers of the threshold), and they seek to put forth a hand on King Ahasuerus, ²² and the thing is known to Mordecai, and he declares [it] to Esther the queen, and Esther speaks to the king in the name of Mordecai, ²³ and the thing is sought out, and found, and both of them are hanged on a tree, and it is written in the scroll of the Chronicles before the king.

CHAPTER 3

¹ After these things has King Ahasuerus exalted Haman son of Hammedatha the Agagite, and lifts him up, and sets his throne above all the heads who [are] with him, ² and all servants of the king, who [are] in the gate of the king, are bowing and doing homage to Haman, for so the king has commanded for him; and Mordecai does not bow nor pay respect. ³ And the servants of the king, who [are] in the gate of the king, say to Mordecai, "Why [are] you transgressing the command of the king?" ⁴ And it comes to pass, in their speaking to him, day by day, and he has not listened to them, that they declare [it] to Haman, to see whether the words of Mordecai stand, for he has declared to them that he [is] a Jew. ⁵ And Haman sees that Mordecai is not bowing and doing homage to

him, and Haman is full of fury, **6** and it is contemptible in his eyes to put forth a hand on Mordecai by himself, for they have declared to him the people of Mordecai, and Haman seeks to destroy all the Jews who [are] in all the kingdom of Ahasuerus—the people of Mordecai. **7** In the first month—it [is] the month of Nisan—in the twelfth year of King Ahasuerus, has one caused to fall Pur (that [is] the lot) before Haman, from day to day, and from month to month, [to] the twelfth, it [is] the month of Adar. **8** And Haman says to King Ahasuerus, "There is one people scattered and separated among the peoples, in all provinces of your kingdom, and their laws [are] diverse from all people, and the laws of the king they are not doing, and for the king it is not profitable to permit them; **9** if to the king [it be] good, let it be written to destroy them, and ten thousand talents of silver I weigh into the hands of those doing the work, to bring [it] into the treasuries of the king." **10** And the king turns aside his signet from off his hand, and gives it to Haman son of Hammedatha the Agagite, adversary of the Jews; **11** and the king says to Haman, "The silver is given to you, and the people, to do with it as [it is] good in your eyes." **12** And scribes of the king are called, on the first month, on the thirteenth day of it, and it is written according to all that Haman has commanded, to lieutenants of the king, and to the governors who [are] over province and province, and to the heads of people and people, province and province, according to its writing, and people and people according to its tongue, in the name of King Ahasuerus it has been written and sealed with the signet of the king, **13** and letters to be sent by the hand of the runners to all provinces of the king, to cut off, to slay, and to destroy all the Jews, from young even to old, infant and women, on one day, on the thirteenth of the twelfth month—it [is] the month of Adar—and to seize their spoil, **14** a copy of the writing to be made law in each and every province is revealed to all the peoples, to be ready for this day. **15** The runners have gone forth, hurried by the word of the king, and the law has been given in Shushan the palace, and the king and Haman have sat down to drink, and the city Shushan is perplexed.

CHAPTER 4

1 And Mordecai has known all that has been done, and Mordecai tears his garments, and puts on sackcloth and ashes, and goes forth into the midst of the city and cries—a cry loud and bitter, **2** and he comes to the front of the gate of the king, but none is to come to the gate of the king with a sackcloth-garment. **3** And in each and every province, the place where the word of the king, even his law, is coming, the Jews have a great mourning, and fasting, and weeping, and lamenting: sackcloth and ashes are spread for many. **4** And young women of Esther come in and her eunuchs, and declare [it] to her, and the queen is exceedingly pained, and sends garments to clothe Mordecai, and to turn aside his sackcloth from off him, and he has not received [them]. **5** And Esther calls to Hatach, of the eunuchs of the king, whom he has stationed before her, and gives him a charge for Mordecai, to know what this [is], and why this [is]. **6** And Hatach goes out to Mordecai, to a broad place of the city, that [is] before the gate of the king, **7** and Mordecai declares to him all that has met him, and the explanation of the money that Haman said to weigh to the treasuries of the king for the Jews, to destroy them, **8** and the copy of the writing of the law that had been given in Shushan to destroy them he has given to him, to show Esther, and to declare [it] to her, and to lay a charge on her to go in to the king, to make supplication to him, and to seek from before him, for her people. **9** And Hatach comes in and declares to Esther the words of Mordecai, **10** and Esther speaks to Hatach, and charges him for Mordecai: **11** "All servants of the king, and people of the provinces of the king, know that any man and woman who comes to the king, into the inner court, who is not called—one law of his [is] to put [them] to death, apart from him to whom the king holds out the golden scepter, then he has lived; and I have not been called to come in to the king these thirty days." **12** And they declare to Mordecai the words of Esther, **13** and Mordecai commands to send back to Esther: "Do not think in your soul to be delivered [in] the house of the king, more than all the Jews, **14** but if you keep entirely silent at this time, respite and deliverance remains to the Jews from another place, and you and the house of your fathers are destroyed; and who knows whether for a time like this you have come to the kingdom?" **15** And Esther commands to send back to Mordecai: **16** "Go, gather all the Jews who are found in

Shushan, and fast for me, and do not eat nor drink three days, by night and by day; also I and my young women fast likewise, and so I go in to the king, that [is] not according to law, and when I have perished—I have perished." **17** And Mordecai passes on, and does according to all that Esther has charged on him.

CHAPTER 5

1 And it comes to pass on the third day, that Esther puts on royalty, and stands in the inner-court of the house of the king in front of the house of the king, and the king is sitting on his royal throne, in the royal-house, opposite the opening of the house, **2** and it comes to pass, at the king's seeing Esther the queen standing in the court, she has received grace in his eyes, and the king holds out to Esther the golden scepter that [is] in his hand, and Esther draws near, and touches the top of the scepter. **3** And the king says to her, "What do you [want], Esther, O queen? and what [is] your request? To the half of the kingdom—and it is given to you." **4** And Esther says, "If to the king [it be] good, the king comes in, and Haman, today, to the banquet that I have made for him"; **5** and the king says, "Hurry Haman—to do the word of Esther"; and the king comes in, and Haman, to the banquet that Esther has made. **6** And the king says to Esther, during the banquet of wine, "What [is] your petition? and it is given to you; and what [is] your request? To the half of the kingdom—and it is done." **7** And Esther answers and says, "My petition and my request [is]: **8** if I have found grace in the eyes of the king, and if to the king [it be] good, to give my petition, and to perform my request, the king comes, and Haman, to the banquet that I make for them, and tomorrow I do according to the word of the king." **9** And Haman goes forth on that day rejoicing and glad in heart, and at Haman's seeing Mordecai in the gate of the king, and he has not risen nor moved for him, then is Haman full of fury against Mordecai. **10** And Haman forces himself, and comes into his house, and sends, and brings in his friends, and his wife Zeresh, **11** and Haman recounts to them the glory of his wealth, and the abundance of his sons, and all that with which the king made him great, and with which he lifted him up above the heads and servants of the king. **12** And Haman says, "Indeed, Esther the queen brought none in with the king, to the feast that she made, except myself, and also for tomorrow I am called to her, with the king, **13** and all this is not profitable to me, during all the time that I am seeing Mordecai the Jew sitting in the gate of the king." **14** And his wife Zeresh says to him, and all his friends, "Let them prepare a tree, in height fifty cubits, and in the morning speak to the king, and they hang Mordecai on it, and go in with the king to the banquet rejoicing"; and the thing is good before Haman, and he prepares the tree.

CHAPTER 6

1 On that night the sleep of the king has fled away, and he commands to bring in the scroll of memorials of the chronicles, and they are read before the king, **2** and it is found written that Mordecai had declared concerning Bigthana and Teresh, two of the eunuchs of the king, of the keepers of the threshold, who sought to put forth a hand on King Ahasuerus. **3** And the king says, "What honor and greatness has been done to Mordecai for this?" And the servants of the king, his ministers, say, "Nothing has been done with him." **4** And the king says, "Who [is] in the court?" And Haman has come into the outer court of the house of the king, to say to the king to hang Mordecai on the tree that he had prepared for him. **5** And the servants of the king say to him, "Behold, Haman is standing in the court"; and the king says, "Let him come in." **6** And Haman comes in, and the king says to him, "What should [I] do with the man in whose honor the king has delighted?" And Haman says in his heart, "To whom does the king delight to do honor more than myself?" **7** And Haman says to the king, "The man in whose honor the king has delighted, **8** let them bring in royal clothing that the king has put on himself, and a horse on which the king has ridden, and that the royal crown be put on his head, **9** and to give the clothing and the horse into the hand of a man of the heads of the king, the chiefs, and they have clothed the man in whose honor the king has delighted, and caused him to ride on the horse in a broad place of the city, and called before him: Thus it is done to the man in whose honor the king has delighted." **10** And the king says to Haman, "Hurry, take the clothing and the horse, as you have spoken, and do so to Mordecai the Jew, who is sitting in the gate of the king; there does not fall a thing of all that you have spoken." **11** And Haman takes the clothing, and the horse, and clothed Mordecai, and causes him to ride in a broad place of the city, and calls before him, "Thus it is done to the man in whose glory the king has delighted." **12** And Mordecai turns back to the gate of the king, and Haman has been hurried to his house mourning, and with covered head, **13** and Haman recounts to his wife Zeresh, and to all his friends, all that has met him, and his wise men and his wife Zeresh say to him, "If Mordecai [is] of the seed of the Jews, before whom you have begun to fall, you are not able for him, but certainly fall before him." **14** They are yet speaking with him, and eunuchs of the king have come, and hurry to bring in Haman to the banquet that Esther has made.

CHAPTER 7

1 And the king comes in, and Haman, to drink with Esther the queen, **2** and the king says to Esther also on the second day, during the banquet of wine, "What [is] your petition, Esther, O queen? and it is given to you; and what [is] your request? To the half of the kingdom—and it is done." **3** And Esther the queen answers and says, "If I have found grace in your eyes, O king, and if to the king [it be] good, let my life be given to me at my petition, and my people at my request; **4** for we have been sold, I and my people, to cut off, to slay, and to destroy; and if for menservants and for maidservants we had been sold I had kept silent—but the adversity is not equal to the loss of the king." **5** And King Ahasuerus says, indeed, he says to Esther the queen, "Who [is] he—this one? and where [is] this one whose heart has filled him to do so?" **6** And Esther says, "The man—adversary and enemy—[is] this wicked Haman"; and Haman has been afraid at the presence of the king and of the queen. **7** And the king has risen, in his fury, from the banquet of wine, to the garden of the house, and Haman has remained to seek for his life from Esther the queen, for he has seen that evil has been determined against him by the king. **8** And the king has turned back out of the garden of the house to the house of the banquet of wine, and Haman is falling on the couch on which Esther [is], and the king says, "Also to subdue the queen with me in the house?" The word has gone out from the mouth of the king, and the face of Haman they have covered. **9** And Harbonah, one of the eunuchs, says before the king, "Also behold, the tree that Haman made for Mordecai, who spoke good for the king, is standing in the house of Haman, in height fifty cubits"; and the king says, "Hang him on it." **10** And they hang Haman on the tree that he had prepared for Mordecai, and the fury of the king has lain down.

CHAPTER 8

1 On that day has King Ahasuerus given to Esther the queen the house of Haman, adversary of the Jews, and Mordecai has come in before the king, for Esther has declared what he [is] to her, **2** and the king turns aside his signet, that he has caused to pass away from Haman, and gives it to Mordecai, and Esther sets Mordecai over the house of Haman. **3** And Esther adds, and speaks before the king, and falls before his feet, and weeps, and makes supplication to him, to cause the evil of Haman the Agagite to pass away, and his scheme that he had devised against the Jews; **4** and the king holds out to Esther the golden scepter, and Esther rises, and stands before the king, **5** and says, "If to the king [it be] good, and if I have found grace before him, and the thing has been right before the king, and I [am] good in his eyes, let it be written to bring back the letters—a scheme of Haman son of Hammedatha the Agagite—that he wrote to destroy the Jews who [are] in all provinces of the king, 6 for how do I endure when I have looked on the evil that finds my people? and how do I endure when I have looked on the destruction of my family?" 7 And King Ahasuerus says to Esther the queen, and to Mordecai the Jew, "Behold, the house of Haman I have given to Esther, and him they have hanged on the tree, because that he put forth his hand on the Jews, 8 and you, write for the Jews, as [it is] good in your eyes, in the name of the king, and seal with the signet of the king—

for the writing that is written in the name of the king, and sealed with the signet of the king, there is none to turn back." 9 And the scribes of the king are called, at that time, in the third month—it [is] the month of Sivan—in the twenty-third [day] of it, and it is written, according to all that Mordecai has commanded, to the Jews, and to the lieutenants, and the governors, and the heads of the provinces, that [are] from Hodu even to Cush, one hundred twenty-seven provinces—province and province according to its writing, and people and people according to its tongue, and to the Jews according to their writing, and according to their tongue. 10 And he writes in the name of King Ahasuerus, and seals with the signet of the king, and sends letters by the hand of the runners with horses, riders of the dromedary, the mules, the young mares, 11 that the king has given to the Jews who [are] in each and every city, to be assembled, and to stand for their life, to cut off, to slay, and to destroy the whole force of the people and province who are distressing them, infants and women, and their spoil to seize. 12 In one day, in all the provinces of King Ahasuerus, on the thirteenth of the twelfth month—it [is] the month of Adar— 13 a copy of the writing to be made law in each and every province is revealed to all the peoples, and for the Jews being ready at this day to be avenged of their enemies. 14 The runners, riding on the dromedary, [and] the mules, have gone out, hurried and pressed by the word of the king, and the law has been given in Shushan the palace. 15 And Mordecai went out from before the king, in royal clothing of blue and white, and a great crown of gold, and a garment of fine linen and purple, and the city of Shushan has rejoiced and been glad; 16 to the Jews has been light, and gladness, and joy, and honor, 17 and in each and every province, and in each and every city, the place where the word of the king, even his law, is coming, gladness and joy [are] to the Jews, a banquet, and a good day; and many of the peoples of the land are becoming Jews, for a fear of the Jews has fallen on them.

CHAPTER 9

1 And in the twelfth month—it [is] the month of Adar—on the thirteenth day of it, in which the word of the king, even his law, has come to be done, in the day that the enemies of the Jews had hoped to rule over them, and it is turned that the Jews rule over those hating them— **2** the Jews have been assembled in their cities, in all provinces of King Ahasuerus, to put forth a hand on those seeking their evil, and no man has stood in their presence, for their fear has fallen on all the peoples. **3** And all heads of the provinces, and the lieutenants, and the governors, and those doing the work that the king has, are lifting up the Jews, for a fear of Mordecai has fallen on them; **4** for great [is] Mordecai in the house of the king, and his fame is going into all the provinces, for the man Mordecai is going on and becoming great. **5** And the Jews strike among all their enemies—a striking of the sword, and slaughter, and destruction—and do with those hating them according to their pleasure, **6** and in Shushan the palace the Jews have slain and destroyed five hundred men; **7** and Parshandatha, and Dalphon, and Aspatha, **8** and Poratha, and Adalia, and Aridatha, **9** and Parmashta, and Arisai, and Aridai, and Vajezatha, **10** ten sons of Haman son of Hammedatha, adversary of the Jews, they have slain, and on the prey they have not put forth their hand. **11** On that day has come the number of the slain in Shushan the palace before the king, **12** and the king says to Esther the queen, "In Shushan the palace the Jews have slain and destroyed five hundred men, and the ten sons of Haman; in the rest of the provinces of the king what have they done? and what [is] your petition? and it is given to you; and what your request again? and it is done." **13** And Esther says, "If [it is] good to the king, let it also be given tomorrow, to the Jews who [are] in Shushan, to do according to the law of today; and the ten sons of Haman they hang on the tree." **14** And the king commands [for it] to be done so; and a law is given in Shushan, and they have hanged the ten sons of Haman. **15** And the Jews who [are] in Shushan are also assembled on the fourteenth day of the month of Adar, and they slay three hundred men in Shushan, and they have not put forth their hand on the prey. **16** And the rest of the Jews, who [are] in the provinces of the king, have been assembled, even to stand for their life, and to rest from their enemies, and to slay seventy-five thousand among those hating them, and they have not put forth their hand on the prey; **17** on the thirteenth day of the month of Adar, even to rest on the fourteenth of it, and to make it a day of banquet and of joy. **18** And the Jews who [are] in Shushan have been assembled, on the thirteenth day of it, and on the fourteenth of it, even to rest on the fifteenth of it, and to make it a day of banquet and of joy. **19** Therefore the Jews of the open places, who are dwelling in cities of the open places, are making the fourteenth day of the month of Adar—joy and banquet, and a good day, and of sending portions to one another. **20** And Mordecai writes these things, and sends letters to all the Jews who [are] in all provinces of King Ahasuerus, who are near and who are far off, **21** to establish on them, to be keeping the fourteenth day of the month of Adar, and the fifteenth day of it, in every year and year, **22** as days on which the Jews have rested from their enemies, and the month that has been turned to them from sorrow to joy, and from mourning to a good day, to make them days of banquet and of joy, and of sending portions to one another, and gifts to the needy. **23** And the Jews have received that which they had begun to do, and that which Mordecai has written to them, **24** because Haman son of Hammedatha the Agagite, adversary of all the Jews, had devised concerning the Jews to destroy them, and had caused to fall Pur—that [is] the lot—to crush them and to destroy them; **25** and in her coming in before the king, he commanded with the letter, "Let his evil scheme that he devised against the Jews return on his own head," and they have hanged him and his sons on the tree, **26** therefore they have called these days Purim—by the name of the lot— therefore, because of all the words of this letter, and what they have seen concerning this, and what has come to them, **27** the Jews have established and received on them, and on their seed, and on all those joined to them, and it does not pass away, to be keeping these two days according to their writing, and according to their season, in every year and year; **28** and these days are remembered and kept in every generation and generation, family and family, province and province, and city and city, and these days of Purim do not pass away from the midst of the Jews, and their memorial is not ended from their seed. **29** And Esther the queen, daughter of Abihail, writes, and Mordecai the Jew, with all might, to establish this second letter of Purim, **30** and he sends letters to all the Jews, to the one hundred twenty-seven provinces of the kingdom of Ahasuerus—words of peace and truth— **31** to establish these days of Purim, in their seasons, as Mordecai the Jew has established on them, and Esther the queen, and as they had established on themselves, and on their seed—matters of the fastings, and of their cry. **32** And a saying of Esther has established these matters of Purim, and it is written in the Scroll.

CHAPTER 10

1 And King Ahasuerus sets a tribute on the land and the islands of the sea; 2 and all the work of his strength, and his might, and the explanation of the greatness of Mordecai with which the king made him great, are they not written on the scroll of the Chronicles of Media and Persia? 3 For Mordecai the Jew [is] second to King Ahasuerus, and a great man of the Jews, and accepted of the multitude of his brothers, seeking good for his people, and speaking peace to all his seed.

JOB

CHAPTER 1

[1] There has been a man in the land of Uz—his name Job— and that man has been perfect and upright—both fearing God, and turning aside from evil. [2] And seven sons and three daughters are borne to him, [3] and his substance is seven thousand sheep, and three thousand camels, and five hundred pairs of oxen, and five hundred female donkeys, and a very abundant service; and that man is greater than any of the sons of the east. [4] And his sons have gone and made a banquet— the house of each [in] his day—and have sent and called to their three sisters to eat and to drink with them; [5] and it comes to pass, when they have gone around the days of the banquet, that Job sends and sanctifies them, and has risen early in the morning, and caused burnt-offerings to ascend—the number of them all—for Job said, "Perhaps my sons have sinned, yet

blessed God in their heart." Thus Job does all the days. [6] And the day is, that sons of God come to station themselves by Yhwh, and there also comes Satan in their midst. [7] And Yhwh says to Satan, "Where do you come from?" And Satan answers Yhwh and says, "From going to and fro in the land, and from walking up and down on it." [8] And Yhwh says to Satan, "Have you set your heart against My servant Job because there is none like him in the land, a man perfect and upright, fearing God, and turning aside from evil?" [9] And Satan answers Yhwh and says, "Is Job fearing God for nothing? [10] Have You not made a hedge for him, and for his house, and for all that he has—all around? [11] You have blessed the work of his hands, and his substance has spread in the land, and yet, put forth Your hand now, and strike against anything that he has—if not, he blesses You to Your face!" [12] And Yhwh says to Satan, "Behold, all that he has [is] in your hand, only do not put forth your hand to him." And Satan goes out from the presence of Yhwh. [13] And the day is, that his sons and his daughters are eating and drinking wine in the house of their brother, the firstborn. [14] And a messenger has come to Job and says, "The oxen have been plowing, and the female donkeys feeding by their sides, [15] and Sheba falls, and takes them, and they have struck the young men by the mouth of the sword, and I have escaped—only I alone—to declare [it] to you." [16] While this [one] is speaking another has also come and says, "Fire of God has fallen from the heavens, and burns among the flock, and among the young men, and consumes them, and I have escaped—only I alone—to declare [it] to you." [17] While this [one] is speaking another also has come and says, "Chaldeans made three heads, and rush on the camels, and take them, and they have struck the young men by the mouth of the sword, and I have escaped—only I alone—to declare [it] to you." [18] While this [one] is speaking another has also come and says, "Your sons and your daughters are eating, and drinking wine, in the house of their brother, the firstborn. [19] And behold, a great wind has come from over the wilderness, and strikes against the four corners of the house, and it falls on the young men, and they are dead, and I have escaped—only I alone—to declare [it] to you." [20] And Job rises, and tears his robe, and shaves his head, and falls to the earth, and pays respect, [21] and he says, "I came forth naked from the womb of my mother, || And naked I return there. Yhwh has given and Yhwh has taken; Let the Name of Yhwh be blessed." [22] In all this Job has not sinned, nor given folly to God.

CHAPTER 2

[1] And the day is, that sons of God come to station themselves by Yhwh, and there also comes Satan in their midst to station himself by Yhwh. [2] And Yhwh says to Satan, "From where have you come?" And Satan answers Yhwh and says, "From going to and fro in the land, and from walking up and down in it." [3] And Yhwh says to Satan, "Have you set your heart to My servant Job because there is none like him in the land, a man perfect and upright, fearing God and turning aside from evil? and still he is keeping hold on his integrity, and you move Me against him to swallow him up for nothing!" [4] And Satan answers Yhwh and says, "A skin for a skin, and all that a man has he gives for his life. [5] Yet, put forth Your hand now, and strike to his bone and to his flesh—if not, he blesses You to Your face!" [6] And Yhwh says to Satan, "Behold, he [is] in your hand; only take care of his life." [7] And Satan goes forth from the presence of Yhwh, and strikes Job with a severe ulcer from the sole of his foot to his crown. [8] And he takes to him a potsherd to scrape himself with it, and he is sitting in the midst of the ashes. [9] And his wife says to him, "You are still keeping hold on your integrity: bless God and die." [10] And he says to her, "As one of the foolish women speaks, you speak; indeed, do we receive the good from God, and we do not receive the bad?" In all this Job has not sinned with his lips. [11] And three of the friends of Job hear of all this evil that has come on him, and they each come in from his place—Eliphaz the Temanite, and Bildad the Shuhite, and Zophar the Naamathite—and they have met together to come to bemoan him, and to comfort him; [12] and they lift up their eyes from afar and have not discerned him, and they lift up their voice and weep, and each tears his robe, and sprinkle dust on their heads—heavenward. [13] And they sit with him on the earth seven days and seven nights, and there is none speaking to him a word when they have seen that the pain has been very great.

CHAPTER 3

[1] After this Job has opened his mouth, and reviles his day. [2] And Job answers and says: [3] "Let the day perish in which I am born, || And the night that has said: A man-child has been conceived. [4] That day—let it be darkness, || Do not let God require it from above, || Nor let light shine on it. [5] Let darkness and death-shade redeem it, || Let a cloud dwell on it, || Let them terrify it as the most bitter of days. [6] That night—let thick darkness take it, || Let it not be united to days of the year, || Let it not come into the number of months. [7] Behold! That night—let it be barren, || Let no singing come into it. [8] Let the cursers of day mark it, || Who are ready to wake up Leviathan. [9] Let the stars of its twilight be dark, || Let it wait for light, and there is none, || And let it not look on the eyelids of the dawn. [10] Because it has not shut the doors || Of the womb that was mine! And hide misery from my eyes. [11] Why do I not die from the womb? I have come forth from the belly and gasp! [12] Why have knees been before me? And what [are] breasts, that I suck? [13] For now, I have lain down, and am quiet, I have slept—then there is rest to me, [14] With kings and counselors of earth, || These building ruins for themselves. [15] Or with princes—they have gold, || They are filling their houses [with] silver. [16] (Or I am not as a hidden abortion, || As infants—they have not seen light.) [17] There the wicked have ceased troubling, || And there the wearied rest in power. [18] Together prisoners have been at ease, || They have not heard the voice of an exactor, [19] Small and great [are] the same there. And a servant [is] free from his lord. [20] Why does He give light to the miserable, and life to the bitter soul? [21] Who are waiting for death, and it is not, || And they seek it above hid treasures. [22] Who are glad—to joy, || They rejoice when they find a grave. [23] To a man whose way has been hidden, || And whom God shuts up? [24] For before my food, my sighing comes, || And my roarings [are] poured out as waters. [25] For I feared a fear and it meets me, || And what I was afraid of comes to me. [26] I was not safe—nor was I quiet—Nor was I at rest—and trouble comes!"

CHAPTER 4

[1] And Eliphaz the Temanite answers and says: [2] "Has one tried a word with you? You are weary! And who is able to keep in words? [3] Behold, you have instructed many, || And feeble hands you make strong. [4] Your words raise up the stumbling one, || And you strengthen bowing knees. [5] But now, it comes to you, || And you are weary; It strikes to you, and you are troubled. [6] Is your reverence not your confidence? Your hope—the perfection of your ways? [7] Now remember, || Who, being innocent, has perished? And where have the upright been cut off? [8] As I have seen—plowers of iniquity, || And sowers of misery, reap it! [9] From the breath of God they perish, || And from the spirit of His anger [are] consumed. [10] The roaring of a lion, || And the voice of a fierce lion, || And teeth of young lions have been broken. [11] An old lion is perishing without prey, || And the whelps of the lioness separate. [12] And a thing is secretly brought to me, || And my ear receives a little of it. [13] In thoughts from visions of the night, || In the falling of deep sleep on men, [14] Fear has met me, and trembling, || And the multitude of my bones caused to fear. [15] And a spirit passes before my face, || The hair of my flesh stands up; [16] It stands, and I do not discern its aspect, || A likeness [is] before my eyes, || Silence! And I hear a voice: [17] Is mortal man more righteous than God? Is a man cleaner than his Maker? [18] Behold, He puts no credence in His servants, || Nor sets praise in His messengers. [19] Also—the inhabitants of houses of clay || (Whose foundation [is] in the dust, || They bruise them before a moth). [20] From morning to evening are beaten down, || Without any regarding, they perish forever. [21] Has their excellence not been removed with them? They die, and not in wisdom!"

CHAPTER 5

[1] "Pray, call, is there any to answer you? And to which of the holy ones do you turn? [2] For provocation slays the perverse, || And envy puts to death the simple, [3] I have seen the perverse taking root, || And I mark his habitation straight away, [4] His sons are far from safety, || And they are bruised in the gate, || And there is no deliverer. [5] Whose harvest the hungry eat, || And even take it from the thorns, || And the designing swallowed their wealth. [6] For sorrow does not come forth from the dust, || Nor does misery spring up from the ground. [7] For man is born to misery, || And the sparks go high to fly. [8] Yet I inquire for God, || And for God I give my word, [9] Doing great things, and there is no searching. Wonderful, until there is no numbering. [10] Who is giving rain on the face of the land, || And is sending waters on the out-places. [11] To set the low on a high place, || And the mourners have been high [in] safety. [12] Making void thoughts of the cunning, || And their hands do not execute wisdom. [13] Capturing the wise in their subtlety, || And the counsel of wrestling ones was hurried, [14] By day they meet darkness, || And as night—they grope at noon. [15] He saves the needy from the sword in their mouth, || And from a strong hand, [16] And there is hope for the poor, || And perverseness has shut her mouth. [17] Behold, the blessedness of mortal man, || God reproves him: And do not despise the discipline of the Mighty, [18] For He pains, and He binds up, || He strikes, and His hands heal. [19] In six distresses He delivers you, || And in seven evil does not strike on you. [20] In famine He has redeemed you from death, || And in battle from the hands of the sword. [21] When the tongue scourges you are hid, || And you are not afraid of destruction, || When it comes. [22] At destruction and at hunger you mock, || And of the beast of the earth, || You are not afraid. [23] (For with sons of the field [is] your covenant, || And the beast of the field || Has been at peace with you.) [24] And you have known that your tent [is] peace, || And inspected your habitation, and do not err, [25] And have known that your seed [is] numerous, || And your offspring as the herb of the earth; [26] You come in full age to the grave, || As the going up of a stalk in its season. [27] Behold, this—we searched it out—it [is] right, listen; And you, know for yourself!"

CHAPTER 6

[1] And Job answers and says: [2] "O that my provocation were thoroughly weighed, || And my calamity in balances || They would lift up together! [3] For now it is heavier than the sands of the sea, || Therefore my words have been rash. [4] For arrows of the Mighty [are] with me, || Whose poison is drinking up my spirit. Terrors of God array themselves [for] me! [5] Does a wild donkey bray over tender grass? Does an ox low over his provender? [6] Is an insipid thing eaten without salt? Is there sense in the drivel of dreams? [7] My soul is refusing to touch! They [are] as my sickening food. [8] O that my request may come, || That God may grant my hope! [9] That God would please—and bruise me, || Loose His hand and cut me off! [10] And yet it is my comfort || (And I exult in pain—He does not spare), || That I have not hidden || The sayings of the Holy One. [11] What [is] my power that I should hope? And what [is] my end that I should prolong my life? [12] Is my strength the strength of stones? Is my flesh bronze? [13] Is my help not with me, || And substance driven from me? [14] To a despiser of his friends [is] shame, || And the fear of the Mighty he forsakes. [15] My brothers have deceived as a brook, || As a stream of brooks they pass away. [16] That are black because of ice, || By them snow hides itself. [17] By the time they are warm they have been cut off, || By its being hot they have been || Extinguished from their place. [18] The paths turn aside of their way, || They ascend into emptiness, and are lost. [19] Passengers of Tema looked expectingly, || Travelers of Sheba hoped for them. [20] They were ashamed that one has trusted, || They have come to it and are confounded. [21] Surely now you have become the same! You see a downfall, and are afraid. [22] Is it because I said, Give to me? And, By your power bribe for me? [23] And, Deliver me from the hand of an adversary? And, Ransom me from the hand of terrible ones? [24] Show me, and I keep silent, || And what I have erred, let me understand. [25] How powerful have been upright sayings, || And what reproof from you reproves? [26] For reproof—do you reckon words? And for wind—sayings of the desperate? [27] You cause anger to fall on the fatherless, || And are strange to your friend. [28] And now, please, look on me, || Even to your face do I lie? [29] Please turn back, let it not be perverseness, || Indeed, turn back again—my righteousness [is] in it. [30] Is there perverseness in my tongue? Does my palate not discern calamity?"

CHAPTER 7

¹ "Is there not warfare to man on earth? And his days as the days of a hired worker? ² As a servant desires the shadow, || And as a hired worker expects his wage, ³ So I have been caused to inherit months of vanity, || And they numbered nights of misery to me. ⁴ If I lay down, then I have said, When do I rise, || And evening has been measured? And I have been full of tossings until dawn. ⁵ My flesh has been clothed [with] worms, || And a clod of dust, || My skin has been shriveled and is loathsome, ⁶ My days swifter than a loom, || And they are consumed without hope. ⁷ Remember that my life [is] a breath, || My eye does not turn back to see good. ⁸ The eye of my beholder does not behold me. Your eyes [are] on me—and I am not. ⁹ A cloud has been consumed, and it goes, || So he who is going down to Sheol does not come up. ¹⁰ He does not turn to his house again, || Nor does his place discern him again. ¹¹ Also I do not withhold my mouth—I speak in the distress of my spirit, I talk in the bitterness of my soul. ¹² Am I a sea [monster], or a dragon, || That You set a watch over me? ¹³ When I said, My bed comforts me, || In my talking He takes away my couch. ¹⁴ And You have frightened me with dreams, || And You terrify me from visions, ¹⁵ And my soul chooses strangling, || Death rather than my bones. ¹⁶ I have wasted away—I do not live for all time. Cease from me, for my days [are] vanity. ¹⁷ What [is] man that You magnify him? And that You set Your heart to him? ¹⁸ And inspect him in the mornings, || [And] in the evenings try him? ¹⁹ How long do You not look from me? You do not desist until I swallow my spittle. ²⁰ I have sinned, what do I do to You, || O watcher of man? Why have You set me for a mark to You, || And I am for a burden to myself—and what? ²¹ You do not take away my transgression, || And [do not] cause my iniquity to pass away, || Because now, I lie down in dust, || And You have sought me—and I am not!"

CHAPTER 8

¹ And Bildad the Shuhite answers and says: ² "Until when do you speak these things? And a strong wind—sayings of your mouth? ³ Does God pervert judgment? And does the Mighty One pervert justice? ⁴ If your sons have sinned before Him, || And He sends them away, || By the hand of their transgression, ⁵ If you seek for God early, || And make supplication to the Mighty, ⁶ If you [are] pure and upright, || Surely now He wakes for you, || And has completed || The habitation of your righteousness. ⁷ And your beginning has been small, || And your latter end is very great. ⁸ For inquire, please, of a former generation, || And prepare for a search of their fathers, ⁹ For we [are] of yesterday, and we do not know, || For our days [are] a shadow on earth. ¹⁰ Do they not show you—speak to you, || And from their heart bring forth words? ¹¹ Does a rush rise without a marsh? A reed increase without water? ¹² While it [is] in its budding—uncropped, || Even before any herb it withers. ¹³ So [are] the paths of all forgetting God, || And the hope of the profane perishes, ¹⁴ Whose confidence is loathsome, || And the house of a spider his trust. ¹⁵ He leans on his house—and it does not stand, || He takes hold on it—and it does not abide. ¹⁶ He [is] green before the sun, || And over his garden his branch goes out. ¹⁷ His roots are wrapped by a heap, || He looks for a house of stones. ¹⁸ If [one] destroys him from his place, || Then it has feigned concerning him, || I have not seen you! ¹⁹ Behold, this [is] the joy of His way, || And from the dust others spring up. ²⁰ Behold, God does not reject the perfect, || Nor takes hold on the hand of evildoers. ²¹ While He fills your mouth with laughter, || And your lips with shouting, ²² Those hating you put on shame, || And the tent of the wicked is not!"

CHAPTER 9

¹ And Job answers and says: ² "Truly I have known that [it is] so, || But how is man righteous with God? ³ If he delights to strive with Him—He does not answer him one of a thousand. ⁴ Wise in heart and strong in power—Who has hardened toward Him and is at peace? ⁵ Who is removing mountains, || And they have not known, || Who has overturned them in His anger. ⁶ Who is shaking earth from its place, || And its pillars move themselves. ⁷ Who is commanding to the sun, and it does not rise, || And the stars He seals up. ⁸ Stretching out the heavens by Himself, || And treading on the heights of the sea, ⁹ Making the Great Bear, Orion, and the Pleiades, || And the inner chambers of the south. ¹⁰ Doing great things until there is no searching, || And wonderful, until there is no numbering. ¹¹ Behold, He goes over by me, and I do not see, || And He passes on, and I do not attend to it. ¹² Behold, He snatches away, who brings it back? Who says to Him, What [are] You doing? ¹³ God does not turn back His anger, || Proud helpers have bowed under Him. ¹⁴ How much less do I answer Him? Choose out my words with Him? ¹⁵ Whom, though I were righteous, I do not answer, || For my judgment I make supplication. ¹⁶ Though I had called and He answers me, I do not believe that He gives ear [to] my voice. ¹⁷ Because He bruises me with a storm, || And has multiplied my wounds for nothing. ¹⁸ He does not permit me to refresh my spirit, || But fills me with bitter things. ¹⁹ If of power, behold, the Strong One; And if of judgment—who convenes me? ²⁰ If I am righteous, my mouth declares me wicked; [If] I am perfect, it declares me perverse. ²¹ I am perfect; I do not know my soul, I despise my life. ²² It is the same thing, therefore I said, || He is consuming the perfect and the wicked. ²³ If a scourge puts to death suddenly, He laughs at the trial of the innocent. ²⁴ Earth has been given || Into the hand of the wicked. He covers the faces of her judges, || If not—where, who [is] he? ²⁵ My days have been swifter than a runner, || They have fled, they have not seen good, ²⁶ They have passed on with ships of reed, || As an eagle darts on food. ²⁷ Though I say, I forget my talking, || I forsake my corner, and I brighten up! ²⁸ I have been afraid of all my griefs, || I have known that You do not acquit me. ²⁹ I become wicked; why [is] this? I labor [in] vain. ³⁰ If I have washed myself with snow-water, || And purified my hands with soap, ³¹ Then You dip me in corruption, || And my garments have detested me. ³² But if a man like myself—I answer Him, || We come together into judgment. ³³ If there were a mediator between us, || He places his hand on us both. ³⁴ He turns aside His rod from off me, || And His terror does not make me afraid, ³⁵ I speak, and do not fear Him, but I am not right with myself."

CHAPTER 10

¹ "My soul has been weary of my life, I leave off my talking to myself, I speak in the bitterness of my soul. ² I say to God, Do not condemn me, || Let me know why You strive [with] me. ³ Is it good for You that You oppress? That You despise the labor of Your hands, || And shine on the counsel of the wicked? ⁴ Do you have eyes of flesh? Do You see as man sees? ⁵ [Are] Your days as the days of man? Your years as the days of a man? ⁶ That You inquire for my iniquity, || And seek for my sin? ⁷ For You know that I am not wicked, || And there is no deliverer from Your hand. ⁸ Your hands have taken pains about me, || And they make me together all around, || And You swallow me up! ⁹ Please remember || That You have made me as clay, || And You bring me back to dust. ¹⁰ Do You not pour me out as milk? And curdle me as cheese? ¹¹ Skin and flesh You put on me, || And fence me with bones and sinews. ¹² Life and kindness You have done with me. And Your inspection has preserved my spirit. ¹³ And these You have laid up in Your heart, I have known that this [is] with You. ¹⁴ If I sinned, then You have observed me, || And do not acquit me from my iniquity, ¹⁵ If I have done wickedly—woe to me, || And righteously—I do not lift up my head, || Full of shame—then see my affliction. ¹⁶ And it rises—as a lion You hunt me. And You turn back—You show Yourself wonderful in me. ¹⁷ You renew Your witnesses against me, and multiply Your anger with me, || Changes and warfare [are] with me. ¹⁸ And why from the womb || Have You brought me forth? I expire, and the eye does not see me. ¹⁹ I am as [if] I had not been, || I am brought from the belly to the grave, ²⁰ Are my days not few? Cease then, and put from me, || And I brighten up a little, ²¹ Before I go, and do not return, || To a land of darkness and death-shade, ²² A land of obscurity as thick darkness, || Death-shade—and no order, || And the shining [is] as thick darkness."

CHAPTER 11

¹ And Zophar the Naamathite answers and says: ² "Is a multitude of words not answered? And is a man of lips justified?

³ Your boastings make men keep silent, || You scorn, and none is causing blushing! ⁴ And you say, My discourse [is] pure, || And I have been clean in Your eyes. ⁵ And yet, O that God had spoken! And opens His lips with you. ⁶ And declares to you secrets of wisdom, for counsel has foldings. And know that God forgets of your iniquity for you. ⁷ Do you find out God by searching? To perfection find out the Mighty One? ⁸ Heights of the heavens—what [can] you do? Deeper than Sheol—what [can] you know? ⁹ Its measure [is] longer than earth, and broader than the sea. ¹⁰ If He passes on, and shuts up, and assembles, || Who then reverses it? ¹¹ For He has known men of vanity, || And He sees iniquity, || And one does not consider [it]! ¹² And empty man is bold, || And man is born [as] the colt of a wild donkey. ¹³ If you have prepared your heart, || And have spread out your hands to Him, ¹⁴ If iniquity [is] in your hand, put it far off, || And do not let perverseness dwell in your tents. ¹⁵ For then you lift up your face from blemish, || And you have been firm, and do not fear. ¹⁶ For you forget misery, || As waters passed away you remember. ¹⁷ And age rises above the noon, || You fly—you are as the morning. ¹⁸ And you have trusted because there is hope, || And searched—in confidence you lie down, ¹⁹ And you have rested, || And none is causing trembling, || And many have begged [at] your face; ²⁰ And the eyes of the wicked are consumed, || And refuge has perished from them, || And their hope [is] a breathing out of soul!"

terrify you? And His dread fall on you? ¹² Your remembrances [are] allegories of ashes, || For high places of clay [are] your heights. ¹³ Keep silent from me, and I speak, || And pass over me what will. ¹⁴ Why do I take my flesh in my teeth? And my soul put in my hand? ¹⁵ Behold, He slays me—I do not wait! Only, I argue my ways to His face. ¹⁶ Also—He [is] to me for salvation, || For the profane do not come before Him. ¹⁷ Hear my word diligently, || And my declaration with your ears. ¹⁸ Now behold, I have set the cause in order, || I have known that I am righteous. ¹⁹ Who [is] he that strives with me? For now I keep silent and gasp. ²⁰ Only two things, O God, do with me, || Then I am not hidden from Your face: ²¹ Put Your hand far off from me, || And do not let Your terror terrify me. ²² And You call, and I answer, || Or—I speak, and You answer me. ²³ How many iniquities and sins do I have? Let me know my transgression and my sin. ²⁴ Why do You hide Your face? And reckon me for an enemy to You? ²⁵ Do You terrify a leaf driven away? And do you pursue the dry stubble? ²⁶ For You write bitter things against me, || And cause me to possess iniquities of my youth, ²⁷ And you put my feet in the stocks, || And observe all my paths—You set a print on the roots of my feet, ²⁸ And he, as a rotten thing, wears away, || A moth has consumed him as a garment."

CHAPTER 12

¹ And Job answers and says: ²"Truly—you [are] the people, and wisdom dies with you. ³ I also have a heart like you, I am not fallen more than you, || And with whom is there not like these? ⁴ I am a laughter to his friend: He calls to God, and He answers him, || A laughter [is] the perfect righteous one. ⁵ A torch—despised in the thoughts of the secure || Is prepared for those sliding with the feet. ⁶ The tents of spoilers are at peace, || And those provoking God have confidence, || Into whose hand God has brought. ⁷ And yet, now ask [one of] the beasts, || And it shows you, || And a bird of the heavens, || And it declares to you. ⁸ Or talk to the earth, and it shows you, || And fishes of the sea recount to you: ⁹ Who has not known in all these, || That the hand of Yhwh has done this? ¹⁰ In whose hand [is] the breath of every living thing, || And the spirit of all flesh of man. ¹¹ Does the ear not try words? And the palate taste food for itself? ¹² With the very aged [is] wisdom, || And [with] length of days [is] understanding. ¹³ With Him [are] wisdom and might, || To Him [are] counsel and understanding. ¹⁴ Behold, He breaks down, and it is not built up, || He shuts against a man, || And it is not opened. ¹⁵ Behold, He keeps in the waters, and they are dried up, || And He sends them forth, || And they overturn the land. ¹⁶ With Him [are] strength and wisdom, || His the deceived and deceiver. ¹⁷ Causing counselors to go away [as] a spoil, || Indeed, He makes fools of judges. ¹⁸ He has opened the bands of kings, || And He binds a girdle on their loins. ¹⁹ Causing ministers to go away [as] a spoil || And strong ones He overthrows. ²⁰ Turning aside the lip of the steadfast, || And the reason of the aged He takes away. ²¹ Pouring contempt on princes, || And the girdle of the mighty He made feeble. ²² Removing deep things out of darkness, || And He brings out to light death-shade. ²³ Magnifying the nations, and He destroys them, || Spreading out the nations, and He quiets them. ²⁴ Turning aside the heart || Of the heads of the people of the land, || And He causes them to wander || In vacancy—no way! ²⁵ They feel darkness, and not light, || He causes them to wander as a drunkard."

CHAPTER 13

¹ "Behold, my eye has seen all, || My ear has heard, and it attends to it. ² According to your knowledge I have known—also I. I am not fallen more than you. ³ Yet I speak for the Mighty One, || And I delight to argue for God. ⁴ And yet, you [are] forgers of falsehood, || Physicians of nothing—all of you, ⁵ O that you would keep perfectly silent, || And it would be to you for wisdom. ⁶ Please hear my argument, || And attend to the pleadings of my lips, ⁷ Do you speak perverseness for God? And do you speak deceit for Him? ⁸ Do you accept His face, if you strive for God? ⁹ Is [it] good that He searches you, || If, as one mocks at a man, you mock at Him? ¹⁰ He surely reproves you, if you accept faces in secret. ¹¹ Does His excellence not

CHAPTER 14

¹ "Man, born of woman! Of few days, and full of trouble! ² As a flower he has gone forth, and is cut off, || And he flees as a shadow and does not stand. ³ Also—on this You have opened Your eyes, and bring me into judgment with You. ⁴ Who gives a clean thing out of an unclean? not one. ⁵ If his days are determined, || The number of his months [are] with You, || You have made his limit, || And he does not pass over; ⁶ Look away from off him that he may cease, || Until he enjoy as a hired worker his day. ⁷ For there is hope for a tree, if it is cut down, || That it changes again, || That its tender branch does not cease. ⁸ If its root becomes old in the earth, || And its stem dies in the dust, ⁹ From the fragrance of water it flourishes, || And has made a crop as a plant. ¹⁰ And a man dies, and becomes weak, || And man expires, and where [is] he? ¹¹ Waters have gone away from a sea, || And a river becomes waste and dry. ¹² And man has lain down, and does not rise, || Until the wearing out of the heavens they do not awaken, || Nor are roused from their sleep. ¹³ O that You would conceal me in Sheol, || Hide me until the turning of Your anger, || Set a limit for me, and remember me. ¹⁴ If a man dies—does he revive? All [the] days of my warfare I wait, until my change comes. ¹⁵ You call, and I answer You; To the work of Your hands You have desire. ¹⁶ But now, You number my steps, || You do not watch over my sin. ¹⁷ My transgression [is] sealed up in a bag, and You sew up my iniquity. ¹⁸ And yet, a falling mountain wastes away, and a rock is removed from its place. ¹⁹ Waters have worn away stones, || Their outpourings wash away the dust of earth, || And You have destroyed the hope of man. ²⁰ You prevail [over] him forever, and he goes, || He is changing his countenance, || And You send him away. ²¹ His sons are honored, and he does not know; And they are little, and he does not attend to them. ²² Only—his flesh is pained for him, || And his soul mourns for him."

CHAPTER 15

¹ And Eliphaz the Temanite answers and says: ²"Does a wise man answer [with] vain knowledge? And fill his belly [with] an east wind? ³ To reason with a word not useful? And speeches—no profit in them? ⁴ Indeed, you make reverence void, and diminish meditation before God. ⁵ For your mouth teaches your iniquity, || And you choose the tongue of the cunning. ⁶ Your mouth declares you wicked, and not I, || And your lips testify against you. ⁷ Are you the first man born? And were you formed before the heights? ⁸ Do you hear of the secret counsel of God? And withdraw wisdom to you? ⁹ What have you known, and we do not know? [What] do you understand, and it is not with us? ¹⁰ Both the gray-headed || And the very aged [are] among us—Greater than your father [in] days. ¹¹ Are the comforts of God too few for you? And a gentle word [is] with you, ¹² Why does your heart take you away? And why are your eyes high? ¹³ Do you turn your spirit against God? And have brought out words from your mouth: ¹⁴

What [is] man that he is pure, || And that he is righteous, one born of woman? ¹⁵ Behold, He puts no credence in His holy ones, || And the heavens have not been pure in His eyes. ¹⁶ Also—surely abominable and filthy || Is man drinking perverseness as water. ¹⁷ I show you—listen to me—And this I have seen and declare, ¹⁸ Which the wise declare—And have not hid—from their fathers. ¹⁹ To them alone was the land given, || And a stranger did not pass over into their midst: ²⁰ All [the] days of the wicked he is paining himself, || And few years have been laid up for the terrible one. ²¹ A fearful voice [is] in his ears, || In peace a destroyer comes to him. ²² He does not believe to return from darkness, || And he watches for the sword. ²³ He is wandering for bread: Where [is] it? He has known that ready at his hand || Is a day of darkness. ²⁴ Adversity and distress terrify him, || They prevail over him as a king ready for a boaster. ²⁵ For he stretched out his hand against God, || And against the Mighty he makes himself mighty. ²⁶ He runs to Him with a neck, || With thick bosses of his shields. ²⁷ For he has covered his face with his fat, || And makes vigor over [his] confidence. ²⁸ And he inhabits cities cut off, houses not dwelt in, || That have been ready to become heaps. ²⁹ He is not rich, nor does his wealth rise, || Nor does he stretch out their continuance on earth. ³⁰ He does not turn aside from darkness, || A flame dries up his tender branch, || And he turns aside at the breath of His mouth! ³¹ Do not let him put credence in vanity, || He has been deceived, || For vanity is his exchange. ³² It is not completed in his day, || And his bending branch is not green. ³³ He shakes off his unripe fruit as a vine, || And casts off his blossom as an olive. ³⁴ For the company of the profane [is] barren, || And fire has consumed tents of bribery. ³⁵ To conceive misery, and to bear iniquity, || Even their heart prepares deceit."

CHAPTER 16

¹ And Job answers and says: ² "I have heard many such things, || Miserable comforters [are] you all. ³ Is there an end to words of wind? Or what emboldens you that you answer? ⁴ I also, like you, might speak, || If your soul were in my soul's stead. I might join against you with words, || And nod at you with my head. ⁵ I might harden you with my mouth, || And the moving of my lips might be sparing. ⁶ If I speak, my pain is not restrained, || And I cease—what goes from me? ⁷ Only, now, it has wearied me; You have desolated all my company, ⁸ And You loathe me, || For it has been a witness, || And my failure rises up against me, || It testifies in my face. ⁹ His anger has torn, and He hates me, || He has gnashed at me with His teeth, || My adversary sharpens His eyes for me. ¹⁰ They have gaped on me with their mouth, || In reproach they have struck my cheeks, || Together they set themselves against me. ¹¹ God shuts me up to the perverse, || And turns me over to the hands of the wicked. ¹² I have been at ease, and He breaks me, || And He has laid hold on my neck, || And He breaks me in pieces, || And He raises me to Him for a mark. ¹³ His archers go around against me. He split my reins, and does not spare, || He pours out my gall to the earth. ¹⁴ He breaks me—breach on breach, || He runs on me as a mighty one. ¹⁵ I have sewed sackcloth on my skin, || And have rolled my horn in the dust. ¹⁶ My face is foul with weeping, || And on my eyelids [is] death-shade. ¹⁷ Not for violence in my hands, || And my prayer [is] pure. ¹⁸ O earth, do not cover my blood! And let there not be a place for my cry. ¹⁹ Also, now, behold, my witness [is] in the heavens, || And my testifier in the high places. ²⁰ My interpreter [is] my friend, || My eye has dropped to God; ²¹ And He reasons for a man with God, || As a son of man for his friend. ²² When a few years come, || Then I go [on] the path of no return."

CHAPTER 17

¹ "My spirit has been destroyed, || My days extinguished—graves [are] for me. ² If not—mockeries [are] with me. And my eye lodges in their provocations. ³ Now place my pledge with You; Who is he that strikes hand with me? ⁴ For You have hidden their heart from understanding, || Therefore You do not exalt them. ⁵ For a portion he shows friendship, || And the eyes of his sons are consumed. ⁶ And He set me up for a proverb of the peoples, || And I am a wonder before them. ⁷ And my eye is dim from sorrow, || And my members—all of them—as a shadow. ⁸ The upright are astonished at this, and the innocent

stirs himself up against the profane. ⁹ And the righteous lays hold [on] his way, || And the clean of hands adds strength. ¹⁰ But please return and come in, all of you, || And I do not find a wise man among you. ¹¹ My days have passed by, || My plans have been broken off, || The possessions of my heart! ¹² They appoint night for day, || Light [is] near because of darkness. ¹³ If I wait—Sheol [is] my house, || In darkness I have spread out my bed. ¹⁴ To corruption I have called: You [are] my father. To the worm: My mother and my sister. ¹⁵ And where [is] my hope now? Indeed, my hope, who beholds it? ¹⁶ You go down [to] the parts of Sheol, || If we may rest together on the dust."

CHAPTER 18

¹ And Bildad the Shuhite answers and says: ² "When do you set an end to words? Consider, and afterward we speak. ³ Why have we been reckoned as livestock? We have been defiled in your eyes! ⁴ He is tearing himself in his anger. Is earth forsaken for your sake? And is a rock removed from its place? ⁵ Also, the light of the wicked is extinguished. And there does not shine a spark of his fire. ⁶ The light has been dark in his tent, || And his lamp over him is extinguished. ⁷ The steps of his strength are restricted, || And his own counsel casts him down. ⁸ For he is sent into a net by his own feet, || And he habitually walks on a snare. ⁹ A trap seizes on the heel, || The designing prevails over him. ¹⁰ His cord is hidden in the earth, || And his trap on the path. ¹¹ Terrors have terrified him all around, || And they have scattered him—at his feet. ¹² His sorrow is hungry, || And calamity is ready at his side. ¹³ It consumes the parts of his skin, || Death's firstborn consumes his parts. ¹⁴ His confidence is drawn from his tent, || And it causes him to step to the king of terrors. ¹⁵ It dwells in his tent—out of his provender, || Sulfur is scattered over his habitation. ¹⁶ From beneath his roots are dried up, || And from above his crop is cut off. ¹⁷ His memorial has perished from the land, || And he has no name on the street. ¹⁸ They thrust him from light to darkness, || And cast him out from the habitable earth. ¹⁹ He has no continuator, || Nor successor among his people, || And none is remaining in his dwellings. ²⁰ At this day, those [in the] west have been astonished, || And those [in the] east have taken fright. ²¹ Only these [are] dwelling places of the perverse, || And this [is] the place God has not known."

CHAPTER 19

¹ And Job answers and says: ² "Until when do you afflict my soul, || And bruise me with words? ³ These ten times you put me to shame, you do not blush. You make yourselves strange to me— ⁴ And also—truly, I have erred, || My error remains with me. ⁵ If, truly, you magnify yourselves over me, || And decide my reproach against me; ⁶ Know now, that God turned me upside down, || And has set around His net against me, ⁷ Behold, I cry out—violence, and am not answered, I cry aloud, and there is no judgment. ⁸ He hedged up my way, and I do not pass over, || And He places darkness on my paths. ⁹ He has stripped my honor from off me, || And He turns the crown from my head. ¹⁰ He breaks me down all around, and I go, || And removes my hope like a tree. ¹¹ And He kindles His anger against me, || And reckons me to Him as His adversaries. ¹² His troops come in together, || And they raise up their way against me, || And encamp around my tent. ¹³ He has put my brothers far off from me, || And my acquaintances have surely been estranged from me. ¹⁴ My neighbors have ceased || And my familiar friends have forgotten me, ¹⁵ Sojourners of my house and my maids, || Reckon me for a stranger; I have been an alien in their eyes. ¹⁶ I have called to my servant, || And he does not answer, || With my mouth I make supplication to him. ¹⁷ My spirit is strange to my wife, || And my favors to the sons of my [mother's] womb. ¹⁸ Also sucklings have despised me, I rise, and they speak against me. ¹⁹ All the men of my counsel detest me, || And those I have loved, || Have been turned against me. ²⁰ To my skin and to my flesh || My bone has cleaved, || And I deliver myself with the skin of my teeth. ²¹ Pity me, pity me, you my friends, || For the hand of God has struck against me. ²² Why do you pursue me as God? And are not satisfied with my flesh? ²³ Who grants now, that my words may be written? Who grants that they may be inscribed in a scroll? ²⁴ With a pen of iron and lead—They may be hewn in a rock forever. ²⁵ That—I have known my Redeemer, || The

living and the Last, || For He raises the dust. ²⁶ And after my skin has been surrounded this [body], || Then from my flesh I see God— ²⁷ Whom I see on my side, || And my eyes have beheld, and not a stranger, || My reins have been consumed in my bosom. ²⁸ But you say, Why do we pursue after him? And the root of the matter has been found in me. ²⁹ Be afraid because of the sword, || For the punishments of the sword [are] furious, || That you may know that [there is] a judgment."

CHAPTER 20

¹ And Zophar the Naamathite answers and says: ² "Therefore my thoughts cause me to answer, || And because of my sensations in me. ³ I hear the discipline of my shame, || And the spirit of my understanding causes me to answer: ⁴ Have you known this from antiquity? Since the placing of man on earth? ⁵ That the singing of the wicked [is] short, || And the joy of the profane for a moment, ⁶ Though his excellence goes up to the heavens, || He strikes his head against a cloud— ⁷ He perishes as his own dung forever, || His beholders say, Where [is] he? ⁸ He flees as a dream, and they do not find him, || And he is driven away as a vision of the night, ⁹ The eye has not seen him, and does not add. And his place does not behold him again. ¹⁰ His sons oppress the poor, || And his hands give back his wealth. ¹¹ His bones have been full of his youth, and it lies down with him on the dust. ¹² Though he sweetens evil in his mouth, hides it under his tongue, ¹³ has pity on it, and does not forsake it, and keeps it back in the midst of his palate, ¹⁴ his food is turned in his bowels, the bitterness of cobras [is] in his heart. ¹⁵ He has swallowed wealth, and vomits it. God drives it out from his belly. ¹⁶ He sucks [the] gall of cobras, the tongue of a viper slays him. ¹⁷ He does not look on streams, || Flowing of brooks of honey and butter. ¹⁸ He is giving back [what] he labored for, and does not consume [it]; As a bulwark [is] his exchange, and he does not exult. ¹⁹ For he oppressed—he forsook the poor, || He has taken a house away violently, || And he does not build it. ²⁰ For he has not known ease in his belly. With his desirable thing he does not deliver himself. ²¹ There is not a remnant to his food, || Therefore his good does not stay. ²² In the fullness of his sufficiency he is constricted. Every perverse hand meets him. ²³ It comes to pass, at the filling of his belly, || He sends forth against him || The fierceness of His anger, || Indeed, He rains on him in his eating. ²⁴ He flees from an iron weapon, || A bow of bronze passes through him. ²⁵ One has drawn, || And it comes out from the body, || And a glittering weapon proceeds from his gall. Terrors [are] on him. ²⁶ All darkness is hid for his treasures, || A fire not blown consumes him, || The remnant is broken in his tent. ²⁷ The heavens reveal his iniquity, || And earth is raising itself against him. ²⁸ The increase of his house is removed, || Poured forth in a day of His anger. ²⁹ This [is] the portion of a wicked man from God. And an inheritance appointed him by God."

CHAPTER 21

¹ And Job answers and says: ² "Hear my word diligently, || And this is your consolation. ³ Bear with me, and I speak, || And after my speaking—you may deride. ⁴ [Is] my complaint [against] man? and if [so], why may my temper not become short? ⁵ Turn to me, and be astonished, || And put hand to mouth. ⁶ Indeed, if I have remembered, then I have been troubled. And my flesh has taken fright. ⁷ Why do the wicked live? They have become old, || Indeed, they have been mighty in wealth. ⁸ Their seed is established, || Before their face with them, || And their offspring before their eyes. ⁹ Their houses [are] peace without fear, || Nor [is] a rod of God on them. ¹⁰ His bullock breeds without fail. His cow brings forth safely, and does not miscarry. ¹¹ They send forth their sucklings as a flock, || And their children skip, ¹² They lift [themselves] up at timbrel and harp, || And rejoice at the sound of a pipe. ¹³ They wear out their days in good, || And in a moment go down [to] Sheol. ¹⁴ And they say to God, Turn aside from us, || And the knowledge of Your ways || We have not desired. ¹⁵ What [is] the Mighty One that we serve Him? And what do we profit when we meet with Him? ¹⁶ Behold, their good [is] not in their hand || (The counsel of the wicked || Has been far from me). ¹⁷ How often is the lamp of the wicked extinguished, || And their calamity comes on them? He apportions pangs in His anger. ¹⁸ They are as straw before wind, || And as chaff a windstorm has

stolen away, ¹⁹ God lays up for his sons his sorrow, || He gives repayment to him—and he knows. ²⁰ His own eyes see his destruction, || And he drinks of the wrath of the Mighty. ²¹ For what [is] his delight in his house after him, || And the number of his months cut off? ²² Does [one] teach knowledge to God, || Since He judges [those] on high? ²³ This [one] dies in his perfect strength, || Wholly at ease and quiet. ²⁴ His breasts have been full of milk, || And marrow moistens his bones. ²⁵ And this [one] dies with a bitter soul, || And has not eaten with gladness. ²⁶ Together they lie down on the dust, || And the worm covers them over. ²⁷ Behold, I have known your thoughts, || And the schemes against me you do wrongfully. ²⁸ For you say, Where [is] the house of the noble? And where the tent—the dwelling places of the wicked? ²⁹ Have you not asked those passing by the way? And do you not know their signs? ³⁰ That the wicked is spared to a day of calamity. They are brought to a day of wrath. ³¹ Who declares his way to his face? And [for] that which he has done, || Who gives repayment to him? ³² And he is brought to the graves, || And a watch is kept over the heap. ³³ The clods of the valley have been sweet to him, || And he draws every man after him, || And there is no numbering before him. ³⁴ And how do you comfort me [with] vanity, || And trespass has been left in your answers?"

CHAPTER 22

¹ And Eliphaz the Temanite answers and says: ² "Is a man profitable to God, || Because a wise man is profitable to himself? ³ Is it a delight to the Mighty One || That you are righteous? is it gain, || That you make your ways perfect? ⁴ Because of your reverence || Does He reason [with] you? He enters with you into judgment: ⁵ Is your wickedness not abundant? And there is no end to your iniquities. ⁶ For you take a pledge of your brother for nothing, || And you strip off the garments of the naked. ⁷ You do not cause the weary to drink water, || And you withhold bread from the hungry. ⁸ As for the man of arm—he has the earth, || And the accepted of face—he dwells in it. ⁹ You have sent widows away empty, || And the arms of the fatherless are bruised. ¹⁰ Therefore snares [are] all around you, || And sudden fear troubles you. ¹¹ Or darkness—you do not see, || And abundance of waters covers you. ¹² Is God not high [in] the heavens? And see the summit of the stars, || That they are high. ¹³ And you have said, How has God known? Does He judge through thickness? ¹⁴ Thick clouds [are] a secret place to Him, || And He does not see, || And He habitually walks [above] the circle of the heavens. ¹⁵ Do you observe the path of the age, || That men of iniquity have trodden, ¹⁶ Who have been cut down unexpectedly? A flood is poured out on their foundation. ¹⁷ Those saying to God, Turn aside from us, || And what does the Mighty One do to them? ¹⁸ And He has filled their houses [with] good (And the counsel of the wicked || Has been far from me). ¹⁹ The righteous see and they rejoice, || And the innocent mocks at them: ²⁰ Surely our substance has not been cut off, || And fire has consumed their excellence. ²¹ Now acquaint yourself with Him, and be at peace, || Thereby your increase [is] good. ²² Please receive a law from His mouth, || And set His sayings in your heart. ²³ If you return to the Mighty you are built up, || You put iniquity far from your tents. ²⁴ So as to set a defense on the dust, || And a covering on a rock of the valleys. ²⁵ And the Mighty has been your defense, || And silver [is] strength to you. ²⁶ For then you delight yourself on the Mighty, || And lift up your face to God, ²⁷ You make supplication to Him, || And He hears you, || And you complete your vows. ²⁸ And you decree a saying, || And it is established to you, || And light has shone on your ways. ²⁹ For they have made low, || And you say, Lift up. And He saves the bowed down of eyes. ³⁰ He delivers the one [who is] not innocent, || Indeed, he has been delivered || By the cleanness of your hands."

CHAPTER 23

¹ And Job answers and says: ² "Also—today my complaint [is] bitter, || My hand has been heavy because of my sighing. ³ O that I had known—and I find Him, || I come to His seat, ⁴ I arrange the cause before Him, || And fill my mouth [with] arguments. ⁵ I know the words He answers me, || And understand what He says to me. ⁶ Does He strive with me in the abundance of power? No! Surely He puts [it] in me. ⁷ There

the upright reason with Him, || And I escape from mine who is judging—forever. [8] Behold, I go forward—and He is not, || And backward—and I do not perceive Him. [9] [To] the left in His working—and I do not see, || He is covered [on] the right, and I do not behold. [10] For He has known the way with me, || He has tried me—I go forth as gold. [11] My foot has laid hold on His step, || I have kept His way, and do not turn aside, [12] The command of His lips, and I do not depart. I have laid up above my allotted portion || The sayings of His mouth. [13] And He [is] in one [mind], || And who turns Him back? And His soul has desired—and He does [it]. [14] For He completes my portion, || And many such things [are] with Him. [15] Therefore, I am troubled at His presence, I consider, and am afraid of Him. [16] And God has made my heart soft, || And the Mighty has troubled me. [17] For I have not been cut off before darkness, || And before me He covered thick darkness."

CHAPTER 24

[1] "For this reason from the Mighty One || Times have not been hidden, || And those knowing Him have not seen His days. [2] They reach the borders, || They have taken a drove away violently, || Indeed, they do evil. [3] They lead away the donkey of the fatherless, || They take in pledge the ox of the widow, [4] They turn aside the needy from the way, || Together have hid the poor of the earth. [5] Behold, wild donkeys in a wilderness, || They have gone out about their work, || Seeking early for prey, || A mixture for himself—food for young ones. [6] They reap his provender in a field, || And they glean the vineyard of the wicked. [7] They cause the naked to lodge without clothing. And there is no covering in the cold. [8] From the inundation of hills they are wet, || And without a refuge—have embraced a rock. [9] They take away violently || The orphan from the breast, || And they lay a pledge on the poor. [10] Naked, they have gone without clothing, || And hungry—have taken away a sheaf. [11] They make oil between their walls, || They have trodden winepresses, and thirst. [12] Men groan because of enmity, || And the soul of pierced ones cries, || And God does not give praise. [13] They have been those rebelling against light, || They have not discerned His ways, || Nor abided in His paths. [14] The murderer rises at the light, || He slays the poor and needy, || And in the night he is as a thief. [15] And the eye of an adulterer || Has observed the twilight, || Saying, No eye beholds me. And he puts the face in secret. [16] He has dug in the darkness—houses; By day they shut themselves up, || They have not known light. [17] When together, morning [is] death-shade to them, || When he discerns the terrors of death-shade. [18] He [is] light on the face of the waters, || Their portion is vilified in the earth, || He does not turn the way of vineyards. [19] Drought—also heat—consume snow-waters, || Sheol—[those who] have sinned. [20] The womb forgets him, || The worm sweetens [on] him, || He is remembered no more, || And wickedness is broken as a tree. [21] Treating evil the barren [who] does not bear, || And he does no good [to] the widow, [22] And [God] has drawn the mighty by His power, || He rises, and none believes in life. [23] He gives to him confidence, and he is supported, || And His eyes [are] on their ways. [24] They were high [for] a little, and they are not, || And they have been brought low. They are shut up as all [others], || And cut off as the head of an ear of grain. [25] And if not now, who proves me a liar, || And makes my word of nothing?"

CHAPTER 25

[1] And Bildad the Shuhite answers and says: [2] "The rule and fear [are] with Him, || Making peace in His high places. [3] Is their [any] number to His troops? And on whom does His light not arise? [4] And what? is man righteous with God? And what? is he pure—born of a woman? [5] Behold—to the moon, and it does not shine, || And stars have not been pure in His eyes. [6] How much less man—a grub, || And the son of man—a worm!"

CHAPTER 26

[1] And Job answers and says: [2] "How you have helped the

powerless, || Saved an arm not strong! [3] How you have given counsel to the unwise, || And made known wise plans in abundance. [4] With whom have you declared words? And whose breath came forth from you? [5] The Rephaim are formed, || Also their inhabitants beneath the waters. [6] Sheol [is] naked before Him, || And there is no covering to destruction. [7] Stretching out the north over desolation, || Hanging the earth on nothing, [8] Binding up the waters in His thick clouds, || And the cloud is not burst under them. [9] Taking hold of the face of the throne, || Spreading His cloud over it. [10] He has placed a limit on the waters, || To the boundary of light with darkness. [11] Pillars of the heavens tremble, || And they wonder because of His rebuke. [12] By His power He has quieted the sea, || And by His understanding struck the proud. [13] He beautified the heavens by His Spirit, || His hand has formed the fleeing serpent. [14] Behold, these [are] the borders of His way, and how little a matter is heard of Him, and who understands the thunder of His might?"

CHAPTER 27

[1] And Job adds to lift up his allegory and says: [2] "God lives! He turned aside my judgment, || And the Mighty—He made my soul bitter. [3] For all the while my breath [is] in me, || And the wind of God in my nostrils. [4] My lips do not speak perverseness, || And my tongue does not utter deceit. [5] Defilement to me—if I justify you, || Until I expire I do not turn aside my integrity from me. [6] On my righteousness I have laid hold, || And I do not let it go, || My heart does not reproach me while I live. [7] My enemy is as the wicked, || And my withstander as the perverse. [8] For what [is] the hope of the profane, || When He cuts off? When God casts off his soul? [9] [Does] God hear his cry, || When distress comes on him? [10] Does he delight himself on the Mighty? Call God at all times? [11] I show you by the hand of God, || That which [is] with the Mighty I do not hide. [12] Behold, you—all of you—have seen, || And why [is] this—you are altogether vain? [13] This [is] the portion of wicked man with God, || And the inheritance of terrible ones || They receive from the Mighty. [14] If his sons multiply—a sword [is] for them. And his offspring [are] not satisfied [with] bread. [15] His remnant are buried in death, || And his widows do not weep. [16] If he heaps up silver as dust, || And prepares clothing as clay, [17] He prepares—and the righteous puts [it] on, || And the innocent apportions the silver. [18] He has built his house as a moth, || And as a shelter a watchman has made. [19] He lies down rich, and he is not gathered, || He has opened his eyes, and he is not. [20] Terrors overtake him as waters, || By night a whirlwind has stolen him away. [21] An east wind takes him up, and he goes, || And it frightens him from his place, [22] And it casts at him, and does not spare, || He diligently flees from its hand. [23] It claps its hands at him, || And it hisses at him from his place."

CHAPTER 28

[1] "Surely there is a source for silver, || And a place for the gold they refine; [2] Iron is taken from the dust, || And bronze [from] the firm stone. [3] He has set an end to darkness, || And he is searching to all perfection, || A stone of darkness and death-shade. [4] A stream has broken out from a sojourner, || Those forgotten of the foot, || They were low, they wandered from man. [5] The earth! Bread comes forth from it, || And its under-part is turned like fire. [6] A place of the sapphire [are] its stones, || And it has dust of gold. [7] A path—a ravenous bird has not known it, || Nor has an eye of the falcon scorched it, [8] Nor have the sons of pride trodden it, || The fierce lion has not passed over it. [9] He sent forth his hand against the flint, || He overturned mountains from the root. [10] Among rocks, he has cleaved brooks, || And his eye has seen every precious thing. [11] He has bound overflowing rivers, || And the hidden thing brings out [to] light. [12] And the wisdom—from where is it found? And where [is] this, the place of understanding? [13] Man has not known its arrangement, || Nor is it found in the land of the living. [14] The deep has said, It [is] not in me, || And the sea has said, It is not with me. [15] Gold is not given for it, || Nor is silver weighed—its price. [16] It is not valued with pure gold of Ophir, || With precious onyx and sapphire, [17] Gold and crystal do not equal it, || Nor [is] its exchange a vessel of fine gold. [18] Corals and pearl are not remembered, || The acquisition of

wisdom [is] above rubies. ¹⁹ The topaz of Cush does not equal it, || It is not valued with pure gold. ²⁰ And the wisdom—from where does it come? And where [is] this, the place of understanding? ²¹ It has been hid from the eyes of all living. And from the bird of the heavens || It has been hidden. ²² Destruction and death have said: With our ears we have heard its fame. ²³ God has understood its way, || And He has known its place. ²⁴ For He looks to the ends of the earth, || He sees under the whole heavens, ²⁵ To make a weight for the wind, || And He meted out the waters in measure. ²⁶ In His making for the rain a limit, || And a way for the brightness of the voices, ²⁷ Then He has seen and declares it, || He has prepared it, and also searched it out, ²⁸ And He says to man: Behold, fear of the Lord, that [is] wisdom, || And to turn from evil [is] understanding."

CHAPTER 29

¹ And Job adds to lift up his allegory and says: ² "Who makes me as [in] months past, || As [in] the days of God's preserving me? ³ In His causing His lamp to shine on my head, || By His light I walk [through] darkness. ⁴ As I have been in days of my maturity, || And the counsel of God on my tent. ⁵ When yet the Mighty One [is] with me. Around me—my young ones, ⁶ When washing my goings with butter, || And the firm rock [is] with me—streams of oil. ⁷ When I go out to the gate by the city, || In a broad place I prepare my seat. ⁸ Youths have seen me, and they have been hidden, || And the aged have risen—they stood up. ⁹ Princes have kept in words, || And they place a hand on their mouth. ¹⁰ The voice of leaders has been hidden, || And their tongue has cleaved to the palate. ¹¹ For the ear heard, and declares me blessed, || And the eye has seen, and testifies [to] me. ¹² For I deliver the afflicted who is crying, || And the fatherless who has no helper. ¹³ The blessing of the perishing comes on me, || And I cause the heart of the widow to sing. ¹⁴ I have put on righteousness, and it clothes me, || My justice as a robe and a crown. ¹⁵ I have been eyes to the blind, || And I [am] feet to the lame. ¹⁶ I [am] a father to the needy, || And the cause I have not known I search out. ¹⁷ And I break the jaw-teeth of the perverse, || And from his teeth I cast away prey. ¹⁸ And I say, I expire with my nest, || And I multiply days as the sand. ¹⁹ My root is open to the waters, || And dew lodges on my branch. ²⁰ My glory [is] fresh with me, || And my bow is renewed in my hand. ²¹ They have listened to me, || Indeed, they wait, and are silent for my counsel. ²² After my word they do not change, || And my speech drops on them, ²³ And they wait for me as [for] rain, || And they have opened wide their mouth || [As] for the spring rain. ²⁴ I laugh at them—they give no credence, || And do not cause the light of my face to fall. ²⁵ I choose their way, and sit [as] head, || And I dwell as a king in a troop, || When he comforts mourners."

CHAPTER 30

¹ "And now, laughed at me, || Have the younger in days than I, || Whose fathers I have loathed to set || With the dogs of my flock. ² Also—the power of their hands, why [is it] to me? On them old age has perished. ³ With want and with harsh famine, || They are gnawing a dry place [in] the recent night, || [In] desolation and ruin, ⁴ Those cropping mallows near a shrub, || And their food [is] root of broom trees. ⁵ They are cast out from the midst || (They shout against them as a thief), ⁶ To dwell in a frightful place of valleys, || Holes of earth and clefts. ⁷ They groan among shrubs, || They are gathered together under nettles. ⁸ Sons of folly—even sons without name, || They have been struck from the land. ⁹ And now, I have been their song, || And I am to them for a byword. ¹⁰ They have detested me, || They have kept far from me, || And from before me have not spared to spit. ¹¹ Because He loosed His cord and afflicts me, || And the bridle from before me, || They have cast away. ¹² A brood arises on the right hand, || They have cast away my feet, || And they raise up against me, || Their paths of calamity. ¹³ They have broken down my path, || They profit by my calamity: He has no helper. ¹⁴ They come as a wide breach, || Under the desolation have rolled themselves. ¹⁵ He has turned terrors against me, || It pursues my abundance as the wind, || And as a thick cloud, || My safety has passed away. ¹⁶ And now, in me my soul pours itself out,

|| Days of affliction seize me. ¹⁷ [At] night my bone has been pierced in me, || And my gnawing [pain] does not lie down. ¹⁸ By the abundance of power, || Is my clothing changed, || As the mouth of my coat it girds me. ¹⁹ Casting me into mire, || And I have become like dust and ashes. ²⁰ I cry to You, || And You do not answer me, I have stood, and You consider me. ²¹ You are turned to be fierce to me, || With the strength of Your hand, || You oppress me. ²² You lift me up, || You cause me to ride on the wind, || And You melt—You level me. ²³ For I have known You bring me back [to] death, || And [to] the house appointed for all living. ²⁴ Surely not against the heap || Does He send forth the hand, || Though they have safety in its ruin. ²⁵ Did I not weep for him whose day is hard? My soul has grieved for the needy. ²⁶ When I expected good, then comes evil, || And I wait for light, and darkness comes. ²⁷ My bowels have boiled, and have not ceased, || Days of affliction have gone before me. ²⁸ I have gone mourning without the sun, || I have risen, I cry in an assembly. ²⁹ I have been a brother to dragons, || And a companion to daughters of the ostrich. ³⁰ My skin has been black on me, || And my bone has burned from heat, ³¹ And my harp becomes mourning, || And my pipe the sound of weeping."

CHAPTER 31

¹ "I made a covenant for my eyes, || And how do I attend to a virgin? ² And what [is] the portion of God from above? And the inheritance of the Mighty from the heights? ³ Is not calamity to the perverse? And strangeness to workers of iniquity? ⁴ Does He not see my ways, || And number all my steps? ⁵ If I have walked with vanity, || And my foot hurries to deceit, ⁶ He weighs me in righteous balances, || And God knows my integrity. ⁷ If my step turns aside from the way, || And my heart has gone after my eyes, || And blemish has cleaved to my hands, ⁸ Let me sow—and another eat, || And let my products be rooted out. ⁹ If my heart has been enticed by a woman, || And I laid wait by the opening of my neighbor, ¹⁰ Let my wife grind to another, || And let others bend over her. ¹¹ For it [is] a wicked thing, and a judicial iniquity; ¹² For it [is] a fire, it consumes to destruction, || And takes root among all my increase, ¹³ If I despise the cause of my manservant, || And of my handmaid, || In their contending with me, ¹⁴ Then what do I do when God arises? And when He inspects, || What do I answer Him? ¹⁵ Did He that made me in the womb not make him? Indeed, One prepares us in the womb. ¹⁶ If I withhold the poor from pleasure, || And consume the eyes of the widow, ¹⁷ And I eat my morsel by myself, || And the orphan has nothing [to] eat of it, ¹⁸ (But from my youth || He grew up with me as [with] a father, || And from the belly of my mother I am led), ¹⁹ If I see [any] perishing without clothing, || And there is no covering for the needy, ²⁰ If his loins have not blessed me, || And from the fleece of my sheep || He does not warm himself, ²¹ If I have waved my hand at the fatherless, || When I see [him] in the gate of my court, ²² Let my shoulder fall from its blade, || And the bone from my arm be broken. ²³ For calamity [from] God [is] a dread to me, || And because of His excellence I am not able. ²⁴ If I have made gold my confidence, || And to the pure gold have said, My trust; ²⁵ If I rejoice because my wealth [is] great, || And because my hand has found abundance, ²⁶ If I see the light when it shines, || And the precious moon walking, ²⁷ And my heart is enticed in secret, || And my hand kisses my mouth, ²⁸ It also [is] a judicial iniquity, || For I had lied to God above. ²⁹ If I rejoice at the ruin of my hater, || And stirred up myself when evil found him, ³⁰ Indeed, I have not permitted my mouth to sin, || To ask with an oath his life. ³¹ If not, say, O men of my tent: O that we had of his flesh, we are not satisfied. ³² A stranger does not lodge in the street, || I open my doors to the traveler. ³³ If I have covered my transgressions as Adam, || To hide my iniquity in my bosom, ³⁴ Because I fear a great multitude, || And the contempt of families frightens me, || Then I am silent, I do not go out of the opening. ³⁵ Who gives to me a hearing? behold, my mark. The Mighty One answers me, || And my adversary has written a bill. ³⁶ If not—on my shoulder I take it up, || I bind it [as] a crown on myself. ³⁷ The number of my steps I tell Him, || As a leader I approach Him. ³⁸ If my land cries out against me, || And together its furrows weep, ³⁹ If I consumed its strength without money, || And the life of its possessors, I have caused to breathe out, ⁴⁰ Instead of wheat let a thorn go forth, || And instead of barley a useless weed!" The words of Job are finished.

CHAPTER 32

¹ And these three men cease from answering Job, for he [is] righteous in his own eyes, ² and the anger of Elihu son of Barachel the Buzite burns, of the family of Ram; his anger has burned against Job, because of his justifying himself more than God; ³ and his anger has burned against his three friends, because that they have not found an answer, and condemn Job. ⁴ And Elihu has waited earnestly beside Job with words, for they are older than he in days. ⁵ And Elihu sees that there is no answer in the mouth of the three men, and his anger burns. ⁶ And Elihu son of Barachel the Buzite answers and says: "I [am] young in days, and you [are] aged; Therefore I have feared, || And am afraid of showing you my opinion. ⁷ I said, Days speak, || And a multitude of years teach wisdom. ⁸ Surely a spirit is in man, || And the breath of the Mighty One || Causes them to understand. ⁹ The multitude are not wise, || Nor do the aged understand judgment. ¹⁰ Therefore I have said: Listen to me, I show my opinion—even I. ¹¹ Behold, I have waited for your words, I give ear to your reasons, || Until you search out sayings. ¹² And to you I attend, || And behold, there is no reasoner for Job, || [Or] answerer of his sayings among you. ¹³ Lest you say, We have found wisdom, || God thrusts him away, not man. ¹⁴ And he has not set words in array for me, || And I do not answer him with your sayings. ¹⁵ (They have broken down, || They have not answered again, || They removed words from themselves. ¹⁶ And I have waited, but they do not speak, || For they have stood still, || They have not answered anymore.) ¹⁷ I answer, even I—my share, || I show my opinion—even I. ¹⁸ For I have been full of words, || The spirit of my breast has distressed me, ¹⁹ Behold, my breast [is] as wine not opened, || It is broken up like new bottles. ²⁰ I speak, and there is refreshment to me, || I open my lips and answer. ²¹ Please do not let me accept the face of any, || Nor give flattering titles to man, ²² For I have not known to give flattering titles, || My Maker takes me away in a little."

CHAPTER 33

¹ "And yet, please, O Job, || Hear my speech and give ear [to] all my words. ² Now behold, I have opened my mouth, || My tongue has spoken in the palate. ³ Of the uprightness of my heart [are] my sayings, || And my lips have clearly spoken knowledge. ⁴ The Spirit of God has made me, || And the breath of the Mighty quickens me. ⁵ If you are able—answer me, || Set in array before me—station yourself. ⁶ Behold, I [am], according to your word, for God, || I have also been formed from the clay. ⁷ Behold, my terror does not frighten you, || And my burden on you is not heavy. ⁸ Surely you have spoken in my ears, || And the sounds of words I hear: ⁹ I [am] pure, without transgression, || I [am] innocent, and I have no iniquity. ¹⁰ Behold, He develops hindrances against me, || He reckons me for an enemy to Him, ¹¹ He puts my feet in the stocks, || He watches all my paths. ¹² Behold, you have not been righteous [in] this, || I answer you, that God is greater than man. ¹³ Why have you striven against Him, || When [for] all His matters He does not answer? ¹⁴ For once God speaks, and twice (he does not behold it), ¹⁵ In a dream—a vision of night, || In the falling of deep sleep on men, || In slumberings on a bed. ¹⁶ Then He uncovers the ear of men, || And seals for their instruction, ¹⁷ To turn aside man [from] doing, || And He conceals pride from man. ¹⁸ He keeps back his soul from corruption, || And his life from passing away by a dart. ¹⁹ And he has been reproved || With pain on his bed, || And the strife of his bones [is] enduring. ²⁰ And his life has nauseated bread, || And his soul desirable food. ²¹ His flesh is consumed from being seen, || And his bones are high, they were not seen! ²² And his soul draws near to the pit, || And his life to those causing death. ²³ If there is a messenger by him, || An interpreter—one of a thousand, || To declare for man his uprightness, ²⁴ Then He favors him and says, || Ransom him from going down to the pit, || I have found an atonement. ²⁵ Fresher [is] his flesh than a child's, || He returns to the days of his youth. ²⁶ He makes supplication to God, || And He accepts him. And he sees His face with shouting, || And He returns to man His righteousness. ²⁷ [Then] he looks on men and says, || I sinned, and I have perverted uprightness, || And it has not been profitable to me. ²⁸ He has ransomed my soul || From going over into the pit, || And my life looks on the

light. ²⁹ Behold, God works all these, || Twice, [even] three times with man, ³⁰ To bring back his soul from the pit, || To be enlightened with the light of the living. ³¹ Attend, O Job, listen to me, || Keep silent, and I speak. ³² If there are words—answer me, || Speak, for I have a desire to justify you. ³³ If there are not—listen to me, || Keep silent, and I teach you wisdom."

CHAPTER 34

¹ And Elihu answers and says: ² "Hear, O wise men, my words, || And, O knowing ones, give ear to me. ³ For the ear tries words, || And the palate tastes to eat. ⁴ Let us choose judgment for ourselves, || Let us know among ourselves what [is] good. ⁵ For Job has said, I have been righteous, || And God has turned aside my right, ⁶ Against my right do I lie? My arrow [is] mortal—without transgression. ⁷ Who [is] a man like Job? He drinks scoffing like water, ⁸ And he has traveled for company || With workers of iniquity, || So as to go with men of wickedness. ⁹ For he has said, It does not profit a man || When he delights himself with God. ¹⁰ Therefore, O men of heart, listen to me; Far be it from God to do wickedness, || And [from] the Mighty to do perverseness, ¹¹ For He repays the work of man to him, || And according to the path of each He causes him to find. ¹² Indeed, truly, God does not do wickedly, || And the Mighty does not pervert judgment. ¹³ Who has inspected for Himself the earth? And who has placed all the habitable world? ¹⁴ If He sets His heart on him, || [If] He gathers His Spirit and His breath to Himself, ¹⁵ All flesh expires together, || And man returns to dust. ¹⁶ And if [there is] understanding, hear this, || Give ear to the voice of my words. ¹⁷ Indeed, does one hating justice govern? Or do you condemn the Most Just? ¹⁸ Who has said to a king, Worthless, || To princes, Wicked? ¹⁹ That has not accepted the person of princes, || Nor has known the rich before the poor, || For all of them [are] a work of His hands. ²⁰ [In] a moment they die, || And at midnight people shake, || And they pass away, || And they remove the mighty without hand. ²¹ For His eyes [are] on the ways of each, || And He sees all his steps. ²² There is no darkness nor death-shade, || For workers of iniquity to be hidden there; ²³ For He does not permit man anymore, || To go to God in judgment, ²⁴ He breaks the mighty—no searching! And He appoints others in their stead. ²⁵ Therefore He knows their works, || And He has overturned by night, || And they are bruised. ²⁶ As wicked He has struck them, || In the place of beholders. ²⁷ Because that against right || They have turned aside from after Him, || And have considered none of His ways, ²⁸ To cause to come to Him || The cry of the poor, || And He hears the cry of the afflicted. ²⁹ And He gives rest, and who makes wrong? And hides the face, and who beholds it? And in reference to a nation and to a man, || [It is] the same. ³⁰ From the reigning of a profane man, || From the snares of a people; ³¹ For has any said to God: I have taken away, || I do not do corruptly, ³² Besides [that which] I see, You show me, || If I have done iniquity—I do not add? ³³ Does He repay by you, that you have refused—That you choose, and not I? And what you have known, speak. ³⁴ Let men of heart say to me, || And a wise man is listening to me: ³⁵ Job—he does not speak with knowledge, || And his words [are] not with wisdom. ³⁶ My Father! Let Job be tried—to victory, || Because of answers for men of iniquity, ³⁷ For he adds to his sin, || He vomits transgression among us, || And multiplies his sayings to God."

CHAPTER 35

¹ And Elihu answers and says: ² "Have you reckoned this for judgment [when] you have said, || My righteousness [is] more than God's? ³ For you say, What does it profit You? What do I profit from my sin? ⁴ I return words, and your friends with you, ⁵ Behold attentively the heavens—and see, || And behold the clouds, || They have been higher than you. ⁶ If you have sinned, what do you do against Him? And your transgressions have been multiplied, || What do you do to Him? ⁷ If you have been righteous, || What do you give to Him? Or what does He receive from your hand? ⁸ For a man like yourself [is] your wickedness, || And for a son of man your righteousness. ⁹ Because of the multitude of oppressions || They cause to cry out, || They cry because of the arm of the mighty. ¹⁰ And none said, Where [is] God my Maker? Giving songs in the night, ¹¹

Teaching us more than the beasts of the earth, || Indeed, He makes us wiser than the bird of the heavens. ¹² There they cry, and He does not answer, || Because of the pride of evildoers. ¹³ Surely God does not hear vanity, || And the Mighty does not behold it. ¹⁴ Indeed, though you say you do not behold Him, || Judgment [is] before Him, and stays for Him. ¹⁵ And now, because there is not, || He has appointed His anger, || And He has not known in great extremity. ¹⁶ And Job opens his mouth [with] vanity, || He multiplies words without knowledge."

CHAPTER 36

¹ And Elihu adds and says: ² "Honor me a little, and I show you, || That yet for God [are] words. ³ I lift up my knowledge from afar, || And I ascribe righteousness to my Maker. ⁴ For my words [are] truly not false, || The perfect in knowledge [is] with you. ⁵ Behold, God [is] mighty, and does not despise, || Mighty [in] power [and] heart. ⁶ He does not revive the wicked, || And appoints the judgment of the poor; ⁷ He does not withdraw His eyes from the righteous, || And [from] kings on the throne, || And causes them to sit forever, and they are high, ⁸ And if prisoners in chains || They are captured with cords of affliction, ⁹ Then He declares to them their work, || And their transgressions, || Because they have become mighty, ¹⁰ And He uncovers their ear for instruction, || And commands that they turn back from iniquity. ¹¹ If they hear and serve, || They complete their days in good, || And their years in pleasantness. ¹² And if they do not listen, || They pass away by the dart, || And expire without knowledge. ¹³ And the profane in heart set the face, || They do not cry when He has bound them. ¹⁴ Their soul dies in youth, || And their life among the defiled. ¹⁵ He draws out the afflicted in his affliction, || And uncovers their ear in oppression. ¹⁶ And He also moved you from a narrow place || [To] a broad place—no constriction under it, || And the sitting beyond of your table has been full of fatness. ¹⁷ And you have fulfilled the judgment of the wicked, || Judgment and justice are upheld because of fury, ¹⁸ Lest He move you with a stroke, || And the abundance of an atonement not turn you aside. ¹⁹ Does He value your riches? He has gold, and all the forces of power. ²⁰ Do not desire the night, || For the going up of peoples in their stead. ²¹ Take heed—do not turn to iniquity, || For you have fixed on this || Rather than [on] affliction. ²² Behold, God sits on high by His power, || Who [is] like Him—a teacher? ²³ Who has appointed to Him His way? And who said, You have done iniquity? ²⁴ Remember that you magnify His work || That men have beheld. ²⁵ All men have looked on it, || Man looks attentively from afar. ²⁶ Behold, God [is] high, || And we do not know the number of His years, || Indeed, there [is] no searching. ²⁷ When He diminishes droppings of the waters, || They refine rain according to its vapor, ²⁸ Which clouds drop, || They distill on man abundantly. ²⁹ Indeed, do [any] understand || The spreadings out of a cloud? The noises of His dwelling place? ³⁰ Behold, He has spread His light over it, || And He has covered the roots of the sea, ³¹ For He judges peoples by them, || He gives food in abundance. ³² By two palms He has covered the light, || And lays a charge over it in meeting, ³³ His shout shows it, || The livestock also, the rising [storm]."

CHAPTER 37

¹ "Also, my heart trembles at this, || And it moves from its place. ² Listen diligently to the trembling of His voice, || Indeed, the sound goes forth from His mouth. ³ He directs it under the whole heavens, || And its light [is] over the skirts of the earth. ⁴ A voice roars after it—He thunders with the voice of His excellence, || And He does not hold them back, || When His voice is heard. ⁵ God thunders with His voice wonderfully, || Doing great things and we do not know. ⁶ For He says to snow: Be [on] the earth. And the small rain and great rain of His power. ⁷ Into the hand of every man he seals, || For the knowledge by all men of His work. ⁸ And the beast enters into [its] lair, || And it continues in its habitations. ⁹ From the inner chamber comes a windstorm, || And from scatterings winds— cold, ¹⁰ From the breath of God is frost given, || And the breadth of waters is constricted, ¹¹ Indeed, by filling He presses out a cloud, || [and] His light scatters a cloud. ¹² And it is turning itself around by His counsels, || For their doing all He commands them, || On the face of the habitable earth. ¹³

Whether for a rod, or for His land, || Or for kindness—He causes it to come. ¹⁴ Hear this, O Job, || Stand and consider the wonders of God. ¹⁵ Do you know when God places them, || And caused the light of His cloud to shine? ¹⁶ Do you know the balancings of a cloud? The wonders of the Perfect in knowledge? ¹⁷ How your garments [are] warm, || In the quieting of the earth from the south? ¹⁸ You have made an expanse with Him || For the clouds—strong as a hard mirror! ¹⁹ Let us know what we say to Him, || We do not set in array because of darkness. ²⁰ Is it declared to Him that I speak? If a man has spoken, surely he is swallowed up. ²¹ And now, they have not seen the light, || It [is] bright in the clouds, || And the wind has passed by and cleanses them. ²² It comes from the golden north, || Fearful splendor [is] beside God. ²³ The Mighty! We have not found Him out, || High in power and judgment, || He does not answer! And abundant in righteousness, ²⁴ Therefore men fear Him, || He does not see any of the wise of heart."

CHAPTER 38

¹ And Yhwh answers Job out of the whirlwind and says: ² "Who [is] this—darkening counsel, || By words without knowledge? ³ Now gird your loins as a man, || And I ask you, and you cause Me to know. ⁴ Where were you when I founded the earth? Declare, if you have known understanding. ⁵ Who placed its measures—if you know? Or who has stretched out a line on it? ⁶ On what have its sockets been sunk? Or who has cast its cornerstone— ⁷ In the singing together of [the] stars of morning, || When all [the] sons of God shout for joy? ⁸ And He shuts up the sea with doors, || In its coming forth, it goes out from the womb. ⁹ In My making a cloud its clothing, || And thick darkness its swaddling band, ¹⁰ And I measure My statute over it, || And place bar and doors, ¹¹ And say, To here you come, and no more, || And a command is placed || On the pride of your billows. ¹² Have you commanded morning since your days? Do you cause the dawn to know its place? ¹³ To take hold on the skirts of the earth, || And the wicked are shaken out of it, ¹⁴ It turns itself as clay of a seal || And they station themselves as clothed. ¹⁵ And their light is withheld from the wicked, || And the arm lifted up is broken. ¹⁶ Have you come to springs of the sea? And in searching the deep || Have you walked up and down? ¹⁷ Were the gates of death revealed to you? And do you see the gates of death-shade? ¹⁸ You have understanding, || Even to the broad places of earth! Declare— if you have known it all. ¹⁹ Where [is] this—the way light dwells? And darkness, where [is] this—its place? ²⁰ That you take it to its boundary, || And that you understand the paths of its house. ²¹ You have known—for then you are born, || And the number of your days [are] many! ²² Have you come to the treasure of snow? Indeed, do you see the treasures of hail, ²³ That I have kept back for a time of distress, || For a day of conflict and battle? ²⁴ Where [is] this, the way light is apportioned? It scatters an east wind over the earth. ²⁵ Who has divided a conduit for the flood? And a way for the lightning of the voices? ²⁶ To cause [it] to rain on a land [with] no man, || A wilderness [with] no man in it. ²⁷ To satisfy a desolate and ruined place, || And to cause to shoot up || The produce of the tender grass? ²⁸ Does the rain have a father? Or who has begotten the drops of dew? ²⁹ From whose belly came forth the ice? And the hoarfrost of the heavens, || Who has begotten it? ³⁰ Waters are hidden as a stone, || And the face of the deep is captured. ³¹ Do you bind the chains of the Pleiades? Or do you open the cords of Orion? ³² Do you bring out the twelve signs in [their] season? And do you comfort the Great Bear over her sons? ³³ Have you known the statutes of the heavens? Or do you appoint || Its dominion in the earth? ³⁴ Do you lift up your voice to the cloud, || And abundance of water covers you? ³⁵ Do you send out lightnings, and they go || And say to you, Behold us? ³⁶ Who has put wisdom in the inward parts? Or who has given understanding to the covered part? ³⁷ Who numbers the clouds by wisdom? And the bottles of the heavens, || Who causes to lie down, ³⁸ In the hardening of dust into hardness, || And clods cleave together? ³⁹ Do you hunt prey for a lion? And fulfill the desire of young lions? ⁴⁰ When they bow down in dens—Abide in a thicket for a covert? ⁴¹ Who prepares for a raven his provision, || When his young ones cry to God? They wander without food.

CHAPTER 39

[1] "Have you known the time of || The bearing of the wild goats of the rock? Do you mark the bringing forth of does? [2] Do you number the months they fulfill? And have you known the time of their bringing forth? [3] They bow down, || They bring forth their young ones safely, || They cast forth their pangs. [4] Their young ones are safe, || They grow up in the field, they have gone out, || And have not returned to them. [5] Who has sent forth the wild donkey free? Indeed, who opened the bands of the wild donkey? [6] Whose house I have made the wilderness, || And his dwellings the barren land, [7] He laughs at the multitude of a city, || He does not hear the cries of an exactor. [8] The range of mountains [is] his pasture, || And he seeks after every green thing. [9] Is a wild ox willing to serve you? Does he lodge by your crib? [10] Do you bind a wild ox in a furrow [with] his thick band? Does he harrow valleys after you? [11] Do you trust in him because his power [is] great? And do you leave your labor to him? [12] Do you trust in him || That he brings back your seed, || And gathers [it to] your threshing-floor? [13] [The] wing of the crying ostriches exults, but as a pinion and feather of a stork? [14] For she leaves her eggs on the earth, || And she warms them on the dust, [15] And she forgets that a foot may press it, || And a beast of the field treads it down. [16] It has hardened her young ones without her, || Her labor [is] in vain, without fear. [17] For God has caused her to forget wisdom, || And He has not given a portion || To her in understanding; [18] At the time she lifts herself up on high, || She laughs at the horse and his rider. [19] Do you give might to the horse? Do you clothe his neck [with] a mane? [20] Do you cause him to rush as a locust? The splendor of his snorting [is] terrible. [21] They dig in a valley, and he rejoices in power, || He goes forth to meet the armor. [22] He laughs at fear, and is not frightened, || And he does not turn back from the face of the sword. [23] Quiver rattles against him, || The flame of a spear, and a javelin. [24] He swallows the ground with trembling and rage, || And does not remain steadfast || Because of the sound of a horn. [25] Among the horns he says, Aha, || And from afar he smells battle, || Roaring of princes and shouting. [26] By your understanding does a hawk fly? Does he spread his wings to the south? [27] At your command does an eagle go up high? Or lift up his nest? [28] He inhabits a rock, || Indeed, he lodges on the tooth of a rock, and fortress. [29] From there he has sought food, || His eyes look attentively to a far-off place, [30] And his brood sucks up blood, || And where the pierced [are]—there [is] he!"

CHAPTER 40

[1] And Yhwh answers Job and says: [2] "Is the striver with the Mighty instructed? The reprover of God, let him answer it." [3] And Job answers Yhwh and says: [4] "Behold, I have been vile, || What do I return to You? I have placed my hand on my mouth. [5] I have spoken once, and I do not answer, || And twice, and I do not add." [6] And Yhwh answers Job out of the whirlwind and says: [7] "Now gird your loins as a man, || I ask you, and you cause Me to know. [8] Do you also make My judgment void? Do you condemn Me, || That you may be righteous? [9] And do you have an arm like God? And do you thunder with a voice like His? [10] Now put on excellence and loftiness, || Indeed, put on splendor and beauty. [11] Scatter abroad the wrath of your anger, || And see every proud one, and make him low. [12] See every proud one—humble him, || And tread down the wicked in their place. [13] Hide them in the dust together, || Bind their faces in secret. [14] And even I praise you, || For your right hand gives salvation to you. [15] Now behold, behemoth, || That I made with you: He eats grass as an ox. [16] Now behold, his power [is] in his loins, || And his strength in the muscles of his belly. [17] He bends his tail as a cedar, || The sinews of his thighs are wrapped together, [18] His bones [are] tubes of bronze, || His bones [are] as a bar of iron. [19] He [is] a beginning of the ways of God, || His Maker [alone] brings His sword near; [20] For mountains bear food for him, || And all the beasts of the field play there. [21] He lies down under shades, || In a secret place of reed and marsh. [22] Shades cover him, [with] their shadow, || Willows of the brook cover him. [23] Behold, a flood oppresses—he does not hurry, || He is confident though Jordan || Comes forth to his mouth. [24] Does [one] take him by his eyes? || Does [one] pierce the nose with snares?"

CHAPTER 41

[1] "Do you draw leviathan with a hook? And do you let down his tongue with a rope? [2] Do you put a reed in his nose? And pierce his jaw with a thorn? [3] Does he multiply supplications to you? Does he speak tender things to you? [4] Does he make a covenant with you? Do you take him for a perpetual servant? [5] Do you play with him as a bird? And do you bind him for your girls? [6] (Companions feast on him, || They divide him among the merchants!) [7] Do you fill his skin with barbed irons? And his head with fish-spears? [8] Place your hand on him, || Remember the battle—do not add! [9] Behold, the hope of him is found a liar, || Also, is one not cast down at his appearance? [10] None so fierce that he awakes him, || And who [is] he [who] stations himself before Me? [11] Who has brought before Me and I repay? Under the whole heavens it [is] Mine. [12] I do not keep silent concerning his parts, || And the matter of might, || And the grace of his arrangement. [13] Who has uncovered the face of his clothing? Who enters within his double bridle? [14] Who opened the doors of his face? Around his teeth [are] terrible. [15] A pride—strong ones of shields, || Shut up—a close seal. [16] They draw near to one another, || And air does not enter between them. [17] They adhere to one another, || They stick together and are not separated. [18] His sneezings cause light to shine, || And his eyes [are] as the eyelids of the dawn. [19] Flames go out of his mouth, sparks of fire escape. [20] Smoke goes forth out of his nostrils, || As a blown pot and reeds. [21] His breath sets coals on fire, || And a flame goes forth from his mouth. [22] Strength lodges in his neck, || And grief exults before him. [23] The flakes of his flesh have adhered—Firm on him—it is not moved. [24] His heart [is] firm as a stone, || Indeed, firm as the lower piece. [25] The mighty are afraid at his rising, || From his breakings they keep themselves free. [26] The sword of his overtaker does not stand, || Spear, dart, and breastplate. [27] He reckons iron as straw, bronze as rotten wood. [28] The son of the bow does not cause him to flee, || Stones of the sling are turned into stubble by him. [29] Darts have been reckoned as stubble, || And he laughs at the shaking of a javelin. [30] Sharp points of clay [are] under him, || He spreads gold on the mire. [31] He causes the deep to boil as a pot, || He makes the sea as a pot of ointment. [32] He causes a path to shine after him, || One thinks the deep to be hoary. [33] There is not on the earth his like, || That is made without terror. [34] He sees every high thing, || He [is] king over all sons of pride."

CHAPTER 42

[1] And Job answers Yhwh and says: [2] "You have known that [for] all things You are able, || And no purpose is withheld from You. [3] [You said], Who [is] this hiding counsel without knowledge? Therefore, I have declared, and do not understand, || Too wonderful for me, and I do not know. [4] Please hear, and I speak; [You said], I ask you, and you cause Me to know. [5] By the hearing of the ear I heard You, || And now my eye has seen You. [6] Therefore I loathe [it], || And I have sighed on dust and ashes." [7] And it comes to pass after Yhwh's speaking these words to Job, that Yhwh says to Eliphaz the Temanite, "My anger has burned against you and against your two friends, because you have not spoken correctly concerning Me, like My servant Job. [8] And now, take seven bullocks and seven rams for yourselves, and go to My servant Job, and you have caused a burnt-offering to ascend for yourselves; and Job My servant prays for you, for surely I accept his face, so as not to do folly with you, because you have not spoken correctly concerning Me, like My servant Job." [9] And they go—Eliphaz the Temanite, and Bildad the Shuhite, Zophar the Naamathite—and do as Yhwh has spoken to them; and Yhwh accepts the face of Job. [10] And Yhwh has turned [to] the captivity of Job in his praying for his friends, and Yhwh adds [to] all that Job has—to double. [11] And all his brothers come to him, and all his sisters, and all his former acquaintances, and they eat bread with him in his house, and bemoan him, and comfort him concerning all the calamity that Yhwh had brought on him, and they each gave to him one kesitah, and each one ring of gold. [12] And Yhwh has blessed the latter end of Job more than his beginning, and he has fourteen thousand of a flock, and six thousand camels, and one thousand pairs of oxen, and one thousand female donkeys. [13] And he has seven sons and three daughters; [14] and he calls the name of the first Jemima, and the name of the second Kezia, and the name of the third

Keren-Happuch. ¹⁵ And there have not been found women [as] beautiful as the daughters of Job in all the land, and their father gives to them an inheritance in the midst of their brothers. ¹⁶ And Job lives after this one hundred and forty years, and sees his sons, and his sons' sons, four generations; ¹⁷ and Job dies, aged and satisfied [with] days.

PSALMS

PSALM 1

¹ O the blessedness of that one, || Who has not walked in the counsel of the wicked, || And has not stood in the way of sinners, || And has not sat in the seat of scorners; ² But his delight [is] in the Law of Yhwh, || And in His law he meditates by day and by night: ³ And he has been as a tree, || Planted by streams of water, || That gives its fruit in its season, || And its leaf does not wither, || And all that he does he causes to prosper. ⁴ Not so the wicked: But [they are] as chaff that wind drives away! ⁵ Therefore the wicked do not rise in judgment, || Nor sinners in the congregation of the righteous, ⁶ For Yhwh is knowing the way of the righteous, || And the way of the wicked is lost!

PSALM 2

¹ Why have nations assembled tumultuously? And peoples meditate vanity? ² Kings of the earth station themselves, and princes have been united together, against Yhwh, and against His Messiah: ³ "Let us draw off Their cords, || And cast Their thick bands from us." ⁴ He who is sitting in the heavens laughs, || The Lord mocks at them. ⁵ Then He speaks to them in His anger, and in His wrath He troubles them: ⁶ "And I have anointed My King, || On Zion—My holy hill." ⁷ I declare concerning a statute: Yhwh said to me, "You [are] My Son, today I have brought You forth. ⁸ Ask of Me and I give nations [as] Your inheritance, || And the ends of the earth [for] Your possession. ⁹ You rule them with a scepter of iron, || You crush them as a vessel of a potter." ¹⁰ And now, O kings, act wisely, || Be instructed, O judges of earth, ¹¹ Serve Yhwh with fear, || And rejoice with trembling. ¹² Kiss the Chosen One [[*or* Son]], lest He is angry, || And you perish [from] the way, || When His anger burns but a little, || O the blessedness of all trusting in Him!

PSALM 3

¹ A Psalm of David, in his fleeing from the face of his son Absalom. Yhwh, how my distresses have multiplied! Many are rising up against me. ² Many are saying of my soul, "There is no salvation for him in God." Selah. ³ And You, O Yhwh, [are] a shield for me, || My glory, and lifter up of my head. ⁴ My voice [is] to Yhwh: I call and He answers me from His holy hill, Selah. ⁵ I have lain down, and I sleep, || I have awoken, for Yhwh sustains me. ⁶ I am not afraid of myriads of people, || That they have set against me all around. ⁷ Rise, O Yhwh! Save me, my God! For You have struck all my enemies [on] the cheek. You have broken the teeth of the wicked. ⁸ This salvation [is] of Yhwh; Your blessing [is] on Your people! Selah.

PSALM 4

¹ To the Overseer. With stringed instruments. A Psalm of David. In my calling answer me, || O God of my righteousness. In adversity You gave enlargement to me; Favor me, and hear my prayer. ² Sons of men! Until when [is] my glory for shame? You love a vain thing, you seek a lie. Selah. ³ And know that Yhwh || Has separated a saintly one to Himself. Yhwh hears in my calling to Him. ⁴ "Tremble, and do not sin"; Say [thus] in your heart on your bed, || And be silent. Selah. ⁵ Sacrifice sacrifices of righteousness, || And trust in Yhwh. ⁶ Many are saying, "Who shows us good?" Lift on us the light of Your face, O Yhwh, ⁷ You have given joy in my heart, || From the time

their grain and their wine || Have been multiplied. ⁸ Together I lie down and sleep in peace, || For You, O Yhwh, alone, || Cause me to dwell in confidence!

PSALM 5

¹ To the Overseer. [Blown] into the pipes. A Psalm of David. Hear my sayings, O Yhwh, || Consider my meditation. ² Be attentive to the voice of my cry, || My King and my God, || For I pray to You habitually. ³ Yhwh, [in] the morning You hear my voice, || [In] the morning I set in array for You, || And I look out [expectantly]. ⁴ For You [are] not a God desiring wickedness, || Evil does not inhabit You. ⁵ The boastful do not station themselves before Your eyes: You have hated all working iniquity. ⁶ You destroy those speaking lies, || Yhwh detests a man of blood and deceit. ⁷ And I, in the abundance of Your kindness, || I enter Your house, || I bow myself toward Your holy temple in Your fear. ⁸ O Yhwh, lead me in Your righteousness, || Because of those observing me, || Make Your way straight before me, ⁹ For there is no stability in their mouth. Their heart [is] mischiefs, || Their throat [is] an open grave, || They make their tongue smooth. ¹⁰ Declare them guilty, O God, || Let them fall from their own counsels, || In the abundance of their transgressions || Drive them away, || Because they have been rebellious against You. ¹¹ And all trusting in You rejoice, || They sing for all time, and You cover them over, || And those loving Your Name exult in You. ¹² For You bless the righteous, O Yhwh, || Surrounding him with favor as a buckler!

PSALM 6

¹ To the Overseer. With stringed instruments, on the eighth. A Psalm of David. O Yhwh, do not reprove me in Your anger, || Nor discipline me in Your fury. ² Favor me, O Yhwh, for I [am] weak, || Heal me, O Yhwh, || For my bones have been troubled, ³ And my soul has been troubled greatly, || And You, O Yhwh, until when? ⁴ Turn back, O Yhwh, draw out my soul, || Save me for Your kindness' sake. ⁵ For in death there is no memorial of You, || In Sheol, who gives thanks to You? ⁶ I have been weary with my sighing, || I meditate [on] my bed through all the night, || I dissolve my couch with my tear. ⁷ My eye is old from provocation, || It is old because of all my adversaries, ⁸ Turn from me all you workers of iniquity, || For Yhwh heard the voice of my weeping, ⁹ Yhwh has heard my supplication, || Yhwh receives my prayer. ¹⁰ All my enemies are greatly ashamed and troubled, || They turn back—ashamed [in] a moment!

PSALM 7

¹ A Shiggaion of David, that he sung to Yhwh concerning the words of Cush, a Benjamite. O Yhwh, my God, in You I have trusted, || Save me from all my pursuers, and deliver me. ² Lest he tear my soul as a lion, || Tearing, and there is no deliverer. ³ O Yhwh, my God, if I have done this, || If there is iniquity in my hands, ⁴ If I have done my well-wisher evil, || And draw my adversary without cause, ⁵ [Then] an enemy pursues my soul, and overtakes, || And treads down my life to the earth, || And places my glory in the dust. Selah. ⁶ Rise, O Yhwh, in Your anger, || Be lifted up at the wrath of my adversaries, || And awake Yourself for me. You have commanded judgment: ⁷ And a congregation of peoples surround You, || And over it turn back on high. ⁸ Yhwh judges the peoples; Judge me, O Yhwh, || According to my righteousness, || And according to my integrity [that is] on me. ⁹ Please let the evil of the wicked be ended, || And establish the righteous, || And a trier of hearts and reins is the righteous God. ¹⁰ My shield [is] on God, || Savior of the upright in heart! ¹¹ God [is] judging right, || And He is not angry at all times. ¹² If [one] does not turn, || He sharpens His sword, || He has bent His bow [and] He prepares it, ¹³ Indeed, He has prepared for Himself || Instruments of death, || He makes His arrows for burning pursuers. ¹⁴ Behold, he travails [with] iniquity, || And he has conceived perverseness, || And has brought forth falsehood. ¹⁵ He has prepared a pit, and he digs it, || And he falls into a ditch he makes ¹⁶ His perverseness returns on his

head, || And his violence comes down on his crown. ¹⁷ I thank Yhwh, || According to His righteousness, || And I praise the Name of Yhwh Most High!

PSALM 8

¹ To the Overseer. On the gittith. A Psalm of David. Yhwh, our Lord, || How majestic [is] Your Name in all the earth, || Who have set Your splendor on the heavens! ² From the mouths of infants and sucklings || You have founded strength, || Because of Your adversaries, || To still an enemy and a self-avenger. ³ For I see Your heavens, a work of Your fingers, || [The] moon and stars that You established. ⁴ What [is] man that You remember him? The son of man that You inspect him? ⁵ You make him a little lower than the gods [[or God]], || And surround him with glory and majesty. ⁶ You cause him to rule || Over the works of Your hands, || You have placed all under his feet. ⁷ Sheep and oxen, all of them, || And also beasts of the field, ⁸ Bird of the heavens, and fish of the sea, || Passing through the paths of the seas! ⁹ Yhwh, our Lord, || How majestic [is] Your Name in all the earth!

PSALM 9

¹ To the Overseer. [Set] on "Death of the Son." A Psalm of David. I confess, O Yhwh, with all my heart, || I recount all Your wonders, ² I rejoice and exult in You, || I praise Your Name, O Most High. ³ In my enemies turning backward, || They stumble and perish from Your face. ⁴ For You have done my judgment and my right. You have sat on a throne, || Judging [with] righteousness. ⁵ You have rebuked nations, || You have destroyed the wicked, || You have blotted out their name for all time and forever. ⁶ The enemy—[your] destructions have been completed forever, || As for cities you have plucked up, || Their memorial has perished with them. ⁷ And Yhwh abides for all time, || He is preparing His throne for judgment. ⁸ And He judges the world in righteousness, || He judges the peoples in uprightness. ⁹ And Yhwh is a tower for the bruised, || A tower for times of adversity. ¹⁰ They trust in You who know Your Name, || For You have not forsaken those seeking You, O Yhwh. ¹¹ Sing praise to Yhwh, inhabiting Zion, || Declare His acts among the peoples, ¹² For He who is seeking for blood || Has remembered them, || He has not forgotten the cry of the afflicted. ¹³ Favor me, O Yhwh, || See my affliction by those hating me, || You who lift me up from the gates of death, ¹⁴ So that I recount all Your praise, || In the gates of the daughter of Zion. I rejoice on Your salvation. ¹⁵ Nations have sunk in a pit they made, || Their foot has been captured in a net that they hid. ¹⁶ Yhwh has been known, || He has done judgment; By a work of his hands || The wicked has been snared. Meditation. Selah. ¹⁷ The wicked turn back to Sheol, || All nations forgetting God. ¹⁸ For the needy is not forgotten forever, || [Nor] the hope of the humble lost for all time. ¹⁹ Rise, O Yhwh, do not let man be strong, || Let nations be judged before Your face. ²⁰ Appoint them to fear, O Yhwh, || Let nations know they [are] men! Selah.

PSALM 10

¹ Why, Yhwh, do You stand at a distance? Do You hide in times of adversity? ² Through the pride of the wicked, || Is the poor inflamed, || They are caught in schemes that they devised. ³ Because the wicked has boasted || Of the desire of his soul, || And he has blessed a dishonest gainer, || He has despised Yhwh. ⁴ The wicked does not inquire according to the height of his face. "There is no God!" [are] all his schemes. ⁵ His ways writhe at all times, || Your judgments [are] on high before him, || All his adversaries—he puffs at them. ⁶ He has said in his heart, "I am not moved, || [And am] not in calamity to generation and generation." ⁷ His mouth is full of oaths, || And deceits, and fraud: Under his tongue [is] perverseness and iniquity, ⁸ He sits in an ambush of the villages, || He slays the innocent in secret places. His eyes secretly watch for the afflicted, ⁹ He lies in wait in a secret place, as a lion in a covert. He lies in wait to catch the poor, || He catches the poor, drawing him into his net. ¹⁰ He is bruised—he bows down, || The afflicted has fallen by his mighty ones. ¹¹ He said in his

heart, "God has forgotten, || He has hid His face, || He has never seen." ¹² Arise, O Yhwh! O God, lift up Your hand! Do not forget the humble. ¹³ Why has the wicked despised God? He has said in his heart, "It is not required." ¹⁴ You have seen, || For You behold perverseness and anger; By giving into Your hand, || The afflicted leave [it] on You, || You have been a helper of the fatherless. ¹⁵ Break the arm of the wicked and the evil, || Seek out his wickedness, find none; ¹⁶ Yhwh [is] King for all time and forever, || The nations have perished out of His land! ¹⁷ You have heard the desire of the humble, O Yhwh. You prepare their heart; You cause Your ear to attend, ¹⁸ To judge the fatherless and bruised: He adds no more to oppress—man of the earth!

PSALM 11

¹ To the Overseer. By David. In Yhwh I trusted, how do you say to my soul, "They moved to your mountain [as] the bird?" ² For behold, the wicked bend a bow, || They have prepared their arrow on the string, || To shoot in darkness at the upright in heart. ³ When the foundations are destroyed, || The righteous—what has he done? ⁴ Yhwh [is] in His holy temple: Yhwh—His throne [is] in the heavens. His eyes see—His eyelids try the sons of men. ⁵ Yhwh tries the righteous. And the wicked and the lover of violence, || His soul has hated, ⁶ He pours on the wicked snares, fire, and brimstone, || And a horrible wind [is] the portion of their cup. ⁷ For Yhwh [is] righteous, || He has loved righteousness, || His countenance sees the upright!

PSALM 12

¹ To the Overseer. On the eighth. A Psalm of David. Save, Yhwh, for the saintly has failed, || For the steadfast have ceased || From the sons of men: ² They each speak vanity with his neighbor, || Lip of flattery! With heart and heart they speak. ³ Yhwh cuts off all lips of flattery, || A tongue speaking great things, ⁴ Who said, "By our tongue we do mightily: Our lips [are] our own; who [is] lord over us?" ⁵ Because of the spoiling of the poor, || Because of the groaning of the needy, || Now I arise, says Yhwh, || I set in safety [him who] breathes for it. ⁶ Sayings of Yhwh [are] pure sayings—Silver tried in a furnace of earth, refined sevenfold. ⁷ You, O Yhwh, preserve them, || You keep us from this generation for all time. ⁸ The wicked walk around continually, || According as vileness is exalted by sons of men!

PSALM 13

¹ To the Overseer. A Psalm of David. Until when, O Yhwh, || Do You forget me forever? Until when do You hide Your face from me? ² Until when do I set counsels in my soul, || [With] sorrow in my heart daily? Until when is my enemy exalted over me? ³ Look attentively; Answer me, O Yhwh, my God, || Enlighten my eyes, lest I sleep in death, ⁴ Lest my enemy say, "I overcame him," || My adversaries rejoice when I am moved. ⁵ And I have trusted in Your kindness, || My heart rejoices in Your salvation. ⁶ I sing to Yhwh, || For He has conferred benefits on me!

PSALM 14

¹ To the Overseer. By David. A fool has said in his heart, "There is no God"; They have done corruptly, || They have done abominable actions, || There is not a doer of good. ² Yhwh has looked from the heavens on the sons of men, || To see if there is a wise one—seeking God. ³ The whole have turned aside, || Together they have been filthy: There is not a doer of good, not even one. ⁴ Have all working iniquity not known? Those consuming my people have eaten bread, || They have not called Yhwh. ⁵ They have feared a fear there, || For God [is] in the generation of the righteous. ⁶ You cause the counsel of the poor to stink, || Because Yhwh [is] his refuge. ⁷ "Who gives the salvation of Israel from Zion?" When Yhwh turns back || [To] a captivity of His people, || Jacob rejoices—Israel is glad!

PSALM 15

[1] A Psalm of David. Yhwh, who sojourns in Your tent? Who dwells in Your holy hill? [2] He who is walking uprightly, || And working righteousness, || And speaking truth in his heart. [3] He has not slandered by his tongue, || He has not done evil to his friend; And he has not lifted up reproach || Against his neighbor. [4] A rejected one [is] despised in his eyes, || And he honors those fearing Yhwh. He has sworn to endure evil, and does not change; [5] He has not given his silver in usury, || And has not taken a bribe against the innocent; Whoever is doing these is not moved for all time!

PSALM 16

[1] A Miktam of David. Preserve me, O God, for I trusted in You. [2] You have said to Yhwh, "You [are] my Lord"; My goodness [is] not above You; [3] For the holy ones who [are] in the land, || And the honorable, all my delight [is] in them. [4] Their griefs are multiplied, [who] have hurried backward; I do not pour out their drink-offerings of blood, || Nor do I take up their names on my lips. [5] Yhwh [is] the portion of my share, and of my cup, || You uphold my lot. [6] Lines have fallen to me in pleasant places, || Indeed, a beautiful inheritance [is] for me. [7] I bless Yhwh who has counseled me; Also [in] the nights my reins instruct me. [8] I placed Yhwh before me continually, || Because [He is] at my right hand I am not moved. [9] Therefore my heart has been glad, || And my glory rejoices, || Also my flesh dwells confidently: [10] For You do not leave my soul to Sheol, || Nor give your Holy One to see corruption. [11] You cause me to know the path of life; In Your presence [is] fullness of joys, || Pleasant things [are] by Your right hand forever!

PSALM 17

[1] A Prayer of David. Hear, O Yhwh, righteousness, attend my cry, || Give ear [to] my prayer, without lips of deceit. [2] My judgment goes out from before You; Your eyes see uprightly. [3] You have proved my heart, || You have inspected by night, || You have tried me, You find nothing; My thoughts do not pass over my mouth. [4] As for doings of man, || Through a word of Your lips I have observed || The paths of a destroyer; [5] To uphold my goings in Your paths, || My steps have not slipped. [6] I called You, for You answer me, || O God, incline Your ear to me, hear my speech. [7] Separate Your kindness wonderfully, O Savior of the confiding, || By Your right hand, from withstanders. [8] Keep me as the apple, the daughter of the eye; Hide me in the shadow of Your wings, [9] From the face of the wicked who spoiled me, || [From] my enemies in soul who go around against me. [10] They have closed up their fat, || Their mouths have spoken with pride: [11] "Our steps have now surrounded [him]"; They set their eyes to turn aside in the land. [12] His likeness as a lion desirous to tear, || As a young lion dwelling in secret places. [13] Arise, O Yhwh, go before his face, || Cause him to bend. Deliver my soul from the wicked, Your sword, [14] From men, Your hand, O Yhwh, || From men of the world, their portion [is] in life, || And [with] Your hidden things You fill their belly, || They are satisfied [with] sons, || And have left their abundance to their sucklings. [15] I—in righteousness, || I see Your face; I am satisfied, in awaking, [with] Your form!

PSALM 18

[1] To the Overseer. By a servant of Yhwh, by David, who has spoken to Yhwh the words of this song in the day Yhwh delivered him from the hand of all his enemies, and from the hand of Saul, and he says: I love You, O Yhwh, my strength. [2] Yhwh [is] my rock, and my bulwark, || And my deliverer, || My God [is] my rock, || I trust in Him: My shield, and the horn of my salvation, || My high tower. [3] I call on Yhwh, the Praised One, || And I am saved from my enemies. [4] Cords of death have surrounded me, || And streams of the worthless make me afraid. [5] Cords of Sheol have surrounded me, || Snares of death have been before me. [6] In my adversity I call Yhwh, ||

And I cry to my God. He hears my voice from His temple, || And My cry comes into His ears before Him. [7] And the earth shakes and trembles, || And foundations of hills are troubled, || And they shake—because He has wrath. [8] Smoke has gone up from His nostrils, || And fire from His mouth consumes, || Coals have been kindled by it. [9] And He inclines the heavens, and comes down, || And thick darkness [is] under His feet. [10] And He rides on a cherub, and flies, || And He flies on wings of wind. [11] He makes darkness His secret place, || Around Him His dwelling place, || Darkness of waters, thick clouds of the skies. [12] From the brightness before Him His thick clouds have passed on, || Hail and coals of fire. [13] And Yhwh thunders in the heavens, || And the Most High gives forth His voice, || Hail and coals of fire. [14] And He sends His arrows and scatters them, || And much lightning, and crushes them. [15] And the streams of waters are seen, || And foundations of the earth are revealed, || From Your rebuke, O Yhwh, || From the breath of the wind of Your anger. [16] He sends from above—He takes me, || He draws me out of many waters. [17] He delivers me from my strong enemy, || And from those hating me, || For they have been stronger than I. [18] They go before me in a day of my calamity || And Yhwh is for a support to me. [19] And He brings me forth to a large place, || He draws me out, because He delighted in me. [20] Yhwh repays me || According to my righteousness, || According to the cleanness of my hands, || He returns to me. [21] For I have kept the ways of Yhwh, || And have not done wickedly against my God. [22] For all His judgments [are] before me, || And I do not turn His statutes from me. [23] And I am perfect with Him, || And I keep myself from my iniquity. [24] And Yhwh returns to me, || According to my righteousness, || According to the cleanness of my hands, || Before His eyes. [25] With the kind You show Yourself kind, || With a perfect man You show Yourself perfect. [26] With the pure You show Yourself pure, || And with the perverse You show Yourself a wrestler, [27] For You save a poor people, || And cause the eyes of the high to fall. [28] For You light my lamp, || My God Yhwh enlightens my darkness. [29] For by You I run [against] a troop! And by my God I leap a wall. [30] God—perfect [is] His way, || The saying of Yhwh is tried, || He [is] a shield to all those trusting in Him. [31] For who [is] God besides Yhwh? And who [is] a rock except our God? [32] God—who is girding me [with] strength, || And He makes my way perfect. [33] Making my feet like does, || And on my high places causes me to stand. [34] Teaching my hands for battle, || And a bow of bronze was brought down by my arms. [35] And You give to me the shield of Your salvation, || And Your right hand supports me, || And Your lowliness makes me great. [36] You enlarge my step under me, || And my ankles have not slipped. [37] I pursue my enemies, and overtake them, || And do not turn back until they are consumed. [38] I strike them, and they are not able to rise, || They fall under my feet, [39] And You gird me [with] strength for battle, || You cause my withstanders to bow under me. [40] As for my enemies—You have given to me the neck, || As for those hating me—I cut them off. [41] They cry, and there is no savior, || On Yhwh, and He does not answer them. [42] And I beat them as dust before wind, || I empty them out as mire of the streets. [43] You deliver me || From the strivings of the people, || You place me for a head of nations, || A people I have not known serve me. [44] At the hearing of the ear they listen to me, || Sons of a stranger feign obedience to me, [45] Sons of a stranger fade away, || And are slain out of their close places. [46] Yhwh lives—and blessed [is] my rock, || And exalted is the God of my salvation. [47] God—who is giving vengeance to me, || And He subdues peoples under me, [48] My deliverer from my enemies, || You raise me above my withstanders, || Deliver me from a man of violence. [49] Therefore I confess You among nations, O Yhwh, || And I sing praise to Your Name, [50] Magnifying the salvation of His king, || And doing kindness to His anointed, || To David, and to his seed—for all time!

PSALM 19

[1] To the Overseer. A Psalm of David. The heavens [are] recounting the glory of God, || And the expanse [is] declaring the work of His hands. [2] Day to day utters speech, || And night to night shows knowledge. [3] There is no speech, and there are no words. Their voice has not been heard. [4] Their line has gone forth into all the earth, || And their sayings to the end of the world, || In them He placed a tent for the sun, [5] And he, as a bridegroom, goes out from his covering, || He rejoices as a mighty one || To run the path. [6] From the end of the heavens

[is] his going out, || And his revolution [is] to their ends, || And nothing is hid from his heat. ⁷ The law of Yhwh [is] perfect, refreshing the soul, || The testimonies of Yhwh [are] steadfast, || Making the simple wise, ⁸ The precepts of Yhwh [are] upright, || Rejoicing the heart, || The command of Yhwh [is] pure, enlightening the eyes, ⁹ The fear of Yhwh [is] clean, standing for all time, || The judgments of Yhwh [are] true, || They have been righteous—together. ¹⁰ They are more desirable than gold, || Indeed, than much fine gold; and sweeter than honey, || Even liquid honey of the comb. ¹¹ Also— Your servant is warned by them, "In keeping them [is] a great reward." ¹² [His] errors—who understands? Declare me innocent from hidden ones, ¹³ Also—keep back Your servant from presumptuous ones, || Do not let them rule over me, || Then I am perfect, || And declared innocent of much transgression. ¹⁴ Let the sayings of my mouth, || And the meditation of my heart, || Be for a pleasing thing before You, || O Yhwh, my rock, and my redeemer!

PSALM 20

¹ To the Overseer. A Psalm of David. Yhwh answers you, || In a day of adversity, || The Name of the God of Jacob sets you on high, ² He sends your help from the sanctuary, || And supports you from Zion, ³ He remembers all your presents, || And reduces your burnt-offering to ashes. Selah. ⁴ He gives to you according to your heart, || And fulfills all your counsel. ⁵ We sing of Your salvation, || And in the Name of our God set up a banner. Yhwh fulfills all your requests. ⁶ Now I have known || That Yhwh has saved His anointed, || He answers him from His holy heavens, || With the saving might of His right hand. ⁷ Some of chariots, and some of horses, || And we of the Name of our God Yhwh || Make mention. ⁸ They have bowed and have fallen, || And we have risen and station ourselves upright. ⁹ O Yhwh, save the king, || He answers us in the day we call!

PSALM 21

¹ To the Overseer. A Psalm of David. Yhwh, the king is joyful in Your strength, || How greatly he rejoices in Your salvation. ² You gave the desire of his heart to him, || And You have not withheld the request of his lips. Selah. ³ For You put blessings of goodness before him, || You set a crown of fine gold on his head. ⁴ He has asked for life from You, || You have given length of days to him, || For all time and forever. ⁵ Great [is] his glory in Your salvation, || You place splendor and majesty on him. ⁶ For You make him blessings forever, || You cause him to rejoice with joy, || By Your countenance. ⁷ For the king is trusting in Yhwh, || And in the kindness of the Most High he is not moved. ⁸ Your hand comes to all Your enemies, || Your right hand finds Your haters. ⁹ You make them as a furnace of fire, || At the time of Your presence. Yhwh swallows them in His anger, || And fire devours them. ¹⁰ You destroy their fruit from earth, || And their seed from the sons of men. ¹¹ For they stretched out evil against You, || They devised a wicked scheme, they do not prevail, ¹² For You make them turn their back, || When You prepare Your strings against their faces. ¹³ Be exalted, O Yhwh, in Your strength, || We sing and we praise Your might!

PSALM 22

¹ To the Overseer. [Set] on "Doe of the Morning." A Psalm of David. My God, My God, why have You forsaken Me? Far from My salvation, || The words of My roaring? ² My God, I call by day, and You do not answer, || And by night, and am not silent. ³ And You [are] holy, || Sitting—the Praise of Israel. ⁴ In You our fathers trusted; They trusted, and You deliver them. ⁵ To You they cried, and were delivered, || In You they trusted, and were not disappointed. ⁶ And I [am] a worm, and no man, || A reproach of man, and despised of the people. ⁷ All beholding Me mock at Me, || They make free with the lip— shake the head, ⁸ "Roll to Yhwh, He delivers Him, || He delivers Him, for He delighted in Him." ⁹ For You [are] He bringing Me forth from the womb, || Causing Me to trust, || On the breasts of My mother. ¹⁰ On You I have been cast from the womb, || From the belly of My mother You [are] My God. ¹¹ Do not be far from Me, || For adversity is near, for there is no helper. ¹² Many

bulls have surrounded Me, || Mighty ones of Bashan have surrounded Me, ¹³ They have opened their mouth against Me, || A lion tearing and roaring. ¹⁴ I have been poured out as waters, || And all my bones have separated themselves, || My heart has been like wax, || It is melted in the midst of My bowels. ¹⁵ My power is dried up as an earthen vessel, || And My tongue is cleaving to My jaws. ¹⁶ And You appoint Me to the dust of death, || For dogs have surrounded Me, || A company of evildoers has surrounded Me, || Piercing My hands and My feet. ¹⁷ I count all My bones—they look expectingly, || They look on Me, ¹⁸ They apportion My garments to themselves, || And they cause a lot to fall for My clothing. ¹⁹ And You, O Yhwh, do not be far off, || O My strength, hurry to help Me. ²⁰ Deliver My soul from the sword, || My only one from the paw of a dog. ²¹ Save Me from the mouth of a lion || And You have answered Me from the horns of the high places! ²² I declare Your Name to My brothers, || In the midst of the assembly I praise You. ²³ You who fear Yhwh, praise Him, || All the seed of Jacob, honor Him, || And be afraid of Him, all you seed of Israel. ²⁴ For He has not despised, nor detested, || The affliction of the afflicted, || Nor has He hidden His face from Him, || And in His crying to Him He hears. ²⁵ Of You My praise [is] in the great assembly. I complete My vows before His fearers. ²⁶ The humble eat and are satisfied, || Those seeking Him praise Yhwh, || Your heart lives forever. ²⁷ Remember and return to Yhwh, || Do all the ends of the earth, || And bow themselves before You, || Do all families of the nations, ²⁸ For to Yhwh [is] the kingdom, || And He is ruling among nations. ²⁹ And the fat ones of earth have eaten, || And they bow themselves, || All going down to dust bow before Him, || And he [who] has not revived his soul. ³⁰ A seed serves Him, || It is declared of the Lord to the generation. ³¹ They come and declare His righteousness, || To a people that is born, that He has made!

PSALM 23

¹ A Psalm of David. Yhwh [is] my shepherd, I do not lack, ² He causes me to lie down in pastures of tender grass, || He leads me by quiet waters. ³ He refreshes my soul, || He leads me in paths of righteousness || For His Name's sake; ⁴ Also— when I walk in a valley of death-shade, || I fear no evil, for You [are] with me, || Your rod and Your staff—they comfort me. ⁵ You arrange a table before me, || In front of my adversaries, || You have anointed my head with oil, || My cup is full! ⁶ Surely goodness and kindness pursue me || All the days of my life, || And my dwelling [is] in the house of Yhwh, || For [the] length of [my] days!

PSALM 24

¹ A Psalm of David. To Yhwh [is] the earth and its fullness, || The world and the inhabitants in it. ² For He has founded it on the seas, || And He establishes it on the floods. ³ Who goes up into the hill of Yhwh? And who rises up in His holy place? ⁴ The clean of hands, and pure of heart, || Who has not lifted up his soul to vanity, || Nor has sworn to deceit. ⁵ He carries away a blessing from Yhwh, || Righteousness from the God of his salvation. ⁶ This [is] a generation of those seeking Him. Seeking Your face, O Jacob! Selah. ⁷ Lift up your heads, O gates! And be lifted up, O perpetual doors! And the King of Glory comes in! ⁸ Who [is] this—"the King of Glory?" Yhwh— strong and mighty, || Yhwh, the mighty in battle. ⁹ Lift up your heads, O gates! And be lifted up, O perpetual doors! And the King of Glory comes in! ¹⁰ Who [is] He—this "King of Glory?" Yhwh of hosts—He [is] the King of Glory! Selah.

PSALM 25

¹ By David. [Aleph-Bet] To You, O Yhwh, I lift up my soul. ² My God, in You I have trusted, || Do not let me be ashamed, || Do not let my enemies exult over me. ³ Also let none waiting on You be ashamed, || Let the treacherous dealers without cause be ashamed. ⁴ Your ways, O Yhwh, cause me to know, || You teach me Your paths. ⁵ Cause me to tread in Your truth, and teach me, || For You [are] the God of my salvation, || Near You I have waited all the day. ⁶ Remember Your mercies, O Yhwh, || And Your kindnesses, for they [are] from the age. ⁷

Sins of my youth, and my transgressions, || Do not remember. According to Your kindness be mindful of me, || For Your goodness' sake, O Yhwh. [8] Good and upright [is] Yhwh, || Therefore He directs sinners in the way. [9] He causes the humble to tread in judgment, || And teaches the humble His way. [10] All the paths of Yhwh [are] kindness and truth, || To those keeping His covenant, || And His testimonies. [11] For Your Name's sake, O Yhwh, || You have pardoned my iniquity, for it [is] great. [12] Who [is] this—the man fearing Yhwh? He directs him in the way He chooses. [13] His soul remains in good, || And his seed possesses the land. [14] The secret of Yhwh [is] for those fearing Him, || And His covenant—to cause them to know. [15] My eyes [are] continually to Yhwh, || For He brings my feet out from a net. [16] Turn to me, and favor me, || For I [am] lonely and afflicted. [17] The distresses of my heart have enlarged themselves, || Bring me out from my distresses. [18] See my affliction and my misery, || And bear with all my sins. [19] See my enemies, for they have been many, || And they have hated me with violent hatred. [20] Keep my soul, and deliver me, || Do not let me be ashamed, for I trusted in You. [21] Integrity and uprightness keep me, || For I have waited [on] You. [22] Redeem Israel, O God, from all his distresses!

PSALM 26

[1] By David. Judge me, O Yhwh, for I have walked in my integrity, || And I have trusted in Yhwh, || I do not slide. [2] Try me, O Yhwh, and prove me, || My reins and my heart [are] purified, [3] For Your kindness [is] before my eyes, || And I have habitually walked in Your truth. [4] I have not sat with vain men, || And I do not enter with pretenders. [5] I have hated the assembly of evildoers, || And I do not sit with the wicked. [6] I wash my hands in innocence, || And I go around Your altar, O Yhwh. [7] To sound with a voice of confession, || And to recount all Your wonders. [8] Yhwh, I have loved the habitation of Your house, || And the place of the Dwelling Place of Your glory. [9] Do not gather my soul with sinners, || And my life with men of blood, [10] In whose hand [is] a wicked scheme, || And their right hand [is] full of bribes. [11] And I walk in my integrity, || Redeem me, and favor me. [12] My foot has stood in uprightness, || In assemblies I bless Yhwh!

PSALM 27

[1] By David. Yhwh [is] my light and my salvation, || Whom do I fear? Yhwh [is] the strength of my life, || Of whom am I afraid? [2] When evildoers come near to me to eat my flesh, || My adversaries and my enemies to me, || They have stumbled and fallen. [3] Though a host encamps against me, || My heart does not fear, || Though war rises up against me, || In this I [am] confident. [4] One [thing] I asked of Yhwh—it I seek: My dwelling in the house of Yhwh, || All the days of my life, || To look on the pleasantness of Yhwh, || And to inquire in His temple. [5] For He hides me in a dwelling place in the day of evil, || He hides me in a secret place of His tent, || He raises me up on a rock. [6] And now my head is lifted up, || Above my enemies—my surrounders, || And I sacrifice in His tent sacrifices of shouting, || I sing, indeed, I sing praise to Yhwh. [7] Hear, O Yhwh, my voice—I call, || And favor me, and answer me. [8] My heart said to You, "They sought my face, || Your face, O Yhwh, I seek." [9] Do not hide Your face from me, || Do not turn Your servant aside in anger, || You have been my help. Do not leave me, nor forsake me, || O God of my salvation. [10] When my father and my mother || Have forsaken me, then Yhwh gathers me. [11] Show me, O Yhwh, Your way, || And lead me in a path of uprightness, || For the sake of my beholders. [12] Do not give me to the will of my adversaries, || For false witnesses have risen against me, || And they breathe out violence to me. [13] I had not believed to look on the goodness of Yhwh || In the land of the living! [14] Look to Yhwh—be strong, || And He strengthens your heart, || Indeed, look to Yhwh!

PSALM 28

[1] By David. To You, O Yhwh, I call, || My rock, do not be silent to me! Lest You are silent to me, || And I have been compared || With those going down to the pit. [2] Hear the voice of my supplications, || In my crying to You, || In my lifting up my hands toward your holy oracle. [3] Do not draw me with the wicked, || And with workers of iniquity, || Speaking peace with their neighbors, || And evil in their heart. [4] Give to them according to their acting, || And according to the evil of their doings. Give to them according to the work of their hands. Return their deed to them. [5] For they do not attend to the doing of Yhwh, || And to the work of His hands. He throws them down, || And does not build them up. [6] Blessed [is] Yhwh, || For He has heard the voice of my supplications. [7] Yhwh [is] my strength, and my shield, || In Him my heart trusted, and I have been helped. And my heart exults, || And I thank Him with my song. [8] Yhwh [is] strength to him, || Indeed, the strength of the salvation of His anointed [is] He. [9] Save Your people, and bless Your inheritance, || And feed them, and carry them for all time!

PSALM 29

[1] A Psalm of David. Ascribe to Yhwh, you sons of the mighty, || Ascribe to Yhwh glory and strength. [2] Ascribe to Yhwh the glory of His Name, || Bow yourselves to Yhwh, || In the beauty of holiness. [3] The voice of Yhwh [is] on the waters, || The God of glory has thundered, || Yhwh [is] on many waters. [4] The voice of Yhwh [is] with power, || The voice of Yhwh [is] with majesty, [5] The voice of Yhwh [is] shattering cedars, || Indeed, Yhwh shatters the cedars of Lebanon. [6] And He causes them to skip as a calf, || Lebanon and Sirion as a son of Reems, [7] The voice of Yhwh is hewing fiery flames, [8] The voice of Yhwh pains a wilderness, || Yhwh pains the wilderness of Kadesh. [9] The voice of Yhwh pains the oaks, || And makes bare the forests, || And in His temple everyone says, "Glory!" [10] Yhwh has sat on the flood, || And Yhwh sits [as] king for all time, [11] Yhwh gives strength to His people, || Yhwh blesses His people with peace!

PSALM 30

[1] A Psalm. A Song of the dedication of the house of David. I exalt You, O Yhwh, || For You have drawn me up, || And have not let my enemies rejoice over me. [2] My God Yhwh, I have cried to You, || And You heal me. [3] Yhwh, You have brought up my soul from Sheol, || You have kept me alive, || From going down [to] the pit. [4] Sing praise to Yhwh, you His saints, || And give thanks at the remembrance of His holiness, [5] For—a moment [is] in His anger, || Life [is] in His goodwill, || At evening remains weeping, and at morning singing. [6] And I have said in my ease, "I am not moved for all time. [7] O Yhwh, in Your good pleasure, || You have caused strength to remain for my mountain," || You have hidden Your face—I have been troubled. [8] To You, O Yhwh, I call, || And to Yhwh I make supplication. [9] "What gain [is] in my blood? In my going down to corruption? Does dust thank You? Does it declare Your truth? [10] Hear, O Yhwh, and favor me, O Yhwh, be a helper to me." [11] You have turned my mourning to dancing for me, || You have loosed my sackcloth, || And gird me [with] joy. [12] So that glory praises You, and is not silent, || O Yhwh, my God, I thank You for all time!

PSALM 31

[1] To the Overseer. A Psalm of David. In You, O Yhwh, I have trusted, || Do not let me be ashamed for all time, || In Your righteousness deliver me. [2] Incline Your ear to me quickly, deliver me, || Be to me for a strong rock, || For a house of bulwarks to save me. [3] For You [are] my rock and my bulwark, || For Your Name's sake lead me and tend me. [4] Bring me out from the net that they hid for me, || For You [are] my strength. [5] Into Your hand I commit my spirit, || You have redeemed me, Yhwh God of truth. [6] I have hated the observers of lying vanities, || And I have been confident toward Yhwh. [7] I rejoice, and am glad in Your kindness, || In that You have seen my affliction, || You have known my soul in adversities. [8] And You have not shut me up, || Into the hand of an enemy, || You have caused my feet to stand in a broad place. [9] Favor me, O Yhwh, for distress [is] to me, || My eye, my soul, and my body || Have become old by provocation. [10] For my life has been

consumed in sorrow || And my years in sighing. My strength has been feeble because of my iniquity, || And my bones have become old. ¹¹ I have been a reproach among all my adversaries, || And to my neighbors exceedingly, || And a fear to my acquaintances, || Those seeing me without—fled from me. ¹² I have been forgotten as dead, out of mind, || I have been as a perishing vessel. ¹³ For I have heard an evil account of many, || Fear [is] all around. In their being united against me, || They have devised to take my life, ¹⁴ And I have trusted on You, || O Yhwh, I have said, "You [are] my God." ¹⁵ In Your hand [are] my times, || Deliver me from the hand of my enemies, || And from my pursuers. ¹⁶ Cause Your face to shine on Your servant, || Save me in Your kindness. ¹⁷ O Yhwh, do not let me be ashamed, || For I have called You, let the wicked be ashamed, || Let them become silent to Sheol. ¹⁸ Let lips of falsehood become mute, || That are speaking against the righteous, || Ancient sayings, in pride and contempt. ¹⁹ How abundant is Your goodness, || That You have laid up for those fearing You, || You have worked for those trusting in You, || Before sons of men. ²⁰ You hide them in the secret place of Your presence, || From schemes of man, || You conceal them in a dwelling place, || From the strife of tongues. ²¹ Blessed [is] Yhwh, || For He has made His kindness marvelous || To me in a city of bulwarks. ²² And I have said in my haste, "I have been cut off from before Your eyes," || But You have heard the voice of my supplications, || In my crying to You. ²³ Love Yhwh, all you His saints, || Yhwh is keeping the faithful, || And repaying a proud doer abundantly. ²⁴ Be strong, and He strengthens your heart, || All you who are waiting for Yhwh!

PSALM 32

¹ An Instruction of David. O the blessedness of him whose transgression [is] forgiven, || Whose sin is covered. ² O the blessedness of a man, || To whom Yhwh does not impute iniquity, || And in whose spirit there is no deceit. ³ When I have kept silence, my bones have become old, || Through my roaring all the day. ⁴ When by day and by night Your hand is heavy on me, || My moisture has been changed || Into the droughts of summer. Selah. ⁵ I cause You to know my sin, || And I have not covered my iniquity. I have said, "I confess to Yhwh concerning My transgressions," || And You have taken away the iniquity of my sin. Selah. ⁶ For every saintly one prays this to You, || In the time to find [You]. Surely at an overflowing of many waters, || They do not come to him. ⁷ You [are] a hiding place for me, || You keep me from distress, || Surround me [with] songs of deliverance. Selah. ⁸ I cause you to act wisely, || And direct you in the way that you go, || I cause My eye to take counsel concerning you. ⁹ Do not be as a horse—as a mule, || Without understanding, || With bridle and bit, its ornaments, to curb, || Not to come near to you. ¹⁰ Many [are] the pains of the wicked; As for him who is trusting in Yhwh, || Kindness surrounds him. ¹¹ Be glad in Yhwh, and rejoice, you righteous, || And sing, all you upright of heart!

PSALM 33

¹ Sing, you righteous, in Yhwh, || [For] praise from upright ones [is] lovely. ² Give thanks to Yhwh with a harp, || With stringed instrument of ten strings sing praise to Him, ³ Sing to Him a new song, || Play skillfully with shouting. ⁴ For the word of Yhwh [is] upright, || And all His work [is] in faithfulness. ⁵ Loving righteousness and judgment, || The earth is full of the kindness of Yhwh. ⁶ By the word of Yhwh || The heavens have been made, || And all their host by the breath of His mouth. ⁷ Gathering the waters of the sea as a heap, || Putting the depths in treasuries. ⁸ All the earth is afraid of Yhwh, || All the inhabitants of the world are afraid of Him. ⁹ For He has spoken, and it is, || He has commanded, and it stands. ¹⁰ Yhwh made void the counsel of nations, || He disallowed the thoughts of the peoples. ¹¹ The counsel of Yhwh stands for all time, || The thoughts of His heart from generation to generation. ¹² O the blessedness of the nation whose God [is] Yhwh, || Of the people He chose, || For an inheritance to Him. ¹³ Yhwh has looked from the heavens, || He has seen all the sons of men. ¹⁴ From the fixed place of His dwelling, || He looked to all inhabitants of the earth; ¹⁵ Who is forming their hearts together, || Who is attending to all their works. ¹⁶ The king is not saved by the multitude of a force. A mighty man is not

delivered, || By abundance of power. ¹⁷ A false thing [is] the horse for safety, || And he does not deliver || By the abundance of his strength. ¹⁸ Behold, the eye of Yhwh [is] to those fearing Him, || To those waiting for His kindness, ¹⁹ To deliver their soul from death, || And to keep them alive in famine. ²⁰ Our soul has waited for Yhwh, || He [is] our help and our shield, ²¹ For our heart rejoices in Him, || For we have trusted in His Holy Name. ²² Let Your kindness, O Yhwh, be on us, || As we have waited for You!

PSALM 34

¹ By David, in his changing his behavior before Abimelech, and he drives him away, and he goes. [Aleph-Bet] I bless Yhwh at all times, || His praise [is] continually in my mouth. ² In Yhwh my soul boasts herself, || The humble hear and rejoice. ³ Ascribe greatness to Yhwh with me, || And we exalt His Name together. ⁴ I sought Yhwh, and He answered me, || And delivered me from all my fears. ⁵ They looked expectingly to Him, || And they became bright, || And their faces are not ashamed. ⁶ This poor [one] called, and Yhwh heard, || And saved him from all his distresses. ⁷ A messenger of Yhwh is encamping, || Around those who fear Him, || And He arms them. ⁸ Taste and see that Yhwh [is] good, || O the blessedness of the man who trusts in Him. ⁹ Fear Yhwh, you His holy ones, || For there is no lack to those fearing Him. ¹⁰ Young lions have lacked and been hungry, || And those seeking Yhwh do not lack any good, ¹¹ Come, children, listen to me, || I teach you the fear of Yhwh. ¹² Who [is] the man that is desiring life? Loving days to see good? ¹³ Keep your tongue from evil, || And your lips from speaking deceit. ¹⁴ Turn aside from evil and do good, || Seek peace and pursue it. ¹⁵ The eyes of Yhwh [are] to the righteous, || And His ears to their cry. ¹⁶ (The face of Yhwh [is] on doers of evil, || To cut off their memorial from earth.) ¹⁷ They cried, and Yhwh heard, || And delivered them from all their distresses. ¹⁸ Yhwh [is] near to the broken of heart, || And He saves the bruised of spirit. ¹⁹ Many [are] the afflictions of the righteous, || Yhwh delivers him out of them all. ²⁰ He is keeping all his bones, || Not one of them has been broken. ²¹ Evil puts the wicked to death, || And those hating the righteous are desolate. ²² Yhwh redeems the soul of His servants, || And none trusting in Him are desolate!

PSALM 35

¹ By David. Strive, Yhwh, with my strivers, fight with my fighters, ² Take hold of shield and buckler, and rise for my help, ³ And draw out spear and lance, || To meet my pursuers. Say to my soul, "I [am] your salvation." ⁴ They are ashamed and blush, those seeking my soul, || Turned backward and confounded, || Those devising my evil. ⁵ They are as chaff before wind, || And a messenger of Yhwh driving away. ⁶ Their way is darkness and slipperiness, || And a messenger of Yhwh—their pursuer. ⁷ For without cause they hid their net [in] a pit for me, || Without cause they dug for my soul. ⁸ Desolation meets him—he does not know, || And his net that he hid catches him, || He falls into it for desolation. ⁹ And my soul is joyful in Yhwh, || It rejoices in His salvation. ¹⁰ All my bones say, "Yhwh, who is like You, || Delivering the poor from the [one] stronger than he, || And the poor and needy from his plunderer." ¹¹ Violent witnesses rise up, || That which I have not known they ask me. ¹² They pay me evil for good, bereaving my soul, ¹³ And I—in their sickness my clothing [is] sackcloth, || I have humbled my soul with fastings, || And my prayer returns to my bosom. ¹⁴ As [if] a friend, as [if] my brother, || I habitually walked, || As a mourner for a mother, || I have bowed down mourning. ¹⁵ And they have rejoiced in my halting, || And have been gathered together, || The strikers were gathered against me, || And I have not known; || They have torn, and they have not ceased; ¹⁶ With profane ones, mockers in feasts, || Gnashing their teeth against me. ¹⁷ Lord, how long do You behold? Keep my soul back from their desolations, || My only one from young lions. ¹⁸ I thank You in a great assembly, || I praise You among a mighty people. ¹⁹ Do not let my enemies rejoice over me [with] falsehood, || Those hating me without cause wink the eye. ²⁰ For they do not speak peace, || And against the quiet of the land, || They devise deceitful words, ²¹ And they enlarge their mouth against me, || They said, "Aha, aha, our eye has seen." ²² You have seen, O Yhwh,

|| Do not be silent, O Lord—do not be far from me, 23 Stir up, and wake to my judgment, || My God, and my Lord, to my plea. 24 Judge me according to Your righteousness, O Yhwh my God, || And they do not rejoice over me. 25 They do not say in their heart, "Aha, our desire." They do not say, "We swallowed him up." 26 They are ashamed and confounded together, || Who are rejoicing at my evil. They put on shame and confusion, || Who are magnifying themselves against me. 27 They sing and rejoice, who are desiring my righteousness, || And they continually say, "Yhwh is magnified, || Who is desiring the peace of His servant." 28 And my tongue utters Your righteousness, || All the day Your praise!

PSALM 36

1 To the Overseer. By a servant of Yhwh, by David. The transgression of the wicked || Is affirming within my heart, "Fear of God is not before his eyes, 2 For he made [it] smooth to himself in his eyes, || To find his iniquity to be hated. 3 The words of his mouth [are] iniquity and deceit, || He ceased to act prudently—to do good. 4 He devises iniquity on his bed, || He stations himself on a way not good, || He does not refuse evil." 5 O Yhwh, Your kindness [is] in the heavens, || Your faithfulness [is] to the clouds. 6 Your righteousness [is] as mountains of God, || Your judgments [are] a great deep. You save man and beast, O Yhwh. 7 How precious [is] Your kindness, O God, || And the sons of men trust || In the shadow of Your wings. 8 They are filled from the fatness of Your house, || And You cause them to drink the stream of Your delights. 9 For a fountain of life [is] with You, || In Your light we see light. 10 Draw out Your kindness to those knowing You, || And Your righteousness to the upright of heart. 11 Do not let a foot of pride meet me, || And do not let a hand of the wicked move me. 12 Workers of iniquity have fallen there, || They have been overthrown, || And have not been able to arise!

PSALM 37

1 By David. [Aleph-Bet] Do not fret because of evildoers, || Do not be envious against doers of iniquity, 2 For they are cut off speedily as grass, || And fade as the greenness of the tender grass. 3 Trust in Yhwh, and do good, || Dwell [in] the land, and enjoy faithfulness, 4 And delight yourself on Yhwh, || And He gives to you the petitions of your heart. 5 Roll your way on Yhwh, || And trust on Him, and He works, 6 And has brought out your righteousness as light, || And your judgment as noonday. 7 Be silent for Yhwh, and stay yourself for Him, || Do not fret because of him || Who is making his way prosperous, || Because of a man doing wicked schemes. 8 Desist from anger, and forsake fury, || Do not fret yourself to only do evil. 9 For evildoers are cut off, || As for those waiting on Yhwh, they possess the land. 10 And yet a little [while], and the wicked is not, || And you have considered his place, and it is not. 11 And the humble possess the land, || And they have delighted themselves || In the abundance of peace. 12 The wicked is devising against the righteous, || And gnashing his teeth against him. 13 The Lord laughs at him, || For He has seen that his day comes. 14 The wicked have opened a sword, || And they have bent their bow, || To cause the poor and needy to fall, || To slaughter the upright of the way. 15 Their sword enters into their own heart, || And their bows are shattered. 16 Better [is] the little of the righteous, || Than the store of many wicked. 17 For the arms of the wicked are shattered, || And Yhwh is sustaining the righteous. 18 Yhwh knows the days of the perfect, || And their inheritance is for all time. 19 They are not ashamed in a time of evil, || And they are satisfied in days of famine. 20 But the wicked perish, and the enemies of Yhwh, || Have been consumed as the preciousness of lambs, || They have been consumed in smoke. 21 The wicked is borrowing and does not repay, || And the righteous is gracious and giving. 22 For His blessed ones possess the land, || And His reviled ones are cut off. 23 The steps of a man [are] from Yhwh, || They have been prepared, || And He desires his way. 24 When he falls, he is not cast down, || For Yhwh is sustaining his hand. 25 I have been young, || I have also become old, || And I have not seen the righteous forsaken, || And his seed seeking bread. 26 All the day he is gracious and lending, || And his seed [is] for a blessing. 27 Turn aside from evil, and do good, and dwell for all time. 28 For Yhwh is loving judgment, || And He does not

forsake His saintly ones, || They have been kept for all time, || And the seed of the wicked is cut off. 29 The righteous possess the land, || And they dwell on it forever. 30 The mouth of the righteous utters wisdom, || And his tongue speaks judgment. 31 The law of his God [is] his heart, || His steps do not slide. 32 The wicked is watching for the righteous, || And is seeking to put him to death. 33 Yhwh does not leave him in his hand, || Nor condemn him in his being judged. 34 Look to Yhwh, and keep His way, || And He exalts you to possess the land, || In the wicked being cut off—you see! 35 I have seen the wicked terrible, || And spreading as a green native plant, 36 And he passes away, and behold, he is not, || And I seek him, and he is not found! 37 Observe the perfect, and see the upright, || For the latter end of each [is] peace. 38 And transgressors were destroyed together, || The latter end of the wicked was cut off. 39 And the salvation of the righteous [is] from Yhwh, || Their strong place in a time of adversity. 40 And Yhwh helps them and delivers them, || He delivers them from the wicked, || And saves them, || Because they trusted in Him!

PSALM 38

1 A Psalm of David. "To Cause to Remember." Yhwh, do not reprove me in Your wrath, || Nor discipline me in Your fury. 2 For Your arrows have come down on me, || And You let down Your hand on me. 3 Soundness is not in my flesh, || Because of Your indignation, || Peace is not in my bones, || Because of my sin. 4 For my iniquities have passed over my head, || As a heavy burden—too heavy for me. 5 Stunk—my wounds have become corrupt, || Because of my folly. 6 I have been bent down, || I have been bowed down—to excess, || I have gone mourning all the day. 7 For my flanks have been full of drought, || And soundness is not in my flesh. 8 I have been feeble and struck—to excess, || I have roared from disquietude of heart. 9 Lord, all my desire [is] before You, || And my sighing has not been hid from You. 10 My heart [is] panting, my power has forsaken me, || And the light of my eyes, || Even they are not with me. 11 My lovers and my friends stand aloof from before my plague. And my neighbors have stood far off. 12 And those seeking my soul lay a snare, || And those seeking my evil || Have spoken mischievous things, || And they meditate [on] deceits all the day. 13 And I, as deaf, do not hear. And as a mute one who does not open his mouth. 14 Indeed, I am as a man who does not hear, || And in his mouth are no reproofs. 15 Because for You, O Yhwh, I have waited, || You answer, O Lord my God. 16 When I said, "Lest they rejoice over me, || In the slipping of my foot they magnified themselves against me." 17 For I am ready to halt, || And my pain [is] continually before me. 18 For I declare my iniquity, || I am sorry for my sin. 19 And my enemies [are] lively, || They have been strong, and those hating me without cause, || Have been multiplied. 20 And those paying evil for good accuse me, || Because of my pursuing good. 21 Do not forsake me, O Yhwh, || My God, do not be far from me, 22 Hurry to help me, O Lord, my salvation!

PSALM 39

1 To the Overseer. For Jeduthun. A Psalm of David. I have said, "I observe my ways, || Against sinning with my tongue, || I keep a curb for my mouth, || While the wicked [is] before me." 2 I was mute [with] silence, || I kept silent from good, and my pain is excited. 3 My heart [is] hot within me, || In my meditating the fire burns, || I have spoken with my tongue. 4 "Cause me to know, O Yhwh, my end, || And the measure of my days—what it [is]," || I know how frail I [am]. 5 Behold, You have made my days handbreadths, || And my age [is] as nothing before You, || Only, every man set up [is] all vanity. Selah. 6 Only, each habitually walks in an image, || Only, [in] vain, they are disquieted, || He heaps up and does not know who gathers them. 7 And now, what have I expected? O Lord, my hope—it [is] of You. 8 Deliver me from all my transgressions, || Do not make me a reproach of the fool. 9 I have been mute, I do not open my mouth, || Because You have done [it]. 10 Turn aside Your stroke from off me, || From the striving of Your hand I have been consumed. 11 With reproofs against iniquity, || You have corrected man, || And dissolve his desirableness as a moth, || Only, every man [is] vanity. Selah. 12 Hear my prayer, O Yhwh, || And give ear [to] my cry, || Do not be silent to my tear, || For I [am] a sojourner with You, ||

225

A settler like all my fathers. 13 Look from me, and I brighten up before I go and am not!

PSALM 40

1 To the Overseer. A Psalm of David. I have diligently expected Yhwh, || And He inclines to me, and hears my cry, 2 And He causes me to come up || From a pit of desolation— from mire of mud, || And He raises up my feet on a rock, || He is establishing my steps. 3 And He puts a new song in my mouth, "Praise to our God." Many see and fear, and trust in Yhwh. 4 O the blessedness of the man || Who has made Yhwh his trust, || And has not turned to the proud, || And those turning aside to lies. 5 You have done much, my God Yhwh; Your wonders and Your thoughts toward us, || There is none to arrange to You, || I declare and speak: They have been more than to be numbered. 6 Sacrifice and present You have not desired, || But a body You have prepared for me, || Burnt and sin-offering You have not asked. 7 Then I said, "Behold, I have come, || In the roll of the scroll it is written of me, 8 I have delighted to do Your pleasure, my God, || And Your law [is] within my heart." 9 I have proclaimed tidings of righteousness || In the great assembly, || Behold, I do not restrain my lips, || O Yhwh, You have known. 10 I have not concealed Your righteousness || In the midst of my heart, || I have told of Your faithfulness and Your salvation, || I have not hidden Your kindness and Your truth, || To the great assembly. 11 You, O Yhwh, do not restrain Your mercies from me, || Your kindness and Your truth continually keep me. 12 For innumerable evils have surrounded me, || My iniquities have overtaken me, || And I have not been able to see; They have been more than the hairs of my head, || And my heart has forsaken me. 13 Be pleased, O Yhwh, to deliver me, || O Yhwh, make haste for my help. 14 They are ashamed and confounded together, || Who are seeking my soul to destroy it, || They are turned backward, || And are ashamed, who are desiring my evil. 15 They are desolate because of their shame, || Who are saying to me, "Aha, aha." 16 All seeking You rejoice and are glad in You, || Those loving Your salvation continually say, "Yhwh is magnified." 17 And I [am] poor and needy, || The Lord devises for me. You [are] my help and my deliverer, O my God, do not linger.

PSALM 41

1 To the Overseer. A Psalm of David. O the blessedness of him || Who is acting wisely to the poor, || In a day of evil Yhwh delivers him. 2 Yhwh preserves him and revives him, || He is blessed in the land, || And You do not give him into the will of his enemies. 3 Yhwh supports [him] on a bed of sickness, || You have turned his bed in his weakness. 4 I said, "O Yhwh, favor me, || Heal my soul, for I sinned against You," 5 My enemies say evil of me: When he dies—his name has perished! 6 And if he came to see—he speaks vanity, || His heart gathers iniquity to itself, || He goes out—at the street he speaks. 7 All hating me whisper together against me, || Against me they devise evil to me: 8 A worthless thing is poured out on him, || And because he lay down he does not rise again. 9 Even my ally, in whom I trusted, || One eating my bread, || Made the heel great against me, 10 And You, Yhwh, favor me, || And cause me to rise, || And I give repayment to them. 11 By this I have known, || That You have delighted in me, || Because my enemy does not shout over me. 12 As for me, in my integrity, || You have taken hold on me, || And cause me to stand before You for all time. 13 Blessed [is] Yhwh, God of Israel, || From age to age. Amen and Amen.

PSALM 42

1 To the Overseer. An Instruction of the sons of Korah. As a deer pants for streams of water, || So my soul pants toward You, O God. 2 My soul thirsted for God, for the living God, || When do I enter and see the face of God? 3 My tear has been bread day and night to me, || In their saying to me all the day, "Where [is] your God?" 4 These I remember, and pour out my soul in me, || For I pass over into the shelter, || I go softly with them to the house of God, || With the voice of singing and confession, || The multitude keeping celebration! 5 Why bow yourself, O my soul? Indeed, are you troubled within me? Wait for God, for I still confess Him: The salvation of my countenance—my God! 6 My soul bows itself in me, || Therefore I remember You from the land of Jordan, || And of the Hermons, from Mount Mizar. 7 Deep is calling to deep || At the noise of Your waterspouts, || All Your breakers and Your billows passed over me. 8 By day Yhwh commands His kindness, || And by night a song [is] with me, || A prayer to the God of my life. 9 I say to God my Rock, "Why have You forgotten me? Why do I go mourning in the oppression of an enemy?" 10 With a sword in my bones || My adversaries have reproached me, || In their saying to me all the day, "Where [is] your God?" 11 Why bow yourself, O my soul? And why are you troubled within me? Wait for God, for I still confess Him, || The salvation of my countenance, and my God!

PSALM 43

1 Judge me, O God, || And plead my cause against a nation not pious, || You deliver me from a man of deceit and perverseness, 2 For you [are] the God of my strength. Why have You cast me off? Why do I go up and down mourning, || In the oppression of an enemy? 3 Send forth Your light and Your truth, || They lead me, they bring me in, || To Your holy hill, and to Your dwelling places. 4 And I go to the altar of God, || To God, the joy of my rejoicing. And I thank You with a harp, O God, my God. 5 Why bow yourself, O my soul? And why are you troubled within me? Wait for God, for I still confess Him, || The salvation of my countenance, and my God!

PSALM 44

1 To the Overseer. An Instruction of the sons of Korah. O God, we have heard with our ears, || Our fathers have recounted to us, || The work You worked in their days, || In the days of old. 2 You, [with] Your hand, have dispossessed nations. And You plant them. You afflict peoples, and send them away. 3 For they did not possess the land by their sword, || And their arm did not give salvation to them, || But Your right hand, and Your arm, || And the light of Your countenance, || Because You had accepted them. 4 You [are] He, my King, O God, || Command the deliverances of Jacob. 5 By You we push our adversaries, || By Your Name we tread down our withstanders, 6 For I do not trust in my bow, || And my sword does not save me. 7 For You have saved us from our adversaries, || And You have put to shame those hating us. 8 In God we have boasted all the day, || And we thank Your Name for all time. Selah. 9 In anger You have cast off and cause us to blush, || And do not go forth with our hosts. 10 You cause us to turn backward from an adversary, || And those hating us, || Have spoiled for themselves. 11 You make us food like sheep, || And You have scattered us among nations. 12 You sell Your people—without wealth, || And have not become great by their price. 13 You make us a reproach to our neighbors, || A scorn and a reproach to our surrounders. 14 You make us an allegory among nations, || A shaking of the head among peoples. 15 All the day my confusion [is] before me, || And the shame of my face has covered me. 16 Because of the voice of a reproacher and reviler, || Because of an enemy and a self-avenger. 17 All this met us, and we did not forget You, || Nor have we dealt falsely in Your covenant. 18 We do not turn our heart backward, || Nor turn aside our step from Your path. 19 But You have struck us in a place of dragons, || And cover us over with death-shade. 20 If we have forgotten the Name of our God, || And spread our hands to a strange God, 21 Does God not search this out? For He knows the secrets of the heart. 22 Surely, for Your sake we have been slain all the day, || Reckoned as sheep of the slaughter. 23 Stir up—why do You sleep, O Lord? Awake, do not cast us off forever. 24 Why do You hide Your face? You forget our afflictions and our oppression, 25 For our soul has bowed to the dust, || Our belly has cleaved to the earth. 26 Arise, a help to us, || And ransom us for your kindness' sake.

PSALM 45

1 To the Overseer. [Set] on "Lilies." An Instruction of the sons of Korah. A Song of Loves. My heart has stirred a good

word, || I am telling my works to the King, || My tongue [is] the pen of a speedy writer. [2] You have been beautified above the sons of men, || Grace has been poured into Your lips, || Therefore God has blessed You for all time. [3] Gird Your sword on the thigh, O Mighty [One], || Your splendor and Your majesty! [4] As for Your majesty—prosper [and] ride! Because of truth, meekness, [and] righteousness, || And Your right hand shows You fearful things. [5] Your arrows [are] sharp—Peoples fall under You—In the heart of the enemies of the King. [6] Your throne, O God, [is for] all time and forever, || A scepter of uprightness || [Is] the scepter of Your kingdom. [7] You have loved righteousness and hate wickedness, || Therefore God, Your God, has anointed You || With oil of joy above Your companions. [8] Myrrh, and aloes, [and] cassia || [Cover] all Your garments; Out of palaces of ivory, || Stringed instruments have made You glad. [9] Daughters of kings [are] among Your precious ones, || A queen has stood at Your right hand, || In pure gold of Ophir. [10] Listen, O daughter, and see, incline your ear, || And forget your people, and your father's house, [11] And the King desires your beauty, || Because He [is] your Lord—bow yourself to Him, [12] And the daughter of Tyre with a present, || The rich of the people appease your face. [13] All glory [is] the daughter of the king within, || Her clothing [is] with filigrees of gold. [14] In various colors she is brought to the King; Afterward, virgins, her companions, || Are brought to You. [15] They are brought with joy and gladness, || They come into the palace of the King. [16] Instead of Your fathers are Your sons, || You appoint them for princes in all the earth. [17] I make mention of Your Name in all generations, || Therefore peoples praise You, || For all time and forever!

PSALM 46

[1] To the Overseer. By sons of Korah. For girls' [voices]. A Song. God [is] our refuge and strength, || A most sure help in adversities. [2] Therefore we do not fear in the changing of earth, || And in the slipping of mountains || Into the heart of the seas. [3] Roar—troubled are its waters, || Mountains shake in its pride. Selah. [4] A river—its streams make glad the city of God, || Your holy place of the dwelling places of the Most High. [5] God [is] in her midst—she is not moved, God helps her at the turn of the morning! [6] Nations have been troubled, || Kingdoms have been moved, || He has given forth His voice—earth melts. [7] Yhwh of Hosts [is] with us, || The God of Jacob [is] a tower for us. Selah. [8] Come, see the works of Yhwh, || Who has done astonishing things in the earth, [9] Causing wars to cease, || To the end of the earth, He shatters the bow, || And He has cut apart the spear, || He burns chariots with fire. [10] Desist, and know that I [am] God, || I am exalted among nations, || I am exalted in the earth. [11] Yhwh of hosts [is] with us, || The God of Jacob [is] a tower for us! Selah.

PSALM 47

[1] To the Overseer. A Psalm of the sons of Korah. All you peoples, clap the hand, || Shout to God with a voice of singing, [2] For Yhwh Most High [is] fearful, || A great King over all the earth. [3] He leads peoples under us, and nations under our feet. [4] He chooses for us our inheritance, || The excellence of Jacob that He loves. Selah. [5] God has gone up with a shout, || Yhwh with the sound of a horn. [6] Praise God—praise—give praise to our king, praise. [7] For God [is] King of all the earth, || Give praise, O understanding one. [8] God has reigned over nations, God has sat on His holy throne, [9] Nobles of peoples have been gathered, || [With] the people of the God of Abraham, || For the shields of earth [are] to God, || Greatly has He been exalted!

PSALM 48

[1] A Song. A Psalm of the sons of Korah. Great [is] Yhwh, and greatly praised, || In the city of our God—His holy hill. [2] Beautiful [for] elevation, || A joy of all the land, [is] Mount Zion, || The sides of the north, the city of [the] great King. [3] God is known for a tower in her high places. [4] For behold, the kings met, they passed by together, [5] They have seen—so they have marveled, || They have been troubled, they were hurried away. [6] Trembling has seized them there, || Pain, as of a travailing woman. [7] By an east wind You shatter ships of Tarshish. [8] As we have heard, so we have seen, || In the city of Yhwh of hosts, || In the city of our God, God establishes her for all time. Selah. [9] We have thought, O God, of Your kindness, || In the midst of Your temple, [10] As [is] Your Name, O God, so [is] Your praise, || Over the ends of the earth, || Righteousness has filled Your right hand. [11] Mount Zion rejoices, || The daughters of Judah are joyful, || For the sake of Your judgments. [12] Surround Zion, and go around her, count her towers, [13] Set your heart to her bulwark, || Consider her high places, || So that you recount to a later generation, [14] That this God [is] our God—For all time and forever, || He leads us over death!

PSALM 49

[1] To the Overseer. A Psalm of the sons of Korah. Hear this, all you peoples, || Give ear, all you inhabitants of the world. [2] Both low and high, together rich and needy. [3] My mouth speaks wise things, || And the meditations of my heart [are] things of understanding. [4] I incline my ear to an allegory, || I open my riddle with a harp: [5] Why do I fear in days of evil? The iniquity of my supplanters surrounds me. [6] Those trusting on their wealth, || And in the multitude of their riches, || Show themselves foolish. [7] A brother ransoms no one at all, || He does not give to God his atonement. [8] And precious [is] the redemption of their soul, || And it has ceased for all time. [9] And still he lives forever, || He does not see the pit. [10] For he sees wise men die, || Together the foolish and brutish perish, || And have left their wealth to others. [11] Their heart [is that] their houses [are] for all time, || Their dwelling places from generation to generation. They proclaimed their names over the lands. [12] And man does not remain in honor, || He has been like the beasts, they have been cut off. [13] This their way [is] folly for them, || And their posterity are pleased with their sayings. Selah. [14] They have set themselves as sheep for Sheol, || Death afflicts them, || And the upright rule over them in the morning, || And their form [is] for consumption. Sheol [is] a dwelling for him. [15] Only, God ransoms my soul from the hand of Sheol, || For He receives me. Selah. [16] Do not fear when one makes wealth, || When the glory of his house is abundant, [17] For at his death he receives nothing, || His glory does not go down after him. [18] For he blesses his soul in his life || (And they praise you when you do well for yourself). [19] It comes to the generation of his fathers, || They do not see the light forever. [20] Man in honor, who does not understand, || Has been like the beasts, they have been cut off!

PSALM 50

[1] A Psalm of Asaph. The God of gods—Yhwh—has spoken, || And He calls to the earth || From the rising of the sun to its going in. [2] From Zion, the perfection of beauty, God shone. [3] Our God comes, and is not silent, || Fire devours before Him, || And around Him it has been very tempestuous. [4] He calls to the heavens from above, || And to the earth, to judge His people. [5] Gather My saints to Me, || Making covenant with Me over a sacrifice. [6] And the heavens declare His righteousness, || For God Himself is judging. Selah. [7] Hear, O My people, and I speak, || O Israel, and I testify against you, || God—I [am] your God. [8] I do not reprove you for your sacrifices, || Indeed, your burnt-offerings || [Are] continually before Me. [9] I do not take a bullock from your house, || [Or] male goats from your folds. [10] For every beast of the forest [is] Mine, || The livestock on the hills of oxen. [11] I have known every bird of the mountains, || And the wild beast of the field [is] with Me. [12] If I am hungry I do not tell [it] to you, || For the world and its fullness [is] Mine. [13] Do I eat the flesh of bulls, || And drink the blood of male goats? [14] Sacrifice to God confession, || And complete your vows to the Most High. [15] And call Me in a day of adversity, || I deliver you, and you honor Me. [16] And to the wicked God has said: What to you—to recount My statutes? That you lift up My covenant on your mouth? [17] Indeed, you have hated instruction, || And cast My words behind you. [18] If you have seen a thief, || Then you are pleased with him, || And your portion [is] with adulterers. [19] You have sent forth

your mouth with evil, || And your tongue joins deceit together, [20] You sit, you speak against your brother, || You give slander against a son of your mother. [21] These you did, and I kept silent, || You have thought that I am like you, || I reprove you, and set in array before your eyes. [22] Now understand this, || You who are forgetting God, || Lest I tear, and there is no deliverer. [23] He who is sacrificing praise honors Me, || As for him who makes a way, || I cause him to look on the salvation of God!

PSALM 51

[1] To the Overseer. A Psalm of David, in the coming of Nathan the prophet to him when he has gone in to Bathsheba. Favor me, O God, according to Your kindness, || According to the abundance of Your mercies, || Blot out my transgressions. [2] Thoroughly wash me from my iniquity, || And cleanse me from my sin, [3] For I know my transgressions, || And my sin [is] continually before me. [4] Against You, You only, I have sinned, || And done evil in Your eyes, || So that You are righteous in Your words, || You are pure in Your judging. [5] Behold, I have been brought forth in iniquity, || And my mother conceives me in sin. [6] Behold, You have desired truth in the inward parts, || And in the hidden part You cause me to know Wisdom. [7] You cleanse me with hyssop and I am clean, || Wash me, and I am whiter than snow. [8] You cause me to hear joy and gladness, || You make bones You have bruised joyful. [9] Hide Your face from my sin. And blot out all my iniquities. [10] Create for me a clean heart, O God, || And renew a right spirit within me. [11] Do not cast me forth from Your presence, || And do not take Your Holy Spirit from me. [12] Restore to me the joy of Your salvation, || And a willing spirit sustains me. [13] I teach transgressors Your ways, || And sinners return to You. [14] Deliver me from blood, O God, God of my salvation, || My tongue sings of Your righteousness. [15] O Lord, you open my lips, || And my mouth declares Your praise. [16] For You do not desire sacrifice, or I give [it], || You do not accept burnt-offering. [17] The sacrifices of God [are] a broken spirit, || A heart broken and bruised, O God, || You do not despise. [18] Do good in Your good pleasure with Zion, || You build the walls of Jerusalem. [19] Then You desire sacrifices of righteousness, || Burnt-offering, and whole burnt-offering, || Then they offer bullocks on your altar!

PSALM 52

[1] To the Overseer. An Instruction of David, in the coming in of Doeg the Edomite, and he declares to Saul and says to him, "David came to the house of Ahimelech." Why do you boast in evil, O mighty one? The kindness of God [is] all the day. [2] Your tongue devises mischiefs, || Like a sharp razor, working deceit. [3] You have loved evil rather than good, || Lying, than speaking righteousness. Selah. [4] You have loved all devouring words, || O you deceitful tongue. [5] Also—God breaks you down forever, || Takes you, and pulls you out of the tent, || And He has uprooted you || Out of the land of the living. Selah. [6] And the righteous see, || And fear, and laugh at him. [7] "Behold, the man who does not make God his strong place, || And trusts in the abundance of his riches, || He is strong in his mischiefs." [8] And I, as a green olive in the house of God, || I have trusted in the kindness of God, || For all time and forever, [9] I thank You for all time, because You have done [it], || And I wait [on] Your Name for [it is] good before Your saints!

PSALM 53

[1] To the Overseer. "On a disease." An Instruction of David. A fool said in his heart, "There is no God." They have done corruptly, || Indeed, they have done abominable iniquity, || There is none doing good. [2] God looked on the sons of men from the heavens, || To see if there is an understanding one, || [One] seeking God. [3] Everyone went back, together they became filthy, || There is none doing good—not even one. [4] Workers of iniquity have not known, || Those eating my people have eaten bread, || They have not called God. [5] There they feared a fear—there was no fear, || For God has scattered the bones of him || Who is encamping against you, || You have put to shame, || For God has despised them. [6] Who gives the salvation of Israel from Zion? When God turns back [to] a captivity of His people, || Jacob rejoices—Israel is glad!

PSALM 54

[1] To the Overseer. With stringed instruments. An Instruction of David, in the coming in of the Ziphim, and they say to Saul, "Is David not hiding himself with us?" O God, save me by Your Name, and judge me by Your might. [2] O God, hear my prayer, || Give ear to the sayings of my mouth, [3] For strangers have risen up against me || And terrible ones have sought my soul, || They have not set God before them. Selah. [4] Behold, God [is] a helper to me, || The Lord [is] with those supporting my soul, [5] Turn back the evil to my enemies, || Cut them off in Your truth. [6] I sacrifice to You with a free-will offering, || I thank Your Name, O Yhwh, for [it is] good, [7] For He delivered me from all adversity, || And my eye has looked on my enemies!

PSALM 55

[1] To the Overseer. With stringed instruments. An Instruction of David. Give ear, O God, [to] my prayer, || And do not hide from my supplication. [2] Attend to me, and answer me, || I mourn in my meditation, and make a noise, [3] Because of the voice of an enemy, || Because of the oppression of the wicked, || For they cause sorrow to move against me, || And in anger they hate me. [4] My heart is pained within me, || And terrors of death have fallen on me. [5] Fear and trembling come to me, || And horror covers me. [6] And I say, "Who gives to me a pinion as a dove?" I fly away and rest, [7] Behold, I move far off, || I lodge in a wilderness. Selah. [8] I hurry escape for myself, || From a rushing wind, from a whirlwind. [9] Swallow up, O Lord, divide their tongue, || For I saw violence and strife in a city. [10] By day and by night they go around it, on its walls. Both iniquity and perverseness [are] in its midst, [11] Mischiefs [are] in its midst. Fraud and deceit do not depart from its street. [12] For an enemy does not reproach me, or I bear [it], || He who is hating me || Has not magnified himself against me, || Or I hide from him. [13] But you, a man—as my equal, || My familiar friend, and my acquaintance. [14] When together we sweeten counsel, || We walk into the house of God in company. [15] Desolations [are] on them, || They go down [to] Sheol—alive, || For wickedness [is] in their dwelling, in their midst. [16] I call to God, and Yhwh saves me. [17] Evening, and morning, and noon, || I meditate, and make a noise, and He hears my voice, [18] He has ransomed my soul in peace || From him who is near to me, || For with the multitude they were with me. [19] God hears and afflicts them, || And He sits of old. Selah. Because they have no changes, and do not fear God, [20] He has sent forth his hands against his well-wishers, || He has defiled his covenant. [21] His mouth has been sweeter than honey, || And his heart [is] war! His words have been softer than oil, || And they [are] drawn [swords]. [22] Cast on Yhwh that which He has given you, || And He sustains you, || He does not permit the moving of the righteous forever. [23] And You, O God, bring them down || To a pit of destruction, || Men of blood and deceit do not reach to half their days, || And I trust in You!

PSALM 56

[1] To the Overseer. [Set] on "A Silent Dove Far Off." A Miktam of David, in the Philistines' taking hold of him in Gath. Favor me, O God, for man swallowed me up, || All the day fighting he oppresses me, [2] My enemies have swallowed up all the day, || For many [are] fighting against me, O Most High, [3] [In] the day I am afraid I am confident toward You. [4] In God I praise His word, in God I have trusted, || I do not fear what flesh does to me. [5] All the day they wrest my words, || All their thoughts [are] for evil concerning me, [6] They assemble, they hide, they watch my heels, || When they have expected my soul. [7] They escape by iniquity, || In anger put down the peoples, O God. [8] You have counted my wandering, || You place my tear in Your bottle, || Are they not in Your scroll? [9] Then turn back my enemies in the day I call. This I have known, that God [is] for me. [10] In God I praise the word, || In Yhwh I praise the word. [11] In God I trusted, || I do not fear what man does

to me, [12] On me, O God, [are] Your vows, || I repay thank-offerings to You. [13] For You have delivered my soul from death, || Do You not [keep] my feet from falling? To habitually walk before God in the light of the living!

PSALM 57

[1] To the Overseer. "Do Not Destroy." A Miktam of David, in his fleeing from the face of Saul into a cave. Favor me, O God, favor me, || For my soul is trusting in You, || And I trust in the shadow of Your wings, || Until the calamities pass over. [2] I call to God Most High, || To God [who] is perfecting for me. [3] He sends from the heavens, and saves me, || He reproached [the one] who is panting after me. Selah. God sends forth His kindness and His truth. [4] My soul [is] in the midst of lions, || I lie down [among] flames—sons of men, || Their teeth [are] a spear and arrows, || And their tongue a sharp sword. [5] Be exalted above the heavens, O God, || Your glory above all the earth. [6] They have prepared a net for my steps, || My soul has bowed down, || They have dug a pit before me, || They have fallen into its midst. Selah. [7] My heart is prepared, O God, || My heart is prepared, || I sing and praise. [8] Awake, my glory, awake, stringed instrument and harp, || I awake the morning dawn. [9] I thank You among the peoples, O Lord, || I praise You among the nations. [10] For Your kindness [is] great to the heavens, || And Your truth to the clouds. [11] Be exalted above the heavens, O God. Your glory above all the earth!

PSALM 58

[1] To the Overseer. "Do Not Destroy." A Miktam of David. Is it true, O silent one, that you speak righteously? Do you judge uprightly, O sons of men? [2] Even in heart you work iniquities, || In the land you ponder the violence of your hands. [3] The wicked have been estranged from the womb, || They have erred from the belly, speaking lies. [4] Their poison [is] as poison of a serpent, || As a deaf cobra shutting its ear, [5] Which does not listen to the voice of whisperers, || A charmer of most skillful charms. [6] O God, break their teeth in their mouth, || Break down the jaw-teeth of young lions, O Yhwh. [7] They are melted as waters, || They go up and down for themselves, || His arrow proceeds as they cut themselves off. [8] He goes on as a snail that melts, || [As] an untimely birth of a woman, || They have not seen the sun. [9] Before your pots discern the bramble, || As living, He whirls away in His burning anger. [10] The righteous rejoices that he has seen vengeance, || He washes his steps in the blood of the wicked. [11] And man says: "Surely fruit [is] for the righteous: Surely there is a God judging in the earth!"

PSALM 59

[1] To the Overseer. "Do Not Destroy." A Miktam of David, in Saul's sending, and they watch the house to put him to death. Deliver me from my enemies, O my God, || Set me on high from my withstanders. [2] Deliver me from workers of iniquity, || And save me from men of blood. [3] For behold, they laid wait for my soul, || Strong ones are assembled against me, || Not my transgression nor my sin, O Yhwh. [4] Without punishment they run and prepare themselves, || Stir up to meet me, and see. [5] And You, Yhwh, God of Hosts, God of Israel, || Awake to inspect all the nations. Do not favor any treacherous dealers of iniquity. Selah. [6] They return at evening, || They make a noise like a dog, || And go around the city. [7] Behold, they belch out with their mouths, || Swords [are] in their lips, for "Who hears?" [8] And You, O Yhwh, laugh at them, || You mock at all the nations. [9] O my Strength, to You I take heed, || For God [is] my tower—the God of my kindness. [10] God goes before me, || He causes me to look on my enemies. [11] Do not slay them, lest my people forget, || Shake them by Your strength, || And bring them down, O Lord our shield. [12] The sin of their mouth [is] a word of their lips, || And they are captured in their pride, || And they recount from the curse and lying. [13] Consume in fury, consume and they are not, || And they know that God is ruling in Jacob, || To the ends of the earth. Selah. [14] And they return at evening, || They make a noise like a dog, || And they go around the city. [15] They wander for food, || If they are not

satisfied—then they murmur. [16] And I sing of Your strength, || And at morning I sing of Your kindness, || For You have been a tower to me, || And a refuge for me in a day of adversity. [17] O my Strength, I sing praise to You, || For God [is] my tower, the God of my kindness!

PSALM 60

[1] To the Overseer. [Set] on "Lily of Testimony." A Miktam of David, to teach, in his striving with Aram-Naharaim and with Aram-Zobah, when Joab turns back and strikes Edom in the Valley of Salt—twelve thousand. O God, You had cast us off, || You had broken us—had been angry! You turn back to us. [2] You have caused the land to tremble, || You have broken it, || Heal its breaches, for it has moved. [3] You have shown Your people a hard thing, || You have caused us to drink wine of trembling. [4] You have given an ensign to those fearing You, || To be lifted up as an ensign || Because of truth. Selah. [5] That Your beloved ones may be drawn out, || Save [with] Your right hand, and answer us. [6] God has spoken in His holiness: I exult—I apportion Shechem, || And I measure the Valley of Succoth, [7] Gilead [is] Mine, and Manasseh [is] Mine, || And Ephraim [is] the strength of My head, || Judah [is] My lawgiver, [8] Moab [is] My pot for washing, || Over Edom I cast My shoe, || Shout, concerning Me, O Philistia. [9] Who brings me [to] a city of bulwarks? Who has led me to Edom? [10] Is it not You, O God? have You cast us off? And do You not go forth, O God, with our hosts? [11] Give to us help from adversity, || And the deliverance of man [is] vain. [12] We do mightily in God, || And He treads down our adversaries!

PSALM 61

[1] To the Overseer. On stringed instruments. By David. Hear, O God, my loud cry, attend to my prayer. [2] I call to You from the end of the land, || In the feebleness of my heart, || You lead me into a rock higher than I. [3] For You have been a refuge for me, || A tower of strength because of the enemy. [4] I sojourn in Your tent for all ages, || I trust in the secret place of Your wings. Selah. [5] For You, O God, have listened to my vows, || You have appointed the inheritance || Of those fearing Your Name. [6] You add days to the days of the king, || His years as generation and generation. [7] He dwells before God for all time, || Appoint kindness and truth—they keep him. [8] So I praise Your Name forever, || When I pay my vows day by day!

PSALM 62

[1] To the Overseer. For Jeduthun. A Psalm of David. Toward God alone [is] my soul silent, || My salvation [is] from Him. [2] He alone [is] my rock, and my salvation, || My tower, I am not much moved. [3] Until when do you devise mischief against a man? All of you are destroyed, || As a wall inclined, a hedge that is cast down. [4] Only—from his excellence || They have consulted to drive away, || They enjoy a lie, they bless with their mouth, || And revile with their heart. Selah. [5] For God alone, be silent, O my soul, || For my hope [is] from Him. [6] He alone [is] my rock and my salvation, || My tower, I am not moved. [7] On God [is] my salvation, and my glory, || The rock of my strength, my refuge [is] in God. [8] Trust in Him at all times, O people, || Pour forth your heart before Him, || God [is] a refuge for us. Selah. [9] Surely vanity the low, a lie the high. In balances to go up || They [are] lighter than a breath. [10] Do not trust in oppression, || And do not become vain in robbery, || Do not set the heart [on] wealth when it increases. [11] Once has God spoken, twice I heard this, || That "strength [is] with God." [12] And with You, O Lord, [is] kindness, || For You repay to each, || According to his work!

PSALM 63

[1] A Psalm of David, in his being in the wilderness of Judah. O God, You [are] my God, earnestly I seek You, || My soul has thirsted for You, || My flesh has longed for You, || In a dry and weary land, without waters. [2] So I have seen You in the

sanctuary, || To behold Your strength and Your glory. ³ Because better [is] Your kindness than life, || My lips praise You. ⁴ So I bless You in my life, || I lift up my hands in Your Name. ⁵ As [with] milk and fatness is my soul satisfied, || And [with] singing lips my mouth praises. ⁶ If I have remembered You on my bed, || I meditate on You in the watches. ⁷ For You have been a help to me, || And I sing in the shadow of Your wings. ⁸ My soul has cleaved after You, || Your right hand has taken hold on me. ⁹ And they who seek my soul for desolation, || Go into the lower parts of the earth. ¹⁰ They cause him to run on the edge of the sword, || They are a portion for foxes. ¹¹ And the king rejoices in God, || Everyone swearing by Him boasts, || But the mouth of those speaking lies is stopped!

PSALM 64

¹ To the Overseer. A Psalm of David. Hear, O God, my voice, in my meditation, || You keep my life from the fear of an enemy, ² Hide me from the secret counsel of evildoers, || From the tumult of workers of iniquity. ³ Who sharpened their tongue as a sword, || They directed their arrow—a bitter word. ⁴ To shoot the perfect in secret places, || Suddenly they shoot him, and do not fear. ⁵ They strengthen an evil thing for themselves, || They recount of the hiding of snares, || They have said, "Who looks at it?" ⁶ They search out perverse things, "We perfected a searching search," || And the inward part of man, and the heart, [are] deep. ⁷ And God shoots them [with] an arrow, || Their wounds have been sudden, ⁸ And they cause him to stumble, || Their own tongue [is] against them, || Every looker on them flees away. ⁹ And all men fear, and declare the work of God, || And they have wisely considered His deed. ¹⁰ The righteous rejoice in Yhwh, || And have trusted in Him, || And all the upright of heart boast!

PSALM 65

¹ To the Overseer. A Psalm of David. A Song. To You, silence [and] praise, O God, in Zion, || And to You a vow is completed. ² Hearer of prayer, all flesh comes to You. ³ Matters of iniquities were mightier than I, || Our transgressions—You cover them. ⁴ O the blessedness of [him whom] You choose, || And draw near, he inhabits Your courts, || We are satisfied with the goodness of Your house, || Your holy temple. ⁵ By fearful things in righteousness You answer us, || O God of our salvation, || The confidence of all far off || The ends of the earth and sea. ⁶ Establishing mountains by His power, || He has been girded with might, ⁷ Restraining the noise of seas, the noise of their billows, || And the multitude of the peoples. ⁸ And the inhabitants of the uttermost parts || Are afraid from Your signs, || You cause the outgoings of morning and evening to sing. ⁹ You have inspected the earth, and water it, || You make it very rich, the stream of God [is] full of water, || You prepare their grain, || When thus You prepare it, ¹⁰ Its ridges have been filled, || Its furrow has been deepened, || You soften it with showers, || Its springing up You bless. ¹¹ You have crowned the year of Your goodness, || And Your paths drop fatness. ¹² The pastures of a wilderness drop, || And You gird the hills with joy. ¹³ The meadows are clothed with the flock, || And valleys are covered with grain, || They shout—indeed, they sing!

PSALM 66

¹ To the Overseer. A Song. A Psalm. Shout to God, all the earth. ² Praise the glory of His Name, || Make honorable His praise. ³ Say to God, "How fearful Your works—By the abundance of Your strength, || Your enemies feign obedience to You. ⁴ All the earth bows to You, || They sing praise to You, they praise Your Name." Selah. ⁵ Come, and see the works of God, || Fearful acts toward the sons of men. ⁶ He has turned a sea to dry land, || Through a river they pass over on foot, || There we rejoice in Him. ⁷ Ruling by His might for all time, || His eyes watch among the nations, || The stubborn do not exalt themselves. Selah. ⁸ Bless our God you peoples, || And sound the voice of His praise, ⁹ Who has placed our soul in life, || And has not permitted our feet to be moved. ¹⁰ For You have tried us, O God, || You have refined us as the refining of silver. ¹¹ You have brought us into a net, || You have placed pressure on our loins. ¹² You have caused man to ride at our head. We have entered into fire and into water, || And You bring us out to a watered place. ¹³ I enter Your house with burnt-offerings, || I complete my vows to You, ¹⁴ For my lips were opened, || And my mouth spoke in my distress: ¹⁵ "I offer to You burnt-offerings of fatlings, || With incense of rams, I prepare a bullock with male goats." Selah. ¹⁶ Come, hear, all you who fear God, || And I recount what He did for my soul. ¹⁷ I have called to Him [with] my mouth, || And exaltation [is] under my tongue. ¹⁸ Iniquity, if I have seen in my heart, || The Lord does not hear. ¹⁹ But God has heard, || He has attended to the voice of my prayer. ²⁰ Blessed [is] God, || Who has not turned aside my prayer, || And His loving-kindness, from me!

PSALM 67

¹ To the Overseer. With stringed instruments. A Psalm. A Song. God favors us and blesses us, || [And] causes His face to shine with us. Selah. ² For the knowledge of Your way in earth, || Your salvation among all nations. ³ Peoples praise You, O God, || Peoples praise You, all of them. ⁴ Nations rejoice and sing, || For You judge peoples uprightly, || And comfort peoples on earth. Selah. ⁵ Peoples confess You, O God, || Peoples confess You—all of them. ⁶ Earth has given her increase, God blesses us—our God, ⁷ God blesses us, and all the ends of the earth fear Him!

PSALM 68

¹ To the Overseer. A Psalm. A Song of David. God rises [and] His enemies are scattered! And those hating Him flee from His face. ² You drive them away as the driving away of smoke, || As the melting of wax before fire, || The wicked perish at the presence of God. ³ And the righteous rejoice, they exult before God, || And they rejoice with gladness. ⁴ Sing to God—praise His Name, || Raise up a highway for Him who is riding in deserts, || In Yah [is] His Name, and exult before Him. ⁵ Father of the fatherless, and judge of the widows, || [Is] God in His holy habitation. ⁶ God—causing the lonely to dwell at home, || Bringing out bound ones into prosperity, || Only—the stubborn have inhabited a dry place. ⁷ O God, in Your going forth before Your people, || In Your stepping through the wilderness, Selah. ⁸ The earth has shaken, || Indeed, the heavens have dropped before God, || This Sinai—before God, the God of Israel. ⁹ You shake out a shower of free-will gifts, O God. Your inheritance, when it has been weary, || You have established it. ¹⁰ Your creature has dwelt in it, || You prepare for the poor in Your goodness, O God. ¹¹ The Lord gives the saying, || The female proclaimers [are] a numerous host. ¹² Kings of hosts utterly flee away, || And a female inhabitant of the house apportions spoil. ¹³ Though you lie between two boundaries, || Wings of a dove covered with silver, || And her pinions with yellow gold. ¹⁴ When the Mighty spreads kings in it, it snows in Salmon. ¹⁵ A hill of God [is] the hill of Bashan, || A hill of heights [is] the hill of Bashan. ¹⁶ Why do you envy, O high hills, || The hill God has desired for His seat? Yhwh also dwells forever. ¹⁷ The chariots of God [are] myriads, thousands of changes, || The Lord [is] among them, in Sinai, in the sanctuary. ¹⁸ You have ascended on high, || You have taken captivity captive, || You have taken gifts for men, || That even the stubborn may rest, O Yah God. ¹⁹ Blessed [is] the Lord, day by day He lays on us. God Himself [is] our salvation. Selah. ²⁰ God Himself [is] to us a God for deliverances, || And Yhwh Lord has the outgoings of death. ²¹ Only—God strikes || The head of His enemies, || The hairy crown of a habitual walker in his guilt. ²² The Lord said: "From Bashan I bring back, || I bring back from the depths of the sea. ²³ So that you dash your foot || In the blood of enemies—the tongue of Your dogs." ²⁴ They have seen Your goings, O God, || Goings of my God, my king, in the sanctuary. ²⁵ Singers have been before, || Behind [are] players on instruments, || Virgins playing with timbrels in the midst. ²⁶ In assemblies bless God, || The Lord—from the fountain of Israel. ²⁷ There [is] little Benjamin, their ruler, || Heads of Judah their defense, || Heads of Zebulun—heads of Naphtali. ²⁸ Your God has commanded your strength, || Be strong, O God, You have worked this for us. ²⁹ Because of Your temple at Jerusalem, || Kings bring a present to You. ³⁰ Rebuke a beast of the reeds, a herd of bulls, || With calves of the peoples, || Each humbling himself with pieces of silver, || You scatter

peoples delighting in conflicts. ³¹ Fat ones come out of Egypt, || Cush causes her hands to run to God. ³² Kingdoms of the earth, sing to God, || Praise the Lord! Selah. ³³ To Him who is riding on the heavens of the heavens of old, || Behold, He gives with His voice a strong voice. ³⁴ Ascribe strength to God, || His excellence [is] over Israel, and His strength in the clouds. ³⁵ Fearful, O God, out of Your sanctuaries, || The God of Israel Himself, || Giving strength and might to the people. Blessed [is] God!

PSALM 69

¹ To the Overseer. [Set] on "Lilies." by David. Save me, O God, for waters have come to the soul. ² I have sunk in deep mire, || And there is no standing, || I have come into the depths of the waters, || And a flood has overflown me. ³ I have been wearied with my calling, || My throat has been burned, || My eyes have been consumed, waiting for my God. ⁴ Those hating me without cause || Have been more than the hairs of my head, || Mighty have been my destroyers, || My lying enemies, || That which I did not take away—I bring back. ⁵ O God, You have known || Concerning my overturn, || And my desolations have not been hid from You. ⁶ Do not let those waiting on You be ashamed because of me, || O Lord, Yhwh of Hosts, || Do not let those seeking You || Blush because of me, || O God of Israel. ⁷ For because of You I have borne reproach, || Shame has covered my face. ⁸ I have been a stranger to my brother, || And a foreigner to sons of my mother. ⁹ For [my] zeal for Your house has consumed me, || And the reproaches of Your reproachers || Have fallen on me. ¹⁰ And I weep in the fasting of my soul, || And it is for a reproach to me. ¹¹ And I make my clothing sackcloth, || And I am for an allegory to them. ¹² Those sitting at the gate meditate concerning me, || And those drinking strong drink, || Play on instruments. ¹³ And my prayer [is] to You, O Yhwh, || A time of good pleasure, O God, || In the abundance of Your kindness, || Answer me in the truth of Your salvation. ¹⁴ Deliver me from the mire, and do not let me sink, || Let me be delivered from those hating me, || And from deep places of waters. ¹⁵ Do not let a flood of waters overflow me, || Nor let the deep swallow me up, || Nor let the pit shut her mouth on me. ¹⁶ Answer me, O Yhwh, for Your kindness [is] good, || Turn to me according to the abundance of Your mercies, ¹⁷ And do not hide Your face from Your servant, || For I am in distress—hurry, answer me. ¹⁸ Be near to my soul—redeem it, || Ransom me because of my enemies. ¹⁹ You have known my reproach, || And my shame, and my blushing, || All my adversaries [are] before You. ²⁰ Reproach has broken my heart, and I am sick, || And I look for a bemoaner, and there is none, || And for comforters, and I have found none. ²¹ And they give gall for my food, || And cause me to drink vinegar for my thirst. ²² Their table before them is for a snare, || And for a repayment—for a trap. ²³ Their eyes are darkened from seeing, || And their loins continually shake You. ²⁴ Pour Your indignation on them, || And the fierceness of Your anger seizes them. ²⁵ Their tower is desolated, || There is no dweller in their tents. ²⁶ For they have pursued him [whom] You have struck, || And recount of the pain of Your pierced ones. ²⁷ Give punishment for their iniquity, || And they do not enter into Your righteousness. ²⁸ They are blotted out of the scroll of life, || And are not written with the righteous. ²⁹ And I [am] afflicted and pained, || Your salvation, O God, sets me on high. ³⁰ I praise the Name of God with a song, || And I magnify Him with thanksgiving, ³¹ And it is better to Yhwh than an ox, || A bullock—horned [and] hoofed. ³² The humble have seen—they rejoice, || You who seek God—and your heart lives. ³³ For Yhwh listens to the needy, || And He has not despised His bound ones. ³⁴ The heavens and earth praise Him, || Seas, and every moving thing in them. ³⁵ For God saves Zion, || And builds the cities of Judah, || And they have dwelt there, and possess it. ³⁶ And the seed of His servants inherit it, || And those loving His Name dwell in it!

PSALM 70

¹ To the Overseer. By David. "To Cause to Remember." O God, [hurry] to deliver me, || O Yhwh, hurry to help me. ² Let them be ashamed and confounded || Who are seeking my soul, || Let them be turned backward and blush || Who are desiring my evil. ³ Let them turn back because of their shame, || Who

are saying, "Aha, aha." ⁴ Let all those seeking You rejoice and be glad in You, || And let those loving Your salvation || Continually say, "God is magnified." ⁵ And I [am] poor and needy, O God, hurry to me, || You [are] my help and my deliverer, || O Yhwh, do not linger!

PSALM 71

¹ In You, O Yhwh, I have trusted, || Do not let me be disappointed for all time. ² You deliver me in Your righteousness, || And cause me to escape, || Incline Your ear to me, and save me. ³ Be a rock to me—a habitation, || To go in continually, || You have given command to save me, || For You [are] my rock and my bulwark. ⁴ O my God, cause me to escape || From the hand of the wicked, || From the hand of the perverse and violent. ⁵ For You [are] my hope, O Lord Yhwh, || My trust from my youth. ⁶ I have been supported from the womb by You, || You cut me out from my mother's bowels, || My praise [is] continually in You. ⁷ I have been as a wonder to many, || And You [are] my strong refuge. ⁸ My mouth is filled [with] Your praise, || All the day [with] Your beauty. ⁹ Do not cast me off at the time of old age, || Do not forsake me according to the consumption of my power. ¹⁰ For my enemies have spoken against me, || And those watching my soul have taken counsel together, ¹¹ Saying, "God has forsaken him, || Pursue and catch him, for there is no deliverer." ¹² O God, do not be far from me, || O my God, make haste for my help. ¹³ They are ashamed, they are consumed, || Who are opposing my soul, || They are covered [with] reproach and blushing, || Who are seeking my evil, ¹⁴ And I continually wait with hope, || And have added to all Your praise. ¹⁵ My mouth recounts Your righteousness, || All the day Your salvation, || For I have not known the numbers. ¹⁶ I come in [the] might of Lord Yhwh, || I mention Your righteousness—Yours alone. ¹⁷ God, You have taught me from my youth, || And until now I declare Your wonders. ¹⁸ And also to old age and grey hairs, || O God, do not forsake me, || Until I declare Your strength to a generation, || Your might to everyone that comes. ¹⁹ And Your righteousness, O God, [is] to the heights, || Because You have done great things, || O God, who [is] like You? ²⁰ Because You have showed me many and sad distresses, || You turn back— You revive me, || And from the depths of the earth, || You turn back—You bring me up. ²¹ You increase my greatness, || And You surround—You comfort me, ²² I also thank You with a vessel of stringed instrument, || Your truth, O my God, I sing to You with a harp, || O Holy One of Israel, ²³ My lips cry aloud when I sing praise to You, || And my soul that You have redeemed, ²⁴ My tongue also utters Your righteousness all the day, || Because ashamed—because confounded, || Have been those seeking my evil!

PSALM 72

¹ By Solomon. O God, give Your judgments to the king, || And Your righteousness to the king's Son. ² He judges Your people with righteousness, || And Your poor with judgment. ³ The mountains bear peace to the people, || And the heights by righteousness. ⁴ He judges the poor of the people, || Gives deliverance to the sons of the needy, || And bruises the oppressor. ⁵ They fear You with the sun, and before the moon, || Generation—generations. ⁶ He comes down as rain on mown grass, || As showers—sprinkling the earth. ⁷ The righteous flourish in His days, || And abundance of peace until the moon is not. ⁸ And He rules from sea to sea, || And from the river to the ends of the earth. ⁹ Desert-dwellers bow before Him, || And His enemies lick the dust. ¹⁰ Kings of Tarshish and of the islands send back a present. Kings of Sheba and Seba bring a reward near. ¹¹ And all kings bow themselves to Him, || All nations serve Him, ¹² For He delivers the needy who cries, || And the poor when he has no helper, ¹³ He has pity on the poor and needy, || And He saves the souls of the needy, ¹⁴ He redeems their soul from fraud and from violence, || And their blood is precious in His eyes. ¹⁵ And He lives, and the gold of Sheba [is] given to Him, || And prayer is continually made for Him, || All day He is continually blessed. ¹⁶ There is a handful of grain in the earth, || On the top of mountains, || Its fruit shakes like Lebanon, || And they flourish out of the city as the herb of the

earth. [17] His Name is for all time, || Before the sun is His Name continued, || And they bless themselves in Him, || All nations pronounce Him blessed. [18] Blessed is Yhwh God, God of Israel, || He alone is doing wonders, [19] And blessed [is] the Name of His glory for all time, || And the whole earth is filled [with] His glory. Amen and amen! [20] The prayers of David son of Jesse have been ended.

PSALM 73

[1] A Psalm of Asaph. Surely God [is] good to Israel, to the clean of heart. And I—as a little thing, || My feet have been turned aside, [2] As nothing, my steps have slipped, || For I have been envious of the boastful, [3] I see the peace of the wicked, || That there are no bands at their death, [4] And their might [is] firm. [5] They are not in the misery of mortals, || And they are not plagued with common men. [6] Therefore pride has encircled them, || Violence covers them as a dress. [7] Their eye has come out from fat. The imaginations of the heart transgressed; [8] They do corruptly, || And they speak in the wickedness of oppression, || They speak from on high. [9] They have set their mouth in the heavens, || And their tongue walks in the earth. [10] Therefore His people return here, || And waters of fullness are wrung out to them. [11] And they have said, "How has God known? And is there knowledge in the Most High?" [12] Behold, these [are] the wicked and easy ones of the age, || They have increased strength. [13] Only—a vain thing! I have purified my heart, || And I wash my hands in innocence, [14] And I am plagued all the day, || And my reproof—every morning. [15] If I have said, "I recount thus," || Behold, I have deceived a generation of Your sons. [16] And I think to know this, || It [is] perverseness in my eyes, [17] Until I come into the sanctuaries of God, || I attend to their latter end. [18] Surely You set them in slippery places, || You have caused them to fall to desolations. [19] How they have become a desolation as in a moment, || They have been ended—consumed from terrors. [20] As a dream from awaking, O Lord, || In awaking, You despise their image. [21] For my heart shows itself violent, || And my reins prick themselves, [22] And I am brutish, and do not know. I have been a beast with You. [23] And I [am] continually with You, || You have laid hold on my right hand. [24] You lead me with Your counsel, || And after, receive me [to] glory. [25] Whom do I have in the heavens? And none have I desired in earth [besides] You. [26] My flesh and my heart have been consumed, || God [is] the rock of my heart and my portion for all time. [27] For behold, those far from You perish, || You have cut off everyone, || Who is going whoring from You. [28] And [the] nearness of God to me [is] good, || I have placed my refuge in Lord Yhwh, || To recount all Your works!

PSALM 74

[1] An Instruction of Asaph. Why, O God, have You cast off forever? Your anger smokes against the flock of Your pasture. [2] Remember Your congregation || [That] You purchased of old, || You redeemed the rod of Your inheritance, || This Mount Zion—You dwelt in it. [3] Lift up Your steps to the continuous desolations, || Everything the enemy did wickedly in the sanctuary. [4] Your adversaries have roared, || In the midst of Your meeting-places, || They have set their ensigns as ensigns. [5] He is known as one bringing in on high || Against a thicket of wood—axes. [6] And now they break down its engravings, || Together, with axe and hatchet, [7] They have sent Your sanctuary into fire, || They defiled the Dwelling Place of Your Name to the earth, [8] They said in their hearts, "Let us oppress them together," || They burned all the meeting-places of God in the land. [9] We have not seen our ensigns, || There is no longer a prophet, || Nor with us is one knowing how long. [10] Until when, O God, does an adversary reproach? Does an enemy despise Your Name forever? [11] Why do You turn back Your hand, || Even Your right hand? Remove [it] from the midst of Your bosom. [12] And God [is] my king of old, || Working salvation in the midst of the earth. [13] You have divided [the] sea by Your strength, || You have shattered heads of dragons by the waters, [14] You have broken the heads of leviathan, || You make him food for the people of desert-dwellers. [15] You have cleaved a fountain and a stream, || You have dried up

perennial flowings. [16] The day [is] Yours, || The night [is] also Yours, || You have prepared a light-giver—the sun. [17] You have set up all the borders of earth, || Summer and winter—You have formed them. [18] Remember this—an enemy reproached Yhwh, || And a foolish people have despised Your Name. [19] Do not give up to a [wild] creature, || The soul of Your turtle-dove, || Do not forget the life of Your poor ones forever. [20] Look attentively to the covenant, || For the dark places of earth, || Have been full of habitations of violence. [21] Do not let the oppressed turn back ashamed, || Let the poor and needy praise Your Name, [22] Arise, O God, plead Your plea, || Remember Your reproach from a fool all the day. [23] Do not forget the voice of Your adversaries, || The noise of Your withstanders is going up continually!

PSALM 75

[1] To the Overseer. "Do not destroy." A Psalm of Asaph. A Song. We have given thanks to You, O God, || We have given thanks, and Your Name [is] near, || They have recounted Your wonders. [2] When I receive an appointment, I judge uprightly. [3] The earth and all its inhabitants are melted, || I have pondered its pillars. Selah. [4] I have said to the boastful, "Do not be boastful," || And to the wicked, "Do not raise up a horn." [5] Do not raise up your horn on high || (You speak with a stiff neck). [6] For not from the east, or from the west, || Nor from the wilderness—[is] elevation. [7] But God [is] judging, || This He makes low—and this He lifts up. [8] For a cup [is] in the hand of Yhwh, || And the wine has foamed, || It is full of mixture, and He pours out of it, || Surely wring out its dregs, || And all the wicked of the earth drink, [9] And I declare [it] for all time, || I sing praise to the God of Jacob. [10] And I cut off all horns of the wicked, || The horns of the righteous are exalted!

PSALM 76

[1] To the Overseer. With stringed instruments. A Psalm of Asaph. A Song. God [is] known in Judah, || His Name [is] great in Israel. [2] And His dwelling place is in Salem, || And His habitation in Zion. [3] There He has shattered arrows of a bow, || Shield, and sword, and battle. Selah. [4] You [are] bright, majestic above hills of prey. [5] The mighty of heart have spoiled themselves, || They have slept their sleep, || And none of the men of might found their hands. [6] From Your rebuke, O God of Jacob, || Both rider and horse have been fast asleep. [7] You, fearful [are] You, || And who stands before You, || Since You have been angry? [8] You have sounded judgment from the heavens, || Earth has feared, and has been still, [9] In the rising of God to judgment, || To save all the humble of earth. Selah. [10] For the fierceness of man praises You, || You gird on the remnant of fierceness. [11] Vow and complete to your God Yhwh, || All you surrounding Him, || They bring presents to the Fearful One. [12] He gathers the spirit of leaders, || Fearful to the kings of earth!

PSALM 77

[1] To the Overseer. For Jeduthun. A Psalm of Asaph. My voice [is] to God, and I cry, || My voice [is] to God, || And He has given ear to me. [2] I sought the Lord in a day of my distress, || My hand has been spread out by night, || And it does not cease, || My soul has refused to be comforted. [3] I remember God, and make a noise, || I meditate, and my spirit is feeble. Selah. [4] You have taken hold of the watches of my eyes, || I have been moved, and I do not speak. [5] I have reckoned the days of old, || The years of the ages. [6] I remember my music in the night, || I meditate with my heart, and my spirit searches diligently: [7] Does the Lord cast off for all ages? Does He add to be pleased no longer? [8] Has His kindness ceased forever? The saying failed from generation to generation? [9] Has God forgotten [His] favors? Has He shut up His mercies in anger? Selah. [10] And I say: "My weakness is, || The changes of the right hand of the Most High." [11] I mention the doings of Yah, || For I remember Your wonders of old, [12] And I have meditated on all Your working, || And I talk concerning Your doings. [13] O God, Your way [is] in holiness, || Who [is] a great god like God? [14] You [are] the God doing wonders. You have made Your

strength known among the peoples, ^{15} You have redeemed Your people with strength, || The sons of Jacob and Joseph. Selah. ^{16} The waters have seen You, O God, || The waters have seen You, || They are afraid—also depths are troubled. ^{17} Thick clouds have poured out waters, || The skies have given forth a noise, || Also—Your arrows go up and down. ^{18} The voice of Your thunder [is] in the spheres, || Lightnings have lightened the world, || The earth has trembled, indeed, it shakes. ^{19} Your way [is] in the sea, || And Your paths in many waters, || And Your tracks have not been known. ^{20} You have led Your people as a flock, || By the hand of Moses and Aaron!

PSALM 78

^{1} An Instruction of Asaph. Give ear, O my people, to my law, || Incline your ear to sayings of my mouth. ^{2} I open my mouth with an allegory, || I bring forth hidden things of old, ^{3} That we have heard and know, || And our fathers have recounted to us. ^{4} We do not hide from their sons, || Recounting praises of Yhwh to a later generation, || And His strength, and His wonders that He has done. ^{5} And He raises up a testimony in Jacob, || And has placed a law in Israel, || That He commanded our fathers, || To make them known to their sons. ^{6} So that a later generation knows, || Sons who are born, rise and recount to their sons, ^{7} And place their confidence in God, || And do not forget the doings of God, || But keep His commands. ^{8} And they are not like their fathers, || A generation apostatizing and being rebellious, || A generation—it has not prepared its heart, || Nor [is] its spirit steadfast with God. ^{9} Sons of Ephraim—armed bearers of bow, || Have turned in a day of conflict. ^{10} They have not kept the covenant of God, || And they have refused to walk in His law, ^{11} And they forget His doings, || And His wonders that He showed them. ^{12} He has done wonders before their fathers, || In the land of Egypt—the field of Zoan. ^{13} He cleft a sea, and causes them to pass over, || Indeed, He causes waters to stand as a heap. ^{14} And leads them with a cloud by day, || And with a light of fire all the night. ^{15} He cleaves rocks in a wilderness, || And gives drink—as the great deep. ^{16} And brings out streams from a rock, || And causes waters to come down as rivers. ^{17} And they still add to sin against Him, || To provoke the Most High in the dry place. ^{18} And they try God in their heart, || To ask food for their lust. ^{19} And they speak against God—they said: "Is God able to array a table in a wilderness?" ^{20} Behold, He has struck a rock, || And waters flow, indeed, streams overflow. "Also, [is] He able to give bread? Does He prepare flesh for His people?" ^{21} Therefore Yhwh has heard, || And He shows Himself angry, || And fire has been kindled against Jacob, || And anger has also gone up against Israel, ^{22} For they have not believed in God, || Nor have they trusted in His salvation. ^{23} And He commands clouds from above, || Indeed, He has opened doors of the heavens. ^{24} And He rains manna on them to eat, || Indeed, He has given grain of the heavens to them. ^{25} Each has eaten food of the mighty, || He sent provision to them to satiety. ^{26} He causes an east wind to journey in the heavens, || And leads a south wind by His strength, ^{27} And He rains on them flesh as dust, || And as sand of the seas—winged bird, ^{28} And causes [it] to fall in the midst of His camp, || Around His dwelling places. ^{29} And they eat, and are greatly satisfied, || And He brings their desire to them. ^{30} They have not been estranged from their desire, || Their food [is] yet in their mouth, ^{31} And the anger of God has gone up against them, || And He slays among their fat ones, || And He caused youths of Israel to bend. ^{32} With all this they have sinned again, || And have not believed in His wonders. ^{33} And He consumes their days in vanity, || And their years in trouble. ^{34} If He slew them, then they sought Him, || And turned back, and earnestly sought God, ^{35} And they remember that God [is] their rock, || And God Most High their redeemer. ^{36} And they deceive Him with their mouth, || And lie to Him with their tongue, ^{37} And their heart has not been right with Him, || And they have not been steadfast in His covenant. ^{38} And He, the Merciful One, pardons iniquity, and does not destroy, || And has often turned back His anger, || And does not awaken all His fury. ^{39} And He remembers that they [are] flesh, || A wind going on—and it does not return. ^{40} How often do they provoke Him in the wilderness, || Grieve Him in the desolate place? ^{41} Indeed, they turn back, and try God, || And have limited the Holy One of Israel. ^{42} They have not remembered His hand || The day He ransomed them from the adversary. ^{43} When He set His signs in Egypt, || And His wonders in the field of Zoan,

^{44} And He turns their streams to blood, || And they do not drink their floods. ^{45} He sends among them the beetle, and it consumes them, || And the frog, and it destroys them, ^{46} And gives their increase to the caterpillar, || And their labor to the locust. ^{47} He destroys their vine with hail, || And their sycamores with frost, ^{48} And delivers their beasts up to the hail, || And their livestock to the burning flames. ^{49} He sends on them the fury of His anger, || Wrath, and indignation, and distress—A discharge of evil messengers. ^{50} He ponders a path for His anger, || He did not keep back their soul from death, || Indeed, He delivered up their life to the pestilence. ^{51} And He strikes every firstborn in Egypt, || The first-fruit of the strong in tents of Ham. ^{52} And causes His people to journey as a flock, || And guides them as a drove in a wilderness, ^{53} And He leads them confidently, || And they have not been afraid, || And the sea has covered their enemies. ^{54} And He brings them to the border of His sanctuary, || This mountain His right hand had acquired, ^{55} And casts out nations from before them, || And causes them to fall in the line of inheritance, || And causes the tribes of Israel to dwell in their tents, ^{56} And they tempt and provoke God Most High, || And have not kept His testimonies. ^{57} And they turn back, || And deal treacherously like their fathers, || They have been turned like a deceitful bow, ^{58} And make Him angry with their high places, || And make Him zealous with their carved images, ^{59} God has heard, and shows Himself angry. And kicks exceedingly against Israel. ^{60} And He leaves the Dwelling Place of Shiloh, || The tent He had placed among men, ^{61} And He gives His strength to captivity, || And His beauty into the hand of an adversary, ^{62} And delivers His people up to the sword, || And showed Himself angry with His inheritance. ^{63} Fire has consumed His young men, || And His virgins have not been praised. ^{64} His priests have fallen by the sword, || And their widows do not weep. ^{65} And the Lord wakes as a sleeper, || As a mighty one crying aloud from wine. ^{66} And He strikes His adversaries backward, || He has put a continuous reproach on them, ^{67} And He kicks against the tent of Joseph, || And has not fixed on the tribe of Ephraim, ^{68} And He chooses the tribe of Judah, || With Mount Zion that He loved, ^{69} And builds His sanctuary as a high place, || Like the earth, He founded it for all time. ^{70} And He fixes on His servant David, || And takes him from the folds of a flock, ^{71} He has brought him in from behind suckling ones, || To rule over Jacob His people, || And over Israel His inheritance. ^{72} And he rules them according to the integrity of his heart, || And leads them by the skillfulness of his hands!

PSALM 79

^{1} A Psalm of Asaph. O God, nations have come into Your inheritance, || They have defiled Your holy temple, || They made Jerusalem become heaps, ^{2} They gave the dead bodies of Your servants || [As] food for the birds of the heavens, || The flesh of Your saints || For the wild beast of the earth. ^{3} They have shed their blood || As water around Jerusalem, || And there is none burying. ^{4} We have been a reproach to our neighbors, || A scorn and a derision to our surrounders. ^{5} Until when, O Yhwh? are You angry forever? Your jealousy burns as fire. ^{6} Pour Your fury on the nations who have not known You, || And on kingdoms that have not called on Your Name. ^{7} For [one] has devoured Jacob, || And they have made his habitation desolate. ^{8} Do not remember for us the iniquities of forefathers, || Hurry, let Your mercies go before us, || For we have been very weak. ^{9} Help us, O God of our salvation, || Because of the glory of Your Name, || And deliver us, and cover over our sins, || For Your Name's sake. ^{10} Why do the nations say, "Where [is] their God?" Let [it] be known among the nations before our eyes, || The vengeance of the blood of Your servants that is shed. ^{11} Let the groaning of the prisoner come in before You, || According to the greatness of Your arm, || Leave the sons of death. ^{12} And return to our neighbors, || Sevenfold to their bosom, their reproach, || With which they reproached You, O Lord. ^{13} And we, Your people, and the flock of Your pasture, || We give thanks to You for all time, || We recount Your praise from generation to generation!

PSALM 80

^{1} To the Overseer. [Set] to "Lilies of Testimony." A Psalm of Asaph. Shepherd of Israel, give ear, || Leading Joseph as a flock, || Inhabiting the cherubim—shine forth, ² Before Ephraim, and Benjamin, and Manasseh, || Wake up Your might, and come for our salvation. ³ O God, cause us to turn back, || And cause Your face to shine, and we are saved. ⁴ Yhwh, God of Hosts, until when? You have burned against the prayer of Your people. ⁵ You have caused them to eat bread of tears, || And cause them to drink || With tears a third time. ⁶ You make us a strife to our neighbors, || And our enemies mock at it. ⁷ God of Hosts, turn us back, || And cause Your face to shine, and we are saved. ⁸ You bring a vine out of Egypt, || You cast out nations, and plant it. ⁹ You have looked before it, and root it, || And it fills the land, ¹⁰ Hills have been covered [with] its shadow, || And its boughs [are] cedars of God. ¹¹ It sends forth its branches to the sea, || And its shoots to the river. ¹² Why have You broken down its hedges, || And everyone passing by the way has plucked it? ¹³ A boar out of the forest tears it, || And a wild beast of the fields grazes it. ¹⁴ God of Hosts, turn back, we implore You, || Look from the heavens, and see, and inspect this vine, ¹⁵ And the root that Your right hand planted, || And the branch You made strong for Yourself, ¹⁶ Burned with fire—cut down, || They perish from the rebuke of Your face. ¹⁷ Let Your hand be on the man of Your right hand || On the son of man You have strengthened for Yourself. ¹⁸ And we do not go back from You, || You revive us, and in Your Name we call. ¹⁹ O Yhwh, God of Hosts, turn us back, || Cause Your face to shine, and we are saved!

PSALM 81

¹ To the Overseer. On the gittith. By Asaph. Cry aloud to God our strength, || Shout to the God of Jacob. ² Lift up a song, and give out a timbrel, || A pleasant harp with stringed instrument. ³ Blow a horn in the month, || In the new moon, at the day of our festival, ⁴ For it [is] a statute to Israel, || An ordinance of the God of Jacob. ⁵ He has placed it—a testimony on Joseph, || In his going forth over the land of Egypt. A lip, I have not known—I hear. ⁶ I turned aside his shoulder from the burden, || His hands pass over from the basket. ⁷ In distress you have called and I deliver you, || I answer you in the secret place of thunder, || I try you by the waters of Meribah. Selah. ⁸ Hear, O My people, and I testify to you, || O Israel, if you listen to me: ⁹ There is not in you a strange god, || And you do not bow yourself to a strange god. ¹⁰ I [am] your God Yhwh, || Who brings you up out of the land of Egypt. Enlarge your mouth, and I fill it. ¹¹ But My people did not listen to My voice, || And Israel has not consented to Me. ¹² And I send them away in the enmity of their heart, || They walk in their own counsels. ¹³ O that My people were listening to Me, || Israel would walk in My ways. ¹⁴ As a little thing I cause their enemies to bow, || And I turn back My hand against their adversaries, ¹⁵ Those hating Yhwh should have feigned [obedience] to Him, || And their time would last for all time. ¹⁶ He causes him to eat of the fat of wheat, || And I satisfy you [with] honey from a rock!

PSALM 82

¹ A Psalm of Asaph. God has stood in the congregation of God, || He judges among the gods. ² Until when do you judge perversely? And lift up the face of the wicked? Selah. ³ Judge the weak and fatherless, || Declare the afflicted and the poor righteous. ⁴ Let the weak and needy escape, || Deliver them from the hand of the wicked. ⁵ They did not know, nor do they understand, || They habitually walk in darkness, || All the foundations of earth are moved. ⁶ I have said, "You [are] gods, || And sons of the Most High—all of you, ⁷ But you die as man, and you fall as one of the heads." ⁸ Rise, O God, judge the earth, || For You have inheritance among all the nations!

PSALM 83

¹ A Song. A Psalm of Asaph. O God, let there be no silence to You, || Do not be silent, nor be quiet, O God. ² For behold, Your enemies roar, || And those hating You have lifted up the head, ³ They take crafty counsel against Your people, || And consult against Your hidden ones. ⁴ They have said, "Come, and we cut them off from [being] a nation, || And the name of Israel is not remembered anymore." ⁵ For they consulted in heart together, || They make a covenant against You, ⁶ Tents of Edom, and Ishmaelites, Moab, and the Hagarenes, ⁷ Gebal, and Ammon, and Amalek, Philistia with inhabitants of Tyre, ⁸ Asshur is also joined with them, || They have been an arm to sons of Lot. Selah. ⁹ Do to them as Midian, || As Sisera, as Jabin, at the Brook of Kishon. ¹⁰ They were destroyed at Endor, || They were dung for the ground! ¹¹ Make their nobles as Oreb and as Zeeb, || And as Zebah and Zalmunna—all their princes, ¹² Who have said, "Let us occupy the pastures of God for ourselves." ¹³ O my God, make them as a rolling thing, || As stubble before wind. ¹⁴ As a fire burns a forest, || And as a flame sets hills on fire, ¹⁵ So You pursue them with Your whirlwind, || And trouble them with Your windstorm. ¹⁶ Fill their faces [with] shame, || And they seek Your Name, O Yhwh. ¹⁷ They are ashamed and troubled forever, || Indeed, they are confounded and lost. ¹⁸ And they know that You—Your Name [is] Yhwh—By Yourself [are] the Most High over all the earth!

PSALM 84

¹ To the Overseer. On the gittith. A Psalm of the sons of Korah. How beloved Your dwelling places, Yhwh of Hosts! ² My soul desired, indeed, it has also been consumed, || For the courts of Yhwh, || My heart and my flesh cry aloud to the living God, ³ Even a sparrow has found a house, || And a swallow a nest for herself, || Where she has placed her brood—Your altars, O Yhwh of Hosts, || My king and my God. ⁴ O the blessedness of those inhabiting Your house, || Yet they praise You. Selah. ⁵ O the blessedness of a man whose strength is in You, || Highways [are] in their heart. ⁶ Those passing through a valley of weeping make it a spring, || The early rain covers it with pools. ⁷ They go from strength to strength, || He appears to God in Zion. ⁸ O Yhwh, God of Hosts, hear my prayer, || Give ear, O God of Jacob. Selah. ⁹ Our shield, see, O God, || And behold the face of Your anointed, ¹⁰ For a day in Your courts [is] good, O Teacher! I have chosen rather to be at the threshold, || In the house of my God, || Than to dwell in tents of wickedness. ¹¹ For Yhwh God [is] a sun and a shield, || Yhwh gives grace and glory. He does not withhold good || To those walking in uprightness. ¹² Yhwh of Hosts! O the blessedness of a man trusting in You.

PSALM 85

¹ To the Overseer. A Psalm of the sons of Korah. You have accepted, O Yhwh, Your land, || You have turned [to] the captivity of Jacob. ² You have carried away the iniquity of Your people, || You have covered all their sin. Selah. ³ You have gathered up all Your wrath, || You have turned back from the fierceness of Your anger. ⁴ Turn back [to] us, O God of our salvation, || And make void Your anger with us. ⁵ Are You angry against us for all time? Do You draw out Your anger || To generation and generation? ⁶ Do You not turn back? You revive us, || And Your people rejoice in You. ⁷ Show us, O Yhwh, your kindness, || And You give to us Your salvation. ⁸ I hear what God, Yhwh, speaks, || For He speaks peace to His people, || And to His saints, and they do not turn back to folly. ⁹ Surely His salvation [is] near to those fearing Him, || That glory may dwell in our land. ¹⁰ Kindness and truth have met, || Righteousness and peace have kissed, ¹¹ Truth springs up from the earth, || And righteousness looks out from the heavens, ¹² Yhwh also gives that which is good, || And our land gives its increase. ¹³ Righteousness goes before Him, || And makes a way for His footsteps!

PSALM 86

¹ A Prayer of David. Incline, O Yhwh, Your ear, || Answer me, for I [am] poor and needy. ² Keep my soul, for I [am] pious, || Save Your servant who is trusting to You, O You, my God. ³ Favor me, O Lord, for I call to You all the day. ⁴ Make glad the soul of Your servant, || For to You, O Lord, I lift up my soul. ⁵ For You, Lord, [are] good and forgiving, || And abundant in kindness to all calling You. ⁶ Hear, O Yhwh, my prayer, || And attend to the voice of my supplications. ⁷ In a day of my distress I call You, || For You answer me. ⁸ There is none like You among the gods, O Lord, || And like Your works there are

none. ⁹ All nations that You have made || Come and bow themselves before You, O Lord, || And give honor to Your Name. ¹⁰ For You [are] great, and doing wonders, || You [are] God alone. ¹¹ Show me, O Yhwh, Your way, || I walk in Your truth, || My heart rejoices to fear Your Name. ¹² I confess You, O Lord my God, with all my heart, || And I honor Your Name for all time. ¹³ For Your kindness [is] great toward me, || And You have delivered my soul from the lowest Sheol. ¹⁴ O God, the proud have risen up against me, || And a company of the terrible sought my soul, || And have not placed You before them, ¹⁵ And You, O Lord, [are] God, merciful and gracious, || Slow to anger, and abundant in kindness and truth. ¹⁶ Look to me, and favor me, || Give Your strength to Your servant, || And give salvation to a son of Your handmaid. ¹⁷ Do with me a sign for good, || And those hating me see and are ashamed, || For You, O Yhwh, have helped me, || Indeed, You have comforted me!

PSALM 87

¹ A Psalm of the sons of Korah. A Song. His foundation [is] in holy mountains. ² Yhwh is loving the gates of Zion || Above all the dwelling places of Jacob. ³ Honorable things are spoken in You, || O city of God. Selah. ⁴ I mention Rahab and Babel to those knowing Me, || Behold, Philistia, and Tyre, with Cush! This [one] was born there. ⁵ And of Zion it is said: Each one was born in her, || And He, the Most High, establishes her. ⁶ Yhwh recounts in the describing of the peoples, "This [one] was born there." Selah. ⁷ Also singers as players on instruments, || All my fountains [are] in You!

PSALM 88

¹ A Song. A Psalm of the sons of Korah. To the Overseer. [Set] on "Sickness to Afflict." An Instruction of Heman the Ezrahite. O Yhwh, God of my salvation, || Daily I have cried, nightly before You, ² My prayer comes in before You, || Incline Your ear to my loud cry, ³ For my soul has been full of evils, || And my life has come to Sheol. ⁴ I have been reckoned with those going down [to] the pit, || I have been as a man without strength. ⁵ Among the dead—free, || As pierced ones lying in the grave, || Whom You have not remembered anymore, || Indeed, they have been cut off by Your hand. ⁶ You have put me in the lowest pit, || In dark places, in depths. ⁷ Your fury has lain on me, || And You have afflicted [with] all Your breakers. Selah. ⁸ You have put my acquaintance far from me, || You have made me an abomination to them, || Shut up—I do not go forth. ⁹ My eye has grieved because of affliction, || I called You, O Yhwh, all the day, || I have spread out my hands to You. ¹⁰ Do You do wonders to the dead? Does Rephaim rise? do they thank You? Selah. ¹¹ Is Your kindness recounted in the grave? Your faithfulness in destruction? ¹² Are Your wonders known in the darkness? And Your righteousness in the land of forgetfulness? ¹³ And I, to You, O Yhwh, I have cried, || And in the morning my prayer comes before You. ¹⁴ Why, O Yhwh, do You cast off my soul? You hide Your face from me. ¹⁵ I [am] afflicted, and expiring from youth, || I have borne Your terrors—I pine away. ¹⁶ Your wrath has passed over me, || Your terrors have cut me off, ¹⁷ They have surrounded me as waters all the day, || They have gone around against me together, ¹⁸ You have put lover and friend far from me, || My acquaintance [is] the place of darkness!

PSALM 89

¹ An Instruction of Ethan the Ezrahite. Of the kind acts of Yhwh, I sing for all time, || From generation to generation I make known Your faithfulness with my mouth, ² For I said, "Kindness is built for all time, || The heavens! You establish Your faithfulness in them." ³ I have made a covenant for My chosen, || I have sworn to My servant David: ⁴ "Even for all time I establish your seed, || And have built your throne to generation and generation." Selah. ⁵ and the heavens confess Your wonders, O Yhwh, || Your faithfulness [is] also in an assembly of holy ones. ⁶ For who in the sky, compares himself

to Yhwh? [Who] is like to Yhwh among sons of the mighty? ⁷ God is very terrible, || In the secret counsel of His holy ones, || And fearful over all surrounding Him. ⁸ O Yhwh, God of Hosts, || Who [is] like You—a strong Yah? And Your faithfulness [is] around You. ⁹ You [are] ruler over the pride of the sea, || In the lifting up of its billows You restrain them. ¹⁰ You have bruised Rahab, as one wounded. You have scattered Your enemies with the arm of Your strength. ¹¹ The heavens [are] Yours, || The earth [is] also Yours, || The habitable world and its fullness, || You have founded them. ¹² North and south You have appointed them, || Tabor and Hermon sing in Your Name. ¹³ You have an arm with might, || Strong is Your hand—high Your right hand. ¹⁴ Righteousness and judgment || [Are] the fixed place of Your throne, || Kindness and truth go before Your face. ¹⁵ O the blessedness of the people knowing the shout, || O Yhwh, they habitually walk in the light of Your face. ¹⁶ They rejoice in Your Name all the day, || And they are exalted in Your righteousness, ¹⁷ For You [are] the beauty of their strength, || And in Your good will is our horn exalted, ¹⁸ For our shield [is] of Yhwh, || And our king to the Holy One of Israel. ¹⁹ Then You have spoken in vision, || To Your saint, indeed, || You say, I have placed help on a mighty one, || Exalted a chosen one out of the people, ²⁰ I have found My servant David, || With My holy oil I have anointed him. ²¹ With whom My hand is established, || My arm also strengthens him. ²² An enemy does not exact on him, || And a son of perverseness does not afflict him. ²³ And I have beaten down his adversaries before him, || And I plague those hating him, ²⁴ And My faithfulness and kindness [are] with him, || And in My Name is his horn exalted. ²⁵ And I have set his hand on the sea, || And his right hand on the rivers. ²⁶ He proclaims to Me: "You [are] my Father, || My God, and the rock of my salvation." ²⁷ I also appoint him firstborn, || Highest of the kings of the earth. ²⁸ For all time I keep for him My kindness, || And My covenant [is] steadfast with him. ²⁹ And I have set his seed forever, || And his throne as the days of the heavens. ³⁰ If his sons forsake My law, || And do not walk in My judgments; ³¹ If they defile My statutes, || And do not keep My commands, ³² I have looked after their transgression with a rod, || And their iniquity with strokes, ³³ And I do not break My kindness from him, || Nor do I deal falsely in My faithfulness. ³⁴ I do not profane My covenant, || And I do not change that which is going forth from My lips. ³⁵ Once I have sworn by My holiness, || I do not lie to David, ³⁶ His seed is for all time, || And his throne [is] as the sun before Me, ³⁷ It is established as the moon for all time, || And the witness in the sky is steadfast. Selah. ³⁸ And You, You have cast off, and reject, || You have shown Yourself angry with Your anointed, ³⁹ Have rejected the covenant of Your servant, || You have defiled his crown to the earth, ⁴⁰ You have broken down all his hedges, || You have made his fortifications a ruin. ⁴¹ Everyone passing by the way has spoiled him, || He has been a reproach to his neighbors, ⁴² You have exalted the right hand of his adversaries, || You have caused all his enemies to rejoice. ⁴³ Also—You turn back the sharpness of his sword, || And have not established him in battle, ⁴⁴ Have caused [him] to cease from his brightness, || And have cast down his throne to the earth. ⁴⁵ You have shortened the days of his youth, || Have covered him over [with] shame. Selah. ⁴⁶ Until when, O Yhwh, are You hidden? Does Your fury burn as fire forever? ⁴⁷ Remember how [short] my lifetime [is]. Why have You created in vain || All the sons of men? ⁴⁸ Who [is] the man that lives, and does not see death? He delivers his soul from the hand of Sheol. Selah. ⁴⁹ Where [are] Your former kindnesses, O Lord, || [Which] You have sworn to David in Your faithfulness? ⁵⁰ Remember, O Lord, the reproach of Your servants, || I have borne in my bosom all the strivings of the peoples, ⁵¹ With which Your enemies reproached, O Yhwh, || With which they have reproached || The steps of Your anointed. ⁵² Blessed [is] Yhwh for all time. Amen and amen!

PSALM 90

¹ A Prayer of Moses, the man of God. Lord, You have been a habitation, || To us—in generation and generation, ² Before mountains were brought forth, || And You form the earth and the world, || Even from age to age You [are] God. ³ You turn man to a bruised thing, || And say, Return, you sons of men. ⁴ For one thousand years in Your eyes [are] as yesterday, || For it passes on, indeed, [as] a watch by night. ⁵ You have inundated them, they are asleep, || In the morning he changes as grass. ⁶ In the morning it flourishes, and has changed, || At

evening it is cut down, and has withered. [7] For we were consumed in Your anger, || And we have been troubled in Your fury. [8] You have set our iniquities before You, || Our hidden things at the light of Your face, [9] For all our days pined away in Your wrath, || We consumed our years as a meditation. [10] The days of our years, in them [are] seventy years, || And if, by reason of might, eighty years, || Yet their enlargement [is] labor and vanity, || For it has been cut off quickly, and we fly away. [11] Who knows the power of Your anger? And according to Your fear—Your wrath? [12] Let [us] know to number our days correctly, || And we bring the heart to wisdom. [13] Turn back, O Yhwh, until when? And regret concerning Your servants. [14] Satisfy us at morning [with] Your kindness, || And we sing and rejoice all our days. [15] Cause us to rejoice according to the days || Wherein You have afflicted us, || The years we have seen evil. [16] Let Your work appear to Your servants, || And Your honor on their sons. [17] And let the pleasantness of our God Yhwh be on us, || And establish on us the work of our hands, || Indeed, establish the work of our hands!

PSALM 91

[1] He who is dwelling || In the secret place of the Most High, || Habitually lodges in the shade of the Mighty, [2] He is saying of Yhwh, "My refuge, and my bulwark, my God, I trust in Him," [3] For He delivers you from the snare of a fowler, || From a calamitous pestilence. [4] He covers you over with His pinion, || And under His wings you trust, || His truth [is] a shield and buckler. [5] You are not afraid of fear by night, || Of arrow that flies by day, [6] Of pestilence that walks in thick darkness, || Of destruction that destroys at noon, [7] One thousand fall at your side, || And a myriad at your right hand, || [But] it does not come near to you. [8] But with your eyes you look, || And you see the reward of the wicked, [9] (For You, O Yhwh, [are] my refuge), || You made the Most High your habitation. [10] Evil does not happen to you, || And a plague does not come near your tent, [11] For He charges His messengers for you, || To keep you in all your ways, [12] On the hands they bear you up, || Lest you strike your foot against a stone. [13] You tread on lion and cobra, || You trample young lion and dragon. [14] Because he has delighted in Me, || I also deliver him—I set him on high, || Because he has known My Name. [15] He calls Me, and I answer him, || I [am] with him in distress, || I deliver him, and honor him. [16] I satisfy him with [the] length of [his] days, || And I cause him to look on My salvation!

PSALM 92

[1] A Psalm. A Song for the Sabbath day. [It is] good to give thanks to Yhwh, || And to sing praises to Your Name, O Most High, [2] To declare Your kindness in the morning, || And Your faithfulness in the nights. [3] On ten strings and on stringed instrument, || On higgaion, with harp. [4] For You have caused me to rejoice, O Yhwh, in Your work, || I sing concerning the works of Your hands. [5] How great Your works have been, O Yhwh, || Your thoughts have been very deep. [6] A brutish man does not know, || And a fool does not understand this— [7] When the wicked flourish as an herb, || And all workers of iniquity blossom—For their being destroyed forever and ever! [8] And You [are] high for all time, O Yhwh. [9] For behold, Your enemies, O Yhwh, || For behold, Your enemies perish, || All workers of iniquity separate themselves. [10] And You exalt my horn as a wild ox, || I have been anointed with fresh oil. [11] And my eye looks on my enemies, || Of those rising up against me, || The evildoers, my ears hear. [12] The righteous flourish as a palm-tree, || He grows as a cedar in Lebanon. [13] Those planted in the house of Yhwh, || In the courts of our God, flourish. [14] Still they bring forth in old age, || They are fat and flourishing, [15] To declare that Yhwh my Rock [is] upright, || And there is no perverseness in Him!

PSALM 93

[1] Yhwh has reigned, || He has put on excellence, || Yhwh put on strength, He girded Himself, || Also—the world is established, unmoved. [2] Your throne is established since then, || You [are] from the age. [3] Floods have lifted up, O Yhwh, || Floods have lifted up their voice, || Floods lift up their breakers. [4] Mightier than the voices of many mighty waters, breakers of a sea, || [Is] Yhwh on high, [5] Your testimonies have been very steadfast, || Holiness befits Your house, O Yhwh, for [the] length of [Your] days!

PSALM 94

[1] God of vengeance—Yhwh! God of vengeance, shine forth. [2] Be lifted up, judging the earth, || Send back a repayment on the proud. [3] Until when do the wicked, O Yhwh—Until when do the wicked exult? [4] They utter—they speak arrogance, || All working iniquity boast [about] themselves. [5] Your people, O Yhwh, they bruise, || And they afflict Your inheritance. [6] They slay widow and sojourner, || And they murder fatherless ones. [7] And they say, "Yah does not see, || And the God of Jacob does not consider." [8] Consider, you brutish among the people, || And you foolish, when do you act wisely? [9] He who plants the ear, does He not hear? He who forms the eye, does He not see? [10] He who is instructing nations, does He not reprove? He who is teaching man knowledge [is] Yhwh. [11] He knows the thoughts of man, that they [are] vanity. [12] O the blessedness of the man || Whom You instruct, O Yah, || And teach him out of Your law, [13] To give rest to him from days of evil, || While a pit is dug for the wicked. [14] For Yhwh does not leave His people, || And does not forsake His inheritance. [15] For judgment turns back to righteousness, || And after it all the upright of heart. [16] Who rises up for me with evildoers? Who stations himself for me with workers of iniquity? [17] Unless Yhwh [were] a help to me, || My soul had almost inhabited silence. [18] If I have said, "My foot has slipped," || Your kindness, O Yhwh, supports me. [19] In the abundance of my thoughts within me, || Your comforts delight my soul. [20] Is a throne of mischief joined [with] You? A framer of perverseness by statute? [21] They decree against the soul of the righteous, || And declare innocent blood wicked. [22] And Yhwh is for a high place to me, || And my God [is] for a rock—my refuge, [23] And He turns back their iniquity on them, || And in their wickedness cuts them off; Our God Yhwh cuts them off!

PSALM 95

[1] Come, we sing to Yhwh, || We shout to the rock of our salvation. [2] We come before His face with thanksgiving, || We shout to Him with psalms. [3] For Yhwh [is] a great God, || And a great King over all gods. [4] In whose hand [are] the deep places of earth, || And the strong places of hills [are] His. [5] Whose is the sea, and He made it, || And His hands formed the dry land. [6] Come in, we bow ourselves, and we bend, || We kneel before Yhwh our Maker. [7] For He [is] our God, and we the people of His pasture, || And the flock of His hand, || Today, if you listen to His voice, [8] Do not harden your heart as [in] Meribah, || As [in] the day of Massah in the wilderness, [9] Where your fathers have tried Me, indeed, have seen My work. [10] Forty years I am weary of the generation, || And I say, "A people erring in heart—they! And they have not known My ways": [11] Where I swore in My anger, "If they come into My rest—!"

PSALM 96

[1] Sing to Yhwh a new song, || Sing to Yhwh all the earth. [2] Sing to Yhwh, bless His Name, || Proclaim His salvation from day to day. [3] Declare His glory among nations, || His wonders among all the peoples. [4] For Yhwh [is] great, and greatly praised, || He [is] fearful over all gods. [5] For all the gods of the peoples [are] nothing, || And Yhwh made the heavens. [6] Splendor and majesty [are] before Him, || Strength and beauty in His sanctuary. [7] Ascribe to Yhwh, O families of the peoples, || Ascribe to Yhwh glory and strength. [8] Ascribe to Yhwh the glory of His Name, || Lift up a present and come into His courts. [9] Bow yourselves to Yhwh, || In the honor of holiness, || Be afraid of His presence, all the earth. [10] Say among nations, "Yhwh has reigned, || Also—the world is established, unmoved, || He judges the peoples in uprightness." [11] The heavens rejoice, and the earth is joyful, || The sea and its fullness roar. [12] The field exults, and all that [is] in it, || Then all trees of the

forest sing, 13 Before Yhwh, for He has come, || For He has come to judge the earth. He judges the world in righteousness, || And the peoples in His faithfulness!

PSALM 97

1 Yhwh has reigned, || The earth is joyful, many islands rejoice. 2 Cloud and darkness [are] around Him, || Righteousness and judgment the basis of His throne. 3 Fire goes before Him, || And burns around His adversaries. 4 His lightnings have lightened the world, || The earth has seen, and is pained. 5 Hills, like wax, melted before Yhwh, || Before the Lord of all the earth. 6 The heavens declared His righteousness, || And all the peoples have seen His glory. 7 All servants of a carved image are ashamed, || Those boasting themselves in idols, || Bow yourselves to Him, all you gods. 8 Zion has heard and rejoices, || And daughters of Judah are joyful, || Because of Your judgments, O Yhwh. 9 For You, Yhwh, [are] Most High over all the earth, || You have been exalted greatly over all gods. 10 You who love Yhwh, hate evil, || He is keeping the souls of His saints, || He delivers them from the hand of the wicked. 11 Light [is] sown for the righteous, || And joy for the upright of heart. 12 Rejoice, you righteous, in Yhwh, || And give thanks at the remembrance of His holiness!

PSALM 98

1 A Psalm. Sing to Yhwh a new song, || For He has done wonders, || His right hand and His holy arm have given salvation to Him. 2 Yhwh has made His salvation known, || Before the eyes of the nations, || He has revealed His righteousness, 3 He has remembered His kindness, || And His faithfulness to the house of Israel, || All the ends of the earth have seen the salvation of our God. 4 Shout to Yhwh, all the earth, || Break forth, and cry aloud, and sing. 5 Sing to Yhwh with harp, || With harp, and voice of praise, 6 With trumpets, and voice of a horn, shout before the King, Yhwh. 7 The sea and its fullness roar, || The world and the inhabitants in it. 8 Floods clap hand, together hills cry aloud, 9 Before Yhwh, || For He has come to judge the earth, || He judges the world in righteousness, || And the people in uprightness!

PSALM 99

1 Yhwh has reigned, peoples tremble, || The Inhabitant of the cherubim, the earth shakes. 2 Yhwh [is] great in Zion, || And He [is] high over all the peoples. 3 They praise Your Name, "Great, and fearful, [it] is holy!" 4 And the strength of the king || Has loved judgment, || You have established uprightness; Judgment and righteousness in Jacob, || You have done. 5 Exalt our God Yhwh, || And bow yourselves at His footstool, He [is] holy. 6 Moses and Aaron among His priests, || And Samuel among those proclaiming His Name. They are calling to Yhwh, || And He answers them. 7 He speaks to them in a pillar of cloud, || They have kept His testimonies, || And He has given the statute to them. 8 O Yhwh, our God, || You have afflicted them, || You have been a forgiving God to them, || And taking vengeance on their actions. 9 Exalt our God Yhwh, || And bow yourselves at His holy hill, || For our God Yhwh [is] holy!

PSALM 100

1 A Psalm of thanksgiving. Shout to Yhwh, all the earth! 2 Serve Yhwh with joy, come before Him with singing. 3 Know that Yhwh [is] God, || He made us, and we are His, || His people—and the flock of His pasture. 4 Enter His gates with thanksgiving, || His courts with praise, || Give thanks to Him, bless His Name. 5 For Yhwh [is] good, || His kindness [is] for all time, || And His faithfulness to generation and generation!

PSALM 101

1 A Psalm of David. I sing kindness and judgment, || To You, O Yhwh, I sing praise. 2 I act wisely in a perfect way, || When do You come to me? I habitually walk in the integrity of my heart, || In the midst of my house. 3 I do not set a worthless thing before my eyes, || I have hated the work of those turning aside, || It does not adhere to me. 4 A perverse heart turns aside from me, || I do not know wickedness. 5 Whoever slanders his neighbor in secret, || Him I cut off, || The high of eyes and proud of heart, || Him I do not endure. 6 My eyes are on the faithful of the land, || To dwell with me, || Whoever is walking in a perfect way, he serves me. 7 He who is working deceit does not dwell in my house, || Whoever is speaking lies is not established before my eyes. 8 At morning I cut off all the wicked of the land, || To cut off from the city of Yhwh || All the workers of iniquity!

PSALM 102

1 A Prayer of the afflicted when he is feeble, and pours out his complaint before Yhwh. O Yhwh, hear my prayer, indeed, my cry comes to You. 2 Do not hide Your face from me, || In a day of my adversity, || Incline Your ear to me, || In the day I call, hurry, answer me. 3 For my days have been consumed in smoke, || And my bones have burned as a firebrand. 4 Struck as the herb, and withered, is my heart, || For I have forgotten to eat my bread. 5 From the voice of my sighing || My bone has cleaved to my flesh. 6 I have been like to a pelican of the wilderness, || I have been as an owl of the dry places. 7 I have watched, and I am || As a bird alone on the roof. 8 All the day my enemies reproached me, || Those mad at me have sworn against me. 9 Because I have eaten ashes as bread, || And have mingled my drink with weeping, 10 From Your indignation and Your wrath, || For You have lifted me up, || And cast me down. 11 My days [are] stretched out as a shadow, || And I am withered as the herb. 12 And You, O Yhwh, abide for all time, || And Your memorial from generation to generation. 13 You rise— You pity Zion, || For the time to favor her, || For the appointed time has come. 14 For Your servants have been pleased with her stones, || And they favor her dust. 15 And nations fear the Name of Yhwh, || And all kings of the earth Your glory, 16 For Yhwh has built Zion, || He has been seen in His glory, 17 He turned to the prayer of the destitute, || And He has not despised their prayer. 18 This is written for a later generation, || And the people created praise Yah. 19 For He has looked || From the high place of His sanctuary. Yhwh looked attentively from the heavens to earth, 20 To hear the groan of the prisoner, || To loose sons of death, 21 To declare in Zion the Name of Yhwh, || And His praise in Jerusalem, 22 In the peoples being gathered together, || And the kingdoms—to serve Yhwh. 23 He has humbled my power in the way, || He has shortened my days. 24 I say, "My God, do not take me up in the midst of my days," || Your years [are] through all generations. 25 You founded the earth before time, || And the heavens [are] the work of Your hands. 26 They perish, and You remain, || And all of them become old as a garment, || You change them as clothing, || And they are changed. 27 And You [are] the same, and Your years are not finished. 28 The sons of Your servants continue, || And their seed is established before You!

PSALM 103

1 By David. Bless, O my soul, Yhwh, || And all my inward parts—His Holy Name. 2 Bless, O my soul, Yhwh, || And do not forget all His benefits, 3 Who is forgiving all your iniquities, || Who is healing all your diseases, 4 Who is redeeming your life from destruction, || Who is crowning you [with] kindness and mercies, 5 Who is satisfying your desire with good, || Your youth renews itself as an eagle. 6 Yhwh is doing righteousness and judgments || For all the oppressed. 7 He makes His ways known to Moses, || His acts to the sons of Israel. 8 Yhwh [is] merciful and gracious, || Slow to anger, and abundant in mercy. 9 He does not strive forever, || Nor does He watch for all time. 10 He has not done to us according to our sins, || Nor according to our iniquities || Has He conferred benefits on us. 11 For as the height of the heavens [is] above the earth, || His kindness has been mighty over those fearing Him. 12 He has put our transgressions far from us—as the distance of east from west. 13 As a father has mercy on sons, || Yhwh has mercy on those fearing Him. 14 For He has known our frame, ||

Remembering that we [are] dust. ¹⁵ Mortal man! His days [are] as grass, || He flourishes as a flower of the field; ¹⁶ For a wind has passed over it, and it is not, || And its place does not discern it anymore. ¹⁷ And the kindness of Yhwh || [Is] from age even to age on those fearing Him, || And His righteousness to sons' sons, ¹⁸ To those keeping His covenant, || And to those remembering His precepts to do them. ¹⁹ Yhwh has established His throne in the heavens, || And His kingdom has ruled over all. ²⁰ Bless Yhwh, you His messengers, || Mighty in power—doing His word, || To listen to the voice of His word. ²¹ Bless Yhwh, all you His hosts, || His ministers—doing His pleasure. ²² Bless Yhwh, all you His works, || In all places of His dominion. Bless, O my soul, Yhwh!

PSALM 104

¹ Bless, O my soul, Yhwh! Yhwh, my God, || You have been very great, || You have put on splendor and majesty. ² Covering Himself [with] light as a garment, || Stretching out the heavens as a curtain, ³ Who is laying the beam of His upper chambers in the waters, || Who is making thick clouds His chariot, || Who is walking on wings of wind, ⁴ Making His messengers—the winds, || His ministers—the flaming fire. ⁵ He has founded earth on its bases, || It is not moved for all time and forever. ⁶ The abyss! You have covered it as with clothing, || Waters stand above hills. ⁷ They flee from Your rebuke, || They hurry away from the voice of Your thunder. ⁸ They go up hills—they go down valleys, || To a place You have founded for them. ⁹ You have set a border, they do not pass over, || They do not turn back to cover the earth. ¹⁰ He is sending forth fountains in valleys, || They go on between hills. ¹¹ They water every beast of the field, || Wild donkeys break their thirst. ¹² The bird of the heavens dwells by them, || From between the branches || They give forth the voice. ¹³ Watering hills from His upper chambers, || The earth is satisfied from the fruit of Your works. ¹⁴ Causing grass to spring up for livestock, || And herb for the service of man, || To bring forth bread from the earth, ¹⁵ And wine—it makes the heart of man glad, || To cause the face to shine from oil, || And bread—it supports the heart of man. ¹⁶ The trees of Yhwh [are] satisfied, || Cedars of Lebanon that He has planted, ¹⁷ Where birds make nests, || The stork—the firs [are] her house. ¹⁸ The high hills [are] for wild goats, rocks [are] a refuge for hyraxes, ¹⁹ He made the moon for seasons, || The sun has known his place of entrance. ²⁰ You set darkness, and it is night, || Every beast of the forest creeps in it. ²¹ The young lions are roaring for prey, || And to seek their food from God. ²² The sun rises, they are gathered, || And they crouch in their dens. ²³ Man goes forth to his work, || And to his service—until evening. ²⁴ How many have been Your works, O Yhwh, || You have made all of them in wisdom, || The earth is full of your possessions. ²⁵ This, the sea, great and broad of sides, || There [are] moving things—innumerable, || Living creatures—small with great. ²⁶ There ships go—[and] leviathan, || That You have formed to play in it. ²⁷ All of them look to You, || To give their food in its season. ²⁸ You give to them—they gather, || You open Your hand—they [are] satisfied [with] good. ²⁹ You hide Your face—they are troubled, || You gather their spirit—they expire, || And they return to their dust. ³⁰ You send out Your Spirit, they are created, || And You renew the face of the ground. ³¹ The glory of Yhwh is for all time, || Yhwh rejoices in His works, ³² Who is looking to earth, and it trembles, || He comes against hills, and they smoke. ³³ I sing to Yhwh during my life, || I sing praise to my God while I exist. ³⁴ My meditation on Him is sweet, || I rejoice in Yhwh. ³⁵ Sinners are consumed from the earth, || And the wicked are no more. Bless, O my soul, Yhwh. Praise Yah!

PSALM 105

¹ Give thanks to Yhwh—call on His Name, || Make His acts known among the peoples. ² Sing to Him—sing praise to Him, || Meditate on all His wonders. ³ Boast yourselves in His Holy Name, || The heart of those seeking Yhwh rejoices. ⁴ Seek Yhwh and His strength, || Seek His face continually. ⁵ Remember His wonders that He did, || His signs and the judgments of His mouth. ⁶ O seed of Abraham, His servant, || O sons of Jacob, His chosen ones. ⁷ He [is] our God Yhwh, || His judgments [are] in all the earth. ⁸ He has remembered His covenant for all time, || The word He commanded to one

thousand generations, ⁹ That He has made with Abraham, || And His oath to Isaac, ¹⁰ And establishes it to Jacob for a statute, || To Israel—a perpetual covenant, ¹¹ Saying, "I give the land of Canaan to you, || The portion of your inheritance," ¹² In their being few in number, || But a few, and sojourners in it. ¹³ And they go up and down, from nation to nation, || From a kingdom to another people. ¹⁴ He has not permitted any to oppress them || And He reproves kings for their sakes. ¹⁵ "Do not strike against My anointed, || And do no evil to My prophets." ¹⁶ And He calls a famine on the land, || He has broken the whole staff of bread. ¹⁷ He has sent a man before them, || Joseph has been sold for a servant. ¹⁸ They have afflicted his feet with chains, || Iron has entered his soul, ¹⁹ Until the time of the coming of His word || The saying of Yhwh has tried him. ²⁰ The king has sent, and looses him, || The ruler of the peoples, and draws him out. ²¹ He has made him lord of his house, || And ruler over all his possessions. ²² To bind his chiefs at his pleasure, || And he makes his elderly wise. ²³ And Israel comes into Egypt, || And Jacob has sojourned in the land of Ham. ²⁴ And He makes His people very fruitful, || And makes it mightier than its adversaries. ²⁵ He turned their heart to hate His people, || To conspire against His servants. ²⁶ He has sent His servant Moses, || Aaron whom He had fixed on. ²⁷ They have set among them the matters of His signs, || And wonders in the land of Ham. ²⁸ He has sent darkness, and it is dark, || And they have not provoked His word. ²⁹ He has turned their waters to blood, || And puts their fish to death. ³⁰ Their land has teemed [with] frogs, || In the inner chambers of their kings. ³¹ He has commanded, and the beetle comes, || Lice into all their border. ³² He has made their showers hail, || A flaming fire [is] in their land. ³³ And He strikes their vine and their fig, || And shatters the trees of their border. ³⁴ He has commanded, and the locust comes, || And the cankerworm—innumerable, ³⁵ And it consumes every herb in their land, || And it consumes the fruit of their ground. ³⁶ And He strikes every firstborn in their land, || The first-fruit of all their strength, ³⁷ And brings them out with silver and gold, || And there is not a feeble one in its tribes. ³⁸ Egypt has rejoiced in their going forth, || For their fear had fallen on them. ³⁹ He has spread a cloud for a covering, || And fire to enlighten the night. ⁴⁰ They have asked, and He brings quails, || And satisfies them [with] bread of the heavens. ⁴¹ He has opened a rock, and waters flow, || They have gone on in dry places—a river. ⁴² For He has remembered His holy word, || With His servant Abraham, ⁴³ And He brings forth His people with joy, || His chosen ones with singing. ⁴⁴ And He gives to them the lands of nations, || And they possess the labor of peoples, ⁴⁵ That they may observe His statutes, || And may keep His laws. Praise Yah!

PSALM 106

¹ Praise Yah, give thanks to Yhwh, for [He is] good, for His kindness [is] for all time! ² Who utters the mighty acts of Yhwh? Sounds all His praise? ³ O the blessedness of those keeping judgment, || Doing righteousness at all times. ⁴ Remember me, O Yhwh, || With the favor of Your people, || Look after me in Your salvation. ⁵ To look on the good of Your chosen ones, || To rejoice in the joy of Your nation, || To boast myself with Your inheritance. ⁶ We have sinned with our fathers, || We have done perversely, we have done wickedly. ⁷ Our fathers in Egypt, || Have not considered wisely Your wonders, || They have not remembered || The abundance of Your kind acts, || And provoke by the sea, at the Sea of Suph. ⁸ And He saves them for His Name's sake, || To make His might known, ⁹ And rebukes the Sea of Suph, and it is dried up, || And causes them to go || Through depths as a wilderness. ¹⁰ And He saves them from the hand || Of him who is hating, || And redeems them from the hand of the enemy. ¹¹ And waters cover their adversaries, || One of them has not been left. ¹² And they believe in His words, they sing His praise, ¹³ They have hurried—forgotten His works, || They have not waited for His counsel. ¹⁴ And they lust greatly in a wilderness, || And try God in a desert. ¹⁵ And He gives to them their request, || And sends leanness into their soul. ¹⁶ And they are envious of Moses in the camp, || Of Aaron, Yhwh's holy one. ¹⁷ Earth opens, and swallows up Dathan, || And covers over the company of Abiram. ¹⁸ And fire burns among their company, || A flame sets the wicked on fire. ¹⁹ They make a calf in Horeb, || And bow themselves to a molten image, ²⁰ And change their glory || Into the form of an ox eating herbs. ²¹ They have forgotten God their Savior, || The doer of great things in Egypt, ²² Of

wonderful things in the land of Ham, || Of fearful things by the Sea of Suph. ²³ And He commands to destroy them, || Unless Moses, His chosen one, || Had stood in the breach before Him, || To turn back His wrath from destroying. ²⁴ And they kick against the desirable land, || They have not given credence to His word. ²⁵ And they murmur in their tents, || They have not listened to the voice of Yhwh. ²⁶ And He lifts up His hand to them, || To cause them to fall in a wilderness, ²⁷ And to cause their seed to fall among nations, || And to scatter them through lands. ²⁸ And they are coupled to Ba'al-Peor, || And eat the sacrifices of the dead, ²⁹ And they provoke to anger by their actions, || And a plague breaks forth on them, ³⁰ And Phinehas stands, and executes judgment, || And the plague is restrained, ³¹ And it is reckoned to him for righteousness, || From generation to generation—for all time. ³² And they cause wrath by the waters of Meribah, || And it is evil to Moses for their sakes, ³³ For they have provoked his spirit, || And he speaks wrongfully with his lips. ³⁴ They have not destroyed the peoples, || As Yhwh had commanded to them, ³⁵ And mix themselves among nations, and learn their works, ³⁶ And serve their idols, || And they are for a snare to them. ³⁷ And they sacrifice their sons and their daughters to the demons, ³⁸ And they shed innocent blood—Blood of their sons and of their daughters, || Whom they have sacrificed to idols of Canaan, || And the land is profaned with blood. ³⁹ And they are defiled with their works, || And commit whoredom in their habitual doings. ⁴⁰ And the anger of Yhwh || Is kindled against His people, || And He detests His inheritance. ⁴¹ And gives them into the hand of nations, || And those hating them rule over them, ⁴² And their enemies oppress them, || And they are humbled under their hand. ⁴³ He delivers them many times, || And they rebel in their counsel, || And they are brought low in their iniquity. ⁴⁴ And He looks on their distress || When He hears their cry, ⁴⁵ And remembers His covenant for them, || And is comforted, || According to the abundance of His kindness. ⁴⁶ And He appoints them for mercies || Before all their captors. ⁴⁷ Save us, O our God Yhwh, and gather us from the nations, || To give thanks to Your Holy Name, || To glory in Your praise. ⁴⁸ Blessed [is] Yhwh, God of Israel, || From age until age. And all the people said, "Amen, praise Yah!"

PSALM 107

¹ "Give thanks to Yhwh, || For [He is] good, for His kindness [is] for all time": ² Let the redeemed of Yhwh say [so], || Whom He redeemed from the hand of an adversary. ³ And has gathered them from the lands, || From east and from west, || From north, and from the sea. ⁴ They wandered in a wilderness, in a desert by the way, || They have not found a city of habitation. ⁵ Hungry—indeed—thirsty, || Their soul becomes feeble in them, ⁶ And they cry to Yhwh in their adversity, || He delivers them from their distress, ⁷ And causes them to tread in a right way, || To go to a city of habitation. ⁸ They confess to Yhwh His kindness, || And His wonders to the sons of men. ⁹ For He has satisfied a longing soul, || And has filled a hungry soul [with] goodness. ¹⁰ Inhabitants of dark places and death-shade, || Prisoners of affliction and of iron, ¹¹ Because they changed the saying of God, || And despised the counsel of the Most High. ¹² And He humbles their heart with labor, || They have been feeble, and there is no helper. ¹³ And they cry to Yhwh in their adversity, || He saves them from their distresses. ¹⁴ He brings them out from the dark place, || And death-shade, || And He draws away their bands. ¹⁵ They confess to Yhwh His kindness, || And His wonders to the sons of men. ¹⁶ For He has broken doors of bronze, || And He has cut bars of iron. ¹⁷ Fools, by means of their transgression, || And by their iniquities, afflict themselves. ¹⁸ Their soul detests all food, || And they come near to the gates of death, ¹⁹ And cry to Yhwh in their adversity, || He saves them from their distresses, ²⁰ He sends His word and heals them, || And delivers [them] from their destructions. ²¹ They confess to Yhwh His kindness, || And His wonders to the sons of men, ²² And they sacrifice sacrifices of thanksgiving, || And recount His works with singing. ²³ Those going down [to] the sea in ships, || Doing business in many waters, ²⁴ They have seen the works of Yhwh, || And His wonders in the deep. ²⁵ And He commands, and appoints a storm, || And it lifts up its billows, ²⁶ They go up [to] the heavens, they go down [to] the depths, || Their soul is melted in evil. ²⁷ They reel to and fro, and move as a drunkard, || And all their wisdom is swallowed up. ²⁸ And they cry to Yhwh in their adversity, || And He brings them out from their

distresses. ²⁹ He calms a whirlwind, || And their billows are hushed. ³⁰ And they rejoice because they are quiet, || And He leads them to the haven of their desire. ³¹ They confess to Yhwh His kindness, || And His wonders to the sons of men, ³² And they exalt Him in [the] assembly of [the] people, || And praise Him in [the] seat of [the] elderly. ³³ He makes rivers become a wilderness, || And fountains of waters become dry land. ³⁴ A fruitful land becomes a barren place, || For the wickedness of its inhabitants. ³⁵ He makes a wilderness become a pool of water, || And a dry land become fountains of waters. ³⁶ And He causes the hungry to dwell there, || And they prepare a city of habitation. ³⁷ And they sow fields, and plant vineyards, || And they make fruits of increase. ³⁸ And He blesses them, and they multiply exceedingly, || And He does not diminish their livestock. ³⁹ And they are diminished, and bow down, || By restraint, evil, and sorrow. ⁴⁰ He is pouring contempt on nobles, || And causes them to wander in vacancy—no way. ⁴¹ And sets the needy on high from affliction, || And places families as a flock. ⁴² The upright see and rejoice, || And all perversity has shut her mouth. ⁴³ Who [is] wise, and observes these? They understand the kind acts of Yhwh!

PSALM 108

¹ A Song. A Psalm of David. My heart is prepared, O God, || I sing, indeed, I sing praise, also my glory. ² Awake, stringed instrument and harp, || I awake the dawn. ³ I thank You among peoples, O Yhwh, || And I praise You among the nations. ⁴ For Your kindness [is] great above the heavens, || And Your truth to the clouds. ⁵ Be exalted above the heavens, O God, || And Your glory above all the earth. ⁶ That Your beloved ones may be delivered, || Save [with] Your right hand, and answer us. ⁷ God has spoken in His holiness: I exult, I apportion Shechem, || And I measure the Valley of Succoth, ⁸ Gilead [is] Mine, Manasseh [is] Mine, || And Ephraim [is] the strength of My head, || Judah [is] My lawgiver, ⁹ Moab [is] a pot for My washing, || On Edom I cast My shoe, || Over Philistia I habitually shout. ¹⁰ Who brings me [into] the fortified city? Who has led me to Edom? ¹¹ Have You not, O God, cast us off? And You do not go out, O God, with our hosts! ¹² Give to us help from adversity, || And the salvation of man is vain. ¹³ We do mightily in God, || And He treads down our adversaries!

PSALM 109

¹ To the Overseer. A Psalm of David. O God of my praise, do not be silent, ² For the mouth of wickedness, and the mouth of deceit, || They have opened against me, || They have spoken with me—A tongue of falsehood, and words of hatred! ³ They have surrounded me about, || And they fight me without cause. ⁴ For my love they oppose me, and I—prayer! ⁵ And they set against me evil for good, || And hatred for my love. ⁶ Appoint the wicked over him, || And an adversary stands at his right hand. ⁷ In his being judged, he goes forth wicked, || And his prayer is for sin. ⁸ His days are few, another takes his oversight, ⁹ His sons are fatherless, and his wife a widow. ¹⁰ And his sons wander continually, || Indeed, they have begged, || And have sought out of their dry places. ¹¹ An exactor lays a snare for all that he has, || And strangers spoil his labor. ¹² He has none to extend kindness, || Nor is there one showing favor to his orphans. ¹³ His posterity is for cutting off, || Their name is blotted out in another generation. ¹⁴ The iniquity of his fathers || Is remembered to Yhwh, || And the sin of his mother is not blotted out. ¹⁵ They are continually before Yhwh, || And He cuts off their memorial from earth. ¹⁶ Because that he has not remembered to do kindness, || And pursues the poor man and needy, || And the struck of heart—to slay, ¹⁷ And he loves reviling, and it meets him, || And he has not delighted in blessing, || And it is far from him. ¹⁸ And he puts on reviling as his robe, || And it comes in as water into his midst, || And as oil into his bones. ¹⁹ It is to him as apparel—he covers himself, || And he girds it on for a continual girdle. ²⁰ This [is] the wage of my accusers from Yhwh, || And of those speaking evil against my soul. ²¹ And You, O Lord Yhwh, || Deal with me for Your Name's sake, || Because Your kindness [is] good, deliver me. ²² For I [am] poor and needy, || And my heart has been pierced in my midst. ²³ I have gone as a shadow when it is stretched out, || I have been driven away as a locust. ²⁴ My knees have been feeble from fasting, || And my flesh has failed

of fatness. ²⁵ And I have been a reproach to them, || They see me, they shake their head. ²⁶ Help me, O Yhwh my God, || Save me, according to Your kindness. ²⁷ And they know that this [is] Your hand, || You, O Yhwh, You have done it. ²⁸ They revile, and You bless, || They have risen, and are ashamed, || And Your servant rejoices. ²⁹ My accusers put on blushing, and are covered, || Their shame [is] as an upper robe. ³⁰ I thank Yhwh greatly with my mouth, || And I praise Him in the midst of many, ³¹ For He stands at the right hand of the needy, || To save from those judging his soul.

PSALM 110

¹ A Psalm of David. A declaration of Yhwh to my Lord: "Sit at My right hand, || Until I make Your enemies Your footstool." ² Yhwh sends the rod of Your strength from Zion, || Rule in the midst of Your enemies. ³ Your people [are] free-will gifts in the day of Your strength, in the honors of holiness, || From the womb, from the morning, || You have the dew of Your youth. ⁴ Yhwh has sworn, and does not relent, "You [are] a priest for all time, || According to the order of Melchizedek." ⁵ The Lord on Your right hand struck kings || In the day of His anger. ⁶ He judges among the nations, || He has completed the carcasses, || Has struck the head over the mighty earth. ⁷ He drinks from a brook in the way, || Therefore He lifts up the head!

PSALM 111

¹ Praise Yah! [Aleph-Bet] I thank Yhwh with the whole heart, || In the secret meeting of the upright, || And of the congregation. ² Great [are] the works of Yhwh, || Sought out by all desiring them. ³ Splendid and majestic is His work, || And His righteousness is standing forever. ⁴ He has made a memorial of His wonders, || Yhwh [is] gracious and merciful. ⁵ He has given prey to those fearing Him, || He remembers His covenant for all time. ⁶ He has declared the power of His works to His people, || To give to them the inheritance of nations. ⁷ The works of His hands [are] true and just, || All His appointments [are] steadfast. ⁸ They are sustained forever and for all time. They are made in truth and uprightness. ⁹ He has sent redemption to His people, || He has appointed His covenant for all time, || His Name [is] holy and fearful. ¹⁰ The fear of Yhwh [is] the beginning of wisdom, || Good understanding have all doing them, || His praise [is] standing forever!

PSALM 112

¹ Praise Yah! [Aleph-Bet] O the blessedness of one fearing Yhwh, || He has greatly delighted in His commands. ² His seed is mighty in the earth, || The generation of the upright is blessed. ³ Wealth and riches [are] in his house, || And his righteousness is standing forever. ⁴ Light has risen in darkness to the upright, || Gracious, and merciful, and righteous. ⁵ The man—good, gracious, and lending, || He sustains his matters in judgment. ⁶ For he is not moved for all time; For the righteous is a continuous memorial. ⁷ He is not afraid of an evil report, || His heart is prepared [and] confident in Yhwh. ⁸ His heart is sustained—he does not fear, || Until he looks on his adversaries. ⁹ He has scattered—has given to the needy, || His righteousness is standing forever, || His horn is exalted with glory. ¹⁰ The wicked sees, and has been angry, || He gnashes his teeth, and has melted, || The desire of the wicked perishes!

PSALM 113

¹ Praise Yah! Praise, you servants of Yhwh. Praise the Name of Yhwh. ² The Name of Yhwh is blessed, || From now on, and for all time. ³ From the rising of the sun to its going in, || The Name of Yhwh [is] praised. ⁴ Yhwh [is] high above all nations, || His glory [is] above the heavens. ⁵ Who [is] as our God Yhwh, || He is exalting [Himself] to sit? ⁶ He is humbling [Himself] to look || On the heavens and on the earth. ⁷ He is raising up the poor from the dust, || He exalts the needy from a dunghill. ⁸ To cause [them] to sit with princes, || With the princes of His

people. ⁹ Causing the barren one of the house to sit, || A joyful mother of sons; praise Yah!

PSALM 114

¹ In the going out of Israel from Egypt, || The house of Jacob from a strange people, ² Judah became His sanctuary, || Israel his dominion. ³ The sea has seen, and flees, || The Jordan turns backward. ⁴ The mountains have skipped as rams, || Heights as sons of a flock. ⁵ What is [ailing] you, O sea, that you flee? O Jordan, you turn back! ⁶ O mountains, you skip as rams! O heights, as sons of a flock! ⁷ From before the Lord be afraid, O earth, || From before the God of Jacob, ⁸ He is turning the rock to a pool of waters, || The flint to a fountain of waters!

PSALM 115

¹ Not to us, O Yhwh, not to us, || But to Your Name give glory, || For Your kindness, for Your truth. ² Why do the nations say, "Where, pray, [is] their God?" ³ And our God [is] in the heavens, || All that He has pleased He has done. ⁴ Their idols [are] silver and gold, work of man's hands, ⁵ They have a mouth, and they do not speak, || They have eyes, and they do not see, ⁶ They have ears, and they do not hear, || They have a nose, and they do not smell, ⁷ Their hands, but they do not handle, || Their feet, and they do not walk; ⁸ Nor do they mutter through their throat, || Their makers are like them, || Everyone who is trusting in them. ⁹ O Israel, trust in Yhwh, "He [is] their help and their shield." ¹⁰ O house of Aaron, trust in Yhwh, "He [is] their help and their shield." ¹¹ You fearing Yhwh, trust in Yhwh, "He [is] their help and their shield." ¹² Yhwh has remembered us, He blesses, || He blesses the house of Israel, || He blesses the house of Aaron, ¹³ He blesses those fearing Yhwh, || The small with the great. ¹⁴ Yhwh adds to you—to you and to your sons. ¹⁵ Blessed [are] you of Yhwh, || Maker of the heavens and earth, ¹⁶ The heavens—the heavens [are] Yhwh's, || And He has given the earth to sons of men; ¹⁷ The dead do not praise Yah, || Nor any going down to silence. ¹⁸ And we, we bless Yah, || From now on, and for all time. Praise Yah!

PSALM 116

¹ I have loved, because Yhwh hears My voice, my supplication, ² Because He has inclined His ear to me, || And during my days I call. ³ Cords of death have surrounded me, || And straits of Sheol have found me, || I find distress and sorrow. ⁴ And in the Name of Yhwh I call: Ah, now, O Yhwh, deliver my soul, ⁵ Yhwh [is] gracious, and righteous, || Indeed, our God [is] merciful, ⁶ Yhwh [is] a preserver of the simple, || I was low, and He gives salvation to me. ⁷ Return, O my soul, to your rest, || For Yhwh has conferred benefits on you. ⁸ For You have delivered my soul from death, || My eyes from tears, my feet from overthrowing. ⁹ I habitually walk before Yhwh || In the lands of the living. ¹⁰ I have believed, for I speak, || I have been greatly afflicted. ¹¹ I said in my haste, "Every man [is] a liar." ¹² What do I return to Yhwh? All His benefits [are] on me. ¹³ I lift up the cup of salvation, || And in the Name of Yhwh I call. ¹⁴ Let me complete my vows to Yhwh, || Now, before all His people. ¹⁵ Precious in the eyes of Yhwh [is] the death of His saints. ¹⁶ Ah, now, O Yhwh, for I [am] Your servant; I [am] Your servant, son of Your handmaid; You have opened my bonds. ¹⁷ I sacrifice a sacrifice of thanks to You, || And in the Name of Yhwh I call. ¹⁸ Let me complete my vows to Yhwh, || Now, before all His people, ¹⁹ In the courts of the house of Yhwh, || In your midst, O Jerusalem, praise Yah!

PSALM 117

¹ Praise Yhwh, all you nations, || Glorify Him, all you peoples! ² For His kindness has been mighty to us, || And the truth of Yhwh [is] for all time. Praise Yah!

PSALM 118

¹ Give thanks to Yhwh, || For [He is] good, for His kindness [is] for all time. ² Now let Israel say, || His kindness [is] for all time. ³ Now let the house of Aaron say, || His kindness [is] for all time. ⁴ Now let those fearing Yhwh say, || His kindness [is] for all time. ⁵ I called Yah from the narrow place, || Yah answered me in a broad place. ⁶ Yhwh [is] for me, || I do not fear what man does to me. ⁷ Yhwh [is] for me among my helpers, || And I look on those hating me. ⁸ Better to take refuge in Yhwh, || Than to trust in man, ⁹ Better to take refuge in Yhwh, || Than to trust in princes. ¹⁰ All nations have surrounded me, || In the Name of Yhwh I surely cut them off. ¹¹ They have surrounded me, || Indeed, they have surrounded me, || In the Name of Yhwh I surely cut them off. ¹² They surrounded me as bees, || They have been extinguished as a fire of thorns, || In the Name of Yhwh I surely cut them off. ¹³ You have severely thrust me to fall, || And Yhwh has helped me. ¹⁴ Yah is my strength and song, || And He is to me for salvation. ¹⁵ A voice of singing and salvation, || [Is] in the tents of the righteous, || The right hand of Yhwh is doing valiantly. ¹⁶ The right hand of Yhwh is exalted, || The right hand of Yhwh is doing valiantly. ¹⁷ I do not die, but live, || And recount the works of Yah, ¹⁸ Yah has severely disciplined me, || And has not given me up to death. ¹⁹ Open gates of righteousness to me, || I enter into them—I thank Yah. ²⁰ This [is] the gate to Yhwh, || The righteous enter into it. ²¹ I thank You, for You have answered me, || And are to me for salvation. ²² A stone the builders refused || Has become head of a corner. ²³ This has been from Yhwh, || It [is] wonderful in our eyes, ²⁴ This [is] the day Yhwh has made, || We rejoice and are glad in it. ²⁵ Ah, now, O Yhwh, please save, || Ah, now, O Yhwh, please prosper. ²⁶ Blessed [is] He who is coming || In the Name of Yhwh, || We blessed you from the house of Yhwh, ²⁷ God [is] Yhwh, and He gives light to us, || Direct the festal-sacrifice with cords, || To the horns of the altar. ²⁸ You [are] my God, and I confess You, || My God, I exalt You. ²⁹ Give thanks to Yhwh, || For [He is] good, for His kindness [is] for all time!

PSALM 119

¹ [Aleph] O the blessedness of those perfect in the way, || They are walking in the Law of Yhwh, ² O the blessedness of those keeping His testimonies, || They seek Him with the whole heart. ³ Indeed, they have not done iniquity, || They have walked in His ways. ⁴ You have commanded us to diligently keep Your precepts, ⁵ O that my ways were prepared to keep Your statutes, ⁶ Then I am not ashamed || In my looking to all Your commands. ⁷ I confess You with uprightness of heart, || In my learning the judgments of Your righteousness. ⁸ I keep Your statutes, do not utterly leave me! ⁹ [Beth] With what does a young man purify his path? To observe—according to Your word. ¹⁰ I have sought You with all my heart, || Do not let me err from Your commands. ¹¹ I have hid Your saying in my heart, || That I do not sin before You. ¹² Blessed [are] You, O Yhwh, teach me Your statutes. ¹³ With my lips I have recounted || All the judgments of Your mouth. ¹⁴ I have rejoiced in the way of Your testimonies, || As over all wealth. ¹⁵ I meditate on Your precepts, || And I attentively behold Your paths. ¹⁶ I delight myself in Your statutes, || I do not forget Your word. ¹⁷ [Gimel] Confer benefits on Your servant, || I live, and I keep Your word. ¹⁸ Uncover my eyes, and I behold wonders out of Your law. ¹⁹ I [am] a sojourner on earth, || Do not hide Your commands from me. ²⁰ My soul has broken for desire || To Your judgments at all times. ²¹ You have rebuked the cursed proud, || Who are erring from Your commands. ²² Remove reproach and contempt from me, || For I have kept Your testimonies. ²³ Princes also sat—they spoke against me, || Your servant meditates on Your statutes, ²⁴ Your testimonies [are] also my delight, || The men of my counsel! ²⁵ [Daleth] My soul has cleaved to the dust, || Quicken me according to Your word. ²⁶ I have recounted my ways, || And You answer me, teach me Your statutes, ²⁷ Cause me to understand the way of Your precepts, || And I meditate on Your wonders. ²⁸ My soul has dropped from affliction, || Establish me according to Your word. ²⁹ Turn aside the way of falsehood from me || And favor me with Your law. ³⁰ I have chosen the way of faithfulness, || I have compared Your judgments, ³¹ I have adhered to Your testimonies, || O Yhwh, do not put me to shame. ³² I run the way of Your commands, || For You enlarge my heart! ³³ [He] Show me, O Yhwh, the way of Your statutes, || And I keep it—[to] the end. ³⁴ Cause me to understand, and I keep Your law, || And observe it with the whole heart. ³⁵ Cause me to tread in the path of Your commands, || For I have delighted in it. ³⁶ Incline my heart to Your testimonies, || And not to dishonest gain. ³⁷ Remove my eyes from seeing vanity, || Quicken me in Your way. ³⁸ Establish Your saying to Your servant, || That [is] concerning Your fear. ³⁹ Remove my reproach that I have feared, || For Your judgments [are] good. ⁴⁰ Behold, I have longed for Your precepts, || Quicken me in Your righteousness, ⁴¹ [Waw] And Your kindness meets me, O Yhwh, || Your salvation according to Your saying. ⁴² And I answer him who is reproaching me a word, || For I have trusted in Your word. ⁴³ And You do not utterly take away || The word of truth from my mouth, || Because I have hoped for Your judgment. ⁴⁴ And I keep Your law continually, || For all time and forever. ⁴⁵ And I habitually walk in a broad place, || For I have sought Your precepts. ⁴⁶ And I speak of Your testimonies before kings, || And I am not ashamed. ⁴⁷ And I delight myself in Your commands, || That I have loved, ⁴⁸ And I lift up my hands to Your commands, || That I have loved, || And I meditate on Your statutes! ⁴⁹ [Zayin] Remember the word to Your servant, || On which You have caused me to hope. ⁵⁰ This [is] my comfort in my affliction, || That Your saying has quickened me. ⁵¹ The proud have utterly scorned me, || I have not turned aside from Your law. ⁵² I remembered Your judgments of old, O Yhwh, || And I comfort myself. ⁵³ Horror has seized me, || Because of the wicked forsaking Your law. ⁵⁴ Your statutes have been songs to me, || In the house of my sojournings. ⁵⁵ I have remembered Your Name in the night, O Yhwh, || And I keep Your law. ⁵⁶ This has been to me, || That I have kept Your precepts! ⁵⁷ [Heth] Yhwh [is] my portion; I have said I would keep Your words, ⁵⁸ I appeased Your face with the whole heart, || Favor me according to Your saying. ⁵⁹ I have reckoned my ways, || And turn back my feet to Your testimonies. ⁶⁰ I have made haste, || And did not delay, to keep Your commands. ⁶¹ Cords of the wicked have surrounded me, || I have not forgotten Your law. ⁶² At midnight I rise to give thanks to You, || For the judgments of Your righteousness. ⁶³ I [am] a companion to all who fear You, || And to those keeping Your precepts. ⁶⁴ Of Your kindness, O Yhwh, the earth is full, || Teach me Your statutes! ⁶⁵ [Teth] You did good with Your servant, O Yhwh, || According to Your word. ⁶⁶ Teach me the goodness of reason and knowledge, || For I have believed in Your commands. ⁶⁷ Before I am afflicted, I am erring, || And now I have kept Your saying. ⁶⁸ You [are] good, and doing good, || Teach me Your statutes. ⁶⁹ The proud have forged falsehood against me, || I keep Your precepts with the whole heart. ⁷⁰ Their heart has been thick as fat, || I have delighted in Your law. ⁷¹ [It is] good for me that I have been afflicted, || That I might learn Your statutes. ⁷² The Law of Your mouth [is] better to me || Than thousands of gold and silver! ⁷³ [Yod] Your hands made me and establish me, || Cause me to understand, and I learn Your commands. ⁷⁴ Those fearing You see me and rejoice, || Because I have hoped for Your word. ⁷⁵ I have known, O Yhwh, || That Your judgments [are] righteous, || And [in] faithfulness You have afflicted me. ⁷⁶ Please let Your kindness be to comfort me, || According to Your saying to Your servant. ⁷⁷ Your mercies meet me, and I live, || For Your law [is] my delight. ⁷⁸ The proud are ashamed, || For [with] falsehood they dealt perversely with me. I meditate on Your precepts. ⁷⁹ Those fearing You turn back to me, || And those knowing Your testimonies. ⁸⁰ My heart is perfect in Your statutes, || So that I am not ashamed. ⁸¹ [Kaph] My soul has been consumed for Your salvation, || I have hoped for Your word. ⁸² My eyes have been consumed for Your word, || Saying, "When does it comfort me?" ⁸³ For I have been as a bottle in smoke, || I have not forgotten Your statutes. ⁸⁴ How many [are] the days of Your servant? When do You execute judgment || Against my pursuers? ⁸⁵ The proud have dug pits for me, || That [are] not according to Your law. ⁸⁶ All Your commands [are] faithfulness, || They have pursued me [with] falsehood, || Help me. ⁸⁷ They have almost consumed me on earth, || And I have not forsaken Your precepts. ⁸⁸ Quicken me according to Your kindness, || And I keep the Testimony of Your mouth! ⁸⁹ [Lamed] For all time, O Yhwh, Your word is set up in the heavens. ⁹⁰ Your faithfulness from generation to generation, || You established earth, and it stands. ⁹¹ According to Your ordinances || They have stood this day, for the whole—Your servants. ⁹² Unless Your law [were] my delights, || Then had I perished in my affliction. ⁹³ I do not forget Your precepts for all time, || For You have quickened me by them. ⁹⁴ I [am] Yours, save me, for I have sought Your precepts. ⁹⁵ Your wicked waited for me to destroy me, || I understand Your testimonies. ⁹⁶ I have seen an end of all perfection, || Your command [is] exceedingly broad! ⁹⁷ [Mem] O how I have loved Your law! It

[is] my meditation all the day. 98 Your command makes me wiser than my enemies, || For it [is] before me for all time. 99 I have acted wisely above all my teachers. For Your testimonies [are] my meditation. 100 Above elderly—I understand more, || For I have kept Your precepts. 101 I restrained my feet from every evil path, || So that I keep Your word. 102 I did not turn aside from Your judgments, || For You have directed me. 103 How sweet Your saying has been to my palate, || Above honey to my mouth. 104 I have understanding from Your precepts, || Therefore I have hated every false path! 105 [Nun] Your word [is] a lamp to my foot, || And a light to my path. 106 I have sworn, and I confirm, || To keep the judgments of Your righteousness. 107 I have been afflicted very much, || O Yhwh, quicken me, according to Your word. 108 Please accept [the] free-will offerings of my mouth, O Yhwh, || And teach me Your judgments. 109 My soul [is] in my hand continually, || And I have not forgotten Your law. 110 The wicked have laid a snare for me, || And I did not wander from your precepts. 111 I have inherited Your testimonies for all time, || For they [are] the joy of my heart. 112 I have inclined my heart || To do Your statutes, for all time—[to] the end! 113 [Samekh] I have hated doubting ones, || And I have loved Your law. 114 You [are] my hiding place and my shield, || I have hoped for Your word. 115 Turn aside from me, you evildoers, || And I keep the commands of my God. 116 Sustain me according to Your saying, || And I live, and You do not put me to shame because of my hope. 117 Support me, and I am saved, || And I look on Your statutes continually. 118 You have trodden down || All going astray from Your statutes, || For their deceit [is] falsehood. 119 Dross! You have caused to cease || All the wicked of the earth; Therefore I have loved Your testimonies. 120 My flesh has trembled from Your fear, || And I have been afraid from Your judgments! 121 [Ayin] I have done judgment and righteousness, || Do not leave me to my oppressors. 122 Make Your servant sure for good, || Do not let the proud oppress me. 123 My eyes have been consumed for Your salvation. And for the saying of Your righteousness. 124 Do with Your servant according to Your kindness. And teach me Your statutes. 125 I [am] Your servant—cause me to understand, || And I know Your testimonies. 126 Time for Yhwh to work! They have made Your law void. 127 Therefore I have loved Your commands || Above gold—even fine gold. 128 Therefore all my appointments I have declared wholly right, || I have hated every path of falsehood! 129 [Pe] Your testimonies [are] wonderful, || Therefore my soul has kept them. 130 The opening of Your words enlightens, || Instructing the simple. 131 I have opened my mouth, indeed, I pant, || For I have longed for Your commands. 132 Look to me, and favor me, || As customary to those loving Your Name. 133 Establish my steps by Your saying, || And any iniquity does not rule over me. 134 Ransom me from the oppression of man, || And I observe Your precepts, 135 Cause Your face to shine on Your servant, || And teach me Your statutes. 136 Streams of waters have come down my eyes, || Because they have not kept Your law! 137 [Tsade] You [are] righteous, O Yhwh, || And Your judgments [are] upright. 138 You have appointed Your testimonies, || Righteous and exceedingly faithful, 139 My zeal has cut me off, || For my adversaries forgot Your words. 140 Your saying [is] tried exceedingly, || And Your servant has loved it. 141 I [am] small, and despised, || I have not forgotten Your precepts. 142 Your righteousness [is] righteousness for all time, || And Your law [is] truth. 143 Adversity and distress have found me, || Your commands [are] my delights. 144 The righteousness of Your testimonies || [Is] to cause me to understand, and I live! 145 [Qof] I have called with the whole heart, || Answer me, O Yhwh, I keep Your statutes, 146 I have called You, save me, || And I keep Your testimonies. 147 I have gone forward in the dawn, and I cry, || I have hoped for Your word. 148 My eyes have gone before the watches, || To meditate on Your saying. 149 Hear my voice, according to Your kindness, || Yhwh, quicken me according to Your judgment. 150 My wicked pursuers have been near, || They have been far off from Your law. 151 You [are] near, O Yhwh, || And all Your commands [are] truth. 152 I have known Your testimonies of old, || That You have founded them for all time! 153 [Resh] See my affliction, and deliver me, || For I have not forgotten Your law. 154 Plead my plea, and redeem me, || Quicken me according to Your saying. 155 Salvation [is] far from the wicked, || For they have not sought Your statutes. 156 Your mercies [are] many, O Yhwh, || Quicken me according to Your judgments. 157 My pursuers and adversaries are many, || I have not turned aside from Your testimonies. 158 I have seen treacherous ones, || And grieve myself, || Because they have not kept Your saying. 159

See, for I have loved Your precepts, || Yhwh, quicken me according to Your kindness. 160 The sum of Your word [is] truth, || And every judgment of Your righteousness [is] for all time! 161 [Shin] Princes have pursued me without cause, || And my heart was afraid because of Your words. 162 I rejoice concerning Your saying, || As one finding abundant spoil. 163 I have hated falsehood, indeed I detest [it], || I have loved Your law. 164 Seven [times] in a day I have praised You, || Because of the judgments of Your righteousness. 165 Those loving Your law have abundant peace, || And they have no stumbling-block. 166 I have waited for Your salvation, O Yhwh, || And I have done Your commands. 167 My soul has kept Your testimonies, || And I love them exceedingly. 168 I have kept Your precepts and Your testimonies, || For all my ways are before You! 169 [Taw] My loud cry comes near before You, O Yhwh; Cause me to understand according to Your word. 170 My supplication comes in before You, || Deliver me according to Your saying. 171 My lips utter praise, || For You teach me Your statutes. 172 My tongue sings of Your saying, || For all Your commands [are] righteous. 173 Your hand is for a help to me, || For I have chosen Your commands. 174 I have longed for Your salvation, O Yhwh, || And Your law [is] my delight. 175 My soul lives, and it praises You, || And Your judgments help me. 176 I wandered as a lost sheep, [so] seek Your servant, || For I have not forgotten Your precepts!

PSALM 120

1 A Song of the Ascents. I have called to Yhwh in my distress, || And He answers me. 2 O Yhwh, deliver my soul from a lying lip, || From a deceitful tongue! 3 What does He give to you? And what does He add to you? O deceitful tongue! 4 Sharp arrows of a mighty one, with coals of broom trees. 5 Woe to me, for I have inhabited Mesech, || I have dwelt with tents of Kedar. 6 My soul has dwelt too much with him who is hating peace. 7 I—peace, and when I speak they [are] for war!

PSALM 121

1 A Song of the Ascents. I lift up my eyes to the hills, || From where does my help come? 2 My help [is] from Yhwh, || Maker of the heavens and earth, 3 He does not permit your foot to be moved, || He who is preserving you does not slumber. 4 Behold, He does not slumber, nor sleep, || He who is preserving Israel. 5 Yhwh [is] He who is preserving you, || Yhwh [is] your shade on your right hand, 6 By day the sun does not strike you, || Nor the moon by night. 7 Yhwh preserves you from all evil, || He preserves your soul. 8 Yhwh preserves your going out and your coming in, || From now on—even for all time!

PSALM 122

1 A Song of the Ascents. By David. I have rejoiced in those saying to me, "We go to the house of Yhwh." 2 Our feet have been standing in your gates, O Jerusalem! 3 Jerusalem—the built one—[Is] as a city that is joined to itself together. 4 For there tribes have gone up, || Tribes of Yah, companies of Israel, || To give thanks to the Name of Yhwh. 5 For there thrones of judgment have sat, || Thrones of the house of David. 6 Ask [for] the peace of Jerusalem, || Those loving you are at rest. 7 Peace is in your bulwark, rest in your high places, 8 For the sake of my brothers and my companions, || Please let me speak, "Peace [be] in you." 9 For the sake of the house of our God Yhwh, || I seek good for you!

PSALM 123

1 A Song of the Ascents. I have lifted up my eyes to You, || O dweller in the heavens. 2 Behold, as eyes of menservants || [Are] to the hand of their masters, || As eyes of a maidservant || [Are] to the hand of her mistress, || So [are] our eyes to our God Yhwh, || Until He favors us. 3 Favor us, O Yhwh, favor us, || For we have been greatly filled with contempt, 4 Our soul has been greatly filled || With the scorning of the easy ones, ||

With the contempt of the arrogant!

PSALM 124

[1] A Song of the Ascents. By David. If Yhwh had not been for us || (Pray, let Israel say), [2] If Yhwh had not been for us, || In the rising up of man against us, [3] Then they had swallowed us alive, || In the burning of their anger against us, [4] Then the waters had overflowed us, || The stream passed over our soul, [5] Then proud waters had passed over our soul. [6] Blessed [is] Yhwh who has not given us, || [As] prey to their teeth. [7] Our soul has escaped as a bird from a snare of fowlers, || The snare was broken, and we have escaped. [8] Our help [is] in the Name of Yhwh, || Maker of the heavens and earth!

PSALM 125

[1] A Song of the Ascents. Those trusting in Yhwh [are] as Mount Zion, || It is not moved—it abides for all time. [2] Jerusalem! Mountains [are] around her, || And Yhwh [is] around His people, || From now on—even for all time. [3] For the rod of wickedness does not rest on the lot of the righteous, || That the righteous do not put forth their hands on iniquity. [4] Do good, O Yhwh, to the good, || And to the upright in their hearts. [5] As for those turning [to] their crooked ways, || Yhwh causes them to go with workers of iniquity. Peace on Israel!

PSALM 126

[1] A Song of the Ascents. In Yhwh's turning back [to] the captivity of Zion, || We have been as dreamers. [2] Then our mouth is filled [with] laughter, || And our tongue [with] singing, || Then they say among nations, "Yhwh did great things with these." [3] Yhwh did great things with us, || We have been joyful. [4] Turn again, O Yhwh, [to] our captivity, || As streams in the south. [5] Those sowing in tears, reap with singing, [6] Whoever goes on and weeps, || Carrying the basket of seed, || Surely comes in with singing, carrying his sheaves!

PSALM 127

[1] A Song of the Ascents. By Solomon. If Yhwh does not build the house, || Its builders have labored at it in vain, || If Yhwh does not watch a city, || A watchman has awoken in vain. [2] Vain for you who are rising early, || Who delay sitting, eating the bread of griefs, || So He gives sleep to His beloved one. [3] Behold, sons [are] an inheritance of Yhwh, || The fruit of the womb [is] a reward. [4] As arrows in the hand of a mighty one, || So [are] the sons of the young men. [5] O the blessedness of the man || Who has filled his quiver with them, || They are not ashamed, || For they speak with enemies in the gate!

PSALM 128

[1] A Song of the Ascents. O the blessedness of everyone fearing Yhwh, || Who is walking in His ways. [2] You surely eat the labor of your hands, || You [are] blessed, and good [is] to you. [3] Your wife [is] as a fruitful vine in the sides of your house, || Your sons as olive plants around your table. [4] Behold, surely thus is the man blessed who is fearing Yhwh. [5] Yhwh blesses you out of Zion, || Look, then, on the good of Jerusalem, || All the days of your life, [6] And see the sons of your sons! Peace on Israel!

PSALM 129

[1] A Song of the Ascents. Often they distressed me from my youth, || Pray, let Israel say: [2] Often they distressed me from my youth, || Yet they have not prevailed over me. [3] Plowers have plowed over my back, || They have made their furrows long. [4] Yhwh [is] righteous, || He has cut apart cords of the wicked. [5] All hating Zion [are] confounded and turn backward.

[6] They are as grass of the roofs, || That withers before it was drawn out, [7] That has not filled the hand of a reaper, || And the bosom of a binder of sheaves. [8] And the passers by have not said, "The blessing of Yhwh [is] on you, || We blessed you in the Name of Yhwh!"

PSALM 130

[1] A Song of the Ascents. I have called You from the depths, Yhwh. [2] Lord, listen to my voice, || Your ears are attentive to the voice of my supplications. [3] If You observe iniquities, Lord Yah, who stands? [4] But forgiveness [is] with You, that You may be feared. [5] I hoped [for] Yhwh—my soul has hoped, || And I have waited for His word. [6] My soul [is] for the Lord, || More than those watching for morning, || Watching for morning! [7] Israel waits on Yhwh, || For kindness [is] with Yhwh, || And redemption [is] abundant with Him. [8] And He redeems Israel from all his iniquities!

PSALM 131

[1] A Song of the Ascents. By David. Yhwh, my heart has not been haughty, || Nor have my eyes been high, || Nor have I walked in great things, || And in things too wonderful for me. [2] Have I not compared, and kept my soul silent, || As a weaned one by its mother? As a weaned one by me [is] my soul. [3] Israel waits on Yhwh, || From now on, and for all time!

PSALM 132

[1] A Song of the Ascents. Remember, Yhwh, for David, all his afflictions; [2] Who has sworn to Yhwh, || He has vowed to the Mighty One of Jacob: [3] "If I enter into the tent of my house, || If I go up on the couch of my bed, [4] If I give sleep to my eyes, || To my eyelids—slumber, [5] Until I find a place for Yhwh, dwelling places for the Mighty One of Jacob." [6] Behold, we have heard it in Ephratah, || We have found it in the fields of the forest. [7] We come into His dwelling places, || We bow ourselves at His footstool. [8] Arise, O Yhwh, to Your rest, || You, and the Ark of Your strength, [9] Your priests put on righteousness, || And Your pious ones cry aloud. [10] For the sake of Your servant David, || Do not turn back the face of Your anointed. [11] Yhwh has sworn truth to David, || He does not turn back from it: "Of the fruit of your body, || I set on the throne for you. [12] If your sons keep My covenant, || And My testimonies that I teach them, || Their sons also forever and ever || Sit on the throne for you." [13] For Yhwh has fixed on Zion, || He has desired [it] for a seat to Himself, [14] "This [is] My rest forever and ever, || Here I sit, for I have desired it. [15] I greatly bless her provision, || I satisfy her poor [with] bread, [16] And I clothe her priests [with] salvation, || And her pious ones sing aloud. [17] There I cause a horn to spring up for David, || I have arranged a lamp for My Anointed. [18] I clothe His enemies [with] shame, || And His crown flourishes on Him!"

PSALM 133

[1] A Song of the Ascents. By David. Behold, how good and how pleasant || The dwelling of brothers—even together! [2] As the good oil on the head, || Coming down on the beard, the beard of Aaron, || That comes down on the skirt of his robes, [3] As dew of Hermon—That comes down on hills of Zion, || For there Yhwh commanded the blessing—Life for all time!

PSALM 134

[1] A Song of the Ascents. Behold, bless Yhwh, all servants of Yhwh, || Who are standing in the house of Yhwh by night. [2] Lift up your hands [in] the sanctuary, || And bless Yhwh. [3] Yhwh blesses you out of Zion, || The Maker of the heavens and earth!

PSALM 135

¹ Praise Yah! Praise the Name of Yhwh, || Praise, you servants of Yhwh, ² Who are standing in the house of Yhwh, || In the courts of the house of our God. ³ Praise Yah! For Yhwh [is] good, || Sing praise to His Name, for [it is] pleasant. ⁴ For Yah has chosen Jacob for Himself, || Israel for His peculiar treasure. ⁵ For I have known that Yhwh [is] great, || Indeed, our Lord [is] above all gods. ⁶ All that Yhwh pleased He has done, || In the heavens and in earth, || In the seas and all deep places, ⁷ Causing vapors to ascend from the end of the earth, || He has made lightnings for the rain, || Bringing forth wind from His treasures. ⁸ Who struck the firstborn of Egypt, || From man to beast. ⁹ He sent tokens and wonders into your midst, O Egypt, || On Pharaoh and on all his servants. ¹⁰ Who struck many nations, and slew strong kings, ¹¹ Even Sihon king of the Amorite, || And Og king of Bashan, || And all kingdoms of Canaan. ¹² And He gave their land as an inheritance, || An inheritance to His people Israel, ¹³ O Yhwh, Your Name [is] for all time, || O Yhwh, Your memorial from generation to generation. ¹⁴ For Yhwh judges His people, || And comforts Himself for His servants. ¹⁵ The idols of the nations [are] silver and gold, || Work of the hands of man. ¹⁶ They have a mouth, and they do not speak, || They have eyes, and they do not see, ¹⁷ They have ears, and they do not give ear, || Nose—there is no breath in their mouth! ¹⁸ Their makers are like them, || Everyone who is trusting in them. ¹⁹ O house of Israel, bless Yhwh, || O house of Aaron, bless Yhwh, ²⁰ O house of Levi, bless Yhwh, || Those fearing Yhwh, bless Yhwh. ²¹ Blessed [is] Yhwh from Zion, || Inhabiting Jerusalem—praise Yah!

PSALM 136

¹ Give thanks to Yhwh, || For [He is] good, for His kindness [is] for all time. ² Give thanks to the God of gods, || For His kindness [is] for all time. ³ Give thanks to the Lord of lords, || For His kindness [is] for all time. ⁴ To Him doing great wonders by Himself alone, || For His kindness [is] for all time. ⁵ To Him making the heavens by understanding, || For His kindness [is] for all time. ⁶ To Him spreading the earth over the waters, || For His kindness [is] for all time. ⁷ To Him making great lights, || For His kindness [is] for all time. ⁸ The sun to rule by day, || For His kindness [is] for all time. ⁹ The moon and stars to rule by night, || For His kindness [is] for all time. ¹⁰ To Him striking Egypt in their firstborn, || For His kindness [is] for all time. ¹¹ And bringing forth Israel from their midst, || For His kindness [is] for all time. ¹² By a strong hand and an outstretched-arm, || For His kindness [is] for all time. ¹³ To Him cutting the Sea of Suph into parts, || For His kindness [is] for all time, ¹⁴ And caused Israel to pass through its midst, || For His kindness [is] for all time, ¹⁵ And shook out Pharaoh and his force in the Sea of Suph, || For His kindness [is] for all time. ¹⁶ To Him leading His people in a wilderness, || For His kindness [is] for all time. ¹⁷ To Him striking great kings, || For His kindness [is] for all time. ¹⁸ Indeed, He slays majestic kings, || For His kindness [is] for all time. ¹⁹ Even Sihon king of the Amorite, || For His kindness [is] for all time. ²⁰ And Og king of Bashan, || For His kindness [is] for all time. ²¹ And He gave their land for inheritance, || For His kindness [is] for all time. ²² An inheritance to Israel His servant, || For His kindness [is] for all time. ²³ Who has remembered us in our lowliness, || For His kindness [is] for all time. ²⁴ And He delivers us from our adversaries, || For His kindness [is] for all time. ²⁵ Giving food to all flesh, || For His kindness [is] for all time. ²⁶ Give thanks to the God of the heavens, || For His kindness [is] for all time!

PSALM 137

¹ By rivers of Babylon—There we sat, || Indeed, we wept when we remembered Zion. ² We hung our harps on willows in its midst. ³ For there our captors asked us the words of a song, || And our spoilers—joy: "Sing to us of a song of Zion." ⁴ How do we sing the song of Yhwh, || On the land of a stranger? ⁵ If I forget you, O Jerusalem, my right hand forgets! ⁶ My tongue cleaves to my palate, || If I do not remember you, || If I do not exalt Jerusalem above my chief joy. ⁷ Remember, Yhwh, for the sons of Edom, || The day of Jerusalem, || Those saying, "Raze, raze to its foundation!" ⁸ O daughter of Babylon, O destroyed one, || O the blessedness of him who repays to you your deed, || That you have done to us. ⁹ O the blessedness of him who seizes, and has dashed your sucklings on the rock!

PSALM 138

¹ By David. I confess You with all my heart, || I praise You before the gods. ² I bow myself toward Your holy temple, || And I confess Your Name, || For Your kindness, and for Your truth, || For You have made Your saying great above all Your Name. ³ In the day I called, when You answer me, || You strengthen me in my soul [with] strength. ⁴ O Yhwh, all kings of earth confess You, || When they have heard the sayings of Your mouth. ⁵ And they sing in the ways of Yhwh, || For the glory of Yhwh [is] great. ⁶ For Yhwh [is] high, and He sees the lowly, || And He knows the haughty from afar. ⁷ If I walk in the midst of distress You quicken me, || You send forth Your hand against the anger of my enemies, || And Your right hand saves me. ⁸ Yhwh perfects for me, || O Yhwh, Your kindness [is] for all time, || Do not let the works of Your hands fall!

PSALM 139

¹ To the Overseer. A Psalm of David. Yhwh, You have searched me, and know. ² You have known my sitting down, || And my rising up, || You have attended to my thoughts from afar. ³ You have fanned my path and my lying down, || And have been acquainted [with] all my ways. ⁴ For there is not a word in my tongue, || Behold, O Yhwh, You have known it all! ⁵ You have besieged me behind and before, || And You place Your hand on me. ⁶ Knowledge too wonderful for me, || It has been set on high, || I am not able for it. ⁷ To where do I go from Your Spirit? And to where do I flee from Your face? ⁸ If I ascend the heavens—You [are] there, || And spread out a bed in Sheol, behold, You! ⁹ I take the wings of morning, || I dwell in the uttermost part of the sea, ¹⁰ Also there Your hand leads me, || And Your right hand holds me. ¹¹ And I say, "Surely darkness bruises me," || Then night [is] light to me. ¹² Also darkness does not hide from You, || And night shines as day, || As [is] darkness so [is] light. ¹³ For You have possessed my reins, || You cover me in my mother's belly. ¹⁴ I confess You, because I have been fearfully distinguished. Your works [are] wonderful, || And my soul is knowing [it] well. ¹⁵ My substance was not hid from You, || When I was made in secret, || Curiously worked in the lower part of earth. ¹⁶ Your eyes saw my unformed substance, || And all of them are written on Your scroll, || The days they were formed—And not one among them. ¹⁷ And how precious Your thoughts have been to me, || O God, how great has been their sum! ¹⁸ I recount them! They are more than the sand, || I have awoken, and I am still with You. ¹⁹ Do You slay, O God, the wicked? Then, men of blood, turn aside from me! ²⁰ Who exchange You for wickedness, || Your enemies [are] lifted up to vanity. ²¹ Do I not hate, Yhwh, those hating You? And grieve myself with Your withstanders? ²² I have hated them [with] perfect hatred, || They have become enemies to me. ²³ Search me, O God, and know my heart, || Try me, and know my thoughts, ²⁴ And see if a grievous way be in me, || And lead me in a perpetual way!

PSALM 140

¹ To the Overseer. A Psalm of David. Deliver me, O Yhwh, from an evil man, || Keep me from one of violence. ² Who have devised evils in the heart, || All the day they assemble [for] wars. ³ They sharpened their tongue as a serpent, || Poison of a viper [is] under their lips. Selah. ⁴ Preserve me, Yhwh, from the hands of the wicked, || Keep me from one of violence, || Who have devised to overthrow my steps. ⁵ The proud hid a snare for me—and cords, || They spread a net by the side of the path, || They have set snares for me. Selah. ⁶ I have said to Yhwh, "You [are] my God, || Hear, Yhwh, the voice of my supplications." ⁷ O Yhwh, my Lord, strength of my salvation, || You have covered my head in the day of armor. ⁸ Do not grant, O Yhwh, the desires of the wicked, || Do not bring forth his wicked scheme, || They are high. Selah. ⁹ The chief of my surrounders, || The perverseness of their lips covers them. ¹⁰ They cause burning coals to fall on themselves, || He casts them into fire, || Into deep pits—they do not arise. ¹¹ A talkative man is not established in the earth, || One of violence—evil hunts to overflowing. ¹² I have known that Yhwh executes || The judgment of the afflicted, || The judgment of

the needy. [13] Surely the righteous give thanks to Your Name, || The upright dwell with Your presence!

PSALM 141

[1] A Psalm of David. O Yhwh, I have called You, hurry to me, || Give ear [to] my voice when I call to You. [2] My prayer is prepared—incense before You, || The lifting up of my hands—the evening present. [3] Set, O Yhwh, a watch for my mouth, || Watch over the door of my lips. [4] Do not incline my heart to an evil thing, || To habitually do actions in wickedness, || Working iniquity with men, || Indeed, I do not eat of their pleasant things. [5] The righteous beat me [in] kindness. And reprove me, || My head does not disallow oil of the head, || For my prayer [is] still about their distress. [6] Their judges have been released by the sides of a rock, || And they have heard my sayings, || For they have been pleasant. [7] As one tilling and ripping up in the land, || Have our bones been scattered at the command of Saul. [8] But to You, O Yhwh, my Lord, [are] my eyes, || In You I have trusted, || Do not make my soul bare. [9] Keep me from the trap they laid for me, || Even snares of workers of iniquity. [10] The wicked fall in their dragnets together, until I pass over!

PSALM 142

[1] An Instruction of David. A Prayer when he is in the cave. My voice [is] to Yhwh, I cry, || My voice [is] to Yhwh, I beg [for] grace. [2] I pour forth my meditation before Him, || I declare my distress before Him. [3] When my spirit has been feeble in me, || Then You have known my path; In the way [in] which I walk, || They have hid a snare for me. [4] Looking on the right hand—and seeing, || And I have none recognizing; Refuge has perished from me, || There is none inquiring for my soul. [5] I have cried to you, O Yhwh, || I have said, "You [are] my refuge, || My portion in the land of the living." [6] Attend to my loud cry, || For I have become very low, || Deliver me from my pursuers, || For they have been stronger than I. [7] Bring forth my soul from prison to confess Your Name, || The righteous surround me about, || When You confer benefits on me!

PSALM 143

[1] A Psalm of David. O Yhwh, hear my prayer, || Give ear to my supplications, || Answer me in Your faithfulness—in Your righteousness. [2] And do not enter into judgment with Your servant, || For no one living is justified before You. [3] For an enemy has pursued my soul, || He has bruised my life to the earth, || He has caused me to dwell in dark places, || As the dead of old. [4] And my spirit has become feeble in me, || My heart has become desolate within me. [5] I have remembered days of old, || I have meditated on all Your acts, || I muse on the work of Your hand. [6] I have spread forth my hands to You, || My soul [is] as a weary land for You. Selah. [7] Hurry, answer me, O Yhwh, || My spirit has been consumed, || Do not hide Your face from me, || Or I have been compared with those going down [to] the pit. [8] Cause me to hear Your kindness in the morning, || For I have trusted in You, || Cause me to know the way that I go, || For I have lifted up my soul to You. [9] Deliver me from my enemies, O Yhwh, || Near You I am covered. [10] Teach me to do Your good pleasure, || For You [are] my God—Your Spirit [is] good, || Lead me into a land of uprightness. [11] You quicken me for Your Name's sake, O Yhwh, || In Your righteousness, You bring out my soul from distress, [12] And in Your kindness cut off my enemies, || And have destroyed all the adversaries of my soul, || For I [am] Your servant!

PSALM 144

[1] By David. Blessed [is] Yhwh my Rock, || Who is teaching My hands for war, || My fingers for battle. [2] My kind one, and my bulwark, || My tower, and my deliverer, || My shield, and in whom I have trusted, || Who is subduing my people under me! [3] Yhwh, what [is] man that You know him? The son of man, that You esteem him? [4] Man has been like a breath, || His days [are] as a shadow passing by. [5] Yhwh, incline Your heavens and come down, || Strike against mountains, and they smoke. [6] Send forth lightning, and scatter them, || Send forth Your arrows, and trouble them, [7] Send forth Your hand from on high, || Free me, and deliver me from many waters, || From the hand of sons of a stranger, [8] Because their mouth has spoken vanity, || And their right hand [is] a right hand of falsehood. [9] O God, I sing to You a new song, || I sing praise to You on a stringed instrument of ten strings. [10] Who is giving deliverance to kings, || Who is freeing His servant David from the sword of evil. [11] Free me, and deliver me || From the hand of sons of a stranger, || Because their mouth has spoken vanity, || And their right hand [is] a right hand of falsehood, [12] Because our sons [are] as plants, || Becoming great in their youth, || Our daughters as hewn stones, || Polished—the likeness of a palace, [13] Our granaries [are] full, bringing out from kind to kind, || Our flocks are bringing forth thousands, || Ten thousands in our out-places, [14] Our oxen are carrying, there is no breach, || And there is no outgoing, || And there is no crying in our broad places. [15] O the blessedness of the people that is thus, || O the blessedness of the people whose God [is] Yhwh!

PSALM 145

[1] A Praise [Song] of David. [Aleph-Bet] I exalt You, my God, O king, || And bless Your Name for all time and forever. [2] Every day I bless You, || And praise Your Name for all time and forever. [3] Yhwh [is] great, and greatly praised, || And there is no searching of His greatness. [4] Generation to generation praises Your works, || And they declare Your mighty acts. [5] The majesty, the glory of Your splendor, || And the matters of Your wonders, I declare. [6] And they tell of the strength of Your fearful acts, || And I recount Your greatness. [7] They send forth the memorial of the abundance of Your goodness. And they sing of Your righteousness. [8] Yhwh [is] gracious and merciful, || Slow to anger, and great in kindness. [9] Yhwh [is] good to all, || And His mercies [are] over all His works. [10] O Yhwh, all Your works confess You, || And Your saints bless You. [11] They tell of the glory of Your kingdom, || And they speak of Your might, [12] To make His mighty acts known to sons of men, || The glory of the majesty of His kingdom. [13] Your kingdom [is] a kingdom of all ages, || And Your dominion [is] in all generations. [[Yhwh [is] faithful in all His words, || And kind in all His works.]] [14] Yhwh is supporting all who are falling, || And raising up all who are bowed down. [15] The eyes of all look to You, || And You are giving their food to them in its season, [16] Opening Your hand, and satisfying || The desire of every living thing. [17] Yhwh [is] righteous in all His ways, || And kind in all His works. [18] Yhwh [is] near to all those calling Him, || To all who call Him in truth. [19] He does the desire of those fearing Him, || And He hears their cry, and saves them. [20] Yhwh preserves all those loving Him, || And He destroys all the wicked. [21] My mouth speaks the praise of Yhwh, || And all flesh blesses His Holy Name, || For all time and forever!

PSALM 146

[1] Praise Yah! Praise, O my soul, Yhwh. [2] I praise Yhwh during my life, || I sing praise to my God while I exist. [3] Do not trust in princes—in a son of man, || For he has no deliverance. [4] His spirit goes forth, he returns to his earth, || In that day his thoughts have perished. [5] O the blessedness of him || Who has the God of Jacob for his help, || His hope [is] on his God Yhwh, [6] Making the heavens and earth, || The sea and all that [is] in them, || Who is keeping truth for all time, [7] Doing judgment for the oppressed, || Giving bread to the hungry. [8] Yhwh is losing the prisoners, || Yhwh is opening (the eyes of) the blind, || Yhwh is raising the bowed down, || Yhwh is loving the righteous, [9] Yhwh is preserving the strangers, || He causes the fatherless and widow to stand, || And He turns the way of the wicked upside down. [10] Yhwh reigns for all time, || Your God, O Zion, to generation and generation, || Praise Yah!

PSALM 147

¹ Praise Yah! For [it is] good to praise our God, || For pleasant—lovely [is] praise. ² Yhwh [is] building Jerusalem, || He gathers the driven away of Israel. ³ Who is giving healing to the broken of heart, || And is binding up their griefs. ⁴ Appointing the number of the stars, || He gives names to all of them. ⁵ Our Lord [is] great, and abundant in power, || There is no narration of His understanding. ⁶ Yhwh is causing the meek to stand, || Making the wicked low to the earth. ⁷ Answer to Yhwh with thanksgiving, || Sing to our God with a harp. ⁸ Who is covering the heavens with clouds, || Who is preparing rain for the earth, || Who is causing grass to spring up [on] mountains, ⁹ Giving to the beast its food, || To the young of the ravens that call. ¹⁰ He does not delight in the might of the horse, || He is not pleased in the legs of a man. ¹¹ Yhwh is pleased with those fearing Him, || With those waiting for His kindness. ¹² Glorify, O Jerusalem, Yhwh, || Praise your God, O Zion. ¹³ For He strengthened the bars of your gates, || He has blessed your sons in your midst. ¹⁴ Who is making your border peace, || He satisfies you [with] the fat of wheat. ¹⁵ Who is sending forth His saying [on] earth, || His word runs very speedily. ¹⁶ Who is giving snow like wool, || He scatters hoarfrost as ashes. ¹⁷ Casting forth His ice like morsels, || Who stands before His cold? ¹⁸ He sends forth His word and melts them, || He causes His wind to blow—the waters flow. ¹⁹ Declaring His words to Jacob, || His statutes and His judgments to Israel. ²⁰ He has not done so to any nation, || As for judgments, they have not known them. Praise Yah!

PSALM 148

¹ Praise Yah! Praise Yhwh from the heavens, || Praise Him in high places. ² Praise Him, all His messengers, || Praise Him, all His hosts. ³ Praise Him, sun and moon, || Praise Him, all stars of light. ⁴ Praise Him, heavens of heavens, || And you waters that are above the heavens. ⁵ They praise the Name of Yhwh, || For He commanded, and they were created. ⁶ And He establishes them forever and for all time, || He gave a statute, and they do not pass over. ⁷ Praise Yhwh from the earth, || Dragons and all deeps, ⁸ Fire and hail, snow and vapor, || Whirlwind doing His word; ⁹ The mountains and all heights, || Fruit tree, and all cedars, ¹⁰ The wild beast, and all livestock, || Creeping thing, and winged bird, ¹¹ Kings of earth, and all peoples, || Chiefs, and all judges of earth, ¹² Young men, and also maidens, || Aged men, with youths, ¹³ They praise the Name of Yhwh, || For His Name alone has been set on high, || His splendor [is] above earth and heavens. ¹⁴ And He exalts the horn of His people, || The praise of all His saints, || Of the sons of Israel, || A people near Him. Praise Yah!

PSALM 149

¹ Praise Yah! Sing to Yhwh a new song, || His praise in an assembly of saints. ² Israel rejoices in his Maker, || Sons of Zion rejoice in their king. ³ They praise His Name in a dance, || Sing praise to Him with timbrel and harp. ⁴ For Yhwh is pleased with His people, || He beautifies the humble with salvation. ⁵ Saints exult in glory, || They sing aloud on their beds. ⁶ The exaltation of God [is] in their throat, || And a two-edged sword in their hand. ⁷ To do vengeance among nations, || Punishments among the peoples. ⁸ To bind their kings with chains, || And their honored ones with chains of iron, ⁹ To do among them the judgment written, || It [is] an honor for all his saints. Praise Yah!

PSALM 150

¹ Praise Yah! Praise God in His holy place, || Praise Him in the expanse of His strength. ² Praise Him in His mighty acts, || Praise Him according to the abundance of His greatness. ³ Praise Him with blowing of horn, || Praise Him with stringed instrument and harp. ⁴ Praise Him with timbrel and dance, || Praise Him with stringed instruments and pipe. ⁵ Praise Him with cymbals of sounding, || Praise Him with cymbals of shouting. ⁶ All that breathes praise Yah! Praise Yah!

PROVERB

CHAPTER 1

¹ Proverbs of Solomon, son of David, king of Israel: ² For knowing wisdom and instruction, || For understanding sayings of intelligence, ³ For receiving the instruction of wisdom, || Righteousness, judgment, and uprightness, ⁴ For giving to simple ones—prudence, || To a youth—knowledge and discretion. ⁵ (The wise hear and increase learning, || And the intelligent obtain counsels.) ⁶ For understanding a proverb and its sweetness, || Words of the wise and their acute sayings. ⁷ Fear of Yhwh [is the] beginning of knowledge, || Fools have despised wisdom and instruction! ⁸ Hear, my son, the instruction of your father, || And do not leave the law of your mother, ⁹ For they [are] a graceful wreath to your head, || And chains to your neck. ¹⁰ My son, if sinners entice you, do not be willing. ¹¹ If they say, "Come with us, we lay wait for blood, || We watch secretly for the innocent without cause, ¹² We swallow them as Sheol—alive, || And whole—as those going down [to] the pit, ¹³ We find every precious substance, || We fill our houses [with] spoil, ¹⁴ You cast your lot among us, || One purse is—to all of us." ¹⁵ My son! Do not go in the way with them, || Withhold your foot from their path, ¹⁶ For their feet run to evil, || And they hurry to shed blood. ¹⁷ Surely in vain is the net spread out before the eyes of any bird. ¹⁸ And they lay wait for their own blood, || They watch secretly for their own lives. ¹⁹ So [are] the paths of every gainer of dishonest gain, || It takes the life of its owners. ²⁰ Wisdom cries aloud in an out-place, || She gives forth her voice in broad places, ²¹ She calls at the head of the multitudes, || In the openings of the gates, || In the city she says her sayings: ²² "Until when, you simple, do you love simplicity? And have scorners desired their scorning? And do fools hate knowledge? ²³ Turn back at my reproof, behold, || I pour forth my spirit to you, || I make known my words with you. ²⁴ Because I have called, and you refuse, || I stretched out my hand, and none is attending, ²⁵ And you slight all my counsel, || And you have not desired my reproof. ²⁶ I also laugh in your calamity, || I deride when your fear comes, ²⁷ When your fear comes as destruction, || And your calamity comes as a windstorm, || When adversity and distress come on you. ²⁸ Then they call me, and I do not answer, || They seek me earnestly, and do not find me. ²⁹ Because that they have hated knowledge, || And have not chosen the fear of Yhwh. ³⁰ They have not consented to my counsel, || They have despised all my reproof, ³¹ And they eat of the fruit of their way, || And they are filled from their own counsels. ³² For the turning of the simple slays them, || And the security of the foolish destroys them. ³³ And whoever is listening to me dwells confidently, || And [is] quiet from fear of evil!"

CHAPTER 2

¹ My son, if you accept my sayings, || And lay up my commands with you, ² To cause your ear to attend to wisdom, || You incline your heart to understanding, ³ For if you call for intelligence, || [And] give forth your voice for intelligence, ⁴ If you seek her as silver, || And search for her as hid treasures, ⁵ Then you understand the fear of Yhwh, || And you find the knowledge of God. ⁶ For Yhwh gives wisdom, || Knowledge and understanding from His mouth. ⁷ Even to lay up substance for the upright, || A shield for those walking uprightly. ⁸ To keep the paths of judgment, || And He preserves the way of His saints. ⁹ Then you understand righteousness, || And judgment, and uprightness—every good path. ¹⁰ For wisdom comes into your heart, || And knowledge is pleasant to your soul, ¹¹ Thoughtfulness watches over you, || Understanding keeps you, ¹² To deliver you from an evil way, || From any speaking contrary things, ¹³ Who are forsaking paths of uprightness, || To walk in ways of darkness, ¹⁴ Who are rejoicing to do evil, || They delight in [the] contrariness of the wicked, ¹⁵ Whose paths [are] crooked, || Indeed, they are perverted in their ways. ¹⁶ To deliver you from the strange woman, || From the stranger who has made her sayings smooth, ¹⁷ Who is forsaking the guide of her youth, || And has forgotten the covenant of her God. ¹⁸ For her house has inclined to death, || And her paths to Rephaim. ¹⁹ None going in to her return, || Nor do they reach

the paths of life. ²⁰ That you go in the way of the good, || And keep the paths of the righteous. ²¹ For the upright inhabit the earth, || And the perfect are left in it, ²² And the wicked are cut off from the earth, || And treacherous dealers plucked out of it!

CHAPTER 3

¹ My son! Do not forget my law, || And let your heart keep my commands, ² For [the] length of [your] days and years, || Life and peace they add to you. ³ Do not let kindness and truth forsake you, || Bind them on your neck, || Write them on the tablet of your heart, ⁴ And find grace and good understanding || In the eyes of God and man. ⁵ Trust to Yhwh with all your heart, || And do not lean to your own understanding. ⁶ In all your ways know Him, || And He makes your paths straight. ⁷ Do not be wise in your own eyes, || Fear Yhwh, and turn aside from evil. ⁸ It is healing to your navel, || And moistening to your bones. ⁹ Honor Yhwh from your substance, || And from the beginning of all your increase; ¹⁰ And your barns are filled [with] plenty, || And your presses break forth [with] new wine. ¹¹ Discipline of Yhwh, my son, do not despise, || And do not be distressed with His reproof, ¹² For whom Yhwh loves He reproves, || Even as a father the son He is pleased with. ¹³ O the blessedness of a man [who] has found wisdom, || And of a man [who] brings forth understanding. ¹⁴ For better [is] her merchandise || Than the merchandise of silver, || And than gold—her increase. ¹⁵ She [is] precious above rubies, || And all your pleasures are not comparable to her. ¹⁶ Length of days [is] in her right hand, || In her left [are] wealth and honor. ¹⁷ Her ways [are] ways of pleasantness, || And all her paths [are] peace. ¹⁸ She [is] a tree of life to those laying hold on her, || And whoever is retaining her [is] blessed. ¹⁹ Yhwh founded the earth by wisdom, || He prepared the heavens by understanding. ²⁰ By His knowledge depths have been broken, || And clouds drop dew. ²¹ My son! Do not let them turn from your eyes, || Keep wisdom and thoughtfulness, ²² And they are life to your soul, and grace to your neck. ²³ Then you go your way confidently, || And your foot does not stumble. ²⁴ If you lie down, you are not afraid, || Indeed, you have lain down, || And your sleep has been sweet. ²⁵ Do not be afraid of sudden fear, || And of the desolation of the wicked when it comes. ²⁶ For Yhwh is at your side, || And He has kept your foot from capture. ²⁷ Do not withhold good from its owners, || When your hand [is] toward God to do [it]. ²⁸ Do not say to your friend, || "Go, and return, and tomorrow I give," || When substance [is] with you. ²⁹ Do not devise evil against your neighbor, || And he sitting confidently with you. ³⁰ Do not strive with a man without cause, || If he has not done you evil. ³¹ Do not be envious of a man of violence, || Nor fix on any of his ways. ³² For the perverted [is] an abomination to Yhwh, || And His secret counsel [is] with the upright. ³³ The curse of Yhwh [is] in the house of the wicked. And He blesses the habitation of the righteous. ³⁴ If He scorns the scorners, || Yet He gives grace to the humble. ³⁵ The wise inherit glory, || And fools are bearing away shame!

CHAPTER 4

¹ Hear, you sons, the instruction of a father, || And give attention to know understanding. ² For I have given to you good learning, do not forsake my law. ³ For I have been a son to my father—tender, || And an only one before my mother. ⁴ And he directs me, and he says to me: "Let your heart retain my words, || Keep my commands, and live. ⁵ Get wisdom, get understanding, || Do not forget, nor turn away || From the sayings of my mouth. ⁶ Do not forsake her, and she preserves you, || Love her, and she keeps you. ⁷ The first thing [is] wisdom—get wisdom, || And with all your getting get understanding. ⁸ Exalt her and she lifts you up, || She honors you when you embrace her. ⁹ She gives a wreath of grace to your head, || She gives you a crown of beauty freely." ¹⁰ Hear, my son, and receive my sayings, || And years of life [are] multiplied to you. ¹¹ I have directed you in a way of wisdom, || I have caused you to tread in paths of uprightness. ¹² In your walking your step is not restricted, || And if you run, you do not stumble. ¹³ Lay hold on instruction, do not desist, || Keep her, for she [is] your life. ¹⁴ Do not enter into the path of the wicked, || And do not be blessed in a way of evildoers. ¹⁵ Avoid

it, do not pass over into it, || Turn aside from it, and pass on. ¹⁶ For they do not sleep if they do no evil, || And their sleep has been taken away violently, || If they do not cause [some] to stumble. ¹⁷ For they have eaten bread of wickedness, || And they drink wine of violence. ¹⁸ And the path of the righteous [is] as a shining light, || Going and brightening until the day is established, ¹⁹ The way of the wicked [is] as darkness, || They have not known at what they stumble. ²⁰ My son, give attention to my words, || Incline your ear to my sayings, ²¹ Do not let them turn aside from your eyes, || Preserve them in the midst of your heart. ²² For they [are] life to those finding them, || And healing to all their flesh. ²³ Above every charge keep your heart, || For out of it [are] the outgoings of life. ²⁴ Turn aside a contrary mouth from you, || And put perverse lips far from you, ²⁵ Your eyes look straightforward, || And your eyelids look straight before you. ²⁶ Ponder the path of your feet, || And all your ways [are] established. ²⁷ Do not incline [to] the right or to the left, || Turn aside your foot from evil!

CHAPTER 5

¹ My son! Give attention to my wisdom, || Incline your ear to my understanding, ² To observe thoughtfulness, || And your lips keep knowledge. ³ For the lips of a strange woman drop honey, || And her mouth [is] smoother than oil, ⁴ And her latter end [is] bitter as wormwood, || Sharp as a sword [with] mouths. ⁵ Her feet are going down to death, || Her steps take hold of Sheol. ⁶ The path of life—lest you ponder, || Her paths have moved—you do not know. ⁷ And now, you sons, listen to me, || And do not turn from sayings of my mouth. ⁸ Keep your way far from off her, || And do not come near to the opening of her house, ⁹ Lest you give your splendor to others, || And your years to the fierce, ¹⁰ Lest strangers be filled [with] your power, || And your labors in the house of a stranger, ¹¹ And you have howled in your latter end, || In the consumption of your flesh and your food, ¹² And have said, "How I have hated instruction, || And my heart has despised reproof, ¹³ And I have not listened to the voice of my teachers, || And have not inclined my ear to my teachers. ¹⁴ As a little thing I have been all evil, || In the midst of an assembly and a congregation." ¹⁵ Drink waters out of your own cistern, || Even flowing ones out of your own well. ¹⁶ Let your fountains be scattered abroad, || In broad places streams of waters. ¹⁷ Let them be to you for yourself, || And not to strangers with you. ¹⁸ Let your fountain be blessed, || And rejoice because of the wife of your youth, ¹⁹ A doe of loves, and a roe of grace! Let her loves satisfy you at all times, || Magnify yourself in her love continually. ²⁰ And why do you magnify yourself, || My son, with a stranger? And embrace the bosom of a strange woman? ²¹ For the ways of each are before the eyes of Yhwh, || And He is pondering all his paths. ²² His own iniquities capture the wicked, || And he is holden with the ropes of his sin. ²³ He dies without instruction, || And magnifies himself in the abundance of his folly!

CHAPTER 6

¹ My son! If you have been guarantor for your friend, || Have struck your hand for a stranger, ² Have been snared with sayings of your mouth, || Have been captured with sayings of your mouth, ³ Do this now, my son, and be delivered, || For you have come into the hand of your friend. Go, trample on yourself, and strengthen your friend, ⁴ Do not give sleep to your eyes, || And slumber to your eyelids, ⁵ Be delivered as a roe from the hand, || And as a bird from the hand of a fowler. ⁶ Go to the ant, O slothful one, || See her ways and be wise; ⁷ Which has no captain, overseer, and ruler, ⁸ She prepares her bread in summer, || She has gathered her food in harvest. ⁹ Until when, O slothful one, do you lie? When do you arise from your sleep? ¹⁰ A little sleep, a little slumber, || A little clasping of the hands to rest, ¹¹ And your poverty has come as a traveler, || And your want as an armed man. ¹² A man of worthlessness, a man of iniquity, || Walking [with] perverseness of mouth, ¹³ Winking with his eyes, speaking with his feet, || Directing with his fingers, ¹⁴ Contrariness [is] in his heart, devising evil at all times, || He sends forth contentions. ¹⁵ Therefore his calamity comes suddenly, || He is broken instantly—and no healing. ¹⁶ These six has Yhwh hated, || Indeed, seven [are] abominations to His soul: ¹⁷ High eyes, || False tongues, || And hands shedding innocent blood, ¹⁸ A heart devising thoughts of vanity,

|| Feet hastening to run to evil, 19 A false witness [who] breathes out lies, || And one sending forth contentions between brothers. 20 Keep, my son, the command of your father, || And do not leave the law of your mother. 21 Bind them on your heart continually, || Tie them on your neck. 22 In your going up and down, it leads you, || In your lying down, it watches over you, || And you have awoken—it talks [with] you. 23 For the command [is] a lamp, || And the Law a light, || And a way of life [are] reproofs of instruction, 24 To preserve you from an evil woman, || From the flattery of the tongue of a strange woman. 25 Do not desire her beauty in your heart, || And do not let her take you with her eyelids. 26 For a harlot consumes to a cake of bread, || And an adulteress hunts the precious soul. 27 Does a man take fire into his bosom, || And are his garments not burned? 28 Does a man walk on the hot coals, || And are his feet not scorched? 29 So [is] he who has gone in to the wife of his neighbor, || None who touches her is innocent. 30 They do not despise the thief, || When he steals to fill his soul when he is hungry, 31 And being found he repays sevenfold, || He gives all the substance of his house. 32 He who commits adultery [with] a woman lacks heart, || He who does it is destroying his soul. 33 He finds a stroke and shame, || And his reproach is not wiped away, 34 For jealousy [is] the fury of a man, || And he does not spare in a day of vengeance. 35 He does not accept the appearance of any atonement, || Indeed, he does not consent, || Though you multiply bribes!

CHAPTER 7

1 My son! Keep my sayings, || And lay up my commands with you. 2 Keep my commands, and live, || And my law as the pupil of your eye. 3 Bind them on your fingers, || Write them on the tablet of your heart. 4 Say to wisdom, "You [are] my sister." And cry to understanding, "Relative!" 5 To preserve you from a strange woman, || From a stranger who has made her sayings smooth. 6 For at a window of my house, || I have looked out through my casement, 7 And I see among the simple ones, || I discern among the sons, || A young man lacking understanding, 8 Passing on in the street, near her corner, || And the way [to] her house he steps, 9 In the twilight—in the evening of day, || In the darkness of night and blackness. 10 And behold, a woman to meet him— (A harlot's dress, and watchful of heart, 11 She [is] noisy, and stubborn, her feet do not rest in her house. 12 Now in an out-place, now in broad places, || And she lies in wait near every corner)— 13 And she laid hold on him and kissed him, || She has hardened her face and says to him, 14 "Sacrifices of peace-offerings [are] by me, || Today I have completed my vows. 15 Therefore I have come forth to meet you, || To earnestly seek your face, and I find you. 16 I decked my bed [with] ornamental coverings, || Carved works—cotton of Egypt. 17 I sprinkled my bed [with] myrrh, aloes, and cinnamon. 18 Come, we are filled [with] love until the morning, || We delight ourselves in loves. 19 For the man is not in his house, || He has gone on a long journey. 20 He has taken a bag of money in his hand, || At the day of the new moon he comes to his house." 21 She turns him aside with the abundance of her speech, || She forces him with the flattery of her lips. 22 He is going after her straight away, he comes as an ox to the slaughter, || And as a chain to the discipline of a fool, 23 Until an arrow splits his liver, || As a bird has hurried to a snare, || And has not known that it [is] for its life. 24 And now, you sons, listen to me, || And give attention to sayings of my mouth. 25 Do not let your heart turn to her ways, || Do not wander in her paths, 26 For many [are] the wounded she caused to fall, || And mighty [are] all her slain ones. 27 The ways of Sheol—her house, || Going down to inner chambers of death!

CHAPTER 8

1 Does wisdom not call? And understanding give forth her voice? 2 At the head of high places by the way, || She has stood between the paths, 3 At the side of the gates, at the mouth of the city, || The entrance of the openings, she cries aloud, 4 "To you, O men, I call, || And my voice [is] to the sons of men. 5 Understand, you simple ones, prudence, || And you fools, understand the heart, 6 Listen, for I speak noble things, || And the opening of my lips [is] uprightness. 7 For my mouth utters truth, || And wickedness [is] an abomination to my lips. 8 All the sayings of my mouth [are] in righteousness, || Nothing in

them is contrary and perverse. 9 All of them [are] plain to the intelligent, || And upright to those finding knowledge. 10 Receive my instruction, and not silver, || And knowledge rather than choice gold. 11 For wisdom [is] better than rubies, || Indeed, all delights are not comparable with it. 12 I, wisdom, have dwelt with prudence, || And I find out a knowledge of purposes. 13 The fear of Yhwh [is] to hate evil; Pride, and arrogance, and an evil way, || And a contrary mouth, I have hated. 14 Counsel and substance [are] mine, || I [am] understanding, I have might. 15 By me kings reign, and princes decree righteousness, 16 By me chiefs' rule, and nobles, || All judges of earth. 17 I love those loving me, || And those seeking me earnestly find me. 18 Wealth and honor [are] with me, || Lasting substance and righteousness. 19 My fruit [is] better than gold, even fine gold, || And my increase than choice silver. 20 I cause to walk in a path of righteousness, || In midst of paths of judgment, 21 To cause my lovers to inherit substance, || Indeed, I fill their treasures. 22 Yhwh possessed me—the beginning of His way, || Before His works since then. 23 I was anointed from the age, from the first, || From former states of the earth. 24 In there being no depths, I was brought forth, || In there being no fountains heavy [with] waters, 25 Before mountains were sunk, || Before heights, I was brought forth. 26 While He had not made the earth, and out-places, || And the top of the dusts of the world. 27 In His preparing the heavens I [am] there, || In His decreeing a circle on the face of the deep, 28 In His strengthening clouds above, || In His making strong fountains of the deep, 29 In His setting for the sea its limit, || And the waters do not transgress His command, || In His decreeing the foundations of earth, 30 Then I am near Him, a workman, || And I am a delight—day by day. Rejoicing before Him at all times, 31 Rejoicing in the habitable part of His earth, || And my delights [are] with the sons of men. 32 And now, you sons, listen to me, || Indeed, blessed are they who keep my ways. 33 Hear instruction, and be wise, and do not slight. 34 O the blessedness of the man listening to me, || To watch at my door's day by day, || To watch at the doorposts of my entrance. 35 For whoever is finding me, has found life, || And brings out goodwill from Yhwh. 36 And whoever is missing me, is wronging his soul, || All hating me have loved death!"

CHAPTER 9

1 Wisdom has built her house, || She has hewn out her pillars—seven. 2 She has slaughtered her slaughter, || She has mingled her wine, || Indeed, she has arranged her table. 3 She has sent forth her girls, || She cries on the tops of the high places of the city: 4 "Who [is] simple? let him turn aside here." Whoever lacks heart: she has said to him, 5 "Come, eat of my bread, || And drink of the wine I have mingled. 6 Forsake the simple and live, || And be blessed in the way of understanding." 7 The instructor of a scorner || Is receiving for it—shame, || And a reprover of the wicked—his blemish. 8 Do not reprove a scorner, lest he hate you, || Give reproof to the wise, and he loves you. 9 Give to the wise, and he is wiser still, || Make known to the righteous, || And he increases learning. 10 The commencement of wisdom [is] the fear of Yhwh, || And a knowledge of the Holy Ones [is] understanding. 11 For by me your days multiply, || And years of life are added to you. 12 If you have been wise, you have been wise for yourself, || And you have scorned—you bear [it] alone. 13 A foolish woman [is] noisy, || Simple, and has not known what. 14 And she has sat at the opening of her house, || On a throne—the high places of the city, 15 To call to those passing by the way, || Who are going straight [on] their paths. 16 "Who [is] simple? let him turn aside here." And whoever lacks heart—she said to him, 17 "Stolen waters are sweet, || And hidden bread is pleasant." 18 And he has not known that Rephaim [are] there, || Her invited ones in deep places of Sheol!

CHAPTER 10

1 Proverbs of Solomon. A wise son causes a father to rejoice, || And a foolish son [is] an affliction to his mother. 2 Treasures of wickedness do not profit, || And righteousness delivers from death. 3 Yhwh does not cause the soul of the righteous to hunger, || And He thrusts away the desire of the wicked. 4 Poor [is] he who is working [with] a slothful hand, || And the hand of the diligent makes rich. 5 Whoever is gathering

in summer [is] a wise son, || Whoever is sleeping in harvest [is] a son causing shame. [6] Blessings [are] for the head of the righteous, || And the mouth of the wicked covers violence. [7] The remembrance of the righteous [is] for a blessing, || And the name of the wicked rots. [8] The wise in heart accepts commands, || And a talkative fool kicks. [9] Whoever is walking in integrity walks confidently, || And whoever is perverting his ways is known. [10] Whoever is winking the eye gives grief, || And a talkative fool kicks. [11] A fountain of life [is] the mouth of the righteous, || And the mouth of the wicked covers violence. [12] Hatred awakens contentions, || And love covers over all transgressions. [13] Wisdom is found in the lips of the intelligent, || And a rod [is] for the back of him who is lacking understanding. [14] The wise lay up knowledge, and the mouth of a fool [is] near ruin. [15] The wealth of the rich [is] his strong city, || The ruin of the poor [is] their poverty. [16] The wage of the righteous [is] for life, || The increase of the wicked for sin. [17] A traveler to life [is] he who is keeping instruction, || And whoever is forsaking rebuke is erring. [18] Whoever is covering hatred with lying lips, || And whoever is bringing out an evil report is a fool. [19] In the abundance of words transgression does not cease, || And whoever is restraining his lips [is] wise. [20] The tongue of the righteous [is] chosen silver, || The heart of the wicked—as a little thing. [21] The lips of the righteous delight many, || And fools die for lack of heart. [22] The blessing of Yhwh—it makes rich, || And He adds no grief with it. [23] To execute inventions [is] as play to a fool, || And wisdom to a man of understanding. [24] The feared thing of the wicked meets him, || And the desire of the righteous is given. [25] As the passing by of a windstorm, || So the wicked is not, || And the righteous is a perpetual foundation. [26] As vinegar to the teeth, || And as smoke to the eyes, || So [is] the slothful to those sending him. [27] The fear of Yhwh adds days, || And the years of the wicked are shortened. [28] The hope of the righteous [is] joyful, || And the expectation of the wicked perishes. [29] The way of Yhwh [is] strength to the perfect, || And ruin to workers of iniquity. [30] The righteous is not moved for all time, || And the wicked do not inhabit the earth. [31] The mouth of the righteous utters wisdom, || And the tongue of contrariness is cut out. [32] The lips of the righteous know a pleasing thing, || And the mouth of the wicked perverseness!

CHAPTER 11

[1] Balances of deceit [are] an abomination to Yhwh, || And a perfect weight [is] His delight. [2] Pride has come, and shame comes, || And wisdom [is] with the lowly. [3] The integrity of the upright leads them, || And the perverseness of the treacherous destroys them. [4] Wealth does not profit in a day of wrath, || And righteousness delivers from death. [5] The righteousness of the perfect makes his way right, || And by his wickedness the wicked fall. [6] The righteousness of the upright delivers them, || And in mischief the treacherous are captured. [7] In the death of a wicked man, hope perishes, || And the expectation of the iniquitous has been lost. [8] The righteous is drawn out from distress, || And the wicked goes in instead of him. [9] A hypocrite corrupts his friend with the mouth, || And the righteous are drawn out by knowledge. [10] A city exults in the good of the righteous, || And in the destruction of the wicked [is] singing. [11] By the blessing of the upright is a city exalted, || And by the mouth of the wicked thrown down. [12] Whoever is despising his neighbor lacks heart, || And a man of understanding keeps silence. [13] A busybody is revealing secret counsel, || And the faithful of spirit is covering the matter. [14] Without counsels a people falls, || And deliverance [is] in a multitude of counselors. [15] An evil [one] suffers when he has been guarantor [for] a stranger, || And whoever hates striking hands [in agreement] is confident. [16] A gracious woman retains honor, || And terrible [men] retain riches. [17] A kind man is rewarding his own soul, || And the fierce is troubling his own flesh. [18] The wicked is getting a lying wage, || And whoever is sowing righteousness—a true reward. [19] Correctly [is] righteousness for life, || And whoever is pursuing evil—for his own death. [20] The perverse of heart are an abomination to Yhwh, || And the perfect of the way [are] His delight. [21] Hand to hand, the wicked is not acquitted, || And the seed of the righteous has escaped. [22] A ring of gold in the nose of a sow—A beautiful woman and stubborn of behavior. [23] The desire of the righteous [is] only good, || The hope of the wicked [is] transgression. [24] There is [one] who is scattering, and yet is increased, || And [one] who is keeping back from uprightness, only to want. [25] A liberal soul

is made fat, || And whoever is watering, he also is watered. [26] Whoever is withholding grain, the people execrate him, || And a blessing [is] for the head of him who is selling. [27] Whoever is earnestly seeking good || Seeks a pleasing thing, || And whoever is seeking evil—it meets him. [28] Whoever is confident in his wealth falls, || And as a leaf, the righteous flourish. [29] Whoever is troubling his own house inherits wind, || And the fool [is] a servant to the wise of heart. [30] The fruit of the righteous [is] a tree of life, || And whoever is taking souls [is] wise. [31] Behold, the righteous is repaid in the earth, || Surely also the wicked and the sinner!

CHAPTER 12

[1] Whoever is loving instruction, is loving knowledge, || And whoever is hating reproof [is] brutish. [2] The good brings forth favor from Yhwh, || And the man of wicked schemes He condemns. [3] A man is not established by wickedness, || And the root of the righteous is not moved. [4] A virtuous woman [is] a crown to her husband, || And as rottenness in his bones [is] one causing shame. [5] The thoughts of the righteous [are] justice, || The counsels of the wicked—deceit. [6] The words of the wicked [are]: "Lay [in] wait for blood," || And the mouth of the upright delivers them. [7] Overthrow the wicked, and they are not, || And the house of the righteous stands. [8] A man is praised according to his wisdom, || And the perverted of heart becomes despised. [9] Better [is] the lightly esteemed who has a servant, || Than the self-honored who lacks bread. [10] The righteous knows the life of his beast, || And the mercies of the wicked [are] cruel. [11] Whoever is tilling the ground is satisfied [with] bread, || And whoever is pursuing vanities is lacking heart, [12] The wicked has desired the net of evildoers, || And the root of the righteous gives. [13] The snare of the wicked [is] in transgression of the lips, || And the righteous goes out from distress. [14] One [is] satisfied [with] good from the fruit of the mouth, || And the deed of man's hands returns to him. [15] The way of a fool [is] right in his own eyes, || And whoever is listening to counsel [is] wise. [16] The fool—his anger is known in a day, || And the prudent is covering shame. [17] Whoever utters faithfulness declares righteousness, || And a false witness—deceit. [18] A rash speaker is like piercings of a sword, || And the tongue of the wise is healing. [19] The lip of truth is established forever, || And a tongue of falsehood for a moment. [20] Deceit [is] in the heart of those devising evil, || But for counselors of peace—joy. [21] No iniquity is desired by the righteous, || And the wicked have been full of evil. [22] Lying lips [are] an abomination to Yhwh, || And steadfast doers [are] his delight. [23] A prudent man is concealing knowledge, || And the heart of fools proclaims folly. [24] The hand of the diligent rules, || And slothfulness becomes tributary. [25] Sorrow in the heart of a man bows down, || And a good word makes him glad. [26] The righteous searches his companion, || And the way of the wicked causes them to err. [27] The slothful does not roast his game, || And the wealth of a diligent man is precious. [28] In the path of righteousness [is] life, || And in the way of [that] path [is] no death!

CHAPTER 13

[1] A wise son—the instruction of a father, || And a scorner—he has not heard rebuke. [2] A man eats good from the fruit of the mouth, || And the soul of the treacherous—violence. [3] Whoever is keeping his mouth, is keeping his soul, || Whoever is opening wide his lips—ruin to him! [4] The soul of the slothful is desiring, and does not have. And the soul of the diligent is made fat. [5] The righteous hates a false word, || And the wicked causes abhorrence, and is confounded. [6] Righteousness keeps him who is perfect in the way, || And wickedness overthrows a sin offering. [7] There is [he] who is making himself rich, and has nothing, || Who is making himself poor, and wealth [is] abundant. [8] The ransom of a man's life [are] his riches, || And the poor has not heard rebuke. [9] The light of the righteous rejoices, || And the lamp of the wicked is extinguished. [10] A vain man causes debate through pride, || And wisdom [is] with the counseled. [11] Wealth from vanity becomes little, || And whoever is gathering by the hand becomes great. [12] Hope prolonged is making the heart sick, || And a tree of life [is] the coming desire. [13] Whoever is despising the word is destroyed for it, || And whoever is fearing the command is repaid. [14] The

law of the wise [is] a fountain of life, || To turn aside from snares of death. ¹⁵ Good understanding gives grace, || And the way of the treacherous [is] hard. ¹⁶ Every prudent one deals with knowledge, || And a fool spreads out folly. ¹⁷ A wicked messenger falls into evil, || And a faithful ambassador is healing. ¹⁸ Whoever is refusing instruction—poverty and shame, || And whoever is observing reproof is honored. ¹⁹ A desire accomplished is sweet to the soul, || And an abomination to fools || [Is] to turn from evil. ²⁰ Whoever is walking with wise men is wise, || And a companion of fools suffers evil. ²¹ Evil pursues sinners, || And good repays the righteous. ²² A good man causes sons' sons to inherit, || And the sinner's wealth [is] laid up for the righteous. ²³ Abundance of food—the tillage of the poor, || And substance is consumed without judgment. ²⁴ Whoever is sparing his rod is hating his son, || And whoever is loving him has hurried his discipline. ²⁵ The righteous is eating to the satiety of his soul, || And the belly of the wicked lacks!

CHAPTER 14

¹ Every wise woman has built her house, || And the foolish breaks it down with her hands. ² Whoever is walking in his uprightness is fearing Yhwh, || And the perverted is despising Him [in] his ways. ³ A rod of pride [is] in the mouth of a fool, || And the lips of the wise preserve them. ⁴ Without oxen a stall [is] clean, || And great [is] the increase by the power of the ox. ⁵ A faithful witness does not lie, || And a false witness breathes out lies. ⁶ A scorner has sought wisdom, and it is not, || And knowledge [is] easy to the intelligent. ⁷ Go from before a foolish man, || Or you have not known the lips of knowledge. ⁸ The wisdom of the prudent [is] to understand his way, || And the folly of fools [is] deceit. ⁹ Fools mock at a guilt-offering, || And among the upright—a pleasing thing. ¹⁰ The heart knows its own bitterness, || And a stranger does not interfere with its joy. ¹¹ The house of the wicked is destroyed, || And the tent of the upright flourishes. ¹² There is a way—right before a man, || And its latter end [are] ways of death. ¹³ Even in laughter is the heart pained, || And the latter end of joy [is] affliction. ¹⁴ The backslider in heart is filled from his ways, || And a good man—from his fruits. ¹⁵ The simple gives credence to everything, || And the prudent attends to his step. ¹⁶ The wise is fearing and turning from evil, || And a fool is transgressing and is confident. ¹⁷ Whoever is short of temper does folly, || And a man of wicked schemes is hated. ¹⁸ The simple have inherited folly, || And the prudent are crowned [with] knowledge. ¹⁹ The evil have bowed down before the good, || And the wicked at the gates of the righteous. ²⁰ The poor is hated even of his neighbor, || And those loving the rich [are] many. ²¹ Whoever is despising his neighbor sins, || Whoever is favoring the humble, || O his blessedness. ²² Do they who are devising evil not err? And kindness and truth [are] to those devising good, ²³ In all labor there is advantage, || And a thing of the lips [is] only to want. ²⁴ The crown of the wise is their wealth, || The folly of fools [is] folly. ²⁵ A true witness is delivering souls, || And a deceitful one breathes out lies. ²⁶ Strong confidence [is] in the fear of Yhwh, || And there is a refuge to His sons. ²⁷ The fear of Yhwh [is] a fountain of life, || To turn aside from snares of death. ²⁸ The honor of a king [is] in the multitude of a people, || And the ruin of a prince in lack of people. ²⁹ Whoever is slow to anger [is] of great understanding, || And whoever is short in temper is exalting folly. ³⁰ A healed heart [is] life to the flesh, || And rottenness to the bones [is] envy. ³¹ An oppressor of the poor reproaches his Maker, || And whoever is honoring Him || Is favoring the needy. ³² The wicked is driven away in his wickedness, || And the righteous [is] trustful in his death. ³³ Wisdom rests in the heart of the intelligent. And it is known in the midst of fools. ³⁴ Righteousness exalts a nation, || And the righteousness of peoples [is] a sin-offering. ³⁵ The favor of a king [is] to a wise servant, || And one causing shame is an object of his wrath!

CHAPTER 15

¹ A soft answer turns back fury, || And a grievous word raises up anger. ² The tongue of the wise makes knowledge good, || And the mouth of fools utters folly. ³ The eyes of Yhwh are in every place, || Watching the evil and the good. ⁴ A healed tongue [is] a tree of life, || And perverseness in it—a breach in the spirit. ⁵ A fool despises the instruction of his father, || And whoever is regarding reproof is prudent. ⁶ Abundant strength [is in] the house of the righteous, || And in the increase of the wicked—trouble. ⁷ The lips of the wise scatter knowledge, || And the heart of fools [is] not right. ⁸ The sacrifice of the wicked [is] an abomination to Yhwh, || And the prayer of the upright [is] His delight. ⁹ The way of the wicked [is] an abomination to Yhwh, || And He loves whoever is pursuing righteousness. ¹⁰ Discipline [is] grievous to him who is forsaking the path, || Whoever is hating reproof dies. ¹¹ Sheol and destruction [are] before Yhwh, || Surely also the hearts of the sons of men. ¹² A scorner does not love his reprover, || He does not go to the wise. ¹³ A joyful heart makes the face glad, || And the spirit is struck by grief of heart. ¹⁴ The heart of the intelligent seeks knowledge, || And the mouth of fools enjoys folly. ¹⁵ All the days of the afflicted [are] evil, || And gladness of heart [is] a perpetual banquet. ¹⁶ Better [is] a little with the fear of Yhwh, || Than much treasure, and tumult with it. ¹⁷ Better [is] an allowance of green herbs and love there, || Than a fatted ox, and hatred with it. ¹⁸ A man of fury stirs up contention, || And the slow to anger appeases strife. ¹⁹ The way of the slothful [is] as a hedge of briers, || And the path of the upright is raised up. ²⁰ A wise son makes a father glad. And a foolish man is despising his mother. ²¹ Folly is joy to one lacking heart, || And a man of intelligence directs [his] going. ²² The making void of purposes [is] without counsel, || And in a multitude of counselors it is established. ²³ Joy [is] to a man in the answer of his mouth, || And a word in its season—how good! ²⁴ A path of life [is] on high for the wise, || To turn aside from Sheol beneath. ²⁵ Yhwh pulls down the house of the proud, || And He sets up the border of the widow. ²⁶ Thoughts of wickedness [are] an abomination to Yhwh, || And sayings of pleasantness [are] pure. ²⁷ A dishonest gainer is troubling his house, || And whoever is hating gifts lives. ²⁸ The heart of the righteous meditates to answer, || And the mouth of the wicked utters evil things. ²⁹ Yhwh [is] far from the wicked, || And He hears the prayer of the righteous. ³⁰ The light of the eyes makes the heart glad, || A good report makes the bone fat. ³¹ An ear that is hearing the reproof of life || Lodges among the wise. ³² Whoever is refusing instruction is despising his soul, || And whoever is hearing reproof || Is getting understanding. ³³ The fear of Yhwh [is] the instruction of wisdom, || And humility [is] before honor!

CHAPTER 16

¹ Arrangements of the heart [are] of man, || An answer of the tongue from Yhwh. ² All the ways of a man are pure in his own eyes, || And Yhwh is pondering the spirits. ³ Roll your works to Yhwh, || And your purposes are established, ⁴ Yhwh has worked all things for Himself, || And also the wicked—for a day of evil. ⁵ Every proud one of heart [is] an abomination to Yhwh, || Hand to hand—he is not acquitted. ⁶ Iniquity is pardoned in kindness and truth, || And in the fear of Yhwh || Turn aside from evil. ⁷ When a man's ways please Yhwh, even his enemies, || He causes to be at peace with him. ⁸ Better [is] a little with righteousness, || Than abundance of increase without justice. ⁹ The heart of man devises his way, || And Yhwh establishes his step. ¹⁰ An oath [is] on the lips of a king, || In judgment his mouth does not trespass. ¹¹ A just beam and balances [are] Yhwh's, || All the stones of the bag [are] His work. ¹² Doing wickedness [is] an abomination to kings, || For a throne is established by righteousness. ¹³ Righteous lips [are] the delight of kings, || And he loves whoever is speaking uprightly, ¹⁴ The fury of a king [is] messengers of death, || And a wise man pacifies it. ¹⁵ In the light of a king's face [is] life, || And his goodwill [is] as a cloud of the spring rain. ¹⁶ To get wisdom—how much better than gold, || And to get understanding—to be chosen [more] than silver! ¹⁷ A highway of the upright [is] to turn from evil, || Whoever is preserving his soul is watching his way. ¹⁸ Pride [is] before destruction, || And before stumbling—a haughty spirit. ¹⁹ Better is humility of spirit with the poor, || Than to apportion spoil with the proud. ²⁰ The wise in any matter finds good, || And whoever is trusting in Yhwh, O his blessedness. ²¹ For the wise in heart is called intelligent, || And sweetness of lips increases learning. ²² Understanding [is] a fountain of life to its possessors, || The instruction of fools is folly. ²³ The heart of the wise causes his mouth to act wisely, || And he increases learning by his lips, ²⁴

Sayings of pleasantness [are] a honeycomb, || Sweet to the soul, and healing to the bone. ²⁵ There is a way right before a man, || And its latter end—ways of death. ²⁶ A laboring man has labored for himself, || For his mouth has caused [him] to bend over it. ²⁷ A worthless man is preparing evil, || And on his lips [is] as a burning fire. ²⁸ A contrary man sends forth contention, || A tale-bearer is separating a familiar friend. ²⁹ A violent man entices his neighbor, || And causes him to go in a way [that is] not good. ³⁰ Consulting his eyes to devise contrary things, || Moving his lips he has accomplished evil. ³¹ Grey hairs [are] a crown of beauty, || It is found in the way of righteousness. ³² Better [is] the [one] slow to anger than the mighty, || And the ruler over his spirit than he who is taking a city. ³³ The lot is cast into the center, || And all its judgment [is] from Yhwh!

CHAPTER 17

¹ Better [is] a dry morsel, and rest with it, || Than a house full of the sacrifices of strife. ² A wise servant rules over a son causing shame, || And he apportions an inheritance in the midst of brothers. ³ A refining pot [is] for silver, and a furnace for gold, || And the trier of hearts [is] Yhwh. ⁴ An evildoer is attentive to lips of vanity, || Falsehood is giving ear to a mischievous tongue. ⁵ Whoever is mocking at the poor || Has reproached his Maker, || Whoever is rejoicing at calamity is not acquitted. ⁶ Sons' sons [are] the crown of old men, || And the glory of sons [are] their fathers. ⁷ A lip of excellence is not fitting for a fool, much less a lip of falsehood for a noble. ⁸ A stone of grace [is] the bribe in the eyes of its possessors, || Wherever it turns, it prospers. ⁹ Whoever is covering transgression is seeking love, || And whoever is repeating a matter || Is separating a familiar friend. ¹⁰ Rebuke comes down on the intelligent || More than one hundred stripes on a fool. ¹¹ An evil man seeks only rebellion, || And a fierce messenger is sent against him. ¹² The meeting of a bereaved bear by a man, || And—not a fool in his folly. ¹³ Whoever is returning evil for good, || Evil does not move from his house. ¹⁴ The beginning of contention [is] a letting out of waters, || And leave the strife before it is meddled with. ¹⁵ Whoever is justifying the wicked, || And condemning the righteous, || Even both of these [are] an abomination to Yhwh. ¹⁶ Why [is] this—a price in the hand of a fool to buy wisdom, || And a heart—there is none? ¹⁷ The friend is loving at all times, || And a brother is born for adversity. ¹⁸ A man lacking heart is striking hands, || He becomes a guarantor before his friend. ¹⁹ Whoever is loving transgression is loving debate, || Whoever is making his entrance high is seeking destruction. ²⁰ The perverse of heart does not find good, || And the [one] turned in his tongue falls into evil. ²¹ Whoever is begetting a fool has affliction for it, || Indeed, the father of a fool does not rejoice. ²² A rejoicing heart does good to the body, || And a struck spirit dries the bone. ²³ The wicked takes a bribe from the bosom, || To turn aside the paths of judgment. ²⁴ The face of the intelligent [is] to wisdom, || And the eyes of a fool—at the end of the earth. ²⁵ A foolish son [is] a provocation to his father, || And bitterness to her bearing him. ²⁶ Also, [it] is not good to fine the righteous, || To strike nobles for uprightness. ²⁷ One acquainted with knowledge is sparing his words, || And the cool of temper [is] a man of understanding. ²⁸ Even a fool keeping silence is reckoned wise, || He who is shutting his lips [seems] intelligent!

CHAPTER 18

¹ He who is separated seeks [his own] desire, || He interferes with all wisdom. ² A fool does not delight in understanding, || But in uncovering his heart. ³ Contempt has also come with the coming of the wicked, || And with shame—reproach. ⁴ The words of a man's mouth [are] deep waters, || The fountain of wisdom [is] a flowing brook. ⁵ Favoring of the face of the wicked [is] not good, || To turn aside the righteous in judgment. ⁶ The lips of a fool enter into strife, || And his mouth calls for stripes. ⁷ The mouth of a fool [is] ruin to him, || And his lips [are] the snare of his soul. ⁸ The words of a tale-bearer [are] as self-inflicted wounds, || And they have gone down [to] the inner parts of the heart. ⁹ He also that is remiss in his work, || He [is] a brother to a destroyer. ¹⁰ The Name of Yhwh [is] a tower of strength, || The righteous runs into it, and

is set on high. ¹¹ The wealth of the rich [is] the city of his strength, || And as a wall set on high in his own imagination. ¹² The heart of man is high before destruction, || And humility [is] before honor. ¹³ Whoever is answering a matter before he hears, || It is folly to him—and shame. ¹⁴ The spirit of a man sustains his sickness, || And who bears a struck spirit? ¹⁵ The heart of the intelligent gets knowledge, || And the ear of the wise seeks knowledge. ¹⁶ The gift of a man makes room for him, || And it leads him before the great. ¹⁷ The first in his own cause [seems] righteous, || [But] his neighbor comes and has searched him. ¹⁸ The lot causes contentions to cease, || And it separates between the mighty. ¹⁹ A brother transgressed against is as a strong city, || And contentions as the bar of a palace. ²⁰ From the fruit of a man's mouth is his belly satisfied, || [From the] increase of his lips he is satisfied. ²¹ Death and life [are] in the power of the tongue, || And those loving it eat its fruit. ²² [Whoever] has found a wife has found good, || And brings out goodwill from Yhwh. ²³ The poor speaks [with] supplications, || And the rich answers fierce things. ²⁴ A man with friends—to show himself friendly, || And there is a lover adhering more than a brother!

CHAPTER 19

¹ Better [is] the poor walking in his integrity, || Than the perverse [in] his lips—who [is] a fool. ² Also, without knowledge the soul [is] not good, || And the hasty in feet is sinning. ³ The folly of man perverts his way, || And his heart is angry against Yhwh. ⁴ Wealth adds many friends, || And the poor is separated from his neighbor. ⁵ A false witness is not acquitted, || Whoever breathes out lies is not delivered. ⁶ Many beg the face of the noble, || And all have made friendship to a man of gifts. ⁷ All the brothers of the poor have hated him, || Surely his friends have also been far from him, || He is pursuing words—they are not! ⁸ Whoever is getting heart is loving his soul, || He is keeping understanding to find good. ⁹ A false witness is not acquitted, || And whoever breathes out lies perishes. ¹⁰ Luxury is not fitting for a fool, || Much less for a servant to rule among princes. ¹¹ The wisdom of a man has deferred his anger, || And his glory [is] to pass over transgression. ¹² The wrath of a king [is] a growl as of a young lion, || And his goodwill as dew on the herb. ¹³ A foolish son [is] a calamity to his father, || And the contentions of a wife [are] a continual dropping. ¹⁴ House and wealth [are] the inheritance of fathers, || And an understanding wife [is] from Yhwh. ¹⁵ Sloth causes deep sleep to fall, || And an indolent soul hungers. ¹⁶ Whoever is keeping the command is keeping his soul, || Whoever is despising His ways dies. ¹⁷ Whoever is lending [to] Yhwh is favoring the poor, || And He repays his deed to him. ¹⁸ Discipline your son, for there is hope, || And do not lift up your soul to put him to death. ¹⁹ A man of great wrath is bearing punishment, || For if you deliver, yet again you add. ²⁰ Hear counsel and receive instruction, || So that you are wise in your latter end. ²¹ The purposes in a man's heart [are] many, || And the counsel of Yhwh—it stands. ²² The desirableness of a man [is] his kindness, || And the poor [is] better than a liar. ²³ The fear of Yhwh [is] to life, || And he remains satisfied—he is not charged with evil. ²⁴ The slothful has hidden his hand in a dish, || Even to his mouth he does not bring it back. ²⁵ Strike a scorner, and the simple acts prudently, || And give reproof to the intelligent, || He understands knowledge. ²⁶ Whoever is spoiling a father causes a mother to flee, || A son causing shame, and bringing confusion. ²⁷ Cease, my son, to hear instruction—To err from sayings of knowledge. ²⁸ A worthless witness scorns judgment, || And the mouth of the wicked swallows iniquity. ²⁹ Judgments have been prepared for scorners, || And stripes for the back of fools!

CHAPTER 20

¹ Wine [is] a scorner—strong drink [is] noisy, || And any going astray in it is not wise. ² The fear of a king [is] a growl as of a young lion, || He who is causing him to be angry is wronging his soul. ³ Cessation from strife is an honor to a man, || And every fool interferes. ⁴ The slothful does not plow because of winter, || He asks in harvest, and there is nothing. ⁵ Counsel in the heart of a man [is] deep water, || And a man of understanding draws it up. ⁶ A multitude of men each proclaim his kindness, || And a man of steadfastness who

finds? [7] The righteous is habitually walking in his integrity, || O the blessedness of his sons after him! [8] A king sitting on a throne of judgment, || Is scattering all evil with his eyes, [9] Who says, "I have purified my heart, || I have been cleansed from my sin?" [10] A stone and a stone, an ephah and an ephah, || Even both of them [are] an abomination to Yhwh. [11] Even by his actions a youth makes himself known, || Whether his work is pure or upright. [12] A hearing ear, and a seeing eye—Yhwh has even made both of them. [13] Do not love sleep, lest you become poor, || Open your eyes—be satisfied [with] bread. [14] "Bad, bad," says the buyer, || And then he boasts himself going his way. [15] Substance, gold, and a multitude of rubies, || Indeed, a precious vessel, [are] lips of knowledge. [16] When a stranger has been guarantor, take his garment, || And pledge it for strangers. [17] The bread of falsehood [is] sweet to a man, || And afterward his mouth is filled [with] gravel. [18] You establish purposes by counsel, || And with plans you make war. [19] The busybody is a revealer of secret counsels, || And do not make yourself guarantor for a deceiver [with] his lips. [20] Whoever is vilifying his father and his mother, his lamp is extinguished in blackness of darkness. [21] An inheritance gotten wrongly at first, || Even its latter end is not blessed. [22] Do not say, "I repay evil," || Wait for Yhwh, and He delivers you. [23] A stone and a stone [are] an abomination to Yhwh, || And balances of deceit [are] not good. [24] The steps of a man [are] from Yhwh, || And man—how does he understand his way? [25] A snare to a man [that] he has swallowed a holy thing, || And to make inquiry after vows. [26] A wise king is scattering the wicked, || And turns the wheel back on them. [27] The breath of man [is] a lamp of Yhwh, || Searching all the inner parts of the heart. [28] Kindness and truth keep a king, || And he has supported his throne by kindness. [29] The beauty of young men is their strength, || And the honor of old men is grey hairs. [30] Blows that wound cleanse away evil, || Also the scourges of the inner parts of the heart!

CHAPTER 21

[1] The heart of a king [is] streams of waters in the hand of Yhwh, || He inclines it wherever He pleases. [2] Every way of a man [is] right in his own eyes, || And Yhwh is pondering hearts. [3] To do righteousness and judgment, || Is chosen of Yhwh rather than sacrifice. [4] Loftiness of eyes, and breadth of heart, || Tillage of the wicked [is] sin. [5] The purposes of the diligent [are] only to advantage, || And of every hasty one, only to want. [6] The making of treasures by a lying tongue, || [Is] a vanity driven away of those seeking death. [7] The spoil of the wicked catches them, || Because they have refused to do judgment. [8] The way of a man who is vile [is] contrary, || And the pure—his work [is] upright. [9] Better to sit on a corner of the roof, || Than [with] a woman of contentions and a house of company. [10] The soul of the wicked has desired evil, his neighbor is not gracious in his eyes. [11] When the scorner is punished, the simple becomes wise, || And in giving understanding to the wise He receives knowledge. [12] The Righteous One is acting wisely || Toward the house of the wicked, || He is overthrowing the wicked for wickedness. [13] Whoever is shutting his ear from the cry of the poor, || He also cries, and is not answered. [14] A gift in secret pacifies anger, || And a bribe in the bosom—strong fury. [15] To do justice [is] joy to the righteous, || But ruin to workers of iniquity. [16] A man who is wandering from the way of understanding, || Rests in an assembly of Rephaim. [17] Whoever [is] loving mirth [is] a poor man, || Whoever is loving wine and oil makes no wealth. [18] The wicked [is] an atonement for the righteous, || And the treacherous dealer for the upright. [19] Better to dwell in a wilderness land, || Than [with] a woman of contentions and anger. [20] A treasure to be desired, and oil, || [Is] in the habitation of the wise, || And a foolish man swallows it up. [21] Whoever is pursuing righteousness and kindness, || Finds life, righteousness, and honor. [22] The wise has gone up a city of the mighty, || And brings down the strength of its confidence. [23] Whoever is keeping his mouth and his tongue, || Is keeping his soul from adversities. [24] Proud, haughty, scorner—his name, || Who is working in the wrath of pride. [25] The desire of the slothful slays him, || For his hands have refused to work. [26] All the day desiring he has desired, || And the righteous gives and does not withhold. [27] The sacrifice of the wicked [is] abomination, || Much more when he brings it in wickedness. [28] A false witness perishes, || And an attentive man speaks forever. [29] A wicked man has hardened by his face, || And the

upright—he prepares his way. [30] There is no wisdom, nor understanding, || Nor counsel against Yhwh. [31] A horse is prepared for a day of battle, || And the deliverance [is] of Yhwh!

CHAPTER 22

[1] A name is chosen rather than much wealth, || Than silver and than gold—good grace. [2] Rich and poor have met together, || Yhwh [is] the Maker of them all. [3] The prudent has seen the evil, and is hidden, || And the simple have passed on, and are punished. [4] The end of humility [is] the fear of Yhwh, riches, and honor, and life. [5] Thorns [and] snares [are] in the way of the perverse, || Whoever is keeping his soul is far from them. [6] Give instruction to a youth about his way, || Even when he is old he does not turn from it. [7] The rich rules over the poor, || And a servant [is] the borrower to the lender. [8] Whoever is sowing perverseness reaps sorrow, || And the rod of his anger wears out. [9] The good of eye—he is blessed, || For he has given of his bread to the poor. [10] Cast out a scorner—and contention goes out, || And strife and shame cease. [11] Whoever is loving cleanness of heart, || His lips [are] grace, || A king [is] his friend. [12] The eyes of Yhwh have kept knowledge, || And He overthrows the words of the treacherous. [13] The slothful has said, "A lion [is] outside, || I am slain in the midst of the broad places." [14] The mouth of strange women [is] a deep pit, || The abhorred of Yhwh falls there. [15] Folly is bound up in the heart of a youth, || The rod of discipline puts it far from him. [16] He [who] is oppressing the poor to multiply his [riches], || Is giving to the rich—only to want. [17] Incline your ear, and hear words of the wise, || And set your heart to my knowledge, [18] For they are pleasant when you keep them in your heart, || They are prepared together for your lips. [19] That your trust may be in Yhwh, || I caused you to know today, even you. [20] Have I not written to you three times || With counsels and knowledge? [21] To cause you to know the certainty of sayings of truth, || To return sayings of truth to those sending you. [22] Do not rob the poor because he [is] poor, || And do not bruise the afflicted in the gate. [23] For Yhwh pleads their cause, || And has spoiled the soul of their spoilers. [24] Do not show yourself friendly with an angry man, || And do not go in with a man of fury, [25] Lest you learn his paths, || And have received a snare to your soul. [26] Do not be among those striking hands, || Among sureties [for] burdens. [27] If you have nothing to pay, || Why does he take your bed from under you? [28] Do not remove a border of ancient times, || That your fathers have made. [29] Have you seen a man speedy in his business? He stations himself before kings, || He does not station himself before obscure men!

CHAPTER 23

[1] When you sit to eat with a ruler, || Diligently consider that which [is] before you, [2] And you have put a knife to your throat, || If you [are] a man of appetite. [3] Have no desire to his delicacies, seeing it [is] lying food. [4] Do not labor to make wealth, || Cease from your own understanding, || Do you cause your eyes to fly on it? Then it is not. [5] For wealth makes wings to itself, || It flies to the heavens as an eagle. [6] Do not eat the bread of an evil eye, || And have no desire to his delicacies, [7] For as he has thought in his soul, so he [is]. "Eat and drink," he says to you, || And his heart [is] not with you. [8] You vomit up your morsel you have eaten, || And have marred your words that [are] sweet. [9] Do not speak in the ears of a fool, || For he treads on the wisdom of your words. [10] Do not remove a border of ancient times, || And do not enter into fields of the fatherless, [11] For their Redeemer [is] strong, || He pleads their cause with you. [12] Bring your heart to instruction, || And your ear to sayings of knowledge. [13] Do not withhold discipline from a youth, || When you strike him with a rod he does not die. [14] You strike him with a rod, || And you deliver his soul from Sheol. [15] My son, if your heart has been wise, || My heart rejoices, even mine, [16] And my reins exult when your lips speak uprightly. [17] Do not let your heart be envious at sinners, || But—in the fear of Yhwh all the day. [18] For is there a posterity? Then your hope is not cut off. [19] Hear, my son, and be wise, || And make your heart blessed in the way, [20] Do not become drunk with wine, || Among gluttonous ones of flesh, [21] For the drunkard and glutton become poor, || And drowsiness

clothes with rags. 22 Listen to your father, who begot you, || And do not despise your mother when she has become old. 23 Buy truth, and do not sell, || Wisdom, and instruction, and understanding, 24 The father of the righteous rejoices greatly, || The begetter of the wise rejoices in him. 25 Your father and your mother rejoice, || Indeed, she bearing you is joyful. 26 Give, my son, your heart to me, || And let your eyes watch my ways. 27 For a harlot [is] a deep ditch, || And a strange woman [is] a narrow pit. 28 She also, as catching prey, lies in wait, || And she increases the treacherous among men. 29 Who has woe? who has sorrow? Who has contentions? who has complaint? Who has wounds without cause? Who has redness of eyes? 30 Those lingering by the wine, || Those going in to search out mixed wine. 31 Do not see wine when it shows itself red, || When it gives its color in the cup, || It goes up and down through the upright. 32 Its latter end—it bites as a serpent, || And it stings as a viper. 33 Your eyes see strange women, || And your heart speaks perverse things. 34 And you have been as one lying down in the heart of the sea, || And as one lying down on the top of a mast. 35 "They struck me, I have not been sick, || They beat me, I have not known. When I awake—I seek it yet again!"

CHAPTER 24

1 Do not be envious of evil men, || And do not desire to be with them. 2 For their heart meditates [on] destruction, || And their lips speak perverseness. 3 A house is built by wisdom, || And it establishes itself by understanding. 4 And the inner parts are filled by knowledge, || [With] all precious and pleasant wealth. 5 The wise [is] mighty in strength, || And a man of knowledge is strengthening power, 6 For you make war for yourself by plans, || And deliverance [is] in a multitude of counselors. 7 Wisdom [is] high for a fool, he does not open his mouth in the gate. 8 Whoever is devising to do evil, || They call him a master of wicked thoughts. 9 The thought of folly [is] sin, || And a scorner [is] an abomination to man. 10 You have showed yourself weak in a day of adversity, || Your power is restricted, 11 If [from] delivering those taken to death, || And you take back those slipping to the slaughter. 12 When you say, "Behold, we did not know this." Is the Ponderer of hearts not He who understands? And the Keeper of your soul He who knows? And He has rendered to man according to his work. 13 My son, eat honey that [is] good, || And the honeycomb [is] sweet to your palate. 14 So [is] the knowledge of wisdom to your soul, || If you have found that there is a posterity || And your hope is not cut off. 15 Do not lay wait, O wicked one, || At the habitation of the righteous. Do not spoil his resting place. 16 For the righteous fall and rise seven [times], || And the wicked stumble in evil. 17 Do not rejoice in the falling of your enemy, || And do not let your heart be joyful in his stumbling, 18 Lest Yhwh see, and [it be] evil in His eyes, || And He has turned His anger from off him. 19 Do not fret yourself at evildoers, do not be envious at the wicked, 20 For there is not a posterity to the evil, || The lamp of the wicked is extinguished. 21 Fear Yhwh, my son, and the king, || Do not mix yourself up with changers, 22 For their calamity rises suddenly, || And the ruin of them both—who knows! 23 These are also for the wise: [It] is not good to discern faces in judgment. 24 Whoever is saying to the wicked, "You [are] righteous," || Peoples execrate him—nations abhor him. 25 And it is pleasant to those reproving, || And a good blessing comes on them. 26 He who is returning straightforward words kisses lips. 27 Prepare your work in an out-place, || And make it ready in the field—go afterward, || Then you have built your house. 28 Do not be a witness against your neighbor for nothing, || Or you have enticed with your lips. 29 Do not say, "As he did to me, so I do to him, || I render to each according to his work." 30 I passed by near the field of a slothful man, || And near the vineyard of a man lacking heart. 31 And behold, it has gone up—all of it—thorns! Nettles have covered its face, || And its stone wall has been broken down. 32 And I see—I set my heart, || I have seen—I have received instruction, 33 A little sleep—a little slumber—A little folding of the hands to lie down. 34 And your poverty has come [as] a traveler, || And your want as an armed man!

CHAPTER 25

1 These are also proverbs of Solomon, that men of Hezekiah king of Judah transcribed: 2 The glory of God [is] to hide a thing, || And the glory of kings [is] to search out a matter. 3 The heavens for height, and the earth for depth, || And the heart of kings—[are] unsearchable. 4 Take away dross from silver, || And a vessel goes forth for the refiner, 5 Take away the wicked before a king, || And his throne is established in righteousness. 6 Do not honor yourself before a king, || And do not stand in the place of the great. 7 For better [that] he has said to you, "Come up here," || Than [that] he humbles you before a noble, || Whom your eyes have seen. 8 Do not go forth to strive, hurry, turn, || What do you do in its latter end, || When your neighbor causes you to blush? 9 Plead your cause with your neighbor, || And do not reveal the secret counsel of another, 10 Lest the hearer put you to shame, || And your evil report not turn back. 11 Apples of gold in imagery of silver, || [Is] the word spoken at its fit times. 12 A ring of gold, and an ornament of pure gold, || [Is] the wise reprover to an attentive ear. 13 As a vessel of snow in a day of harvest, || [So is] a faithful ambassador to those sending him, || And he refreshes the soul of his masters. 14 Clouds and wind without rain, || [Is] a man boasting himself in a false gift. 15 A ruler is persuaded by long-suffering, || And a soft tongue breaks a bone. 16 You have found honey—eat your sufficiency, || Lest you are satiated [with] it, and have vomited it. 17 Withdraw your foot from your neighbor's house, || Lest he is satiated [with] you, and has hated you. 18 A maul, and a sword, and a sharp arrow, || [Is] the man testifying a false testimony against his neighbor. 19 A bad tooth, and a tottering foot, || [Is] the confidence of the treacherous in a day of adversity. 20 Whoever is taking away a garment in a cold day, || [Is as] vinegar on natron, || And a singer of songs on a sad heart. 21 If he who is hating you hungers, cause him to eat bread, || And if he thirsts, cause him to drink water. 22 For you are putting coals on his head, || And Yhwh gives repayment to you. 23 A north wind brings forth rain, || And a secret tongue—indignant faces. 24 Better to sit on a corner of a roof, || Than [with] a woman of contentions, and a house of company. 25 [As] cold waters for a weary soul, || So [is] a good report from a far country. 26 A spring troubled, and a fountain corrupt, || [Is] the righteous falling before the wicked. 27 The eating of much honey is not good, || Nor a searching out of one's own honor—honor. 28 A city broken down without walls, || [Is] a man without restraint over his spirit!

CHAPTER 26

1 As snow in summer, and as rain in harvest, || So honor [is] not fitting for a fool. 2 As a bird by wandering, as a swallow by flying, || So reviling without cause does not come. 3 A whip is for a horse, a bridle for a donkey, || And a rod for the back of fools. 4 Do not answer a fool according to his folly, || Lest you are like to him—even you. 5 Answer a fool according to his folly, || Lest he is wise in his own eyes. 6 He is cutting off feet, he is drinking injury, || Who is sending things by the hand of a fool. 7 The two legs of the lame have been weak, || And an allegory in the mouth of fools. 8 As one who is binding a stone in a sling, || So [is] he who is giving honor to a fool. 9 A thorn has gone up into the hand of a drunkard, || And an allegory in the mouth of fools. 10 The Former of all [is] great, || And He is rewarding a fool, || And is rewarding transgressors. 11 As a dog has returned to its vomit, || A fool is repeating his folly. 12 You have seen a man wise in his own eyes, || More hope of a fool than of him! 13 The slothful has said, || "A lion [is] in the way, || A lion [is] in the broad places." 14 The door turns around on its hinge, || And the slothful on his bed. 15 The slothful has hid his hand in a dish, || He is weary of bringing it back to his mouth. 16 Wiser [is] the slothful in his own eyes, || Than seven [men] returning a reason. 17 Laying hold on the ears of a dog, || [Is] a passer-by making himself wrath for strife [that is] not his own. 18 As [one] pretending to be feeble, || Who is casting sparks, arrows, and death, 19 So has a man deceived his neighbor, || And has said, "Am I not playing?" 20 Fire is going out without wood, || And contention ceases without a tale-bearer, 21 Coal to burning coals, and wood to fire, || And a man of contentions to kindle strife. 22 The words of a tale-bearer [are] as self-inflicted wounds, || And they have gone down [to] the inner parts of the heart. 23 Silver of dross spread over potsherd, || [Are] burning lips and an evil heart. 24 A hater pretends by his lips, || And he places deceit in his heart, 25 When his voice is gracious do not trust in him, || For seven

abominations [are] in his heart. ²⁶ Hatred is covered by deceit, || Its wickedness is revealed in an assembly. ²⁷ Whoever is digging a pit falls into it, || And the roller of a stone, it turns to him. ²⁸ A lying tongue hates its bruised ones, || And a flattering mouth works an overthrow!

CHAPTER 27

¹ Do not boast about tomorrow, || For you do not know what a day brings forth. ² Let another praise you, and not your own mouth, || A stranger, and not your own lips. ³ A stone [is] heavy, and the sand [is] heavy, || And the anger of a fool || Is heavier than them both. ⁴ Fury [is] fierce, and anger [is] overflowing, || And who stands before jealousy? ⁵ Better [is] open reproof than hidden love. ⁶ The wounds of a lover are faithful, || And the kisses of an enemy [are] abundant. ⁷ A satiated soul treads down a honeycomb, || And every bitter thing [is] sweet [to] a hungry soul. ⁸ As a bird wandering from her nest, || So [is] a man wandering from his place. ⁹ Perfume and incense make the heart glad, || And the sweetness of one's friend—from counsel of the soul. ¹⁰ Do not forsake your own friend and the friend of your father, || And do not enter the house of your brother in a day of your calamity, || A near neighbor [is] better than a brother far off. ¹¹ Be wise, my son, and make my heart glad, || And I return a word [to] my reproacher. ¹² The prudent has seen the evil, he is hidden, || The simple have passed on, they are punished. ¹³ Take his garment when a stranger has been guarantor, || And pledge it for a strange woman. ¹⁴ Whoever is greeting his friend with a loud voice, || Rising early in the morning, || It is reckoned a light thing to him. ¹⁵ A continual dropping in a day of rain, || And a woman of contentions are alike, ¹⁶ Whoever is hiding her has hidden the wind, || And the ointment of his right hand calls out. ¹⁷ Iron is sharpened by iron, || And a man sharpens the face of his friend. ¹⁸ The keeper of a fig tree eats its fruit, || And the preserver of his master is honored. ¹⁹ As [in] water the face [is] to face, || So the heart of man to man. ²⁰ Sheol and destruction are not satisfied, || And the eyes of man are not satisfied. ²¹ A refining pot [is] for silver, and a furnace for gold, || And a man according to his praise. ²² If you beat the foolish in a mortar, || Among washed things—with a pestle, || His folly does not turn aside from off him. ²³ Know the face of your flock well, || Set your heart to the droves, ²⁴ For riches [are] not for all time, || Nor a crown to generation and generation. ²⁵ The hay was revealed, and the tender grass seen, || And the herbs of mountains gathered. ²⁶ Lambs [are] for your clothing, || And the price of the field [are] male goats, ²⁷ And a sufficiency of goats' milk [is] for your bread, || For bread to your house, and life to your girls!

CHAPTER 28

¹ The wicked have fled and there is no pursuer, || And the righteous is confident as a young lion. ² By the transgression of a land its heads are many, || And by an understanding man, || Who knows right—it is prolonged. ³ A man—poor and oppressing the weak, || [Is] a sweeping rain, and there is no bread. ⁴ Those forsaking the Law praise the wicked, || Those keeping the Law plead against them. ⁵ Evil men do not understand judgment, || And those seeking Yhwh understand all. ⁶ Better [is] the poor walking in his integrity, || Than the perverse of ways who is rich. ⁷ Whoever is keeping the Law is an intelligent son, || And a friend of gluttons || Causes his father to blush. ⁸ Whoever is multiplying his wealth by biting and usury, || Gathers it for one favoring the poor. ⁹ Whoever is turning his ear from hearing the Law, || Even his prayer [is] an abomination. ¹⁰ Whoever is causing the upright to err in an evil way, || He falls into his own pit, || And the perfect inherits good. ¹¹ A rich man is wise in his own eyes, || And the intelligent poor searches him. ¹² In the exulting of the righteous the glory [is] abundant, || And in the rising of the wicked man is apprehensive. ¹³ Whoever is covering his transgressions does not prosper, || And he who is confessing and forsaking has mercy. ¹⁴ O the blessedness of a man fearing continually, || And whoever is hardening his heart falls into evil. ¹⁵ A growling lion, and a ranging bear, || [Is] the wicked ruler over a poor people. ¹⁶ A leader lacking understanding multiplies oppressions, || Whoever is hating dishonest gain prolongs days. ¹⁷ A man oppressed with the blood of a soul, || Flees to the pit, [and] none takes hold on him [to help]. ¹⁸ Whoever is walking uprightly is saved, || And the perverted of ways falls at once. ¹⁹ Whoever is tilling his ground is satisfied [with] bread, || And whoever is pursuing vanity, || Is filled [with] poverty. ²⁰ A steadfast man has multiplied blessings, || And whoever is hastening to be rich is not acquitted. ²¹ [It] is not good to discern faces, || And a man transgresses for a piece of bread. ²² The man [with] an evil eye [is] troubled for wealth, || And he does not know that want meets him. ²³ Whoever is reproving a man finds grace afterward, || More than a flatterer with the tongue. ²⁴ Whoever is robbing his father or his mother, || And is saying, "It is not transgression," || He is a companion to a destroyer. ²⁵ Whoever is proud in soul stirs up contention, || And whoever is trusting on Yhwh is made fat. ²⁶ Whoever is trusting in his heart is a fool, || And whoever is walking in wisdom is delivered. ²⁷ Whoever is giving to the poor has no lack, || And whoever is hiding his eyes multiplied curses. ²⁸ A man is hidden in the rising of the wicked, || And the righteous multiply in their destruction!

CHAPTER 29

¹ A man often reproved, hardening the neck, || Is suddenly broken, and there is no healing. ² In the multiplying of the righteous the people rejoice, || And in the ruling of the wicked the people sigh. ³ A man loving wisdom makes his father glad, || And a friend of harlots destroys wealth. ⁴ A king establishes a land by judgment, || And one receiving gifts throws it down. ⁵ A man taking a portion above his neighbor, || Spreads a net for his own steps. ⁶ A snare [is] in the transgression of the evil, || And the righteous sing and rejoice. ⁷ The righteous knows the plea of the poor, || The wicked does not understand knowledge. ⁸ Men of scorning ensnare a city, || And the wise turn back anger. ⁹ A wise man is judged by the foolish man, || And he has been angry, || And he has laughed, and there is no rest. ¹⁰ Men of blood hate the perfect, || And the upright seek his soul. ¹¹ A fool brings out all his mind, || And the wise restrains it until afterward. ¹² A ruler who is attending to lying words, || All his ministers [are] wicked. ¹³ The poor and the man of frauds have met together, || Yhwh is enlightening the eyes of them both. ¹⁴ a king that is judging the poor with truth, || His throne is established forever. ¹⁵ A rod and reproof give wisdom, || And a youth let away is shaming his mother. ¹⁶ In the multiplying of the wicked transgression multiplies, || And the righteous look on their fall. ¹⁷ Discipline your son, and he gives you comfort, || Indeed, he gives delights to your soul. ¹⁸ A people is made naked without a vision, || And whoever is keeping the Law, O his blessedness! ¹⁹ By words a servant is not instructed though he understand, || And there is nothing answering. ²⁰ You have seen a man hasty in his words! More hope of a fool than of him. ²¹ Whoever is bringing up his servant delicately, from youth, || [At] his latter end he is also continuator. ²² An angry man stirs up contention, || And a furious man is multiplying transgression. ²³ The pride of man humbles him, || And humility of spirit upholds honor. ²⁴ Whoever is sharing with a thief is hating his own soul, || He hears execration, and does not tell. ²⁵ Fear of man causes a snare, || And the confident in Yhwh is set on high. ²⁶ Many are seeking the face of a ruler, || And the judgment of each [is] from Yhwh. ²⁷ The perverse man [is] an abomination to the righteous, || And the upright in the way [is] an abomination to the wicked!

CHAPTER 30

¹ Words of Agur, son of Jakeh, the burden, a declaration of the man to Ithiel—to Ithiel and Ucal: I have wearied myself [for] God, || I have wearied myself [for] God, and am consumed. ² For I am more brutish than anyone, || And do not have the understanding of a man. ³ Nor have I learned wisdom, || Yet I know the knowledge of the Holy Ones. ⁴ Who went up to the heavens, and comes down? Who has gathered the wind in His fists? Who has bound waters in a garment? Who established all ends of the earth? What [is] His Name? and what [is] His Son's Name? Surely you know! ⁵ Every saying of God [is] tried, || He [is] a shield to those trusting in Him. ⁶ Do not add to His words, lest He reason with you, || And you have been found false. ⁷ Two things I have asked from You, || Do not withhold from me before I die. ⁸ Put vanity and a lying word

far from me, || Do not give poverty or wealth to me, || Cause me to eat the bread of my portion, ⁹ Lest I become satiated, and have denied, || And have said, "Who [is] Yhwh?" And lest I am poor, and have stolen, || And have laid hold of the Name of my God. ¹⁰ Do not accuse a servant to his lord, || Lest he disapprove of you, and you are found guilty. ¹¹ A generation lightly esteems their father, || And does not bless their mother. ¹² A generation—pure in their own eyes, || But not washed from their own filth. ¹³ A generation—how high are their eyes, || Indeed, their eyelids are lifted up. ¹⁴ A generation—their teeth [are] swords, || And their jaw-teeth [are] knives, || To consume the poor from earth, || And the needy from [among] men. ¹⁵ To the leech [are] two daughters—Give! Give! Behold, three things are not satisfied, || Four have not said "Sufficiency"; ¹⁶ Sheol, and a restrained womb, || Earth—it [is] not satisfied [with] water, || And fire—it has not said, "Sufficiency," ¹⁷ An eye that mocks at a father, || And despises to obey a mother, || Ravens of the valley dig it out, || And young eagles eat it. ¹⁸ Three things have been too wonderful for me, || Indeed, four that I have not known: ¹⁹ The way of the eagle in the heavens, || The way of a serpent on a rock, || The way of a ship in the heart of the sea, || And the way of a man in youth. ²⁰ So—the way of an adulterous woman, || She has eaten and has wiped her mouth, || And has said, "I have not done iniquity." ²¹ For three things has earth been troubled, || And for four—it is not able to bear: ²² For a servant when he reigns, || And a fool when he is satisfied with bread, ²³ For a hated one when she rules, || And a maidservant when she succeeds her mistress. ²⁴ Four [are] little ones of earth, || And they are made wiser than the wise: ²⁵ The ants [are] a people not strong, || And they prepare their food in summer, ²⁶ hyraxes [are] a people not strong, || And they place their house in a rock, ²⁷ There is no king to the locust, || And it goes out each one shouting, ²⁸ A spider with two hands takes hold, || And is in the palaces of a king. ²⁹ There are three going well, || Indeed, four are good in going: ³⁰ An old lion—mighty among beasts, || That does not turn back from the face of any, ³¹ A girt one of the loins, || Also a male goat, || And a king—troops with him. ³² If you have been foolish in lifting yourself up, || And if you have devised evil—hand to mouth! ³³ For the churning of milk brings out butter, || And the wringing of the nose brings out blood, || And the forcing of anger brings out strife!

CHAPTER 31

¹ Words of Lemuel, a king, a declaration that his mother taught him: ² "What, my son? and what, son of my womb? And what, son of my vows? ³ Do not give your strength to women, || And your ways to wiping away of kings. ⁴ [It is] not for kings, O Lemuel, || Not for kings, to drink wine, || And for princes—a desire of strong drink. ⁵ Lest he drink, and forget the decree, || And change the judgment of any of the sons of affliction. ⁶ Give strong drink to the perishing, || And wine to the bitter in soul, ⁷ He drinks, and forgets his poverty, || And he does not remember his misery again. ⁸ Open your mouth for the mute, || For the right of all sons of change. ⁹ Open your mouth, judge righteously, || Both the cause of the poor and needy!" ¹⁰ [Aleph-Bet] A woman of worth who finds? Indeed, her price [is] far above rubies. ¹¹ The heart of her husband has trusted in her, || And he does not lack spoil. ¹² She has done him good, and not evil, || All [the] days of her life. ¹³ She has sought wool and flax, || And with delight she works [with] her hands. ¹⁴ She has been as ships of the merchant, || She brings in her bread from afar. ¹⁵ Indeed, she rises while yet night, || And gives food to her household, || And a portion to her girls. ¹⁶ She has considered a field, and takes it, || She has planted a vineyard from the fruit of her hands. ¹⁷ She has girded her loins with might, || And strengthens her arms. ¹⁸ She has perceived when her merchandise [is] good, || Her lamp is not extinguished in the night. ¹⁹ She has sent forth her hands on a spindle, || And her hands have held a distaff. ²⁰ She has spread forth her hand to the poor, || Indeed, she sent forth her hands to the needy. ²¹ She is not afraid of her household from snow, || For all her household are clothed [with] scarlet. ²² She has made ornamental coverings for herself, || Silk and purple [are] her clothing. ²³ Her husband is known in the gates, || In his sitting with [the] elderly of [the] land. ²⁴ She has made linen garments, and sells, || And she has given a girdle to the merchant. ²⁵ Strength and honor [are] her clothing, || And she rejoices at a latter day. ²⁶ She has opened her mouth in

wisdom, || And the law of kindness [is] on her tongue. ²⁷ She [is] watching the ways of her household, || And she does not eat bread of sloth. ²⁸ Her sons have risen up, and pronounce her blessed, || Her husband, and he praises her, ²⁹ "The daughters who have done worthily [are] many, || You have gone up above them all." ³⁰ Favor [is] deceitful, and beauty [is] vain, || A woman fearing Yhwh, she may boast herself. ³¹ Give to her of the fruit of her hands, || And her works praise her in the gates!

ECCLESIASTES

CHAPTER 1

¹ Words of a preacher, son of David, king in Jerusalem: ² Vanity of vanities, said the Preacher, vanity of vanities: the whole [is] vanity. ³ What advantage [is] to man by all his labor that he labors at under the sun? ⁴ A generation is going, and a generation is coming, and the earth is standing for all time. ⁵ Also, the sun has risen, and the sun has gone in, and to its place panting it is rising there. ⁶ Going to the south, and turning around to the north, turning around, turning around, the wind is going, and by its circuits the wind has returned. ⁷ All the streams are going to the sea, and the sea is not full; to a place to where the streams are going, there they are turning back to go. ⁸ All these things are wearying; a man is not able to speak, the eye is not satisfied by seeing, nor is the ear filled from hearing. ⁹ What [is] that which has been? it [is] that which is, and what [is] that which has been done? it [is] that which is done, and there is not an entirely new thing under the sun. ¹⁰ There is a thing of which [one] says: "See this, it [is] new!" Already it has been in the ages that were before us! ¹¹ There is not a remembrance of former [generations]; and also of the latter that are, there is no remembrance of them with those that are at the last. ¹² I, a preacher, have been king over Israel in Jerusalem. ¹³ And I have given my heart to seek and to search out by wisdom concerning all that has been done under the heavens. It [is] a sad travail God has given to the sons of man to be humbled by it. ¹⁴ I have seen all the works that have been done under the sun, and behold, the whole [is] vanity and distress of spirit! ¹⁵ A crooked thing [one] is not able to make straight, and a lacking thing is not able to be numbered. ¹⁶ I spoke with my heart, saying, "I, behold, have magnified and added wisdom above everyone who has been before me at Jerusalem, and my heart has seen wisdom and knowledge abundantly. ¹⁷ And I give my heart to know wisdom, and to know madness and folly: I have known that even this [is] distress of spirit; ¹⁸ for in abundance of wisdom [is] abundance of sadness, and he who adds knowledge adds pain."

CHAPTER 2

¹ I said in my heart, "Pray, come, I try you with mirth, and look on gladness"; and behold, even it [is] vanity. ² Of laughter I said, "Foolish!" And of mirth, "What [is] this it is doing?" ³ I have sought in my heart to draw out with wine my appetite (and my heart leading in wisdom), and to take hold on folly until I see where this [is]—the good to the sons of man of that which they do under the heavens, the number of the days of their lives. ⁴ I made great my works, I built for myself houses, I planted for myself vineyards. ⁵ I made for myself gardens and paradises, and I planted in them trees of every fruit. ⁶ I made for myself pools of water, to water from them a forest shooting forth trees. ⁷ I acquired menservants, and maidservants, and sons of the house were to me; also, I had much substance—herd and flock—above all who had been before me in Jerusalem. ⁸ I also gathered for myself silver and gold, and the peculiar treasure of kings and of the provinces. I prepared for myself men-singers and women-singers, and the luxuries of the sons of man—a wife and wives. ⁹ And I became great, and increased above everyone who had been before me in Jerusalem; also, my wisdom stood with me. ¹⁰ And all that my eyes asked I did not keep back from them; I did not withhold my heart from any joy, for my heart rejoiced because of all my labor, and this has been my portion, from all my labor, ¹¹ and

I have looked on all my works that my hands have done, and on the labor that I have labored to do, and behold, the whole [is] vanity and distress of spirit, and there is no advantage under the sun! 12 And I turned to see wisdom, and madness, and folly, but what [is] the man who comes after the king? that which [is] already—they have done it! 13 And I saw that there is an advantage to wisdom above folly, like the advantage of the light above the darkness. 14 The wise—his eyes [are] in his head, and the fool is walking in darkness, and I also knew that one event happens with them all; 15 and I said in my heart, "As it happens with the fool, it happens also with me, and why am I then more wise?" And I spoke in my heart, that also this [is] vanity: 16 That there is no remembrance to the wise—with the fool—for all time, for that which [is] already, [in] the days that are coming is all forgotten, and how dies the wise? with the fool! 17 And I have hated life, for sad to me [is] the work that has been done under the sun, for the whole [is] vanity and distress of spirit. 18 And I have hated all my labor that I labor at under the sun, because I leave it to a man who is after me. 19 And who knows whether he is wise or foolish? yet he rules over all my labor that I have labored at, and that I have done wisely under the sun! This [is] also vanity. 20 And I turned around to cause my heart to despair concerning all the labor that I labored at under the sun. 21 For there is a man whose labor [is] in wisdom, and in knowledge, and in equity, and to a man who has not labored therein he gives it—his portion! Even this [is] vanity and a great evil. 22 For what has been to a man by all his labor, and by the thought of his heart that he labored at under the sun? 23 For all his days are sorrows, and his travail sadness; even at night his heart has not lain down; this [is] also vanity. 24 There is nothing good in a man who eats, and has drunk, and has shown his soul good in his labor. This also I have seen that it [is] from the hand of God. 25 For who eats and who hurries out more than I? 26 For to a man who [is] good before Him, He has given wisdom, and knowledge, and joy; and to a sinner He has given travail, to gather and to heap up, to give to the good before God. Even this [is] vanity and distress of spirit.

CHAPTER 3

1 To everything—a season, and a time to every delight under the heavens: 2 A time to bring forth, || And a time to die. A time to plant, || And a time to eradicate the planted. 3 A time to slay, || And a time to heal, || And a time to break down, || And a time to build up. 4 A time to weep, || And a time to laugh. A time to mourn, || And a time to skip. 5 A time to cast away stones, || And a time to heap up stones. A time to embrace, || And a time to be far from embracing. 6 A time to seek, || And a time to destroy. A time to keep, || And a time to cast away. 7 A time to tear, || And a time to sew. A time to be silent, || And a time to speak. 8 A time to love, || And a time to hate. A time of war, || And a time of peace. 9 What advantage does the doer have in that which he is laboring at? 10 I have seen the travail that God has given to the sons of man to be humbled by it. 11 The whole He has made beautiful in its season; also, that knowledge He has put in their heart without which man does not find out the work that God has done from the beginning even to the end. 12 I have known that there is no good for them except to rejoice and to do good during their life, 13 indeed, even every man who eats and has drunk and seen good by all his labor, it [is] a gift of God. 14 I have known that all that God does is for all time, to it nothing is to be added, and from it nothing is to be withdrawn; and God has worked that they fear before Him. 15 What is that which has been? already it is, and that which [is] to be has already been, and God requires that which is pursued. 16 And again, I have seen under the sun the place of judgment—there [is] the wicked; and the place of righteousness—there [is] the wicked. 17 I said in my heart, "The righteous and the wicked God judges, for a time [is] to every matter and for every work there." 18 I said in my heart concerning the matter of the sons of man that God might cleanse them, so as to see that they themselves [are] beasts. 19 For an event [is to] the sons of man, and an event [is to] the beasts, even one event [is] to them; as the death of this, so [is] the death of that; and one spirit [is] to all, and the advantage of man above the beast is nothing, for the whole [is] vanity. 20 The whole are going to one place, the whole have been from the dust, and the whole are turning back to the dust. 21 Who knows the spirit of the sons of man that is going up on high, and the spirit of the beast that is going down below to

the earth? 22 And I have seen that there is nothing better than that man rejoice in his works, for it [is] his portion; for who brings him to look on that which is after him?

CHAPTER 4

1 And I have turned, and I see all the oppressions that are done under the sun, and behold, the tear of the oppressed, and they have no comforter; and at the hand of their oppressors [is] power, and they have no comforter. 2 And I am praising the dead who have already died above the living who are yet alive. 3 And better than both of them [is] he who has not yet been, in that he has not seen the evil work that has been done under the sun. 4 And I have seen all the labor, and all the benefit of the work, because for it a man is the envy of his neighbor. Even this [is] vanity and distress of spirit. 5 The fool is clasping his hands, and eating his own flesh: 6 "Better [is] a handful [with] quietness, than two handfuls [with] labor and distress of spirit." 7 And I have turned, and I see a vain thing under the sun: 8 There is one, and there is not a second; even son or brother he has not, and there is no end to all his labor! His eye also is not satisfied with riches, and [he does not say], "For whom am I laboring and bereaving my soul of good?" This also is vanity, it is a sad travail. 9 The two [are] better than the one, in that they have a good reward by their labor. 10 For if they fall, the one raises up his companion, but woe to the one who falls and there is not a second to raise him up! 11 Also, if two lie down, then they have heat, but how has one heat? 12 And if the one strengthens himself, the two stand against him; and the threefold cord is not quickly broken. 13 Better is a poor and wise youth than an old and foolish king, who has not known to be warned anymore. 14 For from a house of prisoners he has come out to reign, for even in his own kingdom he has been poor. 15 I have seen all the living, who are walking under the sun, with the second youth who stands in his place; 16 there is no end to all the people, to all who were before them; also, the latter do not rejoice in him. Surely this also is vanity and distress of spirit.

CHAPTER 5

1 Keep your feet when you go to a house of God, and draw near to hear rather than to give of fools the sacrifice, for they do not know they do evil. 2 Do not cause your mouth to hurry, and do not let your heart hurry to bring out a word before God, for God is in the heavens, and you on the earth, therefore let your words be few. 3 For the dream has come by abundance of business, and the voice of a fool by abundance of words. 4 When you vow a vow to God, do not delay to complete it, for there is no pleasure in fools; that which you vow—complete. 5 Better that you do not vow, than that you vow and do not complete. 6 Do not permit your mouth to cause your flesh to sin, nor say before the messenger that it [is] ignorance. Why is God angry because of your voice and has destroyed the work of your hands? 7 For in the abundance of dreams both vanities and words abound; but fear God. 8 If oppression of the poor, and violent taking away of judgment and righteousness you see in a province, do not marvel at the matter, for a higher than the high is observing, and high ones [are] over them. 9 And the abundance of a land is for all. A king for a field is served. 10 Whoever is loving silver is not satisfied [with] silver, nor he who is in love with stores [with] increase. Even this [is] vanity. 11 In the multiplying of good have its consumers been multiplied, and what benefit [is] to its possessor except the sight of his eyes? 12 Sweet [is] the sleep of the laborer whether he eat little or much; and the sufficiency of the wealthy is not permitting him to sleep. 13 There is a painful evil I have seen under the sun: wealth kept for its possessor, for his evil. 14 And that wealth has been lost in an evil business, and he has begotten a son and there is nothing in his hand! 15 As he came out from the belly of his mother, naked he turns back to go as he came, and he does not take away anything of his labor, that goes in his hand. 16 And this also [is] a painful evil, just as he came, so he goes, and what advantage [is] to him who labors for wind? 17 He also consumes all his days in darkness, and sadness, and wrath, and sickness abound. 18 Behold, that which I have seen: [It is] good, because beautiful, to eat, and to drink, and to see good in all one's labor that he labors at under the sun, the number of the days of his life that God has given

to him, for it [is] his portion. ¹⁹ Every man also to whom God has given wealth and riches, and has given him power to eat of it, and to accept his portion, and to rejoice in his labor, this is a gift of God. ²⁰ For he does not much remember the days of his life, for God is answering through the joy of his heart.

CHAPTER 6

¹ There is an evil that I have seen under the sun, and it [is] great on man: ² A man to whom God gives wealth, and riches, and honor, and there is no lack to his soul of all that he desires, and God does not give him power to eat of it, but stranger eats it; this [is] vanity, and it [is] an evil disease. ³ If a man begets one hundred, and lives many years, and is great, because they are the days of his years, and his soul is not satisfied from the goodness, and also he has not had a grave, I have said, "Better than he [is] the untimely birth." ⁴ For in vanity he came in, and in darkness he goes, and in darkness his name is covered, ⁵ even the sun he has not seen nor known, more rest has this than that. ⁶ And though he had lived one thousand years twice over, yet he has not seen good; does not everyone go to the same place? ⁷ All the labor of man [is] for his mouth, || And yet the soul is not filled. ⁸ For what advantage [is] to the wise above the fool? What to the poor who knows to walk before the living? ⁹ Better [is] the sight of the eyes than the going of the soul. This [is] also vanity and distress of spirit. ¹⁰ What [is] that which has been? already is its name called, and it is known that it [is] man, || And he is not able to contend with him who is stronger than he. ¹¹ For there are many things multiplying vanity; What advantage [is] to man? ¹² For who knows what [is] good for a man in life, the number of the days of the life of his vanity, and he makes them as a shadow? for who declares to man what is after him under the sun?

CHAPTER 7

¹ Better [is] a name than good perfume, || And the day of death than the day of birth. ² Better to go to a house of mourning, || Than to go to a house of banqueting, || For that is the end of all men, || And the living lays [it] to his heart. ³ Better [is] sorrow than laughter, || For by the sadness of the face the heart becomes better. ⁴ The heart of the wise [is] in a house of mourning, || And the heart of fools in a house of mirth. ⁵ Better to hear a rebuke of a wise man, || Than [for] a man to hear a song of fools, ⁶ For as the noise of thorns under the pot, || So [is] the laughter of a fool, even this [is] vanity. ⁷ Surely oppression makes the wise mad, || And a gift destroys the heart. ⁸ Better [is] the latter end of a thing than its beginning, || Better [is] the patient of spirit, than the haughty of spirit. ⁹ Do not be hasty in your spirit to be angry, || For anger in the bosom of fools rests. ¹⁰ Do not say, "What was it, || That the former days were better than these?" For you have not asked wisely of this. ¹¹ Wisdom [is] good with an inheritance, || And an advantage [it is] to those beholding the sun. ¹² For wisdom [is] a defense, money [is] a defense, || And the advantage of the knowledge of wisdom [is], || She revives her possessors. ¹³ See the work of God, || For who is able to make straight that which He made crooked? ¹⁴ In a day of prosperity be in gladness, || And in a day of calamity consider: God has also made this alongside of that, || To the intent that man does not find anything after him. ¹⁵ The whole I have considered in the days of my vanity. There is a righteous one perishing in his righteousness, and there is a wrongdoer prolonging [himself] in his wrong. ¹⁶ Do not be over-righteous, nor show yourself too wise, why are you desolate? ¹⁷ Do not do much wrong, neither be a fool, why do you die within your time? ¹⁸ [It is] good that you lay hold on this, and also, do not withdraw your hand from that, for whoever is fearing God goes out with them all. ¹⁹ The wisdom gives strength to a wise man, more than wealth the rulers who have been in a city. ²⁰ Because there is not a righteous man on earth that does good and does not sin. ²¹ Also to all the words that they speak do not give your heart, that you do not hear your servant reviling you. ²² For many times also has your heart known that you yourself have also reviled others. ²³ All this I have tried by wisdom; I have said, "I am wise," and it [is] far from me. ²⁴ Far off [is] that which has been, and deep, deep, who finds it? ²⁵ I have turned around, also my heart, to know and to search, and to seek out wisdom, and reason, and to know the wrong of folly, and the

madness of foolishness. ²⁶ And I am finding more bitter than death, the woman whose heart [is] nets and snares, her hands [are] bands; the good before God escapes from her, but the sinner is captured by her. ²⁷ See, this I have found, said the Preacher, one to one, to find out the reason ²⁸ (that still my soul had sought, and I had not found), || One man, a teacher, I have found, and a woman among all these I have not found. ²⁹ See, this alone I have found, that God made man upright, and they have sought out many inventions.

CHAPTER 8

¹ Who [is] as the wise? and who knows the interpretation of a thing? The wisdom of man causes his face to shine, and the hardness of his face is changed. ² I [counsel]: keep the command of a king, even for the sake of an oath [to] God. ³ Do not be troubled at his presence, you may go, do not stand in an evil thing, for all that he pleases he does. ⁴ Where the word of a king [is] power [is], and who says to him, "What do you do?" ⁵ Whoever is keeping a command knows no evil thing, and time and judgment the heart of the wise knows. ⁶ For to every delight there is a time and a judgment, for the misfortune of man is great on him. ⁷ For he does not know that which will be, for when it will be who declares to him? ⁸ There is no man ruling over the spirit to restrain the spirit, and there is no authority over the day of death, and there is no discharge in battle, and wickedness does not deliver its possessors. ⁹ All this I have seen so as to give my heart to every work that has been done under the sun; a time that man has ruled over man to his own evil. ¹⁰ And so I have seen the wicked buried, and they went in, even from the Holy Place they go, and they are forgotten in the city whether they had so done. This [is] also vanity. ¹¹ Because sentence has not been done [on] an evil work speedily, therefore the heart of the sons of man is full within them to do evil. ¹² Though a sinner is doing evil one hundred [times], and prolonging [himself] for it, surely also I know that there is good to those fearing God, who fear before Him. ¹³ And good is not to the wicked, and he does not prolong days as a shadow, because he is not fearing before God. ¹⁴ There is a vanity that has been done on the earth, that there are righteous ones to whom it is coming according to the work of the wicked, and there are wicked ones to whom it is coming according to the work of the righteous. I have said that this [is] also vanity. ¹⁵ And I have praised mirth because there is no good to man under the sun except to eat and to drink, and to rejoice, and it remains with him of his labor the days of his life that God has given to him under the sun. ¹⁶ When I gave my heart to know wisdom and to see the business that has been done on the earth (for there is also a spectator in whose eyes sleep is not by day and by night), ¹⁷ then I considered all the work of God, that man is not able to find out the work that has been done under the sun, because though man labor to seek, yet he does not find; and even though the wise man speak of knowing he is not able to find.

CHAPTER 9

¹ But all this I have laid to my heart, so as to clear up the whole of this, that the righteous and the wise, and their works, [are] in the hand of God, neither love nor hatred does man know, the whole [is] before them. ² The whole [is] as to the whole; one event is to the righteous and to the wicked, to the good, and to the clean, and to the unclean, and to him who is sacrificing, and to him who is not sacrificing; as [is] the good, so [is] the sinner, he who is swearing as he who is fearing an oath. ³ This [is] an evil among all that has been done under the sun, that one event [is] to all, and also the heart of the sons of man is full of evil, and madness [is] in their heart during their life, and after it—to the dead. ⁴ But [to] him who is joined to all the living there is confidence, for to a living dog it [is] better than to the dead lion. ⁵ For the living know that they die, and the dead do not know anything, and there is no more reward to them, for their remembrance has been forgotten. ⁶ Their love also, their hatred also, their envy also, has already perished, and they have no more portion for all time in all that has been done under the sun. ⁷ Go, eat your bread with joy, and drink your wine with a glad heart, for already has God been pleased with your works. ⁸ At all times let your garments be white, and do not let oil be lacking on your head. ⁹ See life with the wife

whom you have loved, all the days of the life of your vanity, that He has given to you under the sun, all the days of your vanity, for it [is] your portion in life, even of your labor that you are laboring at under the sun. ¹⁰ All that your hand finds to do, with your power do, for there is no work, and plan, and knowledge, and wisdom in Sheol to where you are going. ¹¹ I have turned so as to see under the sun, that not to the swift [is] the race, nor to the mighty the battle, nor even to the wise bread, nor even to the intelligent wealth, nor even to the skillful grace, for time and chance happen with them all. ¹² For even man does not know his time; as fish that are taken hold of by an evil net, and as birds that are taken hold of by a snare, the sons of man are snared like these at an evil time when it falls on them suddenly. ¹³ This also I have seen: wisdom under the sun, and it is great to me. ¹⁴ A little city, and few men in it, and a great king has come to it, and has surrounded it, and has built against it great bulwarks; ¹⁵ and there has been found in it a poor wise man, and he has delivered the city by his wisdom, and men have not remembered that poor man! ¹⁶ And I said, "Better [is] wisdom than might, and the wisdom of the poor is despised, and his words are not heard." ¹⁷ The words of the wise are heard in quiet, || More than the cry of a ruler over fools. ¹⁸ Better [is] wisdom than weapons of conflict, || And one sinner destroys much good!

CHAPTER 10

¹ Dead flies cause a perfumer's perfume || To send forth a stink; The precious by reason of wisdom—By reason of honor—a little folly! ² The heart of the wise [is] at his right hand, || And the heart of a fool at his left. ³ And also, when he that is a fool || Is walking in the way, his heart is lacking, || And he has said to everyone, "He [is] a fool." ⁴ If the spirit of the ruler goes up against you, do not leave your place, || For yielding quiets great sinners. ⁵ There is an evil I have seen under the sun, || As ignorance that goes out from the ruler, ⁶ He has set the fool in many high places, || And the rich sits in a low place. ⁷ I have seen servants on horses, || And princes walking as servants on the earth. ⁸ Whoever is digging a pit falls into it, || And whoever is breaking a hedge, a serpent bites him. ⁹ Whoever is removing stones is grieved by them, || Whoever is cleaving trees endangered by them. ¹⁰ If the iron has been blunt, || And he has not sharpened the face, || Then he increases strength, || And wisdom [is] advantageous to make right. ¹¹ If the serpent bites without enchantment, || Then there is no advantage to a master of the tongue. ¹² Words of the mouth of the wise [are] gracious, || And the lips of a fool swallow him up. ¹³ The beginning of the words of his mouth [is] folly, || And the latter end of his mouth || [Is] mischievous madness. ¹⁴ And the fool multiplies words: "Man does not know that which is—And that which is after him, who declares to him?" ¹⁵ The labor of the foolish wearies him, || In that he has not known to go to the city. ¹⁶ Woe to you, O land, when your king [is] a youth, || And your princes eat in the morning. ¹⁷ Blessed are you, O land, || When your king [is] a son of nobles, || And your princes eat in due season, || For might, and not for drunkenness. ¹⁸ By slothfulness is the wall brought low, || And by idleness of the hands the house drops. ¹⁹ For mirth they are making a feast, || And wine makes life joyful, || And the silver answers with all. ²⁰ Even in your mind do not revile a king, || And in the inner parts of your bed-chamber do not revile the rich: For a bird of the heavens causes the voice to go, || And a possessor of wings declares the word.

CHAPTER 11

¹ Send forth your bread on the face of the waters, || For in the multitude of the days you find it. ² Give a portion to seven, and even to eight, || For you do not know what evil is on the earth. ³ If the thick clouds are full of rain, || On the earth they empty [themselves]; And if a tree falls in the south or to the north, || The place where the tree falls, there it is. ⁴ Whoever is observing the wind does not sow, || And whoever is looking on the thick clouds does not reap. ⁵ As you do not know what [is] the way of the spirit, || How—bones in the womb of the full one, || So you do not know the work of God who makes the whole. ⁶ In the morning sow your seed, || And at evening do not withdraw your hand, || For you do not know which is right, this or that, || Or whether both of them alike [are] good. ⁷

Sweet also [is] the light, || And good for the eyes to see the sun. ⁸ But if man lives many years, || In all of them let him rejoice, || And remember the days of darkness, || For they are many! All that is coming [is] vanity. ⁹ Rejoice, O young man, in your childhood, || And let your heart gladden you in days of your youth, || And walk in the ways of your heart, || And in the sight of your eyes, || And know that for all these, God brings you into judgment. ¹⁰ And turn aside anger from your heart, || And cause evil to pass from your flesh, || For the childhood and the age [are] vanity!

CHAPTER 12

¹ Remember also your Creator in days of your youth, || While that the evil days do not come, || Nor the years have arrived, that you say, || "I have no pleasure in them." ² While that the sun is not darkened, and the light, || And the moon, and the stars, || And the thick clouds returned after the rain. ³ In the day that keepers of the house tremble, || And men of strength have bowed themselves, || And grinders have ceased, because they have become few. And those looking out at the windows have become dim, ⁴ And doors have been shut in the street. When the noise of the grinding is low, || And [one] rises at the voice of the bird, || And all daughters of song are bowed down. ⁵ Also of that which is high they are afraid, || And of the low places in the way, || And the almond-tree is despised, || And the grasshopper has become a burden, || And want is increased, || For man is going to his perpetual home, || And the mourners have gone around through the street. ⁶ While that the silver cord is not removed, || And the golden bowl broken, || And the pitcher broken by the fountain, || And the wheel broken at the well. ⁷ And the dust returns to the earth as it was, || And the spirit returns to God who gave it. ⁸ Vanity of vanities, said the preacher, the whole [is] vanity. ⁹ And further, because the preacher was wise, he still taught the people knowledge, and gave ear, and sought out—he made right many allegories. ¹⁰ The preacher sought to find out pleasing words, and [that] written [by] the upright—words of truth. ¹¹ Words of the wise [are] as the goads, and as nails planted [by] the masters of collections, they have been given by one Shepherd. ¹² And further, from these, my son, be warned; the making of many scrolls has no end, and much study [is] a weariness of the flesh. ¹³ The end of the whole matter let us hear: "Fear God, and keep His commands, for this [is] the whole of man. ¹⁴ For every work God brings into judgment, with every hidden thing, whether good or bad."

SONG OF SONGS

CHAPTER 1

¹ The Song of Songs, that [is] of Solomon. ² Let him kiss me with kisses of his mouth, || For better [are] your loves than wine. ³ For fragrance [are] your good perfumes. Perfume emptied out—your name, || Therefore have virgins loved you! ⁴ Draw me: we run after you, || The king has brought me into his inner chambers, || We delight and rejoice in you, || We mention your loves more than wine, || Uprightly they have loved you! ⁵ I [am] dark and lovely, daughters of Jerusalem, as tents of Kedar, as curtains of Solomon. ⁶ Do not fear me, because I [am] very dark, || Because the sun has scorched me, || The sons of my mother were angry with me, || They made me keeper of the vineyards, || My vineyard—my own—I have not kept. ⁷ Declare to me, you whom my soul has loved, || Where you delight, || Where you lie down at noon, || For why am I as one veiled, || By the ranks of your companions? ⁸ If you do not know, || O beautiful among women, || Go forth by the traces of the flock, || And feed your kids by the shepherds' dwellings! ⁹ To my joyous one in chariots of Pharaoh, I have compared you, my friend, ¹⁰ Your cheeks have been lovely with garlands, your neck with chains. ¹¹ We make garlands of gold for you, with studs of silver! ¹² While the king [is] in his circle, || My spikenard has given its fragrance. ¹³ A bundle of myrrh [is] my beloved to me, || Between my breasts it lodges. ¹⁴ A cluster of cypress [is] my beloved to me, || In the vineyards of En-Gedi! ¹⁵ Behold, you [are] beautiful, my

friend, || Behold, you [are] beautiful, your eyes [are] doves! [16] Behold, you [are] beautiful, my love, indeed, pleasant, || Indeed, our bed [is] green, [17] The beams of our houses [are] cedars, || Our rafters [are] firs, I [am] a rose of Sharon, a lily of the valleys!

CHAPTER 2

[1] As a lily among the thorns, [2] So [is] my friend among the daughters! [3] As a citron among trees of the forest, || So [is] my beloved among the sons, || In his shade I delighted, and sat down, || And his fruit [is] sweet to my palate. [4] He has brought me to a house of wine, || And his banner over me [is] love, [5] Sustain me with grape-cakes, || Support me with citrons, for I [am] sick with love. [6] His left hand [is] under my head, || And his right embraces me. [7] I have adjured you, daughters of Jerusalem, || By the roes or by the does of the field, || Do not stir up nor wake the love until she pleases! [8] The voice of my beloved! Behold, this—he is coming, || Leaping on the mountains, skipping on the hills. [9] My beloved [is] like to a roe, || Or to a young one of the harts. Behold, this—he is standing behind our wall, || Looking from the windows, || Blooming from the lattice. [10] My beloved has answered and said to me, || "Rise up, my friend, my beautiful one, and come away, [11] For behold, the winter has passed by, || The rain has passed away—it has gone. [12] The flowers have appeared in the earth, || The time of the singing has come, || And the voice of the turtle was heard in our land, [13] The fig tree has ripened her green figs, || And the sweet-smelling vines have given forth fragrance, || Rise, come, my friend, my beautiful one, indeed, come away. [14] My dove, in clefts of the rock, || In a secret place of the ascent, || Cause me to see your appearance, || Cause me to hear your voice, || For your voice [is] sweet, and your appearance lovely." [15] Seize for us foxes, || Little foxes—destroyers of vineyards, || Even our sweet-smelling vineyards. [16] My beloved [is] mine, and I [am] his, || Who is delighting among the lilies, [17] Until the day breaks forth, || And the shadows have fled away, || Turn, be like, my beloved, || To a roe, or to a young one of the harts, || On the mountains of separation!

CHAPTER 3

[1] On my bed by night, I sought him whom my soul has loved; I sought him, and I did not find him! [2] Now let me rise, and go around the city, || In the streets and in the broad places, || I seek him whom my soul has loved! I sought him, and I did not find him. [3] The watchmen have found me || (Who are going around the city), || "Have you seen him whom my soul has loved?" [4] But I passed on a little from them, || Until I found him whom my soul has loved! I seized him, and did not let him go, || Until I brought him to the house of my mother— And the chamber of her that conceived me. [5] I have adjured you, daughters of Jerusalem, || By the roes or by the does of the field, || Do not stir up nor wake the love until she pleases! [6] Who [is] this coming up from the wilderness, || Like palm-trees of smoke, || Perfumed [with] myrrh and frankincense, || From every powder of the merchant? [7] Behold, his couch, that [is] of Solomon, || Sixty mighty ones [are] around it, || Of the mighty of Israel, [8] All of them holding sword, taught of battle, || Each his sword by his thigh, for fear at night. [9] A palanquin King Solomon made for himself, || Of the wood of Lebanon, [10] Its pillars he made of silver, || Its bottom of gold, its seat of purple, || Its midst lined [with] love, || By the daughters of Jerusalem. [11] Go forth, and look, you daughters of Zion, || On King Solomon, with the crown, || With which his mother crowned him, || In the day of his espousals, || And in the day of the joy of his heart!

CHAPTER 4

[1] Behold, you [are] beautiful, my friend, behold, you [are] beautiful, || Your eyes [are] doves behind your veil, || Your hair as a row of the goats that have shone from Mount Gilead, [2] Your teeth as a row of the shorn ones that have come up from the washing, || For all of them are forming twins, || And a bereaved one is not among them. [3] As a thread of scarlet [are]

your lips, || And your speech [is] lovely, || As the work of the pomegranate [is] your temple behind your veil, [4] As the Tower of David [is] your neck, built for an armory, || The chief of the shields are hung on it, || All shields of the mighty. [5] Your two breasts [are] as two fawns, || Twins of a roe, that are feeding among lilies. [6] Until the day breaks forth, || And the shadows have fled away, || I go for myself to the mountain of myrrh, || And to the hill of frankincense. [7] You [are] all beautiful, my friend, || And there is not a blemish in you. Come from Lebanon, O spouse, [8] Come from Lebanon, come in. Look from the top of Amana, || From the top of Shenir and Hermon, || From the habitations of lions, || From the mountains of leopards. [9] You have emboldened me, my sister-spouse, || Emboldened me with one of your eyes, || With one chain of your neck. [10] How beautiful have been your loves, my sister-spouse, || How much better have been your loves than wine, || And the fragrance of your perfumes than all spices. [11] Your lips drop honey, O spouse, || Honey and milk [are] under your tongue, || And the fragrance of your garments || [Is] as the fragrance of Lebanon. [12] A garden shut up [is] my sister-spouse, || A spring shut up—a fountain sealed. [13] Your shoots a paradise of pomegranates, || With precious fruits, [14] Cypresses with nard—nard and saffron, || Cane and cinnamon, || With all trees of frankincense, || Myrrh and aloes, with all chief spices. [15] A fount of gardens, a well of living waters, || And flowings from Lebanon! [16] Awake, O north wind, and come, O south, || Cause my garden to breathe forth, its spices let flow, || Let my beloved come to his garden, || And eat its pleasant fruits!

CHAPTER 5

[1] I have come to my garden, my sister-spouse, || I have plucked my myrrh with my spice, || I have eaten my comb with my honey, || I have drunk my wine with my milk. Eat, O friends, drink, || Indeed, drink abundantly, O beloved ones! [2] I am sleeping, but my heart wakes. The sound of my beloved knocking! "Open to me, my sister, my friend, || My dove, my perfect one, || For my head is filled [with] dew, || My locks [with] drops of the night." [3] I have put off my coat, how do I put it on? I have washed my feet; how do I defile them? [4] My beloved sent his hand from the network, || And my bowels were moved for him. [5] I rose to open to my beloved, || And my hands dripped myrrh, || Indeed, my fingers were flowing [with] myrrh, || On the handles of the lock. [6] I opened to my beloved, || But my beloved withdrew—he passed on, || My soul went forth when he spoke, I sought him, and did not find him. I called him, and he did not answer me. [7] The watchmen who go around the city, || Found me, struck me, wounded me, || Keepers of the walls lifted up my veil from off me. [8] I have adjured you, daughters of Jerusalem, || If you find my beloved—What do you tell him? that I [am] sick with love! [9] What [is] your beloved above [any] beloved, || O beautiful among women? What [is] your beloved above [any] beloved, || That thus you have adjured us? [10] My beloved [is] clear and ruddy, || Conspicuous above a myriad! [11] His head [is] pure gold—fine gold, || His locks flowing, dark as a raven, [12] His eyes as doves by streams of water, || Washing in milk, sitting in fullness. [13] His cheeks [are] as a bed of the spice, towers of perfumes, || His lips—lilies, dripping [and] flowing [with] myrrh, [14] His hands rings of gold, set with beryl, || His heart bright ivory, covered with sapphires, [15] His limbs pillars of marble, || Founded on sockets of fine gold, || His appearance as Lebanon, choice as the cedars. [16] His mouth is sweetness— and all of him desirable, || This [is] my beloved, and this my friend, || O daughters of Jerusalem!

CHAPTER 6

[1] To where has your beloved gone, || O beautiful among women? To where has your beloved turned, || And we seek him with you? [2] My beloved went down to his garden, || To the beds of the spice, || To delight himself in the gardens, and to gather lilies. [3] I [am] my beloved's, and my beloved [is] mine, || Who is delighting himself among the lilies. [4] You [are] beautiful, my friend, as Tirzah, lovely as Jerusalem, || Awe-inspiring as bannered hosts. [5] Turn around your eyes from before me, || Because they have made me proud. Your hair [is] as a row of the goats, || That have shone from Gilead, [6]

Your teeth as a row of the lambs, || That have come up from the washing, || Because all of them are forming twins, || And a bereaved one is not among them. ⁷ As the work of the pomegranate [is] your temple behind your veil. ⁸ Sixty are queens, and eighty concubines, || And virgins without number. ⁹ One is my dove, my perfect one, || She [is] one of her mother, || She [is] the choice one of her that bore her, || Daughters saw, and pronounce her blessed, || Queens and concubines, and they praise her. ¹⁰ "Who [is] this that is looking forth as morning, || Beautiful as the moon—clear as the sun, || Awe-inspiring as bannered hosts?" ¹¹ To a garden of nuts I went down, || To look on the buds of the valley, || To see to where the vine had flourished, || The pomegranates had blossomed— ¹² I did not know my soul, || It made me—chariots of my people Nadib. ¹³ Return, return, O Shulammith! Return, return, and we look on you. What do you see in Shulammith?

CHAPTER 7

¹ As the chorus of "Mahanaim." How beautiful were your feet with sandals, O daughter of Nadib. The turnings of your sides [are] as ornaments, || Work of the hands of a craftsman. ² Your waist [is] a basin of roundness, || It does not lack the mixture, || Your body a heap of wheat, fenced with lilies, ³ Your two breasts as two young ones, twins of a roe, ⁴ Your neck as a tower of the ivory, || Your eyes pools in Heshbon, near the Gate of Bath-Rabbim, || Your face as a tower of Lebanon looking to Damascus, ⁵ Your head on you as Carmel, || And the locks of your head as purple, || The king is bound with the flowings! ⁶ How beautiful and how pleasant you have been, || O love, in delights. ⁷ This your stature has been like to a palm, || And your breasts to clusters. ⁸ I said, "Let me go up on the palm, || Let me lay hold on its boughs," || Indeed, let your breasts now be as clusters of the vine, || And the fragrance of your face as citrons, ⁹ And your palate as the good wine— Flowing to my beloved in uprightness, || Strengthening the lips of the aged! ¹⁰ I [am] my beloved's, and on me [is] his desire. ¹¹ Come, my beloved, we go forth to the field, ¹² We lodge in the villages, we go early to the vineyards, || We see if the vine has flourished, || The sweet smelling-flower has opened. The pomegranates have blossomed, || There I give to you my loves; ¹³ The mandrakes have given fragrance, || And at our openings all pleasant things, || New, indeed, old, my beloved, I laid up for you!

CHAPTER 8

¹ Who makes you as a brother to me, || Suckling the breasts of my mother? I find you outside, I kiss you, || Indeed, they do not despise me, ² I lead you; I bring you into my mother's house, || She teaches me, I cause you to drink of the spiced wine, || Of the juice of my pomegranate, ³ His left hand [is] under my head, || And his right embraces me. ⁴ I have adjured you, daughters of Jerusalem, || How you stir up, || And how you wake the love until she pleases! ⁵ Who [is] this coming from the wilderness, || Hastening herself for her beloved? Under the citron-tree I have awoken you, || There your mother pledged you, || There she [who] bore you gave a pledge. ⁶ Set me as a seal on your heart, as a seal on your arm, || For strong as death is love, || Sharp as Sheol is jealousy, || Its burnings [are] burnings of fire, a flame of Yah! ⁷ Many waters are not able to quench the love, || And floods do not wash it away. If one gives all the wealth of his house for love, || Treading down—they tread on it. ⁸ We have a little sister, and she does not have breasts, || What do we do for our sister, || In the day that it is told of her? ⁹ If she is a wall, we build by her a palace of silver. And if she is a door, || We fashion by her board-work of cedar. ¹⁰ I [am] a wall, and my breasts as towers, || Then I have been in his eyes as one finding peace. ¹¹ Solomon has a vineyard in Ba`al-Hamon, || He has given the vineyard to keepers, || Each brings for its fruit one thousand pieces of silver; ¹² My vineyard—my own—is before me, || The one thousand [is] for you, O Solomon. And the two hundred for those keeping its fruit. O dweller in gardens! ¹³ The companions are attending to your voice, || Cause me to hear. Flee, my beloved, and be like to a roe, ¹⁴ Or to a young one of the harts on mountains of spices!

ISAIAH

CHAPTER 1

¹ The visions of Isaiah's son of Amoz, that he has seen concerning Judah and Jerusalem, in the days of Uzziah, Jotham, Ahaz, Hezekiah, kings of Judah. ² Hear, O heavens, and give ear, O earth, || For Yhwh has spoken: "I have nourished and brought up sons, || And they transgressed against Me. ³ An ox has known its owner, || And a donkey the crib of its master, || Israel has not known, || My people have not understood." ⁴ Oh, sinning nation, a people heavy [with] iniquity, || A seed of evildoers, sons—corrupters! They have forsaken Yhwh, || They have despised the Holy One of Israel, || They have gone away backward. ⁵ Why are you struck anymore? You add apostasy! Every head has become diseased, and every heart [is] sick. ⁶ From the sole of the foot—to the head, || There is no soundness in it, || Wound, and bruise, and fresh striking! They have not been closed nor bound, || Nor have they softened with ointment. ⁷ Your land [is] a desolation, your cities burned with fire, || Your ground—strangers are consuming it before you, || And a desolation as overthrown by strangers! ⁸ And the daughter of Zion has been left, || As a shelter in a vineyard, || As a lodge in a place of cucumbers— as a city besieged. ⁹ Unless Yhwh of Hosts had left a remnant to us, || Shortly—we had been as Sodom, || We had been like to Gomorrah! ¹⁰ Hear the word of Yhwh, you rulers of Sodom, || Give ear to the Law of our God, you people of Gomorrah, ¹¹ "Why the abundance of your sacrifices to Me?" says Yhwh, "I have been satiated [with] burnt-offerings of rams, || And fat of fatlings; And blood of bullocks, and lambs, || And I have not desired male goats. ¹² When you come to appear before Me, || Who has required this of your hand, || To trample My courts? ¹³ Do not add to bring in a vain present, || Incense—it [is] an abomination to Me, || New moon, and Sabbath, calling of convocation! Do not render iniquity—and a restraint! ¹⁴ My soul has hated your new moons and your set seasons, || They have been on Me for a burden, || I have been weary of bearing. ¹⁵ And in your spreading forth your hands, I hide My eyes from you, || Also when you increase prayer, I do not hear, || Your hands have been full of blood. ¹⁶ Wash yourselves, make yourselves pure, || Turn aside the evil of your doings, from before My eyes, || Cease to do evil, learn to do good. ¹⁷ Seek judgment, make the oppressed blessed, || Judge the fatherless, strive [for] the widow. ¹⁸ Now come, and we settle this," says Yhwh, "If your sins are as scarlet, they will be white as snow, || If they are red as crimson, they will be as wool! ¹⁹ If you are willing, and have listened, || The good of the land you consume, ²⁰ And if you refuse, and have rebelled, || You are consumed [by] the sword," || For the mouth of Yhwh has spoken. ²¹ How has a faithful city become a harlot? I have filled it [with] judgment, || Righteousness lodges in it—now murderers. ²² Your silver has become dross, || Your drink defiled with water. ²³ Your princes [are] apostates, and companions of thieves, || Everyone loving a bribe, and pursuing rewards, || They do not judge the fatherless, || And the plea of the widow does not come to them. ²⁴ Therefore—a declaration of the Lord—Yhwh of Hosts, the Mighty One of Israel: "Oh, I relieve Myself from My adversaries, || And avenge Myself against My enemies, ²⁵ And I turn back My hand on you, || And I refine your dross as purity, || And I turn aside all your tin, ²⁶ And I give back your judges as at the first, || And your counselors as in the beginning, || After this you are called, A city of righteousness—a faithful city." ²⁷ Zion is redeemed in judgment, || And her captivity in righteousness. ²⁸ And the destruction of transgressors and sinners [is] together, || And those forsaking Yhwh are consumed. ²⁹ For [men] are ashamed because of the oaks || That you have desired, || And you are confounded because of the gardens || That you have chosen. ³⁰ For you are as an oak whose leaf is fading, || And as a garden that has no water. ³¹ And the strong has been for tow, || And his work for a spark, || And both of them have burned together, || And there is none quenching!

CHAPTER 2

¹ The thing that Isaiah son of Amoz has seen concerning Judah and Jerusalem: ² And it has come to pass, || In the latter end of the days, || The mountain of Yhwh's house is established, || Above the top of the mountains, || And it has been lifted up above the heights, || And all the nations have flowed to it. ³ And many peoples have gone and said, "Come, and we go up to the mountain of Yhwh, || To the house of the God of Jacob, || And He teaches us of His ways, || And we walk in His paths, || For a law goes forth from Zion, || And a word of Yhwh from Jerusalem. ⁴ And He has judged between the nations, || And has given a decision to many peoples, || And they have beat their swords to plowshares, || And their spears to pruning-hooks, || Nation does not lift up sword to nation, || Nor do they learn anymore—war. ⁵ O house of Jacob, come, || And we walk in the light of Yhwh." ⁶ For You have left Your people, the house of Jacob. For they have been filled from the east, || And [are] sorcerers like the Philistines, || And strike hands with the children of strangers. ⁷ And its land is full of silver and gold, || And there is no end to its treasures, || And its land is full of horses, || And there is no end to its chariots, ⁸ And its land is full of idols, || It bows itself to the work of its hands, || To that which its fingers have made, ⁹ And the low bows down, and the high is humbled, || And You do not accept them. ¹⁰ Enter into a rock, and be hidden in dust, || Because of the fear of Yhwh, || And because of the honor of His excellence. ¹¹ The haughty eyes of man have been humbled, || And the loftiness of men has been bowed down, || And Yhwh alone has been set on high in that day. ¹² For a day [is] to Yhwh of Hosts, || For every proud and high one, || And for every lifted up and low one, ¹³ And for all cedars of Lebanon, || The high and the exalted ones, || And for all oaks of Bashan, ¹⁴ And for all the high mountains, || And for all the exalted heights, ¹⁵ And for every high tower, || And for every fortified wall, ¹⁶ And for all ships of Tarshish, || And for all desirable pictures. ¹⁷ And the haughtiness of man has been bowed down, || And the loftiness of men humbled, || And Yhwh alone has been set on high in that day. ¹⁸ And the idols—they completely pass away. ¹⁹ And [men] have entered into caverns of rocks, || And into caves of dust, || Because of the fear of Yhwh, || And because of the honor of His excellence, || In His rising to terrify the earth. ²⁰ In that day man casts his idols of silver, || And his idols of gold, || That they have made for him to worship, || To moles, and to bats, ²¹ To enter into cavities of the rocks, || And into clefts of the high places, || Because of the fear of Yhwh, || And because of the honor of His excellence, || In His rising to terrify the earth. ²² Cease yourselves from man, || Whose breath [is] in his nostrils, || For—in what is he esteemed?

CHAPTER 3

¹ For behold, the Lord, Yhwh of Hosts, || Is turning aside from Jerusalem and from Judah || [Both] stay and staff: Every stay of bread and every stay of water; ² Mighty and man of war, judge and prophet, || And diviner and elderly, ³ Head of fifty, and accepted of faces, || And counselor, and wise craftsmen, || And discerning charmer. ⁴ And I have made youths their heads, || And sucklings rule over them. ⁵ And the people has exacted—man on man, || Even a man on his neighbor, || The youths enlarge themselves against the aged, || And the lightly esteemed against the honored. ⁶ When one lays hold on his brother, || Of the house of his father, [by] the garment, "Come, you are a ruler to us, || And this ruin [is] under your hand." ⁷ He lifts up, in that day, saying, "I am not a binder up, || And in my house is neither bread nor garment, || You do not make me a ruler of the people." ⁸ For Jerusalem has stumbled, and Judah has fallen, || For their tongue and their doings [are] against Yhwh, || To provoke the eyes of His glory. ⁹ The appearance of their faces witnessed against them, || And their sin, as Sodom, they declared, || They have not hidden! Woe to their soul, || For they have done evil to themselves. ¹⁰ Say to the righteous that [it is] good, || Because they eat the fruit of their doings. ¹¹ Woe to the wicked—evil, || Because the deed of his hand is done to him. ¹² My people—its exactors [are] sucklings, || And women have ruled over it. My people—your eulogists are causing to err, || And the way of your paths swallowed up. ¹³ Yhwh has stood up to plead, || And He is standing to judge the peoples. ¹⁴ Yhwh enters into judgment || With [the] elderly of His people, and its heads: "And you, you have consumed the vineyard, || Plunder of the poor [is] in your houses. ¹⁵ Why? Why do you [do this]? you bruise My people, || And you grind the faces of the poor." A

declaration of the Lord, Yhwh of Hosts, || And Yhwh says: ¹⁶ "Because those daughters of Zion have been haughty, || And they walk stretching out the neck, || And deceiving [with] the eyes, || They go walking and mincing, || And they make a jingling with their feet, ¹⁷ The Lord has also scabbed || The crown of the head of daughters of Zion, || And Yhwh exposes their simplicity. ¹⁸ In that day the Lord turns aside || The beauty of the jingling ornaments, || And of the embroidered works, || And of the crescents, ¹⁹ Of the pendants, and the bracelets, and the veils, ²⁰ Of the headdresses, and the ornaments of the legs, || And of the bands, || And of the perfume boxes, and the amulets, ²¹ Of the seals, and of the nose-rings, ²² Of the costly apparel, and of the mantles, || And of the coverings, and of the purses, ²³ Of the mirrors, and of the linen garments, || And of the hoods, and of the veils, ²⁴ And it has been, instead of spice is muck, || And instead of a girdle, a rope, || And instead of curled work, baldness, || And instead of a stomacher a girdle of sackcloth. ²⁵ For instead of glory, your men fall by sword, || And your might in battle. ²⁶ And her openings have lamented and mourned, || Indeed, she has been emptied, she sits on the earth!"

CHAPTER 4

¹ And seven women have taken hold on one man, || In that day, saying, "We eat our own bread, || And we put on our own raiment, || Only, let your name be called over us, || Remove our reproach." ² In that day is the Shoot of Yhwh for desire and for glory, || And the fruit of the earth || For excellence and for beauty to the escaped of Israel. ³ And it has been, he who is left in Zion, || And he who is remaining in Jerusalem, "Holy" is said of him, || Of everyone who is written for life in Jerusalem. ⁴ If the Lord has washed away || The filth of daughters of Zion, || And purges the blood of Jerusalem from her midst, || By the spirit of judgment, and by the spirit of burning. ⁵ Then Yhwh has created || Over every fixed place of Mount Zion, || And over her convocations, || A cloud by day, and smoke, || And the shining of a flaming fire by night, || That over all glory—a safeguard, ⁶ And a covering may be, || For a shadow from drought by day, || And for a refuge, and for a hiding place, || From inundation and from rain!

CHAPTER 5

¹ Now let me sing for my Beloved, || A song of my Beloved as to His vineyard: My beloved has a vineyard in a fruitful hill, ² And He fences it, and casts out its stones, || And plants it [with] a choice vine, || And builds a tower in its midst, || And has also hewn out a winepress in it, || And He waits for the yielding of grapes, || And it yields bad ones! ³ And now, O inhabitant of Jerusalem and man of Judah, || Please judge between Me and My vineyard. ⁴ What [is there] to do still to My vineyard, || That I have not done in it? For what reason have I waited for the yielding of grapes, || And it yields [only] bad ones? ⁵ And now, pray, let Me cause you to know, || That which I am doing to My vineyard, || To turn its hedge aside, || And it has been for consumption, || To break down its wall, || And it has been for a treading-place. ⁶ And I make it a waste, || It is not pruned, nor arranged, || And brier and thorn have gone up, || And I lay a charge on the thick clouds, || From raining on it rain. ⁷ Because the vineyard of Yhwh of Hosts || [Is] the house of Israel, || And the man of Judah His pleasant plant, || And He waits for judgment, and behold, oppression, || For righteousness, and behold, a cry. ⁸ Woe [to] those joining house to house, || They bring field near to field, || Until there is no place, || And you have been settled by yourselves || In the midst of the land! ⁹ Do many houses not become a desolation by the weapons of Yhwh of Hosts? Great and good without inhabitant! ¹⁰ For ten acres of vineyard yield one bath, || And a homer of seed yields an ephah. ¹¹ Woe [to] those rising early in the morning, || They pursue strong drink! Lingering in twilight, wine inflames them! ¹² And harp, and stringed instrument, tambourine, and pipe, || And wine, have been their banquets, || And they do not behold the work of Yhwh, || Indeed, they have not seen the work of His hands. ¹³ Therefore my people removed without knowledge, || And its honorable ones are famished, || And its multitude dried up of thirst. ¹⁴ Therefore Sheol has enlarged herself, || And has opened her mouth without limit. And its honor has gone down, and its

multitude, || And its noise, and its exulting one—into her. **15** And the low is bowed down, and the high humbled, || And the eyes of the haughty become low, **16** And Yhwh of Hosts is high in judgment, || And the Holy God sanctified in righteousness, **17** And lambs have fed according to their leading, || And sojourners consume wastelands of the fat ones. **18** Woe [to] those drawing out iniquity with cords of vanity, || And as [with] thick ropes of the cart—sin. **19** Who are saying, "Let Him hurry, || Let Him hurry His work, that we may see, || And let the counsel of the Holy One of Israel || Draw near and come, and we know." **20** Woe [to] those saying to evil "good," and to good "evil," || Putting darkness for light, and light for darkness, || Putting bitter for sweet, and sweet for bitter. **21** Woe [to] the wise in their own eyes, || And—before their own faces—intelligent! **22** Woe [to] the mighty to drink wine, || And men of strength to mingle strong drink. **23** Declaring righteous the wicked for a bribe, || And the righteousness of the righteous || They turn aside from him. **24** Therefore, as a tongue of fire devours stubble, || And flaming hay falls, || Their root is as muck, || And their flower goes up as dust. Because they have rejected the Law of Yhwh of Hosts, || And despised the saying of the Holy One of Israel. **25** Therefore the anger of Yhwh has burned among His people, || And He stretches out His hand against it, || And strikes it, and the mountains tremble, || And their carcass is as filth in the midst of the out-places. With all this His anger did not turn back, || And still His hand is stretched out! **26** And He lifted up an ensign to the far-off nations, || And hissed to it from the end of the earth, || And behold, with haste, it comes swiftly. **27** There is none weary, nor stumbling in it, || It does not slumber, nor sleep, || Nor has the girdle of its loins been opened, || Nor the strap of its sandals drawn away. **28** Whose arrows [are] sharp, and all its bows bent, || Hooves of its horses have been reckoned as flint, || And its wheels as a windstorm! **29** Its roaring [is] like a lioness, || It roars like young lions, || And it howls, and seizes prey, || And carries away safely, and there is none delivering. **30** And it howls against it in that day as the howling of a sea, || And it has looked attentively to the land, || And behold, darkness—distress, || And light has been darkened by its abundance!

CHAPTER 6

1 In the year of the death of King Uzziah—I see the Lord, sitting on a throne, high and lifted up, and His train is filling the temple. **2** Seraphim are standing above it: each one has six wings; with two [each] covers its face, and with two [each] covers its feet, and with two [each] flies. **3** And this one has called to that, and has said: "Holy, Holy, Holy, [is] Yhwh of Hosts, || The fullness of all the earth [is] His glory!" **4** And the posts of the thresholds are moved by the voice of him who is calling, and the house is full of smoke. **5** And I say, "Woe to me, for I have been silent, || For I [am] a man of unclean lips, || And I am dwelling in [the] midst of a people of unclean lips, || Because the King, Yhwh of Hosts, my eyes have seen." **6** And one of the seraphim flees to me, and in his hand—a burning coal (with tongs he has taken [it] from off the altar), **7** and he strikes against my mouth and says: "Behold, this has struck against your lips, || And your iniquity is turned aside, || And your sin is covered." **8** And I hear the voice of the Lord, saying, "Whom do I send? and who goes for Us?" And I say, "Here I [am], send me." **9** And He says, "Go, and you have said to this people, hearing you hear, and you do not understand, || And seeing you see, and you do not know. **10** Declare the heart of this people fat, || And declare its ears heavy, || And declare its eyes dazzled, || Lest it see with its eyes, || And hear with its ears, and consider with its heart, || And it has turned back, and has health." **11** And I say, "Until when, O Lord?" And He says, "Surely until cities have been ruined without inhabitant, || And houses without man, || And the ground is ruined—a desolation, **12** And Yhwh has put man far off, || And the forsaken part [is] great in the heart of the land. **13** And yet a tenth in it, and it has turned, || And has been for a burning, || As a teil-tree, and as an oak, that in falling, || Has substance in them, || The holy seed [is] its substance!"

CHAPTER 7

1 And it comes to pass in the days of Ahaz, son of Jotham,

son of Uzziah, king of Judah, [that] Rezin king of Aram, and Pekah, son of Remaliah, king of Israel, have gone up to Jerusalem, to battle against it, and he is not able to fight against it. **2** And it is declared to the house of David, saying, "Aram has been led toward Ephraim," and his heart and the heart of his people is moved, like the moving of trees of a forest by the presence of wind. **3** And Yhwh says to Isaiah, "Now go forth to meet Ahaz, you and your son Shear-Jashub, to the end of the conduit of the upper pool, to the highway of the fuller's field, **4** and you have said to him: Take heed, and be quiet, do not fear, || And do not let your heart be timid, || Because of these two tails of smoking brands, || For the fierceness of the anger of Rezin and Aram, || And the son of Remaliah. **5** Because that Aram counseled evil against you, Ephraim and the son of Remaliah, saying, **6** We go up into Judah, and we distress it, || And we divide it to ourselves, || And we cause a king to reign in its midst—The son of Tabeal. **7** Thus said Lord Yhwh: It does not stand, nor will it be! **8** For the head of Aram [is] Damascus, || And the head of Damascus [is] Rezin, || And within sixty-five years || Is Ephraim broken from [being] a people. **9** And the head of Ephraim [is] Samaria, || And the head of Samaria [is] the son of Remaliah. If you do not give credence, || Surely you are not steadfast." **10** And Yhwh adds to speak to Ahaz, saying, **11** "Ask for a sign from your God Yhwh, || Make the request deep, or make [it] high upwards." **12** And Ahaz says, "I do not ask nor try Yhwh." **13** And he says, "Now hear, O house of David, || Is it a little thing for you to weary men, || That you also weary my God? **14** Therefore the Lord Himself gives a sign to you, || Behold, the virgin is conceiving, || And is bringing forth a Son, || And has called His Name Immanuel, **15** He eats butter and honey, || When He knows to refuse evil, and to fix on good. **16** For before the youth knows || To refuse evil, and to fix on good, || The land you are distressed with is forsaken, because of her two kings. **17** Yhwh brings on you, and on your people, || And on the house of your father, || Days that have not come, || Even from the day of the turning aside of Ephraim from Judah, || By the king of Asshur." **18** And it has come to pass in that day, || Yhwh hisses for a fly that [is] in the extremity of the brooks of Egypt, || And for a bee that [is] in the land of Asshur. **19** And they have come, and all of them rested in the desolate valleys, || And in holes of the rocks, and on all the thorns, || And on all the commendable things. **20** In that day the Lord shaves, || By a razor that is hired beyond the river, || By the king of Asshur, || The head, and the hair of the feet, || Indeed, it also consumes the beard. **21** And it has come to pass in that day, || A man keeps alive a heifer of the herd, || And two of the flock, **22** And it has come to pass, || He eats butter from the abundance of the yielding of milk, || For everyone who is left in the heart of the land eats butter and honey. **23** And it has come to pass in that day, || Every place where there are one thousand vines, || At one thousand pieces of silver, || Is for briers and for thorns. **24** He comes there with arrows and with bow, || Because all the land is brier and thorn. **25** And all the hills that are kept in order with a mattock, || There does not come [for] fear of brier and thorn, || And it has been for the sending forth of ox, || And for the treading of sheep!

CHAPTER 8

1 And Yhwh says to me, "Take a great tablet to yourself, and write on it with an engraving tool of man, || To hurry spoil, enjoy prey." **2** And I cause faithful witnesses to testify to me, Uriah the priest, and Zechariah son of Jeberechiah. **3** And I draw near to the prophetess, and she conceives, and bears a son; and Yhwh says to me, "Call his name Maher-shalal-hash-baz, **4** for before the youth knows to cry, My father, and, My mother, one takes away the wealth of Damascus and the spoil of Samaria, before the king of Asshur." **5** And Yhwh adds to speak to me again, saying, **6** "Because that this people has refused || The waters of Shiloah that go softly, || And is rejoicing with Rezin and the son of Remaliah, **7** Therefore, behold, the Lord is bringing up on them, || The waters of the river, the mighty and the great || (The king of Asshur and all his glory), || And it has gone up over all its streams, || And has gone on over all its banks. **8** And it has passed on into Judah, || It has overflown and passed over, || It comes to the neck, || And the stretching out of its wings || Has been the fullness of the breadth of your land, O Immanuel! **9** Be friends, O nations, and be broken, || And give ear, all you far-off ones of earth, || Gird yourselves, and be broken, || Gird yourselves, and be broken. **10** Take counsel, and it is broken, || Speak a word, and it does not stand, || Because of Immanuel!" **11** For thus has Yhwh spoken to me with strength of hand, and instructs me against walking in the way of this people, saying, **12** "You do not say, A confederacy, || To all to whom this people says, A confederacy, || And its fear you do not fear, || Nor declare fearful. **13** Yhwh of Hosts—Him you sanctify, || And He [is] your Fear, and He your Dread, **14** And He has been for a sanctuary, || And for a stone of stumbling, and for a rock of falling, || To the two houses of Israel, || For a trap and for a snare to the inhabitants of Jerusalem. **15** And many among them have stumbled and fallen, || And been broken, and snared, and captured." **16** Bind up the testimony, || Seal the Law among My disciples. **17** And I have waited for Yhwh, || Who is hiding His face from the house of Jacob, || And I have looked for Him. **18** Behold, I, and the children whom Yhwh has given to me, || [Are] for signs and for wonders in Israel, || From Yhwh of Hosts, who is dwelling in Mount Zion. **19** And when they say to you, "Seek to those having familiar spirits, || And to wizards, who chatter and mutter," || Does a people not seek to its God? To the dead on behalf of the living? **20** To the Law and to the testimony! If not, let them say after this manner, "That there is no dawn to it." **21** And it has passed over into it, hardened and hungry, || And it has come to pass, || That it is hungry, and has been angry, || And made light of its king, and of its God, || And has looked upwards. **22** And it looks attentively to the land, || And behold, adversity and darkness! Dimness, distress, and thick darkness are driven away, || But not the dimness for which she is in distress!

CHAPTER 9

1 For [there will be] no gloom on her who [is] distressed as at the former time. The land of Zebulun and the land of Naphtali, || So the latter has honored the way of the sea, || Beyond the Jordan, Galilee of the nations. **2** The people who are walking in darkness || Have seen a great light, || Dwellers in a land of death-shade, || Light has shone on them. **3** You have multiplied the nation, || You have made its joy great, || They have rejoiced before You as the joy in harvest, || As [men] rejoice in their apportioning spoil. **4** Because the yoke of its burden, || And the staff of its shoulder, the rod of its exactor, || You have broken as [in] the day of Midian. **5** For every battle of a warrior [is] with rushing, and raiment rolled in blood, || And it has been for burning—fuel of fire. **6** For a Child has been born to us, || A Son has been given to us, || And the dominion is on His shoulder, || And He calls His Name || Wonderful, Counselor, Mighty God, || Father of Eternity, Prince of Peace. **7** Of the increase of [His] dominion, || And of peace, there is no end, || On the throne of David, and on His kingdom, || To establish it, and to support it, || In judgment and in righteousness, || From now on, even for all time, || The zeal of Yhwh of Hosts does this. **8** The Lord has sent a word into Jacob, || And it has fallen in Israel. **9** And the people have known—all of it, Ephraim, and the inhabitant of Samaria, || In pride and in greatness of heart, saying, **10** "Bricks have fallen, and we build hewn work, || Sycamores have been cut down, and we renew cedars." **11** And Yhwh sets the adversaries of Rezin on high above him, || And he joins his enemies together, **12** Aram from before, and Philistia from behind, || And they devour Israel with the whole mouth. With all this His anger has not turned back, || And His hand is still stretched out. **13** And the people has not turned back to Him who is striking it, || And they have not sought Yhwh of Hosts. **14** And Yhwh cuts off head and tail from Israel, || Branch and reed—the same day. **15** Elderly and accepted of faces—he [is] the head, || And prophet teaching falsehood—he [is] the tail. **16** And the eulogists of this people are causing to err, || And its eulogized ones are consumed. **17** Therefore, the Lord does not rejoice over its young men, || And He does not pity its orphans and its widows, || For everyone [is] profane, and an evildoer, || And every mouth is speaking folly. With all this His anger has not turned back, || And His hand is still stretched out. **18** For wickedness has burned as a fire, || It devours brier and thorn, || And it kindles in thickets of the forest, || And they lift themselves up, an exaltation of smoke! **19** In the wrath of Yhwh of Hosts || The land has been consumed, || And the people is as fuel of fire; A man has no pity on his brother, **20** And cuts down on the right, and has been hungry, || And he devours on the left, || And they have not been satisfied, || They each devour the flesh of his own arm. **21** Manasseh—Ephraim, and Ephraim—Manasseh,

|| Together they [are] against Judah, || With all this His anger has not turned back. And His hand is still stretched out!

CHAPTER 10

1 "Woe [to] those decreeing decrees of iniquity, || And writers who have prescribed perverseness, **2** of My people, || That widows may be their prey, || That they may spoil the fatherless. **3** And what do you do at a day of inspection? And at desolation that comes from afar? Near whom do you flee for help? And where do you leave your glory? **4** It has bowed down without Me || In the place of a bound one, || And they fall in the place of the slain." With all this His anger has not turned back, || And His hand is still stretched out. **5** "Woe [to] Asshur, a rod of My anger, || And My indignation [is] a staff in their hand. **6** I send him against a profane nation, || And concerning a people of My wrath || I charge him, || To spoil spoil, and to seize prey, || And to make it a treading-place as the clay of out places. **7** And he does not think [it] so, || And his heart does not reckon [it] so, || For—to destroy [is] in his heart, || And to cut off nations—not a few. **8** For he says, Are my princes not altogether kings? **9** Is not Calno as Carchemish? Is not Hamath as Arpad? Is not Samaria as Damascus? **10** As my hand has gotten to the kingdoms of a worthless thing, and their carved images, || [Greater] than Jerusalem and than Samaria, **11** Do I not—as I have done to Samaria, || And to her worthless things, || So do to Jerusalem and to her grievous things?" **12** And it has come to pass, || When the Lord fulfills all His work || In Mount Zion and in Jerusalem, || I see concerning the fruit of the greatness || Of the heart of the king of Asshur, || And concerning the glory of the height of his eyes. **13** For he has said, "I have worked by the power of my hand, || And by my wisdom, for I have been intelligent, || And I remove borders of the peoples, || And I have spoiled their chief ones, || And I put down the inhabitants as a mighty one, **14** And my hand gets to the wealth of the peoples as to a nest, || And as a gathering of forsaken eggs || I have gathered all the earth, || And there has not been one moving wing, || Or opening mouth, or whispering." **15** Does the axe glorify itself || Against him who is hewing with it? Does the saw magnify itself || Against him who is shaking it? As a rod waving those lifting it up! As a staff lifting up that which is not wool! **16** Therefore the Lord, the Lord of Hosts, || Sends leanness among his fat ones, || And under his glory || He kindles a burning || As the burning of a fire. **17** And the light of Israel has been for a fire, || And his Holy One for a flame, || And it has burned, and devoured his thorn || And his brier in one day. **18** And the glory of his forest, and his fruitful field, || He consumes from soul even to flesh, || And it has been as the fainting of a standard-bearer. **19** And the rest of the trees of his forest [are] few, || And a youth writes them. **20** And it has come to pass in that day, || The remnant of Israel, || And the escaped of the house of Jacob, || Do not add anymore to lean on its striker, || And have leaned on Yhwh, || The Holy One of Israel, in truth. **21** A remnant returns—a remnant of Jacob, || To the Mighty God. **22** For though your people Israel be as the sand of the sea, || A remnant of it returns, || A consumption determined, || Overflowing [with] righteousness. **23** For a consumption that is determined, || The Lord, Yhwh of Hosts, || Is making in the midst of all the land. **24** Therefore, thus said the Lord, Yhwh of Hosts: "Do not be afraid, My people, inhabiting Zion, because of Asshur, || He strikes you with a rod, || And his staff lifts up against you, in the way of Egypt. **25** For yet a very little [while], || And the indignation has been completed, || And My anger by their wearing out." **26** And Yhwh of Hosts is awaking for him, || A scourge like the striking of Midian at the rock Oreb, || And his rod [is] over the sea, || And he has lifted it in the way of Egypt. **27** And it has come to pass in that day, || His burden is turned from off your shoulder, || And his yoke from off your neck, || And the yoke has been destroyed, because of prosperity. **28** He has come in against Aiath, || He has passed over into Migron, || At Michmash he looks after his vessels. **29** They have gone over the passage, || They have made Geba a lodging place, || Rama has trembled, || Gibeah of Saul fled. **30** Cry aloud [with] your voice, daughter of Gallim, || Give attention, Laish! Answer her, Anathoth. **31** Madmenah has fled away, || The inhabitants of the high places have hardened themselves. **32** Yet today to remain in Nob, || The mountain of the daughter of Zion waves its hand, || The hill of Jerusalem. **33** Behold, the Lord, Yhwh of Hosts, || Is lopping a branch with violence, || And the high of stature are cut down, || And the lofty have become low, **34** And

He has gone around the thickets of the forest with iron, || And Lebanon falls by a mighty one!

CHAPTER 11

1 And a Rod has come out from the stock of Jesse, || And a Branch is fruitful from his roots. **2** The Spirit of Yhwh has rested on Him, || The Spirit of wisdom and understanding, || The Spirit of counsel and might, || The Spirit of knowledge and fear of Yhwh. **3** To refresh Him in the fear of Yhwh, || And He does not judge by the sight of His eyes, || Nor decides by the hearing of His ears. **4** And He has judged the poor in righteousness, || And decided for the humble of earth in uprightness, || And has struck earth with the rod of His mouth, || And He puts the wicked to death with the breath of His lips. **5** And righteousness has been the girdle of His loins, || And faithfulness—the girdle of His reins. **6** "And a wolf has sojourned with a lamb, || And a leopard lies down with a kid, || And calf, and young lion, and fatling [are] together, || And a little youth is leader over them. **7** And cow and bear feed, || Together their young ones lie down, || And a lion eats straw as an ox. **8** And a suckling has played by the hole of a cobra, || And on the den of a viper || The weaned one has put his hand. **9** They do no evil, nor destroy in all My holy mountain, || For the earth has been full with the knowledge of Yhwh, || As the waters are covering the sea." **10** And there has been, in that day, || A Root of Jesse that is standing for an ensign of peoples, || Nations seek Him, || And His rest has been glorious! **11** And it has come to pass in that day, || The Lord adds His power a second time, || To get the remnant of His people that is left, || From Asshur, and from Egypt, || And from Pathros, and from Cush, || And from Elam, and from Shinar, || And from Hamath, and from islands of the sea, **12** And He has lifted up an ensign to nations, || And gathers the driven away of Israel, || And He assembles the scattered of Judah, || From the four wings of the earth. **13** And has turned aside the envy of Ephraim, || And the adversaries of Judah are cut off, || Ephraim does not envy Judah, || And Judah does not distress Ephraim. **14** And they have flown on the shoulder of the Philistines westward, || Together they spoil the sons of the east, || Edom and Moab sending forth their hand, || And sons of Ammon obeying them. **15** And Yhwh has devoted to destruction || The tongue of the Sea of Egypt, || And has waved His hand over the river, || In the terror of His wind, || And has struck it at the seven streams, || And has caused [men] to tread [it] with shoes. **16** And there has been a highway, || For the remnant of His people that is left, from Asshur, || As there was for Israel in the day of his coming up out of the land of Egypt!

CHAPTER 12

1 And you have said in that day: "I thank you, O Yhwh, || Though You have been angry with me, || Your anger turns back, || And You comfort me. **2** Behold, God [is] my salvation, I trust, and do not fear, || For my strength and song [is] Yah—Yhwh, || And He is to me for salvation. **3** And you have drawn waters with joy || Out of the fountains of salvation, **4** And you have said in that day, || Give praise to Yhwh, call on His Name. Make His acts known among the peoples. Make mention that His Name is set on high. **5** Praise Yhwh, for He has done excellence, || This is known in all the earth. **6** Cry aloud, and sing, O inhabitant of Zion, || For the Holy One of Israel [is] great in your midst!"

CHAPTER 13

1 The burden of Babylon that Isaiah son of Amoz has seen: **2** "Lift up an ensign on a high mountain, || Raise the voice to them, wave the hand, || And they go into the openings of nobles. **3** I have given charge to My sanctified ones, || Also I have called My mighty ones for My anger, || Those rejoicing at My excellence." **4** A voice of a multitude in the mountains, || A likeness of a numerous people, || A voice of noise from the kingdoms of nations who are gathered, || Yhwh of Hosts inspecting a host of battle! **5** They are coming in from a far-off land, || From the end of the heavens, || Yhwh and the instruments of His indignation, || To destroy all the land. **6**

Howl, for the Day of Yhwh [is] near, || It comes as destruction from the Mighty. **7** Therefore, all hands fail, || And every heart of man melts. **8** And they have been troubled, || Pains and pangs take them, || They are pained as a travailing woman, || A man marvels at his friend, || The appearance of flames—their faces! **9** Behold, the Day of Yhwh comes, || Fierce, with wrath, and heat of anger, || To make the land become a desolation, || Indeed, He destroys its sinning ones from it. **10** For the stars of the heavens, and their constellations, || Do not cause their light to shine, || The sun has been darkened in its going out, || And the moon does not cause its light to come forth. **11** "And I have appointed evil on the world, || And on the wicked their iniquity, || And have caused the excellence of the proud to cease, || And I make the excellence of the terrible low. **12** I make man more rare than fine gold, || And a common man than pure gold of Ophir. **13** Therefore I cause the heavens to tremble, || And the earth shakes from its place, || In the wrath of Yhwh of Hosts, || And in a day of the heat of His anger. **14** And it has been, as a roe driven away, || And as a flock that has no gatherer, || Each to his people—they turn, || And each to his land—they flee. **15** Everyone who is found is thrust through, || And everyone who is added falls by sword. **16** And their sucklings are dashed to pieces before their eyes, || Their houses are spoiled, and their wives lain with. **17** Behold, I am stirring up the Medes against them, || Who do not esteem silver, || And gold—they do not delight in it. **18** And bows dash young men to pieces, || And they do not pity the fruit of the womb, || Their eye has no pity on sons. **19** And Babylon, the beauty of kingdoms, || The glory, the excellence of the Chaldeans, || Has been as overthrown by God, || With Sodom and with Gomorrah. **20** She does not sit forever, || Nor continue to many generations, || Nor does Arab pitch tent there, || And shepherds do not lie down there. **21** And desert-dwellers have lain down there, || And their houses have been full of howlers, || And daughters of an ostrich have dwelt there, || And goats skip there. **22** And howlers—he has responded in his forsaken habitations, || And dragons in palaces of delight, || And her time [is] near to come, || And her days are not drawn out!"

CHAPTER 14

1 For Yhwh loves Jacob, || And has fixed again on Israel, || And given them rest on their own land, || And the sojourner has been joined to them, || And they have been admitted to the house of Jacob. **2** And peoples have taken them, || And have brought them to their place, || And the house of Israel has inherited them, || On the land of Yhwh, || For menservants and for maidservants, || And they have been captors of their captors, || And have ruled over their exactors. **3** And it has come to pass, || In the day of Yhwh's giving rest to you, || From your grief, and from your trouble, || And from the sharp bondage, || That has been served on you, **4** That you have taken up this allegory || Concerning the king of Babylon, and said, "How the exactor has ceased, **5** The golden one has ceased. Yhwh has broken the staff of the wicked, || The scepter of rulers. **6** He who is striking peoples in wrath, || A striking without intermission, || He who is ruling nations in anger, || Pursuing without restraint! **7** At rest—all the earth has been quiet, || They have broken forth [into] singing. **8** Even firs have rejoiced over you, || Cedars of Lebanon, [saying], Since you have lain down, || The hewer does not come up against us. **9** Sheol beneath has been troubled at you, || To meet your coming in, || It is waking up Rephaim for you, || All chief ones of earth, || It has raised up from their thrones || All kings of nations. **10** All of them answer and say to you, Even you have become weak like us! You have become like to us! **11** Your excellence has been brought down to Sheol, || The noise of your stringed instruments, || The worm has been spread out under you, || Indeed, the worm is covering you. **12** How you have fallen from the heavens, || O shining one, son of the dawn! You have been cut down to earth, || O weakener of nations. **13** And you said in your heart: I go up into the heavens, || I raise my throne above the stars of God, || And I sit on the mountain of meeting in the sides of the north. **14** I go up above the heights of a thick cloud, I am like to the Most High. **15** Only—you are brought down to Sheol, || To the sides of the pit. **16** Your beholders look to you, they attend to you, || Is this the man causing the earth to tremble, || Shaking kingdoms? **17** He has made the world as a wilderness, || And he has broken down his cities, || He did not open the house of his bound ones. **18** All kings of nations—all of them, || Have lain down in glory, each in his house, **19** And you have been cast out of your grave, || As an abominable branch, raiment of the slain, || Thrust through ones of the sword, || Going down to the sons of the pit, || As a carcass trodden down. **20** You are not united with them in burial, || For you have destroyed your land, || You have slain your people, || The seed of evildoers is not named for all time. **21** Prepare slaughter for his sons; Because of the iniquity of their fathers, || They do not rise, nor have possessed the land, || Nor filled the face of the world [with] cities. **22** And I have risen up against them," || A declaration of Yhwh of Hosts, || "And have cut off, in reference to Babylon, || Name and remnant, and continuator and successor," || A declaration of Yhwh. **23** "And have made it for a possession of a hedgehog, || And ponds of waters, || And swept it with the broom of destruction," || A declaration of Yhwh of Hosts! **24** Yhwh of Hosts has sworn, saying, "As I thought—so has it not been? And as I counseled—it stands; **25** To break Asshur in My land, || And I tread him down on My mountain, || And his yoke has turned from off them, || Indeed, his burden turns aside from off their shoulder. **26** This [is] the counsel that is counseled for all the earth, || And this [is] the hand that is stretched out for all the nations. **27** For Yhwh of Hosts has purposed, || And who makes void? And His hand that is stretched out, || Who turns it back?" **28** In the year of the death of King Ahaz was this burden: **29** "Do not rejoice, Philistia, all of you, || That the rod of your striker has been broken, || For from the root of a serpent comes out a viper, || And its fruit [is] a flying, burning serpent. **30** And the firstborn of the poor have delighted, || And the needy lie down in confidence, || And I have put to death your root with famine, || And it slays your remnant. **31** Howl, O gate; cry, O city, || You are melted, Philistia, all of you, || For smoke has come from the north, || And there is none alone in his set places." **32** And what does one answer the messengers of a nation? That Yhwh has founded Zion, || And the poor of His people take refuge in it!

CHAPTER 15

1 The burden of Moab. Because in a night Ar of Moab was destroyed—It has been cut off, || Because in a night Kir of Moab was destroyed—It has been cut off. **2** He has gone up to Bajith and Dibon, || The high places—to weep, || Moab howls on Nebo and on Medeba, || Baldness [is] on all its heads, every beard cut off. **3** In its out-places they girded on sackcloth, || On its pinnacles, and in its broad places, || Everyone howls—going down with weeping. **4** And Heshbon and Elealeh cry, || Their voice has been heard to Jahaz, || Therefore the armed ones of Moab shout, || His life has been grievous to him. **5** My heart [is] toward Moab, || Her fugitives cry to Zoar, a heifer of the third [year], || For—the ascent of Luhith—He goes up in it with weeping, || For in the way of Horonaim, || They wake up a cry of destruction. **6** For the waters of Nimrim are desolations, || For the hay has been withered, || The tender grass has been finished, || There has not been a green thing. **7** Therefore the abundance he made, and their store, || They carry to the Brook of the Willows. **8** For the cry has gone around the border of Moab, || Its howling [is] to Eglaim, || And its howling [is] to Beer-Elim. **9** For the waters of Dimon have been full of blood, || For I set additions on Dimon, || A lion for the escaped of Moab, || And for the remnant of Adamah!

CHAPTER 16

1 Send a lamb [to] the ruler of the land, || From Selah in the wilderness, || To the mountain of the daughter of Zion. **2** And it has come to pass, || As a wandering bird, cast out of a nest, || Are daughters of Moab, [at] fords of Arnon. **3** Bring in counsel, do judgment, || Make your shadow as night in the midst of noon, || Hide outcasts, do not reveal the wanderer. **4** My outcasts sojourn in you, O Moab, || Be a secret hiding place for them, || From the face of a destroyer, || For the extortioner has ceased, || Devastation has been finished, || The tramplers are consumed out of the land. **5** And the throne is established in kindness, || And [One] has sat on it in truth, in the tent of David, || Judging and seeking judgment, and hastening righteousness. **6** We have heard of the pride of Moab—very proud, || His pride, and his arrogance, and his wrath—his boastings [are] not right. **7** Therefore Moab howls for Moab, all of it howls, || It meditates for the grape cakes of Kir-Hareseth,

|| They are surely struck. **8** Because fields of Heshbon languish, || The vine of Sibmah, || Lords of nations beat her choice vines, || They have come to Jazer, || They have wandered in a wilderness, || Her plants have spread themselves, || They have passed over a sea. **9** Therefore I weep with the weeping of Jazer, || The vine of Sibmah, || I water you [with] my tear, || O Heshbon and Elealeh, || For—for your summer fruits, and for your harvest, || The shouting has fallen. **10** And gladness and joy have been removed from the fruitful field, || And they do not sing in vineyards, nor shout, || The treader does not tread wine in the presses, || I have caused shouting to cease. **11** Therefore my bowels sound as a harp for Moab, || And my inward parts for Kir-Haresh. **12** And it has come to pass, when it has been seen, || That Moab has been weary on the high place, || And he has come to his sanctuary to pray, || And is not able. **13** This [is] the word that Yhwh has spoken to Moab from that time, **14** And now Yhwh has spoken, saying, "In three years, as years of a hired worker, || The glory of Moab is lightly esteemed, || With all the great multitude, || And the remnant [is] little, small, not mighty!"

CHAPTER 17

1 The burden of Damascus. Behold, Damascus is taken away from [being] a city, || And it has been a heap—a ruin. **2** The cities of Aroer are forsaken, || They are for droves, and they have lain down, || And there is none troubling. **3** And the fortress has ceased from Ephraim, || And the kingdom from Damascus, || And the remnant of Aram are as the glory of the sons of Israel, || A declaration of Yhwh of Hosts! **4** And it has come to pass in that day, || The glory of Jacob waxes poor, || And the fatness of his flesh waxes lean. **5** And it has come to pass, || As the gathering of the standing grain by the reaper, || And his arm reaps the ears, || And it has come to pass, || As the gathering of the ears in the Valley of Rephaim, **6** And gleanings have been left in him, || As the surrounding of an olive, || Two—three berries on the top of a branch, || Four—five on the fruitful boughs, || A declaration of Yhwh, God of Israel! **7** In that day man looks to His Maker, || Indeed, his eyes look to the Holy One of Israel, **8** And he does not look to the altars. The work of his own hands, || And that which his own fingers made, He does not see—the Asherim and the images. **9** In that day the cities of his strength are || As the forsaken thing of the forest, || And the branch that they have left, || Because of the sons of Israel, || It has also been a desolation. **10** Because you have forgotten the God of your salvation, || And have not remembered the Rock of your strength, || Therefore you plant plants of pleasantness, || And sow it with a strange shoot, **11** You cause your plant to become great in the day, || And make your seed to flourish in the morning, || The harvest [is] a heap in a day of overflowing, || And of mortal pain. **12** Woe [to] the multitude of many peoples, || They sound as the sounding of seas; And the roaring of nations, || As the roaring of mighty waters [that] make a crashing. **13** Nations crash as the roaring of many waters, || And He rebuked them, || And they fled far off, || And were pursued as chaff of hills before wind, || And as a rolling thing before a windstorm. **14** At evening, behold, terror, before morning it is not, || This [is] the portion of our spoilers, || And the lot of our plunderers!

CHAPTER 18

1 Behold, land shadowed [with] wings, || That [is] beyond the rivers of Cush, **2** That is sending ambassadors by sea, || Even with implements of reed on the face of the waters—Go, swift messengers, || To a nation drawn out and peeled, || To a people fearful from its beginning and onward, || A nation meeting out by line, and treading down, || Whose land floods have spoiled. **3** All you inhabitants of the world, || And you dwellers of earth, || At the lifting up of an ensign on hills you look, || And at the blowing of a horn you hear. **4** For thus said Yhwh to me: "I rest, and I look on My settled place, || As a clear heat on an herb. As a thick cloud of dew in the heat of harvest. **5** For before harvest, when the flower is perfect, || And the blossom is producing unripe fruit, || Then [One] has cut the sprigs with pruning hooks, || And the branches He has turned aside, cut down. **6** They are left together to the ravenous bird of the mountains, || And to the beast of the earth, || And the ravenous bird has summered on them, || And every beast of the earth winters on them. **⁷** At that time a present is brought to Yhwh of Hosts, || A nation drawn out and peeled. Even of a people fearful from the beginning until now, || A nation meting out by line, and treading down, || Whose land floods have spoiled, || To the place of the Name of Yhwh of Hosts—Mount Zion!"

CHAPTER 19

¹ The burden of Egypt. Behold, Yhwh is riding on a swift thick cloud, || And He has entered Egypt, || And the idols of Egypt have been moved at His presence, || And the heart of Egypt melts in its midst. **²** And I armed Egyptians against Egyptians, || And they fought, each against his brother, || And each against his neighbor, || City against city, kingdom against kingdom. **³** And the spirit of Egypt has been emptied out in its midst. And I swallow up its counsel, || And they have sought to the idols, || And to the charmers, || And to those having familiar spirits, || And to the wizards. **⁴** And I have delivered the Egyptians || Into the hand of a hard lord, || And a strong king rule over them, || A declaration of the Lord, Yhwh of Hosts. **⁵** And waters have failed from the sea, || And a river is desolated and dried up. **⁶** And they have turned away the flowings, || Brooks of the bulwark have been weak and dried up, || Reed and flag have withered. **⁷** Exposed things by the brook, by the edge of the brook, || And every sown thing of the brook, has withered, || It has been driven away, and is not. **⁸** And the fishers have lamented, || And all casting a hook into the brook have mourned, || And those spreading dragnets on the face of the waters have languished. **⁹** And makers of fine flax have been ashamed, || And weavers of networks. **¹⁰** And its foundations have been struck, || All making wages [are] afflicted in soul. **¹¹** Only, the princes of Zoan [are] fools, || The counsel of the wise ones of the counselors of Pharaoh has become brutish. How do you say to Pharaoh, "I am a son of the wise, a son of kings of antiquity?" **¹²** Where [are] they now, your wise ones? Indeed, let them now tell [it] to you, || And they know what Yhwh of Hosts has counseled against Egypt! **¹³** Princes of Zoan have been foolish, || Princes of Noph have been lifted up, || And they have caused Egypt to err, || The chief of her tribes. **¹⁴** Yhwh has mingled in her midst || A spirit of perverseness, || And they have caused Egypt to err in all its work, || As a drunkard errs in his vomit. **¹⁵** And there is no work to Egypt, || That head or tail, branch or reed, may do. **¹⁶** In that day Egypt is like women, || And it has mourned, and been afraid, || Because of the waving of the hand of Yhwh of Hosts, || That He is waving over it. **¹⁷** And the land of Judah has been to Egypt for a cause of staggering, || Everyone who mentions it, fears for himself, || Because of the counsel of Yhwh of Hosts, || That He is counseling against it. **¹⁸** In that day there are five cities in the land of Egypt, || Speaking the lip of Canaan, || And swearing to Yhwh of Hosts, || "The city of destruction," is said of one. **¹⁹** In that day there is an altar to Yhwh || In the midst of the land of Egypt, || And a standing pillar to Yhwh near its border, **²⁰** And it has been for a sign and for a testimony, || To Yhwh of Hosts in the land of Egypt, || For they cry to Yhwh from the face of oppressors, || And He sends a Savior to them, || Even a great one, and has delivered them. **²¹** And Yhwh has been known to Egypt, || And the Egyptians have known Yhwh in that day, || And done sacrifice and present, || And vowed a vow to Yhwh, and completed [it]. **²²** And Yhwh has struck Egypt, striking and healing, || And they have turned back to Yhwh, || And He has accepted their plea, || And has healed them. **²³** In that day a highway is out of Egypt to Asshur, || And the Assyrians have come into Egypt, || And the Egyptians into Asshur, || And the Egyptians have served with the Assyrians. **²⁴** In that day Israel is third, || With Egypt, and with Asshur, || A blessing in the heart of the earth. **²⁵** In that Yhwh of Hosts blessed it, saying, "Blessed [is] My people—Egypt, || And the work of My hands—Asshur, || And My inheritance—Israel!"

CHAPTER 20

¹ In the year of the coming in of Tartan to Ashdod, when Sargon king of Asshur sends him, and he fights against Ashdod and captures it, **²** at that time Yhwh spoke by the hand of Isaiah son of Amoz, saying, "Go, and you have loosed the sackcloth from off your loins, and you draw your sandal from off your foot," and he does so, going naked and barefoot. **³** And Yhwh says, "As My servant Isaiah has gone naked and barefoot three years, a sign and a wonder for Egypt and for Cush, **⁴** so the king of Asshur leads the captivity of Egypt, and the expulsion of Cush, young and old, naked and barefoot, with seat uncovered—the nakedness of Egypt; **⁵** and they have been frightened and ashamed of Cush their confidence, and of Egypt their beauty, **⁶** and the inhabitant of this island has said in that day—Behold, thus [is] our trust, || To where we have fled for help, || To be delivered from the king of Asshur, || And how do we escape—we?"

CHAPTER 21

¹ The burden of the wilderness of the sea. Like windstorms in the south for passing through, || It has come from the wilderness, || From a fearful land. **²** A hard vision has been declared to me, || The treacherous dealer is dealing treacherously, || And the destroyer is destroying. Go up, O Elam, besiege, O Media, || I have caused all its sighing to cease. **³** Therefore my loins have been filled [with] great pain, || Pangs have seized me as pangs of a travailing woman, || I have been bent down by hearing, || I have been troubled by seeing. **⁴** My heart has wandered, trembling has terrified me, || He has made the twilight of my desire a fear to me, **⁵** Arrange the table, watch in the watchtower, || Eat, drink, rise, you heads, anoint the shield, **⁶** For thus said the Lord to me: "Go, station the watchman, || Let him declare that which he sees." **⁷** And he has seen a chariot—a couple of horsemen, || The rider of a donkey, the rider of a camel, || And he has given attention—He has increased attention! **⁸** And he cries, "A lion, my lord! I am continually standing on a watchtower by day, || And I am stationed on my ward whole nights. **⁹** And behold, this, the chariot of a man is coming, || A couple of horsemen." And he answers and says: "Fallen, fallen has Babylon, || And He has broken all the carved images of her gods to the earth. **¹⁰** O my threshing, and the son of my floor, || That which I heard from Yhwh of Hosts, God of Israel, || I have declared to you!" **¹¹** The burden of Dumah. [One] is calling to me from Seir, "Watchman, what of the night? Watchman, what of the night?" **¹²** The watchman has said, "Morning has come, and also night, || If you inquire, inquire, return, come." **¹³** The burden on Arabia. You lodge in a forest in Arabia, || O caravans of Dedanim. **¹⁴** Inhabitants of the land of Tema || Have brought water to meet the thirsty, || With his bread they came before a fugitive. **¹⁵** For they fled from the face of destructions, || From the face of an outstretched sword, || And from the face of a trodden bow, || And from the face of the grievousness of battle. **¹⁶** For thus said the Lord to me: "Within a year, as years of a hired worker, || All the glory of Kedar has been consumed. **¹⁷** And the remnant of the number of bow-men, || The mighty of the sons of Kedar, are few, || For Yhwh, God of Israel, has spoken!"

CHAPTER 22

¹ The burden of the Valley of Vision. What is [troubling] you now, that you have gone up, || All of you—to the roofs? **²** Full of stirs—a noisy city—an exulting city, || Your pierced are not pierced of the sword, || Nor dead in battle. **³** All your rulers fled from the bow together, || All found of you have been bound, || They have been kept bound together, || They have fled far off. **⁴** Therefore I said, "Look [away] from me, || I am bitter in my weeping, do not hurry to comfort me, || For the destruction of the daughter of my people." **⁵** For a day of noise, and of treading down, || And of perplexity, [is] to the Lord, Yhwh of Hosts, || In the Valley of Vision, digging down a wall, || And crying to the mountain. **⁶** And Elam has carried a quiver, || In a chariot of men—horsemen, || And Kir has exposed a shield. **⁷** And it comes to pass, || The choice of your valleys have been full of chariots, || And the horsemen diligently place themselves at the gate. **⁸** And one removes the covering of Judah, || And in that day you look || To the armor of the house of the forest, **⁹** And you have seen the breaches of the City of David, || For they have become many, || And you gather the waters of the lower pool, **¹⁰** And you numbered the houses of Jerusalem, || And you break down the houses to fortify the wall. **¹¹** And you made a ditch between the two walls, || For the waters of the old pool, || And you have not looked to its Maker, || And you have not seen its Framer of old. **¹²** And the Lord calls, Yhwh of Hosts, || In that day, to weeping and to lamentation, || And to baldness and to girding on of sackcloth, **13** And behold, joy and gladness, slaying of oxen, || And slaughtering of sheep, || Eating of flesh, and drinking of wine, || Eat and drink, for tomorrow we die. **14** And it has been revealed in my ears, || [By] Yhwh of Hosts: This iniquity is not pardoned to you, || Until you die, said the Lord, Yhwh of Hosts. **15** Thus said the Lord, Yhwh of Hosts: "Go forth, go to this steward, || To Shebna, who [is] over the house: **16** What are you [doing] here? And who has [allowed] you here? That you have hewn out a tomb for yourself here? Hewing his tomb on high, || Carving a dwelling for himself in a rock. **17** Behold, Yhwh is casting you up and down, || A casting up and down, O mighty one, **18** And your coverer covering, wrapping around, || Wraps you around, O babbler, || On a land of broad sides—there you die, || And there the chariots of your glory [are] the shame of the house of your lord. **19** And I have thrust you from your station, || And he throws you down from your office. **20** And it has come to pass in that day, || That I have called to My servant, || To Eliakim son of Hilkiah. **21** And I have clothed him with your coat, || And I strengthen him with your girdle, || And I give your garment into his hand, || And he has been for a father to the inhabitant of Jerusalem, || And to the house of Judah. **22** And I have placed the key || Of the house of David on his shoulder, || And he has opened, and none is shutting, || And has shut, and none is opening. **23** And I have fixed him [as] a nail in a steadfast place, || And he has been for a throne of glory || To the house of his father. **24** And they have hanged on him || All the glory of the house of his father, || The offspring and the issue, || All vessels of small quality, || From vessels of basins to all vessels of flagons. **25** In that day—a declaration of Yhwh of Hosts, || The nail that is fixed is moved || In a steadfast place, || Indeed, it has been cut down, and has fallen, || And the burden that [is] on it has been cut off, || For Yhwh has spoken!"

CHAPTER 23

1 The Burden of Tyre. Howl, you ship of Tarshish, || For it has been destroyed, || Without house, without entrance, || From the land of Chittim it was revealed to them. **2** Be silent, you inhabitants of the island, || Trader of Sidon, passing the sea, they filled you. **3** And the seed of Sihor [is] in many waters, || Her increase [is] the harvest of the brook, || And she is a market of nations. **4** Be ashamed, O Sidon; for the sea spoke, || The strength of the sea, saying, "I have not been pained, nor have I brought forth, || Nor have I nourished young men, [nor] brought up virgins." **5** As they are pained [at] the report of Egypt, || So [at] the report of Tyre. **6** Pass over to Tarshish, howl, you inhabitants of the island, **7** Is this your exulting one? Her antiquity [is] from the days of old, || Her own feet carry her far off to sojourn. **8** Who has counseled this against Tyre, || The crowning one, whose traders [are] princes, || Her merchants—the honored of earth? **9** Yhwh of Hosts has counseled it, || To defile the excellence of all beauty, || To make light all the honored of earth. **10** Pass through your land as a brook, || Daughter of Tarshish, || There is no longer a girdle. **11** He has stretched out His hand over the sea, || He has caused kingdoms to tremble, || Yhwh has charged concerning the merchant one, || To destroy her strong places. **12** And He says, "You do not add to exult anymore, || O oppressed one, virgin daughter of Sidon, || To Chittim arise, pass over, || Even there—there is no rest for you." **13** Behold, the land of the Chaldeans—this people was not, || Asshur founded it for desert-dwellers, || They raised its watchtowers, || They lifted up her palaces—He has appointed her for a ruin! **14** Howl, you ships of Tarshish, || For your strength has been destroyed. **15** And it has come to pass in that day, || That Tyre is forgotten seventy years, || According to the days of one king. At the end of seventy years there is to Tyre as the song of the harlot. **16** Take a harp, go around the city, O forgotten harlot, play well, || Multiply song that you may be remembered. **17** And it has come to pass, || At the end of seventy years Yhwh inspects Tyre, || And she has returned to her wage, || And she committed fornication || With all kingdoms of the earth on the face of the ground. **18** And her merchandise and her wage have been holy to Yhwh, || Not treasured up nor stored, || For her merchandise is to those sitting before Yhwh, || To eat to satiety, and for a lasting covering!

CHAPTER 24

1 Behold, Yhwh is emptying the earth, || And is making it desolate, || And has overturned [it on] its face, || And has scattered its inhabitants. **2** And it has been—as a people so a priest, || As the servant so his master, || As the maidservant so her mistress, || As the buyer so the seller, || As the lender so the borrower, || As the usurer so he who is lifting [it] on himself. **3** The earth is utterly emptied, and utterly spoiled, || For Yhwh has spoken this word: **4** The earth has mourned, faded, || The world has languished, faded, || They have languished—the high place of the people of the earth. **5** And the earth has been defiled under its inhabitants, || Because they have transgressed laws, || They have changed a statute, || They have made void a perpetual covenant. **6** Therefore a curse has consumed the earth, || And the inhabitants in it become desolate, || Therefore inhabitants of the earth have been consumed, || And few men have been left. **7** The new wine has mourned, the vine languished, || All the joyful of heart have sighed. **8** The joy of tambourines has ceased, || The noise of exulting ones has ceased, || The joy of a harp has ceased. **9** They do not drink wine with a song, || Strong drink is bitter to those drinking it. **10** It was broken down—a city of emptiness, || Every house has been shut from [its] entrance. **11** In out-places [is] a cry over the wine, || All joy has been darkened, || The joy of the land has been removed. **12** Desolation [is] left in the city, || And the gate is struck [with] ruin. **13** When thus it is in the heart of the land, || In the midst of the peoples, || As the surrounding of the olive, || As gleanings when harvest has been finished, **14** They lift up their voice, || They sing of the excellence of Yhwh, || They have cried aloud from the sea. **15** Therefore honor Yhwh in prosperity, || In islands of the sea, the Name of Yhwh, God of Israel. **16** From the skirt of the earth we heard songs, || The desire of the righteous. And I say, "Leanness [is] to me, || Leanness [is] to me, woe [is] to me." Treacherous dealers dealt treacherously, || Indeed, treachery, treacherous dealers dealt treacherously. **17** Fear, and a snare, and a trap, || [Are] on you, O inhabitant of the earth. **18** And it has come to pass, || He who is fleeing from the noise of the fear falls into the snare, || And he who is coming up from the midst of the snare, || Is captured by the trap, || For windows have been opened on high, || And foundations of the earth are shaken. **19** The earth has been utterly broken down, || The earth has been utterly broken, || The earth has been utterly moved. **20** The earth staggers greatly as a drunkard, || And it has been moved as a lodge, || And its transgression has been heavy on it, || And it has fallen, and does not add to rise. **21** And it has come to pass in that day, || Yhwh lays a charge on the host of the high place in the high place, || And on the kings of the earth on the earth. **22** And they have been gathered—A gathering of bound ones in a pit, || And they have been shut up in a prison, || And after a multitude of days are inspected. **23** And the moon has been confounded, || And the sun has been ashamed, || For Yhwh of Hosts has reigned || In Mount Zion, and in Jerusalem, || And before His elderly—glory!

CHAPTER 25

1 O Yhwh, You [are] my God, I exalt You, I confess Your Name, || For You have done a wonderful thing, || Counsels of old, steadfastness, O steadfast One. **2** For You made of a city a heap, || Of a fortified city a ruin, || A high place of strangers from [being] a city, || It is not built for all time. **3** Therefore a strong people honor You, || A city of the terrible nations fears You. **4** For You have been a stronghold for the poor, || A stronghold for the needy in his distress, || A refuge from storm, a shadow from heat, || When the spirit of the terrible [is] as a storm—a wall. **5** As heat in a dry place, || You humble the noise of strangers, || [As] heat with the shadow of a thick cloud, || The singing of the terrible is humbled. **6** And Yhwh of Hosts has made, || For all the peoples in this mountain, || A banquet of fat things, || A banquet of preserved things, || Fat things full of marrow, || Preserved things—refined. **7** And He has swallowed up in this mountain || The face of the wrapping that is wrapped over all the peoples, || And of the covering that is spread over all the nations. **8** He has swallowed up death in victory, || And Lord Yhwh has wiped [the] tear from off all faces, || And He turns aside the reproach of His people from off all the earth, || For Yhwh has spoken. **9** And [one] has said in that day, "Behold, this [is] our God, || We waited for Him, and He saves us, || This [is] Yhwh, we have waited for Him, || We are glad and rejoice in His salvation!" **10** For the hand of Yhwh rests on this mountain, || And Moab is trodden down under Him, || As straw is trodden down on a dunghill. **11** And He spread out His hands in its midst, || As the swimmer spreads out to swim; And He has humbled his excellence || With the machinations of his hands. **12** And the fortress of the high place of your walls || He has bowed down—He has made low, || He has caused [it] to come to the earth—to dust.

CHAPTER 26

1 In that day this song is sung in the land of Judah: "We have a strong city, || He makes salvation [for] walls and bulwark. **2** Open the gates, || That a righteous nation may enter, || Preserving steadfastness. **3** You keep [him] in peace [whose] imagination [is] stayed—peace! For he is confident in You. **4** Trust in Yhwh forever, || For in Yah—Yhwh [is] a rock of ages, **5** For He bowed down the dwellers on high, || A city set on high He makes low, || He makes it low to the earth, || He causes it to come to the dust, **6** A foot treads it down, || Feet of the poor—steps of the weak. **7** The path for the righteous [is] uprightness, || O upright One, || You ponder the path of the righteous. **8** Also, [in] the path of Your judgments, || O Yhwh, we have waited [for] You, || To Your Name and to Your remembrance || [Is] the desire of the soul. **9** I desired You in the night [with] my soul, || Also, I seek You earnestly [with] my spirit within me, || For when Your judgments [are] on the earth, || The inhabitants of the world have learned righteousness. **10** The wicked finds favor, || He has not learned righteousness, || He deals perversely in a land of straightforwardness, || And does not see the excellence of Yhwh. **11** O Yhwh, Your hand [is] high—they do not see, || They see the zeal of the people, and are ashamed, || Also, the fire consumes Your adversaries. **12** O Yhwh, You appoint peace to us, || For You have also worked all our works for us. **13** O our God Yhwh, lords have ruled us besides You, || Only, by You we make mention of Your Name. **14** Dead—they do not live, || Rephaim, they do not rise, || Therefore You have inspected and destroy them, || Indeed, you destroy all their memory. **15** You have added to the nation, O Yhwh, || You have added to the nation, || You have been honored, || You have put all the ends of the earth far off. **16** O Yhwh, in distress they missed You, || They have poured out a whisper, || Your discipline [is] on them. **17** When a pregnant woman comes near to the birth, || She is pained—she cries in her pangs, || So we have been from Your face, O Yhwh. **18** We have conceived; we have been pained. We have brought forth, as it were, wind, || We do not work salvation in the earth, || Nor do the inhabitants of the world fall. **19** Your dead live—My dead body, they rise. Awake and sing, you dwellers in the dust, || For the dew of herbs [is] your dew, || And you cause the land of Rephaim to fall. **20** Come, My people, enter into your inner chambers, || And shut your doors behind you, || Hide yourself shortly [for] a moment until the indignation passes over. **21** For behold, Yhwh is coming out of His place, || To charge the iniquity of the inhabitant of the earth on him, || And the earth has revealed her blood, || Nor does she cover her slain anymore!"

CHAPTER 27

1 In that day Yhwh lays a charge, || With His sword—the sharp, and the great, and the strong, || On leviathan—a fleeing serpent, || And on leviathan—a crooked serpent, || And He has slain the dragon that [is] in the sea. **2** In that day respond to her, "A desirable vineyard, **3** I, Yhwh, am its keeper, || I water it every moment, || Lest any lay a charge against it, || Night and day I keep it! **4** Fury is not in Me; Who gives Me a brier—a thorn in battle? I step into it, || I burn it at once. **5** Or—he takes hold on My strength, || [That] he makes peace with Me, || [And] he makes peace with Me." **6** He causes those coming in to take root, || Jacob blossoms, and Israel has flourished, || And they have filled the face of the world [with] increase. **7** Has He struck him as the striking of his striker? Does He slay as the slaying of his slain? **8** In measure, in sending it forth, you strive with it, || He has taken away by His sharp wind, || In the day of an east wind, **9** Therefore the iniquity of Jacob is covered by this, || And this [is] all the fruit—To take away his sin, || In his setting all the stones of an altar, || As chalkstones beaten in

pieces, || They do not rise—Asherim and images. **10** For the fortified city [is] alone, || A habitation cast out and forsaken as a wilderness, || There the calf delights, || And there it lies down, || And has consumed its branches. **11** In the withering of its branch it is broken off, || Women are coming in [and] setting it on fire, || For it [is] not a people of understanding, || Therefore its Maker does not pity it, || And its Former does not favor it. **12** And it has come to pass in that day, || Yhwh beats out from the branch of the river, || To the stream of Egypt, || And you are gathered one by one, O sons of Israel. **13** And it has come to pass in that day, || It is blown with a great horn, || And those perishing in the land of Asshur have come in, || And those cast out in the land of Egypt, || And have bowed themselves to Yhwh, || In the holy mountain—in Jerusalem!

CHAPTER 28

1 Woe [to] the proud crown of the drunkards of Ephraim. And the fading flower of the beauty of his glory, || That [is] on the head of the fat valley of the broken down of wine. **2** Behold, a mighty and strong one [is] to the Lord, || As a storm of hail—a destructive shower, || As an inundation of mighty waters overflowing, || He cast down to the earth with the hand. **3** The proud crown of the drunkards of Ephraim is trodden down by feet, **4** And the fading flower of the beauty of his glory || That [is] on the head of the fat valley, || Has been as its first-fruit before summer, || That [is] its beholder sees; He swallows it while it [is] yet in his hand. **5** In that day Yhwh of Hosts is || For a crown of beauty, and for a circlet of glory, || To the remnant of His people. **6** And for a spirit of judgment || To him who is sitting in the judgment, || And for might [to] those turning back the battle to the gate. **7** And even these have erred through wine, || And have wandered through strong drink, || Priest and prophet erred through strong drink, || They have been swallowed up of the wine, || They wandered because of the strong drink, || They have erred in seeing, || They have stumbled judicially. **8** For all tables have been full of vomit, || Filth—without place! **9** By whom does He teach knowledge? And by whom does He cause to understand the report? The weaned from milk, the removed from breasts, **10** For rule on rule, rule on rule, || Line on line, line on line, || A little here, a little there, **11** For by scorned lip, and by another tongue, || Does He speak to this people. **12** To whom He has said, "This [is] the rest, give rest to the weary, || And this—the refreshing": And they have not been willing to hear, **13** And to whom a word of Yhwh has been, || Rule on rule, rule on rule, || Line on line, line on line, || A little here, a little there, || So that they go and have stumbled backward, || And been broken, and snared, and captured. **14** Therefore, hear a word of Yhwh, you men of scorning, || Ruling this people that [is] in Jerusalem. **15** Because you have said: "We have made a covenant with death, || And we have made a provision with Sheol, || An overflowing scourge, when it passes over, || Does not meet us, || Though we have made a lie our refuge, || And have been hidden in falsehood." **16** Therefore, thus said Lord Yhwh: "Behold, I am laying a foundation in Zion, || A stone—a tried stone, a precious corner stone, a settled foundation, || He who is believing does not make haste. **17** And I have put judgment for a line, || And righteousness for a plummet, || And hail sweeps away the refuge of lies, || And waters overflow the secret hiding place. **18** And your covenant with death has been annulled, || And your provision with Sheol does not stand, || An overflowing scourge, when it passes over, || Then you have been to it for a treading-place. **19** From the fullness of its passing over it takes you, || For it passes over morning by morning, || By day and by night, || And it has been only a trembling to consider the report. **20** For the bed has been shorter || Than to stretch one's self out in, || And the covering has been narrower || Than to wrap one's self up in. **21** For as Yhwh rises [at] Mount Perazim, || As He is troubled [at] the valley in Gibeon, || To do His work—strange [is] His work, || And to do His deed—strange [is] His deed." **22** And now, do not show yourselves scorners, || Lest your bands are strong, || For a consumption, that is determined, || I have heard, by the Lord, Yhwh of Hosts, || [Is] for all the land. **23** Give ear, and hear my voice, || Attend, and hear my saying: **24** Does the plowman plow the whole day to sow? He opens and harrows his ground! **25** Has he not, if he has made its face level, || Then scattered fitches, and sprinkles cumin, || And has placed the principal wheat, || And the appointed barley, || And the rye [in] its own border? **26** And his God instructs him for judgment,

|| He directs him. **27** For fitches are not threshed with a sharp-pointed thing, || And the wheel of a cart turned around on cumin, || For fitches are beaten out with a staff, || And cumin with a rod. **28** Bread-[grain] is beaten small, || For he does not severely thresh it forever, || Nor has a wheel of his cart crushed [it], || Nor do his hooves beat it small. **29** Even this from Yhwh of Hosts has gone out, || He has made counsel wonderful, || He has made wisdom great!

CHAPTER 29

1 Woe [to] Ariel, Ariel, || The city of the encampment of David! Add year to year, let festivals go around. **2** And I have sent distress to Ariel, || And it has been lamentation and mourning, || And it has been to me as Ariel. **3** And I encamped, O babbler, against you, || And I laid siege against you—a camp. And I raised up bulwarks against you. **4** And you have been low, || You speak from the earth, || And make your saying low from the dust, || And your voice has been from the earth, || As one having a familiar spirit, || And your saying whispers from the dust, **5** And as small dust has been || The multitude of those scattering you, || And as chaff passing on the multitude of the terrible, || And it has been in an instant—suddenly. **6** You are inspected by Yhwh of Hosts, || With thunder, and with an earthquake, || And great noise, windstorm, and whirlwind, || And flame of devouring fire. **7** And as a dream, a vision of night, || Has been the multitude of all the nations || Who are warring against Ariel, || And all its warriors, and its bulwark, || Even of those distressing her. **8** And it has been, as when the hungry dreams, || And behold, he is eating, || And he has awoken, || And his soul [is] empty, || And as when the thirsty dreams, || And behold, he is drinking, || And he has awoken, || And behold, he is weary, || And his soul is longing, || So is the multitude of all the nations || Who are warring against Mount Zion. **9** Linger and wonder, look, indeed, look, || Be drunk, and not with wine, || Stagger, and not with strong drink. **10** For Yhwh has poured out a spirit of deep sleep on you, || And He closes your eyes—the prophets, || And your heads—the seers—He covered. **11** And the vision of the whole is to you, || As words of the sealed scroll, || That they give to one knowing scrolls, || Saying, "Please read this," || And he has said, "I am not able, for it [is] sealed"; **12** And the scroll is given to him who has not known scrolls, || Saying, "Please read this," || And he has said, "I have not known scrolls." **13** And the Lord says: "Because this people has drawn near with its mouth, || And they have honored Me with its lips, || And it has put its heart far off from Me, || And their fear of Me is a precept taught by men! **14** Therefore, behold, I am adding to do wonderfully with this people, || A wonder, and a marvel, || And the wisdom of its wise ones has perished, || And the understanding of its intelligent ones hides itself." **15** Woe [to] those going deep from Yhwh to hide counsel, || And whose works have been in darkness. And they say, "Who is seeing us? And who is knowing us?" **16** Your perversion! Is the potter esteemed as clay, || That the work says of its maker, "He has not made me?" And the framed thing said of its framer, "He did not understand?" **17** Is it not yet a very little [while], || And Lebanon has turned into a fruitful field, || And the fruitful field is reckoned for a forest? **18** And the deaf have heard the words of a scroll in that day, || And out of thick darkness, and out of darkness, || The eyes of the blind see. **19** And the humble have added joy in Yhwh, || And the poor among men || Rejoice in the Holy One of Israel. **20** For the terrible one has ceased, || And the scorner has been consumed, || And all watching for iniquity have been cut off, **21** Who cause men to sin in word, || And lay a snare for a reprover in the gate, || And turn aside the righteous into emptiness. **22** Therefore, thus said Yhwh, || Who ransomed Abraham, || Concerning the house of Jacob: "Jacob is not ashamed now, || Nor does his face now become pale, **23** For in his seeing his children, || The work of My hand, in his midst, || They sanctify My Name, || And have sanctified the Holy One of Jacob, || And they declare the God of Israel fearful. **24** And the erring in spirit have known understanding, || And murmurers learn doctrine!"

CHAPTER 30

1 Woe [to] apostate sons, || A declaration of Yhwh! To do

counsel, and not from Me, || And to spread out a covering, and not of My Spirit, || So as to add sin to sin. **2** Who are walking to go down to Egypt, || And have not asked My mouth, || To be strong in the strength of Pharaoh, || And to trust in the shadow of Egypt. **3** And the strength of Pharaoh || Has been to you for shame, || And the trust in the shadow of Egypt confusion, **4** For his princes were in Zoan, || And his messengers reach Hanes. **5** He made all ashamed of a people that do not profit, || Not for help, and not for profit, || But for shame, and also for reproach! **6** The burden of the beasts of the south. Into a land of adversity and distress, || Of young lion and of old lion, || From where [are] viper and flying, burning serpent, || They carry their wealth on the shoulder of donkeys, || And their treasures on the hump of camels, || To a people not profitable. **7** Indeed, Egyptians [are] vanity, and help in vain, || Therefore I have cried concerning this: "Their strength [is] to sit still." **8** No, go in, write it on a tablet with them, || And inscribe it on a scroll, || And it is for a latter day, for a witness for all time, **9** That this [is] a people of rebellion, sons—liars, || Sons not willing to hear the Law of Yhwh. **10** Who have said to seers, "Do not see," || And to prophets, "Do not prophesy to us straightforward things, || Speak to us smooth things, prophesy deceits, **11** Turn aside from the way, || Decline from the path, || Cause the Holy One of Israel || To cease from before us." **12** Therefore, thus said the Holy One of Israel: "Because of your kicking against this word, || And you trust in oppression, || And perverseness, and rely on it, **13** Therefore this iniquity is to you as a breach falling, || Swelled out in a wall set on high, || Whose destruction comes suddenly, in an instant. **14** And He has broken it || As the breaking of the potters' bottle, || Beaten down—He does not spare, || Nor is there found, in its beating down, || A potsherd to take fire from the burning, || And to draw out waters from a ditch." **15** For thus said Lord Yhwh, || The Holy One of Israel: "In returning and rest you are saved, || In keeping quiet and in confidence is your might," || And you have not been willing. **16** And you say, "No, for we flee on a horse," || Therefore you flee, || And, "We ride on the swift!" Therefore, your pursuers are swift. **17** One thousand [flee] because of the rebuke of one, || Because of the rebuke of five you flee, || Until you have surely been left as a pole || On the top of the mountain, || And as an ensign on the height. **18** And therefore Yhwh waits to favor you, || And therefore He is exalted to pity you, || For Yhwh [is] a God of judgment, || O the blessedness of all waiting for Him. **19** For the people in Zion dwell in Jerusalem, || Do not weep—weeping, || Pitying, He pities you at the voice of your cry, || When He hears He answers you. **20** And the Lord has given to you bread of adversity, || And water of oppression. And your teachers remove no longer, || And your eyes have seen your teachers, **21** And your ear hears a word behind you, saying, "This [is] the way, go in it," || When you turn to the right, || And when you turn to the left. **22** And you have defiled the covering of Your carved images of silver, || And the ephod of your molten image of gold, || You scatter them as a sickening thing, "Go out," you say to it. **23** And He has given rain [for] your seed, || With which you sow the ground, || And bread, the increase of the ground, || And it has been fat and plentiful, || Your livestock enjoy an enlarged pasture in that day. **24** And the oxen and the young donkeys serving the ground, || Eat fermented provender, || That one is winnowing with shovel and fan. **25** And there has been on every high mountain, || And on every exalted hill, || Streams—conduits of waters, || In a day of much slaughter, in the falling of towers. **26** And the light of the moon has been as the light of the sun, || And the light of the sun is sevenfold, || As the light of seven days, || In the day of Yhwh's binding up the breach of His people, || When He heals the stroke of its wound. **27** Behold, the Name of Yhwh is coming from far, || His anger is burning, and the flame [is] great, || His lips have been full of indignation, || And His tongue [is] as a devouring fire. **28** And His breath [is] as an overflowing stream, || It divides to the neck, || To sift nations with a sieve of vanity, || And a bridle causing to err, || [Is] on the jaws of the peoples. **29** Singing is to you as in a night sanctified for a festival, || And joy of heart as he who is going with a pipe, || To go to the mountain of Yhwh, || To the rock of Israel. **30** And Yhwh has caused || The splendor of His voice to be heard, || And the coming down of His arm || He shows with the raging of anger, || And the flame of a consuming fire, || Scattering, and inundation, and hailstone. **31** For from the voice of Yhwh Asshur [is] broken down, || He strikes with a rod. **32** And every passage of the settled staff, || That Yhwh causes to rest on him, || Has been with tambourines and with harps, || And in battles of shaking He has fought with it. ³³ For Tophet is arranged from former time, || Even it is prepared for the king, || He has made deep, || He has made large, || Its pile [is] fire and much wood, || The breath of Yhwh, || As a stream of brimstone, is burning in it!

CHAPTER 31

¹ Woe [to] those going down to Egypt for help, || And [who] lean on horses, || And trust on chariots, because [they are] many, || And on horsemen, because [they are] very strong, || And have not looked on the Holy One of Israel, || And have not sought Yhwh. ² And He [is] also wise, and brings in evil, || And He has not turned aside His words, || And He has risen against a house of evildoers, || And against the help of workers of iniquity. ³ And the Egyptians [are men], and not God, || And their horses [are] flesh, and not spirit, || And Yhwh stretches out His hand, || And the helper has stumbled, || And the helped one has fallen, || And together all of them are consumed. ⁴ For thus said Yhwh to me: "As the lion and the young lion growl over his prey, || Against whom a multitude of shepherds is called, || He is not frightened from their voice, || And he is not humbled from their noise; So Yhwh of Hosts comes down || To war on Mount Zion, and on her height. ⁵ As birds flying, so does Yhwh of Hosts || Cover over Jerusalem, covering and delivering, || Passing over, and causing to escape." ⁶ Turn back to Him from whom sons of Israel || Have deepened apostasy. ⁷ For in that day each despises His idols of silver, and his idols of gold, || That your hands made to you—a sin. ⁸ And Asshur has fallen by sword, not of the high, || Indeed, a sword—not of the low, consumes him, || And he has fled for himself from the face of a sword, || And his young men become tributary. ⁹ And he passes on [to] his rock from fear, || And his princes have been frightened by the ensign—a declaration of Yhwh, || Who has a light in Zion, || And who has a furnace in Jerusalem!

CHAPTER 32

¹ Behold, a king reigns for righteousness, || As for princes, they rule for judgment. ² And each has been as a hiding place [from] wind, || And as a secret hiding place [from] inundation, || As streams of waters in a dry place, || As a shadow of a heavy rock in a weary land. ³ And the eyes of beholders are not dazzled, || And the ears of hearers attend. ⁴ And the heart of those hurried understands to know, || And the tongue of stammerers hurries to speak clearly. ⁵ A fool is no more called "noble," || And to a miser it is not said, "rich"; ⁶ For a fool speaks folly, || And his heart does iniquity, to do profanity, || And to speak error concerning Yhwh, || To empty the soul of the hungry, || Indeed, he causes the thirsty to lack [their] drink. ⁷ And the miser—his instruments [are] evil, || He has counseled wicked schemes, || To corrupt the poor with lying sayings, || Even when the needy speaks justly. ⁸ And the noble counseled noble things, || And he rises up for noble things. ⁹ Women, easy ones, rise, hear my voice, || Daughters, confident ones, give ear [to] my saying, ¹⁰ In days and a year || You are troubled, O confident ones, || For harvest has been consumed, || The gathering does not come. ¹¹ Tremble, you women, you easy ones, || Be troubled, you confident ones, || Strip and make bare, with a girdle on the loins, ¹² They are lamenting for breasts, || For fields of desire, for the fruitful vine. ¹³ Over the ground of my people thorn [and] brier go up, || Surely over all houses of joy of the exulting city, ¹⁴ The palace has been left, || The multitude of the city forsaken, || Fort and watchtower have been for dens for all time, || A joy of wild donkeys—a pasture of herds; ¹⁵ Until the Spirit is emptied out on us from on high, || And a wilderness has become a fruitful field, || And the fruitful field is reckoned for a forest. ¹⁶ And judgment has dwelt in the wilderness, || And righteousness remains in the fruitful field. ¹⁷ And a work of the righteousness has been peace, || And a service of the righteousness—Keeping quiet and confidence for all time. ¹⁸ And My people have dwelt in a peaceful habitation, || And in steadfast dwelling places, || And in quiet resting places. ¹⁹ And it has hailed in the going down of the forest, || And the city is low in the valley. ²⁰ Blessed [are] you sowing by all waters, || Sending forth the foot of the ox and the donkey!

CHAPTER 33

¹ Woe, spoiler! And you not spoiled, || And treacherous! And they did not deal treacherously with you, || When you finish, O spoiler, you are spoiled, || When you finish dealing treacherously, || They deal treacherously with you. ² O Yhwh, favor us, || We have waited for You, || Be their arm, in the mornings, || Indeed, our salvation in time of adversity. ³ From the voice of a multitude peoples have fled, || From Your exaltation nations have been scattered. ⁴ And Your spoil has been gathered, || A gathering of the caterpillar, || As a running to and fro of locusts || He is running on it. ⁵ Yhwh is set on high, for He is dwelling on high, || He has filled Zion [with] judgment and righteousness, ⁶ And has been the steadfastness of your times, || The strength of salvation, wisdom, and knowledge, || Fear of Yhwh—it [is] His treasure. ⁷ Behold, "Their Ariel," they have cried outside, || Messengers of peace weep bitterly. ⁸ Highways have been desolated, || He who passes along the path has ceased, || He has broken covenant, || He has despised enemies, || He has not esteemed a man. ⁹ The land has mourned, languished, || Lebanon has been confounded, || Sharon has been withered as a wilderness, || And Bashan and Carmel are shaking. ¹⁰ Now I arise, says Yhwh, || Now I am exalted, now I am lifted up. ¹¹ You conceive chaff, you bear stubble; Your spirit—a fire [that] devours you. ¹² And peoples have been [as] burnings of lime, || Thorns, as sweepings, they burn with fire. ¹³ Hear, you far off, that which I have done, || And know, you near ones, My might. ¹⁴ Sinners have been afraid in Zion, || Trembling has seized the profane: Who dwells for us—consuming fire, || Who dwells for us—burnings of the age? ¹⁵ Whoever is walking righteously, || And is speaking uprightly, || Kicking against gain of oppressions, || Shaking his hands from taking hold on a bribe, || Stopping his ear from hearing of blood, || And shutting his eyes from looking on evil, ¹⁶ He inhabits high places, || Strongholds of rock [are] his high tower, || His bread has been given, his waters steadfast. ¹⁷ Your eyes see a king in his beauty, || They see a far-off land. ¹⁸ Your heart meditates [on] terror, || Where [is] he who is counting? Where [is] he who is weighing? Where [is] he who is counting the towers? ¹⁹ You do not see the strong people, || A people deeper of lip than to be understood, || Of a scorned tongue, there is no understanding. ²⁰ See Zion, the city of our meetings, || Your eyes see Jerusalem—a quiet habitation, || A tent not taken down, its pins are not removed forever, || And none of its cords are broken. ²¹ But Yhwh [is] mighty for us there, || A place of rivers—streams of broad sides, || No ship with oars goes into it, || And a mighty ship does not pass over it. ²² For Yhwh, ours who is judging, || Yhwh our lawgiver, || Yhwh our King—He saves us. ²³ Your ropes have been left, || They do not correctly strengthen their mast, || They have not spread out a sail, || Then a prey of much spoil has been apportioned, || The lame have taken spoil. ²⁴ Nor does an inhabitant say, "I was sick"; The people dwelling in it [are] forgiven of [their] iniquity!

CHAPTER 34

¹ Come near, you nations, to hear, || And you peoples, give attention, || The earth and its fullness hear, || The world, and all its productions. ² For to Yhwh [is] wrath against all the nations, || And fury against all their host, || He has devoted them to destruction, || He has given them to slaughter. ³ And their wounded are cast out, || And their carcasses cause their stench to ascend, || And mountains have been melted from their blood. ⁴ And all the host of the heavens have been consumed, || And the heavens have been rolled together as a scroll, || And all their hosts fade, || As the fading of a leaf of a vine, || And as the fading one of a fig tree. ⁵ For My sword was soaked in the heavens, || Behold, it comes down on Edom, || On the people of My curse for judgment. ⁶ A sword [is] to Yhwh—it has been full of blood, || It has been made fat with fatness, || With blood of lambs and male goats. With fat of kidneys of rams, || For to Yhwh [is] a sacrifice in Bozrah, || And a great slaughter in the land of Edom. ⁷ And reems have come down with them, || And bullocks with bulls, || And their land has been soaked from blood, || And their dust is made fat from fatness. ⁸ (For a day of vengeance [is] to Yhwh, || A year of recompenses for Zion's strife, ⁹ And her streams have been turned to pitch, || And her dust to brimstone, || And her land has become burning pitch. ¹⁰ She is not quenched by night and

by day, || Her smoke goes up for all time, || She is desolate from generation to generation, || Forever and ever, none is passing into her. ¹¹ And pelican and hedgehog possess her, || And owl and raven dwell in her, || And He has stretched out over her || A line of vacancy, and stones of emptiness. ¹² They call her nobles [to] the kingdom, || But there are none there, || And all her princes are at an end. ¹³ And thorns have gone up her palaces, || Nettle and bramble [are] in her fortresses, || And it has been a habitation of dragons, || A court for daughters of an ostrich. ¹⁴ And desert-dwellers have met with howlers, || And the goat calls for its companion, || Surely the night-owl has rested there, || And has found a place of rest for herself. ¹⁵ The owl has made her nest there, || Indeed, she lays, and has hatched, || And has gathered under her shadow, || Surely vultures have been gathered there, || Each with its companion. ¹⁶ Seek out of the scroll of Yhwh, and read, || One of these has not been lacking, || None has missed its companion, || For My mouth—it has commanded, || And His Spirit—He has gathered them. ¹⁷ And He has cast a lot for them, || And His hand has apportioned [it] to them by line, || They possess it for all time, || They dwell in it from generation to generation!

CHAPTER 35

¹ They rejoice from the wilderness and dry place, || And the desert rejoices, || And flourishes as the rose, ² Flourishing it flourishes, and rejoices, || Indeed, [with] joy and singing, || The glory of Lebanon has been given to it, || The beauty of Carmel and Sharon, || They see the glory of Yhwh, || The majesty of our God. ³ Strengthen the feeble hands, || Indeed, strengthen the stumbling knees. ⁴ Say to the hurried of heart, "Be strong, || Do not fear, behold, your God; vengeance comes, || The repayment of God, || He Himself comes and saves you." ⁵ Then eyes of the blind are opened, || And ears of the deaf are unstopped, ⁶ Then the lame leap as a deer, || And the tongue of the mute sings, || For waters have been broken up in a wilderness, || And streams in a desert. ⁷ And the mirage has become a pond, || And the thirsty land—fountains of waters, || In the habitation of dragons, || Its place of lying down, || A court for reed and rush. ⁸ And a highway has been there, and a way, || And it is called the "Way of Holiness." The unclean do not pass over it, || And He Himself [is] by them, || Whoever is going in the way—even fools do not err. ⁹ No lion is there, || Indeed, a destructive beast does not ascend it, || It is not found there, || And the redeemed have walked, ¹⁰ And the ransomed of Yhwh return, || And have entered Zion with singing, || And [with] continuous joy on their head, || They attain joy and gladness, || And sorrow and sighing have fled away!

CHAPTER 36

¹ And it comes to pass, in the fourteenth year of King Hezekiah, Sennacherib king of Asshur has come up against all the fortified cities of Judah, and seizes them. ² And the king of Asshur sends Rabshakeh from Lachish to Jerusalem, to King Hezekiah, with a heavy force, and he stands by the conduit of the upper pool, in the highway of the fuller's field, ³ and Eliakim son of Hilkiah goes forth to him, who [is] over the house, and Shebna the scribe, and Joah son of Asaph, the remembrancer. ⁴ And Rabshakeh says to them, "Now say to Hezekiah, Thus said the great king, the king of Asshur: What [is] this confidence in which you have confided? ⁵ I have said, Only a word of the lips! Counsel and might [are] for battle. Now, on whom have you trusted, that you have rebelled against me? ⁶ Behold, you have trusted on the staff of this broken reed—on Egypt—which a man leans on, and it has gone into his hand, and pierced it—so [is] Pharaoh king of Egypt to all those trusting on him. ⁷ And do you say to me, We have trusted in our God Yhwh? is it not He whose high places and whose altars Hezekiah has turned aside, and says to Judah and to Jerusalem, Bow yourselves before this altar? ⁸ And now, please negotiate with my lord the king of Asshur, and I give two thousand horses to you, if you are able to put riders on them for yourself. ⁹ And how do you turn back the face of one captain of the least of the servants of my lord, and trust on Egypt for yourself, for chariot and for horsemen? ¹⁰ And now, without Yhwh have I come up against this land to destroy it? Yhwh said

to me, Go up to this land, and you have destroyed it." ¹¹ And Eliakim says—and Shebna and Joah—to Rabshakeh, "Please speak to your servants [in] Aramaic, for we are understanding; and do not speak to us [in] Jewish, in the ears of the people who [are] on the wall." ¹² And Rabshakeh says, "To your lord, and to you, has my lord sent me to speak these words? is it not for the men—those sitting on the wall to eat their own dung and to drink their own water with you?" ¹³ And Rabshakeh stands and calls with a great voice [in] Jewish, and says, "Hear the words of the great king, the king of Asshur— ¹⁴ thus said the king: Do not let Hezekiah lift you up, for he is not able to deliver you; ¹⁵ and do not let Hezekiah make you trust to Yhwh, saying, Yhwh certainly delivers us, this city is not given into the hand of the king of Asshur. ¹⁶ Do not listen to Hezekiah, for thus said the king of Asshur: Make a blessing with me, and come out to me, and each of you eat of his vine, and each of his fig tree, and each drink the waters of his own well, ¹⁷ until my coming in, and I have taken you to a land like your own land, a land of grain and wine, a land of bread and vineyards; ¹⁸ lest Hezekiah persuades you, saying, Yhwh delivers us. Have the gods of the nations each delivered his land out of the hand of the king of Asshur? ¹⁹ Where [are] the gods of Hamath and Arpad? Where [are] the gods of Sepharvaim, that they have delivered Samaria out of my hand? ²⁰ Who among all the gods of these lands [are] they who have delivered their land out of my hand, that Yhwh delivers Jerusalem out of my hand?" ²¹ And they keep silent, and have not answered him a word, for a command of the king is, saying, "Do not answer him." ²² And Eliakim son of Hilkiah, who [is] over the house, comes in, and Shebna the scribe, and Joah son of Asaph, the remembrancer, to Hezekiah, with torn garments, and they declare to him the words of Rabshakeh.

CHAPTER 37

¹ And it comes to pass, at King Hezekiah's hearing, that he tears his garments, and covers himself with sackcloth, and enters the house of Yhwh, ² and sends Eliakim, who [is] over the house, and Shebna the scribe, and [the] elderly of the priests, covering themselves with sackcloth, to Isaiah son of Amoz the prophet, ³ and they say to him, "Thus said Hezekiah: A day of distress, and rebuke, and despising, [is] this day; for sons have come to the birth, and there is not power to bear. ⁴ It may be your God Yhwh hears the words of Rabshakeh with which the king of Asshur his lord has sent him to reproach the living God, and has decided concerning the words that your God Yhwh has heard, and you have lifted up prayer for the remnant that is found." ⁵ And the servants of King Hezekiah come to Isaiah, ⁶ and Isaiah says to them, "Thus you say to your lord, Thus said Yhwh: Do not be afraid because of the words that you have heard, with which the servants of the king of Asshur have reviled Me. ⁷ Behold, I am giving a spirit in him, and he has heard a report, and has turned back to his land, and I have caused him to fall by the sword in his land." ⁸ And Rabshakeh turns back and finds the king of Asshur fighting against Libnah, for he has heard that he has journeyed from Lachish. ⁹ And he hears concerning Tirhakah king of Cush, saying, "He has come out to fight with you"; and he hears, and sends messengers to Hezekiah, saying, ¹⁰ "Thus you speak to Hezekiah king of Judah, saying, Do not let your God in whom you are trusting lift you up, saying, Jerusalem is not given into the hand of the king of Asshur. ¹¹ Behold, you have heard that which the kings of Asshur have done to all the lands—to devote them—and you are delivered? ¹² Did the gods of the nations deliver them whom my fathers destroyed—Gozan, and Haran, and Rezeph, and the sons of Eden, who [are] in Telassar? ¹³ Where [is] the king of Hamath, and the king of Arpad, and the king of the city of Sepharvaim, Hena, and Ivvah?" ¹⁴ And Hezekiah takes the letters out of the hand of the messengers, and reads them, and Hezekiah goes up to the house of Yhwh, and Hezekiah spreads it before Yhwh. ¹⁵ And Hezekiah prays to Yhwh, saying, ¹⁶ "Yhwh of Hosts, God of Israel, inhabiting the cherubim, You [are] God Himself—You alone—to all kingdoms of the earth, You have made the heavens and the earth. ¹⁷ Incline, O Yhwh, Your ear, and hear; open, O Yhwh, Your eyes and see; and hear all the words of Sennacherib that he has sent to reproach the living God. ¹⁸ Truly, O Yhwh, kings of Asshur have laid waste all the lands and their land, ¹⁹ so as to put their gods into fire—for they [are] no gods, but work of the hands of man, wood and stone—and they destroy them. ²⁰ And now, our God Yhwh, save us from his hand, and all kingdoms

of the earth know that You [are] Yhwh, You alone." **21** And Isaiah son of Amoz sends to Hezekiah, saying, "Thus said Yhwh, God of Israel: That which you have prayed to Me concerning Sennacherib king of Asshur— **22** this [is] the word that Yhwh spoke concerning him: Trampled on you, laughed at you, || Has the virgin daughter of Zion, || The daughter of Jerusalem has shaken the head behind you. **23** Whom have you reproached and reviled? And against whom—lifted up the voice? Indeed, you lift up your eyes on high || Against the Holy One of Israel. **24** By the hand of your servants || You have reviled the Lord, and say: In the multitude of my chariots || I have come up to a high place of hills, || The sides of Lebanon, || And I cut down the height of its cedars, || The choice of its firs, || And I enter the high place of its extremity, || The forest of its Carmel. **25** I have dug and drunk waters, || And I dry up with the sole of my steps || All floods of a bulwark. **26** Have you not heard from afar [that] I did it, || From days of old—that I formed it? Now I have brought it in, || And it is to make desolate, || Ruinous heaps—fortified cities, **27** And their inhabitants are feeble-handed, || They were broken down, and are dried up. They have been the herb of the field, || And the greenness of the tender grass, || Grass of the roofs, || And blasted grain, before it has risen up. **28** And your sitting down, and your going out, || And your coming in, I have known, || And your anger toward Me. **29** Because of your anger toward Me, || And your noise—it came up into My ears, || I have put My hook in your nose, || And My bridle in your lips, || And I have caused you to turn back || In the way in which you came. **30** And this [is] the sign to you, || Self-sown grain [is] food of the year, || And in the second year the spontaneous growth, || And in the third year, sow and reap, || And plant vineyards, and eat their fruit. **31** And it has continued—The escaped of the house of Judah that has been left—To take root beneath, || And it has made fruit upward. **32** For a remnant goes forth from Jerusalem, || And an escape from Mount Zion, || The zeal of Yhwh of Hosts does this. **33** Therefore, thus said Yhwh, || Concerning the king of Asshur: He does not come into this city, || Nor does he shoot an arrow there, || Nor does he come before it [with] shield, || Nor does he pour out a mound against it. **34** In the way that he came, in it he turns back, || And to this city he does not come in, || A declaration of Yhwh, **35** And I have covered over this city, || To save it, for My own sake, || And for the sake of My servant David." **36** And a messenger of Yhwh goes out, and strikes in the camp of Asshur one hundred and eighty-five thousand; and [men] rise early in the morning, and behold, all of them [are] dead corpses. **37** And he journeys, and goes, and Sennacherib king of Asshur turns back, and dwells in Nineveh. **38** And it comes to pass, he is bowing himself in the house of his god Nisroch, and his sons Adrammelech and Sharezer have struck him with the sword, and they have escaped to the land of Ararat, and his son Esar-Haddon reigns in his stead.

CHAPTER 38

1 In those days has Hezekiah been sick to death, and Isaiah son of Amoz, the prophet, comes to him and says to him, "Thus said Yhwh: Give a charge to your house, for you [are] dying, and do not live." **2** And Hezekiah turns around his face to the wall, and prays to Yhwh, **3** and says, "Ah, now, O Yhwh, please remember how I have habitually walked before You in truth, and with a perfect heart, and I have done that which [is] good in your eyes"; and Hezekiah weeps [with] a great weeping. **4** And a word of Yhwh is to Isaiah, saying, **5** "Go, and you have said to Hezekiah, Thus said Yhwh, God of your father David: I have heard your prayer, I have seen your tear, behold, I am adding fifteen years to your days, **6** and out of the hand of the king of Asshur I deliver you and this city, and have covered over this city. **7** And this [is] to you the sign from Yhwh, that Yhwh does this thing that He has spoken. **8** Behold, I am bringing back the shadow of the degrees that it has gone down on the degrees of Ahaz, by the sun, backward ten degrees"; and the sun turns back ten degrees in the degrees that it had gone down. **9** A writing of Hezekiah king of Judah concerning his being sick when he revives from his sickness: **10** "I said in the cutting off of my days, || I go to the gates of Sheol, || I have numbered the remnant of my years. **11** I said, I do not see Yah—Yah! In the land of the living, || I do not behold man anymore, || With the inhabitants of the world. **12** My sojourning has departed, || And been removed from me as a shepherd's tent, || I have drawn together, as a weaver, my life, || By

weakness it cuts me off, || From day to night You end me. **13** I have set [Him] as a lion until morning, || So He breaks all my bones, || From day to night You end me. **14** As a crane—a swallow—so I chatter, || I mourn as a dove, || My eyes have been drawn up on high, || O Yhwh, oppression [is] on me, be my guarantor. **15** What do I say? seeing He spoke to me, || And He Himself has worked, || I go softly all my years for the bitterness of my soul. **16** Lord, [men] live by these, || And by all in them [is] the life of my spirit, || And You save me, make me to also live, **17** Behold, He changed bitterness to peace for me, || And You have delighted in my soul without corruption, || For You have cast all my sins behind Your back. **18** For Sheol does not confess You, || Death does not praise You, || Those going down to the pit do not hope for Your truth. **19** The living, the living, he confesses You, **20** Like myself today; A father makes known to [his] sons of Your faithfulness, || O Yhwh—to save me: And we sing my songs all [the] days of our lives || In the house of Yhwh." **21** And Isaiah says, "Let them take a bunch of figs, and plaster over the ulcer, and he lives." **22** And Hezekiah says, "What [is] the sign that I go up to the house of Yhwh?"

CHAPTER 39

1 At that time, Merodach-Baladan, son of Baladan, king of Babylon, has sent letters and a present to Hezekiah when he hears that he has been sick and has become strong. **2** And Hezekiah rejoices over them, and shows them the house of his spices, the silver, and the gold, and the spices, and the good ointment, and all the house of his vessels, and all that has been found in his treasures; there has not been a thing in his house, and in all his dominion, that Hezekiah has not showed them. **3** And Isaiah the prophet comes to King Hezekiah and says to him, "What did these men say? and from where do they come to you?" And Hezekiah says, "They have come to me from a far-off land—from Babylon." **4** And he says, "What did they see in your house?" And Hezekiah says, "They saw all that [is] in my house; there has not been a thing that I have not showed them among my treasures." **5** And Isaiah says to Hezekiah, "Hear a word of Yhwh of Hosts: **6** Behold, days are coming, and all that [is] in your house, and that your fathers have treasured up until this day, has been carried to Babylon; there is not a thing left, said Yhwh; **7** and of your sons who come forth from you, whom you beget, they take, and they have been eunuchs in a palace of the king of Babylon." **8** And Hezekiah says to Isaiah, "The word of Yhwh that you have spoken [is] good"; and he says, "Because there is peace and truth in my days."

CHAPTER 40

1 "Comfort, comfort My people," says your God. **2** Speak to the heart of Jerusalem, and call to her, || That her warfare has been completed, || That her punishment has been accepted, || That she has received from the hand of Yhwh || Double for all her sins. **3** A voice is crying in a wilderness: "Prepare the way of Yhwh, || Make straight in a desert a highway for our God. **4** Every valley is raised up, || And every mountain and hill become low, || And the crooked place has become a plain, || And the entangled places a valley. **5** And the glory of Yhwh has been revealed, || And all flesh have seen [it] together, || For the mouth of Yhwh has spoken." **6** A voice is saying, "Call," || And he said, "What do I call?" All flesh [is] grass, and all its goodness || [Is] as a flower of the field: **7** Grass has withered, the flower faded, || For the Spirit of Yhwh blew on it, || Surely the people [is] grass; **8** Grass has withered, the flower faded, || But a word of our God rises forever. **9** Get up on a high mountain, O Zion, || Proclaiming tidings, || Lift up your voice with power, O Jerusalem, proclaiming tidings, || Lift up, do not fear, say to cities of Judah, "Behold, your God." **10** Behold, Lord Yhwh comes with strength, || And His arm is ruling for Him, || Behold, His hire [is] with Him, and His wage before Him. **11** He feeds His flock as a shepherd, || He gathers lambs with His arm, || And He carries [them] in His bosom: He leads suckling ones. **12** Who has measured the waters in the hollow of His hand, || And has meted out the heavens by a span, || And comprehended the dust of the earth in a measure, || And has weighed the mountains in scales, || And the hills in a balance? **13** Who has meted out the Spirit of Yhwh, || And [being] His counselor, teaches Him? **14** With whom [did] He consult, || That he causes Him to understand? And teaches Him in the path of judgment, || And teaches Him knowledge? And causes Him to know the way of understanding? **15** Behold, nations [are] as a drop from a bucket, || And have been reckoned as small dust of the balance, || Behold, He takes up islands as a small thing. **16** And Lebanon is not sufficient to burn, || Nor its beasts sufficient for a burnt-offering. **17** All the nations [are] as nothing before Him, || Less than nothing and emptiness, || They have been reckoned to Him. **18** And to whom do you liken God, || And what likeness do you compare to Him? **19** An artisan has poured out the carved image, || And a refiner spreads it over with gold, || And he is refining chains of silver. **20** He who is poor [by] raised-offerings, || Chooses a tree [that is] not rotten, || He seeks a skillful artisan for it, || To establish a carved image—not moved. **21** Do you not know—do you not hear? Has it not been declared from the first to you? Have you not understood || [From] the foundations of the earth? **22** He who is sitting on the circle of the earth, || And its inhabitants [are] as grasshoppers, || He who is stretching out the heavens as a thin thing, || And spreads them as a tent to dwell in. **23** He who is making princes become nothing, || Has made judges of earth formless; **24** Indeed, they have not been planted, || Indeed, they have not been sown, || Indeed, their stock is not taking root in the earth, || And He has also blown on them, and they wither, || And a whirlwind takes them away as stubble. **25** And to whom do you liken Me, || And [to whom] I equal? says the Holy One. **26** Lift up your eyes on high, || And see—who has created these? He who is bringing out their host by number, || He calls to all of them by name, || By the abundance of His strength || And mighty power, || Not one is lacking. **27** Why say, O Jacob, and speak, O Israel, "My way has been hid from Yhwh, || And from my God my judgment passes over?" **28** Have you not known? have you not heard? The God of the age—Yhwh, || Preparer of the ends of the earth, || Is not wearied nor fatigued, || There is no searching of His understanding. **29** He is giving power to the weary, || And to those not strong He increases might. **30** Even youths are wearied and fatigued, || And young men utterly stumble, **31** But those expecting Yhwh pass [to] power, || They raise up the pinion as eagles, || They run and are not fatigued, || They go on and do not faint!

CHAPTER 41

1 Keep silent toward Me, O islands, || And the peoples pass on [to] power, || They come near, then they speak, "Together we draw near to judgment." **2** Who stirred up a righteous one from the east? He calls him to His foot, || He gives nations before him, || And He causes him to rule kings, || He gives [them] as dust [to] his sword, || As driven stubble [to] his bow. **3** He pursues them, he passes over in safety || A path he does not enter with his feet. **4** Who has worked and done, || Calling the generations from the first? I, Yhwh, the first, and with the last I [am] He. **5** Islands have seen and fear, || The ends of the earth tremble, || They have drawn near, indeed, they come. **6** They each help his neighbor, || And to his brother he says, "Be strong." **7** And an artisan strengthens the refiner, || A smoother [with] a hammer, || Him who is beating [on] an anvil, saying, "For joining it [is] good," || And he strengthens it with nails, it is not moved! **8** And you, O Israel, My servant, || Jacob, whom I have chosen, || Seed of Abraham, My lover, **9** Whom I have taken hold of, from the ends of the earth, || And from its near places I have called you, || And I say to you, You [are] My servant, || I have chosen you, and not rejected you. **10** Do not be afraid, for I [am] with you, do not look around, for I [am] your God, || I have strengthened you, || Indeed, I have helped you, indeed, I upheld you, || With the right hand of My righteousness. **11** Behold, all those displeased with you, || They are ashamed and blush, || They are as nothing, indeed, || The men who strive with you perish. **12** You seek them, and do not find them, || The men who debate with you, || They are as nothing, indeed, as nothing, || The men who war with you. **13** For I, your God Yhwh, || Am strengthening your right hand, || He who is saying to you, "Do not fear, I have helped you." **14** Do not fear, O worm Jacob, || You men of Israel, || I helped you, a declaration of Yhwh, || Even your redeemer, the Holy One of Israel. **15** Behold, I have set you for a new sharp threshing instrument, || Possessing teeth, you thresh mountains, || And beat small, and make hills as chaff. **16** You winnow them, and a wind lifts them up, || And a whirlwind scatter them, || And you rejoice in Yhwh, || [And] boast yourself in the Holy One of Israel. **17** The poor and the needy

are seeking water, || And there is none, || Their tongue has failed with thirst, || I, Yhwh, answer them, || The God of Israel—I do not forsake them. **18** I open rivers on high places, || And fountains in midst of valleys, || I make a wilderness become a pond of water, || And a dry land becomes springs of water. **19** I give in a wilderness the cedar, || Shittah, and myrtle, and oil-tree, || I set in a desert the fir-pine and box-wood together. **20** So that they see, and know, || And regard, and act wisely together, || For the hand of Yhwh has done this, || And the Holy One of Israel has created it. **21** Bring your cause near, says Yhwh, || Bring your mighty ones near, says the King of Jacob. **22** They bring [them] near, and declare to us that which happens, || Declare the first things—what they [are], || And we set our heart, and know their latter end, || Or cause us to hear the coming things. **23** Declare the things that are coming hereafter, || And we know that you [are] gods, || Indeed, you may do good or do evil, || And we look around and see [it] together. **24** Behold, you [are] of nothing, and your work of nothing, || An abomination—it fixes on you. **25** I have stirred up [one] from the north, || And he comes, || From the rising of the sun he calls in My Name, || And he comes in [on] prefects as [on] clay, || And as a potter tread down mire. **26** Who has declared from the first, and we know? And formerly, and we say, "Righteous?" Indeed, there is none declaring, || Indeed, there is none proclaiming, || Indeed, there is none hearing your sayings. **27** First to Zion, || Behold, behold them, || And to Jerusalem I give one proclaiming tidings, **28** And I see that there is no man, || Indeed, of these that there is no counselor, || And I ask them, and they return word: **29** "Behold, all of them [are] vanity, || Their works [are] nothing, || Their molten images [are] wind and emptiness!"

CHAPTER 42

1 Behold, My servant, I take hold on Him, || My Chosen One—My soul has accepted, I have put My Spirit on Him, || He brings forth judgment to nations. **2** He does not cry, nor lift up, || Nor cause His voice to be heard in the street. **3** A bruised reed He does not break, || And faded flax He does not quench, || He brings forth judgment to truth. **4** He does not become weak nor bruised, || Until He sets judgment in the earth, || And islands wait with hope for His law. **5** Thus said God, Yhwh, || Creating the heavens, and stretching them out, || Spreading out the earth and its productions, || Giving breath to the people on it, || And spirit to those walking in it. **6** I, Yhwh, called you in righteousness, || And I lay hold on your hand, and keep you, || And I give you for a covenant of a people, || And a light of nations. **7** To open the eyes of the blind, || To bring forth the bound one from prison, || Those sitting in darkness from the house of restraint. **8** I [am] Yhwh, this [is] My Name, || And I do not give My glory to another, || Nor My praise to carved images. **9** The former things, behold, have come, || And I am declaring new things, || Before they spring up I cause you to hear. **10** Sing a new song to Yhwh, || His praise from the end of the earth, || You who are going down to the sea, and its fullness, || Islands, and their inhabitants. **11** The wilderness and its cities lift up [their voice], || Kedar inhabits the villages, || The inhabitants of Sela sing, || They cry from the top of mountains. **12** They ascribe to Yhwh glory, || And they declare His praise in the islands. **13** Yhwh goes forth as a mighty one. He stirs up zeal as a man of war, || He cries; indeed, He shrieks, || He shows Himself mighty against His enemies. **14** I have kept silent from of old, || I keep silent, I refrain Myself, || I cry out as a travailing woman, || I desolate and swallow up together. **15** I make desolate mountains and hills, || And I dry up all their herbs, || And I have made rivers become islands, || And I dry up ponds. **16** And I have caused the blind to go, || In a way they have not known, || I cause them to tread in paths they have not known, || I make a dark place become light before them, || And unleveled places become a plain, || These [are] the things I have done to them, || And I have not forsaken them. **17** Removed backward—utterly ashamed, || Are those trusting in a carved image, || Those saying to a molten image, "You [are] our gods." **18** You deaf, hear; and you blind, look to see. **19** Who [is] blind but My servant? And deaf as My messenger I send? Who [is] blind as he who is at peace, || Indeed, blind, as the servant of Yhwh? **20** Seeing many things, and you do not observe, || Opening ears, and he does not hear. **21** Yhwh has delight for the sake of His righteousness, || He magnifies law, and makes honorable. **22** And this [is] a people seized and spoiled, || Snared in holes all of them, || And they were hidden in houses of restraint, || They have been for a prey, || And there is no deliverer, || A spoil, and none is saying, "Restore." **23** Who among you gives ear [to] this? Attends, and hears afterward? **24** Who has given Jacob for a spoil, || And Israel to the spoilers? Is it not·Yhwh— He against whom we sinned? Indeed, they have not been willing to walk in His ways, || Nor have they listened to His law. **25** And He pours fury on him, || His anger, and the strength of battle, || And it sets him on fire all around, || And he has not known, || And it burns against him, and he does not lay it to heart!

CHAPTER 43

1 And now, thus said Yhwh, Your Creator, O Jacob, and your Fashioner, O Israel: Do not be afraid, for I have redeemed you, || I have called on your name—you [are] Mine. **2** When you pass into waters, I [am] with you, || And into floods, they do not overflow you, || When you go into fire, you are not burned, || And a flame does not burn against you. **3** For I—your God Yhwh, || The Holy One of Israel, your Savior, || I have appointed Egypt your atonement, || Cush and Seba in your stead. **4** Since you were precious in My eyes, || You were honored, and I have loved you, || And I appoint men in your stead, || And peoples instead of your life. **5** Do not be afraid, for I [am] with you, || I bring in your seed from the east, || And I gather you from the west. **6** I am saying to the north, "Give up," || And to the south, "Do not restrain." Bring in My sons from afar, || And My daughters from the end of the earth. **7** Everyone who is called by My Name, || Even for My glory I have created him, || I have formed him, indeed, I have made him. **8** He brought out a blind people who have eyes, || And deaf ones who have ears. **9** All the nations have been gathered together, || And the peoples are assembled, || Who among them declares this, || And causes us to hear former things? They give their witnesses, || And they are declared righteous, || And they hear and say, "Truth." **10** You [are] My witnesses, a declaration of Yhwh, || And My servant whom I have chosen, || So that you know and give credence to Me, || And understand that I [am] He, || Before Me there was no God formed, || And after Me there is none. **11** I [am] Yhwh, || And besides Me there is no savior. **12** I declared, and saved, and proclaimed, || And there is no stranger with you, || And you [are] My witnesses, a declaration of Yhwh, || And I [am] God. **13** Even from the day I [am] He, || And there is no deliverer from My hand, || I work, and who turns it back? **14** Thus said Yhwh, your Redeemer, || The Holy One of Israel: "I have sent to Babylon for your sake, || And caused them to descend—all of them, || And the Chaldeans, whose song [is] in the ships. **15** I [am] Yhwh, your Holy One, || Creator of Israel, your King." **16** Thus said Yhwh, || Who is giving a way in the sea, || And a path in the strong waters. **17** Who is bringing forth chariot and horse, || A force, even a strong one: "They lie down together— they do not rise, || They have been extinguished, || They have been quenched as flax." **18** Do not remember former things, || And do not consider ancient things. **19** Behold, I am doing a new thing, now it springs up, || Do you not know it? Indeed, I put a way in a wilderness, || In a desolate place—floods. **20** The beast of the field honors Me, || Dragons and daughters of an ostrich, || For I have given waters in a wilderness, || Floods in a desolate place, || To give drink to My people—My chosen. **21** I have formed this people for Myself, || They recount My praise. **22** And you have not called Me, O Jacob, || For you have been wearied of Me, O Israel, **23** You have not brought to Me, || The lamb of your burnt-offerings, || And [with] your sacrifices you have not honored Me, || I have not caused you to serve with a present, || Nor wearied you with frankincense. **24** You have not bought Me sweet cane with money, || And have not filled Me [with] the fat of your sacrifices, || Only—you have caused Me to serve with your sins, || You have wearied Me with your iniquities. **25** I [am] He who is blotting out Your transgressions for My own sake, || And I do not remember your sins. **26** Cause Me to remember—we are judged together, || Declare that you may be justified. **27** Your first father sinned, || And your interpreters transgressed against Me, **28** And I defile princes of the sanctuary, || And I give Jacob to destruction, and Israel to revilings!

CHAPTER 44

1 "And now, hear, O Jacob, My servant, || And Israel, whom I have fixed on— **2** Thus said Yhwh, your Maker, and your Former, || From the womb He helps you: Do not fear, My servant Jacob, || And Yeshurun, whom I have fixed on. **3** For I pour waters on a thirsty one, || And floods on a dry land, || I pour My Spirit on your seed, || And My blessing on your offspring. **4** And they have sprung up as among grass, || As willows by conduits of water. **5** This [one] says, For I [am] Yhwh's, || And this calls [himself] by the name of Jacob, || And this [one] writes [with] his hand, For Yhwh, || And surnames himself by the name of Israel." **6** Thus said Yhwh, King of Israel, || And his Redeemer, Yhwh of Hosts: "I [am] the first, and I [am] the last, || And besides Me there is no God. **7** And who [is] as I, call and declare it, || And arrange it for Me, || Since My placing the people of antiquity, || And things that are coming, || And those that come, they declare to them. **8** Do not fear, nor be afraid, || Have I not caused you to hear from that time, and declared? And you [are] My witnesses, || Is there a God besides Me? indeed, there is none, || I have not known another Rock." **9** Framers of a carved image, all of them [are] emptiness, || And their desirable things do not profit, || And they [are] their own witnesses, || They do not see, nor know, that they may be ashamed. **10** Who has formed a god, || And poured out a molten image—not profitable? **11** Behold, all his companions are ashamed, || As for artisans—they [are] of men, || All of them gather together, they stand up, || They fear, they are ashamed together. **12** He has worked iron [with] an axe, || And has worked with coals, || And forms it with hammers, || And works it by his powerful arm, || Indeed, he is hungry, and there is no power, || He does not drink water, and he is wearied. **13** He has worked [with] wood, || He has stretched out a rule, || He marks it out with a line, || He makes it with carving tools, || And he marks it out with a compass, || And makes it according to the form of a man, || According to the beauty of a man, || To remain in the house. **14** Cutting down cedars for himself, || He also takes a cypress, and an oak, || And he strengthens [it] for himself || Among the trees of a forest, || He has planted an ash, and the shower nourishes [it]. **15** And it has been for man to burn, || And he takes of them, and becomes warm, || Indeed, he kindles [it], and has baked bread, || Indeed, he makes a god, and bows himself, || He has made it a carved image, || And he falls down to it. **16** Half of it he has burned in the fire, || By [this] half of it he eats flesh, || He roasts a roasting and is satisfied, || Indeed, he is warm and says: "Aha, I have become warm, I have enjoyed the light." **17** And he has made its remnant for a god—For his carved image, || He falls down to it, and worships, || And prays to it, and he says, "Deliver me, for you [are] my god." **18** They have not known, nor do they understand, || For He has coated their eyes from seeing, || Their heart from acting wisely. **19** And none turn [it] back to his heart, || Nor has knowledge nor understanding to say, "I have burned half of it in the fire, || Indeed, I have also baked bread over its coals, || I roast flesh and I eat, || And I make its remnant for an abomination, || I fall down to the stock of a tree." **20** Feeding on ashes, the heart is deceived, || It has turned him aside, || And he does not deliver his soul, nor says: "Is there not a lie in my right hand?" **21** "Remember these, O Jacob, and Israel, || For you [are] My servant, || I formed you, you [are] a servant to Me, || O Israel, you do not forget Me. **22** I have blotted out, as [by] a thick cloud, || Your transgressions, || And as [by] a cloud, your sins, || Return to Me, for I have redeemed you." **23** Sing, O heavens, for Yhwh has worked, || Shout, O lower parts of earth, || Break forth, O mountains, with singing, || Forest, and every tree in it, || For Yhwh has redeemed Jacob, || And He beautifies Himself in Israel. **24** Thus said Yhwh, your Redeemer, || And your Framer from the womb: "I [am] Yhwh, doing all things, || Stretching out the heavens by Myself, || Spreading out the earth—who [is] with Me? **25** Making void the tokens of devisers, || And makes diviners mad, || Turning the wise backward, || And makes their knowledge foolish. **26** Confirming the word of His servant, || He perfects the counsel of His messengers, || Who is saying of Jerusalem, || She is inhabited, || And of cities of Judah, || They will be built, and her ruins I raise up, **27** Who is saying to the deep, || Be dry, and your rivers I cause to dry up, **28** Who is saying of Cyrus, My shepherd, || And he perfects all My delight, || So as to say of Jerusalem, You are built, || And of the temple, You are founded."

CHAPTER 45

1 Thus said Yhwh, || To His anointed, to Cyrus, || Whose right hand I have laid hold on, || To subdue nations before him, || Indeed, I loose loins of kings, || To open double doors before him, || Indeed, gates are not shut: 2 "I go before you, and make crooked places straight, || I shatter doors of bronze, || And I cut bars of iron apart, 3 And have given to you treasures of darkness, || Even treasures of secret places, || So that you know that I, Yhwh, || Who am calling on your name—[am] the God of Israel. 4 For the sake of My servant Jacob, || And of Israel My chosen, || I also call you by your name, I surname you, || And you have not known Me. 5 I [am] Yhwh, and there is none else, || There is no God except Me, || I gird you, and you have not known Me. 6 So that they know from the rising of the sun, || And from the west, that there is none besides Me, || I [am] Yhwh, and there is none else, 7 Forming light, and creating darkness, || Making peace, and creating calamity, || I [am] Yhwh, doing all these things. 8 Drop, you heavens, from above, || And clouds cause righteousness to flow, || Earth opens, and they are fruitful, || Salvation and righteousness spring up together, || I, Yhwh, have created it. 9 Woe [to] him who is striving with his Former || (A potsherd with potsherds of the ground!) Does clay say to its Framer, What [are] you doing? And your work, He has no hands? 10 Woe [to] him who is saying to a father, What do you beget? Or to a wife, What do you bring forth?" 11 Thus said Yhwh, The Holy One of Israel, and his Former: "Ask Me of the things coming concerning My sons, || Indeed, concerning the work of My hands, you command Me. 12 I made earth, and created man on it, || My hands stretched out the heavens, || And I have commanded all their host. 13 I have stirred him up in righteousness, || And I make all his ways straight, || He builds My city, and sends out My captivity, || Not for price, nor for bribe," said Yhwh of Hosts. 14 Thus said Yhwh: "The labor of Egypt, || And the merchandise of Cush, || And of the Sebaim—men of measure, || Pass over to you, and they are yours, || They go after you, they pass over in chains, || And they bow themselves to you, || They pray to you: Surely God [is] in you, || And there is none else, no [other] God." 15 Surely You [are] a God hiding Yourself, God of Israel—Savior! 16 They have been ashamed, || And they have even blushed—all of them, || Those carving images have gone together in confusion. 17 Israel has been saved in Yhwh, || A perpetual salvation! You are not ashamed nor confounded || For all ages of eternity! 18 For thus said Yhwh, Creator of the heavens, || He is God, || Former of earth, and its Maker, || He established it—He did not create it empty, || For He formed it to be inhabited: "I [am] Yhwh, and there is none else. 19 I have not spoken in secret, in a dark place of the earth, || I have not said to the seed of Jacob, || Seek Me in vain, || I [am] Yhwh, speaking righteousness, || Declaring uprightness. 20 Be gathered, and come in, || Come near together, you escaped of the nations, || They have not known, || Who are lifting up the wood of their carved image, || And praying to a god [that] does not save. 21 Declare, and bring near, || Indeed, they take counsel together, || Who has proclaimed this from of old? [Who] has declared it from that time? Is it not I—Yhwh? And there is no other god besides Me, || A God righteous and saving, there is none except Me. 22 Turn to Me, and be saved, all the ends of the earth, || For I [am] God, and there is none else. 23 I have sworn by Myself, || A word has gone out from My mouth in righteousness, || And it does not return, || That to Me, every knee bow, every tongue swears. 24 Only in Yhwh, one has said, || Do I have righteousness and strength, || He comes to Him, || And all those displeased with Him are ashamed. 25 In Yhwh are all the seed of Israel justified, || And they boast themselves."

CHAPTER 46

1 Bel has bowed down, Nebo is stooping, || Their idols have been for the beast and for livestock, || Your burdens are loaded, a burden to the weary. 2 They have stooped, they have bowed together, || They have not been able to deliver the burden, || And have gone into captivity themselves. 3 "Listen to Me, O house of Jacob, || And all the remnant of Israel, || Who are borne from the belly, || Who are carried from the womb, 4 Even to old age, I [am] He, and to grey hairs I carry, || I made, and I bear, indeed, I carry and deliver. 5 To whom do you liken Me, and make equal? And compare Me, that we

may be like? 6 They are pouring out gold from a bag, || And they weigh silver on the beam, || They hire a refiner, and he makes it a god, || They fall down, indeed, they bow themselves. 7 They lift him up on the shoulder, || They carry him, and cause him to rest in his place, || And he stands, he does not move from his place, || Indeed, one cries to him, and he does not answer, || He does not save him from his adversity. 8 Remember this, and show yourselves men, || Turn [it] back, O transgressors, to the heart. 9 Remember former things of old, || For I [am] Mighty, and there is none else, || God—and there is none like Me. 10 Declaring the latter end from the beginning, || And from of old that which has not been done, || Saying, My counsel stands, || And all My delight I do. 11 Calling a ravenous bird from the east, || The man of My counsel from a far land, || Indeed, I have spoken, indeed, I bring it in, || I have formed [it], indeed, I do it. 12 Listen to Me, you mighty in heart, || Who are far from righteousness. 13 I have brought My righteousness near, || It is not far off, || And My salvation—it does not linger, || And I have given salvation in Zion, || For Israel My glory!"

CHAPTER 47

1 "Come down, and sit on the dust, || O virgin daughter of Babylon, || Sit on the earth, there is no throne, || O daughter of the Chaldeans, || For they no longer cry to you, || O tender and delicate one. 2 Take millstones, and grind flour, || Remove your veil, draw up the skirt, || Uncover the leg, pass over the floods. 3 Your nakedness is revealed, indeed, your reproach is seen, || I take vengeance, and I do not meet a man." 4 Our redeemer [is] Yhwh of Hosts, || His Name [is] the Holy One of Israel. 5 "Sit silent, and go into darkness, || O daughter of the Chaldeans, || For they no longer cry to you, Mistress of kingdoms. 6 I have been angry against My people, I have defiled My inheritance || And I give them into your hand, || You have not appointed mercies for them, || You have made your yoke very heavy on the aged, 7 And you say, I am mistress for all time, || While you have not laid these things to your heart, || You have not remembered the latter end of it. 8 And now, hear this, O luxurious one, || Who is sitting confidently—Who is saying in her heart, I [am], and none else, || I do not sit [as] a widow, nor know bereavement. 9 And these two things come to you, || In a moment, in one day: childlessness and widowhood, || They have come on you according to their perfection, || In the multitude of your sorceries, || In the exceeding might of your charms. 10 And you are confident in your wickedness, || You have said, There is none seeing me, || Your wisdom and your knowledge, || It is turning you back, || And you say in your heart, I [am], and none else. 11 And evil has come in on you, || You do not know its rising, || And disaster falls on you, || You are not able to pacify it, || And desolation comes on you suddenly, || You do not know. 12 Now stand in your charms, || And in the multitude of your sorceries, || In which you have labored from your youth, || It may be you are able to profit, || It may be you terrify! 13 You have been wearied in the multitude of your counsels, || Now stand up and let them save you—The charmers of the heavens, || Those looking on the stars, || Those teaching concerning the months—From those things that come on you! 14 Behold, they have been as stubble! Fire has burned them, || They do not deliver themselves from the power of the flame, || There is not a coal to warm them, a light to sit before it. 15 So they have been to you with whom you have labored, || Your merchants from your youth, || They have each wandered to his passage, || None is saving you!"

CHAPTER 48

1 "Hear this, O house of Jacob, || Who are called by the name of Israel, || And from the waters of Judah came out, || Who are swearing by the Name of Yhwh, || And make mention of the God of Israel, || Not in truth nor in righteousness. 2 For they have been called from the Holy City, || And been supported on the God of Israel, || Yhwh of Hosts [is] His Name. 3 I declared the former things from that time, || And they have gone forth from My mouth, || And I proclaim them, || Suddenly I have done, and it comes. 4 From My knowing that you are

obstinate, || And your neck—a sinew of iron, || And your forehead—bronze, **5** And from that time I declare [it] to you, || Before it comes, I have caused you to hear, || Lest you say, My idol has done them, || And my carved image, || And my molten image commanded them. **6** You have heard, see the whole of it, || And you, do you not declare? I have caused you to hear new things from this time, || And things reserved that you did not know. **7** Now they have been produced and not from that time, || Indeed, before the day, and you have not heard them, || Lest you say, Behold, I have known them. **8** Indeed, you have not heard, || Indeed, you have not known, || Indeed, your ear has not opened from that time, || For I have known you deal treacherously, || And [are] a transgressor from the belly, || One is crying to you. **9** I defer My anger for My Name's sake, || And [for] My praise I restrain for you, || So as not to cut you off. **10** Behold, I have refined you, and not with silver, || I have chosen you in a furnace of affliction. **11** For My sake, for My own sake, I do [it], || For how is it defiled? And I do not give My glory to another. **12** Listen to me, O Jacob, and Israel, My called one, || I [am] He, || I [am] first, and I [am] last; **13** Also, My hand has founded earth, || And My right hand stretched out the heavens, || I am calling to them, they stand together. **14** Be gathered, all of you, and hear, || Who among them declared these things? Yhwh has loved him, || He does His pleasure on Babylon, || And His arm [is on] the Chaldeans. **15** I have spoken, indeed, I have called him, I have brought him in, || And he has made his way prosperous. **16** Come near to Me, hear this, || I have not spoken in secret from the beginning, || From the time of its being, I [am] there, || And now Lord Yhwh has sent Me, and His Spirit." **17** Thus said Yhwh, your Redeemer, || The Holy One of Israel: "I [am] your God Yhwh, teaching you to profit, || Causing you to tread in the way you go. **18** O that you had attended to My commands, || Then your peace is as a river, || And your righteousness as billows of the sea, **19** And your seed is as sand, || And the offspring of your bowels as gravel, || His name would not be cut off nor destroyed before Me." **20** Go out from Babylon, flee from the Chaldeans, || Declare with a voice of singing, || Cause this to be heard, || Bring it forth to the end of the earth, || Say, "Yhwh has redeemed His servant Jacob." **21** And they have not thirsted in wastelands, || He has caused them to go on, || He has caused waters from a rock to flow to them, || Indeed, he cleaves a rock, and waters flow. **22** "There is no peace," said Yhwh, "for the wicked!"

CHAPTER 49

1 Listen, O islands, to Me, || And attend, O peoples, from afar, || Yhwh has called Me from the womb, || From the bowels of My mother || He has made mention of My Name. **2** And He makes My mouth as a sharp sword, || He has hid Me in the shadow of His hand, || And He makes Me for a clear arrow, || He has hid Me in His quiver. **3** And He says to me, "You are My servant, O Israel, || In whom I beautify Myself." **4** And I said, "I labored in vain, || I consumed my power for emptiness and vanity, || But my judgment [is] with Yhwh, || And my wage with my God." **5** "And now," said Yhwh, who is forming Me from the belly—His Servant, || To bring Jacob back to Him || (Though Israel is not gathered, || Yet I am honored in the eyes of Yhwh, || And My God has been My strength). **6** And He says, "It has been a light thing || That You are My Servant || To raise up the tribes of Jacob, || And to bring back the preserved of Israel, || And I have given You for a light to the nations, || To be My salvation to the end of the earth." **7** Thus said Yhwh, Redeemer of Israel, His Holy One, || To the despised in soul, || To the detested of a nation, || To the Servant of rulers: "Kings see, and have risen, princes, and worship, || For the sake of Yhwh, who is faithful, || The Holy of Israel, and He chooses You." **8** Thus said Yhwh: "In a time of good pleasure I answered You, || And in a day of salvation I helped You, || And I keep You, and give You, || For a covenant of the people, || To establish the earth, || To cause to inherit desolate inheritances. **9** To say to the bound, Go out, || To those in darkness, Be uncovered. They feed on the ways, || And their pasture is in all high places. **10** They do not hunger, nor thirst, || Nor do mirage and sun strike them, || For He who is pitying them leads them, || And tends them by fountains of waters. **11** And I have made all My mountains for a way, || And My highways are lifted up. **12** Behold, these come in from afar, || And behold, these from the north, and from the sea, || And these from the land of Sinim." **13** Sing, O heavens, and rejoice,

O earth, || And break forth, O mountains, with singing, || For Yhwh has comforted His people, || And He pities His afflicted ones. **14** And Zion says, "Yhwh has forsaken me, || And my Lord has forgotten me." **15** "Does a woman forget her suckling, || The loved one—the son of her womb? Indeed, these forget—but I do not forget you. **16** Behold, I have carved you on the palms of the hand, || Your walls [are] continually before Me. **17** Those building you have hurried, || Those destroying you, and laying you waste, go out from you. **18** Lift up your eyes, [look] around and see, || All of them have been gathered, || They have come to you. [As] I live," a declaration of Yhwh! "Surely you put on all of them as an ornament, || And you bind them on like a bride. **19** Because your ruins, and your desolate places, || And the land of your ruins, || Are now surely restricted because of inhabitants, || And those consuming you have been far off. **20** Again the sons of your bereavement say in your ears: The place is too narrow for me, || Come near to me—and I dwell. **21** And you have said in your heart: Who has begotten these for me? And I [am] bereaved and barren, || A captive, and turned aside, || And who has nourished these? Behold, I was left by myself, these—where [are] they from?" **22** Thus said Lord Yhwh: "Behold, I lift up My hand to nations, || And I raise up My ensign to peoples, || And they have brought your sons in the bosom, || And your daughters are carried on the shoulder. **23** And kings have been your nursing fathers, || And their princesses—your nursing mothers; Face to the earth—they bow down to you, || And they lick up the dust of your feet, || And you have known that I [am] Yhwh, || That those expecting Me are not ashamed." **24** Is prey taken from the mighty? And the captive of the righteous delivered? **25** For thus said Yhwh: "Even the captive of the mighty is taken, || And the prey of the terrible is delivered, || And I strive with your striver, and I save your sons. **26** And I have caused your oppressors to eat their own flesh, || And they drink their own blood as new wine, || And all flesh has known that I, Yhwh, || Your Savior, and your Redeemer, || [Am] the Mighty One of Jacob!"

CHAPTER 50

1 Thus said Yhwh: "Where [is] this—the bill of your mother's divorce, || Whom I sent away? Or to which of My creditors have I sold you? Behold, you have been sold for your iniquities, || And for your transgressions || Your mother has been sent away. **2** Why have I come, and there is no one? I called, and there is none answering, || Has My hand been at all short of redemption? And is there not power in Me to deliver? Behold, by My rebuke I dry up a sea, || I make rivers a wilderness, || Their fish stink, for there is no water, || And die with thirst. **3** I clothe the heavens [with] blackness, || And I make their covering sackcloth." **4** Lord Yhwh has given to Me || The tongue of taught ones, || To know to aid the weary [by] a word, || He awakens [Me] morning by morning, || He awakens [My] ear to hear as taught ones. **5** Lord Yhwh opened My ear, || And I did not rebel—I did not move backward. **6** I have given My back to those striking, || And My cheeks to those plucking out, || I did not hide My face from shame and spitting. **7** And Lord Yhwh gives help to Me, || Therefore I have not been ashamed, || Therefore I have set My face as a flint, || And I know that I am not ashamed. **8** Near [is] He who is justifying Me, || Who contends with Me? We stand together, who [is] My opponent? Let him come near to Me. **9** Behold, Lord Yhwh gives help to Me, || Who [is] he that declares Me wicked? Behold, all of them wear out as a garment, || A moth eats them. **10** "Who [is] among you, fearing Yhwh, || Listening to the voice of His Servant, || That has walked in dark places, || And there is no brightness for him? Let him trust in the Name of Yhwh, || And lean on his God. **11** Behold, all you kindling a fire, girding on sparks, || Walk in the light of your fire, || And in the sparks you have caused to burn, || This has been to you from My hand, || You lie down in grief!"

CHAPTER 51

1 "Listen to Me, you pursuing righteousness, || Seeking Yhwh, || Look attentively to the rock—you have been hewn, || And to the hole of the pit—you have been dug. **2** Look attentively to your father Abraham, || And to Sarah—she brings you forth, || For—one—I have called him, || And I bless him, and multiply him." **3** For Yhwh has comforted Zion, || He has comforted all her ruins, || And He sets her wilderness as Eden, || And her desert as a garden of Yhwh, || Joy, indeed, gladness is found in her, || Confession, and the voice of song. [4] "Attend to Me, O My people, || And, O My nation, give ear to Me. For a law goes out from Me, || And My judgment to the light, || I cause peoples to rest. [5] My righteousness [is] near, || My salvation has gone out, || And My arms judge peoples, || Islands wait on Me, || Indeed, on My arm they wait with hope. [6] Lift up your eyes to the heavens, || And look attentively to the earth beneath, || For the heavens have vanished as smoke, || And the earth wears out as a garment, || And its inhabitants die as gnats, || And My salvation is for all time, || And My righteousness is not broken. [7] Listen to Me, you who know righteousness, || A people in whose heart [is] My law, || Do not fear the reproach of men, || And do not be frightened of their reviling, [8] For a moth eats them as a garment, || And a worm eats them as wool, || And My righteousness is for all time, || And My salvation from generation to generation." [9] Awake, awake, put on strength, O arm of Yhwh, || Awake, as [in] days of old, generations of the ages, || Are You not it that is hewing down Rahab, || Piercing a dragon? [10] Are You not it that is drying up a sea, || Waters of a great deep? That has made deep places of a sea || A way for the passing of the redeemed? [11] And the ransomed of Yhwh return, || And they have come to Zion with singing, || And continuous joy [is] on their head, || They attain gladness and joy, || Sorrow and sighing have fled away, [12] "I [am] He who comforts you, || Who [are] you—and you are afraid of man? he dies! And of the son of man—he is made [like] grass! [13] And you forget Yhwh your Maker, || Who is stretching out the heavens, and founding earth, || And you continually fear all the day, || Because of the fury of the oppressor, || As he has prepared to destroy. And where [is] the fury of the oppressor? [14] A wanderer has hurried to be loosed, || And he does not die in the pit, || And his bread is not lacking. [15] And I [am] your God Yhwh, || Quieting the sea when its billows roar, || Yhwh of Hosts [is] His Name. [16] And I put My words in your mouth, || And have covered you with the shadow of My hand, || To plant the heavens, and to found earth, || And to say to Zion, You [are] My people." [17] Stir yourself, stir yourself, rise, Jerusalem, || You who have drunk from the hand of Yhwh || The cup of His fury, || The goblet, the cup of trembling, you have drunk, || You have wrung out. [18] There is not a leader to her || Out of all the sons she has borne, || And there is none laying hold on her hand || Out of all the sons she has nourished. [19] These two are meeting you, || Who is moved for you? Spoiling and destruction, famine and sword! By whom do I comfort you? [20] Your sons have been wrapped up, they have lain down, || At the head of all out places, as an antelope [in] a dragnet, || They are full of the fury of Yhwh, || The rebuke of Your God. [21] Therefore, please hear this, || O afflicted and drunken one, and not with wine, [22] Thus said your Lord Yhwh, and your God, || He pleads [for] His people: "Behold, I have taken the cup of trembling out of your hand, || The goblet, the cup of My fury, || You do not add to drink it anymore. [23] And I have put it into the hand of those afflicting you, || Who have said to your soul, || Bow down, and we pass over, || And you make your body as the earth, || And as the street to those passing by!"

CHAPTER 52

[1] Awake, awake, put on your strength, O Zion, || Put on the garments of your beauty, Jerusalem—the Holy City; For the uncircumcised and unclean no longer enter into you again. [2] Shake yourself from dust, arise, sit, O Jerusalem, || Bands of your neck have loosed themselves, || O captive daughter of Zion. [3] For thus said Yhwh: "You have been sold for nothing, || And you are redeemed without money." [4] For thus said Lord Yhwh: "My people went down at first || To Egypt to sojourn there, || And Asshur—he has oppressed it for nothing. [5] And now, what [have] I here," || A declaration of Yhwh, || "That My people are taken for nothing? Its rulers cause howling," || A declaration of Yhwh, || "And My Name is continually despised all the day. [6] Therefore My people know My Name, || Therefore, in that day, || Surely I [am] He who is speaking, behold Me." [7] How lovely on the mountains, || Have been the feet of one proclaiming tidings, || Sounding peace, proclaiming good tidings, || Sounding salvation, || Saying to Zion, "Your God has reigned." [8] The voice of your watchmen! They have lifted up the voice, together they cry aloud, || Because they see eye to eye, || In Yhwh's turning back [to] Zion. [9] Break forth, sing

together, || O ruins of Jerusalem, || For Yhwh has comforted His people, || He has redeemed Jerusalem. [10] Yhwh has made His holy arm bare || Before the eyes of all the nations, || And all the ends of the earth have seen || The salvation of our God. [11] Turn aside, turn aside, go out from there, || Do not touch the unclean, || Go out from her midst, || Be pure, who are carrying the weapons of Yhwh. [12] For you do not go out in haste, || Indeed, you do not go on with flight, || For Yhwh [is] going before you, || And the God of Israel [is] gathering you! [13] "Behold, My Servant acts wisely, || He is high, and has been lifted up, || And has been very high." [14] As many have been astonished at You || (His appearance so marred by man, || And His form by sons of men), [15] So He sprinkles many nations. Kings shut their mouth concerning Him, || For that which was not recounted to them they have seen, || And that which they had not heard they have understood!

CHAPTER 53

[1] Who has given credence to that which we heard? And the arm of Yhwh, || On whom has it been revealed? [2] Indeed, He comes up as a tender plant before Him, || And as a root out of dry land, || He has no form or splendor when we observe Him, || Nor appearance, that we desire Him. [3] He is despised, and left of men, || A Man of pains, and acquainted with sickness, || And as one hiding the face from us, || He is despised, and we did not esteem Him. [4] Surely, He has borne our sicknesses, || And our pains—He has carried them, || And we have esteemed Him [as] plagued, struck of God, and afflicted. [5] And He is pierced for our transgressions, bruised for our iniquities, || The discipline of our peace [is] on Him, || And by His scourging we are healed. [6] All of us, like sheep, have wandered, || Man has turned to his own way, || And Yhwh has laid on Him the punishment of us all. [7] It has been exacted, and He has answered, || And He does not open His mouth, || He is brought as a lamb to the slaughter, || And as a sheep before its shearers is silent, || So He does not open His mouth. [8] By restraint and by judgment He has been taken, || And of His generation who meditates, || That He has been cut off from the land of the living? He is plagued by the transgression of My people, [9] And He appoints His grave with the wicked, || And with the rich at His death, || Because He has done no violence, || Nor [is] deceit in His mouth. [10] And Yhwh has delighted to crush Him, || He has made Him sick; If His soul makes an offering for guilt, || He sees [His] seed—He prolongs [His] days, || And the pleasure of Yhwh prospers in His hand. [11] Of the labor of His soul He sees—He is satisfied, || Through His knowledge My Righteous Servant gives righteousness to many, || And He bears their iniquities. [12] Therefore I give a portion to Him among the many, || And He apportions spoil with the mighty, || Because that He exposed His soul to death, || And He was numbered with transgressors, || And He has borne the sin of many, || And He intercedes for transgressors.

CHAPTER 54

[1] "Sing, O barren, she [who] has not borne! Break forth with singing, and cry aloud, || She [who] has not brought forth! For more [are] the sons of the desolate, || Than the sons of the married one," said Yhwh. [2] "Enlarge the place of your tent, || And they stretch out the curtains of your dwelling places, || Do not restrain—lengthen your cords, || And make your pins strong. [3] For you break forth right and left, || And nations possess your seed, [4] And they cause desolate cities to be inhabited. Do not fear, for you are not ashamed, || Nor blush, for you are not confounded, || For you forget the shame of your youth, || And the reproach of your widowhood || You do not remember anymore. [5] For your Maker [is] your husband, || Yhwh of Hosts [is] His Name, || And your Redeemer [is] the Holy One of Israel, || He is called God of all the earth. [6] For as a woman forsaken and grieved in spirit, || Yhwh has called you, || Even a youthful wife when she is refused," said your God. [7] "In a small moment I have forsaken you, || And in great mercies I gather you, [8] In overflowing wrath I hid My face [for] a moment from you, || And in perpetual kindness I have loved you, || Said your Redeemer—Yhwh! [9] For this [is as] the days of Noah to Me, || In that I have sworn that the waters of Noah || Do not pass over the earth again—So I have sworn, || Wrath is not on you, || Nor rebuke against you. [10] For the mountains

depart, and the hills remove, || And My kindness does not depart from you, || And the covenant of My peace does not remove," || Says Yhwh, your loving one. ¹¹ "O afflicted, storm-tossed, not comforted, || Behold, I am laying your stones with cement, || And have founded you with sapphires, ¹² And have made your pinnacles of agate, || And your gates of carbuncle stones, || And all your border of stones of delight, ¹³ And all your sons are taught of Yhwh, || And the peace of your sons [is] abundant. ¹⁴ You establish yourself in righteousness, || Be far from oppression, for you do not fear, || And from ruin, for it does not come near to you. ¹⁵ Behold, he diligently assembles without My desire, || Whoever has assembled near you falls by you! ¹⁶ Behold, I have created an artisan, || Blowing on a fire of coals, || And bringing out an instrument for his work, || And I have created a destroyer to destroy. ¹⁷ No weapon formed against you prospers, || And every tongue rising against you, || You condemn in judgment. This [is] the inheritance of the servants of Yhwh, || And their righteousness from Me," a declaration of Yhwh!

CHAPTER 55

¹ "Behold, every thirsty one, || Come to the waters, || And he who has no money, || Come, buy and eat, || Indeed, come, buy wine and milk || Without money and without price. ² Why do you weigh money for that which is not bread? And your labor for that which is not for satiety? Listen diligently to Me, and eat good, || And your soul delights itself in fatness. ³ Incline your ear, and come to Me, || Hear, and your soul lives, || And I make a perpetual covenant for you, || The kind blessings of David that are steadfast. ⁴ Behold, I have given him [as] a witness to peoples, || A leader and commander to peoples. ⁵ Behold, a nation you do not know, you call, || And a nation who does not know you runs to you, || For the sake of your God Yhwh, || And for the Holy One of Israel, || Because He has beautified you." ⁶ Seek Yhwh while He may be found, || Call Him while He is near, ⁷ Let the wicked forsake his way, || And the man of iniquity his thoughts, || And he returns to Yhwh, || And He pities him, || And to our God, || For He multiplies to pardon. ⁸ "For My thoughts [are] not your thoughts, || Nor your ways My ways," || A declaration of Yhwh, ⁹ "For [as] high [as] the heavens have been above the earth, || So high have been My ways above your ways, || And My thoughts above your thoughts. ¹⁰ For as the shower comes down, || And the snow from the heavens, || And does not return there, || But has watered the earth, || And has caused it to yield, and to spring up, || And has given seed to the sower, and bread to the eater, ¹¹ So is My word that goes out of My mouth, || It does not return to Me empty, || But has done that which I desired, || And prosperously effected that [for] which I sent it. ¹² For you go forth with joy, || And you are brought in with peace, || The mountains and the hills || Break forth before you [with] singing, || And all trees of the field clap the hand. ¹³ Instead of the thorn comes up fir, || Instead of the brier comes up myrtle, || And it has been to Yhwh for a name, || For a perpetual sign—it is not cut off!"

CHAPTER 56

¹ Thus said Yhwh: "Keep judgment, and do righteousness, || For My salvation [is] near to come, || And My righteousness to be revealed." ² O the blessedness of a man who does this, || And of a son of man who keeps hold on it, || Keeping the Sabbath from defiling it, || And keeping his hand from doing any evil. ³ Do not let a son of the stranger speak, || Who is joined to Yhwh, saying, "Yhwh certainly separates me from His people." Nor let the eunuch say, "Behold, I am a dried-up tree," ⁴ For thus said Yhwh: "To the eunuchs who keep My Sabbaths, || And have fixed on that which I desired, || And are keeping hold on My covenant: ⁵ I have given to them in My house, || And within My walls a station and a name, || Better than sons and than daughters, || I give a continuous name to him || That is not cut off. ⁶ And sons of the stranger, who are joined to Yhwh, || To serve Him, and to love the Name of Yhwh, || To be for servants to Him, || All keeping from defiling the Sabbath, || And those keeping hold on My covenant, ⁷ I have brought them to My holy mountain, || And caused them to rejoice in My house of prayer, || Their burnt-offerings and their sacrifices || [Are] for a pleasing thing on My altar, || For My house is

called a house of prayer for all the peoples." ⁸ A declaration of Lord Yhwh, || Who is gathering the outcasts of Israel: "Again I gather to him—to his gathered ones." ⁹ Every beast of the field, || Come to devour, every beast in the forest. ¹⁰ His watchmen [are] blind—all of them, || They have not known, || All of them [are] mute dogs, they are not able to bark, || Dozing, lying down, loving to slumber. ¹¹ And the dogs [are] strong of desire, || They have not known sufficiency, || And they [are] shepherds! They have not known understanding, || All of them turned to their own way, || Each to his dishonest gain from his quarter: ¹² "Come, I take wine, || And we drink, gulp strong drink, || And tomorrow has been as this day, || Great—exceedingly abundant!"

CHAPTER 57

¹ The righteous has perished, || And there is none laying [it] to heart, || And men of kindness are gathered, || Without any considering that from the face of evil || The righteous one is gathered. ² He enters into peace, they rest on their beds, || [Each] is going straightforward. ³ "And you, come near here, || O sons of a sorceress, seed of an adulterer, || Even you commit whoredom. ⁴ Against whom do you sport yourselves? Against whom do you enlarge the mouth || [And] prolong the tongue? Are you not children of transgression? a false seed? ⁵ Who are inflamed among oaks, under every green tree, || Slaughtering the children in valleys, || Under clefts of the rocks. ⁶ Your portion [is] among the smooth things of a brook, || They [are] your lot, || You have also poured out an oblation to them, || You have caused a present to ascend, || Am I comforted in these things? ⁷ On a mountain, high and exalted, || You have set your bed, || You have also gone up there to make a sacrifice. ⁸ And behind the door, and the post, || You have set up your memorial, || For you have removed from Me, and go up, || You have enlarged your bed, || And cut [a covenant] with them, || You have loved their bed, the station you saw, ⁹ And go joyfully to the king in ointment, || And multiply your perfumes, || And send your ambassadors far off, || And humble yourself to Sheol. ¹⁰ You have labored in the greatness of your way, || You have not said, It is desperate. You have found the life of your hand, || Therefore you have not been sick. ¹¹ And of whom have you been afraid, and fear, || That you lie, and have not remembered Me? You have not laid [it] to your heart, || Am I not silent, even from of old? And you do not fear Me? ¹² I declare your righteousness, and your works, || And they do not profit you. ¹³ When you cry, let your gatherings deliver you, || And wind carries all of them away, || Vanity takes away, || And whoever is trusting in Me inherits the land, || And possesses My holy mountain." ¹⁴ And He has said, "Raise up, raise up, prepare a way, || Lift a stumbling-block out of the way of My people." ¹⁵ For thus said the high and exalted One, || Inhabiting eternity, and His Name [is] holy: "I dwell in the high and holy place, || And with the bruised and humble of spirit, || To revive the spirit of the humble, || And to revive the heart of bruised ones, ¹⁶ For I do not strive for all time, nor am I angry forever, || For the spirit is feeble before Me, || And the souls I have made. ¹⁷ For the iniquity of his dishonest gain, || I have been angry, and I strike him, || Hiding—and am angry, || And he goes on turning back in the way of his heart. ¹⁸ I have seen his ways, and I heal him, indeed, I lead him, || And repay comforts to him and to his mourning ones. ¹⁹ Producing the fruit of the lips, || Peace, peace, to the far off, and to the near, || And I have healed him," said Yhwh. ²⁰ And the wicked [are] as the driven-out sea, || For it is not able to rest, || And its waters cast out filth and mire. ²¹ "There is no peace," said my God, "for the wicked!"

CHAPTER 58

¹ "Call with the throat, do not restrain, lift up your voice as a horn, || And declare to My people their transgression, || And to the house of Jacob their sins; ² They seek Me day by day, || And they desire the knowledge of My ways, || As a nation that has done righteousness, || And has not forsaken the judgment of its God, || They ask of Me judgments of righteousness, || They desire the drawing near of God: ³ Why have we fasted, and You have not seen? We have afflicted our soul, and You do not know. Behold, you find pleasure in the day of your fast, || And exact all your laborers. ⁴ Behold, you fast for strife and

debate, || And to strike with the fist of wickedness, || You do not fast as [this] day, || To sound your voice in the high place. ⁵ Is this like the fast that I choose? The day of a man's afflicting his soul? To bow his head as a reed, || And spread-out sackcloth and ashes? Do you call this a fast, || And a desirable day—to Yhwh? ⁶ Is this not the fast that I chose—To loosen the bands of wickedness, || To shake off the burdens of the yoke, || And to send out the oppressed free, || And draw off every yoke? ⁷ Is it not to deal your bread to the hungry, || And bring home the wandering poor, || That you see the naked and cover him, || And do not hide yourself from your own flesh? ⁸ Then your light breaks forth as the dawn, || And your health springs up in haste, || Your righteousness has gone before you, || The glory of Yhwh gathers you. ⁹ Then you call, and Yhwh answers, || You cry, and He says, Behold Me. If you turn aside the yoke from your midst, || The sending forth of the finger, || And the speaking of vanity, ¹⁰ And bring out your soul to the hungry, || And satisfy the afflicted soul, || Then your light has risen in the darkness, || And your thick darkness [is] as noon. ¹¹ And Yhwh continually leads you, || And has satisfied your soul in drought, || And He arms your bones, || And you have been as a watered garden, || And as an outlet of waters, whose waters do not lie. ¹² And they have built the ancient ruins from you, || You raise up the foundations of many generations, || And one calls you, Repairer of the breach, || Restorer of paths to rest in. ¹³ If you turn your foot from the Sabbath, || [From] doing your own pleasure on My holy day, || And have cried to the Sabbath, A delight, || To the holy of Yhwh, Honored, || And have honored it, without doing your own ways, || Without finding your own pleasure, || And speaking a word. ¹⁴ Then you delight yourself on Yhwh, || And I have caused you to ride on high places of earth, || And have caused you to eat the inheritance of your father Jacob, || For the mouth of Yhwh has spoken!"

CHAPTER 59

¹ Behold, the hand of Yhwh || Has not been shortened from saving, || Nor His ear heavy from hearing. ² But your iniquities have been separating || Between you and your God, || And your sins have hidden || The Presence from you—from hearing. ³ For your hands have been defiled with blood, || And your fingers with iniquity, || Your lips have spoken falsehood, || Your tongue mutters perverseness. ⁴ There is none calling in righteousness, || And there is none pleading in faithfulness, || Trusting on emptiness, and speaking falsehood, || Conceiving perverseness, and bearing iniquity. ⁵ They have hatched eggs of a viper, || And weave webs of a spider, || Whoever is eating their eggs dies, and the crushed hatches a viper. ⁶ Their webs do not become a garment, || Nor do they cover themselves with their works, || Their works [are] works of iniquity, || And a deed of violence [is] in their hands. ⁷ Their feet run to evil, || And they hurry to shed innocent blood, || Their thoughts [are] thoughts of iniquity, || Spoiling and destruction [are] in their highways. ⁸ They have not known a way of peace, || And there is no judgment in their paths, || They have made their paths perverse for themselves, || None treading in it has known peace. ⁹ Therefore judgment has been far from us, || And righteousness does not reach us, || We wait for light, and behold, darkness, || For brightness—in thick darkness we go, ¹⁰ We feel [for] the wall like the blind, || Indeed, we feel as without eyes, || We have stumbled at noon as at twilight, || In desolate places as the dead. ¹¹ We make a noise as bears—all of us, || And we coo severely as doves; We wait for judgment, and there is none, || For salvation—it has been far from us. ¹² For our transgressions have been multiplied before You, || And our sins have testified against us, || For our transgressions [are] with us, || And our iniquities—we have known them. ¹³ Transgressing, and lying against Yhwh, || And removing from after our God, || Speaking oppression and apostasy, || Conceiving and uttering from the heart || Words of falsehood. ¹⁴ And judgment is removed backward, || And righteousness stands far off, || For truth has been feeble in the street, || And straightforwardness is not able to enter, ¹⁵ And the truth is lacking, || And whoever is turning aside from evil, || Is making himself a spoil. And Yhwh sees, and it is evil in His eyes, || That there is no judgment. ¹⁶ And He sees that there is no man, || And is astonished that there is no intercessor, || And His own arm gives salvation to Him, || And His righteousness—it sustained Him. ¹⁷ And He puts on righteousness as a

breastplate, || And a helmet of salvation on His head, || And He puts on garments of vengeance [for] clothing, || And is covered, as [with] an upper-robe, [with] zeal. ¹⁸ According to deeds—so He repays. Fury to His adversaries, [their] deed to His enemies, || To the islands He repays [their] deed. ¹⁹ And from the west they fear the Name of Yhwh, || And from the rising of the sun—His glory, || When an adversary comes in as a flood, || The Spirit of Yhwh has raised an ensign against him. ²⁰ "And the Redeemer has come to Zion, || Even to captives of transgression in Jacob," || A declaration of Yhwh. ²¹ "And I—this [is] My covenant with them," said Yhwh, "My Spirit that [is] on you, || And My words that I have put in your mouth, || Do not depart from your mouth, || And from the mouth of your seed, || And from the mouth of your seed's seed," said Yhwh, "From now on, even for all time!"

CHAPTER 60

¹ Arise, shine, for your light has come, || And the glory of Yhwh has risen on you. ² For behold, the darkness covers the earth, || And thick darkness the peoples, || And Yhwh rises on you, || And His glory is seen on you. ³ And nations have come to your light, || And kings to the brightness of your rising. ⁴ "Lift up your eyes around and see, || All of them have been gathered, they have come to you, || Your sons come from afar, || And your daughters are supported on the side. ⁵ Then you see, and have become bright, || And your heart has been afraid and enlarged, || For the multitude of the sea turn to you, || The forces of nations come to you. ⁶ A multitude of camels covers you, || Dromedaries of Midian and Ephah, || All of them from Sheba come, || They carry gold and frankincense, || And they proclaim the praises of Yhwh. ⁷ All the flock of Kedar are gathered to you, || The rams of Nebaloth serve you, || They ascend My altar for acceptance, || And I beautify the house of My beauty. ⁸ Who [are] these—they fly as a thick cloud, || And as doves to their windows? ⁹ Surely islands wait for Me, || And ships of Tarshish first, || To bring your sons from afar, || Their silver and their gold with them, || To the Name of your God Yhwh, || And to the Holy One of Israel, || Because He has beautified you. ¹⁰ And sons of a stranger have built your walls, || And their kings serve you, || For in My wrath I have struck you, || And in My good pleasure I have pitied you. ¹¹ And your gates have continually opened, || They are not shut by day and by night, || To bring the force of nations to you, || Even their kings are led. ¹² For the nation and the kingdom that does not serve you perishes, || Indeed, the nations are utterly desolated. ¹³ The glory of Lebanon comes to you, || Fir, pine, and box together, || To beautify the place of My sanctuary, || And I make the place of My feet honorable. ¹⁴ And the sons of those afflicting you || Have come to you, bowing down, || And all despising you || Have bowed themselves to the soles of your feet, || And they have cried to you: The City of Yhwh, || Zion of the Holy One of Israel! ¹⁵ Instead of your being forsaken and hated, || And none passing through, || I have made you for a continuous excellence, || A joy of generation and generation. ¹⁶ And you have sucked the milk of nations, || Indeed, you suckle the breast of kings, || And you have known that I, Yhwh, || Your Savior, and Your Redeemer, || [Am] the Mighty One of Jacob. ¹⁷ Instead of the bronze I bring in gold, || And instead of the iron I bring in silver, || And instead of the wood bronze, || And instead of the stone iron, || And I have made your inspection peace, || And your exactors righteousness. ¹⁸ Violence is not heard in your land anymore, || Spoiling and destruction in your borders, || And you have called your walls Salvation, || And your gates Praise. ¹⁹ The sun is no longer your light by day, || And for brightness the moon does not give light to you, || And Yhwh has become to you || A continuous light, and your God your beauty. ²⁰ Your sun goes in no more, || And your moon is not removed, || For Yhwh becomes a continuous light to you. And the days of your mourning have been completed. ²¹ And all your people [are] righteous, || They possess the earth for all time, || A branch of My planting, || A work of My hands, to be beautified. ²² The little one becomes a chief, || And the small one a mighty nation, || I, Yhwh, hurry it in its own time!"

CHAPTER 61

¹ "[The] Spirit of Lord Yhwh [is] on Me, || Because Yhwh

anointed Me || To proclaim tidings to the humble, || He sent Me to bind the broken of heart, || To proclaim liberty to the captives, || And an opening of bands to [those] bound. **2** To proclaim the year of the favor of Yhwh, || And the day of vengeance of our God, || To comfort all mourners. **3** To appoint to mourners in Zion, || To give to them beauty instead of ashes, || The oil of joy instead of mourning, || A covering of praise for a faded spirit, || And He is calling to them, Trees of righteousness, || The planting of Yhwh—to be beautified." **4** And they have built the ancient ruins, || They raise up the desolations of the ancients, || And they have renewed ruined cities, || The desolations of generation and generation. **5** And strangers have stood and fed your flock, || And the sons of a foreigner || [Are] your farmers and your vinedressers. **6** And you are called priests of Yhwh, || It is said of you [that you are] ministers of our God, || You consume the strength of nations, || And you boast yourselves in their glory. **7** Instead of your shame—double [honor], || And [instead of] confusion, || They rejoice in their portion, || Therefore they take possession in their land a second time, || Continuous joy [is] for them. **8** "For I [am] Yhwh, loving judgment, || Hating plunder for a burnt-offering, || And I have given their wage in truth, || And I make a perpetual covenant for them. **9** And their seed has been known among the nations, || And their offspring in the midst of the peoples, || All their beholders acknowledge them, || For they [are] a seed Yhwh has blessed." **10** I greatly rejoice in Yhwh, || My soul rejoices in my God, || For He clothed me with garments of salvation, || [And] covered me with a robe of righteousness, || As a bridegroom prepares ornaments, || And as a bride puts on her jewels. **11** For as the earth brings forth her shoots, || And as a garden causes its sown things to shoot up, || So Lord Yhwh causes righteousness and praise || To shoot up before all the nations!

CHAPTER 62

1 For Zion's sake I am not silent, || And for Jerusalem's sake I do not rest, || Until her righteousness goes out as brightness, || And her salvation burns as a torch. **2** And nations have seen your righteousness, || And all kings your glory, || And He is giving a new name to you, || That the mouth of Yhwh defines. **3** And you have been a crown of beauty in the hand of Yhwh, || And a turban of royalty in the hand of your God, **4** It is not said of you anymore, "Forsaken!" And of your land it is not said anymore, "Desolate," || For to you is cried, "My delight [is] in her," || And to your land, "Married," || For Yhwh has delighted in you, || And your land is married. **5** For a young man marries a virgin, || Your builders marry you, || With the joy of a bridegroom over a bride, || Your God rejoices over you. **6** "On your walls, O Jerusalem, I have appointed watchmen, || All the day and all the night, || Continually, they are not silent." O you remembering Yhwh, do not keep silence for yourselves, **7** And do not give silence to Him, || Until He establishes, and until He makes Jerusalem a praise in the earth. **8** Yhwh has sworn by His right hand, || Even by the arm of His strength: "I do not give your grain anymore [as] food for your enemies, || Nor do sons of a stranger drink your new wine, || For which you have labored. **9** For those gathering it eat it, and have praised Yhwh, || And those collecting it drink it in My holy courts." **10** Pass on, pass on through the gates, || Prepare the way of the people, || Raise up, raise up the highway, clear it from stones, || Lift up an ensign over the peoples. **11** Behold, Yhwh has proclaimed to the end of the earth: "Say to the daughter of Zion, || Behold, your salvation has come, || Behold, His hire [is] with Him, || And His wage before Him." **12** And they have cried to them, "The People of the Holy One! The Redeemed of Yhwh!" Indeed, to you is called, "The sought out one, a city not forsaken!"

CHAPTER 63

1 Who [is] this coming from Edom? With dyed garments from Bozrah? This that is honorable in His clothing, || Traveling in the abundance of His power? "I, speaking in righteousness, mighty to save." **2** Why [is] Your clothing red? And Your garments as treading in a winepress? **3** "I have trodden a wine vat by Myself, || And of the peoples there is no one with Me, ||

And I tread them in My anger, || And I trample them in My fury, || Their strength is sprinkled on My garments, || And I have defiled all My clothing. **4** For the day of vengeance [is] in My heart, || And the year of My redeemed has come. **5** And I look attentively, and there is none helping, || And I am astonished that there is none supporting, || And My own arm gives salvation to Me. And My wrath—it has supported Me. **6** And I tread down peoples in My anger, || And I make them drunk in My fury, || And I bring down their strength to earth." **7** I make mention of the kind acts of Yhwh, || The praises of Yhwh, || According to all that Yhwh has done for us, || And the abundance of the goodness to the house of Israel, || That He has done for them, || According to His mercies, || And according to the abundance of His kind acts. **8** And He says, "Surely they [are] My people, || Sons—they do not lie," and He is to them for a Savior. **9** In all their distress [He is] no adversary, || And the Messenger of His Presence saved them, || In His love and in His pity He redeemed them, || And He lifts them up, || And carries them all the days of old. **10** And they have been rebellious and have grieved His Holy Spirit, || And He turns to them for an enemy, || He Himself has fought against them. **11** And He remembers the days of old, || Moses—his people. Where [is] He who is bringing them up from the sea, || The shepherd of His flock? Where [is] He who is putting in its midst His Holy Spirit? **12** Leading by the right hand of Moses, the arm of His glory, || Cleaving waters from before them, || To make to Himself a continuous Name. **13** Leading them through the depths, || They do not stumble as a horse in a plain. **14** As a beast goes down into a valley, || The Spirit of Yhwh causes him to rest, || So You have led Your people, || To make to Yourself a glorious Name. **15** Look attentively from the heavens, || And see from Your holy and beautiful habitation, || Where [is] Your zeal and Your might? The multitude of Your bowels and Your mercies—Are they restrained? **16** For You [are] our Father, || For Abraham has not known us, || And Israel does not acknowledge us, || You, O Yhwh, [are] our Father, || Our Redeemer from the Age, [is] Your Name. **17** Why cause us to wander, O Yhwh, from Your ways? You harden our heart from Your fear, || Turn back for Your servants' sake, || The tribes of Your inheritance. **18** For a little while Your holy people possessed, || Our adversaries have trodden down Your sanctuary. **19** We have been from of old, || You have not ruled over them, || Your Name is not called on them!

CHAPTER 64

1 Did You not tear the heavens? You came down, || Mountains flowed from Your presence, **2** (As fire kindles stubble—Fire causes water to boil), || To make Your Name known to Your adversaries, || Nations tremble from Your presence. **3** In Your doing fearful things [that] we do not expect, || You came down, || Mountains flowed from Your presence. **4** Even from antiquity [men] have not heard, || They have not given ear, || Eye has not seen a God except You, || He works for those waiting for Him. **5** You have met with the rejoicer || And the doer of righteousness, || In Your ways they remember You, || Behold, You have been angry when we sin, || By them [is] continuance, and we are saved. **6** And we are as unclean—all of us, || And all our righteous acts [are] as garments of menstruation; And we fade as a leaf—all of us. And our iniquities take us away as wind. **7** And there is none calling on Your Name, || Stirring himself up to lay hold on You, || For You have hid Your face from us, || And You melt us away by our iniquities. **8** And now, O Yhwh, You [are] our Father, || We [are] the clay, and You [are] our Framer, || And the work of Your hand—all of us. **9** Do not be angry, O Yhwh, very severely, || Nor remember iniquity forever, || Behold, look attentively, we implore You, || We [are] all Your people. **10** Your holy cities have been a wilderness, || Zion has been a wilderness, || Jerusalem a desolation. **11** Our holy and our beautiful house, || Where our fathers praised You, || Has become burned with fire, || And all our desirable things have become a ruin. **12** Do You refrain Yourself for these, Yhwh? You are silent, and afflict us very severely!

CHAPTER 65

1 "I have been inquired of by those who did not ask, || I have been found by those who did not seek Me, || I have said,

Behold Me, behold Me, || To a nation not calling on My Name. **2** I have spread out My hands all the day || To an apostate people, || Who are going in the way [that is] not good, || After their own thoughts. **3** The people who are continually provoking Me to anger, || To My face, || Sacrificing in gardens, and making incense on the bricks: **4** Who are dwelling among tombs, || And lodge in reserved places, || Who are eating flesh of the sow, || And a piece of abominations—their vessels. **5** Who are saying, Keep to yourself, do not come near to me, || For I have declared you unholy. These [are] smoke in My anger, || A fire burning all the day. **6** Behold, it is written before Me: I am not silent, but have repaid; And I have repaid into their bosom, **7** Your iniquities, and the iniquities of your fathers together," said Yhwh, "Who have made incense on the mountains, || And have reproached Me on the heights, || And I have measured their former work into their bosom." **8** Thus said Yhwh: "As the new wine is found in the cluster, || And one has said, Do not destroy it for a blessing [is] in it, || So I do for My servants' sake, || Not to destroy the whole. **9** And I have brought out a Seed from Jacob, || And from Judah a Possessor of My mountain, || And My chosen ones possess it, || And My servants dwell there. **10** And Sharon has been for the habitation of a flock, || And the Valley of Achor for the lying down of a herd, || For My people who have sought Me. **11** And you [are] those forsaking Yhwh, || Who are forgetting My holy mountain, || Who are setting a table in array for Gad, || And who are filling a mixture for Meni. **12** And I have numbered you for the sword, || And all of you bow down for slaughter, || Because I called, and you have not answered, || I have spoken, and you have not listened, || And you do evil in My eyes, || And on that which I did not desire—fixed." **13** Therefore, thus said Lord Yhwh: "Behold, My servants eat, and you hunger, || Behold, My servants drink, and you thirst, || Behold, My servants rejoice, and you are ashamed, **14** Behold, My servants sing from joy of heart, || And you cry from pain of heart, || And you howl from breaking of spirit. **15** And you have left your name || For an oath for My chosen ones, || And Lord Yhwh has put you to death, || And He gives another name to His servants; **16** So that he who is blessing himself in the earth, || Blesses himself in the God of faithfulness, || And he who is swearing in the earth, || Swears by the God of faithfulness, || Because the former distresses have been forgotten, || And because they have been hid from My eyes. **17** For behold, I am creating new heavens and a new earth, || And the former things are not remembered, || Nor do they ascend on the heart. **18** But rejoice, and rejoice forever, that I [am] Creator, || For behold, I am creating Jerusalem [to be] a rejoicing, || And her people a joy. **19** And I have rejoiced in Jerusalem, || And have rejoiced in My people, || And the voice of weeping is not heard in her anymore, and the voice of crying. **20** There is not a suckling of [mere] days there anymore, || And an aged man who does not complete his days, || For the youth dies one hundred years old, || And the sinner, one hundred years old, is lightly esteemed. **21** And they have built houses, and inhabited, || And planted vineyards, and eaten their fruit. **22** They do not build, and another inhabit, || They do not plant, and another eat, || For as the days of a tree [are] the days of My people, || And My chosen wear out the work of their hands. **23** They do not labor for a vain thing, || Nor do they bring forth for trouble, || For they [are] the seed of the blessed of Yhwh, || And their offspring with them. **24** And it has come to pass, || They do not yet call, and I answer, || They are yet speaking, and I hear. **25** Wolf and lamb feed as one, || And a lion eats straw as an ox, || As for the serpent—its food [is] dust, || They do no evil, nor destroy, || In all My holy mountain," said Yhwh!

CHAPTER 66

1 Thus said Yhwh: "The heavens [are] My throne, || And the earth My footstool, || Where [is] this—the house that you build for Me? And where [is] this—the place—My rest? **2** And My hand has made all these, || And all these things are," || A declaration of Yhwh! "And to this one I look attentively, || To the humble and bruised in spirit, || And who is trembling at My word. **3** Whoever slaughters the ox strikes a man, || Whoever sacrifices the lamb beheads a dog, || Whoever is bringing up a present—The blood of a sow, || Whoever is making mention of frankincense, || Is blessing iniquity. Indeed, they have fixed on their own ways, || And their soul has delighted in their abominations. **4** I also—I fix on their distress, || And I bring in their fears to them, || Because I have called, and there is none

answering, || I spoke, and they have not listened, || And they do evil in My eyes, || And on that which I did not desire—fixed." **5** Hear a word of Yhwh, || You who are trembling at His word: "Your brothers who are hating you, || Who are driving you out for My Name's sake, have said, || Yhwh is honored, and we look on your joy, || But they are ashamed." **6** A voice of noise from the city, || A voice from the temple, || The voice of Yhwh, || Giving repayment to His enemies. **7** "Before she is pained she has brought forth, || Before a pang comes to her, || She has delivered a male. **8** Who has heard anything like this? Who has seen anything like these? Is earth caused to bring forth in one day? Is a nation born at once? For she has been pained, || Zion has also borne her sons. **9** Do I bring to the birth, || And not cause to bring forth?" says Yhwh, || "Am I not He who is causing to beget? I have also restrained," said your God. **10** "Rejoice with Jerusalem, || And be glad in her, all you loving her, || Rejoice with her for joy, || All you who are mourning for her, **11** So that you suckle, and have been satisfied, || From the breast of her consolations, || So that you wring out, and have delighted yourselves || From the abundance of her glory." **12** For thus said Yhwh: "Behold, I am stretching out to her peace as a river, || And the glory of nations as an overflowing stream, || And you have sucked, || You are carried on the side, || And you are dandled on the knees. **13** As one whom his mother comforts, so do I comfort you, || Indeed, you are comforted in Jerusalem." **14** And you have seen, and your heart has rejoiced, || And your bones flourish as tender grass, || And the hand of Yhwh has been known to His servants, || And He has been indignant with His enemies. **15** For behold, Yhwh comes in fire, || And His chariots as a windstorm, || To refresh His anger in fury, || And His rebuke in flames of fire. **16** For by fire and by His sword, || Yhwh does judgment with all flesh. And many have been Yhwh's pierced ones. **17** "Those sanctifying and cleansing themselves [to go] to the gardens, || One after another in the midst, || Eating flesh of the sow, || And of the abomination, and of the muroid, || Are consumed together," || A declaration of Yhwh. **18** "And I—their works and their thoughts, || I come to gather all the nations and tongues, || And they have come and seen My glory. **19** And I have set a sign among them, || And have sent out of them those escaping to the nations || (Tarshish, Pul, and Lud, drawing bow, Tubal and Javan, the islands that are far off), || Who have not heard My fame, nor seen My glory, || And they have declared My glory among nations. **20** And they have brought all your brothers out of all the nations, || A present to Yhwh, || On horses, and on chariot, and on litters, || And on mules, and on dromedaries, || To My holy mountain Jerusalem," said Yhwh, "As the sons of Israel bring the present in a clean vessel, || Into the house of Yhwh. **21** And I also take of them for priests, || For Levites," said Yhwh. **22** "For as the new heavens and the new earth that I am making, || Are standing before Me," || A declaration of Yhwh, || "So your seed and your name remain. **23** And it has been from month to month, || And from Sabbath to Sabbath, || All flesh come to bow themselves before Me," said Yhwh. **24** "And they have gone forth, || And looked on the carcasses of the men || Who are transgressing against Me, || For their worm does not die, || And their fire is not quenched, || And they have been an abhorrence to all flesh!"

JEREMIAH

CHAPTER 1

1 Words of Jeremiah son of Hilkiah, of the priests who [are] in Anathoth, in the land of Benjamin, **2** to whom the word of Yhwh has been in the days of Josiah son of Amon, king of Judah, in the thirteenth year of his reign, **3** and it is in the days of Jehoiakim son of Josiah, king of Judah, until the completion of the eleventh year of Zedekiah son of Josiah, king of Judah, until the expulsion of Jerusalem in the fifth month. **4** And there is a word of Yhwh to me, saying, **5** "Before I form you in the belly, I have known you; and before you come forth from the womb I have separated you; I have made you a prophet to the nations." **6** And I say, "Aah! Lord Yhwh! Behold, I have not known—to speak, for I [am] a youth." **7** And Yhwh says to me, "Do not say, I [am] a youth, for to all to whom I send you—go, and all that I command you—speak. **8** Do not be afraid of their faces, for I [am] with you to deliver you," a declaration of Yhwh. **9** And Yhwh puts forth His hand, and strikes against my mouth, and Yhwh says to me, "Behold, I have put My words in your mouth. **10** See, I have charged you this day concerning the nations, and concerning the kingdoms, to pluck up, and to break down, and to destroy, and to throw down, to build, and to plant." **11** And there is a word of Yhwh to me, saying, "What are you seeing, Jeremiah?" And I say, "I am seeing a rod of an almond tree." **12** And Yhwh says to me, "You have seen well: for I am watching over My word to do it." **13** And there is a word of Yhwh to me a second time, saying, "What are you seeing?" And I say, "I am seeing a blown pot, and its face [is] from the north." **14** And Yhwh says to me, "From the north the evil is loosed against all inhabitants of the land. **15** For behold, I am calling for all families of the kingdoms of the north," a declaration of Yhwh, "And they have come, and each put his throne at the opening of the gates of Jerusalem, and by its walls all around, and by all cities of Judah. **16** And I have spoken My judgments with them concerning all their evil, in that they have forsaken Me, and make incense to other gods, and bow themselves to the works of their own hands. **17** And you, you gird up your loins, and have arisen, and spoken to them all that I command you: do not be frightened because of them, lest I frighten you before them. **18** And I, behold, have given you this day for a fortified city, and for an iron pillar, and for bronze walls over all the land, to the kings of Judah, to its heads, to its priests, and to the people of the land; **19** and they have fought against you, and they do not prevail against you; for I [am] with you," a declaration of Yhwh, "to deliver you."

CHAPTER 2

1 And there is a word of Yhwh to me, saying, **2** "Go, and you have called in the ears of Jerusalem, saying, Thus said Yhwh: I have remembered for you || The kindness of your youth, the love of your espousals, || Your going after Me in a wilderness, in a land not sown. **3** Israel [is] holy to Yhwh, || The first-fruit of His increase, || All consuming him are guilty, || Calamity comes to them," || A declaration of Yhwh. **4** Hear a word of Yhwh, O house of Jacob, || And all you families of the house of Israel— **5** Thus said Yhwh: "What perversity have your fathers found in Me, || That they have gone far off from Me, || And go after vanity, and become vain, **6** And have not said, Where [is] Yhwh, || Who brings us up out of the land of Egypt, || Who leads us in a wilderness, || In a land of deserts and pits, || In a dry land, and of death-shade, || In a land that none has passed through, || Nor has man dwelt there? **7** Indeed, I bring you into a land of fruitful fields, || To eat its fruit and its goodness, || And you come in and defile My land, || And have made My inheritance an abomination. **8** The priests have not said, Where [is] Yhwh? And those handling the Law have not known Me. And the shepherds transgressed against Me, || And the prophets have prophesied by Ba'al, || And have gone after those who do not profit. **9** Therefore, I yet plead with you," || A declaration of Yhwh, || "And I plead with your sons' sons. **10** For pass to the islands of Chittim and see, || And send to Kedar and consider well, || And see if there has been [anything] like this: **11** Has a nation changed gods? (And they [are] no gods!) And My people have changed its glory || For that which does not profit. **12** Be astonished, you heavens, at this, || Indeed, be frightened, be greatly desolated," || A declaration of Yhwh. **13** "For My people have done two evils, || They have forsaken Me, a fountain of living waters, || To hew out for themselves wells— broken wells, || That do not contain the waters. **14** [Is] Israel a servant? Is he a child of the house? Why has he been for a prey? **15** Young lions roar against him, || They have given forth their voice, || And make his land become a desolation, || His cities have been burned without inhabitant. **16** Also sons of Noph and Tahapanes || Consume you—the crown of the head! **17** Do you not do this to yourself? [By] your forsaking your God Yhwh, || At the time He is leading you in the way? **18** And now, why do you [go] in the way of Egypt, || To drink the waters of Sihor? And why do you [go] in the way of Asshur, || To drink the waters of the River? **19** Your wickedness instructs you, || And your backslidings reprove you, || Know and see that an evil and a bitter thing [is] your forsaking your God Yhwh, || And My fear not being on you," || A declaration of Lord Yhwh of Hosts. **20** "For from of old you have broken your yoke, || Drawn away your bands, and say, I do not serve, || For on every high height, and under every green tree, || You are wandering—a harlot. **21** And I planted you [as] a choice vine, wholly of true seed, || And how have you been turned || Into the degenerate shoots of a strange vine to Me? **22** But though

you wash with natron, || And multiply soap to yourself, || Your iniquity is marked before Me," || A declaration of Lord Yhwh. **23** "How can you say, I have not been defiled, || I have not gone after the Ba'alim? See your way in a valley, know what you have done, || A swift dromedary winding her ways, **24** A wild donkey accustomed to a wilderness, || She has swallowed up wind in the desire of her soul, || Her meeting—who turns her back? None seeking her weary themselves, || In her month they find her. **25** Withhold your foot from being unshod, || And your throat from thirst, || And you say, It is incurable, || No, for I have loved strangers, and I go after them. **26** As the shame of a thief when he is found, || So has the house of Israel been put to shame, || They, their kings, their heads, || And their priests, and their prophets, **27** Saying to wood, You [are] my father! And to a stone, You have brought me forth, || For they turned to me the back and not the face, || And in the time of their distress, || They say, Arise, and save us. **28** And where [are] your gods, that you have made to yourself? Let them arise, if they may save you, || In the time of your distress, || For—the number of your cities have been your gods, O Judah, **29** Why do you strive with Me? All of you have transgressed against Me," || A declaration of Yhwh. **30** "I have struck your sons in vain, || They have not accepted instruction, || Your sword has devoured your prophets, || As a destroying lion. **31** O generation, see the word of Yhwh: Have I been a wilderness to Israel? A land of thick darkness? Why have My people said, || We wandered freely, || We do not come to You again. **32** Does a virgin forget her ornaments? A bride her bands? And My people have forgotten Me [for] days without number. **33** Why do you make your ways pleasing to seek love? Therefore, you have even taught the wicked your ways. **34** Also the blood of innocent needy souls || Has been found on your skirts, || I have not found them by digging, || But on all these. **35** And you say, Because I have been innocent, || Surely His anger has turned back from me? Behold, I have been judged with you, || Because of your saying, I have not sinned. **36** What? you are very vile to repeat your way, || You are even ashamed of Egypt, || As you have been ashamed of Asshur, **37** Also you go out from this, || And your hands on your head, || For Yhwh has kicked at your confidences, || And you do not give prosperity to them!"

CHAPTER 3

1 "Saying, Behold, one sends his wife away, || And she has gone from him, || And she has been to another man, || Does he return to her again? Is that land not greatly defiled? And you have committed whoredom with many lovers, || And turn to Me again," || A declaration of Yhwh. **2** "Lift your eyes to the high places, and see, || Where have you not been lain with? You have sat for them on the land, || As an Arab in a wilderness, || And you defile the land, || By your fornications, and by your wickedness. **3** And showers are withheld, and there has been no spring rain. You have the forehead of a whorish woman, || You have refused to be ashamed. **4** Have you not from now on called to Me, || My Father, You [are] the leader of my youth? **5** Does He keep for all time? watch forever? Behold, you have spoken these things, || And you do evil, and prevail." **6** And Yhwh says to me, in the days of Josiah the king, "Have you seen that which backsliding Israel has done? She is going on every high mountain, and to the place of every green tree, and commits fornication there. **7** And I say, after her doing all these, Return to Me, and she has not returned, and her treacherous sister Judah sees it. **8** And I see that for all the causes whereby backsliding Israel committed adultery, I have sent her away, and I give the bill of her divorce to her; and her treacherous sister Judah has not feared, and goes and commits fornication—she also. **9** And it has come to pass, from the vileness of her fornication, that the land is defiled, and she commits fornication with stone and with wood. **10** And even in all this her treacherous sister Judah has not turned back to Me with all her heart, but with falsehood," a declaration of Yhwh. **11** And Yhwh says to me: "Backsliding Israel has justified herself, || More than treacherous Judah. **12** Go, and you have proclaimed these words toward the north, and have said, Return, O backsliding Israel," || A declaration of Yhwh! "I do not cause My anger to fall on you, for I [am] kind," || A declaration of Yhwh, || "I do not watch for all time. **13** Only, know your iniquity, || For you have transgressed against your God Yhwh, || And you scatter your ways to strangers, || Under every green tree, || And you have not listened to My voice," ||

A declaration of Yhwh. **14** "Return, O backsliding sons," || A declaration of Yhwh, "For I have ruled over you, || And taken you—one from a city, and two from a family, || And have brought you to Zion, **15** And I have given shepherds to you || According to My own heart, || And they have fed you with knowledge and understanding. **16** And it has come to pass, when you are multiplied, || And have been fruitful in the land, || In those days," || A declaration of Yhwh, || "They no longer say, The Ark of the Covenant of Yhwh, || Nor does it go up on the heart, || Nor do they remember concerning it, || Nor do they inspect, nor is it made again. **17** At that time they cry to Jerusalem, O throne of Yhwh, || And all the nations have been gathered to her, || For the Name of Yhwh, to Jerusalem, || Nor do they go after the stubbornness of their evil heart anymore. **18** In those days the house of Judah || Goes to the house of Israel, || And they come together from the land of the south, || To the land that I caused your fathers to inherit. **19** And I have said, How do I put you among the sons, || And give a desirable land to you, || A beautiful inheritance of the hosts of nations, || And I say, You call Me—My Father, || And you do not turn back from after Me. **20** But a woman has deceived her friend, || So you have dealt treacherously with Me, || O house of Israel," || A declaration of Yhwh. **21** A voice is heard on high places—weeping, || Supplications of the sons of Israel, || For they have made their way perverse, || They have forgotten their God Yhwh. **22** "Return, O backsliding sons, || I cause your backslidings to cease." "Behold us, we have come to You, || For You [are] our God Yhwh. **23** Surely in vain—from the heights, || The multitude of mountains—Surely the salvation of Israel [is] in our God Yhwh. **24** And the shameful thing has devoured || The labor of our fathers from our youth, || Their flock and their herd, || Their sons and their daughters. **25** We have lain down in our shame, and our confusion covers us, || For we have sinned against our God Yhwh, || We, and our fathers, from our youth even to this day, || Nor have we listened to the voice of our God Yhwh!"

been against her all around, || For she has been rebellious with Me," || A declaration of Yhwh. **18** "Your way and your doings have done these to you, || This [is] your distress, for [it is] bitter, || For it has struck to your heart." **19** My bowels, my bowels! I am pained [in] the walls of my heart, || My heart makes a noise for me, I am not silent, || For I have heard the voice of a horn, || O my soul—a shout of battle! **20** Destruction on destruction is proclaimed, || For all the land has been spoiled, || My tents have suddenly been spoiled, || In a moment—my curtains. **21** Until when do I see an ensign? Do I hear the voice of a horn? **22** "For My people [are] foolish, || They have not known Me, || They [are] foolish sons, || Indeed, they [are] not intelligent, || They [are] wise to do evil, || And they have not known to do good." **23** I looked [to] the earth, and behold—formless and void, || And to the heavens, and they [had] no light. **24** I have looked [to] the mountains, || And behold, they are trembling. And all the hills moved themselves lightly. **25** I have looked, and behold, man is not, || And all birds of the heavens have fled. **26** I have looked, and behold, || The fruitful place [is] a wilderness, || And all its cities have been broken down, || Because of Yhwh, || Because of the fierceness of His anger. **27** For thus said Yhwh: "All the land is a desolation, but I do not make a completion. **28** For this the earth mourns, || And the heavens above have been black, || Because I have spoken—I have purposed, || And I have not relented, || Nor do I turn back from it. **29** From the voice of the horseman, || And of him shooting with the bow, || All the city is fleeing, || They have come into thickets, || And they have gone up on cliffs, || All the city is forsaken, || And there is no one dwelling in them. **30** And you, O spoiled one, what do you do? For you put on scarlet, || For you adorn yourself [with] ornaments of gold. For you tear your eyes with pain, || In vain you make yourself beautiful, || Unhealthy ones have kicked against you, || They seek your life. **31** For I have heard a voice as of a travailing woman, || Distress, as of one bringing forth a firstborn, || The voice of the daughter of Zion, || She laments herself, || She spreads out her hands, || Woe to me now, my soul is weary of slayers!"

CHAPTER 4

1 "If you return, O Israel," || A declaration of Yhwh, || "Return to Me, || And if you turn aside Your abominations from My face, || Then you do not bemoan. **2** And you have sworn— Yhwh lives, || In truth, in judgment, and in righteousness, || And nations have blessed themselves in Him, || And they boast themselves in Him." **3** For thus said Yhwh, || To the man of Judah, and to Jerusalem: "Till for yourselves tillage, || And do not sow to the thorns. **4** Be circumcised to Yhwh, || And turn aside the foreskins of your heart, || O man of Judah, and you inhabitants of Jerusalem, || Lest My fury goes out as fire, and has burned, || And there is none quenching, || Because of the evil of your doings." **5** Declare in Judah, and sound in Jerusalem, and say: "Blow a horn in the land, || Call, Fill up together, || And say, Assemble yourselves and let us go into the fortified cities. **6** Lift up an ensign toward Zion, || Strengthen yourselves, do not stand still, || For I am bringing evil in from the north, || And a great destruction." **7** A lion has gone up from his thicket, || And a destroyer of nations has journeyed, || He has come forth from his place || To make your land become a desolation, || Your cities are laid waste, without inhabitant. **8** For this, gird on sackcloth, lament and howl, || For the fierce anger of Yhwh has not turned back from us. **9** "And it has come to pass in that day," || A declaration of Yhwh, || "The heart of the king perishes, || And the heart of the princes, || And the priests have been astonished, || And the prophets wonder." **10** And I say, "Aah! Lord Yhwh, || Surely you have entirely forgotten this people and Jerusalem, || Saying, Peace is for you, || And a sword has struck to the soul!" **11** At that time it is said of this people, || And of Jerusalem: "A dry wind of high places in the wilderness, || The way of the daughter of My people || (Not for winnowing, nor for cleansing), **12** A full wind from these comes for Me, || Now also, I speak judgments with them." **13** "Behold, he comes up as clouds, || And his chariots as a windstorm, || His horses have been lighter than eagles, || Woe to us, for we have been spoiled." **14** Wash evil from your heart, O Jerusalem, || That you may be saved, || Until when do you lodge in your heart || Thoughts of your strength? **15** For a voice is declaring from Dan, || And sounding sorrow from Mount Ephraim: **16** "Make mention to the nations, || Behold, sound to Jerusalem, || Besiegers are coming from the far-off land, || And they give forth their voice against cities of Judah. **17** As the keepers of a field || They have

CHAPTER 5

1 "Go to and fro in streets of Jerusalem, || And see now and know, || And seek in her broad places, || If you find a man, || If there is one doing judgment, || Seeking steadfastness—Then I am propitious to her. **2** And if they say, Yhwh lives, || Surely they swear to a falsehood." **3** Yhwh, Your eyes, are they not on steadfastness? You have struck them, and they have not grieved, || You have consumed them, || They have refused to receive instruction, || They made their faces harder than a rock, || They have refused to turn back. **4** And I said, "Surely these [are] poor, || They have been foolish, || For they have not known the way of Yhwh, || The judgment of their God. **5** I go to the great, and I speak with them, || For they have known the way of Yhwh, || The judgment of their God." Surely, they have broken the yoke together, || They have drawn away the bands. **6** Therefore a lion out of the forest has struck them, || A wolf of the deserts spoils them, || A leopard is watching over their cities, || Everyone who is going out of them is torn, || For their transgressions have been many, || Their backslidings have been mighty. **7** "I am not propitious to you for this, || Your sons have forsaken Me, || And are satisfied by [those who are] not gods, || I satisfy them, and they commit adultery, || And at the house of a harlot || They gather themselves together. **8** Fed horses—they have been early risers, || They each neigh to the wife of his neighbor. **9** Do I not lay a charge for these?" A declaration of Yhwh, "And on a nation such as this, || Does My soul not avenge itself? **10** Go up on her walls, and destroy, || And I do not make a completion, || Turn her branches aside, || For they [are] not Yhwh's, **11** For the house of Israel has dealt treacherously against Me, || And the house of Judah," || A declaration of Yhwh. **12** They have lied against Yhwh, || And they say, "[It is] not He, || Nor does evil come in against us, || Indeed, we do not see sword and famine. **13** And the prophets become wind, || And the word is not in them, || Thus it is done to them." **14** Therefore, thus said Yhwh, God of Hosts: "Because of your speaking this word, || Behold, I am making My words become fire in your mouth, || And this people wood, || And it has devoured them. **15** Behold, I am bringing against you a nation from afar, || O house of Israel," || A declaration of Yhwh, || "It [is] a strong nation, || It [is] an ancient nation, || A nation whose tongue you do not know, || Nor understand what it speaks. **16** Its quiver [is] as an open tomb, || All of them—mighty ones. **17** And it has consumed your harvest and your bread, || They consume your sons, and your daughters, || It consumes your flock, and your herd, || It consumes your vine and your fig tree, || It makes your fortified cities poor, || In which you are trusting—by the sword. **18** And even in those days," || A declaration of Yhwh, || "I do not make you a completion. **19** And it has come to pass, when you say, Why has our God Yhwh done all these [things] to us? That you have said to them, As you have forsaken Me, || And serve the gods of a foreigner in your land, || So you serve strangers in a land [that is] not yours. **20** Declare this in the house of Jacob, || And sound it in Judah, saying, **21** Now hear this, || O people, foolish and without heart, || They have eyes, and they do not see, || They have ears, and they do not hear. **22** Do you not fear Me?" A declaration of Yhwh; "Are you not pained from My presence? Who has made sand the border of the sea, || A perpetual limit, and it does not pass over it, || They shake themselves, and they are not able, || Indeed, its billows have sounded, and they do not pass over. **23** And this people has an apostatizing and rebelling heart, || They have turned aside, and they go on. **24** And they have not said in their heart, || Now let us fear our God Yhwh, who is giving rain, || The autumn rain and the spring rain, in its season, || He keeps the appointed weeks of harvest for us. **25** Your iniquities have turned these away, || And your sins have kept the good from you. **26** For the wicked have been found among My people. He watches like one who sets snares, || They have set up a trap—they capture men. **27** As a cage full of birds, || So their houses are full of deceit, || Therefore they have been great, and are rich. **28** They have been fat, they have shone, || Indeed, they have surpassed the acts of the evil, || They have not judged judgment, || The judgment of the fatherless—and they prosper, || And they have not judged the judgment of the needy. **29** Do I not inspect for these," || A declaration of Yhwh, || "On a nation such as this, || Does My soul not avenge itself? **30** An astonishing and horrible thing has been in the land: **31** The prophets have prophesied falsely, || And the priests bear rule by their means, || And My people have loved [it] so, || And what do they do at its latter end?"

CHAPTER 6

1 "Strengthen yourselves, sons of Benjamin, || From the midst of Jerusalem, || And blow a horn in Tekoa, || And lift up a flame over Beth-Haccerem, || For evil has been seen from the north, || And great destruction. **2** I have cut off the lovely and delicate one, || The daughter of Zion. **3** Shepherds and their droves come to her, || They have struck tents by her all around, || They have each fed [in] his own station." **4** "Sanctify the battle against her, || Rise, and we go up at noon. Woe to us, for the day has turned, || For the shades of evening are stretched out, **5** Rise, and we go up by night, || And we destroy her palaces." **6** For thus said Yhwh of Hosts: "Cut down her wood, || And pour out a mound against Jerusalem, || She [is] the city to be inspected, || She [is] full of oppression in her midst. **7** As the digging of a well, is [for] its waters, || So she has dug [for] her wickedness, || Violence and spoil is heard in her, || Sickness and striking [are] continually before My face. **8** Be instructed, O Jerusalem, || Lest My soul be alienated from you, || Lest I make you a desolation, || A land [that is] not inhabited." **9** Thus said Yhwh of Hosts: "They surely glean, as a vine, the remnant of Israel, || Put your hand back, as a gatherer to the baskets." **10** To whom do I speak, and testify, and they hear? Behold, their ear [is] uncircumcised, || And they are not able to attend. Behold, a word of Yhwh has been to them for a reproach, || They do not delight in it. **11** And I have been filled with the fury of Yhwh || (I have been weary of containing), "To pour [it] on the suckling in the street, || And on the assembly of youths together, || For even husband with wife are captured, || [The] elderly with one full of days, **12** And their houses have been turned to others, || Fields and wives together, || For I stretch out My hand against the inhabitants of the land," || A declaration of Yhwh. **13** "For from their least to their greatest, || Everyone is gaining dishonest gain, || And from prophet even to priest, || Everyone is dealing falsely, **14** And they heal the breach of the daughter of My people slightly, || Saying, Peace, peace! And there is no peace. **15** They were ashamed when they did abomination! Indeed, they are not at all ashamed, || Indeed, they have not known blushing, || Therefore they fall among those falling, || In the time I have

inspected them, || They stumble," said Yhwh. **16** Thus said Yhwh: "Stand by the ways and see, and ask for paths of old, || Where [is] this—the good way? and go in it, || And find rest for yourselves. And they say, We do not go. **17** And I have raised up watchmen for you, || Attend to the voice of the horn. And they say, We do not attend. **18** Therefore hear, O nations, and know, O congregation, || That which [is] on them. **19** Hear, O earth, behold, I am bringing evil on this people, || The fruit of their plans, || For they gave no attention to My words, || And My law—they kick against it. **20** Why [is] this to Me? frankincense comes from Sheba, || And the sweet cane from a far-off land, || Your burnt-offerings [are] not for acceptance, || And your sacrifices have not been sweet to Me." **21** Therefore, thus said Yhwh: "Behold, I give stumbling blocks to this people, || And fathers and sons have stumbled against them together, || The neighbor and his friend perish." **22** Thus said Yhwh: "Behold, a people has come from a north country, || And a great nation is stirred up from the sides of the earth. **23** They take hold of bow and javelin, || It [is] fierce, and they have no mercy, || Their voice sounds as a sea, || And they ride on horses, || Set in array as a man of war, || Against you, O daughter of Zion." **24** We have heard its sound, our hands have been feeble, || Distress has seized us, pain as of a travailing woman. **25** Do not go forth to the field, || And do not walk in the way, || For the enemy has a sword, || Fear [is] all around. **26** O daughter of my people, || Gird on sackcloth, || And roll yourself in ashes, || Make mourning [as for] an only one, || A most bitter lamentation, || For the spoiler suddenly comes against us. **27** "I have given you a watchtower, || A fortress among My people, || And you know, and have tried their way. **28** All of them are turned aside by apostates, || Walking slanderously—bronze and iron, || All of them are corrupters. **29** The bellows have been burned, || The lead has been consumed by fire, || A refiner has refined in vain, || And the wicked have not been drawn away. **30** They have called them rejected silver, || For Yhwh has kicked against them!"

CHAPTER 7

1 The word that has been to Jeremiah from Yhwh, saying, **2** "Stand in the gate of the house of Yhwh, and you have proclaimed this word there, and have said, Hear a word of Yhwh, all you of Judah, who are coming in at these gates, to bow before Yhwh." **3** Thus said Yhwh of Hosts, God of Israel: "Amend your ways, and your doings, || And I cause you to dwell in this place. **4** Do not trust for yourselves || To the words of falsehood, saying, || The temple of Yhwh! The temple of Yhwh! These [are] the temple of Yhwh! **5** For if you thoroughly amend your ways and your doings, || If you thoroughly do judgment || Between a man and his neighbor, **6** You do not oppress sojourner, fatherless, and widow, || And innocent blood is not shed in this place, || And [you] do not walk after other gods, for evil to yourselves, **7** Then I have caused you to dwell in this place, || In the land that I gave to your fathers, || From age even to age. **8** Behold, you are trusting for yourselves || On the words of falsehood, so as not to profit. **9** Stealing, murdering, and committing adultery, || And swearing to falsehood, and giving incense to Ba`al, || And going after other gods whom you did not know. **10** And you have come in and stood before Me, || In this house on which My Name is called, || And have said, We have been delivered, || In order to do all these abominations. **11** Has this house, || On which My Name is called, || Been a den of burglars in your eyes? Even I, behold, have seen," || A declaration of Yhwh. **12** "But go now to My place that [is] in Shiloh, || Where I caused My Name to dwell at first, || And see that which I have done to it, || For the wickedness of My people Israel. **13** And now, because of your doing all these works," || A declaration of Yhwh, || "And I speak to you, rising early and speaking, || And you have not listened, || And I call you, and you have not answered, **14** I also have done to the house on which My Name is called, || In which you are trusting, || And to the place that I gave to you, and to your fathers, || As I have done to Shiloh. **15** And I have cast you from before My face, || As I have cast out all your brothers, || The whole seed of Ephraim. **16** And you do not pray for this people, || Nor lift up crying and prayer for them, || Nor intercede with Me, for I do not hear you. **17** Are you not seeing what they are doing || In cities of Judah, and in streets of Jerusalem? **18** The sons are gathering wood, || And the fathers are causing the fire to burn, || And the women are kneading dough, || To make cakes to the queen of the heavens, || And to pour out drink-offerings to other gods, || So as to provoke Me to anger. ¹⁹ Are they provoking Me to anger?" A declaration of Yhwh, "Is it not themselves, || For the shame of their own faces?" ²⁰ Therefore, thus said Lord Yhwh: "Behold, My anger and My fury is poured out on this place, || On man, and beast, and on tree of the field, || And on fruit of the ground, || And it has burned, and it is not quenched." ²¹ Thus said Yhwh of Hosts, God of Israel: "Add your burnt-offerings to your sacrifices and eat flesh. ²² For I did not speak with your fathers, || Nor did I command them in the day of My bringing them out of the land of Egypt, || Concerning the matters of burnt-offering and sacrifice, ²³ But this thing I commanded them, saying, || Listen to My voice, || And I have been to you for God, || And you are to Me for a people, || And have walked in all the way that I command you, || So that it is well for you. ²⁴ And they have not listened, nor inclined their ear, || And they walk in the counsels, || [And] in the stubbornness, of their evil hearts, || And are backward and not forward. ²⁵ Even from the day when your fathers || Went out of the land of Egypt until this day, || I send all My servants the prophets to you, || Daily rising early and sending, ²⁶ And they have not listened to Me, || Nor inclined their ear—and they harden their neck, || They have done evil above their fathers. ²⁷ And you have spoken all these words to them, || And they do not listen to you, || And you have called to them, || And they do not answer you. ²⁸ And you have said to them: This [is] the nation that has not listened, || To the voice of its God Yhwh, || Nor have they accepted instruction, || Steadfastness has perished, || Indeed, it has been cut off from their mouth. ²⁹ Cut off your crown, and cast [it] away, || And lift up lamentation on high places, || For Yhwh has rejected, || And He leaves the generation of His wrath. ³⁰ For the sons of Judah || Have done evil in My eyes," || A declaration of Yhwh, || "They have set their abominations in the house || On which My Name is called—to defile it, ³¹ And have built the high places of Tophet, || That [are] in the Valley of the Son of Hinnom, || To burn their sons and their daughters with fire, || Which I did not command, || Nor did it come up on My heart. ³² Therefore, behold, days are coming," || A declaration of Yhwh, || "And it is no longer said, The Tophet, || And, Valley of the Son of Hinnom, || But, Valley of the Slaughter, || And they have buried in Tophet—without place. ³³ And the carcass of this people has been for food || To a bird of the heavens, and to a beast of the earth, || And there is none troubling. ³⁴ And I have caused to cease from cities of Judah, || And from streets of Jerusalem, || The voice of joy, and the voice of gladness, || Voice of bridegroom, and voice of bride, || For the land becomes a desolation!"

CHAPTER 8

¹ "At that time," || A declaration of Yhwh, || "They bring the bones of the kings of Judah, || And the bones of its princes, || And the bones of the priests, || And the bones of the prophets, || And the bones of inhabitants of Jerusalem, || Out of their graves, ² And have spread them to sun, and to moon, || And to all the host of the heavens, that they have loved, || And that they have served, || And that they have walked after, || And that they have sought, || And to which they have bowed themselves, || They are not gathered, nor buried, || They are for dung on the face of the ground. ³ And death is chosen rather than life || By all the remnant who are left of this evil family, || In all the remaining places, to where I have driven them," || A declaration of Yhwh of Hosts. ⁴ "And you have said to them, Thus said Yhwh: Do they fall, and not rise? Does he turn back, and not return? ⁵ Why has this people of Jerusalem || Turned back—a continuous backsliding? They have kept hold on deceit, || They have refused to turn back. ⁶ I have given attention; indeed, I listen, || They do not speak right, || No man has sighed over his wickedness, || Saying, What have I done? Everyone has turned to his courses, || As a horse is rushing into battle. ⁷ Even a stork in the heavens has known her seasons, || And turtle, and swallow, and crane, || Have watched the time of their coming, || And—My people have not known the judgment of Yhwh. ⁸ How do you say, we [are] wise, || And the Law of Yhwh [is] with us? Surely, behold, it has worked falsely, || The false pen of scribes. ⁹ The wise have been ashamed, || They have been frightened, and are captured, || Behold, they kicked against a word of Yhwh, || And what wisdom do they have? ¹⁰ Therefore, I give their wives to others, || Their fields to dispossessors, || For from the least even to the greatest, || Everyone is gaining dishonest gain, ||

From prophet even to priest, everyone is dealing falsely. ¹¹ And they heal the breach of the daughter of My people slightly, || Saying, Peace, peace! And there is no peace. ¹² They were ashamed when they did abomination! Indeed, they are not ashamed at all, || And they have not known blushing, || Therefore, they fall among falling ones, || They stumble in the time of their inspection, said Yhwh. ¹³ I utterly consume them," || A declaration of Yhwh, || "There are no grapes in the vine, || Indeed, there are no figs in the fig tree, || And the leaf has faded, || And the strength they have passes from them. ¹⁴ Why are we sitting still? Be gathered, and we go into the fortified cities, || And we are silent there, || For our God Yhwh has made us silent, || Indeed, He causes us to drink water of gall, || For we have sinned against Yhwh. ¹⁵ Looking for peace—and there is no good, || For a time of healing, and behold—terror. ¹⁶ The snorting of his horses has been heard from Dan, || From the voice of the neighings of his mighty ones, || All the land has trembled, || And they come in and consume the land and its fullness, || The city and the inhabitants in it. ¹⁷ For behold, I am sending serpents among you, || Vipers that have no charmer, || And they have bitten you," || A declaration of Yhwh. ¹⁸ My sorrow [is] beyond comfort, || My heart [is] sick in me. ¹⁹ Behold, the voice of a cry of the daughter of my people from a far-off land, || Is Yhwh not in Zion? is her King not in her? "Why have they provoked Me with their carved images, || With the vanities of a foreigner?" ²⁰ Harvest has passed, summer has ended, || And we have not been saved. ²¹ For a breach of the daughter of my people I have been broken, || I have been dark, || Astonishment has seized me. ²² Is there no balm in Gilead? Is there no physician there? Why has the health of the daughter of my people not gone up?

CHAPTER 9

¹ Who makes my head waters, || And my eye a fountain of tears? And I weep by day and by night, || For the wounded of the daughter of my people. ² Who gives me in a wilderness || A lodging-place for travelers? And I leave my people, and go from them, || For all of them [are] adulterers, || An assembly of treacherous ones. ³ "And they bend their tongue, || Their bow [is] a lie, || And they have not been mighty for steadfastness in the land, || For they have gone forth from evil to evil, || And they have not known Me," || A declaration of Yhwh! ⁴ "You each beware of his friend, || And do not trust any brother, || For every brother utterly supplants, || For every friend slanderously walks, ⁵ And they each mock at his friend, || And they do not speak truth, || They taught their tongue to speak falsehood, || They have labored to commit iniquity. ⁶ your dwelling [is] in the midst of deceit, || Through deceit they refused to know Me," || A declaration of Yhwh. ⁷ Therefore, thus said Yhwh of Hosts: "Behold, I am refining them, and have tried them, || For how do I deal with the daughter of My people? ⁸ Their tongue [is] a slaughtering arrow, || It has spoken deceit in its mouth, || It speaks peace with its neighbor, || And in its heart it lays its ambush, ⁹ Do I not see after them for these things?" A declaration of Yhwh, "Does My soul not avenge itself against a nation such as this?" ¹⁰ I lift up weeping and wailing for the mountains, || And a lamentation for the habitations of the wilderness, || For they have been burned up without any passing over, || Nor have they heard the voice of livestock, || From the bird of the heavens and to the beast—they have fled, || They have gone. ¹¹ "And I make Jerusalem become heaps, || A habitation of dragons, || And I make the cities of Judah a desolation, || Without inhabitant." ¹² Who [is] the wise man? and he understands this, || And he to whom the mouth of Yhwh spoke? And he declares it, || For why has the land perished? It has been burned up as a wilderness, || Without any passing through. ¹³ And Yhwh says: "Because of their forsaking My law that I set before them, || And they have not listened to My voice nor walked in it, ¹⁴ And they walk after the stubbornness of their heart, || And after the Ba'alim, || That their fathers taught them," ¹⁵ Therefore, thus said Yhwh of Hosts, God of Israel: "Behold, I am causing them—this people—to eat wormwood, || And I have caused them to drink water of gall, ¹⁶ And I have scattered them among nations || Which they did not know, they and their fathers, || And have sent the sword after them, || Until I have consumed them." ¹⁷ Thus said Yhwh of Hosts: "Consider, and call for mourning women, || And they come, || And send to the wise women, || And they come, ¹⁸ And they hurry, and lift up a wailing for us. And tears run down our eyes, || And waters flow from our

eyelids. **19** For a voice of wailing is heard from Zion: How we have been spoiled! We have been greatly ashamed, || Because we have forsaken the land, || Because they have cast down our dwelling places." **20** But hear, you women, a word of Yhwh, || And your ear receives a word of His mouth, || And teach your daughters wailing, || And each her neighbor lamentation. **21** For death has come up into our windows, || It has come into our palaces, || To cut off the suckling from outside, || Young men from the broad places. **22** Speak thus, "A declaration of Yhwh, || And the carcass of man has fallen, || As dung on the face of the field, || And as a handful after the reaper, || And there is none gathering." **23** Thus said Yhwh: "Do not let the wise boast himself in his wisdom, || Nor let the mighty boast himself in his might, || Do not let the rich boast himself in his riches, **24** But let the boaster boast himself in this, || In understanding and knowing Me, || For I [am] Yhwh, doing kindness, || Judgment, and righteousness, in the earth, || For I have delighted in these," || A declaration of Yhwh. **25** "Behold, days are coming," || A declaration of Yhwh, || "And I have laid a charge on all circumcised in the foreskin, **26** On Egypt, and on Judah, and on Edom, || And on the sons of Ammon, and on Moab, || And on all cutting the corner [of the beard], || Who are dwelling in the wilderness, || For all the nations [are] uncircumcised, || And all the house of Israel [are] uncircumcised in heart!"

CHAPTER 10

1 Hear the word, O house of Israel, || That Yhwh has spoken for you. **2** Thus said Yhwh: "Do not accustom yourselves to the way of the nations, || And do not be frightened by the signs of the heavens, || For the nations are frightened by them. **3** For the statutes of the peoples are vanity, || For one has cut a tree from a forest, || Work of the hands of a craftsman, with an axe, **4** They beautify it with silver and with gold, || They fix it with nails and with hammers, || And it does not stumble. **5** They [are] stiff as a palm, and they do not speak, || They are surely carried, for they do not step, || Do not be afraid of them, for they do no evil, || Indeed, to do good is also not in them." **6** Because there is none like You, O Yhwh, || You [are] great, and Your Name [is] great in might. **7** Who does not fear You, King of the nations? For it is befitting to You, || For among all the wise of the nations, || And in all their kingdom, there is none like You. **8** And as one they are brutish and foolish, || An instruction of vanities [is] the tree itself. **9** Spread-out silver is brought from Tarshish, || And gold from Uphaz, || Work of an artisan, and of the hands of a refiner, || Their clothing [is] blue and purple, || Work of the skillful—all of them. **10** And Yhwh [is] a God of truth, || He [is] a living God, and a perpetual King, || The earth shakes from His wrath, || And nations do not endure His indignation. **11** Thus you say to them, "The gods who have not made the heavens and earth, || They perish from the earth, || And from under these heavens." **12** The Maker of the earth by His power, || The Establisher of the world by His wisdom, || Who, by His understanding, stretched forth the heavens— **13** When He gives forth His voice, || A multitude of waters [is] in the heavens, || And He causes vapors to come up from the end of the earth, || He has made lightnings for rain, || And brings out wind from His treasures. **14** Every man is brutish by knowledge, || Every refiner is put to shame by a carved image, || For his molten image [is] false. And there is no breath in them. **15** They [are] vanity, work of erring ones, || They perish in the time of their inspection. **16** The Portion of Jacob [is] not like these, || For He [is] the Framer of all things, || And Israel [is] the rod of His inheritance, || Yhwh of Hosts [is] His Name. **17** Gather your merchandise from the land, || O dweller in the bulwark, **18** For thus said Yhwh: "Behold, I am slinging out the inhabitants of the land at this time, || And have been an adversary to them, || So that they are found out." **19** Woe to me for my breaking, || My striking has been grievous, || And I said, "Surely this [is] my sickness, and I bear it." **20** My tent has been spoiled, || And all my cords have been broken, || My sons have gone out from me, and they are not, || There is none stretching out my tent anymore, || And raising up my curtains. **21** For the shepherds have become brutish, || And they have not sought Yhwh, || Therefore they have not acted wisely, || And all their flock is scattered. **22** A voice of a report, behold, it has come, || Even a great shaking from the north country, || To make the cities of Judah a desolation, || A habitation of dragons. **23** I have known, O Yhwh, that not of man [is] his way, || Not of man [is] the going and establishing of his step.

24 Discipline me, O Yhwh, only in judgment, || Not in Your anger, lest You make me small. **25** Pour out Your fury on the nations that have not known You, || And on the families that have not called on Your Name, || For they have eaten up Jacob, || Indeed, they have eaten him up, indeed, they consume him, || And they have made his habitation desolate!

CHAPTER 11

1 The word that has been to Jeremiah from Yhwh, saying, **2** "Hear the words of this covenant, and you have spoken to the men of Judah, and to the inhabitants of Jerusalem, **3** and you have said to them, Thus said Yhwh God of Israel: Cursed [is] the man who does not obey the words of this covenant, **4** That I commanded your fathers, || In the day of My bringing them out from the land of Egypt, || Out of the iron furnace, saying, Listen to My voice, and you have done them, || According to all that I command you, || And you have been to Me for a people, || And I am to you for God, **5** In order to establish the oath that I have sworn to your fathers, || To give to them a land flowing with milk and honey, as this day." And I answer and say, "Amen, O Yhwh." **6** And Yhwh says to me, "Proclaim all these words in the cities of Judah, and in the streets of Jerusalem, saying, || Hear the words of this covenant, || And you have done them. **7** For I certainly testified against your fathers, || In the day of My bringing them up out of the land of Egypt—until this day, || Rising early and testifying, saying, Listen to My voice, **8** And they have not listened nor inclined their ear, || And they each walk in the stubbornness of their evil heart, || And I bring on them all the words of this covenant, || That I commanded to do, and they did not." **9** And Yhwh says to me: "A conspiracy is found in the men of Judah, || And in the inhabitants of Jerusalem. **10** They have turned back to the iniquities of their first fathers, || Who refused to hear My words, || And they have gone after other gods to serve them, || The house of Israel and the house of Judah || Have made void My covenant that I made with their fathers." **11** Therefore, thus said Yhwh: "Behold, I am bringing calamity on them, || That they are not able to go out from, || And they have cried to Me, || And I do not listen to them. **12** And the cities of Judah, and inhabitants of Jerusalem have gone, || And they have cried to the gods, || To whom they are making incense, || And they give no deliverance at all to them, || In the time of their distress. **13** For the number of your cities have been your gods, O Judah, || And [for] the number of the streets of Jerusalem You have placed altars to a shameful thing, || Altars to make incense to Ba'al. **14** And you, you do not pray for this people, || Nor do you lift up cry and prayer for them, || For I do not listen in the time of their calling to Me for their distress. **15** What has My beloved to do in My house, || Her doing wickedness with many, || And does the holy flesh pass over from you? When you do evil, then you exult. **16** An olive, green, beautiful, of good fruit, || Has Yhwh called your name, || At the noise of a great tumult He has kindled fire against it, || And its thin branches have been broken. **17** And Yhwh of Hosts, who is planting you, || Has spoken calamity concerning you, || For the evil of the house of Israel, and of the house of Judah, || That they have done to themselves, || To provoke Me to anger, to make incense to Ba'al." **18** And, O Yhwh, cause me to know, and I know, || Then You have showed me their doings. **19** And I [am] as a trained lamb brought to slaughter, || And I have not known || That they have devised schemes against me: "We destroy the tree with its food, || And cut him off from the land of the living, || And his name is not remembered again." **20** And O Yhwh of Hosts, judging righteousness, || Trying reins and heart, || I see Your vengeance against them, || For I have revealed my cause to You. **21** Therefore, thus said Yhwh concerning the men of Anathoth, who are seeking your life, saying, "Do not prophesy in the Name of Yhwh, and you do not die by our hands." **22** Therefore, thus said Yhwh of Hosts: "Behold, I am seeing after them, || The chosen ones die by sword, || Their sons and their daughters die by famine, **23** And they have no remnant, || For I bring calamity to the men of Anathoth, || The year of their inspection!"

CHAPTER 12

1 You [are] righteous, O Yhwh, || When I plead toward You, || Only, let me speak judgments with You, || Why did the way of the wicked prosper? All treacherous dealers have been at rest. ² You have planted them, || Indeed, they have taken root, || They go on, indeed, they have made fruit, || You [are] near in their mouth, || And far off from their reins. ³ And You, O Yhwh, You have known me, || You see me, and have tried my heart with You, || Draw them away as sheep to slaughter, || And separate them for a day of slaughter. ⁴ Until when does the earth mourn, || And the herb of the whole field wither? For the wickedness of those dwelling in it, || Beast and bird have been consumed, || Because they said, "He does not see our latter end." ⁵ "For you have run with footmen, || And they weary you, || And how you fret yourself with horses! Even in the land of peace, || [In which] you are confident—And how will you do in the rising of Jordan? ⁶ For even your brothers and the house of your father, || Even they dealt treacherously against you, || Even they called after you fully, || Do not trust in them when they speak good things to you. ⁷ I have forsaken My house, || I have left My inheritance, || I have given the beloved of My soul || Into the hand of her enemies. ⁸ My inheritance has been to Me as a lion in a forest, || She gave forth against Me with her voice, || Therefore I have hated her. ⁹ [Is] My inheritance a speckled bird to Me? Is the bird around against her? Come, assemble, every beast of the field, || Come for food. ¹⁰ Many shepherds destroyed My vineyard, || They have trodden down My portion, || They have made My desirable portion || Become a wilderness—a desolation. ¹¹ He has made it become a desolation, || The desolation has mourned to Me, || All the land has been desolated, || But there is no one laying it to heart. ¹² Spoilers have come in on all high places in the plain, || For the sword of Yhwh is consuming, || From the end of the land even to the end of the land, || There is no peace to any flesh. ¹³ They sowed wheat, and have reaped thorns, || They have become sick—they do not profit, || And they have been ashamed of your increases, || Because of the fierceness of the anger of Yhwh." ¹⁴ Thus said Yhwh: "Concerning all My evil neighbors, who are striking against the inheritance that I caused My people—Israel—to inherit: Behold, I am plucking them from off their ground, || And I pluck the house of Judah out of their midst. ¹⁵ And it has been, after My plucking them out, || I turn back, and have pitied them, || And I have brought them back, || Each to his inheritance, and each to his land. ¹⁶ And it has come to pass, || If they learn the ways of My people well, || To swear by My Name, Yhwh lives, || As they taught My people to swear by Ba'al, || Then they have been built up in the midst of My people. ¹⁷ And if they do not listen, || Then I have plucked up that nation, || Plucking up and destroying," || A declaration of Yhwh!

CHAPTER 13

¹ Thus said Yhwh to me: "Go, and you have acquired a girdle of linen for yourself, and have placed it on your loins, and you do not cause it to enter into water." ² And I get the girdle, according to the word of Yhwh, and I place [it] on my loins. ³ And there is a word of Yhwh to me a second time, saying, ⁴ "Take the girdle that you have acquired, that [is] on your loins, and rise, go to the Euphrates, and hide it there in a hole of the rock"; ⁵ and I go and hide it by the Euphrates, as Yhwh commanded me. ⁶ And it comes to pass, at the end of many days, that Yhwh says to me, "Rise, go to the Euphrates, and take the girdle there, that I commanded you to hide there"; ⁷ and I go to the Euphrates, and dig, and take the girdle from the place where I had hid it; and behold, the girdle has been marred, it is not profitable for anything. ⁸ And there is a word of Yhwh to me, saying, "Thus said Yhwh: ⁹ Thus I mar the excellence of Judah, || And the great excellence of Jerusalem. ¹⁰ This evil people, who refuse to hear My words, || Who walk in the stubbornness of their heart, || And go after other gods to serve them, || And to bow themselves to them, || Indeed it is—as this girdle, that is not profitable for anything. ¹¹ For as the girdle cleaves to the loins of a man, || So I caused to cleave to Me || The whole house of Israel, || And the whole house of Judah," || A declaration of Yhwh, || "To be to Me for a people, and for a name, || And for praise, and for beauty, || And they have not listened. ¹² And you have said this word to them, || Thus said Yhwh, God of Israel: Every bottle is full of wine, || And they have said to you: Do we not certainly know that every bottle is full of wine? ¹³ And you have said to them, || Thus said Yhwh: Behold, I am filling all the inhabitants of this land, || And the kings who sit for David on his throne, || And the priests, and the prophets, || And all the inhabitants of Jerusalem, || [With] drunkenness, ¹⁴ And have dashed them against one another, || And the fathers and the sons together," || A declaration of Yhwh, || "I do not pity, nor spare, nor do I have mercy, || So as not to destroy them." ¹⁵ Hear, and give ear—do not be haughty, || For Yhwh has spoken. ¹⁶ Give glory to your God Yhwh, || Before He causes darkness, || And before your feet stumble on dark mountains, || And you have waited for light, || And He has made it for death-shade, || And has appointed [it] for thick darkness. ¹⁷ And if you do not hear it, || My soul weeps in secret places, because of pride, || Indeed, it weeps and wails, || And the tear comes down my eyes, || For the flock of Yhwh has been taken captive. ¹⁸ Say to the king and to the mistress: Make yourselves low—sit still, || For your principalities have come down, || The crown of your beauty. ¹⁹ The cities of the south have been shut up, || And there is none opening, || Judah has been removed—all of her, || She has been completely removed— ²⁰ Lift up your eyes, and see those coming in from the north, || Where [is] the drove given to you, your beautiful flock? ²¹ What do you say when He looks after you? And you have taught them [to be] over you—leaders for head? Do pangs not seize you as a travailing woman? ²² And when you say in your heart, "Why have these met me?" For the abundance of your iniquity || Have your skirts been uncovered, || Have your heels suffered violence. ²³ "Does a Cushite change his skin? and a leopard his spots? Can you also do good, who are accustomed to do evil? ²⁴ And I scatter them as stubble, || Passing away, by a wind of the wilderness. ²⁵ This [is] your lot, the portion of your measures from Me," || A declaration of Yhwh, || "Because you have forgotten Me, || And trust in falsehood. ²⁶ I have also made your skirts bare before your face, || And your shame has been seen. ²⁷ Your adulteries, and your neighings, || The wickedness of your whoredom, on heights in a field, || I have seen your abominations. Woe to you, O Jerusalem, || You are not [yet] made clean—after when [will you be] again?"

CHAPTER 14

¹ That which has been the word of Yhwh to Jeremiah concerning the matters of the scarcities: ² "Judah has mourned, and her gates have languished, || They have mourned to the earth, || And the cry of Jerusalem has gone up. ³ And their majestic ones have sent their little ones to the water, || They have come to ditches, || They have not found water, || They have turned back—their vessels empty! They have been ashamed, || And have blushed and covered their head. ⁴ Because the ground has been broken, || For there has been no rain in the land, || Farmers have been ashamed, || They have covered their head. ⁵ For even the doe in the field has brought forth—to forsake [it!] || For there has been no grass. ⁶ And wild donkeys have stood on high places, || They have swallowed up wind like dragons, || Their eyes have been consumed, for there is no herb." ⁷ Surely our iniquities have testified against us, || O Yhwh, work for Your Name's sake, || For our backslidings have been many, || We have sinned against You. ⁸ O Hope of Israel—its Savior in time of trouble, || Why are You as a sojourner in the land? And as a traveler turned aside to lodge? ⁹ Why are You as one mute? As a mighty one not able to save? And You [are] in our midst, O Yhwh, || And Your Name is called over us, || Do not leave us. ¹⁰ Thus said Yhwh concerning this people: "They have loved to wander well, || They have not restrained their feet, || And Yhwh has not accepted them, || Now He remembers their iniquity, || And inspects their sin." ¹¹ And Yhwh says to me: "You do not pray for this people for good. ¹² When they fast, I do not listen to their cry, and when they cause burnt-offering and present to ascend, I do not accept them; for I am consuming them by sword, and by famine, and by pestilence." ¹³ And I say, "Aah! Lord Yhwh, behold, the prophets are saying to them: You do not see a sword, indeed, famine is not [on] you, for I give true peace to you in this place." ¹⁴ And Yhwh says to me: "The prophets are prophesying falsehood in My Name. I did not send them, nor command them, nor have I spoken to them. A false vision, and divination, and vanity—indeed, they are prophesying the deceit of their own heart to you. ¹⁵ Therefore, thus said Yhwh concerning the prophets who are prophesying in My Name and I have not sent them, and they are saying, Sword and famine is not in this land: By sword and by famine are these prophets consumed. ¹⁶ And the people to whom they are prophesying are cast into out-places of Jerusalem, because of the famine and the sword, and they have none burying them—them, their

wives, and their sons, and their daughters—and I have poured out their evil on them. **17** And you have said this word to them: Tears come down my eyes night and day, || And they do not cease, || For [with] a great breach, || The virgin daughter of my people has been broken, || A very grievous stroke. **18** If I have gone forth to the field, || Then, behold, the pierced of the sword! And if I have entered the city, || Then, behold, the diseased of famine! For both prophet and priest have gone up and down || To a land that they did not know." **19** Have You utterly rejected Judah? Has Your soul loathed Zion? Why have You struck us, || And there is no healing to us? Looking for peace, and there is no good, || And for a time of healing, and behold, terror. **20** We have known, O Yhwh, our wickedness, || The iniquity of our fathers, || For we have sinned against You. **21** Do not despise, for Your Name's sake, || Do not dishonor the throne of Your glory, || Remember, do not break Your covenant with us. **22** Are there any among the vanities of the nations causing rain? And do the heavens give showers? Are You not He, O our God Yhwh? And we wait for you, for You have done all these!

CHAPTER 15

1 And Yhwh says to me: "Though Moses and Samuel should stand before Me, || My soul is not toward this people, || Send from before My face, and they go out. **2** And it has come to pass, when they say to you, || To where do we go out? that you have said to them, || Thus said Yhwh: Those who [are] for death—to death, || And those who are for the sword—to the sword, || And those who are for famine—to famine, || And those who are for captivity—to captivity. **3** And I have appointed four kinds over them," || A declaration of Yhwh, || "The sword to slay, and the dogs to drag, || And the bird of the heavens, || And the beast of the earth, to consume and to devour. **4** And I have given them for a trembling || To all kingdoms of the earth, || Because of Manasseh son of Hezekiah king of Judah, || For that which he did in Jerusalem. **5** For who has pity on you, O Jerusalem? And who bemoans for you? And who turns aside to ask of your welfare? **6** You have left Me," || A declaration of Yhwh, || "You go backward, || And I stretch out My hand against you, || And I destroy you, || I have been weary of relenting, **7** And I scatter them with a fan, || In the gates of the land, || I have bereaved [them], || I have destroyed My people, || They did not turn back from their ways. **8** Its widows have been more to Me than the sand of the seas, || I brought on them—against the mother—A young man—a spoiler—at noon. I caused wrath and trouble to fall on her suddenly. **9** The bearer of seven has languished, || She has breathed out her spirit, || Her sun has gone in while yet day, || It has been ashamed and confounded, || And I give up their remnant to the sword before their enemies," || A declaration of Yhwh. **10** Woe to me, my mother, || For you have borne me, || A man of strife and a man of contention to all the land, || I have not lent on usury, || Nor have they lent on usury to me— All of them are reviling me. **11** Yhwh said, "Did I not direct you for good? Did I not intercede for you in a time of evil, || And in a time of adversity, with the enemy? **12** Does one break iron, || Northern iron and bronze? **13** I give your strength and your treasures for a prey—not for price, || Even for all your sins, and in all your borders. **14** And I have caused your enemies || To pass over into the land [that] You have not known, || For a fire has been kindled in My anger, || It burns against you." **15** You, You have known, O Yhwh, || Remember me, and inspect me, || And take vengeance for me of my pursuers, || In Your long-suffering do not take me away, || Know [that] I have borne reproach for You. **16** Your words have been found, and I eat them, || And Your word is to me for a joy, || And for the rejoicing of my heart, || For Your Name is called on me, O Yhwh, God of Hosts. **17** I have not sat in an assembly of deriders, || Nor do I exult, because of your hand—I have sat alone, || For You have filled me [with] indignation. **18** Why has my pain been continuous? And my wound incurable? It has refused to be healed, || You are surely as a failing stream to me, || Waters [that are] not steadfast. **19** Therefore, thus said Yhwh: "If you turn back, then I bring you back, || You stand before Me, || And if you bring out the precious from the vile, || You are as My mouth! They return to you, || And you do not return to them. **20** And I have made you to this people || For a wall—bronze—fortified, || And they have fought against you, || And they do not prevail against you, || For I [am] with you to save you, || And to deliver you," || A declaration of Yhwh,

21 "And I have delivered you from the hand of evildoers, || And I have ransomed you || From the hand of the terrible!"

CHAPTER 16

1 And there is a word of Yhwh to me, saying, **2** "You do not take a wife to yourself, || Nor do you have sons and daughters in this place." **3** For thus said Yhwh, || Of the sons and of the daughters who are born in this place, || And of their mothers— those bearing them, || And of their fathers—those begetting them in this land: **4** "They die painful deaths, || They are not lamented, nor are they buried, || For they are dung on the face of the ground, || And are consumed by sword and by famine, || And their carcass has been for food || To the bird of the heavens, || And to the beast of the earth." **5** For thus said Yhwh: "Do not enter the house of a mourning-feast, || Nor go to lament nor bemoan for them, || For I have removed My peace from this people," || A declaration of Yhwh, || "The kindness and the mercies. **6** And great and small have died in this land, || They are not buried, and none lament for them, || Nor does any cut himself, nor become bald for them. **7** Nor do they deal out to them for mourning, || To comfort him concerning the dead, || Nor cause them to drink a cup of consolations || For his father and for his mother. **8** You do not enter a house of banqueting, || To sit with them, to eat and to drink," **9** For thus said Yhwh of Hosts, God of Israel: "Behold, I am causing to cease from this place, || Before your eyes, and in your days, || The voice of joy, and the voice of rejoicing, || The voice of bridegroom and voice of bride. **10** And it has come to pass, || When you declare all these words to this people, || And they have said to you, || Why has Yhwh spoken all this great evil against us? indeed, what [is] our iniquity, and what [is] our sin, || That we have sinned against our God Yhwh? **11** Then you have said to them: Because that your fathers have forsaken Me, || A declaration of Yhwh, || And go after other gods, and serve them, || And they bow themselves to them, || And have forsaken Me, and not kept My law, **12** You also have done evil above your fathers, || And behold, you are each walking after the stubbornness of his evil heart, || So as not to listen to Me. **13** And I have cast you from off this land, || On to a land that you have not known, || You and your fathers, || And you have served other gods there by day and by night, || Where I do not give grace to you. **14** Therefore, behold, days are coming," || A declaration of Yhwh, || "And it is not said anymore, || Yhwh lives, who brought up the sons of Israel out of the land of Egypt, **15** But, Yhwh lives, who brought up the sons of Israel out of the land of the north, || And out of all the lands to where He drove them, || And I have brought them back to their land, || That I gave to their fathers. **16** Behold, I am sending for many fishers," || A declaration of Yhwh, || "And they have fished them, || And after this I send for many hunters, || And they have hunted them from off every mountain, || And from off every hill, and from holes of the rocks. **17** For My eyes [are] on all their ways, || They have not been hidden from My face, || Nor has their iniquity been concealed from before My eyes. **18** And I have repaid a first—A second time—their iniquity and their sin, || Because of their defiling My land, || With the carcass of their detestable things, || Indeed, their abominations have filled My inheritance." **19** O Yhwh, my strength, and my fortress, || And my refuge in a day of adversity, || Nations come to You from the ends of the earth, || And say, "Our fathers only inherited falsehood, || Vanity, and none among them is profitable." **20** Does man make gods for himself, || And they—no gods? **21** "Therefore, behold, I am causing them to know at this time, || I cause them to know My hand and My might, || And they have known that My Name [is] Yhwh!"

CHAPTER 17

1 "The sin of Judah is written with a pen of iron, || With the point of a diamond, || Engraved on the tablet of their heart, || And on the horns of your altars, **2** As their sons remember their altars and their Asherim, || By the green tree, by the high hills. **3** O My mountain in the field—your strength, || All your treasures—I give for a prey, || Your high places for sin in all your borders. **4** And you have let go—even through yourself, || Of your inheritance that I gave to you, || And I have caused you to serve your enemies, || In a land that you have not known, || For you have kindled a fire in My anger, || It burns for all time." **5** Thus said Yhwh: "Cursed [is] the man who trusts in man, || And has made flesh his arm, || And whose heart turns from Yhwh. **6** And he has been as a naked thing in a desert, || And does not see when good comes, || And has inhabited parched places in a wilderness, || A salt land, and not inhabited. **7** Blessed [is] the man who trusts in Yhwh, || And whose confidence has been Yhwh. **8** And has been as a tree planted by waters, || And he sends forth his roots by a stream, || And he does not see when heat comes, || And his leaf has been green, || And he is not sorrowful in a year of scarcity, || Nor does he cease from making fruit. **9** The heart [is] deceitful above all things, || And it [is] incurable—who knows it? **10** I, Yhwh, search the heart, try the reins, || Even to give to each according to his way, || According to the fruit of his doings. **11** A partridge hatching, and not bringing forth, || [Is] one making wealth, and not by right, || In the midst of his days he forsakes it, || And in his latter end—he is a fool." **12** A throne of glory on high from the beginning, || The place of our sanctuary, **13** The hope of Israel [is] Yhwh, || All forsaking You are ashamed. "And My apostates are written in the earth, || For they have forsaken Yhwh, || A fountain of living waters." **14** Heal me, O Yhwh, and I am healed, || Save me, and I am saved, || For You [are] my praise. **15** Behold, they are saying to me: "Where [is] the word of Yhwh? pray, let it come." **16** And I did not hurry from feeding after You, || And I have not desired the desperate day, || You have known the produce of my lips, || It has been before Your face, **17** Do not be to me for a terror, || You [are] my hope in a day of calamity. **18** Let my pursuers be ashamed, || And do not let me be ashamed—me! Let them be frightened, || And do not let me be frightened—me! Bring in on them a day of calamity, || And destroy them a second time [with] destruction. **19** Thus said Yhwh to me: "Go, and you have stood in the gate of the sons of the people, by which kings of Judah come in, and by which they go out, and in all gates of Jerusalem, **20** and you have said to them: Hear a word of Yhwh, you kings of Judah, and all Judah, and all inhabitants of Jerusalem, who are coming in by these gates," **21** Thus said Yhwh: "Take heed to yourselves, || And you do not bear a burden on the day of rest, || Nor have you brought [it] in by the gates of Jerusalem. **22** Nor do you take out a burden from your houses on the day of rest, || Indeed, you do not do any work, || And you have sanctified the day of rest, || As I have commanded your fathers. **23** And they have not listened nor inclined their ear, || And they stiffen their neck not to hear, || And not to receive instruction. **24** And it has been, if you certainly listen to Me," || A declaration of Yhwh, || "So as not to bring in a burden by the gates of this city on the day of rest, || And to sanctify the day of rest, || So as not to do any work in it— **25** Then kings and princes have entered by the gates of this city, || Sitting on the throne of David, || Riding in a chariot, and on horses, || They, and their princes, the man of Judah, || And inhabitants of Jerusalem, || And this city has remained for all time. **26** And they have come in from cities of Judah, || And from outskirts of Jerusalem, || And from the land of Benjamin, || And from the low country, || And from the hill-country, || And from the south, || Bringing in burnt-offering, and sacrifice, || And present, and frankincense, || And bringing praise [to] the house of Yhwh. **27** And if you do not listen to Me to sanctify the day of rest, || And so as not to bear a burden, || And to come in at the gates of Jerusalem on the day of rest, || Then I have kindled a fire in its gates, || And it has consumed the high places of Jerusalem, || And it is not quenched!"

CHAPTER 18

1 The word that has been to Jeremiah from Yhwh, saying, **2** "Rise, and you have gone down [to] the potter's house, and there I cause you to hear My words"; **3** and I go down [to] the potter's house, and behold, he is doing a work on the stones, **4** and the vessel that he is making is marred, as clay in the hand of the potter, and he has turned and he makes it another vessel, as it was right in the eyes of the potter to make. **5** And there is a word of Yhwh to me, saying, **6** "O house of Israel, am I not able to do to you as this potter?" A declaration of Yhwh. "Behold, as clay in the hand of the potter, || So [are] you in My hand, O house of Israel. **7** The moment I speak concerning a nation, || And concerning a kingdom, || To pluck up and to break down, and to destroy, **8** And that nation has turned from its evil, || Because I have spoken against it, || Then I have relented of the calamity that I thought to do to it. **9** And the

moment I speak concerning a nation, || And concerning a kingdom, to build, and to plant, **10** And it has done evil in My eyes, || So as not to listen to My voice, || Then I have relented of the good || That I have spoken of doing to it. **11** And now, speak now to men of Judah, || And against inhabitants of Jerusalem, saying, || Thus said Yhwh: Behold, I am framing calamity against you, || And devising a scheme against you; Please turn back, each from his evil way, || And amend your ways and your doings." **12** And they have said, "It is incurable, || For we go after our own plans, || And each of us does the stubbornness of his evil heart." **13** Therefore, thus said Yhwh: "Now ask among the nations, || Who has heard such things? The virgin of Israel has done a very horrible thing. **14** Does snow of Lebanon || Cease from the rock of the field? Will the cold strange [waters] that are flowing be forsaken? **15** But My people have forgotten Me, they make incense to a vein thing, || And they cause them to stumble in their ways—paths of old, || To walk in paths—a way not raised up, **16** To make their land become a desolation, || A continuous hissing, || Everyone passing by it is astonished, || And bemoans with his head. **17** I scatter them before an enemy as with an east wind, || I show them the neck and not the face, || In the day of their calamity." **18** And they say, "Come, || And we devise schemes against Jeremiah, || For law does not perish from the priest, || Nor counsel from the wise, || Nor the word from the prophet, || Come, and we strike him with the tongue, || And we do not attend to any of his words." **19** Give attention, O Yhwh, to me, || And listen to the voice of those contending with me. **20** Is evil repaid instead of good, || That they have dug a pit for my soul? Remember my standing before You to speak good of them, || To turn back Your wrath from them. **21** Therefore, give up their sons to famine, || And cause them to run on the sides of the sword, || And their wives are bereaved and widows, || And their men are slain by death, || Their young men [are] struck by sword in battle, **22** A cry is heard from their houses, || For You suddenly bring a troop against them, || For they dug a pit to capture me, || And they have hidden snares for my feet. **23** And You, O Yhwh, You have known, || All their counsel against me [is] for death, || You do not cover over their iniquity, || Nor blot out their sin from before You, || And they are made to stumble before You, || Work against them in the time of Your anger!

CHAPTER 19

1 Thus said Yhwh: "Go, and you have acquired a potter's earthen vessel, and from [the] elderly of the people, and from [the] elderly of the priests, **2** and you have gone forth to the Valley of the Son of Hinnom, that [is] at the opening of the gate of the pottery, and have proclaimed there the words that I speak to you, **3** and have said, Hear a word of Yhwh, you kings of Judah, and inhabitants of Jerusalem!" Thus said Yhwh of Hosts, God of Israel: "Behold, I am bringing in evil on this place, at which the ears of everyone who is hearing it tingles, **4** because that they have forsaken Me, and make known this place, and make incense in it to other gods, that they did not know, they and their fathers, and the kings of Judah, and they have filled this place [with] innocent blood, **5** and have built the high places of Ba'al to burn their sons with fire, burnt-offerings to Ba'al, that I did not command, nor spoke of, nor did it come up on My heart. **6** Therefore, behold, days are coming," a declaration of Yhwh, "and this place is no longer called The Tophet and Valley of the Son of Hinnom, but Valley of the Slaughter. **7** And I have made void the counsel of Judah and Jerusalem in this place, and have caused them to fall by the sword before their enemies, and by the hand of those seeking their life, and I have given their carcass for food to the bird of the heavens, and to the beast of the earth, **8** and I have made this city for a desolation, and for a hissing, everyone passing by it is astonished, and hisses for all its plagues. **9** And I have caused them to eat the flesh of their sons, and the flesh of their daughters, and they each eat the flesh of his friend, in the siege and in the constriction with which their enemies constrict them, and those seeking their life." **10** "And you have broken the bottle before the eyes of the men who are going with you, **11** and have said to them, Thus said Yhwh of Hosts: Thus I break this people and this city, as one breaks the potter's vessel, that is not able to be repaired again, and in Tophet they bury—without place to bury; **12** so I do to this place—a declaration of Yhwh—and to its inhabitants, so as to make this city as Tophet; **13** and the houses of Jerusalem, and the houses of the kings of

Judah, have been as the place of Tophet—defiled, even all the houses on whose roofs they have made incense to all the host of the heavens, so as to pour out oblations to other gods." **14** And Jeremiah comes in from Tophet, to where Yhwh had sent him to prophesy, and he stands in the court of the house of Yhwh, and he says to all the people: **15** "Thus said Yhwh of Hosts, God of Israel: Behold, I am bringing to this city, and on all its cities, all the calamity that I have spoken against it, for they have hardened their neck to not hear My words!"

CHAPTER 20

1 And Pashhur son of Immer the priest—who [is] also overseer, leader in the house of Yhwh—hears Jeremiah prophesying these things, **2** and Pashhur strikes Jeremiah the prophet, and puts him in the stocks that [are] by the Upper Gate of Benjamin, that [is] by the house of Yhwh. **3** and it comes to pass on the next day, that Pashhur brings Jeremiah out from the stocks, and Jeremiah says to him, "Yhwh has not called your name Pashhur, but Terror on Every Side. **4** For thus said Yhwh: Behold, I am making you for a fear to yourself, || And to all loving you, || And they have fallen by the sword of their enemies, and your eyes are beholding, || And all Judah I give into the hand of the king of Babylon, || And he has removed them to Babylon, || And he has struck them with the sword. **5** And I have given all the strength of this city, || And all its labor, and all its precious things, || Indeed, I give all the treasures of the kings of Judah into the hand of their enemies, || And they have spoiled them, and taken them, || And have brought them into Babylon. **6** And you, Pashhur, and all dwelling in your house, || Go into captivity. And you enter Babylon, || And there you die, and there you are buried, || You and all loving you, || To whom you have prophesied falsely." **7** You have persuaded me, O Yhwh, and I am persuaded; You have hardened me, and prevail, || I have been for a laughter all the day, || Everyone is mocking at me, **8** Because from the time I speak I cry out, I shout, "Violence and destruction!" || For the word of Yhwh has been to me || For reproach and for derision all the day. **9** And I said, "I do not mention Him, || Nor do I speak anymore in His Name," || And it has been in my heart || As a burning fire shut up in my bones, || And I have been weary of containing, || And I am not able. **10** For I have heard the evil report of many, "Fear [is] all around!" "Declare, and we declare it!" All my allies are watching [for] my halting, "Perhaps he is enticed, and we prevail over him, || And we take our vengeance on him." **11** And Yhwh [is] with me, as a mighty, awesome One, || Therefore my persecutors stumble and do not prevail, || They have been exceedingly ashamed, || For they have not acted wisely, || Continuous confusion is not forgotten. **12** And, O Yhwh of Hosts, trier of the righteous, || Beholder of reins and heart, || I see Your vengeance on them, || For I have revealed my cause to you. **13** Sing to Yhwh, praise Yhwh, || For He has delivered the soul of the needy || From the hand of evildoers. **14** Cursed [is] the day in which I was born, || The day that my mother bore me, || Let it not be blessed! **15** Cursed [is] the man who bore tidings [to] my father, || Saying, "A male child has been born to you," || Making him very glad! **16** Then that man has been as the cities, || That Yhwh overthrew, and did not relent, || And he has heard a cry in the morning, || And a shout at noontime. **17** Because he has not put me to death from the womb, || And my mother is to me—my grave, || And her womb [is] a perpetual pregnancy. **18** Why [is] this? I have come out from the womb || To see labor and sorrow, || Indeed, my days are consumed in shame!

CHAPTER 21

1 The word that has been to Jeremiah from Yhwh, in King Zedekiah's sending to him Pashhur son of Malchiah and Zephaniah son of Maaseiah the priest, saying, **2** "Please inquire of Yhwh for us, for Nebuchadnezzar king of Babylon has fought against us; perhaps Yhwh deals with us according to all His wonders, and causes him to go up from off us." **3** And Jeremiah says to them, "Thus you say to Zedekiah, **4** Thus said Yhwh, God of Israel: Behold, I am turning around the weapons of battle || That [are] in your hand, || With which you fight the king of Babylon, || And the Chaldeans, who are laying siege against you, || At the outside of the wall, || And I have gathered them into the midst of this city, **5** And I have fought

against you, || With an outstretched hand, and with a strong arm, || And in anger, and in fury, and in great wrath, **6** And I have struck the inhabitants of this city, || Both man and beast, || They die by a great pestilence. **7** And after this," || A declaration of Yhwh, || "I give Zedekiah king of Judah, || And his servants, and the people, || And those left in this city, || From the pestilence, from the sword, and from the famine, || Into the hand of Nebuchadnezzar king of Babylon, || And into the hand of their enemies, || And into the hand of those seeking their life, || And he has struck them by the mouth of the sword, || He has no pity on them, || Nor does he spare, nor does he have mercy." **8** "And you say to this people, Thus said Yhwh: Behold, I am setting before you the way of life, || And the way of death! **9** Whoever is abiding in this city—dies, || By sword, and by famine, and by pestilence, || And whoever is going forth, || And has fallen to the Chaldeans, || Who are laying siege against you—lives, || And his life has been for a spoil to him. **10** For I have set My face against this city for calamity, || And not for good," || A declaration of Yhwh. "It is given into the hand of the king of Babylon, || And he has burned it with fire. **11** And as for the house of the king of Judah," || Hear a word of Yhwh; **12** O house of David, thus said Yhwh: "Decide judgment in the morning, || And deliver the plundered from the hand of the oppressor, || Lest My fury go forth as fire, || And has burned, and none is quenching, || Because of the evil of your doings. **13** Behold, I [am] against you," || A declaration of Yhwh, || "O inhabitant of the valley, rock of the plain, || Who are saying, Who comes down against us? And who comes into our habitations? **14** And I have laid a charge against you, || According to the fruit of your doings," || A declaration of Yhwh, || "And I have kindled a fire in its forest, || And it has consumed all its outskirts!"

CHAPTER 22

1 Thus said Yhwh: "Go down [to] the house of the king of Judah, and you have spoken this word there, and have said, **2** Hear a word of Yhwh, O king of Judah, who are sitting on the throne of David, you, and your servants, and your people, who are coming in at these gates," **3** Thus said Yhwh: "Do judgment and righteousness, || And deliver the plundered from the hand of the oppressor, || And sojourner, orphan, and widow, you do not oppress nor wrong, || And innocent blood you do not shed in this place. **4** For if you certainly do this thing, || Then kings sitting for David on his throne || Have come in by the gates of this house, || Riding on chariot, and on horses, || He, and his servants, and his people. **5** And if you do not hear these words, || I have sworn by Myself," || A declaration of Yhwh, || "That this house is for a desolation." **6** For thus said Yhwh concerning the house of the king of Judah: "You [are] Gilead to Me—head of Lebanon, || If not—I make you a wilderness, || Cities [that] are not inhabited. **7** And I have separated destroyers for you, || Each with his weapons, || And they have cut down the choice of your cedars, || And have cast them on the fire." **8** And many nations have passed by this city, || And they have each said to his neighbor, "Why has Yhwh done thus to this great city?" **9** And they have said, "Because that they have forsaken || The covenant of their God Yhwh, || And bow themselves to other gods, and serve them." **10** You do not weep for the dead, nor bemoan for him, || Weep severely for the traveler, || For he does not return again, || Nor has he seen the land of his birth. **11** For thus said Yhwh concerning Shallum son of Josiah king of Judah, who is reigning instead of his father Josiah, who has gone forth from this place: "He does not return here again; **12** For he dies in the place to where they have removed him, || And he does not see this land again. **13** Woe to him who is building his house by unrighteousness, || And his upper chambers by injustice, || He lays service on his neighbor for nothing, || And he does not give his wage to him. **14** Who is saying, || I build a large house for myself, || And airy upper chambers, || And he has cut out its windows for himself, || Covered with cedar, and painted with vermillion. **15** Do you reign, because you are fretting yourself in cedar? Your father—did he not eat and drink? Indeed, he did judgment and righteousness, || Then [it is] well with him. **16** He decided the cause of the poor and needy, || Then [it is] well—is it not to know Me?" A declaration of Yhwh. **17** "But your eyes and your heart are not, || Except on your dishonest gain, || And on shedding of innocent blood, || And on oppression, and on doing of violence." **18** Therefore, thus said Yhwh concerning Jehoiakim son of Josiah king of Judah: "They do not lament for him, ||

Oh, my brother! And, Oh, my sister! They do not lament for him, || Oh, lord! And, Oh, his splendor! **19** He is buried [with] the burial of a donkey, || Dragged and cast out there to the gates of Jerusalem. **20** Go up to Lebanon, and cry, || And give forth your voice in Bashan, || And cry from Abarim, || For all loving you have been destroyed. **21** I have spoken to you in your ease, || You have said, I do not listen, || This [is] your way from your youth, || For you have not listened to My voice. **22** Wind consumes all your friends, || And your lovers go into captivity, || Surely then you are ashamed, || And have blushed for all your wickedness. **23** O dweller in Lebanon, making a nest among cedars, || How gracious have you been when pangs come to you, || Pain—as of a travailing woman." **24** "[As] I live," || A declaration of Yhwh, || "Though Coniah son of Jehoiakim king of Judah was a seal on My right hand, surely there I draw you away, **25** And I have given you into the hand of those seeking your life, || And into hands of which you are afraid, || Into the hand of Nebuchadnezzar king of Babylon, || And into the hand of the Chaldeans. **26** And I have cast you, || And your mother who bore you, to another country, || Where you were not born, and you die there. **27** And to the land to where they are lifting up their soul to return, || They do not return there." **28** A grief—a despised broken thing—is this man Coniah? A vessel in which there is no pleasure? Why have they been cast up and down, || He and his seed, || Indeed, were they cast on to a land that they did not know? **29** Earth, earth, earth, hear a word of Yhwh! **30** Thus said Yhwh: "Write this man down [as] childless, || A man—he does not prosper in his days, || For none of his seed prospers, || Sitting on the throne of David, || And ruling in Judah again!"

CHAPTER 23

1 "Woe to shepherds destroying, || And scattering the flock of My pasture," || A declaration of Yhwh. **2** Therefore, thus said Yhwh, God of Israel, || Against the shepherds who feed My people: "You have scattered My flock, and drive them away, || And have not inspected them, || Behold, I am charging on you the evil of your doings," || A declaration of Yhwh. **3** "And I gather the remnant of My flock || Out of all the lands to where I drove them, || And have brought them back to their fold, || And they have been fruitful, and multiplied. **4** And I have raised shepherds for them, || And they have fed them, || And they no longer fear, nor are frightened, || Nor are they lacking," || A declaration of Yhwh. **5** "Behold, days are coming," || A declaration of Yhwh, || "And I have raised a righteous shoot to David, || And a king has reigned and acted wisely, || And done judgment and righteousness in the earth. **6** Judah is saved in His days, and Israel dwells confidently, || And this [is] His Name that Yhwh proclaims Him: Our Righteousness. **7** Therefore, behold, days are coming," || A declaration of Yhwh, || "And they no longer say, Yhwh lives who brought up || The sons of Israel out of the land of Egypt, **8** But—Yhwh lives, who brought up, || And who brought in, the seed of the house of Israel, || From the land of the north, || And from all the lands to where I drove them, || And they have dwelt on their own ground!" **9** In reference to the prophets: My heart has been broken in my midst, || All my bones have fluttered, || I have been as a man—a drunkard, || And as a man—wine has passed over him, || Because of Yhwh, and of His holy words. **10** For the land has been full of adulterers, || For the land has mourned because of these, || The pleasant places of the wilderness have dried up, || And their course is evil, and their might—not right. **11** "For both prophet and priest have been profane, || Indeed, I found their wickedness in My house," || A declaration of Yhwh. **12** "Therefore their way is as slippery places to them, || They are driven into thick darkness, || And they have fallen in it, || For I bring in calamity against them, || The year of their inspection," || A declaration of Yhwh. **13** "And I have seen folly in prophets of Samaria, || They have prophesied by Ba'al, || And cause My people—Israel—to err. **14** And I have seen a horrible thing in prophets of Jerusalem, || Committing adultery, and walking falsely, || Indeed, they strengthened the hands of evildoers, || So that they have not turned back, || Each from his wickedness, || All of them have been as Sodom to me, || And its inhabitants as Gomorrah." **15** Therefore, thus said Yhwh of Hosts, concerning the prophets: "Behold, I am causing them to eat wormwood, || And have caused them to drink water of gall, || For from prophets of Jerusalem || Profanity has gone forth to all the land." **16** Thus said Yhwh of Hosts: "You do not listen to the words || Of the prophets who

are prophesying to you, || They are making you vain things, || They speak a vision of their own heart, || Not from the mouth of Yhwh. **17** Diligently saying to those despising, || The word of Yhwh: Peace is for you, || And [to] everyone walking in the stubbornness of his heart, they have said: Evil does not come to you." **18** For who has stood in the counsel of Yhwh, || And sees and hears His word? Who has regarded My word, and listens? **19** Behold, a whirlwind of Yhwh—Fury has gone out, even a piercing whirlwind, || It stays on the head of the wicked. **20** The anger of Yhwh does not turn back || Until His doing, and until His establishing, || The thoughts of His heart, || In the latter end of the days || You attend to it with understanding. **21** "I have not sent the prophets, and they have run, || I have not spoken to them, and they have prophesied. **22** But if they stood in My counsel, || Then they cause My people to hear My words, || And they turn them back from their evil way, || And from the evil of their doings. **23** [Am] I a God near," || A declaration of Yhwh, || "And not a God far off? **24** Is anyone hidden in secret places, || And I do not see him?" A declaration of Yhwh, "Do I not fill the heavens and the earth?" A declaration of Yhwh. **25** "I have heard that which the prophets said, || Who prophesy falsehood in My Name, saying, || I have dreamed, I have dreamed. **26** Until when is it in the heart of the prophets? The prophets of falsehood, || Indeed, prophets of the deceit of their heart, **27** Who are devising to cause My people || To forget My Name by their dreams, || That they each recount to his neighbor, || As their fathers forgot My Name for Ba'al. **28** The prophet with whom [is] a dream, || Let him recount the dream, || And he with whom [is] My word, || Let him truly speak My word. What does the straw [have to do] with the grain?" A declaration of Yhwh. **29** "Is it not thus? My word [is] as fire," || A declaration of Yhwh. "And as a hammer—it breaks a rock in pieces. **30** Therefore, behold, I [am] against the prophets," || A declaration of Yhwh, || "Each stealing My words from his neighbor. **31** Behold, I [am] against the prophets," || A declaration of Yhwh, || "Who are making their tongue smooth, || And they affirm—an affirmation. **32** Behold, I [am] against the prophets of false dreams," || A declaration of Yhwh, || "And they recount them, and cause My people to err, || By their falsehoods, and by their instability, || And I have not sent them, || Nor have I commanded them, || And they are not profitable to this people at all," || A declaration of Yhwh. **33** "And when this people, or the prophet, || Or a priest, asks you, saying, What [is] the burden of Yhwh? Then you have said to them: You [are] the burden, and I have left you," || A declaration of Yhwh. **34** "And the prophet, and the priest, and the people, || That says, The burden of Yhwh, || I have seen after that man, and after his house. **35** Thus you each say to his neighbor, || And each to his brother: What has Yhwh answered? And what has Yhwh spoken? **36** And you do not mention the burden of Yhwh anymore, || For the burden to each is His word, || And you have overturned the words of the living God, Yhwh of Hosts, our God. **37** Thus you say to the prophet, || What has Yhwh answered you? And what has Yhwh spoken? **38** And if you say, The burden of Yhwh, || Therefore, thus said Yhwh: Because of your saying this word, || The burden of Yhwh, || And I send to you, saying, || You do not say, The burden of Yhwh. **39** Therefore, behold, I have utterly taken you away, || And I have sent you out, || And the city that I gave to you, || And to your fathers, from before My face, **40** And I have put continuous reproach on you, || And continuous shame that is not forgotten!"

CHAPTER 24

1 Yhwh has showed me, and behold, two baskets of figs, appointed before the temple of Yhwh—after the removing by Nebuchadnezzar king of Babylon, of Jeconiah, son of Jehoiakim king of Judah, and the heads of Judah, and the artisan, and the smith, from Jerusalem, when he brings them into Babylon— **2** In one basket [are] very good figs, like the first-ripe figs, and in the other basket [are] very bad figs that are not eaten because of badness. **3** And Yhwh says to me, "What are you seeing, Jeremiah?" And I say, "Figs, the good figs [are] very good, and the bad [are] very bad, that are not eaten because of badness." **4** And there is a word of Yhwh to me, saying, **5** "Thus said Yhwh, God of Israel: Like these good figs so I acknowledge || The expulsion of Judah that I sent from this place, || [To] the land of the Chaldeans—for good. **6** And I have set My eyes on them for good, || And have brought them back to this land, || And built them up, and I do not throw down, || And have planted them, and do not pluck up. **7** And have given to them a heart to know Me, || For I [am] Yhwh, || And they have been to Me for a people, || And I am to them for God, || For they turned back to Me with all their heart. ⁸ And like the bad figs that are not eaten for badness, || Surely thus said Yhwh: So I make Zedekiah king of Judah, || And his heads, and the remnant of Jerusalem, || Who are left in this land, || And who are dwelling in the land of Egypt, ⁹ And I have given them for a trembling, || For evil—to all kingdoms of the earth, || For a reproach, and for an allegory, || For a byword, and for a reviling, || In all the places to where I drive them. ¹⁰ And I have sent the sword against them, || The famine and the pestilence, || Until their consumption from off the ground, || That I gave to them and to their fathers!"

CHAPTER 25

¹ The word that has been to Jeremiah concerning all the people of Judah, in the fourth year of Jehoiakim son of Josiah king of Judah—it [is] the first year of Nebuchadnezzar king of Babylon— ² Which Jeremiah the prophet has spoken concerning all the people of Judah, even to all the inhabitants of Jerusalem, saying, ³ "From the thirteenth year of Josiah son of Amon king of Judah, and to this day—this twenty-third year—the word of Yhwh has been to me, and I speak to you, rising early and speaking, and you have not listened; ⁴ and Yhwh has sent all His servants to you, the prophets, rising early and sending, and you have not listened, nor inclined your ear to hear, saying, ⁵ Please turn back, each from his evil way, and from the evil of your doings, and dwell on the ground that Yhwh has given to you and to your fathers from age to age, ⁶ and you do not go after other gods to serve them, and to bow yourselves to them, nor do you provoke Me to anger with the work of your hands, and I do no evil to you; ⁷ and you have not listened to Me," a declaration of Yhwh, "so as to provoke Me to anger with the work of your hands for evil to you. ⁸ Therefore, thus said Yhwh of Hosts: Because that you have not obeyed My words, ⁹ behold, I am sending, and have taken all the families of the north—a declaration of Yhwh—even to Nebuchadnezzar king of Babylon, My servant, and have brought them in against this land, and against its inhabitants, and against all these surrounding nations, and have devoted them, and appointed them for an astonishment, and for a hissing, and for continuous ruins. ¹⁰ And I have destroyed from them the voice of rejoicing, and the voice of joy, voice of bridegroom and voice of bride, noise of millstones, and the light of lamps. ¹¹ And all this land has been for a desolation, for an astonishment, and these nations have served the king of Babylon seventy years. ¹² And it has come to pass, at the fullness of seventy years, I charge against the king of Babylon, and against that nation," a declaration of Yhwh, "their iniquity, and against the land of the Chaldeans, and have appointed it for continuous desolations. ¹³ And I have brought in on that land all My words that I have spoken against it, all that is written in this scroll, that Jeremiah has prophesied concerning all the nations. ¹⁴ For laid service on them—also them—have many nations and great kings, and I have given repayment to them according to their doing, and according to the work of their hands." ¹⁵ For thus said Yhwh, God of Israel, to me: "Take the wine cup of this fury out of My hand, and you have caused all the nations to drink it to whom I am sending you; ¹⁶ and they have drunk, and shaken themselves and shown themselves [to be] foolish, because of the sword that I am sending among them." ¹⁷ And I take the cup out of the hand of Yhwh, and cause all the nations to drink to whom Yhwh sent me: ¹⁸ Jerusalem, and the cities of Judah, || And its kings, its heads, || To give them to ruin, to astonishment, || To hissing, and to reviling, as [at] this day; ¹⁹ Pharaoh king of Egypt, and his servants, || And his heads, and all his people, ²⁰ And all the mixed people, || And all the kings of the land of Uz, || And all the kings of the land of the Philistines, || And Ashkelon, and Gaza, and Ekron, || And the remnant of Ashdod, ²¹ Edom, and Moab, and the sons of Ammon, ²² And all the kings of Tyre, || And all the kings of Sidon, || And the kings of the island that [is] beyond the sea, ²³ Dedan, and Tema, and Buz, || And all cutting the corners [of the beard], ²⁴ And all the kings of Arabia, || And all the kings of the mixed people, || Who are dwelling in the wilderness, ²⁵ And all the kings of Zimri, || And all the kings of Elam, || And all the kings of Media, ²⁶ And all the kings of the north, || The near and the far off to one another, || And all the kingdoms of the earth, || That [are] on the face of the ground, || And King Sheshach drinks after them. ²⁷ "And you have said to them,

Thus said Yhwh of Hosts, God of Israel: Drink, indeed drink abundantly, || And vomit, and fall, and do not rise, || Because of the sword that I am sending among you. ²⁸ And it has come to pass, || When they refuse to receive the cup out of your hand to drink, || That you have said to them, Thus said Yhwh of Hosts: You certainly drink. ²⁹ For behold, in the city over which My Name is called, || I am beginning to bring ruin, || And are you entirely acquitted? You are not acquitted, for I am proclaiming a sword, || For all inhabitants of the land," || A declaration of Yhwh of Hosts. ³⁰ "And you, you prophesy all these words to them, and have said to them: Yhwh roars from the high place, || And gives forth His voice from His holy habitation, || He surely roars for His habitation, || A shout as those treading [the grapes], || God answers all the inhabitants of the land, ³¹ A rumbling has come to the end of the earth, || For Yhwh has a controversy with nations, || He has executed judgment for all flesh, || He has given the wicked to the sword," || A declaration of Yhwh. ³² Thus said Yhwh of Hosts: "Behold, evil is going out from nation to nation, || And a great whirlwind is stirred up from the sides of the earth. ³³ And the pierced of Yhwh have been in that day, || From the end of the earth even to the end of the earth, || They are not lamented, nor gathered, nor buried, || For they are dung on the face of the ground. ³⁴ Howl, you shepherds, and cry, || And roll yourselves, you majestic of the flock, || For your days have been full || For slaughtering, and [for] your scatterings, || And you have fallen as a desirable vessel. ³⁵ And refuge has perished from the shepherds, || And escape from the majestic of the flock. ³⁶ A voice of the cry of the shepherds, || And a howling of the majestic of the flock, || For Yhwh is spoiling their pasture. ³⁷ And the peaceable habitations have been cut down, || Because of the fierceness of the anger of Yhwh. ³⁸ He has forsaken His covert as a young lion, || Surely their land has become a desolation, || Because of the oppressing fierceness, || And because of the fierceness of His anger!"

CHAPTER 26

¹ In the beginning of the reign of Jehoiakim son of Josiah, king of Judah, this word has been from Yhwh, saying, ² "Thus said Yhwh: Stand in the court of the house of Yhwh, and you have spoken to all [those of] the cities of Judah, who are coming to bow themselves in the house of Yhwh, all the words that I have commanded you to speak to them—you do not diminish a word. ³ Perhaps they listen, and each turns back from his evil way; then I have relented concerning the evil that I am thinking of doing to them, because of the evil of their doings. ⁴ And you have said to them, Thus said Yhwh: If you do not listen to Me, to walk in My law that I set before you, ⁵ to listen to the words of My servants the prophets, whom I am sending to you, indeed, rising early and sending, and you have not listened, ⁶ then I have given up this house as Shiloh, and this city I give up for a reviling to all nations of the earth." ⁷ And the priests, and the prophets, and all the people, hear Jeremiah speaking these words in the house of Yhwh, ⁸ and it comes to pass, at the completion of Jeremiah's speaking all that Yhwh has commanded him to speak to all the people, that the priests, and the prophets, and all the people catch him, saying, "You surely die! ⁹ Why have you prophesied in the Name of Yhwh, saying, This house will be as Shiloh, and this city is desolated, without inhabitant?" And all the people are assembled to Jeremiah in the house of Yhwh. ¹⁰ And the heads of Judah hear these things, and they go up from the house of the king [to] the house of Yhwh, and sit in the opening of the New Gate of Yhwh. ¹¹ And the priests and the prophets speak to the heads, and to all the people, saying, "Judgment of death [is] for this man, for he has prophesied against this city, as you have heard with your ears." ¹² And Jeremiah speaks to all the heads, and to all the people, saying, "Yhwh sent me to prophesy concerning this house, and concerning this city, all the words that you have heard. ¹³ And now, amend your ways, and your doings, and listen to the voice of your God Yhwh, and Yhwh relents concerning the evil that He has spoken against you. ¹⁴ And I, behold, I [am] in your hand, do to me as is good and as is right in your eyes; ¹⁵ only, certainly know that if you are putting me to death, you are surely putting innocent blood on yourselves, and on this city, and on its inhabitants; for Yhwh has truly sent me to you to speak all these words in your ears." ¹⁶ And the heads and all the people say to the priests and to the prophets, "There is not a judgment of death for this man, for he has spoken to us in the Name of our God Yhwh." ¹⁷ And

men from [the] elderly of the land rise up and speak to all the assembly of the people, saying, **18** "Micah the Morashtite has been prophesying in the days of Hezekiah king of Judah, and he says to all the people of Judah, saying, Thus said Yhwh of Hosts: Zion is a plowed field, and Jerusalem is heaps, || And the mountain of the house is for high places of a forest. **19** Did Hezekiah king of Judah and all Judah put him to death? Did he not fear Yhwh? indeed, he appeases the face of Yhwh, and Yhwh relents concerning the calamity that He spoke against them; and we are doing great evil against our souls." **20** And there has also been a man prophesying in the Name of Yhwh, Urijah son of Shemaiah, of Kirjath-Jearim, and he prophesies against this city, and against this land according to all the words of Jeremiah, **21** and King Jehoiakim, and all his mighty ones, and all the heads, hear his words, and the king seeks to put him to death, and Urijah hears, and fears, and flees, and goes to Egypt. **22** And King Jehoiakim sends men to Egypt— Elnathan son of Achbor, and men with him to Egypt— **23** and they bring out Urijah from Egypt, and bring him to King Jehoiakim, and he strikes him with a sword, and casts his corpse to the graves of the sons of the people. **24** Only, the hand of Ahikam son of Shaphan has been with Jeremiah so as not to give him up into the hand of the people to put him to death.

CHAPTER 27

1 In the beginning of the reign of Jehoiakim son of Josiah, king of Judah, this word has been to Jeremiah from Yhwh, saying, **2** "Thus said Yhwh to me: Make bands and yokes for yourself, **3** and you have put them on your neck, and have sent them to the king of Edom, and to the king of Moab, and to the king of the sons of Ammon, and to the king of Tyre, and to the king of Sidon, by the hand of messengers who are coming to Jerusalem, to Zedekiah king of Judah; **4** and you have commanded them for their lords, saying, Thus said Yhwh of Hosts, God of Israel, **5** Thus you say to your lords, I have made the earth with man, and the livestock that [are] on the face of the earth, by My great power, and by My outstretched arm, and I have given it to whom it has been right in My eyes. **6** And now, I have given all these lands into the hand of Nebuchadnezzar king of Babylon, My servant, and I have also given the beast of the field to him to serve him; **7** and all the nations have served him, and his son, and his son's son, until the coming in of the time of his land, also it; and many nations and great kings have made him serve them. **8** And it has come to pass, the nation and the kingdom that does not serve him— Nebuchadnezzar king of Babylon—and that which does not put its neck into the yoke of the king of Babylon, with sword, and with famine, and with pestilence, I lay a charge on that nation—a declaration of Yhwh—until I consume them by his hand. **9** And you, you do not listen to your prophets, and to your diviners, and to your dreamers, and to your observers of clouds, and to your sorcerers who are speaking to you, saying, You do not serve the king of Babylon— **10** For they are prophesying falsehood to you, so as to remove you far from your ground, and I have driven you out, and you have perished. **11** And the nation that causes its neck to enter into the yoke of the king of Babylon, and has served him—I have left it on its ground—a declaration of Yhwh—and it has tilled it, and dwelt in it." **12** And I have spoken to Zedekiah king of Judah according to all these words, saying, "Cause your necks to enter into the yoke of the king of Babylon, and serve him and his people, and live. **13** Why do you die, you and your people, by sword, by famine, and by pestilence, as Yhwh has spoken concerning the nation that does not serve the king of Babylon? **14** And you do not listen to the words of the prophets who are speaking to you, saying, You do not serve the king of Babylon— for they are prophesying falsehood to you. **15** For I have not sent them—a declaration of Yhwh—and they are prophesying falsely in My Name, so as to drive you out, and you have perished, you and the prophets who are prophesying to you." **16** And to the priests, and to all this people, I have spoken, saying, "Thus said Yhwh: You do not listen to the words of your prophets, who are prophesying to you, saying, Behold, the vessels of the house of Yhwh are now brought back from Babylon in haste, for they are prophesying falsehood to you. **17** You do not listen to them; serve the king of Babylon and live! Why is this city a ruin? **18** And if they are prophets, and if a word of Yhwh is with them, let them now intercede with Yhwh of Hosts, so that the vessels that are left in the house of Yhwh,

and [in] the house of the king of Judah, and in Jerusalem, have not gone into Babylon. **19** For thus said Yhwh of Hosts concerning the pillars, and concerning the sea, and concerning the bases, and concerning the rest of the vessels that are left in this city, **20** that Nebuchadnezzar king of Babylon has not taken, in his removing Jeconiah son of Jehoiakim king of Judah from Jerusalem to Babylon with all the nobles of Judah and Jerusalem, **21** surely thus said Yhwh of Hosts, God of Israel, concerning the vessels that are left of the house of Yhwh, and of the house of the king of Judah, and [in] Jerusalem: **22** They are brought to Babylon, and there they are until the day of My inspecting them—a declaration of Yhwh; then I have brought them up, and have brought them back to this place."

CHAPTER 28

1 And it comes to pass, in that year, in the beginning of the reign of Zedekiah king of Judah, in the fourth year, in the fifth month, Hananiah son of Azur the prophet, who [is] of Gibeon, has spoken to me in the house of Yhwh, before the eyes of the priests, and all the people, saying, **2** "Thus spoke Yhwh of Hosts, God of Israel, saying, I have broken the yoke of the king of Babylon; **3** within two years of days I am bringing back to this place all the vessels of the house of Yhwh that Nebuchadnezzar king of Babylon has taken from this place, and carries to Babylon, **4** and Jeconiah son of Jehoiakim, king of Judah, and all the expulsion of Judah, who are entering Babylon, I am bringing back to this place—a declaration of Yhwh; for I break the yoke of the king of Babylon." **5** And Jeremiah the prophet says to Hananiah the prophet, before the eyes of the priests, and before the eyes of all the people who are standing in the house of Yhwh, **6** indeed, Jeremiah the prophet says, "Amen! So may Yhwh do; Yhwh establish your words that you have prophesied, to bring back the vessels of the house of Yhwh and all the expulsion from Babylon, to this place. **7** Only, please hear this word that I am speaking in your ears, and in the ears of all the people. **8** The prophets who have been before me, and before you, from of old, even they prophesy concerning many lands, and concerning great kingdoms, of battle, and of calamity, and of pestilence. **9** The prophet who prophesies of peace, by the word of the prophet coming to pass, the prophet is known [as] one whom Yhwh has truly sent." **10** And Hananiah the prophet takes the yoke from off the neck of Jeremiah the prophet, and breaks it, **11** and Hananiah speaks before the eyes of all the people, saying, "Thus said Yhwh: Thus I break the yoke of Nebuchadnezzar king of Babylon, within two years of days, from off the neck of all the nations"; and Jeremiah the prophet goes on his way. **12** And there is a word of Yhwh to Jeremiah after the breaking, by Hananiah the prophet, of the yoke from off the neck of Jeremiah the prophet, saying, **13** "Go, and you have spoken to Hananiah, saying, Thus said Yhwh: You have broken yokes of wood, and I have made yokes of iron instead of them. **14** For thus said Yhwh of Hosts, God of Israel: I have put a yoke of iron on the neck of all these nations to serve Nebuchadnezzar king of Babylon, and they have served him, and I have also given the beast of the field to him." **15** And Jeremiah the prophet says to Hananiah the prophet, "Now hear, O Hananiah; Yhwh has not sent you, and you have caused this people to trust on falsehood. **16** Therefore, thus said Yhwh: Behold, I am casting you from off the face of the ground; you die this year, for you have spoken apostasy concerning Yhwh." **17** And Hananiah the prophet dies in that year, in the seventh month.

CHAPTER 29

1 And these [are] the words of the letter that Jeremiah the prophet sent from Jerusalem to the remnant of [the] elderly of the expulsion, and to the priests, and to the prophets, and to all the people—whom Nebuchadnezzar removed from Jerusalem to Babylon, **2** after the going forth of Jeconiah the king, and the mistress, and the officers, heads of Judah and Jerusalem, and the craftsman, and the smith, from Jerusalem— **3** by the hand of Eleasah son of Shaphan, and Gemariah son of Hilkiah, whom Zedekiah king of Judah sent to Babylon, to Nebuchadnezzar king of Babylon, saying, **4** "Thus said Yhwh of Hosts, God of Israel, to all the expulsion that I removed from Jerusalem to Babylon: **5** Build houses and abide; and plant gardens and eat their fruit; **6** take wives and beget sons and daughters; and take wives for your sons, and give your daughters to husbands, and they bear sons and daughters; and multiply there, and you are not few; **7** and seek the peace of the city to where I have removed you, and pray to Yhwh for it, for in its peace you have peace. **8** For thus said Yhwh of Hosts, God of Israel: Do not let your prophets who [are] in your midst, and your diviners, lift you up, nor listen to their dreams, that you are causing [them] to dream; **9** for they are prophesying with falsehood to you in My Name; I have not sent them, a declaration of Yhwh. **10** For thus said Yhwh: Surely at the fullness of Babylon—seventy years—I inspect you, and have established My good word toward you, to bring you back to this place. **11** For I have known the thoughts that I am thinking toward you—a declaration of Yhwh; thoughts of peace, and not of evil, to give posterity and hope to you. **12** And you have called Me, and have gone, and have prayed to Me, and I have listened to you, **13** and you have sought Me, and have found, for you seek Me with all your heart; **14** and I have been found by you—a declaration of Yhwh; and I have turned back [to] your captivity, and have gathered you out of all the nations, and out of all the places to where I have driven you—a declaration of Yhwh—and I have brought you back to the place from where I removed you. **15** Because you have said, Yhwh has raised up prophets to us in Babylon, **16** surely thus said Yhwh concerning the king who is sitting on the throne of David, and concerning all the people that are dwelling in this city, your brothers who did not go forth with you in the expulsion— **17** thus said Yhwh of Hosts: Behold, I am sending the sword, the famine, and the pestilence among them, and I have given them up as figs that [are] vile, that are not eaten because of badness. **18** And I have pursued after them with sword, with famine, and with pestilence, and have given them for a trembling to all kingdoms of the earth, for a curse and for an astonishment, and for a hissing, and for a reproach among all the nations to where I have driven them, **19** because that they have not listened to My words—a declaration of Yhwh—that I sent to them by My servants the prophets, rising early and sending, and you did not listen—a declaration of Yhwh. **20** And you, hear a word of Yhwh, all you of the captivity that I have sent from Jerusalem to Babylon— **21** thus said Yhwh of Hosts, God of Israel, concerning Ahab son of Kolaiah, and concerning Zedekiah son of Maaseiah, who are prophesying falsehood to you in My Name: Behold, I am giving them into the hand of Nebuchadnezzar king of Babylon, and he has struck them before your eyes, **22** and because of them a reviling has been taken by all the expulsion of Judah that [are] in Babylon, saying, Yhwh sets you as Zedekiah, and as Ahab, whom the king of Babylon roasted with fire; **23** because that they have done folly in Israel, and commit adultery with the wives of their neighbors, and falsely speak a word in My Name that I have not commanded them, and I [am] He who knows and a witness—a declaration of Yhwh. **24** And you speak to Shemaiah the Nehelamite, saying, **25** Thus said Yhwh of Hosts, God of Israel, saying, Because that you have sent letters in your name to all the people who [are] in Jerusalem, and to Zephaniah son of Maaseiah the priest, and to all the priests, saying, **26** Yhwh has made you priest instead of Jehoiada the priest, for there being inspectors of the house of Yhwh over every man [who] is mad and making himself a prophet, and you have put him in the stocks and in the pillory. **27** And now, why have you not pushed against Jeremiah of Anathoth, who is making himself a prophet to you? **28** Because that he has sent to us [in] Babylon, saying, It [is] long, build houses and abide; and plant gardens and eat their fruit." **29** And Zephaniah the priest reads this letter in the ears of Jeremiah the prophet. **30** And there is a word of Yhwh to Jeremiah, saying, **31** "Send to all the expulsion, saying, Thus said Yhwh concerning Shemaiah the Nehelamite: Because that Shemaiah prophesied to you, and I have not sent him, and he causes you to trust on falsehood, **32** therefore, thus said Yhwh: Behold, I am seeing after Shemaiah the Nehelamite, and after his seed, he has none dwelling in the midst of this people, nor does he look on the good that I am doing to My people," a declaration of Yhwh, "for he has spoken apostasy against Yhwh."

CHAPTER 30

1 The word that has been to Jeremiah from Yhwh, saying, **2** "Thus spoke Yhwh, God of Israel, saying, write for yourself all the words that I have spoken to you on a scroll. **3** For behold, days are coming—a declaration of Yhwh—and I have turned back [to] the captivity of My people Israel and Judah, said Yhwh, and I have caused them to return to the land that I gave to their fathers, and they possess it." **4** And these [are] the words that Yhwh has spoken concerning Israel and concerning Judah: **5** Surely thus said Yhwh: "We have heard a voice of trembling, || Fear—and there is no peace. **6** Now ask and see, is a male bringing forth? Why have I seen every man || [With] his hands on his loins, as a travailing woman, || And all faces have been turned to paleness? **7** Woe! For that day [is] great, without any like it, || Indeed, it [is] the time of Jacob's tribulation, || Yet he is saved out of it. **8** And it has come to pass in that day, || A declaration of Yhwh of Hosts, || I break his yoke from off your neck, || And I draw away your bands, || And strangers lay no more service on him. **9** And they have served their God Yhwh, || And David their king whom I raise up to them. **10** And you, do not be afraid, My servant Jacob, || A declaration of Yhwh, || Nor be frightened, O Israel, || For behold, I am saving you from afar, || And your seed from the land of their captivity, || And Jacob has turned back and rested, || And is quiet, and there is none troubling. **11** For I [am] with you," || A declaration of Yhwh, || "To save you, || For I make an end of all the nations || To where I have scattered you, || Only, I do not make an end of you, || And I have disciplined you in judgment, || And do not entirely acquit you." **12** For thus said Yhwh: "Your breach is incurable, your stroke grievous, **13** There is none judging your cause to bind up, || There are no healing medicines for you. **14** all loving you have forgotten you, || They do not seek you, || For I struck you with the stroke of an enemy, || The discipline of a fierce one, || Because of the abundance of your iniquity, your sins have been mighty! **15** Why do you cry concerning your breach? Your pain [is] incurable, || Because of the abundance of your iniquity, || Your sins have been mighty! I have done these to you. **16** Therefore all consuming you are consumed, || And all your adversaries—all of them—Go into captivity, || And your spoilers have been for a spoil, || And I give up all your plunderers to plunder. **17** For I increase health to you, || And I heal you from your strokes," || A declaration of Yhwh, || "For they have called you an outcast, [saying], || It [is] Zion, || There is none seeking for her." **18** Thus said Yhwh: "Behold, I turn back [to] the captivity of the tents of Jacob, || And I pity his dwelling places, || And the city has been built on its heap, || And the palace remains according to its ordinance. **19** And thanksgiving has gone forth from them, || And the voice of playful ones, || And I have multiplied them and they are not few, || And made them honorable, and they are not small. **20** And his sons have been as before, || And his congregation is established before Me, || And I have seen after all his oppressors. **21** And his majestic one has been of himself, || And his ruler goes forth from his midst, || And I have caused him to draw near, || And he has drawn near to Me, || For who [is] he who has pledged his heart || To draw near to Me?" A declaration of Yhwh. **22** "And you have been to Me for a people, || And I am to you for God." **23** Behold, a whirlwind of Yhwh—Fury has gone forth—a cutting whirlwind, || It stays on the head of the wicked. **24** The fierceness of the anger of Yhwh || Does not turn back until He has done [it], || Indeed, until His establishing the purposes of His heart. In the latter end of the days you consider it!

CHAPTER 31

1 "At that time," a declaration of Yhwh, "I am the God of all families of Israel, || And they are My people." **2** Thus said Yhwh: "A people remaining from the sword || Have found grace in the wilderness || When Israel went to find rest." **3** Yhwh has appeared to me from afar, "I have loved you with perpetual love, || Therefore I have drawn you [with] kindness. **4** I build you again, || And you have been built, || O virgin of Israel, || You put on your tambourines again, || And have gone out in the chorus of the playful. **5** You plant vineyards in mountains of Samaria again, || Planters have planted, and made common. **6** For there is a day, || Watchmen have cried on Mount Ephraim, || Rise, and we go up to Zion, to our God Yhwh"; **7** For thus said Yhwh: "Sing [with] joy for Jacob, || And cry aloud at the head of the nations, || Sound, praise, and say, || Save, O Yhwh, Your people, the remnant of Israel. **8** Behold, I am bringing them in from the north country, || And have gathered them from the sides of the earth, || Blind and lame [are] among them, || Conceiving and travailing one—together, || A great assembly—they return here. **9** They come in with weeping, || And I bring them with supplications, || I cause them to go to streams of waters, || In a right way they do not stumble in it, || For I have been a Father to Israel, || And Ephraim—he [is] My firstborn." **10** Hear a word of Yhwh, O nations, || And declare among the far off in the islands, and say: He who is scattering Israel gathers him, || And has kept His flock as a shepherd, **11** For Yhwh has ransomed Jacob, || And redeemed him from a hand stronger than he. **12** And they have come in, || And have sung in the high place of Zion, || And flowed to the goodness of Yhwh, || For wheat, and for new wine, and for oil, || And for the young of the flock and herd, || And their soul has been as a watered garden, || And they do not add to grieve anymore. **13** "Then a virgin rejoices in a chorus, || Both young men and old men—together, || And I have turned their mourning to joy, || And have comforted them, || And gladdened them above their sorrow, **14** And satisfied the soul of the priests [with] fatness, || And My people are satisfied with My goodness," || A declaration of Yhwh. **15** Thus said Yhwh: "A voice is heard in Ramah, || Wailing [and] the weeping of bitterness, || Rachel is weeping for her sons, || She has refused to be comforted for her sons, because they are not." **16** Thus said Yhwh: "Withhold your voice from weeping, and your eyes from tears, || For there is a reward for your work," || A declaration of Yhwh, || "And they have turned back from the land of the enemy. **17** And there is hope for your latter end," || A declaration of Yhwh, || "And the sons have turned back [to] their border. **18** I have surely heard Ephraim bemoaning himself, || You have disciplined me, || And I am disciplined, as a heifer [that is] not taught, || Turn me back, and I turn back, || For You [are] my God Yhwh. **19** For after my turning back I regretted, || And after my being instructed, I struck on the thigh, || I have been ashamed, I have also blushed, || For I have borne the reproach of my youth. **20** Is Ephraim a precious son to Me? A child of delights? For since My speaking against him, || I still thoroughly remember him, || Therefore My bowels have been moved for him, || I love him greatly," || A declaration of Yhwh. **21** "Set up signs for yourself, || Make heaps for yourself, || Set your heart to the highway, the way you went, || Turn back, O virgin of Israel, || Turn back to these cities of yours. **22** Until when do you withdraw yourself, O backsliding daughter? For Yhwh has prepared a new thing in the land, || Woman surrounds man." **23** Thus said Yhwh of Hosts, God of Israel: "Still they say this word in the land of Judah, || And in its cities, || In My turning back [to] their captivity, || Yhwh blesses you, habitation of righteousness, || Mountain of holiness. **24** And farmers have dwelt in Judah, || And in all its cities together, || And they have journeyed in order. **25** For I have satiated the weary soul, || And I have filled every grieved soul." **26** On this I have awoken, and I behold, and my sleep has been sweet to me. **27** "Behold, days are coming," || A declaration of Yhwh, || "And I have sown the house of Israel, || And the house of Judah, || With seed of man and seed of beast. **28** And it has been, as I watched over them to pluck up, || And to break down, and to throw down, || And to destroy, and to afflict; So I watch over them to build, and to plant," || A declaration of Yhwh. **29** "In those days they no longer say: Fathers have eaten unripe fruit, || And the sons' teeth are blunted. **30** But—each dies for his own iniquity, || Every man who is eating the unripe fruit, || His teeth are blunted. **31** Behold, days are coming," || A declaration of Yhwh, || "And I have made a new covenant || With the house of Israel || And with the house of Judah, **32** Not like the covenant that I made with their fathers, || In the day of My laying hold on their hand, || To bring them out of the land of Egypt, || In that they made My covenant void, || And I ruled over them," || A declaration of Yhwh. **33** "For this [is] the covenant that I make, || With the house of Israel, after those days," || A declaration of Yhwh, || "I have given My law in their inward part, || And I write it on their heart, || And I have been their God, || And they are My people. **34** And they do not teach anymore || Each his neighbor, and each his brother, || Saying, Know Yhwh, || For they all know Me, from their least to their greatest," || A declaration of Yhwh; "For I pardon their iniquity, || And I make no more mention of their sin." **35** Thus said Yhwh, || Who is giving the sun for a light by day, || The statutes of moon and stars for a light by night, || Quieting the sea when its billows roar, || Yhwh of Hosts [is] His Name: **36** "If these statutes depart from before Me," || A declaration of Yhwh, || "Even the seed of Israel ceases || From being a nation before Me [for] all the days." **37** Thus said Yhwh: "If the heavens above can be measured, || And the foundations of earth searched below, ||

Even I kick against all the seed of Israel, || For all that they have done," || A declaration of Yhwh. **38** "Behold, days [are coming]," || A declaration of Yhwh, || "And the city has been built for Yhwh, || From the Tower of Hananeel to the Corner Gate. **39** And the measuring line has gone out again before it, over the height of Gareb, || And it has gone around to Goah. **40** And all the valley of the carcasses and of the ashes, || And all the fields to the Brook of Kidron, || To the corner of the Horse Gate eastward, || [Are] holy to Yhwh, || It is not plucked up, || Nor is it thrown down anymore for all time!"

CHAPTER 32

1 The word that has been to Jeremiah from Yhwh in the tenth year of Zedekiah king of Judah—it [is] the eighteenth year of Nebuchadnezzar— **2** And then the forces of the king of Babylon are laying siege against Jerusalem, and Jeremiah the prophet has been shut up in the court of the prison that [is] in the house of the king of Judah, **3** where Zedekiah king of Judah has shut him up, saying, "Why are you prophesying, saying, Thus said Yhwh: Behold, I am giving this city into the hand of the king of Babylon, and he has captured it; **4** and Zedekiah king of Judah does not escape out of the hand of the Chaldeans, but is certainly given into the hand of the king of Babylon, and his mouth has spoken with his mouth, and his eyes see his eyes, **5** and he leads Zedekiah [to] Babylon, and there he is until My inspecting him—a declaration of Yhwh—because you fight with the Chaldeans, you do not prosper." **6** And Jeremiah says, "A word of Yhwh has been to me, saying, **7** Behold, Hanameel son of Shallum, your uncle, is coming to you, saying, Buy my field that [is] in Anathoth for yourself, for the right of redemption [is] yours to buy." **8** And Hanameel, my uncle's son, comes to me, according to the word of Yhwh, to the court of the prison, and says to me, "Please buy my field that [is] in Anathoth, that [is] in the land of Benjamin, for the right of possession [is] yours, and redemption yours—buy [it] for yourself." And I know that it [is] the word of Yhwh, **9** and I buy the field that [is] in Anathoth from Hanameel, my uncle's son, and I weigh the money to him—seventeen shekels of silver. **10** And I write in a scroll, and seal, and cause witnesses to testify, and weigh the silver in balances; **11** and I take the purchase scroll, the sealed one, according to law and custom, and the open one; **12** and I give the purchase scroll to Baruch son of Neriah, son of Maaseiah, before the eyes of Hanameel, my uncle's son, and before the eyes of the witnesses, those writing in the purchase scroll, before the eyes of all the Jews who are sitting in the court of the prison. **13** And I charge Baruch before their eyes, saying, **14** "Thus said Yhwh of Hosts, God of Israel: Take these scrolls, this purchase scroll, both the sealed one and the open one, and you have put them in an earthen vessel, that they may remain many days. **15** For thus said Yhwh of Hosts, God of Israel: Houses and fields and vineyards are bought in this land again." **16** And I pray to Yhwh after my giving the purchase scroll to Baruch son of Neriah, saying, **17** "Aah! Lord Yhwh, behold, You have made the heavens and the earth by Your great power, and by Your outstretched arm; there is nothing too wonderful for You: **18** doing kindness to thousands, and repaying iniquity of fathers into the bosom of their sons after them; God, the great, the mighty, Yhwh of Hosts [is] His Name; **19** great in counsel, and mighty in act, in that Your eyes are open on all the ways of the sons of Adam, to give to each according to his ways, and according to the fruit of his doings; **20** in that you have done signs and wonders in the land of Egypt to this day, and in Israel, and among men, and You make for Yourself a name as [at] this day. **21** And You bring forth Your people Israel from the land of Egypt, with signs and with wonders, and by a strong hand, and by an outstretched arm, and by great fear, **22** and you give to them this land that you swore to their fathers to give to them, a land flowing with milk and honey, **23** and they come in, and possess it, and they have not listened to Your voice, and have not walked in Your law, all that which You laid a charge on them to do they have not done, and You proclaim all this calamity [to] them. **24** Behold, the [siege] mounds have come to the city to capture it, and the city has been given into the hand of the Chaldeans who are fighting against it, because of the sword, and the famine, and the pestilence; and that which You have spoken has come to pass, and behold, You are seeing. **25** Yet You have said to me, O Lord Yhwh, Buy the field for yourself with money, and cause witnesses to testify—and the city has been given into the hand of the Chaldeans!" **26** And the word of

Yhwh is to Jeremiah, saying, **27** "Behold, I [am] Yhwh, God of all flesh: is anything too wonderful for Me?" **28** Therefore, thus said Yhwh: "Behold, I am giving this city into the hand of the Chaldeans, and into the hand of Nebuchadnezzar king of Babylon, and he has captured it. **29** And the Chaldeans who are fighting against this city have come in, and they have set this city on fire, and have burned it—and the houses on whose roofs they made incense to Ba'al, and poured out drink-offerings to other gods, so as to provoke Me to anger. **30** For the sons of Israel and the sons of Judah have been doing only evil in My eyes from their youth; for the sons of Israel are surely provoking Me with the work of their hands," a declaration of Yhwh. **31** "For this city has been a cause of My anger and a cause of My fury, even from the day that they built it, and to this day—to turn it aside from before My face, **32** because of all the evil of the sons of Israel, and of the sons of Judah that they have done, so as to provoke Me—they, their kings, their heads, their priests, and their prophets, and the men of Judah, and the inhabitants of Jerusalem. **33** And they turn the neck to Me, and not the face, and teaching them, rising early and teaching, and they are not listening to accept instruction. **34** And they set their abominations in the house over which My Name is called, so as to defile it. **35** And they build the high places of Ba'al that [are] in the Valley of the Son of Hinnom, to cause their sons and their daughters to pass through to Molech, which I did not command them, nor did it come up on My heart to do this abomination, so as to cause Judah to sin. **36** And now, therefore, thus said Yhwh, God of Israel, concerning this city, of which you are saying, It has been given into the hand of the king of Babylon by sword, and by famine, and by pestilence: **37** Behold, I am gathering them out of all the lands to where I have driven them in My anger, and in My fury, and in great wrath, and I have brought them back to this place, and have caused them to dwell confidently; **38** and they have been to Me for a people, and I am to them for God; **39** and I have given to them one heart and one way, to fear Me all the days, for the good of them and their sons after them: **40** and I have made a perpetual covenant for them, in that I do not turn back from after them for My doing them good, and I put My fear in their heart, so as not to turn aside from me; **41** and I have rejoiced over them to do them good, and have planted them in this land in truth, with all my heart, and with all My soul." **42** For thus said Yhwh: "As I brought to this people all this great calamity, so I am bringing on them all the good that I am speaking concerning them; **43** and the field has been bought in this land of which you are saying, It [is] a desolation, without man and beast, it has been given into the hand of the Chaldeans. **44** They buy fields with money, so as to write in a scroll, and to seal, and to cause witnesses to testify, in the land of Benjamin, and in outskirts of Jerusalem, and in cities of Judah, and in cities of the hill-country, and in cities of the low country, and in cities of the south, for I return their captivity," a declaration of Yhwh.

CHAPTER 33

1 And there is a word of Yhwh to Jeremiah a second time—and he [is] yet detained in the court of the prison—saying: **2** "Thus said Yhwh who has made it, Yhwh who has formed it, to establish it, Yhwh [is] His Name: **3** Call to Me, and I answer you, indeed, I declare to you great and inaccessible things—you have not known them. **4** For thus said Yhwh, God of Israel, concerning the houses of this city, and concerning the houses of the kings of Judah that are broken down for the [siege] mounds, and for the tool; **5** they are coming to fight with the Chaldeans, and to fill them with the carcasses of men, whom I have struck in My anger, and in My fury, and [for] whom I have hidden My face from this city, because of all their evil: **6** Behold, I am increasing health and cure to it, || And have healed them, and revealed to them || The abundance of peace and truth. **7** And I have turned back the captivity of Judah, || And the captivity of Israel, || And I have built them as at the first, **8** And cleansed them from all their iniquity || That they have sinned against Me, || And I have pardoned all their iniquities || That they have sinned against Me, || And that they transgressed against Me. **9** And it has been for a name of joy to Me, || For praise, and for beauty, to all nations of the earth, || Who hear of all the good that I am doing them, || And they have feared, || And they have trembled for all the good, || And for all the peace, that I am doing to it." **10** Thus said Yhwh: "Again is heard in this place—of which you are saying, It [is] dry, without man and without beast, || In cities of Judah, and in streets of

Jerusalem, || That are desolated, without man, || And without inhabitant, and without beast— **11** A voice of joy and a voice of gladness, || Voice of bridegroom and voice of bride, || The voice of those saying, || Thank Yhwh of Hosts, for Yhwh [is] good, || For His kindness [is] for all time, || Who are bringing in thanksgiving to the house of Yhwh, || For I return the captivity of the land, || As at the first," said Yhwh. **12** Thus said Yhwh of Hosts: "Again there is in this place—that is dry, || Without man and beast, || And in all its cities—a habitation of shepherds, || Causing the flock to lie down. **13** In the cities of the hill-country, || In the cities of the low country, || And in the cities of the south, || And in the land of Benjamin, || And in the outskirts of Jerusalem, || And in the cities of Judah, || Again the flock passes by under the hands of the numberer," said Yhwh. **14** "Behold, days are coming," a declaration of Yhwh, "And I have established the good word || That I spoke to the house of Israel, || And concerning the house of Judah. **15** In those days, and at that time, || I cause a Shoot of righteousness to shoot up to David, || And He has done judgment and righteousness in the earth. **16** In those days Judah is saved, || And Jerusalem dwells confidently, || And this [is] what she is called: Yhwh [is] Our Righteousness." **17** For thus said Yhwh: "A man sitting on the throne of the house of Israel [is] never cut off from David, **18** And to the priests—the Levites, || A man is not cut off from before My face, || Causing a burnt-offering to ascend, || And perfuming a present, and making sacrifice—all the days." **19** And there is a word of Yhwh to Jeremiah, saying, **20** "Thus said Yhwh: If you can break My covenant with the day, || And My covenant with the night, || So that they are not daily and nightly in their season, **21** My covenant is also broken with My servant David, || So that he does not have a son reigning on his throne, || And with the Levites the priests, My ministers. **22** As the host of the heavens is not numbered, || Nor the sand of the sea measured, || So I multiply the seed of My servant David, || And My ministers the Levites." **23** And there is a word of Yhwh to Jeremiah, saying, **24** "Have you not considered what this people have spoken, saying, || The two families on which Yhwh fixed, || He rejects them? And they despise My people, so that they are no longer a people before them!" **25** Thus said Yhwh: "If My covenant [is] not with day and night, || [And if] I have not appointed the statutes of the heavens and earth— **26** I also reject the seed of Jacob, and My servant David, || From taking rulers from his seed || For the seed of Abraham, Isaac, and Jacob, || For I return their captivity, and have pitied them."

CHAPTER 34

1 The word that has been to Jeremiah from Yhwh—and Nebuchadnezzar king of Babylon, and all his force, and all kingdoms of the land of the dominion of his hand, and all the peoples are fighting against Jerusalem, and against all its cities—saying: **2** "Thus said Yhwh, God of Israel: Go, and you have spoken to Zedekiah king of Judah, and have said to him, Thus said Yhwh: Behold, I am giving this city into the hand of the king of Babylon, and he has burned it with fire, **3** and you do not escape out of his hand, for you are certainly caught, and you are given into his hand, and your eyes see the eyes of the king of Babylon, and his mouth speaks with your mouth, and you enter Babylon. **4** Only, hear a word of Yhwh, O Zedekiah king of Judah—thus said Yhwh to you: You do not die by sword, **5** you die in peace, and with the burnings of your fathers, the former kings who have been before you, so they make a burning for you; and, Oh, lord, they lament for you, for the word I have spoken—a declaration of Yhwh." **6** And Jeremiah the prophet speaks all these words to Zedekiah king of Judah in Jerusalem, **7** and the forces of the king of Babylon are fighting against Jerusalem, and against all the cities of Judah that are left—against Lachish, and against Azekah, for these have been left among the cities of Judah, cities of fortresses. **8** The word that has been to Jeremiah from Yhwh, after the making of a covenant by King Zedekiah with all the people who [are] in Jerusalem, to proclaim liberty to them, **9** to each send out his manservant, and each his maidservant—the Hebrew and the Hebrewess—free, so as not to lay service on them—on any Jew, a brother, a man; **10** and all the heads listen, and all the people who have come into the covenant to each send forth his manservant and each his maidservant free, so as not to lay service on them anymore, indeed, they listen, and send them away; **11** and they turn afterward, and cause the menservants and the maidservants to return, whom they had sent forth free, and they subdue them for menservants and for maidservants. ¹² And there is a word of Yhwh to Jeremiah from Yhwh, saying, ¹³ "Thus said Yhwh, God of Israel: I made a covenant with your fathers in the day of My bringing them forth from the land of Egypt, from a house of servants, saying, ¹⁴ At the end of seven years you each send forth his brother, the Hebrew, who is sold to you, and has served you six years, indeed, you have sent him forth from you free: and your fathers did not listen to Me, nor inclined their ear. ¹⁵ And today you turn back and you do that which is right in My eyes, to each proclaim liberty to his neighbor, and you make a covenant before Me in the house over which My Name is called. ¹⁶ And you turn back, and defile My Name, and you each cause his manservant and each his maidservant, whom he had sent forth free (at their pleasure), to return, and you subdue them to be for menservants and for maidservants to you." ¹⁷ Therefore, thus said Yhwh: "You have not listened to Me to proclaim freedom, each to his brother, and each to his neighbor; behold, I am proclaiming to you liberty," a declaration of Yhwh, "to the sword, to the pestilence, and to the famine, and I have given you for a trembling to all kingdoms of the earth. ¹⁸ And I have given the men who are transgressing My covenant, who have not established the words of the covenant that they have made before Me, by the calf, that they have cut in two, and pass through between its pieces— ¹⁹ heads of Judah, and heads of Jerusalem, the officers, and the priests, and all the people of the land who had passed through between the pieces of the calf— ²⁰ indeed, I have given them into the hand of their enemies, and into the hand of those seeking their soul, and their carcass has been for food to the bird of the heavens, and to the beast of the earth. ²¹ And I give Zedekiah king of Judah and his heads into the hand of their enemies, and into the hand of those seeking their soul, and into the hand of the forces of the king of Babylon that are going up from off you. ²² Behold, I am commanding," a declaration of Yhwh, "and have brought them back to this city, and they have fought against it, and captured it, and burned it with fire, and I make the cities of Judah a desolation— without inhabitant."

CHAPTER 35

¹ The word that has been to Jeremiah from Yhwh, in the days of Jehoiakim son of Josiah king of Judah, saying, ² "Go to the house of the Rechabites, and you have spoken with them, and brought them into the house of Yhwh, to one of the chambers, and caused them to drink wine." ³ And I take Jaazaniah son of Jeremiah, son of Habazziniah, and his brothers, and all his sons, and all the house of the Rechabites, ⁴ and bring them into the house of Yhwh, to the chamber of the sons of Hanan son of Igdaliah, a man of God, that [is] near to the chamber of the princes, that [is] above the chamber of Maaseiah son of Shallum, keeper of the threshold; ⁵ and I put before the sons of the house of the Rechabites goblets full of wine, and cups, and I say to them, "Drink wine." ⁶ And they say, "We do not drink wine: for Jonadab son of Rechab, our father, charged us, saying, You do not drink wine, you and your sons—for all time; ⁷ and you do not build a house, and you do not sow seed, and you do not plant a vineyard, nor have of [these]; for you dwell in tents all your days, that you may live many days on the face of the ground to where you are sojourning. ⁸ And we listen to the voice of Jonadab son of Rechab, our father, to all that he commanded us, not to drink wine all our days, we, our wives, our sons, and our daughters; ⁹ nor to build houses to dwell in; and we have no vineyard, and field, and seed; ¹⁰ and we dwell in tents, and we listen, and we do according to all that Jonadab our father commanded us; ¹¹ and it comes to pass, in the coming up of Nebuchadnezzar king of Babylon to the land, that we say, Come, and we enter Jerusalem, because of the force of the Chaldeans, and because of the force of Aram—and we dwell in Jerusalem." ¹² And there is a word of Yhwh to Jeremiah, saying, "Thus said Yhwh of Hosts, God of Israel: ¹³ Go, and you have said to the men of Judah and to the inhabitants of Jerusalem: Do you not receive instruction to listen to My words? A declaration of Yhwh. ¹⁴ The words of Jonadab son of Rechab, when he commanded his sons not to drink wine, have stood, and they have not drunk to this day, for they have obeyed the command of their father; and I have spoken to you, rising early and speaking, and you have not listened to Me. ¹⁵ And I send all My servants the prophets to you, rising early and sending, saying, Please turn back, each from his evil way, and amend your doings, indeed, you do not

walk after other gods, to serve them; and dwell on the ground that I have given to you and to your fathers; and you have not inclined your ear, nor listened to Me. ¹⁶ Because the sons of Jonadab son of Rechab have stood by the command of their father that he commanded them, and this people have not listened to Me, ¹⁷ therefore, thus said Yhwh, God of Hosts, God of Israel: Behold, I am bringing to Judah, and to all inhabitants of Jerusalem, all the calamity that I have spoken against them, because I have spoken to them, and they have not listened, indeed, I call to them, and they have not answered." ¹⁸ And Jeremiah said to the house of the Rechabites: "Thus said Yhwh of Hosts, God of Israel: Because that you have listened to the command of your father Jonadab, and you observe all his commands, and do according to all that he commanded you; ¹⁹ therefore, thus said Yhwh of Hosts, God of Israel: A man of Jonadab son of Rechab is not cut off [from] standing before Me all the days."

CHAPTER 36

¹ And it comes to pass, in the fourth year of Jehoiakim son of Josiah king of Judah, this word has been to Jeremiah from Yhwh, saying, ² "Take a roll of a scroll to yourself, and you have written on it all the words that I have spoken to you concerning Israel, and concerning Judah, and concerning all the nations, from the day I spoke to you, from the days of Josiah, even to this day; ³ perhaps the house of Israel so hears all the evil that I am thinking of doing to them, so that they each turn back from his evil way, and I have been propitious to their iniquity, and to their sin." ⁴ And Jeremiah calls Baruch son of Neriah, and Baruch writes from the mouth of Jeremiah all the words of Yhwh, that He has spoken to him, on a roll of a scroll. ⁵ And Jeremiah commands Baruch, saying, "I am restrained, I am not able to enter the house of Yhwh; ⁶ but you have entered—and you have read in the scroll that you have written from my mouth, the words of Yhwh, in the ears of the people, in the house of Yhwh, in the day of the fast, and you also read them in the ears of all Judah who are coming in from their cities; ⁷ perhaps their supplication so falls before Yhwh, and they each turn back from his evil way, for the anger and the fury that Yhwh has spoken concerning this people [is] great." ⁸ And Baruch son of Neriah does according to all that Jeremiah the prophet commanded him, to read in the scroll the words of Yhwh in the house of Yhwh. ⁹ And it comes to pass, in the fifth year of Jehoiakim son of Josiah king of Judah, in the ninth month, they proclaimed a fast before Yhwh to all the people in Jerusalem, and to all the people who are coming in from cities of Judah to Jerusalem; ¹⁰ and Baruch reads in the scroll the words of Jeremiah in the house of Yhwh, in the chamber of Gemariah son of Shaphan the scribe, in the higher court, at the opening of the New Gate of the house of Yhwh, in the ears of all the people. ¹¹ And Michaiah son of Gemariah, son of Shaphan, hears all the words of Yhwh from off the scroll, ¹² and he goes down [to] the house of the king, to the chamber of the scribe, and behold, there all the heads are sitting: Elishama the scribe, and Delaiah son of Shemaiah, and Elnathan son of Acbor, and Gemariah son of Shaphan, and Zedekiah son of Hananiah, and all the heads. ¹³ And Micaiah declares to them all the words that he has heard when Baruch reads in the scroll in the ears of the people; ¹⁴ and all the heads send to Baruch, Jehudi son of Nethaniah, son of Shelemiah, son of Cushi, saying, "Take in your hand the scroll, which you have read in the ears of the people, and come." And Baruch son of Neriah takes the scroll in his hand and comes to them, ¹⁵ and they say to him, "Please sit down and read it in our ears," and Baruch reads [it] in their ears, ¹⁶ and it comes to pass, when they hear all the words, they have been afraid—one to another—and say to Baruch, "We surely declare all these words to the king." ¹⁷ And they asked Baruch, saying, "Please declare to us, how did you write all these words from his mouth?" ¹⁸ And Baruch says to them, "He pronounces from his mouth all these words to me, and I am writing on the scroll with ink." ¹⁹ And the heads say to Baruch, "Go, be hidden, you and Jeremiah, and let no one know where you [are]." ²⁰ And they go to the king, to the court, and they have laid up the scroll in the chamber of Elishama the scribe, and they declare all the words in the ears of the king. ²¹ And the king sends Jehudi to take the scroll, and he takes it out of the chamber of Elishama the scribe, and Jehudi reads it in the ears of the king, and in the ears of all the heads who are standing by the king; ²² and the king is sitting in the winter-house, in the ninth month, and the stove is

burning before him, ²³ and it comes to pass, when Jehudi reads three or four leaves, he cuts it out with the scribe's knife, and has cast [it] into the fire that [is] on the stove, until the consumption of all the scroll by the fire that [is] on the stove. ²⁴ And the king and all his servants who are hearing all these words have not been afraid, nor torn their garments. ²⁵ And also Elnathan, and Delaiah, and Gemariah have interceded with the king not to burn the scroll, and he has not listened to them. ²⁶ And the king commands Jerahmeel son of Hammelek, and Seraiah son of Azriel, and Shelemiah son of Abdeel, to take Baruch the scribe and Jeremiah the prophet, and Yhwh hides them. ²⁷ And there is a word of Yhwh to Jeremiah—after the king's burning the scroll, even the words that Baruch has written from the mouth of Jeremiah—saying: ²⁸ "Turn, take another scroll to yourself, and write on it all the former words that were on the first scroll that Jehoiakim king of Judah burned, ²⁹ and say to Jehoiakim king of Judah, Thus said Yhwh: You have burned this scroll, saying, Why have you written on it, saying, The king of Babylon surely comes in, and has destroyed this land, and caused man and beast to cease from it? ³⁰ Therefore, thus said Yhwh concerning Jehoiakim king of Judah: He has none sitting on the throne of David, and his carcass is cast out to heat by day, and to cold by night; ³¹ and I have charged on him, and on his seed, and on his servants, their iniquity; and I have brought in on them, and on the inhabitants of Jerusalem, and to the men of Judah, all the evil that I have spoken to them, and they did not listen." ³² And Jeremiah has taken another scroll, and gives it to Baruch son of Neriah the scribe, and he writes on it from the mouth of Jeremiah all the words of the scroll that Jehoiakim king of Judah has burned in the fire; and again there were added to them many words like these.

CHAPTER 37

¹ And King Zedekiah son of Josiah reigns instead of Coniah son of Jehoiakim whom Nebuchadnezzar king of Babylon had caused to reign in the land of Judah, ² and he has not listened—he, and his servants, and the people of the land—to the words of Yhwh that He spoke by the hand of Jeremiah the prophet. ³ And Zedekiah the king sends Jehucal son of Shelemiah, and Zephaniah son of Maaseiah the priest, to Jeremiah the prophet, saying, "Pray, we implore you, for us to our God Yhwh." ⁴ And Jeremiah is coming in and going out in the midst of the people (and they have not put him in the prison-house), ⁵ and the force of Pharaoh has come out of Egypt, and the Chaldeans who are laying siege against Jerusalem hear their report, and go up from off Jerusalem. ⁶ And there is a word of Yhwh to Jeremiah the prophet, saying, ⁷ "Thus said Yhwh, God of Israel: Thus you say to the king of Judah who is sending you to Me, to seek Me: Behold, the force of Pharaoh that is coming out to you for help has turned back to its land, to Egypt, ⁸ and the Chaldeans have turned back and fought against this city, and captured it, and burned it with fire. ⁹ Thus said Yhwh: Do not lift up your souls, saying, The Chaldeans surely go from off us, for they do not go; ¹⁰ for though you had struck all the force of the Chaldeans who are fighting with you, and there were left of them wounded men—they rise, each in his tent, and have burned this city with fire." ¹¹ And it has come to pass, in the going up of the force of the Chaldeans from off Jerusalem, because of the force of Pharaoh, ¹² that Jeremiah goes out from Jerusalem to go [to] the land of Benjamin, to receive a portion there in the midst of the people. ¹³ And it has come to pass, he is at the Gate of Benjamin, and there [is] a master of the ward, and his name is Irijah son of Shelemiah, son of Hananiah; and he catches Jeremiah the prophet, saying, "You are defecting to the Chaldeans!" ¹⁴ And Jeremiah says, "Falsehood! I am not defecting to the Chaldeans"; and he has not listened to him, and Irijah lays hold on Jeremiah, and brings him to the heads, ¹⁵ and the heads are angry against Jeremiah, and have struck him, and put him in the prison-house—the house of Jonathan the scribe, for they had made it for a prison-house. ¹⁶ When Jeremiah has entered into the house of the dungeon, and to the cells, then Jeremiah dwells there many days, ¹⁷ and King Zedekiah sends, and takes him, and the king asks him in his house in secret, and says, "Is there a word from Yhwh?" And Jeremiah says, "There is," and he says, "You are given into the hand of the king of Babylon." ¹⁸ And Jeremiah says to King Zedekiah, "What have I sinned against you, and against your servants, and against this people, that you have put me into a prison-house? ¹⁹ And where [are] your prophets who

prophesied to you, saying, The king of Babylon does not come in against you, and against this land? ²⁰ And now, please listen, O my lord the king; please let my supplication fall before you, and do not cause me to return [to] the house of Jonathan the scribe, that I do not die there." ²¹ And King Zedekiah commands, and they commit Jeremiah into the court of the prison, also to give a cake of bread to him daily from the bakers' street, until the consumption of all the bread of the city, and Jeremiah dwells in the court of the prison.

CHAPTER 38

¹ And Shephatiah son of Mattan, and Gedaliah son of Pashhur, and Jucal son of Shelemiah, and Pashhur son of Malchiah, hear the words that Jeremiah is speaking to all the people, saying, ² "Thus said Yhwh: He who is remaining in this city dies, by sword, by famine, and by pestilence, and he who is going forth to the Chaldeans lives, and his soul has been to him for a prey, and he lives. ³ Thus said Yhwh: This city is certainly given into the hand of the force of the king of Babylon, and he has captured it." ⁴ And the heads say to the king, "Now let this man be put to death, because that he is making feeble the hands of the men of war who are left in this city, and the hands of all the people, by speaking to them according to these words, for this man is not seeking for the peace of this people, but for its calamity." ⁵ And King Zedekiah says, "Behold, he [is] in your hand: for the king is not able [to do] anything against you." ⁶ And they take Jeremiah, and cast him into the pit of Malchiah son of the king, that [is] in the court of the prison, and they send Jeremiah down with cords; and there is no water in the pit, but mire, and Jeremiah sinks in the mire. ⁷ And Ebed-Melech the Cushite, a eunuch who [is] in the king's house, hears that they have put Jeremiah into the pit; and the king is sitting at the Gate of Benjamin, ⁸ and Ebed-Melech goes forth from the king's house, and speaks to the king, saying, ⁹ "My lord, O king, these men have done evil [in] all that they have done to Jeremiah the prophet, whom they have cast into the pit, and he dies in his place because of the famine, for there is no more bread in the city." ¹⁰ And the king commands Ebed-Melech the Cushite, saying, "Take with you thirty men from here, and you have brought up Jeremiah the prophet from the pit, before he dies." ¹¹ And Ebed-Melech takes the men with him, and enters the house of the king, to the place of the treasury, and takes there worn-out shreds of cloth, and worn-out rags, and sends them by cords into the pit to Jeremiah. ¹² And Ebed-Melech the Cushite says to Jeremiah, "Now put the worn-out pieces of cloth and rags under your arms, at the place of the cords," and Jeremiah does so, ¹³ and they draw Jeremiah out with cords, and bring him up out of the pit, and Jeremiah dwells in the court of the prison. ¹⁴ And King Zedekiah sends, and takes Jeremiah the prophet to him, to the third entrance that [is] in the house of Yhwh, and the king says to Jeremiah, "I am asking you something, do not hide anything from me." ¹⁵ And Jeremiah says to Zedekiah, "When I declare [it] to you, do you not surely put me to death? and when I counsel you, you do not listen to me." ¹⁶ And King Zedekiah swears to Jeremiah in secret, saying, "Yhwh lives, He who made this soul for us, I do not put you to death, nor give you into the hand of these men who are seeking your soul." ¹⁷ And Jeremiah says to Zedekiah, "Thus said Yhwh, God of Hosts, God of Israel: If you certainly go forth to the heads of the king of Babylon, then your soul has lived, and this city is not burned with fire, indeed, you have lived, you and your house. ¹⁸ And if you do not go forth to the heads of the king of Babylon, then this city has been given into the hand of the Chaldeans, and they have burned it with fire, and you do not escape from their hand." ¹⁹ And King Zedekiah says to Jeremiah, "I am fearing the Jews who have fallen to the Chaldeans, lest they give me into their hand, and they have insulted me." ²⁰ And Jeremiah says, "They do not give you up; please listen to the voice of Yhwh, to that which I am speaking to you, and it is well for you, and your soul lives. ²¹ And if you are refusing to go forth, this [is] the thing that Yhwh has shown me: ²² That, behold, all the women who have been left in the house of the king of Judah are brought forth to the heads of the king of Babylon, and behold, they are saying: Persuaded you, and prevailed against you, || Have your allies, || Your feet have sunk into mire, || They have been turned backward. ²³ And all your wives and your sons are brought forth to the Chaldeans, and you do not escape from their hand, for you are caught by the hand of the king of Babylon, and this city is burned with fire." ²⁴ And Zedekiah says

to Jeremiah, "Let no man know of these words, and you do not die; 25 and when the heads hear that I have spoken with you, and they have come to you, and have said to you, Now declare to us what you spoke to the king, do not hide [it] from us, and we do not put you to death, and what the king spoke to you, 26 then you have said to them, I am causing my supplication to fall before the king, not to cause me to return to the house of Jonathan, to die there." 27 And all the heads come to Jeremiah, and ask him, and he declares to them according to all these words that the king commanded, and they keep silent from him, for the matter was not heard; 28 and Jeremiah dwells in the court of the prison until the day that Jerusalem has been captured, and he was [there] when Jerusalem was captured.

CHAPTER 39

1 In the ninth year of Zedekiah king of Judah, in the tenth month, Nebuchadnezzar king of Babylon and all his force have come to Jerusalem, and they lay siege against it; 2 in the eleventh year of Zedekiah, in the fourth month, on the ninth of the month, the city has been broken up; 3 and all the heads of the king of Babylon come in, and they sit at the middle gate, Nergal-Sharezer, Samgar-Nebo, Sarsechim, Rab-Saris, Nergal-Sharezer, chief magus, and all the rest of the heads of the king of Babylon. 4 And it comes to pass, when Zedekiah king of Judah and all the men of war have seen them, that they flee and go forth by night from the city, the way of the king's garden, through the gate between the two walls, and he goes forth the way of the plain. 5 And the forces of the Chaldeans pursue after them, and overtake Zedekiah in the plains of Jericho, and they take him, and bring him up to Nebuchadnezzar king of Babylon, to Riblah, in the land of Hamath, and he speaks with him—judgments. 6 And the king of Babylon slaughters the sons of Zedekiah, in Riblah, before his eyes, indeed, the king of Babylon has slaughtered all the nobles of Judah. 7 And he has blinded the eyes of Zedekiah, and he binds him with bronze chains to bring him to Babylon. 8 And the house of the king, and the house of the people, the Chaldeans have burned with fire, and they have broken down the walls of Jerusalem. 9 And the remnant of the people who are left in the city, and those defecting who have defected to him, and the remnant of the people who are left, Nebuzar-Adan, chief of the executioners, has removed [to] Babylon. 10 And Nebuzar-Adan, chief of the executioners, has left in the land of Judah the poor people who have nothing, and he gives vineyards and fields to them in that day. 11 And Nebuchadnezzar king of Babylon gives a charge concerning Jeremiah, by the hand of Nebuzar-Adan, chief of the executioners, saying, 12 "Take him, and place your eyes on him, and do no evil thing to him, but as he speaks to you, so do with him." 13 And Nebuzar-Adan, chief of the executioners, sends, and Nebushazban, chief of the eunuchs, and Nergal-Sharezer, chief magus, and all the chiefs of the king of Babylon, 14 indeed, they send and take Jeremiah out of the court of the prison, and give him to Gedaliah son of Ahikam, son of Shaphan, to carry him home, and he dwells in the midst of the people. 15 And a word of Yhwh has been to Jeremiah—in his being detained in the court of the prison—saying: 16 "Go, and you have spoken to Ebed-Melech the Cushite, saying, Thus said Yhwh of Hosts, God of Israel: Behold, I am bringing in My words to this city for calamity, and not for good, and they have been before you in that day. 17 And I have delivered you in that day—a declaration of Yhwh—and you are not given into the hand of the men of whose face you are afraid, 18 for I certainly deliver you, and you do not fall by sword, and your life has been to you for a spoil, for you have trusted in Me—a declaration of Yhwh."

CHAPTER 40

1 The word that has been to Jeremiah from Yhwh, after Nebuzar-Adan, chief of the executioners, has sent him from Ramah, in his taking him—and he a prisoner in chains—in the midst of all the expulsion of Jerusalem and of Judah, who are removed to Babylon. 2 And the chief of the executioners takes Jeremiah and says to him, "Your God Yhwh has spoken this calamity concerning this place, 3 and Yhwh brings [it] in, and does as He spoke, because you have sinned against Yhwh, and have not listened to His voice, even this thing has been to you.

4 And now, behold, I have loosed you today from the chains that [are] on your hand; if [it is] good in your eyes to come with me [to] Babylon, come, and I keep my eye on you: and if [it is] evil in your eyes to come with me to Babylon, refrain; see, all the land [is] before you, to where [it is] good, and to where [it is] right in your eyes to go—go." 5 And while he does not reply—"Or turn back to Gedaliah son of Ahikam, son of Shaphan, whom the king of Babylon has appointed over the cities of Judah, and dwell with him in the midst of the people, or wherever it is right in your eyes to go—go." And the chief of the executioners gives a ration and gift to him, and sends him away, 6 and Jeremiah comes to Gedaliah son of Ahikam, to Mizpah, and dwells with him in the midst of the people who are left in the land. 7 And all the heads of the forces that [are] in the field hear, they and their men, that the king of Babylon has appointed Gedaliah son of Ahikam over the land, and that he has charged him [with] men, and women, and infants, and of the poor of the land, of those who have not been removed to Babylon; 8 and they come to Gedaliah at Mizpah, even Ishmael son of Nethaniah, and Johanan and Jonathan [the] sons of Kareah, and Seraiah son of Tanhumeth, and the sons of Ephai the Netophathite, and Jezaniah son of the Maachathite, they and their men. 9 And Gedaliah son of Ahikam, son of Shaphan, swears to them and to their men, saying, "Do not be afraid of serving the Chaldeans, abide in the land, and serve the king of Babylon, and it is well for you; 10 and I, behold, I am dwelling in Mizpah to stand before the Chaldeans who have come to us, and you, gather wine, and summer fruit, and oil, and put [them] in your vessels, and dwell in your cities that you have taken." 11 And also all the Jews who [are] in Moab, and among the sons of Ammon, and in Edom, and who [are] in all the lands, have heard that the king of Babylon has given a remnant to Judah, and that he has appointed over them Gedaliah son of Ahikam, son of Shaphan, 12 and all the Jews from all the places to where they have been driven, return and enter the land of Judah, to Gedaliah, to Mizpah, and they gather wine and summer fruit—to multiply abundantly. 13 And Johanan son of Kareah, and all the heads of the forces that [are] in the field, have come to Gedaliah at Mizpah, 14 and they say to him, "Do you really know that Ba'alis king of the sons of Ammon has sent Ishmael son of Nethaniah to strike your soul?" And Gedaliah son of Ahikam has not given credence to them. 15 And Johanan son of Kareah has spoken to Gedaliah in secret, in Mizpah, saying, "Please let me go, and I strike Ishmael son of Nethaniah, and no one knows; why does he strike your soul? and all Judah who are gathered to you have been scattered, and the remnant of Judah has perished." 16 And Gedaliah son of Ahikam says to Johanan son of Kareah, "You do not do this thing, for you are speaking falsehood concerning Ishmael."

CHAPTER 41

1 And it comes to pass, in the seventh month, Ishmael son of Nethaniah, son of Elishama, of the royal seed, and of the chiefs of the king, and ten men with him, have come to Gedaliah son of Ahikam, to Mizpah, and there they eat bread together in Mizpah. 2 And Ishmael son of Nethaniah rises, and the ten men who have been with him, and they strike Gedaliah son of Ahikam, son of Shaphan, with the sword, and he puts him to death whom the king of Babylon has appointed over the land. 3 And all the Jews who have been with him, with Gedaliah, in Mizpah, and the Chaldeans who have been found there—the men of war—Ishmael has struck. 4 And it comes to pass, on the second day of the putting of Gedaliah to death (and no one has known), 5 that men come in from Shechem, from Shiloh, and from Samaria—eighty men—with shaven beards, and torn garments, and cutting themselves, and [with] an offering and frankincense in their hand, to bring [them] to the house of Yhwh. 6 And Ishmael son of Nethaniah goes forth to meet them, from Mizpah, going on and weeping, and it comes to pass, at meeting them, that he says to them, "Come to Gedaliah son of Ahikam." 7 And it comes to pass, at their coming into the midst of the city, that Ishmael son of Nethaniah slaughters them, at the midst of the pit, he and the men who [are] with him. 8 And ten men have been found among them, and they say to Ishmael, "Do not put us to death, for we have things hidden in the field—wheat, and barley, and oil, and honey." And he refrains, and has not put them to death in the midst of their brothers. 9 And the pit to where Ishmael has cast all the carcasses of the men whom he has struck along with Gedaliah, is that which King Asa made because of Baasha king of Israel—

Ishmael son of Nethaniah has filled it with the pierced. **10** And Ishmael takes captive all the remnant of the people who [are] in Mizpah, the daughters of the king, and all the people who are left in Mizpah, whom Nebuzar-Adan, chief of the executioners, has committed [to] Gedaliah son of Ahikam, and Ishmael son of Nethaniah takes them captive, and goes to pass over to the sons of Ammon. **11** And Johanan son of Kareah, and all the heads of the forces that [are] with him, hear of all the evil that Ishmael son of Nethaniah has done, **12** and they take all the men, and go to fight with Ishmael son of Nethaniah, and they find him at the great waters that [are] in Gibeon. **13** And it comes to pass, when all the people who [are] with Ishmael see Johanan son of Kareah, and all the heads of the forces who [are] with him, that they rejoice. **14** And all the people whom Ishmael has taken captive from Mizpah turn around, indeed, they turn back, and go to Johanan son of Kareah. **15** And Ishmael son of Nethaniah has escaped, with eight men, from the presence of Johanan, and he goes to the sons of Ammon. **16** And Johanan son of Kareah, and all the heads of the forces who [are] with him, take all the remnant of the people whom he has brought back from Ishmael son of Nethaniah, from Mizpah—after he had struck Gedaliah son of Ahikam—mighty ones, men of war, and women, and infants, and eunuchs, whom he had brought back from Gibeon, **17** and they go and abide in the habitations of Chimham, that [are] near Beth-Lehem, to go to enter Egypt, **18** from the presence of the Chaldeans, for they have been afraid of them, for Ishmael son of Nethaniah had struck Gedaliah son of Ahikam, whom the king of Babylon had appointed over the land.

CHAPTER 42

1 And they come near—all the heads of the forces, and Johanan son of Kareah, and Jezaniah son of Hoshaiah, and all the people from the least even to the greatest— **2** and they say to Jeremiah the prophet, "Please let our supplication fall before you, and pray for us to your God Yhwh for all this remnant; for we have been left a few out of many, as your eyes see us; **3** and your God Yhwh declares to us the way in which we walk, and the thing that we do." **4** And Jeremiah the prophet says to them, "I have heard: behold, I am praying to your God Yhwh according to your words, and it has come to pass, the whole word that Yhwh answers you, I declare to you—I do not withhold a word from you." **5** And they have said to Jeremiah, "Yhwh is against us for a true and faithful witness, if—according to all the word with which your God Yhwh sends you to us—we do not do so. **6** Whether [it is] good or evil, to the voice of our God Yhwh, to whom we are sending you, we listen; because it is good for us when we listen to the voice of our God Yhwh." **7** And it comes to pass, at the end of ten days, that there is a word of Yhwh to Jeremiah, **8** and he calls to Johanan son of Kareah, and to all the heads of the forces that [are] with him, and to all the people, from the least even to the greatest, **9** and he says to them, "Thus said Yhwh, God of Israel, to whom you sent me, to cause your supplication to fall before Him: **10** If you certainly dwell in this land, then I have built you up, and I do not throw down; and I have planted you, and I do not pluck up; for I have relented concerning the calamity that I have done to you. **11** Do not be afraid of the king of Babylon, whom you are afraid of; do not be afraid of him—a declaration of Yhwh—for I [am] with you, to save you, and to deliver you from his hand. **12** And I give mercies to you, and he has pitied you, and caused you to return to your own ground. **13** And if you are saying, We do not dwell in this land—not to listen to the voice of your God Yhwh, **14** saying, No; but we enter the land of Egypt, that we see no war, and do not hear the sound of a horn, and are not hungry for bread; and we dwell there— **15** And now, therefore, hear a word of Yhwh, O remnant of Judah! Thus said Yhwh of Hosts, God of Israel: If you really set your faces to enter Egypt, and have gone to sojourn there, **16** then it has come to pass, the sword that you are afraid of, overtakes you there, in the land of Egypt; and the hunger, because of which you are sorrowful, cleaves after you there in Egypt, and there you die. **17** Thus are all the men who have set their faces to enter Egypt to sojourn there; they die—by sword, by hunger, and by pestilence, and there is not a remnant and an escaped one to them, because of the calamity that I am bringing in on them; **18** for thus said Yhwh of Hosts, God of Israel: As My anger and My fury have been poured out on the inhabitants of Jerusalem, so My fury is poured out on you in your entering Egypt, and you have been for an execration, and

for an astonishment, and for a reviling, and for a reproach, and you do not see this place anymore. **19** Yhwh has spoken against you, O remnant of Judah, do not enter Egypt: certainly know that I have testified against you today; **20** for you have showed yourselves perverse in your souls, for you sent me to your God Yhwh, saying, Pray for us to our God Yhwh, and according to all that our God Yhwh says, so declare to us, and we have done [it]; **21** and I declare to you today, and you have not listened to the voice of your God Yhwh, and to anything with which He has sent me to you. **22** And now, certainly know that by sword, by famine, and by pestilence you die, in the place that you have desired to go to sojourn there."

CHAPTER 43

1 And it comes to pass, when Jeremiah finishes speaking to all the people all the words of their God Yhwh, with which their God Yhwh has sent him to them—all these words— **2** that Azariah son of Hoshaiah, and Johanan son of Kareah, and all the proud men, speak to Jeremiah, saying, "You are speaking falsehood; our God Yhwh has not sent you to say, Do not enter Egypt to sojourn there; **3** for Baruch son of Neriah is moving you against us, in order to give us up into the hand of the Chaldeans, to put us to death, and to remove us to Babylon." **4** And Johanan son of Kareah, and all the heads of the forces, and all the people, have not listened to the voice of Yhwh, to dwell in the land of Judah; **5** and Johanan son of Kareah, and all the heads of the forces, take all the remnant of Judah who have turned from all the nations to where they were driven to sojourn in the land of Judah, **6** the men, and the women, and the infant, and the daughters of the king, and every person that Nebuzar-Adan, chief of the executioners, had left with Gedaliah son of Ahikam, son of Shaphan, and Jeremiah the prophet, and Baruch son of Neriah, **7** and they enter the land of Egypt, for they have not listened to the voice of Yhwh, and they come as far as Tahpanhes. **8** And there is a word of Yhwh to Jeremiah in Tahpanhes, saying, **9** "Take great stones in your hand, and you have hidden them in the clay in the brick-kiln, that [is] at the opening of the house of Pharaoh in Tahpanhes, before the eyes of the men of Judah, **10** and you have said to them, Thus said Yhwh of Hosts, God of Israel: Behold, I am sending, and I have taken Nebuchadnezzar king of Babylon, My servant, and I have set his throne above these stones that I have hid, and he has stretched out his pavilion over them, **11** and he has come, and struck the land of Egypt—those who [are] for death to death, and those who [are] for captivity to captivity, and those who [are] for the sword to the sword. **12** And I have kindled a fire in the houses of the gods of Egypt, and it has burned them, and he has taken them captive, and covered himself with the land of Egypt, as the shepherd covers himself with his garment, and he has gone forth there in peace; **13** and he has broken the standing pillars of the house of the sun, that [is] in the land of Egypt, and he burns the houses of the gods of Egypt with fire.

CHAPTER 44

1 The word that has been to Jeremiah concerning all the Jews who are dwelling in the land of Egypt—who are dwelling in Migdol, and in Tahpanhes, and in Noph, and in the land of Pathros—saying, **2** "Thus said Yhwh of Hosts, God of Israel: You have seen all the calamity that I have brought in on Jerusalem, and on all the cities of Judah, and behold, they [are] a desolation to this day, and there is none dwelling in them, **3** because of their wickedness that they have done, by provoking Me to anger, by going to make incense, by serving other gods, that they did not know, they, you, and your fathers. **4** And I send to you all My servants the prophets, rising early and sending, saying, please do not do this abomination that I have hated— **5** and they have not listened nor inclined their ear to turn back from their wickedness, not to make incense to other gods, **6** and My fury is poured out, and My anger, and it burns in cities of Judah, and in streets of Jerusalem, and they are for a ruin, for a desolation, as [at] this day. **7** And now, thus said Yhwh of Hosts, God of Israel: Why are you doing great evil to your own souls, to cut off man and woman, infant and suckling, from you, from the midst of Judah, so as not to leave a remnant to you: **8** by provoking Me to anger by the works of your hands, by making incense to other gods in the land of Egypt, to where you are going to sojourn, so as to cut yourselves off, and so as to your being for a reviling and for a reproach among all nations of the earth? **9** Have you forgotten the wickedness of your fathers, and the wickedness of the kings of Judah, and the wickedness of their wives, and your own wickedness, and the wickedness of your wives, that they have done in the land of Judah, and in streets of Jerusalem? **10** They have not been humbled to this day, nor have they been afraid, nor have they walked in My law, and in My statutes, that I have set before you and before your fathers. **11** Therefore, thus said Yhwh of Hosts, God of Israel: Behold, I am setting My face against you for calamity, even to cut off all Judah, **12** and I have taken the remnant of Judah, who have set their faces to enter the land of Egypt to sojourn there, and they have all been consumed in the land of Egypt; they fall by sword [and] are consumed by famine, from the least even to the greatest, they die by sword and by famine, and they have been for an execration, for an astonishment, and for a reviling, and for a reproach. **13** And I have seen after those dwelling in the land of Egypt, as I saw after Jerusalem, with sword, with famine, and with pestilence, **14** and there is not an escaped and remaining one of the remnant of Judah, who are entering into the land of Egypt to sojourn there, even to turn back to the land of Judah, to where they are lifting up their soul to return to dwell, for they do not turn back, except those escaping." **15** And they answer Jeremiah—all the men who are knowing that their wives are making incense to other gods, and all the women who are remaining, a great assembly, even all the people who are dwelling in the land of Egypt, in Pathros—saying: **16** "The word that you have spoken to us in the Name of Yhwh—we are not listening to you; **17** for we certainly do everything that has gone out of our mouth, to make incense to the queen of the heavens, and to pour out drink-offerings to her, as we have done, we, and our fathers, our kings, and our heads, in cities of Judah, and in streets of Jerusalem, and—we are satisfied with bread, and we are well, and we have not seen calamity. **18** And from the time we have ceased to make incense to the queen of the heavens, and to pour out drink-offerings to her, we have lacked all, and we have been consumed by sword and by famine, **19** and when we are making incense to the queen of the heavens, and pouring out drink-offerings to her—have we made cakes for her to idolize her, and to pour out drink-offerings to her, without our husbands?" **20** And Jeremiah says to all the people, concerning the men and concerning the women, and concerning all the people who are answering him, saying, **21** "The incense that you made in the cities of Judah, and in the streets of Jerusalem, you, and your fathers, your kings, and your heads, and the people of the land, has Yhwh not remembered it? indeed, it comes up on His heart. **22** And Yhwh is not able to accept [you] anymore, because of the evil of your doings, because of the abominations that you have done, and your land is for a ruin, and for an astonishment, and for a reviling, without inhabitant, as [at] this day. **23** Because that you have made incense, and because you have sinned against Yhwh, and have not listened to the voice of Yhwh, and have not walked in His law, and in His statutes, and in His testimonies, therefore this calamity has met you as [at] this day." **24** And Jeremiah says to all the people, and to all the women, "Hear a word of Yhwh, all Judah who [are] in the land of Egypt: **25** Thus spoke Yhwh of Hosts, God of Israel, saying, You and your wives both speak with your mouth, and with your hands have fulfilled, saying, We certainly execute our vows that we have vowed, to make incense to the queen of the heavens, and to pour out drink-offerings to her. You certainly establish your vows, and certainly execute your vows. **26** Therefore, hear a word of Yhwh, all Judah who are dwelling in the land of Egypt: Behold, I have sworn by My great Name, said Yhwh, My Name is no longer proclaimed by the mouth of any man of Judah, saying, Lord Yhwh lives—in all the land of Egypt. **27** Behold, I am watching over them for calamity, and not for good, and all the men of Judah who [are] in the land of Egypt have been consumed by sword and by famine, until their consumption. **28** And the escaped of the sword turn back out of the land of Egypt to the land of Judah, few in number, and all the remnant of Judah, who are coming into the land of Egypt to sojourn there, have known whose word is established, Mine or theirs. **29** And this [is] the sign to you—a declaration of Yhwh—that I am seeing after you in this place, so that you know that My words are certainly established against you for calamity— **30** thus said Yhwh: Behold, I am giving Pharaoh-Hophra king of Egypt into the hand of his enemies, and into the hand of those seeking his life, as I have given Zedekiah king of Judah into the hand of Nebuchadnezzar king of Babylon, his enemy, and who is seeking his life."

CHAPTER 45

1 The word that Jeremiah the prophet has spoken to Baruch son of Neriah, in his writing these words on a scroll from the mouth of Jeremiah, in the fourth year of Jehoiakim son of Josiah king of Judah, saying, **2** "Thus said Yhwh, God of Israel, concerning you, O Baruch: **3** You have said, Woe to me, now, for Yhwh has added sorrow to my pain, I have been wearied with my sighing, and I have not found rest. **4** Thus you say to him, Thus said Yhwh: Behold, that which I have built I am throwing down, and that which I have planted I am plucking up, even the whole land itself. **5** And you seek for great things—do not seek, for behold, I am bringing calamity on all flesh—a declaration of Yhwh—and I have given your life to you for a spoil, in all places to where you go."

CHAPTER 46

1 That which has been the word of Yhwh to Jeremiah the prophet concerning the nations, **2** for Egypt, concerning the force of Pharaoh-Necho king of Egypt, that has been by the Euphrates River, in Carchemish, that Nebuchadnezzar king of Babylon has struck, in the fourth year of Jehoiakim son of Josiah king of Judah: **3** "Set shield and buckler in array, || And draw near to battle. **4** Gird the horses, and go up, you horsemen, || And station yourselves with helmets, || Polish the javelins, put on the coats of mail. **5** Why have I seen them dismayed [and] turned backward? And their mighty ones are beaten down, || And they have fled [to] a refuge, || And did not turn their face, || Fear [is] all around—a declaration of Yhwh. **6** The swift do not flee, nor do the mighty escape, || Northward, by the side of the Euphrates River, || They have stumbled and fallen. **7** Who is this? He comes up as a flood, || His waters shake themselves as rivers! **8** Egypt comes up as a flood, || And the waters shake themselves as rivers. And he says, I go up; I cover the land, I destroy the city and the inhabitants in it. **9** Go up, you horses; and boast yourselves, you chariot, || And go forth, you mighty, || Cush and Phut handling the shield, || And Lud handling—treading the bow. **10** And that day [is] to Lord Yhwh of Hosts || A Day of vengeance, || To be avenged of His adversaries, || And the sword has devoured, and been satisfied, || And it has been watered from their blood, || For a sacrifice [is] to Lord Yhwh of Hosts, || In the land of the north, by the Euphrates River. **11** Go up to Gilead, and take balm, || O virgin daughter of Egypt, || You have multiplied medicines in vain, || There is no healing for you. **12** Nations have heard of your shame, || And your cry has filled the land, || For the mighty stumbled on the mighty, || Together they have fallen—both of them!" **13** The word that Yhwh has spoken to Jeremiah the prophet concerning the coming in of Nebuchadnezzar king of Babylon, to strike the land of Egypt: **14** "Declare in Egypt, and sound in Migdol, || And sound in Noph, and in Tahpanhes, say, || Stand firm and prepare yourself, || For a sword has devoured around you, **15** Why has your bull been swept away? He has not stood, because Yhwh thrust him away. **16** He has multiplied the stumbling, || Indeed, one has fallen on his neighbor, || And they say: Rise, and we return to our people, || And to the land of our birth, || Because of the oppressing sword. **17** They have cried there: Pharaoh king of Egypt [is] a desolation, || The appointed time has passed by. **18** [As] I live—an affirmation of the King, || Yhwh of Hosts [is] His Name, || Surely as Tabor [is] among mountains, || And as Carmel by the sea—he comes in, **19** Make goods for yourself for removal, || O inhabitant, daughter of Egypt, || For Noph becomes a desolation, || And has been burned up, without inhabitant. **20** Egypt [is] a very beautiful heifer, || Destruction comes into her from the north. **21** Even her hired ones in her midst [are] as calves of the stall, || For even they have turned, || They have fled together, they have not stood, || For the day of their calamity has come on them, || The time of their inspection. **22** Its voice goes on as a serpent, || For they go with a force, || And they have come in to her with axes, || As hewers of trees. **23** They have cut down her forest, || A declaration of Yhwh, || For it is not searched, || For they have been more than the grasshopper, || And they have no numbering. **24** The daughter of Egypt has been ashamed, ||

She has been given into the hand of the people of the north. **25** Yhwh of Hosts, God of Israel, has said: Behold, I am seeing after Amon of No, || And after Pharaoh, and after Egypt, || And after her gods, and after her kings, || And after Pharaoh, and after those trusting in him, **26** And I have given them into the hand of those seeking their life, || And into the hand of Nebuchadnezzar king of Babylon, || And into the hand of his servants, || And afterward it is inhabited, || As [in] days of old—a declaration of Yhwh. **27** And you, you do not fear, My servant Jacob, || Nor [are] you dismayed, O Israel, || For behold, I am saving you from afar—And your seed from the land of their captivity, || And Jacob has turned back, || And has been at rest, and been at ease, || And there is none disturbing. **28** You do not fear, My servant Jacob, || A declaration of Yhwh, || For I [am] with you, || For I make an end of all the nations || To where I have driven you, || And I do not make an end of you, || And I have reproved you in judgment, || And do not entirely acquit you!"

CHAPTER 47

1 That which has been the word of Yhwh to Jeremiah concerning the Philistines, before Pharaoh strikes Gaza: **2** "Thus said Yhwh: Behold, waters are going up from the north, || And have been for an overflowing stream, || And they overflow the land and its fullness, || The city, and those dwelling in it, || And men have cried out, || And every inhabitant of the land has howled. **3** From the sound of the stamping of the hooves of his mighty ones, || From the rushing of his chariot, || The noise of his wheels, || Fathers have not turned to sons, || From feebleness of hands, **4** Because of the day that has come to spoil all the Philistines, || To cut off every helping remnant from Tyre and from Sidon. For Yhwh is spoiling the Philistines, || The remnant of the island of Caphtor. **5** Baldness has come to Gaza, || Ashkelon has been cut off, || O remnant of their valley, || Until when do you cut yourself? **6** Behold, sword of Yhwh, until when are you not quiet? Be removed to your sheath, rest and cease. **7** How will it be quiet, || And Yhwh has given a charge to it, || Against Ashkelon and against the seashore? He has appointed it there!"

CHAPTER 48

1 Concerning Moab: "Thus said Yhwh of Hosts, God of Israel: Woe to Nebo, for it is spoiled, || Kiriathaim has been captured [and] put to shame, || The high tower has been put to shame, || Indeed, it has been broken down. **2** There is no longer praise of Moab, || In Heshbon they devised evil against her: Come, and we cut it off from [being] a nation, || Also, O Madmen, you are cut off, || A sword goes after you. **3** A voice of a cry [is] from Horonaim, || Spoiling and great destruction. **4** Moab has been destroyed, || Her little ones have caused a cry to be heard. **5** For the ascent of Luhith with weeping, || Weeping goes up, || For in the descent of Horonaim || Adversaries have heard a cry of desolation. **6** Flee, deliver yourselves, || You are as a naked thing in a wilderness. **7** For because of your trusting in your works, || And in your treasures, even you are captured, || And Chemosh has gone out in a removal, || His priests and his heads together. **8** And a spoiler comes to every city, || And no city escapes, || And the valley has perished, || And the plain has been destroyed, as Yhwh said. **9** Give wings to Moab, that she may go forth and flee away, || And her cities are for a desolation, || Without an inhabitant in them. **10** Cursed [is] he who is doing the work of Yhwh slothfully, || And cursed [is] he || Who is withholding his sword from blood. **11** Moab is secure from his youth, || And he [is] at rest for his preserved things, || And he has not been emptied out from vessel to vessel, || And he has not gone into captivity, || Therefore his taste has remained in him, || And his fragrance has not been changed. **12** Therefore, behold, days are coming, || A declaration of Yhwh, || And I have sent wanderers to him, || And they have caused him to wander, || And they empty out his vessels, || And they dash his bottles in pieces. **13** And Moab has been ashamed because of Chemosh, || As the house of Israel has been ashamed || Because of Beth-El, their confidence. **14** How do you say, We [are] mighty, || And men of strength for battle? **15** Moab is spoiled, and has gone up [from] her cities, || And the choice of its young men || Have gone down to slaughter, || An affirmation of the King, || Yhwh

of Hosts [is] His Name. **16** The destruction of Moab is near to come, || And his calamity has hurried exceedingly. **17** Bemoan for him, all you around him, || And all knowing his name, say, || How it has been broken, the staff of strength, || The rod of beauty! **18** Come down from glory, sit in thirst, || O inhabitant, daughter of Dibon, || For a spoiler of Moab has come up to you, || He has destroyed your fortifications. **19** Stand on the way, and watch, O inhabitant of Aroer, || Ask the fugitive and escaped, || Say, What has happened? **20** Moab has been put to shame, || For it has been broken down, || Howl and cry, declare in Arnon, || For Moab is spoiled, **21** And judgment has come to the land of the plain—to Holon, || And to Jahazah, and on Mephaath, **22** And on Dibon, and on Nebo, || And on Beth-Diblathaim, and on Kirathaim, **23** And on Beth-Gamul, and on Beth-Meon, **24** And on Kerioth, and on Bozrah, || And on all cities of the land of Moab, || The far off and the near. **25** The horn of Moab has been cut down, || And his arm has been broken, || A declaration of Yhwh. **26** Declare him drunk, || For he made himself great against Yhwh || And Moab has struck in his vomit, || And he has been for a derision—even he. **27** And was Israel not the derision to you? Was he found among thieves? For since your words concerning him, || You bemoan yourself. **28** Forsake cities, and dwell in a rock, || You inhabitants of Moab, || And be as a dove making a nest in the passages of a pit's mouth. **29** We have heard of the arrogance of Moab, || Exceedingly proud! His haughtiness, and his arrogance, || And his pride, and the height of his heart, **30** I have known, a declaration of Yhwh, || His wrath, and [it is] not right, || His boastings—they have done nothing right. **31** Therefore I howl for Moab, even for Moab—all of it, || I cry for men of Kir-Heres, it mourns, **32** With the weeping of Jazer, I weep for you, O vine of Sibmah, || Your branches have passed over a sea, || They have come to the Sea of Jazer, || On your summer fruits, and on your harvest, || A spoiler has fallen. **33** And joy and gladness have been removed from the fruitful field, || Even from the land of Moab, || And I have caused wine to cease from winepresses, || Shouting does not proceed, || The shouting [is] not shouting! **34** Because of the cry of Heshbon to Elealeh, || They have given their voice to Jahaz, || From Zoar to Horonaim, || A heifer of the third [year], || For even [the] waters of Nimrim become desolations. **35** And I have caused to cease in Moab, || A declaration of Yhwh, || Him who is offering in a high place, || And him who is making incense to his god. **36** Therefore My heart sounds as pipes for Moab, || And My heart sounds as pipes for men of Kir-Heres, || Therefore the abundance he made perished. **37** For every head [is] bald, and every beard diminished, || On all hands—cuttings, and on the loins—sackcloth. **38** On all roofs of Moab, and in her broad-places, || All of it—lamentation, || For I have broken Moab as a vessel in which there is no pleasure," || A declaration of Yhwh. **39** "How it has been broken down! They have howled, || How Moab has turned the neck ashamed! And Moab has been for a derision || And for a terror to all around her." **40** For thus said Yhwh: "Behold, he flees as an eagle, || And has spread his wings to Moab. **41** The cities have been captured, || And the strongholds are caught, || And the heart of the mighty of Moab || Has been in that day as the heart of a distressed woman. **42** And Moab has been destroyed from [being] a people, || For he exerted himself against Yhwh. **43** Fear, and a snare, and a trap, [are] for you, || O inhabitant of Moab—a declaration of Yhwh, **44** Whoever is fleeing because of the fear falls into the snare, || And whoever is coming up from the snare is captured by the trap, || For I bring to her—to Moab—The year of their inspection, || A declaration of Yhwh. **45** In the shadow of Heshbon fugitives have stood powerless, || For fire has gone forth from Heshbon, || And a flame from within Sihon, || And it consumes the corner of Moab, || And the crown of the sons of Shaon. **46** Woe to you, O Moab, || The people of Chemosh have perished, || For your sons were taken with the captives, || And your daughters with the captivity. **47** And I have turned back [to] the captivity of Moab, || In the latter end of the days," || A declaration of Yhwh! "Until now [is] the judgment of Moab."

CHAPTER 49

1 Concerning the sons of Ammon: "Thus said Yhwh: Has Israel no sons? has he no heir? Why has Malcam possessed Gad, || And his people have dwelt in its cities? **2** Therefore, behold, days are coming, || A declaration of Yhwh, || And I have sounded a shout of battle in Rabbah of the sons of

Ammon, || And it has been for a heap—a desolation, || And her daughters are burned with fire, || And Israel has succeeded its heirs, said Yhwh. **3** Howl, Heshbon, for Ai is spoiled, || Cry, daughters of Rabbah, gird on sackcloth, || Lament, and go to and fro by the hedges, || For Malcam goes into captivity, || His priests and his princes together. **4** Why do you boast yourself in valleys? Your valley is flowing, || O backsliding daughter, || Who is trusting in her treasures: Who comes to me? **5** Behold, I am bringing fear in on you, || A declaration of Lord Yhwh of Hosts, || From all around you, || And you have each been driven out before it, || And there is no gatherer of the wandering. **6** And after this I return the captivity of the sons of Ammon, || A declaration of Yhwh.” **7** Concerning Edom: “Thus said Yhwh of Hosts: Is wisdom no longer in Teman? Has counsel perished from the intelligent? Has their wisdom vanished? **8** Flee, turn, go deep to dwell, you inhabitants of Dedan, || For I brought the calamity of Esau on him, || The time I inspected him. **9** If gatherers have come to you, || They do not leave gleanings, || If thieves in the night, || They have destroyed their sufficiency! **10** For I have made Esau bare, || I have uncovered his secret places, || And he is not able to be hidden, || Spoiled [is] his seed, and his brothers, || And his neighbors, and he is not. **11** Leave your orphans—I keep alive, || And your widows—trust on Me, **12** For thus said Yhwh: They whose judgment is not to drink of the cup, || Do certainly drink, || And you [are] he that is entirely acquitted! You are not acquitted, for you certainly drink. **13** For I have sworn by Myself, || A declaration of Yhwh, || That for a desolation, for a reproach, || For a dry place, and for a reviling—is Bozrah, || And all her cities are for continuous ruins. **14** I have heard a report from Yhwh, || And an ambassador is sent among nations, || Gather yourselves and come in against her, || And rise for battle. **15** For behold, I have made you little among nations, || Despised among men. **16** Your terribleness has lifted you up, || The pride of your heart, || O dweller in clefts of the rock, || Holding the high place of the height, || For you make your nest high as an eagle, || From there I bring you down, || A declaration of Yhwh. **17** And Edom has been for a desolation, || Everyone passing by her is astonished, || And hisses because of all her plagues. **18** As the overthrow of Sodom and Gomorrah, || And its neighbors, said Yhwh, || No one dwells there, || Nor does a son of man sojourn in her. **19** Behold, he comes up as a lion, || Because of the rising of the Jordan, || To the enduring habitation, || But I cause to rest, || I cause him to run from off her, || And who is chosen? I lay a charge concerning her, || For who is like Me? and who convenes Me? And who [is] this shepherd who stands before Me? **20** Therefore, hear the counsel of Yhwh, || That He has counseled concerning Edom, || And His plans that He has devised || Concerning the inhabitants of Teman: Do little ones of the flock not drag them out, || Does He not make their habitation desolate? **21** The earth has shaken from the noise of their fall, || The cry—its voice is heard at the Sea of Suph. **22** Behold, He comes up as an eagle, and flies, || And He spreads His wings over Bozrah, || And the heart of the mighty of Edom has been in that day, || As the heart of a travailing woman.” **23** Concerning Damascus: “Hamath and Arpad have been ashamed, || For they have heard an evil report, || They have been melted, sorrow [is] in the sea, || It is not able to be quiet. **24** Damascus has been feeble, || She turned to flee, and fear strengthened her, || Distress and pangs have seized her, as a travailing woman. **25** How it is not left—the city of praise, || The city of My joy! **26** Therefore her young men fall in her broad places, || And all the men of war are cut off in that day, || A declaration of Yhwh of Hosts. **27** And I have kindled a fire against the wall of Damascus, || And it consumed palaces of Ben-Hadad!” **28** Concerning Kedar, and concerning the kingdoms of Hazor that Nebuchadnezzar king of Babylon has struck: “Thus said Yhwh: Arise, go up to Kedar, || And spoil the sons of the east. **29** They take their tents and their flock, || Their curtains, and all their vessels, || And they carry away their camels for themselves, || And they called concerning them, || Fear [is] all around. **30** Flee, bemoan mightily, go deep to dwell, || You inhabitants of Hazor—a declaration of Yhwh, || For Nebuchadnezzar king of Babylon has given counsel against you, || Indeed, he devises a scheme against them. **31** Rise, go up to a nation at rest, || Dwelling confidently, a declaration of Yhwh, || It has no double gates nor bar, || They dwell alone. **32** And their camels have been for a prey, || And the multitude of their livestock for a spoil, || And I have scattered them to every wind, || Who cut off the corner [of the beard], || And from all its passages I bring in their calamity, || A declaration of Yhwh. **33** And Hazor has been for a habitation of dragons, ||

A desolation for all time, || No one dwells there, nor does a son of man sojourn in it!” **34** That which has been the word of Yhwh to Jeremiah the prophet concerning Elam, in the beginning of the reign of Zedekiah king of Judah, saying, **35** “Thus said Yhwh of Hosts: Behold, I am breaking the bow of Elam, || The beginning of their might. **36** And I have brought four winds to Elam, || From the four ends of the heavens, || And have scattered them to all these winds, || And there is no nation to where outcasts of Elam do not come in. **37** And I have frightened Elam before their enemies, || And before those seeking their life, || And I have brought calamity on them, || The heat of My anger, || A declaration of Yhwh, || And I have sent the sword after them, || Until I have consumed them; **38** And I have set My throne in Elam, || And I have destroyed king and princes from there, || A declaration of Yhwh. **39** And it has come to pass, in the latter end of the days, I return the captivity of Elam, || A declaration of Yhwh!”

CHAPTER 50

1 The word that Yhwh has spoken concerning Babylon, concerning the land of the Chaldeans, by the hand of Jeremiah the prophet: **2** “Declare among nations, and sound, || And lift up an ensign, sound, do not hide, || Say, Babylon has been captured, || Bel has been put to shame, || Merodach has been broken, || Her grievous things have been put to shame, || Her idols have been broken. **3** For a nation from the north has come up against her, || It makes her land become a desolation, || And there is not an inhabitant in it. From man even to beast, || They have moved, they have gone. **4** In those days, and at that time,” || A declaration of Yhwh, || “Sons of Israel come in, || They and sons of Judah together, || Going on and weeping they go, || And they seek their God Yhwh. **5** They ask the way [to] Zion, || Their faces [are] toward that place: Come in, and we are joined to Yhwh, || A perpetual covenant—never forgotten. **6** My people have been a perishing flock, || Their shepherds have caused them to err, || Causing them to go back [on] the mountains, || They have gone from mountain to hill, || They have forgotten their crouching-place. **7** All finding them have devoured them, || And their adversaries have said: We are not guilty, || Because that they sinned against Yhwh, || The habitation of righteousness, || And the hope of their fathers—Yhwh. **8** Move from the midst of Babylon, || And go out from the land of the Chaldeans; And be as male goats before a flock. **9** For behold, I am stirring up, || And am causing to come up against Babylon, || An assembly of great nations from [the] land of the north, || And they have set in array against her, || From there she is captured, || Its arrow—as a skillful hero—does not return empty, **10** And Chaldea has been for a spoil, || All her spoilers are satisfied,” || A declaration of Yhwh. **11** “Because you rejoice, because you exult, || O spoilers of My inheritance, || Because you increase as a heifer [at] the tender grass, || And cry aloud as bulls, **12** Your mother has been greatly ashamed, || She who bore you has been confounded, || Behold, the last of nations [is] a wilderness, || A dry land, and a desert. **13** Because of the wrath of Yhwh it is not inhabited, || And it has been a desolation—all of it. Everyone passing by at Babylon is astonished, || And hisses because of all her plagues. **14** Set yourselves in array against Babylon all around, || All you treading a bow, || Shoot at her, have no pity on the arrow, || For she has sinned against Yhwh. **15** Shout against her all around, || She has given forth her hand, || Her foundations have fallen, || Her walls have been thrown down, || For it [is] the vengeance of Yhwh, || Be avenged of her, as she did—do to her. **16** Cut off the sower from Babylon, || And him handling the sickle in the time of harvest, || Because of the oppressing sword, || Each to his people—they turn, || And each to his land—they flee. **17** Israel [is as] a scattered sheep, || Lions have driven [him] away, || At first, the king of Asshur devoured him, || And now, at last, Nebuchadnezzar king of Babylon has broken his bone. **18** Therefore, thus said Yhwh of Hosts, God of Israel: Behold, I am seeing after the king of Babylon, || And after his land, || As I have seen after the king of Asshur; **19** And I have brought Israel back to his habitation, || And he has fed on Carmel and on Bashan; And his soul is satisfied on Mount Ephraim and on Gilead. **20** In those days, and at that time,” || A declaration of Yhwh, || “The iniquity of Israel is sought, and it is not, || And the sin of Judah, and it is not found, || For I am propitious to those whom I leave! **21** Against the land of Merathaim, go up against it, || And to the inhabitants of Pekod, || Dry up and devote their posterity,” ||

A declaration of Yhwh, || "And do according to all that I have commanded you. **22** A noise of battle [is] in the land, || And of great destruction. **23** How it has been cut and broken, || The hammer of the whole earth! How Babylon has been for a desolation among nations! **24** I have laid a snare for you, || And you are also captured, O Babylon, || And you have known, || You have been found, and are also caught, || For you have stirred yourself up against Yhwh. **25** Yhwh has opened His treasury, || And He brings out the weapons of His indignation, || For a work [is] to Lord Yhwh of Hosts, || In the land of the Chaldeans. **26** Come in to her from the extremity, || Open her storehouses, || Raise her up as heaps, and devote her, || Let her have no remnant. **27** Slay all her cows, they go down to slaughter, || Woe [is] on them, for their day has come, || The time of their inspection. **28** A voice of fugitives and escaped ones || [Is] from the land of Babylon, || To declare in Zion the vengeance of our God Yhwh, || The vengeance of His temple. **29** Summon archers to Babylon, all treading the bow, || Encamp against her all around, || Let [her] have no escape; Repay to her according to her work, || According to all that she did—do to her, || For she has been proud against Yhwh, || Against the Holy One of Israel. **30** Therefore her young men fall in her broad places, || And all her men of war are cut off in that day," || A declaration of Yhwh. **31** "Behold, I [am] against you, O pride," || A declaration of Lord Yhwh of Hosts, || "For your day has come, the time of your inspection. **32** And pride has stumbled, || And he has fallen, and has none raising up, || And I have kindled a fire in his cities, || And it has devoured all around him. **33** Thus said Yhwh of Hosts: The sons of Israel are oppressed, || And the sons of Judah together, || And all their captors have kept hold on them, || They have refused to send them away. **34** Their Redeemer [is] strong, || Yhwh of Hosts [is] His Name, || He thoroughly pleads their cause, || So as to cause the land to rest, || And He has given trouble to the inhabitants of Babylon. **35** A sword [is] for the Chaldeans," || A declaration of Yhwh, || "And it [is] on the inhabitants of Babylon, || And on her heads, and on her wise men; **36** A sword [is] on the princes, || And they have become foolish; A sword [is] on her mighty ones, || And they have been broken down; **37** A sword [is] on his horses and on his chariot, || And on all the rabble who [are] in her midst, || And they have become women; A sword [is] on her treasuries, || And they have been spoiled; **38** A sword [is] on her waters, and they have been dried up, || For it [is] a land of carved images, || And they boast themselves in idols. **39** Therefore desert-dwellers dwell with howlers, || Indeed, daughters of the ostrich have dwelt in her, || And it is not inhabited anymore forever, || Nor dwelt in from generation to generation. **40** As the overthrow by God of Sodom, || And of Gomorrah, and of its neighbors," || A declaration of Yhwh, || "None dwell there, || Nor does a son of man sojourn in her. **41** Behold, a people has come from the north, || Even a great nation, || And many kings are stirred up from the sides of the earth. **42** They seize bow and javelin, || They [are] cruel, and they have no mercy, || Their voice sounds as a sea, and they ride on horses, || Set in array as a man for battle, || Against you, O daughter of Babylon. **43** The king of Babylon has heard their report, || And his hands have been feeble, || Distress has seized him; pain as a travailing woman. **44** Behold, he comes up as a lion, || Because of the rising of the Jordan, || To the enduring habitation, || But I cause to rest, I cause them to run from off her. And who is chosen? I lay a charge on her, || For who [is] like Me? And who convenes Me? And who [is] this shepherd who stands before Me? **45** Therefore, hear the counsel of Yhwh, || That He counseled concerning Babylon, || And His plans that He has devised || Concerning the land of the Chaldeans; Do little ones of the flock not drag them out, || Does He not make the habitation desolate over them? **46** From the sound of Babylon having been captured, || The earth has been shaken, || And a cry has been heard among nations!"

CHAPTER 51

1 Thus said Yhwh: "Behold, I am stirring up against Babylon, || And the inhabitants of Leb, My withstanders, || A destroying wind, **2** And I have sent fanners to Babylon, || And they have fanned her, and they empty her land, || For they have been against her, || All around—in the day of evil. **3** Do not let the treader tread his bow, || Nor lift himself up in his coat of mail, || Nor have pity on her young men, || Devote all her host to destruction. **4** And the wounded have fallen in the land of the Chaldeans, || And the pierced-through in her streets. **5** For Israel and Judah are not forsaken || By his God— by Yhwh of Hosts, || For their land has been full of guilt, || Against the Holy One of Israel. **6** Flee from the midst of Babylon, || And let each deliver his soul, || Do not be cut off in her iniquity, || For it [is] a time of vengeance for Yhwh—His, || He is rendering repayment to her. **7** Babylon [is] a golden cup in the hand of Yhwh, || Making all the earth drunk, || Nations have drunk of her wine, || Therefore nations boast themselves. **8** Babylon has suddenly fallen, || Indeed, she is broken, howl for her, || Take balm for her pain, perhaps she may be healed. **9** We healed Babylon, and she was not healed, || Forsake her, and we go, each to his land, || For her judgment has come to the heavens, || And it has been lifted up to the clouds. **10** Yhwh has brought forth our righteousnesses, || Come, and we recount in Zion the work of our God Yhwh. **11** Cleanse the arrows, fill the shields, || Yhwh has stirred up the spirit of the kings of Media, || For His purpose [is] against Babylon to destroy her, || For it [is] the vengeance of Yhwh, || The vengeance of His temple. **12** Lift up an ensign to the walls of Babylon, || Strengthen the watch, || Establish the watchers, prepare the ambush, || For Yhwh has both devised and done that which He spoke, || Concerning the inhabitants of Babylon. **13** O dweller on many waters, abundant in treasures, || Your end has come—the measure of your dishonest gain. **14** Yhwh of Hosts has sworn by Himself, || That, Surely I have filled you [with] men as the cankerworm, || And they have cried against you—shouting. **15** Making [the] earth by His power, || Establishing [the] world by His wisdom, || Who by His understanding stretched out the heavens, **16** At the voice He gives forth, || A multitude of waters [are] in the heavens, || And He causes vapors to come up from the end of the earth, || He has made lightnings for rain, || And He brings out wind from His treasures. **17** Every man has been brutish by knowledge, || Everyone has been put to shame—from refining a carved image, || For his molten image [is] falsehood, || And there is no breath in them. **18** They [are] vanity—a work of errors, || They perish in the time of their inspection. **19** The Portion of Jacob [is] not like these, || For He is forming the whole, || And [Israel is] the tribe of His inheritance, || Yhwh of Hosts [is] His Name. **20** You [are] My shatterer—weapons of war, || And I have broken in pieces nations by you, || And I have destroyed kingdoms by you, **21** And I have broken in pieces horse and its rider by you, || And I have broken in pieces chariot and its charioteer by you, **22** And I have broken in pieces man and woman by you, || And I have broken in pieces old and young by you, || And I have broken in pieces young man and virgin by you, **23** And I have broken in pieces shepherd and his drove by you, || And I have broken in pieces farmer and his team by you, || And I have broken in pieces governors and prefects by you. **24** And I have repaid to Babylon, || And to all inhabitants of Chaldea, || All the evil that they have done in Zion, || Before your eyes," a declaration of Yhwh. **25** "Behold, I [am] against you, O destroying mountain," || A declaration of Yhwh, || "That is destroying all the earth, || And I have stretched out My hand against you, || And I have rolled you from the rocks, || And given you for a burnt mountain. **26** And they do not take out of you a stone for a corner, || And a stone for foundations, || For you are continuous desolations," || A declaration of Yhwh. **27** "Lift up an ensign in the land, || Blow a horn among nations, || Sanctify nations against it, || Summon against it the kingdoms of Ararat, Minni, and Ashkenaz, || Appoint an infant head against it, || Cause the horse to ascend as the rough cankerworm. **28** Sanctify against it the nations with the kings of Media, || Its governors and all its prefects, || And all the land of its dominion. **29** And the land shakes, and it is pained, || For the purposes of Yhwh have stood against Babylon, || To make the land of Babylon a desolation without inhabitant. **30** The mighty of Babylon have ceased to fight, || They have remained in strongholds, || Their might has failed, they have become [as] women, || They have burned her dwelling places, || Her bars have been broken. **31** Runner runs to meet runner, || And announcer to meet announcer, || To announce to the king of Babylon, || For his city has been captured—at the extremity. **32** And the passages have been captured, || And they have burned the reeds with fire, || And the men of war have been troubled. **33** For thus said Yhwh of Hosts, God of Israel: The daughter of Babylon [is] as a threshing-floor, || The time of her threshing—yet a little [while], || And the time of her harvest has come. **34** Devoured us, crushed us, has Nebuchadnezzar king of Babylon, || He has set us [as] an empty vessel, || He has swallowed us as a dragon, || He has filled his belly with my delicacies, || He has driven us away. **35** My wrong, and [that of] my flesh, [is] on Babylon—The inhabitant of Zion says; And my blood [is] on the inhabitants of Chaldea—Jerusalem says. **36** Therefore, thus said Yhwh: Behold, I am pleading your cause, || And I have avenged your vengeance, || And dried up her sea, and made her fountains dry. **37** And Babylon has been for heaps, || A habitation of dragons, || An astonishment, and a hissing, without inhabitant. **38** They roar together as young lions, || They have shaken themselves as lions' whelps. **39** In their heat I make their banquets, || And I have caused them to drink, so that they exult, || And have slept a continuous sleep, || And do not awaken," a declaration of Yhwh. **40** "I cause them to go down as lambs to slaughter, || As rams with male goats. **41** How Sheshach has been captured, || Indeed, the praise of the whole earth is caught, || How Babylon has been for an astonishment among nations. **42** The sea has come up over Babylon, || She has been covered with a multitude of its billows. **43** Her cities have been for a desolation, || A dry land, and a wilderness, || A land—none dwell in them, || Nor does a son of man pass over into them. **44** And I have seen after Bel in Babylon, || And I have brought forth that which he swallowed—from his mouth, || And nations no longer flow to him, || Also the wall of Babylon has fallen. **45** Go forth from her midst, O My people, || And let each deliver his soul, || Because of the fierceness of the anger of Yhwh, **46** And lest your heart be tender, || And you are afraid of the report that is heard in the land, || And the report has come in [one] year, || And after it [another] report in [another] year, || And violence [is] in the land, ruler against ruler; **47** Therefore, behold, days are coming, || And I have seen after the carved images of Babylon. And all its land is ashamed, || And all its pierced ones fall in its midst. **48** And heavens and earth and all that [is] in them || Have cried aloud against Babylon, || For the spoilers come to her from the north," || A declaration of Yhwh. **49** "As Babylon [has caused the] pierced of Israel to fall, || So they of Babylon have fallen, || You pierced of all the earth. **50** You escaped of the sword, go on, do not stand, || Remember Yhwh from afar, || And let Jerusalem come up on your heart. **51** We have been ashamed, for we heard reproach, || Shame has covered our faces, || For strangers have come in against the sanctuaries of the house of Yhwh. **52** Therefore, behold, days are coming," || A declaration of Yhwh, || "And I have seen after her carved images, || And the wounded groan in all her land. **53** Because Babylon goes up to the heavens, || And because she fortifies the high place of her strength, || Spoilers come into her from Me," || A declaration of Yhwh. **54** "A voice of a cry [is] from Babylon, || And of great destruction from the land of the Chaldean. **55** For Yhwh is spoiling Babylon, || And has destroyed her great voice, || And her billows have sounded as many waters, || Their voice has given forth a noise. **56** For a spoiler has come in against her—against Babylon, || And her mighty ones have been captured, || Their bows have been broken, || For the God of recompenses—Yhwh—certainly repays. **57** And I have caused her princes to drink, || And her wise men, her governors, || And her prefects, and her mighty ones, || And they have slept a continuous sleep, || And they do not awaken—an affirmation of the King, || Yhwh of Hosts [is] His Name. **58** Thus said Yhwh of Hosts: The wall of Babylon—The broad one—is made utterly bare, || And her high gates are burned with fire, || And peoples labor in vain, || And nations in fire, and have been weary!" **59** The word that Jeremiah the prophet has commanded Seraiah son of Neriah, son of Maaseiah, in his going with Zedekiah king of Judah to Babylon, in the fourth year of his reign—and Seraiah [is] a quiet prince; **60** and Jeremiah writes all the calamity that comes to Babylon on one scroll—all these words that are written concerning Babylon. **61** And Jeremiah says to Seraiah, "When you enter Babylon, then you have seen, and have read all these words, **62** and have said: Yhwh, You have spoken concerning this place, to cut it off, that there is none dwelling in it, from man even to livestock, for it is a continuous desolation. **63** And it has come to pass, when you finish reading this scroll, you bind a stone to it, and have cast it into the midst of the Euphrates, **64** and said, Thus Babylon sinks, and she does not arise, because of the calamity that I am bringing in against it, and they have been weary." Until now [are the] words of Jeremiah.

CHAPTER 52

1 Zedekiah [is] a son of twenty-one years in his reigning,

and he has reigned eleven years in Jerusalem, and the name of his mother [is] Hamutal daughter of Jeremiah of Libnah. **2** and he does evil in the eyes of Yhwh, according to all that Jehoiakim has done, **3** for because of the anger of Yhwh, it has been in Jerusalem and Judah until He has cast them from before His face, and Zedekiah rebels against the king of Babylon. **4** And it comes to pass, in the ninth year of his reign, in the tenth month, on the tenth of the month, Nebuchadnezzar king of Babylon has come—he and all his force—against Jerusalem, and they encamp against it, and build against it a fortification all around; **5** and the city comes into siege until the eleventh year of King Zedekiah. **6** In the fourth month, on the ninth of the month, when the famine is severe in the city, and there has been no bread for the people of the land, **7** then the city is broken up, and all the men of war flee, and go forth from the city by night, the way of the gate between the two walls that [is] by the king's garden—and the Chaldeans [are] by the city all around—and they go the way of the plain. **8** And the forces of the Chaldeans pursue after the king, and overtake Zedekiah in the plains of Jericho, and all his forces have been scattered from him, **9** and they capture the king, and bring him up to the king of Babylon at Riblah, in the land of Hamath, and he speaks with him—judgments. **10** And the king of Babylon slaughters the sons of Zedekiah before his eyes, and he has also slaughtered all the princes of Judah in Riblah; **11** and he has blinded the eyes of Zedekiah, and he binds him in bronze chains, and the king of Babylon brings him to Babylon, and puts him in the house of inspection to the day of his death. **12** And in the fifth month, on the tenth of the month—it [is] the nineteenth year of King Nebuchadnezzar king of Babylon—Nebuzar-Adan, chief of the executioners, has come; he has stood before the king of Babylon in Jerusalem, **13** and he burns the house of Yhwh, and the house of the king, and all the houses of Jerusalem—even every great house he has burned with fire, **14** and all the forces of the Chaldeans that [are] with the chief of the executioners have broken down all the walls of Jerusalem. **15** And of the poor of the people, and the remnant of the people who are left in the city, and those who are defecting, who have defected to the king of Babylon, and the remnant of the multitude, Nebuzar-Adan, chief of the executioners, has removed; **16** and of the poor of the land, Nebuzar-Adan, chief of the executioners, has left for vinedressers and for farmers. **17** And the pillars of bronze that [are] in the house of Yhwh, and the bases, and the bronze sea that [is] in the house of Yhwh, the Chaldeans have broken, and they carry away all the bronze of them to Babylon; **18** and the pots, and the shovels, and the snuffers, and the bowls, and the spoons, and all the vessels of bronze with which they minister, they have taken away; **19** and the basins, and the fire-pans, and the bowls, and the pots, and the lampstands, and the spoons, and the cups, the gold of that which [is] gold, and the silver of that which [is] silver, the chief of the executioners has taken. **20** The two pillars, the one sea, and the twelve bronze oxen that [are] beneath the bases, that King Solomon made for the house of Yhwh, there was no weighing of the bronze of all these vessels. **21** As for the pillars, eighteen cubits [is] the height of the one pillar, and a cord of twelve cubits goes around it, and its thickness [is] four fingers hollow. **22** And the capital on it [is] of bronze, and the height of the one capital [is] five cubits, and network and pomegranates [are] on the capital all around, the whole [is] of bronze; and like these—the second pillar—and pomegranates. **23** And the pomegranates are ninety-six on a side, all the pomegranates [are] one hundred on the network all around. **24** And the chief of the executioners takes Seraiah the head priest, and Zephaniah the second priest, and the three keepers of the threshold, **25** and he has taken a certain eunuch out of the city, who has been inspector over the men of war, and seven men of those seeing the king's face, who have been found in the city, and the head scribe of the host, who musters the people of the land, and sixty men of the people of the land, who are found in the midst of the city; **26** and Nebuzar-Adan, chief of the executioners, takes them, and brings them to the king of Babylon at Riblah, **27** and the king of Babylon strikes them, and puts them to death in Riblah, in the land of Hamath, and he removes Judah from off its own ground. **28** This [is] the people whom Nebuchadnezzar has removed: in the seventh year, of Jews, three thousand and twenty-three; **29** in the eighteenth year of Nebuchadnezzar—from Jerusalem—eight hundred thirty-two souls; **30** in the twenty-third year of Nebuchadnezzar, Nebuzar-Adan, chief of the guard, has removed of Jewish souls, seven hundred forty-five; all the souls [are] four thousand and six hundred. **31** And it comes to pass, in the thirty-seventh year of the expulsion of Jehoiachin king of Judah, in the twelfth month, on the twenty-fifth of the month, Evil-Merodach king of Babylon has lifted up, in the year of his reign, the head of Jehoiachin king of Judah, and brings him out from the house of restraint, **32** and speaks good things with him, and sets his throne above the throne of the kings who [are] with him in Babylon, **33** and he has changed his prison garments, and he has continually eaten bread before him, all the days of his life. **34** And his allowance—a continual allowance—has been given to him by the king of Babylon, the matter of a day in its day, until [the] day of his death—all [the] days of his life.

LAMENTATIONS

CHAPTER 1

1 [Aleph-Bet] How she has sat alone, || The city abounding with people! She has been as a widow, || The mighty among nations! Princes among provinces, || She has become tributary! **2** She weeps severely in the night, || And her tear [is] on her cheeks, || There is no comforter for her out of all her lovers, || All her friends dealt treacherously by her, || They have been to her for enemies. **3** Removed has Judah because of affliction, || And because of the abundance of her service; She has dwelt among nations, || She has not found rest, || All her pursuers have overtaken her between the straits. **4** The ways of Zion are mourning, || Without any coming at the appointed time, || All her gates are desolate, her priests sigh, || Her virgins are afflicted—and she has bitterness. **5** Her adversaries have become chief, || Her enemies have been at ease, || For Yhwh has afflicted her, || For the abundance of her transgressions, || Her infants have gone captive before the adversary. **6** And all her honor goes out from the daughter of Zion, || Her princes have been as harts—They have not found pasture, || And they go powerless before a pursuer. **7** Jerusalem has remembered || [In] the days of her affliction and her mournings, all her desirable things that were from the days of old, || In the falling of her people into the hand of an adversary, || And she has no helper; Adversaries have seen her, || They have laughed at her cessation. **8** A sin has Jerusalem sinned, || Therefore she has become impure, || All who honored her have esteemed her lightly, || For they have seen her nakedness, || Indeed, she herself has sighed and turns backward. **9** Her uncleanness [is] in her skirts, || She has not remembered her latter end, || And she comes down wonderfully, || There is no comforter for her. See, O Yhwh, my affliction, || For an enemy has exerted himself. **10** His hand has spread out an adversary || On all her desirable things, || For she has seen—Nations have entered her sanctuary, || Concerning which You commanded, || "They do not come into the assembly to you." **11** All her people are sighing—seeking bread, || They have given their desirable things || For food to refresh the body; See, O Yhwh, and behold attentively, || For I have been lightly esteemed. **12** [Is it] nothing to you, all you passing by the way? Look attentively, and see, || If there is any pain like my pain, || That He is rolling to me? Whom Yhwh has afflicted || In the day of the fierceness of His anger. **13** From above He has sent fire into my bone, || And it subdues it, He has spread a net for my feet, || He has turned me backward, || He has made me desolate—all the day sick. **14** Bound has been the yoke of my transgressions by His hand, || They are wrapped together, || They have gone up on my neck, || He has caused my power to stumble, || The Lord has given me into hands, I am not able to rise. **15** The Lord has trodden down all my mighty ones in my midst, || He proclaimed an appointed time against me, || To destroy my young men, || The Lord has trodden a winepress, || To the virgin daughter of Judah. **16** For these I am weeping, || My eye, my eye, is running down with waters, || For a comforter has been far from me, || Refreshing my soul, || My sons have been desolate, || For mighty has been an enemy. **17** Zion has spread forth her hands, || There is no comforter for her, || Yhwh has charged concerning Jacob, || His neighbors [are] his adversaries, || Jerusalem has become impure among them. **18** Yhwh is righteous, || For I have provoked His mouth. Now hear, all you

peoples, and see my pain, || My virgins and my young men have gone into captivity. **19** I called for my lovers, they have deceived me, || My priests and my elderly have expired in the city; When they have sought food for themselves, || Then they give back their soul. **20** See, O Yhwh, for distress [is] to me, || My bowels have been troubled, || My heart has been turned in my midst, || For I have greatly provoked, || From outside the sword has bereaved, || In the house [it is] as death. **21** They have heard that I have sighed, || There is no comforter for me, || All my enemies have heard of my calamity, || They have rejoiced that You have done [it], || You have brought in the day You have called, || And they are like to me. **22** All their evil comes in before You, || And one is doing to them as You have done to me, || For all my transgressions, || For many [are] my sighs, and my heart [is] sick!

CHAPTER 2

1 [Aleph-Bet] How the Lord clouds in His anger the daughter of Zion, || He has cast from the heavens [to] earth the beauty of Israel, || And has not remembered His footstool in the day of His anger. **2** The Lord has swallowed up, || He has not pitied any of the pleasant places of Jacob, || He has broken down in His wrath || The fortresses of the daughter of Judah, || He has caused to come to the earth, || He defiled the kingdom and its princes. **3** He has cut off in the heat of anger every horn of Israel, || He has turned backward His right hand || From the face of the enemy, || And He burns against Jacob as a flaming fire, || It has devoured all around. **4** He has bent His bow as an enemy, || His right hand has stood as an adversary, || And He slays all the desirable ones of the eye, || In the tent of the daughter of Zion, || He has poured out as fire His fury. **5** The Lord has been as an enemy, || He has swallowed up Israel, || He has swallowed up all her palaces, || He has destroyed His fortresses, || And He multiplies in the daughter of Judah || Mourning and moaning. **6** And He shakes as a garden His dwelling place, || He has destroyed His appointed place, || Yhwh has forgotten in Zion the appointed time and Sabbath, || And despises, in the indignation of His anger, king and priest. **7** The Lord has cast off His altar, || He has rejected His sanctuary, || He has shut up into the hand of the enemy || The walls of her palaces, || A noise they have made in the house of Yhwh || Like a day of appointment. **8** Yhwh has devised to destroy the wall of the daughter of Zion, || He has stretched out a line, || He has not turned His hand from destroying, || And He causes bulwark and wall to mourn, || Together—they have been weak. **9** Sunk into the earth have her gates, || He has destroyed and broken her bars, || Her king and her princes [are] among the nations, || There is no law, also her prophets || Have not found vision from Yhwh. **10** Sit on the earth—[the] elderly of Zion's daughter keep silent, || They have caused dust to go up on their head, || They have girded on sackcloth, || The virgins of Jerusalem have || Put their head down to the earth. **11** My eyes have been consumed by tears, || My bowels have been troubled, || My liver has been poured out to the earth, || For the breach of the daughter of my people; In infant and suckling being feeble, || In the broad places of the city, **12** To their mothers they say, || "Where [are] grain and wine?" In their becoming feeble as a pierced one || In the broad places of the city, || In their soul pouring itself out into the bosom of their mothers. **13** What do I testify [to] you, what do I liken to you, || O daughter of Jerusalem? What do I equal to you, and I comfort you, || O virgin daughter of Zion? For great as a sea [is] your breach, || Who gives healing to you? **14** Your prophets have seen for you a false and insipid thing, || And have not revealed concerning your iniquity, || To return your captivity, || And they see for you false burdens and causes of expulsion. **15** Everyone passing by the way clapped hands at you, || They have hissed—and they shake the head || At the daughter of Jerusalem: "Is this the city of which they said: The perfection of beauty, a joy to all the land?" **16** Opened against you their mouth have all your enemies, || They have hissed, indeed, they gnash the teeth, || They have said: "We have swallowed [her] up, || Surely this [is] the day that we looked for, || We have found—we have seen." **17** Yhwh has done that which He devised, || He has fulfilled His saying || That He commanded from the days of old, || He has broken down and has not pitied, || And causes an enemy to rejoice over you, || He lifted up the horn of your adversaries. **18** Their heart has cried to the Lord; O wall of the daughter of Zion, || Cause to go down tears as a stream daily and nightly, do not give rest to yourself, || Do not let the daughter of your eye stand still. **19** Arise, cry aloud in the night, || At the beginning of the watches. Pour out your heart as water, || Before the face of the Lord, || Lift up to Him your hands, for the soul of your infants, || Who are feeble with hunger at the head of all out-places. **20** See, O Yhwh, and look attentively, || To whom You have acted thus, || Do women eat their fruit, infants of a handbreadth? Slain in the sanctuary of the Lord are priest and prophet? **21** Lain on the earth [in] out-places have young and old, || My virgins and my young men have fallen by the sword, || You have slain in a day of Your anger, || You have slaughtered—You have not pitied. **22** You call as [at] a day of appointment, || My fears from all around, || And there has not been in the day of the anger of Yhwh, || An escaped and remaining one, || They whom I stretched out and nourished, || My enemy has consumed!

CHAPTER 3

1 [Aleph-Bet] I [am] the man [who] has seen affliction || By the rod of His wrath. **2** He has led me, and causes to go [in] darkness, and without light. **3** Surely against me He turns back, || He turns His hand all the day. **4** He has worn out my flesh and my skin. He has broken my bones. **5** He has built up against me, || And sets around poverty and weariness. **6** In dark places He has caused me to dwell, || As the dead of old. **7** He has hedged me in, and I do not go out, || He has made heavy my chain. **8** Also when I call and cry out, || He has shut out my prayer. **9** He has hedged my ways with hewn work, || My paths He has made crooked. **10** A bear lying in wait He [is] to me, || A lion in secret hiding places. **11** My ways He is turning aside, and He pulls me in pieces, || He has made me a desolation. **12** He has bent His bow, || And sets me up as a mark for an arrow. **13** He has caused to enter into my reins || The sons of His quiver. **14** I have been a derision to all my people, || Their song all the day. **15** He has filled me with bitter things, || He has filled me [with] wormwood. **16** And He breaks with gravel my teeth, || He has covered me with ashes. **17** And You cast off my soul from peace, || I have forgotten prosperity. **18** And I say, My strength and my hope have perished from Yhwh. **19** Remember my affliction and my mourning, || Wormwood and gall! **20** Remember well, and my soul bows down in me. **21** This I turn to my heart—therefore, I hope. **22** The kindnesses of Yhwh! For we have not been consumed, || For His mercies have not ended. **23** New every morning, abundant [is] Your faithfulness. **24** My portion [is] Yhwh, my soul has said, || Therefore I hope for Him. **25** Yhwh [is] good to those waiting for Him, || To the soul [that] seeks Him. **26** [It is] good when one stays and stands still || For the salvation of Yhwh. **27** [It is] good for a man that he bears a yoke in his youth. **28** He sits alone, and is silent, || For He has laid [it] on him. **29** He puts his mouth in the dust, if so be, there is hope. **30** He gives to his striker the cheek, || He is filled with reproach. **31** For the Lord does not cast off for all time. **32** For though He afflicted, yet He has pitied, || According to the abundance of His kindness. **33** For He has not afflicted with His heart, || Nor does He grieve the sons of men. **34** To bruise under one's feet any bound ones of earth, **35** To turn aside the judgment of a man, || Before the face of the Highest, **36** To subvert a man in his cause, the Lord has not approved. **37** Who [is] this—he has spoken, and it is, || [And] the Lord has not commanded [it]? **38** From the mouth of the Most High does not go forth the evils and the good. **39** Why does a living man sigh habitually, || A man for his sin? **40** We search our ways, and investigate, || And turn back to Yhwh. **41** We lift up our heart on the hands to God in the heavens. **42** We have transgressed and been rebellious, || You have not forgiven. **43** You have covered Yourself with anger, || And pursue us; You have slain—You have not pitied. **44** You have covered Yourself with a cloud, || So that prayer does not pass through. **45** Outcast and refuse You make us || In the midst of the peoples. **46** Opened against us their mouth have all our enemies. **47** Fear and a snare has been for us, || Desolation and destruction. **48** Streams of water go down my eye, || For the destruction of the daughter of my people. **49** My eye is poured out, || And does not cease without intermission, **50** Until Yhwh looks and sees from the heavens, **51** My eye affects my soul, || Because of all the daughters of my city. **52** Hunting—my enemies have hunted me without cause like the bird. **53** They have cut off my life in a pit, || And they cast a stone against me. **54** Waters have flowed over my head, I have said, I have been cut off. **55** I called Your Name, O Yhwh, from the lower pit.

56 You have heard my voice, do not hide Your ear at my breathing—at my cry. **57** You have drawn near in the day I call You, You have said, Do not fear. **58** You have pleaded, O Lord, the pleadings of my soul, || You have redeemed my life. **59** You have seen, O Yhwh, my overthrow, || Judge my cause. **60** You have seen all their vengeance, || All their thoughts of me. **61** You have heard their reproach, O Yhwh, || All their thoughts against me, **62** The lips of my withstanders, || Even their meditation against me all the day. **63** Their sitting down, and their rising up, || Behold attentively, I [am] their song. **64** You return to them the deed, O Yhwh, || According to the work of their hands. **65** You give to them a covered heart, || Your curse to them. **66** You pursue in anger, and destroy them, || From under the heavens of Yhwh!

CHAPTER 4

1 [Aleph-Bet] How the gold has become dim, || Changed the best—the pure gold! Stones of the sanctuary are poured out || At the head of all out-places. **2** The precious sons of Zion, || Who are comparable with fine gold, || How they have been reckoned earthen bottles, || Work of the hands of a potter. **3** Even dragons have drawn out the breast, || They have suckled their young ones, || The daughter of my people has become cruel, || Like the ostriches in a wilderness. **4** The tongue of a suckling has cleaved to his palate with thirst, || Infants asked for bread, they have no dealer [of it] out. **5** Those eating of delicacies have been desolate in out-places, || Those supported on scarlet have embraced dunghills. **6** And greater is the iniquity of the daughter of my people, || Than the sin of Sodom, || That was overturned as [in] a moment, || And no hands were stayed on her. **7** Purer were her Nazarites than snow, || Whiter than milk, ruddier of body than rubies, || Of sapphire their form. **8** Their face has been darker than blackness, || They have not been known in out-places, || Their skin has cleaved to their bone, || It has withered—it has been as wood. **9** Better have been the pierced of a sword || Than the pierced of famine, || For this flow away, pierced through, || Without the increase of the field. **10** The hands of merciful women have boiled their own children, || They have been for food to them, || In the destruction of the daughter of my people. **11** Yhwh has completed His fury, || He has poured out the fierceness of His anger, || And He kindles a fire in Zion, || And it devours her foundations. **12** The kings of earth did not believe, || And any of the inhabitants of the world, || That an adversary and enemy would come || Into the gates of Jerusalem. **13** Because of the sins of her prophets, || The iniquities of her priests, || Who are shedding in her midst the blood of the righteous, **14** They have wandered naked in out-places, || They have been defiled with blood, || Without [any] being able to touch their clothing, **15** "Turn aside—unclean," they called to them, || "Turn aside, turn aside, do not touch," || For they fled—indeed, they have wandered, || They have said among nations: "They do not add to sojourn." **16** The face of Yhwh has divided them, || He does not add to behold them, || They have not lifted up the face of priests, || They have not favored [the] old and elderly. **17** While we exist—consumed are our eyes for our vain help, || In our watchtower we have watched for a nation [that] does not save. **18** They have hunted our steps from going in our broad-places, || Near has been our end, fulfilled our days, || For our end has come. **19** Swifter have been our pursuers, || Than the eagles of the heavens, || On the mountains they have burned [after] us, || In the wilderness they have laid wait for us. **20** The breath of our nostrils—the anointed of Yhwh, || Has been captured in their pits, of whom we said: "We live among nations in his shadow." **21** Rejoice and be glad, O daughter of Edom, || Dwelling in the land of Uz, || Even to you a cup passes over, || You are drunk, and make yourself naked. **22** Completed [is] your iniquity, daughter of Zion, || He does not add to remove you, || He has inspected your iniquity, O daughter of Edom, || He has removed [you] because of your sins!

CHAPTER 5

1 Remember, O Yhwh, what has befallen us, || Look attentively, and see our reproach. **2** Our inheritance has been turned to strangers, || Our houses to foreigners. **3** Orphans we have been—without a father, our mothers [are] as widows. **4** We have drunk our water for money, || Our wood comes for a price. **5** For our neck we have been pursued, || We have labored—there has been no rest for us. **6** [To] Egypt we have given a hand, || [To] Asshur, to be satisfied with bread. **7** Our fathers have sinned—they are not, || We have borne their iniquities. **8** Servants have ruled over us, || There is no deliverer from their hand. **9** With our lives we bring in our bread, || Because of the sword of the wilderness. **10** Our skin as an oven has been burning, || Because of the raging of the famine. **11** Wives in Zion they have humbled, || Virgins—in cities of Judah. **12** Princes have been hanged by their hand, || Elderly faces have not been honored. **13** They have taken young men to grind, || And youths have stumbled with wood. **14** Elderly have ceased from the gate, || Young men from their song. **15** The joy of our heart has ceased, || Our dancing has been turned to mourning. **16** The crown has fallen [from] our head, || Woe [is] now to us, for we have sinned. **17** Our heart has been sick for this, || Our eyes have been dim for these. **18** For the Mount of Zion—that is desolate, || Foxes have gone up on it. **19** You, O Yhwh, remain for all time, || Your throne to generation and generation. **20** Why do You forget us forever? You forsake us for [the] length of [our] days! **21** Turn us back, O Yhwh, to You, || And we turn back, renew our days as of old. **22** For have You utterly rejected us? You have been angry against us—exceedingly?

EZEKIEL

CHAPTER 1

1 And it comes to pass, in the thirtieth year, in the fourth [month], on the fifth of the month, and I [am] in the midst of the expulsion by the river Chebar, the heavens have been opened, and I see visions of God. **2** In the fifth of the month— it is the fifth year of the expulsion of King Jehoiachin— **3** the word of Yhwh has certainly been to Ezekiel son of Buzi the priest, in the land of the Chaldeans, by the river Chebar, and there is on him there a hand of Yhwh. **4** And I look, and behold, a turbulent wind is coming from the north, a great cloud, and fire catching itself, and brightness to it all around, and out of its midst as the color of electrum, out of the midst of the fire. **5** And out of its midst [is] a likeness of four living creatures, and this [is] their appearance; a likeness of man [is] to them, **6** and each had four faces and each of them had four wings, **7** and their feet [are] straight feet, and the sole of their feet [is] as a sole of a calf's foot, and they are sparkling as the color of bright bronze; **8** and on their four sides [each had] hands of man under their wings; and [each] of the four had their faces and their wings; **9** their wings [are] joining to one another, they do not turn around in their going, they each go straight forward. **10** As for the likeness of their faces, [each had] the face of a man, and toward the right the four had the face of a lion, and on the left the four had the face of an ox, and the four had the face of an eagle. **11** And their faces and their wings dividing from above, of each [are] two joining together, and two are covering their bodies. **12** And they each go straight forward, to where the Spirit is to go, they go, they do not turn around in their going. **13** As for the likeness of the living creatures, their appearances [are] as coals of fire—burning as the appearance of lamps; it is going up and down between the living creatures, and brightness [is] to the fire, and lightning is going forth out of the fire. **14** And the living creatures are running, and turning back, as the appearance of the flash. **15** And I see the living creatures, and behold, one wheel [is] in the earth, near the living creatures, at its four faces. **16** The appearance of the wheels and their works [is] as the color of beryl, and the four of them had one likeness, and their appearances and their works [are] as it were the wheel in the midst of the wheel. **17** On their four sides, in their going they go, they do not turn around in their going. **18** As for their rings, they are both high and fearful, and their rings, of the four of them, [are] full of eyes around them. **19** And in the going of the living creatures, the wheels go beside them, and in the living creatures being lifted up from off the earth, the wheels are lifted up. **20** To where the Spirit is to go, they go, there the Spirit [is] to go, and the wheels are lifted up alongside them, for a living spirit [is] in the wheels. **21** In their going, they go; and in their standing, they stand; and in their being lifted up from off the earth, the wheels are lifted up alongside them; for a living spirit [is] in the wheels. **22** And over the heads of the living creatures—a likeness of an expanse, as the color of the fearful ice, stretched out over their heads from above. **23** And under the expanse their wings [are] straight, one toward [its] sister; two [wings] of each are covering them, and two [wings] of each are covering their bodies. **24** And I hear the noise of their wings, as the noise of many waters, as the noise of the Mighty One, in their going—the noise of tumult, as the noise of a camp, in their standing they let their wings fall. **25** And there is a voice from above the expanse, that [is] above their head: in their standing they let their wings fall. **26** And above the expanse that [is] over their head, as an appearance of a sapphire stone, [is] the likeness of a throne, and on the likeness of the throne a likeness, as the appearance of man on it from above. **27** And I see as the color of electrum, as the appearance of fire all around within it, from the appearance of His loins and upward; and from the appearance of His loins and downward, I have seen as the appearance of fire, and brightness [is] all around Him. **28** As the appearance of the bow that is in a cloud in a day of rain, so [is] the appearance of the brightness all around.

CHAPTER 2

1 His appearance [was] of the likeness of the glory of Yhwh, and I see, and fall on my face, and I hear a voice speaking, and He says to me, "Son of man, stand on your feet, and I speak with you." **2** And [the] Spirit comes into me when He has spoken to me, and causes me to stand on my feet, and I hear Him who is speaking to me. **3** And He says to me, "Son of man, I am sending you to the sons of Israel, to rebelling nations who have rebelled against Me; they and their fathers have transgressed against Me, to this very day. **4** And the sons [are] brazen-faced and hard-hearted to whom I am sending you, and you have said to them: Thus said Lord Yhwh. **5** And they— whether they hear, or whether they refrain, for they [are] a house of rebellion—have known that a prophet has been in their midst. **6** And you, son of man, you are not afraid of them, indeed, you are not afraid of their words, for briers and thorns are with you, and you are dwelling near scorpions, you are not afraid of their words, and you are not frightened of their faces, for they [are] a house of rebellion, **7** and you have spoken My words to them, whether they hear or whether they refrain, for they [are] a rebellion. **8** And you, son of man, hear that which I am speaking to you; do not be of rebellion like the house of rebellion, open your mouth and eat that which I am giving to you." **9** And I look, and behold, a hand [is] sent forth to me, and behold, a roll of a scroll [is] in it, **10** and He spreads it before me, and it is written in front and behind, and written on it [are] lamentations, and mourning, and woe!

CHAPTER 3

1 And He says to me, "Son of man, eat that which you find, eat this scroll, and go, speak to the house of Israel." **2** And I open my mouth, and He causes me to eat this scroll. **3** And He says to me, "Son of man, feed your belly, and fill your bowels with this scroll that I am giving to you"; and I eat it, and it is as honey for sweetness in my mouth. **4** And He says to me, "Son of man, go forth, go to the house of Israel, and you have spoken to them with My words. **5** For you [are] not sent to a people deep of lip and heavy of tongue—to the house of Israel; **6** not to many peoples, deep of lip and heavy of tongue, whose words you do not understand. If I had not sent you to them— they listen to you, **7** but the house of Israel are not willing to listen to you, for they are not willing to listen to Me, for all the house of Israel are brazen-faced and strong-hearted. **8** Behold, I have made your face strong against their face, and your forehead strong against their forehead. **9** As an adamant, harder than a rock, I have made your forehead; do not fear them, nor are you frightened before them, for they [are] a house of rebellion." **10** And He says to me, "Son of man, all My words that I speak to you, receive with your heart, and hear with your ears; **11** and go forth, go to the expulsion, to the sons of your people, and you have spoken to them, and have said to them: Thus said Lord Yhwh; whether they hear, or whether they refrain." **12** And a spirit lifts me up, and I hear a noise behind me, a great rushing—"Blessed [is] the glory of Yhwh from His place!" **13** Even a noise of the wings of the living creatures touching one another, and a noise of the wheels alongside them, even a noise of a great rushing. **14** And [the] Spirit has lifted me up, and takes me away, and I go bitterly, in the heat of my spirit, and the hand of Yhwh [is] strong on me. **15** And I come to the expulsion, at Tel-Ahib, who are dwelling at the river Chebar, and where they are dwelling I also dwell [for] seven days, causing astonishment in their midst. **16** And it comes to pass, at the end of seven days, **17** that there is a word of Yhwh to me, saying, "Son of man, I have given you [as] a watchman to the house of Israel, and you have heard a word from My mouth, and have warned them from Me. **18** In My saying to the wicked: You surely die; and you have not warned him, nor have spoken to warn the wicked from his wicked way, so that he lives; he—the wicked—dies in his iniquity, and I require his blood from your hand. **19** And you, because you have warned the wicked, and he has not turned back from his wickedness, and from his wicked way, he dies in his iniquity, and you have delivered your soul. **20** And in the turning back of the righteous from his righteousness, and he has done perversity, and I have put a stumbling-block before him, he dies; because you have not warned him, he dies in his sin, and his righteousness that he has done is not remembered, and I require his blood from your hand. **21** And you, because you have warned him—the righteous—that the righteous does not sin, and he has not sinned, he surely lives, because he has been warned; and you have delivered your soul." **22** And there is a hand of Yhwh on me there, and He says to me, "Rise, go forth to the valley, and there I speak with you." **23** And I rise and go forth to the valley, and behold, there the glory of Yhwh is standing as the glory that I had seen by the river Chebar, and I fall on my face. **24** And [the] Spirit comes into me, and causes me to stand on my feet, and He speaks with me, and says to me, "Go in, be shut up in the midst of your house. **25** And you, son of man, behold, they have put thick bands on you, and have bound you with them, and you do not go forth in their midst; **26** and I cause your tongue to cleave to your palate, and you have been mute, and are not for a reprover to them, for they [are] a house of rebellion. **27** And in My speaking with you, I open your mouth, and you have said to them: Thus said Lord Yhwh; the hearer hears, and the refrainer refrains; for they [are] a house of rebellion."

CHAPTER 4

1 "And you, son of man, take a brick for yourself, and you have put it before you, and have carved a city on it—Jerusalem, **2** and have placed a siege against it, and built a fortification against it, and poured out a mound against it, and placed camps against it, indeed, set battering-rams against it all around. **3** And you, take an iron pan for yourself, and you have made it a wall of iron between you and the city; and you have prepared your face against it, and it has been in a siege, indeed, you have laid siege against it. It [is] a sign to the house of Israel. **4** And you, lie on your left side, and you have placed the iniquity of the house of Israel on it; the number of the days that you lie on it, you bear their iniquity. **5** And I have laid the years of their iniquity on you, the number of days, three hundred and ninety days; and you have borne the iniquity of the house of Israel. **6** And you have completed these, and have lain on your right side, a second time, and have borne the iniquity of the house of Judah forty days—a day for a year—a day for a year I have appointed to you. **7** And to the siege of Jerusalem you prepare your face, and your arm [is] uncovered, and you have prophesied concerning it. **8** And behold, I have put thick bands on you, and you do not turn from side to side until your completing the days of your siege. **9** And you, take for yourself wheat, and barley, and beans, and lentiles, and millet, and spelt, and you have put them in one vessel, and made them for bread for yourself; the number of the days that you are lying on your side—three hundred and ninety days— you eat it. **10** And your food that you eat [is] by weight, twenty shekels daily; from time to time you eat it. **11** And you drink water by measure, a sixth part of the hin; from time to time you drink [it]. **12** And you eat it [as] barley-cake, and it with dung—the filth of man—you bake before their eyes." **13** And Yhwh says, "Thus the sons of Israel eat their defiled bread among the nations to where I drive them." **14** And I say, "Aah! Lord Yhwh, behold, my soul is not defiled, and carcass, and torn thing, I have not eaten from my youth, even until now; nor has abominable flesh come into my mouth." **15** And He says to me, "See, I have given to you bullock's dung instead of

man's dung, and you have made your bread by it." **16** And He says to me, "Son of man, behold, I am breaking the staff of bread in Jerusalem, and they have eaten bread by weight and with fear; and water by measure and with astonishment, they drink; **17** so that they lack bread and water, and have been astonished with one another, and been consumed in their iniquity."

CHAPTER 5

1 "And you, son of man, take a sharp weapon for yourself, take the barber's razor for yourself, and you have caused [it] to pass over your head, and over your beard, and you have taken weighing scales for yourself, and apportioned them. **2** You burn a third part with fire in the midst of the city, at the fullness of the days of the siege; and you have taken the third part, you strike with a weapon around it; and the third part you scatter to the wind, and I draw out a weapon after them. **3** And you have taken there a few in number—and have bound them in your skirts; **4** and you take of them again, and have cast them into the midst of the fire, and have burned them in the fire—out of it comes forth a fire to all the house of Israel." **5** Thus said Lord Yhwh: "This [is] Jerusalem, || I have set her in the midst of the nations, || And the lands [are] around her. **6** And she changes My judgments into wickedness more than the nations, || And My statutes more than the lands that [are] around her, || For they have kicked against My judgments, || And My statutes—they have not walked in them." **7** Therefore, thus said Lord Yhwh: "Because of your multiplying above the nations that [are] around you, || You have not walked in My statutes, || And you have not done My judgments, || According to the judgments of the nations that [are] around you, you have not done." **8** Therefore, thus said Lord Yhwh: "Behold, I [am] against you, even I, || And I have done judgments in your midst, || Before the eyes of the nations. **9** And I have done in you that which I have not done, || And the like of which I do not do again, || Because of all your abominations. **10** Therefore fathers eat sons in your midst, || And sons eat their fathers, || And I have done judgments in you, || And have scattered all your remnant to every wind. **11** Therefore, [as] I live," a declaration of Lord Yhwh, || "Because you have defiled My sanctuary || With all your detestable things, || And with all your abominations, || Therefore I also diminish you, || And My eye does not pity, and I do not spare. **12** Your third part dies by pestilence, || And are consumed by famine in your midst, || And the third part fall by sword around you, || And the third part I scatter to every wind, || And I draw out a sword after them. **13** And My anger has been completed, || And I have caused My fury to rest on them, || And I have been comforted, || And they have known that I, Yhwh, have spoken in My zeal, || In My completing My fury on them. **14** And I give you for a ruin, || And for a reproach among nations that [are] around you, || Before the eyes of everyone passing by. **15** And it has been a reproach and a reviling, || An instruction and an astonishment, || To nations that [are] around you, || In My doing judgments in you, || In anger and fury, and in furious reproofs, || I, Yhwh, have spoken. **16** In My sending the evil arrows of famine among them, || That have been for destruction, || That I send to destroy you, || And I am adding famine on you, || And I have broken your staff of bread. **17** And I have sent famine and evil beasts on you, || And they have bereaved you, || And pestilence and blood pass over on you, || And I bring a sword in against you, || I, Yhwh, have spoken!"

CHAPTER 6

1 And there is a word of Yhwh to me, saying, **2** "Son of man, set your face toward mountains of Israel, and prophesy concerning them: **3** And you have said, Mountains of Israel, || Hear a word of Lord Yhwh! Thus said Lord Yhwh, || To the mountains, and to the hills, || To the streams, and to the valleys: Behold, I am bringing in a sword against you, || And I have destroyed your high places. **4** And your altars have been desolated, || And your images have been broken, || And I have caused your wounded to fall before your idols, **5** And I have put the carcasses of the sons of Israel before your idols, || And I have scattered your bones around your altars. **6** In all your dwellings the cities are laid waste, || And the high places are desolate, || So that your altars are dry and desolate, || Your idols have broken and ceased, || And your images have been cut down, || And your works have been blotted out. **7** And the wounded has fallen in your midst, || And you have known that I [am] Yhwh. **8** And I have caused [some] to remain, || In their being for you the escaped of the sword among nations, || In your being scattered through lands. **9** And your escaped have remembered Me among nations, || To where they have been taken captive, || Because I have been broken with their heart that is going whoring, || That has turned aside from off Me, || And with their eyes they are going whoring after their idols, || And they have been loathsome in their own faces, || For the evils that they have done—all their abominations. **10** And they have known that I [am] Yhwh, || I have not spoken to do this evil to them for nothing. **11** Thus said Lord Yhwh: Strike with your palm, and stamp with your foot, || And say: Aah! For all the evil abominations of the house of Israel, || Which falls by sword, by famine, and by pestilence. **12** The far-off dies by pestilence, || And the near falls by sword, || And the left and the besieged dies by famine, || And I have completed My fury on them. **13** And you have known that I [am] Yhwh, || In their wounded being in the midst of their idols, || Around their altars, || On every high hill, on all tops of mountains, || And under every green tree, and under every thick oak, || The place where they gave refreshing fragrance to all their idols. **14** And I have stretched out My hand against them, || And have made the land a desolation, || Even a desolation from the wilderness to Diblath, || In all their dwellings, || And they have known that I [am] Yhwh!"

CHAPTER 7

1 And there is a word of Yhwh to me, saying, "And you, son of man, || Thus said Lord Yhwh to the ground of Israel: **2** An end, the end has come on the four corners of the land. **3** Now [is] the end for you, || And I have sent My anger on you, || And judged you according to your ways, || And set all your abominations against you. **4** And My eye has no pity on you, nor do I spare, || For I set your ways against you, || And your abominations are in your midst, || And you have known that I [am] Yhwh. **5** Thus said Lord Yhwh: Calamity, a single calamity, behold, it has come. **6** An end has come, the end has come, || It has awoken for you, behold, it has come. **7** The circlet has come to you, O inhabitant of the land! The time has come, a day of trouble [is] near, || And not the shouting of mountains. **8** Now shortly I pour out My fury on you, || And have completed My anger against you, || And judged you according to your ways, || And set all your abominations against you. **9** And My eye does not pity, nor do I spare, || I give to you according to your ways, || And your abominations are in your midst, || And you have known that [it is] I, Yhwh, striking. **10** Behold, the day, behold, it has come, || The circlet has gone forth, || The rod has blossomed, the pride has flourished. **11** The violence has risen to a rod of wickedness, || There is none of them, nor of their multitude, || Nor of their noise, nor is there wailing for them. **12** The time has come, the day has arrived, || The buyer does not rejoice, || And the seller does not become a mourner, || For wrath [is] to all its multitude. **13** For the seller does not turn to the sold thing, || And yet their life [is] among the living, || For the vision [is] to all its multitude, || It does not turn back, || And none strengthens his life by his iniquity. **14** They have blown with a horn to prepare the whole, || And none is going to battle, || For My wrath [is] to all its multitude. **15** The sword [is] outside, || And the pestilence and the famine within, || He who is in a field dies by sword, || And he who is in a city—Famine and pestilence devour him. **16** And their fugitives have escaped away, || And they have been on the mountains || As doves of the valleys, || All of them making a noise—each for his iniquity. **17** All the hands are feeble, and all knees go [as] waters. **18** And they have girded on sackcloth, || And trembling has covered them, || And shame [is] on all faces, || And baldness on all their heads. **19** They cast their silver into out-places, || And their gold becomes impurity. Their silver and gold are not able to deliver them, || In a day of the wrath of Yhwh, || They do not satisfy their soul, || And they do not fill their bowels, || For it has been the stumbling-block of their iniquity. **20** As for the beauty of his ornament, || He set it for excellence, || And the images of their abominations, || Their detestable things—they made in it, || Therefore I have given it to them for impurity, **21** And I have given it into the hand of the strangers for a spoil, || And to the wicked of the land for a prey, || And they have defiled it. **22** And I have turned My face from them, || And they have defiled My hidden place, || Indeed, destroyers have come into it, and defiled it. **23** Make the chain; for the land || Has been full of bloody judgments, || And the city has been full of violence. **24** And I have brought in the wicked of the nations, || And they have possessed their houses, || And I have caused the excellence of the strong to cease, || And those sanctifying them have been defiled. **25** Destruction has come, || And they have sought peace, and there is none. **26** Disaster comes on disaster, and report is on report, || And they have sought a vision from a prophet, || And law perishes from [the] priest, || And counsel from [the] elderly, **27** The king becomes a mourner, || And a prince puts on desolation, || And the hands of the people of the land are troubled, || I deal with them from their own way, || And I judge them with their own judgments, || And they have known that I [am] Yhwh!"

CHAPTER 8

1 And it comes to pass, in the sixth year, in the sixth [month], on the fifth of the month, I am sitting in my house, and [the] elderly of Judah are sitting before me, and there a hand of Lord Yhwh falls on me, **2** and I look, and behold, a likeness as the appearance of fire, from the appearance of His loins and downward—fire, and from His loins and upward, as the appearance of brightness, as the color of electrum. **3** And He puts forth a form of a hand, and takes me by a lock of my head, and [the] Spirit lifts me up between the earth and the heavens, and brings me to Jerusalem in visions of God, to the opening of the inner gate that is facing the north, where the seat of the figure of jealousy [is] that is making jealous, **4** and behold, there the glory of the God of Israel [is] as the appearance that I saw in the valley. **5** And He says to me, "Son of man, now lift up your eyes [toward] the way of the north." And I lift up my eyes [toward] the way of the north, and behold, on the north of the gate of the altar [is] this figure of jealousy, at the entrance. **6** And He says to me, "Son of man, are you seeing what they are doing? the great abominations that the house of Israel is doing here, to keep far off from My sanctuary; and turn again, [and] see great abominations." **7** And He brings me to an opening of the court, and I look, and behold, a hole in the wall; **8** and He says to me, "Son of man, now dig through the wall"; and I dig through the wall, and behold, an opening. **9** And He says to me, "Go in, and see the evil abominations that they are doing here." **10** And I go in, and look, and behold, every form of creeping thing, and detestable beast—and all the idols of the house of Israel—carved on the wall, all around, **11** and seventy men from [the] elderly of the house of Israel—and Jaazaniah son of Shaphan standing in their midst—are standing before them, and each [with] his censer in his hand, and [the] abundance of [the] cloud of the incense is going up. **12** And He says to me, "Have you seen, son of man, that which elderly of the house of Israel are doing in the darkness, each in [the] inner chambers of his imagery, for they are saying, Yhwh is not seeing us, Yhwh has forsaken the land?" **13** And He says to me, "Turn again, [and] see [the] great abominations that they are doing." **14** And He brings me to the opening of the gate of the house of Yhwh that [is] at the north, and behold, there the women are sitting, weeping for Tammuz. **15** And He says to me, "Have you seen, son of man? Turn again, [and] see greater abominations than these." **16** And He brings me into the inner court of the house of Yhwh, and behold, at the opening of the temple of Yhwh, between the porch and the altar, about twenty-five men, their backs toward the temple of Yhwh, and their faces eastward, and they are bowing themselves eastward to the sun. **17** And He says to me, "Have you seen, son of man? has it been a light thing to the house of Judah to do the abomination that they have done here, that they have filled the land with violence, and turn back to provoke Me to anger? and behold, they are putting forth the branch to their nose! **18** And I also deal in fury, my eye does not pity, nor do I spare, and they have cried [with] a loud voice in My ears and I do not hear them."

CHAPTER 9

1 And He cries [with] a loud voice in my ears, saying, "Inspectors of the city have drawn near, and each [with] his destroying weapon in his hand." **2** And behold, six men are coming from the way of the upper gate, that is facing the north, and each [with] his slaughter-weapon in his hand, and one man in their midst is clothed with linen, and a scribe's inkhorn at his loins, and they come in, and stand near the bronze altar. ³ And the glory of the God of Israel has gone up from off the cherub, on which it has been, to the threshold of the house. ⁴ And He calls to the man who is clothed with linen, who has the scribe's inkhorn at his loins, and Yhwh says to him, "Pass on into the midst of the city, into the midst of Jerusalem, and you have made a mark on the foreheads of the men who are sighing and who are groaning for all the abominations that are done in its midst." ⁵ And to the others he said in my ears, "Pass on into the city after him, and strike; your eye does not pity, nor do you spare; ⁶ aged, young man, and virgin, and infant, and women, you slay—to destruction; and against any man on whom [is] the mark you do not go near, and you begin from My sanctuary." ⁷ And they begin among the aged men who [are] before the house, and He says to them, "Defile the house, and fill the courts with the wounded, go forth." And they have gone forth and have struck in the city. ⁸ And it comes to pass, as they are striking, and I am left—that I fall on my face, and cry, and say, "Aah! Lord Yhwh, are You destroying all the remnant of Israel, in Your pouring out Your wrath on Jerusalem?" ⁹ And He says to me, "The iniquity of the house of Israel and Judah [is] very, very great, and the land is full of blood, and the city has been full of perverseness, for they have said: Yhwh has forsaken the land, and Yhwh is not seeing. ¹⁰ And I also, My eye does not pity, nor do I spare; I have put their way on their own head." ¹¹ And behold, the man clothed with linen, at whose loins [is] the inkhorn, is bringing back word, saying, "I have done as You have commanded me."

CHAPTER 10

¹ And I look, and behold, on the expanse that [is] above the head of the cherubim, as a sapphire stone, as the appearance of the likeness of a throne, He has been seen over them. ² And He speaks to the man clothed with linen and says, "Go into the midst of the wheel, to the place of the cherub, and fill your hands with coals of fire from between the cherubim, and scatter over the city." And he goes in before my eyes. ³ And the cherubim are standing on the right side of the house, at the going in of the man, and the cloud has filled the inner court, ⁴ and the glory of Yhwh becomes high above the cherub, over the threshold of the house, and the house is filled with the cloud, and the court has been filled with the brightness of the glory of Yhwh. ⁵ And a noise of the wings of the cherubim has been heard in the outer court, as the voice of God—the Mighty One—in His speaking. ⁶ And it comes to pass, in His commanding the man clothed with linen, saying, "Take fire from between the wheel, from between the cherubim," and he goes in and stands near the wheel, ⁷ that the [one] cherub puts forth his hand from between the cherubim to the fire that [is] between the cherubim, and lifts up, and gives [it] into the hands of him who is clothed with linen, and he receives, and comes forth. ⁸ And there appears in the cherubim the form of a hand of man under their wings, ⁹ and I look, and behold, four wheels near the cherubim, one wheel near one cherub, and another wheel near the other cherub, and the appearance of the wheels [is] as the color of a beryl stone. ¹⁰ And [as for] their appearances, [the] four had one likeness, as it were the wheel in the midst of the wheel. ¹¹ In their going, they go on their four sides; they do not turn around in their going, for to the place to where the head turns, they go after it, they do not turn around in their going. ¹² And all their flesh, and their backs, and their hands, and their wings, and the wheels, are full of eyes all around—[the] wheels [the] four had. ¹³ As for the wheels—they were called "Whirling Wheel" in my ears. ¹⁴ And four faces [are] to each; the face of the first [is] the face of the cherub, and the face of the second [is] the face of man, and of the third the face of a lion, and of the fourth the face of an eagle. ¹⁵ And the cherubim are lifted up, it [is] the living creature that I saw by the river Chebar. ¹⁶ And in the going of the cherubim, the wheels go beside them; and in the cherubim lifting up their wings to be high above the earth, the wheels do not turn around, even they, from being beside them. ¹⁷ In their standing they stand, and in their exaltation, they are exalted with them: for [the] spirit of the living creature [is] in them. ¹⁸ And the glory of Yhwh goes forth from off the threshold of the house, and stands over the cherubim, ¹⁹ and the cherubim lift up their wings, and are lifted up from the earth before my eyes;

in their going forth, the wheels [are] also alongside them, and he stands at the opening of the east gate of the house of Yhwh, and the glory of the God of Israel [is] over them from above. ²⁰ It [is] the living creature that I saw under the God of Israel by the river Chebar, and I know that they are cherubim. ²¹ [The] four—each had four faces, and each had four wings, and the likeness of the hands of man [is] under their wings. ²² And the likeness of their faces, they [are] the faces that I saw by the river Chebar, their appearances and themselves; they each go straight forward.

CHAPTER 11

¹ And [the] Spirit lifts me up, and it brings me to the east gate of the house of Yhwh, that is facing the east, and behold, at the opening of the gate [are] twenty-five men, and I see in their midst Jaazaniah son of Azzur, and Pelatiah son of Benaiah, heads of the people. ² And He says to me, "Son of man, these [are] the men who are devising iniquity, and who are giving evil counsel in this city; ³ who are saying, It [is] not near—to build houses, it [is] the pot, and we [are] the flesh. ⁴ Therefore prophesy concerning them, prophesy, son of man." ⁵ And [the] Spirit of Yhwh falls on me, and He says to me, "Say, Thus said Yhwh: You have said correctly, O house of Israel, || And I have known the steps of your spirit. ⁶ You multiplied your wounded in this city, || And filled its out-places with the wounded. ⁷ Therefore, thus said Lord Yhwh: Your wounded whom you placed in its midst, || They [are] the flesh, and it [is] the pot, || And He has brought you out from its midst. ⁸ You have feared a sword, || And I bring in a sword against you, || A declaration of Lord Yhwh. ⁹ And I have brought you out of its midst, || And given you into the hand of strangers, || And I have done judgments among you. ¹⁰ You fall by the sword, || I judge you on the border of Israel, || And you have known that I [am] Yhwh. ¹¹ It is not for a pot for you, || Nor are you for flesh in its midst, || I judge you at the border of Israel. ¹² And you have known that I [am] Yhwh, || For you have not walked in My statutes, || And you have not done My judgments, || And according to the judgments of the nation's || Who are around you, you have done!" ¹³ And it comes to pass, at my prophesying, that Pelatiah son of Benaiah is dying, and I fall on my face, and cry—a loud voice—and say, "Aah! Lord Yhwh, You are making an end of the remnant of Israel." ¹⁴ And there is a word of Yhwh to me, saying, ¹⁵ "Son of man, your brothers, your brothers, men of your family, and all the house of Israel—all of it—[are] they to whom inhabitants of Jerusalem have said, Keep far off from Yhwh; ¹⁶ it [is] ours, the land has been given for an inheritance; therefore say, Thus said Lord Yhwh: Because I put them far off among nations, || And because I scattered them through lands, I am also for a little sanctuary to them, || In lands to where they have gone in. ¹⁷ Therefore say, Thus said Lord Yhwh: And I have assembled you from the peoples, || And I have gathered you from the lands, || Into which you have been scattered, || And I have given the ground of Israel to you. ¹⁸ And they have gone in there, || And turned aside all its detestable things, || And all its abominations—out of it. ¹⁹ And I have given one heart to them, || And I give a new spirit in your midst, || And I have turned the heart of stone out of their flesh, || And I have given a heart of flesh to them. ²⁰ So that they walk in My statutes, || And keep My judgments, and have done them, || And they have been to Me for a people, || And I am to them for God. ²¹ As for those whose heart is going to the heart || Of their detestable things and their abominations, || I have put their way on their head, || A declaration of Lord Yhwh." ²² And the cherubim lift up their wings, and the wheels [are] alongside them, and the glory of the God of Israel [is] over them above. ²³ And the glory of Yhwh goes up from off the midst of the city, and stands on the mountain, that [is] on the east of the city. ²⁴ And [the] Spirit has lifted me up, and brings me to Chaldea, to the expulsion, in a vision, by [the] Spirit of God, and the vision that I have seen goes up from off me; ²⁵ and I speak to the expulsion all the matters of Yhwh that He has showed me.

CHAPTER 12

¹ And there is a word of Yhwh to me, saying, ² "Son of man, you are dwelling in the midst of the house of rebellion, that have eyes to see, and they have not seen; they have ears to

hear, and they have not heard; for they [are] a house of rebellion. ³ And you, son of man, make your vessels of removal, and remove by day before their eyes, and you have removed from your place to another place before their eyes, it maybe they consider, for they [are] a house of rebellion. ⁴ And you have brought forth your vessels as vessels of removal by day before their eyes, and you go forth in the evening before their eyes, as the goings forth of a removal. ⁵ You dig through the wall before their eyes, and you have brought forth by it. ⁶ Carry on the shoulder before their eyes, bring forth in the darkness, cover your face, and you do not see the earth, for I have given you [as] a sign to the house of Israel." ⁷ And I do so, as I have been commanded; I have brought forth my vessels as vessels of removal by day, and I have dug through the wall with my hand in the evening; I have brought forth in the darkness, I have carried away on the shoulder, before their eyes. ⁸ And there is a word of Yhwh to me, in the morning, saying, ⁹ "Son of man, have they not said to you—the house of Israel—the house of rebellion—What are you doing? ¹⁰ say to them, Thus said Lord Yhwh: This burden [concerns] the prince in Jerusalem, and all the house of Israel who are in their midst. ¹¹ Say: I [am] your sign; as I have done so it is done to them, into a removal, into a captivity, they go. ¹² As for the prince who [is] in their midst, he carries on the shoulder in the darkness, and he goes forth; they dig through the wall to bring forth by it; he covers his face that he may not look on the very surface of the land. ¹³ And I have spread My net for him, and he has been caught in My snare, and I have brought him to Babylon, the land of the Chaldeans, and he does not see it—and he dies there. ¹⁴ And all who are around him to help him, and all his bands, I scatter to every wind, and I draw out a sword after them. ¹⁵ And they have known that I [am] Yhwh, in My scattering them among nations, and I have spread them through lands; ¹⁶ and I have left of them, a few in number, from the sword, from the famine, and from the pestilence, so that they recount all their abominations among the nations to where they have come, and they have known that I [am] Yhwh." ¹⁷ And there is a word of Yhwh to me, saying, ¹⁸ "Son of man, eat your bread in haste, and drink your water with trembling and with fear; ¹⁹ and you have said to the people of the land, Thus said Lord Yhwh concerning the inhabitants of Jerusalem, concerning the land of Israel: They eat their bread with fear, and drink their water with astonishment, because its land is desolate, because of its fullness, because of the violence of all who are dwelling in it. ²⁰ And the cities that are inhabited are laid waste, and the land is a desolation, and you have known that I [am] Yhwh." ²¹ And there is a word of Yhwh to me, saying, ²² "Son of man, what [is] this allegory to you, concerning the land of Israel, saying, The days are prolonged, and every vision has perished? ²³ therefore say to them, Thus said Lord Yhwh: I have caused this allegory to cease, || And they do not use it as an allegory in Israel again, || But speak to them: The days have drawn near, || And every vision has spoken. ²⁴ For there is no longer any vain vision, and flattering divination, || In the midst of the house of Israel. ²⁵ For I, Yhwh, speak, || The word that I speak—it is done, || It is not prolonged anymore, || For in your days, O house of rebellion, I speak a word, and I have done it, || A declaration of Lord Yhwh." ²⁶ And there is a word of Yhwh to me, saying, ²⁷ "Son of man, behold, the house of Israel is saying, The vision that he is seeing [is not] for many days, and he is prophesying of far-off times, ²⁸ therefore say to them, Thus said Lord Yhwh: None of My words are prolonged anymore, || When I speak a word—it is done, || A declaration of Lord Yhwh!"

CHAPTER 13

¹ And there is a word of Yhwh to me, saying, ² "Son of man, prophesy concerning the prophets of Israel who are prophesying, and you have said to those prophesying from their own heart, Hear a word of Yhwh! ³ Thus said Lord Yhwh: Woe to the prophets who are foolish, || Who are going after their own spirit, || And they have seen nothing. ⁴ Your prophets have been || As foxes in the wasteland, O Israel. ⁵ You have not gone up into breaches, || Nor do you make a wall for the house of Israel, || To stand in battle in a day of Yhwh. ⁶ They have seen vanity, and lying divination, || Who are saying: A declaration of Yhwh, || And Yhwh has not sent them, || And they have hoped to establish a word. ⁷ Have you not seen a vain vision, || And spoken a lying divination, || When you say, A declaration of Yhwh, || And I have not spoken? ⁸ Therefore,

thus said Lord Yhwh: Because you have spoken vanity, and seen a lie, || Therefore, behold, I [am] against you, || A declaration of Lord Yhwh. ⁹ And My hand has been on the prophets, || Who are seeing vanity, and who are divining a lie, || They are not in the assembly of My people, || And they are not written in the writing of the house of Israel, || And they do not come to the ground of Israel, || And you have known that I [am] Lord Yhwh. ¹⁰ Because, even because, they caused My people to err, || Saying, Peace! And there is no peace, || And that one is building a wall, || And behold, they are coating it with chalk. ¹¹ Say to those coating with chalk—It falls, || There has been an overflowing shower, || And you, O hailstones, fall, || And a turbulent wind breaks out, ¹² And behold, the wall has fallen! Does one not say to you, Where [is] the coating that you coated? ¹³ Therefore, thus said Lord Yhwh: I have broken with a turbulent wind in My fury, || And an overflowing shower is in My anger, || And hailstones in My fury—to consume. ¹⁴ And I have broken down the wall that you coated with chalk, || And have caused it to come to the earth, || And its foundation has been revealed, || And it has fallen, || And you have been consumed in its midst, || And you have known that I [am] Yhwh. ¹⁵ And I have completed My wrath on the wall, || And on those coating it with chalk, || And I say to you: The wall is not, || And those coating it are not, ¹⁶ [These]—the prophets of Israel, who are prophesying concerning Jerusalem, || And who are seeing a vision of peace for her, || And there is no peace, || A declaration of Lord Yhwh. ¹⁷ And you, son of man, set your face against the daughters of your people, who are prophesying out of their own heart, and prophesy concerning them, ¹⁸ And you have said, Thus said Lord Yhwh: Woe to those sowing [magic] bands for all joints of the arm, || And to those making the veils || For the head of every stature—to hunt souls, || Do you hunt the souls of My people? And do your souls that live remain alive? ¹⁹ Indeed, you pierce Me concerning My people, || For handfuls of barley, || And for pieces of bread, || To put to death souls that should not die, || And to keep alive souls that should not live, || By your lying to My people—listening to lies. ²⁰ Therefore, thus said Lord Yhwh: Behold, I [am] against your [magic] bands, || With which you are hunting there the souls of the flourishing, || And I have torn them from off your arms, || And have sent away the souls that you are hunting, || The souls of the flourishing. ²¹ And I have torn your veils, || And delivered My people out of your hand, || And they are no longer for a prey in your hand, || And you have known that I [am] Yhwh. ²² Because of paining the heart of the righteous with falsehood, || And I have not pained it, || And strengthening the hands of the wicked, || So as not to turn [him] back from his evil way, || To keep him alive, ²³ Therefore, you do not see vanity, || And you do not divine divination again, || And I have delivered My people out of your hand, || And you have known that I [am] Yhwh!"

CHAPTER 14

¹ And men from [the] elderly of Israel come to me, and sit before me. ² And there is a word of Yhwh to me, saying, ³ "Son of man, these men have caused their idols to go up on their heart, and they have put the stumbling-block of their iniquity before their faces; am I inquired of at all by them? ⁴ Therefore, speak with them, and you have said to them, Thus said Lord Yhwh: Everyone of the house of Israel who causes his idols to go up to his heart, and sets the stumbling-block of his iniquity before his face, and has gone to the prophet—I, Yhwh, have given an answer to him for this, for the abundance of his idols, ⁵ in order to catch the house of Israel by their heart, in that they have become estranged from off Me by their idols—all of them. ⁶ Therefore say to the house of Israel, Thus said Lord Yhwh: Turn back, indeed, turn back from your idols, and turn back your faces from all your abominations, ⁷ for everyone of the house of Israel, and of the sojourners who sojourn in Israel, who is separated from after Me, and causes his idols to go up to his heart, and sets the stumbling-block of his iniquity before his face, and has come to the prophet to inquire of him concerning Me, I, Yhwh, have answered him for Myself; ⁸ and I have set My face against that man, and made him for a sign, and for allegories, and I have cut him off from the midst of My people, and you have known that I [am] Yhwh. ⁹ And the prophet, when he is enticed, and has spoken a word—I, Yhwh, have enticed that prophet, and have stretched out My hand against him, and have destroyed him from the midst of My people Israel. ¹⁰ And they have borne their iniquity: as the

iniquity of the inquirer, so is the iniquity of the prophet; **11** so that the house of Israel does not wander from after Me anymore, nor are they defiled with all their transgressions anymore, and they have been to Me for a people, and I am to them for God—a declaration of Lord Yhwh." **12** And there is a word of Yhwh to me, saying, **13** "Son of man, when the land sins against Me to commit a trespass, and I have stretched out My hand against it, and broken the staff of bread for it, and sent famine into it, and cut off man and beast from it— **14** and [despite] these three men [that] have been in its midst: Noah, Daniel, and Job—they [only] deliver their own soul by their righteousness," a declaration of Lord Yhwh. **15** "If I cause an evil beast to pass through the land, and it has bereaved, and it has been a desolation, without any passing through because of the beast— **16** [despite] these three men in its midst—[as] I live," a declaration of Lord Yhwh, "they deliver neither sons nor daughters; they alone are delivered, and the land is a desolation. **17** Or [if] I bring a sword in against that land, and I have said: Sword, pass over through the land, and I have cut off man and beast from it— **18** and [despite] these three men in its midst—[as] I live," a declaration of Lord Yhwh, "they do not deliver sons and daughters, for they alone are delivered. **19** Or [if] I send pestilence to that land, and I have poured out My fury against it in blood, to cut off man and beast from it— **20** and [despite] Noah, Daniel, and Job, in its midst—[as] I live," a declaration of Lord Yhwh, "they deliver neither son nor daughter; they, by their righteousness, [only] deliver their own soul." **21** For thus said Lord Yhwh: "Although My four severe judgments—sword, and famine, and wild beast, and pestilence—I have sent to Jerusalem, to cut off man and beast from it, **22** yet, behold, there has been left an escape in it, who are brought forth, sons and daughters, behold, they are coming forth to you, and you have seen their way, and their doings, and have been comforted concerning the calamity that I have brought in against Jerusalem, all that which I have brought in against it. **23** And they have comforted you, for you see their way and their doings, and you have known that I have not done all that which I have done in her for nothing," a declaration of Lord Yhwh.

CHAPTER 15

1 And there is a word of Yhwh to me, saying, **2** "Son of man, || What is the vine-tree more than any tree? The vine-branch that has been, || Among trees of the forest? **3** Is wood taken from it to use for work? Do they take a pin of it to hang any vessel on it? **4** Behold, it has been given to the fire for fuel, || The fire has eaten its two ends, || And its midst has been scorched! Is it profitable for work? **5** Behold, in its being perfect it is not used for work, || How much less when fire has eaten of it, || And it is scorched, || Has it been used yet for work?" **6** Therefore, thus said Lord Yhwh: "As the vine-tree among trees of the forest, || That I have given to the fire for fuel, || So I have given the inhabitants of Jerusalem. **7** And I have set My face against them, || They have gone forth from the fire, || And the fire consumes them, || And you have known that I [am] Yhwh, || In My setting My face against them. **8** And I have made the land a desolation, || Because they have committed a trespass," || A declaration of Lord Yhwh!

CHAPTER 16

1 And there is a word of Yhwh to me, saying, **2** "Son of man, cause Jerusalem to know her abominations, and you have said, **3** Thus said Lord Yhwh to Jerusalem: Your birth and your nativity || [Are] of the land of the Canaanite, || Your father the Amorite, and your mother a Hittite. **4** As for your nativity, in the day you were born, || Your navel has not been cut, || And you were not washed in water for ease, || And you have not been salted at all, || And you have not been swaddled at all. **5** No eye has had pity on you, to do any of these to you, || To have compassion on you, || And you are cast on the face of the field, || With loathing of your soul || In the day you were born! **6** And I pass over by you, || And I see you trodden down in your blood, || And I say to you in your blood, Live! Indeed, I say to you in your blood, Live! **7** I have made you a myriad as the shoot of the field, || And you are multiplied, and are great, || And come in with an excellent adornment, || Breasts have been formed, and your hair has grown—And you, naked and

bare! **8** And I pass over by you, and I see you, || And behold, your time [is] a time of loves, || And I spread My skirt over you, || And I cover your nakedness, || And I swear to you, and come into a covenant with you, || A declaration of Lord Yhwh, || And you become Mine. **9** And I wash you with water, || And I wash away your blood from off you, || And I anoint you with oil. **10** And I clothe you with embroidery, || And I shoe you with tachash [skin], || And I gird you with fine linen, || And I cover you with figured silk. **11** And I adorn you with adornments, || And I give bracelets for your hands, || And a chain for your neck. **12** And I give a ring for your nose, || And rings for your ears, || And a crown of beauty on your head. **13** And you put on gold and silver, || And your clothing [is] fine linen, || And figured silk and embroidery, || You have eaten fine flour, and honey, and oil, || And you are very, very beautiful, || And go prosperously to the kingdom. **14** And your name goes forth among nations, || Because of your beauty—for it [is] complete, || In My honor that I have set on you, || A declaration of Lord Yhwh. **15** And you trust in your beauty, || And go whoring because of your renown, || And pour out your whoredoms on everyone passing by—to him [that would have] it. **16** And you take from your garments, || And make spotted high-places for yourself, || And go whoring on them, || They are not coming in—nor will it be! **17** And you take your beautiful vessels || Of My gold and My silver that I gave to you, || And make images of a male for yourself, || And go whoring with them, **18** And you take the garments of your embroidery, || And cover them, || And you have set My oil and My incense before them. **19** And My bread, that I gave to you, || Fine flour, and oil, and honey, that I caused you to eat. You have even set it before them, || For a refreshing fragrance—thus it is, || A declaration of Lord Yhwh. **20** And you take your sons and your daughters whom you have born to Me, || And sacrifice them to them for food. Is it a little thing because of your whoredoms, **21** that you slaughter My sons, || And give them up in causing them to pass over to them? **22** And with all your abominations and your whoredoms, || You have not remembered the days of your youth, || When you were naked and bare, || You were trodden down in your blood! **23** And it comes to pass, after all your wickedness || (Woe, woe, to you—a declaration of Lord Yhwh), **24** That you build an arch for yourself, || And make a high place for yourself in every broad place. **25** At every head of the way you have built your high place, || And you make your beauty abominable, || And open wide your feet to everyone passing by, || And multiply your whoredoms, **26** And go whoring to sons of Egypt, || Your neighbors—great of appetite! And you multiply your whoredoms, || To provoke Me to anger. **27** And behold, I have stretched out My hand against you, || And I diminish your portion, || And give you to the desire of those hating you, || The daughters of the Philistines, || Who are ashamed of your wicked way. **28** And you go whoring to sons of Asshur, || Without your being satisfied, || And you go whoring with them, || And also—you have not been satisfied. **29** And you multiply your whoredoms || On the land of Canaan—toward Chaldea, || And even with this you have not been satisfied. **30** How weak [is] your heart, || A declaration of Lord Yhwh, || In your doing all these, || The work of a domineering, whorish woman. **31** In your building your arch at the head of every way, || You have made your high place in every broad place, || And have not been as a whore deriding a wage. **32** The wife who commits adultery—Under her husband—receives strangers. **33** They give a gift to all whores, || And you have given your gifts to all your lovers, || And bribe them to come in to you, || From all around—in your whoredoms. **34** And you are opposite from [other] women in your whoredoms, || That none go whoring after you; And in your giving a wage, || And a wage has not been given to you; Therefore, you are the opposite. **35** Therefore, O whore, hear a word of Yhwh! **36** Thus said Lord Yhwh: Because of your bronze being poured forth, || And your nakedness is revealed in your whoredoms near your lovers, || And near all the idols of your abominations, || And according to the blood of your sons, || Whom you have given to them; **37** Therefore, behold, I am assembling all your lovers, || To whom you have been sweet, || And all whom you have loved, || Besides all whom you have hated; And I have assembled them by you all around, || And have revealed your nakedness to them, || And they have seen all your nakedness. **38** And I have judged you—judgments of adulteresses, || And of women shedding blood, || And have given you blood, fury, and jealousy. **39** And I have given you into their hand, || And they have thrown down your arch, || And they have broken down your high places, || And they have stripped you of your garments, || And they have taken your beautiful vessels, || And they have left you naked and bare. ⁴⁰ And have caused an assembly to come up against you, || And stoned you with stones, || And thrust you through with their swords, ⁴¹ And burned your houses with fire, || And done judgments in you before the eyes of many women, || And I have caused you to cease from going whoring, || And also, you no longer give a wage. ⁴² And I have caused My fury against you to rest, || And My jealousy has turned aside from you, || And I have been quiet, and I am not angry anymore. ⁴³ Because you have not remembered the days of your youth, || And give trouble to Me in all these, || Therefore I also—behold—I put your way on [your own] head, || A declaration of Lord Yhwh, || And you will not have done—have done this wickedness above all your abominations. ⁴⁴ Behold, everyone using the allegory against you, || Uses [this] allegory concerning [you], saying, || As the mother—her daughter! ⁴⁵ You [are] your mother's daughter, || Loathing her husband and her sons, || And you [are] your sisters' sister, || Who loathed their husbands and their sons, || Your mother [is] a Hittite, and your father an Amorite. ⁴⁶ And your older sister [is] Samaria, she and her daughters, || Who is dwelling at your left hand, || And your younger sister, who is dwelling on your right hand, [is] Sodom and her daughters. ⁴⁷ And you have not walked in their ways, || And done according to their abominations, || It has been loathed as a little thing, || Indeed, you do more corruptly than they in all your ways. ⁴⁸ [As] I live—a declaration of Lord Yhwh, || Your sister Sodom has not done—she and her daughters—As you have done—you and your daughters. ⁴⁹ Behold, this has been the iniquity of your sister Sodom, || Arrogancy, fullness of bread, and quiet ease, || Have been to her and to her daughters, || And the hand of the afflicted and needy || She has not strengthened. ⁵⁰ And they are haughty and do abomination before Me, || And I turn them aside when I have seen. ⁵¹ And Samaria has not sinned even half of your sins, || But you multiply your abominations more than they, || And justify your sisters by all your abominations that you have done. ⁵² You also—bear your shame, || That you have adjudged for your sisters, || Because of your sins that you have done more abominably than they, || They are more righteous than you, || And you, also, be ashamed and bear your shame, || In your justifying your sisters. ⁵³ And I have turned back [to] their captivity, || The captivity of Sodom and her daughters, || And the captivity of Samaria and her daughters, || And the captivity of your captives in their midst, ⁵⁴ So that you bear your shame, || And have been ashamed of all that you have done, || In your comforting them. ⁵⁵ And your sisters, Sodom and her daughters, || Return to their former state, || And Samaria and her daughters return to their former state, || And you and your daughters return to your former state. ⁵⁶ And your sister Sodom has not been for a report in your mouth, || In the day of your arrogancy, ⁵⁷ Before your wickedness is revealed, || As [at] the time of the reproach of the daughters of Aram, || And of all her neighbors, the daughters of the Philistines, || Who are despising you all around. ⁵⁸ Your wicked plans and your abominations, || You have borne them, a declaration of Yhwh. ⁵⁹ For thus said Lord Yhwh: I have dealt with you as you have done, || In that you have despised an oath—to break covenant. ⁶⁰ And I have remembered My covenant with you, || In the days of your youth, || And I have established a perpetual covenant for you. ⁶¹ And you have remembered your ways, || And you have been ashamed, || In your receiving your sisters— Your older with your younger, || And I have given them to you for daughters, || And not by your covenant. ⁶² And I have established My covenant with you, || And you have known that I [am] Yhwh. ⁶³ So that you remember, || And you have been ashamed, || And there is not an opening of the mouth to you anymore because of your shame, || In My receiving atonement for you, || For all that you have done, || A declaration of Lord Yhwh!"

CHAPTER 17

¹ And there is a word of Yhwh to me, saying, ² "Son of man, put forth a riddle, and use an allegory to the house of Israel, ³ and you have said, Thus said Lord Yhwh: The great eagle, great-winged, long-pinioned, || Full of feathers, that has diverse colors, || Has come to Lebanon, || And he takes the foliage of the cedar, ⁴ He has cropped the top of its tender twigs, || And he brings it to the land of Canaan. He has placed it in a city of merchants. ⁵ And he takes of the seed of the land, || And puts it in a field of seed, || He took [it] by many waters, || He has set it in a conspicuous place. ⁶ And it springs up, and becomes a spreading vine, humble of stature, || To turn its thin shoots toward itself, || And its roots are under it, || And it becomes a vine, and makes boughs, || And sends forth beautiful branches. ⁷ And there is another great eagle, || Great-winged, and abounding with feathers, || And behold, this vine has bent its roots toward him, || And it has sent out its thin shoots toward him, || To water it from the furrows of its planting, ⁸ On a good field, by many waters, it is planted, to make branches, and to bear fruit, to be for a good vine. ⁹ Say, Thus said Lord Yhwh: It prospers—does he not draw out its roots, || And cut off its fruit, and it is withered? [In] all the leaves of its springing it withers, || And not by great strength, or by numerous people, || To lift it up by its roots. ¹⁰ And behold, the planted thing—does it prosper? When the east wind comes against it, does it not utterly wither? On the furrows of its springing, it withers." ¹¹ And there is a word of Yhwh to me, saying, ¹² "Now say to the house of rebellion, || Have you not known what these [are]? Say, Behold, the king of Babylon has come to Jerusalem, || And he takes its king, and its princes, || And brings them to himself to Babylon. ¹³ And he takes of the seed of the kingdom, || And makes a covenant with him, || And brings him into an oath, || And he has taken the mighty of the land, ¹⁴ That the kingdom may be humble, || That it may not lift itself up, || To keep his covenant—that it may stand. ¹⁵ And he rebels against him, || To send his messengers to Egypt, || To give to him horses, and many people, || Does he prosper? does he who is doing these things escape? And has he broken covenant and escaped? ¹⁶ [As] I live—a declaration of Lord Yhwh, || Does he not—in the place of the king who is causing him to reign, || Whose oath he has despised, || And whose covenant he has broken—die with him in the midst of Babylon? ¹⁷ And not with a great force, and with a numerous assembly, || Does Pharaoh maintain him in battle, || By pouring out a mound, and in building a fortification, || To cut off many souls. ¹⁸ And he despised the oath—to break covenant, || And behold, he has given his hand, || And all these he has done—he does not escape. ¹⁹ Therefore, thus said Lord Yhwh: [As] I live—My oath that he has despised, || And My covenant that he has broken, || Have I not put it on his head? ²⁰ And I have spread out My snare for him, || And he has been caught in My net, || And I have brought him to Babylon, || And judged him there [for the] trespass || That he has trespassed against Me. ²¹ And all his fugitives, with all his bands, || Fall by sword, and those remaining, || They are spread out to every wind, || And you have known that I, Yhwh, have spoken. ²² Thus said Lord Yhwh: I have taken of the foliage of the high cedar, || And I have set [it], || I crop a tender one from the top of its tender shoots, || And I have planted [it] on a high and lofty mountain. ²³ In a mountain—the high place of Israel, I plant it, || And it has borne boughs, and yielded fruit, || And become a good cedar, || And every bird of every [kind of] wing has dwelt under it, || They dwell in the shade of its thin shoots. ²⁴ And all trees of the field have known || That I, Yhwh, have made the high tree low, || I have set the low tree on high, || I have dried up the moist tree, || And I have caused the dry tree to flourish, || I, Yhwh, have spoken, and have done [it]!"

CHAPTER 18

¹ And there is a word of Yhwh to me, saying, ² "What [is it] to you [that] you are using this allegory || Concerning the ground of Israel, saying, || Fathers eat unripe fruit, || And the sons' teeth are blunted? ³ [As] I live," a declaration of Lord Yhwh, "You no longer have the use of this allegory in Israel. ⁴ Behold, all the souls are Mine, || As the soul of the father, || So also the soul of the son—they are Mine, || The soul that is sinning—it dies. ⁵ And a man, when he is righteous, || And has done judgment and righteousness, ⁶ He has not eaten on the mountains, || And has not lifted up his eyes || To idols of the house of Israel, || And did not defile his neighbor's wife, || And did not come near to a separated woman, ⁷ He does not oppress a man, || He returns his pledge to the debtor, || He does not take away plunder, || He gives his bread to the hungry, || And covers the naked with a garment, ⁸ He does not give in usury, and does not take increase, || He turns back his hand from perversity, || He does true judgment between man and man. ⁹ He walks in My statutes, || And he has kept My judgments—to deal truly, || He [is] righteous—he surely lives," || A declaration of Lord Yhwh. ¹⁰ "And he has begotten a son,

|| A burglar—a shedder of blood, || And he has made a brother of one of these, **11** And he has not done all those, || For he has even eaten on the mountains, || And he has defiled his neighbor's wife, **12** He has oppressed the afflicted and needy, || He has taken away plunder violently, || He does not return a pledge, || And he has lifted up his eyes to the idols, || He has done abomination! **13** He has given in usury, and taken increase, || And he lives? He does not live, || He has done all these abominations, || He surely dies, his blood is on him. **14** And—behold, he has begotten a son, || And he sees all the sins of his father, || That he has done, and he fears, || And does not do like them, **15** He has not eaten on the mountains, || And he has not lifted up his eyes || To idols of the house of Israel, || He has not defiled his neighbor's wife, **16** He has not oppressed a man, || He has not bound a pledge, || And he has not taken away plunder, || He has given his bread to the hungry, || And he covered the naked with a garment, **17** He has turned back his hand from the afflicted, || He has not taken usury and increase, || He has done My judgments, || He has walked in My statutes, || He does not die for the iniquity of his father, || He surely lives. **18** His father—because he used oppression, || Violently plundered a brother, || And did that which [is] not good in the midst of his people, || And behold, he is dying in his iniquity. **19** And you have said, Why has the son not borne of the iniquity of the father? And the son has done judgment and righteousness, || He has kept all My statutes, || And he does them, he surely lives. **20** The soul that sins—it dies. A son does not bear of the iniquity of the father, || And a father does not bear of the iniquity of the son, || The righteousness of the righteous is on him, || And the wickedness of the wicked is on him. **21** And the wicked—when he turns back || From all his sins that he has done, || And he has kept all My statutes, || And has done judgment and righteousness, || He surely lives, he does not die. **22** All his transgressions that he has done || Are not remembered to him, || In his righteousness that he has done he lives. **23** Do I take pleasure [or] delight in the death of the wicked?" A declaration of Lord Yhwh, "Is it not in his turning back from his way—And he has lived? **24** And in the turning back of the righteous from his righteousness, || And he has done perversity, || According to all the abominations || That the wicked has done, || Does he then live? All his righteous deeds that he has done are not remembered, || For his trespass that he has trespassed, || And for his sin that he has sinned, || For them he dies. **25** And you have said, The way of the Lord is not pondered. Now hear, O house of Israel, || My way—is it not pondered? Are not your ways unpondered? **26** In the turning back of the righteous from his righteousness, || And he has done perversity, || And he is dying by them, || He dies for his perversity that he has done. **27** And in the turning back of the wicked || From his wickedness that he has done, || And he does judgment and righteousness, || He keeps his soul alive. **28** And he sees and turns back, || From all his transgressions that he has done, || He surely lives, he does not die, **29** And the house of Israel has said, The way of the Lord is not pondered, || My ways—are they not pondered? O house of Israel—are not your ways unpondered? **30** Therefore, I judge each according to his ways, || O house of Israel," || A declaration of Lord Yhwh, || "Turn back, indeed, turn yourselves back, || From all your transgressions, || And iniquity is not for a stumbling-block to you, **31** Cast away all your transgressions from over you, || By which you have transgressed, || And make a new heart and a new spirit for yourselves, || And why do you die, || O house of Israel? **32** For I have no pleasure in the death of the dying," || A declaration of Lord Yhwh, || "Therefore turn back and live!"

CHAPTER 19

1 "And you, lift up a lamentation to princes of Israel, **2** and you have said: What [is] your mother? A lioness, || She has crouched down among lions, || She has multiplied her whelps in the midst of young lions. **3** And she brings up one of her whelps, || He has been a young lion, || And he learns to tear prey, || He has devoured man. **4** And nations hear of him, || He has been caught in their pit, || And they bring him to the land of Egypt in chains. **5** And as she waited, she sees that her hope has perished, || And she takes one of her whelps, || She has made him a young lion. **6** And he goes up and down in the midst of lions, || He has been a young lion, || And he learns to tear prey, || He has devoured man. **7** And he knows his forsaken habitations, || And he has laid waste [to] their cities,

|| And the land and its fullness is desolate, || Because of the voice of his roaring. **8** And surrounding nations set against him from the provinces. And they spread out their net for him, || He has been caught in their pit. **9** And they put him in prison—in chains, || And they bring him to the king of Babylon, || They bring him into bulwarks, || So that his voice is not heard || On mountains of Israel anymore. **10** Your mother, like the vine in your blood, || Is being planted by waters, || She was bearing fruit and full of boughs, || Because of many waters. **11** And she has strong rods for scepters of rulers, || And she is high in stature above—between thick branches, || And it appears in its height || In the multitude of its thin shoots. **12** And she is plucked up in fury, || She has been cast to the earth, || And the east wind has dried up her fruit, || [The] rod of her strength has been broken and withered, || Fire has consumed it. **13** And now she is planted in a wilderness, || In a dry and thirsty land. **14** And fire goes forth from a rod of her boughs, || It has devoured her fruit, || And she has no rod of strength—a scepter to rule, || A lamentation—and she has become for a lamentation!"

CHAPTER 20

1 And it comes to pass, in the seventh year, in the fifth [month], on the tenth of the month, men from [the] elderly of Israel have come in to seek Yhwh, and they sit before me; **2** and there is a word of Yhwh to me, saying, **3** "Son of man, speak to the elderly of Israel, and you have said to them, Thus said Lord Yhwh: Are you coming in to seek Me? [As] I live—I am not sought by you—a declaration of Lord Yhwh. **4** Do you judge them? Do you judge, son of man? Cause them to know the abominations of their fathers, **5** and you have said to them, Thus said Lord Yhwh: In the day of My fixing on Israel, || I lift up My hand, || To the seed of the house of Jacob, || And am known to them in the land of Egypt, || And I lift up My hand to them, || Saying, I [am] your God Yhwh. **6** In that day I lifted up My hand to them, || To bring them forth from the land of Egypt, || To a land that I spied out for them, || Flowing with milk and honey, || It [is] a beauty to all the lands, **7** And I say to them, Let each cast away the detestable things of his eyes, || And do not be defiled with the idols of Egypt, || I [am] your God Yhwh. **8** And they rebel against Me, || And have not been willing to listen to Me, || Each has not cast away the detestable things of their eyes, || And have not forsaken the idols of Egypt, || And I speak—to pour out My fury on them, || To complete My anger against them, || In the midst of the land of Egypt. **9** And I do [it] for My Name's sake, || Not to defile [it] before the eyes of the nations, || In whose midst they [are in], || Before whose eyes I became known to them, || To bring them out from the land of Egypt. **10** And I bring them out of the land of Egypt, || And I bring them into the wilderness, **11** And I give My statutes to them, || And I caused them to know My judgments, || Which the man who does—lives by them. **12** And I have also given My Sabbaths to them, || To be for a sign between Me and them, || To know that I [am] Yhwh who is sanctifying them. **13** And the house of Israel rebels against Me in the wilderness, || They have not walked in My statutes, || And they have despised My judgments, || Which the man who does—lives by them. And they have greatly defiled My Sabbaths, || And I speak—to pour out My fury on them in the wilderness, to consume them. **14** And I do [it] for My Name's sake, || Not to defile [it] before the eyes of the nations, || Before whose eyes I brought them forth. **15** And also, I have lifted up My hand to them in the wilderness, || Not to bring them into the land that I had given, || Flowing with milk and honey, || It [is] a beauty to all the lands, **16** Because they kicked against My judgments, || And they have not walked in My statutes, || And they have defiled My Sabbaths, || For their heart is going after their idols. **17** And My eye has pity on them—against destroying them, || And I have not made an end of them in the wilderness. **18** And I say to their sons in the wilderness: Do not walk in the statutes of your fathers, || And do not observe their judgments, || And do not defile yourselves with their idols. **19** I [am] your God Yhwh, walk in My statutes, || And observe My judgments, and do them, **20** And sanctify My Sabbaths, || And they have been for a sign between Me and you, || To know that I [am] your God Yhwh. **21** And the sons rebel against Me, || They have not walked in My statutes, || And they have not observed My judgments—to do them, || Which the man who does—lives by them. They have defiled My Sabbaths, || And I speak—to pour out My fury on them, || To complete My anger against them in the wilderness. **22** And I have turned back My hand, || And I do [it] for My Name's sake, || Not to defile [it] before the eyes of the nations, || Before whose eyes I brought them out. **23** I also, I have lifted up My hand to them in the wilderness, || To scatter them among nations, || And to spread them through lands. **24** Because they have not done My judgments, || And they have despised My statutes, || And they have defiled My Sabbaths, || And their eyes have been after [the] idols of their fathers. **25** And I also, I have given statutes to them [that are] not good, || And judgments by which they do not live. **26** And I defile them by their own gifts, || By causing every opener of a womb to pass away, || So that I make them desolate, || So that they know that I [am] Yhwh. **27** Therefore, speak to the house of Israel, son of man, and you have said to them, Thus said Lord Yhwh: Still in this your fathers have reviled Me, || In their committing a trespass against Me. **28** And I bring them into the land, || That I lifted up My hand to give to them, || And they see every high hill, and every thick tree, || And they sacrifice their sacrifices there, || And give the provocation of their offering there, || And make their refreshing fragrance there, || And they pour out their drink-offerings there. **29** And I say to them: What [is] the high place to where you are going in?" And its name is called "High Place" to this day. **30** "Therefore, say to the house of Israel, Thus said Lord Yhwh: Are you defiling yourselves in the way of your fathers? And do you go whoring after their detestable things? **31** And in the offering of your gifts, || In causing your sons to pass through fire, || You are defiled by all your idols to this day, || And I am sought by you, O house of Israel? [As] I live—a declaration of Lord Yhwh, I am not sought by you. **32** And that which is going up on your mind, || It is not at all—in that you are saying: We will be as the nations, as the families of the lands, || To serve wood and stone. **33** [As] I live—a declaration of Lord Yhwh, || Do I not, with a strong hand, || And with an outstretched arm, || And with poured out fury—rule over you? **34** And I have brought you forth from the peoples, || And assembled you from the lands || In which you have been scattered, || With a strong hand and with an outstretched arm, || And with poured out fury. **35** And I have brought you into the wilderness of the peoples, || And have been judged with you there face to face. **36** As I was judged with your fathers, || In the wilderness of the land of Egypt, || So I am judged with you, || A declaration of Lord Yhwh. **37** And I have caused you to pass under the rod, || And brought you into the bond of the covenant, **38** And cleared out the rebels from you, || And those transgressing against Me, || I bring them out from the land of their sojournings, || And they do not come to the land of Israel, || And you have known that I [am] Yhwh. **39** And you, O house of Israel, thus said Lord Yhwh: Each go, serve his idols, || And afterward, if you are not listening to Me [anyway], || But you do not defile My holy Name anymore by your gifts, and by your idols. **40** For on My holy mountain, || On the mountain of the height of Israel, || A declaration of Lord Yhwh, || All the house of Israel serves Me there, || All of it, in the land—I accept them there, || And I seek your raised-offerings there, || And with the first-fruit of your gifts, || With all your holy things. **41** With refreshing fragrance I accept you, || In My bringing you out from the peoples, || And I have assembled you from the lands || In which you have been scattered, || And I have been sanctified in you || Before the eyes of the nations. **42** And you have known that I [am] Yhwh, || In My bringing you to the ground of Israel, || To the land that I lifted up My hand || To give it to your fathers, **43** And you have remembered your ways there, || And all your doings, || In which you have been defiled, || And you have been loathsome in your own faces, || For all your evils that you have done. **44** And you have known that I [am] Yhwh, || In My dealing with you for My Name's sake, || Not according to your evil ways, || And according to your corrupt doings, O house of Israel, || A declaration of Lord Yhwh." **45** And there is a word of Yhwh to me, saying, **46** "Son of man, set your face the way of Teman, and prophesy to the south, and prophesy to the forest of the field—the south; **47** and you have said to the forest of the south, Hear a word of Yhwh! Thus said Lord Yhwh: Behold, I am kindling a fire in you, || And it has devoured every moist tree in you, and every dry tree, || The glowing flames are not quenched, || And all faces from south to north have been burned by it. **48** And all flesh has seen, that I, Yhwh, have kindled it—it is not quenched." **49** And I say, "Aah! Lord Yhwh, || They are saying of me, || Is he not using allegories?"

CHAPTER 21

1 And there is a word of Yhwh to me, saying, **2** "Son of man, set your face toward Jerusalem, and prophesy to the holy places, and prophesy to the ground of Israel; **3** and you have said to the ground of Israel, Thus said Yhwh: Behold, I [am] against you, || And have brought out My sword from its scabbard, || And have cut off righteous and wicked from you. **4** Because that I have cut off righteous and wicked from you, || Therefore My sword goes out from its scabbard, || To all flesh, from south to north. **5** And all flesh has known that I, Yhwh, || Have brought out My sword from its scabbard, || It does not turn back anymore. **6** And you, son of man, sigh with breaking of loins, indeed, sigh before their eyes with bitterness, **7** and it has come to pass, when they say to you, Why are you sighing? that you have said: Because of the report, for it is coming, || And every heart has melted, || And all hands have been feeble, || And every spirit is weak, || And all knees go [as] waters, || Behold, it is coming, indeed, it has been, || A declaration of Lord Yhwh." **8** And there is a word of Yhwh to me, saying, **9** "Son of man, prophesy, and you have said, Thus said Yhwh: Say, A sword, a sword is sharpened, and also polished. **10** It is sharpened so as to slaughter a slaughter. It is polished so as to have brightness, || Or do we rejoice? It is despising the scepter of My son [as] every tree. **11** And He gives it for polishing, || For laying hold of by the hand. It is sharpened—the sword—and polished, || To give it into the hand of a slayer. **12** Cry and howl, son of man, || For it has been among My people, || It [is] among all the princes of Israel, || My people have been cast to the sword. Therefore strike on your thigh, **13** Because [it is] a trier, || And what if it is even despising the scepter? It will not be, a declaration of Lord Yhwh. **14** And you, son of man, prophesy, || And strike hand on hand, || And the sword is bent a third time, || The sword of the wounded! It [is] the sword of the wounded—the great one, || That is entering the inner chamber to them. **15** To melt the heart, and to multiply the ruins, || I have set the point of a sword by all their gates. Aah! It is made for brightness, || Wrapped up for slaughter. **16** Take possession of the right, place yourself at the left, || To where your face is appointed. **17** And I also, I strike My hand on My hand, || And have caused My fury to rest; I, Yhwh, have spoken." **18** And there is a word of Yhwh to me, saying, **19** "And you, son of man, appoint two ways for yourself, for the coming in of the sword of the king of Babylon; they come forth from one land, both of them. And create a station; create [it] at the top of the way of the city. **20** Appoint a way for the coming of the sword, || To Rabbath of the sons of Ammon, || And to Judah, in fortified Jerusalem. **21** For the king of Babylon has stood at the head of the way, || At the top of the two ways, to use divination, || He has moved lightly with the arrows, || He has inquired of the teraphim, || He has looked on the liver. **22** The divination [for] Jerusalem has been at his right, || To place battering-rams, || To open the mouth with slaughter, || To lift up a voice with shouting, || To place battering-rams against the gates, || To pour out a mound, to build a fortification. **23** And it has been to them as a false divination in their eyes, || Who have sworn oaths to them, || But he is causing iniquity to be remembered [so they] are caught. **24** Therefore, thus said Lord Yhwh: Because of your causing your iniquity to be remembered, || In your transgressions being revealed, || For your sins being seen, in all your doings, || Because of your being remembered, || You are caught by the hand. **25** And you, wounded, wicked one, || Prince of Israel, whose day has come, || In the time of the iniquity of the end, **26** Thus said Lord Yhwh: Turn aside the turban, and carry away the crown, || This—not this—make high the low, || And make low the high. **27** An overturn, overturn, overturn, I make it, || Also this has not been until the coming of Him, || Whose [is] the judgment, and I have given it. **28** And you, son of man, prophesy, and you have said, Thus said Lord Yhwh concerning the sons of Ammon, and concerning their reproach, and you have said: A sword, a sword, open for slaughter, || Polished to the utmost for brightness! **29** In seeing a vain thing for you, || In divining a lie for you, || To put you on the necks of the wounded of the wicked, whose day has come, || In the time of the iniquity of the end. **30** Turn [it] back to its scabbard; I judge you || In the place where you were produced, || In the land of your birth. **31** And I have poured My indignation on you, || I blow against you with [the] fire of My wrath, || And have given you into the hand of brutish men—craftsmen of destruction. **32** You are fuel for the fire, || Your blood is in the midst of the land, || You are not remembered,

|| For I, Yhwh, have spoken!"

CHAPTER 22

1 And there is a word of Yhwh to me, saying, **2** "And you, son of man, do you judge? do you judge the city of blood? then you have caused it to know all its abominations, **3** and you have said, Thus said Lord Yhwh: The city is shedding blood in its midst, || For the coming in of its time, || And it has made idols on it for defilement. **4** You have been guilty by your blood that you have shed, || And you have been defiled by your idols that you have made, || And you cause your days to draw near, || And have come to your years, || Therefore I have given you [for] a reproach to nations, || And a derision to all the lands. **5** The near and the far-off from you scoff at you, || O defiled of name—abounding in trouble. **6** Behold, princes of Israel—each according to his arm || Have been in you to shed blood. **7** They have made light of father and mother in you, || They dealt oppressively to a sojourner in your midst, || They oppressed fatherless and widow in you. **8** You have despised My holy things, || And you have defiled My Sabbaths. **9** Men of slander have been in you to shed blood, || And they have eaten on the mountains in you, || They have done wickedness in your midst. **10** One has uncovered the nakedness of a father in you, || They humbled the menstruous woman in you. **11** And each has done abomination with the wife of his neighbor, || And each has defiled his daughter-in-law through wickedness, || And each has humbled his sister, his father's daughter, in you. **12** They have taken a bribe to shed blood in you, || You have taken usury and increase, || And cut off your neighbor by oppression, || And you have forgotten Me, || A declaration of Lord Yhwh! **13** And behold, I have struck My hand, || Because of your dishonest gain that you have gained, || And for your blood that has been in your midst. **14** Does your heart stand—are your hands strong, || For the days that I am dealing with you? I, Yhwh, have spoken and have done [it]. **15** And I have scattered you among nations, || And have spread you out among lands, || And consumed your uncleanness out of you. **16** And you have been defiled in yourself || Before the eyes of nations, || And you have known that I [am] Yhwh." **17** And there is a word of Yhwh to me, saying, **18** "Son of man, the house of Israel has been for dross to Me, || All of them [are] bronze, and tin, and iron, and lead, || In the midst of a furnace—silver has been dross, **19** Therefore, thus said Lord Yhwh: Because you have all become dross, || Therefore, behold, I am gathering you into the midst of Jerusalem, **20** A gathering of silver, and bronze, and iron, and lead, and tin, || Into the midst of a furnace—to blow fire on it, to melt it, || So I gather in My anger and in My fury, || And I have let rest, and have melted you. **21** And I have heaped you up, || And blown on you in the fire of My wrath, || And you have been melted in its midst. **22** As the melting of silver in the midst of a furnace, || So you are melted in its midst, || And you have known that I, Yhwh, have poured out My fury on you." **23** And there is a word of Yhwh to me, saying, **24** "Son of man, say to it, You [are] a land, || It [is] not cleansed nor rained on in a day of indignation. **25** A conspiracy of its prophets [is] in its midst, || As a roaring lion tearing prey; They have devoured the soul, || They have taken wealth and glory, || Its widows have multiplied in its midst. **26** Its priests have wronged My law, || And they defile My holy things, || They have not made separation between holy and common, || And they have not made known [the difference] between the unclean and the clean, || And they have hidden their eyes from My Sabbaths, || And I am pierced in their midst. **27** Its princes [are] as wolves in its midst, || Tearing prey, to shed blood, to destroy souls, || For the sake of gaining dishonest gain. **28** And its prophets have coated with chalk for them, || Seeing a vain thing, and divining a lie for them, || Saying, Thus said Lord Yhwh, || And Yhwh has not spoken. **29** The people of the land have used oppression, || And have taken plunder away violently, || And have oppressed humble and needy, || And oppressed the sojourner without judgment. **30** And I seek from them a man making a wall, || And standing in the breach before Me, || In behalf of the land—not to destroy it, || And I have found none. **31** And I pour out My indignation on them, || I have consumed them by [the] fire of My wrath, || I have put their way on their own head, || A declaration of Lord Yhwh!"

CHAPTER 23

1 And there is a word of Yhwh to me, saying, "Son of man, **2** Two women were daughters of one mother, **3** And they go whoring in Egypt, || They have gone whoring in their youth, || There they have bruised their breasts, || And there they have dealt with the loves of their virginity. **4** And their names [are] Aholah the older, || And Aholibah her sister, || And they are Mine, and bear sons and daughters. As for their names—Samaria [is] Aholah, || And Jerusalem [is] Aholibah. **5** And Aholah goes whoring under Me, and she lusts on her lovers, on the neighboring Assyrians, **6** Clothed with blue—governors and prefects, || All of them desirable young men, || Horsemen, riding on horses, **7** And she gives her whoredoms on them, || The choice of the sons of Asshur, || All of them—even all on whom she lusted, || She has been defiled by all their idols. **8** And she has not forsaken her whoredoms out of Egypt, || For with her they lay in her youth, || And they dealt with the loves of her virginity, || And they pour out their whoredoms on her. **9** Therefore I have given her into the hand of her lovers, || Into the hand of sons of Asshur on whom she lusted. **10** They have uncovered her nakedness, || They have taken her sons and her daughters, || And they have slain her by sword, || And she is a name for women, || And they have done judgments with her. **11** And her sister Aholibah sees, || And she makes her unhealthy love more corrupt than she, || And her whoredoms than the whoredoms of her sister. **12** She has lusted on sons of Asshur, || Governors and prefects, || Neighboring ones—clothed in perfection, || Horsemen, riding on horses, || All of them desirable young men. **13** And I see that she has been defiled, || One way [is] to them both. **14** And she adds to her whoredoms, || And she sees men carved on the wall, || Pictures of Chaldeans, carved with vermillion, **15** Girded with a girdle on their loins, || Dyed attire spread out on their heads, || The appearance of rulers—all of them, || The likeness of sons of Babylon, || Chaldea is the land of their birth. **16** And she lusts on them at the sight of her eyes, || And sends messengers to them, to Chaldea. **17** And sons of Babylon come in to her, || To the bed of loves, || And they defile her with their whoredoms, || And she is defiled with them, || And her soul is alienated from them. **18** And she reveals her whoredoms, || And she reveals her nakedness, || And My soul is alienated from off her, || As My soul was alienated from off her sister. **19** And she multiplies her whoredoms, || To remember the days of her youth, || When she went whoring in the land of Egypt. **20** And she lusts on their lovers, || Whose flesh [is] the flesh of donkeys, || And the emission of horses—their emission. **21** You look after the wickedness of your youth, || In dealing out of Egypt your loves, || For the sake of the breasts of your youth. **22** Therefore, O Aholibah, thus said Lord Yhwh: Behold, I am stirring up your lovers against you, || From whom your soul has been alienated, || And have brought them in against you from all around. **23** Sons of Babylon, and of all Chaldea, Pekod, and Shoa, and Koa, || All the sons of Asshur with them, || Desirable young men, governors and prefects, || All of them—rulers and proclaimed ones, || All of them riding on horses. **24** And they have come in against you, || With arms, rider, and wheel, || And with an assembly of peoples; Buckler, and shield, and helmet, || They set against you all around, || And I have set judgment before them, || They have judged you in their judgments. **25** And I have set My jealousy against you, || And they have dealt with you in fury, || They turn aside your nose and your ears, || And your posterity falls by sword, || They take away your sons and your daughters, || And your posterity is devoured by fire. **26** And they have stripped you of your garments, || And have taken your beautiful jewels. **27** And I have caused your wickedness to cease from you, || And your whoredoms out of the land of Egypt, || And you do not lift up your eyes to them, || And you do not remember Egypt again. **28** For thus said Lord Yhwh: Behold, I am giving you into a hand that you have hated, || Into a hand from which you were alienated. **29** And they have dealt with you in hatred, || And they have taken all your labor, || And they have left you naked and bare, || And the nakedness of your whoredoms has been revealed, || And the wickedness of your whoredoms. **30** To do these things to you, || In your going whoring after nations, || Because you have been defiled with their idols, **31** You have walked in the way of your sister, || And I have given her cup into your hand. **32** Thus said Lord Yhwh: You drink the cup of your sister, || The deep and the wide one || (You are for laughter and for scorn), || Abundant to contain. **33** You are filled with drunkenness and sorrow, || A cup of astonishment and desolation, || The cup of your sister Samaria. **34** And you have drunk it, and have drained [it], || And you gnaw its earthen ware, || And you pluck off your own breasts, || For I have spoken, || A declaration of Lord Yhwh, **35** Therefore, thus said Lord Yhwh: Because you have forgotten Me, || And you cast Me behind your back, || Even you also bear your wickedness and your whoredoms." **36** And Yhwh says to me, "Son of man, || Do you judge Aholah and Aholibah? Then declare their abominations to them. **37** For they have committed adultery, || And blood [is] in their hands, || They committed adultery with their idols, || And also their sons whom they bore to Me, || They caused to pass over to them for food. **38** Again, they have done this to Me, || They defiled My sanctuary in that day, || And they have defiled My Sabbaths. **39** And in their slaughtering their sons to their idols || They also come into My sanctuary in that day to defile it, || And behold, thus they have done in the midst of My house, **40** And also that they send to men coming from afar, || To whom a messenger is sent, || And behold, they have come in for whom you have washed, || Painted your eyes, and put on adornment. **41** And you have sat on a couch of honor, || And a table arrayed before it, || And placed My incense and My oil on it. **42** And the voice of a multitude at ease [is] with her, || And Sabeans from the wilderness are brought in to men of the common people, || And they put bracelets on their hands, || And a beautiful crown on their heads. **43** And I say of the worn-out one in adulteries, || Now they commit her whoredoms—she also! **44** And they come in to her, || As the coming in to a whorish woman, || So they have come in to Aholah, || And to Aholibah—the wicked women. **45** As for righteous men, they judge them with the judgment of adulteresses, || And the judgment of women shedding blood, || For they [are] adulteresses, || And blood [is] in their hands. **46** For thus said Lord Yhwh: Bring up an assembly against them, || And give them to trembling and to spoiling. **47** And they have cast the stone of the assembly at them, || And cut them with their swords, || They slay their sons and their daughters, || And they burn their houses with fire. **48** And I have caused wickedness to cease from the land, || And all the women have been instructed, || And they do not do according to your wickedness. **49** And they have put your wickedness on you, || And you bear the sins of your idols, || And you have known that I [am] Lord Yhwh!"

CHAPTER 24

1 And there is a word of Yhwh to me, in the ninth year, in the tenth month, on the tenth of the month, saying, **2** "Son of man, write! Write the name of the day for yourself, this very day; the king of Babylon has leaned toward Jerusalem in this very day. **3** And use an allegory toward the house of rebellion, and you have said to them, Thus said Lord Yhwh: To set on the pot, to set [it] on, and also to pour water into it, **4** To gather its pieces to it, every good piece, || Thigh and shoulder, to fill in the choice of the bones. **5** To take the choice of the flock, || And also to pile the bones under it, || Boil it thoroughly, indeed, cook its bones in its midst. **6** Therefore, thus said Lord Yhwh: Woe [to] the city of blood, || A pot whose scum [is] in it, || And its scum has not come out of it, || By piece of it, by piece of it bring it out, a lot has not fallen on it. **7** For her blood has been in her midst, || She has set it on a clear place of a rock, || She has not poured it on the earth, || To cover it over with dust. **8** To cause fury to come up to take vengeance, || I have put her blood on a clear place of a rock—not to be covered. **9** Therefore, thus said Lord Yhwh: Woe [to] the city of blood, indeed, I make the pile great. **10** Make the wood abundant, || Kindle the fire, consume the flesh, || And make the compound, || And let the bones be burned. **11** And cause it to stand empty on its coals, || So that its bronze is hot and burning, || Its uncleanness has been melted in its midst, || Its scum is consumed. **12** She has wearied herself [with] sorrows, || And the abundance of her scum does not go out of her, || Her scum [is] in the fire. **13** Wickedness [is] in your uncleanness, || Because I have cleansed you, || And you have not been cleansed, || You are not cleansed from your uncleanness again, || Until I have caused My fury to rest on you. **14** I, Yhwh, have spoken, || It has come, and I have done [it], || I do not free, nor do I spare, nor do I regret, || According to your ways, and according to your acts, || They have judged you, || A declaration of Lord Yhwh." **15** And there is a word of Yhwh to me, saying, **16** "Son of man, behold, I am taking the desire of your eyes from you by a stroke, and you do not mourn, nor weep, nor let your tear come. **17** Cease to groan [and] make no mourning [for] the dead, bind your headdress on yourself, and

put your shoes on your feet, and you do not cover over the upper lip, and you do not eat [the] bread of men." **18** And I speak to the people in the morning, and my wife dies in the evening, and I do in the morning as I have been commanded. **19** And the people say to me, "Do you not declare to us what these [are] to us, that you are doing?" **20** And I say to them, "A word of Yhwh has been to me, saying, **21** Say to the house of Israel, Thus said Lord Yhwh: Behold, I am defiling My sanctuary, || The excellence of your strength, || The desire of your eyes, and the pitied of your soul, || And your sons and your daughters whom you have left, fall by sword. **22** And you have done as I have done, || You have not covered over the upper lip, || And you do not eat [the] bread of men. **23** And your headdresses [are] on your heads, || And your shoes [are] on your feet, || You do not mourn nor do you weep, || And you have wasted away for your iniquities, || And you have howled to one another. **24** And Ezekiel has been for a type to you; according to all that he has done you do. In its coming in—you have known that I [am] Lord Yhwh." **25** "And you, son of man, is it not in the day of My taking from them their strength, the joy of their beauty, the desire of their eyes, and the song of their soul—their sons and their daughters? **26** In that day the escaped one comes to you to cause the ears to hear. **27** In that day your mouth is opened with the escaped and you speak, and are not silent anymore, and you have been for a type to them, and they have known that I [am] Yhwh."

CHAPTER 25

1 And there is a word of Yhwh to me, saying, **2** "Son of man, set your face toward the sons of Ammon, and prophesy against them; **3** and you have said to the sons of Ammon: Hear a word of Lord Yhwh! Thus said Lord Yhwh: Because of your saying, Aha, to My sanctuary, || Because it has been defiled, || And to the ground of Israel, || Because it has been desolate, || And to the house of Judah, || Because they have gone into a removal: **4** Therefore, behold, I am giving you to sons of the east for a possession, || And they set their towers in you, || And have placed their dwelling places in you. They eat your fruit, and they drink your milk, **5** And I have given Rabbah for a habitation of camels, || And the sons of Ammon for the crouching of a flock, || And you have known that I [am] Yhwh. **6** For thus said Lord Yhwh: Because of your clapping the hand, || And of your stamping with the foot, || And you rejoice with all your despite in soul || Against the ground of Israel, **7** Therefore, behold, I have stretched out My hand against you, || And have given you for a portion to nations, || And I have cut you off from the peoples, || And caused you to perish from the lands; I destroy you, and you have known that I [am] Yhwh. **8** Thus said Lord Yhwh: Because of the saying of Moab and Seir, Behold, the house of Judah [is] as all the nations; **9** Therefore, behold, I am opening the shoulder of Moab—From the cities—from his cities—from his frontier, || The beauty of the land, Beth-Jeshimoth, Ba'al-Meon, and Kiriathaim, **10** To the sons of the east, with the sons of Ammon, || And I have given it for a possession, || So that the sons of Ammon are not remembered among nations. **11** And I do judgments in Moab, || And they have known that I [am] Yhwh. **12** Thus said Lord Yhwh: Because of the doings of Edom, || In taking vengeance on the house of Judah, || Indeed, they are very guilty, || And they have taken vengeance on them. **13** Therefore, thus said Lord Yhwh: I have stretched out My hand against Edom, || And I have cut off man and beast from it, || And given it up—a ruin, from Teman even to Dedan, || They fall by sword. **14** And I have given My vengeance on Edom, || By the hand of My people Israel, || And they have done in Edom, || According to My anger, and according to My fury, || And they have known My vengeance, || A declaration of Lord Yhwh. **15** Thus said Lord Yhwh: Because of the doings of the Philistines in vengeance, || And they take vengeance with despite in soul, || Destruction [with] continuous enmity, **16** Therefore, thus said Lord Yhwh: Behold, I am stretching out My hand against the Philistines, || And I have cut off the Cherethim, || And destroyed the remnant of the haven of the sea, **17** And done great vengeance on them with furious reproofs, || And they have known that I [am] Yhwh, || In My giving out My vengeance on them!"

CHAPTER 26

¹ And it comes to pass, in the eleventh year, on the first of the month, there has been a word of Yhwh to me, saying, "Son of man, ² Because that Tyre has said of Jerusalem: Aha, she has been broken, || The doors of the peoples, || She has turned around to me, || I am filled—she has been laid waste, ³ Therefore, thus said Lord Yhwh: Behold, I [am] against you, O Tyre, || And have caused many nations to come up against you, || As the sea causes its billows to come up. ⁴ And they have destroyed the walls of Tyre, || And they have broken down her towers, || And I have scraped her dust from her, || And made her for a clear place of a rock. ⁵ She is a spreading place of nets in the midst of the sea, || For I have spoken," || A declaration of Lord Yhwh, || "And she has been for a spoil to nations. ⁶ And her daughters who [are] in the field, are slain by sword, || And they have known that I [am] Yhwh," ⁷ For thus said Lord Yhwh: "Behold, I am bringing Nebuchadnezzar king of Babylon to Tyre, || From the north—a king of kings, || With horse, and with chariot, and with horsemen, || Even an assembly, and a numerous people. ⁸ He slays your daughters in the field by sword, || And he has made a fort against you, || And has poured out a mound against you, || And has raised a buckler against you. ⁹ And he places a battering-ram before him against your walls, || And he breaks your towers with his weapons. ¹⁰ From the abundance of his horses their dust covers you, || From the noise of horseman, and wheel, and rider, || Your walls shake, in his coming into your gates, || As the coming into a city that has been broken-up. ¹¹ He treads all your out-places with [the] hooves of his horses, || He slays your people by sword, || And the pillars of your strength come down to the earth. ¹² And they have spoiled your wealth, || And they have plundered your merchandise, || And they have thrown down your walls, || And they break down your desirable houses, || And your stones, and your wood, and your dust, || They place in the midst of the waters. ¹³ And I have caused the noise of your songs to cease, || And the voice of your harps is heard no more. ¹⁴ And I have given you up for a clear place of a rock, || You are a spreading-place of nets, || You are not built up anymore, || For I, Yhwh, have spoken," || A declaration of Lord Yhwh. ¹⁵ Thus said Lord Yhwh to Tyre: "Do not—from the noise of your fall, || In the groaning of the wounded, || In the slaying of the slaughter in your midst—The islands shake? ¹⁶ And all princes of the sea have come down from off their thrones, || And they have turned their robes aside, || And strip off their embroidered garments, || They put on trembling, || They sit on the earth, || And they have trembled every moment, || And they have been astonished at you, ¹⁷ And have lifted up a lamentation for you, || And said to you: How you have perished, || That are inhabited from the seas, || The praised city, that was strong in the sea, || She and her inhabitants, || Who put their terror on all her inhabitants! ¹⁸ Now the islands tremble [on the] day of your fall; The islands that [are] in the sea have been troubled at your outgoing." ¹⁹ For thus said Lord Yhwh: "In My making you a city dried up, || Like cities that have not been inhabited, || In bringing up the deep against you, || Then the great waters have covered you. ²⁰ And I have caused you to go down, || With those going down to the pit, || To the people of old, || And I have caused you to dwell || In the lower parts of the earth—in ancient ruins, || With those going down to the pit, || So that you are not inhabited, || And I have given beauty in the land of the living. ²¹ I make you a terror, and you are not, || And you are sought, and are not found anymore—for all time," || A declaration of Lord Yhwh!

CHAPTER 27

¹ And there is a word of Yhwh to me, saying, ² "And you, son of man, lift up a lamentation concerning Tyre, and you have said to Tyre: ³ O dweller on the entrances of the sea, || Merchant of the peoples to many islands, Thus said Lord Yhwh: O Tyre, you have said, || I [am] the perfection of beauty. ⁴ Your borders [are] in the heart of the seas, || Your builders have perfected your beauty. ⁵ They have built of firs from Senir all your double-boarded ships for you, || They have taken of cedars from Lebanon to make a mast for you, ⁶ They made your oars of oaks from Bashan, || They have made your bench of ivory, || A branch of Ashurim from islands of Chittim. ⁷ Your sail has been of fine linen with embroidery from Egypt, || To be for your ensign, || Your covering has been of blue and purple from islands of Elishah. ⁸ Inhabitants of Sidon and Arvad have been rowers for you, || Your wise men, O Tyre, have been in

you, || They [are] your pilots. ⁹ The elderly of Gebal and its wise men have been in you, || Strengthening your breach; All ships of the sea and their mariners, || Have been in you, to trade your merchandise. ¹⁰ Persia and Lud and Phut || Have been in your forces—your men of war. They hung up shield and helmet in you, || They have given out your honor. ¹¹ The sons of Arvad, and your force, || [Are] on your walls all around, || And short swordsmen have been in your towers, || They have hung up their shields on your walls all around, || They have perfected your beauty. ¹² Tarshish [is] your merchant, || Because of the abundance of all wealth, || They have given silver, iron, tin, and lead [for] your wares. ¹³ Javan, Tubal, and Meshech—they [are] your merchants, || They have given [the] soul of man, and vessels of bronze, [for] your merchandise. ¹⁴ Those of the house of Togarmah, || They have given horses, and riding steeds, and mules [for] your wares. ¹⁵ Sons of Dedan [are] your merchants, || Many islands [are] the market of your hand, || They sent back horns of ivory and ebony [for] your reward. ¹⁶ Aram [is] your merchant, || Because of the abundance of your works, || They have given emerald, purple, and embroidery, || And fine linen, and coral, and agate for your wares. ¹⁷ Judah and the land of Israel—they [are] your merchants, || They have given wheat of Minnith and Pannag, || And honey, and oil, and balm [for] your merchandise. ¹⁸ Damascus [is] your merchant, || For the abundance of your works, || Because of the abundance of all wealth, || For wine of Helbon, and white wool. ¹⁹ Dan and Javan go about with your wares, || They have given shining iron, cassia, and cane, || It has been in your merchandise. ²⁰ Dedan [is] your merchant, || For clothes of freedom for riding. ²¹ Arabia, and all princes of Kedar, || They [are] the traders of your hand, || For lambs, and rams, and male goats, || In these your merchants. ²² Merchants of Sheba and Raamah—they [are] your merchants, || They have given the chief of all spices, || And every precious stone, and gold [for] your wares. ²³ Haran, and Canneh, and Eden, merchants of Sheba, Asshur—Chilmad—[are] your merchants, ²⁴ They [are] your merchants for perfect things, || For wrappings of blue, and embroidery, || And for treasuries of rich apparel, || With cords bound and girded, for your merchandise, ²⁵ Ships of Tarshish are journeying [with] your merchandise for you, || And you are filled and honored greatly, || In the heart of the seas. ²⁶ Those rowing you have brought you into great waters, || The east wind has broken you in the heart of the seas. ²⁷ Your wealth and your wares, || Your merchandise, your mariners, || And your pilots, strengtheners of your breach, || And the traders of your merchandise, || And all your men of war, who [are] in you, || And in all your assembly that [is] in your midst, || Fall into the heart of the seas in the day of your fall, ²⁸ At the voice of the cry of your pilots the outskirts shake. ²⁹ And all handling an oar come down from their ships, || Mariners [and] all the pilots of the sea stand on the land, ³⁰ And have sounded with their voice for you, || And cry bitterly, and cause dust to go up on their heads, || They roll themselves in ashes; ³¹ And they have made themselves bald for you, || And they have girded on sackcloth, || And they have wept for you, || In bitterness of soul—a bitter mourning. ³² And their sons have lifted up a lamentation for you, || And they have lamented over you, who [is] as Tyre? As the cut-off one in the midst of the sea? ³³ With the outgoing of your wares from the seas, || You have filled many peoples, || With the abundance of your riches, and your merchandise, || You have enriched [the] kings of earth. ³⁴ At the time of [your] being broken by the seas in the depths of the waters, || Your merchandise and all your assembly have fallen in your midst. ³⁵ All inhabitants of the islands have been astonished at you, || And their kings have been severely afraid, || They have been troubled in countenance. ³⁶ Merchants among the peoples have shrieked for you, || You have been terrors, and you are not—for all time!"

CHAPTER 28

¹ And there is a word of Yhwh to me, saying, ² "Son of man, say to the leader of Tyre, Thus said Lord Yhwh: Because your heart has been high, || And you say: I [am] a god, || I have inhabited the habitation of God, || In the heart of the seas, || And you [are] man, and not God, || And you give out your heart as the heart of God, ³ Behold, you [are] wiser than Daniel, || No hidden thing have they concealed from you. ⁴ By your wisdom and by your understanding || You have made wealth for yourself, || And make gold and silver in your

treasuries. **5** By the abundance of your wisdom, || Through your merchandise, || You have multiplied your wealth, || And your heart is high through your wealth. **6** Therefore, thus said Lord Yhwh: Because of your giving out your heart as the heart of God, **7** Therefore, behold, I am bringing in strangers against you, || The terrible of the nations, || And they have drawn out their swords || Against the beauty of your wisdom, || And they have pierced your brightness. **8** They bring you down to destruction, || You die by the deaths of the wounded, in the heart of the seas. **9** Do you really say, I [am] God, || Before him who is slaying you? And you [are] man, and not God, || In the hand of him who is piercing you. **10** You die the deaths of the uncircumcised, || By the hand of strangers, for I have spoken," || A declaration of Lord Yhwh. **11** And there is a word of Yhwh to me, saying, **12** "Son of man, lift up a lamentation for the king of Tyre, || And you have said to him, Thus said Lord Yhwh: You are sealing up a measurement, || Full of wisdom, and perfect in beauty. **13** You have been in Eden, the garden of God, || Every precious stone [was] your covering, || Ruby, topaz, and diamond, beryl, onyx, and jasper, || Sapphire, emerald, and carbuncle, and gold, || The workmanship of your tambourines and of your pipes, || In you in the day of your being produced, have been created; **14** And I established you as the anointed, covering cherub, || You have been in [the] holy mountain of God, || You have walked up and down in [the] midst of [the] stones of fire. **15** You [were] perfect in your ways, || From [the] day of your being created, || Until perversity was found in you. **16** By [the] abundance of your merchandise || They have filled your midst with violence, || And you sin, || And I thrust you from [the] mountain of God, || And I destroy you, O covering cherub, || From [the] midst of [the] stones of fire. **17** Your heart has been high because of your beauty, || You have corrupted your wisdom because of your brightness, || I have cast you to earth, || I have set you before kings, to look on you, **18** From [the] abundance of your iniquity, || By [the] perversity of your merchandise, || You have defiled your sanctuaries, || And I bring forth fire from your midst, || It has devoured you, || And I make you become ashes on the earth, || In [the] eyes of all beholding you. **19** All knowing you among the peoples || Have been astonished at you, || You have been terrors, and you are not—for all time." **20** And there is a word of Yhwh to me, saying, **21** "Son of man, set your face toward Sidon, and prophesy concerning it; **22** and you have said, Thus said Lord Yhwh: Behold, I [am] against you, O Sidon, || And I have been honored in your midst, || And they have known that I [am] Yhwh, || In My doing judgments in her, || And I have been sanctified in her. **23** And I have sent pestilence into her, || And blood into her out-places, || The wounded has been judged in her midst, || By the sword on her all around, || And they have known that I [am] Yhwh. **24** And there is no more pricking brier and paining thorn || For the house of Israel, || Of all around them—despising them, || And they have known that I [am] Lord Yhwh. **25** Thus said Lord Yhwh: In My gathering the house of Israel, || Out of the peoples among whom they were scattered, || I have been sanctified in them, || Before the eyes of the nations, || And they have dwelt on their ground, || That I gave to My servant, to Jacob, **26** And they have dwelt confidently on it, || And built houses, and planted vineyards, || And dwelt confidently—in My doing judgments, || On all those despising them all around, || And they have known that I [am] their God Yhwh!"

CHAPTER 29

1 In the tenth year, in the tenth [month], on the twelfth of the month, a word of Yhwh has been to me, saying, **2** "Son of man, set your face against Pharaoh king of Egypt, and prophesy concerning him, and concerning Egypt—all of it. **3** Speak, and you have said, Thus said Lord Yhwh: Behold, I [am] against you, || Pharaoh king of Egypt! The great dragon that is crouching in the midst of his floods, || Who has said, My flood [is] my own, || And I have made it [for] myself. **4** And I have put hooks in your jaws, || And I have caused the fish of your floods to cleave to your scales, || And I have caused you to come up from the midst of your floods, || And every fish of your floods cleaves to your scales. **5** And I have left you in the wilderness, || You and every fish of your floods, || You fall on the face of the field, || You are not gathered nor assembled, || I have given you for food to the beast of the earth and to the bird of the heavens. **6** And all inhabitants of Egypt have known || That I [am] Yhwh, || Because of their being a staff of reed

to the house of Israel. **7** In their taking hold of you by your hand, || You crush and have torn every shoulder of theirs, || And in their leaning on you you are broken, || And have caused all their thighs to stand. **8** Therefore, thus said Lord Yhwh: Behold, I am bringing in a sword against you, || And have cut off man and beast from you. **9** And the land of Egypt has been for a desolation and a ruin, || And they have known that I [am] Yhwh, || Because he said: The flood [is] mine, and I made [it]. **10** Therefore, behold, I [am] against you, and against your floods, || And have given the land of Egypt for ruins, || A dry place, a desolation, from Migdol to Syene, || And to the border of Cush. **11** A foot of man does not pass over into it, || Indeed, the foot of beast does not pass into it, || Nor is it inhabited forty years. **12** And I have made the land of Egypt a desolation, || In the midst of desolate lands, || And its cities, in the midst of cities [that are] laid waste, || Are a desolation [for] forty years, || And I have scattered the Egyptians among nations, || And I have dispersed them through lands. **13** But thus said Lord Yhwh: At the end of forty years I gather the Egyptians || Out of the peoples to where they have been scattered, **14** And I have turned back [to] the captivity of Egypt, || And I have brought them back || [To] the land of Pathros, to the land of their birth, || And they have been a low kingdom there. **15** It is lowest of the kingdoms, || And it does not lift itself up above the nations anymore, || And I have made them few, || So as not to rule among nations. **16** And it is no longer for confidence to the house of Israel, || Bringing iniquity to remembrance, || By their turning after them, || And they have known that I [am] Lord Yhwh." **17** And it comes to pass, in the twenty-seventh year, in the first [month], on the first of the month, a word of Yhwh has been to me, saying, **18** "Son of man, Nebuchadnezzar king of Babylon, || Has caused his force to serve a great service against Tyre, || Every head [is] bald—every shoulder peeled, || And neither he, nor his force, had reward out of Tyre, || For the service that he served against it. **19** Therefore, thus said Lord Yhwh: Behold, I am giving the land of Egypt to Nebuchadnezzar king of Babylon, || And he has taken away its store, || And has taken its spoil, and taken its prey, || And it has been a reward to his force. **20** I have given to him his wage for which he labored—The land of Egypt, in that they worked for Me, || A declaration of Lord Yhwh. **21** In that day I cause a horn to shoot up for the house of Israel, || And I give an opening to your mouth in their midst, || And they have known that I [am] Yhwh!"

CHAPTER 30

1 And there is a word of Yhwh to me, saying, **2** "Son of man, prophesy, and you have said, Thus said Lord Yhwh: Howl, Aah! For the day! **3** For a day [is] near, a day [is] near to Yhwh! It is a time of cloud [over] the nations. **4** And a sword has come into Egypt, || And there has been great pain in Cush, || In the falling of the wounded in Egypt, || And they have taken its store, || And its foundations have been broken down. **5** Cush, and Phut, and Lud, and all the mixture, and Chub, || And the sons of the land of the covenant fall by sword with them, **6** Thus said Yhwh: And those supporting Egypt have fallen, || And the arrogance of her strength has come down, || From Migdol to Syene, they fall by sword in her, || A declaration of Lord Yhwh. **7** And they have been desolated in the midst of desolate lands, || And its cities are in the midst of cities [that are] laid waste. **8** And they have known that I [am] Yhwh, || In My giving fire against Egypt, || And all her helpers have been broken. **9** In that day messengers go forth from before Me in ships, || To trouble confident Cush, || And there has been great pain among them, || As the day of Egypt, for behold, it has come. **10** Thus said Lord Yhwh: I have caused the multitude of Egypt to cease, || By the hand of Nebuchadnezzar king of Babylon, **11** He and his people with him—the terrible of nations, || Are brought in to destroy the land, || And they have drawn their swords against Egypt, || And have filled the land [with] the wounded. **12** And I have made floods a dry place, || And I have sold the land into the hand of evildoers, || And I have made the land desolate, || And its fullness, by the hand of strangers, || I, Yhwh, have spoken. **13** Thus said Lord Yhwh: And I have destroyed idols, || And caused vain things to cease from Noph, || And there is no longer a prince of the land of Egypt, || And I give fear in the land of Egypt. **14** And I have made Pathros desolate, || And I have given fire against Zoan, || And I have done judgments in No, **15** And I have poured out My fury on Sin, the stronghold of Egypt, || And I have cut off the multitude of No. **16** And I have given fire against Egypt, || Sin is greatly pained, and No is to be broken, || And Noph has daily distresses. **17** The youths of Aven and Pi-Beseth fall by sword, || And these go into captivity. **18** And the day has been dark in Tehaphnehes, || In My breaking the yokes of Egypt there, || And the excellence of her strength has ceased in her, || Her! A cloud covers her, || And her daughters go into captivity. **19** And I have done judgments in Egypt, || And they have known that I [am] Yhwh." **20** And it comes to pass, in the eleventh year, in the first [month], on the seventh of the month, a word of Yhwh has been to me, saying, "Son of man, **21** I have broken the arm of Pharaoh, king of Egypt, || And behold, it has not been bound up to give healing, || To put a bandage to bind it, || To strengthen it—to lay hold on the sword. **22** Therefore, thus said Lord Yhwh: Behold, I [am] against Pharaoh, king of Egypt, || And I have broken his arms, || The strong one and the broken one, || And have caused the sword to fall out of his hand, **23** And I have scattered the Egyptians among nations, || And have spread them through lands, **24** And I have strengthened the arms of the king of Babylon, || And have given My sword into his hand, || And I have broken the arms of Pharaoh, || And he has groaned the groans of a pierced one—before him. **25** And I have strengthened the arms of the king of Babylon, || And the arms of Pharaoh fall down, || And they have known that I [am] Yhwh, || In My giving My sword into the hand of the king of Babylon, || And he has stretched it out toward the land of Egypt. **26** And I have scattered the Egyptians among nations, || And I have spread them through lands, || And they have known that I [am] Yhwh!"

CHAPTER 31

1 And it comes to pass, in the eleventh year, in the third [month], on the first of the month, a word of Yhwh has been to me, saying, **2** "Son of man, say to Pharaoh king of Egypt, and to his multitude: To whom have you been like in your greatness? **3** Behold, Asshur, a cedar in Lebanon, || Beautiful in branch, and shading bough, and high in stature, || And its foliage has been between thickets. **4** Waters have made it great, || The deep has exalted him with its flowings, || Going around its planting, || And it has sent forth its conduits to all trees of the field. **5** Therefore his stature has been higher than all trees of the field, || And his boughs are multiplied, and his branches are long, || Because of many waters in his shooting forth. **6** Every bird of the heavens has made a nest in his boughs, || And every beast of the field has brought forth under his branches, || And all great nations dwell in his shade. **7** And he is beautiful in his greatness, || In the length of his thin shoots, || For his root has been by great waters. **8** Cedars have not hid him in the garden of God, || Firs have not been like to his boughs, || And plane-trees have not been as his branches, || No tree in the garden of God has been like to him in his beauty, **9** I have made him beautiful in the multitude of his thin shoots, || And all trees of Eden that [are] in the garden of God envy him. **10** Therefore, thus said Lord Yhwh: Because that you have been high in stature, || And he yields his foliage between thickets, || And his heart is high in his haughtiness, **11** I give him into the hand of a god of nations, || He deals severely with him, || In his wickedness I have cast him out. **12** And strangers cut him off, || The terrible of nations, and they leave him, || His thin shoots have fallen on the mountains and in all valleys, || And his boughs are broken at all streams of the land, || And all peoples of the land go down from his shade, and they leave him. **13** Every bird of the heavens dwells on his ruin, || And all beasts of the field have been on his boughs, **14** In order that none of the trees of the waters || May become haughty because of their stature, || Nor give their foliage between thickets, || Nor any drinking waters stand up to them in their haughtiness, || For all of them are given up to death, || To the lower earth, || In the midst of the sons of men, || To those going down to the pit. **15** Thus said Lord Yhwh: I have caused mourning in the day of his going down to Sheol, || I have covered the deep over him, and diminish its flowings, || And many waters are restrained, || And I make Lebanon black for him, || And all trees of the field [have been] a covering for him. **16** I have caused nations to shake at the sound of his fall, || In My causing him to go down to Sheol, || With those going down to the pit, || And all trees of Eden are comforted in the lower earth, || The choice and good of Lebanon—All drinking waters. **17** Those with him have also gone down to Sheol, || To the pierced of the sword, || And his arm—they dwelt in his shade

in the midst of nations. **18** To whom have you been thus like, || In glory and in greatness among the trees of Eden? And you have been brought down with the trees of Eden, || To the lower earth, || You lie in the midst of the uncircumcised, || With the pierced of the sword. This [is] Pharaoh, and all his multitude, || A declaration of Lord Yhwh!"

CHAPTER 32

1 And it comes to pass, in the twelfth year, in the twelfth month, on the first of the month, a word of Yhwh has been to me, saying, **2** "Son of man, lift up a lamentation for Pharaoh king of Egypt, and you have said to him: You have been like a young lion of nations, || And you [are] as a dragon in the seas, || And you come forth with your flowings, || And trouble the waters with your feet, || And you foul their flowings. **3** Thus said Lord Yhwh: And I have spread out My net for you, || With an assembly of many peoples, || And they have brought you up in My net. **4** And I have left you in the land, || I cast you out on the face of the field, || And I have caused every bird of the heavens to dwell on you, || And have satisfied every beast of the earth with you. **5** And I have put your flesh on the mountains, || And filled the valleys [with] your heap, **6** And watered the land with your flowing, || From your blood—to the mountains, || And streams are filled with you. **7** And in quenching you I have covered the heavens, || And have made their stars black, || I cover the sun with a cloud, || And the moon does not cause its light to shine. **8** I make all luminaries of light in the heavens black over you, || And I have given darkness over your land, || A declaration of Lord Yhwh, **9** And I have distressed the heart of many peoples, || In My bringing in your destruction among nations, || To lands that you have not known. **10** And I have made many peoples astonished at you, || And their kings are afraid because of you with trembling, || In My brandishing My sword before their faces, || And they have trembled every moment, || Each for his life—in the day of your fall. **11** For thus said Lord Yhwh: A sword of the king of Babylon enters you, **12** I cause your multitude to fall by swords of the mighty, || The terrible of nations—all of them, || And they have spoiled the excellence of Egypt, || And all her multitude has been destroyed. **13** And I have destroyed all her beasts, || From beside many waters, || And a foot of man does not trouble them anymore, || Indeed, the hooves of beasts do not trouble them. **14** Then I cause their waters to sink, || And I cause their rivers to go as oil, || A declaration of Lord Yhwh. **15** In My making the land of Egypt a desolation, || And the land has been desolated of its fullness, || In My striking all the inhabitants in it, || Then they have known that I [am] Yhwh. **16** It [is] a lamentation, and they have lamented her, || Daughters of the nations lament her, || For Egypt, and for all her multitude, they lament her, || A declaration of Lord Yhwh." **17** And it comes to pass, in the twelfth year, on the fifteenth of the month, a word of Yhwh has been to me, saying, **18** "Son of man, || Wail for the multitude of Egypt, || And cause it to go down, || It, and the daughters of majestic nations, || To the lower parts of the earth, || With those going down to the pit. **19** Whom have you surpassed in beauty? Go down, and be laid with [the] uncircumcised. **20** They fall in the midst of the pierced of the sword, || She has been given [to] the sword, || They drew her out, and all her multitude. **21** The gods of the mighty speak to him out of the midst of Sheol, || With his helpers— they have gone down, || They have lain with the uncircumcised, || The pierced of the sword. **22** There [is] Asshur, and all her assembly, || His graves [are] around him, || All of them [are] wounded, who are falling by sword, **23** Whose graves are appointed in the sides of the pit, || And her assembly is around her grave, || All of them wounded, falling by sword, || Because they gave terror in the land of the living. **24** There [is] Elam, and all her multitude, || Around her grave, || All of them wounded, who are falling by sword, || Who have gone down uncircumcised to the lower parts of the earth, || Because they gave their terror in the land of the living, || And they bear their shame with those going down to the pit. **25** They have appointed a bed for her in the midst of the wounded, || With all her multitude, || Her graves [are] around them, || All of them uncircumcised, pierced of the sword, || For their terror was given in the land of the living, || And they bear their shame with those going down to the pit, || He has been set in the midst of the pierced. **26** There [is] Meshech, Tubal, and all her multitude, || Her graves [are] around them, || All of them uncircumcised, pierced by the sword, || For they gave their terror in the land of the living, 27 And they do not lie with the mighty, || Who are falling of the uncircumcised, || Who have gone down to Sheol with their weapons of war, || And they put their swords under their heads, || And their iniquities are on their bones, || For the terror of the mighty [is] in the land of the living. 28 And you are broken in the midst of the uncircumcised, || And lie with the pierced of the sword. 29 There [is] Edom, her kings, and all her princes, || Who have been given up in their might, || With the pierced of the sword, || They lie with the uncircumcised, || And with those going down to the pit. 30 There [are] princes of the north, || All of them, and every Zidonian, || Who have gone down with the pierced in their terror, || They are ashamed of their might, || And they lie uncircumcised with the pierced of the sword, || And they bear their shame with those going down to the pit. 31 Then Pharaoh sees, || And he has been comforted for all his multitude, || The pierced of the sword—Pharaoh and all his force, || A declaration of Lord Yhwh. 32 For I have given his terror in the land of the living, || And he has been laid down in [the] midst of [the] uncircumcised, || With [the] pierced of [the] sword—Pharaoh, and all his multitude, || A declaration of Lord Yhwh!"

CHAPTER 33

1 And there is a word of Yhwh to me, saying, 2 "Son of man, speak to the sons of your people, and you have said to them: When I bring a sword on a land, || And the people of the land have taken one man out of their borders, || And made him their watchman, 3 And he has seen the sword coming against the land, || And has blown with a horn, and has warned the people, 4 And the hearer has heard the voice of the horn, and he has not taken warning, || And the sword comes in, and takes him away, || His blood is on his [own] head. 5 The voice of the horn he heard, || And he has not taken warning, his blood is on him, || And he who took warning has delivered his soul. 6 And the watchman, when he sees the sword coming in, || And he has not blown with a horn, || And the people have not been warned, || And a sword comes in, || And takes away a soul from them, || He is taken away in his iniquity, || And I require his blood from the hand of the watchman. 7 And you, son of man, || I gave you [as] a watchman for the house of Israel, || And you have heard a word from My mouth, || And you have warned them from Me. 8 In My saying to the wicked, O wicked one—you surely die, || And you have not spoken to warn the wicked from his way, || He—the wicked—dies in his iniquity, || And I require his blood from your hand. 9 And you, when you have warned the wicked of his way, to turn back from it, || And he has not turned back from his way, || He dies in his iniquity, || And you have delivered your soul. 10 And you, son of man, say to the house of Israel: You have spoken correctly, saying, || Surely our transgressions and our sins [are] on us, || And we are wasting away in them, || How, then, do we live? 11 Say to them, [As] I live—a declaration of Lord Yhwh, || I do not delight in the death of the wicked, || But in the turning of the wicked from his way, and he has lived. Turn back, turn back, from your evil ways! Indeed, why do you die, O house of Israel? 12 And you, son of man, say to the sons of your people: The righteousness of the righteous does not deliver him in the day of his transgression, || And the wickedness of the wicked, || He does not stumble for it in the day of his turning from his wickedness, || And the righteous is not able to live in it in the day of his sinning. 13 In My saying of the righteous: He surely lives, || And—he has trusted on his righteousness, || And he has done perversity, || All his righteous acts are not remembered, || And for his perversity that he has done, || He dies for it. 14 And in My saying to the wicked: You surely die, || And—he has turned back from his sin, || And has done judgment and righteousness, 15 (The wicked restores a pledge, he repays [for] plunder), || He has walked in the statutes of life, || So as not to do perversity, || He surely lives—he does not die. 16 All his sin—his sins that he has sinned—are not remembered against him, || He has done judgment and righteousness, || He surely lives. 17 And the sons of your people have said: The way of the Lord is not pondered, || As for them—their way is not pondered. 18 In the turning back of the righteous from his righteousness, || And he has done perversity—he dies for it. 19 And in the turning back of the wicked from his wickedness, || And he has done judgment and righteousness—he lives by them. 20 And you have said, The way of the Lord is not pondered; I judge each of you according to his ways, O house of Israel." 21 And it comes to pass, in the twelfth year—in the tenth [month], in the fifth of the month—of our removal, one who is escaped from Jerusalem comes to me, saying, "The city has been struck." 22 And the hand of Yhwh has been to me in the evening, before the coming in of the escaped one, and He opens my mouth until [his] coming in to me in the morning, and my mouth is opened, and I have not been silent again. 23 And there is a word of Yhwh to me, saying, 24 "Son of man, the inhabitants of these ruins on the ground of Israel are speaking, saying, Abraham has been alone—and he possesses the land, and we [are] many—the land has been given to us for a possession. 25 Therefore say to them, Thus said Lord Yhwh: You eat with the blood, || And you lift up your eyes to your idols, || And you shed blood, || Should you then inherit the land? 26 You have stood on your sword, || You have done abomination, || You have each defiled the wife of his neighbor, || Should you then possess the land? 27 Thus you say to them, Thus said Lord Yhwh: [As] I live—do they who [are] in the ruins not fall by the sword? And they who [are] on the face of the field, || I have given for food to the beast, || And they who are in strongholds and in caves die by pestilence. 28 And I have made the land a desolation and an astonishment, || And the excellence of its strength has ceased, || And mountains of Israel have been desolated, || Without anyone passing through. 29 And they have known that I [am] Yhwh, || In My making the land a desolation and an astonishment, || For all their abominations that they have done. 30 And you, son of man, || The sons of your people who are speaking about you, || By the walls, and in openings of the houses, || Have spoken with one another, each with his brother, || Saying, Please come in, || And hear what the word [is] that comes out from Yhwh. 31 And they come in to you as the coming in of a people, || And they sit before you—My people, || And have heard your words, and they do not do them, || For they are making unhealthy loves with their mouth, || Their heart is going after their dishonest gain. 32 And behold, you [are] as a singer of unhealthy loves to them, || A beautiful voice, and playing well on an instrument, || And they have heard your words, and they are not doing them. 33 And in its coming in—behold, it has come, || And they have known that a prophet has been in their midst!"

CHAPTER 34

1 And there is a word of Yhwh to me, saying, 2 "Son of man, prophesy concerning shepherds of Israel, prophesy, and you have said to them, Thus said Lord Yhwh to the shepherds: Woe [to] the shepherds of Israel, || Who have been feeding themselves! Do the shepherds not feed the flock? 3 You eat the fat, and you put on the wool, || You slaughter the fed one, || You do not feed the flock. 4 You have not strengthened the weak, || And you have not healed the sick one, || And you have not bound up the broken, || And have not brought back the driven away, || And you have not sought the lost, || And you have ruled them with might and with rigor. 5 And they are scattered from want of a shepherd, || And are for food to every beast of the field, || Indeed, they are scattered. 6 My flock goes astray on all the mountains, || And on every high hill, || And My flock has been scattered on [the] whole face of the earth, || And there is none inquiring, and none seeking. 7 Therefore, shepherds, hear a word of Yhwh: 8 [As] I live—a declaration of Lord Yhwh, || If not, because of My flock being for a prey, || Indeed, My flock is for food to every beast of the field, || Because there is no shepherd, || And My shepherds have not sought My flock, || And the shepherds feed themselves, || And they have not fed My flock. 9 Therefore, O shepherds, hear a word of Yhwh! 10 Thus said Lord Yhwh: Behold, I [am] against the shepherds, || And have required My flock from their hand, || And caused them to cease from feeding the flock, || And the shepherds feed themselves no more, || And I have delivered My flock from their mouth, || And they are not for food to them. 11 For thus said Lord Yhwh: Behold, I—even I, have required My flock, || And I have sought it out. 12 As a shepherd's searching of his drove, || In the day of his being in the midst of his scattered flock, so I seek My flock, || And have delivered them out of all places, || To where they have been scattered, || In a day of cloud and thick darkness. 13 And I have brought them out from the peoples, || And have gathered them from the lands, || And brought them to their own ground, || And have fed them on mountains of Israel, || By streams, and by all dwellings of the land. 14 I feed them with good pasture, ||

And their habitation is on mountains of the high place of Israel, || There they lie down in a good habitation, || And they enjoy fat pastures on mountains of Israel. **15** I feed My flock, and cause them to lie down, || A declaration of Lord Yhwh. **16** I seek the lost, and bring back the driven away, || And I bind up the broken, and I strengthen the sick, || And I destroy the fat and the strong, || I feed it with judgment. **17** And you, My flock, thus said Lord Yhwh: Behold, I am judging between sheep and sheep, || Between rams and male goats. **18** Is it a little thing for you—[that] you enjoy the good pasture, || And tread down the remnant of your pasture with your feet, || And drink a depth of waters, || And trample the remainder with your feet, **19** And My flock consumes the trodden thing of your feet, || And drinks the trampled thing of your feet? **20** Therefore, thus said Lord Yhwh to them: Behold, I—even I, have judged between fat sheep and lean sheep. **21** Because you thrust away with side and with shoulder, || And push all the diseased with your horns, || Until you have scattered them to the out-place, **22** Therefore I have given safety to My flock, || And they are not for prey anymore, || And I have judged between sheep and sheep. **23** And have raised up one shepherd over them, || And he has fed them—My servant David, || He feeds them, and he is their shepherd, **24** And I, Yhwh, I am their God, || And My servant David [is] prince in their midst, || I, Yhwh, have spoken. **25** And I have made a covenant of peace with them, || And caused evil beasts to cease out of the land, || And they have dwelt confidently in a wilderness, || And they have slept in forests. **26** And I have given them, and the outskirts of My hill, a blessing, || And caused the shower to come down in its season, || They are showers of blessing. **27** And the tree of the field has given its fruit, || And the land gives her increase, || And they have been confident on their land, || And they have known that I [am] Yhwh, || In My breaking the bands of their yoke, || And I have delivered them from the hand of those laying service on them. **28** And they are no longer a prey to nations, || And the beast of the earth does not devour them, || And they have dwelt confidently, || And there is none troubling. **29** And I have raised a plantation of renown for them, || And they are no longer consumed by hunger in the land, || And they no longer bear the shame of the nations. **30** And they have known that I, Yhwh, their God, [am] with them, || And they—the house of Israel—My people, || A declaration of Lord Yhwh. **31** And you, My flock, the flock of My pasture, || You [are] men [and] I [am] your God, || A declaration of Lord Yhwh!"

CHAPTER 35

1 And there is a word of Yhwh to me, saying, **2** "Son of man, set your face against Mount Seir, and prophesy against it, **3** And you have said to it, Thus said Lord Yhwh: Behold, I [am] against you, O Mount Seir, || And have stretched out My hand against you, || And made you a desolation and an astonishment. **4** I make your cities a ruin, and you are a desolation, || And you have known that I [am] Yhwh. **5** Because of your having continuous enmity, || And you saw the sons of Israel, || By the hands of the sword, || In the time of their calamity, || In the time of the iniquity of the end: **6** Therefore, [as] I live—a declaration of Lord Yhwh, || Surely I appoint you for blood, || And blood pursues you, || If you have not hated blood, || Blood also pursues you. **7** And I have given Mount Seir for a desolation and an astonishment, || And have cut off from it him who is passing over and him who is returning, **8** And filled his mountains with his wounded, || Your hills, and your valleys, and all your streams, || The pierced of the sword fall into them. **9** I make you continuous desolations, || And your cities do not return, || And you have known that I [am] Yhwh. **10** Because of your saying: The two nations and the two lands are mine, and we have possessed it, || And Yhwh has been there; **11** Therefore, [as] I live—a declaration of Lord Yhwh, || And I have done according to your anger, || And according to your envy, || With which you have worked, || Because of your hatred against them, || And I have been known among them when I judge you. **12** And you have known that I [am] Yhwh, || I have heard all your despisings that you have spoken || Against mountains of Israel, saying, || A desolation—they were given to us for food. **13** And you magnify yourselves against Me with your mouth, || And have made your words abundant against Me; I have heard. **14** Thus said Lord Yhwh: According to the rejoicing of the whole land, || I make a desolation of you. **15** According to your joy at the inheritance of the house of Israel

because of desolation, || So I do to you—you are a desolation, || O Mount Seir, and all Edom—all of it, || And they have known that I [am] Yhwh!"

CHAPTER 36

1 "And you, son of man, prophesy to mountains of Israel, and you have said, O mountains of Israel, hear a word of Yhwh! **2** Thus said Lord Yhwh: Because the enemy said against you, Aha! The high places of old have also become our possession, **3** therefore, prophesy, and you have said, Thus said Lord Yhwh: Because, even because, of desolating, || And of swallowing you up from all around, || For your being a possession to the remnant of the nations, || And you are taken up on the tip of the tongue, || And [are] an evil report to the people. **4** Therefore, O mountains of Israel, || Hear a word of Lord Yhwh! Thus said Lord Yhwh, to mountains, and to hills, || To streams, and to valleys, || And to ruins that [are] desolate, || And to cities that are forsaken, || That have been for a prey, || And for a scorn, to the remnant of the surrounding nations, **5** Therefore, thus said Lord Yhwh: Have I not, in the fire of My jealousy, || Spoken against the remnant of the nations, || And against Edom—all of it, || Who gave My land to themselves for a possession, || With the joy of the whole heart—with despite of soul, || For the sake of casting it out for a prey? **6** Therefore, prophesy concerning the ground of Israel, || And you have said to mountains, and to hills, || To streams, and to valleys, || Thus said Lord Yhwh: Behold, I, in My jealousy and in My fury, have spoken, || Because you have borne the shame of nations. **7** Therefore, thus said Lord Yhwh: I have lifted up My hand, || Do the nations who [are] surrounding you not bear their own shame? **8** And you, O mountains of Israel, || You give out your branch, || And you bear your fruits for My people Israel, || For they have drawn near to come. **9** For behold, I [am] for you, and have turned to you, || And you have been tilled and sown. **10** And I have multiplied men on you, || All the house of Israel—all of it, || And the cities have been inhabited, || And the ruins are built. **11** And I have multiplied man and beast on you, || And they have multiplied and been fruitful, || And I have caused you to dwell according to your former states, || And I have done better than at your beginnings, || And you have known that I [am] Yhwh. **12** And I have caused man to walk over you—My people Israel, || And they possess you, and you have been their inheritance, || And you no longer add to bereave them. **13** Thus said Lord Yhwh: Because they are saying to you, You [are] a devourer of men, || And you have been a bereaver of your nations, **14** Therefore, you no longer devour man, || And you do not cause your nations to stumble anymore, || A declaration of Lord Yhwh. **15** And I do not proclaim the shame of the nations to you anymore, || And you no longer bear the reproach of peoples, || And your nations do not stumble anymore, || A declaration of Lord Yhwh." **16** And there is a word of Yhwh to me, saying, **17** "Son of man, || The house of Israel are dwelling on their land, || And they defile it by their way and by their doings, || Their way has been as the uncleanness of a separated one before Me. **18** And I pour out My fury on them || For the blood that they shed on the land, || And they have defiled it with their idols. **19** And I scatter them among nations, || And they are spread through lands, || According to their way, and according to their doings, || I have judged them. **20** And one goes to the nations to where they have gone, || And they defile My holy Name by saying to them, || These [are] the people of Yhwh, || And they have gone forth from His land. **21** And I have pity on My holy Name, || That the house of Israel has defiled || Among the nations to where they have gone in. **22** Therefore, say to the house of Israel, Thus said Lord Yhwh: I am not working for your sake, || O house of Israel, but for My holy Name || That you have defiled || Among the nations to where you have gone in. **23** And I have sanctified My great Name, || That is profaned among the nations, || That you have defiled in your midst, || And the nations have known that I [am] Yhwh, || A declaration of Lord Yhwh, || In My being sanctified in you before your eyes. **24** And I have taken you out of the nations, || And have gathered you out of all the lands, || And I have brought you into your land, **25** And I have sprinkled clean water over you, || And you have been clean; I cleanse you from all your uncleannesses, || And from all your idols. **26** And I have given a new heart to you, || And I give a new spirit in your midst, || And I have turned aside the heart of stone out of your flesh, || And I have given a heart of flesh to you. **27** And I give My Spirit in your midst, || And I have done this, so that you walk in My statutes, || And you keep My judgments, and have done them. **28** And you have dwelt in the land that I have given to your fathers, || And you have been to Me for a people, || And I am to you for God. **29** And I have saved you from all your uncleannesses, || And I have called to the grain, and multiplied it, || And I have put no famine on you. **30** And I have multiplied the fruit of the tree, || And the increase of the field, || So that you do not receive a reproach of famine among nations anymore. **31** And you have remembered your ways that [are] evil, || And your doings that [are] not good, || And have been loathsome in your own faces, || For your iniquities, and for your abominations. **32** I am not working for your sake, || A declaration of Lord Yhwh, || Be it known to you, || Be ashamed and confounded, because of your ways, || O house of Israel. **33** Thus said Lord Yhwh: In the day of My cleansing you from all your iniquities, || I have caused the cities to be inhabited, || And the ruins have been built, **34** And the desolate land is tilled, || Instead of which it was a desolation before the eyes of everyone passing by, **35** And they have said: This land, that was desolated, || Has been as the Garden of Eden, || And the cities—the dried up, || And the desolated, and the broken down, || [And the] fortified have remained. **36** And the nations who are left around you have known || That I, Yhwh, have built the thrown down, || I have planted the desolated: I, Yhwh, have spoken, and I have done [it]. **37** Thus said Lord Yhwh: Yet this I am inquired of by the house of Israel to do for them: I multiply them as a flock of men, **38** As a flock of holy ones, as a flock of Jerusalem, || In her appointed times, || So the dried up cities are full of flocks of man, || And they have known that I [am] Yhwh!"

CHAPTER 37

1 There has been a hand of Yhwh on me, and He takes me forth in [the] Spirit of Yhwh, and places me in the midst of the valley, and it is full of bones, **2** and He causes me to pass over by them, all around, and behold, very many [are] on the face of the valley, and behold—very dry. **3** And He says to me, "Son of man, do these bones live?" And I say, "O Lord Yhwh, You have known." **4** And He says to me, "Prophesy concerning these bones, and you have said to them, O dry bones, hear a word of Yhwh! **5** Thus said Lord Yhwh to these bones: Behold, I am bringing a spirit into you, and you have lived, **6** and I have given sinews on you, and cause flesh to come up on you, and covered you over with skin, and given a spirit in you, and you have lived, and you have known that I [am] Yhwh." **7** And I have prophesied as I have been commanded, and there is a noise as I am prophesying, and behold, a rushing, and the bones draw near, bone to its bone. **8** And I beheld, and behold, sinews [are] on them, and flesh has come up, and skin covers them over above—and there is no spirit in them. **9** And He says to me: "Prophesy to the Spirit, prophesy, son of man, and you have said to the Spirit, Thus said Lord Yhwh: Come in from the four winds, O Spirit, and breathe on these slain, and they live." **10** And I have prophesied as He commanded me, and the Spirit comes into them, and they live, and stand on their feet—a very, very great force. **11** And He says to me, "Son of man, these bones are the whole house of Israel; behold, they are saying, Our bones have dried up, || And our hope has perished, || We have been cut off by ourselves. **12** Therefore, prophesy, and you have said to them, Thus said Lord Yhwh: Behold, I am opening your graves, || And have brought you up out of your graves, O My people, || And brought you into the land of Israel. **13** And you have known that I [am] Yhwh, || In My opening your graves, || And in My bringing you up out of your graves, O My people. **14** And I have given My Spirit in you, and you have lived, || And I have caused you to rest on your land, || And you have known that I, Yhwh, have spoken, and I have done [it], || A declaration of Yhwh." **15** And there is a word of Yhwh to me, saying, **16** "And you, son of man, take one stick for yourself, and write on it, || For Judah, and for the sons of Israel, his companions; and take another stick, and write on it, || For Joseph, the stick of Ephraim, and all the house of Israel, his companions, **17** and bring them near to one another, to you, for one stick, and they have become one in your hand. **18** And when sons of your people speak to you, saying, Do you not declare to us what these [are] to you? **19** Speak to them, Thus said Lord Yhwh: Behold, I am taking the stick of Joseph, that [is] in the hand of Ephraim, and the tribes of Israel his companions, and have given them to him, with the stick of Judah, and have made them become one stick, and they have

been one in My hand. **20** And the sticks on which you write have been in your hand before your eyes, **21** and speak to them, Thus said Lord Yhwh: Behold, I am taking the sons of Israel, || From among the nations to where they have gone, || And have gathered them from all around, || And I have brought them into their land. **22** And I have made them become one nation in the land, on mountains of Israel, || And one king is to them all for king, || And they are no longer as two nations, || Nor are they divided anymore into two kingdoms again. **23** Nor are they defiled anymore with their idols, || And with their abominations, || And with any of their transgressions, || And I have saved them out of all their dwellings, || In which they have sinned, || And I have cleansed them, || And they have been to Me for a people, || And I am to them for God. **24** And My servant David [is] king over them, || And they all have one shepherd, || And they go in My judgments, || And they keep My statutes, and have done them. **25** And they have dwelt on the land that I gave to My servant, to Jacob, || In which your fathers have dwelt, || And they have dwelt on it, they and their sons, || And their son's sons—for all time, || And My servant David [is] their prince for all time. **26** And I have made a covenant of peace with them, || It is a perpetual covenant with them, || And I have placed them, and multiplied them, || And placed My sanctuary in their midst for all time. **27** And My dwelling place has been over them, || And I have been to them for God, || And they have been to Me for a people. **28** And the nations have known that I, Yhwh, am sanctifying Israel, || In My sanctuary being in their midst for all time!"

CHAPTER 38

1 And there is a word of Yhwh to me, saying, **2** "Son of man, set your face toward Gog, of the land of Magog, chief prince of [[or prince of Rosh,]] Meshech and Tubal, and prophesy concerning him, **3** and you have said, Thus said Lord Yhwh: Behold, I [am] against you, O Gog, || Chief prince of [[or prince of Rosh,]] Meshech and Tubal, **4** And I have turned you back, || And I have put hooks in your jaws, || And have brought you out, and all your force, || Horses and horsemen, || All of them clothed in perfection, || A numerous assembly, [with] buckler and shield, || All of them handling swords. **5** Persia, Cush, and Phut, with them, || All of them [with] shield and helmet. **6** Gomer and all its bands, || The house of Togarmah [from] the sides of the north, || And all its bands, many peoples with you, **7** Be prepared, indeed, prepare yourself, || You and all your assemblies who are assembled to you, || And you have been for a watch for them. **8** After many days you are appointed, || In the latter end of the years you come into a land brought back from sword—Gathered out of many peoples, || On mountains of Israel, || That have been for a continuous ruin, || And it has been brought out from the peoples, || And all of them have dwelt safely. **9** And you have gone up—you come in as desolation, || You are as a cloud to cover the land, || You and all your bands, and many peoples with you. **10** Thus said Lord Yhwh: And it has come to pass in that day, || Things come up on your heart, || And you have thought an evil thought, **11** And you have said: I go up over a land of open places, || I go to those at rest, dwelling confidently, || All of them are dwelling without walls, || And they have no bar and doors— **12** To take a spoil, and to take a prey, || To turn back your hand on inhabited ruins, || And on a people gathered out of nations, || Making livestock and substance, || Dwelling on a high part of the land. **13** Sheba, and Dedan, and merchants of Tarshish, || And all its young lions say to you, || Are you coming to take spoil? Have you assembled your assembly to take prey? To carry away silver and gold? To take away livestock and substance? To take a great spoil? **14** Therefore, prophesy, son of man, and you have said to Gog, Thus said Lord Yhwh: In that day, in the dwelling of My people Israel safely, || Do you not know? **15** And you have come in out of your place, || From the sides of the north, || You and many peoples with you, || Riding on horses—all of them, || A great assembly, and a numerous force. **16** And you have come up against My people Israel, || As a cloud to cover the land, || It is in the latter end of the days, || And I have brought you in against My land, || In order that the nations may know Me, || In My being sanctified in you before their eyes, O Gog. **17** Thus said Lord Yhwh: Are you he of whom I spoke in former days, || By the hand of My servants, prophets of Israel, || Who were prophesying [for] years in those days, || To bring you in against them? **18** And it has come to pass in that day, || In the day of the coming in of Gog against the land of Israel, || A declaration of Lord Yhwh, || My fury comes up in My face, **19** And in My zeal, in the fire of My wrath, || I have spoken: Is there not a great rushing on the land of Israel in that day? **20** And rushed from My presence have fishes of the sea, || And the bird of the heavens, || And the beast of the field, || And every creeping thing that is creeping on the ground, || And all men who [are] on the face of the ground, || And the mountains have been thrown down, || And the ascents have fallen, || And every wall falls to the earth. **21** And I have called for a sword against him throughout all My mountains, || A declaration of Lord Yhwh, || The sword of each is against his brother. **22** And I have judged him with pestilence and with blood, || And an overflowing rain and hailstones, || I rain fire and brimstone on him, and on his bands, || And on many peoples who [are] with him. **23** And I have magnified Myself, and sanctified Myself, || And I have been known before the eyes of many nations, || And they have known that I [am] Yhwh!"

CHAPTER 39

1 "And you, son of man, prophesy concerning Gog, and you have said, Thus said Lord Yhwh: Behold, I [am] against you, O Gog, || Chief prince of [[or prince of Rosh,]] Meshech and Tubal, **2** And have turned you back, and enticed you, || And caused you to come up from the sides of the north, || And brought you in against mountains of Israel, **3** And have struck your bow out of your left hand, || Indeed, I cause your arrows to fall out of your right. **4** You fall on mountains of Israel, || You, and all your bands, and the peoples who [are] with you, || To ravenous bird—a bird of every wing, || And [to] a beast of the field, I have given you for food. **5** You fall on the face of the field, for I have spoken, || A declaration of Lord Yhwh. **6** And I have sent a fire against Magog, || And against the confident inhabitants of the islands, || And they have known that I [am] Yhwh. **7** And I make My holy Name known in the midst of My people Israel, || And I do not defile My holy Name anymore, || And the nations have known that I, Yhwh, the Holy One, [am] in Israel. **8** Behold, it has come, and it has been done, || A declaration of Lord Yhwh, || It [is] the day of which I spoke. **9** And those dwelling [in the] cities of Israel have gone out, || And they have burned and kindled [a fire], || With armor, and shield, and buckler, || With bow, and with arrows, || And with hand weapon, and with javelin, || And they have caused a fire to burn seven years with them, **10** And they do not take wood out of the field, || Nor do they hew out of the forests, || For they cause the fire to burn with armor, || And they have spoiled their spoilers, || And they have plundered their plunderers, || A declaration of Lord Yhwh. **11** And it has come to pass in that day, I give a place to Gog there—a grave in Israel, the valley of those passing by, east of the sea, and it is stopping those passing by, and they have buried there Gog, and all his multitude, and have cried, O valley of the multitude of Gog! **12** And the house of Israel has buried them—in order to cleanse the land—seven months. **13** Indeed, all the people of the land have buried them, and it has been to them for a name—the day of My being honored—a declaration of Lord Yhwh. **14** And they separate men for continual employment, with those passing through, passing on through the land, burying those who are left on the face of the earth, to cleanse it. At the end of seven months they search. **15** And those passing by have passed through the land, and seen a bone of man, and one has constructed a sign near it until those burying have buried it in the valley of the multitude of Gog. **16** And also the name of the city [is] The Multitude; and they have cleansed the land. **17** And you, son of man, thus said Lord Yhwh: Say to the bird—every wing, and to every beast of the field: Be assembled and come in, || Be gathered from all around, || For My sacrifice that I am sacrificing for you, || A great sacrifice on mountains of Israel, || And you have eaten flesh, and drunk blood. **18** You eat [the] flesh of [the] mighty, || And you drink [the] blood of [the] princes of the earth, || Of rams, of lambs, and of male goats, || Of calves, fatlings of Bashan—all of them. **19** And you have eaten fat to satiety, || And you have drunk blood—to drunkenness, || Of My sacrifice that I sacrificed for you. **20** And you have been satisfied at My table with horse and rider, || Mighty man, and every man of war, || A declaration of Lord Yhwh. **21** And I have given My glory among nations, || And all the nations have seen My judgment that I have done, || And My hand that I have laid on them. **22** And the house of Israel has known that I [am] their God Yhwh, || From that day and

from now on. **23** And the nations have known || That the house of Israel was removed for their iniquity, || Because they have trespassed against Me, || And I hide My face from them, || And give them into the hand of their adversaries, || And they fall by sword—all of them. **24** According to their uncleanness, || And according to their transgressions, I have done with them, || And I hide My face from them. **25** Therefore, thus said Lord Yhwh: Now I bring back the captivity of Jacob, || And I have pitied all the house of Israel, || And have been zealous for My holy Name. **26** And they have forgotten their shame, || And all their trespass that they trespassed against Me, || In their dwelling on their land confidently and none troubling. **27** In My bringing them back from the peoples, || I have assembled them from the lands of their enemies, || And I have been sanctified in them before the eyes of the many nations, **28** And they have known that I [am] their God Yhwh, || In My removing them to the nations, || And I have gathered them to their land, || And I leave none of them there anymore. **29** And I do not hide My face from them anymore, || In that I have poured out My Spirit on the house of Israel, || A declaration of Lord Yhwh!"

CHAPTER 40

1 In the twenty-fifth year of our removal, in the beginning of the year, on the tenth of the month, in the fourteenth year after which the city was struck, on this very same day a hand of Yhwh has been on me, and He brings me in there; **2** in visions of God He has brought me into the land of Israel, and causes me to rest on a very high mountain, and on it [is] as the frame of a city from the south. **3** And He brings me in there, and behold, a man, his appearance as the appearance of bronze, and a thread of flax in his hand, and a measuring-reed, and he is standing at the gate, **4** and the man speaks to me: "Son of man, see with your eyes, || And hear with your ears, || And set your heart to all that I am showing you, || For in order to show [it] you, || You have been brought in here, || Declare all that you are seeing to the house of Israel." **5** And behold, a wall all around on the outside of the house, and a measuring-reed in the hand of the man, six cubits by a cubit and a handbreadth, and he measures the breadth of the building—one reed, and the height—one reed. **6** And he comes to the gate whose front [is] eastward, and he goes up by its steps, and he measures the threshold of the gate—one reed broad, even one threshold—one reed broad, **7** and the little chamber—one reed long and one reed broad, and between the little chambers—five cubits, and the threshold of the gate, from the side of the porch of the gate from within—one reed. **8** And he measures the porch of the gate from within—one reed, **9** and he measures the porch of the gate—eight cubits, and its posts—two cubits, and the porch of the gates from within, **10** and the little chambers of the gate eastward, three on this side and three on that side; the three of them—one measure, and the posts—one measure, on this side and on that side. **11** And he measures the breadth of the opening of the gate—ten cubits, the length of the gate—thirteen cubits; **12** and a border before the little chambers—one cubit, and one cubit [is] the border on this side, and the little chamber—six cubits on this side, and six cubits on that side. **13** And he measures the gate from the roof of the [one] little chamber to the roof of another; the breadth—twenty-five cubits, opening opposite opening. **14** And he makes the posts of sixty cubits, even to the post of the court, the gate all around; **15** and by the front of the gate of the entrance, by the front of the porch of the inner gate—fifty cubits; **16** and narrow windows [are] in the little chambers, and in their posts on the inside of the gate all around—and so to the arches—and windows all around on the inside, and palm-trees [are] on the post. **17** And he brings me into the outer court, and behold, chambers and a pavement made for the court all around—thirty chambers on the pavement— **18** and the pavement to the side of the gates, corresponding to the length of the gates, [is] the lower pavement; **19** and he measures the breadth from before the lower gate, to the front of the inner court, on the outside—one hundred cubits, eastward and northward. **20** As for the gate of the outer court whose front [is] northward, he has measured its length and its breadth; **21** and its little chambers, three on this side and three on that side, and its posts and its arches have been according to the measure of the first gate, its length [is] fifty cubits, and breadth [is] twenty-five by the cubit; **22** and its windows, and its arches, and its palm-trees [are] according to the measure of the gate whose face [is] eastward, and they go up on it by seven steps, and its arches [are] before them. 23 And the gate of the inner court [is] opposite the gate at the north and at the east; and he measures from gate to gate—one hundred cubits. 24 And he causes me to go southward, and behold, a gate southward, and he has measured its posts and its arches according to these measurements; 25 and windows [are] in it and in its arches all around, like these windows, the length—fifty cubits, and the breadth—twenty-five cubits; 26 and seven steps [are] its ascent, and its arches [are] before them, and palm-trees [are] in it, one on this side and one on that side, on its posts; 27 and the gate of the inner court [is] southward, and he measures from gate to gate southward, one hundred cubits. 28 And he brings me into the inner court by the south gate, and he measures the south gate according to these measurements; 29 and its little chambers, and its posts, and its arches [are] according to these measurements, and windows [are] in it and in its arches all around; the length—fifty cubits, and the breadth—twenty-five cubits. 30 As for the arches all around, the length—twenty-five cubits, and the breadth—five cubits; 31 and its arches [are] toward the outer court, and palm-trees [are] on its posts, and eight steps [are] its ascent. 32 And he brings me into the inner court eastward, and he measures the gate according to these measurements; 33 and its little chambers, and its posts, and its arches [are] according to these measurements: and windows [are] in it and in its arches all around, the length—fifty cubits, and the breadth—twenty-five cubits; 34 and its arches [are] toward the outer court, and palm-trees [are] toward its posts, on this side and on that side, and eight steps [are] its ascent. 35 And he brings me into the north gate, and has measured according to these measurements; 36 its little chambers, its posts, and its arches; and windows [are] in it all around: the length—fifty cubits, and the breadth—twenty-five cubits; 37 and its posts [are] toward the outer court, and palm-trees [are] on its posts, on this side and on that side, and eight steps [are] its ascent. 38 And the chamber and its opening [is] by the posts of the gates, there they purge the burnt-offering. 39 And in the porch of the gate [are] two tables on this side and two tables on that side, to slaughter on them the burnt-offering, and the sin-offering, and the guilt-offering; 40 and at the side without, at the going up to the opening of the north gate, [are] two tables; and at the other side that [is] at the porch of the gate, [are] two tables; 41 four tables [are] on this side and four tables on that side, at the side of the gate, eight tables on which they slaughter. 42 And the four tables for burnt-offering [are] of hewn stone: the length—one cubit and a half, and the breadth—one cubit and a half, and the height—one cubit; they place on them the instruments with which they slaughter the burnt-offering and the sacrifice. 43 And the boundaries [are] one handbreadth, prepared within all around: and the flesh of the offering [is] on the tables. 44 And on the outside of the inner gate [are] chambers of the singers, in the inner court, that [are] at the side of the north gate, and their fronts [are] southward, one at the side of the east gate [with] front northward. 45 And he speaks to me: "This chamber, whose front [is] southward, [is] for priests keeping charge of the house; 46 and the chamber, whose front [is] northward, [is] for priests keeping charge of the altar: they [are] sons of Zadok, who are drawing near of the sons of Levi to Yhwh, to serve Him." 47 And he measures the court: the length—one hundred cubits, and the breadth—one hundred cubits, square, and the altar [is] before the house. 48 And he brings me to the porch of the house, and he measures the post of the porch—five cubits on this side and five cubits on that side, and the breadth of the gate—three cubits on this side and three cubits on that side; 49 the length of the porch—twenty cubits, and the breadth—eleven [[or twelve]] cubits; and they go up to it by the [[ten]] steps. And pillars [are] by the posts, one on this side and one on that side.

CHAPTER 41

1 And he brings me into the temple, and he measures the posts, six cubits the breadth on this side and six cubits the breadth on that side—the breadth of the tent. 2 And the breadth of the opening [is] ten cubits; and the sides of the opening [are] five cubits on this side and five cubits on that side; and he measures its length—forty cubits, and the breadth—twenty cubits. 3 And he has gone inward, and measures the post of the opening—two cubits, and the opening—six cubits, and the breadth of the opening—seven cubits. 4 And he measures its

length—twenty cubits, and the breadth—twenty cubits, to the front of the temple, and he says to me, "This [is] the Holy of Holies." 5 And he measures the wall of the house—six cubits, and the breadth of the side-chamber—four cubits, all around the house. 6 And the side-chambers [are] side-chamber by side-chamber, thirty-three times; and they are entering into the wall—which the house has for the side-chambers all around—to be taken hold of, and they are not taken hold of by the wall of the house. 7 And it has become wider when one has turned even higher toward the side-chambers, for the encompassment of the house [is] even higher all around the house: therefore the breadth of the house [goes] upwards, and so the lower [story] goes up to the higher by the middle. 8 And I have looked at the height all around the house: the foundations of the side-chambers [are] the fullness of the reed, six cubits by the joining. 9 The breadth of that wall, of the side-chamber, at the outside, [is] five cubits; and the space remaining of the side-chambers—that of the house, 10 and between the chambers—[is] a breadth of twenty cubits around the house, all around. 11 And the opening of the side-chamber [is] to the remaining [space], one opening northward and one opening southward, and the breadth of the remaining space [is] five cubits all around. 12 As for the building that [is] at the front of the separate place [at] the corner westward, the breadth [is] seventy cubits, and the wall of the building [is] five cubits broad all around, and its length—ninety cubits. 13 And he has measured the house, the length [is] one hundred cubits; and the separate place, and the building, and its walls, the length [is] one hundred cubits; 14 and the breadth of the front of the house, and of the separate place eastward—one hundred cubits. 15 And he has measured the length of the building to the front of the separate place that [is] at its back part, and its galleries on this side and on that side—one hundred cubits. And the inner temple and the porches of the court, 16 the thresholds, and the narrow windows, and the galleries around the three of them, opposite the threshold, [were] paneled with wood all around—and the ground to the windows, and the windows were covered, 17 over above the opening, and to the inner-house, and at the outside, and by all the wall all around inside and outside [by] measurements. 18 And it is made [with] cherubim and palm-trees, and a palm-tree [is] between cherub and cherub, and two faces [are] on the cherub; 19 and the face of a man toward the palm-tree on this side and the face of a young lion toward the palm-tree on that side; it is made to all the house all around. 20 from the earth to above the opening the cherubim and the palm-trees [were] made, and [on] the wall of the temple. 21 The doorpost of the temple [is] square, and of the front of the sanctuary, the appearance [is] as that appearance. 22 Of the altar, the wood [is] three cubits in height, and its length—two cubits; and its corners [are] to it, and its length, and its walls [are] of wood, and he speaks to me, "This [is] the table that [is] before Yhwh." 23 And the temple and the sanctuary had two doors; 24 and the doors had two panels, two turning panels: two on one door, and two panels on the other. 25 And made on them, on the doors of the temple, [are] cherubim and palm-trees as are made on the walls, and a thickness of wood [is] at the front of the porch on the outside. 26 And narrow windows and palm-trees [are] on this side and on that side, at the sides of the porch, and the side-chambers of the house, and the thick places.

CHAPTER 42

1 And he brings me forth to the outer court, the way northward, and he brings me into the chamber that [is] opposite the separate place, and that [is] opposite the building at the north. 2 At the front of the length [is] one hundred cubits [at] the north opening, and the breadth—fifty cubits. 3 Opposite the twenty [cubits] that are of the inner court, and opposite the pavement that [is] of the outer court, [is] gallery [with] face toward gallery, in the three [stories]. 4 And at the front of the chambers [is] a walk of ten cubits in breadth to the inner part, a way of one cubit, and their openings [are] at the north. 5 And the upper chambers [are] short, for the galleries contain more than these, than the lower, and than the middle one, of the building; 6 for they [are] threefold, and they have no pillars as the pillars of the court, therefore it has been kept back—more than the lower and than the middle one—from the ground. 7 As for the wall that [is] at the outside, alongside the chambers, the way of the outer-court at the front of the

chambers, its length [is] fifty cubits; **8** for the length of the chambers that [are] in the outer court [is] fifty cubits, and of those on the front of the temple—one hundred cubits. **9** And under these chambers [is] the entrance from the east, in one's going into them from the outer court. **10** In the breadth of the wall of the court eastward, to the front of the separate place, and to the front of the building, [are] chambers. **11** And the way before them [is] as the appearance of the chambers that [are] northward, according to their length so [is] their breadth, and all their outlets, and according to their fashions, and according to their openings. **12** And according to the openings of the chambers that [are] southward [is] an opening at the head of the way, the way directly in the front of the wall eastward in entering them. **13** And he says to me, "The north chambers, the south chambers, that [are] at the front of the separate place, they [are] holy chambers, where the priests (who [are] near to Yhwh) eat the most holy things, there they place the most holy things, and the present, and the sin-offering, and the guilt-offering, for the place [is] holy. **14** In the priests' going in, they do not come out from the sanctuary to the outer court, and there they place their garments with which they minister, for they [are] holy, and have put on other garments, and have drawn near to that which [is] for the people." **15** And he has finished the measurements of the inner house, and has brought me forth the way of the gate whose front [is] eastward, and he has measured it all around. **16** He has measured the east side with the measuring-reed, five hundred reeds, with the measuring-reed all around. **17** He has measured the north side, five hundred reeds, with the measuring reed all around. **18** The south side he has measured, five hundred reeds, with the measuring-reed. **19** He has turned around to the west side, he has measured five hundred reeds with the measuring-reed. **20** At the four sides he has measured it; it had a wall all around, the length—five hundred, and the breadth—five hundred, to separate between the holy and the profane place.

CHAPTER 43

1 And he causes me to go to the gate, the gate that is looking eastward. **2** And behold, the glory of the God of Israel has come from the way of the east, and His voice [is] as the noise of many waters, and the earth has shone from His glory. **3** And according to the appearance [is] the appearance that I saw, as the appearance that I saw in my coming in to destroy the city, and the appearances [are] as the appearance that I saw at the river Chebar, and I fall on my face. **4** And the glory of Yhwh has come into the house, the way of the gate whose face [is] eastward. **5** And [the] Spirit takes me up, and brings me into the inner court, and behold, the glory of Yhwh has filled the house. **6** And I hear one speaking to me from the house, and a man has been standing near me, **7** and He says to me: "Son of man, the place of My throne, || And the place of the soles of My feet, || Where I dwell in the midst of the sons of Israel for all time, || The house of Israel defiles My holy Name no longer, || They, and their kings, by their whoredom, || And by the carcasses of their kings—their high places. **8** In their putting their threshold with My threshold, || And their doorpost near My doorpost, || And the wall between Me and them, || And they have defiled My holy Name, || By their abominations that they have done, || And I consume them in My anger. **9** Now they put their whoredom far off, || And the carcasses of their kings—from Me, || And I have dwelt in their midst for all time. **10** You, son of man, || Show the house of Israel the house, || And they are ashamed of their iniquities, || And they have measured the measurement. **11** And since they have been ashamed of all that they have done, || The form of the house, and its measurement, || And its outlets, and its inlets, and all its forms, || And all its statutes, even all its forms, || And all its laws—cause them to know, || And write [it] before their eyes, || And they observe all its forms, || And all its statutes, and have done them. **12** This [is] a law of the house: on the top of the mountain, all its border all around [is] most holy; behold, this [is] a law of the house. **13** And these [are] measurements of the altar by cubits: the cubit [is] a cubit and a handbreadth, and the center [is] a cubit, and the breadth a cubit; and its border on its edge around [is] one span, and this [is] the upper part of the altar. **14** And from the center of the ground to the lower border [is] two cubits, and the breadth—one cubit, and from the lesser border to the greater border—four cubits, and the breadth a cubit. **15** And the altar [is] four cubits, and from the altar and upward [are] four horns. **16** And the altar [is]

twelve long by twelve broad, square in its four sides. **17** And the border [is] fourteen long by fourteen broad, at its four sides, and the border around it [is] half a cubit, and the center of it [is] a cubit around, and its steps are looking eastward." **18** And He says to me, "Son of man, thus said Lord Yhwh: These [are] statutes of the altar in the day of its being made to cause burnt-offering to go up on it, and to sprinkle blood on it. **19** And you have given to the priests, the Levites—who [are] of the seed of Zadok, who are near to Me, a declaration of Lord Yhwh, to serve Me—a calf from the herd, for a sin-offering. **20** And you have taken of its blood, and have put it on its four horns, and on the four corners of its border, and on the border all around, and have cleansed it, and purified it. **21** And you have taken the bullock of the sin-offering, and have burned it in the appointed place of the house at the outside of the sanctuary. **22** And on the second day you bring a kid of the goats near, a perfect one, for a sin-offering, and they have cleansed the altar, as they cleansed [it] for the bullock. **23** In your finishing cleansing, you bring a calf near, a son of the herd, a perfect one, and a ram out of the flock, a perfect one. **24** And you have brought them near before Yhwh, and the priests have cast salt on them, and have caused them to go up, a burnt-offering to Yhwh. **25** [For] seven days you prepare a goat daily for a sin-offering; and they also prepare a bullock, a son of the herd, and a ram out of the flock—perfect ones. **26** [For] seven days they purify the altar, and have cleansed it, and filled their hand. **27** And the days are completed, and it has come to pass on the eighth day, and from now on, the priests prepare your burnt-offerings and your peace-offerings on the altar, and I have accepted you—a declaration of Lord Yhwh."

CHAPTER 44

1 And he causes me to turn back the way of the gate of the outer sanctuary that is looking eastward, and it is shut. **2** And Yhwh says to me, "This gate is shut, it is not opened, and none go in by it, for Yhwh, God of Israel, has come in by it, and it has been shut. **3** The prince, who [is] prince, he sits by it to eat bread before Yhwh, he comes in by the way of the porch of the gate, and by its way he goes out." **4** And he brings me in the way of the north gate to the front of the house, and I look, and behold, the glory of Yhwh has filled the house of Yhwh, and I fall on my face. **5** And Yhwh says to me, "Son of man, set your heart, and see with your eyes, and hear with your ears, all that I am speaking with you, all of the statutes of the house of Yhwh, and all of its laws; and you have set your heart to the entrance of the house, with all the outlets of the sanctuary, **6** and have said to [the] rebellion, to the house of Israel, Thus said Lord Yhwh: Enough from you—of all your abominations, O house of Israel. **7** In your bringing in sons of a stranger, uncircumcised of heart, and uncircumcised of flesh, to be in My sanctuary, to defile it, even My house, in your bringing near My bread, fat, and blood, and they break My covenant by all your abominations, **8** and you have not kept [the] charge of My holy things, and you set [others] for keeping My charge in My sanctuary for you. **9** Thus said Lord Yhwh: No son of a stranger, uncircumcised of heart, and uncircumcised of flesh, comes into My sanctuary, even any son of a stranger, who [is] in the midst of the sons of Israel. **10** And the Levites who have gone far off from Me, in the wandering of Israel when they went astray from Me after their idols, and they have borne their iniquity. **11** And they have been servants in My sanctuary, overseers at the gates of the house, and servants at the house; they slay the burnt-offering and the sacrifice for the people, and they stand before them to serve them. **12** Because that they serve them before their idols, and have been for a stumbling-block of iniquity to the house of Israel, therefore I have lifted up My hand against them—a declaration of Lord Yhwh—and they have borne their iniquity. **13** And they do not draw near to Me to act as My priest, and to draw near to any of My holy things, to the Holy of Holies, and they have borne their shame and their abominations that they have done, **14** and I made them keepers of the charge of the house, for all its service and for all that is done in it. **15** And the priests, the Levites, sons of Zadok, who have kept the charge of My sanctuary in the wandering of the sons of Israel from off Me, they draw near to Me to serve Me, and have stood before Me, to bring fat and blood near to Me—a declaration of Lord Yhwh: **16** they come into My sanctuary, and they draw near to My table to serve Me, and they have kept My charge. **17** And it has come to pass, in their going into the gates of the inner court, they put on linen garments; and no wool comes up on them in their ministering in the gates of the inner court and within. **18** Linen headdresses are on their head, and linen trousers are on their loins, they are not restrained with sweat. **19** And in their going forth to the outer court—to the outer court to the people—they strip off their garments, in which they are ministering, and have placed them in the holy chambers, and have put on other garments; and they do not sanctify the people in their own garments. **20** And they do not shave their head, and they do not send forth the lock; they certainly trim their heads. **21** And no priest drinks wine in their coming into the inner court. **22** And they do not take a widow or divorced woman to themselves for wives, but they take virgins of the seed of the house of Israel, and the widow who is widow of a priest. **23** And they direct My people between holy and common, and they cause them to discern between unclean and clean. **24** And concerning controversy, they stand up for judgment; they judge it with My judgments; and they keep My law and My statutes in all My appointed places; and they sanctify My Sabbaths. **25** And he does not come near to any dead man to be defiled, but if for father, and for mother, and for son, and for daughter, for brother, for sister who has not been to a man, they may defile themselves. **26** And after his cleansing, they number seven days to him. **27** And in the day of his coming into the sanctuary, into the inner court, to minister in the sanctuary, he brings his sin-offering near—a declaration of Lord Yhwh. **28** And it has been for an inheritance to them; I [am] their inheritance, and you do not give a possession to them in Israel; I [am] their possession. **29** The present, and the sin-offering, and the guilt-offering, they eat, and every devoted thing in Israel is theirs. **30** And the first of all the first-fruits of all, and every raised-offering of all, of all your raised-offerings, are the priests'; and you give the first of your dough to the priest, to cause a blessing to rest on your house. **31** The priests do not eat any carcass or torn thing, from the bird or from the beast."

CHAPTER 45

1 "And in your causing the land to fall into inheritance, you lift up a raised-offering to Yhwh, a holy [portion] of the land: the length—twenty-five thousand [is] the length, and the breadth—ten thousand; it [is] holy in all its surrounding border. **2** There is of this for the sanctuary five hundred by five hundred, square, around; and fifty cubits of outskirt [is] around it. **3** And by this measure you measure: the length—twenty-five thousand, and the breadth—ten thousand: and the sanctuary is in it, the Holy of Holies. **4** It [is] the holy [portion] of the land; it is for priests, servants of the sanctuary, who are drawing near to serve Yhwh; and it has been a place for their houses, and a holy place for the sanctuary. **5** And of the twenty-five thousand of length, and of the ten thousand of breadth, there is to the Levites, servants of the house, for them—for a possession—twenty chambers. **6** And of the possession of the city you set [an area] of five thousand breadth, and twenty-five thousand lengths, alongside the raised-offering of the holy [portion]; it is for all the house of Israel. **7** And for the prince: on this side and on that side of the raised-offering of the holy place, and of the possession of the city, at the front of the raised-offering of the holy place, and at the front of the possession of the city, from the west corner westward, and from the east corner eastward—and the length [is] corresponding to one of the portions from the west border to the east border— **8** of the land there is for a possession to him in Israel, and My princes do not oppress My people anymore, and they give the land to the house of Israel according to their tribes." **9** Thus said Lord Yhwh: "Enough from you—princes of Israel; turn violence and spoil aside, and do judgment and righteousness; lift up your exactions from off My people—a declaration of Lord Yhwh. **10** You must have just balances, and a just ephah, and a just bath. **11** The ephah and the bath is of one measure, for the bath to carry a tenth of the homer, and the ephah a tenth of the homer: its measurement is according to the homer. **12** And the shekel [is] twenty gerah: twenty shekels, twenty-five shekels, fifteen shekels—is your maneh. **13** This [is] the raised-offering that you lift up; a sixth part of the ephah of a homer of wheat, also you have given a sixth part of the ephah of a homer of barley, **14** and the portion of oil, the bath of oil, a tenth part of the bath out of the cor, a homer of ten baths—for ten baths [are] a homer; **15** and one lamb out of the flock, out of two hundred, out of the watered country of Israel, for a present, and for a burnt-offering, and

for peace-offerings, to make atonement by them—a declaration of Lord Yhwh. **16** All the people of the land are at this raised-offering for the prince in Israel. **17** And on the prince are the burnt-offerings, and the present, and the drink-offering, in celebrations, and in new moons, and in Sabbaths, in all appointed times of the house of Israel: he makes the sin-offering, and the present, and the burnt-offering, and the peace-offerings, to make atonement for the house of Israel." **18** Thus said Lord Yhwh: "In the first [month], on the first of the month, you take a bullock, a son of the herd, a perfect one, and have cleansed the sanctuary: **19** and the priest has taken from the blood of the sin offering, and has put [it] on the doorpost of the house, and on the four corners of the border of the altar, and on the post of the gate of the inner court. **20** And so you do on the seventh of the month, because of each erring one, and because of the simple one—and you have purified the house. **21** In the first [month], on the fourteenth day of the month, you have the Passover, a celebration of seven days, unleavened bread is eaten. **22** And the prince has prepared on that day, for himself, and for all the people of the land, a bullock, a sin-offering. **23** And [on] the seven days of the celebration he prepares a burnt-offering to Yhwh, seven bullocks, and seven rams, perfect ones, daily [for] seven days, and a sin-offering, a kid of the goats, daily. **24** And he prepares a present of an ephah for a bullock, and an ephah for a ram, and a hin of oil for an ephah. **25** In the seventh [month], on the fifteenth day of the month, in the celebration, he does according to these things [for] seven days; as the sin-offering so the burnt-offering, and as the present so also the oil."

CHAPTER 46

1 Thus said Lord Yhwh: "The gate of the inner court that is looking eastward is shut [during] the six days of work, and on the day of rest it is opened, and in the day of the new moon it is opened; **2** and the prince has come in the way of the porch of the gate from the outside, and he has stood by the post of the gate, and the priests have made his burnt-offering, and his peace-offerings, and he has bowed himself by the opening of the gate, and has gone forth, and the gate is not shut until the evening. **3** And the people of the land have bowed themselves at the opening of that gate, on Sabbaths, and on new moons, before Yhwh. **4** And the burnt-offering that the prince brings near to Yhwh on the day of rest [is] six lambs, perfect ones, and a ram, a perfect one. **5** And the present [is] an ephah for a ram, and for the lambs a present, the gift of his hand, and a hin of oil for an ephah. **6** And on the day of the new moon—a bullock, a son of the herd, a perfect one, and six lambs and a ram; they are perfect. **7** And with an ephah for a bullock, and an ephah for a ram, he prepares a present, and for the lambs as his hand attains, and a hin of oil for an ephah. **8** And in the coming in of the prince, he comes in the way of the porch of the gate, and by its way he goes out. **9** And in the coming in of the people of the land before Yhwh at appointed times, he who has come in the way of the north gate to bow himself, goes out the way of the south gate, and he who has come in the way of the south gate, goes out by the way of the north gate: he does not turn back the way of the gate by which he came in, but he goes out opposite it. **10** And in their coming in the prince in their midst comes in, and in their going out he goes out. **11** And in celebrations, and in appointed times, the present is an ephah for a bullock, and an ephah for a ram, and for lambs the gift of his hand, and a hin of oil for an ephah. **12** And when the prince makes a free-will burnt-offering, or free-will peace-offerings, to Yhwh, then he has opened the gate that is looking eastward for himself, and has made his burnt-offering and his peace-offerings as he does in the day of rest, and he has gone out, and has shut the gate after his going out. **13** And you make a daily burnt-offering of a lamb, son of a year, a perfect one, to Yhwh; you make it morning by morning. **14** And you make a present with it morning by morning, a sixth part of the ephah, and a third part of the hin of oil, to temper with the fine flour, a present to Yhwh, by a continuous statute—continually; **15** and they prepare the lamb, and the present, and the oil, morning by morning—a continual burnt-offering." **16** Thus said Lord Yhwh: "When the prince gives a gift to any of his sons, it [is] his inheritance, it [is] for his sons; it [is] their possession by inheritance. **17** And when he gives a gift out of his inheritance to one of his servants, then it has been his until the year of freedom, and it has turned back to the prince, only the inheritance of his sons is theirs. **18** And the prince does not take from the people's inheritance to oppress them—from their possession; he causes his sons to inherit out of his own possession, so that My people are not each scattered from his possession." **19** And he brings me in through the entrance that [is] by the side of the gate, to the holy chambers, to the priests, that are looking northward, and behold, there [is] a place in their two sides westward. **20** And he says to me, "This [is] the place where the priests boil the guilt-offering and the sin-offering, where they bake the present, so as not to bring [it] out to the outer court, to sanctify the people." **21** And he brings me out to the outer court, and causes me to pass over to the four corners of the court, and behold, a court in a corner of the court, [moreover] a court in [every] corner of the corner. **22** In the four corners of the court [are] enclosed courts, forty long and thirty broads, [with] one measure for the four corners. **23** And a row [is] all around in them—around the four of them—and made with boilers under the rows all around. **24** And he says to me, "These [are] the houses of those boiling where the servants of the house boil the sacrifice of the people."

CHAPTER 47

1 And he causes me to turn back to the opening of the house; and behold, water is coming forth from under the threshold of the house eastward, for the front of the house [is] eastward, and the water is coming down from beneath, from the right side of the house, from south of the altar. **2** And he causes me to go out the way of the gate northward, and causes me to turn around the way outside, to the gate that [is] outside, the way that is looking eastward, and behold, water is coming forth from the right side. **3** In the going out of the man eastward—and a line in his hand—then he measures one thousand by the cubit, and he causes me to pass over into the waters—waters [to my] ankles. **4** And he measures one thousand, and causes me to pass over into the waters—waters [to my] knees. And he measures one thousand, and causes me to pass over waters [to my] loins. **5** And he measures one thousand—a stream that I am not able to pass over; for the waters have risen—waters to swim in—a stream that is not passed over. **6** And he says to me, "Have you seen, son of man?" And he leads me, and brings me back to the edge of the stream. **7** In my turning back, then, behold, at the edge of the stream [are] very many trees, on this side and on that side. **8** And he says to me, "These waters are going forth to the east circuit, and have gone down to the desert, and have entered the sea; they are brought forth to the sea, and the waters have been healed. **9** And it has come to pass, every living creature that teems, wherever the streams come, lives: and there has been great abundance of fish, for these waters have come there, and they are healed; and everything to where the stream comes has lived. **10** And it has come to pass, fishers stand by it, from En-Gedi even to En-Eglaim; they are a spreading place for the nets; their fish are of the same kind as the fish of the Great Sea—very many. **11** Its miry and its marshy places—they are not healed; they have been given up to salt. **12** And there comes up by the stream, on its edge, on this side and on that side, every [kind of] fruit-tree whose leaf does not fade, and its fruit is not consumed, it yields first-fruits according to its months, because its waters are coming forth from the sanctuary; and its fruits have been for food, and its leaf for medicine." **13** Thus said Lord Yhwh: "This [is] the border whereby you inherit the land, according to the twelve tribes of Israel; Joseph [has two] portions. **14** And you have inherited it, one as well as another, in that I have lifted up My hand to give it to your fathers; and this land has fallen to you in inheritance. **15** And this [is] the border of the land at the north quarter; from the Great Sea, the way of Hethlon, at the coming in to Zedad: **16** Hamath, Berothah, Sibraim, that [is] between the border of Damascus and the border of Hamath; Hazar-Hatticon, that [is] at the coast of Havran. **17** And the border from the sea has been Hazar-Enan, the border of Damascus, and Zaphon at the north, and the border of Hamath: and [this is] the north quarter. **18** And the east quarter [is] from between Havran, and Damascus, and Gilead, and the land of Israel, [to] the Jordan; you measure from the border on the Eastern Sea: and [this is] the east quarter. **19** And the south quarter southward [is] from Tamar to the waters of Meriboth-Kadesh, the stream to the Great Sea: and [this is] the south quarter southward. **20** And the west quarter [is] the Great Sea, from the border until opposite the coming in to Hamath: this [is] the west quarter. **21** And you have divided this land to yourselves, according to

the tribes of Israel; **22** and it has come to pass, you separate it for an inheritance to yourselves, and to the sojourners who are sojourning in your midst, who have begotten sons in your midst, and they have been to you as native, with the sons of Israel; they are separated with you for an inheritance in the midst of the tribes of Israel. **23** And it has come to pass, in the tribe with which the sojourner sojourns, there you give his inheritance," a declaration of Lord Yhwh.

CHAPTER 48

1 "And these [are] the names of the tribes: from the north end to the side of the way of Hethlon, at the coming in to Hamath, Hazar-Enan, the border of Damascus northward, in the direction of Hamath, and they have been his—east side to west, Dan, one [portion]; 2 and by the border of Dan, from the east side to the west side, Asher, one [portion]; 3 and by the border of Asher, from the east side even to the west side, Naphtali, one [portion]; 4 and by the border of Naphtali, from the east side to the west side, Manasseh, one [portion]; 5 and by the border of Manasseh, from the east side to the west side, Ephraim, one [portion]; 6 and by the border of Ephraim, from the east side even to the west side, Reuben, one [portion]; 7 and by the border of Reuben, from the east side to the west side, Judah, one [portion]; 8 and by the border of Judah, from the east side to the west side is the raised-offering that you lift up, twenty-five thousand [cubits] broad and long, as one of the parts, from the east side to the west side: and the sanctuary has been in its midst. 9 The raised-offering that you lift up to Yhwh [is] twenty-five thousand long and ten thousand broad. 10 And of these is the holy raised-offering for the priests, northward twenty-five thousand, and westward ten thousand [in] breadth, and eastward ten thousand [in] breadth, and southward twenty-five thousand [in] length: and the sanctuary of Yhwh has been in its midst. 11 For the priests who are sanctified of the sons of Zadok, who have kept My charge, who did not err in the erring of the sons of Israel, as the Levites erred, 12 even the raised-offering has been for them, out of the raised-offering of the land, most holy, by the border of the Levites. 13 And [to] the Levites alongside the border of the priests [are] twenty-five thousand [in] length, and ten thousand [in] breadth, all the length [is] twenty-five thousand, and the breadth ten thousand. 14 And they do not sell of it, nor exchange, nor cause the first-fruit of the land to pass away: for [it is] holy to Yhwh. 15 And the five thousand that is left in the breadth, on the front of the twenty-five thousand, is common—for the city, for dwelling, and for outskirt, and the city has been in its midst. 16 And these [are] its measurements: the north side—four thousand and five hundred, and the south side—four thousand and five hundred, and on the east side—four thousand and five hundred, and the west side—four thousand and five hundred. 17 And the outskirt of the city has been northward—two hundred and fifty, and southward—two hundred and fifty, and eastward—two hundred and fifty, and westward—two hundred and fifty. 18 And the remainder in length alongside the raised-offering of the holy [portion is] ten thousand eastward, and ten thousand westwards, and it has been alongside the raised-offering of the holy [portion], and its increase has been for food for those serving the city, 19 even [to] him who is serving the city, they serve it out of all the tribes of Israel. 20 All the raised-offering [is] twenty-five thousand by twenty-five thousand square—you lift up the raised-offering of the holy [portion] with the possession of the city. 21 And the remainder [is] for the prince, on this side and on that side of the raised-offering of the holy [portion], and of the possession of the city, on the front of the twenty-five thousand of the raised-offering to the east border, and westward, on the front of the twenty-five thousand on the west border, alongside the portions of the prince; and the raised-offering of the holy [portion], and the sanctuary of the house, has been in its midst. 22 And from the possession of the Levites, from the possession of the city, in the midst of that which is for the prince, between the border of Judah and the border of Benjamin, there is for the prince. 23 As for the rest of the tribes, from the east side to the west side, Benjamin, one [portion]; 24 and by the border of Benjamin, from the east side to the west side, Simeon, one [portion]; 25 and by the border of Simeon, from the east side to the west side, Issachar, one [portion]; 26 and by the border of Issachar, from the east side to the west side, Zebulun, one [portion]; 27 and by the border of Zebulun, from the east side to the west side, Gad,

one [portion]; 28 and by the border of Gad, at the south side southward, the border has been from Tamar [to] the waters of Meriboth-Kadesh, the stream by the Great Sea. 29 This [is] the land that you separate by inheritance to the tribes of Israel, and these [are] their divisions," a declaration of Lord Yhwh. 30 "And these [are] the outgoings of the city: on the north side, four thousand and five hundred measures; 31 and the gates of the city [are] according to the names of the tribes of Israel; three gates northward—one gate of Reuben, one gate of Judah, one gate of Levi. 32 And on the east side, four thousand and five hundred, and three gates—one gate of Joseph, one gate of Benjamin, one gate of Dan. 33 And the south side, four thousand and five hundred, and three gates—one gate of Simeon, one gate of Issachar, one gate of Zebulun. 34 The west side, four thousand and five hundred, [with] their three gates—one gate of Gad, one gate of Asher, one gate of Naphtali. 35 [It is] eighteen thousand around, and the renown of the city [is] from the day Yhwh [is] there."

DANIEL

CHAPTER 1

¹ In the third year of the reign of Jehoiakim king of Judah, Nebuchadnezzar king of Babylon has come to Jerusalem, and lays siege against it; ² and the Lord gives into his hand Jehoiakim king of Judah, and some of the vessels of the house of God, and he brings them in [to] the land of Shinar, [to] the house of his god, and the vessels he has brought in [to] the treasure-house of his god. ³ And the king says, to Ashpenaz master of his eunuchs, to bring in out of the sons of Israel (even of the royal seed, and of the chiefs), ⁴ boys in whom there is no blemish, and of good appearance, and skillful in all wisdom, and possessing knowledge, and teaching thought, and who have ability to stand in the palace of the king, and to teach them the literature and language of the Chaldeans. ⁵ And the king appoints for them a rate, day by day, of the king's portion of food, and of the wine of his drinking, so as to nourish them three years, that at the end thereof they may stand before the king. ⁶ And there are among them out of the sons of Judah, Daniel, Hananiah, Mishael, and Azariah, ⁷ and the chief of the eunuchs sets names on them, and he sets on Daniel, Belteshazzar; and on Hananiah, Shadrach; and on Mishael, Meshach; and on Azariah, Abed-Nego. ⁸ And Daniel purposes in his heart that he will not defile himself with the king's portion of food, and with the wine of his drinking, and he seeks of the chief of the eunuchs that he may not defile himself. ⁹ And God gives Daniel for kindness and for mercies before the chief of the eunuchs; ¹⁰ and the chief of the eunuchs says to Daniel, "I am fearing my lord the king, who has appointed your food and your drink, for why does he see your faces sadder than [those of] the boys which [are] of your circle? then you have made my head indebted to the king," ¹¹ And Daniel says to the Meltzar, whom the chief of the eunuchs has appointed over Daniel, Hananiah, Mishael, and Azariah, ¹² "Please try your servants [for] ten days; and they give to us from the vegetables and we eat, and water, and we drink; ¹³ and our appearance is seen before you, and the appearance of the boys who are eating the king's portion of food, and as you see—deal with your servants." ¹⁴ And he listens to them, to this word, and tries them ten days: ¹⁵ and at the end of ten days their appearance has appeared better and fatter in flesh then any of the boys who are eating the king's portion of food. ¹⁶ And the Meltzar is taking away their portion of food, and the wine of their drink, and is giving to them vegetables. ¹⁷ As for these four boys, God has given to them knowledge and understanding in every [kind of] literature, and wisdom; and Daniel has given instruction about every [kind of] vision and dreams. ¹⁸ And at the end of the days that the king had said to bring them in, the chief of the eunuchs brings them in before Nebuchadnezzar. ¹⁹ And the king speaks with them, and there has not been found among them all like Daniel, Hananiah, Mishael, and Azariah, and they stand before the king; ²⁰ and [in] any matter of wisdom [and] understanding that the king has sought of them, he finds them ten hands above all the enchanters, the conjurers, who [are] in all his kingdom. ²¹ And Daniel is to the first year of Cyrus the king.

CHAPTER 2

¹ And in the second year of the reign of Nebuchadnezzar, Nebuchadnezzar has dreamed dreams, and his spirit moves itself, and his sleep has been against him; ² and the king says to call for enchanters, and for conjurers, and for sorcerers, and for Chaldeans, to declare to the king his dreams. And they come in and stand before the king; ³ and the king says to them, "I have dreamed a dream, and my spirit is moved to know the dream." ⁴ And the Chaldeans speak to the king [in] Aramaic, "O king, live for all ages, tell the dream to your servants, and we show the interpretation." ⁵ The king has answered and said to the Chaldeans, "The thing is gone from me; if you do not cause me to know the dream and its interpretation, you are made pieces, and your houses are made dunghills; ⁶ and if the dream and its interpretation you show, gifts, and fee, and great glory you receive from before me, therefore the dream and its interpretation you show me." ⁷ They have answered a second time, and are saying, "Let the king tell the dream to his servants, and we show the interpretation." ⁸ The king has answered and said, "Of a truth I know that you are gaining time, because that you have seen that the thing is gone from me, ⁹ [so] that, if you do not cause me to know the dream—one is your sentence, seeing a lying and corrupt word you have prepared to speak before me, until the time is changed, therefore tell the dream to me, then I know that you show me its interpretation." ¹⁰ The Chaldeans have answered before the king, and are saying, "There is not a man on the earth who is able to show the king's matter; therefore, no king, chief, and ruler, has asked such a thing as this of any scribe, and enchanter, and Chaldean; ¹¹ and the thing that the king is asking [is] precious, and there are no others that show it before the king, except the gods, whose dwelling is not with flesh." ¹² Therefore the king has been furious and very angry, and has said to destroy all the wise men of Babylon. ¹³ And the sentence has gone forth, and the wise men are being slain, and they have sought Daniel and his companions to be slain. ¹⁴ Then Daniel has replied [with] counsel and discretion to Arioch chief of the executioners of the king, who has gone forth to slay the wise men of Babylon. ¹⁵ He has answered and said to Arioch the king's captain, "Why [is] the sentence so urgent from before the king?" Then Arioch has made the thing known to Daniel, ¹⁶ and Daniel has gone up, and sought of the king that he would give him time to show the interpretation to the king. ¹⁷ Then Daniel has gone to his house, and to Hananiah, Mishael, and Azariah, his companions, he has made the thing known, ¹⁸ and to seek mercies from before the God of the heavens concerning this secret, that they do not destroy Daniel and his companions with the rest of the wise men of Babylon. ¹⁹ Then to Daniel, in a vision of the night, the secret has been revealed. Then Daniel has blessed the God of the heavens. ²⁰ Daniel has answered and said, "Let the Name of God be blessed from age even to age, for wisdom and might—for they are His. ²¹ And He is changing times and seasons, He is causing kings to pass away, and He is raising up kings; He is giving wisdom to the wise, and knowledge to those possessing understanding. ²² He is revealing deep and hidden things; He has known what [is] in darkness, and light has dwelt with Him. ²³ You, O God of my fathers, I am thanking and praising, for wisdom and might You have given to me; and now, You have caused me to know that which we have sought from You, for the king's matter You have caused us to know." ²⁴ Therefore Daniel has gone up to Arioch, whom the king has appointed to destroy the wise men of Babylon; he has gone, and thus has said to him, "You do not destroy the wise men of Babylon, bring me up before the king, and I show the interpretation to the king." ²⁵ Then Arioch in haste has brought up Daniel before the king, and thus has said to him, "I have found a man of the sons of the expulsion of Judah, who makes known the interpretation to the king." ²⁶ The king has answered and said to Daniel, whose name [is] Belteshazzar, "Are you able to cause me to know the dream that I have seen, and its interpretation?" ²⁷ Daniel has answered before the king and said, "The secret that the king is asking, the wise men, the enchanters, the scribes, the soothsayers, are not able to show to the king; ²⁸ but there is a God in the heavens, a revealer of secrets, and He has made known to King Nebuchadnezzar that which [is] to be in the latter end of the days. Your dream and the visions of your head on your bed are these: ²⁹ You, O king, your thoughts on your bed have come up [concerning] that which [is] to be after this, and the Revealer of secrets has caused you to know that which [is] to be. ³⁰ As for me—not for [any] wisdom that is in me

above any living has this secret been revealed to me; but for the intent that the interpretation to the king they make known, and the thoughts of your heart you know. **31** You, O king, were looking, and behold, a certain great image. This image [is] mighty, and its brightness excellent; it is standing before you, and its appearance [is] terrible. **32** This image! Its head [is] of fine gold, its breasts and its arms of silver, its belly and its thighs of bronze; **33** its legs of iron, its feet, part of them of iron, and part of them of clay. **34** You were looking until that a stone has been cut out without hands, and it has struck the image on its feet, that [are] of iron and of clay, and it has broken them small; **35** then broken small together have been the iron, the clay, the bronze, the silver, and the gold, and they have been as chaff from the summer threshing-floor, and the wind has carried them away, and no place has been found for them: and the stone that struck the image has become a great mountain, and has filled all the land. **36** This [is] the dream, and its interpretation we tell before the king. **37** You, O king, are a king of kings, for the God of the heavens a kingdom, strength, and might, and glory, has given to you; **38** and wherever sons of men are dwelling, the beast of the field, and the bird of the heavens, He has given into your hand, and has caused you to rule over them all; you [are] this head of gold. **39** And after you another kingdom arises lower than those, and another third kingdom of bronze, that rules over all the earth. **40** And the fourth kingdom is strong as iron, because that iron is breaking small, and making feeble, all [things], even as iron that is breaking all these, it beats small and breaks. **41** As for that which you have seen: the feet and toes, part of them potter's clay, and part of them iron, the kingdom is divided: and some of the standing of the iron [is] to be in it, because that you have seen the iron mixed with miry clay. **42** As for the toes of the feet, part of them iron, and part of them clay: some part of the kingdom is strong, and some part of it is brittle. **43** Because you have seen iron mixed with miry clay, they are mixing themselves with the seed of men: and they are not adhering with one another, even as iron is not mixed with clay. **44** And in the days of these kings the God of the heavens raises up a kingdom that is not destroyed for all time, and its kingdom is not left to another people: it beats small and ends all these kingdoms, and it stands for all time. **45** Because that you have seen that out of the mountain a stone has been cut without hands, and it has beaten the iron small, the bronze, the clay, the silver, and the gold; the great God has made known to the king that which [is] to be after this; and the dream [is] true, and its interpretation steadfast." **46** Then King Nebuchadnezzar has fallen on his face, and to Daniel he has done homage, and present, and sweet things, he has said to pour out to him. **47** The king has answered Daniel and said, "Of a truth [it is] that your God is a God of gods, and a Lord of kings, and a revealer of secrets, since you have been able to reveal this secret." **48** Then the king has made Daniel great, and many great gifts he has given to him, and has caused him to rule over all the province of Babylon, and chief of the prefects over all the wise men of Babylon. **49** And Daniel has sought from the king, and he has appointed over the work of the province of Babylon, Shadrach, Meshach, and Abed-Nego, and Daniel [is] in the gate of the king.

CHAPTER 3

1 Nebuchadnezzar the king has made an image of gold, its height sixty cubits, its breadth six cubits; he has raised it up in the Valley of Dura, in the province of Babylon; **2** and Nebuchadnezzar the king has sent to gather the satraps, the prefects, and the governors, the counselors, the treasurers, the judges, the magistrates, and all the rulers of the province, to come to the dedication of the image that Nebuchadnezzar the king has raised up. **3** Then are gathered the satraps, the prefects, and the governors, the counselors, the treasurers, the judges, the magistrates, and all the rulers of the province, to the dedication of the image that Nebuchadnezzar the king has raised up: and they are standing before the image that Nebuchadnezzar has raised up. **4** And a crier is calling mightily: "They are saying to you: O peoples, nations, and languages! **5** at the time that you hear the voice of the horn, the flute, the harp, the lyre, the stringed instrument, the symphony, and all kinds of music, you fall down and pay respect to the golden image that Nebuchadnezzar the king has raised up: **6** and whoever does not fall down and pay respect, in that hour he is cast into the midst of a burning fiery furnace." **7** Therefore at that time, when all the peoples are hearing the voice of the horn, the flute, the harp, the lyre, the stringed instrument, and all kinds of music, falling down are all the peoples, nations and languages, worshiping the golden image that Nebuchadnezzar the king has raised up. **8** Therefore at that time certain Chaldeans have drawn near, and accused the Jews; **9** they have answered, indeed, and are saying to Nebuchadnezzar the king, "O king, live for all ages! **10** You, O king, have made a decree that every man who hears the voice of the horn, the flute, the harp, the lyre, the stringed instrument, and the symphony, and all kinds of music, falls down and pays respect to the golden image; **11** and whoever does not fall down and pay respect, is cast into the midst of a burning fiery furnace. **12** There are certain Jews whom you have appointed over the work of the province of Babylon—Shadrach, Meshach, and Abed-Nego, these men have not made of you, O king, [any] regard; your gods they are not serving, and to the golden image you have raised up—are not making worship." **13** Then Nebuchadnezzar, in anger and fury, has said to bring in Shadrach, Meshach, and Abed-Nego. Then these men have been brought in before the king. **14** Nebuchadnezzar has answered and said to them, "Is [it] a laid plan, O Shadrach, Meshach, and Abed-Nego—my gods you are not serving, and to the golden image that I have raised up you are not worshiping? **15** Now behold, you are ready, so that at the time that you hear the voice of the horn, the flute, the harp, the lyre, the stringed instrument, and the symphony, and all kinds of music, you fall down and pay respect to the image that I have made! But if you do not worship—in that hour you are cast into the midst of a burning fiery furnace; who is that God who delivers you out of my hands?" **16** Shadrach, Meshach, and Abed-Nego have answered, indeed, they are saying to King Nebuchadnezzar, "We have no need concerning this matter to answer you. **17** Behold, it is; our God whom we are serving, is able to deliver us from a burning fiery furnace; and from your hand, O king, He delivers. **18** And behold—not! Be it known to you, O king, that we are not serving your gods, and we do not worship the golden image you have raised up." **19** Then Nebuchadnezzar has been full of fury, and the expression of his face has been changed concerning Shadrach, Meshach, and Abed-Nego; he answered and said to heat the furnace seven times above that which it is seen to be heated; **20** and to certain mighty men who [are] in his force he has said to bind Shadrach, Meshach, and Abed-Nego, to cast into the burning fiery furnace. **21** Then these men have been bound in their coats, their tunics, and their turbans, and their clothing, and have been cast into the midst of the burning fiery furnace. **22** Therefore, because that the word of the king is urgent, and the furnace heated exceedingly, those men who have taken up Shadrach, Meshach, and Abed-Nego—the spark of the fire has killed them. **23** And these three men, Shadrach, Meshach, and Abed-Nego, have fallen down in the midst of the burning fiery furnace—bound. **24** Then Nebuchadnezzar the king has been astonished, and has risen in haste; he has answered and said to his counselors, "Have we not cast three men into the midst of the fire—bound?" They have answered and are saying to the king, "Certainly, O king." **25** He answered and has said, "Behold, I am seeing four men loose, walking in the midst of the fire, and they have no hurt; and the appearance of the fourth [is] like to a son of the gods." **26** Then Nebuchadnezzar has drawn near to the gate of the burning fiery furnace; he has answered and said, "Shadrach, Meshach, and Abed-Nego, servants of God Most High come forth, indeed, come"; then Shadrach, Meshach, and Abed-Nego come forth, from the midst of the fire; **27** and gathered together, the satraps, the prefects, and the governors, and the counselors of the king, are seeing these men, that the fire has no power over their bodies, and the hair of their head has not been singed, and their coats have not changed, and the smell of fire has not passed on them. **28** Nebuchadnezzar has answered and has said, "Blessed [is] the God of Shadrach, Meshach, and Abed-Nego, who has sent His messenger, and has delivered His servants who trusted on Him." And the word of the king changed, and gave up their bodies that they might not serve nor pay respect to any god except to their own God. **29** "And by me a decree is made, that any people, nation, and language, that speaks erroneously concerning the God of Shadrach, Meshach, and Abed-Nego, he is made pieces, and its house is made a dunghill, because that there is no other god who is able thus to deliver." **30** Then the king has caused Shadrach, Meshach, and Abed-Nego, to prosper in the province of Babylon.

CHAPTER 4

¹ "Nebuchadnezzar the king to all peoples, nations, and languages, who are dwelling in all the earth: Your peace be great! ² The signs and wonders that God Most High has done with me, it is good before me to show. ³ How great His signs! And how mighty His wonders! His kingdom [is] a continuous kingdom, and His rule [is] with generation and generation. ⁴ I, Nebuchadnezzar, have been at rest in my house, and flourishing in my palace: ⁵ a dream I have seen, and it makes me afraid, and the conceptions on my bed, and the visions of my head, trouble me. ⁶ And by me a decree is made, to cause all the wise men of Babylon to come up before me, that the interpretation of the dream they may cause me to know. ⁷ Then coming up are the scribes, the enchanters, the Chaldeans, and the soothsayers, and the dream I have told before them, and its interpretation they are not making known to me. ⁸ And at last Daniel has come up before me, whose name [is] Belteshazzar—according to the name of my god—and in whom [is] the spirit of the holy gods, and the dream before him I have told: ⁹ O Belteshazzar, master of the scribes, as I have known that the spirit of the holy gods [is] in you, and no secret presses you, the visions of my dream that I have seen, and its interpretation, tell. ¹⁰ As for the visions of my head on my bed, I was looking, and behold, a tree in the midst of the earth, and its height [is] great: ¹¹ the tree has become great, indeed, strong, and its height reaches to the heavens, and its vision to the end of the whole land; ¹² its leaves [are] beautiful, and its budding great, and food for all [is] in it: under it the beast of the field takes shade, and in its boughs dwell the birds of the heavens, and of it are all flesh fed. ¹³ I was looking, in the visions of my head on my bed, and behold, a sifter, even a holy one, from the heavens is coming down. ¹⁴ He is calling mightily, and thus has said, Cut down the tree, and cut off its branches, shake off its leaves, and scatter its budding, move away let the beast from under it, and the birds from off its branches; ¹⁵ but the stump of its roots leave in the earth, even with a band of iron and bronze, in the tender grass of the field, and with the dew of the heavens is it wet, and with the beasts [is] his portion in the herb of the earth; ¹⁶ his heart from man's is changed, and the heart of a beast is given to him, and seven times pass over him; ¹⁷ by the decree of the sifters [is] the sentence, and by the saying of the holy ones the requirement, to the intent that the living may know that the Most High is ruler in the kingdom of men, and to whom He wills He gives it, and the lowest of men He raises up over it. ¹⁸ This dream I have seen, I King Nebuchadnezzar; and you, O Belteshazzar, tell the interpretation, because that all the wise men of my kingdom are not able to cause me to know the interpretation, and you [are] able, for the spirit of the holy gods [is] in you." ¹⁹ Then Daniel, whose name [is] Belteshazzar, has been astonished about one hour, and his thoughts trouble him; the king has answered and said, "O Belteshazzar, do not let the dream and its interpretation trouble you." Belteshazzar has answered and said, "My lord, the dream—to those hating you, and its interpretation—to your enemies! ²⁰ The tree that you have seen, that has become great and strong, and its height reaches to the heavens, and its vision to all the land, ²¹ and its leaves [are] beautiful, and its budding great, and food for all [is] in it, under it the beast of the field dwells, and on its boughs the birds of the heavens sit. ²² It [is] you, O king, for you have become great and mighty, and your greatness has become great, and has reached to the heavens, and your dominion to the end of the earth; ²³ and that which the king has seen—a sifter, even a holy one, coming down from the heavens, and he has said, Cut down the tree, and destroy it; but the stump of its roots leave in the earth, even with a band of iron and bronze, in the tender grass of the field, and with the dew of the heavens it is wet, and with the beast of the field [is] his portion, until seven times pass over him. ²⁴ This [is] the interpretation, O king, and it [is] the decree of the Most High that has come against my lord the king: ²⁵ and they are driving you away from men, and your dwelling is with the beast of the field, and they cause you to eat the herb as oxen, and they are wetting you by the dew of the heavens, and pass over you seven times, until you know that the Most High is ruler in the kingdom of men, and to whom He wills He gives it. ²⁶ And that which they said—to leave the stump of the roots of the tree; your kingdom abides for you, after that you know that the heavens are ruling. ²⁷ Therefore, O king, let my counsel be acceptable to you, and your sins by righteousness break off, and your perversity by pitying the poor, behold, it is a lengthening of your ease." ²⁸ All—has come on Nebuchadnezzar the king. ²⁹ At the end of twelve months, on the palace of the kingdom of Babylon he has been walking; ³⁰ the king has answered and said, "Is this not that great Babylon that I have built, for the house of the kingdom, in the might of my strength, and for the glory of my honor?" ³¹ While the word is [in] the king's mouth a voice from the heavens has fallen: "They are saying to you: O Nebuchadnezzar the king, the kingdom has passed from you, ³² and from men they are driving you away, and your dwelling [is] with the beast of the field, they cause you to eat the herb as oxen, and pass over you seven times, until you know that the Most High is ruler in the kingdom of men, and to whom He wills He gives it." ³³ In that hour the thing has been fulfilled on Nebuchadnezzar, and from men he is driven, and he eats the herb as oxen, and his body is wet by the dew of the heavens, until his hair has become great as eagles, and his nails as birds. ³⁴ "And at the end of the days I, Nebuchadnezzar, have lifted up my eyes to the heavens, and my understanding returns to me, and I have blessed the Most High, and the Perpetual Living One I have praised and honored, whose dominion [is] a continuous dominion, and His kingdom with generation and generation; ³⁵ and all who are dwelling on the earth are reckoned as nothing, and according to His will He is doing among the forces of the heavens and those dwelling on the earth, and there is none that claps with his hand and says to Him, What have You done? ³⁶ At that time my understanding returns to me, and for the glory of my kingdom, my honor and my brightness return to me, and to me my counselors and my great men seek, and over my kingdom I have been made right, and abundant greatness has been added to me. ³⁷ Now I, Nebuchadnezzar, am praising and exalting and honoring the King of the heavens, for all His works [are] truth, and His paths judgment, and those walking in pride He is able to humble."

CHAPTER 5

¹ Belshazzar the king has made a great feast to one thousand of his great men, and before the one thousand he is drinking wine; ² Belshazzar has said—while tasting the wine—to bring in the vessels of gold and of silver that his father Nebuchadnezzar had taken from the temple that [is] in Jerusalem, that the king may drink with them, and his great men, his wives, and his concubines. ³ Then they have brought in the vessels of gold that had been taken out of the temple of the house of God that [is] in Jerusalem, and the king and his great men, his wives and his concubines, have drunk with them; ⁴ they have drunk wine, and have praised the gods of gold, and of silver, of bronze, of iron, of wood, and of stone. ⁵ In that hour fingers of a man's hand have come forth, and they are writing in front of the lampstand, on the plaster of the wall of the king's palace: and the king is seeing the extremity of the hand that is writing; ⁶ then the king's countenance has changed, and his thoughts trouble him, and the joints of his loins are loosed, and his knees are striking against one another. ⁷ The king calls mightily, to bring up the enchanters, the Chaldeans, and the soothsayers. The king has answered and said to the wise men of Babylon, that, "Any man who reads this writing, and shows me its interpretation, he puts on purple, and a bracelet of gold [is] on his neck, and he rules third in the kingdom." ⁸ Then all the wise men of the king are coming up, and they are not able to read the writing, and to make known the interpretation to the king; ⁹ then King Belshazzar is greatly troubled, and his countenance is changing in him, and his great men are perplexed. ¹⁰ The queen, on account of the words of the king and his great men, has come up to the banquet-house. The queen has answered and said, "O king, live for all ages; do not let your thoughts trouble you, nor your countenance be changed: ¹¹ there is a man in your kingdom in whom [is] the spirit of the holy gods: and in the days of your father, light, and understanding, and wisdom—as the wisdom of the gods—was found in him; and your father King Nebuchadnezzar, chief of the scribes, enchanters, Chaldeans, soothsayers, established him—your father, O king— ¹² because that an excellent spirit, and knowledge, and understanding, interpreting of dreams, and showing of enigmas, and loosing of knots was found in him, in Daniel, whose name the king made Belteshazzar: now let Daniel be called, and the interpretation he shows." ¹³ Then Daniel has been caused to come up before the king; the king has answered and said to Daniel, "You are that Daniel who [is] of the sons of the expulsion of Judah, whom my father the king brought in out of

Judah? **14** And I have heard of you, that the spirit of the gods [is] in you, and light, and understanding, and excellent wisdom have been found in you. **15** And now, caused to come up before me have been the wise men, the enchanters, that they may read this writing, and its interpretation to cause me to know: and they are not able to show the interpretation of the thing: **16** and I have heard of you, that you are able to give interpretations, and to loose knots: now, behold—you are able to read the writing, and its interpretation to cause me to know—purple you put on, and a bracelet of gold [is] on your neck, and you rule third in the kingdom." **17** Then Daniel has answered and said before the king, "Your gifts be to yourself, and give your fee to another; nevertheless, the writing I read to the king, and the interpretation I cause him to know; **18** you, O king, God Most High, a kingdom, and greatness, and glory, and honor, gave to your father Nebuchadnezzar: **19** and because of the greatness that He gave to him, all peoples, nations, and languages were trembling and fearing before him: whom he willed he was slaying, and whom he willed he was keeping alive, and whom he willed he was raising up, and whom he willed he was making low; **20** and when his heart was high, and his spirit was strong to act proudly, he has been caused to come down from the throne of his kingdom, and his glory they have caused to pass away from him, **21** and he is driven from the sons of men, and his heart has been like with the beasts, and with the wild donkeys [is] his dwelling; they cause him to eat the herb like oxen, and by the dew of the heavens is his body wet, until he has known that God Most High is ruler in the kingdom of men, and whom He wills He raises up over it. **22** And you, his son, Belshazzar, have not humbled your heart, though all this you have known; **23** and against the Lord of the heavens you have lifted up yourself; and the vessels of His house they have brought in before you, and you, and your great men, your wives, and your concubines, are drinking wine with them, and gods of silver, and of gold, of bronze, of iron, of wood, and of stone, that are not seeing, nor hearing, nor knowing, you have praised: and the God in whose hand [is] your breath, and all your ways, Him you have not honored. **24** Then from before Him is the extremity of the hand sent, and the writing is noted down; **25** and this [is] the writing that is noted down: Numbered, Numbered, Weighed, and Divided. **26** This [is] the interpretation of the thing: Numbered—God has numbered your kingdom, and has finished it. **27** Weighed—You are weighed in the balances, and have been found lacking. **28** Divided—Your kingdom is divided, and it has been given to the Medes and Persians." **29** Then Belshazzar has spoken, and they have clothed Daniel with purple, and a bracelet of gold [is] on his neck, and they have proclaimed concerning him that he is the third ruler in the kingdom. **30** In that night Belshazzar king of the Chaldeans is slain, **31** and Darius the Mede has received the kingdom when a son of sixty-two years.

CHAPTER 6

1 It has been good before Darius, and he has established over the kingdom satraps—one hundred and twenty—that they may be throughout the whole kingdom, **2** and three presidents higher than they, of whom Daniel [is] first, that these satraps may give to them an account, and the king have no loss. **3** Then this Daniel has been overseer over the presidents and satraps, because that an excellent spirit [is] in him, and the king has thought to establish him over the whole kingdom. **4** Then the presidents and satraps have been seeking to find a cause of complaint against Daniel concerning the kingdom, and any cause of complaint and corruption they are not able to find, because that he [is] faithful, and any error and corruption have not been found in him. **5** Then these men are saying, "We do not find against this Daniel any cause of complaint, except we have found [it] against him in the Law of his God." **6** Then these presidents and satraps have assembled near the king, and thus they are saying to him: "O King Darius, live for all ages! **7** Taken counsel have all the presidents of the kingdom, the prefects, and the satraps, the counselors, and the governors, to establish a royal statute, and to strengthen an interdict, that any who seeks a petition from any god and man until thirty days, except of you, O king, is cast into a den of lions. **8** Now, O king, you establish the interdict, and sign the writing, that it is not to be changed, as a law of Media and Persia, that does not pass away." **9** Therefore King Darius has signed the writing and interdict. **10** And Daniel, when he has known that the writing is signed, has gone up to his house, and the window

being opened for him, in his upper chamber, toward Jerusalem, three times in a day he is kneeling on his knees, and praying, and confessing before his God, because that he was doing [it] before this. **11** Then these men have assembled, and found Daniel praying and pleading grace before his God; **12** then they have come near, indeed, they are saying before the king concerning the king's interdict: "Have you not signed an interdict, that any man who seeks from any god and man until thirty days, except of you, O king, is cast into a den of lions?" The king has answered and said, "The thing [is] certain as a law of Media and Persia, that does not pass away." **13** Then they have answered, indeed, they are saying before the king, that, "Daniel, who [is] of the sons of the expulsion of Judah, has not placed on you, O king, [any] regard, nor on the interdict that you have signed, and three times in a day he is seeking his petition." **14** Then the king, when he has heard the matter, is greatly displeased at himself, and on Daniel he has set the heart to deliver him, and until the going up of the sun he was arranging to deliver him. **15** Then these men have assembled near the king, and are saying to the king, "Know, O king, that the law of Media and Persia [is] that any interdict and statute that the king establishes is not to be changed." **16** Then the king has spoken, and they have brought Daniel, and have cast [him] into a den of lions. The king has answered and said to Daniel, "Your God, whom you are serving continually, delivers you Himself." **17** And a stone has been brought and placed at the mouth of the den, and the king has sealed it with his signet, and with the signet of his great men, that the purpose is not changed concerning Daniel. **18** Then the king has gone to his palace, and he has passed the night fasting, and dahavan have not been brought up before him, and his sleep has fled [from] off him. **19** Then the king rises in the early morning, at the light, and he has gone in haste to the den of lions; **20** and at his coming near to the den, to Daniel, with a grieved voice, he cries. The king has answered and said to Daniel, "O Daniel, servant of the living God, your God, whom you are serving continually, is He able to deliver you from the lions?" **21** Then Daniel has spoken with the king: "O king, live for all ages: **22** my God has sent His messenger, and has shut the lions' mouths, and they have not injured me: because that before Him purity has been found in me; and also before you, O king, injury I have not done." **23** Then was the king very glad for him, and he has commanded Daniel to be taken up out of the den, and Daniel has been taken up out of the den, and no injury has been found in him, because he has believed in his God. **24** And the king has spoken, and they have brought those men who had accused Daniel, and to the den of lions they have cast them, they, their sons, and their wives; and they have not come to the lower part of the den until the lions have power over them, and all their bones they have broken small. **25** Then Darius the king has written to all the peoples, nations, and languages, who are dwelling in all the land: "Your peace be great! **26** From before me a decree is made, that in every dominion of my kingdom they are trembling and fearing before the God of Daniel, for He [is] the living God, and abiding for all ages, and His kingdom that which [is] not destroyed, and His dominion [is] to the end. **27** A deliverer, and rescuer, and doer of signs and wonders in the heavens and in earth [is] He who has delivered Daniel from the paw of the lions." **28** And this Daniel has prospered in the reign of Darius, and in the reign of Cyrus the Persian.

CHAPTER 7

1 In the first year of Belshazzar king of Babylon, Daniel has seen a dream, and the visions of his head on his bed, then he has written the dream, the chief of the things he has said. **2** Daniel has answered and said, "I was seeing in my vision by night, and behold, the four winds of the heavens are coming forth to the Great Sea; **3** and four great beasts are coming up from the sea, diverse from one another. **4** The first [is] like a lion, and it has an eagle's wings. I was seeing until its wings have been plucked, and it has been lifted up from the earth, and on feet as a man it has been caused to stand, and a heart of man is given to it. **5** And behold, another beast, a second, like to a bear, and to the same authority it has been raised, and three ribs [are] in its mouth, between its teeth, and thus they are saying to it, Rise, consume much flesh. **6** After this I was seeing, and behold, another like a leopard, and it has four wings of a bird on its back, and the beast has four heads, and dominion is given to it. **7** After this I was seeing in the visions of the night, and behold, a fourth beast, terrible and fearful, and exceedingly strong; and it has very great iron teeth, it has consumed, indeed, it breaks small, and it has trampled the remnant with its feet; and it [is] diverse from all the beasts that [are] before it; and it has ten horns. [8] I was considering about the horns, and behold, another horn, a little one, has come up between them, and three of the first horns have been eradicated from before it, and behold, eyes as the eyes of man [are] in this horn, and a mouth speaking great things. [9] I was seeing until thrones have been thrown down, and the Ancient of Days is seated, His garment [is] white as snow, and the hair of His head [is] as pure wool, His throne flames of fire, its wheels burning fire. [10] A flood of fire is proceeding and coming forth from before Him, one million serve Him and one hundred million rise up before Him, judgment has been set, and the scrolls have been opened. [11] I was seeing, then, because of the voice of the great words that the horn is speaking, I was seeing until the beast is slain, and his body has been destroyed, and given to the burning fire; [12] and the rest of the beasts have caused their dominion to pass away, and a prolongation in life is given to them, until a season and a time. [13] I was seeing in the visions of the night, and behold, [One] like a Son of Man was coming with the clouds of the heavens, and to the Ancient of Days He has come, and before Him they have brought Him near. [14] And to Him is given dominion, and glory, and a kingdom, and all peoples, nations, and languages serve Him, His dominion [is] a continuous dominion, that does not pass away, and His kingdom that which is not destroyed. [15] My spirit has been pierced—I, Daniel—in the midst of the sheath, and the visions of my head trouble me; [16] I have drawn near to one of those standing, and the certainty I seek from him of all this; and he has spoken to me, indeed, the interpretation of the things he has caused me to know: [17] These great beasts, that [are] four, [are] four kings, they rise up from the earth; [18] and the saints of the Most High receive the kingdom, and they strengthen the kingdom for all time, even for all time and all ages. [19] Then I wished for certainty concerning the fourth beast, that was diverse from them all, exceedingly fearful; its teeth of iron, and its nails of bronze, it has devoured, it breaks small, and it has trampled the remnant with its feet; [20] and concerning the ten horns that [are] in its heads, and of the other that came up, and before which three have fallen, even of that horn that has eyes, and a mouth speaking great things, and whose appearance [is] great above its companions. [21] I was seeing, and this horn is making war with the saints, and has prevailed over them, [22] until the Ancient of Days has come, and judgment is given to the saints of the Highest, and the time has come, and the saints have strengthened the kingdom. [23] Thus he said: The fourth beast is the fourth kingdom in the earth, that is diverse from all kingdoms, and it consumes all the earth, and treads it down, and breaks it small. [24] And the ten horns out of the kingdom [are] ten kings, they rise, and another rises after them, and it is diverse from the former, and it humbles three kings; [25] and it speaks words as an adversary of the Highest, and it wears out the saints of the Highest, and it hopes to change seasons and law; and they are given into its hand, until a time, and times, and a division of a time. [26] And judgment is set, and they cause his dominion to pass away, to perish, and to be destroyed—to the end; [27] and the kingdom, and the dominion, even the greatness of the kingdom under the whole heavens, is given to the people—the saints of the Highest, His kingdom [is] a continuous kingdom, and all dominions serve and obey Him. [28] Here [is] the end of the matter. I, Daniel, [am] greatly troubled [by] my thoughts, and my countenance is changed on me, and I have kept the matter in my heart."

CHAPTER 8

[1] "In the third year of the reign of Belshazzar the king, a vision has appeared to me—I Daniel—after that which had appeared to me at the beginning. [2] And I see in a vision, and it comes to pass, in my seeing, and I [am] in Shushan the palace that [is] in Elam the province, and I see in a vision, and I have been by the stream Ulai. [3] And I lift up my eyes, and look, and behold, a certain ram is standing before the stream, and it has two horns, and the two horns [are] high; and one [is] higher than the other, and the high one is coming up last. [4] I have seen the ram pushing westward, and northward, and southward, and no living creatures stand before it, and there is none delivering out of its hand, and it has done according to

its pleasure, and has exerted itself. [5] And I have been considering, and behold, a young male goat has come from the west, over the face of the whole earth, whom none is touching in the earth; as for the young male goat, a conspicuous horn [is] between its eyes. [6] And it comes to the ram possessing the two horns, that I had seen standing before the stream, and runs to it in the fury of its power. [7] And I have seen it coming near the ram, and it becomes embittered at it, and strikes the ram, and breaks its two horns, and there has been no power in the ram to stand before it, and it casts it to the earth, and tramples it down, and there has been no deliverer to the ram out of its power. [8] And the young male goat has exerted itself very much, and when it is strong, the great horn has been broken; and a vision of four comes up in its place, at the four winds of the heavens. [9] And from one of them has come forth a little horn, and it exerts itself greatly toward the south, and toward the east, and toward the beautiful [land]; [10] indeed, it exerts to the host of the heavens, and causes to fall to the earth of the host, and of the stars, and tramples them down. [11] And to the prince of the host it exerts itself, and the continual [sacrifice] has been taken away by it, and thrown down the base of his sanctuary. [12] And the host is given up, with the continual [sacrifice], through transgression, and it throws down truth to the earth, and it has worked, and prospered. [13] And I hear a certain holy one speaking, and a certain holy one says to the wonderful numberer who is speaking: Until when [is] the vision of the continual [sacrifice], and of the transgression, an astonishment, to make a treading down of both sanctuary and host? [14] And he says to me, Until evening—morning two thousand and three hundred, then is the holy place declared right. [15] And it comes to pass in my seeing—I, Daniel—the vision, that I require understanding, and behold, standing before me [is] as the appearance of a mighty one. [16] And I hear a voice of man between [the banks of] Ulai, and he calls and says: Gabriel, cause this [one] to understand the appearance. [17] And he comes in near my station, and at his coming in I have been afraid, and I fall on my face, and he says to me: Understand, son of man, for at the time of the end [is] the vision. [18] And in his speaking with me, I have been in a trance on my face, on the earth; and he comes against me, and causes me to stand on my station, [19] and says: Behold, I am causing you to know that which is in the latter end of the indignation; for at the appointed time [is] the end. [20] The ram that you have seen possessing two horns, [are] the kings of Media and Persia. [21] And the young male goat, the hairy one, [is] the king of Javan; and the great horn that [is] between its eyes is the first king; [22] and that being broken, four stand up in its place, four kingdoms stand up from the nation, and not in its power. [23] And in the latter end of their kingdom, about the perfecting of the transgressors, a king stands up, fierce of face, and understanding hidden things; [24] and his power has been mighty, and not by his own power; and he destroys wonderful things, and he has prospered, and worked, and destroyed mighty ones, and the people of the Holy Ones. [25] And by his understanding he has also caused deceit to prosper in his hand, and in his heart he exerts himself, and by ease he destroys many; and he stands against the Prince of princes—and he is broken without hand. [26] And the appearance of the evening and of the morning, that is told, is true; and you, hide the vision, for [it is] after many days. [27] And I, Daniel, have been, indeed, I became sick [for] days, and I rise, and do the king's work, and am astonished at the appearance, and there is none understanding."

CHAPTER 9

[1] "In the first year of Darius, son of Ahasuerus, of the seed of the Medes, who has been made king over the kingdom of the Chaldeans, [2] in the first year of his reign, I, Daniel, have understood by scrolls the number of the years (in that a word of Yhwh has been to Jeremiah the prophet), concerning the fulfilling of the desolations of Jerusalem—seventy years; [3] and I set my face toward the Lord God, to seek [by] prayer and supplications, with fasting, and sackcloth, and ashes. [4] And I pray to my God Yhwh, and confess, and say: Ah, now, O Lord God, the great and the fearful, keeping the covenant and the kindness to those loving Him and to those keeping His commands; [5] we have sinned, and done perversely, and done wickedly, and rebelled, to turn aside from Your commands, and from Your judgments: [6] and we have not listened to Your servants, the prophets, who have spoken in Your Name to our

kings, our heads, and our fathers, and to all the people of the land. ⁷ To You, O Lord, [is] the righteousness, and to us the shame of face, as [at] this day, to the men of Judah, and to the inhabitants of Jerusalem, and to all Israel, who are near, and who are far off, in all the lands to where You have driven them, in their trespass that they have trespassed against You. ⁸ O Lord, to us [is] the shame of face, to our kings, to our heads, and to our fathers, in that we have sinned against You. ⁹ To the Lord our God [are] the mercies and the forgivenesses, for we have rebelled against Him, ¹⁰ and have not listened to the voice of our God Yhwh, to walk in His laws, that He has set before us by the hand of His servants the prophets; ¹¹ and all Israel has transgressed Your law, to turn aside so as not to listen to Your voice; and poured on us is the execration, and the oath, that is written in the Law of Moses, servant of God, because we have sinned against Him. ¹² And He confirms His words that He has spoken against us, and against our judges who have judged us, to bring great calamity on us, in that it has not been done under the whole heavens as it has been done in Jerusalem, ¹³ as it is written in the Law of Moses, all this evil has come on us, and we have not appeased the face of our God Yhwh to turn back from our iniquities, and to act wisely in Your truth. ¹⁴ And Yhwh watches for the evil, and brings it on us, for our God Yhwh is righteous concerning all His works that He has done, and we have not listened to His voice. ¹⁵ And now, O Lord our God, who has brought forth Your people from the land of Egypt by a strong hand, and makes for Yourself a name as at this day, we have sinned, we have done wickedly. ¹⁶ O Lord, according to all Your righteous acts, please let Your anger and Your fury turn back from Your city Jerusalem, Your holy mountain, for by our sins, and for the iniquities of our fathers, Jerusalem and Your people [are] for a reproach to all our neighbors; ¹⁷ and now, listen, O our God, to the prayer of Your servant, and to his supplication, and cause Your face to shine on Your sanctuary that [is] desolate, for the Lord's sake. ¹⁸ Incline, O my God, Your ear, and hear, open Your eyes and see our desolations, and the city on which Your Name is called; for not for our righteous acts are we causing our supplications to fall before You, but for Your mercies that [are] many. ¹⁹ O Lord, hear, O Lord, forgive; O Lord, attend and do; do not delay, for Your own sake, O my God, for Your Name is called on Your city, and on Your people. ²⁰ And while I am speaking, and praying, and confessing my sin, and the sin of my people Israel, and causing my supplication to fall before my God Yhwh, for the holy mountain of my God, ²¹ indeed, while I am speaking in prayer, then that one Gabriel, whom I had seen in vision at the commencement, being caused to fly swiftly, is coming to me at the time of the evening present. ²² And he gives understanding, and speaks with me, and says, O Daniel, now I have come forth to cause you to consider understanding wisely; ²³ at the commencement of your supplications the word has come forth, and I have come to declare [it], for you [are] greatly desired, and understand concerning the matter, and consider concerning the appearance. ²⁴ Seventy periods of seven are determined for your people and for your holy city, to shut up the transgression, and to seal up sins, and to cover iniquity, and to bring in continuous righteousness, and to seal up vision and prophet, and to anoint the Holy of Holies. ²⁵ And you know, and consider wisely, from the going forth of the word to restore and to build Jerusalem until Messiah the Leader [is] seven periods of seven, and sixty-two periods of seven: the broad place has been built again, and the rampart, even in the distress of the times. ²⁶ And after the sixty-two periods of seven, Messiah is cut off, but not for Himself, and the people of the leader who is coming destroy the city and the holy place; and its end [is] with a flood, and until the end [is] war, [and] desolations [are] determined. ²⁷ And he has strengthened a covenant with many [for] one period of seven, and [in] the midst of the period of seven he causes sacrifice and present to cease, and by the wing of abominations he is making desolate, even until the consummation, and that which is determined is poured on the desolate one."

CHAPTER 10

¹ In the third year of Cyrus king of Persia, a thing is revealed to Daniel, whose name is called Belteshazzar, and the thing [is] true, and the warfare [is] great: and he has understood the thing, and has understanding about the appearance. ² "In those days, I, Daniel, have been mourning three weeks of days; ³ I have not eaten desirable bread, and no flesh and wine came into my mouth, and I have not anointed myself at all, until the completion of three weeks of days. ⁴ And in the twenty-fourth day of the first month, I have been by the side of the great river, that [is] Hiddekel: ⁵ and I lift up my eyes, and look, and behold, a certain one clothed in linen, and his loins girt with pure gold of Uphaz, ⁶ and his body as a beryl, and his face as the appearance of lightning, and his eyes as lamps of fire, and his arms and his feet as the aspect of bright bronze, and the voice of his words as the voice of a multitude. ⁷ And I, Daniel, have seen the vision by myself, and the men who have been with me have not seen the vision, but a great trembling has fallen on them, and they flee to be hidden; ⁸ and I have been left by myself, and I see this great vision, and there has been no power left in me, and my splendor has been turned in me to corruption, indeed, I have not retained power. ⁹ And I hear the voice of his words, and when I hear the voice of his words, then I have been in a trance on my face, and my face [is] to the earth; ¹⁰ and behold, a hand has come against me, and shakes me on my knees and the palms of my hands. ¹¹ And he says to me: Daniel, man greatly desired, attend to the words that I am speaking to you, and stand on your station, for now I have been sent to you. And when he speaks with me this word, I have stood trembling. ¹² And he says to me: Do not fear, Daniel, for from the first day that you gave your heart to understand, and to humble yourself before your God, your words have been heard, and I have come because of your words. ¹³ And the head of the kingdom of Persia is standing in opposition in front of me [for] twenty-one days, and behold, Michael, first of the chief heads, has come to help me, and I have remained there near the kings of Persia; ¹⁴ and I have come to cause you to understand that which happens to your people in the latter end of the days, for yet the vision [is] after days. ¹⁵ And when he speaks with me about these things, I have set my face toward the earth, and have been silent; ¹⁶ and behold, as the manner of the sons of men, he is striking against my lips, and I open my mouth, and I speak, and say to him who is standing in opposition in front of me: My lord, by the vision my pangs have been turned against me, and I have retained no power. ¹⁷ And how is the servant of this my lord able to speak with this my lord? as for me, from now on there remains in me no power, indeed, breath has not been left in me. ¹⁸ And he adds, and strikes against me, as the appearance of a man, and strengthens me, ¹⁹ and he says: Do not fear, O man greatly desired, peace to you, be strong, indeed, be strong; and when he speaks with me, I have strengthened myself, and I say, Let my lord speak, for you have strengthened me. ²⁰ And he says, Have you known why I have come to you? and now I return to fight with the head of Persia; indeed, I am going forth, and behold, the head of Javan has come; ²¹ but I declare to you that which is noted down in the Writing of Truth, and there is not one strengthening himself with me, concerning these, except Michael your head."

CHAPTER 11

¹ "And I, in the first year of Darius the Mede, my standing [is] for a strengthener, and for a stronghold to him; ² and now, I declare to you truth: Behold, yet three kings are standing for Persia, and the fourth becomes far richer than all, and according to his strength by his riches he stirs up the whole, with the kingdom of Javan. ³ And a mighty king has stood, and he has ruled a great dominion, and has done according to his will; ⁴ and according to his standing is his kingdom broken, and divided to the four winds of the heavens, and not to his posterity, nor according to his dominion that he ruled, for his kingdom is plucked up—and for others apart from these. ⁵ And a king of the south—even of his princes—becomes strong, and prevails against him, and has ruled; a great dominion [is] his dominion. ⁶ And at the end of years they join themselves together, and a daughter of the king of the south comes to the king of the north to do upright things; and she does not retain the power of the arm; and he does not stand, nor his arm; and she is given up, she, and those bringing her in, and her child, and he who is strengthening her in [these] times. ⁷ And [one] has stood up from a branch of her roots, [in] his station, and he comes to the bulwark, indeed, he comes into a stronghold of the king of the north, and has worked against them, and has done mightily; ⁸ and also their gods, with their princes, with their desirable vessels of silver and gold, he brings in captivity [to] Egypt; and he stands more years than the king of the

north. **9** And the king of the south has come into the kingdom, and turned back to his own land; **10** and his sons stir themselves up, and have gathered a multitude of great forces, and he has certainly come in, and overflowed, and passed through, and he turns back, and they stir themselves up to his stronghold. **11** And the king of the south becomes embittered, and has gone forth and fought with him, with the king of the north, and has caused a great multitude to stand, and the multitude has been given into his hand, **12** and he has carried away the multitude, his heart is high, and he has caused myriads to fall, and he does not become strong. **13** And the king of the north has turned back, and has caused a multitude to stand, greater than the first, and at the end of the times a second time he certainly comes in with a great force, and with much substance; **14** and in those times many stand up against the king of the south, and sons of the destroyers of your people lift themselves up to establish the vision—and they have stumbled. **15** And the king of the north comes in, and pours out a mound, and has captured fortified cities; and the arms of the south do not stand, nor the people of his choice, indeed, there is no power to stand. **16** And he who is coming to him does according to his will, and there is none standing before him; and he stands in the desirable land, and [it is] wholly in his hand. **17** And he sets his face to go in with the strength of his whole kingdom, and upright ones with him; and he has worked, and the daughter of women he gives to him, to corrupt her; and she does not stand, nor is for him. **18** And he turns back his face to the islands, and has captured many; and a prince has caused his reproach of himself to cease; without his reproach he turns [it] back to him. **19** And he turns back his face to the strongholds of his land, and has stumbled and fallen, and is not found. **20** And stood up on his station has [one] causing an exactor to pass over the honor of the kingdom, and in a few days he is destroyed, and not in anger, nor in battle. **21** And a despicable one has stood up on his station, and they have not given to him the splendor of the kingdom, and he has come in quietly, and has strengthened the kingdom by flatteries. **22** And the arms of the flood are overflowed from before him, and are broken; and also the leader of the covenant. **23** And after they join themselves to him, he works deceit, and has increased, and has been strong by a few of the nation. **24** Peaceably even into the fertile places of the province He comes, and he has done that which his fathers did not, nor his fathers' fathers; prey, and spoil, and substance, he scatters to them, and against fortifications he devises his plans, even for a time. **25** And he stirs up his power and his heart against the king of the south with a great force, and the king of the south stirs himself up to battle with a very great and mighty force, and does not stand, for they devise plans against him, **26** and those eating his portion of food destroy him, and his force overflows, and many wounded have fallen. **27** And both of the kings' hearts [are] to do evil, and at one table they speak lies, and it does not prosper, for yet the end [is] at a time appointed. **28** And he turns back [to] his land with great substance, and his heart [is] against the holy covenant, and he has worked, and turned back to his land. **29** At the appointed time he turns back, and has come against the south, and it is not as the former, and as the latter. **30** And ships of Chittim have come in against him, and he has been pained, and has turned back, and has been insolent toward the holy covenant, and has worked, and turned back, and he understands concerning those forsaking the holy covenant. **31** And strong ones stand up out of him, and have defiled the sanctuary, the stronghold, and have turned aside the continual [sacrifice], and appointed the desolating abomination. **32** And those acting wickedly [against] the covenant, he defiles by flatteries; and the people knowing their God are strong, and have worked. **33** And the teachers of the people give understanding to many; and they have stumbled by sword, and by flame, by captivity, and by spoil—days. **34** And in their stumbling, they are helped—a little help, and joined to them have been many with flatteries. **35** And some of the teachers stumble for refining by them, and for purifying, and for making white—until the end of the time, for [it is] yet for a time appointed. **36** And the king has done according to his will, and exalts himself, and magnifies himself against every god, and he speaks wonderful things against the God of gods, and has prospered until the indignation has been completed, for that which is determined has been done. **37** And to the God of his fathers he does not attend, nor to the desire of women, indeed, he does not attend to any god, for he magnifies himself against all. **38** And to the god of strongholds, on his station, he gives honor; indeed, to a god whom his fathers did not know he gives honor, with gold, and with silver, and with precious stone, and with desirable things. **39** And he has dealt in the fortresses of the strongholds with a strange god whom he has acknowledged; he multiplies honor, and has caused them to rule over many, and the ground he apportions at a price. **40** And at the time of the end, a king of the south pushes himself forward with him, and a king of the north storms against him, with chariot, and with horsemen, and with many ships; and he has come into the lands, and has overflowed, and passed over, **41** and has come into the desirable land, and many stumble, and these escape from his hand: Edom, and Moab, and the chief of the sons of Ammon. **42** And he sends forth his hand on the lands, and the land of Egypt is not for an escape; **43** and he has ruled over treasures of gold and of silver, and over all the desirable things of Egypt, and Lubim and Cushim [are] at his steps. **44** And reports trouble him out of the east and out of the north, and he has gone forth in great fury to destroy, and to devote many to destruction; **45** and he plants the tents of his palace between the seas and the holy desirable mountain, and has come to his end, and there is no helper to him.

CHAPTER 12

1 "And at that time Michael stands up, the great head, who is standing up for the sons of your people, and there has been a time of distress, such as has not been since there has been a nation until that time, and at that time your people escape, everyone who is found written in the scroll. **2** And the multitude of those sleeping in the dust of the ground awake, some to continuous life, and some to reproaches—to continuous abhorrence. **3** And those teaching shine as the brightness of the expanse, and those justifying the multitude as stars for all time and forever." **4** "And you, O Daniel, hide the things, and seal the scroll until the time of the end, many go to and fro, and knowledge is multiplied." **5** "And I have looked—I, Daniel—and behold, two others are standing, one here at the edge of the flood and one there at the edge of the flood, **6** and he says to the one clothed in linen, who [is] on the waters of the flood, Until when [is] the end of these wonders? **7** And I hear the one clothed in linen, who [is] on the waters of the flood, and he lifts up his right hand and his left to the heavens, and swears by Him who is living for all time, that, After a time, times, and a half, and at the completion of the scattering of the power of the holy people, all these are finished. **8** And I have heard, and I do not understand, and I say, O my lord, what [is] the latter end of these? **9** And he says, Go, Daniel; for hidden and sealed [are] the things until the time of the end. **10** Purify themselves, indeed, make themselves white, indeed, many are refined: and the wicked have done wickedly, and none of the wicked understand, and those acting wisely understand; **11** and from the time of the turning aside of the continuous [sacrifice], and to the giving out of the desolating abomination, [are] one thousand, two hundred, and ninety days. **12** O the blessedness of him who is waiting earnestly, and comes to the one thousand, three hundred, thirty-five days. **13** And you, go on to the end, then you rest, and stand in your lot at the end of the days."

HOSEA

CHAPTER 1

1 A word of Yhwh that has been to Hosea, son of Beeri, in the days of Uzziah, Jotham, Ahaz, Hezekiah, kings of Judah, and in the days of Jeroboam son of Joash, king of Israel: **2** The commencement of Yhwh's speaking by Hosea. And Yhwh says to Hosea, "Go, take a woman of whoredoms for yourself, and children of whoredoms, for the land goes utterly whoring from after Yhwh." **3** And he goes and takes Gomer daughter of Diblaim, and she conceives and bears a son to him; **4** and Yhwh says to him, "Call his name Jezreel, for yet a little, and I have charged the blood of Jezreel on the house of Jehu, and have caused the kingdom of the house of Israel to cease; **5** and it has come to pass in that day that I have broken the bow of Israel in the Valley of Jezreel." **6** And she conceives again, and bears a daughter, and He says to him, "Call her name Lo-Ruhamah [(Not Loved)], for I no longer pity the house of Israel, for I utterly take them away; **7** and I pity the house of Judah, and have saved them by their God Yhwh, and do not save them by bow, and by sword, and by battle, by horses, and by horsemen." **8** And she weans Lo-Ruhamah, and conceives, and bears a son; **9** and He says, "Call his name Lo-Ammi [(Not My People)], for you [are] not My people, and I am not for you; **10** and the number of the sons of Israel has been as the sand of the sea that is not measured nor numbered, and it has come to pass in the place where it is said to them, You [are] not My people, it is said to them, Sons of the Living God; **11** and the sons of Judah and the sons of Israel have been gathered together, and they have appointed one head for themselves, and have gone up from the land, for great [is] the day of Jezreel."

CHAPTER 2

1 "Say to your brothers—Ammi, || And to your sisters—Ruhamah. **2** Plead with your mother—plead || (For she [is] not My wife, and I [am] not her husband), || And she turns her whoredoms from before her, || And her adulteries from between her breasts, **3** Lest I strip her naked. And have set her up as [in] the day of her birth, || And have made her as a wilderness, || And have set her as a dry land, || And have put her to death with thirst. **4** And her sons I do not pity, || For they [are] sons of whoredoms, **5** For their mother has gone whoring, || Their conceiver has acted shamefully, || For she has said, I go after my lovers, || Those giving my bread and my water, || My wool and my flax, my oil and my drink. **6** Therefore, behold, I am hedging up your way with thorns, || And I have made a wall for her, || And her paths she does not find. **7** And she has pursued her lovers, || And she does not overtake them, || And has sought them, and does not find [them], || And she has said: I go, and I return to my first husband, || For—better to me then than now. **8** And she did not know that I had given to her || The grain, and the new wine, and the oil. Indeed, I multiplied silver to her, || And the gold they prepared for Ba'al. **9** Therefore I return, || And I have taken My grain in its season, || And My new wine in its appointed time, || And I have taken away My wool and My flax, covering her nakedness. **10** And now I reveal her dishonor before the eyes of her lovers, || And none deliver her out of My hand. **11** And I have caused all her joy to cease, || Her festival, her new moon, and her Sabbath, || Even all her appointed times, **12** And made desolate her vine and her fig tree, || Of which she said, They [are] a wage to me, || That my lovers have given to me, || And I have made them for a forest, || And a beast of the field have consumed them. **13** And I have charged on her the days of the Ba'alim, || To whom she makes incense, || And puts on her ring and her ornament, || And goes after her lovers, || And forgot Me," a declaration of Yhwh. **14** "Therefore, behold, I am enticing her, || And have caused her to go to the wilderness, || And I have spoken to her heart, **15** And given to her her vineyards from there, || And the Valley of Achor for an opening of hope, || And she has responded there as in the days of her youth, || And as in the day of her coming up out of the land of Egypt. **16** And it has come to pass in that day," || A declaration of Yhwh, || "You call Me: My husband, || And do not call Me anymore: My lord. **17** And I have turned aside the names of the lords from her mouth, || And they are not remembered anymore by their name. **18** And I have made a covenant for them in that day, || With the beast of the field, || And with the bird of the heavens, || And the creeping thing of the ground, || And bow, and sword, and war I break from off the land, || And have caused them to lie down confidently. **19** And I have betrothed you to Me for all time, || And betrothed you to Me in righteousness, || And in judgment, and kindness, and mercies, **20** And betrothed you to Me in faithfulness, || And you have known Yhwh. **21** And it has come to pass in that day, I answer," || A declaration of Yhwh, || "I answer the heavens, and they answer the earth. **22** And the earth answers the grain, || And the new wine, and the oil, || And they answer Jezreel. **23** And I have sowed her to Me in the land, || And I have pitied Lo-Ruhamah, || And I have said to Lo-Ammi, You [are] My people, || And he says, My God!"

CHAPTER 3

1 And Yhwh says to me: "Again, go, love a woman, loved of a friend, and an adulteress, like the loved of Yhwh, the sons of Israel, and they are turning to other gods, and are lovers of grape-cakes." **2** And I buy her for myself for fifteen pieces of silver, and a homer and a lethech of barley; **3** and I say to her, "You remain many days for Me, you do not go whoring, nor become anyone's; and I also [am] for you." **4** For the sons of Israel remain without a king for many days, and there is no prince, and there is no sacrifice, and there is no standing pillar, and there is no ephod and teraphim. **5** Afterward the sons of Israel have turned back, and sought their God Yhwh, and David their king, and have hurried to Yhwh, and to His goodness, in the latter end of the days.

CHAPTER 4

1 "Hear a word of Yhwh, sons of Israel, || For a strife [is] to Yhwh with inhabitants of the land, || For there is no truth, nor kindness, || Nor knowledge of God in the land; **2** Swearing, and lying, and murdering, || And stealing, and committing adultery—have increased, || And blood has touched against blood. **3** Therefore the land mourns, || And every dweller is weak in it, || With the beast of the field, || And with the bird of the heavens, || And the fishes of the sea—they are removed. **4** Only, let no one strive, nor reprove a man, || And your people [are] as those striving with a priest. **5** And you have stumbled in the day, || And a prophet has also stumbled with you in the night, || And I have cut off your mother. **6** My people have been cut off for lack of knowledge, || Because you have rejected knowledge, || I reject you from being priest to Me, || And you forget the Law of your God—I forget your sons, I also! **7** According to their abundance so they sinned against Me, || I change their glory into shame. **8** The sin of My people they eat, || And to their iniquity lift up their soul. **9** And it has been, like people, like priest, || And I have charged on it its ways, || And its habitual doings I return to it. **10** And they have eaten, and are not satisfied, || They have gone whoring, and do not increase, || For they have left off taking heed to Yhwh. **11** Whoredom, and wine, and new wine, take the heart, **12** My people at its staff asks and its rod declares to it, || For a spirit of whoredoms has caused to err, || And they go whoring from under their God. **13** On tops of the mountains they sacrifice, || And on the hills they make incense, || Under oak, and poplar, and terebinth, || For good [is] its shade. **14** Therefore your daughters commit whoredom, || And your spouses commit adultery, || I do not see after your daughters when they commit whoredom, || And after your spouses when they commit adultery, || For they with the harlots are separated, || And with the whores they sacrifice, || A people that does not understand kicks. **15** Though you [are] a harlot, O Israel, || Do not let Judah become guilty, || And do not come to Gilgal, nor go up to Beth-Aven, || Nor swear, Yhwh lives. **16** For Israel has turned aside as a stubborn heifer, || Now Yhwh feeds them as a lamb in a large place. **17** Ephraim is joined to idols, leave him alone. **18** Sour [is] their drink, || They have gone whoring diligently, || Her protectors have thoroughly loved shame. **19** Wind has distressed her with its wings, || And they are ashamed of their sacrifices!

CHAPTER 5

1 "Hear this, O priests, and attend, O house of Israel, || And, O house of the king, give ear, || For the judgment [is] for you, || For you have been a snare on Mizpah, || And a net spread out on Tabor. **2** And to slaughter sinners have gone deep, || And I [am] a chain to them all. **3** I have known Ephraim, || And Israel has not been hid from Me, || For now you have gone whoring, Ephraim, || Israel is defiled. **4** They do not give up their habitual doings, || To turn back to their God, || For a spirit of whoredoms [is] in their midst, || And Yhwh they have not known. **5** And humbled has been the excellence of Israel to his face, || And Israel and Ephraim stumble by their iniquity, || Judah has also stumbled with them. **6** With their flock and with their herd, || They go to seek Yhwh, and do not find, || He has withdrawn from them. **7** Against Yhwh they dealt treacherously, || For they have begotten strange sons, || Now a month consumes them [with] their portions. **8** Blow a horn in Gibeah, a trumpet in Ramah, || Shout, O Beth-Aven, after you, O Benjamin. **9** Ephraim is for a desolation in a day of reproof,

|| I have made known a sure thing among the tribes of Israel. **10** Princes of Judah have been as those removing a border, || I pour out My wrath as water on them. **11** Ephraim is oppressed, broken in judgment, || When he pleased he went after the command. **12** And I [am] as a moth to Ephraim, || And as a rotten thing to the house of Judah. **13** And Ephraim sees his sickness, and Judah his wound, || And Ephraim goes to Asshur, || And sends to a warlike king, || And he is not able to give healing to you, || Nor does he remove a scar from you. **14** For I [am] as a lion to Ephraim, || And as a young lion to the house of Judah, I tear and go, || I carry away, and there is no deliverer. **15** I go—I return to My place, || Until they are desolate, and have sought My face. In their distress they seek Me speedily!"

CHAPTER 6

1 "Come, and we turn back to Yhwh, || For He has torn, and He heals us, || He strikes, and He binds us up. **2** He revives us after two days, || In the third day He raises us up, || And we live before Him. **3** And we know—we pursue to know Yhwh, || His going forth is prepared as the dawn, || And He comes in as a shower to us, || As spring rain [and] autumn rain to the earth." **4** "What do I do to you, O Ephraim? What do I do to you, O Judah? Your goodness [is] as a cloud of the morning, || And as dew rising early—going. **5** Therefore I have hewed by prophets, || I have slain them by sayings of My mouth, || And My judgments go forth to the light. **6** For kindness I desired, and not sacrifice, || And a knowledge of God above burnt-offerings. **7** And they, as Adam, transgressed a covenant, || There they dealt treacherously against Me. **8** Gilead [is] a city of workers of iniquity, || Slippery from blood. **9** And as bands wait for a man, || A company of priest's murder—the way to Shechem, || For they have done wickedness. **10** In the house of Israel I have seen a horrible thing, || There [is] the whoredom of Ephraim—Israel is defiled. **11** Also, O Judah, a harvest is appointed to you, || In My turning back [to] the captivity of My people!"

CHAPTER 7

1 "When I give healing to Israel, || Then the iniquity of Ephraim is revealed, || And the wickedness of Samaria, || For they have worked falsehood, || And a thief comes in, || A troop has stripped off in the street, **2** And they do not say to their heart, || [That] I have remembered all their evil, || Now their doings have surrounded them, || They have been before My face. **3** With their wickedness they make a king glad, || And with their lies—princes. **4** All of them [are] adulterers, || Like a burning oven of a baker, || He ceases from stirring up after kneading the dough, until its leavening. **5** A day of our king! Princes have defiled themselves [with] the poison of wine, || He has drawn out his hand with scorners. **6** For they have drawn near, || Their heart [is] as an oven || In their lying-in wait—their baker sleeps all night, || Morning! He is burning as a flaming fire. **7** All of them are warm as an oven, || And they have devoured their judges, || All their kings have fallen, || There is none calling to Me among them. **8** Ephraim! He mixes himself among peoples, || Ephraim has been an unturned cake. **9** Strangers have devoured his power, || And he has not known, || Also old age has sprinkled [itself] on him, || And he has not known. **10** And the excellence of Israel has been humbled to his face, || And they have not turned back to their God Yhwh, || Nor have they sought Him for all this. **11** And Ephraim is as a simple dove without heart, || Egypt they called on—[to] Asshur they have gone. **12** When they go I spread over them My net, || As the bird of the heavens I bring them down, || I discipline them as their congregation has heard. **13** Woe to them, for they wandered from Me, || Destruction to them, for they transgressed against Me, || And I ransom them, and they have spoken lies against Me, **14** And have not cried to Me with their heart, but howl on their beds; They assemble themselves for grain and new wine, || They turn aside against Me. **15** And I instructed—I strengthened their arms, || And concerning Me they think evil! **16** They turn back—not to the Highest, || They have been as a deceitful bow, || Their princes fall by sword, || From the insolence of their tongue, || This [is] their derision in the land of Egypt!"

CHAPTER 8

1 "To your mouth—a horn, || As an eagle against the house of Yhwh, || Because they transgressed My covenant, || And against My law they have rebelled. **2** To Me they cry, My God, we—Israel—have known You. **3** Israel has cast off good, an enemy pursues him. **4** They have made kings, and not by Me, || They have made princes, and I have not known, || Their silver and their gold they have made to them idols, || So that they are cut off. **5** Your calf has cast off, O Samaria, || My anger has burned against them; Until when are they not capable of purity? **6** For even it [is] of Israel; a craftsman made it, || And it [is] not God, || For the calf of Samaria is fragments! **7** For wind they sow, and a windstorm they reap, || Stalk it has none—a shoot not yielding grain, || If so be it yield—strangers swallow it up. **8** Israel has been swallowed up, || Now they have been among nations, || As a vessel in which is no delight. **9** For they have gone up [to] Asshur, || A wild donkey alone by himself [is] Ephraim, || They have hired lovers! **10** Also though they hire among nations, || Now I gather them, and they are pained a little, || From the burden of a king of princes. **11** Because Ephraim multiplied altars to sin, || They have been to him altars to sin. **12** I write for him numerous things of My law, || As a strange thing they have been reckoned. **13** The sacrifices of My offerings! They sacrifice flesh, and they eat, || Yhwh has not accepted them, || Now He remembers their iniquity, || And inspects their sin, || They return [to] Egypt. **14** And Israel forgets his Maker, and builds temples, || And Judah has multiplied cities of defense, || And I have sent a fire into his cities, || And it has consumed their palaces!"

CHAPTER 9

1 "Do not rejoice, O Israel, do not be joyful like the peoples, || For you have gone whoring from your God, || You have loved a wage near all floors of grain. **2** Floor and winepress do not feed them, || And new wine fails in her, **3** They do not abide in the land of Yhwh, || And Ephraim has turned back [to] Egypt, || And they eat an unclean thing in Asshur. **4** They do not pour out wine to Yhwh, || Nor are they sweet to Him, || Their sacrifices [are] as bread of mourners to them, || All eating it are unclean: For their bread [is] for themselves, || It does not come into the house of Yhwh. **5** What do you do at the day appointed? And at the day of Yhwh's festival? **6** For behold, they have gone because of destruction, || Egypt gathers them, Moph buries them, || The desirable things of their silver, || Nettles possess them—a thorn [is] in their tents. **7** The days of inspection have come in, || The days of repayment have come in, Israel knows! The prophet [is] a fool, || Mad [is] the man of the spirit, || Because of the abundance of your iniquity, || And great [is] the hatred. **8** Ephraim is looking [away] from My God, || The prophet! A snare of a fowler [is] over all his ways, || Hatred [is] in the house of his God. **9** They have gone deep—have done corruptly, || As [in] the days of Gibeah, || He remembers their iniquity, He inspects their sins. **10** As grapes in a wilderness I found Israel, || As the first-fruit in a fig tree, at its beginning, I have seen your fathers, || They have gone in [to] Ba'al-Peor, || And are separated to a shameful thing, || And have become abominable like their love. **11** Ephraim [is] as a bird, their glory flies away, without birth, and without womb, and without conception. **12** For though they nourish their sons, I have made them childless—without man, || Surely also, woe to them when I turn aside from them. **13** Ephraim! When I have looked to the rock, || Is planted in comeliness, || And Ephraim [is] to bring out his sons to a slayer. **14** Give to them, Yhwh—what do You give? Give to them miscarrying womb, and dry breasts. **15** All their evil [is] in Gilgal, || Surely there I have hated them, || Because of the evil of their doings, || Out of My house I drive them, || I no longer love them, || All their heads [are] apostates. **16** Ephraim has been struck, || Their root has dried up, they do not yield fruit, || Indeed, though they bring forth, || I have put to death the desired of their womb. **17** My God rejects them, || Because they have not listened to Him, || And they are wanderers among nations!"

CHAPTER 10

¹ "Israel [is] an empty vine, || He makes fruit like to himself, || According to the abundance of his fruit, || He has multiplied for the altars, || According to the goodness of his land, || They have made good standing-pillars. ² Their heart has been divided, now they are guilty, || He breaks down their altars, || He destroys their standing-pillars. ³ For now they say: We have no king, || Because we have not feared Yhwh, || And the king—what does he do for us? ⁴ They have spoken words, || To swear falsehood in making a covenant, || And flourished as a poisonous herb has judgment, on the furrows of a field. ⁵ For the inhabitants of Samaria fear the calves of Beth-Aven, || Surely its people have mourned on account of it, || And its priests leap about on account of it, || Because of its glory, for it has removed from it, ⁶ Also, it is carried to Asshur, a present to a warlike king, || Ephraim receives shame, || And Israel is ashamed of its own counsel. ⁷ Samaria is cut off! Its king [is] as wrath on the face of the waters. ⁸ And high places of Aven have been destroyed, the sin of Israel. Thorn and bramble go up on their altars, || And they have said to hills, Cover us, || And to heights, Fall on us. ⁹ From the days of Gibeah you have sinned, O Israel, || There they have stood, || Battle does not overtake them in Gibeah, || Because of sons of perverseness. ¹⁰ When I desire, then I bind them, || And peoples have gathered against them, || When they bind themselves to their two iniquities. ¹¹ And Ephraim [is] a trained heifer—loving to thresh, || And I have passed over on the goodness of its neck, || I cause [one] to ride Ephraim, || Judah plows, Jacob harrows for him. ¹² Sow for yourselves in righteousness, || Reap according to loving-kindness, || Till for yourselves tillage of knowledge, || To seek Yhwh, || Until He comes and shows righteousness to you. ¹³ You have plowed wickedness, || Perversity you have reaped, || You have eaten the fruit of lying, || For you have trusted in your way, || In the abundance of your might. ¹⁴ And a tumult rises among your people, || And all your fortresses are spoiled, || As the spoiling of Shalman of Beth-Arbel, || In a day of battle, || Mother against sons dashed in pieces. ¹⁵ Thus has Beth-El done to you, || Because of the evil of your wickedness, || In the dawn a king of Israel is utterly cut off!"

CHAPTER 11

¹ "Because Israel [is] a youth, and I love him, || Out of Egypt I have called for My Son. ² They have called to them correctly, || They have gone from before them, || They sacrifice to lords, || And make incense to carved images. ³ And I have caused Ephraim to go on foot, || Taking them by their arms, || And they have not known that I strengthened them. ⁴ I draw them with cords of man, || With thick cords of love, || And I am to them as a raiser up of a yoke on their jaws, || And I incline to him—I feed [him]. ⁵ He does not return to the land of Egypt, || And Asshur—he [is] his king, || For they have refused to return. ⁶ The sword has been grievous in his cities, || And it has ended his bars, and consumed—from their own counsels. ⁷ And My people are hanging in suspense about My returning, || And to the Most High they call, || Together they do not exalt. ⁸ How do I give you up, O Ephraim? Do I deliver you up, O Israel? How do I make you as Admah? Do I set you as Zeboim? My heart is turned in Me, || My sympathy has been kindled together. ⁹ I do not do the fierceness of My anger, || I do not turn back to destroy Ephraim, || For I [am] God, and not a man—The Holy One in your midst, and I do not enter in enmity. ¹⁰ They go after Yhwh—He roars as a lion, || When He roars, then the sons from the west tremble. ¹¹ They tremble as a sparrow out of Egypt, || And as a dove out of the land of Asshur, || And I have caused them to dwell in their own houses," || A declaration of Yhwh. ¹² "Ephraim has surrounded Me with feigning, || And the house of Israel with deceit. And Judah is again ruling with God, || And [is] faithful with the Holy Ones!"

CHAPTER 12

¹ "Ephraim is enjoying wind, || And is pursuing an east wind, || All the day he multiplies lying and spoiling, || And they make a covenant with Asshur, || And oil is carried to Egypt. ² And Yhwh has a controversy with Judah, || To lay a charge on Jacob according to his ways, || He returns to him according to his doings. ³ In the womb he took his brother by the heel, ||

And by his strength he was a prince with God, ⁴ Indeed, he is a prince to the Messenger, || And he overcomes [by] weeping, || And he makes supplication to Him, || At Bethel He finds him, || And there He speaks with us, ⁵ Even Yhwh, God of the Hosts, Yhwh [is] His memorial. ⁶ And you, through your God, turn, || Keep kindness and judgment, || And wait on your God continually. ⁷ Canaan! In his hand [are] balances of deceit! He has loved to oppress. ⁸ And Ephraim says, || Surely, I have become rich, I have found wealth for myself, || All my labors— they do not find against me iniquity that [is] sin. ⁹ And I—your God Yhwh from the land of Egypt, || Again I turn you back into tents, || As in the days of the appointed time. ¹⁰ And I have spoken to the prophets, || And I have multiplied vision, || And by the hand of the prophets I use allegories. ¹¹ Surely Gilead [is] iniquity, || They have been only vanity, || In Gilead they have sacrificed bullocks, || Also their altars [are] as heaps, on the furrows of a field. ¹² And Jacob flees to the country of Aram, || And Israel serves for a wife, || Indeed, he has kept watch for a wife. ¹³ And by a prophet has Yhwh brought up Israel out of Egypt, || And by a prophet it has been watched. ¹⁴ Ephraim has most bitterly provoked, || And he leaves his blood on himself, || And his Lord turns his reproach back to him!"

CHAPTER 13

¹ "When Ephraim speaks tremblingly, || He has been lifted up in Israel, || When he becomes guilty in Ba'al he dies. ² And now they sin, || And make for themselves a molten image of their silver, || By their own understanding—idols, || A work of artisans—all of it, || Of them they say, who [are] sacrificers among men, The calves let them kiss. ³ Therefore they are as a cloud of the morning, || And as dew, rising early, going away, || As chaff tossed about out of a floor, || And as smoke out of a window. ⁴ And I [am] your God Yhwh from the land of Egypt, || And you do not know a God besides Me, || And a Savior— there is none except Me. ⁵ I have known you in a wilderness, || In a land of droughts. ⁶ They are satiated according to their feedings, || They have been satiated, || And their heart is lifted up, || Therefore they have forgotten Me, ⁷ And I am to them as a lion, || I look out as a leopard by the way. ⁸ I meet them as a bereaved bear, || And I tear the enclosure of their heart, || And I consume them there as a lioness, || A beast of the field tears them. ⁹ You have destroyed yourself, O Israel, || But in Me [is] your help; ¹⁰ Where [is] your king now—And he saves you in all your cities? And your judges of whom you said, || Give a king and heads to me? ¹¹ I give to you a king in My anger, || And I take away in My wrath. ¹² Bound up [is] the iniquity of Ephraim, || Hidden [is] his sin, ¹³ Pangs of a travailing woman come to him, || He [is] not a wise son, || For he does not remain [at] the time for the breaking forth of sons. ¹⁴ Will I ransom them from the hand of Sheol? Will I redeem them from death? Where [is] your plague, O death? Where your destruction, O Sheol? Comfort is hid from My eyes. ¹⁵ Though he produces fruit among brothers, || An east wind comes in, a wind of Yhwh, || From a wilderness it is coming up, || And it dries up his fountain, || And his spring becomes dry, || It—it spoils a treasure—every desirable vessel. ¹⁶ Samaria becomes desolate, || Because she has been rebellious against her God, || They fall by sword, || Their sucklings are dashed in pieces, || And its pregnant ones are ripped up!"

CHAPTER 14

¹ "Turn back, O Israel, to your God Yhwh, || For you have stumbled by your iniquity. ² Take words with you, and turn to Yhwh, || Say to Him, Take away all iniquity, and give good, || And we render the fruit of our lips. ³ Asshur does not save us, we do not ride on a horse, || Nor do we say anymore, Our god, to the work of our hands, || For in You the fatherless find mercy. ⁴ I heal their backsliding, I love them freely, || For My anger has turned back from him. ⁵ I am as dew to Israel, he flourishes as a lily, || And he strikes forth his roots as Lebanon. ⁶ His shoots go on, || And his splendor is as an olive, || And he has fragrance as Lebanon. ⁷ The dwellers return under his shadow, || They revive [as] grain, and flourish as a vine, || His memorial [is] as wine of Lebanon. ⁸ O Ephraim, what have I anymore to do with idols? I have answered, and I look after him: I [am] as a green fir-tree, || Your fruit is found from Me. ⁹ Who [is] wise, and understands these? Prudent, and knows

them? For upright are the ways of Yhwh, || And the righteous go on in them, || And the transgressors stumble therein!"

JOEL

CHAPTER 1

¹ A word of Yhwh that has been to Joel, son of Pethuel: ² Hear this, you aged ones, || And give ear, all you inhabitants of the land, || Has this been in your days? Or in the days of your fathers? ³ Concerning it talk to your sons, || And your sons to their sons, || And their sons to another generation. ⁴ What is left of the palmer-worm, the locust has eaten, || And what is left of the locust, || The cankerworm has eaten, || And what is left of the cankerworm, || The caterpillar has eaten. ⁵ Awake, you drunkards, and weep, || And howl all drinking wine, because of the juice, || For it has been cut off from your mouth. ⁶ For a nation has come up on My land, || Strong, and there is no number, || Its teeth [are] the teeth of a lion, || And it has the jaw-teeth of a lioness. ⁷ It has made My vine become a desolation, || And My fig tree become a splinter, || It has made it thoroughly bare, and has cast down, || Its branches have been made white. ⁸ Wail, as a virgin girds with sackcloth, || For the husband of her youth. ⁹ Present and drink-offering have been cut off from the house of Yhwh, || The priests have mourned, servants of Yhwh. ¹⁰ The field is spoiled, || The ground has mourned, || For the grain is spoiled, || New wine has been dried up, oil languishes. ¹¹ Be ashamed, you farmers, || Howl, vinedressers, for wheat and for barley, || For the harvest of the field has perished. ¹² The vine has been dried up, || And the fig tree languishes, || Pomegranate, also palm, and apple-tree, || All trees of the field have withered, || For joy has been dried up from the sons of men. ¹³ Gird, and lament, you priests, || Howl, you servants of the altar, || Come in, lodge in sackcloth, servants of my God, || For present and drink-offering have been withheld from the house of your God. ¹⁴ Sanctify a fast, proclaim a restraint, || Gather [the] elderly [and] all those inhabiting the land, || [Into the] house of your God Yhwh, ¹⁵ And cry to Yhwh, "Aah! For the day! For [the] Day of Yhwh [is] near, || And it comes as destruction from [the] Almighty. ¹⁶ Is food not cut off before our eyes? Joy and rejoicing from the house of our God? ¹⁷ Scattered things have rotted under their clods, || Storehouses have been desolated, || Granaries have been broken down, || For the grain has withered. ¹⁸ How livestock have sighed! Perplexed have been droves of oxen, || For there is no pasture for them, || Also droves of sheep have been desolated. ¹⁹ To You, O Yhwh, I call, || For fire has consumed lovely places of a wilderness, || And a flame has set on fire all trees of the field. ²⁰ Also the livestock of the field long for You, || For dried up have been streams of water, || And fire has consumed lovely places of a wilderness!"

CHAPTER 2

¹ Blow a horn in Zion, || And shout in My holy hill, || All inhabitants of the earth tremble, || For the Day of Yhwh is coming, for [it is] nearby! ² A Day of darkness and thick darkness, || A Day of cloud and thick darkness, || As darkness spread on the mountains, || A people numerous and mighty, || Like there has not been from of old, || And after it there is not again—Until the years of generation and generation. ³ Before it fire has consumed, || And after it a flame burns, || As the Garden of Eden [is] the land before it, || And after it a wilderness—a desolation! And also, there has not been to it an escape, ⁴ As the appearance of horses [is] its appearance, || And as horsemen, so they run. ⁵ As the noise of chariots, they skip on the tops of the mountains, || As the noise of a flame of fire devouring stubble, || As a mighty people set in array for battle. ⁶ Pained are peoples from its face, || All faces have gathered paleness. ⁷ They run as mighty ones, || As men of war they go up a wall, || And they each go in his own ways, || And they do not change their paths. ⁸ And each does not press his brother, || They each go on in his way, || If they fall by the missile, they are not cut off. ⁹ In the city they run to and fro, || On the wall they run, || Into houses they go up by the windows, || They go in as a thief. ¹⁰ At their face the earth has trembled, || The heavens have shaken, || Sun and moon have

been black, || And stars have gathered up their shining. ¹¹ And Yhwh has given forth His voice before His force, || For His camp [is] very great, || For mighty [is] the doer of His word, || For great [is] the Day of Yhwh—very fearful, || And who bears it? ¹² "And also now," a declaration of Yhwh, || "Turn back to Me with all your heart, || And with fasting, and with weeping, || And with lamentation." ¹³ And tear your heart, and not your garments, || And turn back to your God Yhwh, || For He [is] gracious and merciful, || Slow to anger, and abundant in kindness, || And relenting from evil. ¹⁴ Who knows—He turns back, || Indeed—He has relented, || And He has left behind Him a blessing, || A present and drink-offering of your God Yhwh? ¹⁵ Blow a horn in Zion, || Sanctify a fast—proclaim a restraint. ¹⁶ Gather the people, sanctify an assembly, || Assemble the aged, || Gather infants and sucklings of the breasts, || Let a bridegroom go out from his inner chamber, || And a bride out of her closet. ¹⁷ Let the priests weep between the porch and the altar, servants of Yhwh, || And let them say: "Have pity, O Yhwh, on Your people, || And do not give Your inheritance to reproach, || To the ruling over them of nations, || Why do they say among peoples, Where [is] their God?" ¹⁸ And let Yhwh be zealous for His land, || And have pity on His people. ¹⁹ Let Yhwh answer and say to His people, || "Behold, I am sending to you the grain, || And the new wine, and the oil, || And you have been satisfied with it, || And I make you no longer a reproach among nations, ²⁰ And the northern I put far off from you, || And have driven him to a land dry and desolate, || With his face toward the Eastern Sea, || And his rear to the Western Sea, || And his stink has come up, || And his stench comes up, || For he has exerted himself to work." ²¹ Do not fear, O land! Be glad and rejoice, || For Yhwh has exerted Himself to work. ²² Do not fear, O livestock of the field! For pastures of a wilderness have sprung up, || For the tree has borne its fruit, || Fig tree and vine have given their strength! ²³ And you sons of Zion, || Be glad and rejoice in your God Yhwh, || For He has given to you the Teacher for righteousness, || And causes a shower to come down to you, || Early rain and spring rain [as] in the beginning. ²⁴ And the floors have been full [with] pure grain, || And the presses have overflown [with] new wine and oil. ²⁵ "And I have repaid to you the years that the locust consumed, || The cankerworm, and the caterpillar, and the palmer-worm, || My great force that I sent against you. ²⁶ And you have eaten, eating and being satisfied, || And have praised the Name of your God Yhwh, || Who has dealt with you wonderfully, || And My people are not ashamed for all time. ²⁷ And you have known that I [am] in the midst of Israel, || And I [am] your God Yhwh, and there is none else, || And My people are not ashamed for all time. ²⁸ And it has come to pass afterward, || I pour out My Spirit on all flesh, || And your sons and your daughters have prophesied, || Your old men dream dreams, || Your young men see visions. ²⁹ And also on the menservants and on the maidservants, || In those days I pour out My Spirit. ³⁰ And I have given wonders in the heavens and in the earth: Blood, and fire, and columns of smoke. ³¹ The sun is turned to darkness, and the moon to blood, || Before the coming of the Day of Yhwh, || The great and the fearful. ³² And it has come to pass, || Everyone who calls on the Name of Yhwh is delivered, || For in Mount Zion and in Jerusalem there is an escape, || As Yhwh has said, || And among the remnants whom Yhwh is calling!"

CHAPTER 3

¹ "For behold, in those days, and in that time, || When I turn back [to] the captivity of Judah and Jerusalem, ² Then I have gathered all the nations, || And caused them to go down to the Valley of Jehoshaphat, || And I have been in judgment with them there, || Concerning My people and My inheritance—Israel, || Whom they scattered among nations, || And My land they have apportioned. ³ And for My people they cast a lot, || And they give the young man for a harlot, || And have sold the young woman for wine, || That they may drink. ⁴ And also, what [are] you to Me, O Tyre and Sidon, || And all circuits of Philistia? Are you rendering repayment to Me? And if you are giving repayment to Me, || Swiftly, quickly, I return your repayment on your head. ⁵ In that My silver and My gold you took, || And My desirable things that are good, || You have brought into your temples. ⁶ And sons of Judah, and sons of Jerusalem, || You have sold to the sons of Javan, || To put

them far off from their border. **7** Behold, I am stirring them up out of the place || To where you have sold them, || And I have turned back your repayment on your head, **8** And have sold your sons and your daughters || Into the hand of the sons of Judah, || And they have sold them to Sabeans, || To a nation far off, for Yhwh has spoken." **9** Proclaim this among nations, || Sanctify a war, stir up the mighty ones, || Come near, come up, let all the men of war. **10** Beat your plowshares to swords, || And your pruning-hooks to javelins, || Let the weak say, "I [am] mighty." **11** Hurry, and come in, all you nations around, || And be gathered together, || There cause to come down, O Yhwh, || Your mighty ones. **12** "Let the nations wake and come up to the Valley of Jehoshaphat, || For there I sit to judge all the nations around. **13** Send forth a sickle, || For harvest has ripened, || Come in, come down, for the press has been filled, || Winepresses have overflowed, || For great [is] their wickedness." **14** Multitudes, multitudes [are] in the Valley of Decision, || For near [is] the Day of Yhwh in the Valley of Decision. **15** Sun and moon have been black, || And stars have gathered up their shining. **16** And Yhwh roars from Zion, || And gives forth His voice from Jerusalem, || And the heavens and earth have shaken, || And Yhwh [is] a refuge to His people, || And a stronghold to sons of Israel. **17** "And you have known that I [am] your God Yhwh, || Dwelling in Zion, My holy mountain, || And Jerusalem has been holy, || And strangers do not pass over into it again." **18** And it has come to pass in that day, || The mountains drop down juice, || And the hills flow [with] milk, || And all streams of Judah go [with] water, || And a fountain from the house of Yhwh goes forth, || And has watered the Valley of Shittim. **19** "Egypt becomes a desolation, || And Edom becomes a desolation, a wilderness, || For violence [to] sons of Judah, || Whose innocent blood they shed in their land. **20** And Judah dwells for all time, || And Jerusalem to generation and generation. **21** And I have declared their blood innocent, || [That] I did not declare innocent, || And Yhwh is dwelling in Zion!"

AMOS

CHAPTER 1

1 Words of Amos—who has been among herdsmen of Tekoa—that he has seen concerning Israel, in the days of Uzziah king of Judah, and in the days of Jeroboam son of Joash king of Israel, two years before the shaking; **2** and he says, "Yhwh roars from Zion, || And gives forth His voice from Jerusalem, || And pastures of the shepherds have mourned, || And the top of Carmel has withered!" **3** And thus said Yhwh: "For three transgressions of Damascus, || And for four, I do not reverse it, || Because of their threshing Gilead with sharp-pointed irons, **4** And I have sent a fire against the house of Hazael, || And it has consumed the palaces of Ben-Hadad. **5** And I have broken the bar of Damascus, || And cut off the inhabitant from Bikat-Aven, || And a holder of a scepter from Beth-Eden, || And the people of Aram have been removed to Kir," said Yhwh. **6** Thus said Yhwh: "For three transgressions of Gaza, || And for four, I do not reverse it, || Because of their removing a complete captivity, || To deliver up to Edom, **7** And I have sent a fire against the wall of Gaza, || And it has consumed her palaces; **8** And I have cut off the inhabitant from Ashdod, || And a holder of a scepter from Ashkelon, || And have turned back My hand against Ekron, || And the remnant of the Philistines have perished," said Lord Yhwh. **9** Thus said Yhwh: "For three transgressions of Tyre, || And for four, I do not reverse it, || Because of their delivering up a complete captivity to Edom, || And they did not remember the brotherly covenant, **10** And I have sent a fire against the wall of Tyre, || And it has consumed her palaces." **11** Thus said Yhwh: "For three transgressions of Edom, || And for four, I do not reverse it, || Because of his pursuing his brother with a sword, || And he has destroyed his mercies, || And his anger tears continuously, || And his wrath—he has kept it forever, **12** And I have sent a fire against Teman, || And it has consumed palaces of Bozrah." **13** Thus said Yhwh: "For three transgressions of the sons of Ammon, || And for four, I do not reverse it, || Because of their ripping up the pregnant ones of Gilead, || To enlarge their border, **14** And I have kindled a fire against the wall of Rabbah, || And it has consumed her palaces, || With a shout in a day of battle, || With a whirlwind in a day of windstorm, **15**

And their king has gone in a removal, || He and his heads together," said Yhwh!

CHAPTER 2

1 Thus said Yhwh: "For three transgressions of Moab, || And for four, I do not reverse it, || Because of his burning the bones of the king of Edom to lime, **2** And I have sent a fire against Moab, || And it has consumed the palaces of Kerioth, || And Moab is dying with noise, || With shouting, with voice of a horn. **3** And I have cut off judge from her midst, || And I slay all its heads with him," said Yhwh. **4** Thus said Yhwh: "For three transgressions of Judah, || And for four, I do not reverse it, || Because of their loathing the Law of Yhwh, || And His statutes they have not kept, || And their lies cause them to err, || After which their fathers walked, **5** And I have sent a fire against Judah, || And it has consumed palaces of Jerusalem." **6** Thus said Yhwh: "For three transgressions of Israel, || And for four, I do not reverse it, || Because of their selling the righteous for silver, || And the needy for a pair of sandals. **7** Who are panting for the dust of the earth on the head of the poor, || And the way of the humble they turn aside, || And a man and his father go to the girl, || So as to defile My holy Name. **8** And they stretch themselves on pledged garments near every altar, || And the wine of fined ones they drink [in] the house of their gods. **9** And I have destroyed the Amorite from before them, || Whose height [is] as the height of cedars, || And he [is] strong as the oaks, || And I destroy his fruit from above, || And his roots from beneath. **10** And I have brought you up from the land of Egypt, || And cause you to go in a wilderness forty years, || To possess the land of the Amorite. **11** And I raise of your sons for prophets, || And of your choice ones for Nazarites, || Is this not true, O sons of Israel?" A declaration of Yhwh. **12** "And you cause the Nazarites to drink wine, || And on the prophets you have laid a charge, || Saying, Do not prophesy! **13** Behold, I am pressing you under, || As the full cart presses a sheaf for itself. **14** And refuge has perished from the swift, || And the strong does not strengthens his power, || And the mighty does not deliver his soul. **15** And the handler of the bow does not stand, || And the swift does not deliver [himself] with his feet, || And the rider of the horse does not deliver his soul. **16** And the courageous of heart among the mighty, || Flees naked in that day," || A declaration of Yhwh!

CHAPTER 3

1 Hear this word that Yhwh has spoken concerning you, O sons of Israel, concerning all the family that I brought up from the land of Egypt, saying, **2** "Only you have I known of all families of the earth, || Therefore I charge on you all your iniquities." **3** Do two walk together if they have not met? **4** Does a lion roar in a forest and he has no prey? Does a young lion give out his voice from his habitation, || If he has not caught? **5** Does a bird fall into a snare of the earth, || And there is no trap for it? Does a snare go up from the ground, || And it does not capture prey? **6** Is a horn blown in a city, || And do people not tremble? Is there affliction in a city, || And Yhwh has not done [it]? **7** For Lord Yhwh does nothing, || Except He has revealed His counsel to His servants the prophets. **8** A lion has roared—who does not fear? Lord Yhwh has spoken—who does not prophesy? **9** "Sound to palaces in Ashdod, || And to palaces in the land of Egypt, and say: Be gathered on mountains of Samaria, || And see many troubles within her, || And oppressed ones in her midst. **10** And they have not known to act straightforwardly," || A declaration of Yhwh, || "Who are treasuring up violence and spoil in their palaces." **11** Therefore, thus said Lord Yhwh: "An adversary—and surrounding the land, || And he has brought down your strength from you, || And your palaces have been spoiled." **12** Thus said Yhwh: "As the shepherd delivers from the lion's mouth || Two legs, or a piece of an ear, || So the sons of Israel are delivered, || Who are sitting in Samaria on the corner of a bed, || And in Damascus [on that of] a couch. **13** Hear and testify to the house of Jacob," || A declaration of Lord Yhwh, God of Hosts. **14** "For in the day of My charging the transgressions of Israel on him, I have laid a charge on the altars of Beth-El, || And the horns of the altar have been cut off, || And they have fallen to the earth. **15** And I have struck the winter-house with the summer-house, || And houses of ivory have perished, || And many houses have been consumed," || A declaration of Yhwh!

CHAPTER 4

¹ Hear this word, you cows of Bashan, || Who [are] on the mountain of Samaria, || Who are oppressing the poor, || Who are bruising the needy, || Who are saying to their lords: "Bring in, and we drink." ² Lord Yhwh has sworn by His holiness, || "Behold, days are coming on you, || And He has taken you away with hooks, || And your posterity with fish-hooks. ³ And [by] breaches you go forth, || A woman before her, || And you have cast down the high place," || A declaration of Yhwh. ⁴ "Enter Beth-El, and transgress, || At Gilgal multiply transgression, || And bring in your sacrifices every morning, || Your tithes every third year. ⁵ And burn a thank-offering with leaven as incense, || And proclaim willing gifts, sound! For so you have loved, O sons of Israel," || A declaration of Lord Yhwh. ⁶ "And I also—I have given to you cleanness of teeth in all your cities, || And lack of bread in all your places, || And you have not turned back to Me," || A declaration of Yhwh. ⁷ "And I also—I have withheld from you the rain, || While yet three months to harvest, || And I have sent rain on one city, || And on another city I do not send rain, || One portion is rained on, || And the portion on which it does not rain withers. ⁸ And two or three cities have wandered, || To the same city to drink water, || And they are not satisfied, || And you have not turned back to Me," || A declaration of Yhwh. ⁹ "I have struck you with blasting and with mildew, || The abundance of your gardens and of your vineyards, || And of your figs, and of your olives, || The palmer-worm eats, || And you have not turned back to Me," || A declaration of Yhwh. ¹⁰ "I have sent among you pestilence by the way of Egypt, || I have slain your choice ones by sword, || With your captive horses, || And I cause the stink of your camps to come up—Even into your nostrils, || And you have not turned back to Me," || A declaration of Yhwh. ¹¹ "I have overturned among you, || Like the overturn by God of Sodom and Gomorrah, || And you are as a brand delivered from a burning, || And you have not turned back to Me," || A declaration of Yhwh. ¹² "Therefore, thus I do to you, O Israel, at last, || Because this I do to you, || Prepare to meet your God, O Israel." ¹³ For behold, the Former of mountains, and Creator of wind, || And the Declarer to man what [is] His thought, || He is making dawn obscurity, || And is treading on high places of earth, || Yhwh, God of Hosts, [is] His Name!

CHAPTER 5

¹ Hear this word that I am bearing to you, || A lamentation, O house of Israel: ² "Fallen, not to rise again, has the virgin of Israel, || Left on her land—she has none [to] raise [her] up." ³ For thus said Lord Yhwh: "The city that is going out one thousand, || Leaves one hundred, || And that which is going out one hundred, || Leaves ten to the house of Israel." ⁴ For thus said Yhwh to the house of Israel: "Seek Me, and live, ⁵ And do not seek Beth-El, and do not enter Gilgal, || And do not pass through Beer-Sheba, || For Gilgal utterly removes, || And Beth-El becomes vanity. ⁶ Seek Yhwh, and live, || Lest He prosper as fire [against] the house of Joseph, || And it has consumed, || And there is no quencher for Beth-El— ⁷ You who are turning judgment to wormwood, || And have put down righteousness to the earth!" ⁸ The Maker of the Pleiades and Orion, || And He who is turning death-shade to the morning—And He has made day [as] dark [as] night—Who is calling to the waters of the sea, || And pours them on the face of the earth, || Yhwh [is] His Name; ⁹ Who is brightening up the spoiled against the strong, || And the spoiled comes against a fortress. ¹⁰ They have hated a reprover in the gate, || And they detest a plain speaker. ¹¹ Therefore, because of your trampling on the poor, || And the tribute of grain you take from him, || Houses of hewn work you have built, || And you do not dwell in them, || Desirable vineyards you have planted, || And you do not drink their wine. ¹² For I have known—many [are] your transgressions, || And mighty your sins, || Adversaries of the righteous, taking ransoms, || And you turned aside the needy in the gate. ¹³ Therefore the wise is silent at that time, || For it [is] an evil time. ¹⁴ Seek good, and not evil, that you may live, and it is so; Yhwh, God of Hosts, [is] with you, as you said. ¹⁵ Hate evil, and love good, || And set up judgment in the gate, || It may be Yhwh, God of Hosts, pities the remnant of Joseph. ¹⁶ Therefore, thus said Yhwh, God of Hosts, the Lord: "Lamentation is in all broad places, || And in all out-places they say, Oh! Oh! And called the farmer to mourning, || And the skillful of wailing to lamentation. ¹⁷ And in all vineyards [is] lamentation, || For I pass into your midst," said Yhwh. ¹⁸ Behold, you who are desiring the Day of Yhwh, || Why [is] this to you—the Day of Yhwh? It is darkness, and not light, ¹⁹ As [when] one flees from the face of the lion, || And the bear has met him, || And he has come into the house, || And has leaned his hand on the wall, || And the serpent has bitten him. ²⁰ Is not the Day of Yhwh darkness and not light, || Even thick darkness that has no brightness? ²¹ "I have hated—I have loathed your festivals, || And I am not refreshed by your restraints. ²² For though you cause burnt-offerings and your presents to ascend to Me, || I am not pleased, || And I do not behold the peace-offering of your fatlings. ²³ Turn the noise of your songs aside from Me, || Indeed, I do not hear the praise of your stringed instruments. ²⁴ And judgment rolls on as waters, || And righteousness as a perennial stream. ²⁵ Did you bring sacrifices and offerings near to Me, || In a wilderness forty years, O house of Israel? ²⁶ And you bore Succoth your king, and Chiun your images, || The star of your god, that you made for yourselves. ²⁷ And I removed you beyond Damascus," said Yhwh—God of Hosts [is] His Name.

CHAPTER 6

1 Woe [to] those secure in Zion, || And those confident on the mountain of Samaria, || The marked of the chief of the nations, || And the house of Israel has come to them. 2 Pass over [to] Calneh and see, || And go there [to] Hamath the great, || And go down [to] Gath of the Philistines, || Are [they] better than these kingdoms? [Is] their border greater than your border? 3 Who are putting away the day of evil, || And you bring the seat of violence near, 4 Who are lying down on beds of ivory, || And are spread out on their couches, || And are eating lambs from the flock, || And calves from the midst of the stall, 5 Who are taking part according to the stringed instrument, || Like David they invented for themselves instruments of music; 6 Who are drinking with bowls of wine, || And anoint themselves [with] chief perfumes, || And have not been pained for the breach of Joseph. 7 Therefore they now go at the head of the captives, || And the mourning-feast of stretched-out ones is turned aside. 8 Lord Yhwh has sworn by Himself, || A declaration of Yhwh, God of Hosts: "I am abominating the excellence of Jacob, || And his high places I have hated, || And I have delivered up the city and its fullness." 9 And if there are left ten persons in one house, || It has come to pass—that they have died. 10 And his loved one has lifted him up, even his burner, || To bring forth the bones from the house, || And he said to him who [is] in the sides of the house, || "Is there [any] yet with you?" And he said, "None," || Then he said, "Hush! We must not make mention of the Name of Yhwh." 11 For behold, Yhwh is commanding, || And He has struck the great house [with] breaches, || And the little house [with] clefts. 12 Do horses run on a rock? Does one plow [it] with oxen? For you have turned judgment to gall, || And the fruit of righteousness to wormwood. 13 O you who are rejoicing at nothing, || Who are saying, "Have we not taken to ourselves horns by our strength?" 14 "Surely, behold, I am raising a nation against you, O house of Israel," || A declaration of Yhwh, God of Hosts, || "And they have oppressed you from the coming in to Hamath, || To the stream of the desert."

CHAPTER 7

¹ Thus Lord Yhwh has showed me, and behold, He is forming locusts at the beginning of the ascending of the latter growth, and behold, the latter growth [is] after the mowings of the king [[or King Gog]]; ² and it has come to pass, when it has finished to consume the herb of the land, that I say, "Lord Yhwh, please forgive, || How does Jacob arise—for he [is] small?" ³ Yhwh has relented of this, "It will not be," said Yhwh. ⁴ Thus has Lord Yhwh showed me, and behold, Lord Yhwh is calling to contend by the fire, and it consumes the great deep, indeed, it has consumed the portion, and I say, ⁵ "Lord Yhwh, please cease, || How does Jacob arise—for he [is] small?" ⁶

Yhwh has relented of this, "It also will not be," said Lord Yhwh. **7** Thus has He showed me, and behold, the Lord is standing by a wall [made according to] a plumb-line, and in His hand a plumb-line; **8** and Yhwh says to me, "What are you seeing, Amos?" And I say, "A plumb-line"; and the Lord says: "Behold, I am setting a plumb-line in the midst of My people Israel, I no longer pass over to it. **9** And high places of Isaac have been desolated, || And sanctuaries of Israel are dried up, || And I have risen against the house of Jeroboam with a sword." **10** And Amaziah priest of Beth-El sends to Jeroboam king of Israel, saying, "Amos has conspired against you in the midst of the house of Israel; the land is not able to bear all his words, **11** for thus said Amos: Jeroboam dies by sword, || And Israel certainly removes from off its land." **12** And Amaziah says to Amos, "Seer, go, flee to the land of Judah for yourself, and eat bread there, and there you prophesy; **13** and no longer prophesy [at] Beth-El anymore, for it [is] the king's sanctuary, and it [is] the royal house." **14** And Amos answers and says to Amaziah, "I [am] no prophet, nor [am] I a prophet's son, but I [am] a herdsman, and a cultivator of sycamores, **15** and Yhwh takes me from after the flock, and Yhwh says to me, Go, prophesy to My people Israel. **16** And now, hear a word of Yhwh: You are saying, Do not prophesy against Israel, nor drop [anything] against the house of Isaac, **17** therefore, thus said Yhwh: Your wife goes whoring in the city, || And your sons and your daughters fall by sword, || And your land is apportioned by line, || And you die on an unclean land, || And Israel certainly removes from off its land."

CHAPTER 8

1 Thus has Lord Yhwh showed me, and behold, a basket of summer-fruit. **2** And He says, "What are you seeing, Amos?" And I say, "A basket of summer-fruit." And Yhwh says to me: "The end has come to My people Israel, || I no longer pass over to it anymore. **3** And female singers have howled of a palace in that day," || A declaration of Lord Yhwh, || "Many [are] the carcasses, into any place throw—hush!" **4** Hear this, you who are swallowing up the needy, || To cause the poor of the land to cease, **5** Saying, "When does the new moon pass, || And we sell ground grain? And the Sabbath, and we open out pure grain? To make little the ephah, || And to make great the shekel, || And to use balances of deceit perversely. **6** To purchase the poor with money, || And the needy for a pair of sandals, || Indeed, the refuse of the pure grain we sell." **7** Yhwh has sworn by the excellence of Jacob: "I do not forget any of their works forever. **8** Does the land not tremble for this, || And every dweller in it has mourned? And all of it has come up as a flood. And it has been cast out, and has sunk, || Like the flood of Egypt. **9** And it has come to pass in that day," || A declaration of Lord Yhwh, || "I have caused the sun to go in at noon, || And caused darkness on the land in a day of light, **10** And have turned your festivals to mourning, || And all your songs to lamentation, || And caused sackcloth to come up on all loins, || And on every head—baldness, || And made it as a mourning of an only one, || And its latter end as a day of bitterness. **11** Behold, days are coming," || A declaration of Lord Yhwh, || "And I have sent a famine into the land, || Not a famine of bread, nor a thirst of water, || But of hearing the words of Yhwh. **12** And they have wandered from sea to sea, || And from north even to east, || They go to and fro to seek the word of Yhwh, || And they do not find [it]. **13** In that day the beautiful virgins, || And the young men, faint with thirst. **14** Those swearing by the guilt of Samaria, || And who have said, Your god lives, O Dan, || And, The way of Beer-Sheba lives, || Indeed, they have fallen and do not rise again!"

CHAPTER 9

1 I have seen the Lord standing by the altar, and He says, || "Strike the knob, and the thresholds shake, || And cut them off by the head—all of them, || And I slay their posterity with a sword, || None that flee of them flee away, || Nor a fugitive of them escape. **2** If they dig through into Sheol, || From there My hand takes them, || And if they go up [to] the heavens, || From there I cause them to come down. **3** And if they are hid in the top of Carmel, || From there I search out, and have taken them, || And if they are hid from My eyes in the bottom of the sea, || From there I command the serpent, || And it has bitten

them. **4** And if they go into captivity before their enemies, || From there I command the sword, || And it has slain them, || And I have set My eye on them for evil, || And not for good." **5** And [it is] the Lord, Yhwh of Hosts, || Who is striking against the land, and it melts, || And mourned have all the inhabitants in it, || And all of it has come up as a flood, || And it has sunk—like the flood of Egypt. **6** Who is building His upper chambers in the heavens; As for His troop, || On earth He has founded it, || Who is calling for the waters of the sea, || And pours them out on the face of the land, || Yhwh [is] His Name. **7** "Are you not as sons of Cushim to Me, O sons of Israel?" A declaration of Yhwh. "Did I not bring Israel up out of the land of Egypt? And the Philistines from Caphtor, and Aram from Kir? **8** Behold, [the] eyes of Lord Yhwh [are] on the sinful kingdom, || And I have destroyed it from off the face of the ground, || Only, I do not utterly destroy the house of Jacob," || A declaration of Yhwh. **9** "For behold, I am commanding, || And I have shaken among all the nations the house of Israel, || As [one] shakes with a sieve, || And there does not fall a grain [to] the earth. **10** By sword all sinners of My people die, || Who are saying, || Evil does not overtake, or go before, || For our sakes. **11** In that day I raise the dwelling place of David that is fallen, || And I have repaired their breaches, || And I raise up its ruins, || And I have built it up as in days of old, **12** So that they possess the remnant of Edom, || And all the nations on whom My Name is called," || A declaration of Yhwh—the doer of this. **13** "Behold, days are coming," || A declaration of Yhwh, || "And the plowman has come near to the reaper, || And the treader of grapes to the scatterer of seed, || And the mountains have dropped juice, || And all the hills melt. **14** And I have turned back [to] the captivity of My people Israel, || And they have built desolate cities, and inhabited, || And have planted vineyards, and drunk their wine, || And made gardens, and eaten their fruit. **15** And I have planted them on their own ground, || And they are not plucked up anymore from off their own ground, || That I have given to them," said your God Yhwh!

OBADIAH

CHAPTER 1

1 Thus said Lord Yhwh to Edom || (We have heard a report from Yhwh, || And an ambassador among nations was sent, || "Rise, indeed, let us rise against her for battle"): **2** "Behold, I have made you little among nations, || You [are] despised exceedingly. **3** The pride of your heart has lifted you up, || O dweller in clefts of a rock || (A high place [is] his habitation, || He is saying in his heart: Who brings me down [to] earth?) **4** If you go up high as an eagle, || And if you set your nest between stars, || From there I bring you down," || A declaration of Yhwh. **5** "If thieves have come in to you, || If spoilers of the night, || How have you been cut off! Do they not steal their sufficiency? If gatherers have come in to you, || Do they not leave gleanings? **6** How has Esau been searched out! His hidden things have flowed out, **7** All your allies have sent you to the border, || Forgotten you, prevailed over you, have your friends, || They make your bread a snare under you, || There is no understanding in him! **8** Is it not in that day," a declaration of Yhwh, || "That I have destroyed the wise out of Edom, || And understanding out of the mountain of Esau? **9** And your mighty ones have been broken down, O Teman, || So that everyone of the mountain of Esau is cut off. **10** For slaughter, for violence [to] your brother Jacob, || Shame covers you, || And you have been cut off for all time. **11** In the day of your standing aloof from the opposite [side], || In the day of strangers taking his force captive, || And foreigners have entered his gates, || And have cast a lot for Jerusalem, || Even you [are] as one of them! **12** And—you do not look on the day of your brother, || On the day of his alienation, || Nor do you rejoice over sons of Judah, || In the day of their destruction, || Nor make your mouth great in a day of distress. **13** Nor come into a gate of My people in a day of their calamity, || Nor look, even you, on its misfortune in a day of its calamity, || Nor send forth against its force in a day of its calamity, **14** Nor stand by the breach to cut off its escaped, || Nor deliver up its remnant in a day of distress. **15** For near [is] the Day of Yhwh, on all the nations, || As you have done, it is done to you, || Your deed turns back on your own head. **¹⁶** For—as you have drunk on My holy mountain, || All the nations drink continually, || And they have drunk and have swallowed, || And they have been as [if] they have not been. **¹⁷** And in Mount Zion there is an escape, || And it has been holy, || And the house of Jacob has possessed their possessions. **¹⁸** And the house of Jacob has been a fire, || And the house of Joseph a flame, || And the house of Esau for stubble, || And they have burned among them, || And they have consumed them, || And there is not a remnant to the house of Esau," || For Yhwh has spoken. **¹⁹** And they have possessed the south with the mountain of Esau, || And the low country with the Philistines, || And they have possessed the field of Ephraim, || And the field of Samaria, || And Benjamin with Gilead. **²⁰** And the expulsion of this force of the sons of Israel, || That [is with] the Canaanites to Zarephat, || And the expulsion of Jerusalem that [is] with the Sepharad, || Possess the cities of the south. **²¹** And saviors have gone up on Mount Zion, || To judge the mountain of Esau, || And the kingdom has been to Yhwh!

JONAH

CHAPTER 1

¹ And there is a word of Yhwh to Jonah son of Amittai, saying, **²** "Rise, go to Nineveh, the great city, and proclaim against it that their wickedness has come up before Me." **³** And Jonah rises to flee to Tarshish from the face of Yhwh, and goes down [to] Joppa, and finds a ship going [to] Tarshish, and he gives its fare, and goes down into it, to go with them to Tarshish from the face of Yhwh. **⁴** And Yhwh has cast a great wind on the sea, and there is a great storm in the sea, and the ship has reckoned to be broken; **⁵** and the mariners are afraid, and they each cry to his god, and cast the goods that [are] in the ship into the sea, to make [it] light of them; and Jonah has gone down to the sides of the vessel, and he lies down, and is fast asleep. **⁶** And the chief of the company draws near to him and says to him, "What are you [doing], O sleeper? rise, call to your God, it may be God considers Himself of us, and we do not perish." **⁷** And they each say to his neighbor, "Come, and we cast lots, and we know on whose account this evil [is] on us." And they cast lots, and the lot falls on Jonah. **⁸** And they say to him, "Now declare to us, on whose account [is] this evil on us? what [is] your occupation, and where do you come from? what [is] your country, seeing you are not of this people?" **⁹** And he says to them, "I—a Hebrew, and I fear Yhwh, God of the heavens, who made the sea and the dry land." **¹⁰** And the men fear a great fear, and say to him, "What [is] this you have done!" For the men have known that he is fleeing from the face of Yhwh, for he has told them. **¹¹** And they say to him, "What do we do to you that the sea may cease from us, for the sea is more and more turbulent?" **¹²** And he says to them, "Lift me up, and cast me into the sea, and the sea ceases from you; for I know that on my account this great storm [is] on you." **¹³** And the men row to turn back to the dry land, and are not able, for the sea is more and more turbulent against them. **¹⁴** And they cry to Yhwh, and say, "Ah, now, O Yhwh, please do not let us perish for this man's life, and do not lay innocent blood on us! For You, Yhwh, as You have pleased, You have done." **¹⁵** And they lift up Jonah, and cast him into the sea, and the sea ceases from its raging; **¹⁶** and the men fear Yhwh [with] a great fear, and sacrifice a sacrifice to Yhwh, and vow vows. **¹⁷** And Yhwh appoints a great fish to swallow up Jonah, and Jonah is in the bowels of the fish three days and three nights.

CHAPTER 2

¹ And Jonah prays to his God Yhwh from the bowels of the fish. **²** And he says: "I called, because of my distress, to Yhwh, || And He answers me, || From the belly of Sheol I have cried, || You have heard my voice. **³** When You cast me [into] the deep, || Into the heart of the seas, || Then the flood surrounds me, || All Your breakers and Your billows have passed over me. **⁴** And I said: I have been cast out from before Your eyes || (Yet I add to look to Your holy temple!) **⁵** Waters have surrounded me to the soul, || The deep surrounds me, || The weed is

bound to my head. **⁶** To the cuttings of mountains I have come down, || The earth, her bars [are] behind me for all time. And You bring my life up from the pit, O Yhwh my God. **⁷** In the feebleness of my soul within me, || I have remembered Yhwh, || And my prayer comes to You, || Into Your holy temple. **⁸** Those observing lying vanities forsake their own mercy. **⁹** And I—with a voice of thanksgiving—I sacrifice to You, || That which I have vowed I complete, || Salvation [is] of Yhwh." **¹⁰** And Yhwh speaks to the fish, and it vomits Jonah out on the dry land.

CHAPTER 3

¹ And there is a word of Yhwh to Jonah a second time, saying, **²** "Rise, go to Nineveh, the great city, and proclaim to it the proclamation that I am speaking to you"; **³** and Jonah rises, and he goes to Nineveh, according to the word of Yhwh. And Nineveh has been a great city before God, a journey of three days. **⁴** And Jonah begins to go into the city—a journey of one day—and proclaims and says, "Yet forty days and Nineveh is overturned!" **⁵** And the men of Nineveh believe in God, and proclaim a fast, and put on sackcloth, from their greatest even to their least, **⁶** seeing the word comes to the king of Nineveh, and he rises from his throne, and removes his honorable robe from off him, and spreads out sackcloth, and sits on the ashes, **⁷** and he cries and says in Nineveh by a decree of the king and his great ones, saying, "Man and beast, herd and flock—do not let them taste anything, do not let them feed, do not even let them drink water; **⁸** and let man and beast cover themselves [with] sackcloth, and let them call to God mightily, and let them each turn back from his evil way, and from the violence that [is] in their hands. **⁹** Who knows? He turns back, and God has relented, and has turned back from the heat of His anger, and we do not perish." **¹⁰** And God sees their works, that they have turned back from their evil way, and God relents of the evil that He spoke of doing to them, and He has not done [it].

CHAPTER 4

¹ And it is grievous to Jonah—a great evil—and he is displeased at it; **²** and he prays to Yhwh, and he says, "Ah, now, O Yhwh, is this not my word while I was in my own land—therefore I was beforehand [going] to flee to Tarshish—that I have known that You [are] a God, gracious and merciful, slow to anger, and abundant in kindness, and relenting of evil? **³** And now, O Yhwh, please take my soul from me, for better [is] my death than my life." **⁴** And Yhwh says, "Is doing good displeasing to you?" **⁵** And Jonah goes forth from the city, and sits on the east of the city, and makes a shelter for himself there, and sits under it in the shade, until he sees what is in the city. **⁶** And Yhwh God appoints a gourd, and causes it to come up over Jonah, to be a shade over his head, to give deliverance to him from his affliction, and Jonah rejoices because of the gourd [with] great joy. **⁷** And God appoints a worm at the going up of the dawn on the next day, and it strikes the gourd, and it dries up. **⁸** And it comes to pass, about the rising of the sun, that God appoints a cutting east wind, and the sun strikes on the head of Jonah, and he wraps himself up, and asks for his soul to die, and says, "Better [is] my death than my life." **⁹** And God says to Jonah: "Is doing good displeasing to you, because of the gourd?" And he says, "To do good is displeasing to me—to death." **¹⁰** And Yhwh says, "You have had pity on the gourd, for which you did not labor, neither did you nourish it, which came up [as] a son of night, and perished [as] a son of night, **¹¹** and I—do I not have pity on Nineveh, the great city, in which there are more than one hundred twenty thousand of mankind, who have not known between their right hand and their left—and much livestock?"

MICAH

CHAPTER 1

¹ A word of Yhwh that has been to Micah the Morashite in the days of Jotham, Ahaz, Hezekiah, kings of Judah, that he has seen concerning Samaria and Jerusalem: ² Hear, O peoples, all of them! Attend, O earth, and its fullness, || And Lord Yhwh is against you for a witness, || The Lord from His holy temple. ³ For behold, Yhwh is going out from His place, || And He has come down, || And has trodden on high places of earth. ⁴ The mountains have been melted under Him, || And the valleys split themselves, || As wax from the presence of fire, || As waters cast down by a slope. ⁵ For the transgression of Jacob [is] all this, || And for the sins of the house of Israel. What [is] the transgression of Jacob? Is it not Samaria? And what the high places of Judah? Is it not Jerusalem? ⁶ "And I have set Samaria for a heap of the field, || For plantations of a vineyard, || And poured out into a valley her stones, || And her foundations I uncover. ⁷ And all her carved images are beaten down, || And all her wages are burned with fire, || And all her idols I make a desolation, || For from the wage of a harlot she gathered, and to the wage of a harlot they return." ⁸ For this I lament and howl, || I go spoiled and naked, || I make a lamentation like dragons, || And a mourning like daughters of an ostrich. ⁹ For mortal [are] her wounds, || For it has come to Judah, || It has come to a gate of My people—to Jerusalem. ¹⁰ In Gath do not tell—in Acco do not weep, || In Beth-Aphrah, roll yourself in dust. ¹¹ Pass over for you, O inhabitant of Shaphir, || Naked one of shame. The inhabitant of Zaanan has not gone out, || The lamentation of Beth-Ezel takes from you its standing. ¹² For the inhabitant of Maroth has stayed for good, || For calamity has come down from Yhwh to the gate of Jerusalem. ¹³ Bind the chariot to a swift beast, O inhabitant of Lachish, || The beginning of sin [is] she to the daughter of Zion, || For in you have been found the transgressions of Israel. ¹⁴ Therefore you give presents to Moresheth-Gath, || The houses of Achzib become a lying thing to the kings of Israel. ¹⁵ Yet I bring the possessor to you, O inhabitant of Mareshah, || The glory of Israel comes to Adullam. ¹⁶ Make bald and shave, for your delightful sons, || Enlarge your baldness as an eagle, || For they have removed from you!

CHAPTER 2

¹ Woe [to] those devising iniquity, || And working evil on their beds, || In the morning light they do it, || For their hand is—to God. ² And they have desired fields, || And they have taken violently, || And houses, and they have taken away, || And have oppressed a man and his house, || Even a man and his inheritance. ³ Therefore, thus said Yhwh: "Behold, I am devising against this family calamity, || From which you do not remove your necks, || Nor walk loftily, for it [is] a time of evil. ⁴ In that day [one] takes up for you an allegory, || And he has wailed a wailing of woe, || He has said, We have been utterly spoiled, || The portion of my people He changes, || How He moves toward me! To the backslider our fields He apportions." ⁵ Therefore, you have no caster of a line by lot || In the assembly of Yhwh. ⁶ You do not prophesy—they prophesy, || They do not prophesy to these, || It does not remove shame. ⁷ [Those] named the house of Jacob: "Has the Spirit of Yhwh been shortened? Are these His doings? Do My words not benefit the people that are walking uprightly? ⁸ And recently My people raise up as an enemy, || You strip off the honorable ornament from the outer garment, || From the confident passers by, || You who are turning back from war. ⁹ The women of My people you cast out from its delightful house, || From its sucklings you take away My honor for all time. ¹⁰ Rise and go, for this [is] not the rest, || Because of uncleanness it corrupts, || And corruption is powerful. ¹¹ If one is going [with] the wind, || And [with] falsehood has lied: I prophesy to you of wine, and of strong drink, || He has been the prophet of this people! ¹² I surely gather you, O Jacob, all of you, || I surely bring together the remnant of Israel, || Together I set it as the flock of Bozrah, || As a drove in the midst of its pasture, || It makes a noise because of man. ¹³ The breaker has gone up before them, || They have broken through, || Indeed, they pass through the gate, || Indeed, they go out through it, || And their king passes on before them, || And Yhwh at their head!"

CHAPTER 3

¹ And I say, "Now hear, O heads of Jacob, || And you judge of the house of Israel, || Is it not for you to know the judgment? ² You who are hating good, and loving evil, || Taking violently their skin from off them, || And their flesh from off their bones, ³ And who have eaten the flesh of My people, || And their skin from off them have stripped, || And their bones they have broken, || And they have spread [them] out as in a pot, || And as flesh in the midst of a cauldron." ⁴ Then they cry to Yhwh, || And He does not answer them, || And hides His face from them at that time, || As they have made evil their doings. ⁵ Thus said Yhwh concerning the prophets || Who are causing My people to err, || Who are biting with their teeth, || And have cried "Peace," || And he who does not give to their mouth, || They have sanctified against him war: ⁶ "Therefore you have a night without vision, || And you have darkness without divination, || And the sun has gone in on the prophets, || And the day has been black over them. ⁷ And the seers have been ashamed, || And the diviners have been confounded, || And all of them have covered their lip, || For there is no answer, O God." ⁸ And yet I have been full of power by the Spirit of Yhwh, || And of judgment, and of might, || To declare to Jacob his transgression, || And to Israel his sin. ⁹ Now hear this, O heads of the house of Jacob, || And you judges of the house of Israel, || Who are making judgment abominable, || And pervert all uprightness. ¹⁰ Building up Zion with blood, || And Jerusalem with iniquity. ¹¹ Her heads judge for a bribe, || And her priests teach for hire, || And her prophets divine for silver, || And on Yhwh they lean, saying, || "Is not Yhwh in our midst? Evil does not come in on us." ¹² Therefore, for your sake, Zion is plowed a field, and Jerusalem is heaps, || And the mountain of the house [is] for high places of a forest!

CHAPTER 4

¹ And it has come to pass, || In the latter end of the days, || The mountain of the house of Yhwh || Is established above the top of the mountains, || And it has been lifted up above the hills, || And flowed to it have peoples. ² And gone have many nations and said, || "Come and we go up to the mountain of Yhwh, || And to the house of the God of Jacob, || And He teaches us of His ways, || And we walk in His paths," || For a law goes forth from Zion, || And a word of Yhwh from Jerusalem. ³ And He has judged between many peoples, || And given a decision to mighty nations far off, || They have beaten their swords to plowshares, || And their spears to pruning-hooks, || Nation does not lift up sword to nation, || Nor do they learn war anymore. ⁴ And they have sat each under his vine, || And under his fig tree, || And there is none troubling, || For the mouth of Yhwh of Hosts has spoken. ⁵ For all the peoples walk, || Each in the name of its god—and we, || We walk in the Name of our God Yhwh, || For all time and forever. ⁶ "In that day," a declaration of Yhwh, || "I gather the halting one, || And the driven away one I bring together, || And she whom I have afflicted. ⁷ And I have set the halting for a remnant, || And the far-off for a mighty nation, || And Yhwh has reigned over them in Mount Zion, || From now on, and for all time. ⁸ And you, O Tower of Eder, || Fort of the daughter of Zion, to you it comes, || Indeed, the former rule has come in, || The kingdom to the daughter of Jerusalem." ⁹ Now why do you shout aloud? Is there no king in you? Has your counselor perished, || That pain as of a travailing woman has taken hold of you? ¹⁰ Be pained, and bring forth, O daughter of Zion, || As a travailing woman, || For now you go forth from the city, || And you have dwelt in the field, || And you have gone to Babylon, || There you are delivered, || There Yhwh redeems you from the hand of your enemies. ¹¹ And now, many nations have gathered against you, who are saying: "Let her be defiled, and our eyes look on Zion." ¹² They have not known the thoughts of Yhwh, || Nor have they understood His counsel, || For He has gathered them as a sheaf [into] a threshing-floor. ¹³ Arise, and thresh, O daughter of Zion, || For I make your horn iron, || And I make your hooves bronze, || And you have beaten small many peoples, || And I have devoted to Yhwh their gain, || And their wealth to the Lord of the whole earth!

|| And you walk in their counsels, || For My giving you for a desolation, || And its inhabitants for a hissing, || And you bear the reproach of My people!"

CHAPTER 5

1 Now gather yourself together, O daughter of troops, || He has laid a siege against us, || They strike [the] judge of Israel on the cheek with a rod. **2** "And you, Beth-Lehem Ephratah, || Little to be among the chiefs of Judah! From you He comes forth to Me—to be ruler in Israel, || And His comings forth [are] of old, || From the days of antiquity." **3** Therefore He gives them up until the time she who brings forth has brought forth, || And the remnant of His brothers return to the sons of Israel. **4** And He has stood and delighted in the strength of Yhwh, || In the excellence of the Name of His God Yhwh, || And they have remained, || For now He is great to the ends of the earth. **5** And this [One] has been peace. Asshur, when he comes into our land, || And when he treads in our palaces, || We have raised against him seven shepherds, || And eight anointed of man. **6** And they have afflicted the land of Asshur with the sword, || And the land of Nimrod at its openings, || And He has delivered from Asshur when he comes into our land, || And when he treads in our borders. **7** And the remnant of Jacob has been in the midst of many peoples, || As dew from Yhwh—as showers on the herb, || That does not wait for man, nor stays for the sons of men. **8** Indeed, the remnant of Jacob has been among nations, || In the midst of many peoples, || As a lion among beasts of a forest, || As a young lion among ranks of a flock, || Which if it has passed through, || Has both trodden down and has torn, || And there is no deliverer. **9** High is your hand above your adversaries, || And all your enemies are cut off. **10** "And it has come to pass in that day," || A declaration of Yhwh, || "I have cut off your horses from your midst, || And I have destroyed your chariots, **11** And I have cut off the cities of your land, || And I have thrown down all your fortresses, **12** And have cut off sorcerers out of your hand, || And observers of clouds—you have none. **13** And I have cut off your carved images, || And your standing-pillars out of your midst, || And you do not bow yourself anymore || To the work of your hands. **14** And I have plucked up your Asherim out of your midst, || And I have destroyed your enemies. **15** And I have done vengeance in anger and in fury, || With the nations who have not listened!"

CHAPTER 6

1 Now hear that which Yhwh is saying: "Rise—strive with the mountains, || And cause the hills to hear your voice. **2** Hear, O mountains, the strife of Yhwh, || You strong ones—foundations of earth! For a strife [is] to Yhwh, with His people, || And with Israel He reasons. **3** O My people, what have I done to you? And how have I wearied you? Testify against Me. **4** For I brought you up from the land of Egypt, || And I have ransomed you from the house of servants, || And I send Moses, Aaron, and Miriam before you. **5** O My people, please remember || What Balak king of Moab counseled, || What Balaam son of Beor answered him || (From Shittim to Gilgal), || In order to know the righteous acts of Yhwh." **6** With what do I come before Yhwh? Do I bow to God Most High? Do I come before Him with burnt-offerings? With calves—sons of a year? **7** Is Yhwh pleased with thousands of rams? With myriads of streams of oil? Do I give my firstborn [for] my transgression? The fruit of my body [for] the sin of my soul? **8** He has declared to you, O man, what [is] good; Indeed, what is Yhwh requiring of you, || Except—to do judgment, and love kindness, || And to walk lowly with your God? **9** A voice of Yhwh calls to the city, || And wisdom fears Your Name, || "Hear the rod, and Him who appointed it. **10** Are there yet [in] the house of the wicked || Treasures of wickedness, || And the abhorred meager ephah? **11** Do I reckon [it] pure with balances of wickedness? And with a bag of deceitful stones? **12** Whose rich ones have been full of violence, || And its inhabitants have spoken falsehood, || And their tongue [is] deceitful in their mouth. **13** And I also, I have begun to strike you, || To make desolate, because of your sins. **14** You eat, and you are not satisfied, || And your pit [is] in your midst, || And you remove, and do not deliver, || And that which you deliver, I give to a sword. **15** You sow, and you do not reap, || You tread the olive, || And you do not pour out oil, || And new wine—and you do not drink wine. **16** And the statutes of Omri are kept habitually, || And all the work of the house of Ahab,

CHAPTER 7

1 My woe [is] to me, || For I have been as gatherings of summer-fruit, || As gleanings of harvest, || There is no cluster to eat, || The first-ripe fruit has my soul desired. **2** The kind have perished out of the land, || And upright among men—there are none, || All of them lie in wait for blood, || They each hunt his brother [with] a net. **3** On the evil [are] both hands to do [it] well, || The prince is asking—also the judge—for repayment, || And the great—he is speaking the mischief of his soul, || And they wrap it up. **4** Their best one [is] as a brier, || The upright one—than a thorn-hedge, || The day of your watchmen—Your visitation—has come. Now is their perplexity. **5** Do not believe in a friend, || Do not trust in a leader, || From her who is lying in your bosom keep the openings of your mouth. **6** For a son is dishonoring a father, || A daughter has stood against her mother, || A daughter-in-law against her mother-in-law, || The enemies of each [are] the men of his house. **7** And I—in Yhwh I watch, || I wait for the God of my salvation, || My God hears me. **8** You do not rejoice over me, O my enemy, || When I have fallen, I have risen, || When I sit in darkness Yhwh is a light to me. **9** I bear the indignation of Yhwh, || For I have sinned against Him, || Until He pleads my cause, || And has executed my judgment, || He brings me forth to the light, || I look on His righteousness. **10** And my enemy sees, || And shame covers her, || Who says to me, "Where [is] your God Yhwh?" My eyes look on her, || Now she is for a treading-place, || As mire of the out-places. **11** The day to build your walls! That day—removed is the limit. **12** That day—even to you it comes in, || From Asshur and the cities of the fortress, || And from the fortress even to the river, || And from sea to sea, and mountain to mountain. **13** And the land has been for a desolation, || Because of its inhabitants, || Because of the fruit of their doings. **14** Rule Your people with Your rod, || The flock of Your inheritance, || Dwelling alone [in] a forest in the midst of Carmel, || They enjoy Bashan and Gilead as in days of old. **15** "According to the days of your coming forth out of the land of Egypt, || I show it wonderful things." **16** Nations see, and they are ashamed of all their might, || They lay a hand on the mouth, their ears are deaf. **17** They lick dust as a serpent, as fearful things of earth, || They tremble from their enclosures, || They are afraid of our God Yhwh, || Indeed, they are afraid of You. **18** Who [is] a God like You? taking away iniquity, || And passing by the transgression of the remnant of His inheritance, || He has not retained His anger forever, || Because He delights [in] kindness. **19** He turns back, He pities us, || He subdues our iniquities, || And You cast all their sins into the depths of the sea. **20** You give truth to Jacob, kindness to Abraham, || That You have sworn to our fathers, from the days of antiquity!

NAHUM

CHAPTER 1

1 Burden of Nineveh. The Scroll of the Vision of Nahum the Elkoshite. **2** A God zealous and avenging [is] Yhwh, || An avenger [is] Yhwh, and possessing fury. An avenger [is] Yhwh on His adversaries, || And He is watching for His enemies. **3** Yhwh [is] slow to anger, and great in power, || And Yhwh does not entirely acquit, || In a windstorm and in a storm [is] His way, || And a cloud [is] the dust of His feet. **4** He is pushing against a sea, and dries it up, || Indeed, He has made all the floods dry, || Bashan and Carmel [are] languishing, || Indeed, the flower of Lebanon [is] languishing. **5** Mountains have shaken because of Him, || And the hills have been melted; And the earth [is] lifted up at His presence, || And the world and all dwelling in it. **6** Who stands before His indignation? And who rises up in the heat of His anger? His fury has been poured out like fire, || And the rocks have been broken by Him. **7** Good [is] Yhwh for a strong place in a day of distress. And He knows those trusting in Him. **8** And with a flood passing over, || An end He makes of its place, || And darkness pursues His enemies. **9** What do we devise against Yhwh? He is making an end, distress does not arise twice. **10** For while princes [are] perplexed, || And with their drink are drunken, || They have been consumed as stubble fully dried. **11** From you has come forth a deviser of evil || Against Yhwh—a worthless counselor. **12** Thus said Yhwh: "Though complete, and thus many, || Yet thus they have been cut off, || And he has passed away. Though I afflicted you, I afflict you no longer. **13** And now I break his rod from off you, || And your bands I draw away." **14** And Yhwh has commanded concerning you, || "No more of your name spreads abroad, || I cut off carved and molten image from the house of your gods, || I appoint your grave, for you have been vile." **15** Behold, on the mountains the feet of one proclaiming tidings, sounding peace! Celebrate, O Judah, your festivals, complete your vows, || For the worthless no longer pass over into you, || He has been completely cut off!

CHAPTER 2

1 A scatterer has come up to your face, || Keep the bulwark, watch the way, || Strengthen the loins, strengthen power mightily. **2** For Yhwh has turned back to the excellence of Jacob, || As [to] the excellence of Israel, || For emptiers have emptied them out, || And they have marred their branches. **3** The shield of his mighty ones has become red, || Men of might [are in] scarlet, || With fiery torches [is] the chariot in a day of his preparation, || And the firs have been caused to tremble. **4** In out-places the chariots shine, || They go to and fro in broad places, || Their appearances [are] like torches, || As lightnings they run. **5** He remembers his majestic ones, || They stumble in their goings, || They hurry [to] its wall, || And the covering is prepared. **6** Gates of the rivers have been opened, || And the palace is dissolved. **7** And it is established—she has removed, || She has been brought up, || And her handmaids are leading as the voice of doves, || Tabering on their hearts. **8** And Nineveh [is] as a pool of waters, || From of old it [is]—and they are fleeing! "Stand, stand"; and none is turning! **9** Seize silver, seize gold, || And there is no end to the prepared things, || [To] the abundance of all desirable vessels. **10** She is empty, indeed, emptiness and waste, || And the heart has melted, || And the knees have struck together, || And great pain [is] in all loins, || And the faces of all of them have gathered paleness. **11** Where [is] the habitation of lionesses? And a feeding-place it [is] for young lions || Where a lion has walked, an old lion, || A lion's whelp, and there is none troubling. **12** The lion is tearing parts [for] his whelps, || And is strangling for his lionesses, || And he fills his holes [with] prey, || And his habitations [with] torn flesh. **13** "Behold, I [am] against you," || A declaration of Yhwh of Hosts, || "And I have burned its chariot in smoke, || And a sword consumes your young lions, || And I have cut off your prey from the land, || And the voice of your messengers is not heard anymore!"

CHAPTER 3

1 Woe [to] the city of blood, || She is all full with lies [and] burglary, || Prey does not depart. **2** The sound of a whip, || And the sound of the rattling of a wheel, || And of a prancing horse, and of a bounding chariot, || Of a horseman mounting. **3** And the flame of a sword, and the lightning of a spear, || And the abundance of the wounded, || And the weight of carcasses, || Indeed, there is no end to the bodies, || They stumble over their bodies. **4** Because of the abundance of the fornications of a harlot, || The goodness of the grace of the lady of witchcrafts, || Who is selling nations by her fornications, || And families by her witchcrafts. **5** "Behold, I [am] against you," || A declaration of Yhwh of Hosts, || "And have removed your skirts before your face, || And have showed nations your nakedness, || And kingdoms your shame, **6** And I have cast on you abominations, || And dishonored you, and made you as a sight. **7** And it has come to pass, || Each of your beholders flees from you, || And has said: Nineveh is spoiled, || Who bemoans for her? From where do I seek comforters for you?" **8** Are you better than No-Ammon, || That is dwelling among brooks? Waters she has around her, || Whose bulwark [is] the sea, waters her wall. **9** Cush her might, and Egypt, and there is no end. Put and Lubim have been for your help. **10** Even she becomes an exile, || She has gone into captivity, || Even her sucklings are dashed to pieces || At the top of all out-places, || And for her honored ones they cast a lot, || And all her great ones have been bound

in chains. **11** Even you are drunken, you are hidden, || Even you seek a strong place, because of an enemy. **12** All your fortresses [are] fig trees with first-fruits, || If they are shaken, || They have fallen into the mouth of the eater. **13** Behold, your people [are] women in your midst, || To your enemies thoroughly opened || Have been the gates of your land, || Fire has consumed your bars. **14** Waters of a siege draw for yourself, || Strengthen your fortresses, || Enter into mire, and tread on clay, || Make strong a brick-kiln. **15** There a fire consumes you, || A sword cuts you off, || It consumes you as a cankerworm! Make yourself heavy as the cankerworm, || Make yourself heavy as the locust. **16** Multiply your merchants above the stars of the heavens, || The cankerworm has stripped off, and flees away. **17** Your crowned ones [are] as a locust, || And your princes as great grasshoppers, || That encamp in hedges in a day of cold, || The sun has risen, and it flees away, || And its place where they are is not known. **18** Your friends have slumbered, king of Asshur, || Your majestic ones rest, || Your people have been scattered on the mountains, || And there is none gathering. **19** There is no weakening of your destruction, || Your striking [is] grievous, || All hearing your fame have clapped the hand at you, || For over whom did your wickedness not pass continually?

HABAKKUK

CHAPTER 1

1 The burden that Habakkuk the prophet has seen: **2** Until when, O Yhwh, have I cried, || And You do not hear? I cry to You, "Violence!" And You do not save. **3** Why do You show me iniquity, || And cause [me] to behold perversity? And spoiling and violence [are] before me, || And there is strife, and contention lifts [itself] up, **4** Therefore law ceases, || And judgment does not go forth forever, || For the wicked is surrounding the righteous, || Therefore wrong judgment goes forth. **5** "Look on nations, and behold and marvel greatly. For a work He is working in your days, || You do not believe though it is declared. **6** For behold, I am raising up the Chaldeans, || The bitter and hasty nation, || That is going to the broad places of earth, || To occupy dwelling places not his own. **7** He [is] terrible and fearful, || His judgment and his excellence go forth from him. **8** His horses have been swifter than leopards, || And sharper than evening wolves, || And his horsemen have increased, || Even his horsemen from afar come in, || They fly as an eagle, hastening to consume. **9** All for violence—he comes in, || Their faces swallowing up the east wind, || And he gathers a captivity as the sand. **10** And he scoffs at kings, || And princes [are] a laughter to him, || He laughs at every fortification, || And he heaps up dust, and captures it. **11** Then the spirit has passed on, || Indeed, he transgresses, || And [ascribes] this—his power—to his god." **12** Are You not of old, O Yhwh, my God, my Holy One? We do not die, O Yhwh, || You have appointed him for judgment, || And, O Rock, You have founded him for reproof. **13** Purer of eyes than to behold evil, || You are not able to look on perverseness, || Why do You behold the treacherous? You keep silent when the wicked || Swallow the more righteous than he, **14** And You make man as fishes of the sea, || As a creeping thing [with] none ruling over him. **15** He has brought up each of them with a hook, || He catches it in his net, and gathers it in his dragnet, || Therefore he delights and rejoices. **16** Therefore he sacrifices to his net, || And makes incense to his dragnet, || For by them [is] his portion fertile, and his food fat. **17** Does he therefore empty his net, || And continually not spare to slay nations?

CHAPTER 2

1 On my charge I stand, and I station myself on a bulwark, and I watch to see what He speaks against me, and what I reply to my reproof. **2** And Yhwh answers me and says: "Write a vision, and explain on the tablets, || That he may run who is reading it. **3** For yet the vision [is] for a season, || And it breathes for the end, and does not lie, || If it lingers, wait for it, || For surely it comes, it is not late. **4** Behold, a presumptuous one! His soul is not upright within him, || And the righteous lives by his faith. **5** And also, because the wine

[is] treacherous, || A man is haughty, and does not remain at home, || Who has enlarged his soul as Sheol, || And is as death that is not satisfied, || And gathers to itself all the nations, || And assembles to itself all the peoples, **6** Are these not—all of them—an allegory taken up against him, || And a moral of acute sayings for him, || And say, Woe [to] him who is multiplying [what is] not his? Until when also is he multiplying to himself heavy pledges? **7** Do your usurers not instantly rise up, || And those shaking you awake, || And you have been a spoil to them? **8** Because you have spoiled many nations, || All the remnant of the peoples spoil you, || Because of man's blood, and of violence [to] the land, || [To] the city, and [to] all dwelling in it. **9** Woe [to] him who is gaining evil gain for his house, || To set his nest on high, || To be delivered from the hand of evil, **10** You have counseled a shameful thing to your house, || To cut off many peoples, and your soul [is] sinful. **11** For a stone cries out from the wall, || And a beam from the wood answers it. **12** Woe [to] him who is building a city by blood, || And establishing a city by iniquity. **13** Behold, is it not from Yhwh of Hosts || And peoples are fatigued for fire, || And nations for vanity are weary? **14** For the earth is full of the knowledge of the glory of Yhwh, || As the waters cover over a sea. **15** Woe [to] him who is giving drink to his neighbor, || Pouring out your bottle, and also making drunk, || In order to look on their nakedness. **16** You have been filled—shame without honor, || Drink also, and be uncircumcised, || Turn around to you does the cup of the right hand of Yhwh, || And shameful spewing [is] on your glory. **17** For violence [done to] Lebanon covers you, || And spoil of beasts frightens them, || Because of man's blood, and of violence [to] the land, || [To] the city, and [to] all dwelling in it. **18** What profit has a carved image given || That its former has hewn it? A molten image and teacher of falsehood, || That the former has trusted on his own formation—to make mute idols? **19** Woe [to] him who is saying to wood, Awake, || To a mute stone, Stir up, || It [is] a teacher! Behold, it is overlaid—gold and silver, || And there is no spirit in its midst. **20** And Yhwh [is] in His holy temple, || Be silent before Him, all the earth!"

CHAPTER 3

1 A prayer of Habakkuk the prophet, [set] on shigionoth: **2** O Yhwh, I heard your report, || I have been afraid, O Yhwh, || Your work! In midst of years revive it, || In the midst of years You make known, || In anger You remember mercy. **3** God comes from Teman, || The Holy One from Mount Paran. Pause! His splendor has covered the heavens, || And His praise has filled the earth. **4** And the brightness is as the light, || He has rays out of His hand, || And there—the hiding of His strength. **5** Before Him goes pestilence, || And a burning flame goes forth at His feet. **6** He has stood, and He measures earth, || He has seen, and He shakes off nations, || And mountains of antiquity scatter themselves, || The hills of old have bowed, || The ways of old [are] His. **7** Under sorrow I have seen tents of Cushan, || Curtains of the land of Midian tremble. **8** Has Yhwh been angry against rivers? Against rivers [is] Your anger? [Is] Your wrath against the sea? For You ride on Your horses—Your chariots of salvation. **9** You make Your bow utterly naked, || The tribes have sworn, saying, "Pause!" You cleave the earth [with] rivers. **10** Seen You—pained are mountains, || An inundation of waters has passed over, || The deep has given forth its voice, || It has lifted up its hands high. **11** Sun—moon—has stood—a habitation, || Your arrows go on at the light, || At the brightness, the glittering of Your spear. **12** In indignation You tread earth, || In anger You thresh nations. **13** You have gone forth for the salvation of Your people, || For salvation with Your Anointed, || You have struck the head of the house of the wicked, || Laying bare the foundation to the neck. Pause! **14** You have pierced the head of his leaders with his own rods, || They are tempestuous to scatter me, || Their exultation [is] as to consume the poor in secret. **15** You have proceeded through the sea with Your horses—the clay of many waters. **16** I have heard, and my belly trembles, || At the noise have my lips quivered, || Rottenness comes into my bones, || And in my place I tremble, || That I rest for a day of distress, || At the coming up of the people, he overcomes it. **17** Though the fig tree does not flourish, || And there is no produce among vines, || The work of the olive has failed, || And fields have not yielded food, || The flock has been cut off from the fold, || And there is no herd in the stalls, **18** Yet I, in Yhwh I exult, || I am joyful in the God of my salvation. **19** Yhwh the Lord [is] my strength, || And He makes my feet like does, || And causes me to tread on my high-places. To the overseer with my stringed instruments!

ZEPHANIAH

CHAPTER 1

1 A word of Yhwh that has been to Zephaniah son of Cushi, son of Gedaliah, son of Amariah, son of Hezikiah, in the days of Josiah son of Amoz, king of Judah: **2** "I utterly consume all from off the face of the ground," || A declaration of Yhwh. **3** "I consume man and beast, || I consume bird of the heavens, and fishes of the sea, || And the stumbling-blocks—the wicked, || And I have cut off man from the face of the ground," || A declaration of Yhwh, **4** "And I have stretched out My hand against Judah, || And against all inhabiting Jerusalem, || And cut off from this place the remnant of Ba`al, || The name of the idolatrous priests, with the priests, **5** And those bowing themselves || On the roofs to the host of the heavens, || And those bowing themselves, || Swearing to Yhwh, and swearing by Malcham, **6** And those removing from after Yhwh, || And who have not sought Yhwh, nor implored Him." **7** Hush! Because of Lord Yhwh, || For near [is the] Day of Yhwh, || For Yhwh has prepared a sacrifice, || He has sanctified His invited ones. **8** "And it has come to pass, || In the day of the sacrifice of Yhwh, || That I have laid a charge on the heads, || And on sons of the king, || And on all putting on strange clothing. **9** And I have laid a charge on everyone || Who is leaping over the threshold in that day, || Who are filling the house of their masters || [With] violence and deceit. **10** And there has been in that day," || A declaration of Yhwh, || "The noise of a cry from the Fish Gate, || And of a howling from the Second [Quarter], || And of great destruction from the hills. **11** Howl, you inhabitants of the hollow place, || For all the merchant people have been cut off, || All carrying silver have been cut off. **12** And it has come to pass at that time, || I search Jerusalem with lights, || And I have laid a charge on the men || Who are hardened on their preserved things, || Who are saying in their heart: Yhwh does no good, nor does He do evil. **13** And their wealth has been for a spoil, || And their houses for desolation, || And they have built houses, and do not inhabit, || And they have planted vineyards, || And they do not drink their wine." **14** Near [is] the Great Day of Yhwh, || Near, and hastening exceedingly, || The noise of the Day of Yhwh, || There a mighty one bitterly shrieks. **15** A day of wrath [is] that day, || A day of adversity and distress, || A day of devastation and desolation, || A day of darkness and gloominess, || A day of cloud and thick darkness, **16** A day of horn and shouting against the fortified cities, || And against the high corners. **17** "And I have sent distress to men, || And they have walked as the blind, || For against Yhwh they have sinned, || And poured out is their blood as dust, || And their flesh [is] as dung." **18** Even their silver, even their gold, is not able to deliver them in a day of the wrath of Yhwh, and in the fire of His jealousy is the whole land consumed, for He makes only a hurried end of all the inhabitants of the land!

CHAPTER 2

1 Bend yourselves, indeed, bend, || O nation not desired, **2** Before the bringing forth of a statute, || The day has passed on as chaff, || While the heat of the anger of Yhwh has not yet come in on you, || While [the] Day of the anger of Yhwh has not yet come in on you, **3** Seek Yhwh, all you humble of the land, || Who have done His judgment, || Seek righteousness, seek humility, || It may be you are hidden in the Day of the anger of Yhwh. **4** For Gaza is forsaken, || And Ashkelon [is] for a desolation, || Ashdod! At noon they cast her forth, || And Ekron is rooted up. **5** Behold! O inhabitants of the seacoast, || Nation of the Cherethites, || A word of Yhwh [is] against you, || Canaan, land of the Philistines, || "And I have destroyed you without an inhabitant." **6** And the seacoast has been habitations, || Cottages [for] shepherds, and folds [for] a flock. **7** And the coast has been for the remnant of the house of Judah, || By them they have pleasure, || In houses of Ashkelon they lie down at evening, || For their God Yhwh inspects them, || And He has turned back [to] their captivity. **8** "I have heard the reproach of Moab, || And the revilings of the sons of Ammon, || With which they reproached My people, || And magnify [themselves] against their border. **9** Therefore, [as] I live," || A declaration of Yhwh of Hosts, God of Israel, || "Surely Moab is as Sodom, || And the sons of Ammon as Gomorrah, || An overrunning of nettles and salt-pits, || And a desolation for all time. A remnant of My people seizes them, || And a remnant of My nation inherits them." **10** This [is] to them for their arrogancy, || Because they have reproached, || And they magnify [themselves] against the people of Yhwh of Hosts. **11** Fearful [is] Yhwh against them, || For He made all gods of the land bare, || And all islanders of the nations bow themselves to Him, || Each from his place. **12** "Also you, O Cushim, they [are] pierced of My sword." **13** And He stretches His hand against the north, || And destroys Asshur, || And He sets Nineveh for a desolation, || A dry land like a wilderness. **14** And droves have crouched in her midst, || Every beast of the nation, || Both pelican and hedgehog lodge in her knobs, || A voice sings at the window, || "Destruction [is] at the threshold, || For the cedar-work is exposed." **15** This [is] the exulting city that is dwelling confidently, || That is saying in her heart, || "I [am], and there is none beside me," || How she has been for a desolation, || A crouching-place for beasts, || Everyone passing by her hisses, || He shakes his hand!

CHAPTER 3

1 Woe [to] the rebelling and defiling, || The oppressing city! **2** She has not listened to the voice, || She has not accepted instruction, || In Yhwh she has not trusted, || She has not drawn near to her God. **3** Her heads in her midst [are] roaring lions, || Her judges [are] wolves [as in] evening, || They have not gnawn the bone in the morning. **4** Her prophets unstable—men of treachery, || Her priests have defiled the sanctuary, || They have violated the Law. **5** Yhwh [is] righteous in her midst, || He does not do perverseness, || Morning by morning His judgment He gives to the light, || It has not been lacking, || And the perverse do not know shame. **6** "I have cut off nations, || Desolated have been their chief ones, || I have laid waste their out-places without any passing by, || Destroyed have been their cities, || Without man, without inhabitant. **7** I have said: Only, you fear Me, || You accept instruction, || And her habitation is not cut off, || All that I have appointed for her, || But they have risen early, || They have corrupted all their doings. **8** Therefore, wait for Me," || A declaration of Yhwh, || "For the day of My rising for prey, || For My judgment [is] to gather nations, || To assemble kingdoms, || To pour out on them My indignation, || All the heat of My anger, || For by the fire of My jealousy all the earth is consumed. **9** For then I turn a pure lip to peoples, || To call all of them by the Name of Yhwh, || To serve Him [with] one shoulder. **10** From beyond the rivers of Cush, My suppliants, || The daughter of My scattered ones, || Bring My present. **11** In that day you are not ashamed because of any of your actions, || With which you have transgressed against Me, || For then I turn aside from your midst || The exulting ones of your excellence, || And you are to be haughty no longer, || In My holy mountain. **12** And I have left in your midst a people humble and poor, || And they have trusted in the Name of Yhwh. **13** The remnant of Israel does no perversity, nor speaks lies, || Nor is a deceitful tongue found in their mouth, || For they have delight, and have lain down, || And there is none troubling." **14** Cry aloud, O daughter of Zion, shout, O Israel, || Rejoice and exult with the whole heart, O daughter of Jerusalem. **15** Yhwh has turned aside your judgments, || He has faced your enemy, || The King of Israel, Yhwh, [is] in your midst, || You see evil no more. **16** In that day it is said to Jerusalem, || "Do not fear, O Zion, || Do not let your hands be feeble. **17** Your God Yhwh [is] in your midst, || A mighty one [to] save, || He rejoices over you with joy, || He works in His love, || He delights over you with singing." **18** "I have gathered My afflicted from the appointed place, || They have been bearing reproach from you for her sake. **19** Behold, I am dealing with all afflicting you at that time, || And I have saved the halting one, || And I gather the ones driven out, || And have set them for a praise and for a name, || In all the

land of their shame. **20** At that time I bring you in, || Even at the time of My assembling you, || For I give you for a name, and for a praise, || Among all peoples of the land, || In My turning back [to] your captivity before your eyes," said Yhwh

HAGGAI

CHAPTER 1

1 In the second year of Darius the king, in the sixth month, on the first day of the month, a word of Yhwh has been by the hand of Haggai the prophet, to Zerubbabel son of Shealtiel, governor of Judah, and to Joshua son of Josedech, the high priest, saying, **2** "Thus spoke Yhwh of Hosts, saying, This people—they have said, || The time has not come, || The time the house of Yhwh [is] to be built." **3** And there is a word of Yhwh by the hand of Haggai the prophet, saying, **4** "Is it time for you to dwell in your covered houses, || And this house to lie waste?" **5** And now, thus said Yhwh of Hosts: "Set your heart to your ways. **6** You have sown much, and brought in little, || To eat, and not to satiety, || To drink, and not to drunkenness, || To clothe, and none has heat, || And he who is hiring himself out, || Is hiring himself for a bag pierced through." **7** Thus said Yhwh of Hosts: "Set your heart to your ways. **8** Go up the mountain, and you have brought in wood, || And build the house, and I am pleased with it. And I am honored," said Yhwh. **9** "Looking for much, and behold, little, || And you brought [it] home, and I blew on it—why?" A declaration of Yhwh of Hosts, || "Because of My house that is desolate, || And you are running—each to his house, **10** Therefore, over you the heavens have refrained from dew, || And the land has refrained its increase. **11** And I proclaim drought on the land, || And on the mountains, and on the grain, || And on the new wine, and on the oil, || And on what the ground brings forth, || And on man, and on beast, || And on all labor of the hands." **12** And Zerubbabel son of Shealtiel, and Joshua son of Josedech, the high priest, and all the remnant of the people, listen to the voice of their God Yhwh, and to the words of Haggai the prophet, as their God Yhwh had sent him, and the people are afraid of the face of Yhwh. **13** And Haggai, messenger of Yhwh, in messages of Yhwh, speaks to the people, saying, "I [am] with you, a declaration of Yhwh." **14** And Yhwh stirs up the spirit of Zerubbabel son of Shealtiel, governor of Judah, and the spirit of Joshua son of Josedech, the high priest, and the spirit of all the remnant of the people, and they come in, and work in the house of Yhwh of Hosts their God, **15** in the twenty-fourth day of the sixth month, in the second year of Darius the king.

CHAPTER 2

1 In the seventh [month], on the twenty-first of the month, a word of Yhwh has been by the hand of Haggai the prophet, saying, **2** "Now speak to Zerubbabel son of Shealtiel, governor of Judah, and to Joshua son of Josedech, the high priest, and to the remnant of the people, saying, **3** Who among you has been left that saw this house in its former glory? And what are you seeing it now? Is it not, compared with it, as nothing in your eyes? **4** And now, be strong, O Zerubbabel," || A declaration of Yhwh, || "And be strong, O Joshua, son of Josedech, the high priest, || And be strong, all you people of the land," || A declaration of Yhwh, || "And do, for I [am] with you," || A declaration of Yhwh of Hosts. **5** "The thing that I covenanted with you, || In your coming forth from Egypt, || And My Spirit is remaining in your midst, do not fear." **6** For thus said Yhwh of Hosts: "Yet once more—it [is] a little, || And I am shaking the heavens and the earth, || And the sea, and the dry land, **7** And I have shaken all the nations, || And they have come [to] the desire of all the nations, || And I have filled this house [with] glory," said Yhwh of Hosts. **8** "The silver [is]

Mine, and the gold [is] Mine," || A declaration of Yhwh of Hosts. **⁹** "Greater is the glory of this latter house, || Than of the former," said Yhwh of Hosts, || "And I give peace in this place," || A declaration of Yhwh of Hosts. **¹⁰** On the twenty-fourth of the ninth [month], in the second year of Darius, a word of Yhwh has been by the hand of Haggai the prophet, saying, **¹¹** Thus said Yhwh of Hosts: "Now ask the priests of the Law, saying, **¹²** Behold, [when] one carries holy flesh in the skirt of his garment, and he has come with his skirt against the bread, or against the stew, or against the wine, or against the oil, or against any food—is it holy?" And the priests answer and say, "No." **¹³** And Haggai says, "If the unclean of body comes against any of these, is it unclean?" And the priests answer and say, "It is unclean." **¹⁴** And Haggai answers and says, "So [is] this people, and so [is] this nation before Me," a declaration of Yhwh, "and so [is] every work of their hands, and that which they bring near there—it is unclean. **¹⁵** And now, please lay [it] to your heart, || From this day and onward, || Before the laying of stone to stone in the temple of Yhwh. **¹⁶** From that time [one] has come to a heap of twenty, || And it has been ten, || He has come to the wine vat to draw out fifty measures, || And it has been twenty. **¹⁷** I have struck you with blasting, || And with mildew, and with hail—all the work of your hands, || And there is none of you with Me," || A declaration of Yhwh. **¹⁸** "Now set [it] to your heart, from this day and onward, from the twenty-fourth day of the ninth [month], even from the day that the temple of Yhwh has been founded, set [it] to your heart. **¹⁹** Is the seed yet in the barn? And until now the vine and the fig, || And the pomegranate, and the olive-tree, || Have not borne—from this day I bless." **²⁰** And there is a word of Yhwh a second time to Haggai, on the twenty-fourth of the month, saying, **²¹** "Speak to Zerubbabel governor of Judah, saying, I am shaking the heavens and the earth, **²²** And have overturned the throne of kingdoms, || And I have destroyed the strength of kingdoms of the nations, || And overturned chariot and its charioteers, || And horses and their riders have come down, || Each by the sword of his brother. **²³** In that day," a declaration of Yhwh of Hosts, || "I take you, Zerubbabel, son of Shealtiel, My servant," || A declaration of Yhwh, || "And have set you as a signet, || For I have fixed on you," || A declaration of Yhwh of Hosts!

ZECHARIAH

CHAPTER 1

¹ In the eighth month, in the second year of Darius, a word of Yhwh has been to Zechariah, son of Berechiah, son of Iddo the prophet, saying, **²** "Yhwh was angry against your fathers—wrath! **³** And you have said to them, Thus said Yhwh of Hosts: Return to Me, || A declaration of Yhwh of Hosts, || And I return to you, said Yhwh of Hosts. **⁴** You will not be as your fathers, || To whom the former prophets called, || Saying, Thus said Yhwh of Hosts: Please turn back from your evil ways and from your evil doings, || And they did not listen, || Nor attend to Me—a declaration of Yhwh. **⁵** Your fathers—where [are] they? And the prophets—do they live for all time? **⁶** Only, My words and My statutes, || That I commanded My servants the prophets, || Have they not overtaken your fathers? And they turn back and say: As Yhwh of Hosts designed to do to us, || According to our ways, and according to our doings, || So He has done to us." **⁷** On the twenty-fourth day of the eleventh month (it [is] the month of Sebat), in the second year of Darius, a word of Yhwh has been to Zechariah, son of Berechiah, son of Iddo the prophet. [He was] saying: **⁸** I have seen by night, and behold, one riding on a red horse, and he is standing between the myrtles that [are] in the shade, and behind him [are] horses, red, bay, and white. **⁹** And I say, "What [are] these, my lord?" And the messenger who is speaking with me says to me, "I show you what these [are]." **¹⁰** And the one who is standing between the myrtles answers and says, "These [are] they whom Yhwh has sent to walk up and down in the land." **¹¹** And they answer the Messenger of Yhwh who is standing between the myrtles, and say, "We have walked up and down in the land, and behold, all the land is sitting still, and at rest." **¹²** And the Messenger of Yhwh answers and says, "Yhwh of Hosts! Until when do You not pity Jerusalem, and the cities of Judah, that You have abhorred these seventy years?" **¹³** And Yhwh answers the messenger, who is speaking with me, good words, comfortable words. **¹⁴** And the messenger who is speaking with

me, says to me, "Call, saying, Thus said Yhwh of Hosts: I have been zealous for Jerusalem, || And for Zion [with] great zeal. **¹⁵** And [with] great wrath I am angry against the nations who are at ease, || For I was a little angry, and they assisted—for evil. **¹⁶** Therefore, thus said Yhwh: I have turned to Jerusalem with mercies, || My house is built in it, || A declaration of Yhwh of Hosts, || And a line is stretched over Jerusalem. **¹⁷** Again call, saying, || Thus said Yhwh of Hosts: Again My cities overflow from good, || And Yhwh has again comforted Zion, || And He has fixed again on Jerusalem." **¹⁸** And I lift up my eyes, and look, and behold, four horns. **¹⁹** And I say to the messenger who is speaking with me, "What [are] these?" And he says to me, "These [are] the horns that have scattered Judah, Israel, and Jerusalem." **²⁰** And Yhwh shows me four artisans. **²¹** And I say, "What [are] these coming to do?" And He speaks, saying, "These [are] the horns that have scattered Judah, so that no one has lifted up his head, and these come to trouble them, to cast down the horns of the nations who are lifting up a horn against the land of Judah—to scatter it."

CHAPTER 2

¹ And I lift up my eyes, and look, and behold, a man, and in his hand a measuring line. **²** And I say, "To where are you going?" And he says to me, "To measure Jerusalem, to see how much [is] its breadth and how much its length." **³** And behold, the messenger who is speaking with me is going out, and another messenger is going out to meet him, **⁴** and he says to him, "Run, speak to this young man, saying, || Jerusalem is inhabited [as] open places, || From the abundance of man and beast in her midst. **⁵** And I am to her—a declaration of Yhwh—A wall of fire all around, || And I am for glory in her midst. **⁶** Behold, and flee from the land of the north, || A declaration of Yhwh, || For as the four winds of the heavens, || I have spread you abroad, || A declaration of Yhwh. **⁷** Behold, Zion, be delivered who are dwelling [with] the daughter of Babylon. **⁸** For thus said Yhwh of Hosts: He has sent Me after glory to the nations who are spoiling you, || For he who is coming against you, || Is coming against the pupil of His eye. **⁹** For behold, I am waving My hand against them, || And they have been a spoil to their servants. And you have known that Yhwh of Hosts has sent Me. **¹⁰** Sing, and rejoice, O daughter of Zion, || For behold, I am coming, and have dwelt in your midst, || A declaration of Yhwh. **¹¹** And many nations have been joined to Yhwh in that day, || And they have been to Me for a people, || And I have dwelt in your midst, || And you have known that Yhwh of Hosts has sent Me to you. **¹²** And Yhwh has inherited Judah, || His portion on the holy ground, || And He has fixed again on Jerusalem. **¹³** Hush, all flesh, because of Yhwh, || For He has been roused up from His holy habitation!"

CHAPTER 3

¹ And he shows me Joshua the high priest standing before the Messenger of Yhwh, and Satan standing at his right hand, to be an adversary to him. **²** And Yhwh says to Satan: "Yhwh pushes against you, O Satan, || Indeed, Yhwh pushes against you, || Who is fixing on Jerusalem, || Is this not a brand delivered from fire?" **³** And Joshua was clothed with filthy garments, and is standing before the Messenger. **⁴** And He answers and speaks to those standing before Him, saying, "Turn aside the filthy garments from off him." And He says to him, "See, I have caused your iniquity to pass away from off you, so as to clothe you with costly apparel." **⁵** He also said, "Let them set a pure turban on his head." And they set the pure turban on his head, and clothe him with garments. And the Messenger of Yhwh is standing, **⁶** and the Messenger of Yhwh protests to Joshua, saying, **⁷** "Thus said Yhwh of Hosts: If you walk in My ways, || And if you keep My charge, || Then also you judge My house, || And also you keep My courts, || And I have given to you conductors among these standing by. **⁸** Now hear, O Joshua the high priest, || You and your companions sitting before you || (For men of type [are] they), || For behold, I am bringing in My servant—a Shoot. **⁹** For behold, the stone that I put before Joshua, || On one stone [are] seven eyes, || Behold, I am engraving its engraving, || A declaration of Yhwh of Hosts, || And I have removed the iniquity of that land in one day. **¹⁰** In that day—a declaration of Yhwh of Hosts, || You call, each to his neighbor, || To the place of the vine, || And to the place of the fig tree!"

CHAPTER 4

¹ And the messenger who is speaking with me turns back, and stirs me up as one who is stirred up out of his sleep, ² and he says to me, "What are you seeing?" And I say, "I have looked, and behold, a lampstand of gold—all of it, and its bowl [is] on its top, and its seven lamps [are] on it, and twice seven pipes [are] to the lights that [are] on its top, ³ and two olive-trees [are] by it, one on the right of the bowl and one on its left." ⁴ And I answer and speak to the messenger who is speaking with me, saying, "What [are] these, my lord?" ⁵ And the messenger who is speaking with me answers and says to me, "Have you not known what these [are]?" And I say, "No, my lord." ⁶ And he answers and speaks to me, saying, "This [is] a word of Yhwh to Zerubbabel, saying, || Not by a force, nor by power, || But—by My Spirit, said Yhwh of Hosts. ⁷ Who [are] you, O great mountain || Before Zerubbabel—for a plain! And he has brought forth the top-stone, || Cries of Grace, grace—[are] to it." ⁸ And there is a word of Yhwh to me, saying, ⁹ "Hands of Zerubbabel founded this house, || And his hands finish it, || And you have known that Yhwh of Hosts || Has sent Me to you. ¹⁰ For who trampled on the day of small things, || They have rejoiced, || And seen the tin weight in the hand of Zerubbabel, || These seven [are] the eyes of Yhwh, || They are going to and fro in all the land." ¹¹ And I answer and say to him, "What [are] these two olive-trees, on the right of the lampstand, and on its left?" ¹² And I answer a second time, and say to him, "What [are] the two branches of the olive trees that, by means of the two golden pipes, are emptying out of themselves the oil?" ¹³ And he speaks to me, saying, "Have you not known what these [are]?" And I say, "No, my lord." ¹⁴ And he says, "These [are] the two sons of the oil, who are standing by the Lord of the whole earth."

CHAPTER 5

¹ And I turn back, and lift up my eyes, and look, and behold, a flying scroll. ² And he says to me, "What are you seeing?" And I say, "I am seeing a flying scroll, its length [is] twenty by the cubit, and its breadth [is] ten by the cubit." ³ And he says to me, "This [is] the execration that is going forth over the face of all the land, for everyone who is stealing, on the one side, according to it, has been declared innocent, and everyone who has sworn, on the other side, according to it, has been declared innocent." ⁴ "I have brought it out," a declaration of Yhwh of Hosts, "and it has come into the house of the thief, and into the house of him who has sworn in My Name with a falsehood, and it has remained in the midst of his house, and has consumed it, both its wood and its stones." ⁵ And the messenger who is speaking with me goes forth and says to me, "Now lift up your eyes, and [do you] see what this [is] that is coming forth?" ⁶ And I say, "What [is] it?" And he says, "This— the ephah that is coming forth." And he says, "This [is] their aspect in all the land. ⁷ And behold, a disc of lead lifted up; and this [is] a woman sitting in the midst of the ephah." ⁸ And he says, "This [is] the wicked woman." And he casts her into the midst of the ephah, and casts the weight of lead on its mouth. ⁹ And I lift up my eyes, and see, and behold, two women are coming forth, and wind [is] in their wings; and they have wings like wings of the stork, and they lift up the ephah between the earth and the heavens. ¹⁰ And I say to the messenger who is speaking with me, "To where [are] they causing the ephah to go?" ¹¹ And he says to me, "To build a house for it in the land of Shinar." And it has been prepared and has been placed there on its base.

CHAPTER 6

¹ And I turn back, and lift up my eyes, and look, and behold, four chariots are coming forth from between two of the mountains, and the mountains [are] mountains of bronze. ² In the first chariot [are] red horses, and in the second chariot brown horses, ³ and in the third chariot white horses, and in the fourth chariot strong spotted horses. ⁴ And I answer and say to the messenger who is speaking with me, "What [are]

these, my lord?" ⁵ And the messenger answers and says to me, "These [are] four spirits of the heavens coming forth from presenting themselves before the Lord of the whole earth. ⁶ The brown horses that [are] therein, are coming forth to the land of the north; and the white have come forth to their back part; and the spotted have come forth to the land of the south; ⁷ and the strong ones have come forth, and they seek to go to walk up and down in the earth"; and he says, "Go, walk up and down in the earth"; and they walk up and down in the earth. ⁸ And he calls me, and speaks to me, saying, "See, those coming forth to the land of the north have caused My Spirit to rest in the land of the north." ⁹ And there is a word of Yhwh to me, saying, ¹⁰ "Take of the captivity (who came from Babylon) from Heldai, from Tobijah, and from Jedaiah, and you have come in—you, in that day, indeed, you have come into the house of Josiah son of Zephaniah, ¹¹ and you have taken silver and gold, and have made a crown, and have placed [it] on the head of Joshua son of Josedech, the high priest, ¹² and have spoken to him, saying, || Thus spoke Yhwh of Hosts, saying, || Behold, the Man! A Shoot—[is] His Name, || And from His place He shoots up, || And He has built the temple of Yhwh. ¹³ Indeed, He builds the temple of Yhwh, || And He carries away splendor, || And He has sat and ruled on His throne, || And has been a priest on His throne, || And a counsel of peace is between both. ¹⁴ And the crown is to Helem, and to Tobijah, and to Jedaiah, and to Hen son of Zephaniah, for a memorial in the temple of Yhwh. ¹⁵ And the far-off come in, and they have built in the temple of Yhwh, and you have known that Yhwh of Hosts has sent me to you, indeed, it has come to pass, if you certainly listen to the voice of your God Yhwh."

CHAPTER 7

¹ And it comes to pass, in the fourth year of Darius the king, a word of Yhwh has been to Zechariah, in the fourth of the ninth month, in Chisleu. ² And Beth-El sends Sherezer and Regem-Melech, and its men, to appease the face of Yhwh, ³ speaking to the priests who [are] at the house of Yhwh of Hosts, and to the prophets, saying, "Do I weep in the fifth month—being separated—as I have done these so many years?" ⁴ And there is a word of Yhwh of Hosts to me, saying, ⁵ "Speak to all the people of the land, and to the priests, saying, ⁶ When you fasted with mourning in the fifth and in the seventh [months]—even these seventy years—did you keep the fast [to] Me? And when you eat, and when you drink, is it not you who are eating, and you who are drinking? ⁷ Are [these] not the words that Yhwh proclaimed by the hand of the former prophets, in Jerusalem's being inhabited, and [in] safety, and its cities around it, and the south and the plain—abiding?" ⁸ And there is a word of Yhwh to Zechariah, saying, ⁹ "Thus spoke Yhwh of Hosts, saying, || Judge [with] true judgment, || And do kindness and mercy with one another. ¹⁰ And do not oppress widow, and fatherless, || Sojourner, and poor, || And you do not devise the calamity of one another in your heart. ¹¹ And they refuse to attend, || And they give a stubborn shoulder, || And their ears are made heavy against hearing. ¹² And their heart they have made adamant, || Against hearing the Law, and the words, || That Yhwh of Hosts sent by His Spirit, || By the hand of the former prophets, || And there is great wrath from Yhwh of Hosts. ¹³ And it comes to pass, as He called, || And they have not listened, || So they call, and I do not listen," said Yhwh of Hosts. ¹⁴ "And I toss them on all the nations, || That they have not known, || The land has been desolate behind them, || Of any passing by and turning back, || And they set a desirable land for a desolation!"

CHAPTER 8

¹ And there is a word of Yhwh of Hosts, saying, ² "Thus said Yhwh of Hosts: I have been zealous for Zion with great zeal, || With great heat I have been zealous for her. ³ Thus said Yhwh: I have turned back to Zion, || And I have dwelt in the midst of Jerusalem, || And Jerusalem has been called The City of Truth, || And The Mountain of Yhwh of Hosts, || The Holy Mountain. ⁴ Thus said Yhwh of Hosts: Again old men and old women dwell || In broad places of Jerusalem, || And each his staff in his hand, || Because of abundance of days. ⁵ And broad places of the city are full of boys and girls, || Playing in its broad places. ⁶ Thus said Yhwh of Hosts: Surely it is wonderful in the eyes of

the remnant of this people in those days, || Also in My eyes it is wonderful, || A declaration of Yhwh of Hosts. **7** Thus said Yhwh of Hosts: Behold, I am saving My people from the land of the rising, || And from the land of the going in, of the sun, **8** And I have brought them in, || They have dwelt in the midst of Jerusalem, || And they have been to Me for a people, || And I am to them for God, || In truth and in righteousness. **9** Thus said Yhwh of Hosts: Let your hands be strong, || You who are hearing in these days these words from the mouth of the prophets, || That in the day the house of Yhwh of Hosts has been founded, || The temple [is] to be built. **10** For before those days there has been no hiring of man, || Indeed, a hiring of beasts there is none; And to him who is going out, || And to him who is coming in, || There is no peace because of the adversary, || And I send all men—each against his neighbor. **11** And now, not as [in] the former days [am] I to the remnant of this people, || A declaration of Yhwh of Hosts. **12** Because of the sowing of peace, || The vine gives her fruit, || And the earth gives her increase, || And the heavens give their dew, || And I have caused the remnant of this people || To inherit all these. **13** And it has come to pass, || As you have been a reviling among nations, || O house of Judah, and house of Israel, || So I save you, and you have been a blessing, || Do not fear, let your hands be strong. **14** For thus said Yhwh of Hosts: As I purposed to do evil to you, || When your fathers made Me angry—said Yhwh of Hosts—And I did not relent, **15** So I have turned back, I have purposed, in these days, || To do good with Jerusalem, || And with the house of Judah—do not fear! **16** These [are] the things that you do: Each speak truth with his neighbor, || Judge [with] truth and peaceful judgment in your gates, **17** And do not devise the evil of his neighbor in your heart, || And do not love a false oath, || For all these [are] things that I have hated, || A declaration of Yhwh." **18** And there is a word of Yhwh of Hosts to me, saying, **19** "Thus said Yhwh of Hosts: The fast of the fourth, and the fast of the fifth, and the fast of the seventh, and the fast of the tenth [months], are to the house of Judah for joy and for rejoicing, and for pleasant appointed times, and the truth and the peace they have loved. **20** Thus said Yhwh of Hosts: Yet peoples come, and inhabitants of many cities, **21** Indeed, inhabitants of one || Have gone to another, saying, || We go diligently, || To appease the face of Yhwh, || To seek Yhwh of Hosts—I go, even I. **22** Indeed, many peoples have come in, and mighty nations, || To seek Yhwh of Hosts in Jerusalem, || And to appease the face of Yhwh. **23** Thus said Yhwh of Hosts: In those days ten men of all languages of the nations take hold, || Indeed, they have taken hold on the skirt of a man, a Jew, saying, || We go with you, for we heard God [is] with you!"

CHAPTER 9

1 The burden of a word of Yhwh against the land of Hadrach, and Demmeseh—his place of rest: (When to Yhwh [is] the eye of man, || And of all the tribes of Israel). **2** And also Hamath borders thereon, || Tyre and Sidon, for—very wise! **3** And Tyre builds a bulwark for herself, || And heaps silver as dust, || And gold as mire of out-places. **4** Behold, the Lord dispossesses her, || And He has struck her force in the sea, || And she is consumed with fire. **5** Ashkelon sees and fears, || Also Gaza, and she is exceedingly pained, || Also Ekron—for her expectation dried up, || And a king has perished from Gaza, || And Ashkelon does not remain, **6** "And a foreigner has dwelt in Ashdod, || And I have cut off the excellence of the Philistines. **7** And turned aside his blood from his mouth, || His abominations from between his teeth, || And he has remained, even he, to our God, || And he has been as a leader in Judah, || And Ekron as a Jebusite. **8** And I have pitched a camp for My house, || Because of the passer through, and of the returner, || And an exactor does not pass through against them again, || For now, I have seen with My eyes. **9** Rejoice exceedingly, O daughter of Zion, || Shout, O daughter of Jerusalem, || Behold, your King comes to you, || Righteous and having salvation, || Afflicted—and riding on a donkey, || And on a colt—a son of female donkeys. **10** And I have cut off the chariot from Ephraim, || And the horse from Jerusalem, || Indeed, the bow of battle has been cut off, || And He has spoken peace to nations, || And His rule [is] from sea to sea, || And from the river to the ends of the earth. **11** Also You—by the blood of Your covenant, || I have sent Your prisoners out of the pit, || There is no water in it. **12** Return to a stronghold, || You prisoners of the hope, || Even today a second announcer I restore to you. **13** For I have

trodden for Myself with Judah, || I have filled a bow [with] Ephraim, || And I have stirred up your sons, O Zion, || Against your sons, O Javan, || And I have set you as the sword of a hero." **14** And Yhwh appears for them, || And His arrow has gone forth as lightning, || And Lord Yhwh blows with a horn, || And He has gone with whirlwinds of the south. **15** Yhwh of Hosts covers them over, || And they consumed, and subdued sling-stones, || Indeed, they have drunk, || They have made a noise as wine, || And they have been full as a bowl, || As corners of an altar. **16** And their God Yhwh has saved them in that day, || As a flock of His people, || For stones of a crown are displaying themselves over His ground. **17** For what His goodness! And what His beauty! Grain the young men, || And new wine the virgins—make fruitful!

CHAPTER 10

1 They asked of Yhwh rain || In a time of spring rain, || Yhwh is making lightnings, || And He gives to them rain [in] showers. To each—the herb in the field. **2** Because the teraphim spoke iniquity, || And the diviners have seen a falsehood, || And dreams of the vanity they speak, || [With] vanity they give comfort, || Therefore they have journeyed as a flock, || They are afflicted, for there is no shepherd. **3** "My anger burned against the shepherds, || And I lay a charge against the male goats, || For Yhwh of Hosts has inspected His flock, the house of Judah, || And set them as His splendid horse in battle. **4** From him [is] a cornerstone, || From him a nail, from him a battle-bow, || From him goes forth every exactor together. **5** And they have been as heroes, || Treading in mire of out-places in battle, || And they have fought, for Yhwh [is] with them, || And have put to shame riders of horses. **6** And I have made the house of Judah mighty, || And I save the house of Joseph, || And I have caused them to dwell, for I have loved them, || And they have been as [if] I had not cast them off, || For I [am] their God Yhwh, || And I answer them. **7** And Ephraim has been as a hero, || And their heart has rejoiced as wine, || And their sons see, and they have rejoiced, || Their heart rejoices in Yhwh. **8** I hiss for them, and I gather them, || For I have redeemed them, || And they have multiplied as they multiplied. **9** And I sow them among peoples, || And in far-off places they remember Me, || And they have lived with their sons, || And they have turned back. **10** And I have brought them back from the land of Egypt, || And I gather them from Asshur, || And I bring them into the land of Gilead and Lebanon, || And [space] is not found for them there. **11** And He has passed over through the sea, || And has pressed and struck billows in the sea, || And all depths of a flood have been dried up, || And the excellence of Asshur has been brought down, || And the rod of Egypt turns aside. **12** And I have made them mighty in Yhwh, || And in His Name they walk up and down," || A declaration of Yhwh!

CHAPTER 11

1 Open, O Lebanon, your doors, || And fire devours among your cedars. **2** Howl, O fir, for the cedar has fallen, || For their majestic ones were destroyed, || Howl, you oaks of Bashan, || For the enclosed forest has come down, **3** A voice of the howling of the shepherds! For their robe of honor was destroyed, || A voice of the roaring of young lions! For the excellence of Jordan was destroyed. **4** Thus said my God Yhwh: "Feed the flock of the slaughter, **5** Whose buyers slay them, and are not guilty, || And their sellers say, Blessed [is] Yhwh, || And I am rich, || And their shepherds have no pity on them. **6** For I no longer have pity on inhabitants of the land, || A declaration of Yhwh, || And behold, I am causing man to come forth, || Each into the hand of his neighbor, || And into the hand of his king, || And they have beaten down the land, || And I do not deliver out of their hand." **7** And I feed the flock of slaughter, even you, you afflicted of the flock; and I take two staffs to myself; I have called one Pleasantness, and I have called the other Bands, and I feed the flock. **8** And I cut off the three shepherds in one month, and my soul is grieved with them, and also their soul has abhorred me. **9** And I say, "I do not feed you, the dying, let die; and the cut off, let be cut off; and the remaining ones, let each eat the flesh of its neighbor." **10** And I take my staff Pleasantness, and cut it apart, to make void my covenant that I had made with all the peoples: **11** and it is broken in that day, and the afflicted of the flock who are observing me know well, that it [is] a word of Yhwh. **12** And I say to them: "If good in your eyes, give my hire, and if not, refrain"; and they weigh out my hire—thirty pieces of silver. **13** And Yhwh says to me, "Cast it to the potter"; the good price that I have been prized at by them, and I take the thirty pieces of silver, and cast them [into] the house of Yhwh, to the potter. **14** And I cut apart my second staff, Bands, || To break the unity between Judah and Israel. **15** And Yhwh says to me, "Again take to yourself the instrument of a foolish shepherd. **16** For behold, I am raising up a shepherd in the land, || The cut off he does not inspect, || The shaken off he does not seek, || And the broken he does not heal, || The standing he does not sustain, || And the flesh of the fat he eats, || And their hooves he breaks off. **17** Woe [to] the worthless shepherd, forsaking the flock, || A sword [is] on his arm, and on his right eye, || His arm is utterly dried up, || And his right eye is very dim!"

CHAPTER 12

1 The burden of a word of Yhwh on Israel. A declaration of Yhwh, || Stretching out the heavens, and founding earth, || And forming the spirit of man in his midst: **2** "Behold, I am making Jerusalem a cup of reeling || To all the surrounding peoples, || And it is also against Judah, || In the siege against Jerusalem. **3** And it has come to pass in that day, || I make Jerusalem a burdensome stone to all the peoples, || All loading it are completely pressed down, || And gathered against it have been all nations of the earth. **4** In that day," a declaration of Yhwh, || "I strike every horse with astonishment, || And its rider with madness, || And on the house of Judah I open My eyes, || And every horse of the peoples I strike with blindness. **5** And leaders of Judah have said in their heart, || The inhabitants of Jerusalem [are] strength to me, || In Yhwh of Hosts their God. **6** In that day I make the leaders of Judah || As a hearth of fire among trees, || And as a torch of fire in a sheaf, || And they have consumed—on the right and on the left—all the surrounding peoples, || And Jerusalem has again inhabited her place in Jerusalem. **7** And Yhwh has saved the tents of Judah first, || So that the beauty of the house of David does not become great against Judah, || And the beauty of the inhabitant of Jerusalem. **8** In that day Yhwh covers over the inhabitant of Jerusalem, || And the stumbling among them has been in that day as David, || And the house of David as God— As the Messenger of Yhwh—before them. **9** And it has come to pass in that day, || I seek to destroy all the nations || Who are coming in against Jerusalem, **10** And I have poured on the house of David, || And on the inhabitant of Jerusalem, || The Spirit of grace and supplications, || And they have looked to Me whom they pierced, || And they have mourned over Him, || Like a mourning over the only one, || And they have been in bitterness for Him, || Like a bitterness over the firstborn. **11** In that day, great is the mourning of Jerusalem, || As the mourning of Hadadrimmon in the Valley of Megiddon, **12** And the land has mourned—every family apart, || The family of the house of David apart, || And their women apart; The family of the house of Nathan apart, || And their women apart; **13** The family of the house of Levi apart, || And their women apart; The family of Shimei apart, || And their women apart, **14** All the families that are left, || Every family apart, and their women apart!"

CHAPTER 13

1 "In that day there is a fountain opened || To the house of David || And to the inhabitants of Jerusalem, || For sin and for impurity. **2** And it has come to pass in that day," || A declaration of Yhwh of Hosts, || "I cut off the names of the idols from the land, || And they are not remembered anymore, || And also the prophets and the spirit of uncleanness || I cause to pass away from the land. **3** And it has been, when one prophesies again, || That his parents, his father and his mother, || Have said to him, You do not live, || For you have spoken falsehood in the Name of Yhwh, || And his father and his mother, his parents, || Have pierced him through in his prophesying. **4** And it has come to pass in that day, || The prophets are ashamed, each of his vision, in his prophesying, || And they do not put on a hairy robe to deceive. **5** And [one] has said, I am not a prophet, || A man—I am a tiller of ground, || For ground [is]

my possession from my youth. **6** And [one] has said to him, || What [are] these wounds in your hands? And he has said, Because I was struck [at] home by my lovers. **7** Sword, awake against My Shepherd, || And against a hero—My Fellow," || A declaration of Yhwh of Hosts. "Strike the Shepherd, and the flock is scattered, || And I have put back My hand on the little ones. **8** And it has come to pass, || In all the land," a declaration of Yhwh, || "Two parts in it are cut off—they expire, || And the third is left in it. **9** And I have brought the third into fire, || And refined them like a refining of silver, || And have tried them like a trying of gold, || It calls in My Name, and I answer it, || I have said, It [is] My people, || And it says, Yhwh [is] my God!"

CHAPTER 14

1 Behold, a day has come to Yhwh, || And your spoil has been divided in your midst. **2** And I have gathered all the nations to Jerusalem to battle, || And the city has been captured, || And the houses have been spoiled, || And the women are lain with, || Half the city has gone forth in a removal, || And the remnant of the people are not cut off from the city. **3** And Yhwh has gone forth, || And He has fought against those nations, || As in the day of His fighting in a day of conflict. **4** And His feet have stood, in that day, || On the Mount of Olives, || That [is] eastward before Jerusalem, || And the Mount of Olives has been cleft at its midst, || To the east, and to the west, a very great valley, || And half of the mountain is removed toward the north, || And half toward the south. **5** And you have fled [to] the valley of My mountains, || For the valley of the mountains joins to Azal, || And you have fled as you fled before the shaking, || In the days of Uzziah king of Judah, || And my God Yhwh has come in, || All holy ones [are] with You. **6** And it has come to pass in that day, || The precious light is not, it is dense darkness, **7** And there has been one day, || It is known to Yhwh, not day nor night, || And it has been at evening-time—there is light. **8** And it has come to pass in that day, || Living waters go forth from Jerusalem, || Half of them to the Eastern Sea, || And half of them to the Western Sea, || It is in summer and in winter. **9** And Yhwh has become King over all the earth, || In that day Yhwh is one, and His Name one. **10** All the land is changed as a plain, || From Gebo to Rimmon, south of Jerusalem, || And she has been high, and has dwelt in her place, || Even from the Gate of Benjamin || To the place of the first gate, to the front gate, || And from the Tower of Hananeel, || To the wine-vats of the king. **11** And they have dwelt in her, || And destruction is no more, || And Jerusalem has dwelt confidently. **12** And this is the plague with which Yhwh plagues all the peoples who have warred against Jerusalem: He has consumed away its flesh, || And it is standing on its feet, || And its eyes are consumed in their holes, || And its tongue is consumed in their mouth. **13** And it has come to pass in that day, || A great destruction [from] Yhwh is among them, || And they have each seized the hand of his neighbor, || And his hand has gone up against the hand of his neighbor. **14** And also Judah is fought with in Jerusalem, || And the force of all the surrounding nations has been gathered, || Gold, and silver, and apparel, in great abundance. **15** And so is the plague of the horse, of the mule, || Of the camel, and of the donkey, || And of all the livestock that are in these camps, || As this plague. **16** And it has come to pass, || Everyone who has been left of all the nations, || Who are coming in against Jerusalem, || They have also gone up from year to year, || To bow themselves to the King, Yhwh of Hosts, || And to celebrate the Celebration of the Shelters. **17** And it has come to pass, || That he who does not go up of the families of the land to Jerusalem, || To bow himself to the King, Yhwh of Hosts, || Even on them there is no shower. **18** And if the family of Egypt does not go up, nor come in, || Then on them is the plague || With which Yhwh plagues the nations || That do not go up to celebrate the Celebration of Shelters. **19** This is the punishment of the sin of Egypt, || And the punishment of the sin of all the nations, || That do not go up to celebrate the Celebration of Shelters. **20** In that day "Holy to Yhwh" is [engraved] on bells of the horse, || And the pots in the house of Yhwh || Have been as bowls before the altar. **21** And every pot in Jerusalem and in Judah, || Have been holy to Yhwh of Hosts, || And all those sacrificing have come in, || And have taken of them, and boiled in them, || And in that day there is no merchant anymore in the house of Yhwh of Hosts!

MALACHI

CHAPTER 1

¹ The burden of a word of Yhwh to Israel by the hand of Malachi: ² "I have loved you, said Yhwh, || And you have said, || In what have You loved us? ³ Is not Esau Jacob's brother?" A declaration of Yhwh, || "And I love Jacob, and Esau I have hated, || And I make his mountains a desolation, || And his inheritance for dragons of a wilderness. ⁴ Because Edom says, We have been made poor, || And we return and we build the ruins, || Thus said Yhwh of Hosts: They build, and I destroy, || And [men] have called to them, || O region of wickedness, || O people whom Yhwh defied for all time. ⁵ And your eyes see, and you say, || Yhwh is magnified beyond the border of Israel, ⁶ A son honors a father, and a servant his master. And if I [am] a father, where [is] My glory? And if I [am] a master, where [is] My fear? Said Yhwh of Hosts to you, || O priests, despising My Name! And you have said, In what have we despised Your Name? ⁷ You are bringing defiled bread near on My altar, || And you have said, In what have we defiled You? In your saying, The table of Yhwh—it [is] despicable, ⁸ And when you bring the blind near for sacrifice, [saying], || There is no evil, || And when you bring the lame and sick near, [saying], || There is no evil; Now bring it near to your governor—Does he accept you? or does he lift up your face?" said Yhwh of Hosts. ⁹ "And now, please appease the face of God, || And He favors us; This has been from your own hand, || Does He accept your faces?" said Yhwh of Hosts. ¹⁰ "Who [is] even among you, || And he shuts the double doors? Indeed, you do not kindle My altar for nothing, || I have no pleasure in you," said Yhwh of Hosts, || "And I do not accept a present of your hand. ¹¹ For from the rising of the sun to its going in, || Great [is] My Name among nations, || And in every place incense is brought near for My Name, and a pure present, || For great [is] My Name among nations," said Yhwh of Hosts. ¹² "And you are defiling it in your saying, || The table of Yhwh—it is defiled, || As for its fruit—its food is despicable. ¹³ And you have said, Behold, what a weariness, || And you have puffed at it," said Yhwh of Hosts, || "And you have brought in plunder, || And the lame and the sick, || And you have brought in the present! Do I accept it from your hand?" said Yhwh. ¹⁴ "And a deceiver [is] cursed, who has in his drove a male, || And is vowing, and is sacrificing a marred thing to the Lord, || For I [am] a great King," said Yhwh of Hosts, || "And My Name [is] revered among nations!"

CHAPTER 2

¹ "And now, to you [is] this charge, O priests, ² If you do not listen, and if you do not lay [it] to heart, || To give glory to My Name," said Yhwh of Hosts, || "I have sent the curse against you, || And I have cursed your blessings, || Indeed, I have also cursed it, || Because you are not laying [it] to heart. ³ Behold, I am pushing away the seed before you, || And have scattered dung before your faces, || Dung of your festivals, || And it has taken you away with it. ⁴ And you have known that I have sent this charge to you, || For My covenant being with Levi," said Yhwh of Hosts. ⁵ "My covenant has been of life and of peace with him, || And I make them a fear to him, and he fears Me, || And because of My Name he has been frightened. ⁶ The law of truth has been in his mouth, || And perverseness has not been found in his lips, || In peace and in uprightness he walked with Me, || And he brought back many from iniquity. ⁷ For the lips of a priest preserve knowledge, || And they seek law from his mouth, || For he [is] a messenger of Yhwh of Hosts. ⁸ And you, you have turned from the way, || You have caused many to stumble in the Law, || You have corrupted the covenant of Levi," said Yhwh of Hosts. ⁹ "And I also, I have made you despised and low before all the people, || Because you are not keeping My ways, || And are accepting by superficial things in the Law." ¹⁰ Have we not all one Father? Has not our God created us? Why do we deal treacherously, || Each against his brother, || To defile the covenant of our fathers? ¹¹ Judah has dealt treacherously, || And abomination has been done in Israel and in Jerusalem, || For Judah has defiled the holy thing of Yhwh that He has loved, || And has married the daughter of a strange god. ¹² Yhwh cuts off the man who does it, || Tempter and tempted—from the tents of Jacob, || Even he who is bringing a present near to Yhwh of Hosts. ¹³ And you do this a second time, || Covering the altar of Yhwh with tears, || With weeping and groaning, || Because there is no more turning to the present, || Or receiving of a pleasing thing from your hand. ¹⁴ And you have said, "Why?" Because Yhwh has testified between you || And the wife of your youth, || That you have dealt treacherously against her, || And she [is] your companion, and your covenant-wife. ¹⁵ And He did not make one [only], || And a remnant of the Spirit [is] for him. And what [is] the one [alone]! He is seeking a godly seed. And you have been watchful over your spirit, || And with the wife of your youth, || None deal treacherously. ¹⁶ "For He hates sending away," said Yhwh, God of Israel, || "And he [who] has covered violence with his clothing," said Yhwh of Hosts, || "And you have been watchful over your spirit, || And you do not deal treacherously." ¹⁷ You have wearied Yhwh with your words, || And you have said, "In what have we wearied Him?" In your saying, "Every evildoer [is] good in the eyes of Yhwh, || And He is delighting in them," || Or, "Where [is] the God of judgment?"

CHAPTER 3

¹ "Behold, I am sending My messenger, || And he has prepared a way before Me, || And suddenly the Lord whom you are seeking comes into His temple, || Even the Messenger of the Covenant, || Whom you are desiring, || Behold, He is coming," said Yhwh of Hosts. ² "And who is bearing the day of His coming? And who is standing in His appearing? For He [is] as fire of a refiner, || And as soap of a fuller. ³ And He has sat, a refiner and purifier of silver, || And He has purified the sons of Levi, || And has refined them as gold and as silver, || And they have been bringing a present near to Yhwh in righteousness. ⁴ And the present of Judah and Jerusalem has been sweet to Yhwh, || As in days of old, and as in former years. ⁵ And I have drawn near to you for judgment, || And I have been a witness, || Making haste against sorcerers, and against adulterers, || And against swearers to a falsehood, || And against oppressors of the hire of a hired worker, || Of a widow, and of a fatherless one, || And those turning aside a sojourner, || And who do not fear Me," said Yhwh of Hosts. ⁶ "For I, Yhwh, have not changed, || And you, the sons of Jacob, || You have not been consumed. ⁷ Even from the days of your fathers You have turned aside from My statutes, || And you have not taken heed. Return to Me, and I return to you," said Yhwh of Hosts. "And you have said, || In what do we turn back? ⁸ Does man deceive God? but you are deceiving Me, || And you have said, || In what have we deceived You? The tithe and the raised-offering! ⁹ You are cursed with a curse! And you are deceiving Me—this nation—all of it. ¹⁰ Bring in all the tithe to the treasure-house, || And there is food in My house; When you have tried Me, now, with this," said Yhwh of Hosts, || "Do I not open the windows of the heavens to you? Indeed, I have emptied on you a blessing until there is no space. ¹¹ And I have pushed against the consumer for you, || And He does not destroy the fruit of your ground, || Nor does the vine in the field miscarry to you," said Yhwh of Hosts. ¹² "And all the nations have declared you blessed, || For you are a delightful land," said Yhwh of Hosts. ¹³ "Your words have been hard against Me," said Yhwh, || "And you have said, What have we spoken against You? ¹⁴ You have said, A vain thing to serve God! And what gain when we kept His charge? And when we have gone in black, || Because of Yhwh of Hosts? ¹⁵ And now, we are declaring the proud blessed, || Indeed, those doing wickedness have been built up, || Indeed, they have tempted God, and escape. ¹⁶ Then have those fearing Yhwh spoken to one another, || And Yhwh attends and hears, || And a scroll of memorial is written before Him || Of those fearing Yhwh, || And of those esteeming His Name. ¹⁷ And they have been to Me," said Yhwh of Hosts, || "In the day that I am appointing—a peculiar treasure, || And I have had pity on them, || As one has pity on his son who is serving him. ¹⁸ And you have turned back and considered, || Between the righteous and the wicked, || Between the servant of God and him who is not His servant."

CHAPTER 4

¹ "For behold, the day has come, burning as a furnace, || When all the proud and all those doing wickedness have been stubble, || And the day that came has burned them," said Yhwh of Hosts, || "That there is not left to them root or branch, ² But for you fearing My Name, || The Sun of Righteousness has risen with healing in His wings, || And you have gone forth, || And have bounded as calves of a stall. ³ And you have trodden down the wicked, || For they are ashes under the soles of your feet, || In the day that I am appointing," said Yhwh of Hosts. ⁴ "Remember the Law of My servant Moses, || That I commanded him in Horeb, || For all Israel—statutes and judgments, ⁵ Behold, I am sending Elijah the prophet to you, || Before the coming of the great and fearful Day of Yhwh. ⁶ And he has turned back the heart of fathers to sons, || And the heart of sons to their fathers, || Before I come and have utterly struck the land!"

NEW TESTAMENT

MATTHEW

CHAPTER 1

¹ [The] scroll of the birth of Jesus Christ, Son of David, Son of Abraham. ² Abraham begot Isaac, and Isaac begot Jacob, and Jacob begot Judah and his brothers, ³ and Judah begot Perez and Zerah of Tamar, and Perez begot Hezron, and Hezron begot Ram, ⁴ and Ram begot Amminadab, and Amminadab begot Nahshon, and Nahshon begot Salmon, ⁵ and Salmon begot Boaz of Rahab, and Boaz begot Obed of Ruth, and Obed begot Jesse, ⁶ and Jesse begot David the king. And David the king begot Solomon, of her [who had been] Uriah's, ⁷ and Solomon begot Rehoboam, and Rehoboam begot Abijah, and Abijah begot Asa, ⁸ and Asa begot Jehoshaphat, and Jehoshaphat begot Joram, and Joram begot Uzziah, ⁹ and Uzziah begot Jotham, and Jotham begot Ahaz, and Ahaz begot Hezekiah, ¹⁰ and Hezekiah begot Manasseh, and Manasseh begot Amon, and Amon begot Josiah, ¹¹ and Josiah begot Jeconiah and his brothers, at the Babylonian removal. ¹² And after the Babylonian removal, Jeconiah begot Shealtiel, and Shealtiel begot Zerubbabel, ¹³ and Zerubbabel begot Abiud, and Abiud begot Eliakim, and Eliakim begot Azor, ¹⁴ and Azor begot Sadok, and Sadok begot Achim, and Achim begot Eliud, ¹⁵ and Eliud begot Eleazar, and Eleazar begot Matthan, and Matthan begot Jacob, ¹⁶ and Jacob begot Joseph, the husband of Mary, of whom was begotten Jesus, who is named Christ. ¹⁷ All the generations, therefore, from Abraham to David [are] fourteen generations, and from David to the Babylonian removal fourteen generations, and from the Babylonian removal to the Christ, fourteen generations. ¹⁸ And of Jesus Christ, the birth was thus: for His mother Mary having been betrothed to Joseph, before their coming together she was found to have conceived from the Holy Spirit, ¹⁹ and her husband Joseph being righteous, and not willing to make her an example, resolved to send her away privately. ²⁰ And on his thinking of these things, behold, a messenger of the Lord appeared to him in a dream, saying, "Joseph, son of David, you may not fear to receive your wife Mary, for that which was begotten in her is of [the] Holy Spirit, ²¹ and she will bring forth a Son, and you will call His Name Jesus, for He will save His people from their sins." ²² And all this has come to pass, that it may be fulfilled that was spoken by the Lord through the prophet, saying, ²³ "Behold, the virgin will conceive, and she will bring forth a Son, and they will call His Name Emmanuel," which is, being interpreted, "God with us." ²⁴ And Joseph, having risen from sleep, did as the messenger of the Lord directed him, and received his wife, ²⁵ and did not know her until she brought forth her Son—the firstborn, and he called His Name Jesus.

CHAPTER 2

¹ And Jesus having been born in Beth-Lehem of Judea, in the days of Herod the king, behold, magi from the east came to Jerusalem, ² saying, "Where is He who was born King of the Jews? for we saw His star in the east, and we came to worship Him." ³ And Herod the king having heard, was stirred, and all Jerusalem with him, ⁴ and having gathered all the chief priests and scribes of the people, he was inquiring from them where the Christ is born. ⁵ And they said to him, "In Beth-Lehem of Judea, for thus it has been written through the prophet: ⁶ And you, Beth-Lehem, the land of Judah, you are by no means the least among the leaders of Judah, for out of you will come One leading, who will feed My people Israel." ⁷ Then Herod, having called the magi privately, inquired exactly from them the time of the appearing star, ⁸ and having sent them to Beth-Lehem, he said, "Having gone—inquire exactly for the Child, and whenever you may have found, bring me back word, that I also having come may worship Him." ⁹ And they, having heard the king, departed, and behold, the star, that they saw in the east, went before them, until, having come, it stood over where the Child was. ¹⁰ And having seen the star, they rejoiced with exceedingly great joy, ¹¹ and having come into the house, they found the Child with His mother Mary, and having fallen down they worshiped Him, and having opened their treasures, they presented to Him gifts, gold, and frankincense, and myrrh, ¹² and having been divinely warned in a dream not to return to Herod, through another way they withdrew to their own region. ¹³ And on their having withdrawn, behold, a messenger of the Lord appears in a dream to Joseph, saying, "Having risen, take the Child and His mother, and flee to Egypt, and be there until I may speak to you, for Herod is about to seek the Child to destroy Him." ¹⁴ And he, having risen, took the Child and His mother by night, and withdrew to Egypt, ¹⁵ and he was there until the death of Herod, that it might be fulfilled that was spoken by the Lord through the prophet, saying, "Out of Egypt I called My Son." ¹⁶ Then Herod, having seen that he was deceived by the magi, was very angry, and having sent forth, he slew all the male children in Beth-Lehem, and in all its borders, from two years and under, according to the time that he inquired exactly from the magi. ¹⁷ Then was fulfilled that which was spoken by Jeremiah the prophet, saying, ¹⁸ "A voice in Ramah was heard—weeping and much mourning—Rachel weeping [for] her children, and she would not be comforted because they are not." ¹⁹ And Herod having died, behold, a messenger of the Lord appears in a dream to Joseph in Egypt, ²⁰ saying, "Having risen, take the Child and His mother, and be going to the land of Israel, for they have died—those seeking the life of the Child." ²¹ And he, having risen, took the Child and His mother, and came to the land of Israel, ²² and having heard that Archelaus reigns over Judea instead of his father Herod, he was afraid to go there, and having been divinely warned in a dream, he withdrew to the parts of Galilee, ²³ and coming, he dwelt in a city named Nazareth, that it might be fulfilled that was spoken through the Prophets, that "He will be called a Nazarene."

CHAPTER 3

¹ And in those days John the Immerser comes, proclaiming in the wilderness of Judea, ² and saying, "Convert, for the kingdom of the heavens has come near," ³ for this is he having been spoken of by Isaiah the prophet, saying, "A voice of one crying in the wilderness: Prepare the way of the Lord, || Make His paths straight." ⁴ And this John had his clothing of camel's hair, and a girdle of skin around his loins, and his nourishment was locusts and honey of the field. ⁵ Then were going forth to him Jerusalem, and all Judea, and all the region around the Jordan, ⁶ and they were immersed in the Jordan by him, confessing their sins. ⁷ And having seen many of the Pharisees and Sadducees coming about his immersion, he said to them, "Brood of vipers! Who showed you to flee from the coming wrath? ⁸ bear, therefore, fruits worthy of conversion, ⁹ and do not think to say in yourselves, We have a father—Abraham, for I say to you that God is able to raise children to Abraham out of these stones, ¹⁰ and now also, the axe is laid to the root of the trees, therefore, every tree not bearing good fruit is cut down, and is cast into fire. ¹¹ I indeed immerse you in water for conversion, but He who is coming after me is mightier than I, of whom I am not worthy to carry the sandals, He will immerse you in the Holy Spirit and fire, ¹² whose fan [is] in His hand, and He will thoroughly cleanse His floor, and will gather His wheat into the storehouse, but He will burn the chaff with unquenchable fire." ¹³ Then Jesus comes from Galilee to John at the Jordan, to be immersed by him, ¹⁴ but John was forbidding Him, saying, "I have need to be immersed by You— and You come to me?" ¹⁵ But Jesus answering said to him, "Permit [it] now, for thus it is fitting to us to fulfill all righteousness," then he permits Him. ¹⁶ And having been immersed, Jesus immediately went up from the water, and behold, the heavens were opened to Him, and He saw the Spirit of God descending as a dove, and coming on Him, ¹⁷ and behold, a voice out of the heavens, saying, "This is My Son, the Beloved, in whom I delighted."

CHAPTER 4

¹ Then Jesus was led up to the wilderness by the Spirit, to be tempted by the Devil, ² and having fasted forty days and forty nights, afterward He hungered. ³ And the tempting [one], having come to Him, said, "If You are the Son of God—speak that these stones may become loaves." ⁴ But He answering said, "It has been written: Man does not live on bread alone, but on every word coming forth from the mouth of God." ⁵ Then the Devil takes Him to the [holy] city, and sets Him on the pinnacle of the temple, ⁶ and says to Him, "If You are the Son

of God—cast Yourself down, for it has been written that, His messengers He will charge concerning you, and on hands they will bear you up, that you may not dash your foot on a stone." [7] Jesus said to him again, "It has been written: You will not tempt the Lord your God." [8] Again the Devil takes Him to a very high mountain, and shows to Him all the kingdoms of the world and their glory, [9] and says to Him, "All these I will give to You, if falling down You may worship me." [10] Then Jesus says to him, "Go—Satan, for it has been written: You will worship the Lord your God, and Him only will you serve." [11] Then the Devil leaves Him, and behold, messengers came and were ministering to Him. [12] And Jesus, having heard that John was delivered up, withdrew to Galilee, [13] and having left Nazareth, having come, He dwelt at Capernaum that is by the sea, in the borders of Zebulun and Naphtali, [14] that it might be fulfilled that was spoken through Isaiah the prophet, saying, [15] "Land of Zebulun and land of Naphtali, way of the sea, beyond the Jordan, Galilee of the nations! [16] The people that is sitting in darkness saw a great light, and to those sitting in a region and shadow of death—light arose to them." [17] From that time Jesus began to proclaim and to say, "Convert, for the kingdom of the heavens has come near." [18] And Jesus, walking by the Sea of Galilee, saw two brothers, Simon named Peter and his brother Andrew, casting a drag into the sea—for they were fishers— [19] and He says to them, "Come after Me, and I will make you fishers of men," [20] and they, immediately, having left the nets, followed Him. [21] And having advanced from there, He saw two other brothers, James of Zebedee, and his brother John, in the boat with their father Zebedee, refitting their nets, and He called them, [22] and they, immediately, having left the boat and their father, followed Him. [23] And Jesus was going in all of Galilee teaching in their synagogues, and proclaiming the good news of the kingdom, and healing every disease and every sickness among the people, [24] and His fame went forth to all Syria, and they brought to Him all the ill having manifold oppressing diseases and torments—and demoniacs, and lunatics, and paralytics—and He healed them. [25] And there followed Him many multitudes from Galilee, and Decapolis, and Jerusalem, and Judea, and beyond the Jordan.

CHAPTER 5

[1] And having seen the multitudes, He went up to the mountain, and He having sat down, His disciples came to Him, [2] and having opened His mouth, He was teaching them, saying, [3] "Blessed the poor in spirit—because theirs is the kingdom of the heavens. [4] Blessed the mourning—because they will be comforted. [5] Blessed the meek—because they will inherit the land. [6] Blessed those hungering and thirsting for righteousness—because they will be filled. [7] Blessed the kind—because they will find kindness. [8] Blessed the clean in heart—because they will see God. [9] Blessed the peacemakers—because they will be called sons of God. [10] Blessed those persecuted for righteousness' sake—because theirs is the kingdom of the heavens. [11] Blessed are you whenever they may reproach you, and may persecute, and may say any evil thing against you falsely for My sake— [12] rejoice and be glad, because your reward [is] great in the heavens, for thus they persecuted the prophets who were before you. [13] You are the salt of the earth, but if the salt may lose savor, in what will it be salted? It is good for nothing from now on, except to be cast outside, and to be trodden down by men. [14] You are the light of the world, a city set on a mountain is not able to be hid; [15] nor do they light a lamp and put it under the measure, but on the lampstand, and it shines to all those in the house; [16] so let your light shine before men, that they may see your good works, and may glorify your Father who [is] in the heavens. [17] Do not suppose that I came to throw down the Law or the Prophets—I did not come to throw down, but to fulfill; [18] for truly I say to you, until the heaven and the earth may pass away, one iota or one tittle may not pass away from the Law, until all may come to pass. [19] Therefore whoever may loose one of these commands—the least—and may teach men so, he will be called least in the kingdom of the heavens, but whoever may do and may teach [them], he will be called great in the kingdom of the heavens. [20] For I say to you that if your righteousness may not abound above that of the scribes and Pharisees, you may not enter into the kingdom of the heavens. [21] You heard that it was said to the ancients: You will not murder, and whoever may murder will be in danger of the judgment; [22] but I say to you that everyone who is angry at his brother without cause will be in danger of the judgment, and whoever may say to his brother, Stupid, will be in danger of the Sanhedrin, and whoever may say, Moron, will be in danger of the Gehenna of fire. [23] If, therefore, you may bring your gift to the altar, and there may remember that your brother has anything against you, [24] leave there your gift before the altar, and go—first be reconciled to your brother, and then having come, bring your gift. [25] Be agreeing with your opponent quickly, while you are in the way with him, that the opponent may not deliver you to the judge, and the judge may deliver you to the officer, and you may be cast into prison; [26] truly I say to you, you may not come forth from there until you may pay the last penny. [27] You heard that it was said to the ancients: You will not commit adultery; [28] but I say to you that everyone who is looking on a woman to desire her, already committed adultery with her in his heart. [29] But if your right eye causes you to stumble, pluck it out and cast from you, for it is good to you that one of your members may perish, and not your whole body be cast into Gehenna. [30] And if your right hand causes you to stumble, cut it off, and cast from you, for it is good to you that one of your members may perish, and not your whole body be cast into Gehenna. [31] And it was said that, Whoever may put away his wife, let him give to her a writing of divorce; [32] but I say to you that whoever may put away his wife, except for the matter of whoredom, makes her to commit adultery; and whoever may marry her who has been put away commits adultery. [33] Again, you heard that it was said to the ancients: You will not swear falsely, but you will pay to the Lord your oaths; [34] but I say to you not to swear at all; neither by Heaven, because it is the throne of God, [35] nor by the earth, because it is His footstool, nor by Jerusalem, because it is [the] city of [the] great King, [36] nor may you swear by your head, because you are not able to make one hair white or black; [37] but let your word be, Yes, Yes, No, No, and that which is more than these is of the evil [one]. [38] You heard that it was said: Eye for eye, and tooth for tooth; [39] but I say to you not to resist the evil, but whoever will slap you on your right cheek, turn to him also the other; [40] and whoever is willing to take you to law, and to take your coat—also permit to him the cloak. [41] And whoever will impress you one mile, go with him two; [42] to him who is asking of you be giving, and him who is willing to borrow from you, you may not turn away. [43] You heard that it was said: You will love your neighbor, and will hate your enemy; [44] but I say to you, love your enemies, bless those cursing you, do good to those hating you, and pray for those accusing you falsely, and persecuting you, [45] that you may be sons of your Father in the heavens, because He causes His sun to rise on evil and good, and He sends rain on righteous and unrighteous. [46] For if you may love those loving you, what reward do you have? Do the tax collectors not also do the same? [47] and if you may greet your brothers only, what do you do abundant? do the nations not also do so? [48] you will therefore be perfect, as your Father who [is] in the heavens is perfect."

CHAPTER 6

[1] "Take heed not to do your kindness before men, to be seen by them, and if not—you have no reward from your Father who [is] in the heavens; [2] whenever, therefore, you may do kindness, you may not sound a trumpet before you as the hypocrites do, in the synagogues, and in the streets, that they may have glory from men; truly I say to you, they have their reward! [3] But you, doing kindness, do not let your left hand know what your right hand does, [4] that your kindness may be in secret, and your Father who is seeing in secret will reward you Himself. [5] And when you may pray, you will not be as the hypocrites, because they cherish to pray standing in the synagogues and in the corners of the broad places, that they may be seen of men; truly I say to you that they have their reward. [6] But you, when you may pray, go into your chamber, and having shut your door, pray to your Father who [is] in secret, and your Father who is seeing in secret will reward you. [7] And—praying—you may not use vain repetitions like the nations, for they think that in their speaking much they will be heard, [8] therefore do not be like them, for your Father knows those things that you have need of before your asking Him; [9] therefore pray thus: Our Father who [is] in the heavens, hallowed be Your Name. [10] Your kingdom come, Your will come to pass, as in Heaven also on the earth. [11] Give us today our appointed bread. [12] And forgive us our debts, as we also forgive

our debtors. **13** And may You not lead us into temptation, but deliver us from the evil [one], because Yours is the kingdom, and the power, and the glory for all ages. Amen. **14** For if you may forgive men their trespasses, He also will forgive you—your Father who [is] in the heavens; **15** but if you may not forgive men their trespasses, neither will your Father forgive your trespasses. **16** And when you may fast, do not be as the hypocrites, of sour countenances, for they disfigure their faces, that they may appear to men fasting; truly I say to you that they have their reward. **17** But you, fasting, anoint your head, and wash your face, **18** that you may not appear to men fasting, but to your Father who [is] in secret, and your Father, who is seeing in secret, will reward you. **19** Do not treasure up to yourselves treasures on the earth, where moth and rust disfigure, and where thieves break through and steal, **20** but treasure up to yourselves treasures in Heaven, where neither moth nor rust disfigure, and where thieves do not break through nor steal, **21** for where your treasure is, there will your heart be also. **22** The lamp of the body is the eye, if, therefore, your eye may be perfect, all your body will be enlightened, **23** but if your eye may be evil, all your body will be dark; if, therefore, the light that [is] in you is darkness—the darkness, how great! **24** None is able to serve two lords, for either he will hate the one and love the other, or he will hold to the one, and despise the other; you are not able to serve God and wealth. **25** Because of this I say to you, do not be anxious for your life, what you may eat, and what you may drink, nor for your body, what you may put on. Is not life more than nourishment, and the body than clothing? **26** look to the birds of the sky, for they do not sow, nor reap, nor gather into storehouses, and your heavenly Father nourishes them; are you not much better than they? **27** And who of you, being anxious, is able to add to his age one cubit? **28** and why are you anxious about clothing? consider well the lilies of the field; how do they grow? they do not labor, nor do they spin; **29** and I say to you that not even Solomon in all his glory was clothed as one of these. **30** And if the herb of the field, that today is, and tomorrow is cast into the furnace, God so clothes—not much more you, O you of little faith? **31** therefore you may not be anxious, saying, What may we eat? or, What may we drink? or, [With] what may we be clothed? **32** for the nations seek for all these, for your heavenly Father knows that you have need of all these; **33** but seek first the Kingdom of God and His righteousness, and all these will be added to you. **34** Therefore do not be anxious for tomorrow, for tomorrow will be anxious for its own things; sufficient for the day [is] the evil of it."

CHAPTER 7

1 "Do not judge, that you may not be judged, **2** for in what judgment you judge, you will be judged, and in what measure you measure, it will be measured to you. **3** And why do you behold the speck that [is] in your brother's eye, and do not consider the beam that [is] in your own eye? **4** or, how will you say to your brother, Permit [that] I may cast out the speck from your eye, and behold, the beam [is] in your own eye? **5** Hypocrite, first cast out the beam out of your own eye, and then you will see clearly to cast out the speck out of your brother's eye. **6** You may not give that which is [holy] to the dogs, nor cast your pearls before the pigs, that they may not trample them among their feet, and having turned—may tear you apart. **7** Ask, and it will be given to you; seek, and you will find; knock, and it will be opened to you; **8** for everyone who is asking receives, and he who is seeking finds, and to him who is knocking it will be opened. **9** Or what man is of you, of whom, if his son may ask [for] a loaf—a stone will he present to him? **10** and if he may ask [for] a fish—a serpent will he present to him? **11** if, therefore, you being evil, have known to give good gifts to your children, how much more will your Father who [is] in the heavens give good things to those asking Him? **12** All things, therefore, whatever you may will that men may be doing to you, so also do to them, for this is the Law and the Prophets. **13** Go in through the narrow gate, because wide [is] the gate and broad the way that is leading to the destruction, and many are those going in through it; **14** how narrow [is] the gate and compressed the way that is leading to life, and few are those finding it! **15** But take heed of the false prophets who come to you in sheep's clothing, and inwardly are ravenous wolves. **16** From their fruits you will know them; do [men] gather grapes from thorns? or figs from thistles? **17** so every good tree yields good fruits, but the bad tree yields evil fruits.

18 A good tree is not able to yield evil fruits, nor a bad tree to yield good fruits. **19** Every tree not yielding good fruit is cut down and is cast into fire; **20** therefore from their fruits you will know them. **21** Not everyone who is saying to Me, Lord, Lord, will come into the kingdom of the heavens, but he who is doing the will of My Father who is in the heavens. **22** Many will say to Me in that day, Lord, Lord, have we not prophesied in Your Name? and in Your Name cast out demons? and in Your Name done many mighty things? **23** and then I will acknowledge to them, that—I never knew you, depart from Me you who are working lawlessness. **24** Therefore, everyone who hears these words of Mine, and does them, I will liken him to a wise man who built his house on the rock; **25** and the rain descended, and the streams came, and the winds blew, and they beat on that house, and it did not fall, for it had been founded on the rock. **26** And everyone who is hearing these words of Mine, and is not doing them, will be likened to a foolish man who built his house on the sand; **27** and the rain descended, and the streams came, and the winds blew, and they beat on that house, and it fell, and its fall was great." **28** And it came to pass, when Jesus finished these words, the multitudes were astonished at His teaching, **29** for He was teaching them as having authority, and not as the scribes.

CHAPTER 8

1 And when He came down from the mountain, great multitudes followed Him, **2** and behold, a leper having come, was prostrating to Him, saying, "Lord, if You are willing, You are able to cleanse me"; **3** and having stretched forth the hand, Jesus touched him, saying, "I will, be cleansed," and immediately his leprosy was cleansed. **4** And Jesus says to him, "See, you may tell no one, but go, show yourself to the priest, and bring the gift that Moses commanded for a testimony to them." **5** And Jesus having entered into Capernaum, there came to Him a centurion calling on Him, **6** and saying, "Lord, my young man has been laid in the house a paralytic, fearfully afflicted," **7** and Jesus says to him, "I, having come, will heal him." **8** And the centurion answering said, "Lord, I am not worthy that You may enter under my roof, but only say a word, and my servant will be healed; **9** for I also am a man under authority, having under myself soldiers, and I say to this one, Go, and he goes, and to another, Be coming, and he comes, and to my servant, Do this, and he does [it]." **10** And Jesus having heard, wondered, and said to those following, "Truly I say to you, not even in Israel have I found such great faith; **11** and I say to you that many from east and west will come and recline with Abraham, and Isaac, and Jacob, in the kingdom of the heavens, **12** but the sons of the kingdom will be cast forth into the outer darkness—there will be the weeping and the gnashing of the teeth." **13** And Jesus said to the centurion, "Go, and as you believed let it be to you"; and his young man was healed in that hour. **14** And Jesus having come into the house of Peter, saw his mother-in-law laid, and fevered, **15** and He touched her hand, and the fever left her, and she arose, and was ministering to them. **16** And evening having come, they brought to Him many demoniacs, and He cast out the spirits with a word, and healed all who were ill, **17** that it might be fulfilled that was spoken through Isaiah the prophet, saying, "He took our sicknesses Himself, and bore the diseases." **18** And Jesus having seen great multitudes around Him, commanded to depart to the other side; **19** and a certain scribe having come, said to Him, "Teacher, I will follow You wherever You may go"; **20** and Jesus says to him, "The foxes have holes, and the birds of the sky places of rest, but the Son of Man has nowhere He may lay the head." **21** And another of His disciples said to Him, "Lord, permit me first to depart and to bury my father"; **22** and Jesus said to him, "Follow Me, and permit the dead to bury their own dead." **23** And when He entered into the boat His disciples followed Him, **24** and behold, a great storm arose in the sea, so that the boat was being covered by the waves, but He was sleeping, **25** and His disciples having come to Him, awoke Him, saying, "Lord, save us! We are perishing!" **26** And He says to them, "Why are you fearful, O you of little faith?" Then having risen, He rebuked the winds and the sea, and there was a great calm; **27** and the men wondered, saying, "What kind—is this, that even the wind and the sea obey Him?" **28** And He having come to the other side, to the region of the Gergesenes, there met Him two demoniacs, coming forth out of the tombs, very fierce, so that no one was able to pass over by that way, **29** and behold, they cried out, saying, "What [regards] us and You, [[Jesus,]] Son of God? did You come here to afflict us before the time?" **30** And there was a herd of many pigs feeding far off from them, **31** and the demons were calling on Him, saying, "If You cast us forth, permit us to go away into the herd of the pigs"; **32** and He says to them, "Go." And having come forth, they went into the herd of the pigs, and behold, the whole herd of the pigs rushed down the steep, into the sea, and died in the waters, **33** and those feeding fled, and having gone into the city, they declared all, and the matter of the demoniacs. **34** And behold, all the city came forth to meet Jesus, and having seen Him, they called on [Him] that He might depart from their borders.

CHAPTER 9

1 And having gone into the boat, He passed over, and came to His own city, **2** and behold, they were bringing to Him a paralytic, laid on a bed, and Jesus having seen their faith, said to the paralytic, "Take courage, child, your sins have been forgiven." **3** And behold, certain of the scribes said within themselves, "This One speaks evil." **4** And Jesus, having known their thoughts, said, "Why think evil in your hearts? **5** for which is easier? to say, Your sins are forgiven; or to say, Rise and walk? **6** But that you may know that the Son of Man has power on the earth to forgive sins—(then He says to the paralytic)—Having risen, take up your bed, and go to your house." **7** And he, having risen, went to his house, **8** and the multitudes having seen, wondered, and glorified God, who gave such power to men. **9** And Jesus passing on from there saw a man sitting at the tax office named Matthew, and says to him, "Follow Me," and he, having risen, followed Him. **10** And it came to pass, He reclining in the house, that behold, many tax collectors and sinners having come, were dining with Jesus and His disciples, **11** and the Pharisees having seen, said to His disciples, "Why does your teacher eat with the tax collectors and sinners?" **12** And Jesus having heard, said to them, "They who are whole have no need of a physician, but they who are ill; **13** but having gone, learn what [this] is: Kindness I will, and not sacrifice; for I did not come to call righteous men, but sinners." **14** Then the disciples of John come to Him, saying, "Why do we and the Pharisees fast much, and Your disciples do not fast?" **15** And Jesus said to them, "Can the sons of the bride-chamber mourn, so long as the bridegroom is with them? but days will come when the bridegroom may be taken from them, and then they will fast. **16** And no one puts a patch of undressed cloth on an old garment, for its filling up takes from the garment, and a worse split is made. **17** Nor do they put new wine into old skins, and if not—the skins burst, and the wine runs out, and the skins are destroyed, but they put new wine into new skins, and both are preserved together." **18** While He is speaking these things to them, behold, a ruler having come, was prostrating to Him, saying that "My daughter just now died, but having come, lay Your hand on her, and she will live." **19** And Jesus having risen, followed him, also His disciples, **20** and behold, a woman having a flow of blood [for] twelve years, having come to Him behind, touched the fringe of His garments, **21** for she said within herself, "If only I may touch His garment, I will be saved." **22** And Jesus having turned, and having seen her, said, "Take courage, daughter, your faith has saved you," and the woman was saved from that hour. **23** And Jesus having come into the house of the ruler, and having seen the pipers and the multitude making tumult, **24** He says to them, "Withdraw, for the girl did not die, but sleeps," and they were deriding Him; **25** but when the multitude was put forth, having gone in, He took hold of her hand, and the girl arose, **26** and the fame of this went forth to all the land. **27** And Jesus passing on from there, two blind men followed Him, calling and saying, "Deal kindly with us, Son of David!" **28** And He having come into the house, the blind men came to Him, and Jesus says to them, "Do you believe that I am able to do this?" They say to Him, "Yes, Lord." **29** Then He touched their eyes, saying, "According to your faith let it be to you," **30** and their eyes were opened, and Jesus strictly charged them, saying, "See, let no one know"; **31** but they, having gone forth, spread His fame in all that land. **32** And as they are coming forth, behold, they brought to Him a man mute, a demoniac, **33** and the demon having been cast out, the mute spoke, and the multitude wondered, saying that "It was never so seen in Israel," **34** but the Pharisees said, "By the ruler of the demons He casts out the demons." **35** And Jesus was going up and down all the cities and the villages, teaching in their synagogues, and proclaiming the good news of the kingdom, and healing every disease and every sickness among the people. **36** And having seen the multitudes, He was moved with compassion for them, that they were faint and cast aside, as sheep not having a shepherd; **37** then He says to His disciples, "The harvest indeed [is] abundant, but the workmen few; **38** therefore implore the Lord of the harvest that He may put forth workmen to His harvest."

CHAPTER 10

1 And having called His twelve disciples to Himself, He gave to them power over unclean spirits, so as to be casting them out, and to be healing every disease and every sickness. **2** And of the twelve apostles the names are these: first, Simon, who is called Peter, and his brother Andrew; James of Zebedee, and his brother John; **3** Philip, and Bartholomew; Thomas, and Matthew the tax collector; James of Alpheus, and Lebbeus who was surnamed Thaddeus; **4** Simon the Zealot, and Judas Iscariot, who also delivered Him up. **5** These twelve Jesus sent forth, having given command to them, saying, "Do not go away to the way of the nations, and do not go into a city of the Samaritans, **6** and be going rather to the lost sheep of the house of Israel. **7** And going on, proclaim, saying that the kingdom of the heavens has come near; **8** be healing [those] ailing, raising the dead, cleansing lepers, casting out demons—freely you received, freely give. **9** Do not provide gold, nor silver, nor brass in your girdles, **10** nor leather pouch for the way, nor two coats, nor sandals, nor staff—for the workman is worthy of his nourishment. **11** And into whatever city or village you may enter, inquire who in it is worthy, and abide there, until you may go forth. **12** And coming into the house greet it, **13** and if indeed the house is worthy, let your peace come on it; and if it is not worthy, let your peace return to you. **14** And whoever may not receive you nor hear your words, coming forth from that house or city, shake off the dust of your feet, **15** truly I say to you, it will be more tolerable for the land of Sodom and Gomorrah in the day of judgment than for that city. **16** Behold, I send you forth as sheep in the midst of wolves, therefore be wise as the serpents, and pure as the doves. **17** And take heed of men, for they will give you up to Sanhedrin's, and in their synagogues they will scourge you, **18** and before governors and kings you will be brought for My sake, for a testimony to them and to the nations. **19** And whenever they may deliver you up, do not be anxious how or what you may speak, for it will be given you in that hour what you will speak; **20** for you are not the speakers, but the Spirit of your Father that is speaking in you. **21** And brother will deliver up brother to death, and father child, and children will rise up against parents, and will put them to death, **22** and you will be hated by all because of My Name, but he who has endured to the end, he will be saved. **23** And whenever they may persecute you in this city, flee to the other, for truly I say to you, you may not have finished [going through] the cities of Israel until the Son of Man may come. **24** A disciple is not above the teacher, nor a servant above his lord; **25** sufficient to the disciple that he may be as his teacher, and the servant as his lord; if the master of the house they called Beelzebul, how much more those of his household? **26** You may not, therefore, fear them, for there is nothing covered that will not be revealed, and hid that will not be known; **27** that which I tell you in the darkness, speak in the light, and that which you hear at the ear, proclaim on the housetops. **28** And do not be afraid of those killing the body, and are not able to kill the soul, but rather fear Him who is able to destroy both soul and body in Gehenna. **29** Are not two sparrows sold for an assarion? and one of them will not fall on the ground without your Father; **30** and of you—even the hairs of the head are all numbered; **31** therefore, do not be afraid, you are better than many sparrows. **32** Everyone, therefore, who will confess in Me before men, I also will confess in him before My Father who is in the heavens; **33** and whoever will deny Me before men, I also will deny him before My Father who is in the heavens. **34** You may not suppose that I came to put peace on the earth; I did not come to put peace, but a sword; **35** for I came to set a man at variance against his father, and a daughter against her mother, and a daughter-in-law against her mother-in-law, **36** and the enemies of a man are those of his household. **37** He who is cherishing father or mother above Me, is not worthy of Me, and he who is cherishing son or daughter above Me, is not worthy of Me, **38** and whoever does not receive his cross and follow after Me, is not worthy of Me. **39** He who found his life will lose it, and he who lost his life for

My sake will find it. **40** He who is receiving you receives Me, and he who is receiving Me receives Him who sent Me; **41** he who is receiving a prophet in the name of a prophet, will receive a prophet's reward, and he who is receiving a righteous man in the name of a righteous man, will receive a righteous man's reward, **42** and whoever may give to drink to one of these little ones a cup of cold water only in the name of a disciple, truly I say to you, he may not lose his reward."

CHAPTER 11

1 And it came to pass, when Jesus finished directing His twelve disciples, He departed from there to teach and to preach in their cities. **2** And John having heard in the prison the works of the Christ, having sent two of his disciples, **3** said to Him, "Are You He who is coming, or do we look for another?" **4** And Jesus answering said to them, "Having gone, declare to John the things that you hear and see, **5** blind receive sight, and lame walk, lepers are cleansed, and deaf hear, dead are raised, and poor have good news proclaimed, **6** and blessed is he who may not be stumbled in Me." **7** And as they are going, Jesus began to say to the multitudes concerning John, "What did you go out to the wilderness to view? A reed shaken by the wind? **8** But what did you go out to see? A man clothed in soft garments? behold, those wearing the soft things are in the kings' houses. **9** But what did you go out to see? A prophet? yes, I say to you, and more than a prophet, **10** for this is he of whom it has been written: Behold, I send My messenger before Your face, who will prepare Your way before You. **11** Truly I say to you, there has not risen, among those born of women, [one] greater than John the Immerser, but he who is least in the kingdom of the heavens is greater than he. **12** And from the days of John the Immerser until now, the kingdom of the heavens suffers violence, and violent men seize it by force, **13** for all the Prophets and the Law prophesied until John, **14** and if you are willing to receive [it], he is Elijah who was about to come; **15** he who is having ears to hear—let him hear. **16** And to what will I liken this generation? it is like little children in marketplaces, sitting and calling to others, **17** and saying, We piped to you, and you did not dance, we lamented to you, and you did not strike the breast. **18** For John came neither eating nor drinking, and they say, He has a demon; **19** the Son of Man came eating and drinking, and they say, Behold, a man, a glutton, and a wine-drinker, a friend of tax collectors and sinners; and wisdom was justified of her children." **20** Then He began to reproach the cities in which were done most of His mighty works, because they did not convert. **21** "Woe to you, Chorazin! Woe to you, Bethsaida! Because, if in Tyre and Sidon had been done the mighty works that were done in you, long ago in sackcloth and ashes they had converted; **22** but I say to you, to Tyre and Sidon it will be more tolerable in [the] day of judgment than for you. **23** And you, Capernaum, which were exalted to Heaven, will be brought down to Hades, because if the mighty works that were done in you had been done in Sodom, it had remained to this day; **24** but I say to you, to the land of Sodom it will be more tolerable in [the] day of judgment than to you." **25** At that time Jesus answering said, "I confess to You, Father, Lord of the heavens and of the earth, that You hid these things from wise and understanding ones, and revealed them to babies. **26** Yes, Father, because so it was good pleasure before You. **27** All things were delivered to Me by My Father, and none know the Son, except the Father, nor does any know the Father, except the Son, and he to whom the Son may resolve to reveal [Him]. **28** Come to Me, all you laboring and burdened ones, and I will give you rest; **29** take up My yoke on you, and learn from Me, because I am meek and humble in heart, and you will find rest to your souls, **30** for My yoke [is] easy, and My burden is light."

CHAPTER 12

1 At that time Jesus went on the Sabbaths through the grainfields, and His disciples were hungry, and they began to pluck ears, and to eat, **2** and the Pharisees having seen, said to Him, "Behold, Your disciples do that which it is not lawful to do on a Sabbath." **3** And He said to them, "Did you not read what David did when he was hungry, himself and those with him— **4** how he went into the house of God, and ate the Bread of the Presentation, which it is not lawful to him to eat, nor to those

with him, except to the priests alone? **5** Or did you not read in the Law that on the Sabbaths the priests in the temple profane the Sabbath and are blameless? **6** and I say to you that [One] greater than the temple is here; **7** and if you had known what [this] is: Kindness I will, and not sacrifice—you had not condemned the blameless, **8** for the Son of Man is Lord even of the Sabbath." **9** And having departed from there, He went to their synagogue, **10** and behold, there was a man having the hand withered, and they questioned Him, saying, "Is it lawful to heal on the Sabbaths?" That they might accuse Him. **11** And He said to them, "What man will be of you who will have one sheep, and if this may fall on the Sabbaths into a ditch, will not lay hold on it and raise [it]? **12** How much better, therefore, is a man than a sheep? So that it is lawful on the Sabbaths to do good." **13** Then He says to the man, "Stretch forth your hand," and he stretched [it] forth, and it was restored whole as the other. **14** And the Pharisees having gone forth, held a consultation against Him, how they might destroy Him, **15** and Jesus having known, withdrew from there, and there followed Him great multitudes, and He healed them all, **16** and charged them that they might not make Him apparent, **17** that it might be fulfilled that was spoken through Isaiah the prophet, saying, **18** "Behold, My Servant, whom I chose, || My Beloved, in whom My soul delighted, || I will put My Spirit on Him, || And He will declare judgment to the nations; **19** He will not strive nor cry, || Nor will any hear His voice in the broad places; **20** A bruised reed He will not break, || And smoking flax He will not quench, || Until He may put forth judgment to victory, **21** And in His Name will nations hope." **22** Then was brought to Him a demoniac, blind and mute, and He healed him, so that the blind and mute both spoke and saw. **23** And all the multitudes were amazed and said, "Is this the Son of David?" **24** but the Pharisees having heard, said, "This One does not cast out demons, except by Beelzebul, ruler of the demons." **25** And Jesus, knowing their thoughts, said to them, "Every kingdom having been divided against itself is desolated, and no city or house having been divided against itself stands, **26** and if Satan casts out Satan, against himself he was divided, how then does his kingdom stand? **27** And if I, by Beelzebul, cast out the demons, your sons—by whom do they cast out? because of this they will be your judges. **28** But if I, by the Spirit of God, cast out the demons, then the Kingdom of God has already come to you. **29** Or how is one able to go into the house of the strong man, and to snatch his goods, if first he may not bind the strong man? and then his house he will plunder. **30** He who is not with Me is against Me, and he who is not gathering with Me, scatters. **31** Because of this I say to you, all sin and slander will be forgiven to men, but the slander of the Spirit will not be forgiven to men. **32** And whoever may speak a word against the Son of Man it will be forgiven to him, but whoever may speak against the Holy Spirit, it will not be forgiven him, neither in this age, nor in that which is coming. **33** Either make the tree good, and its fruit good, or make the tree bad, and its fruit bad, for from the fruit is the tree known. **34** Brood of vipers! How are you able to speak good things—being evil? for out of the abundance of the heart the mouth speaks. **35** The good man out of the good treasure of the heart puts forth the good things, and the evil man out of the evil treasure puts forth evil things. **36** And I say to you that every idle word that men may speak, they will give for it a reckoning in [the] day of judgment; **37** for from your words you will be declared righteous, and from your words you will be declared unrighteous." **38** Then certain of the scribes and Pharisees answered, saying, "Teacher, we will to see a sign from You." **39** And He answering said to them, "A generation, evil and adulterous, seeks a sign, and a sign will not be given to it, except the sign of Jonah the prophet; **40** for as Jonah was in the belly of the fish three days and three nights, so will the Son of Man be in the heart of the earth three days and three nights. **41** Men of Nineveh will stand up in the judgment with this generation, and will condemn it, for they converted at the proclamation of Jonah, and behold, [One] greater than Jonah [is] here! **42** A queen of the south will rise up in the judgment with this generation, and will condemn it, for she came from the ends of the earth to hear the wisdom of Solomon, and behold, [One] greater than Solomon [is] here! **43** And when the unclean spirit may go forth from the man, it walks through dry places seeking rest and does not find; **44** then it says, I will return to my house from where I came forth; and having come, it finds [it] unoccupied, swept, and adorned: **45** then it goes, and takes with itself seven other spirits more evil than itself, and having gone in they dwell there, and the last of that man becomes worse than the first; so will it also be to this evil generation." **46** And while He was yet speaking to the multitudes, behold, His mother and brothers had stood outside, seeking to speak to Him, **47** and one said to Him, "Behold, Your mother and Your brothers stand outside, seeking to speak to You." **48** And He answering said to him who spoke to Him, "Who is My mother? and who are My brothers?" **49** And having stretched forth His hand toward His disciples, He said, "Behold, My mother and My brothers! **50** for whoever may do the will of My Father who is in the heavens, He is My brother, and sister, and mother."

CHAPTER 13

1 And in that day Jesus, having gone forth from the house, was sitting by the sea, **2** and gathered together to Him were many multitudes, so that He having gone into the boat sat down, and all the multitude on the beach stood, **3** and He spoke to them many things in allegories, saying, "Behold, the sower went forth to sow, **4** and in his sowing, some indeed fell by the way, and the birds having come, devoured them, **5** and others fell on the rocky places where they did not have much earth, and immediately they sprang forth, through having no depth of earth, **6** and the sun having risen they were scorched, and through having no root, they withered, **7** and others fell on the thorns, and the thorns came up and choked them, **8** and others fell on the good ground, and were giving fruit, some indeed a hundredfold, and some sixty, and some thirty. **9** He who is having ears to hear—let him hear." **10** And the disciples having come near, said to Him, "Why do You speak to them in allegories?" **11** And He answering said to them that, "To you it has been given to know the secrets of the kingdom of the heavens, and to these it has not been given, **12** for whoever has, it will be given to him, and he will have overabundance, and whoever has not, even that which he has will be taken from him. **13** Because of this, in allegories I speak to them, because seeing they do not see, and hearing they do not hear, nor understand, **14** and fulfilled on them is the prophecy of Isaiah that says, With hearing you will hear, and you will not understand, and seeing you will see, and you will not perceive, **15** for the heart of this people was made obtuse, and with the ears they barely heard, and they closed their eyes, lest they might see with the eyes, and might hear with the ears, and understand with the heart, and turn back, and I might heal them. **16** And blessed are your eyes because they see, and your ears because they hear, **17** for truly I say to you that many prophets and righteous men desired to see that which you look on, and they did not see, and to hear that which you hear, and they did not hear. **18** You, therefore, hear the allegory of the sower: **19** Everyone hearing the word of the kingdom, and not understanding—the evil one comes, and snatches that which has been sown in his heart; this is that sown by the way. **20** And that sown on the rocky places, this is he who is hearing the word, and immediately with joy is receiving it, **21** and he has no root in himself, but is temporary, and persecution or tribulation having happened because of the word, immediately he is stumbled. **22** And that sown toward the thorns, this is he who is hearing the word, and the anxiety of this age, and the deceitfulness of the riches, chokes the word, and it becomes unfruitful. **23** And that sown on the good ground: this is he who is hearing the word, and is understanding, who indeed bears fruit, and makes, some indeed a hundredfold, and some sixty, and some thirty." **24** Another allegory He set before them, saying, "The kingdom of the heavens was likened to a man sowing good seed in his field, **25** and while men are sleeping, his enemy came and sowed darnel in the midst of the wheat, and went away, **26** and when the herb sprang up, and yielded fruit, then appeared also the darnel. **27** And the servants of the householder, having come near, said to him, Lord, did you not sow good seed in your field? from where then does it have the darnel? **28** And he says to them, A man, an enemy, did this; and the servants said to him, Will you, then, [that] having gone away we may gather it up? **29** And he said, No, lest—gathering up the darnel—you root up with it the wheat; **30** permit both to grow together until the harvest, and in the time of the harvest I will say to the reapers, Gather up first the darnel, and bind it in bundles, to burn it, and the wheat gather up into my storehouse." **31** Another allegory He set before them, saying, "The kingdom of the heavens is like to a grain of mustard, which a man having taken, sowed in his field, **32** which less, indeed, is than all the seeds, but when it may be grown, is greatest of the herbs, and becomes a tree, so that the birds of the sky come and rest in its branches." **33** Another allegory He spoke to them: "The kingdom of the heavens is like to leaven, which a woman having taken, hid in three measures of meal, until the whole was leavened." **34** All these things Jesus spoke in allegories to the multitudes, and without an allegory He was not speaking to them, **35** that it might be fulfilled that was spoken through the prophet, saying, "I will open in allegories My mouth, || I will utter things having been hidden from the foundation of the world." **36** Then having let away the multitudes, Jesus came into the house, and His disciples came near to Him, saying, "Explain to us the allegory of the darnel of the field." **37** And He answering said to them, "He who is sowing the good seed is the Son of Man, **38** and the field is the world, and the good seed, these are the sons of the kingdom, and the darnel are the sons of the evil one, **39** and the enemy who sowed them is the Devil, and the harvest is [the] full end of the age, and the reapers are messengers. **40** As, then, the darnel is gathered up, and is burned with fire, so will it be in the full end of this age; **41** the Son of Man will send forth His messengers, and they will gather up out of His kingdom all the stumbling-blocks, and those doing the lawlessness, **42** and will cast them into the furnace of the fire; there will be the weeping and the gnashing of the teeth. **43** Then will the righteous shine forth as the sun in the kingdom of their Father. He who is having ears to hear—let him hear. **44** Again, the kingdom of the heavens is like to treasure hid in the field, which a man having found, hid, and from his joy goes, and all, as much as he has, he sells, and buys that field. **45** Again, the kingdom of the heavens is like to a man, a merchant, seeking good pearls, **46** who having found one pearl of great price, having gone away, has sold all, as much as he had, and bought it. **47** Again, the kingdom of the heavens is like to a net that was cast into the sea, and gathered together of every kind, **48** which, when it was filled, having drawn up again on the beach, and having sat down, they gathered the good into vessels, and the bad they cast out, **49** so will it be in the full end of the age, the messengers will come forth and separate the evil out of the midst of the righteous, **50** and will cast them into the furnace of the fire; there will be the weeping and the gnashing of the teeth." **51** Jesus says to them, "Did you understand all these?" They say to Him, "Yes, Lord." **52** And He said to them, "Because of this, every scribe having been discipled in regard to the kingdom of the heavens is like to a man, a householder, who brings forth out of his treasure things new and old." **53** And it came to pass, when Jesus finished these allegories, He removed from there, **54** and having come to His own country, He was teaching them in their synagogue, so that they were astonished, and were saying, "From where to this One this wisdom and the mighty works? **55** is this not the carpenter's Son? Is His mother not called Mary, and His brothers James, and Joses, and Simon, and Judas? **56** and His sisters—are they not all with us? from where, then, to this One all these?" **57** and they were stumbled at Him. And Jesus said to them, "A prophet is not without honor except in his own country, and in his own house": **58** and He did not do many mighty works there, because of their unbelief.

CHAPTER 14

1 At that time Herod the tetrarch heard the fame of Jesus, **2** and said to his servants, "This is John the Immerser, he rose from the dead, and because of this the mighty energies are working in him." **3** For Herod having laid hold on John, bound him, and put him in prison, because of Herodias, his brother Philip's wife, **4** for John was saying to him, "It is not lawful to you to have her," **5** and willing to kill him, he feared the multitude, because as a prophet they were holding him. **6** But the birthday of Herod being kept, the daughter of Herodias danced in the midst, and pleased Herod, **7** after which with an oath he professed to give her whatever she might ask. **8** And she, having been instigated by her mother, says, "Give me here on a plate the head of John the Immerser"; **9** and the king was grieved, but because of the oaths and of those dining with him, he commanded [it] to be given; **10** and having sent, he beheaded John in the prison, **11** and his head was brought on a plate, and was given to the girl, and she brought [it] near to her mother. **12** And his disciples having come, took up the body, and buried it, and having come, they told Jesus, **13** and Jesus having heard, withdrew from there in a boat to a desolate place by Himself, and the multitudes having heard followed Him on land from the cities. **14** And Jesus having come forth, saw a great multitude, and was moved with compassion on them, and healed their sick; **15** and evening having come, His disciples came to Him, saying, "The place is desolate, and the hour has now past, let away the multitudes that, having gone into the villages, they may buy food for themselves." **16** And Jesus said to them, "They have no need to go away—you give them to eat." **17** And they say to Him, "We have nothing here except five loaves and two fishes." **18** And He said, "Bring them to Me here." **19** And having commanded the multitudes to recline on the grass, and having taken the five loaves and the two fishes, having looked up to the sky, He blessed, and having broken, He gave the loaves to the disciples, and the disciples [gave] to the multitudes, **20** and they all ate, and were filled, and they took up what was over of the broken pieces twelve hand-baskets full; **21** and those eating were about five thousand men, apart from women and children. **22** And immediately Jesus constrained His disciples to go into the boat, and to go before Him to the other side, until He might let away the multitudes; **23** and having let away the multitudes, He went up to the mountain by Himself to pray, and evening having come, He was there alone, **24** and the boat was now in the midst of the sea, distressed by the waves, for the wind was contrary. **25** And in the fourth watch of the night Jesus went away to them, walking on the sea, **26** and the disciples having seen Him walking on the sea, were troubled, saying, "It is an apparition," and from the fear they cried out; **27** and immediately Jesus spoke to them, saying, "Take courage! I am; do not be afraid." **28** And Peter answering Him said, "Lord, if it is You, command me to come to You on the waters"; **29** and He said, "Come"; and having gone down from the boat, Peter walked on the waters to come to Jesus, **30** but seeing the vehement wind, he was afraid, and having begun to sink, he cried out, saying, "Lord, save me!" **31** And immediately Jesus, having stretched forth the hand, laid hold of him and says to him, "Little faith! For why did you waver?" **32** and they having gone into the boat, the wind stilled, **33** and those in the boat having come, worshiped Him, saying, "You are truly God's Son." **34** And having passed over, they came into the land of Gennesaret, **35** and having recognized Him, the men of that place sent forth to all that surrounding region, and they brought to Him all who were ill, **36** and were calling on Him that they might only touch the fringe of His garment, and as many as touched were saved.

CHAPTER 15

1 Then they come to Jesus from Jerusalem—scribes and Pharisees—saying, **2** "Why do Your disciples transgress the tradition of the elders? for they do not wash their hands when they may eat bread." **3** And He answering said to them, "Why also do you transgress the command of God because of your tradition? **4** for God commanded, saying, Honor your father and mother; and, He who is speaking evil of father or mother—let him die the death; **5** but you say, Whoever may say to father or mother, An offering [is] whatever you may be profited by me— **6** and he may not honor his father or his mother, and you set aside the command of God because of your tradition. **7** Hypocrites, Isaiah prophesied well of you, saying, **8** This people draws near to Me with their mouth, and with the lips it honors Me, but their heart is far off from Me; **9** and in vain they worship Me, teaching teachings—commands of men." **10** And having called near the multitude, He said to them, "Hear and understand: **11** [it is] not that which is coming into the mouth [that] defiles the man, but that which is coming forth from the mouth, this defiles the man." **12** Then His disciples having come near, said to Him, "Have You known that the Pharisees, having heard the word, were stumbled?" **13** And He answering said, "Every plant that My heavenly Father did not plant will be rooted up; **14** leave them alone, they are guides—blind of blind; and if blind may guide blind, both will fall into a ditch." **15** And Peter answering said to Him, "Explain to us this allegory." **16** And Jesus said, "Are you also yet without understanding? **17** do you not understand that all that is going into the mouth passes into the belly, and is cast forth into the drain? **18** but the things coming forth from the mouth come forth from the heart, and these defile the man; **19** for out of the heart come forth evil thoughts, murders, adulteries, whoredoms, thefts, false witnessings, slanders: **20** these are the things defiling the man; but to eat with unwashed hands does not defile the man." **21** And Jesus having come forth from there, withdrew to the parts of Tyre and Sidon, **22** and behold, a woman, a Canaanite, having come forth from those borders, called to Him, saying,

"Deal kindly with me, Lord, Son of David; my daughter is miserably demonized." **23** And He did not answer her a word; and His disciples having come to Him, were asking Him, saying, "Let her away, because she cries after us"; **24** and He answering said, "I was not sent except to the lost sheep of the house of Israel." **25** And having come, she was worshiping Him, saying, "Lord, help me"; **26** and He answering said, "It is not good to take the children's bread, and to cast to the little dogs." **27** And she said, "Yes, Lord, for even the little dogs eat of the crumbs that are falling from their lords' table"; **28** then answering, Jesus said to her, "O woman, great [is] your faith, let it be to you as you will"; and her daughter was healed from that hour. **29** And having departed from there, Jesus came near to the Sea of Galilee, and having gone up to the mountain, He was sitting there, **30** and there came to Him great multitudes, having with them lame, blind, mute, maimed, and many others, and they cast them at the feet of Jesus, and He healed them, **31** so that the multitudes wondered, seeing mute ones speaking, maimed whole, lame walking, and blind seeing; and they glorified the God of Israel. **32** And Jesus having called near His disciples, said, "I have compassion on the multitude, because now three days they continue with Me, and they do not have what they may eat; and to let them away fasting I will not, lest they faint in the way." **33** And His disciples say to Him, "From where to us in a wilderness [will we get] so many loaves, as to fill so great a multitude?" **34** And Jesus says to them, "How many loaves do you have?" And they said, "Seven, and a few little fishes." **35** And He commanded the multitudes to sit down on the ground, **36** and having taken the seven loaves and the fishes, having given thanks, He broke, and gave to His disciples, and the disciples [gave] to the multitude. **37** And they all ate, and were filled, and they took up what was over of the broken pieces seven baskets full, **38** and those eating were four thousand men, apart from women and children. **39** And having let away the multitudes, He went into the boat, and came to the borders of Magdala.

CHAPTER 16

1 And the Pharisees and Sadducees having come, tempting, questioned Him, to show to them a sign from Heaven, **2** and He answering said to them, "Evening having come, you say, Fair weather, for the sky is red, **3** and at morning, Foul weather today, for the sky is red—gloomy; hypocrites, you indeed know to discern the face of the sky, but the signs of the times you are not able! **4** An evil and adulterous generation seeks a sign, and a sign will not be given to it, except the sign of Jonah the prophet"; and having left them He went away. **5** And His disciples having come to the other side, forgot to take loaves, **6** and Jesus said to them, "Beware, and take heed of the leaven of the Pharisees and Sadducees"; **7** and they were reasoning in themselves, saying, "Because we took no loaves." **8** And Jesus having known, said to them, "Why reason you in yourselves, you of little faith, because you took no loaves? **9** do you not yet understand, nor remember the five loaves of the five thousand, and how many hand-baskets you took up? **10** nor the seven loaves of the four thousand, and how many baskets you took up? **11** how do you not understand that I did not speak to you of bread—to take heed of the leaven of the Pharisees and Sadducees?" **12** Then they understood that He did not say to take heed of the leaven of the bread, but of the teaching of the Pharisees and Sadducees. **13** And Jesus, having come to the parts of Caesarea Philippi, was asking His disciples, saying, "Who do men say I am—the Son of Man?" **14** and they said, "Some, John the Immerser, and others, Elijah, and others, Jeremiah, or one of the prophets." **15** He says to them, "And you—who do you say I am?" **16** and Simon Peter answering said, "You are the Christ, the Son of the living God." **17** And Jesus answering said to him, "Blessed are you, Simon Bar-Jona, because flesh and blood did not reveal [it] to you, but My Father who is in the heavens. **18** And I also say to you that you are Peter, and on this rock I will build My Assembly, and [the] gates of Hades will not prevail against it; **19** and I will give to you the keys of the kingdom of the heavens, and whatever you may bind on the earth will be having been bound in the heavens, and whatever you may loose on the earth will be having been loosed in the heavens." **20** Then He charged His disciples that they may say to no one that He is Jesus the Christ. **21** From that time Jesus began to show to His disciples that it is necessary for Him to go away to Jerusalem, and to suffer many things from the elders, and chief priests, and scribes, and to be put to death, and the third day to rise. **22** And having taken Him aside, Peter began to rebuke Him, saying, "Be kind to Yourself, Lord; this will not be to You"; **23** and He having turned, said to Peter, "Get behind Me, Satan! You are a stumbling-block to Me, for you do not mind the things of God, but the things of men." **24** Then Jesus said to His disciples, "If anyone wills to come after Me, let him disown himself, and take up his cross, and follow Me, **25** for whoever may will to save his life will lose it, and whoever may lose his life for My sake will find it; **26** for what is a man profited if he may gain the whole world, but of his life suffer loss? or what will a man give as an exchange for his life? **27** For the Son of Man is about to come in the glory of His Father, with His messengers, and then He will reward each according to his work. **28** Truly I say to you, there are certain of those standing here who will not taste of death until they may see the Son of Man coming in His kingdom."

CHAPTER 17

1 And after six days Jesus takes Peter, and James, and his brother John, and brings them up to a high mountain by themselves, **2** and He was transfigured before them, and His face shone as the sun, and His garments became white as the light, **3** and behold, Moses and Elijah appeared to them, talking together with Him. **4** And Peter answering said to Jesus, "Lord, it is good to us to be here; if You will, we may make three shelters here: one for You, and one for Moses, and one for Elijah." **5** While he is yet speaking, behold, a bright cloud overshadowed them, and behold, a voice out of the cloud, saying, "This is My Son, the Beloved, in whom I delighted; hear Him." **6** And the disciples having heard, fell on their face, and were exceedingly afraid, **7** and Jesus having come near, touched them, and said, "Rise, do not be afraid," **8** and having lifted up their eyes, they saw no one, except Jesus only. **9** And as they are coming down from the mountain, Jesus charged them, saying, "Say to no one the vision, until the Son of Man may rise out of the dead." **10** And His disciples questioned Him, saying, "Why then do the scribes say that Elijah must come first?" **11** And Jesus answering said to them, "Elijah does indeed come first, and will restore all things, **12** and I say to you, Elijah already came, and they did not know him, but did with him whatever they would, so also the Son of Man is about to suffer by them." **13** Then the disciples understood that He spoke to them concerning John the Immerser. **14** And when they came to the multitude, there came to Him a man, kneeling down to Him, **15** and saying, "Lord, deal kindly with my son, for he is [a] lunatic, and suffers miserably, for he often falls into the fire, and often into the water, **16** and I brought him near to Your disciples, and they were not able to heal him." **17** And Jesus answering said, "O generation, unsteadfast and perverse, until when will I be with you? until when will I bear you? bring him to Me here"; **18** and Jesus rebuked him, and the demon went out of him, and the boy was healed from that hour. **19** Then the disciples having come to Jesus by Himself, said, "Why were we not able to cast him out?" **20** And Jesus said to them, "Through your want of faith; for truly I say to you, if you may have faith as a grain of mustard, you will say to this mountain, Move from here to there, and it will move, and nothing will be impossible to you, **21** [[and this kind does not go forth except in prayer and fasting."]] **22** And while they are living in Galilee, Jesus said to them, "The Son of Man is about to be delivered up into the hands of men, **23** and they will kill Him, and the third day He will rise," and they were exceedingly sorry. **24** And they having come to Capernaum, those receiving the didrachms came near to Peter and said, "Your teacher—does He not pay the didrachmas?" He says, "Yes." **25** And when he came into the house, Jesus anticipated him, saying, "What do you think, Simon? the kings of the earth—from whom do they receive custom or poll-tax? from their sons or from the strangers?" **26** Peter says to Him, "From the strangers." Jesus said to him, "Then the sons are free; **27** but that we may not cause them to stumble, having gone to the sea, cast a hook, and the fish that has come up first take up, and having opened its mouth, you will find a stater, that having taken, give to them for Me and you."

1 At that hour the disciples came near to Jesus, saying, "Who, now, is greater in the kingdom of the heavens?" **2** And Jesus having called near a child, set him in the midst of them, **3** and said, "Truly I say to you, if you may not be turned and become as the children, you may not enter into the kingdom of the heavens; **4** whoever then may humble himself as this child, he is the greater in the kingdom of the heavens. **5** And he who may receive one such child in My Name, receives Me, **6** and whoever may cause to stumble one of those little ones who are believing in Me, it is better for him that a weighty millstone may be hanged on his neck, and he may be sunk in the depth of the sea. **7** Woe to the world from the stumbling-blocks! For there is necessity for the stumbling-blocks to come, but woe to that man through whom the stumbling-block comes! **8** And if your hand or your foot causes you to stumble, cut them off and cast [them] from you; it is good for you to enter into life lame or maimed, rather than having two hands or two feet, to be cast into the continuous fire. **9** And if your eye causes you to stumble, pluck it out and cast from you; it is good for you to enter into life one-eyed, rather than having two eyes to be cast into the Gehenna of fire. **10** Beware! You may not despise one of these little ones, for I say to you that their messengers in the heavens always behold the face of My Father who is in the heavens, **11** [[for the Son of Man came to save the lost.]] **12** What do you think? if a man may have one hundred sheep, and there may go astray one of them, does he not—having left the ninety-nine, having gone on the mountains—seek that which is gone astray? **13** and if it may come to pass that he finds it, truly I say to you that he rejoices over it more than over the ninety-nine that have not gone astray; **14** so it is not [the] will in [the] presence of your Father who is in the heavens that one of these little ones may perish. **15** And if your brother may sin against you, go and show him his fault between you and him alone, if he may hear you, you gained your brother; **16** and if he may not hear, take with you yet one or two, that by the mouth of two witnesses or three every word may stand. **17** And if he may not hear them, say [it] to the assembly, and if also the assembly he may not hear, let him be to you as the heathen man and the tax collector. **18** Truly I say to you, whatever things you may bind on the earth will be having been bound in the heavens, and whatever things you may loose on the earth will be having been loosed in the heavens. **19** Again, I say to you that if two of you may agree on the earth concerning anything, whatever they may ask—it will be done to them from My Father who is in the heavens, **20** for where there are two or three gathered together—to My Name, there am I in the midst of them." **21** Then Peter having come near to Him, said, "Lord, how often will my brother sin against me, and I forgive him—until seven times?" **22** Jesus says to him, "I do not say to you until seven times, but until seventy times seven. **23** Because of this was the kingdom of the heavens likened to a man, a king, who willed to take reckoning with his servants, **24** and he having begun to take account, there was brought near to him one debtor of a myriad of talents, **25** and he having nothing to pay, his lord commanded him to be sold, and his wife, and the children, and all, whatever he had, and payment to be made. **26** The servant then, having fallen down, was prostrating to him, saying, Lord, have patience with me, and I will pay you all; **27** and the lord of that servant having been moved with compassion released him, and the debt he forgave him. **28** And that servant having come forth, found one of his fellow-servants who was owing him one hundred denarii, and having laid hold, he took him by the throat, saying, Pay me that which you owe. **29** His fellow-servant then, having fallen down at his feet, was calling on him, saying, Have patience with me, and I will pay you all; **30** and he would not, but having gone away, he cast him into prison, until he might pay that which was owing. **31** And his fellow-servants having seen the things that were done, were grieved exceedingly, and having come, showed fully to their lord all the things that were done; **32** then having called him, his lord says to him, Evil servant! All that debt I forgave you, seeing you called on me; **33** did it not seem necessary to you to have dealt kindly with your fellow servant, as I also dealt kindly with you? **34** And having been angry, his lord delivered him to the inquisitors, until he might pay all that was owing to him; **35** so also My heavenly Father will do to you, if you may not forgive each one his brother from your hearts thr trespasses."

CHAPTER 18

CHAPTER 19

¹ And it came to pass, when Jesus finished these words, He removed from Galilee, and came to the borders of Judea, beyond the Jordan, ² and great multitudes followed Him, and He healed them there. ³ And the Pharisees came near to Him, tempting Him, and saying to Him, "Is it lawful for a man to put away his wife for every cause?" ⁴ And He answering said to them, "Did you not read that He who made [them] from the beginning, made them a male and a female, ⁵ and said, For this cause will a man leave father and mother, and cleave to his wife, and they will be—the two—for one flesh? ⁶ so that they are no longer two, but one flesh; what therefore God joined together, let no man separate." ⁷ They say to Him, "Why then did Moses command to give a roll of divorce, and to put her away?" ⁸ He says to them, "Moses for your stiffness of heart permitted you to put away your wives, but from the beginning it has not been so. ⁹ And I say to you that whoever may put away his wife, if not for whoredom, and may marry another, commits adultery; and he who married her that has been put away, commits adultery." ¹⁰ His disciples say to Him, "If the case of the man with the woman is so, it is not good to marry." ¹¹ And He said to them, "All do not receive this word, but those to whom it has been given; ¹² for there are eunuchs who from the mother's womb were so born; and there are eunuchs who were made eunuchs by men; and there are eunuchs who kept themselves eunuchs because of the kingdom of the heavens: he who is able to receive [it]—let him receive." ¹³ Then were brought near to Him children that He might put hands on them and pray, and the disciples rebuked them. ¹⁴ But Jesus said, "Permit the children, and do not forbid them to come to Me, for of such is the kingdom of the heavens"; ¹⁵ and having laid [His] hands on them, He departed from there. ¹⁶ And behold, one having come near, said to Him, "Good Teacher, what good thing will I do that I may have continuous life?" ¹⁷ And He said to him, "Why do you call Me good? no one [is] good except one—God; but if you will to enter into life, keep the commands." ¹⁸ He says to Him, "What kind?" And Jesus said, "You will not murder, You will not commit adultery, You will not steal, You will not bear false witness, ¹⁹ Honor your father and mother, and, You will love your neighbor as yourself." ²⁰ The young man says to Him, "All these I kept from my youth; what yet do I lack?" ²¹ Jesus said to him, "If you will to be perfect, go away, sell what you have, and give to the poor, and you will have treasure in Heaven, and come, follow Me." ²² And the young man, having heard the word, went away sorrowful, for he had many possessions; ²³ and Jesus said to His disciples, "Truly I say to you that hardly will a rich man enter into the kingdom of the heavens; ²⁴ and again I say to you, it is easier for a camel to go through the eye of a needle, than for a rich man to enter into the Kingdom of God." ²⁵ And His disciples having heard, were exceedingly amazed, saying, "Who, then, is able to be saved?" ²⁶ And Jesus having earnestly beheld, said to them, "With men this is impossible, but with God all things are possible." ²⁷ Then Peter answering said to Him, "Behold, we left all, and followed You, what then will we have?" ²⁸ And Jesus said to them, "Truly I say to you that you who followed Me, in the regeneration, when the Son of Man may sit on a throne of His glory, will sit—you also—on twelve thrones, judging the twelve tribes of Israel; ²⁹ and everyone who left houses, or brothers, or sisters, or father, or mother, or wife, or children, or fields, for My Name's sake, will receive a hundredfold, and will inherit continuous life; ³⁰ and many first will be last, and last first."

CHAPTER 20

¹ "For the kingdom of the heavens is like to a man, a householder, who went forth with the morning to hire workmen for his vineyard, ² and having agreed with the workmen for a denarius a day, he sent them into his vineyard. ³ And having gone forth about the third hour, he saw others standing in the marketplace idle, ⁴ and to these he said, Go—also you—to the vineyard, and whatever may be righteous I will give you; ⁵ and they went away. Again, having gone forth about the sixth and the ninth hour, he did in like manner. ⁶ And about the eleventh hour, having gone forth, he found others standing idle and says to them, Why have you stood here idle all day? ⁷ they say to him, Because no one hired us; he says to them, Go—you also—to the vineyard, and whatever may be righteous you will receive. ⁸ And evening having come, the lord of the vineyard says to his steward, Call the workmen, and pay them the reward, having begun from the last—to the first. ⁹ And they of

about the eleventh hour having come, each received a denarius. ¹⁰ And the first having come, supposed that they will receive more, and they received, they also, each a denarius, ¹¹ and having received [it], they were murmuring against the householder, saying, ¹² that, These, the last, worked one hour, and you made them equal to us, who were bearing the burden of the day—and the heat. ¹³ And he answering said to one of them, Friend, I do no unrighteousness to you; did you not agree with me for a denarius? ¹⁴ take that which is yours, and go; and I will to give to this, the last, also as to you; ¹⁵ is it not lawful to me to do what I will in my own? is your eye evil because I am good? ¹⁶ So the last will be first, and the first last, for many are called, and few chosen." ¹⁷ And Jesus going up to Jerusalem, took the twelve disciples by themselves in the way and said to them, ¹⁸ "Behold, we go up to Jerusalem, and the Son of Man will be delivered to the chief priests and scribes, ¹⁹ and they will condemn Him to death, and will deliver Him to the nations to mock, and to scourge, and to crucify, and the third day He will rise again." ²⁰ Then came near to Him the mother of the sons of Zebedee, with her sons, prostrating and asking something from Him, ²¹ and He said to her, "What do you will?" She says to Him, "Say that they may sit—these two sons of mine—one on Your right hand and one on the left, in Your kingdom." ²² And Jesus answering said, "You have not known what you ask for yourselves; are you able to drink of the cup that I am about to drink? and with the immersion that I am immersed with, to be immersed?" They say to Him, "We are able." ²³ And He says to them, "Of My cup indeed you will drink, and with the immersion that I am immersed with you will be immersed; but to sit on My right hand and on My left is not Mine to give, but—to those for whom it has been prepared by My Father." ²⁴ And the ten having heard, were much displeased with the two brothers, ²⁵ and Jesus having called them near, said, "You have known that the rulers of the nation's exercise lordship over them, and those [who are] great exercise authority over them, ²⁶ but not so will it be among you, but whoever may will among you to become great, let him be your servant; ²⁷ and whoever may will among you to be first, let him be your servant; ²⁸ even as the Son of Man did not come to be ministered to, but to minister, and to give His life [as] a ransom for many." ²⁹ And they going forth from Jericho, there followed Him a great multitude, ³⁰ and behold, two blind men sitting by the way, having heard that Jesus passes by, cried, saying, "Deal kindly with us, Lord—Son of David." ³¹ And the multitude charged them that they might be silent, and they cried out the more, saying, "Deal kindly with us Lord—Son of David." ³² And having stood, Jesus called them and said, "What do you will [that] I may do to you?" ³³ they say to Him, "Lord, that our eyes may be opened"; ³⁴ and having been moved with compassion, Jesus touched their eyes, and immediately their eyes received sight, and they followed Him.

CHAPTER 21

¹ And when they came near to Jerusalem, and came to Bethphage, to the Mount of Olives, then Jesus sent two disciples, ² saying to them, "Go on into the village in front of you, and immediately you will find a donkey bound, and a colt with her—having loosed, you bring to Me; ³ and if anyone may say anything to you, you will say that the Lord has need of them, and immediately He will send them." ⁴ And all this came to pass, that it might be fulfilled that was spoken through the prophet, saying, ⁵ "Tell the daughter of Zion, Behold, your King comes to you, meek, and mounted on a donkey, and a colt, a foal of a beast of burden." ⁶ And the disciples having gone and having done as Jesus commanded them, ⁷ brought the donkey and the colt, and put on them their garments, and set [Him] on them; ⁸ and the very great multitude spread their own garments in the way, and others were cutting branches from the trees, and were strewing in the way, ⁹ and the multitudes who were going before, and who were following, were crying, saying, "Hosanna to the Son of David, blessed is He who is coming in the Name of the Lord; Hosanna in the highest!" ¹⁰ And He having entered into Jerusalem, all the city was moved, saying, "Who is this?" ¹¹ And the multitudes said, "This is Jesus the prophet, who [is] from Nazareth of Galilee." ¹² And Jesus entered into the temple of God, and cast forth all those selling and buying in the temple, and the tables of the money-changers He overturned, and the seats of those selling the doves, ¹³ and He says to them, "It has been written: My house will be called a house of prayer; but you made it a den of

robbers." **14** And there came to Him blind and lame men in the temple, and He healed them, **15** and the chief priests and the scribes having seen the wonderful things that He did, and the children crying in the temple, and saying, "Hosanna to the Son of David," were much displeased; **16** and they said to Him, "Do You hear what these say?" And Jesus says to them, "Yes, did you never read, that, Out of the mouth of babies and sucklings You prepared praise?" **17** And having left them, He went forth out of the city to Bethany, and lodged there, **18** and in the morning turning back to the city, He hungered, **19** and having seen a certain fig tree on the way, He came to it, and found nothing in it except leaves only, and He says to it, "No more fruit may be from you—throughout the age"; and instantly the fig tree withered. **20** And the disciples having seen, wondered, saying, "How did the fig tree instantly wither?" **21** And Jesus answering said to them, "Truly I say to you, if you may have faith, and may not doubt, not only this of the fig tree will you do, but even if to this mountain you may say, Be lifted up and be cast into the sea, it will come to pass; **22** and all—as much as you may ask in the prayer, believing, you will receive." **23** And He having come into the temple, there came to Him when teaching the chief priests and the elders of the people, saying, "By what authority do You do these things? and who gave You this authority?" **24** And Jesus answering said to them, "I will ask you—I also—one word, which if you may tell Me, I also will tell you by what authority I do these things; **25** the immersion of John, from where was it? From Heaven, or from men?" And they were reasoning with themselves, saying, "If we should say, From Heaven, He will say to us, Why, then, did you not believe him? **26** and if we should say, From men, we fear the multitude, for all hold John as a prophet." **27** And answering Jesus they said, "We have not known." He said to them—He also, "Neither do I tell you by what authority I do these things. **28** And what do you think? A man had two children, and having come to the first, he said, Child, go, today be working in my vineyard. **29** And he answering said, I will not, but at last, having regretted, he went. **30** And having come to the second, he said in the same manner, and he answering said, I [go], lord, and did not go; **31** which of the two did the will of the father?" They say to Him, "The first." Jesus says to them, "Truly I say to you that the tax collectors and the prostitutes go before you into the Kingdom of God, **32** for John came to you in the way of righteousness, and you did not believe him, and the tax collectors and the prostitutes believed him, and you, having seen, did not regret at last—to believe him. **33** Hear another allegory: There was a certain man, a householder, who planted a vineyard, and put a hedge around it, and dug in it a winepress, and built a tower, and gave it out to farmers, and went abroad. **34** And when the season of the fruits came near, he sent his servants to the farmers, to receive the fruits of it, **35** and the farmers having taken his servants, one they scourged, and one they killed, and one they stoned. **36** Again he sent other servants more than the first, and they did to them in the same manner. **37** And at last he sent to them his son, saying, They will respect my son; **38** and the farmers having seen the son, said among themselves, This is the heir, come, we may kill him, and may possess his inheritance; **39** and having taken him, they cast [him] out of the vineyard, and killed him; **40** whenever therefore the lord of the vineyard may come, what will he do to these farmers?" **41** They say to Him, "Evil men—he will grievously destroy them, and will give out the vineyard to other farmers who will give back to him the fruits in their seasons." **42** Jesus says to them, "Did you never read in the Writings: A stone that the builders disallowed, it became head of a corner; from the Lord has this come to pass, and it is wonderful in our eyes? **43** Because of this I say to you that the Kingdom of God will be taken from you, and given to a nation bringing forth its fruit; **44** and he who is falling on this stone will be broken, and on whomsoever it may fall it will crush him to pieces." **45** And the chief priests and the Pharisees having heard His allegories, knew that He speaks of them, **46** and seeking to lay hold on Him, they feared the multitudes, seeing they were holding Him as a prophet.

CHAPTER 22

1 And Jesus answering, again spoke to them in allegories, saying, **2** "The kingdom of the heavens was likened to a man, a king, who made wedding feasts for his son, **3** and he sent forth his servants to call those having been called to the wedding feasts, and they were not willing to come. **4** Again he sent forth other servants, saying, Say to those who have been called: Behold, I prepared my early meal, my oxen and the fatlings have been killed, and all things [are] ready, come to the wedding feasts; **5** and they, having disregarded [it], went away, one to his own field, and the other to his merchandise; **6** and the rest, having laid hold on his servants, mistreated and slew [them]. **7** And the king having heard, was angry, and having sent forth his soldiers, he destroyed those murderers, and their city he set on fire; **8** then he says to his servants, The wedding feast indeed is ready, and those called were not worthy, **9** be going, then, on to the cross-ways, and as many as you may find, call to the wedding feasts. **10** And those servants, having gone forth to the ways, gathered all, as many as they found, both bad and good, and the wedding was filled with those reclining. **11** And the king having come in to view those reclining, saw there a man not clothed with wedding clothes, **12** and he says to him, Friend, how did you come in here, not having wedding clothes? and he was speechless. **13** Then the king said to the servants, Having bound his feet and hands, take him up and cast forth into the outer darkness, there will be the weeping and the gnashing of the teeth; **14** for many are called, and few chosen." **15** Then the Pharisees having gone, took counsel how they might ensnare Him in words, **16** and they send to Him their disciples with the Herodians, saying, "Teacher, we have known that You are true, and the way of God in truth You teach, and You are not caring for anyone, for You do not look to the face of men; **17** tell us, therefore, what do You think? is it lawful to give tribute to Caesar or not?" **18** And Jesus having known their wickedness, said, "Why do you tempt Me, hypocrites? **19** show Me the tribute-coin." And they brought to Him a denarius; **20** and He says to them, "Whose [is] this image and the inscription?" **21** they say to Him, "Caesar's"; then He says to them, "Render therefore the things of Caesar to Caesar, and the things of God to God"; **22** and having heard they wondered, and having left Him they went away. **23** In that day there came near to Him Sadducees who are saying there is not a resurrection, and they questioned Him, saying, **24** "Teacher, Moses said if anyone may die having no children, his brother will marry his wife, and will raise up seed to his brother. **25** And there were with us seven brothers, and the first having married died, and having no seed, he left his wife to his brother; **26** in like manner also the second, and the third, to the seventh, **27** and last of all the woman also died; **28** therefore in the resurrection, of which of the seven will she be wife—for all had her?" **29** And Jesus answering said to them, "You go astray, not knowing the Writings, nor the power of God; **30** for in the resurrection they do not marry, nor are they given in marriage, but are as messengers of God in Heaven. **31** And concerning the resurrection of the dead, did you not read that which was spoken to you by God, saying, **32** I am the God of Abraham, and the God of Isaac, and the God of Jacob? God is not a God of dead men, but of living." **33** And having heard, the multitudes were astonished at His teaching; **34** and the Pharisees, having heard that He silenced the Sadducees, were gathered together to Him; **35** and one of them, a lawyer, questioned, tempting Him, and saying, **36** "Teacher, which [is] the great command in the Law?" **37** And Jesus said to him, "You will love the Lord your God with all your heart, and with all your soul, and with all your understanding— **38** this is a first and great command; **39** and the second [is] like to it: You will love your neighbor as yourself; **40** on these—the two commands—all the Law and the Prophets hang." **41** And the Pharisees having been gathered together, Jesus questioned them, **42** saying, "What do you think concerning the Christ? of whom is He Son?" They say to Him, "Of David." **43** He says to them, "How then does David in the Spirit call Him Lord, saying, **44** The Lord said to my Lord, || Sit at My right hand, || Until I may make Your enemies Your footstool? **45** If then David calls Him Lord, how is He his son?" **46** And no one was able to answer Him a word, nor did any dare question Him from that day [on].

CHAPTER 23

1 Then Jesus spoke to the multitudes, and to His disciples, **2** saying, "On the seat of Moses sat down the scribes and the Pharisees; **3** all, then, as much as they may say to you to observe, observe and do, but according to their works do not do, for they say, and do not do; **4** for they bind together burdens [too] heavy and grievous to bear, and lay [them] on the shoulders of men, but with their finger they will not move them. **5** And all their works they do to be seen by men, and they make broad their phylacteries, and enlarge the fringes of their garments, **6** they also cherish the first couches at the banquets, and the first seats in the synagogues, **7** and the salutations in the marketplaces, and to be called by men, Rabbi, Rabbi. **8** And you may not be called Rabbi, for one is your teacher—the Christ, and you are all brothers; **9** and you may not call [any] your father on the earth, for one is your Father, who is in the heavens, **10** nor may you be called teachers, for one is your teacher—the Christ. **11** And the greater of you will be your servant, **12** and whoever will exalt himself will be humbled, and whoever will humble himself will be exalted. **13** Woe to you, scribes and Pharisees, hypocrites! Because you shut up the kingdom of the heavens before men, for you do not go in, nor do you permit those going in to enter. **14** [[Woe to you, scribes and Pharisees, hypocrites! Because you eat up the houses of the widows, and for a pretense make long prayers, because of this you will receive more abundant judgment.]] **15** Woe to you, scribes and Pharisees, hypocrites! Because you go around the sea and the dry land to make one proselyte, and whenever it may happen—you make him a son of Gehenna twofold more than yourselves. **16** Woe to you, blind guides, who are saying, whoever may swear by the temple, it is nothing, but whoever may swear by the gold of the temple—is debtor! **17** Fools and blind! For which [is] greater, the gold, or the temple that is sanctifying the gold? **18** And, whoever may swear by the altar, it is nothing, but whoever may swear by the gift that is on it—is debtor! **19** Fools and blind! For which [is] greater, the gift, or the altar that is sanctifying the gift? **20** He therefore who swore by the altar, swears by it, and by all things on it; **21** and he who swore by the temple, swears by it, and by Him who is dwelling in it; **22** and he who swore by Heaven, swears by the throne of God, and by Him who is sitting on it. **23** Woe to you, scribes and Pharisees, hypocrites! Because you give tithe of the mint, and the dill, and the cumin, and neglected the weightier things of the Law—judgment, and kindness, and faith; these it was necessary to do, and those not to neglect. **24** Blind guides! Who are straining out the gnat, and are swallowing the camel? **25** Woe to you, scribes and Pharisees, hypocrites! Because you make clean the outside of the cup and the plate, and within they are full of robbery and self-indulgence. **26** Blind Pharisee! First cleanse the inside of the cup and the plate, that the outside of them may also become clean. **27** Woe to you, scribes and Pharisees, hypocrites! Because you are like to whitewashed graves, which outwardly indeed appear beautiful, and within are full of bones of dead men, and of all uncleanness; **28** so also you outwardly indeed appear to men righteous, and within you are full of hypocrisy and lawlessness. **29** Woe to you, scribes and Pharisees, hypocrites! Because you build the graves of the prophets, and adorn the tombs of the righteous, **30** and say, If we had been in the days of our fathers, we would not have been partakers with them in the blood of the prophets. **31** So that you testify to yourselves that you are sons of them who murdered the prophets; **32** and you fill up the measure of your fathers. **33** Serpents! Brood of vipers! How may you escape from the judgment of Gehenna? **34** Because of this, behold, I send to you prophets, and wise men, and scribes, and of them you will kill and crucify, and of them you will scourge in your synagogues, and will pursue from city to city, **35** that on you may come all the righteous blood being poured out on the earth from the blood of Abel the righteous, to the blood of Zacharias son of Barachias, whom you murdered between the temple and the altar: **36** truly I say to you, all these things will come on this generation. **37** Jerusalem, Jerusalem, that are killing the prophets, and stoning those sent to you, how often I willed to gather your children together, as a hen gathers her own chickens under the wings, and you did not will. **38** Behold, your house is left to you desolate; **39** for I say to you, you may not see Me from now on, until you may say, blessed [is] He who is coming in the Name of the Lord."

CHAPTER 24

1 And having gone forth, Jesus departed from the temple, and His disciples came near to show Him the buildings of the temple, **2** and Jesus said to them, "Do you not see all these? truly I say to you, there may not be left here a stone on a stone that will not be thrown down." **3** And when He is sitting on the Mount of Olives, the disciples came near to Him by Himself, saying, "Tell us, when will these be? and what [is] the sign of Your coming, and of the full end of the age?" **4** And Jesus

answering said to them, "Take heed that no one may lead you astray, **5** for many will come in My Name, saying, I am the Christ, and they will lead many astray, **6** and you will begin to hear of wars, and reports of wars; see, do not be troubled, for it is necessary for all [these] to come to pass, but the end is not yet. **7** For nation will rise against nation, and kingdom against kingdom, and there will be famines, and pestilences, and earthquakes, in various places; **8** and all these [are the] beginning of travails; **9** then they will deliver you up to tribulation, and will kill you, and you will be hated by all the nations because of My Name; **10** and then will many be stumbled, and they will deliver up one another, and will hate one another. **11** And many false prophets will arise, and will lead many astray; **12** and because of the abounding of the lawlessness, the love of the many will become cold; **13** but he who endured to the end, he will be saved; **14** and this good news of the kingdom will be proclaimed in all the world, for a testimony to all the nations, and then will the end arrive. **15** Whenever, therefore, you may see the abomination of the desolation, that was spoken of through Daniel the prophet, standing in the holy place (whoever is reading let him observe) **16** then those in Judea—let them flee to the mountains; **17** he on the housetop—do not let him come down to take up anything out of his house; **18** and he in the field—do not let him turn back to take his garments. **19** And woe to those with child, and to those giving suck in those days; **20** and pray that your flight may not be in winter, nor on a Sabbath; **21** for there will then be great tribulation, such as was not from the beginning of the world until now, no, nor may be. **22** And if those days were not shortened, no flesh would have been saved; but because of the chosen will those days be shortened. **23** Then if anyone may say to you, Behold, here [is] the Christ! Or, Here! You may not believe; **24** for there will arise false Christs, and false prophets, and they will give great signs and wonders, so as to lead astray, if possible, also the chosen. **25** Behold, I told you beforehand. **26** If therefore they may say to you, Behold, He is in the wilderness, you may not go forth; Behold, in the inner chambers, you may not believe; **27** for as the lightning comes forth from the east, and appears to the west, so will also be the coming of the Son of Man; **28** for wherever the carcass may be, there the eagles will be gathered together. **29** And immediately after the tribulation of those days, the sun will be darkened, and the moon will not give her light, and the stars will fall from the sky, and the powers of the heavens will be shaken; **30** and then will appear the sign of the Son of Man in the sky; and then will all the tribes of the earth strike the breast, and they will see the Son of Man coming on the clouds of Heaven, with power and much glory; **31** and He will send His messengers with a great sound of a trumpet, and they will gather together His chosen from the four winds, from the ends of the heavens to the ends thereof. **32** And from the fig tree learn the allegory: when its branch may have already become tender, and it may put forth the leaves, you know that summer [is] near, **33** so also you, when you may see all these, you know that it is near—at the doors. **34** Truly I say to you, this generation may not pass away until all these may come to pass. **35** The heaven and the earth will pass away, but My words will not pass away. **36** And concerning that day and the hour no one has known—not even the messengers of the heavens—except My Father only; **37** and as the days of Noah—so will also be the coming of the Son of Man; **38** for as they were, in the days before the flood, eating, and drinking, marrying, and giving in marriage, until the day Noah entered into the Ark, **39** and they did not know until the flood came and took all away, so will also be the coming of the Son of Man. **40** Then two [men] will be in the field: one is received, and one is left; **41** two [women] will be grinding in the mill: one is received, and one is left. **42** Watch therefore, because you have not known in what hour your Lord comes; **43** and know this, that if the master of the house had known in what watch the thief comes, he had watched, and did not permit his house to be broken through; **44** because of this also you, become ready, because in what hour you do not think, the Son of Man comes. **45** Who, then, is the servant, faithful and wise, whom his lord set over his household, to give them the nourishment in season? **46** Blessed that servant, whom his lord, having come, will find doing so; **47** truly I say to you that he will set him over all his substance. **48** And if that evil servant may say in his heart, My lord delays to come, **49** and may begin to beat the fellow-servants, and to eat and to drink with the drunken, **50** the lord of that servant will arrive in a day when he does not expect, and in an hour of which he does not know, **51** and will cut him off, and will appoint his portion with the hypocrites; there will be the weeping and the gnashing of the teeth."

CHAPTER 25

¹ "Then will the kingdom of the heavens be likened to ten virgins, who, having taken their lamps, went forth to meet the bridegroom; ² and five of them were prudent, and five foolish; ³ they who were foolish having taken their lamps, did not take with themselves oil; ⁴ and the prudent took oil in their vessels, with their lamps. ⁵ And the bridegroom lingering, they all nodded and were sleeping, ⁶ and in the middle of the night a cry was made, Behold, the bridegroom comes; go forth to meet him! ⁷ Then all those virgins rose, and trimmed their lamps, ⁸ and the foolish said to the prudent, Give us of your oil, because our lamps are going out; ⁹ and the prudent answered, saying, Lest there may not be sufficient for us and you, go rather to those selling, and buy for yourselves. ¹⁰ And while they are going away to buy, the bridegroom came, and those ready went in with him to the wedding feasts, and the door was shut; ¹¹ and afterward come also the rest of the virgins, saying, Lord, lord, open to us; ¹² and he answering said, Truly I say to you, I have not known you. ¹³ Watch therefore, for you have not known the day nor the hour in which the Son of Man comes. ¹⁴ For—as a man going abroad called his own servants, and delivered to them his substance, ¹⁵ and to one he gave five talents, and to another two, and to another one, to each according to his several ability, went abroad immediately. ¹⁶ And he who received the five talents, having gone, worked with them, and made five other talents; ¹⁷ in like manner also he who [received] the two, he gained, also he, other two; ¹⁸ and he who received the one, having gone away, dug in the earth, and hid his lord's money. ¹⁹ And after a long time comes the lord of those servants, and takes reckoning with them; ²⁰ and he who received the five talents, having come, brought five other talents, saying, Lord, you delivered five talents to me; behold, I gained five other talents besides them. ²¹ And his lord said to him, Well done, good and faithful servant, you were faithful over a few things, I will set you over many things; enter into the joy of your lord. ²² And he also, who received the two talents, having come, said, Lord, you delivered to me two talents; behold, I gained two other talents besides them. ²³ His lord said to him, Well done, good and faithful servant, you were faithful over a few things, I will set you over many things; enter into the joy of your lord. ²⁴ And he also who has received the one talent, having come, said, Lord, I knew you, that you are a hard man, reaping where you did not sow, and gathering from where you did not scatter; ²⁵ and having been afraid, having gone away, I hid your talent in the earth; behold, you have your own! ²⁶ And his lord answering said to him, Evil servant, and slothful, you had known that I reap where I did not sow, and I gather from where I did not scatter! ²⁷ it was necessary [for] you then to put my money to the money-lenders, and having come I had received my own with increase. ²⁸ Take therefore from him the talent, and give to him having the ten talents, ²⁹ for to everyone having will be given, and he will have overabundance, and from him who is not having, even that which he has will be taken from him; ³⁰ and cast forth the unprofitable servant into the outer darkness; there will be the weeping and the gnashing of the teeth. ³¹ And whenever the Son of Man may come in His glory, and all the holy messengers with Him, then He will sit on a throne of His glory; ³² and all the nations will be gathered together before Him, and He will separate them from one another, as the shepherd separates the sheep from the goats, ³³ and He will set the sheep indeed on His right hand, and the goats on the left. ³⁴ Then the King will say to those on His right hand, Come, the blessed of My Father, inherit the kingdom that has been prepared for you from the foundation of the world; ³⁵ for I hungered, and you gave Me to eat; I thirsted, and you gave Me to drink; I was a stranger, and you received Me; ³⁶ naked, and you clothed Me; I was sick, and you looked after Me; I was in prison, and you came to Me. ³⁷ Then will the righteous answer Him, saying, Lord, when did we see You hungering, and we nourished? or thirsting, and we gave to drink? ³⁸ and when did we see You a stranger, and we received? or naked, and we clothed? ³⁹ and when did we see You ailing or in prison, and we came to You? ⁴⁰ And the King answering, will say to them, Truly I say to you, inasmuch as you did [it] to one of these My brothers—the least—you did [it] to Me. ⁴¹ Then will He say also to those on the left hand, Go from Me, the cursed, into the continuous fire that has been prepared for the Devil and his messengers; ⁴² for I hungered, and you gave Me nothing to eat; I thirsted, and you gave Me nothing to drink; ⁴³ I was a stranger, and you did not receive Me; naked, and you did not clothe Me; sick and in prison, and you did not look after Me. ⁴⁴ Then they will answer, they also, saying, Lord, when did we see You hungering, or thirsting, or a stranger, or naked, or sick, or in prison, and we did not minister to You? ⁴⁵ Then will He answer them, saying, Truly I say to you, inasmuch as you did [it] not to one of these, the least, you did [it] not to Me. ⁴⁶ And these will go away into continuous punishment, but the righteous into continuous life."

CHAPTER 26

¹ And it came to pass, when Jesus finished all these words, He said to His disciples, ² "You have known that after two days the Passover comes, and the Son of Man is delivered up to be crucified." ³ Then were gathered together the chief priests, and the scribes, and the elders of the people, into the court of the chief priest who was called Caiaphas; ⁴ and they consulted together that they might take Jesus by guile, and kill [Him], ⁵ and they said, "Not in the celebration, that there may not be a tumult among the people." ⁶ And Jesus having been in Bethany, in the house of Simon the leper, ⁷ there came to Him a woman having an alabaster box of ointment, very precious, and she poured on His head as He is reclining. ⁸ And having seen [it], His disciples were much displeased, saying, "To what purpose [is] this waste? ⁹ for this ointment could have been sold for much, and given to the poor." ¹⁰ And Jesus having known, said to them, "Why do you give trouble to the woman? for a good work she worked for Me; ¹¹ for you always have the poor with you, and you do not always have Me; ¹² for she having put this ointment on My body—for My burial she did [it]. ¹³ Truly I say to you, wherever this good news may be proclaimed in the whole world, what this [one] did will also be spoken of—for a memorial of her." ¹⁴ Then one of the Twelve, who is called Judas Iscariot, having gone to the chief priests, said, ¹⁵ "What are you willing to give me, and I will deliver Him up to you?" And they weighed out to him thirty pieces of silver, ¹⁶ and from that time he was seeking a convenient season to deliver Him up. ¹⁷ And on the first [day] of the Unleavened [Bread] the disciples came near to Jesus, saying to Him, "Where will You [that] we may prepare for You to eat the Passover?" ¹⁸ and He said, "Go away into the city, to such a one, and say to him, The Teacher says, My time is near; near you I keep the Passover with My disciples"; ¹⁹ and the disciples did as Jesus appointed them, and prepared the Passover. ²⁰ And evening having come, He was reclining with the Twelve, ²¹ and while they are eating, He said, "Truly I say to you that one of you will deliver Me up." ²² And being grieved exceedingly, they began to say to Him, each of them, "Is it I, Lord?" ²³ And He answering said, "He who dipped with Me the hand in the dish, he will deliver Me up; ²⁴ the Son of Man indeed goes, as it has been written concerning Him, but woe to that man through whom the Son of Man is delivered up! It were good for him if that man had not been born." ²⁵ And Judas—he who delivered Him up—answering said, "Is it I, Rabbi?" He says to him, "You have said." ²⁶ And while they were eating, Jesus having taken the bread, and having blessed, broke, and was giving [it] to the disciples, and said, "Take, eat, this is My body"; ²⁷ and having taken the cup, and having given thanks, He gave to them, saying, "Drink of it—all; ²⁸ for this is My blood of the New Covenant, that is being poured out for many, for forgiveness of sins; ²⁹ and I say to you that I may not drink from now on this produce of the vine, until that day when I may drink it with you new in the kingdom of My Father." ³⁰ And having sung a hymn, they went forth to the Mount of Olives; ³¹ then Jesus says to them, "All you will be stumbled at Me this night; for it has been written: I will strike the Shepherd, and the sheep of the flock will be scattered abroad; ³² but after My having risen, I will go before you to Galilee." ³³ And Peter answering said to Him, "Even if all will be stumbled at You, I will never be stumbled." ³⁴ Jesus said to him, "Truly I say to you that this night, before rooster-crowing, three times you will deny Me." ³⁵ Peter says to Him, "Even if it may be necessary for me to die with You, I will not deny You"; in like manner also said all the disciples. ³⁶ Then Jesus comes with them to a place called Gethsemane, and He says to the disciples, "Sit here, until having gone away, I will pray over there." ³⁷ And having taken Peter and the two sons of Zebedee, He began to be sorrowful,

and to be very heavy; **38** then He says to them, "Exceedingly sorrowful is My soul—to death; abide here, and watch with Me." **39** And having gone forward a little, He fell on His face, praying, and saying, "My Father, if it be possible, let this cup pass from Me; nevertheless, not as I will, but as You." **40** And He comes to the disciples, and finds them sleeping, and He says to Peter, "So! You were not able to watch with Me one hour! **41** watch, and pray, that you may not enter into temptation: the spirit indeed is forward, but the flesh weak." **42** Again, a second time, having gone away, He prayed, saying, "My Father, if this cup cannot pass away from Me except I drink it, Your will be done"; **43** and having come, He finds them again sleeping, for their eyes were heavy. **44** And having left them, having gone away again, He prayed a third time, saying the same word; **45** then He comes to His disciples and says to them, "Sleep on from now on, and rest! Behold, the hour has come near, and the Son of Man is delivered up into the hands of sinners. **46** Rise, let us go; behold, he who is delivering Me up has come near." **47** And while He is yet speaking, behold, Judas, one of the Twelve came, and with him a great multitude, with swords and sticks, from the chief priests and elders of the people. **48** And he who delivered Him up gave them a sign, saying, "Whomsoever I will kiss, it is He, lay hold on Him"; **49** and immediately, having come to Jesus, he said, "Greetings, Rabbi," and kissed Him; **50** and Jesus said to him, "Friend, for what are you present?" Then having come near, they laid hands on Jesus, and took hold on Him. **51** And behold, one of those with Jesus, having stretched forth the hand, drew his sword, and having struck the servant of the chief priest, he took off his ear. **52** Then Jesus says to him, "Turn back your sword to its place; for all who took the sword will perish by the sword; **53** do you think that I am not able now to call on My Father, and He will place beside Me more than twelve legions of messengers? **54** how then may the Writings be fulfilled, that thus it must happen?" **55** In that hour Jesus said to the multitudes, "Did you come forth as against a robber, with swords and sticks, to take Me? daily I was with you sitting, teaching in the temple, and you did not lay hold on Me; **56** but all this has come to pass, that the Writings of the prophets may be fulfilled"; then all the disciples, having left Him, fled. **57** And those laying hold on Jesus led [Him] away to Caiaphas the chief priest, where the scribes and the elders were gathered together, **58** and Peter was following Him far off, to the court of the chief priest, and having gone in within, he was sitting with the officers, to see the end. **59** And the chief priests, and the elders, and all the council, were seeking false witness against Jesus, that they might put Him to death, **60** and they did not find; and many false witnesses having come near, they did not find; and at last two false witnesses having come near, **61** said, "This One said, I am able to throw down the temple of God, and after three days to build it." **62** And the chief priest having stood up, said to Him, "Nothing You answer? what do these witness against You?" **63** and Jesus was silent. And the chief priest answering said to Him, "I adjure You, by the living God, that You may say to us if You are the Christ—the Son of God." **64** Jesus says to him, "You have said; nevertheless I say to you, hereafter you will see the Son of Man sitting on the right hand of the Power and coming on the clouds of Heaven." **65** Then the chief priest tore his garments, saying, "He has slandered; what need have we yet of witnesses? behold, now you heard His slander; **66** what do you think?" And they answering said, "He is worthy of death." **67** Then they spit in His face and punched Him, and others slapped, **68** saying, "Declare to us, O Christ, who he is that struck You?" **69** And Peter was sitting in the court outside, and there came near to him a certain maid, saying, "And you were with Jesus of Galilee!" **70** And he denied before all, saying, "I have not known what you say." **71** And he having gone forth to the porch, another female saw him, and says to those there, "And this one was with Jesus of Nazareth"; **72** and again he denied with an oath, "I have not known the Man." **73** And after a while those standing near having come, said to Peter, "Truly you also are of them, for even your speech makes you evident." **74** Then he began to curse, and to swear, "I have not known the Man"; and immediately a rooster crowed, **75** and Peter remembered the saying of Jesus, He having said to him, "Before rooster-crowing, you will deny Me three times"; and having gone outside, he wept bitterly.

CHAPTER 27

1 And morning having come, all the chief priests and the elders of the people took counsel against Jesus, so as to put Him to death; **2** and having bound Him, they led [Him] away, and delivered Him up to Pontius Pilate, the governor. **3** Then Judas—he who delivered Him up—having seen that He was condemned, having regretted, brought back the thirty pieces of silver to the chief priests and to the elders, saying, **4** "I sinned, having delivered up innocent blood"; and they said, "What [is that] to us? you will see!" **5** and having cast down the pieces of silver in the temple, he departed, and having gone away, he strangled himself. **6** And the chief priests having taken the pieces of silver, said, "It is not lawful to put them into the treasury, seeing it is the price of blood"; **7** and having taken counsel, they bought the potter's field with them, for the burial of strangers; **8** therefore that field was called, "Field of Blood," to this day. **9** Then was fulfilled that spoken through Jeremiah the prophet, saying, "And I took the thirty pieces of silver, the price of Him who has been priced, whom they of the sons of Israel priced, **10** and gave them for the potter's field, as the Lord appointed to me." **11** And Jesus stood before the governor, and the governor questioned Him, saying, "Are You the King of the Jews?" And Jesus said to him, "You say [it]." **12** And in His being accused by the chief priests and the elders, He did not answer anything; **13** then Pilate says to Him, "Do You not hear how many things they witness against You?" **14** And He did not answer him, not even to one word, so that the governor wondered greatly. **15** And at the celebration the governor had been accustomed to release one to the multitude, a prisoner, whom they willed, **16** and they had a noted prisoner then, called Barabbas, **17** therefore they having been gathered together, Pilate said to them, "Whom do you will [that] I may release to you? Barabbas or Jesus who is called Christ?" **18** for he had known that they had delivered Him up because of envy. **19** And as he is sitting on the judgment seat, his wife sent to him, saying, "Nothing—to you and to that Righteous One, for I suffered many things today in a dream because of Him." **20** And the chief priests and the elders persuaded the multitudes that they might ask for themselves Barabbas, and might destroy Jesus; **21** and the governor answering said to them, "Which of the two will you [that] I may release to you?" And they said, "Barabbas." **22** Pilate says to them, "What then will I do with Jesus who is called Christ?" They all say to him, "Let [Him] be crucified!" **23** And the governor said, "Why, what evil did He do?" And they were crying out the more, saying, "Let [Him] be crucified!" **24** And Pilate having seen that it profits nothing, but rather a tumult is made, having taken water, he washed the hands before the multitude, saying, "I am innocent from the blood of this Righteous One; you will see [to it] yourselves"; **25** and all the people answering said, "His blood [is] on us, and on our children!" **26** Then he released Barabbas to them, and having scourged Jesus, he delivered [Him] up that He may be crucified; **27** then the soldiers of the governor having taken Jesus to the Praetorium, gathered to Him all the band; **28** and having unclothed Him, they put a crimson cloak around Him, **29** and having plaited Him a garland out of thorns they put [it] on His head, and [put] a reed in His right hand, and having kneeled before Him, they were mocking Him, saying, "Hail, the King of the Jews!" **30** And having spit on Him, they took the reed, and were striking on His head; **31** and when they had mocked Him, they took off the cloak from Him, and put His own garments on Him, and led Him away to crucify [Him]. **32** And coming forth, they found a man, a Cyrenian, by name Simon: they impressed him that he might carry His cross; **33** and having come to a place called Golgotha, which is called "Place of [the] Skull," **34** they gave Him vinegar mixed with gall to drink, and having tasted, He would not drink. **35** And having crucified Him, they divided His garments, casting a lot, [[that it might be fulfilled which was spoken by the prophet: "They divided My garments to themselves, and they cast a lot over My clothing";]] **36** and sitting down, they were watching Him there, **37** and they put up over His head, His accusation written: "This is Jesus, the King of the Jews." **38** Then two robbers are crucified with Him, one on the right hand and one on the left, **39** and those passing by kept slandering Him, wagging their heads, **40** and saying, "You that are throwing down the temple, and in three days building [it], save Yourself; if You are the Son of God, come down from the cross." **41** And in like manner also the chief priests mocking, with the scribes and elders, said, **42** "He saved others; He is not able to save Himself! If He is King of Israel, let Him come down now from the cross, and we will believe Him; **43** He has trusted on God, let Him now deliver Him if He wants Him, because He said, I am [the] Son of God"; **44** with the same also the robbers, who were crucified with Him, were reproaching Him. **45** And from the sixth hour darkness came over all the land to the ninth hour, **46** and about the ninth hour Jesus cried out with a great voice, saying, "Eli, Eli, lama sabachthani?" That is, "My God, My God, why did You forsake Me?" **47** And certain of those standing there having heard, said, "He calls Elijah"; **48** and immediately, one of them having run, and having taken a sponge, having filled [it] with vinegar, and having put [it] on a reed, was giving Him to drink, **49** but the rest said, "Let alone, let us see if Elijah comes—about to save Him." **50** And Jesus having again cried with a great voice, yielded the spirit; **51** and behold, the veil of the temple was torn in two from top to bottom, and the earth quaked, and the rocks were split, **52** and the tombs were opened, and many bodies of the holy ones who have fallen asleep, arose, **53** and having come forth out of the tombs after His rising, they went into the holy city, and appeared to many. **54** And the centurion, and those with him watching Jesus, having seen the earthquake, and the things that were done, were exceedingly afraid, saying, "Truly this was God's Son." **55** And there were there many women beholding from afar, who followed Jesus from Galilee, ministering to Him, **56** among whom was Mary the Magdalene, and Mary the mother of James and of Joses, and the mother of the sons of Zebedee. **57** And evening having come, there came a rich man from Arimathea named Joseph, who also himself was discipled to Jesus, **58** he having gone near to Pilate, asked for himself the body of Jesus; then Pilate commanded the body to be given back. **59** And having taken the body, Joseph wrapped it in clean linen, **60** and laid it in his new tomb that he hewed in the rock, and having rolled a great stone to the door of the tomb, he went away; **61** now Mary the Magdalene was there, and the other Mary, sitting opposite the grave. **62** And on the next day that is after the Preparation, the chief priests and the Pharisees were gathered together to Pilate, **63** saying, "Lord, we have remembered that this deceiver said while yet living, After three days I rise; **64** command, then, the grave to be made secure until the third day, lest His disciples, having come by night, may steal Him away, and may say to the people, He rose from the dead, and the last deceit will be worse than the first." **65** And Pilate said to them, "You have a guard, go away, make [it] secure—as you have known"; **66** and they, having gone, made the grave secure, having sealed the stone, together with the guard.

CHAPTER 28

1 Now after [the] Sabbaths, it being dawn, toward the first [day] of the weeks, Mary the Magdalene came, and the other Mary, to see the grave, 2 and behold, there came a great earthquake, for a messenger of the Lord, having come down out of Heaven, having come, rolled away the stone from the door, and was sitting on it, 3 and his countenance was as lightning, and his clothing white as snow, 4 and from the fear of him the keepers shook, and they became as dead men. 5 And the messenger answering said to the women, "Do not fear, for I have known that you seek Jesus who has been crucified; 6 He is not here, for He rose, as He said; come, see the place where the Lord was lying; 7 and having gone quickly, say to His disciples that He rose from the dead; and behold, He goes before you to Galilee, there you will see Him; behold, I have told you." 8 And having gone forth quickly from the tomb, with fear and great joy, they ran to tell His disciples; 9 and as they were going to tell His disciples, then behold, Jesus met them, saying, "Greetings!" And having come near, they laid hold of His feet, and worshiped Him. 10 Then Jesus says to them, "Do not fear, go away, tell My brothers that they may go away to Galilee, and there they will see Me." 11 And while they are going on, behold, certain of the guard having come into the city, reported to the chief priests all the things that happened, 12 and having been gathered together with the elders, having also taken counsel, they gave much money to the soldiers, 13 saying, "Say that His disciples having come by night, stole Him—we being asleep; 14 and if this is heard by the governor, we will persuade him, and you keep free from anxiety." 15 And they, having received the money, did as they were taught, and this account was spread abroad among Jews until this day. 16 And the eleven disciples went to Galilee, to the mountain where Jesus appointed them, 17 and having seen Him, they worshiped Him, but some wavered. 18 And having come near, Jesus spoke to them, saying, "All authority in Heaven and on earth was given to Me; 19 having gone, then, disciple all the nations, immersing them into the Name of the Father, and of

the Son, and of the Holy Spirit, 20 teaching them to observe all, whatever I commanded you, and behold, I am with you all the days—until the full end of the age."

MARK

CHAPTER 1

1 A beginning of the good news of Jesus Christ, Son of God. **2** As it has been written in the Prophets: "Behold, I send My messenger before Your face, || Who will prepare Your way before You. **3** A voice of one calling in the wilderness: Prepare the way of the Lord, || Make His paths straight." **4** John came immersing in the wilderness, and proclaiming an immersion of conversion for forgiveness of sins, **5** and there were going forth to him all the region of Judea, and they of Jerusalem, and they were all immersed by him in the river Jordan, confessing their sins. **6** And John was clothed with camel's hair, and a girdle of skin around his loins, and eating locusts and honey of the field, **7** and he proclaimed, saying, "He comes—who is mightier than I—after me, of whom I am not worthy—having stooped down—to loose the strap of His sandals; **8** I indeed immersed you in water, but He will immerse you in the Holy Spirit." **9** And it came to pass in those days, Jesus came from Nazareth of Galilee, and was immersed by John in the Jordan; **10** and immediately coming up from the water, He saw the heavens dividing, and the Spirit coming down on Him as a dove; **11** and a voice came out of the heavens, "You are My Son, the Beloved, in whom I delighted." **12** And immediately the Spirit puts Him forth into the wilderness, **13** and He was there in the wilderness forty days, being tempted by Satan, and He was with the beasts, and the messengers were ministering to Him. **14** And after the delivering up of John, Jesus came to Galilee, proclaiming the good news of the Kingdom of God, **15** and saying, "The time has been fulfilled, and the Kingdom of God has come near, convert and believe in the good news." **16** And walking by the Sea of Galilee, He saw Simon, and his brother Andrew, casting a drag into the sea, for they were fishers, **17** and Jesus said to them, "Come after Me, and I will make you to become fishers of men"; **18** and immediately, having left their nets, they followed Him. **19** And having gone on there a little, He saw James of Zebedee, and his brother John, and they were in the boat refitting the nets, **20** and immediately He called them, and having left their father Zebedee in the boat with the hired servants, they went away after Him. **21** And they go on to Capernaum, and immediately, on the Sabbaths, having gone into the synagogue, He was teaching, **22** and they were astonished at His teaching, for He was teaching them as having authority, and not as the scribes. **23** And there was in their synagogue a man with an unclean spirit, and he cried out, **24** saying, "What [regards] us and You, Jesus the Nazarene? you came to destroy us; I have known You, who You are—the Holy One of God." **25** And Jesus rebuked him, saying, "Be silenced, and come forth out of him," **26** and the unclean spirit having convulsed him, and having cried with a great voice, came forth out of him, **27** and they were all amazed, so as to reason among themselves, saying, "What is this? what new teaching [is] this? that with authority He also commands the unclean spirits, and they obey Him!" **28** And the fame of Him went forth immediately to all the region of Galilee. **29** And immediately, having come forth out of the synagogue, they went into the house of Simon and Andrew, with James and John, **30** and the mother-in-law of Simon was lying fevered, and immediately they tell Him about her, **31** and having come near, He raised her up, having laid hold of her hand, and the fever left her immediately, and she was ministering to them. **32** And evening having come, when the sun set, they brought to Him all who were ill and who were demoniacs, **33** and the whole city was gathered together near the door, **34** and He healed many who were ill of manifold diseases, and He cast forth many demons, and was not permitting the demons to speak, because they knew Him. **35** And very early, it being yet night, having risen, He went forth, and went away to a desolate place, and was praying there; **36** and Simon and those with him went in quest of Him, **37** and having found Him, they say to Him, "All seek You"; **38** and He says to them, "We may go into the next towns, that there also I may preach, for—for this I came forth." **39** And He was preaching in their synagogues, in all Galilee, and is casting out the demons, **40** and there comes to Him a leper, calling on Him, and kneeling to Him, and saying to Him, "If You may will, You are able to cleanse me." **41** And Jesus having been moved with compassion, having stretched forth the hand, touched him and says to him, "I will, be cleansed"; **42** and He having spoken, immediately the leprosy went away from him, and he was cleansed. **43** And having sternly charged him, immediately He put him forth, **44** and says to him, "See [that] you may say nothing to anyone, but go away, show yourself to the priest, and bring near for your cleansing the things Moses directed, for a testimony to them." **45** And he, having gone forth, began to proclaim much, and to spread the thing abroad, so that He was no longer able to openly enter into the city, but He was outside in desolate places, and they were coming to Him from every quarter.

CHAPTER 2

1 And again He entered into Capernaum, after [some] days, and it was heard that He is in the house, **2** and immediately many were gathered together, so that there was no more room, not even at the door, and He was speaking to them the word. **3** And they come to Him, bringing a paralytic, carried by four, **4** and not being able to come near to Him because of the multitude, they uncovered the roof where He was, and having broken [it] up, they let down the pallet on which the paralytic was lying, **5** and Jesus having seen their faith, says to the paralytic, "Child, your sins have been forgiven you." **6** And there were certain of the scribes sitting there, and reasoning in their hearts, **7** "Why does this One thus speak evil words? who is able to forgive sins except one—God?" **8** And immediately Jesus, having known in His spirit that they thus reason in themselves, said to them, "Why do you reason these things in your hearts? **9** which is easier? To say to the paralytic, Your sins are forgiven; or to say, Rise, and take up your pallet, and walk? **10** That you may know that the Son of Man has authority on the earth to forgive sins—(He says to the paralytic)— **11** I say to you, rise, and take up your pallet, and go away to your house"; **12** and he rose immediately, and having taken up the pallet, he went forth before all, so that all were astonished, and glorify God, saying, "Never thus did we see." **13** And He went forth again by the sea, and all the multitude was coming to Him, and He was teaching them, **14** and passing by, He saw Levi of Alpheus sitting at the tax office, and says to him, "Follow Me," and he, having risen, followed Him. **15** And it came to pass, in His reclining in his house, that many tax collectors and sinners were dining with Jesus and His disciples, for there were many, and they followed Him. **16** And the scribes and the Pharisees, having seen Him eating with the tax collectors and sinners, said to His disciples, "Why—that with the tax collectors and sinners He eats and drinks?" **17** And Jesus, having heard, says to them, "They who are strong have no need of a physician, but they who are ill; I did not come to call righteous men, but sinners." **18** And the disciples of John and those of the Pharisees were fasting, and they come and say to Him, "Why do the disciples of John and those of the Pharisees fast, and Your disciples do not fast?" **19** And Jesus said to them, "Are the sons of the bride-chamber able, while the bridegroom is with them, to fast? As long a time [as] they have the bridegroom with them they are not able to fast; **20** but days will come when the bridegroom may be taken from them, and then they will fast—in those days. **21** And no one sews a patch of undressed cloth on an old garment, and if not—the new, filling it up, takes from the old and the split becomes worse; **22** and no one puts new wine into old skins, and if not—the new wine bursts the skins, and the wine is poured out, and the skins will be destroyed; but new wine is to be put into new skins." **23** And it came to pass—He is going along on the Sabbaths through the grainfields—and His disciples began to make a way, plucking the ears, **24** and the Pharisees said to Him, "Behold, why do they do on the Sabbaths that which is not lawful?" **25** And He said to them, "Did you never read what David did when he had need and was hungry, he and those with him? **26** how he went into the house of God, in [the days of] Abiathar the chief priest, and ate the Bread of the Presentation, which it is not lawful to eat, except to the priests, and he also gave to those who were with him?" **27** And He said to them, "The Sabbath was made for man, not man for the Sabbath, **28** so that the Son of Man is also Lord of the Sabbath."

CHAPTER 3

1 And He entered again into the synagogue, and there was there a man having the hand withered, **2** and they were watching Him, whether on the Sabbaths He will heal him, that they might accuse Him. **3** And He says to the man having the hand withered, "Rise up in the midst." **4** And He says to them, "Is it lawful on the Sabbaths to do good, or to do evil? To save life, or to kill?" But they were silent. **5** And having looked around on them with anger, being grieved for the hardness of their heart, He says to the man, "Stretch forth your hand"; and he stretched forth, and his hand was restored whole as the other; **6** and the Pharisees having gone forth, immediately, with the Herodians, were taking counsel against Him how they might destroy Him. **7** And Jesus withdrew with His disciples to the sea, and a great multitude from Galilee followed Him, and from Judea, **8** and from Jerusalem, and from Idumea and beyond the Jordan; and they around Tyre and Sidon—a great multitude—having heard how He was doing great things, came to Him. **9** And He said to His disciples that a little boat may wait on Him, because of the multitude, that they may not press on Him, **10** for He healed many, so that they threw themselves on Him, in order to touch Him—as many as had plagues; **11** and the unclean spirits, when they were seeing Him, were falling down before Him, and were crying, saying, "You are the Son of God"; **12** and many times He was charging them that they might not make Him apparent. **13** And He goes up to the mountain, and calls near whom He willed, and they went away to Him; **14** and He appointed twelve, that they may be with Him, and that He may send them forth to preach, **15** and to have power to heal the sicknesses, and to cast out the demons. **16** And He put on Simon the name Peter; **17** and James of Zebedee, and John the brother of James, and He put on them names—Boanerges, that is, "Sons of Thunder", **18** and Andrew, and Philip, and Bartholomew, and Matthew, and Thomas, and James of Alpheus, and Thaddeus, and Simon the Zealot, **19** and Judas Iscariot, who also delivered Him up; and they come into a house. **"** And a multitude comes together again, so that they are not even able to eat bread; **21** and those alongside Him having heard, went forth to lay hold on Him, for they said that He was beside Himself, **22** and the scribes who [are] from Jerusalem having come down, said, "He has Beelzebul," and, "By the ruler of the demons He casts out the demons." **23** And having called them near, He said to them in allegories, "How is Satan able to cast out Satan? **24** and if a kingdom is divided against itself, that kingdom cannot be made to stand; **25** and if a house is divided against itself, that house cannot be made to stand; **26** and if Satan rose against himself, and has been divided, he cannot be made to stand, but has an end. **27** No one is able to spoil the vessels of the strong man, having entered into his house, if first he may not bind the strong man, and then he will spoil his house. **28** Truly I say to you that all sins will be forgiven to the sons of men, and slanders with which they might have slandered, **29** but whoever may slander in regard to the Holy Spirit has no forgiveness—throughout the age, but is in danger of continuous judgment; **30** because they said, He has an unclean spirit." **31** Then His brothers and mother come, and standing outside, they sent to Him, calling Him, **32** and a multitude was sitting around Him, and they said to Him, "Behold, Your mother and Your brothers seek You outside." **33** And He answered them, saying, "Who is My mother, or My brothers?" **34** And having looked around in a circle to those sitting around Him, He says, "Behold, My mother and My brothers! **35** for whoever may do the will of God, he is My brother, and My sister, and mother."

CHAPTER 4

1 And again He began to teach by the sea, and there was gathered to Him a great multitude, so that He, having gone into the boat, sat in the sea, and all the multitude was near the sea, on the land, **2** and He taught them many things in allegories, and He said to them in His teaching: **3** "Listen, behold, the sower went forth to sow; **4** and it came to pass, in the sowing, some fell by the way, and the birds of the sky came and devoured it; **5** and other fell on the rocky ground, where it did not have much earth, and immediately it sprang forth, because of having no depth of earth, **6** and the sun having risen, it was scorched, and because of having no root it withered; **7** and other fell toward the thorns, and the thorns came up and choked it, and it gave no fruit; **8** and other fell to the good ground, and was giving fruit, coming up and increasing, and it was bearing, one thirty-fold, and one sixty, and one a hundred." **9** And He said to them, "He who is having ears to hear—let him hear." **10** And when He was alone, those around Him, with the Twelve, asked Him of the allegory, **11** and He said to them, "To you it has been given to know the secret of the Kingdom of God, but to those who are outside, in allegories are all the things done, **12** that seeing they may see and not perceive, and hearing they may hear and not understand, lest they may turn, and the sins may be forgiven them." **13** And He says to them, "Have you not known this allegory? and how will you know all the allegories? **14** He who is sowing sows the word; **15** and these are they by the way where the word is sown: and whenever they may hear, Satan immediately comes, and he takes away the word that has been sown in their hearts. **16** And these are they, in like manner, who are sown on the rocky ground: who, whenever they may hear the word, immediately receive it with joy, **17** and have no root in themselves, but are temporary; afterward tribulation or persecution having come because of the word, immediately they are stumbled. **18** And these are they who are sown toward the thorns: these are they who are hearing the word, **19** and the anxieties of this age, and the deceitfulness of the riches, and the desires concerning the other things, entering in, choke the word, and it becomes unfruitful. **20** And these are they who on the good ground have been sown: who hear the word, and receive, and bear fruit, one thirty-fold, and one sixty, and one a hundred." **21** And He said to them, "Does the lamp come that it may be put under the measure, or under the bed—not that it may be put on the lampstand? **22** for there is not anything hid that may not be revealed, nor was anything kept hid but that it may come to light. **23** If any has ears to hear—let him hear." **24** And He said to them, "Take heed what you hear; in what measure you measure, it will be measured to you; and to you who hear it will be added; **25** for whoever may have, there will be given to him, and whoever has not, also that which he has will be taken from him." **26** And He said, "Thus is the Kingdom of God: as if a man may cast the seed on the earth, **27** and may sleep, and may rise night and day, and the seed springs up and grows, he has not known how; **28** for of itself the earth bears fruit, first a blade, afterward an ear, afterward full grain in the ear; **29** and whenever the fruit may yield itself, immediately he sends forth the sickle, because the harvest has come." **30** And He said, "To what may we liken the Kingdom of God, or in what allegory may we compare it? **31** As a grain of mustard, which, whenever it may be sown on the earth, is less than any of the seeds that are on the earth; **32** and whenever it may be sown, it comes up, and becomes greater than any of the herbs, and makes great branches, so that under its shade the birds of the sky are able to rest." **33** And with many such allegories He was speaking to them the word, as they were able to hear, **34** and without an allegory He was not speaking to them, and by themselves, to His disciples He was expounding all. **35** And He says to them on that day, evening having come, "We may pass over to the other side"; **36** and having let away the multitude, they take Him up as He was in the boat, and other little boats were also with Him. **37** And there comes a great storm of wind, and the waves were beating on the boat, so that it is now being filled, **38** and He Himself was on the stern, sleeping on the pillow, and they wake Him up, and say to Him, "Teacher, are You not caring that we perish?" **39** And having awoken, He rebuked the wind and said to the sea, "Peace, be stilled"; and the wind stilled, and there was a great calm; **40** and He said to them, "Why are you so fearful? how have you no faith?" **41** and they feared a great fear and said to one another, "Who, then, is this, that even the wind and the sea obey Him?"

CHAPTER 5

1 And they came to the other side of the sea, to the region of the Gadarenes, **2** and He having come forth out of the boat, immediately there met Him out of the tombs a man with an unclean spirit, **3** who had his dwelling in the tombs, and not even with chains was anyone able to bind him, **4** because that many times he had been bound with shackles and chains, and the chains had been pulled in pieces by him, and the shackles broken in pieces, and none was able to tame him, **5** and always, night and day, he was in the mountains, and in the tombs, crying and cutting himself with stones. **6** And having seen Jesus from afar, he ran and prostrated to Him, **7** and having called with a loud voice, he said, "What [regards] me and You, Jesus, Son of God the Highest? I adjure You by God, may You not afflict me!" **8** For He said to him, "Come forth, unclean spirit, out of the man!" **9** And He was questioning him, "What [is] your name?" And he answered, saying, "Legion [is] my name, because we are many"; **10** and he was calling on Him much, that He may not send them out of the region. **11** And there was there, near the mountains, a great herd of pigs feeding, **12** and all the demons called on Him, saying, "Send us to the pigs, that into them we may enter"; **13** and immediately Jesus gave them leave, and having come forth, the unclean spirits entered into the pigs, and the herd rushed down the steep place to the sea—and they were about two thousand—and they were choked in the sea. **14** And those feeding the pigs fled, and told in the city, and in the fields, and they came forth to see what it is that has been done; **15** and they come to Jesus, and see the demoniac, sitting, and clothed, and right-minded—him having had the legion—and they were afraid; **16** and those having seen [it], declared to them how it had come to pass to the demoniac, and about the pigs; **17** and they began to call on Him to go away from their borders. **18** And He having gone into the boat, the demoniac was calling on Him that he may be with Him, **19** and Jesus did not permit him, but says to him, "Go away to your house, to your own [friends], and tell them how the Lord did great things to you, and dealt kindly with you"; **20** and he went away, and began to proclaim in the Decapolis how Jesus did great things to him, and all were wondering. **21** And Jesus having passed over in the boat again to the other side, there was gathered a great multitude to Him, and He was near the sea, **22** and behold, there comes one of the chiefs of the synagogue, by name Jairus, and having seen Him, he falls at His feet, **23** and he was calling on Him much, saying, "My little daughter is at the last extremity—that having come, You may lay on her [Your] hands, so that she may be saved, and she will live"; **24** and He went away with him. And there was following Him a great multitude, and they were thronging Him, **25** and a certain woman, being with a flow of blood [for] twelve years, **26** and having suffered many things under many physicians, and having spent all that she had, and having profited nothing, but rather having come to the worse, **27** having heard about Jesus, having come in the multitude behind, she touched His garment, **28** for she said, "If I may even touch His garments, I will be saved"; **29** and immediately the fountain of her blood was dried up, and she knew in the body that she has been healed of the plague. **30** And immediately Jesus having known in Himself that power had gone forth out of Him, having turned in the multitude, said, "Who touched My garments?" **31** and His disciples said to Him, "You see the multitude thronging You, and You say, Who touched Me!" **32** And He was looking around to see her who did this, **33** and the woman, having been afraid, and trembling, knowing what was done on her, came, and fell down before Him, and told Him all the truth, **34** and He said to her, "Daughter, your faith has saved you; go away in peace, and be whole from your plague." **35** As He is yet speaking, there come from the chief of the synagogue's [house, certain], saying, "Your daughter died, why do you still harass the Teacher?" **36** And Jesus immediately, having heard the word that is spoken, says to the chief of the synagogue, "Do not be afraid, only believe." **37** And He did not permit anyone to follow with Him, except Peter, and James, and John the brother of James; **38** and He comes into the house of the chief of the synagogue, and sees a tumult, much weeping and wailing; **39** and having gone in He says to them, "Why do you make a tumult, and weep? the child did not die, but sleeps"; **40** and they were laughing at Him. And He, having put all forth, takes the father of the child, and the mother, and those with Him, and goes in where the child is lying, **41** and having taken the hand of the child, He says to her, "Talitha cumi"; which is, being interpreted, "Girl (I say to you), arise." **42** And immediately the girl arose, and was walking, for she was twelve years [old]; and they were amazed with a great amazement, **43** and He charged them much, that no one may know this thing, and He said that there be given to her to eat.

CHAPTER 6

1 And He went forth from there, and came to His own country, and His disciples follow Him, **2** and Sabbath having come, He began to teach in the synagogue, and many hearing were astonished, saying, "From where [did] this One [hear] these things? and what [is] the wisdom that was given to Him, that also such mighty works are done through His hands? **3** Is this not the carpenter, the Son of Mary, and brother of James, and Joses, and Judas, and Simon? and are His sisters not here with us?" And they were being stumbled at Him. **4** And Jesus said to them, "A prophet is not without honor, except in his own country, and among his relatives, and in his own house"; **5** and He was not able to do any mighty work there, except having put hands on a few sick, He healed [them]; **6** and He wondered because of their unbelief. And He was going around the villages, in a circle, teaching, **7** and He calls near the Twelve, and He began to send them forth two by two, and He was giving them power over the unclean spirits, **8** and He commanded them that they may take nothing for the way, except a staff only—no leather pouch, no bread, no brass in the girdle, **9** but having been shod with sandals, and you may not put on two coats. **10** And He said to them, "Whenever you may enter into a house, remain there until you may depart from there, **11** and as many as may not receive you nor hear you, going out from there, shake off the dust that is under your feet for a testimony to them; [[truly I say to you, it will be more tolerable for Sodom or Gomorrah in [the] day of judgment than for that city."]] **12** And having gone forth they were preaching that [men] might convert, **13** and they were casting out many demons, and they were anointing many sick with oil, and they were healing [them]. **14** And King Herod heard (for His Name became public), and he said, "John the Immerser was raised out of the dead, and because of this the mighty powers are working in him." **15** Others said, "It is Elijah," and others said, "It is a prophet, or as one of the prophets." **16** And Herod having heard, said, "He whom I beheaded—John—this is he; he was raised out of the dead." **17** For Herod himself, having sent forth, laid hold on John, and bound him in the prison, because of Herodias, the wife of his brother Philip, because he married her, **18** for John said to Herod, "It is not lawful for you to have the wife of your brother"; **19** and Herodias was having a quarrel with him, and was willing to kill him, and was not able, **20** for Herod was fearing John, knowing him [to be] a righteous and holy man, and was keeping watch over him, and having heard him, was doing many things, and hearing him gladly. **21** And a seasonable day having come when Herod on his birthday was making a banquet to his great men, and to the chiefs of thousands, and to the first men of Galilee, **22** and the daughter of that Herodias having come in, and having danced, and having pleased Herod and those dining with him, the king said to the girl, "Ask of me whatever you will, and I will give to you," **23** and he swore to her, "Whatever you may ask me, I will give to you—to the half of my kingdom." **24** And she, having gone forth, said to her mother, "What will I ask for myself?" And she said, "The head of John the Immerser"; **25** and having come in immediately with haste to the king, she asked, saying, "I will that you may immediately give me the head of John the Immerser on a plate." **26** And the king, made very sorrowful because of the oaths and of those reclining with him, would not put her away, **27** and immediately the king having sent a guardsman, commanded his head to be brought, **28** and he having gone, beheaded him in the prison, and brought his head on a plate, and gave it to the girl, and the girl gave it to her mother; **29** and having heard, his disciples came and took up his corpse, and laid it in the tomb. **30** And the apostles are gathered together to Jesus, and they told Him all, and how many things they did, and how many things they taught, **31** and He said to them, "Come yourselves apart to a desolate place, and rest a little," for those coming and those going were many, and not even to eat had they opportunity, **32** and they went away to a desolate place, in the boat, by themselves. **33** And the multitudes saw them going away, and many recognized Him, and they ran there by land from all the cities, and went before them, and came together to Him, **34** and having come forth, Jesus saw a great multitude, and was moved with compassion on them, that they were as sheep not having a shepherd, and He began to teach many things. **35** And now the hour being advanced, His disciples having come near to Him, say, "The place is desolate, and the hour is now advanced, **36** let them away, that having gone away into the surrounding fields and villages, they may buy loaves for themselves, for they do not have what they may eat." **37** And He answering said to them, "You give them to eat," and they say to Him, "Having gone away, may we buy two hundred denarii worth of loaves, and give to them to eat?" **38** And He

says to them, "How many loaves do you have? go and see"; and having known, they say, "Five, and two fishes." **39** And He commanded them to make all recline in companies on the green grass, **40** and they sat down in squares, by hundreds, and by fifties. **41** And having taken the five loaves and the two fishes, having looked up to the sky, He blessed, and broke the loaves, and was giving [them] to His disciples, that they may set [them] before them, and the two fishes He divided to all, **42** and they all ate, and were filled, **43** and they took up of broken pieces twelve hand-baskets full, and of the fishes, **44** and those eating of the loaves were about five thousand men. **45** And immediately He constrained His disciples to go into the boat, and to go before [Him] to the other side, to Bethsaida, until He may let the multitude away, **46** and having taken leave of them, He went away to the mountain to pray. **47** And evening having come, the boat was in the midst of the sea, and He alone on the land; **48** and He saw them harassed in the rowing, for the wind was against them, and about the fourth watch of the night He comes to them walking on the sea, and wished to pass by them. **49** And they having seen Him walking on the sea, thought [it] to be an apparition, and cried out, **50** for they all saw Him, and were troubled, and immediately He spoke with them, and says to them, "Take courage! I am; do not be afraid." **51** And He went up to them into the boat, and the wind stilled, and greatly out of measure they were amazed in themselves, and were wondering, **52** for they did not understand concerning the loaves, for their heart has been hard. **53** And having passed over, they came on the land of Gennesaret, and drew to the shore, **54** and they having come forth out of the boat, immediately having recognized Him, **55** they ran around through all that surrounding region, and they began to carry around on the pallets those being ill, where they were hearing that He is, **56** and wherever He was going, to villages, or cities, or fields, in the marketplaces they were laying the ailing, and were calling on Him, that they may touch if it were but the fringe of His garment, and as many as were touching Him were saved.

CHAPTER 7

1 And gathered together to Him are the Pharisees, and certain of the scribes, having come from Jerusalem, **2** and having seen certain of His disciples with defiled hands—that is, unwashed—eating bread, they found fault; **3** for the Pharisees, and all the Jews, if they do not wash the hands to the wrist, do not eat, holding the tradition of the elders, **4** and [coming] from the marketplace, if they do not immerse themselves, they do not eat; and many other things there are that they received to hold, immersions of cups, and pots, and bronze vessels, and couches. **5** Then the Pharisees and the scribes question Him, "Why do Your disciples not walk according to the tradition of the elders, but eat the bread with unwashed hands?" **6** and He answering said to them, "Well did Isaiah prophesy concerning you, hypocrites, as it has been written: This people honors Me with the lips, and their heart is far from Me; **7** and in vain they worship Me, teaching teachings, commands of men; **8** for having put away the command of God, you hold the tradition of men, immersions of pots and cups; and many other such like things you do." **9** And He said to them, "Well do you put away the command of God that you may keep your tradition; **10** for Moses said, Honor your father and your mother; and, He who is speaking evil of father or mother—let him die the death; **11** and you say, If a man may say to father or to mother, Korban (that is, a gift), [is] whatever you may be profited out of mine, **12** and you no longer permit him to do anything for his father or for his mother, **13** setting aside the word of God for your tradition that you delivered; and many such like things you do." **14** And having called near all the multitude, He said to them, "Listen to Me, you all, and understand; **15** there is nothing from outside the man entering into him that is able to defile him, but the things coming out from him, those are the things defiling the man. **16** [[If any has ears to hear—let him hear."]] **17** And when He entered into a house from the multitude, His disciples were questioning Him about the allegory, **18** and He says to them, "So also you are without understanding! Do you not perceive that nothing from outside entering into the man is able to defile him? **19** because it does not enter into his heart, but into the belly, and into the drain it goes out, purifying all the meats." **20** And He said, "That which is coming out from the man, that defiles the man; **21** for from within, out of the heart of men, the evil reasonings come forth, adulteries, whoredoms, murders, **22** thefts, covetous desires, wickedness, deceit, arrogance, an evil eye, slander, pride, foolishness; **23** all these evils come forth from within, and they defile the man." **24** And from there having risen, He went away to the borders of Tyre and Sidon, and having entered into the house, He wished none to know, and He was not able to be hid, **25** for a woman having heard about Him, whose little daughter had an unclean spirit, having come, fell at His feet— **26** and the woman was a Greek, a Syro-Phoenician by nation—and was asking Him that He may cast forth the demon out of her daughter. **27** And Jesus said to her, "First permit the children to be filled, for it is not good to take the children's bread, and to cast [it] to the little dogs." **28** And she answered and says to Him, "Yes, Lord; for the little dogs under the table also eat of the children's crumbs." **29** And He said to her, "Because of this word, go; the demon has gone forth out of your daughter"; **30** and having come away to her house, she found the demon gone forth, and the daughter laid on the bed. **31** And again, having gone forth from the coasts of Tyre and Sidon, He came to the Sea of Galilee, through the midst of the coasts of Decapolis, **32** and they bring to Him a deaf, stuttering man, and they call on Him that He may put the hand on him. **33** And having taken him away from the multitude by Himself, He put His fingers to his ears, and having spit, He touched his tongue, **34** and having looked to the sky, He sighed, and says to him, "Ephphatha," that is, "Be opened"; **35** and immediately his ears were opened, and the string of his tongue was loosed, and he was speaking plain. **36** He charged them that they may tell no one, but the more He was charging them, the more abundantly they were proclaiming [it], **37** and they were being astonished beyond measure, saying, "He has done all things well; He makes both the deaf to hear, and the mute to speak."

CHAPTER 8

1 In those days the multitude being very great, and not having what they may eat, Jesus having called near His disciples, says to them, **2** "I have compassion on the multitude, because now three days they continue with Me, and they have not what they may eat; **3** and if I will let them away fasting to their home, they will faint in the way, for certain of them are come from far." **4** And His disciples answered Him, "From where will anyone be able to feed these here in a wilderness with bread?" **5** And He was questioning them, "How many loaves do you have?" And they said, "Seven." **6** And He commanded the multitude to sit down on the ground, and having taken the seven loaves, having given thanks, He broke, and was giving to His disciples that they may set before [them]; and they set before the multitude. **7** And they had a few small fishes, and having blessed, He said to set them also before [them]; **8** and they ate and were filled, and they took up that which was over of broken pieces—seven baskets; **9** and those eating were about four thousand. And He let them away, **10** and immediately having entered into the boat with His disciples, He came to the parts of Dalmanutha, **11** and the Pharisees came forth, and began to dispute with Him, seeking from Him a sign from Heaven, tempting Him; **12** and having sighed deeply in His spirit, He says, "Why does this generation seek after a sign? Truly I say to you, no sign will be given to this generation." **13** And having left them, having entered again into the boat, He went away to the other side; **14** and they forgot to take loaves, and except one loaf they had nothing with them in the boat, **15** and He was charging them, saying, "Take heed, beware of the leaven of the Pharisees, and of the leaven of Herod," **16** and they were reasoning with one another, saying, "Because we have no loaves." **17** And Jesus having known, says to them, "Why do you reason, because you have no loaves? do you not yet perceive, nor understand, yet have you hardened your heart? **18** Having eyes, do you not see? and having ears, do you not hear? and do you not remember? **19** When I broke the five loaves to the five thousand, how many hand-baskets full of broken pieces did you take up?" They say to Him, "Twelve." **20** "And when the seven to the four thousand, how many hand-baskets full of broken pieces did you take up?" And they said, "Seven." **21** And He said to them, "How do you not understand?" **22** And He comes to Bethsaida, and they bring to Him one blind, and call on Him that He may touch him, **23** and having taken the hand of the blind man, He led him forth outside the village, and having spit on his eyes, having put [His] hands on him, He was questioning him if he beholds anything: **24** and he, having looked up, said, "I behold men, as I see trees, walking." **25**

Afterward again He put [His] hands on his eyes, and made him look up, and he was restored, and discerned all things clearly, **26** and He sent him away to his house, saying, "Neither may you go into the village, nor tell [it] to any in the village." **27** And Jesus went forth, and His disciples, into the villages of Caesarea Philippi, and in the way He was questioning His disciples, saying to them, "Who do men say I am?" **28** And they answered, "John the Immerser, and others Elijah, but others one of the prophets." **29** And He says to them, "And you—who do you say I am?" And Peter answering says to him, "You are the Christ." **30** And He strictly charged them that they may tell no one about it, **31** and began to teach them that it is necessary for the Son of Man to suffer many things, and to be rejected by the elders, and chief priests, and scribes, and to be killed, and to rise again after three days; **32** and openly He was speaking the word. And Peter having taken Him aside, began to rebuke Him, **33** and He, having turned, and having looked on His disciples, rebuked Peter, saying, "Get behind Me, Satan, because you do not mind the things of God, but the things of men." **34** And having called near the multitude, with His disciples, He said to them, "Whoever wills to come after Me—let him disown himself, and take up his cross, and follow Me; **35** for whoever may will to save his life will lose it; and whoever may lose his life for My sake and for the good news' sake, he will save it; **36** for what will it profit a man, if he may gain the whole world, and forfeit his life? **37** Or what will a man give as an exchange for his life? **38** for whoever may be ashamed of Me, and of My words, in this adulterous and sinful generation, the Son of Man will also be ashamed of him when He may come in the glory of His Father with the holy messengers."

CHAPTER 9

1 And He said to them, "Truly I say to you that there are certain of those standing here, who may not taste of death until they see the Kingdom of God having come in power." **2** And after six days Jesus takes Peter, and James, and John, and brings them up to a high mountain by themselves, alone, and He was transfigured before them, **3** and His garments became glittering, exceedingly white, as snow, so as a launderer on the earth is not able to whiten [them]. **4** And there appeared to them Elijah with Moses, and they were talking with Jesus. **5** And Peter answering says to Jesus, "Rabbi, it is good to us to be here; and we may make three shelters, for You one, and for Moses one, and for Elijah one": **6** for he was not knowing what he might say, for they were greatly afraid. **7** And there came a cloud overshadowing them, and there came a voice out of the cloud, saying, "This is My Son, the Beloved, hear Him"; **8** and suddenly, having looked around, they saw no one anymore, but Jesus only with themselves. **9** And as they are coming down from the mountain, He charged them that they may declare to no one the things that they saw, except when the Son of Man may rise out of the dead; **10** and the thing they kept to themselves, questioning together what the rising out of the dead is. **11** And they were questioning Him, saying that the scribes say that Elijah must come first. **12** And He answering said to them, "Elijah indeed, having come first, restores all things; and how has it been written concerning the Son of Man, that He may suffer many things, and be set at nothing? **13** But I say to you that also Elijah has come, and they did to him what they willed, as it has been written of him." **14** And having come to the disciples, He saw a great multitude around them, and scribes questioning with them, **15** and immediately, all the multitude having seen Him, were amazed, and running near, were greeting Him. **16** And He questioned the scribes, "What do you dispute with them?" **17** and one out of the multitude answering said, "Teacher, I brought my son to You, having a mute spirit; **18** and wherever it seizes him, it tears him, and he foams, and gnashes his teeth, and pines away; and I spoke to Your disciples that they may cast it out, and they were not able." **19** And He answering him, said, "O generation unbelieving, until when will I be with you? until when will I suffer you? bring him to Me"; **20** and they brought him to Him, and he having seen Him, immediately the spirit convulsed him, and he, having fallen on the earth, was wallowing—foaming. **21** And He questioned his father, "How much time is it since this came to him?" And he said, "From childhood, **22** and many times it also cast him into fire, and into water, that it might destroy him; but if You are able to do anything, help us, having compassion on us." **23** And Jesus said to him, "If you are able to believe! All things are possible to the one that is believing";

²⁴ and immediately the father of the child, having cried out with tears, said, "I believe, Lord; be helping my unbelief." ²⁵ Jesus having seen that a multitude runs together, rebuked the unclean spirit, saying to it, "Spirit—mute and deaf—I charge you, come forth out of him, and you may no longer enter into him"; ²⁶ and having cried, and convulsed him much, it came forth, and he became as dead, so that many said that he was dead, ²⁷ but Jesus, having taken him by the hand, lifted him up, and he arose. ²⁸ And He having come into the house, His disciples were questioning Him by Himself, "Why were we not able to cast it forth?" ²⁹ And He said to them, "This kind is able to come forth with nothing except with prayer and fasting." ³⁰ And having gone forth there, they were passing through Galilee, and He did not wish that any may know, ³¹ for He was teaching His disciples, and He said to them, "The Son of Man is being delivered into the hands of men, and they will kill Him, and having been killed, the third day He will rise," ³² but they were not understanding the saying, and they were afraid to question Him. ³³ And He came to Capernaum, and being in the house, He was questioning them, "What were you reasoning in the way among yourselves?" ³⁴ and they were silent, for they reasoned with one another in the way who is greater; ³⁵ and having sat down He called the Twelve, and He says to them, "If any wills to be first, he will be last of all, and minister of all." ³⁶ And having taken a child, He set him in the midst of them, and having taken him in His arms, said to them, ³⁷ "Whoever may receive one of such children in My Name, receives Me, and whoever may receive Me, does not receive Me, but Him who sent Me." ³⁸ And John answered Him, saying, "Teacher, we saw a certain one casting out demons in Your Name, who does not follow us, and we forbade him, because he does not follow us." ³⁹ And Jesus said, "Do not forbid him, for there is no one who will do a mighty work in My Name, and will be readily able to speak evil of Me: ⁴⁰ for he who is not against us is for us; ⁴¹ for whoever may give you to drink a cup of water in My Name, because you are Christ's, truly I say to you, he may not lose his reward; ⁴² and whoever may cause to stumble one of the little ones believing in Me, better is it for him if a millstone is hanged around his neck, and he has been cast into the sea. ⁴³ And if your hand may cause you to stumble, cut it off; it is better for you to enter into life maimed, than having the two hands, to go away into Gehenna, into the fire—the unquenchable— ⁴⁴ [[where their worm is not dying, and the fire is not being quenched.]] ⁴⁵ And if your foot may cause you to stumble, cut it off; it is better for you to enter into life lame, than having the two feet to be cast into Gehenna, into the fire—the unquenchable— ⁴⁶ [[where their worm is not dying, and the fire is not being quenched.]] ⁴⁷ And if your eye may cause you to stumble, cast it out; it is better for you to enter into the Kingdom of God one-eyed, than having two eyes, to be cast into the Gehenna of fire— ⁴⁸ where their worm is not dying, and the fire is not being quenched; ⁴⁹ for everyone will be salted with fire, and every sacrifice will be salted with salt. ⁵⁰ The salt [is] good, but if the salt may become saltless, in what will you season [it]? Have in yourselves salt, and have peace in one another."

CHAPTER 10

¹ And having risen from there, He comes to the coasts of Judea, through the other side of the Jordan, and again multitudes come together to Him, and as He had been accustomed, again He was teaching them. ² And the Pharisees, having come near, questioned Him if it is lawful for a husband to put away a wife, tempting Him, ³ and He answering said to them, "What did Moses command you?" ⁴ and they said, "Moses permitted to write a bill of divorce, and to put away." ⁵ And Jesus answering said to them, "For the stiffness of your heart he wrote you this command, ⁶ but from the beginning of the creation God made them a male and a female; ⁷ on this account will a man leave his father and mother, and will cleave to his wife, ⁸ and they will be—the two—for one flesh, so that they are no longer two, but one flesh; ⁹ what God therefore joined together, do not let man separate." ¹⁰ And in the house His disciples again questioned Him of the same thing, ¹¹ and He says to them, "Whoever may put away his wife, and may marry another, commits adultery against her; ¹² and if a woman may put away her husband, and is married to another, she commits adultery." ¹³ And they were bringing to Him children that He might touch them, and the disciples were rebuking those bringing them, ¹⁴ and Jesus having seen, was much displeased,

and He said to them, "Permit the children to come to Me, and do not forbid them, for of such is the Kingdom of God; ¹⁵ truly I say to you, whoever may not receive the Kingdom of God as a child—he may not enter into it"; ¹⁶ and having taken them in His arms, having put [His] hands on them, He was blessing them. ¹⁷ And as He is going forth into the way, one having run and having kneeled to Him, was questioning Him, "Good Teacher, what may I do that I may inherit continuous life?" ¹⁸ And Jesus said to him, "Why do you call Me good? no one [is] good except one—God; ¹⁹ you have known the commands: You may not commit adultery, You may not murder, You may not steal, You may not bear false witness, You may not defraud, Honor your father and mother." ²⁰ And he answering said to Him, "Teacher, all these I have kept from my youth." ²¹ And Jesus having looked on him, loved him, and said to him, "One thing you lack: go away, whatever you have—sell, and give to the poor, and you will have treasure in Heaven, and come, follow Me, having taken up the cross." ²² And he—gloomy at the word—went away sorrowing, for he was having many possessions. ²³ And Jesus having looked around, says to His disciples, "How hardly will they who have riches enter into the Kingdom of God!" ²⁴ And the disciples were astonished at His words, and Jesus again answering says to them, "Children, how hard it is to those trusting on riches to enter into the Kingdom of God! ²⁵ It is easier for a camel to enter through the eye of the needle, than for a rich man to enter into the Kingdom of God." ²⁶ And they were astonished beyond measure, saying to themselves, "And who is able to be saved?" ²⁷ And Jesus, having looked on them, says, "With men it is impossible, but not with God; for all things are possible with God." ²⁸ And Peter began to say to Him, "Behold, we left all, and we followed You." ²⁹ And Jesus answering said, "Truly I say to you, there is no one who left house, or brothers, or sisters, or father, or mother, or wife, or children, or fields, for My sake, and for the good news', ³⁰ who may not receive a hundredfold now in this time, houses, and brothers, and sisters, and mothers, and children, and fields, with persecutions, and in the age that is coming, continuous life; ³¹ and many first will be last, and the last first." ³² And they were in the way going up to Jerusalem, and Jesus was going before them, and they were amazed, and following they were afraid. And having again taken the Twelve, He began to tell them the things about to happen to Him: ³³ "Behold, we go up to Jerusalem, and the Son of Man will be delivered to the chief priests, and to the scribes, and they will condemn Him to death, and will deliver Him to the nations, ³⁴ and they will mock Him, and scourge Him, and spit on Him, and kill Him, and the third day He will rise again." ³⁵ And there come near to Him James and John, the sons of Zebedee, saying, "Teacher, we wish that whatever we may ask for ourselves, You may do for us"; ³⁶ and He said to them, "What do you wish Me to do for you?" ³⁷ and they said to Him, "Grant to us that, one on Your right hand and one on Your left, we may sit in Your glory"; ³⁸ and Jesus said to them, "You have not known what you ask; are you able to drink of the cup that I drink of, and with the immersion that I am immersed with—to be immersed?" ³⁹ And they said to Him, "We are able"; and Jesus said to them, "Of the cup indeed that I drink of, you will drink, and with the immersion that I am immersed with, you will be immersed; ⁴⁰ but to sit on My right and on My left is not Mine to give, but—to those for whom it has been prepared." ⁴¹ And the ten having heard, began to be much displeased at James and John, ⁴² but Jesus having called them near, says to them, "You have known that they who are considered to rule the nations exercise lordship over them, and their great ones exercise authority on them; ⁴³ but not so will it be among you; but whoever may will to become great among you, he will be your minister, ⁴⁴ and whoever of you may will to become first, he will be servant of all; ⁴⁵ for even the Son of Man did not come to be ministered to, but to minister, and to give His life [as] a ransom for many." ⁴⁶ And they come to Jericho, and as He is going forth from Jericho with His disciples and a great multitude, a son of Timaeus—Bartimaeus the blind—was sitting beside the way begging, ⁴⁷ and having heard that it is Jesus the Nazarene, he began to cry out, and to say, "The Son of David—Jesus! Deal kindly with me"; ⁴⁸ and many were rebuking him that he might keep silent, but the more abundantly he cried out, "Son of David, deal kindly with me." ⁴⁹ And Jesus having stood, He commanded him to be called, and they call the blind man, saying to him, "Take courage, rise, He calls you"; ⁵⁰ and he, having cast away his garment, having risen, came to Jesus. ⁵¹ And answering, Jesus says to him, "What do you will I may do to you?" And the blind man said to

Him, "Rabboni, that I may see again"; ⁵² and Jesus said to him, "Go, your faith has saved you": and immediately he saw again, and was following Jesus in the way.

CHAPTER 11

¹ And when they come near to Jerusalem, to Bethphage, and Bethany, to the Mount of Olives, He sends forth two of His disciples, ² and says to them, "Go away into the village that is in front of you, and immediately, entering into it, you will find a colt tied, on which no one of men has sat, having loosed it, bring [it]: ³ and if anyone may say to you, Why do you do this? say that the Lord has need of it, and immediately He will send it here." ⁴ And they went away, and found the colt tied at the door outside, by the two ways, and they loose it, ⁵ and certain of those standing there said to them, "What do you—losing the colt?" ⁶ and they said to them as Jesus commanded, and they permitted them. ⁷ And they brought the colt to Jesus, and cast their garments on it, and He sat on it, ⁸ and many spread their garments in the way, and others were cutting down branches from the trees, and were strewing in the way. ⁹ And those going before and those following were crying out, saying, "Hosanna! Blessed [is] He who is coming in the Name of the Lord; ¹⁰ blessed is the coming kingdom, in the Name of the Lord, of our father David; Hosanna in the highest!" ¹¹ And Jesus entered into Jerusalem, and into the temple, and having looked around on all things, it being now evening, He went forth to Bethany with the Twelve. ¹² And on the next day, they having come forth from Bethany, He hungered, ¹³ and having seen a fig tree far off having leaves, He came, if perhaps He will find anything in it, and having come to it, He found nothing except leaves, for it was not a time of figs, ¹⁴ and Jesus answering said to it, "No longer from you—throughout the age—may any eat fruit"; and His disciples were hearing. ¹⁵ And they come to Jerusalem, and Jesus having gone into the temple, began to cast forth those selling and buying in the temple, and He overthrew the tables of the money-changers and the seats of those selling the doves, ¹⁶ and He did not permit that any might carry a vessel through the temple, ¹⁷ and He was teaching, saying to them, "Has it not been written: My house will be called a house of prayer for all the nations? And you made it a den of robbers!" ¹⁸ And the scribes and the chief priests heard, and they were seeking how they will destroy Him, for they were afraid of Him, because all the multitude was astonished at His teaching; ¹⁹ and when evening came, He was going forth outside the city. ²⁰ And in the morning, passing by, they saw the fig tree having been dried up from the roots, ²¹ and Peter having remembered says to Him, "Rabbi, behold, the fig tree that You cursed is dried up." ²² And Jesus answering says to them, "Have faith from God; ²³ for truly I say to you that whoever may say to this mountain, Be taken up, and be cast into the sea, and may not doubt in his heart, but may believe that the things that he says come to pass, it will be to him whatever he may say. ²⁴ Because of this I say to you, all whatever—praying—you ask, believe that you receive, and it will be to you. ²⁵ And whenever you may stand praying, forgive, if you have anything against anyone, that your Father who is in the heavens may also forgive you your trespasses; ²⁶ [[and, if you do not forgive, neither will your Father who is in the heavens forgive your trespasses."]] ²⁷ And they come again to Jerusalem, and in the temple, as He is walking, there come to Him the chief priests, and the scribes, and the elders, ²⁸ and they say to Him, "By what authority do You do these things? and who gave You this authority that You may do these things?" ²⁹ And Jesus answering said to them, "I will question you—I also—one word; and answer Me, and I will tell you by what authority I do these things; ³⁰ the immersion of John—was it from Heaven or from men? answer Me." ³¹ And they were reasoning with themselves, saying, "If we may say, From Heaven, He will say, Why then did you not believe him? ³² But if we may say, From men..." They were fearing the people, for all were holding that John was indeed a prophet; ³³ and answering they say to Jesus, "We have not known"; and Jesus answering says to them, "Neither do I tell you by what authority I do these things."

CHAPTER 12

¹ And He began to speak to them in allegories: "A man planted a vineyard, and put a hedge around, and dug a wine vat, and built a tower, and gave it out to farmers, and went abroad; ² and he sent to the farmers at the due time a servant, that from the farmers he may receive from the fruit of the vineyard, ³ and they, having taken him, severely beat [him], and sent him away empty. ⁴ And again he sent to them another servant, and having cast stones at that one, they wounded [him] in the head, and sent [him] away—dishonored. ⁵ And again he sent another, and that one they killed; and many others, some beating, and some killing. ⁶ Having yet therefore one son—his beloved—he also sent him to them last, saying, They will respect my son; ⁷ and those farmers said among themselves, This is the heir, come, we may kill him, and the inheritance will be ours; ⁸ and having taken him, they killed, and cast [him] forth outside the vineyard. ⁹ What therefore will the lord of the vineyard do? he will come and destroy the farmers, and will give the vineyard to others. ¹⁰ And this Writing you did not read: A stone that the builders rejected, it became the head of a corner; ¹¹ this was from the Lord, and it is wonderful in our eyes." ¹² And they were seeking to lay hold on Him, and they feared the multitude, for they knew that He spoke the allegory against them, and having left Him, they went away; ¹³ and they send to Him certain of the Pharisees and of the Herodians, that they may ensnare Him in discourse, ¹⁴ and they having come, say to Him, "Teacher, we have known that You are true, and You are not caring for anyone, for You do not look to the face of men, but in truth teach the way of God; is it lawful to give tribute to Caesar or not? may we give, or may we not give?" ¹⁵ And He, knowing their hypocrisy, said to them, "Why do you tempt Me? bring Me a denarius, that I may see"; ¹⁶ and they brought, and He says to them, "Whose [is] this image, and the inscription?" And they said to Him, "Caesar's"; ¹⁷ and Jesus answering said to them, "Give back the things of Caesar to Caesar, and the things of God to God"; and they wondered at Him. ¹⁸ And the Sadducees come to Him, who say there is not a resurrection, and they questioned Him, saying, ¹⁹ "Teacher, Moses wrote to us that if anyone's brother may die, and may leave a wife, and may leave no children, that his brother may take his wife, and raise up seed to his brother. ²⁰ There were then seven brothers, and the first took a wife, and dying, he left no seed; ²¹ and the second took her, and died, not having left seed, and the third in like manner, ²² and the seven took her, and left no seed, last of all the woman also died; ²³ in the resurrection, then, whenever they may rise, of which of them will she be wife—for the seven had her as wife?" ²⁴ And Jesus answering said to them, "Do you not go astray because of this, not knowing the Writings, nor the power of God? ²⁵ for when they may rise out of the dead, they neither marry nor are they given in marriage, but are as messengers who are in the heavens. ²⁶ And concerning the dead, that they rise: have you not read in the Scroll of Moses (at the bush), how God spoke to him, saying, I [am] the God of Abraham, and the God of Isaac, and the God of Jacob; ²⁷ He is not the God of dead men, but a God of living men; you then go greatly astray." ²⁸ And one of the scribes having come near, having heard them disputing, knowing that He answered them well, questioned Him, "Which is the first command of all?" ²⁹ and Jesus answered him, "The first of all the commands—Hear, O Israel: The Lord is our God, the Lord is one; ³⁰ and you will love the Lord your God out of all your heart, and out of all your soul, and out of all your understanding, and out of all your strength—this [is] the first command; ³¹ and the second [is] like [it], this, You will love your neighbor as yourself—there is no other command greater than these." ³² And the scribe said to Him, "Well, Teacher, in truth You have spoken that there is one God, and there is none other but He; ³³ and to love Him out of all the heart, and out of all the understanding, and out of all the soul, and out of all the strength, and to love one's neighbor as one's self, is more than all the whole burnt-offerings and the sacrifices." ³⁴ And Jesus, having seen him that he answered with understanding, said to him, "You are not far from the Kingdom of God"; and no one dared question Him anymore. ³⁵ And Jesus answering said, teaching in the temple, "How do the scribes say that the Christ is son of David? ³⁶ for David himself said in the Holy Spirit, The Lord said to my Lord, || Sit on My right hand, || Until I place Your enemies—Your footstool; ³⁷ therefore David himself calls Him Lord, and from where is He his son?" And the great multitude were hearing Him gladly, ³⁸ and He was saying to them in His teaching, "Beware of the scribes who will to walk in long robes, and love salutations in the marketplaces, ³⁹ and first seats in the synagogues, and first couches at the banquets, ⁴⁰ who are devouring the widows' houses, and for a pretense are making long prayers; these will

receive more abundant judgment." **41** And Jesus having sat down opposite the treasury, was beholding how the multitude puts brass into the treasury, and many rich were putting in much, **42** and having come, a poor widow put in two mites, which are a penny. **43** And having called near His disciples, He says to them, "Truly I say to you that this poor widow has put in more than all those putting into the treasury; **44** for all, out of their abundance, put in, but she, out of her want, put in all that she had—all her living."

CHAPTER 13

1 And as He is going forth out of the temple, one of His disciples says to Him, "Teacher, see! What stones! And what buildings!" **2** and Jesus answering said to him, "See these great buildings? there may not be left a stone on a stone that may not be thrown down." **3** And as He is sitting at the Mount of Olives, opposite the temple, Peter, and James, and John, and Andrew, were questioning Him by Himself, **4** "Tell us when these things will be? and what [is] the sign when all these may be about to be fulfilled?" **5** And Jesus answering them, began to say, "Take heed lest anyone may lead you astray, **6** for many will come in My Name, saying, I am [He], and many they will lead astray; **7** and when you may hear of wars and reports of wars, do not be troubled, for these ought to be, but the end [is] not yet; **8** for nation will rise against nation, and kingdom against kingdom, and there will be earthquakes in various places, and there will be famines and troubles; these [are the] beginning of travails. **9** And take heed to yourselves, for they will deliver you up to Sanhedrins, and to synagogues, you will be beaten, and before governors and kings you will be set for My sake, for a testimony to them; **10** and to all the nations it is first necessary that the good news be proclaimed. **11** And when they may lead you, delivering up, do not be anxious beforehand what you may speak, nor premeditate, but whatever may be given to you in that hour, that speak, for it is not you who are speaking, but the Holy Spirit. **12** And brother will deliver up brother to death, and father child, and children will rise up against parents, and will put them to death, **13** and you will be hated by all because of My Name, but he who has endured to the end—he will be saved. **14** And when you may see the abomination of the desolation, that was spoken of by Daniel the prophet, standing where it should not (whoever is reading let him understand), then those in Judea, let them flee to the mountains; **15** and he on the housetop, do not let him come down into the house, nor come in to take anything out of his house; **16** and he who is in the field, do not let him turn to the things behind, to take up his garment. **17** And woe to those with child, and to those giving suck, in those days; **18** and pray that your flight may not be in winter, **19** for those days will be tribulation, such as has not been from the beginning of the creation that God created, until now, and may not be [again]; **20** and if the Lord did not shorten the days, no flesh had been saved; but because of the chosen, whom He chose to Himself, He shortened the days. **21** And then, if any may say to you, Behold, here [is] the Christ, or, Behold, there, you may not believe; **22** for there will rise false Christs and false prophets, and they will give signs and wonders, to seduce, if possible, also the chosen; **23** and you, take heed; behold, I have foretold you all things. **24** But in those days, after that tribulation, the sun will be darkened, and the moon will not give her light, **25** and the stars of the sky will be falling, and the powers that are in the heavens will be shaken. **26** And then they will see the Son of Man coming in clouds with much power and glory, **27** and then He will send His messengers, and gather together His chosen from the four winds, from the end of the earth to the end of heaven. **28** And from the fig tree learn the allegory: when the branch may already become tender, and may put forth the leaves, you know that the summer is near; **29** so you, also, when you may see these coming to pass, you know that it is near, at the doors. **30** Truly I say to you that this generation may not pass away until all these things may come to pass; **31** the heaven and the earth will pass away, but My words will not pass away. **32** And concerning that day and the hour no one has known—not even the messengers who are in Heaven, not even the Son—except the Father. **33** Take heed, watch and pray, for you have not known when the time is; **34** as a man who is gone abroad, having left his house, and given to his servants the authority, and to each one his work, also commanded the doorkeeper that he may watch; **35** watch, therefore, for you have not known when the lord of the house comes, at evening, or at midnight, or at rooster-crowing, or at the morning; **36** lest, having come suddenly, he may find you sleeping; **37** and what I say to you, I say to all, Watch!"

CHAPTER 14

1 And the Passover and the Unleavened [Bread] were after two days, and the chief priests and the scribes were seeking how, by guile, having taken hold of Him, they might kill Him; **2** and they said, "Not in the celebration, lest there will be a tumult of the people." **3** And He, being in Bethany, in the house of Simon the leper, at His reclining, there came a woman having an alabaster box of ointment, of spikenard, very precious, and having broken the alabaster box, poured [it] on His head; **4** and there were certain much displeased within themselves, and saying, "For what has this waste of the ointment been made? **5** for this could have been sold for more than three hundred denarii, and given to the poor"; and they were murmuring at her. **6** And Jesus said, "Leave her alone; why are you giving her trouble? She worked a good work on Me; **7** for you always have the poor with you, and whenever you may will you are able to do them good, but you do not always have Me; **8** she did what she could, she anticipated to anoint My body for the embalming. **9** Truly I say to you, wherever this good news may be proclaimed in the whole world, what this woman did will also be spoken of—for a memorial of her." **10** And Judas the Iscariot, one of the Twelve, went away to the chief priests that he might deliver Him up to them, **11** and having heard, they were glad, and promised to give him money, and he was seeking how, conveniently, he might deliver Him up. **12** And the first day of the Unleavened [Bread], when they were killing the Passover, His disciples say to Him, "Where will You, [that] having gone, we may prepare, that You may eat the Passover?" **13** And He sends forth two of His disciples and says to them, "Go away into the city, and there a man carrying a pitcher of water will meet you, follow him; **14** and wherever he may go in, say to the master of the house: The Teacher says, Where is the guest-chamber, where the Passover, with My disciples, I may eat? **15** and he will show you a large upper room, furnished, prepared—make ready for us there." **16** And His disciples went forth, and came into the city, and found as He said to them, and they made ready the Passover. **17** And evening having come, He comes with the Twelve, **18** and as they are reclining, and eating, Jesus said, "Truly I say to you that one of you who is eating with Me will deliver Me up." **19** And they began to be sorrowful, and to say to Him one by one, "Is it I?" And another, "Is it I?" **20** And He answering said to them, "One of the Twelve who is dipping with Me in the dish; **21** the Son of Man indeed goes, as it has been written concerning Him, but woe to that man through whom the Son of Man is delivered up; it were good to him if that man had not been born." **22** And as they are eating, Jesus having taken bread, having blessed, broke, and gave to them, and said, "Take, eat; this is My body." **23** And having taken the cup, having given thanks, He gave to them, and they drank of it—all; **24** and He said to them, "This is My blood of the New Covenant, which is being poured out for many; **25** truly I say to you that I may drink no more of the produce of the vine until that day when I may drink it new in the Kingdom of God." **26** And having sung a hymn, they went forth to the Mount of Olives, **27** and Jesus says to them, "All of you will be stumbled at Me this night, because it has been written: I will strike the Shepherd, and the sheep will be scattered abroad; **28** but after My having risen I will go before you to Galilee." **29** And Peter said to Him, "And if all will be stumbled, yet not I." **30** And Jesus said to him, "Truly I say to you that today, this night, before a rooster will crow twice, three times you will deny Me." **31** And he spoke the more vehemently, "If it may be necessary for me to die with You—I will in no way deny You"; and in like manner also said they all. **32** And they come to a spot, the name of which [is] Gethsemane, and He says to His disciples, "Sit here until I may pray"; **33** and He takes Peter, and James, and John with Him, and began to be amazed, and to be very heavy, **34** and He says to them, "My soul is exceedingly sorrowful—to death; remain here, and watch." **35** And having gone forward a little, He fell on the earth, and was praying that, if it be possible, the hour may pass from Him, **36** and He said, "Abba, Father; all things are possible to You; make this cup pass from Me; but not what I will, but what You [will]." **37** And He comes, and finds them sleeping, and says to Peter, "Simon, you sleep! You were not able to watch one hour! **38** Watch and pray, that you may not enter into temptation; the spirit indeed is forward, but the flesh weak." **39** And again having gone away, He prayed, saying the same word; **40** and having returned, He found them sleeping again, for their eyes were heavy, and they had not known what they might answer Him. **41** And He comes the third time and says to them, "Sleep on from now on, and rest—it is over; the hour came; behold, the Son of Man is delivered up into the hands of the sinful; **42** rise, we may go, behold, he who is delivering Me up has come near." **43** And immediately—while He is yet speaking—Judas comes near, one of the Twelve, and with him a great multitude with swords and sticks, from the chief priests, and the scribes, and the elders; **44** and he who is delivering Him up had given a token to them, saying, "Whomsoever I will kiss, it is He, lay hold on Him, and lead Him away safely," **45** and having come, immediately, having gone near Him, he says, "Rabbi, Rabbi," and kissed Him. **46** And they laid on Him their hands, and kept hold on Him; **47** and a certain one of those standing by, having drawn the sword, struck the servant of the chief priest, and took off his ear. **48** And Jesus answering said to them, "As against a robber you came out, with swords and sticks, to take Me! **49** daily I was with you teaching in the temple, and you did not lay hold on Me—but that the Writings may be fulfilled." **50** And having left Him they all fled; **51** and a certain young man was following Him, having cast a linen cloth on [his] naked [body], and the young men lay hold on him, **52** and he, having left the linen cloth, fled from them naked. **53** And they led Jesus away to the chief priest, and all the chief priests, and the elders, and the scribes come together; **54** and Peter followed Him far off, to the inside of the hall of the chief priest, and he was sitting with the officers, and warming himself near the fire. **55** And the chief priests and all the Sanhedrin were seeking testimony against Jesus—to put Him to death, and they were not finding, **56** for many were bearing false testimony against Him, and their testimonies were not alike. **57** And certain having risen up, were bearing false testimony against Him, saying, **58** "We heard Him saying, I will throw down this temple made with hands, and by three days, I will build another made without hands"; **59** and neither so was their testimony alike. **60** And the chief priest, having risen up in the midst, questioned Jesus, saying, "You do not answer anything! Why do these testify against You?" **61** and He was keeping silent and did not answer anything. Again the chief priest was questioning Him and says to Him, "Are You the Christ—the Son of the Blessed?" **62** and Jesus said, "I am; and you will see the Son of Man sitting on the right hand of the Power and coming with the clouds of Heaven." **63** And the chief priest, having torn his garments, says, "What need have we yet of witnesses? **64** You heard the slander, what appears to you?" And they all condemned Him to be worthy of death, **65** and certain began to spit on Him, and to cover His face, and to punch Him, and to say to Him, "Prophesy"; and the officers were striking Him with their palms. **66** And Peter being in the hall beneath, there comes one of the maids of the chief priest, **67** and having seen Peter warming himself, having looked on him, she said, "And you were with Jesus of Nazareth!" **68** and he denied, saying, "I have not known [Him], neither do I understand what you say"; and he went forth outside to the porch, and a rooster crowed. **69** And the maid having seen him again, began to say to those standing near, "This is of them"; **70** and he was again denying. And after a while again, those standing near said to Peter, "Truly you are of them, for you also are a Galilean, and your speech is alike"; **71** and he began to curse, and to swear, "I have not known this Man of whom you speak"; **72** and a second time a rooster crowed, and Peter remembered the saying that Jesus said to him, "Before a rooster crow twice, you may deny Me three times"; and having thought thereon—he was weeping.

CHAPTER 15

1 And immediately, in the morning, the chief priests having made a consultation with the elders, and scribes, and the whole Sanhedrin, having bound Jesus, led [Him] away, and delivered [Him] to Pilate; **2** and Pilate questioned Him, "Are You the King of the Jews?" And He answering said to him, "You say [it]." **3** And the chief priests were accusing Him of many things, [but He answered nothing.] **4** And Pilate again questioned Him, saying, "You do not answer anything? behold, how many things they testify against You!" **5** and Jesus no longer answered anything, so that Pilate wondered. **6** And at every celebration he was releasing to them one prisoner, whomsoever they were asking for; **7** and there was [one] named Barabbas, bound with

those making insurrection with him, who had committed murder in the insurrection. **8** And the multitude having cried out, began to ask for themselves as he was always doing to them, **9** and Pilate answered them, saying, "Will you [that] I will release to you the King of the Jews?" **10** for he knew that the chief priests had delivered Him up because of envy; **11** and the chief priests moved the multitude that he might rather release Barabbas to them. **12** And Pilate answering, again said to them, "What, then, will you [that] I will do to Him whom you call King of the Jews?" **13** and they again cried out, "Crucify Him!" **14** And Pilate said to them, "Why—what evil did He do?" And they cried out the more vehemently, "Crucify Him!" **15** And Pilate, resolving to do that which [was] satisfactory to the multitude, released Barabbas to them, and delivered up Jesus—having scourged [Him]—that He might be crucified. **16** And the soldiers led Him away into the hall, which is [the] Praetorium, and call together the whole band, **17** and clothe Him with purple, and having plaited a garland of thorns, they put [it] on Him, **18** and began to greet Him, "Hail, King of the Jews!" **19** And they were striking Him on the head with a reed, and were spitting on Him, and having bent the knee, were prostrating to Him, **20** and when they [had] mocked Him, they took the purple from off Him, and clothed Him in His own garments, and they led Him forth, that they may crucify Him. **21** And they impress a certain one passing by—Simon, a Cyrenian, coming from the field, the father of Alexander and Rufus—that he may carry His cross, **22** and they bring Him to the place [called] Golgotha, which is, being interpreted, "Place of [the] Skull"; **23** and they were giving Him wine mingled with myrrh to drink, and He did not receive [it]. **24** And having crucified Him, they were dividing His garments, casting a lot on them, what each may take; **25** and it was the third hour, and they crucified Him; **26** and the inscription of His accusation was written above: "The King of the Jews." **27** And they crucify two robbers with Him, one on the right hand and one on His left, **28** [[and the Writing was fulfilled that is saying, "And He was numbered with lawless ones."]] **29** And those passing by were slandering Him, shaking their heads, and saying, "Ha! The [One] throwing down the temple, and building [it] in three days! **30** save Yourself, and come down from the cross!" **31** And in like manner also the chief priests, mocking with one another, with the scribes, said, "He saved others; He is not able to save Himself. **32** The Christ! The King of Israel—let Him come down now from the cross, that we may see and believe"; and those crucified with Him were reproaching Him. **33** And the sixth hour having come, darkness came over the whole land until the ninth hour, **34** and at the ninth hour Jesus cried with a great voice, saying, "Eloi, Eloi, lamma sabachthani?" Which is, being interpreted, "My God, My God, why did You forsake Me?" **35** And certain of those standing by, having heard, said, "Behold, He calls Elijah"; **36** and one having run, and having filled a sponge with vinegar, having also put [it] on a reed, was giving Him to drink, saying, "Let alone, let us see if Elijah comes to take Him down." **37** And Jesus having uttered a loud cry, yielded the spirit, **38** and the veil of the temple was torn in two from top to bottom, **39** and the centurion who was standing opposite Him, having seen that, having so cried out, He yielded the spirit, said, "Truly this Man was [the] Son of God." **40** And there were also women beholding far off, among whom was also Mary the Magdalene, and Mary of James the less, and of Joses, and Salome, **41** who also, when He was in Galilee, were following Him and were ministering to Him, and many other women who came up with Him to Jerusalem. **42** And now evening having come, seeing it was the Preparation, that is, before Sabbath, **43** Joseph of Arimathea, an honorable counselor, who also himself was waiting for the Kingdom of God, came, boldly entered in to Pilate, and asked for the body of Jesus. **44** And Pilate wondered if He were already dead, and having called near the centurion, questioned him if He were long dead, **45** and having known [it] from the centurion, he granted the body to Joseph. **46** And he, having brought fine linen, and having taken Him down, wrapped Him in the linen, and laid Him in a tomb that had been hewn out of a rock, and he rolled a stone to the door of the tomb, **47** and Mary the Magdalene, and Mary of Joses, were beholding where He is laid.

CHAPTER 16

1 And the Sabbath having past, Mary the Magdalene, and Mary of James, and Salome, bought spices, that having come, they may anoint Him, **2** and early in the morning of the first

[day] of the weeks, they come to the tomb, at the rising of the sun, **3** and they said among themselves, "Who will roll away the stone out of the door of the tomb for us?" **4** And having looked, they see that the stone has been rolled away—for it was very great, **5** and having entered into the tomb, they saw a young man sitting on the right hand, clothed in a long white robe, and they were amazed. **6** And he says to them, "Do not be amazed, you seek Jesus the Nazarene, the crucified [One]: He rose—He is not here; behold the place where they laid Him! **7** and go, say to His disciples and Peter that He goes before you to Galilee; there you will see Him, as He said to you." **8** And having come forth quickly, they fled from the tomb, and trembling and amazement had seized them, and they said to no one anything, for they were afraid. [[**9** And He, having risen in the morning of the first of the week, appeared first to Mary the Magdalene, out of whom He had cast seven demons; **10** she having gone, told those who had been with Him, mourning and weeping; **11** and they, having heard that He is alive, and was seen by her, did not believe. **12** And after these things, to two of them, as they are going into a field, walking, He appeared in another form, **13** and they having gone, told [it] to the rest; not even them did they believe. **14** Afterward, as they are reclining, He appeared to the Eleven, and reproached their unbelief and stiffness of heart, because they did not believe those having seen Him being raised; **15** and He said to them, "Having gone into all the world, proclaim the good news to all the creation; **16** he who has believed and has been immersed will be saved; and he who has not believed will be condemned. **17** And signs will accompany those believing these things: they will cast out demons in My Name; they will speak with new tongues; **18** they will take up serpents; and if they may drink any deadly thing, it will not hurt them; they will lay hands on the ailing, and they will be well." **19** The Lord, then, indeed, after speaking to them, was received up to Heaven, and sat on the right hand of God; **20** and they, having gone forth, preached everywhere, the Lord working with [them], and confirming the word, through the signs following. Amen.

LUKE

CHAPTER 1

1 Seeing that many took in hand to set in order a narration of the matters that have been fully assured among us, **2** as they delivered to us, who from the beginning became eyewitnesses, and officers of the word, **3** it seemed good also to me, having followed from the first after all things exactly, to write to you in order, most noble Theophilus, **4** that you may know the certainty of the things wherein you were instructed. **5** There was in the days of Herod, the king of Judea, a certain priest, by name Zacharias, of the division of Abijah, and his wife of the daughters of Aaron, and her name Elizabeth; **6** and they were both righteous before God, going on in all the commands and righteousnesses of the Lord blameless, **7** and they had no child, because that Elizabeth was barren, and both were advanced in their days. **8** And it came to pass, in his acting as priest, in the order of his division before God, **9** according to the custom of the priesthood, his lot was to make incense, having gone into the temple of the Lord, **10** and all the multitude of the people were praying outside, at the hour of the incense. **11** And there appeared to him a messenger of the Lord standing on the right side of the altar of the incense, **12** and Zacharias, having seen, was troubled, and fear fell on him; **13** and the messenger said to him, "Do not fear, Zacharias, for your supplication was heard, and your wife Elizabeth will bear a son to you, and you will call his name John, **14** and there will be joy to you, and gladness, and many will rejoice at his birth, **15** for he will be great before the Lord, and wine and strong drink he may not drink, and he will be full of the Holy Spirit, even from his mother's womb; **16** and he will turn many of the sons of Israel to the Lord their God, **17** and he will go before Him, in the spirit and power of Elijah, to turn hearts of fathers to children, and disobedient ones to the wisdom of righteous ones, to make ready for the Lord, a people prepared." **18** And Zacharias said to the messenger, "Whereby will I know this? for I am aged, and my wife is advanced in her days?" **19** And the messenger answering said to him, "I am Gabriel, who has been standing near before God, and I was sent to speak to you,

and to proclaim this good news to you, **20** and behold, you will be silent, and not able to speak, until the day that these things will come to pass, because you did not believe my words that will be fulfilled in their season." **21** And the people were waiting for Zacharias, and wondering at his lingering in the temple, **22** and having come out, he was not able to speak to them, and they perceived that he had seen a vision in the temple, and he was beckoning to them, and remained mute. **23** And it came to pass, when the days of his service were fulfilled, he went away to his house, **24** and after those days, his wife Elizabeth conceived, and hid herself five months, saying, **25** "Thus the Lord has done to me, in days in which He looked on [me], to take away my reproach among men." **26** And in the sixth month the messenger Gabriel was sent by God, to a city of Galilee, the name of which [is] Nazareth, **27** to a virgin, betrothed to a man, whose name [is] Joseph, of the house of David, and the name of the virgin [is] Mary. **28** And the messenger having come in to her, said, "Greetings, favored one, the Lord [is] with you; blessed [are] you among women"; **29** and she, having seen, was troubled at his word, and was reasoning of what kind this salutation may be. **30** And the messenger said to her, "Do not fear, Mary, for you have found favor with God; **31** and behold, you will conceive in the womb, and will bring forth a Son, and call His Name Jesus; **32** He will be great, and He will be called Son of the Highest, and the Lord God will give Him the throne of His father David, **33** and He will reign over the house of Jacob for all ages; and of His kingdom there will be no end." **34** And Mary said to the messenger, "How will this be, seeing I do not know a husband?" **35** And the messenger answering said to her, "The Holy Spirit will come on you, and the power of the Highest will overshadow you, therefore also the holy-begotten thing will be called Son of God; **36** and behold, Elizabeth, your relative, she also has conceived a son in her old age, and this is the sixth month to her who was called barren; **37** because nothing will be impossible with God." **38** And Mary said, "Behold, the maidservant of the Lord; let it be to me according to your saying," and the messenger went away from her. **39** And Mary having arisen in those days, went into the hill-country, with haste, to a city of Judea, **40** and entered into the house of Zacharias, and greeted Elizabeth. **41** And it came to pass, when Elizabeth heard the salutation of Mary, the baby leapt in her womb; and Elizabeth was filled with the Holy Spirit, **42** and spoke out with a loud voice and said, "Blessed [are] you among women, and blessed [is] the Fruit of your womb; **43** and from where [is] this to me, that the mother of my Lord might come to me? **44** For behold, when the voice of your salutation came to my ears, the baby in my womb leapt in gladness; **45** and blessed [is] she who believed, for there will be a completion to the things spoken to her from the Lord." **46** And Mary said, "My soul magnifies the Lord, **47** And my spirit was glad on God my Savior, **48** Because He looked on the lowliness of His maidservant, || For behold, from now on all the generations will call me blessed, **49** For He who is mighty did great things to me, || And holy [is] His Name, **50** And His kindness [is] to generations of generations, || To those fearing Him; **51** He did powerfully with His arm, || He scattered abroad the proud in the thought of their heart, **52** He brought down the mighty from thrones, || And He exalted the lowly, **53** He filled the hungry with good, || And the rich He sent away empty; **54** He has taken hold of His servant Israel, || To remember kindness, **55** As He spoke to our fathers, || To Abraham and to his seed—throughout the age." **56** And Mary remained with her about three months, and turned back to her house. **57** And to Elizabeth was the time fulfilled for her bringing forth, and she bore a son, **58** and the neighbors and her relatives heard that the Lord was making His kindness great with her, and they were rejoicing with her. **59** And it came to pass, on the eighth day, they came to circumcise the child, and they were calling him by the name of his father, Zacharias, **60** and his mother answering said, "No, but he will be called John." **61** And they said to her, "There is none among your relatives who is called by this name," **62** and they were making signs to his father, what he would wish him to be called, **63** and having asked for a tablet, he wrote, saying, "John is his name"; and they all wondered; **64** and his mouth was opened immediately, and his tongue, and he was speaking, praising God. **65** And fear came on all those dwelling around them, and in all the hill-country of Judea were all these sayings spoken of, **66** and all who heard laid them up in their hearts, saying, "What then will this child be?" And the hand of the Lord was with him. **67** And his father Zacharias was filled with the Holy Spirit, and prophesied, saying, **68** "Blessed [is] the Lord, the God of Israel, || Because

He looked on, || And worked redemption for His people, **69** And raised a horn of salvation to us, || In the house of His servant David, **70** As He spoke by the mouth of His holy prophets, || Which have been from the age; **71** Salvation from our enemies, || And out of the hand of all hating us, **72** To do kindness with our fathers, || And to be mindful of His holy covenant, **73** An oath that He swore to Abraham our father, **74** To give to us, without fear, || Having been delivered out of the hand of our enemies, **75** To serve Him, in holiness and righteousness || Before Him, all the days of our life. **76** And you, child, || Prophet of the Highest will you be called; For you will go before the face of the Lord, || To prepare His ways. **77** To give knowledge of salvation to His people || In forgiveness of their sins, **78** Through the yearnings of our God, || In which the rising from on high looked on us, **79** To give light to those sitting in darkness and death-shade, || To guide our feet to a way of peace." **80** And the child grew, and was strengthened in spirit, and he was in the deserts until the day of his showing to Israel.

CHAPTER 2

1 And it came to pass in those days, there went forth a decree from Caesar Augustus that all the world be registered— **2** this census first came to pass when Quirinius was governor of Syria— **3** and all were going to be registered, each to his proper city, **4** and Joseph also went up from Galilee, out of the city of Nazareth, to Judea, to the city of David, that is called Beth-Lehem, because of his being of the house and family of David, **5** to register himself with Mary his betrothed wife, being with Child. **6** And it came to pass, in their being there, the days were fulfilled for her bringing forth, **7** and she brought forth her Son—the firstborn, and wrapped Him up, and laid Him down in the manger, because there was not a place for them in the guest-chamber. **8** And there were shepherds in the same region, lodging in the field and keeping the night-watches over their flock, **9** and behold, a messenger of the Lord stood over them, and the glory of the Lord shone around them, and they feared [with] a great fear. **10** And the messenger said to them, "Do not fear, for behold, I bring you good news of great joy that will be to all the people, **11** because today in the city of David a Savior was born to you, who is Christ the Lord! **12** And this [is] the sign to you: you will find a Baby wrapped up, lying in the manger." **13** And suddenly there came with the messenger a multitude of the heavenly host, praising God, and saying, **14** "Glory in the highest to God, and on earth peace, among men—good will!" **15** And it came to pass, when the messengers were gone away from them to the heavens, that the men, the shepherds, said to one another, "We may indeed go over to Beth-Lehem and see this thing that has come to pass, that the Lord made known to us!" **16** And they came, having hurried, and found both Mary, and Joseph, and the Baby lying in the manger, **17** and having seen, they made known abroad concerning the saying spoken to them concerning the Child. **18** And all who heard [it] wondered concerning the things spoken to them by the shepherds; **19** and Mary was preserving all these things, pondering [them] in her heart; **20** and the shepherds turned back, glorifying and praising God for all those things they heard and saw, as it was spoken to them. **21** And when eight days were fulfilled to circumcise the Child, then was His Name called Jesus, having been so called by the messenger before His being conceived in the womb. **22** And when the days of their purification were fulfilled, according to the Law of Moses, they brought Him up to Jerusalem, to present to the Lord, **23** as it has been written in the Law of the Lord: "Every male opening a womb will be called holy to the Lord," **24** and to give a sacrifice, according to that said in the Law of the Lord: "A pair of turtle-doves, or two young pigeons." **25** And behold, there was a man in Jerusalem whose name [is] Simeon, and this man is righteous and devout, looking for the comforting of Israel, and the Holy Spirit was on him, **26** and it has been divinely told him by the Holy Spirit—not to see death before he may see the Christ of the Lord. **27** And he came in the Spirit into the temple, and in the parents bringing in the child Jesus, for their doing according to the custom of the Law regarding Him, **28** then he took Him in his arms, and blessed God, and he said, **29** "Now You send Your servant away, O Lord, according to Your word, in peace, **30** because my eyes saw Your salvation, **31** which You prepared before the face of all the peoples, **32** a light to the uncovering of nations, and the glory of Your people

Israel." **33** And Joseph and His mother were wondering at the things spoken concerning Him, **34** and Simeon blessed them and said to His mother Mary, "Behold, this [One] is set for the falling and rising again of many in Israel, and for a sign spoken against— **35** (and also a sword will pass through your own soul)—that the reasonings of many hearts may be revealed." **36** And there was Anna, a prophetess, daughter of Phanuel, of the tribe of Asher, she was much advanced in days, having lived with a husband seven years from her virginity, **37** and she [is] a widow of about eighty-four years, who did not depart from the temple, serving with fasts and supplications, night and day, **38** and she, at that hour, having come in, was confessing, likewise, to the Lord, and was speaking concerning Him to all those looking for redemption in Jerusalem. **39** And when they completed all things according to the Law of the Lord, they turned back to Galilee, to their city of Nazareth; **40** and the Child grew and was strengthened in spirit, being filled with wisdom, and the grace of God was on Him. **41** And His parents were going yearly to Jerusalem, at the Celebration of the Passover, **42** and when He became twelve years old, they having gone up to Jerusalem according to the custom of the celebration, **43** and having finished the days, in their returning the child Jesus remained behind in Jerusalem, and Joseph and His mother did not know, **44** and having supposed Him to be in the company, they went a day's journey, and were seeking Him among the relatives and among the acquaintances, **45** and having not found Him, they turned back to Jerusalem seeking Him. **46** And it came to pass, after three days they found Him in the temple, sitting in the midst of the teachers, both hearing them and questioning them, **47** and all those hearing Him were astonished at His understanding and answers. **48** And having seen Him, they were amazed, and His mother said to Him, "Child, why did You do this to us? behold, Your father and I, sorrowing, were seeking You." **49** And He said to them, "Why [is it] that you were seeking Me? did you not know that it is necessary for Me to be in the things of My Father?" **50** and they did not understand the saying that He spoke to them, **51** and He went down with them, and came to Nazareth, and He was subject to them, and His mother was keeping all these sayings in her heart, **52** and Jesus was advancing in wisdom, and in stature, and in favor with God and men.

CHAPTER 3

1 And in the fifteenth year of the government of Tiberius Caesar—Pontius Pilate being governor of Judea, and Herod tetrarch of Galilee, and his brother Philip, tetrarch of Ituraea and of the region of Trachonitis, and Lysanias tetrarch of Abilene, **2** [and] Annas and Caiaphas being chief priests—there came a word of God to John the son of Zacharias, in the wilderness, **3** and he came to all the region around the Jordan, proclaiming an immersion of conversion for forgiveness of sins, **4** as it has been written in the scroll of the words of Isaiah the prophet: "A voice of one crying in the wilderness: Prepare the way of the Lord, || Make His paths straight; **5** Every valley will be filled, || And every mountain and hill will be made low, || And the crooked will become straightness, || And the rough become smooth ways; **6** And all flesh will see the salvation of God." **7** Then he said to the multitudes coming forth to be immersed by him, "Brood of vipers! Who prompted you to flee from the coming wrath? **8** make, therefore, fruits worthy of conversion, and do not begin to say within yourselves, We have a father—Abraham; for I say to you that God is able to raise children to Abraham out of these stones; **9** and also the axe is already laid to the root of the trees, every tree, therefore, not making good fruit is cut down, and it is cast into fire." **10** And the multitudes were questioning him, saying, "What, then, will we do?" **11** and he answering says to them, "He having two coats, let him impart to him having none; and he having food, let him do in like manner." **12** And there also came tax collectors to be immersed, and they said to him, "Teacher, what will we do?" **13** and he said to them, "Exact no more than that directed you." **14** And also questioning him were those warring, saying, "And we, what will we do?" And he said to them, "Do violence to no one, nor accuse falsely, and be content with your wages." **15** And the people are looking forward, and all are reasoning in their hearts concerning John, whether or not he may be the Christ; **16** John answered, saying to all, "I indeed immerse you in water, but He comes who is mightier than I, of whom I am not worthy to loose the strap of His sandals—He will immerse you in the Holy Spirit and fire; **17** whose winnowing shovel [is] in His hand, and He will thoroughly cleanse His floor, and will gather the wheat into His storehouse, and He will burn the chaff with unquenchable fire." **18** And therefore, indeed, with many other things, exhorting, he was proclaiming good news to the people, **19** and Herod the tetrarch, being reproved by him concerning Herodias, the wife of his brother Philip, and concerning all the evils that Herod did, **20** added also this to all, that he shut up John in the prison. **21** And it came to pass, in all the people being immersed, Jesus also being immersed, and praying, Heaven was opened, **22** and the Holy Spirit came down in a bodily appearance, as if a dove, on Him, and a voice came out of Heaven, saying, "You are My Son, the Beloved, in You I delighted." **23** And Jesus Himself was beginning to be about thirty years of age, being, as was supposed, Son of Joseph, **24** the [son] of Eli, the [son] of Matthat, the [son] of Levi, the [son] of Melchi, the [son] of Janna, the [son] of Joseph, **25** the [son] of Mattathias, the [son] of Amos, the [son] of Nahum, the [son] of Esli, **26** the [son] of Naggai, the [son] of Maath, the [son] of Mattathias, the [son] of Semei, the [son] of Joseph, the [son] of Judah, **27** the [son] of Joanna, the [son] of Rhesa, the [son] of Zerubbabel, the [son] of Shealtiel, **28** the [son] of Neri, the [son] of Melchi, the [son] of Addi, the [son] of Cosam, the [son] of Elmodam, the [son] of Er, **29** the [son] of Jose, the [son] of Eliezer, the [son] of Jorim, the [son] of Matthat, **30** the [son] of Levi, the [son] of Simeon, the [son] of Judah, the [son] of Joseph, the [son] of Jonan, the [son] of Eliakim, **31** the [son] of Melea, the [son] of Mainan, the [son] of Mattatha, the [son] of Nathan, **32** the [son] of David, the [son] of Jesse, the [son] of Obed, the [son] of Boaz, the [son] of Salmon, the [son] of Nahshon, **33** the [son] of Amminadab, the [son] of Aram, the [son] of Esrom, the [son] of Perez, **34** the [son] of Judah, the [son] of Jacob, the [son] of Isaac, the [son] of Abraham, the [son] of Terah, the [son] of Nahor, **35** the [son] of Serug, the [son] of Reu, the [son] of Peleg, the [son] of Eber, **36** the [son] of Salah, the [son] of Cainan, the [son] of Arphaxad, the [son] of Shem, the [son] of Noah, the [son] of Lamech, **37** the [son] of Methuselah, the [son] of Enoch, the [son] of Jared, the [son] of Mahalaleel, **38** the [son] of Cainan, the [son] of Enos, the [son] of Seth, the [son] of Adam, the [son] of God.

CHAPTER 4

1 And Jesus, full of the Holy Spirit, turned back from the Jordan, and was brought in the Spirit into the wilderness, **2** being tempted by the Devil forty days, and He did not eat anything in those days, and they having been ended, He afterward hungered, **3** and the Devil said to Him, "If You are [the] Son of God, speak to this stone that it may become bread." **4** And Jesus answered him, saying, "It has been written, that, Not on bread only will man live, but on every saying of God." **5** And the Devil having brought Him up to a high mountain, showed to Him all the kingdoms of the world in a moment of time, **6** and the Devil said to Him, "To You I will give all this authority, and their glory, because to me it has been delivered, and to whomsoever I will, I give it; **7** You, then, if You may worship me—all will be Yours." **8** And Jesus answering him said, "[[Get behind Me, Satan, for]] it has been written: You will worship the Lord your God, and Him only you will serve." **9** And he brought Him to Jerusalem, and set Him on the pinnacle of the temple, and said to Him, "If You are the Son of God, cast Yourself down from here, **10** for it has been written: To His messengers He will give charge concerning you, to guard over you; **11** and: On hands they will bear you up, lest at any time you may dash your foot against a stone." **12** And Jesus answering said to him, "It has been said, You will not tempt the Lord your God." **13** And having ended all temptation, the Devil departed from Him until a convenient season. **14** And Jesus turned back in the power of the Spirit to Galilee, and a fame went forth through all the surrounding region concerning Him, **15** and He was teaching in their synagogues, being glorified by all. **16** And He came to Nazareth, where He has been brought up, and He went in, according to His custom, on the day of the Sabbaths, into the synagogue, and stood up to read; **17** and there was given over to Him a scroll of Isaiah the prophet, and having unfolded the scroll, He found the place where it has been written: **18** "The Spirit of the Lord [is] on Me, || Because He anointed Me || To proclaim good news to the poor, || Sent Me to heal the broken of heart, || To proclaim to captives deliverance, || And to blind receiving of sight, || To send the bruised away with deliverance, **19** To proclaim the acceptable year of the Lord." **20** And having folded the scroll,

having given [it] back to the officer, He sat down, and the eyes of all in the synagogue were gazing on Him. **21** And He began to say to them, "Today this writing has been fulfilled in your ears"; **22** and all were bearing testimony to Him, and were wondering at the gracious words that are coming forth out of His mouth, and they said, "Is this not the Son of Joseph?" **23** And He said to them, "Certainly you will say to Me this allegory, Physician, heal yourself; as great things as we heard done in Capernaum, do also here in Your country"; **24** and He said, "Truly I say to you, no prophet is accepted in his own country; **25** and of a truth I say to you, many widows were in the days of Elijah, in Israel, when the sky was shut for three years and six months, when great famine came on all the land, **26** and to none of them was Elijah sent, but—to Sarepta of Sidon, to a woman, a widow; **27** and many lepers were in the time of Elisha the prophet, in Israel, and none of them was cleansed, but—Naaman the Syrian." **28** And all in the synagogue were filled with wrath, hearing these things, **29** and having risen, they put Him forth outside the city, and brought Him to the brow of the hill on which their city had been built—to cast Him down headlong, **30** and He, having gone through the midst of them, went away. **31** And He came down to Capernaum, a city of Galilee, and was teaching them on the Sabbaths, **32** and they were astonished at His teaching, because His word was with authority. **33** And in the synagogue was a man having a spirit of an unclean demon, and he cried out with a great voice, **34** "Aah! What [regards] us and You, Jesus, O Nazarene? you came to destroy us; I have known who You are—the Holy One of God!" **35** And Jesus rebuked him, saying, "Be silenced, and come forth out of him"; and the demon having cast him into the midst, came forth from him, having hurt him nothing; **36** and amazement came on all, and they were speaking together with one another, saying, "What [is] this word, that with authority and power He commands the unclean spirits, and they come forth?" **37** and there was going forth a fame concerning Him to every place of the surrounding region. **38** And having risen out of the synagogue, He entered into the house of Simon, and the mother-in-law of Simon was pressed with a great fever, and they asked Him about her, **39** and having stood over her, He rebuked the fever, and it left her, and immediately, having risen, she was ministering to them. **40** And at the setting of the sun, all, as many as had any ailing with manifold diseases, brought them to Him, and He, having put hands on each one of them, healed them. **41** And demons were also coming forth from many, crying out and saying, "You are the Christ, the Son of God"; and rebuking, He did not permit them to speak, because they knew Him to be the Christ. **42** And day having come, having gone forth, He went on to a desolate place, and the multitudes were seeking Him, and they came to Him, and were restraining Him—not to go on from them, **43** and He said to them, "Also to the other cities it is necessary for Me to proclaim good news of the Kingdom of God, because for this I have been sent"; **44** and He was preaching in the synagogues of Galilee.

CHAPTER 5

1 And it came to pass, in the multitude pressing on Him to hear the word of God, that He was standing beside the Lake of Gennesaret, **2** and He saw two boats standing beside the lake, and the fishers, having gone away from them, were washing the nets, **3** and having entered into one of the boats, that was Simon's, He asked him to put back a little from the land, and having sat down, was teaching the multitudes out of the boat. **4** And when He left off speaking, He said to Simon, "Put back into the deep, and let down your nets for a catch"; **5** and Simon answering said to Him, "Master, through the whole night, having labored, we have taken nothing, but at Your saying I will let down the net." **6** And having done this, they enclosed a great multitude of fishes, and their net was breaking, **7** and they beckoned to the partners who [are] in the other boat, having come, to help them; and they came, and filled both the boats, so that they were sinking. **8** And Simon Peter having seen, fell down at the knees of Jesus, saying, "Depart from me, because I am a sinful man, O Lord"; **9** for astonishment seized him, and all those with him, at the catch of the fishes that they took, **10** and in like manner also James and John, sons of Zebedee, who were partners with Simon; and Jesus said to Simon, "Do not fear, from now on you will be catching men"; **11** and they, having brought the boats on the land, having left all, followed Him. **12** And it came to pass, in His being in one of the cities, that behold, a man full of leprosy, and having seen Jesus, having fallen on [his] face, he implored Him, saying, "Lord, if You may will, You are able to cleanse me"; **13** and having stretched forth [His] hand, He touched him, having said, "I will, be cleansed"; and immediately the leprosy went away from him. **14** And He charged him to tell no one, "But having gone away, show yourself to the priest, and bring near for your cleansing according as Moses directed, for a testimony to them"; **15** but the more was the report going abroad concerning Him, and great multitudes were coming together to hear, and to be healed by Him of their sicknesses, **16** and He was withdrawing Himself in the desolate places and was praying. **17** And it came to pass, on one of the days, that He was teaching, and there were sitting by Pharisees and teachers of the Law, who were come out of every village of Galilee, and Judea, and Jerusalem, and the power of the Lord was—to heal them. **18** And behold, men carrying a man on a bed, who has been struck with palsy, and they were seeking to bring him in, and to place before Him, **19** and having not found by what way they may bring him in because of the multitude, having gone up on the housetop, through the tiles they let him down with the little bed, into the midst before Jesus, **20** and He having seen their faith, said to him, "Man, your sins have been forgiven you." **21** And the scribes and the Pharisees began to reason, saying, "Who is this that speaks evil words? who is able to forgive sins, except God only?" **22** And Jesus having known their reasonings, answering, said to them, "What reason you in your hearts? **23** which is easier—to say, Your sins have been forgiven you? or to say, Arise, and walk? **24** And that you may know that the Son of Man has authority on the earth to forgive sins—(He said to the one struck with palsy)—I say to you, arise, and having taken up your little bed, be going on to your house." **25** And immediately having risen before them, having taken up [that] on which he was lying, he went away to his house, glorifying God, **26** and astonishment took all, and they were glorifying God, and were filled with fear, saying, "We saw strange things today." **27** And after these things He went forth, and beheld a tax collector, by name Levi, sitting at the tax office, and said to him, "Follow Me"; **28** and he, having left all, having arisen, followed Him. **29** And Levi made a great entertainment to Him in his house, and there was a great multitude of tax collectors and others who were with them reclining, **30** and the scribes and the Pharisees among them were murmuring at His disciples, saying, "Why do You eat and drink with tax collectors and sinners?" **31** And Jesus answering said to them, "They who are well have no need of a physician, but they that are ill: **32** I did not come to call righteous men, but sinners, to conversion." **33** And they said to Him, "Why do the disciples of John fast often, and make supplications—in like manner also those of the Pharisees—but Yours eat and drink?" **34** And He said to them, "Are you able to make the sons of the bride-chamber—in the Bridegroom being with them—to fast? **35** but days will come, and when the bridegroom may be taken away from them, then they will fast in those days." **36** And He spoke also an allegory to them: "No one puts a patch of new clothing on old clothing, and if otherwise, the new also makes a split, and with the old the patch does not agree, that [is] from the new. **37** And no one puts new wine into old skins, and if otherwise, the new wine will burst the skins, and itself will be poured out, and the skins will be destroyed; **38** but new wine is to be put into new skins, and both are preserved together; **39** and no one having drunk old, immediately wishes new, for he says, The old is better."

CHAPTER 6

1 And it came to pass, on a Sabbath, as He is going through the grainfields, that His disciples were plucking the ears, and were eating, rubbing with the hands, **2** and certain of the Pharisees said to them, "Why do you do that which is not lawful to do on the Sabbaths?" **3** And Jesus answering said to them, "Did you not read even this that David did when he hungered, himself and those who are with him, **4** how he went into the house of God, and took the Bread of the Presentation, and ate, and gave also to those with him, which it is not lawful to eat, except only to the priests?" **5** and He said to them, "The Son of Man is Lord also of the Sabbath." **6** And it came to pass also, on another Sabbath, that He goes into the synagogue, and teaches, and there was there a man, and his right hand was withered, **7** and the scribes and the Pharisees were watching Him, if on the Sabbath He will heal, that they might find an accusation against Him. **8** And He Himself had known their reasonings and said to the man having the withered hand, "Rise, and stand in the midst"; and he having risen, stood. **9** Then Jesus said to them, "I will question you something: is it lawful on the Sabbaths to do good, or to do evil? To save life or to kill?" **10** And having looked around on them all, He said to the man, "Stretch forth your hand"; and he did so, and his hand was restored whole as the other; **11** and they were filled with madness, and were speaking with one another what they might do to Jesus. **12** And it came to pass in those days, He went forth to the mountain to pray, and was passing the night in the prayer of God, **13** and when it became day, He called near His disciples, also having chosen twelve from them, whom He also named apostles: **14** Simon, whom He also named Peter, and his brother Andrew, James and John, Philip and Bartholomew, **15** Matthew and Thomas, James of Alphaeus, and Simon called Zealot, **16** Judas of James, and Judas Iscariot, who also became betrayer. **17** And having come down with them, He stood on a level spot; and a crowd of His disciples, and a great multitude of the people from all Judea, and Jerusalem, and the seacoast of Tyre and Sidon, **18** who came to hear Him and to be healed of their diseases, [gathered]. And those harassed by unclean spirits [also gathered] and were healed. **19** And all the multitude were seeking to touch Him, because power was going forth from Him, and He was healing all. **20** And He, having lifted up His eyes to His disciples, said: "Blessed the poor—because yours is the Kingdom of God. **21** Blessed those hungering now—because you will be filled. Blessed those weeping now—because you will laugh. **22** Blessed are you when men will hate you, and when they will separate you, and will reproach, and will cast forth your name as evil, for the Son of Man's sake— **23** rejoice in that day, and leap, for behold, your reward [is] great in Heaven, for according to these things were their fathers doing to the prophets. **24** But woe to you—the rich, because you have gotten your comfort. **25** Woe to you who have been filled—because you will hunger. Woe to you who are laughing now—because you will mourn and weep. **26** Woe to you when all men will speak well of you—for according to these things were their fathers doing to false prophets. **27** But I say to you who are hearing, love your enemies, do good to those hating you, **28** bless those cursing you, pray for those maligning you; **29** and to him striking you on the cheek, give also the other, and from him taking away from you the mantle, also the coat you may not keep back. **30** And to everyone who is asking of you, be giving; and from him who is taking away your goods, do not be asking again; **31** and as you wish that men may do to you, do also to them in like manner; **32** and—if you love those loving you, what grace is it to you? for also the sinful love those loving them; **33** and if you do good to those doing good to you, what grace is it to you? for also the sinful do the same; **34** and if you lend [to those] of whom you hope to receive back, what grace is it to you? for also the sinful lend to sinners—that they may receive again as much. **35** But love your enemies, and do good, and lend, hoping for nothing again, and your reward will be great, and you will be sons of the Highest, because He is kind to the ungracious and evil; **36** be therefore merciful, as also your Father is merciful. **37** And do not judge, and you may not be judged; do not condemn, and you may not be condemned; release, and you will be released. **38** Give, and it will be given to you; good measure, pressed, and shaken, and running over, they will give into your bosom; for with that measure with which you measure, it will be measured to you again." **39** And He spoke an allegory to them, "Is blind able to lead blind? will they not both fall into a pit? **40** A disciple is not above his teacher, but everyone perfected will be as his teacher. **41** And why do you behold the speck that is in your brother's eye, and do not consider the beam that [is] in your own eye? **42** or how are you able to say to your brother, Brother, permit, I may take out the speck that [is] in your eye—yourself not beholding the beam in your own eye? Hypocrite, first take the beam out of your own eye, and then you will see clearly to take out the speck that [is] in your brother's eye. **43** For there is not a good tree making bad fruit, nor a bad tree making good fruit; **44** for each tree is known from its own fruit, for they do not gather figs from thorns, nor do they crop a grape from a bramble. **45** The good man out of the good treasure of his heart brings forth that which [is] good; and the evil man out of the evil treasure of his heart brings forth that which [is] evil; for out of the abounding of the heart his mouth speaks. **46** And why do you call Me, Lord, Lord, and do not do what I say? **47** Everyone who is coming to Me, and is hearing My words, and is doing them, I will show you to whom he is like: **48** he is like to a man building a house, who dug and deepened, and laid a foundation on the rock, and a flood having come, the stream broke forth on that house, and was not able to shake it, for it had been founded on the rock. **49** And he who heard and did not, is like to a man having built a house on the earth, without a foundation, against which the stream broke forth, and immediately it fell, and the ruin of that house became great."

CHAPTER 7

1 And when He completed all His sayings in the ears of the people, He went into Capernaum; **2** and a certain centurion's servant being ill, was about to die, who was much valued by him, **3** and having heard about Jesus, he sent to Him elders of the Jews, imploring Him, that having come He might thoroughly save his servant. **4** And they, having come near to Jesus, were calling on Him earnestly, saying, "He is worthy to whom You will do this, **5** for he loves our nation, and he built to us the synagogue." **6** And Jesus was going on with them, and now when He is not far distant from the house the centurion sent to Him friends, saying to Him, "Lord, do not be troubled, for I am not worthy that You may enter under my roof; **7** for this reason I did not consider myself worthy to come to You, but say in a word, and my boy will be healed; **8** for I also am a man placed under authority, having under myself soldiers, and I say to this [one], Go, and he goes; and to another, Be coming, and he comes; and to my servant, Do this, and he does [it]." **9** And having heard these things Jesus wondered at him, and having turned to the multitude following Him, He said, "I say to you, not even in Israel did I find so much faith"; **10** and those sent, having turned back to the house, found the ailing servant in health. **11** And it came to pass, on the next day, He was going on to a city called Nain, and there were going with Him many of His disciples, and a great multitude, **12** and as He came near to the gate of the city, then, behold, one dead was being carried forth, an only son of his mother, and she a widow, and a great multitude of the city was with her. **13** And the Lord having seen her, was moved with compassion toward her and said to her, "Do not be weeping"; **14** and having come near, He touched the bier, and those carrying [it] stood still, and He said, "Young man, to you I say, Arise"; **15** and the dead sat up, and began to speak, and He gave him to his mother; **16** and fear took hold of all, and they were glorifying God, saying, "A great prophet has risen among us," and, "God looked on His people." **17** And the account of this went forth in all Judea about Him, and in all the region around. **18** And the disciples of John told him about all these things, **19** and John having called near a certain two of his disciples, sent to Jesus, saying, "Are You He who is coming, or do we look for another?" **20** And having come near to Him, the men said, "John the Immerser sent us to You, saying, Are You He who is coming, or do we look for another?" **21** And in that hour He cured many from diseases, and plagues, and evil spirits, and He granted sight to many blind. **22** And Jesus answering said to them, "Having gone on, report to John what you saw and heard, that blind men see again, lame walk, lepers are cleansed, deaf hear, dead are raised, poor have good news proclaimed"; **23** and blessed is he whoever may not be stumbled in Me." **24** And the messengers of John having gone away, He began to say to the multitudes concerning John: "What have you gone forth into the wilderness to look on? a reed shaken by the wind? **25** but what have you gone forth to see? a man clothed in soft garments? behold, they in splendid clothing, and living in luxury, are in the houses of kings! **26** But what have you gone forth to see? a prophet? Yes, I say to you, and much more than a prophet: **27** this is he concerning whom it has been written: Behold, I send My messenger before Your face, who will prepare Your way before You; **28** for I say to you, there is not a greater prophet, among those born of women, than John the Immerser; but the least in the Kingdom of God is greater than he." **29** And all the people having heard, and the tax collectors, declared God righteous, having been immersed with the immersion of John, **30** but the Pharisees and the lawyers put away the counsel of God for themselves, having not been immersed by him. **31** And the Lord said, "To what, then, will I liken the men of this generation? and to what are they like? **32** they are like to children, to those sitting in a marketplace, and calling to one another, and saying, We piped to you, and you did not dance, we mourned to you, and you did not weep! **33** For John the Immerser came neither eating bread nor drinking wine, and you say, He has a demon; **34** the Son of Man came eating and drinking, and you say, Behold, a man, a glutton, and a wine drinker, a friend of tax collectors and sinners; **35** and the wisdom was justified from all her children." **36** And a certain one of the Pharisees was asking Him that He might eat with him, and having gone into the house of the Pharisee He reclined, **37** and behold, a woman in the city, who was a sinner, having known that He reclines in the house of the Pharisee, having provided an alabaster box of ointment, **38** and having stood behind, beside His feet, weeping, she began to wet His feet with the tears, and with the hairs of her head she was wiping, and was kissing His feet, and was anointing with the ointment. **39** And the Pharisee who called Him, having seen, spoke within himself, saying, "This One, if He were a prophet, would have known who and of what kind [is] the woman who touches Him, that she is a sinner." **40** And Jesus answering said to him, "Simon, I have something to say to you"; and he says, "Teacher, say on." **41** "Two debtors were to a certain creditor; one was owing five hundred denarii, and the other fifty; **42** and they not having [with which] to give back, he forgave both; which of them then, do you say, will love him more?" **43** And Simon answering said, "I suppose that to whom he forgave the more"; and He said to him, "You judged correctly." **44** And having turned to the woman, He said to Simon, "See this woman? I entered into your house; you did not give water for My feet, but this woman wet My feet with tears, and wiped with the hairs of her head; **45** you did not give a kiss to Me, but this woman, from what [time] I came in, did not cease kissing My feet; **46** you did not anoint My head with oil, but this woman anointed My feet with oil; **47** therefore I say to you, her many sins have been forgiven, because she loved much; but to whom is forgiven little, loves little." **48** And He said to her, "Your sins have been forgiven"; **49** and those dining with Him began to say within themselves, "Who is this, who also forgives sins?" **50** and He said to the woman, "Your faith has saved you, be going on to peace."

CHAPTER 8

1 And it came to pass thereafter, that He was going through every city and village, preaching and proclaiming good news of the Kingdom of God, and the Twelve [are] with Him, **2** and certain women who were healed of evil spirits and sicknesses, Mary who is called Magdalene, from whom seven demons had gone forth, **3** and Joanna wife of Chuza, steward of Herod, and Susanna, and many others, who were ministering to Him from their substance. **4** And a great multitude having gathered, and those who from city and city were coming to Him, He spoke by an allegory: **5** "The sower went forth to sow his seed, and in his sowing, some indeed fell beside the way, and it was trodden down, and the birds of the sky devoured it. **6** And other fell on the rock, and having sprung up, it withered, through having no moisture. **7** And other fell amidst the thorns, and the thorns having sprung up with it, choked it. **8** And other fell on the good ground, and having sprung up, it made fruit a hundredfold." Saying these things, He was calling, "He having ears to hear— let him hear." **9** And His disciples were questioning Him, saying, "What may this allegory be?" **10** And He said, "To you it has been given to know the secrets of the Kingdom of God, but to the rest in allegories, that seeing they may not see, and hearing they may not understand. **11** And this is the allegory: the seed is the word of God, **12** and those beside the way are those hearing, then comes the Devil, and takes up the word from their heart, lest having believed, they may be saved. **13** And those on the rock: they who, when they may hear, receive the word with joy, and these have no root, who for a time believe, and in time of temptation fall away. **14** And that which fell to the thorns: these are they who have heard, and going forth, through anxieties, and riches, and pleasures of life, are choked, and do not bear to completion. **15** And that in the good ground: these are they who in an upright and good heart, having heard the word, retain [it], and bear fruit in continuance. **16** And no one having lighted a lamp covers it with a vessel, or puts [it] under a bed; but he puts [it] on a lampstand, that those coming in may see the light, **17** for nothing is secret, that will not become visible, nor hid, that will not be known and become visible. **18** See, therefore, how you hear, for whoever may have, there will be given to him, and whoever may not have, also what he seems to have will be taken from him." **19** And there came to Him His mother and brothers, and they were not able to get to Him because of the multitude, **20** and it was told Him, saying, "Your mother and Your brothers stand outside, wishing to see You"; **21** and He answering said to them, "My mother and My brothers! They are those who are hearing the word of God, and doing." **22** And it came to pass, on one of the days, that He Himself went into a boat with His disciples, and He said to them, "We may go over to the other side of the lake"; and they set forth, **23** and as they are sailing He fell deeply asleep, and there came down a storm of wind to the lake, and they were filling, and were in peril. **24** And having come near, they awoke Him, saying, "Master, Master, we perish!" And He, having arisen, rebuked the wind and the raging of the water, and they ceased, and there came a calm, **25** and He said to them, "Where is your faith?" And they being afraid wondered, saying to one another, "Who, then, is this, that He even commands the winds and the water, and they obey Him?" **26** And they sailed down to the region of the Gadarenes that is opposite Galilee, **27** and He having gone forth on the land, there met Him a certain man, out of the city, who had demons for a long time, and was not clothed with a garment, and was not abiding in a house, but in the tombs, **28** and having seen Jesus, and having cried out, he fell before Him, and with a loud voice, said, "What [regards] me and You, Jesus, Son of God Most High? I implore You, may You not afflict me!" **29** For He commanded the unclean spirit to come forth from the man, for many times it had caught him, and he was being bound with chains and shackles—guarded, and breaking apart the bonds he was driven by the demons into the deserts. **30** And Jesus questioned him, saying, "What is your name?" And he said, "Legion," because many demons were entered into him, **31** and he was calling on Him that He may not command them to go away into the abyss, **32** and there was there a herd of many pigs feeding on the mountain, and they were calling on Him that He might permit them to enter into these, and He permitted them, **33** and the demons having gone forth from the man, entered into the pigs, and the herd rushed down the steep into the lake, and were drowned. **34** And those feeding [them], having seen what was come to pass, fled, and having gone, told [it] to the city, and to the fields; **35** and they came forth to see what was come to pass, and they came to Jesus, and found the man sitting, out of whom the demons had gone forth, clothed, and right-minded, at the feet of Jesus, and they were afraid; **36** and those also having seen [it], told them how the demoniac was saved. **37** And the whole multitude of the region of the Gadarenes asked Him to go away from them, because they were pressed with great fear, and He having entered into the boat, turned back. **38** And the man from whom the demons had gone forth was imploring of Him to be with Him, and Jesus sent him away, saying, **39** "Return to your house, and tell how God did great things to you"; and he went away through all the city proclaiming how Jesus did great things to him. **40** And it came to pass, in the turning back of Jesus, the multitude received Him, for they were all looking for Him, **41** and behold, there came a man whose name [is] Jairus, and he was a chief of the synagogue, and having fallen at the feet of Jesus, was calling on Him to come to his house, **42** because he had an only daughter about twelve years [old], and she was dying. And in His going away, the multitudes were thronging Him, **43** and a woman, being with a flow of blood for twelve years, who, having spent all her living on physicians, was not able to be healed by any, **44** having come near behind, touched the fringe of His garment, and immediately the flow of her blood stood still. **45** And Jesus said, "Who [is] it that touched Me?" And all denying, Peter and those with him said, "Master, the multitudes press You, and throng [You], and You say, Who [is] it that touched Me?" **46** And Jesus said, "Someone touched Me, for I knew power having gone forth from Me." **47** And the woman, having seen that she was not hid, trembling, came, and having fallen before Him, for what cause she touched Him declared to Him before all the people, and how she was healed instantly; **48** and He said to her, "Take courage, daughter, your faith has saved you, be going on to peace." **49** While He is yet speaking, there comes a certain one from the chief of the synagogue's [house], saying to him, "Your daughter has died, do not harass the Teacher"; **50** and Jesus having heard, answered him, saying, "Do not be afraid, only believe, and she will be saved." **51** And having come into the house, He permitted no one to go in, except Peter, and James, and John, and the father of the child, and the mother; **52** and they were all weeping, and beating themselves for her, and He said, "Do not weep, she did not die, but sleeps"; **53** and they were deriding Him, knowing that she died; **54** and He having put all forth outside, and having taken hold of her hand, called,

saying, "Child, arise"; **55** and her spirit came back, and she arose immediately, and He directed that there be given to her to eat; **56** and her parents were amazed, but He charged them to say to no one what had come to pass.

CHAPTER 9

1 And having called together His twelve disciples, He gave them power and authority over all the demons, and to cure diseases, **2** and He sent them to proclaim the Kingdom of God, and to heal the ailing. **3** And He said to them, "Take nothing for the way, neither staff, nor leather pouch, nor bread, nor money; neither have two coats each; **4** and into whatever house you may enter, remain there, and depart from there; **5** and as many as may not receive you, going forth from that city, even the dust from your feet shake off, for a testimony against them." **6** And going forth they were going through the several villages, proclaiming good news, and healing everywhere. **7** And Herod the tetrarch heard of all the things being done by Him, and was perplexed, because it was said by some that John has been raised out of the dead, **8** and by some that Elijah appeared, and by others, that a prophet, one of the ancients, was risen; **9** and Herod said, "I beheaded John, but who is this concerning whom I hear such things?" And he was seeking to see Him. **10** And the apostles having turned back, declared to Him how they did great things, and having taken them, He withdrew by Himself into a city called Bethsaida, **11** and the multitudes having known followed Him, and having received them, He was speaking to them concerning the Kingdom of God, and He cured those having need of service. **12** And the day began to decline, and the Twelve having come near, said to Him, "Let away the multitude, that having gone into the surrounding villages and the fields, they may lodge and may find provision, because here we are in a desolate place." **13** And He said to them, "You give them to eat"; and they said, "We have no more than five loaves and two fishes; except, having gone, we may buy food for all this people"; **14** for they were about five thousand men. And He said to His disciples, "Cause them to recline in companies, in each fifty"; **15** and they did so, and made all to recline; **16** and having taken the five loaves and the two fishes, having looked up to the sky, He blessed them, and broke, and was giving to the disciples to set before the multitude; **17** and they ate, and were all filled, and there was taken up what was over to them of broken pieces, twelve baskets. **18** And it came to pass, as He is praying alone, the disciples were with Him, and He questioned them, saying, "Who do the multitudes say I am?" **19** And they answering said, "John the Immerser; and others, Elijah; and others, that a prophet, one of the ancients, was risen"; **20** and He said to them, "And you—who do you say I am?" And Peter answering said, "The Christ of God." **21** And having charged them, He commanded [them] to say this to no one, **22** saying, "It is necessary for the Son of Man to suffer many things, and to be rejected by the elders, and chief priests, and scribes, and to be killed, and to be raised the third day." **23** And He said to all, "If anyone wills to come after Me, let him disown himself, and take up his cross daily, and follow Me; **24** for whoever may will to save his life will lose it, and whoever may lose his life for My sake, he will save it; **25** for what is a man profited, having gained the whole world, and having lost or having forfeited himself? **26** For whoever may be ashamed of Me and of My words, of this one will the Son of Man be ashamed when He may come in His glory, and the Father's, and the holy messengers'; **27** and I say to you, truly, there are certain of those standing here who will not taste of death until they may see the Kingdom of God." **28** And it came to pass, after these words, as it were eight days, that having taken Peter, and John, and James, He went up to the mountain to pray, **29** and it came to pass, in His praying, the appearance of His face became altered, and His clothing became flashing white. **30** And behold, two men were speaking together with Him, who were Moses and Elijah, **31** who having appeared in glory, spoke of His outgoing that He was about to fulfill in Jerusalem, **32** but Peter and those with him were heavy with sleep, and having awoken, they saw His glory, and the two men standing with Him. **33** And it came to pass, in their parting from Him, Peter said to Jesus, "Master, it is good to us to be here; and we may make three shelters: one for You, and one for Moses, and one for Elijah," not knowing what he says: **34** and as he was speaking these things, there came a cloud, and overshadowed them, and they feared in their entering into the cloud, **35** and a voice came out of the cloud, saying, "This is My Son, the Beloved; hear Him"; **36** and when the voice was past, Jesus was found alone; and they were silent, and declared to no one in those days anything of what they have seen. **37** And it came to pass on the next day, they having come down from the mountain, a great multitude met Him there, **38** and behold, a man from the multitude cried out, saying, "Teacher, I implore You, look on my son, because he is my only begotten; **39** and behold, a spirit takes him, and suddenly he cries out, and it convulses him, with foaming, and it hardly departs from him, bruising him, **40** and I implored Your disciples that they might cast it out, and they were not able." **41** And Jesus answering said, "O generation, unsteadfast and perverse, until when will I be with you, and endure you? bring your son near here"; **42** and as he is yet coming near, the demon threw him down, and convulsed [him], and Jesus rebuked the unclean spirit, and healed the youth, and gave him back to his father. **43** And they were all amazed at the greatness of God, and while all are wondering at all things that Jesus did, He said to His disciples, **44** "Lay to your ears these words, for the Son of Man is about to be delivered up into the hands of men." **45** And they were not knowing this saying, and it was veiled from them, that they might not perceive it, and they were afraid to ask Him about this saying. **46** And there entered a reasoning among them, this—who may be greater of them. **47** and Jesus having seen the reasoning of their heart, having taken hold of a child, set him beside Him, **48** and said to them, "Whoever may receive this child in My Name, receives Me, and whoever may receive Me, receives Him who sent Me, for he who is least among you all—he will be great." **49** And John answering said, "Master, we saw a certain one casting forth the demons in Your Name, and we forbade him, because he does not follow with us"; **50** and Jesus said to him, "Do not forbid, for he who is not against us, is for us." **51** And it came to pass, in the completing of the days of His being taken up, that He fixed His face to go on to Jerusalem, **52** and He sent messengers before His face, and having gone on, they went into a village of Samaritans, to make ready for Him, **53** and they did not receive Him, because His face was going on to Jerusalem. **54** And His disciples James and John having seen, said, "Lord, will You [that] we may command fire to come down from Heaven, and to consume them, as Elijah also did?" **55** and having turned, He rebuked them and said, "You have not known of what spirit you are, **56** for the Son of Man did not come to destroy men's lives, but to save"; and they went on to another village. **57** And it came to pass, as they are going on in the way, a certain one said to Him, "I will follow You wherever You may go, Lord"; **58** and Jesus said to him, "The foxes have holes, and the birds of the sky places of rest, but the Son of Man has nowhere He may recline the head." **59** And He said to another, "Follow Me"; and he said, "Lord, permit me, having gone away, to first bury my father"; **60** and Jesus said to him, "Permit the dead to bury their own dead, and you, having gone away, publish the Kingdom of God." **61** And another also said, "I will follow You, Lord, but first permit me to take leave of those in my house"; **62** and Jesus said to him, "No one having put his hand on a plow, and looking back, is fit for the Kingdom of God."

CHAPTER 10

1 And after these things, the Lord also appointed seventy others, and sent them by twos before His face, to every city and place to where He Himself was about to come, **2** then He said to them, "The harvest [is] indeed abundant, but the workmen few; implore then the Lord of the harvest, that He may put forth workmen to His harvest. **3** Go away; behold, I send you forth as lambs in the midst of wolves; **4** carry no bag, no leather pouch, nor sandals; and greet no one on the way; **5** and into whatever house you enter, first say, Peace to this house; **6** and if indeed there may be there the son of peace, your peace will rest on it; and if not so, it will turn back on you. **7** And remain in that house, eating and drinking the things they have, for worthy [is] the workman of his hire; do not go from house to house, **8** and into whatever city you enter, and they may receive you, eat the things set before you, **9** and heal the ailing in it, and say to them, The Kingdom of God has come near to you. **10** And into whatever city you enter, and they may not receive you, having gone forth to its broad places, say, **11** And the dust that has cleaved to us from your city, we wipe off against you, but know this, that the Kingdom of God has come near to you; **12** and I say to you that it will be more tolerable for Sodom in that day than for that city. **13** Woe to you,

Chorazin; woe to you, Bethsaida; for if the mighty works that were done in you had been done in Tyre and Sidon, they had converted long ago, sitting in sackcloth and ashes; **14** but it will be more tolerable for Tyre and Sidon in the judgment than for you. **15** And you, Capernaum, which were exalted to Heaven, you will be brought down to Hades. **16** He who is hearing you, hears Me; and he who is putting you away, puts Me away; and he who is putting Me away, puts away Him who sent Me." **17** And the seventy turned back with joy, saying, "Lord, and the demons are being subjected to us in Your Name"; **18** and He said to them, "I was beholding Satan having fallen as lightning from Heaven; **19** behold, I give to you the authority to tread on serpents and scorpions, and on all the power of the enemy, and nothing by any means will hurt you; **20** but do not rejoice in this, that the spirits are subjected to you, but rejoice rather that your names were written in the heavens." **21** In that hour Jesus was glad in the Spirit and said, "I confess to You, Father, Lord of Heaven and of earth, that You hid these things from wise men and understanding, and revealed them to babies; yes, Father, because so it became good pleasure before You. **22** All things were delivered up to Me by My Father, and no one knows who the Son is, except the Father, and who the Father is, except the Son, and he to whom the Son may resolve to reveal [Him]." **23** And having turned to the disciples, He said, by themselves, "Blessed the eyes that are perceiving what you perceive; **24** for I say to you that many prophets and kings wished to see what you perceive, and did not see, and to hear what you hear, and did not hear." **25** And behold, a certain lawyer stood up, trying Him, and saying, "Teacher, what having done, will I inherit continuous life?" **26** And He said to him, "In the Law what has been written? how do you read [it]?" **27** And he answering said, "You will love the Lord your God out of all your heart, and out of all your soul, and out of all your strength, and out of all your understanding, and your neighbor as yourself." **28** And He said to him, "You answered correctly; do this, and you will live." **29** And he, willing to declare himself righteous, said to Jesus, "And who is my neighbor?" **30** and Jesus having taken up [the word], said, "A certain man was going down from Jerusalem to Jericho, and fell among robbers, and having stripped him and inflicted blows, they went away, leaving [him] half dead. **31** And by a coincidence a certain priest was going down in that way, and having seen him, he passed over on the opposite side; **32** and in like manner also, a Levite, having been around the place, having come and seen, passed over on the opposite side. **33** But a certain Samaritan, journeying, came along him, and having seen him, he was moved with compassion, **34** and having come near, he bound up his wounds, pouring on oil and wine, and having lifted him up on his own beast, he brought him to an inn, and was careful of him; **35** and on the next day, going forth, taking out two denarii, he gave to the innkeeper and said to him, Be careful of him, and whatever you may spend more, I, in my coming again, will give back to you. **36** Who, then, of these three, seems to you to have become neighbor of him who fell among the robbers?" **37** and he said, "He who did the kindness with him," then Jesus said to him, "Be going on, and you be doing in like manner." **38** And it came to pass, in their going on, that He entered into a certain village, and a certain woman, by name Martha, received Him into her house, **39** and she also had a sister, called Mary, who also, having seated herself beside the feet of Jesus, was hearing the word, **40** and Martha was distracted about much serving, and having stood by Him, she said, "Lord, do You not care that my sister left me alone to serve? say then to her that she may partake along with me." **41** And Jesus answering said to her, "Martha, Martha, you are anxious and disquieted about many things, **42** but of one thing there is need, and Mary chose the good part; that will not be taken away from her."

CHAPTER 11

1 And it came to pass, in His being in a certain place praying, as He ceased, a certain one of His disciples said to Him, "Lord, teach us to pray, as also John taught his disciples." **2** And He said to them, "When you may pray, say: Our Father who is in the heavens, hallowed be Your Name; Your kingdom come, Your will come to pass, as in Heaven also on earth; **3** be giving us daily our appointed bread; **4** and forgive us our sins, for we also ourselves forgive everyone indebted to us; and may You not bring us into temptation, but deliver us from the evil [one]." **5** And He said to them, "Who of you will have a friend, and will go on to him at midnight, and may say to him, Friend, lend me three loaves, 6 seeing a friend of mine came out of the way to me, and I have not what I will set before him, 7 and he from within answering may say, Do not give me trouble, the door has already been shut, and my children are with me in the bed, I am not able, having risen, to give to you. 8 I say to you, even if he will not give to him, having risen, because of his being his friend, yet because of his persistence, having risen, he will give him as many as he needs; 9 and I say to you, ask, and it will be given to you; seek, and you will find; knock, and it will be opened to you; 10 for everyone who is asking receives; and he who is seeking finds; and to him who is knocking it will be opened. 11 And of which of you—the father—[if] the son will ask [for] a loaf, will present to him a stone? and [if] a fish, instead of a fish, will present to him a serpent? 12 and [if] he may ask [for] an egg, will present to him a scorpion? 13 If, then, you, being evil, have known to be giving good gifts to your children, how much more will the Father who is from Heaven give the Holy Spirit to those asking Him!" 14 And He was casting forth a demon, and it was mute, and it came to pass, the demon having gone forth, the mute man spoke, and the multitudes wondered, 15 and certain of them said, "By Beelzebul, ruler of the demons, He casts forth the demons"; 16 and others, tempting, were asking [for] a sign out of Heaven from Him. 17 And He, knowing their thoughts, said to them, "Every kingdom having been divided against itself is desolated; and house against house falls; 18 and if Satan was also divided against himself, how will his kingdom be made to stand? for you say by Beelzebul is My casting forth the demons, 19 but if I, by Beelzebul, cast forth the demons—your sons, by whom do they cast forth? because of this they will be your judges; 20 but if by the finger of God I cast forth the demons, then the Kingdom of God came unaware on you. 21 When the strong man may keep his hall armed, his goods are in peace; 22 but when the stronger than he, having come on [him], may overcome him, he takes away his whole armor in which he had trusted, and he distributes his spoils; 23 he who is not with Me is against Me, and he who is not gathering with Me scatters. 24 When the unclean spirit may go forth from the man, it walks through waterless places seeking rest, and not finding, it says, I will return to my house from where I came forth; 25 and having come, it finds [it] swept and adorned; 26 then it goes, and takes to it seven other spirits more evil than itself, and having entered, they dwell there, and the last of that man becomes worse than the first." 27 And it came to pass, in His saying these things, a certain woman having lifted up the voice out of the multitude, said to Him, "Blessed the womb that carried You, and the breasts that You sucked!" 28 And He said, "Indeed, rather, blessed those hearing the word of God, and keeping [it]!" 29 And the multitudes crowding together on Him, He began to say, "This generation is evil, it seeks after a sign, and a sign will not be given to it, except the sign of Jonah the prophet, 30 for as Jonah became a sign to the Ninevites, so also will the Son of Man be to this generation. 31 A queen of the south will rise up in the judgment with the men of this generation, and will condemn them, because she came from the ends of the earth to hear the wisdom of Solomon; and behold, [One] greater than Solomon [is] here! 32 Men of Nineveh will stand up in the judgment with this generation, and will condemn it, because they converted at the proclamation of Jonah; and behold, [One] greater than Jonah [is] here! 33 And no one having lighted a lamp, puts [it] in a secret place, nor under the measure, but on the lampstand, that those coming in may behold the light. 34 The lamp of the body is the eye, when then your eye may be simple, your whole body is also lightened; and when it may be evil, your body is also darkened; 35 take heed, then, lest the light that [is] in you is darkness; 36 if then your whole body is lightened, not having any part darkened, the whole will be lightened, as when the lamp by the brightness may give you light." 37 And in [His] speaking, a certain Pharisee was asking Him that He might dine with him, and having gone in, He reclined, 38 and the Pharisee having seen, wondered that He did not first immerse Himself before the early meal. 39 And the Lord said to him, "Now you, the Pharisees, make the outside of the cup and of the plate clean, but your inward part is full of robbery and wickedness. 40 Unthinking [ones]! Did He who made the outside not also make the inside? 41 But what you have given [as] alms, and behold, all things are clean to you. 42 But woe to you, the Pharisees, because you tithe the mint, and the rue, and every herb, and you pass by the judgment and the love of God; these things [you] should do, and those not to be neglecting. 43 Woe to you, the Pharisees, because you love the first seats in the synagogues and the salutations in the marketplaces. 44 Woe to you, scribes and Pharisees, hypocrites, because you are as the unseen tombs, and the men walking above have not known." 45 And one of the lawyers answering, says to Him, "Teacher, saying these things, You also insult us"; 46 and He said, "And to you, the lawyers, woe! Because you burden men with burdens [too] grievous to bear, and you yourselves do not touch the burdens with one of your fingers! 47 Woe to you, because you build the tombs of the prophets, and your fathers killed them. 48 Then you testify, and are well pleased with the works of your fathers, because they indeed killed them, and you build their tombs; 49 because of this also the wisdom of God said: I will send to them prophets, and apostles, and some of them they will kill and persecute, 50 that the blood of all the prophets, that is being poured forth from the foundation of the world, may be required from this generation— 51 from the blood of Abel to the blood of Zacharias, who perished between the altar and the house; yes, I say to you, it will be required from this generation. 52 Woe to you, the lawyers, because you took away the key of the knowledge; you yourselves did not enter; and you hindered those coming in." 53 And in His speaking these things to them, the scribes and the Pharisees began fearfully to urge and to press Him to speak about many things, 54 laying wait for Him, and seeking to catch something out of His mouth, that they might accuse Him.

CHAPTER 12

1 At which time the myriads of the multitude having been gathered together, so as to tread on one another, He began to say to His disciples, first, "Take heed to yourselves of the leaven of the Pharisees, which is hypocrisy; 2 and there is nothing covered that will not be revealed, and hid that will not be known; 3 because whatever you said in the darkness will be heard in the light, and what you spoke to the ear in the inner-chambers will be proclaimed on the housetops. 4 And I say to you, my friends, do not be afraid of those killing the body, and after these things are not having anything more to do; 5 but I will show to you whom you may fear: fear Him who, after the killing, is having authority to cast into Gehenna; yes, I say to you, fear Him. 6 Are not five sparrows sold for two assaria? and one of them is not forgotten before God, 7 but even the hairs of your head have all been numbered; therefore, do not fear, you are of more value than many sparrows. 8 And I say to you, everyone who may confess in Me before men, the Son of Man will also confess in him before the messengers of God, 9 and he who has denied Me before men, will be denied before the messengers of God, 10 and everyone who will say a word to the Son of Man, it will be forgiven to him, but the [one] having slandered to the Holy Spirit will not be forgiven. 11 And when they bring you before the synagogues, and the rulers, and the authorities, do not be anxious how or what you may reply, or what you may say, 12 for the Holy Spirit will teach you in that hour what [you] should say." 13 And a certain one out of the multitude said to Him, "Teacher, say to my brother to divide with me the inheritance." 14 And He said to him, "Man, who set Me a judge or a divider over you?" 15 And He said to them, "Observe, and beware of the covetousness, because his life is not in the abundance of one's goods." 16 And He spoke an allegory to them, saying, "Of a certain rich man the field brought forth well; 17 and he was reasoning within himself, saying, What will I do, because I have nowhere I will gather together my fruits? 18 and he said, This I will do, I will take down my storehouses, and I will build greater ones, and I will gather together there all my products and my good things, 19 and I will say to my soul, Soul, you have many good things laid up for many years, be resting, eat, drink, be merry. 20 And God said to him, Unthinking [one]! This night your life is required of you, and what things you prepared—to whom will they be [given]? 21 so [is] he who is treasuring up to himself, and is not rich toward God." 22 And He said to His disciples, "Because of this, to you I say, do not be anxious for your life, what you may eat; nor for the body, what you may put on; 23 life is more than nourishment, and the body than clothing. 24 Consider the ravens, that they do not sow, nor reap, to which there is no barn nor storehouse, and God nourishes them; how much better are you than the birds? 25 and who of you, being anxious, is able to add to his age one cubit? 26 If, then, you are not able for the least—why are you anxious for the rest? 27 Consider the lilies, how do they grow? they do not labor, nor do they spin,

and I say to you, not even Solomon in all his glory was clothed as one of these; **28** and if the herbage in the field, that today is, and tomorrow is cast into an oven, God so clothes, how much more you of little faith? **29** And you—do not seek what you may eat, or what you may drink, and do not be in suspense, **30** for the nations of the world seek after all these things, and your Father has known that you have need of these things; **31** but seek the Kingdom of God, and all these things will be added to you. **32** Do not fear, little flock, because your Father delighted to give you the kingdom; **33** sell your goods, and give alms, make to yourselves bags that do not become old, a treasure unfailing in the heavens, where thief does not come near, nor moth destroy; **34** for where your treasure is, there your heart will be also. **35** Let your loins be girded, and the lamps burning, **36** and you [be] like to men waiting for their lord when he will return out of the wedding feasts, that he having come and knocked, immediately they may open to him. **37** Blessed those servants, whom the lord, having come, will find watching; truly I say to you that he will gird himself, and will cause them to recline, and having come near, will minister to them; **38** and if he may come in the second watch, and in the third watch he may come, and may find [it] so, blessed are those servants. **39** And know this, that if the master of the house had known what hour the thief comes, he would have watched, and would not have permitted his house to be broken through; **40** and you, then, become ready, because at the hour you do not think, the Son of Man comes." **41** And Peter said to Him, "Lord, do You speak this allegory to us, or also to all?" **42** And the Lord said, "Who, then, is the faithful and prudent steward whom the lord will set over his household, to give in season the wheat measure? **43** Blessed that servant, whom his lord, having come, will find doing so; **44** truly I say to you that he will set him over all his goods. **45** And if that servant may say in his heart, My lord delays to come, and may begin to beat the menservants and the maidservants, to eat also, and to drink, and to be drunken, **46** the lord of that servant will come in a day in which he does not look for [him], and in an hour that he does not know, and will cut him off, and he will appoint his portion with the unfaithful. **47** And that servant, who having known his lord's will, and having not prepared, nor having gone according to his will, will be beaten with many stripes, **48** and he who, not having known, and having done things worthy of stripes, will be beaten with few; and to everyone to whom much was given, much will be required from him; and to whom they committed much, more abundantly they will ask of him. **49** I came to cast fire to the earth, and what I wish [is] if it were already kindled! **50** but I have an immersion to be immersed with, and how I am pressed until it may be accomplished! **51** Do you think that I came to give peace in the earth? no, I say to you, but rather division; **52** for there will be from now on five in one house divided—three against two, and two against three; **53** a father will be divided against a son, and a son against a father, a mother against a daughter, and a daughter against a mother, a mother-in-law against her daughter-in-law, and a daughter-in-law against her mother-in-law." **54** And He also said to the multitudes, "When you may see the cloud rising from the west, immediately you say, A shower comes, and it is so; **55** and when a south wind is blowing, you say that there will be heat, and it is; **56** hypocrites! You have known to discern the face of the earth and of the sky, but how do you not discern this time? **57** And why, also, of yourselves, do you not judge what is righteous? **58** For as you are going away with your opponent to the ruler, in the way give diligence to be released from him, lest he may drag you to the judge, and the judge may deliver you to the officer, and the officer may cast you into prison; **59** I say to you, you may not come forth from there until even the last mite you may give back."

vineyard, and he came seeking fruit in it, and he did not find; **7** and he said to the vinedresser, Behold, three years I come seeking fruit in this fig tree, and do not find [it], cut it off, why does it also render the ground useless? **8** And he answering says to him, Lord, permit it also this year, until I may dig around it, and cast in dung; **9** and if indeed it may bear fruit—and if not so, thereafter you will cut it off." **10** And He was teaching in one of the synagogues on the Sabbath, **11** and behold, there was a woman having a spirit of disability [for] eighteen years, and she was bent together, and not able to bend back at all, **12** and Jesus having seen her, called [her] near and said to her, "Woman, you have been loosed from your disability"; **13** and He laid on her [His] hands, and immediately she was set upright, and was glorifying God. **14** And the chief of the synagogue answering—much displeased that on the Sabbath Jesus healed—said to the multitude, "Six days there are in which it is necessary to be working; in these, then, coming, be healed, and not on the day of the Sabbath." **15** Then the Lord answered him and said, "Hypocrite, do not each of you loose his ox or donkey from the stall on the Sabbath, and having led [it] away, water [it]? **16** and this one, being a daughter of Abraham, whom Satan bound eighteen years, behold, did [she] not ought to be loosed from this bond on the day of the Sabbath?" **17** And He saying these things, all who were opposed to Him were being ashamed, and all the multitude were rejoicing over all the glorious things that are being done by Him. **18** And He said, "To what is the Kingdom of God like? and to what will I liken it? **19** It is like to a grain of mustard, which a man having taken, cast into his garden, and it increased, and came to a great tree, and the birds of the heavens rested in its branches." **20** And again He said, "To what will I liken the Kingdom of God? **21** It is like leaven, which a woman, having taken, hid in three measures of meal, until all was leavened." **22** And He was going through cities and villages, teaching, and making progress toward Jerusalem; **23** and a certain one said to Him, "Lord, are those saved few?" And He said to them, **24** "Be striving to go in through the straight gate, because many, I say to you, will seek to go in, and will not be able; **25** from the time the Master of the house may have risen up, and may have shut the door, and you may begin to stand outside, and to knock at the door, saying, Lord, Lord, open to us, and He answering will say to you, I have not known you from where you are, **26** then you may begin to say, We ate before You, and drank, and You taught in our broad places; **27** and He will say, I say to you, I have not known you from where you are; depart from Me, all you workers of the unrighteousness. **28** There will be there the weeping and the gnashing of the teeth when you may see Abraham, and Isaac, and Jacob, and all the prophets, in the Kingdom of God, and yourselves being cast outside; **29** and they will come from east and west, and from north and south, and will recline in the Kingdom of God, **30** and behold, there are last who will be first, and there are first who will be last." **31** On that day there came near certain Pharisees, saying to Him, "Go forth, and be going on from here, for Herod wishes to kill You"; **32** and He said to them, "Having gone, say to that fox, Behold, I cast forth demons, and perfect cures today and tomorrow, and the third [day] I am being perfected; **33** but it is necessary for Me today, and tomorrow, and the [day] following, to go on, because it is not possible for a prophet to perish out of Jerusalem. **34** Jerusalem, Jerusalem, that is killing the prophets, and stoning those sent to her, how often I willed to gather together your children, as a hen [gathers] her brood under the wings, and you did not will. **35** Behold, your house is being left to you desolate, and truly I say to you, you may not see Me, until it may come when you may say, blessed [is] He who is coming in the Name of the Lord."

CHAPTER 13

1 And there were some present at that time, telling Him about the Galileans, whose blood Pilate mingled with their sacrifices; **2** and Jesus answering said to them, "Do you think that these Galileans became sinners beyond all the Galileans, because they have suffered such things? **3** No—I say to you, but if you may not convert, even so will all you perish. **4** Or those eighteen on whom the tower in Siloam fell, and killed them, do you think that these became debtors beyond all men who are dwelling in Jerusalem? **5** No—I say to you, but if you may not convert, all you will perish in like manner." **6** And He spoke this allegory: "A certain one had a fig tree planted in his

CHAPTER 14

1 And it came to pass, on His going into the house of a certain one of the chiefs of the Pharisees, on a Sabbath, to eat bread, that they were watching Him, **2** and behold, there was a certain dropsical man before Him; **3** and Jesus answering spoke to the lawyers and Pharisees, saying, "Is it lawful to heal on the Sabbath?" **4** and they were silent, and having taken hold of [him], He healed him, and let [him] go; **5** and answering them He said, "Of which of you will a donkey or ox fall into a pit, and he will not immediately draw it up on the Sabbath day?" **6** and they were not able to answer Him again to these things. **7** And He spoke an allegory to those called, marking how they were choosing out the first couches, saying to them, **8** "When you may be called by anyone to wedding feasts, you may not recline on the first couch, lest [one] more honorable than you may have been called by him, **9** and he who called you and him having come will say to you, Give to this one [your] place, and then you may begin to occupy the last place with shame. **10** But when you may be called, having gone on, recline in the last place, that when he who called you may come, he may say to you, Friend, come up higher; then you will have glory before those dining with you; **11** because everyone who is exalting himself will be humbled, and he who is humbling himself will be exalted." **12** And He also said to him who called Him, "When you may make an early meal or a dinner, do not be calling your friends, nor your brothers, nor your relatives, nor rich neighbors, lest they may also call you again, and a repayment may come to you; **13** but when you may make a feast, be calling poor, maimed, lame, blind, **14** and you will be blessed, because they have nothing to repay you, for it will be repaid to you in the resurrection of the righteous." **15** And one of those dining with Him, having heard these things, said to Him, "Blessed [is] he who will eat bread in the Kingdom of God"; **16** and He said to him, "A certain man made a great dinner, and called many, **17** and he sent his servant at the hour of the dinner to say to those having been called, Be coming, because now all things are ready. **18** And all began with one [voice] to excuse themselves. The first said to him, I bought a field, and I have need to go forth and see it; I beg of you, have me excused. **19** And another said, I bought five yoke of oxen, and I go on to prove them; I beg of you, have me excused. **20** And another said, I married a wife, and because of this I am not able to come. **21** And that servant having come, told these things to his lord, then the master of the house, having been angry, said to his servant, Go forth quickly into the broad places and lanes of the city, and the poor, and maimed, and lame, and blind, bring in here. **22** And the servant said, Lord, it has been done as you commanded, and still there is room. **23** And the lord said to the servant, Go forth into the ways and hedges, and constrain to come in, that my house may be filled; **24** for I say to you that none of those men who have been called will taste of my dinner." **25** And there were going on with Him great multitudes, and having turned, He said to them, **26** "If anyone comes to Me, and does not hate his own father, and mother, and wife, and children, and brothers, and sisters, and yet even his own life, he is not able to be My disciple; **27** and whoever does not carry his cross, and come after Me, is not able to be My disciple. **28** For who of you, willing to build a tower, does not first, having sat down, count the expense, whether he has the things for completing? **29** lest that he having laid a foundation, and not being able to finish, all who are beholding may begin to mock him, **30** saying, This man began to build, and was not able to finish. **31** Or what king going on to engage with another king in war, does not, having sat down, first consult if he with ten thousand is able to meet him who is coming against him with twenty thousand? **32** and if not so—he being yet a long way off—having sent a delegation, he asks the things for peace. **33** So, then, everyone of you who does not take leave of all that he himself has, is not able to be My disciple. **34** The salt [is] good, but if the salt becomes tasteless, with what will it be seasoned? **35** It is neither fit for land nor for manure—they cast it outside. He who is having ears to hear—let him hear."

CHAPTER 15

1 And all the tax collectors and sinners were coming near to Him, to hear Him, **2** and the Pharisees and the scribes were murmuring, saying, "This One receives sinners, and eats with them." **3** And He spoke to them this allegory, saying, **4** "What man of you having one hundred sheep, and having lost one out of them, does not leave behind the ninety-nine in the wilderness, and go on after the lost one, until he may find it? **5** and having found, he lays [it] on his shoulders rejoicing, **6** and having come into the house, he calls together the friends and the neighbors, saying to them, Rejoice with me, because I found my sheep—the lost one. **7** I say to you that [more] joy will be in Heaven over one sinner converting, rather than over ninety-nine righteous men who have no need of conversion. **8** Or what woman having ten drachmas, if she may lose one drachma, does not light a lamp, and sweep the house, and seek carefully until she may find? **9** and having found, she calls together the female friends and the neighbors, saying, Rejoice with me, for I found the drachma that I lost. **10** So I say to you,

joy comes before the messengers of God over one sinner converting." **11** And He said, "A certain man had two sons, **12** and the younger of them said to the father, Father, give me the portion of the substance falling to [me], and he divided to them the living. **13** And not many days after, having gathered all together, the younger son went abroad to a far country, and there he scattered his substance, living riotously; **14** and he having spent all, there came a mighty famine on that country, and himself began to be in want; **15** and having gone on, he joined himself to one of the citizens of that country, and he sent him into the fields to feed pigs, **16** and he was desirous to fill his belly from the husks that the pigs were eating, and no one was giving to him. **17** And having come to himself, he said, How many hired workers of my father have a superabundance of bread, and I am perishing here with hunger! **18** having risen, I will go on to my father, and will say to him, Father, I sinned—to Heaven, and before you, **19** and I am no longer worthy to be called your son; make me as one of your hired workers. **20** And having risen, he went to his own father, and he being yet far distant, his father saw him, and was moved with compassion, and having ran he fell on his neck and kissed him; **21** and the son said to him, Father, I sinned—to Heaven, and before you, and I am no longer worthy to be called your son. **22** And the father said to his servants, Bring forth the foremost robe, and clothe him, and give a ring for his hand, and sandals for the feet; **23** and having brought the fatted calf, kill [it], and having eaten, we may be merry, **24** because this son of mine was dead, and lived again, and he was lost, and was found; and they began to be merry. **25** And his elder son was in a field, and as, coming, he drew near to the house, he heard music and dancing, **26** and having called near one of the young men, he was inquiring what these things might be, **27** and he said to him, Your brother has arrived, and your father killed the fatted calf, because he received him back in health. **28** And he was angry, and would not go in, therefore his father, having come forth, was pleading him; **29** and he answering said to the father, Behold, so many years I serve you, and never did I transgress your command, and you never gave to me a kid that I might make merry with my friends; **30** but when your son—this one who devoured your living with prostitutes—came, you killed to him the fatted calf. **31** And he said to him, Child, you are always with me, and all my things are yours; **32** but to be merry, and to be glad, it was necessary, because this your brother was dead, and lived again, he was lost, and was found."

CHAPTER 16

1 And He also said to His disciples, "A certain man was rich, who had a steward, and he was accused to him as scattering his goods; **2** and having called him, he said to him, What [is] this I hear about you? render the account of your stewardship, for you may not be steward any longer. **3** And the steward said in himself, What will I do, because my lord takes away the stewardship from me? I am not able to dig, I am ashamed to beg— **4** I have known what I will do, that, when I may be removed from the stewardship, they may receive me to their houses. **5** And having called near each one of his lord's debtors, he said to the first, How much do you owe to my lord? **6** and he said, One hundred baths of oil; and he said to him, Take your bill, and having sat down write fifty. **7** Afterward to another he said, And you, how much do you owe? and he said, One hundred cors of wheat; and he says to him, Take your bill, and write eighty. **8** And the lord commended the unrighteous steward that he did prudently, because the sons of this age are more prudent than the sons of the light in respect to their generation. **9** and I say to you, make to yourselves friends out of the wealth of unrighteousness, that when you may fail, they may receive you into the continuous dwelling places. **10** He who is faithful in the least, [is] also faithful in much; and he who in the least [is] unrighteous, is also unrighteous in much; **11** if, then, in the unrighteous wealth you did not become faithful— who will entrust to you the true? **12** and if in the other's you did not become faithful—who will give to you your own? **13** No servant is able to serve two lords, for either he will hate the one, and he will love the other; or one he will hold to, and of the other he will be heedless; you are not able to serve God and wealth." **14** And also the Pharisees, being lovers of money, were hearing all these things, and were deriding Him, **15** and He said to them, "You are those declaring yourselves righteous before men, but God knows your hearts; because that which is high among men [is] abomination before God; **16** the Law and the Prophets [are] until John; since then the good news of the Kingdom of God is proclaimed, and everyone presses into it; **17** and it is easier for the heaven and the earth to pass away, than one tittle to fall of the Law. **18** Everyone who is sending his wife away, and marrying another, commits adultery; and everyone who is marrying her sent away from a husband commits adultery. **19** And—a certain man was rich, and was clothed in purple and fine linen, making merry sumptuously every day, **20** and there was a certain poor man, by name Lazarus, who was laid at his porch, full of sores, **21** and desiring to be filled from the crumbs that are falling from the table of the rich man; indeed, also the dogs, coming, were licking his sores. **22** And it came to pass, that the poor man died, and that he was carried away by the messengers into the bosom of Abraham—and the rich man also died, and was buried; **23** and having lifted up his eyes in Hades, being in torments, he sees Abraham far off, and Lazarus in his bosom, **24** and having cried, he said, Father Abraham, deal kindly with me, and send Lazarus, that he may dip the tip of his finger in water, and may cool my tongue, because I am distressed in this flame. **25** And Abraham said, Child, remember that you received your good things in your life, and Lazarus in like manner the evil things, and now he is comforted, and you are distressed; **26** and besides all these things, between us and you a great chasm is fixed, so that they who are willing to go over from here to you are not able, nor do they pass through from there to us. **27** And he said, I ask, then, father, that you may send him to the house of my father, **28** for I have five brothers, so that he may thoroughly testify to them, that they also may not come to this place of torment. **29** Abraham says to him, They have Moses and the prophets, let them hear them; **30** and he said, No, father Abraham, but if anyone from the dead may go to them, they will convert. **31** And he said to him, If they do not hear Moses and the prophets, neither will they be persuaded if one may rise out of the dead."

CHAPTER 17

1 And He said to the disciples, "It is impossible for the stumbling blocks not to come, but woe [to him] through whom they come; **2** it is more profitable to him if a weighty millstone is put around his neck, and he has been cast into the sea, than that he may cause one of these little ones to stumble. **3** Take heed to yourselves, and if your brother may sin in regard to you, rebuke him, and if he may change his mind, forgive him, **4** and if seven times in the day he may sin against you, and seven times in the day may return to you, saying, I change my mind, you will forgive him." **5** And the apostles said to the Lord, "Add to us faith"; **6** and the Lord said, "If you had faith as a grain of mustard, you would have said to this sycamine, Be uprooted, and be planted in the sea, and it would have obeyed you. **7** But who is he of you—having a servant plowing or feeding—who, to him having come in out of the field, will say, Having come, recline at once? **8** but will not [rather] say to him, Prepare what I may dine, and having girded yourself around, minister to me, until I eat and drink, and after these things you will eat and drink? **9** Does he have favor to that servant because he did the things directed? I think not. **10** So also you, when you may have done all the things directed you, say, We are unprofitable servants, because that which we owed to do we have done." **11** And it came to pass, in His going on to Jerusalem, that He passed through the midst of Samaria and Galilee, **12** and He entering into a certain village, there ten leprous men met Him, who stood far off, **13** and they lifted up the voice, saying, "Jesus, Master, deal kindly with us"; **14** and having seen [them], He said to them, "Having gone on, show yourselves to the priests"; and it came to pass, in their going on, they were cleansed, **15** and one of them having seen that he was healed turned back, glorifying God with a loud voice, **16** and he fell on [his] face at His feet, giving thanks to Him, and he was a Samaritan. **17** And Jesus answering said, "Were not the ten cleansed, and the nine—where? **18** There were none found who turned back to give glory to God, except this foreigner"; **19** and He said to him, "Having risen, be going on, your faith has saved you." **20** And having been questioned by the Pharisees when the Kingdom of God comes, He answered them and said, "The Kingdom of God does not come with observation; **21** nor will they say, Behold, here; or, Behold, there; for behold, the Kingdom of God is within you." **22** And He said to His disciples, "Days will come when you will desire to see one of the days of the Son of Man and you will not behold [it]; **23** and they will say to you, Behold, here; or, Behold, there;

you may not go away, nor follow; **24** for as the lightning is flashing out of one [part] under the sky [and] shines to the other [part] under the sky, so will the Son of Man also be in His day; **25** and first it is necessary for Him to suffer many things, and to be rejected by this generation. **26** And as it came to pass in the days of Noah, so will it also be in the days of the Son of Man; **27** they were eating, they were drinking, they were marrying, they were given in marriage, until the day that Noah entered into the Ark, and the flood came, and destroyed all; **28** in like manner also, as it came to pass in the days of Lot; they were eating, they were drinking, they were buying, they were selling, they were planting, they were building; **29** and on the day Lot went forth from Sodom, He rained fire and brimstone from the sky, and destroyed all. **30** According to these things it will be, in the day the Son of Man is revealed; **31** in that day, he who will be on the housetop, and his vessels in the house, do not let him come down to take them away; and he in the field, in like manner, do not let him turn backward; **32** remember the wife of Lot. **33** Whoever may seek to save his life, will lose it; and whoever may lose it, will preserve it. **34** I say to you, in that night there will be two [men] on one bed: one will be taken, and the other will be left; **35** two [women] will be grinding at the same place together: one will be taken, and the other will be left; **36** [[two [men] will be in the field: one will be taken, and the other left."]] **37** And they answering say to Him, "Where, Lord?" And He said to them, "Where the body [is], there the eagles will be gathered together."

CHAPTER 18

1 And He also spoke an allegory to them, that it is always necessary to pray and not to faint, **2** saying, "A certain judge was in a certain city—he is not fearing God, and he is not regarding man— **3** and a widow was in that city, and she was coming to him, saying, Do me justice on my opponent, **4** and he would not for a time, but after these things he said in himself, Even if I do not fear God, and do not regard man, **5** yet because this widow gives me trouble, I will do her justice, lest, continuously coming, she may bruise me." **6** And the Lord said, "Hear what the unrighteous judge says: **7** and will God not execute justice to His chosen ones, who are crying to Him day and night—bearing long in regard to them? **8** I say to you that He will execute justice to them quickly; but the Son of Man having come, will He find faith on the earth?" **9** And He also spoke to some who have been trusting in themselves that they were righteous, and have been despising the rest, this allegory: **10** "Two men went up to the temple to pray, one a Pharisee, and the other a tax collector; **11** the Pharisee having stood by himself, thus prayed: God, I thank You that I am not as the rest of men, rapacious, unrighteous, adulterers, or even as this tax collector; **12** I fast twice in the week, I give tithes of all things—as many as I possess. **13** And the tax collector, having stood far off, would not even lift up the eyes to the sky, but was striking on his breast, saying, God be propitious to me—the sinner! **14** I say to you, this one went down declared righteous, to his house, rather than that one: for everyone who is exalting himself will be humbled, and he who is humbling himself will be exalted." **15** And they were also bringing the babies near, that He may touch them, and the disciples having seen, rebuked them, **16** and Jesus having called them near, said, "Permit the little children to come to Me, and do not forbid them, for of such is the Kingdom of God; **17** truly I say to you, whoever may not receive the Kingdom of God as a little child, may not enter into it." **18** And a certain ruler questioned Him, saying, "Good Teacher, what having done—will I inherit continuous life?" **19** And Jesus said to him, "Why do you call Me good? no one [is] good, except one—God; **20** you have known the commands: You may not commit adultery, You may not murder, You may not steal, You may not bear false witness, Honor your father and your mother." **21** And he said, "All these I kept from my youth"; **22** and having heard these things, Jesus said to him, "Yet one thing to you is lacking: all things—as many as you have—sell, and distribute to the poor, and you will have treasure in Heaven, and come, follow Me"; **23** and he, having heard these things, became very sorrowful, for he was exceedingly rich. **24** And Jesus having seen him become very sorrowful, said, "How hardly will those having riches enter into the Kingdom of God! **25** for it is easier for a camel to enter through the eye of a needle, than for a rich man to enter into the Kingdom of God." **26** And those who heard, said, "And who is able to be saved?" **27** and He said, "The things impossible with men are possible with God." **28** And Peter said, "Behold, we left all, and followed You"; **29** and He said to them, "Truly I say to you that there is not one who left house, or parents, or brothers, or wife, or children, for the sake of the Kingdom of God, **30** who may not receive back manifold more in this time, and in the coming age, continuous life." **31** And having taken the Twelve aside, He said to them, "Behold, we go up to Jerusalem, and all things will be accomplished that have been written through the prophets to the Son of Man, **32** for He will be delivered up to the nations, and will be mocked, and insulted, and spit on, **33** and having scourged they will put Him to death, and on the third day He will rise again." **34** And they understood none of these things, and this saying was hid from them, and they were not knowing the things said. **35** And it came to pass, in His coming near to Jericho, a certain blind man was sitting beside the way begging, **36** and having heard a multitude going by, he was inquiring what this may be, **37** and they brought him word that Jesus the Nazarene passes by, **38** and he cried out, saying, "Jesus, Son of David, deal kindly with me"; **39** and those going before were rebuking him, that he might be silent, but he was crying out much more, "Son of David, deal kindly with me!" **40** And Jesus having stood, commanded him to be brought to Him, and he having come near, He questioned him, **41** saying, "What do you will I will do to you?" And he said, "Lord, that I may receive sight." **42** And Jesus said to him, "Receive your sight; your faith has saved you"; **43** and instantly he received sight, and was following Him, glorifying God; and all the people, having seen, gave praise to God.

CHAPTER 19

1 And having entered, He was passing through Jericho, **2** and behold, a man, by name called Zaccheus, and he was a chief tax collector, and he was rich, **3** and he was seeking to see Jesus, who He is, and was not able for the multitude, because he was small in stature, **4** and having run forward before, he went up on a sycamore, that he may see Him, because through that [way] He was about to pass by. **5** And as Jesus came up to the place, having looked up, He saw him and said to him, "Zaccheus, having hurried, come down, for it is necessary for Me to remain in your house today"; **6** and he having hurried came down, and received Him rejoicing; **7** and having seen [it], they were all murmuring, saying, "He went in to lodge with a sinful man!" **8** And Zaccheus having stood, said to the Lord, "Behold, half of my goods, Lord, I give to the poor, and if I took by false accusation anything of anyone, I give back fourfold." **9** And Jesus said to him, "Today salvation came to this house, inasmuch as he also is a son of Abraham; **10** for the Son of Man came to seek and to save the lost." **11** And while they are hearing these things, having added He spoke an allegory, because of His being near to Jerusalem, and of their thinking that the Kingdom of God is immediately about to appear. **12** He therefore said, "A certain man of birth went on to a far country, to take to himself a kingdom, and to return, **13** and having called ten servants of his own, he gave ten minas to them and said to them, Do business—until I come; **14** and his citizens were hating him, and sent a delegation after him, saying, We do not wish this one to reign over us. **15** And it came to pass, on his coming back, having taken the kingdom, that he commanded these servants to be called to him, to whom he gave the money, that he might know what anyone had done in business. **16** And the first came near, saying, Lord, your mina gained ten minas; **17** and he said to him, Well done, good servant, because you became faithful in a very little, be having authority over ten cities. **18** And the second came, saying, Lord, your mina made five minas; **19** and he also said to this one, And you, become [ruler] over five cities. **20** And another came, saying, Lord, behold, your mina, that I had lying away in a napkin; **21** for I was afraid of you, because you are an austere man; you take up what you did not lay down, and reap what you did not sow. **22** And he says to him, Out of your mouth I will judge you, evil servant: you knew that I am an austere man, taking up what I did not lay down, and reaping what I did not sow! **23** and why did you not give my money to the bank, and I, having come, might have received it with interest? **24** And to those standing by he said, Take the mina from him, and give him having the ten minas— **25** (and they said to him, Lord, he has ten minas)— **26** for I say to you that to everyone having will be given, and from him not having, also what he has will be taken from him, **27** but those my enemies, who did

not wish me to reign over them, bring here and slay before me." **28** And having said these things, He went on before, going up to Jerusalem. **29** And it came to pass, as He came near to Bethphage and Bethany, to that called the Mount of Olives, He sent two of His disciples, **30** having said, "Go away into the village in front of [you], in which, entering in, you will find a colt bound, on which no one of men ever sat, having loosed it, bring [it]; **31** and if anyone questions you, Why do you lose [it]? thus you will say to him: The Lord has need of it." **32** And those sent, having gone away, found according as He said to them, **33** and while they are losing the colt, its owners said to them, "Why do you lose the colt?" **34** and they said, "The Lord has need of it"; **35** and they brought it to Jesus, and having cast their garments on the colt, they sat Jesus on it. **36** And as He is going, they were spreading their garments in the way, **37** and as He is coming near now, at the descent of the Mount of Olives, the whole multitude of the disciples began rejoicing to praise God with a great voice for all the mighty works they had seen, **38** saying, "Blessed [is] the King coming in the Name of the Lord; peace in Heaven, and glory in the highest!" **39** And certain of the Pharisees from the multitude said to Him, "Teacher, rebuke Your disciples"; **40** and He answering said to them, "I say to you that if these will be silent, the stones will cry out!" **41** And when He came near, having seen the city, He wept over it, **42** saying, "If you knew, even you, at least in this your day, the things for your peace; but now they were hid from your eyes. **43** Because days will come on you, and your enemies will cast a rampart around you, and surround you around, and press you on every side, **44** and lay you low, and your children within you, and they will not leave in you a stone on a stone, because you did not know the time of your inspection." **45** And having entered into the temple, He began to cast forth those selling in it, and those buying, **46** saying to them, "It has been written, My house is a house of prayer—but you made it a den of robbers." **47** And He was teaching daily in the temple, but the chief priests and the scribes were seeking to destroy Him—also the chiefs of the people— **48** and they were not finding what they will do, for all the people were hanging on Him, hearing Him.

CHAPTER 20

1 And it came to pass, on one of those days, as He is teaching the people in the temple, and proclaiming good news, the chief priests and the scribes, with the elders, came on [Him], **2** and spoke to Him, saying, "Tell us by what authority You do these things? or who is he that gave to You this authority?" **3** And He answering said to them, "I will question you—I also—one thing, and tell Me: **4** the immersion of John, was it from Heaven, or from men?" **5** And they reasoned with themselves, saying, "If we may say, From Heaven, He will say, Why, then, did you not believe him? **6** and if we may say, From men, all the people will stone us, for they are having been persuaded John to be a prophet." **7** And they answered that they did not know from where [it was], **8** and Jesus said to them, "Neither do I say to you by what authority I do these things." **9** And He began to speak to the people this allegory: "A certain man planted a vineyard, and gave it out to farmers, and went abroad for a long time, **10** and at the season he sent a servant to the farmers, that they may give to him from the fruit of the vineyard, but the farmers having beat him, sent [him] away empty. **11** And he added to send another servant, and they also having beaten and dishonored that one, sent [him] away empty; **12** and he added to send a third, and this one also, having wounded, they cast out. **13** And the owner of the vineyard said, What will I do? I will send my son, the beloved, perhaps having seen this one, they will respect [him]; **14** and having seen him, the farmers reasoned among themselves, saying, This is the heir; come, we may kill him, that the inheritance may become ours; **15** and having cast him outside of the vineyard, they killed [him]; what, then, will the owner of the vineyard do to them? **16** He will come, and destroy these farmers, and will give the vineyard to others." And having heard, they said, "Let it not be!" **17** and He, having looked on them, said, "What, then, is this that has been written: A stone that the builders rejected—this became head of a corner? **18** everyone who has fallen on that stone will be broken, and on whom it may fall, it will crush him to pieces." **19** And the chief priests and the scribes sought to lay hands on Him in that hour, and they feared the people, for they knew that He spoke this allegory against them. **20** And having watched [Him], they sent forth ones lying in wait, feigning themselves to be righteous, that they might take hold of His word, to deliver Him up to the rule and to the authority of the governor, **21** and they questioned Him, saying, "Teacher, we have known that You say and teach correctly, and do not receive a person, but in truth teach the way of God. **22** Is it lawful to us to give tribute to Caesar or not?" **23** And He, having perceived their craftiness, said to them, "Why do you tempt Me? **24** show Me a denarius; of whom does it have an image and inscription?" And they answering said, "Of Caesar": **25** and He said to them, "Give back, therefore, the things of Caesar to Caesar, and the things of God to God"; **26** and they were not able to take hold on His saying before the people, and having wondered at His answer, they were silent. **27** And certain of the Sadducees, who are denying that there is a resurrection, having come near, questioned Him, **28** saying, "Teacher, Moses wrote to us if anyone's brother may die, having a wife, and he may die childless—that his brother may take the wife, and may raise up seed to his brother. **29** There were, then, seven brothers, and the first having taken a wife, died childless, **30** and the second took the wife, and he died childless, **31** and the third took her, and in like manner also the seven—they left no children, and they died; **32** and last of all the woman also died: **33** in the resurrection, then, of which of them does she become wife? For the seven had her as wife." **34** And Jesus answering said to them, "The sons of this age marry and are given in marriage, **35** but those accounted worthy to obtain that age, and the resurrection that is out of the dead, neither marry, nor are they given in marriage; **36** for neither are they able to die anymore—for they are like messengers—and they are sons of God, being sons of the resurrection. **37** And that the dead are raised, even Moses showed at the Bush, since he calls the Lord the God of Abraham, and the God of Isaac, and the God of Jacob; **38** and He is not a God of dead men, but of living, for all live to Him." **39** And certain of the scribes answering said, "Teacher, You said well"; **40** and they no longer dared question Him anything. **41** And He said to them, "How do they say the Christ is [the] son of David, **42** and David himself says in [the] Scroll of Psalms, The Lord said to my Lord, || Sit on My right hand, **43** Until I will make Your enemies Your footstool; **44** David, then, calls Him Lord, and how is He his son?" **45** And all the people hearing, He said to His disciples, **46** "Take heed of the scribes, who are wishing to walk in long robes, and are cherishing salutations in the markets, and first seats in the synagogues, and first couches at the banquets, **47** who devour the houses of the widows, and make long prayers for a pretense, these will receive more abundant judgment."

CHAPTER 21

1 And having looked up, He saw those who cast their gifts into the treasury—rich men, **2** and He also saw a certain poor widow casting two mites there, **3** and He said, "Truly I say to you that this poor widow cast in more than all; **4** for all these out of their superabundance cast into the gifts to God, but this one out of her want, all the living that she had, cast in." **5** And [as] some were speaking about the temple, that it has been adorned with good stones and devoted things, He said, **6** "These things that you behold—days will come in which there will not be left a stone on a stone that will not be thrown down." **7** And they questioned Him, saying, "Teacher, when, then, will these things be? and what [is] the sign when these things may be about to happen?" **8** And He said, "See—you may not be led astray, for many will come in My Name, saying, I am [He], and the time has come near; do not then go on after them; **9** and when you may hear of wars and uprisings, do not be terrified, for it is necessary for these things to happen first, but the end [is] not immediately." **10** Then He said to them, "Nation will rise against nation, and kingdom against kingdom, **11** also great shakings, and there will be famines and pestilences in every place; also there will be fearful things and great signs from the sky; **12** and before all these, they will lay on you their hands, and persecute, delivering up to synagogues and prisons, being brought before kings and governors for My Name's sake; **13** and it will become to you for a testimony. **14** Settle, then, to your hearts, not to meditate beforehand to reply, **15** for I will give to you a mouth and wisdom that all your opposers will not be able to refute or resist. **16** And you will be delivered up also by parents, and brothers, and relatives, and friends, and they will put [some] of you to death; **17** and you will be hated by all because of My Name— **18** and a hair out of your head will not

perish; **19** in your patience possess your souls. **20** And when you may see Jerusalem surrounded by encampments, then know that her desolation has come near; **21** then those in Judea, let them flee to the mountains; and those in her midst, let them depart out; and those in the countries, do not let them come in to her; **22** because these are days of vengeance, to fulfill all things that have been written. **23** And woe to those with child, and to those giving suck, in those days; for there will be great distress on the land, and wrath on this people; **24** and they will fall by the mouth of the sword, and will be led captive to all the nations, and Jerusalem will be trodden down by nations, until the times of nations be fulfilled. **25** And there will be signs in sun, and moon, and stars, and on the earth distress of nations with perplexity, sea and wave roaring; **26** men fainting at heart from fear, and expectation of the things coming on the world, for the powers of the heavens will be shaken. **27** And then they will see the Son of Man coming in a cloud, with power and much glory; **28** and these things beginning to happen, bend yourselves back, and lift up your heads, because your redemption draws near." **29** And He spoke an allegory to them: "See the fig tree, and all the trees, **30** when they may now cast forth, having seen, of yourselves you know that now the summer is near; **31** so also you, when you may see these things happening, you know that the Kingdom of God is near; **32** truly I say to you, this generation may not pass away until all may have come to pass; **33** the sky and the earth will pass away, but My words may not pass away. **34** And take heed to yourselves lest your hearts may be weighed down with carousing, and drunkenness, and anxieties of life, and suddenly that day may come on you, **35** for it will come as a snare on all those dwelling on the face of all the earth, **36** watch, then, in every season, praying that you may be accounted worthy to escape all these things that are about to come to pass, and to stand before the Son of Man." **37** And He was teaching in the temple during the days, and during the nights, going forth, He was lodging at [that] called the Mount of Olives; **38** and all the people were coming early to Him in the temple to hear Him.

CHAPTER 22

1 And the Celebration of the Unleavened [Bread] was coming near, that is called Passover, **2** and the chief priests and the scribes were seeking how they may take Him up, for they were afraid of the people. **3** And Satan entered into Judas, who is surnamed Iscariot, being of the number of the Twelve, **4** and he, having gone away, spoke with the chief priests and the magistrates, how he might deliver Him up to them, **5** and they rejoiced, and covenanted to give him money, **6** and he agreed, and was seeking a favorable season to deliver Him up to them without tumult. **7** And the day of the Unleavened [Bread] came, in which it was necessary [for] the Passover to be sacrificed, **8** and He sent Peter and John, saying, "Having gone on, prepare to us the Passover, that we may eat"; **9** and they said to Him, "Where do You will that we might prepare?" **10** And He said to them, "Behold, in your entering into the city, a man will meet you there, carrying a pitcher of water, follow him into the house where he goes in, **11** and you will say to the master of the house, The Teacher says to you, Where is the guest-chamber where I may eat the Passover with My disciples? **12** and he will show you a large upper room furnished, make ready there"; **13** and they, having gone away, found as He has said to them, and they made the Passover ready. **14** And when the hour was come, He reclined, and the twelve apostles with Him, **15** and He said to them, "With desire I desired to eat this Passover with you before My suffering, **16** for I say to you that I may not eat of it no longer until it may be fulfilled in the Kingdom of God." **17** And having taken a cup, having given thanks, He said, "Take this and divide to yourselves, **18** for I say to you that I may not drink of the produce of the vine until the Kingdom of God may come." **19** And having taken bread, having given thanks, He broke and gave to them, saying, "This is My body, that is being given for you, do this in remembrance of Me." **20** In like manner, also, the cup after the dining, saying, "This cup [is] the New Covenant in My blood, that is being poured forth for you. **21** But behold, the hand of him delivering Me up [is] with Me on the table, **22** and, indeed, the Son of Man goes according to what has been determined; but woe to that man through whom He is being delivered up." **23** And they began to reason among themselves who then of them it may be who is about to do this thing. **24** And there happened also a strife among them—who of them is accounted to be greater. **25** And He said to them, "The kings of the nations exercise lordship over them, and those exercising authority on them are called benefactors; **26** but you [are] not so, but he who is greater among you—let him be as the younger; and he who is leading, as he who is ministering; **27** for who is greater? he who is reclining, or he who is ministering? is it not he who is reclining? and I am in your midst as He who is ministering. **28** And you are those who have remained with Me in My temptations, **29** and I appoint to you a kingdom, as My Father appointed to Me, **30** that you may eat and may drink at My table, in My kingdom, and may sit on thrones, judging the twelve tribes of Israel." **31** And the Lord said, "Simon, Simon, behold, Satan asked for himself to sift you as the wheat, **32** and I implored for you that your faith may not fail; and you, when you turned, strengthen your brothers." **33** And he said to Him, "Lord, I am ready to go with You both to prison and to death"; **34** and He said, "I say to you, Peter, a rooster will not crow today, before you may disown knowing Me three times." **35** And He said to them, "When I sent you without bag, and leather pouch, and sandals, did you lack anything?" And they said, "Nothing." **36** Then He said to them, "But now, he who is having a bag, let him take [it] up, and in like manner also a leather pouch; and he who is not having, let him sell his garment, and buy a sword, **37** for I say to you that this which has been written is necessary to be accomplished in Me: And He was reckoned with lawless ones; for also the things concerning Me have an end." **38** And they said, "Lord, behold, here [are] two swords"; and He said to them, "It is sufficient." **39** And having gone forth, He went on, according to custom, to the Mount of Olives, and His disciples also followed Him, **40** and having come to the place, He said to them, "Pray to not enter into temptation." **41** And He was withdrawn from them, as it were a stone's cast, and having fallen on the knees He was praying, **42** saying, "Father, if You are willing, remove this cup from Me, but not My will, but Yours be done." **43** And there appeared to Him a messenger from Heaven strengthening Him; **44** and having been in agony, He was more earnestly praying, and His sweat became, as it were, great drops of blood falling on the ground. **45** And having risen up from the prayer, having come to the disciples, He found them sleeping from the sorrow, **46** and He said to them, "Why do you sleep? having risen, pray that you may not enter into temptation." **47** And while He is speaking, behold, a multitude, and he who is called Judas, one of the Twelve, was coming before them, and he came near to Jesus to kiss Him, **48** and Jesus said to him, "Judas, do you deliver up the Son of Man with a kiss?" **49** And those around Him, having seen what was about to be, said to Him, "Lord, will we strike with a sword?" **50** And a certain one of them struck the servant of the chief priest, and took off his right ear, **51** and Jesus answering said, "Permit thus far," and having touched his ear, He healed him. **52** And Jesus said to those having come on Him—chief priests, and magistrates of the temple, and elders, "Have you come forth with swords and sticks as on a robber? **53** while daily I was with you in the temple, you stretched forth no hands against Me; but this is your hour and the power of the darkness." **54** And having taken Him, they led and brought Him into the house of the chief priest. And Peter was following far off, **55** and they having kindled a fire in the midst of the court, and having sat down together, Peter was sitting in the midst of them, **56** and a certain maid having seen him sitting at the light, and having earnestly looked at him, she said, "And this one was with Him!" **57** and he disowned Him, saying, "Woman, I have not known Him." **58** And after a while, another having seen him, said, "And you are of them!" And Peter said, "Man, I am not." **59** And one hour, as it were, having intervened, a certain other was confidently affirming, saying, "Of a truth this one also was with Him, for he is also a Galilean"; **60** and Peter said, "Man, I have not known what you say"; and immediately, while he is speaking, a rooster crowed. **61** And the Lord, having turned, looked on Peter, and Peter remembered the word of the Lord, how He said to him, "Before a rooster will crow, you may disown Me three times"; **62** and Peter having gone outside, wept bitterly. **63** And the men who were holding Jesus were mocking Him, beating [Him]; **64** and having blindfolded Him, they were striking Him on the face, and were questioning Him, saying, "Prophesy who he is who struck You?" **65** and many other things, slandering, they spoke in regard to Him. **66** And when it became day there was gathered together the eldership of the people, chief priests also, and scribes, and they led Him up to their own Sanhedrin, **67** saying, "If You are the Christ, tell us." And He said to them, "If I may tell you, you will not believe; **68** and if I also question [you], you will not answer Me or send Me away; **69** from now on, there will be the Son of Man sitting on the right hand of the power of God." **70** And they all said, "You, then, are the Son of God?" And He said to them, "You say [it], because I am"; **71** and they said, "What need do we have yet of testimony? for we ourselves heard [it] from His mouth."

CHAPTER 23

1 And having risen, the whole multitude of them led Him to Pilate, **2** and began to accuse Him, saying, "We found this One perverting the nation, and forbidding to give tribute to Caesar, saying Himself to be Christ, a king." **3** And Pilate questioned Him, saying, "You are the King of the Jews?" And He answering him, said, "You say [it]." **4** And Pilate said to the chief priests and the multitude, "I find no fault in this Man"; **5** and they were the more urgent, saying, "He stirs up the people, teaching throughout the whole of Judea—having begun from Galilee—to this place." **6** And Pilate having heard of Galilee, questioned if the Man is a Galilean, **7** and having known that He is from the jurisdiction of Herod, he sent Him back to Herod, he also being in Jerusalem in those days. **8** And Herod rejoiced exceedingly having seen Jesus, for he was wishing to see Him for a long [time], because of hearing many things about Him, and he was hoping to see some sign done by Him, **9** and was questioning Him in many words, and He answered him nothing. **10** And the chief priests and the scribes stood vehemently accusing Him, **11** and Herod with his soldiers having set Him at nothing, and having mocked, having cast radiant apparel around Him, sent Him back to Pilate, **12** and both Pilate and Herod became friends with one another on that day, for they were previously at enmity between themselves. **13** And Pilate having called together the chief priests, and the rulers, and the people, **14** said to them, "You brought this Man to me as perverting the people, and behold, I having examined [Him] before you, found no fault in this Man in those things you bring forward against Him; **15** no, neither Herod, for he sent Him back to us, and behold, nothing worthy of death is having been done by Him; **16** having corrected, therefore, I will release Him," **17** [[for it was necessary for him to release to them one at every celebration,]] **18** and they cried out—the whole multitude— saying, "Away with this One, and release Barabbas to us," **19** who had been cast into prison, because of a certain sedition made in the city, and murder. **20** Pilate again then—wishing to release Jesus—called to them, **21** but they were calling out, saying, "Crucify! Crucify Him!" **22** And he said to them a third time, "Why, what evil did He do? I found no cause of death in Him; having corrected Him, then, I will release [Him]." **23** And they were pressing with loud voices asking Him to be crucified, and their voices, and those of the chief priests, were prevailing, **24** and Pilate gave judgment for their request being done, **25** and he released him who because of sedition and murder has been cast into the prison, whom they were asking for, and he gave up Jesus to their will. **26** And as they led Him away, having taken hold on Simon, a certain Cyrenian, coming from the field, they put the cross on him to carry [it] behind Jesus. **27** And a great multitude of the people were following Him, and of women, who also were beating themselves and lamenting Him, **28** and Jesus having turned to them, said, "Daughters of Jerusalem, do not weep for Me, but weep for yourselves and for your children; **29** for behold, days come in which they will say, Blessed the barren, and wombs that did not bear, and breasts that did not give suck; **30** then they will begin to say to the mountains, Fall on us, and to the hills, Cover us; **31** for if they do these things in the green tree, what may happen in the dry?" **32** And there were also others—two evildoers—with Him, to be put to death; **33** and when they came to the place that is called "[Place] of [the] Skull," there they crucified Him and the evildoers, one on the right hand and one on the left. **34** And Jesus said, "Father, forgive them, for they have not known what they do"; and parting His garments they cast a lot. **35** And the people were standing, looking on, and the rulers were also sneering with them, saying, "He saved others, let Him save Himself, if this be the Christ, the Chosen One of God." **36** And the soldiers were also mocking Him, coming near and offering vinegar to Him, **37** and saying, "If You are the King of the Jews, save Yourself." **38** And there was also an inscription written over Him [[in letters of Greek, and Latin, and Hebrew]]: "This is the King of the Jews." **39** And one of the evildoers who were hanged was slandering Him, saying, "If You are the Christ, save

Yourself and us." **40** And the other answering, was rebuking him, saying, "Do you not even fear God, that you are in the same judgment? **41** and we indeed justly, for we are receiving back [things] worthy of what we did, but this One did nothing out of place"; **42** and he said to Jesus, "Remember me, Lord, when You may come in Your kingdom"; **43** and Jesus said to him, "Truly I say to you, today you will be with Me in Paradise." **44** And it was, as it were, the sixth hour, and darkness came over all the land until the ninth hour, **45** and the sun was darkened, and the veil of the temple was torn in the middle, **46** and having cried with a loud voice, Jesus said, "Father, into Your hands I commit My spirit"; now having said this, He breathed His last. **47** And the centurion having seen what was done, glorified God, saying, "Truly this Man was righteous"; **48** and all the multitudes having come together to this sight, beholding the things that came to pass, turned back striking their breasts; **49** and all His acquaintances stood far off, and women who followed Him from Galilee, beholding these things. **50** And behold, a man, by name Joseph, being a counselor, a man good and righteous, **51** from Arimathea, a city of the Jews, who also himself was expecting the Kingdom of God, he was not consenting to their counsel and deed, **52** he having gone near to Pilate, asked for the body of Jesus, **53** and having taken it down, he wrapped it in fine linen, and placed it in a hewn-out tomb, where no one was yet laid. **54** And it was [the] Day of Preparation, and Sabbath was approaching, **55** and the women who also have come with Him out of Galilee having followed after, beheld the tomb, and how His body was placed, **56** and having turned back, they made ready spices and ointments, and on the Sabbath, indeed, they rested, according to the command.

CHAPTER 24

1 And on the first [day] of the weeks, at early dawn, they came to the tomb, carrying the spices they made ready, and certain [others] with them, **2** and they found the stone having been rolled away from the tomb, **3** and having gone in, they did not find the body of the Lord Jesus. **4** And it came to pass, while they are perplexed about this, that behold, two men stood by them in clothing—flashing [with light]; **5** and on their having become afraid, and having inclined the face to the earth, they said to them, "Why do you seek the living with the dead? **6** he is not here, but was raised; remember how He spoke to you, being yet in Galilee, **7** saying, It is necessary for the Son of Man to be delivered up into the hands of sinful men, and to be crucified, and to rise again [on] the third day." **8** And they remembered His sayings, **9** and having turned back from the tomb, told all these things to the Eleven, and to all the rest. **10** And it was Mary the Magdalene, and Joanna, and Mary of James, and the other women with them, who told these things to the apostles, **11** and their sayings appeared before them as idle talk, and they were not believing them. **12** And Peter having risen, ran to the tomb, and having stooped down he sees the linen clothes lying alone, and he went away to his own home, wondering at that having come to pass. **13** And behold, two of them were going on during that day to a village, being sixty stadia distant from Jerusalem, the name of which [is] Emmaus, **14** and they were conversing with one another about all these things that have happened. **15** And it came to pass in their conversing and reasoning together, that Jesus Himself, having come near, was going on with them, **16** and their eyes were restrained so as not to know Him, **17** and He said to them, "What [are] these words that you exchange with one another, walking, and you are sad?" **18** And one, whose name was Cleopas, answering, said to Him, "Are You alone visiting Jerusalem and have not known the things having come to pass in it in these days?" **19** And He said to them, "What things?" And they said to Him, "The things about Jesus of Nazareth, who became a man—a prophet—powerful in deed and word, before God and all the people, **20** how also the chief priests and our rulers delivered Him up to a judgment of death, and crucified Him; **21** and we were hoping that it is He who is about to redeem Israel, and also with all these things, this third day is passing today since these things happened. **22** And certain of our women also astonished us, coming early to the tomb, **23** and having not found His body, they came, saying to have also seen an apparition of messengers who say He is alive, **24** and certain of those with us went away to the tomb, and found [it] so, even as the women said, and they did not see Him." **25** And He said to them, "O inconsiderate and slow in heart to believe on all

that the prophets spoke! **26** Was it not necessary [for] the Christ to suffer these things, and to enter into His glory?" **27** and having begun from Moses, and from all the Prophets, He was expounding to them in all the Writings the things about Himself. **28** And they came near to the village to where they were going, and He made an appearance of going on further, **29** and they constrained Him, saying, "Remain with us, for it is toward evening," and the day declined, and He went in to remain with them. **30** And it came to pass, in His reclining with them, having taken the bread, He blessed, and having broken, He was giving to them, **31** and their eyes were opened, and they recognized Him, and He became unseen by them. **32** And they said to one another, "Was our heart not burning within us as He was speaking to us in the way, and as He was opening the Writings up to us?" **33** And they, having risen up the same hour, turned back to Jerusalem, and found the Eleven gathered together, and those with them, **34** saying, "The Lord was indeed raised, and was seen by Simon"; **35** and they were expounding the things in the way, and how He was made known to them in the breaking of the bread, **36** and as they are speaking these things, Jesus Himself stood in the midst of them, and says to them, "Peace to you"; **37** and being amazed, and becoming frightened, they were thinking themselves to see a spirit. **38** And He said to them, "Why are you troubled? and why do reasonings come up in your hearts? **39** see My hands and My feet, that I am He; handle Me and see, because a spirit does not have flesh and bones as you see Me having." **40** And having said this, He showed the hands and the feet to them, **41** and while they are not believing from the joy, and wondering, He said to them, "Do you have anything here to eat?" **42** and they gave to Him part of a broiled fish, and of a honeycomb, **43** and having taken, He ate before them, **44** and He said to them, "These [are] the words that I spoke to you, being yet with you, that it is necessary to be fulfilled all the things that are written in the Law of Moses, and the Prophets, and the Psalms, about Me." **45** Then He opened up their understanding to understand the Writings, **46** and He said to them, "Thus it has been written, and thus it was necessary [for] the Christ to suffer, and to rise out of the dead [on] the third day, **47** and conversion and forgiveness of sins is to be proclaimed in His Name to all the nations, beginning from Jerusalem: **48** and you are witnesses of these things. **49** And behold, I send the promise of My Father on you, but you—abide in the city of Jerusalem until you are clothed with power from on high." **50** And He led them forth outside—to Bethany, and having lifted up His hands He blessed them, **51** and it came to pass, in His blessing them, He was parted from them, and was carried up into Heaven; **52** and they, having worshiped Him, turned back to Jerusalem with great joy, **53** and were continually in the temple, praising and blessing God. Amen.

JOHN

CHAPTER 1

1 In the beginning was the Word, and the Word was with God, and the Word was God; **2** this One was in the beginning with God; **3** all things happened through Him, and without Him not even one thing happened that has happened. **4** In Him was life, and the life was the light of men, **5** and the light shined in the darkness, and the darkness did not perceive it. **6** There came a man—having been sent from God—whose name [is] John, **7** this one came for testimony, that he might testify about the Light, that all might believe through him; **8** that one was not the Light, but—that he might testify about the Light. **9** He was the true Light, which enlightens every man, coming into the world; **10** He was in the world, and the world was made through Him, and the world did not know Him: **11** He came to [His] own, and [His] own did not receive Him; **12** but as many as received Him, to them He gave authority to become sons of God—to those believing in His Name, **13** who were begotten, not of blood, nor of will of flesh, nor of will of man, but of God. **14** And the Word became flesh, and dwelt among us, and we beheld His glory, glory as of [the] only begotten of [the] Father, full of grace and truth. **15** John testifies concerning Him, and has cried, saying, "This was He of whom I said, He who is coming after me has come before me, for He was before me." **16** And we all received out of His fullness, and grace for grace;

[17] for the Law was given through Moses, the grace and the truth came through Jesus Christ. [18] No one has ever seen God; the only begotten God who is on the bosom of the Father—He has expounded [Him]. [19] And this is the testimony of John when the Jews sent priests and Levites out of Jerusalem, that they might question him, "Who are you?" [20] and he confessed and did not deny, and confessed, "I am not the Christ." [21] And they questioned him, "What then? Are you Elijah?" And he says, "I am not." "Are you the prophet?" And he answered, "No." [22] Then they said to him, "Who are you, that we may give an answer to those sending us? what do you say concerning yourself?" [23] He said, "I [am] a voice of one crying in the wilderness: Make straight the way of the Lord, as Isaiah the prophet said." [24] And those sent were of the Pharisees, [25] and they questioned him and said to him, "Why, then, do you immerse, if you are not the Christ, nor Elijah, nor the prophet?" [26] John answered them, saying, "I immerse in water, but in the midst of you has stood He whom you have not known, it is this One who is coming after me, who has been before me, [27] of whom I am not worthy that I may loose the strap of His sandal." [28] These things came to pass in Bethabara, beyond the Jordan, where John was immersing. [29] On the next day John sees Jesus coming to him and says, "Behold, the Lamb of God, who is taking away the sin of the world; [30] this is He concerning whom I said, After me comes a Man who has come before me, because He was before me: [31] and I did not know Him, but that He might be revealed to Israel, because of this I came immersing in water." [32] And John testified, saying, "I have seen the Spirit coming down out of Heaven as a dove, and [that] One remained on Him; [33] and I did not know Him, but He who sent me to immerse in water, He said to me, On whomsoever you may see the Spirit coming down, and remaining on Him, this is He who is immersing in the Holy Spirit; [34] and I have seen, and have testified, that this is the Son of God." [35] On the next day, again, John was standing, and two of his disciples, [36] and having looked on Jesus walking, he says, "Behold, the Lamb of God"; [37] and the two disciples heard him speaking, and they followed Jesus. [38] And Jesus having turned, and having beheld them following, says to them, "What do you seek?" And they said to Him, "Rabbi" (which is, being interpreted, Teacher), "where do You remain?" [39] He says to them, "Come and see"; they came and saw where He remains, and they remained with Him that day and the hour was about the tenth. [40] Andrew, the brother of Simon Peter, was one of the two who heard from John, and followed Him; [41] this one first finds his own brother Simon and says to him, "We have found the Messiah," (which is, being interpreted, Anointed One), [42] and he brought him to Jesus: and having looked on him, Jesus says, "You are Simon, the son of Jonas, you will be called Cephas," (which is interpreted, A rock). [43] On the next day He willed to go forth to Galilee, and He finds Philip and says to him, "Follow Me." [44] And Philip was from Bethsaida, the city of Andrew and Peter; [45] Philip finds Nathanael and says to him, "Him of whom Moses wrote in the Law, and the Prophets, we have found, Jesus the Son of Joseph, who [is] from Nazareth!" [46] And Nathanael said to him, "Is any good thing able to be out of Nazareth?" Philip said to him, "Come and see." [47] Jesus saw Nathanael coming to Him, and He says concerning him, "Behold, truly an Israelite, in whom is no guile"; [48] Nathanael says to Him, "From where do You know me?" Jesus answered and said to him, "Before Philip's calling you, being under the fig tree, I saw you." [49] Nathanael answered and says to Him, "Rabbi, You are the Son of God, You are the King of Israel." [50] Jesus answered and said to him, "Because I said to you, I saw you under the fig tree, you believe; you will see greater things than these"; [51] and He says to him, "Truly, truly, I say to you, from now on you will see Heaven opened, and the messengers of God going up and coming down on the Son of Man."

CHAPTER 2

[1] And [on] the third day a wedding happened in Cana of Galilee, and the mother of Jesus was there, [2] and also Jesus was called, and His disciples, to the wedding; [3] and wine having failed, the mother of Jesus says to Him, "They have no wine"; [4] Jesus says to her, "What [is that] to Me and to you, woman? My hour is not yet come." [5] His mother says to the servants, "Whatever He may say to you—do." [6] And there were six water-jugs of stone there, placed according to the purifying of the Jews, holding each two or three measures. [7] Jesus says to them, "Fill the water-jugs with water"; and they filled them—to the brim; [8] and He says to them, "Draw out, now, and carry to the headwaiter"; and they bore. [9] And as the headwaiter tasted the water become wine, and did not know where it is from (but the servants knew, who have drawn the water), the headwaiter calls the bridegroom, [10] and says to him, "Every man, at first, sets forth the good wine; and when they may have drunk freely, then the inferior; you kept the good wine until now." [11] This [is the] beginning of the signs Jesus did in Cana of Galilee, and revealed His glory, and His disciples believed in Him; [12] after this He went down to Capernaum, He, and His mother, and His brothers, and His disciples; and they did not remain there many days. [13] And the Passover of the Jews was near, and Jesus went up to Jerusalem, [14] and He found in the temple those selling oxen, and sheep, and doves, and the money-changers sitting, [15] and having made a whip of small cords, He put all forth out of the temple, also the sheep, and the oxen; and He poured out the coins of the money-changers, and He overthrew the tables, [16] and He said to those selling the doves, "Take these things from here; do not make the house of My Father a house of merchandise." [17] And His disciples remembered that it is written: "The zeal of Your house ate Me up"; [18] the Jews then answered and said to Him, "What sign do You show to us—that You do these things?" [19] Jesus answered and said to them, "Destroy this temple, and in three days I will raise it up." [20] The Jews, therefore, said, "This temple was built [in] forty-six years, and will You raise it up in three days?" [21] but He spoke concerning the temple of His body; [22] when, then, He was raised out of the dead, His disciples remembered that He said this to them, and they believed the Writing, and the word that Jesus said. [23] And as He was in Jerusalem, in the Passover, in the celebration, many believed in His Name, beholding His signs that He was doing; [24] and Jesus Himself was not trusting Himself to them, because of His knowing all [men], [25] and because He had no need that any should testify concerning man, for He Himself was knowing what was in man.

CHAPTER 3

[1] And there was a man of the Pharisees, his name Nicodemus, a ruler of the Jews; [2] this one came to Him by night and said to Him, "Rabbi, we have known that You have come from God—a teacher, for no one is able to do these signs that You do, if God may not be with him." [3] Jesus answered and said to him, "Truly, truly, I say to you, if anyone may not be born from above, he is not able to see the Kingdom of God"; [4] Nicodemus says to Him, "How is a man able to be born, being old? is he able to enter into the womb of his mother a second time, and to be born?" [5] Jesus answered, "Truly, truly, I say to you, if anyone may not be born of water and the Spirit, he is not able to enter into the Kingdom of God; [6] that which has been born of the flesh is flesh, and that which has been born of the Spirit is spirit. [7] You may not wonder that I said to you, It is required for you to be born from above; [8] the Spirit blows where [that] One wills, and you hear [that] One's voice, but you have not known from where [that] One comes, and to where [that] One goes; thus is everyone who has been born of the Spirit." [9] Nicodemus answered and said to Him, "How are these things able to happen?" [10] Jesus answered and said to him, "You are the teacher of Israel and you do not know these things? [11] Truly, truly, I say to you, what We have known We speak, and what We have seen We testify, and you do not receive Our testimony; [12] if I spoke to you of the earthly things, and you do not believe, how, if I will speak to you of the heavenly things, will you believe? [13] and no one has gone up to Heaven, except He who came down out of Heaven—the Son of Man who is in Heaven. [14] And as Moses lifted up the serpent in the wilderness, so it is necessary for the Son of Man to be lifted up, [15] that everyone who is believing in Him may not perish, but may have continuous life, [16] for God so loved the world that He gave the only begotten Son, that everyone who is believing in Him may not perish, but may have continuous life. [17] For God did not send His Son into the world that He may judge the world, but that the world may be saved through Him; [18] he who is believing in Him is not judged, but he who is not believing has been judged already, because he has not believed in the Name of the only begotten Son of God. [19] And this is the judgment, that the light has come into the world, and men

loved the darkness rather than the light, for their works were evil; **20** for everyone who is doing wicked things hates the light, and does not come into the light, that his works may not be detected; **21** but he who is doing the truth comes into the light, that his works may be revealed, that in God they are having been worked." **22** After these things Jesus and His disciples came into the land of Judea, and there He tarried with them, and was immersing; **23** and John was also immersing in Aenon, near to Salem, because there were many waters there, and they were coming and were being immersed— **24** for John was not yet cast into the prison— **25** there arose then a question from the disciples of John with [some] Jews about purifying, **26** and they came to John and said to him, "Rabbi, He who was with you beyond the Jordan, to whom you testified, behold, this One is immersing, and all are coming to Him." **27** John answered and said, "A man is not able to receive anything if it may not have been given him from Heaven; **28** you yourselves testify to me that I said, I am not the Christ, but that I am having been sent before Him; **29** He who is having the bride is bridegroom, and the friend of the bridegroom, who is standing and hearing Him, rejoices with joy because of the voice of the bridegroom; this, then, my joy has been fulfilled. **30** It is necessary [for] Him to increase, and me to become less; **31** He who is coming from above is above all; he who is from the earth, from the earth he is, and from the earth he speaks; He who is coming from Heaven is above all. **32** And what He has seen and heard—this He testifies, and none receives His testimony; **33** he who is receiving His testimony sealed that God is true; **34** for He whom God sent, He speaks the sayings of God; for God does not give the Spirit by measure; **35** the Father loves the Son, and has given all things into His hand; **36** he who is believing in the Son has continuous life; and he who is not believing the Son will not see life, but the wrath of God remains on him "

CHAPTER 4

1 When therefore the Lord knew that the Pharisees heard that Jesus makes and immerses more disciples than John, **2** (though indeed Jesus Himself was not immersing, but His disciples), **3** He left Judea and went away again to Galilee, **4** and it was necessary [for] Him to go through Samaria. **5** He comes, therefore, to a city of Samaria, called Sychar, near to the place that Jacob gave to his son Joseph; **6** and there was there a well of Jacob. Jesus therefore having been weary from the journeying, was thus sitting on the well; it was as it were the sixth hour; **7** there comes a woman out of Samaria to draw water. Jesus says to her, "Give Me to drink"; **8** for His disciples were gone away into the city that they may buy food; **9** the Samaritan woman therefore says to Him, "How do You, being a Jew, ask drink from me, being a Samaritan woman?" For Jews have no dealing with Samaritans. **10** Jesus answered and said to her, "If you had known the gift of God, and who it is who is saying to you, Give Me to drink, you would have asked Him, and He would have given you living water." **11** The woman says to Him, "Lord, You do not even have a vessel to draw with, and the well is deep; from where, then, have You the living water? **12** Are You greater than our father Jacob, who gave us the well, and himself drank out of it, and his sons, and his livestock?" **13** Jesus answered and said to her, "Everyone who is drinking of this water will thirst again; **14** but whoever may drink of the water that I will give him, may not thirst—throughout the age; and the water that I will give him will become in him a well of water, springing up to continuous life." **15** The woman says to Him, "Lord, give me this water, that I may not thirst, nor come here to draw." **16** Jesus says to her, "Go, call your husband, and come here"; **17** the woman answered and said, "I do not have a husband." Jesus says to her, "Well did you say—I do not have a husband; **18** for you have had five husbands, and now, he whom you have is not your husband; you have said this correctly." **19** The woman says to Him, "Lord, I perceive that You are a prophet; **20** our fathers worshiped in this mountain, and You say that in Jerusalem is the place where it is required to worship." **21** Jesus says to her, "Woman, believe Me, that there comes an hour when neither in this mountain, nor in Jerusalem, will you worship the Father; **22** you worship what you have not known; we worship what we have known, because salvation is of the Jews; **23** but there comes an hour, and it now is, when the true worshipers will worship the Father in spirit and truth, for the Father also seeks such to worship Him; **24** God [is] Spirit, and those worshiping Him should

worship in spirit and truth." **25** The woman says to Him, "I have known that Messiah comes, who is called Christ, when that One may come, He will tell us all things"; **26** Jesus says to her, "I who am speaking to you am [He]." **27** And on this came His disciples, and were wondering that He was speaking with a woman, no one, however, said, "What do You seek?" Or "Why do You speak with her?" **28** The woman then left her water-jug and went away into the city, and says to the men, **29** "Come, see a Man who told me all things—as many as I did; is this the Christ?" **30** They went forth therefore out of the city, and were coming to Him. **31** And in the meanwhile His disciples were asking Him, saying, "Rabbi, eat"; **32** and He said to them, "I have food to eat that you have not known." **33** The disciples then said to one another, "Did anyone bring Him anything to eat?" **34** Jesus says to them, "My food is that I may do the will of Him who sent Me, and may finish His work; **35** do not say that it is yet four months, and the harvest comes; behold, I say to you, lift up your eyes, and see the fields, that they are white to harvest already. **36** And he who is reaping receives a reward, and gathers fruit to continuous life, that both he who is sowing and he who is reaping may rejoice together; **37** for in this the saying is the true one, that one is the sower and another the reaper. **38** I sent you to reap on that which you have not labored; others labored, and you have entered into their labor." **39** And many from that city believed in Him, of the Samaritans, because of the word of the woman testifying, "He told me all things—as many as I did." **40** When, then, the Samaritans came to Him, they were asking Him to remain with them, and He remained there two days; **41** and many more believed because of His word, **42** and said to the woman, "We no longer believe because of your speaking; for we ourselves have heard and known that this is truly the Savior of the world—the Christ." **43** And after the two days He went forth from there, and went away to Galilee, **44** for Jesus Himself testified that a prophet will not have honor in his own country; **45** when then, He came to Galilee, the Galileans received Him, having seen all things that He did in Jerusalem in the celebration—for they also went to the celebration. **46** Jesus came, therefore, again to Cana of Galilee, where He made the water wine, and there was a certain attendant, whose son was ailing in Capernaum, **47** he, having heard that Jesus comes out of Judea to Galilee, went away to Him, and was asking Him that He may come down and may heal his son, for he was about to die. **48** Jesus then said to him, "If you may not see signs and wonders, you will not believe." **49** The attendant says to Him, "Lord, come down before my child dies"; **50** Jesus says to him, "Be going on; your son lives." And the man believed the word that Jesus said to him, and was going on, **51** and he now going down, his servants met him, and told, saying, "Your child lives"; **52** he inquired then of them the hour in which he became better, and they said to him, "Yesterday at the seventh hour the fever left him"; **53** then the father knew that [it was] in that hour in which Jesus said to him, "Your son lives," and he himself believed, and his whole house; **54** this again [was] a second sign Jesus did, having come out of Judea to Galilee.

CHAPTER 5

1 After these things there was a celebration of the Jews, and Jesus went up to Jerusalem, **2** and there is in Jerusalem by the sheep-[gate] a pool that is called in Hebrew Bethesda, having five porches, **3** in these were lying a great multitude of the ailing, blind, lame, withered, [[waiting for the moving of the water, **4** for a messenger at a set time was going down in the pool, and was troubling the water, the first then having gone in after the troubling of the water, became whole of whatever sickness he was held.]] **5** and there was a certain man there being in ailment thirty-eight years, **6** him Jesus having seen lying, and having known that he is already a long time, He says to him, "Do you wish to become whole?" **7** The ailing man answered Him, "Lord, I have no man, that, when the water may be troubled, he may put me into the pool, and while I am coming, another goes down before me." **8** Jesus says to him, "Rise, take up your pallet, and be walking"; **9** and immediately the man became whole, and he took up his pallet, and was walking, and it was a Sabbath on that day, **10** the Jews then said to him that has been healed, "It is a Sabbath, it is not lawful to you to take up the pallet." **11** He answered them, "He who made me whole—that One said to me, Take up your pallet, and be walking"; **12** they questioned him, then, "Who is the Man who is saying to you, Take up your bed and be walking?" **13** But he that was healed had not known who He is, for Jesus moved away, a multitude being in the place. **14** After these things, Jesus finds him in the temple and said to him, "Behold, you have become whole; sin no more, lest something worse may happen to you." **15** The man went away, and told the Jews that it is Jesus who made him whole, **16** and because of this were the Jews persecuting Jesus, and seeking to kill Him, because these things He was doing on a Sabbath. **17** And Jesus answered them, "My Father works until now, and I work"; **18** because of this, then, were the Jews seeking the more to kill Him, because not only was He breaking the Sabbath, but He also called God His own Father, making Himself equal to God. **19** Jesus therefore responded and said to them, "Truly, truly, I say to you, the Son is not able to do anything of Himself, if He may not see the Father doing anything; for whatever things He may do, these also the Son does in like manner; **20** for the Father cherishes the Son, and shows to Him all things that He Himself does; and greater works than these He will show Him, that you may wonder. **21** For as the Father raises the dead, and makes alive, so also the Son makes alive whom He wills; **22** for neither does the Father judge anyone, but all the judgment He has given to the Son, **23** that all may honor the Son according as they honor the Father; he who is not honoring the Son, does not honor the Father who sent Him. **24** Truly, truly, I say to you, he who is hearing My word, and is believing Him who sent Me, has continuous life, and he does not come into judgment, but has passed out of death into life. **25** Truly, truly, I say to you, [that] there comes an hour, and it now is, when the dead will hear the voice of the Son of God, and those having heard will live; **26** for as the Father has life in Himself, so He gave also to the Son to have life in Himself, **27** and authority He gave Him also to do judgment, because He is Son of Man. **28** Do not wonder at this, because there comes an hour in which all those in the tombs will hear His voice, **29** and they will come forth; those who did good things to a resurrection of life, and those who practiced evil things to a resurrection of judgment. **30** I am not able of Myself to do anything; according as I hear I judge, and My judgment is righteous, because I do not seek My own will, but the will of the Father who sent Me. **31** If I testify concerning Myself, My testimony is not true; **32** there is another who is testifying concerning Me, and I have known that the testimony that He testifies concerning Me is true; **33** you have sent to John, and he has testified to the truth. **34** But I do not receive testimony from man, but these things I say that you may be saved; **35** he was the burning and shining lamp, and you willed to be glad, for an hour, in his light. **36** But I have the testimony greater than John's, for the works that the Father gave Me, that I might finish them, the works themselves that I do, they testify concerning Me, that the Father has sent Me. **37** And the Father who sent Me has testified Himself concerning Me; you have neither heard His voice at any time, nor have you seen His appearance; **38** and you do not have His word remaining in you, because you do not believe Him whom He sent. **39** You search the Writings, because you think in them to have continuous life, and these are they that are testifying concerning Me; **40** and you do not will to come to Me, that you may have life; **41** I do not receive glory from man, **42** but I have known you, that you do not have the love of God in yourselves. **43** I have come in the Name of My Father, and you do not receive Me; if another may come in his own name, him you will receive; **44** how are you able—you—to believe, receiving glory from one another, and the glory that [is] from God alone you do not seek? **45** Do not think that I will accuse you to the Father; there is [one] who is accusing you, Moses—in whom you have hoped; **46** for if you were believing Moses, you would have been believing Me, for he wrote concerning Me; **47** but if you do not believe his writings, how will you believe My sayings?"

CHAPTER 6

1 After these things Jesus went away beyond the Sea of Galilee (of Tiberias), **2** and there was following Him a great multitude, because they were seeing His signs that He was doing on the ailing; **3** and Jesus went up to the mountain, and He was sitting with His disciples there, **4** and the Passover was near, the celebration of the Jews. **5** Jesus then having lifted up [His] eyes and having seen that a great multitude comes to Him, says to Philip, "From where will we buy loaves, that these may eat?" **6** And this He said, trying him, for He Himself had known what He was about to do. **7** Philip answered Him, "Two

hundred denarii worth of loaves are not sufficient to them, that each of them may receive some little"; **8** one of His disciples—Andrew, the brother of Simon Peter—says to Him, **9** "There is one little boy here who has five barley loaves and two fishes, but these—what are they to so many?" **10** And Jesus said, "Make the men to sit down"; and there was much grass in the place, the men then sat down, in number, as it were, five thousand, **11** and Jesus took the loaves, and having given thanks He distributed [them] to the disciples, and the disciples to those reclining, in like manner, also of the little fishes as much as they wished. **12** And when they were filled, He says to His disciples, "Gather together the broken pieces that are left over, that nothing may be lost"; **13** they gathered together, therefore, and filled twelve hand-baskets with broken pieces, from the five barley loaves that were over to those having eaten. **14** The men, then, having seen the sign that Jesus did, said, "This is truly the Prophet who is coming into the world"; **15** Jesus, therefore, having known that they are about to come, and to seize Him by force that they may make Him king, retired again to the mountain Himself alone. **16** And when evening came, His disciples went down to the sea, **17** and having entered into the boat, they were going over the sea to Capernaum, and darkness had already come, and Jesus had not come to them, **18** the sea also—a great wind blowing—was being raised, **19** having pushed onward, therefore, about twenty-five or thirty stadia, they behold Jesus walking on the sea, and coming near to the boat, and they were afraid; **20** and He says to them, "I am; do not be afraid"; **21** they were willing then to receive Him into the boat, and immediately the boat came to the land to which they were going. **22** On the next day, the multitude that was standing on the other side of the sea, having seen that there was no other little boat there except one—that into which His disciples entered—and that Jesus did not go in with His disciples into the little boat, but His disciples went away alone **23** (and other little boats came from Tiberias, near the place where they ate the bread, the Lord having given thanks), **24** when therefore the multitude saw that Jesus is not there, nor His disciples, they also entered into the boats themselves, and came to Capernaum seeking Jesus; **25** and having found Him on the other side of the sea, they said to Him, "Rabbi, when have You come here?" **26** Jesus answered them and said, "Truly, truly, I say to you, you seek Me, not because you saw signs, but because you ate of the loaves, and were satisfied; **27** do not work for the food that is perishing, but for the food that is remaining to continuous life, which the Son of Man will give to you, for the Father sealed Him—[even] God." **28** Therefore they said to Him, "What may we do that we may work the works of God?" **29** Jesus answered and said to them, "This is the work of God, that you may believe in Him whom He sent." **30** Therefore they said to Him, "What sign, then, do You do, that we may see and may believe You? what do You work? **31** Our fathers ate the manna in the wilderness, according as it is having been written: He gave them bread out of Heaven to eat." **32** Jesus, therefore, said to them, "Truly, truly, I say to you, Moses did not give you the bread out of Heaven, but My Father gives you the true bread out of Heaven; **33** for the bread of God is Him coming down out of Heaven, and giving life to the world." **34** Therefore they said to Him, "Lord, always give us this bread." **35** And Jesus said to them, "I am the bread of life; he who is coming to Me may not hunger, and he who is believing in Me may not thirst—at any time; **36** but I said to you that you also have seen Me, and you do not believe; **37** all that the Father gives to Me will come to Me; and him who is coming to Me, I will never cast outside, **38** because I have come down out of Heaven, not that I may do My will, but the will of Him who sent Me. **39** And this is the will of the Father who sent Me, that all that He has given to Me, I may lose none of it, but may raise it up in the last day; **40** and this is the will of Him who sent Me, that everyone who is beholding the Son, and is believing in Him, may have continuous life, and I will raise him up in the last day." **41** The Jews, therefore, were murmuring at Him, because He said, "I am the bread that came down out of Heaven"; **42** and they said, "Is this not Jesus, the Son of Joseph, whose father and mother we have known? how then does this One say, I have come down out of Heaven?" **43** Jesus answered, therefore, and said to them, "Do not murmur with one another; **44** no one is able to come to Me if the Father who sent Me may not draw him, and I will raise him up in the last day; **45** it is having been written in the Prophets: And they will all be taught of God; everyone, therefore, who heard from the Father, and learned, comes to Me; **46** not that anyone has seen the Father, except He who is from God, He has seen the

Father. **47** Truly, truly, I say to you, he who is believing in Me has continuous life; **48** I am the bread of life; **49** your fathers ate the manna in the wilderness and they died; **50** this is the bread that is coming down out of Heaven, that anyone may eat of it, and not die. **51** I am the living bread that came down out of Heaven; if anyone may eat of this bread he will live—throughout the age; and the bread also that I will give is My flesh, that I will give for the life of the world." **52** The Jews, therefore, were striving with one another, saying, "How is this One able to give us [His] flesh to eat?" **53** Jesus, therefore, said to them, "Truly, truly, I say to you, if you may not eat the flesh of the Son of Man, and may not drink His blood, you have no life in yourselves; **54** he who is eating My flesh, and is drinking My blood, has continuous life, and I will raise him up in the last day; **55** for My flesh is truly food, and My blood is truly drink; **56** he who is eating My flesh, and is drinking My blood, remains in Me, and I in him. **57** According as the living Father sent Me, and I live because of the Father, he also who is eating Me, even that one will live because of Me; **58** this is the bread that came down out of Heaven; not as your fathers ate the manna, and died; he who is eating this bread will live—throughout the age." **59** He said these things in a synagogue, teaching in Capernaum; **60** many, therefore, of His disciples having heard, said, "This word is hard; who is able to hear it?" **61** And Jesus having known in Himself that His disciples are murmuring about this, said to them, "Does this stumble you? **62** if then you may behold the Son of Man going up where He was before? **63** It is the Spirit that is giving life; the flesh does not profit anything; the sayings that I speak to you are spirit, and they are life; **64** but there are certain of you who do not believe"; for Jesus had known from the beginning who they are who are not believing, and who is he who will deliver Him up, **65** and He said, "Because of this I have said to you, No one is able to come to Me if it may not have been given him from My Father." **66** From this [time] many of His disciples went away backward, and were no longer walking with Him, **67** Jesus, therefore, said to the Twelve, "Do you also wish to go away?" **68** Simon Peter, therefore, answered Him, "Lord, to whom will we go? you have sayings of continuous life; **69** and we have believed, and we have known, that You are the Christ, the Son of the living God." **70** Jesus answered them, "Did I not choose you—the Twelve? and of you—one is a devil." **71** And He spoke of Judas, [son] of Simon Iscariot, for he was about to deliver Him up, being one of the Twelve.

CHAPTER 7

1 And Jesus was walking after these things in Galilee, for He did not wish to walk in Judea, because the Jews were seeking to kill Him, **2** and the celebration of the Jews was near—that of Shelters— **3** His brothers, therefore, said to Him, "Depart from here, and go away to Judea, that Your disciples may also behold Your works that You do; **4** for no one does anything in secret, and himself seeks to be in public; if you do these things—reveal Yourself to the world"; **5** for not even His brothers were believing in Him. **6** Jesus, therefore, says to them, "My time is not yet present, but your time is always ready; **7** the world is not able to hate you, but it hates Me, because I testify concerning it that its works are evil. **8** You—go up to this celebration; I do not yet go up to this celebration, because My time has not yet been fulfilled"; **9** and saying these things to them, He remained in Galilee. **10** And when His brothers went up, then also He Himself went up to the celebration, not openly, but as in secret; **11** the Jews, therefore, were seeking Him in the celebration, and said, "Where is that One?" **12** and there was much murmuring about Him among the multitudes, some indeed said, "He is good"; and others said, "No, but He leads the multitude astray"; **13** no one, however, was speaking freely about Him, through fear of the Jews. **14** And it being now the middle of the celebration, Jesus went up to the temple, and He was teaching, **15** and the Jews were wondering, saying, "How has this One known letters—having not learned?" **16** Jesus answered them and said, "My teaching is not Mine, but His who sent Me; **17** if anyone may will to do His will, he will know concerning the teaching, whether it is of God, or—[if] I speak from Myself. **18** He who is speaking from himself seeks his own glory, but he who is seeking the glory of him who sent him, this one is true, and unrighteousness is not in him; **19** has not Moses given you the Law? and none of you does the Law; why do you seek to kill Me?" **20** The multitude answered and said, "You have a demon, who seeks to kill You?"

21 Jesus answered and said to them, "I did one work, and you all wonder, **22** because of this, Moses has given you the circumcision—not that it is of Moses, but of the fathers—and on a Sabbath you circumcise a man; **23** if a man receives circumcision on a Sabbath that the Law of Moses may not be broken, are you angry with Me that I made a man all whole on a Sabbath? **24** Do not judge according to appearance, but the righteous judgment judge." **25** Certain, therefore, of the Jerusalemites said, "Is this not He whom they are seeking to kill? **26** and behold, He speaks freely, and they say nothing to Him; did the rulers truly know that this is the Christ? **27** but this One—we have known where He is from; and the Christ, when He comes, no one knows where He is from." **28** Jesus cried, therefore, in the temple, teaching and saying, "You have both known Me, and you have known from where I am; and I have not come of Myself, but He who sent Me is true, whom you have not known; **29** and I have known Him, because I am from Him, and He sent Me." **30** They were seeking, therefore, to seize Him, and no one laid the hand on Him, because His hour had not yet come, **31** and many out of the multitude believed in Him and said, "The Christ—when He may come—will He do more signs than these that this One did?" **32** The Pharisees heard the multitude murmuring these things concerning Him, and the Pharisees and the chief priests sent officers that they may take Him; **33** Jesus, therefore, said to them, "Yet a short time I am with you, and I go away to Him who sent Me; **34** you will seek Me, and you will not find; and where I am, you are not able to come." **35** The Jews, therefore, said among themselves, "To where is this One about to go that we will not find Him? Is He about to go to the dispersion of the Greeks, and to teach the Greeks? **36** What is this word that He said, You will seek Me, and you will not find? and, Where I am, you are not able to come?" **37** And in the last, the great day of the celebration, Jesus stood and cried, saying, "If anyone thirsts, let him come to Me and drink; **38** he who is believing in Me, according as the Writing said, Rivers of living water will flow out of his belly"; **39** and this He said of the Spirit, which those believing in Him were about to receive; for not yet was the Holy Spirit, because Jesus was not yet glorified. **40** Many, therefore, out of the multitude, having heard the word, said, "This is truly the Prophet"; **41** others said, "This is the Christ"; and others said, "Why, does the Christ come out of Galilee? **42** Did the Writing not say that out of the seed of David, and from Beth-Lehem—the village where David was—the Christ comes?" **43** A division, therefore, arose among the multitude because of Him. **44** And certain of them were willing to seize Him, but no one laid hands on Him; **45** the officers came, therefore, to the chief priests and Pharisees, and they said to them, "Why did you not bring Him?" **46** The officers answered, "Never so spoke man—as this Man." **47** The Pharisees, therefore, answered them, "Have you also been led astray? **48** did anyone out of the rulers believe in Him? or out of the Pharisees? **49** but this multitude, that is not knowing the Law, is accursed." **50** Nicodemus says to them—he who came by night to Him—being one of them, **51** "Does our law judge the Man, if it may not hear from Him first, and know what He does?" **52** They answered and said to him, "Are you also out of Galilee? search and see that a prophet has not risen out of Galilee"; [[**53** and each one went on to his house, but Jesus went on to the Mount of Olives.

CHAPTER 8

1 And at dawn He came again to the temple [courts], **2** and all the people were coming to Him, and having sat down, He was teaching them; **3** and the scribes and the Pharisees bring to Him a woman having been taken in adultery, and having set her in the midst, **4** they say to Him, "Teacher, this woman was taken in the very crime [of] committing adultery, **5** and in the Law, Moses commanded us that such be stoned; You, therefore, what do You say?" **6** and this they said, trying Him, that they might have to accuse Him. And Jesus, having stooped down, with the finger He was writing on the ground, **7** and when they continued asking Him, having bent Himself back, He said to them, "The sinless of you—let him cast the first stone at her"; **8** and again having stooped down, He was writing on the ground, **9** and they having heard, and being convicted by the conscience, were going forth one by one, having begun from the elders—to the last; and Jesus was left alone, and the woman standing in the midst. **10** And Jesus having bent Himself back, and having seen no one but the woman, said to her, "Woman, where are those—your accusers? did no one pass sentence on you?" **11** and she said, "No one, Lord"; and Jesus said to her, "Neither do I pass sentence on you; be going on, and sin no more."]] **12** Again, therefore, Jesus spoke to them, saying, "I am the light of the world; he who is following Me will not walk in the darkness, but he will have the light of life." **13** The Pharisees, therefore, said to Him, "You testify of Yourself, Your testimony is not true"; **14** Jesus answered and said to them, "And if I testify of Myself—My testimony is true, because I have known from where I came, and to where I go, and you have not known from where I come, or to where I go. **15** You judge according to the flesh; I do not judge anyone, **16** and even if I do judge My judgment is true, because I am not alone, but I and the Father who sent Me; **17** and also in your law it has been written that the testimony of two men is true; **18** I am [One] who is testifying of Myself, and the Father who sent Me testifies of Me." **19** They said, therefore, to Him, "Where is Your father?" Jesus answered, "You have neither known Me nor My Father: if you had known Me, you had also known My Father." **20** Jesus spoke these sayings in the treasury, teaching in the temple, and no one seized Him, because His hour had not yet come; **21** therefore Jesus said again to them, "I go away, and you will seek Me, and you will die in your sin; to where I go away, you are not able to come." **22** The Jews, therefore, said, "Will He kill Himself, because He says, To where I go away, you are not able to come?" **23** and He said to them, "You are from beneath, I am from above; you are of this world, I am not of this world; **24** I said, therefore, to you, that you will die in your sins, for if you may not believe that I am, you will die in your sins." **25** They said, therefore, to Him, "You—who are You?" And Jesus said to them, "Even what I spoke of to you at the beginning; **26** many things I have to speak concerning you and to judge, but He who sent Me is true, and I—what things I heard from Him—these I say to the world." **27** They did not know that He spoke to them of the Father; **28** Jesus, therefore, said to them, "When you may lift up the Son of Man then you will know that I am; and I do nothing of Myself, but according as My Father taught Me, these things I speak; **29** and He who sent Me is with Me; the Father did not leave Me alone, because I always do the things pleasing to Him." **30** As He is speaking these things, many believed in Him; **31** Jesus, therefore, said to the Jews who believed in Him, "If you may remain in My word, you are truly My disciples, **32** and you will know the truth, and the truth will make you free." **33** They answered Him, "We are seed of Abraham; and we have been servants to no one at any time; how do You say—You will become free?" **34** Jesus answered them, "Truly, truly, I say to you, everyone who is committing sin, is a servant of sin, **35** and the servant does not remain in the house—throughout the age, the Son remains—throughout the age; **36** if then the Son may make you free, in reality you will be free. **37** I have known that you are seed of Abraham, but you seek to kill Me, because My word has no place in you; **38** I speak that which I have seen with My Father, and you, therefore, do that which you have seen with your father." **39** They answered and said to Him, "Our father is Abraham"; Jesus says to them, "If you were children of Abraham, the works of Abraham you were doing; **40** and now, you seek to kill Me—a Man who has spoken to you the truth I heard from God; Abraham did not do this; **41** you do the works of your father." They said, therefore, to Him, "We have not been born of whoredom; we have one Father—God"; **42** Jesus then said to them, "If God were your father, you were loving Me, for I came forth from God, and am come; for neither have I come of Myself, but He sent Me; **43** why do you not know My speech? because you are not able to hear My word. **44** You are of a father—the Devil, and the desires of your father you will to do; he was a manslayer from the beginning, and he has not stood in the truth, because there is no truth in him; when one may speak the falsehood, he speaks of his own, because he is a liar—also his father. **45** And because I say the truth, you do not believe Me. **46** Who of you convicts Me of sin? and if I speak truth, why do you not believe Me? **47** he who is of God, he hears the sayings of God; because of this you do not hear, because you are not of God." **48** The Jews, therefore, answered and said to Him, "Do we not say well, that You are a Samaritan, and have a demon?" **49** Jesus answered, "I do not have a demon, but I honor My Father, and you dishonor Me; **50** and I do not seek My own glory; there is [One] who is seeking and is judging; **51** truly, truly, I say to you, if anyone may keep My word, he may not see death—throughout the age." **52** The Jews, therefore, said to Him, "Now we have known that You have a demon; Abraham died, and the prophets, and You say, If anyone may keep My word, he will not taste of death—

throughout the age! **53** Are You greater than our father Abraham, who died? and the prophets died; whom do You make Yourself?" **54** Jesus answered, "If I glorify Myself, My glory is nothing; it is My Father who is glorifying Me, of whom you say that He is your God; **55** and you have not known Him, and I have known Him, and if I say that I have not known Him, I will be like you—speaking falsely; but I have known Him, and I keep His word; **56** your father Abraham was glad that he might see My day; and he saw, and rejoiced." **57** The Jews, therefore, said to Him, "You are not yet fifty years old, and You have seen Abraham?" **58** Jesus said to them, "Truly, truly, I say to you, before Abraham's coming—I am"; **59** they took up, therefore, stones that they may cast at Him, but Jesus hid Himself, and went forth out of the temple, going through the midst of them, and so passed by.

CHAPTER 9

1 And passing by, He saw a man blind from birth, **2** and His disciples asked Him, saying, "Rabbi, who sinned, this one or his parents, that he should be born blind?" **3** Jesus answered, "Neither this one sinned nor his parents, but that the works of God may be revealed in him; **4** it is necessary for Me to be working the works of Him who sent Me while it is day; night comes when no one is able to work: **5** when I am in the world, I am [the] light of the world." **6** Saying these things, He spat on the ground, and made clay of the spittle, and rubbed the clay on the eyes of the blind man, and said to him, **7** "Go away, wash at the pool of Siloam," which is, interpreted, Sent. He went away, therefore, and washed, and came seeing; **8** the neighbors, therefore, and those seeing him before, that he was blind, said, "Is this not he who is sitting and begging?" **9** others said, "This is he"; and others, "He is like to him"; he himself said, "I am [he]." **10** They said, therefore, to him, "How were your eyes opened?" **11** he answered and said, "A man called Jesus made clay, and rubbed my eyes, and said to me, Go away to the pool of Siloam, and wash; and having gone away and having washed, I received sight"; **12** they said, therefore, to him, "Where is that One?" He says, "I have not known." **13** They bring him who once [was] blind to the Pharisees, **14** and it was a Sabbath when Jesus made the clay, and opened his eyes. **15** Again, therefore, the Pharisees also were asking him how he received sight, and he said to them, "He put clay on my eyes, and I washed—and I see." **16** Certain of the Pharisees therefore said, "This Man is not from God, because He does not keep the Sabbath"; others said, "How is a man—a sinful one—able to do such signs?" And there was a division among them. **17** They said to the blind man again, "You—what do you say of Him—that He opened your eyes?" **18** and he said, "He is a prophet." The Jews, therefore, did not believe concerning him that he was blind and received sight, until they called the parents of him who received sight, **19** and they asked them, saying, "Is [this] your son, of whom you say that he was born blind? how then does he now see?" **20** His parents answered them and said, "We have known that this is our son, and that he was born blind; **21** and how he now sees, we have not known; or who opened his eyes, we have not known; he is of age, ask him; he himself will speak concerning himself." **22** His parents said these things, because they were afraid of the Jews, for the Jews had already agreed together, that if anyone may confess Him—Christ, he may be put out of the synagogue; **23** because of this his parents said, "He is of age, ask him." **24** They called, therefore, the man who was blind a second time, and they said to him, "Give glory to God, we have known that this Man is a sinner"; **25** he answered, therefore, and said, "If He is a sinner—I have not known, one thing I have known, that, being blind, now I see." **26** And they said to him again, "What did He do to you? how did He open your eyes?" **27** He answered them, "I told you already, and you did not hear; why do you wish to hear [it] again? do you also wish to become His disciples?" **28** They reviled him, therefore, and said, "You are His disciple, and we are Moses' disciples; **29** we have known that God has spoken to Moses, but this One—we have not known where He is from." **30** The man answered and said to them, "Why, in this is a wonderful thing, that you have not known where He is from, and He opened my eyes! **31** and we have known that God does not hear sinners, but if anyone may be a worshiper of God, and may do His will, He hears him; **32** from the age it was not heard that anyone opened eyes of one who has been born blind; **33** if this One were not from God, He were not able to do anything." **34** They answered and said to him, "In sins you were born altogether, and you teach us?" And they cast him forth outside. ³⁵ Jesus heard that they cast him forth outside, and having found him, He said to him, "Do you believe in the Son of God?" ³⁶ he answered and said, "Who is He, Lord, that I may believe in Him?" ³⁷ And Jesus said to him, "You have both seen Him, and He who is speaking with you is He"; ³⁸ and he said, "I believe, Lord," and worshiped Him. ³⁹ And Jesus said, "I came to this world for judgment, that those not seeing may see, and those seeing may become blind." ⁴⁰ And those of the Pharisees who were with Him heard these things, and they said to Him, "Are we also blind?" ⁴¹ Jesus said to them, "If you were blind, you were not having had sin, but now you say—We see, therefore your sin remains."

CHAPTER 10

¹ "Truly, truly, I say to you, he who is not entering through the door to the fold of the sheep, but is going up from another side, that one is a thief and a robber; ² and he who is entering through the door is shepherd of the sheep; ³ the doorkeeper opens to this one, and the sheep hear his voice, and his own sheep he calls by name, and leads them forth; ⁴ and when he may put forth his own sheep, he goes on before them, and the sheep follow him, because they have known his voice; ⁵ and they will not follow a stranger, but will flee from him, because they have not known the voice of strangers." ⁶ Jesus spoke this allegory to them, and they did not know what the things were that He was speaking to them; ⁷ Jesus therefore said again to them, "Truly, truly, I say to you, I am the door of the sheep; ⁸ all, as many as came before Me, are thieves and robbers, but the sheep did not hear them; ⁹ I am the door, if anyone may come in through Me, he will be saved, and he will come in, and go out, and find pasture. ¹⁰ The thief does not come, except that he may steal, and kill, and destroy; I came that they may have life, and may have [it] abundantly. ¹¹ I am the good shepherd; the good shepherd lays His life down for the sheep; ¹² and the hired worker, and not being a shepherd, who's own the sheep are not, beholds the wolf coming, and leaves the sheep, and flees; and the wolf snatches them, and scatters the sheep; ¹³ and the hired worker flees because he is a hired worker, and is not caring for the sheep. ¹⁴ I am the good shepherd, and I know My [sheep], and am known by Mine, ¹⁵ according as the Father knows Me, and I know the Father, and My life I lay down for the sheep, ¹⁶ and other sheep I have that are not of this fold, these also it is necessary for Me to bring, and My voice they will hear, and there will become one flock— one shepherd. ¹⁷ Because of this the Father loves Me, because I lay down My life, that again I may take it; ¹⁸ no one takes it from Me, but I lay it down of Myself; authority I have to lay it down, and authority I have again to take it; this command I received from My Father." ¹⁹ Therefore, again, there came a division among the Jews, because of these words, ²⁰ and many of them said, "He has a demon, and is mad, why do you hear Him?" ²¹ others said, "These sayings are not those of a demoniac; is a demon able to open blind men's eyes?" ²² And the Dedication in Jerusalem came, and it was winter, ²³ and Jesus was walking in the temple, in the porch of Solomon, ²⁴ the Jews, therefore, came around Him and said to Him, "Until when do You hold our soul in suspense? if You are the Christ, tell us freely." ²⁵ Jesus answered them, "I told you, and you do not believe; the works that I do in the Name of My Father, these testify concerning Me; ²⁶ but you do not believe, for you are not of My sheep, ²⁷ according as I said to you: My sheep hear My voice, and I know them, and they follow Me, ²⁸ and I give continuous life to them, and they will not perish— throughout the age, and no one will snatch them out of My hand; ²⁹ My Father, who has given to Me, is greater than all, and no one is able to snatch out of the hand of My Father; ³⁰ I and the Father are one." ³¹ Therefore, again, the Jews took up stones that they may stone Him; ³² Jesus answered them, "I showed you many good works from My Father; because of which work of them do you stone Me?" ³³ The Jews answered Him, saying, "We do not stone You for a good work, but for slander, and because You, being a man, make Yourself God." ³⁴ Jesus answered them, "Is it not having been written in your law: I said, you are gods? ³⁵ if He called them gods to whom the word of God came (and the Writing is not able to be broken), ³⁶ of Him whom the Father sanctified and sent into the world, do you say—You slander, because I said, I am [the] Son of God? ³⁷ if I do not do the works of My Father, do not believe Me; ³⁸ and If I do, even if you may not believe Me, believe the

works, that you may know and may believe that the Father [is] in Me, and I in Him." ³⁹ Therefore they were seeking again to seize Him, and He went forth out of their hand, ⁴⁰ and went away again to the other side of the Jordan, to the place where John was at first immersing, and remained there, ⁴¹ and many came to Him and said, "John, indeed, did no sign, and all things, as many as John said about this One were true"; ⁴² and many believed in Him there.

CHAPTER 11

¹ And there was a certain one ailing, Lazarus, from Bethany, of the village of Mary and Martha her sister— ² and it was Mary who anointed the Lord with ointment, and wiped His feet with her hair, whose brother Lazarus was ailing— ³ therefore the sisters sent to Him, saying, "Lord, behold, he whom You cherish is ailing"; ⁴ and Jesus having heard, said, "This ailment is not to death, but for the glory of God, that the Son of God may be glorified through it." ⁵ And Jesus was loving Martha, and her sister, and Lazarus, ⁶ when, therefore, He heard that he is ailing, then indeed He remained in the place in which He was two days, ⁷ then after this, He says to the disciples, "We may go to Judea again"; ⁸ the disciples say to Him, "Rabbi, the Jews were just seeking to stone You, and again You go there?" ⁹ Jesus answered, "Are there not twelve hours in the day? if anyone may walk in the day, he does not stumble, because he sees the light of this world; ¹⁰ and if anyone may walk in the night, he stumbles, because the light is not in him." ¹¹ He said these things, and after this He says to them, "Our friend Lazarus has fallen asleep, but I go on that I may awake him"; ¹² therefore His disciples said, "Lord, if he has fallen asleep, he will be saved"; ¹³ but Jesus had spoken about his death, but they thought that He speaks about the repose of sleep. ¹⁴ Then, therefore, Jesus said to them freely, "Lazarus has died; ¹⁵ and I rejoice, for your sake (that you may believe), that I was not there; but we may go to him"; ¹⁶ therefore Thomas, who is called Didymus, said to the fellow-disciples, "We may go—we also, that we may die with Him," ¹⁷ Jesus, therefore, having come, found him having already been four days in the tomb. ¹⁸ And Bethany was near to Jerusalem, about fifteen stadia off, ¹⁹ and many of the Jews had come to Martha and Mary, that they might comfort them concerning their brother; ²⁰ Martha, therefore, when she heard that Jesus comes, met Him, and Mary kept sitting in the house. ²¹ Martha, therefore, said to Jesus, "Lord, if You had been here, my brother had not died; ²² but even now, I have known that whatever You may ask of God, God will give to You"; ²³ Jesus says to her, "Your brother will rise again." ²⁴ Martha says to Him, "I have known that he will rise again in the resurrection in the last day"; ²⁵ Jesus said to her, "I am the resurrection, and the life; he who is believing in Me, even if he may die, will live; ²⁶ and everyone who is living and believing in Me will not die—throughout the age; ²⁷ do you believe this?" She says to Him, "Yes, Lord, I have believed that You are the Christ, the Son of God, who is coming into the world." ²⁸ And having said these things, she went away, and called Mary her sister privately, saying, "The Teacher is present, and calls you"; ²⁹ she, when she heard, rises up quickly, and comes to Him; ³⁰ and Jesus had not yet come into the village, but was in the place where Martha met Him; ³¹ the Jews, therefore, who were with her in the house, and were comforting her, having seen Mary that she rose up quickly and went forth, followed her, saying, "She goes away to the tomb, that she may weep there." ³² Mary, therefore, when she came where Jesus was, having seen Him, fell at His feet, saying to Him, "Lord, if You had been here, my brother had not died"; ³³ Jesus, therefore, when He saw her weeping, and the Jews who came with her weeping, groaned in the spirit, and troubled Himself, and He said, ³⁴ "Where have you laid him?" They say to Him, "Lord, come and see"; ³⁵ Jesus wept. ³⁶ The Jews, therefore, said, "Behold, how He was cherishing him!" ³⁷ and certain of them said, "Was not this One, who opened the eyes of the blind man, also able to cause that this one might not have died?" ³⁸ Jesus, therefore, again groaning in Himself, comes to the tomb, and it was a cave, and a stone was lying on it, ³⁹ Jesus says, "Take away the stone"; the sister of him who has died—Martha—says to Him, "Lord, he already stinks, for he is four days dead"; ⁴⁰ Jesus says to her, "Did I not say to you that if you may believe, you will see the glory of God?" ⁴¹ Therefore they took away the stone where the dead was laid, and Jesus lifted His eyes upwards, and said, "Father, I thank You that You heard Me; ⁴²

and I knew that You always hear Me, but because of the multitude that is standing by, I said [it], that they may believe that You sent Me." **43** And saying these things, He cried out with a loud voice, "Lazarus, come forth!" **44** And he who died came forth, feet and hands being bound with grave-clothes, and his face was bound around with a napkin; Jesus says to them, "Loose him, and permit to go." **45** Many, therefore, of the Jews who came to Mary, and beheld what Jesus did, believed in Him; **46** but certain of them went away to the Pharisees, and told them what Jesus did; **47** the chief priests, therefore, and the Pharisees, gathered together [the] Sanhedrin and said, "What may we do? because this Man does many signs? **48** if we may leave Him alone thus, all will believe in Him; and the Romans will come, and will take away both our place and nation." **49** and a certain one of them, Caiaphas, being chief priest of that year, said to them, "You have not known anything, **50** nor reason that it is good for us that one man may die for the people, and not the whole nation perish." **51** And he did not say this of himself, but being chief priest of that year, he prophesied that Jesus was about to die for the nation, **52** and not for the nation only, but that also the children of God, who have been scattered abroad, He may gather together into one. **53** From that day, therefore, they took counsel together that they may kill Him; **54** Jesus, therefore, was no longer freely walking among the Jews, but went away from there into the region near the wilderness, to a city called Ephraim, and there He tarried with His disciples. **55** And the Passover of the Jews was near, and many went up to Jerusalem out of the country before the Passover, that they might purify themselves; **56** therefore they were seeking Jesus and said with one another, standing in the temple, "What appears to you—that He may not come to the celebration?" **57** and both the chief priests and the Pharisees had given a command, that if anyone may know where He is, he may show [it], so that they may seize Him.

CHAPTER 12

1 Jesus, therefore, six days before the Passover, came to Bethany, where Lazarus was, who had died, whom He raised out of the dead; **2** they made, therefore, a dinner to Him there, and Martha was ministering, and Lazarus was one of those reclining together with Him; **3** Mary, therefore, having taken a pound of ointment of spikenard, of great price, anointed the feet of Jesus and wiped His feet with her hair, and the house was filled from the fragrance of the ointment. **4** Therefore one of His disciples—Judas Iscariot, of Simon, who is about to deliver Him up—says, **5** "Why was this ointment not sold for three hundred denarii, and given to the poor?" **6** and he said this, not because he was caring for the poor, but because he was a thief, and had the bag, and what things were put in he was carrying. **7** Jesus, therefore, said, "Permit her; she has kept it for the day of My embalming, **8** for you always have the poor with yourselves, and you do not always have Me." **9** Therefore, a great multitude of the Jews knew that He is there, and they came, not only because of Jesus, but that they may also see Lazarus, whom He raised out of the dead; **10** and the chief priests took counsel, that they may also kill Lazarus, **11** because on account of him many of the Jews were going away, and were believing in Jesus. **12** On the next day, a great multitude that came to the celebration, having heard that Jesus comes to Jerusalem, **13** took the branches of the palms, and went forth to meet Him, and were crying, "Hosanna! Blessed [is] He who is coming in the Name of the Lord—the King of Israel"; **14** and Jesus having found a young donkey sat on it, according as it is written, **15** "Do not fear, daughter of Zion, behold, your King comes, sitting on a colt of a donkey." **16** And His disciples did not know these things at first, but when Jesus was glorified, then they remembered that these things were having been written about Him, and these things they did to Him. **17** The multitude, therefore, who are with Him, were testifying that He called Lazarus out of the tomb, and raised him out of the dead; **18** because of this the multitude also met Him, because they heard of His having done this sign, **19** therefore the Pharisees said among themselves, "You see that you do not gain anything, behold, the world went after Him." **20** And there were certain Greeks out of those coming up that they may worship in the celebration, **21** these then came near to Philip, who [is] from Bethsaida of Galilee, and were asking him, saying, "Lord, we wish to see Jesus"; **22** Philip comes and tells Andrew, and again Andrew and Philip tell Jesus. **23** And Jesus responded to them, saying, "The hour has come that the Son of Man may be

glorified; **24** truly, truly, I say to you, if the grain of the wheat, having fallen to the earth, may not die, itself remains alone; and if it may die, it bears much fruit; **25** he who is cherishing his life will lose it, and he who is hating his life in this world will keep it to continuous life; **26** if anyone may minister to Me, let him follow Me, and where I am, there My servant will be also; and if anyone may minister to Me—the Father will honor him. **27** Now My soul has been troubled; and what will I say—Father, save Me from this hour? But because of this I came to this hour; **28** Father, glorify Your Name." Therefore there came a voice out of Heaven, "I both glorified, and again I will glorify [it]"; **29** the multitude, therefore, having stood and heard, were saying that there has been thunder; others said, "A messenger has spoken to Him." **30** Jesus answered and said, "This voice has not come because of Me, but because of you; **31** now is a judgment of this world, now will the ruler of this world be cast forth; **32** and I, if I may be lifted up from the earth, will draw all men to Myself." **33** And this He said signifying by what death He was about to die; **34** the multitude answered Him, "We heard that the Christ remains out of the Law—throughout the age; and how do You say that it is required that the Son of Man be lifted up? who is this—the Son of Man?" **35** Therefore Jesus said to them, "Yet a short time is the light with you; walk while you have the light, that darkness may not overtake you; and he who is walking in the darkness has not known where he goes; **36** while you have the light, believe in the light, that you may become sons of light." Jesus spoke these things, and having gone away, He was hid from them, **37** yet He, having done so many signs before them, they were not believing in Him, **38** that the word of Isaiah the prophet might be fulfilled, which he said, "Lord, who gave credence to our report? and the arm of the Lord—to whom was it revealed?" **39** Because of this they were not able to believe, that again Isaiah said, **40** "He has blinded their eyes, and hardened their heart, that they might not see with the eyes, and understand with the heart, and turn, and I might heal them"; **41** Isaiah said these things when he saw His glory, and spoke of Him. **42** Still, however, out of the rulers many also believed in Him, but because of the Pharisees they were not confessing, that they might not be put out of the synagogue, **43** for they loved the glory of men more than the glory of God. **44** And Jesus cried and said, "He who is believing in Me, does not believe in Me, but in Him who sent Me; **45** and He who is beholding Me, beholds Him who sent Me; **46** I—light to the world—have come, that everyone who is believing in Me may not remain in the darkness; **47** and if anyone may hear My sayings, and not believe, I do not judge him, for I did not come that I might judge the world, but that I might save the world. **48** He who is rejecting Me, and not receiving My sayings, has one who is judging him, the word that I spoke, that will judge him in the last day, **49** because I did not speak from Myself, but the Father who sent Me, He gave Me a command, what I may say, and what I may speak, **50** and I have known that His command is continuous life; what, therefore, I speak, according as the Father has said to Me, so I speak."

CHAPTER 13

1 And before the Celebration of the Passover, Jesus knowing that His hour has come, that He may depart out of this world to the Father, having loved His own who [are] in the world—to the end He loved them. **2** And dinner having come, the Devil already having put [it] into the heart of Judas of Simon, Iscariot, that he may deliver Him up, **3** Jesus knowing that all things the Father has given to Him—into [His] hands, and that He came forth from God, and He goes to God, **4** rises from the dinner, and lays down His garments, and having taken a towel, He girded Himself; **5** afterward He puts water into the basin, and began to wash the feet of His disciples, and to wipe with the towel with which He was being girded. **6** He comes, therefore, to Simon Peter, and that one says to Him, "Lord, You—do You wash my feet?" **7** Jesus answered and said to him, "That which I do you have not known now, but you will know after these things"; **8** Peter says to Him, "You may not wash my feet—throughout the age." Jesus answered him, "If I may not wash you, you have no part with Me"; **9** Simon Peter says to Him, "Lord, not my feet only, but also the hands and the head." **10** Jesus says to him, "He who has been bathed has no need except to wash his feet, but he is clean altogether; and you are clean, but not all"; **11** for He knew him who is delivering Him up; because of this He said, "You are not all clean." **12** When, therefore, He washed their feet, and took His garments, having reclined again, He said to them, "Do you know what I have done to you? **13** you call Me the Teacher and the Lord, and you say well, for I am; **14** if then I washed your feet—the Lord and the Teacher—you also ought to wash one another's feet. **15** For I gave to you an example, that, according as I did to you, you also may do; **16** truly, truly, I say to you, a servant is not greater than his lord, nor an apostle greater than he who sent him; **17** if you have known these things, you are blessed if you may do them; **18** I do not speak concerning you all; I have known whom I chose for Myself; but that the Writing may be fulfilled: He who is eating the bread with Me, lifted up his heel against Me. **19** From this time I tell you, before its coming to pass, that, when it may come to pass, you may believe that I am; **20** truly, truly, I say to you, he who is receiving whomsoever I may send, receives Me; and he who is receiving Me, receives Him who sent Me." **21** Having said these things, Jesus was troubled in the spirit, and testified and said, "Truly, truly, I say to you that one of you will deliver Me up"; **22** the disciples were looking, therefore, at one another, doubting concerning of whom He speaks. **23** And there was one of His disciples reclining in the bosom of Jesus, whom Jesus was loving; **24** Simon Peter, then, beckons to this one, to inquire who he may be concerning whom He speaks, **25** and that one having leaned back on the breast of Jesus, responds to Him, "Lord, who is it?" **26** Jesus answers, "It is that one to whom I, having dipped the morsel, will give it"; and having dipped the morsel, He gives [it] to Judas of Simon, Iscariot. **27** And after the morsel, then Satan entered into that one. Jesus, therefore, says to him, "What you do—do quickly"; **28** and none of those reclining knew for what intent He said this to him, **29** for certain [of them] were thinking, since Judas had the bag, that Jesus says to him, "Buy what we have need of for the celebration"; or that he may give something to the poor; **30** having received, therefore, the morsel, that one immediately went forth, and it was night. **31** When, therefore, he went forth, Jesus says, "Now was the Son of Man glorified, and God was glorified in Him; **32** if God was glorified in Him, God will also glorify Him in Himself; indeed, He will immediately glorify Him. **33** Little children, yet a little [while] am I with you; you will seek Me, and according as I said to the Jews, I also say to you now: To where I go away, you are not able to come. **34** A new command I give to you, that you love one another; according as I loved you, that you also love one another; **35** in this will all know that you are My disciples, if you may have love one to another." **36** Simon Peter says to Him, "Lord, to where do You go away?" Jesus answered him, "To where I go away, you are not able now to follow Me, but afterward you will follow Me." **37** Peter says to Him, "Lord, why am I not able to follow You now? I will lay down my life for You"; **38** Jesus answered him, "You will lay down your life for Me? truly, truly, I say to you, a rooster will not crow until you may deny Me three times."

CHAPTER 14

1 "Do not let your heart be troubled, believe in God, believe also in Me; **2** in the house of My Father are many rooms; and if not, I would have told you; I go on to prepare a place for you; **3** and if I go on and prepare a place for you, I come again, and will receive you to Myself, that where I am you also may be; **4** and to where I go away you have known, and the way you have known." **5** Thomas says to Him, "Lord, we have not known to where You go away, and how are we able to know the way?" **6** Jesus says to him, "I am the way, and the truth, and the life, no one comes to the Father, if not through Me; **7** if you had known Me, you would also have known My Father, and from this time you have known Him, and have seen Him." **8** Philip says to Him, "Lord, show to us the Father, and it is enough for us"; **9** Jesus says to him, "Such [a] long time am I with you, and you have not known Me, Philip? He who has seen Me has seen the Father; and how do you say, Show to us the Father? **10** Do you not believe that I [am] in the Father, and the Father is in Me? the sayings that I speak to you, I do not speak from Myself, and the Father who is abiding in Me does the works Himself; **11** believe Me, that I [am] in the Father, and the Father in Me; and if not, because of the works themselves, believe Me. **12** Truly, truly, I say to you, he who is believing in Me, the works that I do—that one will also do, and greater than these he will do, because I go on to My Father; **13** and whatever you may ask in My Name, I will do, that the Father may be glorified in the Son; **14** if you ask anything in My Name I will do [it]. **15** If you love Me, keep My commands, **16** and I will ask the Father,

and He will give to you another Comforter, that He may remain with you throughout the age: **17** the Spirit of truth, whom the world is not able to receive, because it does not see nor know [this] One, and you know [this] One, because [this] One remains with you, and will be in you. **18** I will not leave you bereaved, I come to you; **19** yet a little [while] and the world beholds Me no more, and you behold Me, because I live, and you will live; **20** in that day you will know that I [am] in My Father, and you in Me, and I in you; **21** he who is having My commands, and is keeping them, that one it is who is loving Me, and he who is loving Me will be loved by My Father, and I will love him, and will manifest Myself to him." **22** Judas says to Him (not the Iscariot), "Lord, what has come to pass, that You are about to manifest Yourself to us, and not to the world?" **23** Jesus answered and said to him, "If anyone may love Me, he will keep My word, and My Father will love him, and We will come to him, and We will make [an] abode with him; **24** he who is not loving Me does not keep My words; and the word that you hear is not Mine, but the Father's who sent Me. **25** These things I have spoken to you, remaining with you, **26** and the Comforter, the Holy Spirit, whom the Father will send in My Name, He will teach you all things, and remind you of all things that I said to you. **27** Peace I leave to you; My peace I give to you. Not according as the world gives do I give to you. Do not let your heart be troubled, nor let it be afraid. **28** You heard that I said to you, I go away, and I come to you. If you loved Me, you would have rejoiced that I said, I go on to the Father, because My Father is greater than I. **29** And now I have said [it] to you before it comes to pass, that when it may come to pass, you may believe. **30** I will no longer talk much with you, for the ruler of this world comes, and he has nothing in Me; **31** but that the world may know that I love the Father, and according as the Father gave Me command, so I do; arise, we may go from here."

CHAPTER 15

1 "I am the true vine, and My Father is the vinedresser; **2** every branch not bearing fruit in Me, He takes it away, and everyone bearing fruit, He cleanses by pruning it, that it may bear more fruit; **3** you are already clean, because of the word that I have spoken to you; **4** remain in Me, and I in you, as the branch is not able to bear fruit of itself, if it may not remain in the vine, so neither you, if you may not remain in Me. **5** I am the vine, you the branches; he who is remaining in Me, and I in him, this one bears much fruit, because apart from Me you are not able to do anything; **6** if anyone may not remain in Me, he was cast forth outside as the branch, and was withered, and they gather them, and cast into fire, and they are burned; **7** if you may remain in Me, and My sayings may remain in you, whatever you may wish you will ask, and it will be done to you. **8** In this was My Father glorified, that you may bear much fruit, and you will become My disciples. **9** According as the Father loved Me, I also loved you, remain in My love; **10** if you may keep My commands, you will remain in My love, according as I have kept the commands of My Father, and remain in His love; **11** these things I have spoken to you, that My joy in you may remain, and your joy may be full. **12** This is My command, that you love one another, according as I loved you; **13** greater love has no one than this, that anyone may lay down his life for his friends; **14** you are My friends if you may do whatever I command you; **15** I no longer call you servants, because the servant has not known what his lord does, and I have called you friends, because all things that I heard from My Father, I made known to you. **16** You did not choose Me, but I chose you, and appointed you, that you might go away, and might bear fruit, and your fruit might remain, that whatever you may ask of the Father in My Name, He may give you. **17** These things I command you, that you love one another; **18** if the world hates you, you know that it has hated Me before you; **19** if you were of the world, the world would have been cherishing its own, but because you are not of the world, but I chose [you] out of the world—because of this the world hates you. **20** Remember the word that I said to you: A servant is not greater than his lord; if they persecuted Me, they will also persecute you; if they kept My word, they will also keep yours; **21** but all these things will they do to you, because of My Name, because they have not known Him who sent Me; **22** if I had not come and spoken to them, they were not having sin; but now they have no pretext for their sin. **23** He who is hating Me, hates My Father also; **24** if I did not do among them the works that no other has done, they were not having sin, and now they have both seen and hated both Me and My Father; **25** but—that the word may be fulfilled that was written in their law—They hated Me without a cause. **26** And when the Comforter may come, whom I will send to you from the Father—the Spirit of truth, who comes forth from the Father, He will testify of Me; **27** and you also testify, because you are with Me from the beginning."

CHAPTER 16

1 "These things I have spoken to you, that you may not be stumbled. **2** They will put you out of the synagogues, but an hour comes that everyone who has killed you may think to offer service to God; **3** and these things they will do to you, because they did not know the Father, nor Me. **4** But these things I have spoken to you, that when the hour may come, you may remember them, that I said [them] to you, and I did not say these things to you from the beginning, because I was with you; **5** and now I go away to Him who sent Me, and none of you asks Me, To where do you go? **6** but because I have said to you these things, the sorrow has filled your heart. **7** But I tell you the truth; it is better for you that I go away, for if I may not go away, the Comforter will not come to you, and if I go on, I will send Him to you; **8** and having come, He will convict the world concerning sin, and concerning righteousness, and concerning judgment; **9** concerning sin indeed, because they do not believe in Me; **10** and concerning righteousness, because I go away to My Father, and you behold Me no more; **11** and concerning judgment, because the ruler of this world has been judged. **12** I have yet many things to say to you, but you are not able to bear [them] now; **13** and when He may come—the Spirit of truth—He will guide you to all the truth, for He will not speak from Himself, but as many things as He will hear He will speak, and the coming things He will tell you; **14** He will glorify Me, because He will take of Mine, and will tell to you. **15** All things, as many as the Father has, are Mine; because of this I said that He will take of Mine, and will tell to you; **16** a little while, and you do not behold Me, and again a little while, and you will see Me, because I go away to the Father." **17** Therefore [some] of His disciples said to one another, "What is this that He says to us, A little while, and you do not behold Me, and again a little while, and you will see Me, and, Because I go away to the Father?" **18** they said then, "What is this He says—the little while? we have not known what He says." **19** Jesus, therefore, knew that they were wishing to ask Him, and He said to them, "Concerning this do you seek with one another, because I said, A little while, and you do not behold Me, and again a little while, and you will see Me? **20** truly, truly, I say to you that you will weep and lament, and the world will rejoice; and you will be sorrowful, but your sorrow will become joy. **21** The woman, when she may bear, has sorrow, because her hour came, and when she may bear the child, she no longer remembers the anguish, because of the joy that a man was born into the world. **22** And you, therefore, now indeed have sorrow; and again I will see you, and your heart will rejoice, and no one takes your joy from you, **23** and in that day you will question nothing of Me; truly, truly, I say to you, as many things as you may ask of the Father in My Name, He will give you; **24** until now you asked nothing in My Name; ask, and you will receive, that your joy may be full. **25** I have spoken these things in allegories to you, but there comes an hour when I will no longer speak to you in allegories, but will tell you freely of the Father. **26** In that day you will make request in My Name, and I do not say to you that I will ask the Father for you, **27** for the Father Himself cherishes you, because you have cherished Me, and you have believed that I came forth from God; **28** I came forth from the Father, and have come into the world; again I leave the world, and go on to the Father." **29** His disciples say to Him, "Behold, now You speak freely, and You do not speak allegory; **30** now we have known that You have known all things, and have no need that anyone questions You; in this we believe that You came forth from God." **31** Jesus answered them, "Now do you believe? behold, there comes an hour, **32** and now it has come, that you may be scattered, each to his own things, and you may leave Me alone, and I am not alone, because the Father is with Me; **33** these things I have spoken to you, that in Me you may have peace, in the world you will have tribulation, but take courage—I have overcome the world."

CHAPTER 17

1 These things Jesus spoke, and lifted up His eyes to the sky, and said, "Father, the hour has come, glorify Your Son, that Your Son may also glorify You, **2** according as You gave to Him authority over all flesh, that—all that You have given to Him—He may give to them continuous life; **3** and this is the continuous life, that they may know You, the only true God, and Him whom You sent—Jesus Christ; **4** I glorified You on the earth, having completed the work that You have given Me, that I should do. **5** And now, glorify Me, You Father, with Yourself, with the glory that I had with You before the world was; **6** I revealed Your Name to the men whom You have given to Me out of the world; they were Yours, and You have given them to Me, and they have kept Your word; **7** now they have known that all things, as many as You have given to Me, are from You, **8** because the sayings that You have given to Me, I have given to them, and they themselves received, and have known truly, that I came forth from You, and they believed that You sent Me. **9** I ask in regard to them; I do not ask in regard to the world, but in regard to those whom You have given to Me, because they are Yours, **10** and all Mine are Yours, and Yours [are] Mine, and I have been glorified in them; **11** and I am no longer in the world, and these are in the world, and I come to You. Holy Father, keep them in Your Name, whom You have given to Me, that they may be one as We [are one]; **12** when I was with them in the world, I was keeping them in Your Name; I guarded those whom You have given to Me, and none of them were destroyed, except the son of the destruction, that the Writing may be fulfilled. **13** And now I come to You, and these things I speak in the world, that they may have My joy fulfilled in themselves; **14** I have given Your word to them, and the world hated them, because they are not of the world, as I am not of the world; **15** I do not ask that You may take them out of the world, but that You may keep them out of the evil. **16** They are not of the world, as I am not of the world; **17** sanctify them in Your truth, Your word is truth; **18** as You sent Me into the world, I also sent them into the world; **19** and I sanctify Myself for them, that they also may be sanctified in truth themselves. **20** And I do not ask in regard to these alone, but also in regard to those who will be believing in Me through their word, **21** that they all may be one, as You Father [are] in Me, and I in You, that they also may be one in Us, that the world may believe that You sent Me. **22** And I have given to them the glory that You have given to Me, that they may be one as We are one— **23** I in them, and You in Me, that they may be perfected into one, and that the world may know that You sent Me, and loved them as You loved Me. **24** Father, those whom You have given to Me, I will that where I am they also may be with Me, that they may behold My glory that You gave to Me, because You loved Me before the foundation of the world. **25** Righteous Father, also the world did not know You, and I knew You, and these have known that You sent Me, **26** and I made known to them Your Name, and will make known, that the love with which You loved Me may be in them, and I in them."

CHAPTER 18

1 Having said these things, Jesus went forth with His disciples beyond the Brook of Kidron, where [there] was a garden, into which He entered, Himself and His disciples, **2** and Judas also, who delivered Him up, had known the place, because Jesus assembled there with His disciples many times. **3** Judas, therefore, having taken the band and officers out of the chief priests and Pharisees, comes there with torches and lamps, and weapons; **4** Jesus, therefore, knowing all things that are coming on Him, having gone forth, said to them, "Whom do you seek?" **5** they answered Him, "Jesus the Nazarene"; Jesus says to them, "I am"; and Judas who delivered Him up was standing with them. **6** When, therefore, He said to them, "I am," they went away backward, and fell to the ground. **7** Again, therefore, He questioned them, "Whom do you seek?" And they said, "Jesus the Nazarene"; **8** Jesus answered, "I said to you that I am; if, then, you seek Me, permit these to go away"; **9** that the word might be fulfilled that He said, "Those whom You have given to Me, I did not lose even one of them." **10** Simon Peter, therefore, having a sword, drew it, and struck the chief priest's servant, and cut off his right ear—and the name of the servant was Malchus— **11** Jesus, therefore, said to Peter, "Put the sword into the sheath; the cup that the Father has given to Me, may I not drink it?" **12** The band, therefore, and the captain, and the officers of the Jews, took hold on Jesus, and bound Him, **13** and they led Him away to Annas first, for he was father-in-law of Caiaphas, who was chief priest of that year, **14** and Caiaphas was he who gave counsel to the Jews that it is good for one man to perish for the people. **15** And following Jesus was Simon Peter, and the other disciple, and that disciple was known to the chief priest, and he entered with Jesus into the hall of the chief priest, **16** and Peter was standing at the door outside, therefore the other disciple who was known to the chief priest went forth, and he spoke to the doorkeeper, and he brought in Peter. **17** Then the maid, the doorkeeper, says to Peter, "Are you also of the disciples of this Man?" He says, "I am not"; **18** and the servants and the officers were standing, having made a fire of coals, because it was cold, and they were warming themselves, and Peter was standing with them, and warming himself. **19** The chief priests, therefore, questioned Jesus concerning His disciples, and concerning His teaching; **20** Jesus answered him, "I spoke freely to the world, I always taught in a synagogue, and in the temple, where the Jews always come together; and I spoke nothing in secret; **21** why do you question Me? question those having heard what I spoke to them; behold, these have known what I said." **22** And He having said these things, one of the officers standing by gave Jesus a slap, saying, "Thus do You answer the chief priest?" **23** Jesus answered him, "If I spoke ill, testify concerning the ill; and if well, why do you strike Me?" **24** Annas then sent Him bound to Caiaphas the chief priest. **25** And Simon Peter was standing and warming himself, then they said to him, "Are you also of His disciples?" He denied and said, "I am not." **26** One of the servants of the chief priest, being a relative of him whose ear Peter cut off, says, "Did I not see you in the garden with Him?" **27** again, therefore, Peter denied, and immediately a rooster crowed. **28** They led, therefore, Jesus from Caiaphas into the Praetorium, and it was early, and they themselves did not enter into the Praetorium, that they might not be defiled, but that they might eat the Passover; **29** Pilate, therefore, went forth to them and said, "What accusation do you bring against this Man?" **30** they answered and said to him, "If He were not doing evil, we had not delivered Him to you." **31** Pilate, therefore, said to them, "Take Him—you—and judge Him according to your law"; the Jews, therefore, said to him, "It is not lawful to us to put anyone to death"; **32** that the word of Jesus might be fulfilled which He said, signifying by what death He was about to die. **33** Pilate, therefore, entered into the Praetorium again, and called Jesus, and said to Him, "You are the King of the Jews?" **34** Jesus answered him, "Do you say this from yourself? or did others say it to you about Me?" **35** Pilate answered, "Am I a Jew? your nation and the chief priests delivered You up to me; what did You do?" **36** Jesus answered, "My kingdom is not of this world; if My kingdom were of this world, My officers had struggled that I might not be delivered up to Jews; but now My kingdom is not from here." **37** Pilate, therefore, said to Him, "Are You then a king?" Jesus answered, "You say [it], because I am a king; I have been born for this, and I have come into the world for this, that I may testify to the truth; everyone who is of the truth, hears My voice." **38** Pilate says to Him, "What is truth?" And having said this, again he went forth to the Jews and says to them, "I find no fault in Him; **39** and you have a custom that I will release to you one in the Passover; do you determine, therefore, [that] I will release to you the King of the Jews?" **40** therefore they all cried out again, saying, "Not this One—but Barabbas"; and Barabbas was a robber.

CHAPTER 19

1 Then, therefore, Pilate took Jesus and scourged [Him], **2** and the soldiers having plaited a garland of thorns, placed [it] on His head, and they cast a purple garment around Him, **3** and said, "Hail! The King of the Jews"; and they were giving Him slaps. **4** Pilate, therefore, again went forth outside and says to them, "Behold, I bring Him to you outside, that you may know that I find no fault in Him"; **5** Jesus, therefore, came forth outside, bearing the thorny garland and the purple garment; and he says to them, "Behold, the Man!" **6** When, therefore, the chief priests and the officers saw Him, they cried out, saying, "Crucify! Crucify!" Pilate says to them, "Take Him yourselves and crucify, for I find no fault in Him"; **7** the Jews answered him, "We have a law, and according to our law He ought to die, for He made Himself Son of God." **8** When, therefore, Pilate

heard this word, he was more afraid, **9** and entered again into the Praetorium and says to Jesus, "Where are You from?" And Jesus gave him no answer. **10** Pilate, therefore, says to Him, "Do You not speak to me? have You not known that I have authority to crucify You, and I have authority to release You?" **11** Jesus answered, "You would have no authority against Me if it were not having been given you from above; because of this, he who is delivering Me up to you has greater sin." **12** From this [time] Pilate was seeking to release Him, and the Jews were crying out, saying, "If you may release this One, you are not a friend of Caesar; everyone making himself a king speaks against Caesar." **13** Pilate, therefore, having heard this word, brought Jesus outside—and he sat down on the judgment seat—to a place called, "Pavement," and in Hebrew, Gabbatha; **14** and it was the Preparation of the Passover, and as it were the sixth hour, and he says to the Jews, "Behold, your King!" **15** and they cried out, "Take away! Take away! Crucify Him!" Pilate says to them, "Will I crucify your King?" The chief priests answered, "We have no king except Caesar." **16** Then, therefore, he delivered Him up to them, that He may be crucified, and they took Jesus and led [Him] away, **17** and carrying His cross, He went forth to the [place] called "Place of [the] Skull," which is called in Hebrew, Golgotha— **18** where they crucified Him, and with Him two others, on this side and on that side, but Jesus in the middle. **19** And Pilate also wrote a title, and put [it] on the cross, and it was written: "Jesus the Nazarene, the King of the Jews"; **20** therefore many of the Jews read this title, because the place was near to the city where Jesus was crucified, and it was having been written in Hebrew, in Greek, in Latin. **21** The chief priests of the Jews therefore said to Pilate, "Do not write, The King of the Jews, but that this One said, I am King of the Jews"; **22** Pilate answered, "What I have written, I have written." **23** The soldiers, therefore, when they crucified Jesus, took His garments, and made four parts, to each soldier a part, also the coat, and the coat was seamless, from the top woven throughout; **24** they said, therefore, to one another, "We may not tear it, but cast a lot for it, whose it will be"; that the Writing might be fulfilled, that is saying, "They divided My garments to themselves, and they cast a lot for My clothing"; the soldiers, therefore, indeed, did these things. **25** And there stood by the cross of Jesus His mother, and His mother's sister, Mary of Cleopas, and Mary the Magdalene; **26** Jesus, therefore, having seen [His] mother, and the disciple standing by, whom He was loving, He says to His mother, "Woman, behold, your son"; **27** afterward He says to the disciple, "Behold, your mother"; and from that hour the disciple took her to his own [home]. **28** After this, Jesus knowing that all things have now been accomplished, that the Writing may be fulfilled, says, "I thirst"; **29** a vessel, therefore, was placed full of vinegar, and having filled a sponge with vinegar, and having put [it] around a hyssop stalk, they put [it] to His mouth; **30** when, therefore, Jesus received the vinegar, He said, "It has been accomplished." And having bowed the head, gave up the spirit. **31** The Jews, therefore, that the bodies might not remain on the cross on the Sabbath, since it was the Preparation (for that Sabbath day was a great one), asked of Pilate that their legs may be broken, and they [are] taken away. **32** The soldiers, therefore, came, and they indeed broke the legs of the first and of the other who was crucified with Him, **33** and having come to Jesus, when they saw Him already having been dead, they did not break His legs; **34** but one of the soldiers pierced His side with a spear, and immediately there came forth blood and water; **35** and he who has seen has testified, and his testimony is true, and that one has known that he speaks true things, that you also may believe. **36** For these things came to pass, that the Writing may be fulfilled, "A bone of Him will not be broken"; **37** and again another Writing says, "They will look to Him whom they pierced." **38** And after these things, Joseph of Arimathea—being a disciple of Jesus, but concealed, through the fear of the Jews—asked of Pilate, that he may take away the body of Jesus, and Pilate gave leave; he came, therefore, and took away the body of Jesus, **39** and Nicodemus also came—who came to Jesus by night at the first—carrying a mixture of myrrh and aloes, as it were, one hundred pounds. **40** Therefore they took the body of Jesus, and bound it with linen clothes with the spices, according as it was the custom of the Jews to prepare for burial; **41** and there was a garden in the place where He was crucified, and a new tomb in the garden, in which no one was yet laid; **42** therefore, because the tomb was near, there they laid Jesus because of the Preparation of the Jews.

CHAPTER 20

1 And on the first [day] of the weeks, Mary the Magdalene comes early (there being yet darkness) to the tomb, and she sees the stone having been taken away out of the tomb; **2** she runs, therefore, and comes to Simon Peter, and to the other disciple whom Jesus was cherishing, and says to them, "They took away the Lord out of the tomb, and we have not known where they laid Him." **3** Peter, therefore, went forth, and the other disciple, and they were coming to the tomb, **4** and the two were running together, and the other disciple ran forward more quickly than Peter, and came first to the tomb, **5** and having stooped down, sees the linen clothes lying, yet, indeed, he did not enter. **6** Simon Peter, therefore, comes, following him, and he entered into the tomb, and beholds the linen clothes lying [there], **7** and the napkin that was on His head not lying with the linen clothes, but apart, having been folded up, in one place; **8** then, therefore, the other disciple who came first to the tomb entered also, and he saw and believed; **9** for they did not yet know the Writing, that it was necessary for Him to rise again out of the dead. **10** The disciples therefore went away again to their own friends, **11** and Mary was standing near the tomb, weeping outside; as she was weeping, then, she stooped down into the tomb, and beholds two messengers in white, sitting, **12** one at the head and one at the feet, where the body of Jesus had been laid. **13** And they say to her, "Woman, why do you weep?" She says to them, "Because they took away my Lord, and I have not known where they laid Him"; **14** and having said these things, she turned backward, and sees Jesus standing, and she had not known that it is Jesus. **15** Jesus says to her, "Woman, why do you weep? whom do you seek?" She, supposing that He is the gardener, says to Him, "Lord, if You carried Him away, tell me where You laid Him, and I will take Him away"; **16** Jesus says to her, "Mary!" Having turned, she says to Him, "Rabboni!" That is to say, "Teacher." **17** Jesus says to her, "Do not be touching Me, for I have not yet ascended to My Father; and be going on to My brothers, and say to them, I ascend to My Father and your Father, and [to] My God and your God." **18** Mary the Magdalene comes, reporting to the disciples that she has seen the Lord, and [that] He said these things to her. **19** It being, therefore, evening, on that day, the first [day] of the weeks, and the doors having been shut where the disciples were assembled through fear of the Jews, Jesus came and stood in the midst, and says to them, "Peace to you"; **20** and having said this, He showed them His hands and side; the disciples, therefore, rejoiced, having seen the Lord. **21** Jesus, therefore, said to them again, "Peace to you; according as the Father has sent Me, I also send you"; **22** having said this, He breathed on [them], and says to them, "Receive the Holy Spirit; **23** if you may forgive the sins of any, they are forgiven them; if you may retain of any, they have been retained." **24** And Thomas, one of the Twelve, who is called Didymus, was not with them when Jesus came; **25** the other disciples, therefore, said to him, "We have seen the Lord!" And he said to them, "If I may not see the mark of the nails in His hands, and may [not] put my finger into the mark of the nails, and may [not] put my hand into His side, I will not believe." **26** And after eight days, again His disciples were within, and Thomas [was] with them; Jesus comes, the doors having been shut, and He stood in the midst and said, "Peace to you!" **27** then He says to Thomas, "Bring your finger here, and see My hands, and bring your hand, and put [it] into My side, and do not become unbelieving, but believing." **28** And Thomas answered and said to Him, "My Lord and my God!" **29** Jesus says to him, "Because you have seen Me, Thomas, you have believed; blessed [are] those having not seen, and having believed." **30** Many indeed, therefore, other signs Jesus also did before His disciples that are not written in this scroll; **31** and these have been written that you may believe that Jesus is the Christ, the Son of God, and that believing, you may have life in His Name.

CHAPTER 21

1 After these things Jesus Himself again appeared to the disciples on the Sea of Tiberias, and He revealed Himself thus: 2 Simon Peter, and Thomas who is called Didymus, and Nathanael from Cana of Galilee, and the [sons] of Zebedee, and two of His other disciples were together. 3 Simon Peter says to them, "I go away to fish"; they say to him, "We go—we also—with you"; they went forth and immediately entered into the boat, and on that night they caught nothing. 4 And morning having now come, Jesus stood at the shore, yet indeed the disciples did not know that it is Jesus; 5 Jesus, therefore, says to them, "Boys, do you have any meat?" 6 they answered Him, "No"; and He said to them, "Cast the net at the right side of the boat, and you will find [some]"; they cast, therefore, and no longer were they able to draw it, from the multitude of the fishes. 7 That disciple, therefore, whom Jesus was loving says to Peter, "It is the Lord!" Simon Peter, therefore, having heard that it is the Lord, girded on the outer coat (for he was naked), and cast himself into the sea; 8 and the other disciples came by the little boat, for they were not far from the land, but about two hundred cubits away, dragging the net of the fishes; 9 when, therefore, they came to the land, they behold a fire of coals lying [there], and a fish lying on it, and bread. 10 Jesus says to them, "Bring from the fishes that you caught now"; 11 Simon Peter went up, and drew the net up on the land, full of great fishes—one hundred fifty-three; and though they were so many, the net was not split. 12 Jesus says to them, "Come, dine"; and none of the disciples were venturing to inquire of Him, "Who are You?" Knowing that it is the Lord; 13 Jesus, therefore, comes and takes the bread and gives [it] to them, and the fish in like manner; 14 this [is] now a third time Jesus was revealed to His disciples, having been raised from the dead. 15 When, therefore, they dined, Jesus says to Simon Peter, "Simon, [son] of Jonas, do you love Me more than these?" He says to Him, "Yes, Lord; You have known that I cherish You"; He says to him, "Feed My lambs." 16 He says to him again, a second time, "Simon, [son] of Jonas, do you love Me?" He says to Him, "Yes, Lord; You have known that I cherish You"; He says to him, "Tend My sheep." 17 He says to him the third time, "Simon, [son] of Jonas, do you cherish Me?" Peter was grieved that He said to him the third time, "Do you cherish Me?" And he said to Him, "Lord, You have known all things; You know that I cherish You." Jesus says to him, "Feed My sheep; 18 truly, truly, I say to you, when you were younger, you were girding yourself and were walking to where you willed, but when you may be old, you will stretch forth your hands, and another will gird you, and will carry [you] to where you do not will"; 19 and this He said, signifying by what death he will glorify God; and having said this, He says to him, "Follow Me." 20 And having turned, Peter sees the disciple whom Jesus was loving following (who also reclined in the dinner on His breast and said, "Lord, who is he who is delivering You up?") 21 Having seen this one, Peter says to Jesus, "Lord, and what of this one?" 22 Jesus says to him, "If I will him to remain until I come, what [is that] to you? Follow Me." 23 This word, therefore, went forth to the brothers that this disciple does not die, yet Jesus did not say to him that he does not die, but, "If I will him to remain until I come, what [is that] to you?" 24 this is the disciple who is testifying concerning these things, and he wrote these things, and we have known that his testimony is true. 25 And there are also many other things—as many as Jesus did—which, if they may be written one by one, I think the world itself does not even have place for the scrolls written. Amen.

ACTS

CHAPTER 1

1 The former account, indeed, I made concerning all things, O Theophilus, that Jesus began both to do and to teach, **2** until the day in which, having given command through the Holy Spirit to the apostles whom He chose out, He was taken up, **3** to whom He also presented Himself alive after His suffering, in many certain proofs, being seen by them through forty days, and speaking the things concerning the Kingdom of God. **4** And being assembled together with them, He commanded them not to depart from Jerusalem, but to wait for the promise of the Father, "Which you heard from Me; **5** because John, indeed, immersed in water, but you will be immersed in the Holy Spirit not many days after these." **6** They, therefore, indeed, having come together, were questioning Him, saying, "Lord, do You at this time restore the kingdom to Israel?" **7** and He said to them, "It is not yours to know times or seasons that the Father appointed in His own authority; **8** but you will receive power at the coming of the Holy Spirit on you, and you will be witnesses for Me both in Jerusalem, and in all Judea and Samaria, and to the end of the earth." **9** And having said these things—they beholding—He was taken up, and a cloud received Him up from their sight; **10** and as they were looking steadfastly to the sky in His going on, then, behold, two men stood by them in white clothing, **11** who also said, "Men, Galileans, why do you stand gazing into the sky? this Jesus who was received up from you into Heaven, will so come in what manner you saw Him going on to Heaven." **12** Then they returned to Jerusalem from [that] called the Mount of Olives, that is near Jerusalem, a Sabbath's journey; **13** and when they came in, they went up into the upper room, where were abiding both Peter, and James, and John, and Andrew, Philip, and Thomas, Bartholomew, and Matthew, James, of Alphaeus, and Simon the Zealot, and Judas, of James; **14** these were all continuing with one accord in prayer and supplication, with women, and Mary the mother of Jesus, and with His brothers. **15** And in these days, Peter having risen up in the midst of the disciples, said (also the multitude of the names at the same place was, as it were, one hundred and twenty), **16** "Men, brothers, it was necessary [for] this Writing to be fulfilled that the Holy Spirit spoke beforehand through the mouth of David, concerning Judas, who became guide to those who took Jesus, **17** because he was numbered among us, and received the share in this ministry. **18** (This one, indeed, then, purchased a field out of the reward of unrighteousness, and falling headlong, burst apart in the midst, and all his bowels gushed forth, **19** and it became known to all those dwelling in Jerusalem, insomuch that this place is called, in their proper dialect, Aceldama, that is, Field of Blood.) **20** For it has been written in [the] Scroll of Psalms: Let his lodging-place become desolate, and let no one be dwelling in it, and let another take his oversight. **21** It is necessary, therefore, of the men who went with us during all the time in which the Lord Jesus went in and went out among us, **22** beginning from the immersion of John, to the day in which He was received up from us, one of these to become with us a witness of His resurrection." **23** And they set two, Joseph called Barsabas, who was surnamed Justus, and Matthias, **24** and having prayed, they said, "You, Lord, who are knowing the heart of all, show which one You chose of these two, **25** to receive the share of this ministry and apostleship, from which Judas, by transgression, fell, to go on to his proper place"; **26** and they gave their lots, and the lot fell on Matthias, and he was numbered with the eleven apostles.

CHAPTER 2

1 And in the day of the Pentecost being fulfilled, they were all with one accord at the same place, **2** and there came suddenly out of the sky a sound as of a violent rushing wind, and it filled all the house where they were sitting, **3** and there appeared to them divided tongues, as it were of fire; it also sat on each one of them, **4** and they were all filled with the Holy Spirit, and began to speak with other tongues, according as the Spirit was giving them to declare. **5** And there were Jews dwelling in Jerusalem, devout men from every nation of those under the heaven, **6** and the rumor of this having come, the multitude came together, and was confounded, because they were, each one, hearing them speaking in his proper dialect, **7** and they were all amazed, and wondered, saying to one another, "Behold, are not all these who are speaking Galileans? **8** and how do we hear, each in our proper dialect, in which we were born? **9** Parthians, and Medes, and Elamites, and those dwelling in Mesopotamia, in Judea also, and Cappadocia, Pontus, and Asia, **10** Phrygia also, and Pamphylia, Egypt, and the parts of Libya that [are] along Cyrene, and the strangers of Rome, both Jews and proselytes, **11** Cretes and Arabians, we heard them speaking the great things of God in our tongues." **12** And they were all amazed, and were in doubt, saying to one another, "What would this wish to be?" **13** and others mocking said, "They are full of sweet wine"; **14** and Peter having stood up with the Eleven, lifted up his voice and declared to them: "Men—Jews, and all those dwelling in Jerusalem! Let this be known to you, and listen to my sayings, **15** for these are not drunken, as you take it up, for it is the third hour of the day. **16** But this is that which has been spoken through the prophet Joel: **17** And it will be in the last days, says God, || I will pour out of My Spirit on all flesh, || And your sons and your daughters will prophesy, || And your young men will see visions, || And your old men will dream dreams; **18** And also on My menservants, and on My maidservants, || In those days, I

will pour out of My Spirit, || And they will prophesy; **19** And I will give wonders in the sky above, || And signs on the earth beneath blood, and fire, and vapor of smoke, **20** The sun will be turned to darkness, || And the moon to blood, || Before the coming of the Day of the Lord—the great and conspicuous; **21** And it will be, everyone who, if he may have called on the Name of the Lord, will be saved. **22** Men, Israelites! Hear these words: Jesus the Nazarene, a man approved of God among you by mighty works, and wonders, and signs, that God did through Him in the midst of you, according as also you yourselves have known, **23** this One, by the determinate counsel and foreknowledge of God, being given out, having been taken by lawless hands, having been crucified—you slew, **24** whom God raised up, having loosed the travails of death, because it was not possible for Him to be held by it; **25** for David says in regard to Him: I foresaw the Lord always before me—Because He is on my right hand—That I may not be moved; **26** Because of this was my heart cheered, || And my tongue was glad, || And yet—my flesh will also rest on hope, **27** Because You will not leave my soul to Hades, || Nor will You give Your Holy One to see corruption; **28** You made known to me ways of life, || You will fill me with joy with Your countenance. **29** Men, brothers! It is permitted to speak with freedom to you concerning the patriarch David, that he both died and was buried, and his tomb is among us to this day; **30** therefore, being a prophet, and knowing that God swore to him with an oath, out of the fruit of his loins, according to the flesh, to raise up the Christ, to sit on his throne, **31** having foreseen, he spoke concerning the resurrection of the Christ, that His soul was not left to Hades, nor did His flesh see corruption. **32** God raised up this Jesus, of which we are all witnesses; **33** then having been exalted at the right hand of God—also having received the promise of the Holy Spirit from the Father—He poured forth this which you now see and hear; **34** for David did not go up into the heavens, and he says himself: The Lord says to my Lord, || Sit at My right hand, **35** Until I make Your enemies Your footstool; **36** assuredly, therefore, let all the house of Israel know that God made Him both Lord and Christ—this Jesus whom you crucified." **37** And having heard, they were pricked to the heart; they also say to Peter and to the rest of the apostles, "What will we do, men, brothers?" **38** and Peter said to them, "Convert, and each of you be immersed on the Name of Jesus Christ, for forgiveness of sins, and you will receive the gift of the Holy Spirit, **39** for the promise is to you and to your children, and to all those far off, as many as the Lord our God will call." **40** Also with many more other words he was testifying and exhorting, saying, "Be saved from this perverse generation"; **41** then those, indeed, who gladly received his word were immersed, and there were added on that day, as it were, three thousand souls, **42** and they were continuing steadfastly in the teaching of the apostles, and the fellowship, and the breaking of the bread, and the prayers. **43** And fear came on every soul, also many wonders and signs were being done through the apostles, **44** and all those believing were at the same place, and had all things common, **45** and they were selling the possessions and the goods, and were parting them to all, according as anyone had need. **46** Also continuing daily with one accord in the temple, also breaking bread at every house, they were partaking of food in gladness and simplicity of heart, **47** praising God, and having favor with all the people, and the Lord was adding those being saved every day to the Assembly.

CHAPTER 3

1 And Peter and John were going up at the same time into the temple, at the hour of the prayer, the ninth [hour], **2** and a certain man, being lame from the womb of his mother, was being carried, whom they were laying every day at the gate of the temple, called Beautiful, to ask a kindness from those entering into the temple, **3** who, having seen Peter and John about to go into the temple, was begging to receive a kindness. **4** And Peter, having looked steadfastly toward him with John, said, "Look toward us"; **5** and he was giving heed to them, looking to receive something from them; **6** and Peter said, "I have no silver and gold, but what I have, that I give to you; in the Name of Jesus Christ of Nazareth, rise up and be walking." **7** And having seized him by the right hand, he raised [him] up, and instantly his feet and ankles were strengthened, **8** and springing up, he stood, and was walking, and entered with them into the temple, walking and springing, and praising God;

9 and all the people saw him walking and praising God, 10 and they knew him, that this it was who for a kindness was sitting at the Beautiful Gate of the temple, and they were filled with wonder and amazement at what has happened to him. 11 And at the lame man who was healed holding Peter and John, all the people ran together to them in the porch called Solomon's—greatly amazed, 12 and Peter having seen, answered to the people, "Men, Israelites! Why do you wonder at this? or why do you look on us so earnestly, as if by our own power or piety we have made him to walk? 13 The God of Abraham, and of Isaac, and of Jacob, the God of our fathers, glorified His child Jesus, whom you delivered up, and denied Him in the presence of Pilate, he having given judgment to release [Him], 14 and you denied the Holy and Righteous One, and desired a man—a murderer—to be granted to you, 15 and the Prince of life you killed, whom God raised out of the dead, of which we are witnesses; 16 and on the faith of His Name, this one whom you see and have known, His Name made strong, even the faith that [is] through Him gave to him this perfect soundness before you all. 17 And now, brothers, I have known that through ignorance you did [it], as also your rulers; 18 and God, what things He had declared before through the mouth of all His prophets, that the Christ should suffer, He thus fulfilled; 19 convert, therefore, and turn back, for your sins being blotted out, that times of refreshing may come from the presence of the Lord, 20 and He may send Jesus Christ who before has been preached to you, 21 whom Heaven required, indeed, to receive until times of a restitution of all things, of which God spoke through the mouth of all His holy prophets from the age. 22 For Moses, indeed, said to the fathers—The Lord your God will raise up a Prophet to you out of your brothers, like to me; you will hear Him in all things, as many as He may speak to you; 23 and it will be, every soul that may not hear that Prophet will be utterly destroyed out of the people; 24 and also all the prophets from Samuel and those following in order, as many as spoke, also foretold of these days. 25 You are sons of the prophets, and of the covenant that God made to our fathers, saying to Abraham: And in your Seed will all the families of the earth be blessed; 26 to you first, God, having raised up His child Jesus, sent Him, blessing you, in the turning away of each one from your evil ways."

CHAPTER 4

1 And as they are speaking to the people, there came to them the priests, and the magistrate of the temple, and the Sadducees— 2 being grieved because of their teaching the people, and preaching in Jesus the resurrection out of the dead— 3 and they laid hands on them, and put them in custody until the next day, for it was evening already; 4 and many of those hearing the word believed, and the number of the men became, as it were, five thousand. 5 And it came to pass the next day, there were gathered together of them the rulers, and elders, and scribes, to Jerusalem, 6 and Annas the chief priest, and Caiaphas, and John, and Alexander, and as many as were of the family of the chief priest, 7 and having set them in the midst, they were inquiring, "In what power, or in what name did you do this?" 8 Then Peter, having been filled with the Holy Spirit, said to them: "Rulers of the people, and elders of Israel, 9 if we are examined today concerning the good deed to the ailing man, by whom he has been saved, 10 be it known to all of you, and to all the people of Israel, that in the Name of Jesus Christ of Nazareth, whom you crucified, whom God raised out of the dead, in Him has this one stood by before you whole. 11 This is the stone that was set at nothing by you—the builders, that became head of a corner; 12 and there is not salvation in any other, for there is no other name under Heaven that has been given among men, in which it is required of us to be saved." 13 And beholding the openness of Peter and John, and having perceived that they are illiterate men and commoners, they were wondering—they were also taking knowledge of them that they had been with Jesus— 14 and seeing the man standing with them who has been healed, they had nothing to say against [it], 15 and having commanded them to go away out of the Sanhedrin, they took counsel with one another, 16 saying, "What will we do to these men? because that, indeed, a notable sign has been done through them [is] apparent to all those dwelling in Jerusalem, and we are not able to deny [it]; 17 but that it may spread no further toward the people, let us strictly threaten them to no longer speak in this Name to any man." 18 And having called them, they charged them not to

speak at all, nor to teach, in the Name of Jesus, 19 and Peter and John answering to them said, "Whether it is righteous before God to listen to you rather than to God, judge; 20 for we cannot but speak what we saw and heard." 21 And they having further threatened [them], let them go, finding no way how they may punish them, because of the people, because all were glorifying God for that which has been done, 22 for above forty years of age was the man on whom had been done this sign of the healing. 23 And being let go, they went to their own friends, and declared whatever the chief priests and the elders said to them, 24 and they having heard, lifted up the voice to God with one accord and said, "Lord, You [are] God, who made the heaven, and the earth, and the sea, and all that [are] in them, 25 who, through the mouth of Your servant David, said, Why did nations rage, and peoples meditate vain things? 26 the kings of the earth stood up, and the rulers were gathered together against the Lord and against His Christ; 27 for gathered together of a truth against Your holy child Jesus, whom You anointed, were both Herod and Pontius Pilate, with nations and peoples of Israel, 28 to do whatever Your hand and Your counsel determined before to come to pass. 29 And now, Lord, look on their threatenings, and grant to Your servants to speak Your word with all freedom, 30 in the stretching forth of Your hand, for healing, and signs, and wonders, to come to pass through the Name of Your holy child Jesus." 31 And they having prayed, the place was shaken in which they were gathered together, and they were all filled with the Holy Spirit, and were speaking the word of God with freedom, 32 and of the multitude of those who believed, the heart and the soul were one, and not one was saying that anything of the things he had was his own, but all things were in common to them. 33 And with great power the apostles were giving the testimony to the resurrection of the Lord Jesus, great grace was also on them all, 34 for there was not anyone among them who lacked, for as many as were possessors of fields, or houses, selling [them], were bringing the prices of the thing sold, 35 and were laying them at the feet of the apostles, and distribution was being made to each according as anyone had need. 36 And Joses, who was surnamed by the apostles Barnabas—which is, having been interpreted, Son of Comfort—a Levite, of Cyprus by birth, 37 a field being his, having sold [it], brought the money and laid [it] at the feet of the apostles.

CHAPTER 5

1 And a certain man, Ananias by name, with his wife Sapphira, sold a possession, 2 and kept back of the price—his wife also knowing—and having brought a certain part, he laid [it] at the feet of the apostles. 3 And Peter said, "Ananias, why did Satan fill your heart, for you to lie to the Holy Spirit, and to keep back of the price of the place? 4 while it remained, did it not remain yours? and having been sold, was it not in your authority? why [is] it that you put this thing in your heart? you did not lie to men, but to God"; 5 and Ananias hearing these words, having fallen down, expired, and great fear came on all who heard these things, 6 and having risen, the younger men wound him up, and having carried forth, they buried [him]. 7 And it came to pass, about three hours after, that his wife, not knowing what has happened, came in, 8 and Peter answered her, "Tell me if for so much you sold the place"; and she said, "Yes, for so much." 9 And Peter said to her, "How was it agreed by you to tempt the Spirit of the Lord? behold, the feet of those who buried your husband [are] at the door, and they will carry you forth"; 10 and immediately she fell down at his feet, and expired, and the young men having come in, found her dead, and having carried forth, they buried [her] by her husband; 11 and great fear came on all the Assembly, and on all who heard these things. 12 And through the hands of the apostles came many signs and wonders among the people, and they were all with one accord in the porch of Solomon; 13 and of the rest no one was daring to join himself to them, but the people were magnifying them, 14 (and the more were believers added to the Lord, multitudes of both men and women), 15 so as to bring forth the ailing into the broad places, and to lay [them] on beds and pallets, that at the coming of Peter, even [his] shadow might overshadow someone of them; 16 and there were also coming together the people of the surrounding cities to Jerusalem, carrying ailing persons, and those harassed by unclean spirits—who were all healed. 17 And having risen, the chief priest, and all those with him—being the sect of the Sadducees—were filled with zeal, 18 and laid their hands on the

apostles, and put them in a public prison; **19** but through the night a messenger of the Lord opened the doors of the prison, having also brought them forth, he said, **20** "Go on, and standing, speak in the temple to the people all the sayings of this life"; **21** and having heard, they entered into the temple at the dawn, and were teaching. And the chief priest having come, and those with him, they called together the Sanhedrin and all the Senate of the sons of Israel, and they sent to the prison to have them brought, **22** and the officers having come, did not find them in the prison, and having turned back, they told, **23** saying, "We indeed found the prison shut in all safety, and the keepers standing outside before the doors, and having opened—we found no one within." **24** And as the priest, and the magistrate of the temple, and the chief priests, heard these words, they were doubting concerning them to what this would come; **25** and coming near, a certain one told them, saying, "Behold, the men whom you put in the prison are in the temple standing and teaching the people"; **26** then the magistrate having gone away with officers, brought them without violence, for they were fearing the people, lest they should be stoned; **27** and having brought them, they set [them] in the Sanhedrin, and the chief priest questioned them, **28** saying, "Did we not strictly command you not to teach in this Name? and behold, you have filled Jerusalem with your teaching, and you intend to bring on us the blood of this Man." **29** And Peter and the apostles answering, said, "It is required to obey God, rather than men; **30** and the God of our fathers raised up Jesus, whom you slew, having hanged on a tree; **31** this One, God, a Prince and a Savior, has exalted with His right hand, to give conversion to Israel, and forgiveness of sins; **32** and we are His witnesses of these sayings, and the Holy Spirit also, whom God gave to those obeying Him." **33** And they having heard, were cut [to the heart], and were intending to slay them, **34** but a certain one, having risen up in the Sanhedrin—a Pharisee, by name Gamaliel, a teacher of law honored by all the people—commanded to put the apostles forth a little, **35** and said to them, "Men, Israelites, take heed to yourselves about these men, what you are about to do, **36** for before these days Theudas rose up, saying that he was someone, to whom a number of men joined themselves, as it were four hundred, who was slain, and all, as many as were obeying him, were scattered, and came to nothing. **37** After this one, Judas the Galilean rose up, in the days of the census, and drew away people after him, and that one perished, and all, as many as were obeying him, were scattered; **38** and now I say to you, refrain from these men, and leave them alone, because if this counsel or this work may be of men, it will be overthrown, **39** and if it be of God, you are not able to overthrow it, lest perhaps you are also found fighting against God." **40** And to him they agreed, and having called near the apostles, having beaten [them], they commanded [them] not to speak in the Name of Jesus, and let them go; **41** they, indeed, then, departed from the presence of the Sanhedrin, rejoicing that for His Name they were counted worthy to suffer dishonor, **42** also every day in the temple, and in every house, they were not ceasing teaching and proclaiming good news—Jesus the Christ.

CHAPTER 6

1 And in these days, the disciples multiplying, there came a murmuring of the Hellenists at the Hebrews, because their widows were being overlooked in the daily ministry, **2** and the Twelve, having called near the multitude of the disciples, said, "It is not pleasing that we, having left the word of God, minister at tables; **3** look out, therefore, brothers, seven men of you who are testified well of, full of the Holy Spirit and wisdom, whom we may set over this necessity, **4** and we to prayer, and to the ministry of the word, will give ourselves continually." **5** And the thing was pleasing before all the multitude, and they chose Stephen, a man full of faith and the Holy Spirit, and Philip, and Prochorus, and Nicanor, and Timon, and Parmenas, and Nicolaus, a proselyte of Antioch, **6** whom they set before the apostles, and they, having prayed, laid [their] hands on them. **7** And the word of God increased, and the number of the disciples multiplied in Jerusalem exceedingly; a great multitude of the priests were also obedient to the faith. **8** And Stephen, full of faith and power, was doing great wonders and signs among the people, **9** and there arose certain of those of the synagogue, the [one] called Libertines (and Cyrenians, and Alexandrians, and of those from Cilicia, and Asia), disputing with Stephen, **10** and they were not able to resist the wisdom and the Spirit with which he was speaking; **11** then they suborned men, saying, "We have heard him speaking slanderous sayings in regard to Moses and God." **12** They also stirred up the people, and the elders, and the scribes, and having come on [him], they caught him, and brought [him] to the Sanhedrin; **13** they also set up false witnesses, saying, "This one does not cease to speak evil sayings against this holy place and the Law, **14** for we have heard him saying that this Jesus the Nazarean will overthrow this place, and will change the customs that Moses delivered to us"; **15** and gazing at him, all those sitting in the Sanhedrin saw his face as it were the face of a messenger.

CHAPTER 7

1 And the chief priest said, "Are then these things so?" **2** and he said, "Men, brothers, and fathers, listen! The God of glory appeared to our father Abraham, being in Mesopotamia, before his dwelling in Haran, **3** and He said to him, Go forth out of your land, and out of your relatives, and come to a land that I will show you. **4** Then having come forth out of the land of the Chaldeans, he dwelt in Haran, and from there, after the death of his father, He removed him to this land wherein you now dwell, **5** and He gave him no inheritance in it, not even a footstep, and promised to give it to him for a possession, and to his seed after him—he having no child. **6** And God spoke thus, that his seed will be sojourning in a strange land, and they will cause it to serve, and will do it evil [for] four hundred years. **7** And the nation whom they will serve I will judge, said God; And after these things they will come forth and will do Me service in this place. **8** And He gave to him a covenant of circumcision, and so he begot Isaac, and circumcised him on the eighth day, and Isaac [begot] Jacob, and Jacob—the twelve patriarchs; **9** and the patriarchs, having been moved with jealousy, sold Joseph to Egypt, and God was with him, **10** and delivered him out of all his tribulations, and gave him favor and wisdom before Pharaoh king of Egypt, and he set him—governor over Egypt and all his house. **11** And there came a scarcity on all the land of Egypt and Canaan, and great tribulation, and our fathers were not finding sustenance, **12** and Jacob having heard that there was grain in Egypt, sent forth our fathers a first time; **13** and at the second time was Joseph made known to his brothers, and Joseph's family became disclosed to Pharaoh, **14** and Joseph having sent, called for his father Jacob, and all his relatives—with seventy-five souls— **15** and Jacob went down to Egypt, and died, himself and our fathers, **16** and they were carried over into Shechem, and were laid in the tomb that Abraham bought for a price in money from the sons of Emmor, of Shechem. **17** And according as the time of the promise was drawing near, which God swore to Abraham, the people increased and multiplied in Egypt, **18** until another king rose, who had not known Joseph; **19** this one, having dealt subtly with our family, did evil to our fathers, causing to expose their babies, that they might not live; **20** in which time Moses was born, and he was fair to God, and he was brought up [for] three months in the house of his father; **21** and he having been set outside, the daughter of Pharaoh took him up, and reared him to herself for a son; **22** and Moses was taught in all wisdom of the Egyptians, and he was powerful in words and in works. **23** And when forty years were fulfilled to him, it came on his heart to look after his brothers, the sons of Israel; **24** and having seen a certain one suffering injustice, he defended, and did justice to the oppressed, having struck the Egyptian; **25** and he was supposing his brothers to understand that God gives salvation through his hand; and they did not understand. **26** On the succeeding day, also, he showed himself to them as they are striving, and urged them to peace, saying, Men, you are brothers, why do you do injustice to one another? **27** and he who is doing injustice to the neighbor, thrust him away, saying, Who set you a ruler and a judge over us? **28** Do you wish to kill me, as you killed the Egyptian yesterday? **29** And Moses fled at this word, and became a sojourner in the land of Midian, where he begot two sons, **30** and forty years having been fulfilled, there appeared to him in the wilderness of Mount Sinai [the] Messenger of the Lord, in a flame of fire of a bush, **31** and Moses having seen, wondered at the sight; and he drawing near to behold, there came a voice of the Lord to him, **32** I [am] the God of your fathers; the God of Abraham, and the God of Isaac, and the God of Jacob. And Moses having become terrified, did not dare behold, ³³ and the Lord said to him, Loose the sandal of your feet, for the place in which you have stood is holy ground; ³⁴ seeing I have seen the affliction of My people that [is] in Egypt, and I heard their groaning, and came down to deliver them; and now come, I will send you to Egypt. ³⁵ This Moses, whom they refused, saying, Who set you a ruler and a judge? this one God sent [as] a ruler and a redeemer, by the hand of [the] Messenger who appeared to him in the bush; ³⁶ this one brought them forth, having done wonders and signs in the land of Egypt, and in the Red Sea, and in the wilderness forty years; ³⁷ this is the Moses who said to the sons of Israel: The Lord your God will raise up to you a Prophet out of your brothers, like to me, Him will you hear. ³⁸ This is he who was in the assembly in the wilderness, with the Messenger who is speaking to him in Mount Sinai, and with our fathers who received the living oracles to give to us; ³⁹ to whom our fathers did not wish to become obedient, but thrusted away, and turned back in their hearts to Egypt, ⁴⁰ saying to Aaron, Make to us gods who will go on before us, for this Moses, who brought us forth out of the land of Egypt, we have not known what has happened to him. ⁴¹ And they made a calf in those days, and brought a sacrifice to the idol, and were rejoicing in the works of their hands, ⁴² and God turned, and gave them up to do service to the host of Heaven, according as it has been written in the scroll of the Prophets: Did you offer slain beasts and sacrifices to Me forty years in the wilderness, O house of Israel? ⁴³ and you took up the dwelling place of Moloch, and the star of your god Remphan—the figures that you made to worship them, and I will remove your dwelling beyond Babylon. ⁴⁴ The Dwelling Place of the Testimony was among our fathers in the wilderness, according as He directed, who is speaking to Moses, to make it according to the figure that he had seen; ⁴⁵ which also our fathers having in succession received, brought in with Joshua, into the possession of the nations whom God drove out from the presence of our fathers, until the days of David, ⁴⁶ who found favor before God, and requested to find a dwelling place for the God of Jacob; ⁴⁷ and Solomon built Him a house. ⁴⁸ But the Most High does not dwell in sanctuaries made with hands, according as the prophet says: ⁴⁹ Heaven [is] My throne, || And the earth My footstool, || What house will you build to Me? says the Lord; Or what [is] the place of My rest? ⁵⁰ Has My hand not made all these things? ⁵¹ You stiff-necked and uncircumcised in heart and in ears! You always resist the Holy Spirit; as your fathers—also you; ⁵² which of the prophets did your fathers not persecute? and they killed those who declared before about the coming of the Righteous One, of whom you have now become betrayers and murderers, ⁵³ who received the Law by arrangement of messengers, and did not keep [it]." ⁵⁴ And hearing these things, they were cut to the hearts, and gnashed the teeth at him; ⁵⁵ and being full of the Holy Spirit, having looked steadfastly to the sky, he saw the glory of God, and Jesus standing on the right hand of God, ⁵⁶ and he said, "Behold, I see the heavens having been opened, and the Son of Man standing on the right hand of God." ⁵⁷ And they, having cried out with a loud voice, stopped their ears, and rushed with one accord on him, ⁵⁸ and having cast him forth outside of the city, they were stoning [him]—and the witnesses put down their garments at the feet of a young man called Saul— ⁵⁹ and they were stoning Stephen, [as he was] calling and saying, "Lord Jesus, receive my spirit"; ⁶⁰ and having bowed the knees, he cried with a loud voice, "Lord, may You not lay to them this sin"; and having said this, he fell asleep.

CHAPTER 8

¹ And Saul was assenting to his death, and there came in that day a great persecution on the Assembly in Jerusalem, all were also scattered abroad in the regions of Judea and Samaria, except the apostles; ² and devout men carried Stephen away, and made great lamentation over him; ³ and Saul was making havoc of the Assembly, entering into every house, and dragging away men and women, giving them up to prison; ⁴ they then indeed, having been scattered, went abroad proclaiming good news—the word. ⁵ And Philip having gone down to a city of Samaria, was preaching the Christ to them; ⁶ the multitudes were also giving heed to the things spoken by Philip, with one accord, in their hearing and seeing the signs that he was doing, ⁷ for unclean spirits came forth from many who were possessed, crying with a loud voice, and many who have been paralytic and lame were healed, ⁸ and there was

great joy in that city. ⁹ And a certain man, by name Simon, was previously in the city using magic, and amazing the nation of Samaria, saying himself to be a certain great one, ¹⁰ to whom they were all giving heed, from small to great, saying, "This one is the great power of God"; ¹¹ and they were giving heed to him, because of his having amazed them for a long time with deeds of magic. ¹² And when they believed Philip, proclaiming good news, the things concerning the Kingdom of God and the Name of Jesus Christ, they were immersed—both men and women; ¹³ and Simon himself also believed, and having been immersed, he was continuing with Philip, beholding also signs and mighty acts being done, he was amazed. ¹⁴ And the apostles in Jerusalem having heard that Samaria has received the word of God, sent Peter and John to them, ¹⁵ who having come down prayed concerning them, that they may receive the Holy Spirit— ¹⁶ for as yet He was fallen on none of them, and only they have been immersed—into the Name of the Lord Jesus; ¹⁷ then they were laying hands on them, and they received the Holy Spirit. ¹⁸ And Simon, having beheld that through the laying on of the hands of the apostles the Holy Spirit is given, brought money before them, ¹⁹ saying, "Give also to me this authority, that on whomsoever I may lay the hands, he may receive the Holy Spirit." ²⁰ And Peter said to him, "Your silver with you—may it be to destruction! Because you thought to possess the gift of God through money; ²¹ you have neither part nor lot in this thing, for your heart is not right before God; ²² convert, therefore, from this your wickedness, and implore God, if then the purpose of your heart may be forgiven you, ²³ for in the gall of bitterness, and bond of unrighteousness, I perceive you being." ²⁴ And Simon answering, said, "Implore for me to the Lord, that nothing may come on me of the things you have spoken." ²⁵ They indeed, therefore, having testified fully, and spoken the word of the Lord, turned back to Jerusalem; they also proclaimed good news in many villages of the Samaritans. ²⁶ And a messenger of the Lord spoke to Philip, saying, "Arise, and go on toward the south, on the way that is going down from Jerusalem to Gaza." (This is desolate.) ²⁷ And having arisen, he went on, and behold, a man of Ethiopia, a eunuch, a man of rank, of Candace the queen of the Ethiopians, who was over all her treasure, who had come to Jerusalem to worship; ²⁸ he was also returning, and is sitting on his chariot, and he was reading the prophet Isaiah. ²⁹ And the Spirit said to Philip, "Go near, and be joined to this chariot"; ³⁰ and Philip having run near, heard him reading the prophet Isaiah and said, "Do you then know what you read?" ³¹ and he said, "Why, how am I able, if someone may not guide me?" He called Philip also, having come up, to sit with him. ³² And the passage of the Writing that he was reading was this: "He was led as a sheep to slaughter, || And as a lamb before his shearer is silent, || So He does not open His mouth; ³³ In His humiliation His judgment was taken away, || And His generation—who will declare? because His life is taken from the earth." ³⁴ And the eunuch answering Philip said, "I beg you, about whom does the prophet say this? about himself, or about some other one?" ³⁵ and Philip having opened his mouth, and having begun from this Writing, proclaimed good news to him—Jesus. ³⁶ And as they were going on the way, they came on some water, and the eunuch said, "Behold, water; what hinders me to be immersed?" ³⁷ [[And Philip said, "If you believe out of all the heart, it is lawful"; and he answering said, "I believe Jesus Christ to be the Son of God";]] ³⁸ and he commanded the chariot to stand still, and they both went down to the water, both Philip and the eunuch, and he immersed him; ³⁹ and when they came up out of the water, the Spirit of the Lord snatched up Philip, and the eunuch saw him no more, for he was going on his way rejoicing; ⁴⁰ and Philip was found at Azotus, and passing through, he was proclaiming good news to all the cities, until his coming to Caesarea.

CHAPTER 9

¹ And Saul, yet breathing of threatening and slaughter to the disciples of the Lord, having gone to the chief priest, ² asked from him letters to Damascus, to the synagogues, that if he may find any being of The Way, both men and women, he may bring them bound to Jerusalem. ³ And in the going, he came near to Damascus, and suddenly there shone around him a light from Heaven, ⁴ and having fallen on the earth, he heard a voice saying to him, "Saul, Saul, why do you persecute Me?" ⁵ And he said, "Who are You, Lord?" And the Lord said, "I am Jesus whom you persecute; [[hard for you to kick at the

goads"; **6** trembling also, and astonished, he said, "Lord, what do You wish me to do?" And the Lord [said] to him,**]]** "Arise, and enter into the city, and it will be told [to] you what you must do." **7** And the men who are journeying with him stood speechless, indeed hearing the voice but seeing no one, **8** and Saul arose from the earth, and his eyes having been opened, he beheld no one, and leading him by the hand they brought him to Damascus, **9** and he was three days without seeing, and he neither ate nor drank. **10** And there was a certain disciple in Damascus, by name Ananias, and the Lord said to him in a vision, "Ananias"; and he said, "Behold me, Lord"; **11** and the Lord [says] to him, "Having risen, go on to the street that is called Straight, and seek in the house of Judas, [one] by name Saul of Tarsus, for behold, he prays, **12** and he saw in a vision a man, by name Ananias, coming in, and putting a hand on him, that he may see again." **13** And Ananias answered, "Lord, I have heard from many about this man, how many evils he did to Your holy ones in Jerusalem, **14** and here he has authority from the chief priests, to bind all those calling on Your Name." **15** And the Lord said to him, "Go, because this one is a chosen vessel to Me, to carry My Name before nations and kings—also the sons of Israel; **16** for I will show him how many things he must suffer for My Name." **17** And Ananias went away, and entered into the house, and having put on him [his] hands, said, "Saul, brother, the Lord has sent me—Jesus who appeared to you in the way in which you were coming—that you may see again, and may be filled with the Holy Spirit." **18** And immediately there fell from his eyes as it were scales, he also saw again instantly, and having risen, was immersed, **19** and having received nourishment, was strengthened, and Saul was with the disciples in Damascus certain days, **20** and immediately he was preaching the Christ in the synagogues, that He is the Son of God. **21** And all those hearing were amazed and said, "Is this not he who laid waste in Jerusalem those calling on this Name, and here to this intent had come, that he might bring them bound to the chief priests?" **22** And Saul was still more strengthened, and he was confounding the Jews dwelling in Damascus, proving that this is the Christ. **23** And when many days were fulfilled, the Jews took counsel together to kill him, **24** and their counsel against [him] was known to Saul; they were also watching the gates both day and night, that they may kill him, **25** and the disciples having taken him, by night let him down by the wall, letting down in a basket. **26** And Saul, having come to Jerusalem, tried to join himself to the disciples, and they were all afraid of him, not believing that he is a disciple, **27** and Barnabas having taken him, brought [him] to the apostles, and declared to them how he saw the Lord in the way, and that He spoke to him, and how in Damascus he was speaking boldly in the Name of Jesus. **28** And he was with them, coming in and going out in Jerusalem, **29** and speaking boldly in the Name of the Lord Jesus; he was both speaking and disputing with the Hellenists, and they were taking in hand to kill him, **30** and the brothers having known, brought him down to Caesarea, and sent him forth to Tarsus. **31** Then, indeed, the assemblies throughout all Judea, and Galilee, and Samaria, had peace, being built up, and going on in the fear of the Lord, and in the comfort of the Holy Spirit, they were multiplied. **32** And it came to pass that Peter, passing throughout all [quarters], also came down to the holy ones who were dwelling at Lydda, **33** and he found there a certain man, Aeneas by name—for eight years laid on a pallet—who was paralytic, **34** and Peter said to him, "Aeneas, Jesus the Christ heals you; arise and spread for yourself"; and immediately he rose, **35** and all those dwelling at Lydda and Saron saw him, and turned to the Lord. **36** And in Joppa there was a certain female disciple, by name Tabitha (which interpreted, is called Dorcas); this woman was full of good works and kind acts that she was doing; **37** and it came to pass in those days she, having ailed, died, and having bathed her, they laid her in an upper chamber, **38** and Lydda being near to Joppa, the disciples having heard that Peter is in that [place], sent two men to him, calling on him not to delay to come through to them. **39** And Peter having risen, went with them, whom having come, they brought into the upper chamber, and all the widows stood by him weeping, and showing coats and garments, as many as Dorcas was making while she was with them. **40** And Peter having put them all forth outside, having bowed the knees, prayed, and having turned to the body, said, "Tabitha, arise"; and she opened her eyes, and having seen Peter, she sat up, **41** and having given her [his] hand, he lifted her up, and having called the holy ones and the widows, he presented her alive, **42** and it became known throughout all Joppa, and many believed on the Lord; **43** and it came to pass, that he remained many days in Joppa, with a certain one, Simon a tanner.

CHAPTER 10

1 And there was a certain man in Caesarea, by name Cornelius, a centurion from a cohort that is called Italian, **2** pious, and fearing God with all his house, also doing many kind acts to the people, and always imploring God; **3** he saw in a vision openly, as it were the ninth hour of the day, a messenger of God coming in to him, and saying to him, "Cornelius"; **4** and he having looked earnestly on him, and becoming afraid, said, "What is it, Lord?" And he said to him, "Your prayers and your kind acts came up for a memorial before God, **5** and now send men to Joppa, and send for a certain one Simon, who is surnamed Peter; **6** this one lodges with a certain Simon a tanner, whose house is by the sea; this one will speak to you what you must do." **7** And when the messenger who is speaking to Cornelius went away, having called two of his servants, and a pious soldier of those waiting on him continually, **8** and having expounded all things to them, he sent them to Joppa. **9** And on the next day, as these are proceeding on the way, and are drawing near to the city, Peter went up on the housetop to pray, about the sixth hour, **10** and he became very hungry, and wished to eat; and they making ready, there fell on him a trance, **11** and he beholds Heaven opened, and a certain vessel descending to him, as a great sheet, bound at the four corners, and let down on the earth, **12** in which were all the four-footed beasts of the earth, and the wild beasts, and the creeping things, and the birds of the sky, **13** and there came a voice to him: "Having risen, Peter, slay and eat." **14** And Peter said, "Not so, Lord; because at no time did I eat anything common or unclean"; **15** and [there is] a voice again a second time to him: "What God cleansed, you do not declare common"; **16** and this was done three times, and again was the vessel received up to Heaven. **17** And as Peter was perplexed in himself what the vision that he saw might be, then, behold, the men who have been sent from Cornelius, having made inquiry for the house of Simon, stood at the gate, **18** and having called, they were asking if Simon, who is surnamed Peter, lodges here. **19** And Peter thinking about the vision, the Spirit said to him, "Behold, three men seek you; **20** but having risen, go down and go on with them, doubting nothing, because I have sent them"; **21** and Peter having come down to the men who have been sent from Cornelius to him, said, "Behold, I am he whom you seek, what [is] the cause for which you are present?" **22** And they said, "Cornelius, a centurion, a man righteous and fearing God, well testified to, also, by all the nation of the Jews, was divinely warned by a holy messenger to send for you, to his house, and to hear sayings from you." **23** Having called them in, therefore, he lodged them, and on the next day Peter went forth with them, and certain of the brothers from Joppa went with him, **24** and on the next day they entered into Caesarea; and Cornelius was waiting for them, having called together his relatives and near friends, **25** and as it came that Peter entered in, Cornelius having met him, having fallen at [his] feet, worshiped [him]; **26** and Peter raised him, saying, "Stand up; I am also a man myself"; **27** and talking with him he went in, and finds many having come together. **28** And he said to them, "You know how it is unlawful for a man, a Jew, to keep company with, or to come to, one of another race, but God showed to me to call no man common or unclean; **29** therefore also without contradicting I came, having been sent for; I ask, therefore, for what matter you sent for me?" **30** And Cornelius said, "Four days ago until this hour, I was fasting, and [at] the ninth hour praying in my house, and behold, a man stood before me in radiant clothing, **31** and he said, Cornelius, your prayer was heard, and your kind acts were remembered before God; **32** send, therefore, to Joppa, and call for Simon, who is surnamed Peter; this one lodges in the house of Simon a tanner, by the sea, who having come, will speak to you; **33** at once, therefore, I sent to you; you also did well, having come; now, therefore, we are all present before God to hear all things that have been commanded you by God." **34** And Peter having opened his mouth, said, "Of a truth, I perceive that God is not favoring by appearance, **35** but in every nation he who is fearing Him, and is working righteousness, is acceptable to Him; **36** the word that He sent to the sons of Israel, proclaiming good news—peace through Jesus Christ (this One is Lord of all), **37** you have known the word that came throughout all Judea, having begun from Galilee, after the immersion that John preached; **38** Jesus who [is] from Nazareth—how God anointed Him with the Holy Spirit and power; who went through, doing good, and healing all those oppressed by the Devil, because God was with Him; **39** and we are witnesses of all things that He did, both in the country of the Jews, and in Jerusalem—whom they slew, having hanged [Him] on a tree. **40** This One God raised up [on] the third day, and gave Him to become visible, **41** not to all the people, but to witnesses, to those having been chosen before by God—to us who ate with [Him], and drank with Him, after His rising out of the dead; **42** and He commanded us to preach to the people, and to fully testify that it is He who has been ordained judge of living and dead by God— **43** to this One do all the Prophets testify, that through His Name everyone that is believing in Him receives forgiveness of sins." **44** While Peter is yet speaking these sayings, the Holy Spirit fell on all those hearing the word, **45** and those of circumcision [who were] believing were astonished—as many as came with Peter—because the gift of the Holy Spirit has also been poured out on the nations, **46** for they were hearing them speaking with tongues and magnifying God. **47** Then Peter answered, "Is anyone able to forbid the water, that these may not be immersed, who received the Holy Spirit—even as us also?" **48** he commanded them to also be immersed in the Name of the Lord; then they implored him to remain certain days.

CHAPTER 11

1 And the apostles and the brothers who are in Judea heard that the nations also received the word of God, **2** and when Peter came up to Jerusalem, those of circumcision were contending with him, **3** saying, "You went in to uncircumcised men, and ate with them!" **4** And Peter having begun, set [it] forth to them in order, saying, **5** "I was in the city of Joppa praying, and I saw in a trance a vision, a certain vessel coming down, as a great sheet by four corners being let down out of Heaven, and it came to me; **6** at which having looked steadfastly, I was considering, and I saw the four-footed beasts of the earth, and the wild beasts, and the creeping things, and the birds of the sky; **7** and I heard a voice saying to me, Having risen, Peter, slay and eat; **8** and I said, Not so, Lord, because anything common or unclean has at no time entered into my mouth; **9** and a voice answered me a second time out of Heaven, What God cleansed, you do not declare common. **10** And this happened three times, and again was all drawn up to Heaven, **11** and behold, immediately, three men stood at the house in which I was, having been sent from Caesarea to me, **12** and the Spirit said to me to go with them, doubting nothing, and these six brothers also went with me, and we entered into the house of the man, **13** he also declared to us how he saw the messenger standing in his house, and saying to him, Send men to Joppa, and call for Simon, who is surnamed Peter, **14** who will speak sayings by which you will be saved, you and all your house. **15** And in my beginning to speak, the Holy Spirit fell on them, even as also on us in the beginning, **16** and I remembered the saying of the Lord, how He said, John indeed immersed in water, but you will be immersed in the Holy Spirit; **17** if then God gave to them the equal gift as also to us, having believed on the Lord Jesus Christ, I—how was I able to withstand God?" **18** And they, having heard these things, were silent, and were glorifying God, saying, "Then, indeed, God also gave conversion to life to the nations." **19** Those, indeed, therefore, having been scattered abroad, from the tribulation that came after Stephen, went through to Phoenicia, and Cyprus, and Antioch, speaking the word to none except to Jews only; **20** and there were certain of them, men of Cyprus and Cyrene, who having entered into Antioch, were speaking to the Hellenists, proclaiming good news—the Lord Jesus, **21** and the hand of the Lord was with them, a great number also, having believed, turned to the Lord. **22** And the account was heard in the ears of the assembly that [is] in Jerusalem concerning them, and they sent forth Barnabas to go through to Antioch, **23** who, having come, and having seen the grace of God, was glad, and was exhorting all with purpose of heart to cleave to the Lord, **24** because he was a good man, and full of the Holy Spirit, and of faith, and a great multitude was added to the Lord. **25** And Barnabas went forth to Tarsus, to seek for Saul, **26** and having found him, he brought him to Antioch, and it came to pass that they assembled together a whole year in the assembly, and taught a great multitude, and the disciples were first called Christians in Antioch. **27** And in those days there came from Jerusalem prophets to Antioch, **28** and one of them, by name Agabus, having stood up, signified through the Spirit a great scarcity is about to be throughout all the world—which also came to pass in the time of Claudius Caesar— **29** and the disciples, according as anyone was prospering, determined each of them to send for ministry to the brothers dwelling in Judea, **30** which also they did, having sent to the elders by the hand of Barnabas and Saul.

CHAPTER 12

1 And about that time, Herod the king put forth his hands to do evil to certain of those of the Assembly, **2** and he killed James, the brother of John, with the sword, **3** and having seen that it is pleasing to the Jews, he added to lay hold of Peter also—and they were the days of the Unleavened [Bread]— **4** whom also having seized, he put in prison, having delivered [him] to four squads of four soldiers to guard him, intending to bring him forth to the people after the Passover. **5** Peter, therefore, indeed, was kept in the prison, and fervent prayer was being made by the Assembly to God for him, **6** and when Herod was about to bring him forth, the same night was Peter sleeping between two soldiers, having been bound with two chains, guards were also keeping the prison before the door, **7** and behold, a messenger of the Lord stood by, and a light shone in the buildings, and having struck Peter on the side, he raised him up, saying, "Rise in haste," and his chains fell from off [his] hands. **8** The messenger also said to him, "Gird yourself, and bind on your sandals"; and he did so; and he says to him, "Cast your garment around and follow me"; **9** and having gone forth, he was following him, and he did not know that it is true that which is done through the messenger, and was thinking he saw a vision, **10** and having passed through a first ward, and a second, they came to the iron gate that is leading into the city, which opened to them of its own accord, and having gone forth, they went on through one street, and immediately the messenger departed from him. **11** And Peter having come to himself, said, "Now I have known of a truth that the Lord sent forth His messenger, and delivered me out of the hand of Herod, and all the expectation of the people of the Jews"; **12** also, having considered, he came to the house of Mary, the mother of John, who is surnamed Mark, where there were many thronged together and praying. **13** And Peter having knocked at the door of the porch, there came a girl to listen, by name Rhoda, **14** and having known the voice of Peter, from the joy she did not open the porch, but having run in, told of the standing of Peter before the porch, **15** and they said to her, "You are mad"; and she was confidently affirming [it] to be so, and they said, "It is his messenger"; **16** and Peter was continuing knocking, and having opened, they saw him, and were astonished, **17** and having beckoned to them with the hand to be silent, he declared to them how the Lord brought him out of the prison, and he said, "Declare these things to James and to the brothers"; and having gone forth, he went on to another place. **18** And day having come, there was not a little stir among the soldiers what then was become of Peter, **19** and Herod having sought for him, and having not found, having examined the guards, commanded [them] to be led away to punishment, and having gone down from Judea to Caesarea, he was abiding [there]. **20** And Herod was highly displeased with the Tyrians and Sidonians, and with one accord they came to him, and having made a friend of Blastus, who [is] over the bed-chambers of the king, they were asking peace, because of their country being nourished from the king's; **21** and on a set day, Herod having clothed himself in kingly clothing, and having sat down on the judgment seat, was making an oration to them, **22** and the populace were shouting, "The voice of a god, and not of a man!" **23** And immediately a messenger of the Lord struck him in return for that he did not give the glory to God, and having been eaten of worms, he expired. **24** And the word of God grew and multiplied, **25** and Barnabas and Saul turned back out of Jerusalem, having fulfilled the ministry, having also taken John with [them], who was surnamed Mark.

CHAPTER 13

1 And there were certain in Antioch, in the assembly there, prophets and teachers: both Barnabas, and Simeon who is called Niger, and Lucius the Cyrenian, Manaen also—Herod the tetrarch's foster-brother—and Saul; **2** and in their ministering to the Lord and fasting, the Holy Spirit said, "Separate to Me both Barnabas and Saul to the work to which I have called them," **3** then having fasted, and having prayed, and having laid the hands on them, they sent [them] away. **4** These, indeed, then, having been sent forth by the Holy Spirit, went down to Seleucia, and from there they sailed to Cyprus, **5** and having come to Salamis, they declared the word of God in the synagogues of the Jews, and they also had John [as] a servant; **6** and having gone through the island to Paphos, they found a certain magus, a false prophet, a Jew, whose name [is] Bar-Jesus; **7** who was with the proconsul Sergius Paulus, an intelligent man; this one having called for Barnabas and Saul, desired to hear the word of God, **8** and there withstood them Elymas the magus—for so is his name interpreted—seeking to pervert the proconsul from the faith. **9** And Saul—who also [is] Paul—having been filled with the Holy Spirit, and having looked steadfastly on him, **10** said, "O full of all guile, and all recklessness, son of a devil, enemy of all righteousness, will you not cease perverting the right ways of the Lord? **11** and now, behold, a hand of the Lord [is] on you, and you will be blind, not seeing the sun for a season"; and instantly there fell on him a mist and darkness, and he, going around, was seeking some to lead [him] by the hand; **12** then the proconsul having seen what has come to pass, believed, being astonished at the teaching of the Lord. **13** And those around Paul having set sail from Paphos, came to Perga of Pamphylia, and John having departed from them, turned back to Jerusalem, **14** and they having gone through from Perga, came to Antioch of Pisidia, and having gone into the synagogue on the day of the Sabbaths, they sat down, **15** and after the reading of the Law and of the Prophets, the chief men of the synagogue sent to them, saying, "Men, brothers, if there be a word in you of exhortation to the people—say on." **16** And Paul having risen, and having beckoned with the hand, said, "Men, Israelites, and those fearing God, listen: **17** the God of this people Israel chose our fathers, and He exalted the people in their sojourning in the land of Egypt, and He brought them out of it with a high arm; **18** and about a period of forty years He endured their conduct in the wilderness, **19** and having destroyed seven nations in the land of Canaan, He divided their land to them by lot. **20** And after these things, about four hundred and fifty years, He gave judges—until Samuel the prophet; **21** and thereafter they asked for a king, and God gave to them Saul, son of Kish, a man of the tribe of Benjamin, for forty years; **22** and having removed him, He raised up to them David for king, to whom also having testified, He said, I found David, the [son] of Jesse, a man according to My heart, who will do all My will. **23** Of this one's seed, God, according to promise, raised to Israel a Savior—Jesus, **24** John having first preached, before His coming, an immersion of conversion to all the people of Israel; **25** and as John was fulfilling the course, he said, Whom do you suppose I am? I am not [He], but behold, He comes after me, of whom I am not worthy to loose the sandal of [His] feet. **26** Men, brothers, sons of the race of Abraham, and those among you fearing God, to you was the word of this salvation sent, **27** for those dwelling in Jerusalem, and their chiefs, having not known this One, also the voices of the Prophets, which are being read every Sabbath—having judged [Him]—fulfilled, **28** and having found no cause of death, they asked of Pilate that He should be slain, **29** and when they fulfilled all the things written about Him, having taken [Him] down from the tree, they laid Him in a tomb, **30** and God raised Him out of the dead, **31** and He was seen for many days of those who came up with Him from Galilee to Jerusalem, who are His witnesses to the people. **32** And we proclaim good news to you—that the promise made to the fathers, **33** God has completed in full to us their children, having raised up Jesus, as also in the second Psalm it has been written: You are My Son—I have begotten You today. **34** And that He raised Him up out of the dead, to no longer return to corruption, He has said this: I will give to You the holy [blessings] of David [that are] faithful; **35** for what reason He also says in another [place]: You will not give Your Holy One to see corruption; **36** for David, indeed, having served his own generation by the will of God, fell asleep, and was added to his fathers, and saw corruption, **37** but He whom God raised up, did not see corruption. **38** Let it therefore be known to you, men, brothers, that the forgiveness of sins is declared to you through this One, **39** and from all things in the Law of Moses from which you were not able to be declared righteous, everyone who is believing in this One is declared righteous; **40** see, therefore, it may not come on you that has been spoken

in the Prophets: **41** See, you despisers, and wonder, and perish, because I work a work in your days, a work in which you may not believe, though anyone may declare [it] to you." **42** And having gone forth out of the synagogue of the Jews, the nations were calling on [them] that on the next Sabbath these sayings may be spoken to them, **43** and the synagogue having been dismissed, many of the Jews and of the devout proselytes followed Paul and Barnabas, who, speaking to them, were persuading them to remain in the grace of God. **44** And on the coming Sabbath, almost all the city was gathered together to hear the word of God, **45** and the Jews having seen the multitudes, were filled with zeal, and contradicted the things spoken by Paul—contradicting and slandering. **46** And speaking boldly, Paul and Barnabas said, "It was necessary that the word of God be first spoken to you, and seeing you thrust it away, and do not judge yourselves worthy of the continuous life, behold, we turn to the nations; **47** for so the Lord has commanded us: I have set you for a light of nations—for your being for salvation to the end of the earth." **48** And the nations hearing were glad, and were glorifying the word of the Lord, and believed—as many as were appointed to continuous life; **49** and the word of the Lord was spread abroad through all the region. **50** And the Jews stirred up the devout and honorable women, and the first men of the city, and raised persecution against Paul and Barnabas, and put them out from their borders; **51** and having shaken off the dust of their feet against them, they came to Iconium, **52** and the disciples were filled with joy and the Holy Spirit.

CHAPTER 14

1 And it came to pass in Iconium, that they entered together into the synagogue of the Jews, and spoke, so that there believed a great multitude of both Jews and Greeks; **2** and the unbelieving Jews stirred up and made the souls of the nation's evil against the brothers; **3** [for a] long time, indeed, therefore, they abided speaking boldly in the Lord, who is testifying to the word of His grace, and granting signs and wonders to come to pass through their hands. **4** And the multitude of the city was divided, and some were with the Jews, and some with the apostles, **5** and when there was a purpose both of the nations and of the Jews with their rulers to mistreat [them], and to stone them, **6** they having become aware, fled to the cities of Lycaonia, Lystra, and Derbe, and the surrounding region, **7** and there they were proclaiming good news. **8** And a certain man in Lystra, impotent in the feet, was sitting, being lame from the womb of his mother—who never had walked; **9** this one was hearing Paul speaking, who, having steadfastly beheld him, and having seen that he has faith to be saved, **10** said with a loud voice, "Stand up on your feet upright"; and he was springing and walking, **11** and the multitudes having seen what Paul did, lifted up their voice in the speech of Lycaonia, saying, "The gods, having become like men, came down to us"; **12** they were also calling Barnabas Zeus, and Paul Hermes, since he was the leader in speaking. **13** And the priest of the Zeus that is before their city, having brought oxen and garlands to the porches, wished to sacrifice with the multitudes, **14** and having heard, the apostles Barnabas and Paul, having torn their garments, sprung into the multitude, crying **15** and saying, "Men, why do you do these things? and we are similar-feeling men with you, proclaiming good news to you, to turn to the living God from these vanities, who made the heaven, and the earth, and the sea, and all the things in them; **16** who in the past generations permitted all the nations to go on in their ways, **17** though, indeed, He did not leave Himself without witness, doing good—giving rains to us from Heaven, and fruitful seasons, filling our hearts with food and gladness"; **18** and saying these things, they scarcely restrained the multitudes from sacrificing to them. **19** And there came there, from Antioch and Iconium, Jews, and they having persuaded the multitudes, and having stoned Paul, drew him outside of the city, having supposed him to be dead; **20** and the disciples having surrounded him, having risen he entered into the city, and on the next day he went forth with Barnabas to Derbe. **21** Having also proclaimed good news to that city, and having discipled many, they turned back to Lystra, and Iconium, and Antioch, **22** confirming the souls of the disciples, exhorting them to remain in the faith, and that it is required of us to enter into the Kingdom of God through many tribulations, **23** and having appointed to them elders in every assembly by vote, having prayed with fastings, they commended them to the Lord in whom they had believed. **24** And having passed through Pisidia, they came to Pamphylia, **25** and having spoken the word in Perga, they went down to Attalia, **26** and [from] there sailed to Antioch, from where they had been given by the grace of God for the work that they fulfilled; **27** and having come and gathered the assembly together, they declared as many things as God did with them, and that He opened a door of faith to the nations; **28** and they abided there with the disciples [for] not a short time.

CHAPTER 15

1 And certain having come down from Judea, were teaching the brothers, "If you are not circumcised after the custom of Moses, you are not able to be saved"; **2** there having been, therefore, not a little dissension and debate to Paul and Barnabas with them, they arranged for Paul and Barnabas, and certain others of them, to go up to the apostles and elders at Jerusalem about this question; **3** they indeed, then, having been sent forward by the assembly, were passing through Phoenicia and Samaria, declaring the conversion of the nations, and they were causing great joy to all the brothers. **4** And having come to Jerusalem, they were received by the assembly, and the apostles, and the elders; they also declared as many things as God did with them; **5** and there rose up certain of those of the sect of the Pharisees who believed, saying, "It is required to circumcise them, to command them also to keep the Law of Moses." **6** And there were gathered together the apostles and the elders, to see about this matter, **7** and there having been much disputing, Peter having risen up said to them, "Men, brothers, you know that from former days God made choice among us, through my mouth, for the nations to hear the word of the good news, and to believe; **8** and the heart-knowing God bore them testimony, having given to them the Holy Spirit, even as also to us, **9** and also put no difference between us and them, having purified their hearts by faith; **10** now, therefore, why do you tempt God, to put a yoke on the neck of the disciples, which neither our fathers nor we were able to bear? **11** but through the grace of the Lord Jesus Christ, we believe to be saved, even as also they." **12** And all the multitude kept silence and were listening to Barnabas and Paul expounding as many signs and wonders as God did among the nations through them; **13** and after they were silent, James answered, saying, "Men, brothers, listen to me: **14** Simeon expounded how at first God looked on [us] to take a people out of [the] nations for His Name, **15** and to this the words of the Prophets agree, as it has been written: **16** After these things I will return, || And I will rebuild the dwelling place of David that has fallen down, || And I will rebuild its ruins, || And will set it upright— **17** That the remnant of men may seek after the Lord, || And all the nations on whom My Name has been called, || Says the Lord, who is doing all these things. **18** Known from the ages to God are all His works. **19** For this reason I judge: not to trouble those who turn back to God from the nations, **20** but to write to them to abstain from the defilements of the idols, and the whoredom, and the strangled thing, and the blood; **21** for Moses has those preaching him from former generations in every city—being read every Sabbath in the synagogues." **22** Then it seemed good to the apostles and the elders, with the whole assembly, to send to Antioch with Paul and Barnabas chosen men out of themselves—Judas surnamed Barsabas, and Silas, leading men among the brothers— **23** having written through their hand thus: "The apostles, and the elders, and the brothers, to those in Antioch, and Syria, and Cilicia, brothers, who [are] of the nations, greeting; **24** seeing we have heard that some having gone forth from us troubled you with words, subverting your souls, saying to be circumcised and to keep the Law, to whom we gave no charge, **25** it seemed good to us, having come together with one accord, to send to you chosen men, with our beloved Barnabas and Paul— **26** men who have given up their lives for the Name of our Lord Jesus Christ— **27** we have sent, therefore, Judas and Silas, and they are telling the same things by word. **28** For it seemed good to the Holy Spirit, and to us, to lay no more burden on you, except these necessary things: **29** to abstain from things offered to idols, and blood, and a strangled thing, and whoredom; keeping yourselves from which, you will do well; be strong!" **30** They then, indeed, having been let go, went to Antioch, and having brought the multitude together, delivered the letter, **31** and having read [it] they rejoiced for the consolation; **32** Judas also and Silas, also being prophets themselves, through much discourse exhorted the brothers, and confirmed, **33** and having passed some time, they were let go with peace from the brothers to the apostles; **34** [[and it seemed good to Silas to remain there still.]] **35** And Paul and Barnabas continued in Antioch, teaching and proclaiming good news—with many others also—the word of the Lord; **36** and after certain days, Paul said to Barnabas, "Having turned back again, we may look after our brothers, in every city in which we have preached the word of the Lord—how they are." **37** And Barnabas resolved to take with [them] John called Mark, **38** and Paul was not thinking it good to take him with them who withdrew from them from Pamphylia, and did not go with them to the work; **39** there came, therefore, a sharp contention, so that they were parted from one another, and Barnabas having taken Mark, sailed to Cyprus, **40** and Paul having chosen Silas, went forth, having been given up to the grace of God by the brothers; **41** and he went through Syria and Cilicia, confirming the assemblies.

CHAPTER 16

1 And he came to Derbe and Lystra, and behold, a certain disciple was there, by name Timotheus, son of a certain woman, a believing Jewess, but of a father, a Greek, **2** who was well testified to by the brothers in Lystra and Iconium; **3** Paul wished this one to go forth with him, and having taken [him], he circumcised him, because of the Jews who are in those places, for they all knew his father—that he was a Greek. **4** And as they were going on through the cities, they were delivering to them the decrees to keep, that have been judged by the apostles and the elders who [are] in Jerusalem, **5** then, indeed, were the assemblies established in the faith, and were abounding in number every day; **6** and having gone through Phrygia and the region of Galatia, having been forbidden by the Holy Spirit to speak the word in Asia, **7** having gone toward Mysia, they were trying to go on toward Bithynia, and the Spirit did not permit them, **8** and having passed by Mysia, they came down to Troas. **9** And a vision through the night appeared to Paul—a certain man of Macedonia was standing, calling on him, and saying, "Having passed through to Macedonia, help us." **10** And when he saw the vision, immediately we endeavored to go forth to Macedonia, assuredly gathering that the Lord has called us to preach good news to them, **11** having set sail, therefore, from Troas, we came with a straight course to Samothracia, on the next day also to Neapolis, **12** there also to Philippi, which is a principal city of the part of Macedonia—a colony. And we were abiding in this city some days; **13** on the day of the Sabbaths we also went forth outside of the city, by a river, where there used to be prayer, and having sat down, we were speaking to the women who came together, **14** and a certain woman, by name Lydia, a seller of purple, of the city of Thyatira, worshiping God, was hearing, whose heart the Lord opened to attend to the things spoken by Paul; **15** and when she was immersed, and her household, she called on us, saying, "If you have judged me to be faithful to the Lord, having entered into my house, remain"; and she constrained us. **16** And it came to pass in our going on to prayer, a certain maid, having a spirit of Python, met us, who brought much employment to her masters by soothsaying; **17** she having followed Paul and us, was crying, saying, "These men are servants of the Most High God, who declare to us [the] way of salvation!" **18** And this she was doing for many days, but Paul having been grieved, and having turned, said to the spirit, "I command you, in the Name of Jesus Christ, to come forth from her"; and it came forth the same hour. **19** And her masters having seen that the hope of their employment was gone, having caught Paul and Silas, drew [them] into the marketplace, to the rulers, **20** and having brought them to the magistrates, they said, "These men being Jews exceedingly trouble our city; **21** and they proclaim customs that are not lawful for us to receive nor to do, being Romans." **22** And the multitude rose up together against them, and the magistrates having torn their garments from them, were commanding to beat [them] with rods, **23** having also laid on them many blows, they cast them into prison, having given charge to the jailor to keep them safely, **24** who having received such a charge, put them into the inner prison, and fastened their feet in the stocks. **25** And at midnight Paul and Silas praying, were singing hymns to God, and the prisoners were hearing them, **26** and suddenly a great earthquake came, so that the foundations of the prison were shaken, also all the doors were immediately opened, and of all—the bands were loosed; **27** and the jailor having come out of sleep, and having seen the doors of the prison open, having drawn a sword, was about to kill himself, supposing the prisoners to have fled, **28** and Paul cried out with a loud voice, saying, "You may not do yourself any harm, for we are all here!" **29** And having asked for a light, he sprang in, and he fell down before Paul and Silas trembling, **30** and having brought them forth, said, "Lords, what must I do that I may be saved?" **31** and they said, "Believe on the Lord Jesus Christ, and you will be saved—you and your household." **32** And they spoke to him the word of the Lord, and to all those in his household; **33** and having taken them, in that hour of the night, he bathed [them] from the blows, and immediately he and all of his were immersed, **34** having also brought them into his house, he set food before [them], and was glad with all the household, he having believed in God. **35** And day having come, the magistrates sent the rod-bearers, saying, "Let those men go"; **36** and the jailor told these words to Paul, "The magistrates have sent, that you may be let go; now, therefore, having gone forth go on in peace"; **37** and Paul said to them, "Having beaten us publicly uncondemned—men, being Romans—they cast [us] to prison, and now privately they cast us forth! Why no! But having come themselves, let them bring us forth." **38** And the rod-bearers told these sayings to the magistrates, and they were afraid, having heard that they are Romans, **39** and having come, they implored them, and having brought [them] forth, they were asking [them] to go forth from the city; **40** and they, having gone forth out of the prison, entered into [the house of] Lydia, and having seen the brothers, they comforted them, and went forth.

CHAPTER 17

1 And having passed through Amphipolis, and Apollonia, they came to Thessalonica, where the synagogue of the Jews was, **2** and according to the custom of Paul, he went in to them, and for three Sabbaths he was reasoning with them from the Writings, **3** opening and alleging that it was necessary [for] the Christ to suffer, and to rise again out of the dead, and that "this is the Christ—Jesus whom I proclaim to you." **4** And certain of them believed, and attached themselves to Paul and to Silas, also a great multitude of the worshiping Greeks, also not a few of the principal women. **5** And the Jews, having been moved with envy, and having taken to themselves certain evil men of the agitators, and having made a crowd, were setting the city in an uproar; having also assailed the house of Jason, they were seeking them to bring [them] to the populace, **6** and having not found them, they drew Jason and certain brothers to the city rulers, calling aloud, "These, having put the world in commotion, are also present here, **7** whom Jason has received; and all these do contrary to the decrees of Caesar, saying another to be king—Jesus." **8** And they troubled the multitude and the city rulers, hearing these things, **9** and having taken security from Jason and the rest, they let them go. **10** And the brothers immediately, through the night, sent forth both Paul and Silas to Berea, who having come, went into the synagogue of the Jews; **11** and these were more noble than those in Thessalonica; they received the word with all readiness of mind, examining the Writings every day [to see] whether those things were so; **12** therefore, many of them, indeed, believed, and not a few of the honorable Greek women and men. **13** And when the Jews from Thessalonica knew that also in Berea was the word of God declared by Paul, they came there also, agitating the multitudes; **14** and then immediately the brothers sent forth Paul, to go on as it were to the sea, but both Silas and Timotheus were remaining there. **15** And those conducting Paul, brought him to Athens, and having received a command to Silas and Timotheus that with all speed they may come to him, they departed; **16** and Paul waiting for them in Athens, his spirit was stirred in him, beholding the city wholly given to idolatry, **17** therefore, indeed, he was reasoning in the synagogue with the Jews, and with the worshiping persons, and in the marketplace every day with those who met with him. **18** And certain of the Epicurean and of the Stoic philosophers, were meeting together to see him, and some were saying, "What would this seed picker wish to say?" And others, "He seems to be an announcer of strange demons"; because he proclaimed to them Jesus and the resurrection as good news, **19** having also taken him, they brought [him] to the Areopagus, saying, "Are we able to know what this new teaching [is] that is spoken by you, **20** for you bring certain strange things to our ears? we resolve, then, to know what these things would wish

to be"; **21** and all Athenians, and the strangers sojourning, for nothing else were at leisure but to say something, and to hear some newer thing. **22** And Paul, having stood in the midst of the Areopagus, said, "Men, Athenians, in all things I perceive you as over-religious; **23** for passing through and contemplating your objects of worship, I also found an altar on which had been inscribed: To God—unknown; whom, therefore—not knowing—you worship, this One I announce to you. **24** God, who made the world, and all things in it, this One, being Lord of Heaven and of earth, does not dwell in temples made with hands, **25** neither is He served by the hands of men—needing anything, He giving life to all, and breath, and all things; **26** He also made every nation of man of one blood, to dwell on all the face of the earth—having ordained times before appointed, and the bounds of their dwellings— **27** to seek the Lord, if perhaps they felt after Him and found, though, indeed, He is not far from each one of us, **28** for in Him we live, and move, and are; as certain of your poets have also said: For we are also His offspring. **29** Being, therefore, offspring of God, we ought not to think the Godhead to be like to gold, or silver, or stone, [an] engraving of art and imagination of man; **30** therefore indeed God, having overlooked the times of ignorance, now commands all men everywhere to convert, **31** because He set a day in which He is about to judge the world in righteousness, by a Man whom He ordained, having given assurance to all, having raised Him out of the dead." **32** And having heard of a resurrection of the dead, some, indeed, were mocking, but others said, "We will hear you again concerning this"; **33** and so Paul went forth from the midst of them, **34** and certain men having cleaved to him, believed, among whom [is] also Dionysius the Areopagite, and a woman, by name Damaris, and others with them.

CHAPTER 18

1 And after these things, Paul having departed out of Athens, came to Corinth, **2** and having found a certain Jew, by name Aquilas, of Pontus by birth, lately come from Italy, and his wife Priscilla—because of Claudius having directed all the Jews to depart out of Rome—he came to them, **3** and because of being of the same craft, he remained with them, and was working, for they were tentmakers as to craft; **4** and he was reasoning in the synagogue every Sabbath, persuading both Jews and Greeks. **5** And when both Silas and Timotheus came down from Macedonia, Paul was pressed in the Spirit, testifying fully to the Jews Jesus the Christ; **6** and on their resisting and slandering, having shaken [his] garments, he said to them, "Your blood [is] on your head—I am clean; from now on I will go on to the nations." **7** And having departed from there, he went to the house of a certain one, by name Justus, a worshiper of God, whose house was adjoining the synagogue, **8** and Crispus, the ruler of the synagogue believed in the Lord with all his house, and many of the Corinthians hearing were believing, and they were being immersed. **9** And the Lord said through a vision in the night to Paul, "Do not be afraid, but be speaking and you may not be silent; **10** because I am with you, and no one will set on you to do evil [to] you, because I have many people in this city"; **11** and he continued a year and six months, teaching the word of God among them. **12** And Gallio being proconsul of Achaia, the Jews made a rush with one accord on Paul, and brought him to the judgment seat, **13** saying, "This one persuades men to worship God against the Law"; **14** and Paul being about to open [his] mouth, Gallio said to the Jews, "If, indeed, then, it was anything unrighteous, or an act of wicked recklessness, O Jews, according to reason I had borne with you, **15** but if it is a question concerning words and names, and of your law, look [to it] yourselves, for I do not intend to be a judge of these things," **16** and he drives them from the judgment seat; **17** and all the Greeks having taken Sosthenes, the chief man of the synagogue, were beating [him] before the judgment seat, and Gallio was not even caring for these things. **18** And Paul having remained yet a good many days, having taken leave of the brothers, was sailing to Syria—and with him [are] Priscilla and Aquilas—having shorn [his] head in Cenchera, for he had a vow; **19** and he came down to Ephesus, and left them there, and he himself having entered into the synagogue reasoned with the Jews: **20** and they having requested [him] to remain a longer time with them, he did not consent, **21** but took leave of them, saying, "It is necessary for me by all means to keep the coming celebration at Jerusalem, and again I will return to you—God willing." And he sailed from

Ephesus, **22** and having come down to Caesarea, having gone up, and having greeted the assembly, he went down to Antioch. **23** And having stayed some time, he went forth, going successively through the region of Galatia and Phrygia, strengthening all the disciples. **24** And a certain Jew, Apollos by name, an Alexandrian by birth, a man of eloquence, being mighty in the Writings, came to Ephesus; **25** this one was instructed in the way of the Lord, and being fervent in the Spirit, was speaking and teaching exactly the things about the Lord, knowing only the immersion of John; **26** this one also began to speak boldly in the synagogue, and Aquilas and Priscilla having heard of him, took him to [them], and more exactly set forth to him The Way of God, **27** and he resolving to go through into Achaia, the brothers wrote to the disciples, having exhorted them to receive him, who having come, helped them much who have believed through grace, **28** for he was powerfully refuting the Jews publicly, showing through the Writings Jesus to be the Christ.

CHAPTER 19

1 And it came to pass, in Apollos being in Corinth, Paul having gone through the upper parts, came to Ephesus, and having found certain disciples, **2** he said to them, "Having believed, did you receive the Holy Spirit?" And they said to him, "But we did not even hear whether there is any Holy Spirit"; **3** and he said to them, "Into what, then, were you immersed?" And they said, "Into John's immersion." **4** And Paul said, "John, indeed, immersed with an immersion of conversion, saying to the people that they should believe in Him who is coming after him—that is, in the Christ—Jesus"; **5** and they, having heard, were immersed into the Name of the Lord Jesus, **6** and Paul having laid [his] hands on them, the Holy Spirit came on them, they were also speaking with tongues, and prophesying, **7** and all the men were, as it were, twelve. **8** And having gone into the synagogue, he was speaking boldly for three months, reasoning and persuading the things concerning the Kingdom of God, **9** and when certain were hardened and were disbelieving, speaking evil of The Way before the multitude, having departed from them, he separated the disciples, reasoning every day in the school of a certain Tyrannus. **10** And this happened for two years so that all those dwelling in Asia heard the word of the Lord Jesus, both Jews and Greeks, **11** also mighty works—not common—God was working through the hands of Paul, **12** so that even to the ailing were brought from his body handkerchiefs or aprons, and the diseases departed from them; the evil spirits also went forth from them. **13** And certain of the wandering exorcist Jews, took on [them] to name over those having the evil spirits the Name of the Lord Jesus, saying, "We adjure you by Jesus, whom Paul preaches"; **14** and there were certain—seven sons of Sceva, a Jew, a chief priest—who are doing this thing; **15** and the evil spirit, answering, said, "I know Jesus, and I am acquainted with Paul; and you—who are you?" **16** And the man, in whom was the evil spirit, leaping on them, and having overcome them, prevailed against them, so that they fled naked and wounded out of that house, **17** and this became known to all, both Jews and Greeks, who are dwelling at Ephesus, and fear fell on them all, and the Name of the Lord Jesus was being magnified; **18** many also of those who believed were coming, confessing and declaring their acts, **19** and many of those who had practiced the superfluous arts, having brought the scrolls together, were burning [them] before all; and they reckoned together the prices of them, and found [it] fifty thousand pieces of silver, **20** so powerfully was the word of God increasing and prevailing. **21** And when these things were fulfilled, Paul purposed in the Spirit, having gone through Macedonia and Achaia, to go on to Jerusalem, saying, "After my being there, it is also necessary for me to see Rome"; **22** and having sent to Macedonia two of those ministering to him—Timotheus and Erastus—he himself stayed a time in Asia. **23** And there came, at that time, not a little stir about The Way, **24** for a certain one, Demetrius by name, a worker in silver, making silver sanctuaries of Artemis, was bringing to the craftsmen not a little gain, **25** whom, having brought in a crowd together, and those who worked around such things, he said, "Men, you know that by this work we have our wealth; **26** and you see and hear, that not only at Ephesus, but almost in all Asia, this Paul, having persuaded, turned away a great multitude, saying that they who are made by hands are not gods; **27** and not only is this department in danger for us of coming into disregard, but also, that of the great goddess Artemis, the temple is to be reckoned for nothing, and also her greatness is about to be brought down, whom all Asia and the world worships." **28** And having heard, and having become full of wrath, they were crying out, saying, "Great [is] the Artemis of the Ephesians!" **29** and the whole city was filled with confusion; they rushed also with one accord into the theater, having caught Gaius and Aristarchus, Macedonians, Paul's fellow-travelers. **30** And on Paul's resolving to enter in to the populace, the disciples were not permitting him, **31** and also some of the chief men of Asia, being his friends, having sent to him, were pleading [with] him not to venture into the theater himself. **32** Some indeed, therefore, were calling out one thing, and some another, for the assembly was confused, and the greater part did not know for what they had come together; **33** and out of the multitude they put forward Alexander—the Jews thrusting him forward—and Alexander having beckoned with the hand, wished to make defense to the populace, **34** and having known that he is a Jew, one voice came out of all, for about two hours, crying, "Great [is] the Artemis of the Ephesians!" **35** And the public clerk having quieted the multitude, says, "Men, Ephesians, why, who is the man that does not know that the city of the Ephesians is temple-keeper of the great goddess Artemis, and of that which fell down from Zeus? **36** these things, then, being undeniable, it is necessary for you to be quiet, and to do nothing rashly. **37** For you brought these men, who are neither temple-robbers nor slandering of your goddess; **38** if indeed, therefore, Demetrius and the craftsmen with him have a matter with anyone, court [days] are held, and there are proconsuls; let them accuse one another. **39** And if you seek after anything concerning other matters, it will be determined in the legal assembly; **40** for we are also in peril of being accused of insurrection in regard to this day, there being no occasion by which we will be able to give an account of this concourse"; **41** and having said these things, he dismissed the assembly.

CHAPTER 20

1 And after the ceasing of the tumult, Paul having called near the disciples, and having embraced [them], went forth to go on to Macedonia; **2** and having gone through those parts, and having exhorted them with many words, he came to Greece; **3** and having continued three months—a counsel of the Jews having been against him—being about to set forth to Syria, there came [to him] a resolution of returning through Macedonia. **4** And there were accompanying him to Asia, Sopater of Pyrrhus from Berea, and of Thessalonians Aristarchus and Secundus, and Gaius of Derbe, and Timotheus, and of Asians Tychicus and Trophimus; **5** these, having gone before, remained for us in Troas, **6** and we sailed, after the days of the Unleavened [Bread], from Philippi, and came to them to Troas in five days, where we abided seven days. **7** And on the first [day] of the weeks, the disciples having been gathered together to break bread, Paul was discoursing to them, about to depart on the next day, he was also continuing the discourse until midnight, **8** and there were many lamps in the upper chamber where they were gathered together, **9** and there a certain youth was sitting, by name Eutychus, on the window—being borne down by a deep sleep, Paul discoursing long—he having sunk down from the sleep, fell down from the third story, and was lifted up dead. **10** And Paul, having gone down, fell on him, and having embraced [him], said, "Make no tumult, for his life is in him"; **11** and having come up, and having broken bread, and having tasted, for a long time also having talked—until daylight, so he went forth, **12** and they brought up the boy alive, and were comforted in no ordinary measure. **13** And we having gone before to the ship, sailed to Assos, there intending to take in Paul, for so he had arranged, intending himself to go on foot; **14** and when he met with us at Assos, having taken him up, we came to Mitylene, **15** and there having sailed, on the next day we came opposite Chios, and the next day we arrived at Samos, and having remained in Trogyllium, on the following day we came to Miletus, **16** for Paul decided to sail past Ephesus, that there may not be to him a loss of time in Asia, for he was hurrying, if it were possible for him, to be at Jerusalem on the day of the Pentecost. **17** And from Miletus, having sent to Ephesus, he called for the elders of the assembly, **18** and when they were come to him, he said to them, "You know from the first day in which I came to Asia, how I was with you at all times; **19** serving the Lord with all humility, and many tears, and temptations, that befell me in the counsels of the Jews against [me]; **20** how I kept back nothing of what things are profitable, not to declare to you, and to teach you publicly, and in every house, **21** testifying fully both to Jews and Greeks, conversion toward God, and faith toward our Lord Jesus Christ. **22** And now, behold, I—bound in the Spirit—go on to Jerusalem, not knowing the things that will befall me in it, **23** except that the Holy Spirit fully testifies in every city, saying that bonds and tribulations remain for me; **24** but I make account of none of these, neither do I count my life precious to myself, so that I finish my course with joy, and the ministry that I received from the Lord Jesus, to fully testify [to] the good news of the grace of God. **25** And now, behold, I have known that you will no longer see my face, among all you [to] whom I went preaching the Kingdom of God; **26** for this reason I take you to witness this day, that I [am] clear from the blood of all, **27** for I did not keep back from declaring to you all the counsel of God. **28** Take heed, therefore, to yourselves, and to all the flock, among which the Holy Spirit made you overseers, to feed the Assembly of God that He acquired through His own blood, **29** for I have known this, that there will enter in, after my departing, grievous wolves to you, not sparing the flock, **30** and there will arise men of your own selves, speaking perverse things, to draw away the disciples after them. **31** Therefore, watch, remembering that three years, night and day, I did not cease with tears warning each one; **32** and now, I commend you, brothers, to God, and to the word of His grace, that is able to build up, and to give you an inheritance among all those sanctified. **33** I coveted the silver or gold or clothing of no one; **34** and you yourselves know that to my necessities, and to those who were with me, these hands ministered; **35** I showed you all things, that, thus laboring, it is necessary to partake with the ailing, to also be mindful of the words of the Lord Jesus, that He Himself said: It is more blessed to give than to receive." **36** And having said these things, having bowed his knees, with them all, he prayed, **37** and there came a great weeping to all, and having fallen on the neck of Paul, they were kissing him, **38** sorrowing most of all for the word that he had said—that they are about to see his face no longer; and they were accompanying him to the ship.

CHAPTER 21

1 And it came to pass, at our sailing, having been parted from them, having run direct, we came to Coos, and the succeeding [day] to Rhodes, and there to Patara, **2** and having found a ship passing over to Phoenicia, having gone on board, we sailed, **3** and having discovered Cyprus, and having left it on the left, we were sailing to Syria, and landed at Tyre, for there was the ship discharging the cargo. **4** And having found out the disciples, we tarried there seven days, and they said to Paul, through the Spirit, not to go up to Jerusalem; **5** but when it came that we completed the days, having gone forth, we went on, all bringing us on the way, with women and children, to the outside of the city, and having bowed the knees on the shore, we prayed, **6** and having embraced one another, we embarked in the ship, and they returned to their own friends. **7** And we, having finished the course, from Tyre came down to Ptolemais, and having greeted the brothers, we remained one day with them; **8** and on the next day Paul and his company having gone forth, we came to Caesarea, and having entered into the house of Philip the evangelist—who is of the seven— we remained with him, **9** and this one had four daughters, virgins, prophesying. **10** And we remaining many more days, there came down a certain one from Judea, a prophet, by name Agabus, **11** and he having come to us, and having taken up the girdle of Paul, having also bound his own hands and feet, said, "Thus says the Holy Spirit: The man whose is this girdle—so will the Jews in Jerusalem bind, and they will deliver [him] up into the hands of nations." **12** And when we heard these things, we called on [him]—both we, and those of that place—not to go up to Jerusalem, **13** and Paul answered, "Why are you weeping, and crushing my heart? for I am ready, not only to be bound, but also to die at Jerusalem for the Name of the Lord Jesus"; **14** and he not being persuaded, we were silent, saying, "The will of the Lord be done." **15** And after these days, having taken [our] vessels, we were going up to Jerusalem, **16** and there went also of the disciples from Caesarea with us, bringing with them him with whom we may lodge, a certain Mnason of Cyprus, an aged disciple. **17** And we having come to Jerusalem, the brothers gladly received us, **18** and on the next day Paul was going in with us to James, all the elders also came, **19** and

having greeted them, he was expounding, one by one, each of the things God did among the nations through his ministry, **20** and they having heard, were glorifying the Lord. They also said to him, "You see, brother, how many myriads there are of Jews who have believed, and all are zealous of the Law, **21** and they are instructed concerning you, that you teach departure from Moses to all Jews among the nations, saying not to circumcise the children, nor to walk after the customs; **22** what then is it? certainly the multitude must come together, for they will hear that you have come. **23** This, therefore, that we say to you, do. We have four men having a vow on themselves, **24** having taken these, be purified with them, and be at expense with them, that they may shave the head, and all may know that the things of which they have been instructed concerning you are nothing, but you walk—yourself also—keeping the Law. **25** And concerning those of the nations who have believed, we have written, having given judgment, that they observe no such thing, except to keep themselves both from idol-sacrifices, and blood, and a strangled thing, and whoredom." **26** Then Paul, having taken the men, on the following day, having purified himself with them, was entering into the temple, announcing the fulfilment of the days of the purification, until the offering was offered for each one of them. **27** And as the seven days were about to be fully ended, the Jews from Asia having beheld him in the temple, were stirring up all the multitude, and they laid hands on him, **28** crying out, "Men, Israelites, help! This is the man who, against the people, and the Law, and this place, is teaching all everywhere; and further, also, he brought Greeks into the temple, and has defiled this holy place"; **29** for they had seen before Trophimus, the Ephesian, in the city with him, whom they were supposing that Paul brought into the temple. **30** All the city was also moved and there was a running together of the people, and having laid hold on Paul, they were drawing him out of the temple, and immediately were the doors shut, **31** and they seeking to kill him, a rumor came to the chief captain of the band that all Jerusalem has been thrown into confusion, **32** who, at once, having taken soldiers and centurions, ran down on them, and they having seen the chief captain and the soldiers, left off beating Paul. **33** Then the chief captain, having come near, took him, and commanded [him] to be bound with two chains, and was inquiring who he may be, and what it is he has been doing, **34** and some were crying out one thing, and some another, among the multitude, and not being able to know the certainty because of the tumult, he commanded him to be carried into the stronghold, **35** and when he came on the steps, it happened he was carried by the soldiers, because of the violence of the multitude, **36** for the crowd of the people was following after, crying, "Away with him." **37** And Paul being about to be led into the stronghold, says to the chief captain, "Is it permitted to me to say anything to you?" And he said, "Do you know Greek? **38** are you not, then, the Egyptian who made an uprising before these days, and led the four thousand men of the assassins into the desert?" **39** And Paul said, "I, indeed, am a man, a Jew, of Tarsus of Cilicia, a citizen of no insignificant city; and I implore you, permit me to speak to the people." **40** And he having given him leave, Paul having stood on the stairs, beckoned with the hand to the people, and there having been a great silence, he spoke to them in the Hebrew dialect, saying:

CHAPTER 22

1 "Men, brothers, and fathers, hear my defense now to you." **2** and they having heard that he was speaking to them in the Hebrew dialect, they became even more silent, and he says, **3** "I, indeed, am a man, a Jew, having been born in Tarsus of Cilicia, and brought up in this city at the feet of Gamaliel, having been taught according to the exactness of a law of the fathers, being zealous of God, as all you are today. **4** And this Way I persecuted to death, binding and delivering up to prisons both men and women, **5** as also the chief priest testifies to me, and all the eldership; from whom also having received letters to the brothers, to Damascus, I was going on, to bring also those there bound to Jerusalem that they might be punished, **6** and it came to pass, in my going on and coming near to Damascus, about noon, suddenly out of Heaven there shone a great light around me; **7** I also fell to the ground, and I heard a voice saying to me, Saul, Saul, why do you persecute Me? **8** And I answered, Who are You, Lord? and He said to me, I am Jesus the Nazarene whom you persecute— **9** and they who are with me saw the light, and became afraid, and they did not hear the voice of Him who is speaking to me— **10** and I said, What will I do, Lord? and the Lord said to me, Having risen, go on to Damascus, and there it will be told you concerning all things that have been appointed for you to do. **11** And when I did not see from the glory of that light, being led by the hand by those who are with me, I came to Damascus, **12** and a certain one, Ananias, a pious man according to the Law, being testified to by all the Jews dwelling [there], **13** having come to me and stood by [me], said to me, Saul, brother, look up; and the same hour I looked up to him; **14** and he said, The God of our fathers chose you beforehand to know His will, and to see the Righteous One, and to hear a voice out of His mouth, **15** because you will be His witness to all men of what you have seen and heard; **16** and now, why do you linger? having risen, immerse yourself, and wash away your sins, calling on the Name of the Lord. **17** And it came to pass, when I returned to Jerusalem, and while I was praying in the temple, I came into a trance, **18** and I saw Him saying to me, Hurry and go forth in haste out of Jerusalem, because they will not receive your testimony concerning Me; **19** and I said, Lord, they know that I was imprisoning and was scourging those believing on You in every synagogue; **20** and when the blood of your witness Stephen was being poured forth, I was also standing by and assenting to his death, and keeping the garments of those putting him to death; **21** and He said to me, Go, because I will send you to far-off nations." **22** And they were hearing him to this word, and they lifted up their voice, saying, "Away from the earth with such a one; for it is not fit for him to live." **23** And they crying out and casting up their garments, and throwing dust into the air, **24** the chief captain commanded him to be brought into the stronghold, saying, "Let him be examined by scourges," that he might know for what cause they were crying so against him. **25** And as he was stretching him with the straps, Paul said to the centurion who was standing by, "Is it lawful to you to scourge a man, a Roman, uncondemned?" **26** And the centurion having heard, having gone near to the chief captain, told, saying, "Take heed what you are about to do, for this man is a Roman"; **27** and the chief captain having come near, said to him, "Tell me, are you a Roman?" And he said, "Yes"; **28** and the chief captain answered, "I, with a great sum, obtained this citizenship"; but Paul said, "But I have even been born [so]." **29** Immediately, therefore, they departed from him, those being about to examine him, and the chief captain was also afraid, having learned that he is a Roman, and because he had bound him, **30** and the next day, intending to know the certainty for what reason he is accused by the Jews, he loosed him from the bonds, and commanded the chief priests and all their Sanhedrin to come, and having brought down Paul, he set [him] before them.

CHAPTER 23

1 And Paul having earnestly beheld the Sanhedrin, said, "Men, brothers, I have lived to God in all good conscience to this day"; **2** and the chief priest Ananias commanded those standing by him to strike him on the mouth, **3** then Paul said to him, "God is about to strike you, you whitewashed wall, and you sit judging me according to the Law, and violating law, order me to be struck!" **4** And those who stood by said, "Do you revile the chief priest of God?" **5** and Paul said, "I did not know, brothers, that he is chief priest, for it has been written: You will not speak evil of the ruler of your people"; **6** and Paul having known that one part are Sadducees, and the other Pharisees, cried out in the Sanhedrin, "Men, brothers, I am a Pharisee—son of a Pharisee—concerning [the] hope and resurrection of [the] dead I am judged." **7** And he having spoken this, there came a dissension of the Pharisees and of the Sadducees, and the crowd was divided, **8** for Sadducees, indeed, say there is no resurrection, nor messenger, nor spirit, but Pharisees confess both. **9** And there came a great cry, and the scribes of the Pharisees' part having arisen, were striving, saying, "We find no evil in this man; and if a spirit spoke to him, or a messenger, we may not fight against God"; **10** and a great dissension having come, the chief captain having been afraid lest Paul may be pulled to pieces by them, commanded the army, having gone down, to seize him out of their midst, and to bring [him] into the stronghold. **11** And on the following night, the Lord having stood by him, said, "Take courage, Paul, for as you fully testified [to] the things concerning Me at Jerusalem, so you must also testify at Rome." **12** And day having come, certain of the Jews having made a concourse,

cursed themselves, saying neither to eat nor to drink until they may kill Paul; **13** and they were more than forty who made this conspiracy by oath, **14** who having come near to the chief priests and to the elders said, "With a curse we accursed ourselves—to taste nothing until we have killed Paul; **15** now, therefore, you, signify to the chief captain, with the Sanhedrin, that tomorrow he may bring him down to you, as being about to know more exactly the things concerning him; and we, before his coming near, are ready to put him to death." **16** And the son of Paul's sister having heard of the lying in wait, having gone and entered into the stronghold, told Paul, **17** and Paul having called near one of the centurions, said, "Lead this young man to the chief captain, for he has something to tell him." **18** He indeed, then, having taken him, brought him to the chief captain and says, "The prisoner Paul, having called me near, asked [me] to bring to you this young man, having something to say to you." **19** And the chief captain having taken him by the hand, and having withdrawn by themselves, inquired, "What is that which you have to tell me?" **20** and he said, "The Jews agreed to request you, that tomorrow you may bring down Paul to the Sanhedrin, as being about to inquire something more exactly concerning him; **21** you, therefore, may you not yield to them, for there more than forty men of them lie in wait for him, who cursed themselves—not to eat nor to drink until they kill him, and now they are ready, waiting for the promise from you." **22** The chief captain, then, indeed, let the young man go, having charged [him], "Tell no one that you have shown these things to me"; **23** and having called a certain two of the centurions near, he said, "Make ready two hundred soldiers, that they may go on to Caesarea, and seventy horsemen, and two hundred spearmen, from the third hour of the night; **24** also provide beasts, that, having set Paul on, they may bring him safe to Felix the governor"; **25** he having written a letter after this description: **26** "Claudius Lysias, to the most noble governor Felix, greetings: **27** This man having been taken by the Jews, and being about to be killed by them—having come with the army, I rescued him, having learned that he is a Roman; **28** and intending to know the cause for which they were accusing him, I brought him down to their Sanhedrin, **29** whom I found accused concerning questions of their law, and having no accusation worthy of death or bonds; **30** and a plot having been intimated to me against this man— about to be of the Jews—I sent to you at once, having also given command to the accusers to say the things against him before you; be strong." **31** Then, indeed, the soldiers according to that directed them, having taken up Paul, brought him through the night to Antipatris, **32** and on the next day, having permitted the horsemen to go on with him, they returned to the stronghold; **33** those having entered into Caesarea, and delivered the letter to the governor, also presented Paul to him. **34** And the governor having read [it], and inquired of what province he is, and understood that [he is] from Cilicia; **35** "I will hear you," he said, "when your accusers may also have come"; he also commanded him to be kept in the Praetorium of Herod.

CHAPTER 24

1 And after five days the chief priest Ananias came down, with the elders, and a certain orator—Tertullus, and they disclosed to the governor [the things] against Paul; **2** and he having been called, Tertullus began to accuse [him], saying, "Enjoying much peace through you, and worthy deeds being done to this nation through your forethought, **3** always, also, and everywhere we receive it, most noble Felix, with all thankfulness; **4** and that I may not be further tedious to you, I exhort you to hear us concisely in your gentleness; **5** for having found this man a pestilence, and moving a dissension to all the Jews through the world—also a ringleader of the sect of the Nazarenes— **6** who also tried to profane the temple, whom we also took, [[and wished to judge according to our law, **7** and Lysias the chief captain having come near, took away out of our hands with much violence, **8** having commanded his accusers to come to you,]] from whom you may be able, yourself having examined, to know concerning all these things of which we accuse him"; **9** and the Jews also agreed, professing these things to be so. **10** And Paul—the governor having beckoned to him to speak—answered, "Knowing [that] for many years you have been a judge to this nation, I answer more cheerfully the things concerning myself; **11** you being able to know that it is not more than twelve days to me since I went up to worship in Jerusalem, ¹² and neither did they find me reasoning with anyone in the temple, or making a dissension of the multitude, nor in the synagogues, nor in the city; ¹³ nor are they able to prove against me the things concerning which they now accuse me. ¹⁴ And I confess this to you, that, according to The Way that they call a sect, so I serve the God of the fathers, believing all things that have been written in the Law and the Prophets, ¹⁵ having hope toward God, which they themselves also wait for, [that] there is about to be a resurrection of the dead, both of righteous and unrighteous; ¹⁶ and in this I exercise myself, to always have a conscience void of offense toward God and men. ¹⁷ And after many years I came, about to do kind acts to my nation, and offerings, ¹⁸ in which certain Jews from Asia found me purified in the temple, not with multitude, nor with tumult, ¹⁹ whom it is necessary to be present before you, and to accuse, if they had anything against me, ²⁰ or let these same say if they found any unrighteousness in me in my standing before the Sanhedrin, ²¹ except concerning this one voice, in which I cried, standing among them—Concerning a resurrection of the dead I am judged by you today." ²² And having heard these things, Felix delayed them—having known more exactly of the things concerning The Way—saying, "When Lysias the chief captain may come down, I will know fully the things concerning you"; ²³ having also given a direction to the centurion to keep Paul, to let [him] also have liberty, and to forbid none of his own friends to minister or to come near to him. ²⁴ And after certain days, Felix having come with his wife Drusilla, being a Jewess, he sent for Paul, and heard him concerning faith toward Christ, ²⁵ and he reasoning concerning righteousness, and self-control, and the judgment that is about to be, Felix, having become afraid, answered, "For the present be going, and having time, I will call for you"; ²⁶ and at the same time also hoping that money will be given to him by Paul, that he may release him, therefore, also sending for him often, he was conversing with him; ²⁷ and two years having been fulfilled, Felix received a successor, Porcius Festus; Felix also willing to lay a favor on the Jews, left Paul bound.

CHAPTER 25

¹ Festus, therefore, having come into the province, after three days went up to Jerusalem from Caesarea, ² and the chief priest and the principal men of the Jews disclosed to him [the things] against Paul, and were calling on him, ³ asking favor against him, that he may send for him to Jerusalem, making an ambush to put him to death in the way. ⁴ Then, indeed, Festus answered that Paul is kept in Caesarea, and is himself about to go forth speedily, ⁵ "Therefore those able among you," he says, "having come down together, if there be anything in this man—let them accuse him"; ⁶ and having tarried among them more than ten days, having gone down to Caesarea, on the next day having sat on the judgment seat, he commanded Paul to be brought; ⁷ and he having come, there stood around the Jews who have come down from Jerusalem—many and weighty charges they are bringing against Paul, which they were not able to prove, ⁸ he making defense, [said,] "Neither in regard to the Law of the Jews, nor in regard to the temple, nor in regard to Caesar—did I commit any sin." ⁹ And Festus willing to lay on the Jews a favor, answering Paul, said, "Are you willing, having gone up to Jerusalem, to be judged before me there concerning these things?" ¹⁰ and Paul said, "At the judgment seat of Caesar I am standing, where it is necessary for me to be judged; I did no unrighteousness to Jews, as you also very well know; ¹¹ for if I am indeed unrighteous, and have done anything worthy of death, I do not deprecate to die; and if there is none of the things of which these accuse me, no one is able to make a favor of me to them; I appeal to Caesar!" ¹² then Festus, having communed with the council, answered, "To Caesar you have appealed; to Caesar you will go." ¹³ And certain days having passed, Agrippa the king, and Bernice, came down to Caesarea greeting Festus, ¹⁴ and as they were continuing there more days, Festus submitted to the king the things concerning Paul, saying, "There is a certain man, left by Felix, a prisoner, ¹⁵ about whom, in my being at Jerusalem, the chief priests and the elders of the Jews laid information, asking a decision against him, ¹⁶ to whom I answered, that it is not a custom of Romans to make a favor of any man to die, before that he who is accused may have the accusers face to face, and may receive place of defense in regard to the charge laid against [him]. ¹⁷ They, therefore, having come together—I,

making no delay, on the succeeding [day] having sat on the judgment seat, commanded the man to be brought, ¹⁸ concerning whom the accusers, having stood up, were bringing against [him] no accusation of the things I was thinking of, ¹⁹ but certain questions concerning their own religion they had against him, and concerning a certain Jesus who was dead, whom Paul affirmed to be alive; ²⁰ and I, doubting in regard to the question concerning this, asked if he was willing to go on to Jerusalem, and to be judged there concerning these things— ²¹ but Paul having appealed to be kept to the hearing of Sebastus, I commanded him to be kept until I might send him to Caesar." ²² And Agrippa said to Festus, "I was also intending to hear the man myself"; and he said, "Tomorrow you will hear him"; ²³ on the next day, therefore—on the coming of Agrippa and Bernice with much display, and they having entered into the audience chamber, with the chief captains also, and the principal men of the city, and Festus having ordered—Paul was brought forth. ²⁴ And Festus said, "King Agrippa, and all men who are present with us, you see this one, about whom all the multitude of the Jews dealt with me, both in Jerusalem and here, crying out, He ought not to live any longer; ²⁵ and I, having found him to have done nothing worthy of death, and he also himself having appealed to Sebastus, I decided to send him, ²⁶ concerning whom I have no certain thing to write to [my] lord, for what reason I brought him forth before you, and especially before you, King Agrippa, that the examination having been made, I may have something to write; ²⁷ for it seems to me irrational, sending a prisoner, not to also signify the charges against him."

CHAPTER 26

¹ And Agrippa said to Paul, "It is permitted to you to speak for yourself"; then Paul having stretched forth the hand, was making a defense: ² "Concerning all things of which I am accused by Jews, King Agrippa, I have thought myself blessed, being about to make a defense before you today, ³ especially knowing you to be acquainted with all things—both customs and questions—among Jews; for this reason, I implore you to hear me patiently. ⁴ The manner of my life then, indeed, from youth—which from the beginning was among my nation, in Jerusalem—all the Jews know, ⁵ knowing me before from the first (if they may be willing to testify), that after the most exact sect of our worship, I lived a Pharisee; ⁶ and now for the hope of the promise made to the fathers by God, I have stood judged, ⁷ to which our twelve tribes, intently serving night and day, hope to come, concerning which hope I am accused, King Agrippa, by the Jews; ⁸ why is it judged incredible with you if God raises the dead? ⁹ I indeed, therefore, thought with myself that it was necessary [for me] to do many things against the Name of Jesus of Nazareth, ¹⁰ which I also did in Jerusalem, and I shut up many of the holy ones in prison, having received the authority from the chief priests; they also being put to death, I gave my vote against them, ¹¹ and in every synagogue, often punishing them, I was constraining [them] to speak evil, being also exceedingly mad against them, I was also persecuting [them] even to strange cities. ¹² In which things, also, going on to Damascus—with authority and commission from the chief priests— ¹³ at midday, I saw in the way, O king, out of Heaven, above the brightness of the sun, shining around me a light—and those going on with me; ¹⁴ and we all having fallen to the earth, I heard a voice speaking to me, and saying in the Hebrew dialect, Saul, Saul, why do you persecute Me? [It is] hard for you to kick against goads! ¹⁵ And I said, Who are You, Lord? and He said, I am Jesus whom you persecute; ¹⁶ but rise, and stand on your feet, for this I appeared to you, to appoint you an officer and a witness both of the things you saw, and of the things [in which] I will appear to you, ¹⁷ delivering you from the people, and the nations, to whom I now send you, ¹⁸ to open their eyes, to turn [them] from darkness to light, and [from] the authority of Satan to God, for their receiving forgiveness of sins, and a lot among those having been sanctified by faith that [is] toward Me. ¹⁹ After which, King Agrippa, I was not disobedient to the heavenly vision, ²⁰ but to those in Damascus first, and to those in Jerusalem, also to all the region of Judea, and to the nations, I was preaching to convert, and to turn back to God, doing works worthy of conversion; ²¹ because of these things the Jews—having caught me in the temple—were endeavoring to kill [me]. ²² Having obtained, therefore, help from God, until this day, I have stood witnessing both to small and to great,

saying nothing besides the things that both the prophets and Moses spoke of as about to come, **23** that the Christ is to suffer, whether first by a resurrection from the dead, He is about to proclaim light to the people and to the nations." **24** And he thus making a defense, Festus said with a loud voice, "You are mad, Paul; much learning turns you mad!" **25** And he says, "I am not mad, most noble Festus, but of truth and soberness I speak forth the sayings; **26** for the king knows concerning these things, before whom I also speak boldly, for none of these things, I am persuaded, are hidden from him; for this thing has not been done in a corner; **27** do you believe, King Agrippa, the prophets? I have known that you believe!" **28** And Agrippa said to Paul, "In [so] little you persuade me to become a Christian?" **29** and Paul said, "I would have wished to God, both in a little, and in much, not only you, but also all those hearing me today, to become such as I also am—except these bonds." **30** And he having spoken these things, the king rose up, and the governor, Bernice also, and those sitting with them, **31** and having withdrawn, they were speaking to one another, saying, "This man does nothing worthy of death or of bonds"; **32** and Agrippa said to Festus, "This man might have been released if he had not appealed to Caesar."

CHAPTER 27

1 And when our sailing to Italy was determined, they were delivering up both Paul and certain others, prisoners, to a centurion, by name Julius, of the band of Sebastus, **2** and having embarked in a ship of Adramyttium, we, being about to sail by the coasts of Asia, set sail, there being with us Aristarchus, a Macedonian of Thessalonica, **3** on the next [day] also we touched at Sidon, and Julius, courteously treating Paul, permitted [him], having gone on to friends, to receive [their] care. **4** And there, having set sail, we sailed under Cyprus, because of the winds being contrary, **5** and having sailed over the sea down by Cilicia and Pamphylia, we came to Myria of Lycia, **6** and there the centurion having found a ship of Alexandria, sailing to Italy, put us into it, **7** and having sailed slowly many days, and with difficulty coming down by Cnidus, the wind not permitting us, we sailed under Crete, down by Salmone, **8** and hardly passing it, we came to a certain place called Fair Havens, near to which was the city of Lasaea. **9** And much time being spent, and the sailing now being dangerous—because of the fast also being already past—Paul was admonishing, **10** saying to them, "Men, I perceive that with hurt, and much damage, not only of the load and of the ship, but also of our lives—the voyage is about to be"; **11** but the centurion gave more credence to the pilot and to the shipowner than to the things spoken by Paul; **12** and the haven being not well placed to winter in, the greater part gave counsel to sail from there, if somehow they might be able, having attained to Phoenix, to winter [there], [which is] a haven of Crete, looking to the southwest and northwest, **13** and a south wind blowing softly, having thought they had obtained [their] purpose, having lifted anchor, they sailed close by Crete, **14** and not long after, there came down from it a turbulent wind [that] is called the Euroclydon, **15** and the ship being caught, and not being able to bear up against the wind, having given [her] up, we were carried on, **16** and having run under a certain little island called Clauda, we were hardly able to become masters of the boat, **17** which having taken up, they were using helps, undergirding the ship, and fearing lest they may fall into the [sandbars of] Syrtis, having let down the mast—so were carried on. **18** And we, being exceedingly storm-tossed, the succeeding [day] they were making a clearing, **19** and on the third [day] we cast out the tackling of the ship with our own hands, **20** and neither sun nor stars appearing for more days, and not a little storm lying on us, from then on all hope was taken away of our being saved. **21** And there having been long fasting, then Paul having stood in the midst of them, said, "It was necessary, indeed, O men—having listened to me—not to set sail from Crete, and to save this hurt and damage; **22** and now I exhort you to be of good cheer, for there will be no loss of life among you—but of the ship; **23** for this night there stood by me a messenger of God—whose I am, and whom I serve— **24** saying, Do not be afraid Paul; it is necessary for you to stand before Caesar; and behold, God has granted to you all those sailing with you; **25** for this reason be of good cheer, men! For I believe God, that so it will be, even as it has been spoken to me, **26** and on a certain island it is necessary for us to be cast." **27** And when the fourteenth night came—we being carried up

and down in the Adria—toward the middle of the night the sailors were supposing that some country drew near to them; **28** and having sounded they found twenty fathoms, and having gone a little farther, and again having sounded, they found fifteen fathoms, **29** and fearing lest we may fall on rough places, having cast four anchors out of the stern, they were wishing day to come. **30** And the sailors seeking to flee out of the ship, and having let down the boat to the sea, in pretense as [if] out of the prow they are about to cast anchors, **31** Paul said to the centurion and to the soldiers, "If these do not remain in the ship—you are not able to be saved"; **32** then the soldiers cut off the ropes of the boat, and permitted it to fall off. **33** And until the day was about to be, Paul was calling on all to partake of nourishment, saying, "Fourteen days today, waiting, you continue fasting, having taken nothing, **34** for this reason I call on you to take nourishment, for this is for your safety, for of not one of you will a hair fall from the head"; **35** and having said these things, and having taken bread, he gave thanks to God before all, and having broken [it], he began to eat; **36** and all having become of good cheer, also took food themselves, **37** (and we were—all the souls in the ship—two hundred, seventy-six), **38** and having eaten sufficient nourishment, they were lightening the ship, casting forth the wheat into the sea. **39** And when the day came, they were not discerning the land, but were perceiving a certain bay having a beach, into which they took counsel, if possible, to thrust forward the ship, **40** and having taken up the anchors, they were committing [it] to the sea, at the same time—having loosed the bands of the rudders, and having hoisted up the foresail to the wind—they were making for the shore, **41** and having fallen into a place of two seas, they ran the ship aground, and the prow, indeed, having stuck fast, remained immoveable, but the stern was broken by the violence of the waves. **42** And the soldiers' counsel was that they should kill the prisoners, lest anyone having swam out should escape, **43** but the centurion, resolving to save Paul, hindered them from the counsel, and commanded those able to swim, having cast themselves out first—to get to the land, **44** and the rest, some indeed on boards, and some on certain things of the ship; and thus, it came to pass that all came safe to the land.

CHAPTER 28

1 And having been saved, then they knew that the island is called Malta, 2 and the foreigners were showing us no ordinary kindness, for having kindled a fire, they received us all, because of the pressing rain, and because of the cold; 3 but Paul having gathered together a quantity of sticks, and having laid [them] on the fire, a viper—having come out of the heat—fastened on his hand. 4 And when the foreigners saw the beast hanging from his hand, they said to one another, "Certainly this man is a murderer, whom, having been saved out of the sea, the justice did not permit to live"; 5 he then, indeed, having shaken off the beast into the fire, suffered no evil, 6 and they were expecting him to be about to be inflamed, or to suddenly fall down dead, and they, expecting [it] a long time, and seeing nothing uncommon happening to him, changing [their] minds, said he was a god. 7 And in the neighborhood of that place were lands of the principal man of the island, by name Publius, who, having received us, courteously lodged [us for] three days; 8 and it came to pass, the father of Publius was lying, oppressed with fevers and dysentery, to whom Paul, having entered and having prayed, having laid [his] hands on him, healed him; 9 this, therefore, being done, also the others in the island having sicknesses were coming and were healed; 10 who also honored us with many honors, and we setting sail—they were loading [us] with the things that were necessary. 11 And after three months, we set sail in a ship (that had wintered in the island) of Alexandria, with the sign Dioscuri, 12 and having landed at Syracuse, we remained three days, 13 there having gone around, we came to Rhegium, and after one day, a south wind having sprung up, the second [day] we came to Puteoli, 14 where, having found brothers, we were called on to remain with them seven days, and thus we came to Rome; 15 and there, the brothers having heard the things concerning us, came forth to meet us, as far as [the] Forum of Appius, and Three Taverns—whom Paul having seen, having given thanks to God, took courage. 16 And when we came to Rome, the centurion delivered up the prisoners to the captain of the barracks, but Paul was permitted to remain by himself, with the soldier guarding him. 17 And it

came to pass after three days, Paul called together those who are the principal men of the Jews, and they having come together, he said to them: "Men, brothers, I—having done nothing contrary to the people, or to the customs of the fathers—a prisoner from Jerusalem, was delivered up into the hands of the Romans; 18 who having examined me, were willing to release [me], because of their being no cause of death in me, 19 and the Jews having spoken against [it], I was constrained to appeal to Caesar—not as having anything to accuse my nation of; 20 for this cause, therefore, I called for you to see and to speak with [you], for because of the hope of Israel I am bound with this chain." 21 And they said to him, "We neither received letters concerning you from Judea, nor did anyone who came of the brothers declare or speak any evil concerning you, 22 and we think it good from you to hear what you think, for indeed,concerning this sect it is known to us that it is spoken against everywhere"; 23 and having appointed him a day, more of them came to him, to the lodging, to whom he was setting [it] forth, testifying fully the Kingdom of God, persuading them also of the things concerning Jesus, both from the Law of Moses, and the Prophets, from morning until evening, 24 and some, indeed, were believing the things spoken, and some were not believing. 25 And not being agreed with one another, they were going away, Paul having spoken one word, "The Holy Spirit spoke well through Isaiah the prophet to our fathers, 26 saying, Go on to this people and say, With hearing you will hear, and you will not understand, and seeing you will see, and you will not perceive, 27 for the heart of this people was made obtuse, and with the ears they barely heard, and they closed their eyes, lest they may see with the eyes, and may understand with the heart, and should turn, and I may heal them. 28 Be it known, therefore, to you, that the salvation of God was sent to the nations, these also will hear it"; 29 [[and he having said these things, the Jews went away, having much debate among themselves;]] 30 and Paul remained an entire two years in his own hired [house], and was receiving all those coming in to him, 31 preaching the Kingdom of God, and teaching the things concerning the Lord Jesus Christ with all boldness—unforbidden.

ROMANS

CHAPTER 1

1 Paul, a servant of Jesus Christ, a called apostle, having been separated to the good news of God, 2 which He announced before through His prophets in holy writings, 3 concerning His Son—who has come of the seed of David according to the flesh, 4 who is marked out [as the] Son of God in power, according to the Spirit of sanctification, by the resurrection from the dead—Jesus Christ our Lord; 5 through whom we received grace and apostleship, for obedience of faith among all the nations, in behalf of His Name; 6 among whom are also you, the called of Jesus Christ; 7 to all who are in Rome, beloved of God, called holy ones: Grace to you and peace from God our Father and the Lord Jesus Christ! 8 first, indeed, I thank my God through Jesus Christ for you all, that your faith is proclaimed in the whole world; 9 for God is my witness, whom I serve in my spirit in the good news of His Son, how unceasingly I make mention of you, 10 always in my prayers imploring, if by any means now at length I will have a prosperous journey, by the will of God, to come to you, 11 for I long to see you, that I may impart to you some spiritual gift, that you may be established; 12 and that is, that I may be comforted together among you, through faith in one another, both yours and mine. 13 And I do not wish you to be ignorant, brothers, that many times I purposed to come to you—and was hindered until the present time—that some fruit I might have also among you, even as also among the other nations. 14 Both to Greeks and to foreigners, both to wise and to thoughtless, I am a debtor, 15 so, as much as in me is, I am ready also to you who [are] in Rome to proclaim good news, 16 for I am not ashamed of the good news of the Christ, for it is the power of God to salvation to everyone who is believing, both to Jew first, and to Greek. 17 For the righteousness of God in it is revealed from faith to faith, according as it has been written: "And the righteous one will live by faith," 18 for the wrath of God is revealed from Heaven on all impiety and unrighteousness of

men, holding down the truth in unrighteousness. 19 Because that which is known of God is revealed among them, for God revealed [it] to them, 20 for the invisible things of Him from the creation of the world, by the things made being understood, are plainly seen, both His eternal power and Godhead—to their being inexcusable; 21 because, having known God they did not glorify [Him] as God, nor gave thanks, but were made vain in their reasonings, and their unintelligent heart was darkened, 22 professing to be wise, they were made fools, 23 and changed the glory of the incorruptible God into the likeness of an image of corruptible man, and of birds, and of quadrupeds, and of reptiles. 24 For this reason also God gave them up, in the desires of their hearts, to uncleanness, to dishonor their bodies among themselves; 25 who changed the truth of God into the lie, and honored and served the creature rather than the Creator, who is blessed for all ages. Amen. 26 Because of this God gave them up to dishonorable affections, for even their females changed the natural use into that against nature; 27 and in like manner also the males having left the natural use of the female, burned in their longing toward one another; males with males working shame, and the repayment of their error that was fit, in themselves receiving. 28 And according as they did not approve of having God in knowledge, God gave them up to a disapproved mind, to do the things not seemly; 29 having been filled with all unrighteousness, whoredom, wickedness, covetousness, malice; full of envy, murder, strife, deceit, evil dispositions; whisperers, 30 evil-speakers, God-haters, insulting, proud, boasters, inventors of evil things, disobedient to parents, 31 unintelligent, faithless, without natural affection, implacable, unmerciful; 32 who the righteous judgment of God having known—that those practicing such things are worthy of death—not only do them, but also have delight with those practicing them.

CHAPTER 2

1 Therefore, you are inexcusable, O man—everyone who is judging—for in that in which you judge the other, yourself you condemn, for the same things you practice who are judging, 2 and we have known that the judgment of God is according to truth, on those practicing such things. 3 And do you think this, O man, who are judging those who such things are practicing, and are doing them, that you will escape the judgment of God? 4 or the riches of His goodness, and forbearance, and long-suffering, do you despise, not knowing that the goodness of God leads you to conversion? 5 but according to your hardness and impenitent heart, you treasure up wrath to yourself in [the] day of wrath and of the revelation of the righteous judgment of God, 6 who will render to each according to his works; 7 to those, indeed, who in continuance of a good work, seek glory, and honor, and incorruptibility—continuous life; 8 and to those contentious, and disobedient, indeed, to the truth, and obeying the unrighteousness—indignation and wrath, 9 tribulation and distress, on every soul of man that is working the evil, both of Jew first, and of Greek; 10 and glory, and honor, and peace, to everyone who is working the good, both to Jew first, and to Greek. 11 For there is no favor by appearance with God, 12 for as many as sinned without law, will also perish without law, and as many as sinned in law, through law will be judged, 13 for not the hearers of the Law [are] righteous before God, but the doers of the Law will be declared righteous. 14 For when nations that have no law, by nature may do the things of the Law, these not having a law—to themselves are a law, 15 who show the work of the Law written in their hearts, their conscience also witnessing with them, and between one another the thoughts accusing or else defending, 16 in the day when God will judge the secrets of men, according to my good news, through Jesus Christ. 17 Behold, you are named a Jew, and rest on the Law, and boast in God, 18 and know the will, and approve the distinctions, being instructed out of the Law, 19 and have confidence that you yourself are a leader of blind ones, a light of those in darkness, 20 a corrector of foolish ones, a teacher of babies, having the form of the knowledge and of the truth in the Law. 21 You, then, who are teaching another, do you not teach yourself? 22 you who are preaching not to steal, do you steal? you who are saying not to commit adultery, do you commit adultery? you who are abhorring the idols, do you rob temples? 23 you who boast in the Law, through the transgression of the Law do you dishonor God? 24 for evil is spoken of the Name of

God among the nations because of you, according as it has been written. 25 For circumcision, indeed, profits, if you may practice law, but if you may be a transgressor of law, your circumcision has become uncircumcision. 26 If, therefore, the uncircumcision may keep the righteousness of the Law, will not his uncircumcision be reckoned for circumcision? 27 and the uncircumcision, by nature, fulfilling the Law, will judge you who, through letter and circumcision, [are] a transgressor of law. 28 For he is not a Jew who is [so] outwardly, neither [is] circumcision that which is outward in flesh; 29 but a Jew [is] he who is [so] inwardly, and circumcision [is] of the heart, in spirit, not in letter, of which the praise is not of men, but of God.

CHAPTER 3

1 What, then, [is] the superiority of the Jew? or what the profit of the circumcision? 2 much in every way; for first, indeed, that they were entrusted with the oracles of God; 3 for what, if certain were faithless? will their faithlessness make the faithfulness of God useless? 4 let it not be! And let God become true, and every man false, according as it has been written: "That You may be declared righteous in Your words, and may overcome in Your being judged." 5 And if our unrighteousness establishes God's righteousness, what will we say? is God unrighteous who is inflicting the wrath? (I speak after the manner of a man.) 6 Let it not be! Since how will God judge the world? 7 for if the truth of God in my falsehood abounded more to His glory, why am I also yet judged as a sinner? 8 and not, as we are spoken evil of, and as certain affirm us to say, "We may do the evil things, that the good ones may come?" Whose judgment is righteous. 9 What, then? are we better? not at all! For we charged before both Jews and Greeks with being all under sin, 10 according as it has been written: "There is none righteous, not even one; 11 there is none who is understanding, there is none who is seeking after God. 12 All went out of the way, together they became unprofitable, there is none doing good, there is not even one. 13 Their throat [is] an opened grave; with their tongues they used deceit; poison of cobras [is] under their lips— 14 whose mouth is full of cursing and bitterness. 15 Their feet [are] swift to shed blood. 16 Ruin and misery [are] in their ways. 17 And a way of peace they did not know. 18 There is no fear of God before their eyes." 19 And we have known that as many things as the Law says, to those in the Law it speaks, that every mouth may be stopped, and all the world may come under judgment to God; 20 for this reason by works of law will no flesh be declared righteous before Him, for through law is a knowledge of sin. 21 And now apart from law the righteousness of God has been revealed, testified to by the Law and the Prophets, 22 and the righteousness of God [is] through the faith of Jesus Christ to all, and on all those believing—for there is no difference, 23 for all have sinned and fall short of the glory of God— 24 being declared righteous freely by His grace through the redemption that [is] in Christ Jesus, 25 whom God set forth [as] a propitiatory covering, through faith in His blood, for the showing forth of His righteousness, because of the passing over of the former sins in the forbearance of God— 26 for the showing forth of His righteousness in the present time, for His being righteous, and declaring him righteous who [is] of the faith of Jesus. 27 Where then [is] the boasting? it was excluded; by what law? of works? no, but by a law of faith: 28 therefore we reckon a man to be declared righteous by faith, apart from works of law. 29 [Is He] only the God of Jews, and not also of nations? 30 yes, also of nations; since [there is] one God who will declare righteous circumcision by faith, and uncircumcision through faith. 31 Do we then make law useless through faith? let it not be! Indeed, we establish law.

CHAPTER 4

1 What, then, will we say Abraham our father to have found, according to flesh? 2 for if Abraham was declared righteous by works, he has to boast—but not before God; 3 for what does the writing say? "And Abraham believed God, and it was reckoned to him for righteousness"; 4 and to him who is working, the reward is not reckoned of grace, but of debt; 5 and to him who is not working, and is believing on Him who is declaring righteous the impious, his faith is reckoned for righteousness— 6 even as David also speaks of the blessedness of the man to whom God reckons righteousness apart from works: 7 "Blessed [are] they whose lawless acts were forgiven, || And whose sins were covered; 8 Blessed [is] the man || To whom the Lord may not reckon sin." 9 [Is] this blessedness, then, on the circumcision, or also on the uncircumcision—for we say that faith was reckoned to Abraham for righteousness? 10 how then was it reckoned? he being in circumcision, or in uncircumcision? not in circumcision, but in uncircumcision; 11 and he received a sign of circumcision, a seal of the righteousness of faith in the uncircumcision, for his being father of all those believing through uncircumcision, for the righteousness also being reckoned to them, 12 and father of circumcision to those not of circumcision only, but who also walk in the steps of faith, that [is] in the uncircumcision of our father Abraham. 13 For not through law [is] the promise to Abraham, or to his seed, of his being heir of the world, but through the righteousness of faith; 14 for if they who are of law [are] heirs, faith has been made void, and the promise has been made useless; 15 for the Law works wrath; for where law is not, neither [is] transgression. 16 Because of this [it is] of faith, that [it may be] according to grace, for the promise being sure to all the seed, not to that which [is] of the Law only, but also to that which [is] of the faith of Abraham, 17 who is father of us all (according as it has been written: "A father of many nations I have set you,") before Him whom he believed—God, who is quickening the dead, and is calling the things that are not as being. 18 Who, against hope, believed in hope, for his becoming father of many nations according to that spoken: "So will your seed be"; 19 and having not been weak in faith, he did not consider his own body, already become dead (being about one hundred years old), and the deadness of Sarah's womb, 20 and at the promise of God did not stagger in unbelief, but was strengthened in faith, having given glory to God, 21 and having been fully persuaded that what He has promised He is also able to do: 22 for this reason also it was reckoned to him for righteousness. 23 And it was not written on his account alone that it was reckoned to him, 24 but also on ours, to whom it is about to be reckoned—to us believing on Him who raised up Jesus our Lord out of the dead, 25 who was delivered up because of our offenses, and was raised up because of our being declared righteous.

CHAPTER 5

1 Having been declared righteous, then, by faith, we have peace toward God through our Lord Jesus Christ, 2 through whom also we have the access by faith into this grace in which we have stood, and we boast on the hope of the glory of God. 3 And not only [so], but we also boast in the tribulations, knowing that the tribulation works endurance; 4 and the endurance, experience; and the experience, hope; 5 and the hope does not make ashamed, because the love of God has been poured forth in our hearts through the Holy Spirit that has been given to us. 6 For in our being still ailing, Christ in due time died for the impious; 7 for scarcely for a righteous man will anyone die, for the good man perhaps someone also dares to die; 8 and God commends His own love to us, that, in our being still sinners, Christ died for us; 9 much more, then, having been declared righteous now in His blood, we will be saved through Him from the wrath; 10 for if, being enemies, we have been reconciled to God through the death of His Son, much more, having been reconciled, we will be saved in His life. 11 And not only [so], but we are also boasting in God, through our Lord Jesus Christ, through whom we now received the reconciliation; 12 because of this, even as through one man sin entered into the world, and through sin—death; and thus to all men death passed through, for that all sinned; 13 for until law sin was in the world: and sin is not reckoned when there is not law; 14 but death reigned from Adam until Moses, even on those having not sinned in the likeness of Adam's transgression, who is a type of Him who is coming. 15 But not as the offense so also [is] the free gift; for if by the offense of the one the many died, much more the grace of God, and the free gift in grace of the one man Jesus Christ, abound to the many; 16 and not as through one who sinned [is] the free gift, for the judgment indeed [is] of one to condemnation, but the gift [is] of many offenses to a declaration of "Righteous," 17 for if by the offense of the one death reigned through the one,

much more those who are receiving the abundance of grace and of the free gift of righteousness, in life will reign through the one—Jesus Christ. 18 So, then, as through one offense to all men [it is] to condemnation, so also through one declaration of "Righteous" [it is] to all men to justification of life; 19 for as through the disobedience of the one man, the many were constituted sinners: so also through the obedience of the One, will the many be constituted righteous. 20 And law came in, that the offense might abound, and where sin abounded, grace hyper-abounded, 21 that even as sin reigned in death, so also grace may reign, through righteousness, to continuous life, through Jesus Christ our Lord.

CHAPTER 6

1 What, then, will we say? will we continue in sin that grace may abound? 2 let it not be! We who died to sin—how will we still live in it? 3 are you ignorant that we, as many as were immersed into Christ Jesus, were immersed into His death? 4 we were buried together, then, with Him through the immersion into death, that even as Christ was raised up out of the dead through the glory of the Father, so we also might walk in newness of life. 5 For if we have become planted together to the likeness of His death, [so] we also will be of the resurrection; 6 knowing this, that our old man was crucified with [Him], that the body of sin may be made useless, for our no longer serving sin, 7 for he who has died has been set free from sin. 8 And if we died with Christ, we believe that we also will live with Him, 9 knowing that Christ, having been raised up out of the dead, dies no more; death has no more lordship over Him; 10 for in that He died, He died to sin once, and in that He lives, He lives to God; 11 so also you, reckon yourselves to be dead indeed to sin, and living to God in Jesus Christ our Lord. 12 Do not let then sin reign in your mortal body, to obey it in its desires; 13 neither present your members instruments of unrighteousness to sin, but present yourselves to God as living out of the dead, and your members instruments of righteousness to God; 14 for sin will not have lordship over you, for you are not under law, but under grace. 15 What then? will we sin because we are not under law but under grace? let it not be! 16 have you not known that to whom you present yourselves servants for obedience, servants you are to him to whom you obey, whether of sin to death, or of obedience to righteousness? 17 and thanks to God, that you were servants of sin, and—were obedient from the heart to the form of teaching to which you were delivered up; 18 and having been freed from sin, you became servants to righteousness. 19 I speak in a human [way], because of the weakness of your flesh, for even as you presented your members servants to the uncleanness and to the lawlessness—to the lawlessness, so now present your members servants to righteousness—to sanctification, 20 for when you were servants of sin, you were free from righteousness. 21 What fruit, therefore, were you having then, in the things of which you are now ashamed? for the end of those [is] death. 22 And now, having been freed from sin, and having become servants to God, you have your fruit—to sanctification, and the end continuous life; 23 for the wages of sin [is] death, and the gift of God [is] continuous life in Christ Jesus our Lord.

CHAPTER 7

1 Are you ignorant, brothers—for to those knowing law I speak—that the law has lordship over the man as long as he lives? 2 for the married woman to the living husband has been bound by law, and if the husband may die, she has been free from the law of the husband; 3 so then, the husband being alive, she will be called an adulteress if she may become another man's; and if the husband may die, she is free from the law, so as not to be an adulteress, having become another man's. 4 So that, my brothers, you also were made dead to the law through the body of the Christ, for your becoming another's, who was raised up out of the dead, that we might bear fruit to God; 5 for when we were in the flesh, the passions of sins, that [are] through the Law, were working in our members, to bear fruit to death; 6 and now we have ceased from the Law, that being dead in which we were held, so that we may serve in newness of spirit, and not in oldness of letter. 7 What, then, will we say? The Law [is] sin? let it not be! But I

did not know sin except through law, for also the covetousness I had not known if the Law had not said: 8 "You will not covet"; and sin having received an opportunity, through the command, worked in me all covetousness—for apart from law sin is dead. 9 And I was alive apart from law once, and the command having come, sin revived, and I died; 10 and the command that [is] for life, this was found by me for death; 11 for sin, having received an opportunity, through the command, deceived me, and through it, slew [me], 12 so that the Law, indeed, [is] holy, and the command holy, and righteous, and good. 13 That which is good then, has it become death to me? let it not be! But sin, that it might appear sin, through the good, working death to me, that sin might become exceedingly sinful through the command. 14 For we have known that the Law is spiritual, and I am fleshly, sold by sin; 15 for that which I work, I do not acknowledge; for not what I will, this I practice, but what I hate, this I do. 16 And if what I do not will, this I do, I consent to the Law that [it is] good, 17 and now it is no longer I that work it, but sin dwelling in me, 18 for I have known that there does not dwell in me, that is, in my flesh, good: for to will is present with me, and I do not find to work that which is right, 19 for the good that I will, I do not do; but the evil that I do not will, this I practice. 20 And if what I do not will, this I do, it is no longer I that work it, but sin that is dwelling in me. 21 I find, then, the law, that when I desire to do what is right, the evil is present with me, 22 for I delight in the Law of God according to the inward man, 23 and I behold another law in my members, warring against the law of my mind, and bringing me into captivity to the law of sin that [is] in my members. 24 A wretched man I [am]! Who will deliver me out of the body of this death? 25 I thank God—through Jesus Christ our Lord; so then, I myself indeed serve the Law of God with the mind, and with the flesh, the law of sin.

CHAPTER 8

1 There is, then, now no condemnation to those in Christ Jesus, who walk not according to the flesh, but according to the Spirit; 2 for the law of the Spirit of life in Christ Jesus set me free from the law of sin and of death; 3 for what the Law was not able to do, in that it was weak through the flesh, God, His own Son having sent in the likeness of sinful flesh, and for sin, condemned sin in the flesh, 4 that the righteousness of the Law may be fulfilled in us, who do not walk according to the flesh, but according to the Spirit. 5 For those who are according to the flesh, mind the things of the flesh; and those according to the Spirit, the things of the Spirit; 6 for the mind of the flesh [is] death, and the mind of the Spirit—life and peace; 7 because the mind of the flesh [is] enmity to God, for to the Law of God it does not subject itself, 8 for neither is it able; and those who are in the flesh are not able to please God. 9 And you are not in the flesh, but in the Spirit, if indeed the Spirit of God dwells in you; and if anyone does not have the Spirit of Christ—this one is not His; 10 and if Christ [is] in you, the body, indeed, [is] dead because of sin, and the Spirit [is] life because of righteousness, 11 and if the Spirit of Him who raised up Jesus out of the dead dwells in you, He who raised up the Christ out of the dead will also quicken your dying bodies, through His Spirit dwelling in you. 12 So, then, brothers, we are debtors, not to the flesh, to live according to the flesh; 13 for if according to the flesh you live, you are about to die; and if, by the Spirit, the deeds of the body you put to death, you will live; 14 for as many as are led by the Spirit of God, these are the sons of God; 15 for you did not receive a spirit of bondage again for fear, but you received [the] Spirit of adoption in which we cry, "Abba! Father!" 16 [This] One—the Spirit—testifies with our spirit, that we are children of God; 17 and if children, also heirs, heirs, indeed, of God, and heirs together of Christ—if, indeed, we suffer together, that we may also be glorified together. 18 For I reckon that the sufferings of the present time [are] not worthy [to be compared] with the glory about to be revealed in us; 19 for the earnest looking out of the creation expects the revelation of the sons of God; 20 for to vanity was the creation made subject—not of its will, but because of Him who subjected [it]—in hope, 21 that also the creation itself will be set free from the servitude of the corruption to the liberty of the glory of the children of God; 22 for we have known that all the creation groans together, and travails in pain together until now. 23 And not only [so], but also we ourselves, having the first-fruit of the Spirit, we also ourselves groan in ourselves, expecting adoption—the redemption of our body; 24

for in hope we were saved, and hope beheld is not hope; for what anyone beholds, why does he also hope for [it]? 25 and if what we do not behold we hope for, through continuance we expect [it]. 26 And in like manner also, the Spirit helps our weaknesses; for what we may pray for, as it is necessary, we have not known, but [this] One—the Spirit—makes intercession for us with unutterable groanings, 27 and He who is searching the hearts has known what [is] the mind of the Spirit, because according to God He intercedes for holy ones. 28 And we have known that to those loving God all things work together for good, to those who are called according to purpose; 29 because whom He foreknew, He also foreordained, conformed to the image of His Son, that He might be firstborn among many brothers; 30 and whom He foreordained, these also He called; and whom He called, these also He declared righteous; and whom He declared righteous, these also He glorified. 31 What, then, will we say to these things? if God [is] for us, who [is] against us? 32 He who indeed did not spare His own Son, but delivered Him up for us all, how will He not also with Him grant to us all things? 33 Who will lay a charge against the chosen ones of God? God [is] He that is declaring righteous; 34 who [is] he that is condemning? Christ [is] He that died, indeed, rather also, was raised up; who is also on the right hand of God—who also interceded for us. 35 Who will separate us from the love of the Christ? tribulation, or distress, or persecution, or famine, or nakedness, or peril, or sword? 36 According as it has been written: "For Your sake we are put to death all the day long; we were reckoned as sheep of slaughter." 37 But in all these we more than conquer, through Him who loved us; 38 for I am persuaded that neither death, nor life, nor messengers, nor principalities, nor powers, nor things present, 39 nor things about to be, nor height, nor depth, nor any other created thing, will be able to separate us from the love of God that [is] in Christ Jesus our Lord.

CHAPTER 9

1 Truth I say in Christ, I do not lie, my conscience bearing testimony with me in the Holy Spirit, 2 that I have great grief and unceasing pain in my heart— 3 for I was wishing, I myself, to be accursed from the Christ—for my brothers, my relatives, according to the flesh, 4 who are Israelites, whose [is] the adoption, and the glory, and the covenants, and the lawgiving, and the service, and the promises, 5 whose [are] the fathers, and of whom [is] the Christ, according to the flesh, who is God over all, blessed for all ages. Amen. 6 And it is not possible that the word of God has failed; for not all who [are] of Israel are these of Israel; 7 nor because they are seed of Abraham [are] all children, but, "in Isaac a seed be called to you"; 8 that is, the children of the flesh—these [are] not children of God; but the children of the promise are reckoned for seed; 9 for the word of promise [is] this: "According to this time I will come, and there will be to Sarah a son." 10 And not only [so], but also Rebecca, having conceived by one—our father Isaac 11 (for they being not yet born, neither having done anything good or evil, that the purpose of God, according to [divine] selection, might remain; not of works, but of Him who is calling), 12 it was said to her, "The greater will serve the less"; 13 according as it has been written: "Jacob I loved, and Esau I hated." 14 What, then, will we say? unrighteousness [is] with God? let it not be! 15 for to Moses He says, "I will do kindness to whom I do kindness, and I will have compassion on whom I have compassion"; 16 so then—not of him who is willing, nor of him who is running, but of God who is doing kindness; 17 for the Writing says to Pharaoh, "For this very thing I raised you up, that I might show in you My power, and that My Name might be declared in all the land"; 18 so then, to whom He wills, He does kindness, and to whom He wills, He hardens. 19 You will say, then, to me, "Why does He yet find fault? for who has resisted His counsel?" 20 no, but, O man, who are you that are answering again to God? will the thing formed say to Him who formed [it], Why did you make me thus? 21 Does the potter not have authority over the clay, out of the same lump to make one vessel to honor and one to dishonor? 22 And if God, willing to show the wrath and to make known His power, endured, in much long suffering, vessels of wrath fitted for destruction, 23 and that He might make known the riches of His glory on vessels of kindness, that He before prepared for glory, whom also He called—us— 24 not only out of Jews, but also out of nations, 25 as also in Hosea He says, "I will call

what [is] not My people—My people; and her not beloved—Beloved, 26 and it will be—in the place where it was said to them, You [are] not My people; there they will be called sons of the living God." 27 And Isaiah cries concerning Israel, "If the number of the sons of Israel may be as the sand of the sea, the remnant will be saved; 28 for a matter He is finishing, and is cutting short in righteousness, because a matter cut short will the Lord do on the land." 29 and according as Isaiah says before, "Except the Lord of Hosts left to us a seed, we had become as Sodom, and we had been made like Gomorrah." 30 What, then, will we say? that nations who are not pursuing righteousness attained to righteousness, and righteousness that [is] of faith, 31 and Israel, pursuing a law of righteousness, did not arrive at a law of righteousness; 32 why? because—not by faith, but as by works of law; for they stumbled at the stone of stumbling, 33 according as it has been written: "Behold, I place in Zion a stone of stumbling and a rock of offense; and everyone who is believing thereon will not be ashamed."

CHAPTER 10

1 Brothers, the pleasure indeed of my heart, and my supplication that [is] to God for Israel, is—for salvation; 2 for I bear them testimony that they have a zeal of God, but not according to knowledge, 3 for not knowing the righteousness of God, and seeking to establish their own righteousness, they did not submit to the righteousness of God. 4 For Christ is an end of law for righteousness to everyone who is believing, 5 for Moses describes the righteousness that [is] of the Law, that, "The man who did them will live in them," 6 and the righteousness of faith thus speaks: "You may not say in your heart, Who will go up to Heaven?" (that is, to bring Christ down) 7 or, "Who will go down to the abyss?" (that is, to bring up Christ out of the dead). 8 But what does it say? "The saying is near you—in your mouth, and in your heart": that is, the saying of the faith that we preach; 9 that if you may confess with your mouth that Jesus [is] Lord, and may believe in your heart that God raised Him out of the dead, you will be saved, 10 for with the heart [one] believes to righteousness, and with the mouth is confession made to salvation; 11 for the Writing says, "Everyone who is believing on Him will not be ashamed," 12 for there is no difference between Jew and Greek, for the same Lord of all [is] rich to all those calling on Him, 13 for "Everyone who, if he may have called on the Name of the Lord, will be saved." 14 How then will they call on [Him] in whom they did not believe? and how will they believe [on Him] of whom they did not hear? and how will they hear apart from one preaching? 15 and how will they preach, if they may not be sent? according as it has been written: "How beautiful the feet of those proclaiming good tidings of peace, of those proclaiming good tidings of the good things!" 16 But they were not all obedient to the good tidings, for Isaiah says, "Lord, who gave credence to our report?" 17 so then faith [is] by a report, and the report through a saying of God, 18 but I say, did they not hear? yes, indeed, "their voice went forth to all the earth, and their sayings to the ends of the habitable world." 19 But I say, did Israel not know? first Moses says, "I will provoke you to jealousy by [that which is] not a nation, || By an unintelligent nation I will anger you," 20 and Isaiah is very bold and says, "I was found by those not seeking Me; I became visible to those not inquiring after Me"; 21 and to Israel He says, "All the day I stretched out My hands to a people unbelieving and contradicting."

CHAPTER 11

1 I say then, did God cast away His people? let it not be! For I am also an Israelite, of the seed of Abraham, of the tribe of Benjamin: 2 God did not cast away His people whom He knew before; have you not known—in Elijah—what the Writing says? how he pleads with God concerning Israel, saying, 3 "Lord, they killed Your prophets, and they dug down Your altars, and I was left alone, and they seek my life"; 4 but what does the divine answer say to him? "I left to Myself seven thousand men who did not bow a knee to Ba'al." 5 So then also in the present time there has been a remnant according to the [divine] selection of grace; 6 and if by grace, no longer of

works, otherwise grace becomes no longer grace; and if of works, it is no longer grace, otherwise work is no longer work. / What then? What Israel seeks after, this it did not obtain, and the chosen obtained, and the rest were hardened, 8 according as it has been written: "God gave to them a spirit of deep sleep, eyes not to see, and ears not to hear, to this very day," 9 and David says, "Let their table become for a snare, and for a trap, and for a stumbling-block, and for a repayment to them; 10 let their eyes be darkened—not to behold, and You always bow down their back." 11 I say then, did they stumble that they might fall? let it not be! But by their fall the salvation [is] to the nations, to arouse them to jealousy; 12 and if their fall [is] the riches of [the] world, and their diminishment the riches of nations, how much more their fullness? 13 For to you I speak—to the nations—inasmuch as I am indeed an apostle of nations, I glorify my ministry; 14 if I will arouse my own flesh to jealousy by any means, and will save some of them, 15 for if the casting away of them [is] a reconciliation of the world, what the reception—if not life out of the dead? 16 and if the first-fruit [is] holy, the lump also; and if the root [is] holy, the branches also. 17 And if certain of the branches were broken off, and you, being a wild olive tree, were grafted in among them, and became a fellow-partaker of the root and of the fatness of the olive tree— 18 do not boast against the branches; and if you boast, you do not bear the root, but the root you! 19 You will say, then, "The branches were broken off, that I might be grafted in"; right! 20 by unbelief they were broken off, and you have stood by faith; do not be high-minded, but be fearing; 21 for if God did not spare the natural branches—lest perhaps He also will not spare you. 22 Behold, then, goodness and severity of God—on those indeed who fell, severity; and on you, goodness, if you may remain in the goodness, otherwise, you also will be cut off. 23 And those also, if they may not remain in unbelief, will be grafted in, for God is able to graft them in again; 24 for if you, out of the olive tree, wild by nature, were cut out, and contrary to nature, were grafted into a good olive tree, how much rather will they, who [are] according to nature, be grafted into their own olive tree? 25 For I do not wish you to be ignorant, brothers, of this secret—that you may not be wise in your own conceits—that hardness in part to Israel has happened until the fullness of the nations may come in; 26 and so all Israel will be saved, according as it has been written: "There will come forth out of Zion He who is delivering, and He will turn away impiety from Jacob, 27 and this to them [is] the covenant from Me when I may take away their sins." 28 As regards, indeed, the good tidings, [they are] enemies on your account; and as regards the [divine] selection—beloved on account of the fathers; 29 for the gifts and the calling of God are irrevocable; 30 for as you also once did not believe in God, and now found kindness by the unbelief of these, 31 so also these now did not believe, that in your kindness they also may find kindness; 32 for God shut up together the whole to unbelief, that to the whole He might do kindness. 33 O depth of riches, and wisdom and knowledge of God! How unsearchable His judgments, and untraceable His ways! 34 for who knew the mind of the Lord? or who became His counselor? 35 or who first gave to Him, and it will be given back to him again? 36 because of Him, and through Him, and to Him [are] all things; to Him [is] the glory—for all ages. Amen.

CHAPTER 12

1 I call on you, therefore, brothers, through the compassions of God, to present your bodies [as] a sacrifice—living, sanctified, acceptable to God—your intelligent service; 2 and do not be conformed to this age, but be transformed by the renewing of your mind, for your proving what [is] the will of God—the good, and acceptable, and perfect. 3 For I say, through the grace that was given to me, to everyone who is among you, not to think above what it ought to think; but to think so as to think wisely, as to each God dealt a measure of faith, 4 for as in one body we have many members, and all the members do not have the same office, 5 so we, the many, are one body in Christ, and members of one another—each one. 6 And having gifts, different according to the grace that was given to us: whether prophecy, according to the proportion of faith; 7 or ministry, in the ministry; or he who is teaching, in the teaching; 8 or he who is exhorting, in the exhortation; he who is sharing, in simplicity; he who is leading, in diligence; he

who is doing kindness, in cheerfulness. 9 The love unhypocritical: abhorring the evil; cleaving to the good; 10 in the love of brothers, to one another kindly affectioned: in the honor going before one another; 11 in the diligence not slothful; in the spirit fervent; serving the Lord; 12 in the hope rejoicing; in the tribulation enduring; in the prayer persevering; 13 to the necessities of the holy ones communicating; the hospitality pursuing. 14 Bless those persecuting you; bless, and do not curse; 15 to rejoice with the rejoicing, and to weep with the weeping, 16 of the same mind toward one another, not minding the high things, but with the lowly going along; do not become wise in your own conceit; 17 giving back to no one evil for evil; providing right things before all men. 18 If possible—so far as in you—with all men being in peace; 19 not avenging yourselves, beloved, but give place to the wrath, for it has been written: "Vengeance [is] Mine, 20 I will repay again, says the Lord"; if, then, your enemy hungers, feed him; if he thirsts, give him drink; for doing this, you will heap coals of fire on his head. 21 Do not be overcome by the evil, but overcome, in the good, the evil.

CHAPTER 13

1 Let every soul be subject to the higher authorities, for there is no authority except from God, and the authorities existing are appointed by God, 2 so that he who is setting himself against the authority, has resisted against God's ordinance; and those resisting will receive judgment to themselves. 3 For those ruling are not a terror to the good works, but to the evil; and do you wish to not be afraid of the authority? Be doing that which is good, and you will have praise from it, 4 for it is a servant of God to you for good; and if you may do that which is evil, be fearing, for it does not bear the sword in vain; for it is a servant of God, an avenger for wrath to him who is doing that which is evil. 5 For this reason it is necessary to be subject, not only because of the wrath, but also because of the conscience, 6 for because of this you also pay tribute; for they are servants of God, on this very thing attending continually; 7 render, therefore, to all [their] dues; to whom tribute, the tribute; to whom custom, the custom; to whom fear, the fear; to whom honor, the honor. 8 To no one owe anything, except to love one another; for he who is loving the other—he has fulfilled law, 9 for, "You will not commit adultery, You will not murder, You will not steal, You will not bear false testimony, You will not covet"; and if there is any other command, in this word it is summed up, in this: "You will love your neighbor as yourself"; 10 the love to the neighbor works no ill; the love, therefore, [is] the fullness of law. 11 And this, knowing the time, that for us, the hour already [is] to be aroused out of sleep, for now our salvation [is] nearer than when we believed; 12 the night advanced, and the day came near; let us lay aside, therefore, the works of the darkness, and let us put on the armor of the light; 13 as in daytime, let us walk properly; not in reveling and drunkenness, not in promiscuity and licentiousness, not in strife and jealousy; 14 but put on the Lord Jesus Christ, and take no forethought for the flesh—for desires.

CHAPTER 14

1 And receive him who is weak in the faith—not to determinations of reasonings; 2 one believes that he may eat all things—and he who is weak eats herbs; 3 do not let him who is eating despise him who is not eating: and do not let him who is not eating judge him who is eating, for God received him. 4 You—who are you that are judging another's domestic [affairs]? to his own master he stands or falls; and he will be made to stand, for God is able to make him stand. 5 One judges one day above another, and another judges every day [alike]; let each be fully assured in his own mind. 6 He who is regarding the day, he regards [it] to the Lord, and he who is not regarding the day, he does not regard [it] to the Lord. He who is eating, he eats to the Lord, for he gives thanks to God; and he who is not eating, he does not eat to the Lord, and gives thanks to God. 7 For none of us lives to himself, and none dies to himself; 8 for both, if we may live, we live to the Lord; if also we may die, we die to the Lord; both then if we may live, also if we may die, we are the Lord's; 9 for because of this Christ both

died and rose again, and lived again, that He may be Lord both of dead and of living. 10 And you, why do you judge your brother? or again, you, why do you set at nothing your brother? for we will all stand at the judgment seat of the Christ; 11 for it has been written: "I live! Says the Lord—Every knee will bow to Me, and every tongue will confess to God"; 12 so, then, each of us will give reckoning to God concerning himself; 13 therefore, may we judge one another no longer, but rather judge this, not to put a stumbling-stone before the brother, or an offense. 14 I have known, and am persuaded, in the Lord Jesus, that nothing [is] unclean of itself, except to him who is reckoning anything to be unclean—to that one [it is] unclean; 15 and if your brother is grieved through food, you no longer walk according to love; do not destroy with your food that one for whom Christ died. 16 Do not let, then, evil be spoken of your good, 17 for the Kingdom of God is not eating and drinking, but righteousness, and peace, and joy in the Holy Spirit; 18 for he who in these things is serving the Christ, [is] acceptable to God and approved of men. 19 So, then, may we pursue the things of peace, and the things of building up one another. 20 Do not cast down the work of God for the sake of food; all things, indeed, [are] pure, but evil [is] to the man who is eating through stumbling. 21 [It is] not right to eat flesh, nor to drink wine, nor to [do anything] in which your brother stumbles, or is made to fall, or is weak. 22 You have faith! Have [it] to yourself before God; blessed is he who is not judging himself in what he approves, 23 and he who is making a difference, if he may eat, has been condemned, because [it is] not of faith; and all that [is] not of faith is sin.

CHAPTER 15

1 And we ought—we who are strong—to bear the weaknesses of the powerless, and not to please ourselves; 2 for let each one of us please the neighbor for good, for edification, 3 for even the Christ did not please Himself, but according as it has been written: "The reproaches of those reproaching You fell on Me"; 4 for as many things as were written before, for our instruction were written before, that through the endurance, and the exhortation of the Writings, we might have the hope. 5 And may the God of the endurance, and of the exhortation, give to you to have the same mind toward one another, according to Christ Jesus, 6 that with one accord—with one mouth—you may glorify the God and Father of our Lord Jesus Christ; 7 for this reason receive one another, according as also the Christ received us, to the glory of God. 8 And I say Jesus Christ to have become a servant of circumcision for the truth of God, to confirm the promises to the fathers, 9 and the nations for kindness to glorify God, according as it has been written: "Because of this I will confess to You among nations, and to Your Name I will sing praise"; 10 and again it says, "Rejoice you nations, with His people"; 11 and again, "Praise the Lord, all you nations; and laud Him, all you peoples"; 12 and again, Isaiah says, "There will be the root of Jesse, and He who is rising to rule nations—on Him will nations hope"; 13 and the God of the hope will fill you with all joy and peace in the believing, for your abounding in the hope in power of the Holy Spirit. 14 And I am persuaded, my brothers—I myself also—concerning you, that you yourselves also are full of goodness, having been filled with all knowledge, also able to admonish one another; 15 and the more boldly I wrote to you, brothers, in part, as putting you in mind, because of the grace that is given to me by God, 16 for my being a servant of Jesus Christ to the nations, acting as priest in the good news of God, that the offering up of the nations may become acceptable, sanctified by the Holy Spirit. 17 I have, then, a boasting in Christ Jesus, in the things pertaining to God, 18 for I will not dare to speak anything of the things that Christ did not work through me, to obedience of nations, by word and deed, 19 in power of signs and wonders, in power of the Spirit of God; so that I, from Jerusalem, and in a circle as far as Illyricum, have fully preached the good news of the Christ; 20 and so counting it honor to proclaim good news, not where Christ was named—that on another's foundation I might not build— 21 but according as it has been written: "To whom it was not told concerning Him, they will see; and they who have not heard, will understand." 22 For this reason, also, I was hindered many times from coming to you, 23 and now, no longer having place in these parts, and having a longing to come to you for many years, 24 when I may go on to Spain I will come to you, for I hope in going through, to see you, and by you to be set forward there, if of you first, in part, I will be filled. 25 And now, I go on to Jerusalem, ministering to the holy ones; 26 for it pleased Macedonia and Achaia well to make a certain contribution for the poor of the holy ones who [are] in Jerusalem; 27 for it pleased well, and their debtors they are, for if the nations participated in their spiritual things, they ought also, in the fleshly things, to minister to them. 28 This, then, having finished, and having sealed to them this fruit, I will return through you, to Spain; 29 and I have known that coming to you—in the fullness of the blessing of the good news of Christ I will come. 30 And I call on you, brothers, through our Lord Jesus Christ, and through the love of the Spirit, to strive together with me in the prayers for me to God, 31 that I may be delivered from those not believing in Judea, and that my ministry, that [is] for Jerusalem, may become acceptable to the holy ones; 32 that in joy I may come to you, through the will of God, and may be refreshed with you, 33 and the God of peace [be] with you all. Amen.

CHAPTER 16

1 And I commend you to Phoebe our sister—being a servant of the assembly that [is] in Cenchrea— 2 that you may receive her in the Lord, worthily of the holy ones, and may assist her in whatever matter she may have need of you, for she also became a leader of many, and of myself. 3 Greet Priscilla and Aquilas, my fellow-workmen in Christ Jesus— 4 who laid down their own neck for my life, to whom not only I give thanks, but also all the assemblies of the nations— 5 and the assembly at their house; greet Epaenetus, my beloved, who is first-fruit of Achaia to Christ. 6 Greet Mary, who labored much for us; 7 greet Andronicus and Junias, my relatives, and my fellow-captives, who are of note among the apostles, who also have been in Christ before me. 8 Greet Amplias, my beloved in the Lord; 9 greet Arbanus, our fellow-workman in Christ, and Stachys, my beloved; 10 greet Apelles, the approved in Christ; greet those of the [household] of Aristobulus; 11 greet Herodion, my relative; greet those of the [household] of Narcissus, who are in the Lord; 12 greet Tryphaena, and Tryphosa, who are laboring in the Lord; greet Persis, the beloved, who labored much in the Lord. 13 Greet Rufus, the chosen one in the Lord, and his mother and mine, 14 greet Asyncritus, Phlegon, Hermas, Patrobas, Hermes, and the brothers with them; 15 greet Philologus, and Julias, Nereus, and his sister, and Olympas, and all the holy ones with them; 16 greet one another in a holy kiss; the assemblies of Christ greet you. 17 And I call on you, brothers, to mark those who are causing the divisions and the stumbling-blocks, contrary to the teaching that you learned, and turn away from them; 18 for such do not serve our Lord Jesus Christ, but their own belly; and through the good word and fair speech they deceive the hearts of the harmless. 19 For your obedience reached to all; I rejoice, therefore, as regards you, and I wish you to be wise, indeed, as to the good, and pure as to the evil; 20 and the God of peace will bruise Satan under your feet quickly; the grace of our Lord Jesus Christ [be] with you. Amen! 21 Timotheus greets you, my fellow-workman, and Lucius, and Jason, and Sosipater, my relatives; 22 I, Tertius, greet you (who wrote the letter) in the Lord; 23 Gaius greets you, my host, and of the whole Assembly; Erastus greets you, the steward of the city, and Quartus the brother. 24 [[The grace of our Lord Jesus Christ [be] with you all! Amen.]] 25 And to Him who is able to establish you, according to my good news, and the preaching of Jesus Christ, according to the revelation of the secret, having been kept secret in the times of the ages, 26 and now having been revealed, also, through prophetic writings, according to a command of the perpetual God, having been made known to all the nations for obedience of faith— 27 to the only wise God, through Jesus Christ, to Him [be] glory for all ages. Amen.

1 CORINTHIANS

CHAPTER 1

1 Paul, a called apostle of Jesus Christ, through the will of

God, and Sosthenes the brother, 2 to the Assembly of God that is in Corinth, to those sanctified in Christ Jesus, called holy ones, with all those calling on the Name of our Lord Jesus Christ in every place—both theirs and ours: 3 Grace to you and peace from God our Father and the Lord Jesus Christ! 4 I give thanks to my God always concerning you for the grace of God that was given to you in Christ Jesus, 5 that in everything you were enriched in Him, in all discourse and all knowledge, 6 according as the testimony of the Christ was confirmed in you, 7 so that you are not behind in any gift, waiting for the revelation of our Lord Jesus Christ, 8 who also will confirm you to the end—unblamable in the day of our Lord Jesus Christ; 9 faithful [is] God, through whom you were called into the fellowship of His Son Jesus Christ our Lord. 10 And I call on you, brothers, through the Name of our Lord Jesus Christ, that the same thing you may all say, and there may not be divisions among you, and you may be perfected in the same mind, and in the same judgment, 11 for it was signified to me concerning you, my brothers, by those of Chloe, that contentions are among you; 12 and I say this, that each one of you says, "I, indeed, am of Paul," and "I of Apollos," and "I of Cephas," and "I of Christ." 13 Has the Christ been divided? was Paul crucified for you? or were you immersed into the name of Paul? 14 I give thanks to God that I immersed no one of you, except Crispus and Gaius—15 that no one may say that to my own name I immersed; 16 and I also immersed Stephanas' household—further, I have not known if I immersed any other. 17 For Christ did not send me to immerse, but to proclaim good news, not in wisdom of discourse, that the Cross of the Christ may not be made of no effect; 18 for the word of the Cross to those indeed perishing is foolishness, and to us—those being saved—it is the power of God, 19 for it has been written: "I will destroy the wisdom of the wise, and the intelligence of the intelligent I will bring to nothing"; 20 where [is] the wise? where the scribe? where a disputer of this age? did God not make foolish the wisdom of this world? 21 For seeing in the wisdom of God the world through the wisdom did not know God, it pleased God through the foolishness of the preaching to save those believing. 22 Since also Jews ask a sign, and Greeks seek wisdom, 23 also we preach Christ crucified, to Jews, indeed, a stumbling-block, and to Greeks foolishness, 24 and to those called—both Jews and Greeks—Christ the power of God, and the wisdom of God, 25 because the foolishness of God is wiser than men, and the weakness of God is stronger than men; 26 for see your calling, brothers, that not many [are] wise according to the flesh, not many mighty, not many noble; 27 but God chose the foolish things of the world that He may put the wise to shame; and God chose the weak things of the world that He may put the strong to shame; 28 and God chose the base things of the world, and the things despised, and the things that are not, that He may make useless the things that are— 29 that no flesh may glory before Him; 30 but out of Him you are in Christ Jesus, who became to us from God wisdom, righteousness also, and sanctification, and redemption, 31 that, according as it has been written: "He who is glorying—let him glory in the Lord."

CHAPTER 2

1 And I, having come to you, brothers, came—not in superiority of discourse or wisdom—declaring to you the testimony of God, 2 for I decided not to know anything among you, except Jesus Christ, and Him crucified; 3 and I, in weakness, and in fear, and in much trembling, was with you; 4 and my word and my preaching was not in persuasive words of wisdom, but in demonstration of the Spirit and of power— 5 that your faith may not be in the wisdom of men, but in the power of God. 6 And wisdom we speak among the perfect, and wisdom not of this age, nor of the rulers of this age—of those becoming useless, 7 but we speak the hidden wisdom of God in a secret, that God foreordained before the ages to our glory, 8 which no one of the rulers of this age knew, for if they had known, they would not have crucified the Lord of Glory; 9 but according as it has been written: "What eye did not see, and ear did not hear, and on the heart of man did not come up, what God prepared for those loving Him"; 10 but God revealed [them] to us through His Spirit, for the Spirit searches all things, even the depths of God, 11 for who of men has known the things of the man, except the spirit of the man that [is] in him? so also the things of God no one has known, except the

Spirit of God. 12 And we did not receive the spirit of the world, but the Spirit that [is] of God, that we may know the things conferred by God on us, 13 which things we also speak, not in words taught by human wisdom, but in those taught by the Holy Spirit, comparing spiritual things with spiritual things, 14 and the natural man does not receive the things of the Spirit of God, for they are foolishness to him, and he is not able to know [them], because they are discerned spiritually; 15 and he who is spiritual, indeed discerns all things, and he himself is discerned by no one; 16 for who knew the mind of the Lord that he will instruct Him? and we have the mind of Christ.

CHAPTER 3

1 And I, brothers, was not able to speak to you as to spiritual, but as to fleshly—as to babies in Christ; 2 with milk I fed you, and not with meat, for you were not yet able, but not even yet are you now able, 3 for yet you are fleshly, for where [there is] among you envying, and strife, and divisions, are you not fleshly, and walk in the manner of men? 4 for when one may say, "I, indeed, am of Paul," and another, "I—of Apollos," are you not fleshly? 5 Who, then, is Paul, and who Apollos, but servants through whom you believed, and to each as the Lord gave? 6 I planted, Apollos watered, but God was giving growth; 7 so that neither is he who is planting anything, nor he who is watering, but He who is giving growth—God; 8 and he who is planting and he who is watering are one, and each will receive his own reward according to his own labor, 9 for we are fellow-workmen of God; you are God's tillage, God's building. 10 According to the grace of God that was given to me, as a wise master-builder, I have laid a foundation, and another builds on [it], 11 for no one is able to lay another foundation except that which is laid, which is Jesus the Christ; 12 and if anyone builds on this foundation gold, silver, precious stones, wood, hay, straw— 13 the work will become visible of each, for the day will declare [it], because it is revealed in fire, and the work of each, what kind it is, the fire will prove; 14 if the work of anyone remains that he built on [it], he will receive a wage; 15 if the work of any is burned up, he will suffer loss, but himself will be saved, but so as through fire. 16 have you not known that you are a temple of God, and the Spirit of God dwells in you? 17 if anyone ruins the temple of God, God will ruin him; for the temple of God is holy, which you are. 18 Let no one deceive himself; if anyone seems to be wise among you in this age—let him become a fool, that he may become wise, 19 for the wisdom of this world is foolishness with God, for it has been written: "Who is taking the wise in their craftiness"; 20 and again, "The Lord knows the reasonings of the wise, that they are vain." 21 So then, let no one glory in men, for all things are yours, 22 whether Paul, or Apollos, or Cephas, or the world, or life, or death, or things present, or things about to be—all are yours, 23 and you [are] Christ's, and Christ [is] God's.

CHAPTER 4

1 Let a man so reckon us as officers of Christ, and stewards of the secrets of God, 2 and as to the rest, it is required in the stewards that one may be found faithful, 3 and to me it is for a very little thing that by you I may be judged, or by man's Day, but I do not even judge myself, 4 for I have been conscious of nothing for myself, but I have not been declared right in this—and He who is discerning me is the Lord: 5 so, then, judge nothing before the time, until the Lord may come, who will both bring to light the hidden things of the darkness, and will reveal the counsels of the hearts, and then the praise will come to each from God. 6 And these things, brothers, I transferred to myself and to Apollos because of you, that in us you may learn not to think above that which has been written, that you may not be puffed up one for one against the other, 7 for who makes you to differ? and what do you have, that you did not receive? and if you also received, why do you glory as not having received? 8 Already you are having been filled, already you were rich, apart from us you reigned, and I also wish you reigned, that we also may reign together with you, 9 for I think that God set forth us the apostles last—as appointed to death, because we became a spectacle to the world, and messengers, and men; 10 we [are] fools because of Christ, and you wise in Christ; we [are] ailing, and you strong; you

glorious, and we dishonored; 11 to the present hour we both hunger, and thirst, and are naked, and are battered, and wander, 12 and labor, working with [our] own hands; being reviled, we bless; being persecuted, we endure; 13 being spoken evil of, we plead; we became as filth of the world—of all things an outcast—until now. 14 Not [as] putting you to shame do I write these things, but I admonish as my beloved children, 15 for if a myriad of child-conductors you may have in Christ, yet not many fathers; for in Christ Jesus, through the good news, I begot you; 16 I call on you, therefore, become followers of me; 17 because of this I sent to you Timotheus, who is my child, beloved and faithful in the Lord, who will remind you of my ways in Christ, according as everywhere in every assembly I teach. 18 And some were puffed up as if I were not coming to you; 19 but I will come quickly to you, if the Lord may will, and I will not know the word of those puffed up, but the power; 20 for not in word is the Kingdom of God, but in power. 21 what do you wish? Will I come to you with a rod, or in love, also with a spirit of meekness?

CHAPTER 5

1 Whoredom is actually heard of among you, and such whoredom as is not even named among the nations—as that one has the wife of the father! 2 And you are having been puffed up, and did not rather mourn, that he may be removed out of the midst of you who did this work, 3 for I indeed, as being absent as to the body, and present as to the spirit, have already judged, as being present, him who so worked this thing: 4 in the Name of our Lord Jesus Christ—you being gathered together, also my spirit—with the power of our Lord Jesus Christ, 5 to deliver up such a one to Satan for the destruction of the flesh, that the spirit may be saved in the Day of the Lord Jesus. 6 Your glorying [is] not good; have you not known that a little leaven leavens the whole lump? 7 cleanse out, therefore, the old leaven, that you may be a new lump, according as you are unleavened, for our Passover was sacrificed for us also—Christ, 8 so that we may keep the celebration, not with old leaven, nor with the leaven of evil and wickedness, but with unleavened [bread] of sincerity and truth. 9 I wrote to you in the letter, not to keep company with whoremongers— 10 and certainly not with the whoremongers of this world, or with the covetous, or extortioners, or idolaters, seeing you ought then to go forth out of the world— 11 and now, I wrote to you not to keep company with [him], if anyone, being named a brother, may be a whoremonger, or covetous, or an idolater, or a railer, or a drunkard, or an extortioner—do not even eat together with such a one; 12 for what have I also to judge those outside? Do you not judge those within? 13 and judge those without God; and put away the evil from among yourselves.

CHAPTER 6

1 Dare anyone of you, having a matter with the other, go to be judged before the unrighteous, and not before the holy ones? 2 have you not known that the holy ones will judge the world? and if the world is judged by you, are you unworthy of the smaller judgments? 3 have you not known that we will judge messengers? why not then the things of life? 4 of the things of life, indeed, then, if you may have judgment, those despised in the Assembly—these you cause to sit; 5 I speak to your shame: so there is not among you one wise man, not even one, who will be able to discern in the midst of his brothers! 6 but brother with brother goes to be judged, and this before unbelievers! 7 Already, indeed, then, there is altogether a fault among you, that you have judgments with one another; why do you not rather suffer injustice? why not be defrauded? 8 but you do injustice, and you defraud, and these—brothers! 9 have you not known that the unrighteous will not inherit the Kingdom of God? Do not be led astray; neither whoremongers, nor idolaters, nor adulterers, nor effeminate, nor sodomites, 10 nor thieves, nor covetous, nor drunkards, nor revilers, nor extortioners, will inherit the Kingdom of God. 11 And certain of you were these! But you were washed, but you were sanctified, but you were declared righteous, in the Name of the Lord Jesus, and in the Spirit of our God. 12 All things are lawful to me, but all things are not profitable; all things are lawful to me,

but I will not be under authority by any; 13 the meats [are] for the belly, and the belly for the meats. And God will make useless both this and these; and the body [is] not for whoredom, but for the Lord, and the Lord for the body; 14 and God raised both the Lord, and will raise us up through His power. 15 Have you not known that your bodies are members of Christ? having taken, then, the members of the Christ, will I make [them] members of a prostitute? let it not be! 16 have you not known that he who is joined to the prostitute is one body? For it says, "The two will be into one flesh." 17 And he who is joined to the Lord is one spirit; 18 flee the whoredom; every sin—whatever a man may commit—is outside the body, and he who is committing whoredom sins against his own body. 19 Have you not known that your body is a temple of the Holy Spirit in you, which you have from God? and you are not your own, 20 for you were bought with a price; glorify, then, God in your body and in your spirit, which are God's.

CHAPTER 7

1 And concerning the things of which you wrote to me: [it is] good for a man not to touch a woman, 2 and because of the whoredom let each man have his own wife, and let each woman have her proper husband; 3 to the wife let the husband render the due benevolence, and in like manner also the wife to the husband; 4 the wife does not have authority over her own body, but the husband; and in like manner also, the husband does not have authority over his own body, but the wife. 5 Do not defraud one another, except by consent for a time, that you may be free for fasting and prayer, and again may come together, that Satan may not tempt you because of your self-indulgence; 6 and this I say by way of concurrence—not of command, 7 for I wish all men to be even as I myself [am]; but each has his own gift of God, one indeed thus and one thus. 8 And I say to the unmarried and to the widows: it is good for them if they may remain even as I [am]; 9 and if they do not have continence—let them marry, for it is better to marry than to burn; 10 and to the married I announce—not I, but the Lord—do not let a wife separate from a husband: 11 but, and if she may separate, let her remain unmarried, or let her be reconciled to the husband, and do not let a husband send a wife away. 12 And to the rest I speak—not the Lord—if any brother has an unbelieving wife, and she is pleased to dwell with him, do not let him send her away; 13 and a woman who has an unbelieving husband, and he is pleased to dwell with her, do not let her send him away; 14 for the unbelieving husband has been sanctified in the wife, and the unbelieving wife has been sanctified in the husband; otherwise your children are unclean, but now they are holy. 15 And if the unbelieving separates himself—let him separate himself: the brother or the sister is not under servitude in such [cases], and in peace has God called us; 16 for what, have you known, O wife, whether you will save the husband? or what, have you known, O husband, whether you will save the wife? 17 if not, as God distributed to each, as the Lord has called each—so let him walk; and thus I direct in all the assemblies: 18 being circumcised—was anyone called? Do not let him become uncircumcised; in uncircumcision was anyone called? Do not let him be circumcised; 19 the circumcision is nothing, and the uncircumcision is nothing—but a keeping of the commands of God. 20 Each in the calling in which he was called—in this let him remain; 21 a servant—were you called? Do not be anxious; but if also you are able to become free—use [it] rather; 22 for he who [is] in the Lord—having been called a servant—is the Lord's freedman: in like manner also he the freeman, having been called, is servant of Christ: 23 you were bought with a price, do not become servants of men; 24 each, in that in which he was called, brothers, in this let him remain with God. 25 And concerning the virgins, I do not have a command of the Lord; and I give judgment as having obtained kindness from the Lord to be faithful. 26 I suppose, therefore, this to be good because of the present necessity, that [it is] good for a man that the matter be thus: 27 Have you been bound to a wife? Do not seek to be loosed; have you been loosed from a wife? Do not seek a wife. 28 But, and if you may marry, you did not sin; and if the virgin may marry, she did not sin; and such will have tribulation in the flesh: and I spare you. 29 And this I say, brothers, the time from now on is having been shortened—that both those having wives may be as not having; 30 and those weeping, as not weeping; and those rejoicing, as not rejoicing;

and those buying, as not possessing; 31 and those using this world, as not using [it] up; for the [present] form of this world is passing away. 32 And I wish you to be without anxiety; the unmarried is anxious for the things of the Lord, how he will please the Lord; 33 and the married is anxious for the things of the world, how he will please the wife. 34 The wife and the virgin have been distinguished: the unmarried is anxious for the things of the Lord, that she may be holy both in body and in spirit, and the married is anxious for the things of the world, how she will please the husband. 35 And this I say for your own profit: not that I may cast a noose on you, but for the seemliness and devotedness to the Lord, undistractedly, 36 and if anyone thinks [it] to be unseemly to his virgin, if she may be beyond the bloom of age, and it ought to be so, what he wills let him do; he does not sin—let him marry. 37 And he does well who has stood steadfast in the heart—not having necessity—and has authority over his own will, and he has determined this in his heart—to keep his own virgin; 38 so that both he who is giving in marriage does well, and he who is not giving in marriage does better. 39 A wife has been bound by law [for] as long [a] time as her husband may live, and if her husband may sleep, she is free to be married to whom she will—only in the Lord; 40 and she is happier if she may so remain—according to my judgment; and I think I also have the Spirit of God.

CHAPTER 8

1 And concerning the things sacrificed to idols, we have known that we all have knowledge: knowledge puffs up, but love builds up; 2 and if anyone thinks to know anything, he has not yet known anything according as it is required to know; 3 and if anyone loves God, this one has been known by Him. 4 Concerning the eating then of the things sacrificed to idols, we have known that an idol [is] nothing in the world, and that there is no other God except one; 5 for even if there are those called gods, whether in Heaven, whether on earth—as there are many gods and many lords— 6 yet to us [is] one God, the Father, of whom [are] all things, and we to Him; and one Lord, Jesus Christ, through whom [are] all things, and we through Him; 7 but not in all men [is] the knowledge, and certain with conscience of the idol, until now, eat [it] as a thing sacrificed to an idol, and their conscience, being weak, is defiled. 8 But food does not commend us to God, for neither if we may eat are we in advance; nor if we may not eat, are we behind; 9 but see, lest this privilege of yours may become a stumbling-block to the weak, 10 for if anyone may see you that have knowledge in an idol's temple reclining to eat, will not his conscience—he being weak—be emboldened to eat the things sacrificed to idols? 11 For the [one] being weak—the brother for whom Christ died—will perish by your knowledge. 12 and thus sinning in regard to the brothers, and striking their weak conscience—you sin in regard to Christ; 13 for this reason, if food causes my brother to stumble, I may not eat flesh—throughout the age—that I may not cause my brother to stumble.

CHAPTER 9

1 Am I not an apostle? am I not free? Have I not seen Jesus Christ our Lord? Are you not my work in the Lord? 2 if I am not an apostle to others—yet doubtless I am to you; for you are the seal of my apostleship in the Lord. 3 My defense to those who examine me in this: 4 do we not have authority to eat and to drink? 5 Do we not have authority to lead about a sister—a wife—as also the other apostles, and the brothers of the Lord, and Cephas? 6 or do only Barnabas and I have no authority not to work? 7 Who serves as a soldier at his own expense at any time? who plants a vineyard and does not eat of its fruit? or who feeds a flock and does not eat of the milk of the flock? 8 Do I speak these things according to man? or does the Law not also say these things? 9 For in the Law of Moses it has been written: "you will not muzzle an ox treading out grain"; does God care for the oxen? 10 Or by all means does He say [it] because of us? yes, because of us it was written, because in hope ought the plower to plow, and he who is treading [ought] of his hope to partake in hope. 11 If we sowed to you the spiritual things—[is it] great if we reap your fleshly things? 12 if others partake of the authority over you—[do] we not more?

but we did not use this authority, but we bear all things, that we may give no hindrance to the good news of the Christ. 13 Have you not known that those working about the things of the temple eat of the temple, and those waiting at the altar are partakers with the altar? 14 so also the Lord directed to those proclaiming the good news to live of the good news. 15 And I have used none of these things; neither did I write these things that it may be so done in my case, for [it is] good for me rather to die, than that anyone may make my glorying void; 16 for if I may proclaim good news, it is no glorying for me, for necessity is laid on me, and woe is to me if I may not proclaim good news; 17 for if I do this willingly, I have a reward; and if unwillingly—I have been entrusted with a stewardship! 18 What, then, is my reward? That proclaiming good news, without charge I will make the good news of the Christ, not to abuse my authority in the good news; 19 for being free from all men, I made myself servant to all men, that the more I might gain; 20 and to the Jews I became like a Jew, that I might gain Jews; to those under law as under law, that I might gain those under law; 21 to those without law, as without law—(not being without law to God, but within law to Christ)—that I might gain those without law; 22 to the weak I became weak, that I might gain the weak; to all men I have become all things, that by all means I may save some. 23 And I do this because of the good news, that I may become a fellow-partaker of it; 24 have you not known that those running in a race—all indeed run, but one receives the prize? so run that you may obtain; 25 and everyone who is striving is temperate in all things; these, indeed, then, that they may receive a corruptible garland, but we an incorruptible; 26 I, therefore, thus run, not as uncertainly, thus I fight, as not beating air; 27 but I bruise my body, and bring [it] into servitude, lest by any means, having preached to others—I myself may become disapproved.

CHAPTER 10

1 And I do not wish you to be ignorant, brothers, that all our fathers were under the cloud, and all passed through the sea, 2 and all were immersed into Moses in the cloud, and in the sea; 3 and all ate the same spiritual food, 4 and all drank the same spiritual drink, for they were drinking of a spiritual rock following them, and the rock was the Christ; 5 but in the most of them God was not well pleased, for they were strewn in the wilderness, 6 and those things became types of us, for our not passionately desiring evil things, as also these desired. 7 Neither become idolaters, as certain of them, as it has been written: "The people sat down to eat and to drink, and stood up to play"; 8 neither may we commit whoredom, as certain of them committed whoredom, and there fell in one day twenty-three thousand; 9 neither may we tempt the Christ, as also certain of them tempted, and perished by the serpents; 10 neither murmur, as also some of them murmured, and perished by the destroyer. 11 And all these things happened to those persons as types, and they were written for our admonition, to whom the end of the ages came, 12 so that he who is thinking to stand—let him observe, lest he fall. 13 No temptation has taken you—except that of man; and God is faithful, who will not permit you to be tempted above what you are able, but He will make, with the temptation, also the outlet, for your being able to bear [it]. 14 For this reason, my beloved, flee from the idolatry; 15 as to wise men I speak—judge what I say. 16 The cup of the blessing that we bless—is it not the fellowship of the blood of the Christ? the bread that we break—is it not the fellowship of the body of the Christ? 17 because one bread, one body, are we the many—for we all partake of the one bread. 18 See Israel according to the flesh! Are those not eating the sacrifices in the fellowship of the altar? 19 what do I say then? that an idol is anything? or that a sacrifice offered to an idol is anything? 20 [No,] but that the things that the nations sacrifice—they sacrifice to demons and not to God; and I do not wish you to come into the fellowship of the demons. 21 You are not able to drink the cup of the Lord and the cup of demons; you are not able to partake of the table of the Lord and of the table of demons; 22 do we arouse the Lord to jealousy? are we stronger than He? 23 All things are lawful to me, but not all things are profitable; all things are lawful to me, but not all things build up; 24 let no one seek his own—but each another's. 25 Eat whatever is sold in the meat-market, not inquiring, because of the conscience, 26 for the earth and its fullness [are] the Lord's; 27 and if anyone of the

unbelieving calls you, and you wish to go, eat all that is set before you, inquiring nothing, because of the conscience; 28 and if anyone may say to you, "This is a thing sacrificed to an idol," do not eat, because of that one who showed [it], and of the conscience, for the Lord's [is] the earth and its fullness: 29 and conscience, I say, not of yourself, but of the other, for why [is it] that my liberty is judged by another's conscience? 30 and if I partake thankfully, why am I spoken of [as] evil, for that for which I give thanks? 31 Whether, then, you eat, or drink, or do anything, do all to the glory of God; 32 become offenseless, both to Jews and Greeks, and to the Assembly of God; 33 as I also please all in all things, not seeking my own profit, but that of many—that they may be saved.

CHAPTER 11

1 Become followers of me, as I also [am] of Christ. 2 And I praise you, brothers, that in all things you remember me, and according as I delivered to you, you keep the deliverances, 3 and I wish you to know that the Christ is the head of every man, and the head of a woman is the husband, and the head of Christ is God. 4 Every man praying or prophesying, having the head covered, dishonors his head, 5 and every woman praying or prophesying with the head uncovered, dishonors her own head, for it is one and the same thing with her being shaven, 6 for if a woman is not covered—then let her be shorn, and if [it is] a shame for a woman to be shorn or shaven—let her be covered; 7 for a man, indeed, ought not to cover the head, being the image and glory of God, and a woman is the glory of a man, 8 for a man is not of a woman, but a woman [is] of a man, 9 for also was a man not created because of the woman, but a woman because of the man; 10 because of this the woman ought to have [a token of] authority on the head, because of the messengers; 11 but neither [is] a man apart from a woman, nor a woman apart from a man, in the Lord, 12 for as the woman [is] of the man, so also the man [is] through the woman, and all the things [are] of God. 13 Judge in your own selves: is it seemly for a woman to pray to God uncovered? 14 Does not even nature itself teach you, that if a man indeed has long hair, it is a dishonor to him? 15 and a woman, if she has long hair, it is a glory to her, because the hair has been given to her instead of a covering; 16 and if anyone thinks to be contentious, we have no such custom, neither the assemblies of God. 17 And declaring this, I give no praise, because you do not come together for the better, but for the worse; 18 for first, indeed, coming together in an assembly, I hear of divisions being among you, and I partly believe [it], 19 for it is also necessary for sects to be among you, that those approved may become visible among you; 20 you, then, coming together at the same place—it is not to eat the Lord's Dinner; 21 for each takes his own dinner before in the eating, and one is hungry, and another is drunk; 22 why, do you not have houses to eat and to drink in? or do you despise the Assembly of God, and shame those not having? what may I say to you? will I praise you in this? I do not praise! 23 For I received from the Lord that which I also delivered to you, that the Lord Jesus in the night in which He was delivered up, took bread, 24 and having given thanks, He broke, and said, "Take, eat, this is My body that is being broken for you; do this—to the remembrance of Me." 25 In like manner also the cup after the supping, saying, "This cup is the New Covenant in My blood; do this, as often as you may drink [it]—to the remembrance of Me"; 26 for as often as you may eat this bread, and may drink this cup, you show forth the death of the Lord—until He may come; 27 so that whoever may eat this bread or may drink the cup of the Lord unworthily, he will be guilty of the body and blood of the Lord: 28 and let a man be proving himself, and so let him eat of the bread, and let him drink of the cup; 29 for he who is eating and drinking unworthily, he eats and drinks judgment to himself—not discerning the body of the Lord. 30 Because of this many [are] weak and sickly among you, and many sleep; 31 for if we were discerning ourselves, we would not be being judged, 32 and being judged by the Lord, we are disciplined, that we may not be condemned with the world; 33 so then, my brothers, coming together to eat, wait for one another; 34 and if anyone is hungry, let him eat at home, that you may not come together to judgment; and the rest, whenever I may come, I will arrange.

CHAPTER 12

1 And concerning the spiritual things, brothers, I do not wish you to be ignorant; 2 you have known that you were nations, being carried away as you were led to the mute idols; 3 for this reason, I give you to understand that no one, speaking in the Spirit of God, says Jesus [is] accursed, and no one is able to say Jesus [is] Lord, except in the Holy Spirit. 4 And there are diversities of gifts, and the same Spirit; 5 and there are diversities of ministries, and the same Lord; 6 and there are diversities of workings, and it is the same God—who is working all in all. 7 And to each has been given the manifestation of the Spirit for profit; 8 for to one through the Spirit has been given a word of wisdom, and to another a word of knowledge, according to the same Spirit; 9 and to another faith in the same Spirit, and to another gifts of healings in the same Spirit; 10 and to another in-workings of mighty deeds; and to another prophecy; and to another discernings of spirits; and to another [various] kinds of tongues; and to another interpretation of tongues: 11 and the one and the same Spirit works all these, dividing to each individually as He intends. 12 For even as the body is one, and has many members, and all the members of the one body, being many, are one body, so also [is] the Christ, 13 for also in one Spirit we were all immersed into one body, whether Jews or Greeks, whether servants or freemen, and all were made to drink one Spirit, 14 for also the body is not one member, but many. 15 If the foot may say, "Because I am not a hand, I am not of the body," is it not, because of this, not of the body? 16 And if the ear may say, "Because I am not an eye, I am not of the body," is it not, because of this, not of the body? 17 If the whole body [were] an eye, where the hearing? if the whole hearing, where the smelling? 18 and now, God set the members, each one of them in the body, according as He willed, 19 and if all were one member, where [is] the body? 20 and now, indeed, [are] many members, but one body; 21 and an eye is not able to say to the hand, "I have no need of you"; nor again the head to the feet, "I have no need of you." 22 But much more the members of the body seeming to be weaker are necessary, 23 and those that we think to be less honorable of the body, around these we put more abundant honor, and our unseemly things have more abundant seemliness, 24 and our seemly things have no need; but God tempered the body together, having given more abundant honor to the lacking part, 25 that there may be no division in the body, but that the members may have the same anxiety for one another, 26 and whether one member suffers, all the members suffer with [it], or one member is glorified, all the members rejoice with [it]; 27 and you are the body of Christ, and members in particular. 28 And some, indeed, God set in the Assembly: first apostles, secondly prophets, thirdly teachers, afterward powers, afterward gifts of healings, helpings, governings, various kinds of tongues. 29 [Are] all apostles? [Are] all prophets? [Are] all teachers? [Are] all powers? 30 [Do] all have gifts of healings? do all speak with tongues? do all interpret? 31 and earnestly desire the better gifts; and yet I show to you a far [more] excelling way:

CHAPTER 13

1 If I speak with the tongues of men and of messengers, and do not have love, I have become sounding brass, or a clanging cymbal; 2 and if I have prophecy, and know all the secrets, and all the knowledge, and if I have all faith, so as to remove mountains, and do not have love, I am nothing; 3 and if I give away all my goods to feed others, and if I give up my body that I may be burned, and do not have love, I am profited nothing. 4 Love is long-suffering, it is kind, love does not envy, love does not vaunt itself, is not puffed up, 5 does not act unseemly, does not seek its own things, is not provoked, does not impute evil, 6 [does] not rejoice over unrighteousness, and rejoices with the truth; 7 it bears all things, it believes all, it hopes all, it endures all. 8 Love never fails; and whether [there be] prophecies, they will become useless; whether tongues, they will cease; whether knowledge, it will become useless; 9 for we know in part, and we prophesy in part; 10 and when that which is perfect may come, then that which [is] in part will become useless. 11 When I was a child, I was speaking as a child, I was thinking as a child, I was reasoning as a child, and when I have become a man, I have made useless the things of the child; 12 for we now see obscurely through a mirror, and

then face to face; now I know in part, and then I will fully know, as I was also known; 13 and now there remains faith, hope, love—these three; and the greatest of these [is] love.

CHAPTER 14

1 Pursue love, and earnestly seek the spiritual things, and rather that you may prophesy, 2 for he who is speaking in an [unknown] tongue—he does not speak to men, but to God, for no one listens, and he speaks secrets in spirit; 3 and he who is prophesying to men speaks edification, and exhortation, and comfort; 4 he who is speaking in an [unknown] tongue, edifies himself, and he who is prophesying, edifies the Assembly; 5 and I wish you all to speak with tongues, and more that you may prophesy, for greater is he who is prophesying than he who is speaking with tongues, except one may interpret, that the Assembly may receive edification. 6 And now, brothers, if I may come to you speaking tongues, what will I profit you, except I will speak to you either in revelation, or in knowledge, or in prophesying, or in teaching? 7 yet the things without life giving sound—whether pipe or harp—if they may not give a difference in the sounds, how will be known that which is piped or that which is harped? 8 for also, if a trumpet may give an uncertain sound, who will prepare himself for battle? 9 so also you, if you may not give speech easily understood through the tongue—how will that which is spoken be known? for you will be speaking to air. 10 There are, it may be, so many kinds of voices in the world, and none of them is unmeaning. 11 If, then, I do not know the power of the voice, I will be a foreigner to him who is speaking, and he who is speaking is a foreigner to me; 12 so you also, since you are earnestly desirous of spiritual gifts, seek for the building up of the Assembly that you may abound; 13 for this reason he who is speaking in an [unknown] tongue—let him pray that he may interpret; 14 for if I pray in an [unknown] tongue, my spirit prays, and my understanding is unfruitful. 15 What then is it? I will pray [in] the spirit, and I will also pray [with] understanding, I will sing psalms [in] the spirit, and I will also sing psalms [with] understanding; 16 since, if you may bless in spirit, he who is filling the place of the commoner, how will he say the Amen at your giving of thanks, since he has not known what you say? 17 for you, indeed, give thanks well, but the other is not built up! 18 I give thanks to my God—more than you all with tongues speaking— 19 but I wish to speak five words in an assembly through my understanding, that I also may instruct others, rather than myriads of words in an [unknown] tongue. 20 Brothers, do not become children in the understanding, but in the evil be children, and in the understanding become perfect; 21 in the Law it has been written, that, "With other tongues and with other lips I will speak to this people, and even so they will not hear Me, says the Lord"; 22 so that the tongues are for a sign, not to the believing, but to the unbelieving; and the prophecy [is] not for the unbelieving, but for the believing. 23 If, therefore, the whole assembly may come together to the same place, and all may speak with tongues, and there may come in commoners or unbelievers, will they not say that you are mad? 24 and if all may prophesy, and anyone may come in, an unbeliever or commoner, he is convicted by all, he is discerned by all, 25 and so the secrets of his heart become visible, and so having fallen on [his] face, he will worship God, declaring that God really is among you. 26 What then is it, brothers? whenever you may come together, each of you has a psalm, has a teaching, has a tongue, has a revelation, has an interpretation. let all things be for building up; 27 if anyone speaks an [unknown] tongue, by two, or at the most, by three, and in turn, and let one interpret; 28 and if there may be no interpreter, let him be silent in an assembly, and let him speak to himself, and to God. 29 And prophets—let two or three speak, and let the others discern, 30 and if [anything] may be revealed to another [who is] sitting, let the first be silent; 31 for you are able, one by one, all to prophesy, that all may learn, and all may be exhorted, 32 and the spiritual gift of prophets are subject to prophets, 33 for God is not [a God] of tumult, but of peace, as in all the assemblies of the holy ones. 34 Your women, let them be silent in the assemblies, for it has not been permitted to them to speak, but to be subject, as the Law also says; 35 and if they wish to learn anything, let them question their own husbands at home, for it is a shame to women to speak in an assembly. 36 Did the word of God come forth from you? or did it come to you alone? 37 if anyone thinks to be a prophet, or spiritual, let him acknowledge the things that I write to you—that they are commands of the Lord; 38 and if anyone is ignorant—let him be ignorant; 39 so that, brothers, earnestly desire to prophesy, and do not forbid to speak with tongues; 40 let all things be done decently and in order.

CHAPTER 15

1 And I make known to you, brothers, the good news that I proclaimed to you, which you also received, in which you also have stood, 2 through which you are also being saved, if you hold fast [to] the word—what I proclaimed as good news to you—unless you believed in vain. 3 For I delivered to you as most important what I also received: that Christ died for our sins according to the Writings, 4 and that He was buried, and that He has risen on the third day according to the Writings, 5 and that He appeared to Cephas, then to the Twelve, 6 afterward He appeared to above five hundred brothers at once, of whom the greater part remain until now, and some also fell asleep; 7 afterward He appeared to James, then to all the apostles. 8 And last of all—as to the untimely birth—He also appeared to me, 9 for I am the least of the apostles, who am not worthy to be called an apostle, because I persecuted the Assembly of God, 10 and by the grace of God I am what I am, and His grace that [is] toward me did not come in vain, but I labored more abundantly than they all, yet not I, but the grace of God that [is] with me; 11 whether, then, I or they, so we preach, and so you believed. 12 And if Christ is preached, that He has risen out of the dead, how [do] certain among you say that there is no resurrection of [the] dead? 13 and if there is no resurrection of [the] dead, neither has Christ risen; 14 and if Christ has not risen, then our preaching [is] void, and your faith [is] also void, 15 and we are also found [to be] false witnesses of God, because we testified of God that He raised up the Christ, whom He did not raise if then dead persons do not rise; 16 for if dead persons do not rise, neither has Christ risen, 17 and if Christ has not risen, your faith is vain, you are yet in your sins, 18 then, also, those having fallen asleep in Christ perished; 19 if we only have hope in Christ in this life, we are to be most pitied of all men. 20 And now, Christ has risen out of the dead—He became the first-fruits of those sleeping, 21 for since through man [is] death, also through Man [is] a resurrection of the dead, 22 for even as in Adam all die, so also in the Christ all will be made alive, 23 and each in his proper order: Christ, a first-fruit, afterward those who are the Christ's in His coming, 24 then—the end, when He may deliver up the kingdom to God, even the Father, when He may have made all rule useless, and all authority and power. 25 For it is necessary for Him to reign until He may have put all the enemies under His feet. 26 The last enemy is done away with—death. 27 For He put all things under His feet, and when one may say that all things have been subjected, [it is] evident that He is excepted who subjected all things to Him, 28 and when all things may be subjected to Him, then also the Son Himself will be subject to Him, who subjected to Him all things, that God may be the all in all. 29 Seeing what will they do who are immersed for the dead, if the dead do not rise at all? why are they also immersed for the dead? 30 why do we also stand in peril every hour? 31 I die every day, by the glorying of you that I have in Christ Jesus our Lord. 32 If I fought with wild beasts in Ephesus after the manner of a man, what [is] the advantage to me if the dead do not rise? let us eat and drink, for tomorrow we die! 33 Do not be led astray; evil communications corrupt good manners; 34 wake up, as is right, and do not sin; for some have an ignorance of God; I say [it] to you for shame. 35 But someone will say, "How do the dead rise?" 36 unwise! You—what you sow is not quickened except it may die; 37 and that which you sow, you do not sow the body that will be, but a bare grain, it may be of wheat, or of someone of the others, 38 and God gives a body to it according as He willed, and its proper body to each of the seeds. 39 All flesh [is] not the same flesh, but there is one flesh of men, and another flesh of beasts, and another of fishes, and another of birds; 40 and [there are] heavenly bodies and earthly bodies; but one [is] the glory of the heavenly, and another that of the earthly; 41 one glory of sun, and another glory of moon, and another glory of stars, for star differs from star in glory. 42 So also [is] the resurrection of the dead: it is sown in corruption, it is raised in incorruption; 43 it is sown in dishonor, it is raised in glory; it is sown in weakness, it is raised in power; 44 it is sown a natural body, it is raised a spiritual body; there is a natural body, and there is a spiritual body; 45 so also it has been written: "The first man

Adam became a living creature," the last Adam [is] for a life-giving spirit, 46 but that which is spiritual [is] not first, but that which [was] natural, afterward that which [is] spiritual. 47 The first man [is] out of the earth—earthly; the second Man [is] the Lord out of Heaven; 48 as [is] the earthly, such [are] also the earthly; and as [is] the heavenly, such [are] also the heavenly; 49 and according as we bore the image of the earthly, we will also bear the image of the heavenly. 50 And this I say, brothers, that flesh and blood are not able to inherit the Kingdom of God, nor does the corruption inherit the incorruption. 51 Behold, I tell you a secret: we indeed will not all sleep, but we will all be changed; 52 in a moment, in the twinkling of an eye, in the last trumpet, for it will sound, and the dead will be raised incorruptible, and we will be changed; 53 for it is necessary for this corruptible to put on incorruption, and this mortal to put on immortality; 54 and when this corruptible may have put on incorruption, and this mortal may have put on immortality, then will be brought to pass the word that has been written: "Death was swallowed up—to victory; 55 Where, O Death, your sting? where, O Death [[or Hades]], your victory?" 56 and the sting of death [is] sin, and the power of sin the Law; 57 and to God—thanks, to Him who is giving us the victory through our Lord Jesus Christ; 58 so that, my beloved brothers, become steadfast, unmovable, abounding in the work of the Lord at all times, knowing that your labor in the Lord is not vain.

CHAPTER 16

1 And concerning the collection that [is] for the holy ones, as I directed to the assemblies of Galatia, so also you—do; 2 on every first [day] of the week, let each one of you lay by him, treasuring up whatever he may have prospered, that when I may come then collections may not be made; 3 and whenever I may come, whomsoever you may approve, through letters, these I will send to carry your favor to Jerusalem; 4 and if it be worthy for me also to go, with me they will go. 5 And I will come to you when I pass through Macedonia—for I pass through Macedonia— 6 and with you, it may be, I will abide, or even winter, that you may send me forward wherever I go, 7 for I do not wish to see you now in the passing, but I hope to remain a certain time with you, if the Lord may permit; 8 and I will remain in Ephesus until the Pentecost, 9 for a door has been opened to me—great and effectual—and withstanders [are] many. 10 And if Timotheus may come, see that he may become without fear with you, for he works the work of the Lord, even as I, 11 no one, then, may despise him; and send him forward in peace, that he may come to me, for I expect him with the brothers; 12 and concerning Apollos our brother, I begged him much that he may come to you with the brothers, and it was not at all [his] will that he may come now, and he will come when he may find convenient. 13 Watch, stand in the faith; be men, be strong; 14 let all your things be done in love. 15 And I beg you, brothers, you have known the household of Stephanas, that it is the first-fruit of Achaia, and they set themselves to the ministry to the holy ones— 16 that you also be subject to such, and to everyone who is working with [us] and laboring; 17 and I rejoice over the coming of Stephanas, and Fortunatus, and Achaicus, because these filled up the lack of you; 18 for they refreshed my spirit and yours; acknowledge, therefore, those who [are] such. 19 The assemblies of Asia greet you; Aquilas and Priscilla greet you much in the Lord, with the assembly in their house; 20 all the brothers greet you; greet one another in a holy kiss. 21 The salutation of [me], Paul, with my hand; 22 if anyone does not cherish the Lord Jesus Christ—let him be accursed! The Lord has come! 23 The grace of the Lord Jesus Christ [is] with you; 24 my love [is] with you all in Christ Jesus! Amen.

2 CORINTHIANS

CHAPTER 1

1 Paul, an apostle of Jesus Christ, through the will of God, and Timotheus the brother, to the Assembly of God that is in Corinth, with all the holy ones who are in all Achaia: 2 Grace to you and peace from God our Father and the Lord Jesus Christ! 3 Blessed [is] God, even the Father of our Lord Jesus Christ, the Father of mercies, and God of all comfort, 4 who is comforting us in all our tribulation, for our being able to comfort those in any tribulation through the comfort with which we are comforted ourselves by God; 5 because, as the sufferings of the Christ abound to us, so through the Christ our comfort also abounds; 6 and whether we be in tribulation, [it is] for your comfort and salvation, that is worked in the enduring of the same sufferings that we also suffer; whether we are comforted, [it is] for your comfort and salvation; 7 and our hope [is] steadfast for you, knowing that even as you are partakers of the sufferings—so also of the comfort. 8 For we do not wish you to be ignorant, brothers, of our tribulation that happened to us in Asia, that we were exceedingly burdened above [our] power, so that we even despaired of life; 9 but we ourselves have had the sentence of death in ourselves, that we may not be trusting on ourselves, but on God, who is raising the dead, 10 who delivered us out of so great a death, and delivers, in whom we have hoped that even yet He will deliver; 11 you also working together for us by your supplication, that the gift through many persons to us, through many, may be thankfully acknowledged for us. 12 For our glorying is this: the testimony of our conscience, that in simplicity and sincerity of God, not in fleshly wisdom, but in the grace of God, we conducted ourselves in the world, and more abundantly toward you; 13 for no other things do we write to you, but what you either read or also acknowledge, and I hope that you will also acknowledge to the end, 14 according as you also acknowledged us in part, that we are your glory, even as also you [are] ours, in the Day of the Lord Jesus; 15 and in this confidence I was intending to come to you before, that you might have a second favor, 16 and to pass to Macedonia through you, and to come to you again from Macedonia, and to be sent forward by you to Judea. 17 This, therefore, intending, did I then use the lightness; or the things that I counsel, [did] I counsel according to the flesh, that it may be with me Yes, yes, and No, no? 18 and God [is] faithful, that our word to you did not become Yes and No, 19 for the Son of God, Jesus Christ, having been preached through us among you—through me and Silvanus and Timotheus—did not become Yes and No, but in Him it has become Yes; 20 for as many as [are] promises of God, in Him [are] the Yes, and in Him the Amen, for glory to God through us; 21 and He who is confirming you with us into Christ, and anointed us, [is] God, 22 who also sealed us, and gave the deposit of the Spirit in our hearts. 23 And I call on God for a witness on my soul, that sparing you, I did not come to Corinth yet; 24 not that we are lords over your faith, but we are workers together with your joy, for by faith you stand.

CHAPTER 2

1 And I decided this to myself, not to come again to you in sorrow, 2 for if I make you sorry, then who is he who is making me glad, except he who is made sorry by me? 3 and I wrote to you this same thing, that having come, I may not have sorrow from them of whom it was necessary [for] me to have joy, having confidence in you all, that my joy is of you all, 4 for out of much tribulation and pressure of heart I wrote to you through many tears, not that you might be made sorry, but that you might know the love that I have more abundantly toward you. 5 And if anyone has caused sorrow, he has not caused sorrow to me, but in part, that I may not burden you all; 6 sufficient to such a one is this punishment, that [is] by the greater part, 7 so that, on the contrary, [it is] rather for you to forgive and to comfort, lest by over abundant sorrow such a one may be swallowed up; 8 for this reason, I call on you to confirm love to him, 9 for this also I wrote, that I might know your proof, whether you are obedient in regard to all things. 10 And to whom you forgive anything I also; for I also, if I have forgiven anything, to whom I have forgiven [it], because of you—in the person of Christ [I forgive it,] 11 that we may not be over-reached by Satan, for we are not ignorant of his schemes. 12 And having come to Troas for the good news

of the Christ, and a door having been opened to me in the Lord, 13 I have not had rest to my spirit, on my not finding my brother Titus, but having taken leave of them, I went forth to Macedonia; 14 and to God [is] thanks, who at all times is leading us in triumph in the Christ, and the fragrance of His knowledge He is revealing through us in every place; 15 we are a refreshing fragrance to God because of Christ, in those being saved, and in those being lost; 16 to one, indeed, a fragrance of death to death, and to the other, a fragrance of life to life; and who is sufficient for these things? 17 for we are not as the many, adulterating the word of God, but as of sincerity—but as of God; in the presence of God, in Christ we speak.

CHAPTER 3

1 Do we begin again to recommend ourselves, except we need, as some, letters of recommendation to you, or from you? 2 You are our letter, having been written in our hearts, known and read by all men, 3 revealed that you are a letter of Christ ministered by us, not written with ink, but with the Spirit of the living God, not in the tablets of stone, but in fleshy tablets of the heart, 4 and such trust we have through the Christ toward God, 5 not that we are sufficient of ourselves to think anything, as of ourselves, but our sufficiency [is] of God, 6 who also made us sufficient [to be] servants of the New Covenant, not of letter, but of the Spirit; for the letter kills, and the Spirit makes alive. 7 and if the ministry of death, in letters, engraved in stones, came in glory, so that the sons of Israel were not able to look steadfastly into the face of Moses, because of the glory of his face—which was being made useless, 8 how will the ministry of the Spirit not be more in glory? 9 for if the ministry of the condemnation [is] glory, much more does the ministry of righteousness abound in glory; 10 for also even that which has been glorious, has not been glorious—in this respect, because of the superior glory; 11 for if that which is being made useless [is] through glory, much more that which is remaining [is] in glory. 12 Having, then, such hope, we use much freedom of speech, 13 and [are] not as Moses, who was putting a veil on his own face, for the sons of Israel not to look steadfastly into the end of that which is being made useless, 14 but their minds were hardened, for to this day the same veil at the reading of the Old Covenant remains unwithdrawn—which in Christ is being made useless— 15 but until today, when Moses is read, a veil lies on their heart, 16 and whenever they may turn to the Lord, the veil is taken away. 17 And the Lord is the Spirit; and where the Spirit of the Lord [is], there [is] liberty; 18 and we all, with unveiled face, beholding the glory of the Lord in a mirror, are being transformed into the same image, from glory to glory, even as by the Spirit of the Lord.

CHAPTER 4

1 Because of this, having this ministry, according as we received kindness, we do not faint, 2 but renounced for ourselves the hidden things of shame, not walking in craftiness, nor deceitfully using the word of God, but by the manifestation of the truth recommending ourselves to every conscience of men, before God; 3 and if our good news is also veiled, it is veiled in those perishing, 4 in whom the god of this age blinded the minds of the unbelieving, that there does not shine forth to them the enlightening of the good news of the glory of the Christ, who is the image of God; 5 for we do not preach ourselves, but Christ Jesus—Lord, and [we are] ourselves your servants because of Jesus; 6 because [it is] God who said, "Light will shine out of darkness," who shined in our hearts, for the enlightening of the knowledge of the glory of God in the face of Jesus Christ. 7 And we have this treasure in earthen vessels, that the excellence of the power may be of God, and not of us, 8 being in tribulation in every [way], but not crushed; perplexed, but not despairing; 9 persecuted, but not forsaken; cast down, but not destroyed; 10 at all times carrying around in the body the dying of the Lord Jesus, that the life of Jesus may also be revealed in our body, 11 for we who are living are always delivered up to death because of Jesus, that the life of Jesus may also be revealed in our dying flesh, 12 so that, death indeed works in us, and life in you. 13 And having the same spirit of faith, according to that which has been written: "I believed, therefore I spoke"; we also believe, therefore we also

speak; 14 knowing that He who raised up the Lord Jesus, will also raise us up through Jesus, and will present [us] with you, 15 for all things [are] because of you, that the grace having been multiplied, because of the thanksgiving of the more, may abound to the glory of God; 16 for this reason, we do not faint, but if our outward man also decays, yet the inward is renewed day by day; 17 for the momentary light matter of our tribulation works out for us more and more an exceedingly continuous weight of glory— 18 we [are] not looking to the things seen, but to the things not seen; for the things seen [are] temporary, but the things not seen [are] continuous.

CHAPTER 5

1 For we have known that if the tent of our earthly house may be thrown down, we have a building from God, a house not made with hands—perpetual—in the heavens, 2 for also in this we groan, earnestly desiring to clothe ourselves with our dwelling that is from Heaven, 3 if so be that, having clothed ourselves, we will not be found naked, 4 for we also who are in the tent groan, being burdened, seeing we do not wish to unclothe ourselves, but to clothe ourselves, that the mortal may be swallowed up of life. 5 And He who worked us to this very thing [is] God, who also gave to us the deposit of the Spirit; 6 having courage, then, at all times, and knowing that being at home in the body, we are away from home from the Lord— 7 for we walk through faith, not through sight— 8 we have courage, and are well pleased, rather, to be away from the home of the body, and to be at home with the Lord. 9 We are also ambitious for this reason, whether at home or away from home, to be well pleasing to Him, 10 for it is necessary for all of us to have appeared before the judgment seat of the Christ, that each one may receive the things [done] through the body, in reference to the things that he did, whether good or evil; 11 having known, therefore, the fear of the Lord, we persuade men, and we are revealed to God, and I also hope to have been revealed in your consciences; 12 for we do not again recommend ourselves to you, but we are giving occasion to you of glorifying in our behalf, that you may have [something] in reference to those glorifying in face and not in heart; 13 for whether we were beside ourselves, [it was] to God; whether we be of sound mind, [it is] to you, 14 for the love of the Christ constrains us, having judged thus: that if one died for all, then the whole died, 15 and He died for all, that those living may no longer live to themselves, but to Him who died for them, and was raised again. 16 So that we, from now on, have known no one according to the flesh, and even if we have known Christ according to the flesh, yet now we know Him [thus] no longer; 17 so that if anyone [is] in Christ—[he is] a new creature; the old things passed away, behold, all things have become new. 18 And all things [are] of God, who reconciled us to Himself through Jesus Christ, and gave to us the ministry of the reconciliation, 19 how that God was in Christ—reconciling the world to Himself, not reckoning to them their trespasses; and having put in us the word of the reconciliation, 20 in behalf of Christ, then, we are ambassadors, as if God were calling through us, we implore, in behalf of Christ, "Be reconciled to God"; 21 He made Him having not known sin [to be] sin in our behalf, that we may become the righteousness of God in Him.

CHAPTER 6

1 And also working together we call on [you] that you do not receive the grace of God in vain— 2 for He says, "In an acceptable time I heard you, and in a day of salvation I helped you, behold, now [is] a well-accepted time; behold, now, a day of salvation." 3 In nothing giving any cause of offense, that the ministry may not be blamed, 4 but in everything recommending ourselves as God's servants; in much patience, in tribulations, in necessities, in distresses, 5 in stripes, in imprisonments, in insurrections, in labors, in watchings, in fastings, 6 in pureness, in knowledge, in long-suffering, in kindness, in the Holy Spirit, in unhypocritical love, 7 in the word of truth, in the power of God, through the armor of righteousness, on the right and on the left, 8 through glory and dishonor, through evil report and good report, as leading astray, and true; 9 as unknown, and recognized; as dying, and behold, we live; as disciplined, and not put to death; 10 as sorrowful, and always rejoicing; as poor, and making many

rich; as having nothing, and possessing all things. 11 Our mouth has been open to you, O Corinthians, our heart has been enlarged! 12 you are not restricted in us, and you are restricted in your [own] yearnings, 13 and [as] a repayment of the same kind (as to children I say [it]), be enlarged—also you! 14 Do not become yoked with others—unbelievers, for what partaking [is there] to righteousness and lawlessness? 15 and what fellowship to light with darkness? and what concord to Christ with Belial? or what part to a believer with an unbeliever? 16 and what agreement to the temple of God with idols? for you are a temple of the living God, according as God said, "I will dwell in them, and will walk among [them], and I will be their God, and they will be My people, 17 for this reason, come forth out of the midst of them, and be separated, says the Lord, and do not touch an unclean thing, and I will receive you, 18 and I will be for a Father to you, and you will be sons and daughters to Me, says the Lord Almighty."

CHAPTER 7

1 Having, then, these promises, beloved, may we cleanse ourselves from every defilement of flesh and spirit, perfecting sanctification in the fear of God; 2 receive us; no one did we wrong; no one did we ruin; no one did we defraud; 3 I do not say [it] to condemn you, for I have said before that you are in our hearts to die together and to live together; 4 great [is] my freedom of speech to you, great my glory on your behalf; I have been filled with the comfort, I hyper-abound with the joy on all our tribulation, 5 for we also, having come to Macedonia, our flesh has had no relaxation, but on every side we are in tribulation: fightings outside, fears within; 6 but He who is comforting the cast-down—God—He comforted us in the coming of Titus; 7 and not only in his coming, but also in the comfort with which he was comforted over you, declaring to us your longing desire, your lamentation, your zeal for me, so that I rejoiced the more, 8 because even if I made you sorry in the letter, I do not regret—if even I regretted—for I perceive that the letter, even if for an hour, made you sorry. 9 I now rejoice, not that you were made sorry, but that you were made sorry to conversion, for you were made sorry toward God, that you might receive damage from us in nothing; 10 for sorrow toward God works conversion to salvation without regret, and the sorrow of the world works death, 11 for behold, this same thing—your being made sorry toward God—how much diligence it works in you! But defense, but displeasure, but fear, but longing desire, but zeal, but revenge; in everything you approved yourselves to be pure in the matter. 12 If, then, I also wrote to you—not for his cause who did wrong, nor for his cause who suffered wrong, but for our diligence in your behalf being revealed to you before God— 13 because of this we have been comforted in your comfort, and more abundantly the more we rejoiced in the joy of Titus, that his spirit has been refreshed from you all; 14 because if I have boasted anything to him in your behalf, I was not put to shame; but as we spoke to you all things in truth, so also our boasting before Titus became truth, 15 and his yearnings are more abundantly toward you, remembering the obedience of you all, how you received him with fear and trembling; 16 I rejoice, therefore, that in everything I have courage in you.

CHAPTER 8

1 And we make known to you, brothers, the grace of God, that has been given in the assemblies of Macedonia, 2 because in much trial of tribulation the abundance of their joy, and their deep poverty, abounded to the riches of their liberality; 3 because, according to [their] power, I testify, and above [their] power, they were willing of themselves, 4 with much plea calling on us to receive the favor and the fellowship of the ministry to the holy ones, 5 and not according as we expected, but they gave themselves first to the Lord, and to us, through the will of God, 6 so that we exhorted Titus, that, according as he began before, so also he may also finish this favor to you, 7 but even as in everything you abound, in faith, and word, and knowledge, and all diligence, and in your love to us, that also in this grace you may abound; 8 I do not speak according to command, but because of the diligence of others, and proving the genuineness of your love, 9 for you know the grace of our Lord Jesus Christ, that because of you He became poor—

being rich, that you may become rich by that poverty. 10 and I give an opinion in this: for this [is] expedient to you, who not only to do, but also to will, began before—a year ago, 11 and now also finish doing [it], that even as [there is] the readiness of the will, so also the finishing, out of that which you have, 12 for if the willing mind is present, it is well-accepted according to that which anyone may have, not according to that which he does not have; 13 for I do not speak that for others [to be] released, and you pressured, 14 but by equality, at the present time your abundance—for their want, that also their abundance may be for your want, that there may be equality, 15 according as it has been written: "He who [gathered] much, had nothing over; and he who [gathered] little, had no lack." 16 And thanks to God, who is putting the same diligence for you in the heart of Titus, 17 because he indeed accepted the exhortation, and being more diligent, he went forth to you of his own accord, 18 and we sent with him the brother, whose praise in the good news [is] through all the assemblies, 19 and not only so, but who was also appointed by vote by the assemblies, our fellow-traveler, with this favor that is ministered by us, to the glory of the same Lord, and your willing mind; 20 avoiding this, lest anyone may blame us in this abundance that is ministered by us, 21 providing right things, not only before the Lord, but also before men; 22 and we sent our brother with them, whom we proved being diligent many times in many things, and now much more diligent, by the great confidence that is toward you, 23 whether—about Titus—my partner and fellow-worker toward you, whether—our brothers, apostles of assemblies—glory of Christ; 24 the showing therefore of your love, and of our boasting on your behalf, show to them, even in the face of the assemblies.

CHAPTER 9

1 For indeed, concerning the ministry that [is] for the holy ones, it is superfluous for me to write to you, 2 for I have known your readiness of mind, which in your behalf I boast of to Macedonians, that Achaia has been prepared a year ago, and your zeal stirred up the greater part, 3 and I sent the brothers, that our boasting on your behalf may not be made vain in this respect; that, according as I said, you may be ready, 4 lest if Macedonians may come with me, and find you unprepared, we may be put to shame (that we do not say—you) in this same confidence of boasting. 5 Therefore I thought [it] necessary to exhort the brothers, that they may go before to you, and may make up before your formerly announced blessing, that this be ready, as a blessing, and not as covetousness. 6 And [remember] this: he who is sowing sparingly, will also reap sparingly; and he who is sowing in blessings, will also reap in blessings; 7 each one, according as he purposes in heart, not out of sorrow or out of necessity, for God loves a cheerful giver, 8 and God [is] able to cause all grace to abound to you, that in everything always having all sufficiency, you may abound to every good work, 9 according as it has been written: "He dispersed abroad, He gave to the poor, His righteousness remains throughout the age," 10 and may He who is supplying seed to the sower, and bread for food, supply and multiply your seed sown, and increase the fruits of your righteousness, 11 being enriched to all liberality in everything, which works thanksgiving through us to God, 12 because the ministry of this service not only is supplying the wants of the holy ones, but is also abounding through many thanksgivings to God, 13 through the proof of this ministry glorifying God for the subjection of your confession to the good news of the Christ, and [for] the liberality of the fellowship to them and to all, 14 and by their supplication in your behalf, longing after you because of the exceeding grace of God on you; 15 thanks also to God for His unspeakable gift!

CHAPTER 10

1 And I, Paul, myself, call on you—through the meekness and gentleness of the Christ—who in presence [am] indeed humble among you, and being absent, have courage toward you, 2 and I implore [you], that, being present, I may not have courage, with the confidence with which I reckon to be bold against certain reckoning us as walking according to the flesh; 3 for walking in the flesh, we do not war according to the flesh, 4 for the weapons of our warfare [are] not fleshly, but powerful

to God for bringing down of strongholds, 5 bringing down reasonings, and every high thing lifted up against the knowledge of God, and bringing into captivity every thought to the obedience of the Christ, 6 and being in readiness to avenge every disobedience whenever your obedience may be fulfilled. 7 You see the outward appearance. If anyone has trusted in himself to be Christ's, let him reckon this again from himself, that according as he is Christ's, so also we [are] Christ's; 8 for even if I will also boast anything more abundantly concerning our authority, that the Lord gave us for building up, and not for casting you down, I will not be ashamed, 9 that I may not seem as if I would terrify you through the letters, 10 "because the letters indeed," says one, "[are] weighty and strong, and the bodily presence weak, and the speech despicable." 11 This one—let him reckon thus: that such as we are in word, through letters, being absent, such also, being present, [we are] in deed. 12 For we do not make bold to rank or to compare ourselves with certain of those commending themselves, but they, measuring themselves among themselves, and comparing themselves with themselves, are not wise, 13 and we will not boast ourselves in regard to the unmeasured things, but after the measure of the line that the God of measure appointed to us—to reach even to you; 14 for we do not stretch ourselves too much, as not reaching to you, for even to you we came in the good news of the Christ, 15 not boasting of the things not measured, in other men's labors, and having hope—your faith increasing—in you to be enlarged, according to our line—into abundance, 16 to proclaim good news in the [places] beyond you, not in another's line in regard to the things made ready, to boast; 17 and he who is boasting—let him boast in the Lord; 18 for he who is commending himself is not approved, but he whom the Lord commends.

CHAPTER 11

1 O that you were bearing with me a little of the folly, but you also bear with me: 2 for I am zealous for you with zeal of God, for I betrothed you to one Husband, a pure virgin, to present to Christ, 3 and I fear, lest, as the serpent deceived Eve in his subtlety, so your minds may be corrupted from the simplicity that [is] in the Christ; 4 for if, indeed, he who is coming preaches another Jesus whom we did not preach, or you receive another spirit which you did not receive, or other good news which you did not accept—well were you bearing [it], 5 for I reckon that I have been nothing behind the very chiefest apostles, 6 and even if a commoner in speech—yet not in knowledge, but in everything we were made evident in all things to you. 7 Did I do sin—humbling myself that you might be exalted, because I freely proclaimed the good news of God to you? 8 I robbed other assemblies, having taken wages, for your ministry; 9 and being present with you, and having been in want, I was chargeable to no one, for the brothers supplied my lack—having come from Macedonia—and I kept myself burdenless to you in everything, and will keep. 10 The truth of Christ is in me, because this boasting will not be stopped in regard to me in the regions of Achaia; 11 for what reason? because I do not love you? God has known! 12 and what I do, I also will do, that I may cut off the occasion of those wishing an occasion, that in that which they boast they may be found according as we also; 13 for those such [are] false apostles, deceitful workers, transforming themselves into apostles of Christ, 14 and no wonder—for even Satan transforms himself into a messenger of light; 15 [it is] no great thing, then, if his servants also transform themselves as servants of righteousness—whose end will be according to their works. 16 Again I say, may no one think me to be a fool; and if otherwise, receive me even as a fool, that I also may boast a little. 17 That which I speak, I do not speak according to the Lord, but as in foolishness, in this the confidence of boasting; 18 since many boast according to the flesh, I also will boast: 19 for you gladly bear with the fools—being wise, 20 for you bear, if anyone is bringing you under bondage, if anyone devours, if anyone takes away, if anyone exalts himself, if anyone strikes you on the face; 21 I speak in reference to dishonor, how that we were weak, and in whatever anyone is bold—in foolishness I say [it]—I also am bold. 22 Are they Hebrews? I also! Are they Israelites? I also! Are they seed of Abraham? I also! 23 Are they servants of Christ? As [if] beside myself I speak—I [am] more; in labors more abundantly, in stripes above measure, in prisons more frequently, in deaths many times. 24 Five times I received from Jews forty [stripes] except one; 25

three times I was beaten with rods, once I was stoned, three times I was shipwrecked, I have passed a night and a day in the deep; 26 journeys many times, perils of rivers, perils of robbers, perils from [my own] race, perils from nations, perils in city, perils in wilderness, perils in sea, perils among false brothers; 27 in laboriousness and painfulness, many times in watchings, in hunger and thirst, many times in fastings, in cold and nakedness; 28 apart from the things without—the crowding on me that is daily—the care of all the assemblies. 29 Who is weak, and I am not weak? who is stumbled, and I am not burned? 30 If it is necessary to boast, I will boast of the things of my weakness; 31 the God and Father of our Lord Jesus Christ—who is blessed for all ages—has known that I do not lie! 32 In Damascus the governor [under] Aretas the king was watching the city of the Damascenes, wishing to seize me, 33 and I was let down through a window in a rope basket, through the wall, and fled out of his hands.

CHAPTER 12

1 To boast, really, is not profitable for me, for I will come to visions and revelations of the Lord. 2 I have known a man in Christ, fourteen years ago—whether in the body I have not known, whether out of the body I have not known, God has known—such a one being snatched up to the third heaven; 3 and I have known such a man—whether in the body, whether out of the body, I have not known, God has known— 4 that he was snatched up to the paradise, and heard unutterable sayings, that it is not possible for man to speak. 5 Of such a one I will boast, and of myself I will not boast, except in my weaknesses, 6 for if I may wish to boast, I will not be a fool, for I will say truth; but I refrain, lest in regard to me anyone may think anything above what he sees me, or hears anything of me; 7 and that by the exceeding greatness of the revelations I might not be exalted too much, there was given to me a thorn in the flesh, a messenger of Satan, that he might batter me, that I might not be exalted too much. 8 I called on the Lord three times concerning this thing, that it might depart from me, 9 and He said to me, "My grace is sufficient for you, for My power is perfected in weakness"; most gladly, therefore, will I rather boast in my weaknesses, that the power of the Christ may rest on me: 10 for this reason I am well pleased in weaknesses, in damages, in necessities, in persecutions, in distresses—for Christ; for whenever I may be weak, then I am powerful; 11 I have become a fool—boasting; you compelled me; for I ought to have been commended by you, for I was behind the very chiefest apostles in nothing—even if I am nothing. 12 The signs, indeed, of the apostle were worked among you in all patience, in signs, and wonders, and mighty deeds, 13 for what is there in which you were inferior to the rest of the assemblies, except that I myself was not a burden to you? forgive me this injustice! 14 Behold, a third time I am ready to come to you, and I will not be a burden to you, for I do not seek yours, but you, for the children ought not to lay up for the parents, but the parents for the children, 15 and I will most gladly spend and be entirely spent for your souls, even if, loving you more abundantly, I am loved less. 16 And be it [so], I did not burden you, but being crafty, I took you with guile; 17 anyone of those whom I have sent to you—did I take advantage of you by him? 18 I begged Titus, and sent with [him] the brother; did Titus take advantage of you? Did we not walk in the same Spirit? Did we not [walk] in the same steps? 19 Again, [do] you think that we are making defense to you? We speak before God in Christ; and all things, beloved, [are] for your up-building, 20 for I fear lest, having come, I may not find you such as I wish, and I may be found by you such as you do not wish, lest there be strifes, envyings, wraths, revelries, slanders, whisperings, puffings up, insurrections, 21 lest again having come, my God may humble me in regard to you, and I may mourn many of those having sinned before, and having not changed their mind concerning the uncleanness, and whoredom, and licentiousness, that they practiced.

CHAPTER 13

1 I come to you this third time; on the mouth of two or three witnesses will every saying be established; 2 I have said before, and I say [it] before, as being present, the second time,

and being absent, now, I write to those having sinned before, and to all the rest, that if I come again, I will not spare, 3 since you seek a proof of the Christ speaking in me, who is not weak to you, but is powerful in you, 4 for even if He was crucified from weakness, yet He lives from the power of God; for we also are weak in Him, but we will live with Him from the power of God toward you. 5 Try yourselves, if you are in the faith; prove yourselves; do you not know yourselves, that Jesus Christ is in you, if you are not disapproved of in some respect? 6 and I hope that you will know that we are not disapproved of; 7 and I pray before God that you do no evil, not that we may appear approved, but that you may do that which is right, and we may be as disapproved; 8 for we are not able to do anything against the truth, but for the truth; 9 for we rejoice when we may be weak, but you may be powerful; and we also pray for this—your perfection! 10 because of this, these things—being absent—I write, that being present, I may not treat [any] sharply, according to the authority that the Lord gave me for building up, and not for casting down. 11 From now on, brothers, rejoice; be made perfect, be comforted, be of the same mind, be at peace, and the God of love and peace will be with you. 12 Greet one another in a holy kiss. 13 All the holy ones greet you. 14 The grace of the Lord Jesus Christ, and the love of God, and the fellowship of the Holy Spirit, [is] with you all! Amen.

GALATIANS

CHAPTER 1

1 Paul, an apostle—not from men, nor through man, but through Jesus Christ, and God the Father, who raised Him out of the dead— 2 and all the brothers with me, to the assemblies of Galatia: 3 Grace to you and peace from God the Father and our Lord Jesus Christ, 4 who gave Himself for our sins, that He might deliver us out of the present evil age, according to the will of our God and Father, 5 to whom [is] the glory through the ages of the ages. Amen. 6 I wonder that you are so quickly removed from Him who called you in the grace of Christ to another good news— 7 not that there is another, except there are certain who are troubling you, and wishing to pervert the good news of the Christ; 8 but even if we or a messenger out of Heaven may proclaim good news to you different from what we proclaimed to you—let him be accursed! 9 as we have said before, and now say again: if anyone may proclaim to you good news different from what you received—let him be accursed! 10 for do I now persuade men, or God? or do I seek to please men? for if I yet pleased men—I should not be Christ's servant. 11 And I make known to you, brothers, the good news that was proclaimed by me, that it is not according to man, 12 for neither did I receive it from man, nor was I taught [it], but through a revelation of Jesus Christ, 13 for you heard of my behavior once in Judaism, that I was exceedingly persecuting the Assembly of God, and destroying it, 14 and I was advancing in Judaism above many equals in age in my own race, being more abundantly zealous of my fathers' deliverances, 15 and when God was well pleased—having separated me from the womb of my mother, and having called [me] through His grace— 16 to reveal His Son in me, that I might proclaim Him as good news among the nations, I did not immediately confer with flesh and blood, 17 nor did I go up to Jerusalem to those who were apostles before me, but I went away to Arabia, and again returned to Damascus; 18 then, after three years I went up to Jerusalem to inquire about Peter, and remained with him fifteen days, 19 and I did not see [any] other of the apostles, except James, the brother of the Lord. 20 And the things that I write to you, behold, before God—I do not lie; 21 then I came into the regions of Syria and of Cilicia, 22 and was unknown by face to the assemblies of Judea, that [are] in Christ, 23 and they were only hearing that "he who is persecuting us then, now proclaims good news—the faith that he was then destroying"; 24 and they were glorifying God in me.

CHAPTER 2

1 Then after fourteen years again I went up to Jerusalem with Barnabas, having also taken Titus with me; 2 and I went up by revelation, and submitted the good news to them that I preach among the nations, and privately to those esteemed, lest I ran or might run in vain; 3 but not even Titus, who [is] with me, being a Greek, was compelled to be circumcised— 4 and [that] because of the false brothers brought in unaware, who came in secretly to spy out our liberty that we have in Christ Jesus, that they might bring us under bondage, 5 to whom not even for an hour we gave place by subjection, that the truth of the good news might remain to you. 6 And from those who were esteemed to be something—whatever they were then, it makes no difference to me. God does not accept the face of man, for to me those esteemed added nothing, 7 but on the contrary, having seen that I have been entrusted with the good news of the uncircumcision, as Peter with [that] of the circumcision, 8 for He who worked with Peter to the apostleship of the circumcision, worked also in me in regard to the nations, 9 and having known the grace that was given to me, James, and Cephas, and John, who were esteemed to be pillars, they gave to me a right hand of fellowship, and to Barnabas, that we may go to the nations, and they to the circumcision, 10 only, that we should be mindful of the poor, which I also was diligent—this very thing—to do. 11 And when Peter came to Antioch, I stood up against him to the face, because he was blameworthy, 12 for before the coming of some from James, he was eating with the nations, and when they came, he was withdrawing and separating himself, fearing those of circumcision, 13 and the other Jews acted hypocritically with him, so that Barnabas was also carried away by their hypocrisy. 14 But when I saw that they are not walking uprightly to the truth of the good news, I said to Peter before all, "If you, being a Jew, live in the manner of the nations, and not in the manner of the Jews, how do you compel the nations to live like Jews? 15 we by nature Jews, and not sinners of the nations, 16 having also known that a man is not declared righteous by works of law, but through faith from Jesus Christ, we also believed in Christ Jesus, that we might be declared righteous by faith from Christ, and not by works of law, because no flesh will be declared righteous by works of law." 17 And if, seeking to be declared righteous in Christ, we were also ourselves found sinners, [is] Christ then a servant of sin? let it not be! 18 for if the things I threw down, these again I build up, I set myself forth [as] a transgressor; 19 for I died through law that I may live to God; 20 I have been crucified with Christ, and I no longer live, but Christ lives in me; and that which I now live in the flesh—I live in the faith of the Son of God, who loved me and gave Himself for me; 21 I do not make the grace of God void, for if righteousness [is] through law—then Christ died in vain.

CHAPTER 3

1 O thoughtless Galatians, who bewitched you, not to obey the truth—before whose eyes [it] was previously written [about] Jesus Christ having been crucified? 2 I only wish to learn this from you: did you receive the Spirit by works of the Law, or by the hearing of faith? 3 Are you so thoughtless? Having begun in the Spirit, do you now end in the flesh? 4 so many things you suffered in vain! If, indeed, even in vain. 5 He, therefore, who is supplying the Spirit to you and working mighty acts among you—[is it] by works of law or by the hearing of faith? 6 according as Abraham believed God, and it was reckoned to him for righteousness; 7 know, then, that those of faith—these are sons of Abraham, 8 and the Writing, having foreseen that God declares righteous the nations by faith, foretold the good news to Abraham: 9 "All the nations will be blessed in you"; so that those of faith are blessed with the believing Abraham, 10 for as many as are of works of law are under a curse, for it has been written: "Cursed [is] everyone who is not remaining in all things that have been written in the Scroll of the Law—to do them," 11 and [it] is evident that in law no one is declared righteous with God, because "The righteous will live by faith"; 12 and the Law is not by faith, rather, "The man who did them will live in them." 13 Christ redeemed us from the curse of the Law, having become a curse for us, for it has been written: "Cursed is everyone who is hanging on a tree," 14 that the blessing of Abraham may come to the nations in Christ Jesus, that we may receive the promise of the Spirit through faith. 15 Brothers, I say [it] as a man, no one even makes void or adds to a

confirmed covenant of man, 16 and to Abraham were the promises spoken, and to his Seed; He does not say, "And to seeds," as of many, but as of one, "And to your Seed," which is Christ; 17 and this I say, a covenant confirmed before by God to Christ, the Law, that came four hundred and thirty years after, does not set aside, to make void the promise, 18 for if the inheritance [is] by law, [it is] no longer by promise, but God granted [it] to Abraham through promise. 19 Why, then, the Law? It was added on account of the transgressions, until the Seed might come to which the promise has been made, having been set in order through messengers in the hand of a mediator— 20 and the mediator is not of one, but God is one. 21 [Is] the Law, then, against the promises of God? Let it not be! For if a law was given that was able to make alive, truly there would have been righteousness by law, 22 but the Writing shut up the whole under sin, that the promise by faith of Jesus Christ may be given to those believing. 23 And before the coming of faith, we were being kept under law, shut up to the faith about to be revealed, 24 so that the Law became our tutor—to Christ, that we may be declared righteous by faith, 25 and faith having come, we are no longer under a tutor, 26 for you are all sons of God through faith in Christ Jesus, 27 for as many as were immersed into Christ put on Christ; 28 there is neither Jew nor Greek, there is neither servant nor freeman, there is neither male and female, for you are all one in Christ Jesus; 29 and if you [are] of Christ then you are seed of Abraham, and heirs according to promise.

CHAPTER 4

1 And I say, now as much time as the heir is a child, he differs nothing from a servant, [though] being lord of all, 2 but is under tutors and stewards until the time appointed of the father, 3 so we also, when we were children, were in servitude under the elements of the world, 4 and when the fullness of time came, God sent forth His Son, come of a woman, come under law, 5 that He may redeem those under law, that we may receive the adoption as sons; 6 and because you are sons, God sent forth the Spirit of His Son into your hearts, crying, "Abba! Father!" 7 so that you are no longer a servant, but a son, and if a son, also an heir of God through Christ. 8 But then, indeed, having not known God, you were in servitude to those [that are] not by nature gods, 9 and now, having known God—and rather being known by God—how [do] you turn again to the weak and poor elements to which you desire anew to be in servitude? 10 You observe days, and months, and times, and years! 11 I am afraid for you, lest I labored in vain for you. 12 I implore you, brothers, become as I [am]—because I also [am] as you; you did not hurt me; 13 and you have known that through weakness of the flesh I proclaimed good news to you at the first, 14 and you did not despise nor reject my trial that [is] in my flesh, but you received me as a messenger of God— as Christ Jesus; 15 what then was your blessedness? for I testify to you, that if possible, having plucked out your eyes, you would have given [them] to me; 16 so have I become your enemy, being true to you? 17 they are zealous for you—[yet] not well, but they wish to shut us out, that you may be zealous for them; 18 and [it is] good to be zealously regarded, in what is good, at all times, and not only in my being present with you; 19 my little children, of whom I travail in birth again until Christ may be formed in you, 20 indeed I was wishing to be present with you now, and to change my voice, because I am in doubt about you. 21 Tell me, you who are willing to be under law, do you not hear the Law? 22 for it has been written that Abraham had two sons, one by the maidservant and one by the free [woman], 23 but he who [is] of the maidservant has been according to flesh, but he who [is] of the free [woman], through the promise, 24 which things are allegorized, for these are the two covenants: one, indeed, from Mount Sinai, bringing forth to servitude, which is Hagar; 25 for this Hagar is Mount Sinai in Arabia, and corresponds to the Jerusalem that now [is], and is in servitude with her children, 26 and the Jerusalem above is the free [woman], which is mother of us all, 27 for it has been written: "Rejoice, O barren, who is not bearing; break forth and cry, you who are not travailing, because many [are] the children of the desolate—more than of her having the husband." 28 And we, brothers, as Isaac, are children of promise, 29 but as he then who was born according to the flesh persecuted him [born] according to the Spirit, so also now; 30 but what does the Writing say? "Cast forth the maidservant and her son, for the son of the maidservant may not be heir

with the son of the free [woman]"; 31 then, brothers, we are not a maidservant's children, but the free [woman's].

CHAPTER 5

1 In the freedom, then, with which Christ made you free— stand, and do not be held fast again by a yoke of servitude. 2 Behold! I, Paul, say to you, that if you are [to be] circumcised, Christ will profit you nothing; 3 and I testify again to every man circumcised, that he is a debtor to do the whole law; 4 you were voided from the Christ, you who are declared righteous in law; you fell away from grace; 5 for we by the Spirit, by faith, wait for a hope of righteousness, 6 for in Christ Jesus neither circumcision avails anything, nor uncircumcision, but faith working through love. 7 You were running well; who hindered you [so as] not to obey the truth? 8 the persuasion [is] not of Him who is calling you! 9 a little leaven leavens the whole lump; 10 I have confidence in regard to you in the Lord that you will not be otherwise minded; and he who is troubling you will bear the judgment, whoever he may be. 11 And I, brothers, if I still preach circumcision, why am I still persecuted? then the stumbling-block of the Cross has been done away [with]; 12 O that even they would cut themselves off who are unsettling you! 13 For you were called to freedom, brothers, only the freedom [is] not for an occasion to the flesh, but serve one another through the love, 14 for all the Law is fulfilled in one word—in this: "You will love your neighbor as yourself"; 15 and if you bite and devour one another, see that you may not be consumed by one another. 16 And I say, walk in the Spirit, and you may not fulfill the desire of the flesh; 17 for the flesh desires contrary to the Spirit, and the Spirit contrary to the flesh, and these are opposed to one another, that the things that you may will—these you may not do; 18 and if you are led by the Spirit, you are not under law. 19 And the works of the flesh are also evident, which are: adultery, whoredom, uncleanness, licentiousness, 20 idolatry, witchcraft, enmities, strife, jealousy, wraths, rivalries, dissensions, sects, 21 envyings, murders, drunkenness, reveling, and such like, of which I tell you before, as I also said before, that those doing such things will not inherit the Kingdom of God. 22 And the fruit of the Spirit is: love, joy, peace, long-suffering, kindness, goodness, faith, 23 meekness, [and] self-control. Against such there is no law; 24 and those who are of Christ Jesus have crucified the flesh with the affections and the desires; 25 if we may live in the Spirit, we may also walk in the Spirit; 26 let us not become vainglorious— provoking one another, envying one another!

CHAPTER 6

1 Brothers, even if a man may be overtaken in any trespass, you who [are] spiritual restore such a one in a spirit of meekness, considering yourself—lest you also may be tempted. 2 Bear the burdens of one another, and so fill up the law of the Christ, 3 for if anyone thinks [himself] to be something—being nothing—he deceives himself; 4 and let each one prove his own work, and then he will have the glorying in regard to himself alone, and not in regard to the other, 5 for each one will bear his own burden. 6 And let him who is instructed in the word share with him who is instructing in all good things. 7 Do not be led astray: God is not mocked; for what a man may sow—that he will also reap, 8 because he who is sowing to his own flesh, of the flesh will reap corruption; and he who is sowing to the Spirit, of the Spirit will reap continuous life; 9 and in doing good we should not be weary, for at the proper time we will reap—not desponding; 10 therefore, then, as we have opportunity, may we work the good to all, and especially to those of the household of faith. 11 You see in how large letters I have written to you with my own hand; 12 as many as are willing to make a good appearance in the flesh, these constrain you to be circumcised—only that they may not be persecuted for the Cross of the Christ, 13 for neither do those circumcised keep the Law themselves, but they wish you to be circumcised, that they may glory in your flesh. 14 And for me, let it not be—to glory, except in the Cross of our Lord Jesus Christ, through which the world has been crucified to me, and I to the world; 15 for in Christ Jesus neither circumcision avails anything, nor uncircumcision, but a new creation; 16 and as many as walk by this rule—peace on them, and kindness,

and on the Israel of God! 17 From now on, let no one give me trouble, for I carry the scars of the Lord Jesus in my body. 18 The grace of our Lord Jesus Christ [is] with your spirit, brothers! Amen.

EPHESIANS

CHAPTER 1

1 Paul, an apostle of Jesus Christ through the will of God, to the holy ones who are in Ephesus, and to the faithful in Christ Jesus: 2 Grace to you and peace from God our Father and the Lord Jesus Christ! 3 Blessed [is] the God and Father of our Lord Jesus Christ, who blessed us in every spiritual blessing in the heavenly [places] in Christ, 4 according as He chose us in Him before the foundation of the world, for our being holy and unblemished before Him, in love, 5 having foreordained us to the adoption of sons through Jesus Christ to Himself, according to the good pleasure of His will, 6 to the praise of the glory of His grace, in which He made us accepted in the beloved, 7 in whom we have the redemption through His blood, the forgiveness of the trespasses, according to the riches of His grace, 8 in which He abounded toward us in all wisdom and prudence, 9 having made known to us the secret of His will, according to His good pleasure, that He purposed in Himself, 10 in regard to the dispensation of the fullness of the times, to bring into one the whole in the Christ, both the things in the heavens, and the things on the earth—in Him; 11 in whom also we obtained an inheritance, being foreordained according to the purpose of Him who is working all things according to the counsel of His will, 12 for our being to the praise of His glory, [even] those who first hoped in the Christ, 13 in whom you also, having heard the word of the truth—the good news of your salvation—in whom also having believed, you were sealed with the Holy Spirit of the promise, 14 which is a deposit of our inheritance, to the redemption of the acquired possession, to the praise of His glory. 15 Because of this I also, having heard of your faith in the Lord Jesus, and the love to all the holy ones, 16 do not cease giving thanks for you, making mention of you in my prayers, 17 that the God of our Lord Jesus Christ, the Father of the glory, may give to you a spirit of wisdom and revelation in the recognition of Him, 18 the eyes of your understanding being enlightened, for your knowing what is the hope of His calling, and what the riches of the glory of His inheritance in the holy ones, 19 and what the exceeding greatness of His power to us who are believing, according to the working of the power of His might, 20 which He worked in the Christ, having raised Him out of the dead, and sat [Him] at His right hand in the heavenly [places], 21 far above all principality, and authority, and might, and lordship, and every name named, not only in this age, but also in the coming one; 22 and He put all things under His feet, and gave Him—head over all things to the Assembly, 23 which is His body, the fullness of Him who is filling all in all.

CHAPTER 2

1 Also you—being dead in trespasses and sins, 2 in which you once walked according to the age of this world, according to the ruler of the authority of the air, of the spirit that is now working in the sons of disobedience, 3 among whom we also all walked once in the desires of our flesh, doing the wishes of the flesh and of the thoughts, and were by nature children of wrath—as also the others, 4 but God, being rich in kindness, because of His great love with which He loved us, 5 even being dead in the trespasses, made us alive together with the Christ (by grace you are saved), 6 and raised [us] up together, and sat [us] together in the heavenly [places] in Christ Jesus, 7 that He might show, in the ages that are coming, the exceeding riches of His grace in kindness toward us in Christ Jesus, 8 for by grace you are saved, through faith, and this [is] not of yourselves—[it is] the gift of God, 9 not of works, that no one may boast; 10 for we are His workmanship, created in Christ Jesus on good works, which God prepared before, that we may walk in them. 11 For this reason, remember, that you [were] once the nations in the flesh, who are called Uncircumcision by that called Circumcision in the flesh made by hands, 12 that

you were at that time apart from Christ, having been alienated from the commonwealth of Israel, and strangers to the covenants of the promise, having no hope, and without God in the world; 13 but now, in Christ Jesus, you being once far off became near in the blood of the Christ, 14 for He is our peace, who made both one, and broke down the middle wall of the partition of hostility, 15 the enmity in His flesh, having done away [with] the Law of the commands in ordinances, that He might create the two into one new man in Himself, making peace, 16 and might reconcile both in one body to God through the Cross, having slain the enmity by it, 17 and having come, He proclaimed good news—peace to you—the far-off and the near, 18 because through Him we have the access—we both—in one Spirit to the Father. 19 Then, therefore, you are no longer strangers and foreigners, but fellow-citizens of the holy ones, and of the household of God, 20 being built on the foundation of the apostles and prophets, Jesus Christ Himself being chief corner-[stone], 21 in whom all the building fitly framed together increases to a holy temple in the Lord, 22 in whom you also are built together, for a habitation of God in the Spirit.

CHAPTER 3

1 For this cause, I Paul, the prisoner of Christ Jesus for you the nations, 2 if, indeed, you heard of the dispensation of the grace of God that was given to me in regard to you, 3 that by revelation He made known to me the secret, according as I wrote before in few [words]— 4 in regard to which you are able, reading [it], to understand my knowledge in the secret of the Christ, 5 which in other generations was not made known to the sons of men, as it was now revealed to His holy apostles and prophets in the Spirit— 6 that the nations are fellow-heirs, and of the same body, and partakers of His promise in the Christ, through the good news, 7 of which I became a servant, according to the gift of the grace of God that was given to me, according to the working of His power; 8 to me—the less than the least of all the holy ones—was given this grace, among the nations to proclaim good news—the untraceable riches of the Christ, 9 and to cause all to see what [is] the fellowship of the secret that has been hid from the ages in God, who created all things by Jesus Christ, 10 that there might be made known now to the principalities and the authorities in the heavenly [places], through the Assembly, the manifold wisdom of God, 11 according to a purpose of the ages, which He made in Christ Jesus our Lord, 12 in whom we have the freedom and the access in confidence through the faith of Him, 13 for this reason, I ask [you] not to faint in my tribulations for you, which is your glory. 14 For this cause I bow my knees to the Father of our Lord Jesus Christ, 15 of whom the whole family in the heavens and on earth is named, 16 that He may give to you, according to the riches of His glory, to be strengthened through His Spirit with might, in regard to the inner man, 17 that the Christ may dwell through the faith in your hearts, having been rooted and founded in love, 18 that you may be in strength to comprehend, with all the holy ones, what [is] the breadth, and length, and depth, and height, 19 to know also the love of the Christ that is exceeding the knowledge, that you may be filled—to all the fullness of God; 20 and to Him who is able to do exceedingly [and] abundantly above all things that we ask or think, according to the power that is working in us, 21 to Him [is] the glory in the Assembly in Christ Jesus, to all the generations of the age of the ages. Amen.

CHAPTER 4

1 I, the prisoner of the Lord, then call on you to walk worthily of the calling with which you were called, 2 with all lowliness and meekness, with long-suffering, bearing with one another in love, 3 being diligent to keep the unity of the Spirit in the bond of peace; 4 one body and one Spirit, according as you were also called in one hope of your calling; 5 one Lord, one faith, one immersion, 6 one God and Father of all, who [is] over all, and through all, and in you all, 7 and to each one of you was given grace, according to the measure of the gift of Christ, 8 for this reason, it says, "Having gone up on high He led captive captivity, and gave gifts to men." 9 And that, He went up, what is it except that He also went down first into the lower parts of the earth? 10 he who went down is the same

who also went up far above all the heavens, that He may fill all things— 11 and He gave some [as] apostles, and some [as] prophets, and some [as] proclaimers of good news, and some [as] shepherds and teachers, 12 to the perfecting of the holy ones, for a work of ministry, for a building up of the body of the Christ, 13 until we may all come to the unity of faith and of the recognition of the Son of God, to a perfect man, to a measure of stature of the fullness of the Christ, 14 that we may no longer be children, being tossed by waves and being carried around by every wind of the teaching, in the cunning of men, in craftiness, to the scheming of leading astray, 15 and [speaking] truth in love, we may increase to Him [in] all things, who is the head—the Christ; 16 from whom the whole body, being fitly joined together and united, through the supply of every joint, according to the working in the measure of each single part, the increase of the body makes for the building up of itself in love. 17 This, then, I say, and I testify in the Lord: you are no longer to walk, as also the other nations walk, in the vanity of their mind, 18 being darkened in the understanding, being alienated from the life of God, because of the ignorance that is in them, because of the hardness of their heart, 19 who, having ceased to feel, gave themselves up to the licentiousness, for the working of all uncleanness in greediness; 20 and you did not so learn the Christ, 21 if [it] so be [that] you heard Him, and were taught in Him, as truth is in Jesus; 22 concerning the former behavior you are to put off the old man, that is corrupt according to the desires of the deceit, 23 and to be renewed in the spirit of your mind, 24 and to put on the new man, which, according to God, was created in righteousness and kindness of the truth. 25 For this reason, putting away the lying, each speak truth with his neighbor, because we are members of one another; 26 be angry and do not sin; do not let the sun go down on your wrath, 27 neither give place to the Devil; 28 whoever is stealing let him no longer steal, but rather let him labor, working the thing that is good with the hands, that he may have to impart to him having need. 29 Let no corrupt word go forth out of your mouth, but what is good to the necessary building up, that it may give grace to the hearers; 30 and do not make the Holy Spirit of God sorrowful, in which you were sealed to [the] day of redemption. 31 Let all bitterness, and wrath, and anger, and clamor, and slander, be put away from you, with all malice, 32 and become kind to one another, tender-hearted, forgiving one another, according as God also forgave you in Christ.

CHAPTER 5

1 Become, then, followers of God, as beloved children, 2 and walk in love, as the Christ also loved us, and gave Himself for us, an offering and a sacrifice to God for an odor of a refreshing fragrance, 3 and whoredom, and all uncleanness, or covetousness, do not let it even be named among you, as is proper to holy ones; 4 also filthiness, and foolish talking, or jesting—the things not fit—but rather thanksgiving; 5 for you know this, that every whoremonger, or unclean, or covetous person, who is an idolater, has no inheritance in the kingdom of the Christ and God. 6 Let no one deceive you with vain words, for because of these things comes the anger of God on the sons of the disobedience; 7 do not become, then, partakers with them, 8 for you were once darkness, and now light in the Lord; walk as children of light, 9 for the fruit of the light [is] in all goodness, and righteousness, and truth, 10 proving what is well-pleasing to the Lord; 11 and have no fellowship with the unfruitful works of the darkness and rather even convict, 12 for it is a shame even to speak of the things done by them in secret, 13 and all the things reproved by the light are revealed, for everything that is revealed is light; 14 for this reason it says, "Arouse yourself, you who are sleeping, and arise out of the dead, and the Christ will shine on you." 15 See, then, how exactly you walk, not as unwise, but as wise, 16 redeeming the time, because the days are evil; 17 do not become fools because of this, but—understanding what [is] the will of the Lord, 18 and do not be drunk with wine, in which is wastefulness, but be filled in the Spirit, 19 speaking to yourselves in psalms and hymns and spiritual songs, singing and making melody in your heart to the Lord, 20 always giving thanks for all things, in the Name of our Lord Jesus Christ, to the God and Father, 21 subjecting yourselves to one another in the fear of Christ. 22 The wives: [subject yourselves] to your own husbands, as to the Lord, 23 because the husband is head of the wife, as also the Christ [is] head of the Assembly, and

He is Savior of the body, 24 but even as the Assembly is subject to Christ, so also [are] the wives [subject] to their own husbands in everything. 25 The husbands: love your own wives, as the Christ also loved the Assembly, and gave Himself for it, 26 that He might sanctify it, having cleansed [it] with the bathing of the water in the saying, 27 that He might present the Assembly to Himself in glory, having no spot or wrinkle, or any of such things, but that it may be holy and unblemished; 28 so ought the husbands to love their own wives as their own bodies: he who is loving his own wife—he loves himself; 29 for no one ever hated his own flesh, but nourishes and nurtures it, as also the Lord—the Assembly, 30 because we are members of His body, [[of His flesh, and of His bones.]] 31 "For this cause will a man leave his father and mother, and will be joined to his wife, and the two will be into one flesh"; 32 this secret is great, and I speak in regard to Christ and to the Assembly; 33 but you also, everyone in particular—let each so love his own wife as himself, and the wife—that she may revere the husband.

CHAPTER 6

1 The children: obey your parents in the Lord, for this is right; 2 honor your father and mother, 3 which is the first command with a promise, "That it may be well with you, and you may live a long time on the land." 4 And the fathers: do not provoke your children, but nourish them in the instruction and admonition of the Lord. 5 The servants: obey the masters according to the flesh with fear and trembling, in the simplicity of your heart, as to the Christ; 6 not with eye-service as men-pleasers, but as servants of the Christ, doing the will of God out of [your] soul, 7 serving with goodwill, as to the Lord, and not to men, 8 having known that whatever good thing each one may do, this he will receive from the Lord, whether servant or freeman. 9 And the masters! Do the same things to them, letting threatening alone, having also known that your Master is in the heavens, and favor by appearance is not with Him. 10 As to the rest, my brothers, be strong in the Lord, and in the power of His might; 11 put on the whole armor of God, so you are able to stand against the schemes of the Devil, 12 because our wrestling is not with flesh and blood, but with the principalities, with the authorities, with the world-rulers of the darkness of this age, with the spiritual [forces] of evil in the heavenly [places]; 13 because of this take up the whole armor of God, that you may be able to resist in the day of the evil, and having done all things—to stand. 14 Stand, therefore, having your loins girded around in truth, and having put on the breastplate of righteousness, 15 and having the feet shod in the preparation of the good news of peace; 16 in all, having taken up the shield of faith, in which you will be able to quench all the fiery darts of the evil one, 17 and receive the helmet of the salvation, and the sword of the Spirit, which is the word of God, 18 through all prayer and supplication praying at all times in the Spirit, and in this, watching in all perseverance and supplication for all the holy ones— 19 and in behalf of me, that to me may be given a word in the opening of my mouth, in freedom, to make known the secret of the good news, 20 for which I am an ambassador in a chain, that in it I may speak freely—as it is necessary for me to speak. 21 And that you may know—you also—the things concerning me—what I do, Tychicus will make all things known to you, the beloved brother and faithful servant in the Lord, 22 whom I sent to you for this very thing, that you might know the things concerning us, and that he might comfort your hearts. 23 Peace to the brothers, and love, with faith, from God the Father, and the Lord Jesus Christ! 24 The grace with all those loving our Lord Jesus Christ—undecayingly! Amen.

PHILIPPIANS

CHAPTER 1

1 Paul and Timotheus, servants of Jesus Christ, to all the holy ones in Christ Jesus who are in Philippi, with overseers and servants: 2 Grace to you and peace from God our Father and the Lord Jesus Christ! 3 I give thanks to my God on all the remembrance of you, 4 always, in every supplication of mine

for you all, with joy making the supplication, 5 for your contribution to the good news from the first day until now, 6 having been confident of this very thing, that He who began a good work in you, will complete [it] until [the] day of Jesus Christ, 7 according as it is righteous for me to think this in behalf of you all, because of my having you in the heart, both in my bonds, and [in] the defense and confirmation of the good news, all of you being fellow-partakers with me of grace. 8 For God is my witness, how I long for you all with [the] yearnings of Jesus Christ, 9 and this I pray, that your love may abound yet more and more in full knowledge, and all discernment, 10 for your proving the things that differ, that you may be pure and offenseless—to [the] Day of Christ, 11 being filled with the fruit of righteousness, that [is] through Jesus Christ, to the glory and praise of God. 12 And I intend you to know, brothers, that the things concerning me, rather have come to an advancement of the good news, 13 so that my bonds have become evident in Christ in the whole Praetorium, and to all the other places, 14 and the greater part of the brothers in the Lord, having confidence by my bonds, are more abundantly bold to fearlessly speak the word. 15 Certain, indeed, even through envy and contention, and certain also through goodwill, preach the Christ; 16 one, indeed, of rivalry proclaims the Christ, not purely, supposing to add affliction to my bonds, 17 and the other out of love, having known that I am set for defense of the good news: 18 what then? in every way, whether in pretense or in truth, Christ is proclaimed—and I rejoice in this, indeed, and will rejoice. 19 For I have known that this will turn out to me for salvation, through your supplication, and the supply of the Spirit of Christ Jesus, 20 according to my earnest expectation and hope, that I will be ashamed in nothing, and in all freedom, as always, also Christ will now be magnified in my body, whether through life or through death, 21 for to me to live [is] Christ, and to die [is] gain. 22 And if to live in the flesh [is] to me a fruit of work, then what will I choose? I do not know; 23 for I am pressed by the two, having the desire to depart, and to be with Christ, for it is far better, 24 and to remain in the flesh is more necessary on your account, 25 and being persuaded of this, I have known that I will remain and continue with you all, to your advancement and joy of the faith, 26 that your boasting may abound in Christ Jesus in me through my coming again to you. 27 Only conduct yourselves worthily of the good news of the Christ, that, whether having come and seen you, whether being absent I may hear of the things concerning you, that you stand fast in one spirit, with one soul, striving together for the faith of the good news, 28 and not be terrified in anything by those opposing, which is indeed a token of destruction to them, and to you of salvation, and that from God; 29 because to you it was granted, on behalf of Christ, not only to believe in Him, but also to suffer on behalf of Him; 30 having the same conflict, such as you saw in me, and now hear of in me.

CHAPTER 2

1 If, then, any exhortation [is] in Christ, if any comfort of love, if any fellowship of [the] Spirit, if any yearnings and mercies, 2 fulfill my joy, that you may mind the same thing—having the same love—of one soul—minding the one thing, 3 nothing in rivalry or vainglory, but in humility of mind counting one another more excellent than yourselves— 4 do not each look to your own, but each also to the things of others. 5 For let this mind be in you that [is] also in Christ Jesus, 6 who, being in the form of God, thought [it] not something to be seized to be equal to God, 7 but emptied Himself, having taken the form of a servant, having been made in the likeness of men, 8 and having been found in appearance as a man, He humbled Himself, having become obedient to death—even death of a cross, 9 for this reason, also, God highly exalted Him, and gave to Him a Name that [is] above every name, 10 that in the Name of Jesus every knee may bow—of heavenlies, and earthlies, and what are under the earth— 11 and every tongue may confess that Jesus Christ [is] Lord, to the glory of God the Father. 12 So that, my beloved, as you always obey, not as in my presence only, but now much more in my absence, work out your own salvation with fear and trembling, 13 for it is God who is working in you both to will and to work for His good pleasure. 14 Do all things without murmurings and deliberations, 15 that you may become blameless and pure children of God, unblemished in the midst of a crooked and perverse generation, among whom you appear as luminaries

in the world, 16 holding forth the word of life, for rejoicing to me in regard to [the] Day of Christ, that I did not run in vain, nor did I labor in vain; 17 but if I also am poured forth on the sacrifice and service of your faith, I rejoice and am glad with you all, 18 because of this you also rejoice and are glad with me. 19 And I hope, in the Lord Jesus, to send Timotheus to you quickly, that I also may be of good spirit, having known the things concerning you, 20 for I have no one like-minded, who will sincerely care for the things concerning you, 21 for the whole seek their own things, not the things of Christ Jesus, 22 and you know his proof, that as a child [serves] a father, he served with me in regard to the good news; 23 I indeed hope to send him, when I may see through the things concerning me—immediately; 24 and I trust in the Lord that I will also come quickly myself. 25 And I thought [it] necessary to send to you Epaphroditus—my brother and fellow-workman and fellow-soldier, and your apostle and servant to my need, 26 seeing he was longing after you all, and in heaviness, because you heard that he ailed, 27 for he also ailed near to death, but God dealt kindly with him, and not with him only, but also with me, that I might not have sorrow on sorrow. 28 The more eagerly, therefore, I sent him, that having seen him again you may rejoice, and I may be less sorrowful; 29 receive him, therefore, in the Lord, with all joy, and hold such in honor, 30 because on account of the work of the Christ he drew near to death, having hazarded life that he might fill up your deficiency of service to me.

CHAPTER 3

1 As to the rest, my brothers, rejoice in the Lord; indeed, [it] is not tiresome to me to write to you the same things, and for you [is] sure. 2 Look out for the dogs! Look out for the evil-workers! Look out for the mutilation! 3 For we are the circumcision, who are serving God by the Spirit, and glorying in Christ Jesus, and having no trust in flesh, 4 though I also have [cause of] trust in flesh. If any other one thinks to have trust in flesh, I more: 5 circumcisions on the eighth day! Of the race of Israel! Of the tribe of Benjamin! A Hebrew of Hebrews! According to law—a Pharisee! 6 according to zeal—persecuting the Assembly! According to righteousness that is in law—becoming blameless! 7 But what things were gains to me, these I have counted loss, because of the Christ; 8 yes, indeed, and I count all things to be loss, because of the excellence of the knowledge of Christ Jesus my Lord, because of whom I suffered loss of all things, and count them to be refuse, that I may gain Christ, and be found in Him, 9 not having my righteousness, which [is] of law, but that which [is] through faith from Christ—the righteousness that is of God by faith, 10 to know Him, and the power of His resurrection, and the fellowship of His sufferings, being conformed to His death, 11 if anyhow I may attain to the resurrection of the dead. 12 Not that I already obtained, or have already been perfected, but I pursue, if I also may lay hold of that for which I was also laid hold of by Christ Jesus; 13 brothers, I do not reckon myself to have laid hold [of it], but one thing [I do]—indeed forgetting the things behind, and stretching forth to the things before— 14 I pursue to the mark for the prize of the high calling of God in Christ Jesus. 15 As many, therefore, as [are] perfect—let us think this, and if [in] anything you think otherwise, this also will God reveal to you, 16 but to what we have attained—walk by the same rule, think the same thing; 17 together become my followers, brothers, and observe those thus walking, according as you have us—a pattern; 18 for many walk of whom I told you [about] many times—and now also weeping tell—[they are] the enemies of the Cross of the Christ, 19 whose end [is] destruction, whose god [is] the belly, and whose glory [is] in their shame, who are minding the things on earth. 20 For our citizenship is in the heavens, from where we also await a Savior—the Lord Jesus Christ— 21 who will transform the body of our humiliation to its becoming conformed to the body of His glory, according to the working of His power, even to subject all things to Himself.

CHAPTER 4

1 So then, my brothers, beloved and longed for, my joy and garland, so stand in the Lord, beloved. 2 I exhort Euodia, and I exhort Syntyche, to be of the same mind in the Lord; 3

and I also ask you, genuine yoke-fellow, be assisting those women who strove along with me in the good news, with Clement also, and the others, my fellow-workers, whose names [are] in [the] Scroll of Life. 4 Rejoice in the Lord always; again I will say, rejoice! 5 Let your reasonableness be known to all men; the Lord [is] near; 6 be anxious for nothing, but in everything by prayer, and by supplication, with thanksgiving, let your requests be made known to God; 7 and the peace of God, that is surpassing all understanding, will guard your hearts and your thoughts in Christ Jesus. 8 As to the rest, brothers, as many things as are true, as many as [are] revered, as many as [are] righteous, as many as [are] pure, as many as [are] lovely, as many as [are] of good report, if any worthiness, and if any praise, think on these things; 9 the things that you also learned, and receive, and hear, and saw in me, do those, and the God of peace will be with you. 10 And I rejoiced in the Lord greatly, that now at length you flourished again in caring for me, for which also you were caring, and lacked opportunity; 11 I do not say that in respect of want, for I learned in the things in which I am—to be content; 12 I have known both to be abased, and I have known to abound; in everything and in all things I have been initiated, both to be full and to be hungry, both to abound and to be in want. 13 I have strength for all things, in Christ's strengthening me; 14 but you did well, having shared in my tribulation; 15 and you have known, even you Philippians, that in the beginning of the good news when I went forth from Macedonia, no assembly communicated with me in regard to giving and receiving except you only; 16 because in Thessalonica also, both once and again you sent to my need; 17 not that I seek after the gift, but I seek after the fruit that is overflowing to your account; 18 and I have all things, and abound; I am filled, having received from Epaphroditus the things from you—an odor of a refreshing fragrance—a sacrifice acceptable, well-pleasing to God; 19 and my God will supply all your need, according to His riches in glory in Christ Jesus; 20 and to God, even our Father, [is] the glory through the ages of the ages. Amen. 21 Every holy one in Christ Jesus greets you; the brothers with me greet you; 22 all the holy ones greet you, and especially those of Caesar's house. 23 The grace of our Lord Jesus Christ [is] with you all! Amen.

COLOSSIANS

CHAPTER 1

[1] Paul, an apostle of Jesus Christ through the will of God, and Timotheus the brother, [2] to the holy ones in Colossae, and to the faithful brothers in Christ: Grace to you and peace from God our Father and the Lord Jesus Christ! [3] We give thanks to the God and Father of our Lord Jesus Christ, always praying for you, [4] having heard of your faith in Christ Jesus, and of the love that [is] to all the holy ones, [5] because of the hope that is laid up for you in the heavens, which you heard of beforehand by the word of the truth of the good news, [6] which has come to you, as also in all the world, and is bearing fruit, as also in you, from the day in which you heard, and knew the grace of God in truth, [7] as you also learned from Epaphras, our beloved fellow-servant, who is a faithful servant of the Christ for you, [8] who also declared to us your love in the Spirit. [9] Because of this, we also, from the day in which we heard, do not cease praying for you, and asking that you may be filled with the full knowledge of His will in all wisdom and spiritual understanding, [10] to walk worthily of the Lord, pleasing in all, being fruitful in every good work, and increasing in the knowledge of God, [11] in all might being made mighty according to the power of His glory, to all endurance and long-suffering with joy. [12] Giving thanks to the Father who has qualified us for the participation of the inheritance of the holy ones in the light, [13] who rescued us out of the authority of the darkness, and translated [us] into the kingdom of the Son of His love, [14] in whom we have the redemption [[through His blood]], the forgiveness of sins, [15] who is the image of the invisible God, firstborn of all creation, [16] because all things were created in Him, those in the heavens, and those on the earth, those visible, and those invisible, whether thrones, whether lordships, whether principalities, whether authorities; all things have been created through Him and for Him, [17] and He is before all, and all things have consisted in Him. [18] And He is the head of the body—the

Assembly—who is a beginning, a firstborn out of the dead, that He might become first in all [things] Himself, [19] because all the fullness was pleased to dwell in Him, [20] and through Him to reconcile all things to Himself—having made peace through the blood of His Cross—through Him, whether the things on the earth, whether the things in the heavens. [21] And you—once being alienated, and enemies in the mind, in the evil works, yet now He reconciled, [22] in the body of His flesh through death, to present you holy, and unblemished, and unblameable before Himself, [23] if you also remain in the faith, being founded and settled, and not moved away from the hope of the good news, which you heard, which was preached in all the creation that [is] under Heaven, of which I, Paul, became a servant. [24] I now rejoice in my sufferings for you, and fill up the things lacking of the tribulations of the Christ in my flesh for His body, which is the Assembly, [25] of which I became a servant according to the dispensation of God, that was given to me for you, to fulfill the word of God, [26] the secret that has been hid from the ages and from the generations, but now was revealed to His holy ones, [27] to whom God willed to make known what [is] the riches of the glory of this secret among the nations—which is Christ in you, the hope of the glory, [28] whom we proclaim, warning every man, and teaching every man, in all wisdom, that we may present every man perfect in Christ Jesus, [29] for which I also labor, striving according to His working that is working in me in power.

CHAPTER 2

1 For I wish you to know how great a conflict I have for you and those in Laodicea, and as many as have not seen my face in the flesh, 2 that their hearts may be comforted, being united in love, and to all riches of the full assurance of the understanding, to the full knowledge of the secret of the God and Father, and of the Christ, 3 in whom are all the treasures of the wisdom and the knowledge hid, 4 and this I say, that no one may deceive you with enticing words, 5 for if even in the flesh I am absent—yet in the spirit I am with you, rejoicing and beholding your order, and the steadfastness of your faith in regard to Christ; 6 as, then, you received Christ Jesus the Lord, walk in Him, 7 being rooted and built up in Him, and confirmed in the faith, as you were taught—abounding in it in thanksgiving. 8 See that no one will be carrying you away as spoil through philosophy and vain deceit, according to the tradition of men, according to the rudiments of the world, and not according to Christ, 9 because in Him dwells all the fullness of the Godhead bodily, 10 and you are made full in Him, who is the head of all principality and authority, 11 in whom you also were circumcised with a circumcision not made with hands, in the putting off of the body of sins of the flesh by the circumcision of the Christ, 12 being buried with Him in the immersion, in which you also rose with [Him] through the faith of the working of God, who raised Him out of the dead. 13 And you—being dead in the trespasses and the uncircumcision of your flesh—He made alive together with Him, having forgiven you all the trespasses, 14 having blotted out the handwriting in the ordinances that is against us, that was contrary to us, and He has taken it out of the way, having nailed it to the Cross; 15 having stripped the principalities and the authorities, He made a show of them openly—having triumphed over them by it. 16 Let no one, then, judge you in eating or in drinking, or in respect of a celebration, or of a new moon, or of Sabbaths, 17 which are a shadow of the coming things, but the body [is] of the Christ; 18 let no one deceive you of your prize, delighting in humble-mindedness and [in] worship of the messengers, intruding into the things he has not seen, being vainly puffed up by the mind of his flesh, 19 and not holding the Head, from which all the body—gathering supply through the joints and bands, and being knit together—may increase with the increase of God. 20 If, then, you died with the Christ from the rudiments of the world, why, as living in the world, are you subject to ordinances— 21 you may not touch, nor taste, nor handle— 22 which are all for destruction with the using, after the commands and teachings of men, 23 which are, indeed, having a matter of wisdom in self-willed religion, and humble-mindedness, and neglecting of body—not of any value to satisfying the flesh.

CHAPTER 3

1 If, then, you were raised with the Christ, seek the things above, where the Christ is, seated on the right hand of God; 2 mind the things above, not the things on the earth, 3 for you died, and your life has been hid with the Christ in God; 4 when the Christ—our life—may have appeared, then we will also appear with Him in glory. 5 Put to death, then, your members that [are] on the earth—whoredom, uncleanness, passion, evil desire, and the covetousness, which is idolatry— 6 because of which things comes the anger of God on the sons of the disobedience, 7 in which you also—you once walked, when you lived in them; 8 but now put off, even you, the whole—anger, wrath, malice, slander, filthy talking—out of your mouth. 9 Do not lie to one another, having put off the old man with his practices, 10 and having put on the new, which is renewed in regard to knowledge, after the image of Him who created him, 11 where there is not Greek and Jew, circumcision and uncircumcision, foreigner, Scythian, servant, freeman, but Christ [is] all and in all. 12 Put on, therefore, as chosen ones of God, holy and beloved, yearnings of mercies, kindness, humble-mindedness, meekness, long-suffering, 13 bearing with one another, and forgiving each other, if anyone may have a quarrel with anyone, as the Christ also forgave you—so also you; 14 and above all these things, [have] love, which is a bond of the perfection, 15 and let the peace of God rule in your hearts, to which you were also called in one body, and become thankful. 16 Let the word of Christ dwell in you richly, in all wisdom, teaching and admonishing each other, in psalms, and hymns, and spiritual songs, in grace singing in your hearts to the Lord; 17 and all, whatever you may do in word or in work, [do] all things in the Name of the Lord Jesus—giving thanks to the God and Father, through Him. 18 The wives: be subject to your own husbands, as is fit in the Lord; 19 the husbands: love your wives, and do not be bitter with them; 20 the children: obey the parents in all things, for this is well-pleasing to the Lord; 21 the fathers: do not distress your children, lest they be discouraged; 22 the servants: obey those who are masters in all things according to the flesh, not in eye-service as men-pleasers, but in simplicity of heart, fearing God; 23 and all, whatever you may do—out of soul work—as to the Lord, and not to men, 24 having known that you will receive the repayment of the inheritance from the Lord—for you serve the Lord Christ; 25 and he who is doing unrighteously will receive what he did unrighteously, and there is no favor by appearance.

CHAPTER 4

[1] The masters: give that which is righteous and equal to the servants, having known that you also have a Master in the heavens. [2] Continue in the prayer, watching in it in thanksgiving, [3] also praying for us at the same time, that God may open to us a door for the word, to speak the secret of the Christ, because of which I have also been bound, [4] that I may reveal it, as it is necessary for me to speak. [5] Walk in wisdom toward those outside, redeeming the time, [6] your word always being seasoned with salt in grace—to know how it is necessary for you to answer each one. [7] Tychicus will make known to you all the things concerning me—the beloved brother, and faithful servant, and fellow-servant in the Lord— [8] whom I sent to you for this very thing, that he might know the things concerning you, and might comfort your hearts, [9] with Onesimus the faithful and beloved brother, who is of you; they will make known to you all things that [are] here. [10] Aristarchus greets you, my fellow-captive, and Marcus, the nephew of Barnabas (concerning whom you received commands—if he may come to you, receive him), [11] and Jesus who is called Justus, who are of circumcision: these [are the] only fellow-workers for the Kingdom of God who become a comfort to me. [12] Epaphras greets you, who [is] of you, a servant of Christ, always striving for you in the prayers, that you may stand perfect and made full in all the will of God, [13] for I testify to him that he has much zeal for you, and those in Laodicea, and those in Hierapolis. [14] Lucas greets you, the beloved physician, and Demas; [15] those in Laodicea greet you—brothers, and Nymphas, and the assembly in his house; [16] and when the letter may be read with you, cause that it may also be read in the assembly of the Laodiceans, and the [letter] from Laodicea that you also may read; [17] and say to Archippus, "See to the ministry that you received in the Lord, that you may fulfill it." [18] The salutation [is] by my hand, Paul. Remember my bonds. The grace [is] with you! Amen.

1 THESSALONIANS

CHAPTER 1

1 Paul, and Silvanus, and Timotheus, to the assembly of Thessalonians in God the Father and the Lord Jesus Christ: Grace to you and peace from God our Father and the Lord Jesus Christ! 2 We always give thanks to God for you all, making mention of you in our prayers, 3 unceasingly remembering your work of faith, and the labor of the love, and the endurance of the hope, of our Lord Jesus Christ, in the presence of our God and Father, 4 having known, beloved brothers, by God, your [divine] selection, 5 because our good news did not come to you in word only, but also in power, and in the Holy Spirit, and in much assurance, even as you have known of what sort we became among you for your sake, 6 and you became imitators of us and of the Lord, having received the word in much tribulation with joy of the Holy Spirit, 7 so that you became patterns to all those believing in Macedonia and Achaia, 8 for from you has sounded forth the word of the Lord, not only in Macedonia and Achaia, but also in every place your faith toward God went forth, so that we have no need to say anything, 9 for they themselves declare concerning us what entrance we had to you, and how you turned to God from the idols, to serve a living and true God, 10 and to wait for His Son from the heavens, whom He raised out of the dead Jesus, who is rescuing us from the anger that is coming.

CHAPTER 2

[1] For you have known, brothers, that our entrance to you has not been in vain, [2] but having both suffered before, and having been mistreated (as you have known) in Philippi, we were bold in our God to speak to you the good news of God in much conflict, [3] for our exhortation [is] not out of deceit, nor out of uncleanness, nor in guile, [4] but as we have been approved by God to be entrusted with the good news, so we speak, not as pleasing men, but God, who is proving our hearts, [5] for at no time did we come with speech of flattery (as you have known), nor in a pretext for covetousness (God [is] witness), [6] nor seeking glory from men, neither from you nor from others, being able to be burdensome, as Christ's apostles. [7] But we became gentle in your midst, as a nurse may nurture her own children, [8] so being desirous of you, we are well-pleased to impart to you not only the good news of God, but also our own souls, because you have become beloved to us, [9] for you remember, brothers, our labor and travail, for working night and day not to be a burden on any of you, we preached the good news of God to you; [10] you [are] witnesses—God also—how piously and righteously and blamelessly we became to you who believe, [11] even as you have known how we are exhorting each one of you, as a father his own children, and comforting, and testifying, [12] for your walking worthily of God, who is calling you to His own kingdom and glory. [13] And because of this we also continually give thanks to God, that, having received the word of God [by] your hearing from us, you accepted, not the word of men, but as it truly is, the word of God, who also works in you who believe; [14] for you became imitators, brothers, of the assemblies of God that are in Judea in Christ Jesus, because you suffered such things, even you, from your own countrymen, as they also from the Jews, [15] who put to death both the Lord Jesus and their own prophets, and persecuted us, and they are not pleasing God, and [are] contrary to all men, [16] forbidding us to speak to the nations that they might be saved, so as to always fill up their sins, but [God's] anger came on them—to the end! [17] And we, brothers, having been taken from you for the space of an hour—in presence, not in heart—hurried more abundantly to see your face in much desire; [18] for this reason we wished to come to you (I, indeed, Paul), both once and again, and Satan hindered us; [19] for what [is] our hope, or joy, or garland of rejoicing? Are not even you before our Lord Jesus Christ at His coming? [20] for you are our glory and joy.

CHAPTER 3

1 For this reason, enduring no longer, we thought good to be left in Athens alone, 2 and sent Timotheus—our brother, and a servant of God, and our fellow-workman in the good news of the Christ—to establish you, and to comfort you concerning your faith, 3 that no one be moved in these tribulations, for you have known that we are set for this, 4 for even when we were with you, we said to you beforehand that we are about to suffer tribulation, as it also came to pass, and you have known [it]; 5 because of this also, I, no longer enduring, sent to know your faith, lest he who is tempting tempted you, and our labor might be in vain. 6 And Timotheus now having come to us from you, and having declared good news to us of your faith and love, and that you always have a good remembrance of us, desiring much to see us, as we also [to see] you, 7 because of this we were comforted, brothers, over you, in all our tribulation and necessity, through your faith, 8 because now we live, if you may stand fast in the Lord. 9 For what thanks are we able to repay to God for you, for all the joy with which we delight because of you in the presence of our God, 10 exceedingly imploring night and day, that we might see your face, and perfect the things lacking in your faith? 11 And our God and Father Himself, and our Lord Jesus Christ, direct our way to you, 12 and the Lord cause you to increase and to abound in the love to one another, and to all, even as we also to you, 13 in order to have established your hearts, blameless in sanctification before our God and Father, at the coming of our Lord Jesus Christ with all His holy ones.

CHAPTER 4

1 As to the rest, then, brothers, we request, and call on you in the Lord Jesus, as you received from us how it is necessary for you to walk and to please God, that you may abound the more, 2 for you have known what commands we gave you through the Lord Jesus; 3 for this is the will of God—your sanctification: that you abstain from the whoredom, 4 that each of you know to possess his own vessel in sanctification and honor, 5 not in the affection of desire, as also the nations that were not knowing God, 6 that no one goes beyond and defrauds his brother in the matter, because the Lord [is] an avenger of all these, as we also spoke to you before and testified, 7 for God did not call us to uncleanness, but in sanctification. 8 He, therefore, who is despising, does not despise man, but God, who also gave His Holy Spirit to us. 9 And concerning the brotherly love, you have no need of [my] writing to you, for you yourselves are God-taught to love one another, 10 for you do it also to all the brothers who [are] in all Macedonia; and we call on you, brothers, to abound still more, 11 and to study to be quiet, and to do your own business, and to work with your own hands, as we commanded you, 12 that you may walk properly to those outside, and may have lack of nothing. 13 And I do not wish you to be ignorant, brothers, concerning those who have fallen asleep, that you may not sorrow, as also the rest who have no hope, 14 for if we believe that Jesus died and rose again, so also God will bring with Him those asleep through Jesus, 15 for we say this to you in the word of the Lord, that we who are living—who remain over to the coming of the Lord—may not precede those asleep, 16 because the Lord Himself, with a shout, with the voice of a chief-messenger, and with the trumpet of God, will come down from Heaven, and the dead in Christ will rise first; 17 then we who are living, who are remaining over, will be snatched up together with them in [the] clouds to meet the Lord in [the] air, and so we will always be with the Lord; 18 so, then, comfort one another with these words.

CHAPTER 5

1 And concerning the times and the seasons, brothers, you have no need of my writing to you, 2 for you have thoroughly known that the Day of the Lord so comes as a thief in the night, 3 for when they may say, "Peace and security," then sudden destruction comes [on] them, as the travail [on] her who is with child, and they will not escape; 4 but you, brothers, are not in darkness, that the Day may catch you as a thief; 5 you are all sons of light, and sons of day; we are not of night, nor

of darkness, 6 so, then, we may not sleep as also the others, but watch and be sober, 7 for those sleeping, sleep by night, and those making themselves drunk, are drunken by night, 8 and we, being of the day—let us be sober, putting on a breastplate of faith and love, and a helmet—a hope of salvation, 9 because God did not appoint us to anger, but to the acquiring of salvation through our Lord Jesus Christ, 10 who died for us, that whether we wake—whether we sleep—we may live together with Him; 11 for this reason, comfort one another, and build up one another, as also you do. 12 And we ask you, brothers, to know those laboring among you and leading you in the Lord and admonishing you, 13 and to esteem them very abundantly in love, because of their work; be at peace among yourselves; 14 and we exhort you, brothers, admonish the disorderly, comfort the feeble-minded, support the weak, be patient to all; 15 see [that] no one may render evil for evil to anyone, but always pursue that which is good, both to one another and to all; 16 always rejoice; 17 continually pray; 18 give thanks in everything, for this [is] the will of God in Christ Jesus in regard to you. 19 Do not quench the Spirit; 20 do not despise prophesyings; 21 prove all things; hold fast [to] that which is good; 22 abstain from all appearance of evil; 23 and may the God of peace Himself sanctify you wholly, and may your whole spirit and soul and body be preserved, unblameably at the coming of our Lord Jesus Christ; 24 He who is calling you is steadfast, who also will do [it]. 25 Brothers, pray for us. 26 Greet all the brothers with a holy kiss. 27 I charge you [by] the Lord, that the letter be read to all the holy brothers. 28 The grace of our Lord Jesus Christ [is] with you! Amen.

2 THESSALONIANS

CHAPTER 1

1 Paul, and Silvanus, and Timotheus, to the assembly of Thessalonians in God our Father, and the Lord Jesus Christ: 2 Grace to you and peace from God our Father and the Lord Jesus Christ! 3 We always ought to give thanks to God for you, brothers, as it is fitting, because your faith increases greatly, and the love of each one of you all abounds to one another, 4 so that we ourselves glory in you in the assemblies of God, for your endurance and faith in all your persecutions and tribulations that you bear— 5 a token of the righteous judgment of God, for your being counted worthy of the Kingdom of God, for which you also suffer, 6 since [it is] a righteous thing with God to give back to those troubling you—tribulation, 7 and to you who are troubled—rest with us in the revelation of the Lord Jesus from Heaven, with messengers of His power, 8 in flaming fire, giving vengeance to those not knowing God, and to those not obeying the good news of our Lord Jesus Christ, 9 who will suffer justice—continuous destruction—from the face of the Lord, and from the glory of His strength, 10 when He may come to be glorified in His holy ones, and to be wondered at by all those believing—because our testimony was believed among you—in that day; 11 for which we also always pray for you, that our God may count you worthy of the calling, and may fulfill all the good pleasure of goodness, and the work of faith in power, 12 that the Name of our Lord Jesus Christ may be glorified in you, and you in Him, according to the grace of our God and Lord Jesus Christ.

CHAPTER 2

1 And we ask you, brothers, in regard to the coming of our Lord Jesus Christ, and of our gathering together to Him, 2 that you are not quickly shaken in mind, nor be troubled, neither through spirit, neither through word, neither through letters as

through us, as that the Day of the Lord has arrived; 3 do not let anyone deceive you in any way, because if the departure may not come first, the man of lawlessness may [not] be revealed—the son of destruction, 4 who is opposing and is raising himself up above all called god or worshiped, so as for him to have sat down in the temple of God, proclaiming that he is God. 5 Do you not remember that, yet being with you, I said these things to you? 6 and now, you have known what is restraining, for his being revealed in his own time, 7 for the secret of lawlessness already works, only the [One] now restraining [will do so] until He may come out of [the] midst, 8 and then the lawless one will be revealed, whom the Lord will consume with the Spirit of His mouth, and will nullify at the appearance of His coming, 9 whose coming is according to the working of Satan, in all power, and signs, and lying wonders, 10 and in all deceitfulness of the unrighteousness in those perishing, because they did not receive the love of the truth for their being saved, 11 and because of this God will send to them a working of delusion, for their believing the lie, 12 that they may be judged—all who did not believe the truth, but were well pleased in the unrighteousness. 13 And we ought to give thanks to God always for you, brothers, beloved by the Lord, that God chose you from the beginning to salvation, in sanctification of the Spirit, and belief of the truth, 14 to which He called you through our good news, to the acquiring of the glory of our Lord Jesus Christ; 15 so, then, brothers, stand fast, and hold the traditions that you were taught, whether through word, whether through our letter; 16 and may our Lord Jesus Christ Himself, and our God and Father, who loved us, and gave continuous comfort, and good hope in grace, 17 comfort your hearts, and establish you in every good word and work.

CHAPTER 3

1 As to the rest, pray, brothers, concerning us, that the word of the Lord may run and may be glorified, as also with you, 2 and that we may be delivered from the unreasonable and evil men, for not all [are] of the faith; 3 but faithful is the Lord who will establish you, and will guard [you] from the evil [one]; 4 and we now have confidence in the Lord, that which we command you both do and will do; 5 and the Lord direct your hearts to the love of God, and to the endurance of the Christ. 6 And we command you, brothers, in the Name of our Lord Jesus Christ, to withdraw yourselves from every brother walking disorderly, and not after the tradition that you received from us, 7 for you have known how it is necessary to imitate us, because we did not act disorderly among you; 8 nor did we eat bread of anyone for nothing, but in labor and in travail, working night and day, not to be chargeable to any of you; 9 not because we have no authority, but that we might give ourselves to you [as] a pattern, to imitate us; 10 for even when we were with you, this we commanded you, that if anyone is not willing to work, neither let him eat, 11 for we hear of some walking disorderly among you, working nothing, but being busybodies, 12 and such we command and exhort through our Lord Jesus Christ, that working with quietness, they may eat their own bread; 13 and you, brothers, may you not be weary doing well, 14 and if anyone does not obey our word through the letter, note this one, and have no company with him, that he may be ashamed, 15 and do not count as an enemy, but admonish as a brother; 16 and may the Lord of peace Himself always give to you peace in every way; the Lord [is] with you all! 17 The salutation by the hand of me, Paul, which is a sign in every letter; thus I write. 18 The grace of our Lord Jesus Christ [is] with you all! Amen.

1 TIMOTHY

CHAPTER 1

1 Paul, an apostle of Jesus Christ, according to a command of God our Savior, and of the Lord Jesus Christ our hope, 2 to Timotheus—genuine child in faith: Grace, kindness, peace, from God our Father and Christ Jesus our Lord! 3 According as I exhorted you to remain in Ephesus—I going on to Macedonia—that you might charge certain [ones] not to teach any other thing, 4 nor to give heed to fables and endless genealogies, that cause questions rather than [the] stewardship of God which [is] in faith. 5 And the end of the charge is love out of a pure heart, and of a good conscience, and of unhypocritical faith, 6 from which certain [men], having swerved, turned aside to vain discourse, 7 willing to be teachers of law, not understanding either the things they say, nor concerning what they confidently assert, 8 and we have known that the Law [is] good, if anyone may use it lawfully; 9 having known this, that law is not set for a righteous man, but for lawless and insubordinate persons, ungodly and sinners, impious and profane, murderers of fathers and murderers of mothers, manslayers, 10 whoremongers, homosexuals, enslavers, liars, perjured persons, and if there be any other thing that is adverse to sound doctrine, 11 according to the good news of the glory of the blessed God, with which I was entrusted. 12 And I give thanks to Him who enabled me—Christ Jesus our Lord—that He reckoned me steadfast, having put [me] to the ministry, 13 who before was speaking slander, and persecuting, and insulting, but I found kindness, because, being ignorant, I did [it] in unbelief, 14 and the grace of our Lord exceedingly abounded, with faith and love that [is] in Christ Jesus. 15 The word [is] steadfast, and worthy of all acceptance, that Christ Jesus came into the world to save sinners—of whom I am first; 16 but because of this I found kindness, that Jesus Christ might first show forth all long-suffering in me, for a pattern of those about to believe on Him to continuous life. 17 And to the King of the ages, the incorruptible, invisible, only wise God, [is] honor and glory through the ages of the ages! Amen. 18 I commit to you this charge, child Timotheus, according to the prophecies that went before on you, that you may war in them the good warfare, 19 having faith and a good conscience, which some having thrust away, made shipwreck concerning the faith, 20 of whom are Hymenaeus and Alexander, whom I delivered to Satan, that they might be instructed not to speak evil.

CHAPTER 2

1 I exhort, then, first of all, there be made supplications, prayers, intercessions, thanksgivings, for all men— 2 for kings, and all who are in authority, that we may lead a quiet and peaceable life in all piety and gravity, 3 for this [is] right and acceptable before God our Savior, 4 who wills all men to be saved, and to come to the full knowledge of the truth; 5 for [there is] one God, also one mediator of God and of men—the man Christ Jesus, 6 who gave Himself [as] a ransom for all— the testimony in its own times— 7 in regard to which I was set a preacher and apostle—truth I say in Christ, I do not lie—a teacher of nations, in faith and truth. 8 I intend, therefore, that men pray in every place, lifting up holy hands, apart from anger and deliberation; 9 also the women in like manner, in orderly apparel, to adorn themselves with modesty and sobriety, not in braided hair, or gold, or pearls, or clothing of great price, 10 but—which becomes women professing godly piety—through good works. 11 Let a woman learn in quietness in all subjection, 12 and I do not allow a woman to teach, nor to rule a husband, but to be in quietness, 13 for Adam was formed first, then Eve, 14 and Adam was not deceived, but the woman, having been deceived, came into transgression, 15 and she will be saved through the childbearing, if they remain in faith, and love, and sanctification, with sobriety.

CHAPTER 3

1 The word [is] steadfast: If anyone longs for overseership, he desires a right work; 2 it is required, therefore, the overseer to be blameless, a husband of one wife, vigilant, sober, respectable, a friend of strangers, apt to teach, 3 not given to wine, not a striker, but gentle, not contentious, not a lover of money, 4 leading his own house well, having children in subjection with all dignity, 5 (and if anyone has not known [how] to lead his own house, how will he take care of an assembly of God?) 6 not a new convert, lest having been puffed up he may fall to a judgment of the Devil; 7 and it is required of him also to have a good testimony from those outside, that he may not fall into reproach and a snare of the Devil. 8 Servants, in like manner, dignified, not double-tongued, not

given to much wine, not given to shameful gain, 9 having the secret of the faith in a pure conscience, 10 and let these also first be proved, then let them minister, being unblameable. 11 Women, in like manner, dignified, not false accusers, vigilant, faithful in all things. 12 Servants—let them be husbands of one wife, leading the children well, and their own houses, 13 for those who ministered well acquire a good step to themselves, and much boldness in faith that [is] in Christ Jesus. 14 I write to you these things, hoping to come to you soon, 15 and if I delay, that you may know how it is required to conduct yourself in the house of God, which is an assembly of the living God—a pillar and foundation of the truth, 16 and confessedly, great is the secret of piety: who was revealed in flesh, declared righteous in [the] Spirit, seen by messengers, preached among nations, believed on in the world, taken up in glory!

CHAPTER 4

1 And the Spirit expressly says that in latter times some will depart from the faith, giving heed to seducing spirits and teachings of demons, 2 speaking lies in hypocrisy, being seared in their own conscience, 3 forbidding to marry—to abstain from meats that God created to be received with thanksgiving by those believing and acknowledging the truth, 4 because every creature of God [is] good, and nothing [is] to be rejected, with thanksgiving being received, 5 for it is sanctified through the word of God and intercession. 6 Placing these things before the brothers, you will be a good servant of Jesus Christ, being nourished by the words of the faith, and of the good teaching, which you followed after, 7 but reject the profane and old women's fables, and exercise yourself to piety, 8 for bodily exercise is to little profit, but piety is profitable to all things, having promise of the life that now is, and of that which is coming; 9 the word [is] steadfast, and worthy of all acceptance; 10 for this we both labor and are reproached, because we hope on the living God, who is Savior of all men—especially of those believing. 11 Charge these things, and teach; 12 let no one despise your youth, but become a pattern of those believing in word, in behavior, in love, in spirit, in faith, in purity; 13 until I come, give heed to the reading, to the exhortation, to the teaching; 14 do not be careless of the gift in you, that was given you through prophecy, with laying on of the hands of the eldership; 15 be careful of these things; be in these things, that your advancement may be evident in all things; 16 take heed to yourself and to the teaching; remain in them, for doing this thing, you will save both yourself and those hearing you.

CHAPTER 5

1 You may not rebuke an elder, but exhort [him] as a father, younger persons as brothers, 2 aged women as mothers, younger ones as sisters—in all purity; 3 honor widows who are really widows; 4 and if any widow has children or grandchildren, let them first learn to show piety to their own house, and to give back a repayment to the parents, for this is right and acceptable before God. 5 And she who is really a widow and desolate, has hoped on God, and remains in the supplications and in the prayers night and day, 6 but she given to luxury [while] living has died; 7 and charge these things, that they may be blameless; 8 and if anyone does not provide for his own, and especially for those of the household, he has denied the faith, and he is worse than an unbeliever. 9 A widow—do not let her be enrolled under sixty years of age, having been a wife of one husband, 10 being testified to in good works: if she brought up children, if she entertained strangers, if she washed holy ones' feet, if she relieved those in tribulation, if she followed after every good work; 11 and be refusing younger widows, for when they may revel against the Christ, they wish to marry, 12 having judgment, because they cast away the first faith, 13 and also at the same time, they learn [to be] idle, going around the houses; and not only idle, but also tattlers and busybodies, speaking things they should not; 14 I intend, therefore, younger ones to marry, to bear children, to be mistress of the house, to give no occasion to the opposer of reviling; 15 for some already turned aside after Satan. 16 If any believing man or believing woman has widows, let them relieve them, and do not let the assembly be burdened, that it may relieve those [who are] really widows.

17 Let them, the well-leading elders, be counted worthy of double honor, especially those laboring in word and teaching, 18 for the Writing says, "You will not muzzle an ox treading out," and, "Worthy [is] the workman of his reward." 19 Do not receive an accusation against an elder, except on two or three witnesses. 20 Reprove those sinning before all, that the others may also have fear; 21 I fully testify, before God and the Lord Jesus Christ, and the chosen messengers, that you may keep these things, without prejudging, doing nothing by partiality. 22 Be quickly laying hands on no one, nor be having fellowship with [the] sins of others; be keeping yourself pure; 23 no longer be drinking water, but be using a little wine, because of your stomach and of your frequent sicknesses; 24 the sins of certain men are evident beforehand, leading before to judgment, but some also they follow after; 25 in like manner the right works are also evident beforehand, and those that are otherwise are not able to be hid.

CHAPTER 6

1 As many as are servants under a yoke, let them reckon their own masters worthy of all honor, that evil may not be spoken of the Name of God and the teaching; 2 and those having believing masters, do not let them slight [them], because they are brothers, but rather let them serve, because they are steadfast and beloved, who are partaking of the benefit. Be teaching and exhorting these things; 3 if anyone be teaching otherwise, and does not consent to sound words—those of our Lord Jesus Christ—and to the teaching according to piety, 4 he is proud, knowing nothing, but unhealthy about questions and word-striving, out of which come envy, strife, slanders, evil-surmisings, 5 wranglings of men wholly corrupted in mind, and destitute of the truth, supposing the piety to be gain; depart from such; 6 but it is great gain—the piety with contentment; 7 for we brought nothing into the world—because neither are we able to carry out anything; 8 but having food and raiment—with these we will suffice ourselves; 9 and those intending to be rich fall into temptation and a snare, and many desires, foolish and hurtful, that sink men into ruin and destruction, 10 for the love of money is a root of all the evils, which certain [ones] longing for went astray from the faith, and pierced themselves through with many sorrows; 11 and you, O man of God, flee these things, and pursue righteousness, piety, faith, love, endurance, meekness. 12 Be striving the good strife of the faith; be laying hold on the continuous life to which you also were called, and did profess the right profession before many witnesses. 13 I charge you, before God, who is making all things alive, and of Christ Jesus, who testified the right profession before Pontius Pilate, 14 that you keep the command unspotted, unblameable, until the appearing of our Lord Jesus Christ, 15 which He will show in His own times—the blessed and only sovereign, the King of the kings and Lord of the lords, 16 having immortality alone, dwelling in unapproachable light, whom no one of men saw, nor is able to see, to whom [is] honor and perpetual might! Amen. 17 Charge those rich in the present age not to be high-minded, nor to hope in the uncertainty of riches, but in the living God, who is giving to us all things richly for enjoyment— 18 to do good, to be rich in good works, to be ready to impart, willing to communicate, 19 treasuring up to themselves a right foundation for the time to come, that they may lay hold on [that which is] truly life. 20 O Timotheus, guard the thing entrusted, avoiding the profane vain-words and opposition of the falsely-named knowledge, 21 which certain [ones] professing—swerved concerning the faith. The grace [is] with you! Amen.

2 TIMOTHY

CHAPTER 1

1 Paul, an apostle of Jesus Christ, through the will of God, according to a promise of life that [is] in Christ Jesus, 2 to Timotheus, beloved child: Grace, kindness, peace, from God the Father and Christ Jesus our Lord! 3 I am thankful to God,

whom I serve from progenitors in a pure conscience, that I unceasingly have remembrance concerning you in my supplications night and day, 4 desiring to see you greatly, being mindful of your tears, that I may be filled with joy, 5 taking remembrance of the unhypocritical faith that is in you, that first dwelt in your grandmother Lois, and your mother Eunice, and I am persuaded that also in you. 6 For which cause I remind you to stir up the gift of God that is in you through the putting on of my hands, 7 for God did not give us a spirit of fear, but of power, and of love, and of a sound mind; 8 therefore you may not be ashamed of the testimony of our Lord, nor of me His prisoner, but you suffer evil along with the good news according to the power of God, 9 who saved us, and called with a holy calling, not according to our works, but according to His own purpose and grace, that was given to us in Christ Jesus, before the times of the ages, 10 and was made visible now through the appearing of our Savior Jesus Christ, who indeed abolished death, and enlightened life and immortality through the good news, 11 to which I was placed a preacher and an apostle, and a teacher of nations, 12 for which cause these things I also suffer, but I am not ashamed, for I have known in whom I have believed, and have been persuaded that He is able to guard that which I have committed to Him—to that day. 13 Hold the pattern of sound words, which you heard from me, in faith and love that [is] in Christ Jesus; 14 guard the good thing committed through the Holy Spirit that is dwelling in us; 15 you have known this, that they turned from me—all those in Asia, of whom are Phygellus and Hermogenes; 16 may the Lord give kindness to the house of Onesiphorus, because he refreshed me many times, and was not ashamed of my chain, 17 but being in Rome, he sought me very diligently and found [me]; 18 may the Lord give to him to find kindness from the Lord in that day; and you very well know how much he ministered in Ephesus.

CHAPTER 2

1 You, therefore, my child, be strong in the grace that [is] in Christ Jesus, 2 and the things that you heard from me through many witnesses, be committing these things to steadfast men, who will also be sufficient to teach others; 3 you, therefore, suffer evil as a good soldier of Jesus Christ; 4 no one serving as a soldier entangles himself with the affairs of life, that he may please him who enlisted him; 5 and if anyone also may strive, he is not crowned, except he may strive lawfully; 6 it is first necessary [for] the laboring farmer to partake of the fruits; 7 be considering what things I say, for the Lord gives to you understanding in all things. 8 Remember Jesus Christ, raised out of the dead, of the seed of David, according to my good news, 9 in which I suffer evil—to bonds, as an evildoer, but the word of God has not been bound; 10 because of this I endure all things, because of the chosen ones, that they also may obtain salvation that [is] in Christ Jesus, with perpetual glory. 11 The word [is] steadfast: For if we died together—we will also live together; 12 if we endure together— we will also reign together; if we deny [Him], He will also deny us; 13 if we are not steadfast, He remains steadfast; He is not able to deny Himself. 14 Remind [them] of these things, testifying fully before the Lord—not to strive about words to nothing profitable, but to the subversion of those hearing; 15 be diligent to present yourself approved to God—a workman not ashamed, straightly cutting the word of truth; 16 and stand aloof from the profane vain talkings, for they will advance to more impiety, 17 and their word will have pasture as a gangrene, of whom is Hymenaeus and Philetus, 18 who swerved concerning the truth, saying the resurrection to have already been, and overthrows the faith of some; 19 sure, nevertheless, the foundation of God has stood, having this seal: "The Lord has known those who are His," and, "Let him depart from unrighteousness—everyone who is naming the Name of Christ." 20 And in a great house there are not only vessels of gold and of silver, but also of wood and of earth, and some to honor, and some to dishonor: 21 if, then, anyone may cleanse himself from these, he will be a vessel to honor, sanctified and profitable to the master—having been prepared to every good work; 22 and flee the youthful lusts, and pursue righteousness, faith, love, peace, with those calling on the Lord out of a pure heart; 23 and be avoiding the foolish and uninstructed questions, having known that they beget strife, 24 and a servant of the Lord must not quarrel, but to be gentle to all, apt to teach, patient under evil, 25 instructing those

opposing in meekness—if perhaps God may give to them conversion to an acknowledging of the truth, 26 and they may awake out of the Devil's snare, having been caught by him at his will.

CHAPTER 3

1 And know this, that in the last days there will come perilous times, 2 for men will be lovers of themselves, lovers of money, boasters, proud, slanderous, disobedient to parents, unthankful, unkind, 3 without natural affection, implacable, false accusers, without control, barbaric, not lovers of those who are good, 4 traitors, reckless, lofty, lovers of pleasure more than lovers of God, 5 having a form of piety, but having denied its power; and be turning away from these, 6 for of these there are those coming into the houses and leading captive the weak women, loaded with sins, led away with manifold desires, 7 always learning, and never able to come to a knowledge of truth, 8 and even as Jannes and Jambres stood against Moses, so these also stand against the truth, men corrupted in mind, disapproved concerning the faith; 9 but they will not advance any further, for their folly will be evident to all, as theirs also became. 10 And you have followed after my teaching, manner of life, purpose, faith, long-suffering, love, endurance, 11 the persecutions, the afflictions, that befell me in Antioch, in Iconium, in Lystra; what persecutions I endured! And the Lord delivered me out of all. 12 And all who will to live piously in Christ Jesus will also be persecuted, 13 and evil men and impostors will advance to the worse, leading astray and being led astray. 14 And you—remain in the things which you learned and were entrusted with, having known from whom you learned, 15 and because you have known the Holy Writings from infancy, which are able to make you wise—to salvation, through faith that [is] in Christ Jesus. 16 Every Writing [is] God-breathed, and profitable for teaching, for conviction, for correction, for instruction that [is] in righteousness, 17 that the man of God may be fitted—having been completed for every good work.

CHAPTER 4

1 I fully testify, then, before God, and the Lord Jesus Christ, who is about to judge [the] living and dead at His appearing and His Kingdom— 2 preach the word; be earnest in season, out of season; convict, rebuke, exhort, in all long-suffering and teaching, 3 for there will be a season when they will not endure the sound teaching, but they will heap up teachers according to their own desires—having an itching ear, 4 and, indeed, they will turn away from hearing the truth, and they will be turned aside to the fables. 5 But you—watch in all things; suffer evil; do the work of one proclaiming good news; make full assurance of your ministry, 6 for I am already being poured out, and the time of my release has arrived; 7 I have striven the good strife, I have finished the course, I have kept the faith; 8 from now on there is laid up for me the garland of righteousness that the Lord—the Righteous Judge—will give to me in that day, and not only to me, but also to all those loving His appearing. 9 Be diligent to come to me quickly, 10 for Demas forsook me, having loved the present age, and went on to Thessalonica, Crescens to Galatia, Titus to Dalmatia; 11 only Lucas is with me; having taken Mark, bring [him] with you, for he is profitable to me for ministry; 12 and I sent Tychicus to Ephesus; 13 coming, bring the cloak that I left in Troas with Carpus and the scrolls—especially the parchments. 14 Alexander the coppersmith did me much evil; may the Lord repay to him according to his works, 15 of whom you also beware, for he has greatly stood against our words; 16 no one stood with me in my first defense, but all forsook me (may it not be reckoned to them), 17 but the Lord stood by me, and strengthened me, that the preaching might be fully assured through me, and all the nations might hear, and I was freed out of the mouth of a lion, 18 and the Lord will free me from every evil work, and will save [me]—to His heavenly kingdom; to whom [is] the glory through the ages of the ages! Amen. 19 Greet Prisca and Aquilas, and Onesiphorus' household; 20 Erastus remained in Corinth, and I left Trophimus ailing in Miletus; 21 be diligent to come before winter. Eubulus greets you, and Pudens, and Linus, and Claudia, and all the brothers. 22 The Lord Jesus Christ [is] with your spirit. The grace [is]

with you! Amen.

TITUS

CHAPTER 1

1 Paul, a servant of God, and an apostle of Jesus Christ, according to the faith of the chosen ones of God, and an acknowledging of truth that [is] according to piety, 2 on hope of continuous life, which God, who does not lie, promised before times of ages 3 (and He revealed His word in [His] own times), in preaching, which I was entrusted with, according to a charge of God our Savior, 4 to Titus—true child according to a common faith: Grace, [[kindness,]] peace, from God the Father and the Lord Jesus Christ our Savior! 5 For this cause I left you in Crete, that you may arrange the things lacking, and may set elders down in every city, as I appointed to you, 6 if anyone is blameless, a husband of one wife, having believing children, not under accusation of riotous living or insubordinate— 7 for it is required of the overseer to be blameless, as God's steward, not self-pleased, nor prone to anger, not given to wine, not an abuser, not given to shameful gain, 8 but a lover of strangers, a lover of [the] good, sober-minded, righteous, holy, self-controlled, 9 holding—according to the teaching—to the steadfast word, that he may also be able to exhort in the sound teaching, and to convict the deniers; 10 for there are many both insubordinate, vain-talkers, and mind-deceivers—especially those of the circumcision— 11 whose mouths must be covered, who overturn whole households, teaching what things it should not, for [the] sake of shameful gain. 12 A certain one of them, a prophet of their own, said, "Cretans! Always liars, evil beasts, lazy bellies!" 13 this testimony is true; for which cause convict them sharply, that they may be sound in the faith, 14 not giving heed to Jewish fables and commands of men, turning themselves away from the truth. 15 All things, indeed, [are] pure to the pure, and nothing [is] pure to the defiled and unsteadfast, but even the mind and the conscience of them [is] defiled. 16 They profess to know God, but they deny [Him] by their works, being abominable, and disobedient, and disapproved to every good work.

CHAPTER 2

1 But you—speak what is suitable [according] to the sound teaching. 2 Elders [are] to be temperate, dignified, sober, sound in faith, in the love, in the endurance. 3 Aged women, in like manner, in behavior as becomes sacred persons, not false accusers, not enslaved to much wine, teachers of good things, 4 that they may make the young women sober-minded, to be lovers of [their] husbands, lovers of [their] children, 5 sober, pure, keepers of [their own] houses, good, subject to their own husbands, that evil may not be spoken of the word of God. 6 The younger men, in like manner, exhort [them] to be sober-minded. 7 Concerning all things, present yourself [as] a pattern of good works—in the teaching [with] uncorruptedness, dignity, 8 sound discourse [that is] blameless, so that he who is of the contrary may be ashamed, having nothing evil to say concerning you. 9 Servants [are] to be subject to their own masters, to be well-pleasing in all things, not contradicting, 10 not stealing, but showing all good steadfastness, that the teaching of God our Savior they may adorn in all things. 11 For the saving grace of God has appeared to all men, 12 teaching us, that denying the impiety and the worldly desires, we may live soberly, and righteously, and piously in the present age, 13 waiting for the blessed hope and appearing of the glory of our great God and Savior Jesus Christ, 14 who gave Himself for us, that He might ransom us from all lawlessness, and might purify to Himself a special people, zealous of good works. 15 Speak these things, and exhort and convict with all authority; let no one despise you!

CHAPTER 3

1 Remind them to be subject to principalities and authorities, to obey rule, to be ready to every good work, 2 to speak evil of no one, not to be quarrelsome—gentle, showing all meekness to all men, 3 for we, also, were once thoughtless, disobedient, led astray, serving manifold desires and pleasures, living in malice and envy, odious—hating one another; 4 and when the kindness and the love to men of God our Savior appeared 5 (not by works that [are] in righteousness that we did but according to His kindness), He saved us, through a bathing of regeneration, and a renewing of the Holy Spirit, 6 which He poured on us richly, through Jesus Christ our Savior, 7 that having been declared righteous by His grace, we may become heirs according to the hope of continuous life. 8 The word [is] steadfast; and concerning these things I intend you to affirm fully, that they may be thoughtful, to be leading in good works—who have believed God; these are the good and profitable things to men, 9 but stand away from foolish questions, and genealogies, and contentions, and strivings about law—for they are unprofitable and vain. 10 Reject a heretical man, after a first and second admonition, 11 having known that he has been subverted who [is] such, and sins, being self-condemned. 12 When I will send Artemas to you, or Tychicus, be diligent to come to me to Nicopolis, for I have determined to winter there. 13 Diligently send forth Zenas the lawyer and Apollos on their way, that nothing to them may be lacking, 14 and let them learn—ours also—to be leading in good works to the necessary uses, that they may not be unfruitful. 15 All those with me greet you. Greet those cherishing us in faith. The grace [is] with you all!

PHILEMON

CHAPTER 1

1 Paul, a prisoner of Christ Jesus, and Timotheus the brother, to Philemon our beloved and fellow-worker, 2 and Apphia the beloved, and Archippus our fellow-soldier, and the assembly in your house: 3 Grace to you and peace from God our Father and the Lord Jesus Christ! 4 I give thanks to my God, always making mention of you in my prayers, 5 hearing of your love and faith that you have to the Lord Jesus and toward all the holy ones, 6 that the fellowship of your faith may become working in the full knowledge of every good thing that [is] in you toward Christ Jesus; 7 for we have much joy and comfort in your love, because the yearnings of the holy ones have been refreshed through you, brother. 8 For this reason, having in Christ much boldness to command you that which is fit— 9 because of the love I rather plead, being such a one as Paul the aged, and now also a prisoner of Jesus Christ; 10 I beg you concerning my child—whom I begot in my bonds—Onesimus, 11 who once was to you unprofitable, and now is profitable to me and to you, 12 whom I sent again to you—he who is my own heart, 13 whom I intended to retain to myself, that in your behalf he might minister to me in the bonds of the good news, 14 but apart from your mind I willed to do nothing, so that your good deed may not be as of necessity, but of willingness, 15 for perhaps because of this he departed for an hour, that you may have him continuously, 16 no longer as a servant, but above a servant—a beloved brother, especially to me, and how much more to you, both in the flesh and in the Lord! 17 If, then, you have fellowship with me, receive him as me, 18 and if he did hurt to you, or owes anything, charge this to me; 19 I, Paul, wrote with my hand, I will repay; besides, that I may not say that you also owe to me yourself. 20 Yes, brother, may I have profit of you in the Lord; refresh my yearnings in the Lord; 21 I wrote to you having been confident in your obedience, having known that you will also do above what I may say; 22 and at the same time also prepare for me a lodging, for I hope that through your prayers I will be granted to you. 23 Epaphras greets you (my fellow-captive in Christ Jesus), 24 Marcus, Aristarchus, Demas, Lucas, my fellow-workmen! 25 The grace of our Lord Jesus Christ [is] with your spirit! Amen.

HEBREWS

CHAPTER 1

1 In many parts and many ways, God, having spoken long ago to the fathers by the prophets, 2 in these last days speaks to us in [His] Son, whom He appointed heir of all things, through whom He also made the ages; 3 who being the brightness of the glory, and the impress of His subsistence, bearing up also all things by the saying of His might—having made a cleansing of our sins through Himself, sat down at the right hand of the Greatness in the highest, 4 having become so much better than the messengers, as He inherited a more excellent name than them. 5 For to which of the messengers did He ever say, "You are My Son—today I have begotten You?" And again, "I will be to Him for a Father, and He will be to Me for a Son?" 6 and when again He may bring the firstborn into the world, He says, "And let them worship Him—all messengers of God"; 7 and to the messengers, indeed, He says, "The [One] who is making His messengers spirits, and His ministers a flame of fire"; 8 but to the Son: "Your throne, O God, [is] throughout the age of the age; The scepter of righteousness [is the] scepter of Your kingdom; 9 You loved righteousness, and hated lawlessness; Because of this He anointed You—God, Your God—With oil of gladness above Your partners"; 10 and, "You, Lord, founded the earth at the beginning, || And the heavens are a work of Your hands. 11 These will perish, but You remain, || And all will become old as a garment, 12 And You will roll them together as a mantle, and they will be changed, || But You are the same, and Your years will not fail." 13 And to which of the messengers did He ever say, "Sit at My right hand, || Until I may make Your enemies Your footstool?" 14 are they not all spirits of service—being sent forth for ministry because of those about to inherit salvation?

CHAPTER 2

1 Because of this it is more abundantly necessary to take heed to the things heard, lest we may drift away, 2 for if the word being spoken through messengers became steadfast, and every transgression and disobedience received a just repayment, 3 how will we escape, having neglected such great salvation? which having received [that] spoken through the Lord [from] the beginning, was confirmed to us by those having heard, 4 God also bearing joint-witness both with signs and wonders, and manifold powers, and distributions of the Holy Spirit, according to His will. 5 For He did not subject the coming world to messengers, concerning which we speak, 6 and one in a certain place testified fully, saying, "What is man, that You are mindful of him, || Or a son of man, that You look after him? 7 You made him [a] little less than messengers, || You crowned him with glory and honor, || And set him over the works of Your hands, 8 You put all things in subjection under his feet," for in the subjecting to Him all things, He left nothing to Him unsubjected, but now we do not yet see all things subjected to Him, 9 and we see Him who was made [a] little less than messengers—Jesus—because of the suffering of death, having been crowned with glory and honor, that by the grace of God He might taste of death for everyone. 10 For it was fitting to Him, because of whom [are] all things, and through whom [are] all things, bringing many sons to glory, to make the author of their salvation perfect through sufferings, 11 for both He who is sanctifying and those sanctified [are] all of one, for which cause He is not ashamed to call them brothers, 12 saying, "I will declare Your Name to My brothers, || In the midst of an assembly I will sing praise to You"; and again, "I will be trusting on Him"; 13 and again, "Behold, I and the children that God gave to Me." 14 Seeing, then, the children have partaken of flesh and blood, He Himself also took part of the same in like manner, that through death He might destroy him having the power of death—that is, the Devil— 15 and might deliver those, whoever, with fear of death, throughout all their life, were subjects of bondage, 16 for doubtless, He does not lay hold of messengers, but He lays hold of [the] seed of Abraham, 17 for this reason it seemed necessary to Him to be made like the brothers in all things, that He might become a kind and faithful Chief Priest in the things related to God, to make propitiation for the sins of the people, 18 for in that He suffered, Himself being tempted, He is able to help those who are tempted.

CHAPTER 3

1 For this reason, holy brothers, partakers of a heavenly calling, consider the Apostle and Chief Priest of our profession, Christ Jesus, 2 being faithful to Him who appointed Him, as also Moses [was] in all His house. 3 For this One has been counted worthy of more glory than Moses, inasmuch as He who builds it has more honor than the house. 4 For every house is built by someone, and He who built all things [is] God, 5 and Moses [was] indeed steadfast in all His house, as an attendant, for a testimony of those things that were to be spoken— 6 but Christ, as a Son over His house, whose house we are, if we hold fast the boldness and the rejoicing of the hope to the end. 7 For this reason, as the Holy Spirit says, "Today, if you may hear His voice— 8 you may not harden your hearts, as in the provocation, in the day of the temptation in the wilderness, 9 in which your fathers tempted Me, and saw My works [for] forty years; 10 for this reason I was grieved with that generation and said, They always go astray in [their] heart, and these have not known My ways; 11 so I swore in My anger, They will [not] enter into My rest." 12 Watch out, brothers, lest there will be in any of you an evil heart of unbelief in the falling away from the living God, 13 but exhort one another every day, while [it] is called "Today," that none of you may be hardened by the deceitfulness of sin, 14 for we have become partakers of the Christ, if we may hold fast the confidence [we had] at the beginning to the end, 15 as it is said, "Today, if you may hear His voice, you may not harden your hearts, as in the provocation." 16 For who [were those], having heard, [that] provoked, but not all those having come out of Egypt through Moses? 17 But with whom was He grieved forty years? was it not with those who sinned, whose carcasses fell in the wilderness? 18 and to whom did He swear that they will not enter into His rest, except to those who did not believe? 19 And we see that they were not able to enter in because of unbelief.

CHAPTER 4

1 We may fear, then, lest a promise being left of entering into His rest, anyone of you may seem to have come short, 2 for we also are having good news proclaimed, even as they, but the word heard did not profit them, not being mixed with faith in those who heard, 3 for we enter into the rest—we who believed, as He said, "So I swore in My anger, They will [not] enter into My rest"; and yet the works were done from the foundation of the world, 4 for He spoke in a certain place concerning the seventh [day] thus: "And God rested in the seventh day from all His works"; 5 and in this [place] again, "They will [not] enter into My rest"; 6 since then, it remains for some to enter into it, and those who first heard good news did not enter in because of unbelief— 7 again He limits a certain day, "Today," in David saying, after so long a time, as it has been said, "Today, if you may hear His voice, you may not harden your hearts," 8 for if Joshua had given them rest, He would not have spoken after these things concerning another day; 9 there remains, then, a Sabbath rest to the people of God, 10 for he who entered into His rest, he also rested from his works, as God from His own. 11 May we be diligent, then, to enter into that rest, that no one may fall in the same example of the unbelief, 12 for the Word of God is living, and working, and sharper—beyond every two-edged sword—and piercing as far as [the] division of soul and spirit, of joints and also marrows, and a discerner of thoughts and intents of the heart; 13 and there is not a created thing hidden before Him, but all things [are] naked and open to His eyes—with whom is our reckoning. 14 Having, then, a great Chief Priest having passed through the heavens—Jesus the Son of God—may we hold fast the profession, 15 for we do not have a Chief Priest unable to sympathize with our weaknesses, but [One] tempted in all things in like manner, [yet] without sin; 16 we may come near, then, with freedom, to the throne of grace, that we may receive kindness, and find grace—for seasonable help.

CHAPTER 5

1 For every chief priest taken out of men is set in things [pertaining] to God in behalf of men, that he may offer both gifts and sacrifices for sins, 2 being able to be gentle to those being ignorant and going astray, since he is also surrounded with weakness; 3 and because of this [weakness] he ought, just as for the people, so also for himself, to bring forward [sacrifices] for sins; 4 and no one takes the honor to himself, but he who is called by God, as also Aaron. 5 So also the Christ did not glorify Himself to become Chief Priest, but He who spoke to Him: "You are My Son, today I have begotten You"; 6 just as He also says in another [place], "You [are] a priest throughout the age, according to the order of Melchizedek"; 7 who in the days of His flesh having offered up both prayers and supplications with strong crying and tears to Him who was able to save Him from death, and having been heard in respect to that which He feared, 8 though being a Son, [He] learned obedience by the things which He suffered, 9 and having been made perfect, He became the cause of continuous salvation to all those obeying Him, 10 having been called by God a Chief Priest according to the order of Melchizedek, 11 concerning the Word, of whom we have much [to speak], and of hard explanation to say, since you have become dull of hearing, 12 for even owing to be teachers, because of the time, again you have need that one teach you what [are] the elements of the beginning of the oracles of God, and you have become having need of milk, and not of strong food, 13 for everyone who is partaking of milk [is] unskilled in the word of righteousness— for he is an infant, 14 and the strong food is of perfect men, who because of the use are having the senses exercised, to both the discernment of good and of evil.

CHAPTER 6

1 For this reason, having left the word of the beginning of the Christ, we may advance to perfection, not laying again a foundation of conversion from dead works, and of faith on God, 2 of the teaching of immersions, also of laying on of hands, also of [the] resurrection of the dead, and of continuous judgment, 3 and this we will do, if God may permit, 4 for [it is] impossible for those once enlightened, having also tasted of the heavenly gift, and having become partakers of the Holy Spirit, 5 and tasted the good saying of God, also the powers of the coming age, 6 and having fallen away, to renew [them] again to conversion, having crucified to themselves the Son of God again, and exposed to public shame. 7 For the earth, having drunk in the rain coming on it many times, and is bringing forth herbs fit for those because of whom it is also dressed, partakes of blessing from God, 8 but that which is bearing thorns and briers [is] disapproved of, and near to cursing, whose end [is] for burning; 9 but we are persuaded, concerning you, beloved, the things that are better, and accompanying salvation, though even thus we speak, 10 for God is not unrighteous to forget your work, and the labor of love that you showed to His Name, having ministered to the holy ones and ministering; 11 and we desire each one of you to show the same diligence, to the full assurance of the hope to the end, 12 that you may not become slothful, but followers of those who through faith and patient endurance are inheriting the promises. 13 For God, having made promise to Abraham, seeing He was not able to swear by [any] greater, swore by Himself, 14 saying, "Blessing I will indeed bless you, and multiplying I will multiply you"; 15 and so, having patiently endured, he obtained the promise; 16 for men swear by the greater, and the oath [is] for confirmation of the end of all their controversy, 17 in which God, more abundantly willing to show to the heirs of the promise the immutability of His counsel, interposed by an oath, 18 that through two immutable things, in which [it is] impossible for God to lie, we may have a strong comfort, having fled for refuge, to lay hold on the hope being set before [us], 19 which we have, as an anchor of the soul, both sure and steadfast, and entering into that within the veil, 20 to where a forerunner entered for us—Jesus, having become Chief Priest throughout the age after the order of Melchizedek.

CHAPTER 7

1 For this Melchizedek, king of Salem, priest of God Most High, who met Abraham turning back from the striking of the kings, and blessed him, 2 to whom also Abraham divided a tenth of all (first, indeed, being interpreted, "King of righteousness," and then also, "King of Salem," which is, King of Peace), 3 without father, without mother, without genealogy, having neither beginning of days nor end of life, and having been like the Son of God, remains a priest continually. 4 And see how great this one [is], to whom Abraham the patriarch also gave a tenth out of the best of the spoils, 5 and those, indeed, out of the sons of Levi receiving the priesthood, have a command to take tithes from the people according to the Law, that is, their brothers, even though they came forth out of the loins of Abraham; 6 and he who was not reckoned by genealogy of them, received tithes from Abraham, and he has blessed him having the promises, 7 and apart from all controversy, the less is blessed by the better— 8 and here, indeed, men who die receive tithes, and there [he] who is testified to that he was living, 9 and so to speak, through Abraham even Levi who is receiving tithes, has paid tithes, 10 for he was yet in the loins of the father when Melchizedek met him. 11 If indeed, then, perfection were through the Levitical priesthood—for the people under it had received law—what further need, according to the order of Melchizedek, for another priest to arise, and not to be called according to the order of Aaron? 12 for the priesthood being changed, of necessity also, a change comes of the Law, 13 for He of whom these things are said in another tribe has had part, of whom no one gave attendance at the altar, 14 for [it is] evident that out of Judah has arisen our Lord, in regard to which tribe Moses spoke nothing concerning priesthood. 15 And it is yet more abundantly most evident, if according to the likeness of Melchizedek there arises another priest, 16 who did not come according to the law of a fleshly command, but according to the power of an endless life, 17 for He testifies, "You [are] a priest—throughout the age, according to the order of Melchizedek"; 18 for an annulling indeed comes of the command going before because of its weakness, and unprofitableness 19 (for nothing did the law perfect), and the bringing in of a better hope, through which we draw near to God. 20 And inasmuch as [it is] not apart from oath 21 (for those indeed apart from oath have become priests, and He [became priest] with an oath through Him who is saying to Him, "The Lord swore, and will not regret, You [are] a priest throughout the age, according to the order of Melchizedek"), 22 by so much also has Jesus become guarantee of a better covenant, 23 and those indeed are many who have become priests, because by death they are hindered from remaining; 24 and He, because of His remaining throughout the age, has the inviolable priesthood, 25 from where also He is able to save to the very end, those coming through Him to God—ever living to make intercession for them. 26 For also such a Chief Priest was fitting for us—holy, innocent, undefiled, separate from the sinners, and having become higher than the heavens, 27 who has no daily necessity, as the chief priests, to first offer up sacrifice for His own sins, then for those of the people; for this He did once, having offered up Himself; 28 for the Law appoints men [as] chief priests, having weakness, but the word of the oath that [is] after the Law [appoints] the Son having been perfected throughout the age.

CHAPTER 8

1 And the sum concerning the things spoken of [is]: we have such a Chief Priest, who sat down at the right hand of the throne of the Greatness in the heavens, 2 a servant of the holy places, and of the true dwelling place, which the Lord set up, and not man, 3 for every chief priest is appointed to offer both gifts and sacrifices, from where [it is] necessary for this One to also have something that He may offer; 4 for if, indeed, He were on earth, He would not be a priest (there being the priests who are offering the gifts according to the Law, 5 who to an example and shadow serve of the heavenly things, as Moses has been divinely warned, being about to construct the Dwelling Place, for, "See," He says, "[that] you will make all things according to the pattern that was shown to you on the mountain"), 6 but now He has obtained a more excellent service, how much He is also mediator of a better covenant, which has been sanctioned on better promises, 7 for if that first were faultless, a place would not have been sought for a second. 8 For finding fault, He says to them, "Behold, days

come, says the Lord, and I will complete with the house of Israel, and with the house of Judah, a new covenant, 9 not according to the covenant that I made with their fathers, in the day of My taking [them] by their hand, to bring them out of the land of Egypt—because they did not remain in My covenant, and I did not regard them, says the Lord— 10 because this [is] the covenant that I will make with the house of Israel, after those days, says the Lord, giving My laws into their mind, and I will write them on their hearts, and I will be to them for a God, and they will be to Me for a people; 11 and they will not each teach his neighbor, and each his brother, saying, Know the Lord, because they will all know Me—from the small one of them to the great one of them, 12 because I will be merciful to their unrighteousness, and I will remember their sins and their lawlessnesses no more." 13 In the saying "new," He has made the first obsolete, and what is becoming obsolete and growing old [is] near disappearing.

CHAPTER 9

1 It had, indeed, then (even the first dwelling place) ordinances of service, also a worldly sanctuary, 2 for a dwelling place was prepared, the first, in which was both the lampstand, and the table, and the Bread of the Presentation—which is called "Holy"; 3 and after the second veil a dwelling place that is called "Holy of Holies," 4 having a golden censer, and the Ark of the Covenant overlaid all over with gold, in which [is] the golden pot having the manna, and the rod of Aaron that budded, and the tablets of the covenant, 5 and over it cherubim of the glory, overshadowing the propitiatory covering, concerning which we are not to particularly speak now. 6 And these things having been thus prepared, into the first dwelling place, indeed, the priests go in at all times, performing the services, 7 and into the second, once in the year, only the chief priest, not apart from blood, which he offers for himself and the errors of the people. 8 By this the Holy Spirit was making evident that the way of the holy [places] has not yet been revealed, the first dwelling place yet having a standing, 9 which [is] an allegory in regard to the present time, in which both gifts and sacrifices are offered, which are not able, in regard to conscience, to make perfect him who is serving, 10 only on the basis of food, and drinks, and different immersions, and fleshly ordinances—until the time of reformation imposed on [them]. 11 But Christ having come, Chief Priest of the coming good things, through the greater and more perfect dwelling place not made with hands—that is, not of this creation— 12 neither through blood of goats and calves, but through His own blood, entered in once into the holy places, having obtained continuous redemption; 13 for if the blood of bulls, and goats, and ashes of a heifer, sprinkling those defiled, sanctifies to the purifying of the flesh, 14 how much more will the blood of the Christ (who through the perpetual Spirit offered Himself unblemished to God) purify your conscience from dead works to serve the living God? 15 And because of this, He is mediator of a new covenant, that [His] death having come for redemption of the transgressions under the first covenant, those called may receive the promise of the continuous inheritance, 16 for where a covenant [is], [it is] necessary to establish the death of the [one] having made [it], 17 for a covenant is affirmed at death, since it is not in force at all when the [one] having made [it] lives, 18 for which reason, not even the first has been initiated apart from blood, 19 for every command having been spoken, according to law, by Moses, to all the people, having taken the blood of the calves and goats, with water, and scarlet wool, and hyssop, he sprinkled both the scroll itself and all the people, 20 saying, "This [is] the blood of the covenant that God enjoined to you," 21 and he sprinkled both the Dwelling Place and all the vessels of the service with blood in like manner, 22 and with blood almost all things are purified according to the Law, and forgiveness does not come apart from blood-shedding. 23 [It is] necessary, therefore, the pattern indeed of the things in the heavens to be purified with these, and the heavenly things themselves with better sacrifices than these; 24 for the Christ did not enter into holy places made with hands—figures of the true—but into Heaven itself, now to be manifested in the presence of God for us; 25 nor that He may offer Himself many times, even as the chief priest enters into the holy places every year with blood of others, 26 otherwise it was necessary for Him to suffer many times from the foundation of the world, but now He has been revealed once, at the full end of the ages, for [the] annulling of sin through His sacrifice; 27 and as it is reserved for men to die once, and after this—judgment, 28 so also the Christ, having been offered once to bear the sins of many, will appear a second time, apart from a sin-offering, for salvation to those waiting for Him!

CHAPTER 10

1 For the Law having a shadow of the good things coming—not the very image of the matters, every year, by the same sacrifices that they offer continually, is never able to make perfect those coming near, 2 since, would they not have ceased to be offered, because of those serving having no more conscience of sins, having been purified once? 3 but in those [sacrifices] is a remembrance of sins every year, 4 for it is impossible for blood of bulls and goats to take away sins. 5 For this reason, coming into the world, He says, "Sacrifice and offering You did not will, and a body You prepared for Me; 6 in burnt-offerings, and concerning sin-offerings, You did not delight. 7 Then I said, Behold, I come (in a volume of the scroll it has been written concerning Me), to do, O God, Your will"; 8 saying above, "Sacrifice, and offering, and burnt-offerings, and concerning sin-offering You did not will, nor delight in" (which are offered according to the Law), 9 then He said, "Behold, I come to do, O God, Your will"; He takes away the first that He may establish the second; 10 in which will, we have been sanctified through the offering of the body of Jesus Christ once for all, 11 and every priest, indeed, has daily stood serving, and offering the same sacrifices many times, that are never able to take away sins. 12 But He, having offered one sacrifice for sin—to the end, sat down at the right hand of God— 13 as to the rest, expecting until He may place His enemies [as] His footstool, 14 for by one offering He has perfected to the end those being sanctified; 15 and the Holy Spirit also testifies to us, for after that He has said before, 16 "This [is] the covenant that I will make with them after those days, says the Lord, giving My laws on their hearts, and I will write them on their minds," 17 and, "I will remember their sins and their lawlessness no more"; 18 and where [there is] forgiveness of these, there is no longer offering for sin. 19 Having, therefore, brothers, boldness for the entrance into the holy places, by the blood of Jesus, 20 which [is] the way He initiated for us—new and living, through the veil, that is, His flesh— 21 and a Great Priest over the house of God, 22 may we draw near with a true heart, in full assurance of faith, having the hearts sprinkled from an evil conscience, and having the body bathed with pure water; 23 may we hold fast the unwavering profession of the hope (for He who promised [is] faithful), 24 and may we consider to provoke one another to love and to good works, 25 not forsaking the assembling of ourselves together, as [is] a custom of some, but exhorting, and so much the more as you see the Day coming near. 26 For [if] we are sinning willingly after receiving the full knowledge of the truth—there remains no more sacrifice for sins, 27 but a certain fearful looking for of judgment, and fiery zeal, about to devour the opposers; 28 anyone having set aside a law of Moses dies without mercies on the basis of two or three witnesses. 29 Of how much worse punishment will he be counted worthy who trampled on the Son of God, and counted the blood of the covenant a common thing, by which he was sanctified, and having insulted the Spirit of grace? 30 for we have known Him who is saying, "Vengeance [is] Mine, I will repay, says the Lord"; and again, "The Lord will judge His people." 31 [It is] fearful to fall into [the] hands of [the] living God. 32 But call to your remembrance the former days, in which, having been enlightened, you endured much conflict of sufferings; 33 this indeed, being made spectacles with both insults and afflictions, now this, having become partners of those so living, 34 for you also sympathized with my bonds, and the robbery of your goods you received with joy, knowing that you have in yourselves a better substance in the heavens, and an enduring one. 35 You may not cast away, then, your boldness, which has great repayment of reward, 36 for you have need of patience, that having done the will of God, you may receive the promise. 37 "For yet [in] a very, very little [while], He who is coming will come, and will not linger," 38 but, "The righteous will live by faith; and if he may draw back, My soul has no pleasure in him." 39 But we are not of those drawing back to destruction, but of those believing to a preserving of soul.

CHAPTER 11

1 Now faith is [the] substance of things hoped for, [the] proof of matters not being seen, 2 for by this, the elders were well-attested. 3 By faith we understand the ages to have been prepared by a saying of God, in regard to the things seen having not come out of things appearing. 4 By faith Abel offered a better sacrifice to God than Cain, through which he was testified to be righteous, God testifying of his gifts, and through it, he being dead, yet speaks. 5 By faith Enoch was translated—not to see death, and was not found, because God translated him; for before his translation he had been testified to—that he had pleased God well, 6 and apart from faith it is impossible to please [Him], for it is required of him who is coming to God to believe that He exists and [that] He becomes a rewarder to those seeking Him. 7 By faith Noah, having been divinely warned concerning the things not yet seen, having feared, prepared an ark to the salvation of his house, through which he condemned the world, and he became heir of the righteousness according to faith. 8 By faith Abraham, being called, obeyed, to go forth into the place that he was about to receive for an inheritance, and he went forth, not knowing to where he goes. 9 By faith he sojourned in the land of the promise as a strange country, having dwelt in dwelling places with Isaac and Jacob, fellow-heirs of the same promise, 10 for he was looking for the city having the foundations, whose craftsman and constructor [is] God. 11 And by faith Sarah, herself barren, received power to conceive seed even after the time of life, seeing she judged Him who promised faithful; 12 for this reason, also, from one—and that of one who had become dead—were begotten as the stars of the sky in multitude, and innumerable as the sand that [is] by the seashore. 13 All these died in faith, having not received the promises, but having seen them from afar, and having been persuaded, and having greeted [them], and having confessed that they are strangers and sojourners on the earth, 14 for those saying such things make apparent that they seek a country; 15 and if, indeed, they had been mindful of that from which they came forth, they might have had an opportunity to return, 16 but now they long for better, that is, heavenly, for this reason God is not ashamed of them, to be called their God, for He prepared a city for them. 17 By faith Abraham has offered up Isaac, being tried, even the [one] having received the promises offered up his only begotten, 18 of whom it was said, "In Isaac will your Seed be called," 19 reckoning that God is even able to raise up out of the dead, from where also in a figurative sense he received [him]. 20 By faith, concerning coming things, Isaac blessed Jacob and Esau. 21 By faith Jacob, dying, blessed each of the sons of Joseph and worshiped on the top of his staff. 22 By faith Joseph, dying, made mention concerning the outgoing of the sons of Israel, and gave command concerning his bones. 23 By faith Moses, having been born, was hid three months by his parents, because they saw the child beautiful, and were not afraid of the decree of the king. 24 By faith Moses, having become great, refused to be called a son of the daughter of Pharaoh, 25 having chosen rather to be afflicted with the people of God, than to have sin's pleasure for a season, 26 having reckoned the reproach of the Christ greater wealth than the treasures in Egypt, for he looked to the repayment of reward. 27 By faith he left Egypt behind, having not been afraid of the wrath of the king, for as seeing the Invisible One—he endured. 28 By faith he kept the Passover, and the sprinkling of the blood, so that He who is destroying the firstborn might not touch them. 29 By faith they passed through the Red Sea as through dry land, which having made an attempt [to cross], the Egyptians were swallowed up. 30 By faith the walls of Jericho fell, having been surrounded for seven days. 31 By faith Rahab the prostitute did not perish with those who disbelieved, having received the spies with peace. 32 And what yet will I say? for the time will fail me recounting about Gideon, also Barak, and Samson, and Jephthah, also David, and Samuel, and the prophets, 33 who through faith subdued kingdoms, worked righteousness, obtained promises, stopped mouths of lions, 34 quenched the power of fire, escaped the mouth of the sword, were made powerful out of weakness, became strong in battle, caused armies of the foreigners to give way; 35 women received their dead by a resurrection, and others were tortured, not accepting the redemption, that they might receive a better resurrection, 36 and others received trial of mockings and scourgings, and yet of bonds and imprisonment; 37 they were stoned, they were sawn apart, they were tried; they died in the killing of the sword; they went around in sheepskins, in goatskins—being destitute, afflicted, injuriously treated, 38 of whom the world was not worthy; wandering in deserts, and mountains, and caves, and the holes of the earth; 39 and all these, having been testified to through faith, did not receive the promise, 40 God, having provided something better for us, that apart from us they might not be made perfect.

CHAPTER 12

1 Therefore, we also having so great a cloud of witnesses set around us, having put off every weight, and the closely besetting sin, may we run the contest that is set before us through endurance, 2 looking to the Author and Perfecter of the faith—Jesus, who, for the joy set before Him, endured a cross, having despised shame, and sat down at the right hand of the throne of God; 3 for again consider Him who endured such contradiction from the sinners to Himself, that you may not be wearied in your souls—being faint. 4 You did not yet resist to blood—striving with sin; 5 and you have forgotten the exhortation that speaks fully to you as to sons, "My son, do not despise [the] discipline of [the] Lord, nor be faint, being reproved by Him, 6 for whom the Lord loves He disciplines, and He scourges every son whom He receives"; 7 if you endure discipline, God bears Himself to you as to sons, for who is a son whom a father does not discipline? 8 and if you are apart from discipline, of which all have become partakers, then you are bastards, and not sons. 9 Then, indeed, we have had fathers of our flesh, correctors, and we respected [them]; will we not much rather be subject to the Father of the spirits, and live? 10 for they, indeed, for a few days, according to what seemed good to them, were disciplining, but He for profit, to be partakers of His separation; 11 and all discipline for the present, indeed, does not seem to be of joy, but of sorrow, yet afterward it yields the peaceable fruit of righteousness to those exercised through it. 12 For this reason, lift up the hanging down hands and the loosened knees; 13 and make straight paths for your feet, so that which is lame may not be turned aside, but rather be healed; 14 pursue peace with all, and the separation, apart from which no one will see the Lord, 15 observing lest anyone be failing of the grace of God, lest any root of bitterness springing up may give trouble, and through this many may be defiled; 16 lest anyone be a fornicator, or a profane person, as Esau, who in exchange for one morsel of food sold his birthright, 17 for you know that also afterward, wishing to inherit the blessing, he was disapproved of, for he did not find a place of conversion, though having sought it with tears. 18 For you did not come near to the mountain touched and scorched with fire, and to blackness, and darkness, and storm, 19 and a sound of a trumpet, and a voice of sayings, which those having heard begged that a word might not be added to them, 20 for they were not bearing that which is commanded, "And if a beast may touch the mountain, it will be stoned, or shot through with an arrow," 21 and (so terrible was the sight), Moses said, "I am exceedingly fearful, and trembling." 22 But you came to Mount Zion, and to [the] city of the living God, to the heavenly Jerusalem, and to myriads of messengers, 23 to the assembly-place and Assembly of the Firstborn registered in Heaven, and to God the judge of all, and to spirits of righteous men made perfect, 24 and to a mediator of a new covenant—Jesus, and to blood of sprinkling, speaking better things than that of Abel! 25 Watch out lest you refuse Him who is speaking, for if those did not escape who refused him who was divinely speaking on earth—much less we who turn away from Him who [speaks] from Heaven, 26 whose voice shook the earth then, and now He has promised, saying, "Yet once [more]—I shake not only the earth, but also Heaven"; 27 and this, "Yet once [more]," makes evident the removal of the things shaken, as of things having been made, that the things not shaken may remain; 28 for this reason, receiving a kingdom that cannot be shaken, may we have grace, through which we may serve God well-pleasingly, with reverence and fear, 29 for our God [is] also a consuming fire.

CHAPTER 13

1 Let brotherly love remain. 2 Do not be forgetful of hospitality, for through this some entertained messengers unaware. 3 Be mindful of those in bonds, as having been bound

with them, of those maltreated, as yourselves also being in the body. 4 The marriage [is to be] honored by all, and the bed undefiled, for God will judge whoremongers and adulterers. 5 [Be] without covetous behavior, being content with the things present, for He has said, "No, I will not leave, no, nor forsake you," 6 so that we boldly say, "The Lord [is] to me a helper, and I will not fear what man will do to me." 7 Be mindful of those leading you, who spoke to you the word of God, who, considering the outcome of [their] behavior, imitate [their] faith: 8 Jesus Christ—the same yesterday and today and for all ages. 9 Do not be carried away with strange and manifold teachings, for [it is] good that by grace the heart is confirmed, not with meats, in which they who were occupied were not profited; 10 we have an altar from which they who are serving the Dwelling Place have no authority to eat, 11 for of those beasts whose blood is brought for sin into the holy places through the chief priest—of these the bodies are burned outside the camp. 12 For this reason, also Jesus—that He might sanctify the people through [His] own blood—suffered outside the gate; 13 now then, may we go forth to Him outside the camp, bearing His reproach; 14 for we have no abiding city here, but we seek the coming one. 15 Through Him, then, we may always offer up a sacrifice of praise to God, that is, the fruit of lips, giving thanks to His Name. 16 And do not be forgetful of doing good and of fellowship, for God is well-pleased with such sacrifices. 17 Be obedient to those leading you, and be subject, for these watch for your souls, as about to give account, that they may do this with joy, and not sighing, for this [is] unprofitable to you. 18 Pray for us, for we trust that we have a good conscience, willing to behave well in all things, 19 and I call on [you] to do this more abundantly, that I may be restored to you more quickly. 20 And the God of peace, who brought up the Great Shepherd of the sheep out of the dead—by the blood of a perpetual covenant—our Lord Jesus, 21 make you perfect in every good work to do His will, doing in you that which is well-pleasing before Him, through Jesus Christ, to whom [is] the glory through the ages of the ages! Amen. 22 And I beg you, brothers, endure the word of the exhortation, for I have also written to you through few words. 23 Know that the brother Timotheus is released, with whom I will see you, if he may come more shortly. 24 Greet all those leading you, and all the holy ones. Those from Italy greet you. 25 The grace [is] with you all! Amen.

JAMES

CHAPTER 1

1 James, a servant of God and of the Lord Jesus Christ, to the twelve tribes who are in the dispersion: Greetings! 2 Count [it] all joy, my brothers, when you may fall into manifold temptations, 3 knowing that the proof of your faith works endurance, 4 and let the endurance have a perfect work, that you may be perfect and complete, lacking in nothing. 5 And if any of you lacks wisdom, let him ask from God, who is giving to all generously, and not reproaching, and it will be given to him; 6 but let him ask in faith, doubting nothing, for he who is doubting has been like a wave of the sea, driven by wind and tossed; 7 for do not let that man suppose that he will receive anything from the Lord— 8 a soul-split man [is] unstable in all his ways. 9 And let the brother who is low rejoice in his exaltation, 10 but the rich in his becoming low, because he will pass away as a flower of grass; 11 for the sun rose with the burning heat, and withered the grass, and the flower of it fell, and the beauty of its appearance perished, so also the rich in his way will fade away! 12 Blessed [is] the man who endures temptation, because, becoming approved, he will receive the garland of life, which the Lord promised to those loving Him. 13 Let no one who is being tempted say, "I am tempted from God," for God is not tempted by evils, and Himself tempts no one, 14 but each one is tempted, being led away and enticed by his own desires; 15 afterward the desire having conceived, gives birth to sin, and sin having been perfected, brings forth death. 16 Do not be led astray, my beloved brothers. 17 Every good giving, and every perfect gift, is from above, coming down from the Father of lights, with whom is no variation, or

shadow of turning; 18 having willed [it], He begot us with a word of truth, for our being a certain first-fruit of His creatures. 19 So then, my beloved brothers, let every man be swift to hear, slow to speak, slow to anger, 20 for the wrath of a man does not work the righteousness of God; 21 for this reason, having put aside all filthiness and superabundance of evil, receive the implanted word in meekness, that is able to save your souls; 22 and become doers of the word, and not hearers only, deceiving yourselves, 23 because, if anyone is a hearer of the word and not a doer, this one has been like to a man viewing his natural face in a mirror, 24 for he viewed himself, and has gone away, and immediately he forgot what kind of [man] he was; 25 but he who looked into [the] perfect law—that of liberty, and continued there, not becoming a forgetful hearer, but a doer of work—this one will be blessed in his doing. 26 If anyone thinks to be religious among you, not bridling his tongue, but deceiving his heart, the religion of this one [is] vain; 27 religions pure and undefiled with the God and Father is this: to look after orphans and widows in their tribulation—to keep himself unspotted from the world.

CHAPTER 2

1 My brothers, do not hold the faith of the glory of our Lord Jesus Christ in favor by appearance, 2 for if there may come into your synagogue a man with gold ring, in radiant clothing, and there may also come in a poor man in vile clothing, 3 and you may look on him bearing the radiant clothing, and may say to him, "You—sit here well," and may say to the poor man, "You—stand there," or, "Sit here under my footstool," 4 you did not judge fully in yourselves, and became ill-reasoning judges. 5 Listen, my beloved brothers, did God not choose the poor of this world, rich in faith, and heirs of the kingdom that He promised to those loving Him? 6 But you dishonored the poor one. Do the rich not oppress you and themselves draw you to judgment-seats? 7 Do they not themselves speak evil of the good Name having been called on you? 8 If, indeed, you fulfill royal law, according to the Writing: "You will love your neighbor as yourself," you do well; 9 but if you favor by appearance, you work sin, being convicted by the Law as transgressors; 10 for whoever will keep the whole Law, but will stumble in one [point], he has become guilty of all; 11 for He who is saying, "You may not commit adultery," also said, "You may not murder"; but if you will not commit adultery, but will commit murder, you have become a transgressor of law; 12 thus, speak and so act as [one] about to be judged by a law of liberty, 13 for the judgment without mercy [is] to him having not done mercy, and mercy exults over judgment. 14 What [is] the profit, my brothers, if anyone may speak of having faith, but he may not have works? is that faith able to save him? 15 and if a brother or sister may be naked, and may be destitute of daily food, 16 and anyone of you may say to them, "Depart in peace, be warmed, and be filled," but may not give to them the things necessary for the body, what [is] the profit? 17 so also faith, if it may not have works, is dead by itself. 18 But someone may say, "You have faith, and I have works." Show me your faith without works, and I will show you my faith out of works. 19 You believe that God is one; you do well! The demons also believe—and shudder! 20 And do you wish to know, O vain man, that faith apart from works is dead? 21 Was not our father Abraham considered righteous out of works, having brought up his son Isaac on the altar? 22 do you see that faith was working with his works, and faith was perfected out of the works? 23 and the Writing was fulfilled that is saying, "And Abraham believed God, and it was reckoned to him for righteousness"; and, "Friend of God" he was called. 24 You see, then, that man is considered righteous out of works, and not out of faith only; 25 and in like manner also Rahab the prostitute—was she not considered righteous out of works, having received the messengers, and having sent [them] forth by another way? 26 for as the body apart from [the] spirit is dead, so also the faith apart from works is dead.

CHAPTER 3

1 Do not let many be teachers, my brothers, having known that we will receive greater judgment, 2 for we all make many stumbles; if anyone does not stumble in word, this one [is] a perfect man, able to also bridle the whole body; 3 behold, the

bits we put into the mouths of the horses for their obeying us, and we direct their whole body; 4 behold, also the ships, being so great, and being driven by fierce winds, are directed by a very small rudder, wherever the impulse of the [one] steering wills, 5 so also the tongue is a little member, and boasts greatly; behold, how much forest a little fire kindles! 6 and the tongue [is] a fire, the world of the unrighteousness, so the tongue is set in our members, which is spotting our whole body, and is setting on fire the course of nature, and is set on fire by Gehenna. 7 For every nature, both of beasts and of birds, both of creeping things and things of the sea, is subdued, and has been subdued, by the human nature, 8 but no one of men is able to subdue the tongue—[it is] an unruly evil, full of deadly poison; 9 with it we bless the God and Father, and with it we curse the men made according to [the] likeness of God; 10 out of the same mouth comes forth blessing and cursing; it does not need, my brothers, these things to so happen; 11 does the fountain out of the same opening pour forth the sweet and the bitter? 12 is a fig tree able, my brothers, to make olives? or a vine figs? Neither is salty [water able] to have made sweet water. 13 Who [is] wise and intelligent among you? let him show his works out of good behavior in meekness of wisdom, 14 yet, if you have bitter zeal, and rivalry in your heart, do not glory, nor lie against the truth; 15 this wisdom is not descending from above, but earthly, physical, demon-like, 16 for where zeal and rivalry [are], there is insurrection and every evil matter; 17 but the wisdom from above, first, indeed, is pure, then peaceable, gentle, well-convinced, full of kindness and good fruits, uncontentious, and unhypocritical— 18 and the fruit of righteousness in peace is sown to those making peace.

CHAPTER 4

1 From where [are] wars and fightings among you? [Is it] not from here, out of your passions warring in your members? 2 You desire, and do not have, [so] you murder; and you are zealous, and are not able to attain, [so] you fight and war; and you do not have, because of your not asking; 3 you ask, and you do not receive, because you ask badly, that you may spend [it] in your pleasures. 4 Adulterers and adulteresses! Have you not known that friendship of the world is enmity with God? whoever, then, may intend to be a friend of the world, he is designated [as] an enemy of God. 5 Or, do you think that the Writing says emptily, "The Spirit that has dwelt in us yearns with envy," 6 but [God] gives greater grace, for this reason it says, "God sets Himself up against proud ones, and He gives grace to lowly ones." 7 be subject, then, to God; stand up against the Devil, and he will flee from you; 8 draw near to God, and He will draw near to you; cleanse hands, you sinners! And purify hearts, you split-souled! 9 be exceedingly afflicted, and mourn, and weep, let your laughter be turned to mourning, and the joy to heaviness; 10 be made low before the Lord, and He will exalt you. 11 Do not speak against one another, brothers; he who is speaking against a brother, and is judging his brother, speaks against law, and judges law, and if you judge law, you are not a doer of law but a judge. 12 One is the lawgiver, who is able to save and to destroy; you—who are you that judges the other? 13 Go, now, you who are saying, "Today and tomorrow we will go on to such a city, and will pass there one year, and traffic, and make gain," 14 who does not know the thing of tomorrow; for what is your life? for it is a vapor that is appearing for a little [while], and then is vanishing; 15 instead, you [ought] to say, "If the Lord may will, we will live, and do this or that"; 16 but now you glory in your pride; all such glorying is evil; 17 to him, then, knowing to do good, and not doing [it], it is sin to him.

CHAPTER 5

1 Go, now, you rich! Weep, howling over your miseries that are coming on [you]; 2 your riches have rotted, and your garments have become moth-eaten; 3 your gold and silver have rotted, and the rust of them will be to you for a testimony, and will eat your flesh as fire. You have stored up treasure in the last days! 4 behold, the reward of the workmen cries out, of those who in-gathered your fields, which has been fraudulently kept back by you, and the exclamations of those who reaped have entered into the ears of the Lord of Hosts; 5 you lived in luxury on the earth, and were wanton; you

nourished your hearts, as in a day of slaughter; 6 you condemned—you murdered the righteous; he does not resist you. 7 Be patient, then, brothers, until the coming of the Lord; behold, the farmer expects the precious fruit of the earth, being patient for it, until he may receive rain—early and latter; 8 you also be patient; establish your hearts, because the coming of the Lord has drawn near; 9 do not murmur against one another, brothers, that you may not be condemned; behold, the Judge has stood before the door. 10 Brothers, [as] an example of the suffering of evil and of patience, take the prophets who spoke in the Name of the Lord; 11 behold, we call those who are enduring blessed; you heard of the endurance of Job, and you have seen the end from the Lord, that the Lord is very compassionate, and pitying. 12 And before all things, my brothers, do not swear, neither by Heaven, neither by the earth, neither by any other oath, but let your "Yes" be yes, and the "No," no, that you may not fall under judgment. 13 Does anyone suffer evil among you? let him pray; is anyone of good cheer? let him sing psalms; 14 is anyone sick among you? let him call for the elders of the assembly, and let them pray over him, having anointed him with oil, in the Name of the Lord, 15 and the prayer of faith will save the distressed one, and the Lord will raise him up, and if he may have committed sins, they will be forgiven to him. 16 Be confessing to one another the trespasses, and be praying for one another, that you may be healed; very strong is a working supplication of a righteous man; 17 Elijah was a similar-feeling man as us, and with prayer he prayed—not to rain, and it did not rain on the land three years and six months; 18 and again he prayed, and the sky gave rain, and the land brought forth her fruit. 19 Brothers, if anyone among you may go astray from the truth, and anyone may turn him back, 20 let him know that he who turned back a sinner from the straying of his way will save a soul from death, and will cover a multitude of sins.

1 PETER

CHAPTER 1

1 Peter, an apostle of Jesus Christ, to the chosen sojourners of the dispersion of Pontus, Galatia, Cappadocia, Asia, and Bithynia, 2 according to [the] foreknowledge of God the Father, by [the] sanctification of the Spirit, to [the] obedience and sprinkling of the blood of Jesus Christ: Grace and peace be multiplied to you! 3 Blessed [is] the God and Father of our Lord Jesus Christ, who, according to the abundance of His kindness begot us again to a living hope, through the resurrection of Jesus Christ out of the dead, 4 to an incorruptible inheritance, and undefiled, and unfading, reserved for you in the heavens, 5 who, in the power of God are being guarded, through faith, to salvation, ready to be revealed in the last time, 6 in which you are glad, a little now, if it be necessary, being made to sorrow in various trials, 7 so that the proof of your faith—much more precious than gold that is perishing, and being approved through fire—may be found to [result in] praise, and honor, and glory, at the revelation of Jesus Christ, 8 whom, having not seen, you love, in whom, now believing [although] not seeing, you are glad with unspeakable joy and have been filled with glory, 9 receiving the outcome of the faith—salvation of your souls; 10 concerning which salvation [the] prophets sought out and searched out, who prophesied concerning the grace toward you, 11 searching in regard to what or what manner of time the Spirit of Christ that was in them was signifying, testifying beforehand of the sufferings of Christ and the glory after these, 12 to whom it was revealed, that not to themselves, but to us they were ministering these, which now were told to you (through those who proclaimed good news to you), by the Holy Spirit sent from Heaven, to which things messengers desire to look into intently. 13 For this reason, having girded up the loins of your mind, being sober, hope perfectly on the grace that is being brought to you in the revelation of Jesus Christ, 14 as obedient children, not fashioning yourselves to the former desires in your ignorance, 15 but according as He who called you [is] holy, you also, become holy in all behavior, 16 because it has

been written: "Become holy, because I am holy"; 17 and if you call on the Father, who is judging without favoritism according to the work of each, pass the time of your sojourn in fear, 18 having known that, not with corruptible things—silver or gold—were you redeemed from your foolish behavior inherited from our forefathers, 19 but with precious blood, as of a lamb unblemished and unspotted—Christ's— 20 foreknown, indeed, before the foundation of the world, and revealed in the last times because of you, 21 who through Him believe in God who raised [Him] out of the dead, and gave glory to Him, so that your faith and hope may be in God. 22 Having purified your souls in the obedience of the truth through the Spirit to unhypocritical brotherly love, love one another earnestly out of a pure heart, 23 being begotten again, not out of corruptible seed, but incorruptible, through a word of God—living and remaining—throughout the age; 24 because all flesh [is] as grass, and all glory of man as flower of grass; the grass withered, and the flower of it fell away, 25 but the saying of the Lord remains—throughout the age; and this is the saying of good news that was proclaimed to you.

CHAPTER 2

1 Having put aside, then, all evil, and all guile, and hypocrisies, and envyings, and all evil speakings, 2 as newborn babies, desire the reasonable, unspoiled milk, so that you may grow up to salvation, 3 if [it] so be [that] you tasted that the Lord [is] good, 4 to whom coming—a living stone—having indeed been disapproved of by men, but with God—choice [and] precious, 5 and you yourselves are built up as living stones [into] a spiritual house, a holy priesthood, to offer up spiritual sacrifices acceptable to God through Jesus Christ. 6 For this reason, also, it is contained in the Writing: "Behold, I lay in Zion a chief cornerstone, choice, precious, and he who is believing on Him may not be put to shame"; 7 to you, then, who are believing—the preciousness; but to the unbelieving, [the] stone that the builders disapproved of—this One has become the head of [the] corner, 8 and a stone of stumbling and a rock of offense—who are stumbling at the word, being unbelieving—to which they were also set. 9 But you [are] a chosen race, a royal priesthood, a holy nation, a people acquired, that you may show forth the excellencies of Him who called you out of darkness into His wonderful light, 10 who [were] once not a people, but [are] now the people of God; who had not found mercy, but now have found mercy. 11 Beloved, I call on [you], as strangers and sojourners, to keep from the fleshly desires that war against the soul, 12 having your behavior right among the nations, so that whenever they speak against you as evildoers, seeing [your] good works, they may glorify God in [the] day of inspection. 13 Be subject, then, to every human creation, because of the Lord, whether to a king, as the highest, 14 whether to governors, as to those sent through him, for punishment, indeed, of evildoers, and a praise of those doing good; 15 because, so is the will of God, doing good, to put to silence the ignorance of the foolish men— 16 as free, and not having freedom as the cloak of evil, but as servants of God; 17 give honor to all; love the brotherhood; fear God; honor the king. 18 Servants, be subject in all fear to the masters, not only to the good and gentle, but also to the crooked; 19 for this [is] grace: if anyone endures sorrows because of conscience toward God, suffering unrighteously; 20 for what renown [is it], if sinning and being battered, you endure [it]? but if, doing good and suffering [for it], you endure, this [is] grace with God, 21 for to this you were called, because Christ also suffered for you, leaving to you an example, that you may follow His steps, 22 who did not commit sin, nor was guile found in His mouth, 23 who being reviled—was not reviling again, suffering—was not threatening, and was committing Himself to Him who is judging righteously, 24 who Himself bore our sins in His body on the tree, that having died to sins, we may live to righteousness, by whose stripes you were healed; 25 for you were as sheep going astray, but now you turned back to the Shepherd and Overseer of your souls.

CHAPTER 3

1 Wives, be subject to your own husbands in like manner, that even if some are disobedient to the word, they may be won through the behavior of the wives without the word, 2 having beheld your pure behavior in fear, 3 whose adorning—let it not be that which is outward, of braiding of hair, and of putting around of things of gold, or of putting on of garments, 4 but—the hidden man of the heart, by the incorruptible [thing] of the meek and quiet spirit, which is of great value before God, 5 for thus once also the holy women who hoped on God were adorning themselves, being subject to their own husbands, 6 as Sarah was obedient to Abraham, calling him "lord," of whom you became daughters, doing good, and not fearing any terror. 7 Husbands, in like manner, dwelling with [them], according to knowledge, as to a weaker vessel—to the wife—imparting honor, as also being heirs together of the grace of life, that your prayers are not hindered. 8 And finally, be all of one mind, having fellow-feeling, loving as brothers, compassionate, courteous, 9 not giving back evil for evil, or reviling for reviling, but on the contrary, blessing, having known that you were called to this, that you may inherit a blessing; 10 for "he who is willing to love life, and to see good days, let him guard his tongue from evil, and his lips—not to speak guile; 11 let him turn aside from evil, and do good, let him seek peace and pursue it; 12 because the eyes of the Lord [are] on the righteous, and His ears—to their supplication, but the face of the Lord [is] against those doing evil"; 13 and who [is] he who will be doing you evil, if you may become imitators of Him who is good? 14 but if you also should suffer because of righteousness, [you are] blessed! And do not be afraid of their fear, nor be troubled, 15 but sanctify the Lord God in your hearts. And always [be] ready for defense to everyone who is asking of you an account concerning the hope that [is] in you, with meekness and fear, 16 having a good conscience, so that whenever they speak against you as evildoers, they may be ashamed—[those] who are maligning your good behavior in Christ; 17 for if the will of God wills it, [it is] better to suffer doing good, than doing evil; 18 also because Christ suffered once for sin—righteous for unrighteous—that He might lead us to God, indeed having been put to death in the flesh, but having been made alive in the Spirit, 19 by which, having gone, He also preached to the spirits in prison, 20 who sometime [ago] disobeyed when once the long-suffering of God waited, in [the] days of Noah—an ark being prepared—in which few, that is, eight souls, were saved through water, 21 also an antitype to immersion which now saves you—not a putting away of the filth of flesh, but the question of a good conscience in regard to God, through the resurrection of Jesus Christ, 22 who is at the right hand of God, having gone on to Heaven—messengers, and authorities, and powers, having been subjected to Him.

CHAPTER 4

1 Christ, then, having suffered for us in the flesh, you also arm yourselves with the same mind, because he who suffered in the flesh has finished [with] sin, 2 no longer in the desires of men, but in the will of God, to live the rest of the time in the flesh; 3 for the time has sufficiently passed to have carried out the will of the nations, having walked in licentiousness, lusts, excesses of wines, revelings, drinking-bouts, and unlawful idolatries, 4 in which they think it strange—your not running with them to the same excess of wastefulness, slandering [you]— 5 who will give an account to Him who is ready to judge [the] living and [the] dead, 6 for this also was good news proclaimed to dead men, that they may be judged, indeed, according to men in the flesh, but may live according to God in the Spirit. 7 Now the end of all things has come near; be sober-minded, then, and be sober in [your] prayers. 8 Before all things, having earnest love among yourselves, because love covers a multitude of sins; 9 [be] hospitable to one another, without murmuring; 10 each [one], according as he received a gift, ministering it to one another, as good stewards of the manifold grace of God; 11 if anyone speaks, [speak] as oracles of God; if anyone ministers, [minister] as of the strength which God supplies, so that in all things God may be glorified through Jesus Christ, to whom is the glory and the power through the ages of the ages. Amen. 12 Beloved, do not think it strange at the fiery suffering among you that is coming to try you, as if a strange thing were happening to you, 13 but according as you have fellowship with the sufferings of the Christ, rejoice, that you may also rejoice in the revelation of His glory—exulting; 14 if you are reproached in the Name of Christ—[you are] blessed, because the Spirit of glory and of God rests on you; in regard, indeed, to them, is evil spoken of Him, and in regard to you, He is glorified; 15 for let none of you suffer as a

murderer, or thief, or evildoer, or as a meddler into other men's matters; 16 and if as a Christian, do not let him be ashamed, but let him glorify God in this respect; 17 because it is the time of the judgment to have begun from the house of God, and if first from us, what [is] the end of those disobedient to the good news of God? 18 And if the righteous man is scarcely saved, where will the ungodly and sinner appear? 19 so that those also suffering according to the will of God, as to a steadfast Creator, let them commit their own souls in doing good.

CHAPTER 5

1 Elders who [are] among you, I exhort [you], [as] a fellow-elder, and a witness of the sufferings of the Christ, and a partaker of the glory about to be revealed, 2 feed the flock of God that [is] among you, overseeing not by compulsion, but willingly, neither for shameful gain, but eagerly, 3 neither as exercising lordship over the heritages, but becoming patterns for the flock, 4 and the Chief Shepherd having appeared, you will receive the unfading garland of glory. 5 In like manner, you young [ones], be subject to elders, and all subjecting yourselves to one another; clothe yourselves with humble-mindedness, because God resists the proud, but He gives grace to the humble; 6 be humbled, then, under the powerful hand of God, that He may exalt you in good time, 7 having cast all your care on Him, because He cares for you. 8 Be sober, vigilant, because your opponent the Devil walks around as a roaring lion, seeking whom he may swallow up, 9 whom you must resist, steadfast in the faith, having known the same sufferings of your brotherhood to be accomplished in the world. 10 And the God of all grace, who called you to His perpetual glory in Christ Jesus, having suffered a little, Himself make you perfect, establish, strengthen, settle [you]; 11 to Him [is] the glory and the power through the ages and the ages! Amen. 12 Through Silvanus, the faithful brother as I reckon, I wrote through few [words] to you, exhorting and testifying this to be the true grace of God in which you have stood. 13 She in Babylon chosen with you greets you, and my son Marcus. 14 Greet one another in a kiss of love. Peace to you all who [are] in Christ Jesus! Amen.

2 PETER

CHAPTER 1

1 Simeon Peter, a servant and an apostle of Jesus Christ, to those who obtained an equally precious faith with us in the righteousness of our God and Savior Jesus Christ: 2 Grace and peace be multiplied to you in the acknowledgment of God and of Jesus our Lord! 3 As His divine power has given to us all things pertaining to life and piety, through the acknowledgment of Him who called us through glory and virtue, 4 through which the most great and precious promises have been given to us, that through these you may become partakers of a divine nature, having escaped from the corruption [and] lust in the world. 5 And [for] this same [reason] also, having brought in all diligence, supplement your faith with virtue, and with virtue—knowledge, 6 and with knowledge—self-control, and with self-control—endurance, and with endurance—piety, 7 and with piety—brotherly kindness, and with brotherly kindness—love; 8 for these things being in you and abounding, make [you] neither inert nor unfruitful in regard to the knowledge of our Lord Jesus Christ, 9 for he with whom these things are not present is blind, dim-sighted, having become forgetful of the cleansing of his old sins; 10 therefore, rather, brothers, be diligent to make steadfast your calling and [divine] selection, for doing these things you may never stumble; 11 in this way the entrance into the continuous kingdom of our Lord and Savior Jesus Christ will be richly supplemented to you. 12 Therefore, I will always be ready to remind you about these things, although you have known [them] and have been established in the present truth, 13 and I think right, so long as I am in this tent, to stir you up in reminding [you], 14 having known that the laying aside of my tent is soon, even as our Lord Jesus Christ also showed to me. 15 And I will also be diligent [to ensure] that you always have a remembrance to make of these things after my departure. 16 For having not followed out skillfully devised fables, we made known to you the power and coming of our Lord Jesus Christ, but having become eyewitnesses of His majesty— 17 for having received honor and glory from God the Father, such a voice being borne to Him by the Excellent Glory: "This is My Son, the Beloved, in whom I delighted"; 18 and we heard this voice borne out of Heaven, being with Him at the holy mountain. 19 And we have a firmer prophetic word, to which we do well giving heed, as to a lamp shining in a dark place, until day may dawn, and [the] morning star may arise in your hearts; 20 knowing this first, that no prophecy of the Writing comes of private exposition, 21 for prophecy never came by [the] will of man, but men spoke from God, being brought by the Holy Spirit.

CHAPTER 2

1 But there also came false prophets among the people, as there will also be false teachers among you, who will stealthily bring in destructive sects, even denying the Master who bought them, bringing quick destruction to themselves, 2 and many will follow out their destructive ways, because of whom the way of the truth will be spoken of [as] evil, 3 and in covetousness, with forged words, they will make merchandise of you, whose judgment of old is not idle, and their destruction does not slumber. 4 For if God did not spare messengers having sinned, but having cast [them] down to Tartarus with chains of deepest gloom, delivered [them], having been reserved to judgment, 5 and did not spare the old world, but kept the eighth person, Noah, a preacher of righteousness, having brought a flood on the world of the impious, 6 and having turned the cities of Sodom and Gomorrah to ashes, condemned with an overthrow, having set [them as] an example to those about to be impious, 7 and He rescued righteous Lot, worn down by the conduct of the lawless in licentiousness, 8 for the righteous [man] dwelling among them was tormented in [his] righteous soul, day by day, in seeing and hearing unlawful works— 9 the Lord has known to rescue [the] pious out of temptation, and to keep [the] unrighteous being punished to [the] day of judgment, 10 and chiefly those following after the flesh in lust [and] defilement, and despising lordship. Bold, self-pleased, they are not afraid to speak evil of glorious ones, 11 whereas messengers, being greater in strength and power, do not bear a slanderous judgment against them before the Lord; 12 and these, as irrational natural beasts, made to be caught and destroyed—in what things they are ignorant of, slandering—in their destruction will be destroyed; 13 doing unjustly, [they will receive] a reward of unrighteousness, esteeming pleasure in the day, [and] luxury—[they are] spots and blemishes, reveling in their deceits, feasting with you, 14 having eyes full of adultery, and unable to cease from sin, enticing unstable souls, having a heart exercised in covetousnesses, children of a curse, 15 having forsaken a right way, they went astray, having followed in the way of Balaam the [son] of Bosor, who loved a reward of unrighteousness, 16 and had a rebuke of his own iniquity—a mute donkey, having spoken in man's voice, forbid the madness of the prophet. 17 These are wells without water, and clouds driven by a storm, to whom the deepest gloom of darkness has been kept throughout the age; 18 for speaking swollen words of vanity, they entice in desires of the flesh—licentiousness, those who had truly escaped from those conducting themselves in error, 19 promising liberty to them, themselves being servants of corruption, for by whom anyone has been overcome, he has been brought to servitude to this one also; 20 for if having escaped from the defilements of the world, in the acknowledging of the Lord and Savior Jesus Christ, and again being entangled by these things, they have been overcome, the last things have become worse to them than the first, 21 for it were better to them not to have acknowledged the way of righteousness, than having acknowledged [it], to turn back from the holy command delivered to them, 22 and that of the true proverb has happened to them: "A dog turned back on his own vomit," and, "A sow having bathed herself—to rolling in mire."

CHAPTER 3

1 This [is] now, beloved, a second letter I write to you, in both which I stir up your pure mind in reminding [you] 2 to be mindful of the sayings said before by the holy prophets, and of the command of us the apostles of the Lord and Savior, 3 knowing this first, that there will come scoffers in the last days, going on according to their own desires, 4 and saying, "Where is the promise of His coming? for since the fathers fell asleep, all things so remain from the beginning of the creation"; 5 for this they willingly conceal, that the heavens existed long ago, and the earth having been established by the word of God out of water and through water, 6 through which the world then, having been flooded by water, was destroyed; 7 and by the same word, the present heavens and earth, having been stored up for fire, are being preserved until [the] day of judgment and destruction of impious men. 8 And do not let this one thing be concealed from you, beloved, that one day with the Lord [is] as one thousand years and one thousand years as one day; 9 the Lord is not slow in regard to the promise, as some count slowness, but is long-suffering to us, not intending any to be lost, but all to come to conversion, 10 and it will come—the Day of the Lord—as a thief in the night, in which the heavens will pass away with a rushing noise, and the elements will be dissolved with burning heat, and [the] earth and the works in it will not be found. 11 All these, then, being dissolved, what kind of persons ought you to be in holy behaviors and pious acts, 12 waiting for and hurrying the coming of the Day of God, by which the heavens, being on fire, will be dissolved, and the elements will melt with burning heat? 13 And we wait for new heavens and a new earth according to His promise, in which righteousness dwells; 14 for this reason, beloved, waiting for these things, be diligent, spotless and unblameable, to be found by Him in peace, 15 and count the long-suffering of our Lord [as] salvation, according as also our beloved brother Paul—according to the wisdom given to him—wrote to you, 16 as also in all the letters, speaking in them concerning these things, among which are some things [that are] hard to be understood, which the untaught and unstable twist, as also the other Writings, to their own destruction. 17 You, then, beloved, knowing before, take heed, lest, together with the error of the impious being led away, you may fall from your own steadfastness, 18 and increase in grace, and in the knowledge of our Lord and Savior Jesus Christ; to Him [is] the glory both now, and to the day of the age! Amen.

1 JOHN

CHAPTER 1

1 That which was from the beginning, that which we have heard, that which we have seen with our eyes, that which we beheld, and our hands handled, concerning the Word of Life— 2 and the Life appeared, and we have seen, and testify, and declare to you the continuous Life, which was with the Father, and was revealed to us— 3 we declare to you that which we have seen and heard, that you also may have fellowship with us, and our fellowship [is] with the Father, and with His Son Jesus Christ; 4 and these things we write to you, that your joy may be full. 5 And this is the message that we have heard from Him, and announce to you, that God is light, and darkness is not in Him at all; 6 if we may say, "We have fellowship with Him," and may walk in the darkness—we lie, and do not [speak] the truth; 7 and if we may walk in the light, as He is in the light—we have fellowship with one another, and the blood of His Son Jesus Christ cleanses us from every sin; 8 if we may say, "We have no sin," we lead ourselves astray, and the truth is not in us; 9 if we may confess our sins, He is steadfast and righteous that He may forgive us the sins, and may cleanse us from every unrighteousness; 10 if we may say, "We have not sinned," we make Him a liar, and His word is not in us.

CHAPTER 2

1 My little children, these things I write to you that you may not sin: and if anyone may sin, we have an Advocate with the Father, Jesus Christ, [the] Righteous One, 2 and He is [the] propitiation for our sins, and not only for ours, but also for the whole world, 3 and in this we know that we have known Him, if we may keep His commands; 4 he who is saying, "I have known Him," and is not keeping His commands, is a liar, and the truth is not in him; 5 and whoever may keep His word, truly the love of God has been perfected in him; in this we know that we are in Him. 6 He who is saying he remains in Him, himself ought to also walk according as He walked. 7 Beloved, I do not write a new command to you, but an old command, that you had from the beginning—the old command is the word that you heard from the beginning; 8 again, a new command I write to you, which is true in Him and in you, because the darkness is passing away, and the true light now shines; 9 he who is saying he is in the light, and is hating his brother, he is in the darkness until now; 10 he who is loving his brother, he remains in the light, and there is not a stumbling-block in him; 11 but he who is hating his brother, he is in the darkness, and he walks in the darkness, and he has not known where he goes, because the darkness blinded his eyes. 12 I write to you, little children, because sins have been forgiven you through His Name; 13 I write to you, fathers, because you have known Him who [is] from the beginning; I write to you, young men, because you have overcome the evil [one]; I write to you, little youths, because you have known the Father; 14 I wrote to you, fathers, because you have known Him who [is] from the beginning; I wrote to you, young men, because you are strong, and the word of God remains in you, and you have overcome the evil [one]. 15 Do not love the world, nor the things in the world; if anyone loves the world, the love of the Father is not in him, 16 because all that [is] in the world—the desire of the flesh, and the desire of the eyes, and the ostentation of [one's] life—is not of the Father, but of the world, 17 and the world is passing away, and the desire of it, but he who is doing the will of God, he remains—throughout the age. 18 Little youths, it is the last hour; and even as you heard that the antichrist comes, even now antichrists have become many—whereby we know that it is [the] last hour; 19 they went forth out of us, but they were not of us, for if they had been of us, they would have remained with us; but [they went out] so that they might be revealed that they are not all of us. 20 And you have an anointing from the Holy One, and have known all things; 21 I did not write to you because you have not known the truth, but because you have known it, and because no lie is of the truth. 22 Who is the liar, except he who is denying that Jesus is the Christ? this one is the antichrist who is denying the Father and the Son; 23 everyone who is denying the Son, neither has the Father; he who is confessing the Son has the Father also. 24 You, then, that which you heard from the beginning, let it remain in you; if that which you heard from the beginning may remain in you, you also will remain in the Son and in the Father, 25 and this is the promise that He promised us—the continuous life. 26 These things I wrote to you concerning those leading you astray; 27 and you, the anointing that you received from Him, it remains in you, and you have no need that anyone may teach you, but as the same anointing teaches you concerning all, and is true, and is not a lie, and even as was taught you, you will remain in Him. 28 And now, little children, remain in Him, so that when He may have appeared, we may have boldness, and may not be ashamed before Him, at His coming; 29 if you know that He is righteous, know that everyone doing righteousness, has been begotten of Him.

CHAPTER 3

1 See what love the Father has given to us, that we may be called children of God; because of this the world does not know us, because it did not know Him. 2 Beloved, now, we are children of God, and it was not yet revealed what we will be. We have known that if He may have appeared, we will be like Him, because we will see Him as He is; 3 and everyone who is having this hope on Him, purifies himself, even as He is pure. 4 Everyone who is doing sin, he also does lawlessness, and sin is lawlessness, 5 and you have known that He appeared that He may take away our sins, and sin is not in Him; 6 everyone who is remaining in Him does not sin; everyone who is sinning, has not seen Him, nor known Him. 7 Little children, let no one lead you astray; he who is doing righteousness is righteous, even as He is righteous, 8 he who is doing sin, he is of the Devil, because the Devil sins from the beginning; for this

[reason] the Son of God appeared, that He may undo the works of the Devil; 9 everyone who has been begotten of God, he does not sin, because His seed remains in him, and he is not able to sin, because he has been begotten of God. 10 In this are revealed the children of God, and the children of the Devil; everyone who is not doing righteousness, is not of God, and he who is not loving his brother, 11 because this is the message that you heard from the beginning, that we may love one another, 12 not as Cain—he was of the evil one, and he slew his brother. And for [what] reason did he slay him? because his works were evil, and those of his brother [were] righteous. 13 Do not wonder, my brothers, if the world hates you; 14 we have known that we have passed out of death into life, because we love the brothers; he who is not loving [his] brother remains in death. 15 Everyone who is hating his brother is a manslayer, and you have known that no manslayer has continuous life remaining in him; 16 in this we have known love, because He laid down His life for us, and we ought to lay down [our] lives for the brothers; 17 and whoever may have the goods of the world, and may view his brother having need, and may shut up his yearnings from him—how does the love of God remain in him? 18 My little children, may we not love in word nor in tongue, but in work and in truth! 19 and in this we know that we are of the truth, and before Him we will assure our hearts, 20 because if our heart may condemn—because greater is God than our heart, and He knows all things. 21 Beloved, if our heart may not condemn us, we have boldness toward God, 22 and whatever we may ask, we receive from Him, because we keep His commands, and we do the things pleasing before Him, 23 and this is His command, that we may believe in the Name of His Son Jesus Christ, and may love one another, even as He gave command to us, 24 and he who is keeping His commands, remains in Him, and He in him; and in this we know that He remains in us, from the Spirit that He gave us.

CHAPTER 4

1 Beloved, do not believe every spirit, but prove the spirits, if they are of God, because many false prophets have gone forth into the world. 2 In this you know the Spirit of God: every spirit that confesses Jesus Christ having come in the flesh, it is of God, 3 and every spirit that does not confess Jesus Christ having come in the flesh, it is not of God; and this is that of the antichrist, which you heard that it comes, and now it is already in the world. 4 You are of God, little children, and you have overcome them; because greater is He who [is] in you, than he who is in the world. 5 They are of the world, because they speak of this from the world, and the world hears them; 6 we are of God; he who is knowing God hears us; he who is not of God, does not hear us; from this we know the Spirit of truth and the spirit of error. 7 Beloved, may we love one another, because love is of God, and everyone loving has been begotten of God, and knows God; 8 he who is not loving did not know God, because God is love. 9 In this was revealed the love of God in us, because God has sent His only begotten Son into the world, that we may live through Him; 10 in this is love, not that we loved God, but that He loved us, and sent His Son [as] the propitiation for our sins. 11 Beloved, if God so loved us, we also ought to love one another; 12 no one has ever seen God; if we may love one another, God remains in us, and His love is having been perfected in us; 13 in this we know that we remain in Him, and He in us, because of His Spirit He has given us. 14 And we have seen and testify that the Father has sent the Son [as] Savior of the world; 15 whoever may confess that Jesus is the Son of God, God remains in him, and he in God; 16 and we have known and believed the love that God has in us; God is love, and he who is remaining in love, remains in God, and God in him. 17 In this, love has been perfected with us, that we may have boldness in the day of judgment, because even as He is, we also are in this world. 18 There is no fear in love, but perfect love casts out fear, because fear involves punishment, and he who is fearing has not been made perfect in love; 19 we love Him, because He first loved us; 20 if anyone may say, "I love God," and may hate his brother, he is a liar; for he who is not loving his brother whom he has seen, how is he able to love God whom he has not seen? 21 and this [is] the command we have from Him, that he who is loving God, may also love his brother.

CHAPTER 5

1 Everyone who is believing that Jesus is the Christ has been begotten of God, and everyone who is loving Him who begot, also loves him who is begotten of Him. 2 In this we know that we love the children of God, when we may love God and may keep His commands; 3 for this is the love of God, that we may keep His commands, and His commands are not burdensome; 4 because everyone who is begotten of God overcomes the world, and this is the victory that overcame the world—our faith. 5 Who is he who is overcoming the world, if not he who is believing that Jesus is the Son of God? 6 This One is He who came through water and blood—Jesus the Christ, not in water only, but in the water and the blood; and the Spirit is the [One] testifying, because the Spirit is the truth, 7 because [there] are three who are testifying [[in Heaven: the Father, the Word, and the Holy Spirit, and these three are one; 8 and [there] are three who are testifying in the earth]]: the Spirit, and the water, and the blood, and the three are into the one. 9 If we receive the testimony of men, the testimony of God is greater, because this is the testimony of God that He has testified concerning His Son. 10 He who is believing in the Son of God has the testimony in himself; he who is not believing God has made Him a liar, because he has not believed in the testimony that God has testified concerning His Son; 11 and this is the testimony, that God gave continuous life to us, and this life is in His Son; 12 he who is having the Son has life; he who is not having the Son of God does not have life. 13 I wrote these things to you who are believing in the Name of the Son of God, that you may know that you have continuous life, and that you may believe in the Name of the Son of God. 14 And this is the boldness that we have toward Him, that if we may ask anything according to His will, He hears us, 15 and if we have known that He hears us, whatever we may ask, we have known that we have the requests that we have requested from Him. 16 If anyone may see his brother sinning a sin [that is] not to death, he will ask, and He will give life to him—to those not sinning to death; there is sin to death—I do not say that he may ask concerning it; 17 all unrighteousness is sin, and there is sin [that is] not to death. 18 We have known that everyone who has been begotten of God does not sin, but He who was begotten of God keeps him, and the evil one does not touch him; 19 we have known that we are of God, and the whole world lies [under the power] of the evil [one]; 20 but we have known that the Son of God has come, and has given us a mind that we may know Him who is true, and we are in Him who is true, in His Son Jesus Christ; this One is the true God and the continuous Life! 21 Little children, guard yourselves from idols! Amen.

2 JOHN

CHAPTER 1

1 The elder to the chosen lady, and to her children, whom I love in truth, and not only I, but also all those having known the truth, 2 because of the truth that is remaining in us, and will be with us throughout the age, 3 there will be with you grace, mercy, [and] peace from God the Father, and from the Lord Jesus Christ, the Son of the Father, in truth and love. 4 I rejoiced exceedingly that I have found of your children walking in truth, even as we received a command from the Father; 5 and now I implore you, lady, not as writing to you a new command, but which we had from the beginning, that we may love one another, 6 and this is love, that we may walk according to His commands; this is the command, even as you heard from the beginning, that you may walk in it, 7 because many deceivers entered into the world, who are not confessing Jesus Christ coming in flesh; this one is he who is leading astray, and the antichrist. 8 See to yourselves that you may not lose the things that we worked for, but may receive a full reward; 9 everyone who is transgressing, and is not remaining in the teaching of the Christ, does not have God; he who is remaining in the teaching of the Christ, this one has both the Father and the Son; 10 if anyone comes to you, and does not bear this teaching, do not receive him into the house, and do

not say to him, "Greetings!" 11 for he who is saying to him, "Greetings," has fellowship with his evil works. 12 Having many things to write to you, I did not intend [it] with paper and ink, but I hope to come to you, and speak mouth to mouth, that our joy may be full. 13 The children of your chosen sister greet you. Amen.

3 JOHN

CHAPTER 1

1 The elder to Gaius the beloved, whom I love in truth! 2 beloved, I desire you to prosper concerning all things, and to be in health, even as your soul prospers, 3 for I rejoiced exceedingly, brothers coming and testifying of the truth in you, even as you walk in truth; 4 I have no joy greater than these things, that I may hear of my children walking in truth. 5 Beloved, you act faithfully in whatever you may do toward the brothers and the one [among] strangers, 6 who testified of your love before an assembly, whom you will do well, having sent forward worthily of God, 7 because they went forth for [His] Name, receiving nothing from the nations; 8 we, then, ought to receive such, that we may become fellow-workers to the truth. 9 I wrote to the assembly, but he who is loving to be first among them—Diotrephes—does not receive us; 10 because of this, if I may come, I will cause him to remember his works that he does, talking nonsense against us with evil words; and not content with these, neither does he himself receive the brothers, and he forbids those intending [to receive them], and he casts [them] out of the assembly. 11 Beloved, do not be following that which is evil, but that which is good; he who is doing good, he is of God, [but] he who is doing evil has not seen God; 12 testimonies has been given to Demetrius by all, and by the truth itself, and we also—we testify, and you have known that our testimony is true. 13 Many things I had to write, but I do not wish to write to you through ink and pen, 14 and I hope to see you soon, and we will speak mouth to mouth. Peace to you! The friends greet you. Be greeting the friends by name.

JUDE

CHAPTER 1

1 Judas, a servant of Jesus Christ, and brother of James, to those called, having been loved in God [the] Father, and having been kept in Jesus Christ, 2 mercy and peace and love be multiplied to you! 3 Beloved, using all diligence to write to you concerning our common salvation, I had necessity to write to you, exhorting [you] to fight for the faith once delivered to the holy ones, 4 for there came in certain men stealthily, having been written beforehand to this judgment long ago, impious, perverting the grace of our God to licentiousness, and denying our only Master and Lord—Jesus Christ. 5 Now I intend to remind you, you once having known all this, that Jesus, having saved a people out of the land of Egypt, He secondly destroyed those not having believed; 6 messengers also, those who did not keep their own principality, but left their proper dwelling, He has kept in eternal bonds under darkness until [the] judgment of [the] great day, 7 as Sodom and Gomorrah, and the cities around them, in like manner to these [messengers], having given themselves to whoredom, and having gone after other flesh, have been set before [as] an example, undergoing the justice of continuous fire. 8 In like manner, nevertheless, those dreaming indeed defile the flesh, and they disregard lordship, and they speak evil of glorious [ones], 9 yet Michael, the chief messenger, when disputing with the Devil, reasoning about the body of Moses, did not dare to bring against [him] a judgment of slander, but said, "The Lord rebuke you!" 10 But these, indeed, whatever [things] they have not known, they speak evil of; and whatever [they know], like the irrational beasts, they understand naturally—in these they are corrupted; 11 woe to them! Because they went on in the way of Cain, and they rushed to the deceit of Balaam for reward, and in the controversy of Korah they perished. 12 These are stains at your love-feasts, feasting together with you without fear, shepherding themselves; waterless clouds, being carried away by winds; autumnal trees without fruit, having died twice, having been uprooted; 13 wild waves of a sea, foaming up their own shameful [deeds]; stars going astray, for whom the gloom of the darkness throughout the age has been kept. 14 And Enoch, the seventh from Adam, also prophesied to these, saying, "Behold, the Lord has come with myriads of His holy ones, 15 to do judgment against all, and to convict all their impious ones, concerning all their works of impiety that they did impiously, and concerning all the harsh [words] that impious sinners spoke against Him." 16 These are discontented grumblers, walking according to their own lusts; and their mouth speaks swollen words, giving admiration to persons for the sake of profit; 17 but you, beloved, remember the sayings spoken before by the apostles of our Lord Jesus Christ, 18 that they said to you, that in the last time there will be scoffers, following after their own lusts of impieties, 19 these are those causing divisions, natural men, not having the Spirit. 20 But you, beloved, building yourselves up on your most holy faith, praying in the Holy Spirit, 21 keep yourselves in the love of God, waiting for the mercy of our Lord Jesus Christ [resulting] in continuous life; 22 and, indeed, show mercy to those who are doubting, 23 and rescue others by snatching [them] out of fire; but show mercy to others in fear, hating even the coat having been stained from the flesh. 24 And to Him who is able to guard you without stumbling, and to set [you] in the presence of His glory unblemished, in gladness, 25 to the only wise God our Savior, [is] glory and greatness, power and authority, both now and forever! Amen.

REVELATION

CHAPTER 1

1 A revelation of Jesus Christ that God gave to Him to show to His servants what things must quickly come to pass; and He signified [it], having sent through His messenger to His servant John, 2 who testified [to] the word of God, and the testimony of Jesus Christ, as many things as he also saw. 3 Blessed is he who is reading, and those hearing the words of the prophecy, and keeping the things written in it, for the time is near! 4 John, to the seven assemblies that [are] in Asia: Grace to you, and peace, from Him who is, and who was, and who is coming, and from the Seven Spirits that are before His throne, 5 and from Jesus Christ, the faithful witness, the firstborn out of the dead, and the ruler of the kings of the earth; to Him loving us and having released us from our sins in His blood, 6 [He] has also made us kings and priests to His God and Father, to Him—the glory and the power through the ages of the ages! Amen. 7 Behold, He comes with the clouds, and every eye will see Him, even those who pierced Him, and all the tribes of the land will wail because of Him. Yes! Amen! 8 "I am the Alpha and the Omega, beginning and end, says the Lord, who is, and who was, and who is coming—the Almighty." 9 I, John, who [am] also your brother, and fellow-partner in the tribulation, and in the kingdom and endurance of Jesus Christ, was in the island that is called Patmos, because of the word of God, and because of the testimony of Jesus Christ; 10 I was in the Spirit on the Lord's Day, and I heard a great voice behind me, as of a trumpet, saying, 11 "I am the Alpha and the Omega, the First and the Last," and, "Write what you see in a scroll, and send [it] to the seven assemblies that [are] in Asia: to Ephesus, and to Smyrna, and to Pergamos, and to Thyatira, and to Sardis, and to Philadelphia, and to Laodicea." 12 And I turned to see the voice that spoke with me, and having turned, I saw seven golden lampstands, 13 and in the midst of the seven lampstands, [One] like a Son of Man, clothed to the foot, and having been girded around at the breasts with a golden girdle, 14 and His head and hairs [were] white, as if white wool—as snow, and His eyes as a flame of fire; 15 and His feet like to

frankincense-colored brass, as having been fired in a furnace, and His voice as a sound of many waters; 16 and having seven stars in His right hand, and out of His mouth a sharp two-edged sword is proceeding, and His countenance—as the sun shining in its might. 17 And when I saw Him, I fell at His feet as dead, and He placed His right hand on me, saying to me, "Do not be afraid; I am the First and the Last, 18 and He who is living, and I became dead, and behold, I am living through the ages of the ages. Amen! And I have the keys of Hades and of death. 19 Write the things that you have seen, and the things that are, and the things that are about to come after these things; 20 the secret of the seven stars that you have seen on My right hand, and the seven golden lampstands: the seven stars are messengers of the seven assemblies, and the seven lampstands that you have seen are seven assemblies."

CHAPTER 2

1 "To the messenger of the Ephesian assembly write: These things says He who is holding the seven stars in His right hand, who is walking in the midst of the seven golden lampstands: 2 I have known your works, and your labor, and your endurance, and that you are not able to bear evil ones, and that you have tried those saying themselves to be apostles and are not, and have found them liars, 3 and you bore, and have endurance, and have toiled because of My Name, and have not been weary. 4 But I have against you that you left your first love! 5 remember, then, from where you have fallen, and convert, and do the first works; and if not, I come to you quickly, and will remove your lampstand from its place—if you may not convert; 6 but this you have, that you hate the works of the Nicolaitans, that I also hate. 7 He who is having an ear—let him hear what the Spirit says to the assemblies: To him who is overcoming I will give to him to eat of the Tree of Life that is in the midst of the paradise of God. 8 And to the messenger of the assembly of the Smyrneans write: These things says the First and the Last, who became dead and lived: 9 I have known your works, and tribulation, and poverty—yet you are rich—and the slander of those saying themselves to be Jews, and are not, but [are] a synagogue of Satan. 10 Do not be afraid of the things that you are about to suffer; behold, the Devil is about to cast [some] of you into prison, that you may be tried, and you will have tribulation ten days; become faithful to death, and I will give to you the garland of life. 11 He who is having an ear—let him hear what the Spirit says to the assemblies: He who is overcoming may not be injured of the second death. 12 And to the messenger of the assembly in Pergamos write: These things says He who is having the sharp two-edged sword: 13 I have known your works, and where you dwell—where the throne of Satan [is]—and you hold fast My Name, and you did not deny My faith, even in the days in which Antipas [was] My faithful witness, who was put to death beside you, where Satan dwells. 14 But I have a few things against you: that you have there those holding the teaching of Balaam, who taught Balak to cast a stumbling-block before the sons of Israel, to eat idol-sacrifices, and to commit whoredom; 15 so have you, even you, those holding the teaching of the Nicolaitans—which thing I hate. 16 Convert! And if not, I come to you quickly, and will fight against them with the sword of My mouth. 17 He who is having an ear—let him hear what the Spirit says to the assemblies: To him who is overcoming, I will give to him to eat from the hidden manna, and will give to him a white stone, and on the stone a new name written, that no one knew except him who is receiving [it]. 18 And to the messenger of the assembly of Thyatira write: These things says the Son of God, who is having His eyes as a flame of fire, and His feet like to frankincense-colored brass: 19 I have known your works, and love, and ministry, and faith, and your endurance, and your works—and the last [are] more than the first. 20 But I have a few things against you: that you allow the woman Jezebel, who is calling herself a prophetess, to teach, and to lead astray, My servants to commit whoredom, and to eat idol-sacrifices; 21 and I gave to her a time that she might convert from her whoredom, and she did not convert; 22 behold, I will cast her into a bed, and those committing adultery with her into great tribulation—if they may not convert from her works, 23 and I will kill her children in death, and all the assemblies will know that I am He who is searching affections and hearts; and I will give to you—to each—according to your works. 24 And to you I say, and to the rest who are in Thyatira, as many as do not have this teaching, and who did not know the depths of Satan,

as they say—I will not put on you another burden, 25 but hold that which you have, until I may come; 26 and he who is overcoming, and who is keeping My works to the end, I will give to him authority over the nations, 27 and he will rule them with a rod of iron—they will be broken as the vessels of the potter—as I have also received from My Father; 28 and I will give to him the morning star. 29 He who is having an ear—let him hear what the Spirit says to the assemblies."

CHAPTER 3

1 "And to the messenger of the assembly in Sardis write: These things says He who is having the Seven Spirits of God, and the seven stars: I have known your works, and that you have the name that you live, and you are dead; 2 be watching, and strengthen the rest of the things that are about to die, for I have not found your works fulfilled before God. 3 Remember, then, what you have received and heard, and keep [it] and convert: if, then, you may not watch, I will come on you as a thief, and you may not know what hour I will come on you. 4 You have a few names even in Sardis who did not defile their garments, and they will walk with Me in white, because they are worthy. 5 The [one] thus overcoming will be clothed in white garments, and I will not blot out his name from the Scroll of Life, and I will confess his name before My Father, and before His messengers. 6 He who is having an ear—let him hear what the Spirit says to the assemblies. 7 And to the messenger of the assembly in Philadelphia write: These things says the Holy [One], the True [One], having the key of David, the [One] opening and no one will shut, and shutting and no one opens: 8 I have known your works; behold, I have set before you a door having been opened, which no one is able to shut it, because you have little power, and yet have kept My word, and have not denied My Name; 9 behold, I give from the synagogue of Satan—those saying themselves to be Jews, and are not, but lie—behold, I will make them that they may come and prostrate before your feet, and may know that I loved you. 10 Because you kept the word of My endurance, I also will keep you from the hour of the trial that is about to come on all the world, to try those dwelling on the earth. 11 Behold, I come quickly, be holding fast that which you have, that no one may receive your garland. 12 He who is overcoming—I will make him a pillar in the temple of My God, and he may not go outside anymore, and I will write on him the Name of My God, and the name of the city of My God, the New Jerusalem, that comes down out of Heaven from My God—also My new Name. 13 He who is having an ear—let him hear what the Spirit says to the assemblies. 14 And to the messenger of the assembly of the Laodiceans write: These things says the Amen, the Witness—the Faithful and True—the Chief of the creation of God: 15 I have known your works, that you are neither cold nor hot; I wish you were cold or hot. 16 So—because you are lukewarm, and neither cold nor hot, I am about to vomit you out of My mouth; 17 because you say—I am rich, and have grown rich, and have need of nothing, and have not known that you are the wretched, and miserable, and poor, and blind, and naked; 18 I counsel you to buy from Me gold fired by fire, that you may be rich, and white garments that you may be clothed, and the shame of your nakedness may not be revealed, and with eye-salve anoint your eyes, that you may see. 19 As many as I cherish, I convict and discipline; be zealous, then, and convert; 20 behold, I have stood at the door, and I knock; if anyone may hear My voice, and may open the door, I will come in to him, and will dine with him, and he with Me. 21 He who is overcoming—I will give to him to sit with Me in My throne, as I also overcame and sat down with My Father in His throne. 22 He who is having an ear—let him hear what the Spirit says to the assemblies."

CHAPTER 4

1 After these things I saw, and behold, a door opened in the sky, and the first voice that I heard—as of a trumpet speaking with me, saying, "Come up here, and I will show you what must come to pass after these things"; 2 and immediately I was in [the] Spirit, and behold, a throne was set in Heaven, and on the throne is [One] sitting, 3 and He who is sitting was in appearance like a stone, jasper and sardine: and a rainbow was around the throne in appearance like an emerald. 4 And

around the throne [are] twenty-four thrones, and sitting on the thrones I saw twenty-four elders, having been clothed in white garments, and on their heads golden garlands; 5 and out of the throne proceed lightnings, and thunders, and voices; and seven lamps of fire are burning before the throne, which are the Seven Spirits of God, 6 and before the throne—a sea of glass like to crystal, and in the midst of the throne, and around the throne—four living creatures, full of eyes before and behind; 7 and the first living creature—like a lion; and the second living creature—like a calf; and the third living creature has the face as a man; and the fourth living creature—like an eagle flying. 8 And the four living creatures, one by one of them had six wings respectively, around and within [are] full of eyes, and they have no rest day and night, saying, "Holy, Holy, Holy, the Lord God, the Almighty, who was, and who is, and who is coming"; 9 and when the living creatures give glory, and honor, and thanksgiving, to the [One] sitting on the throne, the [One] living through the ages of the ages, 10 the twenty-four elders will fall down before the [One] sitting on the throne, and worship the [One] living through the ages of the ages, and they will cast their garlands before the throne, saying, 11 "Worthy are You, our Lord and God, to receive the glory, and the honor, and the power, because You created all things, and because of Your will they existed and were created."

CHAPTER 5

1 And I saw a scroll on the right hand of Him who is sitting on the throne, written within and on the back, sealed with seven seals; 2 and I saw a strong messenger crying with a great voice, "Who is worthy to open the scroll and to loose its seals?" 3 and no one was able in Heaven, nor on the earth, nor under the earth, to open the scroll, nor to behold it. 4 And I was weeping much, because no one was found worthy to open and to read the scroll, nor to behold it, 5 and one of the elders says to me, "Do not weep; behold, the Lion of the tribe of Judah, the root of David, has overcome to open the scroll, and to loose its seven seals"; 6 and I saw, and behold, in the midst of the throne, and of the four living creatures, and in the midst of the elders, a Lamb standing as having been slain, having seven horns and seven eyes, which are the Seven Spirits of God, which are sent to all the earth, 7 and He came and took the scroll out of the right hand of Him who is sitting on the throne. 8 And when He took the scroll, the four living creatures and the twenty-four elders fell before the Lamb, each one having harps and golden bowls full of incenses, which are the prayers of the holy ones, 9 and they sing a new song, saying, "Worthy are You to take the scroll, and to open its seals, because You were slain, and You purchased us to God in Your blood, out of every tribe, and tongue, and people, and nation, 10 and made them [to be] to our God kings and priests, and they will reign on the earth." 11 And I saw, and I heard the voice of many messengers around the throne, and the living creatures, and the elders—and the number of them was myriads of myriads, and thousands of thousands— 12 saying with a great voice, "Worthy is the Lamb that was slain to receive the power, and riches, and wisdom, and strength, and honor, and glory, and blessing!" 13 and every creature that is in Heaven, and on the earth, and under the earth, and the things that are on the sea, and all things in them, I heard saying, "To Him who is sitting on the throne and to the Lamb— the blessing, and the honor, and the glory, and the might— through the ages of the ages!" 14 and the four living creatures said, "Amen!" And the twenty-four elders fell down and they worship Him who is living through the ages of the ages.

CHAPTER 6

1 And I saw when the Lamb opened one of the seals, and I heard one of the four living creatures saying, as it were a voice of thunder, "Come and behold!" 2 and I saw, and behold, a white horse, and he who is sitting on it is having a bow, and there was given to him a garland, and he went forth overcoming, and that he may overcome. 3 And when He opened the second seal, I heard the second living creature saying, "Come and behold!" 4 and there went forth another horse—fire-colored, and to him who is sitting on it, there was given to him to take peace from the earth, and that they may slay one another, and there was given to him a great sword. 5

And when He opened the third seal, I heard the third living creature saying, "Come and behold!" And I saw, and behold, a black horse, and he who is sitting on it is having a balance in his hand, 6 and I heard a voice in the midst of the four living creatures saying, "A measure of wheat for a denarius, and three measures of barley for a denarius, and you may not injure the oil and the wine." 7 And when He opened the fourth seal, I heard the voice of the fourth living creature saying, "Come and behold!" 8 and I saw, and behold, a pale horse, and he who is sitting on him—his name is Death, and Hades follows with him, and there was given to them authority to kill over the fourth part of the earth with sword, and with hunger, and with death, and by the beasts of the earth. 9 And when He opened the fifth seal, I saw under the altar the souls of those slain because of the word of God, and because of the testimony that they held, 10 and they were crying with a great voice, saying, "Until when, O Master, the Holy and the True, do You not judge and take vengeance of our blood from those dwelling on the earth?" 11 and there was given to each one a white robe, and it was said to them that they may rest themselves yet a short time, until may also be fulfilled their fellow-servants and their brothers, who are about to be killed—even as they. 12 And I saw when He opened the sixth seal, and behold, a great earthquake came, and the sun became black as sackcloth of hair, and the moon became as blood, 13 and the stars of Heaven fell to the earth—as a fig tree casts her unripe figs, being shaken by a great wind— 14 and the sky departed as a scroll rolled up, and every mountain and island were moved out of their places; 15 and the kings of the earth, and the great men, and the rich, and the chiefs of thousands, and the mighty, and every servant, and every freeman, hid themselves in the dens, and in the rocks of the mountains, 16 and they say to the mountains and to the rocks, "Fall on us, and hide us from the face of Him who is sitting on the throne, and from the anger of the Lamb," 17 because the great day of His anger has come, and who is able to stand?

CHAPTER 7

1 And after these things I saw four messengers, standing on the four corners of the earth, holding the four winds of the earth, that the wind may not blow on the earth, nor on the sea, nor on any tree; 2 and I saw another messenger going up from the rising of the sun, having a seal of the living God, and he cried with a great voice to the four messengers, to whom it was given to injure the land and the sea, saying, 3 "Do not injure the land, nor the sea, nor the trees, until we may seal the servants of our God on their foreheads." 4 And I heard the number of those sealed—one hundred forty-four thousand, having been sealed out of every tribe of the sons of Israel: 5 of the tribe of Judah twelve thousand were sealed; of the tribe of Reuben twelve thousand were sealed; of the tribe of Gad twelve thousand were sealed; 6 of the tribe of Asher twelve thousand were sealed; of the tribe of Naphtali twelve thousand were sealed; of the tribe of Manasseh twelve thousand were sealed; 7 of the tribe of Simeon twelve thousand were sealed; of the tribe of Levi twelve thousand were sealed; of the tribe of Issachar twelve thousand were sealed; 8 of the tribe of Zebulun twelve thousand were sealed; of the tribe of Joseph twelve thousand were sealed; of the tribe of Benjamin twelve thousand were sealed. 9 After these things I saw, and behold, a great multitude, which no one was able to number, out of all nations, and tribes, and peoples, and tongues, standing before the throne, and before the Lamb, having been clothed [in] white robes, and palms in their hands, 10 and crying with a great voice, saying, "Salvation to our God, the [One] sitting on the throne, and to the Lamb!" 11 And all the messengers stood around the throne, and the elders and the four living creatures, and they fell on their faces and worshiped God, 12 saying, "Amen! The blessing, and the glory, and the wisdom, and the thanksgiving, and the honor, and the power, and the strength, [are] to our God through the ages of the ages! Amen!" 13 And one of the elders answered, saying to me, "These having been clothed with the white robes, who are they, and from where have they come?" 14 and I have said to him, "Lord, you have known"; and he said to me, "These are those who are coming out of the Great Tribulation, and they washed their robes, and they made their robes white in the blood of the Lamb; 15 because of this they are before the throne of God, and they do service to Him day and night in His temple, and He who is sitting on the throne will dwell over them; 16 they will not

hunger anymore, nor may the sun fall on them, nor any heat, 17 because the Lamb that [is] in the midst of the throne will feed them, and will lead them to living fountains of waters, and God will wipe away every tear from their eyes."

CHAPTER 8

1 And when He opens the seventh seal, there came silence in Heaven about half an hour, 2 and I saw the seven messengers who have stood before God, and there were given to them seven trumpets, 3 and another messenger came, and he stood at the altar, having a golden censer, and there was given to him much incense, that he may give [it] to the prayers of all the holy ones on the golden altar that [is] before the throne, 4 and the smoke of the incenses, with the prayers of the holy ones, went up before God out of the hand of the messenger; 5 and the messenger took the censer, and filled it out of the fire of the altar, and cast [it] to the earth, and there came voices, and thunders, and lightnings, and an earthquake. 6 And the seven messengers who are having the seven trumpets prepared themselves that they may sound the trumpets; 7 and the first messenger sounded the trumpet, and there came hail and fire, mingled with blood, and it was cast to the earth, and the third of the trees were burned up, and all the green grass was burned up. 8 And the second messenger sounded the trumpet, and [something] like a great mountain burning with fire was cast into the sea, and the third of the sea became blood, 9 and the third of the creatures that [are] in the sea died, those having life, and the third of the ships were destroyed. 10 And the third messenger sounded the trumpet, and there fell out of the sky a great star, burning as a lamp, and it fell on the third of the rivers, and on the fountains of waters, 11 and the name of the star is called Wormwood, and the third of the waters become wormwood, and many of the men died [because] of the waters, because they were made bitter. 12 And the fourth messenger sounded the trumpet, and the third of the sun was struck, and the third of the moon, and the third of the stars, that the third of them may be darkened, and that the day may not shine—the third of it, and the night in like manner. 13 And I saw, and I heard one messenger, flying in midair, saying with a great voice, "Woe, woe, woe, to those dwelling on the earth because of the rest of the voices of the trumpet of the three messengers being about to sound trumpets."

CHAPTER 9

1 And the fifth messenger sounded the trumpet, and I saw a star having fallen to the earth out of Heaven, and there was given to him the key of the pit of the abyss, 2 and [he] opened the pit of the abyss, and there came up a smoke out of the pit as smoke of a great furnace, and the sun and the air were darkened from the smoke of the pit. 3 And out of the smoke came forth locusts to the earth, and there was given to them authority, as scorpions of the earth have authority, 4 and it was said to them that they may not injure the grass of the earth, nor any green thing, nor any tree, but only the men who do not have the seal of God on their foreheads, 5 and it was given to them that they may not kill them, but that they may be tormented five months, and their torment—as the torment of a scorpion—when it may strike a man; 6 and in those days men will seek death and they will not find it, and they will desire to die, and death will flee from them. 7 And the likenesses of the locusts—like to horses made ready to battle, and on their heads [something] as garlands like gold, and their faces as faces of men, 8 and they had hair as hair of women, and their teeth were as [those] of lions, 9 and they had breastplates as breastplates of iron, and the noise of their wings—as the noise of chariots of many horses running to battle; 10 and they have tails like to scorpions, and stings were in their tails; and their authority [is] to injure men five months; 11 and they have over them a king—the messenger of the abyss—a name [is] to him in Hebrew, Abaddon, and in the Greek he has a name, Apollyon. 12 The first woe went forth, behold, there yet come two woes after these things. 13 And the sixth messenger sounded the trumpet, and I heard a voice out of the four horns of the altar of gold that is before God, 14 saying to the sixth messenger who had the trumpet, "Loose the four messengers who are bound at the great river Euphrates"; 15 and the four

messengers were loosed, who have been made ready for the hour, and day, and month, and year, that they may kill the third of mankind; 16 and the number of the forces of the horsemen—twice ten thousand ten thousands, and I heard the number of them. 17 And thus I saw the horses in the vision, and those sitting on them, having breastplates of fire, and jacinth, and brimstone; and the heads of the horses [are] as heads of lions, and out of their mouths proceed fire, and smoke, and brimstone; 18 by these three plagues the third of mankind was killed, from the fire, and from the smoke, and from the brimstone, that is proceeding out of their mouths, 19 for the power of the horses are in their mouth, and in their tails, for their tails [are] like serpents, having heads, and they injure with them. 20 And the rest of mankind, who were not killed in these plagues, neither converted from the works of their hands, that they may not worship the demons, and idols, those of gold, and those of silver, and those of brass, and those of stone, and those of wood, that are neither able to see, nor to hear, nor to walk, 21 and they did not convert from their murders, nor from their sorceries, nor from their whoredoms, nor from their thefts.

CHAPTER 10

1 And I saw another strong messenger coming down out of Heaven, clothed with a cloud, and a rainbow on the head, and his face as the sun, and his feet as pillars of fire, 2 and he had in his hand a little scroll opened, and he placed his right foot on the sea, and the left on the land, 3 and he cried with a great voice, as a lion roars, and when he cried, the seven thunders spoke out their voices; 4 and when the seven thunders spoke their voices, I was about to write, and I heard a voice out of Heaven saying to me, "Seal the things that the seven thunders spoke," and, "You may not write these things." 5 And the messenger whom I saw standing on the sea, and on the land, lifted up his hand to the sky, 6 and swore by Him who lives through the ages of the ages, who created the sky and the things in it, and the land and the things in it, and the sea and the things in it that time will not be yet, 7 but in the days of the voice of the seventh messenger, when he may be about to sound the trumpet, and the secret of God may be accomplished, as He declared to His own servants, to the prophets. 8 And the voice that I heard out of Heaven is again speaking with me, and saying, "Go, take the little scroll that is open in the hand of the messenger who has been standing on the sea, and on the land": 9 and I went away to the messenger, saying to him, "Give me the little scroll"; and he says to me, "Take, and eat it up, and it will make your belly bitter, but in your mouth it will be sweet as honey." 10 And I took the little scroll out of the hand of the messenger, and ate it up, and it was in my mouth sweet as honey, and when I ate it my belly was made bitter; 11 and he says to me, "You must again prophesy about many peoples, and nations, and tongues, and kings."

CHAPTER 11

1 And there was given to me a reed like to a rod, [[and the messenger stood,]] saying, "Rise, and measure the temple of God, and the altar, and those worshiping in it; 2 and leave out the court that is outside the temple, and you may not measure it, because it was given to the nations, and they will tread down the holy city forty-two months; 3 and I will give to My two witnesses, and they will prophesy one thousand, two hundred, sixty days, clothed with sackcloth"; 4 these are the two olive [trees], and the two lampstands that stand before the God of the earth; 5 and if anyone may will to injure them, fire proceeds out of their mouth, and devours their enemies, and if anyone may will to injure them, thus it is required of him to be killed. 6 These have authority to shut the sky, that rain may not rain in the days of their prophecy, and they have authority over the waters to turn them to blood, and to strike the land with every plague, as often as they may will. 7 And when they may finish their testimony, the beast that is coming up out of the abyss will make war with them, and overcome them, and kill them, 8 and their body [is] on the street of the great city that is called spiritually Sodom and Egypt, where also their Lord was crucified, 9 and they gaze—[those] of the peoples, and tribes, and tongues, and nations—on their dead bodies three

and a half days, and they will not allow their dead bodies to be put into tombs, 10 and those dwelling on the earth will rejoice over them, and will make merry, and they will send gifts to one another, because these—the two prophets—tormented those dwelling on the earth. 11 And after the three and a half days, [the] Spirit of life from God entered into them, and they stood on their feet, and great fear fell on those beholding them, 12 and they heard a great voice out of Heaven saying to them, "Come up here"; and they went up to Heaven in the cloud, and their enemies beheld them; 13 and in that hour a great earthquake came, and the tenth of the city fell, and seven thousand names of men were killed in the earthquake, and the rest became frightened, and they gave glory to the God of Heaven. 14 The second woe went forth, behold, the third woe comes quickly. 15 And the seventh messenger sounded the trumpet, and there came great voices in Heaven, saying, "The kingdoms of the world became [those] of our Lord and of His Christ, and He will reign through the ages of the ages!" 16 and the twenty-four elders, who are sitting on their thrones before God, fell on their faces and worshiped God, 17 saying, "We give thanks to You, O Lord God, the Almighty, who is, and who was, and who is coming, because You have taken Your great power and reigned; 18 and the nations were angry, and Your anger came, and the time of the dead to be judged, and to give the reward to Your servants, to the prophets, and to the holy ones, and to those fearing Your Name, to the small and to the great, and to destroy those who are destroying the earth." 19 And the temple of God was opened in Heaven, and the Ark of His Covenant was seen in His temple, and there came lightnings, and voices, and thunders, and an earthquake, and great hail.

CHAPTER 12

1 And a great sign was seen in the sky: a woman clothed with the sun, and the moon under her feet, and on her head a garland of twelve stars, 2 and having [a child] in [her] womb she cries out, travailing and being in pain to bring forth. 3 And there was seen another sign in the sky, and behold, a great fire-colored dragon, having seven heads and ten horns, and seven crowns on his heads, 4 and his tail draws the third of the stars of the sky, and he cast them to the earth; and the dragon stood before the woman who is about to bring forth, that when she may bring forth, he may devour her child; 5 and she brought forth a male son, who is about to rule all the nations with a rod of iron, and her child was snatched up to God and to His throne, 6 and the woman fled into the wilderness, where she has a place made ready from God, that there they may nourish her—one thousand, two hundred, sixty days. 7 And there came war in Heaven: Michael and his messengers warred against the dragon, and the dragon and his messengers warred, 8 and they did not prevail, nor was their place found anymore in Heaven; 9 and the great dragon was cast forth— the old serpent, who is called "Devil," and "Satan," who is leading the whole world astray—he was cast forth to the earth, and his messengers were cast forth with him. 10 And I heard a great voice saying in Heaven, "Now came the salvation, and the power, and the kingdom, of our God, and the authority of His Christ, because the accuser of our brothers was cast down, who is accusing them before our God day and night; 11 and they overcame him because of the blood of the Lamb, and because of the word of their testimony, and they did not love their life—to death; 12 because of this be glad, you heavens, and those who dwell in them; woe to those inhabiting the earth and the sea, because the Devil went down to you, having great wrath, having known that he has [a] short time." 13 And when the dragon saw that he was cast forth to the earth, he pursued the woman who brought forth the male, 14 and there were given to the woman two wings of the great eagle, that she may fly into the wilderness, to her place, where she is nourished a time, and times, and half a time, from the face of the serpent; 15 and the serpent cast forth out of his mouth water as a river after the woman, that he may cause her to be carried away by the river, 16 and the earth helped the woman, and the earth opened its mouth and swallowed up the river that the dragon cast forth out of his mouth; 17 and the dragon was angry against the woman, and went away to make war with the rest of her seed, those keeping the commands of God, and having the testimony of Jesus.

CHAPTER 13

1 And I stood on the sand of the sea, and I saw a beast coming up out of the sea, having seven heads and ten horns, and ten crowns on its horns, and on its heads names of slander, 2 and the beast that I saw was like to a leopard, and its feet as of a bear, and its mouth as the mouth of a lion, and the dragon gave to it his power, and his throne, and great authority. 3 And I saw one of its heads as slain to death, and its deadly wound was healed, and all the earth wondered after the beast, 4 and they worshiped the dragon who gave authority to the beast, and they worshiped the beast, saying, "Who [is] like to the beast? who is able to war with it?" 5 And there was given to it a mouth speaking great things, and slanders, and there was given to it authority to make war forty-two months, 6 and it opened its mouth for slander toward God, to slander His Name, and of His dwelling place, and of those who dwell in Heaven, 7 and there was given to it to make war with the holy ones, and to overcome them, and there was given to it authority over every tribe, and tongue, and nation. 8 And all who are dwelling on the earth will worship him, whose names have not been written in the Scroll of Life of the Lamb slain from the foundation of the world; 9 if anyone has an ear—let him hear: 10 if anyone [goes] into captivity, into captivity he goes; if anyone is to be killed with sword, it is necessary of him by sword to be killed; here is the endurance and the faith of the holy ones. 11 And I saw another beast coming up out of the earth, and it had two horns like a lamb, and it was speaking as a dragon, 12 and all the authority of the first beast does it do before it, and it makes the earth and those dwelling in it that they will worship the first beast, whose deadly wound was healed, 13 and it does great signs, that fire also it may make to come down from the sky to the earth before men, 14 and it leads astray those dwelling on the earth, because of the signs that were given it to do before the beast, saying to those dwelling on the earth to make an image to the beast that has the wound of the sword and lived, 15 and there was given to it to give a spirit to the image of the beast, that also the image of the beast may speak, and it may cause as many as will not worship the image of the beast, that they may be killed. 16 And it makes all, the small, and the great, and the rich, and the poor, and the freemen, and the servants, that it may give to them a mark on their right hand or on their foreheads, 17 and that no one may be able to buy, or to sell, except he who is having the mark, or the name of the beast, or the number of his name. 18 Here is the wisdom! He who is having the understanding, let him count the number of the beast, for it is the number of a man, and its number: six hundred sixty-six.

CHAPTER 14

1 And I saw, and behold, a Lamb was standing on Mount Zion, and with Him one hundred forty-four thousand, having the Name of His Father written on their foreheads; 2 and I heard a voice out of Heaven, as a voice of many waters, and as a voice of great thunder, and I heard a voice of harpists harping with their harps, 3 and they sing, as it were, a new song before the throne, and before the four living creatures, and the elders, and no one was able to learn the song except the one hundred forty-four thousand who have been bought from the earth; 4 these are they who were not defiled with women, for they are virgin; these are they who are following the Lamb wherever He may go; these were bought from among men—a first-fruit to God and to the Lamb— 5 and in their mouth there was not found guile, for they are unblemished before the throne of God. 6 And I saw another messenger flying in midair, having continuous good news to proclaim to those dwelling on the earth, and to every nation, and tribe, and tongue, and people, 7 saying in a great voice, "Fear God, and give to Him glory, because the hour of His judgment came, and worship Him who made the sky, and the land, and sea, and fountains of waters." 8 And another messenger followed, saying, "Fallen, fallen is Babylon the great, because of the wine of the wrath of her whoredom she has given to all nations to drink." 9 And a third messenger followed them, saying in a great voice, "If anyone worships the beast and his image, and receives a mark on his forehead or on his hand, 10 he also will drink of the wine of the wrath of God that has been mingled unmixed in the cup of His anger, and he will be tormented in fire and brimstone before the holy messengers, and before the

Lamb, 11 and the smoke of their torment goes up through ages of ages; and they have no rest day and night, who are worshiping the beast and his image, also if any receive the mark of his name. 12 Here is endurance of the holy ones; here [are] those keeping the commands of God, and the faith of Jesus." 13 And I heard a voice out of Heaven saying to me, "Write: Blessed are the dead who are dying in the Lord from this time!" "Yes," says the Spirit, "That they may rest from their labors—and their works follow them!" 14 And I saw, and behold, a white cloud, and on the cloud [One] sitting like [a] Son of Man, having on His head a golden garland, and in His hand a sharp sickle; 15 and another messenger came forth out of the temple crying in a great voice to Him who is sitting on the cloud, "Send forth Your sickle and reap, because the hour of reaping has come to You, because the harvest of the earth has been ripe"; 16 and He who is sitting on the cloud put forth His sickle on the earth, and the earth was reaped. 17 And another messenger came forth out of the temple that [is] in Heaven, having—he also—a sharp sickle, 18 and another messenger came forth out from the altar, having authority over the fire, and he called with a great cry to him having the sharp sickle, saying, "Send forth your sharp sickle, and gather the clusters of the vine of the earth, because her grapes have come to perfection"; 19 and the messenger put forth his sickle to the earth, and gathered the vine of the earth, and cast [it] into the great winepress of the wrath of God; 20 and the winepress was trodden outside of the city, and blood came forth out of the winepress—to the bridles of the horses, one thousand six hundred stadia.

convert—to give to Him glory. 10 And the fifth messenger poured out his bowl on the throne of the beast, and his kingdom became darkened, and they were gnawing their tongues from the pain, 11 and they slandered the God of Heaven, from their pains, and from their sores, and they did not convert from their works. 12 And the sixth messenger poured out his bowl on the great river, the Euphrates, and its water was dried up, that the way of the kings who are from the rising of the sun may be made ready; 13 and I saw [come] out of the mouth of the dragon, and out of the mouth of the beast, and out of the mouth of the false prophet, three unclean spirits like frogs— 14 for they are spirits of demons, doing signs— which go forth to the kings of the earth, and of the whole world, to bring them together to the battle of that great day of God the Almighty. 15 ("Behold, I come as a thief; blessed [is] he who is watching, and keeping his garments, that he may not walk naked, and they may see his unseemliness.") 16 And they brought them together to the place that is called in Hebrew Armageddon. 17 And the seventh messenger poured out his bowl on the air, and there came forth a great voice from the temple of Heaven, from the throne, saying, "It is done!" 18 and there came voices, and thunders, and lightnings; and a great earthquake came, such as has not come since men came on the earth, so mighty an earthquake—so great! 19 And it came—the great city—into three parts, and the cities of the nations fell, and Babylon the great was remembered before God, to give to her the cup of the wine of the wrath of His anger, 20 and every island fled away, and mountains were not found, 21 and great hail (as of talent weight) comes down out of the sky on men, and men slandered God because of the plague of the hail, because its plague is very great.

CHAPTER 15

1 And I saw another sign in the sky, great and wonderful: seven messengers having the seven last plagues, because in these the wrath of God was completed, 2 and I saw as a sea of glass mingled with fire, and those who gain the victory over the beast, and his image, and his mark, [and] the number of his name, standing by the sea of the glass, having harps of God, 3 and they sing the song of Moses, servant of God, and the song of the Lamb, saying, "Great and wonderful [are] Your works, O Lord God, the Almighty, righteous and true [are] Your ways, O King of holy ones! 4 Who may not fear You, O Lord, and glorify Your Name? because You alone [are] holy, because all the nations will come and worship before You, because Your righteous acts were revealed." 5 And after these things I saw, and behold, the temple of the Dwelling Place of the Testimony was opened in Heaven; 6 and the seven messengers having the seven plagues came forth out of the temple, clothed in linen, pure and radiant, and girded around the breasts with golden girdles: 7 and one of the four living creatures gave to the seven messengers seven golden bowls, full of the wrath of God, who is living through the ages of the ages; 8 and the temple was filled with smoke from the glory of God, and from His power, and no one was able to enter into the temple until the seven plagues of the seven messengers may be completed.

CHAPTER 16

1 And I heard a great voice out of the temple saying to the seven messengers, "Go away, and pour out the bowls of the wrath of God into the earth"; 2 and the first went away, and poured out his bowl into the earth, and there came a sore— bad and grievous—to men, those having the mark of the beast, and those worshiping his image. 3 And the second messenger poured out his bowl into the sea, and it became blood as of [one] dead, and every living soul in the sea died. 4 And the third messenger poured out his bowl into the rivers, and into the fountains of the waters, and there came blood, 5 and I heard the messenger of the waters, saying, "Righteous, O Lord, are You, who is, and who was, [[and who will be,]] the Holy [One], because You judged these things, 6 because they poured out [the] blood of holy ones and prophets, and You gave to them blood to drink, for they are worthy"; 7 and I heard another out of the altar, saying, "Yes, Lord God, the Almighty, true and righteous [are] Your judgments." 8 And the fourth messenger poured out his bowl on the sun, and there was given to him to scorch men with fire, 9 and men were scorched with great heat, and they slandered the Name of God, who has authority over these plagues, and they did not

CHAPTER 17

1 And there came one of the seven messengers, who were having the seven bowls, and he spoke with me, saying to me, "Come, I will show to you the judgment of the great whore, who is sitting on the many waters, 2 with whom the kings of the earth committed whoredom; and those inhabiting the earth were made drunk from the wine of her whoredom"; 3 and he carried me away to a wilderness in the Spirit, and I saw a woman sitting on a scarlet-colored beast, full of names of slander, having seven heads and ten horns, 4 and the woman was clothed with purple and scarlet-color, and gilded with gold, and precious stone, and pearls, having a golden cup in her hand full of abominations and uncleanness of her whoredom, 5 and on her forehead was a name written: "Secret, Babylon the Great, the Mother of the Whores, and the Abominations of the earth." 6 And I saw the woman drunken from the blood of the holy ones, and from the blood of the witnesses of Jesus, and I wondered—having seen her—with great wonder; 7 and the messenger said to me, "For this reason did you wonder? I will tell you the secret of the woman and of the beast that [is] carrying her, which has the seven heads and the ten horns. 8 The beast that you saw: it was, and it is not, and it is about to come up out of the abyss, and to go away to destruction, and those dwelling on the earth will wonder, whose names have not been written on the Scroll of Life from the foundation of the world, beholding the beast that was, and is not, although it is. 9 Here [is] the mind that is having wisdom: the seven heads are seven mountains on which the woman sits, 10 and there are seven kings, the five fell, and the one is, the other did not yet come, and when he may come, it is necessary for him to remain a short time; 11 and the beast that was, and is not, he also is eighth, and he is out of the seven, and he goes away to destruction. 12 And the ten horns that you saw are ten kings who did not yet receive a kingdom, but receive authority as kings one hour with the beast; 13 these have one mind, and they will give over their own power and authority to the beast; 14 these will make war with the Lamb, and the Lamb will overcome them, because He is Lord of lords, and King of kings, and those with Him are called, and chosen, and steadfast." 15 And he says to me, "The waters that you saw, where the whore sits, are peoples, and multitudes, and nations, and tongues; 16 and the ten horns that you saw, and the beast, these will hate the whore, and will make her desolate and naked, and will eat her flesh, and will burn her in fire, 17 for God gave into their hearts to do His purpose, and to make one purpose, and to give their kingdom to the beast until the sayings of God may be fulfilled, 18 and the woman that you saw is the great city that is having reign over the kings of the earth."

CHAPTER 18

1 And after these things I saw another messenger coming down out of Heaven, having great authority, and the earth was lightened from his glory, 2 and he cried in might [with] a great voice, saying, "Fallen, fallen is Babylon the great! And she became a habitation of demons, and a hold of every unclean spirit, and a hold of every unclean and hateful bird, 3 because all the nations have drunk of the wine of the wrath of her whoredom, and the kings of the earth committed whoredom with her, and merchants of the earth were made rich from the power of her indulgence." 4 And I heard another voice out of Heaven, saying, "Come forth out of her, My people, that you may not partake with her sins, and that you may not receive of her plagues, 5 because her sins have reached up to Heaven, and God remembered her unrighteousness. 6 Render to her as she also rendered to you, and double to her twofold according to her works; in the cup that she mingled mingle to her double. 7 As much as she glorified herself and indulged, so much torment and sorrow give to her, because in her heart she says, I sit [as] queen, and I am not a widow, and I will not see sorrow; 8 because of this, in one day, will come her plagues: death, and sorrow, and famine; and she will be utterly burned in fire, because strong [is] the Lord God who is judging her; 9 and the kings of the earth will weep over her and strike themselves for her, who committed whoredom and indulged with her, when they may see the smoke of her burning, 10 having stood from afar because of the fear of her torment, saying, Woe, woe, the great city! Babylon, the strong city! Because in one hour your judgment came. 11 And the merchants of the earth will weep and mourn over her, because no one buys their cargo anymore; 12 cargo of gold, and silver, and precious stone, and pearls, and fine linen, and purple, and silk, and scarlet, and all fragrant wood, and every vessel of ivory, and every vessel of most precious wood, and brass, and iron, and marble, 13 and cinnamon, and amomum, and incense, and ointment, and frankincense, and wine, and oil, and fine flour, and wheat, and cattle, and sheep, and of horses, and of chariots, and of bodies and souls of men. 14 And the fruits of the desire of your soul went away from you, and all things—the sumptuous and the radiant—went away from you, and no more at all may you find them. 15 The merchants of these things, who were made rich by her, will stand far off because of the fear of her torment, weeping, and mourning, 16 and saying, Woe, woe, the great city, that was clothed with fine linen, and purple, and scarlet, and gilded in gold, and precious stone, and pearls— 17 because in one hour so much riches were made desolate! And every shipmaster, and all the company on the ships, and sailors, and as many as work the sea, stood far off, 18 and were crying, seeing the smoke of her burning, saying, What [city is] like to the great city? 19 and they cast dust on their heads, and were crying out, weeping and mourning, saying, Woe, woe, the great city! In which were made rich all having ships in the sea, out of her costliness—for in one hour was she made desolate. 20 Be glad over her, O Heaven, and you holy apostles and prophets, because God judged your judgment of her!" 21 And one strong messenger took up a stone as a great millstone, and cast [it] into the sea, saying, "Thus with violence will Babylon be cast, the great city, and may not be found anymore at all; 22 and voice of harpists, and musicians, and pipers, and trumpeters, may not be heard at all in you anymore; and any craftsman of any craft may not be found at all in you anymore; and noise of a millstone may not be heard at all in you anymore; 23 and light of a lamp may not shine at all in you anymore; and voice of bridegroom and of bride may not be heard at all in you anymore; because your merchants were the great ones of the earth, because all the nations were led astray in your sorcery, 24 and in her blood of prophets and of holy ones was found, and of all those who have been slain on the earth."

CHAPTER 19

1 And after these things I heard a great voice of a great multitude in Heaven, saying, "Hallelujah! The salvation, and the glory, and the power [belong] to the Lord our God; 2 because true and righteous [are] His judgments, because He judged the great whore who corrupted the earth in her whoredom, and He avenged the blood of His servants at her hand"; 3 and a second time they said, "Hallelujah"; and her smoke comes up through the ages of the ages! 4 And the twenty-four elders and the four living creatures fell down and they worshiped God who is sitting on the throne, saying, "Amen! Hallelujah!" 5 And a voice out of the throne came forth, saying, "Praise our God, all you His servants, and those fearing Him, both the small and the great"; 6 and I heard as the voice of a great multitude, and as the voice of many waters, and as the voice of mighty thunderings, saying, "Hallelujah! Because our Lord, the God, the Almighty, has reigned! 7 may we rejoice and exult, and give the glory to Him, because the marriage of the Lamb has come, and His wife has made herself ready; 8 and there was given to her that she may be clothed with fine linen, pure and radiant, for the fine linen is the righteous acts of the holy ones." 9 And he says to me, "Write: Blessed [are] they who have been called to the banquet of the marriage of the Lamb"; and he says to me, "These [are] the true words of God"; 10 and I fell before his feet to worship him, and he says to me, "Behold—No! I am your fellow servant, and of your brothers, those having the testimony of Jesus; worship God, for the testimony of Jesus is the spirit of the prophecy." 11 And I saw Heaven having been opened, and behold, a white horse, and He who is sitting on it is called Faithful and True, and in righteousness He judges and makes war, 12 and His eyes [are] as a flame of fire, and on His head [are] many crowns—having a Name written that no one has known, except Himself, 13 and He is clothed with a garment covered with blood, and His Name is called, The Word of God. 14 And the armies in Heaven were following Him on white horses, clothed in fine linen—white and pure; 15 and out of His mouth proceeds a sharp sword, that with it He may strike the nations, and He will rule them with a rod of iron, and He treads the press of the wine of the wrath and the anger of God the Almighty, 16 and He has on the garment and on His thigh the name written: "King of Kings, and Lord of Lords." 17 And I saw one messenger standing in the sun, and he cried [with] a great voice, saying to all the birds that are flying in midair, "Come and be gathered together to the banquet of the great [[or the great banquet of God]], 18 that you may eat flesh of kings, and flesh of chiefs of thousands, and flesh of strong men, and flesh of horses, and of those sitting on them, and the flesh of all—freemen and servants—both small and great." 19 And I saw the beast, and the kings of the earth, and their armies, having been gathered together to make war with Him who is sitting on the horse, and with His army; 20 and the beast was taken, and with him the false prophet who did the signs before him, in which he led astray those who received the mark of the beast, and those who worshiped his image; the two were cast living into the lake of the fire that is burning with brimstone; 21 and the rest were killed with the sword of Him who is sitting on the horse, which is proceeding out of His mouth, and all the birds were filled with their flesh.

CHAPTER 20

1 And I saw a messenger coming down out of Heaven, having the key of the abyss, and a great chain over his hand, 2 and he laid hold on the dragon, the ancient serpent, who is [the] Devil and Satan, and bound him one thousand years, 3 and he cast him into the abyss, and shut him up, and put a seal on him, that he may no longer lead the nations astray, until the one thousand years may be completed; and after these it is necessary for him to be loosed a short time. 4 And I saw thrones, and they [that] sat on them, and judgment was given to them, and the souls of those who have been beheaded because of the testimony of Jesus, and because of the word of God, and who did not worship the beast, nor his image, and did not receive the mark on their forehead and on their hand, and they lived and reigned with the Christ one thousand years; 5 and the rest of the dead did not live again until the one thousand years may be completed; this [is] the first resurrection. 6 Blessed and holy—he who is having part in the first resurrection; the second death has no authority over these, but they will be priests of God and of the Christ, and will reign with Him one thousand years. 7 And when the one thousand years may be completed, Satan will be loosed out of his prison, 8 and he will go forth to lead the nations astray, that are in the four corners of the earth—Gog and Magog—to gather them together to war, of whom the number—as the sand of the sea; 9 and they went up over the breadth of the land, and surrounded the camp of the holy ones, and the

beloved city, and there came down fire from God out of Heaven, and devoured them; 10 and the Devil, who is leading them astray, was cast into the lake of fire and brimstone where the beast and the false prophet [are], and they will be tormented day and night through the ages of the ages. 11 And I saw a great white throne, and Him who is sitting on it, from whose face the earth and the sky fled away, and no place was found for them; 12 and I saw the dead, small and great, standing before God, and scrolls were opened, and another scroll was opened, which is that of the life, and the dead were judged out of the things written in the scrolls—according to their works; 13 and the sea gave up those dead in it, and death and Hades gave up the dead in them, and they were judged, each one according to their works; 14 and death and Hades were cast into the lake of the fire—this [is] the second death; 15 and if anyone was not found written in the Scroll of Life, he was cast into the lake of the fire.

CHAPTER 21

1 And I saw a new heaven and a new earth, for the first heaven and the first earth passed away, and the sea is no more; 2 and I saw the holy city, New Jerusalem, coming down from God out of Heaven, made ready as a bride adorned for her husband; 3 and I heard a great voice out of Heaven, saying, "Behold, the dwelling place of God [is] with men, and He will dwell with them, and they will be His peoples, and God Himself will be with them [as] their God, 4 and God will wipe away every tear from their eyes, and there will be no more death, nor sorrow, nor crying, nor will there be anymore pain, because the first things passed away." 5 And He who is sitting on the throne said, "Behold, I make all things new"; and He says to me, "Write, because these words are true and steadfast"; 6 and He said to me, "It is done! I am the Alpha and the Omega, the Beginning and the End. To him who is thirsting, I will give of the fountain of the water of life freely. 7 The [one] who is overcoming will inherit all things, and I will be his God, and he will be My son. 8 But to fearful, and unsteadfast, and abominable, and murderers, and whoremongers, and sorcerers, and idolaters, and all the liars, their part [is] in the lake that is burning with fire and brimstone, which is the second death." 9 And one of the seven messengers, having the seven bowls that are full of the seven last plagues, came and spoke with me, saying, "Come, I will show you the bride, the wife of the Lamb," 10 and he carried me away in the Spirit to a mountain great and high, and showed me the great city, the holy Jerusalem, coming down out of Heaven from God, 11 having the glory of God, and her light—like a most precious stone, as a jasper stone clear as crystal, 12 also having a great and high wall, having twelve gates, and at the gates twelve messengers, and names written thereon, which are [those] of the twelve tribes of the sons of Israel— 13 at the east three gates, at the north three gates, at the south three gates, at the west three gates; 14 and the wall of the city had twelve foundations, and on them names of the twelve apostles of the Lamb. 15 And he who is speaking with me had a golden reed, that he may measure the city, and its gates, and its wall; 16 and the city lies square, and the length of it is as great as the breadth; and he measured the city with the reed—twelve thousand stadia; the length, and the breadth, and the height of it are equal. 17 And he measured its wall—one hundred forty-four cubits, the measure of a man, that is, of the messenger; 18 and the building of its wall was jasper, and the city [is] pure gold—like to pure glass. 19 And the foundations of the wall of the city have been adorned with every precious stone: the first foundation jasper, the second sapphire, the third chalcedony, the fourth emerald, 20 the fifth sardonyx, the sixth sardius, the seventh chrysolite, the eighth beryl, the ninth topaz, the tenth chrysoprase, the eleventh jacinth, the twelfth amethyst. 21 And the twelve gates [are] twelve pearls, each one of the gates respectively was of one pearl; and the street of the city [is] pure gold—as transparent glass. 22 And I did not see a temple in it, for the Lord God, the Almighty, and the Lamb, are its temple. 23 And the city has no need of the sun, nor of the moon, that they may shine in it; for the glory of God lightens it, and the lamp of it—the Lamb; 24 and the nations will walk by its light, and the kings of the earth bring their glory and honor into it, 25 and its gates will never be shut by day, for night will not be there; 26 and they will bring the glory and the honor of the nations into it; 27 and there may never enter into it anything defiling and doing abomination, and a lie, if not those written in the Lamb's Scroll of Life.

CHAPTER 22

1 And he showed me [the] river of [the] water of life, radiant as crystal, going forth out of the throne of God and of the Lamb 2 in the midst of its street, and of the river on this side and on that—[the] Tree of Life, producing twelve fruits, yielding its fruit according to each month, and the leaves of the tree [are] for the healing of the nations; 3 and there will no longer be any curse, and the throne of God and of the Lamb will be in it, and His servants will serve Him, 4 and they will see His face, and His Name [is] on their foreheads, 5 and there will be no night there, and they have no need of [the] light of a lamp and of [the] light of [the] sun, because the Lord God gives them light, and they will reign through the ages of the ages. 6 And he said to me, "These words [are] steadfast and true, and the Lord God of the holy prophets sent His messenger to show to His servants the things that must come quickly. 7 Behold, I come quickly; blessed [is] he who is keeping the words of the prophecy of this scroll." 8 And I, John, am he who is seeing these things and hearing, and when I heard and beheld, I fell down to worship before the feet of the messenger who is showing me these things; 9 and he says to me, "Behold—No! For I am your fellow servant, and of your brothers the prophets, and of those keeping the words of this scroll; worship God." 10 And He says to me, "You may not seal the words of the prophecy of this scroll, because the time is near. 11 The [one] being unrighteous—let him be unrighteous still; and the filthy—let him be filthy still; and the righteous—let him do righteousness still; and the holy—let him be holy still. 12 Behold, I come quickly, and My reward [is] with Me, to render to each as his work will be; 13 I am the Alpha and the Omega—the Beginning and End—the First and the Last. 14 Blessed are those washing their robes that the authority will be theirs to the Tree of Life, and they may enter into the city by the gates; 15 and outside [are] the dogs, and the sorcerers, and the whoremongers, and the murderers, and the idolaters, and everyone cherishing and doing falsehood. 16 I, Jesus, sent My messenger to testify to you these things concerning the assemblies; I am the root and the offspring of David, the radiant morning star! 17 And the Spirit and the bride say, Come! And he who is hearing—let him say, Come! And he who is thirsting—let him come; and he who is willing—let him take the water of life freely. 18 For I testify to everyone hearing the words of the prophecy of this scroll, if anyone may add to these, God will add to him the plagues that have been written in this scroll, 19 and if anyone may take away from the words of the scroll of this prophecy, God will take away his part from the Scroll of Life, and out of the holy city, and the things that have been written in this scroll." 20 The [One] testifying [to] these things says, "Yes, I come quickly!" Amen. Come, Lord Jesus! 21 The grace of our Lord Jesus Christ [is] with all [[the holy ones. Amen.]]

BOOK OF APOCRYPHA

APOCRYPHAL ESTHER

The Septuagint (LXX) version of Esther contains a number of sections not found in the Hebrew version of the text (chs. 11–16). These Greek chapters are canonical in a variety of traditions.

CHAPTER 11

¹ In the fourth year of the reign of Ptolemy and Cleopatra, Dositheus, who said he was a priest, and of the Levitical race, and Ptolemy his son brought this letter of Purim, which they said Lysimachus the son of Ptolemy had interpreted in Jerusalem. ² In the second year of the reign of Artaxerxes the great, in the first day of the month of Nisan, Mordecai the son of Jair, the son of Semei, the son of Cis, of the tribe of Benjamin: ³ a Jew who dwelt in the city of Shushan, a great man and among the first of the king's court, had a dream. ⁴ Now he was of the number of the captives, whom Nebuchadnezzar king of Babylon had carried away from Jerusalem with Jehoiachin king of Judah: ⁵ And this was his dream: Behold, there were voices, and tumults, and thunders, and earthquakes, and a disturbance on the earth. ⁶ And behold, two great dragons came forth ready to fight against one another. ⁷ And at their cry all nations were stirred up to fight against the nation of the just. ⁸ And that was a day of darkness and danger, of tribulation and distress, and great fear on the earth. ⁹ And the nation of the just was troubled fearing their own evils and was prepared for death ¹⁰ And they cried to God: and as they were crying, a little fountain grew into a very great river, and abounded into many waters. ¹¹ The light and the sun rose up, and the humble were exalted, and they devoured the glorious. ¹² And when Mordecai had seen this, and arose out of his bed, he was thinking what God would do: and he kept it fixed in his mind, desirous to know what the dream should signify.

CHAPTER 12

¹ And he abodes at that time in the king's court with Bagatha and Thara, the king's eunuchs, who were porters of the palace. ² And when he understood their designs, and had diligently searched into their projects, he learned that they went about to lay violent hands on King Artaxerxes, and he told the king thereof. ³ Then the king had them both examined, and after they had confessed, commanded them to be put to death. ⁴ But the king made a record of what was done: and Mordecai also committed the memory of the thing to writing. ⁵ And the king commanded him to abide in the court of the palace, and gave him presents for the information. ⁶ But Haman, the son of Amadathi the Bugite, was in great honor with the king, and sought to hurt Mordecai and his people, because of the two eunuchs of the king who were put to death.

CHAPTER 13

¹ And this was the copy of the letter: Artaxerxes the great king who reigns from India to Ethiopia, to the princes and governors of the one hundred and twenty-seven provinces that are subject to his empire, greetings. ² Whereas I reigned over many nations, and had brought all the world under my dominion, I was not willing to abuse the greatness of my power, but to govern my subjects with clemency and leniency, that they might live quietly without any terror, and might enjoy peace, which is desired by all men. ³ But when I asked my counselors how this might be accomplished, one that excelled the rest in wisdom and fidelity, and was second after the king, Haman by name, ⁴ he told me that there was a people scattered through the whole world, which used new laws, and acted against the customs of all nations, despised the commands of kings, and violated by their opposition the concord of all nations. ⁵ For what reason having learned this, and seeing one

nation in opposition to all mankind using perverse laws, and going against our commands, and disturbing the peace and concord of the provinces subject to us, ⁶ we have commanded that all whom Haman will mark out, who is chief over all the provinces, and second after the king, and whom we honor as a father, will be utterly destroyed by their enemies, with their wives and children, and that none will have pity on them, on the fourteenth day of the twelfth month Adar of this present year: ⁷ that these wicked men going down to Hades in one day, may restore to our empire the peace which they had disturbed. ⁸ But Mordecai implored the Lord, remembering all His works, ⁹ and said, "O Lord, Lord, almighty King, for all things are in Your power, and there is none that can resist Your will, if You determine to save Israel. ¹⁰ You have made the heavens and earth, and all things that are under the cover of Heaven. ¹¹ You are Lord of all, and there is none that can resist Your majesty. ¹² You know all things, and You know that it was not out of pride and contempt, or any desire of glory, that I refused to worship the proud Haman, ¹³ (for I would willingly and readily for the salvation of Israel have kissed even the steps of his feet,) ¹⁴ but I feared lest I should transfer the honor of my God to a man, and lest I should adore anyone except my God. ¹⁵ And now, O Lord, O King, O God of Abraham, have mercy on Your people, because our enemies resolve to destroy us, and extinguish Your inheritance. ¹⁶ Do not despise Your portion, which You have redeemed for Yourself out of Egypt. ¹⁷ Hear my supplication, and be merciful to Your lot and inheritance, and turn our mourning into joy, that we may live and praise Your Name, O Lord, and do not shut the mouths of them that sing to You." ¹⁸ And all Israel with like mind and supplication cried to the Lord, because they saw certain death hanging over their heads.

CHAPTER 14

¹ Queen Esther also, fearing the danger that was at hand, had recourse to the Lord. ² And when she had laid away her royal apparel, she put on garments suitable for weeping and mourning: instead of various precious ointments, she covered her head with ashes and dung, and she humbled her body with fasts: and all the places in which before she was accustomed to rejoice, she filled with her torn hair. ³ And she prayed to the Lord, the God of Israel, saying, "O my Lord, who alone are our King, help me, a desolate woman, and who has no other helper but You. ⁴ My danger is in my hands. ⁵ I have heard from my father that You, O Lord, took Israel from among all nations, and our fathers from all their predecessors, to possess them as a perpetual inheritance, and You have done to them as You have promised. ⁶ We have sinned in Your sight, and therefore You have delivered us into the hands of our enemies: ⁷ For we have worshiped their gods. You are just, O Lord. ⁸ And now they are not content to oppress us with most hard bondage, but attributing the strength of their hands to the power of their idols, ⁹ they design to change Your promises, and destroy Your inheritance, and shut the mouths of them that praise You, and extinguish the glory of Your temple and altar, ¹⁰ that they may open the mouths of nations, and praise the strength of idols, and magnify a carnal king forever. ¹¹ Do not give, O Lord, Your scepter to them that are nothing, lest they laugh at our ruin, but turn their counsel on themselves, and destroy him that has begun to rage against us. ¹² Remember, O Lord, and show Yourself to us in the time of our tribulation, and give me boldness, O Lord, King of gods, and of all power: ¹³ give me a well-ordered speech in my mouth in the presence of the lion, and turn his heart to the hatred of our enemy, that both he himself may perish, and the rest that consent to him. ¹⁴ But deliver us by Your hand, and help me, who has no other helper, but You, O Lord, who has the knowledge of all things. ¹⁵ And You know that I hate the glory of the wicked, and abhor the bed of the uncircumcised, and of every stranger. ¹⁶ You know my necessity, that I abominate the sign of my pride and glory, which is on my head in the days of my public appearance, and detest it as a menstruous rag, and do not wear it in the days of my silence, ¹⁷ and that I have not eaten at Haman's table, nor has the king's banquet pleased me, and that I have not drunk the wine of the drink offerings: ¹⁸ And that Your handmaid has never rejoiced, since I was brought here to this day, but in You, O Lord, the God of Abraham. ¹⁹ O God, who is mighty above all, hear the voice of them that have no other hope, and deliver us from the hand of the wicked, and deliver me from my fear."

CHAPTER 15

1 And he [(Mordecai)] commanded her to go to the king, and petition for her people, and for her country. **2** "Remember," [he said,] "the days of your low estate, how you were brought up by my hand, because Haman—the second after the king—has spoken against us to [put us to] death. **3** And you [must] call on the Lord, and speak to the king for us, and deliver us from death." **4** And on the third day she laid away the garments she wore, and put on her glorious apparel. **5** And glittering in royal robes, after she had called on God the Ruler and Savior of all, she took two maids with her, **6** and she leaned on one of them, as if for delicateness and excessive tenderness she were not able to bear up her own body. **7** And the other maid followed her lady, bearing up her train flowing on the ground. **8** But she with a rosy color in her face, and with gracious and bright eyes, hid a mind full of anguish, and exceeding great fear. **9** So going in she passed through all the doors in order, and stood before the king, where he sat on his royal throne, clothed with his royal robes, and glittering with gold, and precious stones, and he was terrible to behold. **10** And when he had lifted up his countenance, and with burning eyes had shown the wrath of his heart, the queen sunk down, and her color turned pale, and she rested her weary head on her handmaid. **11** And God changed the king's spirit into mildness, and all in haste and in fear he leaped from his throne, and holding her up in his arms, until she came to herself, caressed her with these words: **12** "What is the matter, Esther? I am your brother, do not fear. **13** You will not die, for this law is not made for you, but for all others. **14** Come near then, and touch the scepter." **15** And as she held her peace, he took the golden scepter, and laid it on her neck, and kissed her, and said, "Why do you not speak to me?" **16** She answered, "I saw you, my lord, as a messenger of God, and my heart was troubled for fear of your majesty. **17** For you, my lord, are very admirable, and your face is full of graces." **18** And while she was speaking, she fell down again, and was almost in a swoon. **19** But the king was troubled, and all his servants comforted her.

CHAPTER 16

1 The great King Artaxerxes, from India to Ethiopia, to the governors and princes of one hundred and twenty-seven provinces, which obey our command, sends greetings. **2** Many have abused to pride the goodness of princes, and the honor that has been bestowed on them: **3** and not only endeavor to oppress the king's subjects, but not bearing the glory that is given them, take in hand to practice also against them that gave it. **4** Neither are they content not to return thanks for benefits received, and to violate in themselves the laws of humanity, but they think they can also escape the justice of God who sees all things. **5** And they break out into such great madness, as to endeavor to undermine by lies such as observe diligently the offices committed to them, and do all things in such manner as to be worthy of all men's praise, **6** while, with crafty fraud, they deceive the ears of princes that are well meaning, and judge of others by their own nature. **7** Now this is proved both from ancient histories, and by the things which are done daily, how the good designs of kings are depraved by the evil suggestions of certain men. **8** For what reason we must provide for the peace of all provinces. **9** Neither must you think, if we command different things, that it comes from the levity of our mind, but that we give sentence according to the quality and necessity of times, as the profit of the commonwealth requires. **10** Now that you may more plainly understand what we say, I, Haman, the son of Amadathi, a Macedonian both in mind and country, and having nothing of the Persian blood, but with his cruelty staining our goodness, was received, being a stranger by us: **11** and found our humanity so great toward him, that he was called our father, and was worshiped by all as the next man after the king, **12** but he was so far puffed up with arrogancy, as to go about to deprive us of our kingdom and life. **13** For with certain new and unheard-of devices he has sought the destruction of Mordecai, by whose fidelity and good services our life was saved, and of Esther the partner of our kingdom, with all their nation, **14** thinking that after they were slain, he might work treason against us left alone without friends, and might transfer the kingdom of the Persians to the Macedonians. **15** But we have found that the Jews, who were by

that most wicked man appointed to be slain, are in no fault at all, but to the contrary, use just laws, **16** and are the children of the highest and the greatest, and the ever-living God, by whose benefit the kingdom was given both to our fathers and to us, and is kept to this day. **17** For what reason, know that those letters which he sent in our name are void and of no effect. **18** For which crime both he himself that devised it, and all his relatives hang on gallows, before the gates of this city Shushan—not us, but God repaying him as he deserved. **19** But this edict, which we now send, will be published in all cities, that the Jews may freely follow their own laws. **20** And you will aid them that they may kill those who had prepared themselves to kill them, on the thirteenth day of the twelfth month, which is called Adar. **21** For the Almighty God has turned this day of sadness and mourning into joy to them. **22** For what reason you will also count this day among other festival days, and celebrate it with all joy, that it may be known also in times to come, **23** that all they who faithfully obey the Persians, receive a worthy reward for their fidelity, but they that are traitors to their kingdom, are destroyed for their wickedness. **24** And let every province and city, that will not be partaker of this solemnity, perish by the sword and by fire, and be destroyed in such manner as to be made unpassable, both to men and beasts, for an example of contempt, and disobedience.

APOCRYPHAL PSALMS

Psalm 151 is a short psalm found in most copies of the Septuagint but not in the Hebrew Bible. The Greek title given to this psalm indicates that it is supernumerary. It is also included in some manuscripts of the Peshitta. The psalm concerns the story of David and Goliath. The Eastern Orthodox Church, as well as the Coptic Orthodox Church, Armenian Apostolic Church, and the Armenian Catholic Church accept Psalm 151 as deuterocanonical. Psalms 152–155 are found extant in two Syriac manuscripts and appear to have been composed in the pre-Christian era. Psalms 154 and 155 have also been found in Hebrew in the Dead Sea Scrolls.

PSALM 151

I. This Psalm is ascribed to David and is outside the number. When he slew Goliath in a duel. **1** I was the youngest among my brothers, || and a youth in my father's house. **2** I used to feed my father's flock, || and I found a lion and a wolf, || and slew them and tore them. **3** My hands made an organ, || and my fingers fashioned a harp. **4** Who will show me my Lord? He, my Lord, has become my God. **5** He sent His messenger and took me away from my father's flock, || and anointed me with the oil of anointing. **6** My brothers, the fair and the tall, || in them the Lord had no pleasure. **7** And I went forth to meet the Philistine, || and he cursed me by his idols. **8** But I drew his sword and cut off his head, || and took away the reproach from the sons of Israel.

PSALM 152

II. The Prayer of Hezekiah when enemies surrounded him. **1** With a loud voice glorify God; In the assembly of many proclaim His glory. **2** Amid the multitude of the upright glorify His praise; And speak of His glory with the righteous. **3** Join your soul to the good and to the perfect, || to glorify the Highest. **4** Gather yourselves together to make known His strength; And do not be slow in showing forth His deliverance and His glory to all babies. **5** That the honor of the Lord may be known, wisdom has been given; And to tell of His works it has been made known to men: **6** To make known to babies His strength, || and to make them that lack understanding [[or heart]] to comprehend His glory; **7** Who are far from His entrances and distant from His gates: **8** Because the Lord of Jacob is exalted, || and His glory is on all His works. **9** And a man who glorifies the Highest, in him will He take pleasure; As in one who offers fine meal, || and as in one who offers male goats and calves; **10** And as in one who makes fat the altar with a multitude of burnt-offerings; And as the smell of incense from the hands of the just. **11** From your upright gates will be heard His voice, || and from the voice of the upright admonition. **12** And in their eating will be satisfying in truth, || and in their drinking, when they share together. **13** Their dwelling is in the law of the Highest, || and their speech is to make known His strength. **14** How far from the wicked is speech of Him, || and from all transgressors to know Him! **15** Behold, the eye of the Lord takes pity on the good, || and to them that glorify Him will He multiply mercy, || and from the time of evil will He deliver their soul. **16** Blessed is the Lord, who has delivered the wretched from the hand of the wicked; Who raises up a horn out of Jacob and a judge of the nations out of Israel; **17** That He may prolong His dwelling in Zion, || and may adorn our age in Jerusalem.

PSALM 153

III. When the People obtained permission from Cyrus to return home. **1** O Lord, I have cried to You; Listen to me. **2** I have lifted up my hands to Your holy dwelling-place; Incline Your ear to me. **3** And grant me my request; Do not withhold my prayer from me. **4** Build up my soul, and do not destroy it; And do not lay it bare before the wicked. **5** Them that repay evil things—turn [them] away from me, O judge of truth. **6** O Lord, do not judge me according to my sins, || because no flesh is innocent before You. **7** Make plain to me, O Lord, Your law, || and teach me Your judgments; **8** And many will hear of Your works, || and the nations will praise Your honor. **9** Remember me and do not forget me; And do not lead me into things that are too hard for me. **10** Make the sins of my youth pass from me, || and my discipline—do not let them remember [it] against me. **11** Cleanse me, O Lord, from the evil leprosy, || and let it no longer come to me. **12** Dry up its roots from me, || and do not let its leaves sprout within me. **13** Great are You, O Lord; Therefore, my request will be fulfilled from before You. **14** To whom will I complain that he may give to me? And what can the strength of men add [to me]? **15** From before You, O Lord, is my confidence; I cried to the Lord and He heard me, and healed the breaking of my heart. **16** I slumbered and slept; I dreamed and was helped, and the Lord sustained me. **17** They severely pained my heart; I will return thanks because the Lord delivered me. **18** Now I will rejoice in their shame; I have hoped in You, and I will not be ashamed. **19** Give You honor for all time—even forever and ever! **20** Deliver Israel, Your chosen one, || and them of the house of Jacob Your proved one.

PSALM 154

IV. Spoken by David when he was contending with the lion and the wolf which took a sheep from his flock. **1** O God, O God, come to my aid; Help me and save me; Deliver my soul from the slayer. **2** Will I go down to Sheol by the mouth of the lion? Or will the wolf confound me? **3** Was it not enough for them that they lay in wait for my father's flock, || and tore in pieces a sheep of my father's drove, || but they were also wishing to destroy my soul? **4** Have pity, O Lord, and save Your holy one from destruction; That he may rehearse Your glories in all his times, || and may praise Your great Name: **5** When You have delivered him from the hands of the destroying lion and of the ravening wolf, || and when You have rescued my captivity from the hands of the wild beasts. **6** Quickly, O my Lord, send a deliverer from before You, || and draw me out of the gaping pit, || which imprisons me in its depths.

PSALM 155

V. Spoken by David when returning thanks to God, who had delivered him from the lion and the wolf and he had slain both of them. **1** Praise the Lord, all you nations; Glorify Him, and bless His Name— **2** Who rescued the soul of His chosen one from the hands of death, || and delivered His holy one from

destruction, **3** And saved me from the nets of Sheol, || and my soul from the pit that cannot be fathomed. **4** Because, before my deliverance could go forth from before Him, || I was well nearly torn in two pieces by two wild beasts. **5** But He sent His messenger, || and shut up from me the gaping mouths, || and rescued my life from destruction. **6** My soul will glorify Him and exalt Him, || because of all His kindnesses which He has done and will do to me.

APOCRYPHAL DANIEL

The Septuagint (LXX) version of Daniel contains three sections not found in the Hebrew version of the text. These are known as "The Prayer of Azariah and Song of the Three Holy Children" (often placed as vv. 3:24–90), "Susanna and the Elders" (Ch. 13), and "Bel and the Dragon" (Ch. 14). All three are included in the LSV, with "The Prayer of Azariah" versified as 3B:1–68, which can be read between verses 3:23 and 3:24 of the standard text of *Daniel*. This particular book is an account of the prayer of Azariah (Abednego) while in the midst of the fire and the song that he and his two other companions sung in praise to God while in the furnace. "Susanna and the Elders" portrays the lovely and virtuous wife Susanna as sexually accosted by two conniving elders. They falsely accuse her of adultery, but the prophet Daniel cross-examines them, exposing them as liars, and then they are put to death. "Bel and the Dragon" recounts Daniel's confrontation with the followers of the false god Bel during the reign of King Cyrus of Persia, which results in their execution. Later in the narrative Daniel slays a much-revered dragon and is thrust into a lion's den as a result. God intervenes to deliver him.

SECTION 1: THE PRAYER OF AZARIAH AND SONG OF THE THREE HOLY CHILDREN

CHAPTER 3B

1 They walked in the midst of the fire, praising God, and blessing the Lord. **2** Then Azariah stood and prayed like this— opening his mouth in the midst of the fire, he said: **3** "Blessed are You, O Lord, You God of our fathers! Your Name is worthy to be praised and glorified forevermore; **4** For You are righteous in all the things that You have done. Yes, all Your works are true. Your ways are right, and all Your judgments are truth. **5** In all the things that You have brought on us, and on the holy city of our fathers, Jerusalem, || You have executed true judgments. For according to truth and justice You have brought all these things on us because of our sins. **6** For we have sinned and committed iniquity in departing from You. **7** In all things we have trespassed, and not obeyed Your commands or kept them. We have not done as You have commanded us, that it might go well with us. **8** Therefore all that You have brought on us, and everything that You have done to us, || You have done in true judgment. **9** You delivered us into the hands of lawless enemies, most hateful rebels, || And to an unjust king who is the most wicked in all the world. **10** And now we cannot open our mouth. Shame and reproach have come on Your servants and those who worship You. **11** Do not utterly deliver us up, for Your Name's sake. Do not annul Your covenant. **12** Do not cause Your mercy to depart from us, || For the sake of Abraham who is loved by You, || And for the sake of Isaac Your servant, and Israel Your holy one, **13** To whom You promised that You would multiply their offspring as the stars of the sky, || And as the sand that is on the seashore. **14** For we, O Lord, have become less than any nation, || And are kept under this day in all the world because of our sins. **15** There is not at this time prince, or prophet, or leader, or burnt-offering, || Or sacrifice, or oblation, or incense, or place to offer before You, and to find mercy. **16** Nevertheless, in a contrite heart and a humble spirit let us be accepted, **17** Like the burnt-offerings of rams and bullocks, and like many thousands of fat lambs—So let our sacrifice be in Your sight this day, that we may wholly go after You, || For they will not be ashamed who put their trust in You. **18** And now we follow You with all our heart. We fear You and seek Your face. **19** Do not put us to shame; but deal with us after Your kindness, || And according to the multitude of Your mercy. **20** Deliver us also according to Your marvelous works, and give glory to Your Name, O Lord. Let all those who harm Your servants be confounded. **21** Let them be ashamed of all their power and might, and let their strength be broken. **22** Let them know that You are the Lord, the only God, || And [are] glorious over the whole world." **23** The king's servants who put them in did not stop making the furnace hot with naphtha, pitch, tinder, and small wood, **24** so that the flame streamed out forty-nine cubits above the furnace. **25** It spread and burned those Chaldeans whom it found around the furnace. **26** But the Messenger of the Lord came down into the furnace together with Azariah and his fellows, and He struck the flame of the fire out of the furnace, **27** and made the midst of the furnace as it had been a moist whistling wind, so that the fire did not touch them at all. It neither hurt nor troubled them. **28** Then the three, as out of one mouth, praised, glorified, and blessed God in the furnace, saying, **29** "Blessed are You, O Lord, You God of our fathers, || To be praised and exalted above all forever! **30** Blessed is Your glorious and holy Name, || To be praised and exalted above all forever! **31** Blessed are You in the temple of Your holy glory, || To be praised and glorified above all forever! **32** Blessed are You who see the depths and sit on the cherubim, || To be praised and exalted above all forever. **33** Blessed are You on the throne of Your kingdom, || To be praised and extolled above all forever! **34** Blessed are You in the expanse of Heaven, || To be praised and glorified forever! **35** O all you works of the Lord, bless the Lord! Praise and exalt Him above all forever! **36** O you heavens, bless the Lord! Praise and exalt Him above all forever! **37** O you messengers of the Lord, bless the Lord! Praise and exalt Him above all forever! **38** O all you waters that are above the sky, bless the Lord! Praise and exalt Him above all forever! **39** O all you powers of the Lord, bless the Lord! Praise and exalt Him above all forever! **40** O you sun and moon, bless the Lord! Praise and exalt Him above all forever! **41** O you stars of the heavens, bless the Lord! Praise and exalt Him above all forever! **42** O every shower and dew, bless the Lord! Praise and exalt Him above all forever! **43** O all you winds, bless the Lord! Praise and exalt Him above all forever! **44** O you fire and heat, bless the Lord! Praise and exalt Him above all forever! **45** O you winter and summer, bless the Lord! Praise and exalt Him above all forever! **46** O you dews and storms of snow, bless the Lord! Praise and exalt Him above all forever! **47** O you nights and days, bless the Lord! Praise and exalt Him above all forever! **48** O you light and darkness, bless the Lord! Praise and exalt Him above all forever! **49** O you cold and heat, bless the Lord! Praise and exalt Him above all forever! **50** O you frost and snow, bless the Lord! Praise and exalt Him above all forever! **51** O you lightning and clouds, bless the Lord! Praise and exalt Him above all forever! **52** O let the earth bless the Lord! Let it praise and exalt Him above all forever! **53** O you mountains and hills, bless the Lord! Praise and exalt Him above all forever! **54** O all you things that grow on the earth, bless the Lord! Praise and exalt Him above all forever! **55** O sea and rivers, bless the Lord! Praise and exalt Him above all forever! **56** O you spring, bless the Lord! Praise and exalt Him above all forever! **57** O you whales and all that move in the waters, bless the Lord! Praise and exalt Him above all forever! **58** O all you birds of the air, bless the Lord! Praise and exalt Him above all forever! **59** O all you beasts and cattle, bless the Lord! Praise and exalt Him above all forever! **60** O you children of men, bless the Lord! Praise and exalt Him above all forever! **61** O let Israel bless the Lord! Praise and exalt Him above all forever. **62** O you priests of the Lord, bless the Lord! Praise and exalt Him above all forever! **63** O you servants of the Lord, bless the Lord! Praise and exalt Him above all forever! **64** O you spirits and souls of the righteous, bless the Lord! Praise and exalt Him above all forever! **65** O you who are holy and humble of heart, bless the Lord! Praise and exalt Him above all forever! **66** O Hananiah, Mishael, and Azariah, bless the Lord!

Praise and exalt Him above all forever; For He has rescued us from Hades and saved us from the hand of death! He has delivered us out of the midst of the furnace and burning flame. He has delivered us out of the midst of the fire. **67** O give thanks to the Lord, for He is good; For His mercy is forever. **68** O all you who worship the Lord, bless the God of gods, praise Him, and give Him thanks; for His mercy is forever!"

SECTION 2: SUSANNA AND THE ELDERS

CHAPTER 13

1 A man lived in Babylon, and his name was Jehoiakim. **2** He took a wife, whose name was Susanna, the daughter of Hilkiah, a very fair woman, and one who feared the Lord. **3** Her parents were also righteous and taught their daughter according to the Law of Moses. **4** Now Jehoiakim was a great rich man, and had a fair garden joining to his house. The Jews used to come to him, because he was more honorable than all others. **5** The same year two of the elders of the people were appointed to be judges, such as the Lord spoke of, that wickedness came from Babylon from elders who were judges, who were supposed to govern the people. **6** These were often at Jehoiakim's house. All that had any suits in law came to them. **7** When the people departed away at noon, Susanna went into her husband's garden to walk. **8** The two elders saw her going in every day, and walking; and they were inflamed with lust for her. **9** They perverted their own mind and turned away their eyes, that they might not look to Heaven, nor remember just judgments. **10** And although they both were wounded with lust for her yet dared not show the other his grief. **11** For they were ashamed to declare their lust, that they desired to have to do with her. **12** Yet they watched jealously from day to day to see her. **13** The one said to the other, "Let us go home, now; for it is dinner time." **14** So when they had gone out, they parted company, and turning back again, they came to the same place. After they had asked one another the cause, they acknowledged their lust. Then they appointed a time both together, when they might find her alone. **15** It happened, as they watched on an opportune day, she went in as before with only two maids, and she desired to wash herself in the garden; for it was hot. **16** There was nobody there except the two elders who had hid themselves and watched her. **17** Then she said to her maids, "Bring me oil and washing balls, and shut the garden doors, that I may wash myself." **18** They did as she asked them, and shut the garden doors, and went out themselves at the side doors to fetch the things that she had commanded them. They did not see the elders, because they were hidden. **19** Now when the maids had gone out, the two elders rose up, and ran to her, saying, **20** "Behold, the garden doors are shut, that no man can see us, and we are in love with you. Therefore, consent to us, and lie with us. **21** If you will not, we will testify against you, that a young man was with you; therefore, you sent your maids away from you." **22** Then Susanna sighed, and said, "I am trapped; for if I do this thing, it is death to me. If I do not do it, I cannot escape your hands. **23** It is better for me to fall into your hands, and not do it, than to sin in the sight of the Lord." **24** With that Susanna cried with a loud voice; and the two elders cried out against her. **25** Then one of them ran and opened the garden doors. **26** So when the servants of the house heard the cry in the garden, they rushed in at the side door, to see what had happened to her. **27** But when the elders had told their tale, the servants were greatly ashamed; for there was never such a report made of Susanna. **28** It came to pass on the next day, when the people assembled to her husband Jehoiakim, the two elders came full of their wicked intent against Susanna to put her to death, **29** and said before the people, "Send for Susanna, the daughter of Hilkiah, Jehoiakim's wife." So they sent; **30** and she came with her father and mother, her children, and all her relatives. **31** Now Susanna was a very delicate woman, and beautiful to behold. **32** These wicked men commanded her to be unveiled, for she was veiled, that they might be filled with her beauty. **33** Therefore her friends and all who saw her wept. **34** Then the two elders stood up in the midst of the people and laid their hands on her head. **35** She, weeping, looked up toward Heaven; for her heart trusted in the Lord. **36** The elders said, "As we walked in the garden alone, this woman came in with two maids, shut the garden doors, and sent the maids away. **37** Then a young man, who was hidden there, came to her and lay with her. **38** And we, being in a corner of the garden, saw this wickedness and ran to them. **39** And when we saw them together, we could not hold the man; for he was stronger than we, and opened the doors, and leapt out. **40** But having taken this woman, we asked who the young man was, but she would not tell us. We testify these things." **41** Then the assembly believed them, as those who were elders of the people and judges; so they condemned her to death. **42** Then Susanna cried out with a loud voice, and said, "O perpetual God, You know the secrets, and know all things before they happen, **43** You know that they have testified falsely against me. Behold, I must die, even though I never did such things as these men have maliciously invented against me." **44** The Lord heard her voice. **45** Therefore when she was led away to be put to death, God raised up the holy spirit of a young youth, whose name was Daniel. **46** He cried with a loud voice, "I am clear from the blood of this woman!" **47** Then all the people turned them toward him, and said, "What do these words that you have spoken mean?" **48** So he, standing in the midst of them, said, "Are you all such fools, you sons of Israel, that without examination or knowledge of the truth you have condemned a daughter of Israel? **49** Return again to the place of judgment; for these have testified falsely against her." **50** Therefore all the people turned again in haste, and the elders said to him, "Come, sit down among us, and show it to us, seeing God has given you the honor of an elder." **51** Then Daniel said to them, "Put them far apart from each another, and I will examine them." **52** So when they were put apart from one another, he called one of them, and said to him, "O you who have become old in wickedness, now your sins have returned which you have committed before, **53** in pronouncing unjust judgment, condemning the innocent, and letting the guilty go free; although the Lord says, You will not kill the innocent and righteous. **54** Now then, if you saw her, tell me, under which tree did you see them companying together?" He answered, "Under a mastick tree." **55** And Daniel said, "You have certainly lied against your own head; for even now the messenger of God has received the sentence of God and will cut you in two." **56** So he put him aside, and commanded to bring the other, and said to him, "O you seed of Canaan, and not of Judah, beauty has deceived you, and lust has perverted your heart. **57** Thus you have dealt with the daughters of Israel, and they for fear were intimate with you; but the daughter of Judah would not tolerate your wickedness. **58** Now therefore, tell me, under which tree did you take them being intimate together?" He answered, "Under an evergreen oak tree." **59** Then Daniel said to him, "You have also certainly lied against your own head; for the messenger of God waits with the sword to cut you in two, that he may destroy you." **60** With that, all the assembly cried out with a loud voice, and blessed God, who saves those who hope in him. **61** Then they arose against the two elders, for Daniel had convicted them of false testimony out of their own mouth. **62** According to the Law of Moses they did to them in such sort as they maliciously intended to do to their neighbor. They put them to death, and the innocent blood was saved the same day. **63** Therefore Hilkiah and his wife praised God for their daughter Susanna, with Jehoiakim her husband, and all the relatives, because there was no dishonesty found in her. **64** And from that day out, Daniel was held in high regard in the sight of the people.

SECTION 3: BEL AND THE DRAGON

CHAPTER 14

1 King Astyages was gathered to his fathers, and Cyrus the Persian received his kingdom. **2** Daniel lived with the king and was honored above all his friends. **3** Now the Babylonians had an idol, called Bel, and every day twelve great measures of fine flour, forty sheep, and six firkins of wine were spent on him. **4** And the king honored it and went daily to worship it; but Daniel worshiped his own God. The king said to him, "Why do you not worship Bel?" **5** He said, "Because I may not honor idols made with hands, but only the living God, who has created the sky and the earth, and has sovereignty over all flesh." **6** Then the king said to him, "Do you not think that Bel is a living god? Do you not see how much he eats and drinks every day?" **7** Then Daniel laughed, and said, "O king, do not be deceived; for this is just clay inside, and brass outside, and never ate or drank anything." **8** So the king was angry, and called for his priests, and said to them, "If you do not tell me who this is who devours these expenses, you will die. **9** But if you can show me that Bel devours them, then Daniel will die; for he has spoken blasphemy against Bel." Daniel said to the king, "Let it be according to your word." **10** Now there were seventy priests of Bel, besides their wives and children. The king went with Daniel into Bel's temple. **11** So Bel's priests said, "Behold, we will leave; but you, O king, set out the meat, and mix the wine and set it out, shut the door securely, and seal it with your own signet. **12** When you come in the morning, if you do not find that Bel has eaten everything, we will suffer death, or else Daniel, who speaks falsely against us." **13** They were not concerned, for under the table they had made a secret entrance, whereby they entered in continually, and consumed those things. **14** It happened, when they had gone out, the king set the meat before Bel. Now Daniel had commanded his servants to bring ashes, and they scattered them all over the temple in the presence of the king alone. Then they went out, shut the door, sealed it with the king's signet, and so departed. **15** Now in the night, the priests came with their wives and children, as they usually did, and ate and drank it all. **16** In the morning, the king arose, and Daniel with him. **17** The king said, "Daniel, are the seals whole?" He said, "Yes, O king, they are whole." **18** And as soon as he had opened the door, the king looked at the table, and cried with a loud voice, "You are great, O Bel, and with you is no deceit at all!" **19** Then Daniel laughed, and held the king that he should not go in, and said, "Behold now the pavement, and mark well whose footsteps these are." **20** The king said, "I see the footsteps of men, women, and children." Then the king was angry, **21** and took the priests with their wives and children, who showed him the secret doors, where they came in, and consumed the things that were on the table. **22** Therefore the king killed them, and delivered Bel into Daniel's power, who overthrew him and his temple. **23** In that same place there was a great dragon, which the people of Babylon worshiped. **24** The king said to Daniel, "Will you also say that this is of brass? Behold, he lives, eats, and drinks. You cannot say that he is no living god. Therefore, worship him." **25** Then Daniel said, "I will worship the Lord my God; for He is a living God. **26** But allow me, O king, and I will kill this dragon without sword or staff." The king said, "I allow you." **27** Then Daniel took pitch, fat, and hair, and melted them together, and made lumps of them. He put these in the dragon's mouth, so the dragon ate and burst apart. Daniel said, "Behold, these are the gods you all worship." **28** When the people of Babylon heard that, they took great indignation, and conspired against the king, saying, "The king has become a Jew. He has pulled down Bel, slain the dragon, and put the priests to the sword." **29** So they came to the king, and said, "Deliver Daniel to us, or else we will destroy you and your house." **30** Now when the king saw that they trapped him, being constrained, the king delivered Daniel to them. **31** They cast him into the lion's den, where he was six days. **32** There were seven lions in the den, and they had been giving them two carcasses and two sheep every day, which then were not given to them, intending that they would devour Daniel. **33** Now there was in Jewry the prophet Habakkuk, who had made stew, and had broken bread into a bowl. He was going into the field to bring it to the reapers. **34** But the messenger of the Lord said to Habakkuk, "Go, carry the dinner that you have into Babylon—to Daniel in the lions' den." **35** Habakkuk said, "Lord, I never saw Babylon. I do not know where the den is." **36** Then the messenger of the Lord took him by the crown and lifted him up by the hair of his head, and with the blast of his breath set him in Babylon over the den. **37** Habakkuk cried, saying, "O Daniel, Daniel, take the dinner which God has sent you." **38** Daniel said, "You have remembered me, O God! You have not forsaken those who love you!" **39** So Daniel arose and ate; and the messenger of God immediately set Habakkuk in his own place again. **40** On the seventh day, the king came to mourn for Daniel. When he came to the den, he looked in, and behold, Daniel was sitting. **41** Then the king cried with a loud voice, saying, "Great are You, O Lord, You God of Daniel, and there is no other besides You!" **42** So he drew him out, and cast those that were the cause of his destruction into the den; and they were devoured in a moment before his face.

TOBIT

The Book of Tobit, named after its principal character, combines Jewish piety and morality with folklore in a fascinating story that has enjoyed wide popularity in both Jewish and Christian circles. Prayers, psalms, and words of wisdom, as well as the skillfully constructed story itself, provide valuable insights into the faith and the religious milieu of its unknown author. The book was probably written early in the 2nd century BC; it is not known where.

CHAPTER 1

1 The scroll of the words of Tobit, the son of Tobiel, the son of Ananiel, the son of Aduel, the son of Gabael, of the seed of Asiel, of the tribe of Naphtali; **2** who in the days of Enemessar king of the Assyrians was carried away captive out of Thisbe, which is on the right side of Kedesh Naphtali in Galilee above Asher. **3** I, Tobit, walked in the ways of truth and righteousness all the days of my life, and I did many kind acts to my countrymen and my nation, who went with me into the land of the Assyrians, to Nineveh. **4** When I was in my own country, in the land of Israel, while I was yet young, all the tribe of my father Naphtali fell away from the house of Jerusalem, which was chosen out of all the tribes of Israel, that all the tribes should sacrifice there, and the temple of the habitation of the Highest was hallowed and built therein for all ages. **5** All the tribes which fell away together sacrificed to the heifer Ba'al, and so did the house of my father Naphtali. **6** I alone went often to Jerusalem at the feasts, as it has been ordained to all Israel by a perpetual decree, having the first-fruits and the tenths of my increase, and that which was first shorn; and I gave them to the priests at the altar, the sons of Aaron. **7** I gave a tenth part of all my increase to the sons of Levi, who ministered at Jerusalem. A second tenth part I sold away, and went, and spent it each year at Jerusalem. **8** A third tenth I gave to them to whom it was appropriate, as Deborah my father's mother had commanded me, because I was left an orphan by my father. **9** When I became a man, I took as wife Anna of the seed of our own family. With her, I became the father of Tobias. **10** When I was carried away captive to Nineveh, all my countrymen and my family ate of the bread of the nations; **11** but I kept myself from eating, **12** because I remembered God with all my soul. **13** So the Most High gave me grace and favor in the sight of Enemessar, and I was his purchasing agent. **14** And I went into Media and left ten talents of silver in trust with Gabael, the brother of Gabrias, at Rages of Media. **15** And when Enemessar was dead, Sennacherib his son reigned in his place. In his time, the highways were troubled, and I could no longer go into Media. **16** In the days of Enemessar, I did many kind acts to my countrymen: I gave my bread to the hungry, **17** and my garments to the naked. If I saw any of my race dead, and thrown out on the wall of Nineveh, I buried him. **18** If Sennacherib the king killed any, when he came fleeing from Judea, I buried them privately; for in his wrath he killed many; and the bodies were sought for by the king and were not found. **19** But one of the Ninevites went and showed to the king concerning me, how I buried them, and hid myself; and when I knew that I was sought for to be put to death, I withdrew myself for fear. **20** And all my goods were forcibly taken away, and there was nothing left to me, save my wife Anna and my son Tobias. **21** No more than fifty-five days passed before two of his sons killed him, and they fled into the mountains of Ararat. And Esarhaddon his son reigned in his place; and he appointed Ahikar, my brother Anael's son, over all the accounts of his kingdom, and over all his affairs. **22** Ahikar requested me, and I came to Nineveh. Now Ahikar was cupbearer, keeper of the signet, steward, and overseer of the accounts. Esarhaddon appointed him next to himself, but he was my brother's son.

CHAPTER 2

1 Now when I had come home again, and my wife Anna was restored to me, and my son Tobias, in the Celebration of Pentecost, which is the holy celebration of the seven weeks, there was a good dinner prepared [for] me, and I sat down to eat. **2** I saw abundance of meat, and I said to my son, "Go and bring whatever poor man you find of our countrymen, who is mindful of the Lord. Behold, I wait for you." **3** Then he came, and said, "Father, one of our race is strangled, and has been cast out in the marketplace." **4** Before I had tasted anything, I sprang up, and took him up into a chamber until the sun had set. **5** Then I returned, washed myself, ate my bread in heaviness, **6** and remembered the prophecy of Amos, as he said, "Your feasts will be turned into mourning, and all your mirth into lamentation." **7** So I wept: and when the sun had set, I went and dug a grave, and buried him. **8** My neighbors mocked me, and said, "He is no longer afraid to be put to death for this matter; and yet he fled away. Behold, he buries the dead again." **9** The same night I returned from burying him, and slept by the wall of my courtyard, being polluted; and my face was uncovered. **10** I did not know that there were sparrows in the wall. My eyes were open, and the sparrows dropped warm dung into my eyes, and white films came over my eyes. I went to the physicians, and they did not help me; but Ahikar nourished me, until I went into Elymais. **11** My wife Anna wove cloth in the women's chambers, **12** and sent the work back to the owners. They on their part paid her wages, and also gave her a kid. **13** But when it came to my house, it began to cry, and I said to her, "Where did this kid come from? Is it stolen? Give it back to the owners; for it is not lawful to eat anything that is stolen." **14** But she said, "It has been given to me for a gift more than the wages." I did not believe her, and I asked her to return it to the owners; and I was ashamed of her. But she answered and said to me, "Where are your alms and your righteous deeds? Behold, you and all your works are known."

CHAPTER 3

1 I was grieved and wept, and prayed in sorrow, saying, **2** "O Lord, You are righteous, || And all Your works and all Your ways are mercy and truth, || And You judge true and righteous judgment forever. **3** Remember me and look at me. Do not take vengeance on me for my sins and my ignorance, || And the sins of my fathers who sinned before You. **4** For they disobeyed Your commands. You gave us as plunder, for captivity, for death, || And for a proverb of reproach to all the nations among whom we are dispersed. **5** Now Your judgments are many and true; That You should deal with me according to my sins and the sins of my fathers; Because we did not keep Your commands, || For we did not walk in truth before You. **6** Now deal with me according to that which is pleasing in Your sight. Command my spirit to be taken from me, || That I may be released, and become earth. For it is more profitable for me to die rather than to live, || Because I have heard false reproaches, || And there is much sorrow in me. Command that I be released from my distress, now, || And go to the agelong place. Do not turn Your face away from me." **7** The same day it happened to Sarah, the daughter of Raguel, in Ecbatana of Media, that she also was reproached by her father's maidservants; **8** because that she had been given to seven husbands, and Asmodeus the evil spirit killed them, before they had lain with her. And they said to her, "Do you not know that you strangle your husbands? You have already had seven husbands, and you have not borne the name of any of them. **9** Why do you scourge us? If they are dead, go your ways with them. Let us never see either son or daughter from you." **10** When she heard these things, she was grieved exceedingly, so that she thought about hanging herself. Then she said, "I am the only daughter of my father. If I do this, it will be a reproach to him, and I will bring down his old age with sorrow to the grave." **11** Then she prayed by the window, and said, "Blessed are You, O Lord my God, || And blessed is Your holy and honorable Name forever! Let all Your works praise You forever!

[12] And now, Lord, I have set my eyes and my face toward You. [13] Command that I be released from the earth, || And that I no longer hear reproach. [14] You know, Lord, that I am pure from all sin with man, [15] And that I never polluted my name or the name of my father, || In the land of my captivity. I am the only daughter of my father, || And he has no child that will be his heir, nor brother near him, || Nor son belonging to him, that I should keep myself for a wife to him. Seven husbands of mine are dead already. Why should I live? If it does not please You to kill me, || Command some regard to be had of me, and pity taken of me, || And that I hear no more reproach." [16] The prayer of both was heard before the glory of the great God. [17] Raphael, also, was sent to heal them both, to scale away the white films from Tobit's eyes, and to give Sarah the daughter of Raguel for a wife to Tobias the son of Tobit, and to bind Asmodeus the evil spirit; because it belonged to Tobias that he should inherit her. At that very time, Tobit returned and entered into his house, and Sarah the daughter of Raguel came down from her upper chamber.

CHAPTER 4

[1] In that day Tobit remembered the money which he had left in trust with Gabael in Rages of Media, [2] and he said to himself, I have asked for death; why do I not call my son Tobias, that I may explain to him about the money before I die? [3] And he called him, and said, "My child, if I die, bury me. Do not despise your mother. Honor her all the days of your life, and do that which is pleasing to her, and do not grieve her. [4] Remember, my child, that she has seen many dangers for you, when you were in her womb. When she is dead, bury her by me in one grave. [5] My child, be mindful of the Lord our God all your days, and do not let your will be set to sin and to transgress His commands: do righteousness all the days of your life, and do not follow the ways of unrighteousness. [6] For if you do what is true, your deeds will prosperously succeed for you, and for all those who do righteousness. [7] Give alms from your possessions. When you give alms, do not let your eye be envious. Do not turn your face away from any poor man, and the face of God will not be turned away from you. [8] As your possessions are, give alms of it according to your abundance. If you have little, do not be afraid to give alms according to that little; [9] for you lay up a good treasure for yourself against the day of necessity; [10] because kindness delivers from death, and does not allow you to come into darkness. [11] Alms is a good gift in the sight of the Most High for all that give it. [12] Beware, my child, of all whoredom, and take first a wife of the seed of your fathers. Do not take a strange wife, who is not of your father's tribe; for we are the descendants of the prophets. Remember, my child, that Noah, Abraham, Isaac, and Jacob, our fathers from antiquity, all took wives of their countrymen, and were blessed in their children, and their seed will inherit the land. [13] And now, my child, love your relatives, and do not scorn your countrymen and the sons and the daughters of your people in your heart, to take a wife of them; for in scornfulness is destruction and much trouble, and in naughtiness is decay and great lack; for naughtiness is the mother of famine. [14] Do not let the wages of any man who works for you wait with you but give it to him out of hand. If you serve God, you will be rewarded. Take heed to yourself, my child, in all your works, and be discreet in all your behavior. [15] And what you yourself hate, do to no man. Do not drink wine to drunkenness, and do not let drunkenness go with you on your way. [16] Give of your bread to the hungry, and of your garments to those who are naked. Give alms from all your abundance. Do not let your eye be envious when you give alms. [17] Pour out your bread on the burial of the just and give nothing to sinners. [18] Ask counsel of every man who is wise, and do not despise any counsel that is profitable. [19] Bless the Lord your God at all times and ask of Him that your ways may be made straight, and that all your paths and counsels may prosper; for every nation has no counsel; but the Lord Himself gives all good things, and He humbles whom He will, as He will. And now, my child, remember my commands, and do not let them be blotted out of your mind. [20] And now I explain to you about the ten talents of silver, which I left in trust with Gabael the son of Gabrias at Rages of Media. [21] And do not fear, my child, because we are made poor. You have much wealth, if you fear God, and depart from all sin, and do that which is pleasing in His sight."

CHAPTER 5

[1] Then Tobias answered and said to him, "Father, I will do all things, whatever you have commanded me. [2] But how could I receive the money, since I do not know him?" [3] He gave him the handwriting, and said to him, "Seek a man who will go with you, and I will give him wages, while I yet live; and go and receive the money." [4] He went to seek a man and found Raphael who was a messenger; [5] and he did not know it. He said to him, "Can I go with you to Rages of Media? Do you know those places well?" [6] The messenger said to him, "I will go with you. I know the way well. I have lodged with our brother Gabael." [7] Tobias said to him, "Wait for me, and I will tell my father." [8] He said to him, "Go, and do not wait." And he went in and said to his father, "Behold, I have found someone who will go with me." But he said, "Call him to me, that I may know of what tribe he is, and whether he is a trustworthy man to go with you." [9] So he called him, and he came in, and they saluted one another. [10] And Tobit said to him, "Brother, of what tribe and of what family are you? Tell me." [11] He said to him, "Do you seek a tribe and a family, or a hired man which will go with your son?" And Tobit said to him, "I want to know, brother, your relatives and your name." [12] And he said, "I am Azariah, the son of Ananias the great, of your relatives." [13] And he said to him, "Welcome, brother. Do not be angry with me, because I sought to know your tribe and family. You are my brother, of an honest and good lineage; for I knew Ananias and Jathan, the sons of Shemaiah the great, when we went together to Jerusalem to worship, and offered the firstborn, and the tenths of our increase; and they did not go astray in the error of our countrymen. My brother, you are of a great stock. [14] But tell me, what wages will I give you? A drachma a day, and those things that are necessary for you, as to my son? [15] And moreover, if you both return safe and sound, I will add something to your wages." [16] And so they agreed. And he said to Tobias, "Prepare yourself for the journey. May God prosper you." So, his son prepared what was needful for the journey, and his father said to him, "Go with this man; but God, who dwells in Heaven, will prosper your journey. May His messenger go with you." Then they both departed, and the young man's dog went with them. [17] But Anna his mother wept, and said to Tobit, "Why have you sent our child away? Is he not the staff of our hand, in going in and out before us? [18] Do not be greedy to add money to money; but let it be as refuse compared to our child. [19] For what the Lord has given us to live is enough for us." [20] Tobit said to her, "Do not worry, my sister. He will return safe and sound, and your eyes will see him. [21] For a good messenger will go with him. His journey will be prospered, and he will return safe and sound." [22] So she stopped weeping.

CHAPTER 6

[1] Now as they went on their journey, they came at evening to the River Tigris, and they lodged there. [2] But the young man went down to wash himself, and a fish leaped out of the river, and would have swallowed up the young man. [3] But the messenger said to him, "Grab the fish!" So the young man grabbed the fish, and hauled it up onto the land. [4] And the messenger said to him, "Cut the fish open, and take the heart, the liver, and the bile, and keep them with you." [5] And the young man did as the messenger commanded him; but they roasted the fish and ate it. And they both went on their way, until they drew near to Ecbatana. [6] The young man said to the messenger, "Brother Azariah, of what use is the heart, the liver, and the bile of the fish?" [7] He said to him, "About the heart and the liver: If a demon or an evil spirit trouble anyone, we must burn those and make smoke of them before the man or the woman, and the affliction will flee. [8] But as for the bile, it is good to anoint a man that has white films in his eyes, and he will be healed." [9] But when they drew near to Rages, [10] the messenger said to the young man, "Brother, today we will lodge with Raguel. He is your relative. He has an only daughter named Sarah. I will speak about her, that she should be given to you for a wife. [11] For her inheritance belongs to you, and you only are of her relatives. [12] The maid is fair and wise. And now hear me, and I will speak to her father. When we return from Rages, we will celebrate the marriage; for I know that Raguel may in no way marry her to another according to the Law of Moses, or else he would be liable to death, because it belongs

to you to take the inheritance, rather than any other." **13** Then the young man said to the messenger, "Brother Azariah, I have heard that this maid has been given to seven men, and that they all perished in the bride-chamber. **14** Now I am the only son of my father, and I am afraid, lest I go in and die, even as those before me. For a demon loves her, which harms no man, but those which come to her. Now I fear lest I die and bring my father's and my mother's life to the grave with sorrow because of me. They have no other son to bury them." **15** But the messenger said to him, "Do not you remember the words which your father commanded you, that you should take a wife of your own relatives? Now hear me, brother; for she will be your wife. Do not worry about the demon; for this night she will be given you as wife. **16** And when you come into the bride-chamber, you will take the ashes of incense, and will lay on them some of the heart and liver of the fish and will make smoke with them. **17** The demon will smell it, and flee away, and never come again anymore. But when you go near to her, both of you rise up, and cry to God who is merciful. He will save you and have mercy on you. Do not be afraid, for she was prepared for you from the beginning; and you will save her, and she will go with you. And I suppose that you will have children with her." When Tobias heard these things, he loved her, and his soul was strongly joined to her.

CHAPTER 7

1 They came to Ecbatana and arrived at the house of Raguel. But Sarah met them; and she greeted them, and they her. Then she brought them into the house. **2** Raguel said to Edna his wife, "This young man really resembles Tobit my cousin!" **3** And Raguel asked them, "Where are you two from, countrymen?" They said to him, "We are of the sons of Naphtali, who are captives in Nineveh." **4** He said to them, "Do you know Tobit our brother?" They said, "We know him." Then he said to them, "Is he in good health?" **5** They said, "He is both alive, and in good health." Tobias said, "He is my father." **6** And Raguel sprang up, and kissed him, wept, **7** blessed him, and said to him, "You are the son of an honest and good man." When he had heard that Tobit had lost his sight, he was grieved, and wept; **8** and Edna his wife and Sarah his daughter wept. They received them gladly; and they killed a ram of the flock and served them meat. But Tobias said to Raphael, "Brother Azariah, speak of those things of which you talked about in the way, and let the matter be finished." **9** So he communicated the thing to Raguel. Raguel said to Tobias, "Eat, drink, and make merry: **10** for it belongs to you to take my child. However, I will tell you the truth. **11** I have given my child to seven men of our countrymen, and whenever they came in to her, they died in the night. But for the present be merry." And Tobias said, "I will taste nothing here, until you all make a covenant and enter into that covenant with me." **12** Raguel said, "Take her to yourself from now on according to custom. You are her relative, and she is yours. The merciful God will give all good success to you." **13** And he called his daughter Sarah, and took her by the hand, and gave her to be wife of Tobias, and said, "Behold, take her to yourself after the Law of Moses, and lead her away to your father." And he blessed them. **14** He called Edna his wife, then took a scroll, wrote a contract, and sealed it. **15** Then they began to eat. **16** And Raguel called his wife Edna, and said to her, "Sister, prepare the other chamber, and bring her in there." **17** She did as he asked her, and brought her in there. She wept, and she received the tears of her daughter, and said to her, **18** "Be comforted, my child. May the Lord of the heavens and earth give you favor for this your sorrow. Be comforted, my daughter."

CHAPTER 8

1 When they had finished their supper, they brought Tobias in to her. **2** But as he went, he remembered the words of Raphael, and took the ashes of the incense, and put the heart and the liver of the fish on them and made smoke with them. **3** When the demon smelled that smell, it fled into the uppermost parts of Egypt, and the messenger bound him. **4** But

after they were both shut in together, Tobias rose up from the bed, and said, "Sister, arise, and let us pray that the Lord may have mercy on us." **5** And Tobias began to say, "Blessed are You, O God of our fathers, || And blessed is Your holy and glorious Name forever. Let the heavens bless You, and all Your creatures. **6** You made Adam and gave him Eve his wife for a helper and support. From them came the seed of men. You said, It is not good that the man should be alone. Let Us make him a helper like him. **7** And now, O Lord, I do not take this my sister for lust, but in truth. Command that I may find mercy and grow old with her." **8** She said with him, "Amen." And they both slept that night. **9** Raguel arose, and went and dug a grave, **10** saying, "Lest he also should die." **11** And Raguel came into his house, **12** and said to Edna his wife, "Send one of the maidservants, and let them see if he is alive. If not, we will bury him, and no man will know it." **13** So the maidservant opened the door, and went in, and found them both sleeping, **14** and came out, and told them that he was alive. **15** Then Raguel blessed God, saying, "Blessed are You, O God, with all pure and holy blessing! Let Your saints bless You, and all Your creatures! Let all Your messengers and Your chosen ones bless You forever! **16** Blessed are You, because You have made me glad; and it has not happened to me as I suspected; but You have dealt with us according to Your great mercy. **17** Blessed are You, because You have had mercy on two that were the only begotten children of their parents. Show them mercy, O Lord. Fulfill their life in health with gladness and mercy." **18** He commanded his servants to fill the grave. **19** He kept the wedding feast for them fourteen days. **20** Before the days of the wedding feast were finished, Raguel swore to him that he should not depart until the fourteen days of the wedding feast were fulfilled; **21** and that then he should take half of his goods and go in safety to his father; "and the rest," he said, "when my wife and I die."

CHAPTER 9

1 And Tobias called Raphael, and said to him, **2** "Brother Azariah, take a servant and two camels with you, and go to Rages of Media to Gabael, and receive the money for me, and bring him to the wedding feast, **3** because Raguel has sworn that I must not depart. **4** My father counts the days; and if I wait long, he will be very grieved." **5** So Raphael went on his way, and lodged with Gabael, and gave him the handwriting; so he brought out the bags with their seals, and gave them to him. **6** Then they rose up early in the morning together and came to the wedding feast. Tobias blessed his wife.

CHAPTER 10

1 Tobit his father counted every day. When the days of the journey were expired, and they did not come, **2** he said, "Is he perhaps detained? Or is Gabael perhaps dead, and there is no one to give him the money?" **3** He was very grieved. **4** But his wife said to him, "The child has perished, seeing he waits long." She began to mourn him, and said, **5** "I care about nothing, my child, since I have let you go, the light of my eyes." **6** Tobit said to her, "Hold your peace. Do not worry. He is in good health." **7** And she said to him, "Hold your peace. Do not deceive me. My child has perished." And she went out every day into the way by which they went, and ate no bread in the daytime, and did not stop mourning her son Tobias for whole nights, until the fourteen days of the wedding feast were expired, which Raguel had sworn that he should spend there. Then Tobias said to Raguel, "Send me away, for my father and my mother no longer look to see me." **8** But his father-in-law said to him, "Stay with me, and I will send to your father, and they will declare to him how things go with you." **9** Tobias said, "No. Send me away to my father." **10** Raguel arose, and gave him Sarah his wife, and half his goods, servants and cattle and money; **11** and he blessed them, and sent them away, saying, "The God of Heaven will prosper you, my children, before I die." **12** And he said to his daughter, "Honor your father-in-law and your mother-in-law. They are now your parents. Let me hear a good report of you." Then he kissed her. Edna said to Tobias, "May the Lord of Heaven restore you, dear brother, and grant to me that I may see your children of my daughter Sarah, that I may rejoice before the Lord. Behold, I commit my daughter to you in special trust. Do not cause her grief."

CHAPTER 11

1 After these things Tobias also went his way, blessing God because He had prospered his journey; and he blessed Raguel and Edna his wife. Then he went on his way until they drew near to Nineveh. **2** Raphael said to Tobias, "Do you not know, brother, how you left your father? **3** Let us run forward before your wife and prepare the house. **4** But take in your hand the bile of the fish." So they went their way, and the dog went after them. **5** Anna sat looking around toward the path for her son. **6** She saw him coming, and said to his father, "Behold, your son is coming with the man that went with him!" **7** Raphael said, "I know, Tobias, that your father will open his eyes. **8** Therefore anoint his eyes with the bile, and being pricked with it, he will rub, and will make the white films fall away. Then he will see you." **9** Anna ran to him, and fell on the neck of her son, and said to him, "I have seen you, my child! I am ready to die." They both wept. **10** Tobit went toward the door and stumbled; but his son ran to him, **11** and took hold of his father. He rubbed the bile on his father's eyes, saying, "Cheer up, my father." **12** When his eyes began to hurt, he rubbed them. **13** Then the white films peeled away from the corners of his eyes; and he saw his son and fell on his neck. **14** He wept, and said, "Blessed are You, O God, || And blessed is Your Name forever! Blessed are all Your holy messengers! **15** For You scourged and had mercy on me. Behold, I see my son Tobias." And his son went in rejoicing and told his father the great things that had happened to him in Media. **16** Tobit went out to meet his daughter-in-law at the gate of Nineveh, rejoicing, and blessing God. Those who saw him go marveled, because he had received his sight. **17** Tobit gave thanks before them, because God had shown mercy on him. When Tobit came near to Sarah his daughter-in-law, he blessed her, saying, "Welcome, daughter! Blessed is God who has brought you to us and blessed are your father and your mother." And there was joy among all his relatives who were at Nineveh. **18** Ahikar and Nasbas his brother's son came. **19** Tobias' wedding feast was kept seven days with great gladness.

CHAPTER 12

1 And Tobit called his son Tobias, and said to him, "See, my child, that the man which went with you have his wages, and you must give him more." **2** And he said to him, "Father, it is no harm to me to give him the half of those things which I have brought; **3** for he has led me for you in safety, and he cured my wife, and brought my money, and likewise cured you." **4** The old man said, "It is due to him." **5** And he called the messenger, and said to him, "Take half of all that you all have brought." **6** Then he called them both privately, and said to them, "Bless God, and give Him thanks, and magnify Him, and give Him thanks in the sight of all that live, for the things which He has done with you. It is good to bless God and exalt His Name, showing out with honor the works of God. Do not be slack to give Him thanks. **7** It is good to keep close the secret of a king, but to reveal gloriously the works of God. Do good, and evil will not find you. **8** Good is prayer with fasting, kindness, and righteousness. A little with righteousness is better than much with unrighteousness. It is better to give alms than to lay up gold. **9** Kindness delivers from death, and it purges away all sin. Those who give alms and do righteousness will be filled with life; **10** but those who sin are enemies to their own life. **11** Surely I will keep nothing closed from you. I have said, It is good to keep close the secret of a king, but to reveal gloriously the works of God. **12** And now, when you prayed, and Sarah your daughter-in-law, I brought the memorial of your prayer before the Holy One. When you buried the dead, I was with you likewise. **13** And when you did not delay to rise up, and leave your dinner, that you might go and cover the dead, your good deed was not hidden from me. I was with you. **14** And now God sent me to heal you and your daughter-in-law Sarah. **15** I am Raphael, one of the seven holy messengers, which present the prayers of the saints, and go in before the glory of the Holy One." **16** And they were both troubled and fell on their faces; for they were afraid. **17** And he said to them, "Do not be afraid. You will all have peace; but bless God forever. **18** For I did not come of any favor of my own, but by the will of your God. Therefore, bless Him forever. **19** All these days I appeared to you, I did not eat or drink, but you all saw a vision. **20** Now give

God thanks, because I ascend to Him that sent me. Write in a scroll all the things which have been done." **21** Then they rose up and saw him no longer. **22** They confessed the great and wonderful works of God, and how the messenger of the Lord had appeared to them.

CHAPTER 13

1 And Tobit wrote a prayer for rejoicing, and said, "Blessed is God who lives forever! Blessed is His kingdom! **2** For He scourges and shows mercy. He leads down to the grave and brings up again. There is no one that will escape His hand. **3** Give thanks to Him before the nations, all you sons of Israel! For He has scattered us among them. **4** Declare His greatness there. Extol Him before all the living; because He is our Lord, and God is our Father forever. **5** He will scourge us for our iniquities, || And will again show mercy, || And will gather us out of all the nations among whom you are all scattered. **6** If you turn to Him with your whole heart and with your whole soul, || To do truth before Him, || Then He will turn to you, || And will not hide His face from you. See what He will do with you. Give Him thanks with your whole mouth. Bless the Lord of righteousness. Exalt the perpetual King. I give Him thanks in the land of my captivity, || And show His strength and majesty to a nation of sinners. Turn, you sinners, and do righteousness before Him. Who can tell if He will accept you and have mercy on you? **7** I exalt my God. My soul exalts the King of Heaven and rejoices in His greatness. **8** Let all men speak and let them give Him thanks in Jerusalem. **9** O Jerusalem, the holy city, He will scourge you for the works of your sons, || And will again have mercy on the sons of the righteous. **10** Give thanks to the Lord with goodness, || And bless the perpetual King, || That His dwelling place may be built in you again with joy, || And that He may make glad in you those who are captives, || And love in you forever those who are miserable. **11** Many nations will come from afar to the Name of the Lord God with gifts in their hands, || Even gifts to the King of Heaven. Generations of generations will praise you and sing songs of rejoicing. **12** All those who hate you are cursed. All those who love you forever will be blessed. **13** Rejoice and be exceedingly glad for the sons of the righteous; For they will be gathered together and will bless the Lord of the righteous. **14** Oh blessed are those who love you. They will rejoice for your peace. Blessed are all those who sorrowed for all your scourges; Because they will rejoice for you when they have seen all your glory. They will be made glad forever. **15** Let my soul bless God the great King. **16** For Jerusalem will be built with sapphires, emeralds, and precious stones; Your walls and towers and battlements with pure gold. **17** The streets of Jerusalem will be paved with beryl, carbuncle, and stones of Ophir. **18** All her streets will say, Hallelujah! And give praise, saying, Blessed is God, who has exalted you forever!"

CHAPTER 14

1 Then Tobit finished giving thanks. **2** He was fifty-eight years old when he lost his sight. After eight years, he received it again. He gave alms and he feared the Lord God more and more and gave thanks to Him. **3** Now he grew very old; and he called his son with the six sons of his son, and said to him, "My child, take your sons. Behold, I have grown old, and am ready to depart out of this life. **4** Go into Media, my child, for I surely believe all the things which Jonah the prophet spoke of Nineveh, that it will be overthrown, but in Media there will rather be peace for a season. Our countrymen will be scattered in the earth from the good land. Jerusalem will be desolate, and the house of God in it will be burned up and will be desolate for a time. **5** God will again have mercy on them, and bring them back into the land, and they will build the house, but not like to the former house, until the times of that age are fulfilled. Afterward they will return from the places of their captivity and build up Jerusalem with honor. The house of God will be built in it forever with a glorious building, even as the prophets spoke concerning it. **6** And all the nations will turn to fear the Lord God in truth, and will bury their idols. **7** All the nations will bless the Lord, and His people will give thanks to God, and the Lord will exalt His people; and all those who love the Lord God in truth and righteousness will rejoice, showing mercy to our countrymen. **8** And now, my child, depart from Nineveh, because those things which the prophet Jonah spoke will surely come to pass. **9** But you must keep the law and the ordinances, and show yourself merciful and righteous, that it may be well with you. **10** Bury me decently, and your mother with me. Do not stay at Nineveh. See, my child, what Nadab did to Ahikar that nourished him, how out of light he brought him into darkness, and all the repayment that he made him. Ahikar was saved, but the other had his repayment, and he went down into darkness. Manasseh gave alms and escaped the snare of death which he set for him; but Nadab fell into the snare and perished. **11** And now, my children, consider what kindness does, and how righteousness delivers." While he was saying these things, he gave up the spirit in the bed; but he was one hundred fifty-eight years old. Tobias buried him magnificently. **12** When Anna died, he buried her with his father. But Tobias departed with his wife and his sons to Ecbatana to Raguel his father-in-law, **13** and he grew old in honor, and he buried his father-in-law and mother-in-law magnificently, and he inherited their possessions, and his father Tobit's. **14** He died at Ecbatana of Media, being one hundred twenty-seven years old. **15** Before he died, he heard of the destruction of Nineveh, which Nebuchadnezzar and Ahasuerus took captive. Before his death, he rejoiced over Nineveh.

JUDITH

The Book of Judith relates the story of God's deliverance of the Jewish people. This was accomplished "by the hand of a female"—a constant motif (cf. 8:33; 9:9, 10; 12:4; 13:4, 14, 15; 15:10; 16:5) meant to recall the "hand" of God in the Exodus narrative (cf. Ex. 15:6). The work may have been written around 100 BC. There are four Greek recensions of Judith (Septuagint codices Vaticanus, Sinaiticus, Alexandrinus, and Basiliano-Vaticanus), four ancient translations (Old Latin, Syriac, Sahidic, and Ethiopic), and some late Hebrew versions, apparently translated from the Vulgate. Despite Jerome's claim to have translated an Aramaic text, no ancient Aramaic or Hebrew manuscripts have been found. The oldest extant text of Judith is the preservation of 15:1–7 inscribed on a third-century AD potsherd. Whatever the reasons, the rabbis did not count Judith among their scriptures, and the Reformers adopted that position.

CHAPTER 1

1 In the twelfth year of the reign of Nebuchadnezzar, who reigned over the Assyrians in Nineveh, the great city, in the days of Arphaxad, who reigned over the Medes in Ecbatana, **2** and built around Ecbatana walls of hewn stones three cubits broad and six cubits long, and made the height of the wall seventy cubits, and its breadth fifty cubits; **3** and set its towers at its gates, one hundred cubits high, and its breadth in the foundation was sixty cubits; **4** and made its gates, even gates that were raised to the height of seventy cubits, and their breadth forty cubits, for his mighty army to go out of, and the setting in array of his footmen— **5** even in those days King Nebuchadnezzar made war with King Arphaxad in the great plain. This plain is on the borders of Ragau. **6** There came to meet him all that lived in the hill country, and all that lived by Euphrates, Tigris, and Hydaspes, and in the plain of Arioch the king of the Elymaeans. Many nations of the sons of Chelod assembled themselves to the battle. **7** And Nebuchadnezzar king of the Assyrians sent to all who lived in Persia, and to all who lived westward, to those who lived in Cilicia, Damascus, Libanus, and Antilibanus, and to all who lived along the seacoast, **8** and to those among the nations that were of Carmel and Gilead, and to the higher Galilee and the great plain of Esdraelon, **9** and to all who were in Samaria and its cities, and beyond Jordan to Jerusalem, Betane, Chellus, Kadesh, the river of Egypt, Tahpanhes, Rameses, and all the land of Goshen, **10** until you come above Tanis and Memphis, and to all that lived in Egypt, until you come to the borders of Ethiopia. **11** All those who lived in all the land made light of the command of Nebuchadnezzar king of the Assyrians and did not go with him to the war; for they were not afraid of him, but he was before them as one man. They turned away his messengers from their

presence without effect, and with disgrace. **12** And Nebuchadnezzar was exceedingly angry with all this land, and he swore by his throne and kingdom, that he would surely be avenged on all the coasts of Cilicia, Damascus, and Syria, that he would kill with his sword all the inhabitants of the land of Moab, and the children of Ammon, all Judea, and all that were in Egypt, until you come to the borders of the two seas. **13** And he set the battle in array with his army against King Arphaxad in the seventeenth year; and he prevailed in his battle, and turned to flight all the army of Arphaxad, with all his horses and all his chariots. **14** He became master of his cities, and he came even to Ecbatana, and took the towers, plundered its streets, and turned its beauty into shame. **15** He took Arphaxad in the mountains of Ragau, struck him through with his darts, and utterly destroyed him, to this day. **16** He returned with them to Nineveh, he and all his company of various nations, an exceedingly great multitude of men of war, and there he took his ease and banqueted, he and his army, for one hundred twenty days.

CHAPTER 2

1 In the eighteenth year, the twenty-second day of the first month, there was talk in the house of Nebuchadnezzar king of the Assyrians, that he should be avenged on all the land, even as he spoke. **2** He called together all his servants and all his great men, and communicated with them his secret counsel, and concluded the afflicting of all the land out of his own mouth. **3** They decreed to destroy all flesh which did not follow the word of his mouth. **4** It came to pass, when he had ended his counsel, Nebuchadnezzar king of the Assyrians called Holofernes the chief captain of his army, which was next after himself, and said to him, **5** "The great king, the lord of all the earth, says: Behold, you will go out from my presence, and take with you men who trust in their strength, to one hundred twenty thousand footmen and twelve thousand horses with their riders. **6** And you will go out against all the west country, because they disobeyed the command of my mouth. **7** You will declare to them that they should prepare earth and water, because I will go out in my wrath against them and will cover the whole face of the earth with the feet of my army, and I will give them as plunder to them. **8** Their slain will fill their valleys and brooks, and the river will be filled with their dead until it overflows. **9** I will lead them captives to the utmost parts of all the earth. **10** But you will go out and take all their coasts for me first. If they will yield themselves to you, then you must reserve them for me until the day of their reproof. **11** As for those who are disobedient, your eye will not spare; but you will give them up to be slain and to be plundered in all your land. **12** For as I live, and by the power of my kingdom, I have spoken, and I will do this with my hand. **13** Moreover, you will not transgress anything of the commands of your lord, but you will surely accomplish them, as I have commanded you. You will not defer to do them." **14** So Holofernes went out from the presence of his lord, and called all the governors, the captains, and officers of the army of Asshur. **15** He counted chosen men for the battle, as his lord had commanded him, to one hundred twenty thousand, with twelve thousand archers on horseback. **16** He arranged them as a great multitude is ordered for the war. **17** He took camels and donkeys and mules for their baggage, an exceedingly great multitude, and sheep and oxen and goats without number for their provision, **18** and great store of rations for every man, and exceedingly much gold and silver out of the king's house. **19** He went out, he and all his army, on their journey, to go before King Nebuchadnezzar, and to cover all the face of the earth westward with their chariots, horsemen, and chosen footmen. **20** A great company of various nations went out with them like locusts, and like the sand of the earth. For they could not be counted by reason of their multitude. **21** And they departed out of Nineveh three days' journey toward the plain of Bectileth and encamped from Bectileth near the mountain which is at the left hand of the upper Cilicia. **22** And he took all his army, his footmen, horsemen, and chariots, and went away from there into the hill country, **23** and destroyed Put and Lud, and plundered all the children of Rasses and the children of Ishmael, which were along the wilderness to the south of the land of the Chellians. **24** And he went over Euphrates, and went through Mesopotamia, and broke down all the high cities that were on the River Arbonai, until you come to the sea. **25** And he took possession of the borders of Cilicia, and killed all that resisted him, and came to the borders of Japheth, which were toward the south, opposite Arabia. **26** He surrounded all the children of Midian, and set their tents on fire, and plundered their sheepfolds. **27** He went down into the plain of Damascus in the days of wheat harvest, and set all their fields on fire, and utterly destroyed their flocks and herds, and plundered their cities, laid their plains waste, and struck all their young men with the edge of the sword. **28** And the fear and the dread of him fell on those who lived on the seacoast, on those who were in Sidon and Tyre, those who lived in Sur and Ocina, and all who lived in Jemnaan. Those who lived in Azotus and Ashkelon feared him exceedingly.

CHAPTER 3

1 And they sent to him messengers with words of peace, saying, **2** "Behold, we the servants of Nebuchadnezzar the great king lie before you. Use us as it is pleasing in your sight. **3** Behold, our dwellings, and all our country, and all our fields of wheat, and our flocks and herds, and all the sheepfolds of our tents, lie before your face. Use them as it may please you. **4** Behold, even our cities and those who dwell in them are your servants. Come and deal with them as it is good in your eyes." **5** So the men came to Holofernes and declared to him according to these words. **6** He came down toward the seacoast, he and his army, and set garrisons in the high cities, and took out of them chosen men for allies. **7** They received him, they and all the country around them, with garlands and dances and timbrels. **8** He cast down all their borders and cut down their sacred groves. It had been given to him to destroy all the gods of the land, that all the nations would worship Nebuchadnezzar only, and that all their tongues and their tribes would call on him as god. **9** Then he came toward Esdraelon near to Dotaea, which is opposite the great ridge of Judea. **10** He encamped between Geba and Scythopolis. He was there a whole month, that he might gather together all the baggage of his army.

CHAPTER 4

1 The sons of Israel that lived in Judea heard all that Holofernes the chief captain of Nebuchadnezzar king of the Assyrians had done to the nations, and how he had plundered all their temples and destroyed them utterly. **2** They were exceedingly afraid before him, and were troubled for Jerusalem, and for the temple of the Lord their God; **3** because they had newly come up from the captivity, and all the people of Judea were recently gathered together; and the vessels, the altar, and the house were sanctified after being profaned. **4** And they sent into every coast of Samaria, to Konae, to Beth-Horon, Belmaim, Jericho, to Choba, Aesora, and to the Valley of Salem; **5** and they occupied beforehand all the tops of the high mountains, fortified the villages that were in them, stored supplies for the provision of war; for their fields were newly reaped. **6** Jehoiakim the chief priest, who was in those days at Jerusalem, wrote to those who lived in Bethulia, and Betomesthaim, which is opposite Esdraelon toward the plain that is near to Doesaim, **7** charging them to seize on the ascents of the hill country; because by them was the entrance into Judea, and it was easy to stop them from approaching, since the approach was narrow, with space for two men at the most. **8** And the sons of Israel did as Jehoiakim the chief priest had commanded them, as did the senate of all the people of Israel, which lived at Jerusalem. **9** And every man of Israel cried to God with great earnestness, and with great earnestness they humbled their souls. **10** They, their wives, their children, their cattle, and every sojourner, hireling, and servant bought with their money put sackcloth on their loins. **11** Every man and woman of Israel, and the little children, and the inhabitants of Jerusalem, fell before the temple, and cast ashes on their heads, and spread out their sackcloth before the Lord. They put sackcloth around the altar. **12** They cried to the God of Israel earnestly with one consent, that He would not give their children as prey, their wives as plunder, the cities of their inheritance to destruction, and the sanctuary to being profaned and being made a reproach, for the nations to rejoice at. **13** The Lord heard their voice and looked at their affliction. The people continued fasting many days in all Judea and Jerusalem before

the sanctuary of the Lord Almighty. **14** And Jehoiakim the chief priest, and all the priests that stood before the Lord, and those who ministered to the Lord, had their loins dressed in sackcloth, and offered the continual burnt-offering, the vows, and the free gifts of the people. **15** They had ashes on their hats. They cried to the Lord with all their power, that He would look on all the house of Israel for good.

CHAPTER 5

1 Holofernes, the chief captain of the army of Asshur, was told that the sons of Israel had prepared for war, had shut up the passages of the hill country, had fortified all the tops of the high hills, and had laid impediments in the plains. **2** Then he was exceedingly angry, and he called all the princes of Moab, and the captains of Ammon, and all the governors of the seacoast, **3** and he said to them, "Tell me now, you sons of Canaan, who are these people who dwell in the hill country? What are the cities that they inhabit? How large is their army? Where is their power and their strength? What king is set over them, to be the leader of their army? **4** Why have they turned their backs, that they should not come and meet me, more than all that dwell in the west?" **5** Then Achior, the leader of all the children of Ammon, said to him, "Let my lord now hear a word from the mouth of your servant, and I will tell you the truth concerning these people who dwell in this hill country, near to the place where you dwell. No lie will come out of the mouth of your servant. **6** These people are descended from the Chaldeans. **7** They sojourned before this in Mesopotamia, because they did not want to follow the gods of their fathers, which were in the land of the Chaldeans. **8** They departed from the way of their parents, and worshiped the God of Heaven, the God whom they knew. Their parents cast them out from the face of their gods, and they fled into Mesopotamia, and sojourned there many days. **9** Then their God commanded them to depart from the place where they sojourned, and to go into the land of Canaan. They lived there, and prospered with gold and silver, and with exceedingly much cattle. **10** Then they went down into Egypt, for a famine covered all the land of Canaan. They sojourned there until they had grown up. They became a great multitude there, so that one could not count the population of their nation. **11** Then the king of Egypt rose up against them, and dealt subtly with them, and brought them low, making them labor in brick, and made them slaves. **12** They cried to their God, and He struck all the land of Egypt with incurable plagues; so the Egyptians cast them out of their sight. **13** God dried up the Red Sea before them, **14** and brought them into the way of Sinai Kadesh-Barnea, and they cast out all that lived in the wilderness. **15** They lived in the land of the Amorites, and they destroyed by their strength everyone in Heshbon. Passing over Jordan, they possessed all the hill country. **16** They cast out before them the Canaanite, the Perizzite, the Jebusite, the Shechemite, and all the Girgashites, and they lived in that country many days. **17** And while they did not sin before their God, they prospered, because God who hates iniquity was with them. **18** But when they departed from the way which He appointed them, they were destroyed in many severe battles, and were led captives into a land that was not theirs. The temple of their God was cast to the ground, and their cities were taken by their adversaries. **19** And now they have returned to their God and have come up from the dispersion where they were dispersed, and have possessed Jerusalem, where their sanctuary is, and are seated in the hill country; for it was desolate. **20** And now, my lord and master, if there is any error in this people, and they sin against their God, we will consider what this thing is in which they stumble, and we will go up and overcome them. **21** But if there is no lawlessness in their nation, let my lord now pass by, lest their Lord defend them, and their God be for them, and we will be a reproach before all the earth." **22** It came to pass, when Achior had finished speaking these words, all the people standing around the tent murmured. The great men of Holofernes, and all that lived by the seaside and in Moab, said that he should kill him. **23** For, they said, "We will not be afraid of the sons of Israel, because, behold, they are a people that has no power nor might to make the battle strong. **24** Therefore now we will go up, and they will be a prey to be devoured by all your army, Lord Holofernes."

CHAPTER 6

¹ And when the disturbance of the men that were around the council had ceased, Holofernes the chief captain of the army of Asshur said to Achior and to all the children of Moab before all the people of the foreigners, ² "And who are you, Achior, and the hirelings of Ephraim, that you have prophesied among us as today, and have said that we should not make war with the race of Israel, because their God will defend them? And who is God but Nebuchadnezzar? ³ He will send out his might and will destroy them from the face of the earth, and their God will not deliver them; but we his servants will strike them as one man. They will not sustain the might of our horses. ⁴ For with them we will burn them up. Their mountains will be drunken with their blood. Their plains will be filled with their dead bodies. Their footsteps will not stand before us, but they will surely perish, says King Nebuchadnezzar, lord of all the earth; for he said, The words that I have spoken will not be in vain. ⁵ But you, Achior, hireling of Ammon, who have spoken these words in the day of your iniquity, will see my face no longer from this day, until I am avenged of the race of those that came out of Egypt. ⁶ And then the sword of my army, and the multitude of those who serve me, will pass through your sides, and you will fall among their slain when I return. ⁷ Then my servants will bring you back into the hill country and will set you in one of the cities of the ascents. ⁸ You will not perish until you are destroyed with them. ⁹ And if you hope in your heart that they will not be taken, do not let your countenance fall. I have spoken it, and none of my words will fall to the ground." ¹⁰ Then Holofernes commanded his servants who waited in his tent to take Achior, and bring him back to Bethulia, and deliver him into the hands of the sons of Israel. ¹¹ So his servants took him and brought him out of the camp into the plain, and they moved from the midst of the plains into the hill country and came to the springs that were under Bethulia. ¹² When the men of the city saw them on the top of the hill, they took up their weapons, and went out of the city against them to the top of the hill. Every man that used a sling kept them from coming up and cast stones against them. ¹³ They took cover under the hill, bound Achior, cast him down, left him at the foot of the hill, and went away to their lord. ¹⁴ But the sons of Israel descended from their city, and came to him, untied him, led him away into Bethulia, and presented him to the rulers of their city; ¹⁵ which were in those days Ozias the son of Micah, of the tribe of Simeon, and Chabris the son of Gothoniel, and Charmis the son of Melchiel. ¹⁶ Then they called together all the elders of the city; and all their young men ran together, with their women, to the assembly. They set Achior in the midst of all their people. Then Ozias asked him what had happened. ¹⁷ He answered and declared to them the words of the council of Holofernes, and all the words that he had spoken in the midst of the princes of the children of Asshur, and all the great words that Holofernes had spoken against the house of Israel. ¹⁸ Then the people fell down and worshiped God, and cried, saying, ¹⁹ "O Lord God of Heaven, behold their arrogance, and pity the low estate of our race. Look on the face of those who are sanctified to You this day." ²⁰ They comforted Achior and praised him exceedingly. ²¹ Then Ozias took him out of the assembly into his house and made a feast for the elders. They called on the God of Israel for help all that night.

CHAPTER 7

¹ The next day Holofernes commanded all his army and all the people who had come to be his allies, that they should move their camp toward Bethulia, take beforehand the ascents of the hill country, and make war against the sons of Israel. ² Every mighty man of them moved that day. The army of their men of war was one hundred seventy thousand footmen, plus twelve thousand horsemen, besides the baggage, and the men that were on foot among them: an exceedingly great multitude. ³ They encamped in the valley near Bethulia, by the fountain. They spread themselves in breadth over Doesaim even to Belmaim, and in length from Bethulia to Cyamon, which is near Esdraelon. ⁴ But the sons of Israel, when they saw the multitude of them, were troubled exceedingly, and everyone said to his neighbor, "Now these men will lick up the face of all the earth. Neither the high mountains, nor the valleys, nor the hills will be able to bear their weight." ⁵ Every man took up his weapons of war, and when they had kindled

fires on their towers, they remained and watched all that night. ⁶ But on the second day Holofernes led out all his cavalry in the sight of the sons of Israel which were in Bethulia, ⁷ viewed the ascents to their city, and searched out the springs of the waters, seized on them, and set garrisons of men of war over them. Then he departed back to his people. ⁸ All the rulers of the children of Esau, all the leaders of the people of Moab, and the captains of the seacoast came to him and said, ⁹ "Let our lord now hear a word, that there not be losses in your army. ¹⁰ For this people of the sons of Israel do not trust in their spears, but in the height of the mountains wherein they dwell, for it is not easy to come up to the tops of their mountains. ¹¹ And now, my lord, do not fight against them as men fight who join battle, and there will not so much as one man of your people perish. ¹² Remain in your camp and keep every man of your army safe. Let your servants get possession of the water spring, which flows from the foot of the mountain, ¹³ because all the inhabitants of Bethulia get their water from there. Then thirst will kill them, and they will give up their city. Then we and our people will go up to the tops of the mountains that are near, and will encamp on them, to watch that not one man gets out of the city. ¹⁴ They will be consumed with famine, they and their wives and their children. Before the sword comes against them, they will be laid low in the streets where they dwell. ¹⁵ And you will pay them back with evil, because they rebelled, and did not meet your face in peace." ¹⁶ Their words were pleasing in the sight of Holofernes and in the sight of all his servants; and he ordered them to do as they had spoken. ¹⁷ And the army of the children of Ammon moved, and with them five thousand of the children of Asshur, and they encamped in the valley. They seized the waters and the springs of the waters of the sons of Israel. ¹⁸ The children of Esau went up with the children of Ammon and encamped in the hill country near Doesaim. They sent some of them toward the south, and toward the east, near Ekrebel, which is near Chusi, that is on the brook Mochmur. The rest of the army of the Assyrians encamped in the plain and covered all the face of the land. Their tents and baggage were pitched on it in a great crowd. They were an exceedingly great multitude. ¹⁹ The sons of Israel cried to the Lord their God, for their spirit fainted; for all their enemies had surrounded them. There was no way to escape out from among them. ²⁰ All the army of Asshur remained around them, their footmen and their chariots and their horsemen, thirty-four days. All their vessels of water ran dry for all the inhabitants of Bethulia. ²¹ The cisterns were emptied, and they had no water to drink their fill for one day; for they rationed drink by measure. ²² Their young children were discouraged. The women and the young men fainted for thirst. They fell down in the streets of the city, and in the passages of the gates. There was no longer any strength in them. ²³ All the people, including the young men, the women, and the children, were gathered together against Ozias, and against the rulers of the city. They cried with a loud voice, and said before all the elders, ²⁴ "God be judge between all of you and us, because you have done us great wrong, in that you have not spoken words of peace with the children of Asshur. ²⁵ Now we have no helper; but God has sold us into their hands, that we should be laid low before them with thirst and great destruction. ²⁶ And now summon them and deliver up the whole city as prey to the people of Holofernes, and to all his army. ²⁷ For it is better for us to be made a plunder to them. For we will be servants, and our souls will live, and we will not see the death of our babies before our eyes, and our wives and our children fainting in death. ²⁸ We take to witness against you the heavens and the earth, and our God and the Lord of our fathers, who punishes us according to our sins and the sins of our fathers. Do what we have said today!" ²⁹ And there was great weeping of all with one consent in the midst of the assembly; and they cried to the Lord God with a loud voice. ³⁰ And Ozias said to them, "Brothers, be of good courage! Let us endure five more days, during which the Lord our God will turn His mercy toward us; for He will not forsake us utterly. ³¹ But if these days pass, and no help comes to us, I will do what you say." ³² Then he dispersed the people, every man to his own camp; and they went away to the walls and towers of their city. He sent the women and children into their houses. They were brought very low in the city.

CHAPTER 8

¹ In those days Judith heard about this. She was the

daughter of Merari, the son of Ox, the son of Joseph, the son of Oziel, the son of Elkiah, the son of Ananias, the son of Gideon, the son of Raphaim, the son of Ahitub, the son of Elihu, the son of Eliab, the son of Nathanael, the son of Salamiel, the son of Salasadai, the son of Israel. **²** Her husband was Manasseh, of her tribe and of her family. He died in the days of barley harvest. **³** For he stood over those who bound sheaves in the field, and the heat came on his head, and he fell on his bed, and died in his city Bethulia. So they buried him with his fathers in the field which is between Doesaim and Balamon. **⁴** Judith was a widow in her house three years and four months. **⁵** She made herself a tent on the roof of her house and put on sackcloth on her loins. The garments of her widowhood were on her. **⁶** And she fasted all the days of her widowhood, except the eves of the Sabbaths, the Sabbaths, the eves of the new moons, the new moons, and the feasts and joyful days of the house of Israel. **⁷** She was of an attractive countenance, and exceedingly beautiful to behold. Her husband Manasseh had left her gold, silver, menservants, maidservants, cattle, and lands. She remained on those lands. **⁸** No one said anything evil about her; for she feared God exceedingly. **⁹** She heard the evil words of the people against the governor, because they fainted for lack of water; and Judith heard all the words that Ozias spoke to them, how he swore to them that he would deliver the city to the Assyrians after five days. **¹⁰** So she sent her maid, who was over all things that she had, to summon Ozias, Chabris, and Charmis, the elders of her city. **¹¹** They came to her, and she said to them, "Hear me now, O you rulers of the inhabitants of Bethulia, for your word that you have spoken before the people this day is not right. You have set the oath which you have pronounced between God and you and have promised to deliver the city to our enemies, unless within these days the Lord turns to help you. **¹²** Now who are you that you have tempted God this day, and stand in the place of God among the children of men? **¹³** Now try the Lord Almighty, and you will never know anything. **¹⁴** For you will not find the depth of the heart of man, and you will not perceive the things that he thinks. How will you search out God, who has made all these things, and know His mind, and comprehend His purpose? No, my countrymen, do not provoke the Lord our God to anger! **¹⁵** For if He has not decided to help us within these five days, He has power to defend us in such time as He will, or to destroy us before the face of our enemies. **¹⁶** But do not pledge the counsels of the Lord our God! For God is not as man, that He should be threatened; neither as the son of man, that He should be turned by entreaty. **¹⁷** Therefore let us wait for the salvation that comes from Him and call on Him to help us. He will hear our voice, if it pleases Him. **¹⁸** For there arose none in our age, neither is there any of us today, tribe, or countrymen, or family, or city, which worship gods made with hands, as it was in the former days; **¹⁹** for this reason our fathers were given to the sword, and for plunder, and fell with a great fall before our enemies. **²⁰** But we know no other god besides Him. Therefore, we hope that He will not despise us, nor any of our race. **²¹** For if we are taken so, all Judea will sit on the ground, and our sanctuary will be plundered; and He will require our blood for profaning it. **²²** And the slaughter of our countrymen, and the captivity of the land, and the desolation of our inheritance, He will turn on our heads among the nations, wherever we will be in bondage. We will be an offense and a reproach before those who take us for a possession. **²³** For our bondage will not be ordered to favor; but the Lord our God will turn it to dishonor. **²⁴** And now, countrymen, let us show an example to our countrymen, because their soul hangs on us, and the sanctuary, the house, and the altar rest on us. **²⁵** Besides all this, let us give thanks to the Lord our God, who tries us, even as He did our fathers also. **²⁶** Remember all the things which He did to Abraham, and all the things in which He tried Isaac, and all the things which happened to Jacob in Mesopotamia of Syria, when he kept the sheep of Laban his mother's brother. **²⁷** For He has not tried us in the fire, as He did them, to search out their hearts, neither has He taken vengeance on us; but the Lord does scourge them that come near to Him, to admonish them." **²⁸** And Ozias said to her, "All that you have spoken, you have spoken with a good heart. There is no one who will deny your words. **²⁹** For this is not the first day wherein your wisdom is manifested; but from the beginning of your days all the people have known your understanding, because the disposition of your heart is good. **³⁰** But the people were exceedingly thirsty and compelled us to do as we spoke to them, and to bring an oath on ourselves, which we will not break. **³¹** And now pray for us, because you are a godly woman, and the Lord will send us rain to fill our cisterns, and we will faint no more." **³²** Then Judith said to them, "Hear me, and I will do a thing, which will go down to all generations among the children of our race. **³³** You will all stand at the gate tonight. I will go out with my maid. Within the days after which you said that you would deliver the city to our enemies, the Lord will visit Israel by my hand. **³⁴** But you will not inquire of my act; for I will not declare it to you, until the things are finished that I will do." **³⁵** Then Ozias and the rulers said to her, "Go in peace. May the Lord God be before you, to take vengeance on our enemies." **³⁶** So they returned from the tent and went to their stations.

CHAPTER 9

¹ But Judith fell on her face, and put ashes on her head, and uncovered the sackcloth with which she was clothed. The incense of that evening was now being offered at Jerusalem in the house of God, and Judith cried to the Lord with a loud voice, and said, **²** "O Lord God of my father Simeon, into whose hand You gave a sword to take vengeance on the strangers who loosened the belt of a virgin to defile her, uncovered the thigh to her shame, and profaned the womb to her reproach; for You said, It will not be so; and they did so. **³** Therefore You gave their rulers to be slain, and their bed, which was ashamed for her who was deceived, to be dyed in blood, and struck the servants with their masters, and the masters on their thrones; **⁴** and gave their wives for a prey, and their daughters to be captives, and all their spoils to be divided among Your dear children; which were moved with zeal for You, and abhorred the pollution of their blood, and called on You for aid. O God, O my God, hear me who am also a widow. **⁵** For You did the things that were before those things, and those things, and such as come after; and You planned the things which are now, and the things which are to come. The things which You planned came to pass. **⁶** Yes, the things which You determined stood before You, and said, Behold, we are here; for all Your ways are prepared, and Your judgment is with foreknowledge. **⁷** For behold, the Assyrians are multiplied in their power. They are exalted with horse and rider. They were proud of the strength of their footmen. They have trusted in shield, spear, bow, and sling. They do not know that You are the Lord who breaks the battles. The Lord is Your Name. **⁸** Break their strength in Your power and bring down their force in Your wrath; for they intend to profane Your sanctuary, and to defile the dwelling place where Your glorious Name rests, and to destroy the horn of Your altar with the sword. **⁹** Look at their pride and send Your wrath on their heads. Give into my hand, which am a widow, the might that I have conceived. **¹⁰** Strike by the deceit of my lips the servant with the prince, and the prince with his servant. Break down their arrogance by the hand of a woman. **¹¹** For Your power stands not in multitude, nor Your might in strong men, but You are a God of the afflicted. You are a helper of the minorities, a helper of the weak, a protector of the forsaken, a Savior of those who are without hope. **¹²** Yes, yes, God of my father, and God of the inheritance of Israel, Lord of the heavens and of the earth, Creator of the waters, King of every creature, hear my prayer. **¹³** Make my speech and deceit to be their wound and stripe, who intend hard things against Your covenant, Your holy house, the top of Zion, and the house of the possession of Your children. **¹⁴** Make every nation and tribe of Yours to know that You are God, the God of all power and might, and that there is none other that protects the race of Israel but You."

CHAPTER 10

¹ It came to pass, when she had ceased to cry to the God of Israel, and had finished saying all these words, **²** that she rose up where she had fallen down, called her maid, and went down into the house that she used to live in on the Sabbath days and on her feast days. **³** She pulled off the sackcloth which she had put on, took off the garments of her widowhood, washed her body all over with water, anointed herself with rich ointment, braided the hair of her head, and put a tiara on it. She put on her garments of gladness, which she used to wear in the days of the life of Manasseh her husband. **⁴** She took sandals for her feet, and put her chains around her, and her bracelets, her rings, her earrings, and all her jewelry, and decked herself bravely, to deceive the eyes of all men who would see her. **5** She gave her maid a leather container of wine and a flask of oil, and filled a bag with parched corn, lumps of figs, and fine bread. She packed all her vessels together and laid them on her. **6** They went out to the gate of the city of Bethulia, and found Ozias and the elders of the city, Chabris and Charmis standing by it. **7** But when they saw her, that her countenance was altered, and her apparel was changed, they wondered at her beauty very exceedingly, and said to her, **8** "May the God of our fathers give you favor and accomplish your purposes to the glory of the sons of Israel, and to the exaltation of Jerusalem." Then she worshiped God, **9** and said to them, "Command that they open the gate of the city for me, and I will go out to accomplish the things you spoke with me about." And they commanded the young men to open to her, as she had spoken; **10** and they did so. Then Judith went out, she, and her handmaid with her. The men of the city watched her until she had gone down the mountain, until she had passed the valley, and they could see her no longer. **11** They went straight onward in the valley. The watch of the Assyrians met her; **12** and they took her, and asked her, "Of what people are you? Where are you coming from? Where are you going?" She said, "I am a daughter of the Hebrews. I am fleeing away from their presence, because they are about to be given to you to be consumed. **13** I am coming into the presence of Holofernes the chief captain of your army, to declare words of truth. I will show him a way that he can go and win all the hill country, and there will not be lacking of his men one person, nor one life." **14** Now when the men heard her words, and considered her countenance, the beauty thereof was exceedingly marvelous in their eyes. They said to her, **15** "You have saved your life, in that you have hurried to come down to the presence of our master. Now come to his tent. Some of us will guide you until they deliver you into his hands. **16** But when you stand before him, do not be afraid in your heart, but declare to him according to your words; and he will treat you well." **17** They chose out of them one hundred men, and appointed them to accompany her and her maid; and they brought them to the tent of Holofernes. **18** And there was great excitement throughout all the camp, for her coming was reported among the tents. They came and surrounded her as she stood outside Holofernes' tent, until they told him about her. **19** They marveled at her beauty and marveled at the sons of Israel because of her. Each one said to his neighbor, "Who would despise this people, that have among them such women? For it is not good that one man of them be left, seeing that, if they are let go, they will be able to deceive the whole earth." **20** Those who lay near Holofernes, and all his servants, went out and brought her into the tent. **21** And Holofernes was resting on his bed under the canopy, which was woven with purple, gold, emeralds, and precious stones. **22** And they told him about her; and he came out into the space before his tent, with silver lamps going before him. **23** But when Judith had come before him and his servants, they all marveled at the beauty of her countenance. She fell down on her face, and bowed down to him, but his servants raised her up.

CHAPTER 11

1 Holofernes said to her, "Woman, take courage. Do not be afraid in your heart; for I never hurt anyone who has chosen to serve Nebuchadnezzar, the king of all the earth. **2** And now, if your people who dwell in the hill country had not slighted me, I would not have lifted up my spear against them; but they have done these things to themselves. **3** And now tell me why you fled from them and came to us; for you have come to save yourself. Take courage! You will live tonight, and hereafter; **4** for there is no one that will wrong you, but all will treat you well, as is done to the servants of King Nebuchadnezzar my lord." **5** And Judith said to him, "Receive the words of your servant, and let your handmaid speak in your presence, and I will declare no lie to my lord this night. **6** If you will follow the words of your handmaid, God will bring the thing to pass perfectly with you; and my lord will not fail to accomplish his purposes. **7** As Nebuchadnezzar king of all the earth lives, and as his power lives, who has sent you for the preservation of every living thing, not only do men serve him by you, but also the beasts of the field, the cattle, and the birds of the sky will live through your strength, in the time of Nebuchadnezzar and

of all his house. **8** For we have heard of your wisdom and the subtle plans of your soul. It has been reported in all the earth that you only are brave in all the kingdom, mighty in knowledge, and wonderful in feats of war. **9** And now as concerning the matter which Achior spoke in your council, we have heard his words; for the men of Bethulia saved him, and he declared to them all that he had spoken before you. **10** Therefore, O lord and master, do not neglect his word; but lay it up in your heart, for it is true; for our race will not be punished, neither will the sword prevail against them, unless they sin against their God. **11** And now, that my lord not be defeated and frustrated of his purpose, and that death may fall on them, their sin has overtaken them, with which they will provoke their God to anger, whenever they do wickedness. **12** Since their food failed them, and all their water was scant, they took counsel to lay hands on their cattle, and determined to consume all those things which God charged them by his laws that they should not eat. **13** They are resolved to spend the first-fruits of the corn, and the tenths of the wine and the oil, which they had sanctified and reserved for the priests who stand before the face of our God in Jerusalem; which things it is not fitting for any of the people so much as to touch with their hands. **14** They have sent some to Jerusalem, because they also that dwell there have done this thing, to bring them permission from the council of elders. **15** It will be, when word comes to them and they do it, they will be given to you to be destroyed the same day. **16** Therefore I, your servant, knowing all this, fled away from their presence. God sent me to work things with you, at which all the earth will be astonished, even as many as hear it. **17** For your servant is religious and serves the God of Heaven day and night. Now, my lord, I will stay with you, and your servant will go out by night into the valley. I will pray to God, and He will tell me when they have committed their sins. **18** Then I will come and show it also to you. Then you will go out with all your army, and there will be none of them that will resist you. **19** And I will lead you through the midst of Judea, until you come to Jerusalem. I will set your seat in the midst of it. You will drive them as sheep that have no shepherd, and a dog will not so much as open his mouth before you; for these things were told me according to my foreknowledge, and were declared to me, and I was sent to tell you." **20** Her words were pleasing in the sight of Holofernes and of all his servants. They marveled at her wisdom, and said, **21** "There is not such a woman from one end of the earth to the other, for beauty of face and wisdom of words." **22** Holofernes said to her, "God did well to send you before the people, that might would be in our hands, and destruction among those who slighted my lord. **23** And now you are beautiful in your countenance, and wise in your words. If you will do as you have spoken, your God will be my God, and you will dwell in the house of King Nebuchadnezzar and will be renowned through the whole earth."

CHAPTER 12

1 He commanded that she should be brought in where his silver vessels were set and asked that his servants should prepare some of his own meats for her, and that she should drink from his own wine. **2** And Judith said, "I will not eat of it, lest there be an occasion of stumbling, but provision will be made for me of the things that have come with me." **3** And Holofernes said to her, "But if the things that are with you should fail, from where will we be able to give you more like it? For there is none of your race with us." **4** And Judith said to him, "As your soul lives, my lord, your servant will not spend those things that are with me, until the Lord works by my hand the things that He has determined." **5** Then Holofernes' servants brought her into the tent, and she slept until midnight. Then she rose up toward the morning watch, **6** and sent to Holofernes, saying, "Let my lord now command that they allow your servant to go out to pray." **7** Holofernes commanded his guards that they should not stop her. She stayed in the camp three days and went out every night into the Valley of Bethulia and washed herself at the fountain of water in the camp. **8** And when she came up, she implored the Lord God of Israel to direct her way to the raising up of the children of His people. **9** She came in clean, and remained in the tent, until she ate her food toward evening. **10** It came to pass on the fourth day, that Holofernes made a feast for his own servants only and called none of the officers to the banquet. **11** And he said to Bagoas the eunuch, who had charge over all that he had, "Go now, and persuade this Hebrew woman who is with you that she come to us and eat and drink with us. **12** For behold, it is a shame for our person, if we will let such a woman go, not having had her company; for if we do not draw her to ourselves, she will laugh us to scorn." **13** Bagoas went from the presence of Holofernes, and came in to her, and said, "Let this fair lady not fear to come to my lord, and to be honored in his presence, and to drink wine and be merry with us, and to be made this day as one of the daughters of the children of Asshur, which wait in the house of Nebuchadnezzar." **14** Judith said to him, "Who am I, that I should contradict my lord? For whatever would be pleasing in his eyes, I will do speedily, and this will be my joy to the day of my death." **15** She arose and decked herself with her apparel and all her woman's attire; and her servant went and laid fleeces on the ground for her next to Holofernes, which she had received from Bagoas for her daily use, that she might sit and eat on them. **16** Judith came in and sat down, and Holofernes' heart was ravished with her. His soul was moved, and he exceedingly desired her company. He was watching for a time to deceive her, from the day that he had seen her. **17** Holofernes said to her, "Drink now, and be merry with us." **18** Judith said, "I will drink now, my lord, because my life is magnified in me this day more than all the days since I was born." **19** Then she took and ate and drank before him what her servant had prepared. **20** Holofernes took great delight in her, and drank exceedingly much wine, more than he had drunk at any time in one day since he was born.

CHAPTER 13

1 But when the evening had come, his servants hurried to depart. Bagoas shut the tent outside and dismissed those who waited from the presence of his lord. They went away to their beds; for they were all weary, because the feast had been long. **2** But Judith was left alone in the tent, with Holofernes lying alone on his bed; for he was drunk with wine. **3** Judith had said to her servant that she should stand outside her bedchamber, and wait for her to come out, as she did daily; for she said she would go out to her prayer. She spoke to Bagoas according to the same words. **4** All went away from her presence, and none was left in the bedchamber, small or great. Judith, standing by his bed, said in her heart, O Lord God of all power, look in this hour on the works of my hands for the exaltation of Jerusalem. **5** For now is the time to help Your inheritance, and to do the thing that I have purposed to the destruction of the enemies which have risen up against us. **6** She came to the rail of the bed, which was at Holofernes' head, and took down his scimitar from there. **7** She drew near to the bed, took hold of the hair of his head, and said, "Strengthen me, O Lord God of Israel, this day." **8** She struck twice on his neck with all her might, and took away his head from him, **9** tumbled his body down from the bed, and took down the canopy from the pillars. After a little while she went out and gave Holofernes' head to her maid; **10** and she put it in her bag of food. They both went out together to prayer, according to their custom. They passed through the camp, circled around that valley, and went up to the mountain of Bethulia, and came to its gates. **11** Judith said far off to the watchmen at the gates, "Open, open the gate, now. God is with us, even our God, to show His power yet in Israel, and His might against the enemy, as He has done even this day." **12** It came to pass, when the men of her city heard her voice, they hurried to go down to the gate of their city, and they called together the elders of the city. **13** They all ran together, both small and great, for it was strange to them that she had come. They opened the gate and received them, making a fire to give light, and surrounded them. **14** She said to them with a loud voice, "Praise God! Praise Him! Praise God, who has not taken away His mercy from the house of Israel but has destroyed our enemies by my hand tonight!" **15** Then she took the head out of the bag and showed it, and said to them, "Behold, the head of Holofernes, the chief captain of the army of Asshur, and behold, the canopy, in which he laid in his drunkenness. The Lord struck him by the hand of a woman. **16** And as the Lord lives, who preserved me in my way that I went, my countenance deceived him to his destruction, and he did not commit sin with me, to defile and shame me." **17** All the people were exceedingly amazed, and bowed themselves, and worshiped God, and said with one accord, "Blessed are You, O our God, which have this day brought to nothing the enemies of Your people." **18** Ozias said to her, "Blessed are you, daughter, in the sight of the Most High God, above all the

women on the earth; and blessed is the Lord God, who created the heavens and the earth, who directed you to cut off the head of the prince of our enemies. **19** For your hope will not depart from the heart of men that remember the strength of God forever. **20** May God turn these things to you for a perpetual praise, to visit you with good things, because you did not spare your life by reason of the affliction of our race, but avenged our fall, walking a straight way before our God." And all the people said, "Amen! Amen!"

CHAPTER 14

1 Judith said to them, "Hear me now, my countrymen, and take this head, and hang it on the battlement of your wall. **2** It will be, so soon as the morning appears, and the sun comes up on the earth, you will each take up his weapons of war, and every valiant man of you go out of the city. You will set a captain over them, as though you would go down to the plain toward the watch of the children of Asshur; but you men will not go down. **3** These will take up their full armor and will go into their camp and rouse up the captains of the army of Asshur. They will run together to Holofernes' tent. They will not find him. Fear will fall on them, and they will flee before your face. **4** You men, and all that inhabit every coast of Israel, will pursue them and overthrow them as they go. **5** But before you do these things, summon Achior the Ammonite to me, that he may see and know him that despised the house of Israel, and that sent him to us, as it were to death." **6** And they called Achior out of the house of Ozias; but when he came and saw the head of Holofernes in a man's hand in the assembly of the people, he fell on his face, and his spirit failed. **7** But when they had recovered him, he fell at Judith's feet, and bowed down to her, and said, "Blessed are you in every tent of Judah, and in every nation, which hearing your name will be troubled. **8** Now tell me all the things that you have done in these days." And Judith declared to him in the midst of the people all the things that she had done, from the day that she went out until the time that she spoke to them. **9** But when she finished speaking, the people shouted with a loud voice, and made a joyful noise in their city. **10** But when Achior saw all the things that the God of Israel had done, he believed in God exceedingly, and circumcised the flesh of his foreskin, and was joined to the house of Israel, to this day. **11** But as soon as the morning arose, they hanged the head of Holofernes on the wall, and every man took up his weapons, and they went out by bands to the ascents of the mountain. **12** But when the children of Asshur saw them, they sent word to their leaders; but they went to their captains and tribunes, and to each of their rulers. **13** They came to Holofernes' tent, and said to him that was over all that he had, "Wake our lord up, now; for the slaves have been bold to come down against us to battle, that they may be utterly destroyed." **14** Bagoas went in and knocked at the outer door of the tent; for he supposed that he was sleeping with Judith. **15** But when no one listened to him, he opened it, and went into the bedchamber, and found him cast on the threshold dead, and his head had been taken from him. **16** He cried with a loud voice, with weeping and groaning and a mighty cry, and tore his garments. **17** He entered into the tent where Judith lodged, and he did not find her. He leaped out to the people, and cried aloud, **18** "The slaves have dealt treacherously! One woman of the Hebrews has brought shame on the house of King Nebuchadnezzar; for behold, Holofernes lies on the ground, and his head is not on him!" **19** But when the rulers of the army of Asshur heard the words, they tore their coats, and their soul was troubled exceedingly. There was a cry and an exceedingly great noise in the midst of the camp.

CHAPTER 15

1 When those who were in the tents heard, they were amazed at what happened. **2** Trembling and fear fell on them, and no man dared stay anymore in the sight of his neighbor, but rushing out with one accord, they fled into every way of the plain and of the hill country. **3** Those who had encamped in the hill country around Bethulia fled away. And then the sons of Israel, everyone who was a warrior among them, rushed out on them. **4** Ozias sent to Betomasthaim, Bebai, Chobai, and Chola, and to every coast of Israel, to tell about the things that had been accomplished, and that all should rush on their enemies to destroy them. **5** But when the sons of Israel heard, they all fell on them with one accord, and struck them to Chobai. Yes, and in like manner also they of Jerusalem and of all the hill country came (for men had told them about what happened in their enemies' camp), and those who were in Gilead and in Galilee fell on their flank with a great slaughter, until they were past Damascus and its borders. **6** The rest of the people who lived at Bethulia fell on the camp of Asshur, and plundered them, and were enriched exceedingly. **7** The sons of Israel returned from the slaughter and got possession of that which remained. The villages and the cities that were in the hill country and in the plain country, took many spoils; for there was an exceedingly great supply. **8** Jehoiakim the chief priest, and the elders of the sons of Israel who lived in Jerusalem, came to see the good things which the Lord had showed to Israel, and to see Judith, and to salute her. **9** When they came to her, they all blessed her with one accord, and said to her, "You are the exaltation of Jerusalem! You are the great glory of Israel! You are the great rejoicing of our race! **10** You have done all these things by your hand. You have done with Israel the things that are good, and God is pleased with it. Blessed are you with the Almighty Lord forever." And all the people said, "Amen!" **11** And the people plundered the camp for the space of thirty days: and they gave Holofernes' tent to Judith, along with all his silver cups, his beds, his bowls, and all his furniture. She took them, and placed them on her mule, and prepared her wagons, and heaped them on it. **12** And all the women of Israel ran together to see her; and they blessed her and made a dance among them for her. She took branches in her hand and distributed them to the women who were with her. **13** Then they made themselves garlands of olive, she and those who were with her, and she went before all the people in the dance, leading all the women. All the men of Israel followed in their armor with garlands, and with songs in their mouths.

CHAPTER 16

1 And Judith began to sing this song of thanksgiving in all Israel, and all the people sang with loud voices this song of praise. **2** Judith said, "Begin a song to my God with timbrels. Sing to my Lord with cymbals. Make melody to Him with psalm and praise. Exalt Him and call on His Name. **3** For the Lord is the God that crushes battles. For in His armies in the midst of the people, || He delivered me out of the hand of those who persecuted me. **4** Asshur came out of the mountains from the north. He came with tens of thousands of his army. Its multitude stopped the torrents. Their horsemen covered the hills. **5** He said that he would burn up my borders, || Kill my young men with the sword, || Throw my nursing children to the ground, || Give my infants up as prey, || And make my virgins a plunder. **6** The Almighty Lord brought them to nothing by the hand of a woman. **7** For their mighty one did not fall by young men, || Neither did sons of the Titans strike him. Tall giants did not attack him, || But Judith the daughter of Merari made him weak with the beauty of her countenance. **8** For she put off the apparel of her widowhood || For the exaltation of those who were distressed in Israel. She anointed her face with ointment, || Bound her hair in a tiara, || And took a linen garment to deceive him. **9** Her sandal ravished his eye. Her beauty took his soul prisoner. The scimitar passed through his neck. **10** The Persians quaked at her daring. The Medes were daunted at her boldness. **11** Then my lowly ones shouted aloud. My weak ones were terrified and trembled for fear. They lifted up their voice, and they fled. **12** The sons of ladies pierced them through and wounded them as fugitives' children. They perished by the battle of my Lord. **13** I will sing to my God a new song: O Lord, You are great and glorious, || Marvelous in strength, invincible. **14** Let all Your creation serve You; For You spoke, and they were made. You sent out Your Spirit, || And it built them. There is no one who can resist Your voice. **15** For the mountains will be moved from their foundations with the waters, || And the rocks will melt as wax at your presence, || But You are yet merciful to those who fear You. **16** For all sacrifice is little for a sweet savor, || And all the fat is very little for a whole burnt-offering to You; But he who fears the Lord is great continually. **17** Woe to the nations who rise up against my race! The Lord Almighty will take vengeance on them in the Day of Judgment, || To put fire and worms in their flesh; And they will weep and feel their pain forever." **18** Now when they came to Jerusalem, they worshiped God. When the people were purified, they offered their whole burnt-offerings, their free will

offerings, and their gifts. **19** Judith dedicated all Holofernes' stuff, which the people had given her, and gave the canopy, which she had taken for herself out of his bedchamber, for a gift to the Lord. **20** And the people continued feasting in Jerusalem before the sanctuary for three months, and Judith remained with them. **21** But after these days, everyone departed to his own inheritance. Judith went away to Bethulia, and remained in her own possession, and was honorable in her time in all the land. **22** Many desired her, and no man knew her all the days of her life, from the day that Manasseh her husband died and was gathered to his people. **23** She increased in greatness exceedingly; and she grew old in her husband's house, to one hundred five years, and let her maid go free. Then she died in Bethulia. They buried her in the cave of her husband Manasseh. **24** The house of Israel mourned for her seven days. She distributed her goods before she died to all those who were nearest relatives to Manasseh her husband, and to those who were nearest of her own relatives. **25** There was no one that made the sons of Israel afraid anymore in the days of Judith, nor a long time after her death.

WISDOM

Otherwise known as Wisdom of Solomon

The Book of Wisdom was written as late as fifty years before the coming of Christ. Its author, whose name is not known to us, was probably a member of the Jewish community at Alexandria, in Egypt. He wrote in Greek, in a style patterned on that of Hebrew verse. At times he speaks in the person of Solomon, placing his teachings on the lips of the wise king of Hebrew tradition in order to emphasize their value.

CHAPTER 1

1 Love righteousness, all you who are judges of the earth. Think of the Lord with a good mind. Seek Him in singleness of heart, **2** Because He is found by those who do not tempt Him and is manifested to those who trust Him. **3** For crooked thoughts separate from God. His Power convicts when it is tested and exposes the foolish, **4** Because wisdom will not enter into a soul that devises evil, || Nor dwell in a body that is enslaved by sin. **5** For a holy spirit of discipline will flee deceit, || And will depart from thoughts that are without understanding, || And will be ashamed when unrighteousness has come in. **6** For wisdom is a spirit who loves man, || And she will not hold a blasphemer guiltless for his lips; Because God is [the] witness of his innermost self, || And is [the] true overseer of his heart, and a hearer of his tongue: **7** Because the Spirit of the Lord has filled the world, || And that which holds all things together knows what is said. **8** Therefore no one who utters unrighteous things will be unseen; Neither will justice, when it convicts, pass him by. **9** For in his counsels the ungodly will be searched out, || And the sound of his words will come to the Lord to bring his lawless deeds to conviction; **10** Because a jealous ear listens to all things, || And the noise of murmurings is not hidden. **11** Beware then of unprofitable murmuring and keep your tongue from slander, || Because no secret utterance will go on its way void, || And a lying mouth destroys a soul. **12** Do not court death in the error of your life; And do not draw destruction on yourselves by the works of your hands, **13** Because God did not make death; Neither does He delight when the living perish. **14** For He created all things that they might have being. The generative powers of the world are wholesome, || And there is no poison of destruction in them, || Nor does Hades have royal dominion on earth; **15** For righteousness is immortal, **16** But ungodly men, by their hands and their words, summon death; Deeming him a friend, they wear themselves out [for him]. They made a covenant with him, || Because they are worthy to belong with him.

CHAPTER 2

1 For they said within themselves, with unsound reasoning, "Our life is short and sorrowful. There is no healing when a man comes to his end, || And no one was ever known who was released from Hades, **2** Because we were born by mere chance, || And hereafter we will be as though we had never been; Because the breath in our nostrils is smoke, || And reason is a spark kindled by the beating of our heart, **3** Which being extinguished, the body will be turned into ashes, || And the spirit will be dispersed as thin air. **4** Our name will be forgotten in time. No one will remember our works. Our life will pass away as the traces of a cloud, || And will be scattered as is a mist, when it is chased by the rays of the sun and overcome by its heat. **5** For our allotted time is the passing of a shadow, and our end does not retreat, || Because it is securely sealed, and no one turns it back. **6** Come therefore and let us enjoy the good things that exist. Let us use the creation earnestly as in our youth. **7** Let us fill ourselves with costly wine and perfumes || And let no Spring flower pass us by. **8** Let us crown ourselves with rosebuds before they wither. **9** Let none of us go without his share in our proud revelry. Let us leave signs of mirth everywhere, || Because this is our portion, and this is our lot. **10** Let us oppress the righteous poor. Let us not spare the widow, || Nor give reverence to the gray hair of the old man. **11** But let our strength be a law of righteousness; For that which is weak is proven useless. **12** But let us lie in wait for the righteous man, || Because he annoys us, is contrary to our works, reproaches us with sins against the law, and charges us with sins against our training. **13** He professes to have knowledge of God and calls himself a child of the Lord. **14** He became to us a reproof of our thoughts. **15** He is grievous to us even to look at, || Because his life is unlike other men's, and his paths are strange. **16** We were regarded by him as worthless metal, || And he abstains from our ways as from uncleanness. He calls the latter end of the righteous happy. He boasts that God is his father. **17** Let us see if his words are true. Let us test what will happen at the end of his life. **18** For if the righteous man is God's son, He will uphold him, || And He will deliver him out of the hand of his adversaries. **19** Let us test him with outrage and torture, || That we may find out how gentle he is and test his patience. **20** Let us condemn him to a shameful death, || For he will be overseen according to his words." **21** So they reasoned, and they were led astray; For their wickedness blinded them, **22** And they did not know the mysteries of God, || Neither did they hope for wages of holiness, || Nor did they discern that there is a prize for blameless souls. **23** Because God created man for incorruption || And made Him an image of His own perpetuity; **24** But death entered into the world by the envy of the Devil, || And those who belong to him experience it.

CHAPTER 3

1 But the souls of the righteous are in the hand of God, || And no torment will touch them. **2** In the eyes of the foolish they seemed to have died. Their departure was considered affliction, **3** And their travel away from us ruin; But they are in peace. **4** For even if they are punished in the sight of men, || Their hope is full of immortality. **5** Having borne a little disciplining, they will receive great good, || Because God tested them and found them worthy of Himself. **6** He tested them like gold in the furnace, || And He accepted them as a whole burnt-offering. **7** In the time of their visitation they will shine. They will run back and out like sparks among stubble. **8** They will judge nations and have dominion over peoples. The Lord will reign over them forever. **9** Those who trust Him will understand truth. The faithful will live with Him in love, || Because grace and mercy are with His chosen ones. **10** But the ungodly will be punished even as they reasoned, || Those who neglected righteousness and revolted from the Lord; **11** For he who despises wisdom and discipline is miserable. Their hope is void and their toils unprofitable. Their works are useless. **12** Their wives are foolish and their children are wicked. **13** Their descendants are cursed, || Because the barren woman who is undefiled is happy—she who has not conceived in transgression. She will have fruit in the visitation of souls. **14** So is the eunuch which has done no lawless deed with his hands, || Nor imagined wicked things against the Lord; For a precious gift will be given to him for his faithfulness—a special favor, and a delightful inheritance in the Lord's sanctuary. **15** For good labors have fruit of great renown. The root of understanding cannot fail. **16** But children of adulterers will not come to maturity. The seed of an unlawful bed will vanish away. **17** For if they live long, they will not be esteemed, || And in the end, their old age will be without honor. **18** If they die

quickly, they will have no hope, || Nor consolation in the day of decision. **19** For the end of an unrighteous generation is always grievous.

CHAPTER 4

1 It is better to be childless with virtue, || For immortality is in the memory of virtue, || Because it is recognized both before God and before men. **2** When it is present, people imitate it. They long after it when it has departed. Throughout all time it marches crowned in triumph—Victorious in the competition for the prizes that are undefiled. **3** But the multiplying brood of the ungodly will be of no profit, || And their illegitimate offshoots will not take deep root, || Nor will they establish a sure hold. **4** For even if they grow branches and flourish for a season, || Standing unsure, they will be shaken by the wind. They will be uprooted by the violence of winds. **5** Their branches will be broken off before they come to maturity. Their fruit will be useless—Never ripe to eat and fit for nothing. **6** For unlawfully conceived children are witnesses of wickedness against parents when they are investigated. **7** But a righteous man, even if he dies before his time, will be at rest. **8** For honorable old age is not that which stands in length of time, || Nor is its measure given by number of years, **9** But understanding is gray hair to men, || And an unspotted life is ripe old age. **10** Being found well-pleasing to God, he was loved; While living among sinners he was transported. **11** He was caught away, lest evil should change his understanding, || Or guile deceive his soul. **12** For the witchcraft of worthlessness obscures the things which are good, || And the whirl of desire perverts an innocent mind. **13** Being made perfect quickly, he filled a long time; **14** For his soul was pleasing to the Lord. Therefore, he hurried out of the midst of wickedness. **15** But as for the peoples seeing and not understanding, || They are not considering this: that grace and mercy are with His chosen, || And that He visits His holy ones. **16** But a righteous man who is dead will condemn the ungodly who are living, || And youth that is quickly perfected will condemn the many years of an unrighteous man's old age. **17** For the ungodly will see a wise man's end, || And will not understand what the Lord planned for him, and why He safely kept him. **18** They will see, and they will despise; But the Lord will laugh them to scorn. After this, they will become a dishonored carcass and a reproach among the dead forever, **19** Because He will dash them speechless to the ground || And will shake them from the foundations. They will lie utterly waste. They will be in anguish and their memory will perish. **20** They will come with cowardly fear when their sins are counted. Their lawless deeds will convict them to their face.

CHAPTER 5

1 Then the righteous man will stand in great boldness || Before the face of those who afflicted him, || And those who make his labors of no account. **2** When they see him, they will be troubled with terrible fear, || And will be amazed at the marvel of salvation. **3** They will speak among themselves converting, || And for distress of spirit they will groan, || "This was he whom we used to hold in derision, as an allegory of reproach. **4** We fools considered his life madness, and his end without honor. **5** How was he counted among sons of God? How is his lot among saints? **6** Truly we went astray from the way of truth. The light of righteousness did not shine for us. The sun did not rise for us. **7** We took our fill of the paths of lawlessness and destruction. We traveled through trackless deserts, || But we did not know the Lord's way. **8** What did our arrogance profit us? What good have riches and boasting brought us? **9** Those things all passed away as a shadow, || Like a message that runs by, **10** Like a ship passing through the billowy water, || Which, when it has gone by, there is no trace to be found, || No pathway of its keel in the billows. **11** Or it is like when a bird flies through the air [and] no evidence of its passage is found, || But the light wind, lashed with the stroke of its pinions, || And torn apart with the violent rush of the moving wings, is passed through. Afterward no sign of its coming remains. **12** Or it is like when an arrow is shot at a mark [and] the parted air closes up again immediately, || So that men do not know where it passed through. **13** So we also, as soon as we were born, ceased to be; And we had no sign of virtue to show, but we were utterly consumed in our wickedness." **14** Because the hope of the ungodly man is like chaff carried by the wind, || And as foam vanishing before a tempest; And [it] is scattered like smoke by the wind, || And passes by as the remembrance of a guest that waits but a day. ¹⁵ But the righteous live forever. Their reward is in the Lord, || And the care for them with the Most High. ¹⁶ Therefore they will receive the crown of royal dignity || And the diadem of beauty from the Lord's hand; Because He will cover them with His right hand, || And He will shield them with His arm. ¹⁷ He will take His jealousy as complete armor || And will make the whole creation His weapons to punish His enemies: ¹⁸ He will put on righteousness as a breastplate || And will wear impartial judgment as a helmet. ¹⁹ He will take holiness as an invincible shield. ²⁰ He will sharpen stern wrath for a sword. The world will go with Him to fight against His frenzied enemies. ²¹ Shafts of lightning will fly with true aim. They will leap to the mark from the clouds, as from a well-drawn bow. ²² Hailstones full of wrath will be hurled from an engine of war. The water of the sea will be angered against them. Rivers will sternly overwhelm them. ²³ A mighty blast will encounter them. It will winnow them away like a tempest. So lawlessness will make all the land desolate. Their evildoing will overturn the thrones of princes.

CHAPTER 6

¹ Hear therefore, you kings, and understand. Learn, you judge of the ends of the earth. ² Give ear, you rulers who have dominion over many people, || And [who] make your boast in multitudes of nations, ³ Because your dominion was given to you from the Lord, || And your sovereignty from the Highest. He will search out your works and will inquire about your plans; ⁴ Because, being officers of His kingdom, you did not judge rightly, || Nor did you keep law, nor did you walk according to God's counsel. ⁵ He will come on you awfully and swiftly, || Because a stern judgment comes on those who are in high places. ⁶ For the man of low estate may be pardoned in mercy, || But mighty men will be mightily tested. ⁷ For the Sovereign Lord of all will not be impressed with anyone, || Neither will He show deference to greatness; Because it is He who made both small and great, and cares about them all; ⁸ But the scrutiny that comes on the powerful is strict. ⁹ Therefore, my words are to you, O princes, || That you may learn wisdom and not fall away. ¹⁰ For those who have kept the things that are holy in holiness will be made holy. Those who have been taught them will find what to say in defense. ¹¹ Therefore set your desire on my words. Long for them, and you princes will be instructed. ¹² Wisdom is radiant and does not fade away, || And is easily seen by those who love her || And found by those who seek her. ¹³ She anticipates those who desire her, making herself known. ¹⁴ He who rises up early to seek her will not have difficulty, || For he will find her sitting at his gates. ¹⁵ For to think on her is perfection of understanding, || And he who watches for her will quickly be free from care; ¹⁶ Because she herself goes around, seeking those who are worthy of her, || And in their paths she appears to them graciously, || And in every purpose she meets them. ¹⁷ For her true beginning is desire for instruction; And desire for instruction is love. ¹⁸ And love is observance of her laws. To give heed to her laws confirms immortality. ¹⁹ Immortality brings closeness to God. ²⁰ So then, desire for wisdom promotes to a kingdom. ²¹ If, therefore, you delight in thrones and scepters—you princes of peoples—Honor wisdom, that you may reign forever. ²² But what wisdom is, and how she came into being, I will declare. I will not hide mysteries from you; But I will explore from her first beginning; [I will] bring the knowledge of her into clear light, || And I will not pass by the truth. ²³ Indeed, I will not go with consuming envy, || Because envy will have no fellowship with wisdom. ²⁴ But a multitude of wise men is salvation to the world, || And an understanding king is stability for his people. ²⁵ Therefore be instructed by my words, and you will profit.

CHAPTER 7

¹ I myself am also mortal, like everyone else, || And am a descendant of one formed first and born of the earth. ² I [was] molded into flesh in the time of ten months in my mother's womb, || Being compacted in blood from the seed of man and pleasure that came with sleep. ³ I also, when I was born, drew in the common air, and fell on the related earth, || Uttering,

like all, for my first voice, the same cry. ⁴ I was nursed with care in swaddling clothes. ⁵ For no king had any other first beginning; ⁶ But all men have one entrance into life, and a common departure. ⁷ For this reason I prayed, and understanding was given to me. I asked, and a spirit of wisdom came to me. ⁸ I preferred her before scepters and thrones. I considered riches nothing in comparison to her. ⁹ Neither did I liken to her any priceless gem, || Because all gold in her presence is a little sand, || And silver will be considered as clay before her. ¹⁰ I loved her more than health and beauty, || And I chose to have her rather than light, || Because her bright shining is never laid to sleep. ¹¹ All good things came to me with her, || And innumerable riches are in her hands. ¹² And I rejoiced over them all because wisdom leads them, || Although I did not know that she was their mother. ¹³ As I learned without guile, I impart without grudging. I do not hide her riches. ¹⁴ For she is a treasure for men that does not fail, || And those who use it obtain friendship with God, || Commended by the gifts which they present through discipline. ¹⁵ But may God grant that I may speak His judgment, || And to conceive thoughts worthy of what has been given me; Because He is one who guides even wisdom and who corrects the wise. ¹⁶ For both we and our words are in His hand, || With all understanding and skill in various crafts. ¹⁷ For He Himself gave me an unerring knowledge of the things that are, || To know the structure of the universe and the operation of the elements; ¹⁸ The beginning, end, and middle of times; The alternations of the solstices and the changes of seasons; ¹⁹ The circuits of years and the positions of stars; ²⁰ The natures of living creatures and the raging of wild beasts; The violence of winds and the thoughts of men; The diversities of plants and the virtues of roots. ²¹ All things that are either secret or manifest I learned, ²² For wisdom, that is the architect of all things, taught me. For there is a spirit in her that is quick to understand, || Holy, unique, manifold, subtle, freely moving, clear in utterance, || Unpolluted, distinct, unharmed, loving what is good, keen, unhindered, ²³ Beneficent, loving toward man, steadfast, sure, free from care, all-powerful, all-surveying, || And penetrating through all spirits that are quick to understand, pure, most subtle: ²⁴ For wisdom is more mobile than any motion. Yes, she pervades and penetrates all things by reason of her purity. ²⁵ For she is a breath of the power of God, || And a clear effluence of the glory of the Almighty. Therefore, nothing defiled can find entrance into her. ²⁶ For she is a reflection of continuous light, || An unspotted mirror of the working of God, || And an image of His goodness. ²⁷ She, being one, has power to do all things. Remaining in herself, she renews all things. From generation to generation passing into holy souls, || She makes friends of God and prophets. ²⁸ For God loves nothing as much as one who dwells with wisdom. ²⁹ For she is fairer than the sun, and above all the constellations of the stars. She is better than light. ³⁰ For daylight yields to night, but evil does not prevail against wisdom.

CHAPTER 8

¹ But she reaches from one end to the other with full strength and orders all things well. ² I loved her and sought her from my youth. I sought to take her for my bride. I became enamored by her beauty. ³ She glorifies her noble birth by living with God. The Sovereign Lord of all loves her. ⁴ For she is initiated into the knowledge of God, || And she chooses His works. ⁵ But if riches are a desired possession in life, || What is richer than wisdom, which makes all things? ⁶ And if understanding works, || Who more than wisdom is an architect of the things that exist? ⁷ If a man loves righteousness, the fruits of wisdom's labor are virtues, || For she teaches soberness, understanding, righteousness, and courage. There is nothing in life more profitable for people than these. ⁸ And if anyone longs for wide experience, || She knows the things of old, and infers the things to come. She understands subtleties of speeches and interpretations of dark sayings. She foresees signs and wonders, and the issues of seasons and times. ⁹ Therefore I determined to take her to live with me, || Knowing that she is one who would give me good counsel, || And encourage me in cares and grief. ¹⁰ Because of her, I will have glory among multitudes, || And honor in the sight of elders, though I am young. ¹¹ I will be found keen when I give judgment. I will be admired in the presence of rulers. ¹² When I am silent, they will wait for me. When I open my lips, they will heed what I say. If I continue speaking, they will put their

hands on their mouths. **13** Because of her, I will have immortality, || And leave behind a continuous memory to those who come after me. **14** I will govern peoples. Nations will be subjected to me. **15** Dreaded monarchs will fear me when they hear of me. Among the people, I will show myself to be good and courageous in war. **16** When I come into my house, I will find rest with her. For conversation with her has no bitterness, || And living with her has no pain, but gladness and joy. **17** When I considered these things in myself || And thought in my heart how immortality is in kinship to wisdom, **18** And in her friendship is good delight, || And in the labors of her hands is wealth that does not fail, || And understanding is in her companionship, || And great renown in having fellowship with her words, || I went around seeking how to take her to myself. **19** Now I was a clever child and received a good soul. **20** Or rather, being good, I came into an undefiled body. **21** But perceiving that I could not otherwise possess wisdom unless God gave her to me—Yes, and to know and understand by whom the grace is given—I pleaded with the Lord and implored Him, and with my whole heart I said:

CHAPTER 9

1 "O God of the fathers, and Lord of mercy, who made all things by Your word; **2** And by Your wisdom You formed man, that he should have dominion over the creatures that were made by You, **3** And rule the world in holiness and righteousness, and execute judgment in uprightness of soul; **4** Give me wisdom—her who sits by You on Your thrones. Do not reject me from among Your servants, **5** Because I am Your servant and the son of Your handmaid, || A weak and short-lived man, with little power to understand judgment and laws. **6** For even if a man is perfect among the sons of men, || If the wisdom that comes from You is not with him, he will count for nothing. **7** You chose me to be king of Your people, || And a judge for Your sons and daughters. **8** You gave a command to build a sanctuary on Your holy mountain, || And an altar in the city where You pitch Your tent—A copy of the holy tent which You prepared from the beginning. **9** Wisdom is with You and knows Your works, || And was present when You were making the world, || And understands what is pleasing in Your eyes, || And what is right according to Your commands. **10** Send her from the holy heavens and ask her to come from the throne of Your glory, || That being present with me she may work, || And I may learn what pleases You well. **11** For she knows all things and understands, || And she will guide me soberly in my actions. She will guard me in her glory. **12** So my works will be acceptable. I will judge Your people righteously, || And I will be worthy of my father's throne. **13** For what man will know the counsel of God? Or who will conceive what the Lord wills? **14** For the thoughts of mortals are unstable, and our plans are prone to fail. **15** For a corruptible body weighs down the soul. The earthy frame lies heavy on a mind that is full of cares. **16** We can hardly guess the things that are on earth, || And we find the things that are close at hand with labor; But who has traced out the things that are in the heavens? **17** Who gained knowledge of Your counsel, || Unless You gave wisdom, and sent Your Holy Spirit from the highest? **18** It was so that the ways of those who are on earth were corrected, || And men were taught the things that are pleasing to You. They were saved through wisdom."

CHAPTER 10

1 Wisdom guarded to the end the first formed father of the world, || Who was created alone, and delivered him out of his own transgression, **2** And gave him strength to get dominion over all things. **3** But when an unrighteous man fell away from her in his anger, || He perished himself in the rage with which he killed his brother. **4** When for his cause the earth was drowning with a flood, || Wisdom again saved it, guiding the righteous man's course by a poor piece of wood. **5** Moreover, when nations consenting together in wickedness had been confounded, || Wisdom knew the righteous man, and preserved him blameless to God, || And kept him strong when his heart yearned toward his child. **6** While the ungodly were perishing, wisdom delivered a righteous man, || When he fled from the fire that descended out of Heaven on [the] five cities— **7** To whose wickedness a smoking waste still witnesses, || And

plants bearing fair fruit that does not ripen, || A disbelieving soul has a memorial: a standing pillar of salt. **8** For having passed wisdom by, || Not only were they disabled from recognizing the things which are good, || But they also left behind them for their life a monument of their folly, || To the end that where they stumbled, they might fail even to be unseen; **9** But wisdom delivered those who waited on her out of troubles. **10** When a righteous man was a fugitive from a brother's wrath, || Wisdom guided him in straight paths. She showed him God's Kingdom and gave him knowledge of holy things. She prospered him in his toils and multiplied the fruits of his labor. **11** When in their covetousness men dealt harshly with him, || She stood by him and made him rich. **12** She guarded him from enemies, || And she kept him safe from those who lay in wait. Over his severe conflict, she watched as judge, || That he might know that godliness is more powerful than everyone. **13** When a righteous man was sold, || Wisdom did not forsake him, but she delivered him from sin. She went down with him into a dungeon, **14** And in bonds she did not depart from him, || Until she brought him the scepter of a kingdom, and authority over those that dealt unjustly with him. She also showed those who had mockingly accused him to be false and gave him continuous glory. **15** Wisdom delivered a holy people and a blameless seed from a nation of oppressors. **16** She entered into the soul of a servant of the Lord || And withstood terrible kings in wonders and signs. **17** She rendered to holy men a reward of their toils. She guided them along a marvelous way || And became to them a covering in the daytime, || And a flame of stars through the night. **18** She brought them over the Red Sea and led them through much water; **19** But she drowned their enemies, and she cast them up from the bottom of the deep. **20** Therefore the righteous plundered the ungodly, || And they sang praise to Your holy Name, O Lord, || And extolled with one accord Your hand that fought for them, **21** Because wisdom opened the mouth of the mute, || And made the tongues of babies to speak clearly.

CHAPTER 11

1 She prospered their works in the hand of a holy prophet. **2** They traveled through a desert without inhabitant, || And they pitched their tents in trackless regions. **3** They withstood enemies and repelled enemies. **4** They thirsted, and they called on You, || And water was given to them out of the flinty rock, || And healing of their thirst out of the hard stone. **5** For by what things their enemies were punished, || By these they in their need were benefited. **6** When enemies were troubled with clotted blood instead of a river's ever-flowing fountain, **7** To rebuke the decree for the slaying of babies, You gave them abundant water beyond all hope, **8** Having shown by the thirst which they had suffered how You punished the adversaries. **9** For when they were tried, although disciplined in mercy, || They learned how the ungodly were tormented, being judged with wrath. **10** For You tested these as a father admonishing them; But You searched out those as a stern king condemning them. **11** Yes, and whether they were far off or near, they were equally distressed; **12** For a double grief seized them, || And a groaning at the memory of things past. **13** For when they heard that through their own punishments the others benefited, || They recognized the Lord. **14** For him who long before was thrown out and exposed they stopped mocking. In the end of what happened, they marveled, || Having thirsted in another manner than the righteous. **15** But in return for the senseless imaginings of their unrighteousness, || Wherein they were led astray to worship irrational reptiles and wretched vermin, || You sent on them a multitude of irrational creatures for vengeance, **16** That they might learn that by what things a man sins, by these he is punished. **17** For Your all-powerful hand that created the world out of formless matter || Did not lack means to send on them a multitude of bears, fierce lions, **18** Or newly-created and unknown wild beasts, full of rage, || Either breathing out a blast of fiery breath, or belching out smoke, || Or flashing dreadful sparks from their eyes, **19** Which had power not only to consume them by their violence, || But to destroy them even by the terror of their sight. **20** Yes, and without these they might have fallen by a single breath, || Being pursued by justice, and scattered abroad by the breath of Your power; But You arranged all things by measure, number, and weight. **21** For to be greatly strong is Yours at all times. Who could withstand the might of Your arm? **22** Because the whole world before You is as a grain in a balance, || And as a drop of dew that comes down on the earth in the morning. **23** But You have mercy on all men, || Because You have power to do all things, || And You overlook the sins of men to the end that they may convert. **24** For You love all things that are || And abhor none of the things which You made; For You never would have formed anything if You hated it. **25** How would anything have endured unless You had willed it? Or that which was not called by You, how would it have been preserved? **26** But You spare all things, because they are Yours, || O Sovereign Lord—You lover of lives.

CHAPTER 12

1 For Your incorruptible Spirit is in all things— **2** Why [indeed] You convict little by little those who fall from the right way, || And, putting them in remembrance by the things wherein they sin, You admonish them, || That escaping from their wickedness they may believe in You, O Lord. **3** For truly the old inhabitants of Your holy land, **4** Hating them because they practiced detestable works of enchantments and unholy rites— **5** Merciless slaughters of children and sacrificial banquets of men's flesh and of blood— **6** Allies in an impious fellowship, and murderers of their own helpless babies, || It was Your counsel to destroy [them] by the hands of our fathers, **7** That the land which in Your sight is most precious of all might receive a worthy colony of God's servants. **8** Nevertheless, You even spared these as men, || And You sent hornets as forerunners of Your army, || To cause them to perish little by little; **9** Not that You were unable to subdue the ungodly under the hand of the righteous in battle, || Or by terrible beasts, or by a stern word to make away with them at once; **10** But judging them little by little, You gave them a chance to convert, || Not being ignorant that their nature by birth was evil, their wickedness inborn, || And that their manner of thought would never be changed. **11** For they were a cursed seed from the beginning. It was not through fear of any that You left them unpunished for their sins. **12** For who will say, "What have You done?" Or "Who will withstand Your judgment?" Who will accuse You for the perishing of nations which You caused? Or who will come and stand before You as an avenger for unrighteous men? **13** For there is not any God besides You that cares for all, || That You might show that You did not judge unrighteously. **14** No king or prince will be able to look You in the face || For those whom You have punished. **15** But being righteous, You rule all things righteously, || Deeming it a thing alien from Your power to condemn one that does not deserve to be punished. **16** For Your strength is the beginning of righteousness, || And Your sovereignty over all makes You to forbear all. **17** For when men do not believe that You are perfect in power, || You show Your strength, || And in dealing with those who think this, || You confuse their boldness. **18** But You, being sovereign over strength, || Judge in gentleness and govern us with great forbearance; For the power is Yours whenever You desire it. **19** But You taught Your people by such works as these, || How the righteous must be a lover of men. You made Your sons to have good hope, || Because You give conversion when men have sinned. **20** For if on those who were enemies of Your servants, || And due to death, You took vengeance with so great deliberation and indulgence, || Giving them times and opportunities when they might escape from their wickedness— **21** With how much greater carefulness You judged Your sons, || To whose fathers You gave oaths and covenants of good promises! **22** Therefore, while You discipline us, || You scourge our enemies ten thousand times more, || To the intent that we may ponder Your goodness when we judge, || And when we are judged may look for mercy. **23** Why also the unrighteous that lived in folly of life, || You tormented through their own abominations. **24** For truly they went very far astray in the ways of error, || Taking as gods those animals which even among their enemies were held in dishonor, || Deceived like foolish babies. **25** Therefore, as to unreasoning children, || You sent Your judgment to mock them. **26** But those who would not be admonished by a mocking correction as of children, || Will experience a judgment worthy of God. **27** For through the sufferings they were indignant of, || Being punished in these creatures which they supposed to be gods, || They saw and recognized as the true God Him whom they refused to know. Therefore, the result of condemnation also came on them.

CHAPTER 13

1 For truly all men who had no perception of God were vain by nature || And did not gain power to know Him who exists from the good things that are seen. They did not recognize the Architect from His works. **2** But they thought that either fire, or wind, or swift air, || Or circling stars, or raging water, or luminaries of the heavens were gods that rule the world. **3** If it was through delight in their beauty that they took them to be gods, || Let them know how much better their Sovereign Lord is than these, || For the first Author of beauty created them. **4** But if it was through astonishment at their power and influence, || Then let them understand from them how much more powerful He who formed them is. **5** For from the greatness of the beauty of created things, || Mankind forms the corresponding image of their Maker. **6** But yet for these men there is but small blame, || For they too perhaps go astray while they are seeking God and desiring to find Him. **7** For they diligently search while living among His works, || And they trust their sight that the things that they look at are beautiful. **8** But again even they are not to be excused. **9** For if they had power to know so much, || That they should be able to explore the world, || How is it that they did not find the Sovereign Lord sooner? **10** But they [were] miserable—And their hopes [were] in dead things—Who called them gods which are works of men's hands: Gold and silver, skillfully made, and likenesses of animals, || Or a useless stone, the work of an ancient hand; **11** Yes, and if some woodcutter, having sawn down a tree that is easily moved, || Skillfully strips away all its bark, and fashioning it in attractive form, || Makes a useful vessel to serve his life's needs. **12** Burning the scraps from his handiwork to cook his food, he eats his fill. **13** Taking a discarded scrap which served no purpose, || A crooked piece of wood and full of knots, || He carves it with the diligence of his idleness, || And shapes it by the skill of his idleness. He shapes it in the image of a man, **14** Or makes it like some paltry animal, || Smearing it with something red, || Painting it red, and smearing over every stain in it. **15** Having made a worthy chamber for it, || He sets it in a wall, securing it with iron. **16** He plans for it that it may not fall down, || Knowing that it is unable to help itself; For it is truly an image, and needs [his] help. **17** When he makes his prayer concerning goods and his marriage and children, || He is not ashamed to speak to that which has no life. **18** Yes, for health, he calls on that which is weak. For life, he implores that which is dead. For aid, he supplicates that which has no experience. For a good journey, he asks that which cannot so much as move a step. **19** And for profit in business and good success of his hands, || He asks ability from that which has hands with no ability.

CHAPTER 14

1 Again, one preparing to sail, and about to journey over raging waves, || Calls on a piece of wood more rotten than the vessel that carries him. **2** For the hunger for profit planned it, || And wisdom was the craftsman who built it. **3** Your providence, O Father, guides it along, || Because even in the sea You give a way, || And in the waves a sure path, **4** Showing that You can save out of every danger, || That even a man without skill may put to sea. **5** It is Your will that the works of Your wisdom should not be idle. Therefore, men also entrust their lives to a little piece of wood, || And passing through the surge on a raft come safely to land. **6** For in the old time also, when proud giants were perishing, || The hope of the world, taking refuge on a raft, || Your hand guided the seed of generations of the race of men. **7** For blessed is [the] wood through which comes righteousness; **8** But the idol made with hands is accursed—Itself and he that made it; Because his was the working, || And the corruptible thing was called a god; **9** For both the ungodly and his ungodliness are alike hateful to God; **10** For the deed will truly be punished together with him who committed it. **11** Therefore there will also be a visitation among the idols of the nation, || Because, though formed of things which God created, || They were made an abomination, stumbling blocks to the souls of men, || And a snare to the feet of the foolish. **12** For the devising of idols was the beginning of fornication, || And the invention of them the corruption of life. **13** For they did not exist from the beginning, || And they will not exist forever. **14** For by the vain pride of men they entered into the world, || And therefore a speedy end was planned for them. **15** For a father worn with untimely grief, making an image of the child quickly taken away. || Now honored him as a god which was then a dead man, || And delivered to those that were under him mysteries and solemn rites. **16** Afterward the ungodly custom, in process of time grown strong, was kept as a law, || And the engraved images received worship by the commands of princes. **17** And when men could not honor them in presence because they lived far off, imagining the likeness from afar, || They made a visible image of the king whom they honored, || That by their zeal they might flatter the absent as if present. **18** But worship was raised to a yet higher pitch, || Even by those who did not know him, urged forward by the ambition of the architect; **19** For he, wishing perhaps to please one in authority, || Used his art to force the likeness toward a greater beauty. **20** So the multitude, allured by reason of the grace of his handiwork, || Now consider an object of devotion him that a little while before was honored as a man. **21** And this became an ambush, because men, in bondage either to calamity or to tyranny, || Invested stones and stocks with the incommunicable Name. **22** Afterward it was not enough for them to go astray concerning the knowledge of God, || But also, while they live in a great war of ignorance, they call a multitude of evils peace. **23** For either slaughtering children in solemn rites, || Or celebrating secret mysteries, || Or holding frantic revels of strange ordinances, **24** No longer do they guard either life or purity of marriage, || But one brings on another: Either death by treachery, or anguish by adultery. **25** And all things confusedly are filled with blood and murder, || Theft and deceit, corruption, faithlessness, tumult, perjury, **26** Confusion about what is good, forgetfulness of favors, ingratitude for benefits, || Defiling of souls, confusion of sex, disorder in marriage, adultery and wantonness. **27** For the worship of idols that may not be named || Is a beginning, and cause, and end of every evil. **28** For their worshipers either make merry to madness, || Or prophesy lies, or live unrighteously, or lightly commit perjury. **29** For putting their trust in lifeless idols, when they have sworn a wicked oath, || They do not expect to suffer harm. **30** But for both, the just doom will pursue them, || Because they had evil thoughts of God by giving heed to idols || And swore unrighteously in deceit through contempt for holiness. **31** For it is not the power of them by whom men swear, || But it is the just penalty for those who sin that always visits the transgression of the unrighteous.

CHAPTER 15

1 But You, our God, are gracious and true, || Patient, and ordering all things in mercy. **2** For even if we sin, we are Yours, knowing Your dominion; But we will not sin, knowing that we have been accounted Yours. **3** For to be acquainted with You is perfect righteousness, || And to know Your dominion is the root of immortality. **4** For we were not led astray by any evil plan of men's, || Nor yet by painters' fruitless labor, a form stained with varied colors, **5** The sight of which leads fools into lust. Their desire is for the breathless form of a dead image. **6** Lovers of evil things, and worthy of such hopes, || Are those who make, desire, and worship them. **7** For a potter, kneading soft earth, laboriously molds each article for our service. He fashions out of the same clay both the vessels that minister to clean uses, || And those of a contrary sort, all in like manner. What will be the use of each article of either sort—the potter is the judge. **8** Also, laboring to an evil end, he molds a vain god out of the same clay, || He who, having but a little while before been made of earth, || After a short span goes his way to the earth out of which he was taken, || When he is required to render back the soul which was lent him. **9** However, he has anxious care, not because his powers must fail, || Nor because his span of life is short; But he compares himself with goldsmiths and silversmiths, || And he imitates molders in brass, || And esteems it glory that he molds counterfeits. **10** His heart is ashes. His hope is of less value than earth. His life is of less honor than clay; **11** Because he was ignorant of Him who molded him, || And of Him that inspired into him an active soul || And breathed into him a vital spirit. **12** But he accounted our life to be a game, || And our lifetime a festival for profit; For, he says, one must get gain however one can, even if it is by evil. **13** For this man knows that he sins beyond all others, || Making brittle vessels and graven images out of earthly matter. **14** But most foolish and more miserable than a baby, || Are the enemies of Your people, who oppressed them; **15** Because they even considered all the idols of the nations to be

gods, || Which have neither the use of eyes for seeing, nor nostrils for drawing breath, || Nor ears to hear, nor fingers for handling, and their feet are helpless for walking. **16** For a man made them, and one whose own spirit is borrowed molded them; For no one has power as a man to mold a god like to himself. **17** But, being mortal, he makes a dead thing by the work of lawless hands; For he is better than the objects of his worship, || Since he indeed had life, but they never did. **18** Yes, and they worship the creatures that are most hateful, || For, being compared as to lack of sense, these are worse than all others; **19** Neither, as seen beside other creatures, are they beautiful, so that one should desire them, || But they have escaped both the praise of God and His blessing.

CHAPTER 16

1 For this reason, they were deservedly punished through creatures like those which they worship || And tormented through a multitude of vermin. **2** Instead of this punishment, You, giving benefits to Your people, || Prepared quails for food, a delicacy to satisfy the desire of their appetite, **3** To the end that Your enemies, desiring food, || Might for the hideousness of the creatures sent among them, || Loathe even the necessary appetite; But these, Your people, having suffered lack for a short time, || Might even partake of delicacies. **4** For it was necessary that inescapable lack should come on those oppressors, || But that to these it should only be showed how their enemies were tormented. **5** For even when terrible raging of wild beasts came on Your people, || And they were perishing by the bites of crooked serpents, || Your wrath did not continue to the uttermost; **6** But for admonition they were troubled for a short time, || Having a token of salvation to put them in remembrance of the command of Your law; **7** For he who turned toward it was not saved because of that which was seen, || But because of You, the Savior of all. **8** Yes, and in this You persuaded our enemies || That You are He who delivers out of every evil. **9** For the bites of locusts and flies truly killed them. No healing for their life was found, || Because they were worthy to be punished by such things. **10** But Your children were not overcome by the very teeth of venomous dragons, || For Your mercy passed by where they were and healed them. **11** For they were bitten to put them in remembrance of Your oracles, || And were quickly saved, lest, falling into deep forgetfulness, || They should become unable to respond to Your kindness. **12** For truly it was neither herb nor mollifying plaster that cured them, || But Your word, O Lord, which heals all things. **13** For You have authority over life and death, || And You lead down to the gates of Hades and lead up again. **14** But though a man kills by his wickedness, || He cannot retrieve the spirit that has departed or release the imprisoned soul. **15** But it is not possible to escape Your hand; **16** For ungodly men, refusing to know You, || Were scourged in the strength of Your arm, || Pursued with strange rains, and hails, and relentless storms, || And utterly consumed with fire. **17** For, what was most marvelous, || In the water which quenches all things, the fire burned hotter; For the world fights for the righteous. **18** For at one time the flame lost its fierceness, || That it might not burn up the creatures sent against the ungodly, || But that these themselves as they looked might see || That they were chased through the judgment of God. **19** At another time even in the midst of water it burns above the power of fire, || That it may destroy the produce of an unrighteous land. **20** Instead of these things, You gave Your people messengers' food to eat, || And You provided ready-to-eat bread for them from Heaven without toil, || Having the virtue of every pleasant flavor, || And agreeable to every taste. **21** For Your nature showed Your sweetness toward Your children, || While that bread, serving the desire of the eater, changed itself according to every man's choice. **22** But snow and ice endured fire, and did not melt, || That people might know that fire was destroying the fruits of the enemies, || Burning in the hail and flashing in the rains; **23** And that this fire again, in order that righteous people may be nourished, || Has even forgotten its own power. **24** For the creation, ministering to You its Maker, || Strains its force against the unrighteous for punishment || And slackens it on behalf of those who trust in You, for kindness. **25** Therefore at that time also, converting itself into all forms, || It ministered to Your all-nourishing bounty, according to the desire of those who had need, **26** That Your sons, whom You loved, O Lord, || Might learn that it is not the growth of crops that nourishes a man, || But that Your word preserves those who trust You. **27**

For that which was not marred by fire, || When it was simply warmed by a faint sunbeam melted away, **28** That it might be known that we must rise before the sun to give You thanks || And must plead with You at the dawning of the light; **29** For the hope of the unthankful will melt as the winter's hoarfrost || And will flow away as water that has no use.

CHAPTER 17

1 For Your judgments are great, and hard to interpret; Therefore, undisciplined souls went astray. **2** For when lawless men had supposed that they held a holy nation in their power, || They, prisoners of darkness, and bound in the chains of a long night, || Kept close beneath their roofs, [and] lay exiled from the perpetual providence. **3** For while they thought that they were unseen in [their] secret sins, || They were divided from one another by a dark curtain of forgetfulness, || Stricken with terrible awe, and very troubled by apparitions. **4** For neither did the dark recesses that held them guard them from fears, || But terrifying sounds rang around them, || And dismal phantoms appeared with unsmiling faces. **5** And no force of fire prevailed to give light, || Neither were the brightest flames of the stars strong enough to illuminate that gloomy night; **6** But only the glimmering of a self-kindled fire appeared to them, full of fear. In terror, they considered the things which they saw || To be worse than that sight, on which they could not gaze. **7** The mockeries of their magic arts were powerless now, || And a shameful rebuke of their boasted understanding: **8** For those who promised to drive away terrors and disorders from a sick soul, || These were sick with a ludicrous fearfulness. **9** For even if no troubling thing frightened them, || Yet, scared with the creeping of vermin and hissing of serpents, **10** They perished trembling in fear, || Refusing even to look at the air, which could not be escaped on any side. **11** For wickedness, condemned by a witness within, is a cowardly thing, || And, being pressed hard by conscience, has always added forecasts of the worst. **12** For fear is nothing else but a surrender of the help which reason offers; **13** And from within, the expectation of being less || Makes of greater account the ignorance of the cause that brings the torment. **14** But they, all through the night which was powerless indeed, || And which came on them out of the recesses of powerless Hades, || Sleeping the same sleep, **15** Now were haunted by monstrous apparitions, || And now were paralyzed by their soul's surrendering; For sudden and unexpected fear came on them. **16** So then, whoever it might be, sinking down in his place, || Was kept captive, shut up in that prison which was not barred with iron; **17** For whether he was a farmer, or a shepherd, or a laborer whose toils were in the wilderness, || He was overtaken, and endured that inevitable necessity; For they were all bound with one chain of darkness. **18** Whether there was a whistling wind, || Or a melodious sound of birds among the spreading branches, || Or a measured fall of water running violently, **19** Or a harsh crashing of rocks hurled down, || Or the swift course of animals bounding along unseen, || Or the voice of wild beasts harshly roaring, || Or an echo rebounding from the hollows of the mountains, || All these things paralyzed them with terror. **20** For the whole world was illuminated with clear light, || And was occupied with unhindered works, **21** While over them alone was spread a heavy night, || An image of the darkness that should afterward receive them; But to themselves, they were heavier than darkness.

CHAPTER 18

1 But there was great light for Your holy ones. Their enemies, hearing their voice but not seeing their form, || Counted it a happy thing that they too had suffered, **2** Yet for that they do not hurt them, || Though wronged by them before, they are thankful; And because they had been at variance with them, they begged for pardon. **3** Whereas You provided a burning pillar of fire to be a guide for Your people's unknown journey, || And a harmless sun for their glorious exile. **4** For the Egyptians well deserved to be deprived of light and imprisoned by darkness, || They who had imprisoned Your children, through whom the incorruptible light of the Law was to be given to the race of men. **5** After they had taken counsel to kill the babies of the holy ones, || And when a single child had been abandoned and saved to convict them of their sin, || You took

their multitude of children away from them, || And destroyed all their army together in a mighty flood. **6** Our fathers were made aware of that night beforehand, || That, having sure knowledge, they might be cheered by the oaths which they had trusted. **7** Salvation of the righteous and destruction of the enemies was expected by Your people. **8** For as You took vengeance on the adversaries, || By the same means, calling us to Yourself, You glorified us. **9** For holy children of good men offered sacrifice in secret, || And with one consent they took on themselves the covenant of the divine law, || That they would partake alike in the same good things and the same perils, || The fathers already leading the sacred songs of praise. **10** But the discordant cry of the enemies echoed back, || And a pitiful voice of lamentation for children was spread abroad. **11** Both servant and master were punished with the same just doom, || And the commoner suffering the same as king; **12** Yes, they all together, under one form of death, had corpses without number. For the living were not even sufficient to bury them, || Since at a single stroke, their most cherished offspring was consumed. **13** For while they were disbelieving all things by reason of the enchantments, || On the destruction of the firstborn they confessed the people to be God's son. **14** For while peaceful silence wrapped all things, || And night in her own swiftness was in mid-course, **15** Your all-powerful word leapt from Heaven out of the royal thrones—A stern warrior, into the midst of the doomed land, **16** Bearing Your authentic command as a sharp sword; And standing, it filled all things with death, || And while it touched the heavens it stood on the earth. **17** Then immediately apparitions in dreams troubled them terribly, || And unexpected fears came on them. **18** And each—one thrown here half dead, another there—Made known why he was dying; **19** For the dreams, disturbing them, forewarned them of this, || That they might not perish without knowing why they were afflicted. **20** But experience of death also touched the righteous, || And a multitude were destroyed in the wilderness; However, the wrath did not last long. **21** For a blameless man hurried to be their champion, || Bringing the weapon of his own ministry: Prayer and the atoning sacrifice of incense. He withstood the indignation, and set an end to the calamity, || Showing that he was your servant. **22** And he overcame the anger, || Not by strength of body, not by force of weapons, || But he subdued him who was punishing by word, || By bringing to remembrance oaths and covenants made with the fathers. **23** For when the dead had already fallen in heaps on one another, || Standing between, he stopped the wrath, || And cut off the way to the living. **24** For the whole world was on his long robe, || And the glories of the fathers were on the engraving of the four rows of precious stones, || And Your majesty was on the diadem of his head. **25** The destroyer yielded to these, and they feared; For it was enough only to test the wrath.

CHAPTER 19

1 But indignation without mercy came on the ungodly to the end; For God also foreknew their future, **2** How, having changed their minds to let Your people go, || And having sped them eagerly on their way, || They would change their minds and pursue them. **3** For while they were yet in the midst of their mourning, || And lamenting at the graves of the dead, || They drew on themselves another counsel of folly, || And pursued as fugitives those whom they had begged to leave and driven out. **4** For the doom which they deserved was drawing them to this end, || And it made them forget the things that had happened to them, || That they might fill up the punishment which was yet lacking to their torments, **5** And that Your people might journey on by a marvelous road, || But they themselves might find a strange death. **6** For the whole creation, each part in its diverse kind, || Was made new again, complying with Your commands, || That Your servants might be kept unharmed. **7** Then the cloud that overshadowed the camp was seen, || And dry land rising up out of what had been water, || Out of the Red Sea an unhindered highway, || And a grassy plain out of the violent surge, **8** By which they passed over with all their army, || These who were covered with Your hand, having seen strange marvels. **9** For like horses they roamed at large, || And they skipped about like lambs, || Praising You, O Lord, who was their deliverer. **10** For they still remembered the things that happened in the time of their sojourning, || How instead of bearing cattle, the land brought out lice, || And instead of fish, the river spewed out a multitude of frogs. **11** But afterward, they also saw a new kind of birds, || When, led on by desire, they asked for luxurious delicacies; **12** For, to comfort them, quails came up for them from the sea. **13** Punishments came on the sinners, || Not without the signs that were given beforehand by the force of the thunders; For they justly suffered through their own wickedness, || For the hatred which they practiced toward guests was grievous indeed. **14** For whereas the others did not receive the strangers when they came to them, || The Egyptians made slaves of guests who were their benefactors. **15** And not only so, but God will visit the men of Sodom another way, || Since they received as enemies those who were aliens; **16** Whereas these first welcomed with feastings, || And then afflicted with dreadful toils—Those who had already shared with them in the same rights. **17** And moreover, they were stricken with loss of sight, || Even as were those others at the righteous man's doors, || When, being surrounded with yawning darkness, || They each looked for the passage through his own door. **18** For as the notes of a lute vary the character of the rhythm, || Even so the elements—Changing their order with one another, continuing always in its sound, || As may clearly be conjectured from the sight of the things that have happened. **19** For creatures of the dry land were turned into creatures of the waters, || And creatures that swim moved on the land. **20** Fire kept the mastery of its own power in water, || And water forgot its quenching nature. **21** On the contrary, flames did not consume flesh of perishable creatures that walked among them, || Neither did they melt the ice-like grains of ambrosial food that were apt to melt. **22** For in all things, O Lord, You magnified Your people, || And You glorified them and did not lightly regard them, || Standing by their side in every time and place.

SIRACH

Otherwise known as Ecclesiasticus

The Wisdom of Ben Sira derives its title from the author, "Yeshua [Jesus], son of Eleazar, son of Sira" (50:27). This seems to be the earliest title of the book. The designation Liber Ecclesiasticus, meaning "Church Book," appended to some Greek and Latin manuscripts, is perhaps due to the extensive use the church made of this book in presenting moral teaching to catechumens and to the faithful. The author, a sage who lived in Jerusalem, was thoroughly imbued with love for the wisdom tradition, and also for the law, priesthood, Temple, and divine worship. Written in Hebrew in the early years of the 2nd century BC, the book was finished by approximately 175.

CHAPTER 1

1 All wisdom comes from the Lord and is with Him forever. **2** Who can count the sand of the seas, || The drops of rain, and the days of [the] age? **3** Who will search out the height of the sky, || The breadth of the earth, the deep, and wisdom? **4** Wisdom has been created before all things, || And the understanding of prudence from perpetuity. **5** . . . **6** To whom has the root of wisdom been revealed? Who has known her shrewd counsels? **7** . . . **8** There is one wise, greatly to be feared, sitting on His throne: The Lord. **9** He created her. He saw and measured her. He poured her out on all His works. **10** She is with all flesh according to His gift. He gave her freely to those who love Him. **11** The fear of the Lord is glory, || Exultation, and gladness, and a crown of rejoicing. **12** The fear of the Lord will delight the heart, || And will give gladness, joy, and length of days. **13** Whoever fears the Lord, || It will go well with him at the end. He will be blessed in the day of his death. **14** To fear the Lord is the beginning of wisdom. It was created together with the faithful in the womb. **15** She laid a perpetual foundation with men. She will be trusted among their offspring. **16** To fear the Lord is the fullness of wisdom. She inebriates men with her fruits. **17** She will fill all her house with desirable things, || And her storehouses with her produce. **18** The fear of the Lord is the crown of wisdom, || Making peace and perfect health to flourish. **19** He both saw and measured her. He rained down skill and knowledge of understanding || And exalted the honor of those who hold her fast. **20** To fear the Lord is the root of wisdom. Her branches are length of days. **21** . . . **22** Unjust wrath

can never be justified, || For the sway of his wrath is his downfall. **23** A man that is patient will resist for a season, || And afterward gladness will spring up to him. **24** He will hide his words for a season, || And the lips of many will tell of his understanding. **25** An allegory of knowledge is in the treasures of wisdom; But godliness is an abomination to a sinner. **26** If you desire wisdom, keep the commands || And the Lord will give her to you freely; **27** For the fear of the Lord is wisdom and instruction. Faith and humility are His good pleasure. **28** Do not disobey the fear of the Lord. Do not come to Him with a double heart. **29** Do not be a hypocrite in the mouths of men. Keep watch over your lips. **30** Do not exalt yourself, || Lest you fall and bring dishonor on your soul. The Lord will reveal your secrets || And will cast you down in the midst of the congregation, || Because you did not come to the fear of the Lord || And your heart was full of deceit.

CHAPTER 2

1 My son, if you come to serve the Lord, || Prepare your soul for temptation. **2** Set your heart correctly, || Constantly endure, || And do not hurry in time of calamity. **3** Cling to Him, and do not depart, || That you may be increased at your latter end. **4** Accept whatever is brought on you || And be patient when you suffer humiliation. **5** For gold is tried in the fire, || And acceptable men in the furnace of humiliation. **6** Put your trust in Him, || And He will help you. Make your ways straight || And set your hope on Him. **7** All you who fear the Lord, || Wait for His mercy. Do not turn aside, lest you fall. **8** All you who fear the Lord, || Put your trust in Him, || And your reward will not fail. **9** All you who fear the Lord, || Hope for good things, || And for continuous gladness and mercy. **10** Look at the generations of old, and see: Who ever put his trust in the Lord, and was ashamed? Or who remained in His fear, and was forsaken? Or who called on Him, and He despised him? **11** For the Lord is full of compassion and mercy. He forgives sins and saves in time of affliction. **12** Woe to fearful hearts, to faint hands, || And to the sinner that goes two ways! **13** Woe to the faint heart! For it does not believe. Therefore, it will not be defended. **14** Woe to you who have lost your patience! And what will you all do when the Lord visits you? **15** Those who fear the Lord will not disobey His words. Those who love Him will keep His ways. **16** Those who fear the Lord will seek His good pleasure. Those who love Him will be filled with the Law. **17** Those who fear the Lord will prepare their hearts || And will humble their souls in His sight. **18** We will fall into the hands of the Lord, || And not into the hands of men; For as His majesty is, so also is His mercy.

CHAPTER 3

1 Hear me, your father, O my children, || And do what you hear, that you all may be saved. **2** For the Lord has given the father glory concerning the children || And has confirmed the judgment of the mother concerning the sons. **3** He who honors his father will make atonement for sins. **4** He that gives glory to his mother is as one who lays up treasure. **5** Whoever honors his father will have joy in his own children. He will be heard in the day of his prayer. **6** He who gives glory to his father will have length of days. He who listens to the Lord will bring rest to his mother, **7** And will serve under his parents, as to masters. **8** Honor your father in deed and word, || That a blessing may come on you from him. **9** For the blessing of the father establishes the houses of children, || But the curse of the mother roots out the foundations. **10** Do not glorify yourself in the dishonor of your father, || For your father's dishonor is no glory to you. **11** For the glory of a man is from the honor of his father, || And a mother in dishonor is a reproach to her children. **12** My son, help your father in his old age, || And do not grieve him as long as he lives. **13** If he fails in understanding, have patience with him. Do not dishonor him in your full strength. **14** For the relieving of your father will not be forgotten. Instead of sins it will be added to build you up. **15** In the day of your affliction it will remember you; As fair weather on ice, so will your sins also melt away. **16** He who forsakes his father is as a blasphemer. He who provokes his mother is cursed by the Lord. **17** My son, go on with your business in humility; So you will be loved by an acceptable man. **18** The greater you are, humble yourself [all] the more, || And you will find favor before the Lord. **19** . . . **20** For the power of the Lord is great, || And He is glorified by those who are lowly. **21** Do not seek things that are too hard for you, || And do not search out things that are above your strength. **22** Think about the things that have been commanded you, || For you have no need of the things that are secret. **23** Do not be overly busy in your superfluous works, || For more things are showed to you than men can understand. **24** For the conceit of many has led them astray. Evil opinion has caused their judgment to slip. **25** There is no light without eyes. There is no wisdom without knowledge. **26** A stubborn heart will do badly at the end. He who loves danger will perish in it. **27** A stubborn heart will be burdened with troubles. The sinner will heap sin on sins. **28** The calamity of the proud is no healing, || For a weed of wickedness has taken root in him. **29** The heart of the prudent will understand an allegory. A wise man desires the ear of a listener. **30** Water will quench a flaming fire; Kindness will make atonement for sins. **31** He who repays with kind acts is mindful of that which comes afterward. In the time of his falling, he will find a support.

CHAPTER 4

1 My son, do not deprive the poor of his living. Do not make the needy eyes wait long. **2** Do not make a hungry soul sorrowful || Or provoke a man in his distress. **3** Do not add more trouble to a heart that is provoked. Do not put off giving to him who is in need. **4** Do not reject a suppliant in his affliction. Do not turn your face away from a poor man. **5** Do not turn your eye away from one who asks. Give no occasion to a man to curse you. **6** For if he curses you in the bitterness of his soul, || He who made him will hear his supplication. **7** Endear yourself to the assembly. Bow your head to a great man. **8** Incline your ear to a poor man. Answer him with peaceful words in humility. **9** Deliver him who is wronged from the hand of him that wrongs him; Do not be faint-hearted in giving judgment. **10** Be as a father to the fatherless, || And like a husband to their mother. So you will be as a son of the Most High, || And He will love you more than your mother does. **11** Wisdom exalts her sons || And takes hold of those who seek her. **12** He who loves her loves life. Those who seek her early will be filled with gladness. **13** He who holds her fast will inherit glory. Where he enters, the Lord will bless. **14** Those who serve her minister to the Holy One. The Lord loves those who love her. **15** He who gives ear to her will judge the nations. He who heeds her will dwell securely. **16** If he trusts her, he will inherit her, || And his generations will possess her. **17** For at the first she will walk with him in crooked ways, || And will bring fear and dread on him, || And torment him with her discipline, || Until she may trust his soul, and try him by her judgments. **18** Then she will return him again to the straight way, || And will gladden him, and reveal to him her secrets. **19** If he goes astray, she will forsake him, || And hand him over to his fall. **20** Observe the opportunity and beware of evil. Do not be ashamed of your soul. **21** For there is a shame that brings sin, || And there is a shame that is glory and grace. **22** Do not show partiality against your soul. Do not revere any man to your falling. **23** Do not refrain from speaking when it is for safety. Do not hide your wisdom for the sake of seeming fair. **24** For wisdom will be known by speech, || And instruction by the word of the tongue. **25** Do not speak against the truth and be shamed for your ignorance. **26** Do not be ashamed to confess your sins. Do not fight the river's current. **27** Do not lay yourself down for a fool to tread on. Do not be partial to one that is mighty. **28** Strive for the truth to death, || And the Lord God will fight for you. **29** Do not be hasty with your tongue, || Or slack and negligent in your deeds. **30** Do not be like a lion in your house, || Or suspicious of your servants. **31** Do not let your hand be stretched out to receive || And closed when you should repay.

CHAPTER 5

1 Do not set your heart on your goods. Do not say, "They are sufficient for me." **2** Do not follow your own mind and your strength || To walk in the desires of your heart. **3** Do not say, "Who will have dominion over me?" For the Lord will surely take vengeance on you. **4** Do not say, "I sinned, and what happened to me?" For the Lord is patient. **5** Do not be so confident of atonement that you add sin on sins. **6** Do not say, "His compassion is great. He will be pacified for the multitude of my sins," || For mercy and wrath are with Him, || And His indignation will rest on sinners. **7** Do not wait to turn to the Lord. Do not put off from day to day; For the wrath of the Lord will suddenly come on you, || And you will perish in the time of vengeance. **8** Do not set your heart on unrighteous gains, || For you will profit nothing in the day of calamity. **9** Do not winnow with every wind. Do not walk in every path. This is what the sinner who has a double tongue does. **10** Be steadfast in your understanding. Let your speech be consistent. **11** Be swift to hear and answer with patience. **12** If you have understanding, answer your neighbor; But if not, put your hand over your mouth. **13** Glory and dishonor is in talk. A man's tongue may be his downfall. **14** Do not be called a whisperer. Do not lie in wait with your tongue; For shame is on the thief, || And an evil condemnation is on him who has a double tongue. **15** Do not be ignorant in a great or small matter.

CHAPTER 6

1 Do not become an enemy instead of a friend; For an evil name will inherit shame and reproach. So it is with the sinner who has a double tongue. **2** Do not exalt yourself in the counsel of your soul, || That your soul is not torn in pieces as a bull. **3** You will eat up your leaves, destroy your fruit, || And leave yourself as a dry tree. **4** A wicked soul will destroy him who has it || And will make him a laughing-stock to his enemies. **5** Sweet words will multiply a man's friends. A gracious tongue will multiply courtesies. **6** Let those that are at peace with you be many, || But your advisers one of one thousand. **7** If you want to gain a friend, get him in a time of testing, || And do not be in a hurry to trust him. **8** For there is a friend just for an occasion. He will not continue in the day of your affliction. **9** And there is a friend who turns into an enemy. He will discover strife to your reproach. **10** And there is a friend who is a companion at the table, || But he will not continue in the day of your affliction. **11** In your prosperity he will be as yourself || And will be bold over your servants. **12** If you are brought low, he will be against you, || And will hide himself from your face. **13** Separate yourself from your enemies and beware of your friends. **14** A faithful friend is a strong defense. He who has found him has found a treasure. **15** There is nothing that can be taken in exchange for a faithful friend. His excellency is beyond price. **16** A faithful friend is a life-saving medicine. Those who fear the Lord will find Him. **17** He who fears the Lord directs his friendship properly; For as he is, so is his neighbor also. **18** My son, gather instruction from your youth up. Even when you have gray hair you will find wisdom. **19** Come to her as one who plows and sows || And wait for her good fruit; For your toil will be little in her tillage, || And you will soon eat of her fruit. **20** How exceedingly harsh she is to the unlearned! He who is without understanding will not remain in her. **21** She will rest on him as a mighty stone of trial. He will not hesitate to cast her from him. **22** For wisdom is according to her name. She is not manifest to many. **23** Give ear, my son, and accept my judgment. Do not refuse my counsel. **24** Bring your feet into her chains, || And your neck into her chain. **25** Put your shoulder under her and bear her. Do not be grieved with her bonds. **26** Come to her with all your soul. Keep her ways with your whole power. **27** Search and seek, and she will be made known to you. When you get hold of her, do not let her go. **28** For at the end you will find her rest; And she will be turned into gladness for you. **29** Her chains will be to you for a covering of strength, || And her chains for a robe of glory. **30** For there is a golden ornament on her, || And her bonds [are] a purple ribbon. **31** You will put her on as a robe of glory || And will put her on as a crown of rejoicing. **32** My son, if you are willing, you will be instructed. If you will yield your soul, you will be prudent. **33** If you love to hear, you will receive. If you incline your ear, you will be wise. **34** Stand in the multitude of the elders. Attach yourself to whoever is wise. **35** Be willing to listen to every godly discourse. Do not let the proverbs of understanding escape you. **36** If you see a man of understanding, get to him early. Let your foot wear out the steps of his doors. **37** Let your mind dwell on the ordinances of the Lord || And meditate continually on His commands. He will establish your heart || And your desire for wisdom will be given to you.

CHAPTER 7

1 Do no evil, so no evil will overtake you. **2** Depart from wrong, and it will turn away from you. **3** My son, do not sow on the furrows of unrighteousness, || And you will not reap them sevenfold. **4** Do not seek preeminence from the Lord, || Nor the seat of honor from the king. **5** Do not justify yourself in the presence of the Lord, || And do not display your wisdom before the king. **6** Do not seek to be a judge, || Lest you not be able to take away iniquities, || Lest perhaps you fear the person of a mighty man || And lay a stumbling block in the way of your uprightness. **7** Do not sin against the multitude of the city. Do not cast yourself down in the crowd. **8** Do not commit a sin twice, || For even in one you will not be unpunished. **9** Do not say, "He will look on the multitude of my gifts. When I make an offering to the Highest God, He will accept it." **10** Do not be faint-hearted in your prayer. Do not neglect to give alms. **11** Do not laugh a man to scorn when he is in the bitterness of his soul, || For there is one who humbles and exalts. **12** Do not devise a lie against your brother or do the same to a friend. **13** Do not love to make any manner of lie, for that is not a good habit. **14** Do not babble in the multitude of elders. Do not repeat your words in your prayer. **15** Do not hate hard labor or farm work, which the Most High has created. **16** Do not number yourself among the multitude of sinners. Remember that wrath will not wait. **17** Humble your soul greatly, || For the punishment of the ungodly man is fire and the worm. **18** Do not exchange a friend for something, || Neither a true brother for the gold of Ophir. **19** Do not deprive yourself of a wise and good wife, || For her grace is worth more than gold. **20** Do not abuse a servant who works faithfully, || Or a hireling who gives you his life. **21** Let your soul love a wise servant. Do not defraud him of liberty. **22** Do you have cattle? Look after them. If they are profitable to you, let them stay by you. **23** Do you have children? Correct them and bow their necks from their youth. **24** Do you have daughters? Take care of their bodies, || And do not be overly indulgent toward them. **25** Give your daughter in marriage, || And you will have accomplished a great matter. Give her to a man of understanding. **26** Do you have a wife after your mind? Do not cast her out. But do not entrust yourself to one who is hateful. **27** Give glory to your father with your whole heart, || And do not forget the birth pangs of your mother. **28** Remember that you were born of them. What will you repay them for the things that they have done for you? **29** Fear the Lord with all your soul; Also revere His priests. **30** With all your strength love Him who made you. Do not forsake His ministers. **31** Fear the Lord and honor the priest. Give him his portion, even as it is commanded you: The first-fruits, the trespass offering, the gift of the shoulders, || The sacrifice of sanctification, and the first-fruits of holy things. **32** Also stretch out your hand to the poor man, || That your blessing may be perfected. **33** A gift has grace in the sight of every living man. Do not withhold grace for a dead man. **34** Do not be lacking to those who weep, || And mourn with those who mourn. **35** Do not be slow to visit a sick man, || For by such things you will gain love. **36** In all your words, remember eternity, || And you will never sin.

CHAPTER 8

1 Do not contend with a mighty man, lest perhaps you fall into his hands. **2** Do not strive with a rich man, lest perhaps he overpowers you; For gold has destroyed many and turned away the hearts of kings. **3** Do not contend with a talkative man. Do not heap wood on his fire. **4** Do not jest with a rude man, lest your ancestors be dishonored. **5** Do not reproach a man when he turns from sin. Remember that we are all worthy of punishment. **6** Do not dishonor a man in his old age; For some of us are also growing old. **7** Do not rejoice over one who is dead. Remember that we all die. **8** Do not neglect the discourse of the wise. Be conversant with their proverbs; For from them you will learn instruction || And how to minister to great men. **9** Do not miss the discourse of the aged, || For they also learned from their fathers, || Because from them you will learn understanding, || And [how] to give an answer in time of need. **10** Do not kindle the coals of a sinner, || Lest you be burned with the flame of his fire. **11** Do not rise up from the presence of an insolent man, || Lest he lie in wait as an ambush for your mouth. **12** Do not lend to a man who is mightier than yourself; And if you lend, be as one who has lost. **13** Do not be

a guarantee above your power. If you are a guarantee, think as one who will have to pay. **14** Do not go to law with a judge; For according to his honor they will give judgment for him. **15** Do not go in the way with a rash man, || Lest he be burdensome to you; For he will do according to his own will, || And you will perish with his folly. **16** Do not fight with a wrathful man. Do not travel with him through the desert, || For blood is as nothing in his sight. Where there is no help, he will overthrow you. **17** Do not take counsel with a fool, || For he will not be able to conceal the matter. **18** Do no secret thing before a stranger, || For you do not know what it will cause. **19** Do not open your heart to every man. Do not let him return you a favor.

CHAPTER 9

1 Do not be jealous over the wife of your bosom, || And do not teach her an evil lesson against yourself. **2** Do not give your soul to a woman, || That she should set her foot on your strength. **3** Do not go to meet a woman who plays the prostitute, || Lest perhaps you fall into her snares. **4** Do not use the company of a woman who is a singer, || Lest perhaps you be caught by her attempts. **5** Do not gaze at a maid, || Lest perhaps you be trapped in her penalties. **6** Do not give your soul to prostitutes, || That you may not lose your inheritance. **7** Do not look around you in the streets of the city, || Neither wander in its solitary places. **8** Turn your eye away from a beautiful woman, || And do not gaze at another's beauty. Many have been led astray by the beauty of a woman; And with this, affection is kindled as a fire. **9** Do not sit at all with a woman who has a husband, || Or revel with her at the wine, || Lest perhaps your soul turns away to her, || And with your spirit you slide into destruction. **10** Do not forsake an old friend; For the new one is not comparable to him. A new friend is like new wine: If it becomes old, you will drink it with gladness. **11** Do not envy the glory of a sinner; For you do not know what his overthrow will be. **12** Do not delight in the delights of the ungodly. Remember, they will not go to the grave unpunished. **13** Keep yourself far from the man who has power to kill, || And you will have no suspicion of the fear of death. If you come to him, commit no fault, || Lest he takes your life away. Surely know that you go about in the midst of snares || And walk on the battlements of a city. **14** As well as you can, aim to know your neighbors, || And take counsel with the wise. **15** Let your conversation be with men of understanding. Let all your discourse be in the Law of the Most High. **16** Let just men be companions at your table. Let your glorying be in the fear of the Lord. **17** A work is commended because of the hand of the artisan; So he who rules the people will be considered wise for his speech. **18** A talkative man is dangerous in his city. He who is headlong in his speech will be hated.

CHAPTER 10

1 A wise judge will instruct his people. The government of a man of understanding will be well ordered. **2** As is the judge of his people, || So are his ministers. As the city's ruler is, || So are all those who dwell in it. **3** An uninstructed king will destroy his people. A city will be established through the understanding of the powerful. **4** The authority of the earth is in the Lord's hand. In due time, He will raise up over it one who is profitable. **5** A man's prosperity is in the Lord's hand. He will lay his honor on the person of the scribe. **6** Do not be angry with your neighbor for every wrong. Do nothing by works of violence. **7** Pride is hateful before the Lord and men. Unrighteousness is abhorrent in the judgment of both. **8** Sovereignty is transferred from nation to nation || Because of iniquities, deeds of violence, and greed for money. **9** Why are dirt and ashes proud? Because in life, my body decays. **10** A long disease mocks the physician. He is a king today, and tomorrow he will die. **11** For when a man is dead, || He will inherit creeping things, and beasts, and worms. **12** It is the beginning of pride when a man departs from the Lord. His heart has departed from Him who made him. **13** For the beginning of pride is sin. He who keeps it will pour out abomination. For this reason, the Lord brought strange calamities on them || And utterly overthrew them. **14** The Lord cast down the thrones of rulers || And set the meek in their place. **15** The Lord plucked up the roots of nations || And planted the lowly in their place.

16 The Lord overthrew the lands of nations || And destroyed them to the foundations of the earth. **17** He took some of them away || And destroyed them and made their memorial to cease from the earth. **18** Pride has not been created for men, || Nor wrathful anger for the offspring of women. **19** What manner of seed has honor? The seed of man, those who fear the Lord. What manner of seed has no honor? The seed of man, those who transgress the commands. **20** In the midst of countrymen he who rules them has honor. Those who fear the Lord have honor in his eyes. **21** . . . **22** The rich man, the honorable, and the poor || All glory in the fear of the Lord. **23** It is not right to dishonor a poor man who has understanding. It is not fitting to glorify a man who is a sinner. **24** The great man, the judge, and the mighty man will be glorified. There is not one of them greater than he who fears the Lord. **25** Free men will minister to a wise servant. A man who has knowledge will not complain. **26** Do not flaunt your wisdom in doing your work. Do not glorify yourself in the time of your distress. **27** Better is he who labors and abounds in all things, || Than he who glorifies himself and lacks bread. **28** My son, glorify your soul in humility, || And esteem yourself honor according to your true worth. **29** Who will justify him who sins against his own soul? Who will glorify him who dishonors his own life? **30** A poor man is glorified for his knowledge. A rich man is glorified for his riches. **31** But he who is glorified in poverty, how much more in riches? He who is dishonored in riches, how much more in poverty?

CHAPTER 11

1 The wisdom of the lowly will lift up his head || And make him sit in the midst of great men. **2** Do not commend a man for his beauty. Do not abhor a man for his outward appearance. **3** The bee is little among flying creatures, || But what it produces is the best of confections. **4** Do not boast about the clothes you wear, || And do not exalt yourself in the day of honor; For the Lord's works are wonderful, || And His works are hidden among men. **5** Many kings have sat down on the ground, || But one who was never thought of has worn a crown. **6** Many mighty men have been greatly disgraced. Men of renown have been delivered into other men's hands. **7** Do not blame before you investigate. Understand first, and then rebuke. **8** Do not answer before you have heard. Do not interrupt while someone else is speaking. **9** Do not argue about a matter that does not concern you. Do not sit with sinners when they judge. **10** My son, do not be busy about many matters; For if you meddle much, || You will not be unpunished. If you pursue, you will not overtake, || And you will not escape by fleeing. **11** There is one who toils, labors, and makes haste, || And is even more behind. **12** There is one who is sluggish, and needs help, lacking in strength, and who abounds in poverty, || But the Lord's eyes looked on him for good, || And He raised him up from his low condition, **13** And lifted up his head so that many marveled at him. **14** Good things and evil, life and death, || Poverty and riches, are from the Lord. **15** . . . **16** . . . **17** The Lord's gift remains with the godly. His good pleasure will prosper forever. **18** One grows rich by his diligence and self-denial, || And this is the portion of his reward: **19** When he says, "I have found rest, and now I will eat of my goods!" He does not know how much time will pass || Until he leaves them to others and dies. **20** Be steadfast in your covenant || And be doing it and grow old in your work. **21** Do not marvel at the works of a sinner, || But trust the Lord and stay in your labor; For it is an easy thing in the sight of the Lord || To swiftly and suddenly make a poor man rich. **22** The Lord's blessing is in the reward of the godly. He makes his blessing flourish in an hour that comes swiftly. **23** Do not say, "What use is there of me? What further good things can be mine?" **24** Do not say, "I have enough. What harm could happen to me now?" **25** In the day of good things, || Evil things are forgotten. In the day of evil things, || A man will not remember things that are good. **26** For it is an easy thing in the sight of the Lord || To reward a man in the day of death according to his ways. **27** The affliction of an hour causes delights to be forgotten. In the end, a man's deeds are revealed. **28** Call no man happy before his death. A man will be known in his children. **29** Do not bring every man into your house, || For many are the plots of a deceitful man. **30** Like a decoy partridge in a cage, || So is the heart of a proud man. Like a spy, he looks for your weakness. **31** For he lies in wait to turn things that are good into evil || And assigns blame in things that are praiseworthy. **32** From a spark of fire, a heap of many coals is kindled, || And a sinful man lies in wait for blood. **33** Take heed of an evildoer, for he plans wicked things, || Lest perhaps he ruins your reputation forever. **34** Receive a stranger into your house, || And he will distract you with arguments and estrange you from your own.

CHAPTER 12

1 If you do good, know to whom you do it, || And your good deeds will have thanks. **2** Do good to a godly man, and you will find a reward—If not from him, then from the Highest. **3** No good will come to him who continues to do evil, || Nor to him who gives no alms. **4** Give to the godly man, || And do not help the sinner. **5** Do good to one who is lowly. Do not give to an ungodly man. Keep back his bread, and do not give it to him, || Lest he subdue you with it; For you would receive twice as much evil || For all the good you would have done to him. **6** For the Most High also hates sinners || And will repay vengeance to the ungodly. **7** Give to the good man, and do not help the sinner. **8** A man's friend will not be fully tried in prosperity. His enemy will not be hidden in adversity. **9** In a man's prosperity, his enemies are grieved. In his adversity, even his friend leaves. **10** Never trust your enemy, || For his wickedness is like corrosion in copper. **11** Though he humbles himself and walks bowed down, || Still be careful and beware of him. You will be to him as one who has wiped a mirror, || To be sure it does not completely tarnish. **12** Do not set him next to you, || Lest he overthrow you and stand in your place. Do not let him sit on your right hand, || Lest he seek to take your seat, || And at the last you acknowledge my words, || And be pricked with my sayings. **13** Who will pity a charmer that is bitten by a snake, || Or any who come near wild beasts? **14** Even so, who will pity him who goes to a sinner, || And is associated with him in his sins? **15** For a while he will stay with you, || And if you falter, he will not stay. **16** The enemy will speak sweetly with his lips, || And in his heart plan to throw you into a pit. The enemy may weep with his eyes, || But if he finds opportunity, he will want more blood. **17** If adversity meets you, || You will find him there before you. Pretending to help you, he will trip you. **18** He will shake his head, clap his hands, || Whisper much, and change his countenance.

CHAPTER 13

1 He who touches pitch will be defiled. He who has fellowship with a proud man will become like him. **2** Do not take up a burden above your strength. Have no fellowship with one who is mightier and richer than yourself. What fellowship would the earthen pot have with the kettle? The kettle will strike, || And the pot will be dashed in pieces. **3** The rich man does a wrong and threatens. The poor is wronged and apologizes. **4** If you are profitable, || He will make merchandise of you. If you are in lack, || He will forsake you. **5** If you own something, || He will live with you. He will drain you bare and will not be sorry. **6** Does he need you? Then he will deceive you, || Smile at you, and give you hope. He will speak kindly to you and say, "What do you need?" **7** He will shame you by his meats || Until he has made you bare twice or three times, || And in the end he will laugh you to scorn. Afterward he will see you, || Will forsake you, and shake his head at you. **8** Beware that you are not deceived || And brought low in your mirth. **9** If a mighty man invites you, be reserved, || And he will invite you more. **10** Do not press him, lest you be thrust back. Do not stand far off, lest you be forgotten. **11** Do not try to speak with him as an equal, || And do not believe his many words; For he will test you with much talk || And will examine you in a smiling manner. **12** He who does not keep secrets to himself is unmerciful. He will not hesitate to harm and to bind. **13** Keep them to yourself and be careful, || For you walk in danger of falling. **14** . . . **15** Every living creature loves its own kind, || And every man loves his neighbor. **16** All flesh associates with their own kind. A man will stick to people like himself. **17** What fellowships would the wolf have with the lamb? So is the sinner to the godly. **18** What peace is there between a hyena and a dog? What peace is there between a rich man and the poor? **19** Wild donkeys are the prey of lions in the wilderness; Likewise, poor men are feeding grounds for the rich. **20** Lowliness is an abomination to a proud man; Likewise, a poor man is an abomination to the rich. **21** When a rich man is shaken, || He is supported by his friends, || But when one of low degree is down, || He is pushed away even by his friends. **22** When a rich man falls, there are many helpers. He speaks things not to be spoken, || And men justify him. A man of low degree falls, and men rebuke him. He utters wisdom and is not listened to. **23** A rich man speaks, and all keep silence. They extol what he says to the clouds. A poor man speaks, and they say, "Who is this?" If he stumbles, they will help to overthrow him. **24** Riches are good if they have no sin. Poverty is evil in the mouth of the ungodly. **25** The heart of a man changes his countenance, || Whether it is for good or for evil. **26** A cheerful countenance is a sign of a prosperous heart. Devising proverbs takes strenuous thinking.

CHAPTER 14

1 Blessed is the man who has not slipped with his mouth || And does not suffer from sorrow for sins. **2** Blessed is he whose soul does not condemn him, || And who has not given up hope. **3** Riches are not appropriate for a stingy person. What would an envious man do with money? **4** He who gathers by denying himself gathers for others. Others will revel in his goods. **5** If one is mean to himself, || To whom will he be good? He will not enjoy his possessions. **6** There is none more evil than he who is stingy with himself. This is a punishment for his wickedness. **7** Even if he does good, he does it in forgetfulness. In the end, he reveals his wickedness. **8** A miser is evil. He turns away and disregards souls. **9** A covetous man's eye is not satisfied with his portion. Wicked injustice dries up his soul. **10** A miser begrudges bread, || And it is lacking at his table. **11** My son, according to what you have, treat yourself well, || And bring worthy offerings to the Lord. **12** Remember that death will not wait, || And that the covenant of Hades has not been shown to you. **13** Do good to your friend before you die. According to your ability, reach out and give to him. **14** Do not defraud yourself of a good day. Do not let the portion of a good desire pass you by. **15** Will you not leave your labors to another, || And your toils be divided by lot? **16** Give, take, and treat yourself well, || Because there is no seeking of luxury in Hades. **17** All flesh grows old like a garment, || For the covenant from the beginning is, "You must die." **18** Like the leaves flourishing on a thick tree—Some it sheds, and some grow—So also are the generations of flesh and blood: One comes to an end and another is born. **19** Every work rots and falls away, || And its builder will depart with it. **20** Blessed is the man who meditates on wisdom, || And who reasons by his understanding. **21** He who considers her ways in his heart || Will also have knowledge of her secrets. **22** Go after her like one who tracks || And lie in wait in her ways. **23** He who pries in at her windows || Will also listen at her doors. **24** He who lodges close to her house || Will also fasten a nail in her walls. **25** He will pitch his tent near at hand to her || And will lodge in a lodging where good things are. **26** He will set his children under her shelter || And will rest under her branches. **27** By her he will be covered from heat || And will lodge in her glory.

CHAPTER 15

1 He who fears the Lord will do this. He who has possession of the Law will obtain her. **2** As a mother, she will meet him || And receive him as a wife married in her virginity. **3** She will feed him with bread of understanding || And give him water of wisdom to drink. **4** He will be stayed on her and will not be moved. He will rely on her and will not be confounded. **5** She will exalt him above his neighbors. She will open his mouth in the midst of the congregation. **6** He will inherit joy, a crown of gladness, and a perpetual name. **7** Foolish men will not obtain her. Sinners will not see her. **8** She is far from pride. Liars will not remember her. **9** Praise is not attractive in the mouth of a sinner; For it was not sent to him from the Lord. **10** For praise will be spoken in wisdom; The Lord will prosper it. **11** Do not say, "It is through the Lord that I fell away"; For you will not do the things that He hates. **12** Do not say, "It is He that caused me to err"; For He has no need of a sinful man. **13** The Lord hates every abomination; And those who fear Him do not love them. **14** He Himself made man from the beginning || And left him in the hand of his own counsel. **15** If you will, you will keep the commands. To be faithful is good pleasure. **16** He has set fire and water before you. You will stretch out your hand to whichever you desire. **17** Before man is life and death.

Whichever he likes, it will be given to him. **18** For great is the wisdom of the Lord. He is mighty in power and sees all things. **19** His eyes are on those who fear Him. He knows every work of man. **20** He has not commanded any man to be ungodly. He has not given any man license to sin.

CHAPTER 16

1 Do not desire a multitude of unprofitable children, || Neither delight in ungodly sons. **2** If they multiply, do not delight in them || Unless the fear of the Lord is in them. **3** Do not trust in their life. Do not rely on their condition. For one is better than one thousand, || And to die childless than to have ungodly children. **4** For from one who has understanding, a city will be populated, || But a race of wicked men will be made desolate. **5** I have seen many such things with my eyes. My ear has heard mightier things than these. **6** In the congregation of sinners, a fire will be kindled. In a disobedient nation, wrath is kindled. **7** He was not pacified toward the giants of ancient time, || Who revolted in their strength. **8** He did not spare Lot's neighbors, || Whom He abhorred for their pride. **9** He did not pity the people of perdition || Who were taken away in their sins, **10** Or in like manner, the six hundred thousand footmen || Who were gathered together in the hardness of their hearts. **11** Even if there is one stiff-necked person, || It is a marvel if he will be unpunished, || For mercy and wrath are both with Him who is mighty to forgive, || And He pours out wrath. **12** As His mercy is great, || So is His correction also. He judges a man according to his works. **13** The sinner will not escape with plunder. The perseverance of the godly will not be frustrated. **14** He will make room for every work of mercy. Each man will receive according to his works. **15** The Lord made the king of Egypt so stubborn || That he would not acknowledge the Lord, || In order that the world might know the Lord's works. **16** He shows His mercy to all creation; He has divided His light from darkness with a plumb line. **17** Do not say, "I will be hidden from the Lord," || And "Who will remember me from on high?" I will not be known among so many people, || For what is my soul in a boundless creation? **18** Behold, the Heaven—the Heaven of heavens—The deep, and the earth, will be moved when He visits. **19** The mountains and the foundations of the earth together || Are shaken with trembling when He looks at them. **20** No heart will think about these things. Who could comprehend His ways? **21** Like a tempest which no man can see, || Yes, the majority of His works are hidden. **22** Who will declare His works of righteousness? Who will endure them? For His covenant is far off. **23** He who is lacking in understanding thinks about these things. An unwise and erring man thinks follies. **24** My son, listen to me, learn knowledge, || And heed my words with your heart. **25** I will impart instruction with precision || And declare knowledge exactly. **26** In the judgment of the Lord are His works from the beginning. From the making of them He determined their parts. **27** He arranged His works for all time, || And their beginnings to their generations. They are not hungry or weary, || And they do not cease from their works. **28** No one thrusts aside his neighbor. They will never disobey His word. **29** After this the Lord also looked at the earth || And filled it with His blessings. **30** All manner of living things covered its face, || And into it is their return.

CHAPTER 17

1 The Lord created mankind out of the earth || And turned them back to it again. **2** He gave them days by number, and a set time, || And gave them authority over the things that are on it. **3** He endowed them with strength appropriate for them || And made them according to His own image. **4** He put the fear of man on all flesh || And gave him dominion over beasts and birds. **5** The Lord gave them the five senses, || But He also gave them a sixth—intelligence, || And a seventh—reason, || Which enables them to interpret what comes to them through the senses. **6** He gave them counsel, tongue, eyes, ears, || And heart to have understanding. **7** He filled them with the knowledge of wisdom || And showed them good and evil. **8** He set His eye on their hearts, || To show them the majesty of His works. **9** And He allowed them to take pride forever in His marvelous deeds. **10** And they will praise the Name of His holiness, || That they may declare the majesty of His works. **11** He added to them knowledge || And gave them a law of life for a heritage. ¹² He made a perpetual covenant with them || And showed them His judgments. ¹³ Their eyes saw the majesty of His glory. Their ears heard the glory of His voice. ¹⁴ He said to them, "Beware of all unrighteousness." So, He gave them command—Each man concerning his neighbor. ¹⁵ Their ways are ever before Him. They will not be hidden from His eyes. ¹⁶ From childhood on they tend to be evil; Their heart is like stone, || And they do not seem to be able to make it more human. ¹⁷ He divided the nations of the whole earth. For every nation He appointed a ruler, || But Israel is the Lord's portion. ¹⁸ Israel is His firstborn, || Whom He disciplines as He brings him up. He gives him the light of His love and never neglects him. ¹⁹ All their works are as clear as the sun before Him. His eyes are continually on their ways. ²⁰ Their iniquities are not hidden from Him. All their sins are before the Lord. ²¹ But the Lord is gracious and knows His creatures; So He has spared them rather than abandon them. ²² With Him the kindness of a man is as a signet. He will keep the bounty of a man as the apple of the eye. ²³ Afterward He will rise up, and repay them, || And render their repayment on their head. ²⁴ However, to those who convert He grants a return. He comforts those who are losing patience. ²⁵ Return to the Lord and forsake sins. Make your prayer before His face offend less. ²⁶ Turn to the Most High again || And turn away from iniquity. Greatly hate the abominable thing. ²⁷ Who will give praise to the Highest in Hades, || In place of those who live and return thanks? ²⁸ Thanksgiving perishes from the dead, || As from one who does not exist. He who is in life and health will praise the Lord. ²⁹ How great is the mercy of the Lord, || And His forgiveness to those who turn to Him! ³⁰ For all things cannot be in men, || Because the son of man is not immortal. ³¹ What is brighter than the sun? Yet even this fails. An evil man thinks about flesh and blood. ³² He looks on the power of the height of Heaven, || While all men are earth and ashes.

CHAPTER 18

¹ He who lives forever created all things in common. ² The Lord alone will be justified || And there is no other besides Him. ³ He guides the world with His hand, || And everything obeys Him. He is the King of all things, || And His power separates what is holy from what is not. ⁴ He has given power to declare His works to no one. Who could trace out His mighty deeds? ⁵ Who could measure the strength of His majesty? Who could also proclaim His mercies? ⁶ As for the wondrous works of the Lord, || It is not possible to take from them nor add to them, || Neither is it possible to explore them. ⁷ When a man has finished, || Then he is just at the beginning. When he ceases, || Then he will be in perplexity. ⁸ What is mankind, and what purpose do they serve? What is their good, and what is their evil? ⁹ The number of man's days at the most are one hundred years. ¹⁰ As a drop of water from the sea, and a pebble from the sand, || So are a few years in the day [[or time]] of [the] age. ¹¹ For this reason the Lord was patient over them || And poured out His mercy on them. ¹² He saw and perceived their end, || That it is evil. Therefore, He multiplied His forgiveness. ¹³ The mercy of a man is on his neighbor; But the mercy of the Lord is on all flesh: Reproving, disciplining, teaching, and bringing back, || As a shepherd does his flock. ¹⁴ He has mercy on those who accept disciplining, || And that diligently seek after His judgments. ¹⁵ My son, add no blemish to your good deeds, || And no grief of words in any of your giving. ¹⁶ Does the dew not relieve the scorching heat? So a word is better than a gift. ¹⁷ Behold, is a word not better than a gift? Both are with a gracious man. ¹⁸ A fool is ungracious and abusive. The gift of an envious man consumes the eyes. ¹⁹ Learn before you speak. Take care of your health before you are sick. ²⁰ Before judgment examine yourself, || And in the hour of visitation you will find forgiveness. ²¹ Humble yourself before you become sick. In the time of sins, show conversion. ²² Let nothing hinder you to pay your vow in due time. Do not wait until death to be justified. ²³ Before you make a vow, prepare yourself. Do not be like a man who tempts the Lord. ²⁴ Think about the wrath coming in the days of the end, || And the time of vengeance, when He turns away His face. ²⁵ In the days of fullness remember the time of hunger. Remember poverty and lack in the days of wealth. ²⁶ From morning until evening, the time changes. All things are speedy before the Lord. ²⁷ A wise man is cautious in everything. In days of sinning, he will beware of offense. ²⁸ Every man of understanding knows wisdom. He will give thanks to him who found her. ²⁹ They who were of

understanding in sayings || Also became wise themselves and poured out apt proverbs. ³⁰ Do not go after your lusts. Refrain yourself from your appetites. ³¹ If you give fully to your soul the delight of her desire, || She will make you the laughing-stock of your enemies. ³² Do not make merry in much luxury, || Neither be tied to the expense thereof. ³³ Do not be made a beggar by banqueting on borrowing || When you have nothing in your purse.

CHAPTER 19

¹ A workman who is a drunkard will not become rich. He who despises small things will fall little by little. ² Wine and women will make men of understanding fall away. And he who joins with prostitutes will be more reckless. ³ Moths and worms will have him as their heritage. A reckless soul will be taken away. ⁴ He who is hasty to trust is shallow-minded. He who sins will offend against his own soul. ⁵ He who makes merry in his heart will be condemned: ⁶ He who hates talk has less wickedness. ⁷ Never repeat what is told you, || And you will not be lacking. ⁸ Whether it is of friend or enemy, do not tell it. Unless it is a sin to you, do not reveal it. ⁹ For he has heard you and observed you, || And when the time comes, he will hate you. ¹⁰ Have you heard a word? Let it die with you. Be of good courage: it will not burst you. ¹¹ A fool will travail in pain with a word, || As a woman in labor with a child. ¹² As an arrow that sticks in the flesh of the thigh, || So is a word in a fool's belly. ¹³ Reprove a friend: It may be [that] he did not do it. If he did something, || It may be [that] he may not do it again. ¹⁴ Reprove your neighbor: It may be [that] he did not say it. If he has said it, || It may be [that] he may not say it again. ¹⁵ Reprove a friend: For many times there is slander. Do not trust every word. ¹⁶ There is one who slips, and not from the heart. Who is he who has not sinned with his tongue? ¹⁷ Reprove your neighbor before you threaten him; And give place to the Law of the Highest; And do not be angry. ¹⁸ Fearing the Lord is the first step toward His accepting you; He will love you if you are wise. ¹⁹ Learn the Lord's commands. It is a discipline that gives life. Those who do what pleases Him || Enjoy the fruit of the tree of immortality. ²⁰ All wisdom is the fear of the Lord. In all wisdom is the doing of the Law || And what the knowledge of His omnipotence means. ²¹ If a servant refuses to obey his master, but later does obey, || The master is still angry. ²² The knowledge of wickedness is not wisdom. The prudence of sinners is not counsel. ²³ There is a wickedness, and it is abomination. There is a fool lacking in wisdom. ²⁴ Better is one who has small understanding, and fears, || Than one who has much prudence, and transgresses the Law. ²⁵ There is an exquisite subtlety, and it is unjust. And there is one who perverts favor to gain a judgment. ²⁶ There is one who does wickedly, || Who hangs down his head with mourning, || But inwardly he is full of deceit, ²⁷ Bowing his face down, || And making [it seem] as if he were deaf of one ear. Where he is not known, || He will be beforehand with you. ²⁸ And if for lack of power he is hindered from sinning, || If he finds opportunity, he will do mischief. ²⁹ A man will be known by his look; One who has understanding will be known by his face when you meet him. ³⁰ A man's attire, grinning laughter, || And gait show what he is.

CHAPTER 20

¹ There is a reproof that is not timely; And there is a man who keeps silent and is wise. ² How good it is to reprove, rather than to be angry. He who confesses will be kept back from hurt. ³ Admit when you are wrong, || And you will avoid embarrassment. ⁴ As is the lust of a eunuch to deflower a virgin, || So is he who executes judgments with violence. ⁵ There is one who keeps silent and is found wise; And there is one who is hated for his much talk. ⁶ There is one who keeps silent, || For he has no answer to make; And there is one who keeps silent, as knowing his time. ⁷ A wise man will be silent until his time has come, || But the braggart and fool will miss his time. ⁸ He who uses many words will be abhorred. He who takes authority for himself will be hated in it. ⁹ There is a prosperity that a man finds in misfortunes; And there is a gain that turns to loss. ¹⁰ There is a gift that will not profit you; And there is a gift [that] pays back double. ¹¹ There is an abasement because of glory; And there is one who has lifted up his head

from a low estate. **12** There is one who buys much for a little and pays for it again sevenfold. **13** He who is wise in words will make himself beloved; But the pleasantries of fools will be wasted. **14** The gift of a fool will not profit you; For his eyes are many instead of one. **15** He will give little and insult much. He will open his mouth like a crier. Today he will lend, || And tomorrow he will ask for it back. Such a one is a hateful man. **16** The fool will say, "I have no friend, || And I have no thanks for my good deeds. They who eat my bread are of evil tongue." **17** How often, and of how many, will he be laughed to scorn! **18** A slip on a pavement is better than a slip with the tongue. So the fall of the wicked will come speedily. **19** A man without grace is a tale out of season. It will be continually in the mouth of the ignorant. **20** An allegory from a fool's mouth will be rejected; For he will not speak it in its season. **21** There is one who is hindered from sinning through lack. When he rests, he will not be troubled. **22** There is one who destroys his soul through bashfulness. By a foolish countenance, he will destroy it. **23** There is one who for bashfulness makes promises to his friend; And he makes him his enemy for nothing. **24** A lie is a foul blot in a man. It will be continually in the mouth of the ignorant. **25** A thief is better than a man who is continually lying, || But they will both inherit destruction. **26** The disposition of a liar is dishonor. His shame is with him continually. **27** He who is wise in words will advance himself. And one who is prudent will please great men. **28** He who tills his land will raise his heap high. He who pleases great men will get pardon for iniquity. **29** Presents and gifts blind the eyes of the wise, || And as a muzzle on the mouth, turn away reproofs. **30** Wisdom that is hidden, and treasure that is out of sight—What profit is in them both? **31** Better is a man who hides his folly || Than a man who hides his wisdom.

CHAPTER 21

1 My son, have you sinned? Add no more to it; And ask forgiveness for your past sins. **2** Flee from sin as from the face of a serpent; For if you draw near, it will bite you. Its teeth are lion's teeth, slaying men's souls. **3** All iniquity is as a two-edged sword. Its stroke has no healing. **4** Terror and violence will lay waste riches. So the house of an arrogant man will be laid waste. **5** Supplication from a poor man's mouth reaches to the ears of God, || And his judgment comes speedily. **6** One who hates reproof is in the path of the sinner. He who fears the Lord will turn again in his heart. **7** He who is mighty in tongue is known far away, || But the man of understanding knows when he slips. **8** He who builds his house with other men's money || Is like one who gathers stones for his own tomb. **9** The congregation of wicked men is as a bundle of tow || With a flame of fire at the end of them. **10** The way of sinners is paved with stones, || And at the end of it is the pit of Hades. **11** He who keeps the Law becomes master of its intent. The end of the fear of the Lord is wisdom. **12** He who is not clever will not be instructed. There is a cleverness which makes bitterness abound. **13** The knowledge of a wise man will be made to abound as a flood, || And his counsel as a fountain of life. **14** The inward parts of a fool are like a broken vessel. He will hold no knowledge. **15** If a man of knowledge hears a wise word, || He will commend it and add to it. The wanton man hears it, and it displeases him, || So he puts it away behind his back. **16** The discourse of a fool is like a burden in the way, || But grace will be found on the lips of the wise. **17** The mouth of the prudent man will be sought for in the congregation. They will ponder his words in their heart. **18** As a house that is destroyed, || So is wisdom to a fool. The knowledge of an unwise man is talk without sense. **19** Instruction is as chains on the feet of an unwise man, || And as shackles on the right hand. **20** A fool lifts up his voice with laughter, || But a clever man smiles quietly. **21** Instruction is to a prudent man as an ornament of gold, || And as a bracelet on his right arm. **22** The foot of a fool rushes into a house, || But a man of experience will be ashamed of entering. **23** A foolish man peers into the door of a house, || But a man who is instructed will stand outside. **24** It is a lack of instruction in a man to listen at a door, || But a prudent man will be grieved with the disgrace. **25** The lips of strangers will be grieved at these things, || But the words of prudent men will be weighed in the balance. **26** The heart of fools is in their mouth, || But the mouth of wise men is their heart. **27** When the ungodly curses Satan, || He curses his own soul. **28** A whisperer defiles his own soul || And will be hated wherever he travels.

CHAPTER 22

1 A slothful man is compared to a stone that is defiled. Everyone will hiss at him in his disgrace. **2** A slothful man is compared to the filth of a dunghill. Every man who takes it up will shake out his hand. **3** An uninstructed child is a disgrace to his father, || And a foolish daughter is born to his loss. **4** A prudent daughter will inherit a husband of her own. She who brings shame is the grief of her father. **5** She who is bold brings shame on father and husband. She will be despised by both of them. **6** Unseasonable discourse is as music in mourning, || But stripes and correction are wisdom in every season. **7** He who teaches a fool is as one who glues a potsherd together, || Even as one who wakes a sleeper out of a deep sleep. **8** He who teaches a fool is as one who teaches a man who slumbers. In the end he will say, "What is it?" **9** Children who are brought up well || Do not show the humble origin of their parents. **10** Children who are not brought up well, || Who are arrogant and conceited, || Are a stain on the noblest family. **11** Weep for the dead, for he lacks light. Weep for a fool, for he lacks understanding. Weep more sweetly for the dead, because he has found rest, || But the life of the fool is worse than death. **12** Mourning for the dead lasts seven days, || But for a fool and an ungodly man, all the days of his life. **13** Do not talk much with a foolish man, || And do not go to one that has no understanding: Beware of him, lest you have trouble and be defiled in his onslaught. Turn away from him, and you will find rest, || And you will not be wearied in his madness. **14** What would be heavier than lead? What is its name, but a fool? **15** Sand, salt, and a mass of iron are easier to bear || Than a man without understanding. **16** Timber girded and bound into a building || Will not be released with shaking. So a heart established in due season on well advised counsel || Will not be afraid. **17** A heart settled on a thoughtful understanding || Is as an ornament of plaster on a polished wall. **18** Fences set on a high place || Will not stand against the wind; So a fearful heart in the imagination of a fool || Will not stand against any fear. **19** He who pricks the eye will make tears fall. He who pricks the heart makes it show feeling. **20** Whoever casts a stone at birds scares them away. He who insults a friend will dissolve friendship. **21** If you have drawn a sword against a friend, do not despair, || For there may be a way back. **22** If you have opened your mouth against a friend, do not be afraid, || For there may be reconciliation, || Unless it is for insulting, arrogance, disclosing of a secret, or a treacherous blow—For any friend will flee these things. **23** Gain trust with your neighbor in his poverty, || That in his prosperity you may have gladness. Stay steadfast to him in the time of his affliction, || That you may be heir with him in his inheritance. **24** Before fire is the vapor and smoke of a furnace, || So insults precede bloodshed. **25** I will not be ashamed to shelter a friend. I will not hide myself from his face: **26** If any evil happens to me because of him, || Everyone that hears it will beware of him. **27** Who will set a watch over my mouth, || And a seal of shrewdness on my lips, || That I do not fall from it, || And that my tongue does not destroy me?

CHAPTER 23

1 O Lord, Father and Master of my life, || Do not abandon me to their counsel. Do not let me fall by them. **2** Who will set scourges over my thought, || And a discipline of wisdom over my heart, || That they do not spare me for my errors, || And not overlook their **[[**or**my]]** sins? **3** Otherwise my errors might be multiplied, || And my sins abound, || [And] I fall before my adversaries, || And my enemy rejoice over me. **4** O Lord, Father and God of my life, || Do not give me haughty eyes, **5** And turn evil desire away from me. **6** Let neither gluttony nor lust overtake me. Do not give me over to a shameless mind. **7** Listen, my children, to the discipline of the mouth. He who keeps it will not be taken. **8** The sinner will be overpowered through his lips. By them, the insulter and the arrogant will stumble. **9** Do not accustom your mouth to an oath, || And do not be accustomed to naming the Holy One, **10** For as a servant who is continually scourged will not lack a bruise, || So he also who swears and continually utters the Name || Will not be cleansed from sin. **11** A man of many oaths will be filled with iniquity. The scourge will not depart from his house. If he offends, his sin will be on him. If he disregards it, he has sinned doubly. If he has sworn in vain, he will not be justified, || For his house will be filled with calamities. **12** There is a manner of speech that is clothed with death. Do not let it be found in the heritage of Jacob, || For all these things will be far from the godly, || And they will not wallow in sins. **13** Do not accustom your mouth to gross rudeness, || For it involves sinful speech. **14** Remember your father and your mother, || For you sit in the midst of great men, || That you are not forgetful before them, || And become a fool by your custom; So you may wish that you had not been born, || And curse the day of your nativity. **15** A man who is accustomed to words of reproach || Will not be corrected all the days of his life. **16** Two sorts of people multiply sins, || And the third will bring wrath: A hot mind, as a burning fire, || Will not be quenched until it is consumed; A fornicator, in the body of his flesh, || Will never cease until he has burned out the fire. **17** All bread is sweet to a fornicator. He will not cease until he dies. **18** A man who goes astray from his own bed, || Says in his heart, "Who sees me? Darkness is around me, and the walls hide me. No one sees me. Of whom am I afraid? The Highest will not remember my sins." **19** The eyes of men are his terror. He does not know that the eyes of the Lord || Are ten thousand times brighter than the sun, || Seeing all the ways of men, || And looking into secret places. **20** All things were known to Him before they were created, || And also after they were completed. **21** This man will be punished in the streets of the city. He will be seized where he least expects it. **22** So also is a wife who leaves her husband || And brings in an heir by a stranger. **23** For first, she was disobedient in the Law of the Highest. Second, she trespassed against her own husband. Third, she played the adulteress in whoredom, || And brought in children by a stranger. **24** She will be brought out into the congregation. Her punishment will extend to her children. **25** Her children will not take root. Her branches will bear no fruit. **26** She will leave her memory for a curse. Her reproach will not be blotted out. **27** And those who are left behind || Will know that there is nothing better than the fear of the Lord, || And nothing sweeter than to heed the commands of the Lord.

CHAPTER 24

1 Wisdom will praise her own soul || And will proclaim her glory in the midst of her people. **2** She will open her mouth in the congregation of the Highest || And proclaim her glory in the presence of His power. **3** "I came out of the mouth of the Highest || And covered the earth as a mist. **4** I lived in high places, || And my throne is in the pillar of the cloud. **5** Alone I surrounded the circuit of Heaven || And walked in the depth of the abyss. **6** In the waves of the sea, and in all the earth, || And in every people and nation, I got a possession. **7** With all these I sought rest. In whose inheritance will I lodge? **8** Then the Creator of all things gave me a command. He who created me made my dwelling place to rest, || And said, Let your dwelling place be in Jacob, || And your inheritance in Israel. **9** He created me from the beginning before the world. For all ages, I will not cease to exist. **10** In the holy Dwelling Place, I ministered before Him. So I was established in Zion. **11** In the beloved city, likewise He gave me rest. In Jerusalem was my domain. **12** I took root in a people that was glorified, || Even in the portion of the Lord's own inheritance. **13** I was exalted like a cedar in Lebanon, || And like a cypress tree on the mountains of Hermon. **14** I was exalted like a palm tree on the seashore, || And as rose plants in Jericho, || And as a fair olive tree in the plain. I was exalted as a plane tree. **15** As cinnamon and as palathus, || I have given a scent to perfumes. As choice myrrh, I spread abroad a pleasant fragrance, || As galbanum, onyx, stacte, || And as the smell of frankincense in the Dwelling Place. **16** As the terebinth, I stretched out my branches. My branches are branches of glory and grace. **17** As the vine, I put out grace. My flowers are the fruit of glory and riches. **18** I am the mother of beautiful love, || Of fear, knowledge, and holy hope. Since I am perpetual, || I am given to all my children, who are named by Him. **19** Come to me, all you who desire me, || And be filled with my fruits. **20** For my memorial is sweeter than honey, || And my inheritance [is sweeter] than the honeycomb. **21** Those who eat me will be hungry for more. Those who drink me will be thirsty for more. **22** He who obeys me will not be ashamed. Those who work in me will not sin." **23** All these things are the Scroll of the Covenant of the Highest God, || The Law which Moses commanded us for an inheritance for the assemblies of Jacob. **24** Always be strong in the Lord;

Stay with Him, so that He may make you strong. There is no God but the Lord Almighty, || And no savior except Him. **25** It is He who makes wisdom abundant, || As Pishon, and as Tigris in the days of first-fruits. **26** He makes understanding as full as [the] Euphrates, || And as [the] Jordan in the days of harvest, **27** Who makes instruction shine out as the light, || As [the] Gihon in the days of vintage. **28** The first man did not know her perfectly. In like manner, the last has not explored her. **29** For her thoughts are filled more than the sea, || And her counsels from the great deep. **30** "I came out as a canal stream from a river, || And as an irrigation ditch into a garden. **31** I said, I will water my garden, || And will drench my garden bed. Behold, my stream became a river, || And my river became a sea. **32** I will yet bring instruction to light as the morning || And will make these things clear from far away. **33** I will continue to pour out doctrine like prophecy || And leave it to generations of ages. **34** Behold that I have not labored for myself only, || But for all those who diligently seek her."

CHAPTER 25

1 In three things I was beautified || And stood up beautiful before the Lord and men: The concord of relatives, || And friendship of neighbors, || And a woman and her husband that walk together in agreement. **2** But three sorts [of men] my soul hates, || And I am greatly offended at their life: A poor man that is arrogant, || And a rich man that is a liar, || [And] an old man that is an adulterer lacking understanding. **3** In [your] youth you have not gathered, || And how should you find in your old age? **4** How beautiful a thing is judgment for gray hairs, || And for elders to know counsel! **5** How beautiful is the wisdom of old men, || And thought and counsel to men that are in honor! **6** Much experience is the crown of old men; And their glorying is the fear of the Lord. **7** There are nine things that I have thought of, || And in my heart counted happy; And the tenth I will utter with my tongue: A man that rejoices in his children; A man that lives and looks on the fall of his enemies; **8** Happy is he that dwells with a wife of understanding; And he that has not slipped with his tongue; And he that has not served a man that is unworthy of him; **9** Happy is he that has found prudence; And he that speaks in the ears of those who listen. **10** How great is he that has found wisdom! Yet there is none above him that fears the Lord. **11** The fear of the Lord passes all things: He that holds it—To whom will he be likened? **12** Fearing the Lord is the first step toward loving Him, || And faith is the first step toward loyalty to Him. **13** [Give me] any plague but the plague of the heart; And any wickedness but the wickedness of a woman; **14** Any calamity, but a calamity from those who hate me; And any vengeance, but the vengeance of enemies. **15** There is no head above the head of a serpent; And there is no wrath above the wrath of an enemy. **16** I would rather dwell with a lion and a dragon, || Than keep house with a wicked woman. **17** The wickedness of a woman changes her look || And darkens her countenance as a bear does. **18** Her husband will sit at meat among his neighbors, || And when he hears it he sighs bitterly. **19** All malice is but little to the malice of a woman: Let the portion of a sinner fall on her. **20** [As] the going up a sandy way [is] to the feet of the aged, || So is a wife full of words to a quiet man. **21** Do not throw yourself on the beauty of a woman; And do not desire a woman for her beauty. **22** There is anger, and impudence, and great reproach, || If a woman supports her husband. **23** A wicked woman is a dejection of heart, || And sadness of countenance, and a wounded heart: A woman that will not make her husband happy || Is [as] hands that hang down, and palsied knees. **24** From a woman [was] the beginning of sin; And because of her we all die. **25** Do not give water an outlet; Neither [give] freedom of speech to a wicked woman. **26** If she does not go as you would have her, || Cut her off from your flesh.

CHAPTER 26

1 Happy is the husband of a good wife; And the number of his days will be doubled. **2** A brave woman rejoices her husband; And he will fulfill his years in peace. **3** A good wife is a good portion: She will be given in the portion of such as fear the Lord. **4** Whether a man is rich or poor, || A good heart [makes] a cheerful countenance at all times. **5** Of three things my heart was afraid; And concerning the fourth kind I made supplication: The slander of a city, || And the assembly of a multitude, || And a false accusation: All these are more grievous than death. **6** A grief of heart and sorrow is a woman that is jealous of [another] woman, || And the scourge of a tongue communicating to all. **7** A wicked woman is [as] a yoke of oxen shaken to and fro; He that takes hold of her is as one that grasps a scorpion. **8** A drunken woman [causes] great wrath; And she will not cover her own shame. **9** The whoredom of a woman is in the lifting up of her eyes; And it will be known by her eyelids. **10** Keep strict watch on a headstrong daughter, || Lest she finds liberty for herself, and uses it. **11** Look well after an impudent eye; And do not marvel if it trespasses against you. **12** She will open her mouth as a thirsty traveler, || And drink of every water that is near: She will sit down at every post || And open her quiver against [any] arrow. **13** The grace of a wife will delight her husband; And her knowledge will fatten his bones. **14** A silent woman is a gift of the Lord; And there is nothing worth so much as a well-instructed soul. **15** A modest woman is grace on grace; And there is no price worthy of a continent soul. **16** As the sun when it arises in the highest places of the Lord, || So is the beauty of a good wife in the ordering of a man's house. **17** As the lamp that shines on the holy candlestick, || So is the beauty of the face in ripe age. **18** As the golden pillars are on a base of silver, || So are beautiful feet with the breasts of one that is steadfast. **19** My child, stay healthy while you are young, || And do not give your strength to strangers. **20** Search the whole land for a fertile field, || And plant it with your own seed, || Trusting your own good stock. **21** Then your children will survive || And grow up confident of their good family. **22** A prostitute is like spit; A married woman who has affairs brings death to her lovers. **23** A lawless man will get a godless wife, as he deserves, || But a man who honors the Lord will have a devout wife. **24** A shameless wife enjoys making a disgrace of herself, || But a modest wife will act modestly even alone with her husband. **25** A self-willed woman is a dog, || But a woman with a sense of decency honors the Lord. **26** A wife who honors her husband will seem wise to everyone; But if she dishonors him by her overbearing attitude, || Everyone will know that she is ungodly. The husband of a good wife is fortunate, || Because he will live twice as long. **27** A loud-mouthed, talkative woman is like a trumpet sounding the signal for attack, || And any man who has such a wife will spend his life at war. **28** For two things my heart is grieved; And for the third anger comes on me: A man of war that suffers for poverty; And men of understanding that are counted as refuse; One that turns back from righteousness to sin—The Lord will prepare him for the sword. **29** A merchant will hardly keep himself from wrongdoing; And a huckster will not be acquitted of sin.

CHAPTER 27

1 Many have sinned for a thing indifferent; And he that seeks to multiply [gain] will turn his eye away. **2** A nail will stick fast between the joining of stones; And sin will thrust itself in between buying and selling. **3** Unless [a man] holds on diligently in the fear of the Lord, || His house will soon be overthrown. **4** In the shaking of a sieve, the refuse remains; So is the filth of man in his reasoning. **5** The furnace will prove the potter's vessels; And the trial of a man is in his reasoning. **6** The fruit of a tree declares the farming thereof; So is the utterance of the thought of the heart of a man. **7** Praise no man before [you hear him] reason; For this is the trial of men. **8** If you follow righteousness, you will obtain her, || And put her on, as a long robe of glory. **9** Birds will return to their like; And truth will return to those who practice her. **10** The lion lies in wait for prey; So does sin for those who work iniquity. **11** The discourse of a godly man is always wisdom, || But the foolish man changes as the moon. **12** Among men void of understanding observe the opportunity; But continually stay among the thoughtful. **13** The discourse of fools is an offense; And their laughter is in the wantonness of sin. **14** The talk of a man of many oaths will make the hair stand upright; And their strife makes one stop his ears. **15** The strife of the proud is a shedding of blood; And their reviling of each other is a grievous thing to hear. **16** He that reveals secrets destroys credit || And will not find a friend to his mind. **17** Love a friend and keep faith with him, || But if you reveal his secrets, || You will not pursue after him; **18** For as a man has destroyed his enemy, || So have you destroyed the friendship of your neighbor. **19** And as a bird

which you have released out of your hand, || So have you let your neighbor go, || And you will not catch him again: **20** Do not pursue him, for he has gone far away, || And has escaped as a gazelle out of the snare. **21** For a wound may be bound up, || And after reviling there may be a reconcilement; But he that reveals secrets has lost hope. **22** One that winks with the eye contrives evil things; And no man will remove him from it. **23** When you are present, he will speak sweetly, || And will admire your words; But afterward he will writhe his mouth || And set a trap [for you] in your words. **24** I have hated many things, || But nothing like him; And the Lord will hate him. **25** One that casts a stone on high casts it on his own head; And a deceitful stroke will open wounds. **26** He that digs a pit will fall into it; And he that sets a snare will be taken therein. **27** He that does evil things, they will roll on him, || And he will not know from where they have come to him. **28** Mockery and reproach are from the arrogant; And vengeance, as a lion, will lie in wait for him. **29** They that rejoice at the fall of the godly || Will be taken in a snare; And anguish will consume them before they die. **30** Wrath and anger, these are also abominations; And a sinful man will possess them.

CHAPTER 28

1 He that takes vengeance will find vengeance from the Lord; And he will surely make firm his sins. **2** Forgive your neighbor the hurt that he has done [you]; And then your sins will be pardoned when you pray. **3** Man cherishes anger against man; And does he [then] seek healing from the Lord? **4** On a man like himself he has no mercy; And does he [then] make supplication for his own sins? **5** He being himself flesh nourishes wrath: Who will make atonement for his sins? **6** Remember your last end, || And cease from enmity: [Remember] corruption and death, || And remain in the commands. **7** Remember the commands || And do not be angry with your neighbor; And [remember] the covenant of the Highest, || And wink at ignorance. **8** Abstain from strife, and you will diminish your sins, || For a passionate man will kindle strife, **9** And a man that is a sinner will trouble friends || And will make debate among those who are at peace. **10** As is the fuel of the fire, so will it burn; And as the stoutness of the strife is, [so] will it burn; As is the strength of the man, [so] will be his wrath; And as is his wealth, [so] he will exalt his anger. **11** A contention begun in haste kindles a fire; And a hasty fighting sheds blood. **12** If you blow a spark, it will burn; And if you spit on it, it will be quenched: And both these will come out of your mouth. **13** Curse the whisperer and double-tongued, || For he has destroyed many that were at peace. **14** A third person's tongue has shaken many || And dispersed them from nation to nation; And it has pulled down strong cities || And overthrown the houses of great men. **15** A third person's tongue has cast out brave women || And deprived them of their labors. **16** He that listens to it will not find rest, || Nor will he dwell quietly. **17** The stroke of a whip makes a mark in the flesh; But the stroke of a tongue will break bones. **18** Many have fallen by the edge of the sword: Yet not so many as those who have fallen because of the tongue. **19** Happy is he that is sheltered from it, || Who has not passed through the wrath thereof; Who has not drawn its yoke, || And has not been bound with its bands. **20** For the yoke thereof is a yoke of iron, || And the bands thereof are bands of brass. **21** The death thereof is an evil death; And Hades would be better than it. **22** It will not have rule over godly men; And they will not be burned in its flame. **23** They that forsake the Lord will fall into it; And it will burn among them and will not be quenched: It will be sent out on them as a lion; And as a leopard it will destroy them. **24** See to it that you hedge around your possession with thorns; Bind up your silver and your gold; **25** And make a balance and a weight for your words; And make a door and a bar for your mouth. **26** Take heed lest you slip therein; Lest you fall before one that lies in wait.

CHAPTER 29

1 He that shows mercy will lend to his neighbor; And he that strengthens him with his hand keeps the commands. **2** Lend to your neighbor in time of his need; And pay your neighbor again in due season. **3** Confirm your word and keep faith with him; And at all seasons you will find what you need. **4** Many have reckoned a loan as a windfall || And have given trouble to those that helped them. **5** Until he has received, he will kiss a man's hands; And for his neighbor's money he will speak submissively: And when payment is due, he will prolong the time, || And return words of heaviness, and complain of the times. **6** If he prevails, he will hardly receive the half; And he will count it as a windfall: If not, he has deprived him of his money, || And he has gotten him for an enemy without cause: He will pay him with cursing and railing; And he will pay him disgrace for honor. **7** Many on account of [men's] ill-dealing have turned away; They have feared to be defrauded for nothing. **8** However, be patient with a man in poor estate; And do not let him wait for [your] kindness. **9** Help a poor man for the command's sake; And according to his need, do not send him away empty. **10** Lose [your] money for a brother and a friend; And do not let it rust under the stone to be lost. **11** Bestow your treasure according to the commands of the Highest, || And it will profit you more than gold. **12** Shut up alms in your store-chambers, || And it will deliver you out of all affliction: **13** It will fight for you against your enemy || Better than a mighty shield and a ponderous spear. **14** A good man will be a guarantee for his neighbor; And he that has lost shame will fail him. **15** Do not forget the good offices of your guarantor; For he has given his life for you. **16** A sinner will overthrow the good estate of his guarantor; **17** And he that is of an unthankful mind will fail him that delivered him. **18** Suretyship has undone many that were prospering || And shaken them as a wave of the sea: It has driven mighty men from their homes; And they wandered among strange nations. **19** A sinner that falls into suretyship, || And undertakes contracts for work, || Will fall into lawsuits. **20** Help your neighbor according to your power || And take heed to yourself that you do not fall [the same way]. **21** The chief thing for life is water, and bread, || And a garment, and a house to cover shame. **22** Better is the life of a poor man under a shelter of logs, || Than sumptuous fare in another man's house. **23** With little or with much, be well satisfied. **24** It is a miserable life to go from house to house: And where you are a sojourner, || You will not [dare to] open your mouth. **25** You will entertain, and give to drink, and have no thanks: And in addition to this, you will hear bitter words. **26** "Come here, you sojourner, furnish a table, || And if you have anything in your hand, feed me with it. **27** Go out, you sojourner, from the face of honor; My brother has come to be my guest; I have need of my house." **28** These things are grievous to a man of understanding: The scolding of [the] household, || And the reproaching of the money-lender.

CHAPTER 30

1 He that loves his son will continue to lay stripes on him, || That he may rejoice in him in the end. **2** He that disciplines his son will profit from him || And will boast of him among his acquaintance. **3** He that teaches his son will provoke his enemy to jealousy; And he will rejoice in him before friends. **4** His father dies and is as though he had not died; For he has left one behind him like himself. **5** In his life, he saw and rejoiced [in him]; And when he died, he did not sorrow: **6** He left behind him an avenger against his enemies, || And one to repay kindness to his friends. **7** He that makes too much of his son will bind up his wounds; And his heart will be troubled at every cry. **8** An unbroken horse becomes stubborn; And a son left at large becomes headstrong. **9** Pamper your child, and he will make you afraid: Play with him, and he will grieve you. **10** Do not laugh with him, lest you have sorrow with him; And you will gnash your teeth in the end. **11** Give him no liberty in his youth, || And do not wink at his follies. **12** Bow his neck down in his youth || And beat him on the sides while he is a child, || Lest he wax stubborn, and be disobedient to you; And there will be sorrow to your soul. **13** Discipline your son, and take pains with him, || Lest his shameless behavior be an offense to you. **14** Better is a poor man, being sound and strong of constitution, || Than a rich man that is plagued in his body. **15** Health and a good constitution are better than all gold; And a strong body than wealth without measure. **16** There is no riches better than health of body; And there is no gladness above the joy of the heart. **17** Death is better than a bitter life, || And perpetual rest than a continual sickness. **18** Good things poured out on a mouth that is closed || Are [as] messes of meat laid on a grave. **19** What does an offering profit an idol? For neither will it eat nor smell; So is he that is afflicted of the Lord, **20** Seeing with his eyes and groaning, || As a eunuch embracing a virgin and groaning. **21** Do not give your soul over to sorrow;

And do not afflict yourself in your own counsel. **22** Gladness of heart is the life of a man; And the joyfulness of a man is length of days. **23** Love your own soul and comfort your heart: And remove sorrow far from you; For sorrow has destroyed many, || And there is no profit therein. **24** Envy and wrath shorten [a man's] days; And care brings old age before the time. **25** A cheerful and good heart || Will have a care of his meat and diet.

CHAPTER 31

1 Wakefulness that comes of riches consumes the flesh, || And the anxiety thereof puts away sleep. **2** Wakeful anxiety will crave slumber; And in a severe disease sleep will be broken. **3** A rich man toils in gathering money together; And when he rests, he is filled with his good things. **4** A poor man toils in lack of substance; And when he rests, he becomes needy. **5** He that loves gold will not be justified; And he that follows destruction will himself have his fill [of it]. **6** Many have been given over to ruin for the sake of gold; And their perdition meets them face to face. **7** It is a stumbling block to those who sacrifice to it; And every fool will be taken with that. **8** Blessed is the rich who is found without blemish, || And who does not go after gold. **9** Who is he? and we will call him blessed; For he has done wonderful things among his people. **10** Who has been tried by it, and found perfect? Then let him glory. Who has had the power to transgress, and has not transgressed? And to do evil, and has not done it? **11** His goods will be made sure. And the congregation will declare his alms. **12** Do you sit at a great table? Do not be greedy on it, || And do not say, "There are many things on it." **13** Remember that an evil eye is a wicked thing: What has been created more evil than an eye? Therefore, it sheds tears from every face. **14** Do not stretch your hand wherever it looks || And do not thrust yourself with it into the dish. **15** Consider your neighbor's [liking] by your own; And be discreet in every point. **16** Eat, as [becomes] a man, || Those things which are set before you; And do not eat greedily, lest you be hated. **17** Be first to leave off for manners' sake; And do not be insatiable, lest you offend. **18** And if you sit among many, || Do not reach out your hand before them. **19** How sufficient to a well-mannered man is a very little, || And he does not breathe hard on his bed. **20** Healthy sleep comes of moderate eating; He rises early, and his wits are with him: The pain of wakefulness, and colic, and griping, || Are with an insatiable man. **21** And if you have been forced to eat, || Rise up in the midst thereof, and you will have rest. **22** Hear me, my son, and do not despise me, || And at the end you will find my words [true]: In all your works be quick, || And no disease will come to you. **23** Him that is liberal of his meat the lips will bless; And the testimony of his excellence will be believed. **24** The city will murmur at he who is stingy with his meat; And the testimony of his stinginess will be sure. **25** Do not show yourself valiant in wine, || For wine has destroyed many. **26** The furnace proves the temper [of steel] by dipping; So does wine [prove] hearts in the quarreling of the proud. **27** Wine is as good as life to men, || If you drink it in its measure: What life is there to a man that is without wine? And it has been created to make men glad. **28** Wine drunk in season, to satisfy, || Is joy of heart and gladness of soul: **29** Wine drunk abundantly is bitterness of soul, || With provocation and conflict. **30** Drunkenness increases the rage of a fool to his hurt; It diminishes strength and adds wounds. **31** Do not rebuke your neighbor at a banquet of wine, || Neither set him at nothing in his mirth; Do not speak a word of reproach to him, || And do not press on him by asking back [a debt].

CHAPTER 32

1 Have they made you ruler [of a feast]? Do not be lifted up; Be among them as one of them; Take thought for them, and so sit down. **2** And when you have done all your office, take your place, || That you may be gladdened on their account, || And receive a crown for your well ordering. **3** Speak, you that are the elder, || For it is suitable for you, [but] with sound knowledge; And do not hinder music. **4** Do not pour out talk where there is a performance of music, || And do not display your wisdom out of season. **5** [As] a signet of carbuncle in a setting of gold, || [So] is a concert of music in a banquet of wine. **6** [As] a signet of emerald in a work of gold, || [So] is a strain of music with pleasant wine. **7** Speak, young man, if there is need of you, [Yet] scarcely if you be twice asked. **8** Sum up your speech, many things in few words; Be as one that knows and yet holds his tongue. **9** [If you be] among great men, || Do not behave as their equal; And when another is speaking, || Do not make much babbling. **10** Lightning speeds before thunder; And before a modest man favor will go out. **11** Rise up on time and do not be the last; Get home quickly and do not loiter: **12** Take your pastime there and do what is in your heart; And do not sin by proud speech: **13** And for these things bless Him that made you || And gives you to drink freely of His good things. **14** He that fears the Lord will receive [His] discipline; And those who seek [Him] early will find favor. **15** He that seeks the Law will be filled with that, || But the hypocrite will stumble at that. **16** They that fear the Lord will find judgment || And will kindle righteous acts as a light. **17** A sinful man shuns reproof || And will find a judgment according to his will. **18** A man of counsel will not neglect a thought; A strange and proud man will not crouch in fear, || Even after he has done a thing by himself without counsel. **19** Do nothing without counsel; And when you have once done [it], || Do not convert [from it]. **20** Do not go in a way of conflict; And do not stumble in stony places. **21** Do not be confident in a smooth way. **22** And beware of your own children. **23** In every work trust your own soul; For this is the keeping of the commands. **24** He that believes the Law gives heed to the command; And he that trusts in the Lord will suffer no loss.

CHAPTER 33

1 No evil will happen to him that fears the Lord, || But in temptation He will once again deliver him. **2** A wise man will not hate the Law; But he that is a hypocrite therein is as a ship In a storm. **3** A man of understanding will put his trust in the Law; And the Law is faithful to him, || As when one asks at the oracle. **4** Prepare [your] speech, and so will you be heard; Bind up instruction and make your answer. **5** The heart of a fool is [as] a cartwheel; And his thoughts like a rolling axle-tree. **6** A stallion horse is as a mocking friend; He neighs under everyone that sits on him. **7** Why does one day excel [over] another, || When all the light of every day in the year is of the sun? **8** By the knowledge of the Lord they were distinguished; And He varied seasons and feasts: **9** Some of them He exalted and hallowed, || And some of them He has made ordinary days. **10** And all men are from the ground, || And Adam was created of earth. **11** In the abundance of His knowledge the Lord distinguished them || And made their ways various: **12** Some of them He blessed and exalted, || And some of them He hallowed and brought near to Himself; Some of them He cursed and brought low, || And overthrew them from their place. **13** As the clay of the potter in his hand, || All his ways are according to his good pleasure; So men are in the hand of Him that made them, || To render to them according to His judgment. **14** Good is the opposite of evil, || And life is the opposite of death; So the sinner is the opposite of the godly. **15** And so look on all the works of the Highest: Two and two, one against another. **16** And I awoke last, as one that gleans after the grape gatherers: By the blessing of the Lord I got before them, || And filled my winepress as one that gathers grapes. **17** Consider that I did not labor for myself alone, || But for all those who seek instruction. **18** Hear me, you great men of the people, || And listen with your ears, you rulers of the congregation. **19** To son and wife, to brother and friend, || Do not give power over yourself while you live; And do not give your goods to another, || Lest you convert and make supplication for them [again]. **20** While you yet live, and breath is in you, || Do not give yourself over to anybody. **21** For it is better that your children should supplicate you, || Than that you should look to the hand of your sons. **22** In all your works keep the upper hand; Do not bring a stain on your honor. **23** In the day that you end the days of your life, || And in the time of death, distribute your inheritance. **24** Fodder, a stick, and burdens, for a donkey; Bread, and discipline, and work, for a servant. **25** Set your servant to work, and you will find rest: Leave his hands idle, and he will seek liberty. **26** Yoke and thong will bow the neck: And for an evil servant there are racks and tortures. **27** Send him to labor, that he may not be idle; For idleness teaches much mischief. **28** Set him to work, as is fit for him; And if he does not obey, make his chains heavy. **29** And do not be excessive toward any; And do nothing without judgment. **30** If you have a servant, let him be as yourself, || Because you have

bought him with blood. **31** If you have a servant, treat him as yourself, || For you will have need of him as your own soul: If you treat him ill, and he departs and runs away, || Which way will you go to seek him?

CHAPTER 34

1 Vain and false hopes are for a man void of understanding; And dreams give wings to fools. **2** As one that catches at a shadow, || And follows after the wind, || So is he that sets his mind on dreams. **3** The vision of dreams is [as] this thing against that, || The likeness of a face near a face. **4** Of an unclean thing what will be cleansed? And of that which is false what will be true? **5** Divinations, and soothsaying, and dreams, are vain: And the heart has fantasies, as a woman's in travail. **6** If they are not sent from the Highest in [your] visitation, || Do not give your heart to them. **7** For dreams have led many astray: And they have failed by putting their hope in them. **8** Without lying the Law will be accomplished; And wisdom is perfection to a faithful mouth. **9** A well-instructed man knows many things; And he that has much experience will declare understanding. **10** He that has no experience knows few things, || But he that has wandered will increase [his] skill. **11** In my wandering I have seen many things; And my understanding is more than my words. **12** I was often in danger even to death; And I was preserved because of these things. **13** The spirit of those that fear the Lord will live; For their hope is on Him that saves them. **14** Whoever fears the Lord will not be afraid || And will not play the coward; For He is his hope. **15** Blessed is the soul of him that fears the Lord: To whom does he give heed? and who is his stay? **16** The eyes of the Lord are on those who love Him, || A mighty protection and strong stay, || A cover from the hot blast, and a cover from the noonday, || A guard from stumbling, and a help from falling. **17** He raises up the soul, and enlightens the eyes: He gives healing, life, and blessing. **18** He that sacrifices of a thing wrongfully gotten—His offering is made in mockery; And the mockeries of wicked men are not well-pleasing. **19** The Most High has no pleasure in the offerings of the ungodly; Neither is He pacified for sins by the multitude of sacrifices. **20** [As] one that kills the son before his father's eyes || Is he that brings a sacrifice from the goods of the poor. **21** The bread of the needy is the life of the poor: He that deprives him thereof is a man of blood. **22** [As] one that slays his neighbor || Is he that takes away his living; And [as] a shedder of blood || Is he that deprives a hireling of his hire. **23** One building, and another pulling down—What profit have they had but toil? **24** One praying, and another cursing—Whose voice will the Lord listen to? **25** He that washes himself after [touching] a dead body, and touches it again—What profit does he have in his washing? **26** Even so a man fasting for his sins, and going again, and doing the same—Who will listen to his prayer? And what profit does he have in his humiliation?

CHAPTER 35

1 He that keeps the Law multiplies offerings; He that takes heed to the commands sacrifices a peace offering. **2** He that returns a favor offers fine flour; And he that gives alms sacrifices a thank offering. **3** To depart from wickedness is a thing pleasing to the Lord; And to depart from unrighteousness is an atoning sacrifice. **4** See that you do not appear in the presence of the Lord empty. **5** For all these things [are to be done] because of the command. **6** The offering of the righteous makes the altar fat; And the sweet savor thereof [is] before the Highest. **7** The sacrifice of a righteous man is acceptable; And the memorial thereof will not be forgotten. **8** Glorify the Lord with a good eye, || And do not limit the first-fruits of your hands. **9** In every gift show a cheerful countenance || And dedicate your tithe with gladness. **10** Give to the Most High according as He has given; And as your hand has found, [give] with a good eye. **11** For the Lord rewards, || And He will reward you sevenfold. **12** Do not think to corrupt with gifts, || For He will not receive them: And do not set your mind on an unrighteous sacrifice, || For the Lord is judge, || And with Him is no respect of persons. **13** He will not accept any person against a poor man; And He will listen to the prayer of him that is wronged. **14** He will in no way despise the supplication of the fatherless; Nor the widow, when she pours out her tale. **15** Do the tears of the widow not run down her cheek? And is her cry not against him that has caused them to fall? **16** He that serves [God] according to His good pleasure will be accepted, || And his supplication will reach to the clouds. **17** The prayer of the humble pierces the clouds; And until it comes near, he will not be comforted; And he will not depart, until the Most High will visit; And He will judge righteously and execute judgment. **18** And the Lord will not be slack, || Neither will He be patient toward them, || Until He has crushed the loins of the unmerciful; And He will repay vengeance to the heathen, || Until He has taken away the multitude of the arrogant, || And broken in pieces the scepters of the unrighteous; **19** Until He has rendered to [every] man according to his doings, || And [to] the works of men according to their plans; Until He has judged the cause of His people; And He will make them to rejoice in His mercy. **20** Mercy is seasonable in the time of His afflicting [them], || As clouds of rain in the time of drought.

CHAPTER 36

1 Have mercy on us, O Lord the God of all, and behold; **2** And send Your fear on all the nations: **3** Lift up Your hand against the strange nations; And let them see Your mighty power. **4** As You were sanctified in us before them, || So be magnified in them before us. **5** And let them know You, as we also have known You, || That there is no God but only You, O God. **6** Show new signs and work various wonders; Glorify Your hand and Your right arm. **7** Raise up indignation, and pour out wrath; Take away the adversary, and destroy the enemy. **8** Hasten the time and remember the oath; And let them declare Your mighty works. **9** Let him that escapes be devoured by the rage of fire; And may those who harm Your people find destruction. **10** Crush the heads of the rulers of the enemies, || That say, "There is none but us." **11** Gather all the tribes of Jacob together, || And take them for Your inheritance, as from the beginning. **12** O Lord, have mercy on the people that is called by Your Name, || And on Israel, whom You did liken to a firstborn. **13** Have compassion on the city of Your sanctuary: Jerusalem, the place of Your rest. **14** Fill Zion; exalt Your oracles || And [fill] Your people with Your glory. **15** Give testimony to those that were Your creatures in the beginning || And raise up the prophecies that have been in Your Name. **16** Give reward to those who wait for You: And men will put their trust in Your prophets. **17** Listen, O Lord, to the prayer of Your suppliants, || According to the blessing of Aaron concerning Your people; And all those who are on the earth will know || That You are the Lord, the perpetual God. **18** The belly will eat any meat; Yet one meat is better than another. **19** The mouth tastes meats taken in hunting; So does an understanding heart false speeches. **20** A contrary heart will cause heaviness: And a man of experience will reward him. **21** A woman will receive any man; But one daughter is better than another. **22** The beauty of a woman cheers the countenance; And a man desires nothing so much. **23** If there is mercy and meekness on her tongue, || Her husband is not like the sons of men. **24** He that gets a wife enters on a possession; A help appropriate for him, and a pillar of rest. **25** Where no hedge is, the possession will be laid waste; And he that has no wife will mourn as he wanders up and down. **26** For who will trust a nimble robber || Who skips from city to city? Even so, [who will trust] a man that has no nest, || And [who] lodges wherever he finds himself at nightfall?

CHAPTER 37

1 Every friend will say, "I am also his friend," || But there is a friend who is only a friend in name. **2** Is there not a grief in it even to death, || When a companion and friend is turned to enmity? **3** O wicked imagination, from where did you come, || Rolling in to cover the dry land with deceitfulness? **4** There is a companion who rejoices in the gladness of a friend, || But in time of affliction will be against him. **5** There is a companion who for the belly's sake labors with his friend, || [But] in the face of battle will take up the buckler. **6** Do not forget a friend in your soul; And do not be unmindful of him in your riches. **7** Every counselor extols counsel; But there is [one] who counsels for himself. **8** Let your soul beware of a counselor || And know beforehand what his interest is, || For he will take counsel for himself; Lest he casts the lot on you, **9** And says to you, "Your way is good": And he will stand near you, || To see what will happen to you. **10** Take no counsel with one that looks suspiciously at you; And hide your counsel from such as are jealous of you. **11** [Take no counsel] with a woman about her rival; Neither with a coward about war; Nor with a merchant about exchange; Nor with a buyer about selling; Nor with an envious man about thankfulness; Nor with an unmerciful man about kindness; Nor with a sluggard about any kind of work; Nor with a hireling in your house about finishing [his work]; Nor with an idle servant about much business: Give no heed to these in any matter of counsel, **12** But rather be continually with a godly man, || Whom you will have known to be a keeper of the commands, || Who in his soul is as your own soul, || And who will grieve with you, if you will miscarry. **13** And make the counsel of your heart to stand; For there is none more faithful to you than it. **14** For a man's soul is sometimes accustomed to bring him tidings—More than seven watchmen that sit up high on a watchtower. **15** And above all this, entreat the Highest, || That He may direct your way in truth. **16** Let reason be the beginning of every work, || And let counsel go before every action. **17** As a token of the changing of the heart, **18** Four manner of things rise up: Good and evil, life and death; And that which rules over them continually is the tongue. **19** There is one that is shrewd [and] the instructor of many, || And yet is unprofitable to his own soul. **20** There is [one] that is subtle in words and is hated; He will be destitute of all food: **21** For grace was not given to him from the Lord, || Because he is deprived of all wisdom. **22** There is one that is wise to his own soul, || And the fruits of his understanding are trustworthy in the mouth. **23** A wise man will instruct his own people, || And the fruits of his understanding are trustworthy. **24** A wise man will be filled with blessing, || And all those who see him will call him happy. **25** The life of man is counted by days, || And the days of Israel are innumerable. **26** The wise man will inherit confidence among his people, || And his name will live forever. **27** My son, prove your soul in your life, || And see what is evil for it, and do not give that to it. **28** For all things are not profitable for all men, || Neither does every soul have pleasure in everything. **29** Do not be insatiable in any luxury, || And do not be greedy in the things that you eat. **30** For in multitude of meats there will be disease, || And gorging will come near to colic. **31** Because of gorging many have perished; But he that takes heed will prolong his life.

CHAPTER 38

1 Honor a physician according to your need [of him] || With the honors due to him; For the Lord has truly created him. **2** For from the Most High comes healing; And from the king he will receive a gift. **3** The skill of the physician will lift up his head; And in the sight of great men he will be admired. **4** The Lord created medicines out of the earth; And a prudent man will have no disgust at them. **5** Was water not made sweet with wood, || That the virtue thereof might be known? **6** And He gave men skill, || That they might be glorified in His marvelous works. **7** With them He heals [a man and] takes away his pain. **8** With these the apothecary will make a confection; And his works will not be brought to an end; And from him is peace on the face of the earth. **9** My son, in your sickness do not be negligent; But pray to the Lord, and He will heal you. **10** Put away wrongdoing, || And order your hands correctly, || And cleanse your heart from all manner of sin. **11** Give a sweet savor, and a memorial of fine flour; And make fat your offering, as one that is not. **12** Then give place to the physician, || For the Lord has truly created him; And do not let him go from you, for you have need of him. **13** There is a time when in their very hands is the issue for good. **14** For they will also implore the Lord, || That He may prosper them in [giving] relief and in healing for the maintenance of life. **15** He that sins before his Maker, || Let him fall into the hands of the physician. **16** My son, let your tears fall over the dead, || And as one that suffers grievously begin lamentation; And wind up his body according to his due, || And do not neglect his burial. **17** Make bitter weeping, and make passionate wailing, || And let your mourning be according to his merit—For one day or two, || Lest you be spoken evil of: And so be comforted for your sorrow. **18** For of sorrow comes death, || And sorrow of heart will bow down the strength. **19** In calamity sorrow also remains: And the poor man's life is grievous to the heart. **20** Do not give your heart to sorrow. Put it away, remembering the latter end. **21** Do not forget it, || For there is no returning again: You will not profit him, || And you will hurt yourself. **22** Remember the sentence on him; For so yours will also be; Yesterday for me, and today for you. **23** When the dead is at rest, || Let his remembrance rest; And be comforted for him, || When his spirit departs from him. **24** The wisdom of the scribe comes by opportunity of leisure; And he that has little business will become wise. **25** How will he become wise that holds the plow, || That glories in the shaft of the goad, || That drives oxen, and is occupied in their labors, || And whose discourse is of the stock of bulls? **26** He will set his heart on turning his furrows; And his wakefulness is to give his heifers their fodder. **27** So is every craftsman and master workman, || That passes his time by night as by day; They that cut gravings of signets, || And his diligence is to make great variety; He will set his heart to preserve likeness in his portraiture || And will be wakeful to finish his work. **28** So is the smith sitting by the anvil and considering the unworked iron: The vapor of the fire will waste his flesh; And in the heat of the furnace, he will wrestle [with his work]: The noise of the hammer will be ever in his ear, || And his eyes are on the pattern of the vessel; He will set his heart on perfecting his works, || And he will be wakeful to adorn them perfectly. **29** So is the potter sitting at his work, || And turning the wheel around with his feet, || Who is always anxiously set at his work, || And all his handiwork is by number; **30** He will fashion the clay with his arm || And will bend its strength in front of his feet; He will apply his heart to finish the glazing; And he will be wakeful to make clean the furnace. **31** All these put their trust in their hands; And each becomes wise in his own work. **32** Without these a city will not be inhabited, || And men will not sojourn nor walk up and down [therein]. **33** They will not be sought for in the council of the people, || And in the assembly, they will not mount on high; They will not sit on the seat of the judge, || And they will not understand the covenant of judgment: Neither will they declare instruction and judgment; And where allegories are, they will not be found. **34** But they will maintain the fabric of the world; And in the handiwork of their craft is their prayer.

CHAPTER 39

1 Not so he that has applied his soul || And meditates in the Law of the Most High; He will seek out the wisdom of all the ancients || And will be occupied in prophecies. **2** He will keep the discourse of the men of renown || And will enter in amidst the subtleties of allegories. **3** He will seek out the hidden meaning of proverbs || And be conversant in the dark sayings of allegories. **4** He will serve among great men || And appear before him that rules. He will travel through the land of strange nations; For he has tried good things and evil among men. **5** He will apply his heart to return early to the Lord that made him, || And will make supplication before the Highest, || And will open his mouth in prayer, || And will make supplication for his sins. **6** If the great Lord wills, || He will be filled with the spirit of understanding: He will pour out the words of his wisdom, || And in prayer give thanks to the Lord. **7** He will direct his counsel and knowledge, || And in His secrets he will meditate. **8** He will show out the instruction which he has been taught || And will glory in the Law of the covenant of the Lord. **9** Many will commend his understanding; And so long as the world endures, || It will not be blotted out: His memorial will not depart, || And his name will live from generation to generation. **10** Nations will declare his wisdom, || And the congregation will tell out his praise. **11** If he continues, he will leave a greater name than one thousand, || And if he dies, he adds to that. **12** Yet more I will utter, which I have thought on; And I am filled as the moon at the full. **13** Listen to me, you holy children, || And bud out as a rose growing by a brook of water: **14** And give a sweet savor as frankincense, || And put out flowers as a lily; Spread abroad a sweet smell, || And sing a song of praise; Bless the Lord for all His works. **15** Magnify His Name, and give utterance to His praise || With the songs of your lips, and with harps; And so will you say when you utter [His praise]: **16** "All the works of the Lord are exceedingly good, || And every command will be [accomplished] in his season." **17** None can say, "What is this? What is that?" For in his season, they will all be sought out. At His word the waters stood as a heap, || And the receptacles of waters at the word of His mouth. **18** At His command all His good pleasure is [done]; And there is none that will hinder His salvation. **19** The works of all flesh are before Him; And it is not possible to be hid from His eyes. **20** He sees from age to age; And there is nothing wonderful before Him. **21** None can say, "What is this? What is that?" For all things are created for their uses. **22** His blessing

covered the dry land as a river || And saturated it as a flood. **23** As He has made the waters salty, || So the heathen will inherit His wrath. **24** His ways are plain to the holy, || So are they stumbling blocks to the wicked. **25** Good things are created from the beginning for the good, || So are evil things for sinners. **26** The chief of all things necessary for the life of man || Are water, and fire, and iron, and salt, || And flour of wheat, and honey, and milk, || The blood of the grape, and oil, and clothing. **27** All these things are for good to the godly; So to the sinners they will be turned into evil. **28** There are winds that are created for vengeance, || And in their fury their scourges lay on heavily; In the time of consummation, they pour out their strength || And will appease the wrath of Him that made them. **29** Fire, and hail, and famine, and death—All these are created for vengeance— **30** Teeth of wild beasts, and scorpions and adders, || And a sword punishing the ungodly to destruction. **31** They will rejoice in His command, || And will be made ready on earth when there is need; And in their seasons they will not transgress [His] word. **32** Therefore, I was resolved from the beginning, || And I considered [this, and] left it in writing; **33** All the works of the Lord are good: And He will supply every need in its season. **34** And none can say, "This is worse than that," || For they will all be well approved in their season. **35** And now with all your heart and mouth || Sing praises and bless the Name of the Lord.

CHAPTER 40

1 Great travail is created for every man, || And a heavy yoke is on the sons of Adam, || From the day of their coming out from their mother's womb, || Until the day for their burial in the mother of all things. **2** The expectation of things to come, and the day of death, || [Trouble] their thoughts, and [cause] fear of heart— **3** From him that sits on a lofty throne, || Even to him that is humbled in earth and ashes; **4** From him that wears purple and a crown, || Even to him that is clothed with a hempen gown **5** [There is] wrath, and jealousy, and trouble, and disquiet, || And fear of death, and anger, and strife, And in the time of rest on his bed || His night sleep changes his knowledge. **6** Little or nothing is his resting, || And afterward in his sleep, as in a day of keeping watch, || He is troubled in the vision of his heart, || As one that has escaped from the front of battle. **7** In the very time of his deliverance he awakens, || And marvels that the fear is nothing. **8** [It is so] with all flesh, from man to beast, || And on sinners sevenfold more. **9** Death, and bloodshed, and strife, and sword, || Calamities, famine, suffering, and the scourge— **10** All these things were created for the wicked, || And because of them the flood came. **11** All things that are of the earth return to the earth again, || And [all things that are] of the waters return into the sea. **12** All bribery and injustice will be blotted out; And good faith will stand forever. **13** The goods of the unjust will be dried up like a river, || And like a great thunder in rain will go off in noise. **14** In opening his hands, [a man] will be made glad; So will transgressors utterly fail. **15** The children of the ungodly will not put out many branches; And [they are as] unclean roots on a sheer rock. **16** The sedge [that grows] on every water and bank of a river || Will be plucked up before all grass. **17** Bounty is as a garden of blessings, || And kindness endures forever. **18** The life of one that labors, and is content, will be made sweet; And he that finds a treasure is above both. **19** Children and the building of a city establish a name; And a blameless wife is counted above both. **20** Wine and music make the heart rejoice; And the love of wisdom is above both. **21** The pipe and the lute make pleasant melody; And a pleasant tongue is above both. **22** Your eye will desire grace and beauty; And above both—the green blade of corn. **23** A friend and a companion never meet wrongly; And a wife with her husband is above both. **24** Brothers and help are for a time of affliction; And kindness is a deliverer above both. **25** Gold and silver will make the foot stand sure; And counsel is esteemed above them both. **26** Riches and strength will lift up the heart; And the fear of the Lord is above both: There is nothing lacking in the fear of the Lord, || And there is no need to seek help therein. **27** The fear of the Lord is as a garden of blessing || And [it] covers a man above all glory. **28** My son, do not lead a beggar's life; It is better to die than to beg. **29** A man that looks to the table of another, || His life is not to be counted for a life; He will pollute his soul with another man's meats, || But a man wise and well-instructed will beware thereof. **30** In the mouth of the shameless, begging will be sweet; And in his belly a fire will be kindled.

CHAPTER 41

1 O death, how bitter is the remembrance of you || To a man that is at peace in his possessions, || To the man that has nothing to distract him, || And [who] has prosperity in all things, || And who still has strength to receive meat! **2** O death, your sentence is acceptable to a man that is needy, || And that fails in strength, that is in extreme old age, || And is distracted about all things, and is perverse, and has lost patience! **3** Do not be afraid of the sentence of death; Remember those who have been before you, || And that come after: This is the sentence from the Lord over all flesh. **4** And why do you refuse, || When it is the good pleasure of the Highest? Whether it be ten, or one hundred, or one thousand years, || There is no inquisition of life in the grave. **5** The children of sinners are abominable children, || And they frequent the dwellings of the ungodly. **6** The inheritance of sinners' children will perish, || And a perpetual reproach will be with their posterity. **7** Children will complain of an ungodly father, || Because they will be reproached for his sake. **8** Woe to you, ungodly men, || Which have forsaken the Law of the Highest God! **9** If you are born, you will be born to a curse; If you die, a curse will be your portion. **10** All things that are of the earth will go back to the earth; So the ungodly will go from a curse to perdition. **11** The mourning of men is about their bodies, || But the name of sinners being evil will be blotted out. **12** Have regard for your name, || For it continues with you longer than one thousand great treasures of gold. **13** A good life has its number of days; And a good name continues forever. **14** My children, keep instruction in peace, || But wisdom that is hid, and a treasure that is not seen, || What profit is in them both? **15** Better is a man that hides his foolishness || Than a man that hides his wisdom. **16** Why show reverence to my word, || For it is not good to retain every kind of shame; And not all things are approved by all in good faith. **17** Be ashamed of whoredom before father and mother, || And of a lie before a prince and a mighty man; **18** Of an offense before a judge and ruler; Of iniquity before the congregation and the people; Of unjust dealing before a partner and friend; **19** And of theft in regard of the place where you sojourn, || And in regard of the truth of God and His covenant; And of leaning with your elbow at meat; And of vulgarity in the matter of giving and taking; **20** And of silence before those who salute you; And of looking on a woman that is a prostitute; **21** And of turning your face away from a relative; Of taking away a portion or a gift; And of gazing on a woman that has a husband; **22** Of being over-busy with his maid—And do not come near her bed; Of scolding speeches before friends; And after you have given, do not scold; **23** Of repeating and speaking what you have heard; And of revealing of secrets. **24** So you will be truly modest and find favor in the sight of every man.

CHAPTER 42

1 Do not be ashamed of these things, || And accept no man's person to sin [by it]: **2** Of the Law of the Highest, and His covenant; And of judgment to do justice to the ungodly; **3** Of reckoning with a partner and with travelers; And of a gift from the heritage of friends; **4** Of exactness of balance and weights; And of getting much or little; **5** Of indifferent selling of merchants; And of much correction of children; And of making the side of an evil servant to bleed. **6** Keeping a seal is good where an evil wife is; And where many hands are, shut [things] closed. **7** Whatever you hand over, || Let it be by number and weight; And in giving and receiving, || Let all be in writing. **8** [Do not be ashamed] to instruct the unwise and foolish, || And one of extreme old age that contends with those that are young; And so you will be well instructed indeed, || And approved in the sight of every living man. **9** A daughter is a secret cause of wakefulness to a father; And the care for her puts away sleep in her youth, || Lest she pass the flower of her age; And when she is married, || Lest she should be hated; **10** In her virginity, || Lest she should be defiled || And be with child in her father's house; And when she has a husband, || Lest she should transgress; And when she is married, || Lest she should be barren. **11** Keep a strict watch over a headstrong daughter, || Lest she makes you a laughing-stock to your enemies, || A byword in the city and notorious among the people, || And shame you before the multitude. **12** Do not look on everybody in regard of beauty || And do not sit in the midst of women; **13** For from garments comes a moth, || And from a woman a woman's wickedness. **14** Better is the wickedness of a man || Than a pleasant-dealing woman, || And a woman which puts you to shameful reproach. **15** I will now make mention of the works of the Lord || And will declare the things that I have seen: In the words of the Lord are His works. **16** The sun that gives light looks on all things; And the work of the Lord is full of His glory. **17** The Lord has not given power to the saints || To declare all His marvelous works, || Which the Almighty Lord firmly settled, || That whatever exists might be established in His glory. **18** He searches out the deep, and the heart, || And He has understanding of their cunning plans; For the Most High knows all knowledge, || And He looks into the signs of the world, **19** Declaring the things that are past, || And revealing the traces of hidden things. **20** No thought escapes Him; There is no word hidden from Him. **21** He has ordered the mighty works of His wisdom—[He] who is from age to age: Nothing has been added to them, || Nor diminished from them; And He had no need of any counselor. **22** How desirable are all His works! One may behold [this] even to a spark. **23** All these things live and remain forever in all manner of uses, || And they are all obedient. **24** All things are double—one against another: And He has made nothing imperfect. **25** One thing establishes the good things of another; And who will be filled with beholding His glory?

CHAPTER 43

1 The pride of the height is the expanse in its clearness, || The appearance of Heaven, in the spectacle of its glory. **2** The sun when he appears, || Bringing tidings as he goes out, || Is a marvelous instrument, the work of the Highest: **3** At his noon he dries up the country, || And who will stand against his burning heat? **4** A man blowing a furnace is in works of heat, || [But] the sun [is] three times more: Burning up the mountains, || Breathing out fiery vapors, || And sending out bright beams—he dims the eyes. **5** Great is the Lord that made him; And at His word he hastens his course. **6** The moon is also in all things for her season, || For a declaration of times, and a sign of the world. **7** From the moon is the sign of the feast day—A light that wanes when she has come to the full. **8** The month is called after her name, || Increasing wonderfully in her changing; An instrument of the army on high, || Shining out in the expanse of Heaven; **9** The beauty of Heaven, the glory of the stars, || An ornament giving light in the highest places of the Lord. **10** At the word of the Holy One they will stand in due order, || And they will not faint in their watches. **11** Look on the rainbow and praise Him that made it—Exceedingly beautiful in the brightness thereof. **12** It encircles the Heaven around with a circle of glory; The hands of the Most High have stretched it. **13** By His command He makes the snow to fall speedily || And swiftly sends the lightnings of His judgment. **14** By reason thereof the treasure-houses are opened; And clouds fly out as birds. **15** By His mighty power He makes the clouds strong, || And the hailstones are broken small: **16** And at His appearing the mountains will be shaken, || And at His will the south wind will blow. **17** The voice of His thunder makes the earth to travail; So does the northern storm and the whirlwind. As birds flying down, He sprinkles the snow; And as the lighting of the locust is the falling down thereof: **18** The eye will marvel at the beauty of its whiteness, || And the heart will be astonished at the raining of it. **19** He also pours the hoarfrost on the earth as salt; And when it is congealed, it is [as] points of thorns. **20** The cold north wind will blow, || And the ice will be congealed on the water: It will lodge on every gathering of water, || And the water will put it on as [if] it were a breastplate. **21** It will devour the mountains, and burn up the wilderness, || And consume the green herb as fire. **22** A mist coming speedily is the healing of all things; A dew coming after heat will bring cheerfulness. **23** By His counsel He has stilled the deep, || And planted islands therein. **24** They that sail on the sea tell of the danger thereof; And when we hear it with our ears, we marvel. **25** Therein are also those strange and wondrous works, || A variety of all that has life—the race of sea-monsters. **26** By reason of Him his end has success, || And by His word all things consist. **27** We may say many things, || Yet we will not attain [to them]; And the sum of our words is, "He is all." **28** How will we have strength to glorify Him? For He Himself is the great one above all His works. **29** The Lord is terrible and exceedingly great; And His power is marvelous. **30** When you glorify the Lord, || Exalt Him as much as you can; For even yet He will exceed: And when you exalt Him, put out your full strength: Do not be weary, for you will never attain. **31** Who has seen Him, that he may declare Him? And who will magnify Him as He is? **32** Many things are hidden greater than these; For we have seen but a few of His works. **33** For the Lord made all things; And He gave wisdom to the godly.

CHAPTER 44

1 Let us now praise famous men, || And our fathers that became the father of us. **2** The Lord manifested [in them] great glory, || [Even] His mighty power from the beginning: **3** Such as bore rule in their kingdoms, || And were men renowned for their power, || Giving counsel by their understanding; Such as have brought tidings in prophecies; **4** Leaders of the people by their counsels, || And by their understanding [men of] learning for the people—Wise [were] their words in their instruction; **5** Such as sought out musical tunes, || And set out verses in writing; **6** Rich men furnished with ability, || Living peaceably in their habitations: **7** All these were honored in their generations, || And were a glory in their days. **8** There is of them, that have left a name behind them, || To declare their praises. **9** And there are some which have no memorial, || Who have perished as though they had not been || And have become as though they had not been born—And their children after them. **10** But these were men of mercy, || Whose righteous deeds have not been forgotten. **11** A good inheritance will remain with their seed continually; Their children [are] within the covenants. **12** Their seed stands fast, || And their children for their sakes. **13** Their seed will remain forever, || And their glory will not be blotted out. **14** Their bodies were buried in peace, || And their name lives to all generations. **15** Peoples will declare their wisdom, || And the congregation tells out their praise. **16** Enoch pleased the Lord, and was translated, || [Being] an example of conversion to all generations. **17** Noah was found perfect [and] righteous; In the season of wrath, he was taken in exchange [for the world]; Therefore a remnant was left to the earth when the flood came. **18** Perpetual covenants were made with him, || That all flesh should no longer be blotted out by a flood. **19** Abraham was a great father of a multitude of nations; And there was none found like him in glory, **20** Who kept the Law of the Highest || And was taken into covenant with Him: In his flesh he established the covenant; And when he was tested, he was found faithful. **21** Therefore He assured him by an oath, || That the nations should be blessed in his seed; That He would multiply him as the dust of the earth, || And exalt his seed as the stars, || And cause them to inherit from sea to sea, || And from the River to the utmost part of the earth. **22** In Isaac He also established likewise, for his father Abraham's sake, || The blessing of all men, and the covenant: **23** And He made it rest on the head of Jacob; He acknowledged him in His blessings, || And gave to him by inheritance, and divided his portions; He parted them among [the] twelve tribes.

CHAPTER 45

1 And He brought out of him a man of mercy, || Which found favor in the sight of all flesh; A man beloved of God and men—Even Moses, whose memorial is blessed. **2** He made him like to the glory of the saints || And magnified him in the fears of his enemies. **3** By his words He caused the wonders to cease; He glorified him in the sight of kings; He gave him command for his people || And showed him part of His glory. **4** He sanctified him in his faithfulness and meekness; He chose him out of all flesh. **5** He made him to hear His voice, || And led him into the thick darkness, || And gave him commands face to face—Even the law of life and knowledge, || That he might teach Jacob the covenant, || And Israel His judgments. **6** He exalted Aaron, a holy man like to him, || Even his brother, of the tribe of Levi. **7** He established a perpetual covenant for him || And gave him the priesthood of the people; He beautified him with attractive ornaments || And girded him around with a robe of glory. **8** He clothed him with the perfection of exultation, || And strengthened him with apparel of honor: The linen trousers, the long robe, and the ephod. **9** And He compassed him with pomegranates of gold, || And with many bells around—To send out a sound as he went, || To make a

sound that might be heard in the temple, || For a memorial to the children of his people— **10** With a holy garment, || With gold, and blue, and purple, the work of the embroiderer, || With an oracle of judgment, || With the Lights and Perfections; **11** With twisted scarlet, the work of the craftsman, || With precious stones graven like a signet, || In a setting of gold, the work of the jeweler, || For a memorial engraved in writing, || After the number of the tribes of Israel; **12** With a crown of gold on the miter, || Having graven on it, as on a signet, Holiness, || An ornament of honor, a work of might, || The desires of the eyes, attractive and beautiful. **13** There have never been any such before him; No stranger put them on, || But his sons only, and his offspring perpetually. **14** His sacrifices will be wholly consumed every day—twice continually. **15** Moses consecrated him and anointed him with holy oil: It was to him for a perpetual covenant, || And to his seed, all the days of Heaven, || To minister to Him, and also to execute the priest's office, || And to bless His people in His Name. **16** He chose him out of all living to offer sacrifice to the Lord, || Incense, and a sweet savor, for a memorial, || To make reconciliation for Your people. **17** He gave His commands to him—Authority in the covenants of judgments, || To teach Jacob the testimonies, || And to enlighten Israel in His law. **18** Strangers gathered themselves together against him, || And envied him in the wilderness, || [Even] Dathan and Abiram with their company, || And the congregation of Korah, with wrath and anger. **19** The Lord saw it, and it displeased Him; And in the wrath of His anger they were destroyed: He did wonders on them, || To consume them with flaming fire. **20** And He added glory to Aaron and gave him a heritage: He divided to him the first-fruits of the increase; [And] first he prepared bread in abundance: **21** For they will eat the sacrifices of the Lord, || Which He gave to him and to his seed. **22** However, in the land of the people he will have no inheritance, || And he has no portion among the people; For He Himself is your portion [and] inheritance. **23** And Phinehas the son of Eleazar is the third in glory, || In that he was zealous in the fear of the Lord, || And stood fast in the good forwardness of his soul when the people turned away, || And he made reconciliation for Israel. **24** Therefore there was a covenant of peace established for him, || [That he should be] leader of the saints and of His people; That he and his seed should have the dignity of the priesthood forever. **25** Also [He made] a covenant with David the son of Jesse, of the tribe of Judah; The inheritance of the king is his alone from son to son; So the inheritance of Aaron is also to his seed. **26** [God] give you wisdom in your heart to judge His people in righteousness, || That their good things may not be abolished, || And [that] their glory [may endure] for all their generations.

CHAPTER 46

1 Joshua the son of Nun was valiant in war || And was the successor of Moses in prophecies: Who according to his name was made great for the saving of God's chosen ones, || To take vengeance of the enemies that rose up against them, || That he might give Israel their inheritance. **2** How he was glorified in lifting up his hands, || And in stretching out his sword against the cities! **3** Who before him so stood fast? For the Lord Himself brought his enemies to him. **4** Did the sun not go back by his hand? And did one day not become as two? **5** He called on the Highest [and] Mighty One, || When his enemies pressed him around; And the great Lord heard him. **6** With hailstones of mighty power || He caused war to break violently on the nation, || And in the going down he destroyed those who resisted, || That the nations might know his armor, || How that he fought in the sight of the Lord; For he followed after the Mighty One. **7** Also in the time of Moses he did a work of mercy—He and Caleb the son of Jephunneh, || In that they withstood the adversary, || Hindered the people from sin, || And stilled the murmuring of wickedness. **8** And of six hundred thousand people on foot, || They two alone were preserved to bring them into the heritage, || Even into a land flowing with milk and honey. **9** Also the Lord gave strength to Caleb, || And it remained with him to his old age, || So that he entered on the height of the land, || And his seed obtained it for a heritage: **10** That all the sons of Israel might see || That it is good to walk after the Lord. **11** Also the judges, everyone by His Name—All whose hearts did not go whoring, || And who did not turn away from the Lord—May their memorial be blessed, **12** May their bones again flourish out of their place, || And may the name of those who have been honored be renewed on their children. **13** Samuel, the prophet of the Lord, beloved of his Lord, || Established a kingdom, and anointed princes over His people. **14** By the Law of the Lord he judged the congregation, || And the Lord visited Jacob. **15** By his faithfulness he was proved to be a prophet, || And by his words he was known to be faithful in vision. **16** Also when his enemies pressed around him, || He called on the Lord, the Mighty One, || With the offering of the sucking lamb. **17** And the Lord thundered from Heaven, || And made His voice to be heard with a mighty sound. **18** And He utterly destroyed the rulers of the Tyrians, || And all the princes of the Philistines. **19** Also before the time of his long sleep || He made protestations in the sight of the Lord and [His] anointed: "I have not taken any man's goods, so much as a sandal": And no man did accuse him. **20** And after he fell asleep, he prophesied, || And showed the king his end, || And lifted up his voice from the earth in prophecy, || To blot out the wickedness of the people.

CHAPTER 47

1 And after him, Nathan rose up to prophesy in the days of David. **2** As is the fat when it is separated from the peace offering, || So was David [separated] from the sons of Israel. **3** He played with lions as with kids, || And with bears as with lambs of the flock. **4** In his youth did he not kill a giant, || And take away reproach from the people, || When he lifted up his hand with a sling stone, || And beat down the boasting of Goliath? **5** For he called on the Highest Lord; And He gave him strength in his right hand, || To kill a man mighty in war, || To exalt the horn of His people. **6** So they glorified him for [his] tens of thousands, || And praised him for the blessings of the Lord, || In that there was given to him a diadem of glory. **7** For he destroyed the enemies on every side, || And brought to nothing the Philistines his adversaries, || [And] broke their horn in pieces to this day. **8** In every work of his || He gave thanks to the Holy One Most High with words of glory; With his whole heart he sang praise || And loved Him that made him. **9** He also set singers before the altar, || So as to make sweet melody by their music. **10** He gave beauty to the feasts, || And set in order the seasons to perfection, || While they praised His holy Name, || And the sanctuary sounded from early morning. **11** The Lord took away his sins, || And exalted his horn forever, || And gave him a covenant of kings, || And a throne of glory in Israel. **12** After him, [his] son rose up—a man of understanding; And for his sake he lived at large. **13** Solomon reigned in days of peace, || And God gave to him rest around, || That he might set up a house for His Name || And prepare a sanctuary forever. **14** How wise you were made in your youth || And filled as a river with understanding! **15** Your soul covered the earth, || And you filled it with dark allegories. **16** Your name reached to the isles far off; And you were beloved for your peace. **17** For your songs, and proverbs, and allegories, || And for your interpretations, the countries marveled at you. **18** By the Name of the Lord God, which is called the God of Israel, || You gathered gold as tin and multiplied silver as lead. **19** You bowed your loins to women, || And in your body you were brought into subjection. **20** You blemished your honor and profaned your seed, || To bring wrath on your children; And I was grieved for your folly, **21** So that the sovereignty was divided, || And out of Ephraim a disobedient kingdom ruled. **22** But the Lord will never forsake His mercy; And He will not destroy any of His works, || Nor blot out the posterity of His chosen ones; And the seed of him that loved Him He will not take away; And He gave a remnant to Jacob, || And to David a root out of him. **23** And [so] rested Solomon with his fathers; And of his seed he left behind him Rehoboam—[Even] the foolishness of the people, || And one that lacked understanding, || Who made the people to revolt by his counsel. Also Jeroboam the son of Nebat, || Who made Israel to sin, and gave to Ephraim a way of sin. **24** And their sins were multiplied exceedingly, || To remove them from their land. **25** For they sought out all manner of wickedness, || Until vengeance should come on them.

CHAPTER 48

1 Also there arose Elijah the prophet as fire, || And his word burned like a torch: **2** Who brought a famine on them, || And by his zeal made them few in number. **3** By the word of the Lord he shut up the Heaven: Three times he so brought down fire. **4** How you were glorified, O Elijah, in your wondrous deeds! And who will [have] glory like to you? **5** Who raised up a dead man from death, || And from the place of the dead, by the word of the Most High; **6** Who brought down kings to destruction, || And honorable men from their bed; **7** Who heard rebuke in Sinai, || And judgments of vengeance in Horeb; **8** Who anointed kings for retribution, || And prophets to succeed after him; **9** Who was taken up in a tempest of fire, || In a chariot of fiery horses; **10** Who was recorded for reproofs in their seasons, || To pacify anger, before it broke out into wrath; To turn the heart of the father to the son, || And to restore the tribes of Jacob. **11** Blessed are those who saw you, || And those who have been beautified with love; For we also will surely live. **12** [It was] Elijah who was wrapped in a tempest, || And Elisha was filled with his spirit; And in [all] his days he was not moved by [the fear of] any ruler, || And no one brought him into subjection. **13** Nothing was too high for him; And when he was laid on sleep his body prophesied. **14** As in his life he did wonders, || So in death his works were marvelous. **15** For all this the people did not convert, || And they did not depart from their sins, || Until they were carried away as a plunder from their land || And were scattered through all the earth; And the people were left very few in number, || And a ruler [was left] in the house of David. **16** Some of them did that which was pleasing [to God], || [And] some multiplied sins. **17** Hezekiah fortified his city || And brought in water into the midst of them: He dug the sheer rock with iron || And built up wells for waters. **18** In his days Sennacherib came up, || And sent Rabshakeh, and departed; And he lifted up his hand against Zion || And boasted great things in his arrogance. **19** Then their hearts and their hands were shaken, || And they were in pain, as women in travail; **20** And they called on the Lord, who is merciful, || Spreading out their hands to Him: And the Holy One heard them speedily out of Heaven, || And delivered them by the hand of Isaiah. **21** He struck the camp of the Assyrians, || And His messenger utterly destroyed them. **22** For Hezekiah did that which was pleasing to the Lord || And was strong in the ways of his father David, || Which Isaiah the prophet commanded, || Who was great and faithful in his vision. **23** In his days the sun went backward; And he added life to the king. **24** He saw by an excellent spirit what should come to pass at the end; And he comforted those who mourned in Zion. **25** He showed the things that should be to the end of time, || And the hidden things before they came.

CHAPTER 49

1 The memorial of Josiah is like the composition of incense || Prepared by the work of the apothecary: It will be sweet as honey in every mouth, || And as music at a banquet of wine. **2** He behaved himself uprightly in the conversion of the people || And took away the abominations of iniquity. **3** He set his heart right toward the Lord; In the days of wicked men, || He made godliness to prevail. **4** Except David, and Hezekiah, and Josiah, all committed trespass; For they forsook the Law of the Highest; The kings of Judah failed. **5** For they gave their power to others, || And their glory to a strange nation. **6** They set the chosen city of the sanctuary on fire, || And made her streets desolate, [as it was written] by the hand of Jeremiah. **7** For they mistreated him; And yet he was sanctified in the womb to be a prophet, || To root out, and to afflict, and to destroy; [And] in like manner to build and to plant. **8** [It was] Ezekiel who saw the vision of glory, || Which [God] showed him on the chariot of the cherubim. **9** For truly he remembered the enemies in storm, || And to do good to those who directed their ways correctly. **10** Also of the twelve prophets || May the bones flourish again out of their place. And he comforted Jacob and delivered them by confidence of hope. **11** How will we magnify Zerubbabel? And he was as a signet on the right hand: **12** So was Jesus the son of Josedek: Who in their days built the house, || And exalted a people holy to the Lord, prepared for continuous glory. **13** Also of Nehemiah the memorial is great: Who raised up for us the walls that were fallen, || And set up the gates and bars, and raised up our homes again. **14** No man was created on the earth such as was Enoch; For he was taken up from the earth. **15** Neither was there a man born like to Joseph, || A governor of his countrymen, a support of the people: Yes, his bones were visited. **16** Shem and Seth were glorified among men; And above every living thing in the creation is Adam.

CHAPTER 50

¹ [It was] Simon, the son of Onias, the great priest, || Who in his life repaired the house, || And in his days strengthened the temple: ² And by him was built from the foundation the height of the double [wall], || The lofty underworks of the enclosure of the temple: ³ In his days the cistern of waters was diminished, || The brazen vessel in compass as the sea. ⁴ [It was] he that took thought for his people that they should not fall || And fortified the city against besieging; ⁵ How glorious was he when the people gathered around him || At his coming out of the sanctuary— ⁶ As the morning star in the midst of a cloud, || As the moon at the full; ⁷ As the sun shining out on the temple of the Most High, || And as the rainbow giving light in clouds of glory; ⁸ As the flower of roses in the days of new [fruits], || As lilies at the water spring, || As the shoot of the frankincense tree in the time of summer; ⁹ As fire and incense in the censer, || As a vessel all of beaten gold, || Adorned with all manner of precious stones; ¹⁰ As an olive tree budding out fruits, || And as a cypress growing high among the clouds. ¹¹ When he took up the robe of glory, || And put on the perfection of exultation, || In the ascent of the holy altar, || He made the precinct of the sanctuary glorious. ¹² And when he received the portions out of the priests' hands, || Himself also standing by the hearth of the altar, || His countrymen as a garland around him, || He was as a young cedar in Libanus; And as stems of palm trees compassed around him, ¹³ And all the sons of Aaron in their glory, || And the Lord's offering in their hands, || Before all the congregation of Israel. ¹⁴ And finishing the service at the altars, || That he might adorn the offering of the Highest, the Almighty, ¹⁵ He stretched out his hand to the cup, || And poured out the cup of the grape; He poured out at the foot of the altar || A sweet smelling savor to the Highest, the King of all. ¹⁶ Then the sons of Aaron shouted, || They sounded the trumpets of beaten work, || They made a great noise to be heard, || For a remembrance before the Highest. ¹⁷ Then all the people hurried together || And fell down on the earth on their faces to worship their Lord—The Almighty, God Most High. ¹⁸ The singers also praised Him with their voices; In the whole house sweet melody was made. ¹⁹ And the people implored the Lord Most High, || In prayer before Him that is merciful, || Until the worship of the Lord should be ended; And so, they accomplished His service. ²⁰ Then he went down and lifted up his hands || Over the whole congregation of the sons of Israel, || To give blessing to the Lord with his lips, || And to glory in His Name. ²¹ And he bowed himself down in worship the second time, || To declare the blessing from the Highest. ²² And now bless the God of all, who everywhere does great things, || Who exalts our days from the womb, || And deals with us according to His mercy. ²³ May He grant us joyfulness of heart, || And that peace may be in our days in Israel for the days of [the] age: ²⁴ To entrust His mercy with us; And let Him deliver us in His time! ²⁵ With two nations is my soul vexed, || And the third is no nation: ²⁶ They that sit on the mountain of Samaria, and the Philistines, || And that foolish people that dwells in Shechem. ²⁷ I have written in this scroll the instruction of understanding and knowledge, || I, Jesus, the son of Sirach Eleazar, of Jerusalem, || Who out of his heart poured out wisdom. ²⁸ Blessed is he that will be exercised in these things; And he that lays them up in his heart will become wise. ²⁹ For if he does them, he will be strong for all things; For the light of the Lord is his guide.

CHAPTER 51

A Prayer of Jesus the son of Sirach. ¹ I will give thanks to You, O Lord, O King, || And will praise You, O God my Savior: I give thanks to Your Name, ² For You were my protector and helper, || And You delivered my body out of destruction, || And out of the snare of a slanderous tongue, || From lips that forge lies, || And were my helper before those who stood by; ³ And You delivered me, || According to the abundance of Your mercy, and [greatness] of Your Name, || From the gnashing [of teeth] ready to devour, || Out of the hand of such as sought my life, || Out of the manifold afflictions which I had; ⁴ From the choking of a fire on every side, || And out of the midst of fire which I did not kindle; ⁵ Out of the depth of the belly of the grave, || And from an unclean tongue, and from lying words— ⁶ The slander of an unrighteous tongue to the king. My soul drew near even to death, || And my life was near to the grave beneath. ⁷ They compassed me on every side, || And there was none to help [me]. I was looking for the help of men, and it was not. ⁸ And I remembered Your mercy, O Lord, || And Your working which has been from perpetuity, || How You deliver those who wait for You, || And save them out of the hand of the enemies. ⁹ And I lifted up my supplication from the earth || And prayed for deliverance from death. ¹⁰ I called on the Lord, the Father of my Lord, || That He would not forsake me in the days of affliction, || In the time when there was no help against the proud. ¹¹ I will praise Your Name continually || And will sing praise with thanksgiving; And my supplication was heard; ¹² For You saved me from destruction, || And delivered me from the evil time. Therefore, I will give thanks and praise to You, || And bless the Name of the Lord. ¹³ When I was yet young, before I went abroad, || I sought wisdom openly in my prayer. ¹⁴ Before the temple I asked for her, || And I will seek her out even to the end. ¹⁵ From [her] flower, as from the ripening grape, || My heart delighted in her; My foot trod in uprightness, || From my youth I tracked her out. ¹⁶ I bowed my ear down a little, and received her, || And found for myself much instruction. ¹⁷ I profited in her: To Him that gives me wisdom I will give glory. ¹⁸ For I purposed to practice her, || And I was zealous for that which is good; And I will never be put to shame. ¹⁹ My soul has wrestled in her, || And in my doing I was exact: I spread out my hands to the Heaven above || And mourned my ignorance of her. ²⁰ I set my soul properly to her, || And in pureness I found her. I got myself a heart [joined] with her from the beginning: Therefore, I will not be forsaken. ²¹ My inward part was also troubled to seek her: Therefore, I have gotten a good possession. ²² The Lord gave me a tongue for my reward; And I will praise Him with that. ²³ Draw near to me, you unlearned, || And lodge in the house of instruction. ²⁴ Say, "Why are you lacking in these things, || And your souls are very thirsty?" ²⁵ I opened my mouth, and spoke, || "Get her for yourselves without money. ²⁶ Put your neck under the yoke, || And let your soul receive instruction: She is hard at hand to find. ²⁷ Behold with your eyes, how that I labored but a little, || And found for myself much rest. ²⁸ Get instruction with a great sum of silver || And gain much gold by her. ²⁹ May your soul rejoice in His mercy, || And may you not be put to shame in praising Him. ³⁰ Work your work before the time comes, || And in His time, He will give you your reward."

1 BARUCH

Called Baruch by most, but 1 Baruch in the LSV for distinction, the opening verses ascribe the book to the well-known assistant to Jeremiah (Jer. 32:12; 36:4, 32; 45:1). It is a collection of four very different compositions, ending with a work entitled "The Letter of Jeremiah," which circulated separately in major manuscripts of the Greek tradition. The original language was likely Hebrew, but only the Greek and other versions have been preserved. The setting is Babylon, where Baruch reads his scroll to King Jechoniah (Jehoiachin) and the exiles; they react by sending gifts and the scroll to Jerusalem (1:1–14), presumably by the hand of Baruch (1:7). No certain date can be given for the book, but it may have been edited in final form during the last two centuries BC.

CHAPTER 1

¹ These are the words of the scroll, which Baruch the son of Neriah, the son of Mahseiah, the son of Zedekiah, the son of Hasadiah, the son of Hilkiah, wrote in Babylon, ² in the fifth year, [and] in the seventh day of the month, at the time the Chaldeans took Jerusalem, and burned it with fire. ³ And Baruch read the words of this scroll in the hearing of Jehoiachin the son of Jehoiakim king of Judah, and in the hearing of all the people that came to [hear] the scroll, ⁴ and in the hearing of the mighty men, and of the kings' sons, and in the hearing of the elders, and in the hearing of all the people, from the least to the greatest, even of all those who lived at Babylon by the River Sud. ⁵ And they wept, and fasted, and prayed before the Lord; ⁶ they also made a collection of money according to

every man's power: [7] and they sent [it] to Jerusalem to Jehoiakim the [high] priest, the son of Hilkiah, the son of Salom, and to the priests, and to all the people which were found with him at Jerusalem, [8] at the same time when he took the vessels of the house of the Lord, that had been carried out of the temple, to return [them] into the land of Judah, the tenth day of the [month] Sivan, [namely,] silver vessels, which Zedekiah the son of Josiah king of Judah had made, [9] after Nebuchadnezzar king of Babylon had carried away Jehoiachin, and the princes, and the captives, and the mighty men, and the people of the land, from Jerusalem, and brought them to Babylon. [10] And they said: "Behold, we have sent you money; therefore buy with the money burnt-offerings, and sin offerings, and incense, and prepare an oblation, and offer on the altar of the Lord our God; [11] and pray for the life of Nebuchadnezzar king of Babylon, and for the life of his son Belshazzar, that their days may be as the days of Heaven above the earth: [12] and the Lord will give us strength, and lighten our eyes, and we will live under the shadow of Nebuchadnezzar king of Babylon, and under the shadow of his son Belshazzar, and we will serve them many days, and find favor in their sight. [13] Pray for us also to the Lord our God, for we have sinned against the Lord our God; and to this day the wrath of the Lord and His indignation is not turned from us. [14] And you will read this scroll which we have sent to you, to make confession in the house of the Lord, on the day of the feast and on the days of the solemn assembly." [15] And you will say: To the Lord our God [belongs] righteousness, but to us confusion of face, as at this day, to the men of Judah, and to the inhabitants of Jerusalem, [16] and to our kings, and to our princes, and to our priests, and to our prophets, and to our fathers: [17] for that we have sinned before the Lord, [18] and disobeyed Him, and have not listened to the voice of the Lord our God, to walk in the commands of the Lord that He has set before us: [19] since the day that the Lord brought our fathers out of the land of Egypt, to this present day, we have been disobedient to the Lord our God, and we have dealt unadvisedly in not listening to His voice. [20] Why the plagues cleaved to us, and the curse, which the Lord commanded Moses His servant [to pronounce] in the day that He brought our fathers out of the land of Egypt, to give us a land that flows with milk and honey, as at this day. [21] Nevertheless, we did not listen to the voice of the Lord our God, according to all the words of the prophets, whom He sent to us, [22] but we walked—every man—in the imagination of his own wicked heart, to serve strange gods, and to do that which is evil in the sight of the Lord our God.

CHAPTER 2

[1] Therefore the Lord has made good His word, which He pronounced against us, and against our judges that judged Israel, and against our kings, and against our princes, and against the men of Israel and Judah, [2] to bring on us great plagues, such as never happened under the whole Heaven, as it came to pass in Jerusalem, according to the things that are written in the Law of Moses; [3] That we should eat—every man—the flesh of his own son, and every man the flesh of his own daughter. [4] Moreover, He has given them to be in subjection to all the kingdoms that are around us, to be a reproach and a desolation among all the surrounding people, where the Lord has scattered them. [5] So were they cast down, and not exalted, because we sinned against the Lord our God, in not listening to His voice. [6] To the Lord our God [belongs] righteousness, but to us and to our fathers confusion of face, as at this day. [7] [For] all these plagues have come on us, which the Lord has pronounced against us. [8] Yet we have not entreated the favor of the Lord, in turning everyone from the thoughts of his wicked heart. [9] Therefore the Lord has kept watch over the plagues, and the Lord has brought [them] on us; for the Lord is righteous in all His works which He has commanded us. [10] Yet we have not listened to His voice, to walk in the commands of the Lord that He has set before us. [11] And now, O Lord, You God of Israel, that have brought Your people out of the land of Egypt with a mighty hand, and with signs, and with wonders, and with great power, and with a high arm, and have gotten Yourself a Name, as at this day: [12] O Lord our God, we have sinned, we have been ungodly, we have dealt unrighteously in all Your ordinances. [13] Let Your wrath turn from us, for we are but a few left among the heathen, where You have scattered us. [14] Hear our prayer, O Lord, and our petition, and deliver us

for Your own sake, and give us favor in the sight of them which have led us away captive, [15] that all the earth may know that You are the Lord our God, because Israel and his posterity is called by Your Name. [16] O Lord, look down from Your holy house, and consider us: incline Your ear, O Lord, and hear: [17] open Your eyes, and behold, for the dead that are in the grave, whose breath is taken from their bodies, will give to the Lord neither glory nor righteousness: [18] but the soul that is greatly vexed, which goes stooping and feeble, and the eyes that fail, and the hungry soul, will give You glory and righteousness, O Lord. [19] For we do not present our supplication before You, O Lord our God, for the righteousness of our fathers, and of our kings. [20] For You have sent Your wrath and Your indignation on us, as You have spoken by Your servants the prophets, [saying,] [21] "The Lord says, Bow your shoulders to serve the king of Babylon, and remain in the land that I gave to your fathers. [22] But if you will not hear the voice of the Lord, to serve the king of Babylon, [23] I will cause to cease out of the cities of Judah, and from the region near Jerusalem, the voice of mirth, and the voice of gladness, the voice of the bridegroom, and the voice of the bride: and the whole land will be desolate without inhabitant." [24] But we would not listen to Your voice, to serve the king of Babylon: therefore You have made good Your words that You spoke by Your servants the prophets, [namely,] that the bones of our kings, and the bones of our fathers, should be taken out of their places. [25] And behold, they are cast out to the heat by day, and to the frost by night, and they died in great miseries by famine, by sword, and by pestilence. [26] And the house which is called by Your Name have You laid [waste], as at this day, for the wickedness of the house of Israel and the house of Judah. [27] Yet, O Lord our God, You have dealt with us after all Your kindness, and according to all Your great mercy, [28] as You spoke by Your servant Moses in the day when You commanded him to write Your law before the sons of Israel, saying, [29] "If you will not hear My voice, surely this very great multitude will be turned into a small [number] among the nations, where I will scatter them. [30] For I know that they will not hear Me, because it is a stiff-necked people, but in the land of their captivity they will take it to heart, [31] and will know that I am the Lord their God: and I will give them a heart, and ears to hear: [32] and they will praise Me in the land of their captivity, and think on My Name, [33] and will return from their stiff neck, and from their wicked deeds, for they will remember the way of their fathers, which sinned before the Lord. [34] And I will bring them again into the land which I swore to their fathers, to Abraham, to Isaac, and to Jacob, and they will be lords of it: and I will increase them, and they will not be diminished. [35] And I will make a perpetual covenant with them to be their God, and they will be My people: and I will no longer remove My people Israel out of the land that I have given them."

CHAPTER 3

[1] O Lord Almighty, You God of Israel, the soul in anguish, the troubled spirit, cries to You. [2] Hear, O Lord, and have mercy; for You are a merciful God: yes, have mercy on us, because we have sinned before You. [3] For You sit [as king] forever, and we perish forevermore. [4] O Lord Almighty, You God of Israel, hear now the prayer of the dead Israelites, and of the children of them which were sinners before You, that did not listen to the voice of You their God, for this reason these plagues cleaved to us. [5] Do not remember the iniquities of our fathers, but remember Your power and Your Name [now] at this time. [6] For You are the Lord our God, and You, O Lord, will we praise. [7] For this reason You have put Your fear in our hearts, to the intent that we should call on Your Name, and we will praise You in our captivity, for we have called to mind all the iniquity of our fathers, that sinned before You. [8] Behold, we are yet this day in our captivity, where You have scattered us, for a reproach and a curse, and to be subject to penalty, according to all the iniquities of our fathers, which departed from the Lord our God. [9] Hear, O Israel, the commands of life: give ear to understand wisdom. [10] How is it, O Israel, that you are in your enemies' land, that you have become old in a strange country, that you are defiled with the dead, [11] that you are counted with those who [go down] into the grave? [12] You have forsaken the fountain of wisdom. [13] [For] if you had walked in the way of God, you should have dwelled in peace forever. [14] Learn where is wisdom, where is strength, where is understanding; that you may also know where is length of days, and life, where is the light of the eyes, and peace. [15] Who

has found out her place? and who has come into her treasuries? **16** Where are the princes of the heathen, and such as ruled the beasts that are on the earth; **17** those who had their pastime with the birds of the air, and those who hoarded up silver and gold, wherein men trust; and of whose getting there is no end? **18** For those who made in silver, and were so careful, and whose works are past finding out, **19** they are vanished and gone down to the grave, and others have come up in their steads. **20** Younger men have seen the light and lived on the earth, but the way of knowledge they have not known, **21** neither did they understand the paths thereof, neither have their children embraced it: they are far off from their way. **22** It has not been heard of in Canaan, neither has it been seen in Teman. **23** The sons also of Agar that seek understanding, which are in the land, the merchants of Merran and Teman, and the authors of fables, and the searchers out of understanding; none of these have known the way of wisdom or remembered her paths. **24** O Israel, how great is the house of God! and how large is the place of His possession! **25** [It is] great, and has no end; high, and unmeasurable. **26** There were the giants born that were famous of old, great of stature, [and] expert in war. **27** God did not choose these, nor did He give the way of knowledge to them; **28** so they perished, because they had no wisdom, they perished through their own foolishness. **29** Who has gone up into Heaven, and taken her, and brought her down from the clouds? **30** Who has gone over the sea, and found her, and will bring her for choice gold? **31** There is none that knows her way, nor any that comprehends her path. **32** But He that knows all things knows her, He found her out with His understanding: He that prepared the earth forevermore has filled it with four-footed beasts: **33** He that sends out the light, and it goes; He called it, and it obeyed Him with fear: **34** and the stars shone in their watches, and were glad when He called them, they said, "Here we are." They shone with gladness to Him that made them. **35** This is our God, [and] there will none other be accounted of in comparison of Him. **36** He has found out all the way of knowledge, and has given it to His servant Jacob, and to Israel that is beloved of Him. **37** Afterward she appeared on earth and was conversant with men.

CHAPTER 4

1 This is the scroll of the commands of God, and the law that endures forever: All those who hold it fast [are appointed] to life; but such as leave it will die. **2** Turn, O Jacob, and take hold of it: walk toward her shining in the presence of the light thereof. **3** Do not give your glory to another, nor the things that are profitable to you to a strange nation. **4** O Israel, happy are we, for the things that are pleasing to God are made known to us. **5** Be of good cheer, my people, the memorial of Israel. **6** You were sold to the nations, [but] not for destruction: because you moved God to wrath, you were delivered to your adversaries. **7** For you provoked Him that made you by sacrificing to demons, and not to God. **8** You forgot the perpetual God that brought you up; you also grieved Jerusalem that nursed you. **9** For she saw the wrath that has come on you from God, and said, "Listen, you [women] that dwell about Zion, for God has brought on me great mourning; **10** for I have seen the captivity of my sons and daughters, which the Perpetual has brought on them. **11** For with joy I nourished them, but sent them away with weeping and mourning. **12** Let no man rejoice over me, a widow, and forsaken of many, for the sins of my children I am left desolate, because they turned away from the law of God, **13** and had no regard to His statutes, neither did they walk in the ways of God's commands, nor trod in the paths of discipline in His righteousness. **14** Let those who dwell about Zion come, and remember the captivity of my sons and daughters, which the Perpetual has brought on them. **15** For He has brought a nation on them from far, a shameless nation, and of a strange language, who neither gave reverence to old man, nor pitied child. **16** And they have carried away the dear beloved sons of the widow and left her that was alone desolate of her daughters. **17** But I—how can I help you? **18** For He that brought these plagues on you will deliver you from the hand of your enemies. **19** Go your way, O my children, go your way, for I am left desolate. **20** I have put off the garment of peace and put on myself the sackcloth of my petition: I will cry to the Perpetual as long as I live. **21** Be of good cheer, O my children, cry to God, and He will deliver you from the power and hand of the enemies. **22** For I have trusted in the Perpetual, that He will save you; and joy has come to me from the Holy

One, because of the mercy which will soon come to you from your continuous Savior. **23** For I sent you out with mourning and weeping, but God will give you to me again with joy and gladness forever. **24** For like as now those who dwell about Zion have seen your captivity, so they will shortly see your salvation from our God, which will come on you with great glory, and brightness of the Perpetual. **25** My children, suffer patiently the wrath that has come on you from God, for your enemy has persecuted you; but shortly you will see his destruction, and will tread on their necks. **26** My delicate ones have gone rough ways; they were taken away as a flock carried off by the enemies. **27** Be of good cheer, O my children, and cry to God, for you will be remembered of Him that has brought [these things] on you. **28** For as it was your mind to go astray from God, return and seek Him ten times more. **29** For He that brought these plagues on you will bring you continuous joy again with your salvation." **30** Be of good cheer, O Jerusalem, for He that called you by name will comfort you. **31** Miserable are those who afflicted you and rejoiced at your fall. **32** Miserable are the cities which your children served; miserable is she that received your sons. **33** For as she rejoiced at your fall, and was glad of your ruin, so she will be grieved for her own desolation. **34** And I will take away her exultation in her great multitude, and her boasting will be turned into mourning. **35** For fire will come on her from the Perpetual, long to endure; and she will be inhabited of devils for a great time. **36** O Jerusalem look around you toward the east and behold the joy that comes to you from God. **37** Behold, your sons come, whom you sent away, they come gathered together from the east to the west at the word of the Holy One, rejoicing in the glory of God.

CHAPTER 5

1 Put off, O Jerusalem, the garment of your mourning and affliction, and put on the beauty of the glory that [comes] from God forever. **2** Cast about you the robe of the righteousness which [comes] from God; set a diadem on your head of the glory of the Perpetual. **3** For God will show your brightness to every [region] under Heaven. **4** For your name will be called of God forever, The Peace of Righteousness, and, The Glory of Godliness. **5** Arise, O Jerusalem, and stand on the height, and look around you toward the east, and behold your children gathered from the going down of the sun to the rising thereof at the word of the Holy One, rejoicing that God has remembered them. **6** For they went from you on foot, being led away of their enemies, but God brings them in to you, borne on high with glory, as [on] a royal throne. **7** For God has appointed that every high mountain, and the perpetual hills, should be made low, and the valleys filled up, to make plain the ground, that Israel may go safely in the glory of God. **8** Moreover the woods and every sweet-smelling tree have overshadowed Israel by the command of God. **9** For God will lead Israel with joy in the light of His glory with the mercy and righteousness that comes from Him.

CHAPTER 6

1 A copy of a letter, which Jeremiah sent to them which were to be led captives into Babylon by the king of the Babylonians, to certify them, as it was commanded him of God. **2** Because of the sins which you have committed before God, you will be led away captives to Babylon by Nebuchadnezzar king of the Babylonians. **3** So when you come to Babylon, you will remain there many years, and for a long season, even for seven generations: and after that I will bring you out peaceably from there. **4** But now you will see in Babylon gods of silver, and of gold, and of wood, borne on shoulders, which cause the nations to fear. **5** Beware, therefore, that you in no way become like to the strangers, neither let fear take hold on you because of them, when you see the multitude before them and behind them, worshiping them. **6** But say in your hearts, "O Lord, we must worship You." **7** For My messenger is with you, and I Myself care for your souls. **8** For their tongue is polished by the workman, and they themselves are overlaid with gold and with silver; yet they are but false and cannot speak. **9** And taking gold, as it were for a virgin that loves to be happy, they make crowns for the heads of their gods: **10** and sometimes also the priests carry from their gods gold and silver and bestow it on themselves; **11** and will even give thereof to the common prostitutes: and they deck them as men with garments, [even] the gods of silver, and gods of gold, and of wood. **12** Yet these gods cannot save themselves from rust and moths, though they are covered with purple raiment. **13** They wipe their faces because of the dust of the temple, which is thick on them. **14** And he that cannot put to death one that offends against him holds a scepter, as though he were judge of a country. **15** He also has a dagger in his right hand, and an axe, but cannot deliver himself from war and robbers. **16** Whereby they are not known to be gods: therefore, do not fear them. **17** For like as a vessel that a man uses is worth nothing when it is broken, even so it is with their gods: when they are set up in the temples their eyes are full of dust through the feet of those who come in. **18** And as the courts are made sure on every side on him that offends the king, as being committed to suffer death, [even so] the priests make fast their temples with doors, with locks, and bars, lest they are carried off by robbers. **19** They light the candles, yes, more than for themselves, of which they cannot see one. **20** They are as one of the beams of the temple; and men say their hearts are eaten out, when things creeping out of the earth devour both them and their raiment: **21** they do not feel it when their faces are blackened through the smoke that comes out of the temple: **22** bats, swallows, and birds land on their bodies and heads; and in like manner the cats also. **23** Whereby you may know that they are no gods: therefore, do not fear them. **24** Notwithstanding the gold with which they are beset to make them beautiful, except one wipe off the rust, they will not shine, for not even when they were molten did they feel it. **25** Things wherein there is no breath are bought at any cost. **26** Having no feet, they are borne on shoulders, whereby they declare to men that they are worth nothing. **27** They also that serve them are ashamed, for if they fall to the ground at any time, they cannot rise up again of themselves; neither, if they are bowed down, can they make themselves straight, but the offerings are set before them, as if they were dead men. **28** And the things that are sacrificed to them, their priests sell and spend; and in like manner their wives also lay up part thereof in salt; but to the poor and to the impotent they will give nothing thereof. **29** The menstruous woman and the woman in childbirth touch their sacrifices, knowing, therefore, by these things, that they are not gods, [and so] do not fear them. **30** For how can they be called gods? because women set meat before the gods of silver, gold, and wood. **31** And in their temples the priests sit on seats, having their clothes torn, and their heads and beards shaven, and nothing on their heads. **32** They roar and cry before their gods, as men do at the feast when one is dead. **33** The priests also take off garments from them and clothe their wives and children in addition. **34** Whether it be evil that one does to them, or good, they are not able to repay it: they can neither set up a king, nor put him down. **35** In like manner, they can neither give riches nor money; though a man makes a vow to them, and does not keep it, they will never exact it. **36** They can save no man from death, neither deliver the weak from the mighty. **37** They cannot restore a blind man to his sight, nor deliver any that is in distress. **38** They can show no mercy to the widow, nor do good to the fatherless. **39** They are like the stones that are [hewn] out of the mountain, [these gods] of wood, and that are overlaid with gold and with silver. Those who minister to them will be confounded. **40** How should a man then think or say that they are gods, when even the Chaldeans themselves dishonor them? **41** Who if they will see one mute that cannot speak, they bring him, and entreat him to call on Bel, as though he were able to understand. **42** Yet they cannot perceive this themselves and forsake them, for they have no understanding. **43** The women also with cords around them sit in the ways, burning bran for incense, but if any of them, drawn by some that passes by, lies with him, she reproaches her fellow, that she was not thought as worthy as herself, nor her cord broken. **44** Whatever is done among them is false. How should a man then think or say that they are gods? **45** They are fashioned by carpenters and goldsmiths—they can be nothing else than the workmen will have them to be. **46** And they themselves that fashioned them can never continue long; how then should the things that are fashioned by them? **47** For they have left lies and reproaches to those who come after. **48** For when there comes any war or plague on them, the priests consult with themselves, where they may be hidden with them. **49** How then can men not understand that they are not gods, which can neither save themselves from war, nor from plague? **50** For seeing they are but of wood, and overlaid with gold and with silver, it will be known hereafter that they are false; **51** and it will be manifest to all nations and kings that they are no gods, but the works of men's hands, and that there is no work of God in them. **52** Who then may not know that they are no gods? **53** For neither can they set up a king in a land, nor give rain to men. **54** Neither can they judge their own cause, nor redress a wrong, being unable, for they are as crows between the heavens and earth. **55** For even when fire falls on the house of gods of wood, or overlaid with gold or with silver, their priests will flee away, and escape, but they themselves will be burned apart like beams. **56** Moreover they cannot withstand any king or enemies. How should a man then allow or think that they are gods? **57** Neither are those gods of wood, and overlaid with silver or with gold, able to escape either from thieves or robbers. **58** Whose gold, and silver, and garments with which they are clothed, they that are strong will take from them, and go away with [them]; neither will they be able to help themselves. **59** Therefore it is better to be a king that shows his manhood, or else a vessel in a house profitable for that of which the owner will have need, than such false gods; or even a door in a house, to keep the things safe that are therein, than such false gods; or a pillar of wood in a palace, than such false gods. **60** For sun, and moon, and stars, being bright and sent to do their offices, are obedient. **61** Likewise also, the lightning when it glitters is fair to see; and after the same manner the wind also blows in every country. **62** And when God commands the clouds to go over the whole world, they do as they are told. **63** And the fire sent from above to consume mountains and woods does as it is commanded, but these are to be likened to them neither in show nor power. **64** Why a man should neither think nor say that they are gods, seeing they are neither able to judge causes, nor to do good to men. **65** Knowing, therefore, that they are not gods, do not fear them. **66** For they can neither curse nor bless kings; **67** neither can they show signs in the heavens among the nations, nor shine as the sun, nor give light as the moon. **68** The beasts are better than they, for they can get under a covert and help themselves. **69** In no way then is it manifest to us that they are gods. Therefore, do not fear them. **70** For as a scarecrow in a garden of cucumbers that keeps nothing, so are their gods of wood, and overlaid with gold and with silver. **71** Likewise also, their gods of wood, and overlaid with gold and with silver, are like to a white thorn in an orchard, that every bird sits on; as also to a dead body that is cast out into the dark. **72** And you will know them to be no gods by the bright purple that rots on them: And they themselves afterward will be consumed and will be a reproach in the country. **73** Better therefore is the just man that has no idols, for he will be far from reproach.

1 MACCABEES

The name Maccabee, probably meaning "hammer," is actually applied in the Books of Maccabees to only one man, Judas, third son of the priest Mattathias and first leader of the revolt against the Seleucid kings who persecuted the Jews (1 Mc. 2:4, 66; 2 Mc. 8:5, 16; 10:1, 16). Traditionally the name has come to be extended to the brothers of Judas, his supporters, and even to other Jewish heroes of the period, such as the seven brothers (2 Mc. 7). First Maccabees was written about 100 BC in Hebrew, but the original has not come down to us. Instead, we have an early, pre-Christian, Greek translation full of Hebrew idioms. The author, probably a Jew, is unknown. He was familiar with the traditions and sacred books of his people and had access to much reliable information on their recent history (from 175 to 134 BC). He may well have played some part in it himself in his youth. His purpose in writing is to record the deliverance of Israel that God worked through the family of Mattathias (5:62)—especially through his three sons, Judas, Jonathan, and Simon, and his grandson, John Hyrcanus.

CHAPTER 1

1 It came to pass, after that Alexander the Macedonian, the son of Philip, who came out of the land of Chittim, and struck Darius king of the Persians and Medes, [it came to pass,] after he had struck him, that he reigned in his stead, in former time, over Greece. **2** And he fought many battles, and won many strongholds, and killed the kings of the earth, **3** and went through to the ends of the earth and took spoils of a multitude of nations. And the earth was quiet before him, and he was exalted, and his heart was lifted up, **4** and he gathered together an exceedingly strong army, and ruled over countries and nations and principalities, and they became tributary to him. **5** And after these things he fell sick, and perceived that he should die. **6** And he called his servants, which were honorable, which had been brought up with him from his youth, and he divided to them his kingdom, while he was yet alive. **7** And Alexander reigned twelve years, and he died. **8** And his servants bare rule, each one in his place. **9** And they did all put diadems on themselves after that he was dead, and so did their sons after them many years: and they multiplied evils in the earth. **10** And there came out of them a sinful root, Antiochus Epiphanes, son of Antiochus the king, who had been a hostage at Rome, and he reigned in the one hundred and thirty-seventh year of the kingdom of the Greeks. **11** In those days came there out of Israel transgressors of the law, and persuaded many, saying, let us go and make a covenant with the nations that are around us; for since we were parted from them many evils have befallen us. **12** And the saying was good in their eyes. **13** And certain of the people were forward [here in] land went to the king, and he gave them license to do after the ordinances of the nations. **14** And they built a place of exercise in Jerusalem according to the laws of the nations; **15** and they made themselves uncircumcised, and forsook the holy covenant, and joined themselves to the nations, and sold themselves to do evil. **16** And the kingdom was well ordered in the sight of Antiochus, and he thought to reign over Egypt, that he might reign over the two kingdoms. **17** And he entered into Egypt with a great multitude, with chariots, and with elephants, and with horsemen, and with a great navy; **18** and he made war against Ptolemy king of Egypt; and Ptolemy was put to shame before him and fled; and many fell wounded to death. **19** And they got possession of the strong cities in the land of Egypt; and he took the spoils of Egypt. **20** And Antiochus, after he had struck Egypt, returned in the one hundred and forty-third year, and went up against Israel and Jerusalem with a great multitude, **21** and entered presumptuously into the sanctuary, and took the golden altar, and the candlestick of the light, and all that pertained to that, **22** and the table of the Bread of the Presentation, and the cups to pour with, and the bowls, and the golden censers, and the veil, and the crowns, and the adorning of gold which was on the face of the temple, and he peeled it all off. **23** And he took the silver and the gold and the precious vessels; and he took the hidden treasures which he found. **24** And when he had taken all, he went away into his own land, and he made a great slaughter, and spoke very presumptuously. **25** And there came great mourning on Israel, in every place where they were; **26** and the rulers and elders groaned, the virgins and young men were made feeble, and the beauty of the women was changed. **27** Every bridegroom took up lamentation, she that sat in the marriage chamber was in heaviness. **28** And the land was moved for the inhabitants thereof, and all the house of Jacob was clothed with shame. **29** And after two full years the king sent a chief collector of tribute to the cities of Judah, and he came to Jerusalem with a great multitude. **30** And he spoke words of peace to them in subtlety, and they gave him credence: and he fell on the city suddenly, and struck it very severely, and destroyed much people out of Israel. **31** And he took the spoils of the city, and set it on fire, and pulled down the houses thereof and the walls thereof on every side. **32** And they led captive the women and the children, and the cattle they took in possession. **33** And they built the city of David with a great and strong wall, with strong towers, and it became to them a citadel. **34** And they put there a sinful nation, transgressors of the law, and they strengthened themselves therein. **35** And they stored up arms and food, and gathering together the spoils of Jerusalem, they laid them up there, and they became a severe snare: **36** and it became a place to lie in wait in against the sanctuary, and an evil adversary to Israel continually. **37** And they shed innocent blood on every side of the sanctuary, and defiled the sanctuary. **38** And the inhabitants of Jerusalem fled because of them; and she became a habitation of strangers, and she became strange to those who were born in her, and her children forsook her. **39** Her sanctuary was laid waste like a wilderness, her feasts were turned into mourning, her Sabbaths into reproach, her honor into contempt. **40** According to her glory, so was her dishonor multiplied, and her high estate was turned into mourning. **41**

And King Antiochus wrote to his whole kingdom, that all should be one people, **42** and that each should forsake his own laws. And all the nations agreed according to the word of the king; **43** and many of Israel consented to his worship, and sacrificed to the idols, and profaned the Sabbath. **44** And the king sent letters by the hand of messengers to Jerusalem and the cities of Judah, that they should follow laws strange to the land, **45** and should forbid whole burnt-offerings and sacrifice and drink offerings in the sanctuary; and should profane the Sabbaths and feasts, **46** and pollute the sanctuary and those who were holy; **47** that they should build altars, and temples, and shrines for idols, and should sacrifice swine's flesh and unclean beasts: **48** and that they should leave their sons uncircumcised, that they should make their souls abominable with all manner of uncleanness and profanation; **49** so that they might forget the law, and change all the ordinances. **50** And whoever will not do according to the word of the king, he will die. **51** According to all these words wrote he to his whole kingdom; and he appointed overseers over all the people, and he commanded the cities of Judah to sacrifice, city by city. **52** And from the people were gathered together to them many, everyone that had forsaken the law; and they did evil things in the land; **53** and they made Israel to hide themselves in every place of refuge which they had. **54** And on the fifteenth day of Kislev, in the one hundred and forty-fifth year, they built an abomination of desolation on the altar, and in the cities of Judah on every side they built [idol] altars. **55** And at the doors of the houses and in the streets they burned incense. **56** And they tore in pieces the scrolls of the law which they found and set them on fire. **57** And wherever was found with any a scroll of the Covenant, and if any consented to the law, the king's sentence delivered him to death. **58** So did they in their might to Israel, to those that were found month by month in the cities. **59** And on the twenty-fifth day of the month they sacrificed on the [idol] altar [of God]. **60** And the women that had circumcised their children they put to death according to the command. **61** And they hanged their babies about their necks, and [destroyed] their houses, and those who had circumcised them. **62** And many in Israel were fully resolved and confirmed in themselves not to eat unclean things. **63** And they chose to die, that they might not be defiled with the meats, and that they might not profane the holy covenant: and they died. **64** And there came exceedingly great wrath on Israel.

CHAPTER 2

1 In those days Mattathias rose up, the son of John, the son of Simeon, a priest of the sons of Joarib, from Jerusalem; and he lived at Modin. **2** And he had five sons, John, who was surnamed Gaddis; **3** Simon, who was called Thassi; **4** Judas, who was called Maccabeus; **5** Eleazar, who was called Avaran; Jonathan, who was called Apphus. **6** And he saw the blasphemies that were committed in Judah and in Jerusalem, **7** and he said, "Woe is me! why was I born to see the destruction of my people, and the destruction of the holy city, and to dwell there, when it was given into the hand of the enemy, the sanctuary into the hand of aliens? **8** Her temple is become as a man that was glorious: **9** her vessels of glory are carried away into captivity, her infants are slain in her streets, her young men with the sword of the enemy. **10** What nation has not inherited her palaces, and gotten possession of her spoils? **11** Her adorning is all taken away; instead of a free woman she is become a bond woman: **12** and behold, our holy things and our beauty and our glory are laid waste, and the nations have profaned them. **13** Why should we live any longer?" **14** And Mattathias and his sons tore their clothes, and put on sackcloth, and mourned exceedingly. **15** And the king's officers, that were enforcing the apostasy, came into the city Modin to sacrifice. **16** And many of Israel came to them, and Mattathias and his sons were gathered together. **17** And the king's officers answered and spoke to Mattathias, saying, "You are a ruler and an honorable and great man in this city, and strengthened with sons and relatives: **18** now therefore, come first and do the command of the king, as all the nations have done, and the men of Judah, and those who remain in Jerusalem: and you and your house will be in the number of the king's friends, and you and your sons will be honored with silver and gold and many gifts." **19** And Mattathias answered and said with a loud voice, "If all the nations that are in the house of the king's dominion listen to him, to each one fall away from the worship of his fathers, and have made choice to follow his commands,

20 yet I and my sons and my relatives will walk in the covenant of our fathers. 21 Heaven forbid that we should forsake the law and the ordinances. 22 We will not listen to the king's words, to go aside from our worship, on the right hand, or on the left." 23 And when he had left speaking these words, there came a Jew in the sight of all to sacrifice on the altar which was at Modin, according to the king's command. 24 And Mattathias saw it, and his zeal was kindled, and his reins trembled, and he showed out his wrath according to judgment, and ran, and killed him on the altar. 25 And the king's officer, who compelled men to sacrifice, he killed at that time, and pulled down the altar. 26 And he was zealous for the law, even as Phinehas did to Zimri the son of Salu. 27 And Mattathias cried out in the city with a loud voice, saying, "Whoever is zealous for the law, and maintains the covenant, let him come out after me." 28 And he and his sons fled into the mountains and forsook all that they had in the city. 29 Then many that sought after justice and judgment went down into the wilderness, to dwell there, 30 they, and their sons, and their wives, and their cattle; because evils were multiplied on them. 31 And it was told the king's officers, and the forces that were in Jerusalem, the city of David, that certain men, who had broken the king's command, were gone down into the secret places in the wilderness; 32 and many pursued after them, and having overtaken them, they encamped against them, and set the battle in array against them on the Sabbath day. 33 And they said to them, so far, "Come out, and do according to the word of the king, and you will live." 34 And they said, "We will not come out, neither will we do the word of the king, to profane the Sabbath day." 35 And they hurried to give them battle. 36 And they did not answer them, neither did they cast a stone at them, nor stopped up the secret places, 37 saying, "Let us die all in our innocence: the heavens and earth witness over us, that you put us to death without trial." 38 And they rose up against them in battle on the Sabbath, and they died, they and their wives and their children, and their cattle, to the number of one thousand souls. 39 And Mattathias and his friends knew it, and they mourned over them exceedingly. 40 And one said to another, "If we all do as our countrymen have done, and fight not against the nations for our lives and our ordinances, they will now quickly destroy us from off the earth." 41 And they took counsel on that day, saying, "Whoever will come against us to battle on the Sabbath day, let us fight against him, and we will in no way all die, as our countrymen died in the secret places." 42 Then were gathered together to them a company of Hasidaeans, mighty men of Israel, everyone that offered himself willingly for the law. 43 And all those who fled from the evils were added to them and became a stay to them. 44 And they mustered an army, and struck sinners in their anger, and lawless men in their wrath: and the rest fled to the nations for safety. 45 And Mattathias and his friends went around and pulled down the altars; 46 and they circumcised by force the children that were uncircumcised, as many as they found in the coasts of Israel. 47 And they pursued after the sons of pride, and the work prospered in their hand. 48 And they rescued the law out of the hand of the nations, and out of the hand of the kings, neither suffered they the sinner to triumph. 49 And the days of Mattathias drew near that he should die, and he said to his sons, "Now have pride and rebuke gotten strength, and a season of overthrow, and wrath of indignation. 50 And now, my children, be zealous for the law, and give your lives for the covenant of your fathers. 51 And call to remembrance the deeds of our fathers which they did in their generations; and receive great glory and a perpetual name. 52 Was not Abraham found faithful in temptation, and it was reckoned to him for righteousness? 53 Joseph in the time of his distress kept the command and became lord of Egypt. 54 Phinehas our father, for that he was zealous exceedingly, obtained the covenant of a perpetual priesthood. 55 Joshua for fulfilling the word became a judge in Israel. 56 Caleb for bearing witness in the congregation obtained a heritage in the land. 57 David for being merciful inherited the throne of a kingdom forever and ever. 58 Elijah, for that he was exceedingly zealous for the law, was taken up into Heaven. 59 Hananiah, Azariah, Mishael, believed, and were saved out of the flame. 60 Daniel for his innocence was delivered from the mouth of lions. 61 And so consider you from generation to generation, that none that put their trust in him will lack for strength. 62 And do not be afraid of the words of a sinful man; for his glory will be dung and worms. 63 Today he will be lifted up, and tomorrow he will in no way be found, because he is returned to his dust, and his thought is perished. 64 And you, my children, be strong, and show yourselves men

in behalf of the law; for therein will you obtain glory. 65 And behold, Simon your brother, I know that he is a man of counsel; give ear to him always: he will be a father to you. 66 And Judas Maccabaeus, he has been strong and mighty from his youth: he will be your captain and will fight the battle of the people. 67 And take to yourself all the doers of the law and avenge the wrong of your people. 68 Render a repayment to the nations and take heed to the commands of the law." 69 And he blessed them and was gathered to his fathers. 70 And he died in the one hundred and forty-sixth year, and his sons buried him in the tombs of his fathers at Modin, and all Israel made great lamentation for him.

CHAPTER 3

1 And his son Judas, who was called Maccabaeus, rose up in his stead. 2 And all his countrymen helped him, and so did all those who cleaved to his father, and they fought with gladness the battle of Israel. 3 And he got his people great glory, and put on a breastplate as a giant, and girded his warlike harness about him, and set battles in array, protecting the army with his sword. 4 And he was like a lion in his deeds, and as a lion's whelp roaring for prey. 5 And he pursued the lawless, seeking them out, and he burned up those that troubled his people. 6 And the lawless shrunk for fear of him, and all the workers of lawlessness were severely troubled, and salvation prospered in his hand. 7 And he angered many kings, and made Jacob glad with his acts, and his memorial is blessed forever. 8 And he went around among the cities of Judah, and destroyed the ungodly out of the land, and turned away wrath from Israel: 9 and he was renowned to the utmost part of the earth, and he gathered together such as were ready to perish. 10 And Apollonius gathered the nations together, and a great army from Samaria, to fight against Israel. 11 And Judas perceived it, and he went out to meet him, and struck him, and killed him: and many fell wounded to death, and the rest fled. 12 And they took their spoils, and Judas took the sword of Apollonius, and with that he fought all his days. 13 And Seron, the commander of the army of Syria, heard it said that Judas had gathered a gathering and a congregation of faithful men with him, and of such as went out to war; 14 And he said, I will make myself a name and get me glory in the kingdom; and I will fight against Judas and those who are with him, that set at nothing the word of the king. 15 And there went up with him also a mighty army of the ungodly to help him, to take vengeance on the sons of Israel. 16 And he came near to the going up of Bethhoron, and Judas went out to meet him with a small company. 17 But when they saw the army coming to meet them, they said to Judas, "What? Will we be able, being a small company, to fight against so great and strong a multitude? and we for our part are faint, having tasted no food this day." 18 And Judas said, "It is an easy thing for many to be shut up in the hands of a few; and with Heaven it is all one, to save by many or by few: 19 for victory in battle stands not in the multitude of an army; but strength is from Heaven. 20 They come to us in fullness of insolence and lawlessness, to destroy us and our wives and our children, for to plunder us: 21 but we fight for our lives and our laws. 22 And he himself will defeat them before our face, but as for you, do not be afraid of them." 23 Now when he had left off speaking, he leapt suddenly on them, and Seron and his army were defeated before him. 24 And they pursued them in the going down of Bethhoron to the plain, and there fell of them about eight hundred men; but the residue fled into the land of the Philistines. 25 And the fear of Judas and his countrymen, and the dread of them, began to fall on the nations around them: 26 and his name came near even to the king, and every nation told of the battles of Judas. 27 But when King Antiochus heard these words, he was full of indignation: and he sent and gathered together all the forces of his realm, an exceedingly strong army. 28 And he opened his treasury, and gave his forces pay for a year, and commanded them to be ready for every need. 29 And he saw that the money failed from his treasures, and that the tributes of the country were small, because of the dissension and plague which he had brought on the land, to the end that he might take away the laws which had been from the first days; 30 and he feared that he should not have enough as at other times for the charges and the gifts which he gave previously with a liberal hand, and he abounded above the kings that were before him. 31 And he was exceedingly perplexed in his mind, and he determined to go into Persia, and to take the tributes of the countries, and to

gather much money. **32** And he left Lysias, an honorable man, and one of the seed royal, to be over the affairs of the king from the River Euphrates to the borders of Egypt, **33** and to bring up his son Antiochus, until he came again. **34** And he delivered to him the half of his forces, and the elephants, and gave him charge of all the things that he would have done, and concerning those who lived in Judea and in Jerusalem, **35** that he should send an army against them, to root out and destroy the strength of Israel, and the remnant of Jerusalem, and to take away their memorial from the place; **36** And that he should make strangers to dwell on all their coasts, and should divide their land to them by lot. **37** And the king took the half that remained of the forces, and removed from Antioch, from his royal city, the one hundred and forty-seventh year; and he passed over the River Euphrates and went through the upper countries. **38** And Lysias chose Ptolemy the son of Dorymenes, and Nicanor, and Gorgias, mighty men of the king's friends; **39** and with them he sent forty thousand footmen, and seven thousand horse, to go into the land of Judah, and to destroy it, according to the word of the king. **40** And they removed with all their army and came and pitched near to Emmaus in the plain country. **41** And the merchants of the country heard the fame of them, and took silver and gold exceedingly much, with chains, and came into the camp to take the sons of Israel for servants: and there were added to them the forces of Syria and of the land of the Philistines. **42** And Judas and his countrymen saw that evils were multiplied, and that the forces were encamping in their borders; and they took knowledge of the king's words which he had commanded, to destroy the people and make an end of them; **43** and they said each man to his neighbor, "Let us raise up the ruin of our people, and let us fight for our people and the holy place." **44** And the congregation was gathered together, that they might be ready for battle, and that they might pray, and ask for mercy and compassion. **45** And Jerusalem was without inhabitant as a wilderness, there was none of her offspring that went in or went out; and the sanctuary was trodden down, and the sons of strangers were in the citadel, the nations lodged therein; and joy was taken away from Jacob, and the pipe and the harp ceased. **46** And they gathered themselves together, and came to Mizpeh, near Jerusalem; for in Mizpeh was there a place of prayer previously for Israel. **47** And they fasted that day, and put on sackcloth, and [put] ashes on their heads, and tore their clothes, **48** and laid open the Scroll of the Law, concerning which the nations were accustomed to inquire, seeking the likenesses of their idols. **49** And they brought the priests' garments, and the first-fruits, and the tithes: and they stirred up the Nazarites, who had accomplished their days. **50** And they cried aloud toward Heaven, saying, "What will we do with these men, and where will we carry them away? **51** And your holy place is trodden down and profaned, and your priests are in heaviness and brought low. **52** And behold, the nations are assembled together against us to destroy us: you know what things they imagine against us. **53** How will we be able to stand before them, except you be our help?" **54** And they sounded with the trumpets and cried with a loud voice. **55** And after this Judas appointed leaders of the people, captains of thousands, and captains of hundreds, and captains of fifties, and captains of tens. **56** And he said to those who were building houses, and were betrothing wives, and were planting vineyards, and were fearful, that they should return, each man to his own house, according to the law. **57** And the army removed and encamped on the south side of Emmaus. **58** And Judas said, "Gird yourselves, and be valiant men, and be in readiness against the morning, that you may fight with these nations, that are assembled together against us to destroy us, and our holy place: **59** for it is better for us to die in battle, than to look on the evils of our nation and the holy place. **60** Nevertheless, as may be the will in Heaven, so will he do."

CHAPTER 4

1 And Gorgias took five thousand footmen, and one thousand chosen horse, and the army removed by night, **2** that it might fall on the army of the Jews and strike them suddenly: and the men of the citadel were his guides. **3** And Judas heard thereof, and removed, he and the valiant men, that he might strike the king's army which was at Emmaus, **4** while as yet the forces were dispersed from the camp. **5** And Gorgias came into the camp of Judas by night and found no man; and he sought them in the mountains; for he said, "These men flee from us."

6 And as soon as it was day, Judas appeared in the plain with three thousand men: however, they did not have the armor and swords they desired. **7** And they saw the camp of the nations strong [and] fortified, and horsemen compassing it around; and these were expert in war. **8** And Judas said to the men that were with him, "Do not fear their multitude, neither be afraid of their onset. **9** Remember how our fathers were saved in the Red Sea, when Pharaoh pursued them with an army. **10** And now let us cry to Heaven, if He will have us, and will remember the covenant of our fathers, and destroy this army before our face today: **11** and all the nations will know that there is one who redeems and saves Israel." **12** And the strangers lifted up their eyes and saw them coming near them: **13** and they went out of the camp to battle. And those who were with Judas sounded their trumpets, **14** and joined battle, and the nations were defeated, and fled into the plain. **15** But all the furthest back fell by the sword: and they pursued them to Gazara, and to the plains of Idumaea and Azotus and Jamnia, and there fell of them about three thousand men. **16** And Judas and his army returned from pursuing after them, **17** and he said to the people, "Do not be greedy of the spoils, inasmuch as there is a battle before us; **18** and Gorgias and his army are near to us in the mountain. But stand you now against our enemies, and fight against them, and afterward take the spoils with boldness." **19** While Judas was yet making an end of these words, there appeared a part of them looking out from the mountain: **20** and they saw that their army had been put to flight, and that the Jews were burning the camp; for the smoke that was seen declared what was done. **21** But when they perceived these things, they were severely afraid; and perceiving also the army of Judas in the plain ready for battle, **22** they fled—all of them—into the land of the Philistines. **23** And Judas returned to plunder the camp, and they got much gold, and silver, and blue, and sea purple, and great riches. **24** And they returned home, and sang a song of thanksgiving, and gave praise to Heaven; because [His mercy] is good, because His mercy endures forever. **25** And Israel had a great deliverance that day. **26** But the strangers, as many as had escaped, came and told Lysias all the things that had happened: **27** but when he heard thereof, he was confounded and discouraged, because neither had such things as he desired been done to Israel, nor had such things as the king commanded him come to pass. **28** And in the next year he gathered together sixty thousand chosen footmen, and five thousand horse, that he might subdue them. **29** And they came into Idumaea and encamped at Bethsura; and Judas met them with ten thousand men. **30** And he saw that the army was strong, and he prayed and said, "Blessed are You, O Savior of Israel, who quelled the onset of the mighty man by the hand of Your servant David, and delivered the army of the Philistines into the hands of Jonathan the son of Saul, and of his armor bearer: **31** shut up this army in the hand of Your people Israel, and let them be ashamed for their army and their horsemen: **32** give them faintness of heart, and cause the boldness of their strength to melt away, and let them quake at their destruction: **33** cast them down with the sword of those who love You, and let all that know Your Name praise You with thanksgiving." **34** And they joined battle; and there fell of the army of Lysias about five thousand men, and they fell down near them. **35** But when Lysias saw that his array was put to flight, and the boldness that had come on those who were with Judas, and how they were ready either to live or to die nobly, he removed to Antioch, and gathered together hired soldiers, that he might come again into Judea with even a greater company. **36** But Judas and his countrymen said, "Behold, our enemies are defeated: let us go up to cleanse the holy place, and to dedicate it afresh." **37** And all the army was gathered together, and they went up to Mount Zion. **38** And they saw the sanctuary laid desolate, and the altar profaned, and the gates burned up, and shrubs growing in the courts as in a forest or as on one of the mountains, and the priests' chambers pulled down; **39** and they tore their clothes, and made great lamentation, and put ashes on their heads, **40** and fell on their faces to the ground, and blew with the solemn trumpets, and cried toward Heaven. **41** Then Judas appointed certain men to fight against those that were in the citadel, until he should have cleansed the holy place. **42** And he chose blameless priests, such as had pleasure in the law: **43** and they cleansed the holy place and bare out the stones of defilement into an unclean place. **44** And they took counsel concerning the altar of burnt-offerings, which had been profaned, what they should do with it: **45** and there came into their mind a good counsel, that they should pull it down, lest it should be a reproach to them, because the nations had defiled it: and they pulled down the altar, **46** and laid up the stones in the mountain of the house in a convenient place, until there should come a prophet to give an answer concerning them. **47** And they took whole stones according to the law and build a new altar after the fashion of the former; **48** and they built the holy place, and the inner parts of the house; and they hallowed the courts. **49** And they made the holy vessels new, and they brought the candlestick, and the altar of burnt-offerings and of incense, and the table, into the temple. **50** And they burned incense on the altar, and they lighted the lamps that were on the candlestick, and they gave light in the temple. **51** And they set loaves on the table, and spread out the veils, and finished all the works which they made. **52** And they rose up early in the morning, on the twenty-fifth day of the ninth month, which is the month Kislev, in the one hundred and forty-eighth year, **53** and offered sacrifice according to the law on the new altar of burnt-offerings which they had made. **54** At what time and on what day the nations had profaned it, even on that [day] was it dedicated afresh, with songs and harps and lutes, and with cymbals. **55** And all the people fell on their faces, and worshiped, and gave praise to Heaven, which had given them good success. **56** And they kept the dedication of the altar eight days, and offered burnt-offerings with gladness, and sacrificed a sacrifice of deliverance and praise. **57** And they decked the forefront of the temple with crowns of gold and small shields, and dedicated afresh the gates and the priests' chambers, and made doors for them. **58** And there was exceedingly great gladness among the people, and the reproach of the nations was turned away. **59** And Judas and his countrymen and the whole congregation of Israel ordained, that the days of the dedication of the altar should be kept in their seasons from year to year by the space of eight days, from the twenty-fifth day of the month Kislev, with gladness and joy. **60** And at that season they built up Mount Zion with high walls and strong towers around, lest perhaps the nations should come and tread them down, as they had done previously. **61** And he set there a force to keep it, and they fortified Bethsura to keep it; that the people might have a stronghold near Idumaea.

CHAPTER 5

1 And it came to pass, when the surrounding nations heard that the altar was built, and the sanctuary dedicated as previously, they were exceedingly angry. **2** And they took counsel to destroy the race of Jacob that was in the midst of them, and they began to kill and destroy among the people. **3** And Judas fought against the children of Esau in Idumaea at Akrabattine, because they besieged Israel: and he struck them with a great slaughter, and brought down their pride, and took their spoils. **4** And he remembered the wickedness of the children of Baean, who were to the people a snare and a stumbling block, lying in wait for them in the ways. **5** And they were shut up by him in the towers; and he encamped against them, and destroyed them utterly, and burned with fire the towers of the place, with all that were therein. **6** And he passed over to the children of Ammon, and found a mighty band, and much people, with Timotheus for their leader. **7** And he fought many battles with them, and they were defeated before his face; and he struck them, **8** and got possession of Jazer, and the villages thereof, and returned again into Judea. **9** And the nations that were in Gilead gathered themselves together against the Israelites that were on their borders, to destroy them. And they fled to the stronghold of Dathema, **10** and sent letters to Judas and his countrymen, saying, "The nations that are around us are gathered together against us to destroy us: **11** and they are preparing to come and get possession of the stronghold whereto we have fled for refuge, and Timotheus is the leader of their army. **12** Now therefore come and deliver us from their hand, for many of us are fallen. **13** And all our countrymen that were in the land of Tubias have been put to death; and they have carried into captivity their wives and their children and their stuff; and they destroyed there about one thousand men." **14** While the letters were yet being read, behold, there came other messengers from Galilee with their clothes torn, bringing a report in this way, **15** saying that there were gathered together against them those of Ptolemais, and of Tyre, and of Sidon, and all Galilee of the nations to consume them. **16** Now when Judas and the people heard these words, there assembled together a great congregation, to consult what they should do for their countrymen, that were in

suffering, and were assaulted of them. **17** And Judas said to Simon his brother, "Choose out men, and go and deliver your countrymen that are in Galilee, but my brother Jonathan and I will go into the land of Gilead." **18** And he left Joseph the son of Zechariah, and Azariah, as leaders of the people, with the remnant of the army, in Judea, for to keep it. **19** And he gave command to them, saying, "Take you the charge of this people, and fight no battle with the nations until that we come again." **20** And to Simon were divided three thousand men to go into Galilee, but to Judas eight thousand men [to go] into the land of Gilead. **21** And Simon went into Galilee, and fought many battles with the nations, and the nations were defeated before him. **22** And he pursued them to the gate of Ptolemais; and there fell of the nations about three thousand men, and he took their spoils. **23** And they took to them those that were in Galilee, and in Arbatta, with their wives and their children, and all that they had, and brought them into Judea with great gladness. **24** And Judas Maccabaeus and his brother Jonathan passed over Jordan, and went three days' journey in the wilderness; **25** and they met with the Nabathaeans, and these met them in a peaceful manner, and told them all things that had befallen their countrymen in the land of Gilead: **26** and how that many of them were shut up in Bosora, and Bosor, and Alema, Casphor, Maked, and Carnaim; all these cities are strong and great: **27** and how that they were shut up in the rest of the cities of the land of Gilead, and that tomorrow they have appointed to encamp against the strongholds, and to take them, and to destroy all these men in one day. **28** And Judas and his army turned suddenly by the way of the wilderness to Bosora; and he took the city and killed all the males with the edge of the sword, and took all their spoils, and burned the city with fire. **29** And he left from there by night and went until he came to the stronghold. **30** And the morning came, and they lifted up their eyes, and behold, much people which could not be counted, bearing ladders and engines of war, to take the stronghold; and they were fighting against them. **31** And Judas saw that the battle was begun, and that the cry of the city went up to Heaven, with trumpets and a great sound, **32** and he said to the men of his army, "Fight this day for your countrymen." **33** And he went out behind them in three companies, and they sounded with their trumpets, and cried out in prayer. **34** And the army of Timotheus perceived that it was Maccabaeus, and they fled from before him: and he struck them with a great slaughter: and there fell of them on that day about eight thousand men. **35** And he turned away to Mizpeh and fought against it, and took it, and killed all the males thereof, and took the spoils thereof, and burned it with fire. **36** From there he left, and took Casphor, Maked, Bosor, and the other cities of the land of Gilead. **37** Now after these things Timotheus gathered another army and encamped near Raphon beyond the brook. **38** And Judas sent men to spy on the army; and they brought him word, saying, "All the nations that are around us are gathered together to them, an exceedingly great army. **39** And they have hired Arabians to help them, and are encamping beyond the brook, ready to come against you to battle." And Judas went to meet them. **40** And Timotheus said to the captains of his army, when Judas and his army drew near to the brook of water, "If he passes over first to us, we will not be able to withstand him; for he will mightily prevail against us: **41** but if he be afraid, and encamp beyond the river, we will cross over to him, and prevail against him." **42** Now when Judas came near to the brook of water, he caused the scribes of the people to remain by the brook, and gave command to them, saying, "Permit no man to encamp, but let all come to the battle." **43** And he crossed over the first against them, and all the people after him: and all the nations were defeated before his face, and cast away their arms, and fled to the temple at Carnaim. **44** And they took the city, and burned the temple with fire, together with all that were therein. And Carnaim was subdued, neither could they stand any longer before the face of Judas. **45** And Judas gathered together all Israel, those who were in the land of Gilead, from the least to the greatest, and their wives, and their children, and their stuff, an exceedingly great army, that they might come into the land of Judah. **46** And they came as far as Ephron, and this same city was great, [and it was] in the way as they should go, exceedingly strong: they could not turn away from it on the right hand or on the left but must necessarily pass through the midst of it. **47** And they of the city shut them out and stopped up the gates with stones. **48** And Judas sent to them with words of peace, saying, "We will pass through your land to go into our own land, and none will do you any harm, we will only pass by on our feet."

And they would not open to him. **49** And Judas commanded proclamation to be made in the army, that each man should encamp in the place where he was. **50** And the men of the army encamped and fought against the city all that day and all that night, and the city was delivered into his hands; **51** and he destroyed all the males with the edge of the sword, and razed the city, and took the spoils thereof, and passed through the city over those who were slain. **52** And they went over Jordan into the great plain near Bethshan. **53** And Judas gathered together those that lagged behind, and encouraged the people all the way through, until he came into the land of Judah. **54** And they went up to Mount Zion with gladness and joy, and offered whole burnt-offerings, because not so much as one of them was slain until they returned in peace. **55** And in the days when Judas and Jonathan were in the land of Gilead, and Simon his brother in Galilee before Ptolemais, **56** Joseph the son of Zechariah, and Azariah, rulers of the army, heard of their exploits and of the war, what things they had done; **57** and they said, "Let us also get us a name, and let us go fight against the nations that are around us." **58** And they gave charge to the men of the army that was with them and went toward Jamnia. **59** And Gorgias and his men came out of the city to meet them in battle. **60** And Joseph and Azariah were put to flight and were pursued to the borders of Judea; and there fell on that day of the people of Israel about two thousand men. **61** And there was a great overthrow among the people, because they did not listen to Judas and his countrymen, thinking to do some exploit. **62** But they were not of the seed of those men, by whose hand deliverance was given to Israel. **63** And the man Judas and his countrymen were glorified exceedingly in the sight of all Israel, and of all the nations, wherever their name was heard of; **64** and men gathered together to them, acclaiming them. **65** And Judas and his countrymen went out and fought against the children of Esau in the land toward the south; and he struck Hebron and the villages thereof, and pulled down the strongholds thereof, and burned the towers thereof. **66** And he left to go into the land of the Philistines, and he went through Samaria. **67** In that day certain priests, desiring to do exploits there, were slain in battle, when he went out to battle unadvisedly. **68** And Judas turned toward Azotus, to the land of the Philistines, and pulled down their altars, and burned the carved images of their gods with fire, and took the plunder of their cities, and returned into the land of Judah.

CHAPTER 6

1 And King Antiochus was journeying through the upper countries; and he heard it said that in Elymais in Persia there was a city renowned for riches, for silver and gold; **2** and that the temple which was in it was exceedingly rich, and that therein were golden shields, and breastplates, and arms, which Alexander, son of Philip, the Macedonian king, who reigned first among the Greeks, left behind there. **3** And he came and sought to take the city, and to pillage it; and he was not able, because the thing was known to them of the city, **4** and they rose up against him to battle: and he fled, and left from there with great heaviness, to return to Babylon. **5** And there came one bringing him tidings into Persia, that the armies, which went against the land of Judah, had been put to flight; **6** and that Lysias went first with a strong army, and was put to shame before them; and that they had waxed strong by reason of arms and power, and with store of spoils, which they took from the armies that they had cut off; **7** and that they had pulled down the abomination which he had built on the altar that was in Jerusalem; and that they had compassed about the sanctuary with high walls, as before, and Bethsura, his city. **8** And it came to pass, when the king heard these words, he was astonished and moved exceedingly: and he laid down on his bed, and fell sick for grief, because it had not befallen him as he looked for. **9** And he was there many days, because great grief was renewed on him, and he made account that he should die. **10** And he called for all his friends, and said to them, "Sleep departs from my eyes, and my heart fails for care. **11** And I said in my heart, To what suffering am I come, and how great a flood is it, wherein I now am! for I was gracious and beloved in my power. **12** But now I remember the evils which I did at Jerusalem, and that I took all the vessels of silver and gold that were therein and sent out to destroy the inhabitants of Judah without a cause. **13** I perceive that on this account these evils have come on me, and behold, I perish through great grief in a strange land." **14** And he called for Philip, one of his Friends,

and set him over all his kingdom, **15** and gave him his diadem, and his robe, and his signet ring, to the end he should bring Antiochus his son, and nourish him up that he might be king. **16** And King Antiochus died there in the one hundred and forty-ninth year. **17** And Lysias knew that the king was dead, and he set up Antiochus his son to reign, whom he had nourished up being young, and he called his name Eupator. **18** And those who were in the citadel shut up Israel around the sanctuary, and sought always their hurt, and the strengthening of the nations. **19** And Judas thought to destroy them and called all the people together to besiege them. **20** And they were gathered together, and besieged them in the one hundred and fiftieth year, and he made mounds to shoot from, and engines of war. **21** And there came out some of those who were shut up, and there were joined to them certain ungodly men of Israel. **22** And they went to the king, and said, "How long will you not execute judgment, and avenge our countrymen? **23** We were willing to serve your father, and to walk after his words, and to follow his commands; **24** and for this reason the children of our people besieged the citadel and were alienated from us; but as many of us as they could descend on they killed and plundered our inheritances. **25** And not against us only did they stretch out their hand, but also against all their borders. **26** And behold, they are encamped this day against the citadel at Jerusalem, to take it: and they have fortified the sanctuary and Bethsura. **27** And if you are not beforehand with them quickly, they will do greater things than these, and you will not be able to control them." **28** And when the king heard this, he was angry, and gathered together all his friends, [even the] rulers of his army, and those who were over the horse. **29** And there came to him from other kingdoms, and from isles of the sea, bands of hired soldiers. **30** And the number of his forces was one hundred thousand footmen, and twenty thousand horsemen, and thirty-two elephants trained for war. **31** And they went through Idumaea, and encamped against Bethsura, and fought against it many days, and made engines of war; and they [of Bethsura] came out, and burned them with fire, and fought valiantly. **32** And Judas left from the citadel, and encamped at Bethzacharias, near the king's camp. **33** And the king rose early in the morning and sent his army at full speed along the road to Bethzacharias, and his forces made them ready to battle, and sounded with the trumpets. **34** And they showed the elephants the blood of grapes and mulberries, that they might prepare them for the battle. **35** And they divided the beasts among the phalanxes, and they set by each elephant one thousand men armed with coats of mail, and helmets of brass on their heads; and for each beast were appointed five hundred chosen horsemen. **36** These were ready beforehand, wherever the beast was; and wherever the beast went, they went with him; they did not depart from him. **37** And towers of wood were on them, strong [and] covered, one on each beast, girded fast on him with cunning contrivances; and on each [beast] were thirty-two valiant men that fought on them, beside his Indian **38** (and the residue of the horsemen he set on this side and that side at the two parts of the army), striking terror [into the enemy], and protected by the phalanxes. **39** Now when the sun shone on the shields of gold and brass, the mountains shone with them, and blazed like torches of fire. **40** And a part of the king's army was spread on the high mountains, and some on the low ground, and they went on firmly and in order. **41** And all that heard the noise of their multitude, and the marching of the multitude, and the rattling of the arms, did quake, for the army was exceedingly great and strong. **42** And Judas and his army drew near for battle, and there fell of the king's army six hundred men. **43** And Eleazar, who was [called] Avaran, saw one of the beasts armed with royal breastplates, and he was higher than all the beasts, and the king seemed to be on him; **44** and he gave himself to deliver his people, and to get himself a perpetual name; **45** and he ran on him courageously into the midst of the phalanx, and killed on the right hand and on the left, and they separated apart from him on this side and on that. **46** And he crept under the elephant, and thrust him from beneath, and killed him; and the [elephant] fell to the earth on him, and he died there. **47** And they saw the strength of the kingdom, and the fierce onset of the army, and turned away from them. **48** But they of the king's army went up to Jerusalem to meet them, and the king encamped toward Judea, and toward Mount Zion. **49** And he made peace with them of Bethsura; and he came out of the city, because they had no food there to endure the siege, because it was a Sabbath to the land. **50** And the king took Bethsura and appointed a garrison there to keep it. **51** And he encamped against the sanctuary many days; and set there mounds to shoot from, and engines of war, and instruments for casting fire and stones, and pieces to cast darts, and slings. ⁵² And they also made engines against their engines and fought for many days. ⁵³ But there was no food in the sanctuary, because it was the seventh year, and those who fled for safety into Judea from among the nations had eaten up the residue of the store; ⁵⁴ and there were but a few left in the sanctuary, because the famine prevailed against them, and they were scattered, each man to his own place. ⁵⁵ And Lysias heard it said that Philip, whom Antiochus the king, while he was yet alive, appointed to nourish up his son Antiochus, that he might be king, ⁵⁶ had returned from Persia and Media, and with him the forces that went with the king, and that he was seeking to take the government to himself. ⁵⁷ And he hurried, and gave consent to depart; and he said to the king and the leaders of the army and to the men, "We decay daily, and our food is scant, and the place where we encamp is strong, and the affairs of the kingdom lie on us: ⁵⁸ now therefore let us give the right hand to these men, and make peace with them and with all their nation, ⁵⁹ and covenant with them, that they will walk after their own laws, as previously, for because of their laws which we abolished they were angered, and did all these things." ⁶⁰ And the saying pleased the king and the princes, and he sent to them to make peace; and they accepted thereof. ⁶¹ And the king and the princes swore to them: immediately they came out from the stronghold. ⁶² And the king entered into Mount Zion; and he saw the strength of the place and set at nothing the oath which he had sworn and gave command to pull down the wall around. ⁶³ And he left in haste, and returned to Antioch, and found Philip master of the city; and he fought against him and took the city by force.

CHAPTER 7

¹ In the one hundred and fiftieth year, Demetrius the son of Seleucus came out from Rome and went up with a few men to a city by the sea and reigned there. ² And it came to pass, when he would go into the house of the kingdom of his fathers, that the army laid hands on Antiochus and Lysias, to bring them to him. ³ And the thing was known to him, and he said, "Do not show me their faces." ⁴ And the army killed them. And Demetrius sat on the throne of his kingdom. ⁵ And there came to him all the lawless and ungodly men of Israel; and Alcimus was their leader, desiring to be chief priest; ⁶ and they accused the people to the king, saying, "Judas and his countrymen have destroyed all your friends, and have scattered us from our own land. ⁷ Now therefore send a man whom you trust and let him go and see all the havock which he has made of us, and of the king's country, and [how] he has punished them and all that helped them." ⁸ And the king chose Bacchides, one of the king's friends, who was ruler in the country beyond the river, and was a great man in the kingdom, and faithful to the king. ⁹ And he sent him, and that ungodly Alcimus, and made sure to him the chief priesthood, and he commanded him to take vengeance on the sons of Israel. ¹⁰ And they went and came with a great army into the land of Judah, and he sent messengers to Judas and his countrymen with words of peace deceitfully. ¹¹ And they gave no heed to their words; for they saw that they were come with a great army. ¹² And there were gathered together to Alcimus and Bacchides a company of scribes, to seek for justice. ¹³ And the Hasidaeans were the first among the sons of Israel that sought peace of them; ¹⁴ for they said, "One that is a priest of the seed of Aaron has come with the forces, and he will do us no wrong." ¹⁵ And he spoke with them words of peace, and swore to them, saying, "We will seek the hurt neither of you nor your friends." ¹⁶ And they gave him credence: and he laid hands on sixty men of them, and killed them in one day, according to the word which [the psalmist] wrote, ¹⁷ "The flesh of your saints [they cast out, and] their blood they shed around Jerusalem; And there was no man to bury them." ¹⁸ And the fear and the dread of them fell on all the people, for they said, "There is neither truth nor judgment in them; for they have broken the covenant and the oath which they swore." ¹⁹ And Bacchides left from Jerusalem and encamped in Bezeth; and he sent and took away many of the deserters that were with him, and certain of the people, and he killed them, and [cast them] into the great pit. ²⁰ And he made sure the country to Alcimus and left with him a force to aid him; and Bacchides went away to the king. ²¹ And Alcimus strove for his chief priesthood. ²² And there were gathered to

him all those who troubled their people, and they got the mastery of the land of Judah and did great hurt in Israel. ²³ And Judas saw all the mischief that Alcimus and his company had done among the sons of Israel, [even] above the nations, ²⁴ and he went out into all the surrounding coasts of Judea and took vengeance on the men that had deserted from him, and they were restrained from going out into the country. ²⁵ But when Alcimus saw that Judas and his company waxed strong and knew that he was not able to withstand them, he returned to the king, and brought evil accusations against them. ²⁶ And the king sent Nicanor, one of his honorable princes, a man that hated Israel and was their enemy, and commanded him to destroy the people. ²⁷ And Nicanor came to Jerusalem with a great army; and he sent to Judas and his countrymen deceitfully with words of peace, saying, ²⁸ "Let there be no battle between me and you; I will come with a few men, that I may see your faces in peace." ²⁹ And he came to Judas, and they saluted one another peaceably. And the enemies were ready to take away Judas by violence. ³⁰ And the thing was known to Judas, that he came to him with deceit, and he was severely afraid of him, and would see his face no longer. ³¹ And Nicanor knew that his counsel was discovered; and he went out to meet Judas in battle beside Capharsalama; ³² and there fell of Nicanor's side about five hundred men, and they fled into the city of David. ³³ And after these things Nicanor went up to Mount Zion: and there came some of the priests out of the sanctuary, and some of the elders of the people, to salute him peaceably, and to show him the whole burned sacrifice that was being offered for the king. ³⁴ And he mocked them, and laughed at them, and entreated them shamefully, and spoke haughtily, ³⁵ and swore in a rage, saying, "Unless Judas and his army are now delivered into my hands, it will be that, if I come again in peace, I will burn up this house"; and he went out in a great rage. ³⁶ And the priests entered in and stood before the altar and the temple; and they wept, and said, ³⁷ "You chose this house to be called by Your Name, to be a house of prayer and supplication for Your people: ³⁸ take vengeance on this man and his army, and let them fall by the sword: remember their blasphemies, and do not allow them to live any longer." ³⁹ And Nicanor went out from Jerusalem, and encamped in Bethhoron, and there met him the army of Syria. ⁴⁰ And Judas encamped in Adasa with three thousand men: and Judas prayed and said, ⁴¹ "When those who came from the king blasphemed, your messenger went out, and struck among them one hundred and eighty-five thousand. ⁴² Even so defeat this army before us today and let all the rest know that he has spoken wickedly against Your sanctuary and judge him according to his wickedness." ⁴³ And on the thirteenth day of the month Adar the armies joined battle: and Nicanor's army was defeated, and he himself was the first to fall in the battle. ⁴⁴ Now when his army saw that Nicanor was fallen, they cast away their arms, and fled. ⁴⁵ And they pursued after them a day's journey from Adasa until you come to Gazara, and they sounded an alarm after them with the solemn trumpets. ⁴⁶ And they came out of all the surrounding villages of Judea and closed them in; and these turned them back on those, and they all fell by the sword, and there was not one of them left. ⁴⁷ And they took the spoils, and the plunder, and they struck off Nicanor's head, and his right hand, which he stretched out so haughtily, and brought them, and hanged them up beside Jerusalem. ⁴⁸ And the people were exceedingly glad, and they kept that day as a day of great gladness. ⁴⁹ And they ordained to keep this day year by year, the thirteenth day of Adar. ⁵⁰ And the land of Judah had rest a little while.

CHAPTER 8

¹ And Judas heard of the fame of the Romans, that they are valiant men, and have pleasure in all that join themselves to them and make friends with all such as come to them, ² and that they are valiant men. And they told him of their wars and exploits which they do among the Gauls, and how that they conquered them, and brought them under tribute; ³ and what things they did in the land of Spain, that they might become masters of the mines of silver and gold which were there; ⁴ and how that by their policy and persistence they conquered all the place (and the place was exceedingly far from them), and the kings that came against them from the uttermost part of the earth, until they had defeated them, and struck them very severely; and how the rest give them tribute year by year: ⁵ and Philip, and Perseus, king of Chittim, and those who lifted

up themselves against them, did they defeat in battle, and conquered them: **6** Antiochus also, the great king of Asia, who came against them to battle, having one hundred and twenty elephants, with horse, and chariots, and an exceedingly great army, and he was defeated by them, **7** and they took him alive, and appointed that both he and such as reigned after him should give them a great tribute, and should give hostages, and a parcel [of land], **8** the country of India, and Media, and Lydia, and of the attractive of their countries; and they took them from him, and gave them to King Eumenes: **9** and how they of Greece took counsel to come and destroy them; **10** and the thing was known to them, and they sent against them a captain, and fought against them, and many of them fell down wounded to death, and they made captive their wives and their children, and plundered them, and conquered their land, and pulled down their strongholds, and plundered them, and brought them into bondage to this day: **11** and the residue of the kingdoms and of the isles, as many as rose up against them at any time, they destroyed and made them to be their servants; **12** but with their friends and such as relied on them they stayed friends; and they conquered the kingdoms that were near and those that were far off, and all that heard of their fame were afraid of them: **13** moreover, whoever they will to help and to make kings, these do they make kings; and whoever they will, do they depose; and they are exalted exceedingly: **14** and for all this none of them ever put on a diadem, neither did they clothe themselves with purple, to be magnified by it: **15** and how they had made for themselves a senate house, and day by day three hundred and twenty men sat in council, always consulting for the people, to the end they might be well ordered: **16** and how they commit their government to one man year by year, that he should rule over them, and be lord over all their country, and all are obedient to that one, and there is neither envy nor emulation among them. **17** And Judas chose Eupolemus the son of John, the son of Accos, and Jason the son of Eleazar, and sent them to Rome, to establish friendship and alliance with them, **18** and that they should take the yoke from them; for they saw that the kingdom of the Greeks kept Israel in bondage. **19** And they went to Rome (and the way was exceedingly long), and they entered into the senate house, and answered and said, **20** Judas, who is also [called] Maccabaeus, and his countrymen, and the people of the Jews, have sent us to you, to make a confederacy and peace with you, and that we might be registered your allies and friends. **21** And the thing was well-pleasing in their sight. **22** And this is the copy of the writing which they wrote back again on tablets of brass, and sent to Jerusalem, that it might be with them there for a memorial of peace and confederacy: **23** "Good success be to the Romans, and to the nation of the Jews, by sea and by land forever: the sword also and the enemy be far from them. **24** But if war arise for Rome first, or any of their allies in all their dominion, **25** the nation of the Jews will help them as allies, as the occasion will prescribe to them, with all their heart: **26** and to those who make war on them they will not give, neither supply, food, arms, money, or ships, as it has seemed good to Rome, and they will keep their ordinances without taking anything therefore. **27** In the same manner, moreover, if war comes first on the nation of the Jews, the Romans will help them as allies with all their soul, as the occasion will prescribe to them: **28** and to those who are allies [with their enemies] there will not be given food, arms, money, or ships, as it has seemed good to Rome; and they will keep these ordinances, and that without deceit. **29** According to these words have the Romans made a covenant with the people of the Jews. **30** But if hereafter the one party and the other will take counsel to add or diminish anything, they will do it at their pleasure, and whatever they will add or take away will be established. **31** And as touching the evils which King Demetrius does to them, we have written to him, saying, Why have you made your yoke heavy on our friends and allies the Jews? **32** If, therefore, they plead anymore against you, we will do them justice, and fight with you by sea and by land."

CHAPTER 9

1 And Demetrius heard that Nicanor was fallen with his forces in battle, and he sent Bacchides and Alcimus again into the land of Judah a second time, and the right wing [of his army] with them: **2** and they went by the way that leads to Gilgal, and encamped against Mesaloth, which is in Arbela, and got possession of it, and destroyed many people. **3** And the first month of the one hundred and fifty-second year they encamped against Jerusalem: **4** and they left, and went to Berea, with twenty thousand footmen and two thousand horses. **5** And Judas was encamped at Elasa, and three thousand chosen men with him: **6** and they saw the multitude of the forces, that they were many, and they feared exceedingly: and many slipped away out of the army; there were not left of them more than eight hundred men. **7** And Judas saw that his army slipped away, and that the battle pressed on him, and he was severely troubled in heart, for that he had no time to gather them together, and he waxed faint. **8** And he said to those who were left, "Let us arise and go up against our adversaries, if perhaps we may be able to fight with them." **9** And they would have dissuaded him, saying, "We will in no way be able, but let us rather save our lives now: let us return again, [we] and our countrymen, and fight against them, but we are few." **10** And Judas said, "Do not let it be so that I should do this thing, to flee from them: and if our time has come, let us die in a manly way for our countrymen's sake, and not leave a cause of reproach against our glory." **11** And the army went from the camp, and stood to encounter them, and the horse was parted into two companies, and the slingers and the archers went before the army, and all the mighty men that fought in the front of the battle. **12** But Bacchides was in the right wing; and the phalanx drew near on the two parts, and they blew with their trumpets. **13** And the men of Judas' side, even they sounded with their trumpets, and the earth shook with the shout of the armies, and the battle was joined, and continued from morning until evening. **14** And Judas saw that Bacchides and the strength of his army were on the right side, and there went with him all that were brave in heart, **15** and the right wing was defeated by them, and he pursued after them to Mount Azotus. **16** And those who were on the left wing saw that the right wing was defeated, and they turned and followed on the footsteps of Judas and of those that were with him: **17** and the battle waxed severe, and many on both parts fell wounded to death. **18** And Judas fell, and the rest fled. **19** And Jonathan and Simon took Judas their brother and buried him in the tomb of his fathers at Modin, **20** And they mourned him, and all Israel made great lamentation for him, and mourned many days, and said, **21** "How is the mighty fallen, the savior of Israel!" **22** And the rest of the acts of Judas, and his wars, and the valiant deeds which he did, and his greatness, they are not written; for they were exceedingly many. **23** And it came to pass after the death of Judas, that the lawless put out their heads in all the coasts of Israel, and all those who did iniquity rose up **24** (in those days there was an exceedingly great famine), and the country went over with them. **25** And Bacchides chose out the ungodly men and made them lords of the country. **26** And they sought out and searched for the friends of Judas, and brought them to Bacchides, and he took vengeance on them, and used them despitefully. **27** And there was great suffering in Israel, such as was not since the time that no prophet appeared to them. **28** And all the friends of Judas were gathered together, and they said to Jonathan, **29** Since your brother Judas has died, we have no man like him to go out against our enemies, and Bacchides, and among them of our nation that hate us. **30** Now therefore, we have chosen you this day to be our prince and leader in his stead, that you may fight our battles. **31** And Jonathan took the governance on him at that time and rose up in the stead of his brother Judas. **32** And Bacchides knew it, and he sought to kill him. **33** And Jonathan, and Simon his brother, and all that were with him, knew it; and they fled into the wilderness of Tekoah, and encamped by the water of the pool Asphar. **34** And Bacchides knew it on the Sabbath day, and came, he and all his army, over Jordan. **35** And [Jonathan] sent his brother, a leader of the multitude, and implored his friends the Nabathaeans, that they might leave with them their baggage, which was much. **36** And the children of Jambri came out of Medaba, and took John, and all that he had, and went their way with it. **37** But after these things they brought word to Jonathan and Simon his brother, that the children of Jambri were making a great marriage and were bringing the bride from Nadabath with a great train, a daughter of one of the great nobles of Canaan. **38** And they remembered John their brother, and went up, and hid themselves under the covert of the mountain: **39** and they lifted up their eyes, and saw, and behold, a great ado and much baggage: and the bridegroom came out, and his friends and his countrymen, to meet them with timbrels, and minstrels, and many weapons. **40** And they rose up against them from their ambush, and killed them, and many fell wounded to death, and the remnant fled into the mountain, and they took all their spoils. **41** And the marriage was turned into mourning, and the voice of their minstrels into lamentation. **42** And they avenged fully the blood of their brother and turned back to the marsh of Jordan. **43** And Bacchides heard it, and he came on the Sabbath day to the banks of Jordan with a great army. **44** And Jonathan said to his company, "Let us stand up now and fight for our lives, for it is not [with us] today, as yesterday and the day before. **45** For behold, the battle is before us and behind us; moreover, the water of the Jordan is on this side and on that side, and marsh and wood; and there is no place to escape. **46** Now therefore, cry to Heaven, that you may be delivered out of the hand of your enemies." **47** And the battle was joined, and Jonathan stretched out his hand to strike Bacchides, and he turned away back from him. **48** And Jonathan and those who were with him leapt into the Jordan and swam over to the other side: and they did not pass over Jordan against them. **49** And there fell of Bacchides' company that day about one thousand men; **50** and he returned to Jerusalem. And they built strong cities in Judea, the stronghold that was in Jericho, and Emmaus, and Bethhoron, and Bethel, and Timnath, Pharathon, and Tephon, with high walls and gates and bars. **51** And in them he set a garrison, to vex Israel. **52** And he fortified the city Bethsura, and Gazara, and the citadel, and put forces in them, and store of food. **53** And he took the sons of the chief men of the country for hostages and put them in ward in the citadel at Jerusalem. **54** And in the one hundred and fifty-third year, in the second month, Alcimus commanded to pull down the wall of the inner court of the sanctuary; he pulled down also the works of the prophets; **55** and he began to pull down. At that time was Alcimus stricken, and his works were hindered; and his mouth was stopped, and he was taken with a palsy, and he could no longer speak anything and give order concerning his house. **56** And Alcimus died at that time with great torment. **57** And Bacchides saw that Alcimus was dead, and he returned to the king: and the land of Judah had rest two years. **58** And all the lawless men took counsel, saying, "Behold, Jonathan and they of his part are dwelling at ease, and in security: now therefore we will bring Bacchides, and he will lay hands on them all in one night." **59** And they went and consulted with him. **60** And he went, and came with a great army, and sent letters privily to all his allies that were in Judea, that they should lay hands on Jonathan and those that were with him: and they could not, because their counsel was known to them. **61** And [those who were of Jonathan's part] laid hands on about fifty of the men of the country, that were authors of the wickedness, and he killed them. **62** And Jonathan, and Simon, and those who were with him, got them away to Bethbasi, which is in the wilderness, and he built up that which had been pulled down thereof, and they made it strong. **63** And Bacchides knew it, and he gathered together all his multitude, and sent word to those who were of Judea. **64** And he went and encamped against Bethbasi, and fought against it many days, and made engines of war. **65** And Jonathan left his brother Simon in the city, and went out into the country, and he went with a few men. **66** And he struck Odomera and his relatives, and the children of Phasiron in their tent. **67** And they began to strike them, and to go up with their forces. And Simon and those who were with him went out of the city, and set on fire the engines of war, **68** and fought against Bacchides, and he was defeated by them, and they afflicted him severely; for his counsel was in vain, and his inroad. **69** And they were very angry with the lawless men that gave him counsel to come into the country, and they killed many of them. And he took counsel to depart into his own land. **70** And Jonathan had knowledge thereof, and sent ambassadors to him, to the end that they should make peace with him, and that he should restore to them the captives. **71** And he accepted the thing, and did according to his words, and swore to him that he would not seek his hurt all the days of his life. **72** And he restored to him the captives which he had taken previously out of the land of Judah, and he returned and departed into his own land, and came not anymore into their borders. **73** And the sword ceased from Israel. And Jonathan lived at Michmash; and Jonathan began to judge the people; and he destroyed the ungodly out of Israel.

CHAPTER 10

1 And in the one hundred and sixtieth year, Alexander Epiphanes, the son of Antiochus, went up and took possession of Ptolemais: and they received him, and he reigned there. **2** And King Demetrius heard thereof, and he gathered together exceedingly great forces, and went out to meet him in battle. **3** And Demetrius sent letters to Jonathan with words of peace, so as to magnify him. **4** For he said, "Let us go beforehand to make peace with them, before he makes peace with Alexander against us: **5** for he will remember all the evils that we have done against him, and to his countrymen and to his nation." **6** And he gave him authority to gather together forces, and to provide arms, and that he should be his ally: and he commanded that they should deliver up to him the hostages that were in the citadel. **7** And Jonathan came to Jerusalem and read the letters in the audience of all the people, and of those who were in the citadel: **8** and they were severely afraid, when they heard that the king had given him authority to gather together an army. **9** And they of the citadel delivered up the hostages to Jonathan, and he restored them to their parents. **10** And Jonathan lived in Jerusalem and began to build and renew the city. **11** And he commanded those who did the work to build the walls and Mount Zion around with square stones for defense; and they did so. **12** And the strangers, that were in the strongholds which Bacchides had built, fled away; **13** and each man left his place, and departed into his own land. **14** Only at Bethsura were there left certain of those that had forsaken the law and the commands; for it was a place of refuge to them. **15** And King Alexander heard all the promises which Demetrius had sent to Jonathan: and they told him of the battles and the valiant deeds which he and his countrymen had done, and of the toils which they had endured; **16** And he said, "Will we find such another man? And now we will make him our friend and ally." **17** And he wrote letters, and sent them to him, according to these words, saying, **18** "King Alexander to his brother Jonathan, greetings: **19** We have heard of you, that you are a mighty man of valor, and meet to be our friend. **20** And now we have appointed you this day to be chief priest of your nation, and to be called the king's friend (and he sent to him a purple robe and a crown of gold), and to take our part, and to keep friendship with us." **21** And Jonathan put on the holy garments in the seventh month of the one hundred and sixtieth year, at the Celebration of Shelters, and he gathered together forces, and provided arms in abundance. **22** And Demetrius heard these things, and he was grieved, and said, **23** "What is this that we have done, that Alexander has been beforehand with us in establishing friendship with the Jews, to strengthen himself? **24** I also will write to them words of encouragement and of honor and of gifts, that they may be with me to aid me." **25** And he sent to them according to these words: "King Demetrius to the nation of the Jews, greetings: **26** Forasmuch as you have kept your covenants with us, and continued in our friendship, and have not joined yourselves to our enemies, we have heard of this, and are glad. **27** And now continue still to keep faith with us, and we will repay to you good things in return for your dealings with us, **28** and will grant you many immunities, and give you gifts. **29** And now I free you, and release all the Jews, from the tributes, and from the customs of salt, and from the crowns. **30** And instead of the third part of the seed, and instead of the half of the fruit of the trees, which falls to me to receive, I release it from this day and from now on, so that I will not take it from the land of Judah, and from the three governments which are added to that from the country of Samaria and Galilee, from this day out and for all time. **31** And let Jerusalem be holy and free, and her borders; the tenths and the tolls [also]. **32** I yield up also my authority over the citadel which is at Jerusalem, and give it to the chief priest, that he may appoint in it such men as he will choose to keep it. **33** And every soul of the Jews, that has been carried captive from the land of Judah into any part of my kingdom, I set at liberty without price; and let all remit the tributes of their cattle also. **34** And all the feasts, and the Sabbaths, and new moons, and appointed days, and three days before a feast, and three days after a feast, let them all be days of immunity and release for all the Jews that are in my kingdom. **35** And no man will have authority to exact from any of them, or to trouble them concerning any matter. **36** And let there be enrolled among the king's forces about thirty thousand men of the Jews, and pay will be given to them, as belongs to all the king's forces. **37** And of them some will be placed in the king's great strongholds, and some of them will be placed over the affairs of the kingdom, which are of trust: and let those that are over them, and their rulers, be of themselves, and let them walk after their own laws, even as the king has commanded in the land of Judah. **38** And the three governments that have been added to Judea from the country of Samaria, let them be added to Judea, that they may be reckoned to be under one, that they may not obey other authority than the chief priest's. **39** As for Ptolemais, and the land pertaining to that, I have given it as a gift to the sanctuary that is at Jerusalem, for the expenses that befit the sanctuary. **40** And I give every year fifteen thousand shekels of silver from the king's revenues from the places that are convenient. **41** And all the overplus, which those who manage the king's affairs paid not in as in the first years, they will give from now on toward the works of the house. **42** And besides this, the five thousand shekels of silver, which they received from the uses of the sanctuary from the revenue year by year, this is also released, because it pertains to the priests that minister. **43** And whoever will flee to the temple that is at Jerusalem, and [be found] within all the borders thereof, whether one owes money to the king, or any other matter, let them go free, and all that they have in my kingdom. **44** And for the building and renewing of the works of the sanctuary the expense will be given also out of the king's revenue. **45** And for the building of the walls of Jerusalem, and the fortifying thereof around, will the expense be given also out of the king's revenue, and for the building of the walls in Judea." **46** Now when Jonathan and the people heard these words, they gave no credence to them, nor received them, because they remembered the great evil which he had done in Israel, and that he had afflicted them very severely. **47** And they were well pleased with Alexander, because he was the first that spoke words of peace to them, and they were allies with him always. **48** And King Alexander gathered together great forces, and encamped near Demetrius. **49** And the two kings joined battle, and the army of Alexander fled; and Demetrius followed after him and prevailed against them. **50** And he strengthened the battle exceedingly until the sun went down: and Demetrius fell that day. **51** And Alexander sent ambassadors to Ptolemy king of Egypt according to these words, saying, **52** "Forasmuch as I am returned to my kingdom, and am set on the throne of my fathers, and have gotten the dominion, and have overthrown Demetrius, and have gotten possession of our country; **53** yes, I joined the battle with him, and he and his army were defeated by us, and we sat on the throne of his kingdom: **54** now also let us make friends with one another, and give me now your daughter to wife: and I will be joined with you, and will give both you and her gifts worthy of you." **55** And Ptolemy the king answered, saying, "Happy is the day wherein you returned into the land of your fathers, and sat on the throne of their kingdom. **56** And now I will do to you as you have written, but meet me at Ptolemais, that we may see one another; and I will join with you, even as you have said." **57** And Ptolemy went out of Egypt, himself and Cleopatra his daughter, and came to Ptolemais in the one hundred and sixty-second year: **58** and King Alexander met him, and he bestowed on him his daughter Cleopatra, and celebrated her wedding at Ptolemais with great pomp, as the manner of kings is. **59** And King Alexander wrote to Jonathan, that he should come to meet him. **60** And he went with pomp to Ptolemais, and met the two kings, and gave them and their friends silver and gold, and many gifts, and found favor in their sight. **61** And there were gathered together against him certain pernicious fellows out of Israel, men that were transgressors of the law, to complain against him: and the king gave no heed to them. **62** And the king commanded, and they took off Jonathan's garments, and clothed him in purple: and so they did. **63** And the king made him sit with him, and said to his princes, "Go out with him into the midst of the city, and make proclamation, that no man complains against him of any matter, and let no man trouble him for any manner of cause." **64** And it came to pass, when those who complained against him saw his glory according as [the herald] made proclamation, and [saw] him clothed in purple, they all fled away. **65** And the king gave him honor, and wrote him among his chief friends, and made him a captain, and governor of a province. **66** And Jonathan returned to Jerusalem with peace and gladness. **67** And in the one hundred and sixty-fifth year came Demetrius, son of Demetrius, out of Crete into the land of his fathers: **68** and King Alexander heard thereof, and he grieved exceedingly, and returned to Antioch. **69** And Demetrius appointed Apollonius, who was over Coele-Syria, and he gathered together a great army, and encamped in Jamnia, and sent to Jonathan the chief priest, saying, **70** "You alone lift up yourself against us, but I am had in derision and in reproach because of you. And why do you vaunt your power against us in the mountains? **71** Now therefore, if you trust in your forces, come down to us into the plain, and there let us try the matter together; for with me is the power of the cities. **72** Ask and learn who I am, and the rest that help us; and they say your foot cannot stand before our face; for your fathers have been twice put to flight in their own land. **73** And now you will not be able to withstand the horse and such an army as this in the plain, where is neither stone nor flint, nor place to flee to." **74** Now when Jonathan heard the words of Apollonius, he was moved in his mind, and he chose out ten thousand men, and went out from Jerusalem, and Simon his brother met him for to help him. **75** And he encamped against Joppa: and they of the city shut him out, because Apollonius had a garrison in Joppa: **76** and they fought against it. And they of the city were afraid and opened to him: and Jonathan became master of Joppa. **77** And Apollonius heard, and he gathered an army of three thousand horses, and a great army, and went to Azotus as though he were on a journey, and immediately drew onward into the plain, because he had a multitude of horse, and trusted therein. **78** And he pursued after him to Azotus, and the armies joined battle. **79** And Apollonius had left one thousand horses behind them privily. **80** And Jonathan knew that there was an ambush behind him. And they compassed round his army, and cast their darts at the people, from morning until evening: **81** but the people stood still, as Jonathan commanded them: and their horses were wearied. **82** And Simon drew out his army and joined battle with the phalanx (for the horsemen were spent), and they were defeated by him, and fled. **83** And the horsemen were scattered in the plain, and they fled to Azotus, and entered into Beth-Dagon, their idol's temple, to save themselves. **84** And Jonathan burned Azotus, and the surrounding cities, and took their spoils; and the temple of Dagon, and those who fled into it, he burned with fire. **85** And those who had fallen by the sword, with those who were burned, were about eight thousand men. **86** And from there Jonathan left, and encamped against Ashkelon, and they of the city came out to meet him with great pomp. **87** And Jonathan, with those who were on his side, returned to Jerusalem, having many spoils. **88** And it came to pass, when King Alexander heard these things, he honored Jonathan yet more; and he sent to him a buckle of gold, as the use is to give to such as are of the relatives of the kings: and he gave him Ekron and all the coasts thereof for a possession.

CHAPTER 11

1 And the king of Egypt gathered together great forces, as the sand which is by the seashore, and many ships, and sought to make himself master of Alexander's kingdom by deceit, and to add it to his own kingdom. **2** And he went out into Syria with words of peace, and they of the cities opened to him, and met him; For King Alexander's command was that they should meet him, because he was his father-in-law. **3** Now as he entered into the cities of Ptolemais, he set his forces for a garrison in each city. **4** But when he came near to Azotus, they showed him the temple of Dagon burned with fire, and Azotus and the pasture lands thereof pulled down, and the bodies cast abroad, and those who had been burned, whom he burned in the war, for they had made heaps of them in his way. **5** And they told the king what things Jonathan had done, that they might cast blame on him: and the king held his peace. **6** And Jonathan met the king with pomp at Joppa, and they saluted one another, and they slept there. **7** And Jonathan went with the king as far as the river that is called Eleutherus and returned to Jerusalem. **8** But King Ptolemy became master of the cities on the seacoast, to Selucia which is by the sea, and he devised evil plans concerning Alexander. **9** And he sent ambassadors to King Demetrius, saying, "Come! Let us make a covenant with one another, and I will give you my daughter whom Alexander has, and you will reign over your father's kingdom; **10** for I have changed my mind that I gave my daughter to him, for he sought to kill me." **11** And he cast blame on him, because he coveted his kingdom. **12** And taking his daughter from him, he gave her to Demetrius, and was estranged from Alexander, and their enmity was openly seen. **13** And Ptolemy entered into Antioch and put on himself the diadem of Asia; and he put two diadems on his head, the diadem of Egypt and that of Asia. **14** But King Alexander was in Cilicia at that season, because they of those parts were in revolt. **15** And Alexander heard of it, and he came against him in war: and Ptolemy led out [his army, and] met him with a strong force, and put him to flight. **16** And Alexander fled into Arabia, that he might be sheltered there; but King Ptolemy was exalted. **17** And Zabdiel the Arabian took off Alexander's head and sent it to Ptolemy. **18** And King Ptolemy died the third day after, and those who were in his strongholds were slain by those who were in the strongholds. **19** And Demetrius reigned in the one hundred and sixty-seventh year. **20** In those days Jonathan gathered together them of Judea, to take the citadel that was at Jerusalem: and he made many engines of war against it. **21** And certain that hated their own nation, men that transgressed the law, went to the king, and reported to him that Jonathan was besieging the citadel. **22** And he heard, and was angered; but when he heard it, he set out immediately, and came to Ptolemais, and wrote to Jonathan, that he should not besiege it, and that he should meet him and speak with him at Ptolemais with all speed. **23** But when Jonathan heard this, he commanded to besiege it [still]: and he chose certain of the elders of Israel and of the priests, and put himself in peril, **24** and taking silver and gold and raiment and various presents besides, went to Ptolemais to the king. And he found favor in his sight. **25** And certain lawless men of those who were of the nation made complaints against him, **26** and the king did to him even as his predecessors had done to him and exalted him in the sight of all his friends, **27** and confirmed to him the chief priesthood, and all the other honors that he had before, and gave him preeminence among his chief friends. **28** And Jonathan requested of the king, that he would make Judea free from tribute, and the three provinces, and the country of Samaria; and promised him three hundred talents. **29** And the king consented and wrote letters to Jonathan concerning all these things after this manner: **30** "King Demetrius to his brother Jonathan, and to the nation of the Jews, greetings: **31** The copy of the letter which we wrote to Lasthenes our countryman concerning you, we have written also to you, that you may see it. **32** King Demetrius to Lasthenes his father, greetings: **33** We have determined to do good to the nation of the Jews, who are our friends, and observe what is just toward us, because of their good will toward us. **34** We have confirmed therefore to them the borders of Judea, and also the three governments of Aphaerema and Lydda and Ramathaim ([these] were added to Judea from the country of Samaria), and all things pertaining to them, for all such as do sacrifice in Jerusalem, instead of the king's dues which the king received of them yearly previously from the produce of the earth and the fruits of trees. **35** And as for the other things that pertain to us from now on, of the tenths and the tolls that pertain to us, and the salt pits, and the crowns that pertain to us, all these we will bestow on them. **36** And not one of these things will be annulled from this time out and forever. **37** Now therefore, be careful to make a copy of these things, and let it be given to Jonathan, and let it be set up on the holy mount in an appropriate and conspicuous place." **38** And King Demetrius saw that the land was quiet before him, and that no resistance was made to him, and he sent away all his forces, each man to his own place, except the foreign forces, which he had raised from the isles of the nations: and all the forces of his fathers hated him. **39** Now Tryphon was of those who previously had been of Alexander's part, and he saw that all the forces murmured against Demetrius, and he went to Imalcue the Arabian, who was nourishing up Antiochus the young child of Alexander, **40** and pressed severely on him that he should deliver him to him, that he might reign in his father's stead: and he told him all that Demetrius had done, and the hatred with which his forces hated him; and he dwelt there many days. **41** And Jonathan sent to King Demetrius, that he should cast out of Jerusalem them of the citadel, and those who were in the strongholds; for they fought against Israel continually. **42** And Demetrius sent to Jonathan, saying, "I will not only do this for you and your nation, but I will greatly honor you and your nation, if I find fair occasion. **43** Now therefore you will do well, if you send me men who will fight for me; for all my forces are revolted." **44** And Jonathan sent him three thousand valiant men to Antioch: and they came to the king, and the king was glad at their coming. **45** And they of the city gathered themselves together into the midst of the city, to the number of one hundred and twenty thousand men, and they were inclined to kill the king. **46** And the king fled into the court of the palace, and they of the city seized the passages of the city and began to fight. **47** And the king called the Jews to help him, and they were gathered together to him all at once, and they dispersed themselves in the city, and killed that day to the number of one hundred thousand. **48** And they set the city on fire, and got many spoils that day, and saved the king. **49** And they of the city saw that the Jews had made themselves masters of the city as they would, and they waxed faint in their hearts, and

they cried out to the king with supplication, saying, **50** "Give us your right hand, and let the Jews cease from fighting against us and the city." **51** And they cast away their arms and made peace; and the Jews were glorified in the sight of the king, and before all that were in his kingdom; and they returned to Jerusalem, having many spoils. **52** And King Demetrius sat on the throne of his kingdom, and the land was quiet before him. **53** And he lied in all that he spoke, and estranged himself from Jonathan, and did not repay him according to the benefits with which he had repaid him and afflicted him exceedingly. **54** Now after this, Tryphon returned, and with him the young child Antiochus; and he reigned and put on a diadem. **55** And there were gathered to him all the forces which Demetrius had sent away with disgrace, and they fought against him, and he fled and was put to the rout. **56** And Tryphon took the elephants and became master of Antioch. **57** And the young Antiochus wrote to Jonathan, saying, "I confirm to you the chief priesthood, and appoint you over the four governments, and to be one of the king's friends." **58** And he sent to him golden vessels and furniture for the table, and gave him leave to drink in golden vessels, and to be clothed in purple, and to have a golden buckle. **59** And his brother Simon he made captain from the Ladder of Tyre to the borders of Egypt. **60** And Jonathan went out and took his journey beyond the river and through the cities; and all the forces of Syria gathered themselves to him for to be his allies. And he came to Ashkelon, and they of the city met him honorably. **61** And he departed from there to Gaza, and they of Gaza shut him out; and he laid siege to it, and burned the pasture lands thereof with fire, and plundered them. **62** And they of Gaza made request to Jonathan, and he gave them his right hand, and took the sons of their princes for hostages, and sent them away to Jerusalem; and he passed through the country as far as Damascus. **63** And Jonathan heard that Demetrius' princes were come to Kedesh, which is in Galilee, with a great army, purposing to remove him from his office; **64** and he went to meet them, but Simon his brother he left in the country. **65** And Simon encamped against Bethsura, and fought against it many days, and shut it up: **66** and they made request to him that he would give them his right hand, and he gave it to them; and he put them out from there, and took possession of the city, and set a garrison over it. **67** And Jonathan and his army encamped at the water of Gennesareth, and early in the morning they got them to the plain of Hazor. **68** And behold, an army of strangers met him in the plain, and they laid an ambush for him in the mountains, but themselves met him face to face. **69** But those who lay in ambush rose out of their places and joined battle; and all those who were of Jonathan's side fled: **70** not one of them was left, except Mattathias, the son of Absalom, and Judas the son of Chalphi, captains of the forces. **71** And Jonathan tore his clothes, and put earth on his head, and prayed. **72** And he turned again to them in battle, and put them to the rout, and they fled. **73** And they of his side that fled saw it, and returned to him, and pursued with him to Kedesh to their camp, and they encamped there. **74** And there fell of the strangers on that day about three thousand men: and Jonathan returned to Jerusalem.

CHAPTER 12

1 And Jonathan saw that the time served him, and he chose men, and sent them to Rome, to confirm and renew the friendship that they had with them. **2** And to the Spartans, and to other places, he sent letters after the same manner. **3** And they went to Rome, and entered into the senate house, and said, "Jonathan the chief priest, and the nation of the Jews, have sent us, to renew for them the friendship and the confederacy, as in former time." **4** And they gave them letters to the men in every place, that they should bring them on their way to the land of Judah in peace. **5** And this is the copy of the letters which Jonathan wrote to the Spartans: **6** "Jonathan the chief priest, and the senate of the nation, and the priests, and the rest of the people of the Jews, to their countrymen the Spartans, greetings: **7** Even before this time were letters sent to Onias the chief priest from Arius, who was reigning among you, to signify that you are our countrymen, as the copy written below shows. **8** And Onias entreated honorably the man that was sent, and received the letters, wherein declaration was made of confederacy and friendship. **9** Therefore we also, albeit we need none of these things, having for our encouragement the holy scrolls which are in our hands, **10** have determined to send that we might renew our brotherhood and friendship with you, to the end that we should not become estranged from you altogether, for a long time has passed since you sent to us. **11** We therefore, at all times without ceasing, both in our feasts, and on the other convenient days, remember you in the sacrifices which we offer, and in our prayers, as it is right and appropriate to be mindful of countrymen: **12** and moreover are glad for your glory. **13** But as for ourselves, many afflictions and many wars have encompassed us, and the kings that are around us have fought against us. **14** We were not inclined therefore to be troublesome to you, and to the rest of our allies and friends, in these wars; **15** for we have the help which is from Heaven to help us, and we have been delivered from our enemies, and our enemies have been brought low. **16** We chose, therefore, Numenius the son of Antiochus, and Antipater the son of Jason, and have sent them to the Romans, to renew the friendship that we had with them, and the former confederacy. **17** We commanded them, therefore, to go also to you, and to salute you, and to deliver you our letters concerning the renewing [of friendship] and our brotherhood. **18** And now you will do well if you give us an answer to that. **19** And this is the copy of the letters which they sent to Onias: **20** Arius, king of the Spartans, to Onias the chief priest, greetings: **21** It has been found in writing, concerning the Spartans and the Jews, that they are countrymen, and that they are of the stock of Abraham: **22** and now, since this has come to our knowledge, you will do well to write to us of your prosperity. **23** And we moreover write on our part to you, that your cattle and goods are ours, and ours are yours. We command, therefore, that they make report to you concerning this." **24** And Jonathan heard that Demetrius' princes were returned to fight against him with a greater army than before, **25** and he went from Jerusalem, and met them in the country of Hamath; for he gave them no respite to set foot in his country. **26** And he sent spies into his camp, and they came again, and reported to him that they were appointed in such and such a way to fall on them in the night season. **27** But as soon as the sun was down, Jonathan commanded his men to watch, and to be in arms, that all the night long they might be ready for battle: and he put out sentinels around the camp. **28** And the adversaries heard that Jonathan and his men were ready for battle, and they feared, and trembled in their hearts, and they kindled fires in their camp, **29** but Jonathan and his men did not know it until the morning; for they saw the lights burning. **30** And Jonathan pursued after them and overtook them not; for they were gone over the River Eleutherus. **31** And Jonathan turned toward the Arabians, who are called Zabadaeans, and struck them, and took their spoils. **32** And he came out from there, and came to Damascus, and took his journey through all the country. **33** And Simon went out, and took his journey as far as Ashkelon, and the strongholds that were near to it. And he turned toward Joppa and took possession of it; **34** for he had heard that they were determined to deliver the stronghold to the men of Demetrius; and he set a garrison there to keep it. **35** And Jonathan returned, and called the elders of the people together; and he took counsel with them to build strongholds in Judea, **36** and to make the walls of Jerusalem higher, and to raise a great mound between the citadel and the city, for to separate it from the city, that so it might be all alone, that men might neither buy nor sell. **37** And they were gathered together to build the city, and there fell down part of the wall of the brook that is on the east side, and he repaired that which is called Chaphenatha. **38** And Simon also built Adida in the plain country, and made it strong, and set up gates and bars. **39** And Tryphon sought to reign over Asia and to put on himself the diadem, and to stretch out his hand against Antiochus the king. **40** And he was afraid lest perhaps Jonathan should not permit him, and lest he should fight against him; and he sought a way how to take him, that he might destroy him. And he went and came to Bethshan. **41** And Jonathan came out to meet him with forty thousand men chosen for battle and came to Bethshan. **42** And Tryphon saw that he came with a great army, and he was afraid to stretch out his hand against him: **43** and he received him honorably, and commended him to all his friends, and gave him gifts, and commanded his forces to be obedient to him, as to himself. **44** And he said to Jonathan, "Why have you put all this people to trouble, seeing there is no war between us? **45** And now send them away to their homes but choose for yourself a few men who will be with you, and come you with me to Ptolemais, and I will give it up to you, and the rest of the strongholds and the rest of the forces, and all the king's officers: and I will return and depart; for this is the cause of my coming." **46** And he put

his trust in him, and did even as he said, and sent away his forces, and they departed into the land of Judah. **47** But he reserved to himself three thousand men, of whom he left two thousand in Galilee, but one thousand went with him. **48** Now as soon as Jonathan entered into Ptolemais, they of Ptolemais shut the gates, and laid hands on him; and all those who came in with him they killed with the sword. **49** And Tryphon sent forces and horsemen into Galilee, and into the great plain, to destroy all Jonathan's men. **50** And they perceived that he was taken and had perished, and those who were with him; and they encouraged one another, and went on their way close together, prepared to fight. **51** And those who followed on them saw that they were ready to fight for their lives and turned back again. **52** And they all came in peace into the land of Judah, and they mourned for Jonathan, and those who were with him, and they were severely afraid; and all Israel mourned with a great mourning. **53** And all the nations that were around them sought to destroy them utterly, for they said, "They have no ruler, nor any to help them: now therefore, let us fight against them and take away their memorial from among men."

CHAPTER 13

1 And Simon heard that Tryphon had gathered together a mighty army to come into the land of Judah and destroy it utterly. **2** And he saw that the people trembled and were in great fear; and he went up to Jerusalem, and gathered the people together; **3** and he encouraged them, and said to them, "You yourselves know all the things that I, and my countrymen, and my father's house, have done for the laws and the sanctuary, and the battles and the distresses which we have seen: **4** by reason of this all my countrymen have perished for Israel's sake, and I am left alone. **5** And now be it far from me, that I should spare my own life in any time of affliction; for I am not better than my countrymen. **6** However, I will take vengeance for my nation, and for the sanctuary, and for our wives and children, because all the nations are gathered to destroy us of very [great] hatred." **7** And the spirit of the people revived, as soon as they heard these words. **8** And they answered with a loud voice, saying, "You are our leader instead of Judas and Jonathan your brother. **9** Fight our battles, and all that you will say to us, that will we do." **10** And he gathered together all the men of war, and hurried to finish the walls of Jerusalem, and he fortified it around. **11** And he sent Jonathan the son of Absalom, and with him a great army, to Joppa; and he cast out those who were therein and dwelt there in it. **12** And Tryphon left from Ptolemais with a mighty army to enter into the land of Judah, and Jonathan was with him in ward. **13** But Simon encamped at Adida, near the plain. **14** And Tryphon knew that Simon was risen up instead of his brother Jonathan, and meant to join battle with him, and he sent ambassadors to him, saying, **15** "It is for money which Jonathan your brother owed to the king's treasure, by reason of the offices which he had, that we hold him fast. **16** And now send one hundred talents of silver, and two of his sons for hostages, that when he is set at liberty he may not revolt from us, and we will set him at liberty." **17** And Simon knew that they spoke to him deceitfully; and he sent the money and the children, lest perhaps he should procure to himself great hatred of the people, **18** and they should say, "Because I did not send him the money and the children, he perished." **19** And he sent the children and the hundred talents. And he dealt falsely and did not set Jonathan at liberty. **20** And after this Tryphon came to invade the land, and destroy it, and he went around by the way that leads to Adora: and Simon and his army marched near him to every place, wherever he went. **21** Now they of the citadel sent to Tryphon ambassadors, hastening him to come to them through the wilderness, and to send them food. **22** And Tryphon made ready all his horse to come: and on that night there fell a very great snow, and he came not by reason of the snow. And he left and came into the country of Gilead. **23** But when he came near to Bascama, he killed Jonathan, and he was buried there. **24** And Tryphon returned and went away into his own land. **25** And Simon sent, and took the bones of Jonathan his brother, and buried him at Modin, the city of his fathers. **26** And all Israel made great lamentation over him and mourned for him many days. **27** And Simon built [a monument] on the tomb of his father and his relatives, and raised it aloft to the sight, with polished stone behind and before. **28** And he set up seven pyramids, one near another, for his father, and his mother, and his four relatives. **29** And for these he made cunning devices, setting around them great pillars, and on the pillars he fashioned all manner of arms for a perpetual memory, and beside the arms ships carved, that they should be seen of all that sail on the sea. **30** This is the tomb which he made at Modin, and [it is there] to this day. **31** Now Tryphon dealt deceitfully with the young King Antiochus, and killed him, **32** and reigned in his stead, and put the diadem of Asia on himself, and brought a great calamity on the land. **33** And Simon built the strongholds of Judea, and fenced them about with high towers, and great walls, and gates, and bars; and he laid up food in the strongholds. **34** And Simon chose men, and sent to King Demetrius, to the end he should give the country an immunity, because all that Tryphon did was to plunder. **35** And King Demetrius sent to him according to these words, and answered him, and wrote a letter to him, after this manner: **36** "King Demetrius to Simon the chief priest and friend of kings, and to the elders and nation of the Jews, greetings: **37** The golden crown, and the palm branch, which you sent, we have received: and we are ready to make a steadfast peace with you, yes, and to write to our officers, to grant immunities to you. **38** And whatever things we confirmed to you, they are confirmed; and the strongholds, which you have built, let them be your own. **39** As for any oversights and faults committed to this day, we forgive them, and the crown which you owed us: and if there were any other toll exacted in Jerusalem, let it be exacted no longer. **40** And if there are any among you appropriate to be enrolled in our court, let them be enrolled, and let there be peace between us." **41** In the one hundred and seventieth year was the yoke of the heathen taken away from Israel. **42** And the people began to write in their instruments and contracts, "In the first year of Simon, the great chief priest and captain and leader of the Jews." **43** In those days he encamped against Gazara and compassed it around with armies; and he made an engine of siege, and brought it up to the city, and struck a tower, and took it. **44** And those who were in the engine leaped out into the city; and there was a great uproar in the city: **45** and they of the city tore their clothes and went up on the walls with their wives and children, and cried with a loud voice, making request to Simon to give them his right hand. **46** And they said, "Do not deal with us according to our wickedness, but according to your mercy." **47** And Simon was reconciled to them and did not fight against them: and he put them out of the city, and cleansed the houses wherein the idols were, and so entered into it with singing and giving praise. **48** And he put all uncleanness out of it and placed in it such men as would keep the law, and made it stronger than it was before, and built therein a dwelling place for himself. **49** But they of the citadel in Jerusalem were hindered from going out, and from going into the country, and from buying and selling; and they hungered exceedingly, and a great number of them perished through famine. **50** And they cried out to Simon, that he should give them his right hand; and he gave it to them: and he put them out from there, and he cleansed the citadel from its pollutions. **51** And he entered into it on the twenty-third day of the second month, in the one hundred and seventy-first year, with praise and palm branches, and with harps, and with cymbals, and with lutes, and with hymns, and with songs: because a great enemy was destroyed out of Israel. **52** And he ordained that they should keep that day every year with gladness. And the hill of the temple that was by the citadel he made stronger than before, and there he lived, himself and his men. **53** And Simon saw that John his son was a [valiant] man, and he made him leader of all his forces: and he lived in Gazara.

CHAPTER 14

1 And in the one hundred and seventy-second year, King Demetrius gathered his forces together, and went into Media, to get himself help, that he might fight against Tryphon. **2** And Arsaces, the king of Persia and Media, heard that Demetrius had come into his borders, and he sent one of his princes to take him alive: **3** and he went and struck the army of Demetrius, and took him, and brought him to Arsaces; and he put him in ward. **4** And the land had rest all the days of Simon: and he sought the good of his nation; and his authority and his glory was well-pleasing to them all his days. **5** And amid all his glory he took Joppa for a haven and made it an entrance for the isles of the sea; **6** and he enlarged the borders of his nation and got possession of the country; **7** and he gathered together a great number of captives, and got the dominion of Gazara,

and Bethsura, and the citadel, and he took away from it its uncleanness; and there was none that resisted him. **8** And they tilled their land in peace, and the land gave her increase, and the trees of the plains their fruit. **9** The ancient men sat in the streets, they communed—all of them—together of good things, and the young men put on glorious and warlike apparel. **10** He provided food for the cities, and furnished them with all manner of munition, until the name of his glory was named to the end of the earth. **11** He made peace in the land, and Israel rejoiced with great joy: **12** and each man sat under his vine and his fig tree, and there was none to make them afraid; **13** and there ceased in the land any that fought against them: and the kings were defeated in those days. **14** And he strengthened all those of his people that were brought low: the law he searched out, and every lawless and wicked person he took away. **15** He glorified the sanctuary, and the vessels of the temple he multiplied. **16** And it was heard at Rome that Jonathan was dead, and even to Sparta, and they were exceedingly sorry. **17** But as soon as they heard that his brother Simon was made chief priest in his stead, and ruled the country, and the cities therein, **18** they wrote to him on tablets of brass, to renew with him the friendship and the confederacy which they had confirmed with Judas and Jonathan his relatives; **19** and they were read before the congregation at Jerusalem. **20** And this is the copy of the letters which the Spartans sent: "The rulers of the Spartans, and the city, to Simon the chief priest, and to the elders, and the priests, and the residue of the people of the Jews, our countrymen, greetings: **21** The ambassadors that were sent to our people made report to us of your glory and honor: and we were glad for their coming, **22** and we registered the things that were spoken by them in the public records after this manner: Numenius son of Antiochus, and Antipater son of Jason, the Jews' ambassadors, came to us to renew the friendship they had with us." **23** And it pleased the people to entertain the men honorably, and to put the copy of their words in the public records, to the end that the people of the Spartans might have a memorial thereof: moreover, they wrote a copy of these things to Simon the chief priest. **24** After this Simon sent Numenius to Rome with a great shield of gold of one-thousand-pound weight, in order to confirm the confederacy with them. **25** But when the people heard these things, they said, "What thanks will we give to Simon and his sons? **26** For he and his countrymen and the house of his father have made themselves strong and have chased away in fight the enemies of Israel from them, and confirmed liberty to Israel." **27** And they wrote on tablets of brass, and set them on pillars in Mount Zion: and this is the copy of the writing: "On the eighteenth day of Elul, in the one hundred and seventy-second year, and this is the third year of Simon the chief priest, **28** in Asaramel, in a great congregation of priests and people and princes of the nation, and of the elders of the country, was it notified to us: **29** Forasmuch as oftentimes there have been wars in the country, but Simon the son of Mattathias, the son of the sons of Joarib, and his countrymen, put themselves in danger, and withstood the enemies of their nation, that their sanctuary and the law might be established, and glorified their nation with great glory: **30** and Jonathan assembled their nation together, and became their chief priest, and was gathered to his people: **31** and their enemies purposed to invade their country, that they might destroy their country utterly, and stretch out their hands against their sanctuary: **32** then rose up Simon, and fought for his nation, and spent much of his own substance, and armed the valiant men of his nation, and gave them wages: **33** and he fortified the cities of Judea, and Bethsura that lies on the borders of Judea, where the arms of the enemies were previously, and set there a garrison of Jews: **34** and he fortified Joppa which is on the sea, and Gazara which is on the borders of Azotus, wherein the enemies lived previously, and placed Jews there, and set therein all things convenient for their restoration: **35** and the people saw the faith of Simon, and the glory which he thought to bring to his nation, and they made him their leader and chief priest, because he had done all these things, and for the justice and the faith which he kept to his nation, and for that he sought by all means to exalt his people: **36** and in his days things prospered in his hands, so that the nations were taken away out of their country, and they also that were in the city of David, those who were in Jerusalem, who had made themselves a citadel, out of which they issued, and polluted all things around the sanctuary, and did great hurt to its purity; **37** and he placed Jews therein, and fortified it for the safety of the country and the city, and made high the walls of Jerusalem: **38** and King Demetrius confirmed to him the chief priesthood according to these things, **39** and made him one of his friends, and honored him with great honor; **40** for he had heard it said that the Jews had been called by the Romans friends and allies and countrymen, and that they had met the ambassadors of Simon honorably; **41** and that the Jews and the priests were well pleased that Simon should be their leader and chief priest forever, until there should arise a faithful prophet; **42** and that he should be captain over them, and should take charge of the sanctuary, to set them over their works, and over the country, and over the arms, and over the strongholds; and that he should take charge of the sanctuary, **43** and that he should be obeyed by all, and that all instruments in the country should be written in his name, and that he should be clothed in purple, and wear gold; **44** and that it should not be lawful for any of the people or of the priests to set at nothing any of these things, or to deny the words that he should speak, or to gather an assembly in the country without him, or to be clothed in purple, or wear a buckle of gold; **45** but whoever should do otherwise, or set at nothing any of these things, he should be liable to punishment." **46** All the people consented to ordain for Simon that he should do according to these words; **47** and Simon accepted this, and consented to be chief priest, and to be captain and governor of the Jews and of the priests, and to be protector of all. **48** And they commanded to put this writing on tablets of brass, and to set them up within the precinct of the sanctuary in a conspicuous place; **49** and moreover to put the copies thereof in the treasury, to the end that Simon and his sons might have them.

CHAPTER 15

1 And Antiochus son of Demetrius the king sent letters from the isles of the sea to Simon the priest and governor of the Jews, and to all the nation; **2** and the contents thereof were after this manner: "King Antiochus to Simon the chief priest and governor, and to the nation of the Jews, greetings: **3** Forasmuch as certain pernicious fellows have made themselves masters of the kingdom of our fathers, but my purpose is to claim the kingdom, that I may restore it as it was before; and moreover I have raised a multitude of foreign soldiers, and have prepared ships of war; **4** moreover I am inclined to land in the country, that I may punish those who have destroyed our country, and those who have made many cities in the kingdom desolate: **5** Now therefore, I confirm to you all the exactions which the kings that were before me remitted to you, and whatever gifts besides they remitted to you: **6** and I give you leave to coin money for your country with your own stamp, **7** but that Jerusalem and the sanctuary should be free: and all the arms that you have prepared, and the strongholds that you have built, which you have in your possession, let them remain to you: **8** and everything owing to the king, and the things that will be owing to the king from now on and forevermore, let them be remitted to you: **9** moreover, when we will have established our kingdom, we will glorify you and your nation and the temple with great glory, so that your glory will be made manifest in all the earth." **10** In the one hundred and seventy-fourth year Antiochus went out into the land of his fathers; and all the forces came together to him, so that there were few men with Tryphon. **11** And King Antiochus pursued him, and he came, as he fled, to Dor, which is by the sea: **12** for he knew that troubles were come on him all at once, and that his forces had forsaken him. **13** And Antiochus encamped against Dor, and with him one hundred and twenty thousand men of war, and eight thousand horses. **14** And he compassed the city around, and the ships joined in the attack from the sea; and he vexed the city by land and sea, and suffered no man to go out or in. **15** And Numenius and his company came from Rome, having letters to the kings and to the countries, wherein were written these things: **16** "Lucius, consul of the Romans, to King Ptolemy, greetings: **17** The Jews' ambassadors came to us as our friends and allies, to renew the old friendship and confederacy, being sent from Simon the chief priest, and from the people of the Jews: **18** moreover they brought a shield of gold of one thousand pounds. **19** It pleased us therefore to write to the kings and to the countries, that they should not seek their hurt, nor fight against them, and their cities, and their country, nor be allies with such as fight against them. **20** Moreover it seemed good to us to receive the shield from them. **21** If, therefore, any pernicious fellows have fled from their country to you, deliver them to Simon the chief priest, that he may take vengeance on them according to their law." **22** And

he wrote the same things to Demetrius the king, and to Attalus, and to Arathes, and to Arsaces, **23** and to all the countries, and to Sampsames, and to the Spartans, and to Delos, and to Myndos, and to Sicyon, and to Caria, and to Samos, and to Pamphylia, and to Lycia, and to Halicarnassus, and to Rhodes, and to Phaselis, and to Cos, and to Side, and to Aradus, and Gortyna, and Cnidus, and Cyprus, and Cyrene. **24** But they wrote this copy to Simon the chief priest. **25** But Antiochus the king encamped against Dor the second day, bringing his forces up to it continually, and making engines of war, and he shut up Tryphon from going in or out. **26** And Simon sent him two thousand chosen men to fight on his side; and silver, and gold, and instruments of war in abundance. **27** And he would not receive them but set at nothing all the covenants which he had made with him previously and was estranged from him. **28** And he sent to him Athenobius, one of his friends, to commune with him, saying, "You hold possession of Joppa and Gazara, and the citadel that is in Jerusalem, cities of my kingdom. **29** The borders thereof you have wasted, and done great hurt in the land, and gotten the dominion of many places in my kingdom. **30** Now therefore, deliver up the cities which you have taken, and the tributes of the places of which you have gotten dominion without the borders of Judea: **31** or else give me for them five hundred talents of silver; and for the harm that you have done, and the tributes of the cities, other five hundred talents: or else we will come and subdue you." **32** And Athenobius the king's friend came to Jerusalem; and he saw the glory of Simon, and the cupboard of gold and silver vessels, and his great attendance, and he was amazed; and he reported to him the king's words. **33** And Simon answered, and said to him, "We have neither taken other men's land, nor have we possession of that which pertains to others, but of the inheritance of our fathers; however, it was had in possession of our enemies wrongfully for a certain time. **34** But we, having opportunity, hold fast the inheritance of our fathers. **35** But as touching Joppa and Gazara, which you demand, they did great harm among the people throughout our country, we will give one hundred talents for them." And he did not answer him a word, **36** but returned in a rage to the king, and reported to him these words, and the glory of Simon, and all that he had seen: and the king was exceedingly angry. **37** But Tryphon embarked on board a ship and fled to Orthosia. **38** And the king appointed Cendebaeus chief captain of the seacoast and gave him forces of foot and horse: **39** and he commanded him to encamp before Judea, and he commanded him to build up Kidron, and to fortify the gates, and that he should fight against the people, but the king pursued Tryphon. **40** And Cendebaeus came to Jamnia, and began to provoke the people, and to invade Judea, and to take the people captive, and to kill them. **41** And he built Kidron, and set horsemen there, and forces of foot, to the end that issuing out they might make excursions on the ways of Judea, according as the king commanded him.

CHAPTER 16

1 And John went up from Gazara and told his father Simon what Cendebaeus was doing. **2** And Simon called his two oldest sons, Judas and John, and said to them, I and my countrymen and my father's house have fought the battles of Israel from our youth, even to this day; and things have prospered in our hands, that we should deliver Israel oftentimes. **3** But now I am old, and you moreover, by [His] mercy, are of a sufficient age: be instead of me and my brother and go out and fight for our nation; but let the help which is from Heaven be with you. **4** And he chose out of the country twenty thousand men of war and horsemen, and they went against Cendebaeus, and slept at Modin. **5** And rising up in the morning, they went into the plain, and behold, a great army came to meet them, of footmen and horsemen: and there was a brook between them. **6** And he encamped near them, he and his people: and he saw that the people were afraid to pass over the brook, and he passed over first, and the men saw him, and passed over after him. **7** And he divided the people and [set] the horsemen in the midst of the footmen, but the enemies' horsemen were exceedingly many. **8** And they sounded with the trumpets; and Cendebaeus and his army were put to the rout, and there fell of them many wounded to death, but those who were left fled to the stronghold: **9** at that time was Judas, John's brother, wounded, but John pursued after them, until he came to Kidron, which [Cendebaeus] had built; **10** and they fled to the towers that are in the fields of Azotus; and he burned it with fire; and there fell of them about two thousand men. And he returned into Judea in peace. **11** And Ptolemy the son of Abubus had been appointed captain for the plain of Jericho, and he had much silver and gold; **12** for he was the chief priest's son-in-law. **13** And his heart was lifted up, and he was inclined to make himself master of the country, and he took counsel deceitfully against Simon and his sons, to make away with them. **14** Now Simon was visiting the cities that were in the country, and taking care for the good ordering of them; and he went down to Jericho, himself and Mattathias and Judas his sons, in the one hundred and seventy-seventh year, in the eleventh month, which is the month Sebat: **15** and the son of Abubus received them deceitfully into the little stronghold that is called Dok, which he had built, and made them a great banquet, and hid men there. **16** And when Simon and his sons had drunk freely, Ptolemy and his men rose up, and took their arms, and came in on Simon into the banqueting place, and killed him, and his two sons, and certain of his servants. **17** And he committed a great iniquity, and repaid evil for good. **18** And Ptolemy wrote these things, and sent to the king, that he should send him forces to aid him, and should deliver him, their country, and the cities. **19** And he sent others to Gazara to make away with John: and to the captains of thousands, he sent letters to come to him, that he might give them silver and gold and gifts. **20** And others he sent to take possession of Jerusalem, and the mount of the temple. **21** And one ran before to Gazara and told John that his father and countrymen were perished, and he has sent to kill you also. **22** And when he heard, he was severely amazed; and he laid hands on the men that came to destroy him and killed them; for he perceived that they were seeking to destroy him. **23** And the rest of the acts of John, and of his wars, and of his valiant deeds which he did, and of the building of the walls which he built, and of his doings, **24** behold, they are written in the chronicles of his chief priesthood, from the time that he was made chief priest after his father.

2 MACCABEES

2 Maccabees is a deuterocanonical book which focuses on the Maccabean Revolt against Antiochus IV Epiphanes and concludes with the defeat of the Seleucid empire general Nicanor in 161 BC by Judas Maccabeus, the hero of the work. Unlike 1 Maccabees, 2 Maccabees was written in Koine Greek, probably in Alexandria, Egypt, circa 124 BC. It presents a revised version of the historical events recounted in the first seven chapters of 1 Maccabees, adding material from the Pharisaic tradition, including prayer for the dead and a resurrection on Judgment Day. Jews and Protestants reject most of the doctrinal issues present in the work, while Catholics and Eastern Orthodox consider the work to be deuterocanonical.

CHAPTER 1

1 The countrymen, the Jews that are in Jerusalem and those who are in the country of Judea, send greetings to the countrymen, the Jews that are throughout Egypt, and [wish them] good peace: **2** and may God do good to you, and remember His covenant with Abraham, and Isaac, and Jacob, His faithful servants; **3** and give you all a heart to worship Him and do His pleasure with a great heart and a willing soul; **4** and open your heart in His law and in His statutes, and make peace, **5** and listen to your requests, and be reconciled with you, and not forsake you in an evil time. **6** And now we here are praying for you. **7** In the reign of Demetrius, in the one hundred [and] sixty-ninth year, we the Jews have [already] written to you in the suffering and in the extremity that has come on us in these years, from the time that Jason and his company revolted from the holy land and the kingdom, **8** and set the gate on fire, and shed innocent blood: and we implored the Lord, and were heard; and we offered sacrifice and meal [offering, and] we lighted the lamps, and we set out the Bread of the Presentation. **9** And now [see] that you keep the days of the Celebration of Shelters of the month Kislev. **10** [Written] in the one hundred eighty-eighth year. They that are in Jerusalem and those who are in Judea and the senate and Judas, to Aristobulus, King Ptolemy's teacher, who is also of the stock of the anointed priests, and to the Jews that are in Egypt, send greetings and health. **11** Having been saved by God out of great perils, as men arrayed against a king, we thank Him greatly. **12** For He cast out into Persia those who arrayed themselves [against us] in the holy city. **13** For when the prince had come, [and] the army with him that seemed irresistible, they were cut to pieces in the temple of Nanaea by the treachery of Nanaea's priests. **14** For Antiochus, on the pretense that he would marry her, came into the place, he and his friends that were with him, that they might take a great part of the treasures in name of a dowry. **15** And when the priests of Nanaea's temple had set the treasures out, and he had come there with a small company within the wall of the precincts, they shut to the temple when Antiochus had come in: **16** and opening the secret door of the paneled ceiling, they threw stones and struck down the prince, and they hewed [him and his company] in pieces, and struck off their heads, and cast them to those that were without. **17** Blessed [be] our God in all things, who gave [for a prey] those who had committed impiety. **18** Whereas we are now about to keep the purification of the temple in the [month] Kislev, on the twenty-fifth day, we thought it necessary to certify you thereof, that you also may keep [the] Celebration of Shelters, and [a memorial] of the fire [which was given] when Nehemiah offered sacrifices, after he had built both the temple and the altar. **19** For indeed when our fathers were about to be led into the land of Persia, the godly priests of that time took of the fire of the altar and hid it privily in the hollow of a well that was without water, wherein they made [it] sure, so that the place was unknown to all men. **20** Now after many years, when it pleased God, Nehemiah, having received a charge from the king of Persia, sent in quest of the fire the descendants of the priests that hid it. When they declared to us that they had found no fire, but thick water, **21** he commanded them to draw out thereof and bring [to him]: and when the sacrifices had been offered, Nehemiah commanded the priests to sprinkle with the water both the wood and the things laid immediately. **22** And when it was done, and some time had passed, and the sun shone out, which before was hid with clouds, there was kindled a great blaze, so that all men marveled. **23** And the priests made a prayer while the sacrifice was consuming, both the priests and all [others], Jonathan leading and the rest answering, as Nehemiah did. **24** And the prayer was after this manner: "O Lord, Lord God, the Creator of all things, who are terrible and strong and righteous and merciful, who alone are King and gracious, **25** who alone supplies [every need], who alone are righteous, and almighty, and continuous, You that save Israel out of all evil, who made the fathers [your] chosen, and sanctified them: **26** accept the sacrifice for all Your people Israel, and guard Your own portion, and consecrate it. **27** Gather together our dispersion, set at liberty those who are in bondage among the heathen, look on those who are despised and abhorred, and let the heathen know that You are our God. **28** Torment those who oppress us and in arrogance shamefully entreat us. **29** Plant Your people in Your holy place, even as Moses said." **30** And immediately the priests sang the hymns. **31** And as soon as the sacrifice was consumed, then Nehemiah commanded to pour [on] great stones the water that was left. **32** And when this was done, a flame was kindled; but when the light from the altar shone near it, [all] was consumed. **33** And when the matter became known, and it was told the king of the Persians, that, in the place where the priests that were led away had hid the fire, there appeared the water, with which also Nehemiah and those who were with him purified the sacrifice, **34** then the king, enclosing [the place], made it sacred, after he had proved the matter. **35** And when the king would show favor to any, he would take [from them] many presents and give them some of [this water]. **36** And Nehemiah and those who were with him called this thing Nephthar, which is by interpretation, "Cleansing"; but most men call it Nephthai.

CHAPTER 2

1 It is also found in the records, that Jeremiah the prophet commanded those who were carried away to take of the fire, as has been signified [above]: **2** and how that the prophet charged those who were carried away, having given them the law, that they should not forget the statutes of the Lord, neither be led astray in their minds, when they saw images of gold and silver, and the adornment thereof. **3** And with other such words exhorted he them, that the law should not depart from their heart. **4** And it was [contained] in the writing, that the prophet, being warned of God, commanded that the Dwelling Place and the Ark should follow with him, when he went out into the mountain where Moses went up and saw the heritage of God. **5** And Jeremiah came and found a chamber in the rock, and there he brought in the Dwelling Place, and the Ark, and the altar of incense; and he made fast the door. **6** And some of those that followed with him came there that they might mark the way and could not find it. **7** But when Jeremiah perceived it, he blamed them, saying, "Yes, and the place will be unknown until God gathers the people again together, and mercy comes: **8** and then will the Lord disclose these things, and the glory of the Lord will be seen, and the cloud." As also it was shown with Moses; as also Solomon implored that the place might be consecrated greatly, **9** and it was also declared that he, having wisdom, offered a sacrifice of dedication, and of the finishing of the temple; [so we would have it now.] **10** As Moses prayed to the Lord, and fire came down out of Heaven and consumed the sacrifice, even so prayed Solomon also, and the fire came down and consumed the burnt-offerings **11** (and Moses said, "Because the sin offering had not been eaten, it was consumed in like manner [with the rest]"); **12** and Solomon kept the eight days. **13** And the same things were related both in the public archives and in the records that concern Nehemiah; and how he, founding a library, gathered together the scrolls about the kings and prophets, and the [scrolls] of David, and letters of kings about sacred gifts. **14** And in like manner Judas also gathered together for us all those [writings] that had been scattered by reason of the war that befell, and they are [still] with us. **15** If, therefore, you have need thereof, send some to fetch them to you. **16** Seeing then that we are about to keep the purification, we write to you; you will therefore do well if you keep the days. **17** Now God, who saved all His people, and restored the heritage to all, and the kingdom, and the priesthood, and the hallowing, **18** even as He promised through the law—in God we have hope, that He will quickly have mercy on us, and gather [us] together out of all the earth to the holy place, for He delivered us out of great evils, and purified the place. **19** Now the things concerning Judas Maccabaeus and his countrymen, and the purification of the great temple, and the dedication of the altar, **20** and further the wars against Antiochus Epiphanes, and Eupator his son, **21** and the manifestations that came from Heaven to those that vied with one another in courageous deeds for the religion of the Jews; so that, being but a few, they rescued the whole country, and chased the barbarous multitudes, **22** and recovered again the temple renowned all the world over, and freed the city, and restored the laws which were like to be overthrown, seeing the Lord became gracious to them with all forbearance: **23** [these things, I say,] which have been declared by Jason of Cyrene in five scrolls, we will determine to abridge in one work. **24** For having in view the confused mass of the numbers, and the difficulty which awaits those who would enter into the narratives of the history, by reason of the abundance of the matter, **25** we were careful that they who choose to read may be attracted, and that they who wish well [to our cause] may find it easy to recall [what we have written, and] that all readers may have profit. **26** And although to us, who have taken on us the painful labor of the abridgement, the task is not easy, but [matter] of sweat and watching **27** (even as it is no light thing to him that prepares a banquet, and seeks the benefit of others); yet for the sake of the gratitude of the many we will gladly endure the painful labor, **28** leaving to the historian the exact handling of every particular, and again having no strength to fill in the outlines of our abridgement. **29** For as the master builder of a new house must care for the whole structure, and again he that undertakes to decorate and paint it must seek out the things fit for the adorning thereof; even so I think it is also with us. **30** To occupy the ground, and to indulge in long discussions, and to be curious in particulars, becomes the first author of the history: **31** but to strive after brevity of expression, and to avoid a labored fullness in the treatment, is to be granted to him that would bring a writing into a new form. **32** Here then let us begin the narration, only adding so much to that which has been already said; for it is a foolish thing to make a long prologue to the history, and to abridge the history [itself].

CHAPTER 3

1 When the holy city was inhabited with all peace, and the laws were kept very well, because of the godliness of Onias the chief priest, and his hatred of wickedness, **2** it came to pass that even the kings themselves did honor the place and glorify the temple with the noblest presents; **3** insomuch that even Seleucus the king of Asia of his own revenues bare all the costs belonging to the services of the sacrifices. **4** But one Simon of the tribe of Benjamin, having been made guardian of the temple, fell out with the chief priest about the ruling of the market in the city. **5** And when he could not overcome Onias, he got him to Apollonius [the son] of Thrasaeus, who at that time was governor of Coele-Syria and Phoenicia: **6** and he brought him word how that the treasury in Jerusalem was full of untold sums of money, so that the multitude of the funds was innumerable, and that they did not pertain to the account of the sacrifices, but that it was possible that these should fall under the king's power. **7** And when Apollonius met the king, he informed him of the money of which he had been told; and the king appointed Heliodorus, who was his chancellor, and sent him with a command to accomplish the removal of the previously mentioned money. **8** So out with Heliodorus took his journey, under a color of visiting the cities of Coele-Syria and Phoenicia, but in fact to execute the king's purpose. **9** And when he had come to Jerusalem and had been courteously received by the chief priest of the city, he laid before [the man] account of the information which had been given [him and] declared why he had come; and he inquired if in truth these things were so. **10** And the chief priest explained to him that there were [in the treasury] deposits of widows and orphans, **11** and moreover some [money] belonging to Hyrcanus the [son] of Tobias, a man in very high place, and [that the case] was not as that impious Simon falsely alleged; and that in all there were four hundred talents of silver and two hundred of gold; **12** and that it was altogether impossible that wrong should be done to them that had put trust in the holiness of the place, and in the majesty and inviolable sanctity of the temple, honored over all the world. **13** But Heliodorus, because of the king's commands given him, said that in any case this [money] must be confiscated for the king's treasury. **14** So having appointed a day, he entered in to direct the inquiry concerning these matters; and there was no small distress throughout the whole city. **15** And the priests, prostrating themselves before the altar in their priestly garments, and [looking] toward Heaven, called on him that gave the law concerning deposits, that he should preserve these [treasures] safe for those that had deposited them. **16** And whoever saw the mien of the chief priest was wounded in mind; for his countenance and the change of his color betrayed the distress of his soul. **17** For a terror and a shuddering of the body had come over the man, whereby the pain that was in his heart was plainly shown to those who looked on him. **18** And those who were in the houses rushed flocking out to make a universal supplication, because the place was like to come into contempt. **19** And the women, girded with sackcloth under their breasts, thronged the streets, and the virgins that were kept in ward ran together, some to the gates, others to the walls, and some looked out through the windows. **20** And all, stretching out their hands toward Heaven, made their solemn supplication. **21** Then it would have pitied a man to see the multitude prostrating themselves all mixed together, and the expectation of the chief priest in his severe distress. **22** While therefore they called on the Almighty Lord to keep the things entrusted [to them] safe and sure for those that had entrusted them, **23** Heliodorus went on to execute that which had been decreed. **24** But when he was already present there with his guards near the treasury, the Sovereign of spirits and of all authority caused a great apparition, so that all that had presumed to come [in] with him, stricken with dismay at the power of God, fainted and were severely afraid. **25** For there was seen by them a horse with a terrible rider on him, and adorned with beautiful trappings, and he rushed fiercely and struck at Heliodorus with his forefeet, and it seemed that he that sat on the horse had complete armor of gold. **26** Two others also appeared to him, young men notable in their strength, and beautiful in their glory, and splendid in their apparel, who stood by him on either side, and scourged him unceasingly, inflicting on him many severe stripes. **27** And when he had fallen suddenly to the ground, and great darkness had come over him, [his guards] caught him up and put him into a litter, **28** and carried him, him that had just now entered with a great train and all his guard into the previously mentioned treasury, himself now brought to utter helplessness, manifestly made to recognize the sovereignty of God. **29** And so, while he, through the working of God, speechless and deprived of all hope and deliverance, lay prostrate, **30** they blessed the Lord, that made marvelous his own place; and the temple, which a little before was full of terror and alarm, was filled with joy and gladness after the Almighty Lord appeared. **31** But quickly certain of Heliodorus' familiar friends implored Onias to call on the Most High, and grant life to him who lay quite at the last gasp. **32** And the chief priest, secretly fearing lest the king might come to think that some treachery toward Heliodorus had been perpetrated by the Jews, brought a sacrifice for the deliverance of the man. **33** But as the chief priest was making the atoning sacrifice, the same young men appeared again to Heliodorus, arrayed in the same garments; and they stood up and said, "Give Onias the chief priest great thanks, for his sake the Lord has granted you life; **34** and do you, since you have been scourged from Heaven, publish to all men the sovereign majesty of God." And when they had spoken these words, they vanished out of sight. **35** So Heliodorus, having offered a sacrifice to the Lord and vowed great vows to him that had saved his life, and having graciously received Onias, returned with his army to the king. **36** And he testified to all men the works of the great God which he had seen with his eyes. **37** And when the king asked Heliodorus, what manner of man was fit to be sent yet once again to Jerusalem, he said, **38** "If you have any enemy or conspirator against the state, send him there, and you will receive him back well scourged, if he even escapes with his life; because of a truth there is about the place a power of God. **39** For He that has His dwelling in Heaven Himself has His eyes on that place and helps it; and those who come to hurt it He strikes and destroys." **40** And such was the history of Heliodorus and the keeping of the treasury.

CHAPTER 4

1 But the previously mentioned Simon, he who had given information of the money, and [had betrayed] his country, slandered Onias, [saying] that it was he who had incited Heliodorus, and made himself the author of these evils. **2** And him that was the benefactor of the city, and the guardian of his fellow countrymen, and a zealot for the laws, he dared to call a conspirator against the state. **3** But when the growing enmity [between them] waxed so great, that even murders were perpetrated through one of Simon's trusted followers, **4** Onias, seeing the danger of the contention, and that Apollonius [the son] of Menestheus, the governor of Coele-Syria and Phoenicia, was increasing Simon's malice, **5** went himself to the king, not to be an accuser of his fellow-citizens, but looking to the good of all the people, both public and private; **6** for he saw that without the king's providence it was impossible for the state to obtain peace anymore, and that Simon would not cease from his madness. **7** But when Seleucus was deceased, and Antiochus, who was called Epiphanes, succeeded to the kingdom, Jason the brother of Onias supplanted [his brother] in the chief priesthood, **8** having promised to the king at an audience three hundred and sixty talents of silver, and [out of] another fund eighty talents; **9** and besides this, he undertook to assign one hundred and fifty more, if it might be allowed him through the king's authority to set him up a [Greek] place of exercise and [form] a body of youths [to be trained therein, and] to register the inhabitants of Jerusalem as [citizens] of Antioch. **10** And when the king had given assent, and he had gotten possession of the office, he out with brought over them of his own race to the Greek fashion. **11** And setting aside the royal ordinances of special favor to the Jews, granted by the means of John the father of Eupolemus, who went on the delegation to the Romans for friendship and alliance, and seeking to overthrow the lawful modes of life, he brought in new customs forbidden by the law: **12** for he eagerly established a [Greek] place of exercise under the citadel itself; and caused the noblest of the young men to wear the [Greek] cap. **13** And so there was an extreme of hellenization, and an advance of an alien religion, by reason of the exceeding profaneness of Jason, that ungodly man and no chief priest; **14** so that the priests had no longer any zeal for the services of the altar, but despising the sanctuary, and neglecting the sacrifices, they hastened to enjoy that which was unlawfully provided in the palaestra, after the summons of the discus; **15** making of no account the honors of their fathers, and thinking the glories of the Greeks best of all. **16** By reason of which severe calamity beset them; and the men whose ways of living they earnestly followed, and to whom they desired to be made like in all things, these became their enemies and punished them. **17** For it is not a light thing to do impiously against the laws of God, but these things the time following will declare. **18** Now when certain games that came every fifth year were kept at Tyre, and the king was present, **19** the vile Jason sent sacred envoys, as being Antiochians of Jerusalem, bearing three hundred drachmas of silver to the sacrifice of Hercules, which even the bearers thereof thought not right to use for [any] sacrifice, because it was not fit, but to expend on another charge. **20** And though in the purpose of the sender this [money was for] the sacrifice of Hercules, yet on account of present circumstances it went to the equipment of the galleys. **21** Now when Apollonius the [son] of Menestheus was sent into Egypt for the enthronement of [Ptolemy] Philometor as king, Antiochus, learning that [Ptolemy] had shown himself ill affected toward the state, took thought for the security of his realm; for that reason, going [by sea] to Joppa, he traveled on to Jerusalem. **22** And being magnificently received by Jason and the city, he was brought in with torches and shouting. This done, he afterward led his army down into Phoenicia. **23** Now after a space of three years Jason sent Menelaus, the previously mentioned Simon's brother, to bear the money to the king, and to make reports concerning some necessary matters. **24** But he, being commended to the king, and having glorified himself by the display of his authority, got the chief priesthood for himself, outbidding Jason by three hundred talents of silver. **25** And having received the royal mandates he came [to Jerusalem], bringing nothing worthy the chief priesthood, but having the passion of a cruel tyrant, and the rage of a savage beast. **26** And whereas Jason, who had supplanted his own brother, was supplanted by another and driven as a fugitive into the country of the Ammonites, **27** Menelaus had possession of the office, but of the money that had been promised to the king nothing was duly paid, and that though Sostratus the governor of the citadel demanded it **28** (for to him pertained the gathering of the revenues); for this reason they were both called by the king to his presence. **29** And Menelaus left his own brother Lysimachus for his deputy in the chief priesthood; and Sostratus [left] Crates, who was over the Cyprians. **30** Now while such was the state of things, it came to pass that they of Tarsus and Mallus made insurrection, because they were to be given as a present to Antiochis, the king's concubine. **31** The king therefore came [to Cilicia] in all haste to settle matters, leaving for his deputy Andronicus, a man of high rank. **32** And Menelaus, supposing that he had gotten a favorable opportunity, presented to Andronicus certain vessels of gold belonging to the temple, which he had stolen: other [vessels] also he had already sold into Tyre and the surrounding cities. **33** And when Onias had sure knowledge [of this], he sharply reproved him, having withdrawn himself into a sanctuary at Daphne, that lies by Antioch. **34** For that reason, Menelaus, taking Andronicus apart, begged him to kill Onias. And coming to Onias, and being persuaded to use treachery, and being received as a friend, Andronicus gave him his right hand with oaths [of fidelity, and], though he was suspected, persuaded him to come out of the sanctuary; and out with he dispatched him without regard of justice. **35** For this reason, not only Jews, but many also of the other nations, had indignation and displeasure at the unjust murder of the man. **36** And when the king had come back again from the places in Cilicia, the Jews that were in the city pleaded before him [against Andronicus] (the Greeks also joining with them in hatred of the wickedness), urging that Onias had been wrongfully slain. **37** Antiochus therefore was heartily sorry, and was moved to pity, and wept, because of the sober and well-ordered life of him that was dead; **38** and being inflamed with passion, out with he stripped off Andronicus' purple robe, and tore off his under garments, and when he had led him round through the whole city to that very place where he had committed impiety against Onias, there he put the murderer out of the way, the Lord rendering to him the punishment he had deserved. **39** Now when many sacrileges had been committed in the city by Lysimachus with the consent of Menelaus, and when the report of them was spread abroad outside, the people gathered themselves together against Lysimachus, after many vessels of gold had been already dispersed. **40** And when the multitudes were rising against [him, and] were filled with anger, Lysimachus armed about three thousand men, and with unrighteous violence began [the conflict], one Hauran, a man far gone in years and no less also in madness, leading [the attack]. **41** But when they perceived the assault of Lysimachus, some caught up stones, others logs of wood, and some took handfuls of the ashes that lay near, and they flung them all pell-mell on Lysimachus and those who were with him; ⁴² by reason of which they wounded many of them, and some they struck to the ground, and all [of them] they forced to flee, but the author of the sacrilege himself they killed beside the treasury. ⁴³ But touching these matters there was an accusation laid against Menelaus. ⁴⁴ And when the king had come to Tyre, the three men that were sent by the senate pleaded the cause before him. ⁴⁵ But Menelaus, seeing himself now defeated, promised much money to Ptolemy the [son] of Dorymenes, that he might win over the king. ⁴⁶ After which Ptolemy taking the king aside into a cloister, as it were to take the air, brought him to be of another mind: ⁴⁷ and him that was the cause of all the evil, Menelaus, he discharged from the accusations; but these hapless men, who, if they had pleaded even before Scythians, would have been discharged uncondemned, them he sentenced to death. ⁴⁸ Soon then did those who were spokesmen for the city and the families [of Israel] and the holy vessels suffer that unrighteous penalty. ⁴⁹ For this reason even certain Tyrians, moved with hatred of the wickedness, provided magnificently for their burial. ⁵⁰ But Menelaus through the covetous dealings of those who were in power remained still in his office, growing in wickedness, as a great conspirator against his fellow-citizens.

CHAPTER 5

¹ Now about this time Antiochus made his second inroad into Egypt. ² And it [so] befell that throughout all the city, for the space of almost forty days, there appeared in the midst of the sky horsemen in swift motion, wearing robes inworked with gold and [carrying] spears, equipped in troops for battle; ³ and drawing of swords; and [on the other side] squadrons of horse in array; and encounters and pursuits of both [armies]; and shaking of shields, and multitudes of lances, and casting of darts, and flashing of golden trappings, and girding on of all sorts of armor. ⁴ For that reason, all men implored that the vision might have been given for good. ⁵ But when a false rumor had arisen that Antiochus was deceased, Jason took not less than one thousand men, and suddenly made an assault on the city; and those who were on the wall being routed, and the city being now at length well near taken, Menelaus took refuge in the citadel. ⁶ But Jason slaughtered his own citizens without mercy, not considering that good success against countrymen is the greatest ill success, but supposing himself to be setting up trophies over enemies, and not over fellow countrymen. ⁷ The office [however] he did not get, but, receiving shame as the end of his conspiracy, he passed again a fugitive into the country of the Ammonites. ⁸ At the last therefore he met with a miserable end: having been shut up at the court of Aretas the prince of the Arabians, fleeing from city to city, pursued of all men, hated as an apostate from the laws, and held in abomination as the butcher of his country and his fellow-citizens, he was cast out into Egypt; ⁹ and he that had driven many from their own country into strange lands perished [himself] in a strange land, having crossed the sea to the Lacedaemonians, as thinking to find shelter [there] because they were related; ¹⁰ and he that had cast out a multitude unburied had none to mourn for him, nor had he any funeral at all, or place in the tomb of his fathers. ¹¹ Now when tidings came to the king concerning that which was done, he thought that Judea was in revolt; after which setting out from Egypt in a furious mind, he took the city by force of arms, ¹² and commanded his soldiers to cut down without mercy such as came in their way, and to kill such as went up on the houses; ¹³ and there was killing of young and old, making away of boys, women, and children, slaying of virgins and infants. ¹⁴ And in all the three days [of the slaughter] there were destroyed eighty thousand, [where of] forty thousand [were slain] in close combat, and no fewer were sold than slain. ¹⁵ But not content with this, he presumed to enter into the most holy temple of all the earth, having Menelaus for his guide (him that had proved himself a traitor both to the laws and to his country), ¹⁶ even taking the sacred vessels with his polluted hands, and dragging down with his profane hands the offerings that had been dedicated by other kings to the augmentation and glory and honor of the place. ¹⁷ And Antiochus was lifted up in mind, not seeing that because of the sins of those who lived in the city the Sovereign Lord had been provoked to anger a little, and therefore His eye was [then] turned away from the place. ¹⁸ But had it not so been that they were already bound

by many sins, this man, even as Heliodorus who was sent by Seleucus the king to view the treasury, would, so soon as he pressed forward, have been scourged and turned back from his daring deed. ¹⁹ However, the Lord did not choose the nation for the place's sake, but the place for the nation's sake. ²⁰ For that reason, also the place itself, having shared in the calamities that befell the nation, did afterward share in [its] benefits; and the [place] which was forsaken in the wrath of the Almighty was, at the reconciliation of the great Sovereign, restored again with all glory. ²¹ As for Antiochus, when he had carried away out of the temple one thousand and eight hundred talents, he departed in all haste to Antioch, thinking in his arrogance to make the land navigable and the sea passable by foot, because his heart was lifted up. ²² And moreover he left governors to afflict the race: at Jerusalem, Philip, by race a Phrygian, and in character more barbarous than him that set him there; ²³ and at Gerizim, Andronicus; and besides these, Menelaus, who worse than all the rest exalted himself against his fellow-citizens. And having a malicious mind toward the Jews—his citizens, ²⁴ he sent that lord of pollutions Apollonius with an army of twenty-two thousand, commanding him to kill all those that were of full age, and to sell the women and the younger men. ²⁵ And he, coming to Jerusalem, and playing the man of peace, waited until the holy day of the Sabbath, and finding the Jews at rest from work, he commanded his men to parade in arms. ²⁶ And he put to the sword all those who came out to the spectacle; and running into the city with the armed men he killed great multitudes. ²⁷ But Judas, who is also Maccabaeus, with nine others or thereabout, withdrew himself, and with his company kept himself alive in the mountains after the manner of wild beasts; and they continued feeding on such poor herbs as grew there, that they might not be partakers of the pollution.

CHAPTER 6

¹ And not long after this the king sent out an old man of Athens to compel the Jews to depart from the laws of their fathers, and not to live after the laws of God; ² and also to pollute the sanctuary in Jerusalem, and to call it by the name of Jupiter Olympius, and [to call] the [sanctuary] in Gerizim by the name of Jupiter the Protector of strangers, even as they were that lived in the place. ³ But severe and utterly grievous was the visitation of this evil. ⁴ For the temple was filled with riot and reveling by the heathen, who dallied with prostitutes, and had to do with women within the sacred precincts, and moreover brought inside things that were not befitting; ⁵ and the place of sacrifice was filled with those abominable things which had been prohibited by the laws. ⁶ And a man could neither keep the Sabbath, nor observe the feasts of the fathers, nor so much as confess himself to be a Jew. ⁷ And on the day of the king's birth every month they were led along with bitter constraint to eat of the sacrifices; and when the Festival of Bacchus came, they were compelled to go in procession in honor of Bacchus, wearing wreaths of ivy. ⁸ A decree went out to the neighboring Greek cities, by the suggestion of Ptolemy, that they should observe the same conduct against the Jews and should make them eat of the sacrifices; ⁹ and that they should kill such as did not choose to go over to the Greek rites. So the present misery was for all to see: ¹⁰ for two women were brought up for having circumcised their children; and these, when they had led them publicly around the city, with the babies hung from their breasts, they cast down headlong from the wall. ¹¹ And others, that had run together into the caves nearby to keep the seventh day secretly, being betrayed to Philip, were all burned together, because they hesitated to defend themselves, from regard to the honor of that most solemn day. ¹² I implore, therefore, those that read this scroll, that they not be discouraged because of the calamities, but account that these punishments were not for the destruction, but for the disciplining of our race. ¹³ For indeed that those who act impiously are not left alone any long time, but immediately meet with retribution, is a sign of great beneficence. ¹⁴ For in the case of the other nations the Sovereign Lord does with patience forbear, until that He punishes them when they have attained to the full measure of [their] sins; but not so judged He as touching us, ¹⁵ that He may not take vengeance on us afterward, when we come to the height of our sins. ¹⁶ For that reason, He never withdraws His mercy from us; but though He chastens with calamity, yet He does not forsake His own people. ¹⁷ However, let this that we have spoken suffice to put

[you] in remembrance; but after [these] few words we must come to the narrative. **18** Eleazar, one of the principal scribes, a man already well stricken in years, and of a noble countenance, was compelled to open his mouth to eat swine's flesh. **19** But he, welcoming death with renown rather than life with pollution, advanced of his own accord to the instrument of torture, but first spat out [the flesh], **20** [coming forward] as men should come that are resolute to repel such things as not [even] for the natural love of life is it lawful to taste. **21** But those who had the charge of that forbidden sacrificial feast took the man aside, for the acquaintance which of old times they had with him, and privately implored him to bring flesh of his own providing, such as was befitting for him to use, and to make as if he did eat of the flesh from the sacrifice, as had been commanded by the king; **22** that by so doing he might be delivered from death, and for his ancient friendship with them might be treated kindly. **23** But he, having formed a high resolve, and one that became his years, and the dignity of old age, and the gray hairs which he had reached with honor, and his excellent education from a child, or rather [that became] the holy laws of God's ordaining, declared his mind accordingly, bidding them quickly send him to Hades. **24** "For it does not become our years to deceive," [he said,] "that [through this] many of the young should suppose that Eleazar, the man of eighty years and ten, had gone over to an alien religion; **25** and [so] they, by reason of my deception, and for the sake of this brief and momentary life, should be led astray because of me, and [so] I get to myself a pollution and a stain of my old age. **26** For even if for the present time I will remove from myself the punishment of men, yet I will not escape the hands of the Almighty, either living or dead. **27** For that reason, by courageously parting with my life now, I will show myself worthy of my old age, **28** and leave behind a noble example to the young to die willingly and nobly a glorious death for the reverend and holy laws." And when he had said these words, he went immediately to the instrument of torture. **29** And when they changed the good will they bore toward him a little before into ill will, because these words of his were, as they thought, sheer madness, **30** and when he was at the point to die with the stripes, he groaned aloud and said, "To the Lord, who has the holy knowledge, it is manifest that, whereas I might have been delivered from death, I endure severe pains in my body by being scourged; but in soul I gladly suffer these things for my fear of Him." **31** So this man also died after this manner, leaving his death for an example of nobleness and a memorial of virtue, not only to the young but also to the great body of his nation.

CHAPTER 7

1 And it came to pass that seven brothers also with their mother were at the king's command taken and shamefully handled with scourges and cords, to compel them to taste of the abominable swine's flesh. **2** But one of them made himself the spokesman and said, "What would you ask and learn of us? For we are ready to die rather than transgress the laws of our fathers." **3** And the king fell into a rage and commanded to heat pans and cauldrons: **4** and when these were heated, he commanded to cut out the tongue of him that had been their spokesman, and to scalp him, and to cut off his extremities, the rest of his brothers and his mother looking on. **5** And when he was utterly maimed, [the king] commanded to bring him to the fire, being yet alive, and to fry him in the pan. And as the vapor of the pan spread far, they and their mother also exhorted one another to die nobly, saying, **6** "The Lord God sees, and in truth is entreated for us, as Moses declared in his song, which witnesses against [the people] to their faces, saying, And He will be treated for His servants." **7** And when the first had died after this manner, they brought the second to the mocking; and they pulled off the skin of his head with the hair and asked him, "Will you eat, before your body is punished in every limb?" **8** But he answered in the language of his fathers and said to them, "No." Therefore he also underwent the next torture in succession, as the first had done. **9** And when he was at the last gasp, he said, "You—miscreant—release us out of this present life, but the King of the world will raise us up, who have died for His laws, to a continuous renewal of life." **10** And after him the third was made a laughingstock. And when he was required, he quickly put out his tongue, and stretched out his hands courageously, **11** and nobly said, "From Heaven I possess these; and for His laws' sake I treat these with contempt; and from Him I hope to

receive these back again": **12** insomuch that the king himself and those who were with him were astonished at the young man's soul, for he regarded the pain as nothing. **13** And when he too was dead, they shamefully handled and tortured the fourth in like manner. **14** And having come near to death he said, "It is good to die at the hands of men and look for the hopes which are [given] by God, that we will be raised up again by Him; for as for you, you will have no resurrection to life." **15** And next after him they brought the fifth, and shamefully handled him. **16** But he looked toward the king and said, "Because you have authority among men, though you are [yourself] corruptible, you do what you will; yet do not think that our race has been forsaken of God; **17** but hold on your way, and behold His sovereign majesty, how it will torture you and your seed." **18** And after him they brought the sixth. And when he was at the point to die he said, "Do not be vainly deceived, for we suffer these things for our own doings, as sinning against our own God: marvelous things have come to pass; **19** but do not think that you will be unpunished, having determined to fight against God." **20** But above all was the mother marvelous and worthy of honorable memory; for when she looked on seven sons perishing within the space of one day, she bare [the sight] with good courage for the hopes [that she had set] on the Lord. **21** And she exhorted each one of them in the language of their fathers, filled with a noble temper and stirring up her womanish thought with manly passion, saying to them, **22** "I do not know how you came into my womb, neither was it I that bestowed on you your spirit and your life, and it was not I that brought into order the first elements of each one of you. **23** Therefore the Creator of the world, who fashioned the generation of man and devised the generation of all things, in mercy gives back to you again both your spirit and your life, as you now treat yourselves with contempt for His laws' sake." **24** But Antiochus, thinking himself to be despised, and suspecting the reproachful voice, while the youngest was yet alive did not only make his appeal [to him] by words, but also at the same time promised with oaths that he would enrich him and raise him to high estate, if he would turn from the [customs] of his fathers, and that he would take him for his friend and entrust him with affairs. **25** But when the young man would in no way give heed, the king called to him his mother, and exhorted her that she would counsel the youth to save himself. **26** And when he had exhorted her with many words, she undertook to persuade her son. **27** But bending toward him, laughing the cruel tyrant to scorn, she spoke this in the language of her fathers: "My son, have pity on me that carried you nine months in my womb, and gave you suck three years, and nourished and brought you up to this age, and sustained you. **28** I implore you, my child, to lift your eyes to the Heaven and the earth, and to see all things that are in it, and so to recognize that God made them not of things that were, and [that] the race of men in this way comes into being. **29** Do not be afraid of this butcher, but, proving yourself worthy of your brothers, accept your death, that in the mercy [of God] I may receive you again with your brothers." **30** But before she had yet ended speaking, the young man said, "Whom do you wait for? I do not obey the command of the king, but I listen to the command of the law that was given to our fathers through Moses. **31** But you, that have devised all manner of evil against the Hebrews, will in no way escape the hands of God. **32** For we are suffering because of our own sins; **33** and if for rebuke and disciplining our living Lord has been angered a little while, yet He will again be reconciled with His own servants. **34** But you, O unholy man and of all most vile, do not be vainly lifted up in your wild pride with uncertain hopes, raising your hand against the heavenly children; **35** for not yet have you escaped the judgment of the Almighty God that sees [all things]. **36** For these our brothers, having endured a short pain that brings continuous life, have now died under God's covenant; but you, through the judgment of God, will receive in just measure the penalties of your arrogance. **37** But I, as my brothers, give up both body and soul for the laws of our fathers, calling on God that He may speedily become gracious to the nation; and that you amidst trials and plagues may confess that He alone is God; **38** and that in me and my brothers you may stay the wrath of the Almighty, which has been justly brought on our whole race." **39** But the king, falling into a rage, handled him worse than all the rest, being exasperated at his mocking. **40** So he also died pure [from pollution], putting his whole trust in the Lord. **41** And last of all, after her sons, the mother died. **42** Let it then suffice to have said so much concerning the sacrificial feasts and the [king's] exceeding barbarities.

CHAPTER 8

[1] But Judas, who is also [called] Maccabaeus, and those who were with him, making their way privily into the villages, called to them their countrymen; and taking to them such as had continued in the Jews' religion, gathered together as many as six thousand. [2] And they called on the Lord, [imploring Him] to look on the people that was oppressed by all; and to also have compassion on the sanctuary that had been profaned by the ungodly men; [3] and to have pity on the city also that was suffering ruin and ready to be made level with the ground; and to listen to the blood that cried to Him; [4] and to remember also the lawless slaughter of the innocent infants, and the blasphemies that had been committed against His Name; and to show His hatred of wickedness. [5] And when Maccabaeus had trained his men for service, the heathen at once found him irresistible, for that the wrath of the Lord was turned into pity. [6] And coming unawares he set fire to cities and villages. And in winning back the most important positions, putting to flight no small number of the enemies, [7] he especially took advantage of the nights for such assaults. And his courage was loudly talked of everywhere. [8] But when Philip saw the man gaining ground little by little, and increasing more and more in his prosperity, he wrote to Ptolemy, the governor of Coele-Syria and Phoenicia, that he should support the king's cause. [9] And [Ptolemy] quickly appointed Nicanor the [son] of Patroclus, one of the king's chief friends, and sent him, in command of no fewer than twenty thousand of all nations, to destroy the whole race of Judea; and with him he joined Gorgias also, a captain and one that had experience in matters of war. [10] And Nicanor undertook by [the sale of the] captive Jews to make up for the king the tribute of two thousand talents which he was to pay to the Romans. [11] And immediately he sent to the cities on the seacoast, inviting them to buy Jewish slaves, promising to allow ninety slaves for a talent, not expecting the judgment that was to follow on him from the Almighty. [12] But tidings came to Judas concerning the inroad of Nicanor, and when he communicated to those who were with him the presence of the army, [13] those who were cowardly and distrustful of the judgment of God ran away and left the country. [14] And others sold all that was left over to them, and in addition implored the Lord to deliver those who had been sold [as slaves] by the impious Nicanor before he ever met them; [15] and, if not for their own sakes, yet for the covenants made with their fathers, and because he had called them by his reverend and glorious name. [16] And Maccabaeus gathered his men together, six thousand in number, and exhorted them not to be stricken with dismay at the enemy, nor to fear the great multitude of the heathen who came wrongfully against them; but to contend nobly, [17] setting before their eyes the outrage that had been lawlessly perpetrated on the holy place, and the shameful handling of the city that had been turned to mockery, and further the overthrow of the mode of life received from their ancestors. [18] "For they," he said, "trust to arms, and in addition to deeds of daring; but we trust on the Almighty God, since He is able at a beckoning to cast down those who are coming against us, and even the whole world." [19] And moreover He recounted to them the help given from time to time in the days of their ancestors, both the [help given] in the days of Sennacherib, how that one hundred and eighty-five thousand perished, [20] and the [help given] in the land of Babylon, even the battle that was fought against the Gauls, how that they came to the engagement eight thousand in all, with four thousand Macedonians, and [how that,] the Macedonians being hard-pressed, the six thousand destroyed the one hundred and twenty thousand, because of the help which they had from Heaven, and took great plunder. [21] And when he had with these words made them of good courage, and ready to die for the laws and their country, he divided his army into four parts; [22] appointing his relatives to be leaders with himself of the several bands—Simon, and Joseph, and Jonathan—giving each the command of fifteen hundred men, [23] and moreover Eleazer also: [then,] having read aloud the sacred scroll, and having given as a watchword, The Help of God, leading the first band himself, he joined battle with Nicanor. [24] And, since the Almighty fought on their side, they killed of the enemy above nine thousand, and wounded and disabled the greater part of Nicanor's army and compelled all to flee: [25] and they took the money of those that had come there to buy them. And after they had pursued them for some distance, they returned, being constrained by the time of the day; [26] for it was the day before the Sabbath, and for this reason they made no effort to chase them far. [27] And when they had gathered the arms of the enemy together, and had stripped off their spoils, they occupied themselves about the Sabbath, blessing and thanking the Lord exceedingly, who had saved them to this day, for that He had caused a beginning of mercy to distill on them. [28] And after the Sabbath, when they had given of the spoils to the maimed, and to the widows and orphans, the residue they distributed among themselves and their children. [29] And when they had accomplished these things, and had made a common supplication, they implored the merciful Lord to be wholly reconciled with His servants. [30] And having had an encounter with the forces of Timotheus and Bacchides, they killed above twenty thousand of them, and made themselves masters of strongholds exceedingly high, and divided very much plunder, giving the maimed and orphans and widows, and moreover the aged also, an equal share with themselves. [31] And when they had gathered the arms of the enemy together, they stored them all up carefully in the most important positions, and the residue of the spoils they carried to Jerusalem. [32] And they killed the phylarch of Timotheus' forces, a most unholy man, and one who had done the Jews much hurt. [33] And as they celebrated [the] victory in the city of their fathers, they burned those that had set the sacred gates on fire, and [among them] Callisthenes, who had fled into an outhouse; and [so] they received the suitable reward of their impiety. [34] And the three times-accursed Nicanor, who had brought the thousand merchants to buy the Jews [for slaves], [35] being through the help of the Lord humbled by them who in his eyes were held to be of least account, put off his glorious apparel, and [passing] through the midland, shunning all company like a fugitive slave, arrived at Antioch, having, [as he thought,] had the greatest possible good fortune, though his army was destroyed. [36] And he that had taken on himself to make tribute sure for the Romans by the captivity of the men of Jerusalem published abroad that the Jews had One who fought for them, and that because this was so the Jews were invulnerable, because they followed the laws ordained by Him.

CHAPTER 9

[1] Now about that time it befell that Antiochus had returned in disorder from the region of Persia. [2] For he had entered into the city called Persepolis, and he determined to rob a temple and to hold down the city. After which there was an onset of the multitudes, and [Antiochus and his men] turned to make defense with arms; and it came to pass that Antiochus was put to flight by the people of the country and broke up his camp with disgrace. [3] And while he was at Ecbatana, news was brought him what had happened to Nicanor and the forces of Timotheus. [4] And being lifted up by his passion he thought to make the Jews suffer even for the evildoing of those that had put him to rout. For that reason, the judgment from Heaven even now accompanying him, he gave order to his charioteer to drive without ceasing and dispatch the journey; for so he arrogantly spoke: I will make Jerusalem a common graveyard of Jews, when I come there. [5] But the All-seeing Lord, the God of Israel, struck him with a fatal and invisible stroke; and as soon as he had ceased speaking this word, an incurable pain of the bowels seized him, and bitter torments of the inner parts; [6] and that most justly, for he had tormented other men's bowels with many and strange sufferings. [7] But he in no way ceased from his rude insolence; no, still more was he filled with arrogance, breathing fire in his passion against the Jews, and commanding to hasten the journey. But it came to pass moreover that he fell from his chariot as it rushed along, and having a grievous fall was racked in all the members of his body. [8] And he that but now supposed himself to have the waves of the sea at his bidding, so vainglorious was he beyond the condition of a man, and that thought to weigh the heights of the mountains in a balance, was now brought to the ground and carried in a litter, showing to all that the power was manifestly God's; [9] so that out of the body of the impious man worms swarmed, and while he was still living in anguish and pains, his flesh fell off, and by reason of the stench all the army turned with loathing from his corruption. [10] And the man that a little before supposed himself to touch the stars of the heavens, no one could endure to carry for his intolerable stench. [11] Therefore he began in great part to cease from his arrogance, being broken [in spirit, and] to come to knowledge

under the scourge of God, his pains increasing every moment. **12** And when he himself could not stand his own smell, he said these words: "It is right to be subject to God, and that one who is mortal should not be inclined arrogantly." **13** And the vile man vowed to the Sovereign Lord, who now no longer would have pity on him, saying concerning this **14** that the holy city, to which he was going in haste, to lay it even with the ground and to make it a common graveyard, he would declare free; **15** and as touching the Jews, whom he had decided not even to count worthy of burial, but to cast them out to the beasts with their infants, for the birds to devour, he would make them all equal to citizens of Athens; **16** and the holy sanctuary, which before he had plundered, he would adorn with excellent offerings, and would restore all the sacred vessels many times multiplied, and out of his own revenues would defray the charges that were required for the sacrifices; **17** and, besides all this, that he would become a Jew, and would visit every inhabited place, publishing abroad the might of God. **18** But when his sufferings did in no way cease, for the judgment of God had come on him in righteousness, having given up all hope of himself, he wrote to the Jews the letter written below, having the nature of a supplication, to this effect: **19** "To the worthy Jews, his fellow-citizens, Antiochus, king and general, wishes much joy and health and prosperity. **20** May you and your children fare well; and your affairs will be to your mind. Having my hope in Heaven, **21** I remembered with affection your honor and good will [toward me]. Returning out of the region of Persia, and being taken with a ghastly sickness, I deemed it necessary to take thought for the common safety of all, **22** not despairing of myself, but having great hope to escape from the sickness. **23** But considering that my father also, at what time he led an army into the upper country, appointed his successor, **24** to the end that, if anything fell out contrary to expectation, or if any unwelcome tidings were brought, they [that remained] in the country, knowing to whom the state had been left, might not be troubled; **25** and, besides all this, observing how that the princes that are borderers and neighbors to my kingdom watch opportunities, and look for the future event, I have appointed my son Antiochus [to be] king, whom I often committed and commended to most of you, when I was hastening to the upper provinces; and I have written to him what is written below. **26** I exhort you therefore and implore you, having in your remembrance the benefits done to you in common and separately, to preserve each of you your present good will toward me and my son. **27** For I am persuaded that he, in gentleness and kindness, will follow my purpose and treat you with indulgence." **28** So the murderer and blasphemer, having endured the most intense sufferings, even as he had dealt with other men, ended his life among the mountains by a most piteous fate in a strange land. **29** And Philip his foster brother carried the body [home]; and then, fearing the son of Antiochus, he went himself to Ptolemy Philometor in Egypt.

CHAPTER 10

1 And Maccabaeus and those who were with him, the Lord leading them on, recovered the temple and the city; **2** and they pulled down the altars that had been built in the marketplace by the aliens, and also sacred enclosures. **3** And having cleansed the sanctuary they made another altar of sacrifice; and striking stones and taking fire out of them, they offered sacrifices, after two years, and [burned] incense, and [lighted] lamps, and set out the Bread of the Presentation. **4** And when they had done these things, they fell prostrate and implored the Lord that they might no longer fall into such evils; but that, if ever they should sin, they might be disciplined by Him with forbearance, and not be delivered to blaspheming and barbarous heathen. **5** Now on the same day that the sanctuary was profaned by aliens, on that very day it came to pass that the cleansing of the sanctuary was made, even on the twenty-fifth day of the same month, which is Kislev. **6** And they kept eight days with gladness in the manner [of the Celebration] of Shelters, remembering how that not long before, during the Celebration of Shelters, they were wandering in the mountains and in the caves after the manner of wild beasts. **7** For that reason, bearing wands wreathed with leaves, and fair boughs, and palms also, they offered up hymns of thanksgiving to him that had prosperously brought to pass the cleansing of his own place. **8** They ordained also with a common statute and decree, for all the nation of the Jews, that they should keep these days every year. **9** And such was the end of Antiochus, who was

called Epiphanes. **10** But now we will declare what came to pass under Antiochus [named] Eupator, who proved himself a [true] son of that ungodly man and will gather up briefly the successive evils of the wars. **11** For this man, when he succeeded to the kingdom, appointed one Lysias—chancellor, and supreme governor of Coele-Syria and Phoenicia. **12** For Ptolemy that was called Macron, setting an example of observing justice toward the Jews because of the wrong that had been done to them, endeavored to conduct his dealings with them on peaceful terms. **13** After which being accused by the king before Eupator, and hearing himself called traitor at every turn, because he had abandoned Cyprus which Philometor had entrusted to him, and had withdrawn himself to Antiochus [called] Epiphanes, and failing to uphold the honor of his office, he took poison and made away with himself. **14** But Gorgias, when he was made governor of the district, maintained a force of mercenaries, and at every turn kept up war with the Jews. **15** And together with him the Idumaeans also, being masters of important strongholds, harassed the Jews; and receiving to them those that had taken refuge [there] from Jerusalem, they determined to keep up war. **16** But Maccabaeus and his men, having made solemn supplication and having implored God to fight on their side, rushed on the strongholds of the Idumaeans; **17** and assaulting them vigorously they made themselves masters of the positions, and kept off all that fought on the wall, and killed those that fell in their way, and killed no fewer than twenty thousand. **18** And because no less than nine thousand were fled into two towers exceedingly strong and having all things [needed] for a siege, **19** Maccabaeus, having left Simon and Joseph, and Zacchaeus besides and those who were with him, a force sufficient to besiege them, departed himself to places where he was most needed. **20** But Simon and those who were with him, yielding to covetousness, were bribed by certain of those that were in the towers, and receiving seventy thousand drachmas let some of them slip away. **21** But when word was brought to Maccabaeus of what was done, he gathered the leaders of the people together, and accused [those men] of having sold their countrymen for money, by setting their enemies free [to fight] against them. **22** So he killed these men for having turned traitors, and out with took possession of the two towers. **23** And prospering with his arms in all things he took in hand, he destroyed in the two strongholds more than twenty thousand. **24** Now Timotheus, who had been before defeated by the Jews, having gathered together foreign forces in great multitudes, and having collected the horsemen which belonged to Asia, not a few, came as though he would take Judea by force of arms. **25** But as he drew near, Maccabaeus and his men sprinkled earth on their heads and girded their loins with sackcloth, in supplication to God, **26** and falling down on the step in front of the altar, implored Him to become gracious to them, and be an enemy to their enemies and an adversary to their adversaries, as the law declares. **27** And rising from their prayer they took up their arms and advanced some distance from the city; and when they had come near to their enemies they halted. **28** And when the dawn was now spreading, the two [armies] joined battle; the one part having this, besides [their] virtue, for a pledge of success and victory, that they had fled to the Lord for refuge, the others making their passion their leader in the strife. **29** But when the battle waxed strong, there appeared out of Heaven to their adversaries five men on horses with bridles of gold, [in] splendid [array]; and two of them, leading on the Jews, **30** and taking Maccabaeus in the midst of them, and covering him with their own armor, guarded him from wounds, while on the adversaries they shot out arrows and thunderbolts; by reason of which they were blinded and thrown into confusion, and were cut to pieces, filled with bewilderment. **31** And there were slain twenty thousand and five hundred, beside six hundred horsemen. **32** But Timotheus himself fled into a stronghold called Gazara, a fortress of exceeding strength, Chaereas being in command there. **33** But Maccabaeus and his men were glad and laid siege to the fortress twenty-four days. **34** And those who were within, trusting to the strength of the place, blasphemed exceedingly, and hurled out impious words. **35** But at dawn of the twenty-fifth day certain young men of the company of Maccabaeus, inflamed with passion because of the blasphemies, assaulted the wall with masculine force and with furious passion, and cut down whoever came in their way. **36** And others climbing up in like manner, while [the besieged] were distracted with them [that had made their way] within, set fire to the towers, and kindling fires burned the blasphemers alive; while others broke open the gates, and, having given entrance to the rest of the band, occupied the city. ³⁷ And they killed Timotheus, who was hidden in a cistern, and his brother Chaereas, and Apollophanes. ³⁸ And when they had accomplished these things, they blessed the Lord with hymns and thanksgiving, Him who does great benefits to Israel, and gives them the victory.

CHAPTER 11

¹ Now after a very short time, Lysias, the king's guardian and countryman and chancellor, being severely displeased for the things that had come to pass, ² collected about eighty thousand [footmen] and all his horsemen and came against the Jews, thinking to make the city a place for Greeks to dwell in, ³ and to levy tribute on the temple, as of the other sacred places of the nations, and to put up the chief priesthood to sale every year; ⁴ holding in no account the might of God, but puffed up with his tens of thousands of footmen, and his thousands of horsemen, and his eighty elephants. ⁵ And coming into Judea and drawing near to Bethsuron, which was a strong place and distant from Jerusalem about five leagues, he pressed it hard. ⁶ But when Maccabaeus and his men learned that he was besieging the strongholds, they and all the people with lamentations and tears made supplication to the Lord to send a good messenger to save Israel. ⁷ And Maccabaeus himself took up arms first and exhorted the others to put themselves in danger together with him and help their countrymen; and they went out with him very willingly. ⁸ And as they were there, close to Jerusalem, there appeared at their head one on horseback in white apparel, brandishing weapons of gold. ⁹ And they all together praised the merciful God and were yet more strengthened in heart: being ready to assail not men only but the wildest beasts, and walls of iron, ¹⁰ they advanced in array, having Him that is in Heaven to fight on their side, for the Lord had mercy on them. ¹¹ And hurling [themselves] like lions on the enemy, they killed of them eleven thousand [footmen] and sixteen hundred horsemen and forced all [the rest] to flee. ¹² But the greater part of them escaped wounded [and] naked; and Lysias also himself escaped by shameful flight. ¹³ But as he was a man not void of understanding, weighing with himself the defeat which had befallen him, and considering that the Hebrews could not be overcome, because the Almighty God fought on their side, he sent again [to them], ¹⁴ and persuaded them to come to terms on condition that all their rights were acknowledged, and [promised] that he would also persuade the king to become their friend. ¹⁵ And Maccabaeus gave consent on all the conditions which Lysias proposed to him, being careful of the [common] good; for whatever [requests] Maccabaeus delivered in writing to Lysias concerning the Jews the king allowed. ¹⁶ For the letters written to the Jews from Lysias were to this effect: "Lysias to the people of the Jews, greetings. ¹⁷ John and Absalom, who were sent from you, having delivered the petition written below, made request concerning the things signified therein. ¹⁸ Whatever things therefore had need to be brought before the king I declared [to him, and] what things were possible he allowed. ¹⁹ If then you will preserve your good will toward the state, henceforward I will also endeavor to contribute to [your] good. ²⁰ And on this behalf, I have given order in detail, both to these men and to those [that are sent] from me, to confer with you. ²¹ Farewell. [Written] in the one hundred [and] forty-eighth year, on the twenty-fourth day of the [month] Dioscorinthius." ²² And the king's letter was in these words: "King Antiochus to his brother Lysias, greetings. ²³ Seeing that our father passed to the gods having the wish that the subjects of his kingdom should be undisturbed and give themselves to the care of their own affairs, ²⁴ we, having heard that the Jews do not consent to our father's purpose to turn them to the [customs] of the Greeks, but choose rather their own manner of living, and make request that the [customs] of their law be allowed to them— ²⁵ choosing therefore that this nation also should be free from disturbance, we determine that their temple be restored to them, and that they live according to the customs that were in the days of their ancestors. ²⁶ You will therefore do well to send [messengers] to them and give them the right hand [of friendship], that they, knowing our mind, may be of good heart, and gladly occupy themselves with the conduct of their own affairs." ²⁷ And to the nation the king's letter was after this manner: "King Antiochus to the senate of the Jews and to the other Jews, greetings. ²⁸ If you fare well, we have our desire:

we ourselves are also in good health. ²⁹ Menelaus informed us that your desire was to return home and follow your own business. ³⁰ They therefore that depart home up to the thirtieth day of Xanthicus will have [our] friendship, with full permission ³¹ that the Jews use their own [proper] meats and [observe their own] laws, even as formerly; and none of them will be in any way molested for the things that have been ignorantly done. ³² Moreover I have sent Menelaus also, that he may encourage you. ³³ Farewell. [Written] in the one hundred [and] forty-eighth year, on the fifteenth day of Xanthicus." ³⁴ And the Romans also sent to them a letter in these words: "Quintus Memmius [and] Titus Manius, ambassadors of the Romans, to the people of the Jews, greetings. ³⁵ In regard to the things which Lysias the king's countryman granted you, we also give consent. ³⁶ But as for the things which he judged should be referred to the king, send one out with, after you have advised thereof, that we may publish such [decrees] as befit your case; for we are on our way to Antioch. ³⁷ For that reason, send some with speed, that we also may learn what is your mind. ³⁸ Farewell. [Written] in the one hundred [and] forty-eighth year, on the fifteenth day of Xanthicus."

CHAPTER 12

¹ So when these covenants had been made, Lysias departed to the king, and the Jews went about their farming. ² But [certain] of the governors of districts, Timotheus, and Apollonius the [son] of Gennaeus, and Hieronymus also, and Demophon, and besides them, Nicanor the governor of Cyprus would not permit them to enjoy tranquility and live in peace. ³ And men of Joppa perpetrated this great impiety: they invited the Jews that lived among them to go with their wives and children into the boats which they had provided, as though they had no ill will toward them; ⁴ and when the Jews, relying on the common decree of the city, accepted [the invitation], as men desiring to live in peace and suspecting nothing, they took them out to sea and drowned them—not less than two hundred. ⁵ But when Judas heard of the cruelty done to his fellow-countrymen, giving command to the men that were with him ⁶ and calling on God the righteous Judge, he came against the murderers of his countrymen, and set the haven on fire by night, and burned the boats, and put to the sword those that had fled there. ⁷ But when the town was closed [against him], he withdrew, intending to come again to root out the whole community of the men of Joppa. ⁸ But learning that the men of Jamnia were inclined to do in like manner to the Jews that sojourned among them, ⁹ he fell on the Jamnites also by night, and set fire to the haven together with the fleet, so that the glare of the light was seen at Jerusalem, two hundred and forty furlongs distant. ¹⁰ Now when they had drawn off nine furlongs from there, as they marched against Timotheus, [an army] of Arabians attacked him, no fewer than five thousand [footmen] and five hundred horsemen. ¹¹ And when a severe battle had been fought, and Judas and his company by the help of God had good success, the nomads being overcome implored Judas to grant them friendship, promising to give [him] cattle, and to help his people in all other ways. ¹² So Judas, thinking that they would indeed be profitable in many things, agreed to live in peace with them; and receiving pledges of friendship they departed to their tents. ¹³ And he also fell on a certain city, Gephyrun, strong and fenced about with walls, and inhabited by a mixed multitude of various nations; and it was named Caspin. ¹⁴ But those who were within, trusting to the strength of the walls and to their store of provisions, behaved themselves rudely toward Judas and those who were with him, railing, and furthermore blaspheming and speaking impious words. ¹⁵ But Judas and his company, calling on the great Sovereign of the world, who without rams and cunning engines of war hurled down Jericho in the times of Joshua, rushed wildly against the wall; ¹⁶ and having taken the city by the will of God, they made unspeakable slaughter, insomuch that the adjoining lake, which was two furlongs broad, appeared to be filled with the deluge of blood. ¹⁷ And when they had drawn off seven hundred and fifty furlongs from there, they made their way to Charax, to the Jews that are called Tubieni. ¹⁸ And they did not find Timotheus in occupation of that district, for he had then departed from the district without accomplishing anything, but had left behind a garrison, and that a very strong one, in a certain post. ¹⁹ But Dositheus and Sosipater, who were of Maccabaeus' captains, went out and destroyed those that had been left by Timotheus in the stronghold, above ten thousand

men. 20 And Maccabaeus, ranging his own army by bands, set these two over the bands, and marched in haste against Timotheus, who had with him one hundred and twenty thousand footmen and two thousand and five hundred horsemen. 21 But when Timotheus heard of the inroad of Judas, he at once sent away the women and the children and also the baggage into the [fortress] called Carnion; for the place was hard to besiege and difficult of access by reason of the narrowness of the approaches on all sides. 22 But when the band of Judas, who led the van, appeared in sight, and when terror came on the enemy and fear, because the manifestation of him who sees all things came on them, they fled a main, carried this way and that, so that they were often hurt of their own men, and pierced with the points of their swords. 23 And Judas continued in hot pursuit, putting the wicked wretches to the sword, and he destroyed as many as thirty thousand men. 24 But Timotheus himself, falling in with the company of Dositheus and Sosipater, implored them with much crafty guile to let him go with his life, because he had in [his power] the parents of many [of them] and the relatives of some: otherwise, [he said,] little regard will be shown to these. 25 So when he had with many words confirmed the agreement to restore them without harm, they let him go that they might save their relatives. 26 And [Judas], marching against Carnion and the temple of Atergatis, killed twenty-five thousand persons. 27 And after he had put these to flight and destroyed them, he also marched against Ephron, a strong city, wherein were multitudes of people of all nations; and stalwart young men placed on the walls made a vigorous defense; and there were great stores of engines and darts there. 28 But calling on the Sovereign who with might breaks in pieces the strength of the enemy, they got the city into their hands, and killed as many as twenty-five thousand of those who were within. 29 And setting out from there they marched in haste against Scythopolis, which is distant from Jerusalem six hundred furlongs. 30 But when the Jews that were settled there testified of the good will that the Scythopolitans had shown toward them, and of their kindly bearing [toward them] in the times of their misfortune, 31 they gave thanks, and further exhorted them to remain well-affected toward the race for the future; and they went up to Jerusalem, the Celebration of Weeks being close to hand. 32 But after the [festival] called Pentecost they marched in haste against Gorgias the governor of Idumaea: 33 and he came out with three thousand footmen and four hundred horsemen. 34 And when they had set themselves in array, it came to pass that a few of the Jews fell. 35 And a certain Dositheus, one of Bacenor's company, who was on horseback and a strong man, pressed hard on Gorgias, and taking hold of his cloak drew him along by main force; and while he was inclined to take the accursed man alive, one of the Thracian horsemen bore down on him and disabled his shoulder, and so Gorgias escaped to Marisa. 36 And when those who were with Esdris had been fighting long and were wearied out, Judas called on the Lord to show Himself, fighting on their side and leading the van of the battle; 37 and [then] in the language of his fathers he raised the battle-cry joined with hymns, and rushing unawares on the troops of Gorgias put them to flight. 38 And Judas gathering his army came to the city of Adullam; and as the seventh day was coming on, they purified themselves according to the custom, and kept the Sabbath there. 39 And on the day following, at which time it had become necessary, Judas and his company came to take up the bodies of those who had fallen, and in company with their countrymen to bring them back to the tombs of their fathers. 40 But under the garments of each one of the dead they found consecrated signs of the idols of Jamnia, which the law forbids the Jews to have anything to do with; and it became clear to all that it was for this reason that they had fallen. 41 All therefore, blessing the [works] of the Lord, the righteous Judge, who makes manifest the things that are hid, 42 went themselves to supplication, imploring that the sin committed might be wholly blotted out. And the noble Judas exhorted the multitude to keep themselves from sin, for so much as they had seen before their eyes what things had come to pass because of the sin of those who had fallen. 43 And when he had made a collection—man by man—to the sum of two thousand drachmas of silver, he sent to Jerusalem to offer a sacrifice for sin, doing therein right well and honorably, in that he took thought for a resurrection. 44 For if he were not expecting that those who had fallen would rise again, it was superfluous and idle to pray for the dead. 45 (And if [he did it] looking to an honorable memorial of gratitude laid up for those who die in godliness, holy and godly was the thought.) For that reason, he made the atoning sacrifice for those who had died, that they might be released from their sin.

CHAPTER 13

1 In the one hundred and forty-ninth year, tidings were brought to Judas and his company that Antiochus Eupator was coming with [great] multitudes against Judea, 2 and with him Lysias his guardian and chancellor, each having a Greek force, one hundred and ten thousand footmen, and five thousand and three hundred horsemen, and twenty-two elephants, and three hundred chariots armed with scythes. 3 And Menelaus also joined himself with them, and with great deception encouraged Antiochus, not for the saving of his country, but because he thought that he would be set over the government. 4 But the King of kings stirred up the passion of Antiochus against the wicked wretch; and when Lysias informed him that this man was the cause of all the evils, [the king] commanded to bring him to Beroea, and to put him to death after the manner of that place. 5 Now there is in that place a tower of fifty cubits high, full of ashes, and it had all around it a gallery descending sheer on every side into the ashes. 6 Here him that is guilty of sacrilege or has attained a preeminence in any other evil deeds, they all push forward into destruction. 7 By such a fate it befell the breaker of the law, Menelaus, to die, without obtaining so much as [a grave in] the earth, and that right justly; 8 for since he had perpetrated many sins against the altar, whose fire and whose ashes were holy, in ashes he received his death. 9 Now the king, infuriated in spirit, was coming with intent to inflict on the Jews the very worst of the sufferings that had befallen [them] in his father's time. 10 But when Judas heard of these things, he gave charge to the multitude to call on the Lord day and night, [imploring Him,] if ever at any other time, so now to help those who were at the point to be deprived of the law and their country and the holy temple, 11 and not to permit the people that had been but now a little while revived to fall into the hands of those profane heathen. 12 So when they had all done the same thing together, imploring the merciful Lord with weeping, and fasting, and prostration for three days without ceasing, Judas exhorted them and commanded they should join him. 13 And having gone apart with the elders, he resolved that, before the king's army should enter into Judea and make themselves masters of the city, they should go out and try the matter [in fight] by the help of God. 14 And committing the decision to the Lord of the world and exhorting those who were with him to contend nobly even to death for laws, temple, city, country, commonwealth, he pitched his camp by Modin. 15 And given out to his men the watchword, Victory is God's, with a chosen body of the bravest young men he fell on [the camp] by night [and penetrated] to the king's tent and killed [of] the army as many as two thousand men and brought down the mightiest elephant with him that was in the tower on him. 16 And at last they filled the army with terror and alarm and departed with good success. 17 And this had been accomplished when the day was but now dawning, because of the Lord's protection that gave Judas help. 18 But the king, having had a taste of the exceeding boldness of the Jews, made attempts by stratagem on their positions; 19 and [on] a strong fortress of the Jews at Bethsura, he advanced, was turned back, failed, was defeated, 20 and Judas carried such things as were necessary to those who were within. 21 But Rhodocus, from the Jewish ranks, made known to the enemy the secrets [of his countrymen]. He was sought out, and taken, and shut up in prison. 22 The king treated with them in Bethsura the second time, gave his hand, took theirs, departed, attacked the forces of Judas, was given a worse [outcome], 23 heard that Philip, who had been left as chancellor in Antioch, had become reckless, was confounded, made to the Jews an overture [of peace], submitted himself, and swore to acknowledge all their rights, came to terms with them and offered sacrifice, honored the sanctuary and the place, 24 showed kindness and graciously received Maccabaeus, left Hegemonides governor from Ptolemais even to the Gerrenians, 25 [and] came to Ptolemais. The men of Ptolemais were displeased at the treaty, for they had exceedingly great indignation [against the Jews]: they desired to annul the articles of the agreement. 26 Lysias came forward to speak, made the best defense that was possible, persuaded, pacified, made them well-affected, [and] departed to Antioch. This was the issue of the inroad and departure of the king.

CHAPTER 14

¹ Now after a space of three years tidings were brought to Judas and his company that Demetrius the [son] of Seleucus, having sailed into the haven of Tripolis with a mighty army and a fleet, ² had gotten possession of the country, having made away with Antiochus and his guardian Lysias. ³ But one Alcimus, who had formerly been chief priest, and had willfully polluted himself in the times when there was no mingling [with the nations], considering that there was no deliverance for him in any way, nor any more access to the holy altar, ⁴ came to King Demetrius in about the one hundred [and] fifty-first year, presenting to him a crown of gold and a palm, and beside these some of the festal olive boughs of the temple. And for that day he held his peace; ⁵ but having gotten opportunity to further his own madness, being called by Demetrius into a meeting of his council and asked how the Jews stood affected and what they purposed, he answered to that. ⁶ Those of the Jews that he called Hasidaeans, whose leader is Judas Maccabaeus, keep up war, and are seditious, not suffering the kingdom to find tranquility. ⁷ For that reason, having laid aside my ancestral glory, I mean the chief priesthood, I have now come here; ⁸ first, for the genuine care I have for the things that concern the king, and secondly, because I also have regard to my own fellow-citizens; for, through the unadvised dealing of those of whom I spoke before, our whole race is in no small misfortune. ⁹ But do you, O king, having informed yourself of these things separately, take thought both for our country and for our race, which is surrounded [by enemies], according to the gracious kindness with which you receive all? ¹⁰ For as long as Judas remains alive, it is impossible that the state should find peace. ¹¹ And when he had spoken such words as these, at once the rest of the [king's] friends, having ill will against Judas, inflamed Demetrius yet more. ¹² And then appointing Nicanor, who had been master of the elephants, and making him governor of Judea, he sent him out, ¹³ giving him written instructions to make away with Judas himself and to scatter those who were with him, and to set up Alcimus as chief priest of the great temple. ¹⁴ And those in Judea that had [before] driven Judas into exile thronged to Nicanor in flocks, supposing that the misfortunes and calamities of the Jews would be successes to themselves. ¹⁵ But when [the Jews] heard of Nicanor's inroad and the assault of the heathen, they sprinkled earth [on their heads] and made solemn supplication to him who had established His own people forevermore, and who always, making manifest His presence, upholds [those who are] His own portion. ¹⁶ And when the leader had given [his] commands, he immediately set out from there, and joined battle with them at a village [called] Lessau. ¹⁷ But Simon, the brother of Judas, had encountered Nicanor, yet not until late, having received a check by reason of the sudden consternation caused by his adversaries. ¹⁸ Nevertheless Nicanor, hearing of the manliness of those who were with Judas, and their courage in fighting for their country, shrank from bringing the matter to the decision of the sword. ¹⁹ For that reason, he sent Posidonius, and Theodotus, and Mattathias to give and receive pledges of friendship. ²⁰ So when these proposals had been long considered, and the leader had made the troops acquainted with them, and it appeared that they were all of like mind, they consented to the covenants. ²¹ And they appointed a day on which to meet together by themselves. And a litter was borne forward from each [army]; they set chairs of state; ²² Judas stationed armed men ready in convenient places, lest perhaps there should suddenly be treachery on the part of the enemy; they held such conference as was suitable. ²³ Nicanor waited in Jerusalem, and did nothing to cause disturbance, but dismissed the flocks of people that had gathered together. ²⁴ And he kept Judas always in his presence; he had gained a hearty affection for the man; ²⁵ he urged him to marry and beget children; he married, settled quietly, took part in common life. ²⁶ But Alcimus, perceiving the good will that was between them, and having gotten possession of the covenants that had been made, came to Demetrius and told him that Nicanor was ill-affected toward the state, for he had appointed that conspirator against his kingdom, Judas, to be his successor. ²⁷ And the king, falling into a rage, and being exasperated by the false accusations of that most wicked man, wrote to Nicanor, signifying that he was displeased at the covenants, and commanding him to send Maccabaeus prisoner to Antioch in all haste. ²⁸ And when this message came to Nicanor, he was confounded, and was severely troubled at the thought of annulling the articles that had been agreed on, the man having done no wrong; ²⁹ but because there was no dealing against the king, he watched his time to execute this purpose by stratagem. ³⁰ But Maccabaeus, when he perceived that Nicanor was behaving more harshly in his dealings with him, and that he had become ruler in his customary bearing, understanding that this harshness came not of good, gathered together not a few of his men, and concealed himself from Nicanor. ³¹ But the other, when he became aware that he had been bravely defeated by the stratagem of Judas, came to the great and holy temple, while the priests were offering the usual sacrifices, and commanded them to deliver the man up. ³² And when they declared with oaths that they had no knowledge where the man was whom he sought, ³³ he stretched out his right hand toward the sanctuary and swore this oath: "If you will not deliver up to me Judas as a prisoner, I will lay this temple of God even with the ground, and will break down the altar, and I will erect here a temple to Bacchus for all to see." ³⁴ And having said this, he departed. But the priests, stretching out their hands toward Heaven, called on Him that ever fights for our nation, in these words: ³⁵ "You, O Lord of the universe, who in Yourself have need of nothing, was well pleased that a sanctuary of Your habitation should be set among us; ³⁶ so now, O holy Lord of all hallowing, keep undefiled forever this house that has been lately cleansed." ³⁷ Now information was given to Nicanor against one Razis, an elder of Jerusalem, as being a lover of his countrymen and a man of very good report, and one called "Father of the Jews" for his good will [toward them]. ³⁸ For in the former times when there was no mingling [with the nations] he had been accused of [cleaving to the] Jews' religion, and had endangered body and life with all earnestness for the religion of the Jews. ³⁹ And Nicanor, wishing to make evident the ill will that he bore to the Jews, sent above five hundred soldiers to take him; ⁴⁰ for he thought by taking him to inflict a calamity on them. ⁴¹ But when the troops were on the point of taking the tower, and were forcing the door of the court, and commanded to bring fire and burn the doors, he being surrounded on every side, fell on his sword, ⁴² choosing rather to die nobly than to fall into the hands of the wicked wretches, and suffer outrage unworthy of his own nobleness: ⁴³ but since he missed his stroke through the excitement of the struggle, and the crowds were now rushing within the door, he ran bravely up to the wall and cast himself down courageously among the crowds. ⁴⁴ But as they quickly gave back, a space was made, and he fell on the middle of his side. ⁴⁵ And having yet breath within him, and being inflamed with passion, he rose up, and though his blood gushed out in streams and his wounds were grievous, he ran through the crowds, and standing on a steep rock, ⁴⁶ when as his blood was now well near spent, he drew out his bowels [through the wound, and] taking them in both his hands he shook them at the crowds; and calling on Him who is Lord of the life and the spirit to restore these again, he thus died.

CHAPTER 15

¹ But Nicanor, hearing that Judas and his company were in the region of Samaria, resolved to set on them with all security on the day of rest. ² And when the Jews that were compelled to follow him said, "Do not destroy so savagely and barbarously, but give due glory to the day which He that sees all things has honored and hallowed above [other days]"; ³ then the three times-accursed wretch asked if there were a Sovereign in Heaven that had commanded to keep the Sabbath day. ⁴ And when they declared, "There is the Lord, living Himself [as the] Sovereign in Heaven, who commanded [us] to observe the seventh day"; ⁵ then the other says, "I also am a sovereign on the earth, who [now] command to take up arms and execute the king's business." Nevertheless, he did not prevail to execute his cruel purpose. ⁶ And Nicanor, bearing himself haughtily in all vain pride, had determined to set up a monument of complete victory over Judas and all those who were with him: ⁷ but Maccabaeus still trusted unceasingly, with all hope that he should obtain help from the Lord. ⁸ And he exhorted his company not to be fearful at the inroad of the heathen, but, keeping in mind the help which of old they had oftentimes received from Heaven, so now also to look for the victory which would come to them from the Almighty; ⁹ and comforting them out of the Law and the Prophets, and in addition, putting them in mind of the conflicts that they had

maintained, he made them more eager [for the battle]. **10** And when he had roused their spirit, he gave them [his] commands, at the same time pointing out the disloyalty of the heathen and their breach of their oaths. **11** And arming each one of them, not so much with the sure defense of shields and spears as with the encouragement [that lies] in good words, and moreover relating to them a dream worthy to be believed, he made them all exceedingly glad. **12** And the vision of that [dream] was this: [He saw] Onias, him that was chief priest, a noble and good man, reverend in bearing, yet gentle in manner and well-spoken, and exercised from a child in all points of virtue, with outstretched hands invoking [blessings] on the whole body of the Jews: **13** there on [he saw] a man appear, of venerable age and exceeding glory, and wonderful and most majestic was the dignity around him: **14** and Onias answered and said, "This is the lover of the countrymen, he who prays much for the people and the holy city, Jeremiah the prophet of God": **15** and Jeremiah stretching out his right hand delivered to Judas a sword of gold, and in giving it addressed [him], saying, **16** "Take the holy sword, a gift from God, with which you will strike down the adversaries." **17** And being encouraged by the words of Judas, which were of a lofty strain, and able to incite to virtue, and to stir the souls of the young to manly courage, they determined not to carry on a campaign, but nobly to bear down on [the enemy, and] fighting hand to hand with all courage bring the matter to an issue, because the city and the sanctuary and the temple were in danger. **18** For their fear for wives and children, and furthermore for relatives and countrymen, was in less account with them; but greatest and first was their fear for the consecrated sanctuary. **19** And they also that were shut up in the city were in no light distress, being troubled because of the encounter in the open ground. **20** And when all were now waiting for the decision of the issue, and the enemy had already joined battle, and the army had been set in array, and the elephants brought back to a convenient post, and the horsemen drawn on the flank, **21** Maccabaeus, perceiving the presence of the troops, and the various arms with which they were equipped, and the savageness of the elephants, holding up his hands to Heaven called on the Lord that works wonders, recognizing that [success] comes not by arms, but that, according as [the Lord] will judge, He gains the victory for those who are worthy. **22** And calling on [God], he said after this manner: "You, O Sovereign Lord, sent Your messenger in the time of Hezekiah king of Judea, and he killed of the army of Sennacherib as many as one hundred and eighty-five thousand; **23** so now also, O Sovereign of the heavens, send a good messenger before us to bring terror and trembling: **24** through the greatness of Your arm let them be stricken with dismay that have come here against Your holy people with blasphemy." And as he ended with these words, **25** Nicanor and his company advanced with trumpets and victory songs; **26** but Judas and his company joined battle with the enemy with invocation and prayers. **27** And contending with their hands, and praying to God with their hearts, they killed no less than thirty-five thousand men, being made exceedingly glad by the manifestation of God. **28** And when the engagement was over, and they were returning again with joy, they recognized Nicanor lying dead in full armor; **29** and there arose a shout and tumult, and then they blessed the Sovereign [Lord] in the language of their fathers. **30** And he that in all things was in body and soul the foremost champion of his fellow-citizens, he that kept through life the good will of his youth toward his countrymen, commanded to cut off Nicanor's head, and his hand with the shoulder, and bring them to Jerusalem. **31** And when he had arrived there, and had called his countrymen together and set the priests before the altar, he sent for those who were in the citadel; **32** and showing the head of the vile Nicanor, and the hand of that profane man, which with proud brags he had stretched out against the holy house of the Almighty, **33** and cutting out the tongue of the impious Nicanor, he said that he would give it by pieces to the birds, and hang up the rewards of his madness near the sanctuary. **34** And they all, [looking up] to Heaven, blessed the Lord who had manifested Himself, saying, "Blessed is He that has preserved His own place undefiled." **35** And he hanged Nicanor's head and shoulder from the citadel, a sign, evident to all and manifest, of the help of the Lord. **36** And they all ordained with a common decree in no way to let this day pass undistinguished, but to mark with honor the thirteenth day of the twelfth month (it is called Adar in the Syrian tongue), the day before the day of Mordecai. **37** This then having been the issue of the attempt of Nicanor, and the city having from those

times been held by the Hebrews, I will also here make an end of my scroll. **38** And if [I have written] well and to the point in my story, this is what I myself desired; but if meanly and indifferently, this is all I could attain to. **39** For as it is distasteful to drink wine alone and in like manner again [to drink] water [alone], while the mingling of wine with water at once gives full pleasantness to the flavor; so also, the fashioning of the language delights the ears of those who read the story. And here will be the end

1 ESDRAS

Otherwise known as 3 Esdras

1 Esdras, also called Greek Esdras, Greek Ezra, or 3 Esdras, is an ancient Greek version of the biblical Book of Ezra in use among the early church, and many modern Christians with varying degrees of canonicity. First Esdras is substantially the same as Masoretic Ezra. As part of the Septuagint translation of the Old Testament, it is regarded as deuterocanonical in the churches of the East, but apocryphal in the West. First Esdras is found in Origen's Hexapla. Greek and related versions of the Bible include both Esdras A (English title: 1 Esdras) and Esdras B (Ezra–Nehemiah) in parallel.

CHAPTER 1

1 Josiah held the Passover in Jerusalem to his Lord and offered the Passover [on] the fourteenth day of the first month; **2** having set the priests according to their daily courses, being arrayed in their vestments, in the temple of the Lord. **3** And he spoke to the Levites, the temple-servants of Israel, that they should make themselves holy to the Lord, to set the holy Ark of the Lord in the house that King Solomon the son of David had built, **4** [and he said,] "You will no longer have need to bear it on your shoulders: now therefore, serve the Lord your God, and minister to His people Israel, and prepare after your fathers' houses and relatives, **5** according to the writing of David, king of Israel, and according to the magnificence of his son Solomon: and standing in the holy place according to the several divisions of the families of you the Levites, who [minister] in the presence of your countrymen the sons of Israel, **6** offer the Passover in order, and make the sacrifices ready for your countrymen, and keep the Passover according to the command of the Lord, which was given to Moses." **7** And to the people which were present Josiah gave thirty thousand lambs and kids, and three thousand calves: these things were given of the king's substance, according as he promised, to the people, and to the priests and Levites. **8** And Hilkiah, and Zechariah, and Esyelus, the rulers of the temple, gave to the priests for the Passover two thousand [and] six hundred sheep, and three hundred calves. **9** And Jeconias, and Samaias, and his brother Nathanael, and Sabias, and Ochielus, and Joram, captains over thousands, gave to the Levites for the Passover five thousand sheep, and seven hundred calves. **10** And when these things were done, the priests and Levites, having the unleavened bread, stood in agreeable order according to the countrymen, **11** and according to the several divisions by fathers' houses, before the people, to offer to the Lord, as it is written in the Scroll of Moses: and so [they] did [in] the morning. **12** And they roasted the Passover with fire, as pertains: and they boiled the sacrifices in the brazen vessels and cauldrons with a good savor, **13** and set them before all the people; and afterward they prepared for themselves, and for their relatives the priests, the sons of Aaron. **14** For the priests offered the fat until night: and the Levites prepared for themselves, and for their relatives the priests, the sons of Aaron. **15** The holy singers also, the sons of Asaph, were in their order, according to the appointment of David, Asaph, Zechariah, and Eddinus, who was of the king's retinue. **16** Moreover, the gatekeepers were at every gate; none had need to depart from his daily course, for their relatives the Levites prepared for them. **17** So were the things that belonged to the sacrifices of the Lord accomplished in that day, in holding the

Passover, **18** and offering sacrifices on the altar of the Lord, according to the command of King Josiah. **19** So the sons of Israel, which were present at that time, held the Passover and the Celebration of Unleavened Bread [for] seven days. **20** And such a Passover was not held in Israel since the time of the prophet Samuel. **21** Yes, all the kings of Israel had not held such a Passover as Josiah, and the priests, and the Levites, and the Jews, with all Israel that were present in their dwelling place at Jerusalem. **22** In the eighteenth year of the reign of Josiah this Passover was held. **23** And the works of Josiah were upright before his Lord with a heart full of godliness. **24** Moreover, the things that came to pass in his days have been written in times past, concerning those that sinned, and did wickedly against the Lord above every people and kingdom, and how they grieved Him exceedingly, so that the words of the Lord were confirmed against Israel. **25** Now after all these acts of Josiah, it came to pass that Pharaoh the king of Egypt came to raise war at Carchemish on [the] Euphrates: and Josiah went out against him. **26** But the king of Egypt sent to him, saying, "What have I to do with you, O king of Judea? **27** I am not sent out from the Lord God against you; for my war is on [the] Euphrates: and now the Lord is with me, yes, the Lord is with me hastening me forward. Depart from me and do not be against the Lord." **28** However, Josiah did not turn back to his chariot, but undertook to fight with him, not regarding the words of the prophet Jeremiah [spoken] by the mouth of the Lord, **29** but he joined battle with him in the plain of Megiddo, and the princes came down against King Josiah. **30** Then the king said to his servants, "Carry me away out of the battle; for I am very weak. And immediately his servants carried him away out of the army." **31** Then he got up on his second chariot; and being brought back to Jerusalem he died and was buried in the tomb of his fathers. **32** And in all Jewry they mourned for Josiah; and the prophet Jeremiah lamented for Josiah, and the chief men with the women made lamentation for him, to this day: and this was given out for an ordinance to be done continually in all the nation of Israel. **33** These things are written in the Scroll of the Histories of the Kings of Judea, and each of the acts that Josiah did, and his glory, and his understanding in the Law of the Lord, and the things that he had done before, and the things now [recited], are reported in the Scroll of the Kings of Israel and Judah. **34** And the people took Joachaz, the son of Josiah, and made him king instead of his father Josiah, when he was twenty-three years old. **35** And he reigned in Judah and in Jerusalem three months: and then the king of Egypt deposed him from reigning in Jerusalem. **36** And he set a tax on the people of one hundred talents of silver and one talent of gold. **37** The king of Egypt also made King Jehoiakim, his brother, king of Judea and Jerusalem. **38** And Jehoiakim bound the nobles, but he apprehended his brother Zarakes and brought him up out of Egypt. **39** Jehoiakim was twenty-five years old when he began to reign in Judea and Jerusalem; and he did that which was evil in the sight of the Lord. **40** And Nebuchadnezzar the king of Babylon came up against him, and bound him with a chain of brass, and carried him to Babylon. **41** Nebuchadnezzar also took of the holy vessels of the Lord, and carried them away, and set them up in his own temple at Babylon. **42** But those things that are reported of him, and of his uncleanness and impiety, are written in the Chronicles of the Kings. **43** And his son Jehoiakim reigned in his stead; for when he was made king he was eighteen years old; **44** and he reigned three months and ten days in Jerusalem; and did that which was evil before the Lord. **45** So after a year Nebuchadnezzar sent and caused him to be brought to Babylon with the holy vessels of the Lord, **46** and he made Zedekiah king of Judea and Jerusalem when he was twenty-one years old; and he reigned eleven years: **47** and he also did that which was evil in the sight of the Lord and did not care for the words that were spoken by the prophet Jeremiah from the mouth of the Lord. **48** And after King Nebuchadnezzar had made him to swear by the Name of the Lord, he renounced it, and rebelled; and hardening his neck and his heart, he transgressed the laws of the Lord, the God of Israel. **49** Moreover, the governors of the people and of the priests did many things wickedly, and surpassed all the pollutions of all nations, and defiled the temple of the Lord, which was sanctified in Jerusalem. **50** And the God of their fathers sent by His messenger to call them back, because He had compassion on them and on His dwelling place. **51** But they mocked His messengers; and in the day when the Lord spoke [to them], they scoffed at His prophets, **52** so much so that He, being angry with His people for their great ungodliness, commanded to bring up the kings of the Chaldeans against them, **53** who killed their young men with the sword, around their holy temple, and spared neither young man nor maid, old man nor child; but He delivered all into their hands. **54** And they took all the holy vessels of the Lord, both great and small, with the vessels of the Ark of the Lord, and the king's treasures, and carried them away to Babylon. **55** And they burned the house of the Lord, and broke down the walls of Jerusalem, and burned the towers thereof with fire. **56** And as for her glorious things, they never ceased until they had brought them all to nothing; and the people that were not slain with the sword he carried to Babylon, **57** and they were servants to him and to his children, until the Persians reigned, to fulfill the word of the Lord by the mouth of Jeremiah: **58** "Until the land has enjoyed her Sabbaths, the whole time of her desolation she will keep Sabbath, to fulfill seventy years."

CHAPTER 2

1 In the first year of Cyrus king of the Persians, that the word of the Lord by the mouth of Jeremiah might be accomplished, **2** the Lord stirred up the spirit of Cyrus king of the Persians, and he made proclamation through all his kingdom, and also by writing, **3** saying, "Cyrus king of the Persians says: The Lord of Israel, the Most High Lord, has made me king of the whole world, **4** and commanded me to build Him a house at Jerusalem that is in Judea. **5** If, therefore, there are any of you that are of His people, let the Lord, even his Lord, be with him, and let him go up to Jerusalem that is in Judea, and build the house of the Lord of Israel: He is the Lord that dwells in Jerusalem. **6** Of such therefore as dwell in various places, let those who are in his own place help each one with gold, and with silver, **7** with gifts, also with horses and cattle, besides the other things which have been added by vow for the temple of the Lord which is in Jerusalem." **8** Then the chief of the families of Judah and of the tribe of Benjamin stood up; the priests also, and the Levites, and all they whose spirit the Lord had stirred to go up, to build the house for the Lord which is in Jerusalem. **9** And those who lived around them helped them in all things with silver and gold, with horses and cattle, and with very many gifts that were vowed of a great number whose minds were stirred up. **10** King Cyrus also brought out the holy vessels of the Lord, which Nebuchadnezzar had carried away from Jerusalem, and had set up in his temple of idols. **11** Now when Cyrus king of the Persians had brought them out, he delivered them to his treasurer Mithradates, **12** and they were delivered by him to Sanabassar the governor of Judea. **13** And this was the number of them: one thousand golden cups, one thousand cups of silver, twenty-nine censers of silver, thirty vials of gold, and of silver—two thousand four hundred and ten, and other vessels—one thousand. **14** So all the vessels of gold and of silver were brought up, even five thousand four hundred and sixty-nine, **15** and were carried back by Sanabassar, together with them of the captivity, from Babylon to Jerusalem. **16** But in the time of Artaxerxes king of the Persians, Belemus, and Mithradates, and Tabellius, and Rathumus, and Beeltethmus, and Samellius the scribe, with the others that were in commission with them, dwelling in Samaria and other places, wrote to him against those who lived in Judea and Jerusalem the following letter: **17** "To King Artaxerxes our Lord, Your servants, Rathumus the recorder, and Samellius the scribe, and the rest of their council, and the judges that are in Coele-Syria and Phoenicia. **18** Be it now known to our lord the king, that the Jews that have come up from you to us, having come to Jerusalem, are building that rebellious and wicked city, and are repairing its marketplaces and walls, and are laying the foundation of a temple. **19** Now if this city is built and the walls [thereof] are finished, they will not only refuse to give tribute, but will even stand up against kings. **20** And forasmuch as the things pertaining to the temple are now in hand, we think it suitable not to neglect such a matter, **21** but to speak to our lord the king, to the intent that, if it be your pleasure, search may be made in the scrolls of your fathers: **22** and you will find in the chronicles what is written concerning these things, and will understand that that city was rebellious, troubling both kings and cities, **23** and that the Jews were rebellious, and always raised wars therein of former time; for this reason even this city was laid waste. **24** For that reason, now we declare to you, O lord the king, that if this city is built again, and the walls thereof set up anew, you will from now on have no passage into Coele-Syria and Phoenicia." **25** Then the king wrote back again to Rathumus the recorder, and

Beeltethmus, and Samellius the scribe, and to the rest that were in commission, and lived in Samaria, and Syria, and Phoenicia, after this manner: **26** "I have read the letter which you have sent to me; therefore, I commanded to make search, and it has been found that that city of former time has made insurrection against kings; **27** and the men were given to rebellion and war therein; and that fierce and mighty kings were in Jerusalem, who reigned and exacted tribute in Coele-Syria and Phoenicia. **28** Now therefore, I have commanded to hinder those men from building the city, and heed to be taken that there is nothing done contrary to this [order]; **29** and that those wicked doings proceed no further to the annoyance of kings. **30** Then King Artaxerxes, his letters being read, Rathumus, and Samellius the scribe, and the rest that were in commission with them, removing in haste to Jerusalem with horsemen and a multitude of people in battle array, began to hinder the builders; and the building of the temple in Jerusalem ceased until the second year of the reign of Darius king of the Persians.

CHAPTER 3

1 Now King Darius made a great feast to all his subjects, and to all that were born in his house, and to all the princes of Media and of Persia, **2** and to all the local governors, and captains, and governors that were under him, from India to Ethiopia, in the one hundred [and] twenty-seven provinces. **3** And when they had eaten and drunken, and being satisfied were gone home, then Darius the king went into his bedchamber, and slept, and awoke out of his sleep. **4** Then the three young men of the bodyguard, that kept the king's person, spoke to one another: **5** "Let each of us say one thing which will be strongest; and he whose sentence will seem wiser than the others, to him Darius the king will give great gifts, and great honors in token of victory: **6** as, to be clothed in purple, to drink in gold, and to sleep on gold, and a chariot with bridles of gold, and a turban of fine linen, and a chain around his neck; **7** and he will sit next to Darius because of his wisdom, and will be called cousin of Darius." **8** And then they each wrote his sentence, and set to their seals, and laid [the writing] under [the] pillow of King Darius, **9** and said, "When the king is risen, some will give him the writing; and of whose side the king and the three princes of Persia will judge that his sentence is the wisest, to him will the victory be given, as it is written." **10** The first wrote, "Wine is the strongest." **11** The second wrote, "The king is strongest." **12** The third wrote, "Women are strongest, but above all things Truth bears away the victory." **13** Now when the king was risen up, they took the writing, and gave it to him, and so he read it: **14** and sending out he called all the princes of Persia and of Media, and the local governors, and the captains, and the governors, and the chief officers, **15** and he sat down in the royal seat of judgment, and the writing was read before them. **16** And he said, "Call the young men, and they will explain their own sentences." So they were called, and came in. **17** And they said to them, "Declare to us your mind concerning the things you have written." Then began the first, who had spoken of the strength of wine, **18** and said, "O lords, how exceedingly strong is wine! it causes all men to err that drink it: **19** it makes the mind of the king and of the fatherless child to be all one; of the bondman and of the freeman, of the poor man and of the rich; **20** it also turns every thought into cheer and mirth, so that a man remembers neither sorrow nor debt; **21** and it makes every heart rich, so that a man remembers neither king nor local governor; and it makes all things to speak by talents; **22** and when they are in their cups, they forget their love both to friends and relatives, and a little after draw their swords, **23** but when they awake from their wine, they do not remember what they have done. **24** O lords, is not wine the strongest, seeing that it enforces to do so?" And when he had so spoken, he held his peace.

CHAPTER 4

1 Then the second, that had spoken of the strength of the king, began to say, **2** "O lords, do men not excel in strength, that bear rule over the sea and land, and all things in them? **3** But yet is the king stronger: and he is their lord and has dominion over them; and in whatever he commands them they obey him. **4** If he commands them to make war—the one against the other—they do it; and if he sends them out against the enemies, they go, and overcome mountains, walls, and towers. **5** They kill and are slain, and [still] do not transgress the king's command: if they get the victory, they bring everything to the king, as well as the plunder, as everything else. **6** Likewise for those that are not soldiers, and have nothing to do with wars, but are farming, when they have again reaped that which they had sown, they bring it to the king, and compel one another to pay tribute to the king. **7** And he is but one man: if he commands to kill, they kill; if he commands to spare, they spare; **8** if he commands to strike, they strike; if he commands to make desolate, they make desolate; if he commands to build, they build; **9** if he commands to cut down, they cut down; if he commands to plant, they plant. **10** So all his people and his armies obey him: furthermore, he lies down, he eats and drinks, and takes his rest, **11** and these keep watch around him, neither may anyone depart and do his own business, neither do they disobey him in [anything]. **12** O lords, how should the king not be strongest, seeing that in such sort he is obeyed? And he held his peace. **13** Then the third, who had spoken of women and of truth (this was Zerubbabel), began to speak. **14** "O lords, is not the king great, and men are many, and wine is strong? who is it then that rules them, or has the lordship over them? are they not women? **15** Women have borne the king and all the people that bear rule by sea and land. **16** Even from them they came: and they nourished them up that planted the vineyards, from where the wine comes. **17** These also make garments for men; these bring glory to men; and without women men cannot be. **18** Yes, and if men have gathered together gold, and silver, and any other attractive thing, and see a woman which is attractive in favor and beauty, **19** they let all those things go, and stare after her, and even with open mouth fix their eyes fast on her; and they have all [the] more desire for her than for gold or silver, or any other attractive thing. **20** A man leaves his own father that brought him up, and his own country, and joins with his wife. **21** And with his wife he ends his days, and remembers neither father, nor mother, nor country. **22** By this also you must know that women have dominion over you: do you not labor and toil, and give and bring all to women? **23** Yes, a man takes his sword, and goes out to make excursions, and to rob and to steal, and to sail on the sea and on rivers; **24** and looks on a lion and walks in the darkness; and when he has stolen, plundered, and robbed, he brings it to his love. **25** For that reason, a man loves his wife better than father or mother. **26** Yes, there are many that have run out of their wits for women and become bondmen for their sakes. **27** Many have also perished, have stumbled, and sinned, for women. **28** And now do you not believe me? is the king not great in his power? do all regions not fear to touch him? **29** Yet I saw him and the king's concubine Apame, the daughter of the illustrious Barticus, sitting at the right hand of the king, **30** and taking the crown from the king's head, and setting it on her own head; yes, she struck the king with her left hand: **31** and immediately the king stared and gazed on her with open mouth. If she laughed on him, he also laughed, but if she took any displeasure at him, he was glad to flatter, that she might be reconciled to him again. **32** O lords, how can it be but women should be strong, seeing they do so?" **33** Then the king and the nobles looked on one another, so he began to speak concerning truth. **34** "O lords, are women not strong? great is the earth, high is the Heaven, swift is the sun in his course, for he encircles the heavens around, and fetches his course again to his own place in one day. **35** Is He not great that makes these things? therefore, great is truth, and stronger than all things. **36** All the earth calls on truth, and the Heaven blesses her; all works shake and tremble, but with her is no unrighteous thing. **37** Wine is unrighteous, the king is unrighteous, women are unrighteous, all the children of men are unrighteous, and all such works of theirs are unrighteous; and there is no truth in them; in their unrighteousness also, they will perish. **38** But truth remains and is strong forever; she lives and conquers forevermore. **39** With her there is no accepting of persons or rewards; but she does the things that are just, and [refrains] from all unrighteous and wicked things; and all men do well like of her works. **40** Neither is any unrighteousness in her judgment; and she is the strength, and the kingdom, and the power, and the majesty, of all ages. Blessed is the God of truth." **41** And with that he held his tongue. And all the people then shouted, and said, "Great is truth, and strong above all things." **42** Then the king said to him, "Ask what you will more than is appointed in writing, and we will give it to you, inasmuch as you are found wisest; and you will sit next to me, and will be called my cousin." **43** Then he said to the king, "Remember your vow, which you vowed to build Jerusalem, in the day when you came to your kingdom, **44** and to send away all the vessels that were taken out of Jerusalem, which Cyrus set apart, when he vowed to destroy Babylon, and vowed to send them there again. **45** You also vowed to build up the temple, which the Edomites burned when Judea was made desolate by the Chaldeans. **46** And now, O lord the king, this is that which I require, and which I desire of you, and this is the princely generosity that will proceed from you: I pray therefore that you make good the vow, the performance of which you have vowed to the King of Heaven with your own mouth." **47** Then Darius the king stood up, and kissed him, and wrote letters for him to all the treasurers, and governors, and captains, and local governors, that they should safely bring on their way both him, and all those that should go up with him to build Jerusalem. **48** He also wrote letters to all the governors that were in Coele-Syria and Phoenicia, and to them in Libanus, that they should bring cedar wood from Libanus to Jerusalem, and that they should build the city with him. **49** Moreover, he wrote for all the Jews that should go out of his realm up into Jewry, concerning their freedom, that no officer, no governor, no local governor, nor treasurer, should forcibly enter into their doors; **50** and that all the country which they occupied should be free to them without tribute; and that the Edomites should give over the villages of the Jews which they then held: **51** and that there should be yearly given twenty talents to the building of the temple, until the time that it were built; **52** and ten more talents yearly, for burnt-offerings to be presented on the altar every day, as they had a command to offer seventeen: **53** and that all those who should come from Babylonia to build the city should have their freedom—they as well as their posterity, and all the priests that came. **54** He also wrote [to give them] their charges, and the priests' vestments wherein they minister; **55** and for the Levites he wrote that their charges should be given them until the day that the house were finished, and Jerusalem built up. **56** And he commanded to give to all that kept the city lands and wages. **57** He also sent away all the vessels from Babylon that Cyrus had set apart, and all that Cyrus had given in command, he also charged to be done, and sent to Jerusalem. **58** Now when this young man had gone out, he lifted up his face to Heaven toward Jerusalem, and praised the King of Heaven, **59** and said, "From You comes victory, from You comes wisdom, and Yours is the glory, and I am Your servant. **60** Blessed are You, who have given me wisdom: and to You I give thanks, O Lord of our fathers." **61** And so he took the letters, and went out, and came to Babylon, and told it [to] all his countrymen. **62** And they praised the God of their fathers, because He had given them freedom and liberty **63** to go up, and to build Jerusalem, and the temple which is called by His Name: and they feasted with instruments of music and gladness [for] seven days.

CHAPTER 5

1 After this the chiefs of fathers' houses were chosen to go up according to their tribes, with their wives, and sons, and daughters, with their menservants and maidservants, and their cattle. **2** And Darius sent one thousand horsemen with them, until they had brought them back to Jerusalem safely, and with musical instruments, tabrets, and flutes. **3** And all their countrymen played, and he made them go up together with them. **4** And these are the names of the men which went up, according to their families among their tribes, after their several divisions. **5** The priests, the sons of Phinehas, the sons of Aaron: Jesus the son of Josedek, the son of Saraias, and Jehoiakim the son of Zerubbabel, the son of Salathiel, of the house of David, of the lineage of Phares, of the tribe of Judah; **6** who spoke wise sentences before Darius the king of Persia in the second year of his reign, in the month Nisan, which is the first month. **7** And these are they of Jewry that came up from the captivity, where they lived as strangers, whom Nebuchadnezzar the king of Babylon had carried away to Babylon. **8** And they returned to Jerusalem, and to the other parts of Jewry, every man to his own city, who came with Zerubbabel, with Jesus, Nehemiah, and Zerahiah, Resaias, Eneneus, Mardocheus, Beelsarus, Aspharsus, Reelias, Roimus, and Baana, their leaders. **9** The number of them of the nation, and their leaders: the sons of Phoros, two thousand one hundred and seventy-two; the sons of Saphat, four hundred and seventy-two; **10** the sons of Ares, seven hundred and fifty-

six; **11** the sons of Phaath-Moab, of the sons of Jesus and Joab, two thousand eight hundred and twelve; **12** the sons of Elam, one thousand two hundred and fifty-four; the sons of Zathui, nine hundred and forty-five; the sons of Chorbe, seven hundred and five; the sons of Bani, six hundred and forty-eight; **13** the sons of Bebai, six hundred and twenty-three; the sons of Astad, one thousand three hundred and twenty-two; **14** the sons of Adonikam, six hundred and sixty-seven; the sons of Bagoi, two thousand and sixty-six; the sons of Adinu, four hundred and fifty-four; **15** the sons of Ater, of Ezekias, ninety-two; the sons of Kilan and Azetas, sixty-seven; the sons of Azaru, four hundred and thirty-two; **16** the sons of Annis, one hundred and one; the sons of Arom, of the sons of Bassai, three hundred and twenty-three; the sons of Arsiphurith, one hundred and twelve; **17** the sons of Baiterus, three thousand and five; the sons of Bethlomon, one hundred and twenty-three; **18** they of Netophas, fifty-five; they of Anathoth, one hundred and fifty-eight; they of Bethasmoth, forty-two; **19** they of Kariathiarius, twenty-five; they of Caphira and Beroth, seven hundred and forty-three; **20** the Chadiasai and Ammidioi, four hundred and twenty-two; they of Kirama and Gabbe, six hundred and twenty-one; **21** they of Macalon, one hundred and twenty-two; they of Betolion, fifty-two; the sons of Niphis, one hundred and fifty-six; **22** the sons of Calamolalus and Onus, seven hundred and twenty-five; the sons of Jerechu, three hundred and forty-five; **23** the sons of Sanaas, three thousand three hundred and thirty. **24** The priests: the sons of Jeddu, the son of Jesus, among the sons of Sanasib, nine hundred and seventy-two; the sons of Emmeruth, one thousand and fifty-two; **25** the sons of Phassurus, one thousand two hundred and forty-seven; the sons of Charme, one thousand and seventeen. **26** The Levites: the sons of Jesus, and Kadmiel, and Bannas, and Sudias, seventy-four. **27** The holy singers: the sons of Asaph, one hundred and twenty-eight. **28** The gatekeepers: the sons of Salum, the sons of Atar, the sons of Tolman, the sons of Dacubi, the sons of Ateta, the sons of Sabi, in all one hundred and thirty-nine. **29** The temple servants: the sons of Esau, the sons of Asipha, the sons of Tabaoth, the sons of Keras, the sons of Sua, the sons of Phaleas, the sons of Labana, the sons of Aggaba. **30** The sons of Acud, the sons of Uta, the sons of Ketab, the sons of Accaba, the sons of Subai, the sons of Anan, the sons of Cathua, the sons of Geddur, **31** the sons of Jairus, the sons of Daisan, the sons of Noeba, the sons of Chaseba, the sons of Gazera, the sons of Ozias, the sons of Phinoe, the sons of Asara, the sons of Basthai, the sons of Asana, the sons of Maani, the sons of Naphisi, the sons of Acub, the sons of Achipha, the sons of Asur, the sons of Pharakim, the sons of Basaloth, **32** the sons of Meedda, the sons of Cutha, the sons of Charea, the sons of Barchus, the sons of Serar, the sons of Thomei, the sons of Nasi, the sons of Atipha. **33** The sons of the servants of Solomon: the sons of Assaphioth, the sons of Pharida, the sons of Jeeli, the sons of Lozon, the sons of Isdael, the sons of Saphuthi, **34** the sons of Agia, the sons of Phacareth, the sons of Sabie, the sons of Sarothie, the sons of Masias, the sons of Gas, the sons of Addus, the sons of Subas, the sons of Apherra, the sons of Barodis, the sons of Saphat, the sons of Allon. **35** All the temple-servants, and the sons of the servants of Solomon, were three hundred and seventy-two. **36** These came up from Thermeleth, and Thelersas, Charaathalan leading them, and Allar; **37** and they could not show their families, nor their stock, how they were of Israel: the sons of Dalan the son of Ban, the sons of Nekodan, six hundred and fifty-two. **38** And of the priests, those who usurped the office of the priesthood and were not found: the sons of Obdia, the sons of Akkos, the sons of Jaddus, who married Augia one of the daughters of Zorzelleus, and was called after his name. **39** And when the description of the relatives of these men was sought in the register, and was not found, they were removed from executing the office of the priesthood: **40** for Nehemiah and Attharias said to them that they should not be partakers of the holy things, until there arose up a chief priest wearing Lights and Perfections. **41** So all those of Israel, from twelve years old [and upward], besides menservants and maidservants, were in [number forty] and two thousand three hundred and sixty. **42** Their menservants and handmaids were seven thousand three hundred and thirty-seven; the minstrels and singers, two hundred and forty-five; **43** four hundred and thirty-five camels, seven thousand and thirty-six horses, two hundred and forty-five mules, five thousand five hundred and twenty-five beasts of burden. **44** And certain of the chief men of their families, when they came to the temple of God that is in Jerusalem, vowed to set up the house again in its own place according to their ability, **45** and to give into the holy treasury of the works one thousand pounds of gold, five thousand of silver, and one hundred priestly vestments. **46** And the priests, and the Levites, and those who were of the people lived in Jerusalem and the country; the holy singers also, and the gatekeepers, and all Israel in their villages. **47** But when the seventh month was at hand, and when the sons of Israel were each in his own place, they all came together with one consent into the broad place before the first porch which is toward the east. **48** Then Jesus the son of Josedek arose, and his relatives the priests, and Zerubbabel the son of Salathiel, and his relatives, and they made the altar of the God of Israel ready, **49** to offer burned sacrifices on it, according as it is expressly commanded in the Scroll of Moses the man of God. **50** And certain [ones] were gathered to them out of the other nations of the land, and they erected the altar on its own place, because all the nations of the land were at enmity with them and oppressed them; and they offered sacrifices according to the time and burnt-offerings to the Lord, both morning and evening. **51** They also held the Celebration of Shelters, as it is commanded in the Law, and [offered] sacrifices daily, as was suitable; **52** and after that, the continual oblations, and the sacrifices of the Sabbaths, and of the new moons, and of all the consecrated feasts. **53** And all those who had made any vow to God began to offer sacrifices to God from the new moon of the seventh month, although the temple of God was not yet built. **54** And they gave money to the masons and carpenters, and meat and drink, **55** and carts to them of Sidon and Tyre, that they should bring cedar trees from Libanus, and transport them in floats to the haven of Joppa, according to the command which was written for them by Cyrus king of the Persians. **56** And in the second year after his coming to the temple of God at Jerusalem, in the second month, Zerubbabel the son of Salathiel, and Jesus the son of Josedek, and their relatives, and the Levitical priests, and all those who had come to Jerusalem out of the captivity commenced: **57** and they laid the foundation of the temple of God on the new moon of the second month, in the second year after they had come to Jewry and Jerusalem. **58** And they appointed the Levites from twenty years old over the works of the Lord. Then Jesus arose, and his sons and relatives, and his brother Kadmiel, and the sons of Jesus, Emadabun, and the sons of Joda the son of Iliadun, and their sons and relatives, all the Levites, started the undertaking with one accord, laboring to advance the works in the house of God. So the builders built the temple of the Lord. **59** And the priests stood arrayed in their vestments with musical instruments and trumpets, and the Levites, the sons of Asaph, with their cymbals, **60** singing songs of thanksgiving, and praising the Lord, after the order of David king of Israel. **61** And they sang aloud, praising the Lord in songs of thanksgiving, because His goodness and His glory are forever in all Israel. **62** And all the people sounded trumpets, and shouted with a loud voice, singing songs of thanksgiving to the Lord for the rearing up of the house of the Lord. **63** Also of the Levitical priests, and of the heads of their families, the ancients who had seen the former house, came to the building of this with lamentation and great weeping. **64** But many with trumpets and joy [shouted] with a loud voice, **65** insomuch that the people did not hear the trumpets for the weeping of the people; for the multitude sounded marvelously, so that it was heard far off. **66** For that reason, when the enemies of the tribe of Judah and Benjamin heard it, they came to know what that noise of trumpets should mean. **67** And they perceived that those who were of the captivity built the temple to the Lord, the God of Israel. **68** So they went to Zerubbabel and Jesus, and to the chief men of the families, and said to them, "We will build together with you. **69** For we likewise, as you, obey your Lord, and sacrifice to Him from the days of Asbasareth the king of the Assyrians, who brought us here." **70** Then Zerubbabel, and Jesus, and the chief men of the families of Israel said to them, "It is not for you to build the house to the Lord our God. **71** We ourselves alone will build to the Lord of Israel, according as Cyrus the king of the Persians has commanded us." **72** But the heathen of the land lying heavy on the inhabitants of Judea, and holding them constricted, hindered their building; **73** and by their secret plots, and popular persuasions, and commotions, hindered the finishing of the building all the time that King Cyrus lived; so they were hindered from building for the space of two years, until the reign of Darius.

CHAPTER 6

1 Now in the second year of the reign of Darius, Haggai and Zechariah, the [grand]son of Iddo, the prophets, prophesied to the Jews in Jewry and Jerusalem; in the Name of the Lord, the God of Israel, [they prophesied] to them. **2** Then Zerubbabel the son of Salathiel and Jesus the son of Josedek stood up and began to build the house of the Lord at Jerusalem, the prophets of the Lord being with them, and helping them. **3** At the same time, Sisinnes the governor of Syria and Phoenicia came to them, with Sathrabuzanes and his companions, and said to them, **4** "By whose appointment do you build this house and this roof, and perform all the other things? and who are the builders that perform these things?" **5** Nevertheless, the elders of the Jews obtained favor, because the Lord had visited the captivity; **6** and they were not hindered from building, until such time as communication was made to Darius concerning them, and his answer signified. **7** The copy of the letter which Sisinnes, governor of Syria and Phoenicia, and Sathrabuzanes, with their companions, the rulers in Syria and Phoenicia, wrote and sent to Darius: **8** "To King Darius, greetings: Let all things be known to our lord the king, that having come into the country of Judea, and having entered into the city of Jerusalem, we found in the city of Jerusalem the elders of the Jews that were of the captivity **9** building a house to the Lord, great [and] new, of hewn and costly stones, with timber laid in the walls. **10** And those works are done with great speed, and the work goes on prosperously in their hands, and it is accomplished with all glory and diligence. **11** Then we asked these elders, saying, By whose command do you build this house, and lay the foundations of these works? **12** Therefore, to the intent that we might give knowledge to you by writing who were the chief doers, we questioned them, and we required of them the names in writing of their principal men. **13** So they gave us this answer: We are the servants of the Lord which made the heavens and earth. **14** And as for this house, it was built many years ago by a great and mighty king of Israel and was completed. **15** But when our fathers sinned against the Lord of Israel, who is in Heaven, and provoked Him to wrath, He gave them over into the hands of Nebuchadnezzar king of Babylon, king of the Chaldeans; **16** and they pulled down the house, and burned it, and carried the people away [as] captives to Babylon. **17** But in the first year that Cyrus reigned over the country of Babylon, King Cyrus wrote [an edict] to build up this house. **18** And the holy vessels of gold and of silver, that Nebuchadnezzar had carried away out of the house at Jerusalem, and had set up in his own temple, those Cyrus the king brought out again out of the temple in Babylonia, and they were delivered to Zerubbabel and to Sanabassarus the governor, **19** with command that he should carry away all these vessels and put them in the temple at Jerusalem; and that the temple of the Lord should be built in its place. **20** Then Sanabassarus, having come here, laid the foundations of the house of the Lord which is in Jerusalem; and from that time to this being still a building, it is not yet fully ended. **21** Now therefore, if it seems good, O king, let search be made among the royal archives of our lord the king that are in Babylon: **22** and if it is found that the building of the house of the Lord which is in Jerusalem has been done with the consent of King Cyrus, and it seems good to our lord the king, let him signify to us thereof." **23** Then King Darius commanded to seek among the archives that were laid up at Babylon: and so at Ekbatana the palace, which is in the country of Media, there was found a scroll where these things were recorded: **24** "In the first year of the reign of Cyrus, King Cyrus commanded to build up the house of the Lord which is in Jerusalem, where they sacrifice with continual fire: **25** whose height will be sixty cubits, and the breadth sixty cubits, with three rows of hewn stones, and one row of new wood of that country; and the expenses thereof to be given out of the house of King Cyrus; **26** and that the holy vessels of the house of the Lord, both gold and silver, that Nebuchadnezzar took out of the house at Jerusalem, and carried away to Babylon, should be restored to the house at Jerusalem, and be set in the place where they were before." **27** And also, he commanded that Sisinnes the governor of Syria and Phoenicia, and Sathrabuzanes, and their companions, and those which were appointed rulers in Syria and Phoenicia, should be careful not to meddle with the place, but permit Zerubbabel, the servant of the Lord, and governor of Judea, and the elders of the Jews, to build that house of the Lord in its place. **28** "And I also command to have it built up whole again; and that they look diligently to help those that be of the captivity of Judea, until the house of the Lord is finished; [29] and that out of the tribute of Coele-Syria and Phoenicia a portion be carefully given these men for the sacrifices of the Lord, [that is,] to Zerubbabel the governor, for bullocks, and rams, and lambs; [30] and also corn, salt, wine, and oil—and that continually every year without further question, according as the priests that are in Jerusalem will signify to be daily spent, [31] that drink offerings may be made to the Most High God for the king and for his children, and that they may pray for their lives. [32] And that command [will] be given that whoever will transgress, yes, or neglect anything written here, out of his own [house] will a tree be taken, and he [will] be hanged on it, and all his goods seized for the king. [33] May the Lord therefore, whose Name is there called on, utterly destroy every king and nation that will stretch out his hand to hinder or damage that house of the Lord in Jerusalem. [34] I, Darius the king, have ordained that according to these things it [will] be done with diligence."

CHAPTER 7

[1] Then Sisinnes the governor of Coele-Syria and Phoenicia, and Sathrabuzanes, with their companions, following the commands of King Darius, [2] very carefully oversaw the holy works, assisting the elders of the Jews and rulers of the temple. [3] And so the holy works prospered, while Haggai and Zechariah the prophets prophesied. [4] And they finished these things by the command of the Lord, the God of Israel, and with the consent of Cyrus, Darius, and Artaxerxes, kings of the Persians. [5] [And so] the house was finished by the twenty-third [[or third]] day of the month Adar, in the sixth year of King Darius. [6] And the sons of Israel, the priests, and the Levites, and the others that were of the captivity, that were added [to them], did according to the things [written] in the Scroll of Moses. [7] And for the dedication of the temple of the Lord they offered one hundred bullocks, two hundred rams, [and] four hundred lambs; [8] [and also] twelve male goats for the sin of all Israel, according to the number of the twelve princes of the tribes of Israel. [9] The priests and the Levites also stood arrayed in their vestments, according to their relatives, for the services of the Lord, the God of Israel, according to the Scroll of Moses: and the gatekeepers at every gate. [10] And the sons of Israel that came out of the captivity held the Passover [on] the fourteenth day of the first month, when the priests and the Levites were sanctified together, [11] and all those who were of the captivity; for they were sanctified. For the Levites were all sanctified together, [12] and they offered the Passover for all those of the captivity, and for their relatives the priests, and for themselves. [13] And the sons of Israel that came out of the captivity ate, even all those who had separated themselves from the abominations of the heathen of the land and sought the Lord. [14] And they kept the Celebration of Unleavened Bread seven days, making merry before the Lord, [15] for that He had turned the counsel of the king of Assyria toward them, to strengthen their hands in the works of the Lord, the God of Israel.

CHAPTER 8

[1] And after these things, when Artaxerxes the king of the Persians reigned, Ezra came, the son of Seraiah, the son of Azariah, the son of Hilkiah, the son of Salem, [2] the son of Zadok, the son of Ahitob, the son of Amariah, the son of Ozias, the son of Memeroth, the son of Zerahiah, the son of Savias, the son of Boccas, the son of Abisne, the son of Phinehas, the son of Eleazar, the son of Aaron, the chief priest. [3] This Ezra went up from Babylon, as being a ready scribe in the Law of Moses that was given by the God of Israel. [4] And the king honored him, for he found grace in his sight in all his requests. [5] There also went up with him certain of the sons of Israel, and of the priests, and Levites, and holy singers, and gatekeepers, and temple servants, to Jerusalem, [6] in the seventh year of the reign of Artaxerxes, in the fifth month, this was the king's seventh year; for they went from Babylon on the new moon of the first month, and came to Jerusalem, according to the prosperous journey which the Lord gave them for His sake. [7] For Ezra had very great skill, so that he omitted nothing of the law and commands of the Lord but taught all Israel the ordinances and judgments. [8] Now the commission, which was written from Artaxerxes the king, came to Ezra the priest and reader of the Law of the Lord, of which this that follows is a copy: [9] "King Artaxerxes to Ezra the priest and reader of the Law of the Lord, greetings: [10] Having determined to deal graciously, I have given order that such of the nation of the Jews, and of the priests and Levites, and of those within our realm, as are willing and desirous, should go with you to Jerusalem. [11] Therefore, as many as have a mind [to this purpose], let them depart with you, as it has seemed good both to me and my seven friends the counselors, [12] that they may look to the affairs of Judea and Jerusalem, agreeably to that which is in the Law of the Lord, [13] and carry the gifts to the Lord of Israel to Jerusalem, which my friends and I have vowed; and that all the gold and silver that can be found in the country of Babylonia for the Lord in Jerusalem, [14] with that also which is given of the people for the temple of the Lord their God that is at Jerusalem, be collected: even the gold and silver for bullocks, rams, and lambs, and things pertaining to that, [15] to the end that they may offer sacrifices to the Lord on the altar of the Lord their God, which is in Jerusalem— [16] and whatever you and your relatives are inclined to do with gold and silver, that perform, according to the will of your God. [17] And the holy vessels of the Lord, which are given to you for the use of the temple of your God, which is in Jerusalem, [18] and anything else you will remember for the use of the temple of your God, you will give it out of the king's treasury. [19] And I, King Artaxerxes, have also commanded the keepers of the treasures in Syria and Phoenicia, that whatever Ezra the priest and reader of the Law of the Highest God will send for, they should give it to him with all diligence, [20] to the sum of one hundred talents of silver, likewise also of wheat even to one hundred measures, and one hundred firkins of wine, and salt in abundance. [21] Let all things be diligently performed after the Law of God—to the Highest God—that wrath does not come on the kingdom of the king and his sons. [22] I also command you that no tax, nor any other imposition, be laid on any of the priests, or Levites, or holy singers, or gatekeepers, or temple servants, or any that have employment in this temple, and that no man have authority to impose anything on them. [23] And you, Ezra, according to the wisdom of God, ordain judges and justices, that they may judge in all Syria and Phoenicia all those that know the law of your God; and you will teach those that do not know it. [24] And whoever will transgress the law of your God, and of the king, will be punished diligently, whether it be by death, or other punishment, by penalty of money, or by imprisonment." [25] Then Ezra the scribe said, "Blessed is the only Lord, the God of my fathers, who has put these things into the heart of the king, to glorify His house that is in Jerusalem, [26] and has honored me in the sight of the king, and his counselors, and all his friends and nobles. [27] Therefore, I was encouraged by the help of the Lord my God and gathered together out of Israel men to go up with me. [28] And these are the chiefs, according to their families and the several divisions thereof, that went up with me from Babylon in the reign of King Artaxerxes: [29] of the sons of Phinehas, Gerson; of the sons of Ithamar, Gamael; of the sons of David, Attus the son of Sechenias; [30] of the sons of Phoros, Zechariah, and with him were counted one hundred and fifty men; [31] of the sons of Phaath-Moab, Eliehoenai the son of Zerahiah, and with him two hundred men; [32] of the sons of Zathoes, Sechenias the son of Jezelus, and with him three hundred men; of the sons of Adin, Obeth the son of Jonathan, and with him two hundred and fifty men; [33] of the sons of Elam, Jesias son of Gotholia, and with him seventy men; [34] of the sons of Saphatias, Zerahiah son of Michael, and with him seventy men; [35] of the sons of Joab, Obadiah son of Jehiel, and with him two hundred and twelve men; [36] of the sons of Banias, Salimoth son of Josaphias, and with him one hundred and sixty men; [37] of the sons of Babi, Zechariah son of Bebai, and with him twenty-eight men; [38] of the sons of Azgad, Joannes son of Hakkatan, and with him one hundred and ten men; [39] of the sons of Adonikam, the last, and these are the names of them— Eliphalat, Jeuel, and Shemaiah, and with them seventy men; [40] of the sons of Bigvai, Uthi the son of Istalcurus, and with him seventy men. [41] And I gathered them together to the river called Theras; and there we pitched our tents three days, and I surveyed them. [42] But when I had found there none of the priests and Levites, [43] then I sent to Eleazar, and Iduel, and Maasmas, [44] and Elnathan, and Samaias, and [Jarib], Nathan, Ennatan, Zechariah, and Mosollamus, principal men and men of understanding. [45] And I commanded those who should go to [Iddo], Loddeus the captain, who was in the place of [Casiphia], the treasury; [46] and I commanded them that they

should speak to Loddeus, and to his relatives, and to the treasurers in that place, to send us such men as might execute the priests' office in the house of our Lord. 47 And by the mighty hand of our Lord they brought to us men of understanding of the sons of Mooli the son of Levi, the son of Israel, Asebebias, and his sons, and his relatives, who were eighteen, 48 and Asebias, and Annuus, and Osaias his brother, of the sons of Chanuneus, and their sons were twenty men; 49 and of the temple-servants whom David and the principal men had appointed for the servants of the Levites, two hundred and twenty temple-servants, the catalogue of all their names was shown. 50 And there I vowed a fast for the young men before our Lord, to desire of Him a prosperous journey both for us and for our children, and [for the] cattle that were with us: 51 for I was ashamed to ask of the king footmen, and horsemen, and conduct for protection against our adversaries. 52 For we had said to the king that the power of our Lord would be with those who seek Him, to support them in all ways. 53 And again we implored our Lord as touching these things and found Him favorable [to us]. 54 Then I separated twelve men of the chiefs of the priests: Eserebias, and Assamias, and ten men of their relatives with them; 55 and I weighed them the silver, and the gold, and the holy vessels of the house of our Lord, which the king, and his counselors, and the nobles, and all Israel, had given. 56 And when I had weighed it, I delivered to them six hundred and fifty talents of silver, and silver vessels of one hundred talents, and one hundred talents of gold, 57 and twenty golden vessels, and twelve vessels of brass, even of fine brass, glittering like gold. 58 And I said to them, "You are holy to the Lord and the vessels are holy—both—and the gold and the silver are a vow to the Lord, the Lord of our fathers. 59 Watch and keep them until you deliver them to the chiefs of the priests and Levites, and to the principal men of the families of Israel, in Jerusalem, in the chambers of the house of our Lord." 60 So the priests and the Levites, who received the silver, and the gold, and the vessels which were in Jerusalem, brought them into the temple of the Lord. 61 And from the River Theras we departed [on] the twelfth day of the first month, until we came to Jerusalem, by the mighty hand of our Lord which was on us: and the Lord delivered us from [assault by] the way, from every enemy, and so we came to Jerusalem. 62 And when we had been there three days, the silver and gold was weighed and delivered in the house of our Lord on the fourth day to Marmoth the priest, the son of Urias. 63 And with him was Eleazar the son of Phinehas, and with them were Josabdus the son of Jesus and Moeth the son of Sabannus, the Levites: all [was delivered to them] by number and weight. 64 And all the weight of them was written up the same hour. 65 Moreover, those who had come out of the captivity offered sacrifices to the Lord, the God of Israel, even twelve bullocks for all Israel, [and] ninety-six rams, 66 seventy-two lambs, goats for a peace offering—twelve; all of them a sacrifice to the Lord. 67 And they delivered the king's commands to the king's stewards, and to the governors of Coele-Syria and Phoenicia; and they honored the people and the temple of the Lord. 68 Now when these things were done, the principal men came to me, and said, 69 "The nation of Israel, and the princes, and the priests, and the Levites, have not put away the strange people of the land, nor the uncleanness of the nations—of the Canaanites, Hittites, Perizzites, Jebusites, and the Moabites, Egyptians, and Edomites. 70 For both they and their sons have married with their daughters, and the holy seed is mixed with the strange people of the land; and from the beginning of this matter the rulers and the nobles have been partakers of this iniquity." 71 And as soon as I had heard these things, I tore my clothes and my holy garment, and plucked the hair from off my head and beard, and sat myself down sad and full of heaviness. 72 So all those who were moved at the word of the Lord, the God of Israel, assembled to me, while I mourned for the iniquity, but I sat still full of heaviness until the evening sacrifice. 73 Then rising up from the fast with my clothes and my holy garment torn, and bowing my knees, and stretching out my hands to the Lord, 74 I said, "O Lord, I am ashamed and confounded before Your face, 75 for our sins are multiplied above our heads, and our errors have reached up to Heaven, 76 ever since the time of our fathers; and we are in great sin, even to this day. 77 And for our sins and our fathers' we with our relatives, and our kings, and our priests were given up to the kings of the earth, to the sword, and to captivity, and for a prey with shame, to this day. 78 And now in some measure mercy has been shown to us from You, O Lord, that a root and a name should be left for us in the place of Your sanctuary, 79 and to discover a light for us in the house of the Lord our God, and to give us food in the time of our servitude. 80 Yes, when we were in bondage, we were not forsaken of our Lord, but He made us gracious before the kings of Persia, so that they gave us food, 81 and glorified the temple of our Lord, and raised up the desolate Zion, to give us a sure dwelling in Jewry and Jerusalem. 82 And now, O Lord, what will we say, having these things? For we have transgressed Your commands, which You gave by the hand of Your servants the prophets, saying, 83 The land, which you enter into to possess as a heritage, is a land polluted with the pollutions of the strangers of the land, and they have filled it with their uncleanness. 84 Therefore now, you will not join your daughters to their sons, neither will you take their daughters to your sons, 85 neither will you seek to have peace with them forever, that you may be strong, and eat the good things of the land, and that you may leave it for an inheritance to your children forevermore. 86 And all that has befallen [us] is done to us for our wicked works and great sins, for You, O Lord, made our sins light, 87 and gave to us such a root, [but] we have turned back again to transgress Your law, in mingling ourselves with the uncleanness of the heathen of the land. 88 You were not angry with us to destroy us, until You had left us neither root, seed, nor name. 89 O Lord of Israel, You are true, for we are left a root to this day. 90 Behold, now we are before You in our iniquities, for we cannot stand any longer before You by reason of these things." 91 And as Ezra made his confession in his prayer, weeping and lying flat on the ground before the temple, there gathered to him from Jerusalem a very great crowd of men, and women, and children, for there was great weeping among the multitude. 92 Then Jehoiachin the son of Jeelus, one of the sons of Israel, called out, and said, "O Ezra, we have sinned against the Lord God, we have married strange women of the heathen of the land, and now is all Israel aloft. 93 Let us make an oath to the Lord herein, that we will put away all our wives, which [we have taken] of the strangers, with their children, 94 like as seems good to you, and to as many as obey the Law of the Lord. 95 Arise and execute this, for this matter pertains to you, and we will be with you to do valiantly." 96 So Ezra arose, and took an oath of the chief of the priests and Levites of all Israel to do after these things; and [so] they swore.

CHAPTER 9

1 Then Ezra, rising from the court of the temple, went to the chamber of Jonas the son of Eliasib, 2 and lodged there, and ate no bread nor drank water, mourning for the great iniquities of the multitude. 3 And there was made proclamation in all Jewry and Jerusalem to all those who were of the captivity, that they should be gathered together at Jerusalem, 4 and that whoever did not meet there within two or three days, according as the elders that bore rule appointed, their cattle should be seized to the use of the temple, and himself cast out from the multitude of those who were of the captivity. 5 And in three days all those of the tribe of Judah and Benjamin were gathered together at Jerusalem: this was the ninth month, on the twentieth day of the month. 6 And all the multitude sat together trembling in the broad place before the temple because of the present foul weather. 7 So Ezra arose and said to them, "You have transgressed the Law and married strange wives to increase the sins of Israel. 8 And now make confession and give glory to the Lord, the God of our fathers, 9 and do His will, and separate yourselves from the heathen of the land, and from the strange women." 10 Then the whole multitude cried, and said with a loud voice, "Just as you have spoken, so we will do. 11 But forasmuch as the multitude is great, and it is foul weather, so that we cannot stand outside, this indeed is not a work of one day or two, seeing our sin in these things is spread far: 12 therefore, let the rulers of the multitude stay, and let all those of our habitations that have strange wives come at the time appointed, 13 and with them the rulers and judges of every place, until we turn the wrath of the Lord away from us for this matter." 14 [Then] Jonathan the son of Azael and Ezekias the son of Thocanus took the matter on them accordingly; and Mosollamus, and Levis, and Sabbateus were assessors to them. 15 And those who were of the captivity did according to all these things. 16 And Ezra the priest chose principal men for himself of their families, all by name: and on the new moon of the tenth month, they were shut in together to examine the matter. 17 So their cause that held strange wives was brought to an end by the new moon of the first month. 18 And there

were found of the priests that had come together and had strange wives, **19** of the sons of Jesus the son of Josedek, and his relatives: Mathelas, and Eleazar, and Joribus, and Joadanus. **20** And they gave their hands to put away their wives, and to [offer] rams to make reconciliation for their error. **21** And of the sons of Emmer: Ananias, and Zabdeus, and Manes, and Sameus, and Hiereel, and Azariah. **22** And of the sons of Phaisur: Elionas, Massias, Ishmael, and Nathanael, and Ocidelus, and Saloas. **23** And of the Levites: Jozabdus, and Semeis, and Colius, who was called Calitas, and Patheus, and Judas, and Jonas. **24** Of the holy singers: Eliasibus [and] Bacchurus. **25** Of the gatekeepers: Sallumus and tolbanes. **26** Of Israel, of the sons of Phoros: Hiermas, and Ieddias, and Melchias, and Maelus, and Eleazar, and Asibas, and Banneas. **27** Of the sons of Ela: Matthanias, Zechariah, and Jezrielus, and Oabdius, and Hieremoth, and Aedias. **28** And of the sons of Zamoth: Eliadas, Eliasimus, Othonias, Jarimoth, and Sabathus, and Zardeus. **29** Of the sons of Bebai: Joannes, and Ananias, and Jozabdus, and Ematheis. **30** Of the sons of Mani: Olamus, Mamuchus, Jedeus, Jasubas, and Jasaelus, and Hieremoth. **31** And of the sons of Addi: Naathus, and Moossias, Laccunus, and Naidus, and Matthanias, and Sesthel, Balnuus, and Manasseas. **32** And of the sons of Annas: Elionas, and Aseas, and Melchias, and Sabbeus, and Simon Chosameus. **33** And of the sons of Asom: Maltanneus, and Mattathias, and Sabanneus, Eliphalat, and Manasseh, and Semei. **34** And of the sons of Baani: Jeremias, Momdis, Ismaerus, Juel, Mamdai, and Pedias, and Anos, Carabasion, and Enasibus, and Mamnitamenus, Eliasis, Bannus, Eliali, someis, Selemias, Nathanias. And of the sons of Ezora: Sesis, Ezril, Azaelus, Samatus, Zambri, Josephus. **35** And of the sons of Nooma: Mazitias, Zabadeas, Edos, Juel, Banaias. **36** All these had taken strange wives, and they put them away with their children. **37** And the priests and Levites, and those who were of Israel, lived in Jerusalem, and in the country, on the new moon of the seventh month, and the sons of Israel in their habitations. **38** And the whole multitude were gathered together with one accord into the broad place before the porch of the temple toward the east; **39** and they said to Ezra the priest and reader, "Bring the Law of Moses, that was given of the Lord, the God of Israel." **40** So Ezra the chief priest brought the Law to the whole multitude of both men and women, and to all the priests, to hear the Law on the new moon of the seventh month. **41** And he read in the broad place before the porch of the temple from morning to midday, before both men and women; and all the multitude gave heed to the Law. **42** And Ezra the priest and reader of the Law stood up on the pulpit of wood, which was made [for that purpose]. **43** And there stood up by him Mattathias, Sammus, Ananias, Azariah, Urias, Ezekias, Ba'alsamus, on the right hand; **44** and on his left hand: Phaldeus, Misael, Melchias, Lothasubus, Nabarias, [and] Zechariah. **45** Then Ezra took the Scroll of the Law before the multitude and sat honorably in the first place before all. **46** And when he opened the Law, they all stood straight up. So Ezra blessed the Lord God Most High, the God of armies, Almighty. **47** And all the people answered, "Amen"; and lifting up their hands they fell to the ground and worshiped the Lord. **48** Also Jesus, Annus, Sarabias, Iadinus, Jacubus, Sabateus, Auteas, Maiannas, and Calitas, Azariah, and Jozabdus, and Ananias, Phalias, the Levites, taught the Law of the Lord, and read the Law of the Lord to the multitude, in addition, making them to understand it. **49** Then Attharates said to Ezra the chief priest and reader, and to the Levites that taught the multitude, even to all, **50** "This day is holy to the Lord"—now they all wept when they heard the Law— **51** "go then, and eat the fat, and drink the sweet, and send portions to those who have nothing, **52** for the day is holy to the Lord; and do not be sorrowful, for the Lord will bring you to honor." **53** So the Levites published all things to the people, saying, "This day is holy; do not be sorrowful." **54** Then they went their way, everyone to eat, and drink, and make merry, and to give portions to those who had nothing, and to make great cheer, **55** because they understood the words wherein they were instructed, and for which they had been assembled.

2 ESDRAS

Otherwise known as 4 Esdras

2 Esdras (also called 4 Esdras, Latin Esdras, or Latin Ezra) is the name of an apocalyptic book in many English versions of the Bible. Its authorship is ascribed to Ezra, a scribe and priest of the 5th century BC, although modern scholarship places its composition between 70 and 218 AD. It is reckoned among the apocrypha by Roman Catholics, Protestants, and most Eastern Orthodox Christians. Although 2 Esdras was preserved in Latin as an appendix to the Vulgate and passed down as a unified book, it is generally considered to be a tripartite work.

CHAPTER 1

1 The second scroll of the prophet Ezra, the son of Saraias, the son of Azariah, the son of Hilkiah, the son of Salemas, the son of Zadok, the son of Ahitob, **2** the son of Achias, the son of Phinehas, the son of Eli, the son of Amariah, the son of Aziei, the son of Marimoth, the son of Arna, the son of Ozias, the son of Borith, the son of Abissei, the son of Phinehas, the son of Eleazar, **3** the son of Aaron, of the tribe of Levi, which was captive in the land of the Medes, in the reign of Artaxerxes king of the Persians. **4** And the word of the Lord came to me, saying, **5** "Go your way, and show My people their sinful deeds, and their children their wickedness which they have done against Me, that they may tell their children's children, **6** because the sins of their fathers are increased in them, for they have forgotten Me, and have done sacrifice to strange gods. **7** Did I not bring them out of the land of Egypt, out of the house of bondage? but they have provoked Me to wrath and have despised My counsels. **8** Shake then the hair of your head, and cast all evils on them, for they have not been obedient to My law, but it is a rebellious people. **9** How long will I forbear them, to whom I have done so much good? **10** I have overthrown many kings for their sakes; I have struck down Pharaoh with his servants and all his army. **11** I have destroyed all the nations before them, and in the east, I have scattered the people of two provinces, even of Tyre and Sidon, and have slain all their adversaries. **12** Therefore, speak to them, saying, **13** The Lord says, Of a truth I brought you through the sea, and where there was no path I made highways for you; I gave you Moses for a leader, and Aaron for a priest. **14** I gave you light in a pillar of fire, and I have done great wonders among you; yet you have forgotten Me, says the Lord." **15** The Lord Almighty says, "The quails were for a token to you; I gave you a camp for your protection, nevertheless you murmured there: **16** and you did not triumph in My Name for the destruction of your enemies, but ever to this day you yet murmur. **17** Where are the benefits that I have done for you? When you were hungry and thirsty in the wilderness, did you not cry to Me, **18** saying, Why have You brought us into this wilderness to kill us? It had been better for us to have served the Egyptians, than to die in this wilderness. **19** I had pity on your mourning and gave you manna for food; you ate messengers' bread. **20** When you were thirsty, did I not cleave the rock, and waters flowed out to your fill? for the heat I covered you with the leaves of the trees. **21** I divided fruitful lands among you; I cast out the Canaanites, the Perizzites, and the Philistines, before you: what will I yet do more for you?" Says the Lord. **22** The Lord Almighty says, "When you were in the wilderness, at the bitter river, being thirsty, and blaspheming My Name, **23** I did not give you fire for your blasphemies, but cast a tree in the water, and made the river sweet. **24** What will I do to you, O Jacob? You, Judah, would not obey Me: I will turn Myself to other nations, and I will give My Name to them, that they may keep my statutes. **25** Seeing you have forsaken Me, I will also forsake you; when you ask me to be merciful to you, I will have no mercy on you. **26** Whenever you will call on Me, I will not hear you, for you have defiled your hands with blood, and your feet are swift to commit manslaughter. **27** You have not as it were forsaken Me, but your own selves," says the Lord. **28** The Lord Almighty says, "Have I not pleaded with you as a father his sons, as a mother her daughters, and a nurse her young babies, **29** that you would be My people, and I should be your God; that you would be My children, and I should be your Father? **30** I gathered you together, as a hen [gathers] her chickens under her wings, but now, what will I do to you? I will cast you out from My presence. **31** When you offer oblations to Me, I will turn My face from you, for your solemn feast days, your new moons, and your circumcisions of the flesh, I have rejected. **32** I sent My servants the prophets to you, whom you have taken and slain, and torn their bodies in pieces, whose blood I will require [of your hands]," says the Lord. **33** The Lord Almighty says, "Your house is desolate, I will cast you out as the wind does stubble. **34** And your children will not be fruitful; for they have neglected My command to you and done that which is evil before Me. **35** I will give your houses to a people that will come, which having not heard of Me, yet believe Me; they to whom I have showed no signs will do that which I have commanded. **36** They have seen no prophets, yet they will call their former estate to remembrance. **37** I take to witness the grace of the people that will come, whose little ones rejoice with gladness: and though they do not see Me with bodily eyes, yet in spirit they will believe the thing that I say. **38** And now, O father, behold with glory; and see the people that come from the east, **39** to whom I will give for leaders: Abraham, Isaac, and Jacob, Hosea, Amos, and Micah, Joel, Obadiah, and Jonah, **40** Nahum, and Habakkuk, Zephaniah, Haggai, Zechariah, and Malachi, which is also called the Messenger of the Lord."

CHAPTER 2

1 The Lord says, "I brought this people out of bondage, and I gave them My commands by My servants the prophets; whom they would not hear but set My counsels at nothing. **2** The mother that bears them says to them, Go your way, O my children; for I am a widow and forsaken. **3** I brought you up with gladness, and with sorrow and heaviness I have lost you; for you have sinned before the Lord God and done that which is evil before me. **4** But what will I now do to you? For I am a widow and forsaken: go your way, O my children, and ask mercy of the Lord. **5** As for Me, O father, I call on you for a witness over the mother of [these] children, because they would not keep My covenant, **6** that you bring them to confusion, and their mother to a plunder, that there may be no offspring of them. **7** Let them be scattered abroad among the heathen, let their names be blotted out of the earth; for they have despised My covenant. **8** Woe to you, Asshur, you that hide the unrighteous with you! O you wicked nation, remember what I did to Sodom and Gomorrah, **9** whose land lies in clods of pitch and heaps of ashes: even so I will also do to those who have not listened to Me," says the Lord Almighty. **10** The Lord says to Ezra, "Tell My people that I will give them the kingdom of Jerusalem, which I would have given to Israel. **11** I will also take their glory, and give these the continuous dwelling places, which I had prepared for them. **12** They will have the Tree of Life for an ointment of sweet savor; they will neither labor, nor be weary. **13** Ask, and you will receive: pray for few days for you, that they may be shortened: the kingdom is already prepared for you: watch. **14** Take the heavens and earth to witness, take them to witness; for I have given up the evil, and created the good; for I live," says the Lord. **15** "Mother, embrace your children; I will bring them out with gladness like a dove; establish their feet; for I have chosen you," says the Lord. **16** "And I will raise those who are dead up again from their places and bring them out from their tombs; for I have known My Name in them. **17** Do not be afraid, you mother of the children, for I have chosen you," says the Lord. **18** "For your help I will send My servants Isaiah and Jeremiah, after whose counsel I have sanctified and prepared for you twelve trees laden with various fruits, **19** and as many springs flowing with milk and honey, and seven mighty mountains, after which there grow roses and lilies, whereby I will fill your children with joy. **20** Do right to the widow, judge the fatherless, give to the poor, defend the orphan, clothe the naked, **21** heal the broken and the weak, do not laugh a lame man to scorn, defend the maimed, and let the blind man come to the sight of My glory. **22** Keep the old and young within your walls. **23** Wherever you find the dead, set a sign on them and commit them to the grave, and I will give you the first place in My resurrection. **24** Stay still, O My people, and take your rest, for your quietness will come. **25** Nourish your children, O you good nurse, and establish their feet. **26** As for the servants whom I have given you, not one of them will perish, for I will require them from among your number. **27** Do not be careful excessively, for when the day of suffering and anguish comes, others will weep and be sorrowful, but you will be merry and have abundance. **28** The nations will envy you, but they will be able to do nothing against you," says the Lord. **29** "My hands will cover you, so that your children do not see Gehenna. **30** Be joyful, O you mother, with your children; for I will deliver you," says the Lord. **31** "Remember your children that sleep, for I will bring them out of the secret places of the earth and show mercy to them, for I am merciful," says the Lord Almighty. **32** "Embrace

your children until I come and proclaim mercy to them, for My wells run over, and My grace will not fail." **33** I, Ezra, received a charge from the Lord on Mount Horeb, that I should go to Israel; but when I came to them, they would have none of me, and rejected the command of the Lord. **34** And therefore I say to you, O you nations that hear and understand: look for your Shepherd; He will give you continuous rest; for He is near at hand who will come in the end of the world. **35** Be ready to the rewards of the kingdom, for the continuous light will shine on you forevermore. **36** Flee the shadow of this world, receive the joyfulness of your glory: I call to witness my Savior openly. **37** O receive that which is given to you of the Lord, and be joyful, giving thanks to Him that has called you to heavenly kingdoms. **38** Arise, and stand, and behold the number of those that are sealed in the celebration of the Lord; **39** those who withdrew themselves from the shadow of the world have received glorious garments of the Lord. **40** Look on your number, O Zion, and make up the reckoning of those of you that are clothed in white, which have fulfilled the Law of the Lord. **41** The number of your children, whom you long for, is fulfilled: implore the power of the Lord, that your people, which have been called from the beginning, may be hallowed. **42** I, Ezra, saw on Mount Zion a great multitude, whom I could not number, and they all praised the Lord with songs. **43** And in the midst of them there was a young Man of a high stature, taller than all the rest, and on each of their heads He set crowns and was more exalted. I marveled greatly at this. **44** So I asked the Messenger, and said, "What are these, my Lord?" **45** He answered and said to me, "These are those who have put off the mortal clothing, and put on the immortal, and have confessed the Name of God: now they are crowned, and receive palms." **46** Then I said to the Messenger, "What young Man is He that sets crowns on them, and gives them palms in their hands?" **47** So He answered and said to me, "It is the Son of God, whom they have confessed in the world." Then I began to greatly commend those who stood so stiffly for the Name of the Lord. **48** Then the Messenger said to me, "Go your way, and tell My people what manner of things, and how great wonders of the Lord God you have seen."

CHAPTER 3

1 In the thirty years after the ruin of the city, I, Salathiel (also called Ezra), was in Babylon, and lay troubled on my bed, and my thoughts came up over my heart: **2** for I saw the desolation of Zion, and the wealth of those who lived at Babylon. **3** And my spirit was severely moved, so that I began to speak words full of fear to the Highest, and said, **4** "O Lord that bears rule, did You not speak at the beginning, when You fashioned the earth, and that Yourself alone, and commanded the dust? **5** And it gave You Adam, a body without a soul? yet it was the workmanship of Your hands, and You breathed into him the breath of life, and he was made living before You. **6** And You led him into paradise, which Your right hand planted, before the earth ever came forward. **7** And You gave to him Your one command, which he transgressed, and immediately You appointed death for him and in his generations; and there were born of him nations and tribes, peoples and relatives, out of number. **8** And every nation walked after their own will, and did ungodly things before You, and despised [Your commands, and] You did not forbid them. **9** Nevertheless, again in [the] process of time You brought the flood on those that lived in the world and destroyed them. **10** And it came to pass, that the same fortune befell them; like as death was to Adam, so was the flood to these. **11** Nevertheless, one of them You left—Noah with his household, [even] all the righteous men [that came] of him. **12** And it came to pass, that when those who lived on the earth began to multiply, they also multiplied children, and peoples, and many nations, and again began to be more ungodly than the first. **13** And it came to pass, when they did wickedly before You, You chose one from among them, whose name was Abraham; **14** and You loved him, and only to him did You show the end of the times secretly by night, **15** and made a perpetual covenant with him, promising him that You would never forsake his seed. **16** And to him You gave Isaac, and to Isaac You gave Jacob and Esau. And You set Jacob apart for Yourself, but put [him] by Esau: and Jacob became a great multitude. **17** And it came to pass, that when You led his seed out of Egypt, You brought them up to Mount Sinai. **18** You also bowed the heavens, and shook the earth, and moved the whole world, and made the depths to tremble, and troubled the [course of that] age. **19** And Your glory went through four gates: of fire, and of earthquake, and of wind, and of cold, that You might give the Law to the seed of Jacob, and the command to the generation of Israel. ²⁰ And yet You did not take away from them [their] wicked heart, that Your law might bring out fruit in them. ²¹ For the first Adam bearing a wicked heart transgressed, and was overcome; [and not only him,] but also all of them that are born of him. ²² Therefore disease was made permanent; and the Law was in the heart of the people along with the wickedness of the root; so the good departed away, and that which was wicked dwelt still. ²³ So the times passed away, and the years were brought to an end: then You raised up a servant, called David, ²⁴ whom You commanded to build a city to Your Name, and to offer oblations to You therein of Your own. ²⁵ When this was done [for] many years, then those who inhabited the city did evil, ²⁶ in all things doing even as Adam and all his generations had done; for they also bore a wicked heart: ²⁷ and so You gave Your city over into the hands of Your enemies. ²⁸ And then I said in my heart, Are their deeds any better that inhabit Babylon? and does she therefore have dominion over Zion? ²⁹ For it came to pass when I came here, that I also saw impieties without number, and my soul saw many evildoers in this thirtieth year, so that my heart failed me. ³⁰ For I have seen how You permit them sinning, and have spared the ungodly doers, and have destroyed Your people, and have preserved Your enemies; and You have not signified to any how Your way may be comprehended. ³¹ Are the deeds of Babylon better than those of Zion? ³² Or is there any other nation that knows You besides Israel? or what tribes have so believed Your covenants as these [tribes of] Jacob? ³³ And yet their reward does not appear, and their labor has no fruit, for I have gone here and there through the nations, and I see that they abound [in wealth, and] do not think on Your commands. ³⁴ Therefore, weigh our iniquities in the balance now, and also theirs that dwell in the world, and so it will be found which way the scale inclines. ³⁵ Or when was it that they which dwell on the earth have not sinned in Your sight? or what nation has so kept Your commands? ³⁶ You will find that men [who may be reckoned] by name have kept Your precepts; but nations You will not find."

CHAPTER 4

¹ And the messenger that was sent to me, whose name was Uriel, gave me an answer, ² and said to me, "Your heart has utterly failed you in [regard to] this world, and do you think to comprehend the way of the Highest?" ³ Then I said, "Yes my Lord." And he answered me, and said, "I have been sent to show you three ways, and to set out three similitudes before you: ⁴ of which if you can declare me one, I also will show you the way that you desire to see, and I will teach you why the heart is wicked." ⁵ And I said, "Speak, my Lord." Then he said to me, "Go forth, weigh me a weight of fire, or measure me a measure of wind, or call me again the day that is past." ⁶ Then I answered and said, "Who of the sons [of men] is able to do this, that you should ask me of such things?" ⁷ And he said to me, "If I had asked you, saying, How many dwellings are there in the heart of the sea? Or how many springs are there at the fountain head of the deep? Or how many ways are above the expanse? Or which are the exits of Hades? Or which are the paths of paradise? ⁸ Perhaps you would say to me, I never went down into the deep, nor as yet into Hades, neither did I ever climb up into Heaven. ⁹ Nevertheless, now I have asked you but only of the fire and wind, and of the day, things you have experienced, and without which you cannot be, and yet you have given me no answer about them." ¹⁰ Moreover, he said to me, "Your own things, that are grown up with you, you cannot know; ¹¹ how then can you comprehend the way of the Highest? And how can he that is already worn out with the corrupted world understand incorruption?" ¹² And when I heard these things I fell on my face, and said to him, "It would be better that we were not here at all, than that we should come here and live in the midst of ungodliness, and suffer, and not know why." ¹³ He answered me, and said, "The woods of the trees of the field went out, and took counsel together, ¹⁴ and said, Come! Let us go and make war against the sea, that it may depart away before us, and that we may make ourselves more woods. ¹⁵ The waves of the sea also in like manner took counsel together, and said, Come! Let us go up and subdue the wood of the plain, that we may make ourselves another country there also. ¹⁶ The counsel of the wood was in vain, for the fire came and consumed it; ¹⁷ likewise also, the counsel of

the waves of the sea, for the sand stood up and stopped them. ¹⁸ If you were judge now between these two, whom would you justify, or whom condemn?" ¹⁹ I answered and said, "It is a foolish counsel that they both have taken, for the ground is given to the wood, and the place of the sea [is given] to bear his waves." ²⁰ Then he answered me, and said, "You have given a right judgment, and why do you not judge in your own case? ²¹ For just as the ground is given to the wood, and the sea to his waves, even so those who dwell on the earth may understand nothing but that which is on the earth: and he [only that dwells] above the heavens [may understand the] things that are above the height of the heavens." ²² Then I answered and said, "I implore you, O Lord, why is the power of understanding given to me? ²³ For it was not in my mind to be curious of the ways above, but of such things as pass by us daily, because Israel is given up as a reproach to the heathen, and the people whom you have loved is given over to ungodly nations, and the Law of our forefathers is made of no effect, and the written covenants are nowhere [regarded], ²⁴ and we pass away out of the world as grasshoppers, and our life is as a vapor, neither are we worthy to obtain mercy. ²⁵ What will He then do for His Name whereby we are called? Of these things have I asked." ²⁶ Then he answered me, and said, "If you are [alive] you will see, and if you live long, you will marvel, for the world hastens quickly to pass away. ²⁷ For it is not able to bear the things that are promised to the righteous in the times [to come], for this world is full of sadness and infirmities. ²⁸ For the evil of which you asked me is sown, but the gathering thereof has not yet come. ²⁹ If, therefore, that which is sown has not reaped, and if the place where the evil is sown has not passed away, there cannot come the field where the good is sown. ³⁰ For a grain of evil seed was sown in the heart of Adam from the beginning, and how much wickedness has it brought out to this time! And how much will it yet bring out until the time of threshing comes! ³¹ Now ponder [this] by yourself: how great a fruit of wickedness a grain of evil seed has brought out. ³² When the ears which are without number will be sown, how great a floor they will fill!" ³³ Then I answered and said, "How long? And when will these things come to pass? Why are our years few and evil?" ³⁴ And he answered me, and said, "You do not hasten more than the Highest, for your haste is for your own self, but He that is above hastens on behalf of many. ³⁵ Did the souls of the righteous not ask questions of these things in their chambers, saying, How long are we here? When does the fruit of the threshing time of our reward come?" ³⁶ And to them Jeremiel the chief-messenger gave answer, and said, "When the number is fulfilled of those who are like to you. For He has weighed the world in the balance; ³⁷ and by measure He has measured the times, and by number He has counted the seasons; and He will not move nor stir them until the said measure is fulfilled." ³⁸ Then I answered and said, "O Lord that bears rule, yet even we are all full of impiety: ³⁹ and for our sakes perhaps it is that the threshing time of the righteous is kept back, because of the sins of those who dwell on the earth." ⁴⁰ So he answered me, and said, "Go your way to a woman with child, and ask of her when she has fulfilled her nine months, if her womb may keep the birth any longer within her." ⁴¹ Then I said, "No, Lord, that it cannot." And he said to me, "In the grave the chambers of souls are like the womb: ⁴² for like as a woman that travails hurries to escape the anguish of the travail, even so do these places hasten to deliver those things that are committed to them from the beginning. ⁴³ Then it will be shown to you concerning those things which you desire to see." ⁴⁴ Then I answered and said, "If I have found favor in your sight, and if it is possible, and if I am therefore suitable, ⁴⁵ show me this also, whether there are more to come than are past, or whether the greater part has [already] gone over us. ⁴⁶ For what is gone I know, but what is still to come I do not know." ⁴⁷ And he said to me, "Stand up on the right side, and I will expound the similitude to you." ⁴⁸ So I stood, and saw, and behold, a hot burning oven passed by before me: and it happened, that when the flame was gone by, I looked, and behold, the smoke remained still. ⁴⁹ After this there passed by before me a watery cloud and it sent down much rain with a storm; and when the stormy rain was past, the drops remained therein still. ⁵⁰ Then he said to me, "Consider with yourself; as the rain is more than the drops, and the fire is greater than the smoke, so the quantity which is past did exceed more; but the drops and the smoke remained still." ⁵¹ Then I prayed, and said, "Will I live until that time? Or who will be alive in those days?" ⁵² He answered me, and said, "As for the signs of which you asked me, I may tell you of them in part, but as touching your life, I am not sent to show you; for I do not know it."

CHAPTER 5

¹ "Nevertheless, as concerning the signs, behold, the days will come, that they which dwell on earth will be taken with great amazement, and the way of truth will be hidden, and the land will be barren of faith. ² But iniquity will be increased above that which you now see, or that you have heard of long ago. ³ And the land, that you now see to have rule, will be waste and untrodden, and men will see it desolate. ⁴ But if the Most High grants you to live, you will see that which is after the third [kingdom] to be troubled; and the sun will suddenly shine out in the night, and the moon in the day; ⁵ and blood will drop out of wood, and the stone will give his voice, and the peoples will be troubled; and their goings will be changed; ⁶ and he will rule, whom those who dwell on the earth do not look for, and the birds will take their flight away together; ⁷ and the Sodomite sea will cast out fish, and make a noise in the night, which many have not known, but all will hear the voice thereof. ⁸ There will also be chaos in many places, and the fire will often be sent out, and the wild beasts will change their places, and women will bring out monsters; ⁹ and salt waters will be found in the sweet, and all friends will destroy one another; then sense will hide itself, and understanding withdraw itself into its chamber; ¹⁰ and it will be sought of [by] many, and will not be found; and unrighteousness and incontinency will be multiplied on earth. ¹¹ One land will also ask another, and say, Has righteousness—has a man that does righteousness—gone through you? And it will say, No. ¹² And it will come to pass at that time that men will hope, but will not obtain: they will labor, but their ways will not prosper. ¹³ To show you such signs I have [taken] leave; and if you will pray again, and weep as now, and fast [for] seven days, you will hear yet greater things than these." ¹⁴ Then I awoke, and an extreme trembling went through my body, and my mind was troubled, so that it fainted. ¹⁵ So the messenger that had come to talk with me held me, comforted me, and set me up on my feet. ¹⁶ And in the second night it came to pass, that Phaltiel the captain of the people came to me, saying, "Where have you been? And why is your countenance sad? ¹⁷ Or do you not know that Israel is committed to you in the land of their captivity? ¹⁸ Get up then, and eat some bread, and do not forsake us, as the shepherd [that leaves the flock] in the hands of cruel wolves." ¹⁹ Then I said to him, "Go your ways from me, and do not come near me for seven days, and then you will come to me." And he heard what I said and went from me. ²⁰ And so I fasted seven days, mourning and weeping, just as Uriel the messenger commanded me. ²¹ And after seven days, so it was, that the thoughts of my heart were very grievous to me again, ²² and my soul recovered the spirit of understanding, and I began to speak words before the Most High again, ²³ and said, "O Lord that bears rule, of all the woods of the earth, and of all the trees thereof, You have chosen one vine for Yourself; ²⁴ and of all the lands of the world You have chosen one country for Yourself; and of all the flowers of the world You have chosen one lily for Yourself; ²⁵ and of all the depths of the sea You have filled one river for Yourself; and of all built cities You have hallowed Zion for Yourself; ²⁶ and of all the birds that are created You have named one dove for Yourself; and of all the cattle that are made You have provided one sheep for Yourself; ²⁷ and among all the multitudes of peoples You have gotten one people for Yourself; and to this people, whom You loved, You gave a law that is approved of all. ²⁸ And now, O Lord, why have You given this one people over to many, and have dishonored the one root above others, and have scattered Your only one among many? ²⁹ And they which denied Your promises have trodden them down that believed Your covenants. ³⁰ If You hate Your people so much, they should be punished with Your own hands." ³¹ Now when I had spoken these words, the Messenger that came to me a previous night was sent to me, ³² and said to me, "Hear Me, and I will instruct you; listen to Me, and I will tell you more." ³³ And I said, "Speak, my Lord." Then He said to me, "You are severely troubled in mind for Israel's sake: do you [love] that people better than He that made them?" ³⁴ And I said, "No, Lord, but I have spoken in great grief, for my reins torment me every hour, while I labor to comprehend the way of the Highest, and to seek out part of His judgment." ³⁵ And he said to me, "You cannot." And I said, "Why, Lord, or for what purpose was I born? Or why was my mother's womb not then my grave, that I might not have seen the travail of Jacob, and the wearisome toil of the stock of Israel?" ³⁶ And He said to me, "Number to Me those who have not yet come, gather together to Me the drops that are scattered abroad, make for Me the flowers green again that are withered, ³⁷ open to Me the chambers that are closed, and bring out to Me the winds that in them are shut up, or show Me the image of a voice: and then I will declare to you the travail that you asked to see." ³⁸ And I said, "O Lord that bears rule, who may know these things, but He that does not have his dwelling with men? ³⁹ As for me, I am unwise: how may I then speak of these things of which You asked me?" ⁴⁰ Then He said to me, "Just as you can do none of these things that I have spoken of, even so you cannot find out My judgment, or the end of the love that I have promised to My people." ⁴¹ And I said, "But, behold, O Lord, You have made the promise to those who are in the end: and what will they do that have been before us, or we [that are now], or those who will come after us?" ⁴² And He said to me, "I will liken My judgment to a ring: just as there is no slackness of those who are last, even so there is no swiftness of those who are first." ⁴³ So I answered and said, "Could You not make them [to be] at once that have been made, and that are now, and that are still to come; that You might show Your judgment sooner?" ⁴⁴ Then He answered me, and said, "The creature may not hasten above the Creator; neither may the world hold them at once that will be created therein." ⁴⁵ And I said, "How have You said to Your servant that You will surely make alive at once the creature that You have created? If, therefore, they will be alive at once, and the creature will sustain them, even so it might now also support them to be present at once." ⁴⁶ And He said to me, "Ask the womb of a woman, and say to her, If you bring out ten children, why [do you do it] several times? Pray instead to bring out ten children at once." ⁴⁷ And I said, "She cannot, but must do it by distance of time." ⁴⁸ Then He said to me, "Even so have I given the womb of the earth to those that are sown therein in their several times. ⁴⁹ For just as a young child may not bring out, neither may she that has grown old [bring out] any more, even so—I have disposed the world which I created." ⁵⁰ And I asked, and said, "Seeing You have now showed me the way, I will speak before You: Is our mother, of whom You have told me, still young? Or does she now draw near to age?" ⁵¹ He answered me, and said, "Ask a woman that bears children, and she will tell you. ⁵² Say to her, Why are they whom you have now not brought out like those that were before, but of less stature? ⁵³ And she will also answer you, They that are born in the strength of youth are of one fashion, and those who are born in the time of age, when the womb fails, are otherwise. ⁵⁴ Therefore, also consider yourself, how that you are of less stature than those that were before you. ⁵⁵ And so are those who come after you less than you, as [born] of the creature which now begins to be old and is past the strength of youth." ⁵⁶ Then I said, "Lord, I implore You, if I have found favor in Your sight, show Your servant by whom You visit Your creature."

CHAPTER 6

¹ And He said to me, "In the beginning, when the earth was made, before the portals of the world were fixed, or the gatherings of the winds ever blew, ² before the voices of the thunder sounded, and before the flashes of the lightning shone, or the foundations of paradise were ever laid, ³ before the fair flowers were seen, or the powers of the earthquake were ever established, before the innumerable army of messengers were gathered together, ⁴ or the heights of the air were ever lifted up, before the measures of the expanse were named, or the footstool of Zion was ever established, ⁵ and before the present years were sought out, and or the imaginations of those who now sin were ever estranged, before they were sealed that have gathered faith for a treasure— ⁶ then I considered these things, and they were all made through Me alone, and through none other: as by Me they will also be ended, and by none other." ⁷ Then I answered and said, "What will be the separating apart of the times? Or when will be the end of the first, and the beginning of it that follows?" ⁸ And He said to me, "From Abraham to Abraham, inasmuch as Jacob and Esau were born of him, for Jacob's hand held the heel of Esau from the beginning. ⁹ For Esau is the end of this world, and Jacob is the beginning of it that follows. ¹⁰ The beginning of a man is his hand, and the end of a man is his heel; between the heel and

the hand do not seek anything else, Ezra." **11** I answered then and said, "O Lord that bears rule, If I have found favor in Your sight, **12** I implore You, show Your servant the end of Your signs, of which You showed me part the last night." **13** So He answered and said to me, "Stand up on your feet, and you will hear a mighty sounding voice; **14** and if the place you stand on is greatly moved, **15** when it speaks, do not be afraid, for the word is of the end, and the foundations of the earth will understand, **16** that the speech is of them: they will tremble and be moved, for they know that their end must be changed." **17** And it happened, that when I had heard it I stood up on my feet, and listened, and behold, there was a voice that spoke, and the sound of it was like the sound of many waters. **18** And it said, "Behold, the days come, and it will be that when I draw near to visit those who dwell on the earth, **19** and when I will make inquisition of those who have done hurt unjustly with their unrighteousness, and when the affliction of Zion will be fulfilled, **20** and when the seal will be set on the world that is to pass away, then I will show these signs: the scrolls will be opened before the expanse, and all will see together; **21** and the children of a year old will speak with their voices, [and] the women with child will bring out untimely children at three or four months, and they will live, and dance; **22** and suddenly the sown places will appear unsown, [and] the full storehouses will suddenly be found empty; **23** and the trumpet will give a sound, which when every man hears, they will be suddenly afraid. **24** At that time friends will make war against one another like enemies, and the earth will stand in fear with those that dwell therein; the springs of the springs will stand still, so that for three hours they will not run. **25** And it will be that whoever remains after all these things that I have told you of, he will be saved, and will see My salvation and the end of My world. **26** And they will see the men that have been taken up, who have not tasted death from their birth: and the heart of the inhabitants will be changed and turned into another meaning. **27** For evil will be blotted out, and deceit will be quenched; **28** and faith will flourish, and corruption will be overcome, and the truth, which has been so long without fruit, will be declared." **29** And when He talked with me, behold, little by little the place I stood on rocked to and fro. **30** And He said to me, "These things I came to show you this night. **31** If, therefore, you will pray yet again, and fast [for] seven more days, I will yet tell you greater things than these. **32** For your voice has surely been heard before the Highest, for the Mighty has seen your righteous dealing; He has also previously seen your chastity, which you have had ever since your youth. **33** And therefore He has sent Me to show you all these things, and to say to you, Be of good comfort, and do not fear. **34** And do not be hasty in [regard of the] former times, to think vain things, that you may not hasten in the latter times." **35** And it came to pass after this, that I wept again, and fasted [for] seven days in like manner, that I might fulfill the three weeks which He told me. **36** And in the eighth night my heart was vexed within me again, and I began to speak before the Highest. **37** For my spirit was greatly set on fire, and my soul was in distress. **38** And I said, "O Lord, of a truth You spoke at the beginning of the creation, on the first day, and said this: Let the heavens and earth be made; and Your word perfected the work. **39** And then the Spirit was fluttering, and darkness and silence were on every side; the sound of man's voice was not yet [heard]. **40** Then You commanded a ray of light to be brought out of Your treasures, that Your works might then appear. **41** On the second day again You made the spirit of the expanse and commanded it to separate apart, and to make a division between the waters, that the one part might go up, and the other remain beneath. **42** On the third day You commanded that the waters should be gathered together in the seventh part of the earth: six parts You dried up, and You keep them, to the intent that of these some being both planted and tilled might serve before You. **43** For as soon as Your word went out the work was done. **44** For immediately there came out great and innumerable fruit, and manifold pleasures for the taste, and flowers of inimitable color, and aromas of most exquisite smell: and this was done the third day. **45** On the fourth day You commanded that the sun should shine, and the moon give her light, and the stars should be in their order: **46** and You gave them a charge to do service to man that was to be made. **47** On the fifth day You said to the seventh part, where the water was gathered together, that it should bring out living creatures—birds and fishes: and so it came to pass, **48** that the mute water—and without life—brought out living things as it was told, that the peoples might therefore praise Your wondrous works. **49** Then

You preserved two living creatures, the one You called Behemoth, and the other you called Leviathan; **50** and You separated the one from the other; for the seventh part, namely, where the water was gathered together, might not hold them both. **51** To Behemoth You gave one part, which was dried up on the third day, that he should dwell in it, wherein are one thousand hills, **52** but to Leviathan You gave the seventh part, namely, the moist; and You have kept them to be devoured of whom You will, and when. **53** But on the sixth day You gave command to the earth, that it should bring out cattle, beasts, and creeping things before You: **54** and over these [is] Adam, whom You ordain lord over all the works that You have made; of him we all come—the people whom You have chosen. **55** I have spoken all this before You, O Lord, because You have said that You have made this world for our sakes. **56** As for the other nations, which also come of Adam, You have said that they are nothing, and are like to spittle: and You have likened the abundance of them to a drop that falls from a vessel. **57** And now, O Lord, behold [how] these nations, which are regarded as nothing, are lords over us, and devour us. **58** But we Your people, whom You have called Your firstborn, Your only begotten, and Your fervent lover, are given into their hands. **59** If the world is now made for our sakes, why do we not possess our world for an inheritance? How long will this endure?"

CHAPTER 7

1 And when I had made an end of speaking these words, there was sent to me the Messenger which had been sent to me the nights before, **2** and He said to me, "Get up, Ezra, and hear the words that I have come to tell you." **3** And I said, "Speak, my Lord." Then He said to me, "There is a sea set in a wide place, that it might be broad and vast. **4** But the entrance thereof will be set in a narrow place so as to be like a river; **5** whoever then should desire to go into the sea to look on it, or to rule it, if he did not go through the narrow, how could he come into the broad? **6** Another thing also: there is a city built and set in a plain country, and full of all good things; **7** but the entrance thereof is narrow and is set in a dangerous place to fall, having a fire on the right hand, and on the left a deep water; **8** and there is only one path between them both, even between the fire and the water, [so small] that there could [be] but one man [who could] go there at once. **9** If this city is now given to a man for an inheritance, if the heir does not pass the danger before him, how will he receive his inheritance?" **10** And I said, "It is so, Lord." Then He said to me, "Even so is Israel's portion also. **11** Because for their sakes I made the world; and when Adam transgressed My statutes, then was decreed that [which] now is done. **12** Then the entrances of this world were made narrow, and sorrowful, and toilsome: they are but few and evil, full of perils, and charged with great toils. **13** For the entrances of the greater world are wide, and sure, and bring out fruit of immortality. **14** If then those who live do not enter these narrow and vain things, they can never receive those that are laid up for them. **15** Now therefore, why do you disquiet yourself, seeing you are but a corruptible man? And why are you moved, whereas you are but mortal? **16** And why have you not considered in your mind that which is to come, rather than that which is present?" **17** Then I answered and said, "O Lord that bears rule, behold, You have ordained in Your law that the righteous should inherit these things, but that the ungodly should perish. **18** The righteous will therefore suffer narrow things, and hope for wide, but those who have done wickedly have suffered the narrow things, and yet will not see the wide." **19** And He said to me, "You are not a judge above God, neither have you understanding above the Highest. **20** Yes, rather let many that now are perish, than that the Law of God which is set before them be despised. **21** For God strictly commanded such as came, even as they came, what they should do to live, and what they should observe to avoid punishment. **22** Nevertheless, they were not obedient to Him, but spoke against Him and imagined for themselves vain things, **23** and framed cunning plans of wickedness, and said, moreover, of the Highest, that He is not, and did not know His ways, **24** but they despised His law and denied His covenants; they have not been faithful to His statutes and have not performed His works. **25** Therefore, Ezra, for the empty are empty things, and for the full are the full things. **26** For behold, the time will come, and it will be, when these signs of which I told, you before will come to pass: that the bride will appear, even the city coming out, and she will be seen that now is withdrawn from the earth. **27** And whoever is delivered from the previously mentioned evils will see My wonders. **28** For My Son the Christ will be revealed with those that are with Him and will rejoice with those who remain four hundred years. **29** After these years My Son the Christ will die, and all those that have the breath of life. **30** And the world will be turned into the primordial silence [for] seven days, just as in the first beginning, so that no man will remain. **31** And after seven days, the world that has not yet awaken will be raised up, and that which is corruptible will die. **32** And the earth will restore those that are asleep in her, and so will the dust those that dwell therein in silence, and the secret places will deliver those souls that were committed to them. **33** And the Highest will be revealed on the seat of judgment, and compassion will pass away, and patience will be withdrawn, **34** but only judgment will remain, truth will stand, and faith will wax strong; **35** and the work will follow, and the reward will be shown, and good deeds will awake, and wicked deeds will not sleep. **36** And the pit of torment will appear, and near it will be the place of rest; and the furnace will be shown, and near it the paradise of delight. **37** And then the Highest will say to the nations that are raised from the dead: See and understand whom you have denied, or whom you have not served, or whose commands you have despised. **38** Look on this side and on that: here is delight and rest, and their fire and torments. He will speak this to them in the Day of Judgment: **39** this is a day that has neither sun, nor moon, nor stars, **40** neither cloud, nor thunder, nor lightning, neither wind, nor water, nor air, neither darkness, nor evening, nor morning, **41** neither summer, nor spring, nor heat, nor winter, neither frost, nor cold, nor hail, nor rain, nor dew, **42** neither noon, nor night, nor dawn, neither shining, nor brightness, nor light, save only the splendor of the glory of the Most High, whereby all will see the things that are set before them, **43** for it will endure as it were a week of years. **44** This is My judgment and the ordinance thereof; but only to you have I showed these things." **45** And I answered, I said even then, "O Lord, and I say now: blessed are those who are now alive and keep the [statutes] ordained of You. **46** But as touching them for whom my prayer was made, [what will I say]? For who is there of those who are alive that has not sinned, and who of the sons [of men] that has not transgressed Your covenant? **47** And now I see that the world to come will bring delight to few, but torments to many. **48** For an evil heart has grown up in us, which has led us astray from these [statutes, and] has brought us into corruption and into the ways of death, has showed us the paths of perdition, and removed us far from life—and that, not a few only, but well near all that have been created." **49** And He answered me, and said, "Listen to Me, and I will instruct you; and I will admonish you yet again: **50** for this reason the Most High has not made one world, but two. **51** For whereas you have said that the just are not many, but few, and the ungodly abound, hear [the answer] to that. **52** If you have exceedingly few choice stones, will you set for yourself near them, according to their number, [things of] lead and clay?" **53** And I said, "Lord, how will this be?" **54** And He said to me, "Not only this, but ask the earth, and she will tell you; entreat her, and she will declare to you. **55** For you will say to her, you bring out gold, and silver, and brass, and iron also, and lead, and clay; **56** but silver is more abundant than gold, and brass than silver, and iron than brass, lead than iron, and clay than lead. **57** Therefore judge which things are precious and to be desired, what is abundant or what is rare." **58** And I said, "O Lord that bears rule, that which is plentiful is of less worth, for that which is rarer is more precious." **59** And He answered me, and said, "Weigh within yourself the things that you have thought, for he that has what is hard to get rejoices over him that has what is plentiful. **60** So also is the judgment which I have promised, for I will rejoice over the few that will be saved, inasmuch as these are those who have made My glory now to prevail, and of whom My Name is now named. **61** And I will not grieve over the multitude of those who perish; for these are those who are now like to vapor and have become as flame and smoke; they are set on fire and burn hotly and are quenched." **62** And I answered and said, "O you earth, why have you brought out, if the mind is made out of dust, like as all other created things? **63** For it were better that the dust itself had been unborn, so that the mind might not have been made from it. **64** But now the mind grows with us, and by reason of this we are tormented, because we perish and know it. **65** Let the race of men lament and the beasts of

the field be glad; let all that are born lament, but let the four-footed beasts and the cattle rejoice. **66** For it is far better with them than with us; for they do not look for judgment, neither do they know of torments or of salvation promised to them after death. **67** For what does it profit us, that we will be preserved alive, but yet be afflicted with torment? **68** For all that are born are defiled with iniquities, and are full of sins, and laden with offenses; **69** and if after death we were not to come into judgment, perhaps it had been better for us." **70** And He answered me, and said, "When the Most High made the world, and Adam and all those who came of him, He first prepared the judgment and the things that pertain to the judgment. **71** And now understand from your own words, for you have said that the mind grows with us. **72** Therefore, they that dwell on the earth will be tormented for this reason, that having understanding, they have done iniquity, and receiving commands, have not kept them, and having obtained a law, they dealt unfaithfully with that which they received. **73** What then will they have to say in the judgment, or how will they answer in the last times? **74** For how great a time has the Most High been patient with those who inhabit the world, and not for their sakes, but because of the times which He has foreordained!" **75** And I answered and said, "If I have found grace in Your sight, O Lord, show this to Your servant also, whether after death, even now when each of us gives up his soul, we will be kept in rest until those times come, in which You will renew the creation, or whether we will be tormented immediately." **76** And He answered me, and said, "I will show you this also, but do not join yourself with those who are scorners, nor count yourself with those who are tormented. **77** For you have a treasure of [good] works laid up with the Highest, but it will not be shown to you until the last times. **78** For concerning death the teaching is: When the determinate sentence has gone out from the Highest that a man should die, as the spirit leaves the body to return again to Him who gave it, it adores the glory of the Most High first of all. **79** And if it is one of those that have been scorners and have not kept the way of the Highest, and that have despised His law, and that hate those who fear God, **80** these spirits will not enter into habitations, but will wander and be in torments immediately, ever grieving and sad, in seven ways. **81** The first way, because they have despised the Law of the Highest. **82** The second way, because they cannot now make a good returning that they may live. **83** The third way, they will see the reward laid up for those who have believed the covenants of the Highest. **84** The fourth way, they will consider the torment laid up for themselves in the last days. **85** The fifth way, they will see the dwelling places of the others guarded by messengers, with great quietness. **86** The sixth way, they will see how some of them will immediately pass into torment. **87** The seventh way, which is more grievous than all the previously mentioned ways, because they will pine away in confusion, and be consumed with shame, and will be withered up by fears, seeing the glory of the Highest before whom they have sinned while living, and before whom they will be judged in the last times. **88** Now this is the order of those who have kept the ways of the Highest, when they will be separated from the corruptible vessel. **89** In the time that they lived therein they painfully served the Highest, and were in danger every hour, that they might keep the Law of the Lawgiver perfectly. **90** Here then is the teaching concerning them: **91** First of all, they will see with great joy the glory of Him who takes them up, for they will have rest in seven orders. **92** The first order, because they have labored with great effort to overcome the evil thought which was fashioned together with them, that it might not lead them astray from life into death. **93** The second order, because they see the perplexity in which the souls of the ungodly wander, and the punishment that awaits them. **94** The third order, they see the witness which He that fashioned them bears concerning them, that while they lived they kept the Law which was given them in trust. **95** The fourth order, they understand the rest which, being gathered in their chambers, they now enjoy with great quietness, guarded by messengers, and the glory that awaits them in the last days. **96** The fifth order, they rejoice, [seeing] how they have now escaped from that which is corruptible, and how they will inherit that which is to come, while they see moreover the narrowness and the painfulness from which they have been delivered, and the large room which they will receive with joy and immortality. **97** The sixth order, when it is showed to them how their face will shine as the sun, and how they will be made like to the light of the stars, being from now on incorruptible. **98** The seventh order, which is greater than all the previous orders, because they will rejoice with confidence, and because they will be bold without confusion, and will be glad without fear, for they hasten to behold the face of Him whom in their lifetime they served, and from whom they will receive [their] reward in glory. **99** This is the order of the souls of the just, as from now on is announced to them, and announced are the ways of torture which those who would not give heed will suffer from now on." **100** And I answered and said, "Will time therefore be given to the souls after they are separated from the bodies, that they may see what You have spoken to me?" **101** And He said, "Their freedom will be for seven days, that for seven days they may see the things that you have been told, and afterward they will be gathered together in their habitations." **102** And I answered and said, "If I have found favor in Your sight, show further to me Your servant whether in the Day of Judgment the just will be able to intercede for the ungodly or to entreat the Most High for them, **103** whether fathers for children, or children for parents, or relatives for relatives, or countrymen for countrymen, or friends for those who are most dear." **104** And He answered me, and said, "Since you have found favor in My sight, I will show you this also: the Day of Judgment is a day of decision, and displays to all the seal of truth; even as now a father does not send his son, or a son his father, or a master his slave, or a friend him that is most dear, that in his stead he may be sick, or sleep, or eat, or be healed, **105** so never will anyone pray for another in that day, neither will one lay a burden on another, for then everyone will bear his own righteousness or unrighteousness." **106** And I answered and said, "How do we now find that first Abraham prayed for the people of Sodom, and Moses for the fathers that sinned in the wilderness, **107** and Joshua after him for Israel in the days of Achar, **108** and Samuel in the days of Saul, and David for the plague, and Solomon for those who [should worship] in the sanctuary, **109** and Elijah for those that received rain, and for the dead, that he might live, **110** and Hezekiah for the people in the days of Sennacherib, and many for many? **111** If, therefore now, when corruption is grown up, and unrighteousness increased, the righteous have prayed for the ungodly, why will it not be so then also?" **112** He answered me, and said, "This present world is not the end; the full glory does not remain therein. Therefore, they who were able have prayed for the weak, **113** but the Day of Judgment will be the end of this time, and the beginning of the immortality to come, wherein corruption has passed away, **114** intemperance is at an end, infidelity is cut off, but righteousness has grown, and truth has sprung up. **115** Then no man will be able to have mercy on him that is cast in judgment, nor to thrust down him that has gotten the victory." **116** I answered then and said, "This is my first and last saying, that it had been better that the earth had not given Adam: or else, when it had given [him], to have restrained him from sinning. **117** For what profit is it for all that are in this present time to live in heaviness, and after death to look for punishment? **118** O you Adam! What have you done? For though it was you that sinned, the evil is not fallen on you alone, but on all of us that come of you. **119** For what profit is it to us, if there is promised us an immortal time, whereas we have done the works that bring death? **120** And that there has been promised us a continuous hope, whereas we have become most miserably vain? **121** And that there are reserved habitations of health and safety, whereas we have lived wickedly? **122** And that the glory of the Highest will defend them which have led a pure life, whereas we have walked in the most wicked ways of all? **123** And that there will be showed a paradise, whose fruit endures without decay, wherein is abundance and healing, but we will not enter into it, **124** for we have walked in unpleasant places? **125** And that the faces of them which have used abstinence will shine above the stars, whereas our faces will be blacker than darkness? **126** For while we lived and committed iniquity, we did not consider what we should have to suffer after death." **127** Then He answered and said, "This is the condition of the battle, which man that is born on the earth will fight; **128** that, if he is overcome, he will suffer as you have said, but if he gets the victory, he will receive the thing that I say. **129** For this is the way of which Moses spoke to the people while he lived, saying, Choose life, that you may live. **130** Nevertheless, they did not believe him, nor yet the prophets after him, no, nor Me which have spoken to them, **131** so that there will not be such heaviness in their destruction, as there will be joy over those who are persuaded to salvation." **132** I answered then and said, "I know, Lord, that the Most High is now called merciful, in that He has mercy on them which have not yet come into the world; **133** and compassionate, in

that He has compassion on those that turn to His law; **134** and patient, for that He long endures those that have sinned, as His creatures; **135** and bountiful, for that He is ready to give rather than to exact; **136** and of great mercy, for that He multiplies more and more mercies to those who are present, and that are past, and also to them which are to come **137** (for if He did not multiply [His mercies], the world would not continue with those who dwell therein); **138** and one that forgives, for if He did not forgive of His goodness, that they which have committed iniquities might be eased of them, the ten-thousandth part of men would not remain living; **139** and a judge, [for] if He did not pardon those who were created by His word, and blot out the multitude of offenses, **140** there would perhaps be very few left in an innumerable multitude."

CHAPTER 8

1 And He answered me, and said, "The Most High has made this world for many, but the world to come for few. **2** I will now tell you a similitude, Ezra: [just] as when you ask the earth, it will say to you that it gives very much mold of which earthen vessels are made, and little dust that gold comes of, even so is the course of the present world. **3** There are many created, but few will be saved." **4** And I answered and said, "Swallow down understanding then, O my soul, and let [my heart] devour wisdom. **5** For you have come here without your will and depart when you would not, for there is given to you no more space than only to live a short time. **6** O Lord, You that are over us, permit Your servant, that we may pray before You, and give us seed to our heart, and culture to our understanding, that there may come fruit of it, whereby each one will live that is corrupt, who bears the likeness of a man. **7** For You are alone, and we are all one workmanship of Your hands, just as You have said. **8** Forasmuch as You give life to the body that is fashioned now in the womb, and give it members, Your creature is preserved in fire and water, and [for] nine months Your workmanship endures Your creature which is created in her. **9** But that which keeps and that which is kept will both be kept by Your keeping: and when the womb gives up again that which has grown in it, **10** You have commanded that out of the parts of the body, that is to say, out of the breasts, be given milk, which is the fruit of the breasts, **11** that the thing which is fashioned may be nourished for a time, and afterward You will order it in Your mercy. **12** Yes, You have brought it up in Your righteousness, and nurtured it in Your law, and corrected it with Your judgment. **13** And You will mortify it as Your creature and give it life as Your work. **14** If, therefore, You will lightly and suddenly destroy him which with so great labor was fashioned by Your command, to what purpose was he made? **15** Now therefore, I will speak; touching man in general, You know best; but touching Your people [I will speak], for whose sake I am sorry; **16** and for Your inheritance, for whose cause I mourn; and for Israel, for whom I am heavy; and for the seed of Jacob, for whose sake I am troubled; **17** therefore I will begin to pray before You for myself and for them, for I see the falls of us that dwell in the land, **18** but I have heard the swiftness of the judgment which is to come. **19** Therefore hear my voice, and understand my saying, and I will speak before You." The beginning of the words of Ezra, before he was taken up. And he said, **20** "O Lord, You who remain forever, whose eyes are exalted, and whose chambers are in the air; **21** whose throne is inestimable; whose glory may not be comprehended; before whom the army of messengers stand with trembling, **22** at whose bidding they are changed to wind and fire; whose word is sure, and sayings constant; whose ordinance is strong, and command fearful; **23** whose look dries up the depths, and whose indignation makes the mountains to melt away, and whose truth bears witness: **24** hear, O Lord, the prayer of Your servant, and give ear to the petition of Your handiwork; **25** attend to my words, for so long as I live I will speak, and so long as I have understanding I will answer. **26** Do not look on the sins of Your people, but on those who have served You in truth. **27** Do not regard the doings of those who deal wickedly, but of those who have kept Your covenants in affliction. **28** Do not think on those that have walked ungenuine before You, but remember them which have willingly known Your fear. **29** Do not let it be Your will to destroy them which have lived like cattle, but look on those who have clearly taught Your law. **30** Take no indignation at them which are deemed worse than beasts, but love those who have always put their trust in Your glory. **31** For we and our fathers have passed our lives in ways that bring death, but You, because of us sinners, are called merciful. ³² For if You have a desire to have mercy on us, then You will be called merciful, to us, namely, that have no works of righteousness. ³³ For the just, which have many [good] works laid up with You, will for their own deeds receive reward. ³⁴ For what is man that You should take displeasure at him? or what is a corruptible race that You should be so bitter toward it? ³⁵ For in truth there is no man among those who are born, but he [who] has dealt wickedly; and among them that have lived there is none which have not done wrong. ³⁶ For in this, O Lord, Your righteousness and Your goodness will be declared, if You are merciful to them which have no store of good works." ³⁷ Then He answered me, and said, "You have spoken some things correctly, and according to your words so it will come to pass. ³⁸ For indeed, I will not think on the fashioning of them which have sinned, or their death, their judgment, or their destruction, ³⁹ but I will rejoice over the framing of the righteous, their pilgrimage also, and the salvation and the reward that they will have. ⁴⁰ Therefore, just as I have spoken, so it will be. ⁴¹ For as the farmer sows much seed on the ground, and plants many trees, and yet not all that is sown will come up in due season, neither will all that is planted take root: even so those who are sown in the world will not all be saved." ⁴² I answered then and said, "If I have found favor, let me speak before You. ⁴³ Forasmuch as the farmer's seed, if it does not come up, seeing that it has not received Your rain in due season, or if it is corrupted through too much rain, so perishes, ⁴⁴ likewise man, which is formed with Your hands, and is called Your own image, because he is made like [You], for whose sake You have formed all things, even him you have made like to the farmer's seed. ⁴⁵ Do not be angry with us, but spare Your people, and have mercy on Your inheritance; for You have mercy on Your own creation." ⁴⁶ Then He answered me, and said, "Things present are for those who now are, and things to come for such as will be hereafter. ⁴⁷ For you come far short that you should be able to love My creature more than Me. But you have brought yourself full near to the unrighteous—never! ⁴⁸ Yet in this you will be admirable to the Most High: ⁴⁹ in that you have humbled yourself, as it is appropriate for you, and have not judged yourself [worthy to be] among the righteous, so as to be much glorified. ⁵⁰ For many grievous miseries will fall on those who in the last times dwell in the world, because they have walked in great pride. ⁵¹ But understand for yourself, and of such as are like you—seek out the glory. ⁵² For to you paradise is opened, the Tree of Life planted, the time to come is prepared, bounty is made ready, a city is built, and rest is allowed, goodness is perfected, wisdom being perfect beforehand. ⁵³ The root [of evil] is sealed up from you, weakness is done away from you, and [death] is hidden; Hades and corruption have fled into forgetfulness; ⁵⁴ sorrows have passed away, and in the end, the treasure of immortality is shown. ⁵⁵ Therefore, do not ask any more questions concerning the multitude of them that perish. ⁵⁶ For when they had received liberty, they despised the Most High, thought scorn of His law, and forsook His ways. ⁵⁷ Moreover, they have trodden down His righteous, ⁵⁸ and said in their heart that there is no God; yes, and that knowing they must die. ⁵⁹ For as the things previously stated you will receive, so thirst and pain which are prepared [they will receive], for the Most High did not will that men should come to nothing, ⁶⁰ but they which are created have themselves defiled the Name of Him that made them and were unthankful to Him which prepared life for them. ⁶¹ And therefore My judgment is now at hand, ⁶² which I have not showed to all men, but to you, and a few like you." Then I answered and said, ⁶³ "Behold, O Lord, now You have showed me the multitude of the wonders, which You will do in the last times, but at what time, You have not showed me."

CHAPTER 9

¹ And He answered me, and said, "Measure diligently within yourself: and when you see that a certain part of the signs are past, which have been told to you beforehand, ² then you will understand that it is the very time wherein the Most High will visit the world which was made by Him. ³ And when there will be seen in the world earthquakes, disquietude of peoples, plans of nations, wavering of leaders, disquietude of princes, ⁴ then you will understand that the Highest spoke of these things from the days that were previously from the beginning. ⁵ For just as of all that is made in the world, the beginning is evident and the end manifest, ⁶ so also are the times of the Highest: the

beginnings are manifest in wonders and mighty works, and the end in effects and signs. ⁷ And everyone that will be saved, and will be able to escape by his works, or by faith, whereby he has believed, ⁸ will be preserved from the stated perils, and will see My salvation in My land, and within My borders, which I have sanctified for Myself from the beginning. ⁹ Then those which have now abused My ways will be amazed, and those who have despitefully cast them away will dwell in torments. ¹⁰ For as many as in their life have received benefits, and yet have not known Me, ¹¹ and as many as have scorned My law while they still had liberty, and, when conversion was open to them, did not understand, but despised [it], ¹² must know [it] after death by torment. ¹³ And therefore, no longer be curious how the ungodly will be punished, but inquire how the righteous will be saved, they whose the world [is, and] for whom the world [was created]." ¹⁴ And I answered and said, ¹⁵ "I have said before, and now speak, and will speak it also hereafter, that there are more of them which perish, than of those which will be saved: ¹⁶ just as a wave is greater than a drop." ¹⁷ And He answered me, saying, "Just as the field is, so also the seed; and as the flowers are, such are the colors also; and such as the work is, such is the judgment [on it] also; and as is the farmer, so is his threshing floor also. For there was a time in the world, ¹⁸ even then when I was preparing for those who now live, before the world was made for them to dwell in; and then no man spoke against Me— ¹⁹ there was not any; but now they which are created in this world that is prepared, both with a table that does not fail, and a law which is unsearchable, are corrupted in their manners. ²⁰ So I considered My world, and behold, it was destroyed, and My earth, and behold, it was in peril, because of the plans that had come into it. ²¹ And I saw, and spared them, but not greatly, and saved Myself a grape out of a cluster, and a plant out of a great forest. ²² Let the multitude which was born in vain perish then; and let My grape be saved, and My plant; for I have made them perfect with great labor. ²³ Nevertheless, if you will cease yet seven more days, (however you will not fast in them, ²⁴ but will go into a field of flowers, where no house is built, and eat only of the flowers of the field; and you will taste no flesh, and will drink no wine, but [will eat] flowers only;) ²⁵ and pray to the Most High continually, then I will come and talk with you." ²⁶ So I went my way, just as He commanded me, into the field which is called Ardat; and there I sat among the flowers, and ate of the herbs of the field, and its meat satisfied me. ²⁷ And it came to pass after seven days that I lay on the grass, and my heart was vexed again just as before; ²⁸ and my mouth was opened, and I began to speak before the Lord Most High, and said, ²⁹ "O Lord, You showed Yourself among us, to our fathers in the wilderness, when they went out of Egypt, and when they came into the wilderness, where no man treads and which bears no fruit; ³⁰ and You said, Hear Me, Israel; and mark My words, O seed of Jacob. ³¹ For behold, I sow My law in you, and it will bring out fruit in you, and you will be glorified in it forever. ³² But our fathers, which received the Law, did not keep it, and did not observe the statutes: and the fruit of the Law did not perish, neither could it, for it was Yours; ³³ yet those who received it perished, because they did not keep the thing that was sown in them. ³⁴ And behold, it is a custom that when the ground has received seed, or the sea a ship, or any vessel meat or drink, and when it comes to pass that that which is sown, or that which is launched, ³⁵ or the things which have been received, should come to an end, these come to an end, but the receptacles remain: yet with us it has not happened so. ³⁶ For we that have received the Law will perish by sin, and also our heart which received it. ³⁷ Notwithstanding, the Law does not perish, but remains in its honor." ³⁸ And when I spoke these things in my heart, I looked around me with my eyes, and on the right side I saw a woman, and behold, she mourned and wept with a loud voice, and was greatly grieved in mind, and her clothes were torn, and she had ashes on her head. ³⁹ Then I let my thoughts go wherein I was occupied, and I turned to her, ⁴⁰ and said to her, "Why do you weep? And why are you grieved in your mind?" ⁴¹ And she said to me, "Leave me alone, my lord, that I may mourn myself, and add to my sorrow, for I am severely vexed in my mind, and brought very low." ⁴² And I said to her, "What ails you? Tell me." ⁴³ She said to me, "I, your servant, was barren, and had no child, though I had a husband [for] thirty years. ⁴⁴ And every hour and every day these thirty years I made my prayer to the Most High day and night. ⁴⁵ And it came to pass after thirty years, that God heard me, your handmaid, and looked on my low estate, and considered my trouble, and gave me a son: and I rejoiced in him greatly—me, and my husband, and all my neighbors—and we gave great honor to the Mighty. **46** And I nourished him with great travail. **47** So when he grew up, and I came to take a wife for him, I made him a feast day."

CHAPTER 10

1 "And so it came to pass, that when my son had entered into his wedding chamber, he fell down and died. **2** Then we all overthrew the lights, and all my neighbors rose up to comfort me: and I remained quiet to the second day at night. **3** And it came to pass when they had all ceased to comfort me, to the end I might be quiet, then I arose by night, and fled, and came here into this field, as you see. **4** And now I do not purpose to return into the city, but to stay here, and neither to eat nor drink, but to continually mourn and fast until I die." **5** Then I left the meditations wherein I was, and answered her in anger, and said, **6** "You foolish woman above all others! Do you not see our mourning, and what has happened to us? **7** How Zion, the mother of us all, is full of sorrow, and greatly humbled. **8** It is right to mourn very severely now, seeing we all mourn, and to be sorrowful, seeing we are all in sorrow, but you mourn for one son. **9** For ask the earth, and she will tell you that it is she which should mourn for so many that grow on her. **10** For out of her all had their beginnings, and others will come; and behold, almost all of them walk into destruction, and the multitude of them is utterly rooted out. **11** Who then should make more mourning: she that has lost so great a multitude, or you which are grieved but for one? **12** But if you say to me, My lamentation is not like the earth's, for I have lost the fruit of my womb, which I brought out with pains, and bore with sorrows, **13** but [it is with the] earth after the manner of the earth—the multitude present in it is gone, as it came: **14** then I say to you, just as you have brought out with sorrow, even so the earth has also given her fruit, namely, man, ever since the beginning to Him that made her. **15** Now therefore, keep your sorrow to yourself, and bear with a good courage the adversities which have befallen you. **16** For if you will acknowledge the decree of God to be just, you will both receive your son in time, and will be praised among women. **17** Go your way then into the city to your husband." **18** And she said to me, "I will not do that. I will not go into the city, but I will die here." **19** So I proceeded to speak further to her, and said, **20** "Do not do that, but permit yourself to be prevailed on by reason of the adversities of Zion; and be comforted by reason of the sorrow of Jerusalem. **21** For you see that our sanctuary is laid waste, our altar broken down, our temple destroyed; **22** our lute is brought low, our song is put to silence, our rejoicing is at an end; the light of our candlestick is put out, the Ark of our covenant is plundered, our holy things are defiled, and the name that is called on us is profaned; our freemen are despitefully treated, our priests are burned, our Levites have gone into captivity, our virgins are defiled, and our wives ravished; our righteous men carried away, our little ones betrayed, our young men are brought into bondage, and our strong men have become weak; **23** and, what is more than all, the seal of Zion—for she has now lost the seal of her honor, and is delivered into the hands of those who hate us. **24** Therefore, shake off your great heaviness, and put away from yourself the multitude of sorrows, that the Mighty may be merciful to you again, and the Most High may give you rest, even ease from your travails." **25** And it came to pass, while I was talking with her, behold, her face suddenly shined exceedingly, and her countenance radiated like lightning, so that I was terrified of her, and wondered what this might be; **26** and behold, she suddenly made a great [and] very fearful cry, so that the earth shook at the noise. **27** And I looked, and behold, the woman appeared to me no longer, but there [where she was] a city was built, and a place showed itself from large foundations. Then I was afraid, and cried with a loud voice, and said, **28** "Where is Uriel the messenger, who came to me at the first? For he has caused me to fall into this great trance, and my end is turned into corruption, and my prayer to rebuke." **29** And as I was speaking these words, behold, the messenger who had come to me at the first came to me, and he looked on me; **30** and behold, I lay as one that had been dead, and my understanding was taken from me; and he took me by the right hand, and comforted me, and set me on my feet, and said to me, **31** "What ails you? And why are you so disquieted? And why is your understanding troubled, and the thoughts of your heart?" **32** And I said, "Because you have forsaken me: yet I did according to your words, and went into the field, and behold, I have seen, and yet see, that which I am not able to express." **33** And he said to me, "Stand up like a man, and I will advise you." **34** Then I said, "Speak, my Lord; only do not forsake me, lest I die without hope. **35** For I have seen and heard that [which] I do not understand. **36** Or is my sense deceived, or my soul in a dream? **37** Now therefore, I implore you to show your servant concerning this vision." **38** And he answered me, and said, "Hear me, and I will inform you, and tell you concerning the things of which you are afraid. For the Most High has revealed many secret things to you. **39** He has seen that your way is right, for that you continually mourn for your people and make great lamentation for Zion. **40** Therefore, this is the meaning of the vision: **41** the woman which appeared to you a little while ago—whom you saw mourning, and began to comfort her, **42** but now you no longer see the likeness of the woman, but there appeared to you a city in building, **43** and whereas she told you of the death of her son—this is the solution: **44** this woman, whom you saw, is Zion, whom you now see as a city built. **45** And whereas she said to you that she has been barren [for] thirty years, [it is] because there were three thousand years in the world wherein there was no offering as yet offered in her. **46** And it came to pass after three thousand years, that Solomon built the city and offered offerings: then it was that the barren [woman] bore a son. **47** And whereas she told you that she nourished him with travail: that was the dwelling in Jerusalem. **48** And whereas she said to you, My son coming into his marriage chamber died, and that misfortune befell her: this was the destruction that came to Jerusalem. **49** And behold, you saw her likeness, how she mourned for her son, and you began to comfort her for what has befallen her: these were the things to be opened to you. **50** For now the Highest, seeing that you are grieved, and suffer from your whole heart for her, has showed you the brightness of her glory, and the attractiveness of her beauty: **51** and therefore I commanded you to remain in the field where no house was built, **52** for I knew that the Most High would show this to you. **53** Therefore I commanded you to come into the field where no foundation of any building was. **54** For in the place wherein the city of the Highest was to be shown, the work of no man's building could stand. **55** Therefore, do not fear, nor let your heart be frightened, but go your way in, and see the beauty and greatness of the building, as much as your eyes are able to see, **56** and then you will hear as much as your ears may comprehend. **57** For you are blessed above many, and are called by name with the Highest, like as but few. **58** But tomorrow at night you will remain here; **59** and so the Highest will show you those visions in dreams, of what the Most High will do to those who dwell on the earth in the last days." So I slept that night and another, just as he commanded me.

CHAPTER 11

1 And it came to pass the second night that I saw a dream, and behold, there came up from the sea an eagle which had twelve feathered wings and three heads. **2** And I saw, and behold, she spread her wings over all the earth, and all the winds of the sky blew on her, and the clouds were gathered together against her. **3** And I saw, and out of her wings there grew [other] wings near them; and they became little wings and small. **4** But her heads were at rest: the head in the midst was greater than the other heads yet rested with them. **5** Moreover, I saw, and behold, the eagle flew with her wings, to reign over the earth, and over those who dwell therein. **6** And I saw how all things under Heaven were subject to her, and no man spoke against her, no, not one creature on earth. **7** And I saw, and behold, the eagle rose on her talons, and uttered her voice to her wings, saying, **8** "Do not watch all at once: everyone sleep in his own place, and watch by course; **9** but let the heads be preserved for the last." **10** And I saw, and behold, the voice did not go out of her heads, but from the midst of her body. **11** And I counted her wings that were near the other, and behold, there were eight of them. **12** And I saw, and behold, on the right side there arose one wing, and it reigned over all the earth; **13** and so it was, that when it reigned, the end of it came and it did not appear, so that the place thereof appeared no longer; and following [it], the next rose up and reigned, and it ruled a great time; **14** and it happened, that when it reigned, the end of it also came, so that it appeared no longer, just as the first. **15** And behold, there came a voice to it, and said, **16** "Hear—you that have borne rule over the earth all this time;

this I proclaim to you, before you will appear no longer: **17** none after you will attain to your time, neither to the half thereof." **18** Then the third arose, and had the rule as the others before, and it also appeared no longer. **19** So it went with all the wings, one after another, as that each one bore rule, and then appeared no longer. **20** And I saw, and behold, in process of time the wings that followed were set up on the right side, that they might also rule; and some of them ruled, but within a while they appeared no longer; **21** some of them also rose up, but did not rule. **22** After this I saw, and behold, the twelve wings appeared no longer, nor two of the little wings, **23** and there was no longer left on the eagle's body, but the three heads that rested, and six little wings. **24** And I saw, and behold, two little wings divided themselves from the six, and remained under the head that was on the right side, but four remained in their place. **25** And I saw, and behold, these wings under thought to set themselves up, and to have the rule. **26** And I saw, and behold, there was one set up, but within a while it appeared no longer. **27** A second also, and it was gone sooner than the first. **28** And I saw, and behold, the two that remained also thought in themselves to reign: **29** and while they so thought, behold, there awakened one of the heads that were at rest, [namely, it] that was in the midst; for that was greater than the two [other] heads. **30** And I saw how it joined the two [other] heads with it. **31** And behold, the head was turned with those who were with it, and it ate up the two wings under that thought to have reigned. **32** But this head held the whole earth in possession, and bore rule over those that dwell therein with much oppression; and it had the governance of the world more than all the wings that had been. **33** And after this I saw, and behold, the head that was in the midst also suddenly appeared no longer, just as the wings. **34** But there remained the two heads, which also in like manner reigned over the earth, and over those that dwell therein. **35** And I saw, and behold, the head on the right side devoured it that was on the left side. **36** Then I heard a voice, which said to me, "Look before you, and consider the thing that you see." **37** And I saw, and behold, as it were a lion roused out of the wood roaring; and I heard how that he sent out a man's voice to the eagle, and spoke, saying, **38** "Hear! I will talk with you, and the Highest will say to you, **39** Are you not it that remains of the four beasts, whom I made to reign in My world, that the end of My times might come through them? **40** And the fourth came, and overcame all the beasts that were past, and held the world in governance with great trembling, and the whole circle of the earth with grievous oppression; and for such a long time he lived on the earth with deceit. **41** And you have judged the earth, but not with truth. **42** For you have afflicted the meek, you have hurt the peaceful, you have hated those who speak truth, you have loved liars, and destroyed the dwellings of those who brought out fruit, and cast down the walls of such as did you no harm. **43** Therefore your insolent dealing has come up to the Highest, and your pride to the Mighty. **44** The Most High has also looked on His times, and behold, they are ended, and His ages are fulfilled. **45** And therefore, appear no longer you eagle, nor your horrible wings, nor your evil little wings, nor your cruel heads, nor your hurtful talons, nor all your vain body, **46** that all the earth may be refreshed, and be eased, being delivered from your violence, and that she may hope for the judgment and mercy of Him that made her."

CHAPTER 12

1 And it came to pass while the lion spoke these words to the eagle, I saw, **2** and behold, the head that remained appeared no longer, and the two wings which went over to it arose and set themselves up to reign, and their kingdom was small, and full of uproar. **3** And I saw, and behold, they appeared no longer, and the whole body of the eagle was burned, so that the earth was in great fear: then I awoke by reason of great ecstasy of mind, and from great fear, and said to my spirit, **4** "Behold, you have done this to me, in that you search out the ways of the Highest. **5** Behold, I am yet weary in my mind, and very weak in my spirit; nor is there the least strength in me, because of the great fear with which I was frightened this night. **6** Therefore, I will now implore the Most High, that He will strengthen me to the end." **7** And I said, "O Lord that bears rule, if I have found favor in Your sight, and if I am justified with You above many others, and if my prayer has indeed come up before Your face, **8** strengthen me then and show me, Your servant, the interpretation and plain

meaning of this fearful vision, that You may perfectly comfort my soul. **9** For You have judged me worthy to show me the end of time and the last times." **10** And He said to me, "This is the interpretation of this vision which you saw: **11** the eagle, whom you saw come up from the sea, is the fourth kingdom which appeared in vision to your brother Daniel. **12** But it was not expounded to him, as I now expound it to you or have expounded it. **13** Behold, the days come that there will rise up a kingdom on earth, and it will be feared above all the kingdoms that were before it. **14** Twelve kings will reign in it, one after another, **15** of which the second will begin to reign and will have a longer time than [any of the] twelve. **16** This is the interpretation of the twelve wings, which you saw. **17** And whereas you heard a voice which spoke, not going out from the heads, but from the midst of the body thereof, this is the interpretation: **18** that after the time of that kingdom there will arise no small contentions, and it will stand in peril of falling; nevertheless, it will not then fall, but will be restored again to its first estate. **19** And whereas you saw the eight wings under sticking to her wings, this is the interpretation: **20** that there will arise eight kings in it, whose times will be but small, and their years swift. **21** And two of them will perish when the middle time approaches; four will be kept for awhile until the time of the ending thereof will approach; but two will be kept to the end. **22** And whereas you saw three heads resting, this is the interpretation: **23** in the last days thereof, the Most High will raise up three kingdoms, and renew many things therein, and they will bear rule over the earth, **24** and over those that dwell therein, with much oppression, above all those that were before them. Therefore they are called the heads of the eagle. **25** For these are those who will accomplish her wickedness, and that will finish her last end. **26** And whereas you saw that the great head appeared no longer, [it signifies] that one of them will die on his bed, and yet with pain. **27** But for the two that remained, the sword will devour them. **28** For the sword of the one will devour him that was with him, but he will also fall by the sword in the last days. **29** And whereas you saw two wings under passing over to the head that is on the right side, **30** this is the interpretation: these are they whom the Most High has kept to His end; this is the small kingdom and full of trouble, as you saw. **31** And the lion, whom you saw rising up out of the wood, and roaring, and speaking to the eagle, and rebuking her for her unrighteousness, and all her words which you have heard: **32** this is the Anointed One, whom the Most High has kept to the end of days, who will spring up out of the seed of David, and He will come and speak to them, and reprove them for their wickedness and unrighteousness, and will heap up before them their contemptuous dealings. **33** For at the first He will set them alive in His judgment, and when He has reproved them, He will destroy them. **34** For He will deliver the rest of My people with mercy, those that have been preserved throughout My borders, and He will make them joyful until the coming of the end, even the Day of Judgment, of which I have spoken to you from the beginning. **35** This is the dream that you saw, and this is the interpretation thereof: **36** and you alone have been chosen to know the secret of the Most High. **37** Therefore, write all these things that you have seen in a scroll and put them in a secret place, **38** and you will teach them to the wise of your people, whose hearts you know are able to comprehend and keep these secrets. **39** But wait here yourself yet seven more days, that there may be showed to you whatever it pleases the Most High to show you." And He departed from me. **40** And it came to pass, when all the people saw that the seven days were past, and I had not come into the city again, they gathered themselves all together, from the least to the greatest, and came to me, and spoke to me, saying, **41** "How have we offended you? And what evil have we done against you that you have utterly forsaken us, and sit in this place? **42** For of all the prophets you alone are left to us, as a cluster of the vintage, and as a lamp in a dark place, and as a haven for a ship saved from the tempest. **43** Are the evils which have come to us not sufficient? **44** If you will forsake us, how much better had it been for us if we had also been consumed in the burning of Zion! **45** For we are not better than those who died there." And they wept with a loud voice. And I answered them, and said, **46** "Be of good comfort, O Israel; and do not be sorrowful, you house of Jacob: **47** for the Most High has you in remembrance, and the Mighty has not forgotten you forever. **48** As for me, I have not forsaken you, neither have I departed from you, but have come into this place to pray for the desolation of Zion, and that I might seek mercy for the low estate of your sanctuary. **49** And now go your way, every man to his own house, and after these days I will come to you." **50** So the people went their way into the city, just as I said to them, **51** but I sat in the field seven days, as [the messenger] commanded me; and in those days I ate only of the flowers of the field and had my meat of the herbs.

CHAPTER 13

1 And it came to pass after seven days, I dreamed a dream by night: **2** and behold, there arose a wind from the sea, that it moved all the waves thereof. **3** And I saw, and behold, this wind caused to come up from the midst of the sea as it were the likeness of a Man, and I saw, and behold, that Man flew with the clouds of Heaven; and when He turned His countenance to look, all things trembled that were seen under Him. **4** And whenever the voice went out of His mouth, all those that heard His voice burned, just as the wax melts when it feels the fire. **5** And after this I saw, and behold, there was gathered together a multitude of men, out of number, from the four winds of the sky, to make war against the Man that came out of the sea. **6** And I saw, and behold, He carved Himself a great mountain, and flew on it. **7** But I sought to see the region or place where the mountain was graven, and I could not. **8** And after this I saw, and behold, all they which were gathered together to fight against Him were severely afraid, and yet dared fight. **9** And behold, as He saw the assault of the multitude that came, He neither lifted up His hand, nor held spear, nor any instrument of war, **10** but only I saw how that He sent out of His mouth as it had been a flood of fire, and out of His lips a flaming breath, and out of His tongue He cast out sparks of the storm. **11** And these were all mixed together: the flood of fire, the flaming breath, and the great storm; and they fell on the assault of the multitude which was prepared to fight, and burned all of them up, so that suddenly nothing of [the] innumerable multitude was to be seen, but only dust of ashes and smell of smoke. When I saw this, I was amazed. **12** Afterward I saw the same Man come down from the mountain, and call to Himself another multitude which was peaceful. **13** And many people came to Him, of which some were glad, some were sorry, some of them were bound, and some brought of those who were offered. Then through great fear I awakened, and prayed to the Most High, and said, **14** "You have showed Your servant these wonders from the beginning, and have counted me worthy that You should receive my prayer: **15** and now show me, moreover, the interpretation of this dream. **16** For as I conceive in my understanding, woe to those who will be left in those days! and much more, woe to those who are not left! **17** For those who were not left will be in heaviness, **18** understanding the things that are laid up in the latter days, but not attaining to them. **19** But also woe to them that are left, for this reason; for they will see great perils and many necessities, just as these dreams declare. **20** Yet it is better for one to be in peril and to come into these things, than to pass away as a cloud out of the world, and not to see the things that will happen in the last days." And He answered to me, and said, **21** "I will tell you the interpretation of the vision, and I will also open to you the things of which you have made mention. **22** Whereas you have spoken of those who are left behind, this is the interpretation: **23** He that will endure the peril in that time will keep those who have fallen into danger, even such as have works and faith toward the Almighty. **24** Therefore, know that they which are left behind are more blessed than those who are dead. **25** These are the interpretations of the vision: whereas you saw a Man coming up from the midst of the sea, **26** this is He whom the Most High has kept a great season, which by His own self will deliver His creature; and He will order those who are left behind. **27** And whereas you saw that out of His mouth there came wind, and fire, and storm, **28** and whereas He held neither spear, nor any instrument of war, but destroyed the assault of that multitude which came to fight against Him, this is the interpretation: **29** behold, the days come when the Most High will begin to deliver those who are on the earth. **30** And there will come astonishment of mind on those who dwell on the earth. **31** And one will think to war against another—city against city, place against place, people against people, and kingdom against kingdom. **32** And it will be, when these things will come to pass, and the signs will happen which I showed you before, then My Son will be revealed, whom you saw [as] a Man ascending. **33** And it will be, when all the nations hear His voice, every man will leave his own land and the battle they have against one another. **31** And an innumerable

multitude will be gathered together, as you saw, desiring to come and to fight against Him. **35** But He will stand on the top of Mount Zion. **36** And Zion will come, and will be shown to all men, being prepared and built, just as you saw the mountain graven without hands. **37** And He, My Son, will rebuke the nations which have come for their wickedness, [with plagues] that are like to a tempest; **38** and He will taunt them to their face with their evil thoughts, and the torments with which they will be tormented, which are likened to a flame; and He will destroy them without labor by the Law, which is likened to fire. **39** And whereas you saw that He gathered to Himself another multitude that was peaceful: **40** these are the ten tribes, which were led away out of their own land in the time of Hoshea the king, whom Salmananser the king of the Assyrians led away captive, and he carried them beyond the River, and they were carried into another land. **41** But they took this counsel among themselves, that they would leave the multitude of the heathen, and go out into a further country, where mankind never lived, **42** that they might keep their statutes there, which they had not kept in their own land. **43** And they entered by the narrow passages of the River Euphrates. **44** For the Most High then performed signs for them, and held back the springs of the River until they had passed over. **45** For through that country there was a great way to go, namely, of a year and a half: and the same region is called Arzareth. **46** Then they lived there until the latter time; and now when they begin to come again, **47** the Most High holds back the springs of the River again, that they may go through: therefore you saw the multitude gathered together with peace. **48** But those that are left behind of your people are those who are found within My holy border. **49** It will be, therefore, when He will destroy the multitude of the nations that are gathered together, He will defend the people that remain. **50** And then He will show them very many wonders." **51** Then I said, "O Lord that bears rule, show me this: why I have seen the Man coming up from the midst of the sea." **52** And He said to me, "Just as one can neither seek out nor know what is in the deep of the sea, even so can no man on earth see My Son, or those that are with Him, but in the time of His day. **53** This is the interpretation of the dream which you saw, and for this you only are enlightened herein. **54** For you have forsaken your own [ways, and] applied your diligence to Mine, and have sought out My law. **55** You have ordered your life in wisdom and have called understanding your mother. **56** And therefore I have showed you this; for there is a reward laid up with the Most High; and it will be, after another three days I will speak other things to you and declare to you mighty and wondrous things." **57** Then I went out and passed into the field, greatly giving praise and thanks to the Most High because of His wonders, which He did from time to time, **58** and because He governs the time, and such things as fall in their seasons. And there I sat three days.

CHAPTER 14

1 And it came to pass on the third day, I sat under an oak, and behold, there came a voice out of a bush near me, and said, "Ezra, Ezra." **2** And I said, "Here I am, Lord." And I stood up on my feet. **3** Then He said to me, "In the bush I manifestly revealed Myself, and talked with Moses when My people were in bondage in Egypt: **4** and I sent him, and he led My people out of Egypt; and I brought him up to [the] mountain of Sinai, where I kept him near Me for many days, **5** and told him many wondrous things, and showed him the secrets of the times, and the end of the seasons, and commanded him, saying, **6** You will publish these words openly, and these you will hide. **7** And now I say to you, **8** lay up in your heart the signs that I have showed, and the dreams that you have seen, and the interpretations which you have heard: **9** for you will be taken away from men, and from now on you will remain with My Son, and with such as are like you, until the times are ended. **10** For the world has lost its youth, and the times begin to wax old. **11** For the world is divided into twelve parts, and ten parts of it are already gone, even the half of the tenth part: **12** and there remains of it two parts after the middle of the tenth part. **13** Now therefore, set your house in order, and reprove your people, comfort the lowly among them, and instruct such of them as are wise, and now renounce the life that is corruptible, **14** and let go from you the mortal thoughts, cast yourself away from the burdens of man, put off now your weak nature, **15** and lay aside the thoughts that are most grievous to you, and hasten to depart from these times. **16** For yet worse evils than those which you have seen happen will be done hereafter. [17] For see how much the world will be weaker through age—so much the more will evils increase on those who dwell therein. [18] For the truth will withdraw itself further off, and falsehood will be hard at hand; for now the eagle which you saw in [the] vision hastens to come." [19] Then I answered and said, "I will speak before You, O Lord. [20] Behold, I will go, as You have commanded me, and reprove the people that now are, but those who will be born afterward, who will admonish them? For the world is set in darkness, and those who dwell therein are without light. [21] For Your law is burned, therefore no man knows the things that You have done, or the works that will be done. [22] But if I have found favor before You, send the Holy Spirit to me, and I will write all that has been done in the world since the beginning, even the things that were written in Your law, that men may be able to find the path, and that they which would live in the latter days may live." [23] And He answered me and said, "Go your way, gather the people together, and say to them that they may not seek you for forty days. [24] But prepare many tablets, and take with you Sarea, Dabria, Selemia, Ethanus, and Asiel, these five, which are ready to write swiftly; [25] and come here, and I will light a lamp of understanding in your heart, which will not be put out until the things which you will write are ended. [26] And when you have done this, some things you will publish openly, and some things you will deliver in secret to the wise. Tomorrow at this hour you will begin to write." [27] Then I went out, as He commanded me, and gathered all the people together, and said, [28] "Hear these words, O Israel. [29] At the beginning our fathers were strangers in Egypt, and they were delivered from there, [30] and received the law of life, which they did not keep, which you also have transgressed after them. [31] Then the land, even the land of Zion, was given to you for a possession, but you yourselves, and your fathers, have done unrighteousness, and have not kept the ways which the Most High commanded you. [32] And forasmuch as He is a righteous judge, He took from you for awhile the thing that He had given to you. [33] And now you are here, and your relatives are among you. [34] Therefore, if [it] so be that you will rule over your own understanding, and instruct your hearts, you will be kept alive, and after death you will obtain mercy. [35] For after death the judgment will come when we will live again; and then the names of the righteous will be manifest, and the works of the ungodly will be declared. [36] Therefore, let no man come to me now, nor seek after me these forty days." [37] So I took the five men as He commanded me, and we went out into the field and remained there. [38] And it came to pass on the next day that, behold, a voice called me, saying, "Ezra, open your mouth, and drink what I give you to drink." [39] Then I opened my mouth, and behold, there was given to me a full cup, which was full as it were with water, but the color of it was like fire. [40] And I took it and drank. And when I had drunk of it, my heart uttered understanding, and wisdom grew in my breast, for my spirit retained its memory; [41] and my mouth was opened and no longer shut. [42] The Most High gave understanding to the five men, and they wrote by course the things that were told them, in characters which they did not know, and they sat [for] forty days. Now they wrote in the daytime, and at night they ate bread. [43] As for me, I spoke in the day, and I did not hold my tongue by night. [44] So in forty days ninety-four scrolls were written. [45] And it came to pass, when the forty days were fulfilled, that the Most High spoke to me, saying, "The first that you have written publish openly, and let the worthy and unworthy read it, [46] but keep the seventy last, that you may deliver them to such as are wise among your people, [47] for in them is the spring of understanding, the fountain of wisdom, and the stream of knowledge." [48] And I did so.

CHAPTER 15

[1] "Behold, speak in the ears of My people the words of prophecy, which I will put in your mouth," says the Lord; [2] "and cause them to be written in paper, for they are faithful and true. [3] Do not be afraid of their imaginations against you, do not let the unbelief of them that speak against you trouble you. [4] For all the unbelievers will die in their unbelief. [5] Behold," says the Lord, "I bring calamities on the whole earth: sword, and famine, and death, and destruction. [6] For wickedness has prevailed over every land, and their hurtful works have come to the full. [7] Therefore," says the Lord, [8] "I will no longer hold My peace as touching their wickedness, which they profanely commit, neither will I permit them in these things, which they

wickedly practice. Behold, the innocent and righteous blood cries to Me, and the souls of the righteous cry out continually. [9] I will surely avenge them," says the Lord, "and will receive to Myself all the innocent blood from among them. [10] Behold, My people are led as a flock to the slaughter: I will not permit them to now dwell in the land of Egypt, [11] but I will bring them out with a mighty hand and with a high arm, and will strike Egypt with plagues, as previously, and will destroy all the land thereof. [12] Let Egypt mourn, and the foundations thereof, for the plague of the discipline and the punishment that God will bring on it. [13] Let the farmers that till the ground mourn, for their seeds will fail and their trees will be laid waste through the blasting, and hail, and a terrible storm. [14] Woe to the world and those who dwell therein! [15] For the sword and their destruction draws near, and nation will rise up against nation to battle with weapons in their hands. [16] For there will be sedition among men; and waxing strong against one another, they will not regard their king nor the chief of their great ones, in their might. [17] For a man will desire to go into a city and will not be able. [18] For because of their pride the cities will be troubled, the houses will be destroyed, and men will be afraid. [19] A man will have no pity on his neighbor but will make an assault on their houses with the sword, and plunder their goods, because of the lack of bread, and for great suffering. [20] Behold," says God, "I call together all the kings of the earth, to stir up those who are from the rising of the sun, from the south, from the east, and Libanus, to turn themselves against one another, and repay the things that they have done to them. [21] Just as they yet do this day to My chosen, so I will do also, and repay in their bosom." The Lord God says: [22] "My right hand will not spare the sinners, and My sword will not cease over those who shed innocent blood on the earth. [23] And a fire has gone out from His wrath, and has consumed the foundations of the earth, and the sinners, like the straw that is kindled. [24] Woe to those who sin and do not keep My commands!" says the Lord. [25] "I will not spare them. Go your way, you rebellious children, do not defile My sanctuary. [26] For the Lord knows all those who trespass against Him, therefore He has delivered them to death and destruction. [27] For now the calamities have come on the whole earth, and you will remain in them, for God will not deliver you, because you have sinned against Him. [28] Behold, a horrible vision, and the appearance thereof from the east! [29] And the nations of the dragons of Arabia will come out with many chariots, and from the day that they set out their hissing of them is carried over the earth, so that all they which will hear them may also fear and tremble. [30] Also the Carmonians raging in wrath will go out as the wild boars of the wood, and they will come with great power and join battle with them, and will waste a portion of the land of the Assyrians with their teeth. [31] And then the dragons will have the upper hand, remembering their nature; and if they will turn themselves, conspiring together in great power to persecute them, [32] then these will be troubled, and keep silence through their power, and will turn and flee. [33] And from the land of the Assyrians the ambusher in wait will besiege them, and consume one of them, and on their army will be fear and trembling, and sedition against their kings. [34] Behold, clouds from the east and from the north to the south, and they are very horrible to look on—full of wrath and storm. [35] They will dash one against another, and they will pour out a plentiful storm on the earth, even their own storm; and there will be blood from the sword to the horse's belly, [36] and to the thigh of man, and to the camel's hock. [37] And there will be fearfulness and great trembling on earth: and they that see that wrath will be afraid, and trembling will take hold on them. [38] And after this there will be stirred up great storms from the south, and from the north, and another part from the west. [39] And strong winds will arise from the east, and will shut it up, even the cloud which He raised up in wrath; and the storm that was to cause destruction by the east wind will be violently driven toward the south and west. [40] And great clouds, indeed mighty and full of wrath, will be lifted up—and the storm—that they may destroy all the earth, and those who dwell therein; and they will pour out over every high and eminent one a terrible storm, [41] [with] fire, and hail, and flying swords, and many waters, that all plains may be full, and all rivers, with the abundance of those waters. [42] And they will break down the cities and walls, mountains and hills, trees of the wood, and grass of the meadows, and their corn. [43] And they will go on steadfastly to Babylon and destroy her. [44] They will come to her and surround her; they will pour out the storm and all wrath on her; then the dust and smoke will rise up to the sky, and all those who are around her will mourn her. **45** And those who remain will do service to those who have put her in fear. **46** And you, Asia, that are partaker in the beauty of Babylon, and in the glory of her person: **47** woe to you, you wretch, because you have made yourself like to her; you have decked your daughters in whoredom, that they might please and glory in your lovers, which have always desired you to commit whoredom with! **48** You have followed her that is hateful in all her works and inventions: therefore," says God, **49** "I will send evils on you: widowhood, poverty, famine, sword, and pestilence, to waste your houses to destruction and death. **50** And the glory of your power will be dried up as a flower, when the heat will arise that is sent over you. **51** You will be weakened as a poor woman with stripes, and as one disciplined with wounds, so that you will not be able to receive your mighty ones and [your] lovers. **52** Would I with jealousy have so proceeded against you," says the Lord, **53** "if you had not always slain My chosen, exalting the stroke of your hands, and saying over their dead, when you were drunken, **54** Set out the beauty of your countenance? **55** The reward of a prostitute will be in your bosom, therefore you will receive repayment. **56** Just as you will do to My chosen," says the Lord, "even so God will do to you, and will deliver you into mischief. **57** And your children will die of hunger, and you will fall by the sword, and your cities will be broken down, and all yours will perish by the sword in the field. **58** And those who are in the mountains will die of hunger, and eat their own flesh, and drink [their own] blood, for great hunger of bread, and thirst of water. **59** You, unhappy above all, will come and will receive calamities again. **60** And in the passage, they will rush on the idle city, and will destroy some portion of your land, and mar part of your glory, and will again return to Babylon that was destroyed. **61** And you will be cast down by them as stubble, and they will be to you as fire, **62** and will devour you, and your cities, your land, and your mountains; they will burn up all your woods and your fruitful trees with fire. **63** They will carry your children away captive, and will plunder your wealth, and mar the glory of your face."

CHAPTER 16

1 "Woe to you, Babylon and Asia! woe to you, Egypt and Syria! **2** Gird yourselves with sackcloth and garments of hair, and mourn your children, and lament; for your destruction is at hand. **3** A sword is sent on you, and who is he that may turn it back? **4** A fire is sent on you, and who is he that may quench it? **5** Calamities are sent on you, and who is he that may drive them away? **6** May one drive away a hungry lion in the wood? or may one quench the fire in stubble, when it has once begun to burn? **7** May one turn again the arrow that is shot of a strong archer? **8** The Lord God sends the evils, and who will drive them away? **9** A fire will go out from His wrath, and who is he that may quench it? **10** He will cast lightning, and who will not fear? he will thunder, and who will not tremble? **11** The Lord will threaten, and who will not be utterly broken in pieces at His presence? **12** The earth quakes, and the foundations thereof; the sea arises with waves from the deep, and the waves of it will be troubled, and also the fishes thereof, at the presence of the Lord, and before the glory of His power: **13** for strong is His right hand that bends the bow; His arrows that He shoots are sharp, and will not miss, when they begin to be shot into the ends of the world. **14** Behold, the calamities are sent out, and will not return again, until they come on the earth. **15** The fire is kindled, and will not be put out, until it consumes the foundations of the earth. **16** Just as an arrow which is shot by a mighty archer does not return backward, even so the calamities that are sent out on earth will not return again. **17** Woe is me! woe is me! who will deliver me in those days? **18** The beginning of sorrows, and the great mourning; the beginning of famine, and many will perish; the beginning of wars, and the powers will stand in fear; the beginning of calamities, and all will tremble! what will they do in [all] this when the calamities will come? **19** Behold, famine and plague, suffering and anguish! they are sent as scourges for amendment. **20** But for all these things they will not turn them from their wickedness, nor be always mindful of the scourges. **21** Behold, food will be so cheap on earth that they will think themselves to be in a good case, and even then, calamities will grow on earth: sword, famine, and great confusion. **22** For many of those who dwell on earth will perish of famine; and the other, that escape the famine, will the sword destroy. **23** And the dead will be cast out as dung, and there will be no man

to comfort them, for the earth will be left desolate, and the cities thereof will be cast down. **24** There will be no farmer left to till the earth, and to sow it. **25** The trees will give fruit, and who will gather them? **26** The grapes will ripen, and who will tread them? for in [all] places there will be a great forsaking: **27** for one man will desire to see another, or to hear his voice. **28** For of a city there will be ten left, and two of the field, which have hidden themselves in the thick groves, and in the clefts of the rocks. **29** As in an orchard of olives on every tree there are left three or four olives, **30** or as when a vineyard is gathered there are some clusters left by those who diligently seek through the vineyard; **31** even so in those days there will be three or four left by those who search their houses with the sword. **32** And the earth will be left desolate, and the fields thereof will be for briers, and her ways and all her paths will bring out thorns, because no sheep will pass through there. **33** The virgins will mourn, having no bridegrooms; the women will mourn, having no husbands; their daughters will mourn, having no helpers. **34** In the wars their bridegrooms will be destroyed, and their husbands will perish of famine. **35** Now hear these things, and understand them, you servants of the Lord. **36** Behold, the word of the Lord, receive it: do not disbelieve the things of which the Lord speaks. **37** Behold, the calamities draw near, and are not slack. **38** Just as a woman with child in the ninth month, when the hour of her delivery draws near, within two or three hours sorrowful pains surround her womb, and when the child comes out from the womb, there will be no waiting for [even] a moment: **39** even so the calamities will not be slack to come on the earth, and the world will groan, and sorrows will take hold of it on every side. **40** O My people, hear My word: make ready for the battle, and in those calamities be even as pilgrims on the earth. **41** He that sells, let him be as he that flees away; and he that buys, as one that will lose; **42** he that occupies merchandise, as he that has no profit by it; and he that builds, as he that will not dwell therein; **43** he that sows, as if he should not reap; so also he that prunes [the vines], as he that will not gather the grapes; **44** those who marry, as those who will get no children; and those who do not marry, as the widowed. **45** Because of this, those who labor labor in vain; **46** for strangers will reap their fruits, and plunder their goods, overthrow their houses, and take their children captive, for in captivity and famine they will beget their children; **47** and those who traffic traffic to become a plunder—the more they deck their cities, their houses, their possessions, and their own persons, **48** the more I will hate them for their sins," says the Lord. **49** "Just as a rightly honest and virtuous woman hates a prostitute, **50** so righteousness will hate iniquity when she decks herself, and will accuse her to her face when He comes that will defend him that diligently searches out every sin on earth. **51** Therefore, do not be like them, nor do the works thereof. **52** For yet a little while, and iniquity will be taken away out of the earth, and righteousness will reign over us. **53** Do not let the sinner say that he has not sinned, for he will burn coals of fire on his head, which says, I have not sinned before God and His glory. **54** Behold, the Lord knows all the works of men, their imaginations, their thoughts, and their hearts— **55** [He] who said, Let the earth be made, and it was made; [and,] Let the heaven be made, and it was made; **56** and at His word the stars were established, and He knows the number of the stars; **57** who searches the deep, and the treasures thereof; He has measured the sea, and what it contains; **58** who has shut the sea in the midst of the waters, and with His word He has hanged the earth on the waters; **59** who spreads out the sky like a vault; He has established it on the waters; **60** who has made springs of water in the desert, and pools on the tops of the mountains, to send out rivers from the height to water the earth; **61** who framed man and put a heart in the midst of the body, and gave him breath, life, and understanding— **62** yes, the Spirit of God Almighty. He who made all things, and searches out hidden things in hidden places, **63** surely He knows your imagination, and what you think in your hearts. Woe to those who sin and would gladly hide their sin! **64** Because of this, the Lord will exactly search out all your works, and He will put you all to shame. **65** And when your sins are brought out before men, you will be ashamed, and your own iniquities will stand as your accusers in that day. **66** What will you do? or how will you hide your sins before God and His messengers? **67** Behold, God is the judge— fear Him: depart from your sins, and forget your iniquities, to no longer meddle with them forever, so God will lead you out, and deliver you from all suffering. **68** For behold, the burning wrath of a great multitude is kindled over you, and they will take away certain of you, and feed you with that which is slain to idols. **⁶⁹** And those who consent to them will be held in derision and in reproach and will be trodden under their foot. **⁷⁰** For there will be in various places, and in the next cities, a great insurrection on those that fear the Lord. **⁷¹** They will be like mad men, sparing none, but spoiling and destroying those who still fear the Lord. **⁷²** For they will waste and take away their goods and cast them out of their houses. **⁷³** Then the trial of My chosen ones will be manifested, even as the gold that is tried in the fire. **⁷⁴** Hear, O you My chosen ones," says the Lord: "behold, the days of suffering are at hand, and I will deliver you from them. **⁷⁵** Do not be afraid, neither doubt; for God is your guide. **⁷⁶** And you who keep My commands and precepts," says the Lord God, "do not let your sins weigh you down, and do not let your iniquities lift themselves up. **⁷⁷** Woe to those who are fast bound with their sins, and covered with their iniquities, like as a field is fast bound with bushes, and the path thereof covered with thorns, that no man may travel through! **⁷⁸** It is even shut off and given up to be consumed by fire."

3 MACCABEES

The book of 3 Maccabees is found in most Orthodox Bibles as a part of the deuterocanon. Catholics consider it to be an example of pseudepigrapha and do not regard it as canonical. Protestants, with the exception of the Moravian Brothers who include it in the Apocrypha of the Czech Kralice Bible and Polish Gdańsk Bible, likewise regard it as non-canonical. Despite the title, the book has nothing to do with the Maccabees or their revolt against the Seleucid Empire, as described in 1 Maccabees and 2 Maccabees. Instead, it tells the story of persecution of the Jews under Ptolemy IV Philopator (222–205 BC), some decades before the Maccabean uprising. The name of the book apparently comes from the similarities between this book and the stories of the martyrdom of Eleazar and the Maccabean youths in 2 Maccabees; the chief priest Shimon is also mentioned.

CHAPTER 1

¹ When Philopator learned from those who came back that Antiochus had made himself master of the places which belonged to himself, he sent orders to all his footmen and horsemen, took his sister Arsinoe with him, and marched out as far as the parts of Raphia, where Antiochus and his forces encamped. **²** And one Theodotus, intending to carry out his design, took with him the bravest of the armed men who had been previously committed to his trust by Ptolemy, and got through at night to the tent of Ptolemy, to kill him on his own responsibility, and so to end the war. **³** But Dositheus, called the son of Drimulus, by birth a Jew, afterward a renegade from the laws and observances of his country, carried Ptolemy away, and made an obscure person lie down in his place in the tent. It befell this man to receive the fate which was meant for the other. **⁴** A fierce battle then took place, and the men of Antiochus prevailing, Arsinoe continually went up and down the ranks, and with disheveled hair, with tears and pleadings, begged the soldiers to fight courageously for themselves, their children, and wives; and promised that if they proved conquerors, she would give them each two minas of gold. **⁵** It then happened that their enemies were defeated in hand-to-hand encounter, and that many of them were taken prisoners. **⁶** Having vanquished this attempt, the king then decided to proceed to the neighboring cities and encourage them. **⁷** By doing this, and by making donations to their temples, he inspired his subjects with confidence. **⁸** The Jews sent some of their council and of their elders to him. The greetings, gifts of welcome, and commendations of the past, bestowed by them, filled him with the greater eagerness to visit their city. **⁹** Having arrived at Jerusalem, sacrificed, and offered thank-offerings to the greatest God, and done whatever else was suitable to the sanctity of the place, and entered the inner court, **¹⁰** he was so struck with the magnificence of the place, and so wondered at the orderly arrangements of the temple, that he considered entering the sanctuary itself. **¹¹** And when they told him that this was not permissible, none of the nation, no, nor even the priests in general, but only the supreme chief priest of all, and he only once in a year, being allowed to go in, he would by no means give way. **¹²** Then they read the Law to him; but he persisted in obtruding himself, exclaiming that he should be allowed, and saying, "Be it that they were deprived of this honor, I should not be." **¹³** And he put the question, "Why, when he entered all the temples, did none of the priests who were present forbid him?" **¹⁴** He was thoroughly answered by someone, that he did wrong to boast of this. **¹⁵** "Well; since I have done this," he said, "be the cause what it may, will I not enter with or without your consent?" **¹⁶** And when the priests fell down in their sacred vestments imploring the greatest God to come and help in time of need, and to avert the violence of the fierce aggressor, and when they filled the temple with lamentations and tears, **¹⁷** then those who had been left behind in the city were scared, and rushed out, uncertain of the event. **¹⁸** Virgins, who had been shut up within their chambers, came out with their mothers, scattering dust and ashes on their heads, and filling the streets with outcries. **¹⁹** Women, but recently separated off, left their bridal chambers, left the reserve that suited them, and ran around the city in a disorderly manner. **²⁰** Newborn babies were deserted by the mothers or nurses who waited on them; some here, some there—in houses, or in fields; these now, with a zeal which could not be checked, swarmed into the highest temple. **²¹** Manifold prayers were offered up by those who assembled in this place, on account of the unholy attempt of the king. **²²** Along with these there were some of the citizens who took courage, and would not submit to his obstinacy, and his intention of carrying out his purpose. **²³** Calling out to arms, and to die bravely in defense of the law of their fathers, they created a great uproar in the place, and were with difficulty brought back by the aged and the elders to the station of prayer which they had occupied before. **²⁴** During this time, the multitude kept on praying. **²⁵** The elders who surrounded the king tried in many ways to divert his arrogant mind from the design which he had formed. **²⁶** He, in his hardened mood, insensible to all persuasion, was going onward with the view of carrying out this design. **²⁷** Yet even his own officers, when they saw this, joined the Jews in an appeal to Him who has all power, to aid in the present crisis, and not to wink at such overconfident lawlessness. **²⁸** Such was the frequency and the vehemence of the cry of the assembled crowd, that an indescribable noise ensued. **²⁹** Not the men only, but the very walls and floor seemed to sound out—all things preferring dissolution rather than to see the place defiled.

CHAPTER 2

¹ Then the chief priest Simon bowed his knees near the holy place, and spread out his hands in reverent form, and uttered the following supplication: **²** "O Lord, Lord, King of the heavens, and Ruler of the whole creation, Holy among the holy, sole Governor, Almighty, give ear to us who are oppressed by a wicked and profane one, who celebrates in his confidence and strength. **³** It is You, the Creator of all, the Lord of the universe, who are a righteous Governor, and judge all who act with pride and insolence. **⁴** It was You who destroyed the former workers of unrighteousness, among whom were the giants, who trusted in their strength and daring, by covering them with a measureless flood. **⁵** It was You who made the Sodomites, those workers of exceeding iniquity, men notorious for their vices, an example to following generations, when You covered them with fire and brimstone. **⁶** You made Your power known when You caused the bold Pharaoh, the enslaver of Your people, to pass through the ordeal of many and diverse afflictions. **⁷** And You rolled the depths of the sea over him, when he made pursuit with chariots, and with a multitude of followers, and gave a safe passage to those who put their trust in You, the Lord of the whole creation. **⁸** These saw and felt the works of Your hands, and praised You, the Almighty. **⁹** You, O King, when You created the limitless and measureless earth, chose out this city: You made this place sacred to Your Name, albeit You need nothing. You glorified it with Your illustrious presence, after constructing it to the glory of Your great and honorable Name. **¹⁰** And You promised, out of love, to the people of Israel, that should we fall away from You, and become afflicted, and then come to this house and pray, You would hear our prayer. **¹¹** Truly You are faithful and true. **¹²** And when You often aided our fathers when hard-pressed, and in low estate, and delivered them out of great dangers, **13** see now, holy King, how through our many and great sins we are borne down, and made subject to our enemies, and have become weak and powerless. **14** We being in this low condition, this bold and profane man seeks to dishonor this, Your holy place, consecrated out of the earth to the Name of Your Majesty. **15** Your dwelling place, the Heaven of heavens, is indeed unapproachable to men. **16** But since it seemed good to You to exhibit Your glory among Your people Israel, You sanctified this place. **17** Do not punish us by means of the uncleanness of their men, nor discipline us by means of their profanity, lest the lawless ones should boast in their rage, and exult in exuberant pride of speech, and say, **18** We have trampled on the holy house, as idolatrous houses are trampled on. **19** Blot out our iniquities, and do away with our errors, and show forth Your compassion in this hour. **20** Let Your mercies quickly go before us. Grant us peace, that the cast down and brokenhearted may praise You with their mouth." **21** At that time God, who sees all things, who is beyond all Holy among the holy, heard that prayer, so suitable, and scourged the man greatly uplifted with scorn and insolence. **22** Shaking him to and fro as a reed is shaken with the wind, He cast him on the pavement, powerless, with limbs paralyzed, by a righteous judgment deprived [him] of the faculty of speech. **23** His friends and bodyguards, beholding the swift repayment which had suddenly overtaken him, struck with exceeding terror, and fearing that he would die, speedily removed him. **24** When in [the] course of time he had come to himself, this severe check caused no conversion within him, but he departed with bitter threats. **25** He proceeded to Egypt, grew worse in wickedness through his aforementioned companions in wine, who were lost to all goodness; **26** and not satisfied with countless acts of impiety, his audacity so increased that he raised evil reports there, and many of his friends, watching his purpose attentively, joined in furthering his will. **27** His purpose was to indict a public stigma on our race; for that reason, he erected a pillar at the tower-porch, and caused the following inscription to be engraved on it: **28** "The entrance to their temple is to be refused to all those who will not sacrifice; all the Jews are to be registered among the common people; those who resist are to be forcibly seized and put to death; **29** those who are so registered, are to be marked on their persons by the ivy-leaf symbol of Dionysus, and to be set apart with these limited rights." **30** To do away with the appearance of hating them all, he had it written underneath: "If any of them should choose to enter the community of those initiated in the rites, these should have equal rights with the Alexandrians." **31** Some of those who were over the city, therefore, abhorring any approach to the city of piety, unhesitatingly gave in to the king, and expected to derive some great honor from a future connection with him. **32** A nobler spirit, however, prompted the majority to cling to their religious observances, and by paying money that they might live unmolested, these sought to escape the registration. **33** Cheerfully looking forward to future aid, they abhorred their own apostates, considering them to be national enemies, and were debarring them from the common usages of social intercourse.

CHAPTER 3

1 On discovering this, so incensed was the wicked king that he no longer confined his rage to the Jews in Alexandria. Laying his hand more heavily on those who lived in the country, he gave orders that they should be quickly collected into one place, and most cruelly deprived of their lives. **2** While this was going on, an invidious rumor was uttered abroad by men who had banded together to injure the Jewish race. The purport of their charge was that the Jews kept them away from the ordinances of the law. **3** Now, while the Jews always maintained a feeling of unwavering loyalty toward the kings, **4** yet, as they worshiped God, and observed His law, they made certain distinctions, and avoided certain things. Hence some persons held them in revulsion; **5** although, as they adorned their conversation with works of righteousness, they had established themselves in the good opinion of the world. **6** What all the rest of mankind said, was, however, made of no account by the foreigners, **7** who said much of the exclusiveness of the Jews with regard to their worship and meats; they alleged that they were unsociable men, hostile to the king's interests, refusing to associate with him or his troops. By this way of speaking,

they brought much odium on them. **8** Nor was this unexpected uproar and sudden conflux of people unobserved by the Greeks who lived in the city, concerning men who had never harmed them: yet to aid them was not in their power, since there was oppression all around, but they encouraged them in their troubles, and expected a favorable turn of affairs. **9** He who knows all things, will not, [they said,] disregard so great a people. **10** Some of the neighbors, friends, and fellow dealers of the Jews, even called them secretly to an interview, pledged them their assistance, and promised to do their very utmost for them. **11** Now the king, elated with his prosperous fortune, and not regarding the superior power of God, but thinking to persevere in his present purpose, wrote the following letter to the prejudice of the Jews: **12** "King Ptolemy Philopator, to the commanders and soldiers in Egypt, and in all places, health and happiness! **13** I am right [and] well; and so, too, are my affairs. **14** Since our Asiatic campaign, the particulars of which you know, and which by the aid of the gods, not lightly given, and by our own vigor, has been brought to a successful issue according to our expectation, **15** we resolved, not with strength of spear, but with gentleness and much humanity, as it were to nurse the inhabitants of Coele-Syria and Phoenicia, and to be their willing benefactors. **16** So, having bestowed considerable sums of money on the temples of the several cities, we proceeded even as far as Jerusalem, and went up to honor the temple of these wretched beings who never cease from their folly. **17** To outward appearance they received us willingly, but belied that appearance by their deeds. When we were eager to enter their temple, and to honor it with the most beautiful and exquisite gifts, **18** they were so carried away by their old arrogance, as to forbid us the entrance; while we, out of our forbearance toward all men, refrained from exercising our power on them. **19** And so, exhibiting their enmity against us, they alone among the nations lift up their heads against kings and benefactors, as men unwilling to submit to anything reasonable. **20** We then, having endeavored to make allowance for the madness of these persons, and on our victorious return treating all people in Egypt courteously, acted in a manner which was befitting. **21** Accordingly, bearing no ill-will against their countrymen [at Jerusalem], but rather remembering our connection with them, and the numerous matters with sincere heart from a remote period entrusted to them, we wished to venture a total alteration of their state, by giving them the rights of citizens of Alexandria, and to admit them to the continuous rites of our solemnities. **22** All this, however, they have taken in a very different spirit. With their innate malignity, they have spurned the fair offer; and constantly inclining to evil, **23** have rejected the inestimable rights. Not only so, but by using speech, and by refraining from speech, they abhor the few among them who are heartily disposed toward us, ever deeming that their ignoble course of procedure will force us to do away with our reform. **24** Having then received certain proofs that these [Jews] bear us every sort of ill-will, we must look forward to the possibility of some sudden tumult among ourselves, when these impious men may turn traitors and barbarous enemies. **25** As soon, therefore, as the contents of this letter become known to you, in that same hour we order those [Jews] who dwell among you, with wives and children, to be sent to us, vilified and abused, in chains of iron, to undergo a death, cruel and ignominious, suitable to disaffected men. **26** For by the punishment of them in one body we perceive that we have found the only means of establishing our affairs for the future on a firm and satisfactory basis. **27** Whoever will shield a Jew, whether it be old man, child, or nursing baby, will with his whole house be tortured to death. **28** Whoever will inform against the [Jews], besides receiving the property of the person charged, will be presented with two thousand drachmas from the royal treasury, will be made free, and will be crowned. **29** Whatever place will shelter a Jew, will, when he is hunted out, be put under the ban of fire, and be forever rendered useless to every living being for all time to come." **30** Such was the purport of the king's letter.

CHAPTER 4

1 Wherever this decree was received, the people kept up a revelry of joy and shouting, as if their long-pent-up, hardened hatred, was now to show itself openly. **2** The Jews suffered great throes of sorrow and wept much, while their hearts, all things around being lamentable, were set on fire as they mourned the sudden destruction which was decreed against them. **3** What home, or city, or place at all inhabited, or what streets were there, which their condition did not fill with wailing and lamentation? **4** They were sent out unanimously by the generals in the several cities, with such stern and pitiless feeling, that the exceptional nature of the infliction moved even some of their enemies. These influenced by sentiments of common humanity, and reflecting on the uncertain issue of life, shed tears at this miserable expulsion of theirs. **5** A multitude of aged, gray-haired old men, were driven along with halting [and] bending feet, urged onward by the impulse of a violent, shameless force to quick speed. **6** Girls who had entered the bridal chamber quite lately, to enjoy the partnership of marriage, exchanged pleasure for misery, and with dust scattered on their myrrh-anointed heads, were hurried along unveiled, and, in the midst of outlandish insults, set up a lamentable cry with one accord instead of the marriage hymn. **7** Bound, and exposed to public gaze, they were violently hurried on board ship. **8** The husbands of these, in the prime of their youthful vigor, wore halters around their necks instead of crowns; instead of feasting and youthful celebration, they spent the rest of their nuptial days in wailing, and saw only the grave at hand. **9** They were dragged along by unyielding chains, like wild beasts; of these, some had their necks thrust into the benches of the rowers, while the feet of others were enclosed in hard chains. **10** The planks of the deck above them blocked out the light, and shut out the day on every side, so that they might be treated like traitors during the whole voyage. **11** They were accordingly transported in this vessel, and at the end of it arrived at Schedia. The king had ordered them to be cast into the vast hippodrome, which was built in front of the city. This place was well adapted by its situation to expose them to the gaze of all those coming into the city, and of those who went from the city into the country. So they could hold no communication with his forces, no, [and] were deemed unworthy of any civilized accommodation. **12** When this was done, the king, hearing that their relatives in the city often went out and lamented the melancholy distress of these victims, **13** was full of rage, and commanded that they should be carefully subjected to the same (and not one bit milder) treatment. **14** The whole nation was now to be registered. Every individual was to be specified by name, not for that hard servitude of labor which we have shortly before mentioned, but that he might expose them to the previously mentioned tortures; and finally, in the short space of a day, might eradicate them by his cruelties. **15** The registering of these men was carried on cruelly, zealously, assiduously, from the rising of the sun to its going down, and was not brought to an end in forty days. **16** The king was filled with great and constant joy, and celebrated banquets before the temple idols. His erring heart, far from the truth, and his profane mouth, gave glory to idols, deaf and incapable of speaking or aiding, and uttered unworthy speech against the greatest God. **17** At the end of the above-mentioned interval of time, the registrars brought word to the king that the multitude of the Jews was too great for registration, **18** inasmuch as there were many still left in the land, of whom some were in inhabited houses, and others were scattered around in various places, so that all the commanders in Egypt were insufficient for the work. **19** The king threatened them, and charged them with taking bribes, in order to contrive the escape of the Jews, but was clearly convinced of the truth of what had been said. **20** They said, and proved, that paper and pens had failed them for the carrying out of their purpose. **21** Now this was an active interference of the unconquerable providence which assisted the Jews from Heaven.

CHAPTER 5

1 Then he called Hermon, who had charge of the elephants. Full of rage, altogether fixed in his furious design, **2** he commanded him, with a quantity of unmixed wine and handfuls of incense [infused] to drug the elephants early on the following day. These five hundred elephants were, when infuriated by the copious draughts of frankincense, to be led up to the execution of death on the Jews. **3** The king, after issuing these orders, went to his feasting and gathered together all those of his friends and of the army who hated the Jews the most. **4** The master of the elephants, Hermon, fulfilled his commission punctually. **5** The underlings appointed for the purpose went out about evening and bound the hands of the miserable victims, and took other precautions for their security at night, thinking that the whole race would perish together. **6**

The heathen believed the Jews to be destitute of all protection, for chains bound them around. **7** They invoked the Almighty Lord, and ceaselessly implored with tears their merciful God and Father, Ruler of all, Lord of every power, **8** to overthrow the evil purpose which had gone out against them, and to deliver them by extraordinary manifestation from that death which was in store for them. **9** Their litany so earnest went up to Heaven. **10** Then Hermon, who had filled his merciless elephants with copious draughts of mixed wine and frankincense, came early to the palace to certify the kind thereof. **11** He, however, who has sent His good creature sleep from all time, by night or by day, so gratifying whom He wills, now diffused a portion thereof on the king. **12** By this sweet and profound influence of the Lord he was held fast, and so his unjust purpose was quite frustrated, and his unflinching resolve greatly falsified. **13** But the Jews, having escaped the hour which had been fixed, praised their holy God, and again begged Him who is easily reconciled to display the power of His powerful hand to the overconfident nations. **14** The middle of the tenth hour had well near arrived, when the person who sent invitations, seeing the guests who were invited present, came and shook the king. **15** He gained his attention with difficulty, and hinting that the mealtime was getting past, talked the matter over with him. **16** The king listened to this, and then turning aside to his drinking, commanded the guests to sit down before him. **17** This done, he asked them to enjoy themselves, and to indulge in mirth at this somewhat late hour of the banquet. **18** Conversation grew on, and the king sent for Hermon, and inquired of him, with fierce denunciations, why the Jews had been allowed to outlive that day. **19** Hermon explained that he had done his bidding over night; and in this he was confirmed by his friends. **20** The king, then, with a barbarity exceeding that of Phalaris, said that they might thank his sleep of that day: "Lose no time, and get the elephants ready against tomorrow, as you did before, for the destruction of these accursed Jews." **21** When the king said this, the company present were glad, and approved; and then each man went to his own home. **22** Nor did they employ the night in sleep, so much as in contriving cruel mockeries for those deemed miserable. **23** The morning cock had just crowed, and Hermon, having harnessed the brutes, was stimulating them in the great colonnade. **24** The city crowds were collected together to see the hideous spectacle and waited impatiently for the dawn. **25** The Jews, breathless with momentary suspense, stretched out their hands, and prayed to the greatest God, in mournful strains, to quickly help them again. **26** The sun's rays were not yet shed abroad, and the king was waiting for his friends, when Hermon came to him, calling him out, and saying that his desires could now be realized. **27** The king, receiving him, was astonished at his unusual exit, and overwhelmed with a spirit of oblivion about everything, inquired [regarding] the object of this earnest preparation. **28** But this was the working of that Almighty God who had made him forget all his purpose. **29** Hermon and all his friends pointed out the preparation of the animals. "They are ready, O king, according to your own strict injunction." **30** The king was filled with fierce anger at these words, for, by the providence of God regarding these things, his mind had become entirely confused. He looked hard at Hermon, and threatened him as follows: **31** "Your parents or your children, were they here, should have been furnished [as] a large meal for these wild beasts—not these innocent Jews, who my forefathers and I have loyally served. **32** Had it not been for familiar friendship, and the claims of your office, your life should have gone for theirs. **33** Hermon, being threatened in this unexpected and alarming manner, was troubled in visage, and depressed in countenance. **34** The friends, too, slipped out one by one, and dismissed the assembled multitudes to their respective occupations. **35** The Jews, having heard of these events, praised the glorious God and King of kings, because they too had obtained this help from Him. **36** Now the king arranged another banquet after the same manner and proclaimed an invitation to mirth. **37** And he summoned Hermon to his presence, and said, with threats, "How often, O wretch, must I repeat my orders to you about these same persons? **38** Once more, arm the elephants for the extermination of the Jews tomorrow." **39** His countrymen, who were reclining with him, wondered at his instability, and so expressed themselves: **40** "O king, how long do you make trial of us, as of men deprived of reason? This is the third time that you have ordered their destruction. When the thing is to be done, you change your mind, and recall your instructions. **41** For this reason the feeling of expectation causes tumult in the city: it swarms with factions and is continually at the point of being plundered." **42** The king, just like another Phalaris, a prey to thoughtlessness, made no account of the changes which his own mind had undergone, issuing in the deliverance of the Jews. He swore a fruitless oath, and firmly determined to send them to Hades, crushed by the knees and feet of the elephants. **43** He would also invade Judea, and level its towns with fire and the sword, and destroy that temple which the heathen might not enter, and prevent sacrifices from ever being offered up there. **44** Joyfully his friends broke up, together with his countrymen, and, trusting in his determination, arranged their forces in guard at the most convenient places of the city. **45** And the master of the elephants urged the beasts into an almost maniacal state, drenched them with incense and wine, and decked them with frightful instruments. **46** About early morning, when the city was now filled with an immense number of people at the hippodrome, he entered the palace and called the king to the business at hand. **47** The king's heart teemed with impious rage, and he rushed out with the mass, along with the elephants. With feelings unsoftened, and eyes pitiless, he longed to gaze at the hard and wretched doom of the above-mentioned [Jews]. **48** But the [Jews], when the elephants went out at the gate, followed by the armed force; and when they saw the dust raised by the throng, and heard the loud cries of the crowd, **49** thought that they had come to the last moment of their lives, to the end of what they had tremblingly expected. They gave way, therefore, to lamentations and moans; they kissed each other; those related to each other hung around one another's necks: fathers around their sons, mothers [around] their daughters; other women held their infants to their breasts, which drew what seemed their last milk. **50** Nevertheless, when they reflected on the help previously granted them from Heaven, they prostrated themselves with one accord, even removed the sucking children from the breasts, **51** and sent up an exceedingly great cry asking the Lord of all power to reveal Himself and have mercy on those who now lay at the gates of Hades.

CHAPTER 6

1 And Eleazar, an illustrious priest of the country, who had attained to length of days, and whose life had been adorned with virtue, caused the elders who were around him to cease to cry out to the holy God, and prayed this: **2** "O King, mighty in power, Most High, Almighty God, who regulates the whole creation with Your tender mercy, **3** look on the seed of Abraham, on the children of the sanctified Jacob, Your sanctified inheritance, O Father, now being wrongfully destroyed as strangers in a strange land. **4** You destroyed Pharaoh, with his army of chariots, when that lord of this same Egypt was uplifted with lawless daring and a loud-sounding tongue. Shedding the beams of Your mercy on the race of Israel, You overwhelmed him with his proud army. **5** When Sennacherib, the grievous king of the Assyrians, exulting in his countless army, had subdued the whole land with his spear, and was lifting himself against Your holy city, with boastings [too] grievous to be endured, You, O Lord, demolished him and showed Your might to many nations. **6** When the three friends in the land of Babylon of their own will exposed their lives to the fire rather than serve vain things, You sent a moist coolness through the fiery furnace and brought the fire on all their adversaries. **7** It was You who, when Daniel was hurled—through slander and envy—as a prey to lions down below, brought him back up to [the] light unharmed. **8** When Jonah was pining away in the belly of the sea-bred monster, You looked on him, O Father, and restored him to the sight of his own. **9** And now, You who hate insolence; You who abound in mercy; You who are the protector of all things: appear quickly to those of the race of Israel, who are insulted by abhorred, lawless nations. **10** If our life has been stained with iniquity during our exile, deliver us from the hand of the enemy, and destroy us, O Lord, by the death which You prefer. **11** Do not let the vain-minded congratulate vain idols at the destruction of Your beloved, saying, "Neither did their God deliver them." **12** You, who are All-powerful and Almighty, O Perpetual One, behold! Have mercy on us who are being withdrawn from life, like traitors, by the unreasoning insolence of lawless men. **13** Let the heathen cower before Your invincible might today, O glorious One, who has all power to save the race of Jacob. **14** The whole band of infants and their parents implore You with tears. **15** Let it be shown to all the nations that You are with us,

O Lord, and have not turned Your face away from us; but as You said that You would not forget them even in the land of their enemies, so fulfill this saying, O Lord. **16** Now, at the time that Eleazar had ended his prayer, the king came along to the hippodrome, with the wild beasts, and with his tumultuous power. **17** When the Jews saw this, they uttered a loud cry to Heaven, so that the adjacent valleys resounded, and caused an irrepressible lamentation throughout the army. **18** Then the all-glorious, all-powerful, and true God, displayed His holy countenance, and opened the gates of Heaven, from which two messengers, dreadful of form, came down and were visible to all but the Jews. **19** And they stood opposite and filled the enemies' army with confusion and cowardice, and bound them with immoveable chains. **20** And a cold shudder came over the person of the king, and oblivion paralyzed the vehemence of his spirit. **21** They turned the animals back on the armed forces which followed them, and the animals trod them down and destroyed them. **22** The king's wrath was converted into compassion, and he wept at his own machinations. **23** For when he heard the cry, and saw them all on the verge of destruction, he angrily threatened his friends with tears, saying, **24** "You have governed badly, and have exceeded tyrants in cruelty; and me, your benefactor, you have labored to deprive of my dominion and my life at once, by secretly devising measures injurious to the kingdom. **25** Who has gathered here, unreasonably removing each from his home, those who, in fidelity to us, had held the fortresses of the country? **26** Who has so consigned to unmerited punishments those who in good will toward us from the beginning have in all things surpassed all nations, and who often have engaged in the most dangerous undertakings? **27** Loose, loose the unjust bonds; send them to their homes in peace, and deprecate what has been done. **28** Release the sons of the almighty living God of Heaven, who from our ancestors' times until now has granted a glorious and uninterrupted prosperity to our affairs. **29** He said these things, and they, released the same moment, having now escaped death, praised God their holy Savior. **30** The king then departed to the city, and called his financier to him, and asked him to provide a seven days' quantity of wine and other materials for feasting for the Jews. He decided that they should keep a joyful festival of deliverance in the very place in which they expected to meet with their destruction. **31** Then they who were previously despised and near to Hades, yes, rather advanced into it, partook of the cup of salvation, instead of a grievous and lamentable death. Full of exultation, they parted out the place intended for their fall and burial into banqueting shelters. **32** Ceasing their miserable strain of woe, they took up the subject of their fatherland, singing praise to God, their wonder-working Savior. All groans, all wailing, were laid aside: they formed dances as a sign of serene joy. **33** So also the king—he collected a number of guests for the occasion and returned unceasing thanks with much magnificence for the unexpected deliverance afforded him. **34** Those who had marked them out as for death and for carrion, and had registered them with joy, howled aloud, and were clothed with shame, and had the fire of their rage ingloriously put out. **35** But the Jews, as we just said, instituted a dance, and then gave themselves up to feasting, glad thanksgiving, and psalms. **36** They made a public ordinance to commemorate these things for generations to come, as long as they should be sojourners. Therefore, they established these days as days of mirth, not for the purpose of drinking or luxury, but because God had saved them. **37** They requested the king to send them back to their homes. **38** They were being enrolled from the twenty-fifth of Pachon to the fourth of Epiphi—a period of forty days. The measures taken for their destruction lasted from the fifth of Epiphi until the seventh—that is, three days. **39** The Ruler over all gloriously manifested His mercy during this time and delivered them all together unharmed. **40** They feasted on the king's provision up to the fourteenth day, and then asked to be sent away. **41** The king commended them and wrote the following letter, of magnanimous importance for them, to the commanders of every city:

CHAPTER 7

1 "King Ptolemy Philopator to the commanders throughout Egypt, and to all who are set over affairs—joy and strength. **2** We ourselves and our children are well, and God has directed our affairs as we wish. **3** Certain of our friends vehemently urged us from malice to punish the Jews of our realm in a body, with the infliction of a monstrous punishment. **4** They pretended that our affairs would never be in a good state until this took place. Such, they said, was the hatred borne by the Jews to all other people. **5** They brought them bound in grievous chains as slaves, no, as traitors. Without inquiry or examination, they endeavored to annihilate them. They buckled themselves with a savage cruelty, worse than Scythian custom. **6** For this reason we severely threatened them; yet, with the clemency which we are accustomed to extend to all men, we at length permitted them to live. Finding that the God of Heaven cast a shield of protection over the Jews so as to preserve them, and that He fought for them as a father always fights for his sons, **7** and taking into consideration their constancy and fidelity toward us and toward our ancestors, we have, as we should, acquitted them of every sort of charge. **8** And we have dismissed them to their various homes, bidding all men everywhere to do them no wrong, or unrighteously revile them about the past. **9** Know that should we conceive any evil design, or in any way aggrieve them, we will ever have as our opposite, not man, but the highest God, the ruler of all might. From Him there will be no escape, as the avenger of such deeds. Farewell." **10** When they had received this letter, they were not hurried to depart immediately. They petitioned the king to be allowed to inflict fitting punishment on those of their race who had willingly transgressed the holy God, and the Law of God. **11** They alleged that men who had for their bellies' sake transgressed the ordinances of God, would never be faithful to the interests of the king. **12** The king admitted the truth of this reasoning and commended them. Full power was given them, without warrant or special commission, to destroy those who had transgressed the Law of God boldly in every part of the king's dominions. **13** Their priests, then, as it was suitable, saluted him with good wishes, and all the people echoed with the "Hallelujah." They then joyfully departed. **14** Then they punished and destroyed with ignominy every polluted Jew that fell in their way; **15** slaying therefore, in that day, more than three hundred men, and esteeming this destruction of the wicked a season of joy. **16** They themselves having held fast their God to death, and having enjoyed a full deliverance, departed from the city garlanded with sweet-flowered wreaths of every kind. Uttering exclamations of joy, with songs of praise and melodious hymns, they thanked the God of their fathers, the perpetual Savior of Israel. **17** Having arrived at Ptolemais, called from the specialty of that district Rose-bearing, where the fleet, in accordance with the general wish, waited seven days for them, **18** they partook of a banquet of deliverance, for the king generously granted them separately the means of securing a return home. **19** They were accordingly brought back in peace, while they gave utterance to appropriate thanks; and they determined to keep these days during their sojourn as days of joyfulness. **20** These they registered as sacred on a pillar, when they had dedicated the place of their festivity to be one of prayer. They departed unharmed, free, abundant in joy, preserved by the king's command, by land, by sea, and by river, each to his own home. **21** They had more weight than before among their enemies, and were honored and feared, and no one in any way robbed them of their goods. **22** Every man received back his own, according to inventory, [from] those who had obtained their goods, giving them up with the greatest terror. For the greatest God made perfect wonders for their salvation. **23** Blessed is the Redeemer of Israel to [the] age. Amen.

4 MACCABEES

The book of 4 Maccabees is a homily or philosophic discourse praising the supremacy of pious reason over passion. It is not in the Bible for most churches, but is an appendix to the Greek Bible, and in the canon of the Georgian Orthodox Bible. It was included in the 1688 Romanian Orthodox and the eighteenth-century Romanian Catholic Bibles where it was called "Iosip" (Joseph). It is no longer printed in Romanian Bibles today. The book was ascribed to Josephus by Eusebius and Jerome, and this opinion was accepted for many years, leading to its inclusion in many editions of Josephus' works. Scholars have, however, pointed to perceived differences of language and style. The book is generally dated between 20 and 130 AD, likely in the later half of that range.

CHAPTER 1

1 As I am going to demonstrate a most philosophical proposition, namely, that religious reasoning is absolute master of the passions, I would willingly advise you to give the utmost heed to philosophy. **2** For reason is necessary to everyone as a step to science: and it more especially embraces the praise of prudence, the highest virtue. **3** If then reasoning appears to hold the mastery over the passions which stand in the way of temperance, such as gluttony and lust, **4** it also surely and manifestly has the rule over the affections which are contrary to justice, such as malice; and of those which are hindrances to manliness, as wrath, and pain, and fear. **5** How then is it, perhaps some may say, that reasoning, if it rules the affections, is not also master of forgetfulness and ignorance? They attempt a ridiculous argument. **6** For reasoning does not rule over its own affections, but over such as are contrary to justice, and manliness, and temperance, and prudence; and yet over these, so as to withstand, without destroying them. **7** I might prove to you, from many other considerations, that religious reasoning is sole master of the passions; **8** but I will prove it with the greatest force from the fortitude of Eleazar, and seven brothers, and their mother, who suffered death in defense of virtue. **9** For all these, treating pains with contempt even to death, by this contempt, demonstrated that reasoning has command over the passions. **10** For their virtues, then, it is right that I should commend those men who died with their mother at this time in behalf of rectitude; and for their honors, I may count them happy. **11** For they, winning admiration not only from men in general, but even from the persecutors, for their manliness and endurance, became the means of the destruction of the tyranny against their nation, having conquered the tyrant by their endurance, so that by them their country was purified. **12** But we may now at once enter on the question, having commenced, as is our custom, with laying down the doctrine, and so proceed to the account of these persons, giving glory to the all-wise God. **13** Therefore the question is whether reasoning is absolute master of the passions. **14** Let us determine, then, what reasoning is, and what passion [is], and how many forms of the passions, and whether reasoning bears sway over all of these. **15** Reasoning is, then, intellect accompanied by a life of rectitude, putting foremost the consideration of wisdom. **16** And wisdom is a knowledge of divine and human things, and of their causes. **17** And this is contained in the education of the Law, by means of which we learn divine things reverently, and human things profitably. **18** And the forms of wisdom are prudence, and justice, and manliness, and temperance. **19** The leading one of these is prudence, by whose means, indeed, it is that reasoning bears rule over the passions. **20** Of the passions, pleasure and pain are the two most comprehensive, and they also by nature refer to the soul. **21** And there are many attendant affections surrounding pleasure and pain. **22** Before pleasure is lust, and after pleasure, joy. **23** And before pain is fear, and after pain is sorrow. **24** Wrath is an affection, common to pleasure and to pain, if anyone will pay attention when it comes on him. **25** And there exists in pleasure a malicious disposition, which is the most multiform of all the affections. **26** In the soul it is arrogance, and love of money, and vain pride, and contention, and faithlessness, and the evil eye. **27** In the body it is greediness, and gorging, and solitary gluttony. **28** As pleasure and pain are, therefore, two growths of the body and the soul, so there are many offshoots of these passions. **29** And reasoning, the universal farmer, purging, and pruning these separately, and binding around, and watering, and transplanting, in every way improves the materials of the morals and affections. **30** For reasoning is the leader of the virtues, but it is the sole ruler of the passions. Observe then first, through the very things which stand in the way of temperance, that reasoning is absolute ruler of the passions. **31** Now temperance consists of a command over the lusts. **32** But of the lusts, some belong to the soul, others to the body: and over each of these classes the reasoning appears to bear sway. **33** For where is it, otherwise, that when urged on to forbidden meats, we reject the gratification which would ensue from them? Is it not because reasoning is able to command the appetites? I believe so. **34** Hence it is, then, that when lusting after aquatic animals and birds, and four-footed beasts, and all kinds of food which are forbidden us by the Law, we withhold ourselves through the mastery of reasoning. **35** For the affections of our appetites are resisted by the temperate understanding, and bent back again, and all the impulses of the body are reined in by reasoning.

CHAPTER 2

¹ And what wonder [is it] if the lusts of the soul, after participation with what is beautiful, are frustrated? ² On this ground, therefore, the temperate Joseph is praised in that by reasoning he subdued, on reflection, the indulgence of sense. ³ For, although young, and ripe for sexual intercourse, he abrogated by reasoning the stimulus of his passions. ⁴ And it is not merely the stimulus of sensual indulgence, but that of every desire, that reasoning is able to master. ⁵ For instance, the Law says, "You will not covet your neighbor's wife, nor anything that belongs to your neighbor." ⁶ Now, then, since it is the Law which has forbidden us to desire, I will much more easily persuade you that reasoning is able to govern our lusts, just as it does the affections which are impediments to justice. ⁷ Since in what way is a solitary eater, and a glutton, and a drunkard reclaimed, unless it is clear that reasoning is lord of the passions? ⁸ Therefore, a man who regulates his course by the Law, even if he is a lover of money, immediately puts force on his own disposition; lending to the needy without interest and cancelling the debt of the incoming Sabbath. ⁹ And should a man be parsimonious, he is ruled by the Law acting through reasoning, so that he does not glean his harvest crops, nor vintage: and in reference to other points we may perceive that it is reasoning that conquers his passions. ¹⁰ For the Law conquers even affection toward parents, not surrendering virtue on their account. ¹¹ And it prevails over marriage love, condemning it when transgressing Law. ¹² And it lords it over the love of parents toward their children, for they punish them for vice; and it domineers over the intimacy of friends, reproving them when wicked. ¹³ And do not think it a strange assertion that reasoning can in behalf of the Law conquer even enmity. ¹⁴ It does not allow [one] to cut down the cultivated herbage of an enemy, but preserves it from the destroyers, and collects their fallen ruins. ¹⁵ And reason appears to be master of the more violent passions, such as love of power, and empty boasting, and slander. ¹⁶ For the temperate understanding repels all these malignant passions, as it does wrath, for it masters even this. ¹⁷ So Moses, when angered against Dathan and Abiram, did nothing to them in wrath, but regulated his anger by reasoning. ¹⁸ For the temperate mind is able, as I said, to be superior to the passions, and to transfer some, and destroy others. ¹⁹ For why else does our most wise father Jacob blame Simeon and Levi for having irrationally slain the whole race of the Shechemites, saying, "Cursed be their anger"? ²⁰ For if reasoning did not possess the power of subduing angry affections, he would not have spoken like this. ²¹ For at the time when God created man, He implanted within him his passions and moral nature. ²² And at that time He enthroned above all the holy leader mind, through the medium of the senses. ²³ And He gave a law to this mind, by living according to which it will maintain a temperate, and just, and good, and manly reign. ²⁴ How [is it] then [that] a man might say that if reasoning is master of the passions, it has no control over forgetfulness and ignorance?

CHAPTER 3

¹ The argument is exceedingly ridiculous, for reasoning does not appear to bear sway over its own affections, but over those of the body, ² in such a way as that anyone of you may not be able to root out desire, but reasoning will enable you to avoid being enslaved to it. ³ One may not be able to root out anger from the soul, but it is possible to withstand anger. ⁴ Anyone of you may not be able to eradicate malice, but reasoning has force to work with you to prevent you yielding to malice. ⁵ For reasoning is not an eradicator, but an antagonist of the passions. ⁶ And this may be more clearly comprehended from the thirst of King David. ⁷ For after David had been attacking the Philistines the whole day, he with the soldiers of his nation killed many of them; ⁸ then when evening came, sweating and very weary, he came to the royal tent, around which the entire army of our ancestors was encamped. ⁹ Now all the rest of them were at supper, ¹⁰ but the king, being very much thirsty, although he had numerous springs, could not by their means quench his thirst, ¹¹ but a certain irrational longing for the water in the enemy's camp grew stronger and fiercer on him, and consumed him with languish. ¹² For that reason, his bodyguards being troubled at this longing of the king, two valiant young soldiers, reverencing the desire of the king, put on their armor, and taking a pitcher, got over the ramparts of the enemies: ¹³ and unperceived by the guardians of the gate, they went throughout the whole camp of the enemy in quest. ¹⁴ And having boldly discovered the fountain, they filled out of it the draught for the king. ¹⁵ But he, though parched with thirst, reasoned that a draught regarded of equal value to blood, would be terribly dangerous to his soul. ¹⁶ For that reason, setting up reasoning in opposition to his desire, he poured out the draught to God. ¹⁷ For the temperate mind has power to conquer the pressure of the passions, and to quench the fires of excitement, ¹⁸ and to wrestle down the pains of the body, however excessive; and, through the excellency of reasoning, to abominate all the assaults of the passions. ¹⁹ But the occasion now invites us to give an illustration of temperate reasoning from history. ²⁰ For at a time when our fathers were in possession of undisturbed peace through obedience to the Law, and were prosperous, so that Seleucus Nicanor, the king of Asia, both assigned them money for divine service, and accepted their form of government, ²¹ then certain persons, bringing in new things contrary to the general unanimity, fell into calamities in various ways.

CHAPTER 4

¹ For a certain man named Simon, who was in opposition to Onias, who once held the chief priesthood for life, and was an honorable and good man, after slandering him in every way, he could not injure him with the people, went away as an exile, with the intention of betraying his country. ² When coming to Apollonius, the military governor of Syria, and Phoenicia, and Cilicia, he said, ³ "Having good will to the king's affairs, I have come to inform you that infinite private wealth is laid up in the treasuries of Jerusalem which do not belong to the temple but pertain to King Seleucus." ⁴ Apollonius, acquainting himself with the particulars of this, praised Simon for his care of the king's interests, and going up to Seleucus informed him of the treasure; ⁵ and getting authority over it, and quickly advancing into our country with the accursed Simon and a very heavy force, ⁶ he said that he came with the commands of the king that he should take the private money of the treasure. ⁷ And the nation, indignant at this proclamation, and replying to the effect that it was extremely unfair that those who had committed deposits to the sacred treasury should be deprived of them, resisted as well as they could. ⁸ But Apollonius went away with threats into the temple. ⁹ And the priests, with the women and children, having supplicated God to throw His shield over the holy, despised place, ¹⁰ and Apollonius going up with his armed force to the seizure of the treasure, there appeared from Heaven messengers riding on horseback, all radiant in armor, filling them with much fear and trembling. ¹¹ And Apollonius fell half dead on the court which is open to all nations, and extended his hands to Heaven, and implored the Hebrews, with tears, to pray for him, and propitiate the heavenly army. ¹² For he said that he had sinned, so as to be consequently worthy of death; and that if he were saved, he would celebrate to all men the blessedness of the holy place. ¹³ Onias the chief priest, induced by these words, although for other reasons anxious that King Seleucus should not suppose that Apollonius was slain by human device and not by Divine punishment, prayed for him; ¹⁴ and he being unexpectedly saved, departed to manifest to the king what had happened to him. ¹⁵ But on the death of Seleucus the king, his son Antiochus Epiphanes succeeds to the kingdom: a man of arrogant pride and terrible, ¹⁶ who having deposed Onias from the chief priesthood, appointed his brother Jason to be chief priest, ¹⁷ who had made a covenant to pay three thousand six hundred and sixty talents yearly if he would give him this authority. ¹⁸ And he committed the chief priesthood and rulership over the nation to him. ¹⁹ And he both changed the manner of living of the people and perverted their civil customs into all lawlessness, ²⁰ so that he not only erected a gymnasium on the very citadel of our country, but [neglected] the guardianship of the temple. ²¹ At which Divine vengeance being grieved, instigated Antiochus himself against them. ²² For being at war with Ptolemy in Egypt, he heard that on a report of his death being spread abroad, the inhabitants of Jerusalem had

exceedingly rejoiced, and he quickly marched against them. **23** And having subdued them, he established a decree that if any of them lived according to the laws of his country he should die. **24** And when he could by no means destroy by his decrees the obedience to the law of the nation, but saw all his threats and punishments without effect, **25** for even women, because they continued to circumcise their children, were flung down a precipice along with them, knowing beforehand of the punishment. **26** When, therefore, his decrees were disregarded by the people, he himself compelled by means of tortures everyone of this race, by tasting forbidden meats, to renounce the Jewish religion.

CHAPTER 5

1 The tyrant Antiochus, therefore, sitting in public state with his assessors on a certain lofty place, with his armed troops standing in a circle around him, **2** commanded his spear-bearers to seize everyone of the Hebrews, and to compel them to taste swine's flesh, and things offered to idols. **3** And should any of them be unwilling to eat the accursed food, they were to be tortured on the wheel, and so killed. **4** And when many had been seized, a foremost man of the assembly, a Hebrew, by name Eleazar, a priest by family, by profession a lawyer, and advanced in years, and for this reason known to many of the king's followers, was brought near to him. **5** And Antiochus seeing him, said, **6** "I would counsel you, old man, before your tortures begin, to taste the swine's flesh, and save your life; for I feel respect for your age and gray head, which since you have had so long, you appear to me to be no philosopher in retaining the superstition of the Jews. **7** For that reason, since nature has conferred on you the most excellent flesh of this animal, do you loathe it? **8** It seems senseless not to enjoy what is pleasant, yet not disgraceful; and from notions of sinfulness, to reject the boons of nature. **9** And you will be acting, I think, still more senselessly, if you follow vain conceits about the truth. **10** And you will, moreover, be despising me to your own punishment. **11** Will you not awake from your trifling philosophy, and give up the folly of your notions, and regaining understanding worthy of your age, search into the truth of an expedient course, **12** and reverencing my kindly admonition, have pity on your own years? **13** For bear in mind that if there is any power which watches over this religion of yours, it will pardon you for all transgressions of the Law which you commit through compulsion." **14** While the tyrant incited him in this manner to the unlawful eating of flesh, Eleazar begged permission to speak. **15** And having received power to speak, he began to deliver himself like this: **16** "We, O Antiochus, who are persuaded that we live under a divine law, consider no compulsion to be so forcible as obedience to that law; **17** for this reason we consider that we should not in any point transgress the Law. **18** And indeed, were our law (as you suppose) not truly divine, and if we wrongly think it divine, we should have no right even in that case to destroy our sense of religion. **19** Do not think eating the unclean, then, a trifling offense. **20** For transgression of the Law, whether in small or great matters, is of equal moment, **21** for in either case the Law is equally slighted. **22** But you deride our philosophy, as though we lived irrationally in it. **23** Yet it instructs us in temperance, so that we are superior to all pleasures and lusts; and it exercises us in manliness, so that we cheerfully undergo every grievance. **24** And it instructs us in justice, so that in all our dealings we render what is due; and it teaches us piety, so that we worship the one [and] only God as is appropriate. **25** For it is that reason we do not eat the unclean; for believing that the Law was established by God, we are convinced that the Creator of the world, in giving His laws, sympathizes with our nature. **26** Those things which are convenient to our souls, He has directed us to eat, but those which are repugnant to them, He has interdicted. **27** But, tyrant-like, you not only force us to break the Law, but also to eat, that you may ridicule us as we so profanely eat; **28** but you will not have this cause of laughter against me, **29** nor will I transgress the sacred oaths of my forefathers to keep the Law. **30** No, not if you pluck out my eyes, and consume my entrails. **31** I am not so old, and void of manliness, but that my rational powers are youthful in defense of my religion. **32** Now then, prepare your wheels and kindle a fiercer flame. **33** I will not so pity my old age, as on my account to break the law of my country. **34** I will not betray you, O law, my instructor! or forsake you, O beloved self-control! **35** I will not put you to shame, O philosopher reason! Or deny you, O

honored priesthood, and science of the law. **36** Mouth! you will not pollute my old age, nor the full stature of a perfect life. **37** My fathers will receive me pure, not having cowered before your compulsion, though to death. **38** For you will tyrannize over the ungodly, but you will not lord it over my thoughts about religion, either by your arguments, or through deeds.

CHAPTER 6

1 When Eleazar had answered the exhortations of the tyrant in this manner, the spear-bearers came up and violently dragged Eleazar to the instruments of torture. **2** And first they stripped the old man, adorned as he was with the beauty of piety. **3** Then tying back his arms and hands, they disdainfully abused him with stripes, **4** [while] a herald opposite was crying out, "Obey the commands of the king!" **5** But Eleazar, the high-minded and truly noble, as one tortured in a dream, did not regard it at all. **6** But raising his eyes on high to Heaven, the old man's flesh was stripped off by the scourges, and his blood streamed down, and his sides were pierced through. **7** And falling on the ground, from his body having no power to support the pains, he yet kept his reasoning upright and unbending. **8** Then one of the harsh spear-bearers leaped on his belly as he was falling, to force him upright. **9** But he endured the pains, and despised the cruelty, and persevered through the indignities; **10** and like a noble athlete, the old man, when struck, vanquished his torturers. **11** His countenance sweating, and panting for breath, he was admired by the very torturers for his courage. **12** For that reason, partly in pity for his old age, **13** partly from the sympathy of acquaintance, and partly in admiration of his endurance, some of the attendants of the king said, **14** "Why do you unreasonably destroy yourself, O Eleazar, with these miseries? **15** We will bring you some meat cooked by yourself, and you can save yourself by pretending that you have eaten swine's flesh." **16** And Eleazar, as though the advice more painfully tortured him, cried out, **17** "Do not let us who are children of Abraham be so wickedly advised as by giving way to make use of an inappropriate pretense; **18** for it were irrational, if having lived up to old age in all truth, and having scrupulously guarded our character for it, we should now turn back, **19** and ourselves should become a pattern of impiety to the young, as being an example of eating pollution. **20** It would be disgraceful if we should live for some short time—and that scorned by all men for cowardice— **21** and be condemned by the tyrant for unmanliness, by not contending to the death for our divine law. **22** For this reason, you, O children of Abraham, die nobly for your religion. **23** You spear-bearers of the tyrant, why do you linger?" **24** Beholding him so high-minded against misery, and not changing at their pity, they led him to the fire: **25** then with their wickedly contrived instruments they burned him on the fire and poured stinking fluids down into his nostrils. **26** And he being at length burned down to the bones, and about to expire, raised his eyes toward God, and said, **27** "You know, O God, that when I might have been saved, I am slain for the sake of the Law by tortures of fire. **28** Be merciful to Your people and be satisfied with my punishment on their account. **29** Let my blood be a purification for them and take my life in repayment for theirs." **30** Therefore speaking, the holy man departed, noble in his torments, and even to the agonies of death resisted in his reasoning for the sake of the Law. **31** Confessedly, therefore, religious reasoning is master of the passions. **32** For had the passions been superior to reasoning, I would have given them the witness of this mastery. **33** But now, since reasoning conquered the passions, we befittingly awarded it the authority of first place. **34** And it is but fair that we should allow that the power belongs to reasoning, since it masters external miseries. **35** It would be ridiculous were it not so; and I prove that reasoning has not only mastered pains, but that it is also superior to the pleasures, and withstands them.

CHAPTER 7

1 The reasoning of our father Eleazar, like a first-rate pilot, steering the vessel of piety in the sea of passions, **2** and flouted by the threats of the tyrant, and overwhelmed with the breakers of torture, **3** in no way shifted the rudder of piety until it sailed into the harbor of victory over death. **4** A city has never, when besieged, held out against many and various machines as that holy man did when his pious soul was tried with the fiery trial of tortures and racking, [and when] he moved his besiegers through the religious reasoning that shielded him. **5** For father Eleazar, projecting his disposition, broke the raging waves of the passions as with a jutting promontory. **6** O priest worthy of the priesthood! you did not pollute your sacred teeth, nor make your appetite, which had always embraced the clean and lawful, a partaker of profanity. **7** O harmonizer with the Law, and sage devoted to a divine life! **8** Of such a character should those be who perform the duties of the Law at the risk of their own blood and defend it with generous sweat by sufferings even to death. **9** You, father, have gloriously established our right government by your endurance, and making our past service of much account, prevented its destruction, and, by your deeds, have made the words of philosophy credible. **10** O aged man of more power than tortures, elder more vigorous than fire, greatest king over the passions, Eleazar! **11** For as father Aaron, armed with a censer, hastening through the consuming fire, vanquished the flame-bearing messenger, **12** so Eleazar, the descendant of Aaron, wasted away by the fire, did not give up his reasoning. **13** And what is most wonderful, though an old man, though the labors of his body were now spent, and his muscles were relaxed, and his sinews worn out, he recovered youth. **14** By the spirit of reasoning, and the reasoning of Isaac, he rendered the many-headed instrument powerless. **15** O blessed old age, and venerable gray head, and life obedient to the Law, which the faithful seal of death perfected. **16** If then an old man, through religion, despised tortures even to death, confessedly religious reasoning is ruler of the passions. **17** But perhaps some might say, "It is not all who conquer passions, as all do not possess wise reasoning." **18** But they who have meditated on religion with their whole heart, these alone can master the passions of the flesh— **19** they who believe that they do not die to God; for as our forefathers Abraham, Isaac, [and] Jacob, they live to God. **20** This circumstance, then, is by no means an objection, that some who have weak reasoning are governed by their passions; **21** since what person, walking religiously by the whole rule of philosophy, and believing in God, **22** and knowing that it is a blessed thing to endure all kinds of hardships for virtue, would not, for the sake of religion, master his passion? **23** For only the wise and brave man is lord over his passions. **24** From where it is that even boys, trained with the philosophy of religious reasoning, have conquered still more bitter tortures:

CHAPTER 8

1 For when the tyrant was manifestly vanquished in his first attempt, in being unable to force the old man to eat the unclean thing, then indeed, vehemently swayed with passion, he commanded others of the adult Hebrews to be brought, and if they would eat of the unclean thing, to let them go when they had eaten, but if they objected, to torment them more grievously. **2** The tyrant having given this charge, seven brothers were brought into his presence, along with their aged mother, handsome, and modest, and well-born, and altogether beautiful. **3** When the tyrant saw them encircling their mother as in a dance, he was pleased at them; and being struck with their appropriate and innocent manner, smiled on them, and calling them near, said, **4** "O youths, with favorable feelings I admire the beauty of each of you; and greatly honoring such a numerous a band of brothers, I not only counsel you not to share the madness of the old man who has been tortured before, **5** but I beg you to yield and to enjoy my friendship; for I possess the power, not only of punishing those who disobey my commands, but of doing good to those who obey them. **6** Put confidence in me, then, and you will receive places of authority in my government if you forsake your national ordinance, **7** and, conforming to the Greek mode of life, alter your rule, and revel in youth's delights. **8** For if you provoke me by your disobedience, you will compel me to destroy you—everyone—with terrible punishments by tortures. **9** Have mercy, then, on your own selves, whom I, although an enemy, pity for your age and attractive appearance. **10** Will you not reason on this—that if you disobey, there will be nothing left for you but to die in tortures?" **11** So speaking, he ordered the instruments of torture to be brought forward, that great fear might prevail on them to eat unclean meat. **12** And when the spearman brought forward the wheels, and the racks, and the hooks, and catapults, and cauldrons, pans, and finger-racks, and iron hands and wedges, and bellows, the tyrant continued:

13 "Fear, young men, and the righteousness which you worship will be merciful to you if you err from compulsion." **14** Now, they having listened to these words of persuasion and seeing the fearful instruments, not only were not afraid, but even answered the arguments of the tyrant, and through their good reasoning destroyed his power. **15** Now let us consider the matter: had any of them been weak-spirited and cowardly among them, what reasoning would they have employed but these? **16** "O wretched that we are, and exceedingly senseless! when the king exhorts us, and calls us to his bounty, should we not obey him? **17** Why do we cheer ourselves with vain counsels, and venture on a disobedience bringing death? **18** Will we not fear, O brothers, the instruments of torture, and weigh the threats of torment, and shun this vainglory and destructive pride? **19** Let us have compassion on our age and relent over the years of our mother. **20** And let us bear in mind that we will be dying as rebels. **21** And Divine Justice will pardon us if we fear the king through necessity. **22** Why withdraw ourselves from a most sweet life, and deprive ourselves of this pleasant world? **23** Let us not oppose necessity, nor seek vainglory by our own excruciation. **24** The Law itself is not forward to put us to death if we dread torture. **25** From where has such angry zeal taken root in us, and such fatal obstinacy approved itself to us, when we might live unmolested by the king?" **26** But nothing of this kind did the young men say or think when about to be tortured. **27** For they were well aware of the sufferings and were masters of the pains. **28** . . . **29** So that as soon as the tyrant had ceased counseling them to eat the unclean, they all with one voice, as from the same heart, said:

CHAPTER 9

1 "Why do you delay, O tyrant? for we are more ready to die than to transgress the injunctions of our fathers. **2** And we should be disgracing our fathers if we did not obey the Law and take knowledge for our guide. **3** O tyrant, counselor of law-breaking, do not, hating us as you do, pity us more than we pity ourselves. **4** For we account escape to be worse than death. **5** And you think to scare us, by threatening us with death by tortures, as though you had learned nothing by the death of Eleazar. **6** But if aged men of the Hebrews have died in the cause of religion after enduring torture, more rightly should we younger men die, scorning your cruel tortures, which our aged instructor overcame. **7** Make the attempt, then, O tyrant; and if you put us to death for our religion, do not think that you harm us by torturing us. **8** For we through this mistreatment and endurance will bear off the rewards of virtue. **9** But you, for the wicked and despotic slaughter of us, will, from the Divine vengeance, endure continuous torture by fire." **10** When they had so spoken, the tyrant was not only exasperated against them as being refractory, but enraged with them as being ungrateful. **11** So that, at his bidding, the torturers brought out the oldest of them, and tearing through his tunic, bound his hands and arms on each side with thongs. **12** And when they had labored hard without effect in scourging him, they hurled him on the wheel. **13** And the noble youth, extended on this, became dislocated. **14** And with every member disjointed, he exclaimed in protest: **15** "O most accursed tyrant, and enemy of heavenly justice, and cruel-hearted, I am no murderer, nor sacrilegious man, whom you so mistreated, but a defender of the Divine law." **16** And when the spearmen said, "Consent to eat, that you may be released from your tortures," **17** he answered, "Not so powerful, O accursed ministers, is your wheel, as to stifle my reasoning; cut my limbs, and burn my flesh, and twist my joints. **18** For through all my torments I will convince you that the children of the Hebrews are alone unconquered in behalf of virtue." **19** While he was saying this, they heaped up fuel, and setting fire to it, strained him on the wheel still more. **20** And the wheel was defiled all over with blood, and the hot ashes were quenched by the droppings of gore, and pieces of flesh were scattered around the axles of the machine. **21** And although the framework of his bones was now destroyed, the high-minded and Abrahamic youth did not groan. **22** But, as though transformed by fire into immortality, he nobly endured the racking, saying, **23** "Imitate me, O brothers, [and] never desert your station, nor renounce our courageous brotherhood: fight the holy and honorable fight of religion, **24** by which means our just and paternal Providence, becoming merciful to the nation, will punish the pernicious tyrant." **25** And saying this, the revered youth abruptly closed his life. **26** And when all admired his courageous soul, the spearmen brought forward him who was second in point of age, and having put on iron hands, bound him with pointed hooks to the torture device. **27** And when, on inquiring whether he would eat before he was tortured, they heard his noble sentiment, **28** after they with the iron hands had violently dragged all the flesh from the neck to the chin—the panther-like beasts tore off the very skin of his head, but he, bearing this misery with firmness, said, **29** "How sweet is every form of death for the religion of our fathers!" And he said to the tyrant, **30** "Do you think, most cruel of all tyrants, that you are now tortured more than I, finding your overconfident conception of tyranny conquered by our perseverance in behalf of our religion? **31** For I lighten my suffering by the pleasures which are connected with virtue. **32** But you are tortured with threats for impiety; and you will not escape, most corrupt tyrant, the vengeance of Divine wrath."

CHAPTER 10

1 Now this one, having endured this praiseworthy death, the third was brought along, and exhorted by many to taste and save his life. **2** But he cried out and said, "Do you not know that the father of those who are dead, became the father of me also, and that the same mother bore me, and that I was brought up in the same tenets? **3** I do not renounce the noble relationship of my brothers. **4** Now then, whatever instrument of vengeance you have, apply it to my body, for you are not able to touch, even if you wish it, my soul. **5** But they, highly incensed at his boldness of speech, dislocated his hands and feet with racking engines, and wrenching them from their sockets, dismembered him." **6** And they dragged around his fingers, and his arms, and his legs, and his ankles. **7** And not being able by any means to strangle him, they tore off his skin, together with the extreme tips of his fingers and then dragged him to the wheel, **8** around which his vertebral joints were loosened, and he saw his own flesh torn to shreds, and streams of blood flowing from his entrails. **9** And when about to die, he said, **10** "We, O accursed tyrant, suffer this for the sake of Divine education and virtue. **11** But you, for your impiety and blood shedding, will endure indissoluble torments." **12** And having died worthily of his brothers, they dragged forward the fourth, saying, **13** "Do not share the madness of your brothers, but give regard to the king, and save yourself." **14** But he said to them, "You do not have a fire so scorching as to make me play the coward. **15** By the blessed death of my brothers, and the continuous punishment of the tyrant, and the glorious life of the pious, I will not repudiate the noble brotherhood. **16** Invent, O tyrant, tortures, that you may learn, even through them, that I am the brother of those tormented before." **17** When he had said this, the blood-thirsty, and murderous, and unhallowed Antiochus ordered his tongue to be cut out. **18** But he said, "Even if you take away the organ of speech, yet God hears the silent. **19** Behold, my tongue is extended, cut it off; for by that you will not halt my reasoning. **20** We gladly lose our limbs in behalf of God. **21** But God will swiftly find you, since you cut off the tongue—the instrument of divine melody."

CHAPTER 11

1 And when he had died, disfigured in his torments, the fifth leaped forward, and said, **2** "I do not intend, O tyrant, to get excused from the torment which is in behalf of virtue. **3** But I have come of my own accord, that by my death you may owe heavenly vengeance a punishment for more crimes. **4** O you hater of virtue and of men! What have we done that you so revel in our blood? **5** Does it seem evil to you that we worship the Founder of all things, and live according to His surpassing law? **6** But this is worthy of honors, not torments, **7** had you been capable of the higher feelings of men and possessed the hope of salvation from God. **8** Behold now, being alien from God, you make war against those who are religious toward God." **9** As he said this, the spear-bearers bound him and drew him to the torture device, **10** to which binding him at his knees, and fastening them with iron chains, they bent down his loins on the wedge of the wheel; and his body was then dismembered, scorpion-fashion. **11** With his breath so confined, and his body strangled, he said, **12** "A great favor you bestow on us, O tyrant, by enabling us to manifest our adherence to the Law by means of nobler sufferings." **13** He also being dead,

the sixth, quite a youth, was brought out; and on the tyrant asking him whether he would eat and be delivered, he said, **14** "I am indeed younger than my brothers, but I am as old in understanding; **15** for having been born and reared to the same end, we are also bound to die in behalf of the same cause. **16** So that if you think proper to torment us for not eating the unclean, then torment!" **17** As he said this, they brought him to the wheel, **18** extended on which, with limbs racked and dislocated, he was gradually roasted from beneath. **19** And having heated sharp spits, they approached them to his back; and having transfixed his sides, they burned away his entrails. **20** And he, while tormented, said, "O period good and holy, in which, for the sake of religion, we brothers have been called to the contest of pain, and have not been conquered! **21** For religious understanding, O tyrant, is unconquered. **22** Armed with upright virtue, I will also depart with my brothers. **23** I, too, [am] bearing with myself a great Avenger, O inventor of tortures and enemy of the truly pious! **24** We six youths have destroyed your tyranny. **25** For is not your inability to overrule our reasoning, and to compel us to eat the unclean, your destruction? **26** Your fire is cold to us, your devices are painless, and your violence harmless. **27** For the guards not of a tyrant but of a divine law are our defenders: through this we keep our reasoning unconquered."

CHAPTER 12

1 When he, too, had undergone blessed martyrdom, and died in the cauldron into which he had been thrown, the seventh, the youngest of all, came forward, **2** whom the tyrant pitying, though he had been dreadfully reproached by his brothers, **3** seeing him already encompassed with chains, had him brought nearer, and endeavored to counsel him, saying, **4** "You see the end of the madness of your brothers, for they have died in torture through disobedience; and you, if disobedient, having been miserably tormented, will yourself perish prematurely. **5** But if you obey, you will be my friend, and have a charge over the affairs of the kingdom." **6** And having so exhorted him, he sent for the mother of the boy, that, by condoling with her for the loss of so many sons, he might incline her, through the hope of safety, to render the survivor obedient. **7** And he, after his mother had urged him on in the Hebrew tongue (as we will soon relate), says, **8** "Release me that I may speak to the king and all his friends." **9** And they, rejoicing exceedingly at the promise of the youth, quickly let him go. **10** And he, running up to the pans, said, **11** "Impious tyrant, and most blasphemous man, were you not ashamed, having received prosperity and a kingdom from God, to kill His servants, and to rack the doers of godliness? **12** For this reason the Divine vengeance is reserving you for continuous fire and torments, which will cling to you for all time. **13** Were you not ashamed, man as you are, yet most savage, to cut out the tongues of men of like feeling and origin, and having so abused to torture them? **14** But they, bravely dying, fulfilled their religion toward God. **15** But you will groan according to your deserts for having slain the champions of virtue without cause." **16** "For this reason," he continued, "I myself, being about to die, **17** will not forsake my brothers. **18** And I call on the God of my fathers to be merciful to my race. **19** But you, both living and dead, He will punish." **20** So having prayed, he hurled himself into the pans, and so expired.

CHAPTER 13

1 If then the seven brothers despised troubles even to death, it is confessed on all sides that righteous reasoning is absolute master over the passions. **2** For just as if, had they as slaves to the passions eaten of the unholy, we should have said that they had been conquered; **3** now it is not so, but by means of the reasoning which is praised by God, they mastered their passions. **4** And it is impossible to overlook the leadership of reflection, for it gained the victory over both passions and troubles. **5** How then can we avoid, according to these men, mastery of passion through right reasoning, since they did not draw back from the pains of fire? **6** For just as by means of towers projecting in front of harbors men break the threatening waves, and therefore assure a still course to vessels entering port, **7** so that seven-towered right-reasoning of the young men, securing the harbor of religion, conquered the intemperance of passions. **8** For having arranged a holy choir of piety, they encouraged one another, saying, **9** "Brothers, may we die brotherly for the Law. Let us imitate the three young men in Assyria who despised the equally afflicting furnace. **10** Let us not be cowards in the manifestation of piety." **11** And one said, "Courage, brother"; and another, "Nobly endure." **12** And another, "Remember of what stock you are— and by the hand of our father Isaac who endured to be slain for the sake of piety." **13** And one and all, looking on each other serene and confident, said, "Let us sacrifice with all our heart our souls to God who gave them, and employ our bodies for the keeping of the Law. **14** Let us not fear him who thinks he kills, **15** for great is the trial of soul and danger of continuous torment laid up for those who transgress the command of God. **16** Let us therefore arm ourselves in the self-control, which is divine reasoning. **17** If we suffer like this, Abraham, and Isaac, and Jacob will receive us, and all the fathers will commend us." **18** And as each one of the brothers was hauled away, the rest exclaimed, "Do not disgrace us, O brother, nor falsify those who died before you. **19** Now you are not ignorant of the charm of brotherhood, which the Divine and all-wise Providence has imparted through fathers to children and has engendered through the mother's womb." **20** In which these brothers having remained an equal time, and having been formed for the same period, and been increased by the same blood, and having been perfected through the same principle of life, **21** and having been brought out at equal intervals, and having sucked milk from the same springs, their brotherly souls are reared up lovingly together, **22** and increase [all] the more powerfully by reason of this simultaneous rearing, and by daily companionship, and by other education, and exercise in the law of God. **23** Brotherly love being so sympathetically constituted, the seven brothers had a more sympathetic mutual harmony. **24** For being educated in the same law, and practicing the same virtues, and reared up in a just course of life, they increased this harmony with each other. **25** For a like zeal for what is right and honorable increased their fellow-feeling toward each other. **26** For it acting along with religion, made their brotherly feeling more desirable to them. **27** And yet, although nature, and companionship, and virtuous morals increased their brotherly love, those who were left endured to behold their brothers, who were mistreated for their religion [and] tortured even to death.

CHAPTER 14

1 And more than this, they even urged them on to this mistreatment, so that they not only despised pains themselves, but they even got the better of their affections of brotherly love. **2** O reasoning, more royal than a king and freer than freemen! **3** O sacred and harmonious concord of the seven brothers as concerning piety! **4** None of the seven youths turned cowardly or shrank back from death. **5** But all of them, as though running the road to immortality, hastened on to death through tortures. **6** For just as hands and feet are moved sympathetically with the directions of the soul, so those holy youths agreed to death for religion's sake, as through the immortal soul of religion. **7** O holy seven—harmonious brothers! for as the seven days of creation, about religion, **8** so the youths, circling around the number seven, annulled the fear of torments. **9** We now shudder at the recital of the affliction of those young men, but they not only saw, and not only heard the immediate execution of the threat, but undergoing it, persevered—and that through the pains of fire. **10** And what could be more painful? for the power of fire, being sharp and quick, speedily dissolved their bodies. **11** And do not think it wonderful that reasoning bore rule over those men in their torments, when even a woman's mind despised more manifold pains. **12** For the mother of those seven youths endured the rackings of each of her children. **13** And consider how comprehensive the love for offspring is, which draws everyone to sympathy of affection, **14** where irrational animals possess a similar sympathy and love for their offspring with men. **15** The tame birds frequenting the roofs of our houses, defend their fledglings. **16** Others build their nests and hatch their young in the tops of mountains, and in the precipices of valleys, and the holes and tops of trees, and keep off the intruder. **17** And if not able to do this, they fly circling around them in agony of affection, calling out in their own note, and save their offspring in whatever manner they are able. **18** But why should we point attention to the sympathy toward children shown by irrational

animals? **19** The very bees, at the season of honey-making, attack all who approach, and pierce with their sting, as with a sword, those who draw near their hive, and repel them even to death. **20** But sympathy for her children did not turn away the mother of the young men—[she] who had a spirit related with that of Abraham.

CHAPTER 15

1 O reasoning of the sons, lord over the passions, and religion more desirable to a mother than progeny! **2** The mother, when two things were set before her—religion and the safety of her seven sons for a time on the conditional promise of a tyrant— **3** rather chose the religion which according to God preserves to continuous life. **4** O in what way can I describe ethically the affections of parents toward their children, the resemblance of soul and of form engrafted into the small type of a child in a wonderful manner, especially through the greater sympathy of mothers with the feelings of those born of them! **5** For by how much mothers are by nature weak in disposition and prolific in offspring, by so much the fonder they are of children. **6** And of all mothers the mother of the seven was the fondest of children, who in seven childbirths had deeply engendered love toward them, **7** and through her many pains undergone in connection with each one, was compelled to feel sympathy with them, **8** yet, through fear of God, she neglected the temporary salvation of her children. **9** Not [only] that, but on account of the excellent disposition to the Law, her maternal affection toward them was increased. **10** For they were both just and temperate, and manly, and high-minded, and fond of their brothers, and so fond of their mother that even to death they obeyed her by observing the Law. **11** And yet, though there were so many circumstances connected with love of children to draw on a mother to sympathy, in the case of none of them were the various tortures able to pervert her principle. **12** But she inclined each one separately and all together to death for religion. **13** O holy nature and parental feeling, and reward of bringing up children, and unconquerable maternal affection! **14** At the racking and roasting of each one of them, the observant mother was prevented by religion from changing. **15** She saw her children's flesh dissolving around the fire, and their extremities quivering on the ground, and the flesh of their heads dropped forward down to their beards, like masks. **16** O you mother who was tried at this time with bitterer pangs than those of childbirth! **17** O you only woman who has brought out perfect holiness! **18** Your firstborn, expiring, did not sway you; nor the second, looking miserable in his torments; nor the third, breathing out his soul. **19** Nor did you weep when you beheld the eyes of each of them looking sternly on their tortures, and their nostrils foreboding death! **20** When you saw children's flesh heaped on children's flesh that had been torn off, heads decapitated on heads, dead falling on the dead, and a choir of children turned through torture into a burying ground, you did not lament. **21** Not so do siren melodies or songs of swans attract the hearers to listening [as did the] voices of [you] children calling on your mother in the midst of torments! **22** O with what and what manner of torments was the mother herself tortured as her sons were undergoing the wheel and the fires! **23** But religious reasoning, having strengthened her courage in the midst of sufferings, enabled her to forego, for the time, parental love. **24** Although beholding the destruction of seven children, the noble mother, after one embrace, stripped off [her feelings] through faith in God. **25** For just as in a council-room, beholding in her own soul vehement counselors—nature, and parentage, and love of her children, and the racking of her children— **26** she holding two votes, one for the death, the other for the preservation of her children, **27** did not lean to that which would have saved her children for the safety of a brief space. **28** But this daughter of Abraham remembered his holy fortitude. **29** O holy mother of a nation, avenger of the Law, and defender of religion, and prime bearer in the battle of the affections! **30** O you nobler in endurance than males, and more manly than men in perseverance! **31** For as the Ark of Noah, bearing the world in the world-filling flood, bore up against the waves, **32** so you, the guardian of the Law, when surrounded on every side by the flood of passions, and constricted by violent storms which were the torments of those children, nobly bore up against the storms against religion.

CHAPTER 16

¹ If then, even a woman, and that an aged one and the mother of seven children, endured to see her children's torments even to death, confessedly religious reasoning is master even of the passions. ² I have proved, then, that not only men have obtained the mastery of their passions, but also that a woman despised the greatest torments. ³ And not so fierce were the lions around Daniel, nor the furnace of Mishael burning with most vehement fires as that natural love of children burned within her, when she saw her seven sons tortured. ⁴ But with the reasoning of religion, the mother quenched passions so great and powerful. ⁵ For we must consider this also: that, had the woman been faint-hearted, as being their other, she would have lamented over them, and perhaps might have spoken like this: ⁶ "Ah! wretched me, and many times miserable, who having born seven sons, have become the mother of none. ⁷ O seven useless childbirths, and seven profitless periods of labor, and fruitless giving of suck, and miserable nursing at the breast. ⁸ Vainly, for your sakes, O sons, have I endured many pangs, and the more difficult anxieties of rearing. ⁹ Aah! Of my children, some of you unmarried, and some who have married to no profit, I will not see your children, nor be congratulated as a grandmother. ¹⁰ Ah! That I who had many and fair children, should be a lone widow full of sorrows! ¹¹ Nor, should I die, will I have a son to bury me." But with such a lament as this the holy and God-fearing mother mourned none of them. ¹² Nor did she divert any of them from death, nor grieve for them as for the dead. ¹³ But as one possessed with an adamantine mind, and as one bringing out again her full number of sons to immortality, she rather with supplication exhorted them to death in behalf of religion. ¹⁴ O woman, soldier of God for religion, you, aged and a female, have even conquered a tyrant through endurance; and though but weak, have been found more powerful in deeds and words. ¹⁵ For when you were seized along with your children, you stood looking on Eleazar in torments, and said to your sons in the Hebrew tongue, ¹⁶ "O sons, the contest is noble to which you are being called as a witness for the nation, [to which] you strive zealously for the laws of your country. ¹⁷ For it were disgraceful that this old man should endure pains for the sake of righteousness, and that you who are younger should be afraid of the tortures. ¹⁸ Remember that through God you obtained existence and have enjoyed it. ¹⁹ And on this second account you should bear every affliction because of God, ²⁰ for whom our father Abraham was also forward to sacrifice our progenitor Isaac, and did not shudder at the sight of his own paternal hand descending down with the sword on him. ²¹ And the righteous Daniel was cast to the lions; and Hananiah, and Azariah, and Mishael were slung out into a furnace of fire, yet they endured through God. ²² You, then, having the same faith toward God, do not be troubled. ²³ For it is unreasonable that they who know religion should not stand up against troubles. ²⁴ With these arguments, the mother of seven, exhorting each of her sons, over-persuaded them from transgressing the command of God. ²⁵ And they also saw this, that they who die for God live to God, as Abraham, and Isaac, and Jacob, and all the patriarchs.

CHAPTER 17

¹ And some of the spear-bearers said that when she herself was about to be seized for the purpose of being put to death, she threw herself on the pile, rather than that they should touch her person. ² O you mother, who together with seven children destroyed the violence of the tyrant, and rendered his wicked intentions void, and exhibited the nobleness of faith! ³ For you, as a house bravely built on the pillar of your children, bore the shock of tortures without swaying. ⁴ Be of good cheer, therefore, O holy-minded mother, holding the firm [substance of the] hope of your steadfastness with God. ⁵ The moon does not appear with the stars in the sky as gracious as you are: established honorable before God, and fixed in the expanse with your sons who you illuminated with religion to the stars. ⁶ For your bearing of children was after the fashion of a child of Abraham. ⁷ And, were it lawful for us to paint as on a tablet the religion of your story, the spectators would not shudder at beholding the mother of seven children enduring, for the sake of religion, various tortures even to death. ⁸ And it had been a worthy thing to have inscribed on the tomb itself these words

as a memorial to those of the nation: ⁹ "Here an aged priest, and an aged woman, and seven sons, are buried through the violence of a tyrant, who wished to destroy the society of the Hebrews. ¹⁰ These also avenged their nation, looking to God and enduring torments to death." ¹¹ For it was truly a divine contest which was carried through by them. ¹² For at that time virtue presided over the contest, approving the victory through endurance, namely, immortality [and] continuous life. ¹³ Eleazar was the first to contend, and [then] the mother of the seven children entered the contest, and [then] the brothers contended. ¹⁴ The tyrant was the opposite; and the world and living men were the spectators. ¹⁵ And reverence for God conquered and crowned her own athletes. ¹⁶ Who did not admire those champions of true legislation? who were not astonished? ¹⁷ The tyrant himself, and all their council, admired their endurance; ¹⁸ through which, also, they now stand beside the divine throne, and live a blessed life. ¹⁹ For Moses says, "And all the saints are under Your hands." ²⁰ These, therefore, having been sanctified through God, have been honored not only with this honor, but that also by their means the enemy did not overcome our nation, ²¹ and that the tyrant was punished, and their country purified. ²² For they became the ransom to the sin of the nation, and the Divine Providence saved Israel, previously afflicted, by the blood of those pious ones, and the propitiatory death. ²³ For the tyrant Antiochus, looking to their manly virtue, and to their endurance in torture, proclaimed that endurance as an example to his soldiers. ²⁴ And they proved to him to be noble and brave for land battles and for sieges; and he conquered and stormed the towns of all his enemies.

CHAPTER 18

¹ O Israeli children, descendants of the seed of Abraham, obey this law, and in every way be religious, ² knowing that religious reasoning is lord of the passions, and those not only inward but outward. ³ When those persons were giving up their bodies to pains for the sake of religion, they were not only admired by men, but were deemed worthy of a divine portion. ⁴ And the nation obtained peace through them, and having renewed the observance of the Law in their country, they drove the enemy out of the land. ⁵ And the tyrant Antiochus was both punished on earth and is punished now [that] he is dead; for when he was quite unable to compel the Israelites to adopt foreign customs and to desert the manner of life of their fathers, ⁶ then, departing from Jerusalem, he made war against the Persians. ⁷ And the righteous mother of the seven children also spoke as follows to her offspring: "I was a pure virgin and did not go beyond my father's house, but I took care of the built-up rib. ⁸ No destroyer of the desert [or] ravisher of the plain injured me; nor did the destructive, deceitful snake make plunder of my pure virginity; and I remained with my husband during the period of my prime. ⁹ And these children of mine, having arrived at maturity, their father died: he was blessed! for having sought out a life of fertility in children, he was not grieved with a period of loss of children. ¹⁰ And he used to teach you, when yet with you, the Law and the Prophets. ¹¹ He used to read to you the slaying of Abel by Cain, and the offering up of Isaac, and the imprisonment of Joseph. ¹² And he used to tell you of the zealous Phinehas; and informed you of Hananiah, and Azariah, and Mishael in the fire. ¹³ And he used to glorify Daniel, who was in the den of lions, and pronounce him blessed. ¹⁴ And he used to put you in mind of the Writing of Isaiah, which says, Even if you pass through the fire, it will not burn you. ¹⁵ He chanted to you David, the hymn-writer, who says, Many are the afflictions of the just. ¹⁶ He declared the proverbs of Solomon, who says, He is a Tree of Life to all those who do His will. ¹⁷ He used to verify Ezekiel, who said, Will these dry bones live? ¹⁸ For he did not forget the song which Moses taught, proclaiming, I will kill, and I will make to live. ¹⁹ This is our life, and the length of our days." ²⁰ O that bitter—and yet not bitter—day when the bitter tyrant of the Greeks, quenching fire with fire in his cruel cauldrons, brought with boiling rage the seven sons of the daughter of Abraham to the torture device, and to all his torments! ²¹ He pierced the balls of their eyes, and cut out their tongues, and put them to death with varied tortures. ²² For this reason divine retribution pursued and will [still] pursue the pernicious wretch. ²³ But the children of Abraham, with their victorious mother, are assembled together to the choir of their father, having received pure and immortal souls from God, ²⁴ to whom be glory forever

and ever. Amen.

PRAYER OF MANASSEH

The Prayer of Manasseh (or Manasses) is a short work of 15 verses recording a penitential prayer attributed to King Manasseh of Judah. Most scholars believe that the Prayer of Manasseh was written in Greek in the 1st or 2nd century BC. Another work by the same title, written in Hebrew and containing distinctly different content, was found among the Dead Sea Scrolls.

CHAPTER 1

1 O Lord Almighty, that are in Heaven, You God of our fathers, of Abraham, and Isaac, and Jacob, and of their righteous seed; **2** who have made the heavens and earth, with all the ornament thereof; **3** who have bound the sea by the word of Your command; who have shut up the deep, and sealed it by Your terrible and glorious Name; **4** whom all things fear, yes, tremble before Your power; **5** for the majesty of Your glory cannot be borne, and the anger of Your threatening toward sinners is importable: **6** Your merciful promise is unmeasurable and unsearchable; **7** for You are the Lord Most High, of great compassion, patient and abundant in mercy, and relenting of bringing evils on men. **8** You, O Lord, according to Your great goodness have promised conversion and forgiveness to those who have sinned against You: and of Your infinite mercies have appointed conversion to sinners, that they may be saved. You, therefore, O Lord, that are the God of the just, have not appointed conversion to the just, to Abraham, and Isaac, and Jacob, which have not sinned against You; but You have appointed conversion to me that am a sinner: **9** for I have sinned above the number of the sands of the sea. My transgressions are multiplied, O Lord: my transgressions are multiplied, and I am not worthy to behold and see the height of Heaven for the multitude of my iniquities. **10** I am bowed down with many iron bands, that I cannot lift up my head by reason of my sins, neither do I have any respite, for I have provoked Your wrath and done that which is evil before You: I did not do Your will, neither did I keep Your commands: I have set up abominations and have multiplied detestable things. **11** Now therefore, I bow the knee of my heart, imploring You of grace. **12** I have sinned, O Lord, I have sinned, and I acknowledge my iniquities: **13** but, I humbly implore You, forgive me, O Lord, forgive me, and do not destroy me with my iniquities. Do not be angry with me forever, by reserving evil for me; neither condemn me into the lower parts of the earth. For You, O Lord, are the God of those who convert; **14** and in me You will show all Your goodness, for You will save me, that am unworthy, according to Your great mercy. **15** And I will praise You forever all the days of my life, for all the army of Heaven sings Your praise, and Yours is the glory forever and ever. Amen.

JUBILEES

The Book of Jubilees, sometimes called Lesser Genesis (Leptogenesis), is an ancient Jewish religious work of 50 chapters, considered canonical by the Ethiopian Orthodox Church as well as Beta Israel (Ethiopian Jews), where it is known as the Book of Division. Jubilees is considered one of the pseudepigrapha by Protestant, Roman Catholic, and Eastern Orthodox Churches. It is also not considered canonical within Judaism outside of Beta Israel. It is generally dated to the 2nd century BC and its primary purpose seems to be in promoting the use of a 364-day calendar in Israel (a year equally divided into 52 weeks of seven days each). With no intercalary method given, the year would not synchronize with the seasons in the longterm. The book also reimagines some of the history of Genesis and introduces a concept foreign to Judeo-Christianity in which certain sins are unatonable.

This is the history of the division of the days of the Law and of the Testimony, of the events of the years, of their periods of seven, of their Jubilees throughout all the years of the world, as the Lord spoke to Moses on Mount Sinai when he went up to receive the tablets of the Law and of the command, according to the voice of God as He said to him, "Go up to the top of the mountain."

CHAPTER 1

1 And it came to pass in the first year of the exodus of the sons of Israel out of Egypt, in the third month, on the sixteenth day of the month, that God spoke to Moses, saying, "Come up to Me on the mountain, and I will give you two tablets of stone, of the Law and of the command, which I have written, that you may teach them." **2** And Moses went up into the mountain of God, and the glory of the Lord abode on Mount Sinai, and a cloud overshadowed it [for] six days. **3** And He called to Moses on the seventh day out of the midst of the cloud, and the appearance of the glory of the Lord was like a flaming fire on the top of the mountain. **4** And Moses was on the mountain [for] forty days and forty nights, and God taught him the earlier and the later history of the division of all the days of the Law and of the Testimony. **5** And He said, "Incline your heart to every word which I will speak to you on this mountain and write them in a scroll in order that their generations may see how I have not forsaken them for all the evil which they have worked in transgressing the covenant which I establish between Me and you for their generations this day on Mount Sinai. **6** And thus it will come to pass when all these things come on them, that they will recognize that I am more righteous than they in all their judgments and in all their actions, and they will recognize that I have truly been with them. **7** And write for yourself all these words which I declare to you this day, for I know their rebellion and their stiff neck, before I bring them into the land of which I swore to their fathers, to Abraham, and to Isaac, and to Jacob, saying, To your seed I will give a land flowing with milk and honey. **8** And they will eat and be satisfied, and they will turn to strange gods, to [gods] which cannot deliver them from any of their tribulation: and this witness will be heard for a witness against them. **9** For they will forget all My commands, [even] all that I command them, and they will walk after the nations, and after their uncleanness, and after their shame, and will serve their gods, and these will prove to them an offense, and a tribulation, and an affliction, and a snare. **10** And many will perish, and they will be taken captive, and will fall into the hands of the enemy, because they have forsaken My ordinances and My commands, and the festivals of My covenant, and My Sabbaths, and My holy place which I have hallowed for Myself in their midst, and My Dwelling Place, and My sanctuary, which I have hallowed for Myself in the midst of the land, that I should set My Name on it, and that it should dwell [there]. **11** And they will make to themselves high places, and groves, and graven images, and they will worship, each his own [graven image], so as to go astray, and they will sacrifice their children to demons, and to all the works of the error of their hearts. **12** And I will send witnesses to them that I may witness against them, but they will not hear, and will slay the witnesses also, and they will persecute those who seek the Law, and they will abrogate and change everything so as to work evil before My eyes. **13** And I will hide My face from them, and I will deliver them into the hand of the nations for captivity, and for a prey, and for devouring, and I will remove them from the midst of the land, and I will scatter them among the nations. **14** And they will forget all My law, and all My commands, and all My judgments, and will go astray as to new moons, and Sabbaths, and festivals, and jubilees, and ordinances. **15** And after this they will turn to Me from among the nations with all their heart, and with all their soul, and with all their strength, and I will gather them from among all the nations, and they will seek Me, so that I will be found by them when they seek Me with all their heart and with all their soul. **16** And I will disclose to them abounding peace with righteousness, and I will remove them—the plant of uprightness—with all My heart and with all My soul, and they will be for a blessing and not for a curse, and they will be the head and not the tail. **17** And I will build My sanctuary in their midst, and I will dwell with them, and I will be their God and they will be My people in truth and righteousness. **18** And I will not forsake them nor fail them; for I am the Lord their God." **19** And Moses fell on his face and prayed and said, "O Lord my God, do not forsake Your people and Your inheritance, so that they should wander in the error of their hearts, and do not deliver them into the hands of their enemies, lest they should rule over them and cause them to sin against You. **20** Let Your mercy, O Lord, be lifted up on Your people, and create an upright spirit in them, and do not let the spirit of Belial rule over them to accuse them before You, and to ensnare them from all the paths of righteousness, so that they may perish from before Your face. **21** But they are Your people and Your inheritance, which You have delivered with Your great power from the hands of the Egyptians: create in them a clean heart and a holy spirit, and do not let them be ensnared in their sins from now on [and] forever." **22** And the Lord said to Moses, "I know their contrariness, and their thoughts, and their stubbornness, and they will not be obedient until they confess their own sin and the sin of their fathers. **23** And after this they will turn to Me in all uprightness and with all [their] heart and with all [their] soul, and I will circumcise the foreskin of their heart and the foreskin of the heart of their seed, and I will create in them a holy spirit, and I will cleanse them so that they will not turn away from Me from that day [and] continuously. **24** And their souls will cleave to Me and to all My commands, and they will fulfill My commands, and I will be their Father and they will be My children. **25** And they will all be called children of the living God, and every messenger and every spirit will know, yes, they will know that these are My children, and that I am their Father in uprightness and righteousness, and that I love them. **26** And write down for yourself all these words which I declare to you on this mountain, the first and the last, which will come to pass in all the divisions of the days in the Law, and in the Testimony, and in the periods of seven, and the jubilees continuously, until I descend and dwell with them forever." **27** And He said to the Messenger of the Presence, "Write for Moses from the beginning of creation until My sanctuary has been built among them for all ages. **28** And the Lord will appear to the eyes of all, and all will know that I am the God of Israel and the Father of all the children of Jacob, and King on Mount Zion for all ages. And Zion and Jerusalem will be holy." **29** And the Messenger of the Presence who went before the camp of Israel took the tablets of the divisions of the years—from the time of the creation—of the Law, and of the Testimony of the periods of seven, of the jubilees, according to the individual years, according to all the number of the jubilees [according to the individual years], from the day of the [new] creation when the heavens and the earth will be renewed and all their creation according to the powers of the heavens, and according to all the creation of the earth, until the sanctuary of the Lord will be made in Jerusalem on Mount Zion, and all the luminaries are renewed for healing, and for peace, and for blessing for all the chosen of Israel, and that thus it may be from that day and to all the days of the earth.

CHAPTER 2

1 And the Messenger of the Presence spoke to Moses according to the word of the Lord, saying, Write the complete history of the creation, how in six days the Lord God finished all His works and all that He created, and kept Sabbath on the seventh day and hallowed it for all ages, and appointed it as a sign for all His works. **2** For on the first day He created the heavens which are above, and the earth, and the waters, and all the spirits which serve before Him—the messengers of the presence, and the messengers of sanctification, and the messengers [[of the spirit of fire, and the messengers]] of the spirit of the winds, and the messengers of the spirit of the clouds, and of darkness, and of snow, and of hail, and of hoarfrost, and the messengers of the voices, and of the thunder, and of the lightning, and the messengers of the spirits of cold, and of heat, and of winter, and of spring, and of autumn, and of summer, and of all the spirits of His creatures which are in the heavens and on the earth, [He created] the abysses and the darkness, evening [and night], and the light, dawn and day, which He has prepared in the knowledge of His heart. **3** And we immediately saw His works, and praised Him, and lauded before Him on account of all His works; for He created seven great works on the first day. **4** And on the second day He created the expanse in the midst of the waters, and the waters were divided on that day—half of them went up above and half of them went down below the expanse [that was] in the midst over the face of the whole earth. And this was the only work [God] created on the second day. **5** And on the third day He commanded the waters to pass from off the face of the whole earth into one place, and the dry land to appear. **6** And the waters did so as He commanded them, and they retired from off the face of the earth into one place outside of this expanse, and the dry land appeared. **7** And on that day, He created for them all the seas according to their separate gathering-places, and all the rivers, and the gatherings of the waters in the mountains and on all the earth, and all the lakes, and all the dew of the earth, and the seed which is sown, and all sprouting things, and fruit-bearing trees, and trees of the wood, and the Garden of Eden, in Eden, and all [plants after their kind]. These four great works God created on the third day. **8** And on the fourth day He created the sun, and the moon, and the stars, and set them in the expanse of the heavens, to give light on all the earth, and to rule over the day and the night, and divide the light from the darkness. **9** And God appointed the sun to be a great sign on the earth for days, and for Sabbaths, and for months, and for feasts, and for years, and for Sabbaths of years, and for jubilees, and for all seasons of the years. **10** And it divides the light from the darkness [and] for prosperity, that all things may prosper which shoot and grow on the earth. These three kinds He made on the fourth day. **11** And on the fifth day He created great sea monsters in the depths of the waters, for these were the first things of flesh that were created by His hands, the fish and everything that moves in the waters, and everything that flies—the birds and all their kind. **12** And the sun rose above them to prosper [them], and above everything that was on the earth, everything that shoots out of the earth, and all fruit-bearing trees, and all flesh. These three kinds He created on the fifth day. **13** And on the sixth day He created all the animals of the earth, and all cattle, and everything that moves on the earth. **14** And after all this He created man, a man and a woman He created them, and gave him dominion over all that is on the earth, and in the seas, and over everything that flies, and over beasts and over cattle, and over everything that moves on the earth, and over the whole earth, and over all this He gave him dominion. And these four kinds He created on the sixth day. **15** And there were altogether twenty-two kinds. **16** And He finished all His work on the sixth day—all that is in the heavens and on the earth, and in the seas and in the abysses, and in the light and in the darkness, and in everything. **17** And He gave us a great sign, the Sabbath day, that we should work six days, but keep Sabbath on the seventh day from all work. **18** And all the messengers of the presence, and all the messengers of sanctification, these two great classes—He has hidden us to keep the Sabbath with Him in the heavens and on earth. **19** And He said to us, "Behold, I will separate a people to Myself from among all the peoples, and these will keep the Sabbath day, and I will sanctify them to Myself as My people and will bless them; as I have sanctified the Sabbath day and sanctify [it] to Myself, even so will I bless them, and they will be My people and I will be their God. **20** And I have chosen the seed of Jacob from among all that I have seen, and have written him down as My firstborn son, and have sanctified him to Myself forever and ever; and I will teach them the Sabbath day, that they may keep Sabbath thereon from all work." **21** And thus He created therein a sign in accordance with which they should keep Sabbath with us on the seventh day, to eat and to drink, and to bless Him who has created all things as He has blessed and sanctified to Himself a peculiar people above all peoples, and that they should keep Sabbath together with us. **22** And He caused His commands to ascend as a sweet savor acceptable before Him all the days. **23** There [were] twenty-two heads of mankind from Adam to Jacob, and twenty-two kinds of work were made until the seventh day; this is blessed and holy; and the former is also blessed and holy; and this one serves with that one for sanctification and blessing. **24** And to these [(Jacob and his seed)] it was granted that they should always be the blessed and holy ones of the first testimony and law, even as He had sanctified and blessed the Sabbath day on the seventh day. **25** He created the heavens, and earth, and everything that He created in six days, and God made the seventh day holy for all His works; therefore, He commanded on its behalf that whoever does any work thereon will die, and that he who defiles it will surely die. ²⁶ For that reason, command the sons of Israel to observe this day that they may keep it holy and not do any work thereon, and not to defile it, as it is holier than all other days. ²⁷ And whoever profanes it will surely die, and whoever does any work thereon will surely die forever, that the sons of Israel may observe this day throughout their generations, and not be rooted out of the land; for it is a holy day and a blessed day. ²⁸ And everyone who observes it and keeps Sabbath thereon from all his work will be holy and blessed throughout all days like to us. ²⁹ Declare and say to the sons of Israel the law of this day, both that they should keep Sabbath thereon, and that they should not forsake it in the error of their hearts; [and] that it is not lawful to do any work thereon which is unseemly, to do their own pleasure thereon, and that they should not prepare anything thereon to be eaten or drunk, and [that it is not lawful] to draw water or bring in or take out thereon through their gates any burden, which they had not prepared for themselves on the sixth day in their dwellings. ³⁰ And they will not bring in nor take out from house to house on that day; for that day is more holy and blessed than any jubilee day of the jubilees: on this we kept Sabbath in the heavens before it was made known to any flesh to keep Sabbath thereon on the earth. ³¹ And the Creator of all things blessed it, but He did not sanctify all peoples and nations to keep Sabbath thereon, but Israel alone: them alone He permitted to eat and drink and to keep Sabbath thereon on the earth. ³² And the Creator of all things blessed this day which He had created for a blessing, and a sanctification, and a glory above all days. ³³ This law and testimony was given to the sons of Israel as a law forever to their generations.

CHAPTER 3

¹ And on the six days of the second week we brought, according to the word of God, to Adam all the beasts, and all the cattle, and all the birds, and everything that moves on the earth, and everything that moves in the water, according to their kinds, and according to their types: the beasts on the first day; the cattle on the second day; the birds on the third day; and all that which moves on the earth on the fourth day; and that which moves in the water on the fifth day. ² And Adam named them all by their respective names, and as he called them, so was their name. ³ And on these five days Adam saw all these, male and female, according to every kind that was on the earth, but he was alone and found no helpmate for him. ⁴ And the Lord said to us, "It is not good that the man should be alone: let us make a helpmate for him." ⁵ And the Lord our God caused a deep sleep to fall on him, and he slept, and He took for the woman one rib from among his ribs, and this rib was the origin of the woman from among his ribs, and He built up the flesh in its stead, and built the woman. ⁶ And He awoke Adam out of his sleep and on awaking he rose on the sixth day, and He brought her to him, and he knew her, and said to her, "This is now bone of my bones and flesh of my flesh; she will be called Woman, because she was taken from Man." ⁷ Therefore man and wife will be one, and therefore a man will leave his father and his mother, and cleave to his wife, and they will be one flesh. ⁸ In the first week Adam was created, and the rib—his wife; in the second week He showed her to him: and for this reason, the command was given to keep in their defilement, for a male seven days, and for a female twice seven days. ⁹ And after Adam had completed forty days in the land where he had been created, we brought him into the Garden of Eden to till and keep it, but they brought his wife in on the eightieth day, and after this she entered into the Garden of Eden. ¹⁰ And for this reason the command is written on the heavenly tablets in regard to her that gives birth: "If she bears a male, she will remain in her uncleanness seven days according to the first week of days, and thirty-three days she will remain in the blood of her purifying, and she will not touch any hallowed thing, nor enter into the sanctuary, until she accomplishes these days which [are prescribed] in the case of a male child. ¹¹ But in the case of a female child she will remain in her uncleanness two weeks of days, according to the first two weeks, and sixty-six days in the blood of her purification, and they will be in all eighty days." ¹² And when she had completed these eighty days, we brought her into the Garden of Eden, for it is holier than all the earth besides, and every tree that is planted in it is holy. ¹³ Therefore, there was ordained regarding her who bears a male or a female child the

statute of those days that she should touch no hallowed thing, nor enter into the sanctuary until these days for the male or female child are accomplished. ¹⁴ This is the law and testimony which was written down for Israel, in order that they should observe [it] all the days. ¹⁵ And in the first week of the first jubilee, Adam and his wife were in the Garden of Eden for seven years tilling and keeping it, and we gave him work and we instructed him to do everything that is suitable for tillage. ¹⁶ And he tilled [the garden], and was naked and did not know it, and was not ashamed, and he protected the garden from the birds, and beasts, and cattle, and gathered its fruit, and ate, and put aside the residue for himself and for his wife. ¹⁷ And after the completion of the seven years, which he had completed there, seven years exactly, and in the second month, on the seventeenth day [of the month], the serpent came and approached the woman, and the serpent said to the woman, "Has God commanded you, saying, you will not eat of every tree of the garden?" ¹⁸ And she said to it, "Of all the fruit of the trees of the garden God has said to us, Eat; but of the fruit of the tree which is in the midst of the garden God has said to us, You will not eat thereof, neither will you touch it, lest you die." ¹⁹ And the serpent said to the woman, "You will not surely die, for God knows that on the day you will eat thereof, your eyes will be opened, and you will be as gods, and you will know good and evil." ²⁰ And the woman saw the tree that it was agreeable and pleasant to the eye, and that its fruit was good for food, and she took thereof and ate. ²¹ And when she had first covered her shame with fig-leaves, she gave thereof to Adam and he ate, and his eyes were opened, and he saw that he was naked. ²² And he took fig-leaves and sewed [them] together, and made an apron for himself, and covered his shame. ³² And God cursed the serpent and was angry with it forever. ²⁴ And He was angry with the woman because she listened to the voice of the serpent and ate; and He said to her, "I will greatly multiply your sorrow and your pains; in sorrow you will bring out children, and your return will be to your husband [[or Man]], and he [[or He]] will rule over you." ²⁵ And He also said to Adam, "Because you have listened to the voice of your wife, and have eaten of the tree of which I commanded you that you should not eat thereof, the ground is cursed for your sake: it will bring out thorns and thistles to you, and you will eat your bread in the sweat of your face, until you return to the earth from where you were taken; for earth you are, and to earth you will return." ²⁶ And He made coats of skin for them, and clothed them, and sent them out from the Garden of Eden. ²⁷ And on that day on which Adam went out from the garden, he offered as a sweet savor an offering: frankincense, galbanum, and stacte, and spices in the morning with the rising of the sun from the day when he covered his shame. ²⁸ And on that day the mouth of all beasts, and of cattle, and of birds, and of whatever walks, and of whatever moves was closed, so that they could no longer speak, for they had all spoken with one another with one lip and with one tongue. ²⁹ And He sent out of the Garden of Eden all flesh that was in the Garden of Eden, and all flesh was scattered according to its kinds, and according to its types to the places which had been created for them. ³⁰ And to man alone did He give [the means] to cover his shame, of all the beasts and cattle. ³¹ On this account, it is prescribed on the heavenly tablets as touching all those who know the judgment of the Law, that they should cover their shame, and should not uncover themselves as the nations uncover themselves. ³² And on the new moon of the fourth month, Adam and his wife went out from the Garden of Eden, and they dwelt in the land of 'Eldâ, in the land of their creation. ³³ And Adam called the name of his wife Eve. ³⁴ And they had no son until the first jubilee, and after this he knew her. ³⁵ Now he tilled the land as he had been instructed in the Garden of Eden.

CHAPTER 4

¹ And in the third week in the second jubilee she gave birth to Cain, and in the fourth she gave birth to Abel, and in the fifth she gave birth to her daughter 'Âwân. ² And in the first [year] of the third jubilee, Cain slew Abel because [God] accepted the sacrifice of Abel and did not accept the offering of Cain. ³ And he slew him in the field: and his blood cried from the ground to Heaven, complaining because he had slain him. ⁴ And the Lord reproved Cain because of Abel, because he had slain him, and he made him a fugitive on the earth because of the blood of his brother, and he cursed him on the earth. ⁵ And

on this account, it is written on the heavenly tablets: "Cursed is he who strikes his neighbor treacherously, and let all who have seen and heard it say so; and the man who has seen and not declared [it], let him be accursed as the other." And for this reason, we announce when we come before the Lord our God all the sin which is committed in the heavens and on earth, and in light and in darkness, and everywhere. **7** And Adam and his wife mourned for Abel four weeks of years, and in the fourth year of the fifth week they became joyful, and Adam knew his wife again, and she bore him a son, and he called his name Seth, for he said, "God has raised up a second seed to us on the earth instead of Abel, for Cain slew him." **8** And in the sixth week he begot his daughter 'Azûrâ. **9** And Cain took his sister 'Âwân to be his wife and she bore him Enoch at the close of the fourth jubilee. And in the first year of the first week of the fifth jubilee, houses were built on the earth, and Cain built a city, and called its name after the name of his son Enoch. **10** And Adam knew his wife Eve and she bore nine more sons. **11** And in the fifth week of the fifth jubilee Seth took his sister 'Azûrâ to be his wife, and in the fourth [year of the sixth week] she bore him Enos. **12** He began to call on the Name of the Lord on the earth. **13** And in the seventh jubilee in the third week Enos took his sister Nôâm to be his wife, and she bore him a son in the third year of the fifth week, and he called his name Kenan. **14** And at the close of the eighth jubilee Kenan took his sister Mûalêlêth to be his wife, and she bore him a son in the ninth jubilee, in the first week in the third year of this week, and he called his name Mahalalel. **15** And in the second week of the tenth jubilee Mahalalel took to himself Dînâh to be [his] wife, the daughter of Barâkî'êl, the daughter of his father's brother, and she bore him a son in the third week in the sixth year, and he called his name Jared, for in his days the messengers of the Lord descended on the earth, those who are named the Watchers, that they should instruct the children of men, and that they should do judgment and uprightness on the earth. **16** And in the eleventh jubilee Jared took to himself a wife, and her name was Bâraka, the daughter of Râsûjâl, a daughter of his father's brother, in the fourth week of this jubilee, and she bore him a son in the fifth week, in the fourth year of the jubilee, and he called his name Enoch. **17** And he was the first among men that are born on earth who learned writing, and knowledge, and wisdom, and who wrote down the signs of the heavens according to the order of their months in a scroll, that men might know the seasons of the years according to the order of their separate months. **18** And he was the first to write a testimony, and he testified to the sons of men among the generations of the earth, and recounted the weeks of the jubilees, and made known to them the days of the years, and set in order the months, and recounted the Sabbaths of the years as we made [them] known to him. **19** And what was and what will be he saw in a vision of his sleep, as it will happen to the children of men throughout their generations until the Day of Judgment; he saw and understood everything, and wrote his testimony, and placed the testimony on earth for all the children of men and for their generations. **20** And in the twelfth jubilee, in the seventh week thereof, he took to himself a wife, and her name was Ednî, the daughter of Dânêl, the daughter of his father's brother, and in the sixth year in this week she bore him a son and he called his name Methuselah. **21** And he was moreover with the messengers of God these six jubilees of years, and they showed him everything which is on earth and in the heavens, the rule of the sun, and he wrote down everything. **22** And he testified to the Watchers who had sinned with the daughters of men, for these had begun to unite themselves [with them], so as to be defiled with the daughters of men, and Enoch testified against [them] all. **23** And he was taken from among the children of men, and we conducted him into the Garden of Eden in majesty and honor, and behold, there he wrote down the condemnation and judgment of the world, and all the wickedness of the children of men. **24** And on account of it [God] brought the waters of the flood on all the land of Eden; for there he was set as a sign and that he should testify against all the children of men, that he should recount all the deeds of the generations until the day of condemnation. **25** And he burned the incense of the sanctuary, [even] sweet spices, acceptable before the Lord on the mountain. **26** For the Lord has four places on the earth: the Garden of Eden, and the mountain of the East, and this mountain on which you are this day, Mount Sinai, and Mount Zion [which] will be sanctified in the new creation for a sanctification of the earth; through it the earth will be sanctified from all [its] guilt and its uncleanness throughout the generations of the world. **27** And in the

fourteenth jubilee Methuselah took to himself a wife, Ednâ the daughter of 'Âzrîâl, the daughter of his father's brother, in the third week, in the first year of this week, and he begot a son and called his name Lamech. **28** And in the fifteenth jubilee in the third week Lamech took to himself a wife, and her name was Bêtênôs, the daughter of Bârâkî'îl, the daughter of his father's brother, and in this week she bore him a son and he called his name Noah, saying, "This one will comfort me for my trouble, and all my work, and for the ground which the Lord has cursed." **29** And at the close of the nineteenth jubilee, in the seventh week in the sixth year thereof, Adam died, and all his sons buried him in the land of his creation, and he was the first to be buried in the earth. **30** And he lacked seventy years of one thousand years; for one thousand years are as one day in the testimony of the heavens and therefore it was written concerning the Tree of Knowledge: "On the day that you eat thereof you will die." For this reason, he did not complete the years of this day, for he died during it. **31** At the close of this jubilee Cain was killed after him in the same year, for his house fell on him and he died in the midst of his house, and he was killed by its stones, for with a stone he had killed Abel, and by a stone he was killed in righteous judgment. **32** For this reason it was ordained on the heavenly tablets: "With the instrument with which a man kills his neighbor with the same he will be killed; after the manner that he wounded him, in like manner they will deal with him." **33** And in the twenty-fifth jubilee Noah took to himself a wife, and her name was 'Êmzârâ, the daughter of Râkê'êl, the daughter of his father's brother, in the first year in the fifth week: and in the third year thereof she bore him Shem, in the fifth year thereof she bore him Ham, and in the first year in the sixth week she bore him Japheth.

CHAPTER 5

1 And it came to pass when the children of men began to multiply on the face of the earth and daughters were born to them, that the messengers of God saw them on a certain year of this jubilee, that they were beautiful to look on; and they took wives [for] themselves of all whom they chose, and they bore sons to them and they were giants. **2** And lawlessness increased on the earth and all flesh corrupted its way—men, and cattle, and beasts, and birds, and everything that walks on the earth alike—all of them corrupted their ways and their orders, and they began to devour each other, and lawlessness increased on the earth, and every imagination of the thoughts of all men was evil continually. **3** And God looked on the earth, and behold it was corrupt, and all flesh had corrupted its orders, and all that were on the earth had worked all manner of evil before His eyes. **4** And He said that He would destroy man and all flesh on the face of the earth which He had created. **5** But Noah found grace before the eyes of the Lord. **6** And against the messengers whom He had sent on the earth, He was exceedingly angry, and He gave command to root them out of all their dominion, and He commanded us to bind them in the depths of the earth, and behold, they are bound in the midst of them and are [kept] separate. **7** And a command went out against their sons from before His face that they should be smitten with the sword and be removed from under the heavens. **8** And He said, "My Spirit will not always abide on man, for they are also flesh and their days will be one hundred and twenty years." **9** And He sent His sword into their midst that each should slay his neighbor, and they began to slay each other until they all fell by the sword and were destroyed from the earth. **10** And their fathers were witnesses [of their destruction], and after this they were bound in the depths of the earth forever, until the day of the great condemnation, when judgment is executed on all those who have corrupted their ways and their works before the Lord. **11** And He destroyed all from their places, and there was not left [even] one of them whom He did not judge according to all their wickedness. **12** And He made for all His works a new and righteous nature, so that they should not sin in their whole nature forever but should be all righteous—each in his kind always. **13** And the judgment of all is ordained and written on the heavenly tablets in righteousness—even [the judgment of] all who depart from the path which is ordained for them to walk in; and if they do not walk therein, judgment is written down for every creature and for every kind. **14** And there is nothing in the heavens or on earth, or in light or in darkness, or in Sheol or in the depth, or in the place of darkness [which is not judged]; and all their judgments are ordained, and written, and engraved. **15** In regard to all He will judge, the great according to his greatness, and the small according to his smallness, and each according to his way. ¹⁶ And He is not one who will regard the person [of any], nor is He one who will receive gifts, if He says that He will execute judgment on each: if one gave everything that is on the earth, He will not regard the gifts or the person [of any], nor accept anything at his hands, for He is a righteous judge. ¹⁷ And of the sons of Israel it has been written and ordained [that] if they turn to Him in righteousness, He will forgive all their transgressions and pardon all their sins. ¹⁸ It is written and ordained that He will show mercy to all who turn from all their guilt once each year. ¹⁹ And as for all those who corrupted their ways and their thoughts before the flood, no man's person was accepted save that of Noah alone; for his person was accepted in behalf of his sons, whom [God] saved from the waters of the flood on his account; for his heart was righteous in all his ways, according as it was commanded regarding him, and he had not departed from anything that was ordained for him. ²⁰ And the Lord said that He would destroy everything which was on the earth, both men, and cattle, and beasts, and birds of the air, and that which moves on the earth. ²¹ And He commanded Noah to make himself an ark, that he might save himself from the waters of the flood. ²² And Noah made the Ark in all respects as He commanded him, in the twenty-seventh jubilee of years, in the fifth week in the fifth year [[on the new moon of the first month]]. [1307 A.M.] ²³ And he entered in the sixth [year] thereof [1308 A.M.], in the second month, on the new moon of the second month, until the sixteenth; and he entered, and all that we brought to him, into the Ark, and the Lord closed it from outside on the seventeenth evening. ²⁴ And the Lord opened seven floodgates of [the] heavens, and the mouths of the fountains of the great deep—seven mouths in number. ²⁵ And the floodgates began to pour down water from the heavens forty days and forty nights, and the fountains of the deep also sent up waters, until the whole world was full of water. ²⁶ And the waters increased on the earth: the waters rose fifteen cubits above all the high mountains, and the Ark was lifted up above the earth, and it moved on the face of the waters. ²⁷ And the water prevailed on the face of the earth five months—one hundred and fifty days. ²⁸ And the Ark went and rested on the top of Lûbâr, one of the mountains of Ararat. ²⁹ And [on the new moon] in the fourth month the fountains of the great deep were closed and the floodgates of the heavens were restrained; and on the new moon of the seventh month all the mouths of the abysses of the earth were opened, and the water began to descend into the deep below. ³⁰ And on the new moon of the tenth month the tops of the mountains were seen, and on the new moon of the first month the earth became visible. ³¹ And the waters disappeared from above the earth in the fifth week in the seventh year [1309 A.M.] thereof, and on the seventeenth day in the second month the earth was dry. ³² And on the twenty-seventh thereof he opened the Ark, and sent out from it beasts, and cattle, and birds, and every moving thing.

CHAPTER 6

¹ And on the new moon of the third month he went out from the Ark and built an altar on that mountain. ² And he made atonement for the earth and took a kid and made atonement by its blood for all the guilt of the earth; for everything that had been on it had been destroyed, save those that were in the Ark with Noah. ³ And he placed the fat thereof on the altar, and he took an ox, and a goat, and a sheep and kids, and salt, and a turtle-dove, and the young of a dove, and placed a burnt sacrifice on the altar, and poured an offering mingled with oil thereon, and sprinkled wine and scattered frankincense over everything, and caused an attractive savor to arise, acceptable before the Lord. ⁴ And the Lord smelled the attractive savor, and He made a covenant with him that there should not be a flood to destroy the earth anymore; that all the days of the earth, seed-time and harvest, should never cease; cold and heat, and summer and winter, and day and night should not change their order, nor cease forever. ⁵ "And you: increase and multiply on the earth, and become many on it, and be a blessing on it. The fear of you and the dread of you I will inspire in everything that is on earth and in the sea. ⁶ And behold, I have given to you all beasts, and all winged things, and everything that moves on the earth, and the fish in the waters, and all things for food; as the green herbs, I have given you all things to eat. ⁷ But flesh, with the life thereof, with the blood, you will not eat; for the life of all flesh is in the blood, lest your blood of your lives be required. At the hand of every man, at the hand of every [beast], I will require the blood of man. ⁸ Whoever sheds man's blood by man his blood will be shed, for in the image of God He made man. ⁹ And you: increase and multiply on the earth." ¹⁰ And Noah and his sons swore that they would not eat any blood that was in any flesh, and he made a covenant before the Lord God forever throughout all the generations of the earth in this month. ¹¹ On this account He spoke to you that you should make a covenant with the sons of Israel in this month on the mountain with an oath, and that you should sprinkle blood on them because of all the words of the covenant, which the Lord made with them forever. ¹² And this testimony is written concerning you that you should observe it continually, so that you should not eat on any day any blood of beasts, or birds, or cattle during all the days of the earth, and the man who eats the blood of beast, or of cattle, or of birds during all the days of the earth, he and his seed will be rooted out of the land. ¹³ And command the sons of Israel to eat no blood, so that their names and their seed may continually be before the Lord our God. ¹⁴ And for this law there is no limit of days, for it is forever. They will observe it throughout their generations, so that they may continue supplicating on your behalf with blood before the altar; every day and at the time of morning and evening they will seek forgiveness on your behalf perpetually before the Lord that they may keep it and not be rooted out. ¹⁵ And He gave a sign to Noah and his sons that there should not be a flood on the [whole] earth again. ¹⁶ He set His bow in the cloud for a sign of the perpetual covenant that there should not again be a flood on the earth to destroy it all the days of the earth. ¹⁷ For this reason it is ordained and written on the heavenly tablets that they should celebrate the Celebration of Weeks in this month once a year, to renew the covenant every year. ¹⁸ And this whole festival was celebrated in Heaven from the day of creation until the days of Noah twenty-six jubilees and five weeks of years: and Noah and his sons observed it for seven jubilees and one week of years, until the day of Noah's death, and from the day of Noah's death his sons did away with [it] until the days of Abraham, and they ate blood. ¹⁹ But Abraham observed it, and Isaac, and Jacob, and his children observed it up to your days, and in your days the sons of Israel forgot it until you celebrated it anew on this mountain. ²⁰ And command the sons of Israel to observe this festival in all their generations for a command to them: one day in the year in this month they will celebrate the festival. ²¹ For it is the Celebration of Weeks and the Celebration of First-Fruits: this feast is twofold and of a double nature. According to what is written and engraved concerning it, celebrate it. ²² For I have written in the scroll of the first law, in that which I have written for you, that you should celebrate it in its season, one day in the year, and I explained to you its sacrifices that the sons of Israel should remember and should celebrate it throughout their generations in this month, one day in every year. ²³ And on the new moon of the first month, and on the new moon of the fourth month, and on the new moon of the seventh month, and on the new moon of the tenth month are the days of remembrance, and the days of the seasons in the four divisions of the year. These are written and ordained as a testimony forever. ²⁴ And Noah ordained them for himself as feasts for the generations forever, so that they have thereby become a memorial to him. ²⁵ And on the new moon of the first month he was commanded to make for himself an ark, and on that [day] the earth became dry, and he opened [the Ark], and saw the earth. ²⁶ And on the new moon of the fourth month the mouths of the depths of the abysses beneath were closed. And on the new moon of the seventh month all the mouths of the abysses of the earth were opened, and the waters began to descend into them. ²⁷ And on the new moon of the tenth month the tops of the mountains were seen, and Noah was glad. ²⁸ And on this account, he ordained them for himself as feasts for a memorial forever, and thus they are ordained. ²⁹ And they placed them on the heavenly tablets; each had thirteen weeks; from one to another—their memorial, from the first to the second, and from the second to the third, and from the third to the fourth. ³⁰ And all the days of the command will be fifty-two weeks of days, and [these will make] the entire year complete. ³¹ Thus it is engraved and ordained on the heavenly tablets. And there is no neglecting [this command] for a single year or from year to year. ³² And command the sons of Israel that they observe the

years according to this reckoning—three hundred and sixty-four days, and [these] will constitute a complete year, and they will not disturb its time from its days and from its feasts; for everything will fall out in them according to their testimony, and they will not leave out any day nor disturb any feasts. ³³ But if they neglect and do not observe them according to His command, then they will disturb all their seasons, and the years will be dislodged from this [order], and they will neglect their ordinances. ³⁴ And all the sons of Israel will forget, and will not find the path of the years, and will forget the new moons, and seasons, and Sabbaths, and they will go wrong as to all the order of the years. ³⁵ For I know and from now on will declare it to you, and it is not of My own devising, for the scroll [lies] written before Me, and on the heavenly tablets the division of days is ordained, lest they forget the feasts of the covenant and walk according to the feasts of the nations after their error and after their ignorance. ³⁶ For there will be those who will assuredly make observations of the moon—how [it] disturbs the seasons and comes in from year to year ten days too soon. ³⁷ For this reason the years will come on them when they will disturb [the order] and make an abominable [day] the day of testimony, and an unclean day a feast day, and they will confound all the days, the holy with the unclean, and the unclean day with the holy; for they will go wrong as to the months, and Sabbaths, and feasts, and jubilees. ³⁸ For this reason I command and testify to you that you may testify to them; for after your death your children will disturb [them], so that they will not make the year three hundred and sixty-four days only, and for this reason they will go wrong as to the new moons, and seasons, and Sabbaths, and festivals, and they will eat all kinds of blood with all kinds of flesh.

CHAPTER 7

¹ And in the seventh week in the first year thereof, in this jubilee, Noah planted vines on the mountain on which the Ark had rested, named Lûbâr, one of the Ararat Mountains, and they produced fruit in the fourth year, and he guarded their fruit, and gathered it in this year in the seventh month. ² And he made wine from that and put it into a vessel, and kept it until the fifth year, until the first day, on the new moon of the first month. ³ And he celebrated with joy the day of this feast, and he made a burnt sacrifice to the Lord—one young ox, and one ram, and seven sheep, each a year old, and a kid of the goats, that he might make atonement thereby for himself and his sons. ⁴ And he prepared the kid first and placed some of its blood on the flesh that was on the altar which he had made, and all the fat he laid on the altar where he made the burnt sacrifice, and the ox, and the ram, and the sheep, and he laid all their flesh on the altar. ⁵ And he placed all their offerings mingled with oil on it, and afterward he sprinkled wine on the fire which he had previously made on the altar, and he placed incense on the altar and caused a sweet savor to ascend acceptable before the Lord his God. ⁶ And he rejoiced and drank of this wine—he and his children with joy. ⁷ And it was evening, and he went into his tent, and being drunken, he lay down and slept, and was uncovered in his tent as he slept. ⁸ And Ham saw his father Noah naked and went out and told his two brothers outside. ⁹ And Shem took his garment and arose, he and Japheth, and they placed the garment on their shoulders and went backward and covered the shame of their father, and their faces were backward. ¹⁰ And Noah awoke from his sleep and knew all that his younger son had done to him, and he cursed his son and said, "Cursed be Canaan; he will be an enslaved servant to his brothers." ¹¹ And he blessed Shem and said, "Blessed is the Lord God of Shem, and Canaan will be his servant. ¹² God will enlarge Japheth, and God will dwell in the dwelling of Shem, and Canaan will be his servant." ¹³ And Ham knew that his father had cursed his younger son, and he was displeased that he had cursed his son, and he parted from his father, he and his sons with him—Cush, and Mizraim, and Put, and Canaan. ¹⁴ And he built a city for himself and called its name after the name of his wife Nê'êlâtamâ'ûk. ¹⁵ And Japheth saw it, and became envious of his brother, and he too built a city for himself, and he called its name after the name of his wife 'Adâtanêsês. ¹⁶ And Shem dwelt with his father Noah, and he built a city close to his father on the mountain, and he too called its name after the name of his wife Sêdêqêtêlĕbâb. ¹⁷ And behold, these three cities are near Mount Lûbâr: Sêdêqêtêlĕbâb, fronting the mountain on its east, and Na'êlâtamâ'ûk on the south, [and] 'Adatanêsês toward the west. ¹⁸ And these are the sons of Shem: Elam, and Asshur, and Arphaxad (this [son] was born two years after the flood), and Lud, and Aram. ¹⁹ The sons of Japheth: Gomer, and Magog, and Madai, and Javan, Tubal, and Meshech, and Tiras. These are the sons of Noah. ²⁰ And in the twenty-eighth jubilee Noah began to prescribe on his sons' sons the ordinances and commands, and all the judgments that he knew, and he exhorted his sons to observe righteousness, and to cover the shame of their flesh, and to bless their Creator, and honor father and mother, and love their neighbor, and guard their souls from fornication, and uncleanness, and all iniquity. ²¹ For owing to these three things the flood came on the earth, namely, owing to the fornication wherein the Watchers against the law of their ordinances went whoring after the daughters of men, and took wives [for] themselves of all which they chose: and they made the beginning of uncleanness. ²² And they begot sons, the Nâphîdîm, and they were all different, and they devoured one another: and the Giants slew the Nâphîl, and the Nâphîl slew the Eljô, and the Eljô mankind, and one man another. ²³ And everyone sold himself to work iniquity and to shed much blood, and the earth was filled with iniquity. ²⁴ And after this they sinned against the beasts, and birds, and all that moves and walks on the earth: and much blood was shed on the earth, and every imagination and desire of men they imagined [was] vanity and evil continually. ²⁵ And the Lord destroyed everything from off the face of the earth; because of the wickedness of their deeds, and because of the blood which they had shed in the midst of the earth He destroyed everything. ²⁶ "And we were left, you and I, my sons, and everything that entered with us into the Ark, and behold, I see your works before me that you do not walk in righteousness; for you have begun to walk in the path of destruction, and you are parting from one another, and are envious of one another, and [so it is] that you are not in harmony, my sons, each with his brother. ²⁷ For I see and behold [that] the demons have begun [their] seductions against you and against your children, and now I fear on your behalf that after my death you will shed the blood of men on the earth, and that you, too, will be destroyed from the face of the earth. ²⁸ For whoever sheds man's blood, and whoever eats the blood of any flesh, will all be destroyed from the earth. ²⁹ And there will not be left any man that eats blood or that sheds the blood of man on the earth, nor will there be left to him any seed or descendants living under the heavens; for they will go into Sheol, and they will descend into the place of condemnation. And into the darkness of the deep they will all be removed by a violent death. ³⁰ No blood will be seen on you of all the blood there will be all the days in which you have killed any beasts, or cattle, or whatever flies on the earth; and work a good work for your souls by covering that which has been shed on the face of the earth. ³¹ And you will not be like him who eats with blood, but guard yourselves that none may eat blood before you: cover the blood, for thus I have been commanded to testify to you and your children, together with all flesh. ³² And do not permit the soul to be eaten with the flesh, that your blood, which is your life, may not be required at the hand of any flesh that sheds [it] on the earth. ³³ For the earth will not be clean from the blood which has been shed on it; for [only] through the blood of him that shed it will the earth be purified throughout all its generations. ³⁴ And now, my children, listen: work judgment and righteousness that you may be planted in righteousness over the face of the whole earth, and your glory [will be] lifted up before my God, who saved me from the waters of the flood. ³⁵ And behold, you will go and build cities for yourselves, and plant in them all the plants that are on the earth, and moreover all fruit-bearing trees. ³⁶ For three years the fruit of everything that is eaten will not be gathered: and in the fourth year its fruit will be accounted holy, acceptable before the Most High God, who created the heavens, and earth, and all things. Let them offer in abundance the first of the wine and oil [as] first-fruits on the altar of the Lord, who receives it, and let the servants of the house of the Lord eat what is left before the altar which receives [it]. ³⁷ And in the fifth year make the release so that you release it in righteousness and uprightness, and you will be righteous, and all that you plant will prosper. ³⁸ For thus did Enoch, the father of your father command Methuselah, his son, and Methuselah his son Lamech, and Lamech commanded me all the things which his fathers commanded him. ³⁹ And I also will give you command, my sons, as Enoch commanded his son in the first jubilees: while still living, the seventh in his generation, he commanded and testified to his son and to his sons' sons until the day of

his death."

CHAPTER 8

¹ In the twenty-ninth jubilee, in the first week, in the beginning thereof, Arphaxad took to himself a wife and her name was Râsû'ëjâ, [the daughter of Sûsân,] the daughter of Elam, and she bore him a son in the third year in this week, and he called his name Kâinâm. ² And the son grew, and his father taught him writing, and he went to seek for himself a place where he might seize for himself a city. ³ And he found a writing which former [generations] had carved on the rock, and he read what was thereon, and he transcribed it and sinned owing to it; for it contained the teaching of the Watchers in accordance with which they used to observe the omens of the sun, and moon, and stars in all the signs of the heavens. ⁴ And he wrote it down and said nothing regarding it; for he was afraid to speak to Noah about it lest he should be angry with him on account of it. ⁵ And in the thirtieth jubilee, in the second week, in the first year thereof, he took to himself a wife, and her name was Mêlkâ, the daughter of Madai, the son of Japheth, and in the fourth year he begot a son, and called his name Shelah, for he said, "Truly I have been sent." ⁶ [And in the fourth year he was born], and Shelah grew up and took to himself a wife, and her name was Mû'ak, the daughter of Kêsêd, his father's brother, in the thirty-first jubilee, in the fifth week, in the first year thereof. ⁷ And she bore him a son in the fifth year thereof, and he called his name Eber: and he took to himself a wife, and her name was 'Azûrâd, the daughter of Nêbrôd, in the thirty-second jubilee, in the seventh week, in the third year thereof. ⁸ And in the sixth year thereof, she bore him a son, and he called his name Peleg, for in the days when he was born the children of Noah began to divide the earth among themselves; for this reason he called his name Peleg. ⁹ And they divided [it] secretly among themselves and told it to Noah. ¹⁰ And it came to pass in the beginning of the thirty-third jubilee that they divided the earth into three parts, for Shem, and Ham, and Japheth, according to the inheritance of each, in the first year in the first week, when one of us, who had been sent, was with them. ¹¹ And he called his sons, and they drew near to him, they and their children, and he divided the earth into the lots, which his three sons were to take in possession, and they reached out their hands, and took the writing out of the bosom of their father Noah. ¹² And there came out on the writing as Shem's lot the middle of the earth which he should take as an inheritance for himself and for his sons, for the perpetual generations, from the middle of the mountain range of Râfâ, from the mouth of the water from the River Tînâ, and his portion goes toward the west through the midst of this river, and it extends until it reaches the water of the abysses, out of which this river goes out and pours its waters into the sea Mê'at, and this river flows into the Great Sea. And all that is toward the north is Japheth's, and all that is toward the south belongs to Shem. ¹³ And it extends until it reaches Kârâsô: this is in the bosom of the tongue which looks toward the south. ¹⁴ And his portion extends along the Great Sea, and it extends in a straight line until it reaches the west of the tongue which looks toward the south; for this sea is called the tongue of the Egyptian Sea. ¹⁵ And it turns from here toward the south toward the mouth of the Great Sea on the shore of [its] waters, and it extends to the west to 'Afrâ and it extends until it reaches the waters of the River Gihon, and to the south of the waters of Gihon, to the banks of this river. ¹⁶ And it extends toward the east until it reaches the Garden of Eden, to the south thereof, [to the south] and from the east of the whole land of Eden and of the whole east [thereof], it turns to the east, and proceeds until it reaches the east of the mountain named Râfâ, and it descends to the bank of the mouth of the River Tînâ. ¹⁷ This portion came out by lot for Shem and his sons, that they should possess it forever to his generations forevermore. ¹⁸ And Noah rejoiced that this portion came out for Shem and for his sons, and he remembered all that he had spoken with his mouth in prophecy; for he had said, "Blessed is the Lord God of Shem, and may the Lord dwell in the dwelling of Shem." ¹⁹ And he knew that the Garden of Eden is the Holy of Holies and the dwelling of the Lord, and Mount Sinai—the center of the desert, and Mount Zion—the center of the navel of the earth: these three were created as holy places facing each other. ²⁰ And he blessed the God of gods who had put the word of the Lord into his mouth, and [blessed] the Lord forevermore. ²¹ And he knew that a blessed portion and a blessing had come

to Shem and his sons to the generations forever—the whole land of Eden and the whole land of the Red Sea, and the whole land of the east, and India, and on the Red Sea and the mountains thereof, and all the land of Bashan, and all the land of Lebanon and the islands of Kaftûr, and all the mountains of Sanîr and 'Amânâ, and the mountains of Asshur in the north, and all the land of Elam, Asshur, and Bâbêl, and Sûsân, and Mâ'ëdâi, and all the mountains of Ararat, and all the region beyond the sea, which is beyond the mountains of Asshur toward the north, a blessed and spacious land, and all that is in it is very good. ²² And for Ham came out the second portion, beyond the Gihon toward the south to the right of the Garden, and it extends toward the south and it extends to all the mountains of fire, and it extends toward the west to the Sea of 'Atêl and it extends toward the west until it reaches the Sea of Mâ'ûk—that [sea] into which everything which is not destroyed descends. ²³ And it goes out toward the north to the limits of Gâdir, and it goes out to the coast of the waters of the sea to the waters of the Great Sea until it draws near to the River Gihon and goes along the River Gihon until it reaches the right of the Garden of Eden. ²⁴ And this is the land which came out for Ham as the portion which he was to occupy forever for himself and his sons to their generations forever. ²⁵ And for Japheth came out the third portion beyond the River Tînâ to the north of the outflow of its waters, and it extends northeastward to the whole region of Gog and to all the country east thereof. ²⁶ And it extends northward to the north, and it extends to the mountains of Qêlt toward the north, and toward the Sea of Mâ'ûk, and it goes out to the east of Gâdir as far as the region of the waters of the sea. ²⁷ And it extends until it approaches the west of Fârâ, and it returns toward 'Afêrâg, and it extends eastward to the waters of the Sea of Mê'at. ²⁸ And it extends to the region of the River Tînâ in a northeasterly direction until it approaches the boundary of its waters toward the mountain Râfâ, and it turns toward the north. ²⁹ This is the land which came out for Japheth and his sons as the portion of his inheritance which he should possess for himself and his sons, for their generations forever: five great islands, and a great land in the north. ³⁰ But it is cold, and the land of Ham is hot, and the land of Shem is neither hot nor cold, but it is of blended cold and heat.

CHAPTER 9

¹ And Ham divided among his sons, and the first portion came out for Cush toward the east, and to the west of him for Mizraim, and to the west of him for Put, and to the west of him [and to the west thereof] on the sea for Canaan. ² And Shem also divided among his sons, and the first portion came out for Elam and his sons, to the east of the River Tigris until it approaches the east, the whole land of India, and on the Red Sea on its coast, and the waters of Dêdân, and all the mountains of Mebrî and 'Êlâ, and all the land of Sûsân and all that is on the side of Pharnâk to the Red Sea and the River Tînâ. ³ And for Asshur came out the second portion, all the land of Asshur, and Nineveh, and Shinar, and to the border of India, and it ascends and skirts the river. ⁴ And for Arphaxad came out the third portion, all the land of the region of the Chaldees to the east of the Euphrates, bordering on the Red Sea, and all the waters of the desert close to the tongue of the sea which looks toward Egypt, all the land of Lebanon, and Sanîr, and 'Amânâ to the border of the Euphrates. ⁵ And for Aram there came out the fourth portion, all the land of Mesopotamia between the Tigris and the Euphrates to the north of the Chaldees to the border of the mountains of Asshur and the land of 'Arârâ. ⁶ And there came out for Lud the fifth portion, the mountains of Asshur and all pertaining to them until it reaches the Great Sea, and until it reaches the east of his brother Asshur. ⁷ And Japheth also divided the land of his inheritance among his sons. ⁸ And the first portion came out for Gomer to the east from the north side to the River Tînâ; and in the north there came out for Magog all the inner portions of the north until it reaches to the Sea of Mê'at. ⁹ And for Madai came out as his portion that he should possess from the west of his two brothers to the islands, and to the coasts of the islands. ¹⁰ And for Javan came out the fourth portion, every island and the islands which are toward the border of Lud. ¹¹ And for Tubal there came out the fifth portion in the midst of the tongue which approaches toward the border of the portion of Lud to the second tongue, to the region beyond the second tongue to the third tongue. ¹² And for Meshech came out the sixth

portion, all the region beyond the third tongue until it approaches the east of Gâdîr. **13** And for Tiras there came out the seventh portion: four great islands in the midst of the sea, which reach to the portion of Ham [[and the islands of Kamâtûrî came out by lot for the sons of Arphaxad as his inheritance]]. **14** And thus the sons of Noah divided to their sons in the presence of their father Noah, and he bound them all by an oath, invoking a curse on everyone that sought to seize the portion which had not fallen [to him] by his lot. **15** And they all said, "So be it; so be it," for themselves and their sons forever throughout their generations until the Day of Judgment, on which the Lord God will judge them with a sword and with fire, for all the unclean wickedness of their errors, with which they have filled the earth with transgression, and uncleanness, and fornication, and sin.

CHAPTER 10

1 And in the third week of this jubilee the unclean demons began to lead the children of the sons of Noah astray, and to make [them] to err, and destroy them. **2** And the sons of Noah came to their father Noah, and they told him concerning the demons which were leading astray, and blinding, and slaying his sons' sons. **3** And he prayed before the Lord his God, and said, "God of the spirits of all flesh, || Who has shown mercy to me, || And has saved me and my sons from the waters of the flood, || And has not caused me to perish as you did the sons of perdition, || For Your grace has been great toward me, || And great has been Your mercy to my soul: Let Your grace be lifted up on my sons, || And do not let wicked spirits rule over them || Lest they should destroy them from the earth. **4** But bless me and my sons, || That we may increase, and multiply, and replenish the earth. **5** And You know how Your Watchers, || The fathers of these spirits, acted in my day: And as for these spirits which are living, || Imprison them and hold them fast in the place of condemnation, || And do not let them bring destruction on the sons of Your servant, my God; For these are malevolent, and created in order to destroy. **6** And do not let them rule over the spirits of the living, || For You alone can exercise dominion over them. And do not let them have power over the sons of the righteous || From now on and forevermore." **7** And the Lord our God commanded us to bind all. **8** And the chief of the spirits, Mastêmâ, came and said, "Lord, Creator, let some of them remain before me, and let them listen to my voice, and do all that I will say to them; for if some of them are not left to me, I will not be able to execute the power of my will on the sons of men; for these are for corruption and leading astray before my judgment, for great is the wickedness of the sons of men." **9** And He said, "Let the tenth part of them remain before him, and let nine parts descend into the place of condemnation." **10** And He commanded that one of us should teach Noah all their medicines; for He knew that they would not walk in uprightness, nor strive in righteousness. **11** And we did according to all His words: we bound all the malevolent evil ones in the place of condemnation, and a tenth part of them we left that they might be subject before Satan on the earth. **12** And we explained to Noah all the medicines of their diseases, together with their seductions, how he might heal them with herbs of the earth. **13** And Noah wrote down all things in a scroll as we instructed him concerning every kind of medicine. Thus, the evil spirits were precluded from [hurting] the sons of Noah. **14** And he gave all that he had written to Shem, his eldest son, for he loved him exceedingly above all his sons. **15** And Noah slept with his fathers and was buried on Mount Lûbâr in the land of Ararat. **16** Nine hundred and fifty years he completed in his life—nineteen jubilees, and two weeks, and five years. **17** And in his life on earth he excelled the children of men, save Enoch because of the righteousness wherein he was perfect. For Enoch's office was ordained for a testimony to the generations of the world, so that he should recount all the deeds of generation to generation, until the Day of Judgment. **18** And in the thirty-third jubilee, in the first year in the second week, Peleg took to himself a wife, whose name was Lômnâ, the daughter of Sînâ'ar, and she bore him a son in the fourth year of this week, and he called his name Reu, for he said, "Behold, the children of men have become evil through the wicked purpose of building for themselves a city and a tower in the land of Shinar." **19** For they departed from the land of Ararat eastward to Shinar, for in his days they built the city and the tower, saying, "Go forth; let us ascend thereby into the heavens." **20** And they began to build, and in the fourth week they made brick with fire, and the bricks served them for stone, and the clay with which they cemented them together was asphalt, which comes out of the sea and out of the fountains of water in the land of Shinar. **21** And they built it; forty-three years they were building it; its breadth was two hundred and three bricks, and the height [of a brick] was the third of one; its height amounted to five thousand and four hundred and thirty-three cubits and two palms, and [the extent of one wall was] thirteen stadia [[and of the other thirty stadia]]. **22** And the Lord our God said to us, "Behold, they are one people, and they begin to do [this], and now nothing will be withheld from them. Go forth; let us go down and confound their language that they may not understand one another's speech, and they may be dispersed into cities and nations, and one purpose will no longer abide with them until the Day of Judgment." **23** And the Lord descended, and we descended with Him to see the city and the tower which the children of men had built. **24** And He confounded their language, and they no longer understood one another's speech, and then they ceased to build the city and the tower. **25** For this reason the whole land of Shinar is called Babel, because the Lord confounded all the language of the children of men there, and from there they were dispersed into their cities, each according to his language and his nation. **26** And the Lord sent a mighty wind against the tower and overthrew it on the earth, and behold, it was between Asshur and Babylon in the land of Shinar, and they called its name "Overthrow." **27** In the fourth week, in the first year, in the beginning thereof, in the thirty-fourth jubilee, they were dispersed from the land of Shinar. **28** And Ham and his sons went into the land which he was to occupy, which he acquired as his portion in the land of the south. **29** And Canaan saw the land of Lebanon to the river of Egypt that it was very good, and he did not go into the land of his inheritance to the west [that is to] the sea, and he dwelt in the land of Lebanon, eastward and westward from the border of Jordan and from the border of the sea. **30** And his father Ham, and his brothers Cush and Mizraim, said to him, "You have settled in a land which is not yours, and which did not fall to us by lot: do not do so; for if you do so, you and your sons will fall in the land and [be] accursed through sedition; for by sedition you have settled, and by sedition your children will fall, and you will be rooted out forever. **31** Do not dwell in the dwelling of Shem, for to Shem and to his sons did it come by their lot. **32** Cursed are you and cursed will you be beyond all the sons of Noah, by the curse by which we bound ourselves by an oath in the presence of the Holy Judge, and in the presence of our father Noah." **33** But he did not listen to them and dwelt in the land of Lebanon from Hamath to the entering of Egypt—he and his sons until this day. **34** And for this reason that land is named Canaan. **35** And Japheth and his sons went toward the sea and dwelt in the land of their portion, and Madai saw the land of the sea and it did not please him, and he begged [for] a [portion] from Elam, and Asshur, and Arphaxad, his wife's brother, and he dwelt in the land of Media, near to his wife's brother, until this day. **36** And he called his dwelling-place and the dwelling-place of his sons Media, after the name of their father Madai.

CHAPTER 11

1 And in the thirty-fifth jubilee, in the third week, in the first year thereof, Reu took to himself a wife, and her name was 'Ôrâ, the daughter of 'Ûr, the son of Kêsêd, and she bore him a son, and he called his name Sêrôḥ, in the seventh year of this week in this jubilee. **2** And the sons of Noah began to war on each other, to take captive and to slay each other, and to shed the blood of men on the earth, and to eat blood, and to build strong cities, and walls, and towers, and individuals [began] to exalt themselves above the nation, and to found the beginnings of kingdoms, and to go to war—people against people, and nation against nation, and city against city, and all [began] to do evil, and to acquire arms, and to teach their sons war, and they began to capture cities, and to sell menservants and maidservants. **3** And 'Ûr, the son of Kêsêd, built the city of 'Arâ of the Chaldees, and called its name after his own name and the name of his father. **4** And they made molten images for themselves, and they each worshiped the idol, the molten image which they had made for themselves, and they began to make graven images and unclean statues, and malevolent spirits assisted and seduced [them] into committing transgression and uncleanness. **5** And the prince Mastêmâ exerted himself to do all this, and he sent out other spirits, those which were put under his hand, to do all manner of wrong and sin, and all manner of transgression, to corrupt and destroy, and to shed blood on the earth. **6** For this reason he called the name of Sêrôḫ, Serug, for everyone turned to do all manner of sin and transgression. **7** And he grew up and dwelt in Ur of the Chaldees, near to the father of his wife's mother, and he worshiped idols, and he took to himself a wife in the thirty-sixth jubilee, in the fifth week, in the first year thereof, and her name was Mêlkâ, the daughter of Kâbêr, the daughter of his father's brother. **8** And she bore him Nahor in the first year of this week, and he grew and dwelt in Ur of the Chaldees, and his father taught him the research of the Chaldees to divine and portend, according to the signs of the heavens. **9** And in the thirty-seventh jubilee, in the sixth week, in the first year thereof, he took to himself a wife, and her name was 'Îjâskâ, the daughter of Nêstâg of the Chaldees. **10** And she bore him Terah in the seventh year of this week. **11** And the prince Mastêmâ sent ravens and birds to devour the seed which was sown in the land, in order to destroy the land, and rob the children of men of their labors. Before they could plow in the seed, the ravens picked [it] from the surface of the ground. **12** And for this reason he called his name Terah, because the ravens and the birds reduced them to destitution and devoured their seed. **13** And the years began to be barren, owing to the birds, and they devoured all the fruit of the trees from the trees: it was only with great effort that they could save a little of all the fruit of the earth in their days. **14** And in this thirty-ninth jubilee, in the second week in the first year, Terah took to himself a wife, and her name was 'Êdnâ, the daughter of 'Abrâm, the daughter of his father's sister. **15** And in the seventh year of this week she bore him a son, and he called his name Abram, by the name of the father of his mother, for he had died before his daughter had conceived a son. **16** And the child began to understand the errors of the earth, that all went astray after graven images and after uncleanness, and his father taught him writing, and he was two weeks of years old, and he separated himself from his father that he might not worship idols with him. **17** And he began to pray to the Creator of all things that He might save him from the errors of the children of men, and that his portion should not fall into error after uncleanness and vileness. **18** And the seed-time came for the sowing of seed on the land, and they all went out together to protect their seed against the ravens, and Abram went out with those that went, and the child was a youth of fourteen years. **19** And a cloud of ravens came to devour the seed, and Abram ran to meet them before they settled on the ground and cried to them before they settled on the ground to devour the seed, and said, "Do not descend! Return to the place where you came!" And they proceeded to turn back. **20** And he caused the clouds of ravens to turn back that day seventy times, and of all the ravens throughout all the land where Abram was there settled there not so much as one. **21** And all who were with him throughout all the land saw him cry out, and all the ravens turn back, and his name became great in all the land of the Chaldees. **22** And there came to him this year all those that wished to sow, and he went with them until the time of sowing ceased: and they sowed their land, and that year they brought enough grain home and ate and were satisfied. **23** And in the first year of the fifth week Abram taught those who made implements for oxen, the craftsmen in wood, and they made a vessel above the ground, facing the frame of the plow, in order to put the seed thereon, and the seed fell down from that on the share of the plow, and was hidden in the earth, and they no longer feared the ravens. **24** And after this manner they made [vessels] above the ground on all the frames of the plows, and they sowed and tilled all the land, according as Abram commanded them, and they no longer feared the birds.

CHAPTER 12

1 And it came to pass in the sixth week, in the seventh year thereof, that Abram spoke to his father Terah, saying, "Father!" And he said, "Behold, here I am, my son." **2** And he said, "What help and profit do we have from those idols which you worship, and before which you bow yourself? **3** For there is no spirit in them, for they are mute forms, and a misleading of the heart. Do not worship them: **4** worship the God of Heaven, who causes the rain and the dew to descend on the earth, and does everything on the earth, and has created everything by His

word, and all life is from before His face. **5** Why do you worship things that have no spirit in them? For they are the work of [men's] hands, and you bear them on your shoulders, and you have no help from them, but they are a great cause of shame to those who make them, and a misleading of the heart to those who worship them: do not worship them." **6** And his father said to him, "I also know it, my son, but what will I do with a people who have made me to serve before them? **7** And if I tell them the truth, they will slay me, for their soul cleaved to them to worship them and honor them. Keep silent, my son, lest they slay you." **8** And he spoke these words to his two brothers, and they were angry with him and he kept silent. **9** And in the fortieth jubilee, in the second week, in the seventh year thereof, Abram took to himself a wife, and her name was Sarai, the daughter of his father, and she became his wife. **10** And his brother Haran took to himself a wife in the third year of the third week, and she bore him a son in the seventh year of this week, and he called his name Lot. **11** And his brother Nahor took to himself a wife. **12** And in the sixtieth year of the life of Abram, that is, in the fourth week, in the fourth year thereof, Abram arose by night, and burned the house of the idols, and he burned all that was in the house, and no man knew it. **13** And they arose in the night and sought to save their gods from the midst of the fire. **14** And Haran tried to save them, but the fire flamed over him, and he was burned in the fire, and he died in Ur of the Chaldees before his father Terah, and they buried him in Ur of the Chaldees. **15** And Terah went out from Ur of the Chaldees, he and his sons, to go into the land of Lebanon and into the land of Canaan, and he dwelt in the land of Haran, and Abram dwelt with his father Terah in Haran [for] two weeks of years. **16** And in the sixth week, in the fifth year thereof, Abram sat up throughout the night on the new moon of the seventh month to observe the stars from the evening to the morning, in order to see what the nature of the year would be with regard to the rains, and he was alone as he sat and observed. **17** And a word came into his heart and he said, "All the signs of the stars, and the signs of the moon and of the sun are all in the hand of the Lord. Why do I search [them] out? **18** If He desires, He causes it to rain, morning and evening; and if He desires, He withholds it, and all things are in His hand." **19** And he prayed that night and said, "My God, God Most High, You alone are my God, and I have chosen You and Your dominion. And You have created all things, and all things that exist are the work of Your hands. **20** Deliver me from the hands of evil spirits who have sway over the thoughts of men's hearts, and do not let them lead me astray from You, my God. And establish me and my seed forever so that we do not go astray from now and forevermore." **21** And he said, "Will I return to Ur of the Chaldees who seek my face that I may return to them, or am I to remain here in this place? The right path before You—prosper it in the hands of Your servant that he may fulfill [it] and that I may not walk in the deceitfulness of my heart, O my God." **22** And he made an end of speaking and praying, and behold, the word of the Lord was sent to him through me, saying, "Go forth from your country, and from your relatives, and from the house of your father to a land which I will show you, and I will make you a great and numerous nation. **23** And I will bless you, and I will make your name great, and you will be blessed in the earth, and all [the] families of the earth will be blessed in you, and I will bless that bless you, and curse them that curse you. **24** And I will be God to you and your son, and to your son's son, and to all your seed: do not fear, from now and to all generations of the earth I am your God." **25** And the Lord God said, "Open his mouth and his ears that he may hear and speak with his mouth, with the language which has been revealed," for it had ceased from the mouths of all the children of men from the day of the overthrow [of Babel]. **26** And I opened his mouth, and his ears, and his lips, and I began to speak with him in Hebrew in the tongue of the creation. **27** And he took the scrolls of his fathers, and these were written in Hebrew, and he transcribed them, and he began from then on to study them, and I made known to him that which he could not [understand], and he studied them during the six rainy months. **28** And it came to pass in the seventh year of the sixth week that he spoke to his father and informed him that he would leave Haran to go into the land of Canaan to see it and [then] return to him. **29** And his father Terah said to him, "Go in peace; may the perpetual God make your path straight, and the Lord [[be with you, and]] protect you from all evil, and grant grace, mercy, and favor to you before those who see you, and may none of the children of men have power over you to harm you; go in peace. **30** And if you see a land pleasant to your eyes to dwell in, then arise and take me to you, and take Lot, the son of your brother Haran, with you as your own son: the Lord be with you. **31** And leave your brother Nahor with me until you return in peace, and we all go with you together."

CHAPTER 13

1 And Abram journeyed from Haran, and he took his wife Sarai, and Lot, his brother Haran's son, to the land of Canaan, and he came into Asshur, and proceeded to Shechem, and dwelt near a lofty oak. **2** And he saw, and behold, the land was very pleasant from the entering of Hamath to the lofty oak. **3** And the Lord said to him, "To you and to your seed I will give this land." **4** And he built an altar there, and he offered a burnt sacrifice thereon to the Lord, who had appeared to him. **5** And he left from there to the mountain [with] Bethel on the west and Ai on the east and pitched his tent there. **6** And he saw, and behold, the land was very wide and good, and everything grew thereon—vines, and figs, and pomegranates, oaks, and hollies, and terebinths, and oil trees, and cedars, and cypresses, and date trees, and all trees of the field, and there was water on the mountains. **7** And he blessed the Lord who had led him out of Ur of the Chaldees and had brought him to this land. **8** And it came to pass in the first year, in the seventh week, on the new moon of the first month, that he built an altar on this mountain, and called on the Name of the Lord: "You, the perpetual God, are my God." **9** And he offered a burnt sacrifice to the Lord on the altar that He should be with him and not forsake him all the days of his life. **10** And he left from there and went toward the south, and he came to Hebron, and Hebron was built at that time, and he dwelt there two years, and he went into the land of the south, to Bealoth, and there was a famine in the land. **11** And Abram went into Egypt in the third year of the week, and he dwelt in Egypt five years before his wife was torn away from him. **12** Now Tanis [(Zoan)] in Egypt was at that time built—seven years after Hebron. **11** And it came to pass when Pharaoh seized Sarai, the wife of Abram, that the Lord plagued Pharaoh and his house with great plagues because of Sarai, Abram's wife. **14** And Abram was very glorious by reason of possessions in sheep, and cattle, and donkeys, and horses, and camels, and menservants, and maidservants, and in exceeding silver and gold. And Lot also, his brother's son, was wealthy. **15** And Pharaoh gave back Sarai, the wife of Abram, and he sent him out of the land of Egypt, and he journeyed to the place where he had pitched his tent at the beginning, to the place of the altar, with Ai on the east and Bethel on the west, and he blessed the Lord his God who had brought him back in peace. **16** And it came to pass in the forty-first jubilee, in the third year of the first week, that he returned to this place and offered a burnt sacrifice there, and called on the Name of the Lord, and said, "You, the Most High God, are my God forever and ever." **17** And in the fourth year of this week Lot parted from him, and Lot dwelt in Sodom, and the men of Sodom were sinners exceedingly. **18** And it grieved him in his heart that his brother's son had parted from him, for he had no children. **19** In that year, when Lot was taken captive, the Lord said to Abram after Lot had parted from him, in the fourth year of this week: "Lift up your eyes from the place where you are dwelling—northward, and southward, and westward, and eastward. **20** For all the land which you see I will give to you and to your seed forever, and I will make your seed as the sand of the sea: though a man may number the dust of the earth, yet your seed will not be numbered. **21** Arise, walk in the length of it and the breadth of it, and see it all; for to your seed I will give it." And Abram went to Hebron and dwelt there. **22** And in this year Chedorlaomer, king of Elam, and Amraphel, king of Shinar, and Arioch, king of Sêllâsar and Têrgâl, king of nations, came and slew the king of Gomorrah, and the king of Sodom fled, and many fell through wounds in the Valley of Siddim, by the Salt Sea. **23** And they took Sodom, and Adam, and Zeboim captive, and they took Lot captive also, the son of Abram's brother, and all his possessions, and they went to Dan. **24** And one who had escaped came and told Abram that his brother's son had been taken captive and [Abram] armed his household servants. **25** For Abram, and for his seed, a tenth of the first-fruits to the Lord, and the Lord ordained it as an ordinance forever that they should give it to the priests who served before Him, that they should possess it forever. **26** And to this law there is no limit of days; for He has ordained it for the generations forever that they should give to the Lord the tenth of everything, of the seed, and of the wine, and of the oil, and of the cattle, and of the sheep. **27** And He gave [it] to His priests to eat and to drink with joy before Him. **28** And the king of Sodom came to him and bowed himself before him, and said, "Our Lord Abram, give to us the souls which you have rescued, but let the plunder be yours." **29** And Abram said to him, "I lift up my hands to the Most High God, that from a thread to a shoe-strap I will not take anything that is yours, lest you should say, I have made Abram rich—save only what the young men have eaten, and the portion of the men who went with me—Aner, Eschol, and Mamre. These will take their portion."

CHAPTER 14

1 After these things, in the fourth year of this week, on the new moon of the third month, the word of the Lord came to Abram in a dream, saying, "Do not fear, Abram; I am your defender, and your reward will be exceedingly great." **2** And he said, "Lord Yhwh, what will You give me, seeing I go childless, and the son of Mâsêq, the son of my handmaid, is the Demmesek Eliezer: he will be my heir, and to me You have not given seed." **3** And He said to him, "This [man] will not be your heir, but one that will come out of your own bowels, he will be your heir." **4** And He brought him out abroad, and said to him, "Look toward the heavens and number the stars, if you are able to number them." **5** And he looked toward the heavens and beheld the stars. And He said to him, "So will your seed be." **6** And he believed in the Lord, and it was counted to him for righteousness. **7** And He said to him, "I am the Lord that brought you out of Ur of the Chaldees, to give you the land of the Canaanites to possess it forever; and I will be God to you and to your seed after you." **8** And he said, "Lord Yhwh, whereby will I know that I will inherit [it]?" **9** And He said to him, "Take Me a heifer of three years, and a goat of three years, and a sheep of three years, and a turtle-dove, and a pigeon." **10** And he took all these in the middle of the month; and he dwelt at the oak of Mamre, which is near Hebron. **11** And he built an altar there and sacrificed all these; and he poured their blood on the altar, and divided them in the midst, and laid them over against each other, but he did not divide the birds. **12** And birds came down on the pieces, and Abram drove them away, and did not permit the birds to touch them. **13** And it came to pass, when the sun had set, that an ecstasy fell on Abram, and behold, a horror of great darkness fell on him, and it was said to Abram: "Know for sure that your seed will be a stranger in a land [that is] not theirs, and they will bring them into bondage, and afflict them four hundred years. **14** And the nation to whom they will be in bondage I will also judge, and after that they will come out from there with much substance. **15** And you will go to your fathers in peace and be buried in a good old age. **16** But in the fourth generation they will return here, for the iniquity of the Amorites is not yet full." **17** And he awoke from his sleep, and he arose, and the sun had set; and there was a flame, and behold, a furnace was smoking, and a flame of fire passed between the pieces. **18** And on that day the Lord made a covenant with Abram, saying, "To your seed I will give this land, from the river of Egypt to the great river, the River Euphrates—the Kenites, the Kenizzites, the Kadmonites, the Perizzites, and the Rephaim, the Phakorites, and the Hivites, and the Amorites, and the Canaanites, and the Girgashites, and the Jebusites." **19** And the day passed, and Abram offered the pieces, and the birds, and their fruit-offerings, and their drink-offerings, and the fire devoured them. **20** And on that day we made a covenant with Abram, according as we had covenanted with Noah in this month; and Abram renewed the festival and ordinance for himself forever. **21** And Abram rejoiced and made all these things known to his wife Sarai; and he believed that he would have seed, but she did not bear. **22** And Sarai advised her husband Abram and said to him, "Go in to Hagar, my Egyptian maid: it may be that I will build up seed to you by her." **23** And Abram listened to the voice of his wife Sarai and said to her, "Do [so]." And Sarai took Hagar, her maid, the Egyptian, and gave her to her husband Abram to be his wife. **24** And he went in to her, and she conceived and bore him a son, and he called his name Ishmael, in the fifth year of this week; and this was the eighty-sixth year in the life of Abram.

CHAPTER 15

¹ And in the fifth year of the fourth week of this jubilee, in the third month, in the middle of the month, Abram celebrated the Celebration of the First-Fruits of the grain harvest. ² And he offered new offerings on the altar, the first-fruits of the produce, to the Lord: a heifer, and a goat, and a sheep on the altar as a burnt sacrifice to the Lord; their fruit-offerings and their drink-offerings he offered on the altar with frankincense. ³ And the Lord appeared to Abram and said to him, "I am God Almighty; approve yourself before Me and be perfect. ⁴ And I will make My covenant between Me and you, and I will multiply you exceedingly." ⁵ And Abram fell on his face, and God talked with him, and said, ⁶ "Behold, My ordinance is with you, and you will be the father of many nations. ⁷ Neither will your name be called Abram anymore, but your name from now on, even forever, will be Abraham. For I have made you the father of many nations. ⁸ And I will make you very great, and I will make you into nations, and kings will come out from you. ⁹ And I will establish My covenant between Me and you, and your seed after you, throughout their generations, for a perpetual covenant, so that I may be a God to you, and to your seed after you. ¹⁰ [[And I will give to you and to your seed after you]] the land where you have been a sojourner, the land of Canaan, that you may possess it forever, and I will be their God." ¹¹ And the Lord said to Abraham, "And as for you: keep My covenant, you and your seed after you, and circumcise every male among you, and circumcise your foreskins, and it will be a token of a perpetual covenant between Me and you. ¹² And you will circumcise the child on the eighth day, every male throughout your generations—him that is born in the house, or whom you have bought with money from any stranger, whom you have acquired who is not of your seed. ¹³ He that is born in your house will surely be circumcised, and those whom you have bought with money will be circumcised, and My covenant will be in your flesh for a perpetual ordinance. ¹⁴ And the uncircumcised male who is not circumcised in the flesh of his foreskin on the eighth day, that soul will be cut off from his people, for he has broken My covenant." ¹⁵ And God said to Abraham, "As for Sarai your wife, her name will no longer be called Sarai, but Sarah will be her name. ¹⁶ And I will bless her, and give you a son by her, and I will bless him, and he will become a nation, and kings of nations will proceed from him." ¹⁷ And Abraham fell on his face, and rejoiced, and said in his heart, "Will a son be born to him that is one hundred years old, and will Sarah, who is ninety years old, bring out?" ¹⁸ And Abraham said to God, "O that Ishmael might live before you!" ¹⁹ And God said, "Yes, and Sarah will also bear you a son, and you will call his name Isaac, and I will establish My covenant with him, a perpetual covenant, and for his seed after him. ²⁰ And as for Ishmael, I have also heard you, and behold, I will bless him, and make him great, and multiply him exceedingly, and he will beget twelve princes, and I will make him a great nation. ²¹ But I will establish My covenant with Isaac, whom Sarah will bear to you, in these days, in the next year." ²² And He left off speaking with him, and God went up from Abraham. ²³ And Abraham did according as God had said to him, and he took his son Ishmael, and all that were born in his house, and whom he had bought with his money, every male in his house, and circumcised the flesh of their foreskin. ²⁴ And on the same day Abraham was circumcised, indeed, all the men of his house and all those whom he had bought with money from the children of the stranger were circumcised with him. ²⁵ This law is for all the generations forever, and there is no circumcision of the days, and no omission of one day out of the eight days, for it is a perpetual ordinance, ordained and written on the heavenly tablets. ²⁶ And everyone that is born, the flesh of whose foreskin is not circumcised on the eighth day, does not belong to the children of the covenant which the Lord made with Abraham, but to the children of destruction; nor is there, moreover, any sign on him that he is the Lord's, but [he is destined] to be destroyed and slain from the earth, and to be rooted out of the earth, for he has broken the covenant of the Lord our God. ²⁷ For all the messengers of the presence and all the messengers of sanctification have been so created from the day of their creation, and before the messengers of the presence and the messengers of sanctification, He has sanctified Israel, that they should be with Him and with His holy messengers. ²⁸ And command the sons of Israel and let them observe the sign of this covenant for their generations as a perpetual ordinance, and they will not be rooted out of the land. ²⁹ For the command is ordained for a covenant, that they should observe it forever among all the sons of Israel. ³⁰ For Ishmael, and his sons, and his brothers, and Esau, the Lord did not cause to approach Him, and He did not choose them because they are the children of Abraham, because He knew them, but He chose Israel to be His people. ³¹ And He sanctified it and gathered it from among all the children of men; for there are many nations and many peoples, and all are His, and over all He has placed spirits in authority to lead them astray from Him. ³² But over Israel He did not appoint any messenger or spirit, for He alone is their ruler, and He will preserve them and require them at the hand of His messengers and His spirits, and at the hand of all His powers in order that He may preserve them and bless them, and that they may be His and He may be theirs from now on and forever. ³³ And now I announce to you that the sons of Israel will not keep true to this ordinance, and they will not circumcise their sons according to all this law, for in the flesh of their circumcision they will omit this circumcision of their sons, and all of them, sons of Belial, will leave their sons uncircumcised as they were born. ³⁴ And there will be great wrath from the Lord against the sons of Israel, because they have forsaken His covenant and turned aside from His word, and provoked and blasphemed, inasmuch as they do not observe the ordinance of this law, for they have treated their members like the nations, so that they may be removed and rooted out of the land. And there will no longer be pardon or forgiveness to them for all the sin of this continuous error.

CHAPTER 16

¹ And on the new moon of the fourth month we appeared to Abraham, at the oak of Mamre, and we talked with him, and we announced to him that a son would be given to him by his wife Sarah. ² And Sarah laughed, for she heard that we had spoken these words with Abraham, and we admonished her, and she became afraid, and denied that she had laughed on account of the words. ³ And we told her the name of her son, as his name [(Isaac)] is ordained and written in the heavenly tablets, ⁴ and [that] when we returned to her at a set time, she would have conceived a son. ⁵ And in this month the Lord executed His judgments on Sodom, and Gomorrah, and Zeboim, and all the region of the Jordan, and He burned them with fire and brimstone, and destroyed them until this day, even as I have declared to you all their works, that they are sinners and exceedingly wicked, and that they defile themselves and commit fornication in their flesh, and work uncleanness on the earth. ⁶ And, in like manner, God will execute judgment on the places where they have done according to the uncleanness of the Sodomites, like to the judgment of Sodom. ⁷ But we saved Lot, for God remembered Abraham and sent him out from the midst of the overthrow. ⁸ And he and his daughters committed sin on the earth, such as had not been on the earth since the days of Adam until his time, for the man lay with his daughters. ⁹ And behold, it was commanded and engraved concerning all his seed, on the heavenly tablets, to remove them and root them out, and to execute judgment on them like the judgment of Sodom, and to leave no seed of the man on earth on the day of condemnation. ¹⁰ And in this month Abraham moved from Hebron and departed and dwelt between Kadesh and Shur in the mountains of Gerar. ¹¹ And in the middle of the fifth month he moved from there and dwelt at the Well of the Oath. ¹² And in the middle of the sixth month the Lord visited Sarah and did to her as He had spoken, and she conceived. ¹³ And she bore a son in the third month, and in the middle of the month, at the time of which the Lord had spoken to Abraham, on the festival of the first-fruits of the harvest, Isaac was born. ¹⁴ And Abraham circumcised his son on the eighth day: he was the first that was circumcised according to the covenant which is ordained forever. ¹⁵ And in the sixth year of the fourth week we came to Abraham, to the Well of the Oath, and we appeared to him [[as we had told Sarah that we should return to her, and she would have conceived a son. ¹⁶ And we returned in the seventh month, and found Sarah with child before us,]] and we blessed him, and we announced to him all the things which had been decreed concerning him: that he should not die until he should beget six more sons, and should see [them] before he died, but [that] in Isaac should his name and seed be called, ¹⁷ and [that] all the seed of his sons should be nations, and be reckoned with the nations, but from the sons of Isaac one should become a holy seed and should not be reckoned among

the nations. **18** For he should become the portion of the Most High, and all his seed had fallen into the possession of God, that it should be to the Lord a people for [His] possession above all nations and that it should become a kingdom, and priests, and a holy nation. **19** And we went our way, and we announced to Sarah all that we had told him, and they both rejoiced with exceedingly great joy. **20** And he built an altar there to the Lord who had delivered him, and who was making him rejoice in the land of his sojourning, and he celebrated a festival of joy in this month [for] seven days, near the altar which he had built at the Well of the Oath. **21** And he built shelters for himself and for his servants on this festival, and he was the first to celebrate the Celebration of Shelters on the earth. **22** And during these seven days he brought each day to the altar a burnt-offering to the Lord: two oxen, two rams, seven sheep, one male goat, for a sin-offering, that he might atone for himself and for his seed thereby. **23** And as a thank-offering: seven rams, seven kids, seven sheep, and seven male goats, and their fruit-offerings and their drink-offerings; and he burned all the fat thereof on the altar, a chosen offering to the Lord for a sweet-smelling savor. **24** And morning and evening he burned fragrant substances: frankincense, and galbanum, and stacte, and nard, and myrrh, and spice, and costum; all these seven he offered crushed, mixed together in equal parts, [and] pure. **25** And he celebrated this feast during seven days, rejoicing with all his heart and with all his soul, he and all those who were in his house; and there was no stranger with him, nor any that was uncircumcised. **26** And he blessed his Creator who had created him in his generation, for He had created him according to His good pleasure, for He knew and perceived that from him would arise the Plant of Righteousness for the continuous generations, and from him a holy Seed, so that it should become like Him who had made all things. **27** And he blessed and rejoiced, and he called the name of this festival the Festival of the Lord, a joy acceptable to the Most High God. **28** And we blessed him forever, and all his seed after him throughout all the generations of the earth, because he celebrated this festival in its season, according to the testimony of the heavenly tablets. **29** For this reason it is ordained on the heavenly tablets concerning Israel that they will celebrate the Celebration of Shelters [for] seven days with joy, in the seventh month, acceptable before the Lord—a statute forever throughout their generations every year. **30** And to this there is no limit of days, for it is ordained forever regarding Israel that they should celebrate it and dwell in shelters, and set wreaths on their heads, and take leafy boughs, and willows from the brook. **31** And Abraham took branches of palm trees, and the fruit of attractive trees, and every day going around the altar with the branches seven times [a day] in the morning, he praised and gave thanks to his God for all things in joy.

CHAPTER 17

1 And in the first year of the fifth week Isaac was weaned in this jubilee, and Abraham made a great banquet in the third month, on the day his son Isaac was weaned. **2** And Ishmael, the son of Hagar the Egyptian, was before the face of his father Abraham, in his place, and Abraham rejoiced and blessed God because he had seen his sons and had not died childless. **3** And he remembered the words which He had spoken to him on the day on which Lot had parted from him, and he rejoiced because the Lord had given him seed on the earth to inherit the earth, and he blessed the Creator of all things with all his mouth. **4** And Sarah saw Ishmael playing and dancing and Abraham rejoicing with great joy, and she became jealous of Ishmael and said to Abraham, "Cast out this bondwoman and her son, for the son of this bondwoman will not be heir with my son Isaac." **5** And the thing was grievous in Abraham's sight, because of his maidservant and because of his son, that he should drive them from him. **6** And God said to Abraham, "Do not let it be grievous in your sight, because of the child and because of the bondwoman; in all that Sarah has said to you, listen to her words and do [them], for in Isaac will your name and seed be called. **7** But as for the son of this bondwoman, I will make him a great nation, because he is of your seed." **8** And Abraham rose up early in the morning and took bread and a bottle of water and placed them on the shoulders of Hagar and the child and sent her away. **9** And she departed and wandered in the wilderness of Beersheba, and the water in the bottle was spent, and the child thirsted, and was not able to go on, and fell down. **10** And his mother took him and cast him

under an olive tree, and went and sat her down over against him, at the distance of a bow-shot; for she said, "Let me not see the death of my child," and as she sat, she wept. **11** And a messenger of God, one of the holy ones, said to her, "Why do you weep, Hagar? Arise, take the child, and hold him in your hand, for God has heard your voice, and has seen the child." **12** And she opened her eyes, and she saw a well of water, and she went and filled her bottle with water, and she gave her child to drink, and she arose and went toward the wilderness of Paran. **13** And the child grew and became an archer, and God was with him; and his mother took a wife [for] him from among the daughters of Egypt. **14** And she bore him a son, and he called his name Nebaioth, for she said, "The Lord was near to me when I called on Him." **15** And it came to pass in the seventh week, in the first year thereof, in the first month in this jubilee, on the twelfth of this month, there were voices in Heaven regarding Abraham, that he was faithful in all that He told him, and that he loved the Lord, and that in every affliction he was faithful. **16** And the prince Mastêmâ came and said before God, "Behold, Abraham loves his son Isaac, and he delights in him above all other things; command him to offer him as a burnt-offering on the altar, and You will see if he will do this command, and You will know if he is faithful in everything wherein You try him." **17** And the Lord knew that Abraham was faithful in all his afflictions, for He had tried him through his country and with famine, and had tried him with the wealth of kings, and had tried him again through his wife, when she was torn [from him], and with circumcision, and had tried him through Ishmael and Hagar, his maidservant, when he sent them away. **18** And in everything wherein He had tried him, he was found faithful, and his soul was not impatient, and he was not slow to act, for he was faithful and a lover of the Lord.

CHAPTER 18

1 And God said to him, "Abraham, Abraham"; and he said, "Behold, [here] I am." **2** And He said, "Take your beloved son whom you love, [even] Isaac, and go to the high country, and offer him on one of the mountains which I will point out to you." **3** And he rose early in the morning and saddled his donkey, and took his two young men with him, and his son Isaac, and cleaved the wood of the burnt-offering, and he went to the place on the third day, and he saw the place far off. **4** And he came to a well of water, and he said to his young men, "Abide here with the donkey, and the youth and I will go [over there], and when we have worshiped we will come again to you." **5** And he took the wood of the burnt-offering and laid it on his son Isaac, and he took in his hand the fire and the knife, and both of them went together to that place. **6** And Isaac said to his father, "Father"; and he said, "Here I am, my son." And he said to him, "Behold the fire, and the knife, and the wood, but where is the sheep for the burnt-offering, father?" **7** And he said, "God will provide for Himself a sheep for a burnt-offering, my son." And he drew near to the place of the mount of God. **8** And he built an altar, and he placed the wood on the altar, and bound his son Isaac, and placed him on the wood which was on the altar, and stretched out his hand to take the knife to slay his son Isaac. **9** And I stood before him, and before the prince of the Mastêmâ, and the Lord said, "Command him not to lay his hand on the youth, nor to do anything to him, for I have shown that he fears the Lord." **10** And I called to him from Heaven, and said to him, "Abraham! Abraham!" And he was terrified and said, "Behold, [here] I am." **11** And I said to him, "Do not lay your hand on the youth, neither do anything to him, for now I have shown that you fear the Lord, and have not withheld your son, your firstborn [[or only]] son, from Me." **12** And the prince of the Mastêmâ was put to shame, and Abraham lifted up his eyes and looked, and behold, a single ram was caught by his horns, and Abraham went and took the ram and offered it for a burnt-offering in the place of his son. **13** And Abraham called that place "The Lord has seen," so that it is said, "[in the mount] the Lord has seen": that is Mount Zion. **14** And the Lord called Abraham by his name a second time from Heaven, as He caused us to appear to speak to him in the Name of the Lord. **15** And He said, "By Myself I have sworn, says the Lord, because you have done this thing, and have not withheld your son, your beloved son, from Me, that in blessing I will bless you, and in multiplying I will multiply your seed as the stars of the heavens, and as the sand which is on the seashore. And your Seed will inherit the cities of its enemies, **16** and in your Seed all nations of the earth will be blessed; because you have obeyed My voice, and I have shown to all that you are faithful to Me in all that I have said to you: go in peace." **17** And Abraham went to his young men, and they arose and went together to Beersheba, and Abraham dwelt by the Well of the Oath. **18** And he celebrated this festival every year [for] seven days with joy, and he called it the Festival of the Lord according to the seven days during which he went and returned in peace. **19** And accordingly it has been ordained and written on the heavenly tablets regarding Israel and its seed that they should observe this festival [for] seven days with the joy of festival.

CHAPTER 19

1 And in the first year of the first week, in the forty-second jubilee, Abraham returned and dwelt opposite Hebron, that is Kirjath-Arba, two weeks of years. **2** And in the first year of the third week of this jubilee the days of the life of Sarah were accomplished, and she died in Hebron. **3** And Abraham went to mourn over her and bury her, and we tried him [to see] if his spirit was patient and he was not indignant in the words of his mouth, and he was found patient in this and was not disturbed. **4** For in patience of spirit he conversed with the children of Heth, to the intent that they should give him a place in which to bury his dead. **5** And the Lord gave him grace before all who saw him, and he implored in gentleness the sons of Heth, and they gave him the land of the double cave over against Mamre, that is Hebron, for four hundred pieces of silver. **6** And they implored him, saying, "We will give it to you for nothing," but he would not take it from their hands for nothing, for he gave the price of the place, the money in full, and he bowed down before them twice; and after this he buried his dead in the double cave. **7** And all the days of the life of Sarah were one hundred and twenty-seven years, that is, two jubilees and four weeks and one year: these are the days of the years of the life of Sarah. **8** This is the tenth trial with which Abraham was tried, and he was found faithful, patient in spirit. **9** And he said not a single word regarding the rumor in the land, how that God had said that He would give it to him and to his seed after him, and he begged [for] a place there to bury his dead, for he was found faithful and was recorded on the heavenly tablets as the friend of God. **10** And in the fourth year thereof he took a wife for his son Isaac and her name was Rebekah [[the daughter of Bethuel, the son of Nahor, the brother of Abraham,]] the sister of Laban and daughter of Bethuel; and Bethuel was the son of Mêlcâ, who was the wife of Nahor, the brother of Abraham. **11** And Abraham took to himself a third wife—and her name was Keturah—from among the daughters of his household servants, for Hagar had died before Sarah. **12** And she bore him six sons: Zimram, and Jokshan, and Medan, and Midian, and Ishbak, and Shuah, in the two weeks of years. **13** And in the sixth week, in the second year thereof, Rebekah bore to Isaac two sons, Jacob and Esau, and Jacob was a smooth and upright man, and Esau was fierce, a man of the field, and hairy, and Jacob dwelt in tents. **14** And the youths grew, and Jacob learned to write, but Esau did not learn, for he was a man of the field and a hunter, and he learned war, and all his deeds were fierce. **15** And Abraham loved Jacob, but Isaac loved Esau. **16** And Abraham saw the deeds of Esau, and he knew that in Jacob should his name and seed be called; and he called Rebekah and gave command regarding Jacob, for he knew that she [too] loved Jacob much more than Esau. **17** And he said to her, "My daughter, watch over my son Jacob, for he will be in my stead on the earth, and for a blessing in the midst of the children of men, and for the glory of the whole seed of Shem. **18** For I know that the Lord will choose him to be a people for possession to Himself, above all peoples that are on the face of the earth. **19** And behold, my son Isaac loves Esau more than Jacob, but I see that you truly love Jacob. **20** Add still further to your kindness to him, and let your eyes be on him in love, for he will be a blessing to us on the earth from now on and to all generations of the earth. **21** Let your hands be strong and let your heart rejoice in your son Jacob, for I have loved him far beyond all my sons. He will be blessed forever, and his seed will fill the whole earth. **22** If a man can number the sand of the earth, his seed will also be numbered. **23** And all the blessings with which the Lord has blessed me and my seed will belong to Jacob and his seed always. **24** And in his seed my name will be blessed, and the name of my fathers: Shem, and Noah, and Enoch, and Mahalalel, and Enos, and Seth, and Adam. **25** And

these will serve to lay the foundations of the heavens, and to strengthen the earth, and to renew all the luminaries which are in the expanse." **26** And he called Jacob before the eyes of his mother Rebekah, and kissed him, and blessed him, and said, **27** "Jacob, my beloved son, whom my soul loves, may God bless you from above the expanse, and may He give you all the blessings with which He blessed Adam, and Enoch, and Noah, and Shem; and all the things of which He told me, and all the things which He promised to give me, may He cause to cleave to you and to your seed forever, according to the days of Heaven above the earth. **28** And the spirits of Mastêmâ will not rule over you or over your seed to turn you from the Lord, who is your God from now on and forever. **29** And may the Lord God be a father to you—and you [being] the firstborn son—and to the people always. Go in peace, my son." **30** And they both went out together from Abraham. **31** And Rebekah loved Jacob with all her heart and with all her soul, very much more than Esau, but Isaac loved Esau much more than Jacob.

CHAPTER 20

1 And in the forty-second jubilee, in the first year of the seventh week, Abraham called Ishmael, and his twelve sons, and Isaac and his two sons, and the six sons of Keturah, and their sons. **2** And he commanded them that they should observe the way of the Lord, that they should work righteousness, and each love his neighbor, and act on this manner among all men, that they should each so walk with regard to them as to do judgment and righteousness on the earth, **3** [and] that they should circumcise their sons according to the covenant which He had made with them, and not deviate to the right hand or the left of all the paths which the Lord had commanded us, and that we should keep ourselves from all fornication and uncleanness. **4** "And if any woman or maid may commit fornication among you, burn her with fire, and do not let them commit fornication with her after their eyes and their heart; and do not let them take to themselves wives from the daughters of Canaan, for the seed of Canaan will be rooted out of the land." **5** And he told them of the judgment of the giants, and the judgment of the Sodomites, how they had been judged on account of their wickedness, and had died on account of their fornication, and uncleanness, and mutual corruption through fornication. **6** "And guard yourselves from all fornication and uncleanness, and from all pollution of sin, lest you make our name a curse, and your whole life a hissing, and all your sons be destroyed by the sword, and you become accursed like Sodom, and all your remnant as the sons of Gomorrah. **7** I implore you, my sons: love the God of Heaven, and cleave to all His commands. And do not walk after their idols, and after their uncleanness, **8** and do not make for yourselves molten or graven gods, for they are vanity, and there is no spirit in them, for they are [the] work of [men's] hands, and all who trust in them, trust in nothing. Do not serve them, nor worship them, **9** but serve the Most High God, and worship Him continually. And hope for His countenance always, and work uprightness and righteousness before Him, that He may have pleasure in you and grant you His mercy, and send rain on you morning and evening, and bless all your works which you have worked on the earth, and bless your bread and your water, and bless the fruit of your womb and the fruit of your land, and the herds of your cattle, and the flocks of your sheep. **10** And you will be for a blessing on the earth, and all nations of the earth will desire you, and bless your sons in my name, that they may be blessed as I am." **11** And he gave to Ishmael, and to his sons, and to the sons of Keturah, gifts, and sent them away from his son Isaac, and he gave everything to his son Isaac. **12** And Ishmael and his sons, and the sons of Keturah and their sons, went together and dwelt from Paran to the entering in of Babylon in all the land which is toward the east facing the desert. **13** And these mingled with each other, and their name was called Arabs, and Ishmaelites.

CHAPTER 21

1 And in the sixth year of the seventh week of this jubilee, Abraham called his son Isaac and commanded him, saying, "I have become old, and I do not know the day of my death, and am full of my days. **2** And behold, I am one hundred and seventy-five years old, and throughout all the days of my life I have remembered the Lord and sought with all my heart to do His will, and to walk uprightly in all His ways. ³ My soul has hated idols, [[and I have despised those that served them, and I have given my heart and spirit]] that I might observe to do the will of Him who created me. ⁴ For He is the living God, and He is holy and faithful, and He is righteous beyond all, and there is with Him no accepting of [men's] persons and no accepting of gifts, for God is righteous and executes judgment on all those who transgress His commands and despise His covenant. ⁵ And you, my son, observe His commands, and His ordinances, and His judgments, and do not walk after the abominations, and after the graven images, and after the molten images. ⁶ And eat no blood at all of animals, or cattle, or of any bird which flies in the heavens. ⁷ And if you slay a victim as an acceptable peace-offering, slay it, and pour out its blood on the altar, and all the fat of the offering offer on the altar with fine flour [and the meat-offering] mingled with oil, with its drink-offering—offer them all together on the altar of burnt-offering; it is a sweet savor before the Lord. ⁸ And you will offer the fat of the sacrifice of thank-offerings on the fire which is on the altar, and the fat which is on the belly, and all the fat on the innards and the two kidneys, and all the fat that is on them, and on the loins and liver you will remove together with the kidneys. ⁹ And offer all these for a sweet savor acceptable before the Lord, with its meat-offering and with its drink-offering, for a sweet savor, the bread of the offering to the Lord, ¹⁰ and eat its meat on that day and on the second day, and do not let the sun go down on it on the second day until it is eaten, and let nothing be left over for the third day, for it is not acceptable; and let it no longer be eaten, and all who eat thereof will bring sin on themselves, for thus I have found it written in the scrolls of my forefathers, and in the words of Enoch, and in the words of Noah. ¹¹ And on all your oblations you will scatter salt, and do not let the salt of the covenant be lacking in all your oblations before the Lord. ¹² And as regards the wood of the sacrifices, beware lest you bring [other] wood for the altar in addition to these: cypress, dêfrân, sagâd, pine, fir, cedar, savin, palm, olive, myrrh, laurel, and citron, juniper, and balsam. ¹³ And of these kinds of wood lay on the altar under the sacrifice, such as have been tested as to their appearance, and do not lay any split or dark wood [on it], [but] hard and clean, without fault—a sound and new growth; and do not lay old wood [on it], for there is no longer fragrance in it as before. ¹⁴ Besides these kinds of wood, there is no other that you will place [on the altar], for the fragrance is dispersed, and the smell of its fragrance does not go up to Heaven. ¹⁵ Observe this command and do it, my son, that you may be upright in all your deeds. ¹⁶ And at all times be clean in your body, and wash yourself with water before you approach to offer on the altar, and wash your hands and your feet before you draw near to the altar; and when you are done sacrificing, wash your hands and your feet again. ¹⁷ And let no blood appear on you nor on your clothes; be on your guard, my son, against blood, be on your guard exceedingly; cover it with dust. ¹⁸ And do not eat any blood, for it is the soul; eat no blood whatsoever. ¹⁹ And take no gifts for the blood of man, lest it be shed with impunity, without judgment, for it is the blood that is shed that causes the earth to sin, and the earth cannot be cleansed from the blood of man save by the blood of him who shed it. ²⁰ And take no present or gift for the blood of man, blood for blood, that you may be accepted before the Lord, the Most High God—for He is the defense of the good—and that you may be preserved from all evil, and that He may save you from every kind of death. ²¹ I see, my son, that all the works of the children of men are sin and wickedness, and all their deeds are uncleanness, and an abomination, and a pollution, and there is no righteousness with them. ²² Beware, lest you should walk in their ways, and tread in their paths, and sin a sin to death before the Most High God. Otherwise He will [[hide His face from you, and]] give you back into the hands of your transgression, and root you out of the land, and your seed likewise from under Heaven, and your name and your seed will perish from the whole earth. ²³ Turn away from all their deeds and all their uncleanness, and observe the ordinance of the Most High God, and do His will, and be upright in all things. ²⁴ And He will bless you in all your deeds and will raise up from you the plant of righteousness through all the earth, throughout all generations of the earth, and my name and your name will not be forgotten under Heaven forever. ²⁵ Go, my son, in peace. May the Most High God, my God and your God, strengthen you to do His will, and may He bless all your seed and the residue of your seed for the generations forever, with all righteous blessings, that you may be a blessing on all the earth." ²⁶ And he went out from him rejoicing.

CHAPTER 22

¹ And it came to pass in the first week, in the forty-fourth jubilee, in the second year, that is, the year in which Abraham died, that Isaac and Ishmael came from the Well of the Oath to celebrate the Celebration of Weeks—that is, the celebration of the first-fruits of the harvest—to their father Abraham, and Abraham rejoiced because his two sons had come. ² For Isaac had many possessions in Beersheba, and Isaac was accustomed to go and see his possessions and to return to his father. ³ And in those days Ishmael came to see his father, and they both came together, and Isaac offered a sacrifice for a burnt-offering, and presented it on the altar of his father which he had made in Hebron. ⁴ And he offered a thank-offering and made a feast of joy before his brother Ishmael: and Rebekah made new cakes from the new grain and gave them to her son Jacob to take them to his father Abraham, from the first-fruits of the land, that he might eat and bless the Creator of all things before he died. ⁵ And Isaac, too, sent by the hand of Jacob to Abraham a best thank-offering, that he might eat and drink. ⁶ And he ate, and drank, and blessed the Highest God who has created the heavens and earth, who has made all the fat things of the earth and given them to the children of men that they might eat, and drink, and bless their Creator. ⁷ "And now I give thanks to you, my God, because You have caused me to see this day: behold, I am one hundred and seventy-five years [old], an old man and full of days, and all my days have been peace to me. ⁸ The sword of the adversary has not overcome me in all that You have given me and my children all the days of my life until this day. ⁹ My God, may Your mercy and Your peace be on Your servant and on the seed of his sons, that they may be to You a chosen nation and an inheritance from among all the nations of the earth from now on and to all the days of the generations of the earth—to all the ages." ¹⁰ And he called Jacob and said, "My son Jacob, may the God of all bless you and strengthen you to do righteousness and His will before Him, and may He choose you and your seed that you may become a people for His inheritance according to His will always. And my son Jacob: draw near and kiss me." ¹¹ And he drew near and kissed him, and he said, "Blessed is my son Jacob, and all the sons of God Most High, to all the ages. May God give to you [the] Seed of righteousness; and may He sanctify some of your sons in the midst of the whole earth. May nations serve you, and all the nations bow themselves before your Seed. ¹² Be strong in the presence of men, and exercise authority over all the seed of Seth. Then your ways and the ways of your sons will be justified, so that they will become a holy nation. ¹³ May the Highest God give you all the blessings with which He has blessed me and with which He blessed Noah and Adam. May they rest on the sacred head of your Seed from generation to generation forever. ¹⁴ And may He cleanse you from all unrighteousness and impurity, that you may be forgiven of all [your] transgressions [and] your sins of ignorance. And may He strengthen you and bless you. And may you inherit the whole earth; ¹⁵ and may He renew His covenant with you, that you may be to Him a nation for His inheritance for all the ages, and that He may be to you and to your seed a God in truth and righteousness throughout all the days of the earth. ¹⁶ And my son Jacob: remember my words and observe the commands of your father Abraham: separate yourself from the nations, and do not eat with them, and do not according to their works, and do not become their associate, for their works are unclean, and all their ways are a pollution, and an abomination, and uncleanness. ¹⁷ They offer their sacrifices to the dead, and they worship evil spirits, and they eat over the graves, and all their works are vanity and nothingness. ¹⁸ They have no heart to understand, and their eyes do not see what their works are, and how they err in saying to a piece of wood, You are my God; and to a stone, You are my lord and you are my deliverer. [[And they have no heart.]] ¹⁹ And as for you, my son Jacob: may the Highest God help you, and the God of Heaven bless you and remove you from their uncleanness and from all their error. ²⁰ Beware, my son Jacob, of taking a wife from any seed of the daughters of Canaan, for all his seed is to be rooted out of the earth. ²¹ For, owing to the transgression of Ham, Canaan erred, and all his seed will be destroyed from off the earth and all the residue thereof, and none springing from him will be saved on the Day of Judgment. ²² And as for

all the worshipers of idols and the profane: there will be no hope for them in the land of the living and there will be no remembrance of them on the earth, for they will descend into Sheol, and they will go into the place of condemnation; as the children of Sodom were taken away from the earth, so will all those who worship idols be taken away. 23 Do not fear, my son Jacob, and do not be dismayed, O son of Abraham: may the Highest God preserve you from destruction, and may He deliver you from all the paths of error. 24 I have built this house for myself that I might put my name on it in the earth: [[it is given to you and to your seed forever]], and it will be named the House of Abraham; it is given to you and to your seed forever, for you will build my house and establish my name before God forever: your seed and your name will stand throughout all generations of the earth." 25 And he ceased commanding him and blessing him. 26 And the two lay together on one bed, and Jacob slept in the bosom of Abraham, his father's father, and he kissed him seven times, and his affection and his heart rejoiced over him. 27 And he blessed him with all his heart and said, "The Most High God, the God of all and Creator of all, who brought me out from Ur of the Chaldees that He might give me this land to inherit it forever, and that I might establish a holy Seed—blessed is the Most High forever." 28 And he blessed Jacob and said [to God], "My son, over whom with all my heart and my affection I rejoice, may Your grace and Your mercy be lifted up on him and on his seed always. 29 And do not forsake him, nor set him at nothing from now on and to the days of [all] ages, and may Your eyes be opened on him and on his seed, that You may preserve him, and bless him, and may sanctify him as a nation for Your inheritance; 30 and bless him with all Your blessings from now on and to all the days of [the] ages, and renew Your covenant and Your grace with him and with his seed according to all Your good pleasure to all the generations of the earth."

CHAPTER 23

1 And he placed two of Jacob's fingers on his eyes, and he blessed the God of gods, and he covered his face, and stretched out his feet, and slept the continuous sleep, and was gathered to his fathers. 2 And notwithstanding all this, Jacob was lying in his bosom, and did not know that Abraham, his father's father, was dead. 3 And Jacob awoke from his sleep, and behold, Abraham was cold as ice, and he said, "Father! Father!" But there was none that spoke, and he knew that he was dead. 4 And he arose from his bosom and ran and told his mother Rebekah; and Rebekah went to Isaac in the night and told him; and they went together, and Jacob with them, and a lamp was in his hand, and when they had gone in they found Abraham lying dead. 5 And Isaac fell on the face of his father, and wept, and kissed him. 6 And the voices were heard in the house of Abraham, and his son Ishmael arose, and went to his father Abraham, and wept over his father Abraham—he and all the house of Abraham—and they wept with a great weeping. 7 And his sons Isaac and Ishmael buried him in the double cave near his wife Sarah, and they wept for him forty days, all the men of his house, and Isaac and Ishmael, and all their sons, and all the sons of Keturah in their places, and the days of weeping for Abraham were ended. 8 And he lived three jubilees and four weeks of years—one hundred and seventy-five years—and completed the days of his life, being old and full of days. 9 For the days of the forefathers, of their life, were nineteen jubilees; and after the flood they began to grow less than nineteen jubilees, and to decrease in jubilees, and to grow old quickly, and to be full of their days by reason of manifold tribulation and the wickedness of their ways, with the exception of Abraham. 10 For Abraham was perfect in all his deeds with the Lord, and well-pleasing in righteousness all the days of his life; and behold, he did not complete four jubilees in his life when he had grown old by reason of the wickedness [in the world] and was full of his days. 11 And all the generations which will arise from this time until the Day of the Great Judgment will grow old quickly before they complete two jubilees, and their knowledge will forsake them by reason of their old age. 12 And in those days, if a man lives [for] a jubilee and a half of years, they will say regarding him: "He has lived long, and the greater part of his days are pain, and sorrow, and tribulation, and there is no peace, 13 for calamity follows on calamity, and wound on wound, and tribulation on tribulation, and evil tidings on evil tidings, and sickness on sickness, and all evil judgments such as these, with one another—sickness, and overthrow, and

snow, and frost, and ice, and fever, and chills, and torpor, and famine, and death, and sword, and captivity, and all kinds of calamities and pains." 14 And all these will come on an evil generation, which transgresses on the earth: their works are uncleanness, and fornication, and pollution, and abominations. 15 Then they will say, "The days of the forefathers were many, [even] to one thousand years, and were good, but behold, the days of our life, if a man has lived many, are sixty years and ten, and, if he is strong, eighty years, and those [are] evil and there is no peace in the days of this evil generation." 16 And in that generation the sons will convict their fathers and their elders of sin and unrighteousness, and of the words of their mouth and the great wickedness which they perpetrate, and concerning their forsaking the covenant which the Lord made between them and Him, that they should observe and do all His commands, and His ordinances, and all His laws, without departing either to the right hand or to the left. 17 For all have done evil, and every mouth speaks iniquity, and all their works are an uncleanness and an abomination, and all their ways are pollution, uncleanness, and destruction. 18 Behold, the earth will be destroyed on account of all their works, and there will be no seed of the vine and no oil, for their works are altogether faithless, and they will all perish together: beasts, and cattle, and birds, and all the fish of the sea, on account of the children of men. 19 And they will strive with one another, the young with the old, and the old with the young, the poor with the rich, and the lowly with the great, and the beggar with the prince, on account of the Law and the Covenant, for they have forgotten command, and covenant, and feasts, and months, and Sabbaths, and jubilees, and all judgments. 20 And they will stand [[with bows and]] swords, and war to turn them back into the way, but they will not return until much blood has been shed on the earth by one another. 21 And those who have escaped will not return from their wickedness to the way of righteousness, but they will all exalt themselves to deceit and wealth, that they may each take all that is his neighbor's, and they will name the Great Name, but not in truth and not in righteousness, and they will defile the Holy of Holies with their uncleanness and the corruption of their pollution. 22 And a great punishment will befall the deeds of this generation from the Lord, and He will give them over to the sword, and to judgment, and to captivity, and to be plundered and devoured. 23 And He will wake up against them the sinners of the nations who have neither mercy nor compassion, and who will respect the person of none, neither old nor young, nor anyone, for they are more wicked and strong to do evil than all the children of men. And they will use violence against Israel and transgression against Jacob, and much blood will be shed on the earth, and there will be none to gather and none to bury. 24 In those days they will cry aloud, and call and pray that they may be saved from the hand of the sinners, the nations, but none will be saved. 25 And the heads of the children will be white with grey hair, and a child of three weeks will appear old like a man of one hundred years, and their stature will be destroyed by tribulation and oppression. 26 And in those days the children will begin to study the laws, and to seek the commands, and to return to the path of righteousness. 27 And the days will begin to grow many and increase among those children of men [until] their days draw near to one thousand years, and to a greater number of years than were the number of the days [before]. 28 And there will be no old man nor one who is not satisfied with his days, for all will be [as] children and youths. 29 And they will complete all their days and live in peace and in joy, and there will be no adversary, nor any evil destroyer, for all their days will be days of blessing and healing, 30 and at that time the Lord will heal His servants, and they will rise up and see great peace, and drive out their adversaries. And the righteous will see and be thankful, and rejoice with joy forever and ever, and will see all their judgments and all their curses on their enemies. 31 And their bones will rest in the earth, and their spirits will have much joy, and they will know that it is the Lord who executes judgment and shows mercy to hundreds, and thousands, and to all that love Him. 32 And you, Moses, write down these words, for thus are they written, and they record [them] on the heavenly tablets for a testimony for the generations forever.

CHAPTER 24

1 And it came to pass after the death of Abraham, that the Lord blessed his son Isaac, and he arose from Hebron and went

and dwelt at the Well of the Vision in the first year of the third week of this jubilee [for] seven years. ² And in the first year of the fourth week a famine began in the land, besides the first famine which had been in the days of Abraham. ³ And Jacob prepared lentil stew, and Esau came from the field hungry. And he said to his brother Jacob, "Give me of this red stew." And Jacob said to him, "Sell your birthright to me and I will give you bread and also some of this lentil stew." ⁴ And Esau said in his heart: "I will die; of what profit to me is this birthright?" And he said to Jacob, "I give it to you." ⁵ And Jacob said, "Swear to me, this day," and he swore to him. ⁶ And Jacob gave his brother Esau bread and stew, and he ate until he was satisfied, and Esau despised his birthright; for this reason Esau's name was called Edom on account of the red stew which Jacob gave him for his birthright. ⁷ And Jacob became the elder, and Esau was brought down from his dignity. ⁸ And the famine was over the land, and Isaac departed to go down into Egypt in the second year of this week, and he went to the king of the Philistines, to Gerar, to Abimelech. ⁹ And the Lord appeared to him and said to him, "Do not go down into Egypt; dwell in the land that I will tell you of, and sojourn in this land, and I will be with you and bless you. ¹⁰ For to you and to your seed I will give all this land, and I will establish My oath which I swore to your father Abraham, and I will multiply your seed as the stars of the heavens, and I will give to your seed all this land. ¹¹ And in your Seed will all the nations of the earth be blessed, because your father obeyed My voice, and kept My charge, and My commands, and My laws, and My ordinances, and My covenant; and now obey My voice and dwell in this land." ¹² And he dwelt in Gerar three weeks of years. ¹³ And Abimelech charged concerning him, and concerning all that was his, saying, "Any man that will touch him or anything that is his will surely die." ¹⁴ And Isaac waxed strong among the Philistines, and he got many possessions: oxen, and sheep, and camels, and donkeys, and a great household. ¹⁵ And he sowed in the land of the Philistines and brought in a hundredfold, and Isaac became exceedingly great, and the Philistines envied him. ¹⁶ Now all the wells which the servants of Abraham had dug during the life of Abraham, the Philistines had stopped them after the death of Abraham and filled them with earth. ¹⁷ And Abimelech said to Isaac, "Go from us, for you are much mightier than us"; and Isaac departed from there in the first year of the seventh week and sojourned in the valleys of Gerar. ¹⁸ And they dug the wells of water again which the servants of his father Abraham had dug, and which the Philistines had closed after the death of his father Abraham, and he called their names as his father Abraham had named them. ¹⁹ And the servants of Isaac dug a well in the valley, and found living water, and the shepherds of Gerar strove with the shepherds of Isaac, saying, "The water is ours"; and Isaac called the name of the well "Perversity," because they had been perverse with us. ²⁰ And they dug a second well, and they strove for that also, and he called its name "Enmity." And he arose from there and they dug another well, and for that they did not strive, and he called the name of it "Room," and Isaac said, "Now the Lord has made room for us, and we have increased in the land." ²¹ And he went up from there to the Well of the Oath in the first year of the first week, in the forty-fourth jubilee. ²² And the Lord appeared to him that night, on the new moon of the first month, and said to him, "I am the God of your father Abraham; do not fear, for I am with you, and will bless you and will surely multiply your seed as the sand of the earth, for the sake of my servant Abraham." ²³ And he built an altar there, which his father Abraham had first built, and he called on the Name of the Lord, and he offered sacrifice to the God of his father Abraham. ²⁴ And they dug a well and they found living water. ²⁵ And the servants of Isaac dug another well and did not find water, and they went and told Isaac that they had not found water, and Isaac said, "I have sworn this day to the Philistines and this thing has been announced to us." ²⁶ And he called the name of that place the "Well of the Oath," for there he had sworn to Abimelech, and his friend Ahuzzath, and Phicol, the prefect of his host. ²⁷ And Isaac knew that day that under constraint he had sworn to them to make peace with them. ²⁸ And on that day Isaac cursed the Philistines and said, "Cursed are the Philistines to the day of wrath and indignation from the midst of all nations; may God make them a derision, and a curse, and an object of wrath and indignation in the hands of the sinners—the nations—and in the hands of the Kittim. ²⁹ And whoever escapes the sword of the enemy and the Kittim, may the righteous nation root out in judgment from under Heaven, for they will be the enemies, and enemies of my children,

throughout their generations on the earth. ³⁰ And no remnant will be left to them, nor one that will be saved on the day of the wrath of judgment, for destruction, and rooting out, and expulsion from the earth is the whole seed of the Philistines [reserved], and there will no longer be left for these Caphtorim a name or a seed on the earth. ³¹ For though he ascends into Heaven, from there he will be brought down, and though he makes himself strong on earth, from there he will be dragged out, and though he hides himself among the nations, even from there he will be rooted out, and though he descends into Sheol, there also will his condemnation be great, and there also he will have no peace. ³² And if he goes into captivity, by the hands of those that seek his life they will slay him on the way, and neither name nor seed will be left to him on all the earth, for he will depart into a continuous curse." ³³ And thus is it written and engraved concerning him on the heavenly tablets, to do to him on the Day of Judgment, so that he may be rooted out of the earth.

CHAPTER 25

¹ And in the second year of this week, in this jubilee, Rebekah called her son Jacob and spoke to him, saying, "My son, do not take a wife for yourself of the daughters of Canaan, as your brother Esau, who took two wives of the daughters of Canaan for himself, and they have embittered my soul with all their unclean deeds, for all their deeds are fornication and lust, and there is no righteousness with them, for [their deeds] are evil. ² And I, my son, love you exceedingly, and my heart and my affection bless you every hour of the day and watch of the night. ³ And now, my son, listen to my voice, and do the will of your mother, and do not take a wife for yourself of the daughters of this land, but only of the house of my father, and of my father's relatives; you will take a wife of the house of my father, and the Most High God will bless you, and your children will be a righteous generation and a holy seed." ⁴ And then Jacob spoke to his mother Rebekah, and said to her, "Behold, mother, I am nine weeks of years old, and I neither know nor have I touched any woman, nor have I betrothed myself to any, nor even think of taking a wife for myself of the daughters of Canaan. ⁵ For I remember, mother, the words of our father Abraham, for he commanded me not to take a wife of the daughters of Canaan, but to take a wife for myself from the seed of my father's house and from my relatives. ⁶ I have heard before that daughters have been born to your brother Laban, and I have set my heart on them to take a wife from among them. ⁷ And for this reason I have guarded myself in my spirit against sinning or being corrupted in all my ways throughout all the days of my life, for with regard to lust and fornication, my father Abraham gave me many commands. ⁸ And despite all that he has commanded me, these twenty-two years my brother has striven with me, and spoken frequently to me, and said, My brother, take a sister of my two wives to be [your] wife; but I refuse to do as he has done. ⁹ I swear before you, mother, that all the days of my life I will not take a wife for myself from the daughters of the seed of Canaan, and I will not act wickedly as my brother has done. ¹⁰ Do not fear, mother; be assured that I will do your will, and walk in uprightness, and not corrupt my ways forever." ¹¹ And immediately she lifted up her face to Heaven, and extended the fingers of her hands, and opened her mouth, and blessed the Most High God who had created the heavens and the earth, and she gave Him thanks and praise. ¹² And she said, "Blessed is the Lord God, and may His holy Name be blessed forever and ever, who has given me Jacob as a pure son and a holy seed; for He is Yours, and his seed will be Yours continually and throughout all the generations forevermore. ¹³ Bless him, O Lord, and place in my mouth the blessing of righteousness, that I may bless him." ¹⁴ And at that hour, when the Spirit of righteousness descended into her mouth, she placed both her hands on the head of Jacob, and said, ¹⁵ "Blessed are You, Lord of righteousness and God of the ages. And may He bless you beyond all the generations of men. May He give you, my son, the path of righteousness, and reveal righteousness to your seed. ¹⁶ And may He make your sons many during your life, and may they arise according to the number of the months of the year. And may their sons become many and great beyond the stars of the heavens, and their numbers be more than the sand of the sea. ¹⁷ And may He give them this excellent land—as He said He would give it to Abraham and to his seed after him always—and may they hold it as a possession forever. ¹⁸ And may I see

[born] to you, my son, blessed children during my life, and a blessed and holy seed may all your seed be. **19** And as you have refreshed your mother's spirit during my life, the womb of her that bore you blesses you, and my breasts bless you, and my mouth and my tongue praise you greatly. **20** Increase and spread over the earth, and may your seed be perfect in the joy of the heavens and earth forever; and may your seed rejoice, and on the great day of peace may it have peace. **21** And may your name and your seed endure to all the ages, and may the Most High God be their God, and may the God of righteousness dwell with them, and by them may His sanctuary be built to all the ages. **22** Blessed is he that blesses you, and all flesh that curses you falsely—may it be cursed." **23** And she kissed him and said to him, "May the Lord of the world love you just as the heart of your mother and her affection rejoices in you and blesses you." And she ceased from blessing.

CHAPTER 26

1 And in the seventh year of this week Isaac called Esau, his elder son, and said to him, "I am old, my son, and behold, my eyes are dim in seeing, and I do not know the day of my death. **2** And now take your hunting weapons, your quiver and your bow, and go out to the field, and hunt and catch me [game], my son, and make me savory meat, such as my soul loves, and bring it to me that I may eat, and that my soul may bless you before I die." **3** But Rebekah heard Isaac speaking to Esau. **4** And Esau went out early to the field to hunt, and catch, and bring home to his father. **5** And Rebekah called her son Jacob and said to him, "Behold, I heard your father Isaac speak to your brother Esau, saying, Hunt for me, and make me savory meat, and bring [it] to me that I may eat and bless you before the Lord before I die. **6** And now, my son, obey my voice in that which I command you: go to your flock and fetch me two good kids of the goats, and I will make them savory meat for your father, such as he loves, and you will bring [it] to your father that he may eat and bless you before the Lord before he die, and that you may be blessed." **7** And Jacob said to his mother Rebekah, "Mother, I will not withhold anything which my father would eat, and which would please him: only I fear, my mother, that he will recognize my voice and wish to touch me. **8** And you know that I am smooth, and my brother Esau is hairy, and I will appear before his eyes as an evildoer, and will do a deed which he had not commanded me, and he will be angry with me, and I will bring a curse on myself, and not a blessing." **9** And his mother Rebekah said to him, "Your curse be on me, my son, only obey my voice." **10** And Jacob obeyed the voice of his mother Rebekah, and went and fetched two good and fat kids of the goats, and brought them to his mother, and his mother made them [savory meat] such as he loved. **11** And Rebekah took the attractive raiment of her elder son Esau, which was with her in the house, and she clothed her younger son Jacob [with them], and she put the skins of the kids on his hands and on the exposed parts of his neck. **12** And she gave the meat and the bread which she had prepared into the hand of her son Jacob. **13** And Jacob went in to his father and said, "I am your son: I have done according as you commanded me. Arise, and sit, and eat of that which I have caught, father, that your soul may bless me." **14** And Isaac said to his son, "How have you found [game] so quickly, my son?" **15** And Jacob said, "Because [the Lord] your God caused me to find [it]." **16** And Isaac said to him, "Come near, that I may feel you, my son, if you are my son Esau or not." **17** And Jacob went near to his father Isaac, and he felt him, and said, **18** "The voice is Jacob's voice, but the hands are the hands of Esau," and he did not discern him, because it was a dispensation from Heaven to remove his power of perception, and Isaac did not discern, for his hands were as hairy as [his brother] Esau's, so that he blessed him. **19** And he said, "Are you my son Esau?" and he said, "I am your son," and he said, "Bring [it] near to me that I may eat of that which you have caught, my son, that my soul may bless you." **20** And he brought [it] near to him, and he ate, and he brought him wine and he drank. **21** And his father Isaac said to him, "Come near and kiss me, my son." And he came near and kissed him. **22** And he smelled the smell of his raiment, and he blessed him, and said, "Behold, the smell of my son is as the smell of a [full] field which the Lord has blessed. **23** And may the Lord give you of the dew of the heavens and of the dew of the earth, and plenty of corn and oil: Let nations serve you || And peoples bow down to you. **24** Be lord over your brothers || And let your mother's sons bow down to you; And

may all the blessings with which the Lord has blessed me and blessed my father Abraham || Be imparted to you and to your seed forever. Cursed is he that curses you, || And blessed is he that blesses you." **25** And it came to pass as soon as Isaac had made an end of blessing his son Jacob and Jacob had gone out from his father Isaac, he hid himself, and his brother Esau came in from his hunting. **26** And he also made savory meat, and brought [it] to his father, and said to his father, "Let my father arise and eat of my venison that your soul may bless me." **27** And his father Isaac said to him, "Who are you?" And he said to him, "I am your firstborn, your son Esau: I have done as you have commanded me." **28** And Isaac was very greatly astonished, and said, "Who is he that has hunted, and caught, and brought [it] to me? And I have eaten of all before you came and have blessed him: [and] he will be blessed, and all his seed forever." **29** And it came to pass when Esau heard the words of his father Isaac that he cried with an exceedingly great and bitter cry, and said to his father, "Bless me, me also, father!" **30** And he said to him, "Your brother came with guile, and has taken away your blessing." And he said, "Now I know why his name is named Jacob: behold, he has supplanted me these two times; he took away my birthright, and now he has taken away my blessing." **31** And he said, "Have you not reserved a blessing for me, father?" And Isaac answered and said to Esau, "Behold, I have made him your lord, and I have given all his brothers to him for servants, and I have strengthened him with plenty of corn, and wine, and oil: and what now will I do for you, my son?" **32** And Esau said to his father Isaac, "Have you but one blessing, O father? Bless me, [even] me also, father!" And Esau lifted up his voice and wept. **33** And Isaac answered and said to him, "Behold, your dwelling will be far from the dew of the earth, and far from the dew of the heavens from above. **34** And you will live by your sword, and you will serve your brother. And it will come to pass when you become great, and shake his yoke from off your neck, you will sin a complete sin to death, and your seed will be rooted out from under Heaven." **35** And Esau kept threatening Jacob because of the blessing with which his father blessed him, and he said in his heart, "May the days of mourning for my father now come, so that I may slay my brother Jacob."

CHAPTER 27

1 And the words of her elder son Esau were told to Rebekah in a dream, and Rebekah sent and called her younger son Jacob, and said to him, **2** "Behold, your brother Esau will take vengeance on you so as to kill you. **3** Now, therefore, my son, obey my voice, and arise and flee to my brother Laban, to Haran, and tarry with him a few days until your brother's anger turns away, and he removes his anger from you, and forgets all that you have done; then I will send and fetch you from there." **4** And Jacob said, "I am not afraid; if he wishes to kill me, I will kill him." **5** But she said to him, "Let me not be deprived of both my sons on one day." **6** And Jacob said to his mother Rebekah, "Behold, you know that my father has become old and does not see because his eyes are dull, and if I leave him it will be evil in his eyes, because I leave him and go away from you, and my father will be angry, and will curse me. I will not go; when he sends me, then only will I go." **7** And Rebekah said to Jacob, "I will go in and speak to him, and he will send you away." **8** And Rebekah went in and said to Isaac, "I loathe my life because of the two daughters of Heth, whom Esau has taken to himself as wives; and if Jacob takes a wife from among the daughters of the land such as these, for what further purpose do I live? For the daughters of Canaan are evil." **9** And Isaac called Jacob and blessed him, and admonished him, and said to him, **10** "Do not take a wife for yourself of any of the daughters of Canaan; arise and go to Mesopotamia, to the house of Bethuel, your mother's father, and take a wife for yourself from there of the daughters of Laban, your mother's brother. **11** And may God Almighty bless you, and increase and multiply you, that you may become a company of nations, and give you the blessings of my father Abraham—to you and to your seed after you—that you may inherit the land of your sojournings and all the land which God gave to Abraham. Go, my son, in peace." **12** And Isaac sent Jacob away, and he went to Mesopotamia, to Laban the son of Bethuel the Syrian, the brother of Rebekah, Jacob's mother. **13** And it came to pass after Jacob had arisen to go to Mesopotamia that the spirit of Rebekah was grieved after her son, and she wept. **14** And Isaac said to Rebekah, "My sister, do not weep on account of my son Jacob, for he goes in peace, and in peace he will return. **15** The Highest God will preserve him from all evil and will be with him, for He will not forsake him all his days, **16** for I know that his ways will be prospered in all things wherever he goes, until he returns to us in peace and we see him in peace. **17** Do not fear on his account, my sister, for he is on the upright path and he is a perfect man: and he is faithful and will not perish. Do not weep." **18** And Isaac comforted Rebekah on account of her son Jacob and blessed him. **19** And Jacob went from the Well of the Oath to go to Haran on the first year of the second week, in the forty-fourth Jubilee, and he came to Luz on the mountains, that is, Bethel, on the new moon of the first month of this week, and he came to the place at evening and turned from the way to the west of the road that night: and he slept there, for the sun had set. **20** And he took one of the stones of that place and laid it [at his head] under the tree, and he was journeying alone, and he slept. **21** And he dreamt that night, and behold, a ladder [was] set up on the earth, and the top of it reached to Heaven, and behold, the messengers of the Lord ascended and descended on it: and behold, the Lord stood on it. **22** And He spoke to Jacob and said, "I am the Lord God of your father Abraham and the God of Isaac; the land on which you are sleeping, to you I will give it, and to your seed after you. **23** And your seed will be as the dust of the earth, and you will increase to the west and to the east, to the north and the south, and in you and in your Seed all the families of the nations will be blessed. **24** And behold, I will be with you, and will keep you wherever you go, and I will bring you into this land again in peace, for I will not leave you until I do everything that I told you of." **25** And Jacob awoke from his sleep, and said, "Truly this place is the house of the Lord, and I did not know it." And he was afraid and said, "This place is dreadful, which is none other than the house of God, and this is the gate of Heaven." **26** And Jacob arose early in the morning and took the stone which he had put under his head and set it up as a pillar for a sign, and he poured oil on the top of it. And he called the name of that place Bethel, but the name of the place was Luz at the first. **27** And Jacob vowed a vow to the Lord, saying, "If the Lord will be with me, and will keep me in this way that I go, and give me bread to eat and raiment to put on, so that I come to my father's house again in peace, then the Lord will be my God, and this stone which I have set up as a pillar for a sign in this place will be the Lord's house, and of all that You give me, I will give the tenth to You, my God."

CHAPTER 28

1 And he went on his journey, and came to the land of the east, to Laban, the brother of Rebekah, and he was with him, and served him for his daughter Rachel [for] one week. **2** And in the first year of the third week he said to him, "Give me my wife, for whom I have served you seven years"; and Laban said to Jacob, "I will give you your wife." **3** And Laban made a feast, and took his elder daughter Leah, and gave [her] to Jacob as a wife, and gave her his handmaid Zilpah for a handmaid, and Jacob did not know, for he thought that she was Rachel. **4** And he went in to her, and behold, she was Leah; and Jacob was angry with Laban, and said to him, "Why have you dealt thus with me? Did I not serve you for Rachel and not for Leah? Why have you wronged me? Take your daughter, and I will go, for you have done evil to me." **5** For Jacob loved Rachel more than Leah, for Leah's eyes were weak, but her form was very attractive, but Rachel had beautiful eyes and a beautiful and very attractive form. **6** And Laban said to Jacob, "It is not so done in our country, to give the younger before the elder." And it is not right to do this, for thus it is ordained and written in the heavenly tablets that no one should give his younger daughter before the elder—but he gives the elder one first and after her the younger—and the man who does so, they set down guilt against him in Heaven, and none is righteous that does this thing, for this deed is evil before the Lord. **7** And command the sons of Israel that they do not do this thing; let them neither take nor give the younger before they have given the elder, for it is very wicked. **8** And Laban said to Jacob, "Let the seven days of the celebration of this one pass by, and I will give you Rachel, that you may serve me another seven years, that you may pasture my sheep as you did in the former week." **9** And on the day when the seven days of the celebration of Leah had passed, Laban gave Rachel to Jacob, that he might serve him another seven years, and he gave to Rachel Bilhah,

the sister of Zilpah, as a handmaid. **10** And he served yet another seven years for Rachel, for Leah had been given to him for nothing. **11** And the Lord opened the womb of Leah, and she conceived and bore Jacob a son, and he called his name Reuben, on the fourteenth day of the ninth month, in the first year of the third week. **12** But the womb of Rachel was closed, for the Lord saw that Leah was hated and Rachel loved. **13** And again Jacob went in to Leah, and she conceived, and bore Jacob a second son, and he called his name Simeon, on the twenty-first of the tenth month, and in the third year of this week. **14** And again Jacob went in to Leah, and she conceived, and bore him a third son, and he called his name Levi, in the new moon of the first month, in the sixth year of this week. **15** And again Jacob went in to her, and she conceived, and bore him a fourth son, and he called his name Judah, on the fifteenth of the third month, in the first year of the fourth week. **16** And on account of all this, Rachel envied Leah, for she did not bear, and she said to Jacob, "Give me children"; and Jacob said, "Have I withheld from you the fruits of your womb? Have I forsaken you?" **17** And when Rachel saw that Leah had borne four sons to Jacob—Reuben, and Simeon, and Levi, and Judah—she said to him, "Go in to my handmaid Bilhah, and she will conceive, and bear a son to me." **18** And he went in to her, and she conceived, and bore him a son, and he called his name Dan, on the ninth of the sixth month, in the sixth year of the third week. **19** And Jacob went in again to Bilhah a second time, and she conceived, and bore Jacob another son, and Rachel called his name Naphtali, on the fifth of the seventh month, in the second year of the fourth week. **20** And when Leah saw that she had become sterile and did not bear, she envied [Rachel] and she also gave her handmaid Zilpah to Jacob to be [his] wife, and she conceived, and bore a son, and Leah called his name Gad, on the twelfth of the eighth month, in the third year of the fourth week. **21** And he went in again to her, and she conceived, and bore him a second son, and Leah called his name Asher, on the second of the eleventh month, in the fifth year of the fourth week. **22** And Jacob went in to Leah, and she conceived, and bore a son, and she called his name Issachar, on the fourth of the fifth month, in the fourth year of the fourth week, and she gave him to a nurse. **23** And Jacob went in again to her, and she conceived, and bore two [children], a son and a daughter, and she called the name of the son Zebulun, and the name of the daughter Dinah, in the seventh of the seventh month, in the sixth year of the fourth week. **24** And the Lord was gracious to Rachel, and opened her womb, and she conceived, and bore a son, and she called his name Joseph, on the new moon of the fourth month, in the sixth year in this fourth week. **25** And in the days when Joseph was born, Jacob said to Laban, "Give me my wives and sons, and let me go to my father Isaac, and let me make myself a house, for I have completed the years in which I have served you for your two daughters, and I will go to the house of my father." **26** And Laban said to Jacob, "Tarry with me for your wages, and pasture my flock for me again, and take your wages." **27** And they agreed with one another that he should give him as his wages those of the lambs and kids which were born black, and spotted, and white; [these] were to be his wages. **28** And all the sheep brought out spotted, and speckled, and black, variously marked, and they brought out again lambs like themselves, and all that were spotted were Jacob's and those which were not were Laban's. **29** And Jacob's possessions multiplied exceedingly, and he possessed oxen, and sheep, and donkeys, and camels, and menservants, and maidservants. **30** And Laban and his sons envied Jacob, and Laban took back his sheep from him, and he observed him with evil intent.

CHAPTER 29

1 And it came to pass when Rachel had borne Joseph, that Laban went to shear his sheep, for they were distant from him a three days' journey. **2** And Jacob saw that Laban was going to shear his sheep, and Jacob called Leah and Rachel, and spoke kindly to them that they should come with him to the land of Canaan. **3** For he told them how he had seen everything in a dream, even all that He had spoken to him that he should return to his father's house, and they said, "To every place where you go we will go with you." **4** And Jacob blessed the God of his father Isaac, and the God of Abraham, his father's father, and he arose and mounted his wives and his children, and took all his possessions and crossed the river, and came to the land of Gilead, and Jacob hid his intention from Laban and did not tell him. ⁵ And in the seventh year of the fourth week Jacob turned [his face] toward Gilead in the first month, on the twenty-first thereof. And Laban pursued after him and overtook Jacob in the mountain of Gilead in the third month, on the thirteenth thereof. ⁶ And the Lord did not permit him to injure Jacob, for He appeared to him in a dream by night. And Laban spoke to Jacob, ⁷ and on the fifteenth of those days Jacob made a feast for Laban and for all who came with him, and Jacob swore to Laban that day, and Laban also to Jacob, that neither should cross the mountain of Gilead to the other with evil purpose. ⁸ And he made a heap there for a witness; for that reason the name of that place is called "The Heap of Witness," after this heap. ⁹ But before [that] they used to call the land of Gilead the land of the Rephaim, for it was the land of the Rephaim, and the Rephaim were born [there]—giants whose height was ten, nine, eight, [and] down to seven cubits. ¹⁰ And their habitation was from the land of the children of Ammon to Mount Hermon, and the seats of their kingdom were Karnaim, and Ashtaroth, and Edrei, and Mîsûr, and Beon. ¹¹ And the Lord destroyed them because of the evil of their deeds, for they were very malevolent, and the Amorites dwelt in their stead, wicked and sinful, and there is no people today which has worked to the measure of all their sins, and they have no more length of life on the earth. ¹² And Jacob sent Laban away, and he departed into Mesopotamia, the land of the east, and Jacob returned to the land of Gilead. ¹³ And he passed over the Jabbok in the ninth month, on the eleventh thereof. And on that day his brother Esau came to him, and he was reconciled to him, and departed from him to the land of Seir, but Jacob dwelt in tents. ¹⁴ And in the first year of the fifth week in this jubilee he crossed the Jordan, and dwelt beyond the Jordan, and he pastured his sheep from the sea of the heap to Bethshan, and to Dothan, and to the forest of Akrabbim. ¹⁵ And he sent to his father Isaac of all his substance: clothing, and food, and meat, and drink, and milk, and butter, and cheese, and some dates of the valley; ¹⁶ and also to his mother Rebekah four times a year, between the times of the months, between plowing and reaping, and between autumn and the rain [season], and between winter and spring, to the tower of Abraham. ¹⁷ For Isaac had returned from the Well of the Oath and gone up to the tower of his father Abraham, and he dwelt there apart from his son Esau. ¹⁸ For in the days when Jacob went to Mesopotamia, Esau took to himself Mahalath, the daughter of Ishmael, to be [his] wife, and he gathered together all the flocks of his father and his wives, and went up and dwelt on Mount Seir, and left his father Isaac at the Well of the Oath alone. ¹⁹ And Isaac went up from the Well of the Oath and dwelt in the tower of his father Abraham on the mountains of Hebron, ²⁰ and there Jacob sent all that he sent to his father and his mother from time to time—all they needed—and they blessed Jacob with all their heart and with all their soul.

CHAPTER 30

¹ And in the first year of the sixth week he went up to Salem, to the east of Shechem, in peace, in the fourth month. ² And there they carried off Dinah, the daughter of Jacob, into the house of Shechem, the son of Hamor, the Hivite, the prince of the land, and he lay with her and defiled her, and she was a little girl, a child of twelve years. ³ And he implored his father and her brothers that she might be given to him to be [his] wife. And Jacob and his sons were angry because of the men of Shechem, for they had defiled their sister Dinah, and they spoke to them with evil intent, and dealt deceitfully with them, and deceived them. ⁴ And Simeon and Levi came stealthily to Shechem, and executed judgment on all the men of Shechem, and slew all the men whom they found in it, and left not a single one remaining in it: they slew all in torments because they had dishonored their sister Dinah. ⁵ And thus do not let it be done again from now on that a daughter of Israel is defiled, for judgment is ordained in Heaven against them that they should destroy with the sword all the men of the Shechemites because they had worked shame in Israel. ⁶ And the Lord delivered them into the hands of the sons of Jacob that they might exterminate them with the sword, and execute judgment on them, and that it might not thus be done again in Israel that a virgin of Israel should be defiled. ⁷ And if there is any man in Israel who wishes to give his daughter or his sister to any man who is of the seed of the nations, he will surely die, and they will stone him with stones, for he has worked shame in Israel; and they will burn the woman with fire, because she has

dishonored the name of the house of her father, and she will be rooted out of Israel. ⁸ And do not let an adulteress be found, and no uncleanness, in Israel, throughout all the days of the generations of the earth, for Israel is holy to the Lord, and every man who has defiled [it] will surely die: they will stone him with stones. ⁹ For thus it has been ordained and written in the heavenly tablets regarding all the seed of Israel: he who defiles [it] will surely die, and he will be stoned with stones. ¹⁰ And to this law there is no limit of days, and no forgiveness, nor any atonement, but the man who has defiled his daughter will be rooted out in the midst of all Israel, because he has given of his seed to Moloch, and worked impiously so as to defile it. ¹¹ And you, Moses, command the sons of Israel and exhort them not to give their daughters to the nations, and not to take any of the daughters of the nations for their sons, for this is abominable before the Lord. ¹² For this reason I have written for you in the words of the Law all the deeds of the Shechemites, which they worked against Dinah, and how the sons of Jacob spoke, saying, "We will not give our daughter to a man who is uncircumcised, for that would be a reproach to us." ¹³ And it is a reproach to Israel to those who give and to those who take the daughters of the nations, for this is unclean and abominable to Israel. ¹⁴ And Israel will not be free from this uncleanness if it has a wife of the daughters of the nations or has given any of its daughters to a man who is of any of the nations. ¹⁵ For there will be plague on plague, and curse on curse, and every judgment, and plague, and curse will come [on him] if he does this thing, or hides his eyes from those who commit uncleanness, or those who defile the sanctuary of the Lord, or those who profane His holy Name, [for] the whole nation will be judged together for all the uncleanness and desecration of this [man]. ¹⁶ And there will be no respect of persons, and no receiving at his hands of fruits, and offerings, and burnt-offerings, and fat, nor the fragrance of sweet savor, so as to accept it: and likewise for every man or woman in Israel who defiles the sanctuary. ¹⁷ For this reason I have commanded you, saying, "Testify this testimony to Israel: see how the Shechemites and their sons fared, how they were delivered into the hands of two sons of Jacob, and they slew them under tortures, and it was [reckoned] to them for righteousness, and it is written down to them for righteousness. ¹⁸ And the seed of Levi was chosen for the priesthood, and to be Levites, that they might minister before the Lord, as we, continually, and that Levi and his sons may be blessed forever, for he was zealous to execute righteousness, and judgment, and vengeance on all those who arose against Israel. ¹⁹ And so they inscribe as a testimony in his favor on the heavenly tablets blessing and righteousness before the God of all; ²⁰ and we remember the righteousness which the man fulfilled during his life, at all periods of the year; until one thousand generations they will [still] record it, and it will come to him and to his descendants after him, and he has been recorded on the heavenly tablets as a friend and a righteous man. ²¹ All this account I have written for you and have commanded you to say to the sons of Israel, that they should not commit sin, nor transgress the ordinances, nor break the covenant which has been ordained for them, [but] that they should fulfill it and be recorded as friends. ²² But if they transgress and work uncleanness in every way, they will be recorded on the heavenly tablets as adversaries, and they will be destroyed out of the Scroll of Life, and they will be recorded in the scroll of those who will be destroyed and with those who will be rooted out of the earth. ²³ And on the day when the sons of Jacob slew Shechem, a writing was recorded in their favor in Heaven that they had executed righteousness, and uprightness, and vengeance on the sinners, and it was written for a blessing. ²⁴ And they brought their sister Dinah out of the house of Shechem, and they took everything captive that was in Shechem: their sheep, and their oxen, and their donkeys, and all their wealth, and all their flocks; and they brought them all to their father Jacob. ²⁵ And he reproached them because they had put the city to the sword, for he feared those who dwelt in the land, the Canaanites and the Perizzites. ²⁶ And the dread of the Lord was on all the cities which are around Shechem, and they did not rise to pursue after the sons of Jacob, for terror had fallen on them."

CHAPTER 31

¹ And on the new moon of the month Jacob spoke to all the people of his house, saying, "Purify yourselves and change your

garments, and let us arise and go up to Bethel, where I vowed a vow to Him on the day when I fled from the face of my brother Esau, because He has been with me and has brought me into this land in peace, and put away the strange gods that are among you." **2** And they gave up the strange gods, and that which was in their ears and which was on their necks, and the idols which Rachel stole from her father Laban she wholly gave to Jacob. And he burned and broke them to pieces, and destroyed them, and hid them under an oak which is in the land of Shechem. **3** And he went up on the new moon of the seventh month to Bethel. And he built an altar at the place where he had slept, and he set up a pillar there, and he sent word to his father Isaac to come to him to his sacrifice, and to his mother Rebekah. **4** And Isaac said, "Let my son Jacob come, and let me see him before I die." **5** And Jacob went to his father Isaac and to his mother Rebekah, to the house of his father Abraham, and he took two of his sons with him, Levi and Judah, and he came to his father Isaac and to his mother Rebekah. **6** And Rebekah came out from the tower to the front of it to kiss Jacob and embrace him, for her spirit had revived when she heard: "Behold, your son Jacob has come!" And she kissed him. **7** And she saw his two sons, and she recognized them, and said to him, "Are these your sons, my son?" and she embraced them, and kissed them, and blessed them, saying, "In you the seed of Abraham will become illustrious, and you will prove a blessing on the earth." **8** And Jacob went in to his father Isaac, to the chamber where he lay, and his two sons were with him, and he took the hand of his father, and stooping down, he kissed him, and Isaac clung to the neck of his son Jacob and wept on his neck. **9** And the darkness left the eyes of Isaac, and he saw the two sons of Jacob, Levi and Judah, and he said, "Are these your sons, my son? for they are like you." **10** And he said to him that they were truly his sons: "And you have truly seen that they are truly my sons." **11** And they came near to him, and he turned and kissed them, and embraced them both together. **12** And the spirit of prophecy came down into his mouth, and he took Levi by his right hand and Judah by his left. **13** And he turned to Levi first, and began to bless him first, and said to him, "May the God of all, the very Lord of all the ages, || Bless you and your children throughout all the ages. **14** And may the Lord give greatness and great glory to you and to your seed, || And cause you and your seed, from among all flesh, to approach Him || To serve in His sanctuary as the messengers of the presence and as the holy ones. [Even] as they, may the seed of your sons be for glory, and greatness, and holiness, || And may He make them great to all the ages. **15** And they will be princes and judges, || And chiefs of all the seed of the sons of Jacob; They will speak the word of the Lord in righteousness, || And they will judge all His judgments in righteousness. And they will declare My ways to Jacob, || And My paths to Israel. The blessing of the Lord will be given in their mouths || To bless all the seed of the beloved. **16** Your mother has called your name Levi, || And justly has she called your name; You will be joined to the Lord, || And be the companion of all the sons of Jacob; Let His table be yours || And you and your sons will eat thereof; And may your table be full to all generations, || And your food will not fail to all the ages. **17** And let all who hate you fall down before you, || And let all your adversaries be rooted out and perish; And blessed is he that blesses you || And cursed is every nation that curses you." **18** And to Judah he said, "May the Lord give you strength and power || To tread down all that hate you; You will be a prince—you and one of your sons, || Over the sons of Jacob; May your name and the name of your sons || Go out and traverse every land and region. Then the nations will fear before your face, || And all the nations [[or peoples]] will quake. **19** In you will be the help of Jacob, || And in you will be found the salvation of Israel. **20** And when you sit on the throne of the honor of your righteousness, || There will be great peace for all the seed of the sons of the beloved, || And he that blesses you will be blessed; And all that hate you, and afflict you, and curse you || Will be rooted out and destroyed from the earth and accursed." **21** And turning, he kissed him again and embraced him, and greatly rejoiced, for he had seen the sons of his son Jacob in exceeding truth. **22** And he went out from between his feet and fell down and worshiped him. And he blessed them. And [Jacob] rested there with his father Isaac that night, and they ate and drank with joy. **23** And he made the two sons of Jacob sleep—the one on his right hand and the other on his left, and it was counted to him for righteousness. **24** And Jacob told his father everything during the night, how the Lord had shown him great mercy, and how He had

prospered [him in] all his ways and protected him from all evil. **25** And Isaac blessed the God of his father Abraham who had not withdrawn His mercy and His righteousness from the sons of His servant Isaac. **26** And in the morning, Jacob told his father Isaac the vow which he had vowed to the Lord, and the vision which he had seen, and that he had built an altar, and that everything was ready for the sacrifice to be made before the Lord as he had vowed, and that he had come to set him on a donkey. **27** And Isaac said to his son Jacob, "I am not able to go with you, for I am old and not able to bear the way: go, my son, in peace, for I am one hundred and sixty-five years [old] this day; I am no longer able to journey. Set your mother [on a donkey] and let her go with you. **28** And I know, my son, that you have come on my account, and may this day be blessed on which you have seen me alive, and I also have seen you, my son. **29** May you prosper and fulfill the vow which you have vowed, and do not put off your vow, for you will be called to account as touching the vow. Now, therefore, make sure to perform it, and may He be pleased who has made all things, to whom you have vowed the vow." **30** And he said to Rebekah, "Go with your son Jacob"; and Rebekah went with her son Jacob, and Deborah with her, and they came to Bethel. **31** And Jacob remembered the prayer with which his father had blessed him and his two sons, Levi and Judah, and he rejoiced and blessed the God of his fathers Abraham and Isaac. **32** And he said, "Now I know that I have a continuous hope, and my sons also, before the God of all"; and thus it is ordained concerning the two; and they record it as a perpetual testimony to them on the heavenly tablets how Isaac blessed them.

CHAPTER 32

1 And he stayed that night at Bethel, and Levi dreamed that they had ordained and made him the priest of the Highest God, him and his sons forever; and he awoke from his sleep and blessed the Lord. **2** And Jacob rose early in the morning, on the fourteenth of this month, and he gave a tithe of all that came with him, both of men and cattle, both of gold and every vessel and garment, yes, he gave tithes of all. **3** And in those days Rachel became pregnant with her son Benjamin. And Jacob counted his sons from him upwards and Levi fell to the portion of the Lord, and his father clothed him in the garments of the priesthood and filled his hands. **4** And on the fifteenth of this month, he brought to the altar fourteen oxen from among the cattle, and twenty-eight rams, and forty-nine sheep, and seven lambs, and twenty-one kids of the goats as a burnt-offering on the altar of sacrifice, well pleasing for a sweet savor before God. **5** This was his offering, in consequence of the vow which he had vowed that he would give a tenth, with their fruit-offerings and their drink-offerings. **6** And when the fire had consumed it, he burned incense on the fire over the fire, and for a thank-offering two oxen, and four rams, and four sheep, four male goats, and two sheep of a year old, and two kids of the goats; and thus he did daily for seven days. **7** And he, and all his sons, and his men were eating [this] with joy there for seven days and were blessing and thanking the Lord who had delivered him out of all his tribulation and had given him his vow. **8** And he tithed all the clean animals, and made a burnt sacrifice, but he did [not] give the unclean animals to his son Levi, and he gave him all the souls of the men. **9** And Levi discharged the priestly office at Bethel before his father Jacob in preference to his ten brothers, and he was a priest there, and Jacob gave his vow: thus he tithed the tithe to the Lord again and sanctified it, and it became holy to Him. **10** And for this reason it is ordained on the heavenly tablets as a law for the tithing the tithe again to eat before the Lord from year to year in the place where it is chosen that His Name should dwell, and to this law there is no limit of days forever. **11** This ordinance is written that it may be fulfilled from year to year in eating the second tithe before the Lord in the place where it has been chosen, and nothing will remain over from it from this year to the year following. **12** For in its year the seed will be eaten until the days of the gathering of the seed of the year, and the wine until the days of the wine, and the oil until the days of its season. **13** And all that is left thereof and becomes old, let it be regarded as polluted: let it be burned with fire, for it is unclean. **14** And thus let them eat it together in the sanctuary and do not let them permit it to become old. **15** And all the tithes of the oxen and sheep will be holy to the Lord, and will belong to His priests, which they will eat before Him from year to year, for thus it is ordained and engraved regarding the tithe on the heavenly tablets. **16** And on the following night, on the twenty-second day of this month, Jacob resolved to build that place, and to surround the court with a wall, and to sanctify it and make it holy forever, for himself and his children after him. **17** And the Lord appeared to him by night, and blessed him, and said to him, "Your name will not be called Jacob, but Israel they will name your name." **18** And He said to him again, "I am the Lord who created the heavens and the earth, and I will increase you and multiply you exceedingly, and kings will come out from you, and they will judge everywhere, wherever the foot of the sons of men has trodden. **19** And I will give to your seed all the earth which is under the heavens, and they will judge all the nations according to their desires, and after that, they will get possession of the whole earth and inherit it forever." **20** And He finished speaking with him, and He went up from him, and Jacob looked until He had ascended into Heaven. **21** And he saw in a vision of the night, and behold, a messenger descended from Heaven with seven tablets in his hands, and he gave them to Jacob, and he read them and knew all that was written therein which would befall him and his sons throughout all the ages. **22** And he showed him all that was written on the tablets and said to him, "Do not build this place, and do not make it a perpetual sanctuary, and do not dwell here, for this is not the place. Go to the house of your father Abraham and dwell with your father Isaac until the day of the death of your father. **23** For in Egypt you will die in peace, and you will be buried in this land with honor in the tomb of your fathers, with Abraham and Isaac. **24** Do not fear, for as you have seen and read it, thus it will all be; and write down everything as you have seen and read." **25** And Jacob said, "Lord, how can I remember all that I have read and seen?" And he said to him, "I will bring all things to your remembrance." **26** And he went up from him, and he awoke from his sleep, and he remembered everything which he had read and seen, and he wrote down all the words which he had read and seen. **27** And he celebrated there yet another day, and he sacrificed thereon according to all that he sacrificed on the former days, and called its name "Addition," for this day was added, and the former days he called "The Feast." **28** And thus it was manifested that it should be, and it is written on the heavenly tablets, for that reason it was revealed to him that he should celebrate it and add it to the seven days of the feast. **29** And its name was called "Addition," because that it was recorded among the days of the feast days, according to the number of the days of the year. **30** And in the night, on the twenty-third of this month, Rebekah's nurse Deborah died, and they buried her beneath the city under the oak of the river, and he called the name of this place, "The river of Deborah," and the oak, "The oak of the mourning of Deborah." **31** And Rebekah went and returned to her house, to his father Isaac, and Jacob sent by her hand rams, and sheep, and male goats that she should prepare a meal for his father such as he desired. **32** And he went after his mother until he came to the land of Kabrâtân, and he dwelt there. **33** And Rachel bore a son in the night and called his name "Son of my sorrow," for she suffered in giving him birth, but his father called his name Benjamin, on the eleventh of the eighth month, in the first of the sixth week of this jubilee. **34** And Rachel died there, and she was buried in the land of Ephrath, the same is Beth-Lehem, and Jacob built a pillar on the grave of Rachel, on the road above her grave.

CHAPTER 33

1 And Jacob went and dwelt to the south of Magdalâdrâ'êf. And he went to his father Isaac, he and his wife Leah, on the new moon of the tenth month. **2** And Reuben saw Bilhah, Rachel's maid, the concubine of his father, bathing in water in a secret place, and he loved her. **3** And he hid himself at night, and he entered the house of Bilhah [at night], and he found her sleeping alone on a bed in her house. **4** And he lay with her, and she awoke and saw, and behold, Reuben was lying with her in the bed, and she uncovered the border of her covering and seized him, and cried out, and discovered that it was Reuben. **5** And she was ashamed because of him, and released her hand from him, and he fled. **6** And she lamented exceedingly because of this thing and did not tell it to anyone. **7** And when Jacob returned and sought her, she said to him, "I am not clean for you, for I have been defiled as regards you, for Reuben has defiled me, and has lain with me in the night, and I was asleep, and did not discover [it] until he uncovered my skirt and slept with me." **8** And Jacob was exceedingly angry

with Reuben because he had lain with Bilhah, because he had uncovered his father's skirt. **9** And Jacob did not approach her again because Reuben had defiled her. And as for any man who uncovers his father's skirt: his deed is exceedingly wicked, for he is abominable before the Lord. **10** For this reason it is written and ordained on the heavenly tablets that a man should not lie with his father's wife, and should not uncover his father's skirt, for this is unclean: they will surely die together, the man who lies with his father's wife and the woman also, for they have worked uncleanness on the earth. **11** And there will be nothing unclean before our God in the nation which He has chosen for Himself as a possession. **12** And again, it is written a second time: "Cursed is he who lies with the wife of his father, for he has uncovered his father's shame"; and all the holy ones of the Lord said, "So be it; so be it." **13** And you, Moses, command the sons of Israel that they observe this word, for it [entails] a punishment of death; and it is unclean, and there is no atonement forever to atone for the man who has committed this, but he is to be put to death and slain, and stoned with stones, and rooted out from the midst of the people of our God. **14** For to no man who does so in Israel is it permitted to remain alive a single day on the earth, for he is abominable and unclean. **15** And do not let them say, "Life and forgiveness were granted to Reuben after he had lain with his father's concubine, and to her also though she had a husband, and her husband Jacob, his father, was still alive." **16** For until that time there had not been revealed the ordinance, and judgment, and law in its completeness for all, but in your days [it has been revealed] as a law of seasons and of days, and a continuous law for the perpetual generations. **17** And for this law there is no consummation of days, and no atonement for it, but they must both be rooted out in the midst of the nation: on the day on which they committed it they will slay them. **18** And you, Moses, write [it] down for Israel that they may observe it, and do according to these words, and not commit a sin to death, for the Lord our God is judge, who does not respect persons and does not accept gifts. **19** And tell them these words of the covenant, that they may hear and observe, and be on their guard with respect to them, and not be destroyed and rooted out of the land; for an uncleanness, and an abomination, and a contamination, and a pollution are all they who commit it on the earth before our God. **20** And there is no greater sin than the fornication which they commit on earth, for Israel is a holy nation to the Lord its God, and a nation of inheritance, and a priestly and royal nation, and for [His own] possession; and no such uncleanness will appear in the midst of the holy nation. **21** And in the third year of this sixth week Jacob and all his sons went and dwelt in the house of Abraham, near his father Isaac and his mother Rebekah. **22** And these were the names of the sons of Jacob: the firstborn Reuben, Simeon, Levi, Judah, Issachar, Zebulun—the sons of Leah; and the sons of Rachel: Joseph and Benjamin; and the sons of Bilhah: Dan and Naphtali; and the sons of Zilpah: Gad and Asher; and Dinah, the daughter of Leah, the only daughter of Jacob. **23** And they came and bowed themselves to Isaac and Rebekah, and when they saw them, they blessed Jacob and all his sons, and Isaac rejoiced exceedingly, for he saw the sons of Jacob, his younger son, and he blessed them.

CHAPTER 34

1 And in the sixth year of this week, of this forty-fourth jubilee, Jacob sent his sons to pasture their sheep, and his servants with them, to the pastures of Shechem. **2** And the seven kings of the Amorites assembled themselves together against them, to slay them, hiding themselves under the trees, and to take their cattle as a prey. **3** And Jacob, and Levi, and Judah, and Joseph were in the house with their father Isaac, for his spirit was sorrowful, and they could not leave him; and Benjamin was the youngest, and for this reason remained with his father. **4** And there came the king[s] of Tâphû, and the king[s] of 'Arêsa, and the king[s] of Sêragân, and the king[s] of Sêlô, and the king[s] of Gâ'as, and the king of Bêthôrôn, and the king of Ma'anîsâkîr, and all those who dwell in these mountains [and] who dwell in the woods in the land of Canaan. **5** And they announced this to Jacob, saying, "Behold, the kings of the Amorites have surrounded your sons, and plundered their herds." **6** And he arose from his house—he, and his three sons, and all the servants of his father, and his own servants— and he went against them with six thousand men who carried swords. **7** And he slew them in the pastures of Shechem, and pursued those who fled, and he slew them with the edge of the sword, and he slew ʿArêsa, and Tâphû, and Sêragân, and Sêlô, and Maʿanîsâkîr, and Gâʿas, and he recovered his herds. **8** And he prevailed over them, and imposed tribute on them that they should pay him tribute, five fruit products of their land, and he built Rôbêl and Tamnâtârês, **9** and he returned in peace, and made peace with them, and they became his servants until the day that he and his sons went down into Egypt. **10** And in the seventh year of this week he sent Joseph from his house to the land of Shechem to learn about the welfare of his brothers, and he found them in the land of Dothan. **11** And they dealt treacherously with him, and formed a plot against him to slay him, but changing their minds, they sold him to Ishmaelite merchants, and they brought him down into Egypt, and they sold him to Potiphar, the eunuch of Pharaoh, the chief of the cooks, priest of the city of ʿÊlêw. **12** And the sons of Jacob slaughtered a kid, and dipped the coat of Joseph in the blood, and sent [it] to their father Jacob on the tenth of the seventh month. **13** And he mourned all that night, for they had brought it to him in the evening, and he became feverish with mourning for his death, and he said, "An evil beast has devoured Joseph"; and all the members of his house were grieving and mourning with him that whole day. **14** And his sons and his daughter rose up to comfort him, but he refused to be comforted for his son. **15** And on that day, Bilhah heard that Joseph had perished, and she died mourning [for] him, and she was living in Qafrâtêf and Dinah also, his daughter, died after Joseph had perished. And these three mournings came on Israel in one month. **16** And they buried Bilhah over against the tomb of Rachel, and Dinah also, his daughter, they buried there. **17** And he mourned for Joseph one year, and did not cease, for he said, "Let me go down to the grave mourning for my son." **18** For this reason it is ordained for the sons of Israel that they should afflict themselves on the tenth of the seventh month—on the day that the news which made him weep for Joseph came to Jacob his father—that they should make atonement for themselves thereon with a young goat on the tenth of the seventh month, once a year, for their sins, for they had grieved the affection of their father regarding his son Joseph. **19** And this day has been ordained that they should grieve thereon for their sins, and for all their transgressions, and for all their errors, so that they might cleanse themselves on that day once a year. **20** And after Joseph perished, the sons of Jacob took wives for themselves. The name of Reuben's wife is ʿAdâ; and the name of Simeon's wife is ʿAdîbâʿa, a Canaanite; and the name of Levi's wife is Mêlkâ, of the daughters of Aram, of the seed of the sons of Terah; and the name of Judah's wife, Bêtasûʿêl, a Canaanite; and the name of Issachar's wife, Hêzaqâ; and the name of Zebulun's wife, Nîʿîmân; and the name of Dan's wife, ʿÊglâ; and the name of Naphtali's wife, Rasûʿû, of Mesopotamia; and the name of Gad's wife, Mâka; and the name of Asher's wife, ʿÎjônâ; and the name of Joseph's wife, Asenath, the Egyptian; and the name of Benjamin's wife, ʿÎjasaka. **21** And Simeon converted, and took a second wife from Mesopotamia as his brothers.

CHAPTER 35

1 And in the first year of the first week of the forty-fifth jubilee, Rebekah called her son Jacob and commanded him regarding his father and regarding his brother, that he should honor them all the days of his life. **2** And Jacob said, "I will do everything as you have commanded me, for this thing will be honor and greatness to me, and righteousness before the Lord, that I should honor them. **3** And you, mother, also know from the time I was born until this day, all my deeds and all that is in my heart, that I always think good concerning all. **4** And how should I not do this thing which you have commanded me, that I should honor my father and my brother! **5** Tell me, mother, what perversity have you seen in me and I will turn away from it, and mercy will be on me." **6** And she said to him, "My son, I have not seen in you all my days anything perverse, but [only] upright deeds. And yet I will tell you the truth, my son: I will die this year, and I will not survive this year in my life, for I have seen in a dream the day of my death, that I should not live beyond one hundred and fifty-five years; and behold, I have completed all the days of my life which I am to live." **7** And Jacob laughed at the words of his mother, because his mother had said to him that she should die; and she was sitting opposite to him in possession of her strength, and she was not weak in her strength, for she went in and out and saw, and her

teeth were strong, and no ailment had touched her all the days of her life. **8** And Jacob said to her, "Blessed am I, mother, if my days approach the days of your life, and my strength remains with me thus as your strength: and you will not die, for you are idly jesting with me regarding your death." **9** And she went in to Isaac and said to him, "One petition I make to you: make Esau swear that he will not injure Jacob, nor pursue him with enmity, for you know that Esau's thoughts are perverse from his youth, and there is no goodness in him, for he desires to kill him after your death. **10** And you know all that he has done since the day his brother Jacob went to Haran until this day, how he has forsaken us with his whole heart and has done evil to us; he has taken your flocks to himself and carried off all your possessions from before your face. **11** And when we implored and entreated him for what was our own, he did as a man who was taking pity on us. **12** And he is bitter against you because you blessed Jacob, your perfect and upright son; for there is no evil but only goodness in him, and since he came from Haran to this day, he has not robbed us of anything, for he always brings us everything in its season, and rejoices with all his heart when we take at his hands, and he blesses us, and has not parted from us since he came from Haran until this day, and he continually remains at home with us, honoring us." **13** And Isaac said to her, "I, too, know and see the deeds of Jacob who is with us, how that he honors us with all his heart, but I formerly loved Esau more than Jacob, because he was the firstborn, but now I love Jacob more than Esau, for he has done manifold evil deeds, and there is no righteousness in him, for all his ways are unrighteousness and violence. **14** And now my heart is troubled because of all his deeds, and neither he nor his seed is to be saved, for they are those who will be destroyed from the earth, and who will be rooted out from under the heavens, for he has forsaken the God of Abraham and gone after his wives, and after their uncleanness, and after their error—he and his children. **15** And you command me to make him swear that he will not slay his brother Jacob; even if he swears, he will not abide by his oath, and he will not do good but only evil. **16** But if he desires to slay his brother Jacob, he will be given into Jacob's hands, and he will not escape from his hands. **17** And do not fear on account of Jacob, for the guardian of Jacob is great, and powerful, and honored, and praised more than the guardian of Esau." **18** And Rebekah sent and called Esau, and he came to her, and she said to him, "I have a petition, my son, to make to you, and do you promise to do it, my son?" **19** And he said, "I will do everything that you say to me, and I will not refuse your petition." **20** And she said to him, "I ask you that the day I die, you will take me in and bury me near Sarah, your father's mother, and that you and Jacob will love each other, and that neither will desire evil against the other, but mutual love only, and [so] you will prosper, my sons, and be honored in the midst of the land, and no enemy will rejoice over you, and you will be a blessing and a mercy in the eyes of all those that love you." **21** And he said, "I will do all that you have told me, and I will bury you on the day you die near Sarah, my father's mother, as you have desired, that her bones may be near your bones. **22** And I will also love my brother Jacob above all flesh, for I have no brother in all the earth but him only; and this is no great merit for me if I love him, for he is my brother, and we were sown together in your body, and together we came out from your womb, and if I do not love my brother, whom will I love? **23** And I, myself, beg you to exhort Jacob concerning me and concerning my sons, for I know that he will assuredly be king over me and my sons, for on the day my father blessed him he made him the higher and me the lower. **24** And I swear to you that I will love him, and not desire evil against him all the days of my life, but good only." And he swore to her regarding all this matter. **25** And she called Jacob before the eyes of Esau and gave him command according to the words which she had spoken to Esau. **26** And he said, "I will do your pleasure; believe me that no evil will proceed from me or from my sons against Esau, and I will be first in nothing save in love only." **27** And she and her sons ate and drank that night, and she died—three jubilees and one week and one year old—on that night, and her two sons, Esau and Jacob, buried her in the double cave near Sarah, their father's mother.

CHAPTER 36

1 And in the sixth year of this week Isaac called his two sons, Esau and Jacob, and they came to him, and he said to them, "My sons, I am going the way of my fathers, to the continuous house where my fathers are. ² For that reason, bury me near my father Abraham, in the double cave in the field of Ephron the Hittite, where Abraham purchased a tomb to bury in; in the tomb which I dug for myself, bury me there. ³ And this I command you, my sons, that you practice righteousness and uprightness on the earth, so that the Lord may bring on you all that the Lord said that He would do to Abraham and to his seed. ⁴ And, my sons, love one another—your brother—as a man who loves his own soul, and let each seek in what [way] he may benefit his brother, and act together on the earth; and let them love each other as their own souls. ⁵ And concerning the question of idols, I command and admonish you to reject them, and hate them, and not to love them, for they are full of deception for those that worship them and for those that bow down to them. ⁶ Remember, my sons, the Lord God of your father Abraham, and how I also worshiped Him and served Him in righteousness and in joy, that He might multiply you and increase your seed as the stars of the heavens in multitude and establish you on the earth as the plant of righteousness which will not be rooted out to all the generations forever. ⁷ And now I will make you swear a great oath—for there is no oath which is greater than it, by the glorious, and honored, and great, and splendid, and wonderful, and mighty Name, which created the heavens, and the earth, and all things together—that you will fear Him and worship Him, ⁸ and that each will love his brother with affection and righteousness, and that neither will desire evil against his brother from now on and forever, all the days of your life, so that you may prosper in all your deeds and not be destroyed. ⁹ And if either of you devises evil against his brother, know that from now on everyone that devises evil against his brother will fall into his hand, and will be rooted out of the land of the living, and his seed will be destroyed from under the heavens. ¹⁰ But on the day of turbulence, and execration, and indignation, and anger, with flaming devouring fire as He burned Sodom, so likewise He will burn his land, and his city, and all that is his, and he will be blotted out of the scroll of the discipline of the children of men, and not be recorded in the Scroll of Life, but in that which is appointed to destruction, and he will depart into continuous execration, so that their condemnation may always be renewed in hate, and in execration, and in wrath, and in torment, and in indignation, and in plagues, and in disease forever. ¹¹ I say and testify to you, my sons, according to the judgment which will come on the man who wishes to injure his brother." ¹² And he divided all his possessions between the two on that day, and he gave the larger portion to him that was the firstborn, and the tower and all that was around it, and all that Abraham possessed at the Well of the Oath. ¹³ And he said, "I will give this larger portion to the firstborn." ¹⁴ And Esau said, "I have sold to Jacob and given my birthright to Jacob; let it be given to him, and I have not a single word to say regarding it, for it is his." ¹⁵ And Isaac said, "May a blessing rest on you, my sons, and on your seed this day, for you have given me rest, and my heart is not pained concerning the birthright, lest you should work wickedness on account of it. ¹⁶ May the Highest God bless the man that works righteousness—him and his seed forever." ¹⁷ And he ended commanding them and blessing them, and they ate and drank together before him, and he rejoiced because there was one mind between them, and they went out from him, and rested that day, and slept. ¹⁸ And Isaac slept on his bed that day rejoicing; and he slept the continuous sleep and died one hundred and eighty years old. He completed twenty-five weeks and five years; and his two sons Esau and Jacob buried him. ¹⁹ And Esau went to the land of Edom, to the mountains of Seir, and dwelt there. ²⁰ And Jacob dwelt in the mountains of Hebron, in the tower of the land of the sojournings of his father Abraham, and he worshiped the Lord with all his heart and according to the visible commands according as He had divided the days of his generations. ²¹ And his wife Leah died in the fourth year of the second week of the forty-fifth jubilee, and he buried her in the double cave near his mother Rebekah, to the left of the grave of Sarah, his father's mother. ²² And all her sons and his sons came to mourn over his wife Leah with him, and to comfort him regarding her, for he was lamenting her. ²³ For he loved her exceedingly after her sister Rachel died, for she was perfect and upright in all her ways and honored Jacob, and all the days that she lived with him he did not hear from her mouth a harsh word, for she was gentle, and peaceable, and upright, and honorable. ²⁴ And he remembered all her deeds which she had done during her life, and he lamented her exceedingly, for he loved her with all his

heart and with all his soul.

CHAPTER 37

¹ And on the day that Isaac the father of Jacob and Esau died, the sons of Esau heard that Isaac had given the portion of the elder to his younger son Jacob and they were very angry. ² And they strove with their father, saying, "Why has your father given Jacob the portion of the elder and passed over you, although you are the elder and Jacob the younger?" ³ And he said to them, "Because I sold my birthright to Jacob for a small mess of lentils; and on the day my father sent me to hunt, and catch, and bring him something that he should eat and bless me, he came with guile and brought my father food and drink, and my father blessed him and put me under his hand. ⁴ And now our father has caused us to swear—me and him—that we will not mutually devise evil, either against his brother, and that we will each continue in love and in peace with his brother and not make our ways corrupt." ⁵ And they said to him, "We will not listen to you to make peace with him, for our strength is greater than his strength, and we are more powerful than he; we will go against him and slay him, and destroy him and his sons. And if you will not go with us, we will do harm to you also. ⁶ And now listen to us: let us send to Aram, and Philistia, and Moab, and Ammon, and let us choose for ourselves chosen men who are ardent for battle, and let us go against him and do battle with him, and let us exterminate him from the earth before he grows strong." ⁷ And their father said to them, "Do not go and do not make war with him lest you fall before him." ⁸ And they said to him, "This, too, is exactly your mode of action from your youth until this day, and you are putting your neck under his yoke. We will not listen to these words." ⁹ And they sent to Aram and to 'Adurâm, to the friend of their father, and they hired along with them one thousand fighting men, chosen men of war. ¹⁰ And there came to them from Moab and from the children of Ammon those who were hired, one thousand chosen men; and from Philistia, one thousand chosen men of war; and from Edom and from the Horites, one thousand chosen fighting men; and from the Kittim, mighty men of war. ¹¹ And they said to their father, "Go out with them and lead them, else we will slay you." ¹² And he was filled with wrath and indignation on seeing that his sons were forcing him to go before [them] to lead them against his brother Jacob. ¹³ But afterward he remembered all the evil which lay hidden in his heart against his brother Jacob, and he did not remember the oath which he had sworn to his father and to his mother that he would devise no evil all his days against his brother Jacob. ¹⁴ And notwithstanding all this, Jacob did not know that they were coming against him to battle, and he was mourning for his wife Leah until they approached very near to the tower with four thousand warriors and chosen men of war. ¹⁵ And the men of Hebron sent to him, saying, "Behold, your brother has come against you, to fight you, with four thousand girt with the sword, and they carry shields and weapons"; for they loved Jacob more than Esau. So they told him, for Jacob was a more liberal and merciful man than Esau. ¹⁶ But Jacob would not believe [it] until they came very near to the tower. ¹⁷ And he closed the gates of the tower; and he stood on the battlements, and spoke to his brother Esau, and said, "Noble is the comfort with which you have come to comfort me for my wife who has died. Is this the oath that you swore to your father and again to your mother before they died? you have broken the oath, and on the moment that you swore to your father you were condemned." ¹⁸ And then Esau answered and said to him, "Neither the children of men nor the beasts of the earth have any oath of righteousness which in swearing they have sworn forever, but every day they devise evil against one another, and how each may slay his adversary and enemy. ¹⁹ And you hate me and my children forever. And there is no observing the tie of brotherhood with you. ²⁰ Hear these words which I declare to you, If the boar can change its skin and make its bristles as soft as wool, or if it can cause horns to sprout out on its head like the horns of a stag or of a sheep, then I will observe the tie of brotherhood with you. [[And if the breasts separated themselves from their mother; for you have not been a brother to me.]] ²¹ And if the wolves make peace with the lambs so as not to devour or do them violence, and if their hearts are toward them for good, then there will be peace in my heart toward you. ²² And if the lion

becomes the friend of the ox and makes peace with him, and if he is bound under one yoke with him and plows with him, then I will make peace with you. ²³ And when the raven becomes white as the râzâ, then know that I have loved you and will make peace with you. You will be rooted out, and your sons will be rooted out, and there will be no peace for you." ²⁴ And when Jacob saw that he was [so] evilly disposed toward him with [all] his heart and with all his soul as to slay him, and that he had come springing like the wild boar which comes on the spear that pierces and kills it, and does not recoil from it, ²⁵ then he spoke to his own and to his servants that they should attack him and all his companions.

CHAPTER 38

¹ And after that, Judah spoke to his father Jacob, and said to him, "Bend your bow, father, and send out your arrows, and cast down the adversary, and slay the enemy; and may you have the power, for we will not slay your brother, for he is such as you, and he is like you: let us give him [this] honor." ² Then Jacob bent his bow, and sent out the arrow, and struck his brother Esau [[on his right breast]], and slew him. ³ And again he sent out an arrow and struck ʿAdôrân the Aramaean, on the left breast, and drove him backward and slew him. ⁴ And then the sons of Jacob went out—they and their servants—dividing themselves into companies on the four sides of the tower. ⁵ And Judah went out in front, and Naphtali and Gad with him, and fifty servants with him on the south side of the tower, and they slew all they found before them, and not one individual of them escaped. ⁶ And Levi, and Dan, and Asher went out on the east side of the tower, and fifty [men] with them, and they slew the fighting men of Moab and Ammon. ⁷ And Reuben, and Issachar, and Zebulun went out on the north side of the tower, and fifty men with them, and they slew the fighting men of the Philistines. ⁸ And Simeon, and Benjamin, and Enoch, Reuben's son, went out on the west side of the tower, and fifty [men] with them, and they slew of Edom and of the Horites four hundred men, stout warriors; and six hundred fled, and four of the sons of Esau fled with them, and left their father lying slain, as he had fallen on the hill which is in ʿAdûram. ⁹ And the sons of Jacob pursued after them to the mountains of Seir. And Jacob buried his brother on the hill which is in ʿAdûram, and he returned to his house. ¹⁰ And the sons of Jacob pressed hard on the sons of Esau in the mountains of Seir and bowed their necks so that they became servants of the sons of Jacob. ¹¹ And they sent to their father [to inquire] whether they should make peace with them or slay them. ¹² And Jacob sent word to his sons that they should make peace, and they made peace with them, and placed the yoke of servitude on them, so that they always paid tribute to Jacob and to his sons. ¹³ And they continued to pay tribute to Jacob until the day that he went down into Egypt. ¹⁴ And the sons of Edom have not gotten rid of the yoke of servitude which the twelve sons of Jacob had imposed on them until this day. ¹⁵ And these are the kings that reigned in Edom, in the land of Edom, before any king reigned over the sons of Israel: ¹⁶ and Bâlâq, the son of Beor, reigned in Edom, and the name of his city was Danâbâ; ¹⁷ and Bâlâq died, and Jobab, the son of Zârâ of Bôsêr, reigned in his stead; ¹⁸ and Jobab died, and ʿAsâm, of the land of Têmân, reigned in his stead; ¹⁹ and ʿAsâm died, and ʿAdâth, the son of Barad, who slew Midian in the field of Moab, reigned in his stead, and the name of his city was Avith; ²⁰ and ʿAdâth died, and Salman, from ʿAmâsêqâ, reigned in his stead; ²¹ and Salman died, and Saul of Râʿabôth [by the] river, reigned in his stead; ²² and Saul died, and Baʿêlûnân, the son of Achbor, reigned in his stead; ²³ and Baʿêlûnân, the son of Achbor, died, and ʿAdâth reigned in his stead, and the name of his wife was Maiṭabîth, the daughter of Mâṭarat, the daughter of Mêtabêdzâʿab. ²⁴ These are the kings who reigned in the land of Edom.

CHAPTER 39

¹ And Jacob dwelt in the land of his father's sojournings in the land of Canaan. ² These are the generations of Jacob. And Joseph was seventeen years old when they took him down into the land of Egypt, and Potiphar, [[a eunuch of Pharaoh,]] the chief cook [[or chief executioner]] bought him. ³ And he set Joseph over all his house, and the blessing of the Lord came on the house of the Egyptian on account of Joseph, and the

Lord prospered him in all that he did. ⁴ And the Egyptian committed everything into the hands of Joseph, for he saw that the Lord was with him, and that the Lord prospered him in all that he did. ⁵ And Joseph's appearance was handsome, and his appearance was very beautiful, and his master's wife lifted up her eyes and saw Joseph, and she loved him, and implored him to lie with her. ⁶ But he did not surrender his soul, and he remembered the Lord and the words which his father Jacob used to read from among the words of Abraham, that no man should commit fornication with a woman who has a husband, that the punishment of death has been ordained in the heavens for him before the Highest God, and the sin will be continually recorded against him in the perpetual scrolls before the Lord. ⁷ And Joseph remembered these words and refused to lie with her. ⁸ And she implored him for a year, but he refused and would not listen. ⁹ But she embraced him and held him fast in the house in order to force him to lie with her, and she closed the doors of the house and held him fast, but he left his garment in her hands, and broke through the door, and fled outside from her presence. ¹⁰ And the woman saw that he would not lie with her, and she accused him in the presence of his lord, saying, "Your Hebrew servant, whom you love, sought to force me so that he might lie with me; and it came to pass when I lifted up my voice, that he fled and left his garment in my hands when I held him, and he broke through the door." ¹¹ And the Egyptian saw the garment of Joseph and the broken door, and heard the words of his wife, and cast Joseph into prison into the place where the prisoners were kept whom the king imprisoned. ¹² And he was there in the prison, and the Lord gave Joseph favor in the sight of the chief of the prison guards and compassion before him, for he saw that the Lord was with him, and that the Lord made all that he did to prosper. ¹³ And he committed all things into his hands, and the chief of the prison guards knew of nothing that was with him, for Joseph did everything, and the Lord perfected it. ¹⁴ And he remained there two years. And in those days Pharaoh, king of Egypt, was angry against his two eunuchs, against the chief butler and against the chief baker, and he put them in ward in the house of the chief cook, in the prison where Joseph was kept. ¹⁵ And the chief of the prison guards appointed Joseph to serve them; and he served before them. ¹⁶ And they both dreamed a dream, the chief butler and the chief baker, and they told it to Joseph. ¹⁷ And as he interpreted [the dreams] to them, so it befell them, and Pharaoh restored the chief butler to his office, and he slew the [chief] baker, as Joseph had interpreted to them. ¹⁸ But the chief butler forgot Joseph in the prison, although he had informed him what would befall him, and did not remember to inform Pharaoh how Joseph had told him, for he forgot.

CHAPTER 40

¹ And in those days Pharaoh dreamed two dreams in one night concerning a famine which was to be in all the land, and he awoke from his sleep and called all the interpreters of dreams that were in Egypt, and magicians, and told them his two dreams, and they were not able to declare [the interpretation]. ² And then the chief butler remembered Joseph and spoke of him to the king, and he brought him out from the prison, and he told his two dreams before him. ³ And he said before Pharaoh that his two dreams were one, and he said to him, "Seven years of plenty will come over all the land of Egypt, and after that, seven years of famine—such a famine as has not been in all the land. ⁴ And now let Pharaoh appoint overseers in all the land of Egypt, and let them store up food in every city throughout the days of the years of plenty, and there will be food for the seven years of famine, and the land will not perish through the famine, for it will be very severe." ⁵ And the Lord gave Joseph favor and mercy in the eyes of Pharaoh, and Pharaoh said to his servants, "We will not find such a wise and discreet man as this man, for the Spirit of the Lord is with him." ⁶ And he appointed him the second in all his kingdom and gave him authority over all Egypt, and caused him to ride in the second chariot of Pharaoh. ⁷ And he clothed him with flax garments, and he put a gold chain on his neck, and [a herald] proclaimed before him "'Êl ʿÊl waʿ Abîrĕr," and he placed a ring on his hand, and made him ruler over all his house, and magnified him, and said to him, "Only on the throne will I be greater than you." ⁸ And Joseph ruled over all the land of Egypt, and all the princes of Pharaoh, and all his servants, and all who did the king's business loved him, for he walked in

uprightness, for he was without pride and arrogance, and he had no respect of persons, and did not accept gifts, but he judged all the people of the land in uprightness. ⁹ And the land of Egypt was at peace before Pharaoh because of Joseph, for the Lord was with him, and gave him favor and mercy for all his generations before all those who knew him and those who heard concerning him, and Pharaoh's kingdom was well ordered, and there was no adversary and no evil person [therein]. ¹⁰ And the king called Joseph's name Sĕphântîphâns and gave Joseph the daughter of Potiphar to be [his] wife, the daughter of the priest of Heliopolis, the chief cook [[or chief executioner]]. ¹¹ And on the day that Joseph stood before Pharaoh, he was thirty years old. ¹² And in that year Isaac died. And it came to pass as Joseph had said in the interpretation of his two dreams, according as he had said it, there were seven years of plenty over all the land of Egypt, and the land of Egypt produced abundantly, one measure [producing] eighteen hundred measures. ¹³ And Joseph gathered food into every city until they were full of corn until they could no longer count and measure it for its multitude.

CHAPTER 41

¹ And in the forty-fifth jubilee, in the second week, [and] in the second year, Judah took a wife for his firstborn Er named Tamar, from the daughters of Aram. ² But he hated [her] and did not lie with her, because his mother was of the daughters of Canaan, and he wished to take a wife [for] himself of the countrymen of his mother, but his father Judah would not permit him. ³ And this Er, the firstborn of Judah, was wicked, and the Lord slew him. ⁴ And Judah said to his brother Onan, "Go in to your brother's wife and perform the duty of a husband's brother to her, and raise up seed to your brother." ⁵ And Onan knew that the seed would not be his, [but] his brother's only, and he went into the house of his brother's wife, and spilled the seed on the ground, and he was wicked in the eyes of the Lord, and He slew him. ⁶ And Judah said to his daughter-in-law Tamar, "Remain in your father's house as a widow until my son Shelah is grown up, and I will give you to him to be [his] wife." ⁷ And he grew up, but Bêdsû'êl, the wife of Judah, did not permit her son Shelah to marry. And Bêdsû'êl, the wife of Judah, died in the fifth year of this week. ⁸ And in the sixth year Judah went up to shear his sheep at Timnah. And they told Tamar, "Behold, your father-in-law goes up to Timnah to shear his sheep." ⁹ And she put off her widow's clothes, and put on a veil, and adorned herself, and sat in the gate adjoining the way to Timnah. ¹⁰ And as Judah was going along, he found her, and thought her to be a harlot, and he said to her, "Let me come in to you"; and she said to him, "Come in," and he went in. ¹¹ And she said to him, "Give me my hire"; and he said to her, "I have nothing in my hand except my ring that is on my finger, and my necklace, and my staff which is in my hand." ¹² And she said to him, "Give them to me until you send me my hire"; and he said to her, "I will send a kid of the goats to you"; and he gave them to her, [and he went in to her,] and she conceived by him. ¹³ And Judah went to his sheep, and she went to her father's house. ¹⁴ And Judah sent a kid of the goats by the hand of his shepherd, an Adullamite, and he did not find her; and he asked the people of the place, saying, "Where is the harlot who was here?" And they said to him, "There is no harlot here with us." ¹⁵ And he returned, and informed him, and said to him that he had not found her; "I asked the people of the place, and they said to me, There is no harlot here." And he said, "Let her keep [them] lest we become a cause of derision." ¹⁶ And when she had completed three months, it was manifest that she was with child, and they told Judah, saying, "Behold, your daughter-in-law Tamar is with child by whoredom." ¹⁷ And Judah went to the house of her father, and said to her father and her brothers, "Bring her out, and let them burn her, for she has worked uncleanness in Israel." ¹⁸ And it came to pass when they brought her out to burn her that she sent to her father-in-law the ring, and the necklace, and the staff, saying, "Discern whose these are, for I am with child by him." ¹⁹ And Judah acknowledged [them] and said, "Tamar is more righteous than I am. And therefore, let them not burn her." ²⁰ And for that reason she was not given to Shelah, and he did not approach her again. ²¹ And after that she bore two sons, Perez and Zerah, in the seventh year of this second week. ²² And immediately the seven years of fruitfulness of which Joseph spoke to Pharaoh were accomplished. ²³ And Judah

acknowledged that the deed which he had done was evil, for he had lain with his daughter-in-law, and he esteemed it hateful in his eyes, and he acknowledged that he had transgressed and gone astray, for he had uncovered the skirt of his son, and he began to lament and to supplicate before the Lord because of his transgression. ²⁴ And we told him in a dream that it was forgiven him because he supplicated earnestly, and lamented, and did not commit it again. ²⁵ And he received forgiveness because he turned from his sin and from his ignorance, for he greatly transgressed before our God; and everyone that acts this way, everyone who lies with his mother-in-law, let them burn him with fire that he may burn therein, for there is uncleanness and pollution on them; let them burn them with fire. ²⁶ And you command the sons of Israel that there is no uncleanness among them, for everyone who lies with his daughter-in-law or with his mother-in-law has worked uncleanness; let them burn the man who has lain with her with fire, and likewise the woman, and he will turn away wrath and punishment from Israel. ²⁷ And to Judah we said that his two sons had not lain with her, and for this reason his seed was established for a second generation and would not be rooted out. ²⁸ For in singleness of eye he had gone and sought for punishment, namely, according to the judgment of Abraham, which he had commanded his sons, Judah had sought to burn her with fire.

CHAPTER 42

¹ And in the first year of the third week of the forty-fifth jubilee the famine began to come into the land, and the rain refused to be given to the earth, for none fell whatsoever. ² And the earth grew barren, but in the land of Egypt there was food, for Joseph had gathered the seed of the land in the seven years of plenty and had preserved it. ³ And the Egyptians came to Joseph that he might give them food, and he opened the storehouses where the grain of the first year was, and he sold it to the people of the land for gold ⁴ [[Now the famine was very severe in the land of Canaan]], and Jacob heard that there was food in Egypt, and he sent his ten sons that they should procure food for him in Egypt, but he did not send Benjamin; and they arrived [in Egypt] among those that went [there.] ⁵ And Joseph recognized them, but they did not recognize him, and he spoke to them and questioned them, and he said to them, "Are you not spies, and have you not come to explore the approaches of the land?" And he put them in ward. ⁶ And after that, he set them free again, and detained Simeon alone, and sent off his nine brothers. ⁷ And he filled their sacks with corn, and he put their gold in their sacks, and they did not know. ⁸ And he commanded them to bring their younger brother, for they had told him their father was living and [also] their younger brother. ⁹ And they went up from the land of Egypt and they came to the land of Canaan; and they told their father all that had befallen them, and how the lord of the country had spoken roughly to them and had seized Simeon until they should bring Benjamin. ¹⁰ And Jacob said, "You have bereaved me of my children! Joseph is not, and Simeon is also not, and you will take Benjamin away. Your wickedness has come on me." ¹¹ And he said, "My son will not go down with you lest perhaps he falls sick, for their mother gave birth to two sons, and one has perished, and you will also take this one from me. If perhaps he took a fever on the road, you would bring down my old age with sorrow to death." ¹² For he saw that their money had been returned to each man in his sack, and for this reason he feared to send him. ¹³ And the famine increased and became severe in the land of Canaan, and in all lands except in the land of Egypt, for many of the children of the Egyptians had stored up their seed for food from the time when they saw Joseph gathering seed together, and putting it in storehouses, and preserving it for the years of famine. ¹⁴ And the people of Egypt fed themselves thereon during the first year of their famine. ¹⁵ But when Israel saw that the famine was very severe in the land and there was no deliverance, he said to his sons, "Go again, and procure food for us that we do not die." ¹⁶ And they said, "We will not go; unless our youngest brother goes with us, we will not go." ¹⁷ And Israel saw that if he did not send him with them, they should all perish by reason of the famine. ¹⁸ And Reuben said, "Give him into my hand, and if I do not bring him back to you, slay my two sons instead of his soul." And he said to him, "He will not go with you." ¹⁹ And Judah came near and said, "Send him with me, and if I do not bring him back to you, let me bear

the blame before you all the days of my life." **20** And he sent him with them in the second year of this week, on the first day of the month, and they came to the land of Egypt with all those who went, and [they had] presents in their hands: stacte, and almonds, and terebinth nuts, and pure honey. **21** And they went and stood before Joseph, and he saw his brother Benjamin, and he knew him, and said to them, "Is this your youngest brother?" And they said to him, "It is he." And he said, "The Lord be gracious to you, my son!" **22** And he sent him into his house, and he brought Simeon out to them, and he made a feast for them, and they presented the gift to him which they had brought in their hands. **23** And they ate before him and he gave them all a portion, but the portion of Benjamin was seven times larger than that of any of theirs. **24** And they ate, and drank, and arose, and remained with their donkeys. **25** And Joseph devised a plan whereby he might learn their thoughts as to whether thoughts of peace prevailed among them, and he said to the steward who was over his house: "Fill all their sacks with food, and return their money to them into their vessels, and my cup, the silver cup out of which I drink, put it in the sack of the youngest, and send them away."

CHAPTER 43

1 And he did as Joseph had told him and filled all their sacks for them with food, and put their money in their sacks, and put the cup in Benjamin's sack. **2** And early in the morning they departed, and it came to pass that, when they had gone from there, Joseph said to the steward of his house, "Pursue them, run and seize them, saying, For good you have repaid me with evil; you have stolen from me the silver cup out of which my lord drinks. And bring back their youngest brother to me, and fetch [him] quickly before I go out to my seat of judgment." **3** And he ran after them and said to them according to these words. **4** And they said to him, "God forbid that your servants should do this thing, and steal from the house of your lord any utensil, and also the money which we found in our sacks the first time, we, your servants, brought back from the land of Canaan. **5** How then should we steal any utensil? Behold, here we are and our sacks; search, and wherever you find the cup in the sack of any man among us, let him be slain, and we and our donkeys will serve your lord." **6** And he said to them, "Not so; the man with whom I find [it], him only will I take as a servant, and you will return to your house in peace." **7** And as he was searching in their vessels, beginning with the eldest and ending with the youngest, it was found in Benjamin's sack. **8** And they tore their garments, and loaded their donkeys, and returned to the city, and came to the house of Joseph, and they all bowed themselves on their faces to the ground before him. **9** And Joseph said to them, "You have done evil." And they said, "What will we say and how will we defend ourselves? Our lord has discovered the transgression of his servants; behold, we are the servants of our lord, and our donkeys also." **10** And Joseph said to them, "I also fear the Lord; as for you, go to your homes and let your brother be my servant, for you have done evil. Do you not know that a man delights in his cup as I with this cup? And yet you have stolen it from me." **11** And Judah said, "O my lord, please let your servant speak a word in my lord's ear; your servant's mother bore two brothers to our father; one went away and was lost, and has not been found, and he alone is left of his mother, and your servant, our father, loves him, and his life is also bound up with the life of this [youth]. **12** And it will come to pass, when we go to your servant, our father, and the youth is not with us, that he will die, and we will bring down our father with sorrow to death. **13** Now rather let me, your servant, abide instead of the boy as a bondsman to my lord, and let the youth go with his brothers, for I became a guarantee for him at the hand of your servant, our father, and if I do not bring him back, your servant will bear the blame to our father forever." **14** And Joseph saw that they were all in accord in goodness with one another, and he could not refrain himself, and he told them that he was Joseph. **15** And he conversed with them in the Hebrew tongue and fell on their neck and wept. But they did not recognize him, and they began to weep. **16** And he said to them, "Do not weep over me, but hurry and bring my father to me; and you see that it is my mouth that speaks, and the eyes of my brother Benjamin see. **17** For behold, this is the second year of the famine, and there are still five years without harvest, or fruit, of trees, or plowing. **18** Come down quickly, you and your households, so that you do not perish through the famine, and do not be

grieved for your possessions, for the Lord sent me before you to set things in order that many people might live. **19** And tell my father that I am still alive, and you, behold, you see that the Lord has made me as a father to Pharaoh, and ruler over his house and over all the land of Egypt. **20** And tell my father of all my glory, and all the riches and glory that the Lord has given Me." **21** And by the command of the mouth of Pharaoh he gave them chariots and provisions for the way, and he gave them all many-colored raiment[s] and silver. **22** And to their father he sent raiment, and silver, and ten donkeys which carried corn, and he sent them away. **23** And they went up and told their father that Joseph was alive and was measuring out corn to all the nations of the earth, and that he was ruler over all the land of Egypt. **24** And their father did not believe it, for he was beside himself in his mind, but when he saw the wagons which Joseph had sent, the life of his spirit revived, and he said, "It is enough for me if Joseph lives; I will go down and see him before I die."

CHAPTER 44

1 And Israel took his journey from Haran from his house on the new moon of the third month, and he went on the way of the Well of the Oath, and he offered a sacrifice to the God of his father Isaac on the seventh of this month. **2** And Jacob remembered the dream that he had seen at Bethel, and he feared to go down into Egypt. **3** And while he was thinking of sending word to Joseph to come to him, and that he would not go down, he remained there seven days, if perhaps he should see a vision as to whether he should remain or go down. **4** And he celebrated the harvest festival of the first-fruits with old grain, for in all the land of Canaan there was not [even] a handful of seed, for the famine was over all the beasts, and cattle, and birds, and also over man. **5** And on the sixteenth [day] the Lord appeared to him, and said to him, "Jacob, Jacob"; and he said, "Here I am." And He said to him, "I am the God of your fathers, the God of Abraham and Isaac; do not fear to go down into Egypt, for I will make of you a great nation there. **6** I will go down with you, and I will bring you up [again], and you will be buried in this land, and Joseph will put his hands on your eyes. Do not fear; go down into Egypt." **7** And his sons rose up, and his sons' sons, and they placed their father and their possessions on wagons. **8** And Israel rose up from the Well of the Oath on the sixteenth [day] of this third month, and he went to the land of Egypt. **9** And Israel sent Judah before him to his son Joseph to examine the land of Goshen, for Joseph had told his brothers that they should come and dwell there that they might be near him. **10** And this was the excellent [land] in the land of Egypt, and near to him, for all [of them] and also for the cattle. **11** And these are the names of the sons of Jacob who went into Egypt with their father Jacob: **12** Reuben, the firstborn of Israel; and these are the names of his sons: Enoch, and Pallu, and Hezron, and Carmi—five. **13** Simeon and his sons; and these are the names of his sons: Jemuel, and Jamin, and Ohad, and Jachin, and Zohar, and Shaul, the son of the Zephathite woman—seven. **14** Levi and his sons; and these are the names of his sons: Gershon, and Kohath, and Merari—four. **15** Judah and his sons; and these are the names of his sons: Shela, and Perez, and Zerah—four. **16** Issachar and his sons; and these are the names of his sons: Tola, and Phûa, and Jâsûb, and Shimron—five. **17** Zebulun and his sons; and these are the names of his sons: Sered, and Elon, and Jahleel—four. **18** And these are the sons of Jacob, and their sons, whom Leah bore to Jacob in Mesopotamia—six, and their one sister, Dinah. And all the souls of the sons of Leah, and their sons, who went with their father Jacob into Egypt, were twenty-nine, and their father Jacob being with them, they were thirty. **19** And the sons of Zilpah, Leah's handmaid, the wife of Jacob, whom she bore to Jacob: Gad and Asher. **20** And these are the names of their sons who went with him into Egypt: the sons of Gad: Ziphion, and Haggi, and Shuni, and Ezbon, [and Eri,] and Areli, and Arodi—eight. **21** And the sons of Asher: Imnah, and Ishvah, [and Ishvi], and Beriah, and Serah, their one sister—six. **22** All the souls were fourteen, and all those of Leah were forty-four. **23** And the sons of Rachel, the wife of Jacob: Joseph and Benjamin. **24** And there were born to Joseph in Egypt, before his father came into Egypt, those whom Asenath, daughter of Potiphar priest of Heliopolis, bore to him: Manasseh and Ephraim—three. **25** And the sons of Benjamin: Bela, and Becher, and Ashbel, Gera, and Naaman, and Ehi, and Rosh, and Muppim, and Huppim, and Ard—eleven. **26** And all the souls of Rachel were fourteen. **27** And the sons of Bilhah, the handmaid of Rachel, the wife of Jacob, whom she bore to Jacob, were Dan and Naphtali. **28** And these are the names of their sons who went with them into Egypt: and the sons of Dan were Hushim, and Sâmôn, and Asûdî, and ʻÎjâka, and Salômôn—six. **29** And they died the year in which they entered into Egypt, and there was left to Dan Hushim alone. **30** And these are the names of the sons of Naphtali: Jahziel, and Guni, and Jezer, and Shallum, and ʻÎv. **31** And ʻÎv, who was born after the years of famine, died in Egypt. **32** And all the souls of Rachel were twenty-six. **33** And all the souls of Jacob which went into Egypt were seventy souls. These are his children and his children's children, seventy in all; but five died in Egypt before Joseph and had no children. **34** And in the land of Canaan two sons of Judah died, Er and Onan, and they had no children, and the sons of Israel buried those who perished, and they were reckoned among the seventy nations.

CHAPTER 45

1 And Israel went into the country of Egypt, into the land of Goshen, on the new moon of the fourth month, in the second year of the third week of the forty-fifth jubilee. **2** And Joseph went to meet his father Jacob, to the land of Goshen, and he fell on his father's neck and wept. **3** And Israel said to Joseph, "Now let me die since I have seen you, and now may the Lord God of Israel be blessed, the God of Abraham and the God of Isaac who has not withheld His mercy and His grace from His servant Jacob. **4** It is enough for me that I have seen your face while I am yet alive; yes, the vision which I saw at Bethel is true. Blessed is the Lord my God forever and ever and blessed is His Name." **5** And Joseph and his brothers ate bread before their father and drank wine, and Jacob rejoiced with exceedingly great joy because he saw Joseph eating with his brothers and drinking before him, and he blessed the Creator of all things who had preserved him and had preserved his twelve sons for him. **6** And Joseph had given to his father and to his brothers as a gift the right of dwelling in the land of Goshen, and in Rameses, and all the surrounding region, which he ruled over before Pharaoh. And Israel and his sons dwelt in the land of Goshen, the best part of the land of Egypt; and Israel was one hundred and thirty years old when he came into Egypt, **7** and Joseph nourished his father, and his brothers, and also their possessions with as much bread as they needed for the seven years of the famine. **8** And the land of Egypt suffered by reason of the famine, and Joseph acquired all the land of Egypt for Pharaoh in return for food, and he got possession of the people, and their cattle, and everything for Pharaoh. **9** And the years of the famine were accomplished, and Joseph gave seed and food to the people in the land that they might sow in the eighth year, for the river had overflowed all the land of Egypt. **10** For in the seven years of the famine it had not overflowed and had irrigated only a few places on the banks of the river, but now it overflowed, and the Egyptians sowed the land, and it bore much corn that year. **11** And this was the first year of the fourth week of the forty-fifth jubilee. **12** And Joseph took the fifth part of the corn of the harvest for the king and left four parts for them for food and for seed, and Joseph made it an ordinance for the land of Egypt until this day. **13** And Israel lived in the land of Egypt [for] seventeen years, and all the days which he lived were three jubilees, one hundred and forty-seven years, and he died in the fourth year of the fifth week of the forty-fifth jubilee. **14** And Israel blessed his sons before he died and told them everything that would befall them in the land of Egypt; and he made known to them what would come on them in the last days, and blessed them, and gave two portions to Joseph in the land. **15** And he slept with his fathers, and he was buried in the double cave in the land of Canaan, near his father Abraham in the grave which he dug for himself in the double cave in the land of Hebron. **16** And he gave all his scrolls and the scrolls of his fathers to his son Levi that he might preserve them and renew them for his children until this day.

CHAPTER 46

1 And it came to pass that after Jacob died, the sons of Israel multiplied in the land of Egypt, and they became a great nation, and they were of one accord in heart, so that brother loved brother and every man helped his brother, and they increased abundantly and multiplied exceedingly [for] ten weeks of years, all the days of the life of Joseph. **2** And there was no adversary nor any evil all the days of the life of Joseph which he lived after his father Jacob, for all the Egyptians honored the sons of Israel all the days of the life of Joseph. **3** And Joseph died being one hundred and ten years old; he lived seventeen years in the land of Canaan, and he was a servant [for] ten years, and [he was] in prison [for] three years, and he was under the king [for] eighty years, ruling all the land of Egypt. **4** And he died, and all his brothers, and all that generation. **5** And he commanded the sons of Israel before he died that they should carry his bones with them when they went out from the land of Egypt. **6** And he made them swear regarding his bones, for he knew that the Egyptians would not again bring out and bury him in the land of Canaan, for Mâkamârôn, king of Canaan, while dwelling in the land of Assyria, fought in the valley with the king of Egypt and slew him there, and pursued after the Egyptians to the gates of ʻÊrmôn. **7** But he was not able to enter, for another, a new king, had become king of Egypt, and he was stronger than he, and he returned to the land of Canaan, and the gates of Egypt were closed, and none went out and none came into Egypt. **8** And Joseph died in the forty-sixth jubilee, in the sixth week, in the second year, and they buried him in the land of Egypt, and his brothers died after him. **9** And the king of Egypt went out to war with the king of Canaan in the forty-seventh jubilee, in the second week in the second year, and the sons of Israel brought out all the bones of the children of Jacob save the bones of Joseph, and they buried them in the field in the double cave in the mountain. **10** And most [of them] returned to Egypt, but a few of them remained in the mountains of Hebron, and your father Amram remained with them. **11** And the king of Canaan was victorious over the king of Egypt, and he closed the gates of Egypt. **12** And he devised an evil scheme against the sons of Israel of afflicting them; and he said to the people of Egypt, **13** "Behold, the people of the sons of Israel have increased and multiplied more than we. Come and let us deal wisely with them before they become too many, and let us afflict them with slavery before war comes on us and before they, too, fight against us, otherwise they will join themselves to our enemies; and get them out of our land, for their hearts and faces are toward the land of Canaan." **14** And he set taskmasters over them to afflict them with slavery; and they built strong cities for Pharaoh, Pithom and Raamses, and they built all the walls and all the fortifications which had fallen in the cities of Egypt. **15** And they made them serve with rigor, and the more they dealt evilly with them, the more they increased and multiplied. **16** And the people of Egypt despised the sons of Israel.

CHAPTER 47

1 And in the seventh week, in the seventh year, in the forty-seventh jubilee, your father went out from the land of Canaan, and you were born in the fourth week, in the sixth year thereof, in the forty-eighth jubilee; this was the time of tribulation on the sons of Israel. **2** And Pharaoh, king of Egypt, issued a command regarding them that they should cast all their male children which were born into the river. **3** And they cast them in for seven months until the day that you were born. And your mother hid you for three months, and they told [the Egyptians] regarding her. **4** And she made an ark for you, and covered it with pitch and asphalt, and placed it in the flags on the bank of the river, and she placed you in it [for] seven days, and your mother came by night and suckled you, and by day your sister Miriam guarded you from the birds. **5** And in those days Tharmuth, the daughter of Pharaoh, came to bathe in the river, and she heard your voice crying, and she told her maidens to bring you out, and they brought you to her. **6** And she took you out of the ark, and she had compassion on you. **7** And your sister said to her, "Will I go and call to you one of the Hebrew women to nurse and suckle this baby for you?" And she said, "Go." **8** And she went and called your mother Jochebed, and she gave her wages, and she nursed you. **9** And afterward, when you were grown up, they brought you to the daughter of Pharaoh, and you became her son, and your father Amram taught you writing, and after you had completed three weeks, they brought you into the royal court. **10** And you were three weeks of years at court until the time when you went out from the royal court and saw an Egyptian striking your friend who was of the sons of Israel, and you slew him and hid him in the sand. **11** And on the second day you found two of the sons of Israel striving together, and you said to him who was doing the wrong: "Why do you strike your brother?" **12** And he was angry and indignant, and said, "Who made you a prince and a judge over us? Do you think to kill me as you killed the Egyptian yesterday?" And you were afraid and fled on account of these words.

CHAPTER 48

1 And in the sixth year of the third week of the forty-ninth jubilee you departed and dwelt in the land of Midian [for] five weeks and one year. And you returned into Egypt in the second week, in the second year, in the fiftieth jubilee. **2** And you yourself know what He spoke to you on Mount Sinai, and what prince Mastêmâ desired to do with you when you were returning into Egypt on the way when you met him at the lodging-place. **3** Did he not, with all his power, seek to slay you and deliver the Egyptians out of your hand when he saw that you were sent to execute judgment and vengeance on the Egyptians? **4** And I delivered you out of his hand, and you performed the signs and wonders which you were sent to perform in Egypt against Pharaoh, and against all his house, and against his servants and his people. **5** And the Lord executed a great vengeance on them for Israel's sake, and struck them through blood and frogs, lice and biting flies, and malignant boils breaking out in blisters, and their cattle by death, and by hailstones, thereby He destroyed everything that grew for them, and by locusts which devoured the residue which had been left by the hail, and by darkness, and [by the death] of the firstborn of men and animals, and on all their idols the Lord took vengeance and burned them with fire. **6** And everything was sent through your hand, that you should declare [these things] before they were done, and you spoke with the king of Egypt before all his servants and before his people. **7** And everything took place according to your words; ten great and terrible judgments came on the land of Egypt that you might execute vengeance on it for Israel. **8** And the Lord did everything for Israel's sake, and according to His covenant, which He had ordained with Abraham that He would take vengeance on them as they had brought them into bondage by force. **9** And the prince of the Mastêmâ stood up against you and sought to cast you into the hands of Pharaoh, and he helped the Egyptian sorcerers, and they stood up and worked before you. **10** We indeed permitted them to work the evils, but we did not allow the remedies to be worked by their hands. **11** And the Lord struck them with malignant ulcers, and they were not able to stand, for we destroyed them so that they could not perform a single sign. **12** And notwithstanding all [these] signs and wonders, the prince of the Mastêmâ was not put to shame because he took courage and cried to the Egyptians to pursue after you with all the powers of the Egyptians, with their chariots, and with their horses, and with all the hosts of the peoples of Egypt. **13** And I stood between the Egyptians and Israel, and we delivered Israel out of his hand, and out of the hand of his people, and the Lord brought them through the midst of the sea as if it were dry land. **14** And all the peoples whom he brought to pursue after Israel, the Lord our God cast them into the midst of the sea, into the depths of the abyss beneath the sons of Israel, even as the people of Egypt had cast their children into the river. He took vengeance on one million of them, and one thousand strong and energetic men were destroyed on account of one suckling of the children of your people which they had thrown into the river. **15** And on the fourteenth day, and on the fifteenth, and on the sixteenth, and on the seventeenth, and on the eighteenth, the prince of the Mastêmâ was bound and imprisoned behind the sons of Israel that he might not accuse them. **16** And on the nineteenth [day] we let them loose that they might help the Egyptians and pursue the sons of Israel. **17** And He hardened their hearts and made them stubborn, and the device was devised by the Lord our God that He might strike the Egyptians and cast them into the sea. **18** And on the fourteenth [day] we bound him that he might not accuse the sons of Israel on the day when they asked the Egyptians for vessels and garments, vessels of silver, and vessels of gold, and vessels of bronze, in order to despoil the Egyptians in return for the bondage in which they had forced them to serve. **19** And we did not lead out the sons of Israel from Egypt empty-handed.

CHAPTER 49

1 Remember the command which the Lord commanded you concerning the Passover, that you should celebrate it in its season on the fourteenth of the first month, that you should kill it before it is evening, and that they should eat it by night on the evening of the fifteenth from the time of the setting of the sun. **2** For on this night—the beginning of the festival and the beginning of the joy—you were eating the Passover in Egypt, when all the powers of Mastêmâ had been let loose to slay all the firstborn in the land of Egypt, from the firstborn of Pharaoh to the firstborn of the captive maidservant in the mill, and to the cattle. **3** And this is the sign which the Lord gave them: into every house on the lintels of which they saw the blood of a lamb of the first year, into [that] house they should not enter to slay, but should pass by [it], that all those should be saved that were in the house because the sign of the blood was on its lintels. **4** And the powers of the Lord did everything according as the Lord commanded them, and they passed by all the sons of Israel, and the plague did not come on them to destroy any soul from among them, either of cattle, or man, or dog. **5** And the plague was very grievous in Egypt, and there was no house in Egypt where there was not someone dead, and weeping, and lamentation. **6** And all Israel was eating the flesh of the Passover lamb, and drinking the wine, and was lauding and blessing, and giving thanks to the Lord God of their fathers, and was ready to go out from under the yoke of Egypt and from the evil bondage. **7** And remember this day all the days of your life and observe it from year to year all the days of your life, once a year, on its day, according to all the law thereof, and do not adjourn [it] from day to day, or from month to month. **8** For it is a perpetual ordinance and engraved on the heavenly tablets regarding all the sons of Israel that they should observe it every year, on its day, once a year, throughout all their generations; and there is no limit of days, for this is ordained forever. **9** And the man who is free from uncleanness and does not come to observe it on occasion of its day so as to bring an acceptable offering before the Lord, and to eat and to drink before the Lord on the day of its festival, that man who is clean and close at hand will be cut off, because he did not offer the oblation of the Lord in its appointed season; he will take the guilt on himself. **10** Let the sons of Israel come and observe the Passover on the day of its fixed time, on the fourteenth day of the first month, between the evenings, from the third part of the day to the third part of the night, for two portions of the day are given to the light, and a third part to the evening. **11** That is that which the Lord commanded you that you should observe it between the evenings. **12** And it is not permissible to slay it during any period of the light, but during the period bordering on the evening, and let them eat it at the time of the evening until the third part of the night, and whatever is leftover of all its flesh from the third part of the night and onwards, let them burn it with fire. **13** And they will not cook it with water, nor will they eat it raw, but roast on the fire: they will eat it with diligence, its head with the inwards thereof and its feet they will roast with fire, and not break any bone thereof, for no bone of the sons of Israel will be crushed. **14** For this reason the Lord commanded the sons of Israel to observe the Passover on the day of its fixed time, and they will not break a bone thereof, for it is a festival day, and a day commanded, and there may be no passing over from day to day, and month to month, but on the day of its festival let it be observed. **15** And command the sons of Israel to observe the Passover throughout their days, every year, once a year on the day of its fixed time, and it will come for a memorial well pleasing before the Lord, and no plague will come on them to slay or to strike that year in which they celebrate the Passover in its season in every respect according to His command. **16** And they will not eat it outside the sanctuary of the Lord, but before the sanctuary of the Lord, and all the people of the congregation of Israel will celebrate it in its appointed season. **17** And every man who has come on its day will eat it in the sanctuary of your God before the Lord from twenty years old and upward, for thus it is written and ordained that they should eat it in the sanctuary of the Lord. **18** And when the sons of Israel come into the land which they are to possess, into the land of Canaan, and set up the Dwelling Place of the Lord in the midst of the land in one of their tribes until the sanctuary of the Lord has been built in the land, let them come and celebrate the Passover in the midst of the Dwelling Place of the Lord, and let them slay it before the Lord from year to year. **19** And in the days when the house has been built in the Name of the Lord in the land of their inheritance, they will go there and slay the Passover in the evening, at sunset, at the third part of the day. **20** And they will offer its blood on the threshold of the altar and will place its fat on the fire which is on the altar, and they will eat its flesh roasted with fire in the court of the house which has been sanctified in the Name of the Lord. **21** And they may not celebrate the Passover in their cities, nor in any place except before the Dwelling Place of the Lord, or before His house where His Name has dwelt; and they will not go astray from the Lord. **22** And you, Moses: command the sons of Israel to observe the ordinances of the Passover, as it was commanded to you; declare to them every year and the day of its days, and the festival of unleavened bread, that they should eat unleavened bread [for] seven days, [and] that they should observe its festival, and that they bring an oblation every day during those seven days of joy before the Lord on the altar of your God. **23** For you celebrated this festival when you went out from Egypt until you entered into the wilderness of Shur, for you completed it on the shore of the sea.

CHAPTER 50

1 And after this law I made known to you the days of the Sabbaths in the wilderness of Zin, which is between Elim and Sinai. **2** And I told you of the Sabbaths of the land on Mount Sinai, and I told you of the jubilee years in the Sabbaths of years, but the year thereof I have not told you until you enter the land which you are to possess. **3** And the land will also keep its Sabbaths while they dwell on it, and they will know the jubilee year. **4** For that reason I have ordained for you the year-weeks, and the years, and the jubilees: there are forty-nine jubilees from the days of Adam until this day, and one week and two years, and there are yet forty years more for learning the commands of the Lord, until they pass over into the land of Canaan, crossing the Jordan to the west. **5** And the jubilees will pass by, until Israel is cleansed from all guilt of fornication, and uncleanness, and pollution, and sin, and error, and dwells with confidence in all the land, and there will no longer be an adversary or any evil one, and the land will be clean from that time forevermore. **6** And behold, the command regarding the Sabbaths—I have written [them] down for you and all the judgments of its laws. **7** Six days you will labor, but on the seventh day is the Sabbath of the Lord your God. In it you will do no manner of work—you, and your sons, and your menservants, and your maidservants, and all your cattle, and the sojourner who is also with you. **8** And the man that does any work on it will die: whoever desecrates that day, whoever lies with [his] wife, or whoever says he will do something on it, that he will set out on a journey thereon in regard to any buying or selling, and whoever draws water thereon which he had not prepared for himself on the sixth day, and whoever takes up any burden to carry it out of his tent or out of his house will die. **9** You will do no work whatsoever on the Sabbath day except [to utilize] what you have prepared for yourselves on the sixth day, so as to eat, and drink, and rest, and keep Sabbath from all work on that day, and to bless the Lord your God who has given you a day of festival, and a holy day; and a day of the holy kingdom for all Israel is this day among their days forever. **10** For great is the honor which the Lord has given to Israel that they should eat, and drink, and be satisfied on this festival day, and rest thereon from all labor which belongs to the labor of the children of men, except burning frankincense and bringing oblations and sacrifices before the Lord for days and for Sabbaths. **11** Only this work will be done on the Sabbaths in the sanctuary of the Lord your God, that they may atone for Israel with sacrifice continually from day to day for a memorial well-pleasing before the Lord, and that He may always receive them from day to day according as you have been commanded. **12** And every man who does any work thereon, or goes on a journey, or tills [his] farm, whether in his house or any other place, and whoever lights a fire, or rides on any beast, or travels by ship on the sea, and whoever strikes or kills anything, or slaughters a beast or a bird, or whoever catches an animal, or a bird, or a fish, or whoever fasts or makes war on the Sabbaths: **13** the man who does any of these things on the Sabbath will die, so that the sons of Israel will observe the Sabbaths according to the commands regarding the Sabbaths of the land, as it is written in the tablets, which He gave into My hands that I should write out for you—the laws

of the seasons and the seasons according to the division of their days. The account of the division of the days is completed.

1 ENOCH

The Book of Enoch (also called 1 Enoch) is an ancient Jewish religious work, ascribed by tradition to Enoch, the great-grandfather of Noah. Enoch contains unique material on the origins of supernatural demons and giants, why some messengers fell from Heaven, an explanation of why the Great Flood was morally necessary, and prophetic exposition of the thousand-year reign of the Messiah. It is wholly extant only in the Ge'ez language, with Aramaic fragments from the Dead Sea Scrolls and a few Greek and Latin fragments. Jude 1:14–15 is a direct quote of Enoch 1:9 (see also 1 Enoch 60:8). Enoch is composed of five sections.

SECTION 1: THE BOOK OF THE WATCHERS

CHAPTER 1

1 The words of the blessing of Enoch, with which he blessed the chosen ones and righteous, who will be living in the day of tribulation, when all the wicked and godless are to be removed. **2** And he took up his allegory and spoke—Enoch a righteous man, whose eyes were opened by God, saw the vision of the Holy One in the heavens, which the messengers showed me, and from them I heard everything, and from them I understood as I saw, but not for this generation, but for a remote one which is to come. **3** Concerning the chosen ones, I spoke and took up my allegory concerning them: The Holy Great One will come out from His dwelling, **4** And the perpetual God will tread on the earth, [even] on Mount Sinai, || And appear in the strength of His might from the Heaven of heavens. **5** And all will be smitten with fear, || And the Watchers will quake, || And great fear and trembling will seize them to the ends of the earth. **6** And the high mountains will be shaken, || And the high hills will be made low || And will melt like wax before the flame, **7** And the earth will be wholly split apart, || And all that is on the earth will perish, || And there will be a judgment on all [men]. **8** But with the righteous He will make peace, || And will protect the chosen ones, || And mercy will be on them. And they will all belong to God, || And they will be prospered, || And they will all be blessed. And He will help them all, || And light will appear to them, || And He will make peace with them. **9** And behold, He comes with myriads of His holy ones || And to destroy all the ungodly || And to convict all flesh of all the works of their ungodliness which they have ungodly committed, || And of all the hard things which ungodly sinners have spoken against Him.

CHAPTER 2

1 Observe everything that takes place in the heavens, how they do not change their orbits, and the luminaries which are in the heavens, how they all rise and set in order, each in its season, and do not transgress against their appointed order. **2** Behold the earth and give heed to the things which take place on it from first to last, how steadfast they are, how none of the things on earth change, but all the works of God appear to you. **3** Behold the summer and the winter, how the whole earth is filled with water, and clouds, and dew, and rain lie on it.

CHAPTER 3

1 Observe and see how [in the winter] all the trees seem

as though they had withered and shed all their leaves, 2 except fourteen trees, which do not lose their foliage but retain the old foliage from two to three years until the new comes.

CHAPTER 4

1 And again, observe the days of summer, how the sun is above the earth—over against it. 2 And you seek shade and shelter by reason of the heat of the sun, and the earth also burns with growing heat, and so you cannot tread on the earth, or on a rock by reason of its heat.

CHAPTER 5

1 Observe how the trees cover themselves with green leaves and bear fruit; for what reason, take heed and know with regard to all His works and recognize how He that lives forever has made them so. 2 And all His works go on like this from year to year forever, and all the tasks which they accomplish for Him, and their tasks do not change, but according as God has ordained so it is done. 3 And behold how the sea and the rivers accomplish [their tasks] in like manner and do not change their tasks from His commands. 4 But you have not been steadfast, || Nor done the commands of the Lord, || But you have turned away and spoken proud and hard words || With your impure mouths against His greatness. O you hard-hearted! You will find no peace. 5 Therefore you will execrate your days, || And the years of your life will perish, || And the years of your destruction will be multiplied in continuous execration, || And you will find no mercy. 6 In those days you will make your names a continuous execration to all the righteous, || And by you will all who curse, curse, || And all the sinners and godless will imprecate by you, || And for you, the godless, there will be a curse. And all the [righteous] will rejoice, || And there will be forgiveness of sins, || And every mercy, and peace, and forbearance: There will be salvation to them, an excellent light. And for all of you sinners there will be no salvation, || But a curse will abide on all of you. 7 But for the chosen ones there will be light, and joy, and peace, || And they will inherit the earth. 8 And then wisdom will be bestowed on the chosen ones, || And they will all live and never again sin, || Either through ungodliness or through pride, || But they who are wise will be humble. 9 And they will not transgress again, || Nor will they sin all the days of their life, || Nor will they die of [the divine] anger or wrath, || But they will complete the number of the days of their life. And their lives will be increased in peace, || And the years of their joy will be multiplied, || In continuous gladness and peace, all the days of their life.

CHAPTER 6

1 And it came to pass when the children of men had multiplied that in those days were born to them beautiful and attractive daughters. 2 And the messengers, the children of the heavens, saw and lusted after them, and said to one another, "Come, let us choose wives [for] ourselves from among the children of men and beget children [for] ourselves." 3 And Semjaza, who was their leader, said to them, "Indeed, I fear you will not agree to do this deed, and I alone will have to pay the penalty of a great sin." 4 And they all answered him and said, "Let us all swear an oath, and all bind ourselves by mutual imprecations not to abandon this plan but to do this thing." 5 Then they all swore together and bound themselves by mutual imprecations on it. 6 And they were two hundred in all who descended in the days of Jared on the summit of Mount Hermon, and they called it Mount Hermon, because they had sworn and bound themselves by mutual imprecations on it. 7 And these are the names of their leaders: their leader Semjaza, [and] Araklba, Rameel, Kokablel, Tamlel, Ramlel, Danel, Ezeqeel, Baraqijal, Asael, Armaros, Batarel, Ananel, Zaqiel, Samsapeel, Satarel, Turel, Jomjael, [and] Sariel. 8 These are their chiefs of tens.

CHAPTER 7

1 And all the others took wives to themselves together with them, and each chose one for himself, and they began to go in to them and to defile themselves with them, and they taught them charms and enchantments, and the cutting of roots, and made them acquainted with plants. 2 And they became pregnant, and they bore great giants, whose height was [[three thousand ells]], 3 who consumed all the acquisitions of men. And when men could no longer sustain them, 4 the giants turned against them and devoured mankind. 5 And they began to sin against birds, and beasts, and reptiles, and fish, and to devour one another's flesh, and drink the blood. 6 Then the earth laid accusation against the lawless ones.

CHAPTER 8

1 And Azazel taught men to make swords, and knives, and shields, and breastplates, and made known to them the metals of the earth and the craft of working them, and bracelets, and ornaments, and the use of antimony, and the beautifying of the eyelids, and all kinds of costly stones, and all coloring tinctures. 2 And there arose much godlessness, and they committed fornication, and they were led astray, and became corrupt in all their ways. 3 Semjaza taught enchantments and root-cuttings, 'Armaros the resolving of enchantments, Baraqijal [taught] astrology, Kokabel the constellations, Ezeqeel the knowledge of the clouds, Araqiel the signs of the earth, Shamsiel the signs of the sun, and Sariel the course of the moon. And as men perished, they cried, and their cry went up to Heaven.

CHAPTER 9

1 And then Michael, Uriel, Raphael, and Gabriel looked down from Heaven and saw much blood being shed on the earth, and all lawlessness being worked on the earth. 2 And they said to one another, "The earth made without inhabitant cries the voice of their crying up to the gates of Heaven." 3 And now to you, the holy ones of Heaven, the souls of men make their suit, saying, "Bring our cause before the Most High." 4 And they said to the Lord of the ages, "Lord of lords, God of gods, King of kings, and God of the ages, the throne of Your glory stands to all the generations of the ages, and Your Name [is] holy, and glorious, and blessed to all the ages! 5 You have made all things and have power over all things: and all things are naked and open in Your sight, and You see all things, and nothing can hide itself from You. 6 You see what Azazel has done, who has taught all unrighteousness on earth and revealed the perpetual secrets which were [preserved] in Heaven, which men were striving to learn— 7 and Semjaza, to whom You have given authority to bear rule over his associates. 8 And they have gone to the daughters of men on the earth, and have slept with the women, and have defiled themselves, and revealed to them all kinds of sins. 9 And the women have borne giants, and the whole earth has thereby been filled with blood and unrighteousness. 10 And now, behold, the souls of those who have died are crying and making their suit to the gates of Heaven, and their lamentations have ascended, and they cannot cease because of the lawless deeds which are worked on the earth. 11 And You know all things before they come to pass, and You see these things and You permit them, and You do not say to us what we are to do to them in regard to these."

CHAPTER 10

1 Then the Most High uttered, the Holy and Great One spoke, and sent Uriel to the son of Lamech, and said to him: 2 "Go to Noah and tell him in My Name: Hide yourself! And reveal to him the end that is approaching, that the whole earth will be destroyed, and a deluge is about to come on the whole earth and will destroy all that is on it. 3 And now instruct him that he may escape and his seed may be preserved for all the generations of the world." 4 And again, the Lord said to Raphael, "Bind Azazel hand and foot and cast him into the darkness, and make an opening in the desert, which is in Dudael, and cast him therein. 5 And place rough and jagged rocks over him, and cover him with darkness, and let him abide there forever, and cover his face that he may not see light. 6

And on the Day of the Great Judgment he will be cast into the fire. **7** And heal the earth which the messengers have corrupted, and proclaim the healing of the earth, that they may heal the plague, and that all the children of men may not perish through all the secret things that the Watchers have disclosed and have taught their sons. **8** And the whole earth has been corrupted through the works that were taught by Azazel: to him ascribe all sin." **9** And to Gabriel the Lord said, "Proceed against the bastards and the reprobates, and against the children of fornication, and destroy the children of the Watchers from among men. Send them against one another that they may destroy each other in battle, for they will not have length of days. **10** And no request that they make of you will be granted to their fathers on their behalf, for they hope to live a continuous life, and that each one of them will live five hundred years." **11** And the Lord said to Michael, "Go, bind Semjaza and his associates who have united themselves with women so as to have defiled themselves with them in all their uncleanness. **12** And when their sons have slain one another, and they have seen the destruction of their beloved ones, bind them fast for seventy generations in the valleys of the earth, until the day of their judgment and of their consummation, until the judgment that is forever and ever is consummated. **13** In those days they will be led off to the abyss of fire, and to the torment and the prison in which they will be confined forever. **14** And whoever will be condemned and destroyed will from then on be bound together with them to the end of all generations. **15** And destroy all the spirits of the reprobate and the children of the Watchers, because they have wronged mankind. **16** Destroy all wrong from the face of the earth and let every evil work come to an end; and let the plant of righteousness and truth appear: and it will prove a blessing; the works of righteousness and truth will be planted in truth and joy forevermore. **17** And then all the righteous will escape and will live until they beget thousands of children, and they will complete all the days of their youth and their old age in peace. **18** And then the whole earth will be tilled in righteousness and will all be planted with trees and be full of blessing. **19** And all desirable trees will be planted on it, and they will plant vines on it, and the vine which they plant thereon will yield wine in abundance. And as for all the seed which is sown thereon, each measure [of it] will bear one thousand, and each measure of olives will yield ten presses of oil. **20** And you will cleanse the earth from all oppression, and from all unrighteousness, and from all sin, and from all godlessness: and destroy all the uncleanness that is worked on the earth from off the earth. **21** And all the children of men will become righteous, and all nations will offer adoration and will praise Me, and all will worship Me. **22** And the earth will be cleansed from all defilement, and from all sin, and from all punishment, and from all torment, and I will never again send [them] on it from generation to generation and forever."

CHAPTER 11

1 "And in those days I will open the store chambers of blessing which are in the heavens, so as to send them down on the earth over the work and labor of the children of men. **2** And truth and peace will be associated together throughout all the days of the world and throughout all the generations of men."

CHAPTER 12

1 Before these things Enoch was hidden, and no one of the children of men knew where he was hidden, and where he dwelt, and what had become of him. **2** And his activities had to do with the Watchers, and his days were with the holy ones. **3** And I, Enoch, was blessing the Lord of majesty and the King of the ages, and the Watchers called me—Enoch the scribe—and said to me, **4** "Enoch, you scribe of righteousness, go, declare to the Watchers of the heavens who have left the high Heaven, the holy perpetual place, and have defiled themselves with women, and have done as the children of earth do, and have taken wives to themselves: **5** You have worked great destruction on the earth, and you will have no peace nor forgiveness of sin; **6** and inasmuch as they delight themselves in their children, they will see the murder of their beloved ones, and they will lament over the destruction of their children, and will make supplication continuously; but you will not attain

mercy and peace."

CHAPTER 13

1 And Enoch went and said, "Azazel, you will have no peace: a severe sentence has gone out against you to put you in bonds, **2** and you will not have toleration nor request granted to you, because of the unrighteousness which you have taught, and because of all the works of godlessness, and unrighteousness, and sin which you have shown to men." **3** Then I went and spoke to them all together, and they were all afraid, and fear and trembling seized them. **4** And they implored me to draw up a petition for them that they might find forgiveness, and to read their petition in the presence of the Lord of Heaven. **5** For from that point forward they could not speak [with Him] nor lift up their eyes to Heaven for shame of their sins for which they had been condemned. **6** Then I wrote out their petition, and the prayer in regard to their spirits and their deeds individually, and in regard to their requests that they should have forgiveness and length. **7** And I went off and sat down at the waters of Dan, in the land of Dan, to the south of the west of Hermon, [and there] I read their petition until I fell asleep. **8** And behold, a dream came to me, and visions fell down on me, and I saw visions of discipline, and a voice came bidding me to tell it to the sons of Heaven and reprimand them. **9** And when I awoke, I came to them, and they were all sitting gathered together, weeping in 'Abelsjail, which is between Lebanon and Seneser, with their faces covered. **10** And I recounted before them all the visions which I had seen in sleep, and I began to speak the words of righteousness, and to reprimand the heavenly Watchers.

CHAPTER 14

1 The Scroll of the Words of Righteousness, and of the reprimand of the perpetual Watchers in accordance with the command of the Holy Great One in that vision. **2** I saw in my sleep what I will now say with a tongue of flesh and with the breath of my mouth, which the Great One has given to men to converse with and understand with the heart. **3** As He has created and given to man the power of understanding, the word of wisdom, so He has also created me and given me the power of reprimanding the Watchers, the children of Heaven. **4** I wrote out your petition, and in my vision it appeared like this, that your petition will not be granted to you throughout all the days of the age, and that judgment has been finally passed on you: yes, [your petition] will not be granted to you. **5** And from now on you will not ascend into Heaven for all ages, and in bonds of the earth the decree has gone out to bind you for all the days of the world. **6** And you will have seen the destruction of your beloved sons beforehand and you will have no pleasure in them, but they will fall before you by the sword. **7** And your petition on their behalf will not be granted, nor yet on your own, even though you weep, and pray, and speak all the words contained in the writing which I have written. **8** And the vision was shown to me like this: behold, in the vision clouds invited me and a mist summoned me, and the course of the stars and the lightnings sped toward me, and the winds in the vision caused me to fly and lifted me upward and bore me into Heaven. **9** And I went in until I drew near to a wall which is built of crystals and surrounded by tongues of fire: and it began to frighten me. **10** And I went into the tongues of fire and drew near to a large house which was built of crystals: and the walls of the house were like a tessellated floor [made] of crystals, and its groundwork was of crystal. **11** Its ceiling was like the path of the stars and the lightnings, and between them were fiery cherubim, and their heaven was [as clear as] water. **12** A flaming fire surrounded the walls, and its portals blazed with fire. **13** And I entered into that house, and it was hot as fire and cold as ice: **14** there were no delights of life therein; fear covered me, and trembling took hold of me. **15** And as I quaked and trembled, I fell on my face. And I beheld a vision, and behold, there was a second house, greater than the former, and the entire portal stood open before me, and it was built of flames of fire. **16** And in every respect it so excelled in splendor, and magnificence, and extent that I cannot describe to you its splendor and its extent. **17** And its floor was of fire, and above it were lightnings and the path of the stars, and its ceiling was also flaming fire. **18** And I looked and saw a lofty throne therein:

its appearance was as crystal, and the wheels thereof as the shining sun, and there was the vision of cherubim. **19** And from underneath the throne came streams of flaming fire so that I could not look thereon. **20** And the Great Glory sat thereon, and His raiment shone more brightly than the sun and was whiter than any snow. **21** None of the messengers could enter and behold His face by reason of the magnificence and glory, and no flesh could behold Him. **22** The flaming fire was around Him, and a great fire stood before Him, and none around could draw near Him: myriads of myriads [stood] before Him, yet He needed no counselor. **23** And the most holy ones who were near to Him did not leave by night nor depart from Him. **24** And until then I had been prostrating on my face, trembling: and the Lord called me with His own mouth, and said to me, "Come here, Enoch, and hear My word." **25** And one of the holy ones came to me and waked me, and He made me rise up and approach the door, and I bowed my face downwards.

CHAPTER 15

1 And He answered and said to me, and I heard His voice: "Do not fear, Enoch, you righteous man and scribe of righteousness: approach here and hear My voice. **2** And go, say to the Watchers of the heavens, who have sent you to intercede for them: You should intercede for men, and not men for you! **3** Why have you left the high, holy, and perpetual Heaven, and lain with women, and defiled yourselves with the daughters of men, and taken wives to yourselves, and done like the children of earth, and begotten giants [as your] sons? **4** And though you were holy [and] spiritual, living the continuous life, you have defiled yourselves with the blood of women, and have begotten [children] with the blood of flesh, and, as the children of men, have lusted after flesh and blood as those who die and perish also do. **5** Therefore I have also given them wives that they might impregnate them, and beget children by them, that nothing might be wanting to them on earth. **6** But you were formerly spiritual, living the continuous life, and immortal for all generations of the world. **7** And, therefore, I have not appointed wives for you; for as for the spiritual ones of the heavens, their dwelling is in the heavens. **8** And now the giants, who are produced from the spirits and flesh, will be called evil spirits on the earth, and their dwelling will be on the earth. **9** Evil spirits have proceeded from their bodies, because they are born from men and their beginning and primal origin is from the holy Watchers; they will be evil spirits on earth, and they will be called evil spirits. **10** [[As for the spirits of Heaven, their dwelling will be in Heaven, but as for the spirits of the earth which were born on the earth, their dwelling will be on the earth.]] **11** And the spirits of the giants afflict, oppress, destroy, attack, do battle, and work destruction on the earth, and cause trouble: they take no food, but nevertheless hunger and thirst, and cause offenses. **12** And these spirits will rise up against the children of men and against the women, because they have proceeded from them."

CHAPTER 16

1 From the days of the slaughter, and destruction, and death of the giants—from the souls of whose flesh the spirits, having gone out, will destroy without incurring judgment—they will therefore destroy until the Day of the Consummation, the Great Judgment in which the age will be consummated over the Watchers and the godless; yes, [it] will be wholly consummated. **2** And now as to the Watchers who have sent you to intercede for them, who had previously been in Heaven, [say to them]: **3** "You have been in Heaven, but all the mysteries had not yet been revealed to you, and you knew worthless ones, and you have made these known to the women in the hardness of your hearts, and through these mysteries women and men work much evil on earth." **4** Therefore, say to them: "You have no peace."

CHAPTER 17

1 And they took and brought me to a place in which those who were there were like flaming fire, and they appeared as men when they wished. **2** And they brought me to the place of darkness, and to a mountain the point of whose summit reached to Heaven. **3** And I saw the places of the luminaries, and the treasuries of the stars and of the thunder, and in the uttermost depths where there were a fiery bow, and arrows, and their quiver, and a fiery sword and all the lightnings. **4** And they took me to the living waters, and to the fire of the west, which receives every setting of the sun. **5** And I came to a river of fire in which the fire flows like water and discharges itself into the Great Sea toward the west. **6** I saw the great rivers and came to the great river and to the great darkness and went to the place where no flesh walks. **7** I saw the mountains of the darkness of winter and the place from where all the waters of the deep flow. **8** I saw the mouths of all the rivers of the earth and the mouth of the deep.

CHAPTER 18

1 I saw the treasuries of all the winds: I saw how He had furnished the whole creation and the firm foundations of the earth with them. **2** And I saw the cornerstone of the earth: I saw the four winds which bear [the earth and] the expanse of the heavens. **3** And I saw how the winds stretch out the vaults of the heavens and have their station between the heavens and earth: these are the pillars of the heavens. **4** I saw the winds of the heavens which turn and bring the circumference of the sun and all the stars to their setting. **5** I saw the winds on the earth carrying the clouds. I saw the paths of the messengers. **6** I saw at the end of the earth the expanse of the heavens above. And I proceeded and saw a place which burns day and night, where there are seven mountains of magnificent stones: three toward the east and three toward the south. **7** And as for those toward the east: [one] was of colored stone, and one of pearl, and one of jacinth; and those toward the south [were] of red stone. **8** But the middle one reached to the heavens like the throne of God, of alabaster, and the summit of the throne was of sapphire. **9** And I saw a flaming fire. **10** And beyond these mountains is a region at the end of the great earth: there the heavens were completed. **11** And I saw a deep abyss with columns of heavenly fire, and among them I saw columns of fire fall, which were beyond measure alike toward the height and toward the depth. **12** And beyond that abyss I saw a place which had no expanse of the heavens above, and no firmly founded earth beneath it: there was no water on it, and no birds, but it was a waste and horrible place. **13** I saw seven stars there like great burning mountains, and to me, when I inquired regarding them, **14** the messenger said, "This place is the end of the heavens and earth: this has become a prison for the stars and the host of Heaven. **15** And the stars which roll over the fire are they which have transgressed the command of the Lord in the beginning of their rising, because they did not come out at their appointed times. **16** And He was angry with them and bound them until the time when their guilt should be consummated for ten thousand years."

CHAPTER 19

1 And Uriel said to me, "The messengers who have connected themselves with women will stand here, and their spirits assuming many different forms are defiling mankind and will lead them astray into sacrificing to demons as gods; [[they will stand here]] until the Day of the Great Judgment in which they will be judged until they are made an end of. **2** And also, the women of the messengers who went astray will become sirens." **3** And only I, Enoch, saw the vision, the ends of all things: and no man will see as I have seen.

CHAPTER 20

1 And these are the names of the holy messengers who watch: **2** Uriel, one of the holy messengers, who is over the world and over Tartarus; **3** Raphael, one of the holy messengers, who is over the spirits of men; **4** Raguel, one of the holy messengers who takes vengeance on the world of the luminaries; **5** Michael, one of the holy messengers, namely, he that is set over the best part of mankind and over chaos; **6** Saraqael, one of the holy messengers, who is set over the spirits who sin in the spirit; **7** Gabriel, one of the holy messengers, who is over Paradise, and the serpents, and the cherubim; **8** Remiel, one of the holy messengers, whom God set over those who rise.

CHAPTER 21

1 And I proceeded to where things were chaotic, **2** and I saw something horrible there: I saw neither a heaven above nor a firmly founded earth, but a chaotic and horrible place. **3** And there I saw seven stars of the heavens bound together in it, like great mountains and burning with fire. **4** Then I said, "For what sin are they bound, and on what account have they been cast in here?" **5** Then Uriel, one of the holy messengers who was with me, and was chief over them, spoke and said, "Enoch, why do you ask, and why are you eager for the truth? **6** These are of the number of the stars of the heavens which have transgressed the command of the Lord and are bound here until ten thousand years, the time entailed by their sins, are consummated." **7** And from there I went to another place, which was still more horrible than the former, and I saw a horrible thing: a great fire there which burned and blazed, and the place was cleft as far as the abyss, being full of great descending columns of fire: I could see neither its extent or magnitude, nor could I conjecture. **8** Then I said, "How fearful is the place and how terrible to look on!" **9** Then Uriel answered me, one of the holy messengers who was with me, and said to me, "Enoch, why do you have such fear and fright?" And I answered, "Because of this fearful place, and because of the spectacle of the pain." **10** And he said to me, "This place is the prison of the messengers, and they will be imprisoned here forever."

CHAPTER 22

1 And then I went to another place—the mountain of hard rock. **2** And there were four hollow places in it, deep, and wide, and very smooth. O how smooth the hollow places are, and deep and dark to look at! **3** Then Raphael answered, one of the holy messengers who was with me, and said to me, "These hollow places have been created for this very purpose, that the spirits of the souls of the dead should assemble therein, yes, that all the souls of the children of men should assemble here. **4** And these places have been made to receive them until the day of their judgment and until their appointed period, until the Great Judgment [comes] on them." **5** I saw [the spirit of] a dead man making suit, and his voice went out to Heaven and made suit. **6** And I asked Raphael, the messenger who was with me, and I said to him, "This spirit which makes suit, whose is it, whose voice goes out and makes suit to Heaven?" **7** And he answered me, saying, "This is the spirit which went out from Abel, whom his brother Cain slew, and he makes his suit against him until his seed is destroyed from the face of the earth, and his seed is annihilated from among the seed of men." **8** Then I asked regarding it, and regarding all the hollow places: "Why is one separated from the other?" **9** And he answered me and said to me, "These three have been made that the spirits of the dead might be separated. And such a division has been made [for] the spirits of the righteous, in which there is the bright spring of water. **10** And such has been made for sinners when they die and are buried in the earth and judgment has not been executed on them in their lifetime. **11** Here their spirits will be set apart in this great pain until the Great Day of Judgment; and [there will be] punishment and torment of those who are cursed forever, and retribution for their spirits. **12** There He will bind them forever. And such a division has been made for the spirits of those who make their suit, who make disclosures concerning their destruction, when they were slain in the days of the sinners. **13** Such has been made for the spirits of men who were not righteous but sinners, who were complete in transgression, and they will be companions of the transgressors, but their spirits will not be slain in the Day of Judgment nor will they be raised from there." **14** Then I blessed the Lord of Glory and said, "Blessed is my Lord, the Lord of righteousness, who rules forever."

CHAPTER 23

1 From there I went to another place to the west of the ends

of the earth. **2** And I saw a burning fire which ran without resting and did not cease from its course day or night, but [ran] regularly. **3** And I asked, saying, "What is this which does not rest?" **4** Then Raguel, one of the holy messengers who was with me, answered me and said to me, "This course of fire which you have seen is the fire in the west which persecutes all the luminaries of the heavens."

CHAPTER 24

1 And from there I went to another place of the earth, and he showed me a mountain range of fire which burned day and night. **2** And I went beyond it and saw seven magnificent mountains, all differing from each other, and the stones [thereof] were magnificent and beautiful, magnificent as a whole, of glorious appearance and fair exterior: three toward the east, one founded on the other, and three toward the south, one on the other, and deep rough ravines, not one of which joined with any other. **3** And the seventh mountain was in the midst of these, and it excelled them in height, resembling the seat of a throne: and fragrant trees encircled the throne. **4** And among them was a tree such as I had never yet smelled, neither was any among them nor were others like it: it had a fragrance beyond all fragrance, and its leaves, and blooms, and wood do not wither forever, and its fruit is beautiful, and its fruit resembles the dates of a palm. **5** Then I said, "O how beautiful and fragrant this tree is! And its leaves are fair, and its blooms [are] very delightful in appearance!" **6** Then Michael, one of the holy and honored messengers who was with me and was their leader, answered.

CHAPTER 25

1 And he said to me, "Enoch, why do you ask me regarding the fragrance of the tree, and why do you wish to learn the truth?" **2** Then I answered him, saying, "I wish to know about everything, but especially about this tree." **3** And he answered, saying, "This high mountain which you have seen, whose summit is like the throne of God, is His throne, where the Holy Great One, the Lord of Glory, the perpetual King will sit when He will come down to visit the earth with goodness. **4** And as for this fragrant tree, no mortal is permitted to touch it until the Great Judgment when He will take vengeance on all and bring [everything] to its consummation forever. **5** It will then be given to the righteous and holy. Its fruit will be for food to the chosen ones: it will be transplanted to the holy place, to the temple of the Lord, the perpetual King. **6** Then they will rejoice with joy and be glad, || And they will enter into the holy place; And its fragrance will be in their bones, || And they will live a long life on earth, || Such as your fathers lived: And in their days no sorrow, or plague, || Or torment, or calamity will touch them." **7** Then I blessed the God of Glory, the perpetual King, who has prepared such things for the righteous, and has created them and promised to give to them.

CHAPTER 26

1 And I went from there to the middle of the earth, and I saw a blessed place in which there were trees with branches abiding and blooming. **2** And there I saw a holy mountain, and underneath the mountain to the east there was a stream and it flowed toward the south. **3** And I saw another mountain higher than this toward the east, and between them a deep and narrow ravine: in it also ran a stream underneath the mountain. **4** And to the west thereof there was another mountain, lower than the former and of small elevation, and a deep and dry ravine between them: and another deep and dry ravine was at the extremities of the three mountains. **5** And all the ravines were deep and narrow, [being formed] of hard rock, and trees were not planted on them. **6** And I marveled at the rocks, and I marveled at the ravine, yes, I marveled very much.

CHAPTER 27

¹ Then I said, "For what purpose is this blessed land, which is entirely filled with trees, and this accursed valley between?" ² Then Uriel, one of the holy messengers who was with me, answered and said, "This accursed valley is for those who are accursed forever. Here all the accursed will be gathered together who utter unseemly words with their lips against the Lord and speak hard things of His glory. Here they will be gathered together, and here will be their place of judgment. ³ In the last days there will be the spectacle of righteous judgment on them in the presence of the righteous forever: here the merciful will bless the Lord of Glory, the perpetual King. ⁴ In the days of judgment over the former, they will bless Him for the mercy in accordance with which He has assigned them [their lot]." ⁵ Then I blessed the Lord of Glory and set out His glory and lauded Him gloriously.

CHAPTER 28

¹ And then I went toward the east, into the midst of the mountain range of the desert, and I saw a wilderness and it was solitary, full of trees and plants. ² And water gushed out from above. ³ Rushing like a copious watercourse [which flowed] toward the northwest, it caused clouds and dew to ascend on every side.

CHAPTER 29

¹ And then I went to another place in the desert and approached to the east of this mountain range. ² And there I saw aromatic trees exhaling the fragrance of frankincense and myrrh, and the trees were also similar to the almond tree.

CHAPTER 30

¹ And beyond these, I went far to the east, and I saw another place, a valley [full] of water. ² And therein there was a tree, the color of fragrant trees such as the mastic. ³ And on the sides of those valleys I saw fragrant cinnamon. And beyond these I proceeded to the east.

CHAPTER 31

¹ And I saw other mountains, and among them were groves of trees, and nectar flowed out from them, which is called sarara and galbanum. ² And beyond these mountains I saw another mountain to the east of the ends of the earth, on which were aloe-trees, and all the trees were full of stacte, being like almond-trees. ³ And when one burned it, it smelled sweeter than any refreshing fragrance.

CHAPTER 32

¹ And after these fragrant odors, as I looked toward the north over the mountains, I saw seven mountains full of choice nard, and fragrant trees, and cinnamon, and pepper. ² And then I went over the summits of all these mountains, far toward the east of the earth, and passed above the Erythraean Sea, and went far from it and passed over the messenger Zotiel. ³ And I came to the Garden of Righteousness and saw beyond those trees many large trees growing there and of attractive fragrance, large, very beautiful and glorious, and the Tree of Wisdom of which they eat and know great wisdom. ⁴ That tree is in height like the fir, and its leaves are like [those of] the Carob tree, and its fruit is like the clusters of the vine, very beautiful, and the fragrance of the tree penetrates far. ⁵ Then I said, "How beautiful is the tree, and how attractive is its look!" ⁶ Then Raphael, the holy messenger, who was with me, answered me and said, "This is the Tree of Wisdom, of which your ancient father and your ancient mother, who were before you, have eaten, and they learned wisdom, and their eyes were opened, and they knew that they were naked, and they were driven out of the garden."

CHAPTER 33

¹ And from there I went to the ends of the earth and saw great beasts there, and each differed from the other, and also birds differing in appearance, and beauty, and voice—the one differing from the other. ² And to the east of those beasts I saw the ends of the earth on which the heavens rest, and the portals of the heavens open. ³ And I saw how the stars of the heavens come out, and I counted the portals out of which they proceed, and wrote down all their outlets, of each individual star by itself, according to their number and their names, their courses and their positions, and their times and their months, as Uriel, the holy messenger who was with me, showed me. ⁴ He showed all things to me and wrote them down for me. He also wrote their names, and their laws, and their companies for me.

CHAPTER 34

¹ And from there I went toward the north to the ends of the earth, and there I saw a great and glorious device at the ends of the whole earth. ² And here I saw three portals of heaven open in the heavens: north winds proceed through each of them. When they blow there is cold, hail, frost, snow, dew, and rain. ³ And out of one portal they blow for good, but when they blow through the other two portals, it is with violence and affliction on the earth, and they blow with violence.

CHAPTER 35

¹ And from there I went toward the west, to the ends of the earth, and saw three portals of heaven open there such as I had seen in the east, the same number of portals, and the same number of outlets.

CHAPTER 36

¹ And from there I went to the south, to the ends of the earth, and saw three portals of heaven open there: and then there came dew, rain, and wind. ² And from there I went to the east, to the ends of the heavens, and saw the three eastern portals of heaven open here, and small portals [were] above them. ³ Through each of these small portals the stars of the heavens pass and run their course to the west on the path which is shown to them. ⁴ And as often as I saw, I always blessed the Lord of Glory, and I continued to bless the Lord of Glory who has worked great and glorious wonders, to show the greatness of His work to the messengers, and to spirits, and to men, that they might praise His work and all His creation, that they might see the work of His might, and praise the great work of His hands, and bless Him forever.

SECTION 2: THE BOOK OF ALLEGORIES OF ENOCH

CHAPTER 37

¹ The second vision which he saw, the vision of wisdom, which Enoch the son of Jared, the son of Mahalalel, the son of Cainan, the son of Enos, the son of Seth, the son of Adam, saw. ² And this is the beginning of the words of wisdom which I lifted up my voice to speak and say to those which dwells on earth: "Hear, you men of ancient time, and see, you that come after, the words of the Holy One which I will speak before the Lord of Spirits." ³ It were better to declare [them only] to the men of

ancient time, but even from those that come after we will not withhold the beginning of wisdom. **4** Until the present day such wisdom has never been given by the Lord of Spirits as I have received according to my insight, according to the good pleasure of the Lord of Spirits by whom the lot of continuous life has been given to me. **5** Now three allegories were imparted to me, and I lifted up my voice and recounted them to those that dwell on the earth.

CHAPTER 38

1 The first allegory. When the congregation of the righteous will appear, and sinners will be judged for their sins, and will be driven from the face of the earth, **2** and when the Righteous One will appear before the eyes of the righteous, whose chosen works hang on the Lord of Spirits, and light will appear to the righteous and the chosen ones who dwell on the earth, where then will be the dwelling of the sinners, and where the resting-place of those who have denied the Lord of Spirits? It had been good for them if they had not been born. **3** When the secrets of the righteous will be revealed and the sinners judged, and the godless driven from the presence of the righteous and chosen ones, **4** from that time those that possess the earth will no longer be powerful and exalted, and they will not be able to behold the face of the holy, for the Lord of Spirits has caused His light to appear on the face of the holy, righteous, and chosen ones. **5** Then the kings and the mighty will perish and be given into the hands of the righteous and holy. **6** And from then on none will seek for themselves mercy from the Lord of Spirits, for their life is at an end.

CHAPTER 39

1 [[And it will come to pass in those days those chosen ones and holy children will descend from the high Heaven, and their seed will become one with the children of men. **2** And in those days, Enoch received scrolls of zeal and wrath, and scrolls of disquiet and expulsion.]] "And mercy will not be accorded to them," says the Lord of Spirits. **3** And in those days a whirlwind carried me off from the earth and set me down at the end of the heavens. **4** And there I saw another vision, the dwelling-places of the holy, and the resting-places of the righteous. **5** Here my eyes saw their dwellings with His righteous messengers, and their resting-places with the holy. And they petitioned, and interceded, and prayed for the children of men, and righteousness flowed before them as water, and mercy like dew on the earth; so it is among them forever and ever. **6** And in that place my eyes saw the Chosen One of righteousness and of faith, and I saw His dwelling-place under the wings of the Lord of Spirits. And righteousness will prevail in His days, and the righteous and chosen ones will be without number before Him forever and ever. **7** And all the righteous and chosen ones before Him will be strong as fiery lights, and their mouth will be full of blessing, and their lips extol the Name of the Lord of Spirits, and righteousness will never fail before Him. **8** I wished to dwell there, and my spirit longed for that dwelling-place; and my portion has been there until now, for so it has been established concerning me before the Lord of Spirits. **9** In those days I praised and extolled the Name of the Lord of Spirits with blessings and praises, because He has destined me for blessing and glory according to the good pleasure of the Lord of Spirits. **10** For a long time my eyes regarded that place, and I blessed Him and praised Him, saying, "Blessed is He, and may He be blessed from the beginning and forevermore. **11** And before Him there is no ceasing. He knows before the world was created what is forever and what will be from generation to generation. **12** Those who do not sleep bless You: they stand before Your glory and bless, praise, and extol, saying, Holy, Holy, Holy, is the Lord of Spirits: He fills the earth with spirits." And here my eyes saw all those who do not sleep: they stand before Him, and bless, and say, "Blessed are You and blessed is the Name of the Lord forever and ever." And my face was changed, for I could no longer behold.

CHAPTER 40

1 And after that I saw thousands of thousands and ten

thousand times ten thousand, I saw a multitude beyond number and reckoning, who stood before the Lord of Spirits. **2** And on the four sides of the Lord of Spirits I saw four presences, different from those that do not sleep, and I learned their names, for the messenger that went with me made their names known to me and showed me all the hidden things. **3** And I heard the voices of those four presences as they uttered praises before the Lord of Glory. **4** The first voice blesses the Lord of Spirits forever and ever. **5** And the second voice I heard blessing the Chosen One and the chosen ones who hang on the Lord of Spirits. **6** And the third voice I heard pray and intercede for those who dwell on the earth and supplicate in the Name of the Lord of Spirits. **7** And I heard the fourth voice fending off the devils and forbidding them to come before the Lord of Spirits to accuse them who dwell on the earth. **8** After that I asked the messenger of peace who went with me, who showed me everything that is hidden: "Who are these four presences which I have seen and whose words I have heard and written down?" **9** And he said to me, "This first is Michael, the merciful and long-suffering; and the second, who is set over all the diseases and all the wounds of the children of men, is Raphael; and the third, who is set over all the powers, is Gabriel; and the fourth, who is set over the conversion to hope of those who inherit continuous life, is named Phanuel." **10** And these are the four messengers of the Lord of Spirits and the four voices I heard in those days.

CHAPTER 41

1 And after that I saw all the secrets of the heavens, and how the kingdom is divided, and how the actions of men are weighed in the balance. **2** And there I saw the mansions of the chosen ones and the mansions of the holy, and there my eyes saw all the sinners which deny the Name of the Lord of Spirits being driven from there and being dragged off: and they could not abide because of the punishment which proceeds from the Lord of Spirits. **3** And there my eyes saw the secrets of the lightning and of the thunder, and the secrets of the winds, how they are divided to blow over the earth, and the secrets of the clouds and dew, and there I saw from where they proceed in that place and from where they saturate the dusty earth. **4** And there I saw closed chambers out of which the winds are divided: the chamber of the hail and winds, the chamber of the mist, and of the clouds, and the cloud thereof hovers over the earth from the beginning of the world. **5** And I saw the chambers of the sun and moon, from where they proceed and where they come again, and their glorious return, and how one is superior to the other, and their stately orbit, and how they do not leave their orbit, and they add nothing to their orbit and they take nothing from it, and they keep faith with each other in accordance with the oath by which they are bound together. **6** And first the sun goes out and traverses his path according to the command of the Lord of Spirits, and mighty is His Name forever and ever. **7** And after that I saw the hidden and the visible path of the moon, and she accomplishes the course of her path in that place by day and by night—the one holding a position opposite to the other before the Lord of Spirits. And they give thanks and praise and do not rest, for their thanksgiving is rest to them. **8** For the sun often changes for a blessing or a curse, and the course of the path of the moon is light to the righteous and darkness to the sinners in the Name of the Lord, who made a separation between the light and the darkness, and divided the spirits of men, and strengthened the spirits of the righteous, in the name of His righteousness. **9** For no messenger hinders and no power is able to hinder, for He appoints a judge for them all and He judges them all before Him.

CHAPTER 42

1 Wisdom found no place where she might dwell; then a dwelling-place was assigned to her in the heavens. **2** Wisdom went out to make her dwelling among the children of men and found no dwelling-place: Wisdom returned to her place and took her seat among the messengers. **3** And unrighteousness went out from her chambers; whom she did not seek she found and dwelt with them, as rain in a desert and dew on a thirsty land.

CHAPTER 43

¹ And I saw other lightnings and the stars of the heavens, and I saw how He called them all by their names and they listened to Him. ² And I saw how they are weighed in a righteous balance according to their proportions of light. [I saw] the width of their spaces, and the day of their appearing, and how their revolution produces lightning; and [I saw] their revolution according to the number of the messengers, and [how] they keep faith with each other. ³ And I asked the messenger who went with me, who showed me what was hidden: "What are these?" ⁴ And he said to me, "The Lord of Spirits has showed you their allegorical meaning: these are the names of the holy who dwell on the earth and believe in the Name of the Lord of Spirits forever and ever."

CHAPTER 44

¹ I also saw another phenomenon in regard to the lightnings: how some of the stars arise and become lightnings and cannot part with their new form.

CHAPTER 45

¹ And this is the second allegory concerning those who deny the name of the dwelling of the holy ones and the Lord of Spirits. ² And they will not ascend into the heavens, and they will not come on the earth: such will be the lot of the sinners who have denied the Name of the Lord of Spirits, who are therefore preserved for the day of suffering and tribulation. ³ On that day My Chosen One will sit on the throne of glory and will try their works, and their places of rest will be innumerable. And their souls will grow strong within them when they see My chosen ones, and those who have called on My glorious Name. ⁴ Then I will cause My Chosen One to dwell among them. And I will transform Heaven and make it a continuous blessing and light, and I will transform the earth and make it a blessing, ⁵ and I will cause My chosen ones to dwell on it, but the sinners and evildoers will not set foot thereon. ⁶ For I have provided and satisfied My righteous ones with peace and have caused them to dwell before Me, but for the sinners there is judgment impending with Me, so that I will destroy them from the face of the earth.

CHAPTER 46

¹ And there I saw One who had a head of days, and His head was white like wool, and another being was with Him whose countenance had the appearance of a Man, and His face was full of graciousness, like one of the holy messengers. ² And I asked the messenger who went with me and showed me all the hidden things, concerning that Son of Man, who He was, and from where He was, [and] why He went with the Head of Days? ³ And he answered and said to me, "This is the Son of Man who has righteousness, with whom dwells righteousness, and who reveals all the treasures of that which is hidden, because the Lord of Spirits has chosen Him, and whose lot has the preeminence before the Lord of Spirits in uprightness forever. ⁴ And this Son of Man whom you have seen || Will raise up the kings and the mighty from their seats, [[|| And the strong from their thrones,]] || And will loosen the reins of the strong || And break the teeth of the sinners. ⁵ [[And He will put down the kings from their thrones and kingdoms,]] || Because they do not extol and praise Him, nor humbly acknowledge from where the kingdom was bestowed on them. ⁶ And He will put down the countenance of the strong || And will fill them with shame. And darkness will be their dwelling, || And worms will be their bed, || And they will have no hope of rising from their beds, || Because they do not extol the Name of the Lord of Spirits. ⁷ [[And they raise their hands against the Highest,]] || And tread on the earth and dwell on it. And all their deeds manifest unrighteousness, || And their power rests on their riches, || And their faith is in the gods which they have made with their hands, || And they deny the Name of the Lord of Spirits, ⁸ And they persecute the houses of His

congregations, || And the faithful who hang on the Name of the Lord of Spirits."

CHAPTER 47

¹ And in those days the prayer of the righteous and the blood of the righteous will have ascended from the earth before the Lord of Spirits. ² In those days the holy ones who dwell above in the heavens will unite with one voice, and supplicate, and pray, [[and praise,]] and give thanks, and bless the Name of the Lord of Spirits on behalf of the blood of the righteous which has been shed, and that the prayer of the righteous may not be in vain before the Lord of Spirits, that judgment may be done to them, and that they may not have to suffer forever. ³ In those days I saw the Head of Days when He seated himself on the throne of His glory, and the scrolls of the living were opened before Him, and all His host which is in Heaven above and His counselors stood before Him, ⁴ And the hearts of the holy were filled with joy, because the number of the righteous had been offered, and the prayer of the righteous had been heard, and the blood of the righteous had been required before the Lord of Spirits.

CHAPTER 48

¹ And in that place I saw the fountain of righteousness which was inexhaustible, and many fountains of wisdom were around it. And all the thirsty drank of them, and were filled with wisdom, and their dwellings were with the righteous, and holy, and chosen ones. ² And at that hour that Son of Man was named in the presence of the Lord of Spirits, and His Name before the Head of Days. ³ Yes, before the sun and the signs were created, before the stars of the heavens were made, His Name was named before the Lord of Spirits. ⁴ He will be a staff to the righteous on which to stay themselves and not fall, and He will be the light of the nations, and the hope of those who are troubled of heart. ⁵ All who dwell on earth will fall down and worship before Him and will praise, and bless, and celebrate the Lord of Spirits with song. ⁶ And for this reason He has been chosen and hidden before Him, before the creation of the world and forevermore. ⁷ And the wisdom of the Lord of Spirits has revealed Him to the holy and righteous, for He has preserved the lot of the righteous, because they have hated and despised this world of unrighteousness and have hated all its works and ways in the Name of the Lord of Spirits; for they are saved in His Name, and it has been in regard to their life according to His good pleasure. ⁸ In these days the kings of the earth and the strong who possess the land will have become downcast in countenance because of the works of their hands, for on the day of their anguish and affliction they will not [be able to] save themselves. ⁹ And I will give them over into the hands of My chosen ones as straw in the fire, so they will burn before the face of the holy. They will sink as lead in the water before the face of the righteous, and no trace of them will be found anymore. ¹⁰ And on the day of their affliction there will be rest on the earth, and they will fall before them and not rise again, and there will be no one to take them with his hands and raise them, for they have denied the Lord of Spirits and His Anointed. The Name of the Lord of Spirits be blessed.

CHAPTER 49

¹ For wisdom is poured out like water, and glory does not fail before Him forevermore. ² For He is mighty in all the secrets of righteousness, and unrighteousness will disappear as a shadow and have no continuance, because the Chosen One stands before the Lord of Spirits, and His glory is forever and ever, and His might to all generations. ³ And in Him dwells the Spirit of wisdom, and the Spirit which gives insight, and the Spirit of understanding and of might, and the Spirit of those who have fallen asleep in righteousness. ⁴ And He will judge the secret things, and none will be able to utter a lying word before Him, for He is the Chosen One before the Lord of Spirits according to His good pleasure.

CHAPTER 50

¹ And in those days a change will take place for the holy and chosen ones, and the light of days will abide on them, and glory and honor will turn to the holy, on the day of affliction on which evil will have been treasured up against the sinners. ² And the righteous will be victorious in the Name of the Lord of Spirits, and He will cause the others to witness [this] that they may convert and forgo the works of their hands. ³ They will have no honor through the Name of the Lord of Spirits, yet they will be saved through His Name, and the Lord of Spirits will have compassion on them, for His compassion is great. ⁴ And He is also righteous in His judgment, and also in the presence of His glory unrighteousness will not maintain itself: at His judgment the unconverted will perish before Him. ⁵ "And from now on I will have no mercy on them," says the Lord of Spirits.

CHAPTER 51

¹ And in those days the earth will also give back that which has been entrusted to it, and Sheol will also give back that which it has received, and destruction will give back that which it owes. For in those days the Chosen One will arise, ² and He will choose the righteous and holy from among them, for the day has drawn near that they should be saved. ³ And the Chosen One will sit on My throne in those days, and His mouth will pour out all the secrets of wisdom and counsel, for the Lord of Spirits has given [them] to Him and has glorified Him. ⁴ And in those days the mountains will leap like rams, and the hills will also skip like lambs satisfied with milk, and the faces of [all] the messengers in Heaven will be lit up with joy. ⁵ And the earth will rejoice, and the righteous will dwell on it, and the chosen ones will walk thereon.

CHAPTER 52

¹ And after those days in that place where I had seen all the visions of that which is hidden, I had been carried off in a whirlwind and they had borne me toward the west. ² There my eyes saw all the secret things of Heaven that will be, a mountain of iron, and a mountain of copper, and a mountain of silver, and a mountain of gold, and a mountain of soft metal, and a mountain of lead. ³ And I asked the messenger who went with me, saying, "What things are these which I have seen in secret?" ⁴ And he said to me, "All these things which you have seen will serve the dominion of His Anointed that He may be potent and mighty on the earth." ⁵ And that messenger of peace answered, saying to me, "Wait a little, and all the secret things which surround the Lord of Spirits will be revealed to you. ⁶ And these mountains which your eyes have seen—the mountain of iron, and the mountain of copper, and the mountain of silver, and the mountain of gold, and the mountain of soft metal, and the mountain of lead—all these will be in the presence of the Chosen One as wax before the fire, and like the water which streams down from above, and they will become powerless before His feet. ⁷ And it will come to pass in those days that none will be saved, either by gold or by silver, and none will be able to escape. ⁸ And there will be no iron for war, nor will one clothe oneself with a breastplate. Bronze will be of no service, and tin will not be esteemed, and lead will not be desired. ⁹ And all these things will be destroyed from the surface of the earth when the Chosen One will appear before the face of the Lord of Spirits."

CHAPTER 53

¹ My eyes saw a deep valley with open mouths there, and all who dwell on the earth, and sea, and islands will bring gifts, and presents, and signs of homage to Him, but that deep valley will not become full. ² And their hands commit lawless deeds, and the sinners devour all whom they lawlessly oppress, yet the sinners will be destroyed before the face of the Lord of Spirits, and they will be banished from off the face of His earth, and they will perish forever and ever. ³ For I saw all the messengers of punishment abiding [there] and preparing all the instruments of Satan. ⁴ And I asked the messenger of peace who went with me: "For whom are they preparing these instruments?" ⁵ And he said to me, "They prepare these for the kings and the mighty of this earth, that they may thereby be destroyed. ⁶ And after this the righteous and Chosen One will cause the house of His congregation to appear: from now on they will no longer be hindered in the Name of the Lord of Spirits. ⁷ And these mountains will not stand as the earth before His righteousness, but the hills will be as a fountain of water, and the righteous will have rest from the oppression of sinners."

CHAPTER 54

¹ And I looked and turned to another part of the earth and saw a deep valley with burning fire there. ² And they brought the kings and the mighty and began to cast them into this deep valley. ³ And there my eyes saw how they made these instruments of theirs iron chains of immeasurable weight. ⁴ And I asked the messenger of peace who went with me, saying, "For whom are these chains being prepared?" And he said to me, "These are being prepared for the hosts of Azazel, so that they may take them and cast them into the abyss of complete condemnation, and they will cover their jaws with rough stones as the Lord of Spirits commanded. ⁶ And Michael, and Gabriel, and Raphael, and Phanuel will take hold of them on that great day, and cast them on that day into the burning furnace, that the Lord of Spirits may take vengeance on them for their unrighteousness in becoming subject to Satan and leading those who dwell on the earth astray." ⁷ And in those days punishment will come from the Lord of Spirits, and He will open all the chambers of waters which are above the heavens, and of the fountains which are beneath the earth. ⁸ And all the waters will be joined with the waters: that which is above the heavens is the masculine, and the water which is beneath the earth is the feminine. ⁹ And they will destroy all who dwell on the earth and those who dwell under the ends of the heavens. ¹⁰ And when they have recognized their unrighteousness which they have worked on the earth, then by these they will perish.

CHAPTER 55

¹ And after that the Head of Days regretted and said, "I have destroyed all who dwell on the earth in vain." ² And He swore by His great Name: "From now on I will not do so to all who dwell on the earth, and I will set a sign in the heavens: and this will be a pledge of good faith between Me and them forever, so long as the heavens are above the earth. And this is in accordance with My command. ³ When I have desired to take hold of them by the hand of the messengers on the day of tribulation and pain because of this, I will cause My discipline and My wrath to abide on them," says God, the Lord of Spirits. ⁴ "You mighty kings who dwell on the earth, you will have to behold My Chosen One, how He sits on the throne of glory and judges Azazel, and all his associates, and all his hosts in the Name of the Lord of Spirits."

CHAPTER 56

¹ And I saw there the hosts of the messengers of punishment going, and they held scourges and chains of iron and bronze. ² And I asked the messenger of peace who went with me, saying, "To whom are these who hold the scourges going?" ³ And he said to me, "To their chosen and beloved ones, that they may be cast into the chasm of the abyss of the valley. ⁴ And then that valley will be filled with their chosen and beloved ones, and the days of their lives will be at an end, and the days of their leading astray will no longer be reckoned. ⁵ And in those days the messengers will return and hurl themselves to the east on the Parthians and Medes: they will stir up the kings, so that a spirit of unrest will come on them, and they will rouse them from their thrones, that they may break out as lions from their lairs, and as hungry wolves among their flocks. ⁶ And they will go up and tread underfoot the land of His chosen ones, [[and the land of His chosen ones will be a threshing-floor and a highway before them,]] ⁷ but the city of my righteous will be a hindrance to their horses. And they will begin to fight among themselves, and their right hand will

be strong against themselves, and a man will not know his brother, nor a son his father or his mother, until there is no number of the corpses through their slaughter, and their punishment is not in vain. **8** In those days Sheol will open its jaws, and they will be swallowed up therein, and their destruction will be at an end; Sheol will devour the sinners in the presence of the chosen ones."

CHAPTER 57

1 And it came to pass after this that I saw another host of wagons, and men riding thereon, and coming on the winds from the east, and from the west to the south. **2** And the noise of their wagons was heard, and when this turmoil took place the holy ones from Heaven noted it, and the pillars of the earth were moved from their place, and the sound thereof was heard from one end of the heavens to the other, in one day. **3** And they will all fall down and worship the Lord of Spirits. And this is the end of the second allegory.

CHAPTER 58

1 And I began to speak the third allegory concerning the righteous and chosen ones. **2** Blessed are you, you righteous and chosen ones, || For your lot will be glorious. **3** And the righteous will be in the light of the sun, || And the chosen ones in the light of continuous life: The days of their life will be unending, || And the days of the holy without number. **4** And they will seek the light and find righteousness || With the Lord of Spirits: There will be peace to the righteous in the Name of the Perpetual Lord. **5** And after this it will be said to the holy in Heaven || That they should seek out the secrets of righteousness, || The heritage of faith; For it has become bright as the sun on earth, || And the darkness is past. **6** And there will be a light that never ends, || And they will not come to a limit of days, || For the darkness will have first been destroyed, || And the light [[of uprightness]] established forever before the Lord of Spirits.

CHAPTER 59

1 [[In those days my eyes saw the secrets of the lightnings, and of the lights, and the judgments they execute: and they lighten for a blessing or a curse as the Lord of Spirits wills. **2** And there I saw the secrets of the thunder, and how when it resounds above in the heavens, the sound thereof is heard, and he caused me to see the judgments executed on the earth, whether they are for well-being and blessing, or for a curse according to the word of the Lord of Spirits. **3** And after that all the secrets of the lights and lightnings were shown to me, and they lighten for blessing and for satisfying.]]

CHAPTER 60

1 In the five hundredth year, in the seventh month, on the fourteenth day of the month in the life of Enoch, in that allegory I saw how a mighty quaking made the Heaven of heavens to quake, and the host of the Highest, and the messengers—one million and [even] one hundred million—were disquieted with a great disquiet. **2** And the Head of Days sat on the throne of His glory, and the messengers and the righteous stood around Him. **3** And a great trembling seized me, and fear took hold of me, and my loins gave way, and my reins were dissolved, and I fell on my face. **4** And Michael sent another messenger from among the holy ones and he raised me up, and when he had raised me up my spirit returned, for I had not been able to endure the look of this host, and the commotion and the quaking of Heaven. **5** And Michael said to me, "Why are you disquieted with such a vision? The day of His mercy lasted until this day; and He has been merciful and long-suffering toward those who dwell on the earth. **6** And when the day, and the power, and the punishment, and the judgment come, which the Lord of Spirits has prepared for those who do not bow to the righteous law, and for those who deny the righteous judgment, and for those who take His Name in vain—that day

is prepared: a covenant for the chosen ones, but an inquisition for sinners. When the punishment of the Lord of Spirits will rest on them, it will rest in order that the punishment of the Lord of Spirits may not come in vain, and it will slay the children with their mothers and the children with their fathers. Afterward the judgment will take place according to His mercy and His patience." **7** And on that day two monsters were parted: a female monster named Leviathan, to dwell in the abysses of the ocean over the fountains of the waters, **8** but the male is named Behemoth, who occupied with his breast a waste wilderness named Duidain, on the east of the garden where the chosen ones and righteous dwell, where my grandfather was taken up—the seventh from Adam, the first man whom the Lord of Spirits created. **9** And I sought the other messenger that he should show me the might of those monsters, how they were parted on one day and cast, the one into the abysses of the sea, and the other onto the dry land of the wilderness. **10** And he said to me, "You son of man, herein you seek to know what is hidden." **11** And the other messenger who went with me and showed me what was hidden told me what is first and last in the height of Heaven, and beneath the earth in the depth, and at the ends of the heavens, and on the foundation of the heavens; **12** and the chambers of the winds, and how the winds are divided, and how they are weighed, and [how] the portals of the winds are reckoned, each according to the power of the wind, and the power of the lights of the moon, and according to the power that is fitting, and the divisions of the stars according to their names, and how all the divisions are divided; **13** and the thunders according to the places where they fall, and all the divisions that are made among the lightnings that it may lighten, and their host that they may immediately obey. **14** For the thunder has places of rest [which] are assigned [to it] while it is waiting for its peal; and the thunder and lightning are inseparable, and although not one and undivided, they both go together through the spirit and do not separate. **15** For when the lightning lightens, the thunder utters its voice, and the spirit enforces a pause during the peal, and divides equally between them; for the treasury of their peals is like the sand, and each one of them as it peals is held in with a bridle, and turned back by the power of the spirit, and pushed forward according to the many quarters of the earth. **16** And the spirit of the sea is masculine and strong, and according to the might of his strength he draws it back with a rein, and in like manner it is driven forward and disperses amid all the mountains of the earth. **17** And the spirit of the hoarfrost is his own messenger, and the spirit of the hail is a good messenger. **18** And the spirit of the snow has forsaken his chambers on account of his strength. There is a special spirit therein, and that which ascends from it is like smoke, and its name is frost. **19** And the spirit of the mist is not united with them in their chambers, but it has a special chamber, for its course is glorious both in light and in darkness, and in winter and in summer, and a messenger is in its chamber. **20** And the spirit of the dew has its dwelling at the ends of the heavens, and is connected with the chambers of the rain, and its course is in winter and summer: and its clouds and the clouds of the mist are connected, and the one gives to the other. **21** And when the spirit of the rain goes out from its chamber, the messengers come and open the chamber and lead it out, and when it is diffused over the whole earth it unites with the water on the earth. **22** For the waters are for those who dwell on the earth, for they are nourishment for the earth from the Most High who is in Heaven. Therefore, there is a measure for the rain, and the messengers take it in charge. **23** And these things I saw toward the Garden of the Righteous. **24** And the messenger of peace who was with me said to me, "These two monsters, prepared conformably to the greatness of God, will feed."

CHAPTER 61

1 And I saw in those days how long cords were given to those messengers, and they took wings for themselves and flew, and they went toward the north. **2** And I asked the messenger, saying to him, "Why have those [messengers] taken these cords and gone off?" And he said to me, "They have gone to measure." **3** And the messenger who went with me said to me, "These will bring the measures of the righteous and the ropes of the righteous to the righteous, that they may stay themselves on the Name of the Lord of Spirits forever and ever. **4** The chosen ones will begin to dwell with the chosen ones, and those are the measures which will be given to faith and which will strengthen righteousness. **5** And these measures will reveal all the secrets of the depths of the earth, and those who have been destroyed by the desert, and those who have been devoured by the beasts, and those who have been devoured by the fish of the sea, that they may return and stay themselves on the day of the Chosen One, for none will be destroyed before the Lord of Spirits, and none can be destroyed. **6** And all who dwell above in Heaven received a command, and power, and one voice, and one light like to fire. **7** And they blessed that One [with] their first words, and extolled and lauded with wisdom, and they were wise in utterance and in the spirit of life. **8** And the Lord of Spirits placed the Chosen One on the throne of glory, and He will judge all the works of the holy above in Heaven, and their deeds will be weighed in the balance, **9** and when He will lift up His countenance to judge their secret ways according to the word of the Name of the Lord of Spirits, and their path according to the way of the righteous judgment of the Lord of Spirits, then with one voice they will all speak, and bless, and glorify, and extol, and sanctify the Name of the Lord of Spirits. **10** And He will summon all the host of the heavens, and all the holy ones above, and the host of God, the cherubim, seraphim, and ophanim, and all the messengers of power, and all the messengers of principalities, and the Chosen One, and the other powers on the earth [and] over the water. **11** They will raise one voice on that day and bless, and glorify, and exalt in the Spirit of faith, and in the Spirit of wisdom, and in the Spirit of patience, and in the Spirit of mercy, and in the Spirit of judgment and of peace, and in the Spirit of goodness, and will all say with one voice: Blessed is He and may the Name of the Lord of Spirits be blessed forever and ever! **12** All who do not sleep above in Heaven will bless Him: All the holy ones who are in Heaven will bless Him, || And all the chosen ones who dwell in the garden of life, || And every spirit of light || Who is able to bless, and glorify, and extol, and hallow Your blessed Name, || And all flesh will glorify and bless Your Name beyond measure forever and ever. **13** For great is the mercy of the Lord of Spirits, and He is long-suffering, and all His works and all that He has created He has revealed to the righteous and chosen ones in the Name of the Lord of Spirits."

CHAPTER 62

1 And so the Lord commanded the kings, and the mighty, and the exalted, and those who dwell on the earth, and said, "Open your eyes and lift up your horns if you are able to recognize the Chosen One." **2** And the Lord of Spirits seated Him on the throne of His glory, and the Spirit of righteousness was poured out on Him, and the word of His mouth slays all the sinners, and all the unrighteous are destroyed from before His face. **3** And all the kings, and the mighty, and the exalted, and those who hold the earth will stand up in that day, and they will see and recognize how He sits on the throne of His glory, and righteousness is judged before Him, and no lying word is spoken before Him. **4** Then pain will come on them as on a woman in travail when her child enters the mouth of the womb and she has pain in bringing out. **5** And one portion of them will look on the other, and they will be terrified, and they will be downcast of countenance, and pain will seize them when they see that Son of Man Sitting on the throne of His glory. **6** And the kings, and the mighty, and all who possess the earth will bless, and glorify, and extol Him who rules over all, who was hidden. **7** For from the beginning the Son of Man was hidden, and the Most High preserved Him in the presence of His might and revealed Him to the chosen ones. **8** And the congregation of the chosen and holy ones will be sown, and all the chosen ones will stand before Him on that day. **9** And all the kings, and the mighty, and the exalted, and those who rule the earth will fall down before Him on their faces, and worship and set their hope on that Son of Man, and petition Him, and supplicate for mercy at His hands. **10** Nevertheless, that Lord of Spirits will so press them that they will have to go out from His presence, and their faces will be filled with shame, and the darkness will grow deeper on their faces. **11** And He will deliver them to the messengers for punishment, to execute vengeance on them because they have oppressed His children and His chosen ones, **12** and they will be a spectacle for the righteous and for His chosen ones: they will rejoice over them, because the wrath of the Lord of Spirits rests on them, and His sword is drunk with their blood. **13** And the righteous and chosen ones will be saved on that day, and they will never again see the face of the sinners and unrighteous. **14** And the Lord of Spirits will abide over them, and they will eat, and lie down, and rise up with that Son of Man forever and ever. **15** And the righteous and chosen ones will have risen from the earth and ceased to be of downcast countenance. And they will have been clothed with garments of glory, **16** and these will be the garments of life from the Lord of Spirits: and your garments will not grow old, nor your glory pass away before the Lord of Spirits.

CHAPTER 63

1 In those days the mighty and the kings who possess the earth will implore [Him] to grant them a little respite from His messengers of punishment to whom they were delivered, that they might fall down and worship before the Lord of Spirits and confess their sins before Him. **2** And they will bless and glorify the Lord of Spirits and say, "Blessed is the Lord of Spirits and the Lord of kings, || And the Lord of the mighty and the Lord of the rich, || And the Lord of Glory and the Lord of wisdom, **3** And splendid in every secret thing is Your power from generation to generation, || And Your glory forever and ever. All Your secrets are deep and innumerable, || And Your righteousness is beyond reckoning. **4** We have now learned that we should glorify and bless the Lord of kings and Him who is King over all kings." **5** And they will say, "If only we had rest to glorify, and give thanks, and confess our faith before His glory! **6** And now we long for a little rest but do not find it; We follow hard on and do not obtain [it]; And light has vanished from before us, || And darkness is our dwelling-place forever and ever, **7** For we have not believed before Him || Nor glorified the Name of the Lord of Spirits, || But our hope was in the scepter of our kingdom, || And in our glory. **8** And in the day of our suffering and tribulation || He does not save us, || And we find no respite for confession that our Lord is true in all His works, || And in His judgments and His justice, || And His judgments have no respect of persons. And we pass away from before His face on account of our works, || And all our sins are reckoned up in righteousness." **10** Now they will say to themselves, "Our souls are full of unrighteous gain, but it does not prevent us from descending from the midst thereof into the burden of Sheol." **11** And after that their faces will be filled with darkness and shame before that Son of Man, and they will be driven from His presence, and the sword will abide before His face in their midst. **12** So spoke the Lord of Spirits: "This is the ordinance and judgment with respect to the mighty, and the kings, and the exalted, and those who possess the earth before the Lord of Spirits."

CHAPTER 64

1 And I saw other forms hidden in that place. **2** I heard the voice of the messenger, saying, "These are the messengers who descended to the earth, and revealed what was hidden to the children of men, and seduced the children of men into committing sin."

CHAPTER 65

1 And in those days Noah saw that the earth had sunk down and its destruction was near. **2** And he arose from there and went to the ends of the earth, and he cried aloud to his grandfather Enoch, **3** and with an embittered voice Noah said three times, "Hear me! Hear me! Hear me!" And I said to him, "Tell me what it is that is falling out on the earth that the earth is in such an evil plight and shaken, lest perhaps I will perish with it?" **4** And there was a great commotion on the earth, and a voice was heard from Heaven, and I fell on my face. **5** And my grandfather Enoch came and stood by me, and said to me, "Why have you cried to me with a bitter cry and weeping? **6** Indeed, a command has gone out from the presence of the Lord concerning those who dwell on the earth that their ruin is accomplished because they have learned all the secrets of the messengers, and all the violence of the devils, and all their powers—the most secret ones—and all the power of those who practice sorcery, and the power of witchcraft, and the power of those who make molten images for the whole earth, **7** and how silver is produced from the dust of the earth, and how soft metal originates in the earth. **8** For lead and tin are not produced from the earth like the first: it is a fountain that produces them, and a messenger stands therein, and that messenger is preeminent." **9** And after that, my grandfather Enoch took hold of me by my hand and raised me up, and said to me, "Go, for I have asked the Lord of Spirits concerning this commotion on the earth." **10** And He said to me, "Because of their unrighteousness their judgment has been determined and will not be withheld by Me forever. Because of the sorceries which they have searched out and learned, the earth and those who dwell on it will be destroyed. **11** And these—they have no place of conversion forever, because they have shown them what was hidden, and they are the damned; but as for you, my son, the Lord of Spirits knows that you are pure and guiltless of this reproach concerning the secrets. **12** And He has destined your name to be among the holy, and will preserve you among those who dwell on the earth, and has destined your righteous Seed both for kingship and for great honors, and from your Seed will proceed a fountain of the righteous and holy without number forever."

CHAPTER 66

1 And after that he showed me the messengers of punishment who are prepared to come and let loose all the powers of the waters which are beneath in the earth in order to bring judgment and destruction on all who [abide and] dwell on the earth. **2** And the Lord of Spirits gave command to the messengers who were going out, that they should not cause the waters to rise but should hold them in check, for those messengers were over the powers of the waters. **3** And I went away from the presence of Enoch.

CHAPTER 67

1 And in those days the word of God came to me, and He said to me, "Noah, your lot has come up before Me, a lot without blame, a lot of love and uprightness. **2** And now the messengers are making a wooden [vessel], and when they have completed that task, I will place My hand on it and preserve it, and the seed of life will come out from it, and a change will set in so that the earth will not remain without inhabitant. **3** And I will make your seed firm before Me forever and ever, and I will spread abroad those who dwell with you: it will not be unfruitful on the face of the earth, but it will be blessed and multiply on the earth in the Name of the Lord." **4** And He will imprison those messengers who have shown unrighteousness in that burning valley which my grandfather Enoch had formerly shown to me, in the west among the mountains of gold, and silver, and iron, and soft metal, and tin. **5** And I saw that valley in which there was a great convulsion and a convulsion of the waters. **6** And when all this took place, a smell of sulfur was produced from that fiery molten metal and from the convulsion thereof in that place, and it was connected with those waters, and that valley of the messengers who had led [mankind] astray burned beneath that land. **7** And streams of fire proceed through its valleys where these messengers who had led those who dwell on the earth astray are punished. **8** But in those days those waters will serve for the kings, and the mighty, and the exalted, and those who dwell on the earth, [not] for the healing of the body, but for the punishment of the spirit; now their spirit is full of lust, that they may be punished in their body, for they have denied the Lord of Spirits and see their punishment daily, and yet do not believe in His Name. **9** And in proportion as the burning of their bodies becomes severe, a corresponding change will take place in their spirit forever and ever, for none will utter an idle word before the Lord of Spirits; **10** for the judgment will come on them, because they believe in the lust of their body and deny the Spirit of the Lord. **11** And those same waters will undergo a change in those days, for when those messengers are punished in these waters, these water-springs will change their temperature, and when the messengers ascend, this water of the springs will change and become cold. **12** And I heard Michael answering, and saying, "This judgment with which the messengers are judged is a testimony for the kings and the mighty who possess the earth." **13** Because these waters of judgment minister to the healing of the body of the kings and the lust of their body, therefore, they will not see

and will not believe that those waters will change and become a fire which burns forever.

CHAPTER 68

1 And after that my grandfather Enoch gave me the teaching of all the secrets in the scroll, in the allegories which had been given to him, and he put them together for me in the words of the Scroll of the Allegories. **2** And on that day Michael answered Raphael and said, "The power of the Spirit transports and makes me to tremble because of the severity of the judgment of the secrets, the judgment of the messengers: who can endure the severe judgment which has been executed, and before which they melt away?" **3** And Michael answered again, and said to Raphael, "Who is he whose heart is not softened concerning it, and whose reins are not troubled by this word of judgment [that] has gone out on them because of those who have so led them out?" **4** And it came to pass when he stood before the Lord of Spirits, Michael said this to Raphael: "I will not take their part under the eye of the Lord, for the Lord of Spirits has been angry with them because they do as if they were the Lord. **5** Therefore all that is hidden will come on them forever and ever; for neither messenger nor man will have his portion [in it], but they alone have received their judgment forever and ever."

CHAPTER 69

1 And after this judgment they will terrify and make them to tremble because they have shown this to those who dwell on the earth. **2** And behold the names of those messengers, [[and these are their names: the first of them is Semjaza, the second Artaqifa, and the third Armen, the fourth Kokabel, the fifth Turael, the sixth Rumjal, the seventh Danjal, the eighth Neqael, the ninth Baraqel, the tenth Azazel, the eleventh Armaros, the twelfth Batarjal, the thirteenth Busasejal, the fourteenth Hananel, the fifteenth Turel, and the sixteenth Simapesiel, the seventeenth Jetrel, the eighteenth Tumael, the nineteenth Turel, the twentieth Rumael, the twenty-first Azazel. **3** And these are the chiefs of their messengers, and their names, and their chief ones over hundreds, and over fifties, and over tens.]] **4** The name of the first Jeqon: that is, the one who led astray [all] the sons of God, and brought them down to the earth, and led them astray through the daughters of men. **5** And the second was named Asbeel: he imparted to the holy sons of God evil counsel and led them astray so that they defiled their bodies with the daughters of men. **6** And the third was named Gadreel: it is he who showed the children of men all the blows of death, and he led Eve astray, and showed the shield, and the coat of mail, and the sword for battle, and all the weapons of death to the children of men; **7** and they have proceeded against those who dwell on the earth from that day and forevermore. **8** And the fourth was named Penemue: he taught the children of men the bitter and the sweet, and he taught them all the secrets of their wisdom, **9** and he instructed mankind in writing with ink and paper, and thereby many sinned from age to age and until this day, **10** for men were not created for such a purpose, to give confirmation to their good faith with pen and ink. **11** For men were created exactly like the messengers, to the intent that they should continue pure and righteous, and death, which destroys everything, could not have taken hold of them, but through this knowledge of theirs they are perishing, and through this power it is consuming me. **12** And the fifth was named Kasdeja: this is he who showed the children of men all the wicked striking of spirits and demons, and the striking of the embryo in the womb that it may pass away, and the striking of the soul [by] the bites of the serpent, and the striking which befalls through the noontide heat, the son of the serpent named Taba'et. **13** And this is the task of Kasbeel, the chief of the oath which he showed to the holy ones when he dwelt high above in glory, and its name is Biqa. **14** This [messenger] requested Michael to show him the hidden name, that he might enunciate it in the oath, so that those might quake before that name and oath who revealed all that was in secret to the children of men. **15** And this is the power of this oath, for it is powerful and strong, and he placed this oath of Akae in the hand of Michael. **16** And these are the secrets of this oath, and they are strong through his oath: and Heaven was suspended before the world was created—and forever, **17** and through it the earth was founded on the water, and from the secret recesses of the mountains come beautiful waters, from the creation of the world and continuously. **18** And through that oath the sea was created, and at its foundation He set for it the sand against the time of [its] anger, and it does not dare pass beyond it from the creation of the world [and] continuously. **19** And through that oath the depths are made fast, and abide, and do not stir from their place from age to age. **20** And through that oath the sun and moon complete their course and do not deviate from their ordinance from age to age. **21** And through that oath the stars complete their course, and He calls them by their names, and they answer Him from age to age. **22** [[And in like manner the spirits of the water, and of the winds, and of all zephyrs, and [their] paths from all the quarters of the winds. **23** And the voices of the thunder and the light of the lightnings are preserved; and the chambers of the hail, and the chambers of the hoarfrost, and the chambers of the mist, and the chambers of the rain and the dew are preserved. **24** And all these believe and give thanks before the Lord of Spirits, and glorify [Him] with all their power, and their food is in every act of thanksgiving: they thank, and glorify, and extol the Name of the Lord of Spirits forever and ever.]] **25** And this oath is mighty over them, and their paths are preserved through it, and their course is not destroyed. **26** And there was great joy among them, and they blessed, and glorified, and extolled, because the Name of that Son of Man had been revealed to them. **27** And He sat on the throne of His glory, and the sum of judgment was given to the Son of Man, and He caused the sinners to pass away and be destroyed from off the face of the earth, and those who have led the world astray. **28** They will be bound with chains, and in their gathering place of destruction they will be imprisoned, and all their works will vanish from the face of the earth. **29** And from now on there will be nothing corruptible, for that Son of Man has appeared and has seated Himself on the throne of His glory, and all evil will pass away before His face, and the word of that Son of Man will go out and be strong before the Lord of Spirits.

CHAPTER 70

1 And it came to pass after this that his name during his lifetime was raised aloft to that Son of Man and to the Lord of Spirits from among those who dwell on the earth. **2** And he was raised aloft on the chariots of the Spirit and his name vanished among them. **3** And from that day I was no longer numbered among them: and He set me between the two winds, between the north and the west, where the messengers took the cords to measure for me the place for the chosen ones and righteous. **4** And there I saw the first fathers and the righteous who dwell in that place from the beginning.

CHAPTER 71

1 And it came to pass after this that my spirit was translated, and it ascended into the heavens, and I saw the holy sons of God: they were stepping on flames of fire, their garments were white, and their faces shone like snow. **2** And I saw two streams of fire, and the light of that fire shone like hyacinth, and I fell on my face before the Lord of Spirits. **3** And the messenger Michael, [[one of the chief-messengers,]] seized me by my right hand, and lifted me up, and led me out into all the secrets, and he showed me all the secrets of righteousness. **4** And he showed me all the secrets of the ends of the heavens, and all the chambers of all the stars, and all the luminaries, from where they proceed before the face of the holy ones. **5** And he translated my spirit into the Heaven of heavens, and I saw there as it were a structure built of crystals, and between those crystals, tongues of living fire. **6** And my spirit saw the girdle which girt that house of fire, and on its four sides were streams full of living fire, and they girt that house. **7** And around were seraphim, cherubim, and ophanim: and these are they who do not sleep, and they guard the throne of His glory. **8** And I saw messengers who could not be counted—one million and [even] one hundred million—encircling that house. And Michael, and Raphael, and Gabriel, and Phanuel, and the holy messengers who are above the heavens, go in and out of that house. **9** And they came out from that house, and [also] Michael and Gabriel, Raphael and

Phanuel, and many holy messengers without number, **10** and with them the Head of Days, His head white and pure as wool, and His raiment indescribable. **11** And I fell on my face, and my whole body became relaxed, and my spirit was transfigured; and I cried with a loud voice, with the spirit of power, and blessed, and glorified, and extolled. **12** And these blessings which went out of my mouth were well pleasing before that Head of Days. **13** And that Head of Days came with Michael and Gabriel, Raphael and Phanuel, [and] thousands and myriads of messengers without number. **14** And He came to me and greeted me with His voice, and said to me, "This is the Son of Man who is born to righteousness, and righteousness abides over Him, and the righteousness of the Head of Days does not forsake Him." **15** And He said to me, "He proclaims peace to you in the name of the world to come, for peace has proceeded from there since the creation of the world, and so it will be to you forever and ever. **16** And all will walk in His ways since righteousness never forsakes Him: their dwelling-places will be with Him, and their heritage with Him, and they will not be separated from Him forever and ever. And so there will be length of days with that Son of Man, and the righteous will have peace and an upright way in the Name of the Lord of Spirits forever and ever."

SECTION 3: THE ASTRONOMICAL BOOK

CHAPTER 72

1 The Scroll of the Courses of the Luminaries of the Heavens, the relations of each, according to their classes, their dominion and their seasons, according to their names and places of origin, and according to their months, which Uriel, the holy messenger who was with me, who is their guide, showed me; and he showed me all their laws exactly as they are, and how it is with regard to all the years of the world and continuously, until the new creation is accomplished which endures forever. **2** And this is the first law of the luminaries: the luminary [named] the Sun has its rising in the eastern portals of heaven, and its setting in the western portals of heaven. **3** And I saw six portals in which the sun rises, and six portals in which the sun sets, and the moon rises and sets in these portals, and the leaders of the stars and those whom they lead: six in the east and six in the west, and all following each other in accurately corresponding order: also, many windows to the right and left of these portals. **4** And first there goes out the great luminary named the Sun, and his circumference is like the circumference of heaven, and he is quite filled with illuminating and heating fire. **5** The chariot on which he ascends, the wind drives, and the sun goes down from heaven and returns through the north in order to reach the east and is so guided that he comes to the appropriate portal and shines in the face of heaven. **6** In this way he rises in the first month in the great portal, which is the fourth. **7** And in that fourth portal from which the sun rises in the first month are twelve window-openings, from which proceed a flame when they are opened in their season. **8** When the sun rises in heaven, he comes out through that fourth portal [for] thirty mornings in succession, and sets accurately in the fourth portal in the west of heaven. **9** And during this period the day becomes daily longer and the night nightly shorter to the thirtieth morning. **10** On that day the day is longer than the night by a ninth part, and the day amounts exactly to ten parts and the night to eight parts. **11** And the sun rises from that fourth portal, and sets in the fourth, and returns to the fifth portal of the east [for] thirty mornings, and rises from it, and sets in the fifth portal. **12** And then the day becomes longer by two parts and amounts to eleven parts, and the night becomes shorter and amounts to seven parts. **13** And it returns to the east and enters into the sixth portal, and rises, and sets in the sixth portal [for] thirty-one mornings on account of its sign. **14** On that day the day becomes longer than the night, and the day becomes double the night, and the day becomes twelve parts, and the night is shortened and becomes six parts. **15** And the sun mounts up to make the day shorter and the night longer, and the sun returns to the east and enters into the sixth portal, and rises from it, and sets [for] thirty mornings. **16** And when thirty mornings are accomplished, the day decreases by exactly one part, and becomes eleven parts, and the night seven. **17** And the sun goes out from that sixth portal in the west, and goes to the east, and rises in the fifth portal for thirty mornings, and sets in the west again in the fifth western portal. **18** On that day the day decreases by two parts and amounts to ten parts and the night to eight parts. **19** And the sun goes out from that fifth portal, and sets in the fifth portal of the west, and rises in the fourth portal for thirty-one mornings on account of its sign, and sets in the west. **20** On that day the day is equalized with the night, and the night amounts to nine parts and the day to nine parts. **21** And the sun rises from that portal, and sets in the west, and returns to the east, and rises [for] thirty mornings in the third portal, and sets in the west in the third portal. **22** And on that day the night becomes longer than the day, and night becomes longer than [the previous] night, and day shorter than [the previous] day until the thirtieth morning, and the night amounts exactly to ten parts and the day to eight parts. **23** And the sun rises from that third portal, and sets in the third portal in the west, and returns to the east, and for thirty mornings rises in the second portal in the east, and in like manner sets in the second portal in the west of heaven. **24** And on that day the night amounts to eleven parts and the day to seven parts. **25** And the sun rises on that day from that second portal, and sets in the west in the second portal, and returns to the east into the first portal for thirty-one mornings, and sets in the first portal in the west of heaven. **26** And on that day the night becomes longer and amounts to the double of the day: and the night amounts exactly to twelve parts and the day to six. **27** And the sun has traversed the divisions of his orbit, and turns again on those divisions of his orbit, and enters that portal [for] thirty mornings, and also sets in the west opposite to it. **28** And on that night the night has decreased in length by a ninth part, and the night has become eleven parts and the day seven parts. **29** And the sun has returned and entered into the second portal in the east, and returns on those divisions of his orbit for thirty mornings, rising and setting. **30** And on that day the night decreases in length, and the night amounts to ten parts and the day to eight. **31** And on that day the sun rises from that portal, and sets in the west, and returns to the east, and rises in the third portal for thirty-one mornings, and sets in the west of heaven. **32** On that day the night decreases and amounts to nine parts, and the day to nine parts, and the night is equal to the day, and the year is exactly as to its days three hundred and sixty-four. **33** And the length of the day and of the night, and the shortness of the day and of the night arise through the course of the sun [where] these distinctions are made. **34** So it comes that its course becomes daily longer, and its course nightly shorter. **35** And this is the law and the course of the sun, and his return as often as he returns sixty times and rises—the great luminary, which is named the Sun, forever and ever. **36** And that which rises is the great luminary, and is so named according to its appearance, according as the Lord commanded. **37** As he rises, so he sets, and does not decrease and does not rest, but runs day and night, and his light is sevenfold brighter than that of the moon, but as regards size, they are both equal.

CHAPTER 73

1 And after this law I saw another law dealing with the smaller luminary, which is named the Moon. **2** And her circumference is like the circumference of heaven, and her chariot in which she rides is driven by the wind, and light is given to her in [definite] measure. **3** And her rising and setting change every month: and her days are like the days of the sun, and when her light is uniform it amounts to the seventh part of the light of the sun. **4** And so she rises. And her first phase in the east comes out on the thirtieth morning: and on that day she becomes visible and constitutes for you the first phase of the moon on the thirtieth day, together with the sun in the portal where the sun rises. **5** And the one half of her goes out by a seventh part, and her whole circumference is empty, without light, with the exception of one-seventh part of it, [and] the fourteenth part of her light. **6** And when she receives one-seventh part of the half of her light, her light amounts to one-seventh part and the half thereof. **7** And she sets with the sun, and when the sun rises, the moon rises with him and

receives the half of one part of light, and in that night, in the beginning of her morning, the moon sets with the sun and is invisible that night with the fourteen parts and the half of one of them. **8** And she rises on that day with exactly a seventh part, and comes out, and recedes from the rising of the sun, and in her remaining days she becomes bright in the [remaining] thirteen parts.

CHAPTER 74

1 And I saw another course, a law for her, [and] how according to that law she performs her monthly revolution. **2** And Uriel, the holy messenger who is the leader of them all, showed all these to me, and their positions, and I wrote down them to me, and I wrote down their months as they were, and the appearance of their lights until fifteen days were accomplished. **3** In each seventh part she accomplishes all her light in the east, and in each seventh part accomplishes all her darkness in the west. **4** And in certain months she alters her settings, and in certain months she pursues her own peculiar course. **5** In two months the moon sets with the sun: in those two middle portals, the third and the fourth. **6** She goes out for seven days, and turns around, and returns again through the portal where the sun rises and accomplishes all her light: and she recedes from the sun, and in eight days enters the sixth portal from which the sun goes out. **7** And when the sun goes out from the fourth portal, she goes out seven days, until she goes out from the fifth, and turns back again in seven days into the fourth portal and accomplishes all her light: and she recedes and enters into the first portal in eight days. **8** And she returns again in seven days into the fourth portal from which the sun goes out. **9** So I saw their position—how the moon rose and the sun set in those days. **10** And if five years are added together the sun has a surplus of thirty days, and all the days which accrue to it for one of those five years, when they are full, amount to three hundred and sixty-four days. **11** And the surplus of the sun and of the stars amounts to six days: in five years six days every year comes to thirty days, and the moon falls behind the sun and stars to the number of thirty days. **12** And the sun and the stars bring in all the years exactly, so that they do not advance or delay their position by a single day [and] continuously, but complete the years with perfect justice in three hundred and sixty-four days. **13** In three years there are one thousand and ninety-two days, and in five years one thousand and eight hundred and twenty days, so that in eight years there are two thousand and nine hundred and twelve days. **14** For the moon alone the days amount in three years to one thousand and sixty-two days, and in five years she falls fifty days behind: there is [the sum of these five] to be added to [the] one thousand and sixty-two days. **15** And in five years there are one thousand and seven hundred and seventy days, so that for the moon the days in eight years amount to two thousand and eight hundred and thirty-two days. **16** [For in eight years she falls behind to the amount of eighty days]; all the days she falls behind in eight years are eighty. **17** And the year is accurately completed in conformity with their world-stations and the stations of the sun, which rises from the portals through which it rises and sets [for] thirty days.

CHAPTER 75

1 And the leaders of the heads of the thousands, who are placed over the whole creation and over all the stars, also have to do with the four intercalary days, being inseparable from their office, according to the reckoning of the year, and these render service on the four days which are not reckoned in the reckoning of the year. **2** And owing to them men go wrong therein, for those luminaries truly render service on the world-stations, one in the first portal, one in the third portal of heaven, one in the fourth portal, and one in the sixth portal, and the exactness of the year is accomplished through its separate three hundred and sixty-four stations. **3** For the signs, and the times, and the years, and the days the messenger Uriel showed to me, whom the Lord of Glory has set forever over all the luminaries of the heavens, in the heavens and in the world, that they should rule on the face of the heavens and be seen on the earth, and be leaders for the day and the night—the sun, moon, and stars, and all the ministering creatures which make their revolution in all the chariots of the heavens. **4** In like manner, Uriel showed me twelve doors open in the circumference of the sun's chariot in the heavens, through which the rays of the sun break out: and from them warmth is diffused over the earth when they are opened at their appointed seasons— **5** [[and for the winds and the spirit of the dew when they are opened, standing open in the heavens, at the ends.]] **6** As for the twelve portals in the heavens at the ends of the earth, out of which go out the sun, moon, and stars, and all the works of heaven in the east and in the west, **7** there are many windows open to the left and right of them, and one window at its [appointed] season produces warmth, corresponding [as these do] to those doors from which the stars come out according as He has commanded them, and wherein they set corresponding to their number. **8** And I saw chariots in the heavens, running in the world, above those portals in which revolve the stars that never set. **9** And one is larger than all the rest, and it is that which makes its course through the entire world.

CHAPTER 76

1 And at the ends of the earth I saw twelve portals open to all the quarters [of the heavens], from which the winds go out and blow over the earth. **2** Three of them are open on the face [(the east)] of the heavens, and three in the west, and three on the right [(the south)] of the heavens, and three on the left [(the north)]. **3** And the three first are those of the east, and three are of the north, and three of the south, and three of the west. **4** Through four of these come winds of blessing and prosperity, and from those eight come hurtful winds: when they are sent, they bring destruction on all the earth, and on the water on it, and on all who dwell thereon, and on everything which is in the water and on the land. **5** And the first wind from those portals, called the East Wind, comes out through the first portal which is in the east, inclining toward the south: desolation, drought, heat, and destruction come out from it. **6** And through the second portal in the middle comes what is fitting: and rain, and fruitfulness, and prosperity, and dew come from it. And through the third portal which lies toward the north come cold and drought. **7** And after these, the south winds come out through three portals: through the first portal of them inclining to the east a hot wind comes out. **8** And through the middle portal next to it, fragrant smells, and dew, and rain, and prosperity, and health come out. **9** And through the third portal lying to the west, dew and rain, locusts and desolation come out. **10** And after these, the north winds: from the seventh portal in the east come dew and rain, locusts and desolation. **11** And from the middle portal, health, and rain, and dew, and prosperity come in a direct direction. And through the third portal in the west come cloud, and hoarfrost, and snow, and rain, and dew, and locusts. **12** And after these [four] are the west winds: through the first portal adjoining the north, dew, and hoarfrost, and cold, and snow, and frost come out. **13** And from the middle portal, dew, and rain, and prosperity, and blessing come out. And through the last portal which adjoins the south, drought, and desolation, and burning, and destruction come out. **14** And the twelve portals of the four quarters of the heavens are completed with that, and I have shown all their laws, and all their plagues, and all their benefactions to you, my son Methuselah.

CHAPTER 77

1 And the first quarter is called the East, because it is the first. And the second, the South, because the Highest will descend there—yes, there in quite a special sense will He who is blessed forever descend. **2** And the west quarter is named the Diminished, because all the luminaries of the heavens wane and go down there. **3** And the fourth quarter, named the North, is divided into three parts: the first of them is for the dwelling of men; and the second contains seas of water, and the abysses, and forests, and rivers, and darkness, and clouds; and the third part contains the Garden of Righteousness. **4** I saw seven high mountains, higher than all the mountains which are on the earth: and there comes out hoarfrost, and days, seasons, and years pass away. **5** I saw seven rivers on the earth larger than all the rivers: one of them coming from the west pours its waters into the Great Sea. **6** And these two come from

the north to the sea and pour their waters into the Erythraean Sea in the east. **7** And the remaining four come out on the side of the north to their own sea—two of them to the Erythraean Sea and two into the Great Sea—and discharge themselves there [[or into the desert]]. **8** I saw seven great islands in the sea and in the mainland: two in the mainland and five in the Great Sea.

CHAPTER 78

1 And the names of the sun are the following: the first Orjares, and the second Tomas. **2** And the moon has four names: the first name is Asonja, the second Ebla, the third Benase, and the fourth Erae. **3** These are the two great luminaries; their circumference is like the circumference of heaven, and the size of the circumference of both is alike. **4** In the circumference of the sun there are seven portions of light which are added to it more than to the moon, and it is transferred in definite measures until the seventh portion of the sun is exhausted. **5** And they set and enter the portals of the west, and make their revolution by the north, and come out through the eastern portals on the face of the heavens. **6** And when the moon rises, one-fourteenth part appears in the heavens; on the fourteenth day she accomplishes her light. **7** And fifteen parts of light are transferred to her until the fifteenth day [when] her light is accomplished, according to the sign of the year, and she becomes fifteen parts, and the moon grows by fourteen parts. **8** And in her waning [the moon] decreases on the first day to fourteen parts of her light, on the second to thirteen parts of light, on the third to twelve, on the fourth to eleven, on the fifth to ten, on the sixth to nine, on the seventh to eight, on the eighth to seven, on the ninth to six, on the tenth to five, on the eleventh to four, on the twelfth to three, on the thirteenth to two, on the fourteenth to the half of a seventh, and all her remaining light disappears wholly on the fifteenth. **9** And in certain months the month has twenty-nine days and once twenty-eight. **10** And Uriel showed me another law [regarding] when light is transferred to the moon, and on which side it is transferred to her by the sun. **11** During all the period during which the moon is growing in her light, she is transferring it to herself when opposite to the sun during fourteen days; and when she is illuminated throughout, her light is fully accomplished in the heavens. **12** And on the first day she is called the new moon, for on that day the light rises on her. **13** She becomes a full moon exactly on the day when the sun sets in the west, and from the east she rises at night, and the moon shines the whole night through until the sun rises over against her and the moon is seen over against the sun. **14** On the side from where the light of the moon comes out, there again she wanes until all the light vanishes and all the days of the month are at an end, and her circumference is empty, void of light. **15** And three months she makes of thirty days, and at her time she makes three months of twenty-nine days each, in which she accomplishes her waning in the first period of time, and in the first portal for one hundred and seventy-seven days. **16** And in the time of her going out she appears for three months [of] thirty days each, and for three months she appears [of] twenty-nine each. **17** At night she appears like a man for twenty days each time, and by day she appears like the heavens, and there is nothing else in her except her light [(the light of day)].

CHAPTER 79

1 "And now, my son, I have shown you everything, and the law of all the stars of the heavens is completed." **2** And he showed me all the laws of these for every day, and for every season of bearing rule, and for every year, and for its going out, and for the order prescribed to it every month and every week; **3** and the waning of the moon which takes place in the sixth portal; for in this sixth portal her light is accomplished, and after that there is the beginning of the waning; **4** [and the waning] which takes place in the first portal in its season, until one hundred and seventy-seven days are accomplished, reckoned according to weeks—twenty-five [weeks] and two days. **5** She falls behind the sun and the order of the stars exactly five days in the course of one period, and when this place which you see has been traversed. ⁶ Such is the picture and sketch of every luminary which the chief-messenger Uriel, who is their leader, showed to me.

CHAPTER 80

¹ And in those days the messenger Uriel answered and said to me, "Behold, I have shown you everything, Enoch, and I have revealed everything to you that you should see this sun and this moon, and the leaders of the stars of the heavens and all those who turn them, their tasks, and times, and departures. ² And in the days of the sinners the years will be shortened, and their seed will be late on their lands and fields, and all things on the earth will alter, and will not appear in their time: And the rain will be kept back, || And the heavens will withhold [it]. ³ And in those times the fruits of the earth will be backward, || And will not grow in their time, || And the fruits of the trees will be withheld in their time. ⁴ And the moon will alter her order, || And not appear at her time. ⁵ [[And in those days the sun will be seen, || And he will journey in the evening || On the extremity of the great chariot in the west,]] || And will shine more brightly than accords with the order of light. ⁶ And many chiefs of the stars || Will transgress the order [prescribed]. And these will alter their orbits and tasks, || And not appear at the seasons prescribed to them. ⁷ And the whole order of the stars will be concealed from the sinners, || And the thoughts of those on the earth will err concerning them, [[|| And they will be altered from all their ways,]] || Yes, they will err and take them to be gods. ⁸ And evil will be multiplied on them, || And punishment will come on them so as to destroy all."

CHAPTER 81

¹ And he said to me, "Enoch, observe these heavenly tablets, and read what is written thereon, and mark every individual fact." ² And I observed the heavenly tablets, and read everything which was written [thereon], and understood everything, and read the scroll of all the deeds of mankind, and of all the children of flesh that will be on the earth to the most remote generations. ³ And thereon I blessed the great Lord, the King of glory, forever, in that He has made all the works of the world, and I extolled the Lord because of His patience, and blessed Him because of the children of men. ⁴ And after that I said, "Blessed is the man who dies in righteousness and goodness, concerning whom there is no scroll of unrighteousness written, and against whom no Day of Judgment will be found." ⁵ And those seven holy ones brought me and placed me on the earth before the door of my house, and said to me, "Declare everything to your son Methuselah, and show to all your children that no flesh is righteous in the sight of the Lord, for He is their Creator. ⁶ One year we will leave you with your son, until you give your [last] commands, that you may teach your children, and record [it] for them, and testify to all your children; and in the second year they will take you from their midst. ⁷ Let your heart be strong, || For the good will announce righteousness to the good; The righteous will rejoice with the righteous || And will offer congratulations to one another. ⁸ But the sinners will die with the sinners, || And the apostate goes down with the apostate. ⁹ And those who practice righteousness || Will die on account of the deeds of men || And be taken away on account of the doings of the godless." ¹⁰ And in those days they ceased to speak to me, and I came to my people, blessing the Lord of the world.

CHAPTER 82

¹ And now, my son Methuselah, all these things I am recounting to you and writing down for you! and I have revealed everything to you, and given you scrolls concerning all these; so preserve, my son Methuselah, the scrolls from your father's hand, and [see] that you deliver them to the generations of the world. ² I have given wisdom to you and to your children, [[|| And your children that will be to you,]] || That they may give it to their children for generations—This wisdom that surpasses their thought. ³ And those who understand it will not sleep, || But will listen with the ear that they may learn this wisdom, || And it will please those that eat thereof better than good food. ⁴ Blessed are all the righteous, blessed are all those who walk in the way of righteousness and do not sin as the sinners in the reckoning of all their days in which the sun traverses the heavens, entering into and departing from the portals for thirty days with the heads of thousands of the order of the stars, together with the four which are intercalated, which divide the four portions of the year, which lead them and enter with them four days. ⁵ Owing to them, men will be at fault and not reckon them in the whole reckoning of the year: yes, men will be at fault, and not recognize them accurately. ⁶ For they belong to the reckoning of the year and are truly recorded [thereon] forever, one in the first portal, and one in the third, and one in the fourth, and one in the sixth, and the year is completed in three hundred and sixty-four days. ⁷ And the account thereof is accurate and the recorded reckoning thereof exact, for the luminaries, and months, and festivals, and years, and days, Uriel has shown and revealed to me, to whom the Lord of the whole creation of the world has subjected the host of Heaven. ⁸ And he has power over night and day in the heavens to cause the light to give light to men—sun, moon, and stars, and all the powers of the heavens which revolve in their circular chariots. ⁹ And these are the orders of the stars, which are set in their places, and in their seasons, and festivals, and months. ¹⁰ And these are the names of those who lead them, who watch that they enter at their times, in their orders, in their seasons, in their months, in their periods of dominion, and in their positions. ¹¹ Their four leaders who divide the four parts of the year enter first; and after them the twelve leaders of the orders who divide the months; and for the three hundred and sixty [days] there are heads over thousands who divide the days; and for the four intercalary days there are the leaders which split the four parts of the year. ¹² And these heads over thousands are intercalated between leader and leader, each behind a station, but their leaders make the division. ¹³ And these are the names of the leaders who divide the four parts of the year which are ordained: Milki'el, Hel'emmelek, and Mel'ejal, and Narel. ¹⁴ And the names of those who lead them: Adnar'el, and Ijasusa'el, and 'Elome'el—these three follow the leaders of the orders, and there is one that follows the three leaders of the orders which follow those leaders of stations that divide the four parts of the year. ¹⁵ In the beginning of the year Melkejal rises first and rules, who is named Tam'aini and Sun, and all the days of his dominion while he bears rule are ninety-one days. ¹⁶ And these are the signs of the days which are to be seen on earth in the days of his dominion: sweat, and heat, and stillness; and all the trees bear fruit, and leaves are produced on all the trees, and the harvest of wheat, and the rose-flowers, and all the flowers which come out in the field, but the trees of the winter season become withered. ¹⁷ And these are the names of the leaders which are under them: Berka'el, Zelebs'el, and another who is added, a head of one thousand called Hilujaseph: and the days of the dominion of this [leader] are at an end. ¹⁸ The next leader after him is Hel'emmelek, whom one names the Shining Sun, and all the days of his light are ninety-one days. ¹⁹ And these are the signs of [his] days on the earth: glowing heat and dryness, and the trees ripen their fruits and produce all their fruits ripe and ready, and the sheep pair and become pregnant, and all the fruits of the earth are gathered in, as well as everything that is in the fields and the winepress: these things take place in the days of his dominion. ²⁰ These are the names, and the orders, and the leaders of those heads of thousands: Gida'ljal, Ke'el, and He'el, and the name of the head of one thousand which is added to them, Asfa'el: and the days of his dominion are at an end.

SECTION 4: THE BOOK OF DREAM VISIONS

CHAPTER 83

1 And now, my son Methuselah, I will show you all my visions which I have seen, recounting them before you. **2** I saw two visions before I took a wife, and the one was quite unlike the other: the first when I was learning to write; the second before I took your mother, [when] I saw a terrible vision. **3** And I prayed to the Lord regarding them. I had laid myself down in the house of my grandfather Mahalalel [when] I saw in a vision how heaven collapsed and was borne off and fell to the earth. **4** And when it fell to the earth, I saw how the earth was swallowed up in a great abyss, and mountains were suspended on mountains, and hills sank down on hills, and high trees were torn from their stems, and hurled down, and sunk in the abyss. **5** And a word suddenly fell into my mouth, and I lifted up [my voice] to cry aloud, and said, "The earth is destroyed!" **6** And my grandfather Mahalalel waked me as I lay near him, and said to me, "Why do you cry so, my son, and why do you make such lamentation?" **7** And I recounted to him the whole vision which I had seen, and he said to me, "You have seen a terrible thing, my son, and of grave moment is your dream-vision as to the secrets of all the sin of the earth: it must sink into the abyss and be destroyed with a great destruction. **8** And now, my son, arise and make petition to the Lord of Glory, since you are a believer, that a remnant may remain on the earth, and that He may not destroy the whole earth. **9** My son, all this will come on the earth from Heaven, and there will be great destruction on the earth." **10** After that I arose, and prayed, and implored, and sought, and wrote down my prayer for the generations of the world, and I will show everything to you, my son Methuselah. **11** And when I had gone out below and seen the heavens, and the sun rising in the east, and the moon setting in the west, and a few stars, and the whole earth, and everything as He had known it in the beginning, then I blessed the Lord of judgment and extolled Him because He had made the sun to go out from the windows of the east, and he ascended and rose on the face of the heavens, and set out and kept traversing the path shown to him

CHAPTER 84

1 And I lifted up my hands in righteousness and blessed the Holy and Great One, and spoke with the breath of my mouth, and with the tongue of flesh, which God has made for the children of the flesh of men, that they should speak with [it], and He gave them breath, and a tongue, and a mouth that they should speak with [them]: **2** "Blessed are You, O Lord, || King, great and mighty in Your greatness, || Lord of the whole creation of the heavens, || King of kings and God of the whole world. And Your power, and kingship, and greatness || Abide forever and ever, || And throughout all generations Your dominion; And all the heavens are Your throne forever, || And the whole earth Your footstool forever and ever. **3** For You have made and You rule all things, || And nothing is too hard for You; Wisdom does not depart from the place of Your throne, || Nor turns away from Your presence. And You know, and see, and hear everything, || And there is nothing hidden from You. **4** And now the messengers of Your heavens are guilty of trespass, || And Your wrath abides on the flesh of men until the great Day of Judgment. **5** And now, O God, and Lord, and Great King, I exceedingly implore You to fulfill my prayer, to leave me a posterity on earth, and not destroy all the flesh of man, and make the earth without inhabitant, so that there should be a continuous destruction. **6** And now, my Lord, destroy from the earth the flesh which has aroused Your wrath, but establish the flesh of righteousness and uprightness as a plant of the continuous seed, and do not hide Your face from the prayer of Your servant, O Lord."

CHAPTER 85

1 And after this I saw another dream, and I will show the whole dream to you, my son. **2** And Enoch lifted up [his voice] and spoke to his son Methuselah: "To you, my son, I will speak: hear my words and incline your ear to the dream-vision of your father. **3** Before I took your mother Edna, I saw in a vision on my bed, and behold, a bull came out from the earth, and that bull was white; and after it a heifer came out, and along with

this [heifer] two bulls came out: one of them black and the other red. **4** And that black bull gored the red one and pursued him over the earth, and immediately I could no longer see that red bull. **5** But that black bull grew, and that heifer went with him, and I saw that many oxen proceeded from him which resembled and followed him. **6** And that cow, that first one, went from the presence of that first bull in order to seek that red one, but did not find him, and lamented with a great lamentation over him and sought him. **7** And I looked until that first bull came to her and quieted her, and from that time onward she no longer cried. **8** And after that, she bore another white bull, and after him she bore many bulls and black cows. **9** And I saw in my sleep that white bull likewise grows and becomes a great white bull, and from him proceeded many white bulls, and they resembled him. **10** And they began to beget many white bulls, which resembled them, one following the other, [even] many."

CHAPTER 86

1 "And again, I saw with my eyes as I slept, and I saw the heavens above, and behold, a star fell from Heaven, and it arose, and ate, and pastured among those oxen. **2** And after that I saw the large and the black oxen, and behold, they all changed their stalls, and pastures, and their cattle, and began to live with each other. **3** And again, I saw in the vision, and looked toward the heavens, and behold, I saw many stars descend and cast themselves down from Heaven to that first star, and they became bulls among those cattle and pastured among them. **4** And I looked at them and saw, and behold, they all let out their genitals like horses, and began to cover the cows of the oxen, and they all became pregnant and bore elephants, camels, and donkeys. **5** And all the oxen feared them, and were frightened at them, and began to bite with their teeth, and to devour, and to gore with their horns. **6** And they began, moreover, to devour those oxen; and behold, all the children of the earth began to tremble and quake before them and to flee from them."

CHAPTER 87

1 "And again, I saw how they began to gore each other and to devour each other, and the earth began to cry aloud. **2** And I raised my eyes again to Heaven, and I saw in the vision, and behold, there came out from Heaven beings who were like white men: and four went out from that place and three with them. **3** And those three that had last come out grasped me by my hand and took me up, away from the generations of the earth, and raised me up to a lofty place, and showed me a tower raised high above the earth, and all the hills were lower. **4** And one said to me, Remain here until you see everything that befalls those elephants, camels, and donkeys, and the stars, and the oxen, and all of them."

CHAPTER 88

1 "And I saw one of those four who had come out first, and he seized that first star which had fallen from Heaven, and bound it hand and foot, and cast it into an abyss: now that abyss was narrow, and deep, and horrible, and dark. **2** And one of them drew a sword and gave it to those elephants, and camels, and donkeys: then they began to strike each other, and the whole earth quaked because of them. **3** And as I was beholding in the vision, one of those four who had come out from Heaven stoned [them], and gathered [them], and took all the great stars whose genitals were like those of horses, and bound them all hand and foot, and cast them in an abyss of the earth."

CHAPTER 89

1 "And one of those four went to that white bull and instructed him in a secret, without his being terrified: he was born a bull, and became a man, and built a great vessel for himself, and dwelt thereon; and three bulls dwelt with him in that vessel, and they were enclosed inside. ² And again, I raised my eyes toward the heavens and saw a lofty roof with seven water torrents thereon, and those torrents flowed with much water into an enclosure. ³ And I saw again, and behold, fountains were opened on the surface of that great enclosure, and that water began to swell and rise on the surface, and I saw that enclosure until all its surface was covered with water. ⁴ And the water, the darkness, and mist increased on it; and as I looked at the height of that water, that water had risen above the height of that enclosure, and was streaming over that enclosure, and it stood on the earth. ⁵ And all the cattle of that enclosure were gathered together until I saw how they sank, and were swallowed up, and perished in that water. ⁶ But that vessel floated on the water, while all the oxen, and elephants, and camels, and donkeys sank to the bottom with all the animals, so that I could no longer see them, and they were not able to escape, [but] perished and sank into the depths. ⁷ And again, I saw in the vision until those water torrents were removed from that high roof, and the chasms of the earth were leveled up, and other abysses were opened. ⁸ Then the water began to run down into these until the earth became visible, but that vessel settled on the earth, and the darkness retired, and light appeared. ⁹ But that white bull which had become a man came out of that vessel, and the three bulls with him, and one of those three was white like that bull, and one of them was red as blood, and one black: and that white bull departed from them. ¹⁰ And they began to bring out beasts of the field and birds, so that there arose different genera: lions, tigers, wolves, dogs, hyenas, wild boars, foxes, squirrels, swine, falcons, vultures, kites, eagles, and ravens; and a white bull was born among them. ¹¹ And they began to bite one another, but that white bull which was born among them begot a wild donkey and a white bull with it, and the wild donkeys multiplied. ¹² But that bull which was born from him begot a black wild boar and a white sheep; and the former begot many boars, but that sheep begot twelve sheep. ¹³ And when those twelve sheep had grown, they gave up one of them to the donkeys, and those donkeys again gave up that sheep to the wolves, and that sheep grew up among the wolves. ¹⁴ And the Lord brought the eleven sheep to live with it and to pasture with it among the wolves: and they multiplied and became many flocks of sheep. ¹⁵ And the wolves began to fear them, and they oppressed them until they destroyed their little ones, and they cast their young into a river of much water, but those sheep began to cry aloud on account of their little ones, and to complain to their Lord. ¹⁶ And a sheep which had been saved from the wolves fled and escaped to the wild donkeys; and I saw how the sheep lamented, and cried, and implored their Lord with all their might until that Lord of the sheep descended at the voice of the sheep from a lofty abode, and came to them, and pastured them. ¹⁷ And He called that sheep which had escaped the wolves and spoke with it concerning the wolves that it should admonish them not to touch the sheep. ¹⁸ And the sheep went to the wolves according to the word of the Lord, and another sheep met it and went with it, and the two went and entered together into the assembly of those wolves, and spoke with them, and admonished them not to touch the sheep from now on. ¹⁹ And immediately I saw the wolves, and how they oppressed the sheep exceedingly with all their power; and the sheep cried aloud. ²⁰ And the Lord came to the sheep and they began to strike those wolves: and the wolves began to make lamentation, but the sheep became quiet and then ceased to cry out. ²¹ And I saw the sheep until they departed from among the wolves, but the eyes of the wolves were blinded, and those wolves departed in pursuit of the sheep with all their power. ²² And the Lord of the sheep went with them, as their leader, and all His sheep followed Him: and his face was dazzling, and glorious, and terrible to behold. ²³ But the wolves began to pursue those sheep until they reached a sea of water. ²⁴ And that sea was divided, and the water stood on this side and on that before their face, and their Lord led them and placed Himself between them and the wolves. ²⁵ And as those wolves did not yet see the sheep, they proceeded into the midst of that sea, and the wolves followed the sheep, and [those wolves] ran after them into that sea. ²⁶ And when they saw the Lord of the sheep, they turned to flee before His face, but that sea gathered itself together, and became as it had been created, and the water swelled and rose until it covered those wolves. ²⁷ And I saw until all the wolves who pursued those sheep perished and were drowned. ²⁸ But the sheep escaped from that water and went out into a wilderness, where there was no water and no grass; and they began to open their eyes and to see; and I saw the Lord of the sheep pasturing them and giving them water and grass, and that sheep going and leading them. ²⁹ And that sheep ascended to the summit of that lofty rock, and the Lord of the sheep sent it to them. ³⁰ And after that I saw the Lord of the sheep who stood before them, and His appearance was great, and terrible, and majestic, and all those sheep saw Him and were afraid before His face. ³¹ And they all feared and trembled because of Him, and they cried to that sheep with them [which was among them]: We are not able to stand before our Lord or to behold Him! ³² And that sheep which led them again ascended to the summit of that rock, but the sheep began to be blinded and to wander from the way which he had showed them, but that sheep was not aware. ³³ And the Lord of the sheep was exceedingly wrathful against them, and that sheep discovered it, and went down from the summit of the rock, and came to the sheep, and found the greatest part of them blinded and fallen away. ³⁴ And when they saw it, they feared and trembled at its presence and desired to return to their folds. ³⁵ And that sheep took other sheep with it, and came to those sheep which had fallen away, and began to slay them; and the sheep feared its presence, and so that sheep brought back those sheep that had fallen away, and they returned to their folds. ³⁶ And I saw in this vision until that sheep became a man, and built a house for the Lord of the sheep, and placed all the sheep in that house. ³⁷ And I saw until this sheep which had met that sheep which led them fell asleep: and I saw until all the great sheep perished and little ones arose in their place, and they came to a pasture, and approached a stream of water. ³⁸ Then that sheep, their leader which had become a man, withdrew from them and fell asleep, and all the sheep sought it and cried over it with a great crying. ³⁹ And I saw until they ceased from crying for that sheep and crossed that stream of water, and there arose the two sheep as leaders in the place of those which had led them and fallen asleep. ⁴⁰ And I saw until the sheep came to an attractive place, and a pleasant and glorious land, and I saw until those sheep were satisfied; and that house stood among them in the pleasant land. ⁴¹ And sometimes their eyes were opened, and sometimes blinded, until another sheep arose and led them and brought them all back, and their eyes were opened. ⁴² And the dogs, and the foxes, and the wild boars began to devour those sheep until the Lord of the sheep raised up a ram from their midst, which led them. ⁴³ And that ram began to butt those dogs, foxes, and wild boars on either side until he had destroyed them all. ⁴⁴ And that sheep whose eyes were opened saw that ram, which was among the sheep, until it forsook its glory and began to butt those sheep, and trampled on them, and behaved unseemly itself. ⁴⁵ And the Lord of the sheep sent the lamb to another lamb and raised it to be a ram and leader of the sheep instead of that ram which had forsaken its glory. ⁴⁶ And it went to it and spoke to it alone, and raised it to be a ram, and made it the prince and leader of the sheep, but during all these things those dogs oppressed the sheep. ⁴⁷ And the first ram pursued that second ram, and that second ram arose and fled before it, and I saw until those dogs pulled down the first ram. ⁴⁸ And that second ram arose and led the [little] sheep. And those sheep grew and multiplied, but all the dogs, and foxes, and wild boars feared and fled before it, and that ram butted and killed the wild beasts, and those wild beasts no longer had any power among the sheep and no longer robbed them of anything. ⁴⁹ And that ram begot many sheep and fell asleep; and a little sheep became ram in its stead and became prince and leader of those sheep. ⁵⁰ And that house became great and broad, and it was built for those sheep: [and] a great and lofty tower was built on the house for the Lord of the sheep, and that house was low, but the tower was elevated and lofty, and the Lord of the sheep stood on that tower and they offered a full table before Him. ⁵¹ And again I saw that those sheep again erred and went many ways, and forsook that house of theirs, and the Lord of the sheep called some from among the sheep and sent them to the sheep, but the sheep began to slay them. ⁵² And one of them was saved and was not slain, and it sped away and cried aloud over the sheep; and they sought to slay it, but the Lord of the sheep saved it from the sheep, and brought it up to me, and caused it to dwell there. ⁵³ And He sent many other sheep to those sheep to testify to them and lament over them. ⁵⁴ And after that, I saw that when they forsook the house of the Lord and His tower they fell away entirely, and their eyes were blinded; and I saw how the Lord of the sheep worked much slaughter among them in their herds until those sheep invited that slaughter and betrayed His place. ⁵⁵ And He gave them over into the hands of the lions, and tigers, and wolves, and hyenas, and into the hand of the foxes, and to all the wild beasts, and those wild beasts began to tear those sheep in pieces. **56** And I saw that He forsook their house and their tower and gave them all into the hand of the lions and into the hand of all the wild beasts to tear and devour them. **57** And I began to cry aloud with all my power, and to appeal to the Lord of the sheep, and to represent to Him in regard to the sheep that they were devoured by all the wild beasts. **58** But He remained unmoved, though He saw it, and rejoiced that they were devoured, and swallowed, and robbed, and He left them to be devoured in the hand of all the beasts. **59** And He called seventy shepherds and cast those sheep to them that they might pasture them, and He spoke to the shepherds and their companions: Let each individual among you pasture the sheep from now on and do everything that I will command you to do. And I will deliver them over to you rightly numbered and tell you which of them are to be destroyed: and destroy them. **60** And He gave those sheep over to them. **61** And He called another and spoke to him: Observe and record everything that the shepherds will do to those sheep, for they will destroy more of them than I have commanded them. **62** And every excess and the destruction which will be worked through the shepherds, record—how many they destroy according to My command, and how many according to their own caprice: record against every individual shepherd all the destruction he effects. **63** And read out before Me by number how many they destroy and how many they deliver over for destruction, that I may have this as a testimony against them, and know every deed of the shepherds, that I may comprehend and see what they do, whether or not they abide by My command which I have commanded them. **64** But they will not know it, and you will not declare it to them, nor admonish them, but only record against each individual all the destruction which each of the shepherds effect in his time, and lay it all before Me. **65** And I saw until those shepherds pastured in their season, and they began to slay and to destroy more than they were commanded, and they delivered those sheep into the hand of the lions. **66** And the lions and tigers ate and devoured the greater part of those sheep, and the wild boars ate along with them; and they burned that tower and demolished that house. **67** And I became exceedingly sorrowful over that tower because that house of the sheep was demolished, and afterward I was unable to see if those sheep entered that house. **68** And the shepherds and their associates delivered those sheep over to all the wild beasts to devour them, and each one of them received a definite number in his time: it was written by the other in a scroll how many of them each one of them destroyed. **69** And each one slew and destroyed many more than was prescribed, and I began to weep and lament on account of those sheep. **70** And so in the vision I saw how that one who wrote wrote down everyone that was destroyed by those shepherds' day by day, and he carried [it] up, and laid [it] down, and actually showed the whole scroll to the Lord of the sheep—[even] everything that they had done, and all that each one of them had made away with, and all that they had given over to destruction. **71** And the scroll was read before the Lord of the sheep, and He took the scroll from his hand, and read it, and sealed it, and laid it down. **72** And then I saw how the shepherds pastured for twelve hours, and behold, three of those sheep turned back, and came, and entered, and began to build up all that had fallen down of that house, but the wild boars tried to hinder them, but they were not able. **73** And they began to build again as before, and they reared up that tower, and it was named the high tower; and they began to place a table again before the tower, but all the bread on it was polluted and not pure. **74** And as concerning all this, the eyes of those sheep were blinded so that they did not see, and [the eyes of] their shepherds likewise; and they delivered them in large numbers to their shepherds for destruction, and they trampled the sheep with their feet and devoured them. **75** And the Lord of the sheep remained unmoved until all the sheep were dispersed over the field and mingled with them, and they did not save them out of the hand of the beasts. **76** And this one who wrote the scroll carried it up, and showed it, and read it before the Lord of the sheep, and implored Him on their account as he showed Him all the doings of the shepherds and gave testimony before Him against all the shepherds. **77** And he took the actual scroll, and laid it down beside Him, and departed."

CHAPTER 90

1 "And I saw until thirty-five shepherds undertook the pasturing [of the sheep] in this manner, and they separately completed their periods as did the first; and others received them into their hands, to pasture them for their period, each shepherd in his own period. **2** And after that, I saw in my vision all the birds of the heavens coming: the eagles, the vultures, the kites, the ravens; but the eagles led all the birds, and they began to devour those sheep, and to pick out their eyes, and to devour their flesh. **3** And the sheep cried out because their flesh was being devoured by the birds, and as for me, I looked and lamented in my sleep over that shepherd who pastured the sheep. **4** And I saw until those sheep were devoured by the dogs, and eagles, and kites, and they left neither flesh, nor skin, nor sinew remaining on them until only their bones stood there: and their bones also fell to the earth and the sheep became few. **5** And I saw until twenty-three had undertaken the pasturing and completed fifty-eight times in their several periods. **6** But behold, lambs were borne by those white sheep, and they began to open their eyes and to see, and to cry to the sheep. **7** Yes, they cried to them, but they did not listen to what they said to them, but were exceedingly deaf, and their eyes were very exceedingly blinded. **8** And I saw in the vision how the ravens flew on those lambs, and took one of those lambs, and dashed the sheep in pieces, and devoured them. **9** And I saw until horns grew on those lambs, and the ravens cast down their horns; and I saw until there sprouted a great horn of one of those sheep, and their eyes were opened. **10** And it looked at them [and their eyes opened], and it cried to the sheep, and the rams saw it, and all ran to it. **11** And notwithstanding all this, those eagles, and vultures, and ravens, and kites still kept tearing the sheep, and swooping down on them, and devouring them: still the sheep remained silent, but the rams lamented and cried out. **12** And those ravens fought and battled with it and sought to lay its horn low, but they had no power over it. **13** And I saw until the shepherds, and eagles, and those vultures and kites came, and they cried to the ravens that they should break the horn of that ram, and they battled and fought with it, and it battled with them and cried that its help might come. **14** And I saw until that man, who wrote down the names of the shepherds [and] carried [it] up into the presence of the Lord of the sheep, [[came and helped it and showed it everything: he had come down for the help of that ram.]] **15** And I saw until the Lord of the sheep came to them in wrath, and all who saw Him fled, and they all fell into His shadow from before His face. **16** All the eagles, and vultures, and ravens, and kites were gathered together, and there came with them all the sheep of the field, yes, they all came together, and helped each other to break that horn of the ram. **17** And I saw until that man, who wrote the scroll according to the command of the Lord, opened that scroll concerning the destruction which those twelve last shepherds had worked, and showed before the Lord of the sheep that they had destroyed much more than their predecessors. **18** And I saw until the Lord of the sheep came to them and took in His hand the staff of His wrath, and struck the earth, and the earth split apart, and all the beasts and all the birds of the heavens fell from among those sheep, and were swallowed up in the earth, and it covered them. **19** And I saw until a great sword was given to the sheep, and the sheep proceeded against all the beasts of the field to slay them, and all the beasts and the birds of the heavens fled before their face. **20** And I saw until a throne was erected in the pleasant land, and the Lord of the sheep sat Himself thereon, and the other took the sealed scrolls and opened those scrolls before the Lord of the sheep. **21** And the Lord called those men, [those] seven first white ones, and commanded that they should bring before Him, beginning with the first star which led the way, all the stars whose genitals were like those of horses, and they brought them all before Him. **22** And He spoke to that man who wrote before Him, being one of those seven white ones, and said to him, Take those seventy shepherds to whom I delivered the sheep, and who taking them on their own authority slew more than I commanded them. **23** And behold, I saw [that] they were all bound, and they all stood before Him. **24** And the judgment was first held over the stars, and they were judged and found guilty, and went to the place of condemnation, and they were cast into an abyss, full of fire and flaming, and full of pillars of fire. **25** And those seventy shepherds were judged and found guilty, and they were cast into that fiery abyss. **26** And I saw at that time how a similar abyss was opened in the midst of the earth, full of fire, and they brought those blinded sheep, and they were all judged, and found guilty, and cast into this fiery abyss, and they burned; now this abyss was to the right of that house. ²⁷ And I saw those sheep burning and their bones burning. ²⁸ And I stood up to see until they folded up that old house, and carried off all the pillars, and all the beams and ornaments of the house were at the same time folded up with it, and they carried it off and laid it in a place in the south of the land. ²⁹ And I saw until the Lord of the sheep brought a new house greater and loftier than that first and set it up in the place of the first which had been folded up: all its pillars were new, and its ornaments were new and larger than those of the first, the old one which He had taken away, and all the sheep were within it. ³⁰ And I saw all the sheep which had been left, and all the beasts on the earth, and all the birds of the heavens falling down and doing homage to those sheep, and making petition to and obeying them in everything. ³¹ And thereafter those three who were clothed in white and had seized me by my hand, [who had taken me up before], and the hand of that ram also seizing hold of me, they took me up and set me down in the midst of those sheep before the judgment took place. ³² And those sheep were all white, and their wool was abundant and clean. ³³ And all that had been destroyed and dispersed, and all the beasts of the field, and all the birds of the heavens assembled in that house, and the Lord of the sheep rejoiced with great joy because they were all good and had returned to His house. ³⁴ And I saw until they laid down that sword which had been given to the sheep, and they brought it back into the house, and it was sealed before the presence of the Lord, and all the sheep were invited into that house, but it did not hold them. ³⁵ And their eyes were all opened, and they saw the good, and there was not one among them that did not see. ³⁶ And I saw that that house was large, and broad, and very full. ³⁷ And I saw that a white bull was born, with large horns and all the beasts of the field and all the birds of the air feared him and made petition to him all the time. ³⁸ And I saw until all their generations were transformed, and they all became white bulls; and the first among them became a lamb, and that lamb became a great animal and had great black horns on its head; and the Lord of the sheep rejoiced over it and over all the oxen. ³⁹ And I slept in their midst: and I awoke and saw everything. ⁴⁰ This is the vision which I saw while I slept, and I awoke and blessed the Lord of righteousness and gave Him glory. ⁴¹ Then I wept with a great weeping and my tears were unrestrained until I could no longer endure it: when I saw, they flowed on account of what I had seen, for everything will come and be fulfilled, and all the deeds of men in their order were shown to me. ⁴² On that night I remembered the first dream, and I wept because of it, and was troubled because I had seen that vision."

SECTION 5: THE EPISTLE OF ENOCH

CHAPTER 91

¹ "And now, my son Methuselah, call all your brothers to me and gather together all the sons of your mother to me; for the word calls me, and the Spirit is poured out on me, that I may show you everything that will befall you forever." ² And there on Methuselah went and summoned to himself all his brothers and assembled his relatives. ³ And he spoke to all the children of righteousness and said, "Hear, you sons of Enoch, all the words of your father, and listen to the voice of my mouth; for I exhort you and say to you, beloved: ⁴ Love uprightness and walk therein. And do not draw near to uprightness with a double heart, || And do not associate with those of a double heart, || But walk in righteousness, my sons. And it will guide you on good paths, || And righteousness will be your companion. ⁵ For I know that violence must increase on the earth, || And a great discipline will be executed on the earth, || Yes, it will be cut off from its roots, || And its whole structure will be destroyed. ⁶ And unrighteousness will again be consummated on the earth, || And all the deeds of unrighteousness, and of violence, and transgression || Will prevail in a twofold degree. ⁷ And when sin, and unrighteousness, and blasphemy, and violence || Increase in all kinds of deeds, || And apostasy, and transgression, and

uncleanness increase, || A great discipline will come from Heaven on all these, || And the holy Lord will come out with wrath and discipline || To execute judgment on earth. ⁸ In those days violence will be cut off from its roots, || And the roots of unrighteousness together with deceit, || And they will be destroyed from under the heavens. ⁹ And all the idols of the heathen will be abandoned, || And the temples burned with fire, || And they will remove them from the whole earth, || And they will be cast into the judgment of fire || And will perish in wrath and in grievous judgment forever. ¹⁰ And the righteous will arise from their sleep, || And wisdom will arise and be given to them. [[And after that the roots of unrighteousness will be cut off, || And the sinners will be destroyed by the sword || [And] will be cut off from the blasphemers in every place, || And those who plan violence and those who commit blasphemy || Will perish by the sword.]] ¹² And after that there will be another, the eighth week—That of righteousness—And a sword will be given to it || That a righteous judgment may be executed on the oppressors, || And sinners will be delivered into the hands of the righteous. ¹³ And at its close they will acquire houses through their righteousness, || And a house will be built for the Great King in glory forevermore, || And all mankind will look to the path of uprightness. ¹⁴ And after that, in the ninth week, || The righteous judgment will be revealed to the whole world, || And all the works of the godless will vanish from all the earth, || And the world will be written down for destruction. ¹⁵ And after this, in the tenth week, in the seventh part, || There will be the great continuous judgment, || In which He will execute vengeance among the messengers. ¹⁶ And the first heaven will depart and pass away, || And a new heaven will appear, || And all the powers of the heavens will give sevenfold light. ¹⁷ And after that there will be many weeks without number forever, || And all will be in goodness and righteousness, || And sin will no longer be mentioned forever. ¹⁸ And now I tell you, my sons, || And show you the paths of righteousness and the paths of violence. Yes, I will show them to you again || That you may know what will come to pass. ¹⁹ And now, listen to me, my sons, || And walk in the paths of righteousness, || And do not walk in the paths of violence, || For all who walk in the paths of unrighteousness will perish forever."

CHAPTER 92

¹ The scroll written by Enoch—[[Enoch indeed wrote this complete doctrine of wisdom, [which is] praised of all men and a judge of all the earth]]—for all my children who will dwell on the earth, and for the future generations who will observe uprightness and peace. ² Do not let your spirit be troubled on account of the times; For the Holy and Great One has appointed days for all things. ³ And the righteous one will arise from sleep || And walk in the paths of righteousness, || And all his path and conversation || Will be in continuous goodness and grace. ⁴ He will be gracious to the righteous || And give him continuous uprightness, || And He will give him power || So that he will be [endowed] with goodness and righteousness. And he will walk in perpetual light. ⁵ And sin will perish in darkness forever || And will no longer be seen from that day forevermore.

CHAPTER 93

¹ And after that, Enoch both gave and began to recount from the scrolls. ² And Enoch said, "Concerning the children of righteousness, and concerning the chosen ones of the world, and concerning the plant of uprightness, I will speak these things; yes, I, Enoch, will declare [them] to you, my sons, according to that which appeared to me in the heavenly vision, and which I have known through the word of the holy messengers, and have learned from the heavenly tablets." ³ And Enoch began to recount from the scrolls and said, "I was born the seventh in the first week, while judgment and righteousness still endured. ⁴ And great wickedness will arise after me in the second week, and deceit will have sprung up, and the first end will be in it. And a man will be saved in it; and after it is ended, unrighteousness will grow up, and a law will be made for the sinners. ⁵ And after that, in the third week, at its close, a man will be chosen as the plant of righteous judgment, and his posterity will become the plant of

righteousness forevermore. **6** And after that, in the fourth week, at its close, visions of the holy and righteous will be seen, and a law for all generations and an enclosure will be made for them. **7** And after that, in the fifth week, at its close, the house of glory and dominion will be built forever. **8** And after that, in the sixth week, all who live in it will be blinded, and the hearts of all of them will godlessly forsake wisdom. And a man will ascend in it; and at its close the house of dominion will be burned with fire, and the whole race of the chosen root will be dispersed. **9** And after that, in the seventh week, an apostate generation will arise, and its [wicked] deeds will be many, and all its deeds will be apostate. **10** And at its close the chosen righteous of the continuous plant of righteousness will be selected to receive sevenfold instruction concerning all His creation. **11** [[For who is there of all the children of men that is able to hear the voice of the Holy One without being troubled? And who can think His thoughts? and who is there that can behold all the works of Heaven? **12** And how should there be one who could behold Heaven, and who is there that could understand the things of Heaven, and see a soul or a spirit, and could tell thereof, or ascend and see all their ends and think them or do like them? **13** And who is there of all men that could know what the breadth and the length of the earth is? And to whom has been shown the measure of all of them? **14** Or is there anyone who could discern the length of the heavens and how great its height is, and on what it is founded, and how great the number of the stars is, and where all the luminaries rest?]]"

CHAPTER 94

1 And now I say to you, my sons, love righteousness and walk therein, for the paths of righteousness are worthy of acceptance, but the paths of unrighteousness will suddenly be destroyed and vanish. **2** And the paths of violence and death will be revealed to certain men of a generation, and they will hold themselves far from them, and will not follow them. **3** And now I say to you, the righteous: do not walk in the paths of wickedness, nor in the paths of death, and do not draw near to them, lest you be destroyed. **4** But seek and choose for yourselves righteousness and a chosen life, and walk in the paths of peace, and you will live and prosper. **5** And hold fast my words in the thoughts of your hearts and do not allow them to be effaced from your hearts, for I know that sinners will tempt men to mistreat wisdom, so that no place may be found for her, and no manner of temptation may diminish. **6** Woe to those who build unrighteousness and oppression and lay deceit as a foundation, for they will be suddenly overthrown, and they will have no peace. **7** Woe to those who build their houses with sin, for they will be overthrown from all their foundations, and they will fall by the sword. [[And those who acquire gold and silver will suddenly perish in judgment.]] **8** Woe to you, you rich, for you have trusted in your riches, and you will depart from your riches, because you have not remembered the Highest in the days of your riches. **9** You have committed blasphemy and unrighteousness, and have become ready for the day of slaughter, and the day of darkness, and the Day of the Great Judgment. **10** So I speak and declare to you: He who has created you will overthrow you, and there will be no compassion for your fall, and your Creator will rejoice at your destruction. **11** And your righteous ones will be a reproach to the sinners and the godless in those days.

CHAPTER 95

1 Oh that my eyes were [a cloud of] waters that I might weep over you || And pour down my tears as a cloud of waters—So that I might rest from my troubled heart! **2** Who has permitted you to practice reproaches and wickedness? And so judgment will overtake you sinners. **3** Do not fear the sinners, you righteous, || For the Lord will deliver them into your hands again, || That you may execute judgment on them according to your desires. **4** Woe to you who fulminate anathemas which cannot be reversed: Healing will therefore be far from you because of your sins. **5** Woe to you who repay your neighbor with evil, || For you will be repaid according to your works. **6** Woe to you, lying witnesses, and to those who weigh out injustice, || For you will suddenly perish. **7** Woe to you, sinners, for you persecute the righteous, || For you will be

delivered up and persecuted because of injustice, || And its yoke will be heavy on you.

CHAPTER 96

1 Be hopeful, you righteous, || For the sinners will suddenly perish before you, || And you will have lordship over them according to your desires. **2** [[And in the day of the tribulation of the sinners, || Your children will mount and rise as eagles, || And your nest will be higher than the vultures, || And you will ascend and enter the crevices of the earth, || And the clefts of the rock forever as coneys before the unrighteous, || And the sirens will sigh and weep because of you.]] **3** So do not fear, you that have suffered, || For healing will be your portion, || And a bright light will enlighten you, || And you will hear the voice of rest from Heaven. **4** Woe to you, you sinners, || For your riches make you appear like the righteous, || But your hearts convict you of being sinners, || And this fact will be a testimony against you for a memorial of [your] evil deeds. **5** Woe to you who devour the finest of the wheat, || And drink wine in large bowls, || And tread the lowly underfoot with your might. **6** Woe to you who drink water from every fountain, || For you will suddenly be consumed and wither away, || Because you have forsaken the fountain of life. **7** Woe to you who work unrighteousness, and deceit, and blasphemy: It will be a memorial against you for evil. **8** Woe to you, you mighty, who oppress the righteous with might, || For the day of your destruction is coming. In those days many and good days will come to the righteous—In the day of your judgment.

CHAPTER 97

1 Believe, you righteous, that the sinners will become a shame and perish in the day of unrighteousness. **2** Be it known to you, [you sinners,] that the Highest is mindful of your destruction, and the messengers of Heaven rejoice over your destruction. **3** What will you do, you sinners, and where will you flee on that Day of Judgment, when you hear the voice of the prayer of the righteous? **4** Yes, you will fare like to them, against whom this word will be a testimony: "You have been companions of sinners." **5** And in those days the prayer of the righteous will reach to the Lord, and for you the days of your judgment will come. **6** And all the words of your unrighteousness will be read out before the Great Holy One, and your faces will be covered with shame, and He will reject every work which is grounded on unrighteousness. **7** Woe to you, you sinners, who live in the midst of [the] ocean and on the dry land, whose remembrance is evil against you. **8** Woe to you who acquire silver and gold in unrighteousness, and say, "We have become rich with riches, and have possessions, and have acquired everything we have desired. **9** And now, let us do what we purposed, for we have gathered silver, and there are many farmers in our houses. And our granaries are brimful as with water, **10** yes, and like water your lies will flow away; for your riches will not abide but speedily ascend from you, for you have acquired it all in unrighteousness, and you will be given over to a great curse.

CHAPTER 98

1 And now I swear to you—to the wise and to the foolish—for you will have manifold experiences on the earth. **2** For you men will put on more adornments than a woman, and more colored garments than a virgin. They will be poured out as water in royalty, and in grandeur, and in power, and in silver, and in gold, and in purple, and in splendor, and in food. **3** Therefore they will be wanting in doctrine and wisdom, and they will thereby perish together with their possessions, and with all their glory, and their splendor; and in shame, and in slaughter, and in great destitution, their spirits will be cast into the furnace of fire. **4** I have sworn to you, you sinners, as a mountain has not become a slave, and a hill does not become the handmaid of a woman, even so sin has not been sent on the earth, but man has created it of himself, and they who commit it will fall under a great curse. **5** And barrenness has not been given to the woman, but she dies without children on account of the deeds of her own hands. **6** I have sworn to you,

you sinners, by the Holy Great One, that all your evil deeds are revealed in the heavens, and that none of your deeds of oppression are covered and hidden. **7** And do not think in your spirit nor say in your heart that you do not know and that you do not see that every sin is recorded every day in Heaven in the presence of the Highest. **8** From now on you know that all your oppression with which you oppress is written down every day until the day of your judgment. **9** Woe to you, you fools, for you will perish through your folly; and you transgress against the wise, and so good fortune will not be your portion. **10** And now, know that you are prepared for the day of destruction. For that reason, do not hope to live, you sinners, but you will depart and die; for you know no ransom; for you are prepared for the Day of the Great Judgment, for the day of tribulation and great shame for your spirits. **11** Woe to you, you obstinate of heart, who work wickedness and eat blood: from where do you have good things to eat, and to drink, and to be filled? From all the good things which the Lord, the Highest, has placed in abundance on the earth. Therefore, you will have no peace. **12** Woe to you who love the deeds of unrighteousness: why do you hope for good for yourselves? Know that you will be delivered into the hands of the righteous, and they will cut off your necks, and slay you, and have no mercy on you. **13** Woe to you who rejoice in the tribulation of the righteous, for no grave will be dug for you. **14** Woe to you who set as nothing the words of the righteous, for you will have no hope of life. **15** Woe to you who write down lying and godless words, for they write down their lies that men may hear them and act godlessly toward [their] neighbor. **16** Therefore, they will have no peace, but will die a sudden death.

CHAPTER 99

1 Woe to you who work godlessness, and glory in lying and extol them: you will perish, and no happy life will be yours. **2** Woe to them who pervert the words of uprightness, and transgress the perpetual law, and transform themselves into what they were not: they will be trodden underfoot on the earth. **3** In those days make ready, you righteous, to raise your prayers as a memorial, and place them as a testimony before the messengers, that they may place the sin of the sinners for a memorial before the Highest. **4** In those days the nations will be stirred up, and the families of the nations will arise on the day of destruction. **5** And in those days the destitute will go out and carry off their children, and they will abandon them, so that their children will perish through them: yes, they will abandon their children—sucklings, and not return to them, and will have no pity on their beloved ones. **6** And again I swear to you, you sinners, that sin is prepared for a day of unceasing bloodshed. **7** And they who worship stones, and grave images of gold, and silver, and wood, and clay, and those who worship impure spirits and demons, and all kinds of idols not according to knowledge, will get no manner of help from them. **8** And they will become godless by reason of the folly of their hearts, and their eyes will be blinded through the fear of their hearts and through visions in their dreams. **9** They will become godless and fearful through these, for they will have worked all their work in a lie and will have worshiped a stone. Therefore, they will perish in an instant. **10** But in those days, blessed are all they who accept the words of wisdom, and understand them, and observe the paths of the Highest, and walk in the path of His righteousness, and do not become godless with the godless, for they will be saved. **11** Woe to you who spread evil to your neighbors, for you will be slain in Sheol. **12** Woe to you who make deceitful and false measures, and who cause bitterness on the earth, for they will thereby be utterly consumed. **13** Woe to you who build your houses through the grievous toil of others, and all their building materials are the bricks and stones of sin; I tell you that you will have no peace. **14** Woe to them who reject the measure and agelong heritage of their fathers and whose souls follow after idols, for they will have no rest. **15** Woe to them who work unrighteousness, and help oppression, and slay their neighbors until the Day of the Great Judgment. **16** For He will cast down your glory, and bring affliction on your hearts, and will arouse His fierce indignation, and destroy all of you with the sword; and all the holy and righteous will remember your sins.

CHAPTER 100

1 And in those days in one place the fathers will be smitten together with their sons and brothers will fall in death with one another until the streams flow with their blood. **2** For a man will not withhold his hand from slaying his sons and his sons' sons, and the sinner will not withhold his hand from his honored brother: they will slay one another from dawn until sunset. **3** And the horse will walk up to the breast in the blood of sinners, and the chariot will be submerged to its height. **4** In those days the messengers will descend into the secret places and gather together into one place all those who brought down sin, and the Highest will arise on that Day of Judgment to execute great judgment among sinners. **5** And He will appoint guardians over all the righteous and holy from among the holy messengers to guard them as the apple of [His] eye, until He makes an end of all wickedness and all sin, and though the righteous sleep a long sleep, they have nothing to fear. **6** And [then] the children of the earth will see the wise in security, and will understand all the words of this scroll, and recognize that their riches will not be able to save them in the overthrow of their sins. **7** Woe to you, sinners, on the day of strong anguish—you who afflict the righteous and burn them with fire: you will be repaid according to your works. **8** Woe to you, you obstinate of heart, who watch in order to devise wickedness: therefore, fear will come on you and there will be none to help you. **9** Woe to you, you sinners, on account of the words of your mouth, and on account of the deeds of your hands which your godlessness has worked: you will burn in blazing flames worse than fire. **10** And now, know that He will inquire from the messengers in Heaven regarding your deeds, [and] from the sun, and from the moon, and from the stars in reference to your sins, because on the earth you execute judgment on the righteous. **11** And He will summon every cloud, and mist, and dew, and rain to testify against you, for they will all be withheld from descending on you because of you, and they will be mindful of your sins. **12** And now give presents to the rain that it is not withheld from descending on you, nor yet the dew, when it has received gold and silver from you, that it may descend. **13** When the hoarfrost and snow with their frigidness, and all the snowstorms with all their plagues fall on you, in those days you will not be able to stand before them.

CHAPTER 101

1 Observe the heavens, you children of Heaven, and every work of the Highest, and fear Him and work no evil in His presence. **2** If He closes the windows of the heavens, and withholds the rain and the dew from descending on the earth on your account, what will you do then? **3** And if He sends His anger on you because of your deeds, you cannot petition Him, for you spoke proud and insolent words against His righteousness: therefore, you will have no peace. **4** And do you not see the sailors of the ships, how their ships are tossed to and fro by the waves, and are shaken by the winds, and are in severe trouble? **5** And therefore, they fear because all their excellent possessions go on the sea with them, and they have evil forebodings of heart that the sea will swallow them, and they will perish therein. **6** Are the entire sea, and all its waters, and all its movements, not the work of the Highest, and has He not set limits to its doings, and confined it throughout by the sand? **7** And at His reproof it is afraid and dries up, and all its fish die and all that is in it, but you sinners that are on the earth do not fear Him. **8** Has He not made the heavens, and the earth, and all that is therein? Who has given understanding and wisdom to everything that moves on the earth and in the sea? **9** Do the sailors of the ships not fear the sea? Yet sinners do not fear the Highest.

CHAPTER 102

1 In those days when He has brought a grievous fire on you, where will you flee, and where will you find deliverance? And when He launches out His Word against you will you not be frightened and fear? **2** And all the luminaries will be frightened with great fear, and all the earth will be frightened, and tremble, and be alarmed. **3** And all the messengers will execute their commands and will seek to hide themselves from the presence of the Great Glory, and the children of earth will tremble and quake; and you sinners will be cursed forever, and you will have no peace. **4** Do not fear, you souls of the righteous, and be hopeful, you that have died in righteousness. **5** And do not grieve if your soul has descended into Sheol in grief, and that in your life your body did not fare according to your goodness, but wait for the day of the judgment of sinners and for the day of cursing and discipline. **6** And yet when you die, the sinners speak over you: "As we die, so the righteous die, and what benefit do they reap for their deeds? **7** Behold, so they die even as we, in grief and darkness, and what have they more than we? From now on we are equal. **8** And what will they receive and what will they see forever? Behold, they have also died, and from now on and forever they will see no light." **9** I tell you, you sinners, you are content to eat and drink, and rob and sin, and strip men naked, and acquire wealth and see good days. **10** Have you seen the righteous, how their end falls out, that no manner of violence is found in them until their death? **11** "Nevertheless, they perished and became as though they had not been, and their spirits descended into Sheol in tribulation."

CHAPTER 103

1 Now, therefore, I swear to you, the righteous, by the glory of the Great and Honored and Mighty One in dominion, and by His greatness I swear to you. **2** I know a mystery and have read the heavenly tablets, and have seen the holy scrolls, and have found written therein and inscribed regarding them **3** that all goodness, and joy, and glory are prepared for them and written down for the spirits of those who have died in righteousness, and that manifold good will be given to you in reward for your labors, and that your lot is abundantly beyond the lot of the living. **4** And the spirits of you who have died in righteousness will live and rejoice, and their spirits will not perish, nor their memorial from before the face of the Great One to all the generations of the world. For that reason, no longer fear their insolence. **5** Woe to you, you sinners, when you have died, if you die in the wealth of your sins! And those who are like you say regarding you, "Blessed are the sinners; they have seen all their days. **6** And how they have died in prosperity and in wealth and have not seen tribulation or murder in their life. And they have died in honor, and judgment has not been executed on them during their life." **7** Know that their souls will be made to descend into Sheol, and they will be wretched in their great tribulation. **8** And your spirits will enter into darkness, and chains, and a burning flame where there is grievous judgment; and the Great Judgment will be for all the generations of the world. Woe to you, for you will have no peace. **9** Do not say in regard to the righteous and good who are in life, "In our troubled days we have toiled laboriously, and experienced every trouble, and met with much evil, and been consumed, and have become few and our spirit small. **10** And we have been destroyed and have not found any to help us even with a word. We have been tortured and have not hoped to see life from day to day. **11** We hoped to be the head and have become the tail. We have toiled laboriously and had no satisfaction in our toil. And we have become the food of the sinners and the unrighteous, and they have laid their yoke heavily on us. **12** They who hated us have had dominion over us and struck us; and we have bowed our necks to those that hated us, but they did not pity us. **13** We desired to get away from them that we might escape and be at rest, but we found no place where we should flee and be safe from them. **14** And we complained to the rulers in our tribulation and cried out against those who devoured us, but they did not attend to our cries and would not listen to our voice. **15** And they helped those who robbed us and devoured us and those who made us few; and they concealed their oppression, and they did not remove from us the yoke of those that devoured us, and dispersed us, and murdered us, and they concealed their murder, and did not remember that they had lifted up their hands against us."

CHAPTER 104

1 I swear to you that the messengers in Heaven remember you for good before the glory of the Great One, and your names are written before the glory of the Great One. **2** Be hopeful, for you were previously put to shame through ill and affliction, but now you will shine as the lights of the heavens; you will shine, and you will be seen, and the portals of the heavens will be opened to you. **3** And in your cry, cry for judgment, and it will

appear to you, for all your tribulation will be visited on the rulers, and on all who helped those who plundered you. **4** Be hopeful and do not cast away your hopes, for you will have great joy as the messengers of Heaven. **5** What will you be obliged to do? you will not have to hide on the Day of the Great Judgment, and you will not be found as sinners, and the continuous judgment will be far from you for all the generations of the world. **6** And now, do not fear, you righteous, when you see the sinners growing strong and prospering in their ways: do not be companions with them, but keep far from their violence, for you will become companions of the hosts of Heaven. **7** And, although you sinners say, "All our sins will not be searched out and written down," nevertheless, they will write down all your sins every day. **8** And now I show to you that light and darkness, day and night, see all your sins. **9** Do not be godless in your hearts, and do not lie, and do not alter the words of uprightness, nor charge the words of the Holy Great One with lying, nor take account of your idols, for all your lying and all your godlessness do not issue in righteousness but in great sin. **10** And now I know this mystery, that sinners will alter and pervert the words of righteousness in many ways, and will speak wicked words, and lie, and practice great deceits, and write scrolls concerning their words. **11** But when they write down all my words truthfully in their languages, and do not change or diminish from my words, but write them all down truthfully, all that I first testified concerning them, **12** then—I know another mystery—scrolls will be given to the righteous and the wise to become a cause of joy, and uprightness, and much wisdom. **13** And the scrolls will be given to them, and they will believe in them and rejoice over them, and then all the righteous who have learned from all the paths of uprightness will be repaid.

CHAPTER 105

1 In those days the Lord commanded [them] to summon and testify to the children of earth concerning their wisdom: "Show [it] to them, for you are their guides and a repayment over the whole earth. **2** For My Son and I will be united with them forever in the paths of uprightness in their lives, and you will have peace. Rejoice, you children of uprightness! Amen."

CHAPTER 106

1 And after some days my son Methuselah took a wife for his son Lamech, and she became pregnant by him and bore a son. **2** And his body was white as snow and red as the blooming of a rose, and the hair of his head and his long locks were white as wool, and his eyes beautiful. And when he opened his eyes, he lighted up the whole house like the sun, and the whole house was very bright. **3** And he immediately arose in the hands of the midwife, opened his mouth, and conversed with the Lord of Righteousness. **4** And his father Lamech was afraid of him, and fled, and came to his father Methuselah. **5** And he said to him, "I have begotten a strange son, diverse from and unlike man, and resembling the sons of the God of Heaven, and his nature is different, and he is not like us, and his eyes are as the rays of the sun, and his countenance is glorious. **6** And it seems to me that he is not sprung from me but from the messengers, and I fear that a wonder may be worked on the earth in his days. **7** And now, my father, I am here to petition and implore you that you may go to our father Enoch and learn the truth from him, for his dwelling-place is among the messengers." **8** And when Methuselah heard the words of his son, he came to me at the ends of the earth, for he had heard that I was there, and he cried aloud, and I heard his voice, and I came to him. And I said to him, "Behold, here I am, my son, why have you come to me?" **9** And he answered and said, "I have come to you because of a great cause of anxiety, and I have approached because of a disturbing vision. **10** And now, my father, hear me: a son has been born to my son Lamech, the like of whom there is none, and his nature is not like man's nature, and the color of his body is whiter than snow and redder than the bloom of a rose, and the hair of his head is whiter than white wool, and his eyes are like the rays of the sun, and he opened his eyes and immediately lighted up the whole house. **11** And he arose in the hands of the midwife, and opened his mouth, and blessed the Lord of Heaven. **12** And his father Lamech became afraid, and fled to me, and did not believe that he was sprung from him, but that he was in the likeness of the messengers of Heaven; and behold, I have come to you that you may make the truth known to me." **13** And I, Enoch, answered and said to him, "The Lord will do a new thing on the earth, and I have already seen this in a vision, and I make known to you that in the generation of my father Jared some of the messengers of Heaven transgressed the word of the Lord. **14** And behold, they commit sin, and transgress the law, and have united themselves with women, and commit sin with them, and have married some of them, and have begot children by them. And they will produce giants on the earth, not according to the spirit, but according to the flesh, and there will be a great punishment on the earth, and the earth will be cleansed from all impurity. **15** Yes, there will come a great destruction over the whole earth, and there will be a deluge and a great destruction for one year. **16** And this son who has been born to you will be left on the earth, **17** and his three children will be saved with him when all mankind that are on the earth will die. **18** And now, make [it] known to your son Lamech that he who has been born is truly his son and call his name Noah, for he will be left to you, and he and his sons will be saved from the destruction which will come on the earth on account of all the sin and all the unrighteousness which will be consummated on the earth in his days. **19** And after that there will still be more unrighteousness than that which was first consummated on the earth, for I know the mysteries of the holy ones; for He, the Lord, has showed me and informed me, and I have read [them] in the heavenly tablets."

CHAPTER 107

1 "And I saw written on them that generation on generation will transgress, until a generation of righteousness arises, and transgression is destroyed, and sin passes away from the earth, and all manner of good comes on it. **2** And now, my son, go and make [it] known to your son Lamech that this son which has been born is truly his son, and that [this] is no lie." **3** And when Methuselah had heard the words of his father Enoch—for he had shown everything to him in secret—he returned and showed [them] to him and called the name of that son Noah, for he will comfort the earth after all the destruction.

CHAPTER 108

1 Another scroll which Enoch wrote for his son Methuselah and for those who will come after him and keep the Law in the last days. **2** You who have done good will wait for those days until an end is made of those who work evil and an end of the might of the transgressors. **3** And indeed, wait until sin has passed away, for their names will be blotted out of the Scroll of Life and out of the holy scrolls, and their seed will be destroyed forever, and their spirits will be slain, and they will cry and make lamentation in a place that is a chaotic wilderness, and they will burn in the fire, for there is no earth there. **4** And I saw something like an invisible cloud there, for by reason of its depth I could not look over, and I saw a flame of fire blazing brightly, and things like shining mountains circling and sweeping to and fro. **5** And I asked one of the holy messengers who was with me, and said to him, "What is this shining thing? For it is not a heaven but only the flame of a blazing fire, and the voice of weeping, and crying, and lamentation, and strong pain." **6** And he said to me, "[Into] this place which you see here are cast the spirits of sinners, and blasphemers, and of those who work wickedness, and of those who pervert everything that the Lord has spoken through the mouth of the prophets—[even] the things that will be. **7** For some of them are written and inscribed above in Heaven in order that the messengers may read them and know that which will befall the sinners, and the spirits of the humble, and of those who have afflicted their bodies and been repaid by God, and of those who have been put to shame by wicked men, **8** [those] who love God and loved neither gold, nor silver, nor any of the good things which are in the world, but gave their bodies over to torture. **9** Who, since they came into being, did not long after earthly food, but regarded everything as a passing breath, and lived accordingly, and the Lord tried them much, and their spirits were found pure so that they should bless His Name. **10** And I have recounted all the blessings destined for them in the scrolls. And He has assigned them

their reward, because they have been found to be such as loved Heaven more than their life in the world, and though they were trodden under [the] foot of wicked men, and experienced abuse and reviling from them, and were put to shame, yet they blessed Me. **11** And now I will summon the spirits of the good who belong to the generation of light, and I will transform those who were born in darkness, who in the flesh were not repaid with such honor as their faithfulness deserved. **12** And I will bring out those who have loved My holy Name in shining light, and I will seat each on the throne of his honor. **13** And they will be resplendent for infinite ages, for righteousness is the judgment of God; for He will give faithfulness to the faithful in the habitation of upright paths. **14** And they will see those who were born in darkness led into darkness, while the righteous will be resplendent. **15** And the sinners will cry aloud and see them resplendent, and they will indeed go where days and seasons are prescribed for them."

2 ENOCH

2 Enoch, also called Slavonic Enoch or the Secrets of Enoch, is thought to have been written between the 1st century BC and the 1st century AD. It deals with Enoch's rapture and ascent through the ten heavenly dimensions.

CHAPTER 1

1 There was a wise man, a great craftsman, and the Lord conceived love for him and received him, that he should behold the uppermost dwellings and be an eyewitness of the wise, and great, and inconceivable, and immutable realm of God Almighty, of the very wonderful, and glorious, and bright, and many-eyed station of the Lord's servants, and of the inaccessible throne of the Lord, and of the degrees and manifestations of the incorporeal hosts, and of the ineffable service of the multitude of the elements, and of the various apparition[s] and inexpressible singing of the host of cherubim, and of the boundless light. **2** At that time he said: When my one hundred and sixty-fifth year was completed, I begot my son Methuselah. **3** After this I also lived two hundred years and completed, of all the years of my life, three hundred and sixty-five years. **4** On the first day of the month I was in my house alone, and was resting on my bed, and slept. **5** And when I was asleep, great distress came up into my heart, and I was weeping with my eyes in sleep, and I could not understand what this distress was, or what would happen to me. **6** And two men appeared to me, exceedingly big, so that I never saw such on earth; their faces were shining like the sun, their eyes were also like a burning light, and fire was coming forth from their lips; with clothing . . . in appearance purple, their wings were brighter than gold, their hands whiter than snow. **7** They were standing at the head of my bed and began to call me by my name. **8** And I arose from my sleep and clearly saw those two men standing in front of me. **9** And I saluted them, and was seized with fear, and the appearance of my face was changed from terror, and those men said to me, **10** "Have courage, Enoch, do not fear; the perpetual God sent us to you, and behold, you will ascend with us into Heaven today, and you will tell your sons and all your household all that they will do without you on earth in your house, and let no one seek you until the Lord returns you to them." **11** And I hurried to obey them, and went out from my house, and made for the doors as it was commanded me, and summoned my sons Methuselah, and Regim, and Gaidad, and made all the marvels those men had told me known to them.

CHAPTER 2

1 Listen to me, my children: I do not know where I go, or what will befall me; now therefore, my children, I tell you: do not turn from God before the face of the vain, who did not make the heavens and earth, for these will perish and those who worship them, and may the Lord make your hearts confident in the fear of Him. And now, my children, let no one think to seek me until the Lord returns me to you.

CHAPTER 3

¹ It came to pass, when Enoch had told [this to] his sons, that the messengers took him on to their wings and bore him up on to the first heaven and placed him on the clouds. And there I looked, and again I looked higher, and saw the ether, and they placed me on the first heaven and showed me a very great sea, greater than the earthly sea.

CHAPTER 4

¹ They brought the elders and rulers of the stellar orders before my face, and showed me two hundred messengers who rule the stars and their services to the heavens, and fly with their wings, and come around all those who sail.

CHAPTER 5

¹ And here I looked down and saw the treasure-houses of the snow, and the messengers who keep their terrible storehouses, and the clouds from where they come out and into which they go.

CHAPTER 6

¹ They showed me the treasure-house of the dew, like oil of the olive, and the appearance of its form, as of all the flowers of the earth; furthermore, many messengers guarding the treasure-houses of these things, and how they are made to shut and open.

CHAPTER 7

¹ And those men took me and led me up on to the second heaven, and showed me darkness, greater than earthly darkness, and there I saw prisoners hanging, watched, awaiting the great and boundless judgment, and these messengers were dark-looking, more than earthly darkness, and unceasingly making weeping through all hours. ² And I said to the men who were with me, "For what reason are these unceasingly tortured?" They answered me: "These are God's apostates who did not obey God's commands, but took counsel with their own will, and turned away with their prince who is also fastened on the fifth heaven." ³ And I felt great pity for them, and they saluted me, and said to me, "Man of God, pray for us to the Lord"; and I answered to them: "Who am I, a mortal man, that I should pray for messengers? Who knows where I go, or what will befall me? Or who will pray for me?"

CHAPTER 8

¹ And those men took me there, and led me up on to the third heaven, and placed me there; and I looked downwards and saw the produce of these places, such as has never been known for goodness. ² And I saw all the sweet-flowering trees and beheld their fruits, which were sweet-smelling, and all the foods borne by them bubbling with fragrant exhalation. ³ And in the midst of the trees, that of Life, in that place whereon the Lord rests, when He goes up into paradise; and this tree is of ineffable goodness and fragrance and adorned more than every existing thing; and on all sides it is gold-looking, and vermillion, and fire-like in form and covers all, and it has produce from all fruits. ⁴ Its root is in the garden at the earth's end. ⁵ And paradise is between corruptibility and incorruptibility. ⁶ And two springs come out which send forth honey and milk, and their springs send forth oil and wine, and they separate into four parts, and go around with quiet course, and go down into the Paradise of Eden, between corruptibility and incorruptibility. ⁷ And there they go forth along the earth and have a revolution to their circle even as other elements. ⁸ And here there is no unfruitful tree, and every place is blessed. ⁹ And there are three hundred very bright messengers who keep the garden, and with unceasing sweet singing and never-silent voices serve the Lord throughout all days and hours. ¹⁰ And I said, "How very sweet this place is!" And those men said to me:

CHAPTER 9

¹ "This place, O Enoch, is prepared for the righteous, who endure all manner of offense from those that exasperate their souls, who avert their eyes from iniquity, and make righteous judgment, and give bread to the hungering, and cover the naked with clothing, and raise up the fallen, and help injured orphans, and who walk without fault before the face of the Lord, and serve Him alone, and for them this place is prepared for continuous inheritance."

CHAPTER 10

¹ And those two men led me up on to the northern side, and showed me a very terrible place there, and there were all manner of tortures in that place: cruel darkness and unilluminated gloom, and there is no light there, but murky fire constantly flaming aloft, and there is a fiery river coming forth, and that whole place is fire everywhere, and everywhere there is frost and ice, thirst and shivering, while the bonds are very cruel, and the messengers fearful and merciless, bearing angry weapons [for] merciless torture, and I said, ² "Woe, woe! How very terrible this place is! ³ And those men said to me, "This place, O Enoch, is prepared for those who dishonor God, who practice sin against nature on earth, which is child-corruption after the sodomitic fashion, magic-making, enchantments, and devilish witchcrafts, and who boast of their wicked deeds—stealing, lies, slanders, envy, malice, fornication, murder—and who, cursed, steal the souls of men; who, seeing the poor, take away their goods and themselves wax rich, injuring them for other men's goods; who being able to satisfy the empty, made the hungering to die; being able to clothe, stripped the naked; and who did not know their Creator, and bowed to the soulless and lifeless gods—who cannot see nor hear, vain gods—who also built hewn images and bow down to unclean handiwork; this place is prepared for all these for a continuous inheritance."

CHAPTER 11

¹ Those men took me, and led me up on to the fourth heaven, and showed me all the successive goings, and all the rays of the light of sun and moon. ² And I measure their goings, and compared their light, and saw that the sun's light is greater than the moon's. ³ Its circle and the wheels on which it goes always, like the wind going past with very marvelous speed, and day and night it has no rest. ⁴ Its passage and return are accompanied by four great stars, and each star has one thousand stars under it, to the right of the sun's wheel, and by four to the left, each having one thousand stars under it—eight thousand altogether, issuing with the sun continually. ⁵ And by day, fifteen myriads of messengers attend it, and by night one thousand. ⁶ And six-winged ones issue with the messengers before the sun's wheel into the fiery flames, and one hundred messengers kindle the sun and set it gleaming.

CHAPTER 12

¹ And I looked and saw other flying elements of the sun, whose names are phoenixes and chalkydri, marvelous and wonderful, with feet and tails in the form of a lion, and a crocodile's head, their appearance is empurpled, like the rainbow; their size is nine hundred measures; their wings are like those of messengers, each has twelve, and they attend and accompany the sun, bearing heat and dew as it is commanded to them from God. ² Thus the sun revolves and goes, and rises under the heavens, and its course goes under the earth with the light of its rays unceasingly.

CHAPTER 13

[1] Those men bore me away to the east, and placed me at the sun's gates, where the sun goes forth according to the regulation of the seasons, and the circuit of the months of the whole year, and the number of the hours, day and night. [2] And I saw six gates open, each gate having sixty-one stadia and a quarter of one stadium, and I measured them accurately, and understood their size to be so great, through which the sun goes forth, and goes to the west, and is made even, and rises throughout all the months, and turns back again from the six gates according to the succession of the seasons; thus, the period of the whole year is finished after the returns of the four seasons.

CHAPTER 14

[1] And again those men led me away to the western parts and showed me six great gates open corresponding to the eastern gates, opposite to where the sun sets, according to the number of the days—three hundred and sixty-five and a quarter. [2] Thus again it goes down to the western gates, and draws away its light, the greatness of its brightness, under the earth; for since the crown of its shining is in Heaven with the Lord, and guarded by four hundred messengers, while the sun goes around [the] wheel under the earth, and stands seven great hours in night, and spends half its course under the earth, when it comes to the eastern approach in the eighth hour of the night, it brings its lights, and the crown of shining, and the sun flames forth more than fire.

CHAPTER 15

[1] Then the elements of the sun, called phoenixes and chalkydri, break into song; therefore, every bird flutters with its wings, rejoicing at the giver of light, and they broke into song at the command of the Lord. [2] The giver of light comes to give brightness to the whole world, and the morning guard takes shape, which is the rays of the sun, and the sun of the earth goes out, and receives its brightness to light up the whole face of the earth, and they showed me this calculation of the sun's going. [3] And the gates which it enters, these are the great gates of the calculation of the hours of the year; for this reason, the sun is a great creation, whose circuit lasts twenty-eight years, and begins again from the beginning.

CHAPTER 16

[1] Those men showed me the other course, that of the moon, twelve great gates, crowned from west to east, by which the moon goes in and out of the customary times. [2] It goes in at the first gate to the western places of the sun, by the first gates with thirty-one days exactly, by the second gates with thirty-one days exactly, by the third with thirty days exactly, by the fourth with thirty days exactly, by the fifth with thirty-one days exactly, by the sixth with thirty-one days exactly, by the seventh with thirty days exactly, by the eighth with thirty-one days perfectly, by the ninth with thirty-one days exactly, by the tenth with thirty days perfectly, by the eleventh with thirty-one days exactly, by the twelfth with twenty-eight days exactly. [3] And it goes through the western gates in the order and number of the eastern and accomplishes the three hundred and sixty-five and a quarter days of the solar year, while the lunar year has three hundred fifty-four, and there are twelve days of the solar circle lacking to it, which are the lunar epacts of the whole year. [4] Thus, too, the great circle contains five hundred and thirty-two years. [5] The quarter of a day is omitted for three years, the fourth fulfills it exactly. [6] Therefore they are taken outside of the heavens for three years and are not added to the number of days, because they change the time of the years to two new months toward completion, to two others toward diminution. [7] And when the western gates are finished, it returns and goes to the eastern, to the lights, and thus goes around the heavenly circles day and night, lower than all circles, swifter than the heavenly winds, and spirits, and elements, and messengers flying; each messenger has six wings. [8] It has a sevenfold course in nineteen years.

CHAPTER 17

[1] I saw armed soldiers in the midst of the heavens serving the Lord with drums and pipes, with unceasing voice, with sweet voice, with sweet and unceasing voice and various singing, which it is impossible to describe, and which astonishes every mind, so wonderful and marvelous is the singing of those messengers, and I was delighted listening to it.

CHAPTER 18

[1] The men took me on to the fifth heaven and placed me [there], and there I saw many countless soldiers called Grigori, of human appearance, and their size was greater than that of great giants, and their faces [were] withered, and the silence of their mouths [was] perpetual, and there was no service on the fifth heaven, and I said to the men who were with me, [2] "For what reason are these very withered, and their faces melancholy, and their mouths silent, and for what reason is there no service on this heaven?" [3] And they said to me, "These are the Grigori, who with their prince Satanael rejected the Lord of light, and after them are those who are held in great darkness on the second heaven, and three of them went down on to earth from the Lord's throne, to the place Hermon, and broke through their vows on the shoulder of Mount Hermon, and saw how pleasing the daughters of men are, and took wives to themselves, and polluted the earth with their deeds, who in all times of their age made lawlessness and mixing, and giants are born, and marvelous large men, and great enmity. [4] And therefore God judged them with great judgment, and they weep for their brothers, and they will be punished on [the] Great Day of the Lord." [5] And I said to the Grigori, "I saw your brothers, and their works, and their great torments, and I prayed for them, but the Lord has condemned them to be under the earth until the existing heavens and earth will end forever." [6] And I said, "For what reason do you wait, brothers, and do not serve before the Lord's face, and have not put your services before the Lord's face, lest you utterly anger your Lord?" [7] And they listened to my admonition, and spoke to the four ranks in Heaven, and behold, as I stood with those two men, four trumpets trumpeted together with great voice, and the Grigori broke into song with one voice, and their voice went up before the Lord pitifully and movingly.

CHAPTER 19

[1] And there those men took me and bore me up on to the sixth heaven, and I saw seven bands of messengers there, very bright and very glorious, and their faces shining more than the sun's shining—glistening, and there is no difference in their faces, or behaviour, or manner of dress; and these make the orders, and learn the goings of the stars, and the alteration of the moon, or revolution of the sun, and the good government of the world. [2] And when they see evildoing, they make commandments and instruction, and sweet and loud singing, and all songs of praise. [3] These are the chief-messengers who are above messengers, [who] measure all life in Heaven and on earth, and the messengers who are appointed over seasons and years, the messengers who are over rivers and sea, and who are over the fruits of the earth, and the messengers who are over every grass, giving food to all, to every living thing, and the messengers who write all the souls of men, and all their deeds, and their lives before the Lord's face; six phoenixes, and six cherubim, and six six-winged ones are in their midst, continually singing with one voice, and it is not possible to describe their singing, and they rejoice before the Lord at His footstool.

CHAPTER 20

[1] And those two men lifted me up there on to the seventh heaven, and I saw a very great light there, and fiery troops of great chief-messengers, incorporeal forces, and dominions, orders and governments, cherubim and seraphim, thrones and

many-eyed ones, nine regiments, the Yah-favored stations of light, and I became afraid, and began to tremble with great terror, and those men took me, and led me after them, and said to me, **2** "Have courage, Enoch, do not fear," and showed me the Lord from afar, sitting on His very high throne. For what is there on the tenth heaven, since the Lord dwells there? **3** On the tenth heaven is God, in the Hebrew tongue He is called Aravat. **4** And all the heavenly troops would come and stand on the ten steps according to their rank, and would bow down to the Lord, and would go to their places again in joy and bliss, singing songs in the boundless light with small and tender voices, gloriously serving Him.

CHAPTER 21

1 And the cherubim and seraphim [are] standing around the throne; the six-winged and many-eyed ones do not depart, standing before the Lord's face, doing His will, and they cover His whole throne, singing with a gentle voice before the Lord's face: "Holy, Holy, Holy, Lord, Ruler of Hosts, the heavens and earth are full of Your glory." **2** When I saw all these things, those men said to me, "Enoch, thus far it is commanded us to journey with you," and those men went away from me and thereon I did not see them. **3** And I remained alone at the end of the seventh heaven, and became afraid, and fell on my face, and said to myself, "Woe is me! What has befallen me?" **4** And the Lord sent one of His glorious ones, the chief-messenger Gabriel, and he said to me, "Have courage, Enoch, do not fear; arise before the Lord's face into eternity; arise, come with me." **5** And I answered him, and said in myself: "My Lord, my soul has departed from me from terror and trembling, and I called to the men who led me up to this place, I relied on them, and it is with them I go before the Lord's face." **6** And Gabriel caught me up, as a leaf caught up by the wind, and placed me before the Lord's face. **7** And I saw the eighth heaven, which is called in the Hebrew tongue Muzaloth, changer of the seasons, of drought, and of wet, and of the twelve constellations of the circle of the expanse, which are above the seventh heaven. **8** And I saw the ninth heaven, which is called in Hebrew Kuchavim, where the heavenly homes of the twelve constellations of the circle of the expanse are.

CHAPTER 22

1 On the tenth heaven, which is called Aravoth, I saw the appearance of the Lord's face, like iron made to glow in fire, and brought out, emitting sparks, and it burns. **2** Thus in a moment of eternity I saw the Lord's face, but the Lord's face is ineffable, marvelous and very awful, and very, very terrible. **3** And who am I to tell of the Lord's unspeakable being, and of His very wonderful face? And I cannot tell the quantity of His many instructions, and various voices—the Lord's throne is very great and not made with hands—nor the quantity of those standing around Him, troops of cherubim and seraphim, nor their unceasing singing, nor His immutable beauty. And who will tell of the ineffable greatness of His glory? **4** And I fell prone and bowed down to the Lord, and the Lord said to me with His lips: **5** "Have courage, Enoch, do not fear; arise and stand before My face into eternity." **6** And the chief-general Michael lifted me up and led me to before the Lord's face. **7** And the Lord said to His servants, trying them: "Let Enoch stand before My face into eternity," and the glorious ones bowed down to the Lord, and said, "Let Enoch go according to Your word." **8** And the Lord said to Michael, "Go and take Enoch from out of his earthly garments, and anoint him with My sweet ointment, and put him into the garments of My glory." **9** And Michael did thus, as the Lord told him. He anointed me, and dressed me, and the appearance of that ointment is more than the great light, and His ointment is like sweet dew, and its smell mild, shining like the sun's ray, and I looked at myself, and I was like one of His glorious ones. **10** And the Lord summoned one of His chief-messengers, Pravuel by name, whose knowledge was quicker in wisdom than the other chief-messengers, who wrote all the deeds of the Lord; and the Lord said to Pravuel, "Bring out the scrolls from My storehouses, and a reed of quick-writing, and give it to Enoch, and deliver to him the choice and comforting scrolls out of your hand."

CHAPTER 23

1 And he was telling me all the works of Heaven, earth and sea, and all the elements, their passages and goings, and the thunderings of the thunders, the sun and moon, the goings and changes of the stars, the seasons, years, days, and hours, the risings of the wind, the numbers of the messengers, and the formation of their songs, and all human things, the tongue of every human song and life, the commandments, instructions, and sweet-voiced singings, and all things that it is fitting to learn. **2** And Pravuel told me: "All the things that I have told you, we have written. Sit and write all the souls of mankind, however many of them are born, and the places prepared for them to eternity; for all souls are prepared to eternity, before the formation of the world." **3** And [I wrote] all [this for] two periods of thirty days and thirty nights; and I wrote out all things exactly, and wrote three hundred and sixty-six scrolls.

CHAPTER 24

1 And the Lord summoned me, and said to me, "Enoch, sit down on My left with Gabriel." **2** And I bowed down to the Lord, and the Lord spoke to me: "Enoch, beloved, all that you see, all things that are standing finished, I tell to you even before the very beginning, all that I created from non-being, and visible things from invisible. **3** Hear, Enoch, and take in these words of Mine, for I have not told My secret to My messengers, and I have not told them their rise, nor My endless realm, nor have they understood My creating, which I tell you today. **4** For before all things were visible, I alone used to go around in the invisible things, like the sun from east to west, and from west to east. **5** But even the sun has peace in itself, while I found no peace, because I was creating all things, and I conceived the thought of placing foundations, and of creating visible creation."

CHAPTER 25

1 "I commanded in the very lowest parts that visible things should come down from invisible, and Adoil came down very great, and I beheld him, and behold, he had a belly of great light. **2** And I said to him, Become undone, Adoil, and let the visible come out of you. **3** And he came undone, and a great light came out. And I was in the midst of the great light, and as there is born light from light, there came forth a great age, and [it] showed all creation, which I had thought to create. **4** And I saw that it was good. **5** And I placed a throne for Myself, and took My seat on it, and said to the light, Go up higher and fix yourself high above the throne, and be a foundation to the highest things. **6** And there is nothing else above the light, and then I bent up and looked up from My throne."

CHAPTER 26

1 "And I summoned the very lowest a second time, and said, Let Archas come forth hard, and he came forth hard from the invisible. **2** And Archas came forth, hard, heavy, and very red. **3** And I said, Be opened, Archas, and let there be born from you; and [when] he came undone, a very great and very dark age came forth, bearing the creation of all lower things, and I saw that it was good, and said to him, **4** Go down below, and make yourself firm, and be a foundation for the lower things; and it happened, and he went down and fixed himself, and became the foundation for the lower things, and there is nothing else below the darkness."

CHAPTER 27

1 "And I commanded that there should be taken from light and darkness, and I said, Be thick, and it became thus, and I spread it out with the light, and it became water, and I spread it out over the darkness, below the light, **2** and then I made the waters firm, that is to say, the bottomless, and I made a foundation of light around the water, and created seven circles from inside, and imaged the water like crystal, wet and dry, that is to say, like glass, and the circumcession of the waters and the other elements, ³ and I showed each one of them its road, and the seven stars, each one of them in its heaven, that they go thus, and I saw that it was good. ⁴ And I separated between light and between darkness, that is to say, in the midst of the water here and there, and I said to the light that it should be the day, and to the darkness, that it should be the night, and there was evening and there was morning the first day."

CHAPTER 28

¹ "And then I made the heavenly circle firm, and made the lower water which is under the heavens collect itself together into one whole, and [made] the chaos become dry, and it became so. ² Out of the waves I created rock, hard and big, and from the rock I piled up the dry, and the dry I called Earth, and the midst of the earth I called Abyss, that is to say, the bottomless; I collected the sea in one place and bound it together with a yoke. ³ And I said to the sea, Behold, I give you your perpetual limits, and you will not break loose from your component parts. ⁴ Thus I made the expanse steady. This day I called the first-created [(Sunday)]."

CHAPTER 29

¹ "And for all the heavenly troops I imaged the image and essence of fire, and My eye looked at the very hard, firm rock, and from the gleam of My eye the lightning received its wonderful nature, which is both fire in water and water in fire, and one does not put out the other, nor does the one dry up the other; therefore, the lightning is brighter than the sun, softer than water, and firmer than hard rock. ² And from the rock I cut off a great fire, and from the fire I created the orders of the incorporeal ten troops of messengers, and their weapons are fiery and their raiment a burning flame, and I commanded that each one should stand in his order. ³ And one from out of the order of messengers, having turned away with the order that was under him, conceived an impossible thought: to place his throne higher than the clouds above the earth, that he might become equal in rank to My power. ⁴ And I threw him out from the height with his messengers, and he was continuously flying in the air above the bottomless [pit]."

CHAPTER 30

¹ "On the third day I commanded the earth to make great and fruitful trees grow, and hills, and seed to sow, and I planted Paradise, and enclosed it, and placed flaming messengers as armed guardians, and thus I created renewal. ² Then there came evening, and there came morning—the fourth day [(Wednesday)]. ³ On the fourth day I commanded that there should be great lights on the heavenly circles. ⁴ On the first uppermost circle I placed the stars [and] Kronos [(Saturn)], and on the second Aphrodite [(Venus)], on the third Ares [(Mars)], on the fifth Zeus [(Jupiter)], on the sixth Hermes [(Mercury)], on the lesser seventh the moon, and adorned it with the lesser stars. ⁵ And on the lower I placed the sun for the illumination of day, and the moon and stars for the illumination of night— ⁶ the sun that it should go according to each constellation, twelve, and I appointed the succession of the months and their names and lives, their thunderings, and their hour-markings, how they should succeed. ⁷ Then there came evening, and there came morning—the fifth day [(Thursday)]. ⁸ On the fifth day I commanded the sea, that it should bring forth fishes, and feathered birds of many varieties, and all animals creeping over the earth, going forth over the earth on four legs, and soaring in the air, male and female, and every soul breathing the breath of life. ⁹ And there came evening, and there came morning—the sixth day [(Friday)]. ¹⁰ On the sixth day I commanded My wisdom to create man from seven consistencies: one, his flesh from the earth; two, his blood from the dew; three, his eyes from the sun; four, his bones from stone; five, his intelligence from the swiftness of the messengers and from cloud; six, his veins and his hair from the grass of the earth; seven, his soul from My breath and from the wind. ¹¹ And I gave him seven natures: to the flesh hearing,

the eyes for sight, to the soul smell, the veins for touch, the blood for taste, the bones for endurance, to the intelligence sweetness [(enjoyment)]. ¹² I conceived a cunning saying to say, I created man from invisible and from visible nature, of both are his death, and life, and image; he knows speech like some created thing, small in greatness and again great in smallness, and I placed him on earth, a second messenger, honorable, great and glorious, and I appointed him as ruler to rule on earth and to have My wisdom, and there was none like him of earth of all My existing creatures. ¹³ And I appointed him a name from the four component parts: from east, from west, from south, from north; and I appointed four special stars for him, and I called his name Adam, and showed him the two ways, the light and the darkness, and I told him: ¹⁴ This is good, and that bad, that I should learn whether he has love or hatred toward Me, that it might be clear which in his race love Me. ¹⁵ For I have seen his nature, but he has not seen his own nature; therefore, through not seeing he will sin worse, and I said, After sin what is there but death? ¹⁶ And I put sleep into him, and he fell asleep. And I took a rib from him and created him a wife, that death should come to him by his wife, and I took his last word and called her name mother, that is to say, Eva [(Eve)]."

CHAPTER 31

¹ "Adam has life on earth, and I created a garden in Eden in the east, that he should observe the testament and keep the command. ² I made the heavens open to him, that he should see the messengers singing the song of victory, and the gloomless light. ³ And he was continuously in paradise, and the Devil understood that I wanted to create another world, because Adam was lord on earth, to rule and control it. ⁴ The Devil is the evil spirit of the lower places; as a fugitive from the heavens, he became Satan, as his name was Satanael; thus he became different from the messengers, but his nature did not change his intelligence as far as his understanding of righteous and sinful things. ⁵ And he understood his condemnation and the sin which he had sinned before, therefore he conceived a thought against Adam, in such form he entered and seduced Eve, but did not touch Adam. ⁶ But I cursed ignorance, but what I had blessed previously, those I did not curse: I did not curse man, nor the earth, nor other creatures, but man's evil fruit, and his works."

CHAPTER 32

¹ "I said to him: Earth you are, and into the earth from where I took you, you will go, and I will not ruin you, but send you from where I took you. ² Then I can receive you again at My second coming. ³ And I blessed all My creatures visible and invisible. And Adam was in paradise [for] five and a half hours. ⁴ And I blessed the seventh day, which is the Sabbath [(Saturday)], on which He rested from all His works."

CHAPTER 33

¹ "And I appointed the eighth day also, that the eighth day should be the first-created after my work, and that the first seven revolve in the form of the seven thousand [years], and that at the beginning of the eighth thousand there should be a time of not-counting—endless, with neither years, nor months, nor weeks, nor days, nor hours. ² And now, Enoch, all that I have told you, all that you have understood, all that you have seen of heavenly things, all that you have seen on earth, and all that I have written in scrolls by My great wisdom, all these things I have devised and created from the uppermost foundation to the lower and to the end, and there is no counselor nor inheritor to My creations. ³ I am self-continuous, not made with hands, and without change. ⁴ My thought is My counselor, My wisdom and My word are prepared, and My eyes observe how all things stand here and tremble with terror. ⁵ If I turn away My face, then all things will be destroyed. ⁶ And apply your mind, Enoch, and know Him who is speaking to you, and take there the scrolls which you yourself have written. ⁷ And I give you Samuel and Raguel, who led you up, and the scrolls, and go down to earth, and tell your sons all that I have

told you, and all that you have seen, from the lower heaven up to My throne, and all the troops. **8** For I created all forces, and there is none that resists Me or that does not subject himself to Me. For all subject themselves to My monarchy, and labor for My sole rule. **9** Give them the scrolls of the handwriting, and they will read them, and will know Me as the Creator of all things, and will understand how there is no other God but Me. **10** And let them distribute the scrolls of your handwriting—children to children, generation to generation, nations to nations. **11** And I will give you, Enoch, My intercessor, the chief-general Michael, for the handwritings of your fathers Adam, Seth, Enos, Cainan, Mahalaleel, and your father Jared."

CHAPTER 34

1 "They have rejected My commandments and My yoke; worthless seed has come up, not fearing God, and they would not bow down to Me, but have begun to bow down to vain gods, and denied My unity, and have laden the whole earth with untruths, offenses, abominable lecheries, namely one with another, and all manner of other unclean wickedness, which are disgusting to relate. **2** And therefore I will bring down a deluge on the earth and will destroy all men, and the whole earth will crumble together into great darkness."

CHAPTER 35

1 "Behold, another generation will arise from their seed, much afterward, but of them many will be very insatiate. **2** He who raises that generation will reveal to them the scrolls of your handwriting, of your fathers, to them to whom he must point out the guardianship of the world, to the faithful men and workers of My pleasure, who do not acknowledge My Name in vain. **3** And they will tell another generation, and those others, having read, will be glorified thereafter, more than the first."

CHAPTER 36

1 "Now, Enoch, I give you the term of thirty days to spend in your house, and tell your sons and all your household, that all may hear from My face what is told them by you, that they may read and understand how there is no other God but Me, **2** and that they may always keep My commandments, and begin to read and take in the scrolls of your handwriting. **3** And after thirty days I will send My messenger for you, and he will take you from earth and from your sons to Me."

CHAPTER 37

1 And the Lord called on one of the older messengers, terrible and menacing, and placed him by me, in appearance white as snow, and his hands like ice, having the appearance of great frost, and he froze my face, because I could not endure the terror of the Lord, just as it is not possible to endure a stove's fire, and the sun's heat, and the frost of the air. **2** And the Lord said to me, "Enoch, if your face is not frozen here, no man will be able to behold your face."

CHAPTER 38

1 And the Lord said to those men who first led me up: "Let Enoch go down on to earth with you, and await him until the determined day." **2** And they placed me on my bed by night. **3** And Methuselah, expecting my coming, keeping watch by day and by night at my bed, was filled with awe when he heard my coming, and I told him, "Let all my household come together, that I tell them everything."

CHAPTER 39

1 Oh my children, my beloved ones, hear the admonition of your father, as much as is according to the Lord's will. **2** I have been allowed to come to you today, and announce to you, not from my lips, but from the Lord's lips, all that is, and was, and all that is now, and all that will be until Judgment Day. **3** For the Lord has let me come to you; you therefore hear the words of my lips, of a man made big for you, but I am one who has seen the Lord's face: like iron made to glow from fire, it sends forth sparks and burns. **4** You now look on my eyes, the eyes of a man big with meaning for you, but I have seen the Lord's eyes, shining like the sun's rays and filling the eyes of man with awe. **5** You see now, my children, the right hand of a man that helps you, but I have seen the Lord's right hand filling Heaven as He helped me. **6** You see the compass of my work like your own, but I have seen the Lord's limitless and perfect compass, which has no end. **7** You hear the words of my lips, as I heard the words of the Lord, like great thunder unceasingly with hurling of clouds. **8** And now, my children, hear the discourses of the father of the earth, how fearful and awful it is to come before the face of the ruler of the earth, how much more terrible and awful it is to come before the face of the ruler of Heaven, the controller of quick and dead, and of the heavenly troops. Who can endure that endless pain?

CHAPTER 40

1 And now, my children, I know all things, for this is from the Lord's lips, and my eyes have seen this from beginning to end. **2** I know all things and have written all things into scrolls: the heavens, and their end, and their plenitude, and all the armies and their marchings. **3** I have measured and described the stars, the great countless multitude of them. **4** What man has seen their revolutions and their entrances? For not even the messengers see their number, while I have written all their names. **5** And I measured the sun's circle, and measured its rays, [and] counted the hours; I also wrote down all things that go over the earth; I have written the things that are nourished, and all seed sown and unsown, which the earth produces, and all plants, and every grass and every flower, and their sweet smells, and their names, and the dwelling-places of the clouds, and their composition, and their wings, and how they bear rain and raindrops. **6** And I investigated all things and wrote the road of the thunder and of the lightning, and they showed me the keys and their guardians, their rise, the way they go; it is let out gently in measure by a chain, lest by a heavy chain and violence it hurls the angry clouds down and destroys all things on earth. **7** I wrote the treasure-houses of the snow, and the storehouses of the cold and the frosty airs, and I observed their season's key-holder; he fills the clouds with them and does not exhaust the treasure-houses. **8** And I wrote the resting-places of the winds and observed and saw how their key-holders bear weighing-scales and measures; first, they put them in one weighing-scale, then in the other, the weights, and they let them out according to measure cunningly over the whole earth, lest by heavy breathing they make the earth to rock. **9** And I measured out the whole earth, its mountains, and all hills, fields, trees, stones, rivers; I wrote down all existing things: the height from earth to the seventh heaven, and downwards to the very lowest [part of] Hades, and the judgment-place, and the very great, open, and weeping depth. **10** And I saw how the prisoners are in pain, expecting the limitless judgment. **11** And I wrote down all those being judged by the judge, and all their judgment, and sentences, and all their works.

CHAPTER 41

1 And I saw all forefathers from all time with Adam and Eve, and I sighed, and broke into tears, and said of the ruin of their dishonor: **2** "Woe to me for my infirmity and for that of my forefathers!" And I thought in my heart and said, **3** "Blessed is the man who has not been born or who has been born and will not sin before the Lord's face, that he does not come into this place, nor bears the yoke of this place."

CHAPTER 42

1 I saw the key-holders and guards of the gates of Hades standing like great serpents, and their faces like extinguishing lamps, and their eyes of fire, their sharp teeth, and I saw all the Lord's works, how they are right, while some [of] the works of man are good, and others bad, and in their works are known those who lie evilly.

CHAPTER 43

1 I, my children, measured and wrote out every work, and every measure, and every righteous judgment. **2** As one year is more honorable than another, so is one man more honorable than another: some for great possessions, some for wisdom of heart, some for particular intellect, some for cunning, one for silence of lip, another for cleanliness, one for strength, another for comeliness, one for youth, another for sharp wit, one for shape of body, another for sensibility. Let it be heard everywhere that there is none better than he who fears God; he will be more glorious in [the] time to come.

CHAPTER 44

1 The Lord, having created man with His hands, in the likeness of His own face, the Lord made him small and great. **2** Whoever reviles the ruler's face, and abhors the Lord's face, has despised the Lord's face, and he who vents anger on any man without injury, the Lord's great anger will cut him down; he who spits on the face of man reproachfully will be cut down at the Lord's Great Judgment. **3** Blessed is the man who does not direct his heart with malice against any man, and helps the injured and condemned, and raises the broken down, and will do charity to the needy, **4** because on the Day of the Great Judgment every weight, every measure, and every makeweight will be as in the market, that is to say, they are hung on scales and stand in the market, and everyone will learn his own measure, and according to his measure will take his reward.

CHAPTER 45

1 Whoever hastens to make offerings before the Lord's face, the Lord, for His part, will hasten that offering by granting of his work. **2** But whoever increases his lamp before the Lord's face and does not make true judgment, the Lord will not increase his treasure in the realm of the highest. **3** When the Lord demands bread, or candles, or the flesh of beasts, or any other sacrifice, then that is nothing; but God demands pure hearts, and with all that, only tests the heart of man.

CHAPTER 46

1 Hear, my people, and take in the words of my lips. **2** If anyone brings any gifts to an earthly ruler, and has disloyal thoughts in his heart, and the ruler know this, will he not be angry with him, and will he not refuse his gifts, and will he not give him over to judgment? **3** Or if one man makes himself appear good to another by deceit of tongue, but has evil in his heart, then will the other not understand the treachery of his heart, and himself be condemned, since his untruth was plain to all? **4** And when the Lord will send a great light, then there will be judgment for the just and the unjust, and no one will escape notice there.

CHAPTER 47

1 And now, my children, lay thought on your hearts; mark well the words of your father, which have all come to you from the Lord's lips. **2** Take these scrolls of your father's handwriting and read them. **3** For the scrolls are many, and in them you will learn all the Lord's works, all that has been from the beginning of creation, and will be until the end of time. **4** And if you will observe my handwriting, you will not sin against the Lord, because there is no other except the Lord, neither in Heaven, nor in earth, nor in the very lowest places, nor in one foundation. **5** The Lord has placed the foundations in the unknown and has spread forth heavens visible and invisible; He fixed the earth on the waters and created countless

creatures. **6** And who has counted the water and the foundation of the unfixed, or the dust of the earth, or the sand of the sea, or the drops of the rain, or the morning dew, or the wind's breathings? Who has filled earth, and sea, and the indissoluble winter? **7** "I cut the stars out of fire, and decorated Heaven, and put it in their midst."

CHAPTER 48

1 So the sun goes along the seven heavenly circles, which are the appointment of one hundred and eighty-two thrones that it goes down on a short day, and again one hundred and eighty-two that it goes down on a big day; and he has two thrones on which he rests, revolving here and there above the thrones of the months, from the seventeenth day of the month Sivan it goes down to the month Thevan, [and] from the seventeenth of Thevan it goes up. **2** And thus it goes close to the earth; then the earth is glad and makes its fruits grow, and when it goes away, then the earth is sad, and trees and all fruits have no florescence. **3** All this He measured with a good measurement of hours, and fixed a measure by His wisdom, of the visible and the invisible. **4** From the invisible He made all things visible, Himself being invisible. **5** Thus I make known to you, my children, and distribute the scrolls to your children, into all your generations, and among the nations who will have the sense to fear God: let them receive them, and may they come to love them more than any food or earthly sweets, and read them, and apply themselves to them. **6** And those who do not understand the Lord, who do not fear God, who do not accept, but reject, who do not receive the scrolls—a terrible judgment awaits these. **7** Blessed is the man who will bear their yoke and will drag them along, for he will be released on the Day of the Great Judgment.

CHAPTER 49

1 I swear to you, my children, but I swear not by any oath, neither by Heaven nor by earth, nor by any other creature which God created. **2** The Lord said, "There is no curse [[or oath]] in Me, nor injustice, but truth." **3** If there is no truth in men, let them swear by the words, Yes, yes, or else, No, no. **4** And I swear to you, yes, yes, that there has been no man in his mother's womb, except which [was] already [prepared] beforehand, even to each one there is a place prepared for the repose of that soul, and a measure fixed how much it is intended that a man be tried in this world. **5** Yes, children, do not deceive yourselves, for a place has been previously prepared for every soul of man.

CHAPTER 50

1 I have put every man's work in writing, and none born on earth can remain hidden nor his works remain concealed. I see all things. **2** Now therefore, my children, spend the number of your days in patience and meekness, so that you inherit endless life. **3** Endure every wound, every injury, every evil word and attack for the sake of the Lord. **5** If retaliations befall you, do not return them either to neighbor or enemy, because the Lord will return them for you and be your avenger on the Day of Great Judgment, that there is no avenging here among men. **6** Whoever of you spends gold or silver for his brother's sake, he will receive ample treasure in the world to come. **7** Harm neither widows, nor orphans, nor strangers, lest God's wrath come on you.

CHAPTER 51

1 Stretch out your hands to the poor according to your strength. **2** Do not hide your silver in the earth. **3** Help the faithful man in affliction, and affliction will not find you in the time of your trouble. **4** And every grievous and cruel yoke that comes on you—bear all for the sake of the Lord, and thus you will find your reward in the Day of Judgment. **5** It is good to go morning, midday, and evening into the Lord's dwelling, for the glory of your Creator, **6** because every breathing thing glorifies

Him, and every creature, visible and invisible, returns Him praise.

CHAPTER 52

¹ Blessed is the man who opens his lips in praise of [the] God of Hosts and praises the Lord with his heart. ² Cursed [is] every man who opens his lips for the bringing into contempt and slander of his neighbor, because he brings God into contempt. ³ Blessed is he who opens his lips blessing and praising God. ⁴ Cursed is he before the Lord, all the days of his life, who opens his lips to curse and abuse. ⁵ Blessed is he who blesses all the Lord's works. ⁶ Cursed is he who brings the Lord's creation into contempt. ⁷ Blessed is he who looks down and raises the fallen. ⁸ Cursed is he who looks to and is eager for the destruction of what is not his. ⁹ Blessed is he who keeps the foundations of his fathers made firm from the beginning. ¹⁰ Cursed is he who perverts the decrees of his forefathers. ¹¹ Blessed is he who imparts peace and love. ¹² Cursed is he who disturbs those that love their neighbors. ¹³ Blessed is he who speaks with a humble tongue and heart to all. ¹⁴ Cursed is he who speaks peace with his tongue, while in his heart there is no peace but a sword. ¹⁵ For all these things will be laid bare in the weighing-scales and in the scrolls on the Day of the Great Judgment.

CHAPTER 53

¹ And now, my children, do not say, "Our father is standing before God and is praying for our sins," for there is no helper there of any man who has sinned. ² You see how I wrote all works of every man, before his creation, all that is done among all men for all time, and none can tell or relate my handwriting, because the Lord sees all imaginings of man, how they are vain, where they lie in the treasure-houses of the heart. ³ And now, my children, mark well all the words of your father that I tell you, lest you regret, saying, "Why did our father not tell us?"

CHAPTER 54

¹ At that time, not understanding this, let these scrolls which I have given you be for an inheritance of your peace. ² Hand them to all who want them, and instruct them, that they may see the Lord's very great and marvelous works.

CHAPTER 55

¹ My children, behold, the day of my term and time have approached. ² For the messengers who will go with me are standing before me and urge me to my departure from you; they are standing here on earth, awaiting what has been told them. ³ For tomorrow I will go up on to Heaven, to the uppermost Jerusalem—to my continuous inheritance. ⁴ Therefore I command you: before the Lord's face do all His good pleasure.

CHAPTER 56

¹ Methuselah, having answered his father Enoch, said, "What is agreeable to your eyes, father, that I may make before your face, that you may bless our dwellings, and your sons, and that your people may be made glorious through you, and then that you may thus depart as the Lord said?" ² Enoch answered to his son Methuselah and said, "Hear, child: from the time when the Lord anointed me with the ointment of His glory, there has been no food in me, and my soul does not remember earthly enjoyment, neither do I want anything earthly."

CHAPTER 57

¹ "My child Methuselah, summon all your brothers, and all your household, and the elders of the people, that I may talk to them and depart, as is planned for me." ² And Methuselah hurried, and summoned his brothers Regim, Riman, Uchon, Chermion, Gaidad, and all the elders of the people before the face of his father Enoch; and he blessed them, and said to them:

CHAPTER 58

¹ Listen to me, my children, today. ² In those days when the Lord came down on to earth for Adam's sake, and visited all His creatures which He created Himself, after all these He created Adam, and the Lord called all the beasts of the earth, all the reptiles, and all the birds that soar in the air, and brought them all before the face of our father Adam. ³ And Adam gave the names to all things living on earth. ⁴ And the Lord appointed him ruler over all, and subjected to him all things under his hands, and made them dumb and made them dull that they can be commanded of man, and be in subjection and obedience to him. ⁵ Thus the Lord also created every man lord over all His possessions. ⁶ The Lord will not judge a single soul of beast for man's sake, but adjudicates the souls of men to their beasts in this world, for men have a special place. ⁷ And as every soul of man is according to number, similarly beasts will not perish, nor all souls of beasts which the Lord created, until the Great Judgment, and they will accuse man if he fed them ill.

CHAPTER 59

¹ Whoever defiles the soul of beasts, defiles his own soul. ² For man brings clean animals to make sacrifice for sin, that he may have cure of his soul. ³ And if they bring for sacrifice clean animals, and birds, man has a cure—he cures his soul. ⁴ All is given to you for food; bind it by the four feet, that is to make good the cure—he cures his soul. ⁵ But whoever kills beast without wounds, kills his own souls and defiles his own flesh. ⁶ And he who does any beast any injury whatever, in secret, it is evil practice, and he defiles his own soul.

CHAPTER 60

¹ He who works the killing of a man's soul, kills his own soul, and kills his own body, and there is no cure for him for all time. ² He who puts a man in any snare, will stick in it himself, and there is no cure for him for all time. ³ He who puts a man in any vessel, his retribution will not be wanting at the Great Judgment for all time. ⁴ He who works crookedly or speaks evil against any soul will not make justice for himself for all time.

CHAPTER 61

¹ And now, my children, keep your hearts from every injustice, which the Lord hates. Just as a man asks something for his own soul from God, so let him do to every living soul, because I know all things, how in the great time to come there is much inheritance prepared for men, good for the good, and bad for the bad, without number—many. ² Blessed are those who enter the good houses, for in the bad houses there is no peace nor return from them. ³ Hear, my children, small and great: when man puts a good thought in his heart [and] brings gifts from his labors before the Lord's face, but his hands did not make them, then the Lord will turn His face away from the labor of his hand, and that man cannot find the labor of his hands. ⁴ And if his hands made it, but his heart murmurs, and his heart does not cease making murmur unceasingly, he does not have any advantage.

CHAPTER 62

¹ Blessed is the man who in his patience brings his gifts with faith before the Lord's face, because he will find forgiveness of sins. ² But if he takes back his words before the

time, there is no conversion for him; and if the time passes and he does not do what is promised of his own will, there is no conversion after death. ³ Because every work which man does before the time is all deceit before men and sin before God.

CHAPTER 63

¹ When man clothes the naked and fills the hungry, he will find reward from God. ² But if his heart murmurs, he commits a double evil: ruin of himself and of that which he gives; and for him there will be no finding of reward on account of that. ³ And if his own heart is filled with his food and his own flesh clothed with his own clothing, he commits contempt, and will forfeit all his endurance of poverty, and will not find reward of his good deeds. ⁴ Every proud and grandiose man, and every false speech clothed in untruth, is hateful to the Lord; it will be cut with the blade of the sword of death, and thrown into the fire, and will burn for all time.

CHAPTER 64

¹ When Enoch had spoken these words to his sons, all people far and near heard how the Lord was calling Enoch. They took counsel together: ² "Let us go and kiss Enoch," and two thousand men came together and came to the place [called] Achuzan where Enoch and his sons were. ³ And the elders of the people, the whole assembly, came and bowed down and began to kiss Enoch and said to him: ⁴ "Our father Enoch, may you be blessed of the Lord, the perpetual ruler, and now bless your sons and all the people, that we may be glorified today before your face. ⁵ For you will be glorified before the Lord's face for all time, since the Lord chose you, rather than all men on earth, and designated you writer of all His creation, visible and invisible, and redeemed of the sins of man, and helper of your household."

CHAPTER 65

¹ And Enoch answered all his people, saying, "Hear, my children: before all creatures were created, the Lord created the visible and invisible things. ² And as much time as there was and went past, understand that after all that, He created man in the likeness of His own form, and put into him eyes to see, and ears to hear, and heart to reflect, and intellect with which to deliberate. ³ And the Lord saw all man's works, and created all His creatures, and divided time: from time He fixed the years, and from the years He appointed the months, and from the months He appointed the days, and of days He appointed seven, ⁴ and in those He appointed the hours, [and] measured them out exactly, that man might reflect on time and count years, months, and hours, their alternation, beginning, and end, and that he might count his own life, from the beginning until death, and reflect on his sin, and write his work, [whether] bad and good, because no work is hidden before the Lord, that every man might know his works, and never transgress all His commandments, and keep my handwriting from generation to generation. ⁵ When all creation visible and invisible, as the Lord created it, will end, then every man goes to the Great Judgment, and then all time will perish, and the years, and from then on there will be neither months, nor days, nor hours; they will adhere together and will not be counted. ⁶ There will be one age, and all the righteous who will escape the Lord's Great Judgment will be collected in the Great Age; the Great Age will begin for the righteous, and they will live continuously, and then there will also be among them neither labor, nor sickness, nor humiliation, nor anxiety, nor need, nor brutality, nor night, nor darkness, but great light. ⁷ And they will have a great indestructible wall, and a bright and incorruptible paradise, for all corruptible things will pass away, and there will be continuous life."

CHAPTER 66

¹ And now, my children, keep your souls from all injustice, such as the Lord hates. ² Walk before His face with terror and trembling and serve Him alone. ³ Bow down to the true God, not to dumb idols, but bow down to His similitude, and bring all just offerings before the Lord's face. The Lord hates what is unjust. ⁴ For the Lord sees all things; when man takes thought in his heart, then He counsels the intellects, and every thought is always before the Lord who made the earth firm and put all creatures on it. ⁵ If you look to Heaven, the Lord is there; if you take thought of the sea's deep and all under the earth, the Lord is there. ⁶ For the Lord created all things. Do not bow down to things made by man, leaving the Lord of all creation, because no work can remain hidden before the Lord's face. ⁷ Walk, my children, in long-suffering, in meekness, honesty, in provocation, in grief, in faith, and in truth, in reliance on promises, in sickness, in abuse, in wounds, in temptation, in nakedness, in privation, loving one another, until you go out from this age of ills, that you become inheritors of endless time. ⁸ Blessed are the just who will escape the Great Judgment, for they will shine forth more than the sun sevenfold, for in this world the seventh part is taken off from all: light, darkness, food, enjoyment, sorrow, paradise, torture, fire, frost, and other things; he put all down in writing, that you might read and understand.

CHAPTER 67

¹ When Enoch had talked to the people, the Lord sent out darkness on to the earth, and there was darkness, and it covered those men standing with Enoch, and they took Enoch up on to the highest Heaven where the Lord is; and He received him and placed him before His face, and the darkness went off from the earth, and light came again. ² And the people did not see and understand how Enoch had been taken, and they glorified God, and they found a roll in which was traced "The Invisible God"; and all went to their dwelling places.

CHAPTER 68

¹ Enoch was born on the sixth day of the month Sivan and lived three hundred and sixty-five years. ² He was taken up to Heaven on the first day of the month Sivan and remained in Heaven sixty days. ³ He wrote all these signs of all creation, which the Lord created, and wrote three hundred and sixty-six scrolls, and handed them over to his sons, and remained on earth thirty days, and was taken up to Heaven again on the sixth day of the month Sivan, on the very day and hour when he was born. ⁴ As every man's nature in this life is dark, so also are his conception, birth, and departure from this life. ⁵ At what hour he was conceived, at that hour he was born, and at that hour too he died. ⁶ Methuselah and his brothers, all the sons of Enoch, hurried and erected an altar at that place called Achuzan, from which and where Enoch had been taken up to Heaven. ⁷ And they took sacrificial oxen, and summoned all people, and sacrificed the sacrifice before the Lord's face. ⁸ All people, the elders of the people and the whole assembly, came to the feast and brought gifts to the sons of Enoch. ⁹ And they made a great feast, rejoicing and making merry [for] three days, praising God who had given them such a sign through Enoch, who had found favor with Him, ¹⁰ and that they should hand it on to their sons from generation to generation, from age to age. Amen.

3 ENOCH

3 Enoch, also called Hebrew Enoch, The Revelation of Metatron, or The Book of the Palaces, was likely written in the 1st or 2nd century AD by either Ishmael ben Elisha ha-Kohen or Rabbi Yishmael ben Elisha. Its Jewish author has an otherworldly experience where he ascends into the heavens and beholds the glorified Enoch (Metatron). Metatron has become the heavenly scribe and among the highest-ranking angels.

CHAPTER 1

¹ Rabbi Ishmael said: When I ascended on high to behold the vision of the Merkaba and had entered the six halls, one within the other, ² as soon as I reached the door of the Seventh Hall I stood still in prayer before the Holy One, blessed is He, and, lifting up my eyes on high toward the Divine Majesty, I said, ³ "Lord of the Universe, please, that the merit of Aaron, the son of Amram, the lover of peace and pursuer of peace, who received the crown of priesthood from Your Glory on Mount Sinai, be valid for me in this hour, so that Cassiel, the prince, and the messengers with him may not get power over me nor throw me down from the heavens." ⁴ Immediately the Holy One, blessed is He, sent Metatron to me, his servant the messenger, the Prince of the Presence, and he, spreading his wings, came to meet me with great joy so as to save me from their hand. ⁵ And he took me by his hand in their sight, saying to me: "Enter in peace before the high and exalted King and behold the picture of the Merkaba." ⁶ Then I entered the Seventh Hall, and he led me to the camps of Shekinah and placed me before the Holy One, blessed is He, to behold the Merkaba. ⁷ As soon as the princes of the Merkaba and the flaming seraphim perceived me, they fixed their eyes on me. Trembling and shuddering instantly seized me, and I fell down and was benumbed by the radiant image of their eyes and the splendid appearance of their faces, until the Holy One, blessed is He, rebuked them, saying, ⁸ "My servants, my seraphim, my cherubim, and my ophanim! Cover your eyes before Ishmael, my son, my friend, my beloved one, and my glory, so he does not tremble or shudder!" ⁹ Immediately Metatron, the Prince of the Presence, came and restored my spirit and put me on my feet. ¹⁰ After that moment there was not strength enough in me to say a song before the Throne of Glory of the glorious King, the mightiest of all kings, the most excellent of all princes, until after the hour had passed. ¹¹ After one hour had passed, the Holy One, blessed is He, opened to me the gates of Shekinah, the gates of Peace, the gates of Wisdom, the gates of Strength, the gates of Power, the gates of Speech, the gates of Song, the gates of Holiness, the gates of Chant. ¹² And he enlightened my eyes and my heart by words of psalm, song, praise, exaltation, thanksgiving, extolment, glorification, hymn, and eulogy. And as I opened my mouth, uttering a song before the Holy One, blessed is He, the holy chayyoth beneath and above the Throne of Glory answered and said, "Holy" and, "Blessed is the glory of the Lord from His place!"

CHAPTER 2

¹ R. Ishmael said: In that hour the eagles of the Merkaba, the flaming ophanim and the seraphim of consuming fire, asked Metatron, saying to him: ² "Youth! Why permit one born of woman to enter and behold the Merkaba? From which nation, from which tribe is this one? What is his character?" ³ Metatron answered and said to them: "From the nation of Israel whom the Holy One, blessed is He, chose for His people from among seventy tongues, from the tribe of Levi, whom He set aside as a contribution to His Name and from the seed of Aaron whom the Holy One, blessed is He, chose for his servant and put on him the crown of priesthood on Sinai." ⁴ Immediately they spoke and said, "Indeed, this one is worthy to behold the Merkaba." And they said, "Happy is the people that is in such a case!"

CHAPTER 3

¹ R. Ishmael said: In that hour I asked Metatron, the messenger, the Prince of the Presence: "What is your name?" ² He answered me: "I have seventy names, corresponding to the seventy tongues of the world, and all of them are based on the name Metatron, Messenger of the Presence; but my King calls me Youth."

CHAPTER 4

¹ R. Ishmael said: I asked Metatron and said to him: "Why are you called by the Name of your Creator, by seventy names? You are greater than all the princes, higher than all the messengers, more beloved than all the servants, honored above all the mighty ones in kingship, greatness, and glory:

why do they call you Youth in the high heavens?" ² He answered and said to me: "Because I am Enoch, the son of Jared. ³ For when the generation of the flood sinned and were confounded in their deeds, saying to God, Depart from us, for we do not desire the knowledge of Your ways, then the Holy One, blessed is He, removed me from their midst to be a witness against them in the high heavens to all the inhabitants of the world, that they may not say: The Merciful One is cruel. What sins had they committed, all those multitudes? Or, let it be they sinned—what had their sons and their daughters, their mules and their cattle sinned? And likewise, all the animals, domestic and wild, and the birds in the world that God destroyed from the world? ⁵ Hence the Holy One, blessed is He, lifted me up in their lifetime before their eyes to be a witness against them to the future world. And the Holy One, blessed is He, assigned me for a prince and a ruler among the ministering messengers. ⁶ In that hour three of the ministering messengers, 'Uzza, 'Azza, and 'Azzael came forth and brought charges against me in the high heavens, saying before the Holy One, blessed is He: Did the Ancient Ones not rightly say before You, Do not create man? The Holy One, blessed is He, answered and said to them: I have made, and I will bear, yes, I will carry and will deliver. ⁷ As soon as they saw me, they said before Him: Lord of the Universe, what is this one that he should ascend to the height of heights? Is he not one from among the sons of the sons of those who perished in the days of the flood? What is he doing in the Raqia'? ⁸ Again, the Holy One, blessed is He, answered and said to them: What are you, that you enter and speak in my presence? I delight in this one more than in all of you, and hence he will be a prince and a ruler over you in the high heavens. ⁹ Immediately all stood up and went out to meet me, prostrated themselves before me, and said, Happy are you and happy is your father, for your Creator favors you. ¹⁰ And because I am small and a youth among them in days, months, and years, therefore they call me Youth."

CHAPTER 5

¹ R. Ishmael said: Metatron, the Prince of the Presence, said to me: "From the day when the Holy One, blessed is He, expelled the first Adam from the Garden of Eden and onwards, Shekinah was dwelling on a cherub under the Tree of Life. ² And the ministering messengers were gathering together and going down from Heaven in parties, from the Raqia in companies, and from the heavens in camps to do His will in the whole world. ³ And the first man and his generation were sitting outside the gate of the Garden to behold the radiant appearance of the Shekinah. ⁴ For the splendor of the Shekinah traversed the world from one end to the other with a splendor three hundred sixty-five thousand times that of the globe of the sun. And everyone who made use of the splendor of the Shekinah, on him no flies and no gnats rested, neither was he sick nor did he suffer any pain. No demons got power over him, neither were they able to injure him. ⁵ When the Holy One, blessed is He, went out and went in from the Garden to Eden, from Eden to the Garden, from the Garden to Raqia, and from Raqia to the Garden of Eden, then all and everyone beheld the splendor of His Shekinah and they were not injured, ⁶ until the time of the generation of Enosh who was the head of all idol worshipers of the world. ⁷ And what did the generation of Enosh do? They went from one end of the world to the other, and each one brought silver, gold, precious stones, and pearls in heaps like to mountains and hills, making idols out of them throughout all the world. And they erected the idols in every quarter of the world: the size of each idol was one thousand parasangs. ⁸ And they brought down the sun, the moon, planets, and constellations, and placed them before the idols on their right hand and on their left, to attend them even as they attend the Holy One, blessed is He, as it is written: And all the host of Heaven were standing by Him on His right hand and on His left. ⁹ What power was in them that they were able to bring them down? They would not have been able to bring them down but for 'Uzza, 'Azza, and 'Azzielis who taught them sorceries whereby they brought them down and made use of them. ¹⁰ In that time the ministering messengers brought charges against them before the Holy One, blessed is He, saying before Him: Master of the World! ¹¹ What have You to do with the children of men? As it is written: What is man that You are mindful of him? Mah Adam is not written here, but Mah Enosh, for he is the head of the idol worshipers. Why have You left the highest of the high heavens, which are filled with the

majesty of Your glory and are high, uplifted, and exalted, and the high and exalted Throne in the Raqia' Araboth on high, and have gone and dwell with the children of men who worship idols and equate You to the idols? **12** Now You are on earth and the idols likewise. What have You to do with the inhabitants of the earth who worship idols? **13** Immediately the Holy One, blessed is He, lifted up His Shekinah from the earth, from their midst. **14** In that moment the ministering messengers came, the troops of hosts and the armies of 'Araboth, in one thousand camps and ten thousand hosts: they fetched trumpets, and took the horns in their hands, and surrounded the Shekinah with all kinds of songs. And He ascended to the high heavens, as it is written: God has gone up with a shout, the Lord with the sound of a trumpet."

CHAPTER 6

1 R. Ishmael said: Metatron, the messenger, the Prince of the Presence, said to me: "When the Holy One, blessed is He, desired to lift me up on high, He first sent 'Anaphiel H, the prince, and he took me from their midst in their sight and carried me in great glory on a fiery chariot with fiery horses, servants of glory. And he lifted me up to the high heavens together with the Shekinah. **2** As soon as I reached the high heavens, the holy chayyoth, the ophanim, the seraphim, the cherubim, the wheels of the Merkaba, the galgallim, and the ministers of the consuming fire, perceiving my smell from a distance of three hundred sixty-five thousand myriads of parasangs, said, What smell of one born of woman and what taste of a white drop is this that ascends on high, and behold, he is merely a gnat among those who divide flames of fire? **3** The Holy One, blessed is He, answered and spoke to them: My servants, My hosts, My cherubim, My ophanim, My seraphim! Do not be displeased on account of this! Since all the children of men have denied Me and My great Kingdom and have gone worshiping idols, I have removed My Shekinah from among them and have lifted it up on high. But this one whom I have taken from among them is a chosen one among the inhabitants of the world, and he is equal to all of them in faith, righteousness, and perfection of deed, and I have taken him as a tribute from My world under all the heavens."

CHAPTER 7

1 R. Ishmael said: Metatron, the messenger, the Prince of the Presence, said to me: "When the Holy One, blessed is He, took me away from the generation of the flood, He lifted me on the wings of the wind of Shekinah to the highest Heaven and brought me into the great palaces of the 'Araboth Raqia' on high, **2** where the glorious Throne of Shekinah, the Merkaba, the troops of anger, the armies of vehemence, the fiery shin'anim, the flaming cherubim, and the burning ophanim, the flaming servants, the flashing chashmallim, and the lightening seraphim are. And He placed me there to attend the Throne of Glory day after day."

CHAPTER 8

1 R. Ishmael said: Metatron, the Prince of the Presence, said to me: "Before He appointed me to attend the Throne of Glory, the Holy One, blessed is He, opened to me three hundred thousand gates of understanding, three hundred thousand gates of subtlety, three hundred thousand gates of life, three hundred thousand gates of grace and loving-kindness, three hundred thousand gates of love, three hundred thousand gates of instruction, three hundred thousand gates of meekness, three hundred thousand gates of maintenance, three hundred thousand gates of mercy, [and] three hundred thousand gates of fear of Heaven. **2** In that hour the Holy One, blessed is He, added in me wisdom to wisdom, understanding to understanding, subtlety to subtlety, knowledge to knowledge, mercy to mercy, instruction to instruction, love to love, loving-kindness to loving-kindness, goodness to goodness, meekness to meekness, power to power, strength to strength, might to might, brilliance to brilliance, beauty to beauty, splendor to splendor, and I was honored and adorned with all these good and praiseworthy things more than all the children of Heaven."

CHAPTER 9

1 R. Ishmael said: Metatron, the Prince of the Presence, said to me: "After all these things the Holy One, blessed is He, put His hand on me and blessed me with five hundred thirty-six blessings. **2** And I was raised and enlarged to the size of the length and width of the world. **3** And He caused seventy-two wings to grow on me, thirty-six on each side. And each wing was as the whole world. **4** And He fixed three hundred sixty-five eyes on me: each eye was as the great luminary. **5** And He left no kind of splendor, brilliance, radiance, [or] beauty in of all the lights of the universe that He did not fix on me."

CHAPTER 10

1 R. Ishmael said: Metatron, the Prince of the Presence, said to me: "All these things the Holy One, blessed is He, made for me: He made me a throne, similar to the Throne of Glory. And He spread a curtain of splendor and brilliant appearance over me—of beauty, grace, and mercy, similar to the curtain of the Throne of Glory; and all kinds of lights in the universe were fixed on it. **2** And He placed it at the door of the Seventh Hall and seated me on it. **3** And the herald went forth into every Heaven, saying, This is My servant Metatron. I have made him into a prince and a ruler over all the princes of My kingdoms and over all the children of Heaven, except the eight great princes, the honored and revered ones who are called Lord, by the Name of their King. **4** And every messenger and every prince who has a word to speak in My presence before Me will go into his presence before him and will speak to him instead. **5** And you observe and fulfill every command that he utters to you in My Name. For I have committed the Prince of Wisdom and the Prince of Understanding to him to instruct him in the wisdom of heavenly things and of earthly things, in the wisdom of this world and of the world to come. **6** Moreover, I have set him over all the treasuries of the palaces of Araboth and over all the stores of life that I have in the high heavens."

CHAPTER 11

1 R. Ishmael said: Metatron, the messenger, the Prince of the Presence, said to me: "Henceforth, the Holy One, blessed is He, revealed to me all the mysteries of instruction, and all the secrets of wisdom, and all the depths of the Perfect Law; and all living beings' thoughts of heart, and all the secrets of the universe, and all the secrets of creation were revealed to me even as they are revealed to the Maker of creation. **2** And I watched intently to behold the secrets of the depth and the wonderful mystery. Before a man thought, I knew what was in his thought. **3** And there was no thing above on high nor below in the deep hidden from me."

CHAPTER 12

1 R. Ishmael said: Metatron, the Prince of the Presence, said to me: "By reason of the love with which the Holy One, blessed is He, loved me more than all the children of Heaven, He made me a garment of glory on which were fixed all kinds of lights, and He clad me in it. **2** And He made me a robe of honor on which were fixed all kinds of beauty, splendor, brilliance, and majesty. **3** And He made me a royal crown in which were fixed forty-nine costly stones like to the light of the globe of the sun. **4** For its splendor went forth in the four quarters of the 'Araboth Raqia', and in through the seven heavens, and in the four quarters of the world. And he put it on my head. **5** And He called me The Lesser Yhwh in the presence of all His heavenly household; as it is written: For My Name is in him."

CHAPTER 13

1 R. Ishmael said: Metatron, the messenger, the Prince of the Presence, the glory of all heavens, said to me: "Because of the great love and mercy with which the Holy One, blessed is He, loved and cherished me more than all the children of Heaven, He wrote with His finger with a flaming style on the crown on my head the letters by which the heavens and earth, the seas and rivers, the mountains and hills, the planets and constellations, the lightnings, winds, earthquakes and voices, the snow and hail, the storm-wind and the tempest were created—the letters by which all the needs of the world and all the orders of creation were created. ² And every single letter sent forth time after time as it were lightnings, time after time as it were torches, time after time as it were flames of fire, time after time rays like as the rising of the sun, and the moon and the planets."

CHAPTER 14

¹ R. Ishmael said: Metatron, the messenger, the Prince of the Presence, said to me: "When the Holy One, blessed is He, put this crown on my head, [then] all the princes of kingdoms who are in the height of 'Araboth Raqia' and all the hosts of every heaven trembled before me; and even the princes of the elim, the princes of the er'elim, and the princes of the taphsarim, who are greater than all the ministering messengers who minister before the Throne of Glory, shook, feared, and trembled before me when they beheld me. ² Even Sammael, the prince of the accusers, who is greater than all the princes of kingdoms on high, feared and trembled before me. ³ And even the messenger of fire, and the messenger of hail, and the messenger of the wind, and the messenger of the lightning, and the messenger of anger, and the messenger of the thunder, and the messenger of the snow, and the messenger of the rain, and the messenger of the day, and the messenger of the night, and the messenger of the sun, and the messenger of the moon, and the messenger of the planets, and the messenger of the constellations who rule the world under their hands, feared, and trembled, and were frightened before me when they beheld me. ⁴ These are the names of the rulers of the world: Gabriel, the messenger of the fire, Baradiel, the messenger of the hail, Ruchiel who is appointed over the wind, Baraqiel who is appointed over the lightnings, Za'amiel who is appointed over the vehemence, Ziqiel who is appointed over the sparks, Zi'iel who is appointed over the commotion, Za'aphiel who is appointed over the storm-wind, Ra'amiel who is appointed over the thunders, Ra'ashiel who is appointed over the earthquake, Shalgiel who is appointed over the snow, Matariel who is appointed over the rain, Shimshiel who is appointed over the day, Lailiel who is appointed over the night, Galgalliel who is appointed over the globe of the sun, 'Ophanniel who is appointed over the globe of the moon, Kokbiel who is appointed over the planets, [and] Rahatiel who is appointed over the constellations. ⁵ And they all fell prostrate when they saw me. And they were not able to behold me because of the majestic glory and beauty of the appearance of the shining light of the crown of glory on my head."

CHAPTER 15

¹ R. Ishmael said: Metatron, the messenger, the Prince of the Presence, the glory of all heavens, said to me: "As soon as the Holy One, blessed is He, took me in His service to attend the Throne of Glory, and the wheels of the Merkaba, and the needs of Shekinah, my flesh was immediately changed into flames, my sinews into flaming fire, my bones into coals of burning juniper, the light of my eyelids into [the] splendor of lightnings, my eyeballs into firebrands, the hair of my head into hot flames, all my limbs into wings of burning fire, and the whole of my body into glowing fire. ² And on my right were divisions of fiery flames, on my left firebrands were burning, around me storm-wind and tempest were blowing, and in front of me and behind me was roaring of thunder with earthquake."

CHAPTER 16

¹ R. Ishmael said: Metatron, the messenger, the Prince of the Presence, the glory of all Heaven, said to me: "At first I was sitting on a great throne at the door of the Seventh Hall,

and I was judging the children of Heaven, the household on high by authority of the Holy One, blessed is He. And I divided Greatness, Kingship, Dignity, Rulership, Honor and Praise, and Diadem and Crown of Glory to all the princes of kingdoms, while I was presiding in the Celestial Court, and the princes of kingdoms were standing before me, on my right and on my left by authority of the Holy One, blessed is He. ² But when Acher came to behold the vision of the Merkaba and fixed his eyes on me, he feared and trembled before me and his soul was frightened even to departing from him, because of [the] fear, horror, and dread of me when he beheld me sitting on a throne like a king with all the ministering messengers standing by me as my servants and all the princes of kingdoms adorned with crowns surrounding me. ³ In that moment he opened his mouth and said, Indeed, there are two Divine Powers in Heaven! ⁴ Immediately Bath Qol, the Divine Voice, went forth from Heaven from before the Shekinah and said, Return, you backsliding children, except Acher! ⁵ Then 'Aniyel, the prince—the honored, glorified, beloved, wonderful, revered, and fearful one—came in commission from the Holy One, blessed is He, and gave me sixty strokes with lashes of fire and made me stand on my feet."

CHAPTER 17

¹ R. Ishmael said: Metatron, the messenger, the Prince of the Presence, the glory of all heavens, said to me: "There are seven princes—the great, beautiful, revered, wonderful, and honored ones—who are appointed over the seven heavens. And they are these: Michael, and Gabriel, Shatqiel, and Baradiel, and Shachaqiel, and Baraqiel, and Sidriel. ² And each of them is the prince of the host of one heaven. And each one of them is accompanied by four hundred ninety-six thousand myriads of ministering messengers. ³ Michael, the great prince, is appointed over the seventh heaven, the highest one, which is in the 'Araboth. Gabriel, the prince of the host, is appointed over the sixth heaven which is in Makon. Shataqiel, prince of the host, is appointed over the fifth heaven which is in Ma'on. Shahaqi'el, prince of the host, is appointed over the fourth heaven which is in Zebul. Badariel, prince of the host, is appointed over the third heaven which is in Shehaqim. Barakiel, prince of the host, is appointed over the second heaven which is in the height of Merom. Pazriel, prince of the host, is appointed over the first heaven which is in Wilon, which is in Shamayim. ⁴ Under them is Galgalliel, the prince who is appointed over the globe of the sun, and with him are ninety-six great and honored messengers who move the sun in Raqia'. ⁵ Under them is 'Ophanniel, the prince who is set over the globe of the moon. And with him are eighty-eight messengers who move the globe of the moon three hundred fifty-four thousand parasangs every night at the time when the moon stands in the east at its turning point. And when is the moon sitting in the east at its turning point? Answer: in the fifteenth day of every month. ⁶ Under them is Rahatiel, the prince who is appointed over the constellations. And he is accompanied by seventy-two great and honored messengers. And why is he called Rahatiel? Because he makes the stars run in their orbits and courses three hundred thirty-nine thousand parasangs every night from the east to the west, and from the west to the east. For the Holy One, blessed is He, has made a tent for all of them: for the sun, the moon, the planets, and the stars in which they travel at night from the west to the east. ⁷ Under them is Kokbiel, the prince who is appointed over all the planets. And with him are three hundred sixty-five thousand myriads of ministering messengers, great and honored ones who move the planets from city to city and from province to province in the Raqia' of heavens. ⁸ And over them are seventy-two princes of kingdoms on high corresponding to the seventy-two tongues of the world. And all of them are crowned with royal crowns, and clad in royal garments, and wrapped in royal cloaks. And all of them are riding on royal horses and they are holding royal scepters in their hands. And before each one of them, when he is traveling in Raqia', royal servants are running with great glory and majesty; even as on earth they are traveling in chariots with horsemen and great armies, and in glory and greatness, with praise, song, and honor."

CHAPTER 18

¹ R. Ishmael said: Metatron, the messenger, the Prince of the Presence, the glory of all Heaven, said to me: "The messengers of the first heaven, whenever they see their prince, they dismount from their horses and fall on their faces. And the prince of the first heaven, when he sees the prince of the second heaven, he dismounts, removes the crown of glory from his head and falls on his face. And the prince of the second heaven, when he sees the prince of the third heaven, he removes the crown of glory from his head and falls on his face. And the prince of the third heaven, when he sees the prince of the fourth heaven, he removes the crown of glory from his head and falls on his face. And the prince of the fourth heaven, when he sees the prince of the fifth heaven, he removes the crown of glory from his head and falls on his face. And the prince of the fifth heaven, when he sees the prince of the sixth heaven, he removes the crown of glory from his head and falls on his face. And the prince of the sixth heaven, when he sees the prince of the seventh heaven, he removes the crown of glory from his head and falls on his face. ² And the prince of the seventh heaven, when he sees the seventy-two princes of kingdoms, he removes the crown of glory from his head and falls on his face. ³ And the seventy-two princes of kingdoms, when they see the doorkeepers of the First Hall in the 'Araboth Raqia in the highest, they remove the royal crown from their head and fall on their faces. And the doorkeepers of the First Hall, when they see the doorkeepers of the Second Hall, they remove the crown of glory from their head and fall on their faces. And the doorkeepers of the Second Hall, when they see the doorkeepers of the Third Hall, they remove the crown of glory from their head and fall on their faces. And the doorkeepers of the Third Hall, when they see the doorkeepers of the Fourth Hall, they remove the crown of glory from their head and fall on their faces. And the doorkeepers of the Fourth Hall, when they see the doorkeepers of the Fifth Hall, they remove the crown of glory from their head and fall on their faces. And the doorkeepers of the Fifth Hall, when they see the doorkeepers of the Sixth Hall, they remove the crown of glory from their head and fall on their faces. And the doorkeepers of the Sixth Hall, when they see the doorkeepers of the Seventh Hall, they remove the crown of glory from their head and fall on their faces. ⁴ And the doorkeepers of the Seventh Hall, when they see the four great princes, the honored ones, who are appointed over the four camps of Shekinah, they remove the crowns of glory from their head and fall on their faces. ⁵ And the four great princes, when they see Tag'as, the prince, great and honored with song and praise, at the head of [the] children of Heaven, they remove the crown of glory from their head and fall on their faces. ⁶ And Tag'as, the great and honored prince, when he sees Barattiel, the great prince of three fingers in the height of 'Araboth, the highest Heaven, he removes the crown of glory from his head and falls on his face. ⁷ And Baratiel, the great prince, when he sees Hamon, the great prince, the fearful and honored, pleasant and terrible one who makes all the children of Heaven to tremble, when the time draws near for the saying of the Thrice Holy—as it is written: At the noise of the tumult the peoples are fled; at the lifting up of Yourself the nations are scattered—he removes the crown of glory from his head and falls on his face. ⁸ And Hamon, the great prince, when he sees Tutresiel, the great prince, he removes the crown of glory from his head and falls on his face. ⁹ And Tutresiel-Yhwh, the great prince, when he sees Atrugiel, the great prince, he removes the crown of glory from his head and falls on his face. ¹⁰ And Atrugiel, the great prince, when he sees Na'aririel-Yhwh, the great prince, he removes the crown of glory from his head and falls on his face. ¹¹ And Na'aririel-Yhwh, the great prince, when he sees Sasnigiel, the great prince, he removes the crown of glory from his head and falls on his face. ¹² And Sasnigiel-Yhwh, when he sees Zazriel-Yhwh, the great prince, he removes the crown of glory from his head and falls on his face. ¹³ And Zazriel-Yhwh, the prince, when he sees Geburatiel-Yhwh, the prince, he removes the crown of glory from his head and falls on his face. ¹⁴ And Geburatiel-Yhwh, the prince, when he sees 'Araphiel-Yhwh, the prince, he removes the crown of glory from his head and falls on his face. ¹⁵ And 'Araphiel-Yhwh, the prince, when he sees 'Ashruylu, the prince, who presides in all the sessions of the children of Heaven, he removes the crown of glory from his head and falls on his face. ¹⁶ And Ashruylu-Yhwh, the prince, when he sees Gallisur-Yhwh, the prince, who reveals all the secrets of the Law, he removes the crown of glory from his head and falls on his face. ¹⁷ And Gallisur-Yhwh, the prince, when he sees Zakzakiel-Yhwh, the prince who is appointed to write down the merits of Israel on the Throne of Glory, he removes the crown of glory from his head and falls on his face. ¹⁸ And Zakzakiel-Yhwh, the great prince, when he sees 'Anaphiel-Yhwh, the prince who keeps the keys of the heavenly halls, he removes the crown of glory from his head and falls on his face. Why is he called by the name of 'Anaphiel? Because the bough of his honor and majesty and his crown, and his splendor, and his brilliance cover all the chambers of 'Araboth Raqia on high even as the Maker of the world overshadows them, just as it is written with regard to the Maker of the world: His glory covered the heavens, and the earth was full of His praise—even so do the honor and majesty of 'Anaphiel cover all the glories of 'Araboth the highest. ¹⁹ And when he sees Sother 'Ashiel-Yhwh, the prince, the great, fearful, and honored one, he removes the crown of glory from his head and falls on his face. Why is he called Sother 'Ashiel? Because he is appointed over the four heads of the fiery river beside the Throne of Glory; and every single prince who goes out or enters before the Shekinah, only goes out or enters by his permission. For the seals of the fiery river are entrusted to him. And furthermore, his height is seven thousand myriads of parasangs. And he stirs up the fire of the river; and he goes out and enters before the Shekinah to expound what is written concerning the inhabitants of the world, according as it is written: The judgment was set, and the scrolls were opened. ²⁰ And Sother 'Ashiel, the prince, when he sees Shoqed Chozi, the great prince, the mighty, terrible, and honored one, he removes the crown of glory from his head and falls on his face. And why is he called Shoqed Chozi? Because he weighs all the merits of man in a balance in the presence of the Holy One, blessed is He. ²¹ And when he sees Zehanpuryu-Yhwh, the great prince, the mighty and terrible one, honored, glorified, and feared in all the heavenly household, he removes the crown of glory from his head and falls on his face. Why is he called Zehanpuryu? Because he rebukes the fiery river and pushes it back to its place. ²² And when he sees 'Azbuga-Yhwh, the great prince, glorified, revered, honored, adorned, wonderful, exalted, beloved, and feared among all the great princes who know the mystery of the Throne of Glory, he removes the crown of glory from his head and falls on his face. Why is he called 'Azbuga? Because in the future he will gird the righteous and pious of the world with the garments of life and wrap them in the cloak of life, that they may live a continuous life in them. ²³ And when he sees the two great princes, the strong and glorified ones who are standing above him, he removes the crown of glory from his head and falls on his face. And these are the names of the two princes: Sopheriel-Yhwh Who Kills, the great prince, the honored, glorified, blameless, venerable, ancient, and mighty one; and Sopheriel-Yhwh Who Makes Alive, the great prince, the honored, glorified, blameless, ancient, and mighty one. ²⁴ Why is he called Sopheriel-Yhwh Who Kills? Because he is appointed over the scrolls of the dead, so that everyone, when the day of his death draws near, he writes him in the scrolls of the dead. ²⁵ Why is he called Sopheriel-Yhwh Who Makes Alive? Because he is appointed over the scrolls of the living, so that everyone whom the Holy One, blessed is He, will bring into life, he writes him in the Scroll of the Living, by authority of Maqom. ²⁶ You might perhaps say: Since the Holy One, blessed is He, is sitting on a throne, they are also sitting when writing. Answer: the Writing teaches us: And all the host of Heaven are standing by Him. ²⁷ It is said, The host of Heaven, in order to show us that even the great princes—like whom there is none in the high heavens—do not fulfill the requests of the Shekinah otherwise than standing. ²⁸ But how is it they are able to write when they are standing? It is like this: one is standing on the wheels of the tempest and the other is standing on the wheels of the storm-wind. ²⁹ The one is clad in kingly garments, the other is clad in kingly garments. The one is wrapped in a mantle of majesty and the other is wrapped in a mantle of majesty. The one is crowned with a royal crown and the other is crowned with a royal crown. The one's body is full of eyes and the other's body is full of eyes. ³⁰ The appearance of one is like to the appearance of lightnings and the appearance of the other is like to the appearance of lightnings. The eyes of the one are like the sun in its might and the eyes of the other are like the sun in its might. The one's height is like the height of the seven heavens and the other's height is like the height of the seven heavens. ³¹ The wings of the one are as many as the days of the year and the wings of the other are as many as the days of the year. The wings of the one extend over the breadth of Raqia' and the wings of the other extend over the breadth of Raqia. ³² The lips of the one are as the gates of the east and

the lips of the other are as the gates of the east. The tongue of the one is as high as the waves of the sea and the tongue of the other is as high as the waves of the sea. ³³ From the mouth of the one a flame goes forth and from the mouth of the other a flame goes forth. From the mouth of the one there go forth lightnings and from the mouth of the other there go forth lightnings. ³⁴ From the sweat of the one fire is kindled and from the perspiration of the other fire is kindled. From the one's tongue a torch is burning and from the tongue of the other a torch is burning. ³⁵ On the head of the one there is a sapphire stone and on the head of the other there is a sapphire stone. On the shoulders of the one there is a wheel of a swift cherub and on the shoulders of the other there is a wheel of a swift cherub. ³⁶ One has a burning scroll in his hand, the other has a burning scroll in his hand. The one has a flaming style in his hand, the other has a flaming style in his hand. ³⁷ The length of the scroll is three thousand myriads of parasangs; the size of the style is three thousand myriads of parasangs; the size of every single letter that they write is three hundred sixty-five parasangs."

CHAPTER 19

¹ R. Ishmael said: Metatron, the messenger, the Prince of the Presence, said to me: "Above these three messengers, these great princes, there is one prince, distinguished, honored, noble, glorified, adorned, fearful, valiant, strong, great, magnified, glorious, crowned, wonderful, exalted, blameless, beloved, lordly, high and lofty, ancient and mighty, like to whom there is none among the princes. His name is Rikbiel-Yhwh, the great and revered prince who is standing by the Merkaba. ² And why is he called Rikbiel? Because he is appointed over the wheels of the Merkaba, and they are given in his charge. ³ And how many are the wheels? Eight; two in each direction. And there are four winds compassing them around. And these are their names: the Storm-Wind, the Tempest, the Strong Wind, and the Wind of Earthquake. ⁴ And there are four fiery rivers continually running under them, one fiery river on each side. And around them, between the rivers, four clouds are planted, and they are these: clouds of fire, clouds of lamps, clouds of coal, [and] clouds of brimstone, and they are standing beside their wheels. ⁵ And the feet of the chayyoth are resting on the wheels. And between one wheel and the other, earthquake is roaring, and thunder is thundering. ⁶ And when the time draws near for the recital of the Song, then the multitudes of wheels are moved, the multitude of clouds tremble, all the chieftains are made afraid, all the horsemen rage, all the mighty ones are excited, all the hosts are frightened, all the troops are in fear, all the appointed ones hurry away, all the princes and armies are dismayed, all the servants faint, and all the messengers and divisions travail with pain. ⁷ And one wheel makes a sound to be heard to the other, and one cherub to another, one chayya to another, one seraph to another, saying, Extol Him that rides in 'Araboth, by His Name Yhwh, and rejoice before Him!"

CHAPTER 20

¹ R. Ishmael said: Metatron, the messenger, the Prince of the Presence, said to me: "Above these there is one great and mighty prince. His name is Chayyliel-Yhwh, a noble and revered prince, a glorious and mighty prince, a great and revered prince, a prince before whom all the children of Heaven tremble, a prince who is able to swallow up the whole earth in one moment. ² And why is he called Chayyliel-Yhwh? Because he is appointed over the holy chayyoth and strikes the chayyoth with lashes of fire, and glorifies them when they give praise, and glory, and rejoicing, and he causes them to hurry to say Holy and Blessed is the Glory of Yhwh from his place!"

CHAPTER 21

¹ R. Ishmael said: Metatron, the messenger, the Prince of the Presence, said to me: "Four [are] the chayyoth corresponding to the four winds. Each chayya is as the space of the whole world. And each one has four faces; and each face is as the face of the east. ² Each one has four wings, and each wing is like the cover of the universe. ³ And each one has faces in the middle of faces and wings in the middle of wings. The size of the faces is as the size of two hundred forty-eight faces, and the size of the wings is as the size of three hundred sixty-five wings. ⁴ And each one is crowned with two thousand crowns on his head. And each crown is like to the bow in the cloud. And its splendor is like to the splendor of the globe of the sun. And the sparks that go forth from each one are like the splendor of the morning star in the east."

CHAPTER 22 (A)

¹ R. Ishmael said: Metatron, the messenger, the Prince of the Presence, said to me: "Above these there is one prince: noble, wonderful, strong, and praised with all kinds of praise. His name is Kerubiel-Yhwh, a mighty prince, full of power and strength, a prince of highness, and with him there is a righteous prince of righteousness, and with him a holy prince of holiness, and with him a prince glorified by one thousand hosts, exalted by ten thousand armies. ² At his wrath the earth trembles, at his anger the camps are moved, from fear of him the foundations are shaken, at his rebuke the 'Araboth trembles. ³ His stature is full of burning coals. The height of his stature is as the height of the seven heavens, the breadth of his stature is as the wideness of the seven heavens, and the thickness of his stature is as the seven heavens. ⁴ The opening of his mouth is like a lamp of fire. His tongue is a consuming fire. His eyebrows are like to the splendor of the lightning. His eyes are like sparks of brilliance. His countenance is like a burning fire. ⁵ And there is a crown of holiness on his head on which the Explicit Name is graven—and lightnings go forth from it. And the bow of Shekinah is between his shoulders. And his sword is like to lightning, and on his loins there are arrows like to a flame, and on his armor and shield there is a consuming fire, and on his neck there are coals of burning juniper, and also around him there are coals of burning juniper. ⁷ And the splendor of Shekinah is on his face, and the horns of majesty on his wheels, and a royal diadem on his skull. ⁸ And his body is full of eyes. And wings are covering the whole of his high stature. ⁹ On his right hand a flame is burning, and on his left a fire is glowing; and coals are burning from it. And firebrands go forth from his body. And lightnings are cast forth from his face. With him there is always thunder on thunder, by his side there is always earthquake on earthquake. ¹⁰ And the two princes of the Merkaba are together with him. ¹¹ Why is he called Kerubiel-Yhwh, the prince? Because he is appointed over the chariot of the cherubim. And the mighty cherubim are given in his charge. And he adorns the crowns on their heads and polishes the diadem on their skull. ¹² He magnifies the glory of their appearance. And he glorifies the beauty of their majesty. And he increases the greatness of their honor. He causes the song of their praise to be sung. He intensifies their beautiful strength. He causes the brilliance of their glory to shine forth. He beautifies their excellent mercy and loving-kindness. He frames the fairness of their radiance. He makes their merciful beauty even more beautiful. He glorifies their upright majesty. He extols the order of their praise, to establish the dwelling place of Him who dwells on the cherubim. ¹³ And the cherubim are standing by the holy chayyoth, and their wings are raised up to their heads, and Shekinah is resting on them, and the brilliance of the Glory is on their faces, and song and praise [are] in their mouth, and their hands are under their wings, and their feet are covered by their wings, and horns of glory are on their heads, and the splendor of Shekinah on their face, and Shekinah is resting on them, and sapphire stones are around them, and columns of fire [are] on their four sides, and columns of firebrands beside them. ¹⁴ There is one sapphire on one side and another sapphire on another side, and under the sapphires there are coals of burning juniper. ¹⁵ And one cherub is standing in each direction, but the wings of the cherubim encircle each other above their skulls in glory; and they spread them to sing a song with them to Him that inhabits the clouds and to praise the fearful majesty of the King of kings with them. ¹⁶ And Kerubiel-Yhwh, the prince who is appointed over them, he arrays them in attractive, beautiful, and pleasant orders, and he exalts them in all manner of exaltation, dignity, and glory. And he hastens them in glory and might to do the will of their Creator every moment. For above their lofty heads continually abides the glory of the High King who dwells on the cherubim."

CHAPTER 22 (B)

1 R. Ishmael said: Metatron, the Prince of the Presence said to me: "What is the distance between one bridge and another? Twelve myriads of parasangs. Their ascent is myriads of parasangs, and their descent myriads of parasangs. **2** The distance between the rivers of dread and the rivers of fear is twenty-two myriads of parasangs; between the rivers of hail and the rivers of darkness, thirty-six myriads of parasangs; between the chambers of lightnings and the clouds of compassion, forty-two myriads of parasangs; between the clouds of compassion and the Merkaba, eighty-four myriads of parasangs; between the Merkaba and the cherubim, one hundred forty-eight myriads of parasangs; between the cherubim and the ophanim, twenty-four myriads of parasangs; between the ophanim and the chambers of chambers, twenty-four myriads of parasangs; between the chambers of chambers and the holy chayyoth, forty thousand myriads of parasangs; between one wing of the chayyoth and another, twelve myriads of parasangs; and the breadth of each one wing is of that same measure; and the distance between the holy chayyoth and the Throne of Glory is thirty thousand myriads of parasangs. **3** And from the foot of the Throne to the seat there are forty thousand myriads of parasangs. And the Name of Him that sits on it: let the Name be sanctified! **4** And the arches of the Bozv are set above the 'Araboth, and they are one million and one hundred million parasangs high. Their measure is after the measure of the 'Irin and Qaddishin, that is, the Watchers and the Holy Ones. As it is written: I have set My bow in the cloud. It is not written here: I will set, but: I have set—already—clouds that surround the Throne of Glory. As His clouds pass by, the messengers of hail turn into burning coal. **5** And a fire of the voice goes down from by the holy chayyoth. And because of the breath of that voice, they run to another place, fearing lest it command them to go; and they return lest it injure them from the other side. Therefore, [as it is written:] They run and return. **6** And these arches of the bow are more beautiful and radiant than the radiance of the sun during the summer solstice, and they are whiter than a flaming fire, and they are great and beautiful. **7** Above the arches of the bow are the wheels of the ophanim. Their height is one million and one hundred million units of measure after the measure of the seraphim and the troops."

CHAPTER 23

1 R. Ishmael said: Metatron, the messenger, the Prince of the Presence, said to me: "There are numerous winds blowing under the wings of the cherubim. The Fluttering Wind blows there, as it is written: And the Spirit of God was fluttering on the face of the waters. **2** The Strong Wind blows there, as it is said: And the Lord caused the sea to go back by a strong east wind all that night. **3** The East Wind blows there, as it is written: The east wind brought the locusts. **4** The Wind of Quails blows there, as it is written: And there went forth a wind from the Lord and brought quails. **5** The Wind of Jealousy blows there, as it is written: And the wind of jealousy came on him. **6** The Wind of Earthquake blows there, as it is written: And after that, the wind of the earthquake, but the Lord was not in the earthquake. **7** The Wind of Yhwh blows there, as it is written: And He carried me out by the Spirit of the Lord and set me down. **8** The Evil Wind blows there, as it is written: And the evil wind departed from him. **9** The Wind of Wisdom, and the Wind of Understanding, and the Wind of Knowledge, and the Wind of the Fear of Yhwh blow there, as it is written: And the Spirit of the Lord will rest on Him, || The Spirit of wisdom and understanding, || The Spirit of counsel and might, || The Spirit of knowledge and of the fear. **10** The Wind of Rain blows there, as it is written: The north wind brings forth rain. **11** The Wind of Lightnings blows there, as it is written: He makes lightnings for the rain and brings forth the wind out of His treasuries. **12** The Wind, Breaking the Rocks, blows there, as it is written: The Lord passed by and a great and strong wind split the mountains and broke in pieces the rocks before the Lord. **13** The Wind of Assuagement of the Sea blows there, as it is written: And God made a wind to pass over the earth, and the waters assuaged. **14** The Wind of Wrath blows there, as it is written: And behold, there came a great wind from the wilderness and [it] struck the four corners of the house and it fell. **15** The Storm-Wind blows there, as it is written: Storm-wind, fulfilling His word. **16** And Satan is standing among these winds, for Storm-Wind is nothing else but Satan, and all these winds do not blow but under the wings of the cherubim, as it is written: And He rode on a cherub and flew, yes, and He flew swiftly on the wings of the wind. **17** And where do all these winds go? The Writing teaches us that they go out from under the wings of the cherubim and descend on the globe of the sun, as it is written: The wind goes toward the south and turns around to the north; it turns around continually in its course and the wind returns again to its circuits. And from the globe of the sun they return and descend on the rivers and the seas, on the mountains and on the hills, as it is written: For behold, He that forms the mountains and creates the wind. **18** And from the mountains and the hills they return and descend to the seas and the rivers; and from the seas and the rivers they return and descend on the cities and provinces; and from the cities and provinces they return and descend into the Garden, and from the Garden they return and descend to Eden, as it is written: Walking in the Garden in the wind of day. **19** And in the midst of the Garden they join together and blow from one side to the other and are perfumed with the spices of the Garden even from its remotest parts, until they separate from each other, and, filled with the scent of the pure spices, they bring the fragrance from the remotest parts of Eden and the spices of the Garden to the righteous and godly who in the time to come will inherit the Garden of Eden and the Tree of Life, **20** as it is written: Awake, O north wind; and come you south; blow on my garden, that the spices thereof may flow out. Let my beloved come into his garden and eat his precious fruits."

CHAPTER 24

1 R. Ishmael said: Metatron, the messenger, the Prince of the Presence, the glory of all Heaven, said to me: "The Holy One, blessed is He, has numerous chariots: He has the Chariots of the Cherubim, as it is written: And he rode on a cherub and flew. **2** He has the Chariots of Wind, as it is written: And he flew swiftly on the wings of the wind. **3** He has the Chariots of the Swift Cloud, as it is written: Behold, the Lord rides on a swift cloud. **4** He has the Chariots of Clouds, as it is written: Behold, I come to you in a cloud. **5** He has the Chariots of the Altar, as it is written: I saw the Lord standing on the altar. **6** He has the Chariots of Myriads, as it is written: The chariots of God are myriads, thousands of messengers. **7** He has the Chariots of the Tent, as it is written: And the Lord appeared in the tent in a pillar of cloud. **8** He has the Chariots of the Dwelling Place, as it is written: And the Lord spoke to him out of the Dwelling Place. **9** He has the Chariots of the Propitiatory Covering, as it is written: Then he heard the voice speaking to him from on the propitiatory covering. **10** He has the Chariots of Sapphire Stone, as it is written: And there was under His feet as it were a paved work of sapphire stone. **11** He has the Chariots of Eagles, as it is written: I bare you on eagles' wings. (Eagles are not literally meant here but they that fly swiftly as eagles.) **12** He has the chariots of Shout, as it is written: God has gone up with a shout. **13** He has the Chariots of 'Araboth, as it is written: Extol Him that rides on the 'Araboth. **14** He has the Chariots of Thick Clouds, as it is written: Who makes the thick clouds His chariot. **15** He has the Chariots of the Chayyoth, as it is written: And the chayyoth ran and returned. They run by permission and return by permission, for Shekinah is above their heads. **16** He has the Chariots of Wheels, as it is written: And He said, Go in between the whirling wheels. **17** He has the Chariots of a Swift Cherub, as it is written: Riding on a swift cherub. And at the time when He rides on a swift cherub, as He sets one of His feet on him, before He sets the other foot on his back, He looks through eighteen thousand worlds at one glance. And He discerns and sees into them all and knows what is in all of them and then he sets down the other foot on him, according as it is written: Around eighteen thousand. From where do we know that He looks through every one of them every day? It is written: He looked down from Heaven on the children of men to see if there were any that understood, that seek after God. **18** He has the Chariots of the Ophanim, as it is written: And the ophanim were full of eyes around. **19** He has the Chariots of His Holy Throne, as it is written: God sits on His holy throne. **20** He has the chariots of the Throne of Yah, as it is written: Because a hand is lifted up on the throne of Yah. **21** He has the Chariots of the Throne of Judgment, as it is written: But the Lord of Hosts will be exalted in judgment. **22** He has the

Chariots of the Throne of Glory, as it is written: The throne of glory, set on high from the beginning, is the place of our sanctuary. 23 He has the Chariots of the High and Exalted Throne, as it is written: I saw the Lord sitting on the high and exalted throne."

CHAPTER 25

1 R. Ishmael said: Metatron, the messenger, the Prince of the Presence, said to me: "Above these there is one great prince, revered, high, lordly, fearful, ancient, and strong. 'Ophphanniel-Yhwh is his name. 2 He has sixteen faces, four faces on each side, one hundred wings on each side. And he has eight thousand four hundred sixty-six eyes, corresponding to the days of the year. Two thousand one hundred and ninety and some say two thousand one hundred sixteen on each side. 3 And those two eyes of his face—in each one of them lightnings are flashing, and from each one of them firebrands are burning, and no creature is able to behold them. For anyone who looks at them is burned instantly. 4 His height is as the distance of two thousand five hundred years' journey. No eye can behold and no mouth can tell the mighty power of his strength except the King of kings, the Holy One, blessed is He, alone. 5 Why is he called 'Ophphanniel? Because he is appointed over the ophanim and the ophanim are given in his charge. He stands every day, and attends, and beautifies them. And he exalts and orders their apartment, and polishes their standing-place, and makes their dwellings bright, [and] makes their corners even, and cleanses their seats. And he waits on them early and late, by day and by night, to increase their beauty, to make their dignity great, and to make them diligent in praise of their Creator. 6 And all the ophanim are full of eyes, and they are all full of brightness; seventy-two sapphire stones are fixed on their garments on their right side and seventy-two sapphire stones are fixed on their garments on their left side. 7 And four carbuncle stones are fixed on the crown of every single one, the splendor of which proceeds in the four directions of 'Araboth even as the splendor of the globe of the sun proceeds in all the directions of the universe. And why is it called Carbuncle? Because its splendor is like the appearance of lightning. And tents of splendor, tents of brilliance, [and] tents of brightness as of sapphire and carbuncle enclose them because of the shining appearance of their eyes."

CHAPTER 26

1 R. Ishmael said: Metatron, the messenger, the Prince of the Presence, said to me: "Above these there is one prince, wonderful, noble, great, honorable, mighty, terrible, a chief, and leader, and a swift scribe, glorified, honored, and beloved. 2 He is altogether filled with splendor, full of praise and shining; and he is wholly full of brilliance, of light and of beauty; and the whole of him is filled with goodliness and greatness. 3 His countenance is altogether like that of messengers, but his body is like an eagle's body. 4 His splendor is like to lightnings, his appearance like firebrands, his beauty like to sparks, his honor like fiery coals, his majesty like electrum, his radiance like the light of the planet Venus. The image of him is like to the Greater Light. His height is as the seven heavens. The light from his eyebrows is like the sevenfold light. 5 The sapphire stone on his head is as great as the whole universe and like to the splendor of the very heavens in radiance. 6 His body is full of eyes like the stars of the sky, innumerable and unsearchable. Every eye is like the planet Venus. Yet, there are some of them like the Lesser Light and some of them like to the Greater Light. From his ankles to his knees, they are like to stars of lightning; from his knees to his thighs like to the planet Venus; from his thighs to his loins like to the moon; from his loins to his neck like the sun; from his neck to his skull like to the Imperishable Light. 7 The crown on his head is like to the splendor of the Throne of Glory. The measure of the crown is the distance of five hundred and two years' journey. There is no kind of splendor, no kind of brilliance, no kind of radiance, no kind of light in the universe but is fixed on that crown. 8 The name of that prince is Seraphiel-Yhwh. And why is he called by the name of Seraphiel-Yhwh? Because he is appointed over the seraphim. And the flaming seraphim are given in his charge. And he presides over them by day and by night and teaches them song, praise, proclamation of beauty, might, and majesty, that they may proclaim the beauty of their King in all manner of praise and sanctification. 9 How many are the seraphim? Four, corresponding to the four winds of the world. And how many wings does each one of them have? Six, corresponding to the six days of Creation. And how many faces do they have? Each one of them [has] four faces. 10 The measure of the seraphim and the height of each one of them correspond to the height of the seven heavens. The size of each wing is like the measure of all Raqia'. The size of each face is like that of the face of the east. 11 And each one of them gives forth light like to the splendor of the Throne of Glory, so that not even the holy chayyoth, the honored ophanim, nor the majestic cherubim are able to behold it. For everyone who beholds it, his eyes are darkened because of its great splendor. 12 Why are they called seraphim? Because they burn the writing tablets of Satan: every day Satan is sitting, together with Sammael, the Prince of Rome, and with Dubbiel, the Prince of Persia, and they write the iniquities of Israel on writing tablets which they hand over to the seraphim in order that they may present them before the Holy One, blessed is He, so that He may destroy Israel from the world. But the seraphim know from the secrets of the Holy One, blessed is He, that He does not desire that this people Israel should perish. What do the seraphim do? Every day they receive them from the hand of Satan and burn them in the burning fire beside the high and exalted Throne in order that they may not come before the Holy One, blessed is He, at the time when He is sitting on the Throne of Judgment, judging the whole world in truth."

CHAPTER 27

1 R. Ishmael said: Metatron, the messenger of Yhwh, the Prince of the Presence, said to me: "Above the seraphim there is one prince, exalted above all the princes, wondrous more than all the servants. His name is Radweriel-Yhwh, who is appointed over the treasuries of the scrolls. 2 He fetches forth the Case of Writings with the Scroll of Records in it, and brings it before the Holy One, blessed is He. And he breaks the seals of the case, opens it, takes out the scrolls, and delivers them before the Holy One, blessed is He. And the Holy One, blessed is He, receives them from his hand and gives them in his sight to the Scribes that they may read them in the Great House of Judgment in the height of 'Araboth Raqia', before the heavenly household. 3 And why is he called Radweriel? Because out of every word that goes forth from his mouth a messenger is created: and he stands in the singing company of the ministering messengers and utters a song before the Holy One, blessed is He, when the time draws near for the recitation of the Thrice Holy."

CHAPTER 28

1 R. Ishmael said: Metatron, the messenger, the Prince of the Presence, said to me: "Above all these there are four great princes, Watchers and Holy Ones by name: high, honored, revered, beloved, wonderful, and glorious ones, greater than all the children of Heaven. There is none like to them among all the celestial princes and none their equal among all the servants. For each one of them is equal to all the rest together. 2 And their dwelling is beside the Throne of Glory, and their standing place beside the Holy One, blessed is He, so that the brilliance of their dwelling is a reflection of the brilliance of the Throne of Glory. And the splendor of their countenance is a reflection of the splendor of Shekinah. 3 And they are glorified by the glory of the Divine Majesty and praised by the praise of Shekinah. 4 And not only that, but the Holy One, blessed is He, does nothing in His world without first consulting them, but after that He does it. As it is written: The sentence is by the decree of the watchers and the demand by the word of the holy ones. 5 The watchers are two and the holy ones are two. And how are they standing before the Holy One, blessed is He? It is to be understood that one watcher is standing on one side and the other watcher on the other side, and one holy one is standing on one side and the other on the other side. 6 And they always exalt the humble, and they abase to the ground those that are proud, and they exalt to the height those that are humble. 7 And every day, as the Holy One, blessed is He, is sitting on the Throne of Judgment and judges the whole

world, and the scrolls of the living and the scrolls of the dead are opened before Him, then all the children of Heaven are standing before Him in fear, dread, awe, and trembling. At that time, when the Holy One, blessed is He, is sitting on the Throne of Judgment to execute judgment, His garment is white as snow, and the hair on His head as pure wool, and the whole of His cloak is like the shining light. And He is covered with righteousness all over as with a coat of mail. **8** And those watchers and holy ones are standing before Him like court officers before the judge. And they raise and argue every case and close the case that comes before the Holy One, blessed is He, in judgment, according as it is written: The sentence is by the decree of the watchers and the demand by the word of the holy ones. **9** Some of them argue and others pass the sentence in the Great House of Judgment in 'Araboth. Some of them make the requests from before the Divine Majesty and some close the cases before the Most High. Others finish by going down and executing the sentences on earth below. According as it is written: Behold, a watcher and a holy one came down from Heaven, and cried aloud, and said thus: Hew down the tree, and cut off his branches, shake off his leaves, and scatter his fruit: let the beasts get away from under it, and the birds from his branches. **10** Why are they called watchers and holy ones? By reason that they sanctify the body and the spirit with lashes of fire on the third day of the judgment, as it is written: After two days He will revive us, || On the third [[day]] He will raise us up, || And we will live before Him."

CHAPTER 29

1 R. Ishmael said: Metatron, the messenger, the Prince of the Presence, said to me: "Each one of them has seventy names corresponding to the seventy tongues of the world. And all of them are based on the Name of the Holy One, blessed is He. And every name is written with a flaming style on the Fearful Crown which is on the head of the high and exalted King. **2** And sparks and lightnings go forth from each one of them. And each one of them is beset with horns of splendor around. From each one lights are shining forth, and each one is surrounded by tents of brilliance so that not even the seraphim and the chayyoth who are greater than all the [other] children of Heaven are able to behold them."

CHAPTER 30

1 R. Ishmael said: Metatron, the messenger, the Prince of the Presence, said to me: "Whenever the Great House of Judgment is seated in the 'Araboth Raqia' on high there is no opening of the mouth for anyone in the world except those great princes who are called Yhwh by the Name of the Holy One, blessed is He. **2** How many are those princes? Seventy-two princes of the kingdoms of the world besides the Prince of the World who speaks in favor of the world before the Holy One, blessed is He, every day, at the hour when the scroll is opened in which all the doings of the world are recorded, according as it is written: The judgment was set and the scrolls were opened."

CHAPTER 31

1 R. Ishmael said: Metatron, the messenger, the Prince of the Presence, said to me: "At the time when the Holy One, blessed is He, is sitting on the Throne of Judgment, then Justice is standing on His right, and Mercy on His left, and Truth before His face. **2** And when man enters before Him to judgment, then a staff, as it were, comes forth from the splendor of the Mercy toward him and stands in front of him. Immediately man falls on his face, and all the messengers of destruction fear and tremble before Him, according as it is written: And with mercy will the throne be established, and He will sit on it in truth."

CHAPTER 32

1 R. Ishmael said: Metatron, the messenger, the Prince of the Presence, said to me: "When the Holy One, blessed is He,

opens the Scroll—half of which is fire and half flame—then they go out from before Him in every moment to execute the judgment on the wicked by His sword that is drawn forth out of its sheath and the splendor of which shines like lightning and pervades the world from one end to the other, as it is written: For the Lord will plead by fire and with all flesh by His sword. **2** And all the inhabitants of the world fear and tremble before Him when they behold His sharpened sword like to lightning from one end of the world to the other, and sparks and flashes of the size of the stars of Raqia' going out from it, according as it is written: If I sharpen the lightning of My sword."

CHAPTER 33

1 R. Ishmael said: Metatron, the messenger, the Prince of the Presence, said to me: "At the time that the Holy One, blessed is He, is sitting on the Throne of Judgment, then the messengers of Mercy are standing on His right, the messengers of Peace are standing on His left, and the messengers of Destruction are standing in front of Him. **2** And one scribe is standing beneath Him, and another scribe above Him. **3** And the glorious seraphim surround the Throne on its four sides with walls of lightnings, and the ophanim surround them with firebrands around the Throne of Glory. And clouds of fire and clouds of flames surround them to the right and to the left; and the holy chayyoth carry the Throne of Glory from below: each one with three fingers. The measure of the fingers of each one is eight hundred thousand and seven hundred times one hundred, and sixty-six thousand parasangs. **4** And underneath the feet of the chayyoth seven fiery rivers are running and flowing. And the breadth of each river is three hundred sixty-five thousand parasangs and its depth is two hundred forty-eight thousand myriads of parasangs. Its length is unsearchable and immeasurable. **5** And each river turns around in a bow in the four directions of 'Araboth Raqia', and from there it falls down to Ma'on and is stayed, and from Ma'on to Zebul, from Zebul to Shechaqim, from Shechaqim to Raqia', from Raqia' to Shamayim, and from Shamayim on the heads of the wicked who are in Gehenna, **6** as it is written: Behold, a whirlwind of the Lord, even His fury, is gone, yes, a whirling tempest; it will burst on the head of the wicked."

CHAPTER 34

1 R. Ishmael said: Metatron, the messenger, the Prince of the Presence, said to me: "The hooves of the chayyoth are surrounded by seven clouds of burning coals. The clouds of burning coals are surrounded on the outside by seven walls of flames. The seven walls of flames are surrounded by the outside by seven walls of hailstones. The hailstones are surrounded on the outside by stones of hail. The stones of hail are surrounded on the outside by stones of the wings of the tempest. The stones of the wings of the tempest are surrounded on the outside by flames of fire. The flames of fire are surrounded by the chambers of the whirlwind. The chambers of the whirlwind are surrounded on the outside by the fire and the water. **2** Around the fire and the water are those who utter the Holy. Around those who utter the Holy are those who utter the Blessed. Around those who utter the Blessed are the bright clouds. The bright clouds are surrounded on the outside by coals of burning juniper; and on the outside surrounding the coals of burning juniper there are one thousand camps of fire and ten thousand hosts of flames. And between every camp and every host there is a cloud, so that they may not be burned by the fire."

CHAPTER 35

1 R. Ishmael said: Metatron, the messenger, the Prince of the Presence, said to me: "The Holy One, blessed is He, has five hundred and six thousand myriads of camps in the height of 'Araboth Raqia'. And each camp is composed of four hundred ninety-six thousand messengers. **2** And every single messenger, the height of his stature is as the Great Sea; and the appearance of their countenance as the appearance of the lightning, and their eyes as lamps of fire, and their arms and their feet like in color to polished brass, and the roaring voice of their words like the voice of a multitude. ³ And they are all standing before the Throne of Glory in four rows. And the princes of the army are standing at the head of each row. ⁴ And some of them utter the Holy and others utter the Blessed, some of them run as messengers, others are standing in attendance, according as it is written: One million ministered to Him and one hundred million stood before him, the judgment was set, and the scrolls were opened. ⁵ And in the hour when the time draws near for [them] to say the Holy, then first there goes forth a whirlwind from before the Holy One, blessed is He, and bursts on the camp of Shekinah and there arises a great commotion among them, as it is written: Behold, the whirlwind of the Lord goes forth with fury—a continuing commotion. ⁶ At that moment one million of them are changed into sparks, one million of them into firebrands, one million into flashes, one million into flames, one million into males, one million into females, one million into winds, one million into burning fires, one million into flames, one million into sparks, one million into chashmals of light, until they take on themselves the yoke of the Kingdom of the heavens, the high and lifted up, of the Creator of them all, with fear, dread, awe, and trembling, with commotion, anguish, terror, and trepidation. Then they are changed again into their former shape to always have the fear of their King before them, as they have set their hearts on saying the Song continually, as it is written: And one cried to another and said, Holy, Holy, Holy."

CHAPTER 36

¹ R. Ishmael said: Metatron, the messenger, the Prince of the Presence, said to me: "At the time when the ministering messengers desire to say the Song, then the fiery stream rises with many thousand[s] of thousands and myriads of myriads of messengers of power and strength of fire and it runs and passes under the Throne of Glory, between the camps of the ministering messengers and the troops of 'Araboth. ² And all the ministering messengers first go down into Nehar di-Nur, and they dip themselves in the fire and dip their tongue and their mouth seven times; and after that they go up and put on the garment of 'Machaqe Samal, and cover themselves with cloaks of chashmal, and stand in four rows beside the Throne of Glory, in all the heavens."

CHAPTER 37

¹ R. Ishmael said: Metatron, the messenger, the Prince of the Presence, said to me: "There are four chariots of Shekinah standing in the seven Halls, and the four camps of Shekinah are standing before each one. Between each camp a river of fire is continually flowing. ² Between each river there are bright clouds surrounding them, and pillars of brimstone are put up between each cloud. Flaming wheels are standing between one pillar and another, surrounding them. And between one wheel and another there are flames of fire around. Between one flame and another there are treasuries of lightnings; behind the treasuries of lightnings are the wings of the storm wind. Behind the wings of the storm-wind are the chambers of the tempest; behind the chambers of the tempest there are winds, voices, thunders, sparks on sparks, and earthquakes on earthquakes."

CHAPTER 38

¹ R. Ishmael said: Metatron, the messenger, the Prince of the Presence, said to me: "At the time when the ministering messengers utter the Thrice Holy, then all the pillars of the heavens and their sockets tremble, and the gates of the Halls of 'Araboth Raqia' are shaken, and the foundations of Shechaqim and the universe are moved, and the orders of Ma'on and the chambers of Makon quiver, and all the orders of Raqia', and the constellations, and the planets are dismayed, and the globes of the sun and the moon hurry away, and flee out of their courses, and run twelve thousand parasangs, and seek to throw themselves down from the heavens ² by reason of the roaring voice of their chant, and the noise of their praise, and the sparks and lightnings that go forth from their faces; as it is written: The voice of Your thunder was in the heavens and the lightnings lightened the world, the earth trembled and

shook. ³ Until the Prince of the World calls them, saying, Be quiet in your place! Do not fear because of the ministering messengers who sing the Song before the Holy One, blessed is He. As it is written: When the morning stars sang together, || And all the sons of Heaven [[or God]] shouted for joy."

CHAPTER 39

¹ R. Ishmael said: Metatron, the messenger, the Prince of the Presence, said to me: "When the ministering messengers utter the Holy, then all the explicit names that are graven with a flaming style on the Throne of Glory fly off like eagles, with sixteen wings. And they surround and encircle the Holy One, blessed is He, on the four sides of the place of His Shekinah. ² And the messengers of the host, and the flaming servants, and the mighty ophanim, and the cherubim of the Shekinah, and the holy chayyoth, and the seraphim, and the er'elim, and the taphsarim and the troops of consuming fire, and the fiery armies, and the flaming hosts, and the holy princes, adorned with crowns, clad in kingly majesty, wrapped in glory, girt with loftiness, fall on their faces three times, saying, Blessed is the name of His glorious Kingdom forever and ever."

CHAPTER 40

¹ R. Ishmael said: Metatron, the messenger, the Prince of the Presence, said to me: "When the ministering messengers say Holy before the Holy One, blessed is He, in the proper way, then the servants of His Throne, the attendants of His Glory, go forth with great mirth from under the Throne of Glory. ² And they all carry in their hands—each one of them—one million and one hundred million crowns of stars, similar in appearance to the planet Venus, and put them on the ministering messengers and the great princes who utter the Holy. They put three crowns on each one of them: one crown because they say Holy, another crown because they say Holy, Holy, and a third crown because they say Holy, Holy, Holy, is the Lord of Hosts. ³ And in the moment that they do not utter the Holy in the right order, a consuming fire goes forth from the little finger of the Holy One, blessed is He, and falls down in the midst of their ranks and is divided into four hundred ninety-six thousand parts corresponding to the four camps of the ministering messengers, and consumes them in one moment, as it is written: A fire goes before Him and burns up His adversaries around. ⁴ After that, the Holy One, blessed is He, opens His mouth, and speaks one word, and creates others in their stead—new ones like them. And each one stands before His Throne of Glory, uttering the Holy, as it is written: They are new every morning; great is Your faithfulness."

CHAPTER 41

¹ R. Ishmael said: Metatron, the messenger, the Prince of the Presence, said to me: "Come and behold the letters by which the heavens and the earth were created, the letters by which the mountains and hills were created, the letters by which the seas and rivers were created, the letters by which the trees and herbs were created, the letters by which the planets and the constellations were created, the letters by which the globe of the moon and the globe of the sun, Orion, the Pleiades, and all the different luminaries of Raqia' were created, ² the letters by which the Throne of Glory and the wheels of the Merkaba were created, the letters by which the necessities of the worlds were created, ³ the letters by which wisdom, understanding, knowledge, prudence, meekness, and righteousness were created, by which the whole world is sustained." ⁴ And I walked by his side, and he took me by his hand, and raised me on his wings, and showed me those letters, all of them, that are graven with a flaming style on the Throne of Glory: and sparks go forth from them and cover all the chambers of 'Araboth.

CHAPTER 42

¹ R. Ishmael said: Metatron, the messenger, the Prince of

the Presence, said to me: "Come, and I will show you where the waters are suspended in the highest, where fire is burning in the midst of hail, where lightnings lighten out of the midst of snowy mountains, where thunders are roaring in the celestial heights, where a flame is burning in the midst of the burning fire, and where voices make themselves heard in the midst of thunder and earthquake." **2** Then I went by his side, and he took me by his hand, and lifted me up on his wings, and showed me all those things. I beheld the waters suspended on high in 'Araboth Raqia', by the Name Yah 'Ehye 'Asher 'Ehye, that is, Yah, I am that I am; and [I beheld] their fruits going down from Heaven and watering the face of the world, as it is written: "He waters the mountains from His chambers: the earth is satisfied with the fruit of Your work." **3** And I saw fire, and snow, and hailstone that were mingled together within each other and yet were not damaged, by the name 'Esh 'Okela, as it is written: "For the Lord your God is a consuming fire." **4** And I saw lightnings that were lightening out of mountains of snow and yet were not damaged, by the name Yah Sur 'Olamim, as it is written: "For in Yah, the Lord, the everlasting rock." **5** And I saw thunders and voices that were roaring in the midst of fiery flames and were not damaged, by the name 'El-Shaddai Rabba, as it is written: "I am God Almighty." **6** And I beheld a flame and a glow that were flaming and glowing in the midst of burning fire, and yet were not damaged, by the name Yad 'Al Kes Yah, as it is written: "And he said, For the hand is on the Throne of the Lord." **7** And I beheld rivers of fire in the midst of rivers of water and they were not damaged, by the name 'Ose Shalom, as it is written: "He makes peace in His high places." For He makes peace between the fire and the water, between the hail and the fire, between the wind and the cloud, between the earthquake and the sparks.

CHAPTER 43

1 R. Ishmael said: Metatron said to me: "Come, and I will show you where the spirits of the righteous are that have been created and have returned, and the spirits of the righteous that have not yet been created." **2** And he lifted me up to his side, took me by his hand, and lifted me up near the Throne of Glory by the place of the Shekinah; and he revealed the Throne of Glory to me, and he showed me the spirits that have been created and had returned: and they were flying above the Throne of Glory before the Holy One, blessed is He. **3** After that I went to interpret the following verse of Writing and I found in what is written: "For the spirit clothed itself before me, and the souls I have made"—that means the spirits that have been created in the chamber of creation of the righteous and that have returned before the Holy One, blessed is He; and the words "and the souls I have made" refer to the spirits of the righteous that have not yet been created in the chamber, or Guph.

CHAPTER 44

1 R. Ishmael said: Metatron, the messenger, the Prince of the Presence, said to me: "Come, and I will show you where the spirits of the wicked and the spirits of the intermediate are standing, and the spirits of the intermediate, where they go down, and the spirits of the wicked, where they go down." **2** And he said to me: "The spirits of the wicked go down to Sheol by the hands of two messengers of destruction: their names are Za'aphiel and Simkiel. **3** Simkiel is appointed over the intermediate to support them and purify them because of the great mercy of the Prince of the Place. Za'aphiel is appointed over the spirits of the wicked in order to cast them down from the presence of the Holy One, blessed is He, and from the splendor of the Shekinah to Sheol, to be punished in the fire of Gehenna with staves of burning coal." **4** And I went by his side, and he took me by his hand and showed me all of them with his fingers. **5** And I beheld the appearance of their faces, and behold, it was as the appearance of children of men, and their bodies like eagles. And not only that, but furthermore the color of the countenance of the intermediate was like pale grey on account of their deeds, for there are stains on them until they have become cleaned from their iniquity in the fire. **6** And the color of the wicked was like the bottom of a pot on account of the wickedness of their doings. **7** And I saw the spirits of the

Patriarchs—Abraham, Isaac, and Jacob—and the rest of the righteous whom they have brought up out of their graves and who have ascended to Heaven. And they were praying before the Holy One, blessed is He, saying in their prayer: "Lord of the Universe! How long will You sit on Your Throne like a mourner in the days of his mourning with Your right hand behind You and not deliver Your children and reveal Your Kingdom in the world? And for how long will You have no pity on Your children who are made slaves among the nations of the world? Nor on Your right hand that is behind You with which You stretched out the heavens, and the earth, and the heavens of heavens? When will You have compassion?" **8** Then the Holy One, blessed is He, answered each of them, saying, "Since these wicked sin so and so, and transgress with such and such transgressions against Me, how could I deliver My Great Right Hand in the downfall by their hands?" **9** In that moment Metatron called me and spoke to me: "My servant! Take the scrolls and read their evil doings!" Immediately I took the scrolls and read their doings and there were to be found thirty-six transgressions written down with regard to each wicked one and besides that they have transgressed all the letters in the Torah, as it is written: "Yes, all Israel has transgressed Your law." It is not written "'al torateka" but, "'et torateka," for they have transgressed from Aleph to Taw; they have transgressed forty statutes for each letter. **10** Immediately Abraham, Isaac, and Jacob wept. Then the Holy One, blessed is He, said to them: "Abraham, My beloved, Isaac, My chosen one, Jacob, My firstborn! How can I now deliver them from among the nations of the world?" And immediately Michael, the prince of Israel, cried and wept with a loud voice and said, "Why do You stand far off, O Lord?"

CHAPTER 45

1 R. Ishmael said: Metatron said to me: "Come, and I will show you the curtain of the Divine Majesty which is spread before the Holy One, blessed is He, and whereon are graven all the generations of the world and all their doings, both what they have done and what they will do until the end of all generations." **2** And I went, and he showed it to me, pointing it out with his fingers like a father who teaches his children the letters of Torah. And I saw each generation, the rulers of each generation, and the heads of each generation, the shepherds of each generation, the oppressors of each generation, the keepers of each generation, the scourgers of each generation, the overseers of each generation, the judges of each generation, the court officers of each generation, the teachers of each generation, the supporters of each generation, the chiefs of each generation, the presidents of academies of each generation, the magistrates of each generation, the princes of each generation, the counselors of each generation, the nobles of each generation, and the men of might of each generation, the elders of each generation, and the guides of each generation. **3** And I saw Adam, his generation, their doings and their thoughts; Noah and his generation, their doings and their thoughts; and the generation of the flood, their doings and their thoughts; Shem and his generation, their doings and their thoughts; Nimrod and the generation of the confusion of tongues, and his generation, their doings and their thoughts; Abraham and his generation, their doings and their thoughts; Isaac and his generation, their doings and their thoughts; Ishmael and his generation, their doings and their thoughts; Jacob and his generation, their doings and their thoughts; Joseph and his generation, their doings and their thoughts; the tribes and their generation, their doings and their thoughts; Amram and his generation, their doings and their thoughts; Moses and his generation, their doings and their thoughts; **4** Aaron and Miriam, their works and their doings; the princes and the elders, their works and doings; Joshua and his generation, their works and doings; the judges and their generation, their works and doings; Eli and his generation, their works and doings; Phinehas, their works and doings; Elkanah and his generation, their works and their doings; Samuel and his generation, their works and doings; the kings of Judah with their generations, their works and their doings; the kings of Israel and their generations, their works and their doings; the princes of Israel, their works and their doings; the princes of the nations of the world, their works and their doings; the heads of the councils of Israel, their works and their doings; the heads of the councils in the nations of the world, their generations, their works and their doings; the rulers of

Israel and their generation, their works and their doings; the nobles of Israel and their generation, their works and their doings; the nobles of the nations of the world and their generations, their works and their doings; the men of reputation in Israel, their generation, their works and their doings; the judges of Israel, their generation, their works and their doings; the judges of the nations of the world and their generation, their works and their doings; the teachers of children in Israel, their generations, their works and their doings; the teachers of children in the nations of the world, their generations, their works and their doings; the counselors of Israel, their generation, their works and their doings; the counselors of the nations of the world, their generation, their works and their doings; all the prophets of Israel, their generation, their works and their doings; all the prophets of the nations of the world, their generation, their works and their doings; **5** and all the fights and wars that the nations of the world worked against the people of Israel in the time of their kingdom. And I saw Messiah, son of Joseph, and His generation, and their works and their doings that they will do against the nations of the world. And I saw Messiah, son of David, and His generation, and all the fights and wars, and their works and their doings that they will do with Israel both for good and evil. And I saw all the fights and wars that Gog and Magog will fight in the days of Messiah, and all that the Holy One, blessed is He, will do with them in the time to come. **6** And all the rest of all the leaders of the generations and all the works of the generations both in Israel and in the nations of the world, both what is done and what will be done hereafter to all generations until the end of time, all were graven on the curtain of Maqom. And I saw all these things with my eyes; and after I had seen it, I opened my mouth in praise of Maqom, the Divine Majesty saying thus: "For the King's word has power and who may say to Him: What are You doing? Whosoever keeps the commandments will know no evil thing." And I said, "O Lord, how manifold are Your works!"

CHAPTER 46

1 R. Ishmael said: Metatron said to me: "Come, and I will show you the space of the stars that are standing in Raqia' night by night in fear of the Almighty and I will show you where they go and where they stand." **2** I walked by his side, and he took me by his hand and pointed out all to me with his fingers. And they were standing on sparks of flames around the Merkaba of the Almighty. What did Metatron do? At that moment he clapped his hands and chased them off from their place. Immediately they flew off on flaming wings, rose, and fled from the four sides of the Throne of the Merkaba, and as they flew he told me the names of every single one. As it is written: "He tells the number of the stars, || He gives them all their names," teaching that the Holy One, blessed is He, has given a name to each one of them. **3** And they all enter in counted order under the guidance of Rahatiel to Raqia' ha-Shamayim to serve the world. And they go out in counted order to praise the Holy One, blessed is He, with songs and hymns, according as it is written: "The heavens declare the glory of God." **4** But in the time to come the Holy One, blessed is He, will create them anew, as it is written: "They are new every morning." And they open their mouth and utter a song. Which is the song that they utter? "When I consider Your heavens."

CHAPTER 47

1 R. Ishmael said: Metatron said to me: "Come, and I will show you the souls of the messengers and the spirits of the ministering servants whose bodies have been burned in the fire of the Almighty that goes forth from His little finger. And they have been made into fiery coals in the midst of the fiery river. But their spirits and their souls are standing behind the Shekinah. **2** Whenever the ministering messengers utter a song at a wrong time or as not appointed to be sung, they are burned and consumed by the fire of their Creator and by a flame from their Maker, in the places of the whirlwind, for it blows on them and drives them into the Nehar di-Nur; and there they are made into numerous mountains of burning coal. But their spirit and their soul return to their Creator, and all are standing behind their Master." **3** And I went by his side, and he took me by his hand and showed me all the souls of the

messengers and the spirits of the ministering servants who were standing behind the Shekinah on wings of the whirlwind and walls of fire surrounding them. **4** At that moment Metatron opened the gates of the walls to me within which they were standing behind the Shekinah, and I lifted up my eyes and saw them, and behold, the likeness of each one was as that of messengers and their wings like birds' wings, made out of flames, the work of burning fire. In that moment I opened my mouth in praise of Maqom and said, "How great are Your works, O Lord."

CHAPTER 48 (A)

1 R. Ishmael said: Metatron said to me: "Come, and I will show you the Right Hand of Maqom, laid behind Him because of the destruction of the holy temple, from which all kinds of splendor and light shine forth and by which the nine hundred fifty-five heavens were created, and whom not even the seraphim and the ophanim are permitted to behold until the day of salvation will arrive." **2** And I went by his side, and he took me by his hand and showed me the Right Hand of Maqom, with all manner of praise, rejoicing, and song: and no mouth can tell its praise, and no eye can behold it, because of its greatness, dignity, majesty, glory, and beauty. **3** And not only that, but all the souls of the righteous who are counted worthy to behold the joy of Jerusalem, they are standing by it, praising and praying before it three times every day, saying, "Awake, awake, put on strength, O arm of the Lord," according as it is written: "He caused His glorious arm to go at the right hand of Moses." **4** In that moment the Right Hand of Maqom was weeping. And there went forth from its five fingers five rivers of tears, and they fell down into the Great Sea, and shook the whole world, according as it is written: "The earth is utterly broken down, || The earth is clean dissolved, || The earth is utterly moved, || The earth will stagger like a drunken man, || And will be moved to and fro like a lodge," five times corresponding to the fingers of His Great Right Hand. **5** But when the Holy One, blessed is He, sees that there is no righteous man in the generation, and no pious man on earth, and no justice in the hands of men, and that there is no man like to Moses, and no intercessor as Samuel who could pray before Maqom for the salvation and for the deliverance, and for His Kingdom, that it might be revealed in the whole world, and for His Great Right Hand that He put it before Himself again to work great salvation for Israel by it, **6** then immediately the Holy One, blessed is He, will remember His own justice, favor, mercy, and grace, and He will deliver His Great Arm by Himself, and His righteousness will support Him, according as it is written: "And He saw that there was no man" (that is, like to Moses who prayed countless times for Israel in the desert and averted the Divine decrees from them) "and He wondered that there was no intercessor"—like to Samuel who entreated the Holy One, blessed is He, and called to Him and He answered him and fulfilled his desire, even if it was not fit in accordance with the Divine plan, according as it is written: "Is it not wheat-harvest today? I will call to the Lord." **7** And not only that, but He joined fellowship with Moses in every place, as it is written: "Moses and Aaron among His priests." And again it is written: "Though Moses and Samuel stood before Me, || My own arm brought salvation to Me." **8** The Holy One, blessed is He, said in that hour: "How long will I wait for the children of men to work salvation according to their righteousness for My arm? For My own sake and for the sake of My merit and righteousness I will deliver [with] My arm and redeem My children by it from among the nations of the world, as it is written: For My own sake I will do it. For why should My Name be profaned?" **9** In that moment the Holy One, blessed is He, will reveal His Great Arm and show it to the nations of the world, for its length is as the length of the world and its breadth is as the width of the world. And the appearance of its splendor is like to the splendor of the sunshine in its might, in the summer solstice. **10** Immediately Israel will be saved from among the nations of the world. And Messiah will appear to them and He will bring them up to Jerusalem with great joy. And not only that, but they will eat and drink, for they will glorify the Kingdom of Messiah, the house of David, in the four quarters of the world. And the nations of the world will not prevail against them, as it is written: "The Lord has made His holy arm bare || In the eyes of all the nations, || And all the ends of the earth will see || The salvation of our God." And again: "The Lord alone led him, || And there was no strange god with him." [And again:] "And the Lord will be King over all the earth."

CHAPTER 48 (B)

¹ Metatron has seventy names which the Holy One, blessed is He, took from His own Name and put on him. And they are these: (1) Yehoel Yah, (2) Yehoel, (3) Yophiel, and (4) Yophphiel, and (5) 'Aphphiel, and (6) Margeziel, (7) Gippuyel, (8) Pa'aziel, (9) 'A'ah, (10) Periel, (11) Tatriel, (12) Tabkiel, (13) 'W, (14) Yhwh, (15) Dh, (16) Whyh, (17) 'Ebed, (18) Dibburiel, (19) 'Aph'apiel, (20) Sppiel, (21) Paspasiel, (22) Senegron, (23) Metatron, (24) Sogdin, (25) 'Adrigon, (26) 'Asum, (27) Saqpam, (28) Saqtam, (29) Migon, (30) Mitton, (31) Mottron, (32) Rosphim, (33) Qinoth, (34) Chatatyah, (35) Degazyah, (36) Pspyah, (37) Bsknyh, (38) Mgrg, (39) Barad, (40) Mkrkk, (41) Msprd, (42) Chshg, (43) Chshg, (43) Chshb, (44) Mnrttt, (45) Bsyrym, (46) Mitmon, (47) Titmon, (48) Pisqon, (49) Saphsaphyah', (50) Zrch, (51) Zrchyah, (52) B, (53) Beyah, (54) Hbhbeyah, (55) Pelet, (56) Pltyah, (57) Rabrabyah, (58) Chas, (59) Chasyah, (60) Taphtaphyah, (61) Tamtamyah, (62) Sehasyah, (63) Iruryah, (64) 'Al'alyah, (65) Bazridyah, (66) Satsatkyah, (67) Sasdyah, (68) Razrazyah, (69) Bazrazyah, (70) 'Arimyah, (71) Sbhyah, (72) Sbibkhyh, (73) Simkam, (74) Yahseyah, (75) Ssbibyah, (76) Sabkasbeyah, (77) Qelilqalyah, (78) Kihhh, (79) Hhyh, (80) Wh, (81) Whyh, (82) Zakklkyah, (83) Tutrisyah, (84) Suryah, (85) Zeh, (86) Penirhyah, (87) Z'zi'h, (88) Gal Razayya, (89) Mamlikyah, (90) Ttyah, (91) 'Emeq, (92) Qamyah, (93) Mekapperyah, (94) Perishyah, (95) Sepham, (96) Gbir, (97) Gibboryah, (98) Gor, (99) Goryah, (100) Ziw, (101) 'Okbar, (102) the Lesser Yhwh, after the Name of his Master, "for My Name is in him," (103) Rabibiel, (104) Tumiel, (105) Segansakkiel, the Prince of Wisdom. ² And why is he called by the name Sagnesakiel? Because all the treasuries of wisdom are committed in his hand. ³ And all of them were opened to Moses on Sinai, so that he learned them during the forty days, while he was standing: the Torah in the seventy aspects of the seventy tongues, the Prophets in the seventy aspects of the seventy tongues, the Writings in the seventy aspects of the seventy tongues, the Halakhas in the seventy aspects of the seventy tongues, the Traditions in the seventy aspects of the seventy tongues, the Haggadahs in the seventy aspects of the seventy tongues, and the Toseftas in the seventy aspects of the seventy tongues. ⁴ But as soon as the forty days were ended, he forgot all of them in one moment. Then the Holy One, blessed is He, called Yephiphyah, the Prince of the Law, and [through him] they were given to Moses as a gift. As it is written: "And the Lord gave them to me." And after that it remained with him. And from where do we know that it remained in his memory? Because it is written: "Remember the Law of My servant Moses which I commanded to him in Horeb for all Israel, even My statutes and judgments." The Law of Moses: that is, the Teaching; the Prophets and the Writings—[the] statutes: that is, the Halakhas and Traditions; Judgments: that is, the Haggadahs and the Toseftas. And all of them are given to Moses on high on Sinai. ⁵ These seventy names are a reflection of the Explicit Names on the Merkaba which are graven on the Throne of Glory. For the Holy One, blessed is He, took from His Explicit Names and put seventy names of His on the name of Metatron by which the ministering messengers call the King of the kings of kings, blessed is He, in the high heavens, and twenty-two letters that are on the ring on His finger with which the destinies of the princes of kingdoms on high are sealed in greatness and power and with which the lots of the Messenger of Death are sealed, and the destinies of every nation and tongue. ⁶ Metatron, the messenger, the Prince of the Presence; the messenger, the Prince of the Wisdom; the messenger, the Prince of the Understanding; the messenger, the Prince of the Kings; the messenger, the Prince of the Rulers; the messenger, the Prince of the Glory; the messenger, the Prince of the High Ones; and of the princes—the exalted, great, and honored ones, in Heaven and on earth—said: ⁷ "Yhwh, the God of Israel, is my witness in this thing, that when I revealed this secret to Moses, then all the hosts in every heaven on high raged against me and said to me: ⁸ Why do you reveal this secret to a son of man, born of woman, tainted and unclean, a man of a decaying drop—the secret by which the heavens and earth, the sea and the dry land, the mountains and hills, the rivers and springs, Gehenna of fire and hail, the Garden of Eden and the Tree of Life were created; and by which Adam and Eve, and the cattle,

and the wild beasts, and the bird of the air, and the fish of the sea, and Behemoth and Leviathan, and the creeping things, the worms, the dragons of the sea, and the creeping things of the deserts, and the Torah, and Wisdom, and Knowledge, and Thought, and the Knowledge of things above, and the fear of Heaven were formed? Why do you reveal this to flesh and blood? Have you obtained authority from Maqom? And again: Have you received permission? The Explicit Names went forth from before me with lightnings of fire and flaming chashmallim. ⁹ But they were not appeased until the Holy One, blessed is He, rebuked them and drove them away with rebuke from before Him, saying to them: I delight in, and have set My love on, and have entrusted and committed to Metatron, My servant, alone, for he is one unique among all the children of Heaven." ¹⁰ And Metatron brought them out from his house of treasuries and committed them to Moses, and Moses to Joshua, and Joshua to the elders, and the elders to the prophets, and the prophets to the men of the Great Synagogue, and the men of the Great Synagogue to Ezra, and Ezra the Scribe to Hillel the elder, and Hillel the elder to R. Abbahu, and R. Abbahu to R. Zera, and R. Zera to the men of faith, and the men of faith committed them to give warning and to heal by them all diseases that rage in the world, as it is written: "If you will diligently listen to the voice of the Lord your God and will do that which is right in His eyes, and will give ear to His commandments, and keep all His statutes, I will put none of the diseases on you which I have put on the Egyptians, for I am the Lord that heals you." Ended and finished. Praise be to the Creator of the World.

BOOK OF GIANTS

Once thought to be nothing more than a 3rd century Manichaean corruption of biblical and Jewish legends, a primordial Aramaic form was found among the Dead Sea Scrolls. This much older Book of Giants was composed hundreds of years before Christ's first advent—*at the latest*—and shares Enochian similarities.

CHAPTER 1

[The rebellious Watchers (messengers) descend to earth, bringing secret knowledge and wickedness. Their hybrid offspring are giants.]

[1Q23] ¹ . . . they knew the secrets of . . . ² . . . sin was great in the earth . . . ³ . . . and they killed many . . . ⁴ . . . [they begot] giants . . .

CHAPTER 2

[The messengers observe all the creatures on earth, including human beings.]

[4Q531] ¹ . . . [everything that the] earth produced . . . ² . . . the great fish . . . ³ . . . the sky with all that grew . . . ⁴ . . . [fruit of] the earth and all kinds of grain and all the trees . . . ⁵ . . . beasts and reptiles . . . all creeping things of the earth, ⁶ and they observed all . . . ⁷ . . . every harsh deed and . . . utterance . . . ⁸ . . . male and female, and among humans . . .

CHAPTER 3

[The messengers choose two hundred specimens from each of a variety of creatures on which to perform ungodly acts.]

[1Q23] ¹ . . . [two hundred] donkeys, two hundred mules, two hundred . . . ² . . . rams of the flock, two hundred goats, two hundred . . . ³ . . . [beasts of the] field from every animal,

4 from every [bird] . . . **5** . . . for interbreeding . . .

CHAPTER 4

[Giants, monsters, and corruption fill the earth as a result of angelic interbreeding.]

[4Q531] **1** . . . they defiled . . . **2** . . . [they begot] giants and monsters . . . **3** . . . they begot, and behold, all [the earth was corrupted] . . . **4** . . . with its blood and by the hand of . . . **5** . . . which did not suffice for them and . . . **6** . . . and they were seeking to devour many . . . **7** . . . the monsters attacked it.

CHAPTER 5

[4Q532] **1** . . . flesh . . . **2** . . . all . . . monsters . . . will be . . . **3** . . . they would arise . . . lacking in true knowledge . . . because . . . **4** . . . the earth [grew corrupt] . . . mighty . . . **5** . . . they were considering . . . **6** . . . from the messengers on . . . **7** . . . in the end it will perish and die . . . **8** . . . they caused great corruption in the [earth] . . . **9** . . . [this did not] suffice to . . . **10** "They will be . . ."

CHAPTER 6

[The giants are troubled by dreams and visions which hint at a coming judgment on them. In one dream, a stone tablet is drenched in water and emerges with only three names still inscribed (presumably the names of Noah's sons).]

[2Q26] **1** . . . they drenched the tablet in the water . . . **2** . . . the waters went up over the [tablet] . . . **3** . . . they lifted the tablet out from the water of . . .

CHAPTER 7

[4Q530] **1** . . . [the vision] is for cursing and sorrow. I am the one who confessed . . . **2** . . . the whole group of the castaways that I will go to . . . **3** . . . the spirits of the slain, complaining about their killers and crying out . . . **4** . . . that we will die together and be made an end of . . . **5** . . . much and I will be sleeping, and bread . . . **6** . . . for my dwelling; **7** the vision and also . . . entered into the gathering of the giants . . . [6Q8] **8** . . . Ohya, and he said to Mahway . . . **9** ". . . without trembling. Who showed you all this vision, brother?" **10** . . . "Barakel, my father, was with me." **11** . . . Before Mahway had finished telling what [he had seen] . . . **12** . . . [said] to him, "Now I have heard wonders! If a barren woman gives birth . . ." [4Q530] **13** Thereon Ohya said to Ha[hya], **14** ". . . [will be destroyed] from on the earth and . . . **15** . . . [the] earth." **16** When . . . **17** . . . they wept before [the giants] . . . **18** ". . . your strength . . ." **19** . . . Thereon Ohya [said] to Hahya, **20** . . . Then he answered, "It is not for us, but for Azaiel, **21** for he did . . . [the offspring of] messengers are the giants, **22** [and they would not let all their loved ones] be neglected . . . **23** . . . [we have] not been cast down; you have strength . . .

CHAPTER 8

[A giant boasts about his strength, but realizes he is not stronger than the faithful messengers of Heaven. One of the speakers is apparently the giant hybrid Gilgamesh from Sumerian myth.]

[4Q531] **1** ". . . I am a giant, and by the mighty strength of my arm and my own great strength . . . **2** . . . anyone mortal, and I have made war against them; **3** but I am not . . . able to stand against them, for my opponents . . . **4** . . . reside in

Heaven, and they dwell in the holy places. **5** And not . . . [they] are stronger than me. **6** . . . of the wild beast has come, and they call [me] the wild man," **7** . . . Then Ohya said to him, "I have been forced to have a dream . . . the sleep of my eyes [vanished], to let me see a vision. Now I know that on . . ." **8** . . . Gilgamesh . . .

CHAPTER 9

[Ohya has a dream in which a tree is uprooted, but three roots remain. This is presumably the same message as the dream of the stone tablet.]

[6Q8] **1** . . . three of its roots . . . **2** . . . [while] I was [watching], there came . . . **3** . . . [the roots were moved into] this garden, all of them, and not . . .

CHAPTER 10

[Bothered by the dreams and visions, Ohya suggests the message is actually judgment on another group.]

[4Q530] **1** . . . concerns the death of our souls . . . **2** . . . and all his comrades, [and] Ohya told them what Gilgamesh said to him . . . **3** . . . and it was said . . . ". . . concerning . . . the leader has cursed the potentates." **4** And the giants were glad at his words. Then he turned and left . . .

CHAPTER 11

[Dreamers recount yet more dreams, first to the assembly of monsters, and second to the assembly of giants.]

[4Q530] **1** Thereon two of them had dreams and the sleep of their eye fled from them, **2** and they arose and came to . . . **3** . . . [and recounted] their dreams, and said in the assembly of [the giants and] the monsters, **4** "[In] my dream I was watching this very night, **5** [and within a garden there were] gardeners and they were watering . . . **6** . . . [two hundred trees and] large shoots came out of their root . . . **7** . . . all the water, and the fire burned all [the trees] . . ." **8** . . . They found the giants to tell them [of the dream] . . .

CHAPTER 12

[Mahway is petitioned to seek Enoch for an interpretation of the dream, and then flies to him with the request.]

[4Q530] **1** "[Go to Enoch,] the noted scribe, and he will interpret the dream for us." **2** Thereon his companion Ohya declared [this], and said to the giants, "I too had a dream this night, O giants, and behold, the Ruler of Heaven came down to earth . . . **3** . . . and such is the end of the dream." **4** [Then] all the giants [and monsters] grew afraid and called Mahway. **5** He came to them and the giants pleaded with him and sent him to Enoch . . . **6** They said to him, "Go . . . to you that . . . you have heard his voice." **7** And he said to him, "He will . . . interpret the dreams . . . **8** . . . how long the giants have to live."

CHAPTER 13

[4Q530] **1** . . . [he moved through the air] like strong winds, **2** and flew with his hands like eagles . . . [he left] the inhabited world and passed over Desolation, the great desert . . . **3** . . . and Enoch saw him and hailed him, **4** and Mahway said to him . . . **5** . . . here and there a second time to Mahway . . .

6 "The giants await your words, and all the monsters of the earth. **7** If . . . has been carried . . . from the days of . . . their . . . and they will be added . . . **8** . . . we would know from you their meaning . . . **9** . . . [two hundred] trees that [came down] from Heaven . . ."

CHAPTER 14

[Enoch grants the request and sends Mahway with a stone tablet containing the interpretation.]

[4Q530] **1** The scribe [Enoch] . . . **2** . . . a copy of the second tablet that [Enoch] sent . . . **3** . . . in the very handwriting of Enoch the noted scribe . . . **4** "[In the Name of God the great] and Holy One, to Shemihaza and all [his companions] . . . **5** . . . let it be known to you that not . . . **6** and the things you have done, and that your wives . . . **7** . . . they and their sons and the wives of [their sons] . . . **8** . . . by your licentiousness on the earth, and there has been on you . . . **9** . . . [and the earth is crying out] and complaining about you and the deeds of your children, **10** [and] the harm that you have done to it. **11** . . . until Raphael arrives, behold, destruction [is coming, a great flood, and it will destroy all living things] **12** and whatever is in the deserts and the seas. **13** And the meaning of the matter . . . **14** . . . on you for evil. **15** But now, loosen the bonds binding [you to evil] . . . and pray."

CHAPTER 15

[4Q531] **1** . . . [great fear] seized me and I fell on my face; I heard his voice . . . **2** . . . he dwelt among human beings but he did not learn from them . . .

JASHER

Otherwise known as Sefer haYashar

The Sefer haYashar (first edition 1552) is a Hebrew midrash also known as the Toledot Adam and Dibre ha-Yamim be-'Aruk. The Hebrew title may be transliterated Sefer haYashar, which means "Book of the Correct Record," but it is known in English translation mostly as the Book of Jasher following English tradition. The book is named after the Book of Jasher mentioned in Joshua and 2 Samuel. Although it is presented as the original "Book of Jasher" in the translations such as that of Moses Samuel (1840), it is not accepted as such in rabbinical Judaism, nor does the original Hebrew text make such a claim. However, the writing is of good quality, the chronology largely aligns with the Masoretic account in Genesis, and some scholars believe the midrash may be even older than the 6th century AD.

CHAPTER 1

1 And God said, "Let Us make man in Our image, after Our likeness," and God created man in His own image. **2** And God formed man from the ground, and He blew into his nostrils the breath of life, and man became a living soul endowed with speech. **3** And the Lord said, "It is not good for man to be alone; I will make a helpmate for him." **4** And the Lord caused a deep sleep to fall on Adam, and he slept, and He took away one of his ribs, and He built flesh on it, and formed it, and brought it to Adam, and Adam awoke from his sleep, and behold, a woman was standing before him. **5** And he said, "This is bone of my bones and it will be called Woman, for this has been taken from Man; and Adam called her name Eve, for she was the mother of all living." **6** And God blessed them and called their names Adam and Eve in the day that He created them, and the Lord God said, "Be fruitful, and multiply, and fill the earth." **7** And the Lord God took Adam and his wife, and He placed them in the Garden of Eden to dress it and to keep it; and He commanded them and said to them, "From every tree of the garden you may eat, but from the Tree of the Knowledge of Good and Evil you will not eat, for in the day that you eat thereof you will surely die." **8** And when God had blessed and commanded them, He went from them, and Adam and his wife dwelt in the garden according to the command which the Lord had commanded them. **9** And the serpent, which God had created with them in the earth, came to them to incite them to transgress the command of God which he had commanded them. **10** And the serpent enticed and persuaded the woman to eat from the Tree of Knowledge, and the woman listened to the voice of the serpent, and she transgressed the word of God, and took from the Tree of the Knowledge of Good and Evil, and she ate, and she took from it, and also gave to her husband and he ate. **11** And Adam and his wife transgressed the command of God which He commanded them, and God knew it, and His anger was kindled against them and He cursed them. **12** And the Lord God drove them that day from the Garden of Eden, to till the ground from which they were taken, and they went and dwelt at the east of the Garden of Eden; and Adam knew his wife Eve and she bore two sons and three daughters. **13** And she called the name of the firstborn Cain, saying, "I have obtained a man from the Lord," and the name of the other she called Abel, for she said, "In vanity we came into the earth, and in vanity we will be taken from it." **14** And the boys grew up and their father gave them a possession in the land; and Cain was a tiller of the ground, and Abel a keeper of sheep. **15** And it was at the expiration of a few years that they brought a comparable offering to the Lord, and Cain brought from the fruit of the ground, and Abel brought from the firstlings of his flock from the fat thereof, and God turned and inclined to Abel and his offering, and a fire came down from the Lord from Heaven and consumed it. **16** And to Cain and his offering the Lord did not turn, and He did not incline to it, for he had brought from the inferior fruit of the ground before the Lord, and Cain was jealous against his brother Abel on account of this, and he sought a pretext to slay him. **17** And some time after, Cain and his brother Abel went into the field one day to do their work; and they were both in the field, Cain tilling and plowing his ground, and Abel feeding his flock; and the flock passed that part which Cain had plowed in the ground, and it severely grieved Cain on this account. **18** And Cain approached his brother Abel in anger, and he said to him, "What is there between me and you, that you come to dwell and bring your flock to feed in my land?" **19** And Abel answered his brother Cain and said to him, "What is there between me and you, that you will eat the flesh of my flock and clothe yourself with their wool? **20** And now therefore, put off the wool of my sheep with which you have clothed yourself, and repay me for their fruit and flesh which you have eaten, and when you will have done this, I will then go from your land as you have said." **21** And Cain said to his brother Abel, "Surely if I slay you this day, who will require your blood from me?" **22** And Abel answered Cain, saying, "Surely God who has made us in the earth will avenge my cause, and He will require my blood from you should you slay me, for the Lord is the judge and arbiter, and it is He who will pay back man according to his evil, and the wicked man according to the wickedness that he may do on earth. **23** And now, if you should slay me here, surely God knows your secret views, and will judge you for the evil which you declared to do to me this day." **24** And when Cain heard the words which his brother Abel had spoken, behold, the anger of Cain was kindled against his brother Abel for declaring this thing. **25** And Cain hastened and rose up, and took the iron part of his plowing instrument, with which he suddenly struck his brother and slew him, and Cain spilt the blood of his brother Abel on the earth, and the blood of Abel streamed on the earth before the flock. **26** And after this Cain regretted having slain his brother, and he was sadly grieved, and he wept over him, and it exceedingly vexed him. **27** And Cain rose up and dug a hole in the field, wherein he put his brother's body, and he turned the dust over it. **28** And the Lord knew what Cain had done to his brother, and the Lord appeared to Cain and said to him, "Where is your brother Abel that was with you?" **29** And Cain concealed his true motives, and said, "I do not know, am I my brother's keeper?" And the Lord said to him, "What have you done? The voice of your brother's blood cries to Me from the ground where you have slain him. **30** For you have slain your brother, and have concealed your intentions before Me, and imagined in your heart that I did not see you, nor knew all your actions. **31** But you did this thing and slew your brother for no reason and because he spoke rightly to you, and now, therefore, cursed are you from the ground which opened its mouth to receive your brother's blood from your hand, and wherein you buried him. **32** And it will be when you will till it, it will no longer give you its strength as in the beginning, for the ground will produce thorns and thistles, and you will be moving and wandering in the earth until the day of your death." **33** And at that time Cain went out from the presence of the Lord, from the place where he was, and he went moving and wandering in the land toward the east of Eden, he and all belonging to him. **34** And Cain knew his wife in those days, and she conceived and bore a son, and he called his name Enoch, saying, "In that time the Lord began to give him rest and quiet in the earth." **35** And at that time Cain also began to build a city: and he built the city and he called the name of the city Enoch, according to the name of his son, for in those days the Lord had given him rest on the earth, and he did not move about and wander as in the beginning. **36** And Irad was born to Enoch, and Irad begot Mehujael, and Mehujael begot Methusael.

CHAPTER 2

1 And it was in the one hundred and thirtieth year of the life of Adam on the earth that he knew his wife Eve again, and she conceived and bore a son in his likeness and in his image, and she called his name Seth, saying, "Because God has appointed me another seed in the place of Abel, for Cain has slain him." **2** And Seth lived one hundred and five years, and he begot a son; and Seth called the name of his son Enosh, saying, "Because in that time the sons of men began to multiply, and to afflict their souls and hearts by transgressing and rebelling against God." **3** And it was in the days of Enosh that the sons of men continued to rebel and transgress against God, to increase the anger of the Lord against the sons of men. **4** And the sons of men went, and they served other gods, and they forgot the Lord who had created them in the earth: and in those days the sons of men made images of brass and iron, wood and stone, and they bowed down and served them. **5** And every man made his god and they bowed down to them, and the sons of men forsook the Lord all the days of Enosh and his children; and the anger of the Lord was kindled on account of their works and abominations which they did in the earth. **6** And the Lord caused the waters of the River Gihon to overwhelm them, and He destroyed and consumed them, and He destroyed the third part of the earth, and notwithstanding this, the sons of men did not turn from their evil ways, and their hands were yet extended to do evil in the sight of the Lord. **7** And in those days there was neither sowing nor reaping in the earth; and there was no food for the sons of men and the famine was very great in those days. **8** And the seed which they sowed in those days in the ground became thorns, thistles, and briers; for from the days of Adam this declaration was concerning the earth, of the curse of God, which He cursed the earth on account of the sin which Adam sinned before the Lord. **9** And it was when men continued to rebel and transgress against God, and to corrupt their ways, that the earth also became corrupt. **10** And Enosh lived ninety years and he begot Cainan; **11** And Cainan grew up and he was forty years old, and he became wise and had knowledge and skill in all wisdom, and he reigned over all the sons of men, and he led the sons of men to wisdom and knowledge; for Cainan was a very wise man and had understanding in all wisdom, and with his wisdom he ruled over spirits and demons. **12** And Cainan knew by his wisdom that God would destroy the sons of men for having sinned on earth, and that the Lord would bring on them the waters of the flood in the latter days. **13** And in those days Cainan wrote on tablets of stone what was to take place in time to come, and he put them in his treasures. **14** And Cainan reigned over the whole earth, and he turned some of the sons of men to the service of God. **15** And when Cainan was seventy years old, he begot three sons and two daughters. **16** And these are the names of the children of Cainan: the name of the firstborn Mahalaleel, the second Enan, and the third Mered, and their sisters were Adah and Zillah; these are the five children of Cainan that were born to him. **17** And Lamech, the son of Methusael, became related to Cainan by marriage, and he took his two daughters for his wives, and Adah conceived and bore a son to Lamech, and she called his name Jabal. **18** And she again conceived and bore a son, and called his name Jubal; and Zillah, her sister, was barren in those days and had no offspring. **19** For in those days the sons of men began to trespass against God, and to transgress the commands which He had commanded to Adam, to be fruitful and multiply in the earth. **20** And some of the sons of men caused their wives to drink a draught that would render them barren, in order that they might retain their figures and whereby their beautiful appearance might not fade. **21** And when the sons of men caused some of their wives to drink, Zillah drank with them. **22** And the childbearing women appeared abominable in the sight of their husbands as widows, while their husbands lived, for they were only attached to the barren ones. **23** And in the end of days and years, when Zillah became old, the Lord opened her womb. **24** And she conceived and bore a son, and she called his name Tubal-Cain, saying, "After I had withered away I have obtained him from the Almighty God." **25** And she conceived again and bore a daughter, and she called her name Naamah, for she said, "After I had withered away I have obtained pleasure and delight." **26** And Lamech was old and advanced in years, and his eyes were dim that he could not see, and his son Tubal-Cain was leading him, and it was one day that Lamech went into the field and Tubal Cain his son was with him, and while they were walking in the field, Cain, the son of Adam, advanced toward them; for Lamech was very old and could not see much, and his son Tubal-Cain was very young. **27** And Tubal-Cain told his father to draw his bow, and with the arrows he struck Cain, who was yet far off, and he slew him, for he appeared to them to be an animal. **28** And the arrows entered Cain's body although he was distant from them, and he fell to the ground and died. **29** And the Lord paid back Cain's evil according to his wickedness which he had done to his brother Abel, according to the word of the Lord which He had spoken. **30** And it came to pass when Cain had died, that Lamech and Tubal-Cain went to see the animal which they had slain, and they saw, and behold, their grandfather Cain was fallen dead on the earth. **31** And Lamech was very much grieved at having done this, and in clapping his hands together, he struck his son and caused his death. **32** And the wives of Lamech heard what Lamech had done, and they sought to kill him. **33** And the wives of Lamech hated him from that day, because he slew Cain and Tubal-Cain, and the wives of Lamech separated from him, and would not listen to him in those days. **34** And Lamech came to his wives, and he pressed them to listen to him about this matter. **35** And he said to his wives Adah and Zillah, "Hear my voice, O wives of Lamech, attend to my words, for now you have imagined and said that I slew a man with my wounds, and a child with my stripes, for their having done no violence, but surely know that I am old and grey-headed, and that my eyes are heavy through age, and I did this thing unknowingly." **36** And the wives of Lamech listened to him in this matter, and they returned to him with the advice of their father Adam, but they bore no children to him from that time, knowing that God's anger was increasing in those days against the sons of men, to destroy them with the waters of the flood for their evil doings. **37** And Mahalaleel the son of Cainan lived sixty-five years and he begot Jared, and Jared lived sixty-two years and he begot Enoch.

CHAPTER 3

1 And Enoch lived sixty-five years and he begot Methuselah; and Enoch walked with God after having begot Methuselah, and he served the Lord, and despised the evil ways of men. **2** And the soul of Enoch was wrapped up in the instruction of the Lord, in knowledge and in understanding; and he wisely retired from the sons of men and hid himself from them for many days. **3** And it was at the expiration of many years, while he was serving the Lord and praying before Him in his house, that a messenger of the Lord called to him from Heaven, and he said, "Here I am." **4** And he said, "Rise, go out from your house and from the place where you hide yourself, and appear to the sons of men in order that you may teach them the way in which they should go and the work which they must accomplish to enter in the ways of God." **5** And Enoch rose up according to the word of the Lord, and went out from his house, from his place and from the chamber in which he was concealed; and he went to the sons of men and taught them the ways of the Lord, and at that time assembled the sons of men and acquainted them with the instruction of the Lord. **6** And he ordered it to be proclaimed in all places where the sons of men dwelt, saying, "Where is the man who wishes to know the ways of the Lord and good works? Let him come to Enoch." **7** And all the sons of men then assembled to him, for all who desired this thing went to Enoch, and Enoch reigned over the sons of men according to the word of the Lord, and they came and bowed to him and they heard his word. **8** And the Spirit of

God was on Enoch, and he taught all his men the wisdom of God and His ways, and the sons of men served the Lord all the days of Enoch, and they came to hear his wisdom. **9** And all the kings of the sons of men, both first and last, together with their princes and judges, came to Enoch when they heard of his wisdom, and they bowed down to him, and they also required of Enoch to reign over them, to which he consented. **10** And they assembled one hundred and thirty kings and princes in all, and they made Enoch king over them, and they were all under his power and command. **11** And Enoch taught them wisdom, knowledge, and the ways of the Lord; and he made peace among them, and peace was throughout the earth during the life of Enoch. **12** And Enoch reigned over the sons of men two hundred and forty-three years, and he did justice and righteousness with all his people, and he led them in the ways of the Lord. **13** And these are the generations of Enoch: Methuselah, Elisha, and Elimelech, three sons; and their sisters were Melca and Nahmah, and Methuselah lived eighty-seven years and he begot Lamech. **14** And it was in the fifty-sixth year of the life of Lamech when Adam died; nine hundred and thirty years old was he at his death, and his two sons, with Enoch and his son Methuselah, buried him with great pomp, as at the burial of kings, in the cave which God had told him. **15** And in that place all the sons of men made a great mourning and weeping on account of Adam; it has therefore become a custom among the sons of men to this day. **16** And Adam died because he ate of the Tree of Knowledge—he and his children after him, as the Lord God had spoken. **17** And it was in the year of Adam's death, which was the two hundred and forty-third year of the reign of Enoch, in that time Enoch resolved to separate himself from the sons of men and to hide himself as at first in order to serve the Lord. **18** And Enoch did so, but did not entirely hide himself from them, but kept away from the sons of men three days and then went to them for one day. **19** And during the three days that he was in his chamber, he prayed to, and praised the Lord his God, and the day on which he went and appeared to his subjects he taught them the ways of the Lord, and all they asked him about the Lord he told them. **20** And he did in this manner for many years, and afterward he concealed himself for six days, and appeared to his people one day in seven; and after that once in a month, and then once in a year, until all the kings, princes, and sons of men sought for him, and desired to see the face of Enoch again and to hear his word, but they could not, as all the sons of men were greatly afraid of Enoch, and they feared to approach him on account of the godlike awe that was seated on his countenance; therefore no man could look at him, fearing he might be punished and die. **21** And all the kings and princes resolved to assemble the sons of men, and to come to Enoch, thinking that they might all speak to him at the time when he should come out among them, and they did so. **22** And the day came when Enoch went out and they all assembled and came to him, and Enoch spoke to them the words of the Lord and he taught them wisdom and knowledge, and they bowed down before him and they said, "May the king live! May the king live!" **23** And some time after, when the kings and princes and the sons of men were speaking to Enoch, and Enoch was teaching them the ways of God, behold, a messenger of the Lord then called to Enoch from Heaven, and wished to bring him up to Heaven to make him reign there over the sons of God, as he had reigned over the sons of men on earth. **24** When at that time Enoch heard this, he went and assembled all the inhabitants of the earth, and taught them wisdom and knowledge, and gave them divine instructions, and he said to them, "I have been required to ascend into Heaven; therefore, I do not know the day of my going. **25** And now, therefore, I will teach you wisdom and knowledge and will give you instruction before I leave you, how to act on earth whereby you may live"; and he did so. **26** And he taught them wisdom and knowledge, and gave them instruction, and he reproved them, and he placed before them statutes and judgments to do on earth, and he made peace among them, and he taught them continuous life, and dwelt with them some time teaching them all these things. **27** And at that time the sons of men were with Enoch, and Enoch was speaking to them, and they lifted up their eyes and the likeness of a great horse descended from Heaven, and the horse paced in the air. **28** And they told Enoch what they had seen, and Enoch said to them, "This horse descends on earth on my account; the time has come when I must go from you and I will no longer be seen by you." **29** And the horse descended at that time and stood before Enoch, and all the sons of men that were with Enoch saw him. **30** And Enoch then again ordered a

voice to be proclaimed, saying, "Where is the man who delights to know the ways of the Lord his God? Let him come this day to Enoch before he is taken from us." **31** And all the sons of men assembled and came to Enoch that day; and all the kings of the earth with their princes and counselors remained with him that day; and Enoch then taught the sons of men wisdom and knowledge, and gave them divine instruction, and he commanded them to serve the Lord and walk in His ways all the days of their lives, and he continued to make peace among them. **32** And it was after this that he rose up and rode on the horse; and he went out and all the sons of men went after him—about eight hundred thousand men; and they went with him one day's journey. **33** And the second day he said to them, "Return home to your tents, why will you go? Perhaps you may die"; and some of them went from him, and those that remained went with him six day's journey; and Enoch said to them every day, "Return to your tents, lest you may die"; but they were not willing to return, and they went with him. **34** And on the sixth day some of the men remained and clung to him, and they said to him, "We will go with you to the place where you go; as the Lord lives, only death will separate us." **35** And they urged so much to go with him that he ceased speaking to them; and they went after him and would not return. **36** And when the kings returned, they caused a census to be taken in order to know the number of remaining men that went with Enoch; and it was on the seventh day that Enoch ascended into Heaven in a whirlwind, with horses and chariots of fire. **37** And on the eighth day all the kings that had been with Enoch sent to bring back the number of men that were with Enoch in that place from which he ascended into Heaven. **38** And all those kings went to the place and they found the earth filled with snow there, and on the snow were large stones of snow, and one said to the other, "Come, let us break through the snow and see, perhaps the men that remained with Enoch are dead and are now under the stones of snow," and they searched but could not find him, for he had ascended into Heaven.

CHAPTER 4

1 And all the days that Enoch lived on earth were three hundred and sixty-five years. **2** And when Enoch had ascended into Heaven, all the kings of the earth rose and took his son Methuselah and anointed him, and they caused him to reign over them in the place of his father. **3** And Methuselah acted uprightly in the sight of God, as his father Enoch had taught him, and he likewise during the whole of his life taught the sons of men wisdom, knowledge, and the fear of God, and he did not turn from the good way either to the right or to the left. **4** But in the latter days of Methuselah, the sons of men turned from the Lord: they corrupted the earth, they robbed and plundered each other, and they rebelled against God, and they transgressed, and they corrupted their ways, and would not listen to the voice of Methuselah, but rebelled against him. **5** And the Lord was exceedingly angry against them, and the Lord continued to destroy the seed in those days, so that there was neither sowing nor reaping in the earth. **6** For when they sowed the ground in order that they might obtain food for their support, behold, thorns and thistles were produced which they did not sow. **7** And still the sons of men did not turn from their evil ways, and their hands were still extended to do evil in the sight of God, and they provoked the Lord with their evil ways, and the Lord was very angry, and regretted that He had made man. **8** And He thought to destroy and annihilate them, and He did so. **9** In those days when Lamech the son of Methuselah was one hundred and sixty years old, Seth the son of Adam died. **10** And all the days that Seth lived were nine hundred and twelve years, and he died. **11** And Lamech was one hundred and eighty years old when he took Ashmua, the daughter of Elisha, the son of his uncle Enoch, and she conceived. **12** And at that time the sons of men sowed the ground, and a little food was produced, yet the sons of men did not turn from their evil ways, and they trespassed and rebelled against God. **13** And the wife of Lamech conceived and bore him a son at that time, at the revolution of the year. **14** And Methuselah called his name Noah, saying, "The earth was at rest and free from corruption in his days," and his father Lamech called his name Menachem, saying, "This one will comfort us in our works and miserable toil in the earth," which God had cursed. **15** And the child grew up and was weaned, and he went in the ways of his father Methuselah, perfect and upright with God. **16** And all the sons of men departed from the ways of the Lord in those days as they multiplied on the face of the earth with sons and daughters, and they taught one another their evil practices and they continued sinning against the Lord. 17 And every man made a god for himself, and they robbed and plundered every man—his neighbor as well as his relative, and they corrupted the earth, and the earth was filled with violence. 18 And their judges and rulers went to the daughters of men and took their wives by force from their husbands according to their choice, and the sons of men in those days took from the cattle of the earth, the beasts of the field, and the birds of the air, and taught the mixture of animals of one species with the other, in order with [them] to provoke the Lord; and God saw the whole earth and it was corrupt, for all flesh had corrupted its ways on earth, all men and all animals. 19 And the Lord said, "I will blot out man that I created from the face of the earth, yes, from man to the birds of the air, together with cattle and beasts that are in the field, for I regret that I made them." 20 And all men who walked in the ways of the Lord died in those days before the Lord brought the evil on man which He had declared, for this was from the Lord, that they should not see the evil which the Lord spoke of concerning the sons of men. 21 And Noah found grace in the sight of the Lord, and the Lord chose him and his children to raise up seed from them on the face of the whole earth.

CHAPTER 5

1 And it was in the eighty-fourth year of the life of Noah that Enoch the son of Seth died; he was nine hundred and five years old at his death. 2 And in the one hundred and seventy-ninth year of the life of Noah, Cainan the son of Enosh died, and all the days of Cainan were nine hundred and ten years, and he died. 3 And in the two hundred and thirty-fourth year of the life of Noah, Mahalaleel the son of Cainan died, and the days of Mahalaleel were eight hundred and ninety-five years, and he died. 4 And Jared the son of Mahalaleel died in those days, in the three hundred and thirty-sixth year of the life of Noah; and all the days of Jared were nine hundred and sixty-two years, and he died. 5 And all who followed the Lord died in those days, before they saw the evil which God declared to do on earth. 6 And after the lapse of many years, in the four hundred and eightieth year of the life of Noah, when all those men who followed the Lord had died away from among the sons of men, and only Methuselah was then left, God said to Noah and Methuselah, saying, 7 "Speak, and proclaim to the sons of men, saying, Thus says the Lord, return from your evil ways and forsake your works, and the Lord will relent of the evil that He declared to do to you, so that it will not come to pass. 8 For thus says the Lord, Behold, I give you a period of one hundred and twenty years; if you will turn to Me and forsake your evil ways, then I will also turn away from the evil which I told you, and it will not exist, says the Lord." 9 And Noah and Methuselah spoke all the words of the Lord to the sons of men, day after day, constantly speaking to them. 10 But the sons of men would not listen to them, nor incline their ears to their words, and they were stiff-necked. 11 And the Lord granted them a period of one hundred and twenty years, saying, "If they will return, then God will relent of the evil, so as not to destroy the earth." 12 Noah the son of Lamech refrained from taking a wife in those days to beget children, for he said, "Surely now God will destroy the earth, why then will I beget children?" 13 And Noah was a just man, he was perfect in his generation, and the Lord chose him to raise up seed from his seed on the face of the earth. 14 And the Lord said to Noah, "Take a wife for yourself, and beget children, for I have seen you righteous before Me in this generation. 15 And you will raise up seed, and your children with you, in the midst of the earth"; and Noah went and took a wife, and he chose Naamah the daughter of Enoch, and she was five hundred and eighty years old. 16 And Noah was four hundred and ninety-eight years old when he took Naamah for a wife. 17 And Naamah conceived and bore a son, and he called his name Japheth, saying, "God has enlarged me in the earth"; and she conceived again and bore a son, and he called his name Shem, saying, "God has made me a remnant to raise up seed in the midst of the earth." 18 And Noah was five hundred and two years old when Naamah bore Shem, and the boys grew up and went in the ways of the Lord in all that Methuselah and their father Noah taught them. 19 And Lamech the father of Noah died in those days; yet truly he did not go with all his heart in the ways of his father, and he died in the one hundred and ninety-fifth year of the life of

Noah. 20 And all the days of Lamech were seven hundred and seventy years, and he died. 21 And all the sons of men who knew the Lord died in that year before the Lord brought evil on them; for the Lord willed them to die, so as not to behold the evil that God would bring on their brothers and relatives, as He had so declared to do. 22 At that time the Lord said to Noah and Methuselah, "Stand out and proclaim to the sons of men all the words that I spoke to you in those days; perhaps they may turn from their evil ways, and I will then relent of the evil and will not bring it." 23 And Noah and Methuselah stood out and said in the ears of the sons of men all that God had spoken concerning them. 24 But the sons of men would not listen, neither would they incline their ears to all their declarations. 25 And it was after this that the Lord said to Noah, "The end of all flesh has come before Me on account of their evil deeds, and behold, I will destroy the earth. 26 So take gopher wood, and go to a certain place, and make a large ark for yourself, and place it in that spot. 27 And thus you will make it three hundred cubits its length, fifty cubits broad, and thirty cubits high. 28 And you will make a door for yourself, open at its side, and to a cubit you will finish above, and cover it within and outside with pitch. 29 And behold, I will bring the flood of waters on the earth, and all flesh will be destroyed from under the heavens— all that is on earth will perish. 30 And you and your household will go and gather two of each of all living things, male and female, and will bring them to the Ark, to raise up seed from them on earth. 31 And gather to yourself all food that is eaten by all the animals, that there may be food for you and for them. 32 And you will choose three maidens for your sons from the daughters of men, and they will be wives to your sons." 33 And Noah rose up, and he made the Ark in the place where God had commanded him, and Noah did as God had ordered him. 34 In his five hundred and ninety-fifth year, Noah commenced to make the Ark, and he made the Ark in five years as the Lord had commanded. 35 Then Noah took the three daughters of Eliakim, son of Methuselah, for wives for his sons, as the Lord had commanded Noah. 36 And it was at that time [that] Methuselah the son of Enoch died; he was nine hundred and sixty years old at his death.

CHAPTER 6

1 At that time, after the death of Methuselah, the Lord said to Noah, "Go, you with your household, into the Ark; behold, I will gather all the animals of the earth to you—the beasts of the field and the birds of the air—and they will all come and surround the Ark. 2 And you will go and seat yourself by the doors of the Ark, and all the beasts, the animals, and the birds, will assemble and place themselves before you, and such of them as will come and crouch before you, you will take and deliver into the hands of your sons, who will bring them to the Ark, and all that will stand before you you will leave." 3 And the Lord brought this about on the next day, and animals, beasts, and birds came in great multitudes and surrounded the Ark. 4 And Noah went and seated himself by the door of the Ark, and of all flesh that crouched before him, he brought into the Ark, and all that stood before him he left on earth. 5 And a lioness came with her two whelps, male and female, and the three crouched before Noah, and the two whelps rose up against the lioness and struck her and made her flee from her place, and she went away, and they returned to their places, and crouched on the earth before Noah. 6 And the lioness ran away and stood in the place of the lions. 7 And Noah saw this and wondered greatly, and he rose and took the two whelps and brought them into the Ark. 8 And Noah brought into the Ark from all living creatures that were on earth, so that there was none left except which Noah brought into the Ark. 9 Two and two they came to Noah into the Ark, but from the clean animals and clean birds, he brought seven couples as God had commanded him. 10 And all the animals, and beasts, and birds, were still there, and they surrounded the Ark at every place, and the rain had not descended until seven days after. 11 And on that day, the Lord caused the whole earth to shake, and the sun darkened, and the foundations of the world raged, and the whole earth was moved violently, and the lightning flashed, and the thunder roared, and all the fountains in the earth were broken up, such as was not known to the inhabitants before; and God did this mighty act in order to terrify the sons of men that there might no longer be evil on earth. 12 And still the sons of men would not return from their evil ways, and they increased the anger of the Lord at that time and did not even

direct their hearts to all this. **13** And at the end of seven days, in the six hundredth year of the life of Noah, the waters of the flood were on the earth. **14** And all the fountains of the deep were broken up, and the windows of Heaven were opened, and the rain was on the earth forty days and forty nights. **15** And Noah, and his household, and all the living creatures that were with him came into the Ark on account of the waters of the flood, and the Lord shut him in. **16** And all the sons of men that were left on the earth became exhausted through evil on account of the rain, for the waters were coming more violently on the earth, and the animals and beasts were still surrounding the Ark. **17** And the sons of men assembled together, about seven hundred thousand men and women, and they came to Noah at the Ark. **18** And they called to Noah, saying, "Open [the door] for us that we may come to you in the Ark—and why will we die?" **19** And Noah answered them with a loud voice from the Ark, saying, "Have you not all rebelled against the Lord, and said that He does not exist? And therefore, the Lord brought this calamity on you, to destroy and cut you off from the face of the earth. **20** Is this not the thing that I spoke to you of one hundred and twenty years back, and you would not listen to the voice of the Lord, and now you desire to live on earth?" **21** And they said to Noah, "We are ready to return to the Lord; only open [the door] for us that we may live and not die." **22** And Noah answered them, saying, "Behold, now that you see the trouble of your souls, you wish to return to the Lord; why did you not return during these one hundred and twenty years, which the Lord granted you as the determined period? **23** But now you come and tell me this on account of the troubles of your souls; now also the Lord will not listen to you, neither will He give ear to you on this day, so that you will not now succeed in your wishes." **24** And the sons of men approached in order to break into the Ark, to come in on account of the rain, for they could not bear the rain on them. **25** And the Lord sent all the beasts and animals that stood around the Ark, and the beasts overpowered them and drove them from that place, and every man went his way, and they again scattered themselves on the face of the earth. **26** And the rain was still descending on the earth, and it descended forty days and forty nights, and the waters prevailed greatly on the earth; and all flesh that was on the earth or in the waters died, whether men, animals, beasts, creeping things, or birds of the air, and there only remained Noah and those that were with him in the Ark. **27** And the waters prevailed, and they greatly increased on the earth, and they lifted up the Ark, and it was raised from the earth. **28** And the Ark floated on the face of the waters, and it was tossed on the waters so that all the living creatures within were turned about like stew in a cauldron. **29** And great anxiety seized all the living creatures that were in the Ark, and the Ark was likely to be broken. **30** And all the living creatures that were in the Ark were terrified, and the lions roared, and the oxen lowed, and the wolves howled, and every living creature in the Ark spoke and lamented in its own language, so that their voices reached to a great distance, and Noah and his sons cried and wept in their troubles; they were greatly afraid that they had reached the gates of death. **31** And Noah prayed to the Lord, and cried to Him on account of this, and he said, "O Lord help us, for we have no strength to bear this calamity that has encompassed us, for the waves of the waters have surrounded us, mischievous torrents have terrified us, the snares of death have come before us; answer us, O Lord, answer us! Light up Your countenance toward us and be gracious to us, redeem us and deliver us." **32** And the Lord listened to the voice of Noah, and the Lord remembered him. **33** And a wind passed over the earth, and the waters were still, and the Ark rested. **34** And the fountains of the deep and the windows of the heavens were stopped, and the rain from the heavens was restrained. **35** And the waters decreased in those days, and the Ark rested on the mountains of Ararat. **36** And Noah then opened the windows of the Ark, and Noah still called out to the Lord at that time, and he said, "O Lord who formed the earth, and the heavens, and all that are therein: bring our souls out from this confinement, and from the prison wherein You have placed us, for I am very wearied with sighing." **37** And the Lord listened to the voice of Noah, and said to him, "When you will have completed a full year you will then go out." **38** And at the revolution of the year, when a full year was completed to Noah's dwelling in the Ark, the waters were dried from off the earth, and Noah put off the covering of the Ark. **39** At that time, on the twenty-seventh day of the second month, the earth was dry, but Noah, and his sons, and those that were with him did not go out from the Ark until the Lord told them.

40 And the day came that the Lord told them to go out, and they all went out from the Ark. **41** And they went and returned everyone to his way and to his place, and Noah and his sons dwelt in the land that God had told them, and they served the Lord all their days, and the Lord blessed Noah and his sons on their going out from the Ark. **42** And He said to them, "Be fruitful and fill all the earth; become strong, and increase abundantly in the earth, and multiply therein."

CHAPTER 7

1 And these are the names of the sons of Noah: Japheth, Ham, and Shem; and children were born to them after the flood, for they had taken wives before the flood. **2** These are the sons of Japheth: Gomer, Magog, Madai, Javan, Tubal, Meshech, and Tiras, seven sons. **3** And the sons of Gomer were Askinaz, Rephas, and Tegarmah. **4** And the sons of Magog were Elichanaf and Lubal. **5** And the sons of Madai were Achon, Zeelo, Chazoni, and Lot. **6** And the sons of Javan were Elisha, Tarshish, Chittim, and Dudonim. **7** And the sons of Tubal were Ariphi, Kesed, and Taari. **8** And the sons of Meshech were Dedon, Zaron, and Shebashni. **9** And the sons of Tiras were Benib, Gera, Lupirion, and Gilak. These are the sons of Japheth according to their families, and their numbers in those days were about four hundred and sixty men. **10** And these are the sons of Ham: Cush, Mitzraim, Phut, and Canaan, four sons. And the sons of Cush were Seba, Havilah, Sabta, Raama, and Satecha. And the sons of Raama were Sheba and Dedan. **11** And the sons of Mitzraim were Lud, Anom, and Pathros, Chasloth, and Chaphtor. **12** And the sons of Phut were Gebul, Hadan, Benah, and Adan. **13** And the sons of Canaan were Zidon, Heth, Amori, Gergashi, Hivi, Arkee, Seni, Arodi, Zimodi, and Chamothi. **14** These are the sons of Ham, according to their families, and their numbers in those days were about seven hundred and thirty men. **15** And these are the sons of Shem: Elam, Asshur, Arphaxad, Lud, and Aram, five sons. And the sons of Elam were Shushan, Machul, and Harmon. **16** And the sons of Asshur were Mirus and Mokil. And the sons of Arphaxad were Salah, Anar, and Ashcol. **17** And the sons of Lud were Pethor and Bizayon. And the sons of Aram were Uz, Chul, Gather, and Mash. **18** These are the sons of Shem, according to their families, and their numbers in those days were about three hundred men. **19** These are the generations of Shem: Shem begot Arphaxad, and Arphaxad begot Salah, and Salah begot Eber; and two children were born to Eber, the name of one was Peleg, for in his days the sons of men were divided, and in the latter days, the earth was divided, **20** and the name of the second was Yoktan, meaning that in his day the lives of the sons of men were diminished and lessened. **21** These are the sons of Yoktan: Almodad, Shelaf, Chazarmoves, Yerach, Hadurom, Ozel, Diklah, Obal, Abimael, Sheba, Ophir, Havilah, and Jobab; all these are the sons of Yoktan. **22** And his brother Peleg begot Yen, and Yen begot Serug, and Serug begot Nahor, and Nahor begot Terah, and Terah was thirty-eight years old, and he begot Haran and Nahor. **23** And Cush, the son of Ham, the son of Noah, took a wife in those days in his old age, and she bore a son, and they called his name Nimrod, saying, "At that time the sons of men again began to rebel and transgress against God," and the child grew up, and his father loved him exceedingly, for he was the son of his old age. **24** And the garments of skin which God made for Adam and his wife (when they went out of the garden) were given to Cush. **25** For after the death of Adam and his wife, the garments were given to Enoch, the son of Jared, and when Enoch was taken up to God, he gave them to his son Methuselah. **26** And at the death of Methuselah, Noah took them and brought them to the Ark, and they were with him until he went out of the Ark. **27** And in their going out, Ham stole those garments from his father Noah, and he took them and hid them from his brothers. **28** And when Ham begot his firstborn Cush, he gave him the garments in secret, and they were with Cush [for] many days. **29** And Cush also concealed them from his sons and brothers, and when Cush had begotten Nimrod, he gave him those garments through his love for him, and Nimrod grew up, and when he was twenty years old, he put on those garments. **30** And Nimrod became strong when he put on the garments, and God gave him might and strength, and he was a mighty hunter in the earth, yes, he was a mighty hunter in the field, and he hunted the animals, and he built altars, and he offered the animals on them before the Lord. **31** And Nimrod strengthened himself, and he rose up from among his brothers, and he fought the battles of his brothers against all their surrounding enemies. **32** And the Lord delivered all the enemies of his brothers into his hands, and God prospered him from time to time in his battles, and he reigned on earth. **33** Therefore it became current in those days, when a man ushered out those that he had trained up for battle, he would say to them, "Like God did to Nimrod, who was a mighty hunter in the earth, and who succeeded in the battles that prevailed against his brothers, that he delivered them from the hands of their enemies, so may God strengthen us and deliver us this day." **34** And when Nimrod was forty years old, at that time there was a war between his brothers and the children of Japheth, so that they were in the power of their enemies. **35** And Nimrod went out at that time, and he assembled all the sons of Cush and their families, about four hundred and sixty men, and he hired also from some of his friends and acquaintances about eighty men, and he gave them their hire, and he went with them to battle, and when he was on the road, Nimrod strengthened the hearts of the people that went with him. **36** And he said to them, "Do not fear, neither be alarmed, for all our enemies will be delivered into our hands, and you may do with them as you please." **37** And all the men that went were about five hundred, and they fought against their enemies, and they destroyed them, and subdued them, and Nimrod placed standing officers over them in their respective places. **38** And he took some of their children as security, and they were all servants to Nimrod and to his brothers, and Nimrod and all the people that were with him turned homeward. **39** And when Nimrod had joyfully returned from battle after having conquered his enemies, all his brothers, together with those who knew him before, assembled to make him king over them, and they placed the regal crown on his head. **40** And he set over his subjects and people, princes, judges, and rulers, as is the custom among kings. **41** And he placed Terah the son of Nahor [as] the prince of his host, and he dignified him and elevated him above all his princes. **42** And while he was reigning according to his heart's desire, after having conquered all his surrounding enemies, he advised with his counselors to build a city for his palace, and they did so. **43** And they found a large valley opposite to the east, and they built him a large and extensive city, and Nimrod called the name of the city that he built Shinar, for the Lord had vehemently shaken his enemies and destroyed them. **44** And Nimrod dwelt in Shinar, and he reigned securely, and he fought with his enemies, and he subdued them, and he prospered in all his battles, and his kingdom became very great. **45** And all nations and tongues heard of his fame, and they gathered themselves to him, and they bowed down to the earth, and they brought him offerings, and he became their lord and king, and they all dwelt with him in the city at Shinar, and Nimrod reigned in the earth over all the sons of Noah, and they were all under his power and counsel. **46** And all the earth was of one tongue and words of union, but Nimrod did not go in the ways of the Lord, and he was more wicked than all the men that were before him, from the days of the flood until those days. **47** And he made gods of wood and stone, and he bowed down to them, and he rebelled against the Lord, and taught all his subjects and the people of the earth his wicked ways; and his son Mardon was more wicked than his father. **48** And everyone that heard of the acts of Mardon the son of Nimrod would say concerning him, "From the wicked goes out wickedness"; therefore, it became a proverb in the whole earth, saying, "From the wicked goes out wickedness," and it was current in the words of men from that time to this. **49** And Terah the son of Nahor, prince of Nimrod's host, was in those days very great in the sight of the king and his subjects, and the king and princes loved him, and they elevated him very high. **50** And Terah took a wife, and her name was Amthelo the daughter of Cornebo; and the wife of Terah conceived and bore him a son in those days. **51** Terah was seventy years old when he begot him, and Terah called the name of his son that was born to him Abram, because the king had raised him in those days, and dignified him above all his princes that were with him.

CHAPTER 8

1 And it was during the night that Abram was born that all the servants of Terah, and all the wise men of Nimrod, and his conjurers came, and ate, and drank in the house of Terah, and they rejoiced with him on that night. **2** And when all the wise men and conjurers went out from the house of Terah, they lifted up their eyes toward the heavens that night to look at the stars, and they saw, and behold, one very large star came from the east and ran in the heavens, and he swallowed up the four stars from the four sides of the heavens. **3** And all the wise men of the king and his conjurers were astonished at the sight, and the sages understood this matter, and they knew its meaning. **4** And they said to each other, "This only signifies the child that has been born to Terah this night, who will grow up and be fruitful, and multiply, and possess all the earth, he and his children forever, and he and his seed will slay great kings, and inherit their lands." **5** And the wise men and conjurers went home that night, and in the morning all these wise men and conjurers rose up early and assembled in an appointed house. **6** And they spoke and said to each other, "Behold, the sight that we saw last night is hidden from the king—it has not been made known to him. **7** And should this thing get known to the king in the latter days, he will say to us, Why have you concealed this matter from me, and then we will all suffer death; therefore, now let us go and tell the king the sight which we saw, and the interpretation thereof, and we will then remain clear." **8** And they did so, and they all went to the king and bowed down to him to the ground, and they said, "May the king live, may the king live. **9** We heard that a son was born to Terah the son of Nahor, the prince of your host, and last night we came to his house, and we ate, and drank, and rejoiced with him that night. **10** And when your servants went out from the house of Terah to go to our respective homes to abide there for the night, we lifted up our eyes to the heavens, and we saw a great star coming from the east, and the same star ran with great speed and swallowed up four great stars from the four sides of the heavens. **11** And your servants were astonished at the sight which we saw, and were greatly terrified, and we made our judgment on the sight, and knew by our wisdom the proper interpretation thereof, that this thing applies to the child that is born to Terah, who will grow up, and multiply greatly, and become powerful, and kill all the kings of the earth, and inherit all their lands, he and his seed forever. **12** And now our lord and king, behold, we have truly acquainted you with what we have seen concerning this child. **13** If it seems good to the king to give his father value for this child, we will slay him before he will grow up, and increase in the land, and his evil increase against us, that we and our children perish through his evil." **14** And the king heard their words and they seemed good in his sight, and he sent and called for Terah, and Terah came before the king. **15** And the king said to Terah, "I have been told that a son was born to you last night, and after this manner was observed in the heavens at his birth. **16** And now, therefore, give me the child, that we may slay him before his evil springs up against us, and I will give you for his value, your house full of silver and gold." **17** And Terah answered the king and said to him: "My lord and king, I have heard your words, and your servant will do all that his king desires. **18** But my lord and king, I will tell you what happened to me last night that I may see what advice the king will give his servant, and then I will answer the king on what he has just spoken"; and the king said, "Speak." **19** And Terah said to the king, "Ayon, son of Mored, came to me last night, saying, **20** Give to me the great and beautiful horse that the king gave you, and I will give you silver, and gold, and straw, and provender for its value; and I said to him, Wait until I see the king concerning your words, and behold, whatever the king says, that I will do. **21** And now my lord and king, behold, I have made this thing known to you, and the advice which my king will give to his servant, that I will follow." **22** And the king heard the words of Terah, and his anger was kindled, and he considered him in the manner of a fool. **23** And the king answered Terah, and he said to him, "Are you so silly, ignorant, or deficient in understanding to do this thing—to give your beautiful horse for silver and gold or even for straw and provender? **24** Are you so short of silver and gold, that you should do this thing, because you cannot obtain straw and provender to feed your horse? And what is silver and gold to you, or straw and provender, that you should give away that fine horse which I gave you, like which there is none to be had on the whole earth?" **25** And the king left off speaking, and Terah answered the king, saying, "Like to this the king has spoken to his servant; **26** I implore you, my lord and king, what is this which you said to me, saying, Give your son that we may slay him, and I will give you silver and gold for his value; what will I do with silver and gold after the death of my son? Who will inherit me? Surely then at my death, the silver and gold will return to my king who gave it." **27** And when the king heard the words of Terah, and the allegory which he brought concerning the king, it grieved him greatly and he was vexed at this thing, and his anger burned within him. **28** And Terah saw that the anger of the king was kindled against him, and he answered the king, saying, "All that I have is in the king's power; whatever the king desires to do to his servant, that let him do, yes, even my son, he is in the king's power, without value in exchange, he and his two brothers that are older than he." **29** And the king said to Terah, "No, but I will purchase your younger son for a price." **30** And Terah answered the king, saying, "I implore you, my lord and king, to let your servant speak a word before you, and let the king hear the word of his servant," and Terah said, "Let my king give me three days' time until I consider this matter within myself, and consult with my family concerning the words of my king"; and he pressed the king greatly to agree to this. **31** And the king listened to Terah, and he did so, and he gave him three days' time, and Terah went out from the king's presence, and he came home to his family and spoke to them all the words of the king; and the people were greatly afraid. **32** And it was in the third day that the king sent to Terah, saying, "Send me your son for a price as I spoke to you; and should you not do this, I will send and slay all [that] you have in your house, so that you will not even have a dog remaining." **33** And Terah hastened (as the thing was urgent from the king), and he took a child from one of his servants, which his handmaid had born to him that day, and Terah brought the child to the king and received value for him. **34** And the Lord was with Terah in this matter that Nimrod might not cause Abram's death, and the king took the child from Terah and dashed his head to the ground with all his might, for he thought it had been Abram; and this was concealed from him from that day, and it was forgotten by the king, as it was the will of Providence not to permit Abram's death. **35** And Terah took his son Abram secretly, together with his mother and nurse, and he concealed them in a cave, and he brought them their provisions monthly. **36** And the Lord was with Abram in the cave, and he grew up, and Abram was in the cave ten years, and the king and his princes, soothsayers, and sages thought that the king had killed Abram.

CHAPTER 9

1 And Haran, the son of Terah, Abram's oldest brother, took a wife in those days. **2** Haran was thirty-nine years old when he took her; and the wife of Haran conceived and bore a son, and he called his name Lot. **3** And she conceived again and bore a daughter, and she called her name Milca; and she again conceived and bore a daughter, and she called her name Sarai. **4** Haran was forty-two years old when he begot Sarai, which was in the tenth year of the life of Abram; and in those days Abram and his mother and nurse went out from the cave, as the king and his subjects had forgotten the affair of Abram. **5** And when Abram came out from the cave, he went to Noah and his son Shem, and he remained with them to learn the instruction of the Lord and His ways, and no man knew where Abram was, and Abram served Noah and his son Shem for a long time. **6** And Abram was in Noah's house thirty-nine years, and Abram knew the Lord from three years old, and he went in the ways of the Lord until the day of his death, as Noah and his son Shem had taught him; and all the sons of the earth in those days greatly transgressed against the Lord, and they rebelled against Him, and they served other gods, and they forgot the Lord who had created them in the earth; and at that time the inhabitants of the earth, each man, made for themselves his god—gods of wood and stone which could neither speak, hear, nor deliver—and the sons of men served them and they became their gods. **7** And the king and all his servants, and Terah with all his household were then the first of those that served gods of wood and stone. **8** And Terah had twelve gods of large size, made of wood and stone, after the twelve months of the year, and he served each one monthly, and every month Terah would bring his meat offering and drink offering to his gods; thus Terah did all the days. **9** And that whole generation was wicked in the sight of the Lord, and they thus made every man his god, but they forsook the Lord who had created them. **10** And there was no man found in those days in the whole earth who knew the Lord (for they each served his own God) except Noah and his household, and all those who were under his counsel knew the Lord in those days. **11** And Abram the son of Terah was waxing great in those days in the house of Noah, and no man knew it, and the Lord was with him. **12** And the Lord gave Abram an understanding heart,

and he knew all the works of that generation were vain, and that all their gods were vain and were of no avail. **13** And Abram saw the sun shining on the earth, and Abram said to himself, "Surely now this sun that shines on the earth is God, and I will serve him." **14** And Abram served the sun in that day and he prayed to him, and when evening came, the sun set as usual, and Abram said within himself, "Surely this cannot be God." **15** And Abram still continued to speak within himself, "Who is He who made the heavens and the earth? Who created on earth? Where is He?" **16** And night darkened over him, and he lifted up his eyes toward the west, north, south, and east, and he saw that the sun had vanished from the earth, and the day became dark. **17** And Abram saw the stars and moon before him, and he said, "Surely this is the God who created the whole earth as well as man, and behold, these servants of his are gods around him": and Abram served the moon and prayed to it all that night. **18** And in the morning, when it was light and the sun shone on the earth as usual, Abram saw all the things that the Lord God had made on earth. **19** And Abram said to himself, "Surely these are not gods that made the earth and all mankind, but these are the servants of God," and Abram remained in the house of Noah and there knew the Lord and His ways, and he served the Lord all the days of his life, and all that generation forgot the Lord, and served other gods of wood and stone, and rebelled all their days. **20** And King Nimrod reigned securely, and all the earth was under his control, and all the earth was of one tongue and words of union. **21** And all the princes of Nimrod and his great men took counsel together—Phut, Mitzraim, Cush, and Canaan with their families—and they said to each other, "Come, let us build ourselves a city and a strong tower in it, and its top reaching the heavens, and we will make ourselves famous, so that we may reign over the whole world, in order that the evil of our enemies may cease from us, that we may reign mightily over them, and that we may not become scattered over the earth on account of their wars." **22** And they all went before the king, and they told the king these words, and the king agreed with them in this affair, and he did so. **23** And all the families assembled, consisting of about six hundred thousand men, and they went to seek an extensive piece of ground to build the city and the tower, and they sought in the whole earth and they found none like one valley at the east of the land of Shinar, about two days' walk, and they journeyed there and they dwelt there. **24** And they began to make bricks and burn fires to build the city and the tower that they had imagined to complete. **25** And the building of the tower was a transgression and a sin for them, and they began to build it, and while they were building against the Lord God of Heaven, they imagined in their hearts to war against Him and to ascend into Heaven. **26** And all these people and all the families divided themselves in three parts: the first said, "We will ascend into Heaven and fight against Him"; the second said, "We will ascend to Heaven and place our own gods there and serve them"; and the third part said, "We will ascend to Heaven and strike Him with bows and spears"; and God knew all their works and all their evil thoughts, and He saw the city and the tower which they were building. **27** And when they were building, they built themselves a great city and a very high and strong tower; and on account of its height the mortar and bricks did not reach the builders in their ascent to it until those who went up had completed a full year, and after that, they reached to the builders and gave them the mortar and the bricks; thus it was done daily. **28** And behold, these ascended and others descended the whole day; and if a brick should fall from their hands and get broken, they would all weep over it, and if a man fell and died, none of them would look at him. **29** And the Lord knew their thoughts, and it came to pass when they were building, they cast the arrows toward the heavens, and all the arrows fell on them filled with blood, and when they saw them, they said to each other, "Surely we have slain all those that are in Heaven." **30** For this was from the Lord in order to cause them to err, and in order to destroy them from off the face of the ground. **31** And they built the tower and the city, and they did this thing daily until many days and years were elapsed. **32** And God said to the seventy messengers who stood foremost before Him, to those who were near to Him, saying, "Come, let us descend and confuse their tongues that one man will not understand the language of his neighbor," and they did so to them. **33** And from that day following, they each forgot his neighbor's tongue, and they could not understand to speak in one tongue, and when the builder took lime or stone from the hands of his neighbor which he did not order, the builder would cast it away and throw it on his neighbor [so] that he would die. **34** And they did so many days, and they killed many of them in this manner. **35** And the Lord struck the three divisions that were there, and He punished them according to their works and designs; those who said, "We will ascend to Heaven and serve our gods," became like apes and elephants; and those who said, "We will strike the heavens with arrows," the Lord killed them, one man through the hand of his neighbor; and the third division of those who said, "We will ascend to Heaven and fight against Him," the Lord scattered them throughout the earth. **36** And when those who were left among them knew and understood the calamity which was coming on them, they forsook the building, and they also became scattered on the face of the whole earth. **37** And they ceased building the city and the tower; therefore, He called that place Babel, for there the Lord confounded the language of the whole earth; behold, it was at the east of the land of Shinar. **38** And as to the tower which the sons of men built, the earth opened its mouth and swallowed up one third part thereof, and a fire also descended from Heaven and burned another third, and the other third is left to this day, and it is of that part which was aloft, and its circumference is three days' walk. **39** And many of the sons of men died in that tower—a people without number.

CHAPTER 10

1 And Peleg the son of Eber died in those days, in the forty-eighth year of the life of Abram son of Terah, and all the days of Peleg were two hundred and thirty-nine years. **2** And when the Lord had scattered the sons of men on account of their sin at the tower, behold, they spread out into many divisions, and all the sons of men were dispersed into the four corners of the earth. **3** And all the families each became according to its language, its land, or its city. **4** And the sons of men built many cities according to their families in all the places where they went and throughout the earth where the Lord had scattered them. **5** And some of them built cities in places from which they were afterward rooted out, and they called these cities after their own names, or the names of their children, or after their particular occurrences. **6** And the sons of Japheth the son of Noah went and built themselves cities in the places where they were scattered, and they called all their cities after their names, and the sons of Japheth were divided on the face of the earth into many divisions and languages. **7** And these are the sons of Japheth according to their families: Gomer, Magog, Medai, Javan, Tubal, Meshech, and Tiras; these are the sons of Japheth according to their generations. **8** And the children of Gomer, according to their cities, were the Francum who dwell in the land of Franza, by the River Franza, by the River Senah. **9** And the children of Rephas are the Bartonim, who dwell in the land of Bartonia by the River Ledah, which empties its waters in the great sea Gihon, that is, Oceanus. **10** And the children of Togarmah are ten families, and these are their names: Buzar, Parzunac, Balgar, Elicanum, Ragbib, Tarki, Bid, Zebuc, Ongal, and Tilmaz; all these spread and rested in the north and built themselves cities. **11** And they called their cities after their own names, those are they who abide by the rivers Hithlah and Italac to this day. **12** But the families of Angoli, Balgar, and Parzunac, they dwell by the great river Dubnee; and the names of their cities are also according to their own names. **13** And the children of Javan are the Javanim who dwell in the land of Makdonia, and the children of Medai are the Orelum that dwell in the land of Curson, and the children of Tubal are those that dwell in the land of Tuskanah by the River Pashiah. **14** And the children of Meshech are the Shibashni, and the children of Tiras are Rushash, Cushni, and Ongolis; all these went and built themselves cities; those are the cities that are situated by the sea [of] Jabus by the River Cura, which empties itself in the River Tragan. **15** And the children of Elishah are the Almanim, and they also went and built themselves cities; those are the cities situated between the mountains of Job and Shibathmo; and of them were the people of Lumbardi who dwell opposite the mountains of Job and Shibathmo, and they conquered the land of Italia and remained there to this day. **16** And the children of Chittim are the Romim who dwell in the Valley of Canopia by the River Tibreu. **17** And the children of Dudonim are those who dwell in the cities of the sea [of] Gihon, in the land of Bordna. **18** These are the families of the children of Japheth, according to their cities and languages, when they were scattered after the tower, and they called their cities after their names and occurrences; and these are the names of all their cities,

according to their families, which they built in those days after the tower. **19** And the sons of Ham were Cush, Mitzraim, Phut, and Canaan, according to their generation and cities, **20** All these went and built themselves cities as they found fit places for them, and they called their cities after the names of their fathers Cush, Mitzraim, Phut, and Canaan. **21** And the sons of Mitzraim are the Ludim, Anamim, Lehabim, Naphtuchim, Pathrusim, Casluchim, and Caphturim, seven families. **22** All these dwell by the River Sihor, that is the brook of Egypt, and they built themselves cities and called them after their own names. **23** And the children of Pathros and Casloch intermarried together, and from them went out the Pelishtim, the Azathim, and the Gerarim, the Githim and the Ekronim, five families in all; these also built themselves cities, and they called their cities after the names of their fathers to this day. **24** And the children of Canaan also built themselves cities, and they called their cities after their names, eleven cities and others without number. **25** And four men from the family of Ham went to the land of the plain; these are the names of the four men: Sodom, Gomorrah, Admah, and Zeboyim. **26** And these men built themselves four cities in the land of the plain, and they called the names of their cities after their own names. **27** And they, and their children, and all belonging to them dwelt in those cities, and they were fruitful, and multiplied greatly, and dwelt peaceably. **28** And Seir the son of Hur, son of Hivi, son of Canaan, went and found a valley opposite to Mount Paran, and he built a city there, and he and his seven sons and his household dwelt there, and he called the city which he built Seir, according to his name; that is the land of Seir to this day. **29** These are the families of the children of Ham, according to their languages and cities, when they were scattered to their countries after the tower. **30** And some of the children of Shem son of Noah, father of all the children of Eber, also went and built themselves cities in the places wherein they were scattered, and they called their cities after their names. **31** And the sons of Shem were Elam, Asshur, Arphaxad, Lud, and Aram, and they built themselves cities and called the names of all their cities after their names. **32** And Asshur son of Shem and his children and household went out at that time—a very large body of them—and they went to a distant land that they found, and they met with a very extensive valley in the land that they went to, and they built themselves four cities, and they called them after their own names and occurrences. **33** And these are the names of the cities which the children of Asshur built: Ninevah, Resen, Calach, and Rehobother; and the children of Asshur dwell there to this day. **34** And the children of Aram also went and built themselves a city, and they called the name of the city Uz after their eldest brother, and they dwell therein; that is the land of Uz to this day. **35** And in the second year after the tower, a man from the house of Asshur, whose name was Bela, went from the land of Ninevah to sojourn with his household wherever he could find a place; and they came until opposite the cities of the plain against Sodom, and they dwelt there. **36** And the man rose up and built a small city there, and called its name Bela after his name; that is the land of Zoar to this day. **37** And these are the families of the children of Shem according to their language and cities, after they were scattered on the earth after the tower. **38** And every kingdom, city, and family of the families of the children of Noah built themselves many cities after this. **39** And they established governments in all their cities in order to be regulated by their orders; so all the families of the children of Noah did forever.

CHAPTER 11

1 And Nimrod son of Cush was still in the land of Shinar, and he reigned over it and dwelt there, and he built cities in the land of Shinar. **2** And these are the names of the four cities which he built, and he called their names after the occurrences that happened to them in the building of the tower. **3** And he called the first Babel, saying, "Because the Lord confounded the language of the whole earth there." And the name of the second he called Erech, because from there God dispersed them. **4** And the third he called Eched, saying, "There was a great battle at that place." And the fourth he called Calnah, because his princes and mighty men were consumed there, and they vexed the Lord; they rebelled and transgressed against Him. **5** And when Nimrod had built these cities in the land of Shinar, he placed in them the remainder of his people, his princes and his mighty men that were left in his kingdom. **6** And Nimrod dwelt in Babel, and he renewed his reign there over the rest of his subjects, and he reigned securely, and the subjects and princes of Nimrod called his name Amraphel, saying that at the tower his princes and men fell through his means. 7 And notwithstanding this, Nimrod did not return to the Lord, and he continued in wickedness and teaching wickedness to the sons of men; and his son Mardon was worse than his father and continued to add to the abominations of his father. 8 And he caused the sons of men to sin, therefore it is said, "From the wicked goes out wickedness." 9 At that time there was war between the families of the children of Ham as they were dwelling in the cities which they had built. 10 And Chedorlaomer, king of Elam, went away from the families of the children of Ham, and he fought with them and he subdued them, and he went to the five cities of the plain and he fought against them and he subdued them, and they were under his control. 11 And they served him twelve years, and they gave him a yearly tax. 12 At that time Nahor son of Serug died—in the forty-ninth year of the life of Abram son of Terah. 13 And in the fiftieth year of the life of Abram son of Terah, Abram came out from the house of Noah, and went to his father's house. 14 And Abram knew the Lord, and he went in His ways and instructions, and the Lord his God was with him. 15 And his father Terah was still captain of the host of King Nimrod in those days, and he still followed strange gods. 16 And Abram came to his father's house and saw twelve gods standing there in their temples, and the anger of Abram was kindled when he saw these images in his father's house. 17 And Abram said, "As the Lord lives, these images will not remain in my father's house; so the Lord who created me will do to me if in three days' time I do not break them all." 18 And Abram went from them and his anger burned within him. And Abram hastened and went from the chamber to his father's outer court, and he found his father sitting in the court, and all his servants with him, and Abram came and sat before him. 19 And Abram asked his father, saying, "Father, tell me where is [the] God who created the heavens and earth, and all the sons of men on earth, and who created you and me." And Terah answered his son Abram and said, "Behold, those who created us are all with us in the house." 20 And Abram said to his father, "My lord, please show them to me"; and Terah brought Abram into the chamber of the inner court, and Abram saw, and behold, the whole room was full of gods of wood and stone—twelve great images and others less than they without number. 21 And Terah said to his son, "Behold, these are they which made all [that] you see on earth, and which created me and you, and all mankind." 22 And Terah bowed down to his gods, and he then went away from them, and his son Abram went away with him. 23 And when Abram had gone from them, he went to his mother and sat before her, and he said to his mother, "Behold, my father has shown me those who made the heavens and earth, and all the sons of men. 24 Now, therefore, hasten and fetch a kid from the flock, and make savory meat from it, that I may bring it to my father's gods as an offering for them to eat; perhaps I may thereby become acceptable to them." 25 And his mother did so, and she fetched a kid, and made savory meat thereof, and brought it to Abram, and Abram took the savory meat from his mother and brought it before his father's gods, and he drew near to them that they might eat; and his father Terah did not know of it. 26 And Abram saw on the day when he was sitting among them that they had no voice, no hearing, no motion, and not one of them could stretch out his hand to eat. 27 And Abram mocked them, and said, "Surely the savory meat that I prepared has not pleased them, or perhaps it was too little for them, and for that reason they would not eat; therefore tomorrow I will prepare fresh savory meat, better and more plentiful than this, in order that I may see the result." 28 And it was on the next day that Abram directed his mother concerning the savory meat, and his mother rose and fetched three fine kids from the flock, and she made of them some excellent savory meat, such as her son was fond of, and she gave it to her son Abram; and his father Terah did not know of it. 29 And Abram took the savory meat from his mother and brought it into the chamber before his father's gods; and he came near to them that they might eat, and he placed it before them, and Abram sat before them all day, thinking perhaps they might eat. 30 And Abram viewed them, and behold, they had neither voice nor hearing, nor did one of them stretch out his hand to the meat to eat. 31 And in the evening of that day in that house Abram was clothed with the Spirit of God. 32 And he called out and said, "Woe to my father and this wicked generation, whose hearts are all inclined to vanity, who serve these idols of wood and stone which can neither eat, smell,

hear, nor speak, who have mouths without speech, eyes without sight, ears without hearing, hands without feeling, and legs which cannot move; those that made them and that trust in them are like them." 33 And when Abram saw all these things his anger was kindled against his father, and he hastened and took a hatchet in his hand, and came to the chamber of the gods, and he broke all his father's gods. 34 And when he had finished breaking the images, he placed the hatchet in the hand of the great god which was there before them, and he went out; and his father Terah came home, for he had heard at the door the sound of the striking of the hatchet; so Terah came into the house to know what this was about. 35 And Terah, having heard the noise of the hatchet in the room of images, ran to the room to the images, and he met Abram going out. 36 And Terah entered the room and found all the idols fallen down and broken, and the hatchet in the hand of the largest, which was not broken, and the savory meat which his son Abram had made was still before them. 37 And when Terah saw this his anger was greatly kindled, and he hastened and went from the room to Abram. 38 And he found his son Abram still sitting in the house; and he said to him, "What is this work you have done to my gods?" 39 And Abram answered his father Terah and said, "Not so my lord, for I brought savory meat before them, and when I came near to them with the meat that they might eat, they all at once stretched out their hands to eat before the great one had put out his hand to eat. 40 And the large one saw their works that they did before him, and his anger was violently kindled against them, and he went and took the hatchet that was in the house and came to them and broke them all, and behold, the hatchet is yet in his hand as you see." 41 And Terah's anger was kindled against his son Abram when he spoke this; and Terah said to his son Abram in his anger, "What is this tale that you have told? You speak lies to me. 42 Is there spirit, soul, or power in these gods to do all you have told me? Are they not wood and stone, and have I not made them myself, and can you speak such lies, saying that the large god that was with them struck them? It is you that placed the hatchet in his hands, and then say he struck them all." 43 And Abram answered his father and said to him, "And how can you then serve these idols in whom there is no power to do anything? Can those idols in which you trust deliver you? Can they hear your prayers when you call on them? Can they deliver you from the hands of your enemies, or will they fight your battles for you against your enemies, that you should serve wood and stone which can neither speak nor hear? 44 And now surely it is not good for you nor for the sons of men that are connected with you to do these things; are you so silly, so foolish, or so short of understanding that you will serve wood and stone, and do after this manner, 45 and forget the Lord God who made the heavens and earth, and who created you in the earth, and thereby bring a great evil on your souls in this matter by serving stone and wood? 46 Did our fathers in days of old not sin in this matter, and the Lord God of the universe brought the waters of the flood on them and destroyed the whole earth? 47 And how can you continue to do this and serve gods of wood and stone, who cannot hear, or speak, or deliver you from oppression, thereby bringing down the anger of the God of the universe on you? 48 Now therefore, my father, refrain from this and do not bring evil on your soul and the souls of your household." 49 And Abram hastened and sprang from before his father, and took the hatchet from his father's largest idol, with which Abram broke it and ran away. 50 And Terah, seeing all that Abram had done, hastened to go from his house, and he went to the king, and he came before Nimrod, and stood before him, and he bowed down to the king; and the king said, "What do you want?" 51 And he said, "I implore you, my lord, to hear me: now fifty years back a child was born to me, and thus he has done to my gods and thus he has spoken; and now therefore, my lord and king, send for him that he may come before you, and judge him according to the law, that we may be delivered from his evil." 52 And the king sent three men of his servants, and they went and brought Abram before the king. And Nimrod and all his princes and servants were sitting before him that day, and Terah also sat before them. 53 And the king said to Abram, "What is this that you have done to your father and to his gods?" And Abram answered the king in the words that he spoke to his father, and he said, "The large god that was with them in the house did to them what you have heard." 54 And the king said to Abram, "Had they power to speak, and eat, and do as you have said?" And Abram answered the king, saying, "And if there is no power in them why do you serve them and cause the sons of men to err through your follies? **55** Do you imagine that they can deliver you or do anything small or great, that you should serve them? And why will you not sense the God of the whole universe, who created you and in whose power it is to kill and keep alive? **56** O foolish, simple, and ignorant king, woe to you forever. **57** I thought you would teach your servants the upright way, but you have not done this, but have filled the whole earth with your sins and the sins of your people who have followed your ways. **58** Do you not know, or have you not heard, that this evil which you do, our ancestors sinned therein in days of old, and the perpetual God brought the waters of the flood on them and destroyed them all, and also destroyed the whole earth on their account? And will you and your people rise up now and do like to this work, in order to bring down the anger of the Lord God of the universe, and to bring calamity on you and the whole earth? **59** Now therefore, put away this evil deed which you do, and serve the God of the universe, as your soul is in His hands, and then it will be well with you. **60** And if your wicked heart will not listen to my words to cause you to forsake your evil ways, and to serve the perpetual God, then you will die in shame in the latter days—you, your people, and all who are connected with you, hearing your words or walking in your evil ways." **61** And when Abram had ceased speaking before the king and princes, Abram lifted up his eyes to the heavens, and he said, "The Lord sees all the wicked, and He will judge them."

CHAPTER 12

1 And when the king heard the words of Abram, he ordered him to be put into prison; and Abram was in prison [for] ten days. **2** And at the end of those days the king ordered that all the kings, princes, and governors of different provinces, and the sages, should come before him, and they sat before him, and Abram was still in the house of confinement. **3** And the king said to the princes and sages, "Have you heard what Abram, the son of Terah, has done to his father? Thus he has done to him, and I ordered him to be brought before me, and thus he has spoken; his heart did not misgive him, neither did he stir in my presence, and behold, now he is confined in the prison. **4** And therefore decide what judgment is due to this man who reviled the king—who spoke and did all the things that you heard." **5** And they all answered the king, saying, "The man who reviles the king should be hanged on a tree; but having done all the things that he said, and having despised our gods, he must therefore be burned to death, for this is the law in this matter. **6** If it pleases the king to do this, let him order his servants to kindle a fire both night and day in your brick furnace, and then we will cast this man into it." And the king did so, and he commanded his servants that they should prepare a fire for three days and three nights in the king's furnace, that is in Kasdim; and the king ordered them to take Abram from prison and bring him out to be burned. **7** And all the king's servants, princes, lords, governors, and judges, and all the inhabitants of the land, about nine hundred thousand men, stood opposite the furnace to see Abram. **8** And all the women and little ones crowded on the roofs and towers to see what was happening with Abram, and they all stood together at a distance; and there was not a man left that did not come on that day to behold the scene. **9** And when Abram had come, the conjurers of the king and the sages saw Abram, and they cried out to the king, saying, "Our sovereign lord, surely this is the man whom we know to have been the child at whose birth the great star swallowed the four stars, which we declared to the king now fifty years since. **10** And behold, now his father has also transgressed your commands and mocked you by bringing you another child, which you killed." **11** And when the king heard their words, he was exceedingly angry, and he ordered Terah to be brought before him. **12** And the king said, "Have you heard what the conjurers have spoken? Now tell me truly: what did you do? And if you will speak truth you will be acquitted." **13** And seeing that the king's anger was so greatly kindled, Terah said to the king, "My lord and king, you have heard the truth, and what the sages have spoken is right." And the king said, "How could you do this thing, to transgress my orders and to give me a child that you did not beget, and to take value for him?" **14** And Terah answered the king, "Because my tender feelings were excited for my son at that time, and I took a son of my handmaid, and I brought him to the king." **15** And the king said, "Who advised you to [do] this? Tell me, do not hide it from me, and then you will not die." **16** And Terah was greatly terrified in the king's presence, and he said to the

king, "It was my eldest son Haran who advised me to [do] this"; and Haran was thirty-two years old in those days that Abram was born. **17** But Haran did not advise his father to [do] anything, for Terah said this to the king in order to deliver his soul from the king, for he feared greatly; and the king said to Terah, "Your son Haran who advised you to [do] this will die through fire with Abram; for the sentence of death is on him for having rebelled against the king's desire in doing this thing." **18** And at that time Haran felt inclined to follow the ways of Abram, but he kept it within himself. **19** And Haran said in his heart, "Behold, now the king has seized Abram on account of these things which Abram did, and it will come to pass, that if Abram prevails over the king, I will follow him, but if the king prevails, I will go after the king." **20** And when Terah had spoken this to the king concerning his son Haran, the king ordered Haran to be seized with Abram. **21** And they brought them both, Abram and his brother Haran, to cast them into the fire; and all the inhabitants of the land, and the king's servants, and princes, and all the women, and little ones were there, standing over them that day. **22** And the king's servants took Abram and his brother, and they stripped them of all their clothes excepting their lower garments which were on them. **23** And they bound their hands and feet with linen cords, and the servants of the king lifted them up and cast them both into the furnace. **24** And the Lord loved Abram and He had compassion over him, and the Lord came down and delivered Abram from the fire, and he was not burned. **25** But all the cords with which they bound him were burned, while Abram remained and walked around in the fire. **26** And Haran died when they had cast him into the fire, and he was burned to ashes, for his heart was not perfect with the Lord; and those men who cast him into the fire, the flame of the fire spread over them, and they were burned, and twelve men of them died. **27** And Abram walked in the midst of the fire [for] three days and three nights, and all the servants of the king saw him walking in the fire, and they came and told the king, saying, "Behold, we have seen Abram walking around in the midst of the fire, and even the lower garments which are on him are not burned, but the cord with which he was bound is burned." **28** And when the king heard their words his heart fainted and he would not believe them; so he sent other faithful princes to see this matter, and they went, and saw it, and told it to the king; and the king rose to go and see it, and he saw Abram walking to and fro in the midst of the fire, and he saw Haran's body burned, and the king wondered greatly. **29** And the king ordered Abram to be taken out from the fire; and his servants approached to take him out and they could not, for the fire was around and the flame ascending toward them from the furnace. **30** And the king's servants fled from it, and the king rebuked them, saying, "Hurry and bring Abram out of the fire that you will not die." **31** And the servants of the king again approached to bring Abram out, and the flames came on them and burned their faces so that eight of them died. **32** And when the king saw that his servants could not approach the fire lest they should be burned, the king called to Abram, "O servant of the God who is in Heaven, go out from amidst the fire and come here before me"; and Abram listened to the voice of the king, and he went out from the fire and came and stood before the king. **33** And when Abram came out, the king and all his servants saw Abram coming before the king with his lower garments on him, for they were not burned, but the cord with which he was bound was burned. **34** And the king said to Abram, "How is it that you were not burned in the fire?" **35** And Abram said to the king, "The God of the heavens and earth in whom I trust and who has all in His power, He delivered me from the fire into which you cast me." **36** And Haran, the brother of Abram, was burned to ashes, and they sought for his body, and they found it consumed. **37** And Haran was eighty-two years old when he died in the fire of Kasdim. And the king, princes, and inhabitants of the land, seeing that Abram was delivered from the fire, they came and bowed down to Abram. **38** And Abram said to them, "Do not bow down to me, but bow down to the God of the world who made you, and serve Him and go in His ways, for it is He who delivered me from out of this fire, and it is He who created the souls and spirits of all men, and formed man in his mother's womb, and brought him out into the world, and it is He who will deliver those who trust in Him from all pain." **39** And this thing seemed very wonderful in the eyes of the king and princes, that Abram was saved from the fire and that Haran was burned; and the king gave Abram many presents and he gave him his two head servants from the king's house; the name of one was Oni and the name of the other was Eliezer. **40** And all the kings, princes, and servants gave Abram many gifts of silver, and gold, and pearl, and the king and his princes sent him away, and he went in peace. **41** And Abram went out from the king in peace, and many of the king's servants followed him, and about three hundred men joined him. **42** And Abram returned that day and went to his father's house, he and the men that followed him, and Abram served the Lord his God all the days of his life, and he walked in His ways and followed His law. **43** And from that day forward Abram inclined the hearts of the sons of men to serve the Lord. **44** And at that time Nahor and Abram took wives for themselves, the daughters of their brother Haran; the wife of Nahor was Milca and the name of Abram's wife was Sarai. And Sarai, wife of Abram, was barren; she had no offspring in those days. **45** And at the expiration of two years from Abram's going out of the fire, that is in the fifty-second year of his life, behold, King Nimrod sat in Babel on the throne, and the king fell asleep and dreamed that he was standing with his troops and hosts in a valley opposite the king's furnace. **46** And he lifted up his eyes and saw a man in the likeness of Abram coming out from the furnace, and that he came and stood before the king with his drawn sword, and then sprang to the king with his sword when the king fled from the man, for he was afraid; and while he was running, the man threw an egg on the king's head, and the egg became a great river. **47** And the king dreamed that all his troops sank in that river and died, and the king took flight with three men who were before him and he escaped. **48** And the king looked at these men and they were clothed in princely dresses as the garments of kings, and had the appearance and majesty of kings. **49** And while they were running, the river again turned to an egg before the king, and there came out from the egg a young bird which came before the king, and flew at his head, and plucked out the king's eye. **50** And the king was grieved at the sight, and he awoke out of his sleep and his spirit was agitated; and he felt a great terror. **51** And in the morning, the king rose from his couch in fear, and he ordered all the wise men and magicians to come before him when the king related his dream to them. **52** And a wise servant of the king, whose name was Anuki, answered the king, saying, "This is nothing else but the evil of Abram and his seed which will spring up against my lord and king in the latter days. **53** And behold, the day will come when Abram, and his seed, and the children of his household will war with my king, and they will strike all the king's hosts and his troops. **54** And as to what you have said concerning three men which you saw like to yourself, and which escaped, this means that only you will escape with three kings from the kings of the earth who will be with you in battle. **55** And that which you saw of the river which turned to an egg as at first, and the young bird plucking out your eye, this means nothing else but the seed of Abram which will slay the king in latter days. **56** This is my king's dream, and this is its interpretation, and the dream is true, and the interpretation which your servant has given you is right. **57** Now therefore, my king, surely you know that it is now fifty-two years since your sages saw this at the birth of Abram, and if my king will permit Abram to live in the earth it will be to the injury of my lord and king, for all the days that Abram lives neither you nor your kingdom will be established, for this was known formerly at his birth; and why will my king not slay him, that his evil may be kept from you in latter days?" **58** And Nimrod listened to the voice of Anuki, and he sent some of his servants in secret to go and seize Abram, and bring him before the king to suffer death. **59** And Eliezer, Abram's servant whom the king had given him, was at that time in the presence of the king, and he heard what Anuki had advised the king, and what the king had said to cause Abram's death. **60** And Eliezer said to Abram, "Hasten, rise up and save your soul, that you may not die through the hands of the king, for thus he saw in a dream concerning you, and thus Anuki interpreted it, and thus also Anuki advised the king concerning you." **61** And Abram listened to the voice of Eliezer, and Abram hastened and ran for safety to the house of Noah and his son Shem, and he concealed himself there and found a place of safety; and the king's servants came to Abram's house to seek him, but they could not find him, and they searched throughout the country and he was not to be found, and they went and searched in every direction and he was not to be met with. **62** And when the king's servants could not find Abram they returned to the king, but the king's anger against Abram was stilled, as they did not find him, and the king drove this matter concerning Abram from his mind. **63** And Abram was concealed in Noah's house for one month until the king had forgotten this matter, but Abram was still afraid of the king; and Terah secretly came to see his son Abram in the house of Noah, and Terah was very great in the eyes of the king. **64** And Abram said to his father, "Do you not know that the king thinks to slay me, and to annihilate my name from the earth by the advice of his wicked counselors? **65** Now whom have you here and what have you in this land? Arise, let us go together to the land of Canaan, that we may be delivered from his hand, lest you also perish through him in the latter days. **66** Do you not know or have you not heard that it is not through love that Nimrod gives you all this honor, but it is only for his benefit that he bestows all this good on you? **67** And if he does to you greater good than this, surely these are only vanities of the world, for wealth and riches cannot avail in the day of wrath and anger. **68** Now therefore, listen to my voice, and let us arise and go to the land of Canaan, out of the reach of injury from Nimrod; and serve the Lord who created you in the earth and it will be well with you; and cast away all the vain things which you pursue." **69** And Abram ceased to speak when Noah and his son Shem answered Terah, saying, "The word which Abram has said to you is true." **70** And Terah listened to the voice of his son Abram, and Terah did all that Abram said, for this was from the Lord that the king should not cause Abram's death.

CHAPTER 13

1 And Terah took his son Abram and his grandson Lot, the son of Haran, and his daughter-in-law Sarai, the wife of his son Abram, and all the souls of his household and went with them from Ur-Kasdim to go to the land of Canaan. And when they came as far as the land of Haran they remained there, for it was exceedingly good land for pasture, and of sufficient extent for those who accompanied them. **2** And the people of the land of Haran saw that Abram was good and upright with God and men, and that the Lord his God was with him, and some of the people of the land of Haran came and joined Abram, and he taught them the instruction of the Lord and His ways; and these men remained with Abram in his house, and they adhered to him. **3** And Abram remained in the land three years, and at the expiration of three years the Lord appeared to Abram and said to him, "I am the Lord who brought you out from Ur-Kasdim and delivered you from the hands of all your enemies. **4** And now therefore, if you will listen to My voice and keep My commands, My statutes and My laws, then I will cause your enemies to fall before you, and I will multiply your seed like the stars of the heavens, and I will send My blessing on all the works of your hands, and you will lack nothing. **5** Arise now, take your wife and all belonging to you and go to the land of Canaan and remain there, and I will be God to you there, and I will bless you." And Abram rose and took his wife and all belonging to him, and he went to the land of Canaan as the Lord had told him; and Abram was [over] fifty years old when he went from Haran. **6** And Abram came to the land of Canaan and dwelt in the midst of the city, and he pitched his tent there among the children of Canaan, inhabitants of the land. **7** And the Lord appeared to Abram when he came to the land of Canaan, and said to him, "This is the land which I gave to you and to your seed after you forever, and I will make your seed like the stars of the heavens, and I will give all the lands which you see to your seed for an inheritance." **8** And Abram built an altar in the place where God had spoken to him, and Abram called on the Name of the Lord there. **9** At that time, at the end of three years of Abram's dwelling in the land of Canaan, in that year Noah died, which was the fifty-eighth year of the life of Abram; and all the days that Noah lived were nine hundred and fifty years and he died. **10** And Abram dwelt in the land of Canaan, he, his wife, and all belonging to him, and all those that accompanied him, together with those that joined him from the people of the land; but Abram's brother Nahor, and his father Terah, and Lot the son of Haran, and all belonging to them dwelt in Haran. **11** In the fifth year of Abram's dwelling in the land of Canaan the people of Sodom and Gomorrah and all the cities of the plain revolted from the power of Chedorlaomer, king of Elam, for all the kings of the cities of the plain had served Chedorlaomer for twelve years and given him a yearly tax, but in those days, in the thirteenth year, they rebelled against him. **12** And in the tenth year of Abram's dwelling in the land of Canaan there was war between Nimrod king of Shinar and Chedorlaomer king of Elam, and Nimrod came to fight with Chedorlaomer and to subdue him. **13** For Chedorlaomer was at that time one of the princes of the hosts of Nimrod, and when all the people at the tower were dispersed and those that remained were also scattered on the face of the earth, Chedorlaomer went to the land of Elam and reigned over it and rebelled against his lord. 14 And in those days when Nimrod saw that the cities of the plain had rebelled, he came with pride and anger to war with Chedorlaomer, and Nimrod assembled all his princes and subjects, about seven hundred thousand men, and went against Chedorlaomer, and Chedorlaomer went out to meet him with five thousand men, and they prepared for battle in the Valley of Babel which is between Elam and Shinar. 15 And all those kings fought there, and Nimrod and his people were smitten before the people of Chedorlaomer, and there fell from Nimrod's men about six hundred thousand, and the king's son Mardon fell among them. 16 And Nimrod fled and returned in shame and disgrace to his land, and he was under subjection to Chedorlaomer for a long time, and Chedorlaomer returned to his land and sent princes of his host to the kings that dwelt around him, to Arioch king of Ellasar, and to Tidal king of Goyim, and made a covenant with them, and they were all obedient to his commands. 17 And it was in the fifteenth year of Abram's dwelling in the land of Canaan, which is the seventieth year of the life of Abram, that the Lord appeared to Abram in that year, and He said to him, "I am the Lord who brought you out from Ur-Kasdim to give you this land for an inheritance. 18 Now therefore, walk before Me, and be perfect, and keep My commands, for I will give this land to you and to your seed for an inheritance, from the River Mitzraim to the great river Euphrates. 19 And you will come to your fathers in peace and in good age, and the fourth generation will return here in this land and will inherit it forever"; and Abram built an altar, and he called on the Name of the Lord who appeared to him, and he brought up sacrifices on the altar to the Lord. 20 At that time Abram returned and went to Haran to see his father and mother, and his father's household, and Abram, and his wife, and all belonging to him returned to Haran, and Abram dwelt in Haran [for] five years. 21 And many of the people of Haran, about seventy two men, followed Abram and Abram taught them the instruction of the Lord and His ways, and he taught them to know the Lord. 22 In those days the Lord appeared to Abram in Haran, and He said to him, "Behold, I spoke to you these twenty years back, saying, 23 Go out from your land, from your birthplace and from your father's house, to the land which I have shown you to give it to you and to your children, for there in that land I will bless you, and make you a great nation, and make your name great, and in you the families of the earth will be blessed. 24 Now therefore, arise, go out from this place, you, your wife, and all belonging to you, also everyone born in your house and all the souls you have made in Haran, and bring them out with you from here, and rise to return to the land of Canaan." 25 And Abram arose and took his wife Sarai, and all belonging to him, and all that were born to him in his house, and the souls which they had made in Haran, and they came out to go to the land of Canaan. 26 And Abram went and returned to the land of Canaan, according to the word of the Lord. And Lot, the son of his brother Haran, went with him, and Abram was seventy-five years old when he went out from Haran to return to the land of Canaan. 27 And he came to the land of Canaan according to the word of the Lord to Abram, and he pitched his tent and he dwelt in the plain of Mamre, and his brother's son Lot and all belonging to him were with him. 28 And the Lord appeared to Abram again and said, "To your seed I will give this land"; and he built an altar there to the Lord who appeared to him, which is still in the plains of Mamre to this day.

CHAPTER 14

1 In those days there was a wise man in the land of Shinar who had understanding in all wisdom, and of a beautiful appearance, but he was poor and indigent; his name was Rikayon and he was hard set to support himself. 2 And he resolved to go to Egypt, to Oswiris the son of Anom king of Egypt, to show the king his wisdom; for perhaps he might find grace in his sight, to raise him up and give him maintenance; and Rikayon did so. 3 And when Rikayon came to Egypt, he asked the inhabitants of Egypt concerning the king, and the inhabitants of Egypt told him the custom of the king of Egypt, for it was then the custom of the king of Egypt that he went from his royal palace and was seen abroad only one day in the year, and after that the king would return to his palace to remain there. 4 And on the day when the king went out, he passed judgment in the land, and everyone having a suit came before the king that day to obtain his request. 5 And when Rikayon heard of the custom in Egypt and that he could not come into the presence of the king, he grieved greatly and was very sorrowful. 6 And in the evening Rikayon went out and found a house in ruins, formerly a bake house in Egypt, and he remained there all night in bitterness of soul and pinched with hunger, and sleep was removed from his eyes. 7 And Rikayon considered within himself what he should do in the town until the king made his appearance, and how he might maintain himself there. 8 And he rose in the morning, and walked around, and met in his way those who sold vegetables and various sorts of seed with which they supplied the inhabitants. 9 And Rikayon wished to do the same in order to get a maintenance in the city, but he was unacquainted with the custom of the people, and he was like a blind man among them. 10 And he went and obtained vegetables to sell them for his support, and the rabble assembled around him and ridiculed him, and took his vegetables from him and left him nothing. 11 And he rose up from there in bitterness of soul and went sighing to the bake house in which he had remained all the night before, and he slept there the second night. 12 And on that night he reasoned within himself again how he could save himself from starvation, and he devised a scheme how to act. 13 And he rose up in the morning and acted ingeniously, and went and hired thirty strong men of the rabble, carrying their war instruments in their hands, and he led them to the top of the Egyptian tomb, and he placed them there. 14 And he commanded them, saying, "Thus says the king, strengthen yourselves and be valiant men, and let no man be buried here until two hundred pieces of silver are given, and then he may be buried"; and those men did according to the order of Rikayon to the people of Egypt the whole of that year. 15 And in eight months time Rikayon and his men gathered great riches of silver and gold, and Rikayon took a great quantity of horses and other animals, and he hired more men, and he gave them horses and they remained with him. 16 And when the year came around, at the time the king went out into the town, all the inhabitants of Egypt assembled together to speak to him concerning the work of Rikayon and his men. 17 And the king went out on the appointed day, and all the Egyptians came before him and cried to him, saying, 18 "May the king live forever. What is this thing you do in the town to your servants, not to permit a dead body to be buried until so much silver and gold are given? Was there ever the like to this done in the whole earth, from the days of former kings, yes, even from the days of Adam, to this day, that the dead should not be buried, [except] only for a set price? 19 We know it to be the custom of kings to take a yearly tax from the living, but you do not only do this, but you also exact a tax from the dead day by day. 20 Now, O king, we can no longer bear this, for the whole city is ruined on this account, and do you not know it?" 21 And when the king heard all that they had spoken he was very angry and his anger burned within him at this affair, for he had known nothing of it. 22 And the king said, "Who and where is he that dares to do this wicked thing in my land without my command? Surely you will tell me." 23 And they told him all the works of Rikayon and his men, and the king's anger was aroused, and he ordered Rikayon and his men to be brought before him. 24 And Rikayon took about one thousand children, sons and daughters, and clothed them in silk and embroidery, and he set them on horses and sent them to the king by means of his men, and he also took a great quantity of silver, and gold, and precious stones, and a strong and beautiful horse as a present for the king, with which he came before the king and bowed down to the earth before him; and the king, his servants, and all the inhabitants of Egypt wondered at the work of Rikayon, and they saw his riches and the present that he had brought to the king. 25 And it greatly pleased the king and he wondered at it; and when Rikayon sat before him, the king asked him concerning all his works, and Rikayon spoke all his words wisely before the king, his servants, and all the inhabitants of Egypt. 26 And when the king heard the words of Rikayon and his wisdom, Rikayon found grace in his sight, and he met with grace and kindness from all the servants of the king and from all the inhabitants of Egypt, on account of his wisdom and excellent speeches, and from that time they loved him exceedingly. 27 And the king answered and said to Rikayon, "Your name will no longer be called Rikayon, but Pharaoh will be your name, since you exacted a tax from the dead"; and he called his name Pharaoh. 28 And the king and his subjects loved Rikayon for his wisdom, and they consulted with all the

inhabitants of Egypt to make him prefect under the king. **29** And all the inhabitants of Egypt and its wise men did so, and it was made a law in Egypt. **30** And they made Rikayon Pharaoh prefect under Oswiris king of Egypt, and Rikayon Pharaoh governed over Egypt, daily administering justice to the whole city, but Oswiris the king would judge the people of the land one day in the year when he went out to make his appearance. **31** And Rikayon Pharaoh cunningly usurped the government of Egypt, and he exacted a tax from all the inhabitants of Egypt. **32** And all the inhabitants of Egypt greatly loved Rikayon Pharaoh, and they made a decree to call every king that should reign over them and their seed in Egypt, Pharaoh. **33** Therefore all the kings that reigned in Egypt from that time forward were called Pharaoh to this day.

CHAPTER 15

1 And in that year there was a heavy famine throughout the land of Canaan, and the inhabitants of the land could not remain on account of the famine for it was very grievous. **2** And Abram and all belonging to him rose and went down to Egypt on account of the famine, and when they were at the brook Mitzraim they remained there some time to rest from the fatigue of the road. **3** And Abram and Sarai were walking at the border of the Brook of Mitzraim, and Abram beheld that his wife Sarai was very beautiful. **4** And Abram said to his wife Sarai, "Since God has created you with such a beautiful countenance, I am afraid of the Egyptians lest they should slay me and take you away, for the fear of God is not in these places. **5** Surely then you will do this: say you are my sister to all that may ask you in order that it may be well with me, and that we may live and not be put to death." **6** And Abram commanded the same to all those that came with him to Egypt on account of the famine; also his nephew Lot he commanded, saying, "If the Egyptians ask you concerning Sarai, say she is the sister of Abram." **7** And yet with all these orders Abram did not put confidence in them, but he took Sarai, and placed her in a chest, and concealed it among their vessels, for Abram was greatly concerned about Sarai on account of the wickedness of the Egyptians. **8** And Abram and all belonging to him rose up from the Brook of Mitzraim and came to Egypt; and they had scarcely entered the gates of the city when the guards stood up to them, saying, "Give tithe to the king from what you have, and then you may come into the town"; and Abram and those that were with him did so. **9** And Abram with the people that were with him came to Egypt, and when they came, they brought the chest in which Sarai was concealed and the Egyptians saw the chest. **10** And the king's servants approached Abram, saying, "What have you here in this chest which we have not seen? Now open the chest and give tithe to the king of all that it contains." **11** And Abram said, "I will not open this chest, but all you demand on it I will give." And Pharaoh's officers answered Abram, saying, "It is a chest of precious stones—give us the tenth thereof." **12** Abram said, "All that you desire I will give, but you must not open the chest." **13** And the king's officers pressed Abram, and they reached the chest and opened it with force, and they saw, and behold, a beautiful woman was in the chest. **14** And when the officers of the king beheld Sarai, they were struck with admiration at her beauty, and all the princes and servants of Pharaoh assembled to see Sarai, for she was very beautiful. And the king's officers ran and told Pharaoh all that they had seen, and they praised Sarai to the king; and Pharaoh ordered her to be brought, and the woman came before the king. **15** And Pharaoh beheld Sarai, and she pleased him exceedingly, and he was struck with her beauty, and the king rejoiced greatly on her account, and made presents to those who brought him the tidings concerning her. **16** And the woman was then brought to Pharaoh's house, and Abram grieved on account of his wife, and he prayed to the Lord to deliver her from the hands of Pharaoh. **17** And Sarai also prayed at that time and said, "O Lord God, You told my lord Abram to go from his land and from his father's house to the land of Canaan, and You promised to do well with him if he would perform Your commands; now behold, we have done that which You commanded us, and we left our land and our families, and we went to a strange land and to a people whom we have not known before. **18** And we came to this land to avoid the famine, and this evil accident has befallen me; now therefore, O Lord God, deliver us and save us from the hand of this oppressor, and do well with me for the sake of Your mercy." **19** And the Lord listened to the voice of Sarai, and the Lord sent a messenger to deliver Sarai from the power of Pharaoh. **20** And the king came and sat before Sarai, and behold, a messenger of the Lord was standing over them, and he appeared to Sarai and said to her, "Do not fear, for the Lord has heard your prayer." **21** And the king approached Sarai and said to her, "What is that man to you who brought you here?" and she said, "He is my brother." **22** And the king said, "It is incumbent on us to make him great, to elevate him and to do to him all the good which you will command us"; and at that time the king sent silver, and gold, and precious stones to Abram in abundance, together with cattle, menservants, and maidservants; and the king ordered Abram to be brought, and he sat in the court of the king's house, and the king greatly exalted Abram on that night. **23** And the king approached to speak to Sarai, and he reached out his hand to touch her when the messenger struck him heavily, and he was terrified and he refrained from reaching to her. **24** And when the king came near to Sarai, the messenger struck him to the ground, and acted thus to him the whole night, and the king was terrified. **25** And on that night the messenger heavily struck all the servants of the king and his whole household on account of Sarai, and there was a great lamentation that night among the people of Pharaoh's house. **26** And Pharaoh, seeing the evil that befell him, said, "Surely on account of this woman this thing has happened to me," and he removed himself at some distance from her and spoke pleasing words to her. **27** And the king said to Sarai, "Please tell me concerning the man with whom you came here"; and Sarai said, "This man is my husband, and I said to you that he was my brother for I was afraid, lest you should put him to death through wickedness." **28** And the king kept away from Sarai, and the plagues of the messenger of the Lord ceased from him and his household; and Pharaoh knew that he was smitten on account of Sarai, and the king was greatly astonished at this. **29** And in the morning the king called for Abram and said to him, "What is this you have done to me? Why did you say, She is my sister, owing to which I took her to me for a wife, and this heavy plague has therefore come on me and my household? **30** Now therefore, here is your wife, take her and go from our land lest we all die on her account." And Pharaoh took more cattle, menservants and maidservants, and silver and gold, to give to Abram, and he returned his wife Sarai to him. **31** And the king took a maiden whom he begot by his concubines, and he gave her to Sarai for a handmaid. **32** And the king said to his daughter, "It is better for you, my daughter, to be a handmaid in this man's house than to be mistress in my house, after we have beheld the evil that befell us on account of this woman." **33** And Abram arose, and he and all belonging to him went away from Egypt; and Pharaoh ordered some of his men to accompany him and all that went with him. **34** And Abram returned to the land of Canaan, to the place where he had made the altar, where he at first had pitched his tent. **35** And Lot the son of Haran, Abram's brother, had a heavy stock of cattle, flocks, and herds, and tents, for the Lord was bountiful to them on account of Abram. **36** And when Abram was dwelling in the land, the herdsmen of Lot quarrelled with the herdsmen of Abram, for their property was too great for them to remain together in the land, and the land could not bear them on account of their cattle. **37** And when Abram's herdsmen went to feed their flock, they would not go into the fields of the people of the land, but the cattle of Lot's herdsmen did otherwise, for they were allowed to feed in the fields of the people of the land. **38** And the people of the land saw this occurrence daily, and they came to Abram and quarrelled with him on account of Lot's herdsmen. **39** And Abram said to Lot, "What is this you are doing to me, to make me despicable to the inhabitants of the land, that you order your herdsman to feed your cattle in the fields of other people? Do you not know that I am a stranger in this land among the children of Canaan, and why will you do this to me?" **40** And Abram quarrelled daily with Lot on account of this, but Lot would not listen to Abram, and he continued to do the same and the inhabitants of the land came and told Abram. **41** And Abram said to Lot, "How long will you be to me for a stumbling block with the inhabitants of the land? Now I implore you: let there no longer be quarrelling between us, for we are relatives. **42** But please separate from me, go and choose a place where you may dwell with your cattle and all belonging to you, but keep yourself at a distance from me—you and your household. **43** And do not be afraid in going from me, for if anyone does harm to you, let me know and I will avenge your cause from him, only remove from me." **44** And when Abram had spoken all these words to Lot, then Lot arose and lifted up his eyes toward the plain of Jordan. **45** And he saw that the whole of this place was well watered, and good for man as well as affording pasture for the cattle. **46** And Lot went from Abram to that place, and he pitched his tent there and he dwelt in Sodom, and they were separated from each other. **47** And Abram dwelt in the plain of Mamre, which is in Hebron, and he pitched his tent there, and Abram remained in that place [for] many years.

CHAPTER 16

1 At that time Chedorlaomer king of Elam sent to all the neighboring kings, to Nimrod king of Shinar, who was then under his power, and to Tidal king of Goyim, and to Arioch king of Ellasar, with whom he made a covenant, saying, "Come up to me and assist me, that we may strike all the towns of Sodom and its inhabitants, for they have rebelled against me these thirteen years." **2** And these four kings went up with all their camps, about eight hundred thousand men, and they went as they were, and struck every man they found in their road. **3** And the five kings of Sodom and Gomorrah—Shinab king of Admah, Shemeber king of Zeboyim, Bera king of Sodom, Bersha king of Gomorrah, and Bela king of Zoar—went out to meet them, and they all joined together in the Valley of Siddim. **4** And these nine kings made war in the Valley of Siddim; and the kings of Sodom and Gomorrah were smitten before the kings of Elam. **5** And the Valley of Siddim was full of lime pits and the kings of Elam pursued the kings of Sodom, and the kings of Sodom fled with their camps and fell into the lime pits, and all that remained went to the mountain for safety, and the five kings of Elam came after them and pursued them to the gates of Sodom, and they took all that there was in Sodom. **6** And they plundered all the cities of Sodom and Gomorrah, and they also took Lot, Abram's brother's son, and his property, and they seized all the goods of the cities of Sodom, and they went away; and Unic, Abram's servant, who was in the battle, saw this, and told Abram all that the kings had done to the cities of Sodom, and that Lot was taken captive by them. **7** And Abram heard this, and he rose up with about three hundred and eighteen men that were with him, and he pursued these kings that night and struck them, and they all fell before Abram and his men, and there was none remaining but the four kings who fled, and they each went his own way. **8** And Abram recovered all the property of Sodom, and he also recovered Lot and his property—his wives, and little ones, and all belonging to him—so that Lot lacked nothing. **9** And when he returned from striking these kings, he and his men passed the Valley of Siddim where the kings had made war together. **10** And Bera king of Sodom, and the rest of his men that were with him, went out from the lime pits into which they had fallen, to meet Abram and his men. **11** And Adonizedek king of Jerusalem (the same was Shem) went out with his men to meet Abram and his people with bread and wine, and they remained together in the Valley of Melech. **12** And Adonizedek blessed Abram, and Abram gave him a tenth from all that he had brought from the spoil of his enemies, for Adonizedek was a priest before God. **13** And all the kings of Sodom and Gomorrah who were there, with their servants, approached Abram and begged of him to return them their servants whom he had made captive, and to take to himself all the property. **14** And Abram answered the kings of Sodom, saying, "As the Lord lives who created the heavens and earth, and who redeemed my soul from all affliction, and who delivered me from my enemies this day, and gave them into my hand, I will not take anything belonging to you, that you may not boast tomorrow, saying, Abram became rich from our property that he saved. **15** For the Lord my God in whom I trust said to me, You will lack nothing, for I will bless you in all the works of your hands. **16** And now therefore, behold, here is all belonging to you—take it and go; as the Lord lives I will not take from you from a living soul down to a strap or thread, excepting the expense of the food of those who went out with me to battle, as also the portions of the men who went with me, Anar, Ashcol, and Mamre, they and their men, as well as those who had also remained to watch the baggage, they will take their portion of the spoil." **17** And the kings of Sodom gave Abram according to all that he had said, and they pressed him to take of whatever he chose, but he would not. **18** And he sent the kings of Sodom and the remainder of their men away, and he gave them orders about Lot, and they went to their respective places. **19** And Lot, his brother's son, he also sent away with his property, and he went with them, and Lot returned to his home, to Sodom, and Abram and his people

returned to their home to the plains of Mamre, which is in Hebron. **20** At that time the Lord appeared to Abram again, in Hebron, and He said to him, "Do not fear, your reward is very great before Me, for I will not leave you until I will have multiplied you, and blessed you, and made your seed like the stars in the heavens, which cannot be measured nor numbered. **21** And I will give to your seed all these lands that you see with your eyes, I will give them to them for an inheritance forever, only be strong and do not fear, walk before Me and be perfect." **22** And in the seventy-eighth year of the life of Abram, in that year Reu the son of Peleg died; and all the days of Reu were two hundred and thirty-nine years, and he died. **23** And Sarai, the daughter of Haran, Abram's wife, was still barren in those days; she did not bear either son or daughter to Abram. **24** And when she saw that she bore no children, she took her handmaid Hagar, whom Pharaoh had given her, and she gave her to her husband Abram for a wife. **25** For Hagar learned all the ways of Sarai as Sarai taught her; she was not in any way deficient in following her good ways. **26** And Sarai said to Abram, "Behold, here is my handmaid Hagar, go to her that she may bring out on my knees, that I may also obtain children through her." **27** And at the end of ten years of Abram's dwelling in the land of Canaan, which is the eighty-fifth year of Abram's life, Sarai gave Hagar to him. **28** And Abram listened to the voice of his wife Sarai and he took his handmaid Hagar, and Abram came to her and she conceived. **29** And when Hagar saw that she had conceived she rejoiced greatly, and her mistress was despised in her eyes, and she said within herself, "This can only be that I am better before God than was my mistress Sarai, for all the days that my mistress has been with my lord, she did not conceive, but the Lord has caused me in so short a time to conceive by him." **30** And when Sarai saw that Hagar had conceived by Abram, Sarai was jealous of her handmaid, and Sarai said within herself, "This is surely nothing else but that she must be better than I am " **31** And Sarai said to Abram, "My wrong be on you, for at the time when you prayed before the Lord for children, why did you not pray on my account that the Lord should give me seed from you? **32** And when I speak to Hagar in your presence, she despises my words, because she has conceived, and you will say nothing to her; may the Lord judge between me and you for what you have done to me." **33** And Abram said to Sarai, "Behold, your handmaid is in your hands, do to her as it may seem good in your eyes"; and Sarai afflicted her, and Hagar fled from her to the wilderness. **34** And [the] Messenger of the Lord found her by a well in the place where she had fled, and He said to her, "Do not fear, for I will multiply your seed, for you will bear a son and you will call his name Ishmael; now then, return to your mistress Sarai, and submit yourself under her hands." **35** And Hagar called the place of that well Beer-lahai-roi, it is between Kadesh and the wilderness of Bered. **36** And Hagar returned to her master's house at that time, and at the end of days Hagar bore a son to Abram, and Abram called his name Ishmael; and Abram was eighty-six years old when he begot him.

CHAPTER 17

1 And in those days, in the ninety-first year of the life of Abram, the children of Chittim made war with the children of Tubal, for when the Lord had scattered the sons of men on the face of the earth, the children of Chittim went and embodied themselves in the plain of Canopia, and they built themselves cities there and dwelt by the River Tibreu. **2** And the children of Tubal dwelt in Tuscanah, and their boundaries reached the River Tibreu, and the children of Tubal built a city in Tuscanan, and they called the name Sabinah, after the name of Sabinah son of Tubal, their father, and they dwelt there to this day. **3** And it was at that time [that] the children of Chittim made war with the children of Tubal, and the children of Tubal were smitten before the children of Chittim, and the children of Chittim caused three hundred and seventy men to fall from the children of Tubal. **4** And at that time the children of Tubal swore to the children of Chittim, saying, "You will not intermarry among us, and no man will give his daughter to any of the sons of Chittim." **5** For all the daughters of Tubal were attractive in those days, for no women were then found in the whole earth as attractive as the daughters of Tubal. **6** And all who delighted in the beauty of women went to the daughters of Tubal and took wives from them, and the sons of men, kings and princes, who greatly delighted in the beauty of women, took wives in those days from the daughters of Tubal. **7** And at the end of three years after the children of Tubal had sworn to the children of Chittim not to give them their daughters for wives, about twenty men of the children of Chittim went to take some of the daughters of Tubal, but they found none. **8** For the children of Tubal kept their oaths not to intermarry with them, and they would not break their oaths. **9** And in the days of harvest the children of Tubal went into their fields to get in their harvest, when the young men of Chittim assembled and went to the city of Sabinah, and each man took a young woman from the daughters of Tubal, and they came to their cities. **10** And the children of Tubal heard of it and they went to make war with them, and they could not prevail over them, for the mountain was exceedingly high from them, and when they saw they could not prevail over them they returned to their land. **11** And at the revolution of the year the children of Tubal went and hired about ten thousand men from those cities that were near them, and they went to war with the children of Chittim. **12** And the children of Tubal went to war with the children of Chittim, to destroy their land and to distress them, and in this engagement the children of Tubal prevailed over the children of Chittim, and the children of Chittim, seeing that they were greatly distressed, lifted up the children which they had had by the daughters of Tubal on the wall which had been built, to be before the eyes of the children of Tubal. **13** And the children of Chittim said to them, "Have you come to make war with your own sons and daughters, and have we not been considered your flesh and bones from that time until now?" **14** And when the children of Tubal heard this they ceased to make war with the children of Chittim, and they went away. **15** And they returned to their cities, and the children of Chittim assembled at that time and built two cities by the sea, and they called one Purtu and the other Ariza. **16** And Abram the son of Terah was then ninety-nine years old. **17** At that time the Lord appeared to him and He said to him, "I will make My covenant between me and you, and I will greatly multiply your seed, and this is the covenant which I make between Me and you: that every male child is circumcised—you and your seed after you. **18** At eight days old he will be circumcised, and this covenant will be in your flesh for a perpetual covenant. **19** And now therefore, your name will no longer be called Abram but Abraham, and your wife will no longer be called Sarai but Sarah. **20** For I will bless you both, and I will multiply your seed after you that you will become a great nation, and kings will come out from you."

CHAPTER 18

1 And Abraham rose and did all that God had ordered him, and he took the men of his household and those bought with his money, and he circumcised them as the Lord had commanded him. **2** And there was not one left whom he did not circumcise, and Abraham and his son Ishmael were circumcised in the flesh of their foreskin; Ishmael was thirteen years old when he was circumcised in the flesh of his foreskin. **3** And in the third day Abraham went out of his tent and sat at the door to enjoy the heat of the sun, during the pain of his flesh. **4** And the Lord appeared to him in the plain of Mamre and sent three of His ministering messengers to visit him, and he was sitting at the door of the tent, and he lifted his eyes and saw, and behold, three men were coming from a distance, and he rose up and ran to meet them, and he bowed down to them, and brought them into his house. **5** And he said to them, "If I have now found favor in your sight, turn in and eat a morsel of bread"; and he pressed them and they turned in, and he gave them water and they washed their feet, and he placed them under a tree at the door of the tent. **6** And Abraham ran and took a calf, tender and good, and he hastened to kill it, and gave it to his servant Eliezer to dress. **7** And Abraham came to Sarah in the tent, and he said to her, "Quickly make ready three measures of fine meal, knead it and make cakes to cover the pot containing the meat," and she did so. **8** And Abraham hastened and brought before them butter and milk, beef and mutton, and gave it before them to eat before the flesh of the calf was sufficiently done, and they ate. **9** And when they had finished eating, one of them said to him, "I will return to you according to the time of life, and your wife Sarah will have a son." **10** And afterward the men departed and went their ways, to the places to which they were sent. **11** In those days all the people of Sodom and Gomorrah, and of the whole five cities, were exceedingly wicked and sinful against the Lord and they provoked the Lord with their abominations, and they

strengthened in aging abominably and scornfully before the Lord, and their wickedness and crimes were great before the Lord in those days. **12** And they had a very extensive valley in their land, about half a day's walk, and in it there were fountains of water and a great deal of herbage surrounding the water. **13** And all the people of Sodom and Gomorrah went there four times in the year with their wives, and children, and all belonging to them, and they rejoiced there with timbrels and dances. **14** And in the time of rejoicing they would all rise and lay hold of their neighbor's wives, and some, the virgin daughters of their neighbors, and they enjoyed them, and each man saw his wife and daughter in the hands of his neighbor and did not say a word. **15** And they did so from morning to night, and afterward they returned home—each man to his house and each woman to her tent; so they always did four times in the year. **16** Also when a stranger came into their cities and brought goods which he had purchased with a view to dispose of there, the people of these cities would assemble, men, women, and children, young and old, and go to the man and take his goods by force, giving a little to each man until there was an end to all the goods of the owner which he had brought into the land. **17** And if the owner of the goods quarreled with them, saying, "What is this work which you have done to me?" then they would approach toward him one by one, and each would show him the little which he took and taunt him, saying, "I only took that little which you gave me"; and when he heard this from them all, he would arise and go from them in sorrow and bitterness of soul, when they would all arise and go after him, and drive him out of the city with great noise and tumult. **18** And there was a man from the country of Elam who was leisurely going on the road, seated on his donkey, which carried a fine mantle of varying colors, and the mantle was bound with a cord on the donkey. **19** And the man was on his journey passing through the street of Sodom when the sun set in the evening, and he remained there in order to abide during the night, but no one would let him into his house; and at that time there was a wicked and mischievous man in Sodom, one skillful to do evil, and his name was Hedad. **20** And he lifted up his eyes and saw the traveler in the street of the city, and he came to him and said, "From where do you come and to where do you go?" **21** And the man said to him, "I am traveling from Hebron to Elam where I belong, and as I passed, the sun set and no one would permit me to enter his house, though I had bread, and water, and also straw and provender for my donkey, and am short of nothing." **22** And Hedad answered and said to him, "All that you will want will be supplied by me, but you will not abide in the street all night." **23** And Hedad brought him to his house, and he took off the mantle from the donkey with the cord, and brought them to his house, and he gave the donkey straw and provender while the traveler ate and drank in Hedad's house, and he stayed there that night. **24** And in the morning the traveler rose up early to continue his journey, when Hedad said to him, "Wait, comfort your heart with a morsel of bread and then go," and the man did so; and he remained with him, and they both ate and drank together during the day, when the man rose up to go. **25** And Hedad said to him, "Behold, now the day is declining, you had better remain all night that your heart may be comforted"; and he pressed him so that he tarried there all night, and on the second day he rose up early to go away, when Hedad pressed him, saying, "Comfort your heart with a morsel of bread and then go," and he remained and ate with him also the second day, and then the man rose up to continue his journey. **26** And Hedad said to him, "Behold, now the day is declining, remain with me to comfort your heart and in the morning rise up early and go your way." **27** And the man would not remain, but rose and saddled his donkey, and while he was saddling his donkey the wife of Hedad said to her husband, "Behold, this man has remained with us for two days eating and drinking and he has given us nothing, and now will he go away from us without giving anything?" and Hedad said to her, "Be silent." **28** And the man saddled his donkey to go, and asked Hedad to give him the cord and mantle to tie it on the donkey. **29** And Hedad said to him, "What did you say?" And he said to him, "That you, my lord, will give me the cord and the mantle made with varying colors which you concealed with you in your house to take care of it." **30** And Hedad answered the man, saying, "This is the interpretation of your dream: the cord which you saw means that your life will be lengthened out like a cord, and having seen the mantle colored with all sorts of colors, means that you will have a vineyard in which you will plant trees of all fruits." **31** And the traveler answered, saying,

"Not so my lord, for I was awake when I gave you the cord and also a mantle woven with different colors, which you took off the donkey to put them away for me"; and Hedad answered and said, "Surely I have told you the interpretation of your dream and it is a good dream, and this is the interpretation thereof. **32** Now the sons of men give me four pieces of silver, which is my charge for interpreting dreams, and of you only I require three pieces of silver." **33** And the man was provoked at the words of Hedad, and he cried bitterly, and he brought Hedad to Serak, judge of Sodom. **34** And the man laid his cause before Serak the judge, when Hedad replied, saying, "It is not so, but thus the matter stands"; and the judge said to the traveler, "This man Hedad tells you the truth, for he is famed in the cities for the accurate interpretation of dreams." **35** And the man cried at the word of the judge, and he said, "Not so my Lord, for it was in the day that I gave him the cord and mantle which was on the donkey in order to put them away in his house"; and they both disputed before the judge, the one saying, "Thus the matter was," and the other declaring otherwise. **36** And Hedad said to the man, "Give me four pieces of silver that I charge for my interpretations of dreams; I will not make any allowance; and give me the expense of the four meals that you ate in my house." **37** And the man said to Hedad, "Truly I will pay you for what I ate in your house, only give me the cord and mantle which you concealed in your house." **38** And Hedad replied before the judge and said to the man, "Did I not tell you the interpretation of your dream? The cord means that your days will be prolonged like a cord, and the mantle, that you will have a vineyard in which you will plant all kinds of fruit trees. **39** This is the proper interpretation of your dream—now give me the four pieces of silver that I require as a compensation, for I will make you no allowance." **40** And the man cried at the words of Hedad and they both quarreled before the judge, and the judge gave orders to his servants, who drove them rashly from the house. **41** And they went away quarreling from the judge, when the people of Sodom heard them, and they gathered around them and they exclaimed against the stranger, and they drove him rashly from the city. **42** And the man continued his journey on his donkey with bitterness of soul, lamenting and weeping. **43** And while he was going along, he wept at what had happened to him in the corrupt city of Sodom.

CHAPTER 19

1 And the cities of Sodom had four judges for [the] four cities, and these were their names: Serak in the city of Sodom, Sharkad in Gomorrah, Zabnac in Admah, and Menon in Zeboyim. **2** And Abraham's servant Eliezer applied different names to them, and he converted Serak to Shakra, Sharkad to Shakrura, Zebnac to Kezobim, and Menon to Matzlodin. **3** And by desire of their four judges the people of Sodom and Gomorrah had beds erected in the streets of the cities, and if a man came to these places, they laid hold of him and brought him to one of their beds, and by force made him to lie in them. **4** And as he lay down, three men would stand at his head and three at his feet, and measure him by the length of the bed, and if the man was less than the bed these six men would stretch him at each end, and when he cried out to them, they would not answer him. **5** And if he was longer than the bed, they would draw together the two sides of the bed at each end, until the man had reached the gates of death. **6** And if he continued to cry out to them, they would answer him, saying, "Thus it will be done to a man that comes into our land." **7** And when men heard all these things that the people of the cities of Sodom did, they refrained from coming there. **8** And when a poor man came to their land, they would give him silver and gold, and cause a proclamation in the whole city not to give him a morsel of bread to eat, and if the stranger should remain there some days and die from hunger, not having been able to obtain a morsel of bread, then at his death all the people of the city would come and take their silver and gold which they had given to him. **9** And those that could recognize the silver or gold which they had given him took it back, and at his death they also stripped him of his garments, and they would fight about them, and he that prevailed over his neighbor took them. **10** After that they would carry him and bury him under some of the shrubs in the deserts; so they did all the days to anyone that came to them and died in their land. **11** And in the course of time Sarah sent Eliezer to Sodom to see Lot and inquire after his welfare. **12** And Eliezer went to Sodom, and he met a man

of Sodom fighting with a stranger, and the man of Sodom stripped the poor man of all his clothes and went away. **13** And this poor man cried to Eliezer and supplicated his favor on account of what the man of Sodom had done to him. **14** And he said to him, "Why do you act thus to the poor man who came to your land?" **15** And the man of Sodom answered Eliezer, saying, "Is this man your brother, or have the people of Sodom made you a judge this day, that you speak about this man?" **16** And Eliezer strove with the man of Sodom on account of the poor man, and when Eliezer approached to recover the poor man's clothes from the man of Sodom, he hastened and with a stone struck Eliezer in the forehead. **17** And the blood flowed copiously from Eliezer's forehead, and when the man saw the blood he caught hold of Eliezer, saying, "Give me my hire for having rid you of this bad blood that was in your forehead, for such is the custom and the law in our land." **18** And Eliezer said to him, "You have wounded me and require me to pay you your hire?" And Eliezer would not listen to the words of the man of Sodom. **19** And the man laid hold of Eliezer and brought him to Shakra the judge of Sodom for judgment. **20** And the man spoke to the judge, saying, "I implore you my lord, thus this man has done, for I struck him with a stone that the blood flowed from his forehead, and he is unwilling to give me my hire." **21** And the judge said to Eliezer, "This man speaks truth to you, give him his hire, for this is the custom in our land"; and Eliezer heard the words of the judge, and he lifted up a stone and struck the judge, and the stone struck on his forehead, and the blood flowed copiously from the forehead of the judge, and Eliezer said, "If this then is the custom in your land, [then] you give to this man what I should have given him, for this has been your decision—you decreed it." **22** And Eliezer left the man of Sodom with the judge, and he went away. **23** And when the kings of Elam had made war with the kings of Sodom, the kings of Elam captured all the property of Sodom, and they took Lot captive, with his property, and when it was told to Abraham he went and made war with the kings of Elam, and he recovered from their hands all the property of Lot as well as the property of Sodom. **24** At that time the wife of Lot bore him a daughter, and he called her name Paltith, saying, "Because God had delivered him and his whole household from the kings of Elam"; and Paltith daughter of Lot grew up, and one of the men of Sodom took her for a wife. **25** And a poor man came into the city to seek a maintenance, and he remained in the city some days, and all the people of Sodom caused a proclamation of their custom not to give this man a morsel of bread to eat until he dropped dead on the earth, and they did so. **26** And Paltith the daughter of Lot saw this man lying in the streets starved with hunger, and no one would give him anything to keep him alive, and he was just on the point of death. **27** And her soul was filled with pity on account of the man, and she fed him secretly with bread for many days, and the soul of this man was revived. **28** For when she went out to fetch water, she would put the bread in the water pitcher, and when she came to the place where the poor man was, she took the bread from the pitcher and gave it to him to eat; so she did [for] many days. **29** And all the people of Sodom and Gomorrah wondered how this man could bear starvation for so many days. **30** And they said to each other, "This can only be that he eats and drinks, for no man can bear starvation for so many days or live as this man has without even his countenance changing"; and three men concealed themselves in a place where the poor man was stationed to know who it was that brought him bread to eat. **31** And Paltith daughter of Lot went out that day to fetch water, and she put bread into her pitcher of water, and she went to draw water by the poor man's place, and she took out the bread from the pitcher and gave it to the poor man and he ate it. **32** And the three men saw what Paltith did to the poor man, and they said to her, "It is you then who have supported him, and therefore he has not starved, nor changed in appearance, nor died like the rest." **33** And the three men went out of the place in which they were concealed, and they seized Paltith and the bread which was in the poor man's hand. **34** And they took Paltith and brought her before their judges, and they said to them, "Thus did she do, and it is she who supplied the poor man with bread, therefore he did not die all this time; now therefore, declare to us the punishment due to this woman for having transgressed our law." **35** And the people of Sodom and Gomorrah assembled and kindled a fire in the street of the city, and they took the woman and cast her into the fire and she was burned to ashes. **36** And in the city of Admah there was a woman to whom they did the like. **37** For a traveler came into the city of Admah to abide there all night with the intention of going home in the morning, and he sat opposite the door of the house of the young woman's father to remain there, as the sun had set when he had reached that place; and the young woman saw him sitting by the door of the house. **38** And he asked her for a drink of water, and she said to him, "Who are you?" And he said to her, "I was going on the road this day, and reached here when the sun set, so I will abide here all night, and in the morning I will arise early and continue my journey." **39** And the young woman went into the house and fetched the man bread and water to eat and drink. **40** And this affair became known to the people of Admah, and they assembled and brought the young woman before the judges that they should judge her for this act. **41** And the judge said, "The judgment of death must pass on this woman because she transgressed our law, and therefore this is the decision concerning her." **42** And the people of those cities assembled and brought out the young woman, and anointed her with honey from head to foot, as the judge had decreed, and they placed her before a swarm of bees which were then in their hives, and the bees flew on her and stung her that her whole body was swelled. **43** And the young woman cried out on account of the bees, but no one took notice of her or pitied her, and her cries ascended to Heaven. **44** And the Lord was provoked at this and at all the works of the cities of Sodom, for they had abundance of food, and had tranquility among them, and still would not sustain the poor and the needy, and in those days their evil doings and sins became great before the Lord. **45** And the Lord sent for two of the messengers that had come to Abraham's house to destroy Sodom and its cities. **46** And the messengers rose up from the door of Abraham's tent after they had eaten and drunk, and they reached Sodom in the evening, and Lot was then sitting in the gate of Sodom, and when he saw them, he rose to meet them, and he bowed down to the ground. **47** And he pressed them greatly and brought them into his house, and he gave them victuals which they ate, and they stayed all night in his house. **48** And the messengers said to Lot, "Arise, go out from this place, you and all belonging to you, lest you be consumed in the iniquity of this city, for the Lord will destroy this place." **49** And the messengers laid hold on the hand of Lot, and on the hand of his wife, and on the hands of his children, and all belonging to him, and they brought him out and set him outside the cities. **50** And they said to Lot, "Escape for your life," and he fled and all belonging to him. **51** Then the Lord rained on Sodom, and on Gomorrah, and on all these cities brimstone and fire from the Lord out of Heaven. **52** And he overthrew these cities, all the plain, and all the inhabitants of the cities, and that which grew on the ground; and Ado the wife of Lot looked back to see the destruction of the cities, for her compassion was moved on account of her daughters who remained in Sodom, for they did not go with her. **53** And when she looked back, she became a pillar of salt, and it is yet in that place to this day. **54** And the oxen which stood in that place daily licked up the salt to the extremities of their feet, and in the morning it would spring out afresh, and they again licked it up to this day. **55** And Lot and two of his daughters that remained with him fled and escaped to the cave of Adullam, and they remained there for some time. **56** And Abraham rose up early in the morning to see what had been done to the cities of Sodom; and he looked and beheld the smoke of the cities going up like the smoke of a furnace. **57** And Lot and his two daughters remained in the cave, and they made their father drink wine, and they lay with him, for they said there was no man on earth that could raise up seed from them, for they thought that the whole earth was destroyed. **58** And they both lay with their father, and they conceived and bore sons, and the firstborn called the name of her son Moab, saying, "From my father I conceived him"; he is the father of the Moabites to this day. **59** And the younger also called her son Benami; he is the father of the children of Ammon to this day. **60** And after this, Lot and his two daughters went away from there, and he dwelt on the other side of the Jordan with his two daughters and their sons, and the sons of Lot grew up, and they went and took wives [for] themselves from the land of Canaan, and they begot children, and they were fruitful and multiplied.

CHAPTER 20

1 And at that time Abraham journeyed from the plain of Mamre, and he went to the land of the Philistines, and he dwelt in Gerar; it was in the twenty-fifth year of Abraham's being in the land of Canaan, and the one hundredth year of the life of Abraham, that he came to Gerar in the land of the Philistines. **2** And when they entered the land he said to his wife Sarah, "Say you are my sister to anyone that will ask you in order that we may escape the evil of the inhabitants of the land." **3** And as Abraham was dwelling in the land of the Philistines, the servants of Abimelech, king of the Philistines, saw that Sarah was exceedingly beautiful, and they asked Abraham concerning her, and he said, "She is my sister." **4** And the servants of Abimelech went to Abimelech, saying, "A man from the land of Canaan has come to dwell in the land, and he has a sister that is exceedingly attractive." **5** And Abimelech heard the words of his servants who praised Sarah to him, and Abimelech sent his officers, and they brought Sarah to the king. **6** And Sarah came to the house of Abimelech, and the king saw that Sarah was beautiful, and she pleased him exceedingly. **7** And he approached her and said to her, "What is that man to you with whom you came to our land?" And Sarah answered and said, "He is my brother, and we came from the land of Canaan to dwell wherever we could find a place." **8** And Abimelech said to Sarah, "Behold, my land is before you: place your brother in any part of this land that pleases you, and it will be our duty to exalt and elevate him above all the people of the land since he is your brother." **9** And Abimelech sent for Abraham, and Abraham came to Abimelech. **10** And Abimelech said to Abraham, "Behold, I have given orders that you will be honored as you desire on account of your sister Sarah." **11** And Abraham went out from the king, and the king's present followed him. **12** As at evening time, before men lie down to rest, the king was sitting on his throne, and a deep sleep fell on him, and he lay on the throne and slept until morning. **13** And he dreamed that a messenger of the Lord came to him with a drawn sword in his hand, and the messenger stood over Abimelech and wished to slay him with the sword, and the king was terrified in his dream, and said to the messenger, "In what have I sinned against you that you come to slay me with your sword?" **14** And the messenger answered and said to Abimelech, "Behold, you die on account of the woman which you brought to your house last night, for she is a married woman, the wife of Abraham who came to your house; now therefore, return that man his wife, for she is his wife; and should you not return her, know that you will surely die—you and all belonging to you." **15** And on that night there was a great outcry in the land of the Philistines, and the inhabitants of the land saw the figure of a man standing with a drawn sword in his hand, and he struck the inhabitants of the land with the sword, yes, he continued to strike them. **16** And the messenger of the Lord struck the whole land of the Philistines on that night, and there was a great confusion on that night and on the following morning. **17** And every womb was closed, and all their issues, and the hand of the Lord was on them on account of Sarah, wife of Abraham, whom Abimelech had taken. **18** And in the morning Abimelech rose with terror, and confusion, and with a great dread, and he sent and had his servants called in, and he related his dream to them, and the people were greatly afraid. **19** And one man standing among the servants of the king answered the king, saying, "O sovereign king, restore this woman to her husband, for he is her husband, for the like happened to the king of Egypt when this man came to Egypt. **20** And he said concerning his wife, She is my sister, for such is his manner of doing when he comes to dwell in the land in which he is a stranger. **21** And Pharaoh sent and took this woman for a wife and the Lord brought grievous plagues on him until he returned the woman to her husband. **22** Now therefore, O sovereign king, know what happened last night to the whole land, for there was a very great consternation, and great pain, and lamentation, and we know that it was on account of the woman which you took. **23** Now, therefore, restore this woman to her husband, lest it should befall us as it did to Pharaoh king of Egypt and his subjects, and that we may not die"; and Abimelech hastened, and called, and had Sarah called for, and she came before him, and he had Abraham called for, and he came before him. **24** And Abimelech said to them, "What is this work you have been doing in saying you are brother and sister, and I took this woman for a wife?" **25** And Abraham said, "Because I thought I should suffer death on account of my wife"; and Abimelech took flocks, and herds, and menservants, and maidservants, and one thousand pieces of silver, and he gave them to Abraham, and he returned Sarah to him. **26** And Abimelech said to Abraham, "Behold, the whole land is before you, dwell in it wherever you will choose." **27** And Abraham and his wife Sarah went out from the king's presence with honor and respect, and they dwelt in the land, even in Gerar. **20** And all the inhabitants of the land of the Philistines and the king's servants were still in pain through the plague which the messenger had inflicted on them the whole night on account of Sarah. **29** And Abimelech sent for Abraham, saying, "Now pray to the Lord your God for your servants, that He may put away this mortality from among us." **30** And Abraham prayed on account of Abimelech and his subjects, and the Lord heard the prayer of Abraham, and He healed Abimelech and all his subjects.

CHAPTER 21

1 And it was at that time, at the end of a year and four months of Abraham's dwelling in the land of the Philistines in Gerar, that God visited Sarah, and the Lord remembered her, and she conceived and bore a son to Abraham. **2** And Abraham called the name of the son which was born to him, which Sarah bore to him, Isaac. **3** And Abraham circumcised his son Isaac at eight days old as God had commanded Abraham to do to his seed after him; and Abraham was one hundred, and Sarah ninety years old, when Isaac was born to them. **4** And the child grew up and he was weaned, and Abraham made a great feast on the day that Isaac was weaned. **5** And Shem, and Eber, and all the great people of the land, and Abimelech king of the Philistines, and his servants, and Phicol, the captain of his host, came to eat, and drink, and rejoice at the feast which Abraham made on the day of his son Isaac's being weaned. **6** Also Terah, the father of Abraham, and Nahor his brother, came from Haran, they and all belonging to them, for they greatly rejoiced on hearing that a son had been born to Sarah. **7** And they came to Abraham, and they ate and drank at the feast which Abraham made on the day of Isaac's being weaned. **8** And Terah and Nahor rejoiced with Abraham, and they remained with him many days in the land of the Philistines. **9** At that time Serug the son of Reu died, in the first year of the birth of Isaac son of Abraham. **10** And all the days of Serug were two hundred and thirty-nine years, and he died. **11** And Ishmael the son of Abraham had grown up in those days; he was fourteen years old when Sarah bore Isaac to Abraham. **12** And God was with Ishmael the son of Abraham, and he grew up, and he learned to use the bow and became an archer. **13** And when Isaac was five years old, he was sitting with Ishmael at the door of the tent. **14** And Ishmael came to Isaac and seated himself opposite to him, and he took the bow, and drew it, and put the arrow in it, and intended to slay Isaac. **15** And Sarah saw the act which Ishmael desired to do to her son Isaac, and it grieved her exceedingly on account of her son, and she sent for Abraham, and said to him, "Cast out this bondwoman and her son, for her son will not be heir with my son, for thus he sought to do to him this day." **16** And Abraham listened to the voice of Sarah, and he rose up early in the morning, and he took twelve loaves and a bottle of water which he gave to Hagar, and sent her away with her son, and Hagar went with her son to the wilderness, and they dwelt in the wilderness of Paran with the inhabitants of the wilderness, and Ishmael was an archer, and he dwelt in the wilderness a long time. **17** And afterward he and his mother went to the land of Egypt, and they dwelt there, and Hagar took a wife for her son from Egypt, and her name was Meribah. **18** And the wife of Ishmael conceived and bore four sons and two daughters, and afterward Ishmael, and his mother, and his wife and children went and returned to the wilderness. **19** And they made themselves tents in the wilderness, in which they dwelt, and they continued to travel and then to rest monthly and yearly. **20** And God gave Ishmael flocks, and herds, and tents on account of his father Abraham, and the man increased in cattle. **21** And Ishmael dwelt in deserts and in tents, traveling and resting for a long time, and he did not see the face of his father. **22** And some time after, Abraham said to his wife Sarah, "I will go and see my son Ishmael, for I have a desire to see him, for I have not seen him for a long time." **23** And Abraham rode on one of his camels to the wilderness to seek his son Ishmael, for he heard that he was dwelling in a tent in the wilderness with all belonging to him. **24** And Abraham went to the wilderness, and he reached the tent of Ishmael about noon, and he asked after Ishmael, and he found the wife of Ishmael sitting in the tent with her children, and her husband Ishmael and his mother were not with them. **25** And Abraham asked the wife of Ishmael, saying, "Where has Ishmael gone?" And she said, "He has gone to the field to hunt," and Abraham was still mounted on the camel,

for he would not get off to the ground as he had sworn to his wife Sarah that he would not get off from the camel. **26** And Abraham said to Ishmael's wife, "My daughter, give me a little water that I may drink, for I am fatigued from the journey." **27** And Ishmael's wife answered and said to Abraham, "We have neither water nor bread," and she continued sitting in the tent and did not notice Abraham, neither did she ask him who he was. **28** But she was beating her children in the tent, and she was cursing them, and she also cursed her husband Ishmael and reproached him, and Abraham heard the words of Ishmael's wife to her children, and he was very angry and displeased. **29** And Abraham called to the woman to come out to him from the tent, and the woman came and stood opposite to Abraham, for Abraham was still mounted on the camel. **30** And Abraham said to Ishmael's wife, "When your husband Ishmael returns home say to him that a very old man from the land of the Philistines came here to seek you, and thus was his appearance and figure; **31** I did not ask him who he was, and seeing you were not here he spoke to me and said, When your husband Ishmael returns, tell him thus this man said, When you come home, put away this nail of the tent which you have placed here, and place another nail in its stead." **32** And Abraham finished his instructions to the woman, and he turned and went off on the camel homeward. **33** And after that, Ishmael came from the chase—he and his mother—and returned to the tent, and his wife spoke these words to him, **34** "A very old man from the land of the Philistines came to seek you, and thus was his appearance and figure; I did not ask him who he was, and seeing you were not at home he said to me, When your husband comes home tell him, thus says the old man, Put away the nail of the tent which you have placed here and place another nail in its stead." **35** And Ishmael heard the words of his wife, and he knew that it was his father, and that his wife did not honor him. **36** And Ishmael understood his father's words that he had spoken to his wife, and Ishmael listened to the voice of his father, and Ishmael cast off that woman and she went away. **37** And afterward Ishmael went to the land of Canaan, and he took another wife, and he brought her to his tent to the place where he then dwelt. **38** And at the end of three years Abraham said, "I will again go and see my son Ishmael, for I have not seen him for a long time." **39** And he rode on his camel, and went to the wilderness, and he reached the tent of Ishmael about noon. **40** And he asked after Ishmael, and his wife came out of the tent and she said, "He is not here my lord, for he has gone to hunt in the fields, and to feed the camels," and the woman said to Abraham, "Turn in, my lord, into the tent, and eat a morsel of bread, for your soul must be wearied on account of the journey." **41** And Abraham said to her, "I will not stop for I am in haste to continue my journey, but give me a little water to drink, for I have thirst"; and the woman hastened, and ran into the tent, and she brought out water and bread to Abraham, which she placed before him and she urged him to eat, and he ate and drank, and his heart was comforted, and he blessed his son Ishmael. **42** And he finished his meal, and he blessed the Lord, and he said to Ishmael's wife, "When Ishmael comes home say these words to him: **43** A very old man from the land of the Philistines came here and asked after you, and you were not here; and I brought him out bread and water, and he ate and drank, and his heart was comforted. **44** And he spoke these words to me: When your husband Ishmael comes home, say to him, The nail of the tent which you have is very good, do not put it away from the tent." **45** And Abraham finished commanding the woman, and he rode off to his home, to the land of the Philistines; and when Ishmael came to his tent his wife went out to meet him with joy and a cheerful heart. **46** And she said to him, "An old man came here from the land of the Philistines and thus was his appearance, and he asked after you and you were not here, so I brought out bread and water, and he ate and drank, and his heart was comforted. **47** And he spoke these words to me: When your husband Ishmael comes home, say to him, The nail of the tent which you have is very good, do not put it away from the tent." **48** And Ishmael knew that it was his father, and that his wife had honored him, and the Lord blessed Ishmael.

CHAPTER 22

1 And Ishmael then rose up and took his wife, and his children, and his cattle, and all belonging to him, and he journeyed from there and he went to his father in the land of the Philistines. **2** And Abraham related to his son Ishmael the transaction with the first wife that Ishmael took, according to what she did. **3** And Ishmael and his children dwelt with Abraham many days in that land, and Abraham dwelt in the land of the Philistines a long time. **4** And the days increased and reached twenty six years, and after that, Abraham with his servants and all belonging to him went from the land of the Philistines and removed to a great distance, and they came near to Hebron, and they remained there, and the servants of Abraham dug wells of water, and Abraham and all belonging to him dwelt by the water, and the servants of Abimelech king of the Philistines heard the report that Abraham's servants had dug wells of water in the borders of the land. **5** And they came and quarreled with the servants of Abraham, and they robbed them of the great well which they had dug. **6** And Abimelech king of the Philistines heard of this affair, and he with Phicol the captain of his host and twenty of his men came to Abraham, and Abimelech spoke to Abraham concerning his servants, and Abraham rebuked Abimelech concerning the well of which his servants had robbed him. **7** And Abimelech said to Abraham, "As the Lord lives who created the whole earth, I did not hear of the act which my servants did to your servants until this day." **8** And Abraham took seven ewe lambs and gave them to Abimelech, saying, "Please take these from my hands that it may be a testimony for me that I dug this well." **9** And Abimelech took the seven ewe lambs which Abraham had given to him, for he had also given him cattle and herds in abundance, and Abimelech swore to Abraham concerning the well, therefore he called that well Beersheba, for there they both swore concerning it. **10** And they both made a covenant in Beersheba, and Abimelech rose up with Phicol the captain of his host and all his men, and they returned to the land of the Philistines, and Abraham and all belonging to him dwelt in Beersheba, and he was in that land a long time. **11** And Abraham planted a large grove in Beersheba, and he made four gates to it facing the four sides of the earth, and he planted a vineyard in it, so that if a traveler came to Abraham, he entered any gate which was in his road and remained there, and ate, and drank, and satisfied himself, and then departed. **12** For the house of Abraham was always open to the sons of men that passed and repassed, who came daily to eat and drink in the house of Abraham. **13** And any man who had hunger and came to Abraham's house, Abraham would give him bread that he might eat, and drink, and be satisfied, and anyone that came naked to his house he would clothe with garments as he might choose, and give him silver and gold, and make known to him the Lord who had created him in the earth; Abraham did this all his life. **14** And Abraham, and his children, and all belonging to him dwelt in Beersheba, and he pitched his tent as far as Hebron. **15** And Abraham's brother Nahor, and his father, and all belonging to them dwelt in Haran, for they did not come with Abraham to the land of Canaan. **16** And children were born to Nahor which Milca the daughter of Haran, and sister to Sarah, Abraham's wife, bore to him. **17** And these are the names of those that were born to him: Uz, Buz, Kemuel, Kesed, Chazo, Pildash, Tidlaf, and Bethuel, being eight sons, these are the children of Milca which she bore to Nahor, Abraham's brother. **18** And Nahor had a concubine, and her name was Reumah, and she also bore to Nahor: Zebach, Gachash, Tachash, and Maacha, being four sons. **19** And the children that were born to Nahor were twelve sons besides his daughters, and they also had children born to them in Haran. **20** And the children of Uz the firstborn of Nahor were Abi, Cheref, Gadin, Melus, and their sister Deborah. **21** And the sons of Buz were Berachel, Naamath, Sheva, and Madonu. **22** And the sons of Kemuel were Aram and Rechob. **23** And the sons of Kesed were Anamlech, Meshai, Benon, and Yifi. And the sons of Chazo were Pildash, Mechi, and Opher. **24** And the sons of Pildash were Arud, Chamum, Mered, and Moloch. **25** And the sons of Tidlaf were Mushan, Cushan, and Mutzi. **26** And the children of Bethuel were Sechar, Laban, and their sister Rebekah. **27** These are the families of the children of Nahor that were born to them in Haran; and Aram the son of Kemuel and his brother Rechob went away from Haran, and they found a valley in the land by the River Euphrates. **28** And they built a city there, and they called the name of the city after the name of Pethor the son of Aram, that is Aram Naharayim to this day. **29** And the children of Kesed also went to dwell where they could find a place, and they went and they found a valley opposite to the land of Shinar, and they dwelt there. **30** And they built themselves a city there, and they called the name of the city Kesed after the name of their father, that is the land Kasdim to this day, and

the Kasdim dwelt in that land, and they were fruitful and multiplied exceedingly. **31** And Terah, father of Nahor and Abraham, went and took another wife in his old age, and her name was Pelilah, and she conceived and bore him a son, and he called his name Zoba. **32** And Terah lived twenty-five years after he begot Zoba. **33** And Terah died in that year, that is in the thirty-fifth year of the birth of Isaac son of Abraham. **34** And the days of Terah were two hundred and five years, and he was buried in Haran. **35** And Zoba the son of Terah lived thirty years and he begot Aram, Achlis, and Merik. **36** And Aram son of Zoba, son of Terah, had three wives and he begot twelve sons and three daughters; and the Lord gave riches and possessions, and abundance of cattle, and flocks, and herds to Aram the son of Zoba, and the man increased greatly. **37** And Aram the son of Zoba, and his brother, and all his household journeyed from Haran, and they went to dwell where they should find a place, for their property was too great to remain in Haran; for they could not stop in Haran together with their brothers, the children of Nahor. **38** And Aram the son of Zoba went with his brothers, and they found a valley at a distance toward the eastern country, and they dwelt there. **39** And they also built a city there, and they called the name thereof Aram, after the name of their eldest brother; that is Aram Zoba to this day. **40** And Isaac the son of Abraham was growing up in those days, and his father Abraham taught him the way of the Lord to know the Lord, and the Lord was with him. **41** And when Isaac was thirty-seven years old, his brother Ishmael was going around with him in the tent. **42** And Ishmael boasted of himself to Isaac, saying, "I was thirteen years old when the Lord spoke to my father to circumcise us, and I did according to the word of the Lord which He spoke to my father, and I gave my soul to the Lord, and I did not transgress His word which He commanded my father." **43** And Isaac answered Ishmael, saying, "Why do you boast to me about this, about a little bit of your flesh which you took from your body, concerning which the Lord commanded you? **44** As the Lord lives, the God of my father Abraham, if the Lord should say to my father, Now take your son Isaac and bring him up [as] an offering before Me, I would not refrain but I would joyfully accede to it." **45** And the Lord heard the word that Isaac spoke to Ishmael, and it seemed good in the sight of the Lord, and he thought to try Abraham in this matter. **46** And the day arrived when the sons of God came and placed themselves before the Lord, and Satan also came with the sons of God before the Lord. **47** And the Lord said to Satan, "From where do you come?" And Satan answered the Lord and said, "From going to and fro in the earth, and from walking up and down in it." **48** And the Lord said to Satan, "What is your word to Me concerning all the children of the earth?" And Satan answered the Lord and said, "I have seen all the children of the earth who serve You and remember You when they require anything from You. **49** And when You give them the thing which they require from You, they sit at their ease, and forsake You, and they no longer remember You. **50** Have You seen Abraham the son of Terah, who at first had no children, and he served You and erected altars to You wherever he came, and he brought up offerings on them, and he proclaimed Your Name continually to all the children of the earth? **51** And now that his son Isaac is born to him, he has forsaken You; he has made a great feast for all the inhabitants of the land, and he has forgotten the Lord. **52** For amidst all that he has done, he brought You no offering; neither burnt-offering nor peace offering, neither ox, lamb, nor goat of all that he killed on the day that his son was weaned. **53** Even from the time of his son's birth until now, being thirty-seven years, he built no altar before You, nor brought any offering to You, for he saw that You gave what he requested before You, and therefore he forsook You." **54** And the Lord said to Satan, "Have you thus considered My servant Abraham? For there is none like him on earth, a perfect and an upright man before Me, one that fears God and avoids evil; as I live, were I to say to him, Bring up your son Isaac before Me, he would not withhold him from Me, much more if I told him to bring up a burnt-offering before Me from his flock or herds." **55** And Satan answered the Lord and said, "Then speak to Abraham now as You have said, and you will see whether he will not transgress and cast aside Your words this day."

CHAPTER 23

1 At that time the word of the Lord came to Abraham, and He said to him, "Abraham," and he said, "Here I am." **2** And He said to him, "Now take your son, your only son, whom you love, even Isaac, and go to the land of Moriah, and offer him there for a burnt-offering on one of the mountains which will be shown to you, for there you will see a cloud and the glory of the Lord." **3** And Abraham said within himself, "How will I separate my son Isaac from his mother Sarah in order to bring him up for a burnt-offering before the Lord?" **4** And Abraham came into the tent, and he sat before his wife Sarah, and he spoke these words to her, **5** "My son Isaac has grown up and he has not for some time studied the service of his God; now tomorrow I will go and bring him to Shem and his son Eber, and there he will learn the ways of the Lord, for they will teach him to know the Lord as well as to know that when he prays continually before the Lord, He will answer him; therefore there he will know the way of serving the Lord his God." **6** And Sarah said, "You have spoken well. Go, my lord, and do to him as you have said, but do not remove him at a great distance from me, neither let him remain there too long, for my soul is bound within his soul." **7** And Abraham said to Sarah, "My daughter, let us pray to the Lord our God that He may do good with us." **8** And Sarah took her son Isaac and he remained all that night with her, and she kissed and embraced him, and gave him instructions until morning. **9** And she said to him, "O my son, how can my soul separate itself from you?" And she still kissed him and embraced him, and she gave Abraham instructions concerning him. **10** And Sarah said to Abraham, "O my lord, please take heed of your son, and place your eyes over him, for I have no other son nor daughter but him. **11** O do not forsake him. If he is hungry, give him bread, and if he is thirsty, give him water to drink; do not let him go on foot, neither let him sit in the sun. **12** Neither let him go by himself in the road, neither force him from whatever he may desire, but do to him as he may say to you." **13** And Sarah wept bitterly the whole night on account of Isaac, and she gave him instructions until morning. **14** And in the morning Sarah selected a very fine and beautiful garment from those garments which she had in the house, that Abimelech had given to her. **15** And she dressed her son Isaac with that, and she put a turban on his head, and she enclosed a precious stone in the top of the turban, and she gave them provision for the road, and they went out, and Isaac went with his father Abraham, and some of their servants accompanied them to see them off the road. **16** And Sarah went out with them, and she accompanied them on the road to see them off, and they said to her, "Return to the tent." **17** And when Sarah heard the words of her son Isaac, she wept bitterly, and her husband Abraham wept with her, and their son wept with them a great weeping; also those who went with them wept greatly. **18** And Sarah caught hold of her son Isaac, and she held him in her arms, and she embraced him, and continued to weep with him, and Sarah said, "Who knows if after this day I will ever see you again?" **19** And they still wept together—Abraham, Sarah, and Isaac, and all those that accompanied them on the road wept with them, and afterward Sarah turned away from her son, weeping bitterly, and all her menservants and maidservants returned with her to the tent. **20** And Abraham went with his son Isaac to bring him up as an offering before the Lord as He had commanded him. **21** And Abraham took two of his young men with him, Ishmael the son of Hagar and his servant Eliezer, and they went together with them, and while they were walking in the road the young men spoke these words to themselves, **22** and Ishmael said to Eliezer, "Now my father Abraham is going with Isaac to bring him up for a burnt-offering to the Lord, as He commanded him. **23** Now when he returns he will give all that he possesses to me, to inherit after him, for I am his firstborn." **24** And Eliezer answered Ishmael and said, "Surely Abraham cast you away with your mother and swore that you should not inherit anything of all he possesses, and to whom will he give all that he has, with all his treasures, but to me his servant, who has been faithful in his house, who has served him night and day, and has done all that he desired me? To me he will bequeath at his death all that he possesses." **25** And while Abraham was proceeding with his son Isaac along the road, Satan came and appeared to Abraham in the figure of a very aged man, humble and of contrite spirit, and he approached Abraham and said to him, "Are you silly or brutish that you go this day to do this thing to your only son? **26** For God gave you a son in your latter days, in your old age, and will you go and slaughter him this day because he committed no violence, and will you cause the soul of your only son to perish from the earth? **27** Do you not know and understand that this thing cannot be from the Lord? For the Lord cannot do to man such evil on earth to say to him,

Go slaughter your child." **28** And Abraham heard this and knew that it was the word of Satan who endeavored to draw him aside from the way of the Lord, but Abraham would not listen to the voice of Satan, and Abraham rebuked him so that he went away. **29** And Satan returned and came to Isaac; and he appeared to Isaac in the figure of a young man, handsome and well-favored. **30** And he approached Isaac and said to him, "Do you not know and understand that your old silly father brings you to the slaughter this day for no reason? **31** Now therefore, my son, do not listen nor attend to him, for he is a silly old man, and do not let your precious soul and beautiful figure be lost from the earth." **32** And Isaac heard this, and said to Abraham, "Have you heard, my father, that which this man has spoken? Even thus he has spoken." **33** And Abraham answered his son Isaac and said to him, "Take heed of him and do not listen to his words, nor attend to him, for he is Satan, endeavoring to draw us aside from the commands of God this day." **34** And Abraham still rebuked Satan, and Satan went from them, and seeing he could not prevail over them, he hid himself from them, and he went and passed before them in the road; and he transformed himself into a large brook of water in the road, and Abraham, and Isaac, and his two young men reached that place, and they saw a brook [as] large and powerful as the mighty waters. **35** And they entered the brook and passed through it, and the waters at first reached their legs. **36** And they went deeper in the brook and the waters reached up to their necks, and they were all terrified on account of the water; and while they were going over the brook, Abraham recognized that place, and he knew that there was no water there before. **37** And Abraham said to his son Isaac, "I know this place in which there was no brook nor water, now therefore, it is this Satan who does all this to us, to draw us aside from the commands of God this day." **38** And Abraham rebuked him and said to him, "The Lord rebuke you, O Satan! Go away from us, for we go by the commands of God." **39** And Satan was terrified at the voice of Abraham, and he went away from them, and the place again became dry land as it was at first. **40** And Abraham went with Isaac toward the place that God had told him. **41** And on the third day Abraham lifted up his eyes and saw the place at a distance which God had told him of. **42** And a pillar of fire appeared to him that reached from the earth to the heavens, and a cloud of glory on the mountain, and the glory of the Lord was seen in the cloud. **43** And Abraham said to Isaac, "My son, do you see in that mountain, which we perceive at a distance, that which I see on it?" **44** And Isaac answered and said to his father, "I see, and behold, a pillar of fire and a cloud, and the glory of the Lord is seen on the cloud." **45** And Abraham knew that his son Isaac was accepted before the Lord for a burnt-offering. **46** And Abraham said to Eliezer and to his son Ishmael, "Do you also see that which we see on the mountain which is at a distance?" **47** And they answered and said, "We see nothing more than [that] like the other mountains of the earth." And Abraham knew that they were not accepted before the Lord to go with them, and Abraham said to them, "Abide here with the donkey while my son Isaac and I will go to that mount, and worship there before the Lord, and then return to you." **48** And Eliezer and Ishmael remained in that place as Abraham had commanded. **49** And Abraham took wood for a burnt-offering and placed it on his son Isaac, and he took the fire and the knife, and they both went to that place. **50** And when they were going along Isaac said to his father, "Behold, I see the fire and wood here, and where then is the lamb that is to be the burnt-offering before the Lord?" **51** And Abraham answered his son Isaac, saying, "The Lord has made choice of you, my son, to be a perfect burnt-offering instead of the lamb." **52** And Isaac said to his father, "I will do all that the Lord spoke to you with joy and cheerfulness of heart." **53** And Abraham again said to his son Isaac, "Is there any thought or counsel in your heart concerning this, which is not proper? Please tell me, my son; O my son do not conceal it from me." **54** And Isaac answered his father Abraham and said to him, "O my father, as the Lord lives and as your soul lives, there is nothing in my heart to cause me to deviate either to the right or to the left from the word that He has spoken to you. **55** Neither limb nor muscle has moved or stirred at this, nor is there any thought or evil counsel in my heart concerning this. **56** But I am of joyful and cheerful heart in this matter, and I say, Blessed is the Lord who has chosen me to be a burnt-offering before Him this day." **57** And Abraham greatly rejoiced at the words of Isaac, and they went on and came together to that place that the Lord had spoken of. **58** And Abraham approached to build the altar in that place, and Abraham was weeping, and Isaac took stones and mortar until they had finished building the altar. 59 And Abraham took the wood and placed it in order on the altar which he had built. 60 And he took his son Isaac and bound him in order to place him on the wood which was on the altar, in order to slay him for a burnt-offering before the Lord. 61 And Isaac said to his father, "Bind me securely and then place me on the altar lest I should turn, and move, and break loose from the force of the knife on my flesh and thereof profane the burnt-offering"; and Abraham did so. 62 And Isaac still said to his father, "O my father, when you will have slain me and burned me for an offering, take with you that which will remain of my ashes to bring to my mother Sarah, and say to her, This is the sweet-smelling savor of Isaac; but do not tell her this if she should sit near a well or on any high place, lest she should cast her soul after me and die." 63 And Abraham heard the words of Isaac, and he lifted up his voice and wept when Isaac spoke these words; and Abraham's tears gushed down on his son Isaac, and Isaac wept bitterly, and he said to his father, "Hasten you, O my father, and do with me the will of the Lord our God as He has commanded you." 64 And the hearts of Abraham and Isaac rejoiced at this thing which the Lord had commanded them; but the eye wept bitterly while the heart rejoiced. 65 And Abraham bound his son Isaac, and placed him on the altar on the wood, and Isaac stretched out his neck on the altar before his father, and Abraham stretched out his hand to take the knife to slay his son as a burnt-offering before the Lord. 66 At that time the messengers of mercy came before the Lord and spoke to him concerning Isaac, saying, 67 "O Lord, You are a merciful and compassionate King over all that You have created in Heaven and in earth, and You support them all; therefore give ransom and redemption instead of your servant Isaac, and have pity and compassion on Abraham and his son Isaac who are performing Your commands this day. 68 Have You seen, O Lord, how Isaac, the son of Your servant Abraham, is bound down to the slaughter like an animal? Now therefore, let Your pity be roused for them, O Lord." 69 At that time the Lord appeared to Abraham, and called to him from Heaven, and said to him, "Do not lay your hand on the youth, neither do anything to him, for now I know that you fear God in performing this act, and in not withholding your son, your only son, from Me." 70 And Abraham lifted up his eyes and saw, and behold, a ram was caught in a thicket by his horns; that was the ram which the Lord God had created in the earth in the day that he made earth and Heaven. 71 For the Lord had prepared this ram from that day to be a burnt-offering instead of Isaac. 72 And this ram was advancing to Abraham when Satan caught hold of him and entangled his horns in the thicket, that he might not advance to Abraham, in order that Abraham might slay his son. 73 And Abraham, seeing the ram advancing to him and Satan withholding him, fetched him and brought him before the altar, and he loosened his son Isaac from his binding, and he put the ram in his stead, and Abraham killed the ram on the altar, and brought it up as an offering in the place of his son Isaac. 74 And Abraham sprinkled some of the blood of the ram on the altar, and he exclaimed and said, "This is in the place of my son, and may this be considered as the blood of my son before the Lord this day." 75 And all that Abraham did on this occasion by the altar, he would exclaim and say, "This is in the room of my son, and may it be considered before the Lord in the place of my son this day"; and Abraham finished the whole of the service by the altar, and the service was accepted before the Lord, and was accounted as if it had been Isaac; and the Lord blessed Abraham and his seed on that day. 76 And Satan went to Sarah, and he appeared to her in the figure of a very humble and meek old man, and Abraham was yet engaged in the burnt-offering before the Lord. 77 And he said to her, "Do you not know all the work that Abraham has made with your only son this day? For he took Isaac, and built an altar, and killed him, and brought him up as a sacrifice on the altar, and Isaac cried and wept before his father, but he did not look at him, neither did he have compassion over him." 78 And Satan repeated these words, and he went away from her, and Sarah heard all the words of Satan, and she imagined him to be an old man from among the sons of men who had been with her son and had come and told her these things. 79 And Sarah lifted up her voice, and wept, and cried out bitterly on account of her son; and she threw herself on the ground, and she cast dust on her head, and she said, "O my son! My son Isaac! O that I had died instead of you this day." And she continued to weep and said, "It grieves me for you, O my son, my son Isaac! O that I had died in your stead this day." 80 And she still continued to weep, and said,

"It grieves me for you after I have reared you and have brought you up; now my joy is turned into mourning over you—I that had a longing for you, and cried and prayed to God until I bore you at ninety years old; and now you have served this day for the knife and the fire, to be made an offering. 81 But I console myself with you, my son, in its being the word of the Lord, for you performed the command of your God; for who can transgress the word of our God, in whose hands is the soul of every living creature? 82 You are just, O Lord our God, for all Your works are good and righteous; for I also rejoice with Your word which You commanded, and while my eye weeps bitterly, my heart rejoices." 83 And Sarah laid her head on the bosom of one of her handmaids, and she became as still as a stone. 84 Afterward she rose up and went around making inquiries until she came to Hebron, and she inquired of all those whom she met walking in the road, and no one could tell her what had happened to her son. 85 And she came with her maidservants and menservants to Kirjath-Arba, which is Hebron, and she asked concerning her son, and she remained there while she sent some of her servants to seek where Abraham had gone with Isaac; they went to seek him in the house of Shem and Eber, and they could not find him, and they sought throughout the land and he was not there. 86 And behold, Satan came to Sarah in the shape of an old man, and he came and stood before her, and he said to her, "I spoke falsely to you, for Abraham did not kill his son and he is not dead"; and when she heard the word her joy was so exceedingly violent on account of her son, that her soul went out through joy; she died and was gathered to her people. 87 And when Abraham had finished his service, he returned with his son Isaac to his young men, and they rose up and went together to Beersheba, and they came home. 88 And Abraham sought for Sarah, and could not find her, and he made inquiries concerning her, and they said to him, "She went as far as Hebron to seek you both where you had gone, for thus she was informed." 89 And Abraham and Isaac went to her to Hebron, and when they found that she was dead, they lifted up their voices and wept bitterly over her; and Isaac fell on his mother's face and wept over her, and he said, "O my mother, my mother! How have you left me, and where have you gone? O how, how have you left me!" 90 And Abraham and Isaac wept greatly, and all their servants wept with them on account of Sarah, and they mourned a great and heavy mourning over her.

CHAPTER 24

1 And the life of Sarah was one hundred and twenty-seven years, and Sarah died; and Abraham rose up from before his dead to seek a burial place to bury his wife Sarah; and he went and spoke to the children of Heth, the inhabitants of the land, saying, 2 "I am a stranger and a sojourner with you in your land; give me possession of a burial place in your land, that I may bury my dead from before me." 3 And the children of Heth said to Abraham, "Behold, the land is before you, in the choice of our tombs bury your dead, for no man will withhold you from burying your dead." 4 And Abraham said to them, "If you are agreeable to this, go and entreat for me to Ephron, the son of Zochar, requesting that he may give me the cave of Machpelah, which is in the end of his field, and I will purchase it from him for whatever he desires for it." 5 And Ephron dwelt among the children of Heth, and they went and called for him, and he came before Abraham, and Ephron said to Abraham, "Behold, your servant will do all [that] you require"; and Abraham said, "No, but I will buy the cave and the field which you have for value, in order that it may be for a possession of a burial place forever." 6 And Ephron answered and said, "Behold, the field and the cave are before you, give whatever you desire"; and Abraham said, "Only at full value will I buy it from your hand, and from the hands of those that go in at the gate of your city, and from the hand of your seed forever." 7 And Ephron and all his brothers heard this, and Abraham weighed four hundred shekels of silver to Ephron in the hands of Ephron and in the hands of all his brothers; and Abraham recorded this transaction, and he recorded it and testified to it with four witnesses. 8 And these are the names of the witnesses: Amigal son of Abishna the Hittite, Adichorom son of Ashunach the Hivite, Abdon son of Achiram the Gomerite, [and] Bakdil the son of Abudish the Zidonite. 9 And Abraham took the scroll of the purchase and placed it in his treasures, and these are the words that Abraham wrote in the scroll, namely that: 10 "The cave and the field Abraham bought from Ephron the Hittite,

and from his seed, and from those that go out of his city, and from their seed forever, are to be a purchase to Abraham, and to his seed, and to those that go out from his loins for a possession of a burial place forever"; and he put a signet to it and testified to it with witnesses. **11** And the field, and the cave that was in it, and all that place were made sure to Abraham and to his seed after him, from the children of Heth; behold, it is before Mamre in Hebron, which is in the land of Canaan. **12** And after this Abraham buried his wife Sarah there, and that place and all its boundary became to Abraham and to his seed for a possession of a burial place. **13** And Abraham buried Sarah with pomp as observed at the interment of kings, and she was buried in very fine and beautiful garments. **14** And Shem, his sons Eber and Abimelech, together with Anar, Ashcol, and Mamre were at her bier; and all the noblemen of the land followed her bier. **15** And the days of Sarah were one hundred and twenty-seven years and she died, and Abraham made a great and heavy mourning, and he performed the rites of mourning for seven days. **16** And all the inhabitants of the land comforted Abraham and his son Isaac on account of Sarah. **17** And when the days of their mourning passed by, Abraham sent his son Isaac away, and he went to the house of Shem and Eber to learn the ways of the Lord and His instructions, and Abraham remained there three years. **18** At that time Abraham rose up with all his servants, and they went and returned homeward to Beersheba, and Abraham and all his servants remained in Beersheba. **19** And at the revolution of the year Abimelech king of the Philistines died in that year; he was one hundred and ninety-three years old at his death; and Abraham went with his people to the land of the Philistines, and they comforted the whole household and all his servants, and he then turned and went home. **20** And it was after the death of Abimelech that the people of Gerar took his son Benmalich, and he was only twelve years old, and they made him lie in the place of his father. **21** And they called his name Abimelech after the name of his father, for thus it was their custom to do in Gerar, and Abimelech reigned instead of his father Abimelech, and he sat on his throne. **22** And Lot the son of Haran also died in those days, in the thirty-ninth year of the life of Isaac, and all the days that Lot lived were one hundred and forty years and he died. **23** And these are the children of Lot that were born to him by his daughters: the name of the firstborn was Moab, and the name of the second was Benami. **24** And the two sons of Lot went and took wives [for] themselves from the land of Canaan, and they bore children to them, and the children of Moab were Ed, Mayon, Tarsus, and Kanvil—four sons; these are fathers to the children of Moab to this day. **25** And all the families of the children of Lot went to dwell wherever they should settle, for they were fruitful and increased abundantly. **26** And they went and built themselves cities in the land where they dwelt, and they called the names of the cities which they built after their own names. **27** And Nahor the son of Terah, brother to Abraham, died in those days in the fortieth year of the life of Isaac, and all the days of Nahor were one hundred and seventy-two years and he died and was buried in Haran. **28** And when Abraham heard that his brother was dead, he grieved sadly, and he mourned over his brother many days. **29** And Abraham called for his head servant Eliezer to give him orders concerning his house, and he came and stood before him. **30** And Abraham said to him, "Behold, I am old; I do not know the day of my death, for I am advanced in days; now therefore, rise up, go out, and do not take a wife for my son from this place and from this land, from the daughters of the Canaanites among whom we dwell. **31** But go to my land and to my birthplace, and take a wife for my son from there, and the Lord God of the heavens and earth who took me from my father's house and brought me to this place, and said to me, To your seed I will give this land for an inheritance forever— He will send His messenger before you and prosper your way that you may obtain a wife for my son from my family and from my father's house." **32** And the servant answered his master Abraham and said, "Behold, I go to your birthplace and to your father's house, and will take a wife for your son from there; but if the woman is not willing to follow me to this land, will I take your son back to the land of your birthplace?" **33** And Abraham said to him, "Take heed that you do not bring my son here again, for the Lord before whom I have walked will send His messenger before you and prosper your way." **34** And Eliezer did as Abraham ordered him, and Eliezer swore to Abraham his master on this matter; and Eliezer rose up and took ten camels of the camels of his master, and ten men from his master's servants with him, and they rose up and went to Haran, the city of Abraham and Nahor, in order to fetch a wife for Isaac the son of Abraham; and while they were gone, Abraham sent to the house of Shem and Eber, and they brought his son Isaac from there. **35** And Isaac came home to his father's house, to Beersheba, while Eliezer and his men came to Haran; and they stopped in the city by the watering place, and he made his camels to kneel down by the water, and they remained there. **36** And Eliezer, Abraham's servant, prayed and said, "O God of my master Abraham, please send me good speed this day and show kindness to my master, that You will appoint a wife for my master's son from his family this day." **37** And the Lord listened to the voice of Eliezer for the sake of His servant Abraham, and he happened to meet with the daughter of Bethuel, the son of Milcah, the wife of Nahor, brother to Abraham, and Eliezer came to her house. **38** And Eliezer related to them all his concerns, and that he was Abraham's servant, and they greatly rejoiced at him. **39** And they all blessed the Lord who brought this thing about, and they gave him Rebekah, the daughter of Bethuel, for a wife for Isaac. **40** And the young woman was of very beautiful appearance, she was a virgin, and Rebekah was ten years old in those days. **41** And Bethuel, and Laban, and his children made a feast on that night, and Eliezer and his men came, and ate, and drank, and rejoiced there on that night. **42** And Eliezer rose up in the morning, he and the men that were with him, and he called to the whole household of Bethuel, saying, "Send me away that I may go to my master"; and they rose up and sent away Rebekah and her nurse Deborah, the daughter of Uz, and they gave her silver and gold, menservants and maidservants, and they blessed her. **43** And they sent Eliezer away with his men; and the servants took Rebekah, and he went and returned to his master to the land of Canaan. **44** And Isaac took Rebekah, and she became his wife, and he brought her into the tent. **45** And Isaac was forty years old when he took Rebekah, the daughter of his uncle Bethuel, for a wife.

CHAPTER 25

1 And it was at that time that Abraham again took a wife in his old age, and her name was Keturah, from the land of Canaan. **2** And she bore to him Zimran, Jokshan, Medan, Midian, Ishbak, and Shuach, being six sons. And the children of Zimran were Abihen, Molich, and Narim. **3** And the sons of Jokshan were Sheba and Dedan, and the sons of Medan were Amida, Joab, Gochi, Elisha, and Nothach. And the sons of Midian were Ephah, Epher, Chanoch, Abida, and Eldaah. **4** And the sons of Ishbak were Makiro, Beyodua, and Tator. **5** And the sons of Shuach were Bildad, Mamdad, Munan, and Meban; all these are the families of the children of Keturah the Canaanite woman which she bore to Abraham the Hebrew. **6** And Abraham sent all these away, and he gave them gifts, and they went away from his son Isaac to dwell wherever they should find a place. **7** And all these went to the mountain at the east, and they built themselves six cities in which they dwelt to this day. **8** But the children of Sheba and Dedan, children of Jokshan, with their children, did not dwell with their brothers in their cities, and they journeyed and encamped in the countries and wildernesses to this day. **9** And the children of Midian, son of Abraham, went to the east of the land of Cush, and they found a large valley there in the eastern country, and they remained there and built a city, and they dwelt therein; that is the land of Midian to this day. **10** And Midian dwelt in the city which he built—he and his five sons and all belonging to him. **11** And these are the names of the sons of Midian according to their names in their cities: Ephah, Epher, Chanoch, Abida, and Eldaah. **12** And the sons of Ephah were Methach, Meshar, Avi, and Tzanua. And the sons of Epher were Ephron, Zur, Alirun, and Medin. And the sons of Chanoch were Reuel, Rekem, Azi, Alyoshub, and Alad. **13** And the sons of Abida were Chur, Melud, Kerury, Molchi. And the sons of Eldaah were Miker, and Reba, and Malchiyah, and Gabol; these are the names of the Midianites according to their families; and afterward the families of Midian spread throughout the land of Midian. **14** And these are the generations of Ishmael the son Abraham, whom Hagar, Sarah's handmaid, bore to Abraham. **15** And Ishmael took a wife from the land of Egypt, and her name was Ribah, the same is Meribah. **16** And Ribah bore to Ishmael Nebayoth, Kedar, Adbeel, Mibsam, and their sister Bosmath. **17** And Ishmael cast away his wife Ribah, and she went from him and returned to Egypt to the house of her father, and she dwelt there, for she had been very bad in the sight of Ishmael and in the sight of his father Abraham. **18** And afterward Ishmael took a wife from the land of Canaan, and her name was Malchuth, and she bore to him Nishma, Dumah, Masa, Chadad, Tema, Yetur, Naphish, and Kedma. **19** These are the sons of Ishmael, and these are their names, being twelve princes according to their nations; and afterward the families of Ishmael spread out, and Ishmael took his children and all the property that he had gained, together with the souls of his household and all belonging to him, and they went to dwell where they should find a place. **20** And they went and dwelt near the wilderness of Paran, and their dwelling was from Havilah to Shur, which is before Egypt as you come toward Assyria. **21** And Ishmael and his sons dwelt in the land, and they had children born to them, and they were fruitful and increased abundantly. **22** And these are the names of the sons of Nebayoth, the firstborn of Ishmael: Mend, Send, Mayon. And the sons of Kedar were Alyon, Kezem, Chamad, and Eli. **23** And the sons of Adbeel were Chamad and Jabin. And the sons of Mibsam were Obadiah, Ebedmelech, and Yeush; these are the families of the children of Ribah, the wife of Ishmael. **24** And the sons of Mishma the son of Ishmael were Shamua, Zecaryon, and Obed. And the sons of Dumah were Kezed, Eli, Machmad, and Amed. **25** And the sons of Masa were Melon, Mula, and Ebidadon. And the sons of Chadad were Azur, Minzar, and Ebedmelech. And the sons of Tema were Seir, Sadon, and Yakol. **26** And the sons of Yetur were Merith, Yaish, Alyo, and Pachoth. And the sons of Naphish were Ebed-Tamed, Abiyasaph, and Mir. And the sons of Kedma were Calip, Tachti, and Omir; these were the children of Malchuth the wife of Ishmael according to their families. **27** All these are the families of Ishmael according to their generations, and they dwelt in those lands wherein they had built themselves cities to this day. **28** And Rebekah the daughter of Bethuel, the wife of Abraham's son Isaac, was barren in those days, she had no offspring; and Isaac dwelt with his father in the land of Canaan; and the Lord was with Isaac; and Arphaxad the son of Shem, the son of Noah, died in those days, in the forty-eighth year of the life of Isaac, and all the days that Arphaxad lived were four hundred and thirty-eight years, and he died.

CHAPTER 26

1 And in the fifty-ninth year of the life of Isaac the son of Abraham, his wife Rebekah was still barren in those days. **2** And Rebekah said to Isaac, "Truly I have heard, my lord, that your mother Sarah was barren in her days until my lord Abraham, your father, prayed for her and she conceived by him. **3** Now therefore, stand up, pray also to God and He will hear your prayer and remember us through His mercies." **4** And Isaac answered his wife Rebekah, saying, "Abraham has already prayed for me to God to multiply his seed, now therefore, this barrenness must proceed to us from you." **5** And Rebekah said to him, "But arise now—you also—and pray that the Lord may hear your prayer and grant me children," and Isaac listened to the words of his wife, and Isaac and his wife rose up and went to the land of Moriah to pray there and to seek the Lord, and when they had reached that place, Isaac stood up and prayed to the Lord on account of his wife because she was barren. **6** And Isaac said, "O Lord God of the heavens and earth, whose goodness and mercies fill the earth, You who took my father from his father's house and from his birthplace, and brought him to this land, and said to him, To your seed I will give the land, and You promised him and declared to him, I will multiply your seed as the stars of the heavens and as the sand of the sea: now may Your words be verified which You spoke to my father. **7** For You are the Lord our God; our eyes are toward You to give us seed of men, as You promised us, for You are the Lord our God and our eyes are directed toward You alone." **8** And the Lord heard the prayer of Isaac the son of Abraham, and the Lord was entreated of him and his wife Rebekah conceived. **9** And about seven months later, the children struggled together within her, and it pained her greatly that she was wearied on account of them, and she said to all the women who were then in the land, "Did such a thing happen to you as it has to me?" and they said to her, "No." **10** And she said to them, "Why am I alone in this among all the women that were on earth?" and she went to the land of Moriah to seek the Lord on account of this; and she went to Shem and his son Eber to make inquiries of them in this matter, and that they should seek the Lord in this thing respecting her. **11** And she also asked Abraham to seek and inquire of the Lord about all that had befallen her. **12** And they all inquired of the Lord concerning this matter, and they brought her word from the Lord and told her: "Two children are in your womb, and two nations will rise from them; and one nation will be stronger than the other, and the greater will serve the younger." **13** And when her days to be delivered were completed, she knelt down, and behold, there were twins in her womb as the Lord had spoken to her. **14** And the first came out red all over like a hairy garment, and all the people of the land called his name Esau, saying, "That this one was made complete from the womb." **15** And after that, his brother came, and his hand took hold of Esau's heel; therefore they called his name Jacob. **16** And Isaac, the son of Abraham, was sixty years old when he begot them. **17** And the boys grew up to their fifteenth year, and they came among the society of men. Esau was a scheming and deceitful man, and an expert hunter in the field, and Jacob was a perfect and wise man, dwelling in tents, feeding flocks, and learning the instructions of the Lord and the commands of his father and mother. **18** And Isaac and the children of his household dwelt with his father Abraham in the land of Canaan as God had commanded them. **19** And Ishmael the son of Abraham went with his children and all belonging to them, and they returned there to the land of Havilah, and they dwelt there. **20** And all the children of Abraham's concubines went to dwell in the land of the east, for Abraham had sent them away from his son, and had given them presents, and they went away. **21** And Abraham gave all that he had to his son Isaac, and he also gave him all his treasures. **22** And he commanded him, saying, "Do you not know and understand the Lord is God in Heaven and in earth, and there is no other besides Him? **23** And it was He who took me from my father's house and from my birthplace, and gave me all the delights on earth; who delivered me from the counsel of the wicked, for I trusted in Him. **24** And He brought me to this place, and He delivered me from Ur-Kasdim; and He said to me, To your seed I will give all these lands, and they will inherit them when they keep My commands, My statutes, and My judgments that I have commanded you, and which I will command them. **25** Now therefore, my son, listen to my voice, and keep the commands of the Lord your God, which I commanded you; do not turn from the right way either to the right or to the left, in order that it may be well with you and your children after you forever. **26** And remember the wonderful works of the Lord, and His kindness that He has shown toward us in having delivered us from the hands of our enemies, and the Lord our God caused them to fall into our hands; and now therefore, keep all that I have commanded you, and do not turn away from the commands of your God, and serve none besides Him in order that it may be well with you and your seed after you. **27** And teach your children and your seed the instructions of the Lord and His commands, and teach them the upright way in which they should go in order that it may be well with them forever." **28** And Isaac answered his father and said to him, "I will do that which my lord has commanded, and I will not depart from the commands of the Lord my God; I will keep all that He commanded me"; and Abraham blessed his son Isaac, and also his children; and Abraham taught Jacob the instruction of the Lord and His ways. **29** And it was at that time that Abraham died, in the fifteenth year of the life of Jacob and Esau, the sons of Isaac, and all the days of Abraham were one hundred and seventy-five years, and he died and was gathered to his people in good old age, old and satisfied with days, and his sons Isaac and Ishmael buried him. **30** And when the inhabitants of Canaan heard that Abraham was dead, they all came with their kings, and princes, and all their men to bury Abraham. **31** And all the inhabitants of the land of Haran, and all the families of the house of Abraham, and all the princes and noblemen, and the sons of Abraham by the concubines, all came when they heard of Abraham's death, and they paid back Abraham's kindness, and comforted his son Isaac, and they buried Abraham in the cave which he bought from Ephron the Hittite and his children for the possession of a burial place. **32** And all the inhabitants of Canaan, and all those who had known Abraham, wept for Abraham a whole year, and men and women mourned over him. **33** And all the little children, and all the inhabitants of the land, wept on account of Abraham, for Abraham had been good to them all, and because he had been upright with God and men. **34** And there did not arise a man who feared God like to Abraham, for he had feared his God from his youth, and had served the Lord, and had gone in all His ways during his life, from his childhood to the day of his death. **35** And the Lord was with him and delivered him from the counsel of Nimrod and his people, and when he made war with the four kings of Elam, he conquered them. **36** And he brought all the children of the earth to the service of God, and he taught them the ways of the Lord, and caused them to know the Lord. **37** And he formed a grove, and he planted a vineyard therein, and he had always prepared meat and drink in his tent for those that passed through the land, that they might satisfy themselves in his house. **38** And the Lord God delivered the whole earth on account of Abraham. **39** And it was after the death of Abraham that God blessed his son Isaac and his children, and the Lord was with Isaac as he had been with his father Abraham, for Isaac kept all the commands of the Lord as his father Abraham had commanded him; he did not turn to the right or to the left from the right path which his father had commanded him.

CHAPTER 27

1 And Esau at that time, after the death of Abraham, frequently went in the field to hunt. **2** And Nimrod king of Babel, the same was Amraphel, also frequently went with his mighty men to hunt in the field, and to walk around with his men in the cool of the day. **3** And Nimrod was observing Esau all the days, for a jealousy was formed in the heart of Nimrod against Esau all the days. **4** And on a certain day Esau went in the field to hunt, and he found Nimrod walking in the wilderness with his two men. **5** And all his mighty men and his people were with him in the wilderness, but they removed at a distance from him, and they went from him in different directions to hunt, and Esau concealed himself for Nimrod, and he lurked for him in the wilderness. **6** And Nimrod and his men that were with him did not know him, and Nimrod and his men frequently walked around in the field in the cool of the day, and to know where his men were hunting in the field. **7** And Nimrod and two of his men that were with him came to the place where they were, when Esau started suddenly from his lurking place, and drew his sword, and hastened, and ran to Nimrod, and cut off his head. **8** And Esau fought a desperate fight with the two men that were with Nimrod, and when they called out to him, Esau turned to them and struck them to death with his sword. **9** And all the mighty men of Nimrod, who had left him to go to the wilderness, heard the cry at a distance, and they knew the voices of those two men, and they ran to know the cause of it; then they found their king and the two men that were with him lying dead in the wilderness. **10** And when Esau saw the mighty men of Nimrod coming at a distance, he fled, and thereby escaped; and Esau took the valuable garments of Nimrod, which Nimrod's father had bequeathed to Nimrod, and with which Nimrod prevailed over the whole land, and he ran and concealed them in his house. **11** And Esau took those garments and ran into the city on account of Nimrod's men, and he came to his father's house wearied and exhausted from fight, and he was ready to die through grief when he approached his brother Jacob and sat before him. **12** And he said to his brother Jacob, "Behold, I will die this day, and why then do I want the birthright?" And Jacob acted wisely with Esau in this matter, and Esau sold his birthright to Jacob, for it was so brought about by the Lord. **13** And Esau's portion in the cave of the field of Machpelah, which Abraham had bought from the children of Heth for the possession of a burial ground, Esau also sold to Jacob, and Jacob bought all this from his brother Esau for value given. **14** And Jacob recorded the whole of this in a scroll, and he testified the same with witnesses, and he sealed it, and the scroll remained in the hands of Jacob. **15** And when Nimrod the son of Cush died, his men lifted him up and brought him in consternation, and buried him in his city, and all the days that Nimrod lived were two hundred and fifteen years and he died. **16** And the days that Nimrod reigned over the people of the land were one hundred and eighty-five years; and Nimrod died by the sword of Esau in shame and contempt, and the seed of Abraham caused his death as he had seen in his dream. **17** And at the death of Nimrod his kingdom became divided into many divisions, and all those parts that Nimrod reigned over were restored to the respective kings of the land, who recovered them after the death of Nimrod, and all the people of the house of Nimrod were enslaved for a long time to all the other kings of the land.

CHAPTER 28

1 And in those days, after the death of Abraham, in that year the Lord brought a heavy famine in the land, and while the famine was raging in the land of Canaan, Isaac rose up to go down to Egypt on account of the famine, as his father Abraham had done. **2** And that night the Lord appeared to Isaac and said to him, "Do not go down to Egypt, but rise and go to Gerar, to Abimelech king of the Philistines, and remain there until the famine will cease." **3** And Isaac rose up and went to Gerar, as the Lord commanded him, and he remained there a full year. **4** And when Isaac came to Gerar, the people of the land saw that his wife Rebekah was of a beautiful appearance, and the people of Gerar asked Isaac concerning his wife, and he said, "She is my sister," for he was afraid to say she was his wife lest the people of the land should slay him on account of her. **5** And the princes of Abimelech went and praised the woman to the king, but he did not answer them, neither did he attend to their words. **6** But he heard them say that Isaac declared her to be his sister, so the king reserved this within himself. **7** And when Isaac had remained in the land [for] three months, Abimelech looked out at the window, and he saw, and behold, Isaac was sporting with his wife Rebekah, for Isaac dwelt in the outer house belonging to the king, so that the house of Isaac was opposite the house of the king. **8** And the king said to Isaac, "What is this you have done to us in saying of your wife, She is my sister? how easily might one of the great men of the people have lain with her, and you would then have brought guilt on us." **9** And Isaac said to Abimelech, "Because I was afraid lest I die on account of my wife, therefore I said, She is my sister." **10** At that time Abimelech gave orders to all his princes and great men, and they took Isaac and his wife Rebekah and brought them before the king. **11** And the king commanded that they should dress them in princely garments, and make them ride through the streets of the city, and proclaim before them throughout the land, saying, "This is the man and this is his wife; whoever touches this man or his wife will surely die." And Isaac returned with his wife to the king's house, and the Lord was with Isaac and he continued to wax great and lacked nothing. **12** And the Lord caused Isaac to find favor in the sight of Abimelech, and in the sight of all his subjects, and Abimelech acted well with Isaac, for Abimelech remembered the oath and the covenant that existed between his father and Abraham. **13** And Abimelech said to Isaac, "Behold, the whole earth is before you; dwell wherever it may seem good in your sight until you will return to your land"; and Abimelech gave Isaac fields, and vineyards, and the best part of the land of Gerar, to sow, and reap, and eat the fruits of the ground until the days of the famine should have passed by. **14** And Isaac sowed in that land and received a hundredfold in the same year, and the Lord blessed him. **15** And the man waxed great, and he had possession of flocks, and possession of herds, and a great store of servants. **16** And when the days of the famine had passed away, the Lord appeared to Isaac and said to him, "Rise up, go out from this place and return to your land, to the land of Canaan"; and Isaac rose up and returned to Hebron which is in the land of Canaan, he and all belonging to him as the Lord commanded him. **17** And after this, Shelach the son of Arphaxad died in that year, which is the eighteenth year of the lives of Jacob and Esau; and all the days that Shelach lived were four hundred and thirty-three years and he died. **18** At that time Isaac sent his younger son Jacob to the house of Shem and Eber, and he learned the instructions of the Lord, and Jacob remained in the house of Shem and Eber for thirty-two years, and his brother Esau did not go, for he was not willing to go, and he remained in his father's house in the land of Canaan. **19** And Esau was continually hunting in the fields to bring home what he could get—so Esau did all the days. **20** And Esau was a scheming and deceitful man, one who hunted after the hearts of men and persuaded them through deceit, and Esau was a valiant man in the field, and in the course of time went as usual to hunt; and he came as far as the field of Seir, the same is Edom. **21** And he remained in the land of Seir hunting in the field [for] a year and four months. **22** And Esau saw there in the land of Seir the daughter of a man of Canaan, and her name was Jehudith, the daughter of Beeri, son of Epher, from the families of Heth son of Canaan. **23** And Esau took her for a wife, and he came to her; Esau was forty years old when he took her, and he brought her to Hebron, the land of his father's dwelling place, and he dwelt there. **24** And it came to pass in those days, in the one hundred and tenth year of the life of Isaac, that is in the fiftieth year of the life of Jacob, in that year Shem the son of Noah died; Shem was six hundred years old at his death. **25** And when Shem died

Jacob returned to his father, to Hebron, which is in the land of Canaan. **26** And in the fifty-sixth year of the life of Jacob, people came from Haran, and Rebekah was told concerning her brother Laban, the son of Bethuel. **27** For the wife of Laban was barren in those days and bore no children, and also all his handmaids bore none to him. **28** And afterward the Lord remembered Adinah the wife of Laban, and she conceived and bore twin daughters, and Laban called the names of his daughters, the name of the elder Leah, and the name of the younger Rachel. **29** And those people came and told these things to Rebekah, and Rebekah rejoiced greatly that the Lord had visited her brother and that he was given children.

CHAPTER 29

1 And Isaac the son of Abraham became old and advanced in days, and his eyes became heavy through age; they were dim and could not see. **2** At that time Isaac called to his son Esau, saying, "Please get your weapons, your quiver and your bow, rise up and go out into the field, and get me some venison, and make me savory meat, and bring it to me, that I may eat in order that I may bless you before my death, as I have now become old and gray-headed." **3** And Esau did so; and he took his weapon and went out into the field to hunt for venison, as usual, to bring to his father as he had ordered him, so that he might bless him. **4** And Rebekah heard all the words that Isaac had spoken to Esau, and she hastened and called her son Jacob, saying, "Thus your father spoke to your brother Esau, and thus I heard; now therefore, hasten and make that which I will tell you. **5** Please rise up and go to the flock, and fetch me two fine kids of the goats, and I will get the savory meat for your father, and you will bring the savory meat that he may eat before your brother will have come from the chase, in order that your father may bless you." **6** And Jacob hastened and did as his mother had commanded him, and he made the savory meat and brought it before his father before Esau had come from his chase. **7** And Isaac said to Jacob, "Who are you, my son?" And he said, "I am your firstborn Esau; I have done as you ordered me, now therefore, please rise up, and eat of my hunt, in order that your soul may bless me as you spoke to me." **8** And Isaac rose up, and he ate, and he drank, and his heart was comforted, and he blessed Jacob, and Jacob went away from his father; and as soon as Isaac had blessed Jacob and he had gone away from him, behold, Esau came from his hunt from the field, and he also made savory meat and brought it to his father to eat thereof and to bless him. **9** And Isaac said to Esau, "And who was he that has taken venison and brought it to me before you came, and whom did I bless?" And Esau knew that his brother Jacob had done this, and the anger of Esau was kindled against his brother Jacob that he had acted thus toward him. **10** And Esau said, "Is he not rightly called Jacob? for he has supplanted me twice: he took away my birthright and now he has taken away my blessing"; and Esau wept greatly; and when Isaac heard the voice of his son Esau weeping, Isaac said to Esau, "What can I do, my son? Your brother came with subtlety and took away your blessing"; and Esau hated his brother Jacob on account of the blessing that his father had given him, and his anger was greatly roused against him. **11** And Jacob was very much afraid of his brother Esau, and he rose up and fled to the house of Eber the son of Shem, and he concealed himself there on account of his brother, and Jacob was sixty-three years old when he went out from the land of Canaan from Hebron, and Jacob was concealed in Eber's house [for] fourteen years on account of his brother Esau, and he continued to learn the ways of the Lord and His commands there. **12** And when Esau saw that Jacob had fled and escaped from him, and that Jacob had cunningly obtained the blessing, then Esau grieved exceedingly, and he was also vexed at his father and mother; and he also rose up, and took his wife, and went away from his father and mother to the land of Seir, and he dwelt there; and Esau saw a woman from among the daughters of Heth there whose name was Bosmath, the daughter of Elon the Hittite, and he took her for a wife in addition to his first wife, and Esau called her name Adah, saying the blessing had at that time passed from him. **13** And Esau dwelt in the land of Seir six months without seeing his father and mother, and afterward Esau took his wives, and rose up, and returned to the land of Canaan, and Esau placed his two wives in his father's house in Hebron. **14** And the wives of Esau vexed and provoked Isaac and Rebekah with their works, for they did not walk in the ways of the Lord, but served their father's gods of wood and stone as their father had taught them, and they were more wicked than their father. **15** And they went according to the evil desires of their hearts, and they sacrificed and burned incense to the Ba'alim, and Isaac and Rebekah became weary of them. **16** And Rebekah said, "I am weary of my life because of the daughters of Heth; if Jacob takes a wife from the daughters of Heth such as these, which are of the daughters of the land, what good then is life to me?" **17** And in those days Adah the wife of Esau conceived and bore him a son, and Esau called the name of the son that was born to him Eliphaz, and Esau was sixty-five years old when she bore him. **18** And Ishmael the son of Abraham died in those days, in the sixtieth year of the life of Jacob, and all the days that Ishmael lived were one hundred and thirty-seven years and he died. **19** And when Isaac heard that Ishmael was dead, he mourned for him, and Isaac lamented over him [for] many days. **20** And at the end of fourteen years of Jacob's residing in the house of Eber, Jacob desired to see his father and mother, and Jacob came to the house of his father and mother to Hebron, and in those days Esau had forgotten what Jacob had done to him in having taken the blessing from him in those days. **21** And when Esau saw Jacob coming to his father and mother, he remembered what Jacob had done to him, and he was greatly incensed against him, and he sought to slay him. **22** And Isaac the son of Abraham was old and advanced in days, and Esau said, "Now my father's time is drawing near that he must die, and when he will die I will slay my brother Jacob." **23** And this was told to Rebekah, and she hastened, and sent, and called for her son Jacob, and she said to him, "Arise, go and flee to Haran, to my brother Laban, and remain there for some time until your brother's anger is turned from you and then you will come back." **24** And Isaac called to Jacob and said to him, "Do not take a wife from the daughters of Canaan, for thus our father Abraham commanded us according to the word of the Lord which He had commanded him, saying, To your seed I will give this land; if your children keep My covenant that I have made with you, then I will also perform to your children that which I have spoken to you and I will not forsake them. **25** Now therefore, my son, listen to my voice, to all that I will command you, and refrain from taking a wife from among the daughters of Canaan; arise, go to Haran, to the house of Bethuel your mother's father, and take a wife for yourself from there from the daughters of your mother's brother Laban. **26** Therefore, take heed lest you should forget the Lord your God and all His ways in the land to which you go, and should get connected with the people of the land, and pursue vanity, and forsake the Lord your God. **27** But when you come to the land serve the Lord there; do not turn to the right or to the left from the way which I commanded you and which you learned. **28** And may the Almighty God grant you favor in the sight of the people of the earth, that you may take a wife there according to your choice, one who is good and upright in the ways of the Lord. **29** And may God give to you and your seed the blessing of your father Abraham, and make you fruitful, and multiply you, and may you become a multitude of people in the land where you go, and may God cause you to return to this land, the land of your father's dwelling, with children and with great riches, with joy and with pleasure." **30** And Isaac finished commanding Jacob and blessing him, and he gave him many gifts, together with silver and gold, and he sent him away; and Jacob listened to his father and mother; he kissed them, and arose, and went to Padan-Aram; and Jacob was seventy-seven years old when he went out from the land of Canaan from Beersheba. **31** And when Jacob went away to go to Haran, Esau called to his son Eliphaz, and secretly spoke to him, saying, "Now hasten, take your sword in your hand, and pursue Jacob, and pass before him in the road, and lurk for him, and slay him with your sword in one of the mountains, and take everything belonging to him, and come back." **32** And Eliphaz the son of Esau was an active man and expert with the bow as his father had taught him, and he was a noted hunter in the field and a valiant man. **33** And Eliphaz did as his father had commanded him, and Eliphaz was thirteen years old at that time, and Eliphaz rose up, and went, and took ten of his mother's brothers with him, and pursued Jacob. **34** And he closely followed Jacob, and he lurked for him in the border of the land of Canaan opposite to the city of Shechem. **35** And Jacob saw Eliphaz and his men pursuing him, and Jacob stood still in the place in which he was going, in order to know what this was, for he did not know the thing; and Eliphaz drew his sword and he went on advancing, he and his men, toward Jacob; and Jacob said to them, "What are you doing that you have come here, and what do you intend that you pursue with your swords?" **36** And Eliphaz came near to Jacob, and he answered and said to him, "Thus my father commanded me, and now therefore, I will not deviate from the orders which my father gave me"; and when Jacob saw that Esau had spoken to Eliphaz to employ force, Jacob then approached and supplicated Eliphaz and his men, saying to him, **37** "Behold all that I have and which my father and mother gave to me: take that to yourselves and go from me, and do not slay me, and may this thing be accounted to you [for] righteousness." **38** And the Lord caused Jacob to find favor in the sight of Eliphaz the son of Esau and his men, and they listened to the voice of Jacob, and they did not put him to death, and Eliphaz and his men took all belonging to Jacob, together with the silver and gold that he had brought with him from Beersheba; they left him nothing. **39** And Eliphaz and his men went away from him and they returned to Esau, to Beersheba, and they told him all that had occurred to them with Jacob, and they gave him all that they had taken from Jacob. **40** And Esau was indignant at his son Eliphaz and at his men that were with him, because they had not put Jacob to death. **41** And they answered and said to Esau, "Because Jacob supplicated us in this matter not to slay him, our pity was excited toward him, and we took all belonging to him and brought it to you; and Esau took all the silver and gold which Eliphaz had taken from Jacob and he put them away in his house." **42** At that time when Esau saw that Isaac had blessed Jacob, and had commanded him, saying, "You will not take a wife from among the daughters of Canaan," and that the daughters of Canaan were bad in the sight of Isaac and Rebekah, **43** then he went to the house of his uncle Ishmael, and in addition to his older wives he took Machlath the daughter of Ishmael, the sister of Nebayoth, for a wife.

CHAPTER 30

1 And Jacob went out, continuing his way to Haran, and he came as far as Mount Moriah, and he tarried there all night near the city of Luz; and on that night the Lord appeared to Jacob there, and He said to him, "I am the Lord God of Abraham and the God of your father Isaac; the land on which you lie I will give to you and your seed. **2** And behold, I am with you and will keep you wherever you go, and I will multiply your seed as the stars of the heavens, and I will cause all your enemies to fall before you; and when they will make war with you they will not prevail over you, and I will bring you again to this land with joy, with children, and with great riches." **3** And Jacob awoke from his sleep and he rejoiced greatly at the vision which he had seen; and he called the name of that place Bethel. **4** And Jacob rose up from that place quite glad, and when he walked, his feet felt light to him for joy, and he went from there to the land of the children of the east, and he returned to Haran, and he sat by the shepherd's well. **5** And there he found some men going from Haran to feed their flocks, and Jacob made inquiries of them, and they said, "We are from Haran." **6** And he said to them, "Do you know Laban, the son of Nahor?" and they said, "We know him, and behold, his daughter Rachel is coming along to feed her father's flock." **7** While he was yet speaking with them, Rachel the daughter of Laban came to feed her father's sheep, for she was a shepherdess. **8** And when Jacob saw Rachel, the daughter of Laban, his mother's brother, he ran and kissed her, and lifted up his voice and wept. **9** And Jacob told Rachel that he was the son of Rebekah, her father's sister, and Rachel ran and told her father, and Jacob continued to cry because he had nothing with him to bring to the house of Laban. **10** And when Laban heard that his sister's son Jacob had come, he ran and kissed him, and embraced him, and brought him into the house, and gave him bread, and he ate. **11** And Jacob related to Laban what his brother Esau had done to him, and what his son Eliphaz had done to him in the road. **12** And Jacob resided in Laban's house for one month, and Jacob ate and drank in the house of Laban, and afterward Laban said to Jacob, "Tell me what your wages will be, for how can you serve me for nothing?" **13** And Laban had no sons but only daughters, and his other wives and handmaids were still barren in those days; and these are the names of Laban's daughters which his wife Adinah had bore to him: the name of the elder was Leah and the name of the younger was Rachel; and Leah was tender-eyed, but Rachel was beautiful and well-favored, and Jacob loved her. **14** And Jacob said to Laban, "I will serve you seven years for your younger daughter Rachel"; and Laban consented to this and

Jacob served Laban seven years for his daughter Rachel. **15** And in the second year of Jacob's dwelling in Haran, that is in the seventy-ninth year of the life of Jacob, in that year Eber the son of Shem died; he was four hundred and sixty-four years old at his death. **16** And when Jacob heard that Eber was dead, he grieved exceedingly, and he lamented and mourned over him [for] many days. **17** And in the third year of Jacob's dwelling in Haran, Bosmath, the daughter of Ishmael, the wife of Esau, bore a son to him, and Esau called his name Reuel. **18** And in the fourth year of Jacob's residence in the house of Laban, the Lord visited Laban and remembered him on account of Jacob, and sons were born to him, and his firstborn was Beor, his second was Alib, and the third was Chorash. **19** And the Lord gave Laban riches and honor, sons and daughters, and the man increased greatly on account of Jacob. **20** And in those days Jacob served Laban in all manner of work, in the house and in the field, and the blessing of the Lord was in all that belonged to Laban in the house and in the field. **21** And in the fifth year Jehudith, the daughter of Beeri, the wife of Esau, died in the land of Canaan, and she had no sons but only daughters. **22** And these are the names of her daughters which she bore to Esau: the name of the elder was Marzith, and the name of the younger was Puith. **23** And when Jehudith died, Esau rose up and went to Seir to hunt in the field as usual, and Esau dwelt in the land of Seir for a long time. **24** And in the sixth year Esau took for a wife, in addition to his other wives, Aholibamah, the daughter of Zebeon the Hivite, and Esau brought her to the land of Canaan. **25** And Aholibamah conceived and bore three sons to Esau: Yeush, Yaalan, and Korah. **26** And in those days there was a quarrel in the land of Canaan between the herdsmen of Esau and the herdsmen of the inhabitants of the land of Canaan, for Esau's cattle and goods were too abundant for him to remain in the land of Canaan, in his father's house, and the land of Canaan could not bear him on account of his cattle. **27** And when Esau saw that his quarreling increased with the inhabitants of the land of Canaan, he rose up and took his wives, and his sons, and his daughters, and all belonging to him, and the cattle which he possessed, and all his property that he had acquired in the land of Canaan, and he went away from the inhabitants of the land to the land of Seir, and Esau and all belonging to him dwelt in the land of Seir. **28** But from time to time Esau would go and see his father and mother in the land of Canaan, and Esau intermarried with the Horites, and he gave his daughters to the sons of Seir, the Horite. **29** And he gave his elder daughter Marzith to Anah, the son of Zebeon, his wife's brother, and he gave Puith to Azar, the son of Bilhan the Horite; and Esau dwelt in the mountain, he and his children, and they were fruitful and multiplied.

CHAPTER 31

1 And in the seventh year Jacob's service which he served Laban was completed, and Jacob said to Laban, "Give me my wife, for the days of my service are fulfilled"; and Laban did so, and Laban and Jacob assembled all the people of that place and they made a feast. **2** And in the evening Laban came to the house, and afterward Jacob came there with the people of the feast, and Laban extinguished all the lights that were there in the house. **3** And Jacob said to Laban, "Why do you do this thing to us?" and Laban answered, "Such is our custom to act in this land." **4** And afterward Laban took his daughter Leah, and he brought her to Jacob, and he came to her and Jacob did not know that she was Leah. **5** And Laban gave his daughter Leah his maid Zilpah for a handmaid. **6** And all the people at the feast knew what Laban had done to Jacob, but they did not tell the thing to Jacob. **7** And all the neighbors came to Jacob's house that night, and they ate, and drank, and rejoiced, and played before Leah on timbrels, and with dances, and they responded before Jacob, "Heleah, Heleah." **8** And Jacob heard their words but did not understand their meaning, but he thought such might be their custom in this land. **9** And the neighbors spoke these words before Jacob during the night, and all the lights that were in the house Laban had extinguished that night. **10** And in the morning, when daylight appeared, Jacob turned to his wife and he saw, and behold, it was Leah that had been lying in his bosom, and Jacob said, "Behold, now I know what the neighbors said last night—Heleah, they said, and I did not know it." **11** And Jacob called to Laban, and said to him, "What is this that you did to me? Surely I served you for Rachel, and why did you deceive me and give me Leah?" **12** And Laban answered Jacob, saying, "It is not so done in our place to give the younger before the elder; now therefore, if you desire to take her sister likewise, take her to you for the service which you will serve me for another seven years." 13 And Jacob did so, and he also took Rachel for a wife, and he served Laban seven more years, and Jacob also came to Rachel, and he loved Rachel more than Leah, and Laban gave her his maid Bilhah for a handmaid. 14 And when the Lord saw that Leah was hated, the Lord opened her womb, and she conceived and bore Jacob four sons in those days. 15 And these are their names: Reuben, Simeon, Levi, and Judah, and afterward she stopped bearing. 16 And at that time Rachel was barren, and she had no offspring, and Rachel envied her sister Leah, and when Rachel saw that she bore no children to Jacob, she took her handmaid Bilhah, and she bore Jacob two sons: Dan and Naphtali. 17 And when Leah saw that she had stopped bearing, she also took her handmaid Zilpah, and she gave her to Jacob for a wife, and Jacob also came to Zilpah, and she also bore Jacob two sons: Gad and Asher. 18 And in those days Leah conceived again and bore Jacob two sons and one daughter, and these are their names: Issachar, Zebulun, and their sister Dinah. 19 And Rachel was still barren in those days, and Rachel prayed to the Lord at that time, and she said, "O Lord God, remember me and visit me, I implore You, for now my husband will cast me off, for I have borne him no children. 20 Now O Lord God, hear my supplication before You, and see my affliction, and give me children like one of the handmaids, that I may no longer bear my reproach." 21 And God heard her and opened her womb, and Rachel conceived and bore a son, and she said, "The Lord has taken away my reproach," and she called his name Joseph, saying, "May the Lord add to me another son"; and Jacob was ninety-one years old when she bore him. 22 At that time, Jacob's mother Rebekah sent her nurse Deborah, the daughter of Uz, and two of Isaac's servants to Jacob. 23 And they came to Jacob, to Haran, and they said to him, "Rebekah has sent us to you that you will return to your father's house to the land of Canaan"; and Jacob listened to them in this which his mother had spoken. 24 At that time, the other seven years which Jacob served Laban for Rachel were completed, and it was at the end of fourteen years that he had dwelt in Haran that Jacob said to Laban, "Give me my wives and send me away that I may go to my land, for behold, my mother sent to me from the land of Canaan that I should return to my father's house." 25 And Laban said to him, "Please not so; if I have found favor in your sight, do not leave me; appoint me your wages and I will give them, and remain with me." 26 And Jacob said to him, "This is what you will give me for wages, that I will pass through all your flock this day and take away from them every lamb that is speckled and spotted and such as are brown among the sheep, and among the goats, and if you will do this thing for me I will return, and feed your flock, and keep them as at first." 27 And Laban did so, and Laban removed from his flock all that Jacob had said and gave them to him. 28 And Jacob placed all that he had removed from Laban's flock in the hands of his sons, and Jacob was feeding the remainder of Laban's flock. 29 And when the servants of Isaac which he had sent to Jacob saw that Jacob would not then return with them to his father, to the land of Canaan, they then went away from him, and they returned home to the land of Canaan. 30 And Deborah remained with Jacob in Haran, and she did not return with the servants of Isaac to the land of Canaan, and Deborah resided with Jacob's wives and children in Haran. 31 And Jacob served Laban six years longer, and when the sheep brought out, Jacob removed from them such as were speckled and spotted, as he had determined with Laban, and Jacob did so at Laban's for six years, and the man increased abundantly, and he had cattle, and maidservants, and menservants, camels, and donkeys. 32 And Jacob had two hundred droves of cattle, and his cattle were of large size, and of beautiful appearance, and were very productive, and all the families of the sons of men desired to get some of the cattle of Jacob, for they were exceedingly prosperous. 33 And many of the sons of men came to procure some of Jacob's flock, and Jacob gave them a sheep for a manservant or a maidservant or for a donkey or a camel, or whatever Jacob desired from them they gave him. 34 And Jacob obtained riches, and honor, and possessions by means of these transactions with the sons of men, and the children of Laban envied him of this honor. 35 And in the course of time he heard the words of Laban's sons, saying, "Jacob has taken away all that was our father's, and of that which was our father's he has acquired all this glory." 36 And Jacob beheld the countenance of Laban and of his children, and behold, it was not toward him in those days as it had been before. 37 And the Lord appeared to Jacob at the expiration of the six years, and said to him, "Arise, go out out of this land, and return to the land of your birthplace and I will be with you." 38 And Jacob rose up at that time, and he mounted his children, and wives, and all belonging to him on camels, and he went out to go to the land of Canaan to his father Isaac. 39 And Laban did not know that Jacob had gone from him, for Laban had been sheep-shearing that day. 40 And Rachel stole her father's images, and she took them, and she concealed them on the camel on which she sat, and she went on. 41 And this is the manner of the images: in taking a man who is the firstborn, and slaying him, and taking the hair off his head, and taking salt and salting the head and anointing it in oil, then taking a small tablet of copper or a tablet of gold and writing the name on it, and placing the tablet under his tongue, and taking the head with the tablet under the tongue and putting it in the house, and lighting up lights before it and bowing down to it. 42 And at the time when they bow down to it, it speaks to them in all matters that they ask of it through the power of the name which is written in it. 43 And some make them in the figures of men, of gold and silver, and go to them in times known to them, and the figures receive the influence of the stars, and tell them future things, and in this manner were the images which Rachel stole from her father. 44 And Rachel stole these images which were her father's in order that Laban might not know through them where Jacob had gone. 45 And Laban came home and asked concerning Jacob and his household, and he was not to be found, and Laban sought his images to know where Jacob had gone, and could not find them, and he went to some other images, and he inquired of them and they told him that Jacob had fled from him to his father's, to the land of Canaan. 46 And Laban then rose up and he took his brothers and all his servants, and he went out and pursued Jacob, and he overtook him in Mount Gilead. 47 And Laban said to Jacob, "What is this you have done to me to flee and deceive me, and lead my daughters and their children as captives taken by the sword? 48 And you did not permit me to kiss them and send them away with joy, and you stole my gods and went away." 49 And Jacob answered Laban, saying, "Because I was afraid lest you would take your daughters by force from me; and now with whomsoever you find your gods he will die." 50 And Laban searched for the images and he examined in all Jacob's tents and furniture but could not find them. 51 And Laban said to Jacob, "We will make a covenant together and it will be a testimony between me and you; if you will afflict my daughters, or will take other wives besides my daughters, even God will be a witness between me and you in this matter." 52 And they took stones and made a heap, and Laban said, "This heap is a witness between me and you," therefore he called the name thereof Gilead. 53 And Jacob and Laban offered a sacrifice on the mount, and they ate there by the heap, and they tarried in the mount all night, and Laban rose up early in the morning, and he wept with his daughters, and he kissed them, and he returned to his place. 54 And he hastened and sent off his son Beor, who was seventeen years old, with Abichorof the son of Uz, the son of Nahor, and ten men were with them. 55 And they hastened, and went, and passed on the road before Jacob, and they came by another road to the land of Seir. 56 And they came to Esau and said to him, "Thus says your brother and relative, your mother's brother Laban, the son of Bethuel, saying, 57 Have you heard what your brother Jacob has done to me, who first came to me naked and bare, and I went to meet him, and brought him to my house with honor, and I made him great, and I gave him my two daughters for wives and also two of my maids? 58 And God blessed him on my account, and he increased abundantly, and had sons, daughters, and maidservants. 59 He also has an immense stock of flocks and herds, camels and donkeys, also silver and gold in abundance; and when he saw that his wealth increased, he left me while I went to shear my sheep, and he rose up and fled in secrecy. 60 And he lifted his wives and children on camels, and he led away all his cattle and property which he acquired in my land, and he lifted up his countenance to go to his father Isaac, to the land of Canaan. 61 And he did not permit me to kiss my daughters and their children, and he led my daughters as captives taken by the sword, and he also stole my gods and he fled. 62 And now I have left him in the mountain of the Brook of Jabuk, him and all belonging to him; he lacks nothing. 63 If it is your wish to go to him, go then and there you will find him, and you can do to him as your soul desires"; and Laban's messengers came and told Esau all these things. 64 And Esau heard all the words of Laban's messengers, and his anger was greatly kindled against Jacob, and he remembered his hatred, and his anger burned within him. **65** And Esau hastened and took his children, and servants, and the souls of his household, being sixty men, and he went and assembled all the children of Seir the Horite and their people, being three hundred and forty men, and took all this number of four hundred men with drawn swords, and he went to Jacob to strike him. **66** And Esau divided this number into several parts, and he took the sixty men of his children, and servants, and the souls of his household as one head and gave them in [the] care of his eldest son Eliphaz. **67** And he gave the remaining heads to the care of the six sons of Seir the Horite, and he placed every man over his generations and children. **68** And the whole of this camp went as it was, and Esau went among them toward Jacob, and he conducted them with speed. **69** And Laban's messengers departed from Esau and went to the land of Canaan, and they came to the house of Rebekah, the mother of Jacob and Esau. **70** And they told her, saying, "Behold, your son Esau has gone against his brother Jacob with four hundred men, for he heard that he was coming, and he has gone to make war with him, and to strike him, and to take all that he has." **71** And Rebekah hastened and sent seventy-two men from the servants of Isaac to meet Jacob on the road, for she said, "Perhaps Esau may make war with me in the road when he meets him." **72** And these messengers went on the road to meet Jacob, and they met him in the road of the brook on the opposite side of the brook Jabuk, and Jacob said when he saw them, "This camp is destined to me from God," and Jacob called the name of that place Machnayim. **73** And Jacob knew all his father's people, and he kissed them, and embraced them, and came with them, and Jacob asked them concerning his father and mother, and they said they were well. **74** And these messengers said to Jacob, "Your mother Rebekah has sent us to you, saying, I have heard, my son, that your brother Esau has gone out against you on the road with men from the children of Seir the Horite. **75** And therefore, my son, listen to my voice and see with your counsel what you will do, and when he comes up to you, supplicate him, and do not speak rashly to him, and give him a present from what you possess, and from what God has favored you with. **76** And when he asks you concerning your affairs, conceal nothing from him; perhaps he may turn from his anger against you and you will thereby save your soul—you and all belonging to you—for it is your duty to honor him, for he is your elder brother." **77** And when Jacob heard the words of his mother which the messengers had spoken to him, Jacob lifted up his voice and wept bitterly, and did as his mother then commanded him.

CHAPTER 32

1 And at that time Jacob sent messengers to his brother Esau toward the land of Seir, and he spoke words of supplication to him. **2** And he commanded them, saying, "Thus you will say to my lord, to Esau: Thus says your servant Jacob: Do not let my lord imagine that my father's blessing with which he blessed me has proved beneficial to me. **3** For I have been with Laban these twenty years, and he deceived me and changed my wages ten times, as it has all been already told to my lord. **4** And I served him in his house very laboriously, and afterward God saw my affliction, my labor, and the work of my hands, and He caused me to find grace and favor in His sight. **5** And afterward, through God's great mercy and kindness, I acquired oxen, and donkeys, and cattle, and menservants, and maidservants. **6** And now I am coming to my land and my home, to my father and mother who are in the land of Canaan; and I have sent to let my lord know all this in order to find favor in the sight of my lord, so that he may not imagine that I have obtained wealth of myself, or that the blessing with which my father blessed me has benefited me." **7** And those messengers went to Esau and found him on the borders of the land of Edom going toward Jacob, and four hundred men of the children of Seir the Horite were standing with drawn swords. **8** And the messengers of Jacob told Esau all the words that Jacob had spoken to them concerning Esau. **9** And Esau answered them with pride and contempt, and said to them, "Surely I have heard and truly it has been told to me what Jacob has done to Laban, who exalted him in his house and gave him his daughters for wives, and he begot sons and daughters, and abundantly increased in wealth and riches in Laban's house through his means. **10** And when he saw that his wealth was abundant and his riches great, he fled from Laban's house with

all belonging to him, and he led Laban's daughters away from the face of their father, as captives taken by the sword without telling him of it. **11** And not only to Laban has Jacob done this, but he has also done so to me and has twice supplanted me, and will I be silent? **12** Now I have therefore come this day with my camps to meet him, and I will do to him according to the desire of my heart." **13** And the messengers returned and came to Jacob, and said to him, "We came to your brother, to Esau, and we told him all your words, and thus he has answered us, and behold, he comes to meet you with four hundred men. **14** Now then, know and see what you will do and pray before God to deliver you from him." **15** And when he heard the words of his brother which he had spoken to the messengers of Jacob, Jacob was greatly afraid, and he was distressed. **16** And Jacob prayed to the Lord his God, and he said, "O Lord God of my fathers, Abraham and Isaac: You said to me when I went away from my father's house, saying, **17** I am the Lord God of your father Abraham and the God of Isaac; I give this land to you and your seed after you, and I will make your seed as the stars of the heavens, and you will spread out to the four sides of [the] heavens, and in you and in your Seed all the families of the earth will be blessed. **18** And you established Your words and gave to me riches, and children, and cattle—as the utmost wishes of my heart, You gave to Your servant; You gave to me all that I asked from You, so that I lacked nothing. **19** And afterward You said to me, Return to your parents and to your birthplace and I will still do well with you. **20** And now that I have come, and You delivered me from Laban, I will fall into the hands of Esau who will slay me, yes, together with the mothers of my children. **21** Now therefore, O Lord God, please also deliver me from the hands of my brother Esau, for I am greatly afraid of him. **22** And if there is no righteousness in me, do it for the sake of Abraham and my father Isaac. **23** For I know that through kindness and mercy I have acquired this wealth; now therefore, I implore You to deliver me this day with Your kindness and to answer me." **24** And Jacob ceased praying to the Lord, and he divided the people that were with him with the flocks and cattle into two camps, and he gave half to the care of Damasek, the son of Eliezer, Abraham's servant, for a camp, with his children, and the other half he gave to the care of his brother Elianus the son of Eliezer, to be for a camp with his children. **25** And he commanded them, saying, "Keep yourselves at a distance with your camps, and do not come too near each other, and if Esau comes to one camp and slays it, the other camp at a distance from it will escape him." **26** And Jacob tarried there that night, and during the whole night he gave his servants instructions concerning the forces and his children. **27** And the Lord heard the prayer of Jacob on that day, and the Lord then delivered Jacob from the hands of his brother Esau. **28** And the Lord sent three messengers of the messengers of Heaven, and they went before Esau and came to him. **29** And these messengers appeared to Esau and his people as two thousand men, riding on horses furnished with all sorts of war instruments, and they appeared in the sight of Esau and all his men to be divided into four camps, with four chiefs to them. **30** And one camp went on and they found Esau coming with four hundred men toward his brother Jacob, and this camp ran toward Esau and his people and terrified them, and Esau fell off the horse in alarm, and all his men separated from him in that place, for they were greatly afraid. **31** And the whole of the camp shouted after them when they fled from Esau, and all the warlike men answered, saying, **32** "Surely we are the servants of Jacob, who is the servant of God, and who then can stand against us?" And Esau said to them, "O then, my lord and brother Jacob is your lord, whom I have not seen for these twenty years, and now that I have come to see him this day, do you treat me in this manner?" **33** And the messengers answered him, saying, "As the Lord lives, were Jacob of whom you speak not your brother, we would not have let one remaining from you and your people, but only on account of Jacob we will do nothing to them." **34** And this camp passed from Esau and his men and it went away, and Esau and his men had gone from them about a league when the second camp came toward him with all sorts of weapons, and they also did to Esau and his men as the first camp had done to them. **35** And when they had left it to go on, behold, the third camp came toward him and they were all terrified, and Esau fell off the horse, and the whole camp cried out, and said, "Surely we are the servants of Jacob, who is the servant of God, and who can stand against us?" **36** And Esau again answered them, saying, "O then, Jacob my lord and your lord is my brother, and for twenty years I have not seen his countenance and hearing this day that he was coming, I went this day to meet him, and do you treat me in this manner?" **37** And they answered him, and said to him, "As the Lord lives, were Jacob not your brother as you have said, we would not have left a remnant from you and your men, but on account of Jacob of whom you speak being your brother, we will not meddle with you or your men." **38** And the third camp also passed from them, and he still continued his road with his men toward Jacob, when the fourth camp came toward him, and they also did to him and his men as the others had done. **39** And when Esau beheld the evil which the four messengers had done to him and to his men, he became greatly afraid of his brother Jacob, and he went to meet him in peace. **40** And Esau concealed his hatred against Jacob, because he was afraid of his life on account of his brother Jacob, and because he imagined that the four camps that he had lighted on were Jacob's servants. **41** And Jacob tarried that night with his servants in their camps, and he resolved with his servants to give a present to Esau from all that he had with him, and from all his property; and Jacob rose up in the morning, he and his men, and they chose from among the cattle a present for Esau. **42** And this is the amount of the present which Jacob chose from his flock to give to his brother Esau: and he selected two hundred and forty head from the flocks, and he selected from the camels and donkeys thirty each, and of the herds he chose fifty cows. **43** And he put them all in ten droves, and he placed each sort by itself, and he delivered them into the hands of ten of his servants, each drove by itself. **44** And he commanded them, and said to them, "Keep yourselves at a distance from each other, and put a space between the droves, and when Esau and those who are with him will meet you and ask you, saying, Whose are you, and where do you go, and to whom belongs all this before you, you will say to them, We are the servants of Jacob, and we come to meet Esau in peace, and behold, Jacob comes behind us. **45** And that which is before us is a present sent from Jacob to his brother Esau. **46** And if they will say to you, Why does he delay behind you, from coming to meet his brother and to see his face, then you will say to them, Surely he comes joyfully behind us to meet his brother, for he said, I will appease him with the present that goes to him, and after this I will see his face—perhaps he will accept me." **47** So the whole present passed on in the hands of his servants, and went before him on that day, and he lodged that night with his camps by the border of the Brook of Jabuk, and he rose up in the midst of the night, and he took his wives, and his maidservants, and all belonging to him, and he made them pass over the ford Jabuk that night. **48** And when he made all belonging to him pass over the brook, Jacob was left by himself, and a Man met him, and he wrestled with Him that night until the breaking of the day, and the hollow of Jacob's thigh was out of joint through wrestling with Him. **49** And at the break of day the Man left Jacob there, and He blessed him and went away, and Jacob passed the brook at the break of day, and he halted on his thigh. **50** And the sun rose on him when he had passed the brook, and he came up to the place of his cattle and children. **51** And they went on until midday, and while they were going, the present was passing on before them. **52** And Jacob lifted up his eyes and looked, and behold, Esau was at a distance, coming along with many men, about four hundred, and Jacob was greatly afraid of his brother. **53** And Jacob hastened and divided his children to his wives and his handmaids, and he put his daughter Dinah in a chest, and delivered her into the hands of his servants. **54** And he passed before his children and wives to meet his brother, and he bowed down to the ground. He bowed down seven times until he approached his brother, and God caused Jacob to find grace and favor in the sight of Esau and his men, for God had heard the prayer of Jacob. **55** And the fear of Jacob and his terror fell on his brother Esau, for Esau was greatly afraid of Jacob for what the messengers of God had done to Esau, and Esau's anger against Jacob was turned into kindness. **56** And when Esau saw Jacob running toward him, he also ran toward him, and he embraced him, and he fell on his neck, and they kissed and wept. **57** And God put fear and kindness toward Jacob in the hearts of the men that came with Esau, and they also kissed Jacob and embraced him. **58** And also Eliphaz, the son of Esau, with his four brothers, sons of Esau, wept with Jacob, and they kissed him and embraced him, for the fear of Jacob had fallen on them all. **59** And Esau lifted up his eyes and saw the women with their offspring, the children of Jacob, walking behind Jacob and bowing along the road to Esau. **60** And Esau said to Jacob, "Who are these with you, my brother? are they

your children or your servants?" and Jacob answered Esau and said, "They are my children which God has graciously given to your servant." **61** And while Jacob was speaking to Esau and his men, Esau beheld the whole camp, and he said to Jacob, "From where did you get the whole of the camp that I met last night?" and Jacob said, "To find favor in the sight of my lord, it is that which God graciously gave to your servant." **62** And the present came before Esau, and Jacob pressed Esau, saying, "Please take the present that I have brought to my lord," and Esau said, "Why is this my purpose? keep that which you have to yourself." **63** And Jacob said, "It is incumbent on me to give all this, since I have seen your face, that you still live in peace." **64** And Esau refused to take the present, and Jacob said to him, "I implore you, my lord, if I have now found favor in your sight, then receive my present at my hand, for I have therefore seen your face, as though I had seen a godlike face, because you were pleased with me." **65** And Esau took the present, and Jacob also gave silver, and gold, and bdellium to Esau, for he pressed him so much that he took them. **66** And Esau divided the cattle that were in the camp, and he gave the half to the men who had come with him, for they had come on hire, and the other half he delivered to the hands of his children. **67** And the silver, and gold, and bdellium he gave in the hands of his eldest son Eliphaz, and Esau said to Jacob, "Let us remain with you, and we will go slowly along with you until you come to my place with me, that we may dwell there together." **68** And Jacob answered his brother and said, "I would do as my lord speaks to me, but my lord knows that the children are tender, and the flocks and herds with their young who are with me only go slowly, for if they went swiftly they would all die, for you know their burdens and their fatigue. **69** Therefore, let my lord pass on before his servant, and I will go on slowly for the sake of the children and the flock, until I come to my lord's place—to Seir." **70** And Esau said to Jacob, "I will place with you some of the people that are with me to take care of you in the road, and to bear your fatigue and burden," and he said, "What need is there of that my lord, if I may find grace in your sight? **71** Behold, I will come to you, to Seir, to dwell there together as you have spoken; go then with your people for I will follow you." **72** And Jacob said this to Esau in order to remove Esau and his men from him, so that afterward Jacob might go to his father's house, to the land of Canaan. **73** And Esau listened to the voice of Jacob, and Esau returned with the four hundred men that were with him on their road to Seir, and that day Jacob and all belonging to him went as far as the extremity of the land of Canaan in its borders, and he remained there some time.

CHAPTER 33

1 And some time after Jacob went away from the borders of the land, he came to the land of Shalem, that is the city of Shechem, which is in the land of Canaan, and he rested in front of the city. **2** And he bought a parcel of the field which was there from the children of Hamor, the people of the land, for five shekels. **3** And Jacob built himself a house there, and he pitched his tent there, and he made shelters for his cattle; therefore he called the name of that place Succoth. **4** And Jacob remained in Succoth a year and six months. **5** At that time some of the women of the inhabitants of the land went to the city of Shechem to dance and rejoice with the daughters of the people of the city, and when they went out, then Rachel and Leah, the wives of Jacob, with their families, also went to behold the rejoicing of the daughters of the city. **6** And Dinah, the daughter of Jacob, also went along with them and saw the daughters of the city, and they remained there before these daughters while all the people of the city were standing by them to behold their rejoicings, and all the great people of the city were there. **7** And Shechem, the son of Hamor, the prince of the land, was also standing there to see them. **8** And Shechem beheld Dinah, the daughter of Jacob, sitting with her mother before the daughters of the city, and the young woman pleased him greatly, and he asked his friends and his people there, saying, "Whose daughter is that sitting among the women, whom I do not know in this city?" **9** And they said to him, "Surely this is the daughter of Jacob, the son of Isaac the Hebrew, who has dwelt in this city for some time, and when it was reported that the daughters of the land were going out to rejoice, she went with her mother and maidservants to sit among them as you see." **10** And Shechem beheld Dinah, the daughter of Jacob, and when he looked at her his soul became fixed on Dinah. **11** And he sent and had her taken by force, and Dinah came to the house of Shechem, and he seized her forcibly, and lay with her, and humbled her, and he loved her exceedingly, and placed her in his house. ¹² And they came and told the thing to Jacob, and when Jacob heard that Shechem had defiled his daughter Dinah, Jacob sent twelve of his servants to fetch Dinah from the house of Shechem, and they went and came to the house of Shechem to take Dinah away from there. ¹³ And when they came, Shechem went out to them with his men and drove them from his house, and he would not permit them to come before Dinah, but Shechem was sitting with Dinah, kissing and embracing her before their eyes. ¹⁴ And the servants of Jacob came back and told him, saying, "When we came, he and his men drove us away, and thus Shechem did to Dinah before our eyes." ¹⁵ And Jacob knew, moreover, that Shechem had defiled his daughter, but he said nothing, and his sons were feeding his cattle in the field, and Jacob remained silent until their return. ¹⁶ And before his sons came home, Jacob sent two maidens from his servants' daughters to take care of Dinah in the house of Shechem and to remain with her, and Shechem sent three of his friends to his father Hamor the son of Chiddekem, the son of Pered, saying, "Get this young woman [for] me for a wife." ¹⁷ And Hamor the son of Chiddekem the Hivite came to the house of his son Shechem, and he sat before him, and Hamor said to his son, "Shechem, is there then no woman among the daughters of your people that you will take a Hebrew woman who is not of your people?" ¹⁸ And Shechem said to him, "Only her must you get for me, for she is delightful in my sight"; and Hamor did according to the word of his son, for he was greatly beloved by him. ¹⁹ And Hamor went out to Jacob to commune with him concerning this matter, and when he had gone from the house of his son Shechem, before he came to Jacob to speak to him, behold, the sons of Jacob had come from the field as soon as they heard the thing that Shechem the son of Hamor had done. ²⁰ And the men were very much grieved concerning their sister, and they all came home fired with anger, before the time of gathering in their cattle. ²¹ And they came and sat before their father, and they spoke to him kindled with wrath, saying, "Surely death is due to this man and to his household, because the Lord God of the whole earth commanded Noah and his children that man will never rob, nor commit adultery; now behold, Shechem has both ravaged and committed fornication with our sister, and not one of all the people of the city spoke a word to him. ²² Surely you know and understand that the judgment of death is due to Shechem, and to his father, and to the whole city on account of the thing which he has done." ²³ And while they were speaking before their father in this matter, behold, Hamor the father of Shechem came to speak to Jacob the words of his son concerning Dinah, and he sat before Jacob and before his sons. ²⁴ And Hamor spoke to them, saying, "The soul of my son Shechem longs for your daughter; please give her to him for a wife and intermarry with us; give us your daughters and we will give you our daughters, and you will dwell with us in our land, and we will be as one people in the land. ²⁵ For our land is very extensive, so dwell and trade therein and get possessions in it, and do therein as you desire, and no one will prevent you by saying a word to you." ²⁶ And Hamor ceased speaking to Jacob and his sons, and behold, his son Shechem had come after him, and he sat before them. ²⁷ And Shechem spoke before Jacob and his sons, saying, "May I find favor in your sight that you will give me your daughter, and whatever you say to me I will do for her. ²⁸ Ask me for abundance of dowry and gift, and I will give it, and whatever you will say to me I will do that, and whoever he is that will rebel against your orders, he will die; only give me the young woman for a wife." ²⁹ And Simeon and Levi answered Hamor and his son Shechem deceitfully, saying, "All you have spoken to us we will do for you. ³⁰ And behold, our sister is in your house, but keep away from her until we send to our father Isaac concerning this matter, for we can do nothing without his consent. ³¹ For he knows the ways of our father Abraham, and whatever he says to us we will tell you—we will conceal nothing from you." ³² And Simeon and Levi spoke this to Shechem and his father in order to find a pretext, and to seek counsel what was to be done to Shechem and to his city in this matter. ³³ And when Shechem and his father heard the words of Simeon and Levi, it seemed good in their sight, and Shechem and his father came out to go home. ³⁴ And when they had gone, the sons of Jacob said to their father, saying, "Behold, we know that death is due to these wicked ones and to their city, because they transgressed that which God had commanded to Noah, and his children, and

his seed after them. ³⁵ And also because Shechem did this thing to our sister Dinah in defiling her, for such vileness will never be done among us. ³⁶ Now therefore, know and see what you will do and seek counsel and pretext [regarding] what is to be done to them, in order to kill all the inhabitants of this city." ³⁷ And Simeon said to them, "Here is a proper suggestion for you: tell them to circumcise every male among them as we are circumcised, and if they do not wish to do this, we will take our daughter from them and go away. ³⁸ And if they consent to do this and will do it, then when they are sunk down with pain, we will attack them with our swords, as on one who is quiet and peaceable, and we will slay every male person among them." ³⁹ And Simeon's advice pleased them, and Simeon and Levi resolved to do to them as it was proposed. ⁴⁰ And on the next morning Shechem and his father Hamor came to Jacob and his sons again to speak concerning Dinah, and to hear what answer the sons of Jacob would give to their words. ⁴¹ And the sons of Jacob spoke deceitfully to them, saying, "We told our father Isaac all your words, and your words pleased him. ⁴² But he spoke to us, saying, Thus his father Abraham commanded him from God, the Lord of the whole earth, that: Any man who is not of his descendants that should wish to take one of his daughters will cause every male belonging to him to be circumcised, as we are circumcised, and then we may give him our daughter for a wife. ⁴³ Now we have made known to you all our ways that our father spoke to us, for we cannot do this of which you spoke to us, to give our daughter to an uncircumcised man, for it is a disgrace to us. ⁴⁴ But herein will we consent to you to give you our daughter, and we will also take your daughters to ourselves, and will dwell among you, and be one people as you have spoken, if you will listen to us, and consent to be like us, to circumcise every male belonging to you, as we are circumcised. ⁴⁵ And if you will not listen to us, to have every male circumcised as we are circumcised, as we have commanded, then we will come to you, and take our daughter from you, and go away." ⁴⁶ And Shechem and his father Hamor heard the words of the sons of Jacob, and the thing pleased them exceedingly, and Shechem and his father Hamor hastened to do the wishes of the sons of Jacob, for Shechem was very fond of Dinah, and his soul was riveted to her. ⁴⁷ And Shechem and his father Hamor hastened to the gate of the city, and they assembled all the men of their city and spoke to them the words of the sons of Jacob, saying, ⁴⁸ "We came to these men, the sons of Jacob, and we spoke to them concerning their daughter, and these men will consent to do according to our wishes, and behold, our land is of great extent for them, and they will dwell in it, and trade in it, and we will be one people; we will take their daughters, and we will give our daughters to them for wives. ⁴⁹ But only on this condition will these men consent to do this thing: that every male among us must be circumcised as they are circumcised, as their God commanded them, and when we will have done according to their instructions to be circumcised, then they will dwell among us, together with their cattle and possessions, and we will be as one people with them." ⁵⁰ And when all the men of the city heard the words of Shechem and his father Hamor, then all the men of their city were agreeable to this proposal, and they obeyed to be circumcised, for Shechem and his father Hamor were greatly esteemed by them, being the princes of the land. ⁵¹ And on the next day, Shechem and his father Hamor rose up early in the morning, and they assembled all the men of their city into the middle of the city, and they called for the sons of Jacob, who circumcised every male belonging to them on that day and the next. ⁵² And they circumcised Shechem and his father Hamor, and the five brothers of Shechem, and then everyone rose up and went home, for this thing was from the Lord against the city of Shechem, and Simeon's counsel was from the Lord in this matter in order that the Lord might deliver the city of Shechem into the hands of Jacob's two sons.

CHAPTER 34

¹ And the number of all the males that were circumcised were six hundred and forty-five men, and two hundred and forty-six children. ² But Chiddekem, son of Pered, the father of Hamor, and his six brothers, would not listen to Shechem and his father Hamor; and they would not be circumcised, for the proposal of the sons of Jacob was loathsome in their sight, and their anger was greatly roused at this, that the people of the city had not listened to them. ³ And in the evening of the second day they found eight small children who had not been

circumcised, for their mothers had concealed them from Shechem, and his father Hamor, and from the men of the city. **4** And Shechem and his father Hamor sent to have them brought before them to be circumcised when Chiddekem and his six brothers sprang at them with their swords and sought to slay them. **5** And they also sought to slay Shechem and his father Hamor, and they sought to slay Dinah with them on account of this matter. **6** And they said to them, "What is this thing that you have done? are there no women among the daughters of your brothers the Canaanites that you wish to take to yourselves daughters of the Hebrews, whom you did not know before, and will do this act which your fathers never commanded you? **7** Do you imagine that you will succeed through this act which you have done? and what will you answer in this affair to your brothers the Canaanites who will come tomorrow and ask you concerning this thing? **8** And if your act will not appear just and good in their sight, what will you do for your lives, and me for our lives, in your not having listened to our voices? **9** And if the inhabitants of the land and all your brothers, the children of Ham, will hear of your act, saying, **10** On account of a Hebrew woman, Shechem, and his father Hamor, and all the inhabitants of their city did that with which they had been unacquainted and which their ancestors never commanded them; where then will you fly, or where conceal your shame, all your days before your brothers, the inhabitants of the land of Canaan? **11** Now therefore, we cannot bear up against this thing which you have done, neither can we be burdened with this yoke on us, which our ancestors did not command us. **12** Behold, tomorrow we will go and assemble all our brothers, the Canaanite brothers who dwell in the land, and we will all come and strike you and all those who trust in you, that there will not be a remnant left from you or them." **13** And when Hamor and his son Shechem and all the people of the city heard the words of Chiddekem and his brothers, they were terribly afraid for their lives at their words, and they converted of what they had done. **14** And Shechem and his father Hamor answered their father Chiddekem and his brothers, and they said to them, "All the words which you spoke to us are true. **15** Now do not say, nor imagine in your hearts, that on account of the love of the Hebrews we did this thing that our ancestors did not command us. **16** But because we saw that it was not their intention and desire to accede to our wishes concerning their daughter as to our taking her, except on this condition, so we listened to their voices and did this act which you saw in order to obtain our desire from them. **17** And when we will have obtained our request from them, we will then return to them and do to them that which you say to us. **18** We implore you then to wait and tarry until our flesh will be healed and we again become strong, and we will then go together against them, and do to them that which is in your hearts and in ours." **19** And Dinah the daughter of Jacob heard all these words which Chiddekem and his brothers had spoken, and what Hamor, and his son Shechem, and the people of their city had answered them. **20** And she hastened and sent one of her maidens—that her father had sent to take care of her in the house of Shechem—to Jacob her father and to her brothers, saying, **21** "Thus Chiddekem and his brothers advised concerning you, and thus Hamor, and Shechem, and the people of the city answered them." **22** And when Jacob heard these words he was filled with wrath, and he was indignant at them, and his anger was kindled against them. **23** And Simeon and Levi swore and said, "As the Lord lives, the God of the whole earth, by this time tomorrow there will not be a remnant left in the whole city." **24** And twenty young men had concealed themselves who were not circumcised, and these young men fought against Simeon and Levi, and Simeon and Levi killed eighteen of them, and two fled from them and escaped to some lime pits that were in the city, and Simeon and Levi sought for them, but could not find them. **25** And Simeon and Levi continued to go around in the city, and they killed all the people of the city at the edge of the sword, and they left none remaining. **26** And there was a great consternation in the midst of the city, and the cry of the people of the city ascended to Heaven, and all the women and children cried aloud. **27** And Simeon and Levi slew all the city; they did not leave [even one] male remaining in the whole city. **28** And they slew Hamor and his son Shechem at the edge of the sword, and they brought Dinah away from the house of Shechem, and they went from there. **29** And the sons of Jacob went and returned, and came on the slain, and spoiled all their property which was in the city and the field. **30** And while they were taking the spoil, three hundred men stood up, and threw dust at them, and struck them with stones; then Simeon

turned to them and he slew them all with the edge of the sword, and Simeon turned before Levi, and came into the city. **31** And they took away their sheep, and their oxen, and their cattle, and also the remainder of the women and little ones, and they led all these away, and they opened a gate, and went out, and came to their father Jacob with vigor. **32** And when Jacob saw all that they had done to the city, and saw the spoil that they took from them, Jacob was very angry at them, and Jacob said to them, "What is this that you have done to me? behold, I obtained rest among the Canaanite inhabitants of the land, and none of them meddled with me. **33** And now you have done [this] to make me obnoxious to the inhabitants of the land, among the Canaanites and the Perizzites, and I am but of a small number, and they will all assemble against me and slay me when they hear of your work with their brothers, and my household and I will be destroyed." **34** And Simeon, and Levi, and all their brothers with them answered their father Jacob and said to him, "Behold, we live in the land, and will Shechem do this to our sister? why are you silent at all that Shechem has done? and will he deal with our sister as with a harlot in the streets?" **35** And the number of women whom Simeon and Levi took captives from the city of Shechem, whom they did not slay, was eighty-five who had not known a man. **36** And among them was a young woman of beautiful appearance and well-favored, whose name was Bunah, and Simeon took her for a wife, and the number of the males which they took captives and did not slay was forty-seven men, and the rest they slew. **37** And all the young men and women that Simeon and Levi had taken captives from the city of Shechem were servants to the sons of Jacob and to their children after them until the day of the sons of Jacob going out from the land of Egypt. **38** And when Simeon and Levi had gone out from the city, the two young men that were left, who had concealed themselves in the city, and did not die among the people of the city, rose up, and these young men went into the city and walked around in it, and found the city desolate without man, and only women weeping, and these young men cried out and said, "Behold, this is the evil which the sons of Jacob the Hebrew did to this city in their having destroyed one of the Canaanite cities this day, and they were not afraid of their lives in all the land of Canaan." **39** And these men left the city and went to the city of Tapnach, and they came there and told the inhabitants of Tapnach all that had befallen them, and all that the sons of Jacob had done to the city of Shechem. **40** And the information reached Jashub king of Tapnach, and he sent men to the city of Shechem to see those young men, for the king did not believe them in this account, saying, "How could two men lay waste such a large town as Shechem?" **41** And the messengers of Jashub came back and told him, saying, "We came to the city, and it is destroyed—there is not a man there, only weeping women; neither is any flock or cattle there, for the sons of Jacob took away all that was in the city." **42** And Jashub wondered at this, saying, "How could two men do this thing, to destroy such a large city, and not one man was able to stand against them? **43** For the like has not been from the days of Nimrod, and not even from the remotest time has the like taken place"; and Jashub, king of Tapnach, said to his people, "Be courageous and we will go and fight against these Hebrews, and do to them as they did to the city, and we will avenge the cause of the people of the city." **44** And Jashub, king of Tapnach, consulted with his counselors about this matter, and his advisers said to him, "You will not prevail over the Hebrews alone, for they must be powerful to do this work to the whole city. **45** If two of them laid waste the whole city, and no one stood against them, surely if you will go against them, they will all rise against us and destroy us likewise. **46** But if you will send to all the kings that surround us, and let them come together, then we will go with them and fight against the sons of Jacob; then you will prevail against them." **47** And Jashub heard the words of his counselors, and their words pleased him and his people, and he did so; and Jashub king of Tapnach sent to all the kings of the Amorites that surrounded Shechem and Tapnach, saying, **48** "Go up with me and assist me, and we will strike Jacob the Hebrew and all his sons, and destroy them from the earth, for thus he did to the city of Shechem, and do you not know of it?" **49** And all the kings of the Amorites heard the evil that the sons of Jacob had done to the city of Shechem, and they were greatly astonished at them. **50** And the seven kings of the Amorites assembled with all their armies, about ten thousand men with drawn swords, and came to fight against the sons of Jacob; and Jacob heard that the kings of the Amorites had assembled to fight against his sons, and Jacob was greatly afraid, and it distressed him. **51** And Jacob exclaimed against Simeon and Levi, saying, "What is this act that you did? why have you injured me, to bring all the children of Canaan against me to destroy me and my household? for I was at rest, even my household and I, and you have done this thing to me, and provoked the inhabitants of the land against me by your proceedings." **52** And Judah answered his father, saying, "Was it for nothing [that] my brothers Simeon and Levi killed all the inhabitants of Shechem? Surely it was because Shechem had humbled our sister and transgressed the command of our God to Noah and his children, for Shechem took our sister away by force and committed adultery with her. **53** And Shechem did all this evil and not one of the inhabitants of his city interfered with him to say, Why will you do this? surely my brothers went and struck the city for this [reason], and the Lord delivered it into their hands, because its inhabitants had transgressed the commands of our God. Is it then for nothing that they have done all this? **54** And now why are you afraid or distressed, and why are you displeased at my brothers, and why is your anger kindled against them? **55** Surely our God who delivered the city of Shechem and its people into their hand will also deliver into our hands all the Canaanite kings who are coming against us, and we will do to them as my brothers did to Shechem. **56** Now be tranquil about them and cast away your fears, but trust in the Lord our God, and pray to Him to assist us, and deliver us, and deliver our enemies into our hands." **57** And Judah called to one of his father's servants, "Go now and see where those kings who are coming against us are situated with their armies." **58** And the servant went and looked far off, and went up opposite Mount Sihon, and saw all the camps of the kings standing in the fields, and he returned to Judah and said, "Behold, the kings are situated in the field with all their camps—a people exceedingly numerous, like to the sand on the seashore." **59** And Judah said to Simeon, and Levi, and to all his brothers, "Strengthen yourselves and be sons of valor, for the Lord our God is with us; do not fear them. **60** Stand ready, each man, girt with his weapons of war, his bow and his sword, and we will go and fight against these uncircumcised men; the Lord is our God; He will save us." **61** And they rose up, and each girded on his weapons of war, great and small, eleven sons of Jacob, and all the servants of Jacob with them. **62** And all the servants of Isaac who were with Isaac in Hebron, all came to them equipped in all sorts of war instruments, and the sons of Jacob and their servants, being one hundred and twelve men, went toward these kings, and Jacob also went with them. **63** And the sons of Jacob sent to their father Isaac, the son of Abraham, to Hebron, the same is Kirjath-Arba, saying, **64** "We implore you: pray for us to the Lord our God to protect us from the hands of the Canaanites who are coming against us, and to deliver them into our hands." **65** And Isaac the son of Abraham prayed to the Lord for his sons, and he said, "O Lord God, You promised my father, saying, I will multiply your seed as the stars of the heavens; and You also promised me. And establish Your word now that the kings of Canaan are coming together to make war with my children because they committed no violence. **66** Now therefore, O Lord God, God of the whole earth, please pervert the counsel of these kings that they may not fight against my sons. **67** And impress the hearts of these kings and their people with the terror of my sons and bring down their pride that they may turn away from my sons. **68** And deliver my sons and their servants from them with Your strong hand and outstretched arm, for power and might are in Your hands to do all this." **69** And the sons of Jacob and their servants went toward these kings, and they trusted in the Lord their God, and while they were going, their father Jacob also prayed to the Lord and said, "O Lord God, powerful and exalted God, who has reigned from days of old, from then until now and forever: **70** You are He who stirs up wars and causes them to cease; in Your hand are power and might to exalt and to bring down; O may my prayer be acceptable before You that You may turn to me with Your mercies to impress the hearts of these kings and their people with the terror of my sons, and terrify them and their camps, and deliver all those that trust in You with Your great kindness, for it is You who can bring people under us and reduce nations under our power."

CHAPTER 35

1 And all the kings of the Amorites came and took their stand in the field to consult with their counselors what was to be done with the sons of Jacob, for they were still afraid of them, saying, "Behold, two of them slew the whole of the city of Shechem." **2** And the Lord heard the prayers of Isaac and Jacob, and He filled the hearts of all these kings' advisers with great fear and terror that they unanimously exclaimed, **3** "Are you silly this day, or is there no understanding in you, that you will fight with the Hebrews, and why will you take a delight in your own destruction this day? **4** Behold, two of them came to the city of Shechem without fear or terror, and they killed all the inhabitants of the city, that no man stood up against them, and how will you be able to fight with them all? **5** Surely you know that their God is exceedingly fond of them, and has done mighty things for them, such as have not been done from days of old, and among all the gods of [the] nations there is none [that] can do like to His mighty deeds. **6** Surely He delivered their father Abraham, the Hebrew, from the hand of Nimrod, and from the hand of all his people who had many times sought to slay him. **7** He also delivered him from the fire in which King Nimrod had cast him, and his God delivered him from it. **8** And who else can do the like? surely it was Abraham who slew the five kings of Elam when they had touched his brother's son who in those days dwelt in Sodom; **9** and he took his servant that was faithful in his house and a few of his men, and they pursued the kings of Elam in one night, and killed them, and restored to his brother's son all his property which they had taken from him. **10** And surely you know the God of these Hebrews is much delighted with them, and they are also delighted with Him, for they know that He delivered them from all their enemies. **11** And behold, through his love toward his God, Abraham took his only and precious son and intended to bring him up as a burnt-offering to his God, and had it not been for God who prevented him from doing this, he would then have done it through his love for his God. **12** And God saw all his works, and swore to him, and promised him that He would deliver his sons and all his seed from every trouble that would befall them, because he had done this thing, and through his love for his God stifled his compassion for his child. **13** And have you not heard what their God did to Pharaoh king of Egypt, and to Abimelech king of Gerar, through taking Abraham's wife, who said of her, She is my sister, lest they might slay him on account of her, and think of taking her for a wife? and God did to them and their people all that you heard of. **14** And behold, we ourselves saw with our [own] eyes that Esau, the brother of Jacob, came to him with four hundred men with the intention of slaying him, for he called to mind that he had taken his father's blessing away from him. **15** And he went to meet him when he came from Syria, to strike the mother with the children, and who delivered him from his hands but his God in whom he trusted? he delivered him from the hand of his brother and also from the hands of his enemies, and He will surely protect them again. **16** Who does not know that it was their God who inspired them with strength to do to the town of Shechem the calamity which you heard of? **17** Could it then be with their own strength that two men could destroy such a large city as Shechem had it not been for their God in whom they trusted? he said and did to them all this to slay the inhabitants of the city in their city. **18** And can you then prevail over those who have come out together from your city to fight with the whole of them, even if one thousand times as many more should come to your assistance? **19** Surely you know and understand that you do not come to fight with them, but you come to war with their God who chose them, and you have therefore all come this day to be destroyed. **20** Now therefore, refrain from this calamity which you are endeavoring to bring on yourselves, and it will be better for you not to go to battle with them, although they are but few in numbers, because their God is with them." **21** And when the kings of the Amorites heard all the words of their advisers, their hearts were filled with terror, and they were afraid of the sons of Jacob and would not fight against them. **22** And they inclined their ears to the words of their advisers, and they listened to all their words, and the words of the counselors greatly pleased the kings, and they did so. **23** And the kings turned and refrained from the sons of Jacob, for they dared not approach them to make war with them, for they were greatly afraid of them, and their hearts melted within them from their fear of them. **24** For this proceeded from the Lord to them, for He heard the prayers of His servants Isaac and Jacob, for they trusted in Him; and all these kings returned with their camps on that day, each to his own city, and they did not fight with the sons of Jacob at that time. **25** And the sons of Jacob kept their station that day until evening opposite Mount Sihon, and seeing that these kings did not come to fight against them, the sons of Jacob returned home.

CHAPTER 36

¹ At that time the Lord appeared to Jacob, saying, "Arise, go to Bethel and remain there, and make an altar there to the Lord who appears to you, who delivered you and your sons from affliction." ² And Jacob rose up with his sons and all belonging to him, and they went and came to Bethel according to the word of the Lord. ³ And Jacob was ninety-nine years old when he went up to Bethel, and Jacob, and his sons, and all the people that were with him remained in Bethel in Luz, and he built an altar there to the Lord who appeared to him, and Jacob and his sons remained in Bethel six months. ⁴ At that time Deborah the daughter of Uz, the nurse of Rebekah, who had been with Jacob, died, and Jacob buried her beneath Bethel under an oak that was there. ⁵ And Rebekah the daughter of Bethuel, the mother of Jacob, also died at that time in Hebron, the same is Kirjath-Arba, and she was buried in the cave of Machpelah which Abraham had bought from the children of Heth. ⁶ And the life of Rebekah was one hundred and thirty-three years, and she died; and when Jacob heard that his mother Rebekah was dead, he wept bitterly for his mother, and made a great mourning for her, and for her nurse Deborah beneath the oak, and he called the name of that place Allon-bachuth. ⁷ And Laban the Syrian died in those days, for God struck him because he transgressed the covenant that existed between him and Jacob. ⁸ And Jacob was one hundred years old when the Lord appeared to him, and blessed him, and called his name Israel; and Rachel, the wife of Jacob, conceived in those days. ⁹ And at that time Jacob and all belonging to him journeyed from Bethel to go to his father's house, to Hebron. ¹⁰ And while they were going on the road and there was yet but a little way to come to Ephrath, Rachel bore a son, and she had hard labor, and she died. ¹¹ And Jacob buried her in the way to Ephrath, which is Beth-Lehem, and he set a pillar on her grave which is there to this day; and the days of Rachel were forty-five years and she died. ¹² And Jacob called the name of his son that was born to him, which Rachel bore to him, Benjamin, for he was born to him in the land on the right hand. ¹³ And it was after the death of Rachel that Jacob pitched his tent in the tent of her handmaid Bilhah. ¹⁴ And Reuben was jealous for his mother Leah on account of this, and he was filled with anger, and he rose up in his anger, and went, and entered the tent of Bilhah, and there he removed his father's bed. ¹⁵ At that time the portion of birthright, together with the kingly and priestly offices, was removed from the sons of Reuben, for he had profaned his father's bed, and the birthright was given to Joseph, the kingly office to Judah, and the priesthood to Levi, because Reuben had defiled his father's bed. ¹⁶ And these are the generations of Jacob who were born to him in Padan-Aram, and the sons of Jacob were twelve. ¹⁷ The sons of Leah were Reuben the firstborn, and Simeon, Levi, Judah, Issachar, Zebulun, and their sister Dinah; and the sons of Rachel were Joseph and Benjamin. ¹⁸ The sons of Zilpah, Leah's handmaid, were Gad and Asher; and the sons of Bilhah, Rachel's handmaid, were Dan and Naphtali; these are the sons of Jacob which were born to him in Padan-Aram. ¹⁹ And Jacob, and his sons, and all belonging to him journeyed and came to Mamre, which is Kirjath-Arba, that is in Hebron, where Abraham and Isaac sojourned; and Jacob with his sons and all belonging to him dwelt with his father in Hebron. ²⁰ And his brother Esau, and his sons, and all belonging to him went to the land of Seir and dwelt there, and had possessions in the land of Seir, and the children of Esau were fruitful and multiplied exceedingly in the land of Seir. ²¹ And these are the generations of Esau that were born to him in the land of Canaan, and the sons of Esau were five. ²² And Adah bore to Esau his firstborn Eliphaz, and she also bore Reuel to him; and Aholibamah bore Jeush, Yaalam, and Korah to him. ²³ These are the children of Esau who were born to him in the land of Canaan; and the sons of Eliphaz, the son of Esau, were Teman, Omar, Zepho, Gatam, Kenaz, and Amalex; and the sons of Reuel were Nachas, Zerach, Shamah, and Mizzah; ²⁴ and the sons of Jeush were Timnah, Alvah, [and] Jetheth; and the sons of Yaalam were Alah, Phinor, and Kenaz; ²⁵ and the sons of Korah were Teman, Mibzar, Magdiel, and Eram; these are the families of the sons of Esau according to their chiefdoms in the land of Seir. ²⁶ And these are the names of the sons of Seir the Horite, inhabitants of the land of Seir: Lotan, Shobal, Zibeon, Anah, Dishan, Ezer, and Dishon, being seven sons. ²⁷ And the children of Lotan were Hori, Heman, and their sister Timna (that is Timna who came to Jacob and his sons, and they would not give ear to her, and she went and became a concubine to Eliphaz the son of Esau, and she bore Amalek to him). ²⁸ And the sons of Shobal were Alvan, Manahas, Ebal, Shepho, and Onam; and the sons of Zibeon were Ajah and Anah (this was that Anah who found the Yemim in the wilderness when he fed the donkeys of Zibeon his father. ²⁹ And while he was feeding his father's donkeys, he led them to the wilderness at different times to feed them. ³⁰ And there was a day that he brought them to one of the deserts on the seashore, opposite the wilderness of the people, and while he was feeding them, behold, a very heavy storm came from the other side of the sea and rested on the donkeys that were feeding there, and they all stood still. ³¹ And afterward about one hundred and twenty great and terrible animals came out from the wilderness at the other side of the sea, and they all came to the place where the donkeys were, and they placed themselves there. ³² And those animals, from their middle downward, were in the shape of the children of men, and from their middle upward, some had the likeness of bears, and some the likeness of the keephas, with tails behind them from between their shoulders reaching down to the earth, like the tails of the ducheephas, and these animals came, and mounted, and rode on these donkeys, and led them away, and they went away to this day. ³³ And one of these animals approached Anah and struck him with his tail, and then fled from that place. ³⁴ And when he saw this work, he was exceedingly afraid for his life, and he fled and escaped to the city. ³⁵ And he related to his sons and brothers all that had happened to him, and many men went to seek the donkeys but could not find them, and Anah and his brothers no longer went to that place from that day following, for they were greatly afraid for their lives). ³⁶ And the children of Anah, the son of Seir, were Dishon and his sister Aholibamah, and the children of Dishon were Hemdan, Eshban, Ithran, and Cheran, and the children of Ezer were Bilhan, Zaavan, and Akan, and the children of Dishon were Uz and Aran. ³⁷ These are the families of the children of Seir the Horite, according to their chiefdoms in the land of Seir. ³⁸ And Esau and his children dwelt in the land of Seir the Horite, the inhabitant of the land, and they had possessions in it, and were fruitful and multiplied exceedingly, and Jacob, and his children, and all belonging to them dwelt with their father Isaac in the land of Canaan as the Lord had commanded their father Abraham.

CHAPTER 37

¹ And in the one hundred and fifth year of the life of Jacob, that is the ninth year of Jacob's dwelling with his children in the land of Canaan, he came from Padan-Aram. ² And in those days Jacob journeyed with his children from Hebron, and they went and returned to the city of Shechem, they and all belonging to them, and they dwelt there, for the children of Jacob obtained good and fat pasture land for their cattle in the city of Shechem, the city of Shechem having then been rebuilt, and there were about three hundred men and women in it. ³ And Jacob, and his children, and all belonging to him dwelt in the part of the field which Jacob had bought from Hamor the father of Shechem when he came from Padan-Aram before Simeon and Levi had smitten the city. ⁴ And all those kings of the Canaanites and Amorites that surrounded the city of Shechem heard that the sons of Jacob had come to Shechem again and dwelt there. ⁵ And they said, "Will the sons of Jacob the Hebrew come to the city again and dwell therein after they have smitten its inhabitants and driven them out? will they now return and also drive out those who are dwelling in the city or slay them?" ⁶ And all the kings of Canaan assembled again, and they came together to make war with Jacob and his sons. ⁷ And Jashub king of Tapnach also sent to all his neighboring kings, to Elan king of Gaash, and to Ihuri king of Shiloh, and to Parathon king of Chazar, and to Susi king of Sarton, and to Laban king of Bethchoran, and to Shabir king of Othnay-mah, saying, ⁸ "Come up to me and assist me, and let us strike Jacob the Hebrew, and his sons, and all belonging to him, for they have come to Shechem again to possess it and to slay its inhabitants as before." ⁹ And all these kings assembled together and came with all their camps—a people exceedingly plentiful like the sand on the seashore—and they were all opposite to Tapnach. ¹⁰ And Jashub king of Tapnach went out

to them with all his army, and he encamped with them opposite to Tapnach outside the city, and they divided all these kings into seven divisions, being seven camps against the sons of Jacob. **11** And they sent a declaration to Jacob and his sons, saying, "Come out to us, all of you, that we may have an interview together in the plain, and revenge the cause of the men of Shechem whom you slew in their city, and you will now return to the city of Shechem again, and dwell therein, and slay its inhabitants as before." **12** And the sons of Jacob heard this and their anger was exceedingly kindled at the words of the kings of Canaan, and ten of the sons of Jacob hastened and rose up, and each of them girded on his weapons of war; and there were one hundred and two of their servants with them equipped in battle array. **13** And all these men, the sons of Jacob with their servants, went toward these kings, and their father Jacob was with them, and they all stood on the heap of Shechem. **14** And Jacob prayed to the Lord for his sons, and he spread out his hands to the Lord, and he said, "O God, You are [the] almighty God, You are our Father, You formed us and we are the works of Your hands; please deliver my sons through Your mercy from the hand of their enemies who are coming to fight with them this day and save them from their hand, for in Your hand is power and might to save the few from the many. **15** And give to my sons, Your servants, strength of heart and might to fight with their enemies, to subdue them, and make their enemies fall before them, and do not let my sons and their servants die through the hands of the children of Canaan. **16** But if it seems good in Your eyes to take away the lives of my sons and their servants, take them in Your great mercy through the hands of Your ministers, that they may not perish this day by the hands of the kings of the Amorites." **17** And when Jacob ceased praying to the Lord, the earth shook from its place, and the sun darkened, and all these kings were terrified, and a great consternation seized them. **18** And the Lord listened to the prayer of Jacob, and the Lord impressed the hearts of all the kings and their hosts with the terror and awe of the sons of Jacob, **19** for the Lord caused them to hear the voice of chariots, and the voice of mighty horses from the sons of Jacob, and the voice of a great army accompanying them. **20** And these kings were seized with great terror at the sons of Jacob, and while they were standing in their quarters, behold, the sons of Jacob advanced on them with one hundred and twelve men, with a great and tremendous shouting. **21** And when the kings saw the sons of Jacob advancing toward them, they were still more panic-stricken, and they were inclined to retreat from before the sons of Jacob as at first, and not to fight with them. **22** But they did not retreat, saying, "It would thus be a disgrace to us to retreat twice from before the Hebrews." **23** And the sons of Jacob came near and advanced against all these kings and their armies, and they saw, and behold, it was a very mighty people, [as] numerous as the sand of the sea. **24** And the sons of Jacob called to the Lord and said, "Help us, O Lord! Help us and answer us, for we trust in You! And let us not die by the hands of these uncircumcised men who have come against us this day." **25** And the sons of Jacob girded on their weapons of war, and they took in their hands—each man—his shield and his javelin, and they approached to battle. **26** And Judah, the son of Jacob, ran first before his brothers, and ten of his servants with him, and he went toward these kings. **27** And Jashub, king of Tapnach, also came out first with his army before Judah, and Judah saw Jashub and his army coming toward him, and Judah's wrath was kindled, and his anger burned within him, and he approached to battle in which Judah ventured his life. **28** And Jashub and all his army were advancing toward Judah, and he was riding on a very strong and powerful horse, and Jashub was a very valiant man, and covered with iron and brass from head to foot. **29** And while he was on the horse, he shot arrows with both hands from before and behind, as was his manner in all his battles, and he never missed the place to which he aimed his arrows. **30** And when Jashub came to fight with Judah, and was darting many arrows against Judah, the Lord bound the hand of Jashub, and all the arrows that he shot rebounded on his own men. **31** And notwithstanding this, Jashub kept advancing toward Judah, to challenge him with the arrows, but the distance between them was about thirty cubits, and when Judah saw Jashub darting out his arrows against him, he ran to him with his wrath-excited might. **32** And Judah took up a large stone from the ground, and its weight was sixty shekels, and Judah ran toward Jashub and struck him on his shield with the stone, [so] that Jashub was stunned with the blow and fell off from his horse to the ground. **33** And the shield burst apart out of the hand of

Jashub, and through the force of the blow sprang to the distance of about fifteen cubits, and the shield fell before the second camp. **34** And the kings that came with Jashub saw at a distance the strength of Judah, the son of Jacob, and what he had done to Jashub, and they were terribly afraid of Judah. **35** And they assembled near Jashub's camp, seeing his confusion, and Judah drew his sword and struck forty-two men of the camp of Jashub, and the whole of Jashub's camp fled before Judah, and no man stood against him, and they left Jashub and fled from him, and Jashub was still prostrate on the ground. **36** And Jashub seeing that all the men of his camp had fled from him, hastened and rose up with terror against Judah, and stood on his legs opposite Judah. **37** And Jashub had a duel with Judah, placing shield toward shield, and Jashub's men all fled, for they were greatly afraid of Judah. **38** And Jashub took his spear in his hand to strike Judah on his head, but Judah had quickly placed his shield to his head against Jashub's spear, so that the shield of Judah received the blow from Jashub's spear, and the shield was split in too. **39** And when Judah saw that his shield was split, he hastily drew his sword and struck Jashub at his ankles and cut off his feet, [so] that Jashub fell on the ground, and the spear fell from his hand. **40** And Judah hastily picked up Jashub's spear, with which he severed his head and cast it next to his feet. **41** And when the sons of Jacob saw what Judah had done to Jashub, they all ran into the ranks of the other kings, and the sons of Jacob fought with the army of Jashub, and the armies of all the kings that were there. **42** And the sons of Jacob caused fifteen thousand of their men to fall, and they struck them as if striking at gourds, and the rest fled for their lives. **43** And Judah was still standing by the body of Jashub, and stripped Jashub of his coat of mail. **44** And Judah also took off the iron and brass that was around Jashub, and behold, nine men of the captains of Jashub came along to fight against Judah. **45** And Judah hastened and took up a stone from the ground, and with it struck one of them on the head, and his skull was fractured, and the body also fell from the horse to the ground. **46** And the eight captains that remained, seeing the strength of Judah, were greatly afraid and they fled, and Judah pursued them with his ten men, and they overtook them and slew them. **47** And the sons of Jacob were still striking the armies of the kings, and they slew many of them, but those kings daringly kept their stand with their captains, and did not retreat from their places, and they exclaimed against those of their armies that fled from before the sons of Jacob, but none would listen to them, for they were afraid for their lives lest they should die. **48** And all the sons of Jacob, after having smitten the armies of the kings, returned and came before Judah, and Judah was still slaying the eight captains of Jashub, and stripping off their garments. **49** And Levi saw Elon, king of Gaash, advancing toward him, with his fourteen captains to strike him, but Levi did not know it for certain. **50** And Elon with his captains approached nearer, and Levi looked back and saw that battle was given to him in the rear, and Levi ran with twelve of his servants, and they went and slew Elon and his captains with the edge of the sword.

CHAPTER 38

1 And Ihuri king of Shiloh came up to assist Elon, and when he approached Jacob, Jacob drew his bow that was in his hand and struck Ihuri with an arrow which caused his death. **2** And when Ihuri king of Shiloh was dead, the four remaining kings fled from their station with the rest of the captains, and they endeavored to retreat, saying, "We have no more strength with the Hebrews after their having killed the three kings and their captains who were more powerful than we are." **3** And when the sons of Jacob saw that the remaining kings had removed from their station, they pursued them, and Jacob also came from the heap of Shechem, from the place where he was standing, and they went after the kings and they approached them with their servants. **4** And the kings and the captains with the rest of their armies, seeing that the sons of Jacob approached them, were afraid for their lives and fled until they reached the city of Chazar. **5** And the sons of Jacob pursued them to the gate of the city of Chazar, and they struck a great striking among the kings and their armies, about four thousand men, and while they were striking the army of the kings, Jacob was occupied with his bow confining himself to striking the kings, and he slew them all. **6** And he slew Parathon king of Chazar at the gate of the city of Chazar, and afterward he struck Susi king of Sarton, and Laban king of Bethchorin, and

Shabir king of Machnaymah, and he slew them all with arrows, an arrow to each of them, and they died. **7** And the sons of Jacob seeing that all the kings were dead and that they were broken up and retreating, continued to carry on the battle with the armies of the kings opposite the gate of Chazar, and they still struck about four hundred of their men. **8** And three men of the servants of Jacob fell in that battle, and when Judah saw that three of his servants had died, it grieved him greatly, and his anger burned within him against the Amorites. **9** And all the men that remained of the armies of the kings were greatly afraid for their lives, and they ran and broke the gate of the walls of the city of Chazar, and they all entered the city for safety. **10** And they concealed themselves in the midst of the city of Chazar, for the city of Chazar was very large and extensive, and when all these armies had entered the city, the sons of Jacob ran after them to the city. **11** And four mighty men, experienced in battle, went out from the city and stood against the entrance of the city, with drawn swords and spears in their hands, and they placed themselves opposite the sons of Jacob, and would not permit them to enter the city. **12** And Naphtali ran and came between them, and struck two of them with his sword, and cut off their heads with one stroke. **13** And he turned to the other two, and behold, they had fled, and he pursued them, overtook them, struck them, and slew them. **14** And the sons of Jacob came to the city and saw, and behold, there was another wall to the city, and they sought for the gate of the wall and could not find it, and Judah sprang on the top of the wall, and Simeon and Levi followed him, and they all three descended from the wall into the city. **15** And Simeon and Levi slew all the men who had run into the city for safety, and also the inhabitants of the city with their wives and little ones, they slew with the edge of the sword, and the cries of the city ascended up to Heaven. **16** And Dan and Naphtali sprang on the wall to see what caused the noise of lamentation, for the sons of Jacob felt anxious about their brothers, and they heard the inhabitants of the city speaking with weeping and supplications, saying, "Take all that we possess in the city and go away, only do not put us to death." **17** And when Judah, Simeon, and Levi had ceased striking the inhabitants of the city, they ascended the wall and called to Dan and Naphtali, who were on the wall, and to the rest of their brothers, and Simeon and Levi informed them of the entrance into the city, and all the sons of Jacob came to fetch the spoil. **18** And the sons of Jacob took the spoil of the city of Chazar, the flocks and herds, and the property, and they took all that could be captured, and went away from the city that day. **19** And on the next day the sons of Jacob went to Sarton, for they heard that the men of Sarton who had remained in the city were assembling to fight with them for having slain their king, and Sarton was a very high and fortified city, and it had a deep rampart surrounding the city. **20** And the pillar of the rampart was about fifty cubits and its breadth forty cubits, and there was no place for a man to enter the city on account of the rampart, and the sons of Jacob saw the rampart of the city, and they sought an entrance in it but could not find it. **21** For the entrance to the city was at the rear, and every man that wished to come into the city came by that road and went around the whole city, and afterward he entered the city. **22** And the sons of Jacob seeing [that] they could not find the way into the city, their anger was greatly kindled, and the inhabitants of the city seeing that the sons of Jacob were coming to them were greatly afraid of them, for they had heard of their strength and what they had done to Chazar. **23** And the inhabitants of the city of Sarton could not go out toward the sons of Jacob after having assembled in the city to fight against them, lest they might thereby get into the city, but when they saw that they were coming toward them, they were greatly afraid of them, for they had heard of their strength and what they had done to Chazar. **24** So the inhabitants of Sarton quickly took away the bridge of the road of the city from its place before the sons of Jacob came, and they brought it into the city. **25** And the sons of Jacob came and sought the way into the city and could not find it, and the inhabitants of the city went up to the top of the wall, and saw, and behold, the sons of Jacob were seeking an entrance into the city. **26** And the inhabitants of the city reproached the sons of Jacob from the top of the wall, and they cursed them, and the sons of Jacob heard the reproaches, and they were greatly incensed, and their anger burned within them. **27** And the sons of Jacob were provoked at them, and they all rose and sprang over the rampart with the force of their strength, and through their might passed the forty cubits' breadth of the rampart. **28** And

when they had passed the rampart, they stood under the wall of the city, and they found all the gates of the city enclosed with iron doors. **29** And the sons of Jacob came near to break open the doors of the gates of the city, and the inhabitants did not let them, for from the top of the wall they were casting stones and arrows on them. **30** And the number of the people that were on the wall was about four hundred men, and when the sons of Jacob saw that the men of the city would not let them open the gates of the city, they sprang and ascended the top of the wall, and Judah went up first to the east part of the city. **31** And Gad and Asher went up after him to the west corner of the city, and Simeon and Levi to the north, and Dan and Reuben to the south. **32** And the men who were on the top of the wall, the inhabitants of the city, seeing that the sons of Jacob were coming up to them, they all fled from the wall, descended into the city, and concealed themselves in the midst of the city. **33** And Issachar and Naphtali that remained under the wall approached and broke the gates of the city and kindled a fire at the gates of the city, [so] that the iron melted, and all the sons of Jacob came into the city—they and all their men— and they fought with the inhabitants of the city of Sarton, and struck them with the edge of the sword, and no man stood up before them. **34** And about two hundred men fled from the city, and they all went and hid themselves in a certain tower in the city, and Judah pursued them to the tower, and he broke down the tower, which fell on the men, and they all died. **35** And the sons of Jacob went up the road of the roof of that tower, and they saw, and behold, there was another strong and high tower at a distance in the city, and the top of it reached to [the] heavens, and the sons of Jacob hastened and descended, and went with all their men to that tower, and found it filled with about three hundred men, women, and little ones. **36** And the sons of Jacob struck a great striking among those men in the tower, and they ran away and fled from them. **37** And when Simeon and Levi pursued them, twelve mighty and valiant men came out to them from the place where they had concealed themselves. **38** And those twelve men maintained a strong battle against Simeon and Levi, and Simeon and Levi could not prevail over them, and those valiant men broke the shields of Simeon and Levi, and when one of them struck at Levi's head with his sword, Levi hastily placed his hand to his head, for he was afraid of the sword, and the sword struck Levi's hand, and it came close to the hand of Levi being cut off. **39** And Levi seized the sword of the valiant man in his hand, and took it forcibly from the man, and he struck at the head of the powerful man with it, and he severed his head. **40** And eleven men approached to fight with Levi, for they saw that one of them was killed, and the sons of Jacob fought, but the sons of Jacob could not prevail over them, for those men were very powerful. **41** And the sons of Jacob seeing that they could not prevail over them, Simeon gave a loud and tremendous shriek, and the eleven powerful men were stunned at the voice of Simeon's shrieking. **42** And Judah at a distance knew the voice of Simeon's shouting, and Naphtali and Judah ran with their shields to Simeon and Levi, and found them fighting with those powerful men, unable to prevail over them as their shields were broken. **43** And Naphtali saw that the shields of Simeon and Levi were broken, and he took two shields from his servants and brought them to Simeon and Levi. **44** And on that day Simeon, Levi, and Judah fought—all three—against the eleven mighty men until the time of sunset, but they could not prevail over them. **45** And this was told to Jacob, and he was severely grieved, and he prayed to the Lord, and he and his son Naphtali went against these mighty men. **46** And Jacob approached and drew his bow, and came near to the mighty men, and slew three of their men with the bow, and the remaining eight turned back, and behold, the war waged against them in the front and rear, and they were greatly afraid for their lives, and could not stand before the sons of Jacob, and they fled from before them. **47** And in their flight they met Dan and Asher coming toward them, and they suddenly fell on them, and fought with them, and slew two of them, and Judah and his brothers pursued them, and struck the remainder of them, and slew them. **48** And all the sons of Jacob returned and walked around the city, searching if they could find any men, and they found about twenty young men in a cave in the city, and Gad and Asher struck them all, and Dan and Naphtali descended on the rest of the men who had fled and escaped from the second tower, and they struck them all. **49** And the sons of Jacob struck all the inhabitants of the city of Sarton, but they left the women and little ones in the city and did not slay them. **50** And all the inhabitants of the city of Sarton were powerful men: one of them would pursue one thousand, and two of them would not flee from ten thousand of the rest of men. ⁵¹ And the sons of Jacob slew all the inhabitants of the city of Sarton with the edge of the sword, [so] that no man stood up against them, and they left the women in the city. ⁵² And the sons of Jacob took all the spoil of the city, and captured what they desired, and they took flocks, and herds, and property from the city, and the sons of Jacob did to Sarton and its inhabitants as they had done to Chazar and its inhabitants, and they turned and went away.

CHAPTER 39

¹ And when the sons of Jacob went from the city of Sarton, they had gone about two hundred cubits when they met the inhabitants of Tapnach coming toward them, for they went out to fight with them, because they had smitten the king of Tapnach and all his men. ² So all that remained in the city of Tapnach came out to fight with the sons of Jacob, and they thought to retake from them the plunder and the spoil which they had captured from Chazar and Sarton. ³ And the rest of the men of Tapnach fought with the sons of Jacob in that place, and the sons of Jacob struck them, and they fled before them, and they pursued them to the city of Arbelan, and they all fell before the sons of Jacob. ⁴ And the sons of Jacob returned and came to Tapnach to take away the spoil of Tapnach, and when they came to Tapnach they heard that the people of Arbelan had gone out to meet them to save the spoil of their brothers, and the sons of Jacob left ten of their men in Tapnach to plunder the city, and they went out toward the people of Arbelan. ⁵ And the men of Arbelan went out with their wives to fight with the sons of Jacob, for their wives were experienced in battle, and they went out, about four hundred men and women. ⁶ And all the sons of Jacob shouted with a loud voice, and they all ran toward the inhabitants of Arbelan with a great and tremendous voice. ⁷ And the inhabitants of Arbelan heard the noise of the shouting of the sons of Jacob, and their roaring like the noise of lions and like the roaring of the sea and its waves. ⁸ And fear and terror possessed their hearts on account of the sons of Jacob, and they were terribly afraid of them, and they retreated and fled before them into the city, and the sons of Jacob pursued them to the gate of the city, and they came on them in the city. ⁹ And the sons of Jacob fought with them in the city, and all their women were engaged in slinging against the sons of Jacob, and the combat was very severe among them the whole of that day until evening. ¹⁰ And the sons of Jacob could not prevail over them, and the sons of Jacob had almost perished in that battle, and the sons of Jacob cried to the Lord and greatly gained strength toward evening, and the sons of Jacob struck all the inhabitants of Arbelan by the edge of the sword—men, women, and little ones. ¹¹ And also the remainder of the people who had fled from Sarton, the sons of Jacob struck them in Arbelan, and the sons of Jacob did to Arbelan and Tapnach as they had done to Chazar and Sarton, and when the women saw that all the men were dead, they went on the roofs of the city and struck the sons of Jacob by showering down stones like rain. ¹² And the sons of Jacob hastened and came into the city, and seized all the women, and struck them with the edge of the sword, and the sons of Jacob captured all the spoil and plunder, flocks, and herds, and cattle. ¹³ And the sons of Jacob did to Machnaymah as they had done to Tapnach, to Chazar, and to Shiloh, and they turned from there and went away. ¹⁴ And on the fifth day the sons of Jacob heard that the people of Gaash had gathered against them to battle, because they had slain their king and their captains, for there had been fourteen captains in the city of Gaash, and the sons of Jacob had slain them all in the first battle. ¹⁵ And the sons of Jacob girded on their weapons of war that day, and they marched to battle against the inhabitants of Gaash, and in Gaash there was a strong and mighty people of the people of the Amorites, and Gaash was the strongest and best fortified city of all the cities of the Amorites, and it had three walls. ¹⁶ And the sons of Jacob came to Gaash, and they found the gates of the city locked and about five hundred men standing at the top of the outermost wall, and a people [as] numerous as the sand on the seashore were set in ambush for the sons of Jacob from outside the city, at the rear thereof. ¹⁷ And the sons of Jacob approached to open the gates of the city, and while they were drawing near, behold, those who were set in ambush at the rear of the city came out from their places and surrounded the sons of Jacob. ¹⁸ And the sons of Jacob were enclosed between the people of Gaash, and the battle was

both to their front and rear, and all the men that were on the wall were casting from the wall arrows and stones on them. ¹⁹ And Judah, seeing that the men of Gaash were getting too heavy for them, gave a most piercing and tremendous shriek and all the men of Gaash were terrified at the voice of Judah's cry, and men fell from the wall at his powerful shriek, and all those that were from outside and within the city were greatly afraid for their lives. ²⁰ And when the sons of Jacob still came near to break the doors of the city, the men of Gaash threw stones and arrows on them from the top of the wall and made them flee from the gate. ²¹ And the sons of Jacob returned against the men of Gaash who were with them from outside the city, and they struck them terribly, as striking against gourds, and they could not stand against the sons of Jacob, for fright and terror had seized them at the shriek of Judah. ²² And the sons of Jacob slew all those men who were outside the city, and the sons of Jacob still drew near to effect an entrance into the city and to fight under the city walls, but they could not for all the inhabitants of Gaash who remained in the city had surrounded the walls of Gaash in every direction, so that the sons of Jacob were unable to approach the city to fight with them. ²³ And [when] the sons of Jacob came near to one corner to fight under the wall, the inhabitants of Gaash threw arrows and stones on them like showers of rain, and they fled from under the wall. ²⁴ And the people of Gaash who were on the wall, seeing that the sons of Jacob could not prevail over them from under the wall, reproached the sons of Jacob in these words, saying, ²⁵ "What is the matter with you in the battle that you cannot prevail? can you then do to the mighty city of Gaash and its inhabitants as you did to the cities of the Amorites that were not so powerful? Surely you did those things to those weak ones among us, and slew them in the entrance of the city, for they had no strength when they were terrified at the sound of your shouting. ²⁶ And will you now then be able to fight in this place? Surely you will all die here, and we will avenge the cause of those cities that you have laid waste." ²⁷ And the inhabitants of Gaash greatly reproached the sons of Jacob, and reviled them with their gods, and continued to cast arrows and stones on them from the wall. ²⁸ And Judah and his brothers heard the words of the inhabitants of Gaash and their anger was greatly roused, and Judah was jealous for his God in this matter, and he called out and said, "O Lord, help! Send help to us and our brothers!" ²⁹ And he ran at a distance with all his might, with his drawn sword in his hand, and he sprang from the earth, and by force of his strength mounted the wall, and his sword fell from his hand. ³⁰ And Judah shouted on the wall, and all the men that were on the wall were terrified, and some of them fell from the wall into the city and died, and those who were yet on the wall, when they saw Judah's strength, they were greatly afraid and fled for their lives into the city for safety. ³¹ And some were emboldened to fight with Judah on the wall, and they came near to slay him when they saw there was no sword in Judah's hand, and they thought of casting him from the wall to his brothers, and twenty men of the city came up to assist them, and they surrounded Judah, and they all shouted over him, and approached him with drawn swords, and they terrified Judah, and Judah cried out to his brothers from the wall. ³² And Jacob and his sons drew the bow from under the wall and struck three of the men that were on the top of the wall, and Judah continued to cry, and he exclaimed, "O Lord help us! O Lord deliver us!" And he cried out with a loud voice on the wall, and the cry was heard at a great distance. ³³ And after this cry he again repeated to shout, and all the men who surrounded Judah on the top of the wall were terrified, and they each threw his sword from his hand at the sound of Judah's shouting and his tremor, and they fled. ³⁴ And Judah took the swords which had fallen from their hands, and Judah fought with them and slew twenty of their men on the wall. ³⁵ And about eighty men and women still ascended the wall from the city, and they all surrounded Judah, and the Lord impressed the fear of Judah in their hearts, that they were unable to approach him. ³⁶ And Jacob and all who were with him drew the bow from under the wall, and they slew ten men on the wall, and they fell below the wall near Jacob and his sons. ³⁷ And the people on the wall seeing that twenty of their men had fallen, they still ran toward Judah with drawn swords, but they could not approach him, for they were greatly terrified at Judah's strength. ³⁸ And when one of their mighty men whose name was Arud approached to strike Judah on the head with his sword, Judah hastily put his shield to his head, and the sword hit the shield, and it was split in two. ³⁹ And this mighty man ran for his life after he had struck Judah, at the fear of

Judah, and his feet slipped on the wall and he fell among the sons of Jacob who were below the wall, and the sons of Jacob struck him and slew him. **40** And Judah's head pained him from the blow of the powerful man, and Judah had nearly died from it. **41** And Judah cried out on the wall owing to the pain produced by the blow, when Dan heard him, and his anger burned within him, and he also rose up, and went at a distance, and ran, and sprang from the earth, and mounted the wall with his wrath-excited strength. **42** And when Dan came on the wall near to Judah, all the men on the wall who had stood against Judah fled, and they went up to the second wall, and they threw arrows and stones on Dan and Judah from the second wall, and endeavored to drive them from the wall. **43** And the arrows and stones struck Dan and Judah, and they had nearly been killed on the wall, and wherever Dan and Judah fled from the wall, they were attacked with arrows and stones from the second wall. **44** And Jacob and his sons were still at the entrance of the city below the first wall, and they were not able to draw their bow against the inhabitants of the city, as they could not be seen by them, being on the second wall. **45** And when Dan and Judah could no longer bear the stones and arrows that fell on them from the second wall, they both sprang on the second wall near the people of the city, and when the people of the city who were on the second wall saw that Dan and Judah had come to them on the second wall, they all cried out and descended below between the walls. **46** And Jacob and his sons heard the noise of the shouting from the people of the city, and they were still at the entrance of the city, and they were anxious about Dan and Judah who were not seen by them—they being on the second wall. **47** And Naphtali went up with his wrath-excited might and sprang on the first wall to see what caused the noise of shouting which they had heard in the city, and Issachar and Zebulun drew near to break the doors of the city, and they opened the gates of the city, and came into the city. **48** And Naphtali leaped from the first wall to the second, and came to assist his brothers, and the inhabitants of Gaash who were on the wall, seeing that Naphtali was the third who had come up to assist his brothers, they all fled and descended into the city, and Jacob, and all his sons, and all their young men came into the city to them. **49** And Judah, and Dan, and Naphtali descended from the wall into the city and pursued the inhabitants of the city, and Simeon and Levi were from outside the city and did not know that the gate was opened, and they went up from there to the wall and came down to their brothers into the city. **50** And the inhabitants of the city had all descended into the city, and the sons of Jacob came to them in different directions, and the battle waged against them from the front and the rear, and the sons of Jacob struck them terribly, and slew about twenty thousand of them—men and women; not one of them could stand up against the sons of Jacob. **51** And the blood flowed plentifully in the city, and it was like a brook of water, and the blood flowed like a brook to the outer part of the city and reached the desert of Bethchorin. **52** And the people of Bethchorin saw at a distance the blood flowing from the city of Gaash, and about seventy men from among them ran to see the blood, and they came to the place where the blood was. **53** And they followed the track of the blood and came to the wall of the city of Gaash, and they saw the blood issue from the city, and they heard the voice of crying from the inhabitants of Gaash, for it ascended to Heaven, and the blood was continuing to flow abundantly like a brook of water. **54** And all the sons of Jacob were still striking the inhabitants of Gaash, and were engaged in slaying them until evening—about twenty thousand men and women—and the people of Chorin said, "Surely this is the work of the Hebrews, for they are still carrying on war in all the cities of the Amorites." **55** And those people hastened and ran to Bethchorin, and each took his weapons of war, and they cried out to all the inhabitants of Bethchorin, who also girded on their weapons of war to go and fight with the sons of Jacob. **56** And when the sons of Jacob had finished striking the inhabitants of Gaash, they walked around the city to strip all the slain, and coming into the innermost part of the city and farther on, they met three very powerful men, and there was no sword in their hand. **57** And the sons of Jacob came up to the place where they were, and the powerful men ran away, and one of them had taken Zebulun, who he saw was a young youth and of short stature, and with his might dashed him to the ground. **58** And Jacob ran to him with his sword and Jacob struck him below his loins with the sword, and cut him in two, and the body fell on Zebulun. **59** And the second one approached and seized Jacob to fell him to the ground, and Jacob turned to him and shouted to him

while Simeon and Levi ran and struck him on the hips with the sword and felled him to the ground. **60** And the powerful man rose up from the ground with wrath-excited might, and Judah came to him before he had gained his footing, and struck him on the head with the sword, and his head was split, and he died. **61** And the third powerful man, seeing that his companions were killed, ran from before the sons of Jacob, and the sons of Jacob pursued him in the city; and while the powerful man was fleeing, he found one of the swords of the inhabitants of the city, and he picked it up, and turned to the sons of Jacob, and fought them with that sword. **62** And the powerful man ran to Judah to strike him on the head with the sword, and there was no shield in the hand of Judah; and while he was aiming to strike him, Naphtali hastily took his shield and put it to Judah's head, and the sword of the powerful man hit the shield of Naphtali and Judah escaped the sword. **63** And Simeon and Levi ran on the powerful man with their swords and struck at him forcibly with their swords, and the two swords entered the body of the powerful man and divided it in two, lengthwise. **64** And the sons of Jacob struck the three mighty men at that time, together with all the inhabitants of Gaash, and the day was about to decline. **65** And the sons of Jacob walked around Gaash and took all the spoil of the city; they did not even permit the little ones and women to live, and the sons of Jacob did to Gaash as they had done to Sarton and Shiloh.

CHAPTER 40

1 And the sons of Jacob led away all the spoil of Gaash and went out of the city by night. **2** They were going out marching toward the fortress of Bethchorin, and the inhabitants of Bethchorin were going to the fortress to meet them, and on that night the sons of Jacob fought with the inhabitants of Bethchorin in the fortress of Bethchorin. **3** And all the inhabitants of Bethchorin were mighty men: one of them would not flee from before one thousand men, and they fought on that night on the fortress, and their shouts were heard on that night from afar, and the earth quaked at their shouting. **4** And all the sons of Jacob were afraid of those men, as they were not accustomed to fight in the dark, and they were greatly confounded, and the sons of Jacob cried to the Lord, saying, "Give help to us, O Lord! Deliver us that we may not die by the hands of these uncircumcised men." **5** And the Lord listened to the voice of the sons of Jacob, and the Lord caused great terror and confusion to seize the people of Bethchorin, and they fought among themselves—the one with the other—in the darkness of night, and struck each other in great numbers. **6** And the sons of Jacob, knowing that the Lord had brought a spirit of perverseness among those men, and that each man fought with his neighbor, went out from among the bands of the people of Bethchorin and went as far as the descent of the fortress of Bethchorin, and farther, and they tarried there securely with their young men on that night. **7** And the people of Bethchorin fought the whole night—one man with his brother, and the other with his neighbor—and they cried out in every direction on the fortress, and their cry was heard at a distance, and the whole earth shook at their voice, for they were powerful above all the people of the earth. **8** And all the inhabitants of the cities of the Canaanites, the Hittites, the Amorites, the Hivites, and all the kings of Canaan, and also those who were on the other side of the Jordan, heard the noise of the shouting on that night. **9** And they said, "Surely these are the battles of the Hebrews who are fighting against the seven cities who came near to them; and who can stand against those Hebrews?" **10** And all the inhabitants of the cities of the Canaanites and all those who were on the other side of the Jordan were greatly afraid of the sons of Jacob, for they said, "Behold, the same will be done to us as was done to those cities, for who can stand against their mighty strength?" **11** And the cries of the Chorinites were very great on that night, and continued to increase; and they struck each other until morning, and [large] numbers of them were killed. **12** And the morning appeared, and all the sons of Jacob rose up at daybreak and went up to the fortress, and they struck those who remained of the Chorinites in a terrible manner, and they were all killed in the fortress. **13** And the sixth day appeared, and all the inhabitants of Canaan saw at a distance all the people of Bethchorin lying dead in the fortress of Bethchorin and scattered around as the carcasses of lambs and goats. **14** And the sons of Jacob led all the spoil which they had captured from Gaash and went to Bethchorin, and they found the city full of people like the sand of the sea, and they fought with them, and the sons of Jacob struck them there until evening time. **15** And the sons of Jacob did to Bethchorin as they had done to Gaash and Tapnach, and as they had done to Chazar, to Sarton, and to Shiloh. **16** And the sons of Jacob took the spoil of Bethchorin and all the spoil of the cities with them, and on that day they went home to Shechem. **17** And the sons of Jacob came home to the city of Shechem and remained outside the city, and then they rested there from the war and tarried there all night. **18** And all their servants, together with all the spoil that they had taken from the cities, they left outside the city, and they did not enter the city, for they said, "Perhaps there may still be more fighting against us, and they may come to besiege us in Shechem." **19** And Jacob, and his sons, and their servants remained on that night and the next day in the portion of the field which Jacob had purchased from Hamor for five shekels, and all that they had captured was with them. **20** And all the plunder which the sons of Jacob had captured was in the portion of the field—immense as the sand on the seashore. **21** And the inhabitants of the land observed them from afar, and all the inhabitants of the land were afraid of the sons of Jacob who had done this thing, for no king from the days of old had ever done the like. **22** And the seven kings of the Canaanites resolved to make peace with the sons of Jacob, for they were greatly afraid for their lives, on account of the sons of Jacob. **23** And on that day, being the seventh day, Japhia king of Hebron sent secretly to the king of Ai, and to the king of Gibeon, and to the king of Shalem, and to the king of Adulam, and to the king of Lachish, and to the king of Chazar, and to all the Canaanite kings who were under their subjection, saying, **24** "Go up with me, and come to me that we may go to the sons of Jacob, and I will make peace with them, and form a treaty with them, lest all your lands be destroyed by the swords of the sons of Jacob as they did to Shechem and the cities around it, as you have heard and seen. **25** And when you come to me, do not come with many men, but let every king bring his three head captains, and every captain bring three of his officers. **26** And all of you come to Hebron, and we will go together to the sons of Jacob and supplicate them that they will form a treaty of peace with us." **27** And all those kings did as the king of Hebron had sent to them, for they were all under his counsel and command, and all the kings of Canaan assembled to go to the sons of Jacob, to make peace with them; and the sons of Jacob returned and went to the portion of the field that was in Shechem, for they did not put confidence in the kings of the land. **28** And the sons of Jacob returned and remained in the portion of the field [for] ten days, and no one came to make war with them. **29** And when the sons of Jacob saw that there was no appearance of war, they all assembled and went to the city of Shechem, and the sons of Jacob remained in Shechem. **30** And at the expiration of forty days, all the kings of the Amorites assembled from all their places and came to Hebron, to Japhia, king of Hebron. **31** And the number of kings that came to Hebron to make peace with the sons of Jacob was twenty-one kings, and the number of captains that came with them was sixty-nine, and their men were one hundred and eighty-nine, and all these kings and their men rested by Mount Hebron. **32** And the king of Hebron went out with his three captains and nine men, and these kings resolved to go to the sons of Jacob to make peace. **33** And they said to the king of Hebron, "Go before us with your men, and speak for us to the sons of Jacob, and we will come after you and confirm your words," and the king of Hebron did so. **34** And the sons of Jacob heard that all the kings of Canaan had gathered together and rested in Hebron, and the sons of Jacob sent four of their servants as spies, saying, "Go and spy on these kings, and search and examine their men whether they are few or many, and if they are but few in number, number them all and come back." **35** And the servants of Jacob went secretly to these kings, and did as the sons of Jacob had commanded them, and on that day they came back to the sons of Jacob, and said to them, "We came to those kings, and they are but few in number, and we numbered them all, and behold, they were two hundred and eighty-eight kings and men." **36** And the sons of Jacob said, "They are but few in number, therefore we will not all go out to them"; and in the morning the sons of Jacob rose up and chose sixty-two of their men, and ten of the sons of Jacob went with them; and they girded on their weapons of war, for they said, "They are coming to make war with us," for they did not know that they were coming to make peace with them. **37** And the sons of Jacob

went with their servants to the gate of Shechem, toward those kings, and their father Jacob was with them. **38** And when they had come out, behold, the king of Hebron and his three captains and nine men with him were coming along the road against the sons of Jacob, and the sons of Jacob lifted up their eyes, and saw at a distance Japhia, king of Hebron, with his captains, coming toward them, and the sons of Jacob took their stand at the place of the gate of Shechem, and did not proceed. **39** And the king of Hebron continued to advance, he and his captains, until he came near to the sons of Jacob, and he and his captains bowed down to them to the ground, and the king of Hebron sat with his captains before Jacob and his sons. **40** And the sons of Jacob said to him, "What has befallen you, O king of Hebron? why have you come to us this day? what do you require from us?" and the king of Hebron said to Jacob, "I implore you, my lord: all the kings of the Canaanites have come to make peace with you this day." **41** And the sons of Jacob heard the words of the king of Hebron, and they would not consent to his proposals, for the sons of Jacob had no faith in him, for they imagined that the king of Hebron had spoken deceitfully to them. **42** And the king of Hebron knew from the words of the sons of Jacob that they did not believe his words, and the king of Hebron approached nearer to Jacob, and said to him, "I implore you, my lord, to be assured that all these kings have come to you on peaceable terms, for they have not come with all their men, neither did they bring their weapons of war with them, for they have come to seek peace from my lord and his sons." **43** And the sons of Jacob answered the king of Hebron, saying, "Send to all these kings, and if you speak truth to us, let them each come before us individually, and if they come to us unarmed, we will then know that they seek peace from us." **44** And Japhia, king of Hebron, sent one of his men to the kings, and they all came before the sons of Jacob, and bowed down to them to the ground, and these kings sat before Jacob and his sons, and they spoke to them, saying, **45** "We have heard all that you did to the kings of the Amorites with your sword and exceedingly mighty arm, so that no man could stand up before you, and we were afraid of you for the sake of our lives, lest it should befall us as it did to them, **46** So we have come to you to form a treaty of peace between us, and now, therefore, contract a covenant of peace and truth with us that you will not meddle with us, inasmuch as we have not meddled with you." **47** And the sons of Jacob knew that they had really come to seek peace from them, and the sons of Jacob listened to them, and formed a covenant with them. **48** And the sons of Jacob swore to them that they would not meddle with them, and all the kings of the Canaanites also swore to them, and the sons of Jacob made them tributary from that day forward. **49** And after this, all the captains of these kings came with their men before Jacob, with presents in their hands for Jacob and his sons, and they bowed down to him to the ground. **50** And these kings then urged the sons of Jacob and begged of them to return all the spoil they had captured from the seven cities of the Amorites, and the sons of Jacob did so, and they returned all that they had captured, the women, the little ones, the cattle, and all the spoil which they had taken, and they sent them off, and they each went away to his city. **51** And all these kings again bowed down to the sons of Jacob, and they sent or brought them many gifts in those days, and the sons of Jacob sent off these kings and their men, and they went peaceably away from them to their cities, and the sons of Jacob also returned to their home, to Shechem. **52** And there was peace from that day forward between the sons of Jacob and the kings of the Canaanites, until the sons of Israel came to inherit the land of Canaan.

CHAPTER 41

1 And at the revolution of the year the sons of Jacob journeyed from Shechem, and they came to Hebron, to their father Isaac, and they dwelt there, but they fed their flocks and herds daily in Shechem, for there was good and fat pasture there in those days, and Jacob, and his sons, and all their household dwelt in the Valley of Hebron. **2** And it was in those days, in that year, being the one hundred and sixth year of the life of Jacob, in the tenth year of Jacob's coming from Padan-Aram, that Leah the wife of Jacob died; she was fifty-one years old when she died in Hebron. **3** And Jacob and his sons buried her in the cave of the field of Machpelah, which is in Hebron, which Abraham had bought from the children of Heth for the possession of a burial place. **4** And the sons of Jacob dwelt with their father in the Valley of Hebron, and all the inhabitants of the land knew their strength and their fame went throughout the land. **5** And Joseph the son of Jacob, and his brother Benjamin, the sons of Rachel, the wife of Jacob, were yet young in those days, and did not go out with their brothers during their battles in all the cities of the Amorites. **6** And when Joseph saw the strength of his brothers, and their greatness, he praised them and extolled them, but he ranked himself greater than them, and extolled himself above them; and his father Jacob also loved him more than any of his sons, for he was a son of his old age, and through his love toward him he made him a coat of many colors. **7** And when Joseph saw that his father loved him more than his brothers, he continued to exalt himself above his brothers, and he brought to his father evil reports concerning them. **8** And the sons of Jacob, seeing the whole of Joseph's conduct toward them, and that their father loved him more than any of them, hated him and could not speak peaceably to him all the days. **9** And Joseph was seventeen years old, and he was still magnifying himself above his brothers, and thought of raising himself above them. **10** At that time he dreamed a dream, and he came to his brothers and told them his dream, and he said to them, "I dreamed a dream, and behold, we were all binding sheaves in the field, and my sheaf rose and placed itself on the ground and your sheaves surrounded it and bowed down to it." **11** And his brothers answered him and said to him, "What does this dream that you dreamed mean? do you imagine in your heart to reign or rule over us?" **12** And he still came, and told the thing to his father Jacob, and Jacob kissed Joseph when he heard these words from his mouth, and Jacob blessed Joseph. **13** And when the sons of Jacob saw that their father had blessed Joseph and had kissed him, and that he loved him exceedingly, they became jealous of him and hated him [even] more. **14** And after this, Joseph dreamed another dream and related the dream to his father in the presence of his brothers, and Joseph said to his father and brothers, "Behold, I have again dreamed a dream, and behold, the sun, and the moon, and the eleven stars bowed down to me." **15** And his father heard the words of Joseph and his dream, and seeing that his brothers hated Joseph on account of this matter, Jacob therefore rebuked Joseph before his brothers on account of this thing, saying, "What does this dream which you have dreamed mean—and this magnifying yourself before your brothers who are older than you are? **16** Do you imagine in your heart that I, and your mother, and your eleven brothers will come and bow down to you, that you speak these things?" **17** And his brothers were jealous of him on account of his words and dreams, and they continued to hate him, and Jacob reserved the dreams in his heart. **18** And one day the sons of Jacob went to feed their father's flock in Shechem, for they were still herdsmen in those days; and while the sons of Jacob were feeding in Shechem that day, they delayed, and the time of gathering in the cattle was passed, and they had not arrived. **19** And Jacob saw that his sons were delayed in Shechem, and Jacob said within himself, "Perhaps the people of Shechem have risen up to fight against them, therefore they have delayed coming this day." **20** And Jacob called his son Joseph and commanded him, saying, "Behold, your brothers are feeding in Shechem this day, and behold, they have not yet come back; now therefore, go and see where they are, and bring word back to me concerning the welfare of your brothers and the welfare of the flock." **21** And Jacob sent his son Joseph to the Valley of Hebron, and Joseph came for his brothers to Shechem, and could not find them, and Joseph went around the field which was near Shechem to see where his brothers had turned, and he missed his road in the wilderness, and did not know which way he should go. **22** And a messenger of the Lord found him wandering in the road toward the field, and Joseph said to the messenger of the Lord, "I seek my brothers; have you not heard where they are feeding?" and the messenger of the Lord said to Joseph, "I saw your brothers feeding here, and I heard them say they would go to feed in Doesan." **23** And Joseph listened to the voice of the messenger of the Lord, and he went to his brothers in Doesan and found them in Doesan feeding the flock. **24** And Joseph advanced to his brothers, and before he had come near to them, they had resolved to slay him. **25** And Simeon said to his brothers, "Behold, the man of dreams is coming to us this day, and now therefore, come and let us kill him and cast him into one of the pits that are in the wilderness, and when his father will seek him from us, we will say an evil beast has devoured him." **26** And Reuben heard the words of his brothers concerning Joseph, and he said to them, "You

should not do this thing, for how can we look up to our father Jacob? Cast him into this pit to die there but do not stretch out a hand on him to spill his blood"; and Reuben said this in order to deliver him from their hand, to bring him back to his father. **27** And when Joseph came to his brothers, he sat before them, and they rose on him, and seized him, and struck him to the earth, and stripped the coat of many colors which he had on. **28** And they took him and cast him into a pit, and there was no water in the pit, but serpents and scorpions. And Joseph was afraid of the serpents and scorpions that were in the pit. And Joseph cried out with a loud voice, and the Lord hid the serpents and scorpions in the sides of the pit, and they did no harm to Joseph. **29** And Joseph called out from the pit to his brothers, and said to them, "What have I done to you, and in what have I sinned? why do you not fear the Lord concerning me? am I not of your bones and flesh, and is your father Jacob not my father? why do you do this thing to me this day, and how will you be able to look up to our father Jacob?" **30** And he continued to cry out and call to his brothers from the pit, and he said, "O Judah, Simeon, and Levi, my brothers! Lift me up from the place of darkness in which you have placed me, and come this day to have compassion on me, you children of the Lord, and sons of my father Jacob! And if I have sinned to you, are you not the sons of Abraham, Isaac, and Jacob? if they saw an orphan, they had compassion over him, or one that was hungry, they gave him bread to eat, or one that was thirsty, they gave him water to drink, or one that was naked, they covered him with garments!" **31** And how then will you withhold your pity from your brother, for I am of your flesh and bones, and if I have sinned to you, surely you will do this on account of my father! **32** And Joseph spoke these words from the pit, and his brothers could not listen to him, nor incline their ears to the words of Joseph, and Joseph was crying and weeping in the pit. **33** And Joseph said, "O that my father knew, this day, the act which my brothers have done to me, and the words which they have spoken this day to me." **34** And all his brothers heard his cries and weeping in the pit, and his brothers went and removed themselves from the pit, so that they might not hear the cries of Joseph and his weeping in the pit.

CHAPTER 42

1 And they went and sat on the opposite side, about the distance of a bow-shot, and they sat there to eat bread, and while they were eating, they held counsel together what was to be done with him, whether to slay him or to bring him back to his father. **2** When they were holding the counsel, they lifted up their eyes and saw, and behold, there was a company of Ishmaelites coming at a distance by the road of Gilead, going down to Egypt. **3** And Judah said to them, "What gain will it be to us if we slay our brother? Perhaps God will require him from us; this then is the counsel proposed concerning him, which you will do to him: behold, this company of Ishmaelites going down to Egypt. **4** Now therefore, come let us dispose of him to them, and do not let our hand be on him, and they will lead him along with them, and he will be lost among the people of the land, and we will not put him to death with our own hands." And the proposal pleased his brothers, and they did according to the word of Judah. **5** And while they were discoursing about this matter, and before the company of Ishmaelites had come up to them, seven trading men of Midian passed by them, and as they passed, they were thirsty, and they lifted up their eyes and saw the pit in which Joseph was confined, and they looked, and behold, every species of bird was on him. **6** And these Midianites ran to the pit to drink water, for they thought that it contained water, and on coming before the pit they heard the voice of Joseph crying and weeping in the pit, and they looked down into the pit, and they saw, and behold, there was a youth of handsome appearance and well-favored. **7** And they called to him and said, "Who are you and who brought you here? And who placed you in this pit in the wilderness?" and they all helped to raise Joseph up and they drew him out, and brought him up from the pit, and took him, and went away on their journey, and passed by his brothers. **8** And these said to them, "Why do you do this, to take our servant from us and to go away? surely we placed this youth in the pit because he rebelled against us, and you come and bring him up and lead him away; now then, give us back our servant." **9** And the Midianites answered and said to the sons of Jacob, "Is this your servant, or does this man attend you? Perhaps you are all his servants, for he is more handsome and well-favored than any of you, and why do you all speak falsely to us? **10** Now therefore, we will not listen to your words, nor attend to you, for we found the youth in the pit in the wilderness, and we took him; we will therefore go on." **11** And all the sons of Jacob approached them, and rose up to them, and said to them, "Give us back our servant, and why will you all die by the edge of the sword?" And the Midianites cried out against them, and they drew their swords, and approached to fight with the sons of Jacob. **12** And behold, Simeon rose up from his seat against them, and sprang on the ground, and drew his sword, and approached the Midianites, and he gave a terrible shout before them, so that his shouting was heard at a distance, and the earth shook at Simeon's shouting. **13** And the Midianites were terrified on account of Simeon and the noise of his shouting, and they fell on their faces, and were excessively alarmed. **14** And Simeon said to them, "I am truly Simeon, the son of the Hebrew Jacob, who has, with my brother alone, destroyed the city of Shechem and the cities of the Amorites; so will God moreover do to me, that if all your brothers, the people of Midian, and also the kings of Canaan, were to come with you, they could not fight against me. **15** Now therefore, give us back the youth whom you have taken, lest I give your flesh to the birds of the skies and the beasts of the earth." **16** And the Midianites were more afraid of Simeon, and they approached the sons of Jacob with terror and fright, and with pathetic words, saying, **17** "Surely you have said that the young man is your servant, and that he rebelled against you, and therefore you placed him in the pit; what then will you do with a servant who rebels against his master? Now therefore, sell him to us, and we will give you all that you require for him"; and the Lord was pleased to do this in order that the sons of Jacob should not slay their brother. **18** And the Midianites saw that Joseph was of a handsome appearance and well-favored; they desired him in their hearts and were urgent to purchase him from his brothers. **19** And the sons of Jacob listened to the Midianites and they sold their brother Joseph to them for twenty pieces of silver, and their brother Reuben was not with them, and the Midianites took Joseph and continued their journey to Gilead. **20** They were going along the road, and the Midianites regretted what they had done, in having purchased the young man, and one said to the other, "What is this thing that we have done, in taking this youth from the Hebrews, who is of handsome appearance and well-favored? **21** Perhaps this youth is stolen from the land of the Hebrews, and why then have we done this thing? and if he should be sought for and found in our hands, we will die through him. **22** Now surely hardy and powerful men have sold him to us, the strength of one of whom you saw this day; perhaps they stole him from his land with their might and with their powerful arm and have therefore sold him to us for the small value which we gave to them." **23** And while they were thus discoursing together, they looked, and behold, the company of Ishmaelites which was coming at first, and which the sons of Jacob saw, was advancing toward the Midianites, and the Midianites said to each other, "Come, let us sell this youth to the company of Ishmaelites who are coming toward us, and we will take for him the little that we gave for him, and we will be delivered from his evil." **24** And they did so, and they reached the Ishmaelites, and the Midianites sold Joseph to the Ishmaelites for twenty pieces of silver which they had given for him to his brothers. **25** And the Midianites went on their road to Gilead, and the Ishmaelites took Joseph and they let him ride on one of the camels, and they were leading him to Egypt. **26** And Joseph heard that the Ishmaelites were proceeding to Egypt, and Joseph lamented and wept at this thing that he was to be so far removed from the land of Canaan, from his father, and he wept bitterly while he was riding on the camel, and one of their men observed him, and made him go down from the camel and walk on foot, and notwithstanding this, Joseph continued to cry and weep, and he said, "O my father, my father!" **27** And one of the Ishmaelites rose up and struck Joseph on the cheek, and still he continued to weep; and Joseph was fatigued in the road, and was unable to proceed on account of the bitterness of his soul, and they all struck him and afflicted him in the road, and they terrified him in order that he might cease from weeping. **28** And the Lord saw the ambition of Joseph and his trouble, and the Lord brought down on those men darkness and confusion, and the hand of everyone that struck him became withered. **29** And they said to each other, "What is this thing that God has done to us in the road?" and they did not know that this befell them on account of Joseph. And the men proceeded on the road, and they passed along the road of Ephrath where Rachel was buried. **30**

And Joseph reached his mother's grave, and Joseph hastened and ran to his mother's grave, and fell on the grave and wept. **31** And Joseph cried aloud on his mother's grave, and he said, "O my mother, my mother! O you who gave birth to me! Awake now, and rise, and see your son—how he has been sold for a slave, and [there is] no one to pity him! **32** O rise and see your son, weep with me on account of my troubles, and see the heart of my brothers! **33** Arouse my mother, arouse! Awake from your sleep for me and direct your battles against my brothers! O how they have stripped me of my coat, and sold me already twice for a slave, and separated me from my father, and there is no one to pity me! **34** Arouse and lay your cause against them before God, and see whom God will justify in the judgment, and whom He will condemn! **35** Rise, O my mother, rise! Awake from your sleep and see my father—how his soul is with me this day, and comfort him and ease his heart!" **36** And Joseph continued to speak these words, and Joseph cried aloud and wept bitterly on his mother's grave; and he ceased speaking, and from bitterness of heart he became still as a stone on the grave. **37** And Joseph heard a voice speaking to him from beneath the ground, which answered him with bitterness of heart, and with a voice of weeping and praying in these words: **38** "My son, my son Joseph! I have heard the voice of your weeping and the voice of your lamentation; I have seen your tears; I know your troubles, my son, and it grieves me for your sake, and abundant grief is added to my grief. **39** Now therefore, my son, my son Joseph: hope on the Lord, and wait for Him, and do not fear, for the Lord is with you; He will deliver you from all trouble. **40** Rise, my son; go down to Egypt with your masters, and do not fear, for the Lord is with you, my son." And she continued to speak like to these words to Joseph, and she was still. **41** And Joseph heard this, and he wondered greatly at this, and he continued to weep; and after this one of the Ishmaelites observed him crying and weeping on the grave, and his anger was kindled against him, and he drove him from there, and he struck him and cursed him. **42** And Joseph said to the men, "May I find grace in your sight to take me back to my father's house, and he will give you abundance of riches." **43** And they answered him, saying, "Are you not a slave, and where is your father? and if you had a father you would not already twice have been sold for a slave for so little value"; and their anger was still roused against him, and they continued to strike him and to punish him, and Joseph wept bitterly. **44** And the Lord saw Joseph's affliction, and the Lord again struck these men, and punished them, and the Lord caused darkness to envelope them on the earth, and the lightning flashed, and the thunder roared, and the earth shook at the voice of the thunder and of the mighty wind, and the men were terrified and did not know where they should go. **45** And the beasts and camels stood still, and they led them, but they would not go; they struck them, and they crouched on the ground; and the men said to each other, "What is this that God has done to us? what are our transgressions, and what are our sins that this thing has thus befallen us?" **46** And one of them answered and said to them, "Perhaps on account of the sin of afflicting this slave this thing has happened to us this day; now therefore, strongly implore him to forgive us, and then we will know on whose account this calamity befalls us, and if God will have compassion over us, then we will know that all this comes to us on account of the sin of afflicting this slave." **47** And the men did so, and they supplicated Joseph and pressed him to forgive them, and they said, "We have sinned to the Lord and to you, now therefore, graciously request of your God that He will put away this death from among us, for we have sinned against Him." **48** And Joseph did according to their words, and the Lord listened to Joseph, and the Lord put away the plague which He had inflicted on those men on account of Joseph, and the beasts rose up from the ground and they conducted them, and they went on, and the raging storm abated, and the earth became tranquilized, and the men proceeded on their journey to go down to Egypt, and the men knew that this calamity had befallen them on account of Joseph. **49** And they said to each other, "Behold, we know that it was on account of his affliction that this calamity befell us; now therefore, why will we bring this death on our souls? Let us hold counsel what to do to this slave." **50** And one answered and said, "Surely he told us to bring him back to his father; now therefore, come, let us take him back, and we will go to the place that he will tell us and take from his family the price that we gave for him, and then we will go away." **51** And one answered again and said, "Behold, this counsel is very good, but we cannot do so for the way is very far from us, and we cannot go out of our road." **52** And one more answered and said to them, "This is the counsel to be adopted, we will not swerve from it; behold, we are going to Egypt this day, and when we will have come to Egypt, we will sell him there at a high price, and we will be delivered from his evil." **53** And this thing pleased the men and they did so, and they continued their journey to Egypt with Joseph.

CHAPTER 43

1 And when the sons of Jacob had sold their brother Joseph to the Midianites, their hearts were smitten on account of him, and they regretted their acts, and they sought for him to bring him back, but could not find him. **2** And Reuben returned to the pit in which Joseph had been put, in order to lift him out, and restore him to his father, and Reuben stood by the pit, and he did not hear a word, and he called out, "Joseph! Joseph!" And no one answered or uttered a word. **3** And Reuben said, "Joseph has died through fright, or some serpent has caused his death"; and Reuben descended into the pit, and he searched for Joseph and could not find him in the pit, and he came out again. **4** And Reuben tore his garments and he said, "The child is not there, and how will I reconcile my father concerning him if he is dead?" and he went to his brothers and found them grieving on account of Joseph, and counseling together how to reconcile their father concerning him, and Reuben said to his brothers, "I came to the pit, and behold, Joseph was not there! What then will we say to our father, for my father will only seek the youth from me?" **5** And his brothers answered him, saying, "Thus and thus we did, and afterward our hearts struck us on account of this act, and we now sit to seek a pretext how we will reconcile our father to it." **6** And Reuben said to them, "What is this you have done to bring down the grey hairs of our father in sorrow to the grave? the thing that you have done is not good." **7** And Reuben sat with them, and they all rose up and swore to each other not to tell this thing to Jacob, and they all said, "The man who will tell this to our father or his household, or who will report this to any of the children of the land, we will all rise up against him and slay him with the sword." **8** And the sons of Jacob feared each other in this matter, from the youngest to the oldest, and no one spoke a word, and they concealed the thing in their hearts. **9** And afterward they sat down to determine and invent something to say to their father Jacob concerning all these things. **10** And Issachar said to them, "Here is an idea for you, if it seems good in your eyes to do this thing: take the coat which belongs to Joseph, and tear it, and kill a kid of the goats, and dip it in its blood. **11** Then send it to our father, and when he sees it, he will say an evil beast has devoured him; therefore, tear his coat, and behold, his blood will be on his coat, and by your doing this we will be free of our father's murmurings." **12** And Issachar's advice pleased them, and they listened to him, and they did according to the word of Issachar which he had counseled them. **13** And they hastened, and took Joseph's coat, and tore it, and they killed a kid of the goats and dipped the coat in the blood of the kid, and then trampled it in the dust, and they sent the coat to their father Jacob by the hand of Naphtali, and they commanded him to say these words: **14** "We had gathered in the cattle and had come as far as the road to Shechem and farther when we found this coat on the road in the wilderness dipped in blood and in dust; now therefore, discern whether it is your son's coat or not." **15** And Naphtali went, and he came to his father, and he gave him the coat, and he spoke to him all the words which his brothers had commanded him. **16** And Jacob saw Joseph's coat, and he knew it, and he fell on his face to the ground and became as still as a stone, and afterward he rose up and cried out with a loud and weeping voice, and he said, "It is the coat of my son Joseph!" **17** And Jacob hastened and sent one of his servants to his sons who went to them and found them coming along the road with the flock. **18** And the sons of Jacob came to their father about evening, and behold, their garments were torn and dust was on their heads, and they found their father crying out and weeping with a loud voice. **19** And Jacob said to his sons, "Tell me, truthfully, what evil you have suddenly brought on me this day!" and they answered their father Jacob, saying, "We were coming along this day after the flock had been gathered in, and we came as far as the city of Shechem by the road in the wilderness, and we found this coat filled with blood on the ground, and we knew it, and we sent [it] to you [to see] if you could discern it." **20** And Jacob heard the words of his sons and he cried out with a loud voice, and he said, "It is the

coat of my son! An evil beast has devoured him! Joseph is torn in pieces, for I sent him this day to see whether it was well with you and well with the flocks, and to bring me word from you again, and he went as I commanded him, and this has happened to him this day while I thought my son was with you." **21** And the sons of Jacob answered and said, "He did not come to us, neither have we seen him from the time of our going out from you until now." **22** And when Jacob heard their words, he cried out aloud again, and he rose up and tore his garments, and he put sackcloth on his loins; then he wept bitterly, and mourned, and lifted up his voice in weeping, and exclaimed and said these words, **23** "My son Joseph, O my son Joseph! I sent you this day after the welfare of your brothers, and behold, you have been torn in pieces; through my hand this has happened to my son! **24** It grieves me for you, my son Joseph, it grieves me for you! How sweet you were to me during life, and now how exceedingly bitter is your death to me! **25** O that I had died in your stead, my son Joseph, for it grieves me sadly for you my son, O my son, my son! My son Joseph, where are you, and where have you been drawn? arouse, arouse from your place, and come and see my grief for you, O my son Joseph! **26** Come now and number the tears gushing from my eyes down my cheeks, and bring them up before the Lord, that His anger may turn from me. **27** O my son Joseph, how did you fall by the hand of one by whom no one had fallen from the beginning of the world to this day, for you have been put to death by the striking of an enemy, inflicted with cruelty, but surely I know that this has happened to you on account of the multitude of my sins. **28** Arouse now and see how bitter my trouble is for you my son, although I did not rear you, nor fashion you, nor give you breath and soul, but it was God who formed you, and built your bones, and covered them with flesh, and breathed into your nostrils the breath of life, and then gave you to me. **29** Now truly God who gave you to me has taken you from me, and such then has befallen you." **30** And Jacob continued to speak like to these words concerning Joseph, and he wept bitterly; he fell to the ground and became still. **31** And all the sons of Jacob, seeing their father's trouble, regretted what they had done, and they also wept bitterly. **32** And Judah rose up and lifted his father's head from the ground, and placed it on his lap, and he wiped his father's tears from his cheeks, and Judah wept an exceedingly great weeping while his father's head was reclining on his lap, still as a stone. **33** And the sons of Jacob saw their father's trouble, and they lifted up their voices and continued to weep, and Jacob was yet lying on the ground still as a stone. **34** And all his sons, and his servants, and his servant's children rose up and stood around him to comfort him, and he refused to be comforted. **35** And the whole household of Jacob rose up and mourned a great mourning on account of Joseph and their father's trouble, and the intelligence reached Isaac, the son of Abraham, the father of Jacob, and he wept bitterly on account of Joseph, he and all his household, and he went from the place where he dwelt in Hebron, and his men with him, and he comforted his son Jacob, and he refused to be comforted. **36** And after this, Jacob rose up from the ground, and his tears were running down his cheeks, and he said to his sons, "Rise up and take your swords and your bows, and go out into the field, and seek whether you can find my son's body and bring it to me that I may bury it. **37** Please also seek among the beasts and hunt them, and that which will first come before you, seize [it] and bring it to me—perhaps the Lord will pity my affliction this day; and prepare before you that which tore my son in pieces, and bring it to me, and I will avenge the cause of my son." **38** And his sons did as their father had commanded them, and they rose up early in the morning, and each took his sword and his bow in his hand, and they went out into the field to hunt the beasts. **39** And Jacob was still crying aloud, and weeping, and walking to and fro in the house, and striking his hands together, saying, "My son Joseph! My son Joseph!" **40** And the sons of Jacob went into the wilderness to seize the beasts, and behold, a wolf came toward them, and they seized him, and brought him to their father, and they said to him, "This is the first we have found, and we have brought him to you as you commanded us, and we could not find your son's body." **41** And Jacob took the beast from the hands of his sons, and he cried out with a loud and weeping voice, holding the beast in his hand, and he spoke with a bitter heart to the beast, "Why did you devour my son Joseph, and how did you have no fear of the God of the earth, or of my trouble for my son Joseph? **42** And you devoured my son for nothing, because he committed no violence, and thereby rendered me culpable on his account, therefore God will require him that is persecuted." **43** And the Lord opened the mouth of the beast in order to comfort Jacob with its words, and it answered Jacob and spoke these words to him: **44** "As God lives who created us in the earth, and as your soul lives, my lord: I did not see your son, neither did I tear him to pieces, but from a distant land I also came to seek my son who went from me this day, and I do not know whether he is living or dead. **45** And I came into the field to seek my son this day, and your sons found me, and seized me, and increased my grief, and have brought me before you this day, and I have now spoken all my words to you. **46** And now therefore, O son of man, I am in your hands, and do to me this day as it may seem good in your sight, but by the life of God who created me, I did not see your son, nor did I tear him to pieces, neither has the flesh of man entered my mouth all the days of my life." **47** And when Jacob heard the words of the beast he was greatly astonished and sent the beast out from his hand, and she went her way. **48** And Jacob was still crying aloud and weeping for Joseph day after day, and he mourned for his son many days.

CHAPTER 44

1 And the sons of Ishmael who had bought Joseph from the Midianites, who had bought him from his brothers, went to Egypt with Joseph, and they came on the borders of Egypt, and when they came near to Egypt, they met four men of the sons of Medan, the son of Abraham, who had gone out from the land of Egypt on their journey. **2** And the Ishmaelites said to them, "Do you desire to purchase this slave from us?" and they said, "Deliver him over to us," and they delivered Joseph over to them, and they beheld him, that he was a very handsome youth and they purchased him for twenty shekels. **3** And the Ishmaelites continued their journey to Egypt and the Medanim also returned to Egypt that day, and the Medanim said to each other, "Behold, we have heard that Potiphar, an officer of Pharaoh, captain of the guard, seeks a good servant who will stand before him to attend him, and to make him overseer over his house and all belonging to him. **4** Now therefore, come, let us sell him to him for what we may desire if he is able to give to us that which we will require for him." **5** And these Medanim went, and came to the house of Potiphar, and said to him, "We have heard that you seek a good servant to attend you: behold, we have a servant that will please you if you can give to us that which we may desire, and we will sell him to you." **6** And Potiphar said, "Bring him before me, and I will see him, and if he pleases me I will give to you that which you may require for him." **7** And the Medanim went, and brought Joseph, and placed him before Potiphar, and he saw him, and he pleased him exceedingly, and Potiphar said to them, "Tell me what you require for this youth?" **8** And they said, "We desire four hundred pieces of silver for him," and Potiphar said, "I will give it [to] you if you bring me the record of his sale to you, and will tell me his history, for perhaps he may be stolen, for this youth is neither a slave, nor the son of a slave, but I observe in him the appearance of an attractive and handsome person." **9** And the Medanim went and brought to him the Ishmaelites who had sold him to them, and they told him, saying, "He is a slave and we sold him to them." **10** And Potiphar heard the words of the Ishmaelites in his giving the silver to the Medanim, and the Medanim took the silver and went on their journey, and the Ishmaelites also returned home. **11** And Potiphar took Joseph and brought him to his house that he might serve him, and Joseph found favor in the sight of Potiphar, and he placed confidence in him, and made him overseer over his house, and he delivered all that belonged to him over into his hand. **12** And the Lord was with Joseph and he became a prosperous man, and the Lord blessed the house of Potiphar for the sake of Joseph. **13** And Potiphar left all that he had in the hand of Joseph, and Joseph was one that caused things to come in and go out, and everything was regulated by his wish in the house of Potiphar. **14** And Joseph was eighteen years old, a youth with beautiful eyes and of handsome appearance, and like to him was not in the whole land of Egypt. **15** At that time, while he was in his master's house going in and out of the house and attending his master, Zelicah, his master's wife, lifted up her eyes toward Joseph and she looked at him, and behold, he was a handsome and well-favored youth. **16** And she coveted his beauty in her heart, and her soul was fixed on Joseph, and she enticed him day after day, and Zelicah persuaded Joseph daily, but Joseph did not lift up his eyes to behold his master's wife. **17** And Zelicah said to him, "How

attractive is your appearance and form, truly I have looked at all the slaves, and have not seen so beautiful a slave as you are"; and Joseph said to her, "Surely He who created me in my mother's womb created all mankind." **18** And she said to him, "How beautiful are your eyes with which you have dazzled all the inhabitants of Egypt, men and women"; and he said to her, "How beautiful they are while we are alive, but should you behold them in the grave, surely you would move away from them." **19** And she said to him, "How beautiful and pleasing are all your words; please take the harp which is in the house now, and play [it] with your hands, and let us hear your words." **20** And he said to her, "How beautiful and pleasing are my words when I speak the praise of my God and His glory"; and she said to him, "How very beautiful is the hair of your head; behold, the golden comb which is in the house, please take it and curl the hair of your head." **21** And he said to her, "How long will you speak these words? cease to utter these words to me, and rise and attend to your domestic affairs." **22** And she said to him, "There is no one in my house, and there is nothing to attend to but to your words and to your wish"; yet notwithstanding all this, she could not bring Joseph to her, neither did he place his eye on her, but directed his eyes below to the ground. **23** And Zelicah desired Joseph in her heart, that he should lie with her, and at the time that Joseph was sitting in the house doing his work, Zelicah came and sat before him, and she enticed him daily with her discourse to lie with her, or ever to look at her, but Joseph would not listen to her. **24** And she said to him, "If you will not do according to my words, I will punish you with the punishment of death, and put an iron yoke on you." **25** And Joseph said to her, "Surely God who created man loosens the chains of prisoners, and it is He who will deliver me from your prison and from your judgment." **26** And when she could not prevail over him, to persuade him, and her soul being still fixed on him, her desire threw her into a grievous sickness. **27** And all the women of Egypt came to visit her, and they said to her, "Why are you in this declining state? you that lack nothing—surely your husband is a great and esteemed prince in the sight of the king, should you lack anything of what your heart desires?" **28** And Zelicah answered them, saying, "This day it will be made known to you from where this disorder springs in which you see me," and she commanded her maidservants to prepare food for all the women, and she made a banquet for them, and all the women ate in the house of Zelicah. **29** And she gave them knives to peel the citrons to eat them, and she commanded that they should dress Joseph in costly garments, and that he should appear before them, and Joseph came before their eyes, and all the women looked on Joseph and could not take their eyes from off him, and they all cut their hands with the knives that they had in their hands, and all the citrons that were in their hands were filled with blood. **30** And they did not know what they had done but they continued to look at the beauty of Joseph and did not turn their eyelids from him. **31** And Zelicah saw what they had done, and she said to them, "What is this work that you have done? behold, I gave you citrons to eat and you have all cut your hands." **32** And all the women saw their hands, and behold, they were full of blood, and their blood flowed down on their garments, and they said to her, "This slave in your house has overcome us, and we could not turn our eyelids from him on account of his beauty." **33** And she said to them, "Surely this happened to you in the moment that you looked at him, and you could not contain yourselves from him; how then can I refrain when he is constantly in my house, and I see him day after day going in and out of my house? how then can I keep from declining or even from perishing on account of this?" **34** And they said to her, "The words are true, for who can see this beautiful form in the house and refrain from him, and is he not your slave and attendant in your house, and why do you not tell him that which is in your heart, and permit your soul to perish through this matter?" **35** And she said to them, "I am daily endeavoring to persuade him, and he will not consent to my wishes, and I promised him everything that is good, and yet I could meet with no return from him; I am therefore in a declining state as you see." **36** And Zelicah became very sick on account of her desire toward Joseph, and she was desperately lovesick on account of him, and all the people of the house of Zelicah and her husband knew nothing of this matter, that Zelicah was sick on account of her love for Joseph. **37** And all the people of her house asked her, saying, "Why are you sick and declining, and lack nothing?" and she said to them, "I do not know this thing which is daily increasing on me." **38** And all the women and her friends came to see her daily, and they spoke with her, and she said to them, "This can only be through the love for Joseph"; and they said to her, "Entice him and seize him secretly, perhaps he may listen to you, and put off this death from you." **39** And Zelicah became worse from her love for Joseph, and she continued to decline until she scarcely had strength to stand. **40** And on a certain day Joseph was doing his master's work in the house, and Zelicah came secretly and suddenly fell on him, and Joseph rose up against her, and he was more powerful than her, and he brought her down to the ground. **41** And Zelicah wept on account of the desire of her heart toward him, and she supplicated him with weeping, and her tears flowed down her cheeks, and she spoke to him in a voice of supplication and in bitterness of soul, saying, **42** "Have you ever heard, seen, or known of so beautiful a woman as I am, or better than myself, who speaks daily to you, fall into a decline through love for you, confer all this honor on you, and still you will not listen to my voice? **43** And if it is through fear of your master lest he punish you, as the king lives, no harm will come to you from your master through this thing; now therefore, please listen to me, and consent for the sake of the honor which I have conferred on you, and put off this death from me, and why should I die for your sake?" and she ceased to speak. **44** And Joseph answered her, saying, "Refrain from me, and leave this matter to my master; behold, my master does not know what there is with me in the house, for he has delivered all that belongs to him into my hand, and how will I do these things in my master's house? **45** For he has also greatly honored me in his house, and he has also made me overseer over his house, and he has exalted me, and there is no one greater in this house than I am, and my master has kept back nothing from me, excepting you who are his wife. How then can you speak these words to me, and how can I do this great evil and sin to God and to your husband? **46** Now therefore, refrain from me, and speak no more such words as these, for I will not listen to your words." But Zelicah would not listen to Joseph when he spoke these words to her, but she daily enticed her to listen to her. **47** And it was after this that the brook of Egypt was filled above all its sides, and all the inhabitants of Egypt went out, and also the king and princes went out with timbrels and dances, for it was a great rejoicing in Egypt, and a holiday at the time of the inundation of the sea Sihor, and they went there to rejoice all day long. **48** And when the Egyptians went out to the river to rejoice, as was their custom, all the people of the house of Potiphar went with them, but Zelicah would not go with them, for she said, "I am indisposed," and she remained alone in the house, and no other person was with her in the house. **49** And she rose up and ascended to her temple in the house, and dressed herself in princely garments, and she placed on her head precious stones of onyx stones, inlaid with silver and gold, and she beautified her face and skin with all sorts of women's purifying liquids, and she perfumed the temple and the house with cassia and frankincense, and she spread myrrh and aloes, and afterward she sat in the entrance of the temple, in the passage of the house through which Joseph passed to do his work, and behold, Joseph came from the field and entered the house to do his master's work. **50** And he came to the place through which he had to pass, and he saw all the work of Zelicah, and he turned back. **51** And Zelicah saw Joseph turning back from her, and she called out to him, saying, "What ails you Joseph? come to your work, and behold, I will make room for you until you will have passed to your seat." **52** And Joseph returned, and came to the house, and passed from there to the place of his seat, and he sat down to do his master's work as usual, and behold, Zelicah came to him and stood before him in princely garments, and the scent from her clothes was spread to a distance. **53** And she hastened and caught hold of Joseph and his garments, and she said to him, "As the king lives, if you will not perform my request you will die this day," and she hastened, and stretched out her other hand, and drew a sword from beneath her garments, and she placed it on Joseph's neck, and she said, "Rise and perform my request, and if not, you die this day." **54** And Joseph was afraid of her at her doing this thing, and he rose up to flee from her, and she seized the front of his garments, and in the terror of his flight the garment which Zelicah seized was torn, and Joseph left the garment in the hand of Zelicah, and he fled and got out, for he was in fear. **55** And when Zelicah saw that Joseph's garment was torn, and that he had left it in her hand and had fled, she was afraid for her life, lest the report should spread concerning her, and she rose up and acted with cunning, and put off the garments in which she was dressed,

and she put on her other garments. **56** And she took Joseph's garment, and she laid it beside her, and she went and seated herself in the place where she had sat in her sickness before the people of her house had gone out to the river, and she called a young youth who was then in the house, and she ordered him to call the people of the house to her. **57** And when she saw them, she said to them with a loud voice and lamentation, "See what [kind of] a Hebrew your master has brought to me in the house, for he came to lie with me this day! **58** For when you had gone out, he came to the house, and seeing that there was no person in the house, he came to me, and caught hold of me, with intent to lie with me. **59** And I seized his garments, and tore them, and called out against him with a loud voice, and when I had lifted up my voice, he was afraid for his life, and left his garment before me, and fled." **60** And the people of her house spoke nothing, but their wrath was very much kindled against Joseph, and they went to his master and told him the words of his wife. **61** And Potiphar came home enraged, and his wife cried out to him, saying, "What is this thing that you have done to me in bringing a Hebrew servant into my house, for he came to me this day to sport with me; thus he did to me this day." **62** And Potiphar heard the words of his wife, and he ordered Joseph to be punished with severe stripes, and they did so to him. **63** And while they were striking him, Joseph called out with a loud voice, and he lifted up his eyes to Heaven, and he said, "O Lord God, you know that I am innocent of all these things, and why will I die this day through falsehood by the hand of these uncircumcised [and] wicked men whom You know?" **64** And while Potiphar's men were beating Joseph, he continued to cry out and weep, and there was a child there eleven months old, and the Lord opened the mouth of the child, and he spoke these words before Potiphar's men who were striking Joseph, saying, **65** "What do you want of this man, and why do you do this evil to him? my mother speaks falsely and utters lies; thus was the transaction." **66** And the child told them accurately all that happened, and all the words of Zelicah to Joseph day after day he declared to them. **67** And all the men heard the words of the child and they wondered greatly at the child's words, and the child ceased to speak and became still. **68** And Potiphar was very much ashamed at the words of his son, and he commanded his men not to beat Joseph anymore, and the men ceased beating Joseph. **69** And Potiphar took Joseph and ordered him to be brought to justice before the priests, who were judges belonging to the king, in order to judge him concerning this affair. **70** And Potiphar and Joseph came before the priests who were the king's judges, and he said to them, "Please decide what judgment is due to a servant, for thus he has done." **71** And the priests said to Joseph, "Why did you do this thing to your master?" and Joseph answered them, saying, "Not so my lords, thus was the matter"; and Potiphar said to Joseph, "Surely I entrusted into your hands all that belonged to me, and I withheld nothing from you except my wife, and how could you do this evil?" **72** And Joseph answered, saying, "Not so my lord; as the Lord lives, and as your soul lives, my lord, the word which you heard from your wife is untrue, for this was the affair this day. **73** A year has elapsed to me since I have been in your house; have you seen any iniquity in me, or anything which might cause you to demand my life?" **74** And the priests said to Potiphar, "Send, please, and let them bring Joseph's torn garment before us, and let us see the tear in it, and if it will be that the tear is in front of the garment, then his face must have been opposite to her and she must have caught hold of him to come to her, and your wife did all that she has spoken with deceit." **75** And they brought Joseph's garment before the priests who were judges, and they saw, and behold, the tear was in front of Joseph, and all the judging priests knew that she had pressed him, and they said, "The judgment of death is not due to this slave, for he has done nothing, but his judgment is that he should be placed in the prison-house on account of the report which through him has gone out against your wife." **76** And Potiphar heard their words, and he placed him in the prison-house, the place where the king's prisoners are confined, and Joseph was in the house of confinement [for] twelve years. **77** And notwithstanding this, his master's wife did not turn from him, and she did not cease from speaking to him day after day to listen to her, and at the end of three months Zelicah continued going to Joseph, to the house of confinement, day by day, and she enticed him to listen to her, and Zelicah said to Joseph, "How long will you remain in this house? but now listen to my voice, and I will bring you out of this house." **78** And Joseph answered her, saying, "It is better for me to remain in this house than to listen to your words to sin against God"; and she said to him, "If you will not perform my wish, I will pluck out your eyes, add chains to your feet, and will deliver you into the hands of them whom you did not know before." 79 And Joseph answered her and said, "Behold, the God of the whole earth is able to deliver me from all that you can do to me, for He opens the eyes of the blind, and loosens those that are bound, and preserves all strangers who are unacquainted with the land." 80 And when Zelicah was unable to persuade Joseph to listen to her, she left off going to entice him; and Joseph was still confined in the house of confinement. 81 And Joseph's father Jacob and all his brothers who were in the land of Canaan still mourned and wept in those days on account of Joseph, for Jacob refused to be comforted for his son Joseph, and Jacob cried aloud, and wept, and mourned all those days.

CHAPTER 45

1 And it was at that time in that year, which is the year of Joseph's going down to Egypt after his brothers had sold him, that Reuben the son of Jacob went to Timnah and took to himself Eliuram for a wife, the daughter of Avi the Canaanite, and he came to her. 2 And Eliuram the wife of Reuben conceived and bore him Hanoch, Palu, Chetzron, and Carmi, four sons; and his brother Simeon took his sister Dinah for a wife, and she bore to him Memuel, Yamin, Ohad, Jachin, and Zochar, five sons. 3 And afterward he came to Bunah the Canaanite woman, the same is Bunah whom Simeon took captive from the city of Shechem, and Bunah was before Dinah and attended on her, and Simeon came to her, and she bore Saul to him. 4 And at that time Judah went to Adulam, and he came to a man of Adulam, and his name was Hirah, and Judah saw the daughter of a man from Canaan there, and her name was Aliyath, the daughter of Shua, and he took her, and came to her, and Aliyath bore Er, Onan, and Shiloh to Judah, three sons. 5 And Levi and Issachar went to the land of the east, and they took to themselves for wives the daughters of Jobab the son of Yoktan, the son of Eber; and Jobab the son of Yoktan had two daughters; the name of the elder was Adinah, and the name of the younger was Aridah. 6 And Levi took Adinah, and Issachar took Aridah, and they came to the land of Canaan, to their father's house, and Adinah bore Gershon, Kehas, and Merari to Levi, three sons. 7 And Aridah bore Tola, Puvah, Job, and Shomron to Issachar, four sons; and Dan went to the land of Moab and took Aphlaleth, the daughter of Chamudan the Moabite, for a wife, and he brought her to the land of Canaan. 8 And Aphlaleth was barren, she had no offspring, and afterward God remembered Aphlaleth the wife of Dan, and she conceived and bore a son, and she called his name Chushim. 9 And Gad and Naphtali went to Haran and took from there the daughters of Amuram the son of Uz, the son of Nahor, for wives. 10 And these are the names of the daughters of Amuram: the name of the elder was Merimah, and the name of the younger Uzith; and Naphtali took Merimah, and Gad took Uzith, and they brought them to the land of Canaan, to their father's house. 11 And Merimah bore to Naphtali Yachzeel, Guni, Jazer, and Shalem, four sons; and Uzith bore to Gad Zephion, Chagi, Shuni, Ezbon, Eri, Arodi, and Arali, seven sons. 12 And Asher went out and took Adon the daughter of Aphlal, the son of Hadad, the son of Ishmael, for a wife, and he brought her to the land of Canaan. 13 And Adon the wife of Asher died in those days—she had no offspring; and it was after the death of Adon that Asher went to the other side of the river and took for a wife Hadurah the daughter of Abimael, the son of Eber, the son of Shem. 14 And the young woman was of a beautiful appearance, and a woman of sense, and she had been the wife of Malkiel the son of Elam, the son of Shem. 15 And Hadurah bore a daughter to Malkiel, and he called her name Serach, and Malkiel died after this, and Hadurah went and remained in her father's house. 16 And after the death of the wife of Asher he went and took Hadurah for a wife and brought her to the land of Canaan, and he also brought her daughter Serach with them, and she was three years old, and the young woman was brought up in Jacob's house. 17 And the young woman was of a beautiful appearance, and she went in the sanctified ways of the children of Jacob; she lacked nothing, and the Lord gave her wisdom and understanding. 18 And Hadurah the wife of Asher conceived and bore to him Yimnah, Yishvah, Yishvi, and Beriah, four sons. 19 And Zebulun went to Midian and took for a wife Merishah the daughter of Molad, the son of Abida, the

son of Midian, and brought her to the land of Canaan. 20 And Merushah bore to Zebulun Sered, Elon, and Yachleel, three sons. 21 And Jacob sent to Aram the son of Zoba, the son of Terah, and he took Mechalia the daughter of Aram for his son Benjamin, and she came to the land of Canaan to the house of Jacob; and Benjamin was ten years old when he took Mechalia the daughter of Aram for a wife. 22 And Mechalia conceived and bore to Benjamin Bela, Becher, Ashbel, Gera, and Naaman, five sons; and afterward Benjamin went and took for a wife Aribath the daughter of Shomron, the son of Abraham, in addition to his first wife, and he was eighteen years old; and Aribath bore to Benjamin Achi, Vosh, Mupim, Chupim, and Ord, five sons. 23 And in those days Judah went to the house of Shem and took Tamar the daughter of Elam, the son of Shem, for a wife for his firstborn Er. 24 And Er came to his wife Tamar, and she became his wife, and when he came to her, he outwardly destroyed his seed, and his work was evil in the sight of the Lord, and the Lord slew him. 25 And it was after the death of Er, Judah's firstborn, that Judah said to Onan, "Go to your brother's wife and marry her as the next brother and raise up seed to your brother." 26 And Onan took Tamar for a wife and he came to her, and Onan also did like to the work of his brother, and his work was evil in the sight of the Lord, and He slew him also. 27 And when Onan died, Judah said to Tamar, "Remain in your father's house until my son Shiloh will have grown up," and Judah no longer delighted in Tamar to give her to Shiloh, for he said, "Perhaps he will also die like his brothers." 28 And Tamar rose up, and went, and remained in her father's house, and Tamar was in her father's house for some time. 29 And at the revolution of the year, Aliyath the wife of Judah died; and Judah was comforted for his wife, and after the death of Aliyath, Judah went up with his friend Hirah to Timnah to shear their sheep. 30 And Tamar heard that Judah had gone up to Timnah to shear the sheep, and that Shiloh was grown up, and Judah did not delight in her. 31 And Tamar rose up and put off the garments of her widowhood, and she put a veil on her, and she entirely covered herself, and she went and sat in the public thoroughfare, which is on the road to Timnah. 32 And Judah passed and saw her, and he took her and came to her, and she conceived by him, and at the time of being delivered, behold, there were twins in her womb, and he called the name of the first Perez, and the name of the second Zerah.

CHAPTER 46

1 In those days Joseph was still confined in the prison-house in the land of Egypt. 2 At that time the attendants of Pharaoh were standing before him—the chief of the butlers and the chief of the bakers which belonged to the king of Egypt. 3 And the butler took wine and placed it before the king to drink, and the baker placed bread before the king to eat, and the king drank of the wine and ate of the bread—he and his servants and ministers that ate at the king's table. 4 And while they were eating and drinking, the butler and the baker remained there, and Pharaoh's ministers found many flies in the wine which the butler had brought, and stones of niter were found in the baker's bread. 5 And the captain of the guard placed Joseph as an attendant over Pharaoh's officers, and Pharaoh's officers were in confinement [for] one year. 6 And at the end of the year, they both dreamed dreams in one night in the place of confinement where they were, and in the morning Joseph came to them to attend to them as usual, and he saw them, and behold, their countenances were dejected and sad. 7 And Joseph asked them, "Why are your countenances sad and dejected this day?" and they said to him, "We dreamed a dream, and there is no one to interpret it"; and Joseph said to them, "Please relate your dream to me, and God will give you an answer of peace as you desire." 8 And the butler related his dream to Joseph, and he said, "I saw in my dream, and behold, a large vine I saw before me, and on that vine I saw three branches, and the vine quickly blossomed and reached a great height, and its clusters were ripened and became grapes. 9 And I took the grapes, and pressed them in a cup, and placed it in Pharaoh's hand, and he drank"; and Joseph said to him, "The three branches that were on the vine are three days. 10 Yet within three days, the king will order you to be brought out and he will restore you to your office, and you will give the king his wine to drink as at first when you were his butler; but let me find favor in your sight [so] that you will remember me before Pharaoh when it will be well with you, and do kindness to me, and get me brought out from this prison, for I was stolen away

from the land of Canaan and was sold for a slave in this place. 11 And also that which was told you concerning my master's wife is false, for they placed me in this dungeon for nothing"; and the butler answered Joseph, saying, "If the king deals well with me as at first, as you last interpreted to me, I will do all that you desire and get you brought out of this dungeon." 12 And the baker, seeing that Joseph had accurately interpreted the butler's dream, also approached and related the whole of his dream to Joseph. 13 And he said to him, "In my dream I saw, and behold, [there were] three white baskets on my head, and I looked, and behold, there were all manner of baked meats for Pharaoh in the uppermost basket, and behold, the birds were eating them from off my head." 14 And Joseph said to him, "The three baskets which you saw are three days: yet within three days Pharaoh will take off your head, and hang you on a tree, and the birds will eat your flesh from off you as you saw in your dream." 15 In those days the queen was about to deliver, and on that day she bore a son to the king of Egypt, and they proclaimed that the king had gotten his firstborn son, and all the people of Egypt, together with the officers and servants of Pharaoh, greatly rejoiced. 16 And on the third day of his birth Pharaoh made a feast for his officers and servants, for the hosts of the land of Zoar and of the land of Egypt. 17 And all the people of Egypt and the servants of Pharaoh came to eat and drink with the king at the celebration of his son, and to rejoice at the king's rejoicing. 18 And all the officers of the king and his servants were rejoicing at that time for eight days at the feast, and they made merry with all sorts of musical instruments, with timbrels and with dances in the king's house for eight days. 19 And the butler, to whom Joseph had interpreted his dream, forgot Joseph, and he did not mention him to the king as he had promised, for this thing was from the Lord in order to punish Joseph because he had trusted in man. 20 And after this Joseph remained in the prison-house [for] two years, until he had completed twelve years.

CHAPTER 47

1 And Isaac the son of Abraham was still living in the land of Canaan in those days; he was very aged—one hundred and eighty years old—and his son Esau, the brother of Jacob, was in the land of Edom, and he and his sons had possessions in it among the children of Seir. 2 And Esau heard that his father's time was drawing near to die, and he and his sons and household came to the land of Canaan, to his father's house, and Jacob and his sons went out from the place where they dwelt in Hebron, and they all came to their father Isaac, and they found Esau and his sons in the tent. 3 And Jacob and his sons sat before his father Isaac, and Jacob was still mourning for his son Joseph. 4 And Isaac said to Jacob, "Bring your sons to me here and I will bless them"; and Jacob brought his eleven children before his father Isaac. 5 And Isaac placed his hands on all the sons of Jacob, and he took hold of them, and embraced them, and kissed them one by one, and Isaac blessed them on that day, and he said to them, "May the God of your fathers bless you and increase your seed like the stars of the heavens for number." 6 And Isaac also blessed the sons of Esau, saying, "May God cause you to be a dread and a terror to all that will behold you, and to all your enemies." 7 And Isaac called Jacob and his sons, and they all came and sat before Isaac, and Isaac said to Jacob, "The Lord God of the whole earth said to me, To your seed I will give this land for an inheritance if your children keep My statutes and My ways, and I will perform to them the oath which I swore to your father Abraham. 8 Now therefore, my son, teach your children and your children's children to fear the Lord, and to go in the good way which will please the Lord your God, for if you keep the ways of the Lord and His statutes, the Lord will also keep His covenant with Abraham to you, and will do well with you and your seed all the days." 9 And when Isaac had finished commanding Jacob and his children, he gave up the spirit and died, and was gathered to his people. 10 And Jacob and Esau fell on the face of their father Isaac, and they wept, and Isaac was one hundred and eighty years old when he died in the land of Canaan, in Hebron, and his sons carried him to the cave of Machpelah, which Abraham had bought from the children of Heth for a possession of a burial place. 11 And all the kings of the land of Canaan went with Jacob and Esau to bury Isaac, and all the kings of Canaan showed Isaac great honor at his death. 12 And the sons of Jacob and the sons of Esau went around barefooted, walking and lamenting until they reached

Kirjath-Arba. 13 And Jacob and Esau buried their father Isaac in the cave of Machpelah, which is in Kirjath-Arba in Hebron, and they buried him with very great honor, as at the funeral of kings. 14 And Jacob and his sons, and Esau and his sons, and all the kings of Canaan made a great and heavy mourning, and they buried him and mourned for him [for] many days. 15 And at the death of Isaac, he left his cattle, and his possessions, and all belonging to him to his sons; and Esau said to Jacob, "Now behold, all that our father has left we will divide it in two parts, and I will have the choice," and Jacob said, "We will do so." 16 And Jacob took all that Isaac had left in the land of Canaan, the cattle and the property, and he placed them in two parts before Esau and his sons, and he said to Esau, "Behold, all this is before you, choose for yourself the half which you will take." 17 And Jacob said to Esau, "Now hear what I will speak to you, saying, The Lord God of the heavens and earth spoke to our fathers Abraham and Isaac, saying, To your seed I will give this land for an inheritance forever. 18 Now therefore, all that our father has left is before you, and behold, all the land is before you: choose from them what you desire. 19 If you desire the whole land, take it for you and your children forever, and I will take these riches, and if you desire the riches, take it to you, and I will take this land for me and for my children to inherit it forever." 20 And Nebayoth, the son of Ishmael, was then in the land with his children, and Esau went on that day and consulted with him, saying, 21 "Thus Jacob has spoken to me, and thus he has answered me; now give your advice and we will hear." 22 And Nebayoth said, "What is this that Jacob has spoken to you? behold, all the children of Canaan are dwelling securely in their land, and Jacob says he will inherit it with his seed all the days. 23 Go now, therefore, and take all your father's riches and leave your brother Jacob in the land as he has spoken." 24 And Esau rose up and returned to Jacob, and he did all that Nebayoth the son of Ishmael had advised; and Esau took all the riches that Isaac had left: the souls, the beasts, the cattle, and the property, and all the riches; he gave nothing to his brother Jacob; and Jacob took all the land of Canaan, from the brook of Egypt to the River Euphrates, and he took it for a perpetual possession, and for his children and for his seed after him forever. 25 Jacob also took from his brother Esau the cave of Machpelah, which is in Hebron, which Abraham had bought from Ephron for a possession of a burial place for him and his seed forever. 26 And Jacob wrote all these things in the scroll of purchase, and he signed it, and he testified all this with four faithful witnesses. 27 And these are the words which Jacob wrote in the scroll, saying, "The land of Canaan and all the cities of the Hittites, the Hivites, the Jebusites, the Amorites, the Perizzites, and the Gergashites— all the seven nations from the river of Egypt to the River Euphrates— 28 and the city of Hebron, Kirjath-Arba, and the cave which is in it, Jacob bought the whole from his brother Esau for value, for a possession and for an inheritance for his seed after him forever." 29 And Jacob took the scroll of purchase, and the signature, [and] the command, and the statutes, and the revealed scroll, and he placed them in an earthen vessel in order that they should remain for a long time, and he delivered them into the hands of his children. 30 Esau took all that his father had left him after his death from his brother Jacob, and he took all the property, from man and beast, camel and donkey, ox and lamb, silver and gold, stones and bdellium, and all the riches which had belonged to Isaac the son of Abraham; there was nothing left which Esau did not take to himself from all that Isaac had left after his death. 31 And Esau took all this, and he and his children went home to the land of Seir the Horite, away from his brother Jacob and his children. 32 And Esau had possessions among the children of Seir, and Esau did not return to the land of Canaan from that day forward. 33 And the whole land of Canaan became an inheritance to the sons of Israel for a perpetual inheritance, and Esau inherited the mountain of Seir with all his children.

CHAPTER 48

1 In those days, after the death of Isaac, the Lord commanded and caused a famine on the whole earth. 2 At that time Pharaoh king of Egypt was sitting on his throne in the land of Egypt, and he lay in his bed and dreamed dreams, and Pharaoh saw in his dream that he was standing by the side of the river of Egypt. 3 And while he was standing, he saw, and behold, seven fat-fleshed and well-favored cows came up out of the river. 4 And seven other cows, lean-fleshed and ill-

favored, came up after them, and the seven ill-favored ones swallowed up the well-favored ones, and still their appearance was ill as at first. **5** And he awoke, and he slept again, and he dreamed a second time, and he saw, and behold, seven ears of corn came up on one stalk, rank and good, and seven thin ears blasted with the east wind sprang up after them, and the thin ears swallowed up the full ones, and Pharaoh awoke out of his dream. **6** And in the morning the king remembered his dreams, and his spirit was sadly troubled on account of his dreams, and the king hastened, and sent and called for all the magicians of Egypt and the wise men, and they came and stood before Pharaoh. **7** And the king said to them, "I have dreamed dreams, and there is none to interpret them"; and they said to the king, "Relate your dreams to your servants and let us hear them." **8** And the king related his dreams to them, and they all answered and said with one voice to the king, "May the king live forever; and this is the interpretation of your dreams: **9** the seven good cows which you saw denote seven daughters that will be born to you in the latter days, and the seven cows which you saw come up after them and swallow them up are for a sign that the daughters which will be born to you will all die in the lifetime of the king. **10** And that which you saw in the second dream of seven full good ears of corn coming up on one stalk, this is their interpretation: that you will build seven cities for yourself in the latter days throughout the land of Egypt; and that which you saw of the seven blasted ears of corn springing up after them and swallowing them up while you beheld them with your eyes is for a sign that the cities which you will build will all be destroyed in the latter days, in the lifetime of the king." **11** And when they spoke these words the king did not incline his ear to their words, neither did he fix his heart on them, for the king knew in his wisdom that they did not give a proper interpretation of the dreams; and when they had finished speaking before the king, the king answered them, saying, "What is this thing that you have spoken to me? surely you have uttered falsehood and spoken lies; now therefore, give the proper interpretation of my dreams that you may not die." **12** And the king commanded after this, and again he sent and called for other wise men, and they came and stood before the king, and the king related his dreams to them, and they all answered him according to the first interpretation, and the king's anger was kindled and he was very angry, and the king said to them, "Surely you speak lies and utter falsehood in what you have said." **13** And the king commanded that a proclamation should be issued throughout the land of Egypt, saying, "It is resolved by the king and his great men that any wise man who knows and understands the interpretation of dreams, and will not come this day before the king, will die. **14** And the man that will declare to the king the proper interpretation of his dreams, there will be given to him all that he will require from the king." And all the wise men of the land of Egypt came before the king, together with all the magicians and sorcerers that were in Egypt, and in Goshen, in Rameses, in Tachpanches, in Zoar, and in all the places on the borders of Egypt, and they all stood before the king. **15** And all the nobles, and the princes, and the attendants belonging to the king came together from all the cities of Egypt, and they all sat before the king, and the king related his dreams before the wise men and the princes, and all that sat before the king were astonished at the vision. **16** And all the wise men who were before the king were greatly divided in their interpretation of his dreams; some of them interpreted them to the king, saying, "The seven good cows are seven kings who will be raised over Egypt from the king's issue. **17** And the seven bad cows are seven princes who will stand up against them in the latter days and destroy them; and the seven ears of corn are the seven great princes belonging to Egypt who will fall in the hands of the seven less powerful princes of their enemies in the wars of our lord the king." **18** And some of them interpreted to the king in this manner, saying, "The seven good cows are the strong cities of Egypt, and the seven bad cows are the seven nations of the land of Canaan who will come against the seven cities of Egypt in the latter days and destroy them. **19** And that which you saw in the second dream of seven good and bad ears of corn is a sign that the government of Egypt will return to your seed again as at first. **20** And in his reign the people of the cities of Egypt will turn against the seven cities of Canaan who are stronger than they are and will destroy them, and the government of Egypt will return to your seed." **21** And some of them said to the king, "This is the interpretation of your dreams: the seven good cows are seven queens whom you will take for wives in the latter days, and the seven bad cows

denote that those women will all die in the lifetime of the king. **22** And the seven good and bad ears of corn which you saw in the second dream are fourteen children, and it will be in the latter days that they will stand up and fight among themselves, and seven of them will strike the seven that are more powerful." **23** And some of them said these words to the king, saying, "The seven good cows denote that seven children will be born to you, and they will slay seven of your children's children in the latter days; and the seven good ears of corn which you saw in the second dream are those princes against whom seven other less powerful princes will fight and destroy them in the latter days and avenge your children's cause, and the government will return to your seed again." **24** And the king heard all the words of the wise men of Egypt and their interpretation of his dreams and none of them pleased the king. **25** And the king knew in his wisdom that they did not altogether speak correctly in all these words, for this was from the Lord to frustrate the words of the wise men of Egypt in order that Joseph might go out from the house of confinement, and in order that he should become great in Egypt. **26** And the king saw that none among all the wise men and magicians of Egypt spoke correctly to him, and the king's wrath was kindled, and his anger burned within him. **27** And the king commanded that all the wise men and magicians should go out from before him, and they all went out from before the king with shame and disgrace. **28** And the king commanded that a proclamation be sent throughout Egypt to slay all the magicians that were in Egypt, and not one of them should be permitted to live. **29** And the captains of the guards belonging to the king rose up, and each man drew his sword, and they began to strike the magicians of Egypt, and the wise men. **30** And after this, Merod, chief butler to the king, came and bowed down before the king and sat before him. **31** And the butler said to the king, "May the king live forever, and may his government be exalted in the land. **32** You were angry with your servant in those days, now two years past, and placed me in the ward, and I was in the ward for some time, I and the chief of the bakers. **33** And there was a Hebrew servant with us belonging to the captain of the guard, his name was Joseph, for his master had been angry with him and placed him in the house of confinement, and he attended us there. **34** And some time after, when we were in the ward, we dreamed dreams in one night—I and the chief of the bakers; we dreamed, each man according to the interpretation of his dream. **35** And we came in the morning and told them to that servant, and he interpreted our dreams to us; he correctly interpreted to each man according to his dream. **36** And it came to pass as he interpreted to us, so was the event; there did not fall to the ground any of his words. **37** And now therefore, my lord and king, do not slay the people of Egypt for nothing; behold, that slave is still confined in the house by the captain of the guard, his master, in the house of confinement. **38** If it pleases the king, let him send for him that he may come before you and he will make the correct interpretation of the dream which you dreamed known to you." **39** And the king heard the words of the chief butler, and the king ordered that the wise men of Egypt should not be slain. **40** And the king ordered his servants to bring Joseph before him, and the king said to them, "Go to him and do not terrify him lest he may be confused and will not know [how] to speak properly." **41** And the servants of the king went to Joseph, and they brought him out of the dungeon hastily, and the king's servants shaved him, and he changed his prison garment and came before the king. **42** And the king was sitting on his royal throne in a princely dress girt around with a golden ephod, and the fine gold which was on it sparkled, and the carbuncle, and the ruby, and the emerald, together with all the precious stones that were on the king's head, dazzled the eye, and Joseph greatly wondered at the king. **43** And the throne on which the king sat was covered with gold and silver, and with onyx stones, and it had seventy steps. **44** And it was their custom throughout the land of Egypt that every man who came to speak to the king, if he was a prince or one that was estimable in the sight of the king, he ascended to the king's throne as far as the thirty-first step, and the king would descend to the thirty-sixth step, and speak with him. **45** If he was one of the common people, he ascended to the third step, and the king would descend to the fourth and speak to him, and their custom was, moreover, that any man who understood to speak in all the seventy languages, he ascended the seventy steps, and went up and spoke until he reached the king. **46** And any man who could not complete the seventy, he ascended as many steps as the languages which he knew to speak in. **47** And it was customary in those days in Egypt that no one should reign over them, except [one] who understood to speak in the seventy languages. **48** And when Joseph came before the king, he bowed down to the ground before the king, and he ascended to the third step, and the king sat on the fourth step and spoke with Joseph. **49** And the king said to Joseph, "I dreamed a dream, and there is no interpreter to interpret it properly, and I commanded this day that all the magicians of Egypt and the wise men thereof should come before me, and I related my dreams to them, and no one has properly interpreted them to me. **50** And after this I heard this day concerning you that you are a wise man and can correctly interpret every dream that you hear." **51** And Joseph answered Pharaoh, saying, "Let Pharaoh relate his dreams that he dreamed; surely the interpretations belong to God"; and Pharaoh related his dreams to Joseph, the dream of the cows and the dream of the ears of corn, and the king ceased speaking. **52** And Joseph was then clothed with the Spirit of God before the king, and he knew all the things that would befall the king from that day forward, and he knew the proper interpretation of the king's dream, and he spoke before the king. **53** And Joseph found favor in the sight of the king, and the king inclined his ears and his heart, and he heard all the words of Joseph. And Joseph said to the king, "Do not imagine that they are two dreams, for it is only one dream, for that which God has chosen to do throughout the land He has shown to the king in his dream, and this is the proper interpretation of your dream: **54** the seven good cows and ears of corn are seven years, and the seven bad cows and ears of corn are also seven years; it is one dream. **55** Behold, [during] the seven years that are coming there will be a great plenty throughout the land, and after that the seven years of famine will follow them—a very grievous famine; and all the plenty will be forgotten from the land, and the famine will consume the inhabitants of the land. **56** The king dreamed one dream, and the dream was therefore repeated to Pharaoh because the thing is established by God, and God will shortly bring it to pass. **57** Now therefore, I will give you counsel and deliver your soul and the souls of the inhabitants of the land from the evil of the famine: seek throughout your kingdom for a very discreet and wise man who knows all the affairs of government and appoint him to superintend over the land of Egypt. **58** And let the man whom you place over Egypt appoint officers under him that they gather in all the food of the good years that are coming and let them lay up corn and deposit it in your appointed stores. **59** And let them keep that food for the seven years of famine that it may be found for you, and your people, and your whole land, and that you and your land are not cut off by the famine. **60** Let all the inhabitants of the land, every man, also be ordered that they gather in the produce of his field, of all sorts of food, during the seven good years, and that they place it in their stores, that it may be found for them in the days of the famine and that they may live on it. **61** This is the proper interpretation of your dream, and this is the counsel given to save your soul and the souls of all your subjects." **62** And the king answered and said to Joseph, "Who says and who knows that your words are correct?" And he said to the king, "This will be a sign for you respecting all my words that they are true and that my advice is good for you: **63** behold, your wife sits on the stool of delivery this day, and she will bear you a son and you will rejoice with him; when your child will have gone out from his mother's womb, your firstborn son that has been born these two years back will die, and you will be comforted in the child that will be born to you this day." **64** And Joseph finished speaking these words to the king, and he bowed down to the king, and he went out, and when Joseph had gone out from the king's presence, those signs which Joseph had spoken to the king came to pass on that day. **65** And the queen bore a son on that day and the king heard the glad tidings about his son, and he rejoiced, and when the reporter had gone out from the king's presence, the king's servants found the firstborn son of the king fallen dead on the ground. **66** And there was great lamentation and noise in the king's house, and the king heard it, and he said, "What is the noise and lamentation that I have heard in the house?" and they told the king that his firstborn son had died; then the king knew that all Joseph's words that he had spoken were correct, and the king was consoled for his son by the child that was born to him on that day as Joseph had spoken.

CHAPTER 49

1 After these things the king sent for and assembled all his officers and servants, and all the princes and nobles belonging to the king, and they all came before the king. **2** And the king said to them, "Behold, you have seen and heard all the words of this Hebrew man, and all the signs which he declared would come to pass, and not any of his words have fallen to the ground. **3** You know that he has given a proper interpretation of the dream and it will surely come to pass; now therefore, take counsel and know what you will do and how the land will be delivered from the famine. **4** Seek now and see whether the same can be found in whose heart there is wisdom and knowledge, and I will appoint him over the land. **5** For you have heard what the Hebrew man has advised concerning this to save the land from the famine, and I know that the land will not be delivered from the famine but with the advice of the Hebrew man—him that advised me." **6** And they all answered the king and said, "The counsel which the Hebrew has given concerning this is good; now therefore, our lord and king, behold, the whole land is in your hand, do that which seems good in your sight. **7** Him whom you choose, and whom you in your wisdom know to be wise and capable of delivering the land with his wisdom, the king will appoint him to be under him over the land." **8** And the king said to all the officers: "I have thought that since God has made known to the Hebrew man all that He has spoken, there is none so discreet and wise in the whole land as he is; if it seems good in your sight, I will place him over the land, for he will save the land with his wisdom." **9** And all the officers answered the king and said, "But surely it is written in the laws of Egypt, and it should not be violated, that no man will reign over Egypt, nor be the second to the king, but one who has knowledge in all the languages of the sons of men. **10** Now therefore, our lord and king, behold, this Hebrew man can only speak the Hebrew language, and how then can he be over us—the second under government—a man who does not even know our language? **11** Now please send for him, and let him come before you, and prove him in all things, and do as you see fit." **12** And the king said, "It will be done tomorrow, and the thing that you have spoken is good"; and all the officers came on that day before the king. **13** And on that night the Lord sent one of His ministering messengers, and he came into the land of Egypt to Joseph, and the messenger of the Lord stood over Joseph, and behold, Joseph was lying in the bed at night in his master's house in the dungeon, for his master had put him back into the dungeon on account of his wife. **14** And the messenger roused him from his sleep, and Joseph rose up and stood on his legs, and behold, the messenger of the Lord was standing opposite to him; and the messenger of the Lord spoke with Joseph, and he taught him all the languages of man in that night, and he called his name Jehoseph. **15** And the messenger of the Lord went from him, and Joseph returned and lay on his bed, and Joseph was astonished at the vision which he saw. **16** And it came to pass in the morning that the king sent for all his officers and servants, and they all came and sat before the king, and the king ordered Joseph to be brought, and the king's servants went and brought Joseph before Pharaoh. **17** And the king came out and ascended the steps of the throne, and Joseph spoke to the king in all languages, and Joseph went up to him and spoke to the king until he arrived before the king in the seventieth step, and he sat before the king. **18** And the king greatly rejoiced on account of Joseph, and all the king's officers rejoiced greatly with the king when they heard all the words of Joseph. **19** And the thing seemed good in the sight of the king and the officers, to appoint Joseph to be second to the king over the whole land of Egypt, and the king spoke to Joseph, saying, **20** "Now, you gave me counsel to appoint a wise man over the land of Egypt in order to save the land from the famine with his wisdom; now therefore, since God has made all this known to you, and all the words which you have spoken, there is not a discreet and wise man like you throughout the land. **21** And your name will no longer be called Joseph, but Zaphnath-Paaneah will be your name; you will be second to me, and all the affairs of my government will be according to your word, and at your word my people will go out and come in. **22** Also from under your hand my servants and officers will receive their salary which is given to them monthly, and all the people of the land will bow down to you; only in my throne will I be greater than you." **23** And the king took off his ring from his hand and put it on the hand of Joseph, and the king dressed Joseph in a princely garment, and he put a golden crown on his head, and he put a golden chain on his neck. **24** And the king commanded his servants and they made him ride in the second chariot belonging to the king that went opposite to the king's chariot, and he caused him to ride on a great and strong horse from the king's horses and to be conducted through the streets of the land of Egypt. **25** And the king commanded that all those that played on timbrels, harps, and other musical instruments should go out with Joseph; one thousand timbrels, one thousand mecholoth, and one thousand nebalim went after him, **26** and [also] five thousand men with drawn swords glittering in their hands, and they went marching and playing before Joseph; and twenty thousand of the great men of the king girt with girdles of skin covered with gold marched at the right hand of Joseph, and twenty thousand at his left; and all the women and young girls went on the roofs or stood in the streets playing and rejoicing before Joseph, and they gazed at the appearance of Joseph and at his beauty. **27** And the king's people went before him and behind him, perfuming the road with frankincense, and with cassia, and with all sorts of fine perfume, and they scattered myrrh and aloes along the road, and twenty men proclaimed these words before him throughout the land in a loud voice: **28** "Do you see this man whom the king has chosen to be his second? all the affairs of government will be regulated by him, and he that transgresses his orders or that does not bow down before him to the ground will die, for he rebels against the king and his second." **29** And when the heralds had ceased proclaiming, all the people of Egypt bowed down to the ground before Joseph and said, "May the king live!" Also, "May his second live!" And all the inhabitants of Egypt bowed down along the road, and when the heralds approached them, they bowed down, and they rejoiced with all sorts of timbrels, mechol, and nebal before Joseph. **30** And Joseph lifted up his eyes to Heaven [from] on his horse, and called out and said, "He raises the poor man from the dust; He lifts up the needy from the dunghill. O Lord of Hosts, happy is the man who trusts in You." **31** And Joseph passed throughout the land of Egypt with Pharaoh's servants and officers, and they showed him the whole land of Egypt and all the king's treasures. **32** And Joseph returned and came on that day before Pharaoh, and the king gave to Joseph a possession in the land of Egypt, a possession of fields and vineyards, and the king gave to Joseph three thousand talents of silver and one thousand talents of gold, and onyx stones, and bdellium, and many gifts. **33** And on the next day the king commanded all the people of Egypt to bring offerings and gifts to Joseph, and that he that violated the command of the king should die; and they made a high place in the street of the city, and they spread out garments there, and whoever brought anything to Joseph put it into the high place. **34** And all the people of Egypt cast something into the high place: one man a golden earring, and the other rings and earrings, and different vessels of gold, and silver work, and onyx stones, and bdellium he cast on the high place; everyone gave something of what he possessed. **35** And Joseph took all these and placed them in his treasuries, and all the officers and nobles belonging to the king exalted Joseph, and they gave him many gifts, seeing that the king had chosen him to be his second. **36** And the king sent to Potiphera, the son of Ahiram priest of On, and he took his young daughter Osnath and gave her to Joseph for a wife. **37** And the young woman was very beautiful, a virgin, one whom man had not known, and Joseph took her for a wife; and the king said to Joseph, "I am Pharaoh, and beside you none will dare to lift up his hand or his foot to regulate my people throughout the land of Egypt." **38** And Joseph was thirty years old when he stood before Pharaoh, and Joseph went out from before the king, and he became the king's second in Egypt. **39** And the king gave Joseph one hundred servants to attend him in his house, and Joseph also sent and purchased many servants and they remained in the house of Joseph. **40** Joseph then built a very magnificent house for himself like the houses of kings, before the court of the king's palace, and he made a large temple in the house, very elegant in appearance and convenient for his residence; [for] three years Joseph was erecting his house. **41** And Joseph made a very elegant throne of abundant gold and silver for himself, and he covered it with onyx stones and bdellium, and he made on it the likeness of the whole land of Egypt, and the likeness of the river of Egypt that waters the whole land of Egypt; and Joseph sat securely on his throne in his house and the Lord increased Joseph's wisdom. **42** And all the inhabitants of Egypt and Pharaoh's servants and his princes loved Joseph exceedingly, for this thing was from the Lord to Joseph. **43** And Joseph had an army that made war, going out in hosts and

troops to the number of forty thousand six hundred men, capable of bearing arms to assist the king and Joseph against the enemy, besides the king's officers, and his servants, and [the] inhabitants of Egypt without number. **44** And Joseph gave to his mighty men, and to all his host, shields, and javelins, and caps, and coats of mail, and stones for slinging.

CHAPTER 50

1 At that time the children of Tarshish came against the sons of Ishmael and made war with them, and the children of Tarshish spoiled the Ishmaelites for a long time. **2** And the children of Ishmael were small in number in those days, and they could not prevail over the children of Tarshish, and they were severely oppressed. **3** And the old men of the Ishmaelites sent a record to the king of Egypt, saying, "Please send officers and hosts to your servants to help us fight against the children of Tarshish, for we have been consuming away for a long time." **4** And Pharaoh sent Joseph with the mighty men and host which were with him, and also his mighty men from the king's house. **5** And they went to the land of Havilah to the children of Ishmael, to assist them against the children of Tarshish, and the children of Ishmael fought with the children of Tarshish, and Joseph struck the Tarshishites, and he subdued all their land, and the children of Ishmael dwell therein to this day. **6** And when the land of Tarshish was subdued, all the Tarshishites fled and came on the border of their brothers, the children of Javan, and Joseph returned to Egypt with all his mighty men and host; not one man of them [was] missing. **7** And at the revolution of the year, in the second year of Joseph's reigning over Egypt, the Lord gave great plenty throughout the land for seven years as Joseph had spoken, for the Lord blessed all the produce of the earth in those days for seven years, and they ate and were greatly satisfied. **8** And at that time Joseph had officers under him, and they collected all the food of the good years, and heaped corn year by year, and they placed it in the treasuries of Joseph. **9** And at any time when they gathered the food, Joseph commanded that they should bring the corn in the ears, and also bring with it some of the soil of the field, that it should not spoil. **10** And Joseph did according to this year by year, and he heaped up corn like the sand of the sea for abundance, for his stores were immense and could not be numbered for abundance. **11** And also all the inhabitants of Egypt gathered all sorts of food in their stores in great abundance during the seven good years, but they did not do to it as Joseph did. **12** And all the food which Joseph and the Egyptians had gathered during the seven years of plenty was secured for the land in stores for the seven years of famine, for the support of the whole land. **13** And each man of the inhabitants of Egypt filled his store and his concealed place with corn to be for support during the famine. **14** And Joseph placed all the food that he had gathered in all the cities of Egypt, and he closed all the stores and placed sentinels over them. **15** And Joseph's wife Osnath the daughter of Potiphera bore him two sons, Manasseh and Ephraim, and Joseph was thirty-four years old when he begot them. **16** And the boys grew up and they went in his ways and in his instructions; they did not deviate from the way which their father taught them, either to the right or left. **17** And the Lord was with the boys, and they grew up and had understanding and skill in all wisdom and in all the affairs of government, and all the king's officers and his great men of the inhabitants of Egypt exalted the boys, and they were brought up among the king's children. **18** And the seven years of plenty that were throughout the land were at an end, and the seven years of famine came after them as Joseph had spoken, and the famine was throughout the land. **19** And all the people of Egypt saw that the famine had commenced in the land of Egypt, and all the people of Egypt opened their stores of corn for the famine prevailed over them. **20** And they found all the food that was in their stores full of vermin and not fit to eat, and the famine prevailed throughout the land, and all the inhabitants of Egypt came and cried before Pharaoh, for the famine was heavy on them. **21** And they said to Pharaoh, "Give food to your servants, and why will we die through hunger before your eyes, even we and our little ones?" **22** And Pharaoh answered them, saying, "And why do you cry to me? did not Joseph command that the corn should be laid up during the seven years of plenty for the years of famine? and why did you not listen to his voice?" **23** And the people of Egypt answered the king, saying, "As your soul lives, our lord, your servants have done all that Joseph ordered, for your servants also gathered in all the produce of their fields during the seven years of plenty and laid it in the stores to this day. ²⁴ And when the famine prevailed over your servants we opened our stores, and behold, all our produce was filled with vermin and was not fit for food." ²⁵ And when the king heard all that had befallen the inhabitants of Egypt, the king was greatly afraid on account of the famine, and he was very terrified; and the king answered the people of Egypt, saying, "Since all this has happened to you, go to Joseph [and] do whatever he will say to you; do not transgress his commands." ²⁶ And all the people of Egypt went out and came to Joseph, and they said to him, "Give food to us, and why will we die before you through hunger? for we gathered in our produce during the seven years as you commanded, and we put it in store, and thus it has befallen us." ²⁷ And when Joseph heard all the words of the people of Egypt and what had befallen them, Joseph opened all his stores of the produce and he sold it to the people of Egypt. ²⁸ And the famine prevailed throughout the land, and the famine was in all countries, but in the land of Egypt there was produce for sale. ²⁹ And all the inhabitants of Egypt came to Joseph to buy corn, for the famine prevailed over them, and all their corn was spoiled, and Joseph sold it to all the people of Egypt daily. ³⁰ And all the inhabitants of the land of Canaan, and the Philistines, and those beyond the Jordan, and the children of the east, and all the cities of the lands far and near heard that there was corn in Egypt, and they all came to Egypt to buy corn, for the famine prevailed over them. ³¹ And Joseph opened the stores of corn and placed officers over them, and daily they stood and sold to all that came. ³² And Joseph knew that his brothers would also come to Egypt to buy corn, for the famine prevailed throughout the earth. And Joseph commanded all his people that they should cause it to be proclaimed throughout the land of Egypt, saying, ³³ "It is the pleasure of the king, of his second and of their great men, that any person who wishes to buy corn in Egypt will not send his servants to Egypt to purchase, but his sons, and also any Egyptian or Canaanite who will come from any of the stores from buying corn in Egypt and will go and sell it throughout the land, he will die, for no one will buy but for the support of his household. ³⁴ And any man leading two or three beasts will die, for a man will only lead his own beast." ³⁵ And Joseph placed sentinels at the gates of Egypt and commanded them, saying, "Any person who may come to buy corn, do not allow him to enter until his name, and the name of his father, and the name of his father's father is written down, and whatever is written by day, send their names to me in the evening that I may know their names." ³⁶ And Joseph placed officers throughout the land of Egypt, and he commanded them to do all these things. ³⁷ And Joseph did all these things and made these statutes in order that he might know when his brothers should come to Egypt to buy corn; and Joseph's people caused it to be proclaimed in Egypt daily according to these words and statutes which Joseph had commanded. ³⁸ And all the inhabitants of the east and west country, and of all the earth, heard of the statutes and regulations which Joseph had enacted in Egypt, and the inhabitants of the extreme parts of the earth came and bought corn in Egypt day after day, and then they went away. ³⁹ And all the officers of Egypt did as Joseph had commanded, and all that came to Egypt to buy corn, the gatekeepers would write their names and their fathers' names, and daily bring them before Joseph in the evening.

CHAPTER 51

¹ And afterward Jacob heard that there was corn in Egypt, and he called to his sons to go to Egypt to buy corn, for the famine also prevailed on them, and he called to his sons, saying, ² "Behold, I hear that there is corn in Egypt, and all the people of the earth go there to purchase [some], now therefore, why will you show yourselves satisfied before the whole earth? Also go down to Egypt and buy us a little corn among those that come there that we may not die." ³ And the sons of Jacob listened to the voice of their father, and they rose up to go down to Egypt in order to buy corn among the rest that came there. ⁴ And their father Jacob commanded them, saying, "When you come into the city, do not enter in one gate together on account of the inhabitants of the land." ⁵ And the sons of Jacob went out and they went to Egypt, and the sons of Jacob did everything as their father had commanded them, and Jacob did not send Benjamin, for he said, "Lest an accident might befall him on the road like his brother"; and ten of

Jacob's sons went out. ⁶ And while the sons of Jacob were going on the road, they regretted what they had done to Joseph, and they spoke to each other, saying, "We know that our brother Joseph went down to Egypt, and now we will seek him where we go, and if we find him we will take him from his master for a ransom, and if not, by force, and we will die for him." ⁷ And the sons of Jacob agreed to this thing and strengthened themselves on account of Joseph, to deliver him from the hand of his master, and the sons of Jacob went to Egypt; and when they came near to Egypt they separated from each other, and they came through ten gates of Egypt, and the gatekeepers wrote their names on that day and brought them to Joseph in the evening. ⁸ And Joseph read the names from the hand of the gatekeepers of the city, and he found that his brothers had entered at the ten gates of the city, and at that time Joseph commanded that it should be proclaimed throughout the land of Egypt, saying, ⁹ "Go out, all you store guards, [and] close all the corn stores, and let only one remain open that those who come may purchase from it." ¹⁰ And all the officers of Joseph did so at that time, and they closed all the stores and left only one open. ¹¹ And Joseph gave the written names of his brothers to him that was set over the open store, and he said to him, "Whoever will come to you to buy corn, ask his name, and when men of these names will come before you, seize them and send them," and they did so. ¹² And when the sons of Jacob came into the city, they joined together in the city to seek Joseph before they bought themselves corn. ¹³ And they went to the walls of the harlots, and they sought Joseph in the walls of the harlots for three days, for they thought that Joseph would come in the walls of the harlots, for Joseph was very handsome and well-favored, and the sons of Jacob sought Joseph for three days, and they could not find him. ¹⁴ And the man who was set over the open store sought for those names which Joseph had given him, and he did not find them. ¹⁵ And he sent to Joseph, saying, "These three days have passed, and those men whose names you gave to me have not come"; and Joseph sent servants to seek the men in all Egypt, and to bring them before Joseph. ¹⁶ And Joseph's servants went and came into Egypt and could not find them, and they went to Goshen and they were not there, and then they went to the city of Rameses and could not find them. ¹⁷ And Joseph continued to send sixteen servants to seek his brothers, and they went and spread themselves in the four corners of the city, and four of the servants went into the house of the harlots, and they found the ten men there seeking their brother. ¹⁸ And those four men took them and brought them before him, and they bowed down to him to the ground, and Joseph was sitting on his throne in his temple, clothed with princely garments, and on his head was a large crown of gold, and all the mighty men were sitting around him. ¹⁹ And the sons of Jacob saw Joseph, and his figure, and comeliness, and dignity of countenance seemed wonderful in their eyes, and they again bowed down to him to the ground. ²⁰ And Joseph saw his brothers, and he knew them, but they did not know him, for Joseph was very great in their eyes, therefore they did not know him. ²¹ And Joseph spoke to them, saying, "Where do you come from?" and they all answered and said, "Your servants have come from the land of Canaan to buy corn, for the famine prevails throughout the earth, and your servants heard that there was corn in Egypt, so they have come among the others coming to buy corn for their support." ²² And Joseph answered them, saying, "If you have come to purchase as you say, why do you come through ten gates of the city? it can only be that you have come to spy through the land." ²³ And they all answered Joseph together and said, "Not so my lord, we are right; your servants are not spies, but we have come to buy corn, for your servants are all brothers, the sons of one man in the land of Canaan, and our father commanded us, saying, When you come to the city, do not enter together at one gate on account of the inhabitants of the land." ²⁴ And Joseph answered them again and said, "That is the thing which I spoke to you: you have come to spy through the land! Therefore, you all came through ten gates of the city; you have come to see the nakedness of the land. ²⁵ Surely everyone that comes to buy corn goes his way, and you are already three days in the land, and what do you do in the walls of harlots in which you have been for these three days? surely spies do like to these things." ²⁶ And they said to Joseph, "Far be it from our lord to speak thus, for we are twelve brothers, the sons of our father Jacob in the land of Canaan, the son of Isaac, the son of Abraham the Hebrew, and behold, the youngest is with our father in the land of Canaan this day, and one is not, for he was lost from us, and we thought perhaps he might be in this land, so we are seeking him throughout the land and have even come to the houses of harlots to seek him there." **27** And Joseph said to them, "And have you then sought him throughout the earth that there only remained Egypt for you to seek him in? And what also should your brother do in the houses of harlots, although he was in Egypt? have you not said that you are from the sons of Isaac, the son of Abraham, and what will the sons of Jacob do then in the houses of harlots?" **28** And they said to him, "Because we heard that Ishmaelites stole him from us, and it was told to us that they sold him in Egypt, and your servant, our brother, is very handsome and well-favored, so we thought he would surely be in the houses of harlots, therefore your servants went there to seek him and give ransom for him." **29** And Joseph still answered them, saying, "Surely you speak falsely and utter lies to say of yourselves that you are the sons of Abraham; as Pharaoh lives, you are spies! Therefore, you have come to the houses of harlots that you should not be known." **30** And Joseph said to them, "And now if you find him, and his master requires of you a great price, will you give it for him?" and they said, "It will be given." **31** And he said to them, "And if his master will not consent to part with him for a great price, what will you do to him on his account?" and they answered him, saying, "If he will not give him to us we will slay him, and take our brother, and go away." **32** And Joseph said to them, "That is the thing which I have spoken to you: you are spies, for you have come to slay the inhabitants of the land, for we heard that two of your brothers struck all the inhabitants of Shechem in the land of Canaan on account of your sister, and you now come to do the same in Egypt on account of your brother. **33** Only hereby will I know that you are true men: if you will send home one from among you to fetch your youngest brother from your father and to bring him here to me, and by doing this thing I will know that you are right." **34** And Joseph called to seventy of his mighty men, and he said to them, "Take these men and bring them into the ward." **35** And the mighty men took the ten men; they laid hold of them and put them into the ward, and they were in the ward [for] three days. **36** And on the third day Joseph had them brought out of the ward, and he said to them, "Do this for yourselves if you are true men, so that you may live: one of your brothers will be confined in the ward while you go and take home the corn for your household to the land of Canaan, and fetch your youngest brother, and bring him here to me that I may know that you are true men when you do this thing." **37** And Joseph went out from them, and came into the chamber, and wept a great weeping, for his pity was excited for them, and he washed his face, and returned to them again, and he took Simeon from them and ordered him to be bound, but Simeon was not willing to have [this] done so, for he was a very powerful man and they could not bind him. **38** And Joseph called to his mighty men and seventy valiant men came before him with drawn swords in their hands, and the sons of Jacob were terrified at them. **39** And Joseph said to them, "Seize this man and confine him in prison until his brothers come to him," and Joseph's valiant men hastened, and they all laid hold of Simeon to bind him, and Simeon gave a loud and terrible shriek, and the cry was heard at a distance. **40** And all the valiant men of Joseph were terrified at the sound of the shriek that they fell on their faces, and they were greatly afraid and fled. **41** And all the men that were with Joseph fled, for they were greatly afraid for their lives, and only Joseph and his son Manasseh remained there, and Manasseh the son of Joseph saw the strength of Simeon, and he was exceedingly angry. **42** And Manasseh, the son of Joseph, rose up to Simeon, and Manasseh struck Simeon [with] a heavy blow, with his fist against the back of his neck, and Simeon was stilled of his rage. **43** And Manasseh laid hold of Simeon, and he violently seized him, and he bound him and brought him into the house of confinement, and all the sons of Jacob were astonished at the act of the youth. **44** And Simeon said to his brothers, "None of you must say that this is the striking of an Egyptian, but it is the striking of the house of my father." **45** And after this Joseph ordered him to be called who was set over the storehouse, to fill their sacks with corn as much as they could carry, and to restore every man's money into his sack, and to give them provision for the road, and thus he did to them. **46** And Joseph commanded them, saying, "Take heed lest you transgress my orders to bring your brother as I have told you, and it will be when you bring your brother here to me, then I will know that you are true men, and you will traffic in the land, and I will restore your brother to you, and you will return to your father in peace." **47** And they all answered and said, "According as our lord speaks, so we will do," and they bowed down to him to the ground. **48** And every man lifted his corn on his donkey, and they went out to go to the land of Canaan to their father; and they came to the inn and Levi spread his sack to give provender to his donkey when he saw, and behold, his money in full weight was still in his sack. **49** And the man was greatly afraid, and he said to his brothers, "My money is restored, and behold, it is even in my sack," and the men were greatly afraid, and they said, "What is this that God has done to us?" **50** And they all said, "And where is the Lord's kindness with our fathers, with Abraham, Isaac, and Jacob, that the Lord has delivered us into the hands of the king of Egypt this day to contrive against us?" **51** And Judah said to them, "Surely we are guilty sinners before the Lord our God in having sold our brother, our own flesh, and why do you say, Where is the Lord's kindness with our fathers?" **52** And Reuben said to them, "Did I not say to you, Do not sin against the youth? And you would not listen to me. now God requires him from us, and how dare you say, Where is the Lord's kindness with our fathers, while you have sinned to the Lord." **53** And they tarried overnight in that place, and they rose up early in the morning and loaded their donkeys with their corn, and they led them, and went on, and came to their father's house in the land of Canaan. **54** And Jacob and his household went out to meet his sons, and Jacob saw, and behold, their brother Simeon was not with them, and Jacob said to his sons, "Where is your brother Simeon whom I do not see?" and his sons told him all that had befallen them in Egypt.

CHAPTER 52

1 And they entered their house, and every man opened his sack, and they saw, and behold, every man's bundle of money was there, at which they and their father were greatly terrified. **2** And Jacob said to them, "What is this that you have done to me? I sent your brother Joseph to inquire after your welfare and you said to me, A wild beast devoured him. **3** And Simeon went with you to buy food and you say the king of Egypt has confined him in prison, and you wish to take Benjamin to cause his death also and to bring down my grey hairs with sorrow to the grave on account of Benjamin and his brother Joseph. **4** Now therefore, my son will not go down with you, for his brother is dead and he is left alone, and mischief may befall him by the way in which you go as it befell his brother." **5** And Reuben said to his father, "You will slay my two sons if I do not bring your son and place him before you"; and Jacob said to his sons, "Abide here and do not go down to Egypt, for my son will not go down with you to Egypt, nor die like his brother." **6** And Judah said to them, "Refrain from him until the corn is finished, and he will then say, Take your brother down [with you], when he will find his own life and the life of his household in danger from the famine." **7** And in those days the famine was severe throughout the land, and all the people of the earth went and came to Egypt to buy food, for the famine prevailed greatly among them, and the sons of Jacob remained in Canaan a year and two months until their corn was finished. **8** And it came to pass after their corn was finished, the whole household of Jacob was pinched with hunger, and all the infants of the sons of Jacob came together and they approached Jacob, and they all surrounded him, and they said to him, "Give bread to us, and why will we all perish through hunger in your presence?" **9** Jacob heard the words of his son's children, and he wept a great weeping, and his pity was roused for them, and Jacob called to his sons and they all came and sat before him. **10** And Jacob said to them, "And have you not seen how your children have been weeping over me this day, saying, Give bread to us, and there is none? now therefore, return and buy a little food for us." **11** And Judah answered and said to his father, "If you will send our brother with us we will go down and buy corn for you, and if you will not send him then we will not go down, for surely the king of Egypt specifically commanded us, saying, You will not see my face unless your brother is with you, for the king of Egypt is a strong and mighty king, and behold, if we will go to him without our brother we will all be put to death. **12** Do you not know, and have you not heard, that this king is very powerful and wise, and there is not [one] like him in all the earth? behold, we have seen all the kings of the earth and we have not seen one like that king, the king of Egypt; surely among all the kings of the earth there is none greater than Abimelech king of the Philistines, yet the king of Egypt is greater and mightier than he, and Abimelech can only be compared to one of his officers. **13** Father, you have not seen his palace, and his throne, and all his servants standing before him; you have not seen that king on his throne in his pomp and royal appearance, dressed in his kingly robes with a large golden crown on his head; you have not seen the honor and glory which God has given to him, for there is not [one] like him in all the earth. **14** Father, you have not seen the wisdom, the understanding, and the knowledge which God has given in his heart, nor heard his sweet voice when he spoke to us. **15** We do not know, father, who made him acquainted with our names and all that befell us, yet he also asked after you, saying, Is your father still living, and is it well with him? **16** You have not seen the affairs of the government of Egypt regulated by him, without inquiring of Pharaoh, his lord; you have not seen the awe and fear which he impressed on all the Egyptians. **17** And also when we went from him, we threatened to do to Egypt like to the rest of the cities of the Amorites, and we were exceedingly angry against all his words which he spoke concerning us as spies, and now when we will come before him again his terror will fall on us all, and not one of us will be able to speak to him either a small or great thing. **18** Now therefore, father, please send the youth with us, and we will go down and buy you food for our support, and not die through hunger." And Jacob said, "Why have you dealt so ill with me to tell the king you had a brother? what is this thing that you have done to me?" **19** And Judah said to his father Jacob, "Give the youth into my care and we will rise up, and go down to Egypt, and buy corn, and then return, and it will be when we return, if the youth is not with us, then let me bear your blame forever. **20** Have you seen all our infants weeping over you through hunger and there is no power in your hand to satisfy them? now let your pity be roused for them and send our brother with us and we will go. **21** For how will the Lord's kindness to our ancestors be manifested to you when you say that the king of Egypt will take away your son? as the Lord lives, I will not leave him until I bring him and place him before you; but pray for us to the Lord, that He may deal kindly with us to cause us to be received favorably and kindly before the king of Egypt and his men, for had we not delayed, surely we would have now returned a second time with your son." **22** And Jacob said to his sons, "I trust in the Lord God that He may deliver you and give you favor in the sight of the king of Egypt and in the sight of all his men. **23** Now therefore, rise up, and go to the man, and take a present for him in your hands from what can be obtained in the land, and bring it before him, and may the Almighty God give you mercy before him that he may send your brothers Benjamin and Simeon with you." **24** And all the men rose up, and they took their brother Benjamin, and they took a large present of the best of the land in their hands, and they also took a double portion of silver. **25** And Jacob strictly commanded his sons concerning Benjamin, saying, "Take heed of him in the way in which you are going, and do not separate yourselves from him in the road, neither in Egypt." **26** And Jacob rose up from his sons, and spread out his hands, and prayed to the Lord on account of his sons, saying, "O Lord God of the heavens and earth, remember Your covenant with our father Abraham; remember it with my father Isaac, and deal kindly with my sons, and do not deliver them into the hands of the king of Egypt; please do it, O God, for the sake of Your mercies, and redeem all my children, and rescue them from Egyptian power, and send them their two brothers." **27** And all the wives of the sons of Jacob and their children lifted up their eyes to Heaven, and they all wept before the Lord and cried to Him to deliver their fathers from the hand of the king of Egypt. **28** And Jacob wrote a record to the king of Egypt and gave it into the hand of Judah and into the hands of his sons for the king of Egypt, saying, **29** "From your servant Jacob, son of Isaac, son of Abraham the Hebrew, the prince of God, to the powerful and wise king, the revealer of secrets, king of Egypt, greetings. **30** Be it known to my lord the king of Egypt, the famine was severe on us in the land of Canaan, and I sent my sons to you to buy us a little food from you for our support. **31** For my sons surrounded me, and I, being very old, cannot see with my eyes, for my eyes have become very heavy through age, as well as with daily weeping for my son, for Joseph who was lost from before me, and I commanded my sons that they should not enter the gates of the city when they came to Egypt on account of the inhabitants of the land. **32** And I also commanded them to go around Egypt to seek for my son Joseph, [for] perhaps they might find him there, and they did so, and you considered them as spies of the land. **33** Have we not heard concerning you that you interpreted Pharaoh's dream and spoke truly to him? how then do you not know in your wisdom

whether my sons are spies or not? **34** Now therefore, my lord and king, behold, I have sent my son before you as you did speak to my sons; I implore you to put your eyes on him until he is returned to me with his brothers in peace. **35** For do you not know, or have you not heard, that which our God did to Pharaoh when he took my mother Sarah, and what he did to Abimelech king of the Philistines on account of her, and also what our father Abraham did to the nine kings of Elam, how he struck them all with a few men that were with him? **36** And also what my two sons Simeon and Levi did to the eight cities of the Amorites, how they destroyed them on account of their sister Dinah? **37** And also on account of their brother Benjamin they consoled themselves for the loss of his brother Joseph; what will they then do for him when they see the hand of any people prevailing over them for his sake? **38** Do you not know, O king of Egypt, that the power of God is with us, and also that God always hears our prayers and does not forsake us all the days? **39** And when my sons told me of your dealings with them, I did not call to the Lord on account of you, for then you would have perished with your men before my son Benjamin came before you, but I thought that as my son Simeon was in your house, perhaps you might deal kindly with him; therefore, I did not do this thing to you. **40** Now therefore, behold, my son Benjamin comes to you with my sons: take heed of him and put your eyes on him, and then God will place His eyes over you and throughout your kingdom. **41** Now I have told you all that is in my heart, and behold, my sons are coming to you with their brother; examine the face of the whole earth for their sake and send them back with their brothers in peace." **42** And Jacob gave the record to his sons into the care of Judah to give it to the king of Egypt.

CHAPTER 53

1 And the sons of Jacob rose up and took Benjamin and all of the presents, and they went and came to Egypt, and they stood before Joseph. **2** And Joseph beheld his brother Benjamin with them, and he saluted them, and these men came to Joseph's house. **3** And Joseph commanded the superintendent of his house to give [food] to his brothers to eat, and he did so to them. **4** And at midday Joseph sent for the men to come before him with Benjamin, and the men told the superintendent of Joseph's house concerning the silver that was returned in their sacks, and he said to them, "It will be well with you, do not fear," and he brought their brother Simeon to them. **5** And Simeon said to his brothers, "The lord of the Egyptians has acted very kindly to me; he did not keep me bound, as you saw with your [own] eyes, for when you went out from the city, he let me free and dealt kindly with me in his house." **6** And Judah took Benjamin by the hand, and they came before Joseph, and they bowed down to him to the ground. **7** And the men gave the present to Joseph and they all sat before him, and Joseph said to them, "Is it well with you? Is it well with your children? Is it well with your aged father?" and they said, "It is well," and Judah took the record which Jacob had sent and gave it into the hand of Joseph. **8** And Joseph read the letter and knew his father's writing, and he wished to weep, and he went into an inner room, and he wept a great weeping; then he went out. **9** And he lifted up his eyes and beheld his brother Benjamin, and he said, "Is this your brother of whom you spoke to me?" And Benjamin approached Joseph, and Joseph placed his hand on his head and said to him, "May God be gracious to you, my son." **10** And when Joseph saw his brother, the son of his mother, he wished to weep again, and he entered the chamber, and he wept there, and he washed his face, and went out, and refrained from weeping, and he said, "Prepare food." **11** And Joseph had a cup from which he drank, and it was of silver beautifully inlaid with onyx stones and bdellium, and Joseph struck the cup in the sight of his brothers while they were sitting to eat with him. **12** And Joseph said to the men, "I know by this cup that Reuben the firstborn, Simeon, and Levi, and Judah, Issachar, and Zebulun are children from one mother; seat yourselves to eat according to your births." **13** And he also placed the others according to their births, and he said, "I know that this youngest brother of yours has no brother, and I, like him, have no brother: he will therefore sit down to eat with me." **14** And Benjamin went up before Joseph and sat on the throne, and the men beheld the acts of Joseph, and they were astonished at them; and the men ate and drank at that time with Joseph, and he then gave presents to them, and Joseph gave one gift to Benjamin, and Manasseh and Ephraim saw the acts of their father, and they also gave presents to him, and Osnath gave him one present, and there were five presents in the hand of Benjamin. **15** And Joseph brought them out wine to drink, and they would not drink, and they said, "From the day on which Joseph was lost we have not drunk wine, nor eaten any delicacies." **16** And Joseph swore to them, and he pressed them hard, and they drank plentifully with him on that day, and afterward Joseph turned to his brother Benjamin to speak with him, and Benjamin was still sitting on the throne before Joseph. **17** And Joseph said to him, "Have you begotten any children?" and he said, "Your servant has ten sons, and these are their names: Bela, Becher, Ashbal, Gera, Naaman, Achi, Rosh, Mupim, Chupim, and Ord, and I called their names after my brother whom I have not seen." **18** And he ordered them to bring his map of the stars before him, whereby Joseph knew all the times, and Joseph said to Benjamin, "I have heard that the Hebrews are acquainted with all wisdom: do you know anything of this?" **19** And Benjamin said, "Your servant is also knowing in all the wisdom which my father taught me," and Joseph said to Benjamin, "Now look at this instrument and understand where your brother Joseph is in Egypt, who you said went down to Egypt." **20** And Benjamin beheld that instrument with the map of the stars of the heavens, and he was wise and looked therein to know where his brother was, and Benjamin divided the whole land of Egypt into four divisions, and he found that he who was sitting on the throne before him was his brother Joseph, and Benjamin wondered greatly, and when Joseph saw that his brother Benjamin was so much astonished, he said to Benjamin, "What have you seen, and why are you astonished?" **21** And Benjamin said to Joseph, "I can see by this that my brother Joseph sits here with me on the throne," and Joseph said to him, "I am your brother Joseph; do not reveal this thing to your brothers; behold, I will send you with them when they go away, and I will command them to be brought back into the city again, and I will take you away from them. **22** And if they dare their lives and fight for you, then I will know that they have converted from what they did to me, and I will make myself known to them, and if they forsake you when I take you, then you will remain with me, and I will wrangle with them, and they will go away, and I will not become known to them." **23** At that time Joseph commanded his officer to fill their sacks with food, and to put each man's money into his sack, and to put the cup in the sack of Benjamin, and to give them provision for the road, and they did so to them. **24** And on the next day the men rose up early in the morning, and they loaded their donkeys with their corn, and they went out with Benjamin, and they went to the land of Canaan with their brother Benjamin. **25** They had not gone far from Egypt when Joseph commanded him that was set over his house, saying, "Rise, pursue these men before they get too far from Egypt, and say to them, Why have you stolen my master's cup?" **26** And Joseph's officer rose up, and he reached them, and he spoke to them all the words of Joseph; and when they heard this thing they became exceedingly angry, and they said, "He with whom your master's cup will be found will die, and we will also become slaves." **27** And they hastened, and each man brought down his sack from his donkey, and they looked in their bags and the cup was found in Benjamin's bag, and they all tore their garments, and they returned to the city, and they struck Benjamin in the road, continually striking him until he came into the city, and they stood before Joseph. **28** And Judah's anger was kindled, and he said, "This man has only brought me back to destroy Egypt this day." **29** And the men came to Joseph's house, and they found Joseph sitting on his throne, and all the mighty men standing at his right and left. **30** And Joseph said to them, "What is this act that you have done, that you took away my silver cup and went away? but I know that you took my cup in order to know thereby in what part of the land your brother was." **31** And Judah said, "What will we say to our lord, what will we speak, and how will we justify ourselves? God has found the iniquity of all your servants this day, therefore He has done this thing to us this day." **32** And Joseph rose up, and caught hold of Benjamin, and took him from his brothers with violence, and he came to the house and locked the door at them, and Joseph commanded him that was set over his house that he should say to them, "Thus says the king, Go to your father in peace; behold, I have taken the man in whose hand my cup was found."

CHAPTER 54

1 And when Judah saw the dealings of Joseph with them, Judah approached him and broke open the door, and came with his brothers before Joseph. **2** And Judah said to Joseph, "Do not let it seem grievous in the sight of my lord: may your servant please speak a word before you?" and Joseph said to him, "Speak." **3** And Judah spoke before Joseph, and his brothers were standing there before them; and Judah said to Joseph, "Surely when we first came to our lord to buy food, you considered us as spies of the land, and we brought Benjamin before you, and you still make sport of us this day. **4** Now therefore, let the king hear my words, and please send our brother that he may go along with us to our father, lest your soul perish this day with all the souls of the inhabitants of Egypt. **5** Do you not know what two of my brothers, Simeon and Levi, did to the city of Shechem and to seven cities of the Amorites on account of our sister Dinah, and also what they would do for the sake of their brother Benjamin? **6** And I with my strength, who am greater and mightier than both of them, come on you and your land this day if you are unwilling to send our brother. **7** Have you not heard what our God who made choice of us did to Pharaoh on account of our mother Sarah, whom he took away from our father, that He struck him and his household with heavy plagues, that even to this day the Egyptians relate this wonder to each other? so will our God do to you on account of Benjamin whom you have taken from his father this day, and on account of the evils which you heap over us in your land this day; for our God will remember His covenant with our father Abraham and bring calamity on you, because you have grieved the soul of our father this day. **8** Now therefore, hear my words that I have spoken to you this day and send our brother that he may go away lest you and the people of your land die by the sword, for you cannot all prevail over me." **9** And Joseph answered Judah, saying, "Why have you opened your mouth wide and why do you boast over us, saying, Strength is with you? as Pharaoh lives, if I command all my valiant men to fight with you, surely you and these brothers of yours would sink in the mire." **10** And Judah said to Joseph, "Surely it is fitting [for] you and your people to fear me; as the Lord lives, if I once draw my sword I will not sheathe it again until I will have slain all Egypt this day, and I will commence with you and finish with your master Pharaoh." **11** And Joseph answered and said to him, "Surely strength does not belong to you alone—I am stronger and mightier than you; surely if you draw your sword I will put it to your neck and the necks of all your brothers." **12** And Judah said to him, "Surely if I open my mouth against you this day I would swallow you up [so] that you are destroyed from off the earth and perish this day from your kingdom." And Joseph said, "Surely if you open your mouth, I have power and might to close your mouth with a stone until you will not be able to utter a word; see how many stones are before us. Truly I can take a stone, and force it into your mouth, and break your jaws." **13** And Judah said, "God is witness between us that we have not so far desired to battle with you: only give us our brother and we will go from you"; and Joseph answered and said, "As Pharaoh lives, if all the kings of Canaan came together with you, you should not take him from my hand. **14** Now therefore, go your way to your father, and your brother will be for a slave to me, for he has robbed the king's house." And Judah said, "What is it to you or to the character of the king? Surely the king sends out from his house, throughout the land, silver and gold, either in gifts or expenses, and you still talk about your cup which you placed in our brother's bag and say that he has stolen it from you? **15** God forbid that our brother Benjamin or any of the seed of Abraham should do this thing to steal from you, or from anyone else, whether king, prince, or any man. **16** Now therefore, cease this accusation lest the whole earth hear your words, saying, For a little silver the king of Egypt wrangled with the men, and he accused them and took their brother for a slave." **17** And Joseph answered and said, "Take this cup for yourself, and go from me, and leave your brother for a slave, for it is the judgment of a thief to be a slave." **18** And Judah said, "Why are you not ashamed of your words, to leave our brother and to take your cup? Surely if you give us your cup, or one thousand times as much, we will not leave our brother for the silver which is found in the hand of any man, that we will not die over him." **19** And Joseph answered, "And why did you forsake your brother and sell him for twenty pieces of silver to this day, and why then will you not do the same to this brother of yours?" **20** And Judah said, "The Lord is witness between me and you that we do not desire your battles; now therefore, give us our brother and we will go from you without quarreling." **21** And

Joseph answered and said, "If all the kings of the land should assemble, they will not be able to take your brother from my hand"; and Judah said, "What will we say to our father when he sees that our brother does not come with us, and will grieve over him?" **22** And Joseph answered and said, "This is the thing which you will tell to your father, saying, The rope has gone after the bucket." **23** And Judah said, "Surely you are a king, and why do you speak these things, giving a false judgment? woe to the king who is like to you." **24** And Joseph answered and said, "There is no false judgment in the word that I spoke on account of your brother Joseph, for all of you sold him to the Midianites for twenty pieces of silver, and you all denied it to your father and said to him, An evil beast has devoured him, Joseph has been torn to pieces." **25** And Judah said, "Behold, the fire of Shem burns in my heart; now I will burn all your land with fire"; and Joseph answered and said, "Surely your sister-in-law Tamar, who killed your sons, extinguished the fire of Shechem." **26** And Judah said, "If I pluck out a single hair from my flesh, I will fill all Egypt with its blood." **27** And Joseph answered and said, "Such is your custom to do as you did to your brother whom you sold, and you dipped his coat in blood and brought it to your father in order that he might say an evil beast devoured him and here is his blood." **28** And when Judah heard this thing he was exceedingly angry and his anger burned within him, and there was a stone before him in that place, the weight of which was about four hundred shekels, and Judah's anger was kindled and he took the stone in one hand, and cast it toward the heavens, and caught it with his left hand. **29** And afterward he placed it under his legs, and he sat on it with all his strength, and the stone was turned into dust from the force of Judah. **30** And Joseph saw the act of Judah and he was very much afraid, but he commanded his son Manasseh and he also did with another stone like to the act of Judah, and Judah said to his brothers, "Do not let any of you say this man is an Egyptian, but by his doing this thing he is of our father's family." **31** And Joseph said, "Strength is not given to you alone, for we are also powerful men, and why will you boast over us all?" and Judah said to Joseph, "Please send our brother and do not ruin your country this day." **32** And Joseph answered and said to them, "Go and tell your father an evil beast has devoured him as you said concerning your brother Joseph." **33** And Judah spoke to his brother Naphtali, and he said to him, "Hurry, go now and number all the streets of Egypt and come and tell me"; and Simeon said to him, "Do not let this thing be a trouble to you; now I will go to the mount, and take up one large stone from the mount, and level it at everyone in Egypt, and kill all that are in it." **34** And Joseph heard all these words that his brothers spoke before him, and they did not know that Joseph understood them, for they imagined that he did not know [how] to speak Hebrew. **35** And Joseph was greatly afraid at the words of his brothers lest they should destroy Egypt, and he commanded his son Manasseh, saying, "Go now, hurry and gather to me all the inhabitants of Egypt, and all the valiant men together, and let them come to me now on horseback, and on foot, and with all sorts of musical instruments," and Manasseh went and did so. **36** And Naphtali went as Judah had commanded him, for Naphtali was lightfooted as one of the swift stags, and he would go on the ears of corn and they would not break under him. **37** And he went and numbered all the streets of Egypt, and found them to be twelve, and he came hastily and told Judah, and Judah said to his brothers, "Hasten, and every man put his sword on his loins, and we will come over Egypt and strike them all, and do not let a remnant remain." **38** And Judah said, "Behold, I will destroy three of the streets with my strength, and you will each destroy one street"; and when Judah was speaking this thing, behold, the inhabitants of Egypt and all the mighty men came toward them with all sorts of musical instruments and with loud shouting. **39** And their number was five hundred cavalry, and ten thousand infantry, and four hundred men who could fight without sword or spear, only with their hands and strength. **40** And all the mighty men came with great storming and shouting, and they all surrounded the sons of Jacob and terrified them, and the ground quaked at the sound of their shouting. **41** And when the sons of Jacob saw these troops, they were greatly afraid for their lives, and Joseph did so in order to terrify the sons of Jacob to become tranquilized. **42** And Judah, seeing some of his brothers terrified, said to them, "Why are you afraid while the grace of God is with us?" and when Judah saw all the people of Egypt surrounding them at the command of Joseph to terrify them, only Joseph commanded them, saying, "Do not touch any of them." **43** Then Judah hastened and drew his sword, and

uttered a loud and bitter scream, and he struck with his sword, and he sprang on the ground, and he still continued to shout against all the people. **44** And when he did this thing, the Lord caused the terror of Judah and his brothers to fall on the valiant men and all the people that surrounded them. **45** And they all fled at the sound of the shouting, and they were terrified and fell on one another, and many of them died as they fell, and they all fled from before Judah and his brothers and from before Joseph. **46** And while they were fleeing, Judah and his brothers pursued them to the house of Pharaoh, and they all escaped, and Judah sat before Joseph again, and roared at him like a lion, and gave a great and tremendous shriek at him. **47** And the shriek was heard at a distance, and all the inhabitants of Succoth heard it, and all Egypt quaked at the sound of the shriek, and also the walls of Egypt and of the land of Goshen fell in from the shaking of the earth, and Pharaoh also fell from his throne on the ground, and also all the pregnant women of Egypt and Goshen miscarried when they heard the noise of the shaking, for they were terribly afraid. **48** And Pharaoh sent word, saying, "What is this thing that has happened in the land of Egypt this day?" and they came and told him all the things from beginning to end, and Pharaoh was alarmed, and he wondered and was greatly afraid. **49** And his fright increased when he heard all these things, and he sent to Joseph, saying, "You have brought the Hebrews to me to destroy all Egypt; what will you do with that thievish slave? send him away and let him go with his brothers, and do not let us perish through their evil, even we—you and all Egypt. **50** And if you do not desire to do this thing, cast off all my valuable things from yourself, and go with them to their land, if you delight in it, for they will destroy my whole country this day and slay all my people; even all the women of Egypt have miscarried through their screams; see what they have done merely by their shouting and speaking; moreover, if they fight with the sword, they will destroy the land; now therefore, choose that which you desire, whether me or the Hebrews, whether Egypt or the land of the Hebrews." **51** And they came and told Joseph all the words of Pharaoh that he had said concerning him, and Joseph was greatly afraid at the words of Pharaoh, and Judah and his brothers were still standing before Joseph indignant and enraged, and all the sons of Jacob roared at Joseph like the roaring of the sea and its waves. **52** And Joseph was greatly afraid of his brothers and on account of Pharaoh, and Joseph sought a pretext to make himself known to his brothers, lest they should destroy all Egypt. **53** And Joseph commanded his son Manasseh, and Manasseh went and approached Judah, and placed his hand on his shoulder, and the anger of Judah was stilled. **54** And Judah said to his brothers, "Let no one of you say that this is the act of an Egyptian youth, for this is the work of my father's house." **55** And Joseph, seeing and knowing that Judah's anger was stilled, approached to speak to Judah in the language of mildness. **56** And Joseph said to Judah, "Surely you speak truth and have verified your assertions concerning your strength this day, and may your God who delights in you increase your welfare; but truly tell me why from among all your brothers you wrangle with me on account of the youth, as none of them have spoken one word to me concerning him." **57** And Judah answered Joseph, saying, "Surely you must know that I was security for the youth to his father, saying if I did not bring him to him I should bear his blame forever. **58** Therefore I have approached you from among all my brothers, for I saw that you were unwilling to permit him to go from you; now therefore, may I find grace in your sight that you will send him to go with us, and behold, I will remain as a substitute for him, to serve you in whatever you desire, for wherever you will send me I will go to serve you with great energy. **59** Send me now to a mighty king who has rebelled against you, and you will know what I will do to him and to his land; although he may have cavalry and infantry or an exceedingly mighty people, I will slay them all and bring the king's head before you. **60** Do you not know, or have you not heard, that our father Abraham with his servant Eliezer struck all the kings of Elam with their hosts in one night? They did not leave one remaining. and ever since that day our father's strength was given to us for an inheritance—for us and our seed forever." **61** And Joseph answered and said, "You speak truth, and falsehood is not in your mouth, for it was also told to us that the Hebrews have power and that the Lord their God delights much in them, and who then can stand before them? **62** However, on this condition I will send your brother: if you will bring before me his brother, the son of his mother, of whom you said that he had gone from you down to Egypt; and it will come to pass when you bring his brother to me [that] I will take him in his stead, because not one of you were security for him to your father, and when he will come to me, I will then send with you his brother for whom you have been security." **63** And Judah's anger was kindled against Joseph when he spoke this thing, and his eyes dropped blood with anger, and he said to his brothers, "How does this man seek his own destruction and that of all Egypt this day?" **64** And Simeon answered Joseph, saying, "Did we not tell you at first that we did not know the particular spot to which he went, and whether he was dead or alive, and why does my lord speak about these things?" **65** And Joseph, observing the countenance of Judah, discerned that his anger began to kindle when he spoke to him, saying, "Bring your other brother to me instead of this brother." **66** And Joseph said to his brothers, "Surely you said that your brother was either dead or lost; now if I should call him this day and he should come before you, would you give him to me instead of his brother?" **67** And Joseph began to speak and call out, "Joseph, Joseph! Come before me this day, and appear to your brothers, and sit before them." **68** And when Joseph spoke this thing before them, they each looked a different way to see from where Joseph would come before them. **69** And Joseph observed all their acts, and said to them, "Why do you look here and there? I am Joseph whom you sold to Egypt; now therefore, do not let it grieve you that you sold me, for God sent me before you as a support during the famine." **70** And his brothers were terrified at him when they heard the words of Joseph, and Judah was exceedingly terrified at him. **71** And when Benjamin heard the words of Joseph he was before them in the inner part of the house, and Benjamin ran to his brother Joseph, and embraced him, and fell on his neck, and they wept. **72** And when Joseph's brothers saw that Benjamin had fallen on his brother's neck and wept with him, they also fell on Joseph and embraced him, and they wept a great weeping with Joseph. **73** And the voice was heard in the house of Joseph that they were Joseph's brothers, and it pleased Pharaoh exceedingly, for he was afraid of them lest they should destroy Egypt. **74** And Pharaoh sent his servants to Joseph to congratulate him concerning his brothers who had come to him, and all the captains of the armies and troops that were in Egypt came to rejoice with Joseph, and all Egypt rejoiced greatly about Joseph's brothers. **75** And Pharaoh sent his servants to Joseph, saying, "Tell your brothers to fetch all belonging to them and let them come to me, and I will place them in the best part of the land of Egypt," and they did so. **76** And Joseph commanded him that was set over his house to bring out gifts and garments to his brothers, and he brought out to them many garments, being robes of royalty, and many gifts, and Joseph divided them among his brothers. **77** And he gave to each of his brothers a change of garments of gold and silver, and three hundred pieces of silver, and Joseph commanded them all to be dressed in these garments, and to be brought before Pharaoh. **78** And Pharaoh, seeing that all of Joseph's brothers were valiant men and of beautiful appearance, greatly rejoiced. **79** And afterward they went out from the presence of Pharaoh to go to the land of Canaan, to their father, and their brother Benjamin was with them. **80** And Joseph rose up and gave eleven chariots from Pharaoh to them, and Joseph gave his chariot to them, on which he rode on the day of his being crowned in Egypt, to fetch his father to Egypt; and Joseph sent to all his brothers' children garments according to their numbers, and one hundred pieces of silver to each of them, and he also sent garments to the wives of his brothers from the garments of the king's wives, and he sent them. **81** And he gave to each of his brothers ten men to go with them to the land of Canaan to serve them, to serve their children and all belonging to them in coming to Egypt. **82** And Joseph sent by the hand of his brother Benjamin ten suits of garments for his ten sons, a portion above the rest of the children of the sons of Jacob. **83** And he sent to each fifty pieces of silver, and ten chariots on the account of Pharaoh, and he sent to his father ten donkeys laden with all the luxuries of Egypt, and ten female donkeys laden with corn, and bread, and nourishment for his father, and to all that were with him as provisions for the road. **84** And he sent to his sister Dinah garments of silver, and gold, and frankincense, and myrrh, and aloes, and women's ornaments in great plenty, and he sent the same from the wives of Pharaoh to the wives of Benjamin. **85** And he gave to all his brothers, also to their wives, all sorts of onyx stones, and bdellium, and from all the valuable things among the great people of Egypt; nothing of all the costly things was left but what Joseph sent of to his father's household. **86** And he sent his brothers away, and they went, and he sent his brother

Benjamin with them. **87** And Joseph went out with them to accompany them on the road to the borders of Egypt, and he commanded them concerning his father and his household to come to Egypt. **88** And he said to them, "Do not quarrel on the road, for this thing was from the Lord to keep a great people from starvation, for there will still be five years of famine in the land." **89** And he commanded them, saying, "When you come to the land of Canaan, do not come suddenly before my father in this affair, but act in your wisdom." **90** And Joseph ceased to command them, and he turned and went back to Egypt, and the sons of Jacob went to the land of Canaan with joy and cheerfulness to their father Jacob. **91** And they came to the borders of the land, and they said to each other, "What will we do in this matter before our father, for if we suddenly come to him and tell him the matter, he will be greatly alarmed at our words and will not believe us." **92** And they went along until they came near to their houses, and they found Serach, the daughter of Asher, going out to meet them, and the young girl was very good and subtle, and knew how to play on the harp. **93** And they called to her and she came before them, and she kissed them, and they took her and gave a harp to her, saying, "Go now before our father, and sit before him, and strike on the harp, and speak these words." **94** And they commanded her to go to their house, and she took the harp and hastened before them, and she came and sat near Jacob. **95** And she played well and sang, and uttered in the sweetness of her words, "My uncle Joseph is living, and he rules throughout the land of Egypt, and is not dead." **96** And she continued to repeat and utter these words, and Jacob heard her words, and they were agreeable to him. **97** He listened while she repeated them twice and three times, and joy entered the heart of Jacob at the sweetness of her words, and the Spirit of God was on him, and he knew all her words to be true. **98** And Jacob blessed Serach when she spoke these words before him, and he said to her, "My daughter, may death never prevail over you, for you have revived my spirit; only speak yet before me as you have spoken, for you have gladdened me with all your words." **99** And she continued to sing these words, and Jacob listened and it pleased him, and he rejoiced, and the Spirit of God was on him. **100** While he was still speaking with her, behold, his sons came to him with horses, and chariots, and royal garments, and servants running before them. **101** And Jacob rose up to meet them, and he saw his sons dressed in royal garments, and he saw all the treasures that Joseph had sent to them. **102** And they said to him, "Be informed that our brother Joseph is living, and it is he who rules throughout the land of Egypt, and it is he who spoke to us as we told you." **103** And Jacob heard all the words of his sons, and his heart palpitated at their words, for he could not believe them until he saw all that Joseph had given them, and what he had sent him, and all the signs which Joseph had spoken to them. **104** And they opened out before him and showed him all that Joseph had sent; they gave to each what Joseph had sent him, and he knew that he had spoken the truth, and he rejoiced exceedingly on account of his son. **105** And Jacob said, "It is enough for me that my son Joseph is still living; I will go and see him before I die." **106** And his sons told him all that had befallen them, and Jacob said, "I will go down to Egypt to see my son and his offspring." **107** And Jacob rose up and put on the garments which Joseph had sent him, and after he had washed and shaved his hair, he put the turban on his head which Joseph had sent him. **108** And all the people of Jacob's house and their wives put on the garments which Joseph had sent to them, and they greatly rejoiced at Joseph, that he was still living and that he was ruling in Egypt, **109** and all the inhabitants of Canaan heard of this thing, and they came and rejoiced much with Jacob that he was still living. **110** And Jacob made a feast for them for three days, and all the kings of Canaan and nobles of the land ate, and drank, and rejoiced in the house of Jacob.

CHAPTER 55

1 And it came to pass after this that Jacob said, "I will go and see my son in Egypt and will then come back to the land of Canaan of which God had spoken to Abraham, for I cannot leave the land of my birthplace." **2** Behold, the word of the Lord came to him, saying, "Go down to Egypt with all your household and remain there; do not fear to go down to Egypt, for I will make you a great nation there." **3** And Jacob said within himself, "I will go and see my son—whether the fear of his God is yet in his heart amidst all the inhabitants of Egypt."

⁴ And the Lord said to Jacob, "Do not fear about Joseph, for he still retains his integrity to serve Me, as will seem good in your sight," and Jacob rejoiced exceedingly concerning his son. ⁵ At that time Jacob commanded his sons and household to go to Egypt according to the word of the Lord to him, and Jacob rose up with his sons and all his household, and he went out from the land of Canaan from Beersheba with joy and gladness of heart, and they went to the land of Egypt. ⁶ And it came to pass when they came near Egypt, Jacob sent Judah before him to Joseph that he might show him a situation in Egypt, and Judah did according to the word of his father, and he hastened, and ran, and came to Joseph, and they assigned a place for them in the land of Goshen for all his household, and Judah returned and came along the road to his father. ⁷ And Joseph harnessed the chariot, and he assembled all his mighty men, and his servants, and all the officers of Egypt in order to go and meet his father Jacob, and Joseph's mandate was proclaimed in Egypt, saying, "All that do not go to meet Jacob will die." ⁸ And on the next day Joseph went out with all Egypt—a great and mighty host, all dressed in garments of fine linen, and purple, and with instruments of silver and gold, and with their instruments of war with them. ⁹ And they all went to meet Jacob with all sorts of musical instruments, with drums and timbrels, scattering myrrh and aloes all along the road, and they all went after this fashion, and the earth shook at their shouting. ¹⁰ And all the women of Egypt went on the roofs of Egypt and on the walls to meet Jacob, and Pharaoh's regal crown was on the head of Joseph, for Pharaoh had sent it to him to put on at the time of his going to meet his father. ¹¹ And when Joseph came within fifty cubits of his father, he descended from the chariot and he walked toward his father, and when all the officers of Egypt and her nobles saw that Joseph had gone on foot toward his father, they also descended and walked on foot toward Jacob. ¹² And when Jacob approached the camp of Joseph, Jacob observed the camp that was coming toward him with Joseph, and it gratified him, and Jacob was astonished at it. ¹³ And Jacob said to Judah, "Who is that man whom I see in the camp of Egypt dressed in kingly robes with a very red garment on him and a royal crown on his head, who has descended from his chariot and is coming toward us?" and Judah answered his father, saying, "He is your son Joseph, the king"; and Jacob rejoiced in seeing the glory of his son. ¹⁴ And Joseph came near to his father and he bowed to his father, and all the men of the camp bowed to the ground with him before Jacob. ¹⁵ And behold, Jacob ran and hastened to his son Joseph, and he fell on his neck and kissed him, and they wept, and Joseph also embraced his father and kissed him, and they wept and all the people of Egypt wept with them. ¹⁶ And Jacob said to Joseph, "Now I will die cheerfully after I have seen your face, that you are still living and with glory." ¹⁷ And the sons of Jacob, and their wives, and their children, and their servants, and all the household of Jacob wept exceedingly with Joseph, and they kissed him and wept with him. ¹⁸ And afterward Joseph and all his people returned home to Egypt, and Jacob, and his sons, and all the children of his household came with Joseph to Egypt, and Joseph placed them in the best part of Egypt, in the land of Goshen. ¹⁹ And Joseph said to his father and to his brothers, "I will go up and tell Pharaoh, saying, My brothers, and my father's household, and all belonging to them have come to me, and behold, they are in the land of Goshen." ²⁰ And Joseph did so and took from his brothers Reuben, Issachar, Zebulun, and his brother Benjamin, and he placed them before Pharaoh. ²¹ And Joseph spoke to Pharaoh, saying, "My brothers, and my father's household, and all belonging to them, together with their flocks and cattle have come to me from the land of Canaan to sojourn in Egypt, for the famine was severe on them." ²² And Pharaoh said to Joseph, "Place your father and brothers in the best part of the land; do not withhold from them anything that is good, and cause them to eat of the fat of the land." ²³ And Joseph answered, saying, "Behold, I have stationed them in the land of Goshen, for they are shepherds; therefore let them remain in Goshen to feed their flocks apart from the Egyptians." ²⁴ And Pharaoh said to Joseph, "Do with your brothers all that they will say to you"; and the sons of Jacob bowed down to Pharaoh, and they went out from him in peace, and afterward Joseph brought his father before Pharaoh. ²⁵ And Jacob came and bowed down to Pharaoh, and Jacob blessed Pharaoh, and he then went out; and Jacob, and all his sons, and all his household dwelt in the land of Goshen. ²⁶ In the second year, that is in the one hundred and thirtieth year of the life of Jacob, Joseph maintained his father, and his brothers, and all his

father's household with bread according to their little ones, all the days of the famine; they lacked nothing. ²⁷ And Joseph gave the best part of the whole land to them; they had the best [part] of Egypt all the days of Joseph; and Joseph also gave to them and to the whole of his father's household clothes and garments year by year; and the sons of Jacob remained securely in Egypt all the days of their brother. ²⁸ And Jacob always ate at Joseph's table; Jacob and his sons did not leave Joseph's table day or night, besides what Jacob's children consumed in their houses. ²⁹ And all Egypt ate bread during the days of the famine from the house of Joseph, for all the Egyptians sold all belonging to them on account of the famine. ³⁰ And Joseph purchased all the lands and fields of Egypt for bread on the account of Pharaoh, and Joseph supplied all Egypt with bread all the days of the famine, and Joseph collected all the silver and gold that came to him for the corn which they bought throughout the land, and he accumulated much gold and silver, besides an immense quantity of onyx stones, bdellium, and valuable garments which they brought to Joseph from every part of the land when their money was spent. ³¹ And Joseph took all the silver and gold that came into his hand, about seventy-two talents of gold and silver, and also onyx stones and bdellium in great abundance, and Joseph went and concealed them in four parts, and he concealed one part in the wilderness near the Red Sea, and one part by the River Perath, and the third and fourth part he concealed in the desert opposite to the wilderness of Persia and Media. ³² And he took part of the gold and silver that was left and gave it to all his brothers, and to all his father's household, and to all the women of his father's household, and the rest he brought to the house of Pharaoh, about twenty talents of gold and silver. ³³ And Joseph gave all the gold and silver that was left to Pharaoh, and Pharaoh placed it in the treasury, and the days of the famine ceased after that in the land, and they sowed and reaped in the whole land, and they obtained their usual quantity year by year; they lacked nothing. ³⁴ And Joseph dwelt securely in Egypt, and the whole land was under his advice, and his father and all his brothers dwelt in the land of Goshen and took possession of it. ³⁵ And Joseph was very aged, advanced in days, and his two sons, Ephraim and Manasseh, continually remained in the house of Jacob, together with the children of the sons of Jacob, their brothers, to learn the ways of the Lord and His law. ³⁶ And Jacob and his sons dwelt in the land of Egypt in the land of Goshen, and they took possession in it, and they were fruitful and multiplied in it.

CHAPTER 56

¹ And Jacob lived in the land of Egypt seventeen years, and the days of Jacob and the years of his life were one hundred and forty-seven years. ² At that time Jacob was attacked with that sickness of which he died, and he sent and called for his son Joseph from Egypt, and his son Joseph came from Egypt and Joseph came to his father. ³ And Jacob said to Joseph and to his sons, "Behold, I die, and the God of your ancestors will visit you and bring you back to the land which the Lord swore to give to you and to your children after you; now therefore, when I am dead, bury me in the cave which is in Machpelah in Hebron in the land of Canaan, near my ancestors." ⁴ And Jacob made his sons swear to bury him in Machpelah, in Hebron, and his sons swore to him concerning this thing. ⁵ And he commanded them, saying, "Serve the Lord your God, for He who delivered your fathers will also deliver you from all trouble." ⁶ And Jacob said, "Call all your children to me," and all the children of Jacob's sons came and sat before him, and Jacob blessed them, and he said to them, "The Lord God of your fathers will grant you one thousand times as much and bless you, and may He give you the blessing of your father Abraham"; and all the children of Jacob's sons went out on that day after he had blessed them. ⁷ And on the next day Jacob called for his sons again, and they all assembled, and came to him, and sat before him, and on that day Jacob blessed his sons before his death: he blessed each man according to his blessing; behold, it is written in the Scroll of the Law of the Lord pertaining to Israel. ⁸ And Jacob said to Judah, "I know, my son, that you are a mighty man for your brothers; reign over them, and your sons will reign over their sons forever. ⁹ Only teach your sons the bow and all the weapons of war in order that they may fight the battles of their brother who will

rule over his enemies." **10** And Jacob commanded his sons again on that day, saying, "Behold, I will be gathered to my people this day; carry me up from Egypt and bury me in the cave of Machpelah as I have commanded you. **11** Nevertheless, please take heed that none of your sons carry me, only yourselves, and this is the manner you will do to me: when you carry my body to go with it to the land of Canaan to bury me, **12** Judah, Issachar, and Zebulun will carry my bier at the eastern side; Reuben, Simeon, and Gad at the south; Ephraim, Manasseh, and Benjamin at the west; Dan, Asher, and Naphtali at the north. **13** Do not let Levi carry with you, for he and his sons will carry the Ark of the Covenant of the Lord with the Israelites in the camp; neither let my son Joseph carry, for as a king so let his glory be; nevertheless, Ephraim and Manasseh will be in their stead. **14** Thus you will do to me when you carry me away; do not neglect anything of all that I command you; and it will come to pass when you do this to me that the Lord will remember you favorably and your children after you forever. **15** And you, my sons, each honor his brother and his relative, and command your children and your children's children after you to serve the Lord God of your ancestors all the days **16** in order that you may prolong your days in the land—you, and your children, and your children's children forever—when you do what is good and upright in the sight of the Lord your God, to go in all His ways. **17** And you, my son Joseph, please forgive the prongs of your brothers and all their misdeeds in the injury that they heaped on you, for God intended it for you and your children's benefit. **18** And O, my son, do not leave your brothers to the inhabitants of Egypt, neither hurt their feelings, for behold, I consign them to the hand of God and in your hand to guard them from the Egyptians"; and the sons of Jacob answered their father, saying, "O, our father, all that you have commanded us, so we will do—but may God be with us." **19** And Jacob said to his sons, "So may God be with you when you keep all His ways; do not turn from His ways either to the right or the left in performing what is good and upright in His sight. **20** For I know that many and grievous troubles will befall you in the latter days in the land—yes, your children and children's children; only serve the Lord and He will save you from all trouble. **21** And it will come to pass when you will go after God to serve Him and will teach your children after you, and your children's children, to know the Lord, then the Lord will raise up to you and your children a servant from among your children, and the Lord will deliver you from all affliction through his hand, and bring you out of Egypt, and bring you back to the land of your fathers to inherit it securely." **22** And Jacob ceased commanding his sons and he drew his feet into the bed; he died and was gathered to his people. **23** And Joseph fell on his father, and he cried out and wept over him, and he kissed him, and he called out in a bitter voice, and he said, "O my father, my father!" **24** And his son's wives and all his household came and fell on Jacob, and they wept over him, and cried in a very loud voice concerning Jacob. **25** And all the sons of Jacob rose up together, and they tore their garments, and they all put sackcloth on their loins, and they fell on their faces, and they cast dust on their heads toward the heavens. **26** And the thing was told to Osnath, Joseph's wife, and she rose up and put on a sack, and she and all the Egyptian women with her came and mourned and wept for Jacob. **27** And also all the people of Egypt who knew Jacob all came on that day when they heard this thing, and all Egypt wept for many days. **28** And also from the land of Canaan women came to Egypt when they heard that Jacob was dead, and they wept for him in Egypt for seventy days. **29** And it came to pass after this that Joseph commanded his servants, the doctors, to embalm his father with myrrh, and frankincense, and all manner of incense and perfume, and the doctors embalmed Jacob as Joseph had commanded them. **30** And all the people of Egypt, and the elders, and all the inhabitants of the land of Goshen wept and mourned over Jacob, and all his sons and the children of his household lamented and mourned over their father Jacob [for] many days. **31** And after the days of his weeping had passed away, at the end of seventy days, Joseph said to Pharaoh, "I will go up and bury my father in the land of Canaan as he made me swear, and then I will return." **32** And Pharaoh sent Joseph, saying, "Go up and bury your father as he said, and as he made you swear"; and Joseph rose up with all his brothers to go to the land of Canaan to bury their father Jacob as he had commanded them. **33** And Pharaoh commanded that it should be proclaimed throughout Egypt, saying, "Whoever does not go up with Joseph and his brothers to the land of Canaan to bury Jacob will die." **34** And all Egypt heard of Pharaoh's

proclamation, and they all rose up together, and all the servants of Pharaoh, and the elders of his house, and all the elders of the land of Egypt went up with Joseph, and all the officers and nobles of Pharaoh went up as the servants of Joseph, and they went to bury Jacob in the land of Canaan. **35** And the sons of Jacob carried the bier on which he lay; according to all that their father commanded them, so his sons did for him. **36** And the bier was of pure gold, and it was inlaid around with onyx stones and bdellium; and the covering of the bier was gold-woven work, joined with threads, and over them were hooks of onyx stones and bdellium. **37** And Joseph placed a large golden crown on the head of his father Jacob, and he put a golden scepter in his hand, and they surrounded the bier as was the custom of kings during their lives. **38** And all the troops of Egypt went before him in this array, at first all the mighty men of Pharaoh and the mighty men of Joseph, and after them the rest of the inhabitants of Egypt, and they were all girded with swords and equipped with coats of mail, and the trappings of war were on them. **39** And all the weepers and mourners went at a distance opposite to the bier, going, and weeping, and lamenting, and the rest of the people went after the bier. **40** And Joseph and his household went together near the bier barefooted and weeping, and the rest of Joseph's servants went around him; each man had his ornaments on him, and they were all armed with their weapons of war. **41** And fifty of Jacob's servants went in front of the bier, and they scattered along the road myrrh, and aloes, and all manner of perfume, and all the sons of Jacob that carried the bier walked on the perfumery, and the servants of Jacob went before them scattering the perfume along the road. **42** And Joseph went up with a heavy camp, and they did after this manner every day until they reached the land of Canaan, and they came to the threshing floor of Atad, which was on the other side of Jordan, and they mourned an exceedingly great and heavy mourning in that place. **43** And all the kings of Canaan heard of this thing and they all went out, each man from his house—thirty-one kings of Canaan—and they all came with their men to mourn and weep over Jacob. **44** And all these kings beheld Jacob's bier, and behold, Joseph's crown was on it, and they also put their crowns on the bier, and encircled it with crowns. **45** And all these kings made a great and heavy mourning in that place with the sons of Jacob and Egypt over Jacob, for all the kings of Canaan knew the valor of Jacob and his sons. **46** And the report reached Esau, saying, "Jacob died in Egypt, and his sons and all Egypt are carrying him to the land of Canaan to bury him." **47** And Esau heard this thing, and he was dwelling in Mount Seir, and he rose up with his sons, and all his people, and all his household, a people exceedingly great, and they came to mourn and weep over Jacob. **48** And it came to pass when Esau came, he mourned for his brother Jacob, and all Egypt and all Canaan rose up again and mourned a great mourning with Esau over Jacob in that place. **49** And Joseph and his brothers brought their father Jacob from that place, and they went to Hebron to bury Jacob in the cave by his fathers. **50** And they came to Kirjath-Arba, to the cave, and as they came, Esau stood with his sons against Joseph and his brothers as a hindrance in the cave, saying, "Jacob will not be buried therein, for it belongs to us and to our father." **51** And Joseph and his brothers heard the words of Esau's sons, and they were exceedingly angry, and Joseph approached to Esau, saying, "What is this thing which they have spoken? surely my father Jacob bought it from you for great riches after the death of Isaac, now twenty-five years ago, and he also bought all the land of Canaan from you, and from your sons, and [from] your seed after you. **52** And Jacob bought it for his sons and his seed after him for an inheritance forever, and why do you speak these things this day?" **53** And Esau answered, saying, "You speak falsely and utter lies, for I did not sell anything belonging to me in all this land as you say, neither did my brother Jacob buy all belonging to me in this land." **54** And Esau spoke these things in order to deceive Joseph with his words, for Esau knew that Joseph was not present in those days when Esau sold all belonging to him in the land of Canaan to Jacob. **55** And Joseph said to Esau, "Surely my father inserted these things with you in the record of purchase, and testified to the record with witnesses, and behold, it is with us in Egypt." **56** And Esau answered, saying to him, "Bring the record—all that you will find in the record, so we will do." **57** And Joseph called to his brother Naphtali, and he said, "Hasten quickly, do not linger, and now run to Egypt and bring all the records—the record of the purchase, the sealed record and the open record, and also all the first records in which all the transactions of the birthright are written; fetch [them]. **58** And you will bring them to us here [so] that we may know from them all the words of Esau and his sons which they spoke this day." **59** And Naphtali listened to the voice of Joseph and he hastened and ran to go down to Egypt, and Naphtali was lighter on foot than any of the stags that were on the wilderness, for he would go on ears of corn without crushing them. **60** And when Esau saw that Naphtali had gone to fetch the records, he and his sons increased their resistance against the cave, and Esau and all his people rose up against Joseph and his brothers to battle. **61** And all the sons of Jacob and the people of Egypt fought with Esau and his men, and the sons of Esau and his people were smitten before the sons of Jacob, and the sons of Jacob slew of Esau's people forty men. **62** And Chushim the son of Dan, the son of Jacob, was with Jacob's sons at that time, but he was about one hundred cubits distant from the place of battle, for he remained with the children of Jacob's sons by Jacob's bier to guard it. **63** And Chushim was mute and deaf, [but] he still understood the voice of consternation among men. **64** And he asked, saying, "Why do you not bury the dead, and what is this great consternation?" and they answered him [with] the words of Esau and his sons; and he ran to Esau in the midst of the battle, and he slew Esau with a sword, and he cut off his head, and it sprang to a distance, and Esau fell among the people of the battle. **65** And when Chushim did this thing the sons of Jacob prevailed over the sons of Esau, and the sons of Jacob buried their father Jacob by force in the cave, and the sons of Esau beheld it. **66** And Jacob was buried in Hebron, in the cave of Machpelah which Abraham had bought from the sons of Heth for the possession of a burial place, and he was buried in very costly garments. **67** And no king had such honor paid him as Joseph paid to his father at his death, for he buried him with great honor like to the burial of kings. **68** And Joseph and his brothers made a mourning of seven days for their father.

CHAPTER 57

1 And it was after this that the sons of Esau waged war with the sons of Jacob, and the sons of Esau fought with the sons of Jacob in Hebron, and Esau was still lying dead and not buried. **2** And the battle was heavy between them, and the sons of Esau were smitten before the sons of Jacob, and the sons of Jacob slew eighty men of the sons of Esau, and not one died of the people of the sons of Jacob; and the hand of Joseph prevailed over all the people of the sons of Esau, and he took Zepho, the son of Eliphaz, the son of Esau, and fifty of his men captive, and he bound them with chains of iron, and gave them into the hand of his servants to bring them to Egypt. **3** And it came to pass when the sons of Jacob had taken Zepho and his people captive, all those that remained were greatly afraid for their lives from the house of Esau lest they should also be taken captive, and they all fled with Eliphaz the son of Esau and his people, with Esau's body, and they went on their road to Mount Seir. **4** And they came to Mount Seir and they buried Esau in Seir, but they had not brought his head with them to Seir, for it was buried in that place where the battle had been in Hebron. **5** And it came to pass when the sons of Esau had fled from before the sons of Jacob, the sons of Jacob pursued them to the borders of Seir, but they did not slay a single man from among them when they pursued them, for Esau's body which they carried with them excited their confusion, so they fled and the sons of Jacob turned back from them and came up to the place where their brothers were in Hebron, and they remained there on that day and on the next day until they rested from the battle. **6** And it came to pass on the third day, they assembled all the sons of Seir the Horite, and they assembled all the children of the east, a multitude of people like the sand of the sea, and they went and came down to Egypt to fight with Joseph and his brothers in order to deliver their brothers. **7** And Joseph and all the sons of Jacob heard that the sons of Esau and the children of the east had come on them to battle in order to deliver their brothers. **8** And Joseph, and his brothers, and the strong men of Egypt went out and fought in the city of Rameses, and Joseph and his brothers dealt out a tremendous blow among the sons of Esau and the children of the east. **9** And they slew of them six hundred thousand men, and they slew among them all the mighty men of the children of Seir the Horite; there were only a few of them left, and they also slew a great many of the children of the east and of the children of Esau; and Eliphaz the son of Esau and the children of the east all fled before Joseph and his brothers. **10** And Joseph and his

brothers pursued them until they came to Succoth, and they yet slew thirty men of them in Succoth, and the rest escaped and they each fled to his city. **11** And Joseph, and his brothers, and the mighty men of Egypt turned back from them with joy and cheerfulness of heart, for they had smitten all their enemies. **12** And Zepho the son of Eliphaz and his men were still slaves in Egypt to the sons of Jacob, and their pains increased. **13** And when the sons of Esau and the sons of Seir returned to their land, the sons of Seir saw that they had all fallen into the hands of the sons of Jacob and the people of Egypt on account of the battle of the sons of Esau. **14** And the sons of Seir said to the sons of Esau, "You have seen and therefore you know that this camp was on your account, and not one mighty man or an adept in war remains. **15** Now therefore, go out from our land; go from us to the land of Canaan to the land of the dwelling of your fathers; why will your children inherit the effects of our children in latter days?" **16** And the children of Esau would not listen to the children of Seir, and the children of Seir considered to make war with them. **17** And the children of Esau secretly sent to Angeas king of Africa, the same is Dinhabah, saying, **18** "Send some of your men to us and let them come to us, and we will fight together with the children of Seir the Horite, for they have resolved to fight with us to drive us away from the land." **19** And Angeas king of Dinhabah did so, for he was friendly to the children of Esau in those days, and Angeas sent five hundred valiant infantry to the children of Esau, and [also] eight hundred cavalry. **20** And the children of Seir sent to the children of the east and to the children of Midian, saying, "You have seen what the children of Esau have done to us, on whose account we are almost all destroyed, in their battle with the sons of Jacob. **21** Now therefore, come to us and assist us, and we will fight them together, and we will drive them from the land and be avenged of the cause of our brothers who died for their sakes in their battle with their brothers, the sons of Jacob." **22** And all the children of the east listened to the children of Seir, and they came to them—about eight hundred men with drawn swords—and the children of Esau fought with the children of Seir at that time in the wilderness of Paran. **23** And the children of Seir then prevailed over the sons of Esau, and the children of Seir slew on that day of the children of Esau in that battle about two hundred men of the people of Angeas king of Dinhabah. **24** And on the second day the children of Esau came again to fight a second time with the children of Seir, and the battle was severe on the children of Esau this second time, and it troubled them greatly on account of the children of Seir. **25** And when the children of Esau saw that the children of Seir were more powerful than they were, some men of the children of Esau turned and assisted the children of Seir, their enemies. **26** And there fell yet of the people of the children of Esau in the second battle fifty-eight men of the people at Angeas king of Dinhabah. **27** And on the third day the children of Esau heard that some of their brothers had turned from them to fight against them in the second battle; and the children of Esau mourned when they heard this thing. **28** And they said, "What will we do to our brothers who turned from us to assist the children of Seir, our enemies?" and the children of Esau sent to Angeas king of Dinhabah again, saying, **29** "Send other men to us again that with them we may fight with the children of Seir, for they have already twice been heavier than we were." **30** And Angeas again sent to the children of Esau about six hundred valiant men, and they came to assist the children of Esau. **31** And in ten days' time the children of Esau again waged war with the children of Seir in the wilderness of Paran, and the battle was very severe on the children of Seir, and the children of Esau prevailed over the children of Seir at this time, and the children of Seir were smitten before the children of Esau, and the children of Esau slew from them about two thousand men. **32** And all the mighty men of the children of Seir died in this battle, and there only remained their young children that were left in their cities. **33** And all Midian and the children of the east went themselves to escape from the battle, and they left the children of Seir and fled when they saw that the battle was severe on them, and the children of Esau pursued all the children of the east until they reached their land. **34** And the children of Esau slew yet of them about two hundred and fifty men, and from the people of the children of Esau there fell in that battle about thirty men, but this evil came on them through their brothers turning from them to assist the children of Seir the Horite, and the children of Esau again heard of the evil doings of their brothers, and they again mourned on account of this thing. **35** And it came to pass after the battle, the children of Esau turned back and came home to Seir, and the children of Esau slew those who had remained in the land of the children of Seir; they also slew their wives and little ones; they did not leave a soul alive except fifty young boys and young girls whom they allowed to live, and the children of Esau did not put them to death, and the boys became their slaves, and they took the young girls for wives. **36** And the children of Esau dwelt in Seir in the place of the children of Seir, and they inherited their land and took possession of it. **37** And the children of Esau took all belonging to the children of Seir in the land, also their flocks, their bullocks, and their goods, and the children of Esau took all belonging to the children of Seir, and the children of Esau dwelt in Seir in the place of the children of Seir to this day, and the children of Esau divided the land into divisions to the five sons of Esau, according to their families. **38** And it came to pass in those days that the children of Esau resolved to crown a king over them in the land of which they possessed. And they said to each other, "Not so, for he will reign over us in our land, and we will be under his counsel and he will fight our battles against our enemies," and they did so. **39** And all the children of Esau swore, saying that none of their brothers should ever reign over them, but a strange man who is not of their brothers, for the souls of all the children of Esau were embittered—every man against his son, brother, and friend—on account of the evil they sustained from their brothers when they fought with the children of Seir. **40** Therefore the sons of Esau swore, saying from that day forward they would not choose a king from their brothers, but one from a strange land to this day. **41** And there was a man there from the people of Angeas king of Dinhabah; his name was Bela the son of Beor, who was a very valiant man, beautiful, and handsome, and wise in all wisdom, and a man of sense and counsel; and there was none of the people of Angeas like to him. **42** And all the children of Esau took him and anointed him, and they crowned him for a king, and they bowed down to him, and they said to him, "May the king live, may the king live!" **43** And they spread out the sheet, and they brought him, each man, earrings of gold and silver or rings or bracelets, and they made him very rich in silver and in gold, in onyx stones and bdellium, and they made him a royal throne, and they placed a regal crown on his head, and they built a palace for him and he dwelt therein, and he became king over all the children of Esau. **44** And the people of Angeas took their hire for their battle from the children of Esau, and they went and returned at that time to their master in Dinhabah. **45** And Bela reigned over the children of Esau thirty years, and the children of Esau dwelt in the land instead of the children of Seir, and they dwelt securely in their stead to this day.

CHAPTER 58

1 And it came to pass in the thirty-second year of the Israelites going down to Egypt, that is in the seventy-first year of the life of Joseph, in that year Pharaoh king of Egypt died, and his son Magron reigned in his stead. **2** And before his death Pharaoh commanded Joseph to be a father to his son Magron, and that Magron should be under the care of Joseph and under his counsel. **3** And all Egypt consented to this thing that Joseph should be king over them, for all the Egyptians loved Joseph as before now, only Magron the son of Pharaoh sat on his father's throne, and he became king in those days in his father's stead. **4** Magron was forty-one years old when he began to reign, and he reigned [for] forty years in Egypt, and all Egypt called his name Pharaoh after the name of his father as it was their custom to do in Egypt to every king that reigned over them. **5** And it came to pass when Pharaoh reigned in his father's stead, he placed the laws of Egypt and all the affairs of government in the hand of Joseph as his father had commanded him. **6** And Joseph became king over Egypt, for he superintended over all Egypt, and all Egypt was under his care and under his counsel, for all Egypt inclined to Joseph after the death of Pharaoh, and they loved him exceedingly to reign over them. **7** But there were some people among them who did not like him, saying, "No stranger will reign over us"; still the whole government of Egypt devolved in those days on Joseph, after the death of Pharaoh, he being the regulator, doing as he liked throughout the land without anyone interfering. **8** And all Egypt was under the care of Joseph, and Joseph made war with all his surrounding enemies, and he subdued them; Joseph also subdued all the land and all the Philistines to the borders of Canaan, and they were all under his power and they gave a yearly tax to Joseph. **9** And Pharaoh king of Egypt sat on his throne in his father's stead, but he was under the control and counsel of Joseph as he was at first under the control of his father. **10** Neither did he reign but in the land of Egypt alone, [but only] under the counsel of Joseph, but Joseph reigned over the whole country at that time, from Egypt to the great river Perath. **11** And Joseph was successful in all his ways, and the Lord was with him, and the Lord gave Joseph additional wisdom, and honor, and glory, and love toward him in the hearts of the Egyptians and throughout the land, and Joseph reigned over the whole country [for] forty years. **12** And all the countries of the Philistines, and Canaan, and Zidon, and on the other side of Jordan brought presents to Joseph all his days, and the whole country was in the hand of Joseph, and they brought a yearly tribute to him as it was regulated, for Joseph had fought against all his surrounding enemies and subdued them, and the whole country was in the hand of Joseph, and Joseph sat securely on his throne in Egypt. **13** And all his brothers, the sons of Jacob, also dwelt securely in the land all the days of Joseph, and they were fruitful and multiplied exceedingly in the land, and they served the Lord all their days as their father Jacob had commanded them. **14** And it came to pass at the end of many days and years when the children of Esau were dwelling quietly in their land with Bela, their king, that the children of Esau were fruitful and multiplied in the land, and they resolved to go and fight with the sons of Jacob and all Egypt, and to deliver their brother Zepho, the son of Eliphaz, and his men, for they were still slaves to Joseph in those days. **15** And the children of Esau sent to all the children of the east, and they made peace with them, and all the children of the east came to them to go with the children of Esau to Egypt to battle. **16** And there also came to them [those] of the people of Angeas, king of Dinhabah, and they also sent to the children of Ishmael and they also came to them. **17** And all this people assembled and came to Seir to assist the children of Esau in their battle, and this camp was very large and heavy with people, numerous as the sand of the sea, about eight hundred thousand men, infantry and cavalry, and all these troops went down to Egypt to fight with the sons of Jacob, and they encamped by Rameses. **18** And Joseph went out with his brothers with the mighty men of Egypt, about six hundred men, and they fought with them in the land of Rameses; and the sons of Jacob again fought with the children of Esau at that time, in the fiftieth year of the sons of Jacob going down to Egypt, that is the thirtieth year of the reign of Bela over the children of Esau in Seir. **19** And the Lord gave all the mighty men of Esau and the children of the east into the hand of Joseph and his brothers, and the people of the children of Esau and the children of the east were smitten before Joseph. **20** And of the people of Esau and the children of the east that were slain, there fell before the sons of Jacob about two hundred thousand men, and their king, Bela the son of Beor, fell with them in the battle, and when the children of Esau saw that their king had fallen in battle and was dead, their hands became weak in the combat. **21** And Joseph, and his brothers, and all Egypt were still striking the people of the house of Esau, and all Esau's people were afraid of the sons of Jacob and fled from before them. **22** And Joseph, and his brothers, and all Egypt pursued them a day's journey, and they slew yet from them about three hundred men, continuing to strike them in the road; and afterward they turned back from them. **23** And Joseph and all his brothers returned to Egypt; not one man was missing from them, but of the Egyptians there fell twelve men. **24** And when Joseph returned to Egypt he ordered Zepho and his men to be additionally bound, and they bound them in irons and they increased their grief. **25** And all the people of the children of Esau and the children of the east each returned in shame to his city, for all the mighty men that were with them had fallen in battle. **26** And when the children of Esau saw that their king had died in battle, they hastened and took a man from the people of the children of the east; his name was Jobab the son of Zarach, from the land of Botzrah, and they caused him to reign over them instead of Bela, their king. **27** And Jobab sat on the throne of Bela as king in his stead, and Jobab reigned in Edom over all the children of Esau ten years, and the children of Esau no longer went to fight with the sons of Jacob from that day forward, for the sons of Esau knew the valor of the sons of Jacob, and they were greatly afraid of them. **28** But from that day forward the children of Esau hated the sons of Jacob, and the hatred and enmity were very strong between them all the days, to this day. **29** And it came to pass after this, at the end of ten years, Jobab, the son of Zarach, from Botzrah, died, and the children of Esau took a man whose name was Chusham, from the land of Teman, and they made him king over them instead of Jobab, and Chusham reigned in Edom over all the children of Esau for twenty years. **30** And Joseph, king of Egypt, and his brothers, and all the sons of Israel dwelt securely in Egypt in those days, together with all the children of Joseph and his brothers, having no hindrance or evil accident and the land of Egypt was at that time at rest from war in the days of Joseph and his brothers.

CHAPTER 59

1 And these are the names of the sons of Israel who dwelt in Egypt who had come with Jacob (all the sons of Jacob came to Egypt, every man with his household). **2** The children of Leah were Reuben, Simeon, Levi, Judah, Issachar, and Zebulun, and their sister Dinah. **3** And the sons of Rachel were Joseph and Benjamin. **4** And the sons of Zilpah, the handmaid of Leah, were Gad and Asher. **5** And the sons of Bilhah, the handmaid of Rachel, were Dan and Naphtali. **6** And these were their offspring that were born to them in the land of Canaan before they came to Egypt with their father Jacob. **7** The sons of Reuben were Chanoch, Pallu, Chetzron, and Carmi. **8** And the sons of Simeon were Jemuel, Jamin, Ohad, Jachin, Zochar, and Saul, the son of the Canaanite woman. **9** And the children of Levi were Gershon, Kehas, and Merari, and their sister Jochebed who was born to them in their going down to Egypt. **10** And the sons of Judah were Er, Onan, Shelah, Perez, and Zarach. **11** And Er and Onan died in the land of Canaan; and the sons of Perez were Chezron and Chamul. **12** And the sons of Issachar were Tola, Puvah, Job, and Shomron. **13** And the sons of Zebulun were Sered, Elon, and Jachleel. And the son of Dan was Chushim. **14** And the sons of Naphtali were Jachzeel, Guni, Jetzer, and Shilam. **15** And the sons of Gad were Ziphion, Chaggi, Shuni, Ezbon, Eri, Arodi, and Areli. **16** And the children of Asher were Jimnah, Jishvah, Jishvi, Beriah, and their sister Serach; and the sons of Beriah were Cheber and Malchiel. **17** And the sons of Benjamin were Bela, Becher, Ashbel, Gera, Naaman, Achi, Rosh, Mupim, Chupim, and Ord. **18** And the sons of Joseph that were born to him in Egypt were Manasseh and Ephraim. **19** And all the souls that went out from the loins of Jacob were seventy souls; these are they who came to Egypt with their father Jacob to dwell there: and Joseph and all his brothers dwelt securely in Egypt, and they ate of the best of Egypt all the days of the life of Joseph. **20** And Joseph lived in the land of Egypt [for] ninety-three years, and Joseph reigned over all Egypt [for] eighty years. **21** And when the days of Joseph drew near that he should die, he sent and called for his brothers and all his father's household, and they all came together and sat before him. **22** And Joseph said to his brothers and to the whole of his father's household, "Behold, I die, and God will surely visit you and bring you up from this land to the land which He swore to your fathers to give to them. **23** And it will be when God will visit you to bring you up from here to the land of your fathers, then bring up my bones with you from here." **24** And Joseph made the sons of Israel to swear for their seed after them, saying, "God will surely visit you and you will bring up my bones with you from here." **25** And it came to pass after this that Joseph died in that year, the seventy-first year of the Israelites going down to Egypt. **26** And Joseph was one hundred and ten years old when he died in the land of Egypt, and all his brothers and all his servants rose up and embalmed Joseph as was their custom, and his brothers and all Egypt mourned over him for seventy days. **27** And they put Joseph in a coffin filled with spices and all sorts of perfume, and they buried him by the side of the river, that is Sihor, and his sons, and all his brothers, and the whole of his father's household made a seven days' mourning for him. **28** And it came to pass after the death of Joseph, all the Egyptians began to rule over the sons of Israel in those days, and Pharaoh, king of Egypt, who reigned in his father's stead, took all the laws of Egypt and conducted the whole government of Egypt under his counsel, and he reigned securely over his people.

CHAPTER 60

1 And when the year came round, being the seventy-second year from the Israelites going down to Egypt, after the death of Joseph, Zepho, the son of Eliphaz, the son of Esau, fled from Egypt, he and his men, and they went away. **2** And he came to Africa, which is Dinhabah, to Angeas king of Africa, and Angeas received them with great honor, and he made Zepho the captain of his host. **3** And Zepho found favor in the sight of Angeas and in the sight of his people, and Zepho was captain of the host to Angeas king of Africa for many days. **4** And Zepho enticed Angeas king of Africa to collect all his army to go and fight with the Egyptians and with the sons of Jacob, and to avenge of them the cause of his brothers. **5** But Angeas would not listen to Zepho to do this thing, for Angeas knew the strength of the sons of Jacob and what they had done to his army in their warfare with the children of Esau. **6** And Zepho was very great in those days in the sight of Angeas and in the sight of all his people, and he continually enticed them to make war against Egypt, but they would not. **7** And it came to pass in those days there was in the land of Chittim a man in the city of Puzimna whose name was Uzu, and he became degenerately deified by the children of Chittim, and the man died and had no son, only one daughter whose name was Jania. **8** And the young woman was exceedingly attractive, beautiful and intelligent, there was none seen like to her for beauty and wisdom throughout the land. **9** And the people of Angeas king of Africa saw her and they came and praised her to him, and Angeas sent to the children of Chittim, and he requested to take her to himself for a wife, and the people of Chittim consented to give her to him for a wife. **10** And when the messengers of Angeas were going out from the land of Chittim to take their journey, behold, the messengers of Turnus king of Bibentu came to Chittim, for Turnus king of Bibentu also sent his messengers to request Jania for him, to take to himself for a wife, for all his men had also praised her to him, therefore he sent all his servants to her. **11** And the servants of Turnus came to Chittim, and they asked for Jania to be taken to Turnus, their king, for a wife. **12** And the people of Chittim said to them, "We cannot give her, because Angeas king of Africa desired her to take her to himself for a wife before you came, and that we should give her to him, and now therefore, we cannot do this thing to deprive Angeas of the young woman in order to give her to Turnus. **13** For we are greatly afraid of Angeas lest he come in battle against us and destroy us, and your master Turnus will not be able to deliver us from his hand." **14** And when the messengers of Turnus heard all the words of the children of Chittim, they turned back to their master and told him all the words of the children of Chittim. **15** And the children of Chittim sent a memorial to Angeas, saying, "Behold, Turnus has sent for Jania to take her to himself for a wife, and thus we have answered him; and we heard that he has collected his whole army to go to war against you, and he intends to pass by the road of Sardunia to fight against your brother Lucus, and after that he will come to fight against you." **16** And Angeas heard the words of the children of Chittim which they sent to him in the record, and his anger was kindled, and he rose up and assembled his whole army, and he came through the islands of the sea, the road to Sardunia, to his brother Lucus king of Sardunia. **17** And Niblos, the son of Lucus, heard that his uncle Angeas was coming, and he went out to meet him with a heavy army, and he kissed him and embraced him, and Niblos said to Angeas, "When you ask my father after his welfare, when I will go with you to fight with Turnus, ask of him to make me captain of his host," and Angeas did so, and he came to his brother and his brother came to meet him, and he asked him after his welfare. **18** And Angeas asked his brother Lucus after his welfare, and to make his son Niblos captain of his host, and Lucus did so, and Angeas and his brother Lucus rose up and they went toward Turnus to battle, and there was with them a great army and a heavy people. **19** And he came in ships, and they came into the province of Ashtorash, and behold, Turnus came toward them, for he went out to Sardunia, and intended to destroy it and afterward to pass on from there to Angeas to fight with him. **20** And Angeas and his brother Lucus met Turnus in the Valley of Canopia, and the battle was strong and mighty between them in that place. **21** And the battle was severe on Lucus king of Sardunia, and all his army fell, and his son Niblos also fell in that battle. **22** And his uncle Angeas commanded his servants, and they made a golden coffin for Niblos, and they put him into it, and Angeas again waged battle toward Turnus, and Angeas was stronger than he, and he slew him, and he struck all his people with the edge of the sword, and Angeas avenged the cause of his brother's son Niblos and the cause of the army of his brother Lucus. **23** And when Turnus died, the hands of those that survived the battle became weak, and they fled from before Angeas and his brother Lucus. **24** And Angeas and his brother

Lucus pursued them to the high road, which is between Alphanu and Romah, and they slew the whole army of Turnus with the edge of the sword. 25 And Lucus king of Sardunia commanded his servants that they should make a coffin of brass, and that they should place therein the body of his son Niblos, and they buried him in that place. 26 And they built a high tower on it there on the high road, and they called its name after the name of Niblos to this day, and they also buried Turnus king of Bibentu there in that place with Niblos. 27 And behold, on the high road between Alphanu and Romah the grave of Niblos is on one side and the grave of Turnus on the other, and [there is] a pavement between them to this day. 28 And when Niblos was buried, his father Lucus returned with his army to his land, Sardunia, and his brother Angeas, king of Africa, went with his people to the city of Bibentu, that is the city of Turnus. 29 And the inhabitants of Bibentu heard of his fame, and they were greatly afraid of him, and they went out to meet him with weeping and supplication, and the inhabitants of Bibentu entreated of Angeas not to slay them nor destroy their city; and he did so, for Bibentu was reckoned as one of the cities of the children of Chittim in those days; therefore he did not destroy the city. 30 But from that day forward the troops of the king of Africa would go to Chittim to spoil and plunder it, and whenever they went, Zepho the captain of the host of Angeas would go with them. 31 And it was after this that Angeas turned with his army and they came to the city of Puzimna, and Angeas took Jania the daughter of Uzu from there for a wife and brought her to his city, to Africa.

CHAPTER 61

1 And it came to pass at that time, Pharaoh king of Egypt commanded all his people to make a strong palace in Egypt for him. 2 And he also commanded the sons of Jacob to assist the Egyptians in the building, and the Egyptians made a beautiful and elegant palace for a royal habitation, and he dwelt therein, and he renewed his government and reigned securely. 3 And Zebulun the son of Jacob died in that year, that is the seventy-second year of the going down of the Israelites to Egypt, and Zebulun died one hundred and fourteen years old, and was put into a coffin and given into the hands of his children. 4 And in the seventy-fifth year his brother Simeon died; he was one hundred and twenty years old at his death, and he was also put into a coffin and given into the hands of his children. 5 And Zepho the son of Eliphaz, the son of Esau, captain of the host to Angeas king of Dinhabah, was still daily enticing Angeas to prepare for battle to fight with the sons of Jacob in Egypt, and Angeas was unwilling to do this thing, for his servants had related to him all the might of the sons of Jacob, what they had done to them in their battle with the children of Esau. 6 And Zepho was enticing Angeas daily in those days to fight with the sons of Jacob in those days. 7 And after some time Angeas listened to the words of Zepho and consented to him to fight with the sons of Jacob in Egypt, and Angeas got all his people in order, a people [as] numerous as the sand which is on the seashore, and he formed his resolution to go to Egypt to battle. 8 And among the servants of Angeas was a youth fifteen years old, Balaam the son of Beor was his name, and the youth was very wise and understood the art of witchcraft. 9 And Angeas said to Balaam, "Please conjure for us with the witchcraft that we may know who will prevail in this battle to which we are now proceeding." 10 And Balaam ordered that they should bring him wax, and he made thereof the likeness of chariots and horsemen representing the army of Angeas and the army of Egypt, and he put them in the cunningly prepared waters that he had for that purpose, and he took the boughs of myrtle trees in his hand, and he exercised his cunning, and he joined them over the water, and there appeared to him in the water the resembling images of the hosts of Angeas falling before the resembling images of the Egyptians and the sons of Jacob. 11 And Balaam told this thing to Angeas, and Angeas despaired and did not arm himself to go down to Egypt to battle, and he remained in his city. 12 And when Zepho the son of Eliphaz saw that Angeas despaired of going out to battle with the Egyptians, Zepho fled from Angeas from Africa, and he went and came to Chittim. 13 And all the people of Chittim received him with great honor, and they hired him to fight their battles all the days, and Zepho became exceedingly rich in those days, and the troops of the king of Africa still spread themselves in those days, and the children of Chittim assembled and went to Mount Cuptizia on account of the troops of Angeas, king of Africa, who

were advancing on them. 14 And it was one day that Zepho lost a young heifer, and he went to seek it, and he heard it lowing around the mountain. 15 And Zepho went, and he saw, and behold, there was a large cave at the bottom of the mountain, and there was a great stone there at the entrance of the cave, and Zepho split the stone, and he came into the cave, and he looked, and behold, a large animal was devouring the ox; from the middle upward it resembled a man, and from the middle downward it resembled an animal, and Zepho rose up against the animal and slew it with his swords. 16 And the inhabitants of Chittim heard of this thing, and they rejoiced exceedingly, and they said, "What will we do to this man who has slain this animal that devoured our cattle?" 17 And they all assembled to consecrate one day in the year to him, and they called the name thereof Zepho after his name, and they brought drink offerings to him year after year on that day, and they brought gifts to him. 18 At that time Jania the daughter of Uzu, wife of King Angeas, became sick, and her sickness was heavily felt by Angeas and his officers, and Angeas said to his wise men, "What will I do to Jania and how will I heal her from her sickness?" And his wise men said to him, "Because the air of our country is not like the air of the land of Chittim, and our water is not like their water, therefore the queen has become sick from this. 19 For through the change of air and water she became sick, and also because in her country she only drank the water which came from Purmah, which her ancestors had brought up with bridges." 20 And Angeas commanded his servants, and they brought to him in vessels of the waters of Purmah belonging to Chittim, and they weighed those waters with all the waters of the land of Africa, and they found those waters lighter than the waters of Africa. 21 And Angeas saw this thing, and he commanded all his officers to assemble the hewers of stone in thousands and tens of thousands, and they hewed stone without number, and the builders came and they built an exceedingly strong bridge, and they transported the spring of water from the land of Chittim to Africa, and those waters were for Jania the queen and for all her concerns, to drink from and to bake, wash and bathe with [them], and also to water with [them] all seed from which food can be obtained, and all fruit of the ground. 22 And the king commanded that they should bring of the soil of Chittim in large ships, and they also brought stones to build with, and the builders built palaces for Jania the queen, and the queen became healed of her sickness. 23 And at the revolution of the year the troops of Africa continued coming to the land of Chittim to plunder as usual, and Zepho son of Eliphaz heard their report, and he gave orders concerning them, and he fought with them, and they fled before him, and he delivered the land of Chittim from them. 24 And the children of Chittim saw the valor of Zepho, and the children of Chittim resolved and they made Zepho king over them, and he became king over them, and while he reigned, they went to subdue the children of Tubal, and all the surrounding islands. 25 And their king, Zepho, went at their head, and they made war with Tubal and the islands and subdued them, and when they returned from the battle they renewed his government for him, and they built a very large palace for him for his royal habitation and seat, and they made a large throne for him, and Zepho reigned over the whole land of Chittim and over the land of Italia [for] fifty years.

CHAPTER 62

1 In that year, being the seventy-ninth year of the Israelites going down to Egypt, Reuben the son of Jacob died in the land of Egypt; Reuben was one hundred and twenty-five years old when he died, and they put him into a coffin, and he was given into the hands of his children. 2 And in the eightieth year his brother Dan died; he was one hundred and twenty years [old] at his death, and he was also put into a coffin and given into the hands of his children. 3 And in that year Chusham king of Edom died, and Hadad the son of Bedad reigned after him for thirty-five years; and in the eighty-first year Issachar the son of Jacob died in Egypt, and Issachar was one hundred and twenty-two years old at his death, and he was put into a coffin in Egypt and given into the hands of his children. 4 And in the eighty-second year his brother Asher died; he was one hundred and twenty-three years old at his death, and he was placed in a coffin in Egypt and given into the hands of his children. 5 And in the eighty-third year Gad died; he was one hundred and twenty-five years old at his death, and he was put into a coffin in Egypt, and given into the hands of his children. 6 And it came

to pass in the eighty-fourth year, that is the fiftieth year of the reign of Hadad son of Bedad, king of Edom, that Hadad assembled all the children of Esau, and he got his whole army in readiness, about four hundred thousand men, and he directed his way to the land of Moab, and he went to fight with Moab and to make them tributary to him. **7** And the children of Moab heard this thing, and they were very much afraid, and they sent to the children of Midian to assist them in fighting with Hadad son of Bedad, king of Edom. **8** And Hadad came to the land of Moab, and Moab and the children of Midian went out to meet him, and they placed themselves in battle array against him in the field of Moab. **9** And Hadad fought with Moab, and there fell of the children of Moab and the children of Midian many slain ones, about two hundred thousand men. **10** And the battle was very severe on Moab, and when the children of Moab saw that the battle was severe on them, they weakened their hands, and turned their backs, and left the children of Midian to carry on the battle. **11** And the children of Midian did not know the intentions of Moab, but they strengthened themselves in battle and fought with Hadad and all his host, and all Midian fell before him. **12** And Hadad struck all Midian with a heavy striking, and he slew them with the edge of the sword; he left none remaining of those who came to assist Moab. **13** And when all the children of Midian had perished in battle and the children at Moab had escaped, Hadad made all Moab tributary to him at that time, and they came under his hand, and they gave a yearly tax as it was ordered, and Hadad turned and went back to his land. **14** And at the revolution of the year, when the rest of the people of Midian that were in the land heard that all their brothers had fallen in battle with Hadad for the sake of Moab, because the children of Moab had turned their backs in battle and left Midian to fight, then five of the princes of Midian resolved with the rest of their brothers who remained in their land to fight with Moab to avenge the cause of their brothers. **15** And the children of Midian sent to all their brothers, the children of the east, and all their brothers; all the children of Keturah came to assist Midian to fight with Moab. **16** And the children of Moab heard this thing, and they were greatly afraid that all the children of the east had assembled together against them for battle, and they, the children of Moab, sent a memorial to the land of Edom to Hadad the son of Bedad, saying, **17** "Come to us now, and assist us, and we will strike Midian, for they all assembled together and have come against us with all their brothers, the children of the east, to battle, to avenge the cause of Midian that fell in battle." **18** And Hadad son of Bedad, king of Edom, went out with his whole army and went to the land of Moab to fight with Midian, and Midian and the children of the east fought with Moab in the field of Moab, and the battle was very fierce between them. **19** And Hadad struck all the children of Midian and the children of the east with the edge of the sword, and at that time Hadad delivered Moab from the hand of Midian, and those that remained of Midian and of the children of the east fled before Hadad and his army, and Hadad pursued them to their land, and struck them with a very heavy slaughter, and the slain fell in the road. **20** And Hadad delivered Moab from the hand of Midian, for all the children of Midian had fallen by the edge of the sword, and Hadad turned and went back to his land. **21** And from that day forward the children of Midian hated the children of Moab, because they had fallen in battle for their sake, and there was a great and mighty enmity between them all the days. **22** And all that were found of Midian in the road of the land of Moab perished by the sword of Moab, and all that were found of Moab in the road of the land of Midian perished by the sword of Midian; thus Midian did to Moab and Moab to Midian for many days. **23** And it came to pass at that time that Judah the son of Jacob died in Egypt, in the eighty-sixth year of Jacob's going down to Egypt, and Judah was one hundred and twenty-nine years old at his death, and they embalmed him and put him into a coffin, and he was given into the hands of his children. **24** And in the eighty-ninth year Naphtali died; he was one hundred and thirty-two years old, and he was put into a coffin, and given into the hands of his children. **25** And it came to pass in the ninety-first year of the Israelites going down to Egypt, that is in the thirtieth year of the reign of Zepho the son of Eliphaz, the son of Esau, over the children of Chittim, the children of Africa came on the children of Chittim to plunder them as usual, but they had not come on them for these thirteen years. **26** And they came to them in that year, and Zepho the son of Eliphaz went out to them with some of his men and struck them desperately, and the troops of Africa fled from before Zepho and the slain fell before him, and Zepho and

his men pursued them, going on and striking them until they were near to Africa. **27** And Angeas king of Africa heard the thing which Zepho had done, and it vexed him exceedingly, and Angeas was afraid of Zepho all the days.

CHAPTER 63

1 And in the ninety-third year Levi the son of Jacob died in Egypt, and Levi was one hundred and thirty-seven years old when he died, and they put him into a coffin, and he was given into the hands of his children. **2** And it came to pass after the death of Levi, when all Egypt saw that the sons of Jacob, the brothers of Joseph, were dead, all the Egyptians began to afflict the children of Jacob, and to embitter their lives from that day to the day of their going out from Egypt, and they took from their hands all the vineyards and fields which Joseph had given to them, and all the elegant houses in which the people of Israel lived, and all the fat of Egypt; the Egyptians took everything from the sons of Jacob in those days. **3** And the hand of all Egypt became more grievous in those days against the sons of Israel, and the Egyptians injured the Israelites until the sons of Israel were wearied of their lives on account of the Egyptians. **4** And it came to pass in those days, in the one hundred and second year of Israel's going down to Egypt, that Pharaoh king of Egypt died, and his son Melol reigned in his stead, and all the mighty men of Egypt and all that generation which knew Joseph and his brothers died in those days. **5** And another generation rose up in their stead, which had not known the sons of Jacob, and all the good which they had done to them, and all their might in Egypt. **6** Therefore all Egypt began from that day out to embitter the lives of the sons of Jacob and to afflict them with all manner of hard labor, because they had not known their ancestors who had delivered them in the days of the famine. **7** And this was also from the Lord, for the sons of Israel, to benefit them in their latter days, in order that all the sons of Israel might know the Lord their God, **8** and in order to know the signs and mighty wonders which the Lord would do in Egypt on account of His people Israel, in order that the sons of Israel might fear the Lord God of their ancestors and walk in all His ways—they and their seed after them [for] all the days. **9** Melol was twenty years old when he began to reign, and he reigned ninety-four years, and all Egypt called his name Pharaoh after the name of his father as it was their custom to do to every king who reigned over them in Egypt. **10** At that time all the troops of Angeas king of Africa went out to spread along the land of Chittim as usual for plunder. **11** And Zepho the son of Eliphaz, the son of Esau, heard their report, and he went out to meet them with his army, and he fought them there in the road. **12** And Zepho struck the troops of the king of Africa with the edge of the sword and left none remaining of them, and not even one returned to his master in Africa. **13** And Angeas heard of this which Zepho the son of Eliphaz had done to all his troops, that he had destroyed them, and Angeas assembled all his troops, all the men of the land of Africa, a people numerous like the sand by the seashore. **14** And Angeas sent to his brother Lucus, saying, "Come to me with all your men and help me to strike Zepho and all the children of Chittim who have destroyed my men," and Lucus came with his whole army, a very great force, to assist his brother Angeas to fight with Zepho and the children of Chittim. **15** And Zepho and the children of Chittim heard this thing, and they were greatly afraid, and a great terror fell on their hearts. **16** And Zepho also sent a letter to the land of Edom to Hadad the son of Bedad king of Edom and to all the children of Esau, saying, **17** "I have heard that Angeas king of Africa is coming to us with his brother for battle against us, and we are greatly afraid of him, for his army is very great, particularly as he comes against us with his brother and his army likewise. **18** Now therefore, come up with me also and help me, and we will fight together against Angeas and his brother Lucus, and you will save us out of their hands, but if not, know that we will all die." **19** And the children of Esau sent a letter to the children of Chittim and to Zepho their king, saying, "We cannot fight against Angeas and his people for a covenant of peace has been between us these many years, from the days of Bela the first king, and from the days of Joseph the son of Jacob, king of Egypt, with whom we fought on the other side of the Jordan when he buried his father." **20** And when Zepho heard the words of his brothers, the children of Esau, he refrained from them, and Zepho was greatly afraid of Angeas. **21** And Angeas and his brother Lucus arrayed all their forces, about eight hundred thousand men, against the children of Chittim. 22 And all the children of Chittim said to Zepho, "Pray for us to the God of your ancestors; perhaps He may deliver us from the hand of Angeas and his army, for we have heard that He is a great God and that He delivers all who trust in Him." 23 And Zepho heard their words, and Zepho sought the Lord, and he said, 24 "O Lord God of my ancestors Abraham and Isaac, this day I know that you are a true God, and all the gods of the nations are vain and useless. 25 Now this day remember for me Your covenant with our father Abraham, which our ancestors related to us, and do graciously with me this day for the sake of our fathers Abraham and Isaac, and save me and the children of Chittim from the hand of the king of Africa who comes against us for battle." 26 And the Lord listened to the voice of Zepho, and He had regard for him on account of Abraham and Isaac, and the Lord delivered Zepho and the children of Chittim from the hand of Angeas and his people. 27 And Zepho fought Angeas king of Africa and all his people on that day, and the Lord gave all the people of Angeas into the hands of the children of Chittim. 28 And the battle was severe on Angeas, and Zepho struck all the men of Angeas and his brother Lucus with the edge of the sword, and there fell from them to the evening of that day about four hundred thousand men. 29 And when Angeas saw that all his men perished, he sent a letter to all the inhabitants of Africa to come to him, to assist him in the battle, and he wrote in the letter, saying, "Let all who are found in Africa come to me from ten years old and upward; let them all come to me, and behold, if he does not come, he will die, and the king will take all that he has, with his whole household." 30 And all the rest of the inhabitants of Africa were terrified at the words of Angeas, and there went out of the city about three hundred thousand men and boys, from ten years upward, and they came to Angeas. 31 And at the end of ten days Angeas renewed the battle against Zepho and the children of Chittim, and the battle was very great and strong between them. 32 And from the army of Angeas and Lucus, Zepho sent many of the wounded to his land, about two thousand men, and Sosiphtar, the captain of the host of Angeas, fell in that battle. 33 And when Sosiphtar had fallen, the African troops turned their backs to flee, and they fled, and Angeas and his brother Lucus were with them. 34 And Zepho and the children of Chittim pursued them, and they struck them still heavily on the road, about two hundred men, and they pursued Azdrubal the son of Angeas who had fled with his father, and they struck twenty of his men in the road, and Azdrubal escaped from the children of Chittim, and they did not slay him. 35 And Angeas and his brother Lucus fled with the rest of their men, and they escaped and came into Africa with terror and consternation, and Angeas feared all the days lest Zepho the son of Eliphaz should go to war with him.

CHAPTER 64

1 And at that time Balaam the son of Beor was with Angeas in the battle, and when he saw that Zepho prevailed over Angeas, he fled from there and came to Chittim. 2 And Zepho and the children of Chittim received him with great honor, for Zepho knew Balaam's wisdom, and Zepho gave many gifts to Balaam and he remained with him. 3 And when Zepho had returned from the war, he commanded all the children of Chittim to be numbered who had gone into battle with him, and behold, not one was missed. 4 And Zepho rejoiced at this thing, and he renewed his kingdom, and he made a feast to all his subjects. 5 But Zepho did not remember the Lord and did not consider that the Lord had helped him in battle and that He had delivered him and his people from the hand of the king of Africa, but still walked in the ways of the children of Chittim and the wicked children of Esau to serve other gods which his brothers, the children of Esau, had taught him; it is therefore said, "From the wicked goes out wickedness." 6 And Zepho reigned over all the children of Chittim securely, but did not know the Lord who had delivered him and all his people from the hand of the king of Africa; and the troops of Africa no longer came to Chittim to plunder as usual, for they knew of the power of Zepho who had smitten them all at the edge of the sword, so Angeas was afraid of Zepho the son of Eliphaz and of the children of Chittim [for] all the days. 7 At that time, when Zepho had returned from the war, and when Zepho had seen how he prevailed over all the people of Africa and had smitten them in battle at the edge of the sword, then Zepho advised with the children of Chittim to go to Egypt to fight with the sons of Jacob and with Pharaoh king of Egypt, 8 for Zepho heard that the

mighty men of Egypt were dead, and that Joseph and his brothers, the sons of Jacob, were dead, and that all their children, the sons of Israel, remained in Egypt. 9 And Zepho considered to go to fight against them and all Egypt, to avenge the cause of his brothers, the children of Esau, whom Joseph with his brothers and all Egypt had smitten in the land of Canaan when they went up to bury Jacob in Hebron. 10 And Zepho sent messengers to Hadad son of Bedad, king of Edom, and to all his brothers, the children of Esau, saying, 11 "Did you not say that you would not fight against the king of Africa, for he is a member of your covenant? behold, I fought with him and struck him and all his people. 12 Now therefore, I have resolved to fight against Egypt and the children of Jacob who are there, and I will be revenged of them for what Joseph, his brothers, and [his] ancestors did to us in the land of Canaan when they went up to bury their father in Hebron. 13 Now then, if you are willing to come to me to assist me in fighting against them and Egypt, then we will avenge the cause of our brothers." 14 And the children of Esau listened to the words of Zepho, and the children of Esau gathered themselves together, a very great people, and they went to assist Zepho and the children of Chittim in battle. 15 And Zepho sent to all the children of the east and to all the children of Ishmael with words like to these, and they gathered themselves and came to the assistance of Zepho and the children of Chittim in the war on Egypt. 16 And all these kings, the king of Edom, and the children of the east, and all the children of Ishmael, and Zepho the king of Chittim went out and arrayed all their hosts in Hebron. 17 And the camp was very heavy, extending in length a distance of three days' journey, a people [as] numerous as the sand on the seashore which cannot be counted. 18 And all these kings and their hosts went down, and came against all Egypt in battle, and encamped together in the Valley of Pathros. 19 And all Egypt heard their report, and they also gathered themselves together, all the people of the land of Egypt, and of all the cities belonging to Egypt, about three hundred thousand men. 20 And the men of Egypt also sent to the sons of Israel who were in the land of Goshen in those days to come to them in order to go and fight with these kings. 21 And the men of Israel assembled and were about one hundred and fifty men, and they went into battle to assist the Egyptians. 22 And the men of Israel and of Egypt went out, about three hundred thousand men and one hundred and fifty men, and they went toward these kings to battle, and they placed themselves from outside the land of Goshen opposite Pathros. 23 And the Egyptians did not believe in Israel to go with them in their camps together for battle, for all the Egyptians said, "Perhaps the sons of Israel will deliver us into the hand of the children of Esau and Ishmael, for they are their brothers." 24 And all the Egyptians said to the sons of Israel, "Remain together here in your position and we will go and fight against the children of Esau and Ishmael, and if these kings should prevail over us, then come altogether on them and assist us," and the sons of Israel did so. 25 And Zepho the son of Eliphaz, the son of Esau, king of Chittim, and Hadad the son of Bedad, king of Edom, and all their camps, and all the children of the east, and children of Ishmael, a people [as] numerous as sand, encamped together in the Valley of Pathros opposite Tachpanches. 26 And Balaam the son of Beor, the Syrian, was there in the camp of Zepho, for he came with the children of Chittim to the battle, and Balaam was a man highly honored in the eyes of Zepho and his men. 27 And Zepho said to Balaam, "Try by divination for us that we may know who will prevail in the battle—we or the Egyptians." 28 And Balaam rose up and tried the art of divination, and he was skillful in the knowledge of it, but he was confused and the work was destroyed in his hand. 29 And he tried it again, but it did not succeed, and Balaam despaired of it, and left it, and did not complete it, for this was from the Lord in order to cause Zepho and his people to fall into the hand of the sons of Israel who had trusted in the Lord, the God of their ancestors, in their war. 30 And Zepho and Hadad put their forces in battle array, and all the Egyptians went alone against them, about three hundred thousand men, and not one man of Israel was with them. 31 And all the Egyptians fought with these kings opposite Pathros and Tachpanches, and the battle was severe against the Egyptians. 32 And the kings were stronger than the Egyptians in that battle, and about one hundred and eighty men of Egypt fell on that day, and about thirty men of the forces of the kings, and all the men of Egypt fled from before the kings, so the children of Esau and Ishmael pursued the Egyptians, continuing to strike them to the place where the camp of the sons of Israel was. **33** And all the Egyptians cried to the sons of Israel, saying, "Hasten to us, and assist us, and save us from the hand of Esau, Ishmael, and the children of Chittim." **34** And the one hundred and fifty men of the sons of Israel ran from their station to the camps of these kings, and the sons of Israel cried to the Lord their God to deliver them. **35** And the Lord listened to Israel, and the Lord gave all the men of the kings into their hand, and the sons of Israel fought against these kings, and the sons of Israel struck about four thousand of the kings' men. **36** And the Lord threw a great consternation in the camp of the kings, so that the fear of the sons of Israel fell on them. **37** And all the hosts of the kings fled from before the sons of Israel, and the sons of Israel pursued them, continuing to strike them to the borders of the land of Cush. **38** And the sons of Israel slew of them in the road yet two thousand [more] men, and not one of the sons of Israel fell. **39** And when the Egyptians saw that the sons of Israel had fought with the kings with such few men, and that the battle was so very severe against them, **40** all the Egyptians were greatly afraid for their lives on account of the strong battle, and all Egypt fled, every man hiding himself from the arrayed forces, and they hid themselves in the road, and they left the Israelites to fight. **41** And the sons of Israel inflicted a terrible blow on the kings' men, and they returned from them after they had driven them to the border of the land of Cush. **42** And all Israel knew the thing which the men of Egypt had done to them, that they had fled from them in battle and had left them to fight alone, **43** so the sons of Israel also acted with cunning, and as the sons of Israel returned from battle, they found some of the Egyptians in the road and struck them there. **44** And while they slew them, they said to them these words: **45** "Why did you go from us and leave us, being a few people, to fight against these kings who had a great people to strike us, that you might thereby deliver your own souls?" **46** And of some which the Israelites met on the road, they, the sons of Israel, spoke to each other, saying, "Strike, strike, for he is an Ishmaelite, or an Edomite, or from the children of Chittim!" And they stood over him and slew him, and they knew that he was an Egyptian. **47** And the sons of Israel did these things cunningly against the Egyptians, because they had deserted them in battle and had fled from them. **48** And the sons of Israel slew of the men of Egypt in the road in this manner about two hundred men. **49** And all the men of Egypt saw the evil which the sons of Israel had done to them, so all Egypt feared the sons of Israel greatly, for they had seen their great power and that not one man of them had fallen. **50** So all the sons of Israel returned with joy on their road to Goshen, and the rest of Egypt returned—each man to his place.

CHAPTER 65

1 And it came to pass after these things that all the counselors of Pharaoh, king of Egypt, and all the elders of Egypt assembled, and came before the king, and bowed down to the ground, and they sat before him. **2** And the counselors and elders of Egypt spoke to the king, saying, **3** "Behold, the people of the sons of Israel are greater and mightier than we are, and you know all the evil which they did to us in the road when we returned from battle. **4** And you have also seen their strong power, for this power is to them from their fathers, for but a few men stood up against a people [as] numerous as the sand and struck them at the edge of the sword, and not one of them has fallen, so that if they had been numerous, they would then have utterly destroyed them. **5** Now therefore, give us counsel [regarding] what to do with them until we gradually destroy them from among us, lest they become too numerous for us in the land. **6** For if the sons of Israel should increase in the land, they will become an obstacle to us, and if any war should happen to take place, they will join our enemy against us with their great strength and fight against us, destroy us from the land, and go away from it." **7** So the king answered the elders of Egypt and said to them, "This is the plan advised against Israel, from which we will not depart: **8** behold, Pithom and Rameses are in the land, cities unfortified against battle; it is necessary for you and us to build them and to fortify them. **9** Now therefore, go also, and act cunningly toward them, and proclaim a voice in Egypt and in Goshen at the command of the king, saying, **10** All you men of Egypt, Goshen, Pathros, and all their inhabitants: the king has commanded us to build Pithom and Rameses and to fortify them for battle; who among you of all Egypt, of the sons of Israel and of all the inhabitants of the cities, are willing to build with us, will each have his wages

given to him daily at the king's order; so first go and do cunningly, and gather yourselves, and come to Pithom and Rameses to build. **11** And while you are building, cause a proclamation of this kind to be made throughout Egypt every day at the command of the king. **12** And when some of the sons of Israel will come to build with you, you will give them their wages daily for a few days. **13** And after they will have built with you for their daily hire, drag yourselves away from them daily one by one in secret, and then you will rise up and become their taskmasters and officers, and afterward you will leave them to build without wages, and should they refuse, then force them with all your might to build. **14** And if you do this, it will be well with us to strengthen our land against the sons of Israel, for on account of the fatigue of the building and the work, the sons of Israel will decrease, because you will deprive them from their wives day by day." **15** And all the elders of Egypt heard the counsel of the king, and the counsel seemed good in their eyes, and in the eyes of the servants of Pharaoh, and in the eyes of all Egypt, and they did according to the word of the king. **16** And all the servants went away from the king, and they caused a proclamation to be made in all Egypt, in Tachpanches, and in Goshen, and in all the cities which surrounded Egypt, saying, **17** "You have seen what the children of Esau and Ishmael did to us, who came to war against us and wished to destroy us. **18** Now therefore, the king commanded us to fortify the land, to build the cities [of] Pithom and Rameses, and to fortify them for battle if they should come against us again. **19** Whoever of you from all Egypt and from the sons of Israel will come to build with us, he will have his daily wages given by the king as his command is to us." **20** And when Egypt and all the sons of Israel heard all that the servants of Pharaoh had spoken, [many] came from the Egyptians and the sons of Israel to build Pithom and Rameses with the servants of Pharaoh, but none of the children of Levi came with their brothers to build. **21** And all the servants of Pharaoh and his princes came at first with deceit to build with all Israel as daily hired laborers, and they gave to Israel their daily hire at the beginning. **22** And the servants of Pharaoh built with all Israel and were employed in that work with Israel for a month. **23** And at the end of the month, all the servants of Pharaoh began to withdraw secretly from the people of Israel daily. **24** And Israel went on with the work at that time, but they received their daily hire then, because some of the men of Egypt were yet carrying on the work with Israel at that time; therefore, the Egyptians gave Israel their hire in those days in order that they, the Egyptians, their fellow-workmen, might also take the pay for their labor. **25** And at the end of a year and four months all the Egyptians had withdrawn from the sons of Israel, so that the sons of Israel were left alone engaged in the work. **26** And after all the Egyptians had withdrawn from the sons of Israel they returned and became oppressors and officers over them, and some of them stood over the sons of Israel as taskmasters to receive from them all that they gave them for the pay of their labor. **27** And the Egyptians did in this manner to the sons of Israel day by day in order to afflict [them] in their work. **28** And all the sons of Israel were engaged in the labor alone, and the Egyptians refrained from giving any pay to the sons of Israel from that time forward. **29** And when some of the men of Israel refused to work on account of the wages not being given to them, then the exactors and the servants of Pharaoh oppressed them, and struck them with heavy blows, and made them return by force to labor with their brothers; thus all the Egyptians did to the sons of Israel all the days. **30** And all the sons of Israel were greatly afraid of the Egyptians in this matter, and all the sons of Israel returned and worked alone without pay. **31** And the sons of Israel built Pithom and Rameses, and all the sons of Israel did the work, some making bricks and some building, and the sons of Israel built and fortified all the land of Egypt and its walls, and the sons of Israel were engaged in work for many years until the time came when the Lord remembered them and brought them out of Egypt. **32** But the children of Levi were not employed in the work with their brothers of Israel from the beginning to the day of their going out from Egypt. **33** For all the children of Levi knew that the Egyptians had spoken all these words with deceit to the Israelites, therefore the children of Levi refrained from approaching to the work with their brothers. **34** And the Egyptians did not direct their attention to make the children of Levi work afterward since they had not been with their brothers at the beginning; therefore the Egyptians left them alone. **35** And the hands of the men of Egypt were directed with continued severity against the sons of Israel in that work, and the Egyptians made the sons of Israel work with rigor. **36** And the Egyptians embittered the lives of the sons of Israel with hard work in mortar and bricks, and also in all manner of work in the field. **37** And the sons of Israel called Melol, the king of Egypt, "Meror, king of Egypt," because in his days the Egyptians had embittered their lives with all manner of work. **38** And all the work wherein the Egyptians made the sons of Israel labor, they exacted with rigor in order to afflict the sons of Israel, but the more they afflicted them, the more they increased and grew, and the Egyptians were grieved because of the sons of Israel.

CHAPTER 66

1 At that time Hadad the son of Bedad, king of Edom, died, and Samlah from Mesrekah, from the country of the children of the east, reigned in his place. **2** In the thirteenth year of the reign of Pharaoh king of Egypt, which was the one hundred and twenty-fifth year of the Israelites going down into Egypt, Samlah had reigned over Edom eighteen years. **3** And when he reigned, he drew out his hosts to go and fight against Zepho the son of Eliphaz and the children of Chittim, because they had made war against Angeas king of Africa and had destroyed his whole army. **4** But he did not engage with him, for the children of Esau prevented him, saying, "He was their brother," so Samlah listened to the voice of the children of Esau, and turned back with all his forces to the land of Edom, and did not proceed to fight against Zepho the son of Eliphaz. **5** And Pharaoh king of Egypt heard this thing, saying, "Samlah king of Edom has resolved to fight the children of Chittim, and afterward he will come to fight against Egypt." **6** And when the Egyptians heard this matter, they increased the labor on the sons of Israel, lest the Israelites should do to them as they did to them in their war with the children of Esau in the days of Hadad. **7** So the Egyptians said to the sons of Israel, "Hasten and do your work, and finish your task, and strengthen the land, lest the children of Esau, your brothers, should come to fight against us, for they will come against us on your account." **8** And the sons of Israel did the work of the men of Egypt day by day, and the Egyptians afflicted the sons of Israel in order to lessen them in the land. **9** But as the Egyptians increased the labor on the sons of Israel, so the sons of Israel increased and multiplied, and all Egypt was filled with the sons of Israel. **10** And in the one hundred and twenty-fifth year of Israel's going down into Egypt, all the Egyptians saw that their counsel did not succeed against Israel, but that they increased and grew, and the land of Egypt and the land of Goshen were filled with the sons of Israel. **11** So all the elders of Egypt and its wise men came before the king, and bowed down to him, and sat before him. **12** And all the elders of Egypt and the wise men thereof said to the king, "May the king live forever; you counseled us the counsel against the sons of Israel, and we did to them according to the word of the king. **13** But in proportion to the increase of the labor so do they increase and grow in the land, and behold, the whole country is filled with them. **14** Now therefore, our lord and king, the eyes of all Egypt are on you to give them advice with your wisdom, by which they may prevail over Israel to destroy them or to diminish them from the land"; and the king answered them, saying, "Give counsel in this matter that we may know what to do to them." **15** And an officer, one of the king's counselors, whose name was Job, from Mesopotamia, in the land of Uz, answered the king, saying, **16** "If it pleases the king, let him hear the counsel of his servant"; and the king said to him, "Speak." **17** And Job spoke before the king, the princes, and before all the elders of Egypt, saying, **18** "Behold, the counsel of the king which he advised formerly respecting the labor of the sons of Israel is very good, and you must not ever remove that labor from them. **19** But this is the advice counseled by which you may lessen them if it seems good to the king to afflict them: **20** behold, we have feared war for a long time, and we said, When Israel becomes fruitful in the land, they will drive us from the land if a war should take place. **21** If it pleases the king, let a royal decree go out and let it be written in the laws of Egypt, which will not be revoked, that every male child born to the Israelites, his blood will be spilled on the ground. **22** And by your doing this, when all the male sons of Israel will have died, the evil of their wars will cease; let the king do so, and send for all the Hebrew midwives and order them to execute it in this matter"; so the thing pleased the king and the princes, and the king did according to the word of Job. **23** And the king sent for the

Hebrew midwives to be called, of which the name of one was Shephrah, and the name of the other Puah. **24** And the midwives came before the king and stood in his presence. **25** And the king said to them, "When you do the office of a midwife to the Hebrew women and see them on the stools, if it is a son, then you will kill him, but if it is a daughter, then she will live. **26** But if you will not do this thing, then I will burn you and all your houses up with fire." **27** But the midwives feared God and did not listen to the king of Egypt nor to his words, and when the Hebrew women brought out a son or daughter to the midwife, then the midwife did all that was necessary for the child and let it live; thus the midwives did all the days. **28** And this thing was told to the king, and he sent and called for the midwives, and he said to them, "Why have you done this thing and have saved the children alive?" **29** And the midwives answered and spoke together before the king, saying, **30** "Do not let the king think that the Hebrew women are as the Egyptian women, for all the sons of Israel are vigorous, and before the midwife comes to them they are delivered, and as for us, your handmaids, for many days no Hebrew woman has brought out on us, for all the Hebrew women are their own midwives, because they are vigorous." **31** And Pharaoh heard their words and believed them in this matter, and the midwives went away from the king, and God dealt well with them, and the people multiplied and waxed exceedingly.

CHAPTER 67

1 There was a man in the land of Egypt of the seed of Levi, whose name was Amram the son of Kehas, the son of Levi, the son of Israel. **2** And this man went and took a wife, namely Jochebed the daughter of Levi, his father's sister, and she was one hundred and twenty-six years old, and he came to her. **3** And the woman conceived and bore a daughter, and she called her name Miriam, because in those days the Egyptians had embittered the lives of the sons of Israel. **4** And she conceived again, and bore a son, and she called his name Aaron, for in the days of her conception, Pharaoh began to spill the blood of the male sons of Israel. **5** In those days Zepho the son of Eliphaz, son of Esau, king of Chittim, died, and Janeas reigned in his stead. **6** And the time that Zepho reigned over the children of Chittim was fifty years, and he died and was buried in the city of Nabna in the land of Chittim. **7** And Janeas, one of the mighty men of the children of Chittim, reigned after him and he reigned fifty years. **8** And it was after the death of the king of Chittim that Balaam the son of Beor fled from the land of Chittim, and he went and came to Egypt, to Pharaoh king of Egypt. **9** And Pharaoh received him with great honor, for he had heard of his wisdom, and he gave him presents, and made him for a counselor, and aggrandized him. **10** And Balaam dwelt in Egypt, in honor with all the nobles of the king, and the nobles exalted him, because they all coveted to learn his wisdom. **11** And in the one hundred and thirtieth year of Israel's going down to Egypt, Pharaoh dreamed that he was sitting on his kingly throne, and he lifted up his eyes and saw an old man standing before him, and there were scales in the hands of the old man, such scales as are used by merchants. **12** And the old man took the scales and hung them before Pharaoh. **13** And the old man took all the elders of Egypt and all its nobles and great men, and he tied them together and put them in one scale. **14** And he took a milk kid and put it into the other scale, and the kid exceeded over all. **15** And Pharaoh was astonished at this dreadful vision, why the kid should exceed over all, and Pharaoh awoke, and behold, it was a dream. **16** And Pharaoh rose up early in the morning, and called all his servants, and related the dream to them, and the men were greatly afraid. **17** And the king said to all his wise men, "Now interpret the dream which I dreamed [so] that I may know it." **18** And Balaam the son of Beor answered the king and said to him, "This means nothing else but [that] a great calamity that will spring up against Egypt in the latter days. **19** For a son will be born to Israel who will destroy all Egypt and its inhabitants and bring out the Israelites from Egypt with a mighty hand. **20** Now therefore, O king, take counsel on this matter that you may destroy the hope of the sons of Israel and their expectation before this calamity arises against Egypt." **21** And the king said to Balaam, "And what will we do to Israel? surely after a certain manner we at first counseled against them and could not prevail over them. **22** Now therefore, also give advice against them by which we may prevail over them." **23** And Balaam answered the king, saying, "Send now and call your two counselors, and we will see what their advice is on this matter and afterward your servant will speak." **24** And the king sent for and called his two counselors Reuel the Midianite and Job the Uzite, and they came and sat before the king. **25** And the king said to them, "Behold, you have both heard the dream which I have dreamed and the interpretation thereof; now therefore, give counsel, and know, and see what is to be done to the sons of Israel whereby we may prevail over them before their evil will spring up against us." **26** And Reuel the Midianite answered the king and said, "May the king live, may the king live forever. **27** If it seems good to the king, let him desist from the Hebrews and leave them, and do not let him stretch out his hand against them. **28** For these are they whom the Lord chose in days of old, and took as the lot of His inheritance from among all the nations of the earth and the kings of the earth; and who is there that stretched his hand against them with impunity, of whom their God was not avenged? **29** Surely you know that when Abraham went down to Egypt, Pharaoh, the former king of Egypt, saw his wife Sarah and took her for a wife, because Abraham said, She is my sister, for he was afraid, lest the men of Egypt should slay him on account of his wife. **30** And when the king of Egypt had taken Sarah, then God struck him and his household with heavy plagues until he restored to Abraham his wife Sarah—then he was healed. **31** And Abimelech the Gerarite, king of the Philistines, God punished on account of Sarah, [the] wife of Abraham, in stopping up every womb from man to beast **32** when their God came to Abimelech in the dream of night and terrified him in order that He might restore to Abraham Sarah whom he had taken, and afterward all the people of Gerar were punished on account of Sarah, and Abraham prayed to his God for them, and He was entreated by him, and He healed them. **33** And Abimelech feared all this evil that came on him and his people, and he returned to Abraham his wife Sarah, and gave him many gifts with her. **34** He also did so to Isaac when he had driven him from Gerar, and God had done wonderful things to him, that all the water courses of Gerar were dried up, and their productive trees did not bring out **35** until Abimelech of Gerar, and Ahuzzath, one of his friends, and Pichol, the captain of his host, went to him, and bent, and bowed down to the ground before him. **36** And they requested of him to supplicate for them, and he prayed to the Lord for them, and the Lord was entreated by him, and He healed them. **37** Jacob also, the plain man, was delivered through his integrity from the hand of his brother Esau, and the hand of Laban the Syrian, his mother's brother, who had sought his life, [and] likewise from the hand of all the kings of Canaan who had come together against him and his children to destroy them, and the Lord delivered them out of their hands, that they turned on them and struck them, for who had ever stretched out his hand against them with impunity? **38** Surely the former Pharaoh, your father's father, raised Joseph the son of Jacob above all the princes of the land of Egypt when he saw his wisdom, for through his wisdom he rescued all the inhabitants of the land from the famine, **39** after which he ordered Jacob and his children to come down to Egypt in order that through their virtue the land of Egypt and the land of Goshen might be delivered from the famine. **40** Now therefore, if it seems good in your eyes, cease from destroying the sons of Israel, but if it is not your will that they will dwell in Egypt, send them out from here [so] that they may go to the land of Canaan, the land where their ancestors sojourned." **41** And when Pharaoh heard the words of Jethro, he was very angry with him, so that he rose from the king's presence with shame, and went to Midian, his land, and took Joseph's stick with him. **42** And the king said to Job the Uzite, "What do you say, Job? And what is your advice respecting the Hebrews?" **43** So Job said to the king, "Behold, all the inhabitants of the land are in your power: let the king do as it seems good in his eyes." **44** And the king said to Balaam, "What do you say, Balaam? Speak your word [so] that we may hear it." **45** And Balaam said to the king, "Of all that the king has counseled against the Hebrews they will be delivered, and the king will not be able to prevail over them with any counsel. **46** For if you think to lessen them by the flaming fire, you cannot prevail over them, for surely their God delivered their father Abraham from Ur of the Chaldeans; and if you think to destroy them with a sword, surely their father Isaac was delivered from it, and a ram was placed in his stead. **47** And if you think to lessen them with hard and rigorous labor, you will not prevail even in this, for their father Jacob served Laban in all manner of hard work and prospered. **48** Now therefore, O king, hear my words, for this is the counsel which is counseled against them, by which you will prevail over them, and from which you should not depart: **49** if it pleases the king, let him order all their children which will be born from this day forward to be thrown into the water, for by this you can wipe away their name, for none of them, nor of their fathers, were tried in this manner." **50** And the king heard the words of Balaam, and the thing pleased the king and the princes, and the king did according to the word of Balaam. **51** And the king ordered a proclamation to be issued and a law to be made throughout the land of Egypt, saying, "Every male child born to the Hebrews from this day forward will be thrown into the water." **52** And Pharaoh called to all his servants, saying, "Go now, and seek throughout the land of Goshen where the sons of Israel are, and see that every son born to the Hebrews will be cast into the river, but you will let every daughter live." **53** And when the sons of Israel heard this thing which Pharaoh had commanded, to cast their male children into the river, some of the people separated from their wives and others adhered to them. **54** And from that day forward, when the time of delivery arrived for those women of Israel who had remained with their husbands, they went to the field to deliver, and brought out in the field, and left their children on the field, and returned home. **55** And the Lord who had sworn to their ancestors to multiply them sent one of His ministering messengers which are in Heaven to wash each child in water, to anoint and swathe it, and to put two smooth stones into its hands from one of which it sucked milk and from the other honey, and He caused its hair to grow to its knees, by which it might cover itself to comfort it and to cleave to it, through His compassion for it. **56** And when God had compassion over them and had desired to multiply them on the face of the land, He ordered His earth to receive them to be preserved therein until the time of their growing up, after which the earth opened its mouth, and vomited them out, and they sprouted out from the city like the herb of the earth and the grass of the forest, and they each returned to his family and to his father's house, and they remained with them. **57** And the babies of the sons of Israel were on the earth like the herb of the field through God's grace to them. **58** And when all the Egyptians saw this thing, they went out, each to his field with his yoke of oxen and his plowshare, and they plowed it up as one plows the earth at seed-time. **59** And when they plowed, they were unable to hurt the infants of the sons of Israel, so the people increased and waxed exceedingly. **60** And Pharaoh ordered his officers to go to Goshen daily to seek for the babies of the sons of Israel. **61** And when they had sought and found one, they took it from its mother's bosom by force and threw it into the river, but they left the female child with its mother; thus the Egyptians did to the Israelites all the days.

CHAPTER 68

1 And it was at that time the Spirit of God was on Miriam the daughter of Amram, the sister of Aaron, and she went out and prophesied about the house, saying, "Behold, [at] this time a son will be born to us from my father and mother, and he will save Israel from the hands of Egypt." **2** And when Amram heard the words of his daughter, he went and took his wife back to the house after he had driven her away at the time when Pharaoh ordered every male child of the house of Jacob to be thrown into the water. **3** So Amram took his wife Jochebed three years after he had driven her away, and he came to her, and she conceived. **4** And at the end of seven months from her conception she brought out a son, and the whole house was filled with great light as of the light of the sun and moon at the time of their shining. **5** And when the woman saw that the child was good and pleasing to the sight, she hid it for three months in an inner room. **6** In those days the Egyptians conspired to destroy all the Hebrews there. **7** And the Egyptian women went to Goshen where the sons of Israel were, and they carried their young ones on their shoulders, their babies who could not yet speak. **8** And in those days, when the women of the sons of Israel brought out, each woman had hidden her son from before the Egyptians, [so] that the Egyptians might not know of their bringing out and might not destroy them from the land. **9** And the Egyptian women came to Goshen and their children who could not speak were on their shoulders, and when an Egyptian woman came into the house of a Hebrew woman her baby began to cry. **10** And when it cried, the child that was in the inner room answered it, so the Egyptian women went and told it at the house of Pharaoh. **11** And Pharaoh sent his officers to take the children and slay them; thus the Egyptians did to the Hebrew women all the days. ¹² And it was at that time, about three months from Jochebed's concealment of her son, that the thing was known in Pharaoh's house. ¹³ And the woman hastened to take her son away before the officers came, and she took an ark of bulrushes for him, and daubed it with slime and with pitch, and put the child therein, and she laid it in the flags by the river's brink. ¹⁴ And his sister Miriam stood far off to know what would be done to him and what would become of her words. ¹⁵ And God sent out a terrible heat in the land of Egypt at that time, which burned up the flesh of man like the sun in his circuit, and it greatly oppressed the Egyptians. ¹⁶ And all the Egyptians went down to bathe in the river on account of the consuming heat which burned up their flesh. ¹⁷ And Bathia, the daughter of Pharaoh, also went to bathe in the river, owing to the consuming heat, and her maidens walked at the riverside, and all the women of Egypt as well. ¹⁸ And Bathia lifted up her eyes to the river, and she saw the ark on the water, and sent her maid to fetch it. ¹⁹ And she opened it and saw the child, and behold, the baby wept, and she had compassion on him, and she said, "This is one of the Hebrew children." ²⁰ And all the women of Egypt walking on the riverside desired to give him suck, but he would not suck, for this thing was from the Lord in order to restore him to his mother's breast. ²¹ And at that time his sister Miriam was among the Egyptian women at the riverside, and she saw this thing, and she said to Pharaoh's daughter, "Will I go and fetch a nurse of the Hebrew women that she may nurse the child for you?" ²² And Pharaoh's daughter said to her, "Go," and the young woman went and called the child's mother. ²³ And Pharaoh's daughter said to Jochebed, "Take this child away and suckle it for me, and I will pay you your wages, two bits of silver daily"; and the woman took the child and nursed it. ²⁴ And at the end of two years, when the child grew up, she brought him to the daughter of Pharaoh, and he was as a son to her, and she called his name Moses, for she said, "Because I drew him out of the water." ²⁵ And his father Amram called his name Chabar, for he said, "It was for him that he associated with his wife whom he had turned away." ²⁶ And his mother Jochebed called his name Jekuthiel, because, she said, "I have hoped for him to the Almighty, and God restored him to me." ²⁷ And his sister Miriam called him Jered, for she descended after him to the river to know what his end would be. ²⁸ And his brother Aaron called his name Abi Zanuch, saying, "My father left my mother and returned to her on his account." ²⁹ And Kehas, the father of Amram, called his name Abigdor, because on his account God repaired the breach of the house of Jacob, [so] that they could no longer throw their male children into the water. ³⁰ And their nurse called him Abi Socho, saying, "He was hidden in his dwelling place for three months on account of the children of Ham." ³¹ And all Israel called his name Shemaiah, son of Nethanel, for they said, "In his days God has heard their cries and rescued them from their oppressors." ³² And Moses was in Pharaoh's house, and was to Bathia, Pharaoh's daughter, as a son, and Moses grew up among the king's children.

CHAPTER 69

¹ And the king of Edom died in those days, in the eighteenth year of his reign, and was buried in his temple which he had built for himself as his royal residence in the land of Edom. ² And the children of Esau sent to Pethor, which is on the river, and they fetched a young man of beautiful eyes and handsome aspect from there whose name was Saul, and they made him king over them in the place of Samlah. ³ And Saul reigned over all the children of Esau in the land of Edom for forty years. ⁴ And when Pharaoh king of Egypt saw that the counsel which Balaam had advised respecting the sons of Israel did not succeed, but that they were still fruitful, multiplied, and increased throughout the land of Egypt, ⁵ then Pharaoh commanded in those days that a proclamation should be issued throughout Egypt to the sons of Israel, saying, "No man who will diminish anything of his daily labor. ⁶ And the man who will be found deficient in his labor which he performs daily, whether in mortar or in bricks, then his youngest son will be put in their place." ⁷ And the labor of Egypt strengthened on the sons of Israel in those days, and behold, if one brick was deficient in any man's daily labor, the Egyptians took his youngest boy by force from his mother and put him into the building in the place of the brick which his father had left wanting. ⁸ And the men of Egypt did so to all the sons of Israel day by day, all the days

for a long period. ⁹ But at that time the tribe of Levi did not work with the Israelites, their brothers, from the beginning, for the children of Levi knew the cunning of the Egyptians which they exercised at first toward the Israelites.

CHAPTER 70

¹ And in the third year from the birth of Moses, Pharaoh was sitting at a banquet when Alparanith the queen was sitting at his right and Bathia at his left, and the youth Moses was lying on her bosom, and Balaam the son of Beor with his two sons, and all the princes of the kingdom were sitting at [the] table in the king's presence. ² And the youth stretched out his hand on the king's head, and took the crown from the king's head, and placed it on his own head. ³ And when the king and princes saw the work which the boy had done, the king and princes were terrified, and one man expressed astonishment to his neighbor. ⁴ And the king said to the princes who were before him at the table, "What do you speak and what do you say, O you princes, in this matter, and what is to be the judgment against the boy on account of this act?" ⁵ And Balaam the son of Beor, the magician, answered before the king and princes, and he said, "Remember now, O my lord and king, the dream which you dreamed many days since, and that which your servant interpreted to you. ⁶ Now therefore, this is a child from the Hebrew children, in whom is the Spirit of God, and do not let my lord the king imagine that this youngster did this thing without knowledge. ⁷ For he is a Hebrew boy, and wisdom and understanding are with him although he is still a child, and with wisdom he has done this and chosen the kingdom of Egypt for himself. ⁸ For this is the manner of all the Hebrews to deceive kings and their nobles, to do all these things cunningly in order to make the kings of the earth and their men tremble. ⁹ Surely you know that their father Abraham acted thus, who deceived the army of Nimrod king of Babel and Abimelech king of Gerar, and that he possessed the land of the children of Heth for himself and all the kingdoms of Canaan, ¹⁰ and that he descended into Egypt and said of his wife Sarah, She is my sister, in order to mislead Egypt and her king. ¹¹ His son Isaac also did so when he went to Gerar and dwelt there, and his strength prevailed over the army of Abimelech king of the Philistines. ¹² He also thought of making the kingdom of the Philistines stumble in saying that his wife Rebekah was his sister. ¹³ Jacob also dealt treacherously with his brother and took his birthright and his blessing from his hand. ¹⁴ Then he went to Padan-Aram to the house of Laban, his mother's brother, and cunningly obtained from him his daughter, his cattle, and all belonging to him, and fled away and returned to the land of Canaan to his father. ¹⁵ His sons sold their brother Joseph, who went down into Egypt, and became a slave, and was placed in the prison-house for twelve years ¹⁶ until the former Pharaoh dreamed dreams, and withdrew him from the prison-house, and magnified him above all the princes in Egypt on account of his interpreting his dreams to him. ¹⁷ And when God caused a famine throughout the land, he sent for and brought his father, and all his brothers, and the whole of his father's household, and supported them without price or reward, and bought the Egyptians for slaves. ¹⁸ Now therefore, my lord king, behold, this child has risen up in their stead in Egypt to do according to their deeds and to trifle with every king, prince, and judge. ¹⁹ If it pleases the king, let us now spill his blood on the ground, lest he grow up and take away the government from your hand, and the hope of Egypt perish after he will have reigned." ²⁰ And Balaam said to the king, "Let us moreover call for all the judges of Egypt and the wise men thereof, and let us know if the judgment of death is due to this boy as you said, and then we will slay him." ²¹ And Pharaoh sent and called for all the wise men of Egypt and they came before the king, and a messenger of the Lord came among them, and he was like one of the wise men of Egypt. ²² And the king said to the wise men, "Surely you have heard what this Hebrew boy who is in the house has done, and thus Balaam has judged in the matter. ²³ Now you also judge and see what is due to the boy for the act he has committed." ²⁴ And the messenger, who seemed like one of the wise men of Pharaoh, answered and said as follows before all the wise men of Egypt and before the king and the princes: ²⁵ "If it pleases the king, let the king send for men who will bring an onyx stone and a coal of fire before him, and place them before the child, and if the child will stretch out his hand and take the onyx stone, then we will know that the youth has done all that he has done with

wisdom, and we must slay him. **26** But if he stretches out his hand on the coal, then we will know that it was not with knowledge that he did this thing, and he will live." **27** And the thing seemed good in the eyes of the king and the princes, so the king did according to the word of the messenger of the Lord. **28** And the king ordered the onyx stone and coal to be brought and placed before Moses. **29** And they placed the boy before them, and the youth endeavored to stretch out his hand to the onyx stone, but the messenger of the Lord took his hand and placed it on the coal, and the coal became extinguished in his hand, and he lifted it up, and put it into his mouth, and burned part of his lips and part of his tongue, and he became heavy in mouth and tongue. **30** And when the king and princes saw this, they knew that Moses had not acted with wisdom in taking off the crown from the king's head. **31** So the king and princes refrained from slaying the child, so Moses remained in Pharaoh's house, growing up, and the Lord was with him. **32** And while the boy was in the king's house, he was robed in purple and he grew among the children of the king. **33** And when Moses grew up in the king's house, Bathia the daughter of Pharaoh considered him as a son, and all the household of Pharaoh honored him, and all the men of Egypt were afraid of him. **34** And daily he went out and came into the land of Goshen where his brothers, the sons of Israel, were, and Moses saw them daily in shortness of breath and hard labor. **35** And Moses asked them, saying, "Why is this labor meted out to you day by day?" **36** And they told him all that had befallen them, and all the injunctions which Pharaoh had put on them before his birth. **37** And they told him all the counsels which Balaam the son of Beor had counseled against them, and what he had also counseled against him in order to slay him when he had taken the king's crown from off his head. **38** And when Moses heard these things, his anger was kindled against Balaam, and he sought to kill him, and he was in ambush for him day by day. **39** And Balaam was afraid of Moses, and he and his two sons rose up and went out from Egypt, and they fled and delivered their souls, and they went to the land of Cush, to Kikianus, king of Cush. **40** And Moses was in the king's house, going out and coming in; the Lord gave him favor in the eyes of Pharaoh, and in the eyes of all his servants, and in the eyes of all the people of Egypt, and they loved Moses exceedingly. **41** And the day arrived when Moses went to Goshen to see his brothers, and he saw the sons of Israel in their burdens and hard labor, and Moses was grieved on their account. **42** And Moses returned to Egypt, and came to the house of Pharaoh, and came before the king, and Moses bowed down before the king. **43** And Moses said to Pharaoh, "Please my lord, I have come to seek a small request from you: do not turn my face away empty"; and Pharaoh said to him, "Speak." **44** And Moses said to Pharaoh, "Let there be given to your servants, the sons of Israel who are in Goshen, one day to rest therein from their labor." **45** And the king answered Moses and said, "Behold, I have lifted up your face in this thing to grant your request." **46** And Pharaoh ordered a proclamation to be issued throughout Egypt and Goshen, saying, **47** "To you, all the sons of Israel, thus says the king: for six days you will do your work and labor, but on the seventh day you will rest and will not perform any work; thus you will do all the days as the king and Moses the son of Bathia have commanded." **48** And Moses rejoiced at this thing which the king had granted to him, and all the sons of Israel did as Moses ordered them, **49** for this thing was from the Lord to the sons of Israel, for the Lord had begun to remember the sons of Israel to save them for the sake of their fathers. **50** And the Lord was with Moses and his fame went throughout Egypt. **51** And Moses became great in the eyes of all the Egyptians, and in the eyes of all the sons of Israel [because of his] seeking good for his people Israel and speaking words of peace regarding them to the king.

CHAPTER 71

1 And when Moses was eighteen years old, he desired to see his father and mother and he went to them, to Goshen, and when Moses had come near Goshen, he came to the place where the sons of Israel were engaged in work, and he observed their burdens, and he saw an Egyptian striking one of his Hebrew brothers. **2** And when the man who was beaten saw Moses, he ran to him for help, for the man Moses was greatly respected in the house of Pharaoh, and he said to him, "My lord, attend to me! This Egyptian came to my house in the night, bound me, and came to my wife in my presence, and

now he seeks to take my life away." **3** And when Moses heard this wicked thing, his anger was kindled against the Egyptian, and he turned this way and the other, and when he saw there was no man there, he struck the Egyptian, and hid him in the sand, and delivered the Hebrew from the hand of him that struck him. **4** And the Hebrew went to his house, and Moses returned to his home, and went out and came back to the king's house. **5** And when the man had returned home, he thought of repudiating his wife, for it was not right in the house of Jacob for any man to come to his wife after she had been defiled. **6** And the woman went and told her brothers, and the woman's brothers sought to slay him, and he fled to his house and escaped. **7** And on the second day Moses went out to his brothers, and saw, and behold, two men were quarreling, and he said to the wicked one, "Why do you strike your neighbor?" **8** And he answered him and said to him, "Who has set you for a prince and judge over us? do you think to slay me as you slew the Egyptian?" and Moses was afraid, and he said, "Surely the thing is known?" **9** And Pharaoh heard of this affair and he ordered Moses to be slain, so God sent His messenger and he appeared to Pharaoh in the likeness of a captain of the guard. **10** And the messenger of the Lord took the sword from the hand of the captain of the guard, and took his head off with it, for the likeness of the captain of the guard was turned into the likeness of Moses. **11** And the messenger of the Lord took hold of the right hand of Moses, and brought him out from Egypt, and placed him from outside the borders of Egypt, a distance of forty days' journey. **12** And only his brother Aaron remained in the land of Egypt, and he prophesied to the sons of Israel, saying, **13** "Thus says the Lord God of your ancestors: Throw away, each man, the abominations of his eyes, and do not defile yourselves with the idols of Egypt." **14** And the sons of Israel rebelled and would not listen to Aaron at that time. **15** And the Lord thought to destroy them were it not that the Lord remembered the covenant which He had made with Abraham, Isaac, and Jacob. **16** In those days the hand of Pharaoh continued to be severe against the sons of Israel, and he crushed and oppressed them until the time when God sent out His word and took notice of them.

CHAPTER 72

1 And it was in those days that there was a great war between the children of Cush and the children of the east and Aram, and they rebelled against the king of Cush in whose hands they were. **2** So Kikianus king of Cush went out with all the children of Cush, a people [as] numerous as the sand, and he went to fight against Aram and the children of the east, to bring them under subjection. **3** And when Kikianus went out, he left Balaam the magician, with his two sons, to guard the city, and the lowest sort of the people of the land. **4** So Kikianus went out to Aram and the children of the east, and he fought against them and struck them, and they all fell down wounded before Kikianus and his people. **5** And he took many of them [as] captives, and he brought them under subjection as at first, and he encamped on their land to take tribute from them as usual. **6** And Balaam the son of Beor, when the king of Cush had left him to guard the city and the poor of the city, he rose up and advised with the people of the land to rebel against King Kikianus, not to let him enter the city when he should come home. **7** And the people of the land listened to him, and they swore to him, and they made him king over them and his two sons for captains of the army. **8** So they rose up and raised the walls of the city at the two corners, and they built an exceedingly strong building. **9** And at the third corner they dug ditches without number between the city and the river which surrounded the whole land of Cush, and they made the waters of the river burst out there. **10** At the fourth corner they collected numerous serpents by their incantations and enchantments, and they fortified the city and dwelt therein, and no one went out or in before them. **11** And Kikianus fought against Aram and the children of the east and he subdued them as before, and they gave him their usual tribute, and he went and returned to his land. **12** And when Kikianus the king of Cush approached his city and all the captains of the forces with him, they lifted up their eyes and saw that the walls of the city were built up and greatly elevated, so the men were astonished at this. **13** And they said to one another, "It is because they saw that we were delayed in battle, and were greatly afraid of us, therefore they have done this thing, and raised the city walls, and fortified them so that the kings of Canaan might not come in battle against them." **14** So the king and the troops approached the city door, and they looked up, and behold, all the gates of the city were closed, and they called out to the sentinels, saying, "Open to us [so] that we may enter the city." **15** But the sentinels refused to open to them by the order of Balaam the magician, their king; they did not permit them to enter their city. **16** So they raised a battle with them opposite the city gate, and one hundred and thirty men of the army of Kikianus fell on that day. **17** And on the next day they continued to fight, and they fought at the side of the river; they endeavored to pass but were not able, so some of them sank in the pits and died. **18** So the king ordered them to cut down trees to make rafts on which they might pass to them, and they did so. **19** And when they came to the place of the ditches, the waters revolved by mills, and two hundred men on ten rafts were drowned. **20** And on the third day they came to fight at the side where the serpents were, but they could not approach there, for the serpents slew one hundred and seventy of their men, and they ceased fighting against Cush, and they besieged Cush for nine years—no person came out or in. **21** At the time that the war and the siege were against Cush, Moses fled from Egypt from Pharaoh who sought to kill him for having slain the Egyptian. **22** And Moses was eighteen years old when he fled from Egypt from the presence of Pharaoh, and he fled and escaped to the camp of Kikianus, which at that time was besieging Cush. **23** And Moses was nine years in the camp of Kikianus king of Cush, all the time that they were besieging Cush, and Moses went out and came in with them. **24** And the king, and princes, and all the fighting men loved Moses, for he was great and worthy; his stature was like a noble lion, his face was like the sun, and his strength was like that of a lion, and he was a counselor to the king. **25** And at the end of nine years, Kikianus was seized with a mortal disease, and his sickness prevailed over him, and he died on the seventh day. **26** So his servants embalmed him, and carried him, and buried him opposite the city gate to the north of the land of Egypt. **27** And they built an elegant, strong, and high building over him, and they placed great stones below. **28** And the king's scribes engraved on those stones all the might of their King Kikianus and all his battles which he had fought; behold, they are written there at this day. **29** Now after the death of Kikianus king of Cush it grieved his men and troops greatly on account of the war, **30** so they said to one another, "Give us counsel [regarding] what we are to do at this time, as we have resided in the wilderness away from our homes [for] nine years. **31** If we say we will fight against the city, many of us will fall wounded or killed, and if we remain here in the siege we will also die. **32** For now all the kings of Aram and of the children of the east will hear that our king is dead, and they will suddenly attack us in a hostile manner, and will fight against us, and leave no remnant of us. **33** Now therefore, let us go and make a king over us, and let us remain in the siege until the city is delivered up to us." **34** And on that day they wished to choose a man for king from the army of Kikianus, and they found no object of their choice comparable to Moses to reign over them. **35** And they hastened, and stripped off each man's garments, and cast them on the ground, and they made a great heap and placed Moses thereon. **36** And they rose up, and blew with trumpets, and called out before him, and said, "May the king live, may the king live!" **37** And all the people and nobles swore to him to give him Adoniah the queen, the Cushite, wife of Kikianus, for a wife, and they made Moses king over them on that day. **38** And all the people of Cush issued a proclamation on that day, saying, "Every man must give something to Moses of what is in his possession." **39** And they spread out a sheet on the heap and every man cast something into it of what he had: one a gold earring and the other a coin. **40** The children of Cush also cast onyx stones, bdellium, pearls, and marble on the heap for Moses—also silver and gold in great abundance. **41** And Moses took all the silver and gold, all the vessels, and the bdellium and onyx stones, which all the children of Cush had given to him, and he placed them among his treasures. **42** And on that day Moses reigned over the children of Cush in the place of Kikianus king of Cush.

CHAPTER 73

1 In the fifty-fifth year of the reign of Pharaoh king of Egypt, that is in the one hundred and fifty-seventh year of the Israelites going down into Egypt, Moses reigned in Cush. **2** Moses was twenty-seven years old when he began to reign over Cush, and he reigned forty years. **3** And the Lord granted Moses favor and grace in the eyes of all the children of Cush, and the children of Cush loved him exceedingly, so Moses was favored by the Lord and by men. **4** And in the seventh day of his reign, all the children of Cush assembled, and came before Moses, and bowed down to him to the ground. **5** And all the children spoke together in the presence of the king, saying, "Give us counsel that we may see what is to be done to this city. **6** For it is now nine years that we have been besieging around the city and have not seen our children and our wives." **7** So the king answered them, saying, "If you will listen to my voice in all that I will command you, then the Lord will give the city into our hands and we will subdue it. **8** For if we fight with them as in the former battle which we had with them before the death of Kikianus, many of us will fall down wounded as before. **9** Now therefore, behold, here is counsel for you in this matter: if you will listen to my voice, then the city will be delivered into our hands." **10** So all the forces answered the king, saying, "All that our lord will command—that we will do." **11** And Moses said to them, "Pass through and proclaim a voice in the whole camp to all the people, saying, **12** Thus says the king, Go into the forest and bring with you of the young ones of the stork—each man [must have] a young one in his hand. **13** And any person transgressing the word of the king, who will not bring his young one, he will die, and the king will take all belonging to him. **14** And when you will bring them, they will be in your keeping; you will rear them until they grow up, and you will teach them to dart on, as is the way of the young ones of the hawk." **15** So all the children of Cush heard the words of Moses, and they rose up and caused a proclamation to be issued throughout the camp, saying, **16** "To you—all the children of Cush: the king's order is that you all go to the forest together and catch the young storks there; each man [must have] his young one in his hand, and you will bring them home. **17** And any person violating the order of the king will die, and the king will take all that belongs to him." **18** And all the people did so, and they went out to the wood, and climbed the fir trees, and caught—each man [with] a young one in his hand—all the young of the storks, and they brought them into the desert, and reared them by order of the king, and taught them to dart on, similar to the young hawks. **19** And after the young storks were reared, the king ordered them to be starved for three days, and all the people did so. **20** And on the third day, the king said to them, "Strengthen yourselves and become valiant men, and each man put on his armor, and gird his sword on him, and each man ride his horse, and each take his young stork in his hand. **21** And we will rise up and fight against the city at the place where the serpents are"; and all the people did as the king had ordered. **22** And each man took his young one in his hand, and they went away, and when they came to the place of the serpents, the king said to them, "Each man send out his young stork on the serpents." **23** And each man sent out his young stork at the king's order, and the young storks ran on the serpents, and devoured them all, and destroyed them out of that place. **24** And when the king and people had seen that all the serpents were destroyed in that place, all the people set up a great shout. **25** And they approached, and fought against the city, and took it, and subdued it, and they entered the city. **26** And there died on that day one thousand and one hundred men of the people of the city—all that inhabited the city—but of the people besieging, not [even] one died. **27** So all the children of Cush each went to his home, to his wife and children, and to all belonging to him. **28** And Balaam the magician, when he saw that the city was taken, he opened the gate and he and his two sons and eight brothers fled and returned to Egypt, to Pharaoh king of Egypt. **29** They are the sorcerers and magicians who are mentioned in the Scroll of the Law, standing against Moses when the Lord brought the plagues on Egypt. **30** So Moses took the city by his wisdom, and the children of Cush placed him on the throne instead of Kikianus king of Cush. **31** And they placed the royal crown on his head, and they gave him Adoniah the Cushite queen, wife of Kikianus, for a wife. **32** And Moses feared the Lord God of his fathers, so that he did not come to her, nor did he turn his eyes to her, **33** for Moses remembered how Abraham had made his servant Eliezer swear, saying to him, "You will not take a woman from the daughters of Canaan for my son Isaac." **34** Also what Isaac did when Jacob had fled from his brother, when he commanded him, saying, "You will not take a wife from the daughters of Canaan, nor make alliance with any of the children of Ham. **35** For the Lord our God gave Ham, the son of Noah, and his children, and all his seed, as slaves to the children of Shem, and to the children of Japheth, and to their seed after them for slaves—agelong." **36** Therefore Moses did not turn his heart nor his eyes to the wife of Kikianus all the days that he reigned over Cush. **37** And Moses feared the Lord his God all his life, and Moses walked before the Lord in truth, with all his heart and soul; he did not turn from the right way all the days of his life; he did not decline from the way, either to the right or to the left, in which Abraham, Isaac, and Jacob had walked. **38** And Moses strengthened himself in the kingdom of the children of Cush, and he guided the children of Cush with his usual wisdom, and Moses prospered in his kingdom. **39** And at that time Aram and the children of the east heard that Kikianus king of Cush had died, so Aram and the children of the east rebelled against Cush in those days. **40** And Moses gathered all the children of Cush, a people very mighty, about thirty thousand men, and he went out to fight with Aram and the children of the east. **41** And they went at first to the children of the east, and when the children of the east heard their report, they went to meet them, and engaged in battle with them. **42** And the war was severe against the children of the east, so the Lord gave all the children of the east into the hand of Moses, and about three hundred men fell down slain. **43** And all the children of the east turned back and retreated, so Moses and the children of Cush followed them, and subdued them, and put a tax on them, as was their custom. **44** So Moses and all the people with him passed from there to the land of Aram for battle. **45** And the people of Aram also went to meet them, and they fought against them, and the Lord delivered them into the hand of Moses, and many of the men of Aram fell down wounded. **46** And Aram were also subdued by Moses and the people of Cush, and also gave their usual tax. **47** And Moses brought Aram and the children of the east under subjection to the children of Cush; and Moses and all the people who were with him turned to the land of Cush. **48** And Moses strengthened himself in the kingdom of the children of Cush, and the Lord was with him, and all the children of Cush were afraid of him.

CHAPTER 74

1 In the end of years Saul king of Edom died, and Ba'al Chanan the son of Achbor reigned in his place. **2** In the sixteenth year of the reign of Moses over Cush, Ba'al Chanan the son of Achbor reigned in the land of Edom over all the children of Edom for thirty-eight years. **3** In his days Moab rebelled against the power of Edom, having been under Edom since the days of Hadad the son of Bedad who struck them and Midian and brought Moab under subjection to Edom. **4** And when Ba'al Chanan the son of Achbor reigned over Edom, all the children of Moab withdrew their allegiance from Edom. **5** And Angeas king of Africa died in those days, and his son Azdrubal reigned in his stead. **6** And in those days Janeas king of the children of Chittim died, and they buried him in his temple which he had built for a residence for himself in the plain of Canopia, and Latinus reigned in his stead. **7** In the twenty-second year of the reign of Moses over the children of Cush, Latinus reigned over the children of Chittim forty-five years. **8** And he also built a great and mighty tower for himself, and he built an elegant temple for his residence therein, to conduct his government, as was the custom. **9** In the third year of his reign he caused a proclamation to be made to all his skillful men who made many ships for him. **10** And Latinus assembled all his forces, and they came in ships, and went therein to fight with Azdrubal son of Angeas, king of Africa, and they came to Africa and engaged in battle with Azdrubal and his army. **11** And Latinus prevailed over Azdrubal, and Latinus took from Azdrubal the aqueduct which his father had brought from the children of Chittim when he took Janiah the daughter of Uzi for a wife, so Latinus overthrew the bridge of the aqueduct, and struck the whole army of Azdrubal [with] a severe blow. **12** And the remaining strong men of Azdrubal strengthened themselves, and their hearts were filled with envy, and they courted death, and again engaged in battle with Latinus king of Chittim. **13** And the battle was severe on all the men of Africa, and they all fell wounded before Latinus and his people, and Azdrubal the king also fell in that battle. **14** And King Azdrubal had a very beautiful daughter whose name was Ushpezena, and all the men of Africa embroidered her likeness on their garments on account of her great beauty and attractive appearance. **15** And the men of Latinus saw Ushpezena, the daughter of Azdrubal, and praised her to Latinus, their king. **16**

And Latinus ordered her to be brought to him, and Latinus took Ushpezena for a wife, and he turned back on his way to Chittim. **17** And it was after the death of Azdrubal son of Angeas, when Latinus had turned back to his land from the battle, that all the inhabitants of Africa rose up and took Anibal the son of Angeas, the younger brother of Azdrubal, and made him king over the whole land of Africa instead of his brother. **18** And when he reigned, he resolved to go to Chittim to fight with the children of Chittim, to avenge the cause of his brother Azdrubal and the cause of the inhabitants of Africa, and he did so. **19** And he made many ships, and he came therein with his whole army, and he went to Chittim. **20** So Anibal fought with the children of Chittim, and the children of Chittim fell wounded before Anibal and his army, and Anibal avenged his brother's cause. **21** And Anibal continued the war for eighteen years with the children of Chittim, and Anibal dwelt in the land of Chittim and encamped there for a long time. **22** And Anibal struck the children of Chittim very severely, and he slew their great men and princes, and he struck about eighty thousand men of the rest of the people. **23** And at the end of days and years, Anibal returned to his land of Africa, and he reigned securely in the place of his brother Azdrubal.

CHAPTER 75

1 At that time, in the one hundred and eightieth year of the Israelites going down into Egypt, there went out from Egypt valiant men, thirty thousand on foot, from the sons of Israel, who were all of the tribe of Joseph, of the children of Ephraim the son of Joseph. **2** For they said the period was completed which the Lord had appointed to the sons of Israel in the times of old, which he had spoken to Abraham. **3** And these men girded themselves, and each man put his sword at his side, and every man [put] his armor on him, and they trusted in their strength, and they went out together from Egypt with a mighty hand. **4** But they brought no provision for the road, only silver and gold; they did not even bring bread for that day in their hands, for they thought of getting their provision for pay from the Philistines, and if not, they would take it by force. **5** And these men were very mighty and valiant men: one man could pursue one thousand and two could rout ten thousand, so they trusted in their strength and went together as they were. **6** And they directed their course toward the land of Gath, and they went down and found the shepherds of Gath feeding the cattle of the children of Gath. **7** And they said to the shepherds, "Give us some of the sheep for pay [so] that we may eat, for we are hungry, for we have eaten no bread this day." **8** And the shepherds said, "Are they our sheep or cattle that we should give them to you even for pay?" so the children of Ephraim approached to take them by force. **9** And the shepherds of Gath shouted over them that their cry was heard at a distance, so all the children of Gath went out to them. **10** And when the children of Gath saw the evil doings of the children of Ephraim, they returned and assembled the men of Gath, and each man put on his armor and came out to the children of Ephraim for battle. **11** And they engaged with them in the Valley of Gath, and the battle was severe, and they struck from each other a great many on that day. **12** And on the second day the children of Gath sent to all the cities of the Philistines [so] that they should come to their aid, saying, **13** "Come up to us and help us [so] that we may strike the children of Ephraim who have come out from Egypt to take our cattle and to fight against us without cause." **14** Now the souls of the children of Ephraim were exhausted with hunger and thirst, for they had eaten no bread for three days. And forty thousand men went out from the cities of the Philistines to the assistance of the men of Gath. **15** And these men were engaged in battle with the children of Ephraim, and the Lord delivered the children of Ephraim into the hands of the Philistines. **16** And they struck all the children of Ephraim—all who had gone out from Egypt; none were remaining except ten men who had run away from the engagement. **17** For this calamity was from the Lord against the children of Ephraim, for they transgressed the word of the Lord in going out from Egypt before the period had arrived which the Lord in the days of old had appointed to Israel. **18** And there also fell a great many of the Philistines, about twenty thousand men, and their brothers carried them and buried them in their cities. **19** And the slain of the children of Ephraim remained forsaken in the Valley of Gath for many days and years, and were not brought to burial, and the valley was filled with men's bones. **20** And the men who had escaped from the battle came to Egypt and told all the sons of Israel all that had befallen them. **21** And their father Ephraim mourned over them for many days, and his brothers came to console him. **22** And he came to his wife and she bore a son, and he called his name Beriah, for she was unfortunate in his house.

CHAPTER 76

1 And Moses the son of Amram was still king in the land of Cush in those days, and he prospered in his kingdom, and he conducted the government of the children of Cush in justice, in righteousness, and [in] integrity. **2** And all the children of Cush loved Moses all the days that he reigned over them, and all the inhabitants of the land of Cush were greatly afraid of him. **3** And in the fortieth year of the reign of Moses over Cush, Moses was sitting on the royal throne while Adoniah the queen was before him, and all the nobles were sitting around him. **4** And Adoniah the queen said before the king and the princes, "What is this thing which you, the children of Cush, have done for this long time? **5** Surely you know that for forty years that this man has reigned over Cush he has not approached me, nor has he served the gods of the children of Cush. **6** Now therefore, hear, O you children of Cush, and let this man no longer reign over you as he is not of our flesh. **7** Behold, my son Menacrus is grown up: let him reign over you, for it is better for you to serve the son of your lord, than to serve a stranger, a slave of the king of Egypt." **8** And all the people and nobles of the children of Cush heard the words which Adoniah the queen had spoken in their ears. **9** And all the people were preparing until the evening, and in the morning, they rose up early and made Menacrus, son of Kikianus, king over them. **10** And all the children of Cush were afraid to stretch out their hand against Moses, for the Lord was with Moses, and the children of Cush remembered the oath which they swore to Moses; therefore, they did no harm to him. **11** But the children of Cush gave many presents to Moses and sent him from them with great honor **12** So Moses went out from the land of Cush, and went home and ceased to reign over Cush, and Moses was sixty-six years old when he went out of the land of Cush, for the thing was from the Lord, for the period had arrived which He had appointed in the days of old, to bring out Israel from the affliction of the children of Ham. **13** So Moses went to Midian, for he was afraid to return to Egypt on account of Pharaoh, and he went and sat at a well of water in Midian. **14** And the seven daughters of Reuel the Midianite went out to feed their father's flock. **15** And they came to the well and drew water to water their father's flock. **16** So the shepherds of Midian came and drove them away, and Moses rose up, and helped them, and watered the flock. **17** And they came home to their father Reuel and told him what Moses did for them. **18** And they said, "An Egyptian man has delivered us from the hands of the shepherds; he drew up water for us and watered the flock." **19** And Reuel said to his daughters, "And where is he? Why have you left the man?" **20** And Reuel sent for him, and fetched him, and brought him home, and he ate bread with him. **21** And Moses related to Reuel that he had fled from Egypt, and that he reigned over Cush [for] forty years, and that afterward they had taken the government from him and had sent him away in peace with honor and with presents. **22** And when Reuel had heard the words of Moses, Reuel said within himself, "I will put this man into the prison-house, whereby I will conciliate the children of Cush, for he has fled from them." **23** And they took and put him into the prison-house, and Moses was in prison [for] ten years, and while Moses was in the prison-house, Zipporah the daughter of Reuel took pity over him, and supported him with bread and water all the time. **24** And all the sons of Israel were yet in the land of Egypt serving the Egyptians in all manner of hard work, and the hand of Egypt continued in severity over the sons of Israel in those days. **25** At that time the Lord struck Pharaoh king of Egypt, and he was afflicted with the plague of leprosy from the sole of his foot to the crown of his head; this plague was from the Lord on Pharaoh king of Egypt at that time, owing to the cruel treatment of the sons of Israel. **26** For the Lord had listened to the prayer of His people, the sons of Israel, and their cry reached Him on account of their hard work. **27** Still His anger did not turn from them, and the hand of Pharaoh was still stretched out against the sons of Israel, and Pharaoh hardened his neck before the Lord, and increased his yoke over the sons of Israel, and embittered their lives with all manner of hard work. **28** And when the Lord had inflicted the plague on Pharaoh

king of Egypt, he asked his wise men and sorcerers to cure him. **29** And his wise men and sorcerers said to him that if the blood of little children were put into the wounds he would be healed. **30** And Pharaoh listened to them and sent his ministers to Goshen to the sons of Israel to take their little children. **31** And Pharaoh's ministers went and took the infants of the sons of Israel from the bosoms of their mothers by force, and they brought them to Pharaoh daily, a child each day, and the physicians killed them and applied them to the plague; thus they did all the days. **32** And the number of the children which Pharaoh slew was three hundred and seventy-five. **33** But the Lord did not listen to the physicians of the king of Egypt, and the plague went on increasing mightily. **34** And Pharaoh was afflicted with that plague [for] ten years, yet the heart of Pharaoh was [still] more hardened against the sons of Israel. **35** And at the end of ten years the Lord continued to afflict Pharaoh with destructive plagues. **36** And the Lord struck him with a bad tumor and sickness of the stomach, and that plague turned to a severe boil. **37** At that time the two ministers of Pharaoh came from the land of Goshen where all the sons of Israel were, and went to the house of Pharaoh, and said to him, "We have seen the sons of Israel slackened in their work and negligent in their labor." **38** And when Pharaoh heard the words of his ministers, his anger was kindled against the sons of Israel exceedingly, for he was greatly grieved at his bodily pain. **39** And he answered and said, "Now that the sons of Israel know that I am sick, they turn and scoff at us; now therefore, harness my chariot for me, and I will go to Goshen myself and will see the scoff of the sons of Israel with which they are deriding me"; so his servants harnessed the chariot for him. **40** And they took him and made him ride on a horse, for he was not able to ride by himself; **41** And he took ten horsemen and ten footmen with him and went to the sons of Israel, to Goshen. **42** And when they had come to the border of Egypt, the king's horse passed into a narrow place, elevated in the hollow part of the vineyard, fenced on both sides, the low, plain country being on the other side. **43** And the horses ran rapidly in that place and pressed each other, and the other horses pressed the king's horse. **44** And the king's horse fell into the low plain while the king was riding on it, and when he fell, the chariot turned over the king's face and the horse lay on the king, and the king cried out, for his flesh was very sore. **45** And the flesh of the king was torn from him, and his bones were broken, and he could not ride, for this thing was from the Lord to him, for the Lord had heard the cries of His people, the sons of Israel, and their affliction. **46** And his servants carried him on their shoulders, a little at a time, and they brought him back to Egypt, and the horsemen who were with him also came back to Egypt. **47** And they placed him in his bed, and the king knew that his end had come to die, so Aparanith the queen, his wife, came and cried before the king, and the king wept a great weeping with her. **48** And all his nobles and servants came on that day, and saw the king in that affliction, and wept a great weeping with him. **49** And the princes of the king and all his counselors advised the king to cause one to reign in his stead in the land, whomsoever he should choose from his sons. **50** And the king had three sons and two daughters which Aparanith the queen, his wife, had borne to him besides the king's children of concubines. **51** And these were their names: the firstborn Othri, the second Adikam, and the third Morion, and their sisters, the name of the elder Bathia and of the other Acuzi. **52** And Othri, the firstborn of the king, was an idiot, precipitate and hurried in his words. **53** But Adikam was a cunning and wise man and knowing in all the wisdom of Egypt, but of unseemly aspect, thick in flesh, and very short in stature; his height was one cubit. **54** And when the king saw his son Adikam intelligent and wise in all things, the king resolved that he should be king in his stead after his death. **55** And he took a wife for him, Gedudah daughter of Abilot, and he was ten years old, and she bore four sons to him. **56** And afterward he went and took three wives and begot eight sons and three daughters. **57** And the disorder greatly prevailed over the king, and his flesh stank like the flesh of a carcass cast on the field in summertime, during the heat of the sun. **58** And when the king saw that his sickness had greatly strengthened itself over him, he ordered his son Adikam to be brought to him, and they made him king over the land in his place. **59** And at the end of three years, the king died in shame, disgrace, and disgust, and his servants carried him and buried him in the tomb of the kings of Egypt in Zoan Mizraim. **60** But they did not embalm him as was usual with kings, for his flesh was putrid, and they could not approach to embalm him on account of the stench, so they buried him in haste. ⁶¹ For this calamity was from the Lord to him, for the Lord had paid him back evil for the evil which he had done to Israel in his days. ⁶² And he died with terror and with shame, and his son Adikam reigned in his place.

CHAPTER 77

¹ Adikam was twenty years old when he reigned over Egypt; he reigned four years. ² In the two hundred and sixth year of Israel's going down to Egypt Adikam reigned over Egypt, but he did not continue as long in his reign over Egypt as his fathers had continued their reigns. ³ For his father Melol reigned ninety-four years in Egypt, but he was sick [for] ten years and died, for he had been wicked before the Lord. ⁴ And all the Egyptians called the name of Adikam Pharaoh like the name of his fathers, as was their custom to do in Egypt. ⁵ And all the wise men of Pharaoh called the name of Adikam Ahuz ([he] is called Ahuz for short in the Egyptian language). ⁶ And Adikam was exceedingly ugly, and he was a cubit and a span, and he had a great beard which reached to the soles of his feet. ⁷ And Pharaoh sat on his father's throne to reign over Egypt, and he conducted the government of Egypt in his wisdom. ⁸ And while he reigned, he exceeded his father and all the preceding kings in wickedness, and he increased his yoke over the sons of Israel. ⁹ And he went with his servants to Goshen, to the sons of Israel, and he strengthened the labor over them and he said to them, "Complete your work—each day's task—and do not let your hands slacken from our work from this day forward as you did in the days of my father." ¹⁰ And he placed officers over them from among the sons of Israel, and over these officers he placed taskmasters from among his servants. ¹¹ And he placed over them a measure of bricks for them to do according to that number, day by day, and he turned back and went to Egypt. ¹² At that time the taskmasters of Pharaoh ordered the officers of the sons of Israel according to the command of Pharaoh, saying, ¹³ "Thus says Pharaoh: Do your work each day, and finish your task, and observe the daily measure of bricks; do not diminish anything. ¹⁴ And it will come to pass that if you are deficient in your daily bricks, I will put your young children in their place." ¹⁵ And the taskmasters of Egypt did so in those days as Pharaoh had ordered them. ¹⁶ And whenever any deficiency was found in the sons of Israel's measure of their daily bricks, the taskmasters of Pharaoh would go to the wives of the sons of Israel and take infants of the sons of Israel according to the number of deficient bricks; they would take them by force from their mother's laps and put them in the building instead of the bricks ¹⁷ while their fathers and mothers were crying over them and weeping when they heard the weeping voices of their infants in the wall of the building. ¹⁸ And the taskmasters prevailed over Israel [so] that the Israelites should place their [own] children in the building, so that a man placed his son in the wall and put mortar over him while his eyes wept over him and his tears ran down on his child. ¹⁹ And the taskmasters of Egypt did so to the babies of Israel for many days, and no one pitied or had compassion over the babies of the sons of Israel. ²⁰ And the number of all the children killed in the building was two hundred and seventy, some whom they had built on instead of the bricks which had been left deficient by their fathers, and some whom they had drawn out dead from the building. ²¹ And the labor imposed on the sons of Israel in the days of Adikam exceeded in hardship that which they performed in the days of his father. ²² And the sons of Israel sighed every day on account of their heavy work, for they had said to themselves, "Behold, when Pharaoh will die, his son will rise up and lighten our work!" ²³ But they increased the latter work more than the former, and the sons of Israel sighed at this and their cry ascended to God on account of their labor. ²⁴ And in those days God heard the voice of the sons of Israel and their cry, and God remembered His covenant with them which He had made with Abraham, Isaac, and Jacob. ²⁵ And God saw the burden of the sons of Israel and their heavy work in those days, and He determined to deliver them. ²⁶ And Moses the son of Amram was still confined in the dungeon in those days, in the house of Reuel the Midianite, and Zipporah the daughter of Reuel secretly supported him with food day by day. ²⁷ And Moses was confined in the dungeon in the house of Reuel for ten years. ²⁸ And at the end of ten years, which was the first year of the reign of Pharaoh over Egypt in the place of his father, ²⁹ Zipporah said to her father Reuel, "No person inquires or seeks after the Hebrew man whom you bound in prison now ten years. ³⁰ Now therefore, if it seems good in your sight, let us send and see whether he is living or dead," but her father did not know that she had supported him. ³¹ And her father Reuel answered and said to her, "Has such a thing ever happened that a man should be shut up in a prison without food for ten years, and that he should live?" ³² And Zipporah answered her father, saying, "Surely you have heard that the God of the Hebrews is great and awful, and does wonders for them at all times. ³³ It was He who delivered Abraham from Ur of the Chaldeans, and Isaac from the sword of his father, and Jacob from the Messenger of the Lord who wrestled with him at the ford of Jabbuk. ³⁴ He has also done many things with this man: He delivered him from the river in Egypt, and from the sword of Pharaoh, and from the children of Cush—so He can also deliver him from famine and make him live." ³⁵ And the thing seemed good in the sight of Reuel, so he did according to the word of his daughter and sent to the dungeon to ascertain what became of Moses. ³⁶ And he saw, and behold, the man Moses was living in the dungeon, standing on his feet, praising and praying to the God of his ancestors. ³⁷ And Reuel commanded Moses to be brought out of the dungeon, so they shaved him, and he changed his prison garments and ate bread. ³⁸ And afterward Moses went into the garden of Reuel which was behind the house, and there he prayed to the Lord his God who had done mighty wonders for him. ³⁹ And it was that while he prayed, he looked opposite to him, and behold, a sapphire stick was placed in the ground, which was planted in the midst of the garden. ⁴⁰ And he approached the stick and looked, and behold, the Name of the Lord God of Hosts was engraved thereon, written and developed on the stick. ⁴¹ And he read it, and stretched out his hand, and plucked it like a forest tree from the thicket, and the stick was in his hand. ⁴² And this is the stick with which all the works of our God were performed after He had created the heavens and earth, and all the host of them, seas, rivers, and all their fishes. ⁴³ And when God had driven Adam from the garden of Eden, he took the stick in his hand and went and tilled the ground from which he was taken. ⁴⁴ And the stick came down to Noah and was given to Shem and his descendants until it came into the hand of Abraham the Hebrew. ⁴⁵ And when Abraham had given all he had to his son Isaac, he also gave this stick to him. ⁴⁶ And when Jacob had fled to Padan-Aram, he took it into his hand, and when he returned to his father, he had not left it behind him. ⁴⁷ Also when he went down to Egypt, he took it into his hand and gave it to Joseph, one portion above his brothers, for Jacob had taken it by force from his brother Esau. ⁴⁸ And after the death of Joseph, the nobles of Egypt came into the house of Joseph, and the stick came into the hand of Reuel the Midianite, and when he went out of Egypt, he took it in his hand and planted it in his garden. ⁴⁹ And all the mighty men of the Kinites tried to pluck it when they endeavored to get his daughter Zipporah, but they were unsuccessful. ⁵⁰ So that stick remained planted in the garden of Reuel until he came who had a right to it and took it. ⁵¹ And when Reuel saw the stick in the hand of Moses, he wondered at it, and he gave him his daughter Zipporah for a wife.

CHAPTER 78

¹ At that time Ba'al Channan son of Achbor, king of Edom, died, and he was buried in his house in the land of Edom. ² And after his death the children of Esau sent to the land of Edom and took a man from there who was in Edom, whose name was Hadad, and they made him king over them in the place of Ba'al Channan, their king. ³ And Hadad reigned over the children of Edom [for] forty-eight years. ⁴ And when he reigned, he resolved to fight against the children of Moab, to bring them under the power of the children of Esau as they were before, but he was not able, because the children of Moab heard this thing, and they rose up and hastened to choose a king over them from among their brothers. ⁵ And afterward they gathered a great people together and sent to their brothers, the children of Ammon, for help to fight against Hadad king of Edom. ⁶ And Hadad heard the thing which the children of Moab had done, and was greatly afraid of them, and refrained from fighting against them. ⁷ In those days Moses the son of Amram took Zipporah the daughter of Reuel, the Midianite, for a wife in Midian. ⁸ And Zipporah walked in the ways of the daughters of Jacob; she was nothing short of the righteousness of Sarah, Rebekah, Rachel, and Leah. ⁹ And Zipporah conceived and bore a son and he called his name Gershom, for he said, "I was a

stranger in a foreign land"; but he did not circumcise his foreskin at the command of his father-in-law Reuel. **10** And she conceived again and bore a son, but circumcised his foreskin, and he called his name Eliezer, for Moses said, "Because the God of my fathers was my help and delivered me from the sword of Pharaoh." **11** And Pharaoh king of Egypt greatly increased the labor of the sons of Israel in those days and continued to make his yoke heavier on the sons of Israel. **12** And he ordered a proclamation to be made in Egypt, saying, "No longer give straw to the people to make bricks with; let them go and gather straw themselves as they can find it. **13** Also, let them give the number of bricks which they must make each day, and diminish nothing from them, for they are idle in their work." **14** And the sons of Israel heard this, and they mourned and sighed, and they cried to the Lord on account of the bitterness of their souls. **15** And the Lord heard the cries of the sons of Israel and saw the oppression with which the Egyptians oppressed them. **16** And the Lord was jealous for His people and His inheritance, and heard their voice, and resolved to take them out of the affliction of Egypt, to give them the land of Canaan for a possession.

CHAPTER 79

1 And in those days Moses was feeding the flock of Reuel the Midianite, his father-in-law, beyond the wilderness of Sin, and the stick which he took from his father-in-law was in his hand. **2** And it came to pass one day that a kid of goats strayed from the flock, and Moses pursued it, and it came to the mountain of God, to Horeb. **3** And when he came to Horeb, the Lord appeared there to him in the bush, and he found the bush burning with fire, but the fire had no power over the bush to consume it. **4** And Moses was greatly astonished at this sight, why the bush was not consumed, and he approached to see this mighty thing, and the Lord called to Moses out of the fire and commanded him to go down to Egypt, to Pharaoh king of Egypt, to send the sons of Israel from his service. **5** And the Lord said to Moses, "Go; return to Egypt, for all those men who sought your life are dead, and you will speak to Pharaoh to send out the sons of Israel from his land." **6** And the Lord commanded him to do signs and wonders in Egypt before the eyes of Pharaoh and the eyes of his subjects in order that they might believe that the Lord had sent him. **7** And Moses listened to all that the Lord had commanded him, and he returned to his father-in-law and told him the thing, and Reuel said to him, "Go in peace." **8** And Moses rose up to go to Egypt, and he took his wife and sons with him, and he was at an inn in the road, and a messenger of God came down and sought an occasion against him. **9** And he wished to kill him on account of his firstborn son, because he had not circumcised him, and had transgressed the covenant which the Lord had made with Abraham. **10** For Moses had listened to the words of his father-in-law which he had spoken to him, [so as] not to circumcise his firstborn son, therefore he did not circumcise him. **11** And Zipporah saw the messenger of the Lord seeking an occasion against Moses, and she knew that this thing was owing to his not having circumcised her son Gershom. **12** And Zipporah hastened and took of the sharp rock stones that were there, and she circumcised her son, and delivered her husband and her son from the hand of the messenger of the Lord. **13** And Aaron the son of Amram, the brother of Moses, was in Egypt walking at the riverside on that day. **14** And the Lord appeared to him in that place, and He said to him, "Go now toward Moses in the wilderness," and he went and met him in the mountain of God, and he kissed him. **15** And Aaron lifted up his eyes and saw Zipporah the wife of Moses and her children, and he said to Moses, "Who are these to you?" **16** And Moses said to him, "They are my wife and sons, which God gave to me in Midian"; and the thing grieved Aaron on account of the woman and her children. **17** And Aaron said to Moses, "Send the woman and her children away that they may go to her father's house," and Moses listened to the words of Aaron, and did so. **18** And Zipporah returned with her children, and they went to the house of Reuel, and remained there until the time arrived when the Lord had visited His people and brought them out from Egypt from the hand of Pharaoh. **19** And Moses and Aaron came to Egypt to the community of the sons of Israel, and they spoke to them all the words of the Lord, and the people rejoiced an exceedingly great rejoicing. **20** And Moses and Aaron rose up early on the next day, and they went to the house of Pharaoh, and they took the stick of God in their hands. **21** And when they

came to the king's gate, two young lions were confined there with iron instruments, and no person went out or came in from before them, unless those whom the king ordered to come, when the conjurers came and withdrew the lions by their incantations, and this brought them to the king. **22** And Moses hastened and lifted up the stick on the lions, and he loosed them, and Moses and Aaron came into the king's house. **23** The lions also came with them in joy, and they followed them and rejoiced as a dog rejoices over his master when he comes from the field. **24** And when Pharaoh saw this thing, he was astonished at it, and he was greatly terrified at the report, for their appearance was like the appearance of the children of God. **25** And Pharaoh said to Moses, "What do you require?" and they answered him, saying, "The Lord God of the Hebrews has sent us to you, to say, Send out My people that they may serve Me." **26** And when Pharaoh heard their words he was greatly terrified before them, and he said to them, "Go today and come back to me tomorrow," and they did according to the word of the king. **27** And when they had gone, Pharaoh sent for Balaam the magician, and to his sons Jannes and Jambres, and to all the magicians, and conjurers, and counselors which belonged to the king, and they all came and sat before the king. **28** And the king told them all the words which Moses and his brother Aaron had spoken to him, and the magicians said to the king, "But how did the men come to you with the lions which were confined at the gate?" **29** And the king said, "Because they lifted up their rod against the lions and loosed them, and came to me, and the lions also rejoiced at them as a dog rejoices to meet his master." **30** And Balaam the son of Beor, the magician, answered the king, saying, "These are nothing other than magicians like ourselves. **31** Now therefore, send for them, and let them come, and we will try them," and the king did so. **32** And in the morning Pharaoh sent for Moses and Aaron to come before the king, and they took the rod of God, and came to the king, and spoke to him, saying, **33** "Thus said the Lord God of the Hebrews: Send My people that they may serve Me." **34** And the king said to them, "But who will believe you that you are the messengers of God and that you come to me by His order? **35** Now therefore, give a wonder or sign in this matter, and then the words which you speak will be believed." **36** And Aaron hastened and threw the rod out of his hand before Pharaoh and before his servants, and the rod turned into a serpent. **37** And the sorcerers saw this, and each man cast his rod on the ground and they became serpents. **38** And the serpent of Aaron's rod lifted up its head and opened its mouth to swallow the rods of the magicians. **39** And Balaam the magician answered and said, "This thing has been from the days of old, that a serpent should swallow its fellow, and that living things devour each other. **40** Now therefore, restore it to a rod as it was at first, and we will also restore our rods as they were at first, and if your rod will swallow our rods, then we will know that the Spirit of God is in you, and if not, you are only a craftsman like ourselves." **41** And Aaron hastened, and stretched out his hand, and caught hold of the serpent's tail, and it became a rod in his hand, and the sorcerers did the same with their rods, and each man took hold of the tail of his serpent, and they became rods as at first. **42** And when they were restored to rods, the rod of Aaron swallowed up their rods. **43** And when the king saw this thing, he ordered the scroll of records that related to the kings of Egypt to be brought, and they brought the scroll of records, the chronicles of the kings of Egypt, in which all the idols of Egypt were inscribed, for they thought of finding the Name of the Lord therein, but they did not find it. **44** And Pharaoh said to Moses and Aaron, "Behold, I have not found the Name of your God written in this scroll, and I do not recognize His Name." **45** And the counselors and wise men answered the king, "We have heard that the God of the Hebrews is a son of the wise, the son of ancient kings." **46** And Pharaoh turned to Moses and Aaron and said to them, "I do not know the Lord whom you have declared; neither will I send His people." **47** And they answered and said to the king, "The Lord God of gods is His Name, and He proclaimed His Name over us from the days of our ancestors, and sent us, saying, Go to Pharaoh and say to him, Send My people that they may serve Me. **48** Now therefore, send us [so] that we may take a journey for three days in the wilderness, and may sacrifice to Him there, for from the days of our going down to Egypt, He has not taken from our hands either burnt-offering, oblation, or sacrifice, and if you will not send us, His anger will be kindled against you, and He will strike Egypt either with the plague or with the sword." **49** And Pharaoh said to them, "Tell me now of His power and His might"; and they said to him, "He created the heavens and the earth, the seas and all their fishes; He formed the light, created the darkness, caused rain on the earth and watered it, and made the herbage and grass to sprout; He created man, and beast, and the animals of the forest, the birds of the air, and the fish of the sea, and by His mouth they live and die. **50** He surely created you in your mother's womb, and put into you the breath of life, and reared you, and placed you on the royal throne of Egypt, and He will take your breath and soul from you, and return you to the ground from where you were taken." **51** And the anger of the king was kindled at their words, and he said to them, "But who among all the gods of the nations can do this? my river is my own, and I have made it for myself." **52** And he drove them from him, and he ordered the labor on Israel to be more severe than it was yesterday and before. **53** And Moses and Aaron went out from the king's presence, and they saw the sons of Israel in an evil condition, for the taskmasters had made their labor exceedingly heavy. **54** And Moses returned to the Lord and said, "Why have you mistreated Your people? for since I came to speak to Pharaoh—the reason You sent me—he has exceedingly mistreated the sons of Israel." **55** And the Lord said to Moses, "Behold, you will see that with an outstretched hand and heavy plagues, Pharaoh will send the sons of Israel from his land." **56** And Moses and Aaron dwelt in Egypt among their brothers, the sons of Israel. **57** And as for the sons of Israel: the Egyptians embittered their lives with the heavy work which they imposed on them.

CHAPTER 80

1 And at the end of two years, the Lord sent Moses to Pharaoh again to bring out the sons of Israel, and to send them out of the land of Egypt. **2** And Moses went and came to the house of Pharaoh, and he spoke to him the words of the Lord who had sent him, but Pharaoh would not listen to the voice of the Lord, and God roused His might in Egypt on Pharaoh and his subjects, and God struck Pharaoh and his people with very great and severe plagues. **3** And the Lord sent by the hand of Aaron and turned all the waters of Egypt into blood, with all their streams and rivers. **4** And when an Egyptian came to drink and draw water, he looked into his pitcher, and behold, all the water was turned into blood; and when he came to drink from his cup, the water in the cup became blood. **5** And when a woman kneaded her dough and cooked her victuals, their appearance was turned to that of blood. **6** And the Lord sent again and caused all their waters to bring out frogs, and all the frogs came into the houses of the Egyptians. **7** And when the Egyptians drank, their bellies were filled with frogs and they danced in their bellies as they dance when in the river. **8** And all their drinking water and cooking water turned to frogs; also, when they lay in their beds their perspiration bred frogs. **9** Notwithstanding all this, the anger of the Lord did not turn from them, and His hand was stretched out against all the Egyptians to strike them with every heavy plague. **10** And He sent and struck their dust to lice, and the lice became in Egypt to the height of two cubits on the earth. **11** The lice were also very numerous in the flesh of man and beast in all the inhabitants of Egypt; the Lord also sent the lice on the king and queen, and it grieved Egypt exceedingly on account of the lice. **12** Notwithstanding this, the anger of the Lord did not turn away, and His hand was still stretched out over Egypt. **13** And the Lord sent all kinds of beasts of the field into Egypt, and they came and destroyed all Egypt—man, and beast, and trees, and all things that were in Egypt. **14** And the Lord sent fiery serpents, scorpions, mice, weasels, toads, together with others creeping in dust— **15** flies, hornets, fleas, bugs, and gnats, each swarm according to its kind. **16** And all reptiles and winged animals according to their kind came to Egypt and grieved the Egyptians exceedingly. **17** And the fleas and flies came into the eyes and ears of the Egyptians. **18** And the hornet came on them and drove them away, and they removed from it into their inner rooms, and it pursued them. **19** And when the Egyptians hid themselves on account of the swarm of animals, they locked their doors after them, and God ordered the Sulanuth, which was in the sea, to come up and go into Egypt. **20** And she had long arms—ten cubits in length of the cubit of a man. **21** And she went on the roofs and uncovered the raftering and flooring, and cut them, and stretched out her arm into the house, and removed the lock and the bolt, and opened the houses of Egypt. **22** Afterward, the swarm of animals came into the houses of Egypt, and the swarm of animals destroyed

the Egyptians, and it grieved them exceedingly. **23** Notwithstanding this, the anger of the Lord did not turn away from the Egyptians, and His hand was yet stretched out against them. **24** And God sent the pestilence, and the pestilence pervaded Egypt, in the horses and donkeys, and in the camels, in herds of oxen and sheep, and in man. **25** And when the Egyptians rose up early in the morning to take their cattle to pasture, they found all their cattle dead. **26** And there remained of the cattle of the Egyptians only one in ten, and of the cattle belonging to Israel in Goshen not one died. **27** And God sent a burning inflammation in the flesh of the Egyptians, which burst their skins, and it became a severe itch in all the Egyptians from the soles of their feet to the crowns of their heads. **28** And many boils were in their flesh [so] that their flesh wasted away until they became rotten and putrid. **29** Notwithstanding this, the anger of the Lord did not turn away, and His hand was still stretched out over all Egypt. **30** And the Lord sent a very heavy hail, which struck their vines, and broke their fruit trees, and dried them up that they fell on them. **31** Also every green herb became dry and perished, for a mingling fire descended amidst the hail; therefore, the hail and the fire consumed all things. **32** Also men and beasts that were found abroad perished by the flames of fire and of the hail, and all the young lions were exhausted. **33** And the Lord sent and brought numerous locusts into Egypt: the Chasel, Salom, Chargol, and Chagole—locusts each after its kind, which devoured all that the hail had left remaining. **34** Then the Egyptians rejoiced at the locusts, although they consumed the produce of the field, and they caught them in abundance and salted them for food. **35** And the Lord turned a mighty wind of the sea which took away all the locusts, even those that were salted, and thrust them into the Red Sea; not one locust remained within the boundaries of Egypt. **36** And God sent darkness over Egypt [so] that the whole land of Egypt and Pathros became dark for three days, so that a man could not see his hand when he lifted it to his mouth. **37** At that time many of the people of Israel died who had rebelled against the Lord, and who would not listen to Moses and Aaron, and did not believe in them, that God had sent them, **38** and who had said, "We will not go out from Egypt lest we perish with hunger in a desolate wilderness," and who would not listen to the voice of Moses. **39** And the Lord plagued them in the three days of darkness, and the Israelites buried them in those days without the Egyptians knowing of them or rejoicing over them. **40** And the darkness was very great in Egypt for three days, and any person who was standing when the darkness came remained standing in his place, and he that was sitting remained sitting, and he that was lying continued lying in the same state, and he that was walking remained sitting on the ground in the same spot; and this thing happened to all the Egyptians until the darkness had passed away. **41** And the days of darkness passed away, and the Lord sent Moses and Aaron to the sons of Israel, saying, "Celebrate your feast and make your Passover, for behold, I come in the midst of the night among all the Egyptians, and I will strike all their firstborn, from the firstborn of a man to the firstborn of a beast, and when I see your Passover, I will pass over you." **42** And the sons of Israel did according to all that the Lord had commanded Moses and Aaron—thus they did in that night. **43** And it came to pass in the middle of the night that the Lord went out in the midst of Egypt and struck all the firstborn of the Egyptians, from the firstborn of man to the firstborn of beast. **44** And Pharaoh rose up in the night, he, and all his servants, and all the Egyptians, and there was a great cry throughout Egypt in that night, for there was not a house in which there was not a corpse. **45** Also the likenesses of the firstborn of Egypt, which were carved in the walls of their houses, were destroyed and fell to the ground. **46** Even the bones of their firstborn, who had died before this and whom they had buried in their houses, were raked up by the dogs of Egypt on that night, and dragged before the Egyptians, and cast before them. **47** And all the Egyptians saw this evil which had suddenly come on them, and all the Egyptians cried out with a loud voice. **48** And all the families of Egypt wept on that night, each man for his son and each man for his daughter, being the firstborn, and the tumult of Egypt was heard at a distance on that night. **49** And Bathia the daughter of Pharaoh went out with the king on that night to seek Moses and Aaron in their houses, and they found them in their houses eating, and drinking, and rejoicing with all Israel. **50** And Bathia said to Moses, "Is this the reward for the good which I have done to you, who have reared you and stretched you out, and you have brought this calamity on me and my father's house?" **51** And Moses said to her, "Surely the

Lord brought ten plagues on Egypt; did any evil accrue to you from any of them? did one of them affect you?" and she said, "No." ⁵² And Moses said to her, "Although you are the firstborn to your mother, you will not die, and no calamity will reach you in the midst of Egypt." ⁵³ And she said, "What advantage is it to me when I see the king, my brother, and all his household and subjects in this calamity, whose firstborn perish with all the firstborn of Egypt?" ⁵⁴ And Moses said to her, "Surely your brother and his household and subjects, the families of Egypt, would not listen to the words of the Lord, therefore this calamity came on them." ⁵⁵ And Pharaoh king of Egypt approached Moses, and Aaron, and some of the sons of Israel who were with them in that place, and he prayed to them, saying, ⁵⁶ "Rise up and take your brothers, all the sons of Israel who are in the land, with their sheep and oxen, and all belonging to them—they will leave nothing remaining; only pray for me to the Lord your God." ⁵⁷ And Moses said to Pharaoh, "Behold, though you are your mother's firstborn, yet do not fear, for you will not die, for the Lord has commanded that you will live in order to show you His great might and strong outstretched arm." ⁵⁸ And Pharaoh ordered the sons of Israel to be sent away, and all the Egyptians strengthened themselves to send them, for they said, "We are all perishing." ⁵⁹ And all the Egyptians sent the Israelites out with great riches—sheep, and oxen, and precious things—according to the oath of the Lord between him and our Father Abraham. ⁶⁰ And the sons of Israel delayed going out at night, and when the Egyptians came to them to bring them out, they said to them, "Are we thieves that we should go out at night?" ⁶¹ And the sons of Israel asked of the Egyptians vessels of silver, and vessels of gold, and garments, and the sons of Israel stripped the Egyptians. ⁶² And Moses hastened, and rose up, and went to the river of Egypt, and brought up the coffin of Joseph from there, and took it with him. ⁶³ Each man [of] the sons of Israel also brought up his father's coffin with him, and each man [brought up] the coffins of his tribe.

CHAPTER 81

¹ And the sons of Israel journeyed from Rameses to Succoth, about six hundred thousand men on foot, besides the little ones and their wives. ² Also a mixed multitude went up with them, and flocks and herds, even many cattle. ³ And the sojourning of the sons of Israel, who dwelt in the land of Egypt in hard labor, was two hundred and ten years. ⁴ And at the end of two hundred and ten years, the Lord brought out the sons of Israel from Egypt with a strong hand. ⁵ And the sons of Israel traveled from Egypt, and from Goshen, and from Rameses, and encamped in Succoth on the fifteenth day of the first month. ⁶ And the Egyptians buried all their firstborn whom the Lord had smitten, and all the Egyptians buried their slain for three days. ⁷ And the sons of Israel traveled from Succoth and encamped in Ethom, at the end of the wilderness. ⁸ And on the third day after the Egyptians had buried their firstborn, many men rose up from Egypt and went after Israel to make them return to Egypt, for they regretted that they had sent the Israelites away from their servitude. ⁹ And one man said to his neighbor, "Surely Moses and Aaron spoke to Pharaoh, saying, We will go a three days' journey in the wilderness and sacrifice to the Lord our God. ¹⁰ Now therefore, let us rise up early in the morning and cause them to return, and it will be that if they return with us to Egypt to their masters, then we will know that there is faith in them, but if they will not return, then we will fight with them and make them come back with great power and a strong hand." ¹¹ And all the nobles of Pharaoh rose up in the morning, and with them about seven hundred thousand men, and they went out from Egypt on that day and came to the place where the sons of Israel were. ¹² And all the Egyptians saw, and behold, Moses, and Aaron, and all the sons of Israel were sitting before Pi-Hahiroth, eating, and drinking, and celebrating the celebration of the Lord. ¹³ And all the Egyptians said to the sons of Israel, "Surely you said, We will go on a journey for three days in the wilderness, and sacrifice to our God, and return. ¹⁴ Now therefore, this day makes five days since you went, why do you not return to your masters?" ¹⁵ And Moses and Aaron answered them, saying, "Because the Lord our God has testified to us, saying, You will never return to Egypt; but we will journey ourselves to a land flowing with milk and honey as the Lord our God had sworn to our ancestors to give to us." ¹⁶ And when the nobles of Egypt saw that the sons of Israel did not listen to them to return to Egypt, they girded themselves

to fight with Israel. ¹⁷ And the Lord strengthened the hearts of the sons of Israel over the Egyptians [so] that they gave them a severe beating, and the battle was severe on the Egyptians, and all the Egyptians fled from before the sons of Israel, for many of them perished by the hand of Israel. ¹⁸ And the nobles of Pharaoh went to Egypt and told Pharaoh, saying, "The sons of Israel have fled and will no longer return to Egypt, and Moses and Aaron spoke to us in this manner." ¹⁹ And Pharaoh heard this thing, and his heart and the hearts of all his subjects were turned against Israel, and they regretted that they had sent Israel; and all the Egyptians advised Pharaoh to pursue the sons of Israel to make them come back to their burdens. ²⁰ And each man said to his brother, "What is this which we have done, that we have sent Israel from our servitude?" ²¹ And the Lord strengthened the hearts of all the Egyptians to pursue the Israelites, for the Lord desired to overthrow the Egyptians in the Red Sea. ²² And Pharaoh rose up and harnessed his chariot, and he ordered all the Egyptians to assemble; not one man was left except the little ones and the women. ²³ And all the Egyptians went out with Pharaoh to pursue the sons of Israel, and the camp of Egypt was an exceedingly large and heavy camp, about one million men. ²⁴ And the whole of this camp went and pursued the sons of Israel to bring them back to Egypt, and they reached them encamping by the Red Sea. ²⁵ And the sons of Israel lifted up their eyes and beheld all the Egyptians pursuing them, and the sons of Israel were greatly terrified at them, and the sons of Israel cried to the Lord. ²⁶ And on account of the Egyptians, the sons of Israel divided themselves into four divisions, and they were divided in their opinions, for they were afraid of the Egyptians, and Moses spoke to each of them. ²⁷ The first division was of the children of Reuben, Simeon, and Issachar, and they resolved to cast themselves into the sea, for they were exceedingly afraid of the Egyptians. ²⁸ And Moses said to them, "Do not fear, stand still and see the salvation of the Lord which He will effect this day for you." ²⁹ The second division was of the children of Zebulun, Benjamin, and Naphtali, and they resolved to go back to Egypt with the Egyptians. ³⁰ And Moses said to them, "Do not fear, for as you have seen the Egyptians this day, so you will see them no more forever." ³¹ The third division was of the children of Judah and Joseph, and they resolved to go to meet the Egyptians to fight with them. ³² And Moses said to them, "Stand in your places, for the Lord will fight for you, and you will remain silent." ³³ And the fourth division was of the children of Levi, Gad, and Asher, and they resolved to go into the midst of the Egyptians to confound them, and Moses said to them, "Remain in your stations and do not fear, only call to the Lord that He may save you out of their hands." ³⁴ After this, Moses rose up from amidst the people, and he prayed to the Lord and said, ³⁵ "O Lord God of the whole earth, save Your people now whom You brought out from Egypt, and do not let the Egyptians boast that power and might are theirs." ³⁶ So the Lord said to Moses, "Why do you cry to Me? speak to the sons of Israel that they will proceed, and you will stretch out your rod on the sea and divide it, and the sons of Israel will pass through it." ³⁷ And Moses did so, and he lifted up his rod on the sea and divided it. ³⁸ And the waters of the sea were divided into twelve parts, and the sons of Israel passed through on foot, with shoes, as a man would pass through a prepared road. ³⁹ And the Lord manifested His wonders to the sons of Israel in Egypt and in the sea by the hand of Moses and Aaron. ⁴⁰ And when the sons of Israel had entered the sea, the Egyptians came after them, and the waters of the sea resumed on them, and they all sank in the water, and not one man was left except Pharaoh, who gave thanks to the Lord and believed in Him; therefore, the Lord did not cause him to perish at that time with the Egyptians. ⁴¹ And the Lord ordered a messenger to take him from among the Egyptians, who cast him on the land of Ninevah and he reigned over it for a long time. ⁴² And on that day the Lord saved Israel from the hand of Egypt, and all the sons of Israel saw that the Egyptians had perished, and they beheld the great hand of the Lord, in what He had performed in Egypt and in the sea. ⁴³ Then Moses and the sons of Israel sang this song to the Lord on the day when the Lord caused the Egyptians to fall before them. ⁴⁴ And all Israel sang in concert, saying, "I will sing to the Lord for He is greatly exalted, || The horse and his rider He has cast into the sea; Behold, it is written in the Scroll of the Law of God." ⁴⁵ After this the sons of Israel proceeded on their journey and encamped in Marah, and the Lord gave to the sons of Israel statutes and judgments in that place in Marah, and the Lord commanded the sons of Israel to walk in all His ways and to serve Him. ⁴⁶ And they journeyed from Marah and came to Elim, and there were twelve springs of water and seventy date trees in Elim, and the children encamped there by the waters. 47 And they journeyed from Elim and came to the wilderness of Sin on the fifteenth day of the second month after their departure from Egypt. 48 At that time the Lord gave the manna to the sons of Israel to eat, and the Lord caused food to rain from Heaven for the sons of Israel day by day. 49 And the sons of Israel ate the manna for forty years, all the days that they were in the wilderness, until they came to the land of Canaan to possess it. 50 And they proceeded from the wilderness of Sin and encamped in Alush. 51 And they proceeded from Alush and encamped in Rephidim. 52 And when the sons of Israel were in Rephidim, Amalek the son of Eliphaz, the son of Esau, the brother of Zepho, came to fight with Israel. 53 And he brought with him eight hundred and one thousand men, magicians and conjurers, and he prepared for battle with Israel in Rephidim. 54 And they carried on a great and severe battle against Israel, and the Lord delivered Amalek and his people into the hands of Moses and the sons of Israel, and into the hand of Joshua the son of Nun, the Ephrathite, the servant of Moses. 55 And the sons of Israel struck Amalek and his people at the edge of the sword, but the battle was very severe on the sons of Israel. 56 And the Lord said to Moses, "Write this thing as a memorial for you in a scroll, and place it in the hand of Joshua the son of Nun, your servant, and you will command the sons of Israel, saying, When you will come to the land of Canaan, you will utterly efface the remembrance of Amalek from under Heaven." 57 And Moses did so, and he took the scroll and wrote on it these words, saying, 58 "Remember what Amalek has done to you in the road when you went out from Egypt, 59 who met you in the road and struck your rear, even those that were feeble behind you when you were faint and weary. 60 Therefore, it will be when the Lord your God will have given you rest from all your surrounding enemies in the land which the Lord your God gives you for an inheritance to possess it, that you will blot out the remembrance of Amalek from under Heaven—you will not forget it. 61 And the king who will have pity on Amalek, or on his memory, or on his seed, behold, I will require it of him, and I will cut him off from among his people." 62 And Moses wrote all these things in a scroll, and he commanded the sons of Israel respecting all these matters.

CHAPTER 82

1 And the sons of Israel proceeded from Rephidim, and they encamped in the wilderness of Sinai in the third month from their going out from Egypt. 2 At that time Reuel the Midianite, the father-in-law of Moses, came with his daughter Zipporah and her two sons, for he had heard of the wonders of the Lord which He had done to Israel, that He had delivered them from the hand of Egypt. 3 And Reuel came to Moses, to the wilderness where he was encamped, where the mountain of God was. 4 And Moses went out to meet his father-in-law with great honor, and all Israel was with him. 5 And Reuel and his children remained among the Israelites for many days, and Reuel knew the Lord from that day forward. 6 And in the third month from the sons of Israel's departure from Egypt, on the sixth day thereof, the Lord gave to Israel the Ten Commandments on Mount Sinai. 7 And all Israel heard all these commands, and all Israel rejoiced exceedingly in the Lord on that day. 8 And the glory of the Lord rested on Mount Sinai, and He called to Moses, and Moses came in the midst of a cloud and ascended the mountain. 9 And Moses was on the mount [for] forty days and forty nights; he ate no bread and drank no water, and the Lord instructed him in the statutes and judgments in order to teach the sons of Israel. 10 And the Lord wrote the Ten Commandments which He had commanded the sons of Israel on two tablets of stone, which He gave to Moses to command the sons of Israel. 11 And at the end of forty days and forty nights, when the Lord had finished speaking to Moses on Mount Sinai, then the Lord gave the tablets of stone to Moses, written with the finger of God. 12 And when the sons of Israel saw that Moses tarried to come down from the mount, they gathered around Aaron, and said, "As for this man Moses, we do not know what has become of him. 13 Now therefore, rise up; make a god for us who will go before us, so that you will not die." 14 And Aaron was greatly afraid of the people, and he ordered them to bring him gold, and he made it into a molten calf for the people. 15 And the Lord said to Moses before he had come down from the mount, "Get down, for your people

whom you brought out from Egypt have corrupted themselves. 16 They have made a molten calf for themselves and have bowed down to it; now therefore, leave Me [so] that I may consume them from off the earth, for they are a stiff-necked people." 17 And Moses implored the countenance of the Lord, and he prayed to the Lord for the people on account of the calf which they had made, and afterward he descended from the mount and in his hands were the two tablets of stone which God had given him to command the Israelites. 18 And when Moses approached the camp and saw the calf which the people had made, the anger of Moses was kindled, and he broke the tablets under the mount. 19 And Moses came to the camp, and he took the calf and burned it with fire, and he ground it until it became fine dust, and scattered it on the water, and gave it to the Israelites to drink. 20 And there died of the people by the swords of each other about three thousand men who had made the calf. 21 And the next day Moses said to the people, "I will go up to the Lord; perhaps I may make atonement for your sins which you have sinned to the Lord." 22 And Moses went up to the Lord again, and he remained with the Lord [for] forty days and forty nights. 23 And during the forty days Moses entreated the Lord in behalf of the sons of Israel, and the Lord listened to the prayer of Moses, and the Lord was entreated of him on behalf of Israel. 24 Then the Lord spoke to Moses to hew two [new] stone tablets and to bring them up to the Lord, who would write on them the Ten Commandments. 25 Now Moses did so, and he came down, and hewed the two tablets, and went up to Mount Sinai to the Lord, and the Lord wrote the Ten Commandments on the tablets. 26 And Moses remained with the Lord yet forty days and forty nights, and the Lord instructed him in statutes and judgments to impart to Israel. 27 And the Lord commanded him respecting the sons of Israel that they should make a sanctuary for the Lord, that His Name might rest therein, and the Lord showed him the likeness of the sanctuary and the likeness of all its vessels. 28 And at the end of the forty days, Moses came down from the mount and the two tablets were in his hand. 29 And Moses came to the sons of Israel and spoke to them all the words of the Lord, and he taught them laws, statutes, and judgments which the Lord had taught him. 30 And Moses told the sons of Israel the word of the Lord, that a sanctuary should be made for Him to dwell among the sons of Israel. 31 And the people rejoiced greatly at all the good which the Lord had spoken to them through Moses, and they said, "We will do all that the Lord has spoken to you." 32 And the people rose up like one man, and they made generous offerings to the sanctuary of the Lord, and each man brought the offering of the Lord for the work of the sanctuary, and for all its service. 33 And all the sons of Israel—each man—brought of all that was found in his possession for the work of the sanctuary of the Lord: gold, silver, and brass, and everything that was serviceable for the sanctuary. 34 And all the wise men who were experienced in work came and made the sanctuary of the Lord according to all that the Lord had commanded, every man in the work in which he had been experienced; and all the wise men in heart made the sanctuary, and its furniture, and all the vessels for the holy service as the Lord had commanded Moses. 35 And the work of the sanctuary of the Dwelling Place was completed at the end of five months, and the sons of Israel did all that the Lord had commanded Moses. 36 And they brought the sanctuary and all its furniture to Moses; like to the representation which the Lord had shown to Moses, so the sons of Israel did. 37 And Moses saw the work, and behold, they did it as the Lord had commanded him, so Moses blessed them.

CHAPTER 83

1 And in the twelfth month, in the twenty-third day of the month, Moses took Aaron and his sons, and he dressed them in their garments, and anointed them, and did to them as the Lord had commanded him, and Moses brought up all the offerings which the Lord had on that day commanded him. 2 Afterward Moses took Aaron and his sons and said to them, "For seven days you will remain at the door of the Dwelling Place, for thus I am commanded." 3 And Aaron and his sons did all that the Lord had commanded them through Moses, and they remained for seven days at the door of the Dwelling Place. 4 And on the eighth day, being the first day of the first month, in the second year from the Israelites' departure from Egypt, Moses erected the sanctuary, and Moses put up all the furniture of the Dwelling Place and all the furniture of the sanctuary, and

lie did all that the Lord had commanded him. 5 And Moses called to Aaron and his sons, and they brought the burnt-offering and the sin offering for themselves and the sons of Israel as the Lord had commanded Moses. 6 On that day the two sons of Aaron, Nadab and Abihu, took strange fire and brought it before the Lord who had not commanded them, and a fire went out from before the Lord and consumed them, and they died before the Lord on that day. 7 Then on the day when Moses had completed to erect the sanctuary, the princes of the sons of Israel began to bring their offerings before the Lord for the dedication of the altar. 8 And each prince brought up their offerings for one day, a prince each day for twelve days. 9 And all the offerings which they brought, each man in his day: one silver charger weighing one hundred and thirty shekels, one silver bowl of seventy shekels after the shekel of the sanctuary, both of them full of fine flour, mingled with oil for a meat offering, 10 one spoon weighing ten shekels of gold, full of incense, 11 one young bullock, one ram, one lamb of the first year for a burnt-offering, 12 and one kid of the goats for a sin offering. 13 And for a sacrifice of a peace offering: two oxen, five rams, five male goats, five lambs of a year old. 14 Thus the twelve princes of Israel did day by day, each man in his day. 15 And it was after this, in the thirteenth day of the month, that Moses commanded the sons of Israel to observe the Passover. 16 And the sons of Israel kept the Passover in its season in the fourteenth day of the month; as the Lord had commanded Moses, so the sons of Israel did. 17 And in the second month, on the first day thereof, the Lord spoke to Moses, saying, 18 "Number the heads of all the males of the sons of Israel from twenty years old and upward, you, and your brother Aaron, and the twelve princes of Israel." 19 And Moses did so, and Aaron came with the twelve princes of Israel, and they numbered the sons of Israel in the wilderness of Sinai. 20 And the numbers of the sons of Israel by the houses of their fathers, from twenty years old and upward, were six hundred and three thousand, five hundred and fifty. 21 But the children of Levi were not numbered among their brothers, the sons of Israel. 22 And the number of all the males of the sons of Israel from one month old and upward was twenty-two thousand, two hundred and seventy-three. 23 And the number of the children of Levi from one month old and above was twenty-two thousand. 24 And Moses placed the priests and the Levites, each man to his service and to his burden, to serve the sanctuary of the Dwelling Place as the Lord had commanded Moses. 25 And on the twentieth day of the month, the cloud was taken away from the Dwelling Place of testimony. 26 At that time the sons of Israel continued their journey from the wilderness of Sinai, and they took a journey of three days, and the cloud rested on the wilderness of Paran; there the anger of the Lord was kindled against Israel, for they had provoked the Lord in asking Him for meat that they might eat. 27 And the Lord listened to their voice and gave them meat which they ate for one month. 28 But after this the anger of the Lord was kindled against them, and He struck them with a great slaughter, and they were buried there in that place. 29 And the sons of Israel called that place Kebroth Hattaavah, because there they buried the people that lusted after flesh. 30 And they departed from Kebroth Hattaavah and pitched [their tents] in Hazeroth, which is in the wilderness of Paran. 31 And while the sons of Israel were in Hazeroth, the anger of the Lord was kindled against Miriam on account of Moses, and she became leprous—white as snow. 32 And she was confined outside the camp for seven days until she had been received again after her leprosy. 33 Afterward the sons of Israel departed from Hazeroth and pitched in the end of the wilderness of Paran. 34 At that time, the Lord spoke to Moses to send twelve men from the sons of Israel, one man to a tribe, to go and explore the land of Canaan. 35 And Moses sent the twelve men, and they came to the land of Canaan to search and examine it, and they explored the whole land from the wilderness of Sin to Rechob as you come to Chamoth. 36 And at the end of forty days they came to Moses and Aaron, and they brought him word as it was in their hearts, and ten of the men brought up an evil report to the sons of Israel regarding the land which they had explored, saying, "It is better for us to return to Egypt than to go to this land, a land that consumes its inhabitants." 37 But Joshua the son of Nun, and Caleb the son of Jephuneh, who were of those that explored the land, said, "The land is exceedingly good. 38 If the Lord delight in us, then He will bring us to this land and give it to us, for it is a land flowing with milk and honey." 39 But the sons of Israel would not listen to them, and they listened to the words of the ten men who had brought up an evil report of the

land. 40 And the Lord heard the murmurings of the sons of Israel, and He was angry and swore, saying, 41 "Surely not [even] one man of this wicked generation will see the land from twenty years old and upward except Caleb the son of Jephuneh and Joshua the son of Nun. 42 But surely this wicked generation will perish in this wilderness, and their children will come to the land and they will possess it"; so the anger of the Lord was kindled against Israel, and He made them wander in the wilderness for forty years until the end of that wicked generation, because they did not follow the Lord. 43 And the people dwelt in the wilderness of Paran a long time, and afterward they proceeded to the wilderness by the way of the Red Sea.

CHAPTER 84

1 At that time Korah the son of Jetzer, the son of Kehas, the son of Levi, took many men of the sons of Israel, and they rose up and quarreled with Moses, and Aaron, and the whole congregation. 2 And the Lord was angry with them, and the earth opened its mouth and swallowed them up with their houses, and all belonging to them, and all the men belonging to Korah. 3 And after this, God made the people go around by the way of Mount Seir for a long time. 4 At that time the Lord said to Moses, "Do not provoke a war against the children of Esau, for I will not give to you of anything belonging to them, as much as the sole of the foot could tread on, for I have given Mount Seir for an inheritance to Esau." 5 Therefore the children of Esau fought against the children of Seir in former times, and the Lord had delivered the children of Seir into the hands of the children of Esau and destroyed them from before them, and the children of Esau dwelt in their place to this day. 6 Therefore the Lord said to the sons of Israel, "Do not fight against the children of Esau, your brothers, for nothing in their land belongs to you, but you may buy food from them for money and eat it, and you may buy water from them for money and drink it." 7 And the sons of Israel did according to the word of the Lord. 8 And the sons of Israel went around the wilderness, going around by the way of Mount Sinai for a long time, and did not touch the children of Esau, and they continued in that district for nineteen years. 9 At that time Latinus king of the children of Chittim died in the forty-fifth year of his reign, which is the fourteenth year of the sons of Israel's departure from Egypt. 10 And they buried him in his place which he had built for himself in the land of Chittim, and Abimnas reigned in his place for thirty-eight years. 11 And the sons of Israel passed the boundary of the children of Esau in those days, at the end of nineteen years, and they came and passed the road of the wilderness of Moab. 12 And the Lord said to Moses, "Do not besiege Moab, and do not fight against them, for I will give you nothing of their land." 13 And the sons of Israel passed the road of the wilderness of Moab for nineteen years, and they did not fight against them. 14 And in the thirty-sixth year of the sons of Israel's departing from Egypt, the Lord struck the heart of Sihon, king of the Amorites, and he waged war, and went out to fight against the children of Moab. 15 And Sihon sent messengers to Beor the son of Janeas, the son of Balaam, counselor to the king of Egypt, and to his son Balaam, to curse Moab, in order that it might be delivered into the hand of Sihon. 16 And the messengers went and brought Beor the son of Janeas and his son Balaam from Pethor in Mesopotamia, so Beor and his son Balaam came to the city of Sihon and they cursed Moab and their king in the presence of Sihon king of the Amorites. 17 So Sihon went out with his whole army, and he went to Moab and fought against them, and he subdued them, and the Lord delivered them into his hands, and Sihon slew the king of Moab. 18 And Sihon took all the cities of Moab in the battle; he also took Heshbon from them, for Heshbon was one of the cities of Moab, and Sihon placed his princes and his nobles in Heshbon, and Heshbon belonged to Sihon in those days. 19 Therefore the allegory speakers Beor and his son Balaam uttered these words, saying, "Come to Heshbon; the city of Sihon will be built and established. 20 Woe to you Moab! You are lost, O people of Kemosh! Behold, it is written on the Scroll of the Law of God." 21 And when Sihon had conquered Moab, he placed guards in the cities which he had taken from Moab, and a considerable number of the children of Moab fell in battle into the hand of Sihon, and he made a great capture of them—sons and daughters—and he slew their king; so Sihon turned back to his own land. 22 And Sihon gave numerous presents of silver and gold to Beor and his son Balaam, and he

dismissed them, and they went to Mesopotamia to their home and country. ²³ At that time all the sons of Israel passed from the road of the wilderness of Moab, and returned, and surrounded the wilderness of Edom. ²⁴ So the whole congregation came to the wilderness of Sin in the first month of the fortieth year from their departure from Egypt, and the sons of Israel dwelt there in Kadesh, of the wilderness of Sin, and Miriam died there, and she was buried there. ²⁵ At that time Moses sent messengers to Hadad king of Edom, saying, "Thus says your brother Israel: Please let me pass through your land; we will not pass through field or vineyard; we will not drink the water of the well; we will walk in the king's road." ²⁶ And Edom said to him, "You will not pass through my country," and Edom went out to meet the sons of Israel with a mighty people. ²⁷ And the children of Esau refused to let the sons of Israel pass through their land, so the Israelites removed from them and did not fight against them. ²⁸ For before this, the Lord had commanded the sons of Israel, saying, "You will not fight against the children of Esau," therefore the Israelites removed from them and did not fight against them. ²⁹ So the sons of Israel departed from Kadesh, and all the people came to Mount Hor. ³⁰ At that time the Lord said to Moses, "Tell your brother Aaron that he will die there, for he will not come to the land which I have given to the sons of Israel." ³¹ And Aaron went up to Mount Hor at the command of the Lord in the fortieth year, in the fifth month, in the first day of the month. ³² And Aaron was one hundred and twenty-three years old when he died in Mount Hor.

CHAPTER 85

¹ And King Arad the Canaanite, who dwelt in the south, heard that the Israelites had come by the way of the spies, and he arranged his forces to fight against the Israelites. ² And the sons of Israel were greatly afraid of him, for he had a great and heavy army, so the sons of Israel resolved to return to Egypt. ³ And the sons of Israel turned back about the distance of three days' journey to Maserath Beni Jaakon, for they were greatly afraid on account of King Arad. ⁴ And the sons of Israel would not get back to their places, so they remained in Beni Jaakon for thirty days. ⁵ And when the children of Levi saw that the sons of Israel would not turn back, they were jealous for the sake of the Lord, and they rose up and fought against the Israelites, their brothers, and slew a great body of them, and forced them to turn back to their place, Mount Hor. ⁶ And when they returned, King Arad was still arranging his host for battle against the Israelites. ⁷ And Israel vowed a vow, saying, "If You will deliver this people into my hand, then I will utterly destroy their cities." ⁸ And the Lord listened to the voice of Israel, and He delivered the Canaanites into their hand, and He utterly destroyed them and their cities, and [Israel] called the name of the place Hormah. ⁹ And the sons of Israel journeyed from Mount Hor and pitched [their tents] in Oboth, and they journeyed from Oboth and they pitched at Ije-abarim in the border of Moab. ¹⁰ And the sons of Israel sent to Moab, saying, "Let us now pass through your land into our place," but the children of Moab would not permit the sons of Israel to pass through their land, for the children of Moab were greatly afraid lest the sons of Israel should do to them as Sihon king of the Amorites had done to them, who had taken their land and had slain many of them. ¹¹ Therefore Moab would not permit the Israelites to pass through his land, and the Lord commanded the sons of Israel, saying that they should not fight against Moab, so the Israelites removed from Moab. ¹² And the sons of Israel journeyed from the border of Moab, and they came to the other side of Arnon, the border of Moab, between Moab and the Amorites, and they pitched in the border of Sihon, king of the Amorites, in the wilderness of Kedemoth. ¹³ And the sons of Israel sent messengers to Sihon, king of the Amorites, saying, ¹⁴ "Let us pass through your land; we will not turn into the fields or into the vineyards; we will go along by the king's highway until we will have passed your border," but Sihon would not permit the Israelites to pass. ¹⁵ So Sihon collected all the people of the Amorites and went out into the wilderness to meet the sons of Israel, and he fought against Israel in Jahaz. ¹⁶ And the Lord delivered Sihon king of the Amorites into the hand of the sons of Israel, and Israel struck all the people of Sihon with the edge of the sword and avenged the cause of Moab. ¹⁷ And the sons of Israel took possession of the land of Sihon, from Aram to Jabuk, to the children of Ammon, and they took all the spoil of the cities. ¹⁸ And Israel took all these cities,

and Israel dwelt in all the cities of the Amorites. ¹⁹ And all the sons of Israel resolved to fight against the children of Ammon, to take their land also. ²⁰ So the Lord said to the sons of Israel, "Do not besiege the children of Ammon, nor stir up battle against them, for I will give nothing to you of their land," and the sons of Israel listened to the word of the Lord and did not fight against the children of Ammon. ²¹ And the sons of Israel turned and went up by the way of Bashan to the land of Og, king of Bashan, and Og the king of Bashan went out to meet the Israelites in battle, and he had many valiant men with him, and a very strong force from the people of the Amorites. ²² And Og king of Bashan was a very powerful man, but his son Naaron was exceedingly powerful, even stronger than he was. ²³ And Og said in his heart, "Behold, now the whole camp of Israel takes up a space of seven miles; now I will strike them at once, without sword or spear." ²⁴ And Og went up Mount Jahaz and took one large stone from there, the length of which was seven miles, and he placed it on his head, and resolved to throw it on the camp of the sons of Israel, to strike all the Israelites with that stone. ²⁵ And the Messenger of the Lord came and pierced the stone on the head of Og, and the stone fell on the neck of Og [so] that Og fell to the earth on account of the weight of the stone on his neck. ²⁶ At that time the Lord said to the sons of Israel, "Do not be afraid of him, for I have given him, and all his people, and all his land into your hand, and you will do to him as you did to Sihon." ²⁷ And Moses went down to him with a small number of the sons of Israel, and Moses struck Og with a stick at the ankles of his feet and slew him. ²⁸ Afterward the sons of Israel pursued the children of Og and all his people, and they beat and destroyed them until there was no remnant left of them. ²⁹ Afterward Moses sent some of the sons of Israel to spy out Jaazer, for Jaazer was a very famous city. ³⁰ And the spies went to Jaazer and explored it, and the spies trusted in the Lord, and they fought against the men of Jaazer. ³¹ And these men took Jaazer and its villages, and the Lord delivered them into their hand, and they drove out the Amorites who had been there. ³² And the sons of Israel took the land of the two kings of the Amorites, sixty cities which were on the other side of [the] Jordan, from the Brook of Arnon to Mount Hermon. ³³ And the sons of Israel journeyed and came into the plain of Moab, which is on this side of [the] Jordan, by Jericho. ³⁴ And the children of Moab heard all the evil which the sons of Israel had done to the two kings of the Amorites, to Sihon and Og, so all the men of Moab were greatly afraid of the Israelites. ³⁵ And the elders of Moab said, "Behold, the two kings of the Amorites, Sihon and Og, who were more powerful than all the kings of the earth, could not stand against the sons of Israel; how then can we stand before them? ³⁶ Surely they sent us a message before now to pass through our land on their way, and we would not permit them, now they will turn on us with their heavy swords and destroy us"; and Moab was distressed on account of the sons of Israel, and they were greatly afraid of them, and they counseled together what was to be done to the sons of Israel. ³⁷ And the elders of Moab resolved and took one of their men, Balak the son of Zippor, the Moabite, and made him king over them at that time, and Balak was a very wise man. ³⁸ And the elders of Moab rose up and sent to the children of Midian to make peace with them, for a great battle and enmity had existed between Moab and Midian in those days, from the days of Hadad the son of Bedad, king of Edom, who struck Midian in the field of Moab, to these days. ³⁹ And the children of Moab sent to the children of Midian, and they made peace with them, and the elders of Midian came to the land of Moab to make peace in behalf of the children of Midian. ⁴⁰ And the elders of Moab counseled with the elders of Midian what to do in order to save their lives from Israel. ⁴¹ And all the children of Moab said to the elders of Midian, "Now therefore, the sons of Israel lick up all that are around us as the ox licks up the grass of the field, for thus they did to the two kings of the Amorites who are stronger than we are." ⁴² And the elders of Midian said to Moab, "We have heard that at the time when Sihon king of the Amorites fought against you, when he prevailed over you and took your land, he had sent to Beor the son of Janeas and to his son Balaam from Mesopotamia, and they came and cursed you; therefore the hand of Sihon prevailed over you [so] that he took your land. ⁴³ Now therefore, send to his son Balaam also, for he still remains in his land, and give him his hire [so] that he may come and curse all the people of whom you are afraid"; so the elders of Moab heard this thing, and it pleased them to send to Balaam the son of Beor. ⁴⁴ So Balak the son of Zippor, king of Moab, sent messengers to Balaam, saying, ⁴⁵ "Behold, there is a people having come out from Egypt: behold, they cover the face of the earth, and they abide near me. **46** Now therefore, come and curse this people for me, for they are too mighty for me; perhaps [then] I will prevail to fight against them and drive them out, for I heard that he whom you bless is blessed, and whom you curse is cursed." **47** So the messengers of Balak went to Balaam and brought Balaam to curse the people to fight against Moab. **48** And Balaam came to Balak to curse Israel, and the Lord said to Balaam, "Do not curse this people for it is blessed." **49** And Balak urged Balaam to curse Israel day by day, but Balaam did not listen to Balak on account of the word of the Lord which He had spoken to Balaam. **50** And when Balak saw that Balaam would not accede to his wish, he rose up and went home, and Balaam also returned to his land, and he went from there to Midian. **51** And the sons of Israel journeyed from the plain of Moab and pitched by the Jordan from Beth-Jesimoth even to Abel-Shittim, at the end of the plains of Moab. **52** And when the sons of Israel dwelt in the plain of Shittim, they began to commit whoredom with the daughters of Moab. **53** And the sons of Israel approached Moab, and the children of Moab pitched their tents opposite to the camp of the sons of Israel. **54** And the children of Moab were afraid of the sons of Israel, and the children of Moab took all their daughters and their wives of beautiful aspect and attractive appearance and dressed them in gold, and silver, and costly garments. **55** And the children of Moab seated those women at the door of their tents in order that the sons of Israel might see them and turn to them, and not fight against Moab. **56** And all the children of Moab did this thing to the sons of Israel, and every man placed his wife and daughter at the door of his tent, and all the sons of Israel saw the act of the children of Moab, and the sons of Israel turned to the daughters of Moab and coveted them, and they went to them. **57** And it came to pass that when a Hebrew came to the door of the tent of Moab, and saw a daughter of Moab, and desired her in his heart, and spoke with her at the door of the tent that he desired, while they were speaking together the men of the tent would come out and speak to the Hebrew like to these words: **58** "Surely you know that we are brothers: we are all the descendants of Lot and the descendants of his brother Abraham; why then will you not remain with us, and why will you not eat our bread and our sacrifice?" **59** And when the children of Moab had thus overwhelmed him with their speeches, and enticed him by their flattering words, they seated him in the tent, and cooked and sacrificed for him, and he ate of their sacrifice and of their bread. **60** Then they gave him wine, and he drank and became intoxicated, and they placed a beautiful young woman before him, and he did with her as he liked, for he did not know what he was doing since he had drunk of wine abundantly. **61** Thus the children of Moab did to Israel in that place, in the plain of Shittim, and the anger of the Lord was kindled against Israel on account of this matter, and He sent a pestilence among them, and there died of the Israelites twenty-four thousand men. **62** Now there was a man of the children of Simeon whose name was Zimri, the son of Salu, who connected himself with the Midianite Cosbi, the daughter of Zur, king of Midian, in the sight of all the sons of Israel. **63** And Phinehas the son of Eleazar, the son of Aaron the priest, saw this wicked thing which Zimri had done, and he took a spear, and rose up, and went after them, and pierced them both, and slew them, and the pestilence ceased from the sons of Israel.

CHAPTER 86

1 At that time after the pestilence, the Lord spoke to Moses, and to Eleazar the son of Aaron the priest, saying, **2** "Number the heads of the whole community of the sons of Israel, from twenty years old and upward, all that went out in the army." **3** And Moses and Eleazar numbered the sons of Israel after their families, and the number of all Israel was seven hundred thousand, seven hundred and thirty. **4** And the number of the children of Levi, from one month old and upward, was twenty-three thousand, and among these there was not a man of those numbered by Moses and Aaron in the wilderness of Sinai. **5** For the Lord had told them that they would die in the wilderness, so they all died, and not one had been left of them except Caleb the son of Jephuneh, and Joshua the son of Nun. **6** And it was after this that the Lord said to Moses, "Say to the sons of Israel to avenge on Midian the cause of their brothers, the sons of Israel." **7** And Moses did so, and the sons of Israel chose from among them twelve thousand men, being one thousand to a

tribe, and they went to Midian. **8** And the sons of Israel warred against Midian, and they slew every male, also the five princes of Midian, and they slew Balaam the son of Beor with the sword. **9** And the sons of Israel took the wives of Midian captive, with their little ones, and their cattle, and all belonging to them. **10** And they took all the spoil and all the prey, and they brought it to Moses and to Eleazar in the plains of Moab. **11** And Moses, and Eleazar, and all the princes of the congregation went out to meet them with joy. **12** And they divided all the spoil of Midian, and the sons of Israel had been avenged on Midian for the cause of their brothers, the sons of Israel.

CHAPTER 87

1 At that time the Lord said to Moses, "Behold, your days are approaching to an end; now take Joshua the son of Nun, your servant, and place him in the Dwelling Place, and I will command him," and Moses did so. **2** And the Lord appeared in the Dwelling Place in a pillar of cloud, and the pillar of cloud stood at the entrance of the Dwelling Place. **3** And the Lord commanded Joshua the son of Nun and said to him, "Be strong and courageous, for you will bring the sons of Israel to the land which I swore to give them, and I will be with you." **4** And Moses said to Joshua, "Be strong and courageous, for you will make the sons of Israel inherit the land, and the Lord will be with you; He will not leave you nor forsake you; do not be afraid nor disheartened." **5** And Moses called to all the sons of Israel and said to them, "You have seen all the good which the Lord your God has done for you in the wilderness. **6** Now therefore, observe all the words of this law and walk in the way of the Lord your God; do not turn from the way which the Lord has commanded you, either to the right or to the left." **7** And Moses taught the sons of Israel statutes, and judgments, and laws to do in the land as the Lord had commanded him. **8** And he taught them the way of the Lord and His laws; behold, they are written on the Scroll of the Law of God which He gave to the sons of Israel by the hand of Moses. **9** And Moses finished commanding the sons of Israel, and the Lord spoke to him, saying, "Go up to Mount Abarim and die there, and be gathered to your people as your brother Aaron was gathered." **10** And Moses went up as the Lord had commanded him, and he died there in the land of Moab by the order of the Lord, in the fortieth year from the Israelites going out from the land of Egypt. **11** And the sons of Israel wept for Moses in the plains of Moab for thirty days, and the days of weeping and mourning for Moses were completed.

CHAPTER 88

1 And it was after the death of Moses that the Lord spoke to Joshua the son of Nun, saying, **2** "Rise up and pass the Jordan to the land which I have given to the sons of Israel, and you will make the sons of Israel inherit the land. **3** Every place on which the sole of your feet will tread will belong to you, from the wilderness of Lebanon to the great river; the river of Perath will be your boundary. **4** No man will stand up against you all the days of your life; as I was with Moses, so I will be with you; only be strong and of good courage to observe all the Law which Moses commanded you; do not turn from the way, either to the right or to the left, in order that you may prosper in all that you do." **5** And Joshua commanded the officers of Israel, saying, "Pass through the camp and command the people, saying, Prepare provisions for yourselves, for in three more days you will pass the Jordan to possess the land." **6** And the officers of the sons of Israel did so, and they commanded the people and they did all that Joshua had commanded. **7** And Joshua sent two men to spy out the land of Jericho, and the men went and spied out Jericho. **8** And at the end of seven days they came to Joshua in the camp and said to him, "The Lord has delivered the whole land into our hands, and the inhabitants thereof have melted with fear because of us." **9** And it came to pass after that, that Joshua rose up in the morning and all Israel with him, and they journeyed from Shittim, and Joshua and all Israel with him passed the Jordan; and Joshua was eighty-two years old when he passed the Jordan with Israel. **10** And the people went up from Jordan on the tenth day of the first month, and they encamped in Gilgal at the eastern corner of Jericho. **11** And the sons of Israel kept the Passover in Gilgal, in the plains of Jericho, on the fourteenth day of the month as it is written in the Law of Moses. **12** And the manna ceased at that time on the next day of the Passover, and there was no more manna for the sons of Israel, and they ate of the produce of the land of Canaan. **13** And Jericho was entirely closed against the sons of Israel—no one came out or went in. **14** And it was in the second month, on the first day of the month, that the Lord said to Joshua, "Rise up; behold, I have given Jericho into your hand with all the people thereof; and all your fighting men will go around the city once each day: thus you will do for six days. **15** And the priests will blow on trumpets, and when you will hear the sound of the trumpet, all the people will give a great shouting [so] that the walls of the city will fall down; all the people will go up—every man against his opponent." **16** And Joshua did so according to all that the Lord had commanded him. **17** And on the seventh day they went around the city seven times, and the priests blew on trumpets. **18** And at the seventh round, Joshua said to the people, "Shout! For the Lord has delivered the whole city into our hands. **19** Only the city and all that it contains will be accursed to the Lord, and keep yourselves from the accursed thing, lest you make the camp of Israel accursed and trouble it. **20** But all the silver, and gold, and brass, and iron will be consecrated to the Lord; they will come into the treasury of the Lord." **21** And the people blew on trumpets and made a great shouting, and the walls of Jericho fell down, and all the people went up, every man straight before him, and they took the city and utterly destroyed all that was in it, both man and woman, young and old, ox, and sheep, and donkey, with the edge of the sword. **22** And they burned the whole city with fire; only the vessels of silver and gold, and brass and iron, they put into the treasury of the Lord. **23** And Joshua swore at that time, saying, "Cursed be the man who builds Jericho; he will lay the foundation thereof in his firstborn, and in his youngest son he will set up the gates thereof." **24** And Achan the son of Carmi, the son of Zabdi, the son of Zerah, son of Judah, dealt treacherously in the accursed thing, and he took of the accursed thing and hid it in the tent, and the anger of the Lord was kindled against Israel. **25** And it was after this when the sons of Israel had returned from burning Jericho, Joshua also sent men to spy out Ai and to fight against it. **26** And the men went up and spied out Ai, and they returned and said, "Do not let all the people go up with you to Ai; only let about three thousand men go up and strike the city, for the men thereof are but few." **27** And Joshua did so, and there went up with him of the sons of Israel about three thousand men, and they fought against the men of Ai. **28** And the battle was severe against Israel, and the men of Ai struck thirty-six men of Israel, and the sons of Israel fled from before the men of Ai. **29** And when Joshua saw this thing, he tore his garments and fell on his face to the ground before the Lord, he, with the elders of Israel, and they put dust on their heads. **30** And Joshua said, "Why, O Lord, did You bring this people over the Jordan? what will I say after the Israelites have turned their backs against their enemies? **31** Now therefore, all the Canaanites, inhabitants of the land, will hear this thing, and surround us and cut off our name." **32** And the Lord said to Joshua, "Why do you fall on your face? rise, get up, for the Israelites have sinned and taken of the accursed thing; I will no longer be with them unless they destroy the accursed thing from among them." **33** And Joshua rose up, and assembled the people, and brought the Lights by the order of the Lord, and the tribe of Judah was taken, and Achan the son of Carmi was taken. **34** And Joshua said to Achan, "Tell me, my son, what have you done?" And Achan said, "I saw among the spoil a fancy garment of Shinar, and two hundred shekels of silver, and a wedge of gold of fifty shekels weight; I coveted them and took them, and behold, they are all hid in the earth in the midst of the tent." **35** And Joshua sent men who went and took them from the tent of Achan, and they brought them to Joshua. **36** And Joshua took Achan and these utensils, and his sons and daughters, and all belonging to him, and they brought them into the Valley of Achor. **37** And Joshua burned them there with fire, and all the Israelites stoned Achan with stones, and they raised a heap of stones over him; therefore, he called that place the Valley of Achor, so the Lord's anger was appeased, and afterward Joshua came to the city and fought against it. **38** And the Lord said to Joshua, "Do not fear, neither be dismayed: behold, I have given Ai, her king, and her people into your hand, and you will do to them as you did to Jericho and her king—only the spoil thereof and the cattle thereof you will take for a prey for yourselves; lay an ambush for the city behind it." **39** So Joshua did according to the word of the Lord, and he chose thirty thousand valiant men from among the sons of war, and he sent them, and they lay in ambush for the city. **40** And he commanded them, saying, "When you will see us, we will flee before them with cunning, and they will pursue us, you will then rise out of the ambush and take the city," and they did so. **41** And Joshua fought, and the men of the city went out toward Israel not knowing that they were lying in ambush for them behind the city. **42** And Joshua and all the Israelites pretended themselves [to be] wearied out before them, and they fled by the way of the wilderness with cunning. **43** And the men of Ai gathered all the people who were in the city to pursue the Israelites, and they went out and were drawn away from the city—not one remained; and they left the city open and pursued the Israelites. **44** And those who were lying in ambush rose up out of their places, and hastened to come to the city, and took it, and set it on fire, and the men of Ai turned back, and behold, the smoke of the city ascended to the skies, and they had no means of retreating either one way or the other. **45** And all the men of Ai were in the midst of Israel, some on this side and some on that side, and they struck them so that not one of them remained. **46** And the sons of Israel took Melosh king of Ai alive, and they brought him to Joshua, and Joshua hanged him on a tree, and he died. **47** And the sons of Israel returned to the city after having burned it, and they struck all those that were in it with the edge of the sword. **48** And the number of those that had fallen of the men of Ai, both man and woman, was twelve thousand; only the cattle and the spoil of the city they took to themselves, according to the word of the Lord to Joshua. **49** And all the kings on this side Jordan, all the kings of Canaan, heard of the evil which the sons of Israel had done to Jericho and to Ai, and they gathered themselves together to fight against Israel. **50** Only the inhabitants of Gibeon were greatly afraid of fighting against the Israelites lest they should perish, so they acted cunningly, and they came to Joshua and to all Israel, and said to them, "We have come from a distant land; now therefore, make a covenant with us." **51** And the inhabitants of Gibeon outwitted the sons of Israel, and the sons of Israel made a covenant with them, and they made peace with them, and the princes of the congregation swore to them, but afterward the sons of Israel knew that they were neighbors to them and were dwelling among them. **52** But the sons of Israel did not slay them, for they had sworn to them by the Lord, and they became hewers of wood and drawers of water. **53** And Joshua said to them, "Why did you deceive me, to do this thing to us?" and they answered him, saying, "Because it was told to your servants all that you had done to all the kings of the Amorites, and we were greatly afraid for our lives, and we did this thing." **54** And Joshua appointed them on that day to hew wood and to draw water, and he divided them for slaves to all the tribes of Israel. **55** And when Adonizedek king of Jerusalem heard that the sons of Israel had done to Jericho and to Ai, he sent to Hoham king of Hebron, and to Piram king at Jarmuth, and to Japhia king of Lachish, and to Deber king of Eglon, saying, **56** "Come up to me and help me [so] that we may strike the sons of Israel and the inhabitants of Gibeon who have made peace with the sons of Israel." **57** And they gathered themselves together, and the five kings of the Amorites went up with all their camps—a mighty people [as] numerous as the sand of the seashore. **58** And all these kings came and encamped before Gibeon, and they began to fight against the inhabitants of Gibeon, and all the men of Gibeon sent to Joshua, saying, "Come up quickly to us and help us, for all the kings of the Amorites have gathered together to fight against us." **59** And Joshua and all the fighting people went up from Gilgal, and Joshua came suddenly to them, and struck these five kings with a great slaughter. **60** And the Lord confounded them before the sons of Israel, who struck them with a terrible slaughter in Gibeon, and pursued them along the way that goes up to Beth-Horon to Makkedah, and they fled from before the sons of Israel. **61** And while they were fleeing, the Lord sent hailstones on them from Heaven, and more of them died by the hailstones than by the slaughter of the sons of Israel. **62** And the sons of Israel pursued them, and they still struck them in the road, going on and striking them. **63** And when they were striking, the day was declining toward evening, and Joshua said in the sight of all the people, "Sun, stand still on Gibeon, and moon, in the Valley of Ajalon, until the nation will have avenged itself on its enemies." **64** And the Lord listened to the voice of Joshua, and the sun stood still in the midst of the heavens, and it stood still thirty-six moments, and the moon also stood still and did not hasten to go down [for] a whole day. **65** And there was no day like that, before it or after it, [in] that the Lord listened to the voice of a man, for the Lord fought for Israel.

CHAPTER 89

[1] Then Joshua spoke this song on the day that the Lord had given the Amorites into the hand of Joshua and the sons of Israel, and he said in the sight of all Israel, [2] "You have done mighty things, O Lord, || You have performed great deeds; Who is like You? my lips will sing to Your Name— [3] My goodness and my fortress, my high tower, || I will sing a new song to You, || I will sing to You with thanksgiving; You are the strength of my salvation. [4] All the kings of the earth will praise You, || The princes of the world will sing to You, || The sons of Israel will rejoice in Your salvation, || They will sing and praise Your power. [5] To You, O Lord, we confided; We said You are our God, || For You were our shelter and strong tower against our enemies. [6] To You we cried and were not ashamed; In You we trusted and were delivered; When we cried to You, You heard our voice, || You delivered our souls from the sword, || You showed Your grace to us, || You gave Your salvation to us, || You made our hearts rejoice with Your strength. [7] You went out for our salvation, || With Your arm You redeemed Your people; You answered us from the heavens of Your holiness, || You saved us from tens of thousands of people. [8] The sun and moon stood still in [the] heavens, || And You stood in Your wrath against our oppressors || And commanded Your judgments over them. [9] All the princes of the earth stood up, || The kings of the nations had gathered themselves together; They were not moved at Your presence, || They desired Your battles. [10] You rose against them in Your anger || And brought down Your wrath on them; You destroyed them in Your anger || And cut them off in Your heart. [11] Nations have been consumed with Your fury, || Kingdoms have declined because of Your wrath, || You wounded kings in the day of Your anger. [12] You poured out Your fury on them—Your wrathful anger took hold of them; You turned their iniquity on them || And cut them off in their wickedness. [13] They spread a trap, they fell therein, || In the net they hid, their foot was caught. [14] Your hand was ready for all Your enemies who said, || Through their sword they possessed the land, || Through their arm they dwelt in the city; You filled their faces with shame, || You brought their horns down to the ground, || You terrified them in Your wrath, || And destroyed them in Your anger. [15] The earth trembled and shook at the sound of Your storm over them, || You did not withhold their souls from death, || And brought down their lives to the grave. [16] You pursued them in Your storm, || You consumed them in Your whirlwind, || You turned their rain into hail; They fell into deep pits so that they could not rise. [17] Their carcasses were like rubbish cast out in the middle of the streets. [18] They were consumed and destroyed in Your anger, || You saved your people with Your might. [19] Therefore our hearts rejoice in You, || Our souls exalt in Your salvation. [20] Our tongues will relate Your might, || We will sing and praise Your wondrous works. [21] For You saved us from our enemies, || You delivered us from those who rose up against us, || You destroyed them from before us || And depressed them beneath our feet. [22] Thus all Your enemies will perish O Lord, || And the wicked will be like chaff driven by the wind, || And Your beloved will be like trees planted by the waters." [23] So Joshua and all Israel with him returned to the camp in Gilgal after having smitten all the kings, so that not [even] a remnant was left of them. [24] And the five kings fled alone on foot from battle, and hid themselves in a cave, and Joshua sought for them in the field of battle and did not find them. [25] And afterward it was told to Joshua, saying, "The kings have been found, and behold, they are hidden in a cave." [26] And Joshua said, "Appoint men to be at the mouth of the cave to guard them, lest they escape"; and the sons of Israel did so. [27] And Joshua called to all Israel and said to the officers of battle, "Place your feet on the necks of these kings," and Joshua said, "So the Lord will do to all your enemies." [28] And afterward Joshua commanded that they should slay the kings, and cast them into the cave, and to put great stones at the mouth of the cave. [29] And afterward Joshua went to Makkedah with all the people that were with him on that day, and he struck it with the edge of the sword. [30] And he utterly destroyed the souls and all belonging to the city, and he did to the king and people thereof as he had done to Jericho. [31] And he passed from there to Libnah, and fought against it, and the Lord delivered it into his hand, and Joshua struck it with the edge of the sword, and all the souls thereof, and he did to it and to the king thereof as he had done to Jericho. [32] And from there he passed on to Lachish to fight against it, and Horam king of Gaza went up to assist the men of Lachish, and Joshua struck him and his people until there was none left to him. [33] And Joshua took Lachish and all the people thereof, and he did to it as he had done to Libnah. [34] And Joshua passed from there to Eglon, and he took that also, and he struck it and all the people thereof with the edge of the sword. [35] And from there he passed to Hebron, and fought against it, and took it, and utterly destroyed it, and he returned from there with all Israel to Debir, and he fought against it and struck it with the edge of the sword. [36] And he destroyed every soul in it—he left none remaining; and he did to it and the king thereof as he had done to Jericho. [37] And Joshua struck all the kings of the Amorites from Kadesh-Barnea to Azah, and he took their country at once, for the Lord had fought for Israel. [38] And Joshua came to the camp with all Israel, to Gilgal. [39] When at that time Jabin king of Chazor heard all that Joshua had done to the kings of the Amorites, Jabin sent to Jobat king of Midian, and to Laban king of Shimron, to Jephal king of Achshaph, and to all the kings of the Amorites, saying, [40] "Come quickly to us and help us [so] that we may strike the sons of Israel before they come on us and do to us as they have done to the other kings of the Amorites." [41] And all these kings listened to the words of Jabin, king of Chazor, and they went out with all their camps, seventeen kings, and their people were as numerous as the sand on the seashore, together with horses and innumerable chariots, and they came and pitched [their tents] together at the waters of Merom, and they were gathered together to fight against Israel. [42] And the Lord said to Joshua, "Do not fear them, for about this time tomorrow I will deliver them all up slain before you: you will hamstring their horses and burn their chariots with fire." [43] And Joshua with all the men of war came suddenly on them and struck them, and they fell into their hands, for the Lord had delivered them into the hands of the sons of Israel. [44] So the sons of Israel pursued all these kings with their camps and struck them until there was none left of them, and Joshua did to them as the Lord had spoken to him. [45] And Joshua returned at that time to Chazor, and struck it with the sword, and destroyed every soul in it, and burned it with fire; and Joshua passed from Chazor to Shimron, and struck it, and utterly destroyed it. [46] From there he passed to Achshaph and he did to it as he had done to Shimron. [47] From there he passed to Adulam and he struck all the people in it, and he did to Adulam as he had done to Achshaph and to Shimron. [48] And he passed from them to all the cities of the kings which he had smitten, and he struck all the people that were left of them and utterly destroyed them. [49] Only their plunder and cattle the Israelites took to themselves as a prey, but every human being they struck; they did not permit a soul to live. [50] As the Lord had commanded Moses, so Joshua and all Israel did; they did not fail in anything. [51] So Joshua and all the sons of Israel struck the whole land of Canaan as the Lord had commanded them, and struck all their kings, being thirty-one kings, and the sons of Israel took their whole country, [52] besides the kingdoms of Sihon and Og, which are on the other side Jordan, of which Moses had smitten many cities, and Moses gave them to the Reubenites, and the Gadites, and to half the tribe of Manasseh. [53] And Joshua struck all the kings that were on this side of the Jordan to the west, and he gave them for an inheritance to the nine tribes and to the half tribe of Israel. [54] For five years Joshua carried on the war with these kings, and he gave their cities to the Israelites, and the land became tranquil from battle throughout the cities of the Amorites and the Canaanites.

CHAPTER 90

[1] At that time, in the fifth year after the sons of Israel had passed over [the] Jordan, after the sons of Israel had rested from their war with the Canaanites, at that time great and severe battles arose between Edom and the children of Chittim, and the children of Chittim fought against Edom. [2] And Abianus king of Chittim went out in that year, that is in the thirty-first year of his reign, and a great force with him of the mighty men of the children of Chittim, and he went to Seir to fight against the children of Esau. [3] And Hadad the king of Edom heard of his report, and he went out to meet him with a heavy people and a strong force, and he engaged in battle with him in the field of Edom. [4] And the hand of Chittim prevailed over the children of Esau, and the children of Chittim slew twenty-two thousand men of the children of Esau, and all the children of Esau fled from before them. [5] And the children of Chittim

pursued them, and they reached Hadad king of Edom who was running before them, and they caught him alive and brought him to Abianus king of Chittim. **6** And Abianus ordered him to be slain, and Hadad king of Edom died in the forty-eighth year of his reign. **7** And the children of Chittim continued their pursuit of Edom, and they struck them with a great slaughter, and Edom became subject to the children of Chittim. **8** And the children of Chittim ruled over Edom, and Edom came under the hand of the children of Chittim and became one kingdom from that day. **9** And from that time on they could no longer lift up their heads, and their kingdom became one with the children of Chittim. **10** And Abianus placed officers in Edom, and all the children of Edom became subject and tributary to Abianus, and Abianus turned back to his own land, Chittim. **11** And when he returned, he renewed his government, and built for himself a spacious and fortified palace for a royal residence, and reigned securely over the children of Chittim and over Edom. **12** In those days, after the sons of Israel had driven away all the Canaanites and the Amorites, Joshua was old and advanced in years, **13** and the Lord said to Joshua, "You are old, advanced in life, and a great part of the land remains to be possessed. **14** Now therefore, divide this land for an inheritance to the nine tribes and to the half tribe of Manasseh," and Joshua rose up and did as the Lord had spoken to him. **15** And he divided the whole land to the tribes of Israel as an inheritance according to their divisions. **16** But to the tribe at Levi he gave no inheritance—the offerings of the Lord are their inheritance as the Lord had spoken of them by the hand of Moses. **17** And Joshua gave Mount Hebron to Caleb the son of Jephuneh, one portion above his brothers, as the Lord had spoken through Moses. **18** Therefore Hebron became an inheritance to Caleb and his children to this day. **19** And Joshua divided the whole land by lots to all Israel for an inheritance as the Lord had commanded him. **20** And the sons of Israel gave cities to the Levites from their own inheritance, and suburbs for their cattle and property; as the Lord had commanded Moses, so the sons of Israel did, and they divided the land by lot whether great or small. **21** And they went to inherit the land according to their boundaries, and the sons of Israel gave to Joshua the son of Nun an inheritance among them. **22** By the word of the Lord they gave to him the city which he required, Timnath-Serah in Mount Ephraim, and he built the city and dwelt therein. **23** These are the inheritances which Eleazar the priest, and Joshua the son of Nun, and the heads of the fathers of the tribes portioned out to the sons of Israel by lot in Shiloh, before the Lord, at the door of the Dwelling Place, and they ceased dividing the land. **24** And the Lord gave the land to the Israelites, and they possessed it as the Lord had spoken to them and as the Lord had sworn to their ancestors. **25** And the Lord gave to the Israelites rest from all their enemies around them, and no man stood up against them, and the Lord delivered all their enemies into their hands, and not one thing failed of all the good which the Lord had spoken to the sons of Israel—the Lord performed everything. **26** And Joshua called to all the sons of Israel, and he blessed them and commanded them to serve the Lord, and afterward he sent them away, and each man went to his city, and each man to his inheritance. **27** And the sons of Israel served the Lord all the days of Joshua, and the Lord gave them rest from all around them, and they dwelt securely in their cities. **28** And it came to pass in those days that Abianus king of Chittim died in the thirty-eighth year of his reign, that is the seventh year of his reign over Edom, and they buried him in his place which he had built for himself, and Latinus reigned in his stead [for] fifty years. **29** And during his reign, he brought out an army, and he went and fought against the inhabitants of Britannia and Kernania, the children of Elisha son of Javan, and he prevailed over them and made them tributary. **30** He then heard that Edom had revolted from under the hand of Chittim, and Latinus went to them, and struck them, and subdued them, and placed them under the hand of the children of Chittim, and Edom became one kingdom with the children of Chittim all the days. **31** And for many years there was no king in Edom, and their government was with the children of Chittim and their king. **32** And it was in the twenty-sixth year after the sons of Israel had passed the Jordan, that is the sixty-sixth year after the sons of Israel had departed from Egypt, that Joshua was old, advanced in years, being one hundred and eight years old in those days. **33** And Joshua called to all Israel, to their elders, their judges and officers, after the Lord had given to all the Israelites rest from all their surrounding enemies, and Joshua said to the elders of Israel, and to their judges, "Behold, I am old, advanced in years, and

you have seen what the Lord has done to all the nations whom He has driven away from before you, for it is the Lord who has fought for you. **34** Now therefore, strengthen yourselves to keep and to do all the words of the Law of Moses, not to deviate from it to the right or to the left, and not to come among those nations who are left in the land; neither will you make mention of the name of their gods, but you will cleave to the Lord your God as you have done to this day." **35** And Joshua greatly exhorted the sons of Israel to serve the Lord all their days. **36** And all the Israelites said, "We will serve the Lord our God all our days—we, and our children, and our children's children, and our seed forever." **37** And Joshua made a covenant with the people on that day, and he sent the sons of Israel away, and each man went to his inheritance and to his city. **38** And it was in those days, when the sons of Israel were dwelling securely in their cities, that they buried the coffins of the tribes of their ancestors, which they had brought up from Egypt—each man in the inheritance of his children; the sons of Israel buried the twelve sons of Jacob—each man in the possession of his children. **39** And these are the names of the cities wherein they buried the twelve sons of Jacob, whom the sons of Israel had brought up from Egypt. **40** And they buried Reuben and Gad on this side of the Jordan, in Romia, which Moses had given to their children. **41** And they buried Simeon and Levi in the city [of] Mauda, which he had given to the children of Simeon, and the suburb of the city was for the children of Levi. **42** And they buried Judah in the city of Benjamin opposite Beth-Lehem. **43** And they buried the bones of Issachar and Zebulun in Zidon, in the portion which fell to their children. **44** And Dan was buried in the city of his children, in Eshtael. And they buried Naphtali and Asher in Kadesh-Naphtali, each man in his place which he had given to his children. **45** And they buried the bones of Joseph in Shechem, in the part of the field which Jacob had purchased from Hamor, and which became an inheritance for Joseph. **46** And they buried Benjamin in Jerusalem opposite the Jebusite, which was given to the children of Benjamin; the sons of Israel buried their fathers—each man in the city of his children. **47** And at the end of two years, Joshua the son of Nun died, [being] one hundred and ten years old-, and the-time which Joshua judged Israel was twenty-eight years, and Israel served the Lord all the days of his life. **48** And the other affairs of Joshua, and his battles, and his reproofs with which he reproved Israel, and all which he had commanded them, and the names of the cities which the sons of Israel possessed in his days, behold, they are written in the scroll of the words of Joshua to the sons of Israel, and in the scroll of the Wars of the Lord, which Moses, and Joshua, and the sons of Israel had written. **49** And the sons of Israel buried Joshua in the border of his inheritance, in Timnath-Serah, which was given to him in Mount Ephraim. **50** And Eleazar the son of Aaron died in those days, and they buried him in a hill belonging to his son Phinehas, which was given [to] him in Mount Ephraim.

CHAPTER 91

1 At that time, after the death of Joshua, the children of the Canaanites were still in the land, and the Israelites resolved to drive them out. **2** And the sons of Israel asked of the Lord, saying, "Who will first go up for us to the Canaanites to fight against them?" and the Lord said, "Judah will go up." **3** And the children of Judah said to Simeon, "Go up with us into our lot, and we will fight against the Canaanites, and we will likewise go up with you in your lot," so the children of Simeon went with the children of Judah. **4** And the children of Judah went up and fought against the Canaanites, so the Lord delivered the Canaanites into the hands of the children of Judah, and they struck them in Bezek—ten thousand men. **5** And they fought with Adonibezek in Bezek, and he fled from before them, and they pursued him and caught him, and they took hold of him and cut off his thumbs and great toes. **6** And Adonibezek said, "Seventy kings having their thumbs and great toes cut off gathered their meat under my table; as I have done, so God has paid me back," and they brought him to Jerusalem and he died there. **7** And the children of Simeon went with the children of Judah, and they struck the Canaanites with the edge of the sword. **8** And the Lord was with the children of Judah, and they possessed the mountain, and the children of Joseph went up to Bethel, the same is Luz, and the Lord was with them. **9** And the children of Joseph spied out Bethel, and the watchmen saw a man going out from the city, and they caught him and said to him, "Show us the entrance of the city now and we will show kindness to you." **10** And that man showed them the entrance of the city, and the children of Joseph came and struck the city with the edge of the sword. **11** And they sent the man away with his family, and he went to the Hittites and built a city, and he called the name thereof Luz, so all the Israelites dwelt in their cities, and the children of Israel dwelt in their cities, and the sons of Israel served the Lord all the days of Joshua, and all the days of the elders, who had lengthened their days after Joshua, and saw the great work of the Lord which He had performed for Israel. **12** And the elders judged Israel after the death of Joshua for seventeen years. **13** And all the elders also fought the battles of Israel against the Canaanites, and the Lord drove the Canaanites from before the sons of Israel in order to place the Israelites in their land. **14** And He accomplished all the words which He had spoken to Abraham, Isaac, and Jacob, and the oath which He had sworn, to give the land of the Canaanites to them and to their children. **15** And the Lord gave them the whole land of Canaan to the sons of Israel as He had sworn to their ancestors, and the Lord gave them rest from those around them, and the sons of Israel dwelt securely in their cities. **16** Blessed is the Lord forever—amen and amen! **17** Strengthen yourselves and let the hearts of all you that trust in the Lord be of good courage.

TESTAMENT OF ISAAC

The Testament of Isaac begins with Isaac being told of his impending death by an angel, and his message to his son in response. Isaac is portrayed as foretelling both the Twelve Tribes of Israel and Jesus—the latter thought by some to be a later Christian addition to an older, perhaps second-century AD Jewish text.

This is the going forth from the body of Isaac the patriarch. He died on the twenty-fourth of Mesore in the peace of God. Amen.

CHAPTER 1

1 Now the patriarch Isaac writes his testament and addresses his words of instruction to his son Jacob and to all those gathered around him. **2** The blessings of the patriarch will be on those who come after us, even those who listen to these words, to these words of instruction and these medicines of life, so that the grace of God may be with all those who believe. **3** This is the end of obedience, as it is written: You have heard a word, let it abide with you—which means that a man should strive patiently with what he hears. **4** God gives grace to those who believe; he who believes the words of God and of His saints will be an inheritor of the Kingdom of God. **5** God has been with the generations gone by, which have passed away, because of their innocence and their faith toward God. He will also be with the generations to come.

CHAPTER 2

1 Now it came to pass, when the time had come for the Patriarch Isaac to go forth from the body, God sent to him the messenger of his father Abraham at dawn on the twenty-second of Mesore. **2** He said to him, "Greetings, son of promise!" Now it was the daily custom of the righteous old man Isaac to converse with the messengers. **3** He lifted his face up to the face of the messenger: he saw him assuming the likeness of his father Abraham; and he opened his mouth and raised his voice and cried out in great joy, "I have seen your face like someone who has seen the face of God." **4** The messenger said to him, "Listen, my beloved Isaac: I have been sent for you by God to take you to the heavens and set you beside your father Abraham, so that you can see all the saints; for your father is expecting you and is coming for you himself. **5** Behold, a throne has been set up for you close to your father

Abraham, and your lot and your beloved son Jacob's lot will surpass that of all others in the whole of God's creation; that is why you have been given forevermore the name of Patriarch and Father of the World." **6** But the God-loving old man Isaac said to the messenger, "I am astonished by you, for you are my father." **7** The messenger answered, "My beloved Isaac, I am the messenger that ministers to your father Abraham. But rejoice now, for I am to take you out of sorrow into gladness, out of suffering to rest forever. **8** I am to transport you from prison to a place where you can range at will—to a place of joy and gladness; I am to take you to where there is light, and merriment, and rejoicing, and abundance that never fails. **9** So then, draw up your testament and a statement for your household, for I am to translate you to rest for all eternity. **10** Blessed is your father who begot you; blessed are you also; blessed is your son Jacob; and blessed are your descendants that will come after you."

CHAPTER 3

1 Now Jacob heard them talking together, but he said nothing. Our father Isaac said to the messenger with a heavy heart, "What will I do about the light of my eyes, my beloved son Jacob? **2** For I am afraid of what Esau might do to him—you know the situation." **3** The messenger said to him, "My beloved Isaac, if all the nations on earth were gathered together, they would not be able to bring these blessings pronounced over Jacob to nothing. **4** When you blessed him, the Father, and the Son, and the Holy Spirit blessed him; and Michael, and Gabriel, and all the messengers, and all the heavenly ones, and the spirits of all the righteous, and your father Abraham all answered, Amen. **5** Therefore, the sword will not touch his body, but he will be held in high honor and grow great and spread far and wide, and twelve thrones will spring from him." **6** Our father Isaac said to the messenger, "You have given me much comfort, but do not let Jacob know in case he is distressed." **7** The messenger said to him, "My beloved Isaac, blessed is every righteous man who goes forth from the body; blessed are they when they meet with God. **8** Woe, woe, woe—three times woe—to the sinner, because he has been born into this world; great sufferings will come to him. **9** Isaac, beloved of God, give these instructions, therefore, to your sons, and the instructions your father has given you. **10** Hide nothing from Jacob, so that he can write them as instructions for the generations that will come after you, and those who love God may live their lives in accordance with them. **11** And take care that I am able to fetch you with joy, without delay. The peace of my Lord that He has given me, I give to you, as I go to Him who sent me."

CHAPTER 4

1 And when the messenger had said this, he rose from the bed on which Isaac was sleeping. He went back to the worlds on high while our father Isaac watched him go, astonished at the vision he had seen. **2** And he said, "I will not see daylight before I am sent for." And while he was thinking this, behold, Jacob got up and came to the door of the room. **3** The messenger had cast a sleep over him so that he should not hear them; and he got up and ran to where his father slept and said to him, "My father, whom have you been talking to?" **4** Our father Isaac said to him, "You have heard, my son: your aged father has been sent for to be taken from you," and Jacob put his arms around his father's neck and wept, saying, "Ah me! My strength has left me! Today you have made me an orphan, my father." **5** Our father Isaac embraced his son Jacob and wept; and both wept together until they could weep no more. **6** And Jacob said, "Take me with you, father Isaac." But Isaac replied, "I would not have it so, my son; wait until you are sent for, my loved one. I remember on the day when the whole earth was shaken from end to end talking to my lord and father Abraham, and I had no strength to do anything. **7** What God has ordained, He has ordained for each one by sure authority; His ordinances are immutable. **8** But I know, and I am glad that I am to go to God, and I am strengthened by a guiding spirit; for this is a way that no one can escape. **9** Listen, my son. Where is the first creation of the hands of God—our father Adam and our mother Eve? Where is Abel, and after him Mahalalel, and Jared, and our father Enoch, and Methuselah, and our father Noah, and his sons Shem, Ham, and Japheth? **10** After these Arphaxad, and Cainan, and Shelah, and Eber, and Reu, and Serug, and Nahor, and Terah, and my blessed father Abraham, and his brother Lot? **11** All these experienced death except the perfect one, our father Enoch. **12** After these, forty-two generations more will pass until Christ comes, born of a pure virgin called Mary. **13** He will spend thirty years preaching in the world. At the end of all this, He will choose twelve men and reveal to them His mysteries and teach them about the archetype of His body and His true blood by means of bread and wine: **14** and the bread will become the body of God and the wine will become the blood of God. **15** And then He will ascend the tree of the Cross and die for the whole creation, and rise on the third day and despoil Hades, and deliver all mankind from the enemy. **16** The generations to come will be saved by His body and by His blood until the end of time. **17** The sacrifices of Christians will not cease until the end of time, whether offered secretly or openly; **18** and the Antichrist will not appear so long as they offer up their sacrifice. **19** Blessed is every man who performs that service and believes in it, because the archetypal service is in the heavens; and they will celebrate with the Son of God in His kingdom."

CHAPTER 5

1 While the God-loving old man, our father Isaac, was saying this, all his household gathered around him and wept. **2** His son told all his relations, and they came to him in tears. **3** Now our father Isaac had made for himself a bedroom in his house; and when his sight began to fail, he withdrew into it and remained there for one hundred years, fasting daily until evening, and offering for himself and his household a young animal for their soul. **4** And he spent half the night in prayer and praise of God. **5** Thus he lived an ascetic life for one hundred years. And he kept three periods of forty days as fasts each year, neither drinking wine nor eating fruit nor sleeping on his bed. **6** And he prayed and gave thanks to God continually.

CHAPTER 6

1 Now when it became generally known that the man of God had regained his sight, people gathered to him from everywhere, listening to his words of life; for they realized that [the] Holy Spirit of God was speaking in him. **2** The great ones who came said to him, "You can now see clearly enough: how come it [is] that after your sight had failed you have now regained it?" **3** The God-loving old man smiled and said to them, "My sons and brothers, the God of my father Abraham has brought this about to comfort me in my old age." **4** But the priest of God said to him, "Tell me what I ought to do, my father Isaac." **5** Our father Isaac said to him, "Keep your body holy, for the temple of God is set in it. Do not engage in controversy with other men in case an angry word escapes your mouth. Be on your guard against evil-speaking, against vainglory, and against uttering any thoughtless word; and see that your hands do not reach out after what is not yours. **6** Do not offer a sacrifice with a blemish in it; and wash yourself with water when you approach the altar. Do not mix the thoughts of the world with the thoughts of God when you stand before Him. **7** Do your utmost to be at peace with everyone. When you stand before God and offer your sacrifice—when you come to offer it on the altar— **8** you should recite privately one hundred prayers to God and make this confession to God, saying, Oh God, the incomprehensible, the unfathomable, the unattainable, the pure treasure, purify me in love, for I am flesh and blood and I run defiled to You, that You may purify me. **9** I come burdened, and I ask that You may lighten my burden. A fire will burn wood, and Your mercy will take away my iniquities. Forgive me—I that am a sinner; I forgive the whole creation that You have made, I have no complaint against anyone: **10** I am at peace with all that is made in Your image. **11** I am unmoved by all the evil reasonings that have been brought before me. I am Your servant and the son of Your maidservant: I am the one who sins, You are the one who forgives. **12** Forgive me and enable me to stand in Your holy place. Let my sacrifice be acceptable before You. **13** Do not reject me because of my sins, but receive me to You, in spite of my many sins, like a sheep that has gone astray. **14** God who

has been with our father Adam, and Abel, and Noah, and our father Abraham, and his son Isaac, who has been with Jacob, be with me also, and receive my sacrifice from my hand. **15** As you recite all this, take your sacrifice and offer it; and strive heavenwards because of the sacrifice of God, so that you do not displease Him. For the work of the priest is no small thing."

CHAPTER 7

1 Every priest today, and until the end of time, must be temperate as regards his food, and drink, and sleep; neither should he talk about events connected with this world, nor listen to anyone who is talking about them. **2** Rather should he spend his whole life occupied with prayer, and vigils, and recitation until our God sends for him in peace. **3** Every man on earth, be he priest or monk—for after a long time they will love the life of holy retreat—must renounce the world and all its evil cares and join in the holy service the messengers render in purity to God. **4** And they will be honored before God and His messengers because of their holy sacrifices and their angelic service, which is like the archetype that is rendered in the heavens. **5** And the messengers will be their friends, because of their perfect faith and their purity; and great is their honor before God. **6** In a word, whether great or small, sinlessness is required of us. **7** The chief sins worthy of conversion are these: You will not kill with the sword; You will not kill with the tongue either; **8** You will not commit fornication with your body; You will not commit fornication with your thoughts; You will not go in to the young to defile them; **9** You will not be envious; You will not be angry until the sun has set; **10** You will not be proud in disposition; You will not rejoice over your neighbour's fall; You will not slander; **11** You will not look at a woman with a lustful eye; and, Do not readily listen to slander. **12** We need to beware of these things, and of others like them, until each one of us is secure from the wrath that will be revealed from Heaven."

CHAPTER 8

1 Now when the people gathered about him heard him, they cried out aloud, saying, "This is appropriate and right. Amen." But the God-loving old man was silent: he drew up his blanket [and] he covered his face. **2** And the people and the priest were silent, so that he could rest himself a little while. **3** But the messenger of his father Abraham came to him and took him up into the heavens. He saw terrors and tumults spread abroad on this side and on that; and it was a terror and a tumult fearful to behold. **4** Some had the face of a camel, others had the face of a lion; some had the face of a dog, others had but one eye and had tongs in their hands, three ells long, all of iron. **5** I looked, and behold, a man was brought, and those who brought him went with him. When they reached the beasts, those who went with him withdrew to one side. The lion advanced toward him, tore him apart into little pieces, and swallowed him; **6** it then vomited him up, and he became like himself again; and the next beast treated him in just the same way. **7** In short, they passed him on from one to the other; each one would tear him into pieces, swallow him, and then vomit him up; and he would become like himself again. **8** I said to the messenger, "What sin has this man committed, my lord, that all this is done to him?" The messenger said to me, "This man you are looking at now had a quarrel with his neighbour, and he died without their being reconciled. **9** See, he has been handed over to five chief tormentors: they spend a year tormenting him for every hour he spent quarreling with his neighbour." **10** The messenger also said to me, "My beloved Isaac, do you think these are the only ones? Believe me Isaac, beloved of God, there are six hundred thousand tormentors. **11** They spend a year tormenting a man for every hour that he spends sinning—if he did not convert, that is, before he went forth from the body."

CHAPTER 9

1 He led me on and brought me to a fiery river, the waters of which were an ell high, and its noise like the noise of Heaven's thunder. **2** And I saw a host of souls submerged in it;

and those who were in that river cried out and wept aloud, and there was a great commotion and much groaning. **3** But it is a discerning fire that does not touch the righteous, yet burns up sinners and boils them in the stench that surrounds them. **4** I also saw the pit of the abyss, the smoke of which went up in clouds; I saw men sunk in it grinding their teeth, crying out and wailing, and each one was groaning. **5** The messenger said to me, "Look and see these others too." And when I had looked at them the messenger said to me, "These are those who have committed the sin of Sodom; these are indeed in great distress." I also saw pits full of worms that do not sleep; I saw Abdemerouchos who is in charge of the punishments, made all of fire, threatening the tormentors in Gehenna, and saying, "Beat them until they know that God is." I saw a house built of fiery stone, and there were grown men underneath it, crying out and wailing. The messenger said to me, "Look with your eyes and contemplate the punishments." I said to the messenger, "My eyes could not endure it; for how long must these punishments go on?" He said to me, "Until the merciful God has pity."

CHAPTER 10

1 After this the messenger took me up into the heavens; I saw my father Abraham, and I made obeisance to him. **2** He saluted me, with all the saints, and the saints honored me because of my father; they walked with me and took me to my [heavenly] Father—I worshiped Him with all the saints. **3** Songs of praise rang out: "You are Holy, You are Holy, You are Holy. King, Lord of Hosts, the heavens and the earth are full of Your holy glory." **4** The Lord said to my father from the holy place, "[It] is good that you have come, Abraham, you righteous root and faithful saint; it is good that you have come to our city. Whatever you may want to ask now, make your requests in the name of your beloved son Isaac, and they will be yours indeed." **5** My father Abraham said, "Yours is the power, O Lord Almighty." The Lord said to Abraham, "As for all those who are given the name of my beloved Isaac, let each one of them copy out his testament and honor it, and feed a poor man with bread in the name of my beloved Isaac on the day of his holy commemoration; I will grant them to you as sons in My kingdom." **6** Abraham said, "My almighty Lord, if a man cannot copy out his testament, can You not in Your mercy accept him, for You are merciful and compassionate?" **7** The Lord said to Abraham, "Let him feed a poor man with bread, and I will give him to you as a gift and as a son in My Kingdom, and he will come with you to the first hour of the thousand years." **8** Abraham said, "Suppose he is poor and has no means of getting bread?" **9** The Lord said, "Let him spend the night of my beloved Isaac's commemoration without sleep, and I will give him to you as a gift and an inheritor in My Kingdom." **10** My father Abraham said, "Suppose he is weak and has no strength, can You not in Your mercy accept him in love?" **11** The Lord said to him, "Let him offer up a little incense in the name of your beloved son Isaac, and I will give him to you as a son in My Kingdom. **12** If he has no means of getting incense, let him seek out a copy of his testament and read it on my beloved Isaac's day. **13** If he cannot read it, let him go and listen to others who can. If he is unable to do any of these things, let him go into his house and say one hundred prayers, and I will give him to you as a son in My Kingdom. **14** But the most essential thing of all is that he should offer a sacrifice in my beloved Isaac's name, for his body was offered as a sacrifice. **15** Yet not only will I give you everyone called by my beloved Isaac's name as a son in My Kingdom, [but] I will also give you everyone who does one of the things I have mentioned. **16** And I will give you everyone who concerns himself about Isaac's life and his testament, or does any compassionate act, such as giving someone a cup of water to drink, or who copies out his testament with his own hand, and those who read it with all their heart in faith, believing everything that I have said. **17** My power and the power of My beloved Son and the Holy Spirit will be with them, and I will give them to you as sons in My Kingdom. Peace to all of you, all My saints."

CHAPTER 11

1 Now when He had said this, songs of praise rang out: "You are Holy, You are Holy, You are Holy. King, Lord of Hosts, the

heavens and the earth are full of Your holy glory." **2** The Father said to Michael from the holy place, "Michael, My steward, go quickly and gather together the messengers and all the saints, so that they may come and meet My beloved Isaac." **3** And Michael sounded the trumpet at once. All the saints gathered with the messengers and came to the couch of our father Isaac. **4** The Lord mounted His chariot, and the seraphim were in front of Him with the messengers. And when they came to our father Isaac's couch, our father Isaac beheld our Lord's face immediately turned toward him full of joy. **5** He cried out, "It is good that You have come, my Lord, and Your great chief-messenger Michael! It is good that you have come, my father Abraham, and all the saints."

CHAPTER 12

1 Now when he had said this, Jacob embraced his father; he kissed his mouth and wept. Our father Isaac fixed his eyes on him and motioned to him to be silent. **2** Our father Isaac said to the Lord, "Remember my beloved Jacob." The Lord said to him, "My power will be with him; and when the time comes and I become man and die and rise from the dead on the third day, I will put your name in everyone's mind, and they will invoke you as their father." **3** Isaac said to Jacob, "My beloved son, this is the last commandment I give you today: keep a sharp eye on yourself; do not dishonor the image of God; for what you do to the image of man, you do to the image of God, and God will do it to you, too, in the place where you will meet Him. This is the beginning and the end." **4** Now when he had said this, our Lord brought his soul out of his body, and it was white as snow. **5** He greeted it [and] set it on the chariot with Him; He took it up into the heavens, with the seraphim making music before Him, and all the messengers and the saints. **6** He freely granted him the good things of His Kingdom forever, and all the requests our father Abraham had asked of the Lord He freely granted him as a covenant forever.

CHAPTER 13

1 This is the going forth from the body of our father Isaac, the patriarch, on the twenty-fourth of the month Mesore. **2** And the day on which his father Abraham offered him as a sacrifice is the eighteenth of Mechir. **3** The heavens and the earth are full of the soothing fragrance of our father Isaac, like choice silver: this is the sacrifice of our father Isaac the patriarch. **4** When Abraham offered him as a sacrifice to God, the soothing fragrance of Isaac's sacrifice went up into the heavens. **5** Blessed is every man who performs an act of mercy in the name of these patriarchs, for they will be their sons in the kingdom of the heavens. **6** For our Lord has made a covenant with them forever, that everyone who performs an act of mercy on the day of their commemoration will be given to them as a son in the kingdom of the heavens forever. **7** And they will come to the first hour of the thousand years, in accordance with the promise of our Lord, even our God and our Savior Jesus Christ, **8** through whom every glory is due to Him, and His good Father, and the Holy Spirit, the giver of life to all creation and one in being with the Father and the Son, now and always, forever and ever. Amen.

TESTAMENT OF JACOB

The Testament of Jacob is the tale of Jacob's visitation by the archangel Michael who tells him of his impending death. Jacob is then taken on a visit to Heaven, where he sees the torment of the sinful dead, and then meets his deceased grandfather Abraham. In this Testament it is the angels that Jacob meets who deliver most of the sermonizing material. It was probably written in the 2nd or 3rd century AD.

CHAPTER 1

[1] In the Name of the Father, the Son, and the Holy Spirit—the one God. [2] We begin, with the help of God Most High and through His intercession, to write the account of the life of our father, the patriarch Jacob, son of the patriarch Isaac, on the twenty-eighth day of the month of Mesore. [3] May the blessing of his prayer guard and protect us from the temptations of the unyielding adversary. Amen! Amen! Amen! [4] He said, "Come, listen, my beloved ones and my brothers who love the Lord, to what has been received." [5] Now when the time of our father Jacob, father of fathers, son of Isaac, son of Abraham, approached and drew near for him to go forth from his body, this faithful one was advanced in years and distinction. [6] So the Lord sent Michael to him, the chief of the messengers, who said to him, "O Israel, my beloved, of noble lineage, write down your spoken legacy and your instruction for your household and give them a covenant; also concern yourself with the proper ordering of your household, for the time has drawn near for you to go to your fathers to rejoice with them forever." [7] So when our father Jacob, the faithful one, heard this from the messenger, he answered and said, as was his custom every day to speak in this manner with the messengers, [8] "Let the will of the Lord be done." And God pronounced a blessing on our father Jacob. [9] Jacob had a secluded place which he would enter to offer his prayers before the Lord in the night and in the day. [10] The messengers would visit him and guard him and strengthen him in all things. [11] God blessed him and multiplied his people in the land of Egypt at the time when he went down to the land of Egypt to meet his son Joseph. [12] His eyes had become dull from weeping, but when he went down to Egypt he saw clearly when he beheld his son. [13] So Jacob-Israel bowed with his face to the ground, then fell on the neck of his son Joseph and kissed him, while weeping and saying, "I can die now, my son, because I have seen your face once more in my lifetime; O my beloved son."

CHAPTER 2

[1] Joseph continued to rule over all Egypt, while Jacob stayed in the land of Goshen for seventeen years and became very old, so that his lifespan was completed. [2] He continually kept all the commandments and feared the Lord. [3] His eyes grew dim and his lifetime was so nearly finished that he could not see a single person because of his advanced age and decline. [4] Then he lifted his eyes toward the light of Isaac, but he was afraid and became disturbed. [5] So the messenger said to him, "Do not fear, O Jacob; [6] I am the messenger who has been walking with you and guarding you from your infancy. [7] I announced that you would receive the blessing of your father and of Rebekah, your mother. [8] I am the one who is with you, O Israel, in all your acts and in everything which you have witnessed. [9] I saved you from Laban when he was endangering you and pursuing you. [10] At that time I gave you all his possessions and blessed you, your wives, your children, and your flocks. [11] I am the one who saved you from the hand of Esau. [12] I am the one who accompanied you to the land of Egypt, O Israel, and a very great people was given to you. [13] Blessed is your father Abraham, for he has become the friend of God—may He be exalted—because of his generosity and love of strangers. [14] Blessed is your father Isaac who begot you, for he was a perfect sacrifice, acceptable to God. [15] Blessed are you also, O Jacob, for you have seen God face to face. [16] You saw the messenger of God—may He be exalted—and you saw the ladder standing firm on the ground with its top in the heavens. [17] Then you beheld the Lord sitting at its top with a power which no one could describe. [18] You spoke out and said, This is the house of God and this is the gate of Heaven. [19] Blessed are you, for you have come near to God and He is strong among mankind, so now do not be troubled, O chosen one of God. [20] Blessed are you, O Israel, and blessed is all your progeny. [21] For all of you will be called The Patriarchs to the end of the age and of the epochs; you are the people and the lineage of the servants of God. [22] Blessed is the nation which will strive for your purity and will see your good works. Blessed is the man who will remember you on the day of your noble festival. [23] Blessed is the one who will perform acts of mercy in honor of your several names, and will give someone a cup of water to drink, or will come with an offering to the sanctuary, or will take in strangers, or visit the sick and console their children, or will clothe a naked one in honor of your several names. [24] Such a one will neither lack any of the good things of this world, nor life everlasting in the world to come. [25] Moreover, whoever will have caused the stories of your several lives and sufferings to be written at his own expense, or will have written them by his own hand, or will have read them soberly, or will hear them in faith, or will remember your deeds—such persons will have their sins forgiven and their trespasses pardoned, and they will go on account of you and your progeny into the kingdom of the heavens. [26] And now rise up, Jacob, for you will be translated from hardship and pain of heart to continuous rest, and you will enter into the repose which will not pass away, into mercy, continuous light, and spiritual joy. [27] So now make your statement to your household, and peace be on you, for I am about to go to Him who sent me."

CHAPTER 3

[1] So when the messenger had made this statement to our father Jacob, he ascended from him into Heaven, as Jacob bid him farewell. [2] Those who were around Jacob heard him as he thanked God and glorified Him with praise. [3] And all the members of his household, great and small, gathered around him, weeping over him, deeply grieving and saying, "You are going away and leaving us as orphans." [4] And they kept on saying to him, "O our beloved father, what will we do, for we are in a strange land?" [5] So Jacob said to them, "Do not fear; God Himself appeared to me in Upper Mesopotamia and said to me: I am the God of your fathers; do not fear, for I am with you forever and with your descendants who will come after you. [6] This land in which you are I am about to give to you and to your descendants after you forever. [7] And do not be afraid to go down to Egypt. [8] I will make a great people for you and your descendants will increase and multiply forever. [9] Joseph will put his hand on your eyes and your people will multiply in the land of Egypt. [10] Afterward they will come to this place and will be without care. I will do good to them for your sake, though for the time being they will be displaced from here."

CHAPTER 4

[1] After this, the time for Jacob-Israel to leave his body had arrived. [2] So he summoned Joseph and said to him, "If indeed you have found grace, place your blessed hand under my side and swear an oath before the Lord that you will place my body in the tomb of my fathers." [3] Then Joseph said to him, "I will do exactly what you command me, O beloved of God." [4] But he said to Joseph, "I want you to swear to me." [5] So Joseph swore to Jacob, his father, to the effect that he would carry his body to the tomb of his fathers, and Jacob accepted the oath of his son. [6] Afterward, this report reached Joseph: "Your father has become uneasy." [7] So he took his two sons, Ephraim and Manasseh, and went before his father Jacob. [8] Joseph said to him, "These are my sons whom God has given me in the land of Egypt to come after me." [9] Israel said, "Bring them closer to me here." [10] For the eyes of Israel had become dim from his advanced age so that he could not see. [11] So Joseph brought his sons closer and Jacob kissed them. Then Joseph commanded them, namely Ephraim and Manasseh, to bow down before Jacob to the ground. [12] Joseph took Manasseh and put him at Israel's right hand and Ephraim at his left hand. [13] But Israel reversed his hands and let his right hand rest on the head of Ephraim and his left hand on the head of Manasseh. [14] He blessed them and gave them back to their father and said, "May the God under whose authority my fathers, Abraham and Isaac, served in reverence, the God who has strengthened me from my youth up to the present time when the messenger has saved me from all my afflictions, may he bless these boys, Manasseh and Ephraim. [15] May my name be on them, also the names of my holy fathers, Abraham and Isaac." [16] After this, Israel said to Joseph, "I will die, and all of you will return to the land of your fathers and God will be with you. [17] And you have personally received a mighty favor, greater than that of your brothers, for I have taken this arrow with my bow and my sword from the Amorites."

CHAPTER 5

1 Then Jacob sent for all his children and said to them, "Gather around me that I may inform you of everything which will come on you and what will overtake each one of you in the last days." **2** So they gathered around Israel from the eldest to the youngest of them. **3** Then Jacob-Israel spoke up and said to his sons, "Listen, O sons of Jacob, listen to your father Israel, from Reuben my firstborn to Benjamin." **4** Then he told them what would come on the twelve children, calling each one of them and his tribe by name; **5** and he blessed them with the celestial blessing. **6** After this they were silent for a short time in order that he might rest. So the heavens rejoiced that he could observe the places of repose. **7** And behold, there approached numerous tormentors differing in their aspects. They were prepared to torment the sinners, who are these: adulterers, male and female; those lusting after males; the vicious who degrade the semen given by God; **8** the astrologers and the sorcerers; the evildoers and the worshipers of idols who hold onto abominations; and the slanderers who pass judgment with two tongues. **9** And as to all these sinners, their punishment is the fire which will not be extinguished and the outer darkness where there is weeping and gnashing of teeth.

CHAPTER 6

1 And when the days of their mourning were finished, Pharaoh was still weeping over Jacob because of his regard for Joseph. **2** Then Joseph addressed the nobles of Pharaoh and said to them, "Since I have found favor with you, will you speak on my behalf to Pharaoh the king, and say to him that Jacob made me take an oath that when he went out from his body I would bury his body in the tomb of my fathers in the land of Canaan, in that very place?" **3** So Pharaoh said to Joseph, "Go in peace and bury your father in accordance with the oath which he required of you. **4** And take chariots and horses with you, the best of my kingdom and from my own household as you desire." **5** So Joseph worshiped God in the presence of Pharaoh, went forth from him, and set out to bury his father. **6** And there set out with him the slaves of Pharaoh, the elders of Egypt, all the household of Joseph, and his brothers and all Israel. **7** They all went up with him into the chariots, and the entourage moved along like a great army. **8** They descended into the land of Canaan to the riverbank across the Jordan and they mourned for him in that place with very great grief indeed. **9** They maintained that great grief for him for seven days. **10** So when the inhabitants of Dan heard about the mourning in their land, they said, "This great mourning is that of the Egyptians." **11** To this day [[they call that place "the Mourning of the Egyptians"]]. **12** Then Israel was carried forward and was buried in the land of Canaan in the second tomb. **13** This is the one which Abraham had bought with authorization for burials from Ephron opposite Mature. **14** After that, Joseph returned to the land of Egypt with his brothers and all the entourage of Pharaoh. **15** And Joseph lived after the death of his father many years. **16** He continued to rule over Egypt, though Jacob had died and was left behind with his own people.

CHAPTER 7

1 This is what we have transmitted: We have described the demise of and the mourning for the father of fathers, Jacob-Israel, to the extent of our ability to do this; **2** also as it is written in the spiritual scrolls of God and as we have found it in the ancient treasury of knowledge of our fathers, the holy, pure apostles. **3** And if you wish to know the life history and get new knowledge of the father of fathers, Jacob, then take a father who is attested in the Old Testament. **4** Moses is the one who wrote it, the first of the prophets, the author of the Law. Read from it and enlighten your insights. **5** You will find this and more in it, written for your sake. **6** You will find that God and His messengers were their friends while they were in their bodies, and that God kept on speaking to them many times in various passages from the Scroll. **7** Also He says in many passages with regard to the patriarch Jacob, the father of

fathers, in the Scroll, thus, "My son, I will bless your descendants like the stars of the heavens." **8** And our father Jacob would speak to his son Joseph and say to him, "My God appeared to me in the land of Canaan at Luz and blessed me and said to me, I will bless you and multiply you and make you a mighty people. **9** They will go out [to war] like the other nations of this earth and your descendants will increase forever." **10** This is what we have heard, O my brothers and my loved ones, from our fathers, the patriarchs. **11** And it is incumbent on us that we have zeal for their deeds, their purity, their faith, their love of mankind, and their acceptance of strangers; **12** in order that we may lay claim to be their sons in the kingdom of the heavens, so that they will intercede for us before God that we may be saved from the torture of Gehenna. **13** These are the ones whom the Arabs have designated as the holy fathers. **14** Jacob instructed his sons with regard to punishment, and he would call them the sword of the Lord, which is the river of fire, prepared with its waves to engulf the evildoers and the impure. **15** These are the things the power of which the father of fathers, Jacob, expounded and taught to all his sons that the wise ones might hear and pursue righteousness in mutual love with mercy and compassion. **16** For mercy saves people from penalties and mercy overcomes a multitude of wrongs. Truly, one who shows mercy to the poor, that one makes a loan to God. **17** So now, my beloved sons, do not slacken from prayer and fasting ever at any time, and by the life of the religion you will drive away the demons. **18** O my dear son, avoid the evil ways of the world, which are anger and depravity and all vicious deeds. **19** And beware of injustice and blasphemy and abduction. **20** For the unjust will not inherit the Kingdom of God, nor will the adulterers, nor the accursed, nor those who commit outrages and have sexual intercourse with males, nor the gluttons, nor the worshipers of idols, nor those who utter imprecations, nor those who pollute themselves outside of pure marriage; and others whom we have not presented or even mentioned will not come near the Kingdom of God. **21** O my sons, honor the saints, for they are the ones who will intercede for you. **22** O my sons, be generous to strangers and you will be given exactly what was given to the great Abraham, the father of fathers, and to our father Isaac, his son. **23** O my sons, do for the poor what will increase compassion for them here and now, so that God will give you the bread of life forever in the Kingdom of God. **24** For to the one who has given a poor person bread in this world God will give a portion from the Tree of Life. **25** Clothe the poor person who is naked on the earth, so that God may clothe you with the apparel of glory in the kingdom of the heavens, and you will be the sons of our holy fathers, Abraham, Isaac, and Jacob in Heaven forever. **26** Be concerned with the reading of the word of God in His scrolls here below, and remember the saints who have written of their lives, their sufferings, and their prostrations in prayer. **27** In the future, it will not be prevented that they should be inscribed in the Scroll of Life in the kingdom of the heavens. **28** And you will be counted among the saints, those who pleased God in their lifetime and will rejoice with the messengers in the land of continuous life.

CHAPTER 8

1 You will honor the memory of our fathers, the patriarchs, at this time each year and on this same day, which is the twenty-eighth of the month of Mesore. **2** This is what we have found written in the ancient documents of our fathers, the saints who were pleasing to God. **3** Because of their intercession and their prayer, we will have all things, namely a share and a place in the kingdom of the heavens which belongs to our Lord and our God and our Master and our Savior, Jesus the Messiah. **4** He is the one whom we ask to forgive us for our mistakes and our errors and to overlook our misdeeds. **5** May He be kind to us on the day of His judgment and let us hear the voice filled with joy, kindness, and gladness, saying, "Come to Me, O blessed ones of My Father, inherit the kingdom which was yours from before the creation of the world." **6** And may we be worthy to receive His divine secrets, which are the means to the pardon of our sins. **7** May He help us toward the salvation of our souls, and may He ward off from us the blows of the wicked enemy. **8** May He let us stand at His right hand on the great and terrible day for the intercession of the mistress of intercessions, the source of purity, generosity, and blessings, the mother of salvation, and for the intercession of all the martyrs, saints, doers of pleasing deeds, and everyone who has pleased the Lord with his pious deeds and his good will. **9** Amen! Amen! Amen! And praise to God always, forever, [and] perpetually.

TESTAMENT OF JOB

The Testament of Job is a book likely written in the 1st century BC or the 1st century AD (thus part of a tradition often called "intertestamental literature" by Christian scholars). The earliest surviving manuscript is in Coptic of the 5th century; other early surviving manuscripts are in Greek and Old Slavonic. Similar to other apocryphal testaments, it is an account of the last events and words of the protagonist (here, Job).

CHAPTER 1

1 On the day he became sick and knew that he would have to leave his bodily abode, he called his seven sons and his three daughters together and spoke to them as follows: **2** Form a circle around me, children, and hear, and I will relate to you what the Lord did for me and all that happened to me. **3** For I am your father Job. **4** Know then, my children, that you are the generation of a chosen one and take heed of your noble birth. **5** For I am of the sons of Esau. My brother is Nahor, and your mother is Dinah. I have become your father by her. **6** For my first wife died with my other ten children in bitter death. **7** Hear now, children, and I will reveal to you what happened to me. **8** I was a very rich man living in the east, in the land of Uz, and before the Lord had named me Job, I was called Jobab. **9** The beginning of my trial was thus: near my house there was the idol of one worshiped by the people; and I saw burnt-offerings constantly brought to him as a god. **10** Then I pondered and said to myself, "Is this he who made the heavens and earth, the sea, and all of us? How will I know the truth?" **11** And in that night as I lay asleep, a voice came and called: "Jobab! Jobab! rise up, and I will tell you who is the One whom you wish to know. **12** This, however, to whom the people bring burnt-offerings and libations, is not God, but this is the power and work of the Seducer by which he deceives the people." **13** And when I heard this, I fell on the earth and I prostrated myself, saying, **14** "O my Lord, who speaks for the salvation of my soul—please, if this is the idol of Satan, please, let me go on and destroy it and purify this spot. **15** For there is none that can forbid me doing this, as I am the king of this land, so that those that live in it will no longer be led astray." **16** And the voice that spoke out of the flame answered to me: "You can purify this spot. **17** But behold, I announce to you what the Lord ordered me to tell you, for I am the chief-messenger of the God." **18** And I said, "Whatever will be told to His servant, I will hear." **19** And the chief-messenger said to me, "Thus speaks the Lord: If you undertake to destroy and take away the image of Satan, he will set himself with wrath to wage war against you, and he will display all his malice against you. **21** He will bring on you many severe plagues and take from you all that you have. **21** He will take away your children and will inflict many calamities on you. **22** Then you must wrestle like an athlete and resist pain, [being] sure of your reward, [and] overcome trials and afflictions. **23** But when you endure, I will make your name renowned throughout all generations of the earth until the [very] end of the world. **24** And I will restore you to all that you had, and the double part of what you will lose will be given to you in order that you may know that God does not consider the person but gives to each who deserves the good. **25** And also to you will it be given, and you will put on a crown of amaranth. **26** And at the resurrection you will awaken for continuous life. Then you will know that the Lord is just, and true, and mighty." **27** Immediately, my children, I replied: "I will from love of God endure all that will come on me until death, and I will not shrink back." **28** Then the messenger put his seal on me and left me.

CHAPTER 2

1 After this I rose up in the night and took fifty slaves and went to the temple of the idol and destroyed it to the ground. **2** And so I went back to my house and gave orders that the door should he firmly locked, saying to my doorkeepers: **3** "If somebody will ask for me, bring no report to me, but tell him: He investigates urgent affairs. He is inside." **4** Then Satan disguised himself as a beggar and knocked heavily at the door, saying to the doorkeeper: **5** "Report to Job and say that I desire to meet him," **6** and the doorkeeper came in and told me that, but heard from me that I was studying. **7** The evil one, having failed in this, went away and took on his shoulder an old, torn basket and went and spoke to the doorkeeper, saying, "Tell Job: Give me bread from your hands that I may eat." **8** And when I heard this, I gave her burnt bread to give it to him, and I made known to him: "Do not expect to eat of my bread, for it is forbidden to you." **9** But the doorkeeper, being ashamed to hand him the burnt and ashy bread, as she did not know that it was Satan, took of her own fine bread and gave it to him. **10** But he took it, and knowing what occurred, said to the maiden, "Go on, bad servant, and bring me the bread that was given you to hand to me." **11** And the servant cried and spoke in grief: "You speak the truth, saying that I am a bad servant, because I have not done as I was instructed by my master." **12** And he turned back and brought him the burnt bread and said to him, "Thus says my lord: You will not eat of my bread anymore, for it is forbidden to you. **13** And he gave me this in order that the charge may not be brought against me that I did not give to the enemy who asked." **14** And when Satan heard this, he sent the servant back to me, saying, "As you see this bread all burnt, so I will soon burn your body to make it like this." **15** And I replied, "Do what you desire to do and accomplish whatever you plot. For I am ready to endure whatever you bring on me." **16** And when the Devil heard this, he left me, and walking up to under the [highest] Heaven, he took from the Lord the oath that he might have power over all my possessions. **17** And after having taken the power, he went and instantly took away all my wealth.

CHAPTER 3

1 For I had one hundred and thirty thousand sheep, and of these I separated seven thousand for the clothing of orphans, and widows, and of needy and sick ones. **2** I had a herd of eight hundred dogs who watched my sheep, and besides these two hundred to watch my house. **3** And I had nine mills working for the whole city and ships to carry goods, and I sent them into every city, and into the villages to the feeble, and sick, and to those that were unfortunate. **4** And I had three hundred and forty thousand nomadic donkeys, and of these I set aside five hundred, and the offspring of these I order to be sold and the proceeds to be given to the poor and the needy. **5** For from all the lands the poor came to meet me. **6** For the four doors of my house were opened, each, being in charge of a watchman who had to see whether there were any people coming, asking [for] alms, and whether they would see me sitting at one of the doors so that they could leave through the other and take whatever they needed. **7** I also had thirty immovable tables set at all hours for the strangers alone, and I also had twelve tables spread for the widows. **8** And if anyone came asking for alms, he found food on my table to take all he needed, and I turned nobody away to leave my door with an empty stomach. **9** I also had three thousand five hundred yokes of oxen, and I selected of these five hundred and had them tend to the plowing. **10** And with these I had done all the work in each field by those who would take it in charge, and I laid aside the income of their crops for the poor on their table. **11** I also had fifty bakeries from which I sent [the bread] to the table for the poor. **12** And I had slaves selected for their service. **13** There were also some strangers who saw my good will; they wished to serve as waiters themselves. **14** Others, being in distress and unable to obtain a living, came with the request, saying, **15** "Please, since we can also fill this office of servants and have no possession, have pity on us and advance money to us in order that we may go into the great cities and sell merchandise. **16** And the surplus of our profit we may give as help to the poor, and then we will return to you your own [money]." **17** And when I heard this, I was glad that they should take this altogether from me for the farming of charity for the poor. **18** And I gave them what they wanted with a willing heart, and I accepted their written bond, but would not take any other security from them except the written document. **19** And they went abroad and gave to the poor as far as they were successful. **20** Frequently, however, some of their goods were lost on the road or on the sea, or they would be robbed of them. **21** Then they would come and say, "Please act generously toward us in order that we may see how we can restore to you your own." **22** And when I heard this, I had sympathy with them, and handed their bond to them, and often, having read it before them, tore it up and released them of their debt, saying to them, **23** "What I have consecrated for the benefit of the poor, I will not take from you." **24** And so I accepted nothing from my debtor. **25** And when a man with cheerful heart came to me, saying, "I am not in need to be compelled to be a paid worker for the poor, **26** but I wish to serve the needy at your table," and he consented to work, and he ate his share, **27** so I gave him his wages nevertheless, and I went home rejoicing. **28** And when he did not wish to take it, I forced him to do so, saying, "I know that you are a laboring man who looks for and waits for his wages, and you must take it." **29** I never deferred paying the wages of the hireling or any other, nor kept back in my house for a single evening his hire that was due to him. **30** Those that milked the cows and the ewes signaled to the passers by that they should take their share. **31** For the milk flowed in such plenty that it curdled into butter on the hills and by the roadside; and by the rocks and the hills the cattle lay which had given birth to their offspring. **32** For my servants grew weary keeping the meat of the widows and the poor and dividing it into small pieces. **33** For they would curse and say, "Oh that we had of his flesh that we could be satisfied," although I was very kind to them. **34** I also had six harps, [and six slaves to play the harps,] and also a cithara, [and] a decachord, and I struck it during the day. **35** And I took the cithara, and the widows responded after their meals. **36** And with the musical instrument I reminded them of God, that they should give praise to the Lord. **37** And when my maidservants would murmur, then I took the musical instruments and played as much as they would have done for their wages, and gave them respite from their labor and sighs.

CHAPTER 4

1 And my children, after having taken charge of the service, took their meals each day along with their three sisters beginning with the older brother, and made a feast. **2** And I rose in the morning and offered fifty rams and nineteen sheep as a sin-offering for them, and what remained as a residue was consecrated to the poor. **3** And I said to them, "Take these as residue and pray for my children. **4** Perhaps my sons have sinned before the Lord, speaking in haughtiness of spirit: We are children of this rich man. All these goods are ours; why should we be servants of the poor? **5** And speaking thus in a haughty spirit they may have provoked the anger of God, for overbearing pride is an abomination before the Lord." **6** So I brought oxen as offerings to the priest at the altar, saying, "May my children never think evil toward God in their hearts." **7** While I lived in this manner, the Seducer could not bear to see the good [I did], and he demanded the warfare of God against me. **8** And he came on me cruelly. **9** First he burned up the large number of sheep, then the camels, then he burned up the cattle and all my herds; or they were captured not only by enemies but also by such as had received benefits from me. **10** And the shepherds came and announced that to me. **11** But when I heard it, I gave praise to God and did not blaspheme. **12** And when the Seducer learned of my fortitude, he plotted new things against me. **13** He disguised himself as [the] king of Persia and besieged my city, and after he had led off all that were therein, he spoke to them in malice, saying in boastful language, **14** "This man Job, who has obtained all the goods of the earth and left nothing for others, has destroyed and torn down the temple of god. **15** Therefore I will repay to him what he has done to the house of the great god. **16** Now come with me and we will pillage all that is left in his house." **17** And they answered and said to him: "He has seven sons and three daughters. **18** Take heed lest they flee into other lands and they may become our tyrants and then come over us with force and kill us." **19** And he said, "Do not be afraid at all. I have destroyed his flocks and his wealth by fire, and I have captured the rest, and behold, I will kill his children." **20** And having spoken thus, he went and threw the house on my children and killed them. **21** And my fellow-citizens, seeing that what was said by him had become true, came and pursued me, and robbed me of all that was in my house. **22** And I saw with mine own eyes the pillage of my house, and men without culture and without honor sat at my table and on my couches, and I could not

remonstrate against them. **23** For I was exhausted like a woman with her loins let loose from multitude of pains, remembering chiefly that this warfare had been predicted to me by the Lord through His messenger. **24** And I became like one who, when seeing the rough sea and the adverse winds, while the lading of the vessel in mid-ocean is too heavy, casts the burden into the sea, saying, **25** "I wish to destroy all this only in order to come safely into the city so that I may take as profit the rescued ship and the best of my things." **26** Thus I managed my own affairs. **27** But there came another messenger and announced to me the ruin of my own children, and I was shaken with terror. **28** And I tore my clothes and said, "The Lord has given, the Lord has taken. As it has deemed best to the Lord, thus it has come to be. May the Name of the Lord be blessed."

CHAPTER 5

1 And when Satan saw that he could put me to despair, he went and asked of the Lord [for] my body in order to inflict plague on me, for the evil one could not bear my patience. **2** Then the Lord delivered me into his hands to use my body as he wanted, but He gave him no power over my soul. **3** And he came to me as I was sitting on my throne, still mourning over my children. **4** And he resembled a great hurricane and turned over my throne and threw me on the ground. **5** And I continued lying on the floor for three hours, and he struck me with a hard plague from the top of my head to the toes of my feet. **6** And I left the city in great terror and woe and sat down on a dunghill, my body being worm-eaten. **7** And I wet the earth with the moistness of my sore body, for matter flowed off my body, and many worms covered it. **8** And when a single worm crept off my body, I put it back, saying, "Remain on the spot where you have been placed until He who has sent you will order you elsewhere." **9** Thus I endured for several years, sitting on a dunghill outside of the city while being plague-stricken. **10** And I saw with my own eyes my longed-for children [carried by messengers to Heaven], **11** and my humbled wife who had been brought to her bridal chamber in such great luxuriousness and with spearmen as bodyguards. I saw her do a water-carrier's work like a slave in the house of a common man in order to win some bread and bring it to me. **12** And in my sore affliction I said, "Oh that these braggart city rulers whom I should not have thought to be equal with my shepherd dogs should now employ my wife as servant!" **13** And after this I took courage again. **14** Yet afterward they withheld even the bread that she should only have her own nourishment. **15** But she took it and divided it between herself and me, saying woefully, "Woe to me! Very soon he may no longer have bread to eat, and he cannot go to the market to ask [for] bread from the bread-sellers in order to bring it to me that he may eat." **16** And when Satan learned this, he took the guise of a bread-seller, and it was as if by chance that my wife met him and asked him for bread thinking that it was that sort of man. **17** But Satan said to her, "Give me the value, and then take what you wish." **18** Immediately she answered, saying, "Where will I get money? Do you not know what misfortune happened to me? If you have pity, show it to me; if not, you will see." **19** And he replied, saying, "If you did not deserve this misfortune, you would not have suffered all this. **20** Now, if there is no silver piece in your hand, give me the hair of your head and take three loaves of bread for it, so that you may live on these for three days." **21** Then she said to herself: "What is the hair of my head in comparison with my starving husband?" **22** And so after having pondered over the matter, she said to him, "Rise and cut off my hair." **3** Then he took a pair of scissors and took off the hair of her head in the presence of all, and gave her three loaves of bread. **24** Then she took them and brought them to me. And Satan went behind her on the road, hiding himself as he walked and troubling her heart greatly.

CHAPTER 6

1 And immediately my wife came near me, and crying aloud and weeping she said, "Job! Job! How long will you sit on the dunghill outside of the city, still pondering for a while and expecting to obtain your hoped-for salvation? **2** And I have been wandering from place to place, roaming around as a hired servant; behold, the memory has already died away from earth. **3** And my sons and the daughters that I carried on my bosom and the labors and pains that I sustained have been for nothing. **4** And you sit in the fetid state of soreness and worms, passing the nights in the cold air. **5** And I have undergone all trials, and troubles, and pains day and night, until I succeeded in bringing bread to you. **6** For your surplus of bread is no longer allowed to me; and as I can scarcely take my own food and divide it between us, I pondered in my heart that it was not right that you should be in pain and hunger for bread. **7** And so I ventured to go to the market without bashfulness, and when the bread-seller told me: Give me money, and you will have bread; I disclosed to him our state of distress. **8** Then I heard him say: If you have no money, hand me the hair of your head, and take three loaves of bread in order that you may live on these for three days. **9** And I yielded to the wrong and said to him: Rise and cut off my hair! And he rose and in disgrace cut off with the scissors the hair of my head on the marketplace while the crowd stood by and wondered. **10** Who would then not be astonished, saying, Is this Sitis, the wife of Job, who had fourteen curtains to cover her inner sitting room, and doors within doors so that he was greatly honored who would be brought near her? And now behold, she barters off her hair for bread! **11** Who had camels laden with goods, and they were brought into remote lands to the poor, and now she sells her hair for bread! **12** Behold her who had seven tables immovably set in her house at which each poor man and each stranger ate, and now she sells her hair for bread! **13** Behold her who had the basin with which to wash her feet made of gold and silver, and now she walks on the ground and [[sells her hair for bread!]] **14** Behold her who had her garments made of byssus interwoven with gold, and now she exchanges her hair for bread! **15** Behold her who had couches of gold and of silver, and now she sells her hair for bread! **16** In short then, Job, after the many things that have been said to me, I now say in one word to you: **17** since the feebleness of my heart has crushed my bones, rise then and take these loaves of bread and enjoy them, and then speak some word against the Lord and die! **18** For I too would exchange the torpor of death for the sustenance of my body." **19** But I replied to her, "Behold, I have been plague-stricken for these seven years, and I have withstood the worms of my body, and I was not weighed down in my soul by all these pains. **20** And as to the word which you say: Speak some word against God and die; together with you I will sustain the evil which you see, and let us endure the ruin of all that we have. **21** Yet you desire that we should say some word against God and that He should be exchanged for the great Pluto. **22** Why do you not remember those great goods which we possessed? If these goods come from the lands of the Lord, should we not also endure evils and be high-minded in everything until the Lord will have mercy again and show pity to us? **23** Do you not see the Seducer stand behind you and confound your thoughts in order that you should deceive me?" **24** And he turned to Satan and said, "Why do you not come openly to me? Stop hiding yourself you wretched one! **25** Does the lion show his strength in the weasel cage? Or does the bird fly in the basket? I now tell you: go away and wage your war against me." **26** Then he went off from behind my wife and placed himself before me, crying, and he said, "Behold, Job, I yield and give way to you who are but flesh while I am a spirit. **27** You are plague-stricken, but I am in great trouble. **28** For I am like a wrestler contesting with a wrestler who has, in single-handed combat, torn down his antagonist and covered him with dust and broken every limb of his, whereas the other one who lies beneath, having displayed his bravery, gives forth sounds of triumph testifying to his own superior excellence. **29** Thus you, O Job, are beneath and stricken with plague and pain, and yet you have carried the victory in the wrestling-match with me, and behold, I yield to you." Then he left me embarrassed. **30** Now my children, you must also show a firm heart in all the evil that happens to you, for firmness of heart is greater than all things.

CHAPTER 7

1 At this time the kings heard what had happened to me and they rose and came to me—each from his land—to visit me and to comfort me. **2** And when they came near me, they cried with a loud voice and each tore his clothes. **3** And after they had prostrated themselves, touching the earth with their heads, they sat down next to me for seven days and seven nights, and none spoke a word. **4** They were four in number: Eliphaz, the king of Teman, and Bildad, and Zophar, and Elihu. **5** And when they had taken their seat, they conversed about what had happened to me. **6** Now when they had come to me for the first time and I had shown them my precious stones, they were astonished and said, **7** "If of us three kings all our possessions would be brought together into one, it would not come up to the precious stones of Jobab's kingdom. For you are of greater nobility than all the people of the east." **8** And when, therefore, they now came to the land of Uz to visit me, they asked in the city: "Where is Jobab, the ruler of this whole land?" **9** And they told them concerning me: "He sits on the dunghill outside of the city, for he has not entered the city for seven years." **10** And then they again inquired concerning my possessions, and there was revealed to them all what happened to me. **11** And when they had learned this, they went out of the city with the inhabitants, and my fellow-citizens pointed me out to them. **12** But these remonstrated and said, "Surely this is not Jobab." **13** And while they hesitated, Eliphaz, the King of Teman, said, "Come, let us step near and see." **14** And when they came near, I remembered them, and I wept very much when I learned the purpose of their journey. **15** And I threw earth on my head, and while shaking my head I revealed to them that I was [Job]. **16** And when they saw me shake my head, they threw themselves down on the ground, all overcome with emotion. **17** And while their hosts were standing around, I saw the three kings lie on the ground for three hours like dead. **18** Then they rose and said to each other, "We cannot believe that this is Jobab." **19** And finally, after they had inquired after everything concerning me and searched for my flocks and other possessions for seven days, they said, **20** "Do we not know how many goods were sent by him to the cities and the villages around to be given to the poor, aside from all that was given away by him within his own house? How then could he have fallen into such a state of perdition and misery?" **21** And after the seven days Elihu said to the kings, "Come, let us step near and examine him accurately, whether he is truly Jobab or not." **22** And they, being not four stadia distant from his fetid body, rose and stepped near, carrying perfume in their hands, while their soldiers went with them and threw fragrant incense around them so that they could come near me. **23** And after they had thus passed three hours, covering the way with aroma, they drew near. **24** And Eliphaz began and said, "Are you, indeed, Job, our fellow-king? Are you the one who owned the great glory? **25** Are you he who once shone like the sun of day on the whole earth? Are you he who once resembled the moon and the stars, radiant throughout the night?" **26** And I answered him and said, "I am," and thereon all wept and lamented, and they sang a royal song of lamentation, their whole army joining them in a chorus. **27** And again Eliphaz said to me, "Are you he who had ordered seven thousand sheep to be given for the clothing of the poor? Where then has the glory of your throne gone? **28** Are you he who had ordered three thousand cattle to do the plowing of the field for the poor? Where then has your glory gone? **29** Are you he who had golden couches, and now you sit on a dunghill? [[Where then has your glory gone?]] **30** Are you he who had sixty tables set for the poor? Are you he who had censers for the fine perfume made of precious stones, and now you are in a fetid state? Where then has your glory gone? **31** Are you he who had golden candelabras set on silver stands, and now must you long for the natural gleam of the moon? [[Where then has your glory gone?]] **32** Are you the one who had ointment made of the spices of frankincense, and now you are in a state of repulsiveness? [[Where then has your glory gone?]] **33** Are you he who laughed the wrongdoers and sinners to scorn and now you have become a laughingstock to all? [[Where then has your glory gone?]]" **34** And when Eliphaz had cried and lamented for a long time, while all the others joined him, so that the commotion was very great, I said to them, **35** "Be silent and I will show you my throne, and the glory of its splendor: my glory will be everlasting. **36** The whole world will perish, and its glory will vanish, and all those who hold fast to it will remain beneath, but my throne is in the upper world and its glory and splendor will be to the right of the Savior in the heavens. **37** My throne exists in the life of the holy ones and its glory in the imperishable world. **38** For rivers will be dried up and their arrogance will go down to the depth of the abyss, but the streams of my land in which my throne is erected will not dry up but will remain unbroken in strength. **39** The kings perish, and the rulers vanish, and their glory and pride are as the shadow in a looking-glass, but my kingdom lasts forever and ever, and its glory and beauty are in the chariot of my Father."

CHAPTER 8

1 When I spoke thus to them, Eliphaz became angry and said to the other friends, "For what purpose is it that we have come here with our hosts to comfort him? Behold, he scolds us. Therefore, let us return to our countries. **2** This man sits here in misery, worm-eaten amidst an unbearable state of putrefaction, and yet he challenges its saving: Kingdoms will perish and their rulers, but my kingdom, he says, will last forever." **3** Eliphaz then rose in great commotion, and turning away from them in great fury, said, "I go on. We have indeed come to comfort him, but he declares war to us in view of our armies." **4** But then Bildad seized him by the hand and said, "One ought not to speak thus to an afflicted man, and especially to one stricken down with so many plagues. **5** Behold, we, being in good health, dared not approach him on account of the offensive odor, except with the help of plenty of fragrant aroma. But you, Eliphaz, are forgetful of all this. **6** Let me speak plainly. Let us be magnanimous and learn what the cause is. Must he, in remembering his former days of happiness, not become mad in his mind? **7** Who should not be altogether perplexed seeing himself thus lapse into misfortune and plagues? But let me step near him that I may find by what cause he is thus." **8** And Bildad rose and approached me, saying, "Are you Job?" And he said, "Is your heart still in good keeping?" **9** And I said, "I did not hold fast to the earthly things, since the earth, with all that inhabit it, is unstable. But my heart holds fast to Heaven, because there is no trouble in Heaven." **10** Then Bildad rejoined and said, "We know that the earth is unstable, for it changes according to season. At times it is in a state of peace, and at times it is in a state of war. But of Heaven we hear that it is perfectly steady. **11** But are you truly in a state of calmness? Therefore let me ask and speak, and when you answer me to my first word, I will have a second question to ask, and if again you answer in well-set words, it will be manifest that your heart has not been unbalanced." **12** And he said, "On what do you set your hope?" And I said, "On the living God." **13** And he said to me, "Who deprived you of all you possessed, and who inflicted you with these plagues?" And I said, "God." **14** And he said, "If you still place your hope on God, how can He do wrong in judgment, having brought on you these plagues and misfortunes, and having taken from you all your possessions? **15** And since He has taken these, it is clear that He has given you nothing. No king will disgrace his soldier who has served him well as bodyguard." **16** [[And I answered, saying,]] "Who understands the depths of the Lord and of His wisdom to be able to accuse God of injustice?" **17** [And Bildad said,] "Answer me, O Job, to this. Again, I say to you: if you are in a state of calm reason, teach me if you have wisdom: **18** why do we see the sun rise in the east and set in the west? And again, when rising in the morning we find him rise in the east. Tell me your thought about this." **19** Then I said, "Why will I betray the mighty mysteries of God? And should my mouth stumble in revealing things belonging to the Master? Never! **20** Who are we that we should pry into matters concerning the upper world while we are only of flesh, no, earth and ashes! **21** In order that you know that my heart is sound, hear what I ask you: **22** through the stomach comes food, and water you drink through the mouth, and then it flows through the same throat, and when the two go down to become excrement, they again part; who effects this separation?" **23** And Bildad said, "I do not know." And I rejoined and said to him, "If you do not even understand the exits of the body, how can you understand the celestial circuits?" **24** Then Zophar rejoined and said, "We do not inquire after our own affairs, but we desire to know whether you are in a sound state, and behold, we see that your reason has not been shaken. **25** What now do you wish that we should do for you? Behold, we have come here and brought the physicians of three kings, and if you wish, you may be cured by them." **26** But I answered and said, "My cure and my restoration come from God, the Maker of physicians."

CHAPTER 9

1 And when I spoke thus to them, behold, there my wife Sitis came running, dressed in rags from the service of the master by whom she was employed as slave though she had been forbidden to leave, lest the kings, on seeing her, might take her as captive. **2** And when she came, she threw herself prostrate to their feet, crying and saying, "Remember, Eliphaz and you other friends, what I once was with you, and how I have changed, how I am now dressed to meet you." **3** Then the kings broke forth in great weeping and, being in double perplexity, they kept silent. But Eliphaz took his purple mantle and cast it around her to wrap her up with it. **4** But she asked him, saying, "I ask as a favor of you, my lords, that you order your soldiers that they should dig among the ruins of our house which fell on my children, so that their bones could be brought in a perfect state to the tombs. **5** For as we have, owing to our misfortune, no power at all, and so we may at least see their bones. **6** For I have, like a brute, the motherly feeling of wild beasts that my ten children should have perished on one day and I could not give a decent burial to one of them." **7** And the kings gave order that the ruins of my house should be dug up. But I prohibited it, saying, **8** "Do not go to the trouble in vain; for my children will not be found, for they are in the keeping of their Maker and Ruler." **9** And the kings answered and said, "Who will deny that he is out of his mind and raves? **10** For while we desire to bring the bones of his children back, he forbids us to do so, saying, They have been taken and placed [in] the keeping of their Maker. Therefore, prove the truth to us." **11** But I said to them, "Raise me that I may stand up," and they lifted me, holding up my arms from both sides. **12** And I stood upright, and first pronounced the praise of God and after the prayer I said to them: "Look with your eyes to the east." **13** And they looked and saw my children with crowns near the glory of the King, the Ruler of Heaven. **14** And when my wife Sitis saw this, she fell to the ground and prostrated [herself] before God, saying, "Now I know that my memory remains with the Lord." **15** And after she had spoken this, and the evening came, she went to the city, back to the master whom she served as slave, and lay herself down at the manger of the cattle and died there from exhaustion. **16** And when her despotic master searched for her and did not find her, he came to the fold of his herds, and there he saw her stretched out on the manger dead, while all the animals around were crying about her. **17** And all who saw her wept and lamented, and the cry extended throughout the whole city. **18** And the people brought her down and wrapped her up and buried her by the house which had fallen on her children. **19** And the poor of the city made a great mourning for her and said, "Behold this Sitis whose like in nobility and in glory is not found in any woman. Aah! she was not found worthy of a proper tomb!" **20** The dirge for her you will find in the record.

CHAPTER 10

1 But Eliphaz and those that were with him were astonished at these things, and they sat down with me and replying to me, spoke in boastful words concerning me for twenty-seven days. **2** They repeated it again and again that I suffered deservedly thus for having committed many sins, and that there was no hope left for me, but I retorted to these men in zest of contention myself. **3** And they rose in anger, ready to part in wrathful spirit. But Elihu conjured them to stay yet a little while until he would have shown them what it was. **4** "For," he said, "you passed so many days allowing Job to boast that he is just. But I will no longer permit it. **5** For from the beginning I continued crying over him, remembering his former happiness. But now he speaks boastfully, and in overbearing pride he says that he has his throne in the heavens. **6** Therefore, hear me, and I will tell you what the cause of his destiny is." **7** Then, imbued with the spirit of Satan, Elihu spoke hard words which are written down in the records left of Elihu. **8** And after he had ended, God appeared to me in a storm and in clouds, and spoke, blaming Elihu and showing me that he who had spoken was not a man, but a wild beast. **9** And when God had finished speaking to me, the Lord spoke to Eliphaz: "You and your friends have sinned in that you have not spoken the truth concerning My servant Job. **10** Therefore rise up and make him bring a sin-offering for you in order that your sins may be forgiven; for were it not for him, I would have destroyed you." **11** And so they brought to me all that belonged to a sacrifice, and I took it and brought a sin-offering for them, and the Lord received it favorably and forgave them their wrong. **12** Then when Eliphaz, Bildad, and Zophar saw that God had graciously pardoned their sin through His servant Job, but that He did not stoop to pardon Elihu, then Eliphaz began to sing a hymn while the others responded, their soldiers also joining while standing by the altar. **13** And Eliphaz spoke thus: "The sin is removed, and our injustice gone, **14** But Elihu, the evil one, will have no remembrance among the living; His luminary is extinguished and has lost its light. **15** The glory of his lamp will announce itself for him, || For he is the son of darkness, and not of light. **16** The doorkeepers of the place of darkness || Will give him their glory and beauty as share. His kingdom has vanished, his throne has decayed, || And the honor of his stature is in Hades. **17** For he has loved the beauty of the serpent and the scales of the dragon—His gall and his venom belong to the Northern One. **18** For he did not own himself to the Lord nor did he fear Him, || But he hated those whom He has chosen. **19** Thus God forgot him, and the holy ones forsook him, || His wrath and anger will be to him desolation, || And he will have no mercy in his heart nor peace, || Because he had the venom of an adder on his tongue. **20** The Lord is righteous, and His judgments are true. With Him there is no preference of person, || For He judges all alike. **21** Behold, the Lord comes! Behold, the holy ones have been prepared! The crowns and the prizes of the victors precede them! **22** Let the saints rejoice, and let their hearts exult in gladness, || For they will receive the glory which is in store for them. Chorus: **23** Our sins are forgiven, our injustice has been cleansed, || But Elihu has no remembrance among the living." **24** After Eliphaz had finished the hymn, we rose and went back to the city, each to the house where they lived. **25** And the people made a feast for me in gratitude and delight of God, and all my friends came back to me. **26** And all those who had seen me in my former state of happiness, asked me, saying, "What are those three ones among us here?"

CHAPTER 11

1 But I, being desirous to take up my work of benevolence for the poor again, asked them, saying, **2** "Give me each a lamb for the clothing of the poor in their state of nakedness, and four drachmas of silver or gold." **3** Then the Lord blessed all that was left to me, and after a few days I became rich again in merchandise, in flocks and all things which I had lost, and I received all in double number again. **4** Then I also took your mother as wife and became the father of you ten in place of the ten children that had died. **5** And now, my children, let me admonish you: "Behold, I die. You will take my place. **6** Only do not forsake the Lord. Be charitable toward the poor; Do not disregard the feeble. Do not take wives from strangers to yourselves. **7** Behold, my children, I will divide what I possess among you, so that each may have control over his own and have full power to do good with his share." **8** And after he had spoken thus, he brought all his goods and divided them among his seven sons, but he gave nothing of his goods to his daughters. **9** Then they said to their father, "Our lord and father! Are we not also your children? Why, then, do you not also give us a share of your possessions?" **10** Then Job said to his daughters, "Do not become angry my daughters. I have not forgotten you. Behold, I have preserved for you a possession better than that which your brothers have taken." **11** And he called his daughter, whose name was Day, and said to her, "Take this double ring used as a key, and go to the treasure-house, and bring me the golden casket, that I may give you your possession." **12** And she went and brought it to him, and he opened it and took out three-stringed girdles about the appearance of which no man can speak. **13** For they were not earthly work, but celestial sparks of light flashed through them like the rays of the sun. **14** And he gave one string to each of his daughters and said, "Put these as girdles around you in order that all the days of your life may encircle you and endow you with every good thing." **15** And the other daughter, whose name was Kassiah, said, "Is this the possession of which you say it is better than that of our brothers? Now how can we live on this?" **16** And their father said to them, "Not only do you have here [what is] sufficient to live on, but these bring you into a better world to live in—in the heavens. **17** Or do you not know, my children, the value of these things here? Hear then! When the Lord had deemed me worthy to have compassion on me and to take the plagues and the worms off my body, He called me and handed these three strings to me. **18** And He said to me, Rise and gird up your loins like a man. I will demand of you and you will declare it to Me. **19** And I took them and girt them around my loins, and immediately the worms left my body, and likewise the plagues, and my whole body took new strength through the Lord, and thus I passed on, as though I had never suffered. **20** But I also forgot the pains in my heart. Then the Lord spoke to me in His great power and showed to

me all that was and will be. **21** Now then, my children, in keeping these, you will not have the enemy plotting against you nor [evil] intentions in your mind because this is a charm from the Lord. **22** Rise then and gird these around you before I die in order that you may see the messengers come at my parting so that you may behold, with wonder, the powers of God." **23** Then the one whose name was Day rose and girt herself; and immediately she departed her body as her father had said, and she put on another heart, as if she never cared for earthly things. **24** And she sang angelic hymns in the voice of messengers, and she chanted forth the angelic praise of God while dancing. **25** Then the other daughter, Kassia by name, put on the girdle, and her heart was transformed, so that she no longer wished for worldly things. **26** And her mouth assumed the dialect of the heavenly rulers and she sang the doxology of the work of the High Place, and if anyone wishes to know the work of the heavens, he may take an insight into the hymns of Kassia. **27** Then the other daughter, by the name of Amalthea's Horn, girt herself and her mouth spoke in the language of those on high; for her heart was transformed, being lifted above the worldly things. **28** She spoke in the dialect of the cherubim, singing the praise of the Ruler of the cosmic powers and extolling their **[[or His]]** glory. **29** And he who desires to follow the vestiges of the "Glory of the Father" will find them written down in the Prayers of Amalthea's Horn.

CHAPTER 12

1 After these three had finished singing hymns, I, Nahor, brother of Job, sat down next to him as he lay down. **2** And I heard the marvelous things of the three daughters of my brother, one always succeeding the other amidst awful silence. **3** And I wrote down this scroll containing the hymns, except the hymns and signs of the [holy] word, for these were the great things of God. **4** And Job lay down from sickness on his couch, yet without pain and suffering, because his pain did not take strong hold of him on account of the charm of the girdle which he had wound around himself. **5** But after three days Job saw the holy messengers come for his soul, and instantly he rose and took the cithara and gave it to his daughter Day, **6** and he gave a censer to Kassia, and he gave a timbrel to Amalthea's Horn in order that they might bless the holy messengers who came for his soul. **7** And they took these, and sang, and played on the psaltery, and praised and glorified God in the holy dialect. **8** And after this He came—He who sits on the great chariot—and kissed Job, while his three daughters looked on, but the others did not see it. **9** And He took the soul of Job and He soared upward, taking her [(the soul)] by the arm and carrying her on the chariot, and He went toward the east. **10** His body, however, was brought to the grave while the three daughters marched ahead, having put on their girdles and singing hymns in praise of God. **11** Then Nahor, his brother, and his seven sons, with the rest of the people and the poor, the orphans and the feeble ones, held a great mourning over him, saying, **12** "Woe to us! For today the strength of the feeble, the light of the blind, the father of the orphans has been taken from us! **13** The receiver of strangers has been taken—the leader of the erring, the cover of the naked, the shield of the widows. Who should not mourn for the man of God?" **14** And as they were mourning in this and in that form, they would not permit him to be put into the grave. **15** After three days, however, he was finally put into the grave, like one in sweet slumber, and he received the name of the beautiful who will remain renowned throughout all generations of the world. **16** He left seven sons and three daughters, and there were no daughters found on earth as fair as the daughters of Job. **17** The name of Job was formerly Jobab, and he was called Job by the Lord. **18** He had lived eighty-five years before his plague, and after the plague he took the double share of all; hence he also doubled his years, which were one hundred seventy years. Thus, he lived two hundred fifty-five years altogether, **19** and he saw sons of his sons to the fourth generation. It is written that he will rise up with those whom the Lord will reawaken. To our Lord be glory. Amen.

TESTAMENT OF MOSES

The Testament of Moses, also called the Assumption of Moses, is thought to have been composed in the 1st century BC or 1st century AD, in Hebrew or a similar Semitic language, and then translated into Koine. The surviving manuscript is actually a 6th century Latin translation of the Greek. There is speculation that a missing portion of the work includes the dispute between Michael and Satan over the body of Moses, which is also found in Jude 1:9. The book is backward and forward-looking, and apocalyptic in nature, dealing with Moses' handoff to Joshua prior to death.

CHAPTER 1

1 And it came to pass in the one hundred and twentieth year of the life of Moses, **2** that is, the two thousand five hundredth year from the creation of the world, **6** that he called Joshua the son of Nun to himself, a man approved of the Lord, **7** that he might be the minister of the people and of the Dwelling Place of the testimony with all its holy things, **8** and that he might bring the people into the land given to their fathers, **9** that it should be given to them according to the covenant and the oath, which he spoke in the Dwelling Place to give [it] by Joshua, saying these words to Joshua: **10** "Be strong and of good courage, according to your might so as to do what has been commanded that you may be blameless to God"— **11** so says the Lord of the world. **12** For He has created the world on behalf of His people. **13** But He was not pleased to manifest this purpose of creation from the foundation of the world, in order that the nations might thereby be convicted, indeed, [that] by [their] arguments they might convict one another to their own humiliation. **14** Accordingly, He designed and devised me, and He prepared me before the foundation of the world, that I should be the mediator of His covenant. **15** And now I declare to you that the time of the years of my life is fulfilled and I am passing away to sleep with my fathers even in the presence of all the people. **16** Now receive this writing that you may know how to preserve the scrolls which I will deliver to you, **17** and you will set these in order, and anoint them with oil of cedar, and put them away in earthen vessels in the place which He made from the beginning of the creation of the world, **18** that His Name should be called on until the day of conversion in the visitation with which the Lord will visit them in the consummation of the end of the days.

CHAPTER 2

1 And now they will go by means of you into the land which He determined and promised to give to their fathers, **2** in which you will bless, and give to them individually, and confirm to them their inheritance in me, and establish the kingdom for them, and appoint prefectures for them according to the good pleasure of their Lord, in judgment and righteousness. **3** And in the sixth year after they enter into the land, that thereafter they will be ruled by chiefs and kings for eighteen years, and for nineteen years the ten tribes will be apostates. **4** And the twelve tribes will go down and transfer the Dwelling Place of the testimony. Then the God of Heaven will make the court of His Dwelling Place and the tower of His sanctuary, and the two holy tribes will be established [there], **5** but the ten tribes will establish kingdoms for themselves according to their own ordinances. **6** And they will offer sacrifices throughout twenty years, **7** and seven will entrench the walls, and I will protect nine, but [four] will transgress the covenant of the Lord and profane the oath which the Lord made with them. **8** And they will sacrifice their sons to strange gods, and they will set up idols in the sanctuary, to worship them. **9** And in the house of the Lord they will work impiety and engrave every [form] of beast—many abominations.

CHAPTER 3

1 And in those days a king from the east will come against them and cover their land with [his] cavalry **2** And he will burn their colony with fire, together with the holy temple of the Lord,

and he will carry away all the holy vessels. **3** And he will cast forth all the people, and he will take them to the land of his nativity, yes, he will take the two tribes with him. **4** Then the two tribes will call on the ten tribes and will be indignant as a lioness on the dusty plains, being hungry and thirsty. **5** And they will cry aloud: "Righteous and holy is the Lord, for, inasmuch as you have sinned, we too, in like manner, have been carried away with you, together with our children." **6** Then the ten tribes will mourn on hearing the reproaches of the two tribes, **7** and they will say, "What have we done to you, brothers? Surely this tribulation has not come on all the house of Israel?" **8** And all the tribes will mourn, crying to Heaven and saying, **9** "God of Abraham, God of Isaac, and God of Jacob, remember Your covenant which You made with them, and the oath which You swore to them by Yourself, that their seed should never fail in the land which You have given them." **10** Then they will remember me, saying, in that day, tribe to tribe and each man to his neighbour: **11** "Is this not that which Moses declared to us then in prophecies, who suffered many things in Egypt, and in the Red Sea, and in the wilderness for forty years, **12** and assuredly called the heavens and earth to witness against us, that we should not transgress His commandments, in the which he was a mediator to us? **13** Behold these things have befallen us after his death according to his words and according to his declaration, as he declared to us at that time— yes, behold, these have taken place even to our being carried away captive into the country of the east, **14** who will also be in bondage for about seventy-seven years."

CHAPTER 4

1 Then there will enter one who is over them, and he will spread forth his hands, and kneel on his knees, and pray on their behalf, saying, **2** "Lord of all, King on the lofty throne, who rules the world, and willed that this people should be Your chosen people: then You willed that You should be called their God, according to the covenant which You made with their fathers, **3** and yet they have gone into captivity with their wives and their children into another land, and around the gates of strange peoples, and where there is great vanity. **4** Regard and have compassion on them, O Lord of Heaven." **5** Then God will remember them on account of the covenant which He made with their fathers, and He will also manifest His compassion in those times. **6** And He will put it into the mind of a king to have compassion on them, and he will send them off to their land and country. **7** Then some portions of the tribes will go up, and they will come to their appointed place, and they will entrench the place, restoring [it]. **8** And the two tribes will continue in their prescribed faith, sad and lamenting because they will not be able to offer sacrifices to the Lord of their fathers. **9** And the ten tribes will increase and multiply among the nations during the time of their captivity.

CHAPTER 5

1 And when the times of discipline draw near and vengeance arises through the kings who share in their guilt and punish them, **2** they themselves will also be divided as to the truth. **3** For what reason it has come to pass: "They will turn aside from righteousness and approach iniquity, and they will defile the house of their worship with pollutions," and "they will go whoring after strange gods." **4** For they will not follow the truth of God, but some will pollute the altar with the very gifts which they offer to the Lord, who are not priests but slaves, sons of slaves. **5** And many will respect rich persons in those times, and will receive gifts, and wrest judgment [on receiving presents]. **6** And on this account the colony and the borders of their habitation will be filled with lawless deeds and iniquities: they will forsake the Lord; they will be impious judges; they will be ready to judge for money as each may wish.

CHAPTER 6

1 Then kings will be raised up to them bearing rule, and they will call themselves high priests of God; they will assuredly work iniquity in the Holy of Holies. **2** And an insolent king will succeed them who will not be of the race of the priests, a man bold and shameless, and he will judge them as they will deserve. **3** And he will cut off their chief men with the sword, and will destroy [them] in secret places, so that no one may know where their bodies are. **4** He will slay the old and the young, and he will not spare. **5** Then the fear of him will be bitter to them in their land. **6** And he will execute judgments on them as the Egyptians executed on them for thirty-four years, and he will punish them. **7** And he will beget children, who succeeding him will rule for shorter periods. **8** Into their parts cohorts and a powerful king of the west will come, who will conquer them; **9** and he will take them captive, and burn a part of their temple with fire, [and] will crucify some around their colony.

CHAPTER 7

1 And when this is done the times will be ended, in a moment the [second] course will be [ended], the four hours will come. **2** They will be forced . . . **3** And, in the time of these, scornful and impious men will rule, saying that they are just. **4** And these will conceal the wrath of their minds, being treacherous men, self-pleasers, impostors in all their own affairs, and lovers of banquets at every hour of the day, gluttons, gourmands . . . **5** . . . **6** devourers of the goods of the poor, saying that they do so on the ground of their justice, but [in reality] to destroy them, complainers, deceitful, concealing themselves lest they should be recognized, impious, filled with lawlessness and iniquity from sunrise to sunset, **8** saying, "We will have feastings and luxury, eating and drinking, yes, we will drink our fill, we will be as princes." **9** And though their hands and their minds touch unclean things, yet their mouth will speak great things, and they will furthermore say, **10** "Do not touch me lest you should pollute me in the place where I stand."

CHAPTER 8

1 And there will come on them a second visitation and wrath, such as has not befallen them from the beginning until that time, in which He will stir up against them a king of the kings of the earth and one that rules with great power, who will crucify those who confess to their circumcision: **2** and he will torture those who conceal [it] and deliver them up to be bound and led into prison. **3** And their wives will be given to the gods among the nations, and their young sons will be operated on by the physicians in order to bring forward their foreskin. **4** And others among them will be punished by tortures, and fire, and sword, and they will be forced to bear their idols in public, [which are as] polluted as the [shrines] that contain them. **5** And they will likewise be forced by those who torture them to enter their inmost sanctuary, and they will be forced by goads to blaspheme the Name with insolence, [and] finally, after these things, the laws and what they had above their altar [as well].

CHAPTER 9

1 Then in that day there will be a man of the tribe of Levi, whose name will be Taxo, who having seven sons will speak to them exhorting [them]: **2** "Observe, my sons; behold, a second ruthless [and] unclean visitation has come on the people, and a punishment merciless and far exceeding the first. **3** For what nation, or what region, or what people of those who are impious toward the Lord, who have done many abominations, have suffered calamities as great as have befallen us? **4** Now therefore, my sons, hear me; for observe and know that neither [our] fathers nor their forefathers tempted God, so as to transgress His commands. **5** And you know that this is our strength, and thus we will do. **6** Let us fast for the space of three days, and on the fourth let us go into a cave which is in the field, and let us die rather than transgress the commands of the Lord of lords, the God of our fathers. **7** For if we do this and die, our blood will be avenged before the Lord."

CHAPTER 10

1 And then His kingdom will appear throughout all His creation, || And then Satan will no longer be, || And sorrow will depart with him. **2** Then the hands of the messenger will be filled, || And he will be appointed chief, || And he will immediately avenge them of their enemies. **3** For the heavenly One will arise from His royal throne, || And He will go forth from His holy habitation, || And His wrath will burn on account of His sons. **4** And the earth will tremble: It will be shaken to its confines, || And the high mountains will be made low, || And the hills will be shaken and fall. **5** And the horns of the sun will be broken, || And he will be turned into darkness; And the moon will not give her light, || And will be turned wholly into blood; And the circle of the stars will be disturbed. **6** And the sea will retire into the abyss, || And the fountains of waters will fail, || And the rivers will dry up. **7** For the Highest will arise, the Perpetual God alone, || And He will appear to punish the nations, || And He will destroy all their idols. **8** Then you, O Israel, will be happy, || And you will mount up on the neck [and wings] of the eagle, || And [the days of your mourning] will be ended. **9** And God will exalt you, || And He will cause you to approach to the heaven of the stars, || And He will establish your habitation among them. **10** And you will look from on high and will see your enemies in Gehenna, || And you will recognize them and rejoice, || And you will give thanks and confess your Creator. **11** And you, Joshua [the son of] Nun, must keep these words and this scroll, **12** for from my death—[my] assumption—until His advent there will be two hundred fifty times. **13** And this is their course which they will pursue until they are consummated. **14** And I will go to sleep with my fathers. **15** For what reason, Joshua—you, [son of] Nun—be of good courage; God has chosen [you] to be my successor in the same covenant.

CHAPTER 11

1 And when Joshua had heard the words of Moses that were written in his writing, as well as all that he had previously said, he tore his clothes and cast himself at Moses' feet. **2** And Moses comforted him and wept with him. **3** And Joshua answered him and said, **4** "Why do you comfort me, lord Moses? And how will I be comforted in regard to that which you have spoken—the bitter word which has gone forth from your mouth, which is full of tears and lamentation, in that you depart from this people? **5** And now what place will receive you? **6** Or what will be the sign that marks [your] grave? **7** Or who will dare to move your body from there as a man from place to place? **8** For when they die, all men have their graves on earth according to their age, but your grave is from the rising to the setting sun, and from the south to the confines of the north: all the world is your grave. **9** My lord, you are departing, and who will feed this people? **10** Or who is there that will have compassion on them, and who will be their guide by the way? **11** Or who will pray for them, not omitting a single day, in order that I may lead them into the land of [their] forefathers? **12** Therefore, how am I to control this people as a father [his] only son, or as a mistress [her] virgin daughter, who is being prepared to be handed over to the husband she will revere, while she guards her person from the sun, and [takes care] that her feet are not unshod for running on the ground? **13** And how will I supply them with food and drink according to the pleasure of their will? **14** For of them there will be six hundred thousand men, for these have multiplied to this degree through your prayers, [my] lord Moses. **15** And what wisdom or understanding do I have that I should judge or answer by word in the house of the Lord? **16** And the kings of the Amorites will also be emboldened to attack us then; [and] believing that there is no longer among them the sacred spirit who was worthy of the Lord, manifold and incomprehensible, the lord of the word, who was faithful in all things, God's chief prophet throughout the earth, the most perfect teacher in the world, that he is no longer among them, they will say, Let us go against them. **17** If the enemy has but once worked impiously against their Lord, they have no advocate to offer prayers on their behalf to the Lord, as Moses the great messenger did, who every hour day and night had his knees fixed to the earth, praying to and looking for help from Him that rules all the world with compassion and righteousness, calling to mind the covenant of the fathers, and propitiating the Lord with the oath. **18** For they will say, He is not with them; therefore, let us go and destroy them from off the face of the earth. **19** What then will become of this people, my lord Moses?"

CHAPTER 12

1 And when Joshua had finished [these] words, he again cast himself at the feet of Moses. **2** And Moses took his hand and raised him into the seat before him, and answered and said to him, **3** "Joshua, do not despise yourself, but set your mind at ease, and listen to my words. **4** All the nations which are in the earth God has created as He has us; He has foreseen [both] them and us from the beginning of the creation of the earth to the end of the age, and nothing has been neglected by Him even to the least thing, but He has foreseen all things and caused all to come forth. **5** All things which are to be in this earth the Lord has foreseen, and behold, they are brought forward [into the light] . . . **6** . . . [[The Lord]] has appointed me on their behalf to pray for their sins and make intercession for them. **7** For [it was] not because of any virtue or strength of mine, but in His compassion and longsuffering was He pleased to call me. **8** For I say to you, Joshua: it is not on account of the godliness of this people that you will root out the nations. **9** The lights of the heavens [and] the foundations of the earth have been made and approved by God and are under the signet ring of His right hand. **10** Therefore, those who do and fulfill the commandments of God will increase and be prospered, **11** but those who sin and set the commandments at nothing will be without the blessings previously mentioned, and they will be punished by the nations with many torments. **12** But to wholly root out and destroy them is not permitted. **13** For God, who has foreseen all things forever, will go forth; and His covenant has been established and the oath which . . ."

TESTAMENT OF SOLOMON

The Testament of Solomon is the account of his receiving a ring of great power from the archangel Michael that enables him to systematically overcome and enslave a series of demons. He then forces these demons to help build the First Temple in Jerusalem. It is thought by most that the text was developed and organized in the medieval period, but at least some of the core material likely dates from the 1st century AD or earlier because of early citations and even an early reference to the title.

[The] Testament of Solomon, son of David, who was king in Jerusalem, and [who] mastered and controlled all spirits of the air, on the earth, and under the earth. By means of them he also worked all the transcendent works of the Temple, also telling of the authorities they wield against men, and by what messengers these demons are brought to nothing. Of the sage Solomon. Blessed are You, O Lord God, who gave Solomon such authority. Glory to You and might to the ages! Amen.

CHAPTER 1

1 And behold, when the temple of the city of Jerusalem was being built and the craftsmen were working there, the demon Ornias came among them toward sunset; **2** and he took away half of the pay of the chief-deviser's little boy, as well as half his food. He also continued to suck the thumb of his right hand every day. **3** And the child grew thin, although he was very much loved by the king. **4** So King Solomon called the boy one day, and questioned him, saying, "Do I not love you more than all the artisans who are working in the temple of God? **5** Do I not give you double wages and a double supply of food? How is it that day by day and hour by hour you grow thinner?" **6** But the child said to the king, "Please, O king. Listen to what has befallen all that your child has. After we are all released from our work on the temple of God, after sunset, when I lie down to rest, one of the evil demons comes and takes away from me

one half of my pay and one half of my food. **7** Then he also takes hold of my right hand and sucks my thumb. And behold, my soul is oppressed, and so my body waxes thinner every day."

CHAPTER 2

1 Now when I, Solomon, heard this, I entered the temple of God, and prayed with all my soul, night and day, that the demon might be delivered into my hands, and that I might gain authority over him. **2** And it came about through my prayer that grace was given to me from the Lord of Hosts by His chief-messenger Michael. **3** [He brought me] a little ring, having a seal consisting of an engraved stone, and said to me, "Take, O Solomon—king, son of David—the gift which the Lord God, the Highest of Hosts, has sent you. With it you will lock up all demons of the earth, [both] male and female; and with their help you will build up Jerusalem. **4** [But] you [must] wear this seal of God. And this engraving of the seal of the ring sent to you is a Pentalpha." **5** And I, Solomon, was overjoyed, and praised and glorified the God of the heavens and earth. And on the next day I called the boy, and gave him the ring, **6** and said to him, "take this, and at the hour in which the demon will come to you, throw this ring at the chest of the demon, and say to him: In the Name of God, King Solomon calls you here. **7** And then come running to me, without having any misgivings or fear in respect of anything you may hear on the part of the demon."

CHAPTER 3

1 So the child took the ring and went off; and behold, at the customary hour Ornias, the fierce demon, came like a burning fire to take the pay from the child. **2** But the child, according to the instructions received from the king, threw the ring at the chest of the demon, and said, "King Solomon calls you here." **3** And then he went off running to the king. But the demon cried out aloud, saying, "Child, why have you done this to me? Take the ring off me, and I will render the gold of the earth to you. Only take this off me, and refrain from leading me away to Solomon." **4** But the child said to the demon, "As the Lord God of Israel lives, I will not allow you [this], so come here." **5** And the child came running, rejoicing, to the king, and said, "I have brought the demon, O king, as you commanded me, O my master. **6** And behold, he stands before the gates of the court of your palace, crying out, and supplicating with a loud voice, offering me the silver and gold of the earth if I will only bring him to you."

CHAPTER 4

1 And when Solomon heard this, he rose up from his throne, and went outside into the vestibule of the court of his palace; **2** and there he saw the demon, shuddering and trembling. **3** And he said to him, "Who are you?" And the demon answered: "I am called Ornias." **4** And Solomon said to him, "Tell me, O demon, to which of the twelve signs you are subject." And he answered: "To the Water-pourer [[*or* Aquarius]]. And those who are consumed with desire for the noble virgins on earth . . . these I strangle. **5** But in case there is no disposition to sleep, I am changed into three forms. Whenever men come to be enamored with women, I transform myself into a beautiful female; and I take hold of the men in their sleep and play with them. **6** And after a while I take to my wings again and hasten to the heavenly regions. **7** I also appear as a lion, and I am commanded by all the demons. I am an offspring of the chief-messenger Uriel, the power of God."

CHAPTER 5

1 I, Solomon, having heard the name of the chief-messenger, prayed and glorified God, the Lord of the heavens and earth. **²** And I sealed the demon and set him to work at stone-cutting, so that he might cut the stones in the temple, which, lying along the shore, had been brought by the Sea of Arabia. **³** But he, fearful of the iron, continued and said to me, "Please, King Solomon, let me go free, and I will bring you all the demons." **⁴** And as he was not willing to be subject to me, I pleaded [with] the chief-messenger Uriel to come and assist me; and I immediately beheld the chief-messenger Uriel coming down to me from the heavens.

CHAPTER 6

¹ And the messenger commanded the whales of the sea to come out of the abyss. And he cast his destiny on the ground, and that [destiny] made the great demon subject [to him]. **²** And he commanded the great demon and bold Ornias to cut stones at the temple. **³** And accordingly I, Solomon, glorified the God of Heaven and Maker of the earth. **⁴** And he commanded Ornias to come with his destiny, and gave him the seal, saying, "Away with you, and bring the prince of all the demons here to me."

CHAPTER 7

¹ So Ornias took the finger-ring, and went off to Beelzebul, who has kingship over the demons. He said to him, "Here! Solomon calls you." **²** But Beelzebul, having heard, said to him, "Tell me, who is this Solomon of whom you speak to me?" Then Ornias threw the ring at the chest of Beelzebul, saying, "Solomon the king calls you." **³** But Beelzebul cried aloud with a mighty voice, and shot out a great burning flame of fire; and he arose, and followed Ornias, and came to Solomon. **⁴** And when I saw the prince of demons, I glorified the Lord God, Maker of the heavens and earth, and I said, "Blessed are You, Lord God Almighty, who has given wisdom to Your servant Solomon, the assessor of the wise, and has subjected all the power of the Devil to me." **⁵** And I questioned him, and said, "Who are you?" The demon replied: "I am Beelzebul, the exarch of the demons. And all the demons have their chief seats close to me. **⁶** And it is I who make the apparition of each demon manifest." **⁷** And he promised to bring all the unclean spirits to me in bonds. And I again glorified the God of the heavens and earth, as I always give thanks to Him.

CHAPTER 8

¹ I then asked of the demon if there were females among them. And when he told me that there were, I said that I desired to see them. **²** So Beelzebul went off at high speed, and brought to me Onoskelis, who had a very pretty shape, and the skin of a lovely woman; and she tossed her head. **³** And when she had come, I said to her, "Tell me, who are you?" But she said to me, "I am called Onoskelis, a spirit worked . . . lurking on the earth. **⁴** There is a golden cave where I lie. But I have a place that always shifts. At one time I strangle men with a noose; at another, I creep up from the nature to the arms. **⁵** But my most frequent dwelling-places are the precipices, caves, [and] ravines. Oftentimes, however, I consort with men in the semblance of a woman, and above all with those of a dark skin. **⁶** For they share my star with me, since it is they who privily or openly worship my star, without knowing that they harm themselves, and but whet my appetite for further mischief. **⁷** For they wish to provide money by means of memory, but I supply a little to those who worship me fairly." **⁸** And I, Solomon, questioned her about her birth, and she replied: "I was born of an untimely voice, the so-called echo of a man's filth dropped in a wood." **⁹** And I said to her, "Under what star do you pass?" And she answered me: "Under the star of the full moon, for the reason that the moon travels over most things." **¹⁰** Then I said to her, "And what messenger is it that frustrates you?" And she said to me, "He that in you [[or through you]] is reigning." **¹¹** And I thought that she mocked me, and I commanded a soldier to strike her, but she cried aloud and said, "I am [subjected] to you, O king, by the wisdom of God given to you, and by the messenger Joel." **¹²** So I commanded her to spin the hemp for the ropes used in the building of the house of God; and accordingly, when I had

sealed and bound her, she was so overcome and brought to nothing as to stand night and day spinning the hemp.

CHAPTER 9

¹ And I immediately commanded another demon to be led to me; and instantly the demon Asmodeus approached me, bound, and I asked him, "Who are you?" **²** But he shot a glance of anger and rage at me, and said, "And who are you?" And I said to him, "Thus punished as you are, [this is how] you answer me?" **³** But he, with rage, said to me, "But how will I answer you, for you are a son of man, whereas I was born of a messenger's seed by a daughter of man, so that no word of our heavenly kind addressed to the earth-born can be overconfident. **⁴** For what reason also my star is bright in the sky, and some men call it the Wagon [[or Ursa Major]], and some the Dragon's Child. I keep near to this star. **⁵** So do not ask me many things; for your kingdom also after a short time is to be disrupted, and your glory is but for a season. **⁶** And your tyranny over us will be short; and then we will have free range over mankind again, so as that they will revere us as if we were gods, not knowing, men that they are, the names of the messengers set over us." **⁷** And I, Solomon, on hearing this, bound him more carefully, and ordered him to be flogged with thongs of ox-hide, and to humbly tell me what was his name and what [was] his business. **⁸** And he answered me thus: "I am called Asmodeus among mortals, and my business is to plot against the newly wedded, so that they may not know one another. **⁹** And I utterly sever them by many calamities, and I waste away the beauty of virgin women, and estrange their hearts." And I said to him, "Is this your only business?" **¹⁰** And he answered me: "I transport men into fits of madness and desire, when they have wives of their own, so that they leave them, and go off by night and day to others that belong to other men, with the result that they commit sin, and fall into murderous deeds." **¹¹** And I adjured him by the Name of the Lord of Hosts, saying, "Fear God, Asmodeus, and tell me by what messenger you are frustrated." **¹²** But he said, "By Raphael, the chief-messenger that stands before the throne of God. But the liver and gall of a fish put me to flight, when smoked over ashes of the tamarisk." **¹³** I asked him again, and said, "Do not hide anything from me. For I am Solomon, son of David, King of Israel. Tell me the name of the fish which you revere." **¹⁴** And he answered: "It is the Glanos by name, and is found in the rivers of Assyria, for what reason it is that I roam around in those parts." **¹⁵** And I said to him, "Do you have nothing else [to say] concerning yourself, Asmodeus?" **¹⁶** And he answered: "The power of God knows, which has bound me with the indissoluble bonds of that one's seal, that whatever I have told you is true. Please, King Solomon, do not condemn me to [go into] water." **¹⁷** But I smiled, and said to him, "As the Lord God of my fathers lives, I will lay iron on you to wear. But you will also make the clay for the entire construction of the temple, treading it down with your feet." **¹⁸** And I ordered them to give him ten water-jars to carry water in. And the demon groaned terribly and did the work I ordered him to do. **¹⁹** And I did this because that fierce demon Asmodeus even knew the future. And I, Solomon, glorified God, who gave wisdom to me, His servant Solomon. **²⁰** And I hung the liver of the fish and its gall on the spike of a reed and burned it over Asmodeus because of his being so strong, and his unbearable malice was thus frustrated.

CHAPTER 10

¹ And I summoned Beelzebul, the prince of demons, to stand before me again, and I sat him down on a raised seat of honor and said to him, "Why are you alone, prince of the demons?" **²** And he said to me, "Because I alone am left of the messengers of Heaven that came down. For I was first messenger in the first heaven being entitled Beelzebul. And now I control all those who are bound in Tartarus. **³** But I too have a child, and he haunts the Red Sea. And on any suitable occasion he comes up to me again, being subject to me, and reveals to me what he has done, and I support him." **⁴** I, Solomon, said to him, "Beelzebul, what is your employment?" **⁵** And he answered me: "I destroy kings. I ally myself with foreign tyrants. And my own demons I set on to men, in order that the latter may believe in them and be lost. **⁶** And the chosen servants of God, priests and faithful men, I excite to desires for wicked sins, and evil heresies, and lawless deeds; and they obey me, and I bear them on to destruction. **7** And I inspire men with envy, and murder, and for wars, and sodomy, and other evil things. And I will destroy the world." **8** So I said to him, "Bring to me your child, who is, as you say, in the Red Sea." **9** But he said to me, "I will not bring him to you, but another demon called Ephippas will come to me. I will bind him, and he will bring him up to me from the deep." **10** And I said to him, "How does your son come to be in the depth of the sea, and what is his name?" **11** And he answered me: "Do not ask me, for you cannot learn from me. However, he will come to you by any command, and will tell you openly." **12** I said to him, "Tell me by what messenger you are frustrated." **13** And he answered: "By the holy and precious Name of the Almighty God, called by the Hebrews by a row of numbers, of which the sum is six hundred forty-four, and among the Greeks it is Emmanuel. And if one of the Romans adjures me by the great name of the power Eleéth, I disappear at once." **14** I, Solomon, was astounded when I heard this; and I ordered him to saw up Theban marbles. And when he began to saw the marbles, the other demons cried out with a loud voice, howling because of their king, Beelzebul. **15** But I, Solomon, questioned him, saying, "If you would gain a respite, discourse to me about the things in Heaven." **16** And Beelzebul said, "Hear, O king, if you burn gum, and incense, and bulb of the sea, with nard and saffron, and light seven lamps in an earthquake, you will firmly fix your house. **17** And if, being pure, you light them at dawn in the sun gleaming, then you will see the heavenly dragons, how they wind themselves along and drag the chariot of the sun." **18** And I, Solomon, having heard this, rebuked him, and said, "Silence for this moment, and continue to saw the marbles as I commanded you."

CHAPTER 11

1 And I, Solomon, praised God, and commanded another demon to present himself to me, **2** and one came before me who carried his face high up in the air, but the rest of the spirit curled away like a snail. **3** And it broke through the few soldiers, and also raised a terrible dust on the ground, and carried it upwards, and then hurled it back again to frighten us, and asked what questions I could ask as a rule. **4** And I stood up, and spat on the ground in that spot, and sealed [it] with the ring of God. And immediately the dust-wind stopped. **5** Then I asked him, saying, "Who are you, O wind?" Then he once more shook up a dust, and answered me: "What would you have [of me], King Solomon?" **6** I answered him: "Tell me what you are called, and I would will to ask you a question. But so far I give thanks to God who has made me wise to answer their evil plots." **7** But [the demon] answered me: "I am the spirit of the ashes (Tephras)." **8** And I said to him, "What is your pursuit?" And he said, "I bring darkness on men, and set fire to fields, and I bring homesteads to nothing. But I am most busy in summer. **9** However, when I get an opportunity, I creep into corners of the wall, by night and day. For I am offspring of the great one, and nothing less." **10** Accordingly I said to him, "Under what star do you lie?" And he answered: "In the very tip of the moon's horn, when it is found in the south. My star is there. **11** For I have been commanded to restrain the convulsions of the tertian fever; and this is why many men pray for the tertian fever using these three names: Bultala, Thallal, Melchal. And I heal them." **12** And I said to him, "I am Solomon; when therefore you would do harm, by whose aid do you do it?" But he said to me, "By the messenger's, by whom also the third day's fever is lulled to rest." **13** So I questioned him, and said, "And by what name?" And he answered: "That of the chief-messenger Azael." **14** And I summoned the chief-messenger Azael, and set a seal on the demon, and commanded him to seize great stones and toss them up to the workmen on the higher parts of the temple. **15** And, being compelled, the demon began to do what he was commanded to do.

CHAPTER 12

1 And I again glorified God who gave me this authority and ordered another demon to come before me, **2** and seven spirits came, females, bound and woven together—lovely in appearance and beautiful. **3** And I, Solomon, seeing them, questioned them and said, "Who are you?" **4** But they, with one accord, said with one voice: "We are of the thirty-three elements of the cosmic ruler of the darkness." **5** And the first said, "I am Deception." The second said, "I am Strife." The third: "I am Klothod, which is Battle." The fourth: "I am Jealousy." The fifth: "I am Power." The sixth: "I am Error." **6** The seventh: "I am the worst of all, and our stars are in Heaven. Seven stars humble in sheen, and all together. And we are called, as it were, goddesses. **7** We change our place—all and together, and together we live, sometimes in Lydia, sometimes in Olympus, sometimes in a great mountain." **8** So I, Solomon, questioned them one by one, beginning with the first, and going down to the seventh. **9** The first said, "I am Deception, I deceive and weave snares here and there. I whet and excite heresies. But I have a messenger who frustrates me, Lamechalal." **10** Likewise also the second said, "I am Strife, strife of strifes. I bring timbers, stones, hangers—my weapons on the spot. But I have a messenger who frustrates me, Baruchiachel." **11** Likewise also the third said, "I am called Klothod, which is Battle, and I cause the well-behaved to scatter and fall foul of one another. And why do I say so much? I have a messenger that frustrates me: Marmarath." **12** Likewise also the fourth said, "I cause men to forget their sobriety and moderation. I part them and split them into parties; for Strife follows me hand in hand. I tear the husband from the sharer of his bed, and children from parents, and brothers from sisters. But why tell so much to my disdain? I have a messenger that frustrates me, the great Balthial." **13** Likewise also the fifth said, "I am Power. By power I raise up tyrants and tear down kings. I furnish power to all rebels. I have a messenger that frustrates me, Asteraôth." **14** Likewise also the sixth said, "I am Error, O King Solomon. And I will make you to err, as I have before made you to err, when I caused you to slay your own brother. I will lead you into error, so as to pry into graves, and teach them that dig; and I lead errant souls away from all piety, and many other evil traits are mine. But I have a messenger that frustrates me, Uriel." **15** Likewise also the seventh said, "I am the worst, and I make you worse off than you were, because I will impose the bonds of Artemis. But the locust will set me free, for by means thereof it is fated that you will achieve my desire . . . For if one were wise, he would not turn his steps toward me." **16** So I, Solomon, having heard and wondered, sealed them with my ring; and since they were so considerable, I commanded them to dig the foundations of the temple of God. **17** For the length of it was two hundred fifty cubits. And I commanded them to be industrious, and with one murmur of joint protest they began to perform the tasks enjoined.

CHAPTER 13

1 But I, Solomon, glorified the Lord, and commanded another demon to come before me, **2** and a demon having all the limbs of a man was brought to me, but without a head. **3** And I, seeing him, said to him, "Tell me, who are you?" And he answered: "I am a demon." So I said to him, "Which?" **4** And he answered me: "I am called Envy. For I delight to devour heads, being desirous to secure a head for myself, but I do not eat enough, but am anxious to have such a head as you have." **5** I, Solomon, on hearing this, sealed him, stretching out my hand against his chest, **6** whereon the demon leapt up, and threw himself down, and gave a groan, saying, "Woe is me! where have I come to? O traitor Ornias, I cannot see!" **7** So I said to him, "I am Solomon. Tell me then how you manage to see." **8** And he answered me: "By means of my feelings." **9** I then, Solomon, having heard his voice come up to me, asked him how he managed to speak. And he answered me: "I, O King Solomon, am wholly voice, for I have inherited the voices of many men. For in the case of all men who are called dumb, it is I who smashed their heads when they were children and had reached their eighth day. **10** Then when a child is crying in the night, I become a spirit, and glide by means of his voice . . . **11** In the crossways I also have many services to render, and my encounter is fraught with harm. **12** For in an instant I grasp a man's head, and with my hands, as with a sword, I cut it off, and put it on myself. **13** And in this way, by means of the fire which is in me, it is swallowed up through my neck. It is I that send grave and incurable mutilations on men's feet, and inflict sores." **14** And I, Solomon, on hearing this, said to him, "Tell me how you discharge forth the fire? Out of what sources do you emit it?" **15** And the spirit said to me, "From the Daystar. For here that Elburion, to whom men offer prayers and kindle lights, has not yet been found. And his name is invoked by the seven demons before me. And he cherishes them." **16** But I said to him, "Tell me his name." But he answered: "I cannot tell you. For if I tell his name, I render myself incurable. But he will come in response to his name." **17** And on hearing this, I, Solomon, said to him, "Tell me then by what messenger you are frustrated." **18** And he answered: "By the fiery flash of lightning." **19** And I bowed myself before the Lord God of Israel, and commanded him to remain in the keeping of Beelzebul until I should come.

CHAPTER 14

1 Then I ordered another demon to come before me, and a hound came into my presence having a very large shape, and it spoke with a loud voice, and said, "Greetings, lord, King Solomon!" **2** And I, Solomon, was astounded. I said to it, "Who are you, O hound?" And it answered: "I do indeed seem to be a hound to you, but before you were, O King Solomon, I was a man that worked many unholy deeds on earth. **3** I was surpassingly educated in letters, and was so mighty that I could hold the stars of the heavens back. **4** And I prepared many divine works. For I do harm to men who follow after our star and turn them . . . **5** And I seize the frenzied men by the larynx, and so destroy them." **6** And I, Solomon, said to him, "What is your name?" And he answered: "Staff" (Rabdos). **7** And I said to him, "What is your employment? And what results can you achieve?" **8** And he replied, "Give me your man, and I will lead him away into a mountainous spot, and will show him a green stone tossed to and fro, with which you may adorn the temple of the Lord God." **9** And I, Solomon, on hearing this, ordered my servant to set off with him, and to take the finger-ring bearing the seal of God with him. **10** And I said to him, "Whoever will show you the green stone, seal him with this finger-ring, and mark the spot with care, and bring me the demon here." **11** And the demon showed him the green stone, and he sealed it, and brought the demon to me. **12** And I, Solomon, decided to confine with my seal on my right hand the two—the headless demon [and] likewise the hound that was so huge; he should be bound as well. **13** And I commanded the hound to keep the fiery spirit safe so that lamps, as it were, might cast their light through its maw on the artisans at work by day and night. **14** And I, Solomon, took from the mine of that stone two hundred shekels for the supports of the table of incense, which was similar in appearance. **15** And I, Solomon, glorified the Lord God, and then closed around the treasure of that stone. **16** And again I ordered the demons to cut marble for the construction of the house of God. **17** And I, Solomon, prayed to the Lord, and asked the hound, saying, "By what messenger are you frustrated?" And the demon replied, "By the great Brieus."

CHAPTER 15

1 And I praised the Lord God of the heavens and earth and commanded another demon to come forward to me, and one in the form of a roaring lion came before me. **2** And he stood and answered me, saying, "O king, in the form which I have, I am a spirit quite incapable of being perceived. **3** I leap on all men who lie prostrate with sickness, coming stealthily along; and I render the man weak, so that his habit of body is enfeebled. But I also have another glory, O king: **4** I cast out demons, and I have legions under my control. And I am capable of being received in my dwelling-places, along with all the demons belonging to the legions under me." **5** But I, Solomon, on hearing this, asked him: "What is your name?" But he answered: "Lion-bearer, Rath in kind." **6** And I said to him, "How are you to be frustrated along with your legions? What messenger is it that frustrates you?" **7** And he answered: "If I tell you my name, I do not only bind myself, but also the legions of demons under me." **8** So I said to him, "I adjure you in the Name of the God of Hosts to tell me by what name you are frustrated along with your host." **9** And the spirit answered me: "The Great Among Men, who is to suffer many things at the hands of men, whose name is the figure six hundred forty-four, which is Emmanuel; it is He who has bound us, and who will then come and plunge us from the steep under water. He

is spread abroad in the three letters which bring Him down." **10** And I, Solomon, on hearing this, glorified God, and condemned his legion to carry wood from the thicket. **11** And I condemned the lion-shaped one himself to saw up the wood small with his teeth, for burning in the unquenchable furnace for the temple of God.

CHAPTER 16

1 And I worshiped the Lord God of Israel and commanded another demon to come forward, and a dragon came before me, three-headed, of fearful aspect. **2** And I questioned him: "Who are you?" And he answered me: "I am a caltrop-like spirit, whose activity [is] in three lines. **3** But I blind children in women's wombs and twirl their ears around. And I make them deaf and mute. **4** And I have again in my third head means of slipping in. And I strike men in the limbless part of the body, and cause them to fall down, and foam, and grind their teeth. **5** But I have my own way of being frustrated, Jerusalem being signified in writing, to the place called [Place] of [the] Skull." **6** For there is appointed beforehand the Messenger of the great counsel, and now He will openly dwell on the Cross. He frustrates me, and I am subject to Him. **7** But in the place where you sit, O King Solomon, stands a column in the air, of purple . . . The demon called Ephippas has brought [it] up from the Red Sea, from inner Arabia. **8** It is he that will be shut up in a skin-bottle and brought before you. **9** But at the entrance of the temple, which you have begun to build, O King Solomon, lies much stored gold, which you can dig up and carry off." **10** And I, Solomon, sent my servant, and found it to be as the demon told me. And I sealed him with my ring and praised the Lord God." **11** So I said to him, "What are you called?" And the demon said, "I am the crest of dragons." And I commanded him to make bricks in the temple. He had human hands.

CHAPTER 17

1 And I adored the Lord God of Israel and commanded another demon to present himself, and a spirit in woman's form came before me that had a head without any limbs, and her hair was dishevelled. **2** And I said to her, "Who are you?" But she answered: "No, who are you? And why do you want to hear concerning me? But, as you would learn, here I stand bound before your face. **3** Go then into your royal storehouses and wash your hands. Then sit down again before your tribunal, and ask me questions, and you will learn, O king, who I am." **4** And I, Solomon, did as she enjoined me, and restrained myself because of the wisdom dwelling in me, in order that I might hear of her deeds, and reprehend them, and manifest them to men. **5** And I sat down, and said to the demon, "What are you?" And she said, "I am called Obizuth among men; and I do not sleep by night, but go my rounds over all the world, and visit women in childbirth. **6** And divining the hour, I take my stand; and if I am lucky, I strangle the child. But if not, I retire to another place. For I cannot retire unsuccessfully for a single night. **7** For I am a fierce spirit, of myriad names and many shapes. And now here, now there I roam. And to westward parts I go my rounds. **8** But as it now is, though you have sealed me around with the ring of God, you have done nothing. I am not standing before you, and you will not be able to command me. **9** For I have no work other than the destruction of children, and the making their ears to be deaf, and the working of evil to their eyes, and the binding their mouths with a bond, and the ruin of their minds, and paining of their bodies." **10** When I, Solomon, heard this, I marveled at her appearance, for I beheld all her body to be in darkness. **11** But her glance was altogether bright and greenish, and her hair was tossed wildly like a dragon's; and the whole of her limbs were invisible. **12** And her voice was very clear as it came to me. And I cunningly said, "Tell me by what messenger you are frustrated, O evil spirit?" **13** But she answered me: "By the messenger of God called Afarôt, which is interpreted Raphael, by whom I am frustrated now and for all time. **14** His name, if any man knows it, and writes the same on a woman in childbirth, then I will not be able to enter her. Of this name the number is six thousand four hundred and one." **15** And I, Solomon, having heard this, and having glorified the Lord, ordered her hair to be bound, and that she should be hung up in front of the temple of God, that all the sons of Israel, as they passed, might see it, and glorify the Lord God of Israel, who had given me this authority, with wisdom and power from God, by means of this signet.

CHAPTER 18

1 And I again ordered another demon to come before me, and this came, rolling itself along—one in appearance like to a dragon, but having the face and hands of a man. 2 And all its limbs, except the feet, were those of a dragon; and it had wings on its back. 3 And when I beheld it, I was astonished, and said, "Who are you, demon, and what are you called? And from where have you come? Tell me." 4 And the spirit answered and said, "This is the first time I have stood before you, O King Solomon. I am a spirit made into a god among men, but now brought to nothing by the ring and wisdom given to you by God. 5 Now I am the so-called winged dragon, and I do not chamber with many women, but only with a few that are of fair shape, which possess the name of Xuli, of this star. 6 And I pair with them in the guise of a spirit winged in form, committing sodomy. 7 And she on whom I have leapt goes heavy with child, and that which is born of her becomes desire. 8 But since such offspring cannot be carried by men, the woman in question breaks wind. Such is my role. 9 Suppose then that I alone am satisfied, and all the other demons molested and disturbed by you will speak the whole truth. 10 But those composed of fire will cause the material of the logs which is to be collected by them for the building in the temple to be burned up by fire." 11 And as the demon said this, I saw the spirit going forth from his mouth, and it consumed the wood of the frankincense-tree, and it burned up all the logs which we had placed in the temple of God. 12 And I, Solomon, saw what the spirit had done, and I marveled. 13 And, having glorified God, I asked the dragon-shaped demon, and said, "Tell me, by what messenger are you frustrated?" 14 And he answered: "By the great messenger who has his seal in the second heaven, which is called in Hebrew Bazazeth." And I, Solomon, having heard this, and having invoked his messenger, condemned him to saw up marbles for the building of the temple of God.

CHAPTER 19

1 And I praised God and commanded another demon to come before me, 2 and another spirit came before my face, as it were a woman in the form she had. But on her shoulders, she had two other heads with hands. 3 And I asked her, and said, "Tell me, who are you?" And she said to me, "I am Enêpsigos, who also have a myriad of names." 4 And I said to her, "By what messenger are you frustrated?" But she said to me, "What do you seek, what do you ask? I undergo changes, I am called like the goddess. And I change again, and pass into possession of another shape. 5 And do not be desirous, therefore, to know all that concerns me. But since you are before me for this much, listen. I have my abode in the moon, and for that reason I possess three forms. 6 At times I am magically invoked by the wise as Kronos. 7 At other times, in connection with those who bring me down, I come down and appear in another shape. 8 The measure of the element is inexplicable and undefinable, and not to be frustrated. I then, changing into these three forms, come down and become such as you see me; but I am frustrated by the messenger Rathanael, who sits in the third heaven. 9 This then is why I speak to you. That temple cannot contain me." 10 Therefore I, Solomon, prayed to my God, and I invoked the messenger of whom Enêpsigos spoke to me, and used my seal. 11 And I sealed her with a triple chain, and [placed] the fastening of the chain beneath her. 12 I used the seal of God, and the spirit prophesied to me, saying, "This is what you, King Solomon, do to us. But after a time, your kingdom will be broken, and again in season this temple will be split apart; and all Jerusalem will be undone by the King of the Persians, and Medes, and Chaldaeans. 13 And the vessels of this temple, which you make, will be put to servile uses of the gods; and along with them all the jars, in which you shut us up, will be broken by the hands of men. 14 And then we will go forth in great power here and there, and be disseminated all over the world. 15 And we will lead the inhabited world astray for a long season, until the Son of God is stretched on the Cross. 16 For never before does a king arise like Him—one frustrating us all, whose mother will

not have contact with man. 17 Who else can receive such authority over spirits, except He, whom the first Devil will seek to tempt, but will not prevail over? The number of His Name is six thousand four hundred forty-two, which is Emmanuel. 18 For what reason, O King Solomon, your time is evil, and your years short and evil, and your kingdom will be given to your servant." 19 And I, Solomon, having heard this, glorified God. And though I marveled at the apology of the demons, I did not credit it until it came true. 20 And I did not believe their words, but when they were realized, then I understood, and at my death I wrote this Testament to the sons of Israel, and gave it to them, so that they might know the powers of the demons and their shapes, and the names of their messengers, by which these messengers are frustrated. 21 And I glorified the Lord God of Israel and commanded the spirits to be bound with indissoluble bonds.

CHAPTER 20

1 And having praised God, I commanded another spirit to come before me, and another demon came before my face, having the shape of a horse in front, but [that] of a fish in back. 2 And he had a mighty voice, and said to me, "O King Solomon, I am a fierce spirit of the sea, and I am greedy for gold and silver. 3 I am such a spirit as rounds itself and comes over the expanses of the water of the sea, and I trip up the men who sail thereon. 4 For I round myself into a wave, and transform myself, and then throw myself on ships and come right in on them. 5 And that is my business, and my way of getting hold of money and men. For I take the men, and whirl them around with myself, and hurl the men out of the sea. 6 For I am not covetous of men's bodies, but cast them up out of the sea so far. 7 But since Beelzebul, ruler of the spirits of air and of those under the earth, and lord of earthly ones, has a joint kingship with us in respect of the deeds of each one of us, I therefore went up from the sea, to get a certain outlook in his company. 8 But I also have another character and role. I transform myself into waves and come up from the sea. 9 And I show myself to men, so that those on earth call me Kunospaston, because I assume the human form. 10 And my name is a true one. For by my passage up into men, I send forth a certain nausea. 11 I came then to take counsel with the prince Beelzebul, and he bound me and delivered me into your hands. 12 And I am here before you because of this seal, and you now torment me. 13 Behold now, in two or three days the spirit that [now] converses with you will fail, because I will have no water." 14 And I said to him, "Tell me by what messenger you are frustrated." And he answered: "By Lameth." And I glorified God. 15 I commanded the spirit to be thrown into a vial along with ten jugs of seawater of two measures each. 16 And I sealed them around, above the marbles, and asphalt, and pitch in the mouth of the vessel. And having sealed it with my ring, I ordered it to be deposited in the temple of God.

CHAPTER 21

1 And I ordered another spirit to come before me, 2 and another enslaved spirit came before my face, having the obscure form of a man, with gleaming eyes, and bearing a blade in his hand. 3 And I asked: "Who are you?" But he answered: "I am a lascivious spirit, engendered of a giant man who dies in the massacre in the time of the giants." 4 I said to him, "Tell me what you are employed in on earth, and where you have your dwelling." 5 And he said, "My dwelling is in fruitful places, but my procedure is this: I seat myself beside the men who pass along among the tombs, and in untimely season I assume the form of the dead; 6 and if I catch anyone, I immediately destroy him with my sword. But if I cannot destroy him, I cause him to be possessed with a demon, and to devour his own flesh, and the hair to fall off his chin." 7 But I said to him, "Be then in fear of the God of Heaven and of earth, and tell me by which messenger you are frustrated." 8 And he answered: "He destroys me who is to become Savior, a Man whose figure, if anyone will write it on his forehead, he will defeat me, and I will quickly retreat in fear. 9 And, indeed, if anyone writes this sign on him, I will be in fear." And I, Solomon, on hearing this, and having glorified the Lord God, shut this demon up like the rest.

CHAPTER 22

1 And I commanded another demon to come before me, and thirty-six spirits came before my face, their heads shapeless like dogs, but in themselves they were human in form, with faces of donkeys, faces of oxen, and faces of birds. **2** And I, Solomon, on hearing and seeing them, wondered, and I asked them and said, "Who are you?" **3** But they, of one accord with one voice, said, "We are the thirty-six elements, the world-rulers of this darkness. **4** But, O King Solomon, you will not wrong us nor imprison us, nor lay command on us; but since the Lord God has given you authority over every spirit, in the air, and on the earth, and under the earth, therefore we also present ourselves before you like the other spirits, from ram and bull, from both twin and crab, lion and virgin, scales and scorpion, archer, goat-horned, water-pourer, and fish." **5** Then I, Solomon, invoked the Name of the Lord of Hosts, and questioned each in turn as to what was its character. **6** And I commanded each one to come forward and tell of its actions. **7** Then the first one came forward, and said, "I am the first decan of the ecliptic, and I am called the ram, and with me are these two." **8** So I put the question to them: "Who are you called?" The first said, "I, O lord, am called Ruax, and I cause the heads of men to be idle, and I pillage their brows. But let me only hear the words, Michael, imprison Ruax, and I immediately retreat." **9** And the second said, "I am called Barsafael, and I cause those who are subject to my hour to feel the pain of migraine. If only I hear the words, Gabriel, imprison Barsafael, I immediately retreat." **10** The third said, "I am called Arôtosael. I do harm to eyes, and grievously injure them. Only let me hear the words, Uriel, imprison Arôtosael, I immediately retreat." **11** The fifth said, "I am called Iudal, and I bring about a block in the ears and deafness of hearing. If I hear, Uruel Iudal, I immediately retreat." **12** The sixth said, "I am called Sphendonaêl. I cause tumors of the parotid gland, and inflammations of the tonsils, and tetanic recurvation. If I hear, Sabrael, imprison Sphendonaêl, I immediately retreat." **13** And the seventh said, "I am called Sphandôr, and I weaken the strength of the shoulders, and cause them to tremble; and I paralyze the nerves of the hands, and I break and bruise the bones of the neck. And I suck out the marrow. But if I hear the words, Araêl, imprison Sphandôr, I immediately retreat." **14** And the eighth said, "I am called Belbel. I distort the hearts and minds of men. If I hear the words, Araêl, imprison Belbel, I immediately retreat." **15** And the ninth said, "I am called Kurtaêl. I send colics in the bowels. I induce pains. If I hear the words, Iaôth, imprison Kurtaêl, I immediately retreat." **16** The tenth said, "I am called Metathiax. I cause the reins to ache. If I hear the words, Adônaêl, imprison Metathiax, I immediately retreat." **17** The eleventh said, "I am called Katanikotaêl. I create strife and wrongs in men's homes and send on them hard temper. If anyone would be at peace in his home, let him write on seven leaves of laurel the name of the messenger that frustrates me, along with these names: Iae, Ieô, sons of hosts, in the Name of the great God let him shut up Katanikotaêl. Then let him wash the laurel-leaves in water, and sprinkle his house with the water, from within to the outside. And I immediately retreat." **18** The twelfth said, "I am called Saphathoraél, and I inspire partisanship in men, and delight in causing them to stumble. If anyone will write on paper these names of messengers, Iacô, Iealô, Iôelet, Sabaôth, Ithoth, Bae, and having folded it up, wear it around his neck or against his ear, I immediately retreat and dissipate the drunken fit." **19** The thirteenth said, "I am called Bobêl, and I cause nervous sickness by my assaults. If I hear the name of the great Adonaêl, imprison Bothothêl, I immediately retreat." **20** The fourteenth said, "I am called Kumeatêl, and I inflict shivering fits and torpor. If only I hear the words: Zôrôêl, imprison Kumentaêl, I immediately retreat." **21** The fifteenth said, "I am called Roêlêd. I cause cold, and frost, and pain in the stomach. Let me only hear the words: Lax, do not remain, do not be warmed, for Solomon is fairer than eleven fathers, I [immediately] retreat." **22** The sixteenth said, "I am called Atrax. I inflict on men fevers, irremediable and harmful. If you would imprison me, chop up coriander and smear it on the lips, reciting the following charm: The fever which is from dirt—I exorcise you by the throne of the Highest God, retreat from dirt and retreat from the creature fashioned by God. And I immediately retreat." **23** The seventeenth said, "I am called Ieropaêl. On the stomach of men I sit, and cause convulsions in the bath and in the road; and wherever I am found, or find a man, I throw him down. But if anyone will say to the afflicted, into their ear, these names three times over, into the right ear: Ludarizê, Sabunê, Denôê, I immediately retreat." **24** The eighteenth said, "I am called Buldumêch. I separate wife from husband and bring about a grudge between them. If anyone writes down the names of your sires, Solomon, on paper and places it in the ante-chamber of his house, I retreat there. And the legend written will be as follows: The God of Abram, and the God of Isaac, and the God of Jacob commands you—retreat from this house in peace. And I immediately retreat." **25** The nineteenth said, "I am called Naôth, and I take my seat on the knees of men. If anyone writes on paper: Phnunoboêol, depart Nathath, and you do not touch the neck, I immediately retreat." **26** The twentieth said, "I am called Marderô. I send on men incurable fever. If anyone writes on the page of a scroll: Sphênêr, Raphael, retreat, do not drag me around, do not flay me, and ties it around his neck, I immediately retreat." **27** The twenty-first said, "I am called Alath, and I cause coughing and hard-breathing in children. If anyone writes on paper: Rorêx, pursue Alath, and fastens it around his neck, I immediately retreat." **28** The twenty-third said, "I am called Nefthada. I cause the reins to ache, and I bring about dysuria. If anyone writes on a plate of tin the words: Lathôth, Uruêl, Nephthada, and fastens it around the loins, I immediately retreat." **29** The twenty-fourth said, "I am called Akton. I cause ribs and lumbar muscles to ache. If one engraves on copper material, taken from a ship which has missed its anchorage, this: Marmaraôth, Sabaôth, pursue Akton, and fastens it round the loin, I immediately retreat." **30** The twenty-fifth said, "I am called Anatreth, and I tear burnings and fevers into the entrails. But if I hear: Arara, Charara, I immediately retreat." **31** The twenty-sixth said, "I am called Enenuth. I steal away men's minds, and change their hearts, and make a man toothless. If one writes: Allazoôl, pursue Enenuth, and ties the paper around him, I immediately retreat." **32** The twenty-seventh said, "I am called Phêth. I make men consumptive and cause hemorrhaging. If one exorcises me in wine, sweet-smelling and unmixed by the eleventh age, and says: I exorcise you by the eleventh age to stop, I demand, Phêth (Axiôphêth), then gives it to the patient to drink, I then immediately retreat." **33** The twenty-eighth said, "I am called Harpax, and I send sleeplessness on men. If one writes Kokphnêdismos, and binds it around the temples, I immediately retreat." **34** The twenty-ninth said, "I am called Anostêr. I engender uterine mania and pains in the bladder. If one powders into pure oil three seeds of laurel and smears it on, saying, I exorcise you, Anostêr, stop by Marmaraô, I immediately retreat." **35** The thirtieth said, "I am called Alleborith. If in eating fish one has swallowed a bone, then he must take a bone from the fish and cough, and I immediately retreat." **36** The thirty-first said, "I am called Hephesimireth, and cause lingering disease. If you throw salt, rubbed in the hand, into oil and smear it on the patient, saying, Seraphim, cherubim, help me! I immediately retreat." **37** The thirty-second said, "I am called Ichthion. I paralyze muscles and contuse them. If I hear Adonaêth, help! I immediately retreat." **38** The thirty-third said, "I am called Agchoniôn. I lie among swaddling-clothes and in the precipice. And if anyone writes on fig-leaves Lycurgos, taking away one letter at a time, and writes it reversing the letters, I immediately retreat—Lycurgos, ycurgos, curgos, urgos, gos, os." **39** The thirty-fourth said, "I am called Autothith. I cause grudges and fighting. Therefore, I am frustrated by Alpha and Omega, if written down." **40** The thirty-fifth said, "I am called Phthenoth. I cast an evil eye on every man. Therefore, the eye, much suffering, if it is drawn, frustrates me." **41** The thirty-sixth said, "I am called Bianakith. I have a grudge against the body. I lay waste houses, I cause flesh to decay, and all else that is similar. If a man writes on the front-door of his house: Mêltô, Ardu, Anaath, I flee from that place."

CHAPTER 23

1 And I, Solomon, when I heard this, glorified the God of the heavens and earth. And I commanded them to fetch water in the temple of God. **2** And I furthermore prayed to the Lord God to cause the demons outside, that hamper humanity, to be bound and made to approach the temple of God. **3** I condemned some of these demons to do the heavy work of the construction of the temple of God. **4** Others I shut up in prisons. Others I ordered to wrestle with fire in [the making of] gold and silver, sitting down by lead and spoon, **5** and to make places ready for the other demons in which they should be confined. **6** And I, Solomon, had much quiet in all the earth, and spent my life in profound peace, honored by all men and by all under Heaven. **7** And I built the entire temple of the Lord God. And my kingdom was prosperous, and my army was with me. **8** And for the rest, the city of Jerusalem had repose, rejoicing and delighted. **8** And all the kings of the earth came to me from the ends of the earth to behold the temple which I built to the Lord God. **9** And having heard of the wisdom given to me, they paid homage to me in the temple, bringing gold, and silver, and many and various precious stones, and bronze, and iron, and lead, and cedar logs. **10** And woods did not decay [that] they brought me for the equipment of the temple of God. **11** And among them the queen of the south, being a witch, also came in great concern and bowed low to the earth before me. **12** And having heard my wisdom, she glorified the God of Israel, and she made formal trial of all my wisdom, of all love in which I instructed her, according to the wisdom imparted to me. And all the sons of Israel glorified God.

CHAPTER 24

1 And behold, in those days one of the workmen of ripe old age threw himself down before me, and said, "King Solomon, pity me, because I am old." **2** So I commanded him to stand up, and said, "Tell me, old man, all you will." **3** And he answered: "I implore you king, I have an only-born son, and he insults and beats me openly, and plucks out the hair of my head, and threatens me with a painful death. Therefore, I implore you: avenge me." **4** And I, Solomon, on hearing this, felt compunction as I looked at his old age; and I commanded the child to be brought to me. **5** And when he was brought, I questioned him whether it was true. And the youth said, "I was not so filled with madness as to strike my father with my hand. Be kind to me, O king. **6** For I have not dared to commit such impiety, poor wretch that I am." **7** But I, Solomon, on hearing this from the youth, exhorted the old man to reflect on the matter, and accept his son's apology. **8** However, he would not, but said he would rather let him die. And as the old man would not yield, I was about to pronounce sentence on the youth, when I saw the demon Ornias laughing. **9** I was very angry at the demon's laughing in my presence; and I ordered my men to remove the other parties and bring Ornias forward before my tribunal. **10** And when he was brought before me, I said to him, "Accursed one, why did you look at me and laugh?" **11** And the demon answered: "Please, king, it was not because of you I laughed, but because of this ill-fated old man and the wretched youth—his son. **12** For after three days his son will die untimely; and behold, the old man desires to unfairly make away with him." **13** But I, Solomon, having heard this, said to the demon, "Is that which you speak true?" And he answered: "It is true, O king." **14** And I, on hearing that, commanded them to remove the demon, and that they should bring the old man with his son before me again. **15** I commanded them to make friends with one another again, and I supplied them with food. **16** And then I told the old man after three days to bring his son to me again here; "and," I said, "I will attend to him." And they saluted me and went their way. **17** And when they were gone, I ordered Ornias to be brought forward, and said to him, "Tell me how you know this"; and he answered: "We demons ascend into the expanse of Heaven, and fly around among the stars. **18** And we hear the sentences which go forth on the souls of men, and immediately we come, and whether by force of influence, or by fire, or by sword, or by some accident, we veil our act of destruction; **19** and if a man does not die by some untimely disaster or by violence, then we demons transform ourselves in such a way as to appear to men and be worshiped in our human nature." **20** I therefore, having heard this, glorified the Lord God, and I questioned the demon again, saying, "Tell me how you can ascend into Heaven, being demons, and intermingle amidst the stars and holy messengers." **21** And he answered: "Just as things are fulfilled in Heaven, so also on earth the types of all of them. **22** For there are principalities, authorities, world-rulers, and we demons fly around in the air; and we hear the voices of the heavenly beings, and survey all the powers. **23** And as having no ground on which to descend and rest, we lose strength and fall off like leaves from trees. **24** And men seeing us imagine that the stars are falling from [the] sky. **25** But it is not really so, O king; but we fall because of our weakness, and because we have nothing

anywhere to lay hold of; and so we suddenly fall down like lightnings in the depth of night. **26** And we set cities in flames and the fields [on] fire. For the stars have firm foundations in the heavens like the sun and the moon." **27** And I, Solomon, having heard this, ordered the demon to be guarded for five days. **28** And after the five days I recalled the old man and was about to question him, but he came to me with dark countenance. **29** And I said to him, "Tell me, old man, where is your son? And what does this [gloomy] appearance mean?" **30** And he answered: "Behold, I have become childless and sit by my son's grave in despair. For it is already two days that he is dead." But I, Solomon, on hearing that, and knowing that the demon Ornias had told me the truth, glorified the God of Israel.

CHAPTER 25

1 And the queen of the south saw all this, and marveled, glorifying the God of Israel; and she beheld the temple of the Lord being built. **2** And she gave a siklos of gold and one hundred myriads of silver and choice bronze, and she went into the temple. **3** And [she beheld] the altar of incense and the brazen supports of this altar, and the gems of the lamps flashing forth of different colors, and of the lampstand of stone, and of emerald, and hyacinth, and sapphire; **4** and she beheld the vessels of gold, and silver, and bronze, and wood, and the folds of skins dyed red with madder. **5** And she saw the bases of the pillars of the temple of the Lord. All were of one gold . . . **6** . . . apart from the demons whom I condemned to labor. And there was peace in the circle of my kingdom and over all the earth.

CHAPTER 26

1 And it came to pass, when I was in my kingdom, the king of the Arabians, Adares, sent me a letter, and the writing of the letter was written as follows: **2** "To King Solomon, greetings! Behold, we have heard, and it has been heard to all the ends of the earth, concerning the wisdom given in you, and that you are a man merciful from the Lord. **3** And understanding has been granted to you over all the spirits of the air, and on earth, and under the earth. **4** Now indeed, there is present in the land of Arabia a spirit of the following kind: at early dawn there begins to blow a certain wind until the third hour. **5** And its blast is harsh and terrible, and it slays man and beast. And no spirit can live on earth against this demon. **6** Please then, forasmuch as the spirit is a wind, contrive something according to the wisdom given in you by the Lord your God, and deign to send a man [who is] able to capture it. **7** And behold, King Solomon, I, and my people, and all my land will serve you to death. **8** And all Arabia will be at peace with you, if you will perform this act of righteousness for us. **9** For what reason, please do not despise our humble prayer, and do not permit the territory subordinated to your authority to be utterly brought to nothing. **10** Because we are suppliants—both I, and my people, and all my land. **11** Farewell to my lord. All health [be to you]!" **12** And I, Solomon, read this letter; and I folded it up and gave it to my people, and said to them, "After seven days you will remind me of this letter." **13** And Jerusalem was built, and the temple was being completed. And there was a stone, the end stone of the corner lying there—great, chosen out, one which I desired to lay in the head of the corner of the completion of the temple. **14** And all the workmen, and all the demons helping them, came to the same place to bring up the stone and lay it on the pinnacle of the holy temple, and were not strong enough to stir it and lay it on the corner allotted to it. **15** For that stone was exceedingly great and useful for the corner of the temple. **16** And after seven days, being reminded of the letter of Adares, king of Arabia, I called my servant and said to him, "Order your camel and take a leather flask for yourself, and also take this seal. **17** And go away into Arabia to the place in which the evil spirit blows; and take the flask there, and the signet-ring in front of the mouth of the flask, and [hold them] toward the blast of the spirit. **18** And when the flask is blown out, you will understand that the demon is [in it]. **19** Then quickly tie up the mouth of the flask, and seal it securely with the seal-ring, and lay it carefully on the camel, and bring it to me here. **20** And if on the way it offers you gold, or silver, or treasure in return for letting it go, see that you are not persuaded. But arrange [it] without using an oath to release it. **21** And then if it points out to the places where gold or silver are, mark the places and seal them with this seal. And bring the demon to me. And now depart, and farewell." **22** Then the youth did as was commanded him. And he ordered his camel, and laid a flask on it, and set off into Arabia. **23** And the men of that region would not believe that he would be able to catch the evil spirit. **24** And when it was dawn, the servant stood before the spirit's blast, and laid the flask on the ground, and the finger-ring on the mouth of the flask. **25** And the demon blew through the middle of the finger-ring into the mouth of the flask, and going in, blew out the flask. **26** But the man promptly stood up to it and drew the mouth of the flask tight with his hand in the Name of the Lord God of Hosts. **27** And the demon remained within the flask. And after that, the youth remained in that land three days to make trial. **28** And the spirit no longer blew against that city. And all the Arabs knew that he had safely shut the spirit in. **29** Then the youth fastened the flask on the camel, and the Arabs sent him forth on his way with much honor and precious gifts, praising and magnifying the God of Israel. **30** But the youth brought in the bag and laid it in the middle of the temple. And on the next day, I, King Solomon, went into the temple of God and sat in deep distress regarding the stone of the end of the corner. **31** And when I entered the temple, the flask stood up and walked around some seven steps and then fell on its mouth and paid homage to me. **32** And I marveled that even along with the bottle the demon still had power and could walk around; and I commanded it to stand up. **33** And the flask stood up and stood on its feet all blown out. And I questioned him, saying, "Tell me, who are you?" **34** And the spirit within said, "I am the demon called Ephippas, that is in Arabia." **35** And I said to him, "Is this your name?" And he answered: "Yes; wheresoever I will, I descend, and set fire, and do [it] to death." **36** And I said to him, "By what messenger are you frustrated?" And he answered: "By the only-ruling God that even has authority over me to be heard— **37** He that is to be born of a virgin and crucified by the Jews on a cross, whom the messengers and chief-messengers worship. **38** He frustrates me and weakens me of my great strength, which has been given to me by my father the Devil." **39** And I said to him, "What can you do?" And he answered: "I am able to remove mountains, to overthrow the oaths of kings. I wither trees and make their leaves to fall off." **40** And I said to him, "Can you raise this stone, and lay it for the beginning of this corner which exists in the fair plan of the temple?" **41** And he said, "Not only raise this, O king, but also, with the help of the demon who presides over the Red Sea, I will bring up the pillar of air, and will stand it where you will in Jerusalem." **42** Saying this, I laid stress on him, and the flask became as if depleted of air. And I placed it under the stone, and [the spirit] girded himself up, and lifted it up [to the] top of the flask. **43** And the flask went up the steps, carrying the stone, and laid it down at the end of the entrance of the temple. **44** And I, Solomon, beholding the stone raised aloft and placed on a foundation, said, "Truly the Writing is fulfilled, which says: The stone which the builders rejected on trial, that same has become the head of the corner. **45** For this is not mine to grant, but God's, that the demon should be strong enough to lift up such a great stone and deposit it in the place I wished." **46** And Ephippas led the demon of the Red Sea with the column. And they both took the column and raised it aloft from the earth. **47** And I outwitted these two spirits, so that they could not shake the entire earth in a moment of time. **48** And then I sealed around on this side and that with my ring, and said, "Watch." **49** And the spirits have remained upholding it until this day, for proof of the wisdom given to me. And there the pillar was hanging of enormous size, in midair, supported by the winds. **50** And thus the spirits appeared underneath, like air, supporting it. And if one looks fixedly, the pillar is a little oblique, being supported by the spirits; and it is so today.

CHAPTER 27

1 And I, Solomon, questioned the other spirit which came up with the pillar from the depth of the Red Sea. **2** And I said to him, "Who are you, and what calls you? And what is your business? For I hear many things about you." **3** And the demon answered: "I, O King Solomon, am called Abezithibod. I am a descendant of the chief-messenger. **4** When once I sat in the

first heaven, of which the name is Ameleouth, I was then a fierce and winged spirit, and with a single wing I was plotting against every spirit under Heaven. **5** I was present when Moses went in before Pharaoh, king of Egypt, and I hardened his heart. **6** I am he whom Jannes and Jambres invoked, striving with Moses in Egypt. I am he who fought against Moses with wonders with signs." **7** I therefore said to him, "How were you found in the Red Sea?" **8** And he answered: "In the exodus of the sons of Israel I hardened the heart of Pharaoh. **9** And I excited his heart and that of his ministers. And I caused them to pursue after the sons of Israel. **10** And Pharaoh followed with [me] and all the Egyptians. Then I was present there, and we followed together. **11** And we all came up on the Red Sea. And it came to pass when the sons of Israel had crossed over, the water returned and hid all the host of the Egyptians and all their might. **12** And I remained in the sea, being kept under this pillar. But when Ephippas came, being sent by you, shut up in the vessel of a flask, he fetched me up to you." **13** I, therefore, Solomon, having heard this, glorified God and adjured the demons not to disobey me, but to remain supporting the pillar. **14** And they both swore, saying, "[As] the Lord your God lives, we will not let go of this pillar until the world's end. But on whatever day this stone falls, then will be the end of the world."

CHAPTER 28

1 And I, Solomon, glorified God, and adorned the temple of the Lord with all pleasant appearance. **2** And I was glad in spirit in my kingdom, and there was peace in my days. And I took wives of my own from every land, who were numberless. **3** And I marched against the Jebusites, and there I saw a Jebusite man's daughter, and fell violently in love with her, and desired to take her to be [my] wife along with my other wives. **4** And I said to their priests, "Give me the Shunammite to be [my] wife." **5** But the priests of Moloch said to me, "If you love this maiden, go in and worship our gods, the great god Remphan and the god called Moloch." **6** I, therefore, was in fear of the glory of God, and did not follow to worship. **7** And I said to them, "I will not worship a strange god. What is this proposal, that you compel me to do so much?" But they said, ". . . by our fathers." **8** And when I answered that I would on no account worship strange gods, they told the maiden not to sleep with me until I complied and sacrificed to the gods. **9** I then was moved, but crafty Eros brought and laid by her five grasshoppers for me, saying, "Take these grasshoppers, and crush them together in the name of the god Moloch; and then I will sleep with you." **10** And I actually did this. And at once the Spirit of God departed from me, and I became weak as well as foolish in my words. **11** And after that I was obliged by her to build a temple of idols to Ba'al, and to Rapha, and to Moloch, and to the other idols. **12** I then, wretch that I am, followed her advice, and the glory of God yet departed from me, and my spirit was darkened, and I became the sport of idols and demons. **13** For this reason I wrote out this Testament, that you who get possession of it may pity, and attend to the last things, and not to the first, **14** so that you may find grace forever and ever. Amen.

PSALMS OF SOLOMON

The apocryphal psalms attributed to Solomon were likely written in the 1st or 2nd centuries BC. While they do not belong to any current canon, they have been found in copies of the Peshitta and Septuagint.

PSALM 1

1 I cried to the Lord when I was in distress, || To God when sinners assailed. **2** Suddenly the alarm of war was heard before me; [I said], "He will listen to me, for I am full of righteousness." **3** I thought in my heart that I was full of righteousness, || Because I was well off and had become rich in children. **4** Their wealth spread to the whole earth, || And their glory to the end of the earth. **5** They were exalted to the stars; They said they would never fall. **6** But they became insolent in their prosperity, || And they were without understanding, **7** Their sins were in secret, || And even I had no knowledge [of them]. **8** Their transgressions [went] beyond those of the heathen before them; They utterly polluted the holy things of the Lord.

PSALM 2

1 A Psalm of Solomon. Concerning Jerusalem. When the sinner waxed proud, with a battering-ram he cast down fortified walls, || And You did not restrain [him]. **2** Alien nations ascended Your altar, || They trampled [it] proudly with their sandals, **3** Because the sons of Jerusalem had defiled the holy things of the Lord, || [And] had profaned with iniquities the offerings of God. **4** Therefore He said, "Cast them far from Me"; **5** It was set at nothing before God, || It was utterly dishonored; **6** The sons and the daughters were in grievous captivity, || Their neck [was] sealed, [it was] branded among the nations. **7** He has done to them according to their sins, || For He has left them in the hands of them that prevailed. **8** He has turned His face away from pitying them—Young, and old, and their children together; **9** For they had done evil, one and all, in not listening. **10** And the heavens were angry, || And the earth abhorred them; **11** For no man on it had done what they did, **12** And the earth recognized all Your righteous judgments, O God. **13** They set the sons of Jerusalem to be mocked at in return for [the] harlots in her; Every wayfarer entered in in the full light of day. **14** They made a mockery with their transgressions, as they themselves were frequent to do; In the full light of day they revealed their iniquities. **15** And the daughters of Jerusalem were defiled in accordance with Your judgment, || Because they had defiled themselves with unnatural intercourse. I am pained in my bowels and my inward parts for these things. **16** And yet, I will justify You, O God, in uprightness of heart, || For in Your judgments is Your righteousness [displayed], O God. **17** For You have rendered to the sinners according to their deeds, || Yes, according to their sins, which were very wicked. **18** You have uncovered their sins, that Your judgment might be manifest; **19** You have wiped out their memorial from the earth. God is a righteous judge, || And He is no respecter of persons. **20** For the nations reproached Jerusalem, trampling it down; Her beauty was dragged down from the throne of glory. **21** She girded on sackcloth instead of beautiful raiment, || A rope [was] around her head instead of a crown. **22** She put off the glorious diadem which God had set on her, || In dishonor her beauty was cast on the ground. **23** And I saw and entreated the Lord and said, || "Long enough, O Lord, has Your hand been heavy on Israel in bringing the nations on [them]. **24** For they have made sport unsparingly in wrath and fierce anger; **25** And they will make an utter end, unless You, O Lord, rebuke them in Your wrath. **26** For they have not done it in zeal, but in lust of soul, || Pouring out their wrath on us with a view to plunder. **27** Do not delay, O God, to repay them on [their] heads, || To turn the pride of the dragon into dishonor." **28** And I did not have long to wait before God showed me the insolent one || Slain on the mountains of Egypt, || Esteemed of less account than the least on land and sea; **29** His body, [too,] borne here and there on the billows with much insolence, || With none to bury [him], because He had rejected him with dishonor. **30** He did not consider that he was man, || And did not consider the latter end; **31** He said, "I will be lord of land and sea"; And he did not recognize that it is God who is great, || Mighty in His great strength. **32** He is King over the heavens, || And judges kings and kingdoms, **33** Who sets me up in glory, || And brings down the proud to continuous destruction in dishonor, || Because they did not know Him. **34** And now behold, you princes of the earth, || The judgment of the Lord, || For [He is] a great and righteous King, || Judging [all] that is under Heaven. **35** Bless God, you that fear the Lord with wisdom, || For the mercy of the Lord will be on them that fear Him, in the Judgment, **36** So that He will distinguish between the righteous and the sinner, || [And] repay the sinners forever according to their deeds, **37** And have mercy on the righteous, [delivering him] from the affliction of the sinner, || And repaying the sinner for what he has done to the righteous. **38** For the Lord is good to them that call on Him in patience, || Doing according to His mercy to His pious ones, || Establishing [them] at all times before Him in strength. **39**

Blessed is the Lord forever before His servants.

PSALM 3

1 A Psalm of Solomon. Concerning the righteous. Why do you sleep, O my soul, || And do not bless the Lord? **2** Sing a new song, || To God who is worthy to be praised. Sing and be wakeful against His awaking, || For a psalm [sung] to God from a glad heart is good. **3** The righteous remember the Lord at all times, || With thanksgiving and declaration of the righteousness of the Lord's judgments. **4** The righteous does not despise the disciplining of the Lord; His will is always before the Lord. **5** The righteous stumbles and holds the Lord righteous: He falls and looks out for what God will do to him; **6** He seeks out from where his deliverance will come. **7** The steadfastness of the righteous is from God their deliverer; There does not lodge in the house of the righteous sin on sin. **8** The righteous continually searches his house, || To utterly remove [all] iniquity [done] by him in error. **9** He makes atonement for [sins of] ignorance by fasting and afflicting his soul, || **10** And the Lord counts guiltless every pious man and his house. **11** The sinner stumbles and curses his life, || The day when he was begotten, and his mother's travail. **12** He adds sins to sins, while he lives; He falls—truly grievous is his fall—and rises no longer. **13** The destruction of the sinner is forever, || And he will not be remembered when the righteous is visited. **14** This is the portion of sinners forever. **15** But they that fear the Lord will rise to continuous life, || And their life [will be] in the light of the Lord, and will come to an end no more.

PSALM 4

1 A Conversation of Solomon with the Men-pleasers. Why do you sit, O profane [man], in the council of the pious, || Seeing that your heart is far removed from the Lord, || Provoking the God of Israel with transgressions? **2** Extravagant in speech, extravagant in outward seeming beyond all [men], || Is he that is severe of speech in condemning sinners in judgment. **3** And his hand is first on him as [though he acted] in zeal, || And [yet] he is himself guilty in respect of manifold sins and of wantonness. **4** His eyes are on every woman without distinction; His tongue lies when he makes contract with an oath. **5** By night and in secret he sins as though unseen, || With his eyes he talks to every woman of evil compacts. **6** He is swift to enter every house with cheerfulness as though guileless. **7** Let God remove those that live in hypocrisy in the company of the pious, || [Even] the life of such a one with corruption of his flesh and destitution. **8** Let God reveal the deeds of the men-pleasers, || The deeds of such a one with laughter and derision; **9** That the pious may count righteous the judgment of their God, || When sinners are removed from before the righteous, **10** [Even the] man-pleaser who utters law guilefully. **11** And their eyes [are fixed] on any man's house that is [still] secure, || That they may, like [the] Serpent, destroy the wisdom of . . . with words of transgressors, **12** His words are deceitful that [he] may accomplish [his] wicked desire. **13** He never ceases from scattering [families] as though [they were] orphans, || Yes, he lays waste a house on account of [his] lawless desire. **14** He deceives with words, [saying,] "There is none that sees, or judges." **15** He fills one [house] with lawlessness, || And [then] his eyes [are fixed] on the next house, || To destroy it with words that give wing to [desire]. [Yet] with all these his soul, like Sheol, is not satisfied. **16** Let his portion, O Lord, be dishonored before You; Let him go forth groaning and come home cursed. **17** Let his life be [spent] in anguish, and destitution, and want, O Lord; Let his sleep be [beset] with pains and his awaking with perplexities. **18** Let sleep be withdrawn from his eyelids at night; Let him fail dishonorably in every work of his hands. **19** Let him come home empty-handed to his house, || And his house be void of everything with which he could satisfy his appetite. **20** [Let] his old age [be spent] in childless loneliness until his removal. **21** Let the flesh of the men-pleasers be torn by wild beasts, || And [let] the bones of the lawless [lie] dishonored in the sight of the sun. **22** Let ravens peck out the eyes of the hypocrites. **23** For they have laid waste many houses of men, in dishonor, || And scattered [them] in [their] lust; **24** And they have not remembered God, || Nor feared God in all these things; **25** But they have provoked God's anger and vexed Him. May He remove them from off the earth, || Because with deceit they deceived the souls of the flawless. **26** Blessed are they that fear the Lord in their flawlessness; **27** The Lord will deliver them from guileful men and sinners, || And deliver us from every stumbling-block of the lawless [men]. **28** Let God destroy them that insolently work all unrighteousness, || For a great and mighty judge is the Lord our God in righteousness. **29** Let Your mercy, O Lord, be on all them that love You.

PSALM 5

1 A Psalm of Solomon. O Lord God, I will praise Your Name with joy, || In the midst of them that know Your righteous judgments. **2** For You are good and merciful, the refuge of the poor; **3** When I cry to You, do not silently disregard me. **4** For no man takes spoil from a mighty man. **5** Who, then, can take anything of all that You have made, except You Yourself give? **6** For man and his portion [lie] before You in the balance; He cannot add to, so as to enlarge, what has been prescribed by You. **7** O God, when we are in distress, we call on You for help, || And You do not turn back our petition, for You are our God. **8** Do not cause Your hand to be heavy on us, || Lest through necessity we sin. **9** Even though You do not restore us, we will not keep away; But we will come to You. **10** For if I hunger, I will cry to You, O God; And You will give to me. **11** You nourish birds and fish, || In that You give rain to the plains that green grass may spring up, || To prepare fodder in the plain for every living thing; **12** And if they hunger, they lift up their face to You. **13** You nourish kings, and rulers, and peoples, O God; And who is the help of the poor and needy, if not You, O Lord? **14** And You will listen—for who is good and gentle but You— Making glad the soul of the humble by opening Your hand in mercy. **15** Man's goodness is [bestowed] grudgingly and . . . And if he repeats [it] without murmuring, even that is marvelous. **16** But Your gift is great in goodness and wealth, || And he whose hope is [set] on You will have no lack of gifts. **17** Your mercy is on the whole earth, O Lord, in goodness. **18** Happy is he whom God remembers in [granting to him] a due sufficiency; **19** If a man abounds over much, he sins. **20** Sufficient are moderate means with righteousness, || And hereby the blessing of the Lord [becomes] abundance with righteousness. **21** They that fear the Lord rejoice in good [gifts], || And Your goodness is on Israel in Your kingdom. Blessed is the glory of the Lord, for He is our King.

PSALM 6

1 In Hope. Of Solomon. Happy is the man whose heart is fixed to call on the Name of the Lord; **2** When he remembers the Name of the Lord, he will be saved. **3** His ways are made even by the Lord, || And the works of his hands are preserved by the Lord his God. **4** At what he sees in his bad dreams, his soul will not be troubled; **5** When he passes through rivers and the tossing of the seas, he will not be dismayed. **6** He arises from his sleep, and blesses the Name of the Lord: **7** When his heart is at peace, he sings to the Name of his God, || And he entreats the Lord for all his house. **8** And the Lord hears the prayer of everyone that fears God, || And the Lord accomplishes every request of the soul that hopes for Him. **9** Blessed is the Lord, who shows mercy to those who love Him in sincerity.

PSALM 7

1 Of Solomon. Of turning. Do not make Your dwelling far from us, O God; Lest they assail us that hate us without cause. **2** For You have rejected them, O God; Do not let their foot trample on Your holy inheritance. **3** Discipline us Yourself in Your good pleasure; But do not give [us] up to the nations; **4** For, if You send pestilence, || You Yourself give it charge concerning us; For You are merciful, || And will not be angry to the point of consuming us. **5** While Your Name dwells in our midst, we will find mercy; **6** And the nations will not prevail against us. For You are our shield, || **7** And when we call on You, You listen to us; **8** For You will pity the seed of Israel forever || And You will not reject [them], || But we [will be] under Your yoke forever, || And [under] the rod of Your

disciplining. **9** You will establish us in the time that You help us, || Showing mercy to the house of Jacob on the day wherein You promised [to help them].

PSALM 8

1 Of Solomon. Of the chief Musician. My ear has heard distress and the sound of war; The sound of a trumpet announcing slaughter and calamity, **2** The sound of many people as of an exceedingly high wind, || As a tempest with mighty fire sweeping through the Negeb. **3** And I said in my heart, "Surely God judges us"; **4** I hear a sound [moving] toward Jerusalem, the holy city. **5** My loins were broken at what I heard, my knees tottered: **6** My heart was afraid, my bones were dismayed like flax. **7** I said, "They establish their ways in righteousness." I thought on the judgments of God since the creation of the heavens and earth; I held God righteous in His judgments which have been from of old. **8** God laid bare their sins in the full light of day; All the earth came to know the righteous judgments of God. **9** In secret places underground their iniquities [were committed] to provoke [Him] to anger; **10** They worked confusion, son with mother and father with daughter; **11** They committed adultery, every man with his neighbor's wife. They concluded covenants with one another with an oath touching these things; **12** They plundered the sanctuary of God, as though there was no avenger. **13** They trod the altar of the Lord, [coming straight] from all manner of uncleanness; And with menstrual blood they defiled the sacrifices, as [though these were] common flesh. **14** They left no sin undone, wherein they did not surpass the heathen. **15** Therefore God mingled for them a spirit of wandering; And gave them a cup of undiluted wine to drink, that they might become drunken. **16** He brought him that is from the end of the earth, that strikes mightily; **17** He decreed war against Jerusalem, and against her land. **18** The princes of the land went to meet him with joy; They said to him, "Blessed is your way! Come, enter in with peace." **19** They made the rough ways even, before his entering in; They opened the gates to Jerusalem, they crowned its walls. **20** As a father [enters] the house of his sons, [so] he entered [Jerusalem] in peace; He established his feet [there] in great safety. **21** He captured her fortresses and the wall of Jerusalem; **22** For God Himself led him in safety, while they wandered. **23** He destroyed their princes and everyone wise in counsel; He poured out the blood of the inhabitants of Jerusalem like the water of uncleanness. **24** He led away their sons and daughters, whom they had begotten in defilement. **25** They did according to their uncleanness, even as their fathers [had done]: **26** They defiled Jerusalem and the things that had been hallowed to the Name of God. **27** [But] God has shown Himself righteous in His judgments on the nations of the earth; **28** And the pious [servants] of God are like innocent lambs in their midst. **29** Worthy to be praised is the Lord that judges the whole earth in His righteousness. **30** Behold, now, O God, You have shown us Your judgment in Your righteousness; **31** Our eyes have seen Your judgments, O God. We have justified Your Name that is honored forever; **32** For You are the God of righteousness, judging Israel with disciplining. **33** Turn, O God, Your mercy on us, and have pity on us; **34** Gather together the dispersed of Israel, with mercy and goodness; **35** For Your faithfulness is with us. And [though] we have stiffened our neck, yet You are our chastener; **36** Do not overlook us, O our God, lest the nations swallow us up, as though there were none to deliver. **37** But You are our God from the beginning, || And on You is our hope [set], O Lord; **38** And we will not depart from You, || For Your judgments on us are good. **39** Ours and our children be Your good pleasure forever; O Lord our Savior, we will never more be moved. **40** The Lord is worthy to be praised for His judgments with the mouth of His pious ones; And blessed is Israel of the Lord forever.

PSALM 9

1 Of Solomon. For rebuke. When Israel was led away captive into a strange land, || When they fell away from the Lord who redeemed them, **2** They were cast away from the inheritance, which the Lord had given them. Among every nation [were] the dispersed of Israel according to the word of God, **3** That You might be justified, O God, in Your righteousness by reason of our transgressions: **4** For You are a just judge over all the peoples of the earth. **5** For from Your knowledge none that does unjustly is hidden, **6** And the righteous deeds of Your pious ones [are] before You, O Lord, || Where, then, can a man hide himself from Your knowledge, O God? **7** Our works are subject to our own choice and power || To do right or wrong in the works of our hands; **8** And in Your righteousness You visitest the sons of men. **9** He that does righteousness lays up life for himself with the Lord; And he that does wrongly forfeits his life to destruction; **10** For the judgments of the Lord are [given] in righteousness to [every] man and [his] house. To whom are You good, O God, except to them that call on the Lord? **12** He cleanses a soul from sins when it makes confession, when it makes acknowledgement; **13** For shame is on us and on our faces on account of all these things. **14** And to whom does He forgive sins, except to them that have sinned? **15** You bless the righteous, and do not reprove them for the sins that they have committed; And Your goodness is on them that sin, when they convert. **16** And now, You are our God, and we the people whom You have loved: Behold and show pity, O God of Israel, for we are Yours; And do not remove Your mercy from us, lest they assail us. **17** For You chose the seed of Abraham before all the nations, || And set Your Name on us, O Lord, **18** And You will not reject [us] forever. You made a covenant with our fathers concerning us; **19** And we hope in You, when our soul turns [to You]. May the mercy of the Lord be on the house of Israel forever and ever.

PSALM 10

1 A Hymn of Solomon. Happy is the man whom the Lord remembers with reproving, || And whom He restrains from the way of evil with strokes, || That he may be cleansed from sin, that it may not be multiplied. **2** He that makes his back ready for strokes will be cleansed, || For the Lord is good to them that endure disciplining. **3** For He makes straight the ways of the righteous, || And does not pervert [them] by His disciplining **4** And the mercy of the Lord [is] on them that love Him in truth, || And the Lord remembers His servants in mercy. **5** For the testimony [is] in the law of the perpetual covenant, || The testimony of the Lord [is] on the ways of men in [His] visitation. **6** Just and kind is our Lord in His judgments forever, || And Israel will praise the Name of the Lord in gladness. **7** And the pious will give thanks in the assembly of the people; And God will have mercy on the poor in the gladness of Israel; **8** For God is good and merciful forever, || And the assemblies of Israel will glorify the Name of the Lord. May the salvation of the Lord be on the house of Israel to everlasting gladness!

PSALM 11

1 Of Solomon. To expectation. Blow on the trumpet in Zion to summon [the] saints, **2** Cause the voice of him that brings good tidings to be heard in Jerusalem; For God has had pity on Israel in visiting them. **3** Stand on the height, O Jerusalem, and behold your children, || From the East and the West, gathered together by the Lord; **4** From the North they come in the gladness of their God, || From the isles far off God has gathered them. **5** He has abased high mountains into a plain for them; **6** The hills fled at their entrance. The woods gave them shelter as they passed by; **7** Every sweet-smelling tree God caused to spring up for them, || That Israel might pass by in the visitation of the glory of their God. **8** Put on, O Jerusalem, your glorious garments; Make your holy robe ready; For God has spoken good concerning Israel, forever and ever. **9** Let the Lord do what He has spoken concerning Israel and Jerusalem; Let the Lord raise up Israel by His glorious Name. May the mercy of the Lord be on Israel forever and ever.

PSALM 12

1 Of Solomon. Against the tongue of transgressors. O Lord, deliver my soul from [the] lawless and wicked man, || From the tongue that is lawless and slanderous, and speaks lies and deceit. **2** Manifoldly twisted are the words of the tongue of the wicked man, || Even as among a people a fire that burns up their beauty. **3** So he delights to fill houses with a lying tongue, || To cut down the trees of gladness which sets transgressors on fire, **4** To involve households in warfare by means of slanderous lips. May God remove far from the innocent the lips of transgressors by [bringing them to] want || And may the bones of slanderers be scattered [far] away from them that fear the Lord! **5** In flaming fire, make the slanderous tongue perish [far] away from the pious! **6** May the Lord preserve the quiet soul that hates the unrighteous; And may the Lord establish the man that follows peace at home. **7** May the salvation of the Lord be on His servant Israel forever; And let the sinners perish together at the presence of the Lord; But let the Lord's pious ones inherit the promises of the Lord.

PSALM 13

1 A Psalm of Solomon. Comfort for the righteous. The right hand of the Lord has covered me; The right hand of the Lord has spared us. **2** The arm of the Lord has saved us from the sword that passed through, || From famine and the death of sinners. **3** Ghastly beasts ran on them: They tore their flesh with their teeth, || And crushed their bones with their molars, || But the Lord delivered us from all these things. **4** The righteous was troubled on account of his errors, || Lest he should be taken away along with the sinners; **5** For the overthrow of the sinner is terrible; But not one of all these things touches the righteous. For not alike are the disciplining of the righteous [for sins done] in ignorance, || And the overthrow of the sinners. **7** The righteous is disciplined secretly, || Lest the sinner rejoice over the righteous. **8** For He corrects the righteous as a beloved son, || And his discipline is as that of a firstborn. **9** For the Lord spares His pious ones, || And blots out their errors by His disciplining. For the life of the righteous will be forever, **10** But sinners will be taken away into destruction, || And their memorial will be found no longer. **11** But the mercy of the Lord is on the pious, || And His mercy on them that fear Him.

PSALM 14

1 A Hymn of Solomon. Faithful is the Lord to them that love Him in truth, || To them that endure His disciplining, || To them that walk in the righteousness of His commandments, || In the law which He commanded us that we might live. **2** The pious of the Lord will live by it forever; The Paradise of the Lord, the trees of life, are His pious ones. **3** Their planting is rooted forever; They will not be plucked up all the days of Heaven. For the portion and the inheritance of God is Israel. **4** But not so are the sinners and transgressors, || Who love [the brief] day [spent] in companionship with their sin; Their delight is in fleeting corruption, **5** And they do not remember God. For the ways of men are known before Him at all times, || And He knows the secrets of the heart before they come to pass. **6** Therefore their inheritance is Sheol and darkness and destruction, || And they will not be found in the day when the righteous obtain mercy; **7** But the pious of the Lord will inherit life in gladness.

PSALM 15

1 A Psalm of Solomon. With a Song. When I was in distress, I called on the Name of the Lord, || I hoped for the help of the God of Jacob and was saved; **2** For the hope and refuge of the poor are You, O God. **3** For who, O God, is strong except to give thanks to You in truth? **4** And wherein is a man powerful except in giving thanks to Your Name **5** A new psalm with song in gladness of heart, || The fruit of the lips with the well-tuned instrument of the tongue, || The first-fruits of the lips from a pious and righteous heart— **6** He that offers these things will never be shaken by evil; The flame of fire and the wrath against the unrighteous will not touch him **7** When it goes forth from the face of the Lord against sinners, || To destroy all the substance of sinners, **8** For the mark of God is on the righteous that they may be saved. Famine, and sword, and pestilence [will be] far from the righteous, **9** For they will flee away from the pious as men pursued in war; But they will pursue sinners and overtake [them], || And they that do lawlessness will not escape the judgment of God; As by enemies experienced [in war], they will be overtaken, 10 For the mark of destruction is on their forehead. 11 And the inheritance of sinners is destruction and darkness, || And their iniquities will pursue them to Sheol beneath. 12 Their inheritance will not be found of their children, 13 For sins will lay waste the houses of sinners. And sinners will perish forever in the day of the Lord's judgment 14 When God visits the earth with His judgment. 15 But they that fear the Lord will find mercy therein, || And will live by the compassion of their God; But sinners will perish forever.

PSALM 16

1 A Hymn of Solomon. For Help to the Pious. When my soul slumbered, [being far] from the Lord, || I had all but slipped down to the pit || When [I was] far from God; 2 My soul had been well nearly poured out to death—Near to the gates of Sheol with the sinner 3 When my soul departed from the Lord God of Israel—Had the Lord not helped me with His everlasting mercy. 4 He pricked me as a horse is pricked, that I might serve Him; My Savior and helper at all times saved me. 5 I will give thanks to You, O God, for You have helped me to [my] salvation, || And have not counted me with sinners to [my] destruction. 6 Do not remove Your mercy from me, O God, || Nor Your memorial from my heart until I die. 7 Rule me, O God, [keeping me back] from wicked sin, || And from every wicked woman that causes the simple to stumble. 8 And do not let the beauty of a lawless woman deceive me, || Nor anyone that is subject to unprofitable sin. 9 Establish the works of my hands before You, || And preserve my goings in the remembrance of You. 10 Protect my tongue and my lips with words of truth; Put anger and unreasoning wrath far from me. 11 Remove murmuring and impatience in affliction far from me || When, if I sin, You discipline me that I may return [to You]. 12 But support my soul with goodwill and cheerfulness; When You strengthen my soul, what is given [to me] will be sufficient for me. 13 For if You do not give strength, || Who can endure discipline with poverty? 14 When a man is rebuked by means of his corruption, || Your testing [of him] is in his flesh and in the affliction of poverty. 15 If the righteous endures in all these [trials], he will receive mercy from the Lord.

PSALM 17

1 A Psalm of Solomon. With Song. Of the King. O Lord, You are our King forever and ever, || For our soul glories in You, O God. 2 How long are the days of man's life on the earth? As are his days, so is the hope [set] on him. 3 But we hope in God, our deliverer; For the might of our God is forever with mercy, 4 And the kingdom of our God is forever over the nations in judgment. 5 You, O Lord, chose David [to be] king over Israel, || And swore to him touching his seed that never should his kingdom fail before You. 6 But, for our sins, sinners rose up against us; They assailed us and thrust us out; What You had not promised to them, they took away [from us] with violence. 7 They did not glorify Your honorable Name at all; They set a [worldly] monarchy in place of [that which was] their excellency; 8 They laid waste the throne of David in tumultuous arrogance. But You, O God, cast them down and removed their seed from the earth, 9 In that there rose up against them a man that was alien to our race. 10 According to their sins You repaid them, O God, || So that it befell them according to their deeds. 11 God showed them no pity; He sought out their seed and does not let one of them go free. 12 Faithful is the Lord in all His judgments || Which He does on the earth. 13 The lawless one laid waste our land so that none inhabited it, || They destroyed young and old and their children together. 14 In the heat of His anger He sent them away, even to the west, || And [He exposed] the rulers of the land unsparingly to derision. 15 Being an alien the enemy acted proudly, || And his heart was alien from our God. 16 And all things, [whatever he did in] Jerusalem, || As also the nations [in the cities to their gods]. 17 And the children of the covenant in the midst of the mingled peoples [surpassed them in evil]. There was not among them one that worked in the midst of Jerusalem mercy and truth. 18 They that loved the synagogues of the pious fled from them, || As sparrows that fly from their nest. 19 They wandered in deserts that their lives might be saved from harm, || And precious in the eyes of them that lived abroad was any that

escaped alive from them. 20 They were scattered over the whole earth by lawless [men]. 21 For the heavens withheld the rain from dropping on the earth, || Springs were stopped perennially out of the deeps [that ran down] from lofty mountains; For there was none among them that worked righteousness and justice; From the chief of them to the least [of them]—all were sinful; 22 The king was a transgressor, and the judge disobedient, and the people sinful. 23 Behold, O Lord, and raise up to them their king, the Son of David, || At the time in which You see, O God, that He may reign over Your servant Israel; 24 And gird Him with strength, that He may shatter unrighteous rulers, 25 And that He may purge Jerusalem from nations that trample [her] down to destruction. 26 Wisely, righteously, He will thrust out sinners from [the] inheritance, || [And] will destroy the pride of the sinner as a potter's vessel. With a rod of iron, He will break in pieces all their substance; 21 He will destroy the godless nations with the word of His mouth; At His rebuke nations will flee before Him, || And He will reprove sinners for the thoughts of their heart. 28 And He will gather together a holy people, whom He will lead in righteousness, || And He will judge the tribes of the people that has been sanctified by the Lord His God. 29 And He will not permit unrighteousness to lodge any more in their midst, || Nor will there dwell with them any man that knows wickedness, 30 For He will know them, that they are all sons of their God. And He shall divide them according to their tribes on the land, 31 And neither sojourner nor alien will sojourn with them any more. He will judge peoples and nations in the wisdom of His righteousness. Selah. 32 And He will have the heathen nations to serve Him under His yoke; And He will glorify the Lord in a place to be seen of all the earth; 33 And He will purge Jerusalem, making it holy as of old: 34 So that nations will come from the ends of the earth to see His glory, || Bringing as gifts her sons who had fainted, 35 And to see the glory of the Lord, with which God has glorified her. And He [will be] a righteous King, taught of God, over them, 36 And there will be no unrighteousness in His days in their midst, || For all will be holy and their King the anointed of the Lord. 37 For He will not put His trust in horse, and rider, and bow, || Nor will He multiply for Himself gold and silver for war, || Nor will He gather confidence from a multitude for the day of battle. 38 The Lord Himself is His King, the hope of him that is mighty through [his] hope in God. All nations [will be] in fear before Him, 39 For He will strike the earth with the word of His mouth forever. 40 He will bless the people of the Lord with wisdom and gladness, 41 And He Himself [will be] pure from sin, so that He may rule a great people. He will rebuke rulers and remove sinners by the might of His word; 42 And [relying] on His God, throughout His days He will not stumble; For God will make Him mighty by means of [His] Holy Spirit, || And wise by means of the spirit of understanding, with strength and righteousness. 43 And the blessing of the Lord [will be] with Him; He will be strong and not stumble; 44 His hope [will be] in the Lord: who then can prevail against Him? [He will be] mighty in His works, and strong in the fear of God; 45 [He will be] shepherding the flock of the Lord faithfully and righteously, || And will permit none among them to stumble in their pasture. 46 He will lead them all correctly, || And there will be no pride among them that any among them should be oppressed. 47 This [will be] the majesty of the King of Israel whom God knows; He will raise Him up over the house of Israel to correct him. 48 His words [will be] more refined than costly gold, the choicest; In the assemblies He will judge the peoples, the tribes of the sanctified. 49 His words [will be] like the words of the holy ones in the midst of sanctified peoples. 50 Blessed are they that will be in those days, || In that they will see the good fortune of Israel which God will bring to pass in the gathering together of the tribes. 51 May the Lord hasten His mercy on Israel! May He deliver us from the uncleanness of unholy enemies! The Lord Himself is our King forever and ever.

PSALM 18

1 A Psalm of Solomon. Again, of the Anointed of the Lord. Lord, your mercy is over the works of Your hands forever; Your goodness is over Israel with a rich gift. 2 Your eyes look on them, so that none of them suffers want; 3 Your ears listen to the hopeful prayer of the poor. Your judgments [are executed] on the whole earth in mercy; 4 And Your love [is] toward the seed of Abraham, the sons of Israel. Your discipline is on us as [on] a firstborn, only-begotten son, 5 To turn back the obedient

soul from folly [that is worked] in ignorance. **6** May God cleanse Israel against the day of mercy and blessing, || Against the day of choice when He brings back His anointed. **7** Blessed will they be that will be in those days, || In that they will see the goodness of the Lord which He will perform for the generation that is to come, **8** Under the rod of disciplining of the Lord's anointed in the fear of his God, || In the spirit of wisdom and righteousness and strength; **9** That he may direct [every} man in the works of righteousness by the fear of God, || That he may establish them all before the Lord— **10** A good generation [living] in the fear of God in the days of mercy. Selah. **11** Great is our God and glorious, dwelling in the highest, **12** Who has established the lights [of Heaven] in [their] courses for determining seasons from year to year, || And they have not turned aside from the way which He appointed them; **13** In the fear of God [they pursue] their path every day, || From the day God created them and forevermore. **14** And they have not erred since the day He created them. Since the generations of old they have not withdrawn from their path, || Unless God commanded them [to do so] by the command of His servants.

the world return to its nature of former times, and the age revert to primeval silence? And will the multitude of souls be taken away, and the nature of man not again be named? And where is all that which You said regarding us?"

CHAPTER 4

1 And the Lord said to me: "This city will be delivered up for a time, || And the people will be disciplined during a time, || And the world will not be given over to oblivion." **[[2** "Do you think that this is that city of which I said, On the palms of My hands I have graven you? **3** This building now built in your midst is not that which is revealed with Me, that which [was] prepared beforehand here from the time when I took counsel to make Paradise, and showed Adam before he sinned, but when he transgressed the commandment, it was removed from him, as also Paradise. **4** And after these things I showed it to My servant Abraham by night among the portions of the victims. **5** And again I also showed it to Moses on Mount Sinai when I showed to the likeness of the Dwelling Place and all its vessels. **6** And now, behold, it is preserved with Me, as Paradise. **7** Go, therefore, and do as I command you."**]]**

2 BARUCH

2 Baruch is a Jewish text, likely pseudepigraphical, thought to have been written in the 1st or 2nd century AD. It is also known as the Syriac Apocalypse of Baruch (used to distinguish it from the Greek Apocalypse of Baruch—3 Baruch). The Apocalypse proper occupies the first 77 chapters of the book. Chapters 78–87 are usually referred to as the "Letter of Baruch to the Nine and a Half Tribes."

CHAPTER 1

1 And it came to pass in the twenty-fifth year of Jehoiachin, king of Judah, that the word of the Lord came to Baruch, the son of Neriah, and said to him: **2** "Have you seen all that this people are doing to Me, that the evils which these two tribes which remained have done are greater than [those of] the ten tribes which were carried away captive? **3** For the former tribes were forced by their kings to commit sin, but these two of themselves have been forcing and compelling their kings to commit sin. **4** For this reason, behold, I bring calamity on this city and on its inhabitants, and it will be removed from before Me for a time, and I will scatter this people among the nations that they may do good to the nations. And My people will be disciplined, and the time will come when they will seek for the prosperity of their times."

CHAPTER 2

1 "For I have said these things to you that you may bid Jeremiah, and all those that are like you, to retire from this city. **2** For your works are to this city as a firm pillar, || And your prayers as a strong wall."

CHAPTER 3

1 And I said, "O Lord, my Lord, have I come into the world for this purpose that I might see the calamities of my mother? No, my Lord. **2** If I have found grace in Your sight, first take my spirit that I may go to my fathers and not behold the destruction of my mother. For two things vehemently constrain me: for I cannot resist You, and my soul, moreover, cannot behold the calamities of my mother. **4** But one thing I will say in Your presence, O Lord. **5** What, therefore, will there be after these things? for if You destroy Your city, and deliver up Your land to those that hate us, how will the name of Israel be remembered again? **6** Or how will one speak of Your praises? or to whom will that which is in Your law be explained? Or will

CHAPTER 5

1 And I answered and said, "So then I am destined to grieve for Zion, || For Your enemies will come to this place and pollute Your sanctuary, || And lead Your inheritance into captivity, || And make themselves masters of those whom You have loved, || And they will depart again to the place of their idols, || And will boast before them: And what will You do for Your great Name?" **2** And the Lord said to me: "My Name and My glory are to all eternity; And My judgment will maintain its right in its own time. **3** And you will see with your eyes || That the enemy will not overthrow Zion, || Nor will they burn Jerusalem, || But be the ministers of the Judge for the time. **4** But you go and do whatever I have said to you." **5** And I went and took Jeremiah, and Adu, and Seriah, and Jabish, and Gedaliah, and all the honorable men of the people, and I led them to the Valley of Kidron, and I narrated to them all that had been said to me. **6** And they lifted up their voice, and they all wept. **7** And we sat there and fasted until the evening.

CHAPTER 6

1 And it came to pass on the next day that, behold, the army of the Chaldees surrounded the city, and at the time of the evening, I, Baruch, left the people, and I went forth and stood by the oak. **2** And I was grieving over Zion and lamenting over the captivity which had come on the people. **3** And behold, suddenly a strong spirit raised me, and bore me aloft over the wall of Jerusalem. **4** And I beheld, and behold, four messengers standing at the four corners of the city, each of them holding a torch of fire in his hands. **5** And another messenger began to descend from Heaven, and said to them, "Hold your lamps, and do not light them until I tell you. **6** For I am first sent to speak a word to the earth, and to place in it what the Lord the Most High has commanded me." **7** And I saw him descend into the Holy of Holies, and take from there the veil, and holy Ark, and the propitiatory covering, and the two tablets, and the holy raiment of the priests, and the altar of incense, and the forty-eight precious stones with which the priest was adorned, and all the holy vessels of the Dwelling Place. **8** And he spoke to the earth with a loud voice: "Earth, earth, earth! Hear the word of the mighty God, || And receive what I commit to you, || And guard them until the last times, || So that, when you are ordered, you may restore them, || So that strangers may not get possession of them. **9** For the time comes when Jerusalem will also be delivered for a time, || Until it is said that it is again restored forever." **10** And the earth opened its mouth and swallowed them up.

CHAPTER 7

1 And after these things I heard that messenger saying to those messengers who held the lamps: "Destroy, therefore, and overthrow its wall to its foundations, lest the enemy should boast and say, || We have overthrown the wall of Zion, || And we have burned the place of the mighty God." **2** And they have seized the place where I had been standing before.

CHAPTER 8

1 Now the messengers did as he had commanded them, and when they had broken up the corners of the walls, a voice was heard from the interior of the temple, after the wall had fallen, saying, **2** "Enter, you enemies; || And come, you adversaries; For He who kept the house has forsaken [it]." **3** And I, Baruch, departed. **4** And it came to pass after these things that the army of the Chaldees entered and seized the house, and all that was around it. And they led the people away captive and slew some of them, and bound Zedekiah the king, and sent him to the king of Babylon.

CHAPTER 9

1 And I, Baruch, came, and Jeremiah, whose heart was found pure from sins, who had not been captured in the seizure of the city. **2** And we tore our garments, we wept, and mourned, and fasted seven days.

CHAPTER 10

1 And it came to pass after seven days, that the word of God carne to me, and said to me: **2** "Tell Jeremiah to go and support the captivity of the people to Babylon. **3** But remain here amid the desolation of Zion, and I will show to you after these days what will befall at the end of days." **4** And I spoke to Jeremiah as the Lord commanded me. **5** And he, indeed, departed with the people, but I, Baruch, returned and sat before the gates of the temple, and I lamented with the following lamentation over Zion and said, **6** "Blessed is he who was not born, || Or he, who having been born, has died. **7** But as for us who live, woe to us, || Because we see the afflictions of Zion, || And what has befallen Jerusalem. **8** I will call the Sirens from the sea, || And you Lilin, come from the desert, || And you Shedim and dragons from the forests: Awake and gird up your loins to mourning, || And take up the dirges with me, || And make lamentation with me. **9** You farmers, do not sow again; And, O earth, why do you give your harvest fruits? Keep within you the sweets of your sustenance. **10** And you, vine, why further do you give your wine? For an offering will not be made again from there in Zion, || Nor will first-fruits be offered again. **11** And you, O heavens, withhold your dew, || And do not open the treasuries of rain; **12** And you, O sun, withhold the light of your rays; And you, O moon, extinguish the multitude of your light. For why should light rise again || Where the light of Zion is darkened? **13** And you—you bridegrooms—do not enter in, || And do not let the brides adorn themselves with garlands; And, you women, do not pray that you may bear. **14** For the barren will above all rejoice, || And those who have no sons will be glad, || And those who have sons will have anguish. **15** For why should they bear in pain, || Only to bury in grief? **16** Or why, again, should mankind have sons? Or why should the seed of their kind be named again, || Where this mother is desolate, || And her sons are led into captivity? **17** From this time forward, do not speak of beauty, || And do not discourse of gracefulness. **18** Moreover, you priests, take the keys of the sanctuary, || And cast them into the height of Heaven, || And give them to the Lord and say, || Guard Your house Yourself, || For behold, we are found false stewards. **19** And you—you virgins who weave fine linen || And silk with gold of Ophir—Take all [these] things with haste || And cast [them] into the fire, || That it may bear them to Him who made them, || And the flame send them to Him who created them, || Lest the enemy get possession of them."

CHAPTER 11

1 Moreover, I, Baruch, say this against you, Babylon: "If

you had prospered, || And Zion had dwelt in her glory, || Yet the grief to us had been great || That you should be equal to Zion. 2 But now, behold, the grief is infinite, || And the lamentation measureless, || For behold, you are prospered || And Zion desolate. 3 Who will be judge regarding these things? Or to whom will we complain regarding that which has befallen us? O Lord, how have You borne [it]? 4 Our fathers went to rest without grief, || And behold, the righteous sleep in the earth in tranquility; 5 For they did not know this anguish, || Nor yet had they heard of that which had befallen us. 6 Would that you had ears, O earth, || And that you had a heart, O dust, || That you might go and announce in Sheol, || And say to the dead: 7 Blessed are you more than we who live."

CHAPTER 12

1 "But I will say this as I think, || And speak against you— the land that is prospering. **2** The noonday does not always burn, || Nor do the rays of the sun constantly give light. **3** And do not expect to rejoice, || Nor condemn greatly. **4** For assuredly in its season the [divine] wrath will be awakened against you, || Which is now restrained by long-suffering as it were by a rein." **5** And when I had said these things, I fasted seven days.

CHAPTER 13

1 And it came to pass after these things that I, Baruch, was standing on Mount Zion, and behold, a voice came forth from the height and said to me: **2** "Stand on your feet, Baruch, and hear the word of the mighty God. **3** Because you have been astonished at what has befallen Zion, you will therefore be assuredly preserved to the consummation of the times, that you may be for a testimony. **4** So that, if ever those prosperous cities say: **5** Why has the mighty God brought this retribution on us? Say to them, You and those like you will have seen this evil and retribution which is coming on you and on your people in its [appointed] time that the nations may be thoroughly smitten. **6** And then they will be in anguish. **7** And if they say at that time: **8** For how long? you will say to them: You who have drunk the strained wine, || Drink also of its dregs—The judgment of the Lofty One || Who has no respect of persons; **9** On this account He formerly had no mercy on His own sons, || But afflicted them as His enemies, because they sinned, **10** Then, therefore, they were disciplined || That they might be sanctified. **11** But now, you peoples and nations, you are guilty || Because you have always trodden down the earth, || And used the creation unrighteously. **12** For I have always benefited you. And you have always been ungrateful for the beneficence."

CHAPTER 14

1 And I answered and said, "Behold, You have shown me the methods of the times, and that which will be. And You have said to me that the retribution which was spoken of by You will be endured by the nations. **2** And now I know that those who have sinned are many, and they have lived . . . and departed from the world, but that few nations will be left in those times to whom . . . the words [which] You said. **3** And what advantage [is there] in this or what worse than [these?] **4** But I will again speak in Your presence: **5** What have they profited who had knowledge before You and have not walked in vanity as the rest of the nations, and have not said to the dead, give us life, but always feared You, and have not left Your ways? **6** And behold, they have been carried off, nor on their account have You had mercy on Zion. **7** And if others did evil, it was due to Zion that on account of the works of those who worked good works she should be forgiven and should not be overwhelmed on account of the works of those who worked unrighteousness. **8** But who, O Lord, my Lord, will comprehend Your judgment, || Or who will search out the profoundness of Your way? Or who will think out the weight of Your path? **9** Or who will be able to think out Your incomprehensible counsel? Or who of those that are born has ever found || The beginning or end of

Your wisdom? **10** For we have all been made like a breath. **11** For as the breath ascends involuntarily, and again dies, so it is with the nature of men, who do not depart according to their own will, and do not know what will befall them in the end. **12** For the righteous justly hope for the end, and without fear depart from this habitation, because they have with You a store of works preserved in treasuries. **13** On this account also, these without fear leave this world, and trusting with joy they hope to receive the world which You have promised them. **14** But as for us—woe to us, who are also now shamefully entreated, and at that time look forward [only] to calamities. **15** But You know accurately what You have done by means of Your servants; for we are not able to understand that which is good as You are, our Creator. **16** But again I will speak in Your presence, O Lord, my Lord. **17** When of old there was no world with its inhabitants, You devised and spoke with a word, and immediately the works of creation stood before You. **18** And You said that You would make for Your world man as the administrator of Your works, that it might be known that he was by no means made on account of the world, but the world on account of him. **19** And now I see that as for the world which was made on account of us, behold, it abides; but we, on account of whom it was made, depart."

CHAPTER 15

1 And the Lord answered and said to me: "You are rightly astonished regarding the departure of man, but you have not judged well regarding the calamities which befall those who sin. **2** And as regards what you have said, that the righteous are carried off and the impious are prospered, **3** and as regards what you have said, Man does not know Your judgment—on this account hear, and I will speak to you, and listen, and I will cause you to hear My words. **5** Man would not rightly have understood My judgment, unless he had accepted the law, and I had instructed him in understanding. **6** But now, because he transgressed willfully, yes, just on this ground that he knows, he will be tormented. **7** And as regards what you said touching the righteous, that on account of them this world has come, so also again, that which is to come will come on their account. **8** For this world is to them a strife and a labor with much trouble; and that accordingly which is to come—a crown with great glory."

CHAPTER 16

1 And I answered and said, **2** "Lord, my Lord, behold, the years of this time are few and evil, and who is able in his short time to acquire that which is measureless?"

CHAPTER 17

1 And the Lord answered and said to me: "With the Highest account is not taken of time nor of a few years. **2** For what did it profit Adam that he lived nine hundred and thirty years and transgressed that which he was commanded? Therefore, the multitude of time that he lived did not profit him, but brought death and cut off the years of those who were born from him, wherein Moses suffered loss in that he lived only one hundred and twenty years, and inasmuch he was subject to Him who formed him, brought the law to the seed of Jacob, and lighted a lamp for the nation of Israel?"

CHAPTER 18

1 And I answered and said, "He that lighted has taken from the light, and there are but few that have imitated him. **2** But those many whom he has lighted have taken from the darkness of Adam and have not rejoiced in the light of the lamp."

CHAPTER 19

1 And He answered and said to me: "For what reason at that time he appointed for them a covenant and said, Behold,

I have placed before you life and death, || And he called the heavens and earth to witness against them. **2** For he knew that his time was but short, || But that the heavens and earth always endure. **3** But after his death they sinned and transgressed, || Though they knew that they had the law reproving [them], || And the light in which nothing could err, || Also the spheres which testify, and Me. **4** Now regarding everything that is, it is I that judge, but do not take counsel in your soul regarding these things, nor afflict yourself because of those which have been. **5** For now it is the consummation of time that should be considered, whether of business, or of prosperity, or of shame, and not the beginning thereof. **6** Because if a man is prospered in his beginnings and shamefully entreated in his old age, he forgets all the prosperity that he had. **7** And again, if a man is shamefully entreated in his beginnings, and at his end is prospered, he does not remember again his evil entrapment. **8** And again listen: though each one was prospered all that time—all the time from the day on which death was decreed against those who transgress—and in his end was destroyed, everything would have been in vain."

CHAPTER 20

1 "Therefore, behold! the days come, || And the times will hasten more than the former, || And the seasons will speed by more than those that are past, || And the years will pass more quickly than the present [years]. **2** Therefore I have now taken Zion away, || That I may the more speedily visit the world in its season. **3** Now therefore, hold fast in your heart everything that I command you, || And seal it in the recesses of your mind. **4** And then I will show you the judgment of My might, || And My ways which are unsearchable. **5** Go therefore and sanctify yourself seven days, and eat no bread, nor drink water, nor speak to anyone. **6** And afterward come to that place and I will reveal Myself to you, and speak true things with you, and I will give you commandment regarding the method of the times; for they are coming and do not tarry."

CHAPTER 21

1 And I went there and sat in the Valley of Kidron in a cave of the earth, and I sanctified my soul there, and I ate no bread, yet I was not hungry, and I drank no water, yet I did not thirst, and I was there until the seventh day, as He had commanded me. **2** And afterward I came to that place where He had spoken with me. **3** And it came to pass at sunset that my soul took much thought, and I began to speak in the presence of the Mighty One, and said, **4** "O You that have made the earth, hear me, that have fixed the expanse by the word, and have made firm the height of the Heaven by the Spirit, that have called from the beginning of the world that which did not yet exist, and they obey You. **5** You that have commanded the air by Your nod and have seen those things which are to be as those things which You are doing. **6** You that rule with great thought the hosts that stand before You; also the countless holy beings, which You made from the beginning, of flame and fire, which stand around Your throne, You rule with indignation. **7** To You only does this belong that You should immediately do whatever You wish. **8** [You] who cause the drops of rain to rain by number on the earth, and alone knows the consummation of the times before they come, have respect to my prayer. **9** For You alone are able to sustain all who are, and those who have passed away, and those who are to be, those who sin, and those who are righteous (as living and being past finding out). **10** For You alone live [as] immortal and past finding out, and know the number of mankind. **11** And if in time many have sinned, yet others—not a few—have been righteous. **12** You know where You preserve the end of those who have sinned, or the consummation of those who have been righteous. **13** For if there were this life only, which belongs to all men, nothing could be more bitter than this. **14** For of what profit is strength that turns to sickness, || Or fullness of food that turns to famine, || Or beauty that turns to ugliness. **15** For the nature of man is always changeable. **16** For what we were formerly now we no longer are and what we now are we will not afterward remain. **16** For if a consummation had not been prepared for all, in vain would have been their beginning. But regarding everything that comes from You, You inform me, and regarding everything about which I ask You, You enlighten me. **19** How long will that which is corruptible remain, and how long will the time of mortals be prospered, and until what time will those who transgress in the world be polluted with much wickedness? **20** Therefore command in mercy and accomplish all that You said You would bring, that Your might may be made known to those who think that Your long-suffering is weakness. **21** And show to those who do not know, that everything that has befallen us and our city until now has been according to the long-suffering of Your power, because on account of Your Name You have called us a beloved people. **22** Therefore, henceforth, bring mortality to an end. **23** And reprove the messenger of death accordingly, and let Your glory appear, and let the might of Your beauty be known, and let Sheol be sealed so that from this time forward it may not receive the dead, and let the treasuries of souls restore those which are enclosed in them. **24** For there have been many years like those that are desolate from the days of Abraham, and Isaac, and Jacob, and of all those who are like them, who sleep in the earth, on whose account You said that You had created the world. **25** And now quickly show Your glory, and do not defer what has been promised by You." **26** And [when] I had completed the words of this prayer I was greatly weakened.

CHAPTER 22

1 And it came to pass after these things that, behold, the heavens were opened, and I saw, and power was given to me, and a voice was heard from on high, and it said to me: **2** "Baruch, Baruch, why are you troubled? **3** He who travels by a road but does not complete it, or who departs by sea but does not arrive at the port, can he be comforted? **4** Or he who promises to give a present to another, but does not fulfill it, is it not robbery? **5** Or he who sows the earth, but does not reap its fruit in its season, does he not lose everything? **6** Or he who plants a plant unless it grows until the time suitable to it, does he who planted it expect to receive fruit from it? **7** Or a woman who has conceived, if she brings forth untimely, does she not assuredly slay her infant? **8** Or he who builds a house, if he does not roof it and complete it, can it be called a house? Tell Me that first."

CHAPTER 23

1 And I answered and said, "Not so, O Lord, my Lord." **2** And He answered and said to me, "Why are you therefore troubled about that which you do not know, and why are you ill at ease about things in which you are ignorant? **3** For as you have not forgotten the people who now are and those who have passed away, so I remember those who are appointed to come. **4** Because when Adam sinned and death was decreed against those who should be born, then the multitude of those who should be born was numbered, and for that number a place was prepared where the living might dwell and the dead might be guarded. Therefore, before the number previously mentioned is fulfilled, the creature will not live again [[for My Spirit is the creator of life]], and Sheol will receive the dead. **6** And again it is given to you to hear what things are to come after these times. **7** For My redemption has truly drawn near and is not far distant as before."

CHAPTER 24

1 "For behold! the days come and the scrolls will be opened in which are written the sins of all those who have sinned, and again also the treasuries in which the righteousness of all those who have been righteous in creation is gathered. 2 For it will come to pass at that time that you will see—and the many that are with you—the long-suffering of the Highest, which has been throughout all generations, who has been long-suffering toward all who are born, [both] those who sin and [those who] are righteous." 3 And I answered and said, "But, behold! O Lord, no one knows the number of those things which have passed nor yet of those things which are to come. 4 For I indeed know that which has befallen us, but I do not know what will happen to our enemies, and when You will visit Your works."

CHAPTER 25

1 And He answered and said to me: "You, too, will be preserved until that time until that sign which the Highest will work for the inhabitants of the earth in the end of days. **2** This will therefore be the sign: **3** when a stupor will seize the inhabitants of the earth, and they will fall into many tribulations, and again when they will fall into great torments. And it will come to pass when they say in their thoughts by reason of their much tribulation: The Mighty One no longer remembers the earth—yes, it will come to pass when they abandon hope, that the time will then awake."

CHAPTER 26

1 And I answered and said, "Will that tribulation which is to come continue [for] a long time, and will that necessarily comprise many years?"

CHAPTER 27

1 And He answered and said to me: "That time is divided into twelve parts, and each one of them is reserved for that which is appointed for it. **2** In the first part there will be the beginning of commotions. **3** And in the second part [there will be] slayings of the great ones. **4** And in the third part the fall of many by death. **5** And in the fourth part the sending of the sword. **6** And in the fifth part famine and the withholding of rain. **7** And in the sixth part earthquakes and terrors. **8** [And in the seventh part] . . . **9** And in the eighth part a multitude of specters and attacks of the Shedim. **10** And in the ninth part the fall of fire. **11** And in the tenth part plunder and much oppression. **12** And in the eleventh part wickedness and unchastity. **13** And in the twelfth part confusion from the mingling together of all those things previously mentioned. **14** For these parts of that time are reserved and will be mingled with one another and minister to one another. **15** For some will leave out some of their own, and receive [in its stead] from others, and some complete their own and that of others, so that those may not understand who are on the earth in those days that this is the consummation of the times."

CHAPTER 28

1 "Nevertheless, whoever understands will then be wise. **2** For the measure and reckoning of that time are two parts a week of seven weeks." **3** And I answered and said, "It is good for a man to come and behold, but it is better that he should not come lest he fall. **4** [[But I will say this also: **5** Will He who is incorruptible despise those things which are corruptible, and whatever befalls in the case of those things which are corruptible, so that He might look only to those things which are not corruptible?]] **6** But if, O Lord, those things will assuredly come to pass which You have foretold to me, so also show this to me if indeed I have found grace in Your sight. **7** Is it in one place or in one of the parts of the earth that those things have come to pass, or will the whole earth experience [them]?"

CHAPTER 29

1 And He answered and said to me: "Whatever will then befall [will befall] the whole earth; therefore, all who live will experience [them]. **2** For at that time I will only protect those who are found in those same days in this land. **3** And it will come to pass when all is accomplished that was to come to pass in those parts, that the Messiah will then begin to be revealed. **4** And Behemoth will be revealed from his place and Leviathan will ascend from the sea—those two great monsters which I created on the fifth day of creation, and will have kept until that time; and then they will be for food for all that are left. **5** The earth will also yield its fruit ten-thousandfold, and on each vine, there will be one thousand branches, and each branch will produce one thousand clusters, and each cluster produce one thousand grapes, and each grape produce a cor of wine. **6** And those who have hungered will rejoice: moreover also, they will behold marvels every day. **7** For winds will go forth from before Me to bring every morning the fragrance of aromatic fruits, and at the close of the day clouds distilling the dew of health. **8** And it will come to pass at that same time that the treasury of manna will again descend from on high, and they will eat of it in those years, because these are they who have come to the consummation of time."

CHAPTER 30

1 "And it will come to pass after these things, when the time of the advent of the Messiah is fulfilled, that He will return in glory. **2** Then all who have fallen asleep in hope of Him will rise again. And it will come to pass at that time that the treasuries will be opened in which is preserved the number of the souls of the righteous, and they will come forth, and a multitude of souls will be seen together in one assemblage of one thought, and the first will rejoice and the last will not be grieved. **3** For they know that the time has come of which it is said that it is the consummation of the times. **4** But the souls of the wicked, when they behold all these things, will then waste away more. **5** For they will know that their torment has come, and their perdition has arrived."

CHAPTER 31

1 And it came to pass after these things that I went to the people and said to them: "Assemble to me all your elders and I will speak words to them." **2** And they all assembled in the Valley of the Kidron. **3** And I answered and said to them: "Hear, O Israel, and I will speak to you, || And give ear, O seed of Jacob, and I will instruct you. **4** Do not forget Zion, || But hold in remembrance the anguish of Jerusalem. **5** For behold, the days come || When everything that is will become the prey of corruption || And be as though it had not been."

CHAPTER 32

1 "But as for you, if you prepare your hearts so as to sow in them the fruits of the law, it will protect you in that time in which the Mighty One is to shake the whole creation. **2** [[Because after a short time the building of Zion will be shaken in order that it may be built again. But that building will not remain, but will again after a time be rooted out, and will remain desolate until the time. **4** And afterward it must be renewed in glory and perfected forevermore.]] **5** Therefore we should not be distressed so much over the calamity which has now come as over that which is still to be. **6** For there will be a greater trial than these two tribulations when the Mighty One will renew His creation. **7** And now do not draw near to me for a few days, nor seek me until I come to you." **8** And it came to pass when I had spoken all these words to them, that I, Baruch, went my way, and when the people saw me setting out, they lifted up their voice and lamented and said, **9** "To where are you departing from us, Baruch, and are you forsaking us as a father who forsakes his orphan children, and departs from them?"

CHAPTER 33

1 "Are these the commands which your companion, Jeremiah the prophet, commanded you, and said to you: Look to this people until I go and make ready the rest of the brothers in Babylon against whom has gone forth the sentence that they should be led into captivity? And now if you also forsake us, it was good for us all to die before you, then that you should withdraw from us."

CHAPTER 34

1 And I answered and said to the people: "Far be it from me to forsake you or to withdraw from you, **2** but I will only go to the Holy of Holies to inquire of the Mighty One concerning you and concerning Zion, If In some respect I should receive more illumination: and after these things I will return to you."

CHAPTER 35

1 And I, Baruch, went to the holy place, and sat down on the ruins and wept, and said, **2** "O that my eyes were springs, || And my eyelids a fount of tears. **3** For how will I lament for Zion, || And how will I mourn for Jerusalem? **4** Because in that place where I am now prostrate, || Of old the high priest offered holy sacrifices, || And placed an incense of fragrant odors thereon. **5** But now our glorying has been made into dust, || And the desire of our soul into sand."

CHAPTER 36

1 And when I had said these things, I fell asleep there, and I saw a vision in the night. **2** And behold, a forest of trees planted on the plain, and lofty and rugged Rocky Mountains surrounded it, and that forest occupied much space. **3** And behold, over against it arose a vine, and from under it there went forth a fountain peacefully. **4** Now that fountain came to the forest and was [stirred] into great waves, and those waves submerged that forest, and suddenly they rooted out the greater part of that forest and overthrew all the mountains which were around it. **5** And the height of the forest began to be made low, and the top of the mountains was made low, and that fountain prevailed greatly, so that it left nothing of that great forest save one cedar only. **6** Also, when it had cast it down and had destroyed and rooted out the greater part of that forest, so that nothing was left of it, nor could its place be recognized, then that vine began to come with the fountain in peace and great tranquility, and it came to a place which was not far from that cedar, and they brought the cedar which had been cast down to it. **7** And I beheld, and behold, that vine opened its mouth and spoke and said to that cedar: "Are you not that cedar which was left of the forest of wickedness, and by whose means wickedness persisted, and was worked all those years, and never for good? **8** And you kept conquering that which was not yours, and to that which was yours you never showed compassion, and you kept extending your power over those who were far from you, and those who drew near you, you held fast in the toils of your wickedness, and you always uplifted yourself as one that could not be rooted out! **9** But now your time has sped, and your hour has come. **10** Do you also therefore depart, O cedar, after the forest, which departed before you, and become dust with it, and let your ashes be mingled together? **11** And now recline in anguish and rest in torment until your last time comes, in which you will come again, and be tormented still more."

CHAPTER 37

1 And after these things I saw that cedar burning, and the vine growing, itself and all around it, the plain full of unfading flowers. **2** And I indeed awoke and arose.

CHAPTER 38

1 And I prayed and said, "O Lord, my Lord, You always enlighten those who are led by understanding. **2** Your law is life, and Your wisdom is right guidance. **3** Therefore make known to me the interpretation of this vision. **4** For You know that my soul has always walked in Your law, and from my [earliest] days I did not depart from Your wisdom."

CHAPTER 39

1 And He answered and said to me: "Baruch, this is the interpretation of the vision which you have seen. **2** As you have seen the great forest, which lofty and rugged mountains surrounded, this is the word. **3** Behold! the days come, and this kingdom will be destroyed which once destroyed Zion, and it will be subjected to that which comes after it. **4** Moreover, that also again after a time will be destroyed, and another, a third, will arise, and that also will have dominion for its time, and will be destroyed. **5** And after these things a fourth kingdom will arise, whose power will be harsh and evil far beyond those which were before it, and it will rule many times as the forests on the plain, and it will hold fast for times, and will exalt itself more than the cedars of Lebanon. **6** And by it the truth will be hidden, and all those who are polluted with iniquity will flee to it, as evil beasts flee and creep into the forest. **7** And it will come to pass when the time of its consummation—that it should fall—has approached, then the principate of My Messiah will be revealed, which is like the fountain and the vine, and when it is revealed, it will root out the multitude of its host. **8** And as touching that which you have seen, the lofty cedar, which was left of that forest, and the fact that the vine spoke those words with it which you heard, this is the word."

CHAPTER 40

1 "The last leader of that time will be left alive, when the multitude of his hosts will be put to the sword, and he will be bound, and they will take him up to Mount Zion, and My Messiah will convict him of all his impieties, and will gather and set before him all the works of his hosts. **2** And afterward he will put him to death, and protect the rest of My people which will be found in the place which I have chosen. **3** And His principate will stand forever, until the world of corruption is at an end, and until the times previously mentioned are fulfilled. **4** This is your vision, and this is its interpretation."

CHAPTER 41

1 And I answered and said, "For whom and for how many will these things be? or who will be worthy to live at that time? **2** For I will speak before You everything that I think, and I will ask of You regarding those things which I meditate. **3** For behold, I see many of Your people who have withdrawn from Your covenant, and cast from themselves the yoke of Your law. **4** But others again I have seen who have forsaken their vanity and fled for refuge beneath Your wings. **5** What therefore will be to them? or how will the last time receive them? **6** Or perhaps the time of these will assuredly be weighed, and as the beam inclines will they be judged accordingly?"

CHAPTER 42

1 And He answered and said to me: "I will also show these things to you. **2** As for what you said—To whom will these things be, and how many [will they be]? To those who have believed there will be the good which was spoken of formerly, and to those who despise there will be the contrary of these things. **3** And as for what you said regarding those who have drawn near and those who have withdrawn this in the word. **4** As for those who were before subject, and afterward withdrew and mingled themselves with the seed of mingled peoples, the time of these was the former, and was accounted as something exalted. **5** And as for those who before did not know but afterward knew life, and mingled [only] with the seed of the people which had separated itself, the time of these [is] the latter, and is accounted as something exalted. **6** And time will succeed to time and season to season, and one will receive from another, and then with a view to the consummation, everything will be compared according to the measure of the times and the hours of the seasons. **7** For corruption will take those that belong to it, and life those that belong to it. **8** And the dust will be called, and there will be said to it: Give back that which is not yours and raise up all that you have kept until its time."

CHAPTER 43

1 "But you, Baruch, direct your heart to that which has been said to you, || And understand those things which have been shown to you; For there are many continuous consolations for

you. **2** For you will depart from this place, || And you will pass from the regions which are now seen by you, || And you will forget whatever is corruptible, || And will not again recall those things which happen among mortals. **3** Therefore go and command your people, and come to this place, and afterward fast seven days, and then I will come to you and speak with you."

CHAPTER 44

1 And I, Baruch, went from there, and came to my people, and I called my firstborn son and [the Gedaliahs] my friends, and seven of the elders of the people, and I said to them: "Behold, I go to my fathers || According to the way of all the earth. **3** But do not withdraw from the way of the law, || But guard and admonish the people which remain, || Lest they withdraw from the commandments of the Mighty One. **4** For you see that He whom we serve is just, || And our Creator is no respecter of persons. **5** And see what has befallen Zion, || And what has happened to Jerusalem. **6** For the judgment of the Mighty One will [thereby] be made known, || And His ways, which, though past finding out, are right. **7** For if you endure and persevere in His fear, || And do not forget His law, || The times will change over you for good, || And you will see the consolation of Zion. **8** Because whatever is now is nothing, || But that which will be is very great. **9** For everything that is corruptible will pass away, || And everything that dies will depart, || And all the present time will be forgotten, || Nor will there be any remembrance of the present time, which is defiled with evils. **10** For that which runs now runs to vanity, || And that which prospers will quickly fall and be humiliated. **11** For that which is to be will be the object of desire, || And for that which comes afterward will we hope; For it is a time that does not pass away, **12** And the hour comes which abides forever. And the new world [comes] which does not turn to corruption those who depart to its blessedness, || And has no mercy on those who depart to torment, || And does not lead to perdition those who live in it. **13** For these are they who will inherit that time which has been spoken of, || And theirs is the inheritance of the promised time. **14** These are they who have acquired for themselves treasures of wisdom, || And with them are found stores of understanding, || And they have not withdrawn from mercy, || And they have preserved the truth of the law. **15** For the world to come will be given to them, || But the dwelling of the rest, who are many, will be in the fire."

CHAPTER 45

1 "Therefore, so far as you are able, instruct the people, for that labor is ours. **2** For if you teach them, you will restore them."

CHAPTER 46

1 And my son and the elders of the people answered and said to me: "Has the Mighty One humiliated us to such a degree || As to take you from us quickly? **2** And we will truly be in darkness, || And there will be no light to the people who are left, **3** For where again will we seek the law, || Or who will distinguish between death and life for us?" **4** And I said to them, "I cannot resist the throne of the Mighty One; Nevertheless, there will not be wanting to Israel a wise man || Nor a son of the law to the race of Jacob. **5** But only prepare your hearts, that you may obey the law, || And be subject to those who in fear are wise and understanding; And prepare your souls that you may not depart from them. **6** For if you do these things, || Good tidings will come to you, [[|| Which I before told you of; Nor will you fall into the torment, of which I testified to you before." **7** (But with regard to the word that I was to have taken, I did not make [it] known to them or to my son.)]]

CHAPTER 47

1 And when I had gone forth and dismissed them, I went there and said to them: "Behold! I go to Hebron; for the Mighty

One has sent me there." **2** And I came to that place where the word had been spoken to me, and I sat there, and fasted seven days.

CHAPTER 48

1 And it came to pass after the seventh day, that I prayed before the Mighty One and said, **2** "O my Lord, You summon the advent of the times, || And they stand before You; You cause the power of the ages to pass away, || And they do not resist You; You arrange the method of the seasons, || And they obey You. **3** You alone know the duration of the generations, || And You do not reveal Your mysteries to many. **4** You make known the multitude of the fire, || And You weigh the lightness of the wind. **5** You explore the limit of the heights, || And You scrutinize the depths of the darkness. **6** You care for the number which pass away that they may be preserved, || And You prepare an abode for those that are to be. **7** You remember the beginning which You have made, || And the destruction that is to be, You do not forget. **8** With nods of fear and indignation You command the flames, || And they change into spirits, || And with a word You give life to that which was not, || And with mighty power You hold that which has not yet come. **9** You instruct created things in Your understanding, || And You make wise the spheres so as to minister in their orders. **10** Innumerable armies stand before You || And minister in their orders quietly at Your nod. **11** Hear Your servant || And give ear to my petition. **12** For in a short time are we born, || And in a short time we return. **13** But with You hours are as an age, || And days as generations. **14** Therefore, do not be angry with man, for he is nothing; **15** And do not take account of our works; For what are we? For behold, by Your gift we come into the world, || And we do not depart of our own will. **16** For we did not say to our parents, Beget us, || Nor did we send to Sheol and say, Receive us. **17** What therefore is our strength that we should bear Your wrath, || Or what are we that we should endure Your judgment? **18** Protect us in Your compassions, || And help us in Your mercy. **19** Behold the little ones that are subject to You, || And save all that draw near to You: And do not destroy the hope of our people, || And do not cut short the times of our aid. **20** For this is the nation which You have chosen, || And these are the people to whom You find no equal. **21** But now I will speak before You, || And I will say as my heart thinks. **22** We trust in You, for behold, Your law is with us, || And we know that we will not fall so long as we keep Your statutes. **23** [[We are blessed for all time at all events in this— That we have not mingled with the nations.]] **24** For we are all one celebrated people, || Who have received one law from One: And the law which is among us will aid us, || And the surpassing wisdom which is in us will help us." **25** And when I had prayed and said these things, I was greatly weakened. **26** And He answered and said to me: "You have prayed simply, O Baruch, || And all your words have been heard. **27** But My judgment exacts its own || And My law exacts its rights. **28** For from your words I will answer you, || And from your prayer I will speak to you. **29** For this is as follows: he that is corrupted is not at all; he has both worked iniquity so far as deceit could do anything, and has not remembered My goodness, nor accepted My long-suffering. **30** Therefore, you will surely be taken up, as I before told you. **31** For that time will arise which brings affliction; for it will come and pass by with quick vehemence, and it will be turbulent, coming in the heat of indignation. **32** And it will come to pass in those days that all the inhabitants of the earth will be moved against one another, because they do not know that My judgment has drawn near. **33** For there will not be found many wise at that time, || And the intelligent will be but a few: Moreover, even those who know will most of all be silent. **34** And there will be many rumors and tidings—not a few, || And the doing of illusions will be manifest, || And promises—not a few—will be recounted, || Some of them [will prove] idle, || And some of them will be confirmed. **35** And honor will be turned into shame, || And strength humiliated into contempt, || And integrity destroyed, || And beauty will become ugliness. **36** And many will say to many at that time: Where has the multitude of intelligence hidden itself, || And to where has the multitude of wisdom removed itself? **37** And while they are meditating on these things, || Then envy will arise in those who had not thought anything of themselves || And passion will seize him that is peaceful, || And many will be stirred up in anger to injure many, || And they will rouse up armies in order to shed blood,

|| And in the end they will perish together with them. **38** And it will come to pass at the same time, || That a change of times will manifestly appeal to every man, || Because in all those times they polluted themselves || And they practiced oppression, || And every man walked in his own works, || And did not remember the Law of the Mighty One. **39** Therefore a fire will consume their thoughts, || And in flame the meditations of their reins will be tried; For the Judge will come and will not tarry. **40** Because each of the inhabitants of the earth knew when he was transgressing. But they did not know My Law by reason of their pride. **41** But many will then assuredly weep, || Yes, over the living more than over the dead." **42** And I answered and said, "O Adam, what have you done to all those who are born from you? And what will be said to the first Eve who listened to the serpent? **43** For all this multitude are going to corruption, || Nor is there any numbering of those whom the fire devours. **44** But again I will speak in Your presence. **45** You, O Lord, my Lord, know what is in Your creature. **46** For You commanded the ancient dust to produce Adam, and You know the number of those who are born from him, and how far they have sinned before You, who have existed and not confessed You as their Creator. **47** And as regards all these their end will convict them, and Your law which they have transgressed will repay them on Your day." **48** [["But now let us dismiss the wicked and inquire about the righteous. **49** And I will recount their blessedness and not be silent in celebrating their glory, which is reserved for them. **50** For assuredly as in a short time in this transitory world in which you live you have endured much labor, so in that world to which there is no end, you will receive great light."]]

CHAPTER 49

1 "Nevertheless, I will again ask from You, O Mighty One, yes, I will ask You who made all things. **2** In what shape will those live who live in Your day? Or how will the splendor of those who [are] after that time continue? **3** Will they then resume this form of the present, || And put on these entangling members, || Which are now involved in evils, || And in which evils are consummated, || Or will You perhaps change these things which have been in the world || As also the world?"

CHAPTER 50

1 And He answered and said to me: "Hear, Baruch, this word, and write in the remembrance of your heart all that you will learn. **2** For the earth will then assuredly restore the dead, [[which it now receives, in order to preserve them.]] It will make no change in their form, but as it has received, so will it restore them, and as I delivered them to it, so also will it raise them. **3** For then it will be necessary to show the living that the dead have come to life again, and that those who had departed have returned [again]. **4** And it will come to pass, when they have individually recognized those whom they now know, then judgment will grow strong, and those things which before were spoken of will come."

CHAPTER 51

1 "And it will come to pass, when that appointed day has gone by, that then will the aspect of those who are condemned be afterward changed, and the glory of those who are justified. **2** For the aspect of those who now act wickedly will become worse than it is, as they will suffer torment. **3** Also, the glory of those who have now been justified in My law, who have had understanding in their life, and who have planted in their heart the root of wisdom, then their splendor will be glorified in changes, and the form of their face will be turned into the light of their beauty, that they may be able to acquire and receive the world which does not die, which is then promised to them. **4** For over this, above all, those who come will then lament that they rejected My law and stopped their ears that they might not hear wisdom or receive understanding. **5** When, therefore, they see those over whom they are now exalted, [but] who will then be exalted and glorified more than they, they will respectively be transformed, the latter into the splendor of messengers, and the former will yet more waste away in wonder at the visions and in the beholding of the forms. **6** For they will first behold and afterward depart to be tormented. **7** But those who have been saved by their works, || And to whom the law has now been a hope, || And understanding an expectation, || And wisdom a confidence, || Will wondrously appear in their time. **8** For they will behold the world which is now invisible to them, || And they will behold the time which is now hidden from them: **9** And time will no longer age them. **10** For they will dwell in the heights of that world, || And they will be made like to the messengers, || And be made equal to the stars, || And they will be changed into every form they desire, || From beauty into loveliness, || And from light into the splendor of glory. **11** For there will be spread before them the extents of Paradise, || And there will be shown to them the beauty of the majesty of the living creatures which are beneath the throne, || And all the armies of the messengers, who are now held fast by My word, || Lest they should appear, and are held fast by a command, that they may stand in their places until their advent comes. **12** Moreover, there will then be excellency in the righteous surpassing that in the messengers. **13** For the first will receive the last, those whom they were expecting, || And the last, those of whom they used to hear that they had passed away. **14** For they have been delivered from this world of tribulation, || And laid down the burden of anguish. **15** For what then have men lost their life, || And for what have those who were on the earth exchanged their soul? **16** For then they did not choose for themselves this time, || Which, beyond the reach of anguish, could not pass away, || But they chose for themselves that time, || Whose issues are full of lamentations and evils, || And they denied the world which does not age those who come to it, || And they rejected the time of glory, || So that they will not come to the honor of which I told you before."

CHAPTER 52

1 And I answered and said, "How can we forget those for whom woe is then reserved? **2** And why therefore do we again mourn for those who die? Or why do we weep for those who depart to Sheol? **3** Let lamentations be reserved for the beginning of that coming torment, || And let tears be laid up for the advent of the destruction of that time. **4** [[But even in the face of these things I will speak. **5** And as for the righteous, what will they do now? **6** Rejoice in the suffering which you now suffer; For why do you look for the decline of your enemies? **7** Make ready your soul for that which is reserved for you, || And prepare your souls for the reward which is laid up for you."]]

CHAPTER 53

1 And when I had said these things, I fell asleep there, and I saw a vision, and behold, a cloud was ascending from a very great sea, and I kept gazing on it, and behold, it was full of white and black waters, and there were many colors in those same waters, and as it were the likeness of great lightning was seen at its summit. **2** And I saw the cloud passing swiftly in quick courses, and it covered all the earth. **3** And it came to pass after these things that that cloud began to pour on the earth the waters that were in it. **4** And I saw that there was not one and the same likeness in the waters which descended from it. **5** For in the first beginning they were black and many, and afterward I saw that the waters became bright, but they were not many, and after these things again I saw black [waters], and after these things again bright, and again black and again bright. **6** Now this was done twelve times, but the black were always more numerous than the bright. **7** And it came to pass at the end of the cloud, that behold, it rained black waters, and they were darker than had been all those waters that were before, and fire was mingled with them, and where those waters descended, they worked devastation and destruction. **8** And after these things I saw how that lightning which I had seen on the summit of the cloud, seized hold of it and hurled it to the earth. **9** Now that lightning shone exceedingly, so as to illuminate the whole earth, and it healed those regions where the last waters had descended and worked devastation. **10** And it took hold of the whole earth and had dominion over it. **11** And I saw after these things, and behold, twelve rivers were ascending from the sea, and they began to surround that lightning and to become subject to it. **12** And by reason of my

fear I awoke.

CHAPTER 54

1 And I implored the Mighty One, and said, "You alone, O Lord, know of the former times—the deep things of the world, || And the things which befall in their times You bring about by Your word, || And against the works of the inhabitants of the earth You hasten the beginnings of the times, || And You alone know the end of the seasons. **2** [You] for whom nothing is too hard, || But who does everything easily by a nod: **3** [You] to whom the depths come as the heights, || And whose word the beginnings of the ages serve: **4** [You] who reveal to those who fear You what is prepared for them, || That from then on they may be comforted. **5** You show great acts to those who do not know; You break up the enclosure of those who are ignorant, || And light up what is dark, || And reveal what is hidden to the pure, || [[Who in faith have submitted themselves to You and Your law.]] **6** You have shown this vision to Your servant; Also reveal its interpretation to me. **7** For I know that as regards those things wherein I implored You, I have received a response, || And as regards what I implored, You revealed to me with what voice I should praise You, || And from what members I should cause praises and hallelujahs to ascend to You. **8** For if my members were mouths, || And the hairs of my head voices, || Even so I could not give You the reward of praise, || Nor laud You as is befitting, || Nor could I recount Your praise, || Nor tell the glory of Your beauty. **9** For what am I among men, || Or why am I reckoned among those who are more excellent than I, || That I have heard all these marvelous things from the Highest, || And numberless promises from Him who created me? **10** Blessed is my mother among those that bear, || And praised among women is she that bore me. **11** For I will not be silent in praising the Mighty One, || And with the voice of praise I will recount His marvelous deeds. **12** For who does like to Your marvelous deeds, O God, || Or who comprehends Your deep thought of life? **13** For with Your counsel You govern all the creatures which Your right hand has created, || And You have established every fountain of light beside You, || And You have prepared the treasures of wisdom beneath Your throne. **14** And justly do they perish who have not loved Your law, || And the torment of judgment will await those who have not submitted themselves to Your power. **15** For though Adam first sinned || And brought untimely death on all, || Yet of those who were born from him || Each one of them has prepared for his own soul torment to come, || And again each one of them has chosen for himself glories to come. **16** [[For assuredly he who believes will receive reward. **17** But now, as for you, you wicked that now are, || Turn to destruction, because you will be speedily visited, in that formerly you rejected the understanding of the Highest. **18** For His works have not taught you, || Nor has the skill of His creation—which is at all times—persuaded you.]] **19** Adam is therefore not the cause, save only of his own soul, || But each of us has been the Adam of his own soul. **20** But You, O Lord, expound to me regarding those things which You have revealed to me, || And inform me regarding that which I implored You. **21** For at the consummation of the world vengeance will be taken on those who have done wickedness according to their wickedness, || And You will glorify the faithful according to their faithfulness. **22** For those who are among Your own You rule, || And those who sin You blot out from among Your own."

CHAPTER 55

1 And it came to pass when I had finished speaking the words of this prayer, that I sat there under a tree, that I might rest in the shade of the branches. **2** And I wondered and was astonished, and pondered in my thoughts regarding the multitude of goodness which sinners who are on the earth have rejected, and regarding the great torment which they have despised, though they knew that they should be tormented because of the sin they had committed. And when I was pondering on these things and the like, behold, the messenger Ramiel who presides over true visions was sent to me, and he said to me: **4** "Why does your heart trouble you, Baruch, || And why does your thought disturb you? **5** For if owing to the report which you have only heard of judgment you are so moved, || What [will you be] when you will see it manifestly with your eyes? **6** And if with the expectation with which you do expect the day of the Mighty One you are so overcome, || What [will you be] when you will come to its advent? **7** And, if at the word of the announcement of the torment of those who have done foolishly you are so wholly distraught, || How much more when the event will reveal marvelous things? **8** And if you have heard tidings of the good and evil things which are then coming and are grieved, || What—when you will behold what the majesty will reveal, || Which will convict these and cause those to rejoice?"

CHAPTER 56

1 "Nevertheless, because you have implored the Highest to reveal to you the interpretation of the vision which you have seen, I have been sent to tell you. **2** And the Mighty One has assuredly made known to you the methods of the times that have passed, and of those that are destined to pass in His world from the beginning of its creation even to its consummation, of those things which [are] deceit and of those which [are] in truth. **3** For as you saw a great cloud which ascended from the sea, and went and covered the earth, this is the duration of the age which the Mighty One made when he took counsel to make the world. **4** And it came to pass when the word had gone forth from His presence, that the duration of the world had come into being in a small degree, and was established according to the multitude of the intelligence of Him who sent it. **5** And as you previously saw on the summit of the cloud black waters which descended previously on the earth, this is the transgression with which Adam the first man transgressed. **6** For [since] when he transgressed || Untimely death came into being, || Grief was named || And anguish was prepared, || And pain was created, || And trouble consummated, || And disease began to be established, || And Sheol kept demanding that it should be renewed in blood, || And the begetting of children was brought about, || And the passion of parents produced, || And the greatness of humanity was humiliated, || And goodness languished. **7** What therefore can be blacker or darker than these things? **8** This is the beginning of the black waters which you have seen. **9** And from these black [waters] again were black derived, and the darkness of darkness was produced. **10** For he became a danger to his own soul: even to the messengers. **11** For moreover, at that time when he was created, they enjoyed liberty. **12** And he became a danger; some of them descended and mingled with the women. **13** And then those who did so were tormented in chains. **14** But the rest of the multitude of the messengers, of which there is [no] number, restrained themselves. **15** And those who dwelt on the earth perished together [with them] through the waters of the deluge. **16** These are the black first waters."

CHAPTER 57

1 "And after these [waters] you saw bright waters: this is the fount of Abraham, also his generations and advent of his son, and of his son's son, and of those like them. **2** Because at that time the unwritten law was named among them, || And the works of the commandments were then fulfilled, || And belief in the coming judgment was then generated, || And hope of the world that was to be renewed was then built up, || And the promise of the life that should come hereafter was implanted. **3** These are the bright waters, which you have seen."

CHAPTER 58

1 "And the black third waters which you have seen, these are the mingling of all sins, which the nations afterward worked after the death of those righteous men, and the wickedness of the land of Egypt, wherein they did wickedly in the service with which they made their sons to serve. **2** Nevertheless, these also perished at last."

CHAPTER 59

1 "And the bright fourth waters which you have seen are the advent of Moses, and Aaron, and Miriam, and Joshua the son of Nun, and Caleb, and of all those like them. **2** For at that time the lamp of the perpetual law shone on all those who sat in darkness, which announced to them that believe the promise of their reward, and to them that deny, the torment of fire which is reserved for them. **3** But also the heavens at that time were shaken from their place, and those who were under the throne of the Mighty One were perturbed, when He was taking Moses to Himself. **4** For He showed him many admonitions together with the principles of the law and the consummation of the times, as also to you, and likewise the pattern of Zion and its measures, in the pattern of which the sanctuary of the present time was to be made. **5** But then He also showed to him the measures of the fire, also the depths of the abyss, and the weight of the winds, and the number of the drops of rain; **6** and the suppression of anger, and the multitude of long-suffering, and the truth of judgment; **7** and the root of wisdom, and the riches of understanding, and the fount of knowledge; **8** and the height of the air, and the greatness of Paradise, and the consummation of the ages, and the beginning of the Day of Judgment; **9** and the number of the offerings, and the earths which have not yet come; **10** and the mouth of Gehenna, and the station of vengeance, and the place of faith, and the region of hope; **11** and the likeness of future torment, and the multitude of innumerable messengers, and the flaming hosts, and the splendor of the lightnings, and the voice of the thunders, and the orders of the chiefs of the messengers, and the treasuries of light, and the changes of the times, and the investigations of the law. **12** These are the bright fourth waters which you have seen."

CHAPTER 60

1 "And the black fifth waters which you have seen raining are the works which the Amorites worked, and the spells of their incantations which they worked, and the wickedness of their mysteries, and the mingling of their pollution. **2** But even Israel was then polluted by sins in the days of the judges, though they saw many signs which were from Him who made them."

CHAPTER 61

1 "And the bright sixth waters which you saw, this is the time in which David and Solomon were born. **2** And there was at that time the building of Zion, || And the dedication of the sanctuary, || And the shedding of much blood of the nations that sinned then, || And many offerings which were offered then in the dedication of the sanctuary. **3** And peace and tranquility existed at that time, || **4** And wisdom was heard in the assembly; And the riches of understanding were magnified in the congregations, || **5** And the holy festivals were fulfilled in blessedness and in much joy. **6** And the judgment of the rulers was then seen to be without guile, || And the righteousness of the precepts of the Mighty One was accomplished with truth. **7** And the land [which] was then beloved by the Lord, || And because its inhabitants did not sin, it was glorified beyond all lands, || And the city Zion ruled then over all lands and regions. **8** These are the bright waters which you have seen."

CHAPTER 62

1 "And the black seventh waters which you have seen, this is the perversion [brought about] by the counsel of Jeroboam, who took counsel to make two calves of gold; **2** and all the iniquities which kings who were after him iniquitously worked. **3** And the curse of Jezebel and the worship of idols which Israel practiced at that time. **4** And the withholding of rain, and the famines which occurred until women ate the fruit of their wombs. **5** And the time of their captivity which came on the nine and a half tribes, because they were in many sins. **6** And Shalmanezzar king of Assyria came and led them away captive. **7** But regarding the nations, it is tedious to tell how they always worked impiety and wickedness, and never worked righteousness. **8** These are the black seventh waters which you have seen."

CHAPTER 63

[1] "And the bright eighth waters which you have seen, this is the rectitude and uprightness of Hezekiah king of Judah, and the grace [of God] which came on him [2] when Sennacherib was stirred up in order that he might perish, and his wrath troubled him in order that he might thereby perish, for the multitude also of the nations which were with him. [3] When, moreover, Hezekiah the king heard those things which the king of Assyria was devising, to come and seize him and destroy his people—the two and a half tribes which remained—moreover, that he wished to overthrow Zion also, Hezekiah then trusted in his works, and had hope in his righteousness, and spoke with the Mighty One and said, [4] For behold, Sennacherib is prepared to destroy us, and he will be boastful and uplifted when he has destroyed Zion." [5] And the Mighty One heard him, for Hezekiah was wise, and He had respect to his prayer, because he was righteous. [6] And thereon the Mighty One commanded His messenger Ramiel who speaks with you. [7] And I went forth and destroyed their multitude, the number of whose chiefs alone was one hundred and eighty-five thousand, and each one of them had an equal number [at his command]. [8] And at that time I burned their bodies within, but their raiment and arms I preserved outwardly, in order that the still more wonderful deeds of the Mighty One might appear, and that His Name might thereby be spoken of throughout the whole earth. [9] And Zion was saved and Jerusalem delivered: Israel was also freed from tribulation. [10] And all those who were in the holy land rejoiced, and the Name of the Mighty One was glorified so that it was spoken of. [11] These are the bright waters which you have seen."

CHAPTER 64

[1] "And the black ninth waters which you have seen, this is all the wickedness which was in the days of Manasseh the son of Hezekiah. [2] For he worked much impiety, and he slew the righteous, and he wrested judgment, and he shed the blood of the innocent, and he violently polluted wedded women, and he overturned the altars, and destroyed their offerings, and drove forth their priests lest they should minister in the sanctuary. [3] And he made an image with five faces: four of them looked to the four winds, and the fifth on the summit of the image as an adversary of the zeal of the Mighty One. [4] And then wrath went forth from the presence of the Mighty One to the intent that Zion should be rooted out, as also it befell in your days. But also, against the two and a half tribes went forth a decree that they should also be led away captive, as you have now seen. [5] And the impiety of Manasseh increased to such a degree that it removed the praise of the Highest from the sanctuary. [7] On this account Manasseh was at that time named the impious, and finally his abode was in the fire. [8] For though his prayer was heard with the Highest, finally, when he was cast into the brazen horse and the brazen horse was melted, it served as a sign to him for the hour. [9] For he had not lived perfectly, for he was not worthy—but that from then on he might know by whom finally he should be tormented. [10] For he who is able to benefit is also able to torment."

CHAPTER 65

[1] "Thus, moreover, Manasseh acted impiously, and thought that in his time the Mighty One would not inquire into these things. [2] These are the black ninth waters which you have seen."

CHAPTER 66

[1] "And the bright tenth waters which you have seen: this is the purity of the generations of Josiah king of Judah, who was the only one at the time who submitted himself to the Mighty One with all his heart and with all his soul. [2] And he cleansed the land from idols, and hallowed all the vessels which had been polluted, and restored the offerings to the altar, and raised the horn of the holy, and exalted the righteous, and

honored all that were wise in understanding, and brought back the priests to their ministry, and destroyed and removed the magicians, and enchanters, and necromancers from the land. [3] And not only did he slay the impious that were living, but they also took from the graves the bones of the dead and burned them with fire. [4] [[And the festivals and the Sabbaths he established in their sanctity]], and their polluted ones he burned in the fire, and the lying prophets which deceived the people, these he also burned in the fire, and the people who listened to them when they were living, he cast them into the Brook of Kidron, and heaped stones on them. [5] And he was zealous with zeal for the Mighty One with all his soul, and he alone was firm in the law at that time, so that he left none that was uncircumcised, or that worked impiety in all the land, all the days of his life. [6] Therefore he will receive a continuous reward, and he will be glorified with the Mighty One beyond many at a later time. [7] For on his account and on account of those who are like him were the honorable glories, of which you were told before, created and prepared. These are the bright waters which you have seen."

CHAPTER 67

[1] "And the black eleventh waters which you have seen: this is the calamity which is now befalling Zion. [2] Do you think that there is no anguish to the messengers in the presence of the Mighty One, that Zion was so delivered up, and that, behold, the nations boast in their hearts, and assemble before their idols and say, She is trodden down who oftentimes trod down, and she has been reduced to servitude who reduced [other nations to servitude]? [3] Do you think that in these things the Most High rejoices, or that His Name is glorified? [4] [[But how will it serve toward His righteous judgment?]] [5] Yet after these things the dispersed among the nations will be taken hold of by tribulation, and in shame they will dwell in every place. [6] Because so far as Zion is delivered up and Jerusalem laid waste, idols will prosper in the cities of the nations, and the vapor of the smoke of the incense of the righteousness which is by the law is extinguished in Zion; and in the region of Zion in every place, behold, there is the smoke of impiety. [7] But the king of Babylon will arise who has now destroyed Zion, and he will boast over the people, and he will speak great things in his heart in the presence of the Highest. [8] But he will also fall at last. These are the black waters."

CHAPTER 68

[1] "And the bright twelfth waters which you have seen: this is the word. For after these things, a time will come when your people will fall into distress, so that they will all run the risk of perishing together. [3] Nevertheless, they will be saved, and their enemies will fall in their presence. [4] And they will have in [due] time much joy. [5] And at that time, after a short interval, Zion will again be rebuilt, and its offerings will again be restored, and the priests will return to their ministry, and also the nations will come to glorify it. [6] Nevertheless, not fully as in the beginning. [7] But it will come to pass after these things that there will be the fall of many nations. [8] These are the bright waters which you have seen."

CHAPTER 69

[1] "For the last waters which you have seen which were darker than all that were before them, those which were after the twelfth number, which were collected together, belong to the whole world. [2] For the Most High made division from the beginning, because He alone knows what will befall. [3] For as to the enormities and the impieties which should be worked before Him, He foresaw six kinds of them. [4] And of the good works of the righteous which should be accomplished before Him, He foresaw six kinds of them, beyond those which He should work at the consummation of the age. [5] On his account there were not black waters with black, nor bright with bright; for it is the consummation."

CHAPTER 70

1 "Therefore hear the interpretation of the last black waters which are to come: this [is] the word. **2** Behold! the days come, and it will be when the time of the age has ripened, || And the harvest of its evil and good seeds has come, || That the Mighty One will bring on the earth and its inhabitants and on its rulers || Perturbation of spirit and stupor of heart. **3** And they will hate one another, || And provoke one another to fight, || And the mean will rule over the honorable, || And those of low degree will be extolled above the famous. **4** And the many will be delivered into the hands of the few, || And those who were nothing will rule over the strong, || And the poor will have abundance beyond the rich, || And the impious will exalt themselves above the heroic. **5** And the wise will be silent, || And the foolish will speak, || Neither will the thought of men be then confirmed, || Nor the counsel of the mighty, || Nor will the hope of those who hope be confirmed. **6** And when those things which were predicted have come to pass, || Then confusion will fall on all men, || And some of them will fall in battle, || And some of them will perish in anguish, || **7** And some of them will be destroyed by their own. Then the peoples of the Highest, whom He has prepared before, || Will come and make war with the leaders that will then be left. **8** And it will come to pass that whoever gets safe out of the war will die in the earthquake, || And whoever gets safe out of the earthquake will be burned by the fire, || And whoever gets safe out of the fire will be destroyed by famine. **9** [[And it will come to pass that whoever of the victors and the vanquished gets safe out of and escapes all these things previously mentioned will be delivered into the hands of My servant Messiah.]] **10** For all the earth will devour its inhabitants."

CHAPTER 71

1 "And the holy land will have mercy on its own, and it will protect its inhabitants at that time. **2** This is the vision which you have seen, and this is the interpretation. **3** For I have come to tell you these things, because your prayer has been heard with the Highest."

CHAPTER 72

1 "Now also hear regarding the bright lightning which is to come at the consummation after these black [waters]: this is the word. **2** After the signs have come of which you were told before, when the nations become turbulent, and the time of My Messiah is come, He will both summon all the nations, and some of them He will spare, and some of them He will slay. **3** Therefore these things will come on the nations which are to be spared by Him. **4** Every nation which does not know Israel and has not trodden down the seed of Jacob, will indeed be spared. **5** And this because some out of every nation will be subjected to your people. **6** But all those who have ruled over you, or have known you, will be given up to the sword."

CHAPTER 73

1 "And it will come to pass, when He has brought low everything that is in the world, || And has sat down in peace for the age on the throne of His kingdom, || That joy will then be revealed, || And rest will appear. **2** And then healing will descend in dew, || And disease will withdraw, || And anxiety, and anguish, and lamentation will pass from among men, || And gladness will proceed through the whole earth. **3** And no one will die untimely again, || Nor will any adversity suddenly befall. **4** And judgments, and abusive talk, and contentions, and revenges, || And blood, and passions, and envy, and hatred, || And whatever things are like these will go into condemnation when they are removed. **5** For it is these very things which have filled this world with evils, || And on account of these the life of man has been greatly troubled. **6** And wild beasts will come from the forest and minister to men || And asps and dragons will come forth from their holes to submit themselves to a little child. **7** And women will no longer then have pain when they bear, || Nor will they suffer torment when they yield the fruit of the womb."

CHAPTER 74

1 "And it will come to pass in those days that the reapers will not grow weary, || Nor those that build be toil-worn; For the works will of themselves speedily advance || Together with those who do them in much tranquility. **2** For that time is the consummation of that which is corruptible, || And the beginning of that which is not corruptible. **3** Therefore those things which were predicted will belong to it: Therefore, it is far away from evils, and near to those things which do not die. **4** This is the bright lightning which came after the last dark waters."

CHAPTER 75

1 And I answered and said, "Who can understand, O Lord, Your goodness? For it is incomprehensible. **2** Or who can search into Your compassions, || Which are infinite? **3** Or who can comprehend Your intelligence? **4** Or who is able to recount the thoughts of Your mind? **5** Or who of those who are born can hope to come to those things, || Unless he is one to whom You are merciful and gracious? **6** Because, assuredly, if You did not have compassion on man, || Those who are under Your right hand, || They could not come to those things, || But those who are in the numbers named can be called. **7** But if, indeed, we who exist know why we have come, || And submit ourselves to Him who brought us out of Egypt, || We will come again and remember those things which have passed, || And will rejoice regarding that which has been. **8** But if now we do not know why we have come, || And do not recognize the principate of Him who brought us up out of Egypt, || We will come again and seek after those things which have been now, || And be grieved with pain because of those things which have befallen."

CHAPTER 76

1 And He answered and said to me: "[[Inasmuch as the revelation of this vision has been interpreted to you as you requested]], hear the word of the Highest that you may know what is to befall you after these things. **2** For you will surely depart from this earth, nevertheless not to death, but you will be preserved to the consummation of the times. **3** Therefore go up to the top of that mountain, and there will pass before you all the regions of that land, and the figure of the inhabited world, and the top of the mountains, and the depth of the valleys, and the depths of the seas, and the number of the rivers, that you may see what you are leaving, and to where you are going. **4** Now this will befall after forty days. Therefore, go now during these days and instruct the people so far as you are able, that they may learn so as not to die at the last time, but may learn in order that they may live at the last times."

CHAPTER 77

1 And I, Baruch, went there and came to the people, and assembled them together from the greatest to the least, and said to them: **2** "Hear, you sons of Israel, behold how many you are who remain of the twelve tribes of Israel. **3** For to you and to your fathers the Lord gave a law more excellent than to all peoples. **4** And because your brothers transgressed the commandments of the Highest, || He brought vengeance on you and on them, || And He did not spare the former, || And the latter He also gave into captivity: And He did not leave a residue of them, **5** But behold! you are here with me. **6** If, therefore, you direct your ways correctly, || You also will not depart as your brothers departed, || But they will come to you. **7** For He is merciful whom you worship, || And He is gracious in whom you hope, || And He is true, so that He will do good and not evil. **8** Have you not seen here what has befallen Zion? **9** Or do you perhaps think that the place had sinned, || And that on this account it was overthrown? Or that the land had worked foolishness, || And that therefore it was delivered up? **10** And do you not know that on account of you who sinned, || That which did not sin was overthrown, || And, on account of those who worked wickedly, || That which did not work foolishness was delivered up to enemies?" **11** And the whole people answered and said to me: "So far as we can recall the good things which the Mighty One has done to us, we do recall them; and those things which we do not remember He in His mercy knows. **12** Nevertheless, do this for us your people: also write to our brothers in Babylon a letter of doctrine and a scroll of hope, that you may confirm them also before you depart from us. **13** For the shepherds of Israel have perished, || And the lamps which gave light are extinguished, || And the fountains have withheld their stream from which we used to drink. **14** And we are left in the darkness, || And amid the trees of the forest, || And the thirst of the wilderness." **15** And I answered and said to them: "Shepherds, and lamps, and fountains come from the law: And though we depart, yet the law abides. **16** If, therefore, you have respect to the law, || And are intent on wisdom, || A lamp will not be wanting, || And a shepherd will not fail, || And a fountain will not dry up. **17** Nevertheless, as you said to me, I will also write to your brothers in Babylon, and I will send by means of men, and I will write in like manner to the nine and a half tribes, and send by means of a bird." **18** And it came to pass on the twenty-first day in the eighth month that I, Baruch, came and sat down under the oak under the shadow of the branches, and no man was with me, but I was alone. **19** And I wrote these two letters: one I sent by an eagle to the nine and a half tribes; and the other I sent to those that were at Babylon by means of three men. **20** And I called the eagle and spoke these words to it: **21** "The Most High has made you that you should be higher than all birds. **22** And now go and do not tarry in [any] place, nor enter a nest, nor settle on any tree, until you have passed over the breadth of the many waters of the Euphrates River, and have gone to the people that dwell there, and cast down this letter to them. **23** Remember, moreover, that, at the time of the deluge, Noah received from a dove the fruit of the olive, when he sent it forth from the Ark. **24** Yes, also the ravens ministered to Elijah, bearing him food, as they had been commanded. **25** Solomon also, in the time of his kingdom, wherever he wished to send or seek for anything, commanded a bird, and it obeyed him as he commanded it. **26** And now, do not let it weary you, and do not turn to the right hand nor the left, but fly and go by a direct way, that you may preserve the command of the Mighty One, according as I spoke to you."

THE EPISTLE OF BARUCH, THE SON OF NERIAH, WHICH HE WROTE TO THE NINE AND A HALF TRIBES

CHAPTER 78

1 These are the words of that letter which Baruch the son of Neriah sent to the nine and a half tribes, which were across the River Euphrates, in which these things were written. **2** Thus says Baruch the son of Neriah to the brothers carried into captivity: "Mercy and peace." I bear in mind, my brothers, the love of Him who created us, who loved us from of old, and never hated us, but above all educated us. **3** And truly I know, that behold, all of us—the twelve tribes—are bound by one bond, inasmuch as we are born from one father. **4** For what reason I have been more careful to leave you the words of this letter before I die, that you may be comforted regarding the calamities which have come on you, and that you may also be grieved regarding the evil that has befallen your brothers; and again, also, that you may justify His judgment which **5** He has decreed against you that you should be carried away captive— for what you have suffered is disproportioned to what you have done—in order that, at the last times, you may be found worthy of your fathers. **6** Therefore, if you consider that you have now suffered those things for your good, that you may not finally be condemned and tormented, then you will receive continuous

hope; if above all you destroy from your heart vain error, on account of which you departed hence. **7** For if you so do these things, He will continually remember you, He who always promised on our behalf to those who were more excellent than we, that He will never forget or forsake us, but with much mercy will again gather together those who were dispersed.

CHAPTER 79

1 Now, my brothers, first learn what befell Zion: how that Nebuchadnezzar king of Babylon came up against us. **2** For we have sinned against Him who made us, and we have not kept the commandments which He commanded us, yet He has not disciplined us as we deserved. **3** For what befell you we also suffer in a preeminent degree, for it befell us also.

CHAPTER 80

1 And now, my brothers, I make known to you that when the enemy had surrounded the city, the messengers of the Highest were sent, and they overthrew the fortifications of the strong wall, and they destroyed the firm iron corners, which could not be rooted out. **2** Nevertheless, they hid all the vessels of the sanctuary, lest the enemy should get possession of them. **3** And when they had done these things, they delivered thereon to the enemy the overthrown wall, and the plundered house, and the burnt temple, and the people who were overcome because they were delivered up, lest the enemy should boast and say: "Thus by force we have been able to lay waste even the house of the Highest in war." They have also bound your brothers and led [them] away to Babylon, and have caused them to dwell there. **5** But we have been left here, being very few. **6** This is the tribulation about which I wrote to you. **7** For assuredly I know that [the consolation of] the inhabitants of Zion consoles you; so far as you knew that it was prospered, [your consolation] was greater than the tribulation which you endured in having to depart from it.

CHAPTER 81

1 But regarding consolation, hear the word. **2** For I was mourning regarding Zion, and I prayed for mercy from the Highest, and I said, **3** "How long will these things endure for us? And will these calamities always come on us?" **4** And the Mighty One did according to the multitude of His mercies, || And the Most High according to the greatness of His compassion, || And He revealed to me the word, that I might receive consolation, || And He showed me visions that I should not again endure anguish, || And He made known to me the mystery of the times, || And He showed me the advent of the hours.

CHAPTER 82

1 Therefore, my brothers, I have written to you that you may comfort yourselves regarding the multitude of your tribulations. **2** For know that our Maker will assuredly avenge us on all our enemies, according to all that they have done to us, also that the consummation which the Highest will make is very near, and His mercy that is coming, and the consummation of His judgment, is by no means far off. **3** For behold, we see now the multitude of the prosperity of the nations, || Though they act impiously, || But they will be like a vapor: **4** And we behold the multitude of their power, || Though they do wickedly, || But they will be made like to a drop: **5** And we see the firmness of their might, || Though they resist the Mighty One every hour, || But they will be accounted as spittle. **6** And we consider the glory of their greatness, || Though they do not keep the statutes of the Highest, || But they will pass away as smoke. **7** And we meditate on the beauty of their gracefulness, || Though they have to do with pollutions, || But as grass that withers, they will fade away. **8** And we consider the strength of their cruelty, || Though they do not remember the end, || But as a wave that passes, they will be broken. **9**

And we remark [regarding] the boastfulness of their might, || Though they deny the beneficence of God, who gave [it] to them, || But they will pass away as a passing cloud.

CHAPTER 83

1 For the Highest will assuredly hasten His times, || And He will assuredly bring on His hours. **2** And He will assuredly judge those who are in His world, || And will visit in truth all things by means of all their hidden works. **3** And He will assuredly examine the secret thoughts, || And that which is laid up in the secret chambers of all the members of mail, || And will make manifest in the presence of all with reproof. **4** Let none therefore of these present things ascend into your hearts, but above all let us be expectant, because that which is promised to us will come. **5** And let us not now look to the delights of the nations in the present, but let us remember what has been promised to us in the end. **6** For the ends of the times, and of the seasons, and whatever is with them will assuredly pass by together. **7** Moreover, the consummation of the age will then show the great might of its ruler, when all things come to judgment. **8** Therefore, prepare your hearts for that which before you believed, lest you come to be in bondage in both worlds, so that you be led away captive here and be tormented there. **9** For that which exists now, or which has passed away, or which is to come, in all these things, neither is the evil fully evil, nor again the good fully good. **10** For all healthinesses of this time are turning into diseases, **11** And all might of this time is turning into weakness, || And all the force of this time is turning into impotence, **12** And every energy of youth is turning into old age and consummation. And every beauty of gracefulness of this time is turning faded and hateful, **13** And every proud dominion of the present is turning into humiliation and shame, **14** And every praise of the glory of this time is turning into the shame of silence, || And every vain splendor and insolence of this time is turning into voiceless ruin. **15** And every delight and joy of this time is turning to worms and corruption, **16** And every clamor of the pride of this time is turning into dust and stillness. **17** And every possession of riches of this time is being turned into Sheol alone, **18** And all the plunder of passion of this time is turning into involuntary death, || And every passion of the lusts of this time is turning into a judgment of torment. **19** And every artifice and craftiness of this time is turning into a proof of the truth, || **20** And every sweetness of ointments of this time is turning into judgment and condemnation, **21** And every love of lying is turning to insult through truth. [[**22** Since therefore all these things are done now, does anyone think that they will not be avenged? But the consummation of all things will come to the truth.]]

CHAPTER 84

1 Behold! I have therefore made known to you [these things] while I live, for I have said [it] that you should learn the things that are excellent; for the Mighty One has commanded me to instruct you: and I will set before you some of the commandments of His judgment before I die. **2** Remember that formerly Moses assuredly called the heavens and earth to witness against you and said, "If you transgress the law you will be dispersed, but if you keep it you will be kept." **3** And other things he also used to say to you when you, the twelve tribes, were together in the desert. **4** And after his death you cast them away from you. On this account there came on you what had been predicted. **5** And now Moses used to tell you before they befell you, and behold, they have befallen you, for you have forsaken the law. **6** Behold, I also say to you after you have suffered, that if you obey those things which have been said to you, you will receive from the Mighty One whatever has been laid up and reserved for you. **7** Moreover, let this letter be for a testimony between me and you, that you may remember the commandments of the Mighty One, and that there may also be a defense for me in the presence of Him who sent me. **8** And remember the law and Zion, and the holy land and your brothers, and the covenant of your fathers, and do not forget the festivals and the Sabbaths. And deliver this letter and the traditions of the law to your sons after you, as your fathers also delivered [them] to you. **9** And at all times make request perseveringly and pray diligently with your whole heart that the Mighty One may be reconciled to you, and that He may not reckon the multitude of your sins, but remember the rectitude of your fathers. **11** For if He does not judge us according to the multitude of His mercies, woe to all of us who are born.

CHAPTER 85

1 Know, moreover, that in former times and in the generations of old our fathers had helpers, righteous men and holy prophets, [but] no longer. **2** We were in our own land, [[and they helped us when we sinned]], and they prayed for us to Him who made us, because they trusted in their works, and the Mighty One heard their prayer and was gracious to us. **3** But now the righteous have been gathered and the prophets have fallen asleep, and we have also gone forth from the land, and Zion has been taken from us, and we have nothing now except the Mighty One and His law. **4** If, therefore, we direct and dispose our hearts, we will receive everything that we lost, and much better things than we lost by many times. **5** For what we have lost was to corruption, and what we will receive will not be corruptible. [[**6** Moreover, I also have written thus to our brothers to Babylon, that I also may attest to them those very things.]] **7** And let all those things previously mentioned always be before your eyes, because we are still in the spirit and the power of our liberty. **8** Again, moreover, the Most High is also long-suffering toward us here, and He has shown to us that which is to be, and has not concealed from us what will befall in the end. **9** Therefore, before judgment exacts its own, and truth that which is its due, let us prepare our soul that we may enter into possession of, and not be taken possession of, and that we may hope and not be put to shame, and that we may rest with our fathers and not be tormented with our enemies. **10** And the strength of the creation is already exhausted, and the advent of the times is very short, yes, they have passed by; and the pitcher is near to the cistern, and the ship to the port, and the course of the journey to the city, and life to consummation. **11** And again prepare your souls, so that when you sail and ascend from the ship you may have rest and not be condemned when you depart. **12** For behold, when the Most High will bring to pass all these things, there will not again be there an opportunity for returning, nor a limit to the times, nor adjournment to the hours, nor change of ways, nor place for prayer, nor sending of petitions, nor receiving of knowledge, nor giving of love, nor place of conversion, nor supplication for offenses, nor intercession of the fathers, nor prayer of the prophets, nor help of the righteous. **13** There, there, is the sentence of corruption, the way of fire, and the path which brings to Gehenna. **14** On this account there is one law by one, one age and an end for all who are in it. **15** Then He will preserve those to whom He finds He may be gracious, and at the same time destroy those who are polluted with sins.

CHAPTER 86

1 When you therefore receive this—my letter—read it in your congregations with care. **2** And meditate thereon, above all on the days of your fasts. **3** And bear me in mind by means of this letter, as I also bear you in mind in it, and always farewell.

CHAPTER 87

1 And it came to pass when I had ended all the words of this letter, and had written it sedulously to its close, **2** that I folded it, and sealed it carefully, and bound it to the neck of the eagle, and dismissed and sent it. Here ends the Scroll of Baruch, the son of Neriah.

3 BARUCH

3 Baruch, also called the Greek Apocalypse of Baruch, is a visionary, probably pseudepigraphic text thought by most to have been written some time between the fall of Jerusalem in

70 AD and the 3rd century AD. Scholars disagree on whether it was written by a Jew or a Christian, or whether a clear distinction can be made in this era. It is self-attributed to the scribe of Jeremiah, Baruch ben Neriah, and does not form part of the biblical canon of either Jews or Christians. It is extant in certain Greek and Old Slavonic manuscripts.

A narrative and revelation of Baruch, concerning those ineffable things which he saw by command of God. Bless You, O Lord. A revelation of Baruch, who stood on the River Gel weeping over the captivity of Jerusalem, when Abimelech was also preserved by the hand of God, at the farm of Agrippa. And he was sitting thus at the beautiful gates, where the Holy of Holies lay.

CHAPTER 1

1 Truly I, Baruch, was weeping in my mind and sorrowing on account of the people, and that Nebuchadnezzar the king was permitted by God to destroy His city, saying, **2** "Lord, why did You set Your vineyard on fire, and lay it waste? Why did You do this? And why, Lord, did You not repay us with another discipline, but delivered us to nations such as these, so that they reproach us and say, Where is their God?" **3** And behold, as I was weeping and saying such things, I saw a messenger of the Lord coming and saying to me, "Understand, O man, greatly beloved, and do not trouble yourself so greatly concerning the salvation of Jerusalem, for thus says the Lord God, the Almighty. **4** For He sent me before you, to make known and to show to you all [the things] of God. **5** For your prayer was heard before Him, and entered into the ears of the Lord God." **6** And when he had said these things to me, I was silent. **7** And the messenger said to me, "Cease to provoke God, and I will show you other mysteries, greater than these." And I Baruch said, "As the Lord God lives, if you will show me, and I hear a word of yours, I will not continue to speak any longer. **8** God will add to my judgment in the Day of Judgment, if I speak hereafter." And the messenger of the powers said to me, "Come, and I will show you the mysteries of God."

CHAPTER 2

1 And he took me and led me where the expanse has been set fast, and where there was a river which no one can cross, nor any strange breeze of all those which God created. **2** And he took me and led me to the first heaven and showed me a door of great size. **3** And he said to me, "Let us enter through it," and we entered as though borne on wings, a distance of about thirty days' journey. And he showed me a plain within the heaven; and there were men dwelling thereon, with the faces of oxen, and the horns of stags, and the feet of goats, and the haunches of lambs. **4** And I, Baruch, asked the messenger, "Make known to me, please, what is the thickness of the heaven in which we journeyed, or what is its extent, or what is the plain, in order that I may also tell the sons of men?" **5** And the messenger whose name is Phamael said to me, "This door which you see is the door of Heaven, and as great as is the distance from earth to Heaven, so great also is its thickness; and again as great as is the distance [[from north to south, so great]] is the length of the plain which you saw." **6** And again the messenger of the powers said to me, "Come, and I will show you greater mysteries." **7** But I said, "Please show me what these men are." And he said to me, "These are they who built the tower of strife against God, and the Lord banished them."

CHAPTER 3

1 And the messenger of the Lord took me and led me to [the] second heaven. **2** And he also showed me a door there like the first and said, "Let us enter through it." **3** And we entered, being borne on wings a distance of about sixty days' journey. **4** And he also showed me a plain there, and it was full of men, whose appearance was like that of dogs, and whose feet were like those of stags. **5** And I asked the messenger: "Please, Lord, tell me who these are." **6** And he said, "These are they who gave counsel to build the tower, for they whom you

see drove forth multitudes of both men and women to make bricks; among whom, a woman making bricks was not allowed to be released in the hour of child-birth, but brought forth while she was making bricks, and carried her child in her apron, and continued to make bricks. **7** And the Lord appeared to them and confused their speech, when they had built the tower to the height of four hundred and sixty-three cubits. **8** And they took a gimlet, and sought to pierce the heaven, saying, Let us see [whether] the heaven is made of clay, or of brass, or of iron. **9** When God saw this, He did not permit them, but struck them with blindness and confusion of speech, and rendered them as you see."

CHAPTER 4

1 And I, Baruch, said, "Behold, Lord, you showed me great and wonderful things; and now show me all things for the sake of the Lord." **2** And the messenger said to me, "Come, let us proceed." **3** [And I proceeded] with the messenger from that place about one hundred- and eighty-five-days' journey. **4** And he showed me a plain and a serpent, which appeared to be two hundred plethra in length. And he showed me Hades, and its appearance was dark and abominable. **5** And I said, "Who is this dragon, and who is this monster around him?" **6** And the messenger said, "The dragon is he who eats the bodies of those who spend their life wickedly, and he is nourished by them. And this is Hades, which itself also closely resembles him, in that it also drinks about a cubit from the sea, which does not sink at all." **7** Baruch said, "And how?" And the messenger said, "Listen, the Lord God made three hundred and sixty rivers, of which the chief of all are Alphias, Abyrus, and the Gericus; and because of these the sea does not sink." **8** And I said, "Please show me which is the tree which led Adam astray." And the messenger said to me, "It is the vine, which the messenger Sammael planted, at which the Lord God was angry, and He cursed him and his plant, while also on this account He did not permit Adam to touch it, and therefore the Devil being envious deceived him through his vine." [[**9** And I, Baruch, said, "Since also the vine has been the cause of such great evil, and is under judgment of the curse of God, and was the destruction of the first created, how is it now so useful?" And the messenger said, "You ask correctly. **10** When God caused the deluge on earth, and destroyed all flesh, and four hundred and nine thousand giants, and the water rose fifteen cubits above the highest mountains, then the water entered into Paradise and destroyed every flower; but it wholly removed the shoot of the vine outside the bounds and cast it outside. **11** And when the earth appeared out of the water, and Noah came out of the Ark, he began to plant of the plants which he found. But he also found the shoot of the vine; and he took it, and was reasoning in himself, What then is it? **12** And I came and spoke to him the things concerning it. And he said, Will I plant it, or what will I do? **13** Since Adam was destroyed because of it, let me not also meet with the anger of God because of it. **14** And saying these things he prayed that God would reveal to him what he should do concerning it. **15** And when he had completed the prayer which lasted forty days, and having implored many things and wept, he said, Lord, I entreat You to reveal to me what I will do concerning this plant. But God sent His messenger Sarasael, and said to him, Arise, Noah, and plant the shoot of the vine, for thus says the Lord: Its bitterness will be changed into sweetness, and its curse will become a blessing, and that which is produced from it will become the blood of God; and as through it the human race obtained condemnation, so again through Jesus Christ, the Immanuel, they will receive in Him the upward calling, and the entry into Paradise.]] **16** Know therefore, O Baruch, that as Adam through this very tree obtained condemnation, and was divested of the glory of God, so also the men who now drink insatiably the wine which is begotten of it, transgress worse than Adam, and are far from the glory of God, and are surrendering themselves to the continuous fire. **17** For [no] good comes through it. For those who drink it to excess do these things: neither does a brother pity his brother, nor a father his son, nor children their parents, but from the drinking of wine come all evils, such as murders, adulteries, fornications, perjuries, thefts, and such like. And nothing good is established by it."

CHAPTER 5

¹ And I, Baruch, said to the messenger, "Let me ask you one thing, Lord. ² Since you said to me that the dragon drinks one cubit out of the sea, say to me also, how great is his belly?" ³ And the messenger said, "His belly is Hades; and as far as a plummet is thrown [by] three hundred men, so great is his belly. Come, then, that I may show you also greater works than these."

CHAPTER 6

¹ And he took me and led me where the sun goes forth; ² and he showed me a chariot and four, under which burned a fire, and in the chariot was sitting a man, wearing a crown of fire, [and] the chariot [was] drawn by forty messengers. ³ And behold, a bird circling before the sun, about nine cubits away. ⁴ And I said to the messenger, "What is this bird?" And he said to me, "This is the guardian of the earth." ⁵ And I said, "Lord, how is he the guardian of the earth? Teach me." ⁶ And the messenger said to me, "This bird flies alongside of the sun, and expanding his wings, receives its fiery rays. For if he were not receiving them, the human race would not be preserved, nor any other living creature. ⁷ But God appointed this bird to that." And he expanded his wings, and I saw on his right wing very large letters, as large as the space of a threshing-floor, the size of about four thousand modii; and the letters were of gold. ⁸ And the messenger said to me, "Read them." ⁹ And I read, and they ran thus: Neither earth nor Heaven bring me forth, but wings of fire bring me forth. ¹⁰ And I said, "Lord, what is this bird, and what is his name?" ¹¹ And the messenger said to me, "His name is called Phoenix." [And I said,] "And what does he eat?" And he said to me, "The manna of Heaven and the dew of earth." ¹² And I said, "Does the bird excrete?" And he said to me, "He excretes a worm, and the excrement of the worm is cinnamon, which kings and princes use. ¹³ But wait and you will see the glory of God." And while he was conversing with me, there was as a thunderclap, and the place was shaken on which we were standing. ¹⁴ And I asked the messenger, "My Lord, what is this sound?" And the messenger said to me, "Even now the messengers are opening the three hundred and sixty-five gates of Heaven, and the light is being separated from the darkness." ¹⁵ And a voice came which said, "Light giver, give to the world radiance." ¹⁶ And when I heard the noise of the bird, I said, "Lord, what is this noise?" ¹⁷ And he said, "This is the bird who awakens from slumber the cocks on earth. For as men do through the mouth, so also does the cock signify to those in the world, in his own speech. For the sun is made ready by the messengers, and the cock crows."

CHAPTER 7

¹ And I said, "And where does the sun begin its labors, after the cock crows?" ² And the messenger said to me, "Listen, Baruch: all things, whatever I showed you, are in the first and second heaven, and in the third heaven the sun passes through and gives light to the world. But wait, and you will see the glory of God." ³ And while I was conversing with him, I saw the bird, and he appeared in front, and grew less and less, and at length returned to his full size. ⁴ And behind him I saw the shining sun, and the messengers which draw it, and a crown on its head, the sight of which we were not able to gaze on and behold. ⁵ And as soon as the sun shone, the phoenix also stretched out his wings. ⁶ But I, when I beheld such great glory, was brought low with great fear, and I fled and hid in the wings of the messenger. ⁷ And the messenger said to me, "Do not fear, Baruch, but wait and you will also see their setting."

CHAPTER 8

¹ And he took me and led me toward the west; and when the time of the setting came, I again saw the bird coming before it, and as soon as it came, I saw the messengers, and they lifted the crown from its head. ² But the bird stood exhausted and with wings contracted. ³ And beholding these things, I said, "Lord, why did they lift the crown from the head of the sun, and why is the bird so exhausted?" ⁴ And the messenger said to me, "The crown of the sun, when it has run through the day, four messengers take it, and bear it up to Heaven, and renew it, because it and its rays have been defiled on earth; moreover, it is so renewed each day." ⁵ And I Baruch said, "Lord, and why are its beams defiled on earth?" ⁶ And the messenger said to me, "Because it beholds the lawlessness and unrighteousness of men, namely fornications, adulteries, thefts, extortions, idolatries, drunkenness, murders, strife, jealousies, evil-speakings, murmurings, whisperings, divinations, and such like [these], which are not well-pleasing to God. On account of these things is it defiled, and therefore is it renewed. ⁷ But you ask concerning the bird, how it is exhausted: because by restraining the rays of the sun through the fire and burning heat of the whole day, it is exhausted thereby. ⁸ For, as we said before, unless his wings were screening the rays of the sun, no living creature would be preserved."

CHAPTER 9

¹ And they having retired, the night also fell, and at the same time the chariot of the moon came, along with the stars. ² And I, Baruch, said, "Lord, show me it also, I implore of you, how it goes forth, where it departs, and in what form it moves along." ³ And the messenger said, "Wait and you will also see it shortly." And on the next day I also saw it in the form of a woman, and [she was] sitting on a wheeled chariot. And before it there were oxen and lambs in the chariot, and a multitude of messengers in like manner. ⁴ And I said, "Lord, what are the oxen and the lambs?" ⁵ And he said to me, "They are also messengers." And again I asked, "Why is it that it at one time increases, but at another time decreases?" ⁶ And [he said to me], "Listen, O Baruch: this which you see had been written by God beautiful as no other. ⁷ And at the transgression of the first Adam, it was near to Sammael when he took the serpent as a garment. ⁸ And it did not hide itself but increased, and God was angry with it, and afflicted it, and shortened its days." ⁹ And I said, "And how does it not also shine always, but only in the night?" ¹⁰ And the messenger said, "Listen: as in the presence of a king, the courtiers cannot speak freely, so the moon and the stars cannot shine in the presence of the sun; for the stars are always suspended, but they are screened by the sun, and the moon, although it is uninjured, is consumed by the heat of the sun."

CHAPTER 10

¹ And when I had learned all these things from the chief-messenger, he took [me] and led me into [the] fourth heaven. ² And I saw a monotonous plain, and in the middle of it a pool of water. ³ And there were multitudes of birds in it of all kinds, but not like those here on earth. ⁴ But I saw a crane as great as great oxen; and all the birds were great beyond those in the world. ⁵ And I asked the messenger, "What is the plain, and what the pool, and what the multitudes of birds around it?" ⁶ And the messenger said, "Listen, Baruch: the plain which contains the pool in it and other wonders is the place where the souls of the righteous come, when they hold converse, living together in choirs. ⁷ But the water is that which the clouds receive, and rain on the earth, and the fruits increase." ⁸ And I said again to the messenger of the Lord, "But [what] are these birds?" And he said to me, "They are those which continually sing praise to the Lord." ⁹ And I said, "Lord, and how do men say that the water which descends in rain is from the sea?" ¹⁰ And the messenger said, "The water which descends in rain—this is also from the sea, and from the waters on earth; but that which stimulates the fruits is [only] from the latter source. ¹¹ Know therefore, henceforth, that from this source is what is called the dew of Heaven."

CHAPTER 11

¹ And the messenger took me and led me from there to [the] fifth heaven. And the gate was closed. ² And I said, "Lord, is this gateway not open that we may enter?" And the messenger said to me, "We cannot enter until Michael comes, who holds the keys of the Kingdom of Heaven; but wait and you will see the glory of God." ³ And there was a great sound, as thunder. And I said, "Lord, what is this sound?" ⁴ And he

said to me, "Even now Michael, the commander of the messengers, comes down to receive the prayers of men." **5** And behold a voice came, "Let the gates be opened." **6** And they opened them, and there was a roar as of thunder. **7** And Michael came, and the messenger who was with me came face to face with him and said, "Greetings, my commander, and that of all our order." **8** And the commander Michael said, "Greetings you also, our brother, and the interpreter of the revelations to those who pass through life virtuously." And having saluted one another thus, they stood still. **9** And I saw the commander Michael say, "Greetings you also, our brother, and the interpreter of the revelations to those who pass through life virtuously." **10** And having saluted one another thus, they stood still. And I saw the commander Michael, holding an exceedingly great vessel; its depth was as great as the distance from Heaven to earth, and its breadth as great as the distance from north to south. **11** And I said, "Lord, what is that which Michael the chief-messenger is holding?" **12** And he said to me, "This is where the merits of the righteous enter, and such good works as they do, which are escorted before the heavenly God."

CHAPTER 12

1 And as I was conversing with them, behold, messengers came bearing baskets full of flowers. **2** And they gave them to Michael. And I asked the messenger, "Lord, who are these, and what are the things brought here from beside them?" **3** And he said to me, "These are messengers [who] are over the righteous." **4** And the chief-messenger took the baskets and cast them into the vessel. **5** And the messenger said to me, "These flowers are the merits of the righteous." **6** And I saw other messengers bearing baskets which were [neither] empty nor full. **7** And they began to lament, and did not venture to draw near, because they did not have the prizes complete. **8** And Michael cried and said, "Come here, also, you messengers; bring what you have brought." And Michael was exceedingly grieved, and the messenger who was with me, because they did not fill the vessel.

CHAPTER 13

1 And then other messengers came in like manner, weeping and lamenting, and saying with fear, "Behold, how we are over-clouded, O Lord, for we were delivered to evil men, and we wish to depart from them." **2** And Michael said, "You cannot depart from them, in order that the enemy may not prevail to the end; but say to me what you ask." **3** And they said, "Please, Michael our commander, transfer us from them, for we cannot abide with wicked and foolish men, for there is nothing good in them, but every kind of unrighteousness and greed. **4** For we do not behold them entering [[into [the] assembly at all, nor among spiritual fathers, nor]] into any good work. **5** But where there is murder, there also are they in the midst, and where are fornications, adulteries, thefts, slanders, perjuries, jealousies, drunkenness, strife, envy, murmurings, whispering, idolatry, divination, and such like [these], then are they workers of such works, and of others worse. **6** For what reason we entreat that we may depart from them." **7** And Michael said to the messengers, "Wait until I learn from the Lord what will come to pass."

CHAPTER 14

1 And in that very hour Michael departed, and the doors were closed. **2** And there was a sound like thunder. And I asked the messenger, "What is the sound?" **3** And he said to me, "Michael is even now presenting the merits of men to God."

CHAPTER 15

1 And in that very hour Michael descended, and the gate was opened; and he brought oil. **2** And as for the messengers which brought the baskets which were full, he filled them with oil, saying, "Take it away, reward our friends a hundredfold, and those who have laboriously worked good works. For those

who sowed virtuously, also reap virtuously." **3** And he also said to those bringing the half-empty baskets, "Come here you also; take away the reward according as you brought, and deliver it to the sons of men." [[**4** Then he also said to those who brought the full and to those who brought the half-empty baskets: "Go and bless our friends, and say to them that thus says the Lord, You are faithful over a few things, I will set you over many things; enter into the joy of your Lord."

CHAPTER 16

1 And turning, he also said to those who brought nothing: "Thus says the Lord, Do not be sad of countenance, and do not weep, nor leave the sons of men alone. **2** But since they angered Me in their works, go and make them envious and angry and provoked against a people that is no people, a people that has no understanding. **3** Further, besides these, send forth the caterpillar and the unwinged locust, and the mildew, and the common locust, [and] hail with lightnings and anger, and punish them severely with the sword and with death, and their children with demons. **4** For they did not listen to My voice, nor did they observe My commandments, nor do them, but were despisers of My commandments, and insolent toward the priests who proclaimed My words to them."

CHAPTER 17

1 And while he yet spoke, the door was closed, and we withdrew. **2** And the messenger took me and restored me to the place where I was at the beginning. **3** And having come to myself, I gave glory to God, who counted me worthy of such honor. **4** For what reason you also, brothers, who obtained such a revelation, yourselves also glorify God, so that He also may glorify you, now and ever, and to all eternity. Amen.

4 BARUCH

4 Baruch, also called the Paralipomena of Jeremiah (meaning "things left out of Jeremiah"), appears as the title in several Ancient Greek manuscripts of the work. It is part of a larger Ethiopian Orthodox book that includes Lamentations and additions to Lamentations. 4 Baruch is usually dated to the first half of the 2nd century AD.

CHAPTER 1

1 It came to pass whenever the sons of Israel were taken captive by the king of the Chaldeans, that God spoke to Jeremiah, saying, "Jeremiah, my chosen one, arise and depart from this city, you and Baruch, since I am going to destroy it because of the multitude of the sins of those who dwell in it. **2** For your prayers are like a solid pillar in its midst, and like an impenetrable wall surrounding it. **3** Now then, arise and depart before the host of the Chaldeans surrounds it." **4** And Jeremiah answered, saying, "I implore You, Lord, permit me, Your servant, to speak in Your presence." **5** And the Lord said to him: "Speak, My chosen one Jeremiah." **6** And Jeremiah spoke, saying, "Lord Almighty, would You deliver the chosen city into the hands of the Chaldeans, so that the king with the multitude of his people might boast and say: I have prevailed over the holy city of God? **7** No, my Lord, but if it is Your will, let it be destroyed by Your hands." **9** "For neither the king nor his host will be able to enter it unless I first open its gates. **10** Arise, then, and go to Baruch, and tell him these words. **11** And when you have arisen at the sixth hour of the night, go out on the city walls and I will show you that unless I first destroy the city, they cannot enter it." **12** When the Lord had said this, He departed from Jeremiah.

CHAPTER 2

¹ And Jeremiah ran and told these things to Baruch; and as they went into the temple of God, Jeremiah tore his garments and put dust on his head and entered the holy place of God. ² And when Baruch saw him with dust sprinkled on his head and his garments torn, he cried out in a loud voice, saying, "Father Jeremiah, what are you doing? What sin has the people committed?" ³ For whenever the people sinned, Jeremiah would sprinkle dust on his head and would pray for the people until their sin was forgiven. ⁴ So Baruch asked him, saying, "Father, what is this?" ⁵ And Jeremiah said to him: "Refrain from rending your garments—rather, let us tear our hearts! And let us not draw water for the trough, but let us weep and fill them with tears! For the Lord will not have mercy on this people." ⁶ And Baruch said, "Father Jeremiah, what has happened?" ⁷ And Jeremiah said, "God is delivering the city into the hands of the king of the Chaldeans, to take the people captive into Babylon." ⁸ And when Baruch heard these things, he also tore his garments and said, "Father Jeremiah, who has made this known to you?" ⁹ And Jeremiah said to him: "Stay with me awhile, until the sixth hour of the night, so that you may know that this word is true." ¹⁰ Therefore they both remained near the altar, weeping, and their garments were torn.

captive." ⁴ But taking the keys of the temple, Jeremiah went outside the city and threw them away in the presence of the sun, saying, "I say to you, Sun, take the keys of the temple of God and guard them until the day in which the Lord asks you for them. ⁵ For we have not been found worthy to keep them, for we have become unfaithful guardians." ⁶ While Jeremiah was still weeping for the people, they brought him out with the people and dragged them into Babylon. ⁷ But Baruch put dust on his head and sat and wailed this lamentation, saying, "Why has Jerusalem been devastated? Because of the sins of the beloved people || She was delivered into the hands of enemies || Because of our sins and those of the people. ⁸ But do not let the lawless ones boast and say: We were strong enough to take the city of God by our might; But it was delivered to you because of our sins. ⁹ And God will pity us and cause us || To return to our city, || But you will not survive! ¹⁰ Blessed are our fathers, Abraham, Isaac and Jacob, || For they departed from this world || And did not see the destruction of this city." ¹¹ When he had said this, Baruch departed from the city, weeping and saying, "Grieving because of you, Jerusalem, I went out from you." ¹² And he remained sitting in a tomb, while the messengers came to him and explained to him everything that the Lord revealed to him through them.

CHAPTER 3

¹ And when the hour of the night arrived, as the Lord had told Jeremiah they came up together on the walls of the city, Jeremiah and Baruch. ² And behold, there came a sound of trumpets; and messengers emerged from Heaven holding torches in their hands, and they set them on the walls of the city. ³ And when Jeremiah and Baruch saw them, they wept, saying, "Now we know that the word is true!" ⁴ And Jeremiah implored the messengers, saying, "I implore you, do not destroy the city yet, until I say something to the Lord." ⁵ And the Lord spoke to the messengers, saying, "Do not destroy the city until I speak to My chosen one, Jeremiah." ⁶ Then Jeremiah spoke, saying, "I beg You, Lord, bid me to speak in Your presence." ⁷ And the Lord said, "Speak, My chosen one Jeremiah." ⁸ And Jeremiah said, "Behold, Lord, now we know that You are delivering the city into the hands of its enemies, and they will take the people away to Babylon. What do You want me to do with the holy vessels of the temple service?" ¹⁰ And the Lord said to him: "Take them and consign them to the earth, saying, Hear, Earth, the voice of Your Creator who formed you in the abundance of waters, who sealed you with seven seals for seven epochs, and after this you will receive your ornaments— ¹¹ guard the vessels of the temple service until the gathering of the beloved!" ¹² And Jeremiah spoke, saying, "I implore You, Lord, show me what I should do for Abimelech the Ethiopian, for he has done many kindnesses to Your servant Jeremiah. ¹³ For he pulled me out of the miry pit; and I do not wish that he should see the destruction and desolation of this city, but that You should be merciful to him and that he should not be grieved." ¹⁴ And the Lord said to Jeremiah: "Send him to the vineyard of Agrippa, and I will hide him in the shadow of the mountain until I cause the people to return to the city. ¹⁵ And you, Jeremiah, go with your people into Babylon and stay with them, preaching to them, until I cause them to return to the city. ¹⁶ But leave Baruch here until I speak with him." ¹⁷ When He had said these things, the Lord ascended from Jeremiah into Heaven. ¹⁸ But Jeremiah and Baruch entered the holy place, and taking the vessels of the temple service, they consigned them to the earth as the Lord had told them. ¹⁹ And immediately the earth swallowed them. ²⁰ And they both sat down and wept. ²¹ And when morning came, Jeremiah sent Abimelech, saying, "Take a basket and go to the estate of Agrippa by the mountain road, and bring back some figs to give to the sick among the people; for the favor of the Lord is on you and His glory is on your head." ²² And when he had said this, Jeremiah sent him away; and Abimelech went as he told him.

CHAPTER 4

¹ And when morning came, behold, the host of the Chaldeans surrounded the city. ² And the great messenger trumpeted, saying, "Enter the city, host of the Chaldeans; for behold, the gate is opened for you. ³ Therefore let the king enter, with his multitudes, and let him take all the people

CHAPTER 5

¹ But Abimelech took the figs in the burning heat; and coming on a tree, he sat under its shade to rest a bit. ² And leaning his head on the basket of figs, he fell asleep and slept for sixty-six years; and he was not awakened from his slumber. ³ And afterward, when he awoke from his sleep, he said, "I slept sweetly for a little while, but my head is heavy because I did not get enough sleep." ⁴ Then he uncovered the basket of figs and found them dripping milk. ⁵ And he said, "I would like to sleep a little longer, because my head is heavy. But I am afraid that I might fall asleep and be late in awakening and my father Jeremiah would think badly of me; for if he were not in a hurry, he would not have sent me today at daybreak. ⁶ So I will get up, and proceed in the burning heat; for isn't there heat, isn't there toil every day?" ⁷ So he got up and took the basket of figs and placed it on his shoulders, and he entered into Jerusalem and did not recognize it—neither his own house, nor the place—nor did he find his own family or any of his acquaintances. ⁸ And he said, "The Lord be blessed, for a great trance has come over me today! ⁹ This is not the city Jerusalem—and I have lost my way because I came by the mountain road when I arose from my sleep; and since my head was heavy because I did not get enough sleep, I lost my way. ¹⁰ It will seem incredible to Jeremiah that I lost my way!" ¹¹ And he departed from the city; and as he searched he saw the landmarks of the city, and he said, "Indeed, this is the city; I lost my way." ¹² And again he returned to the city and searched, and found no one of his own people; and he said, "The Lord be blessed, for a great trance has come over me!" ¹³ And again he departed from the city, and he stayed there grieving, not knowing where he should go. ¹⁴ And he put down the basket, saying, "I will sit here until the Lord takes this trance from me." ¹⁵ And as he sat, he saw an old man coming from the field; and Abimelech said to him: "I say to you, old man, what city is this?" ¹⁶ And he said to him: "It is Jerusalem." ¹⁷ And Abimelech said to him: "Where is Jeremiah the priest, and Baruch the secretary, and all the people of this city, for I could not find them?" ¹⁸ And the old man said to him: "Are you not from this city, seeing that you remember Jeremiah today, because you are asking about him after such a long time? ¹⁹ For Jeremiah is in Babylon with the people; for they were taken captive by King Nebuchadnezzar, and Jeremiah is with them to preach the good news to them and to teach them the word." ²⁰ As soon as Abimelech heard this from the old man, he said, "If you were not an old man, and if it were not for the fact that it is not lawful for a man to scold one older than himself, I would laugh at you and say that you are out of your mind— since you say that the people have been taken captive into Babylon. ²¹ Even if the heavenly torrents had descended on them, there has not yet been time for them to go into Babylon! ²² For how much time has passed since my father Jeremiah sent me to the estate of Agrippa to bring a few figs, so that I might give them to the sick among the people? ²³ And I went and got them, and when I came to a certain tree in the burning heat, I sat to rest a little; and I leaned my head on the basket and fell asleep. ²⁴ And when I awoke, I uncovered the basket

of figs, supposing that I was late; and I found the figs dripping milk, just as I had collected them. **25** But you claim that the people have been taken captive into Babylon. **26** But that you might know, take the figs and see!" **27** And he uncovered the basket of figs for the old man, and he saw them dripping milk. **28** And when the old man saw them, he said, "O my son, you are a righteous man, and God did not want you to see the desolation of the city, so He brought this trance on you. **29** For behold it is sixty-six years today since the people were taken captive into Babylon. **30** But that you might learn, my son, that what I tell you is true—look into the field and see that the ripening of the crops has not appeared. **31** And notice that the figs are not in season, and be enlightened." **32** Then Abimelech cried out in a loud voice, saying, "I bless You, God of the heavens and earth, the Rest of the souls of the righteous in every place!" **33** Then he said to the old man: "What month is this?" **34** And he said, "Nisan," which is Abib. **35** And taking some of [the] figs, he gave them to the old man and said to him: "May God illuminate your way to the city above—Jerusalem."

CHAPTER 6

1 After this, Abimelech went out of the city and prayed to the Lord. **2** And behold, a messenger of the Lord came and took him by the right hand and brought him back to where Baruch was sitting, and he found him in a tomb. **3** And when they saw each other, they both wept and kissed each other. **4** But when Baruch looked up, he saw with his own eyes the figs that were covered in Abimelech's basket. **5** And lifting his eyes to Heaven, he prayed, saying, **6** "You are the God who gives a reward to those who love You. Prepare yourself, my heart, and rejoice and be glad while you are in your dwelling place, saying to your fleshly house, Your grief has been changed to joy; for the Sufficient One is coming and will deliver you in your dwelling place—for there is no sin in you. **7** Revive in your dwelling place, in your virginal faith, and believe that you will live! **8** Look at this basket of figs—for behold, they are sixty-six years old and have not become shrivelled or rotten, but they are dripping milk. **9** So it will be with you, my flesh, if you do what is commanded of you by the messenger of righteousness. **10** He who preserved the basket of figs, the same will again preserve you by his power." **11** When Baruch had said this, he said to Abimelech: "Stand up and let us pray that the Lord may make known to us how we will be able to send to Jeremiah in Babylon the report about the shelter provided for you on the way." **12** And Baruch prayed, saying, "Lord God, our strength is the chosen light which comes forth from Your mouth. **13** We implore and beg of Your goodness—You whose great Name no one is able to know—hear the voice of Your servants and let knowledge come into our hearts. **14** What will we do, and how will we send this report to Jeremiah in Babylon?" **15** And while Baruch was still praying, behold a messenger of the Lord came and said all these words to Baruch: "Agent of the light, do not be anxious about how you will send to Jeremiah; for an eagle is coming to you at the hour of light tomorrow, and you will direct him to Jeremiah. **16** Therefore, write in a letter: Say to the sons of Israel: Let the stranger who comes among you be set apart and let fifteen days go by; and after this I will lead you into your city, says the Lord. **17** He who is not separated from Babylon will not enter into the city; and I will punish them by keeping them from being received back by the Babylonians, says the Lord." **18** And when the messenger had said this, he departed from Baruch. **19** And Baruch sent to the market of the nations and got papyrus and ink and wrote a letter as follows: Baruch, the servant of God, writes to Jeremiah in the captivity of Babylon: **20** Greetings! Rejoice, for God has not allowed us to depart from this body grieving for the city which was laid waste and outraged. **21** For what reason the Lord has had compassion on our tears, and has remembered the covenant which He established with our fathers Abraham, Isaac, and Jacob. **22** And he sent His messenger to me, and he told me these words which I send to you. **23** These, then, are the words which the Lord, the God of Israel, spoke, who led us out of Egypt, out of the great furnace: Because you did not keep My ordinances, but your heart was lifted up, and you were haughty before Me, in anger and wrath I delivered you to the furnace in Babylon. **24** If, therefore, says the Lord, you listen to My voice, from the mouth of Jeremiah My servant, I will bring the one who listens up from Babylon; but the one who does not listen will become a stranger to Jerusalem and to Babylon. **25** And you will test them by means of the water of the Jordan; whoever

does not listen will be exposed—this is the sign of the great seal.

CHAPTER 7

1 And Baruch got up and departed from the tomb and found the eagle sitting outside the tomb. **2** And the eagle said to him in a human voice: "Greetings, Baruch, steward of the faith." **3** And Baruch said to him: "You who speak are chosen from among all the birds of Heaven, for this is clear from the gleam of your eyes; tell me, then, what are you doing here?" **4** And the eagle said to him: "I was sent here so that you might send whatever message you want through me." **5** And Baruch said to him: "Can you carry this message to Jeremiah in Babylon?" **6** And the eagle said to him: "Indeed, it was for this reason I was sent." **7** And Baruch took the letter, and fifteen figs from Abimelech's basket, and tied them to the eagle's neck and said to him: "I say to you, king of the birds, go in peace with good health and carry the message for me. **8** Do not be like the raven which Noah sent out and which never came back to him in the Ark; but be like the dove which, the third time, brought a report to the righteous one. **9** So you also, take this good message to Jeremiah and to those in bondage with him, that it may be well with you. Take this papyrus to the people and to the chosen one of God. **10** Even if all the birds of Heaven surround you and want to fight with you, struggle—the Lord will give you strength. **11** And do not turn aside to the right or to the left, but straight as a speeding arrow, go in the power of God, and the glory of the Lord will be with you the entire way." **12** Then the eagle took flight and went away to Babylon, having the letter tied to his neck; and when he arrived, he rested on a post outside the city in a desert place. **13** And he kept silent until Jeremiah came along, for he and some of the people were coming out to bury a corpse outside the city. **14** For Jeremiah had petitioned King Nebuchadnezzar, saying, "Give me a place where I may bury those of my people who have died"; and the king gave it to him. **15** And as they were coming out with the body, and weeping, they came to where the eagle was. **16** And the eagle cried out in a loud voice, saying, "I say to you, Jeremiah the chosen one of God, go and gather together the people and come here so that they may hear a letter which I have brought to you from Baruch and Abimelech." **17** And when Jeremiah heard this, he glorified God; and he went and gathered together the people along with their wives and children, and he came to where the eagle was. **18** And the eagle came down on the corpse, and it revived. **19** Now this took place so that they might believe. **20** And all the people were astounded at what had happened, and said, "This is the God who appeared to our fathers in the wilderness through Moses, and now he has appeared to us through the eagle." **21** And the eagle said, "I say to you, Jeremiah, come, untie this letter and read it to the people"—so he untied the letter and read it to the people. **22** And when the people heard it, they wept and put dust on their heads, and they said to Jeremiah: "Deliver us and tell us what to do that we may once again enter our city." **23** And Jeremiah answered and said to them: "Do whatever you heard from the letter, and the Lord will lead us into our city." **24** And Jeremiah wrote a letter to Baruch, saying thus: My beloved son, do not be negligent in your prayers, imploring God on our behalf, that He might direct our way until we come out of the jurisdiction of this lawless king. **25** For you have been found righteous before God, and He did not let you come here, lest you see the affliction which has come on the people at the hands of the Babylonians. **26** For it is like a father with an only son, who is given over for punishment; and those who see his father and console him cover his face, lest he see how his son is being punished, and be even more ravaged by grief. **27** For thus God took pity on you and did not let you enter Babylon lest you see the affliction of the people. **28** For since we came here, grief has not left us, for sixty-six years today. **29** For many times when I went out I found some of the people hung up by King Nebuchadnezzar, crying and saying, "Have mercy on us, God-Zar!" **30** When I heard this, I grieved and cried with double mourning, not only because they were hung up, but because they were calling on a foreign god, saying, "Have mercy on us." **31** But I remembered days of festivity which we celebrated in Jerusalem before our captivity; and when I remembered, I groaned, and returned to my house wailing and weeping. **32** Now, then, pray in the place where you are—you and Abimelech—for this people, that they may listen to my voice and to the decrees of my mouth, so that we may depart from here. **33** For I tell you that the entire time that we have spent here they have kept us in subjection, saying, "Recite for us a song from the songs of Zion—the song of your God." **34** And we reply to them: "How will we sing for you since we are in a foreign land?" **35** And after this, Jeremiah tied the letter to the eagle's neck, saying, "Go in peace, and may the Lord watch over both of us." **36** And the eagle took flight and came to Jerusalem and gave the letter to Baruch; and when he had untied it he read it and kissed it and wept when he heard about the distresses and afflictions of the people. **37** But Jeremiah took the figs and distributed them to the sick among the people, and he kept teaching them to abstain from the pollutions of the nations of Babylon.

CHAPTER 8

1 And the day came in which the Lord brought the people out of Babylon. **2** And the Lord said to Jeremiah: "Rise up—you and the people—and come to the Jordan and say to the people: Let anyone who desires the Lord forsake the works of Babylon. **3** As for the men who took wives from them and the women who took husbands from them—those who listen to you will cross over, and you take them into Jerusalem; but those who do not listen to you, do not lead them there." **4** And Jeremiah spoke these words to the people, and they arose and came to the Jordan to cross over. **5** As he told them the words that the Lord had spoken to him, half of those who had taken spouses from them did not wish to listen to Jeremiah, but said to him: "We will never forsake our wives, but we will bring them back with us into our city." **6** So they crossed the Jordan and came to Jerusalem. **7** And Jeremiah and Baruch and Abimelech stood up and said, "No man joined with Babylonians will enter this city!" **8** And they said to one another: "Let us arise and return to Babylon—to our place." And they departed. **9** But while they were coming to Babylon, the Babylonians came out to meet them, saying, "You will not enter our city, for you hated us and you left us secretly; therefore you cannot come in with us. **10** For we have taken a solemn oath together in the name of our god to receive neither you nor your children, since you left us secretly." **11** And when they heard this, they returned and came to a desert place some distance from Jerusalem and built a city for themselves and named it Samaria. **12** And Jeremiah sent to them, saying, "Convert, for the messenger of righteousness is coming and will lead you to your exalted place."

CHAPTER 9

1 Now those who were with Jeremiah were rejoicing and offering sacrifices on behalf of the people for nine days. **2** But on the tenth, Jeremiah alone offered sacrifice. **3** And he prayed a prayer, saying, "Holy, Holy, Holy, Fragrant Aroma of the living trees, True Light that enlightens me until I ascend to You; **4** For Your mercy, I beg You—for the sweet voice of the two seraphim, I beg—for another fragrant aroma. **5** And may Michael, chief-messenger of righteousness, who opens the gates to the righteous, be my guardian until he causes the righteous to enter. **6** I beg You, almighty Lord of all creation, unbegotten and incomprehensible, in whom all judgment was hidden before these things came into existence." **7** When Jeremiah had said this, and while he was standing near the altar with Baruch and Abimelech, he became as one whose soul had departed. **8** And Baruch and Abimelech were weeping and crying out in a loud voice: "Woe to us! For our father Jeremiah has left us—the priest of God has departed!" **9** And all the people heard their weeping, and they all ran to them and saw Jeremiah lying on the ground as if dead. **10** And they tore their garments and put dust on their heads and wept bitterly. **11** And after this they prepared to bury him. **12** And behold, there came a voice, saying, "Do not bury the one who yet lives, for his soul is returning to his body!" **13** And when they heard the voice they did not bury him, but stayed around his dwelling place for three days, saying, "When will he arise?" **14** And after three days his soul came back into his body and he raised his voice in the midst of them all and said, "Glorify God with one voice! All of you glorify God and the Son of God who awakens us—Messiah Jesus—the Light of all the ages, the inextinguishable Lamp, the Life of faith. **15** But after these times there will be four hundred

seventy-seven years more, and He comes to earth. **16** And the Tree of Life planted in the midst of paradise will cause all the unfruitful trees to bear fruit, and will grow and sprout forth. **17** And the trees that had sprouted and became haughty, and said, We have supplied our power to the air, He will cause them to wither, with the grandeur of their branches, and He will cause them to be judged—that firmly rooted tree! **18** And what is crimson will become white as wool—the snow will be blackened—the sweet waters will become salty, and the salty sweet, in the intense light of the joy of God. **19** And He will bless the isles so that they become fruitful by the word of the mouth of His Messiah. **20** For He will come, and He will go out and choose for Himself twelve apostles to proclaim the news among the nations—He whom I have seen adorned by His Father and coming into the world on the Mount of Olives—and He will fill the hungry souls." **21** When Jeremiah was saying this concerning the Son of God—that He is coming into the world— the people became very angry and said, "This is a repetition of the words spoken by Isaiah son of Amos, when he said, I saw God and the Son of God. **22** Come, then, and let us not kill him by the same sort of death with which we killed Isaiah, but let us stone him with stones." **23** And Baruch and Abimelech were greatly grieved because they wanted to hear in full the mysteries that he had seen. **24** But Jeremiah said to them: "Be silent and do not weep, for they cannot kill me until I describe for you everything I saw." **25** And he said to them: "Bring a stone here to me." **26** And he set it up and said, "Light of the ages, make this stone to become like me in appearance, until I have described to Baruch and Abimelech everything I saw." **27** Then the stone, by God's command, took on the appearance of Jeremiah. **28** And they were stoning the stone, supposing that it was Jeremiah! **29** But Jeremiah delivered to Baruch and to Abimelech all the mysteries he had seen, and immediately he stood in the midst of the people desiring to complete his ministry. **30** Then the stone cried out, saying, "O foolish sons of Israel, why do you stone me, supposing that I am Jeremiah? Behold, Jeremiah is standing in your midst!" **31** And when they saw him, immediately they rushed on him with many stones, and his ministry was fulfilled. **32** And when Baruch and Abimelech came, they buried him, and taking the stone they placed it on his tomb and inscribed it thus: This is the stone that was the ally of Jeremiah.

APOCRYPHON OF EZEKIEL

The Apocryphon of Ezekiel, also called 2 Ezekiel, was likely composed in the 1st century BC or 1st century AD, with later Christian interpolations. It is quoted in a number of early works. Fragment 1 comes from the Dead Sea Scrolls and was quoted in the letter of Bar-Naba and the Revelation of Peter. Fragment 2 is identified from a quotation of the Apocryphon found in 1 Clement chapter 8. Fragment 3 was identified with Ezekiel by Tertullian. Fragment 4 was attributed to Jesus by Justin Martyr, and sourced from the Apocryphon by other early writers. Fragment 5 is found in the writings of Clement of Alexandria, among others. Fragment 6 was attributed to Ezekiel by Epiphanius but is dissimilar to the other fragments.

FRAGMENT 1

1 These are the words of Ezekiel. And the word of the Lord came to me, saying, "Son of man, prophesy and say, Behold, the day of the destruction of the nations is coming; **2** . . . Egypt, and there will be anguish in Put, and a sword in Egypt . . . will shake, Cush and Put, and the mighty ones of Egypt, also some of the children of the covenant, and Arabia will fall at the gates of Egypt. **3** And . . . will perish . . . by the sword of Egypt . . . will be devastated . . . you will not die . . . **4** For I am the Lord, who redeems My people, giving the covenant to them." **5** And I said, "O Lord, I have seen many from Israel who have loved Your Name and walked in the ways of righteousness. **6** So, when will these things come to pass? And how will they be rewarded for their piety?" **7** And the Lord said to me, "I will make it manifest . . . the sons of Israel to see, and they will know that I am the Lord." **8** And He said, "Son of man, prophesy over these bones, and speak to the bone, and let them be joined bone to its bone, and joint to its joint." And it was so. **9** And He said a second time, "Prophesy, and let sinews come on them and let skin cover them." And it was so. **10** And He said, "Again, prophesy to the four winds of the heavens, and let them blow on the slain." And it was so. **11** And a great multitude of men came to life. And they blessed the Lord of Hosts who had given life to them. **12** And I said, "O Lord, when will these things be completed?" And the Lord said to me, ". . . and after many days, a piece of wood falls down and rises again [[and when blood drips from a tree]]." **13** . . . and . . . Lord. And all the people arose and stood on their feet to give thanks . . . and to praise the Lord of Hosts. **14** And I also spoke with them . . . And the Lord said to me, "Son of man, say to them . . . in their graves they will lie until . . . from your tombs and from the earth . . . that the yoke of Egypt . . . land, and they will know that I am the Lord." **15** And He said to me, "Look, son of man, at the land of Israel." And I said, "I have seen, O Lord, and behold it is a wasteland. When will You gather them together?" **16** And the Lord said, "A son of Belial is planning to oppress My people, but I will not permit him. His dominion will not persist; and from the impure, no seed will survive, nor will new wine come from the caper bush, nor will a hornet make honey . . . and I will slay the wicked in Memphis. **17** But I will bring My sons out of Memphis, and I will turn toward their remnant. As they will say, There was peace and quiet, they will say, The land will be as it was in the days of . . . old. Therefore, I will arouse wrath on them from the four winds of the heavens . . . like a devouring fire as . . . and he will show no mercy on the poor, but he will bring them to Babel." **18** And Babel is but a cup in the hand of the Lord, in her time He will cast her away . . . in Babel and it will be . . . a dwelling place for demons . . . desolation and . . . will pasture . . . to Babel . . . instead of my grief make my soul rejoice. **19** And the days will hasten quickly until men say, "Are not the days hastening so that the sons of Israel might take possession?" **20** And the Lord said to me, "I will not turn your face away, Ezekiel. Behold, I am cutting short the days and the years . . . a few, just [as] you said to Me . . . For the mouth of the Lord has spoken these things. **21** . . . And My people will be . . . with a cheerful heart and with a willing soul . . . and hide a little while . . . and from the breaches . . ." **22** . . . the vision which Ezekiel saw . . . the brightness of the chariot, and the four living creatures, a living creature . . . and as they moved they did not turn back. **23** Every living creature moved on two wheels, and its two legs . . . on . . . in one there was breath. **24** And their faces were one beside the other. And the appearance of the faces: one of a lion, one of an eagle, one of a calf, and one of a man. **25** And the hand of a man was joined to the backs of the living creatures and attached to their wings . . . and the wheels . . . wheel joined to wheel when they moved, and from both sides of the wheels were streams of fire, **26** and in the midst of the coals were living creatures like flaming coals . . . and the wheels, the living creatures and the wheels. **27** Now there was . . . over their heads an expanse, like an awesome gleam of crystal. And a voice came from above the expanse . . .

FRAGMENT 2

1 Convert, house of Israel, from your lawless ways. **2** I say to you—My people—even if the list of your sins stretches from Heaven to earth, and if they are as black as they can be, and you turn to Me, and with all of your heart say, "Father," I will forgive you, and look on you as holy.

FRAGMENT 3

1 Look at the cow, she has calved, and yet she is pregnant . . .

FRAGMENT 4

1 In this manner, our Lord Jesus Christ also said, "It is what I have seen you doing that I will judge you for."

FRAGMENT 5

1 "And I will bind up the lame persons, and I will heal the sick, and I will bring back the wandering. **2** And I will feed them on My holy mountain, and I will be their Shepherd, and I will be closer to them than a garment is to their skin. **3** They will call Me, and I will say, Behold, here I am. And if they cross, they will not slip," says the Lord.

FRAGMENT 6

[[**1** A certain king had everyone in his kingdom drafted, and had no civilians with an exception of two: one lame and one blind, and each one lived by himself in his own home. **2** And when the king was preparing a wedding feast for his own son, he invited everyone in his kingdom, but he despised the two civilians, the lame man and the blind man. **3** And they were indignant within themselves and resolved to carry out a plot against the king. Now the king had a garden. **4** And the blind man addressed the lame man from a distance, saying, "How much would our crumb of bread have been among the crowds who were invited to the celebration? So come on, let us retaliate [against] him for what he did to us!" "How?" asked the other. **5** And [the blind man] said, "Let us go into his garden, and there, ruin the other things in the garden." But [the lame man] said, "But how can I, for I am lame and unable to crawl?" **6** And the blind man said, "Am I able to do anything myself, since I am unable to see where I am going? But let us use trickery." **7** Plucking the nearby grass and braiding a rope, [the lame man] threw [it] to the blind man, and said, "Grab [it], and come here to me by rope." **8** And he did as he had urged. When he neared, [the lame man] said, "Come here. You be [my] feet and carry me, and I will be your eyes, guiding you from on top to the right and to the left." **9** So by doing this, they went down into the garden. And whether they did any damage or not, nevertheless their footprints were visible in the garden. **10** Now when the celebrants dispersed from the wedding feast, going down into the garden, they were surprised to find the footprints in the garden. **11** So they reported these things to the king, saying, "Everyone in your kingdom is a soldier and no one is a civilian. So why are there civilian footprints in the garden?" **12** And [the king] was astounded. So he summoned the lame man and the blind man. **13** And he asked the blind man, "Did you not come down into the garden?" But [the blind man] replied, "Who—me, lord? You see my handicap, you know that I cannot see where I walk." **14** Then approaching the lame man, [the king] also asked him, "Did you come down into my garden?" **15** And answering, he said, "O lord, do you wish to embitter my soul over my handicap?" **16** And finally the judgment was delayed. What then did the righteous judge do? **17** Realizing in what manner the two had joined together, he put the lame man on the blind man and examined them both under the lash. **18** And they were unable to deny [it]. They each convicted the other. **19** The lame man, on the one hand, said to the blind man, "Did you not pick me up and carry me?" **20** And the blind man said to the lame man, "Did you yourself not become my eyes?"]

DIDACHE

Didache, which means "Teaching," is a very early Christian treatise purporting to have been written by the Twelve Apostles per the opening line. It is thought to have been written between 50 and 150 AD. The document covers basic Christian principles of godly living, conversion, and ritual.

The Lord's teaching to the heathen by the Twelve Apostles.

1 There are two Ways, one of Life and one of Death, and there is a great difference between the two Ways. **2** The Way of Life is this: "First, you will love the God who made you, secondly, your neighbor as yourself; and whatever you would not have done to yourself, do not do to another." **3** Now, the teaching of these words is this: "Bless those that curse you, and pray for your enemies, and fast for those that persecute you. For what credit is it to you if you love those that love you? Do not even the heathen do the same?" But, for your part, "love those that hate you," and you will have no enemy. **4** "Abstain from carnal and bodily lusts." "If any man strikes you on the right cheek, turn to him the other cheek also," and you will be perfect. "If any man impresses you to go with him one mile, go with him two. If any man takes your coat, give him your shirt also. If any man will take from you what is yours, do not refuse it"—not even if you can. **5** Give to everyone that asks you, and do not refuse, for the Father's will is that we give to all from the gifts we have received. Blessed is he that gives according to the mandate; for he is innocent. Woe to him who receives; for if any man receive alms under pressure of need he is innocent; but he who receives it without need will be tried as to why he took and for what, and being in prison, he will be examined as to his deeds, and "he will not come out from there until he pays the last penny." **6** But concerning this it was also said, "Let your alms sweat into your hands until you know to whom you are giving."

ransom for your sins. **7** You will not hesitate to give, nor will you grumble when you give, for you will know who the good Paymaster of the reward is. **8** You will not turn the needy away, but will share everything with your brother, and will not say that it is your own, for if you are sharers in the imperishable, how much more in the things which perish? **9** You will not withhold your hand from your son or from your daughter, but you will teach them the fear of God from their youth up. **10** You will not command in your bitterness your slave or your handmaid, who hope in the same God, lest they cease to fear the God who is over you both; for He does not come to call men with respect of persons, but those whom the Spirit has prepared. **11** But you who are slaves, be subject to your master, as to God's representative, in reverence and fear. **12** You will hate all hypocrisy, and everything that is not pleasing to the Lord. **13** You will not forsake the commands of the Lord, but you will keep what you received, "adding nothing to it and taking nothing away." **14** In the congregation you will confess your transgressions, and you will not go yourself to prayer with an evil conscience. This is the Way of Life.

CHAPTER 2

1 But the second command of the teaching is this: **2** "You will not murder; you will not commit adultery"; you will not commit sodomy; you will not commit fornication; you will not steal; you will not use magic; you will not use love potions; you will not procure abortion, nor commit infanticide; "you will not covet your neighbor's goods"; **3** you will not commit perjury, "you will not bear false witness"; you will not speak evil; you will not bear malice. **4** You will not be double-minded nor double-tongued, for to be double-tongued is the snare of death. **5** Your speech will not be false, nor vain, but completed in action. **6** You will not be covetous nor extortionate, nor a hypocrite, nor malignant, nor proud; you will make no evil plan against your neighbor. **7** You will hate no man; but some you will reprove, and for some you will pray, and some you will love more than your own life.

CHAPTER 3

1 My child, flee from every evil man and from all like him. **2** Do not be proud, for pride leads to murder, nor jealous, nor contentious, nor passionate, for from all these murders are engendered. **3** My child, do not be lustful, for lust leads to fornication, nor a speaker of base words, nor a lifter up of the eyes, for from all these is adultery engendered. **4** My child, do not regard omens, for this leads to idolatry; neither be an enchanter, nor an astrologer, nor a magician, neither wish to see these things, for from them all is idolatry engendered. **5** My child, do not be a liar, for lying leads to theft, nor a lover of money, nor vainglorious, for from all these things are thefts engendered. **6** My child, do not be a grumbler, for this leads to blasphemy, nor stubborn, nor a thinker of evil, for from all these are blasphemies engendered, **7** but be "meek, for the meek will inherit the earth"; **8** be long-suffering, and merciful, and guileless, and quiet, and good, and always fearing the words which you have heard. **9** You will not exalt yourself, nor let your soul be presumptuous. Your soul will not consort with the lofty, but you will walk with righteous and humble men. **10** Receive the accidents that befall you as good, knowing that nothing happens without God.

CHAPTER 4

1 My child, you will remember, day and night, him who speaks the word of God to you, and you will honor him as the Lord, for where the Lord's nature is spoken of, there He is present. **2** And you will seek daily the presence of the holy ones, that you may find rest in their words. **3** You will not desire a schism, but will reconcile those that strive. You will give righteous judgment; you will favor no man's person in reproving transgression. **4** You will not be of two minds whether it will be or not. **5** Do not be one who stretches out his hands to receive, but shuts them when it comes to giving. **6** Of whatever you have gained by your hands you will give a

CHAPTER 5

1 But the Way of Death is this: first of all, it is wicked and full of cursing, murders, adulteries, lusts, fornications, thefts, idolatries, witchcrafts, charms, robberies, false witness, hypocrisies, a double heart, fraud, pride, malice, stubbornness, covetousness, foul speech, jealousy, impudence, haughtiness, boastfulness. **2** Persecutors of the good, haters of truth, lovers of lies, not knowing the reward of righteousness, not cleaving to the good nor to righteous judgment, spending wakeful nights not for good but for wickedness, from whom meekness and patience is far, lovers of vanity, following after reward, unmerciful to the poor, not working for him who is oppressed with toil, without knowledge of Him who made them, murderers of children, corrupters of God's creatures, turning away the needy, oppressing the distressed, advocates of the rich, unjust judges of the poor, altogether sinful; may you be delivered, my children, from all these.

CHAPTER 6

1 See "that no one make you to err" from this Way of the teaching, for he teaches you without God. **2** For if you can bear the whole yoke of the Lord, you will be perfect, but if you cannot, do what you can. **3** And concerning food, bear what you can, but keep strictly from that which is offered to idols, for it is the worship of dead gods.

CHAPTER 7

1 Concerning immersion, immerse thus: having first rehearsed all these things, "immerse in the Name of the Father, and of the Son, and of the Holy Spirit," in running water; **2** but if you have no running water, immerse in other water, and if you cannot in cold, then in warm. **3** But if you have neither, pour water three times on the head "in the Name of the Father, Son, and Holy Spirit." **4** And before the immersion let the immerser and him who is to be immersed fast, and any others who are able. And you will bid him who is to be immersed to fast one or two days before.

CHAPTER 8

1 Do not let your fasts be with the hypocrites, for they fast on Mondays and Thursdays, but you fast on Wednesdays and Fridays. **2** And do not pray as the hypocrites, but as the Lord commanded in His good news, pray thus: "Our Father who is in Heaven, hallowed be Your Name, Your Kingdom come, Your will be done, as in Heaven so also on earth; give us today our daily bread, and forgive us our debt as we forgive our debtors, and do not lead us into trial, but deliver us from the evil [one], for Yours is the power and the glory for all time." **3** Pray thus three times a day.

CHAPTER 9

[1] And concerning the Thanksgiving, hold Thanksgiving thus: [2] first concerning the cup: "We give thanks to You, our Father, for the Holy Vine of Your child David, which You made known to us through Your Child Jesus. To You be glory for all time." [3] And concerning the broken bread: "We give You thanks, our Father, for the life and knowledge which You made known to us through Your Child Jesus. To You be glory for all time. [4] As this broken bread was scattered on the mountains, but was brought together and became one, so let Your Assembly be gathered together from the ends of the earth into Your Kingdom, for Yours is the glory and the power through Jesus Christ for all time." [5] But let none eat or drink of Your Thanksgiving except those who have been immersed in the Lord's Name. For concerning this also the Lord said, "Do not give that which is holy to the dogs."

CHAPTER 10

[1] But after you are satisfied with food, thus give thanks: [2] "We give thanks to You, O Holy Father, for Your Holy Name which You made to dwell in our hearts, and for the knowledge, and faith, and immortality which You made known to us through Your Child Jesus. To You be glory for all time. [3] You, Lord Almighty, created all things for Your Name's sake, and gave food and drink to men for their enjoyment, that they might give thanks to You, but You have blessed us with spiritual food and drink and continuous light through Your Child. [4] Above all we give thanks to You for that You are mighty. To You be glory for all time. [5] Remember, Lord, Your Assembly, to deliver it from all evil and to make it perfect in Your love, and gather it together in its holiness from the four winds to Your Kingdom which You have prepared for it. For Yours is the power and the glory for all time. [6] Let grace come and let this world pass away. Hosanna to the God of David. If any man is holy, let him come! If any man is not, let him convert: Maranatha! Amen!" [7] But permit the prophets to hold Thanksgiving as they will.

CHAPTER 11

[1] Whoever then comes and teaches you all these things previously mentioned, receive him. [2] But if the teacher himself is perverted and teaches another doctrine to destroy these things, do not listen to him, but if his teaching is for the increase of righteousness and knowledge of the Lord, receive him as the Lord. [3] And concerning the apostles and prophets, act thus according to the ordinance of the good news. [4] Let every apostle who comes to you be received as the Lord, [5] but do not let him stay more than one day, or if need be a second as well; but if he stays three days, he is a false prophet. [6] And when an apostle goes forth let him accept nothing but bread until he reaches his night's lodging; but if he asks for money, he is a false prophet. [7] Do not test or examine any prophet who is speaking in [the] Spirit, "for every sin will be forgiven, but this sin will not be forgiven." [8] But not everyone who speaks in a spirit is a prophet, except [if] he has the behavior of the Lord. From his behavior, then, the false prophet and the true prophet will be known. [9] And no prophet who orders a meal in [the] Spirit will eat of it: otherwise, he is a false prophet. [10] And every prophet who teaches the truth, if he does not do what he teaches, is a false prophet. [11] But no prophet who has been tried and is genuine, though he enacts a worldly mystery of the Assembly, if he does not teach others to do what he does himself, will be judged by you; for he has his judgment with God, for so also did the prophets of old. [12] But whoever will say in a spirit "Give me money, or something else," you will not listen to him; but if he tells you to give on behalf of others in want, let none judge him.

CHAPTER 12

[1] Let everyone who "comes in the Name of the Lord" be received; but when you have tested him you will know him, for you will have understanding of true and false. [2] If he who

comes is a traveler, help him as much as you can, but he will not remain with you more than two days, or, if need be, three. [3] And if he wishes to settle among you and has a craft, let him work for his bread. [4] But if he has no craft provide for him according to your understanding, so that no man will live among you in idleness because he is a Christian. [5] But if he will not do so, he is making traffic of Christ; beware of such.

CHAPTER 13

[1] But every true prophet who wishes to settle among you is "worthy of his food." [2] Likewise, a true teacher is himself worthy, like the workman, of his food. [3] Therefore you will take the first-fruit of the produce of the winepress and of the threshing-floor, and of oxen and sheep, and will give them as the first-fruits to the prophets, for they are your chief priests. [4] But if you do not have a prophet, give to the poor. [5] If you make bread, take the first-fruits, and give it according to the command. [6] Likewise, when you open a jar of wine or oil, give the first-fruits to the prophets. [7] Of money also and clothes, and of all your possessions, take the first-fruits, as it seems best to you, and give according to the command.

CHAPTER 14

[1] On the Lord's Day come together, break bread, and hold Thanksgiving, after confessing your transgressions that your offering may be pure; [2] but let none who has a quarrel with his fellow join in your meeting until they are reconciled, that your sacrifice is not defiled. [3] For this is that which was spoken by the Lord, "In every place and time offer Me a pure sacrifice, for I am a great King," says the Lord, "and My Name is wonderful among the heathen."

CHAPTER 15

[1] Therefore, appoint for yourselves overseers and servants worthy of the Lord—meek men, and not lovers of money, and truthful and approved, for they also minister to you the ministry of the prophets and teachers. [2] Therefore do not despise them, for they are your honorable men together with the prophets and teachers. [3] And do not reprove one another in wrath, but in peace as you find in the good news, and let none speak with any who has done a wrong to his neighbor, nor let him hear a word from you until he converts. [4] But perform your prayers, and kindness, and all your acts as you find in the good news of our Lord.

CHAPTER 16

[1] "Watch" over your life; do not "let your lamps" be quenched; and do not "let your loins" be ungirded; but be "ready," for you have not known "the hour in which our Lord comes." [2] But be frequently gathered together seeking the things which are profitable for your souls, for the whole time of your faith will not profit you except you be found perfect at the last time; [3] for in the last days the false prophets and the corrupters will be multiplied, and the sheep will be turned into wolves, and love will change to hate; [4] for as lawlessness increases they will hate one another, and persecute, and betray, and then the deceiver of the world will appear as a son of God, and he will do signs and wonders, and the earth will be given over into his hands, and he will commit iniquities which have never been since the world began. [5] Then the creation of mankind will come to the fiery trial and "many will be offended" and be lost, but "they who endure" in their faith "will be saved" by the curse itself. [6] And "then will appear the signs" of the truth. First, the sign spread out in [the] sky, then the sign of the sound of the trumpet, and thirdly the resurrection of the dead: [7] but not of all the dead, but as it was said, "The Lord will come and all His holy ones with Him." [8] Then the world will "see the Lord coming on the clouds of Heaven."

REVELATION OF PETER

Otherwise known as the Apocalypse of Peter

The Revelation of Peter was listed in the Muratorian Canon among the two apocalypses (the other being the Revelation of John). It was also supported by Clement of Alexandria. The translation that follows comes from the Ethiopic text. A Greek fragment discovered at Akhmîm differs considerably (cf. chs. 2, 4), but seems less supported—the Ethiopic thought to be older. Two other small Greek fragments have been found (Bodleian and Rainer).

CHAPTER 1

1 The second coming of Christ and resurrection of the dead who died because of their sins, for that they did not keep the command of God their creator. **2** And he [(Peter)] pondered thereon, that he might perceive the mystery of the Son of God, the merciful and lover of mercy. **3** And when the Lord was seated on the Mount of Olives, His disciples came to Him. **4** And we implored and entreated Him separately and pleaded [to] Him, saying to Him, "Declare to us what are the signs of Your coming and of the end of the world, that we may perceive and mark the time of Your coming and instruct them that come after us, to whom we preach the word of Your good news, and whom we set over Your Assembly, that when they hear it they may take heed to themselves and mark the time of Your coming." **5** And our Lord answered us, saying, "Take heed that no man deceive you, and that you not be doubters and serve other gods. Many will come in My Name, saying, I am the Christ. Do not believe them, neither draw near to them. For the coming of the Son of God will not be plain, but as the lightning that shines from the east to the west, so I will come on the clouds of Heaven with a great host in My majesty; I will come in My majesty with My cross going before My face; I will come in My majesty—shining sevenfold more than the sun—with all My holy ones, My messengers. And My Father will set a crown on My head, that I may judge the quick and the dead and reward every man according to his works. **6** And you, take the likeness thereof from the fig tree: so soon as the shoot thereof has come forth and the twigs grown, the end of the world will come." **7** And I, Peter, answered and said to Him, "Interpret to me concerning the fig tree, whereby we will perceive it; for throughout all its days the fig tree sends forth shoots, and every year it brings forth its fruit for its master. What, then, does the allegory of the fig tree mean? We do not know it." **8** And the Master answered and said to me, "Do you not understand that the fig tree is the house of Israel? Even as a man that planted a fig tree in his garden, and it brought forth no fruit. And he sought the fruit thereof many years and when he did not find it, he said to the keeper of his garden: Root up this fig tree [so] that it does not make our ground to be unfruitful. And the gardener said to God: [Allow us] to rid it of weeds and dig the ground around it and water it. If then it does not bear fruit, we will immediately remove its roots out of the garden and plant another in place of it. Have you not understood that the fig tree is the house of Israel? Truly I say to you, when the twigs thereof have sprouted forth in the last days, then pretend Christs will come and awake expectation, saying, I am the Christ that has now come into the world. And when they [(Israel)] will perceive the wickedness of their deeds, they will turn away after them and deny him [whom our fathers praised], even the first Christ whom they crucified and therein sinned a great sin. But this deceiver [(the Antichrist)] is not the Christ. And when they reject him, he will slay with the sword, and there will be many martyrs. Then the twigs of the fig tree—that is, the house of Israel—will shoot forth; many will become martyrs at his hand. Enoch and Elijah will be sent to teach them that this is the deceiver which must come into the world and do signs and wonders to deceive. And therefore, they that die by his hand will be martyrs, and will be reckoned among the good and righteous martyrs who have pleased God in their life." **9** And He showed me in His right hand the souls of all men, and on the palm of His right hand the image of that which will be accomplished at the last day: and how the righteous and the sinners will be separated, and how they do that are upright in heart, and how the evildoers will be rooted out throughout all ages. We beheld how the sinners wept in great affliction and sorrow, until all that saw it with their eyes wept, whether righteous or messengers, and He Himself also. **10** And I asked Him and said to him, "Lord, permit me to speak Your word concerning the sinners: It were better for them if they had not been created." And the Savior answered and said to me, "Peter, why do you speak thus, that it were better for them to not have been created? You resist God. You would not have more compassion than He for His image, for He has created them and brought them forth out of not being. Now because you have seen the lamentation which will come on the sinners in the last days, therefore your heart is troubled; but I will show you their works, whereby they have sinned against the Highest. **11** Now behold what will come on them in the last days, when the Day of God and the Day of the decision of the judgment of God comes. From the east to the west all the children of men will be gathered together before My Father that lives forever. And He will command Hades to open its bars of adamant and give up all that is therein. **12** And He will command the wild beasts and the birds to restore all the flesh that they have devoured, because He wills those men should appear; for nothing perishes before God, and nothing is impossible with Him, because all things are His. **13** For all things come to pass on the day of decision, on the Day of Judgment, at the word of God: and as all things were done when He created the world and commanded all that is therein, and it was done—even so will it be in the last days; for all things are possible with God. And, therefore, He says in the Writing: Son of man, prophesy on the several bones and say to the bones: Bone to bone, in joints, sinew, nerves, flesh, and skin, and hair thereon, [[and soul, and spirit]]. **14** And the great Uriel will give them soul and spirit at the command of God; for God has set him over the rising again of the dead at the Day of Judgment. **15** Behold and consider the corns of wheat that are sown in the earth. As things dry and men sow them in the earth without soul, so they live again and bear fruit, and the earth restores them as a pledge entrusted to it. **16** [[And this that dies, that is sown as seed in the earth, and will become alive and be restored to life, is man.]] **17** How much more will God raise up on the Day of Decision them that believe in Him and are chosen of Him, for whose sake He made the world? And the earth will restore all things on the Day of Decision, for it will also be judged with them, and the Heaven with it. **18** And at the Day of Judgment this will come on them that have fallen away from faith in God and that have committed sin: floods of fire will be let loose, and darkness and obscurity will come up and clothe and veil the whole world, and the waters will be changed and turned into coals of fire, and all that is in them will burn, and the sea will become fire. Under the sky will be a sharp fire that cannot be quenched, and [it] flows to fulfill the judgment of wrath. And the stars will fly in pieces by flames of fire, as if they had not been created, and the powers [[or expanses]] of the heavens will pass away for lack of water and will be as though they had not been. And the lightnings of the sky will no longer be, and by their enchantment they will frighten the world [[or The sky will turn to lightning and the lightnings thereof will frighten the world. The spirits of the dead bodies will also be like to them]] and will become fire at the command of God. **19** And so soon as the whole creation dissolves, the men that are in the east will flee to the west, [and those in the west] to the east; they that are in the south will flee to the north, and they that are in the [north to the] south. And in all places the wrath of a fearful fire will overtake them, and an unquenchable flame driving them will bring them to the judgment of wrath, to the stream of unquenchable fire that flows, flaming with fire, and when the waves thereof part themselves from one another, burning, there will be a great gnashing of teeth among the children of men. **20** Then they will all behold Me coming on a continuous cloud of brightness—and the messengers of God that are with Me. And I will sit on the throne of My glory at the right hand of My heavenly Father; and He will set a crown on My head. And when the nations behold it, they will weep, every nation apart. **21** Then He will command them to enter into the river of fire while the works of each of them will stand before them—to every man according to his deeds. As for the chosen ones that have done good, they will come to Me and not see death by the devouring fire. But the unrighteous, the sinners, and the hypocrites will stand in the depths of darkness that will not pass away, and their discipline is the fire, and messengers bring forward their sins and prepare for them a place wherein they will be punished agelong [[everyone according to his transgression]]. **22** Uriel, the messenger of God, will bring forth the souls of those sinners who perished in the flood, and of all that dwelt in all idols, in every molten image, in every [object of] love, and in pictures, and of those that dwelt on all hills, and in stones, and by the wayside, whom men called gods: they will burn them with them in continuous fire; and after that, all of them—with their dwelling places—are destroyed. They will be punished agelong."

CHAPTER 2

1 "Then men and women will come to the place prepared for them. By their tongues with which they have blasphemed the way of righteousness they will be hanged up. There is spread under them unquenchable fire, and they do not escape it. **2** Behold, another place: therein is a pit, great and full. In it are they that have denied righteousness; and messengers of punishment punish them and there kindle on them the fire of their torment. **3** And again, behold—women: they hang them up by their neck and by their hair; they will cast them into the pit. These are they which plaited their hair, not for good [[or not to make them beautiful]] but to turn them to fornication, that they might ensnare the souls of men to perdition. And the men that lay with them in fornication will be hung by their loins in that place of fire; and they will say to one another: We did not know that we should come to continuous punishment. **4** And the murderers and them that have made common cause with them they will cast into the fire, in a place full of venomous beasts, and they will be tormented without rest, feeling their pains; and their worms will be as many in number as a dark cloud. And the messenger Azrael will bring forth the souls of them that have been slain, and they will behold the torment of them that slew them, and say to one another: Righteousness and justice is the judgment of God. For we heard, but we did not believe, that we should come into this place of continuous judgment. **5** And near by this flame will be a great and very deep pit, and into it flows from above all manner of torment, foulness, and issue. And women are swallowed up therein up to their necks and tormented with great pain. These are they that have caused their children to be born untimely and have corrupted the work of God that created them. Over against them will be another place where their children sit alive, and they cry to God. And lightnings go forth from those children and pierce the eyes of them that for fornication's sake have caused their destruction. **6** Other men and women will stand above them, naked; and their children stand over against them in a place of delight, and sigh and cry to God because of their parents, saying, These are they that have despised, and cursed, and transgressed Your commands and delivered us to death: they have cursed the messenger that formed us, and have hanged us up, and withheld from us the light which You have given to all creatures. And the milk of their mothers flowing from their breasts will congeal, and from it will come beasts devouring flesh, which will come forth, and turn, and torment them agelong with their husbands, because they forsook the commands of God and slew their children. As for their children, they will be delivered to the messenger Temlakos. And they that slew them will be tormented continuously, for God wills it so. **7** Azrael, the messenger of wrath, will bring men and women—the half of their bodies burning—and cast them into a place of darkness, even the Gehenna of men; and a spirit of wrath will punish them with all manner of torment, and a worm that does not sleep will devour their entrails: and these are the persecutors and betrayers of My righteous ones. **8** And beside them that are there, will be other men and women, gnawing their tongues; and they will torment them with red-hot iron and burn their eyes. These are they that slander and doubt of My righteousness. Other men and women whose works were done in deceitfulness will have their lips cut off, and fire enters into their mouth and their entrails. These are the false witnesses [[or these are they that caused the martyrs to die by their lying]]. **9** And beside them, in a place near at hand, on the stone will be a pillar of fire, and the pillar is sharper than swords. And there will be men and women clad in rags and filthy garments, and they will be cast thereon, to suffer the judgment of a torment that does not cease: these are they that trusted in their riches and despised the widows and the woman with fatherless children . . . before

God. **10** And into another place hard by, full of filth, they cast men and women up to the knees. These are they that lent money and took usury. **11** And other men and women cast themselves down from a high place and return again and run, and devils drive them. And they put them to the end of their wits, and they cast themselves down. And thus they do continually, and are tormented continuously. These are they which have cut their flesh as [apostles] of a man: and the women that were with them . . . and these are the men that defiled themselves together as women. **12** And beside them will be a brazier, and beneath them the messenger Azrael will prepare a place of much fire: and all the idols of gold and silver, all idols, the work of men's hands, and the semblances of images of cats and lions, of creeping things and wild beasts, and the men and women that have prepared the images thereof, will be in chains of fire and will be punished because of their error before the idols, and this is their judgment forever. **13** And beside them will be other men and women, burning in the fire of the judgment, and their torment is continuous. These are they that have forsaken the command of God and followed the persuasions of devils."

CHAPTER 3

1 "And there will be another place—very high. [[There will be a furnace and a brazier wherein fire will burn. The fire that will burn will come from one end of the brazier.]] The men and women whose feet slip will go rolling down into a place where fear is. And again, while the fire that is prepared flows, they mount up, and fall down again, and continue to roll down. Thus they will be tormented continuously. These are they that did not honor their father and mother, and of their own accord withheld themselves from them. Therefore, they will be punished continuously. **2** Furthermore, the messenger Azrael will bring children and maidens to show them those that are tormented. They will be punished with pains, with hanging up, and with a multitude of wounds which flesh-devouring birds will inflict on them. These are they that boast themselves in their sins, and do not obey their parents, and do not follow the instruction of their fathers, and do not honor them that are more aged than they. **3** Beside them will be girls clad in darkness for a garment and they will be severely punished, and their flesh will be torn in pieces. These are they that did not keep their virginity until they were given in marriage, and with these torments they will be punished, and will feel them. **4** And again, other men and women, gnawing their tongues without ceasing, and being tormented with continuous fire—these are the servants which were not obedient to their masters; and this then is their continuous judgment. **5** And hard by this place of torment will be men and women mute and blind, whose raiment is white. They will crowd on one another and fall on coals of unquenchable fire. These are they that give alms and say, We are righteous before God, whereas they have not sought after righteousness. **6** Azrael, the messenger of God, will bring them forth out of this fire and establish a judgment of decision. This then is their judgment: a river of fire will flow and all [those in] judgment will be drawn down into the middle of the river. And Uriel will set them there. **7** And there are wheels of fire and men and women hung thereon by the strength of the whirling thereof. And they that are in the pit will burn: now these are the sorcerers and sorceresses. Those wheels will be in a decision by fire without number. **8** Thereafter the messengers will bring My chosen ones and righteous which are perfect in all uprightness, and bear them in their hands, and clothe them with the raiment of the life that is above. They will see their desire on them that hated them, when he punishes them, and the torment of everyone will be continuous according to his works. **9** And all they that are in torment will say with one voice: Have mercy on us, for now we know the judgment of God, which He declared to us formerly, and we did not believe. And the messenger Tatirokos will come and punish them with yet greater torment, and say to them: Now do you convert, when it is no longer the time for conversion, and nothing of life remains. And they will say: The judgment of God is righteous, for we have heard and perceived that His judgment is good; for we are repaid according to our deeds. **10** Then I will give to My chosen ones and righteous the immersion and the salvation for which they have implored Me, in the field of Acherusa [[or Elysium]]. They will adorn the portion of the righteous with flowers, and I will go . . . I will rejoice with them. I will cause the peoples to enter into My continuous Kingdom and show them that continuous thing [[*or* life]] whereon I have made them to set their hope, even I and My Father which is in Heaven. ¹¹ I have spoken this to you, Peter, and declared it to you. Therefore, go forth and go to the land [[*or* city]] of the west. [[And enter into the vineyard which I will tell you of, in order that by the sufferings of the Son who is without sin the deeds of corruption may be sanctified. As for you, you are chosen according to the promise which I have given you. Therefore, spread My good news throughout all the world in peace. Truly men will rejoice: My words will be the source of hope and of life, and suddenly the world will be ravished.]]"

CHAPTER 4

¹ And my Lord Jesus Christ our King said to me, "Let us go to the holy mountain." And His disciples went with Him, praying. And behold, there were two men there, and we could not look on their faces, for a light came from them, shining more than the sun, and their raiment was also shining, and cannot be described, and nothing is sufficient to be compared to them in this world. And the sweetness of them . . . that no mouth is able to utter the beauty of their appearance, for their aspect was astonishing and wonderful. And the other, great, I say, shines in his aspect above crystal. Like the flower of roses is the appearance of the color of his aspect and of his body. Their head was a marvel. And on his [[*or* their]] shoulders and on their foreheads was a crown of nard woven of fair flowers. As the rainbow in the water [[*or* in the time of rain]], so was their hair. And such was the comeliness of their countenance, adorned with all manner of ornament. And when we saw them all of a sudden, we marveled. And I drew near to the Lord Jesus Christ and said to Him, "O my Lord, who are these?" And He said to me, "They are Moses and Elijah." And I said to Him, "[What about] Abraham, and Isaac, and Jacob, and the rest of the righteous fathers?" And He showed us a great garden, open, full of fair trees and blessed fruits, and of the fragrance of perfumes. The fragrance thereof was pleasant and came even to us. And thereof I saw much fruit. And my Lord and God Jesus Christ said to me, "Have you seen the companies of the fathers? ² As is their rest, such also is the honor and the glory of them that are persecuted for My righteousness' sake." And I rejoiced, and believed, and understood that which is written in the scroll of my Lord Jesus Christ. And I said to Him, "O my Lord, will You that I make three shelters here, one for You, and one for Moses, and one for Elijah?" And He said to me in wrath: "Satan makes war against you and has veiled your understanding; and the good things of this world prevail against you. Your eyes, therefore, must be opened and your ears unstopped that [you may perceive] a dwelling place not made with men's hands, which My heavenly Father has made for Me and for the chosen ones." And we beheld it and were full of gladness. ³ And behold, suddenly there came a voice from Heaven, saying, "This is My beloved Son in whom I am well pleased." And then came a great and exceeding white cloud over our heads and carried away our Lord, and Moses, and Elijah. And I trembled and was afraid: and we looked up and the sky opened, and we beheld men in the flesh, and they came and greeted our Lord, and Moses, and Elijah and went into another heaven. And the word of the Writing was fulfilled: "This is the generation that seeks Him and seeks the face of the God of Jacob." And great fear and commotion was there in Heaven and the messengers pressed on one another that the word of the Writing might be fulfilled which says: "Open the gates, you princes." ⁴ Thereafter the sky that had been open was shut. ⁵ And we prayed and went down from the mountain, glorifying God, who has written the names of the righteous in Heaven in the Scroll of Life.

3 CORINTHIANS

The Epistle of the Corinthians to Paul, and his purported response, are here in the LSV referred to as "3 Corinthians." These letters are considered by most to have been written in the 2nd century, probably very early, as a pseudonymous response to the burgeoning Gnostic heresies. The later Acts of Paul included 3 Corinthians. 3 Corinthians was included in Syrian and Armenian canons.

[They] prayed that a messenger be sent to Philippi. For the Corinthians were in great trouble concerning Paul, that he would depart out of the world before it was time. For there were certain men who came to Corinth, Simon and Cleobius, saying [that] there is no resurrection of the flesh, but that of the spirit only; and that the body of man is not the creation of God; and also concerning the world, that God did not create it, and that God does not know the world, and that Jesus Christ was not crucified, but it was [only] an appearance, and that he, [saying He] was not born of Mary, nor of the seed of David. And in a word, there were many things which they had taught in Corinth, deceiving many other men, [and deceiving] themselves. When therefore the Corinthians heard that Paul was at Philippi, they sent a letter to Paul, to Macedonia, by the deacons Threptus and Eutychus. And the letter was after this manner:

CHAPTER 1

¹ Stephanus and the elders that are with him, even Daphnus, and Eubulus, and Theophilus, and Zenon, to Paul their perpetual brother: greetings in the Lord. ² There have come to Corinth two men, Simon and Cleobius, which are overthrowing the faith of many with evil words, ³ which you [must] prove and examine: ⁴ for we have never heard such words from you nor from the other apostles: ⁵ but all that we have received from you or from them, that do we hold fast. ⁶ Since therefore the Lord has had mercy on us, that while you are still in the flesh, we may hear these things again from you; ⁷ if it be possible, either come to us or write to us. ⁸ For we believe, according as it has been revealed to Theonoe, that the Lord has delivered you out of the hand of the lawless one. ⁹ Now the things which these men say and teach are these: ¹⁰ They say that we must not use the prophets, ¹¹ and that God is not almighty, ¹² and that there will be no resurrection of the flesh, ¹³ and that man was not made by God, ¹⁴ and that Christ has not come in the flesh, neither was born of Mary, ¹⁵ and that the world is not of God, but of the messengers. ¹⁶ Therefore, brother, please use all diligence to come to us, that the assembly of the Corinthians may remain without offense, and the madness of these men may be made plain. Farewell—always in the Lord.

CHAPTER 2

¹ The deacons Threptus and Eutychus brought the letter to Philippi, ² so that Paul received it, being in bonds because of Stratonice the wife of Apollophanes, and he forgot his bonds, and was severely afflicted, ³ and cried out, saying, "It were better for me to die and to be with the Lord, than to continue in the flesh and to hear such things and the calamities of false doctrine, so that trouble comes on trouble. ⁴ And over and above this so great affliction I am in bonds and behold these evils whereby the devices of Satan are accomplished." ⁵ Paul therefore, in great affliction, wrote a letter, answering thus:

CHAPTER 3

¹ Paul, a prisoner of Jesus Christ, to the brothers which are in Corinth: greetings. ² Being in the midst of many tribulations, I do not marvel if the teachings of the evil one run abroad apace. ³ For my Lord Jesus Christ will hasten His coming and will set at nothing them that falsify His words. ⁴ For I delivered to you in the beginning the things which I received of the holy apostles which were before me, who were at all times with Jesus Christ: ⁵ namely, that our Lord Jesus Christ was born of Mary which is of the seed of David according to the flesh, the Holy Spirit being sent forth from Heaven from the Father to her by the messenger Gabriel, ⁶ that He might come down into this world and redeem all flesh by His flesh, and raise us up from the dead in the flesh, like as He has shown to us in Himself for an example. ⁷ And because man was formed by His Father, ⁸ therefore he was sought when he was lost, that he might be restored by adoption. ⁹ For to this end God Almighty, who made the heavens and earth, first sent the prophets to the Jews, that

they might be drawn away from their sins. **10** For He designed to save the house of Israel: therefore, He conferred a portion of the Spirit of Christ on the prophets and sent them to the Jews first, and they proclaimed the true worship of God for a long space of time. **11** But the prince of iniquity, desiring to be God, laid hands on them and slew them, and bound all flesh by evil lusts [[and the end of the world by judgment drew near]]. **12** But God Almighty, who is righteous, would not cast away His own creation, but had compassion on them from Heaven, **13** and sent His Spirit into Mary in Galilee, [[**14** who believed with all her heart and received the Holy Spirit in her womb, that Jesus might come into the world,]] **15** that by that flesh whereby that wicked one had brought in death, by the same he should be shown to be overcome. **16** For by His own body Jesus Christ saved all flesh [[and restored it to life]], **17** that He might show forth the temple of righteousness in His body. **18** In whom we are saved [[or in whom, if we believe, we are set free]]. **19** Therefore, they are not children of righteousness but children of wrath, who reject the wisdom of God, saying that the heavens and the earth and all that are in them are not the work of God. **20** Therefore, they are children of wrath, for they are cursed, following the teaching of the serpent, **21** whom you drive out from you and flee from their doctrine. [[**22** for you are not children of disobedience, but of the well-beloved Assembly. **23** Therefore is the time of the resurrection proclaimed to all.]] **24** And as for that which they say—that there is no resurrection of the flesh—they indeed will have no resurrection to life, but to judgment, **25** because they do not believe in Him that is risen from the dead, not believing nor understanding, **26** for they do not know, O Corinthians, the seeds of wheat or of other seeds, how they are cast bare into the earth and are corrupted and rise again by the will of God with bodies, and clothed. **27** And not only that [body] which is cast in rises again, but manifold more blessing itself. **28** And if we must not take an example from seeds only, but from more noble bodies, **29** you know how Jonah the son of Amathi, when he would not preach to the men of Nineveh, but fled, was swallowed by the sea-monster; **30** and after three days and three nights God heard the prayer of Jonah out of the lowest [part of] Hades, and no part of him was consumed, not even a hair nor an eyelash. **31** How much more, O you of little faith, will He raise up you that have believed in Christ Jesus, like as He Himself arose. **32** Likewise also, a dead man was cast on the bones of the prophet Elisha by the sons of Israel, and he arose—both body, and soul, and bones, and spirit; how much more will you which have been cast on the body, and bones, and Spirit of the Lord [[or how much more, O you of little faith, will you which have been cast on Him]] arise again in that day having your flesh whole, even as He arose? [[**33** Likewise also, concerning the prophet Elijah, he raised up the widow's son from death: how much more will the Lord Jesus raise you up from death at the sound of the trumpet, in the twinkling of an eye? For He has showed us an example in His own body.]] **34** If then, you receive any other doctrine, God will be witness against you; and let no man trouble me, **35** for I bear these bonds that I may win Christ, and I therefore bear His marks in my body that I may attain to the resurrection of the dead. **36** And whoever receives the rule which He has received by the blessed prophets and the holy good news, will receive a repayment from the Lord, and when he rises from the dead will obtain continuous life. **37** But whoever transgresses these things, with him is the fire, and with them that walk in like manner [[or with them that go before in the same way, who are men without God]], **38** which are a generation of vipers, **39** whom you reject in the power of the Lord, **40** and peace, grace, and love will be with you.

1 CLEMENT

Though the author of the First Epistle of Clement is anonymous, it was thought to have been written by Clement of Rome (possibly consecrated by the Apostle Peter) and is highly regarded, at one point even considered for inclusion in the New Testament canon. Internal evidence places the date of composition around the end of the 1st century, although some even suspect before 70 AD.

The Assembly of God which sojourns at Rome, to the Assembly of God which sojourns at Corinth, to them that are called and sanctified in the will of God through our Lord Jesus Christ: Grace and peace be multiplied to you from Almighty God through Jesus Christ.

CHAPTER 1

1 On account of the sudden and repeated calamities and misfortunes, brothers, that have come on us, we suppose that we have the more slowly given heed to the things that are disputed among you, beloved, and to the foul and unholy sedition, alien and foreign to the chosen ones of God, which a few headstrong and self-willed persons have kindled to such a degree of madness, that your venerable and famous name, worthy to be loved of all men, is greatly blasphemed. **2** For who that has tarried among you has not approved your most virtuous and firm faith, has not admired your sober and seemly piety in Christ, has not proclaimed your splendid disposition of hospitality, has not deemed blessed your perfect and unerring knowledge? **3** For you did all things without respect of persons, and walked in the laws of God, submitting yourselves to them that have the rule over you, and giving the due honor to the elders that are among you. Young men you prescribed to think such things as are sober and grave. Women you exhorted to perform all things in a blameless, and honorable, and pure conscience, loving dutifully their own husbands; and you taught them to manage the affairs of their houses with gravity, keeping in the rule of obedience, being temperate in all things.

CHAPTER 2

1 And you were all humble, boasting of nothing, submitting yourselves rather than subjecting others, more gladly giving than receiving, content with the provision that God had given you; and attending diligently to His words, you received them into your very hearts, and His sufferings were before your eyes. **2** Thus a deep and rich peace was given to all, and an insatiable longing for doing good, and a plentiful outpouring of the Holy Spirit was on all of you. **3** And you, being filled with a holy desire, with excellent zeal and pious confidence, stretched out your arms to Almighty God, imploring Him to be merciful to you, if you had in anything unwillingly done wrong. **4** You contended day and night for the whole brotherhood, that in His mercy and good pleasure the number of His chosen ones might be saved. **5** You were simple and sincere, without malice toward one another: **6** all sedition and all schism were abominable to you. You grieved over the transgressions of your neighbor, judging his shortcomings your own. **7** You did not relent of any well-doing, "being ready to every good work"; **8** and being adorned with a very virtuous and holy habit of life, you did all things in His fear. The commands and ordinances of the Lord were written on the breadth of your heart.

CHAPTER 3

1 All honor and enlargement were given to you, and then was fulfilled that which is written: "The beloved ate and drank, and was enlarged and grew fat and kicked." **2** From this came emulation and envy, strife and sedition, persecution and disorder, war and captivity. **3** Thus the mean men were lifted up against the honorable; those of no regard against those of good regard; the foolish against the wise; the young against the elder. **4** Through this, justice and peace are far off, because each of you leaves off the fear of God and is dimsighted in his faith, nor walks in the laws of His commands, nor behaves as becomes a citizen of Christ; but each walks according to his own evil lusts, having taken up unjust and unholy envy, by which death also entered into the world.

CHAPTER 4

1 For it is thus written: "And it came to pass after certain days, that Cain brought of the fruits of the ground a sacrifice to God, and Abel brought also of the firstlings of the sheep and of their fat. **2** And God had respect to Abel and to his gifts; but to Cain and his gifts he had no regard. **3** And Cain was grieved greatly, and his countenance fell. [4] And God said to Cain, Why are you very sorrowful, and why has your countenance fallen? If you have rightly offered, but have not rightly divided, have you not sinned? [5] Hold your peace; your gift returns to you, and you will be master over it. [6] And Cain said to Abel, Let us pass over into the field. And it came to pass while they were in the field, Cain rose up against his brother Abel and slew him." [7] You see, brothers, jealousy and envy worked the slaughter of a brother. [8] Through envy our father Jacob fled from the face of his brother Esau. [9] Envy caused Joseph to be persecuted to death, and to enter into bondage. [10] Envy compelled Moses to flee from the face of Pharaoh, king of Egypt, because he heard his countryman say, "Who made you a judge or a decider over us? Will you kill me, as you did the Egyptian yesterday?" [11] Through envy Aaron and Miriam pitched their tents outside the camp. [12] Envy brought down Dathan and Abiram alive to the grave, because they contended against Moses, the servant of God. [13] Through envy David suffered jealousy not only of foreigners, but was also persecuted by Saul, king of Israel.

CHAPTER 5

[1] But let us pass from ancient examples and come to those who have in the times nearest to us wrestled for the faith. [2] Let us take the noble examples of our own generation. Through jealousy and envy the greatest and most just pillars of the Assembly were persecuted, and even came to death. [3] Let us place before our eyes the good apostles. [4] Peter, through unjust envy, endured not one or two but many labors, and at last, having delivered his testimony, departed to the place of glory due to him. [5] Through envy Paul, too, showed by example the prize that is given to patience: [6] seven times was he cast into chains; he was banished; he was stoned; having become a herald, both in the east and in the west, he obtained the noble renown due to his faith; [7] and having preached righteousness to the whole world, and having come to the extremity of the west, and having borne witness before rulers, he departed at length out of the world, and went to the holy place, having become the greatest example of patience.

CHAPTER 6

[1] To these men, who walked in holiness, there was gathered a great multitude of the chosen ones, who, having suffered, through envy, many insults and tortures, became a most excellent example among us. [2] Through envy women were persecuted, even the Danaides and Dircae, who, after enduring dreadful and unholy insults, attained to the sure course of the faith; and they who were weak in body received a noble reward. [3] Envy has estranged the minds of wives from their husbands, and changed the saying of our father Adam: "This is now bone of my bone, and flesh of my flesh." [4] Envy and strife have overthrown mighty cities and rooted out great nations.

CHAPTER 7

[1] These things we urge you, beloved, not only by way of admonition to you, but as also putting ourselves in mind. For we are in the same arena, and the same contest is imposed on us. [2] For what reason, let us leave empty and vain thoughts, and come to the glorious and venerable rule of our holy calling. [3] Let us consider what is good, and pleasing, and acceptable before Him who made us. [4] Let us look steadfastly to the blood of Christ and see how precious in the sight of God His blood is, which, having been poured out for our salvation, brought to the whole world the grace of conversion. [5] Let us go back to all generations and learn that in every generation God has granted a place for conversion to such as wished to return to Him. [6] Noah preached conversion, and as many as listened to him were saved. [7] Jonah prophesied destruction to the Ninevites, and they, converting from their sins, appeased God through prayer, and, though alien from God, obtained salvation.

CHAPTER 8

[1] The ministers of the grace of God spoke by the Holy Spirit concerning conversion; [2] and the Lord of all, Himself spoke concerning conversion with an oath: "As I live, says the Lord, I do not desire the death of a sinner, as I desire his conversion"; adding to that an excellent saying: [3] "Convert, O house of Israel, from your iniquity: Say to the sons of My people, Though your sins reach from earth to Heaven, and though they are redder than scarlet, and blacker than sackcloth, and you turn to Me with your whole heart and say, My Father, I will listen to you as to a holy people." [4] And in another place He speaks in this way: "Wash, and be clean; take away the wickedness from your souls from before My eyes; cease from your evil deeds, learn to do well; seek judgment; deliver him that is oppressed; give judgment for the orphan, and justify the widow; and come and let us reason together," He says, "and though your sins be as purple, I will make them white as snow; and though they are as scarlet, I will make them white as wool. And if you are willing and listen to Me, you will eat the good things of the earth; but if you are not willing, and do not listen, the sword will devour you; for the mouth of the Lord has said this." [5] Desiring, therefore, that all His beloved ones should partake of conversion, He has confirmed it by His almighty will.

CHAPTER 9

[1] For what reason, let us submit ourselves to His excellent and glorious will, and, becoming suppliants of His mercy and goodness, let us fall before Him and go ourselves to His mercies, having laid aside the vain toil, and the strife, and the jealousy that leads to death. [2] Let us look steadfastly at those that have ministered with perfectness to His excellent glory. [3] Let us take as example Enoch, who, having been found just by reason of obedience, was translated, and his death was not found. [4] Noah, having been found faithful, preached, by his ministry, regeneration to the world, and by him God preserved the animals that entered with one consent into the Ark.

CHAPTER 10

[1] Abraham, who was called the friend, was found faithful, inasmuch as he became obedient to the words of God. [2] This man, by obedience, went out from his land and his countrymen, and the house of his father, that, by leaving a scant land, and weak countrymen, and a small house, he might inherit the promises of God. [3] For He says to him, "Go out from your land, and your countrymen, and the house of your father, to the land that I will show you, and I will make you a great nation, and bless you, and magnify your name, and you will be blessed; and I will bless them that bless you, and curse them that curse you, and in you all the tribes of the earth will be blessed." [4] And again, when he separated from Lot, God said to him, "Lift up your eyes, and look from the place where you are now to the north and to the south, and to the east and to the sea; for all the land which you see, I will give it to you and to your seed for all time, [5] and I will make your seed as the dust of the earth: if any man can number the dust of the earth, your seed will also be numbered." [6] And again He says, "God brought forth Abraham, and said to him: Look up to Heaven and number the stars, if you are able to number them, so will your seed be. And Abraham believed God, and it was counted to him for righteousness." [7] Through faith and hospitality a son was given to him in old age, and through obedience he offered him a sacrifice to God on one of the mountains that he showed him.

CHAPTER 11

[1] By hospitality and goodness Lot was saved out of Sodom when the whole region around was judged with fire and brimstone; the Lord making it manifest that He does not leave them that hope on Him, but appoints to punishment and torment them that turn in another way. [2] For his wife, who went out together with him, being of another mind, and not being in concord with him, was on that account placed as a sign, so that she became a pillar of salt even to this day; that it might be known to all that the double-minded, and they who doubt

concerning the power of God, are for a judgment and a sign to all generations.

CHAPTER 12

[1] Through faith and hospitality the harlot Rahab was saved; [2] for when spies were sent to Jericho by Jesus [(Joshua)], the son of Nun, the king of the land knew that they had come to spy out his country, and sent out men to apprehend them that they might be taken and put to death. [3] But the hospitable Rahab having received them, hid them in an upper story under the stalks of flax. [4] Therefore, when the men from the king came on her, and said, "There came to you men who are spies of this land of ours; bring them out, for the king so commands it"; she answered, "The two men whom you are seeking entered in to me, but they departed quickly and are on their way"; but she did not show the men to them. [5] And she said to the men, "I know for certain that the Lord your God has given over this city to you; for the fear and trembling of you has fallen on them that inhabit it. Therefore, when it has happened to you to take it, save me and the house of my father." [6] And they say to her, "So will it be, even as you have spoken to us. Therefore, when you have perceived that we are coming, you will gather together all your household under your roof, and they will be saved; but as many as will be found outside the house will be destroyed." [7] And they proceeded further to give her a sign, that she should hang scarlet from her house, making it manifest beforehand that through the blood of the Lord there will be redemption to all who believe and hope on God. [8] Behold, beloved, how there was not only faith, but prophecy in the woman.

CHAPTER 13

[1] Let us therefore, brothers, be humble, laying aside all boasting and pride, and folly and wrath, and let us do that which is written; for the Holy Spirit says, "Do not let the wise boast in his wisdom, nor the strong in his strength, nor the rich in his riches; but let him that boasts make his boast in the Lord, even by seeking Him and doing judgment and justice." Let us especially remember the words of our Lord Jesus Christ which He spoke when teaching gentleness and long-suffering, for He spoke thus: [2] "Show mercy, that you may obtain mercy; forgive, that it may be forgiven to you; as you do, so will it be done to you; as you give, so will it be given to you; as you judge, so will you be judged; as you are kindly affectioned, so will kindness be showed to you; with whatsoever measure you measure, with the same will it be measured to you." [3] With this command and with these exhortations let us strengthen ourselves, that we may walk obedient to His holy words with all humility. For the Holy Writing says, [4] "On whom will I have respect but on him that is meek and quiet, and that trembles at My words?"

CHAPTER 14

[1] It is therefore appropriate and right, men and brothers, that we should be obedient to God rather than follow them that in pride and disorderliness are leaders of detestable sedition. [2] For we will incur no slight harm, but rather a great danger, if we rashly give ourselves up to the wills of men who launch out into strife and sedition so as to estrange us from that which is good. [3] Let us, therefore, show kindness toward them according to the mercy and sweetness of Him that made us. [4] For it is written: "The men of kindness will inherit the land. The innocent will be left on it; but they that are lawless will be destroyed out of it." [5] And again it says, "I saw the unrighteous man exalted on high and lifted up like the cedars of Lebanon. And I passed by, and behold, he was not; I sought his place and did not find it. Keep innocence, and regard righteousness; for there is a remnant that remains to the man of peace."

CHAPTER 15

[1] Let us therefore cleave to them who live in peace and

godliness, not to them who hypocritically profess to desire peace. [2] For He says in a certain place, "This people honors Me with their lips, but their heart is far from Me." [3] And again, "They blessed with their mouth, but they cursed with their heart. [4] And again it says, "They loved Him with their mouth, and with their tongue they lied against Him. For their heart was not right with Him, nor were they faithful in His covenant. [5] Let the crafty lips be put to silence, and may the Lord destroy all the deceitful lips, even the haughty tongue, they who said, Let us magnify our tongue, our lips are our own; who is master over us?" [6] "On account of the misery of the poor, and on account of the groaning of the needy, I will now arise, says the Lord; I will set him in safety, I will deal confidently with him."

CHAPTER 16

[1] For Christ belongs to them that are humble, not to them that exalt themselves over His flock. [2] Our Lord Jesus Christ, who is the scepter of the majesty of God, did not come in the arrogance of boasting and pride, though He was able to do so; but in humility, even as the Holy Spirit spoke concerning Him. [3] For it says, "Lord, who has believed our report, and to whom has the arm of the Lord been revealed? Like a child we have delivered our message before Him; He is as a root in a thirsty land. There is no form nor glory in Him, and we beheld Him, and He had neither form nor comeliness, but His form was despised, lacking comeliness, beyond the form of the sons of men. He was a man stricken and in toil, knowing how to bear infirmity, for His face was turned away; it was dishonored and held in no reputation. [4] He bears our sins and suffers pain on our account, and we esteemed Him as one in toil, stricken, and afflicted. [5] He was wounded for our sins, and for our transgressions He suffered infirmity; the discipline of our peace was on Him, and by His stripes we were healed. [6] All we, like sheep, have gone astray, everyone has erred in his own way, [7] and the Lord has given Him up for our sins; and He, through affliction, does not open His mouth. He was led like a sheep to the slaughter, and as a lamb before its shearers is silent, so He does not open His mouth. [8] In His humiliation His judgment was taken away, and who will declare His generation? For His life is taken from the earth; [9] for the iniquity of My people He has come to death. [10] And I will give the wicked in return for His burial, and the rich for His death, for He did not sin, neither was guile found in His mouth: and the Lord wills to purify from Him [with] stripes. [11] If You make an offering for sin Your soul will prolong its days. [12] And the Lord wills to take away from the travail of His soul, to show Him light and to form Him by knowledge, to justify the righteous man who serves many well; and He will bear their sins Himself. [13] For what reason He will receive the inheritance of many, and will divide the spoils of the strong, because His soul was delivered up to death, and He was numbered among the transgressors, [14] and He bore the sins of many, and was given up for their sins." [15] And again He says, "I am a worm and no man—a reproach of men and despised of the people; [16] all they who saw Me mocked Me, they spoke with their lips, they shook the head; He hoped in God, let Him deliver Him, let Him save Him, because He desires Him." [17] See, beloved, what is the example that has been given to us; for if the Lord so humbled Himself, what will we do who have, through His mercy, come under the yoke of His grace?

CHAPTER 17

[1] Let us also be imitators of them who went around in goatskins and sheepskins, preaching the coming of Christ; we mean Elijah, and Elisha, and Ezekiel the prophets, and beside them those who have obtained a good report. [2] Abraham obtained an exceedingly good report, and was called the friend of God, and says, looking steadfastly to the glory of God in humility, "I am but earth and ashes." [3] And, moreover, concerning Job, it is thus written: "Job was a just man and blameless, truthful, one that feared God and abstained from all evil." [4] But he himself, accusing himself, says, "No one is pure from pollution, though his life is but for one day." [5] Moses was called faithful in all his house, and by his ministry God judged His people Israel by stripes and punishment. But he, though he was greatly glorified, did not speak haughtily, but said, when the oracle was given to him out of the bush, "Who am I that You send me? I am weak of voice and slow of tongue." [6] And

again he says, "I am but as the smoke from a pot."

CHAPTER 18

¹ But what will we say of David, who obtained a good report; to whom God said, "I have found a man after My own heart, David, the son of Jesse; I have anointed him with My continuous mercy. ² But he himself says to God, "Have mercy on me, O God, according to Your great mercy, according to the multitude of Your compassion do away with my iniquity; ³ wash me thoroughly from my iniquity, and cleanse me from my sin. For I know my iniquity, and my sin is ever before me. ⁴ Against You only have I sinned, and done this evil in Your sight, that You might be justified in Your words, and overcome when You are judged. ⁵ Behold, I was fashioned in wickedness, and in sin my mother conceived me. ⁶ Behold, You have loved truth; You have shown me the secret and hidden things of Your wisdom. ⁷ You will sprinkle me with hyssop, and I will be clean. You will wash me, and I will be whiter than snow. ⁸ You will make me to hear of joy and gladness; the bones that have been humiliated will rejoice. ⁹ Turn away Your face from my sins and blot out all my misdeeds. ¹⁰ Create in me a new heart, O Lord, and renew a right spirit within me. ¹¹ Do not cast me away from Your presence, and do not take Your Holy Spirit from me. ¹² Give me the joy of Your salvation again, and establish me with Your guiding Spirit. ¹³ I will teach sinners Your ways; the ungodly will be converted to You. ¹⁴ Deliver me from blood-guiltiness, O God, You God of my salvation; ¹⁵ my tongue will rejoice in Your righteousness. O Lord, You will open my mouth, and my lips will show forth Your praise. ¹⁶ For if You had desired sacrifice, I would have given it; in whole burnt-offerings You will not delight. ¹⁷ The sacrifice of God is a broken spirit; a broken and a contrite heart God will not despise "

CHAPTER 19

¹ The humility of men so many in number and so great, and who have obtained such a good report, and their subjection through obedience, has made not only us but the generations before us better, namely, those who in fear and truth have received His oracles. ² Since, therefore, we have become the partakers in many great and glorious actions, let us finally return to that goal of peace that was given us from the beginning; let us look steadfastly to the Father and Creator of the whole world, and let us cleave to the glorious and excellent gifts and benefits of His peace. ³ Let us behold Him in spirit and look with the eyes of the soul to His long-suffering will. Let us consider how gentle He is toward all His creation.

CHAPTER 20

¹ The heavens, being put in motion by His appointment, are subject to Him in peace; ² night and day they accomplish the course ordered by Him, in nothing hindering one another. ³ The sun, and the moon, and the dances of the stars according to His appointment, in harmony and without any violation of order, roll on the courses appointed to them. ⁴ The fruitful earth brings forth in due season, according to His will, abundant nourishment for men and beasts; doubting nothing, nor changing in anything from the things that are decreed by Him. ⁵ The unsearchable things of the abyss, and the secret ordinances of the lower parts of the earth, are held together by the same command. ⁶ The hollow of the vast sea, gathered together by His hand into its reservoirs, does not transgress the bounds placed around it; but even as He has appointed to it, so it does; ⁷ for He said, "You will come thus far, and your waves will be broken within you." ⁸ The ocean, impassable to men, and the worlds that are beyond it, are governed by the same commands of their Master. ⁹ The seasons of spring and summer, autumn and winter, in peace succeed one another. ¹⁰ The fixed stations of the winds, each in their due time, perform their services without offense. The ever-flowing fountains, made for enjoyment and health, offer their breasts without fail to sustain the lives of men. Even the smallest of animals come together in peace and harmony. ¹¹ All these things the great Maker and Master of all things has appointed to be in peace and harmony, doing good to all things, but more especially to

us, who have fled for refuge to His mercies, through our Lord Jesus Christ, ¹² to whom be glory and majesty forever and ever. Amen.

CHAPTER 21

¹ Beware, beloved, lest His many blessings come to be a condemnation to all of us, unless, walking worthily of Him, we do what is honorable and well pleasing before Him with oneness of mind. ² For He says in a certain place, "The Spirit of the Lord is a candle, searching out the secret places of the heart." ³ Let us see how near He is at hand, and how none of our thoughts and reasonings escape Him. ⁴ It is right, therefore, that we should not desert from His will. ⁵ Let us offend against men who are foolish, and senseless, and puffed up in the pride of their own speech, rather than against God. ⁶ Let us have respect to our Lord Jesus Christ, whose blood was given for us. Let us revere them that are over us. Let us honor our elders. Let us instruct the young in the discipline of the fear of God. Let us direct our wives to that which is good; ⁷ let them show forth the lovely habit of chastity and exhibit the pure disposition of meekness. Let them make manifest by their conversation the government of their tongues; let them show love, not according to partiality, but equally to all that fear the Lord in holiness. ⁸ Let your children be partakers of the discipline of Christ; let them learn how much humility avails before God; what power a pure love has with God; how His fear is honorable and great, preserving all who, with a pure mind, walk in holiness before Him. ⁹ For He is a searcher out of thoughts and counsels, His breath is in us, and when He wills He will take it away.

CHAPTER 22

¹ The faith which is in Christ assures all these things. For He Himself, through the Holy Spirit, thus calls to us: "Come, you children, listen to Me, I will teach you the fear of the Lord. ² What man is he that wishes for life and would gladly see good days? ³ Keep your tongue from evil, and your lips that they speak no guile. ⁴ Turn away from evil and do good; ⁵ seek peace and pursue it. ⁶ The eyes of the Lord are over the just, and His ears are open to their prayer. But the face of the Lord is against them that do evil, to destroy their memorial out of the land. ⁷ The righteous cried, and the Lord heard him, and delivered him out of all his troubles." ⁸ "Many are the afflictions of the sinner, but they that hope in the Lord, mercy will surround them."

CHAPTER 23

¹ The Father whose mercies are over all things, who loves to do good, has yearnings of compassion for them that fear Him, and with gentleness and kindness bestows His favor on them that come to Him with a pure mind. ² For what reason let us not be double-minded, nor let our hearts form vain imaginations concerning His excellent and glorious gifts. ³ Do not let that Writing be applicable to us which says, "Wretched are the double-minded, even they that doubt in their heart and say, We have heard these things in the time of our fathers; and behold, we have grown old, and none of them has happened to us." ⁴ O foolish ones! compare yourselves to a tree. Take, for example, the vine: first it sheds its leaves, then comes the bud, then the leaf, then the flower, after that the unripe grape, then the ripe grape. See how in a short time the fruit of the tree attains to maturity. ⁵ Of a truth, quickly and suddenly will His will be fulfilled; the Writing also bearing witness that He will come quickly, and will not tarry; and the Lord will come suddenly into His temple, even the Holy One, whom you expect.

CHAPTER 24

¹ Let us consider, beloved, how the Master shows to us continually the resurrection that is about to be, of which He has made our Lord Jesus Christ the first-fruit, having raised Him from the dead. ² Let us look, beloved, at the resurrection that

is always taking place— ³ day and night show the resurrection to us; the night is lulled to rest, the day arises; the day departs, the night comes on. ⁴ Let us consider the fruits, in what way a grain of corn is sown. ⁵ The sower goes forth and casts it into the ground, and when the seeds are cast into the ground, they that fell into the ground dry and naked are dissolved; then after their dissolution, the mighty power of the providence of the Lord raises them up, and from one seed many grow up and bring forth fruits.

CHAPTER 25

¹ Let us consider the wonderful sign that happens in the region of the east, even about Arabia. ² There is a bird which is called the phoenix. This, being the only one of its kind, lives for five hundred years. And when the time of its death draws near, it makes for itself a nest of frankincense, and myrrh, and the other perfumes, into which, when its time is fulfilled, it enters, and then dies. ³ But as its flesh rots, a certain worm is produced, which being nourished by the moisture of the dead animal, puts forth feathers. Then, when it has become strong, it takes the nest wherein are the bones of its ancestor, and bearing them, it flies from the region of Arabia to that of Egypt, to the city which is called Heliopolis; ⁴ there, in daytime, in the sight of all, it flies up, and places them on the altar of the sun, and having done so, returns back. ⁵ The priests, therefore, look into the registers of the times, and find that it has come at the completion of the five-hundredth year.

CHAPTER 26

¹ Will we then think it great and wonderful, if the Maker of all things will make a resurrection of those who, in the confidence of a good faith, have piously seized Him, when even by means of a bird He shows the greatness of His promises? ² For He says in a certain place, "And You will raise me up, and I will give thanks to You"; and again: "I slumbered and slept; I rose up because You are with me. ³ And again Job says, "You will raise up this flesh of mine, which has suffered all these things."

CHAPTER 27

¹ In this hope, therefore, let our souls be bound to Him who is faithful in His promises and just in His judgments. ² He who has commanded men not to lie, much more will He not lie, for nothing is impossible with God, except to lie. ³ Let our faith, therefore, be kindled in Him afresh within us, and let us consider that all things are near to Him. ⁴ By the word of His majesty He constituted all things, and by a word He is able to destroy them. ⁵ "Who will say to Him, What have You done? or who will resist the might of His strength?" He will do all things when He wills and as He wills, and none of the things decreed by Him will pass away. ⁶ All things are before Him, and nothing has escaped His counsel, ⁷ seeing that "the heavens declare the glory of God, and the expanse shows the work of His hands: day to day utters speech, and night to night proclaims knowledge; and there is no speech nor language where their voices are not heard."

CHAPTER 28

¹ Therefore, since all things are seen and heard by Him, let us fear Him and abandon the filthy desires for evil deeds, that we may be sheltered by His mercy from the judgments to come. ² For, to where can any of us fly from His mighty hand, and what world will receive any of them that desert from Him? ³ For the Writing says in a certain place: "To where will I go, and where will I conceal myself from Your face? If I ascend into Heaven, You are there; if I depart into the uttermost parts of the earth, Your right hand is there; if I will make my bed in the abyss, Your Spirit is there." ⁴ To where then will we depart, and where will we fly from Him that embraces all things?

CHAPTER 29

¹ Therefore, let us approach Him with holiness of spirit, lifting pure and undefiled hands to Him; loving the kind and compassionate Father who has made us a part of His chosen ones. ² For it is thus written: "When the Most High divided the nations, when He dispersed the sons of Adam, He settled the boundaries of the nations according to the number of the messengers of God. The portion of the Lord was His people Jacob." ³ Israel was the measurement of His inheritance. And in another place it says, "Behold, the Lord takes to Himself a nation from the midst of the nations, even as a man takes the first-fruits of his threshingfloor; and there will go forth from that nation the Holy of Holies."

CHAPTER 30

¹ Since, therefore, we are a portion of the Holy One, let us do all such things as pertain to holiness, avoiding evil-speaking, foul and impure embraces, drunkenness, disorderliness, abominable desires, detestable adultery, execrable pride; ² "for God," it says, "resists the proud, but gives grace to the humble." ³ Let us cleave, therefore, to them to whom grace has been given from God. Let us clothe ourselves with concord, being humble, temperate, keeping ourselves far from all whispering and evil-speaking, justified by our deeds, and not by our words. ⁴ For it says, "He who says many things will, in return, hear many things. Does he that is eloquent think himself to be just? ⁵ Does he that is born of woman and lives but for a short time think himself to be blessed? Do not be abundant in speech." ⁶ Let our praise be in God, and not for ourselves, for God hates the self-praisers. ⁷ Let the testimony of right actions be given us from others, even as it was given to our fathers who were just. ⁸ Audacity, self-will, and boldness belong to them who are accursed of God; but moderation, humility, and meekness, to them that are blessed of God.

CHAPTER 31

¹ Therefore, let us cleave to His blessing, and let us see what the ways of blessing are. Let us consult the records of the things that happened from the beginning. ² On what account was our father Abraham blessed? Was it not that he worked righteousness and truth through faith? ³ Isaac, with confidence, knowing the future, willingly became a sacrifice. ⁴ Jacob, with humility, flying from his brother, went out from his own land and journeyed to Laban and served as a slave, and there were given to him the twelve tribes of Israel.

CHAPTER 32

¹ If anyone will consider these things with sincerity and one by one, he will recognize the magnificence of the gifts that were given by him. ² For from Jacob came the priests and all the Levites that serve the altar of God. From him came our Lord Jesus Christ according to the flesh; from him came the kings, and rulers, and governors of the tribe of Judah; and the remainder of his tribes are of no small glory, since God has promised, "Your seed will be as the stars of the heavens." ³ Therefore, all these have been glorified and magnified, not through themselves, or through their works, or through the righteousness that they have done, but through His will. ⁴ And we who through His will have been called in Christ Jesus are justified, not by ourselves, or through our wisdom, or understanding, or godliness, or the works that we have done in holiness of heart, but by faith, by which all men from the beginning have been justified by Almighty God, to whom be glory through the ages of the ages. Amen.

CHAPTER 33

¹ What, then, will we do, brothers? Will we cease from well-doing, and abandon charity? May the Master never allow that this should happen to us! but let us rather with diligence and

zeal hasten to fulfill every good work. ² For the Maker and Lord of all things rejoices in His works. ³ By His supreme power He founded the heavens, and by His incomprehensible understanding He ordered them. He separated the earth from the water that surrounded it, and fixed it on the firm foundation of His own will. The animals which inhabit therein He commanded to be by His ordinance. Having made beforehand the sea and the animals that are therein, He shut them in by His own power. ⁴ Man, the most excellent of all animals, infinite in faculty, He moulded with His holy and faultless hands, in the impress of His likeness. ⁵ For thus says God: "Let Us make man in Our own image, and after Our own likeness. And God made man. He made them male and female." ⁶ Therefore, when He had finished all things, He praised and blessed them, and said, "Be fruitful, and multiply." ⁷ Let us see, therefore, how all the just have been adorned with good works. Yes, the Lord Himself rejoiced when He had adorned Himself with His works. ⁸ Having, therefore, this example, let us come in without shrinking to His will; let us work with all our strength the work of righteousness.

CHAPTER 34

¹ The good workman boldly receives the bread of his labor, but the slothful and remiss does not look his employer in the face. ² It is therefore right that we should be zealous in well-doing, for from Him are all things; ³ for He tells us beforehand: "Behold, the Lord comes, and His reward is before His face, to give to everyone according to his work." ⁴ He exhorts us, therefore, with this reward in view, to strive with our whole heart not to be slothful or remiss toward every good work. ⁵ Let our glorying and our confidence be in Him; let us submit ourselves to His will; let us consider the whole multitude of His messengers, how they stand by and serve His will. ⁶ For the Writing says, "Ten thousand times ten thousand stood beside Him, and thousands of thousands served Him; and they cried, Holy, Holy, Holy, Lord of Hosts! all creation is full of His glory." ⁷ And let us, being gathered together in harmony and a good conscience, cry earnestly, as it were with one mouth, to Him, that we may become partakers of His great and glorious promises; ⁸ for He says, "Eye has not seen, and ear has not heard, neither has there entered into the heart of man, what things He has prepared for them that wait for Him."

CHAPTER 35

¹ Behold, beloved, how blessed and wonderful are the gifts of God— ² life in immortality, cheerfulness in righteousness, truth in liberty, faith in confidence, temperance in sanctification; and all these things have already come within our cognizance. ³ What therefore are the things that are prepared for them that abide in patience? The Maker and Father of the worlds, the All-Holy One, He knows how many and how beautiful they are. ⁴ Let us, therefore, strive to be found in the number of them that await Him, that we may partake of the promised gifts. ⁵ And how will this be, beloved? If our mind is established by faith toward God; if we seek out what is pleasant and acceptable in His sight; if we perform such things as harmonize with His blameless will, and follow in the way of truth, casting from us all unrighteousness and lawlessness, covetousness, strife, malice and fraud, whispering and evil-speaking, hatred of God, pride and insolence, vainglory and intractableness. ⁶ For they who do these things are hateful to God, and not only they who do them, but also they who have pleasure in them that do them. ⁷ For the Writing says: "But to the sinner God has said, Why do you speak of My ordinances, and take My covenant in your mouth? ⁸ But you have hated instruction and have cast My words behind you. When you saw a thief you went with him and have cast in your portion with the adulterers; your mouth has abounded with evil, and your tongue has contrived deceit. You sat and spoke against your brother and have slandered the son of your mother. ⁹ You have done this, and I kept silence. You thought, O wicked one, that I was like to you; ¹⁰ but I will convict you and will set yourself before you. ¹¹ Consider this, you who forget God, lest He seize you as a lion, and there is none to save you. ¹² The sacrifice of praise will honor Me; and there is the way by which I will show him the salvation of God."

CHAPTER 36

¹ This is the way, beloved, in which we found our salvation—even Jesus Christ, the Chief Priest of our oblations, the champion and defender of our weakness. ² Through Him we look steadfastly to the heights of the heavens; through Him we behold, as in a glass, the immaculate and lofty countenance of God the Father; through Him the eyes of our heart were opened; through Him our foolish and darkened understanding springs up again to His marvelous light; through Him the Lord has willed us to taste of immortal knowledge, "who, being the brightness of His glory, is so far better than the messengers, as He has, by inheritance, obtained a more excellent Name than they." ³ For it is thus written: "Who makes His messengers spirits, || His ministers a flame of fire." ⁴ But of His Son the Lord has thus said, "You are My Son, today have I begotten You. Ask of Me, and I will give You the heathen for Your inheritance, || And the uttermost parts of the world for Your possession." ⁵ And, again, He says to Him: "Sit on My right hand || Until I make Your enemies Your footstool." ⁶ Who then are the enemies? Even the wicked, and they who resist the will of God.

CHAPTER 37

¹ Let us, therefore, men and brothers, carry on our warfare with all earnestness in His faultless ordinances. ² Let us consider those who fight under our rulers, how orderly, and obediently, and submissively they perform what is commanded them. ³ All are not prefects, or commanders of thousands, or commanders of hundreds, or commanders of fifties, or such-like; but each in his own rank performs what has been ordered by the king or the commanders. ⁴ The great cannot exist without the small, nor the small without the great. There is a certain mixture in all things, and from there arises their use. ⁵ Let us take, for example, our body: the head is nothing without the feet, nor the feet without the head. The smallest members of the body are necessary and useful to the whole body, and all unite and work with harmonious obedience for the preservation of the whole body.

CHAPTER 38

¹ Therefore, let our whole body be saved in Christ Jesus, and let each be subject to his neighbor according to the gift which he has received. ² Do not let the strong man despise the weak; and let the weak pay regard to the strong. Let him that is rich minister to him that is poor. Let him that is poor praise God that He has given to him one by whom his want may be supplied. Let the wise show his wisdom, not in words, but in good deeds; let him that is humble not bear witness to himself, but leave another to bear witness to him. Let him that is pure in the flesh not boast of it, knowing that it is another that gives him the power of continence. ³ Let us consider, brothers, of what matter we are made, of what sort and who we are that have come into the world, as it were out of the tomb and darkness. He that made and fashioned us has brought us into this world, having prepared beforehand His benefactions, even before we were born. ⁴ Therefore, having all these things from Him, we should in all respects give thanks to Him, to whom be glory through the ages of the ages. Amen.

CHAPTER 39

¹ The senseless and unwise, the foolish and unruly, make a mockery of us, wishing to exalt themselves in their own imagination. ² For what can a mortal do? or what strength has he that is born of earth? ³ For it is written: "There was no form before my eyes, only I heard a breath and a voice. ⁴ For what? will a mortal be pure before the Lord? or is a man blameless from his works? seeing that He puts no trust in His servants, and even beholds iniquity in His messengers; ⁵ yes, the Heaven is not pure in His sight. Away, you who dwell in houses of clay, of whom are we also even of the same clay. He has smitten them even as it were a moth, and in a single day they are no

ause they could not help themselves, they perished: among them, and they died, because they had no all, now, and see if there is anyone that will obey will behold any of the holy messengers. For anger roys the fool, and envy puts him to death that is gone out of the way. **8** I have beheld the foolish casting forth roots, but immediately his habitation was eaten up. **9** Let his sons be far from safety, let them be mocked at the gates of their inferiors, and there will be none to deliver them. For that which had been prepared for them the just will eat, and they will not be delivered out of their troubles."

CHAPTER 40

1 Therefore, since these things have been made manifest before to us, and since we have looked into the depths of the divine knowledge, we should do everything in order, whatever the Lord has commanded us to do at the appointed seasons, and to perform the offerings and services. **2** He has not commanded these to be done at random or in disorder, but at fixed times and seasons. **3** But when and by whom He wishes them to be fulfilled He Himself has decided by His supreme will, that all things, being done piously, according to His good pleasure, might be acceptable to His will. **4** Therefore, they who at the appointed seasons make their offerings are acceptable and blessed; for while following the laws of the Master they do not completely sin. **5** For to the Chief Priest were assigned special services, and to the priests a special place has been appointed; and on the Levites special duties are imposed. But he that is a layman is bound by the ordinances of laymen.

CHAPTER 41

1 Let each of you, brothers, in his own order, give thanks to God, continuing in a good conscience, not transgressing the fixed rule of his ministry, with all gravity. **2** Not in every place, brothers, are sacrifices offered continually, either in answer to prayer, or concerning sin and neglect, but in Jerusalem only; and even there the offering is not made in every place, but before the temple in the court of the altar, after that which is offered has been diligently examined by the chief priest and the appointed ministers. **3** They, therefore, who do anything contrary to that which is according to His will have death for their punishment. **4** You see, brothers, by as much as we have been thought worthy of greater knowledge, by so much the more are we exposed to danger.

CHAPTER 42

1 The apostles received the good news for us from our Lord Jesus Christ; our Lord Jesus Christ received it from God. **2** Christ, therefore, was sent out from God, and the apostles from Christ; and both these things were done in good order, according to the will of God. **3** They, therefore, having received the promises, having been fully persuaded by the resurrection of our Lord Jesus Christ, and having been confirmed by the word of God, with the full persuasion of the Holy Spirit, went forth preaching the good tidings that the Kingdom of God was at hand. **4** Preaching, therefore, through the countries and cities, they appointed their first-fruits to be overseers and servants over such as should believe, after they had proved them in the Spirit. **5** And this they did in no new way, for in truth it had in long past time been written concerning overseers and servants; for the Writing, in a certain place, says in this way: "I will establish their overseers in righteousness, and their servants in faith."

CHAPTER 43

1 And wherein is it wonderful, if they who, in Christ, were entrusted by God with this work appointed the previously mentioned officers? since even the blessed Moses, the faithful servant in all his house, signified in the sacred scrolls all the things that were commanded to him, whom also the prophets have followed, bearing witness together to the laws which were appointed by him. **2** For he, when a strife arose concerning the priesthood, and when the tribes contended which of them should be adorned with that glorious name, commanded the twelve chiefs of the tribes to bring to him rods, each inscribed with the name of a tribe; and when he had taken them, he bound them together, and sealed them with the seals of the heads of the tribes, and laid them up on the table of God, in the Dwelling Place of the testimony. **3** And when he had closed the Dwelling Place, he sealed the keys, and likewise the rods, **4** and said to them, "Men and brothers, of whatever tribe the rod will bud, this has God chosen to be His priest, and to serve Him." **5** And when morning had come, he called together all Israel, even six hundred thousand men, and showed to the heads of the tribes the seals, and opened the Dwelling Place of the testimony and brought forth the rods, and the rod of Aaron was found not only to have budded, but also bearing fruit. **6** What do you think, beloved? did Moses not know beforehand that this was about to happen? Most assuredly he knew it, but, that there might be no disorder in Israel, he did thus that the Name of the true and only God might be glorified, to whom be glory through the ages of the ages. Amen.

CHAPTER 44

1 Our apostles, too, by the instruction of our Lord Jesus Christ, knew that strife would arise concerning the dignity of an overseer; **2** and on this account, having received perfect foreknowledge, they appointed the above-mentioned as overseers and servants: and then gave a rule of succession, in order that, when they had fallen asleep, other men, who had been approved, might succeed to their ministry. **3** Those who were thus appointed by them, or afterward by other men of good regard, with the consent of the whole Assembly, who have blamelessly ministered to the flock of Christ with humility, quietly, and without illiberality, and who for a long time have obtained a good report from all, these, we think, have been unjustly deposed from the ministry. **4** For it will be no small sin in us if we depose from the office of overseer those who blamelessly and piously have made the offerings. **5** Happy are the elders who finished their course before and died in mature age after they had borne fruit; for they do not fear lest anyone should remove them from the place appointed for them. **6** For we see that you have removed some men of honest conversation from the ministry, which had been blamelessly and honorably performed by them.

CHAPTER 45

1 You are contentious, brothers, and are zealous concerning things that do not pertain to salvation. **2** Look diligently into the Writings, which are the true sayings of the Holy Spirit. **3** You know how that nothing unjust or corrupt has been written in them; for you will not find in them the just expelled by holy men. **4** The just were persecuted, but it was by the lawless; they were thrown into prison, but it was by the unholy; they were stoned, but it was by sinners; they were slain, but it was by wicked men, even by those who had taken up an unjust envy against them. **5** They, therefore, when they suffered all these things, suffered them with a good report. **6** For what will we say, brothers? was it by those that feared God that Daniel was cast into the den of lions? **7** Was it by those who practiced the magnificent and glorious worship of the Highest that Hananiah, Azariah, and Mishael were shut up in the fiery furnace? Let us not suppose that such was the case. Who, then, were the men who did these things? Abominable men and full of all wickedness were inflamed to such a degree of wrath that they cast into tortures those who, with a holy and blameless purpose, served God, not knowing that the Highest is a champion and defender of those who with a pure conscience serve His most excellent Name, to whom be glory through the ages of the ages. Amen. **8** But they, abiding steadfastly in their confidence, have inherited honor and glory, and have both been exalted and made beautiful by God, in the memory that is made of them through the ages of the ages. Amen.

CHAPTER 46

[1] We should also cleave to such examples, brothers. [2] For it is written: "Cleave to them that are holy, for they that cleave to them will be made holy." [3] And again, in another place it says, "With the guiltless man you will be guiltless, and with the excellent you will be excellent, and with him that is crooked you will be perverse." [4] Therefore, let us cleave to the guiltless and the just, for they are the chosen ones of God. [5] Why are there strivings, and anger, and division, and war among you? [6] Do we not have one God and one Christ? Is the Spirit of grace, which was poured out on us, not one? Is our calling in Christ not one? [7] Why do we tear apart and split apart the members of Christ, and make sedition against our body, and come to such a degree of madness that we forget we are members of one another? Remember the words of our Lord Jesus, [8] for He said, "Woe to that man; it were good for him if he had never been born, rather than that he should cause one of My chosen ones to offend. It were better for him that a millstone were tied around him, and that he were cast into the sea, rather than that he should cause one of My little ones to offend. [9] This schism of yours has perverted many, [and] has cast many into despondency, many into doubt, [and] all of us into grief, and, as yet, your sedition remains.

CHAPTER 47

[1] Take into your hands the letter of the blessed apostle Paul. [2] What did he first write to you in the beginning of his good news? [3] Of a truth, he warned you spiritually, in a letter, concerning himself, and concerning Cephas and Apollos, because even then there were factions among you; [4] but the faction of that time brought less sin on you; for you inclined to apostles of good regard, and to a man approved among them. [5] But now consider who they are that have perverted you and have diminished the glory of your famous brotherly love. [6] It is disgraceful, brothers, yes, very disgraceful, and unworthy of the conduct which is in Christ, that it should be reported that the most firm and ancient assembly of the Corinthians has, on account of one or two persons, made sedition against its elders. [7] And this report did not only come to us, but also to the nations, who do not go with us, so that you heap blasphemies on the Name of the Lord through your folly, and in addition cause danger to yourselves.

CHAPTER 48

[1] Therefore, let us remove this thing as quickly as possible, and let us fall before the feet of the Master, and implore Him with tears, that He will have mercy and be reconciled to us, and restore us again to the grave and pure conversation of brotherly love. [2] For this is a gate of righteousness opened to life, as it is written: "Open to me the gates of righteousness; I will go in to them, and give thanks to the Lord: [3] this is the gate of the Lord; the righteous will enter thereby." [4] Now, since many gates have been opened, the gate of righteousness is that which is in Christ. Happy are all they that enter therein, and who keep their path straight in holiness and righteousness, quietly performing all their duties. [5] If a man is faithful, if he is mighty to expound knowledge, if he is wise in the interpretation of words, if he is pure in his deeds, [6] by so much the more should he be humble, and by as much as he seems to be greater, by so much the more should he seek the common advantage of all, and not of himself alone.

CHAPTER 49

[1] Let him that has the love which is in Christ keep the commands of Christ. [2] Who can describe sufficiently the bond of the love of God? [3] Who is sufficient to speak as he should of the excellence of its beauty? [4] The height to which love leads up is unspeakable. [5] Love joins us to God; love hides a multitude of sins; love bears all things; is long suffering in all things. In love there is nothing illiberal, nothing haughty. Love has no schism; love does not make sedition; love does all things in harmony; in love all the chosen ones of God have been made perfect. Without love nothing is acceptable to God. [6] In love, our Master has taken us to Himself. Through the love that He has for us, Jesus Christ our Lord has given His blood for us, by the will of God, His flesh for our flesh, His soul for our soul.

CHAPTER 50

[1] You see, brothers, how great and wonderful a thing love is, and how there is no describing its perfection. [2] Who is sufficient to be found in it, except those whom God will have deemed worthy? Therefore, let us pray and ask from His mercy that we may live in love, without human partiality, blameless. [3] All the generations from Adam, even to this day, have gone by, but they who have been made perfect in love according to the grace of God, inhabit the abode of the pious and will be made manifest in the visitation of the Kingdom of Christ. [4] For it is written: "Enter into the secret chambers but a little while, until My anger and wrath have passed, and I will remember the good day, and will raise you up from your tombs." [5] Blessed are we, beloved, if we do the commands of God in the harmony of love, so that through love our sins may be forgiven us. [6] For it is written: "Blessed are they whose iniquities are forgiven, and whose sins are covered. Blessed is the man to whom the Lord does not impute sin, and in whose mouth, there is no guile." [7] This blessedness comes to them who are chosen by God, through Jesus Christ our Lord, to whom be glory through the ages of the ages. Amen.

CHAPTER 51

[1] Therefore, whatever errors we have committed through the assaults of the adversary, let us ask pardon for these; and they who have been leaders of the sedition and division should consider the common ground of our hope. [2] For they who have their conversation in fear and love wish that they themselves, rather than their neighbors, should fall into suffering; and would rather that they should undergo condemnation themselves, than that the harmony which has been honorably and justly handed down to us should do so. [3] For it is better that a man should make confession concerning his sins, than that he should harden his heart, even as the heart of them was hardened who made sedition against Moses, the servant of God—[they] whose condemnation was manifest; [4] for they went down alive into Hades, and death swallowed them up. [5] Pharaoh and his army, and all the leaders of Egypt, their chariots and their riders, through no other cause were sunk in the Red Sea, and perished there, than through the hardening of their foolish hearts, after that the signs and wonders happened in Egypt through the hand of Moses, the servant of God.

CHAPTER 52

[1] The Lord of all things, brothers, is in need of nothing; neither does He require anything of anyone, except to confess to Him. [2] For the chosen one, David, says, "I will confess to the Lord, and that will please Him more than a young calf that puts forth horns and hooves. Let the poor behold and rejoice at that." [3] And again he says, "Offer to the Lord the sacrifice of praise: pay your vows to the Highest. And call on Me in the day of your affliction, and I will deliver you, and you will glorify Me. [4] For the sacrifice to God is a broken spirit."

CHAPTER 53

[1] You know, beloved, and know well, the sacred Writings, and have looked into the oracles of God; therefore, call these things to remembrance. [2] For, when Moses had gone up into the mount, and had tarried there forty days and forty nights in fasting and humiliation, the Lord said to Him, "Moses, Moses, come down quickly from here, for your people, whom you brought out of the land of Egypt, have worked iniquity. They have quickly gone astray out of the way that you command them and have made molten images for themselves." [3] And the Lord said to him, "I have spoken to you once and twice, saying, I have beheld this people, and behold, it is a stiff-necked people. Leave Me alone, that I may destroy them, and I will

their name from under Heaven, and make of you a [n]at and wonderful, and far more numerous than [an]d Moses said, "Be it far from You, O Lord. Forgive [peo]ple their sin, or also wipe my name out of the Scroll of [th]e Living." **5** Oh, the great love! Oh, the unsurpassable perfection! The servant is bold toward the Lord: he asks forgiveness for the people or demands otherwise that he himself should be destroyed together with them.

CHAPTER 54

1 Who among you is noble? who is compassionate? who is filled with love? **2** Let him speak in this way: "If through me sedition and strife arise, I will depart, I will go away to wherever you will, and I will do that which is commanded by the majority, only let the flock of Christ be at peace together with the appointed elders." **3** He who does this will gain for himself great glory in the Lord, and every place will receive him, "for the earth is the Lord's, and the fullness thereof." **4** These things they have done who are citizens of the Kingdom of God, which does not need to be converted of, and these things they will yet do.

CHAPTER 55

1 But, to bring forward examples from the nations, also many kings and leaders, when a time of pestilence had arisen, being warned by oracles, gave themselves to death, that they might deliver their citizens by their blood. Many went out from their own cities, that there might no longer be sedition therein. **2** We know that many among us gave themselves up to bonds, that they might deliver others. Many have given themselves up to slavery, and, having received their own price, have with those fed others. **3** Many women, waxing strong through the grace of God, have performed many manly deeds. **4** The blessed Judith, when the city was besieged, asked of the elders that she should be permitted to go forth into the camp of the aliens. **5** She therefore delivered herself to danger and went out through love of her country and of her people, who were besieged. And the Lord delivered Holofernes into the hands of a woman. **6** To no smaller danger did Esther, being perfect in faith, expose herself, that she might deliver the twelve tribes of Israel who were about to perish. For by fasting and humiliation she implored the Master, who overlooks all things, the God of Ages, who, seeing the humiliation of her soul, delivered the people for whose sake she put herself in danger.

CHAPTER 56

1 Therefore, let us pray for those who have fallen into any transgression, that moderation and humility may be given to them, to the end that they should submit themselves, I do not say to us, but to the will of God; for so they will obtain a fruitful and perfect remembrance and compassion before God and His holy ones. **2** Let us accept, brothers, that discipline at which no one needs to be offended. The admonition which we make toward one another is exceedingly good and useful, for it joins us to the will of God. **3** For thus speaks the holy word: "The Lord has disciplined me with disciplines, but He has not given me over to death." **4** "For whom the Lord loves He disciplines, and scourges every son whom He receives." **5** "The righteous will discipline me in pity and will rebuke me, but do not let the oil of sinners anoint my head." **6** And again it says: "Blessed is the man whom the Lord has rebuked; do not refuse the admonition of the Almighty, for He makes you to grieve, and again He restores you; **7** He has smitten, and His hands have healed you; **8** six times He will deliver you from calamity, and the seventh time evil will not touch you. **9** In the time of famine He will deliver you from death, in war He will redeem you from the hand of iron. **10** From the scourge of the tongue He will hide you, and you will not be afraid when evils approach. **11** The unjust and the sinner you will laugh to scorn; **12** and of the wild beasts you will not be afraid, for the wild beasts will be at peace with you. **13** Then you will know that your house will be at peace; the habitation of your dwelling place will not fail. **14** You will know that your seed is abundant, your children like all the herb of the field. **15** You will come to your tomb like a ripe ear of corn reaped in due season, like the heap of a threshing-floor that is gathered at its proper time." **16** You see, beloved, that there is a protection for them that are disciplined by the Master, for God chastens us because He is good, to the end that we should be admonished by His holy discipline.

CHAPTER 57

1 Therefore, you that have laid the foundation of the sedition: submit yourselves to the elders, and be disciplined to conversion, bending the knees of your hearts. **2** Learn to submit yourselves, laying aside the vain and haughty self-will of your tongues; for it is better that you should be small and approved in the flock of Christ, rather than that, seeming to be superior to others, you should be cast out of His hope. **3** For thus says the most excellent Wisdom: "Behold, I will send on you the language of My Spirit; I will teach you My word. **4** Since I called and you did not listen, and prolonged My words, and you did not attend [to them], but made My counsels of no effect, and were not obedient to My reproofs, therefore I will laugh at your destruction, I will exult when desolation comes on you; when perturbation has suddenly come on you, and ruin is at hand like a whirlwind, when tribulation and oppression comes on you. **5** For the time will come when you will call on Me, and I will not listen to you; the wicked will seek Me, and will not find Me. They hated wisdom and did not choose the fear of the Lord; they were not willing to attend to My counsels, they mocked at My rebukes. **6** For what reason they will eat the fruits of their own way; they will be filled with their own unrighteousness. **7** For because they wronged the innocent they will be slain, and judgment will destroy the unrighteous; but he who listens to Me will abide, trusting in hope, and will rest securely from all evil."

CHAPTER 58

1 Let us, therefore, submit to His all-holy and glorious Name, and escape the threats that have been before spoken by Wisdom against the disobedient, that we may abide trusting in the most holy Name of His greatness. **2** Accept this advice of ours, and it will not be regretted by you. For as God lives, and as the Lord Jesus Christ lives, and the Holy Spirit—the confidence and hope of the chosen ones—He who observes in humility with earnest obedience, and not complaining, the ordinances and commands given by God, he will be reckoned and counted in the number of them that are saved by Jesus Christ, through whom is the glory to Him through the ages of the ages. Amen.

CHAPTER 59

1 But if some should be disobedient to the things spoken by Him through us, let them know that they will entangle themselves in no small transgression and danger, **2** but that we will be guiltless of this sin; and we will ask, making our prayer and supplication with earnestness, that the Maker of all things may keep uninjured in all the world the number of those that have been numbered as His chosen ones, through His beloved Son, Jesus Christ, through whom He has called us from darkness to light, and from ignorance to a knowledge of the glory of His Name. **3** That we may hope in Your Name, which is the first of all things, open the eyes of our heart to know You, who are alone highest among the highest, holy among the holy, who puts down the haughtiness of the proud, who scatters the reasonings of the nations, who exalts the humble on high, and lowers the lofty, who makes rich and makes poor, who kills and makes to live, the only benefactor of spirits, and God of all flesh, who looks into the abysses, who beholds the works of men, who is the helper of those in danger, the Savior of those who are in despair, the creator and overseer of every soul, who makes the nations to multiply on earth, and out of all has chosen those that love You through Your beloved Son Jesus Christ, through whom You have taught us, have sanctified us, have honored us. **4** We ask You, Lord, to be our helper and assister; save those of us who are in affliction, have compassion on the humble, raise the fallen, appear to those who are in need, heal the sinners, convert those of Your people who are wandering from the way, feed the hungry, ransom our prisoners, raise up the sick, encourage the feeble-hearted, let all the nations know that You are God alone and Jesus Christ Your Son, and that we are Your people and the sheep of Your pasture.

CHAPTER 60

¹ You have made manifest the perpetual constitution of the world by the things that happen. You, Lord, who are faithful in all generations, have founded the world. You who are just in Your judgments, who are wonderful in strength and greatness; You who are wise in creating and prudent in establishing the things that are made; You that are good in the things that are seen and faithful among them that trust on You, merciful and compassionate, forgive us our transgressions and unrighteousness, our sins and our negligence. ² Do not take into account every sin of Your servants and handmaids, but purify us with the purification of Your truth, and make straight our steps in holiness, and righteousness, and singleness of heart, that we may so walk and do such things as are right and well pleasing before You, and before our rulers. ³ Yes, Lord, cause Your face to appear to us in peace to our good, that we may be sheltered by Your mighty hand, and preserved from all sin by Your lofty arm, and deliver us from those that hate us unjustly. ⁴ Give unity and peace both to us and to all that dwell on the earth, as You gave to our fathers when they called on You with faith and truth, so that we should become obedient to Your all-powerful and most excellent Name, and to those who rule and govern us on the earth.

CHAPTER 61

¹ You, Lord, have given the authority of the Kingdom to them through Your almighty and unspeakable power, so that we, knowing the estimation and honor given to them by You, might submit ourselves to them, in no way opposing Your will; to whom give, O Lord, health, peace, concord, stability, so that they may discharge the rule given to them by You without offense; ² for You, heavenly Lord, perpetual King, give to the sons of men glory, and honor, and authority over the things that are on the earth. You, Lord, direct their counsel according to what is good and pleasing before You, that, fulfilling with peace, and meekness, and piety the authority given to them by You, they may obtain mercy from You. ³ You who alone are able to do these and greater good things among us, to You do we give thanks through the Chief Priest and protector of our souls, Jesus Christ, through whom to You be the glory and majesty, now and to all generations, through the ages of the ages. Amen.

CHAPTER 62

¹ Concerning the things that pertain to our religion, and the things that are most useful to a virtuous life, for those who are willing to live piously and righteously, we have sufficiently charged you, men and brothers. ² For we have handled every argument concerning faith and conversion, and genuine love and temperance, and moderation and patience, reminding you that you must, by righteousness, and truth, and long-suffering, approve yourselves with piety to Almighty God, being of one mind, without malice, in love and peace with earnest obedience, even as our fathers, who were previously mentioned, approved themselves with humility both with regard to God the Father and Creator, and to all men. ³ And these things we have so much the more gladly put you in mind of, inasmuch as we knew plainly that we wrote to men who are faithful and of high regard, and who have looked into the oracles of the instruction of God.

CHAPTER 63

¹ It is right, therefore, that those who have attended to so great and so many examples should submit their necks, and fill the place of obedience, so that being at peace from the vain sedition we may attain, without any blame, to the end set before us in truth. ² For you will afford us joy and rejoicing if, becoming obedient to the things that have been written by us, you put an end, by the suggestion of the Holy Spirit, to the unlawful wrath of your discord, according to the supplication which we have made concerning peace and unity in this letter. ³ But we have also sent men to you who are faithful and prudent, who from youth up to old age have behaved blamelessly among us, who also will be witnesses between yourselves and us; ⁴ and this we have done that you may know that our whole thought has been and is this: that you may speedily be at peace among yourselves.

CHAPTER 64

¹ Finally, may my God, who overlooks all things, who is the Master of spirits and Lord of all flesh, who has chosen our Lord Jesus Christ, and us through Him to be a peculiar people, give to every soul that is called after His glorious and holy Name, faith, fear, peace, patience, long-suffering, continence, purity, sobriety, to the well-pleasing of His Name, through our Chief Priest and protector, Jesus Christ, through whom be ascribed to Him glory and greatness, strength and honor, both now and through the ages of the ages. Amen.

CHAPTER 65

¹ See that you quickly send back to us in peace and with joy Claudius Ephebus and Valerius Bito, together also with Fortunatus, who were sent to you from us, that they may the more quickly bring us news of your peace and order, which we pray for and desire, so that we may the sooner have joy concerning your good order. ² The grace of our Lord Jesus Christ be with you, and with all who everywhere are called of God through Him, to whom through Him be glory, honor, might, majesty, and continuous dominion, through the ages of the ages. Amen.

2 CLEMENT

Like 1 Clement, the Second Epistle of Clement has an anonymous author and is ascribed to Clement of Rome by tradition, but unlike 1 Clement, the ascription of 2 Clement to Clement of Rome is more dubious. It was considered for canonization early on and is in fact included in some Coptic Bibles. It was likely written in the late 1st century or early 2nd century.

CHAPTER 1

¹ Brothers, we should so think of our Lord Jesus Christ as of God, as of the Judge of quick and dead, and we should not think lightly concerning our salvation; ² for if we think little concerning Him, we also expect that we will receive little; and if we listen to it as though it were a small thing, we err, not knowing from where we are called, nor by whom, nor to what place, nor what great things Jesus Christ has endured to suffer on our behalf. ³ What repayment, therefore, will we give to Him, or what fruit worthy of that which He has given to us? How many things that help to holiness has He given to us? ⁴ For He has given us the light, He has called us sons as though He were our father, He has saved us when we were ready to perish. ⁵ What praise, therefore, will we give to Him, or what repayment of reward for the things that we have received? ⁶ For we were maimed in our understanding, worshiping stocks and stones, and gold, and silver, and iron, the work of men, and our whole life was nothing but death. We, therefore, who were surrounded with darkness, and who had our sight filled with such gloom, have recovered our sight, having, according to His will, laid aside the cloud that was around us. ⁷ For He has had compassion on us, and, pitying us, has saved us, having beheld in us much wandering and destruction, when we had no hope of salvation except that which is from Him. ⁸ For

d us when as yet we were not, and has willed us to were nothing.

CHAPTER 2

[1] "Rejoice, you barren that do not bear; break forth and shout, you that do not travail, for the desolate has many more children than she that has a husband." In that He said, "Rejoice, you barren that do not bear," He has spoken of us, for our assembly was barren before that children were given to her. [2] But in that He said, "Shout, you that do not travail," He means that we should offer our prayers to God with simplicity, that we do not faint like women in travail. [3] But in that He said, "The children of the desolate are many more than they of her that has a husband," He means that our people seemed to be deserted of God, and now, after that we have believed, we have become more in number than they which seemed to have God. [4] And another Writing says, "I did not come to call the righteous but sinners." [5] He means this, that it is necessary to save them that are perishing. [6] For this is great and wonderful—not to establish the things that are standing, but the things that are falling; [7] thus Christ willed to save the things that were perishing, and He saved many, having come and called us who were already perishing.

CHAPTER 3

[1] Therefore, since He has showed such compassion to us—first, that He has caused that we who live should not sacrifice to gods that are dead, neither worship them, but know through Him the Father of truth—what is this knowledge of Him except the not denying Him through whom we know Him? [2] For He Himself says, "Whoever has confessed Me before men, I will confess Him before My Father." [3] This, therefore, is our reward if we confess Him through whom we have been saved. [4] But whereby will we confess Him? Even by doing what He commands, and not disobeying His commands, and honoring Him not only with our lips but with our whole heart and whole understanding. [5] For He says in Isaiah, "This people honor Me with their lips, but their heart is far from Me."

CHAPTER 4

[1] Therefore, let us not only call Him Lord, for that will not save us. [2] For He says, "It is not everyone that says to Me, Lord, Lord, that will be saved, but he that does righteousness." [3] For what reason, brothers, let us confess Him in our deeds, by loving one another, by not committing adultery, and not speaking ill of each other, neither being envious, but by being continent, compassionate, kind. We should also sympathize with one another, and to abstain from covetousness; it is by these works that we acknowledge Him, and not by the contrary; [4] and we should not fear men but rather God. [5] For what reason, if we do these things, the Lord has said, "Though you have been gathered together with Me in My bosom and do not do My commands, I will cast you from Me, and I will say to you, Depart from Me; I do not know from where you are, you workers of iniquity."

CHAPTER 5

[1] For what reason, brothers, having left our sojourning in this world, let us do the will of Him who called us, and let us not fear to depart from this world. [2] For the Lord says, "You will be as lambs in the midst of wolves." [3] But Peter answered and says to Him, "What, then, if the wolves tear the sheep?" [4] Jesus says to Peter, "Do not let the lambs after that they are dead fear the wolves; and do not fear them that kill you but can do nothing more to you, but fear Him who, after you are dead, has authority over body and soul, even to cast them into the Gehenna of fire." [5] And you know, brothers, that the sojourning of our flesh in this world is but short and for a little while, but the promise of Christ is great and wonderful, even the rest of the kingdom which is to come, and of continuous life. [6] What,

therefore, will we do that we may attain to them, except to lead a holy and just life, and to deem the things of this world to be alien to us, and not to desire them? [7] For while we desire to obtain these things, we fall from the right way.

CHAPTER 6

[1] For the Lord says, "No servant can serve two masters." If, therefore, we wish to serve both God and wealth, it is inexpedient for us; [2] for what advantage is it if a man gains the whole world, but loses his soul? [3] Now this life and the life to come are two enemies. [4] This life preaches adultery, corruption, covetousness, and deceit; but the life that is to come renounces these things. [5] We cannot, therefore, be friends to both; it is necessary for us then to renounce the one and to use thc other. [6] Therefore, let us consider that it is better to hate the things that are here, as being small, and short-lived, and corruptible, but to love the things that are there, as being good and incorruptible. [7] If, therefore, we do the will of Christ, we will find rest; but if not, nothing will deliver us from continuous punishment, if we do not obey His commands. [8] For the Writing says in Ezekiel: "If Noah, and Job, and Daniel should rise up, they will not deliver their children in the captivity." [9] If, therefore, such righteous men as these cannot by their righteousness deliver their children, with what confidence will we, if we do not keep our immersion pure and undefiled, come to the Kingdom of God? or who will be our advocate unless we are found having the works that are holy and just?

CHAPTER 7

[1] For what reason, my brothers, let us strive, knowing that the contest is at hand. We know, too, that many put in for corruptible contests, but all are not crowned, but they only who have labored much and fought a good fight. [2] Therefore, let us contend that we may all be crowned. [3] Let us run in the straight course, in the incorruptible contest; and let us be many that put into it; and let us so contend that we may also be crowned. And if we cannot all be crowned, let us at least come near to the crown. [4] It is necessary for us to know that he who contends in a corruptible contest, if he is found acting unfairly is flogged, and taken away, and cast out of the course. [5] What do you think? what will he suffer that acts unfairly in an incorruptible contest? [6] For of them who have not kept their seal he says, "Their worm will not die, and their fire will not be quenched, and they will be for a spectacle to all flesh."

CHAPTER 8

[1] Therefore, while we are on the earth, let us convert. [2] For we are as clay in the hands of the workman. In like manner as the potter, if while he is making a vessel, it turns wrongly in his hands, or is crushed, can mould it again, but if he has once cast it into the fiery furnace, he can no longer amend it; so let us, so long as we are in this world, convert with all our hearts of the wickedness that we have committed in the flesh, that we may be saved of the Lord while as yet we have time for conversion. [3] For after we have departed out of this world, we are no longer able there to confess or convert. [4] For what reason, brothers, if we have done the will of the Father, and preserved our flesh pure, and kept the commands of the Lord, we will receive continuous life. [5] For the Lord says in the Gospel, "If you have not kept that which is little, who will give you that which is great? for I say to you, he that is faithful in that which is least is also faithful in much." [6] Does he not, therefore, say this, "Keep your flesh pure and your seal unspotted, that you may inherit continuous life?"

CHAPTER 9

[1] And do not let any one of you say that this flesh of ours is not judged nor raised again. [2] Consider this: in what were you saved, in what did you recover your sight, if not in this flesh? [3] We should, therefore, guard our flesh as the temple of

God; **4** for in the same manner as you were called in the flesh, in the flesh you will also come. **5** There is one Christ, our Lord who saved us, who being spirit at the first, was made flesh, and thus called us. So we will also receive the reward in this flesh. **6** Therefore, let us love one another, that we may all come to the Kingdom of God. **7** While we have opportunity to be healed, let us give ourselves up to God who heals, giving a repayment to Him. **8** And of what kind? conversion from a sincere heart. **9** For He foreknows all things and knows the things that are in our hearts. **10** Therefore, let us give Him praise, not from the mouth alone, but also from the heart, that He may receive us as sons. **11** For of a truth the Lord has said, "My brothers are they who do the will of My Father."

CHAPTER 10

1 For what reason, my brothers, let us do the will of the Father who has called us, that we may live; and let us rather pursue virtue, and abandon vice which leads us into sins, and let us fly from ungodliness lest evil seize us; for if we are zealous to do good, peace will pursue us. **2** For this reason it is not possible that a man should find peace. **3** For they introduce the fear of men, choosing rather the present enjoyment that is here than the future promise. **4** For they are ignorant of how great a torment the enjoyment of this world brings, and what delight the future promise has. **5** And if they themselves alone did these things, it would be endurable; but now they continue to instruct innocent souls in evil, not knowing that they will have a twofold condemnation—both themselves and they that listen to them.

CHAPTER 11

1 Therefore, let us serve God with a pure heart, and we will be righteous; but if we do not serve Him, because we do not believe the promise of God, we will be wretched. **2** For the prophetic word says, "Wretched are the double-minded who doubt in their heart, and say, We have heard these things of old, even in the time of our fathers, but we have seen none of them, though we expect them from day to day. **3** You fools, compare yourselves to a tree; take for an example the vine: in the first place it sheds its leaves, then there comes a shoot, after that the unripe grape, then the mature cluster. **4** In like manner My people, in time past, has had disorder and trouble, but afterward it will receive the things that are good." **5** For what reason, my brothers, let us not be double-minded, but let us abide in hope, that we may obtain our reward. **6** Faithful is He that has promised that He will give to each the repayment of his works. **7** If, therefore, we do righteousness before God, we will enter into His Kingdom, and receive the promises which "ear has not heard nor eye seen, neither have entered into the heart of man."

CHAPTER 12

1 Let us, therefore, in love and righteousness expect the Kingdom of God every hour, since we do not know the day of the appearing of God. **2** For the Lord Himself, when He was asked by a certain man when His Kingdom should come, replied, "When two will be one, and that which is without as that which is within, and the male with the female neither male nor female." **3** Now two are one when we speak the truth to one another, and there is, without hypocrisy, one soul in two bodies. **4** And by that which is without being as that which is within, He means this: He calls the soul that which is within, and the body that which is without; in like manner, therefore, as your body is visible, let your soul be made manifest by good deeds. **5** And by the male with the female neither male nor female, He means this: When a brother seeing a sister does not in any way regard her as a female, nor does she regard him as a male; **6** "when you do these things," He says, "the Kingdom of My Father will come."

CHAPTER 13

1 My brothers, therefore let us convert immediately; let us be sober and followers of what is good, for we are burdened with much folly and wickedness. Let us wipe out from among us our former sins and convert sincerely and be saved. And let us not be pleasers of men, nor let us wish to please one another alone, but let us also please them that are outside by our righteous conduct, that the Name may not be blasphemed on our account. **2** For the Lord says, "My Name is continually blasphemed among all the nations"; and again, "Why is My Name blasphemed, whereby it is blasphemed? in that you do not do the things that I will." **3** For the nations, when they hear from our mouth the oracles of God, admire them as beautiful and weighty; but afterward perceiving our deeds, that they are not worthy of the words that we say, they turn thereafter to blasphemy, saying that the matter is but fable and deceit. **4** For when they hear from us that God says, "There is no thanks for you if you love them that love you, but there is thanks for you if you love your enemies and them that hate you"; when they hear these things, they wonder at the excess of the goodness. But when they see that we do not only not love those that hate us, but do not even love those that love us, they turn us to ridicule, and the Name is blasphemed.

CHAPTER 14

1 For what reason, my brothers, by doing the will of our Father, God, we will be of the first, the spiritual Assembly, which was founded before the sun and moon were made; but if we do not do the will of the Lord, we will be of the Writing that says, "My house has become a den of thieves." Therefore, let us choose to be of the Assembly of life that we may be saved. **2** But I do not think that you are ignorant that the living Assembly is the body of Christ. For the Writing says: "God made man, male and female." Now, the male signifies Christ, the female the Assembly. You also know that both the Scrolls and the apostles say that the Assembly is not new, but was from the beginning; for it was of a spiritual kind, as was also our Jesus, but was made manifest in the last days that it might save us. **3** But the Assembly, though spiritual, was manifested in the flesh of Christ, showing to us that if anyone keep it in his flesh, and does not corrupt it, he will receive it in the Holy Spirit; for this flesh is the counterpart of the Spirit; no one, therefore, who corrupts the copy will receive the original in exchange. He therefore means this, my brothers: "Keep the flesh pure, that you may partake of the Spirit." **4** But if we say that the flesh is the Assembly, and the spirit, Christ, he then who does injury to the flesh does injury to the Assembly. Such a one therefore will not partake of the spirit, which is Christ. **5** Such life and immortality is this flesh able to partake of by the union of the Holy Spirit with it. Nor can any say or declare what the Lord has prepared for His chosen ones.

CHAPTER 15

1 Now, I do not think that I have given advice of little importance concerning temperance, which, if a man practices, he will not regret it, but will save both himself and me who advise him. For it is no small service to convert a wandering and perishing soul to salvation. **2** For we are able to give this repayment in return to God who created us, if he who speaks and hears both speaks and hears with faith and love. **3** Therefore, let us remain with righteousness and holiness in the things in which we have believed, that we may with boldness ask of God, who says, "While you are still speaking, I will say, Behold, I am here." **4** For this saying is the token of a great promise. For the Lord says of Himself that He is more ready to give than him that asks. **5** Therefore, since we partake in so much goodness, let us not grudge ourselves the attaining of so many good things; for by so much as His words bring pleasure to those who do them, by so much do they bring condemnation to those who disobey them.

CHAPTER 16

1 For what reason, brothers, since we have received no

rtunity for conversion, let us, while we have time, ... God who has called us, while we still have one who ... us. [2] For if we bid farewell to the luxuries of this ... nquer our soul so that we do not fulfill evil lusts, ...take of the mercy of Jesus. [3] But know that the Day ... Judgment is already coming as a burning furnace, and certain of the heavens will be melted, and the whole earth will be as lead melting on the fire; and then both the secret and open deeds of men will be made manifest. [4] Therefore, kindness is good, as showing conversion from sin; better is fasting than prayer, and kindness than both; for love covers a multitude of sins, and prayer that goes forth from a good conscience saves from death. Happy is everyone who is found full of these things, for kindness becomes a lightening of sin.

CHAPTER 17

[1] Therefore, let us convert with our whole heart lest any of us perish by the way. For if we have received commands and make this our business—to tear men away from idols and instruct them—how much more should a soul not perish that has already come to a knowledge of God? [2] Therefore, let us endeavor to elevate with regard to what is good them that are weak, to the end that we may all be saved; and let us convert one another and reprove one another. [3] And let us not seem to attend and believe now only, while we are being admonished by the elders, but also when we have departed to our homes, let us remember the commands of the Lord; and let us not, on the other hand, be drawn aside by the lusts of the world, but let us endeavor, by coming more frequently, to make progress in the commands of the Lord, to the end that we all being of one mind may be gathered together to life. [4] For the Lord has said, "I come to gather together all the nations, tribes, and tongues." And He says this of the day of His appearing, when He will come and repay each of us according to his works. [5] And the unbelieving will behold His glory and strength, and will be astonished when they see the kingdom of the world in the hands of Jesus, and will say, "Woe to us, for You were and we did not know it, and did not believe, nor did we obey the elders who preached to us concerning our salvation." And their worm will not die, nor their fire be quenched, and they will be for a spectacle to all flesh. [6] He speaks of that Day of Judgment when they will see punished those among us who have lived ungodly and set at nothing the commands of Jesus Christ. [7] But the just, who have done well, and have abided the tests, and have hated the luxuries of the soul, when they behold those who have missed the way and have denied Jesus either by words or deeds, how they are punished with dreadful tortures in unquenchable fire, will give glory to their God, saying that there will be a hope for him who has served God with his whole heart.

CHAPTER 18

[1] Therefore, let us be of those who give thanks, of those who have served God, and not of the ungodly who are judged. [2] For I myself, being in all respects a sinner, and not having yet escaped temptation, but being still in the midst of the snares of the Devil, yet endeavor to follow after righteousness, that I may be able, at any rate, to be near it, fearing the judgment to come

CHAPTER 19

[1] For what reason, my brothers and sisters, after the reading of the words of the God of truth, I also read an exhortation to you, to the end that you should attend to what has been written, that you may both save yourselves and him who preaches among you; for I ask of you, as my reward, that you should convert with your whole heart, gaining for yourselves salvation and life. For by so doing, we will offer an aim to all the young, who are willing to labor cheerfully for the worship and goodness of God. [2] And do not let those of us who are unlearned be vexed or offended when one exhorts us and turns us from sin to righteousness. For we at times when doing what is wrong, do not know it, from the doubt and unbelief that is in our hearts, and are blinded in our understanding by vain lusts. [3] Therefore, let us practice righteousness, that we may be saved at the last. Blessed are they who obey these commands, for if for a short time they suffer in the world that now is, they will gather hereafter the immortal fruit of the resurrection. [4] Therefore, do not let the pious man be vexed if he is afflicted in the times that now are—a blessed time awaits him. He will live above again with the fathers and will rejoice without sorrow continuously.

CHAPTER 20

1 And do not let even that trouble your mind, that we see the unjust prosperous and the servants of God in misery. 2 Let us have faith, my brothers and sisters. We are making trial of the living God and contending in the present life that we may be crowned in the life to come. 3 For none of the just receive a speedy reward, but wait for it. 4 For if God gave speedily the reward of the righteous, we should immediately practice gain and not godliness; for we should seem to be righteous, not on account of what is pious, but on account of what is profitable. And on this account the divine judgment has overtaken a spirit that is not righteous, and has burdened it with chains. 5 Now to the only God, the invisible, the Father of truth, who has sent to us the Savior and leader of immortality, through whom He has made known to us the truth and the heavenly life—to Him be the glory through the ages of the ages. Amen

Made in the USA
Middletown, DE
12 August 2024

59011017R00431